BOURNE END

HEMEL HEMPSTEAD
ST. ALBANS
HATFIELD
M10

BOVINGDON
4 5 6 7 21/6A 21A 9 10 LONDON COLNEY A1(M) 11 12 13 CUFFL
20 8 22 POTTERS BAR 24
CHIPPERFIELD 6 ABBOTS LANGLEY
GREAT MISSENDEN
CHESHAM M25 23/1

LITTLE CHALFONT 19 5
20 21 22 23 24 25 26 27 28 29
AMERSHAM WATFORD BOREHAMWOOD BARNET NEW BARNET
CHORLEYWOOD 18 BUSHEY
EAST BARNET SOUTHGA
TYLERS GREEN 17 M1

CHALFONT ST. GILES RICKMANSWORTH 4
36 37 38 39 40 41 42 43 44 45
LOUDWATER CHALFONT COMMON NORTHWOOD STANMORE EDGWARE FINCHLEY WO GRE
BEACONSFIELD M25 2
M40 HAREFIELD PINNER HENDON
GERRARDS CROSS HARROW
WOOBURN 56 57 58 59 60 61 62 63 64 65
FARNHAM COMMON DENHAM RUISLIP HAMPSTEAD
16/1A 1

STOKE POGES UXBRIDGE NORTHOLT WEMBLEY WILLESDEN
74 75 76 77 78 79 80 81 82 83
PADDINGTON MARYLEBONE
MAIDENHEAD IVER HAYES SOUTHALL ACTON WESTMINS
7 SLOUGH
6 M4 WEST DRAYTON HAMMERSMITH
ETON LANGLEY M4 2 1
92 5 93 15/4B 94 4 95 3 96 97 98 99 100
8/9 DATCHET 4A KEW BATTERSEA
WINDSOR London Heathrow HOUNSLOW BRIX
14
OLD WINDSOR RICHMOND WANDSWORTH
WRAYSBURY FELTHAM TWICKENHAM
WINKFIELD 112 113 114 115 116 117 118 119 120
ASHFORD WIMBLEDON STREATHAM
EGHAM STAINES TEDDINGTON
MERTON MITCHA
VIRGINIA WATER 1 KINGSTON UPON THAMES
ASCOT M3 132 12/2 133 134 135 136 137 138 139 140
CHERTSEY SURBITON
WALTON-ON-THAMES 11
BAGSHOT M3 WEYBRIDGE ESHER SUTTON
3 OTTERSHAW EWELL PUR
150 151 152 153 154 155 156 157 158
CHOBHAM EPSOM
BISLEY BYFLEET OXSHOTT BANSTEAD
STOKE D'ABERNON COULSDON
10 ASHTEAD
WOKING M25 9
166 167 168 169 170 171 9 172 173 174
RIPLEY FETCHAM LEATHERHEAD TADWORTH
MAYFORD WALTON ON THE HILL
MYTCHETT 7
GREAT BOOKHAM
NORMANDY EAST HORSLEY 182 183 8 184
STOUGHTON REIGATE REDHI
TONGHAM EAST CLANDON
GUILDFORD DORKING BROCKHAM

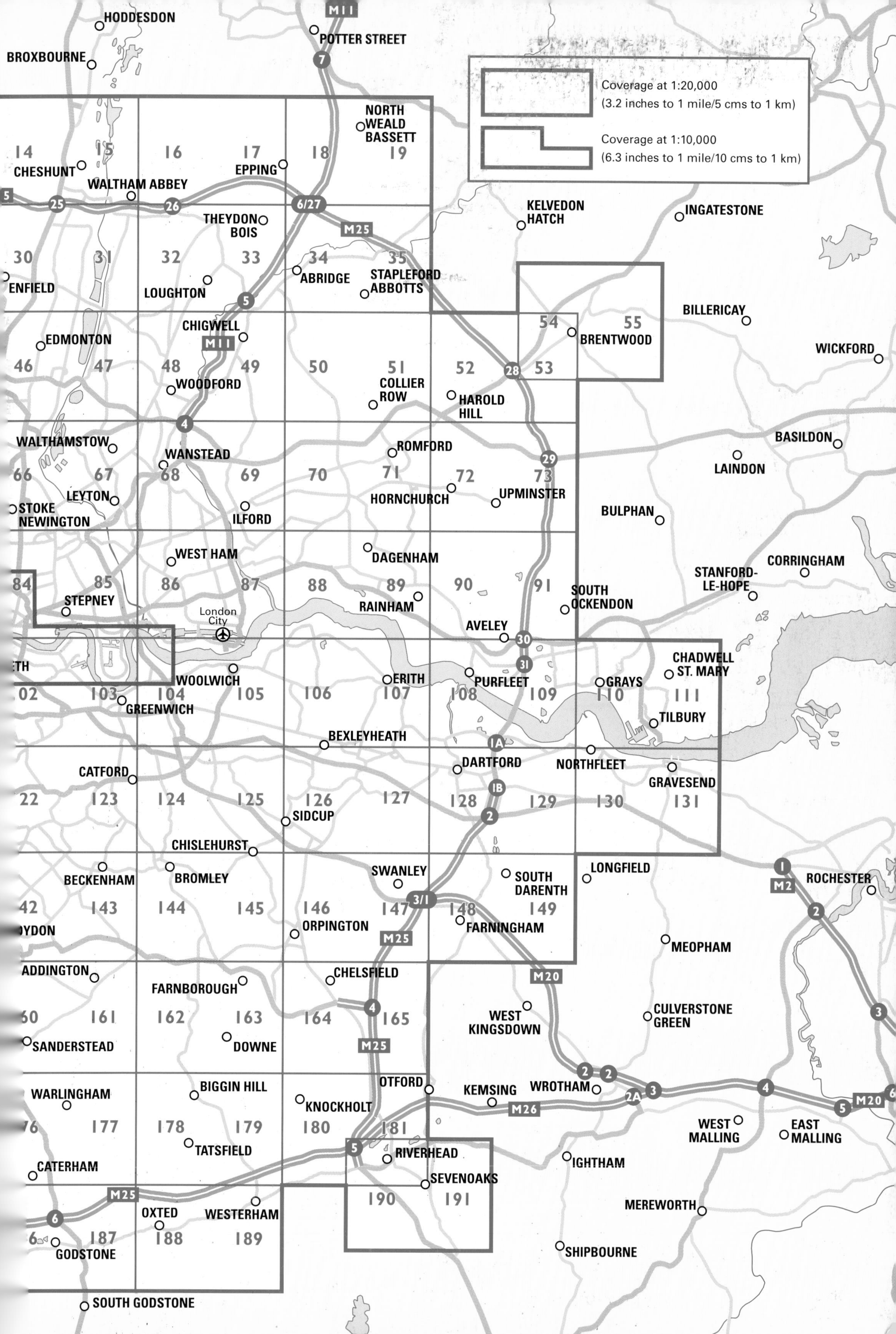
Coverage at 1:20,000
(3.2 inches to 1 mile/5 cms to 1 km)
Coverage at 1:10,000
(6.3 inches to 1 mile/10 cms to 1 km)
M11
HODDESDON
POTTER STREET
BROXBOURNE
NORTH WEALD BASSETT
14
15
16
17
18
19
CHESHUNT
EPPING
WALTHAM ABBEY
KELVEDON HATCH
INGATESTONE
M25
THEYDON BOIS
30
31
32
33
34
35
ENFIELD
LOUGHTON
ABRIDGE
STAPLEFORD ABBOTTS
BILLERICAY
54
55
BRENTWOOD
CHIGWELL
EDMONTON
WICKFORD
46
47
48
49
50
51
52
53
COLLIER ROW
HAROLD HILL
WOODFORD
WALTHAMSTOW
ROMFORD
BASILDON
WANSTEAD
LAINDON
66
67
68
69
70
71
72
73
LEYTON
UPMINSTER
STOKE NEWINGTON
HORNCHURCH
BULPHAN
ILFORD
WEST HAM
DAGENHAM
CORRINGHAM
STANFORD-LE-HOPE
84
85
86
87
88
89
90
91
SOUTH OCKENDON
STEPNEY
RAINHAM
London City
AVELEY
CHADWELL ST. MARY
WOOLWICH
ERITH
PURFLEET
GRAYS
02
103
104
105
106
107
108
109
110
111
GREENWICH
TILBURY
BEXLEYHEATH
DARTFORD
NORTHFLEET
CATFORD
GRAVESEND
22
123
124
125
126
127
128
129
130
131
SIDCUP
CHISLEHURST
LONGFIELD
SWANLEY
SOUTH DARENTH
ROCHESTER
M2
BECKENHAM
BROMLEY
42
143
144
145
146
147
148
149
FARNINGHAM
ORPINGTON
YDON
MEOPHAM
M20
ADDINGTON
CHELSFIELD
FARNBOROUGH
WEST KINGSDOWN
CULVERSTONE GREEN
60
161
162
163
164
165
SANDERSTEAD
DOWNE
OTFORD
WARLINGHAM
BIGGIN HILL
KEMSING
WROTHAM
M26
KNOCKHOLT
WEST MALLING
EAST MALLING
76
177
178
179
180
181
TATSFIELD
RIVERHEAD
IGHTHAM
CATERHAM
SEVENOAKS
190
191
MEREWORTH
OXTED
WESTERHAM
187
188
189
GODSTONE
SHIPBOURNE
SOUTH GODSTONE

Collins Street Atlas

M25 LONDON MASTER

CONTENTS

MAIN LONDON MAPS
Key to main London Maps ii-iii
Key to map symbols iii
M25 route planning map 2-3
Main London maps 4-191

CENTRAL LONDON MAPS
Key to central London Maps 192-193
Key to map symbols 193
Central London maps 194-205

INFORMATION PAGES
Index to places of interest 206-207
Index to place names 208-211
Index to railway stations 211-213
Index to hospitals 214
Index to street names 215-349

Published by Collins
An imprint of HarperCollins*Publishers*
77-85 Fulham Palace Road, Hammersmith, London W6 8JB

London Underground Map by permission of Transport Trading Limited
Registered User No. 01/3468

HarperCollins website: www.**fire**and**water**.com
Bartholomew website: www.bartholomewmaps.com
e-mail: roadcheck@harpercollins.co.uk

Mapping generated from Bartholomew digital databases

ISBN 0 00 711584 9 Spiral OM10846
ISBN 0 00 712962 9 Hardback OM11056
ISBN 0 00 712963 7 Paperback OM11055

Printed in Italy ADD

WHEATHAMPSTEAD
WELWYN GARDEN CITY
HERTFORD
HODDESDON
HATFIELD
BROXBOURNE
HEMEL HEMPSTEAD
ST. ALBANS
BOURNE END
BOVINGDON
LONDON COLNEY
4 5 6
CHIPPERFIELD
21/6A 21A
9 10 11 POTTERS BAR
12 13 CUFFLEY 14 CHESHUNT 15 16 EPPIN
CHESHAM
20
ABBOTS LANGLEY
23/1 24 25 26
LITTLE CHALFONT
AMERSHAM 20 21 22 WATFORD 23 24 BUSHEY 25 26 BOREHAMWOOD 27 BARNET 28 NEW BARNET 29 30 ENFIELD 31 32 LOUGHTON 33
CHORLEYWOOD
EAST BARNET
THEYDON BOIS
CHALFONT ST. GILES RICKMANSWORTH SOUTHGATE CHIGWELL
36 37 38 39 40 41 42 43 44 45 46 EDMONTON 47 48 WOODFORD 49
BEACONSFIELD CHALFONT COMMON NORTHWOOD STANMORE EDGWARE FINCHLEY WOOD GREEN WANSTEAD
HAREFIELD PINNER HENDON WALTHAMSTOW
GERRARDS CROSS HARROW STOKE NEWINGTON LEYTON
FARNHAM COMMON 56 57 58 59 60 61 62 63 64 65 66 67 68 69 ILFO
DENHAM RUISLIP HAMPSTEAD
STOKE POGES UXBRIDGE NORTHOLT WEMBLEY WILLESDEN WEST HAM
74 75 76 77 78 79 80 81 PADDINGTON 82 83 84 85 86 87
SLOUGH IVER HAYES SOUTHALL ACTON MARYLEBONE STEPNEY London City
LANGLEY WEST DRAYTON HAMMERSMITH WESTMINSTER
ETON 92 93 94 95 96 97 98 99 100 LAMBETH 101 102 103 104 WOOLWICH
WINDSOR DATCHET KEW BATTERSEA GREENWICH
London Heathrow HOUNSLOW BRIXTON
OLD WINDSOR RICHMOND WANDSWORTH CATFORD
WRAYSBURY FELTHAM TWICKENHAM CHISLEHURST
112 113 114 115 116 117 118 119 120 121 122 123 124
EGHAM ASHFORD TEDDINGTON WIMBLEDON STREATHAM
STAINES MERTON MITCHAM BECKENHAM BROMLEY
VIRGINIA WATER KINGSTON UPON THAMES
132 133 134 135 136 137 138 139 140 141 142 143 144
CHERTSEY SURBITON CROYDON
WALTON-ON-THAMES
OTTERSHAW WEYBRIDGE ESHER SUTTON ADDINGTON FARNBOROUGH
EWELL
150 151 152 153 154 155 156 157 158 159 160 161 162
CHOBHAM EPSOM PURLEY SANDERSTEAD D
BYFLEET OXSHOTT BANSTEAD
BISLEY STOKE D'ABERNON COULSDON WARLINGHAM BIGGIN
WOKING ASHTEAD
166 167 168 169 170 171 172 173 174 175 176 177 178 TATSFIE
RIPLEY LEATHERHEAD TADWORTH CATERHAM
MAYFORD FETCHAM
WALTON ON THE HILL OXTED WEST
EAST HORSLEY GREAT BOOKHAM
STOUGHTON 7/8 182 183 184 185 186 187 188
EAST CLANDON REIGATE REDHILL GODSTONE
DORKING BROCKHAM
GUILDFORD SOUTH GODSTONE MARLPIT HILL
COMPTON GOMSHALL WESTCOTT BLINDLEY HEATH EDENBRID
SHALFORD ABINGER HAMMER NORTH HOLMWOOD LEIGH SALFORDS
LINGFIELD
GODALMING SHAMLEY GREEN HOLMBURY ST MARY BEARE GREEN HORLEY NEWCHAPEL
MILFORD GRAFHAM JAYES PARK CHARLWOOD Gatwick (London)

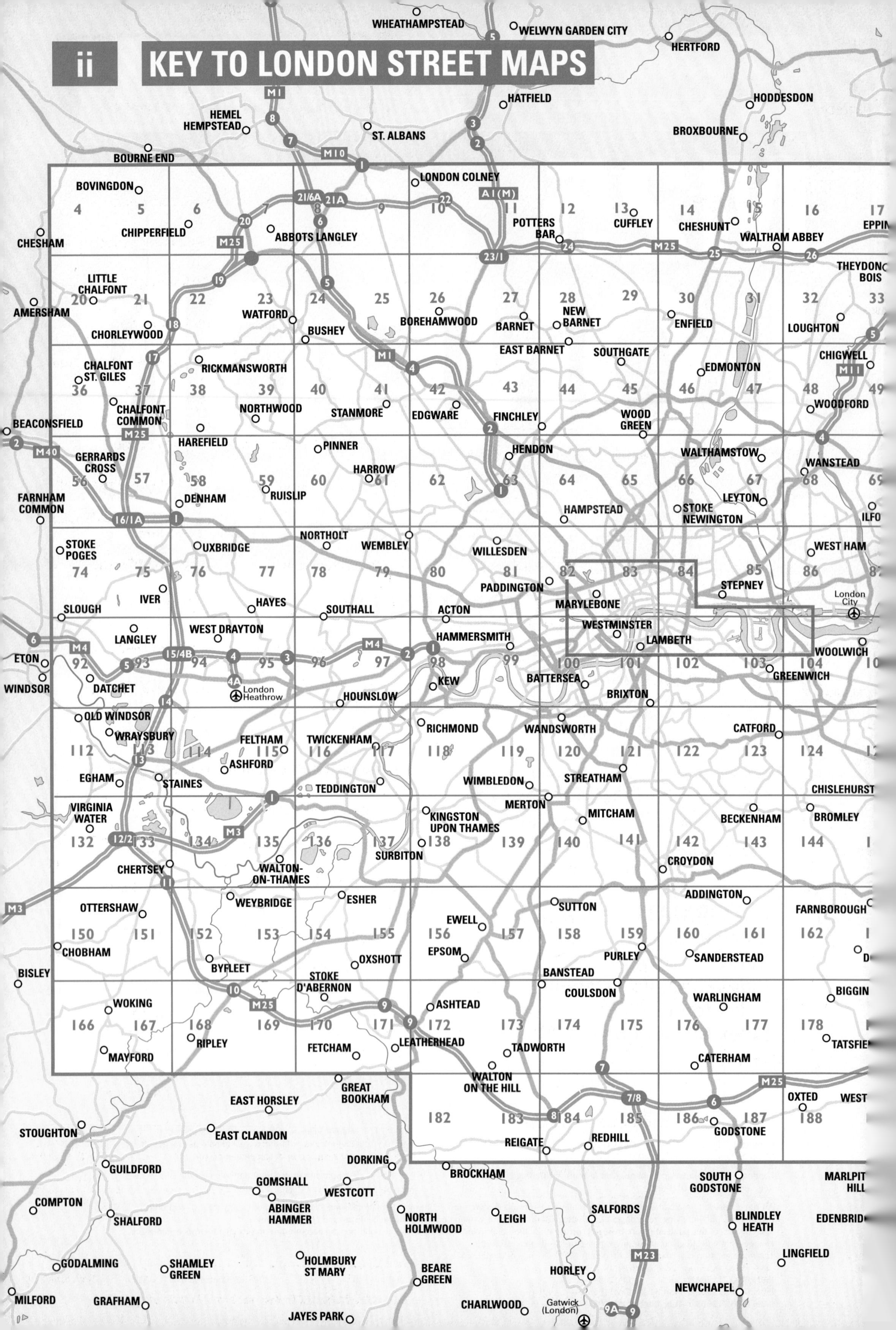

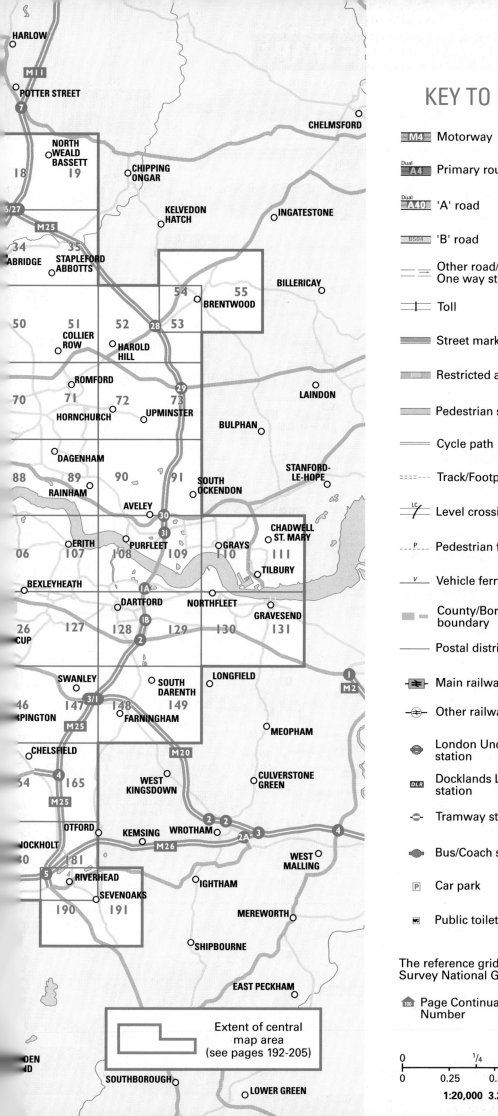

KEY TO MAIN MAP SYMBOLS

M4	Motorway		Leisure & tourism
Dual A4	Primary route		Shopping
Dual A40	'A' road		Administration & law
B504	'B' road		Health & welfare
	Other road/ One way street		Education
	Toll		Industry & commerce
	Street market	✝ ✝	Cemetery
	Restricted access road		Golf course
	Pedestrian street		Public open space/ Allotments
	Cycle path		Park/Garden/Sports ground
	Track/Footpath		Wood/Forest
LC	Level crossing	♀ ♀	Orchard
P	Pedestrian ferry	USA	Embassy
V	Vehicle ferry	Pol	Police station
	County/Borough boundary	Fire Sta	Fire station
	Postal district boundary	PO	Post Office
➤➤	Main railway station	Lib	Library
➤	Other railway station	i	Tourist information centre
	London Underground station	▲	Youth hostel
DLR	Docklands Light Railway station	□	Tower block
	Tramway station	⊕	Heliport
	Bus/Coach station	+	Church
P	Car park	☾	Mosque
WC	Public toilet	✡	Synagogue

The reference grid on this atlas coincides with the Ordnance Survey National Grid System. The grid interval is 500 metres.

🏠 100	Page Continuation Number	AT	Grid Reference	- 03	OS National Grid Kilometre Square

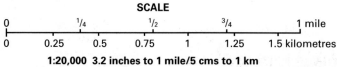

SCALE

0   1/4   1/2   3/4   1 mile

0   0.25   0.5   0.75   1   1.25   1.5 kilometres

1:20,000 3.2 inches to 1 mile/5 cms to 1 km

M1
The North
Luton ✈   13
21

A405
St Albans   3¾
London North West
M1 South
21ᴬ

A1081
St Albans   3
22

Hatfield A1(M)   6
Barnet A1081   3
London North West A1
Services   23

21   **21ᴬ**   **22**   **A1(M)**   **23**   ● SOUTH MIMMS SERVICES

A405   A1081

Hemel Hempstead 5
Aylesbury   20
A41
20

Hemel Hempstead 5
Aylesbury   20
A41
20

M1
The North
Luton ✈   13
21

A405
Watford   4¼
Harrow (M1 South)
21ᴬ

St Albans   3¾
A1081
22

A1 (M) Hatfield   6
A1081 Barnet   3
A1
London North West
Services
23

20   A41   ○   A41   A411   A405   ●

Watford   3½
A41
19

19

A404

Amersham   7
Chorleywood   7½
A404
18

Rickmansworth 2
Chorleywood   ½
Amersham   7
A404
18

18   A404

Maple Cross   1
A412
17

Maple Cross   1
Rickmansworth 2
A412
17

17   A405

M40
Uxbridge   3
London West
Birmingham 100
Oxford   38
16

M40

M40 (West)
Birmingham 100
Oxford (A40) 38
M40 (East)
Uxbridge   3
London (West)
16

16   **M40**   A40

M4
Heathrow ✈ Terminals
1, 2 & 3   3½
London West
Slough   5
Reading   25
The West
15

M4
The West
Slough   5
Reading   25
London West
Heathrow ✈ Terminals
1, 2 & 3   3½
15

M4   **15**   **M4**

A3113
Heathrow ✈
Terminal 4   3½
& Cargo   3
14

14

A3113
Heathrow ✈
Terminal 4   3½
& Cargo   3
14

A3113

13   A30

A30
Staines   2
13

A308   A30

A30
London West
Staines   2
13

B376   ○   A308

M3
Sunbury   6
Southampton 56
Basingstoke 27
12

River Thames

12   **M3**

M3

A320
Chertsey   2
Woking   5
11

A317

M3
Basingstoke 27
Southampton 56
Sunbury   6
12

11   A317

A3
London South West
Guildford   8
Kingston   12
10

Leatherhead   2
A243
Dorking   7½
A24
9

A320
Woking   5
A317
Chertsey   2
11

10   A3

A3
London South West
Guildford   8
10

A245

A243   A244   A243   A24

A217
Reigate   2
Sutton   8
Redhill (A25) 3½
8

9   A24

8 A217

Leatherhead A243 2
Dorking (A24) 6½
9

A217
Reigate
Sutton
Kingston (A240)

B2122   A24

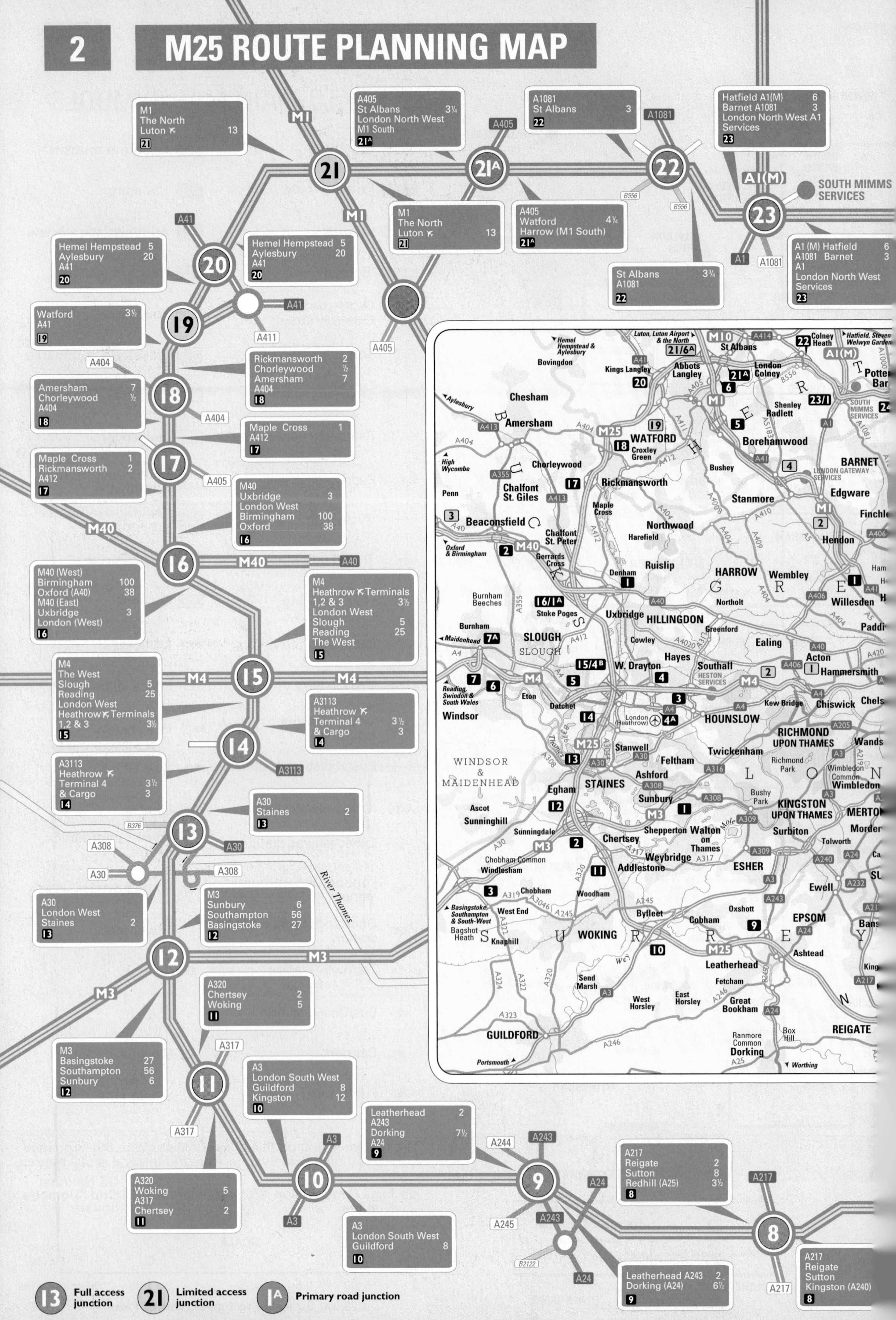

13 Full access junction   **21** Limited access junction   **1ᴬ** Primary road junction

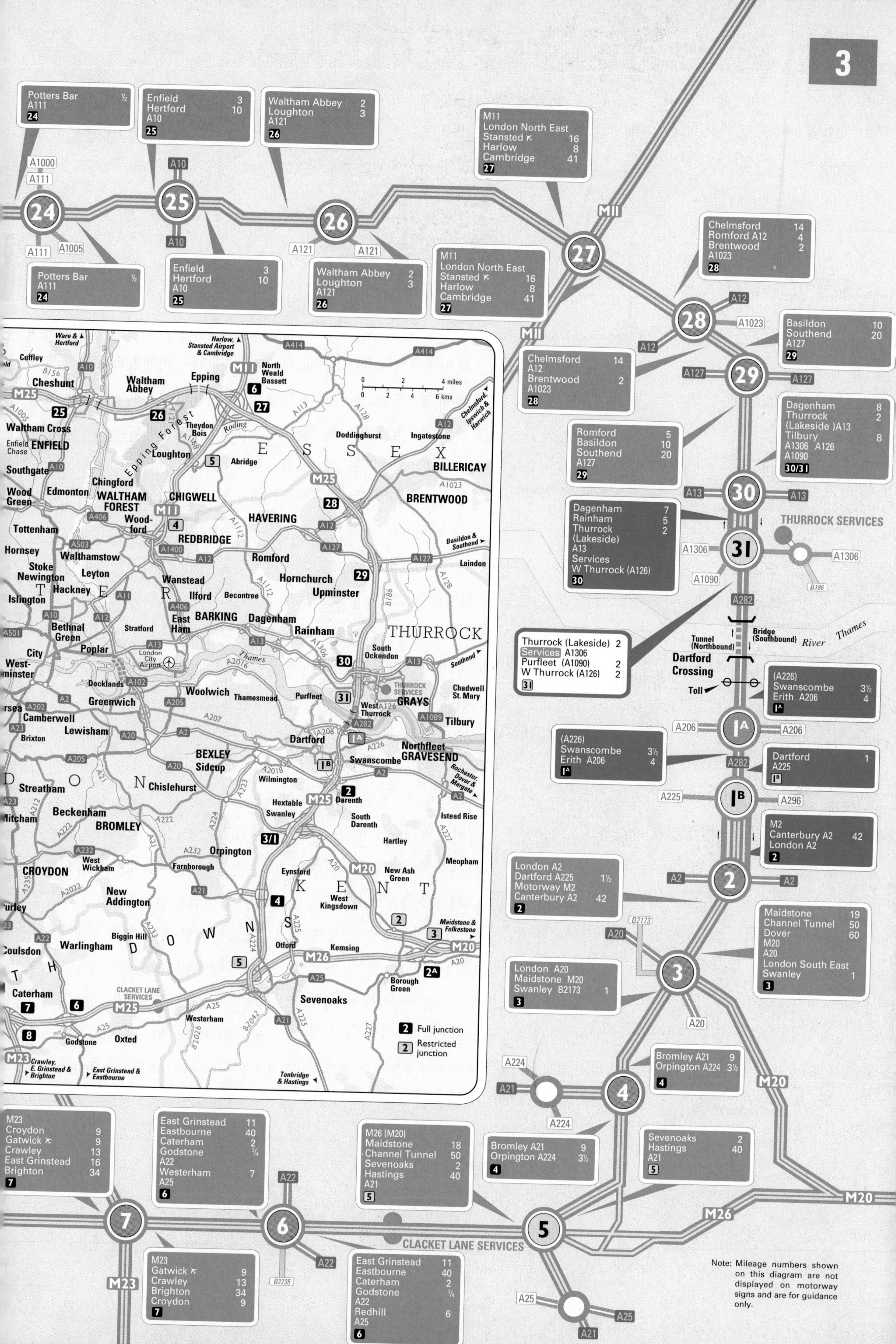

Potters Bar ½ A111 24
Enfield 3 Hertford 10 A10 25
Waltham Abbey 2 Loughton 3 A121 26
M11 London North East Stansted 16 Harlow 8 Cambridge 41 27
A1000
A111
A10
A111
A1005
A121
M11
24
25
26
27
Potters Bar ½ A111 24
Enfield 3 Hertford 10 A10 25
Waltham Abbey 2 Loughton 3 A121 26
M11 London North East Stansted 16 Harlow 8 Cambridge 41 27
Chelmsford 14 Romford A12 4 Brentwood 2 A1023 28
A12
28
A1023
A12
Chelmsford 14 A12 Brentwood 2 A1023 28
Basildon 10 Southend 20 A127 29
A127
29
A127
Dagenham 8 Thurrock 2 (Lakeside) A13 Tilbury 8 A1306 A126 A1090 30/31
Romford 5 Basildon 10 Southend 20 A127 29
A13
30
A13
THURROCK SERVICES
Dagenham 7 Rainham 5 Thurrock 2 (Lakeside) A13 Services W Thurrock (A126) 30
A1306
31
A1306
A1090
B186
A282
Tunnel (Northbound)
Bridge (Southbound)
River Thames
Dartford Crossing
Thurrock (Lakeside) 2 Services A1306 Purfleet (A1090) 2 W Thurrock (A126) 2 31
Toll
(A226) Swanscombe 3½ Erith A206 4 1A
A206
1A
A206
(A226) Swanscombe 3½ Erith A206 4 1A
A282
Dartford 1 A225 1B
A225
1B
A296
M2 Canterbury A2 42 London A2 2
London A2 Dartford A225 1½ Motorway M2 Canterbury A2 42 2
A2
2
A2
Maidstone 19 Channel Tunnel 50 Dover 60 M20 A20 London South East Swanley 1 3
B2173
A20
3
London A20 Maidstone M20 Swanley B2173 1 3
A20
Bromley A21 9 Orpington A224 3½ 4
A224
A21
4
M20
A224
Bromley A21 9 Orpington A224 3½ 4
Sevenoaks 2 Hastings 40 A21 5
M23 Croydon 9 Gatwick 9 Crawley 13 East Grinstead 16 Brighton 34 7
East Grinstead 11 Eastbourne 40 Caterham 2 Godstone ¾ A22 Westerham 7 A25 6
M26 (M20) Maidstone 18 Channel Tunnel 50 Sevenoaks 2 Hastings 40 A21 5
A22
7
6
5
M20
M26
CLACKET LANE SERVICES
M23
A22
B2235
M23 Gatwick 9 Crawley 13 Brighton 34 Croydon 9 7
East Grinstead 11 Eastbourne 40 Caterham 2 Godstone ¾ A22 Redhill 6 A25 6
A25
A25
A21
Note: Mileage numbers shown on this diagram are not displayed on motorway signs and are for guidance only.
Ware & Hertford
Harlow, Stansted Airport & Cambridge
Cuffley
Cheshunt
Waltham Abbey
Epping
North Weald Bassett
0 2 4 miles
0 2 4 6 kms
Chelmsford, Ipswich & Harwich
Waltham Cross
Enfield Chase
ENFIELD
Epping Forest
Theydon Bois
Loughton
Abridge
Doddinghurst
Ingatestone
E S S E X
BILLERICAY
Southgate
Chingford
Wood Green
Edmonton
WALTHAM FOREST
CHIGWELL
BRENTWOOD
Woodford
HAVERING
Tottenham
REDBRIDGE
Basildon & Southend
Hornsey
Walthamstow
Romford
Laindon
Stoke Newington
Leyton
Wanstead
Hornchurch
Islington
Hackney
Ilford
Becontree
Upminster
East Ham
BARKING
Dagenham
Bethnal Green
Stratford
Rainham
THURROCK
City
Poplar
London City Airport
South Ockendon
West-minster
Thames
Southend
Docklands
THURROCK SERVICES
Chadwell St. Mary
Woolwich
Thamesmead
Purfleet
GRAYS
Greenwich
West Thurrock
Tilbury
Camberwell
Lewisham
Dartford
Northfleet
Brixton
BEXLEY
GRAVESEND
Sidcup
Swanscombe
Rochester, Dover & Margate
Streatham
Chislehurst
Wilmington
Darenth
Beckenham
Hextable
Swanley
South Darenth
Istead Rise
BROMLEY
Mitcham
Hartley
Orpington
West Wickham
Meopham
CROYDON
Farnborough
Eynsford
New Ash Green
New Addington
K E N T
West Kingsdown
Purley
Biggin Hill
Maidstone & Folkestone
Coulsdon
Warlingham
D O W N S
Otford
Kemsing
Caterham
CLACKET LANE SERVICES
Sevenoaks
Borough Green
Westerham
Godstone
Oxted
Crawley, E. Grinstead & Brighton
East Grinstead & Eastbourne
Tonbridge & Hastings
2 Full junction
2 Restricted junction

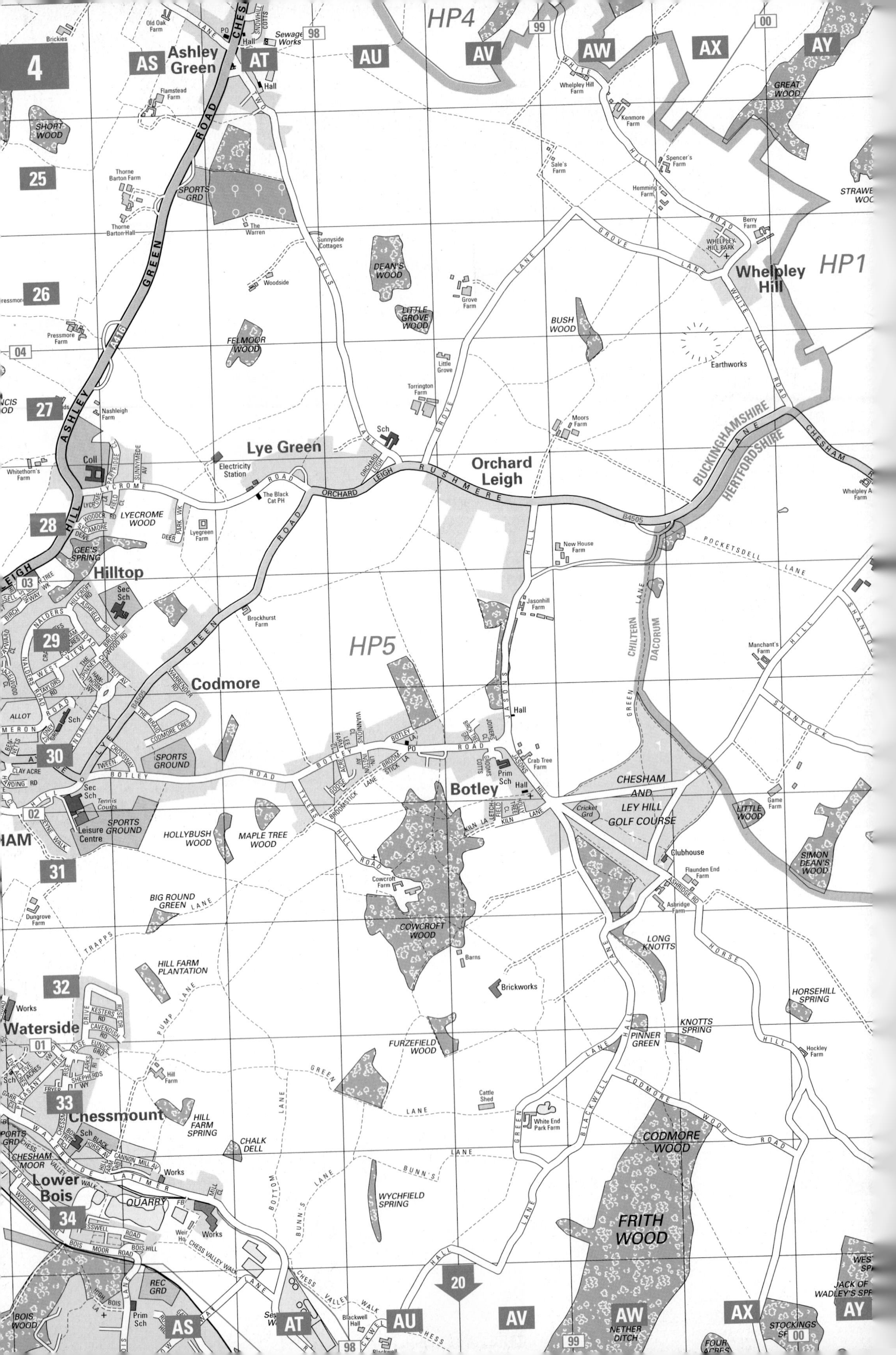
4
Ashley Green
Lye Green
Orchard Leigh
Whelpley Hill
Hilltop
Codmore
Botley
Waterside
Chessmount
Lower Bois
HP4
HP1
HP5
Short Wood
Dean's Wood
Little Grove Wood
Felmoor Wood
Bush Wood
Lyecrome Wood
Gee's Spring
Hollybush Wood
Maple Tree Wood
Cowcroft Wood
Big Round Green
Hill Farm Plantation
Furzefield Wood
Hill Farm Spring
Chalk Dell
Wychfield Spring
Codmore Wood
Frith Wood
Long Knotts
Knotts Spring
Pinner Green
Horsehill Spring
Simon Dean's Wood
Little Wood
Great Wood
Chesham and Ley Hill Golf Course
Buckinghamshire
Hertfordshire
Earthworks
Sports Grd
Sports Ground
Leisure Centre
Rec Grd
Bois Wood
Nether Ditch
20

Bovingdon
Hogpits Bottom
Flaunden
Belsize
HP3
WD4
WD3
H.M. THE MOUNT PRISON
BOX LANE
CHESHAM ROAD
HEMPSTEAD
LONGCROFT LANE
FLAUNDEN LANE
BULSTRODE LANE
TOWER HILL
VENUS HILL
HOGPITS BOTTOM
BRAGMANS LANE
WOODMAN'S WOOD
LOWER PLANTATION
ROSEHALL WOOD
PLOUGH WOOD
DEBARDINE WOOD
SHORTRIDGE WOOD
BURY WOOD
COLESHILL WOOD
HANGING WOOD
TOP SPRING
OLDCROFT WOOD
HANGINGLANE WOOD
PENMAN'S GREEN
Felden
Chipperfield
Sarratt

6
Felden
Apsley
HP3
SHENDISH HOUSE
GOLF COURSE
GREAT
WOOD
SCATTERDELLS
WOOD
Kings
Langley
WD4
Chipperfield
CHIPPERFIELD COMMON
Belsize
Commonwood
Bucks
Hill
WD3
Sarratt
BERRYBUSHES
WOOD
5
22

7
BP
BQ
BR
BS
BT
BU
BV
08
09
10
Highwood Hall Farm
Herts Farm
The Swan PH
POTTERS CROUCH PLANTATION
APPSPOND
LONG DEANS
HP3
Bedmond House
Rose Acre
25
WELLFIELD SPRING
Radio Station
Hyde Meadow Farm
HYDE LANE SPRING
Hyde Springs
Hyde Lane Farm
Hart Hall Farm
Verulam Farm
NEWLANDS
DEADMAN WOOD
Serge Hill
26
NEW PLANTATION
Pimlico House
Hyde Farm
Little Abbots
Hart Hall
Green End Farm
White House Farm
BEDMOND WOOD
White Hart PH
Whitehouse Farm
04
PIECORNER WOOD
HANGING WOOD
27
Bedmond
Hilltop Farm
Bell Inn PH
FURZEFIELD WOOD
JOB'S WOOD
Ninnings Farm
Millhouse Farm
Searches Farm
ASH VIEW MOBILE HOME PARK
MOOR WOOD
BEDMOND PLAYING FIELDS
Prim Sch
LONG SPRING
Poultry Farm
WD5
28
Tenements Farm
Benmore Farm
Glasshouse
GREAT NOTLEY
M25
03
Junction 21 M25
Junction 6A M1
STOWES WOOD
Numbers Farm
Ovaltine Dairy Farm
29
Works
Mansion House Farm
LITTLE NOTLEY
ST. ALBANS THREE RIVERS
LONG WOOD
COVERED RESERVOIR
8
CEM
30
ROUND WOOD
KINGS LANGLEY
Fortunes Farm
BLOOM WOOD
02
Sch
ABBOTS LANGLEY
MANOR HOUSE GROUNDS
Youth Cen
Manor Lo
Garston Manor Rehab. Cen
Sports Centre
31
THE RETREAT
GRAND UNION CANAL
Sch
Clinic
WD25
Junction 20
TANNERS WOOD
LEAVESDEN COUNTRY PARK
32
Garston Manor Sch
Prim Sch
Works
Hall
Health Cen
Prim Sch
01
WOODSIDE STADIUM
Leisure Cen
HILL FARM IND EST
Comm Cen
Prim Sch
PITCH
33
Hunton Bridge
SOUTH WAY PLAYING FLD
Woodside
ALBAN WOOD
WOODSIDE PLAYING FIELDS
Cricket Ground
Leisure Centre
The Kings Head PH
Leavesden Studios
Comm Cen
A405
KINGSWAY (NORTH ORBITAL ROAD)
Langleybury
SPORTS GROUND
THE ROOKERY
Hazelwood
A41
Leavesden Studios
34
Medical Cen
Sec Sch
Home Farm
Leavesden Green
Kingswood
23
Garston
BP
BQ
BR
BS
BT
BU
BV
NORTH WATFORD CEMETERY
STANBOROUGH PARK
WESTERN AVENUE
NORTH WESTERN
08
09
10

8
Potters Crouch
Chiswell Green
AL2
How Wood
Bricket Wood
WD5
WD25
Kingswood
Garston
Meriden
Junction 21A
Junction 21 M25
Junction 6A M1
Junction 6
M1
M25
NORTH ORBITAL ROAD
A405
ST. ALBANS ROAD
WATFORD ROAD
BRICKET WOOD COMMON
MUTCHETTS WOOD
BUILDING RESEARCH ESTABLISHMENT
PENFOLD PARK GOLF COURSE
GARSTON PARK
WOODSIDE STADIUM
WOODSIDE PLAYING FIELDS
THE GDNS OF THE ROSE
BLACKGREEN WOOD
SMUG OAK GREEN BUSINESS CENTRE
Noke Lane Business Centre
The Noke Thistle Hotel
7
24

9
CD
CE
CF
CG
CH
CJ
CK
15
16
17
AL1
AL4
AL2
WD7
WD25
VERULAM GOLF COURSE
NORTH ORBITAL TRADING ESTATE
Sopwell House
Sopwell Home Farm
CHALKDELL WOOD
Hedges Farm
NORTH ORBITAL ROAD
A414
LONDON ROAD
A1081
Aylett Nursery
SHENLEY LANE
VERULAM R.F.C.
COLUMBANS SPORTS GRD
SPORTS GROUND
SPORTS GRD
COPPICE WOOD
Park Street
PARK STREET
Radlett Aerodrome (Disused)
GRAVEL PIT
NAPSBURY HOSPITAL
Napsbury Farm
Tennis Courts
SPORTS GROUND
LONDON COLNEY
MORRIS PLAYING FLD
Prim Sch
Lib
Comm Cen
PARK INDUSTRIAL ESTATE
FROGMORE HOME PARK
Frogmore
RADLETT ROAD
BROAD COLNEY LAKES NATURE RESERVE
Fir Tree Farm
Broad Colney Bridge
River Colne
Superstore
ALL SAINTS PASTORAL CENTRE
The Red Cow PH
M25
VENTURA PARK
QUARRY
COLNEY PARK
Old Parkbury
Works
Colney Street Farm
The George & Dragon PH
Colney Street
Colney Street Bridge
Pumping Sta
SPORTS GRDS
Bowl Grn
Tenn Cts
HARPERBURY HOSPITAL
Harper Lane Rail Depot
Houndswood Farm
The Black Horse PH
RADLETT GOLF RANGE
HOUND'S WOOD
NINE ACRES
Harper Lodge Farm and Stables
Netherwylde Farm
Hill Farm
Wild Farm
Moat
WATLING STREET
A5183
COW BANKS
SHENLEY MANOR
SHENLEY PARK
PORTERS PARK GOLF COURSE
SAND PLANTATION
Cricket Ground
WALLED GDN
Clubhouse
Starveacres
Sewage Works
RADLETT
Pol
Fire Sta
Auriol Farm
10
25
26
27
28
29
30
31
32
33
34
01
02
03
04

CL
CM
CN
CP
CQ
CR
CS
19
20
21
SAND AND
GRAVEL PIT
Highfield Hall
ST. ALBANS
HERTSMERE
Warren Farm
THE WARREN
FREDERICK'S WOOD
WELWYN HATFIELD
HERTSMERE
Tyttenhanger Farm
COPPICE WOOD
(SITE OF SPECIAL SCIENTIFIC INTEREST)
A414 NORTH
LONDON COLNEY BYPASS
A1081
25
26
27
28
29
30
31
32
33
34
GARDEN WOOD
Tyttenhanger House
THE NEW PLANTATION
Coursers Farm
COURSERS ROAD
River Colne
Prim Sch
Rec Cen
Tenn Cts
Works
MORRIS PLAYING FLD
BIG MAYFIELD WOOD
Bowmansgreen Farm
LONDON COLNEY
ALLOT
Works
Lib
Comm Cen
04
AL4
WALSING
WOO
COLLYER ROAD
Prim Sch
BROAD COLNEY LAKES NATURE RESERVE
RIDGEVIEW LODGE
Junction 22
The Bell PH
Superstore
PO
AL2
B5378
03
BELL LANE
ST. ALBANS ROAD
ROUND WOOD
Gordon Hall Building
Tennis Courts
Pav
UNIVERSITY COLLEGE LONDON SPORTS GROUNDS
Tennis Courts
Salisbury Hall
Salisbury Hall Farm
MOAT
DE HAVILLAND MOSQUITO AIRCRAFT MUSEUM
Redwell Wood Farm
REDWE
WOOD
M25
B556
9
LANE
SHENLEYBURY
FARM CLOSE
02
DELL GROVE
Sch
Ridgehill
PACKHORSE LANE
Southridge Animal Centre R.S.P.C.A.
SHENLEYBURY COTTS
ST. ALBANS
HERTSMERE
WD7
RECTORY LANE
COMBE WOOD
COW BANKS
NORTH AVENUE
BLACK LION HILL
Rectory Farm
Shenley Hill Stud Farm
Rabley Park Farm
Rabley Park
FB
Wild Farm
Moat
01
KING CHARLES
SHENLEY MANOR
GRACE AVENUE
PORTERS PARK DRIVE
SHENLEY PARK
The Black Lion PH
Shenley Hill
Catherine Bourne
St. Catherine's Farm
MIMMS LANE
DEEVES HALL
Ravenscroft Court
SPORTS GRD
Shenley
WD6
LITTLERIDGE WOOD
Tenn Cts
Hall
Pol
Prim Sch
WALLED GDN
Cricket Ground
Pav
SPORTS GRD
SAND PLANTATION
BIG PURSLEY WOOD
Ridge Farm
The Garden Nursery
PO
Tokonoma Bonsai
Pursley Farm
CROSSOAKS LANE
Rid
RADLETT
ALLOT
SPORTS GRD
Pav
Cricket Ground
26
LITTLE PURSLEY WOOD
Crossoaks Farm
THE GORSE
Auriol Farm
WOODHALL
CROSS OAKS WOOD

11
12
25
26
27
28
29
30
31
32
33
34
27
CT
CU
CV
CW
CX
CY
CZ
22
23
24
03
04
02
01
A1000
A1(M)
M25
BUSH WOOD
DIXONS HILL ROAD
DIXONS HILL CLOSE
WELHAM MANOR
Sibthorpe Arms PH
Hall
Potterells Farm
Comm Cen
REC GRD
STATION ROAD
Rockwater Nursery
Bell Bar Nursery
M.K.M. Nurseries
Nursery
BULLS LANE
THE LEGG
PELPIN'S WOOD
ROUND WOOD
Tennis Courts
Clubhouse
Home Farm
Sec Sch
BROOKMANS PARK GOLF COURSE
BROOKMANS PARK
GOLF CLUB ROAD
PEPLINS WY
PEPLINS CL
PEPLINS WAY
BRADMORE WAY
Prim Sch
PO
Lib
BRAD GRN
BROOKMANS AVENUE
MOFFATS LANE
MOFFATS CL
GEORGE'S
CALDER
THE GR
GOBIONS OPEN SPACE
GOBIONS GARDEN
GOBIONS POND
WESTLAND DRIVE
OAKLANDS AVENUE
BLUEBRIDGE ROAD
BLUEBRIDGE AV
THE GARDENS
Blue Bridge
AL9
Deep Bottom
SWALLOW HOLE
TH MYMMS PARK
North Mymms Park Training Centre
Cricket Club
Cricket Ground
Home Farm
Water End
SWANLAND ROAD
WARRENGATE ROAD
BRADMORE LANE
BRICK KILN WOOD
WISE'S LANE
Pumping Sta
CANGSLEY WOOD
Royal Veterinary College (Hawkshead House)
HAWKSHEAD LANE
Hawkshead Bridge
HAWKSHEAD ROAD
Royal Veterinary College
WELWYN HATFIELD
HERTSMERE
HAWKSHEAD WOOD
MYMMSHALL WOOD
Pav
Tennis Courts
SPORTS GROUND
PILVAGE WOOD
Site of Motte & Baileys
Mimmshall Brook
POTTERS BAR GOLF COURSE
Depot
CRANBORNE ROAD
Works
FURZEFIELD WOOD
KING GEORGE V PLAYING FLDS
CRANBORNE INDUSTRIAL ESTATE
Sports Cen
SPORTS GRD
Clubho
Warrengate Farm
Mimms Hall Farm
WARRENGATE LANE
Cricket Ground
GRN MEADOW
THE HEATH
MANOR
WESTWOOD CL
THE AVENUE
Clubhouse
MOUNT
MANOR ROAD
BILLY
RITZ COURT
PARK DR
MUTTON LANE
B556
WINDMORE AV
DEEPDENE
TEMPLE COURT
Widmore Hall
WROXHAM GARDENS
Prim Sch
CAMBRIDGE DRIVE
OULTON CRES
ORMESBY DR
OULTON CRES
SUFFOLK RD
BOROUGH WAY
MIMMS HALL ROAD
Comm Cen
Superstore
LAUREL FIELDS
NEVILLE
CLIVE CLOSE
STATION CLOSE
DARKES
LADBROOKE DRIVE
POTTERS BAR
POTTERS BAR
METRO
Comm Cen
THE CLOSE
BIRCH
GROVE
EN6
AUCKLAND
KIMPTONS MEAD
KIMPTONS CL
SHILLITOE AVENUE
RUSHFIELD
UPDALE CL
BROOKLANDS GDNS
ALLANDALE
SHERWOOD AVENUE
DRAYTON AV
ELMSCROFT GDNS
ABERDALE GARDENS
HEATHER WAY
WESTON CL
THE DRIVE
ALLOT
DALESIDE DR
FAIRACRES CL
ELMROYD
SUNNYBANK
THE BYWAY
BRACKEN
AVENUE
ELMFIELD ROAD
SANTERS
THE SHRUBLANDS
OAKROYD AVENUE
Fire Sta
Amb Sta
War Meml
CEM
Town Farm
Catherine Bourne
CECIL ROAD
BROOKSIDE
GOWAR FLD
BLANCHE LANE
South Mimms
Prim Sch
ST. GILES AV
ST ALBANS ROAD
GREYHOUND LANE
HAMILTON
Bignell's Corner
Depot
Bridgefoot
Bridgefoot House
BRIDGEFOOT LANE
Dugdale Hill
DUGDALE HILL
Sec Sch
Rydal Mount
Rydal Mount Stables
BAKER STREET
SAWYERS LANE
Prim Sch
Prim Schs
THE GREENWAY
FIELD VIEW RD
MEADOW WAY
SUNNYBANK RD
WASH LA
Forte Posthouse South Mimms
Depot
South Mimms Services
Works
Natl Inst. for Biological Standards & Control
Cancer
Blanche Farm
BLANCHE LANE
ST. ALBANS
Junction 1 A1(M)
BENTLEY HEATH LANE
Elm Farm
Bentley Heath Farm
Bentley Heath
Garden Centre

12
DA
DB
DC
DD
DE
DF
DG
26
27
28
M.K.M. Nurseries
Nursery
Glasshouse
The Cock o' the North PH
Kentish Lane Farm
Barbers Lodge Farm
Water Tower
COV RES
Tenn Cts
Brookmans Park Transmitting Station
THE LEGG
ROUND WOOD
Tennis Courts
Home Farm
Clubhouse
Sec Sch
25
BROOKMANS PARK
GOLF COURSE
GEORGE'S WOOD
BROOKMANS PARK
26
AVENUE
GEORGE'S WOOD ROAD
NORTH ROAD
KENTISH LANE
BROOMBARNS WOOD
COLDHARBOUR PLANTATION
Rowbourne Hill
GREAT
04
GOBIONS OPEN SPACE
GOBIONS GARDEN
GOBIONS POND
27
AL9
Blue Bridge
Deep Bottom
SWALLOW HOLE
GOBIONS WOOD
SHEPHERDS WAY
SPORTS GROUND
Tenn Cen
Tennis Courts
Queenswood Sch
THE RIDGEWAY
GREAT NORTH ROAD
A1000
28
HAWKSHEAD ROAD
SWANLEY BAR LANE
03
Royal Veterinary College (Boltons Park Farm)
LEGGATTS WOOD
Leggatts Park
WELL WOOD
WELL ROAD
NYN POND
THE VINEYARD
29
WELWYN HATFIELD
HERTSMERE
POTTERS BAR
11
GOLF COURSE
30
Cricket Ground
Sch
Prim Sch
SPORTS GRD
JUDGES HILL
NORTHAW PLACE
Northaw House
The Sun PH
Stud Farm
War Meml
Two Brewers PH
Schs
SPORTS GRD
Northaw
Springfield
SPORTS GROUND
Pav
Tennis Courts
02
Sec Sch
Clubhouse
MOUNT GRACE ROAD
31
BILLY LOWS LANE
Morven (NT)
Sch
Chequers PH
EN6
THE CAUSEWAY
COOPERS LANE
Little Heath Riding Stables
FISH POND
HOOK WOOD
Prim Sch
Comm Cen
Works
RITZ COURT
PARKFIELD OPEN SPACE
Pol
Clinic
Lib
Elec Sta
BUS GAR
Superstore
POTTERS BAR
32
POTTERS BAR
OAKMERE PARK
FIVE ACRE WOOD
Prim Sch
Youth & Comm Cen
Oshwal House
Oshwal Centre
FIR WOOD
Cricket Club
Bowls Club
Superstore
Offices
Med Cen
Prim Sch
01
Amb Sta
Fire Sta
War Meml
CEM
ALLOT
ALLOT
HIGH STREET
SOUTHGATE ROAD
33
MUTTON LANE
Hooke Hill
Foxhole Hill
Prim Sch
Prim Schs
Rydal Mount
POND WOOD
WELWYN HATFIELD
HERTSMERE
ENFIELD
POTTERS BAR COMMUNITY HOSP
34
Turkey Brook
THE RIDGEWAY
A1005
New Cottage Farm
Nursery
Prep. Sch
Water Tower
M25
BENTLEY HEATH LANE
Elm Farm
Bentley Heath Farm
Chase Farm
28
Fenny Shade Hill
STAGG HILL
BARNET ROAD
Bentley Heath
Ganwick Corner
Duke of
Plumridge Hill
DA
DB
DC
DD
DE
DF
DG
26
27
28

DH
DJ
DK
DL
DM
DN
DP
29
30
31
GOLF COURSE
Clubhouse
Newgate Street
Boswell's Livery Stables
Ponsbourne Riding Centre
LONG GROVE
DERRYS WOOD
BAISLEY WOOD
CALVES CROFT
Turnford Brook
Cuffley Brook
NEW PARK ROAD
Sch
Hall
REC GRD
Tenn Cts
Home Farm
Tolmers Park Farm
Tolmers Park
St. Lawrence Farm
Tanfield Stud Farm
SG13
VILLAGE STREET
DARNICLE HILL
Darnicle Hill Nursery
Newgate Street Bridge
HAMMOND STREET
25
26
27
28
29
30
31
32
33
34
04
03
02
01
SHAMBROOK
RICHARDSON CRES
GLADDING ROAD
EVERETT CL
LOVERING RD
BLOOMFIELD ROAD
MARKHAM ROAD
WILKINSON CL
BURGES CL
DAHLIA CL
Postern Bridge
Justice Hill
WOOD
Grimes Bottom
Cuffley Camp
FB
Burleigh Farm
NEWGATE STREET ROAD
Ashfield Nurseries
Nursery
Theobold Nursery
Tolmers Scout Camp
WORMLEY WOOD
HOME WOOD
TOLMERS ROAD
CARBONE HILL
HOMEWOOD LA
Carbone Bottom
BROOKSIDE
HOMEWOOD
CRESCENT
TOLMERS AVENUE
BRADGATE
FARM CL
WARWICK AV
COULTER CL
BRADGATE CL
HANYARDS LANE
THE RIDGEWAY
RIDGEWAY
HANDPOST HILL ROAD
SUTHERLAND AV
SUTHERLAND WY
THE DRIVEWAY
TOLMERS RISE
ORCHARD CL
HILL LEYS
THRUSH LANE
STARLING LA
OAK LA
ACORN LA
THE MEADWAY
CHESHUNT COMMON
CHILTERN CL
ORCHARD WY
Prim Sch
WOODLAND WY
MILLCREST ROAD
ROBINSON AVENUE
NEWGATE STREET
ROBINSON AVENUE
THE CHASE
THE DRIVE
BEEHIVE
OAKTREE CL
GOFF OAK AV
CROUCH LANE
Elm Farm
Rosebury Farm
Springfield Nursery
Weald View Nursery
Rags Brook
Westgate Nursery
Longmead Nursery
JAMES
The Goff's Oak PH
SPORTS GRD
Pav
Tenn Cts
Hall
Lib
PO
WESLEY CL
ISABELLE CL
DOVERFIELD
MYLES
GOFFS
Thornton's Farm
Hempshill Brook
Cuffley Hills Farm
CRANFIELD CRES
BACONS DR
KINGSMEAD
PLOUGH HILL
Health Cen
Hall
Lib
Cuffley
TOLMERS GDNS
CUFFLEY
KING JAMES AV
CHURCH CL
STATION ROAD
PO
CUFFLEY ROAD
B156
Youth Cen
Brook Farm
SOPERS ROAD
Works
JAMES AVENUE
LAMBS CL
PEMBROKE DRIVE
MOORHURST AV
ULWORTH
GREEN WY
AVENUE
BROADFIELDS
POLLARDS
Goffs Oak
Prim Sch
14
Poynden Farm
Theobalds
EN7
SILVER STREET
KINGSWELL RIDE
BURLEIGH WAY
KINGSWELL
COLESDALE
THEOBALDS ROAD
SOUTH DR
Prim Sch
EAST RIDGEWAY
WELWYN HATFIELD
BROXBOURNE
Cuffley Brook
Pumping Sta
Tenn Club
KING GEORGE'S FIELD
Clubho
Wells Farm
Coles Hill
Colesdale Farm
WEST ROAD
NORTHAW ROAD
NORTHAW BROOK
Soper's Viaduct
JONES ROAD
BURNT FARM RIDE
Burnt Farm
OLD PARK
(PRIVATE ROAD)
CATTLINS
DYSONS OSIERS
CATTLEGATE HILL
NURSERY PLANTATION
Northaw Brook
CATTLEGATE WOOD
Robin Hill
WOODGATE AV
OAKWELL DR
COOPERS LANE ROAD
Cattlegate Farm
Cattlegate
Barvin Hill
EN2
Woodhurst Farm
TILEKILN OSIERS
HERTFORDSHIRE
M25
CINDER ASH
Turkey Brook
Owls Hall Farm
The Paddocks
Glasshouse
South Hill
CATTLEGATE ROAD
Oak Hill Farm
Glasgow Stud
Garden Centre
Culver Garden Centre
Country World
CREWS HILL
Turkey Brook
BURNT FM RIDE
Nursery
Sloeman's Farm
Holly Hill Farm
Clubhouse
Woldens Nursery & Garden Centre
Browns of Crews Hill Nurseries
WHITEWEBBS ROAD
29
CREWS HILL GOLF COURSE
THEOBALDS
ROSEWOOD DR
WROXHAM GDNS
BEECH
CYPRESS AV
GOLF RIDE
Kings Oak Riding Stables
Crews Hills
WHITEWEBBS WOOD
WHITEWEBBS
Holy Brook
THE
LODGE

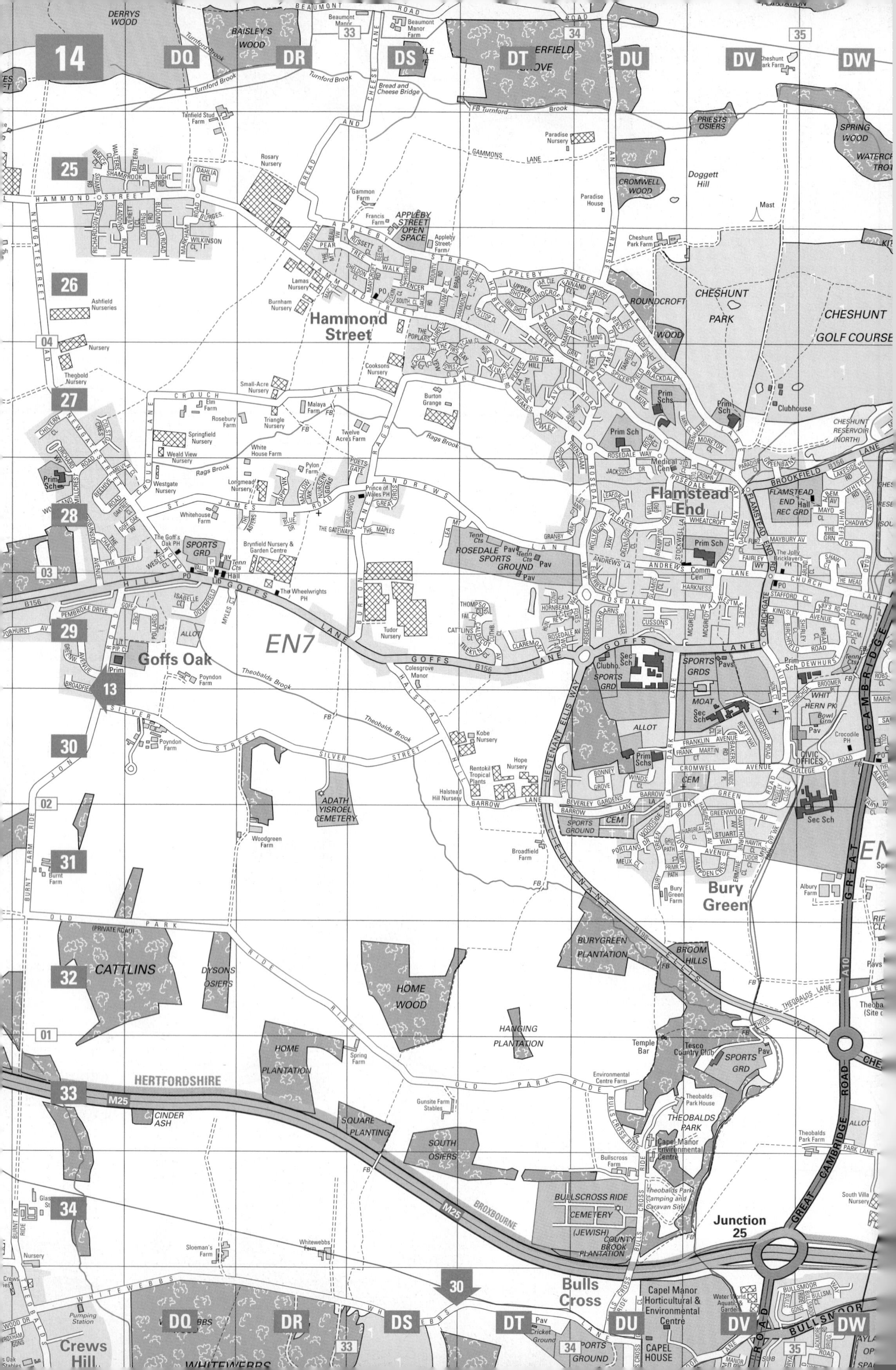

14
DQ
DR
DS
DT
DU
DV
DW
Hammond Street
Flamstead End
Goffs Oak
Bury Green
EN7
Bulls Cross
Crews Hill
CHESHUNT PARK
CHESHUNT GOLF COURSE
CATTLINS
HOME WOOD
HOME PLANTATION
HANGING PLANTATION
THEOBALDS PARK
BULLSCROSS RIDE CEMETERY (JEWISH)
HERTFORDSHIRE
BROXBOURNE
M25
Junction 25
13
30

15
Wormley
EN10
Turnford
Turnford Place
Cheshunt Marriott Hotel
College
NAZEING MARSH
Kings Weir
Turnford Marsh
Aquaduct Lock
HOLYFIELD LAKE
LEE VALLEY PARK
Sailing Club
Weir
Clayton Hill
Paynes Farm Nursery
Langridge Nursery
Larksmead Nursery
St. Leonards Farm
Netherkidd Farm
COLEMAN'S LANE
COLEMAN'S SHAW
Coach & Horses PH
Holyfield Marsh
Holyfield Hill Farm
Elec Station
THE NIGHTLEYS
NORTH METROPOLITAN PIT
SEVENTY ACRES
Hayes Hill Farm
Hayes Hill
Holyfield
North Lodge Farm
GALLEYHILL WOOD
Peartree Farm
Marsh
Grubbs Hill
HOMEFIELD WOOD
CHESHUNT LAKE
Turnershill Marsh
Holyfield Fishery
Holyfield Farm
EN9
Monkhams Hall
KENNEL WOOD
Nightingales
16
Young Mariners Base
Hooks Marsh
Thistly Marsh
CHESHUNT
Poultry Farm
Cheshunt Junction
Waltham Common Lock
WALTHAM ABBEY WOODS
LEE VALLEY PARK
Hall Marsh
Hall Marsh Scrape
BOWYER'S WATER
Cornmill Meadows
Mile Nursery
Langley Nursery
Lea Valley Nursery
Abbey View Nursery
CROOKED MILE
Crooked Mile Roundabout
GRUNDY PARK
HOSP
Marsh Bridge
Waltham Marsh
WALTHAM CROSS
Cheshunt Marsh
Britannia Nursery
Waltham Lock
Small Lee Bridge
HERTFORDSHIRE
ESSEX
BROXBOURNE
EPPING FOREST
WALTHAM ABBEY (Ruins)
ABBEY GARDENS
TOWN HALL
Abbey View Roundabout
LWR ISLAND
TOWN MEAD
LARSENS REC GRD
Waltham Abbey FC
Swim Pool
SPORTS GROUND
Holdbrook
Freezy Water
M25
31
RAMMEY MARSH
Sewardstone Roundabout
Quinton Hill Farm
Cobbin's Brook
DX DY DZ EA EB EC ED
36 37 38
25 26 27 28 29 30 31 32 33 34
01 02 03 04

16
EE
EF
EG
EH
EJ
EK
EL
Bumble's Green
Nazeing Gate
NAZEINGWOOD COMMON
Holyfield
Aimes Green
EN9
Upshire
Copthall Green
WALTHAM ABBEY
WARLIES PARK
GALLEYHILL WOOD
DEERPARK WOOD
COPY WOOD
STOCKING GROVE
LONGCROFT GROVE
FERNHALL WOOD
BROOKMEADOW WOOD
OXLEYS WOOD
POTKILN WOOD
CONYBURY WOOD
KENNEL WOOD
LONGFIELD SHAW
COLEMAN'S SHAW
BRAMBLY SHAW
STABLE SHAW
MAPLE SPRINGS
BROADGATE SPRINGS
BRAYSHILL SPRING
GALLEYHILL GREEN
THE SPRINGS
COBBIN POND
CLAY PIGEON RANGE
BREACH BARN MOBILE HOME PARK
CLAVERHAMBURY ROAD
WALTHAM LANE
ST. LEONARDS ROAD
HOLYFIELD ROAD
GALLEY HILL
PICK HILL
UPSHIRE ROAD
HORSESHOE HILL
CROWN HILL
LONG STREET
COBBINSEND ROAD
FERNHALL LANE
WOODGREEN ROAD
WOODREDON FARM LANE
SOUTHEND LANE
HONEY LANE
SEWARDSTONE ROAD
M25
A121
15
32
01
02
03
04
25
26
27
28
29
30
31
32
33
34
40
41
42

EM
EN
EP
EQ
ER
ES
ET
43
44
45
Epping Green
EPPING LONG GRN
Prim Sch
Cobbin's Brook
Hayleys Manor Farm
UPLAND ROAD
Pinch Timber Farm
EPPING ROAD
Epping Bury Farm Centre
Hunters Hall Farm
Chambers Manor Farm
EPPING BURY FARM CENTRE NATURE TRAIL
NABHILL GROVE
ORANGE WOOD
BALLHILL WOOD
Gills Farm
Cobbin's Bridge
WINTRY WOOD
ORANGE FIELD PLANTATION
ORANGE PEEL
GILLS PLANTATION
LINDSEY STREET
B181
Bury Farm
Shaftesbury Farm
Elec Sta
SPRATT'S HEDGEROW WOOD
SPRATT'S HEDGEROW
BURY LANE
B182
CM16
POND FIELD PLANTATION
JENKINS'S PLANTATION
BOLT CELLAR LANE
Prim Sch
SPORTS GRD
ALLOT
LITTLE ROOKERY WOOD
FITCHES PLANTATION
EPPING CEM
Sec Sch
EPPING
Halls
Lib
Coll
Prim Sch
Fire Sta
Superstore
Sports Cen
CIVIC OFFICES
HIGH STREET
The Wood House
The White House
Home Farm
Paris Hall
New Farm
COPPED HALL GDNS
Copped Hall (Ruins)
GRIFFIN'S WOOD
Griffin's Wood
Bowls Club
Cricket Ground
Cricket Club
Tenn Cts
Creeds Farm
Post House Hotel
Bell Common
Ivy Chimneys
THE SELVAGE
Cricket Club
BELL COMMON TUNNEL
Forest Gate PH
IVY CHIMNEYS ROAD
Prim Sch
Works
EPPING
THEYDON BOWER
Bower Hill
M25
FB
Warren Wood
THE WARREN
LORETO CONVENT
EPPING THICKS
THE SELVAGE
Great Gregories Farm
Gardners Farm
Lodge
Warren Lodge
Ambresbury Banks
Clubhouse
THEYDON BOIS GOLF COURSE
Little Bronx Livery & Riding Stables
EPPING FOREST
Piercing Hill
LITTLE GREGORIES LANE
Junction 6
Junction 27
Long Running
Coll
Forest Lodge
B1393
18
25
26
27
28
29
30
31
32
33
34
04
03
02
01

33

EU
EV
EW
EX
EY
EZ
FA
25
26
27
28
29
30
31
32
33
34
04
03
02
01
47
48
49
Thornwood
NORTH WEALD AIRFIELD
WEALD HALL LANE SEWAGE WORKS
Thames Water Sewage Treatment Plant
Rugby Ground
Golf Range
DRIVING RANGE
WOODSIDE COMMERCIAL ESTATE
WINTRY WOOD
THE LOWER FOREST
EPPING PLAIN
NORTH WEALD GOLF COURSE
ROUGHTALLEY'S WOOD
GERNON BUSHES
ST. MARGARET'S HOSPITAL
SPENCER CLOSE HOSPITAL
Coopersale
CM16
BIRCHING
COPPICE
POSTERNIANE SPRING
HAWKSHILL WOOD
REDYN'S WOOD
FORTY ACRES
MOUNT QUARTER
ONGAR DOWN
GRAVEL PIT WOOD
Bower Hill
EPPING
Fiddlers Hamlet
Mount End
BEACHET WOOD
Hobbs Cross Road Sewage Works
HOBBS CROSS GOLF CENTRE
THE ROUGH PATCH
Theydon Mount
LONG PLANTATION
ICEHOUSE PLANTATION
BARBER'S WOOD
Junction 6 (M11)
Junction 27 (M25)
M11
M25
17
34

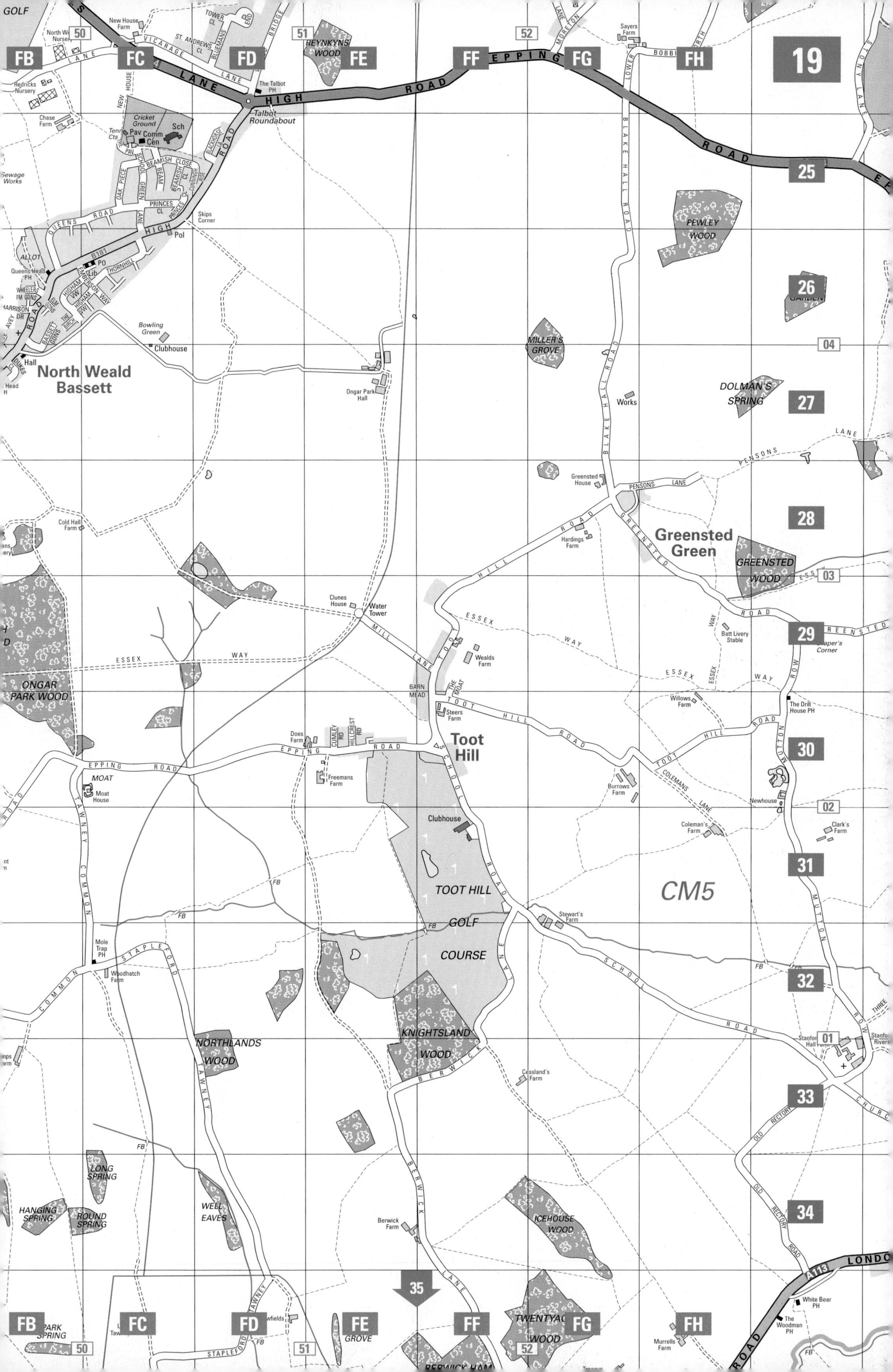

19
North Weald
Bassett
Toot
Hill
Greensted
Green
CM5
TOOT HILL
GOLF
COURSE
KNIGHTSLAND
WOOD
NORTHLANDS
WOOD
ONGAR
PARK WOOD
PEWLEY
WOOD
MILLER'S
GROVE
DOLMAN'S
SPRING
GREENSTED
WOOD
REYNKYNS
WOOD
ICEHOUSE
WOOD
LONG
SPRING
HANGING
SPRING
ROUND
SPRING
WELL
EAVES
HIGH ROAD
EPPING ROAD
BLAKE HALL ROAD
TOOT HILL ROAD
SCHOOL ROAD
SCHOOL LANE
MILL LANE
ESSEX WAY
PENSONS LANE
GREENSTED ROAD
MUTTON ROW
COLEMANS LANE
BERWICK LANE
TAWNEY COMMON
STAPLEFORD TAWNEY
OLD RECTORY ROAD
LOWER BOBBINGWORTH
Talbot Roundabout
The Talbot PH
Water Tower
Clunes House
Ongar Park Hall
Cold Hall Farm
Moat House
Mole Trap PH
Woodhatch Farm
Does Farm
Freemans Farm
Clubhouse
Wealds Farm
Steers Farm
Greensted House
Hardings Farm
Works
Sayers Farm
Batt Livery Stable
Willows Farm
The Drill House PH
Burrows Farm
Coleman's Farm
Newhouse
Clark's Farm
Stewart's Farm
Cessland's Farm
Berwick Farm
Murrells Farm
White Bear PH
The Woodman PH
Skips Corner
Bowling Green
Chase Farm
Redricks Nursery
New House Farm
A113
35
FB FC FD FE FF FG FH
50 51 52
25 26 27 28 29 30 31 32 33 34
04 03 02 01

20
Lower Bois
Chesham Bois
Latimer
Little Chalfont
AS
AT
AU
AV
AW
AX
AY
98
99
00
97
96
4
36
35
37
38
39
40
41
42
43
44
HP5
HP6
HP7
HP8
FRITH WOOD
NETHER DITCH
WESTLAND SPRING
JACK OF WADLEY'S SPRING
STOCKINGS SPRING
FOUR ACRES
STAR CLUMP
TOOLEY'S CROFT
SPORTS GROUND
PARKFIELD WOOD
THE GROVE
RECTORY PLANTATION
Training Centre
CONF CEN
Latimer House
DUCK COVER
Weir
River Chess
Great Water
Latimer Park Farm
LANE WOOD
MARKET READING WOOD
ROUND WOOD
BLACKWELL STUBBS
REC GRD
Sewage Works
Blackwell Hall
Blackwell Farm
Ivy House Farm
Quill Hall Farm
Raans Farm
WYCHFIELD
CHESS VALLEY WALK
LATIMER ROAD
BOIS MOOR ROAD
QUARRY
Works
Weir Ho
WOODSIDE ROAD
A416
A404
A413
WHITE LION ROAD
AMERSHAM ROAD
STATION RD
CHALFONT & LATIMER
WEST WOOD
SPORTS GROUND
Tennis Club
Prim Sch
Sec Sch
Coll
Bendrose Farm
HOBB'S DELL
Little Kimblewick Farm
SNELL'S WOOD
Snell's Farm
LITTLE CHALFONT GOLF COURSE
STONYDEAN WOOD
LOUDHAM'S WOOD
Burton's Farm
BURTON'S WOOD
Nightingales
Five Diamonds
DOGGETT'S WOOD
NIGHTINGALES WOOD
Rowood Farm
Offices
Clubhouse
The Gate House
The Sheiling
POLLARDS WOOD
Pollards Park House
Elmswell House
SPORTS GROUND
Warren Farm
BAILEY WOOD
HAREWOOD DOWNS GOLF COURSE
The Ivy House PH
Harewood Downs House
STRATTON COPSE
Depot
Coke's Farm
STANLEY WOOD
CEM
WILLOW WOOD
HOVEL WOOD
DAY'S WOOD
HIGH WOOD
BOW WOOD
Lower Bottom House Farm
Upper Bottom House Farm
Vache Farm
LONDON ROAD EAST
LONDON ROAD WEST
BYPASS
STANLEY HILL
River Misbourne
AMERSHAM
Amb Sta
Fire Sta
Youth Club
Comm Cen
Swim Pool
Health Cen
Lib
Cricket Grd
ALLOT
B4442
NIGHTINGALES LANE
The Chequers PH

21
5
22
37
01
02
03
BA
BB
BC
BD
BE
BF
AZ
35
36
37
38
39
40
41
42
43
44
99
98
97
96
HANGING CROFT
PLOUGH WOOD
HILLMEADS SPRING
Moonshine Farm
Great Sarratt Hall Farm
Great Sarratt Hall
Mast
R.A.F. Chenies
DACORUM
THREE RIVERS
TOP SPRING
OLDCROFT WOOD
DAFFODIL SPRING
Sarratt
The Boot PH
Martin Top Farm
BRAMBLE CROFT
HANGINGLANE WOOD
LIMESHILL WOOD
OLDFIELD SPRING
BALDWIN'S WOOD
WALLACE'S WOOD
Valley Farm
DAWES COMMON
Ward's Nurseries
SANDFIELD WOOD
Cricketers Inn PH
Adams Nurseries
Watercress Beds
Moor Cottage
Mill Farm
MOUNT WOOD
River Chess
Chenies Place
ALLOT
End Farm
PLACEHOUSE COPSE
CONEY WOOD
Greathouse Farm
Manor House
Sch
Mountwood Farm
Sarratt Bottom Cottages
NICHOLAS SPRING
Goldingtons
Model Farm
Bedford Arms PH
Chenies
TURVEYLANE WOOD
Weir
SCRUBBS WOOD
BLUNTS WOOD
Football Ground
Chenies Garden Centre
Cricket Ground
Pav
WYBURN WOOD
AMERSHAM ROAD
A404
Sarratmill Bridge
Water Works
MEAD SPRING
Weirs
CHILTON'S WOOD
CHILTERN
OLD HANGING WOOD
Great Greenstreet Farm
Little Greenstreet Farm
WD3
HALSEY'S WOOD
Stubbs Farm
BUCKINGHAMSHIRE
HERTFORDSHIRE
CHENIES ROAD
Sec Sch
Field Study Centre
Tennis Club
DELL WOOD
MILLFIELD PLANTATION
WHITELANDS WOOD
HILLAS WOOD
CARPENTER'S WOOD
CEM
The Gate PH
RICKMANSWORTH ROAD
Highlands Water Gardens
Solesbridge Mill Water Gardens
Prim Sch
LITTLE LADY'S WOOD
Junction 18
White Horse PH
Arts Centre
CHORLEYWOOD COMMON
CHORLEYWOOD GOLF COURSE
Newhouse Farm
Clubhouse
CHORLEYWOOD
The Cedars
HOME WOOD
Black Horse PH
Lib
Chorleywood
CROSSLANE WOOD
Fairfield Farm & Livery Stables
Roughwood Park
Berry Farm
THE SCREEN
SOLOMON'S WOOD
The Hall Farm
West Herts Riding School
PHEASANTS WOOD
Penn Farm
Chorleywood Bottom
The Swillet
Bullsland Farm
Heronsgate
M25

22
Commonwood
Bucks Hill
Sarratt
Loudwater
Junction 19
Junction 18
WD3
WD4
BG
BH
BJ
BK
BL
BM
BN
05
06
07
35
36
37
38
39
40
41
42
43
44
99
98
97
96
6
21
38
Plough Wood
Hillmeads Spring
Commonwood Common
Beechen Bottom
Conference Centre
High Spring
Juniper Hill
Sports Ground
Templepan Wood
Great Wood
Sheepyard Spring
Sawpit Spring
Birch Spring
Dartpath Wood
Scrubbs Wood
Blunts Wood
Willow Wood
Welling Grove
Harrocks Wood
Merlin's Wood
Mead Spring
Beechengrove Wood
Millfield Plantation
Long Spring
Upper Plantation
Round Spring
Waterdell Spring
Little Lady's Wood
Parrot's Dell
Copthorne Wood
Home Wood
Solomon's Wood
Pheasants Wood
The Screen
Rickmansworth Masonic Sch
Chorleywood Road Cemetery
Fortune Common
Croxley Green
Sandfield Wood
M25
A404
Chorleywood Road
Sarratt Road
Red Lion Lane
Church Lane
Dimmocks Lane
Templepan Lane
Chandlers Lane
White Shack Lane
Fir Tree
Rousebarn Lane
Redhall Lane
Solesbridge Lane
Loudwater Lane
Scots Hill
Sports Ground
River Chess
Chess Valley Walk
Great Sarratt Hall
Ward's Nurseries
Adams Nurseries
Green End Farm
Micklefield Hall
Micklefield Hall Farm
Mickleford Green Farm
New Model Farm
Newhall Farm
Buckshill Bottom
Little Westwood Farm
Great Westwood Farm
Yew Court Farm
Potten's Farm
Stevens Nurseries
Chandler's Farm
Clarendon Arms PH
Country Place
Blacketts Nurseries
Cottage Farm
Redhall Farm
Coltspring Riding Stables
Coltyard Farm
York Ho Sch
Model Farm
Waterdell House
Thurlwood House
Croxley House
Killingdown Farm
Whitestocks Farm
Walden Lodge
Loudwater House
Loudwater Farm
Glen Chess
Mont Au Source
Highlands Water Gardens
Solesbridge Mill Water Gardens
Watercress Beds
Sarrattmill Bridge
Water Works
Weir
Weirs
Black Horse PH
White Horse PH
The Gate PH
Cricketers Inn PH
The Boot PH
Coach & Horses PH
Artichoke PH
Scotsbridge PH
Prim Sch
Sec Sch
Sch
Hall
Pav
Clubhouse
Hockey Grd
Playing Field
Cricket Grd
Berry Farm
West Herts Riding School
Rickmansworth Park
Rickmansworth
Baldwins Lane Recreation Ground
Baytree Farm
Bucks Hill Farm
Model Farm
Dellfield
Sarratt Bottom Cottages
Poultry Houses
White House
The Grove Lodge
Sheepcote Spring
Dell Wood

Langleybury
THE ROOKERY
BP
BQ
BR
BS
BT
BU
BV
08
09
10
7
Leavesden Green
Kingswood
Garston
HEATH WOOD
GROVE
PARK
PLAYING FIELD
Hunton Bridge Interchange
M25 LINK ROAD
NORTH WESTERN AVENUE
NORTH WESTERN AV
HEMPSTEAD ROAD
NORTH ORBITAL ROAD
KINGSWAY
THREE RIVERS
WATFORD
WD24
NORTH WATFORD
NORTH WATFORD CEMETERY
STANBOROUGH PARK
CALLOWLAND REC GRD
CHESLYN GDNS
CHARLOTTE'S VALE
ROUGH WOOD
SPORTS GROUND
WHIPPENDELL WOOD
WEST HERTFORDSHIRE GOLF COURSE
Jacotts Hill
CASSIOBURY PARK
PADDLING POOLS
Watercress Beds
GRAND UNION CANAL
River Gade
THE COLOSSEUM
TOWN HALL
WATFORD
WD17
WATFORD JUNCTION
WATFORD NORTH
MOWAT INDUSTRIAL EST
EMPIRE CENTRE
Harlequin Centre
Charter Place
WATFORD HIGH STREET
WEST WATFORD
VICARAGE RD CEMETERY
WATFORD GENERAL HOSP
WATFORD FC
WATFORD STADIUM HALT (MATCH DAYS ONLY) (Closed)
WATFORD WEST (Closed)
WD18
Holywell
HOLYWELL IND EST
CROXLEY GREEN (Closed)
CROXLEY
DURRANTS SPORTS GROUND
LONG VALLEY WOOD
COMMON MOOR
KING GEORGE V PLAYING FIELDS
Electricity Transmission Station
WATFORD FIELDS
OXHEY PARK
WOLSEY BUSINESS PARK
MOOR PARK
RICKMANSWORTH ROAD
WATFORD ROAD
ST. ALBANS ROAD
BEECHEN GROVE
EXCHANGE RD
WIGGENHALL ROAD
EASTBURY ROAD
DEACONS HILL
A41
A411
A412
A4178
A4145
A4125
A405
24
35
36
37
38
39
40
41
42
43
44
96
97
98
99

24
BW
BX
BY
BZ
CA
CB
CC
8
12
13
14
GARSTON PARK
CRAB WOOD
PEARTREE WOOD
MUNDEN SPRING
HERTSMERE
Munden House
Garston
NORTH WATFORD CEMETERY
STANBOROUGH PARK
Meriden
River Colne
University of Hertfordshire
ALDENHAM GOLF COURSE & COUNTRY CLUB
HERTSMERE
WATFORD
WESTERN AVENUE
NORTH WESTERN AVENUE
(COLNE WAY)
NORTH WATFORD
JACK NICKLAUS GOLF CENTRE
Junction 5
Berrygrove Interchange
Aldenham
Round Bush
WD25
MOWAT INDUSTRIAL EST
EMPIRE CENTRE
WATFORD JUNCTION
23
ELTON WAY (NORTH WESTERN AVENUE)
(OTTERSPOOL WAY)
Watford Hilton National Hotel
HartSpring Leisure Cen
The David Lloyd Club
WINFIELD MOBILE HOME PARK
Three Compasses PH
Patchetts Equestrian Centre
Delrow House
Holland Farm
WD17
RADLETT ROAD PLAYING FIELDS
SCOTTS WOOD
BUSHEY HALL GOLF COURSE
The Purcell School
METROPOLITAN POLICE BUSHEY SPORTS GROUND
BUSHEY JEWISH CEMETERY
PLAYING FIELD
The Lincolnsfields Centre
SPORTS GROUND
The U.S. International University-Europe
WD23
West Herts Coll
ICEDALE WOODS
Harlequin Centre
WATFORD HIGH STREET
WATFORD GENERAL HOSP
VICARAGE RD CEMETERY
Colne Valley Water Company
Gas Works
OXHEY
OXHEY PARK
SPORTS GROUND
Wiggenhall Bridge
Council Depot
BURIAL GRD
BUSHEY
BUSHEY GOLF COURSE & COUNTRY CLUB
KING GEORGE REC GROUND
Haydon Hill House
Watford Borough Council Nursery
Watford Equestrian
Open Air Pool
40

25
CD
CE
CF
CG
CH
CJ
CK
15
16
17
9
26
41
35
36
37
38
39
40
41
42
43
44
99
98
97
96
RADLETT
WD7
WD6
Letchmore Heath
ELSTREE
ELSTREE AERODROME
HILFIELD PARK RESERVOIR
ALDENHAM COUNTRY PARK
ALDENHAM RESERVOIR
ALDENHAM PARK WOODLAND
ALDENHAM PARK
THE GORSE
SAND PLANTATION
GOLF COURSE
ELSTREE GOLF COURSE
DRIVING RANGE
COBDEN HILL
WATLING STREET
WATFORD ROAD
ELSTREE ROAD
BARNET LANE
ALLUM LANE
THEOBALD STREET
SHENLEY HILL
TYLERS WAY (NORTH WESTERN AV)
M1
A5183
A411
KENDAL WOOD
LITTLE KENDALS WOOD
MOSES DELL
COBDENHILL DELL
WELLHOUSE DELL
SCRUBBITTS WOOD
FIR SPRING
Tabard R.F.C.
Radlett Cricket Club
Tenn & Squash Club
The Haberdasher's Aske's Sch for Boys
The Haberdasher's Aske's Sch for Girls
Aldenham Sch
Lister Institute
Sewage Works
Flying Club
Hangars
Boathouse
DAM
Sailing Club
Elstree Hill Open Space
Edgwarebury Hotel
Centennial Park
Convent
Bhaktivedanta Manor
Three Horseshoes PH
Battle Axes PH
Waggon & Horses PH
Medburn Bridge
Hertsmere Council Cemetery
Clubhouse
Prim Sch
Prep Sch
Starveacres
Woodhall Farm
Organ Hall Farm
Kendal Hall Farm
Little Kendals Farm
Battlers Green Farm
Hilfield Farm
Hilfield Castle
Caldecote Farm
Berkeley Cottage
Gas Pumping Sta

BOREHAMWOOD
ELSTREE
Green Street
Well End
WD7
WD6
BIRCH WOOD
BIG PURSLEY WOOD
LITTLE PURSLEY WOOD
CROSS OAKS WOOD
SCRATCH WOOD
FROGHALL WOOD
DEACONS HILL OPEN SPACE
ABERFORD PARK
MEADOW PARK
RIPON PARK
KING GEORGES PLAYING FLD
AYCLIFFE ROAD PITCHES
SPORTS GROUND
B.B.C. Elstree Studios
De Havilland College
Metropolis Centre
Boulevard 25 Retail Park
HERTSMERE BOROUGH COUNCIL CEMETERY
ELSTREE & BOREHAMWOOD
A5135
A411
A1 BARNET BY-PASS
BARNET LANE
Stirling Corner
CL
CM
CN
CP
CQ
CR
CS
35
36
37
38
39
40
41
42
43
44
19
20
21
96
97
98
99

10
25
42

27
CT
CU
CV
CW
CX
CY
CZ
11
43
M25
Junction 23
(M25)
Junction 1
A1(M)
South Mimms
Dancers Hill
Bentley Heath
WROTHAM PARK
DYRHAM PARK GOLF COURSE
DYRHAM PARK
BRIDGEDOWN GOLF COURSE
OLD FOLD MANOR GOLF COURSE
Kitt's End
Monken Hadley
Battle of Barnet 1471
EN5
High Barnet
Hadley
BARNET
CHIPPING BARNET
BARNET GENERAL HOSP
WROTHAM PARK OPEN SPACE
ARKLEY LANE OPEN SPACE
ARKLEY GOLF COURSE
ARKLEY RISE ESTATE OPEN SPACE
Arkley
Barnet Gate
WHITINGS HILL OPEN SPACE
Ducks Island
GRANGE PLAYING FIELDS
KING GEORGE'S FIELD
Underhill
KING GEORGE V PLAYING FIELDS
SOUTH HERTS GOLF
N20
HERTFORDSHIRE
HERTSMERE
BARNET
28
35
36
37
38
39
40
41
42
43
44
22
23
24
96
97
98
99

28
DA
DB
DC
DD
DE
DF
DG
M25
Junction 24
12
POTTER COMMUNITY HOSP
THE RIDGEWAY
A1005
WELWYN HATFIELD
ENFIELD
POND WOOD
New Cottage Farm
Nursery
Prep. Sch
Water Tower
Fenny Shade Hill
CHASE WOOD
Chase Farm
FIR WOOD
Plumridge Hill
PLUMRIDGE WOOD
Plumridge Farm
35
Bentley Heath
Bentley Heath Farm
Elm Farm
Garden Centre
Ganwick Corner
Duke of York PH
Pav
Cricket Ground
Mausoleum
36
Wrotham Park
Tennis Courts
Open Air Pool
WROTHAM PARK
99
37
Home Farm
38
Three Oak Hill
Hornbeam Hills
HERTFORDSHIRE
Cockshot Hill
Deadman's Bottom
Ganwick Farm
SPOILBANK WOOD
HERTSMERE
Salmon's Brook
Slopers Pond Farm
STAGG HILL
A111
WAGGON ROAD
NORTH ROAD
A1000
ENFIELD
West Lodge Park Hotel
BARTRAMS QUASH
CLAREMONT ROAD
COURTLEIGH AV
KINGWELL ROAD
Monken Mead Brook
Tenn Club
Prim Sch
HADLEY WOOD
LANCASTER AVENUE
CRESCENT WEST
CRESCENT EAST
Great Broadgates Hill
BEECH HILL
FERNY HILL
Ferny Hill Farm
Clubhouse
BEECH HILL PARK
HADLEY WOOD GOLF COURSE
FERNYHILL WOOD
Green Brook
FISH PONDS
Sewit's Hill
COVERT WAY OPEN SPACE
EN4
BEECH HILL LAKE
COCKFOSTERS ROAD
Water Tower
OAK WOOD
COV RES
Monument
98
HADLEY HIGHSTONE
39
Monken Hadley
Battle of Barnet 1471
27
Rectory Farm
Jun Sch
War Memorial
CAMLET WAY
Bournwell Hill
MONKEN HADLEY COMMON
Priddeon's Hill
Newman's Hill
40
HADLEY GREEN
Hadley
97
BAKERS HILL
THE TUDOR GOLF COURSE
TUDOR SPORTS GRD
KING GEORGE'S FIELD
41
BARNET
EN5
Sec Sch
Prim Sch
Middlesex Uni
GAMES ROAD
SPORTS GROUND
SPORTS GROUND
Gas Works
VICTORIA REC GRD
BARNET TRADING EST
THE OLD BULL ARTS CEN
Barnet Coll
Sports Cen
42
HIGH BARNET
Sec Sch
MEADWAY
POTTERS ROAD
NEW BARNET
EAST BARNET ROAD
STATION ROAD
A110
COCKFOSTERS
TRENT PARK CEM
CHIPPING BARNET
96
BARNET HILL
GREAT NORTH ROAD
A1000
NEW BARNET
Fire Sta
43
BARNET FC
Clubhouse
Underhill SPORTS GROUND
Cinema
BROOKHILL ROAD
CAT HILL
A110
Middlesex Uni
Sec Sch
Prim Sch
LONGMORE AVENUE
B193
44
BARNET PLAYING FIELDS
KING GEORGE V PLAYING FIELDS
WYATTS FARM OPEN SPACE
EAST BARNET
OAK HILL PARK
Oak Hill Theological Coll
Bandstand
Miniature Golf Course
Bowl Grn
Sec Sch
OAKLEIGH PARK
44
26
27
28
SOUTH HERTS GOLF
OAKLANDS ROAD

M25
29
30
31
DH
DJ
DK
DL
DM
DN
DP
13
South Hill
CATTLEGATE
Turkey Brook
CREWS HILL
Glasgow Stud
Oak Hill Farm
Garden Centre
Culver Garden Centre
Country World
BURNT FM RIDE
Sloeman's Farm
Holly Hill Farm
Clubhouse
ROAD
Nursery
Woldens Nursery & Garden Centre
Browns of Crews Hill Nurseries
WHITEWEBBS
Pumping Station
35
CREWS HILL GOLF COURSE
Woldens Nurseries
Crews Hills
WHITEWEBBS PARK
Holyhill Brook
THE RIDGEWAY
BEECH AV
ROSEWOOD DR
CYPRESS AV
WROXHAM GDNS
Kings Oak Riding Stables
TINGEYS TOP LANE
Whitewoods Water Garden Centre
Botany Bay
EAST LODGE
WILDWOOD
Pav
Cricket Ground
Kings Oak Plain
Glasshouses
36
SPORTS GROUND
LITTLE BEECHILL WOOD
Hill Side Nursery
Botany Bay Farm
A1005
Works
Prim Sch
99
FLASH
STRAYFIELD ROAD
Brayside Farm
Anglo Aquarium Plant
Cricket Ground
Queenswood Farm
37
Rectory Farm
Turkey Brook
FARM ROAD
Kingswood
Clay Hill
Clay Hill House
Bandstand
CHASE
Rendlesham Viaduct
HILLY FIELDS PARK
Cuckolds Hill
RECTORY
EN2
Park Farms
KING'S OAK PRIVATE HOSPITAL
CHASE FARM HOSPITAL
LAVENDER HILL CEMETERY
38
CAMLET MOAT
HADLEY ROAD
Royal Chace Hotel
Parkside Farm
Pumping Station
OAK AVENUE
ALLOT
MOAT WOOD
Camlet Hill
RIDE WOOD
Vicarage Farm
Amb Sta
98
Leeging Beech Gutter
RIDGE CREST
LAVENDER HILL
GORDON HILL
39
Salmon's Brook
SPORTS GROUND
FISH POND
WILLIAMS WOOD
ICEHOUSE WOOD
Hog Hill
30
Holtwhites Hotel
Middlesex University
NUFFIELD HOSP
40
SHAWS WOOD
THE RIDGEWAY
CHASE GREEN
TRENT PARK GOLF COURSE
SPORTS GROUND
SNAKES LANE
ALLOT
Merryhills Brook
SLADES HILL
WINDMILL HILL
A110
97
41
CHASE GRN GDNS
Triangular WOOD
ENFIELD ROAD
World's End
ENFIELD CHASE
South Lodge Farm
Trent Park Equestrian Centre
Prim Sch
ENFIELD GOLF COURSE
Clubhouse
SPORTS GROUND
BOXER'S LAKE
42
TOWN PARK
Clubhouse
OAKWOOD
Sec Sch
Prim Sch
CHEYNE WALK
GRANGE PARK
96
BUSH HILL PARK GOLF COURSE
43
SPORTS GROUND
N21
PRIORY
Sch Clinic
OAKWOOD PARK
Pitch 'n' Putt
OAKWOOD
YACHTING POND
Hillel Sch
44
Salmon's Brook
Hounsden Gutter
Chaseside Works
45
Sch
ALLOT
N14
WINCHMORE HILL
Bowling Green
Tenn Cts
GREEN DRAGON LANE
RIDGE AVENUE
GREEN LANES
Tenn & Squash Club

30
DQ
DR
DS
DT
DU
DV
DW
33
34
35
14
M25
Junction 25
BULLSCROSS RIDE
CEMETERY (JEWISH)
COUNTY BROOK PLANTATION
Bulls Cross
Capel Manor Horticultural & Environmental Centre
CAPEL HOUSE
Crews Hill
WHITEWEBBS WOOD
WHITEWEBBS PARK
WHITEWEBBS GOLF COURSE
White Webbs House
SPORTS GROUND
EN2
Clay Hill
HILLY FIELDS PARK
BRAMLEY HOUSE
Forty Hill
FORTY HALL COUNTRY PARK
FORTY HALL & MUSEUM
GOUGH PARK
Bullsmoor
CEMETERY
Crematorium
TURKEY STREET
ENFIELD CEMETERY (JEWISH)
QUEEN ELIZABETH STADIUM
EN1
ENFIELD PLAYING FIELDS
ENFIELD
BASEBALL GROUND
ENFIELD TOWN
ENFIELD CHASE
ENFIELD RETAIL PK
SOUTHBURY ROAD
GREAT CAMBRIDGE ROAD
A10
A110
A105
A1010
HERTFORD ROAD
MARTINBRIDGE INDUSTRIAL ESTATE
Middlesex University
BUSH HILL PARK
BUSH HILL PARK GOLF COURSE
TOWN PARK
GRANGE PARK
N21
JUBILEE PARK
ST. GEORGE'S FIELD
Enfield Coll
29
35
36
37
38
39
40
41
42
43
44
46
96
97
98
99

DX
DY
DZ
EA
EB
EC
ED
36
37
38
15
Holdbrook
WALTHAM CROSS
ELEANOR CROSS RD
MONARCH'S WAY
QUEENSGATE
SPORTS GRD
LWR ISLAND
MEAD
Depot
ABBEY MEAD IND PK
CEM
SPORTS GRD
Waltham Abbey FC
Swim Pool
SPORTS GROUND
M25
Freezy Water
Works
MOLLISON AVENUE
A1055
RAMMEY MARSH
Cobbin's Brook
LODGE LANE
BEECHFIELD WALK
Quinton Hill Farm
Sewardstone Roundabout
35
EN9
INNOVA BUSINESS PARK
INNOVA WAY
Small River Lee or Lea
River Lee Navigation
36
Darrens Nursery
Beechview Nursery
AVEY LANE
99
Felicia Nursery
Providence Nursery
Enfield Lock
ENFIELD LOCK
ENFIELD
EPPING FOREST
OSIERS
37
SOHAM LANE OPEN SPACE
Prim Sch
Cattlegate Flood Relief Channel
Hawes Lane Nursery
HAWES LANE
Grange Hill Nursery
Sewardstone Nursery
Sewardstone Hall
SEWARDSTONE
The Plough PH
Mott Street Nursery
THOMPSON'S WOOD
38
ALBANY PARK
EN3
Sports Hall
PRINCE OF WALES OPEN SPACE
SEWARDSTONE MARSH
LEE VALLEY PARK
Barnfield Riding Stables
Brookfield Nursery
98
THE ARENA
Elec Sta
Electricity Station
ENFIELD ENERGY CEN
PLAYING FIELD
LEE VALLEY PARK
Pumping Sta
The Royal Oak PH
GODWIN CL
Netherhouse Farm
Hannah Nursery
39
Northfield Nursery
Sewardstone
32
BLIND LANE
BRIMSDOWN INDUSTRIAL ESTATE
KING GEORGE'S RESERVOIR
Chapelfield Nursery
Barn Hill
Marshfield Nursery
Luthers Farm
40
FERNHILL WOOD
BRIMSDOWN SPORTS GROUND
Woodlands Stables
Amesbury Mead Farm
Santa Maria Nursery
97
Sewardstone Lodge
MILL LANE
Daws Hill Nursery
DAWS HILL
Brimsdown
DURANTS PARK
Willowside Stud
NEW-FIELD
Carrolls Farm
41
WEST ESSEX GOLF COURSE
Clubhouse
Picks Farm
GILWELL PARK
BANCHET FIELD
ALMA ROAD OPEN SPACE
CENTENARY ESTATE
CARP LAKES
THE QUICK
The Scout Association
GILWELL LANE
42
Weir
THE ROUGH
COVERED RESERVOIR
PONDERS END IND EST
Lido
Fox & Hounds PH
E4
Sewardstone
96
KING GEORGE'S RESERVOIR
GILWELL LANE
Yardley Hill
Bury Farm
SEWARDSTONE GREEN
Works
43
WOODMAN'S GLADE
Pitch & Putt
Chapping Wall
Overflow Channel
Ponders End Mills
WHARF ROAD
VALLEY LINK IND EST
Pumping Sta
HAWKWOOD CRESCENT
ALLOT
PLAYING FLD
Waltham Forest Council Nursery
THE HAWK WOOD
CHINGFORD GOLF COURSE
44
A110
LEA VALLEY ROAD
A112
EPPING GLADE
CHINGFORD PLAIN
RIVERSIDE IND EST
MERIDIAN WAY
47
Obelisk
POLE HILL
FOREST AVENUE
Clubhouse
DX
DY
DZ
EA
EB
EC
ED
36
37
38
LEISURE
CHINGFORD
RANGERS ROAD

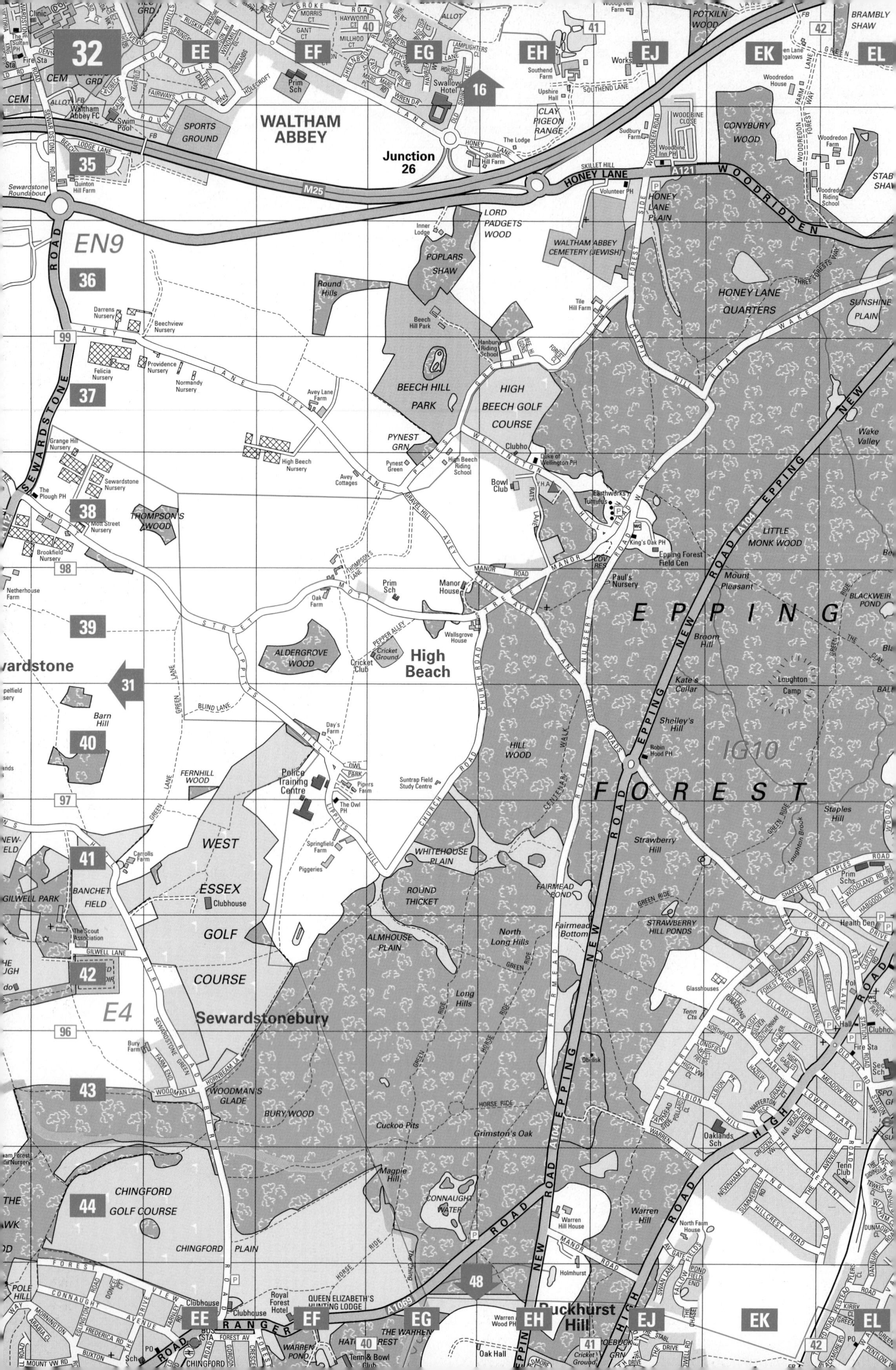
EE
EF
EG
EH
EJ
EK
EL
40
41
42
16
WALTHAM
ABBEY
SPORTS
GROUND
Prim
Sch
Swallow
Hotel
Junction
26
M25
HONEY LANE
A121
WOODRIDDEN
Southend
Farm
SOUTHEND LANE
Upshire
Hall
CLAY
PIGEON
RANGE
The Lodge
Skillet
Hill Farm
SKILLET HILL
Volunteer PH
Woodbine
Inn PH
WOODBINE
CLOSE
Sudbury
Farm
CONYBURY
WOOD
Woodredon
House
Woodredon
Farm
Woodredon
Riding
School
BRAMBLY
SHAW
POTKILN
WOOD
Works
Sewardstone
Roundabout
Quinton
Hill Farm
Waltham
Abbey FC
Swim
Pool
CEM
EN9
35
36
37
38
39
40
41
42
43
44
99
98
97
96
LORD
PADGETS
WOOD
Inner
Lodge
POPLARS
SHAW
WALTHAM ABBEY
CEMETERY (JEWISH)
HONEY
LANE
PLAIN
HONEY LANE
QUARTERS
SUNSHINE
PLAIN
Round
Hills
Beech
Hill Park
Hanbury
Riding
School
Tile
Hill Farm
BEECH HILL
PARK
HIGH
BEECH GOLF
COURSE
Darrens
Nursery
Beechview
Nursery
Felicia
Nursery
Providence
Nursery
Normandy
Nursery
Avey Lane
Farm
AVEY LANE
PYNEST
GRN
Pynest
Green
High Beech
Riding
School
Clubho
Duke of
Wellington PH
Bowl
Club
Grange Hill
Nursery
High Beech
Nursery
Avey
Cottages
Sewardstone
Nursery
The
Plough PH
SEWARDSTONE
Mott Street
Nursery
THOMPSON'S
WOOD
Brookfield
Nursery
Netherhouse
Farm
Earthworks
Tumulus
King's Oak PH
Epping Forest
Field Cen
Paul's
Nursery
LITTLE
MONK WOOD
Wake
Valley
Mount
Pleasant
BLACKWEIR
POND
MANOR ROAD
Prim
Sch
Manor
House
Oak
Farm
MOTT STREET
Wallsgrove
House
E P P I N G
F O R E S T
Broom
Hill
Kate's
Cellar
Loughton
Camp
Shelley's
Hill
Robin
Hood PH
IG10
ALDERGROVE
WOOD
Cricket
Ground
Cricket
Club
High
Beach
PEPPER ALLEY
CHURCH ROAD
LIPPITTS HILL
BLIND LANE
GREEN LANE
Day's
Farm
wardstone
31
Barn
Hill
HILL
WOOD
FERNHILL
WOOD
Police
Training
Centre
OWL
PARK
Pipers
Farm
The Owl
PH
Suntrap Field
Study Centre
EPPING NEW ROAD
A104
CROSS ROADS
Staples
Hill
Strawberry
Hill
WHITEHOUSE
PLAIN
Springfield
Farm
Piggeries
Carrolls
Farm
WEST
ESSEX
GOLF
COURSE
Clubhouse
BANCHET
FIELD
GILWELL PARK
The Scout
Association
GILWELL LANE
ROUND
THICKET
FAIRMEAD
POND
STRAWBERRY
HILL PONDS
Fairmead
Bottom
North
Long Hills
ALMHOUSE
PLAIN
Glasshouses
Health Cen
Prim
Schs
STAPLES ROAD
Long
Hills
Tenn
Cts
Sewardstonebury
E4
Bury
Farm
HORNBEAM LA
WOODMAN LA
WOODMAN'S
GLADE
BURY WOOD
Cuckoo Pits
Grimston's Oak
HORSE RIDE
Obelisk
Oaklands
Sch
Fire Sta
Hall
Clubho
Tenn
Club
Magpie
Hill
CHINGFORD
GOLF COURSE
CONNAUGHT
WATER
Warren
Hill House
Warren
Hill
North Farm
House
CHINGFORD
PLAIN
MANOR ROAD
Holmhurst
48
Royal
Forest
Hotel
QUEEN ELIZABETH'S
HUNTING LODGE
A1069
RANGERS ROAD
BURY ROAD
THE WARREN
FOREST
WARREN
POND
Tenn & Bowl
Club
Warren
Wood PH
Oak Hall
Buckhurst
Hill
HIGH ROAD
Cricket
Ground
CHINGFORD
Clubhouse
CONNAUGHT AVENUE
FOREST VIEW
POLE
HILL
FREDERICA RD
BUXTON RD
MOUNT VW RD

33
EM
EN
EP
EQ
ER
ES
ET
43
44
45
17
49
34
35
36
37
38
39
40
41
42
43
44
96
97
98
99
EPPING FOREST
THEYDON BOIS GOLF COURSE
LITTLE GREGORIES LANE
Little Bronx Livery & Riding Stables
Junction 6 (M
Junction 27 (
Ambresbury Banks
Warren Lodge
EPPING ROAD
B1393
Long Running
Jacks Hill
COPPICE ROW
B172
Oak Hill
HORSE RIDE
GREEN RIDE
Dulsmead Hollow
COPLEY PLAIN
FURZE GROUND
THE DITCHES RIDE
GOLDINGS HILL
A121
BROADSTROOD PLAIN
GREGSON'S RIDE
GOLDING'S HILL PONDS
Oak Hill Farm
Birch Hall
Birch Hall Farm
Sixteen String Jack PH
THEYDON PLAIN
THE COPPICE
BIRCH WOOD
RED OAK WOOD
GAUNT'S WOOD
Ripley Grange
Debden Green
DEBDEN LANE
LOUGHTON LANE
LOUGHTON GOLF COURSE
Clubhouse
PIERCING HILL
Coll
Prim Sch
Hall
PO
THEYDON GREEN
Tenn Club
SPORTS GRD
Cricket Club
ALLOTS
Youth Cen
QUEEN MARY & WESTFIELD COLLEGE SPORTS GROUND
Pav
THEYDON BOIS
Theydon Bois
ABRIDGE ROAD
B172
Parsonage Farm
Blunts Farm
COOPERSALE LANE
Depot
Thrifts Hall Farm
CM16
THEYDON PARK ROAD
THEYDON BOIS CEMETERY
Theydon Hall Farm
Theydon Hall
M11
LONG SHAW
BROADFIELD SHAW
FB
RM4
THEYDON MEAD
Debden
Sec Sch
WILLINGALE ROAD
CLAY'S LANE
ENGLANDS LANE
HILLYFIELDS
HILLYFIELDS OPEN SPACE
RECTORY LANE
A1168
Plume of Feathers PH
CEM
ALLOTMENTS
SPORTS GROUND
Printing Works
Tenn Cts
Clubhouse
PROSPECT BUSINESS PARK
Bowl Grn
DEBDEN
LANGSTON ROAD
OAKWOOD HILL INDUSTRIAL ESTATE
LORRY PK
CHIGWELL LANE
Sir Winston Churchill PH
Sports Cen
Coll
Lib
St. Lukes Sch
BORDERS LANE
Thea
Amb Sta
Clinic
LOUGHTON
Prim Schs
CHEQUERS ROAD
LUSHES ROAD
OAKWOOD HILL
Loughton Bridge
Junction 5
River Roding
RIVERSIDE WALK
IG7
DRIVING RANGE
Woolston Hall
Open Air Pool
EPPING FOREST GOLF COURSE
A113
LONDON ROAD
ABRIDGE ROAD
ABRIDGE PARK
SPORTS GRD
GRAVEL LANE
A1112
Great Downs Farm
Turnours Hall
Marchings
Marchings Farm
Taylor May's Farm
Pettits Hall
PUDDING LANE
Home Farm
Rolls Park
Rolls Park Farm
CHIGWELL LANE

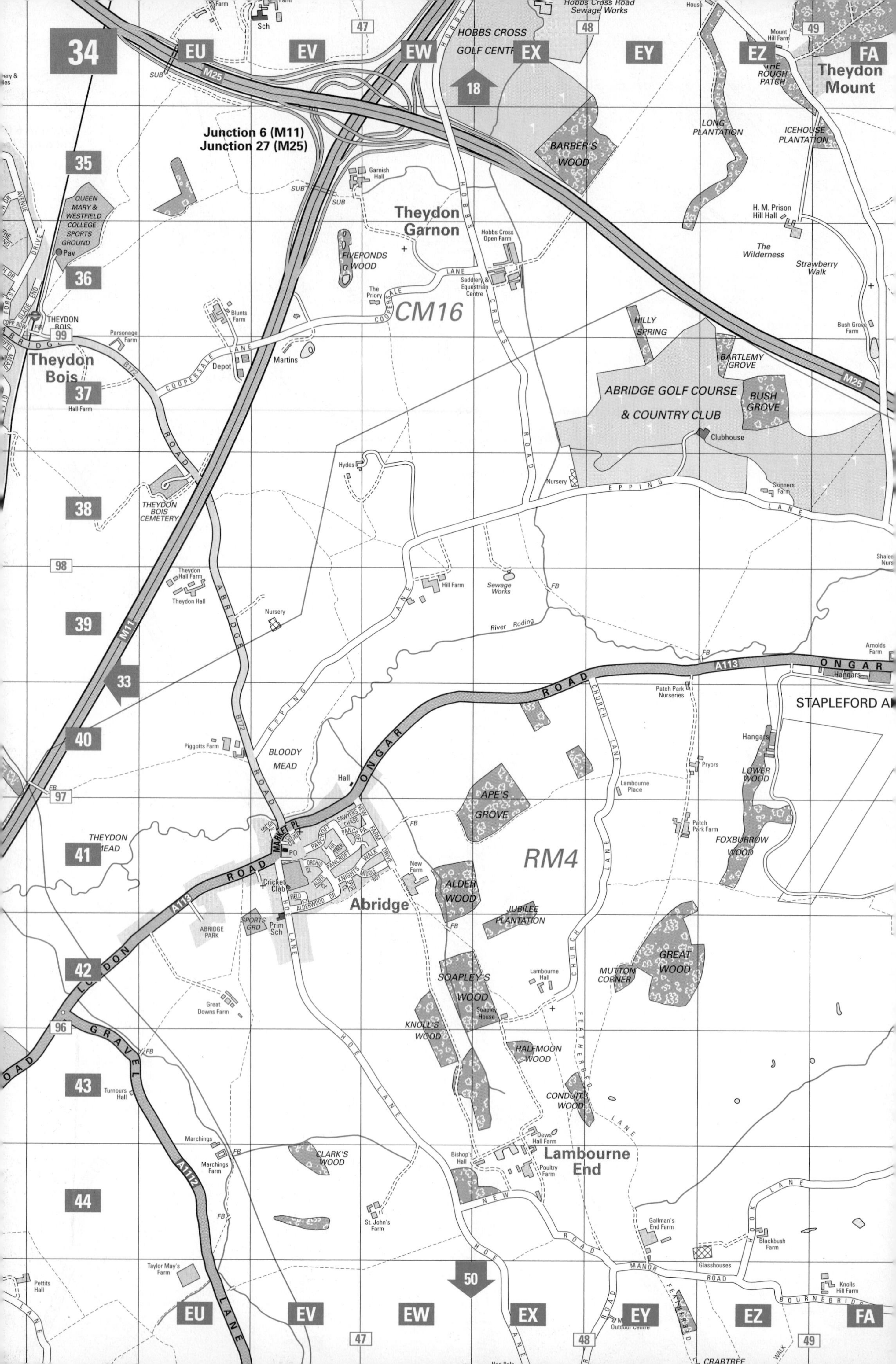

EU
EV
EW
EX
EY
EZ
FA
47
48
49
18
HOBBS CROSS GOLF CENTRE
Hobbs Cross Road Sewage Works
Theydon Mount
THE ROUGH PATCH
Mount Hill Farm
M25
Junction 6 (M11)
Junction 27 (M25)
35
36
37
38
39
40
41
42
43
44
99
98
97
96
QUEEN MARY & WESTFIELD COLLEGE SPORTS GROUND
Pav
Garnish Hall
Theydon Garnon
BARBER'S WOOD
LONG PLANTATION
ICEHOUSE PLANTATION
H. M. Prison Hill Hall
The Wilderness
Strawberry Walk
FIVEPONDS WOOD
Hobbs Cross Open Farm
Saddlery & Equestrian Centre
The Priory
COOPERSALE LANE
CM16
Blunts Farm
THEYDON BOIS
Parsonage Farm
Theydon Bois
Depot
Martins
HILLY SPRING
BARTLEMY GROVE
Bush Grove Farm
ABRIDGE GOLF COURSE & COUNTRY CLUB
BUSH GROVE
Clubhouse
Hall Farm
Hydes
Nursery
EPPING LANE
Skinners Farm
THEYDON BOIS CEMETERY
HOBBS CROSS ROAD
Theydon Hall Farm
Theydon Hall
Hill Farm
Sewage Works
FB
Nursery
River Roding
M11
33
ABRIDGE ROAD
B172
Arnolds Farm
A113
ONGAR ROAD
Hangars
Patch Park Nurseries
STAPLEFORD A
Piggotts Farm
BLOODY MEAD
CHURCH LANE
Pryors
LOWER WOOD
Hall
APE'S GROVE
Lambourne Place
THEYDON MEAD
MARKET PL
PO
Patch Park Farm
FOXBURROW WOOD
RM4
New Farm
Cricket Club
ALDER WOOD
Abridge
JUBILEE PLANTATION
SPORTS GRD
Prim Sch
ABRIDGE PARK
LONDON ROAD
HOE LANE
SOAPLEY'S WOOD
Lambourne Hall
MUTTON CORNER
GREAT WOOD
Great Downs Farm
KNOLL'S WOOD
Soapley House
GRAVEL LANE
HALFMOON WOOD
Turnours Hall
CONDUIT WOOD
FEATHERBED LANE
Marchings
Marchings Farm
CLARK'S WOOD
Dews Hall Farm
Bishop's Hall
Lambourne End
Poultry Farm
NEW ROAD
A1112
St. John's Farm
Gallman's End Farm
HOOK LANE
Blackbush Farm
Glasshouses
MANOR ROAD
Taylor May's Farm
50
Knolls Hill Farm
BOURNEBRIDGE
Pettits Hall
Outdoor Centre
CRABTREE

35
FB
FC
FD
FE
FF
FG
FH
50
51
52
19
LONG SPRING
ROUND SPRING
WELL EAVES
Berwick Farm
ICEHOUSE WOOD
PARK SPRING
Little Tawney Farm
Howfields
THE GROVE
BERWICK HAM
TWENTYACRE WOOD
Murrells Farm
Traceys Farm
White Bear PH
TENACRE WOOD
DOG KENNEL SPRING
CM5
THE MOORS
BOB'S BARN WOOD
LANGFORD BOTTOM
STONYROCKS PLANTATION
BROOM WOOD
99
36
37
38
39
40
41
42
43
44
Great Tawney Hall
Stapleford Tawney
SHALES MORE
RAILMEAD PLANTATION
Mitchells Farm
Shonk's Mill Bridge
HOOK WOOD
98
EPPING FOREST
BRENTWOOD
River Roding
Suttons Manor Clinic
Sutton's Farm
LONDON RD
LONDON ROAD
A113
M25
Howletts Hall
AYE ETCH
Dabbs Farm
Yew Tree Farm
Passingford Bridge
Waters Farm
ALBYNS LANE
RM4
Navestock
97
Green Farm
Grafton Farm
Hammonds Farm
Bons Farm
Albyns Farm
Albyns Hall
The Rabbits PH
40 Acre Farm
CURTISMILL GREEN
Lodge Farm
CURTIS MILL GREEN
Church Farm
Brook Farm
Jenkins Farm
96
Battles Hall
Stapleford Abbotts
Prim Sch
Village Hall
Belmont Farm
Stapleford Hall Farm
Tyseahill Farm
Spring Farm
MURTHERING LANE
Bourne Brook
Olives Farm
THE PADDOCKS
STAPLEFORD ABBOTTS GOLF COURSE
MOAT
WATTON'S GREEN
High House Farm
Woodlands Farm
Brook Farm
Skips Corner Farm
Nursery
TYSEA HILL
HORSEMAN
51
Nuper's Hatch
STAPLEFORD ROAD
GUTTERIDGE LA
CHURCH LANE
CURTIS MILL LANE
B175
FB

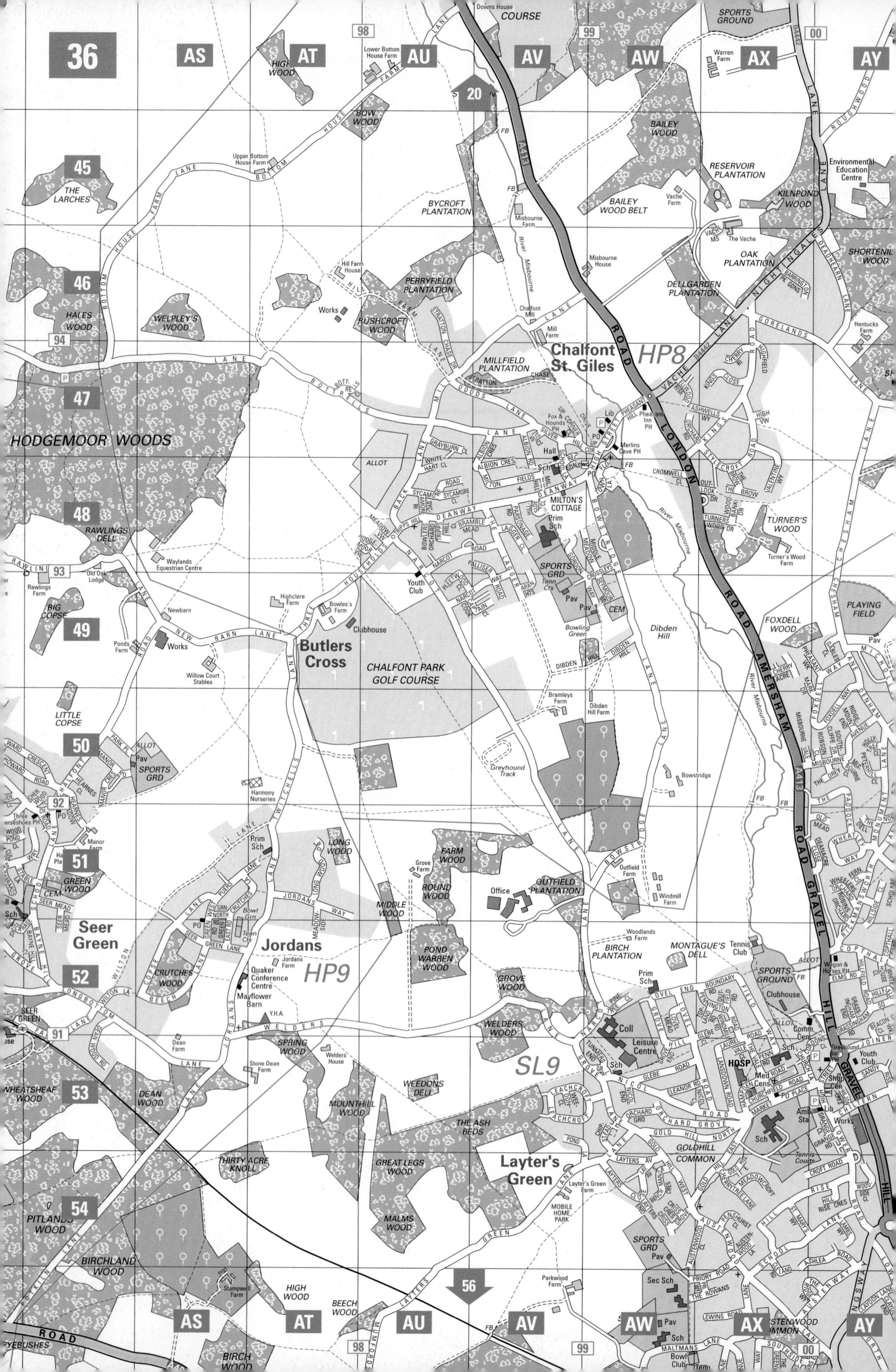
36
AS
AT
AU
AV
AW
AX
AY
98
99
00
20
45
46
47
48
49
50
51
52
53
54
56
94
93
92
91
Downs House
COURSE
SPORTS GROUND
HIGH WOOD
Lower Bottom House Farm
Warren Farm
BOW WOOD
BAILEY WOOD
RESERVOIR PLANTATION
Environmental Education Centre
KILNPOND WOOD
THE LARCHES
Upper Bottom House Farm
BOTTOM HOUSE FARM LANE
BYCROFT PLANTATION
Misbourne Farm
BAILEY WOOD BELT
Vache Farm
The Vache
OAK PLANTATION
SHORTENILS WOOD
Misbourne House
River Misbourne
Hill Farm House
PERRYFIELD PLANTATION
DELLGARDEN PLANTATION
HALES WOOD
WELPLEY'S WOOD
Works
RUSHCROFT WOOD
Chalfont Mill
Mill Farm
Hentucks Farm
Chalfont St. Giles
HP8
MILLFIELD PLANTATION
HODGEMOOR WOODS
Fox & Hounds PH
Pheasant Inn PH
Merlins Cave PH
Lib
Hall
Sch
ALLOT
MILTON'S COTTAGE
Prim Sch
TURNER'S WOOD
Turner's Wood Farm
RAWLINGS DELL
Waylands Equestrian Centre
Old Oak Lodge
Rawlings Farm
SPORTS GRD
Youth Club
Tenn Cts
Pav
CEM
BIG COPSE
Highclere Farm
Bowles's Farm
Newbarn
Clubhouse
Bowling Green
Dibden Hill
FOXDELL WOOD
PLAYING FIELD
Ponds Farm
NEW BARN LANE
Butlers Cross
CHALFONT PARK GOLF COURSE
Willow Court Stables
Bramleys Farm
Dibden Hill Farm
LITTLE COPSE
Greyhound Track
Bowstridge
Harmony Nurseries
Three Horseshoes PH
Manor Farm
LONG WOOD
FARM WOOD
Grove Farm
ROUND WOOD
Outfield Farm
Windmill Farm
GREEN WOOD
Office
OUTFIELD PLANTATION
MIDDLE WOOD
Seer Green
Bowl Grn
Woodlands Farm
BIRCH PLANTATION
MONTAGUE'S DELL
Tennis Club
Jordans
POND WARREN WOOD
HP9
CRUTCHES WOOD
Jordans Farm
Quaker Conference Centre
Mayflower Barn
GROVE WOOD
SPORTS GROUND
Clubhouse
Wagon & Horses PH
Y.H.A.
WELDERS LANE
WELDERS WOOD
Coll
Leisure Centre
Comm Cen
Dean Farm
SPRING WOOD
Welders House
SL9
HOSP
Med Cens
Greyhound Inn PH
Youth Club
Stone Dean Farm
WEEDONS DELL
Shop Cen
WHEATSHEAF WOOD
DEAN WOOD
MOUNTHILL WOOD
THE ASH BEDS
Amb Sta
Works
GOLDHILL COMMON
Tennis Courts
THIRTY ACRE KNOLL
GREAT LEGS WOOD
Layter's Green
Layter's Green Farm
MOBILE HOME PARK
PITLANDS WOOD
MALMS WOOD
SPORTS GRD
BIRCHLAND WOOD
Stampwell Farm
HIGH WOOD
Parkwood Farm
Sec Sch
BEECH WOOD
STENWOOD COMMON
PYEBUSHES
BIRCH WOOD
Bowl Club
LONDON ROAD
AMERSHAM ROAD
GRAVEL HILL
A413
B4442

37
Chorleywood Bottom
The Swillet
Heronsgate
Mill End
Junction 17
NEWLAND PARK
Brunel University Buckinghamshire College
CHILTERN OPEN AIR MUSEUM
SPORTS GROUND
BOTTOM WOOD
LADYWALK WOOD
FIVE PLANTATIONS
POLLARDSHILL WOOD
Maple Cross
MAPLE CROSS INDUSTRIAL ESTATE
WD3
BEECHEN WOOD
KILN WOOD
FRANKLINS SPRING
PLAYING FIELDS
Maple Lodge Sewage Treatment Works
ROBERT'S WOOD
ROUND ROCKET PLANTATION
QUARRY & LANDFILL SITE
SL9
MIDDLE WOOD
BLOOM WOOD
LYNSTERS LAKE
PYNESFIELD LAKE
CHALFONT ST. PETER
HOGTROUGH WOOD
GERRARDS CROSS GOLF COURSE
GRAVEL PIT
Horseshoe Bay
UB9
TRAINING CENTRE DURDENT COURT
NOCKHILL WOOD
JUNIPER WOOD
M25
DENHAM WAY
NORTH ORBITAL ROAD
A412
A405
21
38
57
45
46
47
48
49
50
51
52
53
54

38
37
22
58
45
46
47
48
49
50
51
52
53
54
BG
BH
BJ
BK
BL
BM
BN
05
06
07
94
93
92
91
Mill End
Moneyhill
RICKMANSWORTH
CROXLEY
Batchworth
Batchworth Heath
MOOR PARK GOLF COURSE
BATCHWORTH PARK GOLF COURSE
WD3
UB9
Hill End
HAREFIELD
HAREFIELD HOSPITAL
PHEASANTS WOOD
SOLOMON'S WOOD
WILLIAM PENN MULTISPORTS ARENA
UXBRIDGE ROAD
A412
A404
A405
M25
RIVERSIDE DRIVE
SCOTS HILL
MOOR LANE
LONDON ROAD
BATCHWORTH LAKE
BURY LAKE
THE AQUADROME
GRAND UNION CANAL
STOCKER'S LAKE (NATURE RESERVE)
SPRINGWELL LAKE
SPRINGWELL CHALK PIT
CHALK PIT
GARRETT WOOD
HIGH WOOD
COCKS WOOD
HERTFORDSHIRE
THREE RIVERS
HILLINGDON
WOODCOCK HILL CEMETERY
HAREFIELD ROAD INDUSTRIAL ESTATE
CHORLEYWOOD ROAD CEMETERY
MAPLE CROSS INDUSTRIAL ESTATE
Maple Lodge Sewage Treatment Works
LYNSTERS LAKE
PYNESFIELD LAKE
PARK WOOD
MOUNT PLEASANT SPORTS GRD
WATTS COMMON
TAYLORS MEADOW
PEARSON'S WOOD
BISHOP'S WOOD
LONG SPRING
POORFIELD
LOCKWELL WOOD
FRENCH GROVE
BATTLERS WELLS WOOD
COVERED RESERVOIR
FURZEFIELD
DEADMAN'S GROVE
ASHAIN SPRING
SCARLET SPRING
KILN POND
CLAYPITS
DELL
RAVENERS SPRING
HIGHBONES
Shooting School
Horseshoe Bay
Sailing Club
Juniper Dell
Greenbroom Spring
Sandfield Spring
Bush Spring

39
BP
BQ
BR
BS
BT
BU
BV
Holywell
HOLYWELL IND EST
WATFORD STADIUM HALT (MATCH DAYS ONLY)
Electricity Transmission Station
LONG VALLEY WOOD
COMMON MOOR
KING GEORGE V PLAYING FIELDS
SPORTS GROUND
WOLSEY BUSINESS PARK
MOOR PARK INDUSTRIAL ESTATE
VALE INDUSTRIAL ESTATE
TOLPITS LANE
THE EBURY WAY CYCLE PATH
EASTBURY ROAD
BROOKDENE AVENUE
Brightwells Spring
HAMPERMILL LAKE
RUNNING TRACK
Merchant Taylor's Sch
Tolpits Plantation
The Withey Bed Wood
HAMPERMILL LANE
WD19
HAMPERMILL WOOD
BIG WOOD
Ox Pasture Spring
SOUTH OXHEY PLAYING FIELDS
OXHEY PARK GOLF COURSE
Warren Dell
SANDY LODGE ROAD
SANDY LODGE LANE
GOLF COURSE
MOOR PARK
SANDY LODGE GOLF COURSE
Hampermill Spring
Round Spring
OLD FURZE FIELD
YOUNG HANGINGS
OLD HANGINGS
OXHEY
THE PLANTATION
BECK MASON'S WOOD
OXHEY WOOD
SOUTH OXHEY
Moor Park
MOOR PARK ESTATE
BATHEND CLUMP
Eastbury
H.M.S. Warrior
WESTBURY AVENUE
BATCHWORTH LANE
PRESTWICK ROAD
THREE RIVERS
NORTHWOOD
WILD WOODS
NANS WOOD
SANDY LANE
WATFORD ROAD
A4125
RICKMANSWORTH ROAD
St. Helen's Sch
Northwood Coll
THE GRAVEL PITS
GREEN LANE
HIGH STREET
HA6
HOGS BACK OPEN SPACE
HILLINGDON
PINNER WOOD
PINNER HILL GOLF COURSE
PINNERWOOD PARK
HA5
PINNER GREEN
NORTHWOOD GOLF COURSE
PINNER ROAD
A404
NORTHWOOD & PINNER COTTAGE HOSP
Northwood Hills
HASTE HILL GOLF COURSE
NORTHWOOD CEMETERY
RUISLIP NATURE RESERVE
COPSE WOOD
DUCKS HILL
A4180
POOR'S FIELD
ST VINCENT'S ORTHOPAEDIC HOSPITAL
08
09
10
23
40
45
46
47
48
49
50
51
52
53
54
59
91
92
93
94

40
BW
BX
BY
BZ
CA
CB
CC
24
12
13
14
45
46
47
48
49
50
51
52
53
54
39
60
91
92
93
94
BUSHEY
BUSHEY GOLF COURSE & COUNTRY CLUB
WATFORD HEATH
MERRY HILL
WD19
WD23
HA5
CARPENDERS PARK
HARTSBOURNE GOLF COURSE & COUNTRY CLUB
SOUTH OXHEY
OXHEY PARK GOLF COURSE
SOUTH OXHEY PLAYING FIELDS
GRIM'S DYKE GOLF COURSE
HATCH END
PINNER HILL GOLF COURSE
PINNERWOOD PARK
PINNER GREEN
PINNER PARK
SHAFTESBURY PLAYING FIELDS
SADDLERS MEAD REC GROUND
HATCH END PLAYING FIELD
RAGHUVANSHI CHARITABLE TRUST SPORTS GROUND
CARPENDERS PARK CEMETERY
SHERWOODS WOOD
MARGEHOLES WOOD
SPOILBANKS
GOLF DRIVING RANGE
NANSCOT WOOD
SANDPIT WOOD
MUTTON WOOD
STONY WOOD
WEALD WOOD
LEVELS WOOD
GRIMSTONE LAKE
PINNER WOOD
HERTFORDSHIRE
HARROW
THREE RIVERS
HERTSMERE
HILLINGDON
EASTBURY ROAD
PRESTWICK ROAD
OXHEY LANE
UXBRIDGE ROAD
UXBRIDGE RD
RICKMANSWORTH RD
ST THOMAS' DRIVE
LONDON ROAD
HIGH STREET
CHALK HILL
PINNER ROAD
OXHEY DRIVE
BROOKDENE AVENUE
HAYLING ROAD
CARPENDERS AVENUE
PENROSE AVENUE
HARROW WAY
GEORGE V AVENUE
MERRY HILL ROAD
SPARROWS HERNE
A4125
A4008
A411
A410
A404
B4542
CARPENDERS PARK
HATCH END
HEADSTONE LANE
BUSHEY

41
CD
CE
CF
CG
CH
CJ
CK
15
16
17
25
M1
ALDENHAM RESERVOIR
SPORTS GROUND
ELSTREE ROAD
BARNET A411
ELSTREE HILL OPEN SPACE
ELSTREE HILL SOUTH A5183
WATFORD BYPASS
A41 BYPASS
CENTENNIAL PARK
CENTENNIAL AVENUE
ELSTREE OPEN SPACE
WD6
HERTSMERE
HARROW
45
46
47
48
49
42
50
51
52
53
54
61
94
93
92
91
Junction 4
Edgwarebury Hotel
Caldecote Farm
Berkeley Cottage
Gas Pumping Sta
CONVENT
Coll
B.U.P.A. HOSPITAL
Surgery
Prim Sch
BUSHEY HEATH
HEATHBOURNE ROAD
MAGPIE HALL RD
COMMON ROAD
THE COMMON A4140
STANMORE COMMON
ROYAL NATIONAL ORTHOPAEDIC HOSP
Mike Heaffey Sports & Rehabilitation Centre
Aspire Centre
Brockley Grange
Site of Sulloniace Roman Settlement
BROCKLEY HILL
EDGWARE WAY
WATLING STREET (ROMAN ROAD)
PEAR WOOD
Wood Farm
Lime House
THE GROVE
Works
The Cedars
High Sch for Girls
BENTLEY PRIORY
GROVE FIELDS
LITTLE COMMON
FISH POND
Cricket Ground
Harrow R.F.C.
CLOISTERS WOOD
Tennis Courts
BROCKLEY HILL GOLF PARK
GOVT OFFICES
Clubhouse
SPUR ROAD
Canons Corner
STANMORE HALL
BENTLEY PRIORY OPEN SPACE
BENTLEY PRIORY NATURE RESERVE
HERIOTS WOOD
DEER PARK
HA7
Retirement Home
The Old Barn
The Kiln
Priory House
Hare PH
Country Club
Lower Priory Farm
Suzanne's Riding School
HA3
BROOKSHILL
Abercorn Arms PH
Prim Schs.
LONDON ROAD A410
GLANLEAM ROAD
STANMORE
Sec Sch
BOOT POND
STANMORE
UXBRIDGE ROAD A410
CHURCH RD
THE BDY
STANMORE PARK
Hall
Lib
Tenn Club
HARROW WEALD CEMETERY
HARROW WEALD LAKE
Weald College
Stanmore College
TEMPLE POND
MARSH LANE
A4140
N London Collegiate Sch
Swim Pool
Sports Hall
HA8
KING GEORGE V MEML GDNS
CANONS PARK
CANONS PARK SPORTS GROUND
THE LAKE
Gas Works
STANMORE MARSH
PLAYING FIELD
STANMORE GOLF COURSE
ALLOTMENTS
Clubhouse
GOVT BUILDINGS
HONEYPOT LANE
SPORTS GROUND
PRINCE EDWARD PLAYING FIELD
Fire Sta
HARROW WEALD
RECREATION GROUND
Superstore
Bowl Club
HIGH ROAD
HIGH STREET
A409
ELMS ROAD
COLLEGE HILL ROAD
Health Cen
BELMONT CIRCLE
BELMONT
Kenton Lane Farm
CENTENARY PARK
SPORTS GRD
Pitch 'n' Putt
QUEENSBURY
Clock Tower
Comm Cen
WEALDSTONE
CEM
BYRON REC GRD
REC GRD
Prim Sch
Sec Sch
CONVENT
SPORTS GROUND
Works
ESTATE
GEORGE

42
CL
CM
CN
CP
CQ
CR
CS
19
20
21
26
BARNET LANE
A411
Deacons Hill
DEACONS HILL OPEN SPACE
SCRATCH WOOD
FROGHALL WOOD
BOYS HILL WOOD
THISTLE WOOD
GRAVEL PIT WOOD
Stirling Corner
Elstree Manor
Edgwarebury Hotel
45
ELSTREE OPEN SPACE
WD6
HERTSMERE
M1
BARNET
46
Junction 4
CLUMP OF TREES WOOD
TARGET WOOD
MILL HILL GOLF COURSE
NUT WOOD
London Gateway Services
Bury Farm
EDGWAREBURY CEMETERY
REC GRD
SPORTS GRD
HEMMINGS WOOD
STONEY WOOD LAKE
Travelodge Hotel
47
A41 (WATFORD BYPASS)
FISH POND
48
EDGWAREBURY PARK
SPORTS GROUND Canons Corner
GOVT OFFICES
SPUR ROAD
EDGWARE WAY (WATFORD BYPASS)
Apex Corner
49
A410
STANMORE
41
STONEGROVE
CONVENT
A5100
50
STONEGROVE PARK
N London Collegiate Sch
EDGWARE
SELVAGE LANE
HALE LANE
51
KING GEORGE V MEML GDNS
CANONS PARK
THE BASIN
HIGH STREET
STATION ROAD
BUS STA
Broadwalk Shop Cen
BUS DEPOT
HA8
ALLOTMENTS
LYNDHURST PARK
DEANSBROOK ROAD
A5109
52
CANONS PARK
SPORTS GROUND
Edgware Town F.C.
EDGWARE COMMUNITY HOSPITAL
Hendon Coll
SPORTS GROUND
WATLING PARK
GOVT BUILDINGS
CHANDOS RECREATION GROUND
HA7
BURNT OAK
53
PRINCE EDWARD PLAYING FIELD
SPORTS GROUND
ADASTRAL ESTATE
A4140
HONEYPOT LANE
BURNT OAK BROADWAY
SILKSTREAM PARK
54
BRIXTON EST
MONTROSE PLAYING FIELDS
COLINDALE HOSP
COLINDALE BUSINESS PK
BLOOD TRANSFUSION CENTRE
62
QUEENSBURY
NW9
COLINDALE
Superstore
Yaohan Plaza

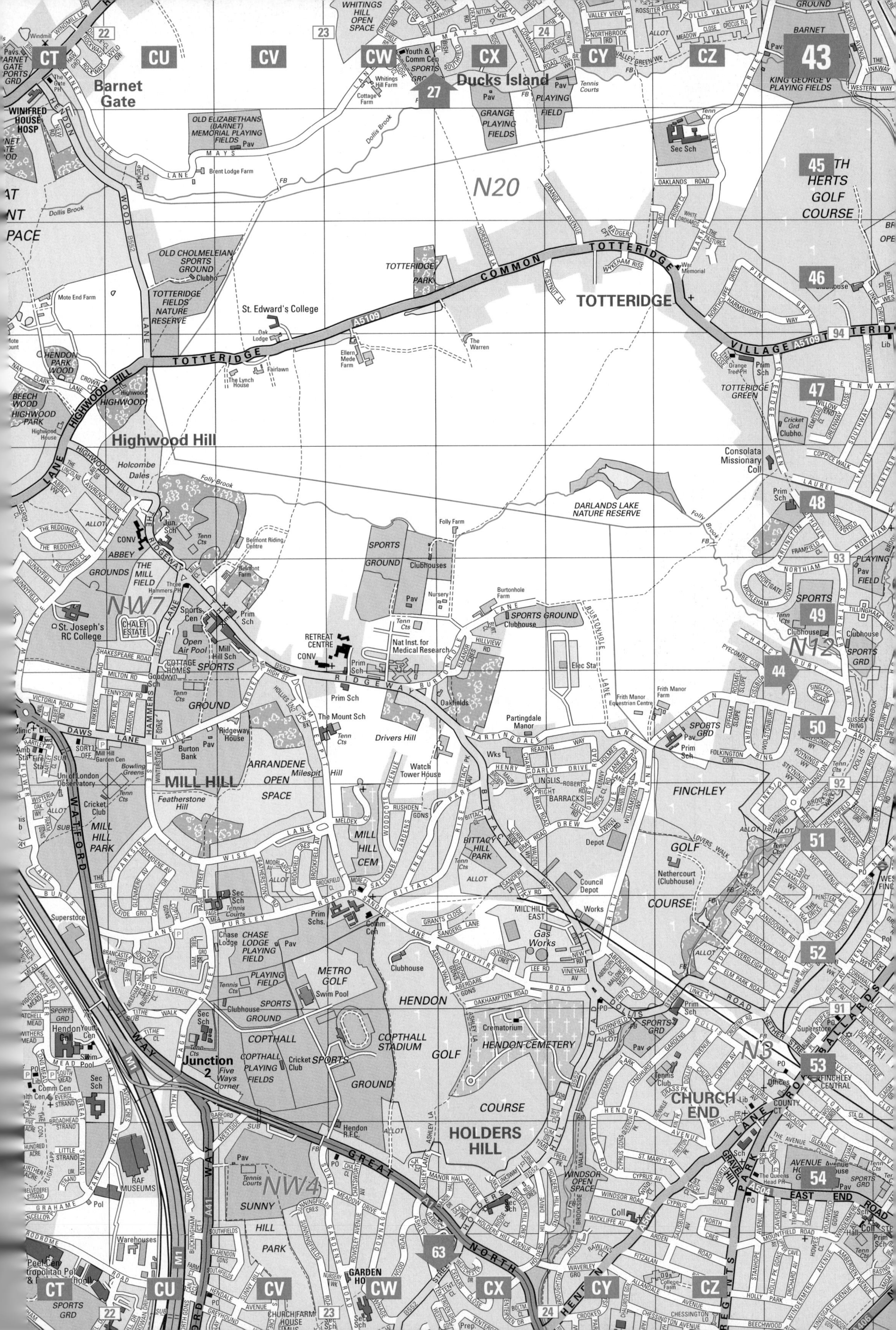

44
DA
DB
DC
DD
DE
DF
DG
28
EAST BARNET
OAK HILL PARK
Oak Hill Theological Coll
SOUTH HERTS GOLF COURSE
WYATTS FARM OPEN SPACE
BROOK FARM OPEN SPACE
N20
DAME ALICE OWEN'S GRD
OAKLEIGH PARK
EN4
TOTTERIDGE VILLAGE
TOTTERIDGE LANE
OAKLEIGH ROAD
TOTTERIDGE & WHETSTONE
WHETSTONE
BRUNSWICK PARK
SWAN LANE OPEN SPACE
NORTH MIDDLESEX GOLF COURSE
BETHUNE GOLF COURSE
FRIARY PARK
FRIERN BARNET
N12
WOODSIDE PARK
43
NORTH FINCHLEY
FINCHLEY
COPPETTS WOOD
WEST FINCHLEY
FINCHLEY MEMORIAL HOSP
GLEBELANDS OPEN SPACE
NORTH CIRCULAR ROAD
VICTORIA PARK FINCHLEY
N3
MUSWELL HILL SPORTS GROUND
COPPETTS WOOD HOSP
FINCHLEY CENTRAL
CHURCH END
ST. PANCRAS & ISLINGTON CEMETERY
COLDFALL WOOD
N2
AVENUE HOUSE GRDS
64
45
46
47
48
49
50
51
52
53
54
94
93
92
91
26
27

45
DH
DJ
DK
DL
DM
DN
DP
29
30
31
OAKWOOD PARK
YACHTING POND
WINCHMORE HILL
GROVELANDS PARK
BOATING LAKE
N14
N21
N13
N11
N22
OSIDGE
SOUTHGATE
Southgate Technical Coll
SOUTHGATE CEMETERY
HOSPITAL (CLOSED)
WOODCROFT SPORTS GROUND
PALMERS GREEN
ARNOS PARK
NEW SOUTHGATE
BROOMFIELD PARK
BOWES PARK
THE PAULIN GROUND
CLOWES SPORTS GROUND
BARROWELL GRN OPEN SPACE
HAZELWOOD SPORTS GRD
TATEM PARK REC GRD
HOLLY-WOOD GDNS
TILE KILN LANE OPEN SPACE
TOTTENHALL SPORTS GROUND
BOUNDARY PLAYING FIELDS
NEW RIVER SPORTS CENTRE
MUSWELL HILL GOLF COURSE
SCOUT PARK
Middlesex Uni
Coll of N E London
WOODSIDE PARK
PLAYING FIELD
WOOD GREEN
NOEL PARK
TRAIN DEPOT
ALEXANDRA PALACE
ALEXANDRA PARK
SPORTS GROUND
HORNSEY WATER TREATMENT WORKS
HORNSEY
MUSWELL HILL
LORDSHIP RECREATION GROUND
BELMONT REC GRD
DOWNHILLS PARK
46
47
48
49
50
51
52
53
54
65
91
92
93
94
CHASE SIDE
THE BOURNE
BOURNE HILL
HIGH STREET
CANNON HILL
ALDERMANS HILL
GREEN LANES
HEDGE LANE
NORTH CIRCULAR ROAD
BOWES ROAD
TELFORD ROAD
WATERFALL ROAD
BOUNDS GREEN ROAD
HIGH ROAD
LORDSHIP LANE
WESTBURY AVENUE
THE BROADWAY
ALEXANDRA PARK ROAD
PALACE GATES ROAD
WOOD GREEN
TURNPIKE LANE
A111
A1004
A1003
A1110
A406
A105
A109
A1080
A10

46
DQ
DR
DS
DT
DU
DV
DW
33
34
35
30
N21
45
46
47
48
49
50
51
52
53
54
94
93
92
91
RIDGE AVENUE
GREEN LANES
THE PAULIN GROUND
EDMONTON CEMETERY
FIRS FARM PLAYING FIELDS
CLOWES SPORTS GROUND
CHURCH STREET REC GRD
CHURCHFIELD REC GRD
JUBILEE PARK
LOWER EDMONTON
EDMONTON GREEN
N9
EDMONTON FEDERATION CEMETERY (JEWISH)
TOTTENHAM PARK CEMETERY
MONTAGU RECREATION GROUND
WESTERN SYNAGOGUE CEMETERY
EDMONTON
PYMMES PARK
N18
TATEM PARK REC GRD
HOLLYWOOD GDNS
HAZELWOOD
N13
45
NORTH MIDDLESEX HOSPITAL
STERLING WAY
ANGEL ROAD
CONDUIT LANE
MERIDIAN WAY
UPPER EDMONTON
TOTTENHALL SPORTS GROUND
BOUNDARY PLAYING FIELDS
NEW RIVER SPORTS CENTRE
SPORTS GROUND
THE ROYAL LONDON ESTATE
WHITE HART LANE
TOTTENHAM HOTSPUR FC
TOTTENHAM CEMETERY
N17
TOTTENHAM
BRUCE CASTLE PARK
TOWER GDNS
THE ROUNDWAY
LORDSHIP LANE
NOEL PARK
LORDSHIP RECREATION GROUND
N22
BELMONT REC GRD
DOWNHILLS PARK
66
DOWN LANE REC GRD
LEE VALLEY TECHNOPARK
TOTTENHAM HALE
TOTTENHAM MARSHES
WATERMEAD WAY
LOCKWOOD RESERVOIR
LEE VALLEY
HIGH ROAD
FORE STREET
HERTFORD ROAD
GREAT CAMBRIDGE ROAD
NORTH CIRCULAR ROAD
WESTBURY AVENUE

47
DX
DY
DZ
EA
EB
EC
ED
36
37
38
31
Gas Works
VALLEY LINK IND EST
RIVERSIDE IND EST
MERIDIAN
SOUTH ROUTE
A1055
LEISURE
Cinema
Sports Cen
SPORTS PITCH
GOLF
Tenn Cts
Pav
GOLF RANGE
COURSE
Works
WILLIAM
GIRLING
RESERVOIR
Overflow Channel
PICKETTS LOCK LANE
Pickett's Lock
Storage Tanks
Filter Beds
DEEPHAMS SEWAGE TREATMENT WORKS
LEE PARK WAY (PRIVATE ROAD)
River Lee Diversion
River Lee Navigation
LEE VALLEY PARK
Pumping Station
Refuge Plant
ASH WHARF
ADVENT WAY
LEA VALLEY VIADUCT
SOUTHEND ROAD
Sunday Market
Superstores
TRADING ESTATE
Roller Skating Cen
HASTINGWOOD TRADING ESTATE
Lee Valley Watersports
BANBURY RESERVOIR
Lee Flood Relief Channel
VALLEY ROAD
A110
KINGS HEAD HILL
SEWARDSTONE ROAD
A112
Pumping Sta
LEA VALLEY PLAYING FIELDS
Golf Range
Clubho
MANSFIELD HILL
MANSFIELD PARK
WALTHAM WAY
A1037
ENFIELD
WALTHAM FOREST
OLD CHURCH ROAD
CHINGFORD MOUNT CEMETERY
War Memorial
RIDGEWAY PARK
Youth Cen
Prim Sch
Green Man PH
Clubhouse
CHINGFORD
Sec Sch
Fire Sta
THE HAWK WOOD
POLE HILL
Obelisk
CHINGFORD GOLF COURSE
CHINGFORD PLAIN
Clubhouse
RANGERS ROAD
STATION ROAD
THE GRN KINGS
Lib
Hall
E4
FRIDAY HILL
PIMP HALL PARK
Pimp Hall Nurseries
LARKSHALL ROAD
B160
NEW ROAD
HATCH LA
A1009
CHINGFORD HATCH
Larkshall PH
Glasshouse
LARKSWOOD PLAYING FIELDS
LARKS WOOD
JUBILEE SPORTS GRD
Tenn Club
HIGHAMS PARK
THE HIGHAMS PARK
BOATING LAKE
HALE END
Royal Oak PH
WOODFORD R.F.C.
County Hotel
EPPING FOREST
WOODFORD GOLF COURSE
The Lops
The Ching
Wheelwright PH
Cricket Ground
CHINGFORD LANE
HALL LANE
Old Hall Tavern PH
CHINGFORD HALL PARK
Prim Schs
Health Cen
SOUTH CHINGFORD
CHINGFORD IND CEN
Superstore
CHINGFORD MOUNT ROAD
WAR MEML REC GRD
Waltham Forest Coll
Prim Sch
AINSLIE WOOD
ROLLS SPORTS GRD
Cricket & Tenn Club
HIGHAMS PARK IND EST
CHINGFORD HALL EST
Comm Cen
AVENUE IND EST
SALISBURY HALL BLADES PLAYING FIELDS
Superstore
SPORTS GRD
Fairways Cen
FAIRWAY GOLF RANGE
BRITANNIA SPORTS GROUND
NORTH CIRCULAR RD
A406
Crooked Billet Roundabout
WALTHAMSTOW GREYHOUND STADIUM
THE LONDON HOSPITAL SPORTS GRD
WADHAM LODGE SPORTS GROUND
Sec Sch
SOUTHEND RD
SOUTHEND ROAD
LRT SPORTS GRD
WADHAM LODGE SPORTS GRD
Comm Cen
WINCHESTER ROAD
FULBOURNE ROAD
William Morris Sch
Sec Sch
BILLET ROAD
HIGHAM HILL REC GRD
HIGHAM HILL
Comm Cen
Clinic
ALLOT
E17
LLOYD PARK
Sec Sch
Swim Pool
WALTHAM FOREST ATHLETICS GRD
WALTHAMSTOW
CHESTNUTS SHOWGROUND
TOWN HALL
ASSEMBLY HALL
Waltham Forest Coll
THORPE COOMBE HOSP
HALLINGBURY COURT
Health Cen
FOREST ROAD
A503
WALTHAMSTOW FOREST
COV RES
Hyland Ho Sch
ALLOTMENTS
CHILDREN'S BOATING POND
WOODFORD NEW ROAD
A104
EPPING FOREST
REDBRIDGE
UPLANDS BUSINESS PARK
HIGHAMS LODGE BUSINESS CEN
WINNS AVENUE
HOE STREET
45
46
47
48
49
50
51
52
53
54
91
92
93
94

48
EE
EF
EG
EH
EJ
EK
EL
40
41
42
32
47
68
CHINGFORD GREEN
FRIDAY HILL
HIGHAMS PARK
HALE END
WOODFORD GREEN
Woodford Wells
WOODFORD
SOUTH WOODFORD
Buckhurst Hill
E4
IG9
IG8
E18
LORD'S BUSHES
RAY PARK
RODING VALLEY PARK
EPPING FOREST
WALTHAMSTOW FOREST
Junction 4

49
EM
EN
EP
EQ
ER
ES
ET
EPPING
FOREST
GOLF
33
ABRIDGE
ROLLS PARK
Rolls Park Farm
Home Farm
Pettits Hall
Taylor May's Farm
PUDDING LANE
River Roding
RIVERSIDE
SPORTS GROUND
LOUGHTON FC
The David Lloyd Club
Pool
M11
IG7
Chigwell House
Pav
SPORTS GROUND
Bramstones
Rodings
RODING LANE
CHIGWELL LANE
Chigwell Hall
Pavs.
METROPOLITAN POLICE SPORTS GRD
CEM
Olde King's Head PH
Sec Sch
Cricket Grd
Prim Sch
Old Farm
Burnt House
Fulham's Farm
Brownings Farm
GRAVEL LANE
Chigwell Row
CHIGWELL ROW WATER WORKS
Filter Beds
RESERVOIR
Settling Tanks
RES
Chase Farm Riding Stables
The Maypole PH
Miller's Farm
GREEN LANE
Ross Bridge
Oaks Farm
Chigwell Brook
Chigwell
HIGH ROAD
HAINAULT ROAD
CHIGWELL
New Barns Farm
Hillside
White Ridge
COV RES
VICARAGE LANE
AMBOURNE ROAD
LAMBOURNE ROAD
REC GRD
Forest House
Sch and Training Cen
PLAYING FIELD
Chig Well (Site of)
Nursery Farm
CHIGWELL CEMETERY
FROGHALL LANE
GRANGE HILL
Gas Trans. Sta
SPORTS GROUND
Luxborough Nursery
Chigwell Nursery
Cedar Court Lodge
CHIGWELL GOLF COURSE
Clubhouse
A113
A123
A1112
B173
MANOR ROAD
FENCEPIECE ROAD
CONVENT OF THE SACRED HEART
Bald Hind PH
Grange Hill
L.R.T. DEPOT
BROCKET WAY
MANFORD WAY
Health Cen
Comm Cen
Lib
Fire Sta
Prim Sch
Sec Sch
Redbridge House (Guide Dogs for the Blind)
Prince Regent Hotel
Kennels
Orchard House
SPORTS GRD
Clubhouse
Claybury Hospital (Closed)
Woodford Bridge
Claybury Hall
Forest House
HOSPITAL HILL WOOD
Claybury Woods
Hospital Hill
COCKED HAT PLANTATION
Tomswood Hill
TOMSWOOD ROAD
P & O Nedlloyd
HAINAULT
HAINAULT RECREATION GROUND
FOREST ROAD PLAYING FIELD
ILFORD WANDERERS R.F.C.
FAIRLOP OAK PLAYING FIELD
SPORTS GROUND
BRACKEN INDUSTRIAL ESTATE
FOREST INDUSTRIAL PARK
Old Maypole PH
Works
SPORTS GROUND
Sailing Centre
Forest Farm
FAIRLOP WATER
FAIRLOP
Sports Cen
Fullwell Cross
IG6
FAIRLOP WATER GOLF COURSE
ASH PLANTATION
OWEN WATERS HO
COCKED HAT PLANTATION
Clinic
Youth Cen
Sec Sch
IG5
CLAYHALL
TIPTREE ESTATE
GARDEN OF REST
BARKINGSIDE CEM
BARKINGSIDE REC GRD
Riding School
PAINTERS
IG2
ALDBOROUGH
Aldborough Hall Farm
Cinema
BARKINGSIDE
43
44
45
91
92
93
94
45
46
47
48
49
50
51
52
53
54
69

Lambourne End
Clark's Wood
Marchings Farm
Bishop's Hall
Poultry Farm
St. John's Farm
Gallman's End Farm
Blackbush Farm
Glasshouses
Knolls Hill Farm
Taylor May's Farm
Pettits Hall
Mansfield Outdoor Centre
Crabtree Hill
Hop Pole Farm
The Camelot PH
Brownings Farm
Willow Park Farm
Harmes Farm
Banks Farm
Three Corners Plain
Taylor's Plain
Spurgate Plain
Spurgate Brook
Weddrell's Plain
Burnt House
Fulham's Farm
IG7
Chigwell Row
Girl Guides Camp Site
Chigwell Row Water Works
Reservoir
Settling Tanks
Chase Farm Riding Stables
Miller's Farm
The Maypole PH
Two Brewers PH
HAINAULT FOREST COUNTRY PARK
Cabin Hill
Cabin Plain
Sandhills
Lower Sandhills
Park Farm
Epping Forest
Redbridge
Essex
The Lake
Foxburrows Farm
Elec Sta
HAINAULT FOREST GOLF COURSE
Dog Kennel Hill
Mile Plantation
Lower Park Farm
Willoughby's Hill
Havering Park
Playing Field
Sch and Training Cen
Chig Well (Site of)
Fairview
Prim Sch
Health Cen
Comm Cen
Lib
Fire Sta
Sec Sch
Hainault Industrial Estate
Sports Ground
Clubhouse
Practice Ground
Five Oaks Lane
IG6
Forest Road Playing Field
Hainault Recreation Ground
Fairlop Oak Playing Field
Bracken Industrial Estate
Sailing Centre
Fairlop Water
RM6
RM5
Forest Farm
Hainault Farm
Seven Kings Water
Hainault Road
Whalebone Lane North
Romford Road
Hog Hill Rd
Collier Row
Gobions Farm
Youth Cen
Nursery
Collier Row FC
Works
Bowling Alley
Whites Farm
Mark's Gate
Furze House Farm
Redbridge
Barking & Dagenham
Riding School
Painters Road
Mill Farm
World War II Gun Emplacements
Sports Ground
Marks Gate Cem
Aldborough Hall Farm
IG2
EU
EV
EW
EX
EY
EZ
FA
A1112
B173
B174

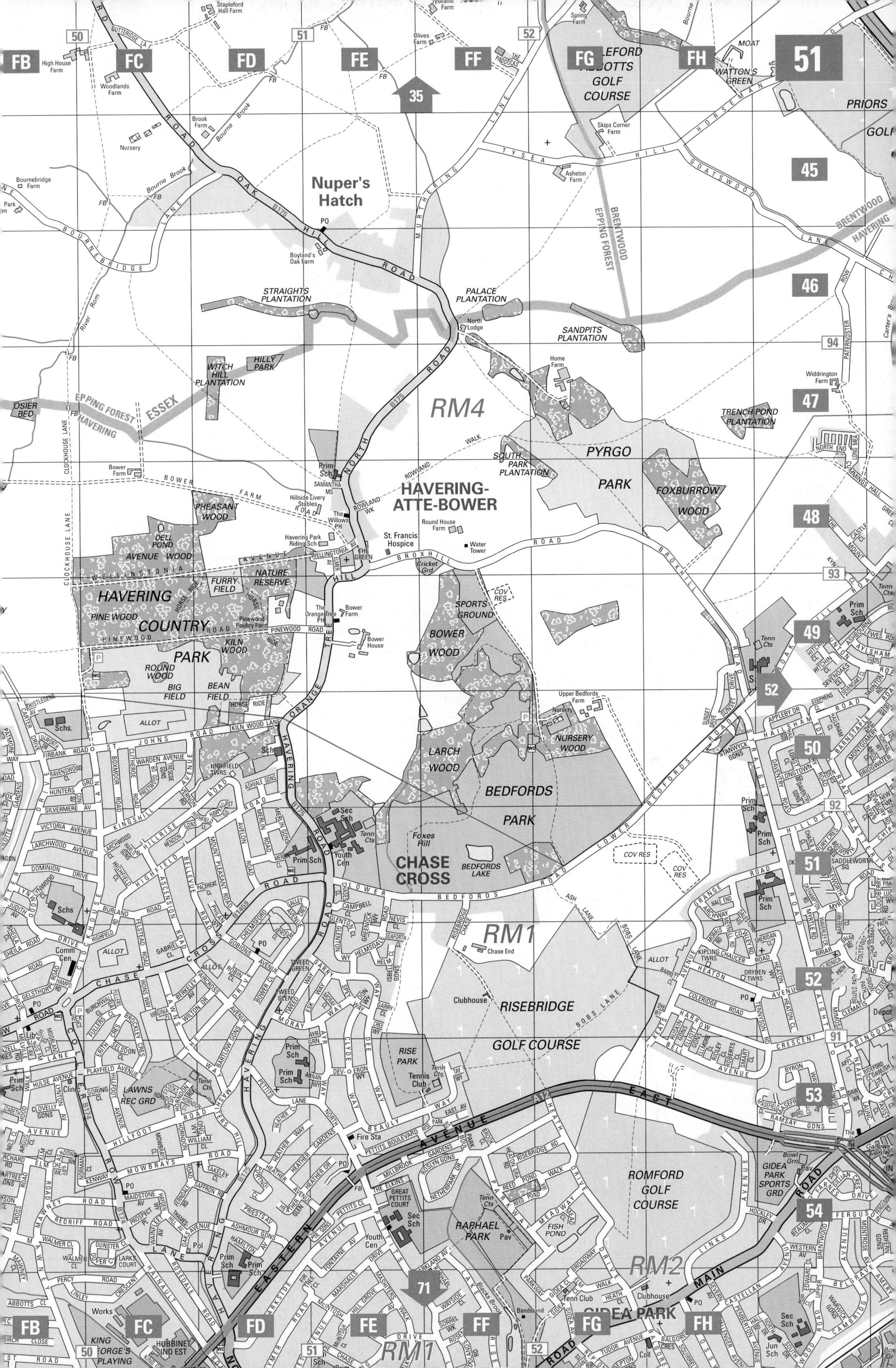

FB
FC
FD
FE
FF
FG
FH
51
50
52
35
71
RM4
RM1
RM2
Nuper's Hatch
HAVERING-ATTE-BOWER
CHASE CROSS
GIDEA PARK
PYRGO PARK
BEDFORDS PARK
HAVERING COUNTRY PARK
STAPLEFORD ABBOTTS GOLF COURSE
RISEBRIDGE GOLF COURSE
ROMFORD GOLF COURSE
RAPHAEL PARK
RISE PARK
LAWNS REC GRD
GIDEA PARK SPORTS GRD
PRIORS
STRAIGHTS PLANTATION
PALACE PLANTATION
SANDPITS PLANTATION
WITCH HILL PLANTATION
HILLY PARK
SOUTH PARK PLANTATION
TRENCH POND PLANTATION
FOXBURROW WOOD
PHEASANT WOOD
DELL POND
AVENUE WOOD
NATURE RESERVE
FURRY FIELD
PINE WOOD
KILN WOOD
ROUND WOOD
BIG FIELD
BEAN FIELD
BOWER WOOD
LARCH WOOD
NURSERY WOOD
SPORTS GROUND
BEDFORDS LAKE
Foxes Hill
OSIER BED
EPPING FOREST
ESSEX
HAVERING
BRENTWOOD
NORTH ROAD
OAK HILL ROAD
ORANGE TREE HILL
HAVERING ROAD
BROXHILL ROAD
LOWER BEDFORDS ROAD
CHASE CROSS ROAD
EASTERN AVENUE
MAIN ROAD
TYSEA HILL
HORSEMAN
GOATSWOOD LANE
BOURNEBRIDGE LANE
CLOCKHOUSE LANE
BOWER FARM ROAD
PINEWOOD ROAD
WELLINGTONIA AVENUE
ST. JOHNS ROAD
KILN WOOD LANE
MURTHERING LANE
PATERNOSTER ROW
BOBS LANE
ASH LANE
St. Francis Hospice
Round House Farm
Water Tower
Upper Bedfords Farm
Bower House
Bower Farm
Home Farm
North Lodge
Boyland's Oak Farm
Asheton Farm
Skips Corner Farm
Widdrington Farm
Brook Farm
Woodlands Farm
High House Farm
Bournebridge Farm
Stapleford Hall Farm
Olives Farm
Spring Farm
Chase End
Clubhouse
Fire Sta
Tennis Club
Youth Cen
Sec Sch
Prim Sch
Comm Cen
Works
HUBBINET IND EST
KING GEORGE'S PLAYING

52
FJ
FK
FL
FM
FN
FP
FQ
PRIORS GOLF COURSE
CURTIS PLANTATION
WABBING'S PLANTATION
SEVENACRE PLANTATION
ESSEX
BRENTWOOD
HAVERING
LOCKSMITH WOOD
GOLDSMITH WOOD
Frieze Hall
The Chequers PH
Weald Bridge
Hou Hatch
Old Macdonalds Farm
Wrightsbridge Farm
Wealdside
Rochetts Farm
St. Vincent's Hamlet
Pentowan Farm
SPICE PITS WOOD
NOAK HILL SPORTS GRD
Widdrington Farm
Noak Hill
TRENCH POND PLANTATION
THE OSIERS
BURNT WOOD
FOXBURROW
The Bear PH
Manor Farm
DAGNAM PARK
FIR WOOD
COCK WOOD
MAYLANDS GOLF COURSE
ALDER WOOD
HATTER'S WOOD
DUCK WOOD NATURE RESERVE
Clubhouse
Maylands
CENTRAL PARK
HAROLD HILL
LONG WOOD
SALE WOOD
SHOULDER OF MUTTON WOOD
RM3
HAROLD PARK
The Saxon King PH
PLAYING FIELD
Paine's Bridge
HAROLD HILL INDUSTRIAL ESTATE
BATES INDUSTRIAL EST
Harold Court
Roots & Shoots Nursery
Ivy Lodge Farm
The Shepherd & Dog PH
Cockabourne Bridge
Pages Farm
HAROLD WOOD HOSPITAL
HAROLD WOOD
AVENUE INDUSTRIAL ESTATE
Gallows Corner
The Plough PH
ROMFORD GOLF COURSE
GIDEA PARK SPORTS GRD
RM2
HAROLD WOOD PARK
Prospect Farm
Tyes Farm
Abattoir
72
COLCHESTER ROAD
A12
SOUTHEND ARTERIAL ROAD
MAIN ROAD
M25
45
46
47
48
49
50
51
52
53
54
91
92
93
94
54
55
56

53
FR
FS
FT
FU
FV
FW
FX
57
58
59
CM15
CM14
CM13
WEALD
COUNTRY
PARK
SOUTH
WEALD LAKE
BELVEDERE
FIELD
LARCH
WOOD
FOX
WOOD
LANGTONS
WOOD
FOXDOWN
WOOD
THE FOREST
LODGE FIELD
THE
PARK
Langtons
Farm
Calcott
Hall Farm
HIGH
WOOD
LARKINS
PLAYING
FIELDS
THE
SPINNEY
South
Weald
Tower Arms
PH
VICARAGE
WOOD
LOWER
VICARAGE
WOOD
Bennett's
Farm
Old
Vicarage
Junction
28
BRENTWOOD BYPASS
Post House
Hotel
BROOK
STREET
BRENTWOOD
LITTLE
HIGHWOOD
HOSP
HIGHWOOD
HOSP
CONVENT
OF MERCY
Anglia
Polytechnic Uni
ESSEX COUNTY
CRICKET
GRD
ESSEX
NUFFIELD
HOSP
BRENTWOOD
COMM HOSP
SPORTS
GROUND
Sawyer's
Hall Farm
Superstore
Shop Cen
CATH
COUNTY CT
COUNCIL
OFF
B.T.
Offices
LONDON
ROAD
CEM
GAS
WORKS
IND EST
KING GEORGES
FIELDS
Clubhouse
Bowling
Greens
WARLEY
WARLEY
HOSPITAL
CEMETERY
DONKEY LANE
PLANTATION
HART'S
WOOD
KENT'S
WOOD
BARRACK WOOD
CLEMENT'S
WOOD
WARLEY
PLAYING FIELDS
MARILLAC
HOSPITAL
B.U.P.A.
HARTSWOOD
HOSP
DEVIL'S HEAD
PLANTATION
LITTLE
WARLEY
COMMON
ELLEN'S
WOOD
HOLDEN'S
WOOD
DRIVING
RANGE
Brentwood
Ski Cen
WARLEY
GAP
Tomlins
Nursery
Mascalls
LOWER BELT
BACHELOR'S
WALK
Leverton
House
Leverton
Hall
Boyles
Court Farm
Great
Ropers
Horse & Groom
PH
Headley
Arms PH
BRENTWOOD
HAVERING
ESSEX
TOP
PLANTATION
TYLERS
SHAW
WORMWALK
SHAW
JERMAINS
WOOD
JACKSONS
WOOD
Tylers
Hall
WARLEY
PLACE NATURE
RESERVE
Warley
Lea Farm
Thatchers Arms
PH
Great
Warley
Stonyhills
Farm
Stonyhills
House
Coombe
Lodge
FOXBURROW
WOOD
COOMBE
WOOD
Tooks
Farm
Pump
Farm
HOLDEN'S
WOOD
RUSHY
PIECE
WARLEY
PARK
GOLF
COURSE
Clubhouse
Clap Gate
Farm
Little Warley
Lodge
Home
Farm
Hole
Farm
Suttons
73
54
45
46
47
48
49
50
51
52
53
54
94
93
92
91
A12
A128
A1023
B186
M25

54
Bentley
Crow Green
PILGRIM'S HATCH
WEALD COUNTRY PARK
South Weald
BRENTWOOD
CM14
CM15
BROOK STREET
WARLEY
52
53
FS
FT
FU
FV
FW
FX
FY
58
59
60
41
42
43
44
45
46
47
48
49
50
96
95
94
93
Junction 28
WARLEY HOSPITAL
SHENFIELD COMMON
DONKEY LANE PLANTATION

FZ
GA
GB
GC
GD
GE
GF
61
62
63
41
42
43
44
45
46
47
48
49
50
96
95
94
93
ICEHOUSE WOOD
Fitzwalter's Farm
Chain Bridge
Chainbridge Farm
HOME WOOD
Begrums Farm
Jordans Farm
Arnold's Farm
MOUNTNESSING
BRENTWOOD BYPASS
CHELMSFORD ROAD
ROMAN ROAD
LOWER ROAD
ARNOLDS FARM LANE
OLD CHURCH LANE (SHIP LANE)
OLD CHURCH ROAD
ARNOLD'S WOOD
ARNOLD'S SHAW
BRICKLEY SHAW
Elec Sta
WASH ROAD
River Wid
Wynbarns Farm
Rose Inn PH
Sports Cen
Sec Sch
REC GRD
ALEXANDER LANE
Works
OLIVER ROAD
LONG RIDINGS
SPORTS GROUND
Prim Sch
PLAYING FLDS
Comm Cen
Clinic
ALLOT
COLLIN'S SHAW
COCK WOOD
COURAGE PLAYING FIELDS
Cricket Club
Eagle & Child PH
HUTTON ROAD
RAYLEIGH ROAD
A129
A1023
A12
A128
HUTTON
Hutton Stud Farm
Bushwood
HAMBROS BANK SPORTS GROUND
Martines Farm
Essex Fire & Rescue H.Q.
SHENFIELD
HUTTON MOUNT
HUTTON FC
Cricket Ground
Humes Farm
Hutton Hall
MOAT
CHURCH SHAW
HUTTON VILLAGE
BLOOD TRANSFUSION SERVICE
Lido
Tenn Cts
Creasey's Farm
Brindles Farm
THRIFT WOOD (SCOUT CAMP)
SPORTS GROUND
HALL WOOD
PRIMSTOCK
LITTLE BLADEN'S WOOD
Filter Beds
Ingrave Hall
Site of St Nicholas's Church
BIRCHES WOOD
SUTTON SHAW
BLADEN'S WOOD
Heatleys
Fountains Head PH
HIGHFIELD WOOD
CM13
BRENTWOOD ROAD
HARTSWOOD GOLF COURSE
MIDDLE ROAD
Salmond's Farm
INGRAVE
LONG PLANTATION
Clubhouse
THORNDON PARK
Heron Hall
Heron Hall Farm
COV RES

Layter's Green
Hedgerley
Gerrards Cross
Fulmer
Farnham Common
BULSTRODE PARK
STOKE COMMON
OXFORD ROAD
SL9
SL2
SL3
M40

57
WD3
37
GERRARDS CROSS GOLF COURSE
CHALFONT PARK
NOCKHILL WOOD
JUNIPER WOOD
TRAINING CENTRE DURDENT COURT
THREE RIVERS
SOUTH BUCKS
GREAT HALINGS WOOD
SQUARE COPSE
ROUND COPSE
QUARTERS WOOD
OAKEND WOOD
NORTHMOOR HILL (NATURE RESERVE)
BATTLESFORD WOOD
RANSTON COVERT
DENHAM MARSH WOOD
DENHAM AERODROME
WADLEY COVERT
NIGHTINGALE WOOD
HOLLY HILL WOOD
Rank Film Laboratories
Denham Green
NEWSTEAD WOOD
DENHAM GOLF COURSE
COLLSELS WOOD
Higher Denham
MILL WOOD
GALLOWS WOOD
TOM WILLIAM'S WOOD
BRADBURY'S ISLAND
MARTINSFIELD SPORTS GRD
UB9
LITTLE GALLOWS WOOD
THE RANCHO
CAPS WOOD
BAKER'S WOOD
BUCKINGHAM
Tatling End
NABOTH
GALDWINS WOOD
BROADSPRING WOOD
HAWKS WOOD
FURZENEY WOOD
Junction 16 (M25)
Junction 1a (M40)
Holly Bush
Denham
GOSSAMS WOOD
BROWN'S WOOD
OLDHOUSE WOOD
PARKSPRING WOOD
MOUNT FIDGET WOOD
LONG COPPICE
LANGLEY COMMON
BRIDGETTINE CONVENT
Langley Corner
M25
M40
A40
A412
A413
55
56
57
58
59
60
61
62
63
64
75
89
88
87
86
01
02
03
AZ
BA
BB
BC
BD
BE
BF

BG
BH
BJ
BK
BL
BM
BN
05
06
07
38
ASHAIN SPRING
SCARLET SPRING
KILN POND
CLAYPITS
DELL
Shooting School
HIGHBONES
Knightscote Farm
Langley Farm
Football Ground
Cricket Ground
NORTH BREAKSPEAR ROAD
Bourne Farm
Warren Farm
SOUTH HAREFIELD
Park Lodge Farm Centre
BAYHURST WOOD COUNTRY PARK
Grand Union Canal
TOWING PATH
Broadwater Farm
55
56
57
58
59
60
61
62
63
64
89
88
87
86
NORTH ORBITAL ROAD
A412
Wyatts Covert Caravan Site
NORTHMOOR (NATURE RESERVE)
BATTLESFORD WOOD
RANSTON COVERT
Rank Film Laboratories
SPORTS GRD
Denham Lock
Widewater Lock
HAREFIELD MOOR
UB9
Horse & Barge PH
COV RES
Pumping Sta
MOORHALL ROAD
BROADWATER PARK
Green Bridge
SOUTH BUCKS
HILLINGDON
Savay Farm
SAVAY LANE
Denham Green
NEWSTEAD WOOD
TILEHOUSE
Medical Centre
PUBLIC TIP
Highway Farm
NEW YEARS GREEN
St. Leonard's Farm
Pylon Farm
High View Farm
Braemer Farm
Newyears Green
NEWYEARS GREEN COVERT
Activities Centre
Dews Farm
DENHAM
ALTCAR COVERT
CRUISE COVERT
Clubhouse
BUCKINGHAMSHIRE GOLF COURSE
DENHAM COUNTRY PARK
UXBRIDGE GOLF COURSE
Glaxo Research Farm
SKIP LANE
Works
Depot
COPTHALL COVERT
MOAT
The Prescotts
Denham Place
FLAGMOOR COVERT
COWMOOR COVERT
Denham Court
Wellers Mead
Hall
VILLAGE ROAD
River Misbourne
OXFORD ROAD
A40
Harvil Farm
Copthall Farm
BREAKSPEAR ROAD SOUTH
Weir
ST. JOHN'S COVERT
PRIORY COVERT
Denham
SPORTS GROUND
Little Acres Farm
DENHAM COUNTRY PARK
Fray's River
Lea Cottage
The Lea
Glasshouses
Farm
Junction 1
M40
WESTERN AVENUE
A40
New House Farm
Depot
Comm Cen
WEATHERLYS COVERT
SWAKELEYS ROAD
RIVERSIDE WALK
THE CLUMP
Sec Sch
Tennis Club
PARK WOOD
Common Plantation
Cornerfields
Ivy House Farm
Oxford Road Nursery
Denham Utd. FC
Dog & Duck PH
PLAYING FIELD
Uxbridge Alderglade Nature Reserve
Fray's Bridge
Shire Ditch
A4020
DENHAM ROAD
Kingcup Farm
Brickfield Farm
76
UXBRIDGE COMMON
Ski Slopes
Hillingdon Ski Centre
UXBRIDGE STADIUM
HILLINGDON HOUSE FARM SPORTS GROUND
UB10
Cricket Club
Open Air Pool
Copse Hill Farm
Southlands Manor
Osborne Farm
B483
PARK ROAD

59
Northwood Hills
NORTH CEMETERY
RUISLIP NATURE RESERVE
HILL GOLF COURSE
39
COPSE WOOD
HA6
YOUNG WOOD
Youngwood Farm
BESS WOOD
POOR'S FIELD
ST. VINCENT'S ORTHOPAEDIC HOSPITAL
RUISLIP LIDO
Ruislip Lido Miniature Railway
PARK WOOD
RUISLIP COMMON
Breakspear Crematorium
SPORTS GROUNDS
DUCKS HILL ROAD
BURY STREET
HIGH STREET
WEST END ROAD
A4180
CUCKOO HILL
HA5
EASTCOTE VILLAGE
Haydon Hall
EASTCOTE HO GRD
Grangewood Sch
Eastcote Hockey & Badminton Club
KINGS COLLEGE PLAYING FIELDS
HA4
Cricket Club
GOVERNMENT OFFICES
Swim Pool & Fitness Cen
WARRENDER PARK
EASTCOTE
RUISLIP
BURIAL GRD
RUISLIP GOLF COURSE
DRIVING RANGE
RUISLIP MANOR
Windmill Hill
CAVENDISH REC GRD
PINE GDNS
SPORTS GROUND
BESSINGBY FIELD
WEST RUISLIP
Barracks
ICKENHAM
Compass Arts Thea
Ruislip R.F.C.
NEW POND FARM FIELDS
RUISLIP GARDENS
DEPOT
Ickenham Marsh
Warehouse Hangar
Hangars
ODYSSEY BUSINESS PARK
SOUTH RUISLIP
NORTHOLT AERODROME
77
Master Brewer Hotel
FREEZELAND COVERT
Yeading Brook
Canal Feeder
BP
BQ
BR
BS
BT
BU
BV
08
09
10
55
56
57
58
59
60
61
62
63
64
86
87
88
89

BW
BX
BY
BZ
CA
CB
CC
12
13
14
40
55
56
57
58
59
60
61
62
63
64
86
87
88
89
78
PINNER GREEN
PINNER
PINNER MEMORIAL PARK
LITTLE COMMON
CEM
PINNER VILLAGE GARDENS
PINNER NEW CEMETERY
HEADSTONE MANOR
RECREATION GROUND
NORTH HARROW
HEADSTO
EASTCOTE VILLAGE
EASTCOTE
CUCKOO HILL
HA5
HA2
HA4
THE CROFT PLAYING FIELD
WARRENDER PARK
RAYNERS LANE
WEST HARROW
WEST HARROW REC GRD
ROXBOURNE PARK
CAVENDISH REC GRD
PINE GDNS
BESSINGBY FIELD
RECREATION GROUND
NEWTON PARK WEST
NEWTON FM ECOLOGY PK
SOUTH HARROW
ALEXANDRA PARK
SOUTH RUISLIP
DEANE PARK
VICTORIA RETAIL PARK
FROGMORE ESTATE
SOLID WASTE TRANSFER STATION
NORTHOLT RECREATION GRD
PLAYING FIELD
ODYSSEY BUSINESS PARK
LORD HALSBURY MEMORIAL GRD
SPORTS GROUND
EARLSMEAD STADIUM
HILLINGDON
HARROW
EALING
UXBRIDGE RD
GEORGE V AVENUE
PINNER ROAD
ALEXANDRA AVENUE
NORTHOLT ROAD
WEST END ROAD
VICTORIA ROAD
EASTCOTE ROAD
FIELD END ROAD
PETTS HILL
A404
A4090
A312
A4180

61
CD
CE
CF
CG
CH
CJ
CK
15
16
17
41
55
56
57
58
59
60
61
62
63
64
79
86
87
88
89
BELMONT
QUEENSBURY
HA7
WEALDSTONE
WEALDSTONE CEM
WAVERLEY INDUSTRIAL ESTATE
HARROW & WEALDSTONE
CIVIC CENTRE
CIVIC AMENITY SITE
HAWTHORN CENTRE
HA3
KENTON RECREATION GROUND
KENTON
KENTON ROAD
WOODCOCK PARK
HARROW
HARROW REC
CEM
ST. ANN'S CENTRE
HARROW ON THE HILL
HA1
HARROW HILL GOLF COURSE
University of Westminster
NORTHWICK PARK HOSPITAL
NORTHWICK PARK
Northwick Park Pavilion
THE GROVE OPEN SPACE
MINIATURE RIFLE RANGE
HARROW SCHOOL PLAYING FIELDS
Harrow School Farm
HARROW SCHOOL GOLF COURSE
JOHN BILLAM SPORTS GRD
PRESTON
PRESTON PARK
SOUTH KENTON
NORTH WEMBLEY
ROXETH
ST. ANDREW'S AT HARROW HOSP
CLEMENTINE CHURCHILL HOSPITAL
CHASEWOOD PARK
SPORTS GROUND
WEMBLEY COMMERCIAL CENTRE
HA9
FORTY FARM SPORTS GROUND
G.E.C. ESTATE
VALE FARM SPORTS GROUND
WEMBLEY FC
KING EDWARD VII PARK
EALING NORTHERN SPORTS GRD
UB6
SUDBURY
BARHAM PARK
HA0
SUDBURY HILL
SUDBURY HILL HARROW
SUDBURY & HARROW ROAD
SUDBURY TOWN
WEMBLEY CENTRAL
NORTH WEMBLEY
WHITTON AVENUE WEST
EASTCOTE AVENUE
HARROW ROAD
WATFORD ROAD
EAST LANE
GREENFORD ROAD

QUEENSBURY
KINGSBURY
FRYENT
COUNTRY
PARK
FRYENT COUNTRY PARK
BARN HILL
OPEN SPACE
PRESTON
WEMBLEY
PARK
WEMBLEY
KYNGTON
CHURCH
END
COLINDALE HOSP
KINGSBURY HOSPITAL
SILVER
JUBILEE
PARK
WEST HENDON
PLAYING FIELDS
WOODCOCK
PARK
PRESTON
PARK
HA7
HA8
HA3
HA9
NW9
NW10
KENTON
ROAD
HONEYPOT
LANE
FRYENT
WAY
FORTY
AVENUE
FORTY
LANE
HARROW
ROAD
HIGH
ROAD
EDGWARE
ROAD
KINGSBURY
ROAD
SALMON
STREET
BLACKBIRD HILL
NEASDEN
LANE
WEMBLEY PARK DRIVE
WEMBLEY
ARENA
CL
CM
CN
CP
CQ
CR
CS

CT
CU
CV
CW
CX
CY
CZ
22
23
24
43
63
55
56
57
58
59
60
61
62
63
64
81
86
87
88
89
HOLDERS HILL
SUNNY HILL PARK
GARDEN HOSP
N3
THE HYDE
HENDON
MALCOLM PARK
NW4
HENDON PARK
Brent Cross Shopping Centre
Junction 1
BRENT RESERVOIR
CLITTERHOUSE PLAYING FIELDS
NW11
HOOP LANE CEMETERY (JEWISH)
GOLDERS GREEN
CHILDS HILL
DOLLIS HILL
CRICKLEWOOD
GLADSTONE PARK
NW2
UNIVERSITY COLLEGE SCHOOL SPORTS GRD
HAMPSTEAD CEMETERY
WILLESDEN
NORTH CIRCULAR ROAD
HENDON WAY
EDGWARE ROAD
CRICKLEWOOD BROADWAY
FINCHLEY ROAD
WATFORD WAY
A406
A41
A5
M1

64
DA
DB
DC
DD
DE
DF
DG
N3
N2
N6
NW11
NW3
EAST FINCHLEY
FORTIS GREEN
HAMPSTEAD GARDEN SUBURB
GOLDERS GREEN
CHILDS HILL
HAMPSTEAD HEATH
HAMPSTEAD
WEST HAMPSTEAD
PARLIAMENT HILL
HIGHGATE WOOD
HIGHGATE GOLF COURSE
HAMPSTEAD GOLF CLUB
HAMPSTEAD HEATH EXTENSION
EAST FINCHLEY CEMETERY
HOOP LANE CEMETERY (JEWISH)
HAMPSTEAD CEMETERY
GOLDERS HILL PARK
SANDY HEATH
WEST HEATH
KENWOOD
THE IVEAGH BEQUEST - KENWOOD HOUSE
ATHLONE HOUSE
HIGHGATE PONDS
HIGHGATE MEN'S POND
HAMPSTEAD PONDS
VALE OF HEALTH
BIG WOOD
LITTLE WOOD
COLDFALL WOOD
CHERRY TREE WOOD
TURNERS WOOD
NORTH WOOD
LYTTELTON PLAYING FIELDS
NAT HOSP FOR NEUROLOGY & NEUROSURGERY
QUEEN MARY'S HOSP
ROYAL FREE HOSP
NORTH CIRCULAR ROAD
FINCHLEY ROAD
FALLODEN WAY
LYTTELTON ROAD
AYLMER ROAD
GREAT NORTH ROAD
ARCHWAY ROAD
NORTH END ROAD
NORTH END WAY
HEATH STREET
SPANIARDS ROAD
HAMPSTEAD LANE
HAMPSTEAD HIGH ST
ROSSLYN HILL
HAVERSTOCK HILL
EAST END ROAD
FORTIS GREEN
HENDON WAY
FORTUNE GREEN ROAD
WEST END LANE
MILL LANE
GOSPEL OAK EST
LISMORE CIRCUS
ST. DOMINIC'S PRIORY
Camden Arts Centre
FINCHLEY ROAD & FROGNAL
WEST HAMPSTEAD (THAMESLINK)
FREUD MUSEUM
TAVISTOCK CEN
ATHLETICS TRACK
26
27
28
44
63
82

DH
DJ
DK
DL
DM
DN
DP
65
29
30
31
45
55
56
57
58
59
60
61
62
63
64
66
83
86
87
88
89
NOEL PARK
LORDSHIP RECREATION GROUND
ALEXANDRA PALACE
ALEXANDRA PARK
N22
MUSWELL HILL
HORNSEY
WEST GREEN
BELMONT REC GRD
DOWNHILLS PARK
CHESTNUTS REC GRD
ST. ANN'S HOSPITAL
N8
PRIORY PARK
HORNSEY CENTRAL HOSP
CROUCH END PLAYING FIELDS
QUEEN'S WOOD
HARRINGAY
CROUCH END
STROUD GREEN
HIGHGATE
FINSBURY PARK
N4
AMERICAN GDNS
N19
WHITTINGTON HOSPITAL
HIGHGATE CEMETERY
WATERLOW PARK
UPPER HOLLOWAY
ARCHWAY
TUFNELL PARK
DARTMOUTH PARK
HOLLOWAY
H.M. PRISON HOLLOWAY
LOWER HOLLOWAY
N7
N5
KENTISH TOWN
HIGHBURY
CANONBURY
PENTONVILLE PRISON
WEST RESERVOIR
SPORTS GROUND
ARSENAL

66
NOEL PARK
DQ
DR
DS
DT
DU
DV
DW
33
34
35
46
55
56
57
58
59
60
61
62
63
64
65
84
86
87
88
89
N22
N17
N15
N16
N4
N5
E5
E8
LORDSHIP RECREATION GROUND
TOTTENHAM MARSH
RESERVOIR
BRUCE GROVE
TOTTENHAM HALE
LOCKWOOD INDUSTRIAL PARK
LEE VALLEY TECHNOPARK
MILMEAD INDUSTRIAL CENTRE
DOWN LANE REC GRD
WEST GREEN
DOWNHILLS PARK
BELMONT REC GRD
MONUMENT WAY
FERRY LANE
LOW MAYNARD RESERVOIR
BOWLING ALLEY
HIGH CROSS CENTRE
RESERVOIR NUMBER TWO
RESERVOIR NUMBER ONE
RESERVOIR NUMBER THREE
RESERVOIR NUMBER FOUR
RESERVOIR NUMBER FIVE
WARWICK RESERVOIR EAST
WARWICK RESERVOIR WEST
MARKFIELD REC GRD
Markfield Beam Engine
CHESTNUTS REC GRD
ST. ANN'S HOSPITAL
SEVEN SISTERS
SOUTH TOTTENHAM
WEST GREEN ROAD
SEVEN SISTERS ROAD
HARRINGAY GREEN LANES
RAILWAY FLDS
FINSBURY PARK
AMERICAN GDNS
EAST RESERVOIR
WEST RESERVOIR
COPPERMILL PLAYING FIELD
SPRINGHILL SPORTS GRD
SPRINGFIELD PARK
Walthamstow Marsh Nature Reserve
CLAPTON COMMON
STAMFORD HILL
STAMFORD HILL ESTATE
UPPER CLAPTON
ABNEY PARK CEMETERY
STOKE NEWINGTON
CLISSOLD PARK
NORTH MILLFIELDS RECREATION GROUND
SHACKLEWELL
HACKNEY DOWNS
BUTTERFIELD GREEN
HIGHBURY
CANONBURY
HIGHBURY & ISLINGTON
KINGSLAND
HACKNEY
HACKNEY CENTRAL
HACKNEY DOWNS
DALSTON LANE
AMHURST ROAD
STOKE NEWINGTON HIGH ST
STAMFORD HILL
HIGH ROAD
UPPER CLAPTON ROAD
LOWER CLAPTON ROAD
GREEN LANES
BLACKSTOCK ROAD
BALLS POND ROAD
ST. PAUL'S ROAD

67
DX
DY
DZ
EA
EB
EC
ED
36
37
38
47
55
56
57
58
59
60
61
62
63
64
68
85
86
87
88
89
HIGHAM HILL
LLOYD PARK
WALTHAMSTOW
FOREST ATHLETICS GRD
CHESTNUTS SHOWGROUND
TOWN HALL
ASSEMBLY HALL
THORPE COOMBE HOSP
UPLANDS BUSINESS PARK
HIGHAMS LODGE BUSINESS CEN
EPPING FOREST
CHILDREN'S BOATING POND
UPPER WALTHAMSTOW
E17
DOUGLAS EYRE PLAYING FIELDS
WALTHAMSTOW CENTRAL
WALTHAMSTOW QUEENS ROAD
Selbourne Walk Shop Cen
WALTHAMSTOW CEM
ST. JAMES'S PARK
LOW HALL SPORTS GROUND
CIVIC AMENITY TIP
ALLOTMENTS
LEYTON IND VILLAGE
FOREST BUSINESS PK
ROXWELL TRADING PK
DORMA TRADING PK
CROMWELL IND EST
WHIPPS CROSS HOSPITAL
LEYTONSTONE
E11
SNARESBROOK
LEYTON MIDLAND ROAD
E10
LEYTON
LEYTON GRANGE EST
SEYMOUR ROAD PLAYING FIELD
MARSH LANE PLAYING FIELD
LEA VALLEY GOLF COURSE
LEYTON MARSHES
Lea Valley Riding Cen
NATURE RESERVE
LEA BRIDGE
HACKNEY MARSH
SIDMOUTH PARK
LEYTON ORIENT F.C.
ST. PATRICK'S RC CEMETERY
New Spitalfields Market
RECREATION GROUND
ETON MANOR SPORTS GROUND
Lea Valley Sports Centre
WICK FIELD
LEE VALLEY PARK
EASTWAY CYCLE CIRCUIT
EASTWAY COMMERCIAL CENTRE
HACKNEY WICK
STADIUM (CLOSED)
CLAPTON PARK
LOWER CLAPTON
HOMERTON
MABLEY GREEN
E9
DRAPERS FIELD REC. GRD
WALTHAM FOREST
NEWHAM
LONDON INTERNATIONAL FREIGHT TERMINAL
STRATFORD
E15
JEWISH CEMETERY
Flood Relief Channel
River Lee or Lea
River Lee Navigation
Dagenham Brook
Channelsea River
FOREST ROAD
LEA BRIDGE ROAD
HOE STREET
HIGH ROAD LEYTON
LEYTONSTONE HIGH ROAD
CHURCH ROAD
MARKHOUSE ROAD
BLACKHORSE ROAD
WOOD STREET
WHIPPS CROSS ROAD
EASTWAY
RUCKHOLT ROAD
ORIENT WAY
A503
A104
A112
A1006
A106
A12
A102
B112

68
EE
EF
EG
EH
EJ
EK
EL
IG8
40
41
42
SOUTH WOODFORD
48
E18
EPPING FOREST
SPORTS GROUND
55
56
57
58
59
60
61
62
63
64
67
86
87
88
89
Junction 4
RODING HOSP
RECREATION GROUND
IG4
SNARESBROOK
SNARESBROOK CROWN COURT
HOLLOW POND
EAGLE POND
WHIPPS CROSS HOSPITAL
EPPING FOREST
RUGBY FOOTBALL GROUND
EASTERN AVENUE
WANSTEAD
WANSTEAD GOLF COURSE
LEYTONSTONE
E11
GREEN MAN ROUNDABOUT
WANSTEAD FLATS
BUSH WOOD
THE BASIN
WANSTEAD GOLF COURSE
WANSTEAD PARK
SHOULDER OF MUTTON POND
HERONRY POND
PERCH POND
ORNAMENTAL WATERS
ALDERSBROOK
CITY OF LONDON CEMETERY
WANSTEAD FLATS
JEWISH CEMETERY
WEST HAM CEMETERY
MANOR PARK CEMETERY
MANOR PARK
E7
FOREST GATE
WOODGRANGE PARK CEMETERY
PLASHET JEWISH CEMETERY
E15
STRATFORD
NORTH CIRCULAR ROAD
WOODFORD NEW ROAD
HOLLYBUSH HILL
WHIPPS CROSS ROAD
HERMON HILL
CHIGWELL ROAD
SNARESBROOK ROAD
BLAKE HALL ROAD
CENTRE ROAD
ALDERSBROOK ROAD
LEYTONSTONE ROAD
HIGH ROAD
ROMFORD ROAD
WOODGRANGE ROAD
DAMES ROAD

69
EM
EN
EP
EQ
ER
ES
ET
43
44
45
49
55
56
57
58
59
60
61
62
63
64
70
86
87
88
89
IG6
IG2
IG1
IG3
CLAYHALL
BARKINGSIDE
FAIRLOP WATER GOLF COURSE
ALDBOROUGH HATCH
GANTS HILL
NEWBURY PARK
SEVEN KINGS
VALENTINES PARK
CRANBROOK
ILFORD
LOXFORD
BARKINGSIDE CEM
GARDEN OF REST
CLAYHALL PARK
SEVEN KINGS PARK
SOUTH PARK
KING GEORGE HOSPITAL
KING GEORGE HOSP
GOODMAYES HOSPITAL
GOODMAYES PARK REC GRD
MAYESBROOK PARK
BARKING PARK
LITTLE ILFORD PARK
MELBOURNE FIELD
KNOX SPORTS FIELD
CRICKLEFIELD ATHLETIC GRD
ILFORD CEMETERY
THE LAKE
BOATING LAKE
EASTERN AVENUE
CRANBROOK ROAD
HIGH ROAD
GREEN LANE
ILFORD LANE
LONGBRIDGE ROAD
WOODFORD AVENUE
NORTH SOUTH WOODFORD TO BARKING RELIEF ROAD
WINSTON WAY
ILFORD HILL
GRIGGS APP
AVENUE
PAINTERS ROAD
A12
A118
A123
A124
A406
A1083
A1400

EU
EV
EW
EX
EY
EZ
FA
47
48
49
50
55
56
57
58
59
60
61
62
63
64
69
88
Mark's Gate
IG2
IG3
RM6
RM8
RM9
CHADWELL HEATH
GOODMAYES
BECONTREE
SEVEN KINGS
KING GEORGE HOSPITAL
GOODMAYES HOSPITAL
CHADWELL HEATH HOSP
Redbridge College
Barking College
Barking Coll
EASTERN AVENUE
HIGH ROAD
GREEN LANE
LONGBRIDGE ROAD
WOOD LANE
WHALEBONE LANE NORTH
WHALEBONE LANE SOUTH
HEATHWAY
PAINTERS ROAD
BILLET ROAD
GOODMAYES LANE
BARLEY LANE
HAINAULT ROAD
PADNALL ROAD
PORTERS AVENUE
VALENCE AVENUE
BECONTREE AVENUE
ST. CHADS PARK
KINGS PARK
GOODMAYES PARK
MAYESBROOK PARK
PARSLOES PARK
VALENCE PARK
WESTLANDS PLAYING FIELDS
WEST HAM UNITED FC TRAINING GROUND
GOLF DRIVING RANGE
MARKS GATE CEM
MIRRAVALE TRADING ESTATE
VALENCE HO MUS
VALENCE MOAT
BOATING LAKE
FORD'S SPORTS GROUND
World War II Gun Emplacements
BARKING & DAGENHAM
REDBRIDGE
A12
A118
A124
A1083
A1112
A1153
A1240
B177

71
FB
FC
FD
FE
FF
FG
FH
50
51
52
ROMFORD GOLF COURSE
RM2
GIDEA PARK
RAPHAEL PARK
KING GEORGE'S PLAYING FIELDS
HUBBINET IND EST
RM1
VICTORIA HOSP
LODGE FARM PARK
55
56
57
58
59
60
61
62
63
64
Ardleigh Green
ROMFORD
SPRING GARDENS IND EST
COTTONS PARK
OLDCHURCH HOSPITAL
ROMFORD STADIUM
RM7
Romford Gas Works
HYLANDS PARK
RM11
Havering College
JUTSUMS PARK
OLDCHURCH PARK
ROMFORD CEMETERY
RUSH GREEN
CROWLANDS SPORTS GROUND
72
FORD SPORTS GROUND
RONEO COR.
HORNCHURCH
BARKING & DAGENHAM
Barking College of Technology
CENTRAL PARK
FELS FIELD
WHITE HART LAKES
EASTBROOKEND CEMETERY
HARROW LODGE PARK
BOATING LAKE
THE CHASE NATURE RESERVE
EASTBROOKEND COUNTRY PARK
RM10
STERLING INDUSTRIAL ESTATE
RM12
ELM PARK
Rhone-Poulenc Rorer
DAGENHAM EAST
PONDFIELD PARK
89
A118
A124
A125

72
ROMFORD GOLF COURSE
GIDEA PARK SPORTS GRD
AVENUE INDUSTRIAL ESTATE
HAROLD WOOD
FJ
FK
FL
FM
FN
FP
FQ
54
55
56
52
RM2
RM3
RM11
RM12
SOUTHEND ARTERIAL ROAD
A127
MAIN ROAD
HAROLD WOOD PARK
Prospect Farm
Ingrebourne Farm
Tyes Farm
Abattoir
The Shepherd & Dog PH
Cockabourne Bridge
Palms Hotel
Mount Pleasant Farm
Havering College of Further Educ
Ardleigh Green
SPORTS GRD
HAYNES PARK
GIDEA PARK
ELLIOT PLAYING FIELDS
Lillyputts Farm
ST. MARY'S CONVENT
EMERSON PARK
THORPE LODGE
Havering College
HYLANDS PARK
FIELDERS SPORTS GRD
LANGTON GDNS
UPMINSTER GOLF COURSE
ST. ANDREW'S PARK
Sixth Form Coll
HIGH STREET
A124
UPMINSTER ROAD
HORNCHURCH
HORNCHURCH CEM
UPMINSTER BRIDGE
HORNCHURCH STADIUM
UPMINSTER
ST. MARY'S LANE
UPMINSTER PARK
71
Ingrebourne River
The Ravensbourne
ELM PARK
ST. GEORGES HOSPITAL
GAYNES PARKWAY
Hacton
Hacton House
Park Corner Farm
White Hart PH
Lodge Farm
Rainham Lodge Farm
Gardners Cor Hall
PARKLANDS OPEN SPACE
Corbets Tey Sch
Harwood Hall
Stables
90
57
58
59
60
61
62
63
64
86
87
88
89
Boathouse
Swim Pool
Sports Centre
Bowls Centre
Cricket Club

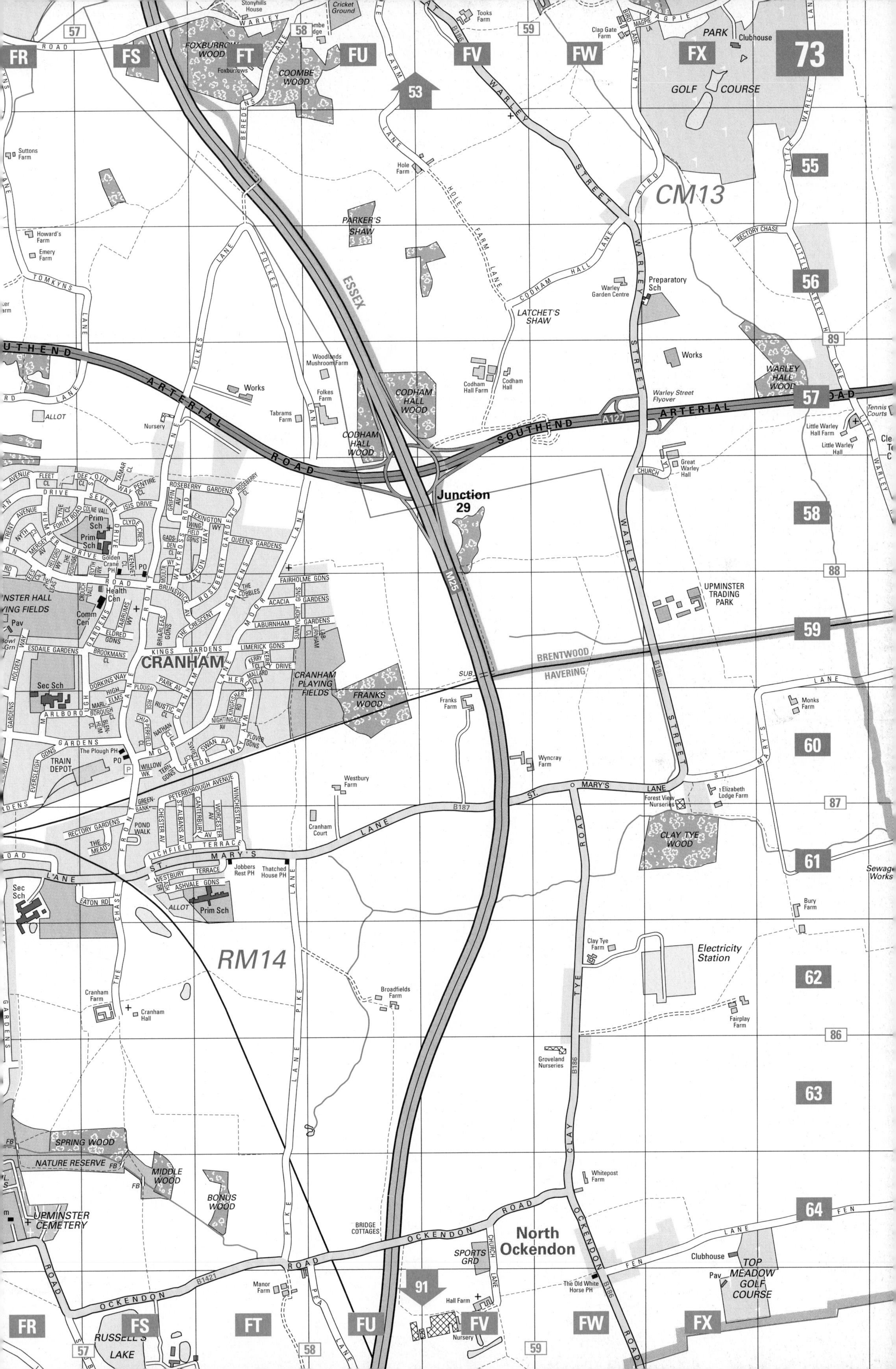
73
53
91
CM13
RM14
CRANHAM
North Ockendon
Junction 29
M25
ESSEX
BRENTWOOD
HAVERING
SOUTHEND ARTERIAL ROAD
WARLEY STREET
ST. MARY'S LANE
CLAY TYE ROAD
OCKENDON ROAD
PIKE LANE
FOXBURROW WOOD
COOMBE WOOD
PARKER'S SHAW
LATCHET'S SHAW
CODHAM HALL WOOD
FRANKS WOOD
CLAY TYE WOOD
WARLEY HALL WOOD
SPRING WOOD
MIDDLE WOOD
BONUS WOOD
NATURE RESERVE
UPMINSTER CEMETERY
CRANHAM PLAYING FIELDS
UPMINSTER TRADING PARK
PARK GOLF COURSE
TOP MEADOW GOLF COURSE
Electricity Station
Warley Street Flyover
TRAIN DEPOT
RUSSELL'S LAKE
FR
FS
FT
FU
FV
FW
FX
55
56
57
58
59
60
61
62
63
64
86
87
88
89

74
AS
AT
AU
AV
AW
AX
AY
98
99
00
56
STOKE COMMON
BROCKHURST WOOD
INGRAM'S COPSE
FRAME WOOD
Penn Wood
Fernacres Farm
Fernacres House
Black Firs
Dar Alshams
FULMER COMMON ROAD
Cricket Grd
Tenn Cts
Mill House Farm
Framewood Manor
Wexham Place
FULMER COMMON
65
66
67
68
69
70
71
72
73
74
84
83
82
81
Farnham Common
PARSON'S WOOD
OLD ORCHARD WOOD
HOME WOOD
Eight Acres Farm
SPORTS GRD
Offices
UPTON WOOD
UPTON LAKE
Upton Farm
STOKE POGES
FARNHAM PARK
GOLF
COURSE
Clubhouses
Tithe Farm
SEFTON PARK
Home Farm
Prim Sch
Hockley Hole
The Stag PH
Wexham Street
DOG KENNEL FIELD
Twin Trees Farm
CUCKOO PEN
Clinic
NUFFIELD HOSP
The Plough PH
ROWLEY WOOD
ROWLEYFIELD LARCHES
ROWLEY SLIP
WALK WOOD
SPORTS GROUND
Clubhouse
WEXHAM PARK GOLF COURSE
GROTES WOOD
GALLIONS WOOD
Grange Farm
Berry Farm
The Clock House
STOKE POGES GOLF COURSE
Monument
Stoke Park Farm
The Manor House
GRAY'S FIELD
Monument to Thomas Gray
Snitterfield Farm
Glasshouse
SPRING WOOD
HOLLYBUSH WOOD
Bell Farm
ROWLEY LAKE
Stoke Park House (Clubhouse)
GARDEN OF REMEMBRANCE
Stoke Green
The Red Lion PH
WEXHAM PARK HOSPITAL
Amb Sta
SL3
STOKE PARK PLAYING FIELD
Tumulus
Stoke Place Hotel and Country Club
Cricket Club
Central Nursery
The Lodge
STONE'S WOOD
BUCKINGHAMSHIRE
THE LANES GOLF COURSE
SL2
REC GRD
GRANVILLE PLAYING FIELD
Stokeplace Farm
Slough Town FC
All Souls Farm
Crematorium
SLOUGH
SOUTH BUCKS
The Green Man PH
CEMETERY
GEORGE GREEN
GODOLPHIN PLAYING FIELDS
SL1
ROCHFORDS GDNS
Slough Nursery
Grand Union Canal
Gas Works
SALT HILL PARK
SLOUGH
Thames Valley Uni
BUS STA
Superstore
Works
Lavender Farm
Southend Farm
BLOOM PARK
Ice Arena
TOWN HALL
Sports Centre
MONTEM REC GRD
Queensmere Shop Centre
Observatory Shop Centre
92
WELLINGTON ST
A4
UXBRIDGE ROAD
A412
A355
B416
CHERRY AVENUE
SUTTON AVENUE

AZ
BA
BB
BC
BD
BE
BF
57
65
66
67
68
69
70
71
72
73
74
76
93
UB9
SL0
BROWN'S WOOD
PARKSPRING WOOD
MOUNT FIDGET WOOD
BRIDGETTINE CONVENT
Alderbourne Farm
Saul's Farm
Ways Farm
Cherry Orchard Farm
OLDHOUSE WOOD
LONG COPPICE
Sevenhills Farm
PLAYING FIELD
Dromenagh Farm
THE CLUMP
Kingcup Farm
Southlands Manor
Round Coppice Farm
Copse Hill Farm
LANGLEY COMMON
STRAWBERRY WOOD
Langley Corner
Pinewood Film Studios
NATURE RESERVE
Heatherden Hall
Park Lodge Farm
Brackenwood
BROOM WARREN
Stag & Hounds PH
Medical Cen
SPORTS GRD
Health Cen
Hall
Lib
Prim Sch
PO
Warren Lodge
Warren House
Warren House Farm
BLACK PARK COUNTRY PARK
DIAMOND WOOD
CHESTNUT WOOD
Centenary Lodge Visitors Centre
FOXES GUTTER
COLUMN LARCHES
Five Points
Crooked Billet PH
Fernleigh
SPORTS GROUND
IVER HEATH
Home Cottage Farm
CHANDLERS HILL
Perivale Livery Stables
Moorwards
Woodlands Park
Mansfield Farm
Watergate Farm
Bangors Park Farm
Norwood Grange
LANGLEY PARK WOOD
RHODODENDRON GARDENS
LANGLEY PARK COUNTRY PARK
ROUGHGROUND WOOD
ARBORETUM
Environmental Studies Centre
Langley Park House
Ashen Cross
Treal Farm
SPORTS GROUND
Eureham Centre
Sports Centre
Nursery
Whip & Collar PH
Coppins Farm
Coppins Cottages
Lower Delaford
Delaford Manor
Iver Lodge
Shreding Green
Gurkha PH
Shredding Green Farm
Love Hill House Farm
IVER
SPORTS GROUND
ALLOT
Delaford Park
Huntsmoor Park Farm
FARLOWS LAKE
Water Treatment Works
THE RIDGEWAY ESTATE
Works
Moat House
Glasshouse
Clubhouse
IVER GOLF COURSE
THE ORCHARDS RESIDENTIAL PARK
Grand Union Canal (Slough Arm)
TOWING PATH
BUCKINGHAMSHIRE
SOUTH BUCKS
SLOUGH
CARAVAN SITE
Depot
CANAL ESTATE
Chequer Bridge
LANGLEY BUSINESS CENTRE
Sewage Works
THORNEY PARK GOLF COURSE
M25
A412
A4007
B470
DENHAM ROAD
CHURCH ROAD
SLOUGH ROAD
SEVEN HILLS ROAD
PINEWOOD ROAD
BANGORS ROAD NORTH
BANGORS ROAD SOUTH
WOOD LANE
BILLET LANE
NORWOOD LANE
SWALLOW STREET
HIGH STREET
LANGLEY PARK ROAD
THORNEY LANE
IVER LANE
RIDGEWAY
01
02
03
81
82
83
84

76
BG
BH
BJ
BK
BL
BM
BN
58
94
75
05
06
07
65
66
67
68
69
70
71
72
73
74
84
83
82
81
UB9
UB8
UB7
UB10
SL0
UXBRIDGE
UXBRIDGE MOOR
COWLEY
IVER
YIEWSLEY
HILLINGDON
WEST DRAYTON
HILLINGDON HOUSE FARM SPORTS GROUNDS
HILLINGDON COURT PARK
HILLINGDON GOLF COURSE
HILLINGDON & UXBRIDGE CEMETERY
HILLINGDON HOSPITAL
Brunel University
Halls of Residence
UNIVERSITY PLAYING FIELDS
HUNTSMOOR PARK
FARLOWS LAKE
COWLEY LAKE
LITTLE BRITAIN LAKE
THORNEY PARK GOLF COURSE
Electricity Sub Station
Sewage Works
Water Treatment Works
Uxbridge College
UXBRIDGE COMMON
HIGHBRIDGE INDUSTRIAL ESTATE
MIDAS INDUSTRIAL ESTATE
CHILTERN BUSINESS VILLAGE
SARUM COMPLEX
COWLEY BUSINESS PARK
BRIDGE WORKS
TOMO INDUSTRIAL EST
RAINBOW INDUSTRIAL ESTATE
THE RIDGEWAY ESTATE
HORTON IND PARK
LAWN FIELDS
The Pavilions
CIVIC OFFICES
R.A.F. Uxbridge
ROCKINGHAM REC GRD
COWLEY HALL REC GRD
COLHAM GREEN REC GRD
Grand Union Canal (Slough Arm)
Coal Depot
Gas Works
Warehouses
DENHAM ROAD
OXFORD ROAD
HIGH STREET
COWLEY ROAD
HILLINGDON ROAD
HILLINGDON HILL
PARK ROAD
ST. JOHNS ROAD
ROCKINGHAM RD
FALLING LANE
A4007
A4020
A408
A412
M25
Colham Roundabout
Apple Tree Roundabout
PARK VIEW RD

77
BP
BQ
BR
BS
BT
BU
BV
59
NORTHOLT AERODROME
HA4
NORTH HILLINGDON
CUTTHROAT WOOD
GUTTERIDGE WOOD
NATURE RESERVE
THE GORSE
SPORTS GROUND
HOME COVERT
HARE PLANTATION
POLE HILL OPEN SPACE
LANE COVERT
WEST LONDON SHOOTING GROUNDS
UB5
YEADING BROOK MEADOWS NATURE RESERVE
GROSVENOR PLAYING FIELD
HAYES SHRUB
HAYES PARK
GRANGE PK
UB4
BELMORE PLAYING FIELDS
YEADING
78
HAYES END
RECREATION GROUND
ROSEDALE PARK
GRASSY MEADOW
BOTANIC GDNS
HAYES STADIUM
HAYES
BARRA HALL PARK
BELL HOUSE FLD
UB3
Uxbridge Coll
PARK COURSE
STOCKLEY PARK
UB11
E.M.I. SPORTS GROUND
95
HAYES TOWN
WARREN PARK
ELYSTAN BUSINESS CENTRE
HAYES METRO CENTRE
HEATHROW INTERCHANGE
PROVIDENT INDUSTRIAL ESTATE
ABENGLEN INDUSTRIAL ESTATE
WARNFORD IND EST
ADLER IND EST
Grand Union Canal
WESTERN AVENUE
A40
UXBRIDGE ROAD
A4020
HAYES BYPASS
DAWLEY ROAD
A437
65
66
67
68
69
70
71
72
73
74
81
82
83
84
08
09
10

BW
BX
BY
BZ
CA
CB
CC
HA4
60
65
66
67
68
69
70
71
72
73
74
77
96
12
13
14
81
82
83
84
SOLID WASTE TRANSFER STATION
FROGMORE ESTATE
NORTHOLT RECREATION GRD
PLAYING FIELD
LORD HALSBURY MEMORIAL REC GRD
HILLINGDON
EALING
WESTERN AVENUE
A40
NORTHOLT
ISLIP MANOR PARK
LONDON GOLF CENTRE
SPORTS GROUND
BELVUE PARK
EALING GOLF RANGE
KELVIN INDUSTRIAL ESTATE
THE METROPOLITAN CENTRE
UB5
WEST LONDON SHOOTING GROUNDS
LIME TREE PARK
PLAYING FIELDS
RECTORY PARK
SMITHS FARM EST
CHURCH ROAD
A312
MANDEVILLE ROAD
RUISLIP ROAD
B455
WEST END ROAD
THE PARKWAY (HAYES BYPASS)
YEADING
UB4
BELMORE PLAYING FIELDS
GREENFORD
RAVENOR PARK
GREENFORD PARK REC GRD
GREENFORD PARK CEMETERY
KING GEORGE'S FIELD
JUBILEE PARK
SPORTS GROUND
WARREN PARK
BROOKSIDE
UXBRIDGE ROAD
THE BROADWAY
A4020
HIGH STREET
UB1
SOUTHALL
SOUTHALL PARK
DORMER'S WELLS
WEST MIDDLESEX GOLF COURSE
GREENFORD ROAD
HAYES METRO CENTRE
ELYSTAN BUSINESS CENTRE
HEATHROW INTERCHANGE
BROOK INDUSTRIAL ESTATE
GRAND UNION CANAL (PADDINGTON BRANCH)
SECURE PARKING
A3005
SOUTH ROAD
BARRATT INDUSTRIAL PARK
SOUTHALL RAILWAY CENTRE
WINDMILL LANE

79
CD
CE
CF
CG
CH
CJ
CK
15
16
17
61
65
66
67
68
69
70
71
72
73
74
80
81
82
83
84
97
SUDBURY
HA0
UB6
W5
W7
W13
PERIVALE
EALING
HANWELL
WHITTON AVENUE WEST
EASTCOTE AVENUE
HARROW ROAD
HIGH ROAD
BRIDGEWATER ROAD
EALING ROAD
HANGER LANE
WESTERN AVENUE
A40
A4005
A4020
A4127
B452
B455
B456
GREENFORD ROAD
UXBRIDGE ROAD
THE BROADWAY
NEW BROADWAY
BOSTON ROAD
LWR BOSTON RD
SUDBURY GOLF COURSE
HORSENDEN HILL GOLF COURSE
HORSENDEN HILL
HORSENDEN WOOD
SPORTS GROUND
BERKELEY FIELDS
GREAT BRAMSTONES
HOME MEAD
GRAND UNION CANAL (PADDINGTON BRANCH)
ALPERTON CEMETERY
ONE TREE HILL REC GRD
PERIVALE WOOD
Westway Cross Shopping Park
OLDFIELD REC GRD
PERIVALE INDUSTRIAL PARK
PERIVALE NEW BUSINESS CENTRE
WADSWORTH BUSINESS CENTRE
FLEETWAY BUSINESS PARK
SHERATON BUSINESS CEN
CAPITAL BUSINESS CEN
METROPOLITAN POLICE TRAFFIC UNIT
ALPERTON SPORTS GROUND
EALING CENTRAL SPORTS GRD
ATHLETICS STADIUM
PERIVALE PARK SPORTS GROUND
PERIVALE PARK GOLF COURSE
EALING GOLF COURSE
PITSHANGER PARK
CLEVELAND PARK
CUCKOO PARK
DRAYTON GREEN
HANGER HILL PARK
BARCLAYS BANK SPORTS GROUND
CHURCHFIELDS RECREATION GROUND
KENSINGTON & CHELSEA CEMETERY
HANWELL CEMETERY
WALPOLE PARK
PITSHANGER MANOR MUS
Thames Valley Uni
EALING COMMON
EALING HOSPITAL N.H.S. TRUST
Ealing Broadway Shop Cen
Ealing Studios
GOLF COURSE
River Brent

WEMBLEY
80
CL
CM
CN
CP
CQ
CR
CS
19
20
21
62
TOKYNGTON
CHURCH END
65
66
67
68
69
70
71
72
73
74
79
81
82
83
84
HA0
HA9
W3
W5
ALPERTON
STONEBRIDGE
PARK ROYAL
NORTH ACTON
WEST ACTON
ACTON
EAST ACTON
EALING
EALING COMMON
HARLESDEN
NORTH CIRCULAR ROAD
WESTERN AVENUE
HANGER LANE
EALING ROAD
GUNNERSBURY AVENUE
UXBRIDGE ROAD
HIGH STREET
HORN LANE
VICTORIA ROAD
CENTRAL MIDDLESEX HOSPITAL
GUINNESS SPORTS GRD
Park Royal Guinness Brewery
NORTHFIELDS INDUSTRIAL ESTATE
PREMIER PARK
TOWNSEND INDUSTRIAL ESTATE
ONE TREE HILL REC GRD
STONEBRIDGE REC GRD
TOKYNGTON RECREATION GROUND
GIBBONS REC GRD
HANGER HILL PARK
BARCLAYS BANK SPORTS GROUND
NORTH ACTON PLAYING FIELDS
NORTH THAMES GAS BOARD SPORTS GRD
ACTON PARK
ACTON CEMETERY
98

CT
CU
CV
CW
CX
CY
CZ
NW2
63
WILLESDEN
WILLESDEN CEMETERY
WILLESDEN GREEN
WILLESDEN COMMUNITY HOSP
ROUNDWOOD PARK
NW10
KING EDWARD VII SPORTS GRD
BRONDESBURY
BRONDESBURY PARK
KILBURN
NW6
PADDINGTON OLD CEMETERY
QUEEN'S PARK
KENSAL RISE
KENSAL GREEN
WEST KILBURN
ST. MARY'S RC CEMETERY
KENSAL GREEN CEMETERY
GRAND UNION CANAL (Paddington Branch)
KENSAL TOWN
MAIDA HILL
W9
W10
NORTH POLE INTERNATIONAL DEPOT
LITTLE WORMWOOD SCRUBS REC GRD
OLD OAK COMMON
WORMWOOD SCRUBS
ST CHARLES HOSP
PRINCESS LOUISE HOSP
LINFORD CHRISTIE STADIUM
QUEEN CHARLOTTE & CHELSEA HOSP
HAMMERSMITH HOSPITAL
H.M. PRISON WORMWOOD SCRUBS
NORTH KENSINGTON
WESTWAY
WESTBOURNE GREEN
NOTTING HILL
W11
SHEPHERD'S BUSH
W12
HOLLAND PARK
KENSINGTON
W8
NOTTING HILL GATE
65
66
67
68
69
70
71
72
73
74
82
99
22
23
24

DA
DB
DC
DD
DE
DF
DG
WEST HAMPSTEAD
BELSIZE PARK
SOUTH HAMPSTEAD
KILBURN
PRIMROSE HILL
NW6
NW8
NW1
REGENT'S PARK
ST. JOHN'S WOOD
LORD'S CRICKET GROUND
LONDON ZOO
MAIDA VALE
MAIDA HILL
W9
LISSON GROVE
MARYLEBONE
WESTBOURNE GREEN
PADDINGTON
BAYSWATER
W2
KENSINGTON GARDENS
HYDE PARK
THE SERPENTINE
KENSINGTON
HOLLAND PARK
W8
NOTTING HILL GATE
BAYSWATER ROAD
KENSINGTON ROAD
KNIGHTSBRIDGE
OXFORD STREET where marked is closed to through traffic (except buses & taxis) from 7a.m.-7p.m. Monday - Saturday
64
65
66
67
68
69
70
71
72
73
74
81
100
26
27
28

83
DH
DJ
DK
DL
DM
DN
DP
65
KENTISH TOWN
CALEDONIAN PARK
PENTONVILLE PRISON
BARNSBURY
CANONBURY
66
67
68
69
70
71
72
73
74
84
KING'S CROSS
CAMDEN TOWN
ISLINGTON
N1
N5
N7
PENTONVILLE
SOMERS TOWN
ST. PANCRAS
BRITISH LIB
EUSTON
FINSBURY
CLERKENWELL
WC1
CORAM'S FIELDS
BLOOMSBURY
BRITISH MUSEUM
HOLBORN
LINCOLN'S INN FIELDS
SOHO
STRAND
WC2
CHARING CROSS
EMBANKMENT
ALDWYCH
VICTORIA EMBANKMENT
RIVER
THAMES
SOUTHWARK
SE1
EC1
EC4
ST. PAUL'S CATH
BART'S HOSP
BARBICAN
TATE MODERN
SHAKESPEARE GLOBE
WATERLOO
ST. JAMES'S
ST. JAMES'S PARK
GREEN PARK
BUCKINGHAM PALACE
PICCADILLY CIRCUS
OXFORD CIRCUS
MIDDLESEX HOSP
THE BOROUGH
101
29
30
31

N5
HIGHBURY
DQ
DR
DS
DT
DU
DV
DW
33
34
35
66
65
67
68
69
70
71
72
73
74
83
82
81
84
102
CANONBURY
DOUGLAS EST
KINGSLAND
DALSTON
HACKNEY
LONDON FIELDS
E8
N1
DE BEAUVOIR TOWN
SOUTH HACKNEY
ST. JOSEPH'S HOSPICE
REGENT'S CANAL
HAGGERSTON PARK
HAGGERSTON
HOXTON
SHOREDITCH PARK
E2
BETHNAL GREEN
GEFFRYE MUSEUM
MILDMAY MISS. HOSP
MOORFIELDS EYE HOSP
ST. LUKE'S
EC1
CLERKENWELL
SHOREDITCH
BROADGATE
BARBICAN
BART'S HOSP
EC2
ST. PAUL'S CATH
WHITECHAPEL
ROYAL LONDON HOSP
E1
STEPNEY
EC4
EC3
RIVER THAMES
TOWER OF LONDON
TATE MODERN
SHAKESPEARE GLOBE THEATRE
LONDON BRIDGE HOSP
GUY'S HOSPITAL
SOUTHWARK
SE1
THE BOROUGH
WAPPING
SHADWELL
TOWER BRIDGE EXPERIENCE
THE POOL
DALSTON LANE
GRAHAM ROAD
BALLS POND RD
KINGSLAND ROAD
HACKNEY ROAD
CAMBRIDGE HEATH RD
MARE ST
NEW NORTH ROAD
ESSEX ROAD
CITY ROAD
OLD STREET
GREAT EASTERN ST
COMMERCIAL ST
COMMERCIAL ROAD
WHITECHAPEL ROAD
LONDON WALL
MOORGATE
BISHOPSGATE
HOUNDSDITCH
MINORIES
TOWER BR APP
EAST SMITHFIELD
THE HIGHWAY
CABLE ST
BLACKFRIARS RD
SOUTHWARK BR
TOOLEY ST
ST. THOMAS ST
BOROUGH HIGH ST
UPPER STREET
ALDERSGATE
NEWGATE ST
HOLBORN VIADUCT

85
DX
DY
DZ
EA
EB
EC
ED
HOMERTON
E9
HACKNEY WICK
67
VALLEY PARK
STRATFORD
E15
LONDON INTERNATIONAL FREIGHT TERMINAL
VICTORIA PARK
HERTFORD UNION CANAL
OLD FORD
BOW
E3
MILE END
MILE END PARK
TOWER HAMLETS CEMETERY PARK
BROMLEY
LEE VALLEY PARK
WEST HAM
MILE END STADIUM
LIMEHOUSE
E14
POPLAR
CANARY WHARF
ISLE
WEST INDIA DOCKS
RIVER THAMES
SE16
THE DOME
NORTH GREENWICH
EAST INDIA DOCK BASIN
LIMMO PENINSULA ECOLOGICAL PARK
CANNING TOWN
65
66
67
68
69
70
71
72
73
74
86
103
36
37
38
81
82
83
84

EE
EF
EG
EH
EJ
EK
EL
40
41
42
E7
E15
E13
E16
E6
SE10
FOREST GATE
STRATFORD
WEST HAM
WEST HAM PARK
PLAISTOW
UPTON
UPTON PARK
CANNING TOWN
CUSTOM HOUSE
SILVERTOWN
ROYAL VICTORIA DOCK
EXCEL
THE DOME
NORTH GREENWICH
WOODGRANGE PARK
GRANGE PARK CEMETERY
PLASHET JEWISH CEMETERY
PLASHET PARK
EAST HAM MEM HOSP
EAST LONDON CEMETERY
MEMORIAL RECREATION GROUND
HERMIT RD REC GRD
NEWHAM GENERAL HOSPITAL
TERENCE McMILLAN STADIUM
BECKTON DISTRICT PARK NORTH
BECKTON DISTRICT PARK SOUTH
KING GEORGE V PARK
CANNING TOWN REC GRD
BRAMPTON PARK
PRIORY PARK
UPTON PARK WEST HAM UTD F.C.
PLAISTOW HOSP
THREE MILLS GREEN
VALLEY PARK
EAST INDIA DOCK BASIN NATURE RESERVE
LIMMO PENINSULA ECOLOGICAL PARK
THAMES BARRIER PARK
LYLE PARK
MERIDIAN GARDENS
THAMESIDE INDUSTRIAL EST
Royal Albert Dock Regatta Centre
Newham Coll of F.E.
ROMFORD ROAD
BARKING ROAD
NEWHAM WAY
PLAISTOW ROAD
HIGH STREET
GREENGATE ST
PRINCE REGENT LANE
UPTON LANE
STOPFORD ROAD
MANOR ROAD
WEST HAM LANE
NEW PLAISTOW RD
BROADWAY
THE GROVE
LEYTONSTONE
SILVERTOWN WAY
NORTH WOOLWICH ROAD
LOWER LEA CROSSING
VICTORIA DOCK RD
CONNAUGHT BRIDGE
EAST INDIA DOCK RD
ASPEN WAY
BLACKWALL TUNNEL
RIVER
WOOLWICH REACH
THAMES FLOOD
CUSTOM HOUSE
PRINCE REGENT
ROYAL VICTORIA
ROYAL ALBERT
WEST HAM
PLAISTOW
UPTON PARK
CANNING TOWN
SILVERTOWN & LONDON CITY AIRPORT
London City Airport Pier
Millennium Pier
Thames Wharf
Blackwall Beach
A118
A114
A112
A124
A13
A1011
A1020
B167
B165
65
66
67
68
69
70
71
72
73
74
81
82
83
84
85
104

EM
EN
EP
EQ
ER
ES
ET
43
44
45
LITTLE ILFORD PARK
LOXFORD PARK
LOXFORD
69
THE LAKE
Lido
BARKING PARK REC GRD
BARKING PARK
Indoor Bowl Club
Bowling Greens
LONGBRIDGE ROAD
BARRINGTON PLAYING FLDS
SPORTS GROUND
Gasholder
NORTHERN RELIEF ROAD
FANSHAWE AV
BARKING
Barking Coll
Health Centre
65
BOATING LAKE
Pitch 'n' Putt
MAYESBROOK PARK
SPORTS GRD
UPNEY
66
MEADOW EST
84
RIPPLESIDE BURIAL GROUND
67
RIPPLE ROAD
BARKING ROAD REC GRD
ABBEY RETAIL PARK
Superstores
RODING TRADING EST
Vicarage Fld Shop Cen
TOWN HALL
SPORTS GRD
Sports Cen
ST. PAULS
A123
A124
A406
A13
A117
A1153
IG11
GREAT FIELDS PARK
BARKING INDUSTRIAL PARK
ALFREDS WAY IND ESTATE
WAYSIDE COMMERCIAL EST
ALFREDS WAY (BARKING BY PASS)
Mill Pond
HAND TROUGH CREEK
CUCKHOLD'S HAVEN
FLANDERS RD PLAYING FLDS
TOWN HALL ANNEXE
Lib
Depot
Works
LONG REACH CT
Fire Sta
LYON BUSINESS PARK
68
83
ABBEY WHARF INDUSTRIAL ESTATE
KATELLA TRADING EST
SPORTS GRD
River Roding
ALLOTMENTS
GOOSELEY'S PLAYING FIELDS
NEWHAM WAY
SPORTS GROUND
Refuse Transfer Sta
Cinema
RIVERSIDE INDUSTRIAL ESTATE
69
City Farm & Ecology Park
RIVER ROAD BUSINESS PARK
88
Filter Beds
BECKTON REACH SEWAGE TREATMENT WORKS
Long Mark
Long Reach
TRAFALGAR BUSINESS CENTRE
70
CREEKMOUTH
Nature Reserve
Superstores
RETAIL PARK
Newham Riding Centre
Northern Outfall Sewer
Dry Ski Slope
ALPINE BUSINESS CEN
Northern Outfall Sewage Works
Incinerator
Power Ho
BUZZARD CREEK INDUSTRIAL ESTATE
82
71
Warpools Reach
Sludge Beds
Pump Sta
BARKING FLOOD BARRIER
Gravel Works
Barking or False Point
Pier
NEWHAM
BARKING & DAGENHAM
A1020
DOCKS ROAD
Gas Works
BECKTON
Travel Inn
Shopping Cen
MANOR WAY
DLR DEPOT
72
NEW BECKTON PARK
East Ham Utd FC
GALLIONS REACH
MARGARET NESS OR TRIPCOCK POINT
81
Thamesmere Lake
Superstore
73
BECKTON PARK
CYPRUS
Uni of East London
GALLIONS ROUNDABOUT
Pumping Sta
ALBERT DOCK
ALBERT BASIN
AIRPORT
KING GEORGE V DOCK
Newham Coll of Further Ed
Motor Cross Track
THAMESMEAD
74
Warehouses
BASIN SOUTH
105
SE28
BIRCHMERE
EASTERN WAY
CENTRAL WAY
A112
STANDARD INDUSTRIAL ESTATE
NORTH WOOLWICH
ROYAL VICTORIA GDNS
Sewage Works
North Woolwich Pier
Woolwich Ferry Pier
GALLIONS REACH
WOOLWICH CROWN
H.M. PRISON
BROADWATER

MAYESBROOK PARK
BARKING FC
SPORTS GRD
EU
EV
EW
EX
EY
EZ
FA
47
48
49
70
PARSLOES PARK
Barking Coll
BOATING LAKE
Pitch 'n' Putt
PORTERS AVENUE
A1153
LODGE AVENUE
Roundhouse PH
BECONTREE
IVYHOUSE ROAD
DAGENHAM HEATHWAY
HEATHWAY
Shopping Centre
65
66
67
68
69
70
71
72
73
74
84
83
82
81
87
106
A123
RIPPLESIDE BURIAL GROUND
MAYBROOK MEADOW EST
BARKING INDUSTRIAL PARK
ALFREDS WAY
ALFREDS WAY IND ESTATE
WAYSIDE COMMERCIAL EST
RENWICK IND ESTATE
TRAIN DEPOT
RIPPLESIDE COMMERCIAL ESTATE
MAYBELLS COMM EST
CASTLE GREEN
GORESBROOK SPORTS GROUND
GORESBROOK PARK
BARKING R.F.C.
DAGENHAM LEISURE PK
Leisure Cen
RIPPLE ROAD
A13
THAMES AVENUE
FORD MOTOR W
DAGENHAM DOCK
RM9
Freight Depot
BOX LANE
GREAT FLEETE WAY
CHOATS ROAD
CHOATS MANOR WAY
IG11
POWER STATION
COAL DEPOT
HINDMANS WAY
Horse Shoe Corner
THUNDERER ROAD
Oil Storage Depot
Power Station
Depot
Jetty
Landing Stage
RIVERSIDE INDUSTRIAL ESTATE
City Farm & Ecology Park
RIVER ROAD BUSINESS PARK
TRAFALGAR BUSINESS
CREEKMOUTH
Superstore
BUZZARD CREEK INDUSTRIAL ESTATE
Gravel Works
BARKING FLOOD BARRIER
Barking or False Point
Pier
BARKING & DAGENHAM
LEVISHAM
BEXLEY
GREENWICH
CROSSNESS LIGHTHOUSE
THAMESMEAD NORTH
Ecology Study Area
Crossway Lake
RIVERSIDE GOLF COURSE
SE2
COVERED RESERVOIRS
Crossness Sewage Treatment Works
Sludge Incinerator
SPORTS GROUND
Thamesmere Lake
Superstore
Shop Cen
MANORWAY GREEN
MOORINGS
CENTRAL WAY
CARLYLE ROAD
Thamesmead Town FC
CROSSWAY PARK
THAMESMEAD
SPORTS GRD
EASTERN WAY
A2016
ERITH MARSHES
SOUTHMERE PARK
LAKESIDE CENTRE
SOUTHMERE
BIRCHMERE PARK
SE28
WOODLAND WAY
DA18
HARROW MANORWAY
Health Cen
H.M. PRISON

89
FB
FC
FD
FE
FF
FG
FH
50
51
52
71
PARK
Dagenham FC
VICTORIA RD
Rhone-Poulenc Rd
DAGENHAM EAST
PONDFIELD PARK
FOXLANDS ROAD
WESTERN AVENUE
MAYSWOOD
AURIEL AVENUE
ALDBOROUGH ROAD
MANOR ROAD
MANOR ROAD SPORTS GRD
Pavs.
Sports Club
Bretons Equestrian Centre
SPORTS GROUND
BRITTONS PLAYING FIELD
RAINHAM ROAD
A125
RAINHAM ROAD SOUTH
DAGENHAM ROAD
Pumping Sta
Dagenham Beam Bridge
Newtons Corner
THOROGOOD WAY
ALLOT
RM10
THE LEYS
OLD DAGENHAM PARK
ARENA
Clubhouse
Comm Cen
BEAM
BARKING & DAGENHAM
HAVERING
Beam River
SOUTH HORNCHURCH
ELM PARK
Superstore
Prim Sch
Sec Sch
65
66
67
68
69
70
71
72
73
74
84
83
82
81
90
RM12
HORNCHURCH COUNTRY PARK
AIRFIELD WOOD
FLIGHTWAY WOOD
FARMFIELD WOOD
LOWFIELD WOOD
Albyns Farm
RM13
INGREBOURNE RIVER
RAINHAM
The Albion PH
Dovers Corner
Cherry Tree PH
SPORTS GROUND
NEW ROAD
A1306
CAR COMPOUND
Depot
LINK ROAD
A1311
CONSUL AVENUE
COURIER
HORNCHURCH MARSHES
Riverside Sewage Works
Rainham Creek
Works
ALBRIGHT INDUSTRIAL ESTATE
DENVER INDUSTRIAL ESTATE
CONTAINER DEPOT
FAIRVIEW INDUSTRIAL PARK
Rainham Sunday Market
THAMES AVENUE
FIESTA DRIVE
THAMES GATEWAY
A13
SALAMONS WAY
FERRY LANE
COLDHARBOUR LANE
Hornchurch Shoot
Old Man's Head
Jetty
DA17
Wharf
Power Station (Closed)
Jenningtree Point
JENNINGTREE POINT LIGHTHOUSE
Depots
Pier
ERITH
107
RAINHAM MARSHES
Silt Lagoons
Common Watercourse
WENNINGTON MARSHES
WENNINGTON ROAD
B1335
Rainham Hall
The Bell Inn PH
Clock Tower
Lib
Health Cen
REC GRD
Swim Pool
South Hall Farm
Southall Bridge
East Hall Farm
UPMINSTER ROAD
CEM

FJ
FK
FL
FM
FN
FP
FQ
54
55
56
72
Hacton
White Hart PH
Park Corner Farm
PARK FARM ROAD
Lodge Farm
Rainham Lodge Farm
Gardners Cor Hall
Central Farm
Corbets Tey Sch
PARKLANDS OPEN SPACE
Harwood Hall
Corbets Tey
Stables
PARKLAND AVENUE
HARWOOD HALL LANE
Superstore
Prim Sch
Prim Schs
MAYBANK AVENUE
MORECAMBE
DEWEY PATH
65
66
67
68
69
70
71
72
73
74
84
83
82
81
RM12
RM13
HORNCHURCH COUNTRY PARK
AIRFIELD WOOD
PINEWOOD
FLIGHTWAY WOOD
FARMFIELD WOOD
LOWFIELD WOOD
ABBEY WOOD
BERWICK POND
WESTERN PATHWAY
EASTERN PATHWAY
WATERMEADOW
INGREBOURNE RIVER
INGREBOURNE VALLEY GREEN
Albyns Farm
ST MATTHEWS
NHAM
REFUSE TRANSFER STATION
Gerpins Farm
LITTLE GERPINS LANE
GERPINS LANE
Berwick Ponds Farm
SAND AND GRAVEL PIT
Berwick Manor
Berwick Manor Farm
White Post Corner
WARWICK LANE
BERWICK POND ROAD
LAUNDERS LANE
WARWICK WOOD
WHITE POST WOOD
RM1
SAND GRAVE
RAINHAM CEMETERY (JEWISH)
SPRING FARM PARK
Pav
Tennis Cts
Saxon Horn PH
UPMINSTER ROAD NORTH
ABBEY WOOD LANE
LAKE AVENUE
LAKESIDE AVENUE
THORN LANE
KING EDWARD AVENUE
FAIRVIEW AVENUE
STOKE ROAD
PARSONAGE ROAD
FARM ROAD
ALLEN ROAD
BRISCOE ROAD
KENWAY
Prim Sch
CEM
Pol
Works
89
NEW ROAD
A1306
Health Cen
ALLOT
Sec Sch
Swim Pool
Prim Sch
Home
Bowl Grn
REC GRD
LAMBS LANE SOUTH
LAMBS LANE NORTH
South Hall Farm
Southall Bridge
NEW COTTAGES
East Hall Farm
EAST HALL LANE
CHURCH LANE
WENNINGTON ROAD
Wennington Hall
The Willows
Hall
THE GREEN
Fire Sta
Wennington
New Farm
SANDY LANE
B1335
Sandy Lane Farm
MOAT
Bretts Farm
Sir Henry Gurnett PH
The Marisco PH
Moor Hall
PO
RAINHAM MARSHES
Silt Lagoons
Common Watercourse
GATEWAY
A13
LONDON ROAD
A1306
108
Works
PURFLEET
Nursery
Clubhouse
SPORTS GROUND
WENNINGTON MARSHES
BUCHANAN CL
TOPLANDS AV
BLENHEIM GDNS
LOWLANDS
GRANGE ROAD
ARNHEM

FR
FS
FT
FU
FV
FW
FX
57
58
59
73
North Ockendon
OCKENDON ROAD
B1421
FEN LANE
Clubhouse
Pav
TOP MEADOW GOLF COURSE
65
66
67
68
69
70
71
72
73
74
84
83
82
81
UPMINSTER CEMETERY
MIDDLE WOOD
BONUS WOOD
NATURE RESERVE
MEML GDNS
Crem
Whitepost Farm
COTTAGES
SPORTS GRD
CHURCH LANE
Hall Farm
Nursery
Manor Farm
The Old White Horse PH
B186
RUSSELL'S LAKE
Outdoor Pursuits Centre
COYS LAKE
STUBBERS LANE
SUNNINGS LANE
PEA LANE
HAVERING
THURROCK
M25
DENNIS RD
DENNISES LANE
DENNIS ROAD
SAND AND GRAVEL PIT
FREEMAN'S SHAW
Kemp's Farm
Groves Barns
THE WILDERNESS
CLAY PIT
Tumulus
South Ockendon Hall
MOAT
South Ockendon Hall Farm
GREEN LANE
CHEELSON RD
WILSMAN RD
NELSON RD
NORTH ROAD
HALL LANE
Prim Sch
PO
Royal Oak PH
War Mem
THE GRN
ALLOT
WEST ROAD
OCKENDON
Comm Cen
Bowl Grn
Pav
SOUTH OCKENDON REC GRD
Tenn Cts
WHITEHALL WOOD
BELHUS WOODS COUNTRY PARK
LITTLE BRICKKILN WOOD
BRICKKILN WOOD
Water Brook
FB
Works
FORD AVELEY PLANT
ROSEMARY CL
LARKSPUR CL
VIOLA CL
CELANDINE CL
MAYFLOWER CL
TAMARISK
BIRCH CRESCENT
HORNBEAM CHASE
ASPEN WAY
JUNIPER DR
ROSEWOOD CL
MAGNOLIA CL
MEDLAR DRIVE
POPLAR CL
HOLLY DRIVE
BRANDON GROVES
LABURNUM GROVE
SYCAMORE WAY
MAPLE DR
LAUREL DR
HAZEL DR
COPPER BEECH RD
GARTH RD
NURSERY CL
MOLLANDS LANE
Bensons Farm
Little Mollands Farm
AVONTAR ROAD
ARDMORE RD
ARCANY RD
ARISDALE AVENUE
ARISDALE AV
ARCHERS CT
SOUTH OCKENDON
South Ockendon Garden Centre
BELHUS PARK
RM15
LONG POND
OAK WOOD
ASH PLANTATION
ROOKERY
The Ockendon Complex
Sec Sch
Sch
HAMBLE LANE
ERRIFF DRIVE
BONNYGATE WOOD
Prim Sch
ANNALEE ROAD
Jack o'Lantern PH
Lib
Hall
BUCKLES LANE
ALDHAM DR
OAK-LANDS DR
MOSS RD
FOYLE DRIVE
EASINGTON WAY
DEVERON WAY
DUNKELLIN WAY
HUMBER AVENUE
HUMBER
DARENTH LANE
DILKES PARK
Knight of Aveley PH
Health Cen
Comm Cen
AFTON DRIVE
BROXBURN DRIVE
South Ockendon Centre
VERBENA CL
CRUICK AVENUE
SOUTH ROAD
LITTLE PALMER'S SHAW
GREAT PALMER'S SHAW
SPORTS GROUND
THE SHRUBBERY
BELHUS PARK GOLF COURSE
Swimming Pool
Clubhouse
Driving Range
GATEHOPE DRIVE
The Archer PH
FAIRHAM AVENUE
DANBURY CRESCENT
Prim Sch
Pav
SPORTS GROUND
Tennis Cts
FORTIN CLOSE
Sch
Prim Sch
CAWDOR AVENUE
The Troubadour PH
CARNACH GREEN
Hill Farm
NORTH STIFFORD
STIFFORD ROAD
B1335
Works
CHERWELL GROVE
CLAYBURN GDNS
MILLARD'S GARDEN
BRANNETT'S WOOD
CULLEN SQUARE
Stifford Bridge
HANGMAN'S WOOD
AVELEY
BYPASS
MARTIN ROAD
CRESCENT
PARK LANE
STANFORD GDNS
ALLOT
Prince Albert PH
Prim Sch
Junction 30
Depot
LOW WELL WOOD
Mar Dyke
STIFFORD HILL
The Dog & Partridge PH
HIGH
Hall
Stifford Interchange
Police Dog Training
BACK LANE
PILGRIMS LANE
CLOCKHOUSE LANE
SPORTS GROUND
HERWOOD
BRICKBARN WOOD
COMBE WOOD
109
LOW WELL WOOD
A13
ARTERIAL ROAD NORTH
THURROCK
PILGRIMS CARAVAN PARK
Gas Works
DUDLEY CLOSE
SPORTS GRD
LAKESIDE COACH PARK
Clinic
Pav
Thurrock Services
ARENA ESSEX RACEWAY

92
AS
AT
AU
AV
AW
AX
AY
98
99
00
74
75
76
77
78
79
80
81
82
83
84
112
SLOUGH
SALT HILL
Thames Valley Uni
WELLINGTON
Queensmere Shop Centre
Observatory Shop Centre
TOWN HALL
Ice Arena
Sports Centre
MONTEM REC GRD
UXBRIDGE
BLOOM PARK
UPTON HOSP
UPTON
LASCELLES PLAYING FIELD
Upton Park
HERSCHEL PARK
SL1
SL3
SL4
SUSSEX PLACE
LONDON ROAD
KEDERMISTER PARK
UPTON COURT PARK
MOTOCROSS TRACK
AGARS PLOUGH PLAYING FIELDS
ETON GOLF COURSE
ATHLETICS CENTRE
B.M.X. TRACK
SLOUGH R.F.C.
Clubhouse
DITTON PARK
DEFENCE RESEARCH AGENCY
KINGS OAK
Riding Court Farm
Offices
FISH POND
M4
Eton College
PLAYING FIELDS
THE HOME PARK RECREATION GROUND
DATCHET GOLF COURSE
Victoria Bri
KING EDWARD VII AVENUE
WINDSOR & ETON RIVERSIDE
WINDSOR CASTLE
EAST LAWN
WINDSOR & ETON CENTRAL
WINDSOR ROYAL STATION
GOLF COURSE
WINDSOR
Victoria Barracks
THE HOME PARK
FROGMORE GARDENS
Royal Mausoleum
Frogmore House
Prince Consort's Home Farm
ROYAL GARDENS
Windsor Hall
Glasshouses
Shaw Farm
Clayhall Farm
PRINCESS MARGARET HOSP
GARRISON SPORTS GROUND
GREAT PARK
RIVER THAMES
SUMPTERMEAD AIT
DATCHET
SPORTS GROUND
DATCHET CEMETERY
The Rising Sun PH
MILL PLACE CARAVAN PARK
Southlea
Southlea Farm
Albert Bridge
NICKCROFT AIT
NEW CUT
HAM ISLAND
Sludge Lagoon
Sludge Beds
Filter Beds
Pumping Sta
Ham Bridge
Manor Farm
St. George's Farm
Old Windsor Lock
The Lord Nelson PH
Sunnymeads
Sailing Club
REMENHAM PARK
ALBERT ROAD
A308
A332
A4
B470
B376
B3026
B3022

93
AZ
BA
BB
BC
BD
BE
BF
01
02
03
75
IVER GOLF COURSE
Clubhouse
Glasshouse
Moat House
THE ORCHARDS RESIDENTIAL PARK
Grand Union Canal (Slough Arm)
TOWING PATH
BUCKINGHAMSHIRE
SOUTH BUCKS
SLOUGH
CANAL ESTATE
Depot
Chequer Bridge
Works
IVER
THORNEY PARK GOLF COURSE
LANGLEY
LANGLEY BUSINESS CENTRE
College
SPORTS GRD
Market
Hall
LANGLEY MEMORIAL GROUND
Prim Sch
Tennis Courts
Withy Bridge
RICHINGS PARK
Glasshouses
SPORTS GRD
Clubhouse
Bowl Grn
Tower Arms PH
Lib
Tenn Cts
NORTH PARK ROAD
RICHINGS PARK GOLF COURSE
Clubhouse
HOME WOOD
SL0
Old Slade Farm
Junction 15 (M25)
Junction 4B (M4)
Swimming Pool
HARVEY PARK
AXIS PARK
Warehouses
Health Centre
Sutton Court Farm
Garden Centre
OAK PLANTATION
M4
SLOUGH OLD WOOD
Heathrow Marriott Hotel
Comm Cen
Sewage Works
Filter Beds
Junction 5
BRANDS HILL
Heathrow Ambassador Hotel
COLNBROOK BYPASS
A4
REC GRD
Brook Farm
COLNBROOK
Comm Cen
Tanhouse Farm
Greyhound PH
Depot
94
Sailing Club
THE QUEEN MOTHER RESERVOIR
Prim Sch
Colnbrook Bridge
GRAVEL PIT
SPORTS GRD
Warehouses
GOLF DRIVING RANGE
POYLE
Longford Roundabout
Mad Bridge
Moor Bridge
UB7
Poyle Channel
Poyle Lodge
BRITANNIA INDUSTRIAL EST
Manor Farm
POYLE TECH CEN
MCKAY TRADING ESTATE
TRIDENT INDUSTRIAL ESTATE
BEDFONT COURT ESTATE
Poyle Farm
Golden Cross PH
HILLINGDON
Works
Ashgood Farm
Berkyn Manor Farm
Crown PH
Five Bells PH
Horton
Sailing Club
Arthur Jacob Nature Reserve
Weir
STANWELL ROAD
HORTON ROAD
Lintells Bridge
Junction 14
M25
AIRPORT WAY
A3113
SURREY
WINDSOR & MAIDENHEAD
COPPERMILL ROAD
Inlet Pier
113
WRAYSBURY
TW19
SPORTS GROUND
STANWELL MOOR
Hall
76
77
78
79
80
81
82
83
84

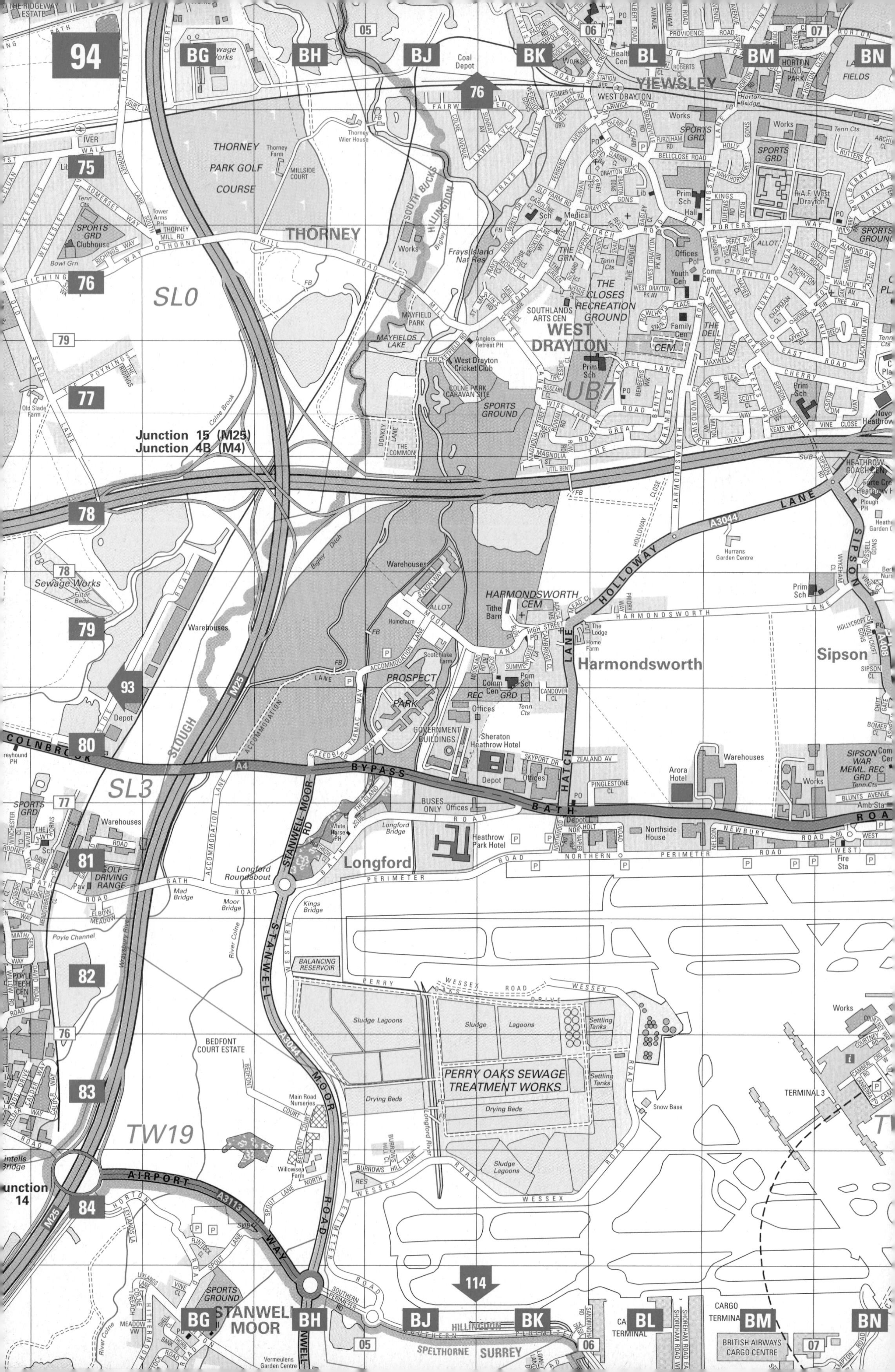
BG
BH
BJ
BK
BL
BM
BN
76
YIEWSLEY
WEST DRAYTON
THORNEY PARK GOLF COURSE
THORNEY
SL0
WEST DRAYTON
UB7
Junction 15 (M25)
Junction 4B (M4)
HARMONDSWORTH CEM
Harmondsworth
Sipson
PROSPECT PARK
SL3
Longford
PERRY OAKS SEWAGE TREATMENT WORKS
TW19
STANWELL MOOR
TERMINAL 3
BRITISH AIRWAYS CARGO CENTRE
SPELTHORNE
SURREY
114
93

BP
BQ
BR
BS
BT
BU
BV
08
09
10
STOCKLEY PARK
Grand Union Canal
Starveall Bridge
Stockley Bridge
ADLER IND EST
ABERGLEN INDUSTRIAL ESTATE
E.M.I. SPORTS GROUND
77
WARNFORD IND EST
HAYES TOWN
BOTWELL GRN
PROVIDENT INDUSTRIAL ESTATE
PETER JAMES BUSINESS CENTRE
HAYES & HARLINGTON
Speedmarque Centre
THE SQUIRRELS TRADING ESTATE
INTERNATIONAL TRADING EST
SECURE PARKING
75
76
77
78
79
80
81
82
83
84
96
115
GOVERNMENT BUILDINGS
BOURNE FARM FIELD
ALLOTMENTS
PINKWELL PARK
UB3
NORTH HYDE ROAD
STATION ROAD
HIGH STREET
CHERRY LANE CEMETERY
Frog's Ditch Farm
SAM PHILIP REC GRD
Western International Market
HARLEQUIN CENTRE
David Lloyd Club
M4
Junction 4
Junction 3
IMPERIAL COLLEGE SPORTS GROUND
LITTLE HARLINGTON FIELD
SIPSON MEADOW
SPORTS GROUND
HARLINGTON
CRANE MEADOW
CRANFORD PARK
TRAVELLERS SITE
BRITISH AIRWAYS SPORTS GROUND
Concorde Centre
PARKWAY TRADING ESTATE
REDWOOD ESTATE
AIR LINKS INDUSTRIAL ESTATE
AVENUE PARK
CRANFORD
TW5
Junction 4A
Edwardian Int Hotel
Marriott Hotel
Sheraton Skyline Hotel
Hotel Ibis
Renaissance Hotel
Heathrow Airport Visitors Cen
BATH ROAD
A4
NORTHERN PERIMETER
CUSTOM HOUSE
HEATHROW AIRPORT (LONDON)
TW4
RIVER CRANE
Maintenance Area
Hangar
Perishable Handling Facility
Speedbird House
Boadicea House
Comet House
HASLEMERE HEATHROW ESTATE
HEATHROW INT TRADING ESTATE
RIFLE RANGE
GREEN LANE OPEN SPACE
TERMINAL 1
HEATHROW TERMINALS 1, 2 & 3
TERMINAL 2
HATTON CROSS
HATTON
BALANCING RESERVOIR
GREAT SOUTH-WEST ROAD
A30
THE PARKWAY
A312
RADIUS PARK
TW14
Hounslow Urban Farm
MERCURY CENTRE
DONKEY WOOD
HOUNSLOW HEATH GOLF COURSE
HEATHROW TERMINAL 4
BEDFONT

96
BW
BX
BY
BZ
CA
CB
CC
12
13
14
SOUTHALL
UB1
78
BROADWAY
HIGH STREET
UXBRIDGE
75
76
77
79
80
81
82
83
84
Junction 3
THE PARKWAY
HAYES
GRAND UNION CANAL
(PADDINGTON BRANCH)
EALING
Gas Works
SECURE PARKING
HEATHROW INTERCHANGE
BROOK INDUSTRIAL ESTATE
BARRATT INDUSTRIAL PARK
SOUTHALL RAILWAY CENTRE
MIDDLESEX BUSINESS CENTRE
TENTELOW LANE SPORTS GROUND
UB2
NORWOOD GREEN
NORTH HYDE
AIRLINKS
GOLF
COURSE
Heston Services
WESTERN INTERNATIONAL MARKET
HARLEQUIN CENTRE
SOUTHALL REC GRD
BRITISH AIRWAYS SPORTS GROUND
PARKWAY TRADING ESTATE
SPITFIRE ESTATE
AIR LINKS INDUSTRIAL ESTATE
Thorncliffe Hotel
95
TW5
HESTON
HESTON PARK
HESTON INDUSTRIAL MALL
SUTTON PLAYING FIELD
SPORTS GROUND
OSTE
LAMPTON
LAMPTON PARK
HOUNSLOW CIVIC CENTRE
GREAT WEST ROAD
BATH ROAD
A4
A312
A3005
A3006
A4127
A315
HOUNSLOW WEST
BEAVERSFORD PARK
HOUNSLOW WEST
Cavalry Barracks
TW4
RIFLE RANGE
GREEN LANE OPEN SPACE
HOUNSLOW
HOUNSLOW CENTRAL
Treaty Centre
DERBY ESTATE
HOUNSLOW HEATH
DONKEY WOOD
CENTRAL PARK EST
MERCURY CENTRE
116
TW3
INWOOD
SOUTH WEST
CAUSEWAY
STAINES ROAD
WELLINGTON ROAD N
WELLINGTON ROAD S

97
CD
CE
CF
CG
CH
CJ
CK
15
16
17
HANWELL
HANWELL CEMETERY
EALING HOSPITAL N.H.S. TRUST
WALPOLE PARK
LAMMAS PARK
LAMMAS
SOUTH EALING
W7
W13
W5
TW7
TW8
TW9
TW1
BRENT RIVER PARK
ELTHORNE PARK
ELTHORNE PARK EXTENSION
WATERSIDE TRADING CENTRE
SPORTS CENTRE
GROUND
LONG WOOD
M4
WYKE GREEN GOLF COURSE
OSTERLEY PARK
BOSTON MANOR
BOSTON MANOR PARK
LONDON PLAYING FIELDS
Grand Union Canal
LITTLE EALING
SOUTH EALING CEMETERY
PHOENIX PARK
Junction 2
BRENTFORD
BRENTFORD FC
BRENTSIDE EXECUTIVE CENTRE
BRENTFORD BUSINESS CENTRE
WEST CROSS CENTRE
MACFARLANE SPORT FIELD
Centaurs R.F.C.
Grasshoppers R.F.C.
Gillette Corner
GREAT WEST ROAD
LONDON ROAD
SYON LANE
SYON PARK
SYON HOUSE
Battles of Brentford 1016 & 1642
Duke of Northumberland Estate
RIVER THAMES
Syon Reach
ROYAL BOTANIC GARDENS
KEW
KEW PALACE
QUEEN'S COTTAGE GARDENS
WATER LILY POND
ARBORETUM
PAGODA VISTA
SPRING GROVE
Brunel University (Osterley Campus)
WEST MIDDLESEX UNIVERSITY HOSP
WOODLANDS
ISLEWORTH
ISLEWORTH AIT
REDLEES PARK
MOGDEN WATER TREATMENT WORKS
Filter Beds
ROYAL MID-SURREY GOLF COURSE (OLD DEER PARK)
OBSERVATORY GARDENS
Kew Observatory
OLD DEER PARK RECREATION GROUND
RICHMOND ATHLETIC GROUND
ROYAL HOSP
London Welsh R.F.C.
RICHMOND GREEN
Richmond Palace Remains
Richmond Lock
ST. MARGARETS
TWICKENHAM ROAD
IVYBRIDGE ESTATE
WORTON HALL INDUSTRIAL ESTATE
75
76
77
78
79
80
81
82
83
84
98
117

98
CL
CM
CN
CP
CQ
CR
CS
EAST ACTON
ACTON PARK
W5
80
EALING COMMON
ACTON HOSP
SPORTS GROUND
POPEFIELD PLAYING FIELDS
SOUTHFIELDS PLAYING FIELDS
ACTON TOWN
SOUTH ACTON
BEDFORD PARK
GUNNERSBURY PARK MUSEUM
W3
GUNNERSBURY PARK
GUNNERSBURY
SOUTH EALING CEMETERY
LITTLE EALING
CLAYPONDS HOSP
KENSINGTON CEMETERY
GUNNERSBURY TRIANGLE NATURE RESERVE
CHISWICK PARK
Junction 1
Junction 2
CHISWICK HIGH ROAD
TW8
W4
KEW BRIDGE STEAM MUS
BRENTFORD FC
BRENTFORD
BRENTFORD AIT
OLIVER'S ISLAND
KEW GREEN
KEW
KEW PALACE
CHISWICK
CHISWICK HOUSE GROUNDS
CHISWICK HOUSE
GROVE PARK
PUBLIC RECORD OFFICE
RIVER THAMES
ROYAL BOTANIC GARDENS
CHISWICK CEMETERY
UNI WEST. SPORTS GRD
DUKE'S MEADOW
CIVIL SERVICE SPORTS GROUND
DUKE'S MEADOW GOLF COURSE
Battles of Brentford 1016 & 1642
SYON HOUSE
QUEEN'S COTTAGE GARDENS
TW9
KEW GARDENS
NORTH SHEEN
NORTH SHEEN CEMETERY
HAMMERSMITH CEMETERY
MORTLAKE
HOUNSLOW
RICHMOND UPON THAMES
ROYAL MID-SURREY GOLF COURSE
RICHMOND ATHLETIC GROUND
ROYAL HOSP
LOWER MORTLAKE ROAD
UPPER RICHMOND ROAD WEST
RICHMOND
RICHMOND GREEN
EAST SHEEN
SW14
PESTHOUSE COMMON
EAST SHEEN COMMON (N T)
118
PALEWELL COMMON
BARNES HOSP
75
76
77
78
79
80
81
82
83
84
97
19
20
21

99
CT
CU
CV
CW
CX
CY
CZ
22
23
24
SHEPHERD'S BUSH
81
W12
W8
W6
W14
SW5
SW6
SW13
SW15
SW18
KENSINGTON
HOLLAND PARK
HOLLAND HOUSE
75
76
77
78
79
80
81
82
83
84
100
119
RANGERS STADIUM QPR F.C.
UXBRIDGE ROAD
GOLDHAWK ROAD
HOLLAND PARK AVENUE
HOLLAND ROAD
KENSINGTON HIGH ST
KENSINGTON (OLYMPIA)
OLYMPIA
COMMONWEALTH INST
RAVENSCOURT PARK
THE STAMFORD
STAMFORD BROOK
KING STREET
GLENTHORNE RD
HAMMERSMITH ROAD
HAMMERSMITH FLYOVER
HAMMERSMITH
TALGARTH ROAD
WEST CROMWELL ROAD
WEST KENSINGTON
BARONS COURT
EARLS COURT
EARLS COURT EXHIBITION CENTRE
HAMMERSMITH CEMETERY
THE QUEENS TENNIS CLUB
CHARING CROSS HOSP
FULHAM PALACE ROAD
LILLIE ROAD
DAWES ROAD
FULHAM CEMETERY
NORTH END ROAD
WEST BROMPTON
PARSONS GREEN
EEL BROOK COMMON
FULHAM BROADWAY
KINGS ROAD
NEW KINGS ROAD
HURLINGHAM PARK
HURLINGHAM CLUB GDNS
SOUTH PARK
CHISWICK LODGE HOSP
CHISWICK EYOT
CASTELNAU
HARROD'S SPORTS GRD
LEG OF MUTTON NATURE RESERVE
BARN ELMS WILDFOWL RESERVE
BARN ELMS PLAYING FIELDS
BARN ELMS SCHOOL SPORTS CENTRE
RIVERSIDE STUDIOS
HAMMERSMITH & FULHAM
RICHMOND UPON THAMES
RIVER THAMES
CRAVEN COTTAGE FULHAM F.C.
BISHOP'S PARK
FULHAM
FULHAM PALACE GARDENS
PUTNEY BRIDGE
BARNES
BARNES COMMON
PUTNEY HOSP
LOWER RICHMOND ROAD
UPPER RICHMOND ROAD
SOUTH CIRCULAR ROAD
PUTNEY HIGH ST
PUTNEY
PUTNEY BRIDGE ROAD
WANDSWORTH PARK
WANDSWORTH
WANDSWORTH
ROEHAMPTON
ROEHAMPTON LANE
ROCKS LANE
QUEENS RIDE
WEST HILL

DA
DB
DC
DD
DE
DF
DG
KENSINGTON GARDENS
HYDE PARK
ROUND POND
THE SERPENTINE
KENSINGTON PALACE
SERPENTINE GALLERY
KENSINGTON
HOLLAND PARK
W8
SW7
SOUTH KENSINGTON
NATURAL HISTORY MUSEUM
SCIENCE MUSEUM
VICTORIA & ALBERT MUSEUM
ROYAL ALBERT HALL
KNIGHTSBRIDGE
HARRODS
BELGRAVIA
BROMPTON
SW3
SW5
EARLS COURT
EARLS COURT EXHIBITION CENTRE
SW10
WEST BROMPTON
BROMPTON CEMETERY
CHELSEA
ROYAL HOSPITAL CHELSEA
ROYAL MARSDEN HOSP
ROYAL BROMPTON HOSP
CHELSEA & WEST. HOSP
STAMFORD BRIDGE CHELSEA F.C.
WALHAM GREEN
PARSONS GREEN
EEL BROOK COMMON
SANDS END
BATTERSEA PARK
CHELSEA REACH
BATTERSEA REACH
SW6
SW11
SW15
SW18
HURLINGHAM PARK
HURLINGHAM CLUB GDNS
SOUTH PARK
CLAPHAM JUNCTION
WANDSWORTH
LONDON WESTLAND HELIPORT
CROMWELL ROAD
KENSINGTON ROAD
KING'S ROAD
FULHAM ROAD
CHEYNE WALK
CHELSEA EMBANKMENT
WANDSWORTH BRIDGE
BATTERSEA BRIDGE
ALBERT BRIDGE
ST. JOHN'S HILL
LAVENDER HILL
CLAPHAM COMMON
BOLINGBROKE HOSP
26
27
28
75
76
77
78
79
80
81
82
83
84
99
120

101
DH
DJ
DK
DL
DM
DN
DP
29
30
31
83
75
76
77
78
79
80
81
82
83
84
102
121
GREEN PARK
ST. JAMES'S PARK
ST. JAMES'S
BUCKINGHAM PALACE
WESTMINSTER
VICTORIA
PIMLICO
SW1
HOUSES OF PARLIAMENT
ST. THOMAS' HOSP
WATERLOO
WATERLOO INTERNATIONAL
SOUTHWARK
SE1
THE BOROUGH
LAMBETH
SE11
VAUXHALL
KENNINGTON
RIVER THAMES
NINE ELMS
SW8
SOUTH LAMBETH
SW9
STOCKWELL
CLAPHAM
SW4
BRIXTON
SE24
SE5
CAMBERWELL
RUSKIN PARK
KENNINGTON PARK
THE FOSTERS OVAL (SURREY C.C.C.)
MYATT'S FIELDS
NEW COVENT GARDEN MARKET
BATTERSEA POWER STATION (DISUSED)
TATE BRITAIN
ELEPHANT & CASTLE
ST. GEORGE'S CATHEDRAL
IMPERIAL WAR MUSEUM
LAMBETH PALACE
LAMBETH BR
VAUXHALL BR
WESTMINSTER BR
GROSVENOR ROAD
WANDSWORTH ROAD
CLAPHAM ROAD
BRIXTON ROAD
KENNINGTON ROAD
CAMBERWELL NEW ROAD
COLDHARBOUR LANE
CLAPHAM HIGH STREET
LANDOR ROAD UNIT
TRINITY HOSPICE
G'S COLLEGE HOSPITAL
ST. MARY'S CATHEDRAL

102
DQ
DR
DS
DT
DU
DV
DW
SE1
SOUTHWARK
WAPPING
THE POOL
THE BOROUGH
GUY'S HOSPITAL
LONDON BRIDGE
TOOLEY ST
ST. THOMAS ST
TOWER BRIDGE EXPERIENCE
BRUNEL ENGINE HOUSE
JAMAICA ROAD
BERMONDSEY
NEWINGTON
ELEPHANT & CASTLE
NEW KENT ROAD
DOVER STREET
GREAT DOVER STREET
SOUTHWARK PARK ROAD
SOUTHWARK PARK
SE17
WALWORTH
OLD KENT ROAD
BURGESS PARK
KENNINGTON PARK
CAMBERWELL
CAMBERWELL NEW ROAD
CAMBERWELL CH ST
PECKHAM ROAD
NORTH PECKHAM ESTATE
PECKHAM
PECKHAM HIGH ST
QUEENS ROAD
ROTHERHITHE NEW ROAD
SE5
SE15
THE MAUDSLEY HOSPITAL
KING'S COLLEGE HOSPITAL
RUSKIN PARK
SW9
COLDHARBOUR LANE
DENMARK HILL
DOG KENNEL HILL
EAST DULWICH
EAST DULWICH ROAD
PECKHAM RYE
PECKHAM RYE COMMON
PECKHAM RYE PARK
NUNHEAD
SE22
SE24
KING'S COLLEGE HOSP DULWICH
SPORTS GROUND
75
76
77
78
79
80
81
82
83
84
101
122
33
34
35

DX
DY
DZ
EA
EB
EC
ED
103
THE DOME
36
37
38
85
ISLE
OF
DOGS
WEST INDIA DOCKS
CANARY WHARF
Canada Square
NORTH GREENWICH
SE10
75
76
77
78
79
80
81
82
83
84
104
123
SE16
ECOLOGICAL PARK
RUSSIA DOCK WOODLAND
ROTHERHITHE
GREENLAND DOCK
SOUTH DOCK
Surrey Docks Water Sports Cen
CUBITT TOWN
MILLWALL
MILLWALL OUTER DOCK
MUDCHUTE PARK
E14
London Arena
Daily Telegraph Print Works
TOWER HAMLETS
SOUTHWARK
LEWISHAM
GREENWICH
GREENWICH REACH
DEPTFORD
SE8
Royal Naval Yd
DEPTFORD PARK
PEPYS PARK
CUTTY SARK
GIPSY MOTH IV
Univ of Greenwich
QUEEN'S HOUSE
NATIONAL MARITIME MUSEUM
GREENWICH PARK
FLAMSTEED HOUSE (Old Royal Observatory)
One Tree Hill
The Wilderness (Deer Park)
BLACKHEATH
BLACKHEATH HILL
SHOOTER'S HILL
SE14
NEW CROSS
NEW CROSS GATE
Goldsmiths College (Univ of Lon)
FORDHAM PARK
TELEGRAPH HILL PARK
ST JOHN'S
HILLY FIELDS
LEWISHAM
Lewisham Centre
SE4
SE13
BROCKLEY
BROCKLEY CEMETERY
LADYWELL CEMETERY
LADYWELL
MANOR PARK
MANOR HOUSE GARDENS
EVELYN STREET
CREEK ROAD
LOAMPIT VALE
LOAMPIT HILL
LEWISHAM WAY
MOLESWORTH STREET
LEE HIGH ROAD
WESTFERRY ROAD
MANCHESTER ROAD
BLACKWALL TUNNEL

104
EE
EF
EG
EH
EJ
EK
EL
E16
40
41
42
THE DOME
NORTH GREENWICH
SE10
RIVER THAMES
WOOLWICH REACH
THAMES FLOOD BARRIER
SILVERTOWN
THAMES BARRIER PARK
LYLE PARK
NORTH WOOLWICH ROAD
86
75
76
77
78
79
80
81
82
83
84
103
124
NEW CHARLTON
MERIDIAN TRADING ESTATE
ANCHORAGE POINT IND EST
GREENWICH INDUSTRIAL EST
CABLE TRADE PARK
WOOLWICH ROAD
GREENWICH DISTRICT HOSP
EAST GREENWICH PLEASAUNCE
WESTCOMBE PARK
MARYON PARK
MARYON WILSON PARK
CHARLTON
SE7
CHARLTON PARK
THE VALLEY (CHARLTON ATHLETIC FC)
HORNFAIR PARK
RECTORY FIELD
GREENWICH
GREENWICH PARK
NATIONAL MARITIME MUSEUM
One Tree Hill
FLAMSTEED HOUSE
The Gardens
THE WILDERNESS (DEER PARK)
RANGER'S HOUSE
SHOOTER'S HILL ROAD
BLACKHEATH
SE3
KIDBROOKE
KIDBROOKE PARK ROAD
ROCHESTER WAY RELIEF RD
SPORTS GROUND
KIDBROOKE GREEN (NAT RES)
BLACKHEATH PARK
BLACKHEATH HOSP
LEE
SE13
SE12
MANOR HOUSE GARDENS
MANOR PARK
SUTCLIFFE PARK
FOOTBALL PITCHES
UNI OF GREENWICH ATHLETIC GRD
LEE HIGH ROAD
ELTHAM ROAD
BURNT ASH
WOOLWICH REACH
RUSSIAN SUBMARINE
Holiday Inn Express

105
EM
EN
EP
EQ
ER
ES
ET
43
44
45
87
125
75
76
77
78
79
80
81
82
83
84
106
THAMESMEAD
THAMESMEAD WEST
KING GEORGE V DOCK
GALLIONS REACH
NEWHAM
GREENWICH
NORTH WOOLWICH
ROYAL VICTORIA GDNS
WOOLWICH FREE FERRY
WOOLWICH FOOT TUNNEL
SE28
H.M. PRISON BELMARSH
WOOLWICH CROWN CT
BROADWATER GRN
WOOLWICH
BARRACK FIELD
WOOLWICH ARSENAL
PLUMSTEAD
PLUMSTEAD GARDENS
PLUMSTEAD COMMON
WINN'S COMMON
SE18
SE2
WOOLWICH CEM
WOOLWICH CEMETERY
SHREWSBURY PARK
SHOOTER'S HILL GOLF COURSE
SHOOTER'S HILL
EAST WICKHAM
EAST WICKHAM OPEN SPACE
HILLVIEW CEMETERY
Royal Military Academy
CASTLEWOOD THERAPY CENTRE
ELTHAM COMMON
MEMORIAL HOSPITAL
CASTLE WOOD
JACK WOOD
OXLEAS MEADOW
OXLEAS WOOD
ELTHAM COMMON
SHEPHERDLEAS WOOD
ELTHAM PARK NORTH
ELTHAM PARK SOUTH
ELTHAM WARREN GOLF COURSE
ELTHAM CEMETERY
FALCONWOOD
FALCONWOOD FIELD
DA16
DA15
WELLING
SE9
GREENWICH
BEXLEY
SHOOTER'S HILL
BELLEGROVE ROAD
WELLING WAY
ROCHESTER WAY
ROCHESTER WAY RELIEF ROAD
EAST ROCHESTER WAY
EASTERN WAY
WESTERN WAY
PLUMSTEAD HIGH STREET
WICKHAM LANE
BOSTALL
WOOLWICH NEW ROAD
BERESFORD ST
PLUMSTEAD ROAD
GRAND DEPOT ROAD
WOOLWICH COMMON
ACADEMY ROAD

106
THAMESMEAD
EU
EV
EW
EX
EY
EZ
FA
47
48
49
88
SOUTHMERE PARK
ERITH MARSHES
LAKESIDE CENTRE
SOUTHMERE
BIRCHMERE PARK
SE28
DA18
WOODLAND WAY
ABBEY WOOD PARK
75
H.M. PRISON BELMARSH
THISTLEBROOK INDUSTRIAL EST
76
ABBEY WOOD
79
77
PLUMSTEAD GARDENS
LESSNESS ABBEY WOOD
78
SE2
BOSTALL HEATH
WINN'S COMMON
BOSTALL HILL
WEST HEATH
CLAM FIELD RECREATION GROUND
BOSTALL WOODS
GOLDIE LEIGH HOSPITAL
SE18
105
WOOLWICH CEM
WOOLWICH CEMETERY
PLUMSTEAD CEMETERY
80
EAST WICKHAM
EAST WICKHAM OPEN SPACE
DA16
81
STEVENS PARK
DA7
82
83
WELLING
84
DANSON
PARK
126
BEXLEYHEATH CEMETERY
DA6
BEXLEYHEATH
BROADWAY
BROADWAY SHOP CENTRE
ARNSBERG WAY
ROCHESTER WAY
BLACKFEN
A206
A207
A209
A221
A2
A2016
A2041
B213

RAINHAM MARSHES
Silt Lagoons
JENNINGTREE POINT LIGHTHOUSE
Power Station (Closed)
FB
FC
FD
FE
FF
FG
FH
89
75
WENNINGTON MARSHES
RM13
76
FREIGHTMASTER ESTATE
Warehouse
HELIPAD
Coldharbour Point
77
HAVERING
BEXLEY
ERITH RANDS
ERITH REACH
RIVER THAMES
78
79
108
80
81
82
83
84
BELVEDERE INDUSTRIAL ESTATE
Erith Oil Works
BELVEDERE
FRANK'S PARK
Erith Coll of Technology
LESSNESS HEATH
ERITH CEMETERY
EUROPA TRADING ESTATE
ERITH
ERITH & DISTRICT HOSP
ERITH REC GRD
ERITH STADIUM
DA8
THE CHURCH TRADING EST
SLADE POWER IND EST
ANCHOR BAY IND EST
MANFORD IND EST
The Saltings
Sailing Club
DARENT INDUSTRIAL PARK
NORTHUMBERLAND HEATH
SLADE GREEN
SPORTS GROUND
CRAYFORD MARSHES
Howbury Farm
HOWBURY LANE REC GRDS
RAIL DEPOT
The Grange
Chemical Works
BURSTED WOOD
BARNEHURST
BARNEHURST GOLF COURSE
Perry Street Farm
Depot & Civic Amenity Site
DA1
BAKERS FIELD
MARTENS GROVE PARK
SHENSTONE PARK
BARNES CRAY
CRAYFORD MARSHES
ACORN INDUSTRIAL PARK
Stanham Farm
127
BRONZE AGE WAY
FRASER ROAD
BEXLEY ROAD
QUEEN'S ROAD
SOUTH RD
NORTHEND ROAD
MANOR ROAD
THAMES ROAD
PERRY STREET
CRAYFORD HIGH ST
WATLING STREET
LONDON ROAD
CRAYFORD WAY
A206
A2016
A2000
A220
A207
50
51
52

108
FJ
FK
FL
FM
FN
FP
FQ
90
107
128
75
76
77
78
79
80
81
82
83
84
54
55
56
RM13
DA8
DA1
RM19
WENNINGTON MARSHES
AVELEY MARSHES
RIFLE RANGES
PURFLEET
Crayford Ness
DARENT INDUSTRIAL PARK
FLOOD BARRIER
DARTFORD SALT MARSHES
CRAYFORD MARSHES
Longreach Sewage Treatment Works
Littlebrook Power Station
DARTFORD FRESH MARSHES
GLAXOWELLCOME
MILLSIDE INDUSTRIAL ESTATE
VICTORIA INDUSTRIAL PARK
BARNES CRAY
UNIVERSITY WAY
DARTFORD NORTHERN BYPASS
LONDON ROAD
THAMES
ARTERIAL ROAD
Junction 1a

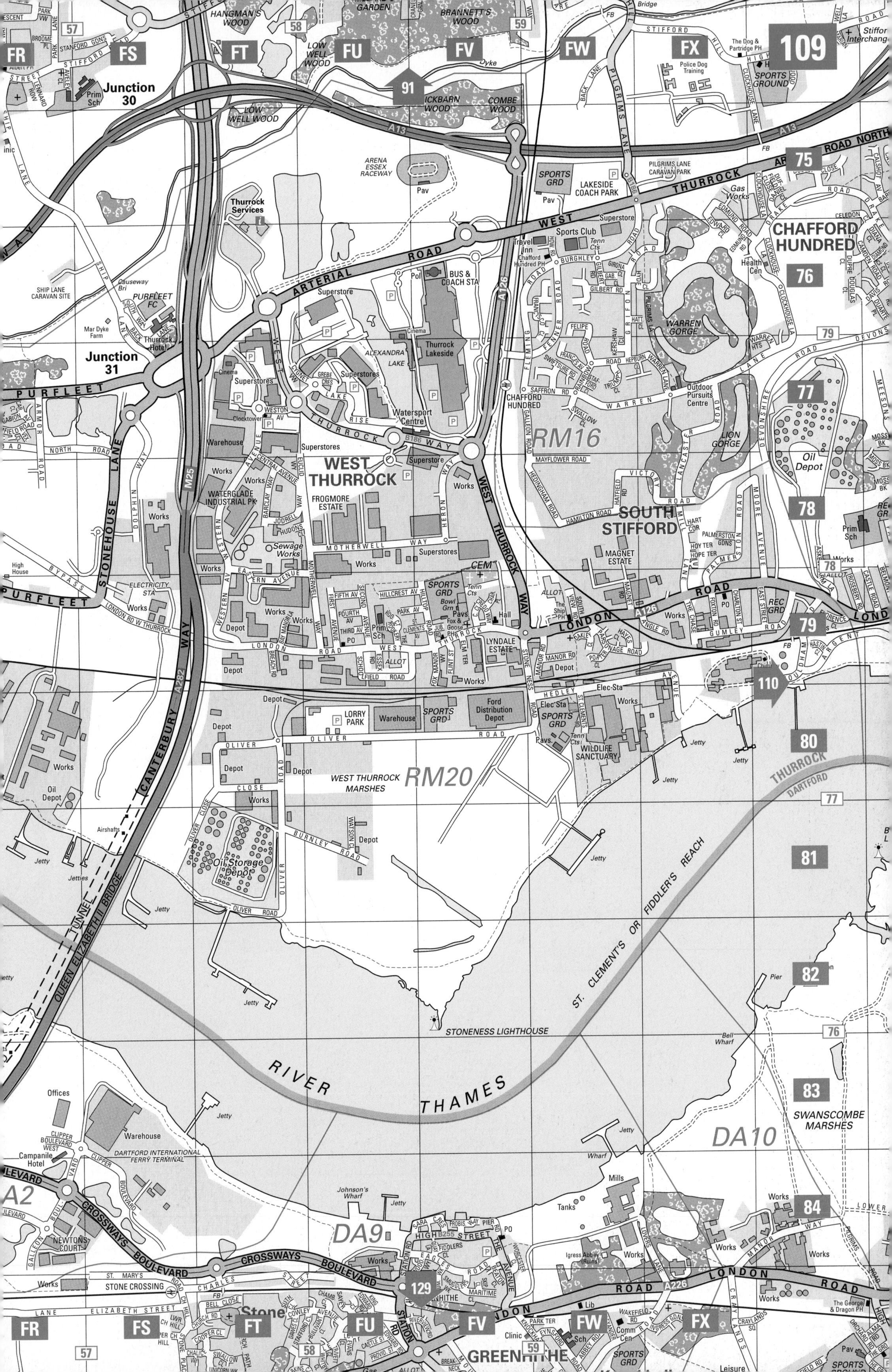

109
FR
FS
FT
FU
FV
FW
FX
58
59
57
91
HANGMAN'S WOOD
BRANNETT'S WOOD
LOW WELL WOOD
ICKBARN WOOD
COMBE WOOD
STIFFORD
Stifford Interchange
The Dog & Partridge PH
Police Dog Training
SPORTS GROUND
CLOCKHOUSE LANE
BACK LANE
PILGRIMS LANE
Junction 30
Prim Sch
A13
ARENA ESSEX RACEWAY
Pav
SPORTS GRD
LAKESIDE COACH PARK
PILGRIMS LANE CARAVAN PARK
75
ARTERIAL ROAD NORTH
WEST THURROCK ARTERIAL ROAD
Thurrock Services
Gas Works
CHAFFORD HUNDRED
76
Health Cen
Superstore
Sports Club
Travel Inn
Chafford Hundred PH
BURGHLEY
GILBERT RD
BUS & COACH STA
Superstore
SHIP LANE CARAVAN SITE
Causeway Bri
PURFLEET FC
Mar Dyke Farm
Thurrock Hotel
Junction 31
Cinema
Thurrock Lakeside
ALEXANDRA LAKE
WARREN GORGE
79
FELIPE ROAD
KERSHAW CL
HEPBURN
WARREN LANE
Outdoor Pursuits Centre
DEVONSHIRE
77
PURFLEET
Superstores
Cinema
Clocktower
WESTON AV
GREBE CRES
LAKE RISE
Watersport Centre
THURROCK WAY
B186
CHAFFORD HUNDRED
SAFFRON RD
WARREN
RM16
LION GORGE
Oil Depot
NORTH ROAD
Warehouse
Superstores
WEST THURROCK
Superstore
Works
WATERGLADE INDUSTRIAL PK
CENTRAL AVENUE
BARCLAY WAY
JODRELL
HUDSONS CL
FROGMORE ESTATE
HERON WAY
WEST THURROCK WAY
MAYFLOWER ROAD
HEDINGHAM ROAD
HAMILTON ROAD
VICTORY ROAD
HATFIELD
LANCASTER
MOORE AVENUE
SOUTH STIFFORD
78
Prim Sch
DOLPHIN WAY
Works
Sewage Works
MOTHERWELL WAY
Superstores
CEM
MAGNET ESTATE
HART COR
PALMERSTON GDNS
HOY TER
HOPE TER
PALMERSTON
High House
BYPASS
STONEHOUSE LANE
ELECTRICITY STA
EASTERN AVENUE
FIFTH AV
HILLCREST AV
SPORTS GRD
Bowl Grn
Tenn Cts
Hall
ALLOT
The Ship PH
LONDON ROAD
A126
CHARLTON ST
EAST STREET
REC GRD
PO
GUMLEY
79
PURFLEET
Works
LONDON RD W THURROCK
WESTERN AV
Depot
FOURTH AV
THIRD AV
PARK AV
Prim Sch
Fox & Goose PH
Pavs
LYNDALE ESTATE
STONE NESS
MANOR RD
PARSONAGE ROAD
Depot
FB
OUDHAM
ARGENT
110
LONDON ROAD WEST
BREACH RD
FIELD ROAD
FOX MANOR
FLINT ST
ELM TER
Works
Depot
HEDLEY AVENUE
Elec Sta
Elec-Sta
Works
LORRY PARK
Warehouse
SPORTS GRD
Ford Distribution Depot
SPORTS GRD
Tenn Cts
Pavs
WILDLIFE SANCTUARY
Jetty
80
OLIVER ROAD
Depot
Depot
WEST THURROCK MARSHES
RM20
CANTERBURY WAY
A282
M25
THURROCK
DARTFORD
77
Works
Oil Depot
CLOSE
Works
BURNLEY ROAD
WATSON CL
Depot
Airshafts
Oil Storage Depot
Jetty
81
Jetties
TUNNEL
QUEEN ELIZABETH II BRIDGE
Jetty
OLIVER ROAD
ST. CLEMENT'S OR FIDDLER'S REACH
Pier
82
Jetty
STONENESS LIGHTHOUSE
Bell Wharf
76
RIVER THAMES
83
Offices
Jetty
SWANSCOMBE MARSHES
Warehouse
CLIPPER BOULEVARD WEST
DARTFORD INTERNATIONAL FERRY TERMINAL
Campanile Hotel
Jetty
DA10
Wharf
A2
Mills
Johnson's Wharf
Jetty
Tanks
Works
84
DA9
HIGH STREET
B255
PIER
PO
CROSSWAYS BOULEVARD
NEWTONS COURT
Works
Igress Abbey (Ruins)
Works
Works
Works
LONDON ROAD
A226
ST. MARY'S
STONE CROSSING
CHARLES STREET
Works
129
MARITIME CL
THE AVENUE
WORCESTER
Lib
WAKEFIELD RD
CRAYLANDS SQ
The George & Dragon PH
ELIZABETH STREET
BELL CLOSE
Stone
GREENHITHE
Clinic
PARK TER
Comm Cen
Sch
SPORTS GRD
Leisure
Pav
SPORTS
FR
FS
FT
FU
FV
FW
FX
57
58
59

FY
FZ
GA
GB
GC
GD
GE
Stifford Interchange
Hogg Lane Roundabout
ARTERIAL ROAD NORTH STIFFORD
THURROCK
RM16
CHAFFORD HUNDRED
Gas Works
WARREN GORGE
LION GORGE
Oil Depot
SOUTH TIFFORD
ELIZABETH ROAD
HOGG LANE
GRAYS
RM17
ORSETT ROAD
PALMERS AV
LONDON ROAD
DEVONSHIRE ROAD
SOUTHEND ROAD
LODGE LANE
STANFORD ROAD
THURROCK ATHLETICS STADIUM
KING GEORGE'S FIELD
Blackshots Leisure Centre
Sockett's Heath
Little Thurrock
HANGMAN'S WOOD
GRAYS NEW CEMETERY
EAST THURROCK RD
BROADWAY
DOCK ROAD
GRAYS PARK
CIVIC OFFICES
Thurrock Yacht Club
MANOR WAY IND EST
LITTLE THURROCK MARSHES
THURROCK PARK IND EST
RIVER THAMES
BROADNESS LIGHTHOUSE
NORTHFLEET HOPE
Radar Mast
BROADNESS SALT MARSHES
SWANSCOMBE MARSHES
DA10
DA11
BOTANY MARSHES
Timber Yard
Elec Sta
Warehouses
TILBURY DOCKS
KENT
GRAVESHAM
DARTFORD
NORTHFLEET INDUSTRIAL ESTATE
GALLEY HILL ROAD
EBBSFLEET INDUSTRIAL ESTATE
ROBINS CREEK
SWANSCOMBE
75
76
77
78
79
80
81
82
83
84
109
130
61
62
63

111
GF
GG
GH
GJ
GK
GL
GM
64
65
66
75
76
77
78
79
80
81
82
83
84
131
Whitecroft's Farm
Heath Place
ORSETT GOLF COURSE
Brook Farm
Walton's Hall
Sutton's Farm
Whittakers Nursery
The Fox PH
Orsett Heath
GEORGE TILBURY HO
GODDERHAM HO
POOLE HO
OLD HOUSE WOOD
ASHEN SHAW
RAINBOW WOOD
GRAVEL PIT
HOLFORD ROAD
Works
BUCKINGHAM HILL ROAD
WALTONS HALL ROAD
Linford
SS17
Merie Loots Farm
George Dragon
PORTS GRD
SPORTS GROUND
Greyhound PH
GREYHOUND LA
CHADWELL ST. MARY
BRENTWOOD ROAD
Sec Sch
TERRELS HEATH
Prim Sch
Thurrock Technical College
A1089
A128
A126
ST. MARY'S CEM
ALLOT
Lib
PO
High House
HIGH HOUSE LANE
Becksland
Muckingford
Ashlea Farm
MUCKINGFORD ROAD
Mill House Farm
Mill House
COAL ROAD
LINFORD ROAD
RIVER VIEW
Chadwell Place
CHADWELL BYPASS
B149
Hutts Hill
Works
Poultry Farm
SHROVE HILL WOOD
Blue Anchor Cottage
BLUE ANCHOR LANE
Holford Farm
TURNPIKE LANE
LOW STREET LANE
SANDY LANE
Hall
The Kings Head PH
Manor Farm
RECTORY ROAD
Hob Hill
Hobhill Farm
BIGGIN LANE
Tally Ho Riding School
Broom Hill
Biggin Farm
West Tilbury
Gunhill Farm
West Tilbury Hall
CHURCH ROAD
GUN HILL
TILBURY MARSHES
HALLHILL COMMON
Low Street
STATION ROAD
COOPERS SHAW ROAD
Tilbury FC
ST. CHAD'S ROAD
PARSONAGE COMMON
KARTING TRACK
KING GEORGE'S FIELD
Pav
SPORTS GROUND
TILBURY
WEST TILBURY MARSHES
EAST TILBURY MARSHES
WALTHAM COMMON
RM18
Electricity Station
Works
CALCUTTA RD
DOCK ROAD
FERRY ROAD
Civic Cen
Leisure Cen
Sports Hall
Health Cen
ANCHOR FLDS PK
MONTREAL RD
CUSTOM HOUSE
Offices
Tilbury Energy & Environmental Centre
Chimney
Conveyor Belt
Tilbury B Power Station
Sewage Works
Filter Beds
Mercy Creek
MOAT
Tilbury Fort
The Worlds End PH
FORT ROAD
Warehouses
DRY DOCK
Cold Storage
Works
Tidal Basin
Pier
Jetty
LOWER ROAD
RIVER THAMES
THURROCK
GRAVESHAM
GRAVESEND
REACH
GRAVESEND

AS
AT
AU
AV
AW
AX
AY
92
85
86
87
88
89
90
91
92
93
94
74
73
72
71
98
99
00
132
OLD WINDSOR
SL4
TW20
SL5
Englefield Green
Egham Wick
Ripley Springs
GREAT PARK
REVIEW GROUND
WINDSOR GREAT PARK
THE LONG WALK
ALBERT ROAD
A308
STRAIGHT ROAD
DATCHET RD
CRIMP HILL
CRIMP HILL ROAD
BISHOPSGATE ROAD
PRIEST HILL
A328
ST. JUDE'S ROAD
LONDON ROAD
EGHAM HILL
WINDSOR ROAD
RIVER THAMES
NEW CUT
HAM LANE
WICK LANE
WICK ROAD
ROYAL GARDENS
NEWMEADOWS PLANTATION
PETERSHILL COPSE
Peter's Hill
MOAT
BEAR'S RAILS
RUSH POND
PRINCE OF WALES POND
WITHY BED
DUKE OF YORK PLANTATION
OLD WINDSOR WOOD
LIDDELL PLANTATION
OLD COVERT
WILD BOAR ENCLOSURE
GORE PLANTATION
Cookes Hill
Spring Hill
Bishops Gate
Royal Lodge
CONSERVATORY COVERT
GREENBROOM COVERT
KING GEORGE VI CORONATION GROVE
COW POND
CUMBERLAND LODGE
WILDERNESS
CHAPEL WOOD
THE SAVILL GARDENS
SMITH'S LAWN
FUZZY CLUMP
ALDER COVERT
OBELISK POND
SCARLETOAK PLANTATION
POLO GROUND
Breakheart Hill
FRANK'S PLANTATION
WEEDEN'S FIELD
JOHNSON'S POND
HEATHER GARDEN
DARKHOLE CLUMP
Temple Hill
CORK CLUMP
Prince Consort's Statue
ANUGRAHA CONFERENCE CENTRE
Beech Hill
Park Place
Prep Sch
SPORTS GROUND
Beaumont College Farm
War Memorial
RUNNYMEDE
WINDSOR & MAIDENHEAD
SURREY
Brunel University, Runnymede Campus
Cooper's Hill
COOPER'S HILL SLOPES NT
COOPER'S HILL COPPICE
Air Forces Memorial
Brunel University (Hall of Residence)
RUNNYMEDE PARK
John F Kennedy Memorial
Magna Carta Monument
MAGNA CARTA ISLAND
RATS CROFT EYOT
FRIARY ISLAND
MANOR FARM ESTATE
REMENHAM PARK
Old Windsor Lock
Ham Bridge
Sludge Beds
Filter Beds
Sailing Club
St. George's Farm
Manor Farm
The Priory
Priory Stables
St. Jude's Cemetery
University of London - Royal Holloway College
Castle Hill
Round Oak
Lubbock House
Meadow Cottage Farm
Parkside House
Glasshouse
Sec Sch
Prim Sch
Med. Cen
Health Cen
Pav
Tenn Cts

113
93
WRAYSBURY
RESERVOIR
TW19
SL3
Junction 14
Junction 13
RUBBISH DUMP
STAINES MOOR
KING GEORGE VI RESERVOIR
114
HERON LAKE
QUEENSMEAD LAKE
Hythe End
RUNNYMEDE PLEASURE GROUND
RUNNYMEDE NT
WINDSOR ROAD
Runnymede Hotel
THE GLANTY
THE CAUSEWAY
CLARENCE ST
HIGH ST
Pooley Green
EGHAM
Egham Hythe
TW18
Thorpe Lea
STAINES
STAINES PARK
Sweep's Bridge
Penton Hook Farm
133
AZ
BA
BB
BC
BD
BE
BF
85
86
87
88
89
90
91
92
93
94
74
73
72
71
01
02
03

BG
BH
BJ
BK
BL
BM
BN
94
85
86
87
88
89
90
91
92
93
94
113
134
05
06
07
74
73
72
71
AIRPORT WAY
STANWELL MOOR
SPORTS GROUND
Hall
Vermeulens Garden Centre
Warehouse
HILLINGDON
SPELTHORNE
SURREY
SOUTHERN PERIMETER RD
CARGO TERMINAL
BRITISH AIRWAYS CARGO CENTRE
Works
BEDFONT ROAD
BLACKBURN TRADING ESTATE
CAMGATE CENTRE
STANWELL
RECREATION GROUND
HAWS LANE
PARK ROAD
KING GEORGE VI RESERVOIR
STAINES RESERVOIRS
TW19
STANWELL MOOR RD
A3044
GRAVEL PIT
Bonehead Ditch
River Colne
Lower Mill Farm
Hithermoor Farm
ASHFORD HOSPITAL
SPORTS GROUND
BURIAL GROUND
Superstore
Fire Sta
LONDON ROAD
A30
STAINES BYPASS
Crooked Billet Roundabout
STAINES
STAINES CEM
SHORTWOOD POND
SHORTWOOD COMMON
Shortwood Farm
Hengrove Farm
New Inn Farm
REC GROUND
Prim Sch
Sec Sch
Sch
Clinic
ASHFORD
ASHFORD MANOR GOLF COURSE
Clubhouse
FORDBRIDGE PARK
Ford Bridge
KINGSTON ROAD
A308
Electricity Station
GRAVEL PIT
River Ash
STAINES PARK MINI RAILWAY
Leisure Cen
COUNCIL OFF.
Elmsleigh Centre
BUS STA
Thames Lodge Hotel
Boathouse
Staines Town FC
Sweep's Bridge
Penton Hook Farm
Sweep's Ditch
TRUSS'S ISLAND
FISHING TEMPLE
TEMPLE GARDENS
SPORTS GROUND
TW18
QUEEN MARY
A320
Penton

HATTON
HATTON CROSS
BP
BQ
BR
BS
BT
BU
BV
08
09
10
95
TW6
HEATHROW TERMINAL 4
TERMINAL 4
Hangars
Heathrow Hilton Hotel
TW14
HATTON CEM
BEDFONT RECREATION GROUND
DUKE OF NORTHUMBERLAND'S RIVER
HOUNSLOW HEATH
DONKEY WOOD
MERCURY CENTRE
THE GRIFFIN CENTRE
85
86
87
88
89
90
91
92
93
94
74
73
72
71
STAINES ROAD
GREAT SOUTH WEST ROAD
HARLINGTON ROAD WEST
HARLINGTON ROAD EAST
HOUNSLOW ROAD
FAGGS ROAD
Clockhouse Roundabout
EAST BEDFONT
BEDFONT LAKES COUNTRY PARK
Interpretation Centre
H.M. Young Offenders Institution & Remand Centre
FELTHAM ARENAS
GLEBELANDS PLAYING FIELDS
BEDFONT LANE REC GRD
GROSVENOR PARK
FELTHAM
FELTHAM BUSINESS COMPLEX
HANWORTH PARK
Hanworth Park House
TW13
116
LOWER FELTHAM
ASHFORD IND EST
TW15
LAKESIDE SPORTS GROUND
FELTHAMHILL
KING GEORGE'S FIELD
Staines R.F.C.
RESERVOIR
Staines Reservoirs Aqueduct
TW16
KEMPTON PARK (RACE DAYS ONLY)
RACECOURSE
ASHFORD COMMON WATER TREATMENT WORKS
Junction 1
135
SUNBURY
HIGH STREET
CHERTSEY ROAD
CADBURY ROAD
STAINES ROAD WEST
A308
A244
A315
B377
B3377
HILLINGDON
HOUNSLOW
SPELTHORNE
SURREY

116
BW
BX
BY
BZ
CA
CB
CC
96
85
86
87
88
89
90
91
92
93
94
115
136
12
13
14
74
73
72
71
TW4
TW13
TW12
TW16
HOUNSLOW HEATH
HOUNSLOW HEATH GOLF COURSE
DONKEY WOOD
Metropolitan Police Training Centre
CENTRAL PARK EST
MERCURY CENTRE
THE GRIFFIN CENTRE
STAINES ROAD
HARLINGTON ROAD WEST
HARLINGTON ROAD EAST
HOUNSLOW ROAD
HANWORTH ROAD
UXBRIDGE ROAD
HAMPTON ROAD WEST
GREAT CHERTSEY ROAD
TWICKENHAM RD
CRANE PARK
BOROUGH CEMETERY
HEATHFIELD REC GRD
TWICKENHAM CEMETERY
WHITTON
SPORTS GROUND
CREMATORIUM
HANWORTH PARK
Hanworth Park House
FELTHAM
FELTHAM BUSINESS COMPLEX
Feltham R.F.C.
RECTORY MEADOW
HANWORTH
HANWORTH TRADING ESTATE
Apex Retail Park
TWICKENHAM PARK GOLF COURSE
FULWELL PARK
FULWELL GOLF COURSE
RESERVOIR
Staines Reservoirs Aqueduct
KEMPTON PARK
RACECOURSE
HALF MOON COVERT
TWICKENHAM R.F.C. Clubhouse
PLAYING FIELD
CARLISLE PARK
HAMPTON
HYDES FIELD
Portlane Bridge
UPPER SUNBURY

CD
CE
CF
CG
CH
CJ
CK
TW9
TW6
TW1
TW10
TW2
TW11
KT2
MOGDEN WATER TREATMENT WORKS
ST. MARGARETS
IVYBRIDGE ESTATE
TWICKENHAM TRADING EST
THE RUGBY FOOTBALL UNION TWICKENHAM
Royal Military Sch of Music
RICHMOND UPON THAMES COLLEGE
HOUNSLOW
RICHMOND UPON THAMES
OLD DEER PARK RECREATION GROUND
RICHMOND GREEN
Richmond Palace Remains
RICHMOND
PLEASURE GDNS
MARBLE HILL
MARBLE HILL HOUSE
MARBLE HILL PARK
RIVER THAMES
GLOVER'S ISLAND
PETERSHAM MEADOWS
PETERSHAM
KING HENRY VIII MOUND
EEL PIE ISLAND
TWICKENHAM
TWICKENHAM RIFLE CLUB
HAM HOUSE (NT)
HAM HOUSE GARDENS
KING GEORGE'S FIELD
SPORTS GROUND
THE COPSE
SANDY LANE EST
HAM
ST. MICHAEL'S CONVENT
HAM COMMON
THE CASSEL HOSPITAL
RICHMOND GOLF COURSE SUDBROOK PARK
Thames Young Mariners Base
Ham Riverside Lands
STRAWBERRY HILL
STRAWBERRY HILL GOLF COURSE
St. Mary's Uni Coll
TEDDINGTON CEM
Teddington Lock
Teddington Weir
Teddington Studios
SHELL SPORTS GRD
TROWLOCK ISLAND
TEDDINGTON
BROOM ROAD REC GRD
STEVEN'S EYOT
CANBURY GDNS
Kingston Coll
CANAL PLANTATION
NATIONAL PHYSICAL LABORATORY
BUSHY HOUSE
ROUND PLANTATION
BUSHY
BROOM CLUMPS
HALF MOON PLANTATION
LEG OF MUTTON POND
HAMPTON WICK
WATERHOUSE WOODLAND
Open During Daylight Hours Only
97
85
86
87
88
89
90
91
92
93
94
118
137
15
16
17
71
72
73
74
A316
A305
A3004
A307
A310
A311
A313
A309
B358
B360

TW9
118
CL
CM
CN
CP
CQ
CR
CS
19
20
21
98
NORTH SHEEN
EAST SHEEN
SW14
UPPER RICHMOND ROAD WEST
SHEEN ROAD
RICHMOND GREEN
Richmond Palace Remains
85
86
87
88
89
90
91
92
93
94
117
74
73
72
71
RICHMOND
PESTHOUSE COMMON
EAST SHEEN COMMON (N T)
EAST SHEEN CEMETERY
RICHMOND CEMETERY
PALEWELL COMMON
PALEWELL PLAYING FIELDS
TECK PLANTATION
SHEEN WOOD
ADAM'S POND
The Bog
CYCLE PATH
HORSE RIDE
SHEEN CROSS WOOD
POLO FIELD
SAWYER'S HILL
CONDUIT WOOD
BISHOP'S PONDS
Richmond Gate
BARN WOOD POND
SAW PIT PLANTATION
JUBILEE PLANTATION
WHITE LODGE PLANTATIONS
DUCHESS WOOD
White Lodge (The Royal Ballet Sch)
KIDNEY WOOD
SIDMOUTH WOOD
RICHMOND
PARK
DEER PARK
QUEEN ELIZABETH'S PLANTATION
LEG OF MUTTON POND
PEN PONDS
KING GEORGE V JUBILEE PLANTATION
TREEBOX WOOD
SPANKER'S HILL WOOD
TW10
POND PLANTATION
LAWN PLANTATION
Tercentenary Plantation
MARTIN'S POND
PRINCE CHARLES'S SPINNEY
GIBBET WOOD
Robin Hood Gate
Pond Slade
HAM CROSS PLANTATION
ISABELLA PLANTATION
PEG'S POND
THOMSON'S POND
STILL POND
HIGH WOOD
Deer Fold
Broomfield Hill
BROOMFIELD HILL PLANTATION
Kingston Uni (Dorich House)
Ham Bottom
Ham Cross
Ham Dip
PETERSHAM
PETERSHAM MEADOWS
PETERSHAM PARK
TERRACE GDNS
TERRACE FIELD
Royal Star & Garter Home
KING HENRY VIII MOUND
RICHMOND GOLF COURSE SUDBROOK PARK
The Wilderness
HAM COMMON
HAM GATE AVENUE
Parkgate House
GLOVER'S ISLAND
TW1
RIVER THAMES
Ham Polo Club
THE COPSE
CORONATION PLANTATION
DANN'S POND
Thatchedhouse Lodge
GALLOW'S POND
Kings Clump
Dark Hill
Ladderstile Gate
Kingston Gate
KINGSTON HILL
Kingston University (Kingston Hill)
Kingston University (Coombehurst)
COOMBE HILL GOLF COURSE
COOMBE WOOD GOLF COURSE
THE WATERGARDENS
KINGSTON PARK EST
COOMBE
COOMBE WOOD GOLF COURSE
KT2
138
KINGSTON HOSPITAL
NORBITON
TROWLOCK ISLAND
STEVEN'S EYOT
BROOM ROAD REC GRD
CANBURY GDNS
Kingston Coll
ROBIN HOOD WAY

119
CT
CU
CV
CW
CX
CY
CZ
22
23
24
99
85
86
87
88
89
90
91
92
93
94
120
139
ROEHAMPTON
PUTNEY
SW15
PUTNEY HEATH
WANDSWORTH
EAST PUTNEY
SOUTHFIELDS
SW18
WIMBLEDON PARK
SW19
WIMBLEDON COMMON
WIMBLEDON
PUTNEY VALE
COPSE HILL
SW20
COTTENHAM PARK
MERTON
ROEHAMPTON GOLF COURSE
ROEHAMPTON PRIORY HOSPITAL
QUEEN MARY'S UNI HOSP
ROEHAMPTON PLAYING FIELDS
Roehampton Institute London
Froebel College
Digby Stuart College
Uni of Greenwich (Downshire House)
Uni of Greenwich (Manresa House)
Wandsworth Adult Ed Coll
MARYFIELD CONVENT
ST. MARY'S CONVENT
RICHMOND PARK GOLF COURSE
Kingsfarm Plantation
PUTNEY VALE CEMETERY
Crematorium
Superstore
WINDMILL MUSEUM
LONDON SCOTTISH GOLF COURSE
ROYAL WIMBLEDON GOLF COURSE
Queen's Mere
King's Mere
Scio Pond
Jerry's Hill
Caesar's Camp
CANNIZARO PARK
Cannizaro House (Hotel)
RUSHMERE POND
LADY JANE'S WOOD
BLUEGATE GRAVEL PIT (DISUSED)
HOOKHAMSLADE POND
Farm Bog
Farm Ravine
Gravelly Hill
Queen's Butt (Site off)
Stag Bog
Silent Pools
Fishponds Wood Nature Reserve
Mill Corner
Shadwell Wood
Tibbet's Corner
ROYAL HOSPITAL
Whitelands Training Coll
Roehampton Institute of Adult Ed
Southlands Coll
PARKSIDE CLINIC
ATHLETICS TRACK
GOLF COURSE
ALL ENGLAND LAWN TENNIS & CROQUET CLUB
MUS OF LOCAL HISTORY
WOLFSON MED. REHAB CENTRE
ATKINSON MORLEY'S HOSPITAL
OBERON PLAYING FIELD
SPORTS GROUND
DUNDONALD REC GRD
KING GEORGE'S PARK
WIMBLEDON PARK
KINGSTON ROAD
UPPER RICHMOND ROAD
WEST HILL
KINGSTON VALE
ROEHAMPTON LANE
PUTNEY HILL
WIMBLEDON PARK SIDE
PARKSIDE
HIGH ST WIMBLEDON
WIMBLEDON HILL RD
THE BROADWAY
DURNSFORD ROAD
MERTON ROAD
BUCKHOLD ROAD
SOUTH CIRCULAR ROAD
WANDSWORTH BRIDGE ROAD
A3
A205
A219
A218
A238
A306
B281
B235

120
DA
DB
DC
DD
DE
DF
DG
WANDSWORTH
SW18
SW11
SW19
SW17
SOUTHFIELDS
EARLSFIELD
SUMMERSTOWN
WIMBLEDON PARK
UPPER TOOTING
BALHAM
TOOTING GRAVENEY
COLLIER'S WOOD
SOUTH WIMBLEDON
MERTON
WANDSWORTH COMMON
WANDSWORTH CEMETERY
CENTRAL LONDON GOLF CENTRE
SPRINGFIELD HOSPITAL
STREATHAM CEMETERY
LAMBETH CEMETERY
WIMBLEDON CEMETERY
WIMBLEDON STADIUM
ST. GEORGE'S HOSPITAL
H.M. PRISON WANDSWORTH
BOLINGBROKE HOSP
KING GEORGE'S PARK
GARRATT PARK
WANDLE PARK
LONDON ROAD CEMETERY
FIGGE'S MARSH
DUNDONALD REC GRD
SOUTH PARK GDNS
GREENLEA PARK
SPENCER PARK
ST. JOHN'S CEN
100
140
119
85
86
87
88
89
90
91
92
93
94
26
27
28
71
72
73
74
TRINITY ROAD
GARRATT LANE
MERTON ROAD
DURNSFORD ROAD
HAYDONS ROAD
MERTON HIGH STREET
TOOTING HIGH STREET
MITCHAM ROAD
UPPER TOOTING ROAD
BALHAM HIGH ROAD
WEST HILL
WANDSWORTH HIGH ST
BURNTWOOD LANE
THE BROADWAY
KINGSTON ROAD
MERANTUN WAY

121
DH
DJ
DK
DL
DM
DN
DP
29
30
31
101
85
86
87
88
89
90
91
92
93
94
122
141
CLAPHAM COMMON
SW4
CLAPHAM PARK
BRIXTON
H.M. PRISON BRIXTON
SW2
BROCKWELL PARK
SE24
HERNE HILL
STREATHAM HILL
TULSE HILL
SE21
TOOTING BEC COMMON
STREATHAM PARK
STREATHAM
SE27
WEST NORWOOD
WEST NORWOOD CEMETERY
STREATHAM COMMON
SW16
NORWOOD GROVE RECREATION GROUND
STREATHAM VALE
SE19
NORWOOD NEW TOWN
BIGGIN WOOD
NORBURY PARK
NORBURY
NATIONAL WESTMINSTER BANK SPORTS GROUND
POYNDERS ROAD
CHRISTCHURCH ROAD
SOUTH CIRCULAR ROAD
STREATHAM HIGH ROAD
BRIXTON HILL
TULSE HILL
NORWOOD ROAD
KNIGHTS HILL
DULWICH ROAD
STREATHAM COMMON NORTH
CROWN LANE
BEC ROAD
MITCHAM LANE
CLAPHAM PARK ROAD
ACRE LANE
CAVENDISH ROAD
BALHAM HILL
THURLOW PARK ROAD

122
DQ
DR
DS
DT
DU
DV
DW
SE24
SE15
SE22
SE21
SE27
SE26
SE19
SE20
HERNE HILL
BROCKWELL PARK
DULWICH
DULWICH PARK
EAST DULWICH
PECKHAM RYE COMMON
PECKHAM RYE PARK
CAMBERWELL OLD CEMETERY
TULSE HILL
WEST DULWICH
DULWICH & SYDENHAM HILL GOLF COURSE
SYDENHAM HILL WOOD (NATURE RESERVE)
DULWICH WOOD
UPPER SYDENHAM
WEST NORWOOD CEMETERY
WEST NORWOOD
NORWOOD PARK
NORWOOD
NORWOOD NEW TOWN
CRYSTAL PALACE PARK
CRYSTAL PALACE ATHLETICS STADIUM
UPPER NORWOOD
PENGE
SOUTH BANK UNIVERSITY SPORTS GROUND
HORNIMAN GDNS
DULWICH PICTURE GALL
KING'S COLL HOSP
HERNE HILL STADIUM
BELAIR PARK
SYDENHAM WELLS PARK
WESTOW PARK
BEAULIEU HEIGHTS
SYLVAN ESTATE
SOUTH NORWOOD
HALF MOON LANE
DULWICH COMMON
THURLOW PARK ROAD
CROXTED ROAD
LORDSHIP LANE
CRYSTAL PALACE PARADE
WESTWOOD HILL
CRYSTAL PALACE PARK ROAD
ANERLEY HILL
CENTRAL HILL
BEULAH HILL
KNIGHTS HILL
DULWICH WOOD PK
KIRKDALE
DARTMOUTH ROAD
LONDON ROAD
A205
A215
A2199
A2214
A2216
A212
A214
A234
85
86
87
88
89
90
91
92
93
94
71
72
73
74
33
34
35
102
121
142

DX
DY
DZ
EA
EB
EC
ED
123
103
85
86
87
88
89
90
91
92
93
94
124
143
36
37
38
71
72
73
74
HILLY FIELDS
BROCKLEY
BROCKLEY CEMETERY
LADYWELL CEMETERY
SE4
LADYWELL
LADYWELL FIELDS
UNIVERSITY LEWISHAM HOSP
LEWISHAM PARK
SE13
HITHER GREEN
MANOR PARK
MANOR HOUSE GARDENS
HONOR OAK SPORTS GRD
HONOR OAK PARK
CATFORD GREYHOUND STADIUM
BLYTHE HILL FIELDS
BROCKLEY HILL PARK
MOUNTFIELD PARK PLAYING FIELDS
CATFORD
CATFORD BRIDGE
BROWNHILL ROAD
SOUTH CIRCULAR ROAD
STANSTEAD ROAD
FOREST HILL
PRIVATE BANKS SPORTS GRD
SE6
SE23
FORSTER MEMORIAL PARK
BELL GREEN
BELLINGHAM
LOWER SYDENHAM
MAYOW PARK
SOUTHEND
SOUTHEND PARK
HOME PARK
NAT WEST BANK SPORTS GRD
LLOYDS BANK SPORTS GRD
C.G.U. CUACO SPORTS GRD
H.S.B.C. GROUP SPORTS GRD
NEW BECKENHAM
BR3
BECKENHAM PLACE PARK
GOLF COURSE
ASH PLANTATION
SUMMERHOUSE HILL WOOD
BR2
LEWISHAM BOROUGH SPORTS GROUND
MIDLAND BANK SPORTS GROUND
WARREN AVE PLAYING FIELDS
CATOR PARK
ALEXANDRA REC GRD
BECKENHAM
BECKENHAM JUNCTION
SHORTLANDS GOLF COURSE
BROMLEY PARK
THE SLOANE HOSPITAL
RAVENSBOURNE
LEWISHAM BROMLEY
DOWNHAM FIELDS
SPORTS GROUND

124
EE
EF
EG
EH
EJ
EK
EL
40
41
42
104
85
86
87
88
89
90
91
92
93
94
123
144
73
74
72
71
SE13
SE12
SE6
BR1
BR2
HITHER GREEN
GROVE PARK
MOTTINGHAM
ELTHAM
DOWNHAM
PLAISTOW
SUNDRIDGE
ELMSTEAD
BROMLEY PARK
MANOR PARK
SUTCLIFFE PARK
HITHER GREEN CEMETERY
NORTHBROOK PARK
CHINBROOK MEADOWS
SUNDRIDGE PARK GOLF COURSE
ELMSTEAD WOOD
ROCKPIT WOOD
LOGSHILL WOOD
LOWER MARVELS WOOD
MARVELS WOOD
GROVE PARK CEMETERY
MOTTINGHAM SPORTS GROUND
UNI OF WESTMINSTER SPORTS GROUND
UNI OF GREENWICH ATHLETIC GRD
CIVIL SERVICE SPORTS GROUNDS
OLD COLFEIANS SPORTS GROUND
MIDDLE PARK FIELD
QUEENSCROFT REC GRD
KING JOHN PLAYING FIELDS
DOWNHAM PLAYING FIELDS
DOWNHAM FIELDS
SHAFTESBURY PARK REC GRD
KING'S MEADOW PLAYING FIELDS
WARREN AVE PLAYING FIELDS
LEWISHAM BOROUGH SPORTS GROUND
MIDLAND BANK SPORTS GROUND
SHORTLANDS GOLF CO
THE SLOANE HOSPITAL
Sundridge Park Management Cen
SOUTH CIRCULAR ROAD
ST. MILDREDS ROAD
WESTHORNE AVENUE
ELTHAM ROAD
SIDCUP ROAD
BURNT ASH HILL
BARING ROAD
BURNT ASH LANE
BROMLEY HILL
LONDON ROAD
KIDBROOKE PARK ROAD
ROCHESTER WAY
MOTTINGHAM LANE
GROVE PARK ROAD
CHINBROOK ROAD
A20
A205
A210
A212
A2212
A21
A2213
B226

EM
EN
EP
EQ
ER
ES
ET
DA16
125
105
85
86
87
88
89
90
91
92
93
94
126
145
43
44
45
ROCHESTER WAY RELIEF ROAD
ELTHAM PARK SOUTH
ELTHAM WARREN GOLF COURSE
ELTHAM
Crematorium
EAST ROCHESTER WAY
SPORTS GROUND
Environment Curriculum Service
BEXLEY ROAD
BLACKFEN ROAD
ELTHAM HIGH ST
AVERY HILL
AVERY HILL PARK
University of Greenwich Avery Hill Campus
CAMBRIDGE MISSION SPORTS GROUND
CHARLTON ATHLETIC FC TRAINING GRD
FOOTSCRAY PLAYING FIELDS
MILLWALL FC TRAINING GRD
GAELIC ATH. ASSOC. SPORTS GRD
BLACKFEN
HOLLY OAK WOOD PK
DA15
LAMORBEY
ROYAL BLACKHEATH GOLF COURSE
TARN BIRD SANCTUARY
SE9
THE TARN
FAIRY HILL REC GRD
NEW ELTHAM
PLAYING FIELD
St Olave's Prep. Sch
SPORTS GROUND
OLD FARM PARK
KING GEORGE'S REC GRD
SIDCUP ROAD
FOOTSCRAY ROAD
LONGLANDS
JACK NICKLAUS GOLF CENTRE
FLAMINGO PK SPORTS GRD
LONGLANDS REC GRD
SIDCUP BYPASS
MAIN ROAD
SIDCUP
DA14
THE COURSE
BELMONT LANE OPEN SPACE
Kemnal Manor Stables
Beaver's Wood
DOG RACING TRACK
CHISLEHURST CEMETERY
Hoblands Wood
Thompson's Nursery
Frogpool Manor Farm
SIDCUP PLACE
QUEEN MARY'S HOSP
WHITE HORSE HILL
RED HILL
HIGH STREET
Ravensbourne Coll
CHISLEHURST WEST
WHYTES WOODLAND
Bird Sanctuary
BR7
OLD ELTHAMIANS SPORTS GRD
UNIVERSITY COLLEGE LONDON SPORTS GRD
SCADBURY PARK
NATURE RESERVE
CHISLEHURST
CAMDEN PARK
CHISLEHURST GOLF COURSE
CHISLEHURST COMMON
PERRY STREET
BROMLEY LANE
BROMLEY ROAD
Perry Street Shaw
Bushy Clump
Icehouse Wood
PARK WOOD
Scadbury Moated Manor House Site
Holbrook Wood
Field Study Centre
Frognal Corner
Little Wood
Plantation

126
EU
EV
EW
EX
EY
EZ
FA
106
DANSON
PARK
THE LAKE
The Boathouse Function Suite
BEXLEYHEATH
DA6
BEXLEYHEATH GOLF COURSE
PLAYING FIELD
ROCHESTER WAY
EAST ROCHESTER WAY
A2
BLACKFEN ROAD
A210
BLACKFEN
HOLLY OAK WOOD PK
DA15
PENHILL PARK
BEXLEY PARK WOOD
RIVERSIDE WALK
SIDCUP GOLF COURSE
MARLBOROUGH PARK
LAMORBEY PARK
Rose Bruford College
HURST ROAD
A222
RUTLAND SHAW
ABBEYHILL PARK
KING GEORGE'S REC GRD
SIDCUP
125
GOLDSMITH COLLEGE SPORTS GRD
THE ALDERS
WARING PARK
Sidcup Arts Cen
NORTH CRAY WOOD
STABLE MEADOW
DA14
FOOTS CRAY MEADOW
Foots Cray Place
GATTONS WOOD
SIDCUP HIGH STREET
SIDCUP PLACE
SPORTS GROUNDS
David Lloyd Club
SIDCUP TECHNOLOGY CENTRE
QUEEN MARY'S HOSP
GARDEN SHAW
FOOTS CRAY
Coca Cola & Schweppes Beverages Limited
RUXLEY CORNER INDUSTRIAL ESTATE
NORTH CRAY ROAD
A223
MAIDSTONE ROAD
RUXLEY WOOD
SIDCUP BYPASS
A20
SCADBURY PARK NATURE RESERVE
LITTLE WOOD
Scadbury Moated Manor House Site
Irish Plantation
SEVENOAKS WAY
146
RUXLEY PARK
CRAY VALLEY
85
86
87
88
89
90
91
92
93
94
47
48
49
71
72
73
74

FB
FC
FD
FE
FF
FG
FH
127
DA1
BARNES CRAY
CRAYFORD MARSHES
107
85
CRAYFORD
CRAYFORD STADIUM
ACORN INDUSTRIAL PARK
MARTENS GROVE PARK
SHENSTONE PARK
BIGS HILL WOOD
WATLING STREET
LONDON ROAD (WATLING STREET)
BOURNE ROAD
HALL PLACE
HALL PLACE GARDENS
SPORTS GROUND
RUGBY GRD
ST. MARY'S REC GRD
OLD BEXLEY
86
87
DARTFORD
North West Kent College of Technology
DARTFORD ROAD (WATLING
SHEPHERDS LANE
EAST ROCHESTER WAY
ROCHESTER WAY
THE OLD ORCHARD
CHURCHFIELD WOOD
QUARRY
DARTFORD HEATH
DARTFORD BYPASS
OLD BEXLEY LANE
88
DARTFORD GOLF COURSE
89
University of Greenwich
Coldblow
DARTFORD ROAD
VICARAGE ROAD
BEXLEY HOSPITAL
CAVEY'S SPRING
Electricity Station
128
90
JOYDEN'S WOOD
Hook Green
91
Wilm
DA2
ROWHILL WOOD
Joydens Wood
92
Rowhill Grange
93
ROWHILL WOOD
THE
BIRCHWOOD PARK
GOLF COURSE
Hextable
HEXTABLE GDNS
94
147
KENT
DARTFORD
SEVENOAKS
Swanley Village
50
51
52
71
72
73
74

128
FJ
FK
FL
FM
FN
FP
FQ
NES CRAY
CRAYFORD MARSHES
DARTFORD FRESH MARSHES
MILLSIDE INDUSTRIAL ESTATE
GLAXOWELLCOME
VICTORIA INDUSTRIAL PARK
108
Junction 1a
BOW ARROW LANE CEM
ARCHERY HOUSE
Uni of Greenwich
STONE HOUSE HOSPITAL
DARTFORD
New Town
EAST HILL CEM
LIVINGSTONE HOSP
North West Kent College of Technology
SPORTS GROUND
CENTRAL PARK
WELLCOME SPORTS GROUND
DA1
WATLING STREET CEM
Leigh City Tech. Coll
BROOKLANDS LAKE
DARTFORD GOLF COURSE
BRICKHILL WOOD
University of Greenwich
OAKFIELD PARK
DARTFORD TRADE PARK
127
DARTFORD BYPASS
Junction 2
Wilmington
Hawley
Darenth
GRAVEL PIT
THE ALDERS
DEER PARK
ST. JOHN'S JERUSALEM
Sutton at Hone
Swanley Village
148
M25
A2
A225
A2026
A2018
A296
A282
B2174
B258
B2200
B2228
85
86
87
88
89
90
91
92
93
94
54
55
56
71
72
73
74

129
FR
FS
FT
FU
FV
FW
FX
57
58
59
Johnson's Wharf
Jetty
Mills
DA9
109
CROSSWAYS BOULEVARD
NEWTONS COURT
STONE CROSSING
Works
ST. MARY'S
CHARLES STREET
ELIZABETH STREET
Stone
HIGH STREET
GREENHITHE
STATION RD
LONDON ROAD
A226
Igress Abbey (Ruins)
Lib
Prim Sch
Comm Cen
SPORTS GRD
Knockhall
REC GRD
The George & Dragon PH
85
Leisure Centre
SPORTS GROUND
SWANSCOMBE HERITAGE PARK
NAT RES
86
CEM
REC GRD
74
Clinic
87
DA10
ALLOT
Gas Works
TA Cen
The Bull PH
War Memorial
STONE REC GRD
Tenn Cts
Pavs
Prim Sch
STONE CEM
Greenhithe Technical Centre
Stone Castle
Works
BLUEWATER PARKWAY
THE VILLAGE
Bluewater Shopping Centre
WATER CIRCUS
LIME TREE AV
OAK TREE AV
Western Cross Farm
Alkerden Farm
MOUNTS ROAD
WATLING STREET
A296
BEAN ROAD
B255
88
CHALK PIT
Works
73
CHALK PIT
89
A2
DARTFORD BYPASS
DARENTH WOOD
DARENTH WOOD ROAD
Knoxfield Caravan Park
Arrow Riding Centre
BURIAL GRD
THE THRIFT
Caravan Site
130
The Royal Oak PH
COV RES
90
Bean Farm
Bean
Badger's Mount
DA2
LADIES WOOD
72
SANDY LANE
Youth Club
Prim Sch
PO
BEACON COUNTRY PARK
Cherwell Farm
LORDS WOOD
Bets 91
The C Arms
Farm (closed)
BETSHAM ROAD
B262
92
Mates Farm
Manor House Farm
HIGHCROSS ROAD
Hall
FB
GREEN STREET GREEN ROAD
Manor Farm Garden Centre
Prim Sch
ALLOT
Cricket Club
71
93
SANDBANKS
The Ship PH
Green Street Green
ST. MARGARET'S ROAD
St. Margaret's Farm
Westwood Farm
Wheatsheaf PH
HOOK GREEN
94
B260
Walnut Tree Farm
Chalkcroft
Ryecroft Farm
149
GILL'S ROAD
Gill's Farm
YECROFTS WOOD
DARTFORD SEVENOAKS
South Darenth
QUARRY
SPORTS GRD

SWANSCOMBE
NORTHFLEET
DA10
DA11
DA13
Betsham
Southfleet
Hook Green
Redstreet
Northfleet Green
Perry Street
Istead Ri
TILBURY DOCKS
NORTHFLEET URBAN COUNTRY PARK
SWANSCOMBE HERITAGE PARK
BLUE CIRCLE SPORTS GRD
SPRINGHEAD ENTERPRISE PARK
NORTHFLEET INDUSTRIAL ESTATE
EBBSFLEET INDUSTRIAL ESTATE
WOMBWELL PARK
SPRINGFIELD REC GRD
NORTHFLEET CEMETRY
CHALK PIT
QUARRY
MADAM WOOD
COURT WOOD
Electricity Station
Electricity Sub Station
Sewage Works
Springhead Nurseries
RECYCLING CENTRE
WATLING STREET
LONDON ROAD
GALLEY HILL ROAD
STONEBRIDGE ROAD
SOUTHFLEET ROAD
SPRINGHEAD ROAD
THAMES WAY
STATION ROAD
HOOK GREEN ROAD
HIGHCROSS ROAD
DOWNS ROAD
NEW BARN ROAD
DARTFORD
GRAVESHAM
FY
FZ
GA
GB
GC
GD
GE
61
62
63
74
73
72
71
85
86
87
88
89
90
91
92
93
94
110
129

GF
GG
GH
GJ
GK
GL
GM
64
65
66
111
RIVER THAMES
THURROCK
GRAVESHAM
GRAVESEND
85
86
87
88
89
90
91
92
93
94
Tidal Basin
Tilbury Fort
The Worlds End PH
Filter Beds
Jetty
Pier
Works
Wharf
Town Pier
ST. ANDREWS ART CENTRE
Customhouse Pier
HERITAGE CEN
IMPERIAL RETAIL PARK
IMPERIAL BUS EST
Superstores
St. Georges Shop Cen
HOSP.
OVERCLIFFE
CLIVE RD
MILTON
A226
RIVERSIDE LEISURE AREA
Milton
Gas Works
MARINA
CANAL
Denton Wharf
Quarantine Station
Electricity Station
Tennis Courts
EASTCOURT MARSHES
DISUSED CANAL
DENTON MARSHES
Sewage Works
Filter Beds
Youth Cen
Denton
WESTCOURT MARSHES
GREAT CLAYLANE MARSHES
74
Windmill Hill
GRAVEL PIT
CIVIC CEN
SPORTS GROUND
OLD GRAVESENDIANS SPORTS GRD
Bowling Green
Sports Centre
ROCHESTER ROAD
Chalk
HIGHAM ROAD
73
The White Hart PH
Coll
Sec Sch
Prim Sch
GRAVESEND CEMETERY
WOODLANDS PARK
Cricket Ground
Kent & Essex PH
The Woodlands PH
OLD ROAD EAST
OLD ROAD WEST
Prep. Sch
CONVENT
Admiral Beatty PH
Westcourt
Kings Farm
DA12
Parrock Farm
MID KENT GOLF COURSE
Clubhouse
WROTHAM ROAD
A227
SINGLEWELL ROAD
JENNY LEE SMITH GOLF COURSE
72
Tourist Railway
Leisure Centre
Comm Cen
Hospice
Superstore
MIKE SPRING COURT
Riverview Park
Youth Cen
Ifield Sch
Sports Club
COV RES
ABBOTS FLD
Singlewell
Tollgate Motel
Tollgate Stables
WATLING STREET
A2
Hartshill
71
Westwood Farm
CLAYLANE WOOD
Ifield Rectory
Ifield Court Cottages
Ifield Court
Kever Court Farm
Services
HUNTONDOWN WOOD
GREYHOUND RACING TRACK
TWENTY ACRE WOOD
GRAVEHILL WOOD
THE BURNET
Scalers Hill House
Scaler's Hill
HENHURST RD
CHURCH ROAD

132
AS
AT
AU
AV
AW
AX
AY
Egham Wick
112
POLO GROUND
FRANK'S PLANTATION
WEEDEN'S FIELD
JOHNSON'S POND
SCARLETOAK PLANTATION
EGHAM WICK PLANTATION
DARKHOLE CLUMP
OXHED CLUMP
HEATHER GARDEN
High Flyer's Hill
WINTER GARDEN
WICK POND
The Punch Bowl
THE VALLEY GARDENS
VIRGINIA WATER PLANTATION
VIRGINIA WATER
Botany Bay Point
FROSTFARM PLANTATION
BLACKNEST
LONDON ROAD
A30
A329
SL5
BELVEDERE WOOD
The American Comm Sch
Royal Holloway College
Callow Hill
GREAT WOOD
VIRGINIA WATER
HOLLOW LANE
CHRISTCHURCH ROAD
KING'S COPSE
WAVERLEY COPSE
GENERAL'S COPSE
DUKE'S COPSE
GU25
Broom Hill
Clubhouse
WENTWORTH POND
WENTWORTH
Wentworth
GOLF COURSE
BEECH WOOD
Knowle Hill
KNOWLE GROVE
GREAT WOOD
KING GEORGE V PLAYING FIELD
PLAYING FLD
Burnt Hill
LONGCROSS
Depots
GU24
Little Arm
Ship Hill
Long Arm
CHERTSEY COMMON
BOG WOOD
DICKEN'S WOOD
BARROWHILLS
MILITARY GOLF COURSE
Longcross
Flutters Hill
Oystershell Hill
Rushy Pond
CHOBHAM COMMON
150
M3
B386
95
96
97
98
99
100
101
102
103
104

AZ
BA
BB
BC
BD
BE
BF
01
02
03
113
95
96
97
98
99
100
101
102
103
104
134
151
TW20
TW18
KT16
Stroude
THORPE
Thorpe Green
THORPE GREEN
LYNE
CHERTSEY
ADDLESTONE MOOR
Great Fosters Hotel
MOAT
LONGSIDE LAKE
THORPE INDUSTRIAL EST
Crabtree Corner
Tasis England
SPORTS GROUND
THE MOAT
WATER GARDENS
MANOR LAKE
THORPE PARK
ST. ANN'S LAKE
Abbey Lake
Mountbatten Pavilion
Britannia Arena
PENTON HOOK MARINA
PENTON HOOK ISLAND
TRUSS'S ISLAND
PENTON PARK (Caravan Park)
LALEHAM BURWAY
Junction 2 (M3), Junction 12 (M25)
ANCHOR COPSE
ST. ANNS HILL PARK
Sewage Works
Sludge Lagoons
ELM FARM CARAVAN PARK
THE ROUGH
RECREATION GROUND
LYNE COPSE
HERSHAM COPSE
FAN GROVE
FANGROVE CARAVAN PARK
Great Cockrow Railway
Cockcrow Hill
RUNNYMEDE HOSP
ST. PETER'S HOSP
FOXHILLS GOLF COURSE
Foxhills Country Club
HOME WOOD
Botleys Mansion
Kitchenride Corner
Junction 11
ADDLESTONE CEMETERY
ABBEY MOOR GOLF COURSE
GOGMORE FM PK
Chertsey Town FC
Cricket Club
Abbey Bridge
CHERTSEY MUS
M25
M3
A320
B386
B388
B389
B375
A317
STAINES ROAD
CHERTSEY LANE
GUILDFORD ROAD
MILL HOUSE LANE
THORPE BYPASS
HOLLOWAY HILL
ST. PETER'S WAY

BG
BH
BJ
BK
BL
BM
BN
05
06
07
114
TW18
QUEEN
MARY
RESERVOIR
SPORTS GROUND
Penton Hook Lock
PENTON HOOK ISLAND
PENTON HOOK
PENTON HOOK MARINA
Yacht Basin
PENTON PARK
(Caravan Park)
MANOR LAKE
Mountbatten Pavilion
Abbey Lake
LALEHAM GOLF COURSE
LALEHAM BURWAY
RESERVOIR
Water Works
LALEHAM
LALEHAM PARK
Laleham Abbey
LALEHAM PARK SPORTS GROUND
Camp Site
GRAVEL PIT
Laleham Nurseries
Littleton Park Nurseries
Shepperton Studios
Squires Bridge
REC GRD
Gas Pipeline Sta
ROUND COPSE
Intake Channel
Pumping Sta
Sailing Club
Charlton Quarry
KT16
M3
133
95
96
97
98
99
100
101
102
103
104
69
68
67
66
ABBEYFIELDS REC GRD
Abbey Bridge
Abbey River
Abbey Chase House
Chertsey Lock
CHERTSEY
CHERTSEY ROAD
RENFREE
Riversleigh Farm
Dumsey Eyot
RECREATION GROUND
SPELTHORNE
RUNNYMEDE
Dockett Eddy
Dockett Point
CHERTSEY MEADS
PHARAOH'S ISLAND
LOCK ISLAND
HAMHAUGH ISLAND
Hamhaugh Point
The Bull Dogs
FORDWATER TRADING EST
Fordwater Bridge
SPORTS GROUND
KT15
WOBURN PARK
St. George's College
ADDLESTONE MOOR
ADDLESTONE CEMETERY
ABBEY MOOR GOLF COURSE
Woburn Hill Nursery
VICTORY PARK
152
ADDLESTONE
WEYBRIDGE TRADING ESTATE
WEYBRIDGE BUSINESS PARK
Black Boy Bridge
Weybridge Lock
M25
Junction 11
Simplemarsh Farm
Woodside Farm
CONVENT
A317
A320
A318
B375
B376
HOSP
WEYBRI

135
BP
BQ
BR
BS
BT
BU
BV
08
09
10
115
136
153
95
96
97
98
99
100
101
102
103
104
69
68
67
66
LITTLETON
TW17
SUNBURY
SUNBURY PARK
TW16
UPPER HALLIFORD
KT12
KT13
WALTON-ON THAMES
ASHLEY PARK
DESBOROUGH ISLAND
D'OYLY CARTE ISLAND
BROAD WATER
OATLANDS PARK
Junction 1
ASHFORD COMMON WATER TREATMENT WORKS
SUNBURY GOLF COURSE
HAZELWOOD GOLF COURSE
SHEPPERTON BUSINESS PARK
SHEPPERTON
LONDON IRISH RUGBY GROUND
GAFLAC SPORTS GROUND
CEDARS REC GRD
SUNBURY CEM
Sunbury Locks
Gas Works
GRAVEL PIT
APPLE COURT GREEN
Shepperton Marina
Shepperton Moat House
BISHOP DUPPA'S REC GRD
LAS PALMAS ESTATE
THAMES MEADOW
COWAY SALE
ELM GROVE REC GRD
GEORGE FROUDE PK
RIVERSIDE ARTS CENTRE
Oatlands Park Hotel
PLAYING FIELDS
ST. MAUR'S CONV
UPPER HALLIFORD BYPASS
GASTON BRIDGE ROAD
WALTON BRIDGE RD
OATLANDS DRIVE
HERSHAM ROAD
NEW ZEALAND AVENUE
HEPWORTH WAY
CHURCH ST
TERRACE
STAINES ROAD
WINDMILL ROAD
HALLIFORD ROAD
WALTON LANE
ASHLEY ROAD
QUEENS ROAD
M3
A308
A3050
A244
B375
B376
B365
B3366

HAMPTON
TW12
TW16
SUNBURY
MOLESEY RESERVOIRS
BESSBOROUGH RESERVOIR
KNIGHTS RESERVOIR
WEST MOLESEY
KT12
QUEEN ELIZABETH II RESERVOIR
ISLAND BARN RESERVOIR
KT10
Lower Green
RYDENS
SANDOWN PARK RACECOURSE
STAIN HILL RESERVOIRS
RACECOURSE
RIVER THAMES
116
135
154

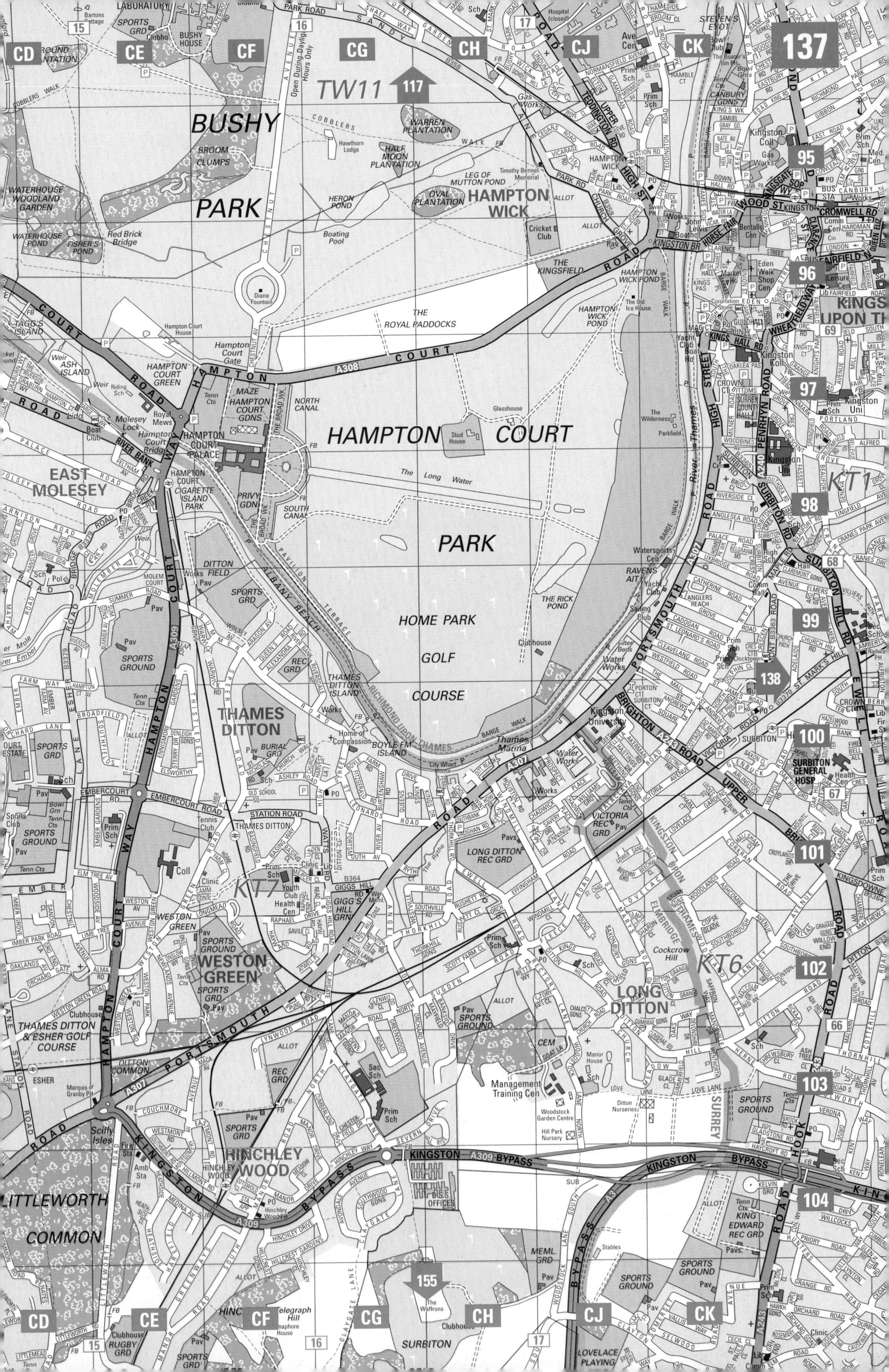
CD
CE
CF
CG
CH
CJ
CK
TW11
117
BUSHY
PARK
BROOM CLUMPS
WATERHOUSE WOODLAND GARDEN
WATERHOUSE POND
FISHER'S POND
Red Brick Bridge
HERON POND
Boating Pool
WARREN PLANTATION
HALF MOON PLANTATION
LEG OF MUTTON POND
OVAL PLANTATION
HAMPTON WICK
Timothy Bennet Memorial
Diana Fountain
THE ROYAL PADDOCKS
HAMPTON COURT ROAD
A308
Hampton Court House
Hampton Court Gate
HAMPTON COURT GREEN
MAZE
HAMPTON COURT GDNS
NORTH CANAL
HAMPTON COURT
Stud House
Glasshouse
HAMPTON COURT PALACE
The Long Water
PRIVY GDN
SOUTH CANAL
PARK
HOME PARK
GOLF
COURSE
THE RICK POND
THE KINGSFIELD
HAMPTON WICK POND
The Old Ice House
BARGE WALK
River Thames
The Wilderness
Parkfield
RAVENS AIT
TAGG'S ISLAND
ASH ISLAND
Molesey Lock
Royal Mews
Hampton Court Bridge
EAST MOLESEY
HAMPTON COURT CIGARETTE ISLAND PARK
DITTON FIELD
SPORTS GRD
SPORTS GROUND
ALBANY REACH
PAVILION TERRACE
THAMES DITTON ISLAND
RICHMOND UPON THAMES
BOYLE FM ISLAND
Thames Marina
City Wharf House
THAMES DITTON
HAMPTON COURT WAY
A309
PORTSMOUTH ROAD
A307
WESTON GREEN
KT7
THAMES DITTON & ESHER GOLF COURSE
DITTON COMMON
ESHER
Marquis of Granby PH
Scilly Isles
HINCHLEY WOOD
KINGSTON BYPASS
LITTLEWORTH COMMON
LONG DITTON REC GRD
VICTORIA REC GRD
LONG DITTON
KT6
Cockcrow Hill
ELMBRIDGE
KINGSTON UPON THAMES
SURREY
Management Training Cen
Woodstock Garden Centre
Hill Park Nursery
Ditton Nurseries
CEM
D.S.S. OFFICES
MEML. GRD
155
The Waffrons
SURBITON
Telegraph Hill
KING EDWARD REC GRD
SURBITON GENERAL HOSP
Kingston University
Kingston Uni
Kingston Coll
KINGSTON UPON THAMES
KT1
KINGSTON BR
HORSE FAIR
CROMWELL RD
Bentalls Cen
Eden Walk Shop Cen
Market Ho
TEDDINGTON RD
HIGH ST
95
96
97
98
99
100
101
102
103
104
138
15
16
17
66
67
68
69

138
CL
CM
CN
CP
CQ
CR
CS
19
20
21
118
95
96
97
98
99
100
101
102
103
104
69
68
67
66
137
156
COOMBE
COOMBE WOOD GOLF COURSE
KT2
KINGSTON HOSPITAL
NORBITON
KINGSTON UPON THAMES
KT1
KINGSTON CEMETERY
KT8
River Thames
HAMPTON WICK POND
Bentalls Cen
Eden Walk Shop Cen
Kingston Coll
Kingston Uni
SURBITON CEMETERY
Sewage Works
BERRYLANDS
KT3
NEW MALDEN
GREEN LANE REC GRD
HOGSMILL PUBLIC OPEN SPACE
KT5
SURBITON
SURBITON GENERAL HOSP
KT6
FISHPONDS OPEN SPACE
ALEXANDRA REC GRD
HOGSMILL OPEN SPACE
MALDEN MANOR
OLD MALDEN
MAORI SPORTS GROUND
TOLWORTH HOSPITAL
TOLWORTH
KINGSTON UNIVERSITY SPORTS GRD
RIVERHILL SPORTS GRD
WANDGAS ATHLETIC GROUND
KING GEORGES FIELD
KT9
KING EDWARD REC GRD
KING GEORGE'S TRADING EST
HOOK RISE SOUTH IND PK
SURREY
KINGSTON UPON THAMES
Cockcrow Hill
KINGSTON BYPASS
COOMBE LANE WEST
CAMBRIDGE ROAD
KINGSTON ROAD
MALDEN WAY
EWELL ROAD
SURBITON HILL RD
PORTSMOUTH ROAD
UPPER BRIGHTON ROAD
HOOK ROAD
LONDON ROAD
KINGSTON HILL

CT
CU
CV
CW
CX
CY
CZ
139
119
140
157
95
96
97
98
99
100
101
102
103
104
22
23
24
66
67
68
69
COPSE HILL
WOLFSON MED. REHAB CENTRE
ATKINSON MORLEY'S HOSPITAL
SW20
COTTENHAM PARK
OBERON PLAYING FIELD
RAYNES PARK SPORTS GRD
RAYNES PARK
PRINCE GEORGE'S PLAYING FIELD
MESSINES PLAYING FLD
JOSEPH HOOD RECREATION GROUND
BUSHEY MEAD
CANNON HILL COMMON
WEST BARNES
MOTSPUR PARK
UNIVERSITY OF LONDON ATHLETIC GROUND
B.B.C. SPORTS GRD
THE SIR JOSEPH HOOD MEMORIAL PLAYING FIELDS
MORDEN CEMETERY
MERTON & SUTTON JOINT CEMETERY
Sewage Treatment Works
OLD BLUES R.F.C.
RAYNES PARK PLAYING FIELDS
MORDEN PARK
MORDEN PARK SPORTS GROUND
MORDEN PLAYING FIELDS
SM4
KING GEORGE'S FIELD
DUNDONALD REC GRD
NELSON HOSP
JOHN INNES REC GRD
SW19
MERTON PARK
MERTON
MORDEN
MORDEN SOUTH
MOSTYN GARDENS
SOUTH MERTON
REIGATE AVENUE REC GRD
SUTTON CEMETERY
SM3
KIMPTON TRADE BUSINESS CENTRE
ST. ANTHONY'S HOSP
GARTH ROAD IND CEN
MANOR PARK REC GRD
MALDEN GRN
WORCESTER PARK
KT4
NORTH CHEAM
CUDDINGTON
SM1
COLLINGWOOD PARK
COOMBE LANE
KINGSTON ROAD
BUSHEY ROAD
GRAND DRIVE
EPSOM ROAD
LONDON ROAD
CENTRAL ROAD
CHEAM COMMON ROAD
MALDEN ROAD
STONECOT HILL
KINGSTON BYPASS

140
DA
DB
DC
DD
DE
DF
DG
SOUTH WIMBLEDON
COLLIER'S WOOD
MERTON
MERTON PARK
MORDEN
SW19
MORDEN HALL PARK
PHIPPS BRIDGE
MITCHAM
CR4
ST. HELIER
SM4
SM5
SM3
SM1
ROSEHILL
BENHILTON
THE WRYTHE
CARSHALTON
120
139
158
26
27
28
66
67
68
69
95
96
97
98
99
100
101
102
103
104
MERTON HIGH STREET
MERANTUN WAY
KINGSTON ROAD
MORDEN ROAD
LONDON ROAD
WESTERN ROAD
CHRISTCHURCH RD
MORDEN HALL ROAD
ST. HELIER AVENUE
BISHOPSFORD ROAD
CENTRAL ROAD
EPSOM ROAD
REIGATE AVENUE
ST. DUNSTAN'S HILL
OLDFIELDS ROAD
CARSHALTON ROAD
COMMONSIDE WEST
CRICKET GRN
MADEIRA RD
CRANMER RD
LONDON ROAD CEMETERY
FIGGE'S MARSH
DUNDONALD REC GRD
NELSON HOSP
JOHN INNES REC GRD
MOSTYN GARDENS
MERTON NURSERY ROAD PLAYING FIELDS
ABBEY REC GRD
MERTON INDUSTRIAL PARK
LOMBARD BUSINESS PARK
NELSON TRADING EST
GREENLEA PARK
ROCK TERRACE REC GRD
BURIAL GROUND
RAVENSBURY PARK
MORDEN PLAYING FIELDS
SPORTS GROUND
MORDEN PARK SPORTS GROUND
MORDEN REC GRD
MORETON GREEN
THOMAS WALL PARK
WATERMEADS NT.
POULTER PARK
GROVE FARM IND EST
WILLOW BUSINESS CENTRE
MITCHAM GARDEN VILLAGE
MILL GREEN
CARSHALTON SPORTS ARENA
ST. HELIER OPEN SPACE
REIGATE AVENUE REC GRD
ROSEHILL PARK EAST
GREENSHAW WOOD
ROSEHILL RECREATION GROUND
ST. HELIER HOSP
QUEEN MARY'S HOSP FOR CHILDREN
SUTTON CEMETERY
KIMPTON TRADE CENTRE
SUTTON COMMON
ROYSTON PARK
LIMES GRN
DALE PARK
THE WRYTHE REC GRD
COLLINGWOOD PARK
Snuff Mill Environmental Cen
Morden Hall
Morden Lodge
Wandle Ind Mus
River Wandle

141
DH
DJ
DK
DL
DM
DN
DP
SE19
STREATHAM VALE
NORBURY
NORBURY PARK
NATIONAL WESTMINSTER BANK SPORTS GROUND
STREATHAM PARK CEMETERY
PLAYING FIELDS
SW16
POLLARDS HILL
GREEN LANE SPORTS GROUND
CR7
THORNTON HEATH
SHERWOOD PK
PLAYING FIELD
COMMON
CROYDON CEMETERY
MAYDAY HOSPITAL
BROAD GREEN
QUEEN'S ROAD CEMETERY
CR0
WADDON
WANDLE PARK
SM6
HACKBRIDGE
BEDDINGTON
BEDDINGTON PARK
THE GRANGE GARDENS
CROYDON SUB STATION
DUPPAS HILL
LONDON ROAD
MITCHAM ROAD
PURLEY WAY
CROYDON ROAD
A23
A236
A232
A235
A212
A213
B272
121
159
95
96
97
98
99
100
101
102
103
104
142
29
30
31
66
67
68
69

142
DQ
DR
DS
DT
DU
DV
DW
UPPER NORWOOD
122
33
34
35
95
96
97
98
99
100
101
102
103
104
141
160
66
67
68
69
THE LAWNS
BEAULIEU HEIGHTS
SOUTH NORWOOD GROUNDS
SPORTS GROUND
SOUTH NORWOOD LAKE
ORCHARD SCHOOL SPORTS CENTRE
SE20
ANERLEY
BETTS PARK
GREEN LANE SPORTS GROUND
GRANGEWOOD PARK
SOUTH NORWOOD
BECKENHAM CEMETERY
CR7
SE25
SELHURST PARK
THORNTON HEATH
SOUTH NORWOOD REC GRD
CROYDON SPORTS ARENA
MAYDAY HOSPITAL
QUEEN'S ROAD CEMETERY
SELHURST
WOOD SIDE
BROAD GREEN
ASHBURTON PARK
CR0
ADDISCOMBE
CROYDON
WANDLE PARK
WHITGIFT PLAYING FIELDS
SHIRLEY PARK
GOLF COURSE
LLOYD PARK
PARK HILL
SPORTS GROUND
DUPPAS HILL
Croydon Flyover
Whitgift Centre
EAST CROYDON
WEST CROYDON
SANDILANDS
WOODSIDE
NORWOOD JUNCTION
HOCKEY PITCH
A212
A213
A214
A215
A222
A232
A235
A236
A2039

143
DX
DY
DZ
EA
EB
EC
ED
36
37
38
123
BECKENHAM
BECKENHAM JUNCTION
THE SLOANE HOSPITAL
BROMLEY PARK
SHORTLANDS GOLF COURSE
95
96
97
98
99
100
101
102
103
104
144
161
BECKENHAM HOSPITAL
CROYDON RD REC GROUND
BR3
KELSEY PARK
ELMERS END
GREASE PARK
HARVINGTON PLAYING FIELD
EDEN PARK
Langley Court (Research Laboratories)
PARK LANGLEY
UPPER ELMERS END
CROUCH OAK WOOD
MONKS ORCHARD
COLD SHAW
HIGH BROOM WOOD
BETHLEM ROYAL HOSPITAL
LANGLEY PARK SPORTS GRD
PLAYING FIELD
THE ROOKERY
LANGLEY PARK GOLF COURSE
WEST WICKHAM
BLAKE REC GRD
GLADE WOOD
PARKFIELDS REC GRD
CR0
SPRING PARK WOOD
FOXES WOOD
KENNEL WOOD
SPRING PARK
SPARROWS DEN PLAYING FIELDS
Old Beccehamian R.F.C.
BR4
CONEY HALL REC GRD
Schiller International University
SHIRLEY
PINEWOODS
A234
A222
A214
A232
A2022
A2015
B230
BECKENHAM ROAD
CROYDON ROAD
ELMERS END ROAD
HIGH STREET
BROMLEY ROAD
HAYES LANE
WICKHAM ROAD
SOUTH EDEN PARK RD
BECKENHAM ROAD
GLEBE WAY
ADDINGTON ROAD
SHIRLEY ROAD
SHIRLEY CHURCH ROAD
PICKHURST LANE

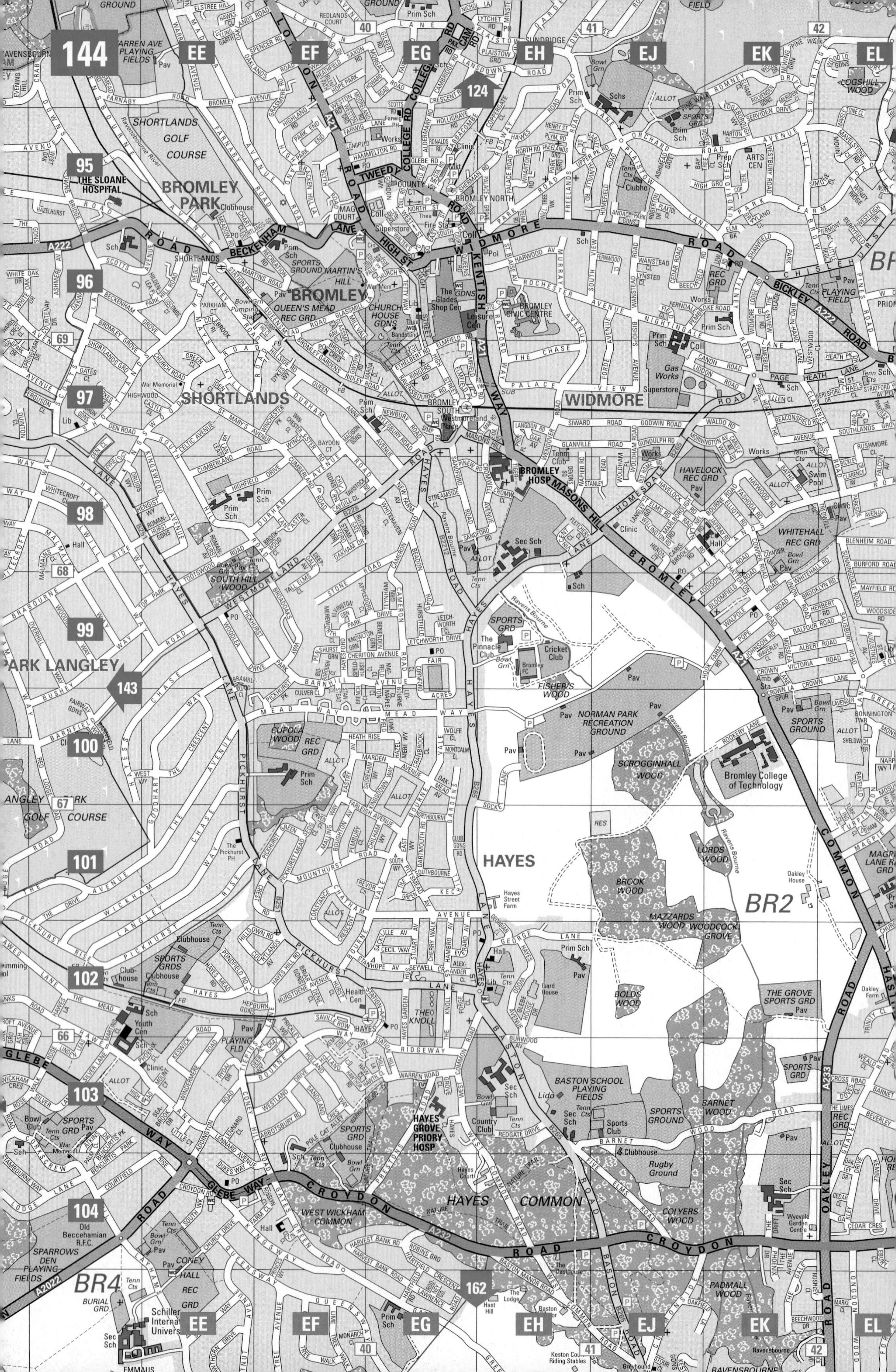
EE
EF
EG
EH
EJ
EK
EL
124
40
41
42
95
96
97
98
99
100
101
102
103
104
69
68
67
66
143
162
SHORTLANDS GOLF COURSE
BROMLEY PARK
THE SLOANE HOSPITAL
BROMLEY
SHORTLANDS
WIDMORE
PARK LANGLEY
HAYES
BR2
BR4
BROMLEY HOSP
BROMLEY CIVIC CENTRE
The Glades Shop Cen
QUEEN'S MEAD REC GRD
CHURCH HOUSE GDNS
MARTIN'S HILL
SOUTH HILL WOOD
HAVELOCK REC GRD
WHITEHALL REC GRD
NORMAN PARK RECREATION GROUND
SCROGGINHALL WOOD
Bromley College of Technology
FISHER'S WOOD
LORDS WOOD
BROOK WOOD
MAZZARDS WOOD
WOODCOCK GROVE
BOLDS WOOD
THE GROVE SPORTS GRD
CUPOLA WOOD
HAYES GROVE PRIORY HOSP
BASTON SCHOOL PLAYING FIELDS
BARNET WOOD
COLYERS WOOD
PADMALL WOOD
HAYES COMMON
WEST WICKHAM COMMON
SPARROWS DEN PLAYING FIELDS
CONEY HALL REC GRD
THE KNOLL
LOGSHILL WOOD
Old Beccehamian R.F.C.
Rugby Ground
Wyevale Garden Centre
Keston Court Riding Stables
A21
A222
A232
A233
A2022
B265
B251
B228
CROYDON ROAD
BECKENHAM LANE
WIDMORE ROAD
BICKLEY ROAD
MASONS HILL
HAYES LANE
HAYES ROAD
PICKHURST LANE
OAKLEY ROAD
GLEBE WAY
BROMLEY COMMON
BASTON ROAD
WEST WICKHAM
HAYES COMMON

145
CAMDEN PARK
CHISLEHURST GOLF COURSE
CHISLEHURST COMMON
NATURE RESERVE
PARK WOOD
Icehouse Wood
Holbrook Wood
The Larches
Scadbury Moated Manor House Site
BROMLEY ROAD
ST PAULS CRAY ROAD
CHISLEHURST
BICKLEY
Bickley Junction
Chislehurst Junction
Petts Wood Junction
BR7
HAWKWOOD ESTATE NT
PETTS WOOD NT
ST. PAUL'S CRAY COMMON
Edlmann Memorial Wood
Willett Memorial Wood
HOBLINGWELL WOOD
HOBLINGWELL WOOD REC GRD
ST. PAUL'S CRAY
CHALKPIT WOOD
BANSOME WOOD
BIRCH WOOD
GOSHILL WOOD
POND WOOD
Marjorie McClure Sch
Bickley Manor Hotel
Bromley High Sch
BLACKBROOK WOOD
THORNET WOOD
JUBILEE COUNTRY PARK
GREAT THRIFT
PETTS WOOD
BR5
POVEREST
COVET WOOD
POVEREST REC GRD
SOUTHBOROUGH
SOUTHBOROUGH OPEN SPACE
SOUTHBOROUGH RECREATION GROUND
BROMLEY GOLF COURSE
Bromley Common
PLAYING FIELD
SPARROW WOOD
SPARROW COMMON
ROUNDABOUT WOOD
CROFTON HEATH
CLAY WOOD
GUMPING COMMON
PETTS WOOD REC GRD
NOBODY'S WOOD
POKERIDDEN WOOD
ORPINGTON
BR6
CROFTON ROAD
SPUR ROAD
STATION ROAD
CHISLEHURST ROAD
ORPINGTON ROAD
PERRY HALL ROAD
FARNBOROUGH HOSPITAL
FARNBOROUGH REC GRD
NEWSTEAD WOOD
DARRICK COMMON
DARRICK WOOD
163
125
146
EM EN EP EQ ER ES ET
43 44 45

NATURE RESERVE
EU
EV
EW
EX
EY
EZ
FA
126
EDGINGTON
SIDCUP
A20 BYPASS
BROMLEY
RUXLEY WOOD
Ruxley Manor Nursery
MAIDSTONE ROAD
Scadbury Moated Manor House Site
Plantation
Field-Study Centre
Youth Cen
Ski Centre
Sports Club
RUXLEY PARK GOLF COURSE
DRIVING RANGE
Clubhouse
CRAY VALLEY GOLF COURSE
Barnfield Bank
COOKHAM
95
96
97
98
99
100
101
102
103
104
MIDFIELD WAY
SEVENOAKS WAY
A224
CRAYFIELD IND PARK
Superstore
HOBLINGWELL WOOD REC GRD
ST. PAUL'S CRAY
CHAPMANS LANE
Pilgrim Hill
Lower Hockenden Farm
Simon's Field Shaw
Hogspring Cottages
The Small House
PAULS CRAY HILL PARK
HIGHLANDS WOOD
BR5
HOCKENDEN WOOD
SPRINGVALE RETAIL PARK
MURRAY BUSINESS CEN
Gas Works
STAR LANE
CEM
ST MARY CRAY
SANDWAY PK
NUGENT IND PARK
BLACKSMITHS LANE
THE WARREN
Sheepcote Farm
Ringland Farm
CHILD'S WOOD
POVEREST
145
ST MARY CRAY
CRAY AVENUE
Shawcroft Sch
CROCKENHILL ROAD
B258
Blueberry Farm
Kevington Farm
Waldens Farm
Crouch Farm
ST. MARY CRAY REC GRD
RIVERSIDE GDNS
Derry Downs
GRIGG'S CROSS
KYNASTON WOOD
POVEREST REC GRD
ALLOT
Walden Manor
Depot
Heather's Holdings
Bleak House Farm
PERRY HALL ROAD
A208
PRIORY GARDENS
BROMLEY MUS
GRASSMEADE RECREATION GROUND
COCKMANNINGS ROAD
EAST HALL ROAD
Eastwood Farm
GRIFF'S WOOD
PINGTON
BR6
RAMSDEN
Walnut Shop Cen
Mkt
Leisure Cen
HOLLINGBOURNE TWR
BEKESBOURNE TWR
Piggery
SPUR ROAD
A232
COURT ROAD (ORPINGTON BYPASS)
HIGH STREET
BUS STA
SAGE WENTS
Byways Nurseries
PLAYING FIELD
SKIBBS LANE
Cookham Hill Farm
Cookham Farm
COOKHAM HILL
Goddington
Goddington House
GODDINGTON PARK
ROUNDS SMALLAMS
Bowling Green
164
LILLY'S WOOD
BLACK BUSH WOOD
CHELSFIELD LANE
ORPINGTON HOSPITAL
A223
47
48
49
66
67
68
69

SWANLEY
Hextable
Swanley Village
Crockenhill
Hulberry
BR8
Junction 3 (M25)
Junction 1 (M20)
PEDHAM PLACE GOLF CENTRE
LULLINGSTONE PARK
127
148
165

Sutton at Hone
Swanley Village
FARNINGHAM WOOD NATURE RESERVE
Junction 3 (M25)
Junction 1 (M20)
PEDHAM PLACE GOLF CENTRE
Farningham
DA4
Eynsford
EYNSFORD CASTLE
FRANKS
WESTMINSTER FIELD
FIREPOUND SHAW
OLIVERS SHAW
ALCHIN'S WOOD
SANDHOLE SHAW
POLLY SHAW
FOUNTAIN HOY
Eynsford Hill
Broom Hill
Tweed Hill
RAM'S WOOD
THE FOLLY
MORETON IND EST
PEDHAM PLACE IND EST
TEARDROP IND EST
Fort Farningham (Site Of)
Lullingstone Roman Villa (Remains Of)
ST JOHN'S JERUSALEM
GORSE HILL (MAIN ROAD)
LONDON ROAD A20
DARTFORD ROAD A225
HIGH STREET A225
STATION ROAD
SWANLEY VILLAGE ROAD
SHIP LANE
CALFSTOCK LANE
FRANKS LANE
EGLANTINE LANE
DONKEY LANE
CROCKENHILL LANE
SPAREPENNY LANE
BUTTON STREET
FARNINGHAM HILL ROAD
FJ FK FL FM FN FP FQ
54 55 56
95 96 97 98 99 100 101 102 103 104
69 68 67 66
128 147

149
129
South Darenth
Pinden
Mile End Green
Longfield
Dean Bottom
Hartley Green
DA3
TN15
New Ash Green
Fawkham Green
HORTON WOOD
CHURCHDOWN WOOD
PENNIS WOOD
REDLIBBETS GOLF COURSE
SAXTEN'S WOOD
CHOAKS WOOD
GROVE WOOD
HATCHFIELD WOOD
HOPKINS SPRING WOOD
YEWFIELD SHAW
RYECROFTS WOOD
GABRIELSPRING WOOD
FAWKHAM MANOR HOSPITAL
CORINTHIAN SPORTS GRD GOLF COURSE
BRANDS HATCH MOTOR RACING
BRANDS HATCH KARTING
QUARRY
DARTFORD SEVENOAKS

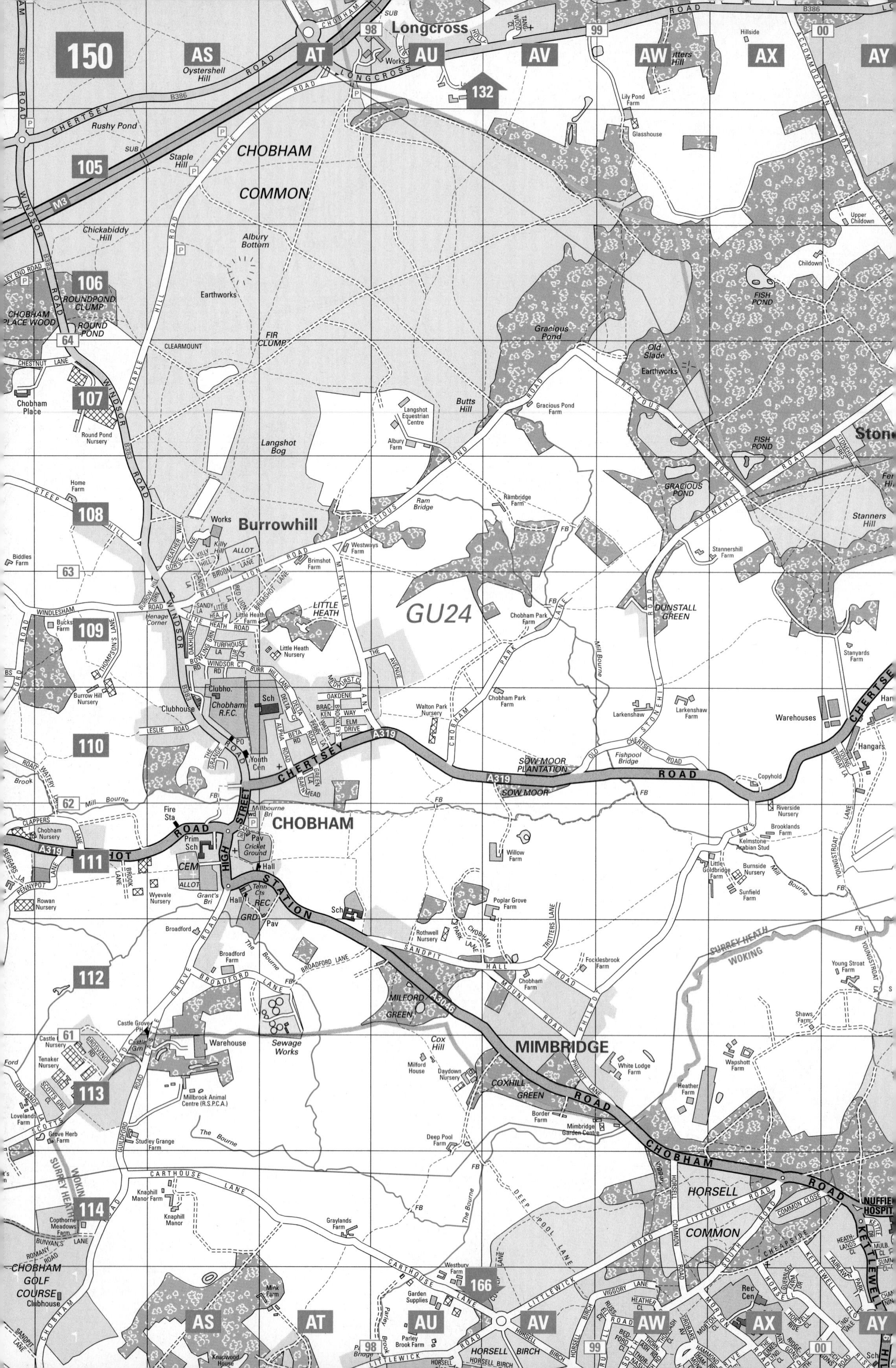
150
Longcross
132
CHOBHAM COMMON
Oystershell Hill
Rushy Pond
Staple Hill
Chickabiddy Hill
Albury Bottom
Earthworks
ROUNDPOND CLUMP
CHOBHAM PLACE WOOD
ROUND POND
FIR CLUMP
CLEARMOUNT
CHESTNUT LANE
Chobham Place
Round Pond Nursery
Langshot Bog
Langshot Equestrian Centre
Albury Farm
Butts Hill
Gracious Pond
Gracious Pond Farm
Old Slade
FISH POND
Lily Pond Farm
Glasshouse
Hillside
Upper Childown
Childown
GRACIOUS POND
Stanners Hill
Stannershill Farm
DUNSTALL GREEN
Home Farm
Burrowhill
Works
Ram Bridge
Rambridge Farm
Westways Farm
Brimshot Farm
Biddles Farm
LITTLE HEATH
GU24
Chobham Park Farm
Henage Corner
Bucks Farm
Little Heath Nursery
Burrow Hill Nursery
Clubhouse
Chobham R.F.C.
Walton Park Nursery
Larkenshaw
Larkenshaw Farm
Warehouses
Hangars
Youth Cen
SOW MOOR PLANTATION
SOW MOOR
Fishpool Bridge
Copyhold
Riverside Nursery
Brooklands Farm
Kelmstone Arabian Stud
CHOBHAM
Millbourne Bri
Chobham Nursery
Rowan Nursery
Wyevale Nursery
Grant's Bri
Cricket Ground
Willow Farm
Little Goldbridge Farm
Burnside Nursery
Sunfield Farm
Poplar Grove Farm
Rothwell Nursery
Broadford
Broadford Farm
Chobham Farm
Focklesbrook Farm
Young Stroat Farm
Shaws Farm
MILFORD GREEN
Sewage Works
Castle Grove PH
Warehouse
Castle Nursery
Tenaker Nursery
Cox Hill
Milford House
Daydown Nursery
MIMBRIDGE
White Lodge Farm
Wapshott Farm
Heather Farm
COXHILL GREEN
Border Farm
Mimbridge Garden Centre
Millbrook Animal Centre (R.S.P.C.A.)
Lovelands Farm
Grove Herb Farm
Studley Grange Farm
The Bourne
Deep Pool Farm
HORSELL COMMON
Knaphill Manor Farm
Knaphill Manor
Copthorne Meadows Farm
Graylands Farm
NUFFIELD HOSPITAL
CHOBHAM GOLF COURSE
Clubhouse
Mink Farm
Westbury Farm
Garden Supplies
166
Parley Brook Farm
Knapwood House
HORSELL BIRCH
Rec Cen
SURREY HEATH
WOKING
M3
A319
A3046
B386
B383
CHERTSEY ROAD
WINDSOR ROAD
STAPLE HILL
LONGCROSS ROAD
ACCOMMODATION ROAD
GRACIOUS POND ROAD
STONEHILL ROAD
STEEP HILL
WINDLESHAM ROAD
HIGH STREET
STATION ROAD
BROADFORD LANE
SANDPIT HALL ROAD
MOUNT ROAD
PHILPOT LANE
CHOBHAM ROAD
CARTHOUSE LANE
LITTLEWICK ROAD
DEEP POOL LANE
GUILDFORD ROAD
CASTLE GROVE ROAD
BOTTOM ROAD
KETTLEWELL
AS AT AU AV AW AX AY
98 99 00
105 106 107 108 109 110 111 112 113 114
64 63 62 61

151
OTTERSHAW
ROW TOWN
WOODHAM
SHEERWATER
KT16
KT15
OTTERSHAW PARK
NEW ZEALAND GOLF COURSE
HORSELL COMMON
WEST BYFLEET GOLF COURSE
Pyrford
Junction 11
ST. PETER'S HOSP
HOSPITAL (CLOSED)
BROX COPSE
GREAT WOOD
BIRCH WOOD
HOYT WOOD
BASINGSTOKE CANAL
133
152
167

152
BG
BH
BJ
BK
BL
BM
BN
05
06
07
134
Junction 11
105
106
107
108
109
110
111
112
113
114
64
63
62
61
151
168
ABBEY MOOR GOLF COURSE
Clubho.
Woodside Farm
PETER'S
A317
Simplemarsh Farm
CONVENT
Prim Sch
Sports Cen
Sec Sch
CHURCH
HIGH STREET
CHERTSEY
BRIGHTON ROAD
VICTORY PARK
Bowl Grn
Superstore
Health Cen
Comm Cen
Pol
CIVIC CEN
Lib
SPORTS GRD
ADDLESTONE
St. George's College
Tennis Cen
Woburn Hill Nursery
Works
MEADOWLANDS PARK
WEYBRIDGE TRADING ESTATE
WEYBRIDGE
WEYBRIDGE BUSINESS PARK
Black Boy Bridge
Weybridge Lock
Hamhaugh Point
Hamm Court Farm
HOSP
BALFOUR RD
ROAD
RUNNYMEDE
ELMBRIDGE
MEADOWS
CEM
Sec Sch
PLAYING FIELDS
Brooklands College
Brooklands Farm
Crickets Hill
Conduit Hill
Weybridge Junction
Crockford Park Nurseries
Crockford Bridge Farm
Crockford Bridge
MILL POND
Coxes Lock
WEY MEADOWS
SAYES COURT PUBLIC OPEN SPACE
ALLOT
KT15
NEW HAW
A318
Addlestone Junction
Clubhouse
DRIVING RANGE
SURREY GOLF AND FITNESS
Works
Nine Arches Bridge
Water Works
SEVEN ARCHES APPROACH
Seven Arches Bridge
Wey Manor Farm
ROW TOWN
Southern Wood Farm
Tenn Cts
Rodwell Farm
Hall's Farm
Glasshouse
Coomelands Farm
CENTRAL VETERINARY LABORATORY
The Bourne
RIVER WEY NAVIGATION
BYFLEET ROAD
Electricity Station
BROOKLANDS MUSEUM
Memorial
BROOKLANDS
Offices
BROOKLANDS BUSINESS PARK
AIRFIELD (DISUSED)
Grange Farm
Charwood Farm
Fallow Farm
M25
BYFLEET & NEW HAW
Byfleet Junction
BROOKLANDS INDUSTRIAL ESTATE
Restricted Access 7am-7pm
WELLINGTON WAY
HEATHERVALE CARAVAN PARK
HEATHERVALE REC GRD
Botton Lock
WOODHAM
PLAYING FIELD
Scotland Lock
CAMPHILL INDUSTRIAL ESTATE
BYFLEET TECHNICAL CENTRE
OYSTER LANE
Superstores
SPORTS GRD
Cricket Grd
Byfleet Bus Cen
PARVIS ROAD
Plough Bridge
Plough Bridge Farm
BASINGSTOKE CANAL
WEST BYFLEET
DARTNELL PARK
A245
OLD WOOD
OLDWOOD POND
TINS WOOD
Sheerwater Bridge
Health Cen
Superstore
Clubhouse
OLD WOKING ROAD
KT14
BROADOAKS GOVERNMENT OFFICES
WEST BYFLEET
DODD'S WOOD
West Hall
Tennis Courts
Murray's Bridge
PLAYING FIELD
BYFLEET
Manor Farm
Glasshouses
Manor Farm Estate
Bluegates Hole
Byfleet Mill
Manor House
THE ISLAND
Park Barn Farm
COMMON MEADOWS
River Wey
Squash & Fitness Cen
GU23
Dodd's Bridge
Broad Ditch
WOKING
GUILDFORD
Nursery
Pyrford
Lees Farm
Sewage Works
BUXTON

153
BP
BQ
BR
BS
BT
BU
BV
08
09
10
135
154
169
BROAD WATER
Oatlands Park Hotel
PLAYING FIELDS
ASHLEY PARK
OATLANDS PARK
BURWOOD PARK
OATLANDS
QUEENS ROAD
A3050
A317
A244
HERSHAM
BYPASS
WALTON-ON-THAMES
Fenner House
Offices
Amb Sta
Fire Sta
Sec Sch
Prim Sch
105
106
107
108
109
110
111
112
113
114
64
63
62
61
Air Products
Haine's Bridge
KT13
KT12
KT11
The Heath
WALTON COMMON
UPPER COMMON
Squire's Garden Centre
Burhill Kennels
CEM
Rabbit Lane House
Tenn Cts
Tenn Club
WARREN POND
SPORTS GROUND
HAWKS HOCKEY CLUB
Clubhouse
Pav
Hill Farm Nursery
Ingram House
OLD BURHILL GOLF COURSE
NEW BURHILL GOLF COURSE
Riverside Farm
Southwood Manor Farm
COVERED RESERVOIRS
Water Tower
FLAGSTAFF HOUSE CONFERENCE CENTRE
ST. GEORGE'S HILL
UPPER POND
ST. GEORGE'S HILL GOLF COURSE
WHITELEY VILLAGE
SPORTS GRD
Strawberry Hill
Dick Turpin's Cottage
River Mole
Norwood Farm
SPORTS GROUND
School
SCHOOL
DRIVING RANGE
Fairmile Hotel
West Gate Lodge
Beards Hill
NOTRE DAME CONVENT
Seven Hills Estate
Cricket Club
Chestnut Lodge Farm
Chestnut Lodge
Hook's Corner
Chippings Farm
OLD COMMON
Walton Firs Scout Camp
MANOR POND
FOXHOLM COVERT
COBHAM BUS MUS
SILVER MERE
Squash Club
Clubho.
SILVERMERE GOLF COURSE
Driving Range
Home Farm
Superstore
COBHAM HOSP
Prim Sch
Hilton National Cobham
Cobham Br
Weir
PAINSHILL PARK
BELL WOOD
Long Orchard Farm
Bramble Hedge Farm
Heyswood Girl Guide Camp
THE BROOM
Gothic Temple
Wood Hill
THE LAKE
WHEEL ISLAND
Red Hill
The Tower
Oak Pollard
Foxwarren Park
Cobham FC
Health Cen
Youth Cen
Lib
Nursery
R. Mole
COBHAM
ROSE LODGE WOOD
The Running
BYFLEET ROAD
A245
ESHER ROAD
PORTSMOUTH ROAD
A3
SEVEN HILLS ROAD
B365
BETWEEN STREETS
HIGH ST
RIVER HILL
MILL RD
STOKE ROAD
REDHILL ROAD
B366
GUILDFORD
BURWOOD ROAD
BURHILL ROAD
SOUTH LODGE ROAD
ELVEDON
FAIRMILE LANE
OLD COMMON ROAD
CAMP END ROAD
RODONA ROAD
HORSESHOE RIDGE
RAVENSCROFT ROAD
YAFFLE ROAD
LINDEN ROAD
WOOD LANE
CAVENDISH ROAD
GRANVILLE ROAD
GODOLPHIN ROAD
EGERTON ROAD
GOWER ROAD
WHITE KNIGHTS RD
CHESTNUT AV
OCTAGON ROAD
CIRCLE
NORTH AV
SOUTH RD
WEST AV
KELVEDON AVENUE
CRANLEY ROAD
ERISWELL ROAD
PATMORE LANE
ALBURY ROAD
FARMLEIGH GRO
THE QUILLOT
BROADWATER RD N
BROADWATER ROAD S
CHARGATE CLOSE
ONSLOW ROAD
KILRUE LANE
HERONRY
KENWOOD DRIVE
EASTWICK DRIVE
WESTCAR LANE
BURWOOD CRESCENT
VAUX CRESCENT
CLARENCE CL
TRENCHARD CL
QUEENS ROAD
FOXHOLES
FAIRLAWN
NETHERBY PARK
BROOM WAY
BEECHWOOD AV
CONIFERS
ASHLEY ROAD
STATION AVENUE
MAYFIELD GDNS
WOODSIDE AVENUE
CHARLTON AV
BURWOOD PARK ROAD
WEST GROVE
GARRICK CLOSE
GROVE
ADELAIDE ROAD
RYDENS ROAD
SILVERDALE AVENUE
PINE GROVE
HEATHSIDE
DANESWOOD CL
TOWERS WALK
PORTSMOUTH ROAD
HOGSHILL LANE
LEIGH ROAD
TARTAR ROAD
CANADA ROAD
QUEENS RIDE
PENNYFIELD
WYNDHAM AVENUE
NORTHFIELD ROAD
RIVERVIEW GDNS
BRIDGE WAY
ANVIL LANE
DOWNSIDE
ALLOT
REC GRD
Offices
Hall
Sch
Pol
PO
Cricket Club
Tenn Cts
Bowl Grn
TA Cen

154
HERSHAM
ESHER
WEST END
KT12
KT11
CLAREMONT LANDSCAPE GARDEN
Claremont Park
ESHER COMMON
FAIRMILE COMMON
OXSHOTT HEATH
Fairmile
NEW BURHILL GOLF COURSE
MOORE PLACE GOLF COURSE
CLARE HILL GOLF COURSE
WEST END COMMON
HERSHAM RIVERSIDE PARK
CORONATION PLAYING FIELDS
PRINCESS ALICE HOSPICE
LITTLE HEATH COMMON
KNOWLE HILL PARK
COBHAM
OXSHOTT
136
153
170
BW
BX
BY
BZ
CA
CB
CC

155
CLAYGATE
SURBITON GOLF COURSE
HINCHLEY WOOD
CHESSINGTON WORLD OF ADVENTURE
Malden Rushett
PRINCE'S COVERTS
OXSHOTT
THE FOREST
KT10
KT9
KT22
KT21
LEATHERHEAD ROAD
ESHER BYPASS
KINGSTON BYPASS
HOOK ROAD
FAIROAK LANE
RUSHETT LANE
LITTLEWORTH COMMON
CLAYGATE COMMON
SIXTY ACRE WOOD
BARWELL LAKE
CHESSINGTON GOLF CENTRE
BARWELL BUSINESS PARK
SILVERGLADE BUSINESS PARK
LEATHERHEAD GOLF COURSE
137
156
171

156
KINGSTON BYPASS
CL
CM
CN
CP
CQ
CR
CS
138
155
172
KT9
KT19
KT18
KT21
19
20
21
105
106
107
108
109
110
111
112
113
114
64
63
62
61
CHESSINGTON
CHESSINGTON NORTH
CHESSINGTON SOUTH
CHESSINGTON GOLF CENTRE
BARWELL BUSINESS PARK
CHURCH FIELDS
KING GEORGES FIELD
KING GEORGE'S TRADING EST
HOOK RISE SOUTH IND PK
HOOK ROAD
LEATHERHEAD ROAD
COX LANE
MOOR LANE
CHESSINGTON ROAD
RUXLEY LANE
CASTLE HILL
BUTCHERS GROVE
HORTON PARK COUNTRY CLUB GOLF COURSE
HOOK ARENA SPORTS GROUND
GREAT WOOD
HOGSMILL RIVERSIDE OPEN SPACE
KING GEORGE V REC GRD
OLD HAILEYBURIANS R.F.C.
WEST EWELL
ST. EBBA'S HOSPITAL
PLAYING FIELD
REC GRD
HORTON
HORTON COUNTRY PARK
FOUR ACRE WOOD
POND WOOD
SURREY
KINGSTON UPON THAMES
EPSOM & EWELL
Bonesgate Stream
CHESSINGTON WOOD
EPSOM & EWELL NEW COTTAGE HOSP
WEST PARK HOSPITAL
SPORTS GROUND
Equestrian Centre
Horton Park Children's Farm
Hospital Closed
COURT REC GRD
NONSUCH INDUSTRIAL ESTATE
LONGMEAD BUSINESS PARK
CHRIST CHURCH ROAD
WEST STREET
HIGH STREET
EAST STREET
UPPER HIGH ST
SOUTH STREET
ASHLEY CEN
TOWN HALL
ROSEBERY PARK
EPSOM
EPSOM COMMON
STEW POND
GREAT POND
Woodcock Corner
FOREST
NEWTON WOOD
The Rye
EPSOM GENERAL HOSP
WOODCOTE GREEN
STAMFORD GRN
WORCESTER PARK ROAD
KINGSTON ROAD

CT
CU
CV
CW
CX
CY
CZ
KT4
CUDDINGTON
REC GRD
STONELEIGH
NORTH CHEAM
SM1
COLLINGWOOD PARK
WEST SUTTON
SM3
CHEAM REC GRD
OAK PLANTATION
NONSUCH PARK
Nonsuch Mansion House
CHEAM PARK
CHEAM
Diana's Dyke
Cuddington Church (Site of)
PLAYING FIELDS
EWELL BYPASS
LONDON ROAD
EWELL ROAD
HIGH ST
ST. DUNSTAN'S HILL
BELMONT RISE
SUTTON WATER SERVICES
PERRETS FIELD
SEARS PARK
OVERTON PARK REC GRD
SM2
EAST EWELL
EWELL
Nescot
SPORTS GROUND
KT17
CUDDINGTON GOLF COURSE
SM7
BANSTEAD DOWN GOLF COURSE
NORTH LOOE
SURREY
EPSOM & EWELL
SUTTON
REIGATE ROAD
ALEXANDRA REC GRD
RIFLE RANGE
BANSTEAD
FIR TREE ROAD
WINKWORTH ROAD
Epsom College
COLLEGE ROAD
EPSOM DOWNS
NORK
BRIGHTON ROAD
A24
A217
A232
A240
A2022
A2043
B2200
B288
B284
139
105
106
107
108
109
110
111
112
113
114
158
173
22
23
24
61
62
63
64

158
DA
DB
DC
DD
DE
DF
DG
140
157
174
SM1
SM2
SM5
SM7
SUTTON
CARSHALTON
CARSHALTON BEECHES
BELMONT
BANSTEAD DOWNS
WOODMANSTERNE
LITTLE WOODCOTE
COLLINGWOOD PARK
ROYSTON PARK
THE WRYTHE REC GRD
THE GROVE
CARSHALTON PARK
CARSHALTON WAR MEMORIAL HOSP
OVERTON PARK REC GRD
SUTTON HOSPITAL
ROYAL MARSDEN HOSP
WELLFIELD PLANTATION
PLAYING FIELD
OAKS SPORTS CENTRE GOLF COURSE
THE OAKS PARK
DOWNVIEW PRISON
HIGHDOWN PRISON
BANSTEAD COMMON
GOLF COURSE
RIFLE RANGE
SPORTS GROUND
RIFFET WOOD
BIG WOOD
CLOCKHOUSE REC GRD
WOODMANSTERNE PARK RECREATION GROUND
CARSHALTON ROAD
BRIGHTON ROAD
BELMONT RISE
ST. DUNSTAN'S HILL
WOODMANSTERNE ROAD
WOODMANSTERNE LANE
CROYDON LANE
WINKWORTH ROAD
BANSTEAD ROAD
SUTTON LANE
POUND STREET
HIGH ST
A232
A217
A2022
B278
105
106
107
108
109
110
111
112
113
114
26
27
28
61
62
63
64

159
BEDDINGTON
BEDDINGTON PARK
WALLINGTON
SM6
SOUTH BEDDINGTON
BANDON HILL CEMETERY
MELLOWS PARK
ROUNDSHAW PARK
ROUNDSHAW PLAYING FIELD
ROUNDSHAW OPEN SPACE
DUPPAS HILL
CR0
PURLEY WAY PLAYING FIELDS
CR2
HALING PARK
SOUTH CROYDON
SOUTH CROYDON REC GRD
PURLEY OAKS
WOODCOTE
PURLEY
CR8
ROTARY FIELD
FOXLEY WOOD
RIDDLESDOWN WOOD
HIGHER DRIVE REC GRD
WOODCOTE GROVE REC GRD
CR5
WOODCOTE PARK GOLF COURSE
REEDHAM
KENLEY
SMITHAM
COULSDON COURT
CROYDON ROAD
PURLEY WAY
STAFFORD ROAD
BRIGHTON ROAD
WOODCOTE ROAD
FOXLEY LANE
GODSTONE ROAD
DOWNS COURT ROAD
MITCHLEY
DUPPAS HILL RD
PARK LANE
DH
DJ
DK
DL
DM
DN
DP
141
160
175
105
106
107
108
109
110
111
112
113
114
29
30
31
61
62
63
64

160
DQ
DR
DS
DT
DU
DV
DW
33
34
35
142
105
106
107
108
109
110
111
112
113
114
159
176
64
63
62
61
SOUTH CROYDON
CR0
CR2
CR8
SANDERSTEAD
PURLEY DOWNS GOLF COURSE
CROHAM HURST GOLF COURSE
CROHAM HURST
SELSDON PARK HOTEL GOLF COURSE
LLOYD PARK
COOMBE PARK
SPORTS GROUND
PLAYING FIELD
WHITGIFT PLAYING FIELDS
SHIRLEY PARK GOLF COURSE
ADDINGTON
COOMBE WOOD
BALLARDS PLANTATION
LITTLEHEATH WOODS
THRIFT WOOD
SANDERSTEAD PLANTATION
MITCHLEY WOOD
RAGGED WOOD
AINSLEY BERRY SHAW
COOMBES WOOD
RIDDLESDOWN WOOD
FOXLEY WOOD
KINGS WO
NEWLANDS WOOD
DUPPAS HILL
HALING GROVE
HALING PARK
PURLEY WAY PLAYING FIELDS
PURLEY BEECHES
HIGHER DRIVE REC GRD
SOUTH CROYDON REC GRD
REC GRD
PARK HILL
COOMBE ROAD
BRIGHTON ROAD
ADDINGTON ROAD
GODSTONE ROAD
MITCHLEY AVENUE
DOWNS COURT ROAD
LIMPSFIELD ROAD
SELSDON ROAD
CROHAM ROAD
CROHAM VALLEY ROAD
BALLARDS WAY
PURLEY DOWNS ROAD
RIDDLESDOWN ROAD
SANDERSTEAD ROAD
PARK LANE
HIGH ST
SOUTH CROYDON
SANDERSTEAD
PURLEY OAKS
RIDDLESDOWN
KENLEY
PURLEY
PURLEY HOSP
Selsdon Park Hotel
Croydon Flyover

161
DX
DY
DZ
EA
EB
EC
ED
143
BR4
CR0
CR6
177
105
106
107
108
109
110
111
112
113
114
162
36
37
38
64
63
62
61
ADDINGTON
NEW ADDINGTON
FORESTDALE
FARLEIGH
ADDINGTON VALE
ADDINGTON GOLF COURSE
ADDINGTON PALACE GOLF COURSE
ADDINGTON COURT (PUBLIC) GOLF COURSE
FARLEIGH COURT GOLF COURSE
KENT GATE WAY
SELSDON PARK ROAD
ADDINGTON ROAD
GRAVEL HILL
FEATHERBED LANE
LODGE LANE
KING HENRY'S DRIVE
PARKWAY
ADDINGTON VILLAGE
Addington Palace Sports Centre
Addington Palace (Royal Sch of Church Music)
ADDINGTON PARK
SPRING PARK PLAYING FIELD
SPARROWS DEN PLAYING FIELDS
Shirley Wanderers R.F.C.
Old Beccehamian R.F.C.
Schiller Internat Univers
EMMAUS CONF. CENTRE
CONEY HALL REC GRD
ROWDOWN FIELDS
SPORTS GROUND
FOXHILL SHAW
BIRCH WOOD
Fox Hill
CASTLE HILL RUFFS
ROWDOWN WOOD
BRADMANSHILL WOOD
Mickleham Way Electricity Sta
FALCONWOOD MEADOW
Featherbed Lane Water Works
REC GRD
NORTH DOWN REC GRD
SELSDON WOOD NT
STEVEN'S LARCH
BEARS WOOD
FRITH WOOD
BIRCHEN SHAW
PUPLET WOOD
FRYLANDS WOOD
THREECORNER GROVE
DUMPSEY DERRY
CRAB WOOD
CHAPEL HILL
COLDBLOW SHAW
BOGRAMS WOOD
LIMEKILN SHAW
HODGE GROVE
HOGCROFT SHAW
MOSSYHILL SHAW
OAKEN SHAW
MOSESHILL SHAW
WELLS SHAW
BEECHES SHAW
GREENHILL SHAW
BROOM WOOD
HILLOCKS WOOD
GREAT PARK WOOD
LITTLE FARLEIGH GREEN
LITTLE GREAT HILL
FIVE ACRE SHAW
MILNE PARK
KENNEL WOOD
THREEHALFPENNY WOOD
FOXES WOOD
PINEWOODS
Haggler's Dean
Farleigh Dean
Farleigh Court
Farleigh Court Manor House
Farleigh Cottages
Elm Farm
Farleigh House Farm
Little Farleigh Green Farm
Scotshall Farm
White Bear Inn PH
Fickleshole Farm
Fairchildes Farm
North Lodge
South Lodge
Cox's Cottage
Harrow Inn PH
Croydon R.F.C.
CROYDON
BROMLEY
TANDRIDGE
SURREY

162
EE
EF
EG
EH
EJ
EK
EL
40
41
42
HAYES
COMMON
WICKHAM COMMON
COLYERS WOOD
Rugby Ground
CROYDON ROAD
GLEBE WAY
A232
144
SPARROWS DEN PLAYING FIELDS
R.F.C.
BR4
A2022
CONEY HALL REC GRD
Schiller International University
BURIAL GRD
105
Sec Sch
EMMAUS CONF. CENTRE
QUEENSWAY
Prim Sch
BASTON MANOR ROAD
Baston Manor
Keston Court Riding Stables
PADMALL WOOD
RAVENSBOURNE OPEN SPACE
KESTON COMMON
FORESTDRIVE
106
WELL WOOD
Rouse Farm
Keston
Earthworks
64
LONG SHAW
COOPER'S WOOD
North Pole Farm
Elm Farm
Raithes Organic Worm Farm
Fortune Bank Farm
JACKASS SHAW
LEAFY GROVE
107
CASTLE HILL RUFFS
FULLER'S WOOD
JAMES'S WOOD
Nash Farm
Layham's Cattery
BR2
WESTERHAM ROAD
A233
BRADMANSHILL WOOD
Five Oaks Equestrian Centre
War Bank
108
Mickleham Way Electricity Sta
RUSHFIELD SHAW
BROOMFIELDBANK SHAW
Keston Court Farm
Scout Camp
NEW ADDINGTON
63
Metropolitan Police Dog Training Centre
ROWDOWN WOOD
Glebe Farm
Keston Fruit Farm
Leaves Green
109
ADDINGTON VALE
161
Layham's Farm
Racing Circuit
Kimberley Farm
110
Works
Prim Schs.
Gas Works
FURZE BOTTOM
The Vale Farm
62
Clubhouse
SPORTS GROUND
Holmshaw Farm
HOPPERSNATCH SHAW
Crown Inn PH
111
MILNE PARK
Greyhound Training Kennels
Bradmore
Greenacres Riding School
Colinette Farm
High House Farm
Milking Lane Farm
Higham's Hill
Highams Hill Farm
112
Croydon R.F.C.
Prim Sch
Sec Sch
THREECORNER GROVE
TERMINAL
HELIPAD
61
SHEEPBARN LANE
JEWELS WOOD
CHAPEL HILL
113
BOGRAMS WOOD
REC GRD
Barracks (Disused)
Hangars
LONDON BIGGIN HILL AIRPORT
SOW WOOD
North Lodge
South Lodge
Fairchildes Farm
White Bear Inn PH
Cox's Cottage
Blackman's Cottages
CR6
TN16
114
CUDHAM LODGE WOODS
AIRPORT INDUSTRIAL ESTATE
GREAT HILL SHAW
FIVE ACRE SHAW
178
Skid Hill House
BIGGIN HILL BUSINESS PARK
Hangar
MAIN ROAD
TANDRIDGE
BROMLEY

FARNBOROUGH
Green Street Green
Downe
Hazelwood
Single Street
Cudham
BR6
TN14
HIGH ELMS GOLF COURSE
ORPINGTON HOSPITAL
FARNBOROUGH HOSPITAL
DARWIN MUSEUM
WEST KENT GOLF COURSE
NEW YEARS WOOD
CUCKOO WOOD
DARRICK WOOD
NINHAMS WOOD
GREAT MOLLOMS WOOD
LITTLE MOLLOMS WOOD
HOMEFIELD SPRING
FOXBERRY WOOD
BROOM WOOD
HIGH WOOD
KANGLES WOOD
FOXBURROW WOOD
HOOK WOOD
NEWLANDS WOOD
BIRCHES CROFT
JOCKEY'S WOOD
HAZEL WOOD
LORDFIELD SHAW
HANG GROVE
TWENTY ACRE SHAW
SQUARE SHAW
DOWNE BANK (NATURE RESERVE)
THOMPSON WOOD
SPENCERS GROVE
BIRD HOUSE WOOD
BURNT GORSE
WHITELANDS WOOD
THE ROOKERY
NATURE FIELD
BLACKLANDS
CHURCH END PLANTATION
COCKSETT PLANTATION
RAMUS WOOD
BROOM BANK
COVERED RESERVOIRS
ROUNDS WOOD
SEVENOAKS WAY
FARNBOROUGH COMMON
A21
A223
B2158
EM EN EP EQ ER ES ET
43 44 45
61 62 63 64
145 164 179
105 106 107 108 109 110 111 112 113 114

EU
EV
EW
EX
EY
EZ
FA
Goddington
GODDINGTON PARK
146
ROUNDS SMALLAMS
LILLY'S WOOD
BLACK BUSH WOOD
CHELSFIELD PARK HOSPITAL
CHELSFIELD
CHELSFIELD GREEN
BR6
Maypole
CHELSFIELD REC GRD
GLENTRAMMON REC GRD
HIGH BEECHES
CHELSFIELD PARK SPORTS GRD
ELEVEN OAKS
CHELSFIELD HILL WOOD
ROUNDS WOOD
CHELSFIELD LAKES GOLF COURSE
CONEYEARTH WOOD
KNOCKHOLT
SEVENOAKS ROAD
COURT ROAD (ORPINGTON BYPASS)
163
LITTLE MOLLOMS
Pratt's Bottom
BROKE HILL GOLF COURSE
WATERCROFTS WOOD
ROCK FIELD SHAW
CHARM WOOD
PRATTS GROVE
RUSHMOOR HILL WOOD
PRATT'S BOTTOM WOOD
HOOK WOOD
BIRTHDAY WOOD
FOXBERRY WOOD
HOMEFIELD SPRING
LOWER BROOMS WOOD
UPPER BROOMS WOOD
LATTICE COPPICE
BROOM WOOD
HIGH WOOD
KANGLES WOOD
BIRCHINGBANK WOOD
PERRY WOOD
LOWER RANDLE'S WOOD
DEERLEAP WOOD
CHALKHURST WOOD
Halstead
NEW YEARS WOOD
HAYMAN'S WOOD
NEWLANDS WOOD
PIECE WOOD
BIRCHES CROFT
LONG BOTTOM SHAW
HAWFIELD WOOD
180
Knockholt Pound
CHAPEL CROFT
JOCKEY'S WOOD
105
106
107
108
109
110
111
112
113
114
47
48
49
61
62
63
64

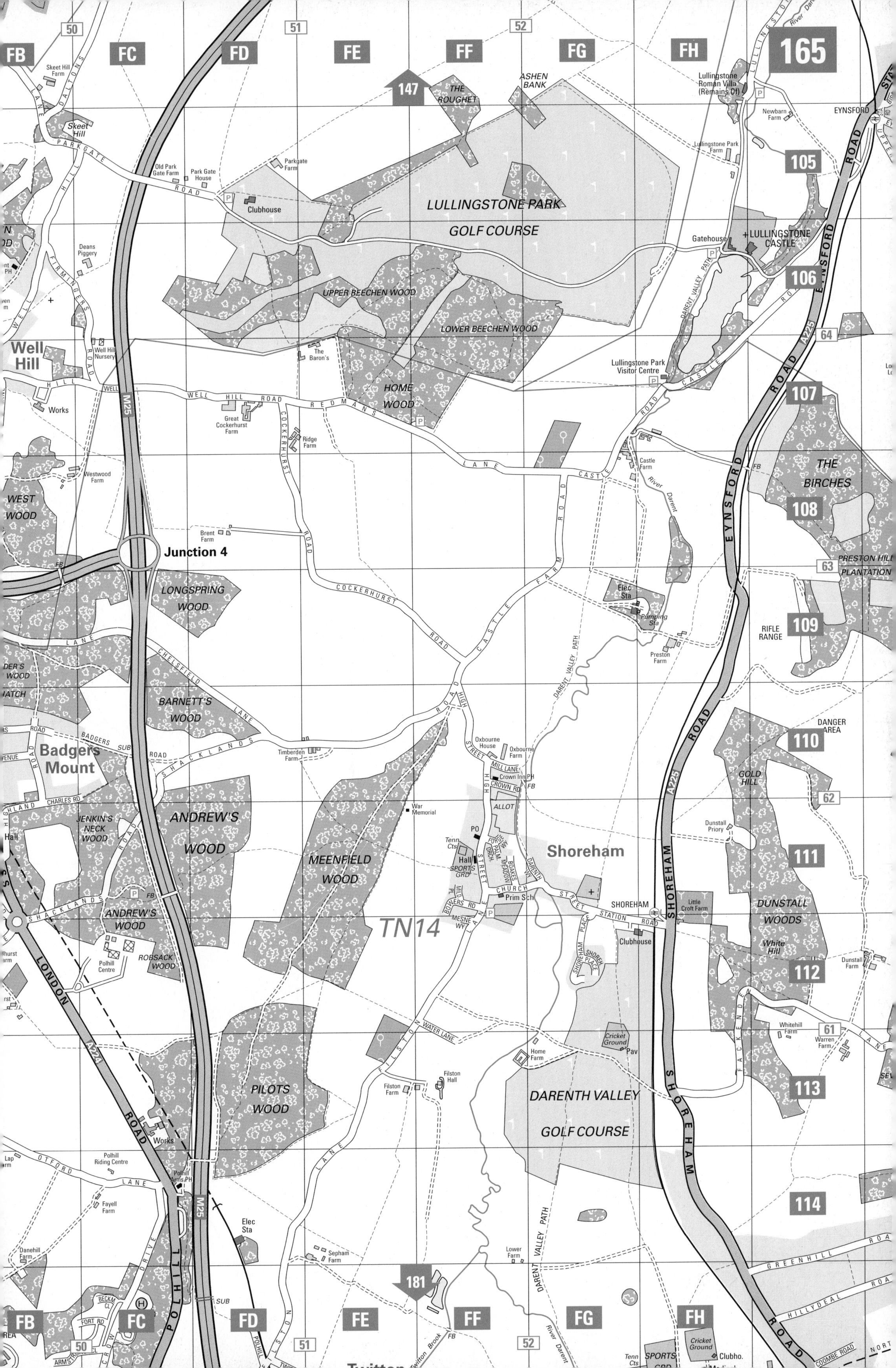

Lullingstone Roman Villa (Remains Of)
EYNSFORD
Skeet Hill Farm
Skeet Hill
THE ROUGHET
ASHEN BANK
Parkgate Farm
Old Park Gate Farm
Park Gate House
Clubhouse
LULLINGSTONE PARK GOLF COURSE
Newbarn Farm
Lullingstone Park Farm
Gatehouse
LULLINGSTONE CASTLE
Deans Piggery
UPPER BEECHEN WOOD
LOWER BEECHEN WOOD
Well Hill
Well Hill Nursery
The Baron's
Lullingstone Park Visitor Centre
HOME WOOD
Works
Great Cockerhurst Farm
Ridge Farm
Castle Farm
River Darent
Westwood Farm
THE BIRCHES
WEST WOOD
Brent Farm
Junction 4
PRESTON HILL PLANTATION
LONGSPRING WOOD
Elec Sta
Pumping Sta
RIFLE RANGE
Preston Farm
BARNETT'S WOOD
DANGER AREA
Badgers Mount
Timberden Farm
Oxbourne House
Oxbourne Farm
Crown Inn PH
GOLD HILL
JENKIN'S NECK WOOD
ANDREW'S WOOD
War Memorial
ALLOT
Dunstall Priory
MEENFIELD WOOD
Shoreham
DUNSTALL WOODS
White Hill
Prim Sch
SHOREHAM
Little Croft Farm
Clubhouse
TN14
Dunstall Farm
ANDREW'S WOOD
ROBSACK WOOD
Polhill Centre
Whitehill Farm
Warren Farm
Cricket Ground
Pav
Home Farm
PILOTS WOOD
Filston Farm
Filston Hall
DARENTH VALLEY GOLF COURSE
Works
Polhill Riding Centre
Polhill Arms PH
Fayell Farm
Elec Sta
Danehill Farm
Sepham Farm
Lower Farm
Cricket Ground
Clubho.
LONDON ROAD
SHOREHAM ROAD
EYNSFORD ROAD
POLHILL
M25
A224
A225
DARENT VALLEY PATH
FB FC FD FE FF FG FH
50 51 52
61 62 63 64
147
181
105 106 107 108 109 110 111 112 113 114

AS
AT
AU
AV
AW
AX
AY
150
98
99
00
115
116
117
118
119
120
121
122
123
124
CHOBHAM GOLF COURSE
HORSELL COMMON
LITTLEWICK COMMON
GOLDSWORTH PARK REC GRD
GOLDSWORTH PARK TRADING ESTATE
TRACIOUS COPSE
GU21
Goldsworth Park
Knaphill
WATERERS PARK
LOCKFIELD DRIVE
AMSTEL WAY
Mount Hermon
St. John's
Hook Heath
WOKING CEMETERY
Crematorium
WOKING GOLF COURSE
BROOKWOOD LYE
WEST HILL GOLF COURSE
GU24
GU22
Mayford
HOE VALLEY LINEAR PARK
Fisher's Hill
WORPLESDON GOLF COURSE
SMART'S HEATH
PREY HEATH
WORPLESDON
Burdenshot Hill
BRIDLEY COPSE
Beech Hill
Pye Hill
SUTTON GREEN GOLF COURSE
GU3
WHITMOOR

167
AZ
BA
BB
BC
BD
BE
BF
01
02
03
151
168
WEST BYFLEET
GOLF COURSE
Pyrford
PYRFORD COMMON
THE ROUGH
Pyrford Court
The Bothy
WOKING
Maybury
Superstores
WOKING BUSINESS PARK
SHEERWATER BUSINESS CENTRE
GENESIS BUSINESS PARK
GU22
HOEBRIDGE GOLF CENTRE
Clubhouse
Monument Hill
Fox Hill
Hoebridge Farm
Roundbridge Farm
Sewage Works
Filter Beds
Pumping Sta
Woking Park Farm
OLDHILL COPSE
Old Woking
HIGH STREET
BROADMEAD ROAD
River Wey
River Wey Navigation NT
Broadmead Cut
Papercourt Lock
Papercourt Farm
Newark Priory (Remains)
Newark Lock
Newark Mill Bridge
Church Farm
Lady Place
Wheelers Farm
Homewood Farm
GARLICK'S ARCH COPSE
Sailing Club
Devonia Farm
GU23
SAND PIT
Send
Send Marsh
GU4
Westfield
Moorlane Farm
Fisher's Farm
Lower Westfield Farm
Runtley Wood Farm
Cricketshill Farm
Cricket Ground
Triggs Lock
Triggs Lock Bridge
Tudor Barn Farm
Sendbar
Boughton Farm
Aldertons
Prews Farm
Cartbridge House
SEND ROAD
SEND BARNS LANE
PORTSMOUTH ROAD
CEM
115
116
117
118
119
120
121
122
123
124
59
58
57
56

Pyrford
Pyrford Green
Pyrford Village
PYRFORD GOLF COURSE
THE WISLEY GOLF COURSE
Wisley
WISLEY COMMON
WISLEY GARDEN (R.H.S.)
OCKHAM COMMON
Elm Corner
WALSHAM MEADOW
RIPLEY GREEN
Ripley
OCKHAM PARK
PARK WOOD
Send Marsh
GARLICK'S ARCH COPSE
LOVELAND'S COPSE
ROBOROW WOOD
BACHELOR'S COPSE
BRAMBLERIDE COPSE
PEATMOOR WOOD
COMMON MEADOWS
BUXTON WOOD
KT14
GU22
M25
PORTSMOUTH ROAD
RIPLEY BYPASS
NEWARK LANE
HIGH STREET
152
167

169
PAINSHILL PARK
BP
BQ
BR
BS
BT
BU
BV
08
09
10
153
PORTSMOUTH ROAD
Junction 10
OCKHAM COMMON
CHATLEY WOOD
CHATLEY HEATH
HATCHFORD WOOD
HATCHFORD PARK
THE LAKE
KT11
River Mole
COBHAM
Downside
DOWNSIDE COMMON
M25
Pointers Green
LITTLE BRICKFIELD COPSE
BRICKFIELD COPSE
NORTON WOOD
Martyr's Green
ELMBRIDGE
GUILDFORD
OLD OAK COMMON
THE NEW PRESERVE
PEAKED ROUGH
ROUNDABOUT
CHAFFERS COPSE
HOOK WOOD
STUMPS GROVE
TRULLIBER COPSE
CLAMP ROUGH
GALLOWS GROVE
EFFINGHAM JUNCTION
KT24
THE DRIFT GOLF COURSE
BARNSTHORNS WOOD
EFFINGHAM COMMON
THE FOREST
BEAUMONT PLANTATION
NEW BARN WOOD
BUSHY THICKET
THICKET COPSE
LITTLE MORNSHILL WOOD
115
116
117
118
119
120
121
122
123
124
170
56
57
58
59

170
BW
BX
BY
BZ
CA
CB
CC
154
COBHAM
Stoke D'Abernon
KT11
Downside
KNOWLE HILL PARK
LITTLE HEATH COMMON
WATERCUT COPSE
THE FURZE
THE COPSE
PARK WOOD
BIG ROUNDABOUT
LITTLE ROUNDABOUT
COBHAM CEM
SPORTS GROUND
DOWNSIDE COMMON
BEAUMONT PLANTATION
MUGGERIDGE WOOD
WRENS HILL WOOD
THORNETS WOOD
DOWN WOOD
SPRING MEADOW WOOD
CHASEMORE WOOD
LADY CHEWTONS WOOD
OLD PARKS COPSE
HEATHFIELD COPSE
LITTLE WOOD
BUSHEY COPSE
WITHY BED
PEAKED ROUGH
NEW BARN WOOD
HUNDRED POUND BRI WOOD
THE BIRCHES
GREAT BOOKHAM COMMON NT
LITTLE BOOKHAM COMMON
BANK'S COMMON NT
THICKET COPSE
BUSHY
LITTLE MORNSHILL WOOD
GREAT MORNSHILL WOOD
KT24
KT23
BOOKHAM INDUSTRIAL ESTATE
PIKES POOL
HERONS REACH
MALLARDS MERE
OAKEN WOOD
THORNET WOOD
Little Bookham
GREAT BOOKHAM
M25
A245
169
115
116
117
118
119
120
121
122
123
124
12
13
14
56
57
58
59

171
KT9
KT21
KT22
LEATHERHEAD GOLF COURSE
ASHTEAD COMMON
Pachesham Park
WOODLANDS PARK
TEAZLE WOOD
PACHESHAM GOLF CENTRE
Leatherhead Common
Lower Ashtead
ASHTEAD
LEATHERHEAD
FETCHAM
Junction 9
RANDALLS PARK CEMETERY
FETCHAM PARK UTD. FC
MILL POND
Beaverbrook Roundabout
ASHTEAD HOSP
LEATHERHEAD BYPASS
KINGSTON ROAD
OXSHOTT ROAD
RANDALLS ROAD
YOUNG STREET
GUILDFORD ROAD
REIGATE ROAD
EPSOM ROAD

EPSOM COMMON
CL
CM
CN
CP
CQ
CR
CS
NEWTON WOOD
156
115
TEAD COMMON
116
WOOD FIELD
ASHTEAD
117
118
ASHTEAD
119
171
120
ASHTEAD HOSP
EPSOM GENERAL HOSP
WOODCOTE GREEN
WOODCOTE
FISH POND
HALFMOON CLUMP
WORLDS END
WOODCOTE PARK GOLF COURSE
THE GROVE
Woodcote Park Hotel Country Club
ASHTEAD PARK
Ashtead Park
City of London Freemen's School
KT21
LANGLEY BOTTOM WOOD
LANGLEY VALE
THE WARREN
EPSOM & EWELL
MOLE VALLEY
KT18
Chase Farm Stud
Esso House
121
122
ADDLESTEAD WOOD
M25
LITTLE HURST WOOD
123
Tyrrell's Wood
TYRRELL'S WOOD
HAMBLETON WOOD
HEADLEY COURT
Beaverbrook Roundabout
124
HOOK WOOD
GREAT HURST WOOD
PIGNUT WOOD
OYSTER HILL NT
KT22
NOWER WOOD
182
TYRRELL'S WOOD GOLF COURSE
COSTAL WOOD
Headley
19
20
21

CT
CU
CV
CW
CX
CY
CZ
22
23
24
157
KT17
EPSOM DOWNS
Epsom College
Clubhouse
NORK
SM7
PARK WOOD
NORK PARK
SPORTS GROUND
Nork Park Farm
PARK WOOD
TATTENHAM WAY RECREATION GROUND
BUCKLE'S GAP
EPSOM DOWNS GOLF COURSE
Grandstand
EPSOM RACE COURSE
EPSOM DOWNS
The Hill
Tattenham Corner
TATTENHAM CORNER
LANGLEY VALE
WALTON DOWNS
EPSOM & EWELL
REIGATE & BANSTEAD
BURGH HEATH
COVERED RESERVOIR
Superstore
CANONS WOOD
Canons Farm
PAGES ACRE
RUFFETT WOOD
115
116
117
118
119
120
121
122
123
124
174
59
58
57
56
Legal & General House
B.U.P.A. WINSCOMBE
St. Monica's
KT20
KINGSWOOD
Kingswood Warren
TADWORTH
THE CHILDRENS TRUST TADWORTH
PIT WOOD
Police Training School
Wingfield Stud Farm
SANDHILL WOOD
Ebbisham Farm
Walton Manor
WALTON ON THE HILL
MERE POND
BANSTEAD HEATH
WORKHOUSE POND
Cricket Ground
Clubhouse
The Clock Tower Riding Centre
BEECHEN
COPSE
183
BANSTEAD

174
DA
DB
DC
DD
DE
DF
DG
158
WINKWORTH A2022
CROYDON
BANSTEAD SM7
WOODMANSTERNE
WOODMANSTERNE PARK RECREATION GROUND
CLOCKHOUSE REC GRD
BIG WOOD
Weston Acres
Nicola Farm
THE SHRUBBERY
SCRATCH WOOD
Courtlands Farm
Place Farm
Mint Farm
The Mint PH
Tall Trees
New Place
Little Haugh
GREAT SOLOM'S WOOD
SOLOM'S COURT
CHALK WORKS
PARK DOWNS
DEPOT
NATURE RESERVE
BANSTEAD WOOD
CHIPSTEAD GOLF COURSE
Clubhouse
How Hills
CHIPSTEAD
COVERED RESERVOIR
PAGES ACRE
RUFFETT WOOD
CANONS WOOD
Canons Farm
Perrotts Farm
LUNCH WOOD
FAMES ROUGH
CHIPSTEAD BOTTOM
WELL COPSE
CHIPHOUSE WOOD
SPORTS GROUND
Legal & General House
B.U.P.A. WINSCOMBE
St Monica's
Chipstead Bottom
OUTWOOD SHAW
POORFIELD WOOD
EMBERS SHAW
CHIPSTEAD MEADS REC GRD
Chipstead R.F.C.
Tennis Club
STARROCK SHAW
KINGSWOOD
KT20
OUTWOOD
THE LONG PLANTATION
THE BELT
Shabden Park
SPORTS GRD
Chipstead FC
Cricket Ground
THE GROVE
Noke Farm
Hooley
FOURTEEN ACRE SHAW
Eyhurst Farm
Eyhurst Park
KINGSWOOD GOLF COURSE AND COUNTRY CLUB
Kingswood Warren
KINGSWOOD
SMUGGLERS PIT PLANTATION
Clubhouse
THE RUFFETT
ROUND WOOD
RUFFETTS WOOD
WHITE HILL
Pigeonhouse Farm
TOP SHAW
ROUND WOOD
Manor Park
South Lodge
HEDGELAND SHAW
Well House PH
WELLFIELD SHAW
HOMEFIELD SHAWS
Reeves Rest
BEECHEN
COPSE
MILLFIELD WOOD
Mugswell
184
Park Farm
HARPS OAK SHAW
BOARS GREEN
LONG WOOD
LITTLE WOOD
Windmill
173
115
116
117
118
119
120
121
122
123
124
26
27
28
56
57
58
59

175
DH
DJ
DK
DL
DM
DN
DP
159
WOODCOTE PARK GOLF COURSE
COULSDON
CR8
KENLEY
115
116
117
118
119
120
121
122
123
124
176
185
COULSDON COURT PUBLIC GOLF COURSE
HARTLEY BUSHES
COULSDON MANOR GOLF COURSE
ULLSWATER BUSINESS PARK
STONYFIELD SHAW
FARTHING OR FAIRDEAN DOWNS
GRANGE PARK
Old Coulsdon
INWOOD
BETTS MEAD RECREATION GROUND
CR5
MARLFIELD SHAW
TWINERS WOOD
DUNSTAN'S WOOD
POSTERN WOOD
Special Unit
SMITHAM
COULSDON SOUTH
STAR SHAW
THREE CORNERED SHAW
PETERSHOLE SHAW
DEVILS DEN WOOD
DITCHES SHAW
BOXERS WOOD
HAPPY VALLEY PARK
SPARKLIE WOOD
FIGGS WOOD
THE GULLET
HOSPITAL (closed)
NETHERNE WOOD
COULSDON COMMON
SPORTS GROUND
CROYDON
TANDRIDGE
SURREY
REIGATE & BANSTEAD
RIFLE RANGES
HAPPY VALLEY GOLF COURSE
BROAD WOOD
PILES WOOD
CHURCH GREEN
RH1
GRASSCUTS SHAW
LORD'S WOOD
CARAVAN PARK
FURZEFIELD WOOD
ALDERSTEAD HEATH
SPARTICLES WOOD
Chaldon
FRYERN BROOM WOOD
CR3
Rook Hill
WILLEY BROOM WOOD
BROTHERS FIELD
Merstham Tunnel
Airshafts
Junction 7
29
30
31
56
57
58
59
BRIGHTON ROAD
A23
A237
B2030
B2031
B2032
B276

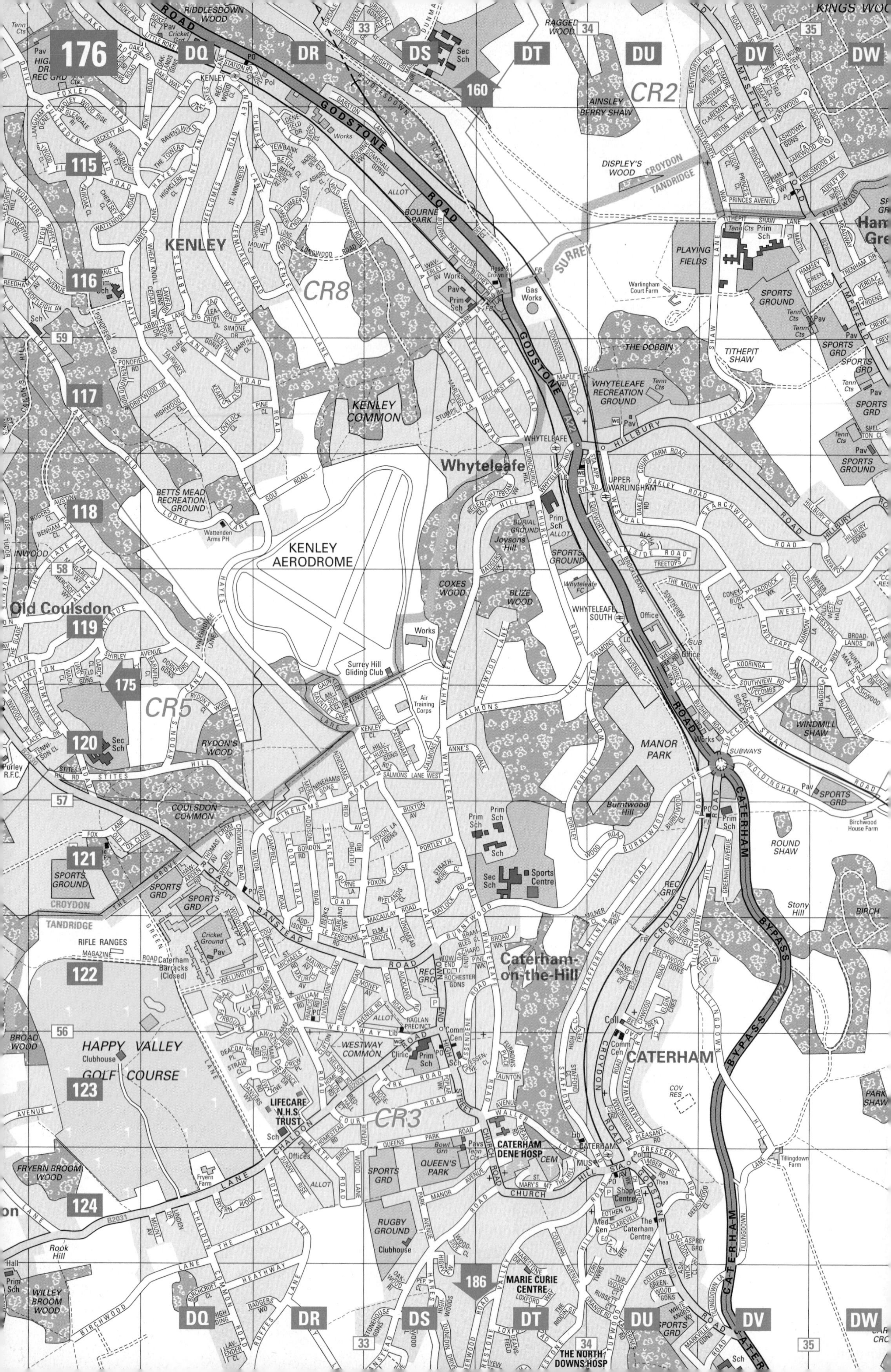

176
DQ
DR
DS
DT
DU
DV
DW
160
175
186
CR2
CR3
CR5
CR8
KENLEY
Whyteleafe
Old Coulsdon
Caterham-on-the-Hill
CATERHAM
KENLEY AERODROME
KENLEY COMMON
RIDDLESDOWN WOOD
RAGGED WOOD
AINSLEY BERRY SHAW
DISPLEY'S WOOD
CROYDON
TANDRIDGE
SURREY
GODSTONE ROAD
PLAYING FIELDS
SPORTS GROUND
THE DOBBIN
TITHEPIT SHAW
WHYTELEAFE RECREATION GROUND
UPPER WARLINGHAM
WHYTELEAFE SOUTH
BETTS MEAD RECREATION GROUND
Surrey Hill Gliding Club
Air Training Corps
COXES WOOD
BLIZE WOOD
Joysons Hill
MANOR PARK
Burntwood Hill
RYDON'S WOOD
COULSDON COMMON
RIFLE RANGES
Caterham Barracks (Closed)
HAPPY VALLEY
GOLF COURSE
BROAD WOOD
FRYERN BROOM WOOD
WILLEY BROOM WOOD
Rook Hill
LIFECARE N.H.S. TRUST
WESTWAY COMMON
QUEEN'S PARK
CATERHAM DENE HOSP
RUGBY GROUND
MARIE CURIE CENTRE
THE NORTH DOWNS HOSP
WINDMILL SHAW
ROUND SHAW
Stony Hill
CATERHAM BYPASS
Purley R.F.C.
Tillingdown Farm
Birchwood House Farm
Warlingham Court Farm

177
DX
DY
DZ
EA
EB
EC
ED
161
187
178
36
37
38
115
116
117
118
119
120
121
122
123
124
59
58
57
56
FARLEIGH
HOGCROFT SHAW
MOSSHILL SHAW
OAKEN SHAW
MOSESHILL SHAW
Farleigh Court
Farleigh Cottages
Farleigh Court Manor House
Little Farleigh Green Farm
LITTLE FARLEIGH GREEN
White Bear Inn PH
Fairchildes Farm
Cox's Cottage
LITTLE GREAT HILL
GT FARLEIGH GRN
LITTLEPARK WOOD
GREAT PARK WOOD
THE GRIPES
Scotshall Farm
FIVE ACRE SHAW
GREAT HILL SHAW
MIDDLEY SHAW
HONEYOAK WOOD
Harrow Inn PH
Pinel House
SPORTS GROUND
SPORTS GRD
CREWE'S WOOD
MOUNT HOPPER
Bowl Grn
Pav
Clubhouse
Sec Sch
SPORTS GROUND
HOLT WOOD
Smugglers Hole
BURIAL GRD
Slades Farm
CR6
The Bull PH
CHELSHAM COMMON
Kennel Farm
BULL GREEN
Ledgers Farm
Chelsham
SPORTS GROUND
Prim Sch
MILL COMMON
HENLEY WOOD
WASHPOND SHAW
OLDBURY SHAW
GREENLAWN MEMORIAL PARK
Superstore
Amb Sta
Chelsham Place Farm
Hare & Hounds PH
Knights Garden Centre
COV RES
Chelsham Court
Chelsham Court Farm
Broom Lodge Farm
BIRCHEN SHAW
CONY CROOK
ARLINGHAM
Highlands Farm
WORMS HEATH
Radio Sta
Masts
SLINES GREEN
SLINES OAK
HALLILOO PLANTATION
DUKE'S DENE GOLF COURSE
Clubhouse
LUMBERDINE WOOD
ASHEN SHAW
TTERSHILL SHAW
High Breach
Beech Farm
Dukes Hill House
Warren Barn Farm
Hovings Hole
Woldingham Garden Village
Knights Garden Centre
WOLDINGHAM
THE USHES
Woldingham
Prim Sch
Clubhouse
SPORTS GRD
Tenn Club
PO
Hall
CR3
Woldingham Equestrian Centre
Marden Park Farm
THE GREEN
GREENHILL SHAW
Botley Hill Farmhouse PH
Mast
LITTLE CHURCH WOOD
Whistlers Wood Farm
Water Tower
Masts
WHISTLERS WOOD
HELL SHAW
TITSEY PLANTATION
TEMPLEHILL PLANTATION
GREAT CHURCH WOOD NATURE RESERVE
NORTH DOWNS GOLF COURSE
Sch
Whistlers Court
CHALK PITS
FARLEIGH ROAD
HARROW ROAD
CREWE'S LANE
CREWE'S FARM LANE
GREEN HILL LANE
LIMPSFIELD ROAD
CHELSHAM COMMON RD
CHURCH LANE
LEDGERS ROAD
WASHPOND LANE
CHELSHAM COURT ROAD
FARM ROAD
BEECH WAY
CROYDON ROAD
SLINES NEW ROAD
BUTLERS DENE ROAD
LUNGHURST ROAD
SLINES OAK ROAD
UPLAND RD
VANGUARD WAY
LONG HILL ROAD
STATION ROAD
PARK VIEW ROAD
CHURCH ROAD
HIGH DRIVE
NORTHDOWN ROAD
SOUTHFIELDS
SOUTHVIEW ROAD
UPPER COURT ROAD
RIDGE
FAIRCHILDES LANE
FAIRCHILDES ROAD
HESIERS ROAD
SCOTSHALL LANE
HIGH LANE
BEECHWOOD LA
DUKES HILL
PLANTATION LANE
WOLDINGHAM ROAD
PARK LEY ROAD
BEULAH WALK
HILLTOP WALK
CAMP ROAD

178
BIGGIN HILL
Tatsfield
Titsey
CR6
PARK WOOD GOLF COURSE
AIRPORT INDUSTRIAL ESTATE
SURREY
TANDRIDGE
BROMLEY
162
177
188

179
43
44
45
EM
EN
EP
EQ
ER
ES
ET
BR6
163
SPENCERS GROVE
BIRD HOUSE WOOD
Down Scout Camp
Clock Tower
Open Air Pool
BROMLEY CROFT
STRAKES SHAW
Single Street
TWENTY ACRE SHAW
LUXTED ROAD
SINGLE STREET
BIRDHOUSE
Sports Centre
Chavic Park Farm Riding School
Prim Sch
The Old Jail PH
JAIL
LANE
Brickyard Farm
Littlewood Farm
Homeleigh Farm
Berry's Green
BERRY'S LANE
BERRY'S GREEN
RESTAVON PARK
BLACKBUSH SHAW
Church Hill Farm
CHURCH HILL
CUDHAM ROAD
Bottom Farm
Cudham Court Farm
SPORTS GRD
Tenn Cts
Blacksmiths Arms PH
Cudham
Cudham Hall
Angas Home
HILL
Cudham Parish Hall
CUDHAM LANE SOUTH
NEW BARN LANE
CACKETS LANE
Cacket's Farm
Cacket's Cottages
Cottage Farm
HOOK WOOD
FOXBURROW WOOD
NEW YEARS WOOD
New Year Cottage
BIRCHES CROFT
NEW YEARS LANE
115
JOCKEY'S WOOD
COPHALL WOOD
Shelleys
116
Letts Green
SHELLEYS
Parsonage Farm
Underhill Farm
Corkers Farm
Rosehaugh Farm
Maple Farm
BROOM WOOD
Horns Green
59
Kno
BASTON WOOD
117
erfield
PIMLICO WOOD
Foal Farm
Clubhouse
CHERRY LODGE GOLF COURSE
Warren Farm
THE GROVE
Cedar Farm
LITTLE JOCKEYS WOOD
TN14
New Barn Farm
Thrift Farm
THRIFT LANE
KNOCKHOLT WOOD
BURLINGS
ROAD
Little Rosemary Farm
Beeches Farm
Mountross Farm
118
The Tally Ho PH
MAIN
Hazlet Wood Farm
Saunderstead
Park Farm
Silverbeach Farm
Buckhurst Farm
MAIN ROAD
CLARENCE ROAD
WOODBURY ROAD
STONINGS
58
DOWNS
Fox & Hounds PH
WITHINS WOOD
Stud Farm
Leecroft
OLD HARROW LANE
CUDHAM FRITH
KENT
SOUTH
119
South Street
A233
GRAY'S WOOD
SHELLEM WOOD
BOMBERS LANE
Milena Stables
THE SEVENOAKS BROMLEY
180
Brasted Hill Farm
NOWER
BRASTED
SHOOT WOO
TN16
Great South Street Farm
Southwood Farm
VIEWLANDS AV
HOGTROUGH
120
THE NOWER
WESTERHAM
JOELAND'S WOOD
GRAYS
SILVER-STEAD LA
SILVERSTEAD LANE
57
Westerham Riding School
Gray's Farm
BUCKHURST
KENT
Hawley Corner
The Spinning Wheel PH
BROMLEY
SEVENOAKS
BROOMCOCKS WOOD
121
NORTH DOWNS WAY
Hogtrough Hill
Westerham Heights Nurseries
AVENUE
Works
CHESTNUT
Little Betsom's Farm
ROUND SHAW
PILGRIMS
Court Lodge Farm
122
Highover
THE
Betsom's Hill
WHITELANDS SHAW
PILGRIMS WAY
Cerne Easter
56
Sch
Pumping Sta
Pav
PLAY FLD
Betsomhill Farm
LONDON
CROYDON
HOLYWELL SHAW
123
PARK WOOD
Gaysham
GREEN
Force Green Farm
FORCE
M25
HARTLEY WOOD
124
Charmans Farm
Park Farm
River Darent
WESTERHAM WOOD
BEGGARS
189
ASH
ELM RD
HARTLEY ROAD
LON RD
OAK
Horizons Centre
Works
Mountwood
A25
Fountain Cottages
ROAD
Prim Sch

180
BR6
EU
EV
EW
EX
EY
EZ
FA
47
48
49
164
179
115
116
117
118
119
120
121
122
123
124
59
58
57
56
TN14
TN16
Knockholt
Knockholt Pound
Chevening
Sundridge
Brasted
CHEVENING PARK
NEWLANDS WOOD
HAYMAN'S WOOD
BIRCHES CROFT
LONG BOTTOM SHAW
HAWFIELD WOOD
JOCKEY'S WOOD
COPHALL WOOD
Letts Green
BROOM WOOD
BASTON WOOD
LITTLE JOCKEYS WOOD
KNOCKHOLT WOOD
COOPER'S WOOD
ASHPLATT
SAND BANKS
SUMMERHOUSE WOOD
PARK WOOD
HAGBUSH WOOD
Sundridge Hill
ROUGHFIELDS WOOD
SHOOTFIELD WOOD
THE NOWER
JOELAND'S WOOD
Hogtrough Hill
CHAPEL CROFT
LEES WOOD
ASHFIELD WOOD
STAR HILL WOOD
MINNY WOOD
THE SPINNEY
HOME WOOD
CLAYPIT SHAW
COMBEBANK WOOD
COMBE WOOD
THE ROOKERIES
THE WARREN
Chevening Cross
Junction
M25
A25
B2211
Knockholt Beeches
Masts
War Meml
Sec Sch
The Crown PH
Court Lodge
Homefield
Blueberry Farm
The Spinney Nurseries
Singles Cross
Whiteleggs Garden Centre
Comm Cen
Clinic
Ivy Farm
Bowl Grn
Football Pitch
Mast
Chine Farm
Warehouses
Harrow Inn PH
Aldwyn House
Meadow Farm
Warren Farm
Rose Cottage Farm
Curry Farm
Works
New Stables Farm
The Mill House
The Grange
Shelleys
Beeches
Mountross Farm
The Tally Ho PH
Hazlet Wood Farm
Keepers Cottage
Shootfield
Home Farm
Well
Chevening House
BURIAL GRD
Grove House
Brasted Hill Farm
Oveny Green Farm
Combe Bank Farm
Farm
Ovenden Lodge
Court Lodge Farm
Combe Bank Wood
Sch
Pav
SPORTS GROUND
Little Coombe Bank
Offices
Council Depot
Pumping Sta
Warren Farm
The Lamb PH
Bowling Green
White Horse PH
Hall
The Old Rectory
Prim Sch
Pumping Station
Tanners
The Old Rectory
PYM ORCHARD
Stanhope Arms PH
Mill Farm
Depot
Mill
White Hart Inn PH
Orchard Farm
Brasted Place
Brasted Place Farm
Bull Inn PH
Tennis Courts
SPORTS GRD
Charmans Farm
Park Farm
Horizons Centre
Works
Mountwood
Fountain Cottages
Long Barn
River Darent
NEW YEARS LANE
SHELLEYS LANE
MAIN ROAD
SUNDRIDGE LANE
BLUEBERRY LANE
RANDLES LANE
SINGLES CROSS LANE
POUND LANE
HALSTEAD HILL
OLD LONDON ROAD
HARROW ROAD
CHEVENING LANE
BIRCHWOOD LA
STAR HILL ROAD
NORTH DOWNS WAY
LORD CHATHAM'S RIDE
PILGRIMS WAY
OVENDEN ROAD
COMBE BANK DRIVE
CHEVENING ROAD
NOWER LANE
BRASTED LANE
BRASTED HILL
HOGTROUGH HILL
STONEINGS
SOUTH MAIN ROAD
THE SEVENOAKS ROAD
BROMLEY
KENT
VIEWLANDS AV
STATION ROAD
COLES LANE
RECTORY LANE
CHURCH ROAD
HIGH STREET
MAIN ROAD
CHAPMANS ROAD
MANOR RD
WOODSIDE ROAD
CHART LANE
WILKINS WAY
THE CARRIAGEWAY
WEST END
GREYSTONE PK
ST. MARTINS MEADOW

FB
FC
FD
FE
FF
FG
FH
165
115
116
117
118
119
120
121
122
123
124
191
190
50
51
52
59
58
57
56
Twitton
OTFORD
Otford
TN14
Dunton Green
Longford
Chipstead
Riverhead
Bessels Green
TN13
SEVENOAKS
CHALK PIT
OLD GROVE
DEFENCE RESEARCH AGENCY
HELIPAD
Morants Court Cross
EDWARD SHAW
ALDER SHAW
RAKEFIELD WOOD
BLUEBELL WOOD
HOME WOOD
RYE WOOD
ORCHARD HEY
OTFORD CEMETERY
GRAVEL PIT
EAST LAKE
SEVENOAKS WILDFOWL RESERVE
WEST LAKE
CHIPSTEAD LAKE
RIVERHEAD PARKLAND
MONTREAL PARK
ANT WOOD
ASH PLAT WOOD
OBELISK WOOD
COLD ARBOR WOOD
LITTLE BRITAIN'S WOOD
MIDDLINGS WOOD
SEVENOAKS HOSP
THE MOORS
RIVERSIDE RETAIL PARK
SEVENOAKS BUSINESS CEN
KNOLE PADDOCK
KNOLE ENVIROMENT PARK
M25
M26
A25
A224
A225
B2042
B2020
POLHILL
LONDON ROAD
SEVENOAKS ROAD
OTFORD ROAD
STATION ROAD
HIGH STREET
PILGRIMS WAY
MORANTS COURT ROAD
BRADBOURNE VALE ROAD
WESTERHAM ROAD
AMHERST HILL
DARTFORD ROAD
ST. JOHN'S HILL
ST. BOTOLPH'S ROAD
SEAL ROAD

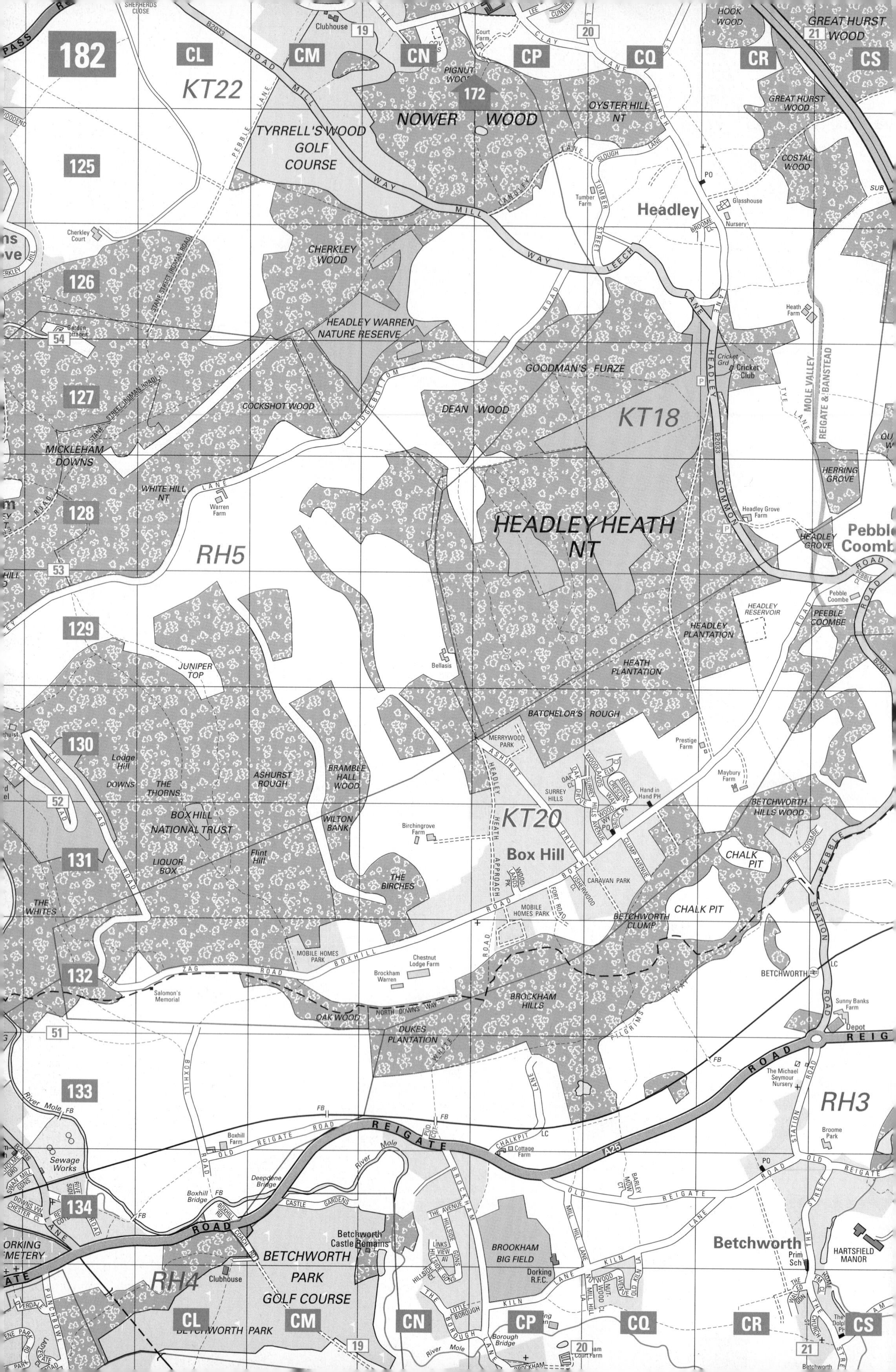

182
CL
CM
CN
CP
CQ
CR
CS
KT22
KT18
KT20
RH5
RH3
RH4
NOWER WOOD
TYRRELL'S WOOD GOLF COURSE
OYSTER HILL NT
GREAT HURST WOOD
HOOK WOOD
COSTAL WOOD
Headley
CHERKLEY WOOD
Cherkley Court
HEADLEY WARREN NATURE RESERVE
GOODMAN'S FURZE
COCKSHOT WOOD
DEAN WOOD
MICKLEHAM DOWNS
WHITE HILL NT
Warren Farm
HEADLEY HEATH NT
HERRING GROVE
HEADLEY GROVE
Pebble Coombe
HEADLEY PLANTATION
HEADLEY RESERVOIR
HEATH PLANTATION
PEEBLE COOMBE
JUNIPER TOP
Bellasis
BATCHELOR'S ROUGH
MERRYWOOD PARK
Lodge Hill
DOWNS
THE THORNS
ASHURST ROUGH
BRAMBLE HALL WOOD
BOX HILL NATIONAL TRUST
WILTON BANK
SURREY HILLS
Hand in Hand PH
BETCHWORTH HILLS WOOD
Box Hill
LIQUOR BOX
Flint Hill
Birchingrove Farm
THE BIRCHES
CHALK PIT
CARAVAN PARK
THE WHITES
MOBILE HOMES PARK
BETCHWORTH CLUMP
Chestnut Lodge Farm
Brockham Warren
Salomon's Memorial
BROCKHAM HILLS
OAK WOOD
NORTH DOWNS WAY
DUKES PLANTATION
BETCHWORTH
Sunny Banks Farm
Depot
The Michael Seymour Nursery
Broome Park
River Mole
Sewage Works
Boxhill Farm
Deepdene Bridge
Boxhill Bridge
Cottage Farm
REIGATE ROAD
A25
Betchworth Castle Remains
BETCHWORTH PARK GOLF COURSE
BROOKHAM BIG FIELD
Dorking R.F.C.
Clubhouse
Betchworth
HARTSFIELD MANOR
DORKING CEMETERY
BETCHWORTH PARK
Borough Bridge
125
126
127
128
129
130
131
132
133
134
172
19
20
21
51
52
53
54

CT
CU
CV
CW
CX
CY
CZ
22
23
24
173
184
125
126
127
128
129
130
131
132
133
134
54
53
52
51
BANSTEAD HEATH
WALTON ON THE HILL
WALTON HEATH GOLF COURSE
WALTON HEATH
KT20
CHUSSEX PLAIN
LITTLE HEATH
Walton Oaks Offices
Pollenarium
M25
LOWER KINGSWOOD
Mogador
GAS STATION
MARGERY WOOD NT
COVERED RESERVOIR
ROUND WOOD
DEWRIDING PLANTATION
Thistle Hill
Lady Hill
Buckland Hills
NORTH DOWNS WAY
Mount Hill
Conybury Hill
PILGRIMS' WAY
Juniper Hill
Colley Hill
THE HORSESHOE
THE SADDLE
KNOB
QUEEN'S PARK
FOUR ACRE UPPER WOODS
THE BEECHES
NORTHLAND SHAW
BUSHY SHAW
COLLEYLAND SHAW
BUSHFIELD COPPICE
RH2
COLLEY COPSE
COLLEY WOOD
Buckland
TAP WOOD
SAND AND GRAVEL PIT
MOLE VALLEY
REIGATE & BANSTEAD
ROUND ALDERS
BUCKLAND ROAD
A25
WEST STREET
SAND AND GRAVEL PIT
THE ALDERS
REIGATE HEATH GOLF COURSE
REIGATE HEATH
REIGATE
PRIORY POND
SPORTS GROUND
MILL POND
TRUMPETS
Dungate Manor
Heathfield Farm
Skimmington Castle PH
Wonham Mill
Sandhills
Wonham Hill
Dungate's Farm
Kemp's Farm
Glebe House
Petty's Farm
The Sloughs
Dowde's Farm
Underhill Farm
BRIGHTON ROAD
A217
GRUB WOOD
Windmill Court
BEECHEN COPSE
Clubhouse
MERE POND
Ebbisham Farm
Walton Manor
CHEQUERS LANE
B2220
DORKING ROAD
B2032

184
DA
DB
DC
DD
DE
DF
DG
26
27
28
174
183
125
126
127
128
129
130
131
132
133
134
54
53
52
51
Clubhouse
Well House PH
Wellfield Shaw
Top Shaw
Reeves Rest
Manor Park
South Lodge
Hedgel Shaw
Beechen Copse
Sports Grd
Millfield Wood
Mugswell
Southerns Farm
Long Wood
Little Wood
Park Farm
Upper Gatton Wood
Boars Green Shaw
Boars Green Farm
Windmill Court
Holly Lodge Mobile Home Park
Furzefield Copse
CR5
Grub Wood
Gatwick Wood
Colts Bushes
Upper Gatton Park
Dell Wood
Furzefield Shaw
Home Field Farm
Highways Livery Stables
Ashtead Hill
Lower Kingswood
Orchard Cottage Riding Stables
Jubilee Plantations
Park Shaw
Rec Grd
Kingswood Grange
Kingswood Manor
KT20
The Crossways
Majority Plantation
Crossways Farm
Manships Shaw
Kingswood Hill
Glebe Shaw
Gatton Field Shaw
Catsbrain East
Gatton Bottom
Gatton
Reigate Golf Course
Whitehall Farm
Clubhouse
Grove Shaw
The Mint Arms PH
Gatlands Shaw
Tower Wood
High Beeches
M25
Catsbrain Shaw
Sec Sch
Covered Reservoir
Margery Hall Stud
Margery
Margery Farm
Margery Wood NT
Gatton Park
Tennis Courts
Junction 8
Halfmoon Clump
Hop Garden Pond
Engine Pond
Reigate Hill
Two Acre Wood
Blackhorse Wood
Great Buck Wood
The Burpit
RH2
Sports Ground
The Lake
Margery Hall
Mast
Wingate Hill
Serpentine Wood
Water Tower
Kingswood Hall
Colley Hill
Queen's Park
Four Acre Upper Woods
Rock Farm
Greenclump Hill
Temple Wood
The Beeches
Reigate Hill NT
Nutwood NT
Stables
Coles Meads
East Surrey Coll
Broadleas
Yew Tree PH
Colley Copse
Coll Wood
Sports Ground
Wray Common
Squash Club
Club
Cricket Ground
Comm Cen
Fire Brigade Headquarters
Fire Sta
Prim Sch
Bowls Club
TA Centre
Sports Cen
Johnston House
Allot
Works
Surgery
Superstore
Sec Sch
Castle Keep
Site of Reigate Castle
Town Hall
Cricket Ground
Sports Ground
Reigate Cemetery
Reigate Pol H.Q.
Art Coll
County Ct
Station Rd
Queensway
Belfry Shop Cen
Redhill
Sports Ground
Bus Garage
Site of Priory
Old Reigatians R.F.C.
Priory Pond
Reigate
Redhill Common
The Garibaldi PH
Redstone Manor
Airshaft
Brighton Road
A217
Reigate Road
A25
A23
A242
B2034
Gatton Road
Croydon Road
London Road
High Street
Church Street
Bell Street
Blackborough Road
Rectory Road
Babylon Lane
Chipstead Lane
Mint Lane
Wray Park Road
Doods Road
Hatchlands Road
Park Road
Redstone Hill

185
175
186
CR3
RH1
South Merstham
Warwick Wold
Nutfield
BLETCHINGLEY
Holmethorpe
Junction 8 (M23), Junction 7 (M25)
M23
M25
A23
A25
SPARTICLES WOOD
ALDERSTEAD HEATH
FURZEFIELD WOOD
FRYERN BROOM WOOD
Rook Hill
WILLEY BROOM WOOD
SIX BROTHERS FIELD
RIDGEBUSHES WOOD
THE SHRUBBERY
COVERED RESERVOIR
Mersham Tunnel
Airshafts
Ockley Hill
OCKLEY WOOD
BEDLAMS BANK
HERONSWOOD MERE
WITHY SHAW
GATTON PARK
THE GROVE
PENDELL WOOD
GRUBS WOOD
SPRING BOTTOM
QUARRY WOOD
ROCKY SHAW
BLACK BUSHES
White Hill
SAND PIT
SEWAGE WORKS
MERCERS PARK COUNTRY PARK
SAND & SILICON WORKS
QUARRYSIDE BUSINESS PARK
COCKLEY PLANTATION
SAND AND GRAVEL PIT
PUBLIC TIP
PARK WOOD
NUTFIELD CEMETERY
NORTH PARK
SPORTS GRD
NUTFIELD PRIORY LAKE
COOMBES COPPICE
STANLEY'S WOOD
Castle Hill
STENERS HILL
Stockers Hill
Furze Hill
FOX HOLE
REDSTONE CEMETERY

186
DQ
DR
DS
DT
DU
DV
DW
176
185
CR3
RH1
MARIE CURIE CENTRE
THE NORTH DOWNS HOSP
Tyler's Green
Godstone
BLETCHINGLEY
BLETCHINGLEY GOLF COURSE
CATERHAM BYPASS
GODSTONE HILL
OXTED ROAD
BLETCHINGLEY ROAD
HIGH STREET
GODSTONE
M25
M23
A25
A22
SPORTS GRD
QUEEN'S PARK
RUGBY GROUND
OLDPARK SHAW
TEN ACRE SHAW
TUPWOOD SCRUBS
FOSTERDOWN WOOD
Fosterdown Fort
Gravelly Hill
GRUBS WOOD
White Hill
QUARRY HANGERS
SPRING BOTTOM
QUARRY WOOD
ROCKY SHAW
BLACK BUSHES
CONDUIT SHAW
KITCHEN COPSE
PENDELL WOOD
RIDGEBUSHES WOOD
WILLEY BROOM WOOD
FRYERN BROOM WOOD
EIGHT ACRE WOOD
ELM PLATT
SAND PIT
COCKLEY PLANTATION
COOMBES COPPICE
STANLEY'S WOOD
HARLINGS SHAW
GRAVELHILL WOOD
TILBURSTOWHILL PLANTATION
ELEVEN ACRE SHAW
CROOKEDFIELD SHAW
Tilburstow Hill
KENNEL SHAW
DIALBANK WOOD
125
126
127
128
129
130
131
132
133
134
33
34
35
50
51
52
53
54

DX
DY
DZ
EA
EB
EC
ED
36
37
38
177
125
126
127
128
129
130
131
132
133
134
188
54
53
52
51
ROOKERY SHAW
TEMPLEHILL PLANTATION
GREAT CHURCH WOOD NATURE RESERVE
NORTH DOWNS GOLF COURSE
LITTLE CHURCH WOOD
WHISTLERS WOOD
HELL SHAW
TITSEY PLANTATION
MARDEN PARK
STUBBS COPSE
CHALK PITS
OXTED QUARRY
CHALK PIT
BEECH PLANTATION NT
OXTED DOWNS NT
SPORTS GROUND
THE RUMPS
WHITFIELD PLANTATION
HAZEL SHAW
SOUTH HAWKE
HORSE SHAW
HANGING WOOD
RYE SHAW
LODGE WOOD
ARMITAGE WOOD
HAMFIELD SHAW
FIVE ACRE SHAW
CHALKPIT WOOD
OXTED & LIMPSFIELD HOSP
RYE WOOD
ROBINS GROVE WOOD
THE ABBEYS
THE BOGS
MASTER PARK
OXTED
THE MOUNT
PALMERS WOOD OILFIELD
FLOWER WOOD
SAND PIT
BUSHEY CROFT REC GRD
TANDRIDGE GOLF COURSE
MOORE'S SHAW
GLEBE WATER
THE BIRCHES
Beechwood Hill
NEW BUSTONS WOOD
BUSTONS WOOD
BROADHAM GREEN
RH8
OLDPARK WOOD
CASTLEHILL WOOD
ROUND WOOD
STONEPIT SHAW
MAIZENHALL SHAW
Tandridge
REDDINGS WOOD
DEAN SHAW
SOUTHLANDS SHAWS
HOPGARDEN WOOD
SOUTHLANDS WOOD
STOW COPPICE
M25
A22
A25
B2236
GODSTONE ROAD
OXTED ROAD
GODSTONE BYPASS
EASTBOURNE ROAD
TANDRIDGE LANE
TANDRIDGE HILL LANE
BARROW GREEN ROAD
GANGERS HILL
HOGTROUGH LANE
CHALKPIT LANE
GORDONS WAY
JACKASS LANE
SOUTHLANDS LANE
BROADHAM GREEN ROAD
TANHOUSE ROAD
SPRING LANE
POPES LANE
BROOK LANE
FLOWER LANE
CHURCH LANE
LEIGH PLACE LANE
THE RIDGE
Clubhouse
Airshaft
Works
Tandridge Hill Farm
Barrow Green Court
Barrow Green Farm
Blunt House
Tandridge Priory
Riding Centre
Knights Garden Centre
Round Lodge
Little Court Farm
Tandridge Court
Tandridge Court Farm
Tandridge Hall Farm
Barley Mow PH
Prim Sch
Tandridge Hall
Sewage Works
Filter Beds
Leigh Mill House
Leigh Place
The Glebe House
Chaldens Farm
Flint Hall Farm
Whistlers Court
Flint House
Masts
Southlands
Southlands Lodge
Perrysfield Farm
Perrysfield
Stockett's Manor
Rose Farm
Newhouse Farm
Oxted Place
Haycutter PH
Health Centre
Stonehall Farm
Stonehamme
Mill Barn
Coll
Superstore
Swim Pool
Gas Holder
Sch
Prim Schs
Tennis Courts

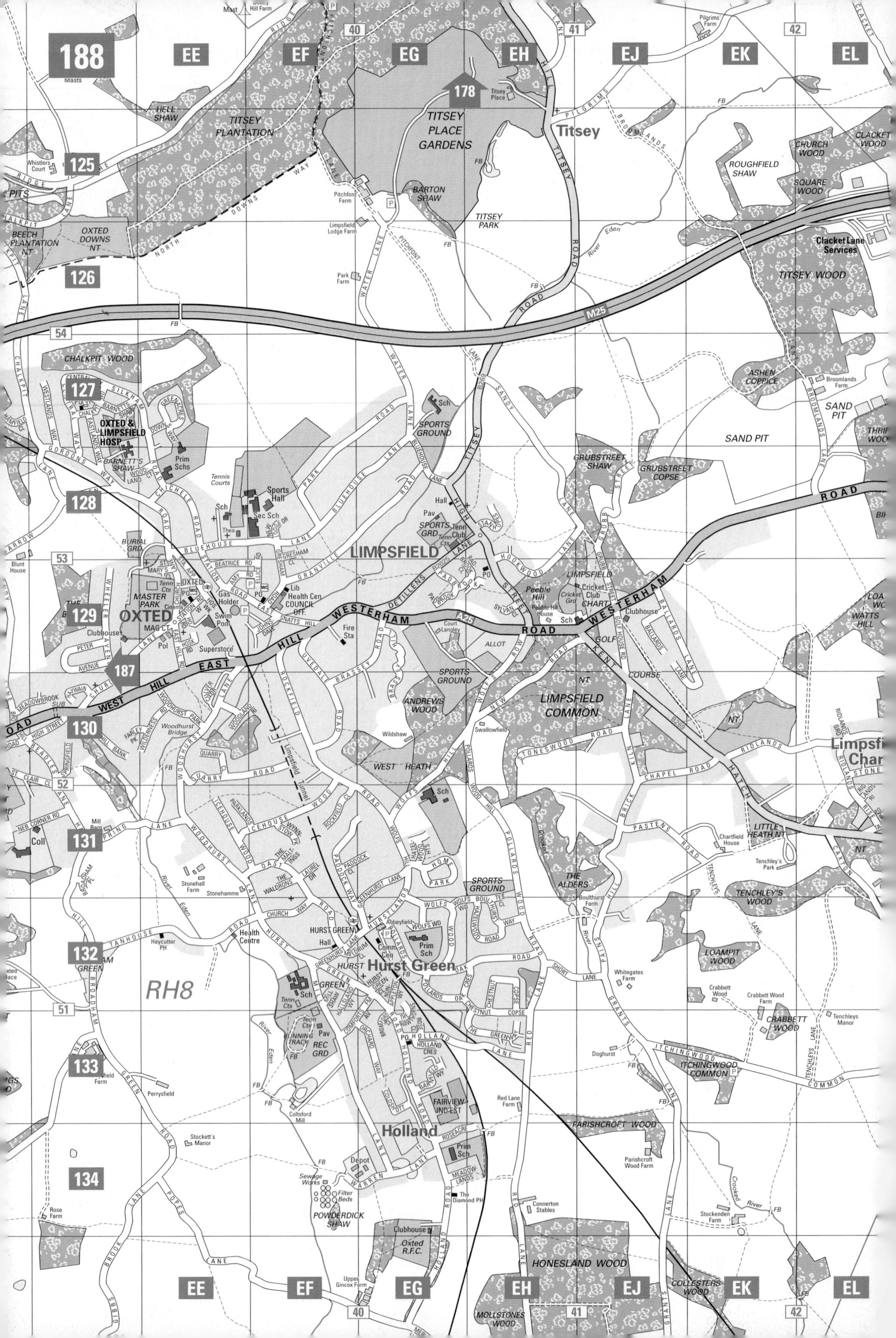

EM
EN
EP
EQ
ER
ES
ET
43
44
45
179
M25
A233
A25
B2024
B2026
B269
Gaysham
Force
HARTLEY WOOD
WESTERHAM WOOD
Charmans Farm
Park Farm
River Darent
Horizons Centre
Works
Mountwood
Fountain Cottages
Clubhouse
Pav
Cricket Grd
Sch
PONDS
WESTERHAM GOLF COURSE
125
126
127
128
129
130
131
132
133
134
54
53
52
51
CLACKET GREEN
ROWTYE WOOD
WET WOOD
DEVIL OF KENT
SAND PIT
Green Croft Farm
WESTERHAM
Prim Sch
ALLOT
Offices
KING GEORGE'S FIELD
Bowl Club
Lib
BURIAL GRD
THE GREEN
Statues
QUEBEC HOUSE
MKT. SQ
VICARAGE HILL
QU. SQ
BRASTED ROAD
WESTERHAM ROAD
LONDON ROAD
CROYDON ROAD
BEGGARS LANE
Dunsdale Farm House
The Granary
Dunsdale House
Dunsdale Wood Farm
DUNSDALE WOOD
FARLEY COMMON
Farley Grange
RANDOLPH'S LA
Westwood Farm
Works
Covers Farm
Cross Dyke
KENT
SURREY
HIGH STREET
WESTERHAM ROAD
The Grasshopper PH
Moorhouse Farm
MOORHOUSE BANK
Moor House
MOORHOUSE BANK COMMON NT
SPORTS GRD
Athletic Club
CRONKLANDS
LODGES WOOD
SQUERRYES COURT
Squerryes Home Farm
Cenotaph
SQUERRYES PARK
SPRING SHAW
Glebe House
Hosey Hill
TN16
Gillhams Farm
Piper's Farm
MANNING'S WOOD
PIPERS GREEN
STANHILL WOOD
Valance End
FRENCH STREET
BURIAL GRD
HOSEY COMMON
TOWER WOOD
Tower
French Street Farm
French Street House
THE HIGH CHART
Goodley Stock
GOODLEY STOCK ROAD
NT
Cobb Cottage
Moorcroft Place
Crockham House
MAPLETON ROAD
HOSEY COMMON ROAD
Kent Hatch
THE CHART
LONG WALK
French Street Nursery
KENT HATCH ROAD
SCEARN BANK
NT
COV RES
Kent Hatch House
CROCKHAMHILL COMMON
Chartwell NT
Chartwell House
Marie Curie Research Institute
The Warren
Hopland
Chartwell Farm
BUDDLES WOOD
BROWN'S OVEN WOOD
ROUNDMEAD SHAW
TREVEREUX HILL
Trevereux
The Red House
Crockham Hill Farm
Froghole Farm
FROGHOLE LANE
Mariners
Froghole
Little Court
GUDGE WOOD
COV RES
PUDDLEDOCK LANE
TANDRIDGE
SEVENOAKS
Kent Brook
FB
OAKDALE LA
SMITHS LANE
Prim Sch
PO
Hall
Woodmote
Coachmans
CHANDLER WOOD
DERBY WOOD
TIES WOOD
SWAYNESLAND ROAD
Swaynesland
Crockham Hill
TN8
DEANERY RD
MAIN ROAD
SPOUT LANE
DAIRY LANE
Hurst Farm
Old Dairy Farm
Pav
SPORTS GRD
Tenn Cts
DENNETTSLAND ROAD
POOTINGS ROAD
Dennett Lodge Farm
Grange Farm
PERRY WOOD
PRIORY WOOD
ROW WOOD
LONGCROFT WOOD
HATCROFT WOOD
Redland Farm
GUILDABLES WOOD
Kent Brook

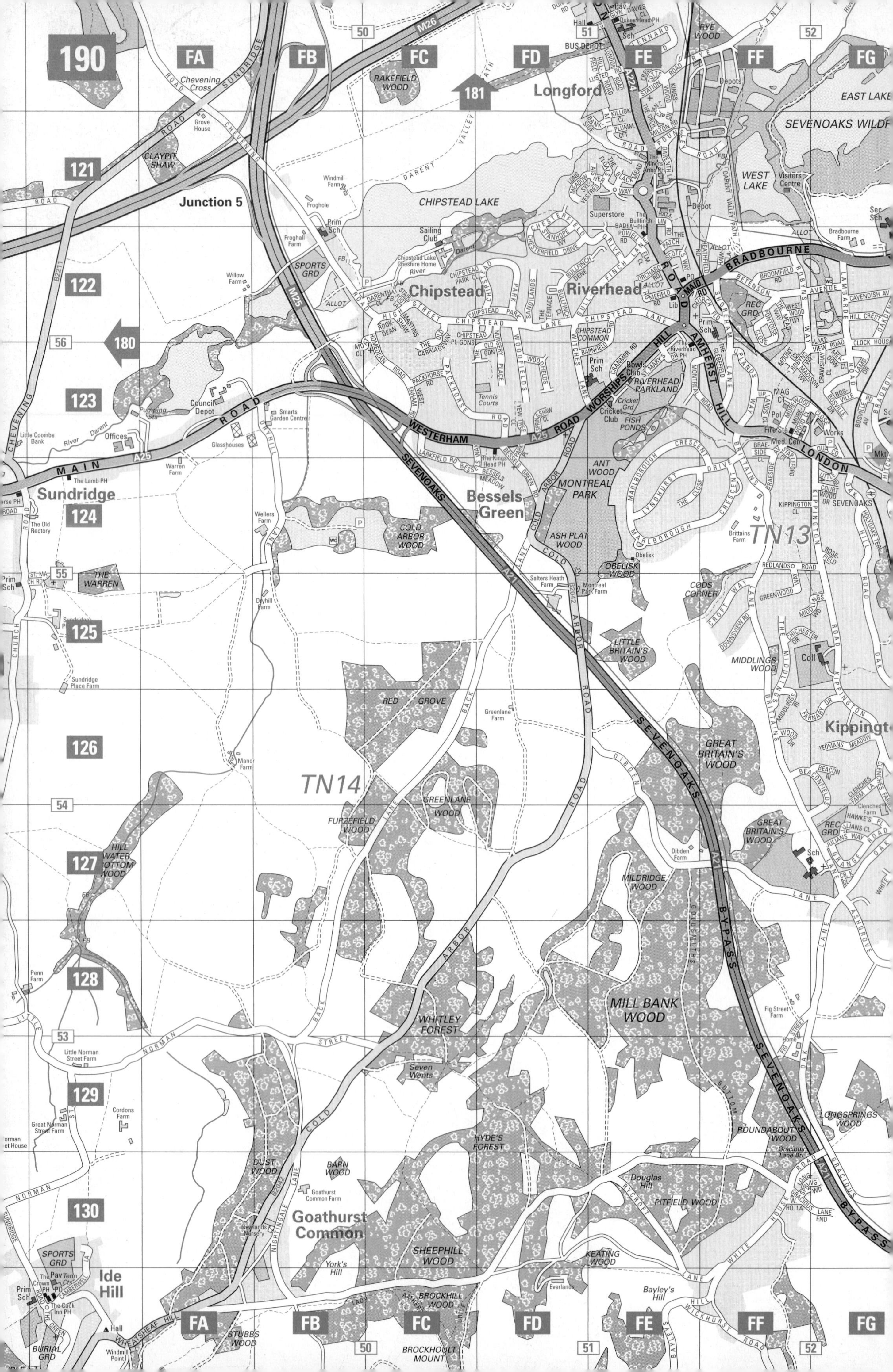
FA
FB
FC
FD
FE
FF
FG
Longford
Chipstead
Riverhead
Sundridge
Bessels Green
Kippingt
TN13
TN14
Goathurst Common
Ide Hill
Junction 5
CHIPSTEAD LAKE
SEVENOAKS WILDF
EAST LAKE
WEST LAKE
MONTREAL PARK
RIVERHEAD PARKLAND
MILL BANK WOOD
WHITLEY FOREST
HYDE'S FOREST
GREAT BRITAIN'S WOOD
SHEEPHILL WOOD
PITFIELD WOOD
181
180
121
122
123
124
125
126
127
128
129
130
50
51
52
53
54
55
56

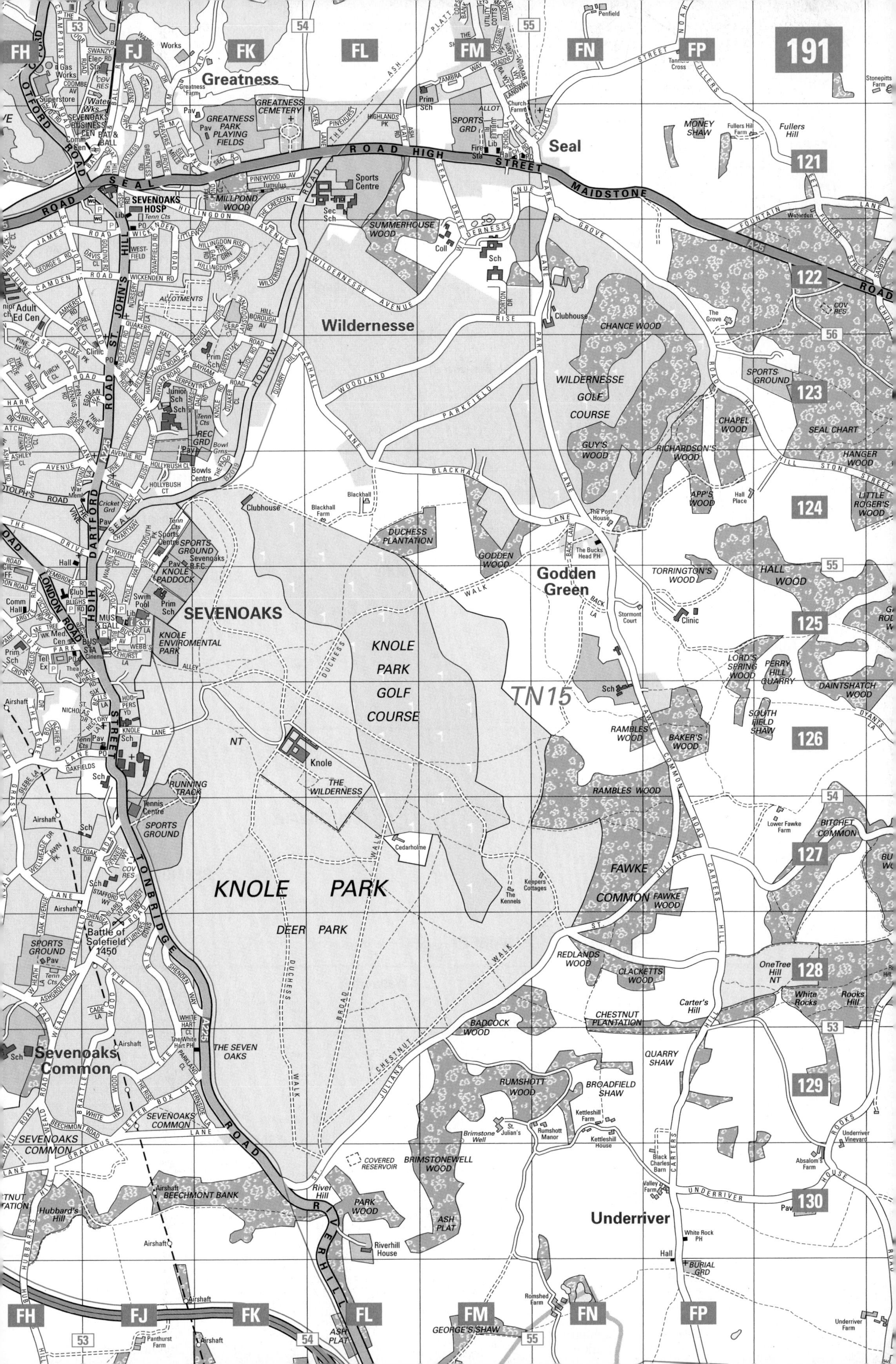
Greatness
Seal
Wildernesse
SEVENOAKS
Godden Green
KNOLE PARK
DEER PARK
KNOLE PARK GOLF COURSE
WILDERNESSE GOLF COURSE
TN15
Sevenoaks Common
SEVENOAKS COMMON
Underriver
FAWKE COMMON
SEAL CHART
Knole
Riverhill House
River Hill
Battle of Solefield 1450
SEAL ROAD
HIGH STREET
MAIDSTONE ROAD
LONDON ROAD
DARTFORD ROAD
ST. JOHN'S HILL
TONBRIDGE ROAD
RIVERHILL
OTFORD ROAD
SEVENOAKS HOSP
FH
FJ
FK
FL
FM
FN
FP
53
54
55
56
121
122
123
124
125
126
127
128
129
130

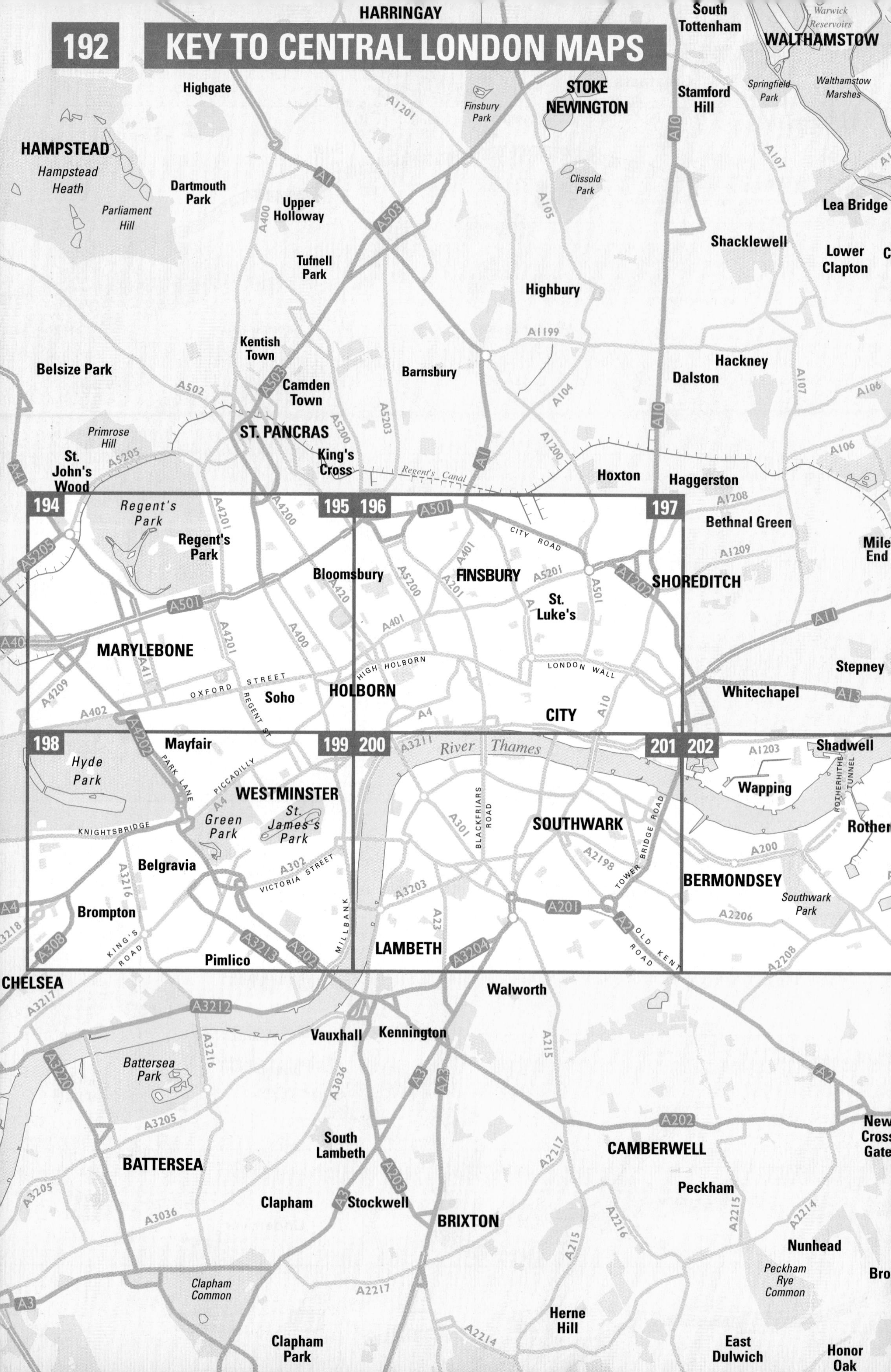

HARRINGAY

South Tottenham

WALTHAMSTOW

Warwick Reservoirs

Highgate

Finsbury Park

STOKE NEWINGTON

Stamford Hill

Springfield Park

Walthamstow Marshes

HAMPSTEAD

Hampstead Heath

Parliament Hill

Dartmouth Park

Upper Holloway

Clissold Park

Lea Bridge

Shacklewell

Lower Clapton

Tufnell Park

Highbury

Belsize Park

Kentish Town

Barnsbury

Hackney

Dalston

Camden Town

Primrose Hill

St. John's Wood

ST. PANCRAS

King's Cross

Regent's Canal

Hoxton

Haggerston

Bethnal Green

Mile End

194
Regent's Park

195   196
Bloomsbury

FINSBURY

197
SHOREDITCH

St. Luke's

MARYLEBONE

OXFORD STREET

Soho

HIGH HOLBORN

HOLBORN

LONDON WALL

CITY

Stepney

Whitechapel

198
Hyde Park

Mayfair

199   200
River Thames

WESTMINSTER

St. James's Park

201   202
Wapping

Shadwell

Green Park

KNIGHTSBRIDGE

SOUTHWARK

Rother

Belgravia

VICTORIA STREET

Brompton

KING'S ROAD

Pimlico

LAMBETH

BERMONDSEY

Southwark Park

OLD KENT ROAD

CHELSEA

Walworth

Vauxhall

Kennington

Battersea Park

South Lambeth

CAMBERWELL

New Cross Gate

BATTERSEA

Peckham

Clapham

Stockwell

BRIXTON

Nunhead

Clapham Common

Peckham Rye Common

Bro

Clapham Park

Herne Hill

East Dulwich

Honor Oak

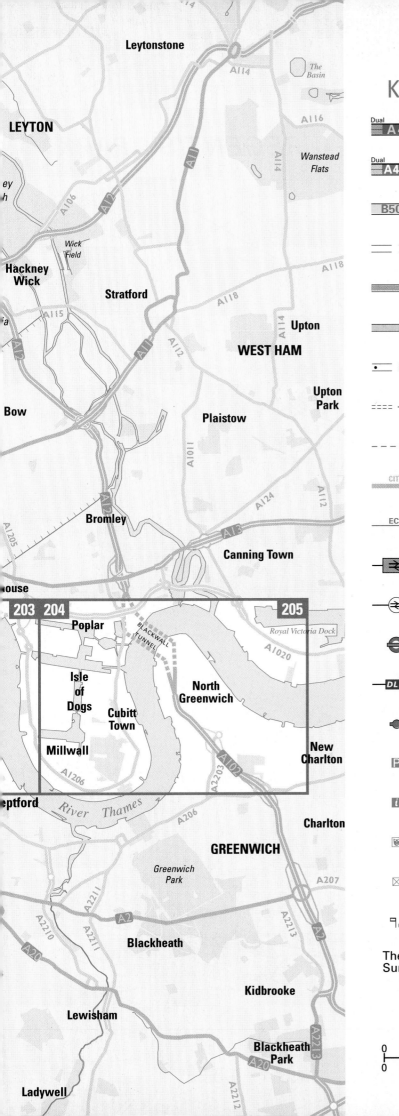

KEY TO CENTRAL MAP SYMBOLS

Dual A4	Primary route	Leisure & tourism
Dual A40	'A' road	Shopping
B504	'B' road	Administration & law
→	Other road/ One way street	Health & welfare
	Street market	Education
	Pedestrian street	Industry & commerce
•—	Access restriction	Public open space
==== ----	Track/Footpath	Park/Garden/Sports ground
- - - - -	Ferry	Cemetery
CITY	Borough boundary	POL Police station
EC2	Postal district boundary	Fire Sta Fire station
⊕	Main railway station	PO Post Office
⊕	Other railway station	Lib Library
🚇	London Underground station	▲ Monument/Statue
DLR	Docklands Light Railway station	🎥 Cinema
	Bus/Coach station	+ Church
P	Car park	☾ Mosque
i	Tourist information centre	✡ Synagogue
☖	Theatre	■ Other place of worship Mormon
⊠	Hotel	WC Public toilet
⌐ USA	Embassy	□ Tower block

The reference grid on this atlas coincides with the Ordnance Survey National Grid System. The grid interval is 250 metres.

◄195 Page Continuation Number   **10** Grid Reference

SCALE

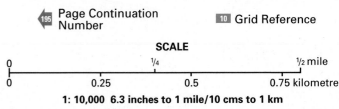

1: 10,000 6.3 inches to 1 mile/10 cms to 1 km

194
82
198
A
B
C
D
E
F
G
1
2
3
4
5
6
7
8
9
10
REGENT'S PARK
ST. JOHN'S WOOD
NW8
LORD'S CRICKET GROUND
M.C.C. MUSEUM
LORD'S TAVERN
LISSON GROVE
MARYLEBONE
W1
W2
PADDINGTON
PADDINGTON GREEN
LILESTONE ESTATE
CHURCH STREET ESTATE
LISSON GREEN ESTATE
TOWNSHEND ESTATE
BOATING LAKE
QUEEN MARY'S GARDENS
OPEN AIR THEATRE
THE HOLME
Bandstand
LONDON BUSINESS SCH
REGENT'S COLLEGE
Clarence Gate
London Central Mosque
WINFIELD HOUSE
HOSP OF ST. JOHN & ST. ELIZABETH
WELLINGTON HOSP N
WELLINGTON HOSP S
CONVENT OF MERCY
MADAME TUSSAUD'S
PLANETARIUM
BAKER STREET
MARYLEBONE
EDGWARE ROAD
MARBLE ARCH
LANCASTER GATE
Speaker's Corner
WALLACE COLLECTION
SELFRIDGES
ST. MARY'S HOSP
Paddington Basin
Royal Lancaster
Hilton
Marlborough Gate
Victoria Gate
The Fountains
BROOK GATE
WELLINGTON ROAD
PRINCE ALBERT ROAD
PARK ROAD
ST. JOHN'S WOOD ROAD
LISSON GROVE
EDGWARE ROAD
MARYLEBONE ROAD
GLOUCESTER PLACE
BAKER ST
OXFORD STREET
BAYSWATER ROAD
SUSSEX GARDENS
PRAED ST
SEYMOUR ST
PARK LANE
OUTER CIRCLE
INNER CIRCLE
THE (NORTH CARRIAGE DRIVE) RING
OXFORD ST where marked is closed to through traffic (except buses & taxis) from 7a.m. - 7p.m. Monday - Saturday

197
H
J
K
L
M
N
P
84
HOXTON
N1
ST. LUKE'S
SHOREDITCH
EC2
BROADGATE
BARBICAN
EC3
CITY
1
2
3
4
5
6
7
8
9
10
201
SHOREDITCH PARK
HOXTON STREET
KINGSLAND RD
HACKNEY RD
COLUMBIA RD
NEW NORTH RD
EAST RD
CITY RD
OLD STREET
SHEPHERDESS WALK
PROVOST ESTATE
PITFIELD ESTATE
ARDEN ESTATE
CRANSTON ESTATE
GEFFRYE MUSEUM
HACKNEY COMM COLL
MOORFIELDS EYE HOSP
ST. LUKE'S ESTATE
BUNHILL FIELDS
BUNHILL FIELDS BURIAL GRD
THE HON. ARTILLERY COMPANY
WESLEY'S HOUSE
GREAT EASTERN STREET
SHOREDITCH HIGH STREET
COMMERCIAL STREET
BETHNAL GREEN TECH. COLL
ARNOLD CIRCUS
OLD SPITALFIELDS MARKET
LIVERPOOL STREET
MOORGATE
FINSBURY SQ.
FINSBURY CIRCUS
LONDON WALL
CHISWELL STREET
BISHOPSGATE
HOUNDSDITCH
MIDDLESEX STREET
WHITECHAPEL HIGH ST
ALDGATE
ALDGATE HIGH ST
MINORIES
LEMAN STREET
MANSELL ST
FENCHURCH
LEADENHALL
CORNHILL
BANK
Bank of England
Royal Ex (LIFFE)
Stock Exch
ST. PAUL'S CATHEDRAL
CHEAPSIDE
MANSION HOUSE
CANNON
MONUMENT
GRACECHURCH ST
EASTCHEAP
GREAT TOWER ST
LOWER THAMES ST
TOWER HILL
TOWER GATEWAY
TOWER OF LONDON
ROYAL MINT
Southwark Bridge Steps
SHAKESPEARE'S GLOBE THEATRE
Swan Lane Pier
Site of Billingsgate Old Mkt
London Commodity Ex
A501
A5201
A1200
A10
A1208
A1202
A1210
A1211
B144
B101
B100
B134
A3

198
194
W2
82
100
HYDE PARK
KENSINGTON GARDENS
OXFORD STREET where marked is closed to through traffic (except buses & taxis) from 7a.m. - 7p.m. Monday - Saturday
BAYSWATER ROAD
THE (NORTH CARRIAGE DRIVE) RING
THE (WEST CARRIAGE DRIVE) RING
PARK LANE
A4202
A402
LANCASTER GATE
Marlborough Gate
Victoria Gate
Royal Lancaster
The Fountains
Speke's Monument
Peter Pan
THE LONG WATER
Bird Sanctuary
THE SERPENTINE
The Lido
Pier
Clubhouse
SERPENTINE ROAD
SERPENTINE GALLERY
ROTTEN ROW
PUTTING GREEN
Albert Memorial
Coalbrookdale Gate
Alexandra Gate
Prince of Wales Gate
Rutland Gate
Edinburgh Gate
Albert Gate
SOUTH CARRIAGE DRIVE
HYDE PARK CORNER
HYDE PARK BARRACKS
BROOK GATE
GROSVENOR GATE
Centre Fountain
STANHOPE GATE
CURZON GATE
ACHILLES WAY
Achilles Statue
Bandstand
War Memorial
Queen Elizabeth Gate
APSLEY HOUSE WELLINGTON MUS
Marble Arch
Speakers' Corner
CUMBERLAND GATE
The Dorchester
KENSINGTON RD
A315
KNIGHTSBRIDGE
A4
SW7
IMPERIAL COLL
ROYAL COLL OF MUSIC
ALBERT HALL
SCIENCE MUSEUM
NATURAL HISTORY MUSEUM
EARTH GALLERIES
VICTORIA & ALBERT MUSEUM
BROMPTON
Brompton Oratory
Holy Trinity
CROMWELL ROAD
SOUTH KENSINGTON
THURLOE PL
PELHAM STREET
HARRODS
BROMPTON ROAD
SLOANE STREET
A3216
BELGRAVE SQUARE
BELGRAVIA
B310
B319
PONT STREET
CADOGAN PLACE
SW3
KING'S ROAD
SLOANE SQ
FULHAM ROAD
A308
A3218
B304
ROYAL MARSDEN HOSP
ROYAL BROMPTON HOSP
SAMUEL LEWIS TRUST DWELLINGS
SUTTON EST
GUINNESS TRUST BLDGS
DUKE OF YORK'S HEADQUARTERS
PETER JONES
LOWER SLOANE ST
PIMLICO RD
A3214
CHELSEA BARRACKS
CHELSEA BRIDGE RD
BURTON'S
B302
A3217
EATON SQUARE
INCHBALD SCH OF DESIGN
Francis Holland Sch
CHELSEA COLL OF ART & DESIGN
KING'S COLL
RANELAGH GARDENS
A B C D E F G
1 2 3 4 5 6 7 8 9 10

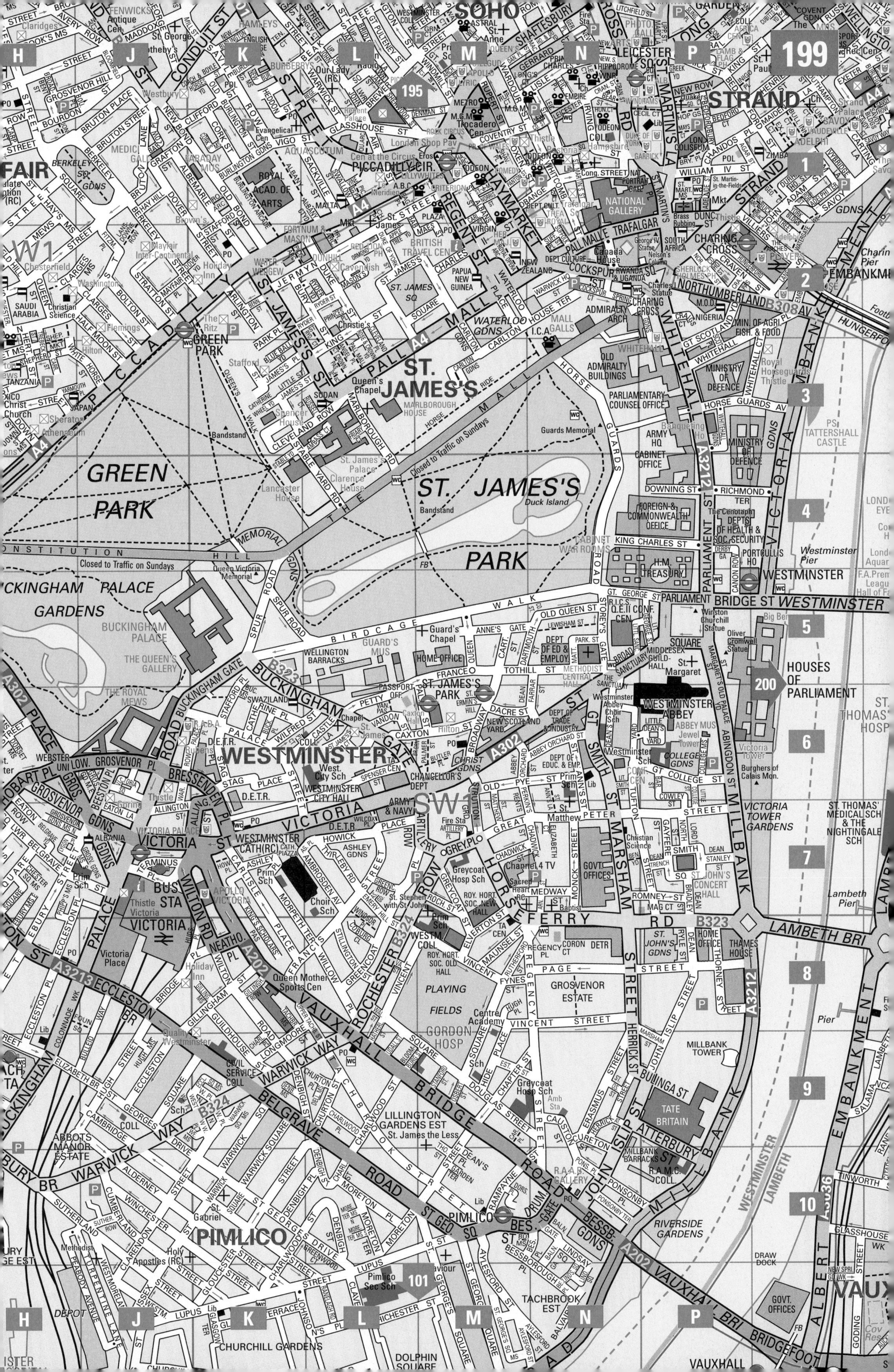
SOHO
STRAND
MAYFAIR
W1
PICCADILLY CIR.
PICCADILLY
ROYAL ACAD. OF ARTS
NATIONAL GALLERY
TRAFALGAR SQ
CHARING CROSS
EMBANKMENT
HUNGERFORD
ST. JAMES'S
ST. JAMES'S PARK
GREEN PARK
CONSTITUTION HILL
BUCKINGHAM PALACE GARDENS
BUCKINGHAM PALACE
THE QUEEN'S GALLERY
THE ROYAL MEWS
THE MALL
PALL MALL
HORSE GUARDS PARADE
WHITEHALL
MINISTRY OF DEFENCE
DOWNING ST
FOREIGN & COMMONWEALTH OFFICE
H.M. TREASURY
PARLIAMENT ST
WESTMINSTER
BRIDGE ST
BIRDCAGE WALK
WELLINGTON BARRACKS
GUARD'S MUS
HOME OFFICE
WESTMINSTER ABBEY
HOUSES OF PARLIAMENT
VICTORIA TOWER GARDENS
WESTMINSTER
SW1
VICTORIA ST
WESTMINSTER CATH (RC)
VICTORIA
VICTORIA PALACE
BUS STA
VAUXHALL BRIDGE ROAD
HORSEFERRY RD
LAMBETH BRI
MILLBANK
MILLBANK TOWER
TATE BRITAIN
GROSVENOR ESTATE
PLAYING FIELDS
LILLINGTON GARDENS EST
BELGRAVE ROAD
WARWICK WAY
PIMLICO
CHURCHILL GARDENS
TACHBROOK EST
RIVERSIDE GARDENS
VAUXHALL BRI
ST. THOMAS' HOSP
ALBERT EMBANKMENT
VICTORIA EMBANKMENT
195
200
101
H
J
K
L
M
N
P
1
2
3
4
5
6
7
8
9
10

200
A
B
C
D
E
F
G
1
2
3
4
5
6
7
8
9
10
STRAND
196
199
101
VICTORIA EMBANKMENT
RIVER THAMES
WESTMINSTER
LAMBETH
SOUTHWARK
KING'S REACH
BLACKFRIARS
BLACKFRIARS BRI
H.M.S. PRESIDENT
H.Q.S. WELLINGTON Master Mariners'
EMBANKMENT
CHARING CROSS
TRAFALGAR
WHITEHALL
HUNGERFORD BRIDGE
WATERLOO BRI
SOMERSET HOUSE
KING'S COLL UNI OF LON
ROYAL FESTIVAL HALL
QUEEN ELIZABETH HALL & PURCELL ROOM
HAYWARD GALLERY
ROYAL NATIONAL
NAT FILM THEA
The London Television Centre
STAMFORD STREET
UPPER GROUND
LONDON NAUTICAL SCH
PEABODY ESTATE
IMAX
WATERLOO EAST
WATERLOO
WATERLOO INTERNATIONAL
LONDON EYE
County Hall
London Aquarium
JUBILEE GDNS
Shell Centre
MINISTRY OF DEFENCE
DOWNING ST
H.M. TREASURY
WESTMINSTER BRI
WESTMINSTER ABBEY
HOUSES OF PARLIAMENT
Big Ben
VICTORIA TOWER GARDENS
ST. THOMAS' HOSP
LAMBETH PALACE GDNS
ARCHBISHOP'S PARK
LAMBETH
LAMBETH BRI
MILLBANK
MILLBANK TOWER
TATE BRITAIN
THAMES HOUSE
RIVERSIDE GARDENS
YORK ROAD
WESTMINSTER BRIDGE ROAD
LAMBETH NORTH
BAYLIS ROAD
THE CUT
THE YOUNG VIC
THE OLD VIC
SOUTHWARK UNION
NELSON SQUARE
ST. GEORGE'S CIRCUS
BOROUGH
ST. GEORGE'S ROAD
GERALDINE MARY HARMSWORTH PARK
IMPERIAL WAR MUS
KENNINGTON ROAD
KENNINGTON LANE
KENNINGTON PARK ROAD
KENNINGTON
NEWINGTON BUTTS
LAMBETH WALK
LAMBETH HIGH ST
BLACK PRINCE ROAD
SE11
VAUXHALL
VAUXHALL BRI
ALBERT EMBANKMENT
Lilian Baylis Sec Sch
COUNTY COURT
CITY & GUILDS LONDON ART SCH
SOUTHWARK COLL
ALBERTA EST
A3200
A301
A302
A3203
A3036
A3204
A23
A201
A3212
A3211
A202
A3
B323
B308

201
197
202
102
H
J
K
L
M
N
P
1
2
3
4
5
6
7
8
9
10
CITY
CANNON ST
MONUMENT
FENCHURCH ST
TOWER HILL
TOWER OF LONDON
Tower Pier
London Bridge City Pier
H.M.S. BELFAST
St. Katharine's Pier
Alderman Stairs
TOWER BRIDGE
TOWER BRIDGE ROAD
TOWER BRIDGE APP
TOWER BRIDGE EXPERIENCE
BUTLER'S WHARF
George's Stairs
DESIGN MUSEUM
TOWER HAMLETS
SOUTHWARK
CITY
LOWER THAMES ST
UPPER THAMES ST
Swan Lane Pier
Southwark Bridge Steps
Bankside Jetty
SHAKESPEARE'S GLOBE THEATRE
Financial Times
CLINK PRISON MUS
Glaziers Hall
LONDON BRIDGE HOSPITAL
SOUTHWARK CATHEDRAL
Hay's Galleria
SOUTHWARK CROWN COURT
GLA HEADQUARTERS (Under Construction)
WILLIAM CURTIS ECOLOGICAL PARK
LAMBETH COLL
LONDON BRIDGE
BRITAIN AT WAR
LONDON DUNGEON
OPERATING THEA MUS
GEORGE INN PH
GUY'S HOSP
TOOLEY ST
DUKE ST HILL
BOROUGH HIGH ST
SOUTHWARK BRIDGE ROAD
SOUTHWARK ST
UNION ST
MARSHALSEA RD
BOROUGH
THE BOROUGH
St. George the Martyr
LONG LANE
GREAT DOVER STREET
BERMONDSEY STREET
ST. THOMAS STREET
LEATHERMARKET GARDENS
Leather Mkt
TABARD GARDENS
SE1
ABBEY STREET
JAMAICA RD
DRUID ST
QUEEN ELIZABETH STREET
BERMONDSEY
Town Hall
BERMONDSEY SPA
GRANGE ROAD
GRANGE WALK
TOWER BRIDGE ROAD
OLD KENT ROAD
NEW KENT ROAD
ELEPHANT & CASTLE
NEWINGTON
WALWORTH
WALWORTH ROAD
SE17
SURREY SQUARE PARK
FARADAY GARDENS
DUNTON ROAD
ROLLS ROAD
HARPER ROAD
FALMOUTH ROAD
DEPOT
CUMING MUS
Superstore
Offices
Works

202
A
B
C
D
E
F
G
1
2
3
4
5
6
7
8
9
10
84
201
102
FENCHURCH ST
CROSSWALL
PORTSOKEN ST
PRESCOT STREET
PINCHIN STREET
SHADWELL
CABLE STREET
English Martyrs
TOWER GATEWAY
DLR
ROYAL MINT ST
DOCK ST
SHEARSMITH HO
HATTON HO
GUILDHALL UNI
TOWER HILL
MINORIES
MANSELL ST
ROYAL MINT CT
ENSIGN ST
Prim Schs
Comm Cen
Old Town Hall
B126
Clinic
Sixth Form Cen
Swim Pool
Fire Sta
Comm Cen
REDCASTLE
HIGHWAY
A1203
THE HIGHWAY
Evangelical
St. Paul
NEWLANDS QUAY
SHADWELL BASIN
SHADWELL
Chapel
TOWER OF LONDON
TOWER BRIDGE APP
EAST SMITHFIELD
London Commodity Ex
Int Ho
COMMODITY QUAY
ST. KATHARINE'S DOCK
Ivory Ho
EAST DOCK
THOMAS MORE ST
B107
E1
PENNINGTON STREET
News International
Tobacco Dock
TOBACCO QUAY
PRINCES CT
VAUGHAN WAY
NESHAM ST
ASHER WAY
KENNET STREET
Superstore
WAPPING
WAPPING LANE
RAINE ST
St. Peter
Prim Sch
Health Cen
OSWELL HO
Lib
MILK YARD
RIVERSIDE MAN.
PROSPECT PL
PROSPECT OF WHITBY PH
Pier
NEW CRANE PL
New Crane Stairs
Tower Pier
Thistle Tower
St. Katharine's Pier
Alderman Stairs
TOWER HAMLETS
SOUTHWARK
TOWER BRIDGE
ST. KATHARINE'S WAY
HERMITAGE WALL
WAPPING HIGH STREET
John Orwell (Wapping) Sports Cen
St. Patrick (RC)
WAPPING
Wapping Dock Stairs
WATERSIDE GARDENS
TOWER BRIDGE EXPERIENCE
BUTLER'S WHARF
George's Stairs
DESIGN MUSEUM
LAMBETH COLL
UPPER POOL
THE POOL
LOWER POOL
Wapping Old Stairs
Wapping New Stairs
TEA & COFFEE MUS
TOM BLAU GALL
Mill Stairs
East Lane Stairs
Fountain Stairs
Cherry Garden Pier
King's Stairs
THE ANGEL PH
Princes Stairs
MAYFLOWER PH
BRUNEL ENGINE HOUSE
St. Mary with All Saints
ROTHERHITHE
ADAMS GARDENS EST
KING'S STAIRS GARDENS
BERMONDSEY WALL WEST
BERMONDSEY WALL EAST
POMEROY PURDY GALLERY
ST. JOHN'S ESTATE
JAMAICA ROAD
A200
Most Holy Trinity (RC)
DICKENS ESTATE
St. Michael's RC Sch
MILLPOND EST
St. Peter (RC)
BRUNEL
ROTHERHITHE TUNNEL APP.
Civic Cen
CANADA ESTATE
ST. SAVIOUR'S EST
ABBEY STREET
ARNOLD EST
BERMONDSEY
KIRBY ESTATE
NEW PLACE SQUARE
St. Crispin
St. James
NECKINGER EST
BERMONDSEY
Town Hall
SPA ROAD
THE SURREY QUAYS CEN
LOCKWOOD SQUARE
SOUTHWARK PARK
SOUTHWARK
Seven Islands Leisure Cen
HOWLAND ESTATE
Free Church
LOWER ROAD
A220
BERMONDSEY SPA
VAUBAN ESTATE
EVELINE LOWE EST
Works
MARDEN SQUARE
Baptist
Lido
CAFE GALLERY
Swedish Seamen's
Aylwin Sch
Cherry Gdn Sch
Health Cen
Offices
SOUTHWARK PARK ROAD
LONGFIELD ESTATE
Spa Sch
St. Anne & St. Augustine
MANOR ESTATE
Methodist
RAYMOUTH RD
TRADING ESTATE
St. Gertrude (RC)
B203
LYNTON EST
Primary Sch
RENNIE ESTATE
SE1
PATERSON PARK
St. Augustine
ROLLS ROAD
B204
Superstore
LONGLAND COURT
St. Philip & St. Mark
Fire Sta
SOUTH BERMONDSEY
NEW ROTHERHITHE ROAD
A2208
CATLIN STREET
MAWBEY ESTATE
SIX BRIDGES TRADING EST
Bacon's Coll
Lewisham Lions Cen
OLD KENT ROAD
VERNEY ROAD
STOCKHOLM RD

LIMEHOUSE
RIVER THAMES
ROTHERHITHE
DEPTFORD
E14
SE8
LIMEHOUSE REACH
HERON QUAYS
WESTFERRY ROAD
SALTER ROAD
REDRIFF ROAD
LOWER ROAD
EVELYN STREET
PLOUGH WAY
GROVE STREET
GREENLAND DOCK
SOUTH DOCK
SURREY QUAYS
SURREY WATER
RUSSIA DOCK WOODLAND
ECOLOGICAL PARK
Stave Hill
MELLISH SPORTS GROUND
SPORTS GROUND
PEPYS PARK
DEPTFORD PARK
SIR JOHN MCDOUGAL GDNS
Daily Telegraph
MILLWALL
WEST INDIA
Surrey Quays Retail Centre
MAST LEISURE PK
CANNON WHARF BUSINESS CENTRE
Royal Naval Yd
Duke Shore Wharf
Lavender Wharf
Limehouse Hole Stairs
Sunderland Wharf
Ordnance Wharf
Lawrence Wharf
Columbia Wharf
West India Dock Pier
Express Wharf
New Atlas Wharf
Greenland Pier
South Lock
St. George's Stairs
Landing Stage
Palmer's Wharf
Payne's Wharf
Borthwick Wharf
Free Trade Wharf
Victoria Wharf
Stone Stairs
Ratcliffe Cross Stairs
TOWER HAMLETS
SOUTHWARK
LEWISHAM
H
J
K
L
M
N
P
1
2
3
4
5
6
7
8
9
10
85
103
204

POPLAR
E14
ISLE OF DOGS
CUBITT TOWN
MILLWALL
CANARY WHARF
WEST INDIA DOCKS
MILLWALL INNER DOCK
MILLWALL OUTER DOCK
POPLAR DOCK
BLACKWALL BASIN
MUDCHUTE PARK
MILLWALL PARK
ISLAND GARDENS
POPLAR HIGH STREET
ASPEN WAY
WESTFERRY ROAD
MANCHESTER ROAD
MARSH WALL
PRESTONS ROAD
EAST FERRY ROAD
LIMEHARBOUR
WEST INDIA QUAY
HERON QUAYS
SOUTH QUAY
CROSSHARBOUR & LONDON ARENA
MUDCHUTE
BLACKWALL
Billingsgate Fish Mkt
Daily Telegraph
LONDON ARENA
Superstore
Royal Naval Yd
GREENWICH REACH
BLACKWALL REACH
GREENWICH FOOT TUNNEL
85
103
203

205
EXCEL
ROYAL VICTORIA
E16
ROYAL VICTORIA DOCK
SILVERTOWN WAY
NORTH WOOLWICH ROAD
A1020
RIVER THAMES
THE DOME
SKYSCAPE
NORTH GREENWICH
COACH STA
SE10
Millennium Pier
London City Airport Pier
Thames Wharf
Phoenix Wharf
Manhattan Wharf
Blackwall Pier
Blackwall Beach
Trinity Buoy Wharf
LYLE PARK
Works
Gas Works
Superstores
Warehouses
Holiday Inn Express
GREENWICH INDUSTRIAL ESTATE
MERIDIAN TRADE ESTATE
Greenwich Yacht Club
Clubhouse
Slipway
Pontoon
Jetty
THAMES PATH
JOHN HARRISON WAY
WEST PARKSIDE
EAST PARKSIDE
MILLENNIUM WAY
BUGSBY'S WAY
PEARTREE WAY
BLACKWALL LANE
A2203
TUNNEL APPROACH
A102
WOOLWICH ROAD
A206
TUNNEL AVENUE
MAURITIUS ROAD
SALUTATION ROAD
MORDEN WHARF ROAD
EAST GREENWICH PLEASAUNCE
COUNCIL DEPOT
WESTCOMBE PARK
86
104
1
2
3
4
5
6
7
8
9
10
H
J
K
L
M
N
P

The following is a comprehensive listing of the places of interest which appear in this atlas. Bold references can be found within the Central London enlarged section (pages 194-205).

The following is a comprehensive listing of all named places which appear in this atlas. Bold references can be found within the Central London enlarged section (pages 194-205). Postal information is either London postal district or non-London post town form. For an explanation of post town abbreviations please see page 215.

Place	Page	Grid
North Beckton E6	86	EL70
North Cheam, Sutt.	139	CW104
North Cray, Sid.	126	FA90
North Finchley N12	44	DD50
North Harrow, Har.	60	CA58
North Hillingdon, Uxb.	77	BQ66
North Hyde, Sthl.	96	BY77
North Kensington W10	81	CW72
North Looe, Epsom	157	CW113
North Ockendon, Upmin.	73	FV64
North Sheen, Rich.	98	CN82
North Watford, Wat.	23	BV37
North Weald Bassett, Epp.	19	FB27
North Wembley, Wem.	61	CH61
North Woolwich E16	104	EL75
Northaw, Pot.B.	12	DF30
Northfleet, Grav.	130	GD86
Northfleet Green, Grav.	130	GC92
Northolt, Nthlt.	78	BZ66
Northumberland Heath, Erith	107	FC80
Northwood, Nthwd.	39	BR51
Northwood Hills, Nthwd.	39	BT54
Norwood SE19	122	DR93
Norwood Green, Sthl.	96	CA77
Norwood New Town SE19	122	DQ93
Notting Hill W11	81	CY73
Nunhead SE15	102	DW83
Nuper's Hatch, Rom.	51	FE45
Nutfield, Red.	185	DM133

O

Place	Page	Grid
Oakleigh Park N20	44	DD46
Oakwood N14	29	DK44
Oatlands Park, Wey.	153	BR105
Ockham, Wok.	168	BN121
Old Bexley, Bex.	127	FB87
Old Coulsdon, Couls.	175	DN119
Old Ford E3	85	DZ67
Old Malden, Wor.Pk.	138	CR102
Old Oak Common NW10	81	CT71
Old Windsor, Wind.	112	AU86
Old Woking, Wok.	167	BA121
Orchard Leigh, Chesh.	4	AV28
Orpington, Orp.	145	ES102
Orsett Heath, Grays	111	GG75
Osidge N14	45	DH46
Osterley, Islw.	96	CC80
Otford, Sev.	181	FG116
Ottershaw, Cher.	151	BC106
Oxhey, Wat.	24	BW44
Oxshott, Lthd.	155	CD113
Oxted, Oxt.	187	ED129

P

Place	Page	Grid
Pachesham Park, Lthd.	171	CG116
Paddington W2	82	DB71
Palmers Green N13	45	DM48
Park Langley, Beck.	143	EC99
Park Royal NW10	80	CN69
Park Street, St.Alb.	9	CD26
Parrock Farm, Grav.	131	GK91
Parsons Green SW6	100	DA81
Patchetts Green, Wat.	24	CC39
Pebble Coombe, Tad.	182	CS128
Peckham SE15	102	DU81
Penge SE20	122	DW94
Pentonville N1	**196**	**D1**
Perivale, Grnf.	79	CJ67
Perry Street, Grav.	130	GE88
Petersham, Rich.	118	CL88
Petts Wood, Orp.	145	ER99
Pilgrim's Hatch, Brwd.	54	FU42
Pimlico SW1	**199**	**K10**
Pinden, Dart.	149	FW96
Pinner, Pnr.	60	BY56
Pinner Green, Pnr.	40	BW54
Pinnerwood Park, Pnr.	40	BW52
Plaistow E13	86	EF69
Plaistow, Brom.	124	EF93
Plumstead SE18	105	ES78
Ponders End, Enf.	30	DW43
Pooley Green, Egh.	113	BC92
Poplar E14	**204**	**B2**
Potters Bar, Pot.B.	12	DA32
Potters Crouch, St.Alb.	8	BX25
Poverest, Orp.	145	ET99
Poyle, Slou.	93	BE81
Pratt's Bottom, Orp.	164	EV110
Preston, Wem.	62	CL59
Primrose Hill NW8	82	DF67
Purfleet, Purf.	108	FP77
Purley, Pur.	159	DM111
Putney SW15	99	CY84
Putney Heath SW15	119	CW86
Putney Vale SW15	119	CT90
Pyrford, Wok.	167	BE115
Pyrford Green, Wok.	168	BH117
Pyrford Village, Wok.	168	BG118

Q

Place	Page	Grid
Queensbury, Har.	61	CK55

R

Place	Page	Grid
Radlett, Rad.	25	CH35
Rainham, Rain.	89	FG69
Ramsden, Orp.	146	EW102
Rayners Lane, Har.	60	BZ60
Raynes Park SW20	139	CV97
Redbridge, Ilf.	69	EM58
Redhill, Red.	184	DG134
Redstreet, Grav.	130	GB93
Regent's Park NW1	**194**	**G1**
Reigate, Reig.	184	DA134
Richings Park, Iver	93	BD75
Richmond, Rich.	118	CL86
Rickmansworth, Rick.	38	BL45
Ridge, Pot.B.	10	CS34
Ridgehill, Rad.	10	CQ30
Ripley, Wok.	168	BJ122
Ripley Springs, Egh.	112	AY93
Riverhead, Sev.	190	FD122
Riverview Park, Grav.	131	GK92
Roehampton SW15	119	CU85
Romford, Rom.	71	FF57
Rosehill, Sutt.	140	DB102
Rosherville, Grav.	131	GF85
Rotherhithe SE16	**203**	**H6**
Round Bush, Wat.	24	CC38
Row Town, Add.	151	BF108
Rowley Green, Barn.	27	CT42
Roxeth, Har.	61	CD61
Ruislip, Ruis.	59	BS59
Ruislip Common, Ruis.	59	BR57
Ruislip Gardens, Ruis.	59	BS63
Ruislip Manor, Ruis.	59	BU61
Rush Green, Rom.	71	FC59
Rydens, Walt.	136	BW103

S

Place	Page	Grid
Saint George's Hill, Wey.	153	BQ110
Saint Helier, Cars.	140	DD101
Saint James's SW1	**199**	**L3**
Saint John's SE8	103	EA82
Saint John's, Wok.	166	AV118
Saint John's Wood NW8	82	DD69
Saint Luke's EC1	**197**	**J4**
Saint Margarets, Twick.	117	CG85
Saint Mary Cray, Orp.	146	EW99
Saint Pancras WC1	**195**	**P3**
Saint Paul's Cray, Orp.	146	EU96
Saint Vincent's Hamlet, Brwd.	52	FP46
Sanderstead, S.Croy.	160	DT111
Sands End SW6	100	DC81
Sarratt, Rick.	22	BG35
Seal, Sev.	191	FN121
Selhurst SE25	142	DS100
Selsdon, S.Croy.	160	DW110
Send, Wok.	167	BC124
Send Marsh, Wok.	167	BF124
Seven Kings, Ilf.	69	ES59
Sevenoaks, Sev.	191	FJ125
Sevenoaks Common, Sev.	191	FH129
Sewardstone E4	31	EC39
Sewardstonebury E4	32	EE42
Shacklewell N16	66	DT63
Shadwell E1	**202**	**F1**
Sheerwater, Wok.	151	BC113
Shenfield, Brwd.	55	GA45
Shenley, Rad.	10	CN33
Shepherd's Bush W12	81	CW74
Shepperton, Shep.	134	BN101
Shirley, Croy.	143	DX104
Shooter's Hill SE18	105	EQ81
Shoreditch E1	**197**	**P5**
Shoreham, Sev.	165	FG111
Shortlands, Brom.	144	EE97
Shreding Green, Iver	75	BB72
Sidcup, Sid.	125	ET91
Silvertown E16	104	EJ75
Single Street, West.	179	EN115
Singlewell, Grav.	131	GK93
Sipson, West Dr.	94	BN79
Slough, Slou.	74	AS74
Snaresbrook E11	68	EE57
Sockett's Heath, Grays	110	GD76
Soho W1	**195**	**M10**
Somers Town NW1	**195**	**M2**
South Acton W3	98	CN76
South Beddington, Wall.	159	DK107
South Chingford E4	47	DZ50
South Croydon, S.Croy.	160	DQ107
South Darenth, Dart.	149	FR95
South Hackney E9	84	DW66
South Hampstead NW6	82	DB66
South Harefield, Uxb.	58	BJ56
South Harrow, Har.	60	CB62
South Hornchurch, Rain.	89	FE67
South Kensington SW7	100	DB76
South Lambeth SW8	101	DL81
South Merstham, Red.	185	DJ130
South Mimms, Pot.B.	11	CT32
South Norwood SE25	142	DT97
South Ockendon, S.Ock.	91	FW70
South Oxhey, Wat.	40	BW48
South Ruislip, Ruis.	60	BW63
South Stifford, Grays	109	FW78
South Street, West.	179	EM119
South Tottenham N15	66	DS57
South Weald, Brwd.	54	FS47
South Wimbledon SW19	120	DB94
South Woodford E18	48	EF54
Southall, Sthl.	78	BX74
Southborough, Brom.	145	EM100
Southend SE6	123	EB
Southfields SW18	120	DA
Southfleet, Grav.	130	GB
Southgate N14	45	DJ
Southlea, Slou.	92	AV
Southwark SE1	**200**	**C**
Spring Grove, Islw.	97	CF
Staines, Stai.	114	BG
Stamford Hill N16	66	DS
Stanmore, Stan.	41	CG
Stanwell, Stai.	114	BL
Stanwell Moor, Stai.	114	BG
Stapleford Abbotts, Rom.	35	FC
Stapleford Tawney, Rom.	35	FC
Stepney E1	84	DW
Stockwell SW9	101	DK
Stoke D'Abernon, Cob.	170	BZ1
Stoke Green, Slou.	74	AU
Stoke Newington N16	66	DS
Stoke Poges, Slou.	74	AT
Stone, Green.	129	FT
Stonebridge NW10	80	CP
Stonehill, Cher.	150	AY1
Stoneleigh, Epsom	157	CU1
Strand WC2	**195**	**P**
Stratford E15	85	EC
Strawberry Hill, Twick.	117	CE
Streatham SW16	121	DL
Streatham Hill SW2	121	DM
Streatham Park SW16	121	DJ
Streatham Vale SW16	121	DK
Stroud Green N4	65	DM
Stroude, Vir.W.	133	AZ
Sudbury, Wem.	61	CG
Summerstown SW17	120	DB
Sunbury, Sun.	135	BU
Sundridge, Brom.	124	EJ
Sundridge, Sev.	180	EZ12
Sunnymeads, Stai.	92	AY
Surbiton, Surb.	138	CM1
Sutton, Sutt.	158	DB1
Sutton at Hone, Dart.	148	FN
Swanley, Swan.	147	FE
Swanley Village, Swan.	148	FJ
Swanscombe, Swans.	130	FZ
Swillet, The, Rick.	21	BB4
Sydenham SE26	122	DW

T

Place	Page	Grid
Tadworth, Tad.	173	CV12
Tandridge, Oxt.	187	EA13
Tatling End, Ger.Cr.	57	BB6
Tatsfield, West.	178	EL12
Tattenham Corner, Epsom	173	CV1
Teddington, Tedd.	117	CG9
Thames Ditton, T.Ditt.	137	CF10
Thamesmead SE28	87	ET
Thamesmead North SE28	88	EX7
Thamesmead West SE18	105	EQ7
Theydon Bois, Epp.	33	ET3
Theydon Garnon, Epp.	34	EW3
Theydon Mount, Epp.	18	FA3
Thorney, Iver	94	BH7
Thornton Heath, Th.Hth.	141	DP9
Thornwood, Epp.	18	EW2
Thorpe, Egh.	133	BC9
Thorpe Green, Egh.	133	BA9
Thorpe Lea, Egh.	113	BB9
Tilbury, Til.	111	GG8
Titsey, Oxt.	188	EH12
Tokyngton, Wem.	80	CP6
Tolworth, Surb.	138	CN10
Toot Hill, Ong.	19	FF3
Tooting Graveney SW17	120	DE9
Tottenham N17	46	DS5
Tottenham Hale N17	66	DV5
Totteridge N20	43	CY4
Tufnell Park N7	65	DK6
Tulse Hill SE21	122	DQ8
Turnford, Brox.	15	DZ2
Twickenham, Twick.	117	CG8
Twitton, Sev.	181	FF11
Tyler's Green, Gdse.	186	DV12
Tyrrell's Wood, Lthd.	172	CM123

U

Place	Page	Grid
Underhill, Barn.	28	DA43
Underriver, Sev.	191	FN13
Upminster, Upmin.	72	FQ6
Upper Clapton E5	66	DV6
Upper Edmonton N18	46	DU5
Upper Elmers End, Beck.	143	DZ9
Upper Halliford, Shep.	135	BS97
Upper Holloway N19	65	DJ6
Upper Norwood SE19	122	DR94
Upper Sydenham SE26	122	DU91
Upper Tooting SW17	120	DE9
Upper Walthamstow E17	67	EB5
Upshire, Wal.Abb.	16	EJ32
Upton E7	86	EH6
Upton, Slou.	92	AU7
Upton Park E6	86	EJ6
Upton Park, Slou.	92	AT7
Uxbridge, Uxb.	76	BK6
Uxbridge Moor, Iver	76	BG67
Uxbridge Moor, Uxb.	76	BG67

V

Vauxhall SE11	101	DL78
Virginia Water, Vir.W.	132	AW97

W

Waddon, Croy.	141	DN103
Walham Green SW6	100	DB80
Wallington, Wall.	159	DJ106
Waltham Abbey, Wal.Abb.	32	EF35
Waltham Cross, Wal.Cr.	15	DZ33
Walthamstow E17	47	EB54
Walton on the Hill, Tad.	183	CT125
Walton-on-Thames, Walt.	135	BT103
Walworth SE17	**201**	**H10**
Wandsworth SW18	119	CZ85
Wanstead E11	68	EH59
Wapping E1	**202**	**C2**
Warley, Brwd.	54	FV50
Warlingham, Warl.	177	DX118
Warwick Wold, Red.	185	DN129
Water End, Hat.	11	CV26
Watford, Wat.	23	BT41
Watford Heath, Wat.	40	BY46
Wealdstone, Har.	61	CF55
Well End, Borwd.	26	CR38
Well Hill, Orp.	165	FB107
Welling, Well.	106	EU83
Wembley, Wem.	62	CL63
Wembley Park, Wem.	62	CM61
Wennington, Rain.	90	FK73
Wentworth, Vir.W.	132	AS100
West Acton W3	80	CN72
West Barnes, N.Mal.	139	CU99
West Brompton SW10	100	DB79
West Byfleet, W.Byf.	152	BH113
West Drayton, West Dr.	94	BK76
West Dulwich SE21	122	DR90
West End, Esher	154	BZ107
West Ewell, Epsom	156	CS108
West Green N15	66	DQ56
West Ham E15	86	EF66
West Hampstead NW6	64	DB64
West Harrow, Har.	60	CC59
West Heath SE2	106	EX79
West Hendon NW9	62	CS59
West Kilburn W9	81	CZ69
West Molesey, W.Mol.	136	BZ99
West Norwood SE27	122	DQ90
West Thurrock, Grays	109	FU78
West Tilbury, Til.	111	GL79
West Watford, Wat.	23	BU42
West Wickham, W.Wick.	143	EC103
Westbourne Green W2	82	DA71
Westcourt, Grav.	131	GL89
Westerham, West.	189	EQ126
Westfield, Wok.	167	AZ122
Westminster SW1	**199**	**K6**
Weston Green, T.Ditt.	137	CF102
Wexham Street, Slou.	74	AW67
Weybridge, Wey.	152	BN105
Whelpley Hill, Chesh.	4	AX26
Whetstone N20	44	DB47
Whitechapel E1	84	DU72
Whiteley Village, Walt.	153	BS110
Whitton, Twick.	116	CB87
Whyteleafe, Cat.	176	DS118
Widmore, Brom.	144	EH97
Wildernesse, Sev.	191	FL122
Willesden NW10	81	CT65
Willesden Green NW10	81	CV66
Wilmington, Dart.	128	FK91
Wimbledon SW19	119	CY93
Wimbledon Park SW19	119	CZ90
Winchmore Hill N21	45	DM45
Windmill Hill, Grav.	131	GG88
Windsor, Wind.	92	AS82
Wisley, Wok.	168	BL116
Woking, Wok.	167	AZ118
Woldingham, Cat.	177	EB122
Woldingham Garden Village, Cat.	177	DY121
Wombwell Park, Grav.	130	GD89
Wood Green N22	45	DL53
Woodcote, Epsom	172	CQ116
Woodcote, Pur.	159	DK111
Woodford, Wdf.Grn.	48	EH51
Woodford Bridge, Wdf.Grn.	48	EL52
Woodford Green, Wdf.Grn.	48	EF49
Woodford Wells, Wdf.Grn.	48	EH49
Woodham, Add.	151	BF111
Woodlands, Islw.	97	CE82
Woodmansterne, Bans.	174	DE115
Woodside, Croy.	142	DU99
Woodside, Wat.	7	BU33
Woolwich SE18	105	EN78
Worcester Park, Wor.Pk.	139	CT103
World's End, Enf.	29	DN41
Wraysbury, Stai.	113	AZ86
Wrythe, The, Cars.	140	DE103

Y

Yeading, Hayes	77	BV69
Yiewsley, West Dr.	76	BL74

INDEX TO RAILWAY STATIONS

The following is a comprehensive listing of all underground, light railway and mainline stations that appear in this atlas. Bold references can be found within the Central London enlarged section (pages 194-205).

A

Abbey Wood	106	EW76
Acton Central	80	CR74
Acton Main Line	80	CQ72
Acton Town	98	CN75
Addington Village	161	EA107
Addiscombe	142	DU102
Addlestone	152	BK105
Albany Park	126	EX89
Aldgate	**197**	**P9**
Aldgate East	84	DT72
Alexandra Palace	45	DL54
All Saints	85	EB73
Alperton	80	CL67
Ampere Way	141	DM102
Anerley	142	DV95
Angel	**196**	**E1**
Angel Road	46	DW50
Apsley	6	BL25
Archway	65	DJ61
Arena	142	DW99
Arnos Grove	45	DJ50
Arsenal	65	DN62
Ashford	114	BM91
Ashtead	172	CL117
Avenue Road	143	DX96

B

Baker Street	**194**	**E5**
Balham	121	DH88
Bank	**197**	**K9**
Banstead	157	CZ114
Barbican	**197**	**H6**
Barking	87	EQ66
Barkingside	69	ER56
Barnehurst	107	FC82
Barnes	99	CU83
Barnes Bridge	98	CS82
Barons Court	99	CY78
Bat & Ball	191	FJ121
Battersea Park	101	DH80
Bayswater	82	DB73
Beckenham Hill	123	EC92
Beckenham Junction	143	EA95
Beckenham Road	143	DY95
Beckton	87	EN71
Beckton Park	87	EM73
Becontree	88	EX65
Beddington Lane	141	DJ100
Belgrave Walk	140	DD98
Bellingham	123	EB90
Belmont	158	DB110
Belsize Park	64	DE64
Belvedere	106	FA76
Bermondsey	**202**	**C6**
Berrylands	138	CP98
Betchworth	182	CS132
Bethnal Green	84	DV70
Bexley	126	FA88
Bexleyheath	106	EY83
Bickley	144	EL97
Birkbeck	142	DW97
Blackfriars	**196**	**F10**
Blackheath	104	EF82
Blackhorse Lane	142	DU101
Blackhorse Road	67	DX56
Blackwall	**204**	**E1**
Bond Street	**195**	**H9**
Bookham	170	BZ123
Borough	**201**	**J5**
Boston Manor	97	CG77
Bounds Green	45	DK52
Bow Church	85	EA69
Bow Road	85	EA69
Bowes Park	45	DL52
Brent Cross	63	CX59
Brentford	97	CJ79
Brentwood	54	FW48
Bricket Wood	8	CA30
Brimsdown	31	DY40
Brixton	101	DN84
Brockley	103	DY83
Bromley North	144	EG95
Bromley South	144	EG97
Bromley-by-Bow	85	EC69
Brondesbury	81	CZ66
Brondesbury Park	81	CY67
Brookmans Park	11	CY27
Bruce Grove	46	DT54
Buckhurst Hill	48	EK47
Burnt Oak	42	CQ53
Bush Hill Park	30	DT44
Bushey	24	BX44
Byfleet & New Haw	152	BK110

C

Caledonian Road	83	DM65
Caledonian Road & Barnsbury	83	DM66
Cambridge Heath	84	DV68
Camden Road	83	DJ66
Camden Town	83	DH67
Canada Water	**202**	**G5**
Canary Wharf	**204**	**B3**
Canning Town	86	EE72
Cannon Street	**197**	**K10**
Canonbury	66	DQ64
Canons Park	42	CL52
Carpenters Park	40	BX48
Carshalton	158	DF105
Carshalton Beeches	158	DF107
Castle Bar Park	79	CF71
Caterham	176	DU124
Catford	123	EA87
Catford Bridge	123	EA87
Chadwell Heath	70	EX59
Chafford Hundred	109	FV77
Chalfont & Latimer	20	AX39
Chalk Farm	82	DG66
Chancery Lane	**196**	**D7**
Charing Cross	**200**	**A2**
Charlton	104	EJ78
Cheam	157	CY108
Chelsfield	164	EV106
Chertsey	133	BF102
Cheshunt	15	DZ30
Chessington North	156	CL106
Chessington South	155	CK108
Chigwell	49	EP48
Chingford	48	EE45
Chipstead	174	DF118
Chislehurst	145	EN96
Chiswick	98	CQ80
Chiswick Park	98	CQ77
Chorleywood	21	BD42
Church Street	142	DQ103
City Thameslink	**196**	**F9**
Clapham Common	101	DJ84
Clapham High Street	101	DK83
Clapham Junction	100	DE84
Clapham North	101	DL83
Clapham South	121	DH86
Clapton	66	DV61
Claygate	155	CE107
Clock House	143	DY95
Cobham & Stoke D'Abernon	170	BY117
Cockfosters	28	DG42
Colindale	62	CS55
Colliers Wood	120	DD94
Coombe Lane	160	DW106
Coulsdon South	175	DK116
Covent Garden	**196**	**A10**
Crayford	127	FE86
Crews Hill	13	DM34
Cricklewood	63	CX63
Crofton Park	123	DZ85
Crossharbour & London Arena	**204**	**C6**
Crouch Hill	65	DM59
Croxley	23	BP44
Crystal Palace	122	DU93
Cuffley	13	DM29
Custom House	86	EH73
Cutty Sark	103	EC79
Cyprus	87	EN73

D

Dagenham Dock	88	EZ69
Dagenham East	71	FC64
Dagenham Heathway	88	EZ65
Dalston Kingsland	66	DS64
Dartford	128	FL86

Datchet	92	AV81
Debden	33	EQ42
Denham	58	BG59
Denham Golf Club	57	BD59
Denmark Hill	102	DR82
Deptford	103	EA80
Deptford Bridge	103	EA81
Devons Road	85	EB70
Dollis Hill	63	CU64
Drayton Green	79	CF72
Drayton Park	65	DN64
Dundonald Road	119	CZ94
Dunton Green	181	FE119

E

Ealing Broadway	79	CK73
Ealing Common	80	CM74
Earls Court	100	DA78
Earlsfield	120	DC88
East Acton	81	CT72
East Croydon	142	DR103
East Dulwich	102	DS84
East Finchley	64	DE56
East Ham	86	EL66
East India	85	ED73
East Putney	119	CY85
Eastcote	60	BW59
Eden Park	143	EA99
Edgware	42	CP51
Edgware Road	**194**	**B7**
Edmonton Green	46	DU47
Effingham Junction	169	BU123
Egham	113	BA92
Elephant & Castle	**201**	**H8**
Elm Park	71	FG63
Elmers End	143	DX98
Elmstead Woods	124	EL93
Elstree	26	CN42
& Borehamwood		
Eltham	125	EM85
Elverson Road	103	EB82
Embankment	**200**	**A2**
Emerson Park	72	FK59
Enfield Chase	30	DQ41
Enfield Lock	31	DY37
Enfield Town	30	DS41
Epping	18	EU31
Epsom	156	CR113
Epsom Downs	173	CV115
Erith	107	FE78
Esher	137	CD103
Essex Road	84	DQ66
Euston	**195**	**M3**
Euston Square	**195**	**L4**
Ewell East	157	CV110
Ewell West	156	CS109

F

Fairlop	49	ER53
Falconwood	105	ER84
Farningham Road	148	FP96
Farringdon	**196**	**F6**
Feltham	115	BV88
Fenchurch Street	**197**	**N10**
Fieldway	161	EB108
Finchley Central	44	DA53
Finchley Road	82	DC65
Finchley Road	64	DC64
& Frognal		
Finsbury Park	65	DN61
Forest Gate	68	EG64
Forest Hill	122	DW89
Fulham Broadway	100	DA80
Fulwell	117	CD91

G

Gallions Reach	87	EP73
Gants Hill	69	EN58
Garston	24	BX35
George Street	142	DQ103
Gerrards Cross	56	AY57
Gidea Park	71	FH56
Gipsy Hill	122	DS92
Gloucester Road	100	DC77
Golders Green	64	DA60
Goldhawk Road	99	CW75
Goodge Street	**195**	**M6**
Goodmayes	70	EU60
Gordon Hill	29	DP39
Gospel Oak	64	DG63
Grange Hill	49	ER49
Grange Park	29	DP43
Gravel Hill	161	DY107
Gravesend	131	GH86
Grays	110	GA79
Great Portland Street	**195**	**J5**
Green Park	**199**	**J2**
Greenford	79	CD67
Greenhithe	129	FU85
Greenwich	103	EC80
Grove Park	124	EH90

H

Gunnersbury	98	CP78

H

Hackbridge	141	DH103
Hackney Central	84	DV65
Hackney Downs	66	DV64
Hackney Wick	85	EA65
Hadley Wood	28	DC38
Hainault	49	ES52
Hammersmith	99	CW77
Hampstead	64	DC63
Hampstead Heath	64	DE63
Hampton	136	CA95
Hampton Court	137	CE98
Hampton Wick	137	CJ95
Hanger Lane	80	CL69
Hanwell	79	CE73
Harlesden	80	CR68
Harold Wood	52	FM53
Harringay	65	DN58
Harringay Green Lanes	65	DP58
Harrington Road	142	DV98
Harrow & Wealdstone	61	CE56
Harrow on the Hill	61	CE58
Hatch End	40	CA52
Hatton Cross	95	BT84
Haydons Road	120	DC92
Hayes	144	EG102
Hayes & Harlington	95	BT76
Headstone Lane	40	CB53
Heathrow Terminal 4	115	BP85
Heathrow Terminals 1,2,3	95	BP83
Hendon	63	CU58
Hendon Central	63	CW57
Herne Hill	121	DP86
Heron Quays	**204**	**A3**
Hersham	136	BY104
High Barnet	28	DA42
High Street Kensington	100	DB75
Highams Park	47	ED51
Highbury & Islington	83	DP65
Highgate	65	DH58
Hillingdon	59	BP64
Hinchley Wood	137	CF104
Hither Green	124	EE86
Holborn	**196**	**B7**
Holland Park	81	CZ74
Holloway Road	65	DM64
Homerton	85	DX65
Honor Oak Park	123	DX86
Hornchurch	72	FK62
Hornsey	65	DM56
Hounslow	116	CB85
Hounslow Central	96	CB83
Hounslow East	96	CC82
Hounslow West	96	BY82
How Wood	8	CC28
Hurst Green	188	EF132
Hyde Park Corner	**198**	**G4**

I

Ickenham	59	BQ63
Ilford	69	EP62
Island Gardens	**204**	**D10**
Isleworth	97	CF82
Iver	93	BF75

K

Kempton Park	115	BV94
(Race days only)		
Kenley	160	DQ114
Kennington	**200**	**F10**
Kensal Green	81	CW69
Kensal Rise	81	CX68
Kensington (Olympia)	99	CY76
Kent House	143	DY95
Kentish Town	65	DJ64
Kentish Town West	83	DH65
Kenton	61	CH58
Kew Bridge	98	CM78
Kew Gardens	98	CN81
Kidbrooke	104	EH83
Kilburn	81	CZ65
Kilburn High Road	82	DB67
Kilburn Park	82	DA68
King's Henry's Drive	161	EB109
King's Cross	**196**	**A1**
King's Cross St. Pancras	**195**	**P2**
King's Cross Thameslink	**196**	**A2**
Kings Langley	7	BQ31
Kingsbury	62	CN57
Kingston	138	CL95
Kingswood	173	CZ121
Knightsbridge	**198**	**E5**
Knockholt	164	EY109

L

Ladbroke Grove	81	CY72
Ladywell	123	EB85

Lambeth North	**200**	**D6**
Lancaster Gate	82	DD73
Langley	93	BA75
Latimer Road	81	CX73
Leatherhead	171	CG121
Lebanon Road	142	DS103
Lee	124	EF86
Leicester Square	**195**	**N10**
Lewisham	103	EC83
Leyton	67	EC62
Leyton Midland Road	67	EC60
Leytonstone	68	EE60
Leytonstone High Road	68	EE61
Limehouse	85	DY72
Liverpool Street	**197**	**M7**
Lloyd Park	160	DT105
London Bridge	**201**	**L3**
London Fields	84	DV66
Longcross	132	AT102
Loughborough Junction	101	DP83
Loughton	32	EL43
Lower Sydenham	123	DZ92

M

Maida Vale	82	DB69
Malden Manor	138	CS101
Manor House	66	DQ59
Manor Park	68	EK63
Mansion House	**197**	**J10**
Marble Arch	**194**	**E9**
Maryland	86	EE65
Marylebone	**194**	**D5**
Maze Hill	104	EE79
Merstham	185	DJ128
Merton Park	140	DA95
Mile End	85	DZ69
Mill Hill Broadway	42	CS51
Mill Hill East	43	CY52
Mitcham	140	DE98
Mitcham Junction	140	DG99
Monument	**197**	**L10**
Moor Park	39	BR48
Moorgate	**197**	**K7**
Morden	140	DB97
Morden Road	140	DB96
Morden South	140	DA99
Mornington Crescent	83	DJ68
Mortlake	98	CQ83
Motspur Park	139	CV99
Mottingham	125	EM88
Mudchute	**204**	**C8**

N

Neasden	62	CS64
New Addington	161	EC110
New Barnet	28	DD43
New Beckenham	123	DZ94
New Cross	103	DZ80
New Cross Gate	103	DY81
New Eltham	125	EQ88
New Malden	138	CS97
New Southgate	45	DH50
Newbury Park	69	ER58
Norbiton	138	CN95
Norbury	141	DM95
North Acton	80	CR71
North Dulwich	122	DR85
North Ealing	80	CM72
North Greenwich	**205**	**H4**
North Harrow	60	CB57
North Sheen	98	CN84
North Wembley	61	CK62
North Woolwich	105	EN75
Northfields	97	CJ76
Northfleet	130	GB86
Northolt	78	CA65
Northolt Park	60	CB63
Northumberland Park	46	DV52
Northwick Park	61	CH59
Northwood	39	BS52
Northwood Hills	39	BU54
Norwood Junction	142	DU98
Notting Hill Gate	82	DA74
Nunhead	102	DW82

O

Oakleigh Park	44	DD45
Oakwood	29	DJ43
Ockendon	91	FV69
Old Street	**197**	**L3**
Orpington	145	ES103
Osterley	97	CD80
Oval	101	DN79
Oxford Circus	**195**	**K9**
Oxshott	154	CC113
Oxted	188	EE129

P

Paddington	82	DD72

Station	Page	Grid
Palmers Green	45	DM49
Park Royal	80	CN70
Park Street	9	CD26
Parsons Green	100	DA81
Peckham Rye	102	DU82
Penge East	122	DW93
Penge West	122	DV93
Perivale	79	CG68
Petts Wood	145	EQ99
Phipps Bridge	140	DD97
Piccadilly Circus	**199**	**M1**
Pimlico	**199**	**M10**
Pinner	60	BY56
Plaistow	86	EG68
Plumstead	105	ER77
Ponders End	31	DY43
Poplar	**204**	**B1**
Potters Bar	11	CZ32
Preston Road	62	CL60
Prince Regent	86	EJ73
Pudding Mill Lane	85	EB67
Purfleet	108	FN78
Purley	159	DN111
Purley Oaks	160	DR109
Putney	99	CY84
Putney Bridge	99	CZ83

Q

Station	Page	Grid
Queen's Park	81	CZ68
Queens Road Peckham	102	DW81
Queensbury	62	CM55
Queenstown Road (Battersea)	101	DH81
Queensway	82	DB73

R

Station	Page	Grid
Radlett	25	CG35
Rainham	89	FG70
Ravensbourne	123	ED94
Ravenscourt Park	99	CV77
Rayners Lane	60	BZ59
Raynes Park	139	CW96
Rectory Road	66	DT62
Redbridge	68	EK58
Redhill	184	DG133
Reedham	159	DM113
Reeves Corner	141	DP103
Regent's Park	**195**	**H5**
Reigate	184	DA133
Richmond	98	CL84
Rickmansworth	38	BK45
Riddlesdown	160	DQ113
Roding Valley	48	EK49
Romford	71	FE58
Rotherhithe	**202**	**G4**
Royal Albert	86	EL73
Royal Oak	82	DB71
Royal Victoria	86	EG73
Ruislip	59	BT60
Ruislip Gardens	59	BU63
Ruislip Manor	59	BU60
Russell Square	**195**	**P5**

S

Station	Page	Grid
St. Helier	140	DA100
St. James Street	67	DY57
St. James's Park	**199**	**M6**
St. John's	103	EA82
St. John's Wood	82	DD68
St. Margarets (TW1)	117	CH86
St. Mary Cray	146	EV98
St. Pancras	**195**	**P2**
St. Paul's	**197**	**H9**
Sanderstead	160	DR109
Sandilands	142	DT103
Selhurst	142	DS99
Seven Kings	69	ES60
Seven Sisters	66	DS57
Sevenoaks	190	FG124
Shadwell	84	DV73
Shenfield	55	GA45
Shepherd's Bush	99	CX75
Shepperton	135	BQ99
Shoreditch	84	DT70
Shoreham	165	FH111
Shortlands	144	EE96
Sidcup	126	EU89
Silver Street	46	DT50
Silvertown & London City Airport	86	EL74
Slade Green	107	FG81
Sloane Square	**198**	**F9**
Slough	74	AT74
Smitham	175	DL115
Snaresbrook	68	EG57
South Acton	98	CQ76
South Bermondsey	**202**	**F10**
South Croydon	160	DR106
South Ealing	97	CK76
South Greenford	79	CE69
South Hampstead	82	DC66
South Harrow	60	CC62
South Kensington	**198**	**A8**
South Kenton	61	CJ60
South Merton	139	CZ97
South Quay	**204**	**B4**
South Ruislip	60	BW64
South Tottenham	66	DT57
South Wimbledon	120	DB94
South Woodford	48	EH54
Southall	96	BZ75
Southbury	30	DV42
Southfields	119	CZ88
Southgate	45	DK46
Southwark	**200**	**F3**
Staines	114	BG92
Stamford Brook	99	CT77
Stamford Hill	66	DS59
Stanmore	41	CK49
Stepney Green	85	DX70
Stockwell	101	DL82
Stoke Newington	66	DT61
Stone Crossing	129	FS85
Stonebridge Park	80	CP66
Stoneleigh	157	CU106
Stratford	85	ED65
Strawberry Hill	117	CF90
Streatham	121	DK92
Streatham Common	121	DK94
Streatham Hill	121	DL89
Sudbury & Harrow Road	61	CH64
Sudbury Hill	61	CE63
Sudbury Hill Harrow	61	CE63
Sudbury Town	79	CH65
Sunbury	135	BU95
Sundridge Park	124	EH94
Sunnymeads	92	AY83
Surbiton	138	CL100
Surrey Quays	**203**	**H8**
Sutton	158	DC107
Sutton Common	140	DB103
Swanley	147	FD98
Swanscombe	130	FZ85
Swiss Cottage	82	DD66
Sydenham	122	DW91
Sydenham Hill	122	DT90
Syon Lane	97	CG80

T

Station	Page	Grid
Tadworth	173	CW122
Tattenham Corner	173	CV118
Teddington	117	CG93
Temple	**196**	**C10**
Thames Ditton	137	CF101
Theobalds Grove	15	DX32
Therapia Lane	141	DL101
Theydon Bois	33	ET36
Thornton Heath	142	DQ98
Tilbury Town	111	GF82
Tolworth	138	CP103
Tooting	120	DF93
Tooting Bec	120	DG90
Tooting Broadway	120	DE92
Tottenham Court Road	**195**	**N8**
Tottenham Hale	66	DU56
Totteridge & Whetstone	44	DC47
Tower Gateway	**197**	**P10**
Tower Hill	**201**	**P1**
Tufnell Park	65	DJ63
Tulse Hill	121	DP89
Turkey Street	30	DW37
Turnham Green	98	CS77
Turnpike Lane	65	DP55
Twickenham	117	CG87

U

Station	Page	Grid
Upminster	72	FQ61
Upminster Bridge	72	FM61
Upney	87	ET66
Upper Halliford	135	BS96
Upper Holloway	65	DK61
Upper Warlingham	176	DU118
Upton Park	86	EJ67
Uxbridge	76	BK66

V

Station	Page	Grid
Vauxhall	101	DL78
Victoria	**199**	**J8**
Virginia Water	132	AY99

W

Station	Page	Grid
Waddon	159	DN105
Waddon Marsh	141	DM102
Wallington	159	DH107
Waltham Cross	15	DZ34
Walthamstow Central	67	EA57
Walthamstow Queens Road	67	EA57
Walton-on-Thames	153	BU105
Wandle Park	141	DN103
Wandsworth Common	120	DF87
Wandsworth Road	101	DJ82
Wandsworth Town	100	DB84
Wanstead	68	EH58
Wanstead Park	68	EH63
Wapping	**202**	**F3**
Warren Street	**195**	**K4**
Warwick Avenue	82	DC70
Waterloo	**200**	**D4**
Waterloo East	**200**	**E3**
Waterloo International	**200**	**C4**
Watford	23	BT41
Watford High Street	24	BW42
Watford Junction	23	BV40
Watford North	24	BW37
Wellesley Road	142	DR103
Welling	106	EU82
Wembley Central	62	CL64
Wembley Park	62	CN62
Wembley Stadium	62	CM64
West Acton	80	CN72
West Brompton	100	DA78
West Byfleet	152	BG112
West Croydon	142	DQ102
West Drayton	76	BL74
West Dulwich	122	DR88
West Ealing	79	CH73
West Finchley	44	DB51
West Ham	86	EE69
West Hampstead	82	DA65
West Hampstead (Thameslink)	82	DA65
West Harrow	60	CC58
West India Quay	**204**	**A1**
West Kensington	99	CZ78
West Norwood	121	DP91
West Ruislip	59	BQ61
West Sutton	158	DA105
West Wickham	143	EC101
Westbourne Park	81	CZ71
Westcombe Park	104	EG78
Westferry	85	EA73
Westminster	**199**	**P5**
Weybridge	152	BN107
White City	81	CW73
White Hart Lane	46	DT52
Whitechapel	84	DV71
Whitton	116	CC87
Whyteleafe	176	DT117
Whyteleafe South	176	DU119
Willesden Green	81	CW65
Willesden Junction	81	CT69
Wimbledon	119	CZ93
Wimbledon Chase	139	CY96
Wimbledon Park	120	DA90
Winchmore Hill	45	DP46
Woking	167	AZ117
Woldingham	177	DX122
Wood Green	45	DN54
Wood Street	67	EC56
Woodford	48	EH51
Woodgrange Park	68	EK64
Woodmansterne	175	DH116
Woodside	142	DV100
Woodside Park	44	DB49
Woolwich Arsenal	105	EP77
Woolwich Dockyard	105	EM77
Worcester Park	139	CU102
Worplesdon	166	AV124
Wraysbury	113	BA86

The following is a comprehensive listing of all hospitals which appear in this atlas. Bold references can be found within the Central London enlarged section (pages 194-205).

General Abbreviations

ll	Alley	Cor	Corner	Gdn	Garden	Ms	Mews	Shop	Shopping
llot	Allotments	Coron	Coroners	Gdns	Gardens	Mt	Mount	Sq	Square
mb	Ambulance	Cors	Corners	Govt	Government	Mus	Museum	St.	Saint
pp	Approach	Cotts	Cottages	Gra	Grange	N	North	St	Street
rc	Arcade	Cov	Covered	Grd	Ground	NT	National Trust	Sta	Station
v/Ave	Avenue	Crem	Crematorium	Grds	Grounds	Nat	National	Sts	Streets
dy	Broadway	Cres	Crescent	Grn	Green	PH	Public House	Sub	Subway
k	Bank	Ct	Court	Grns	Greens	PO	Post Office	Swim	Swimming
ldgs	Buildings	Cts	Courts	Gro	Grove	Par	Parade	TA	Territorial Army
oul	Boulevard	Ctyd	Courtyard	Gros	Groves	Pas	Passage	TH	Town Hall
owl	Bowling	Dep	Depot	Gt	Great	Pav	Pavilion	Tenn	Tennis
r/Bri	Bridge	Dev	Development	Ho	House	Pk	Park	Ter	Terrace
us	Business	Dr	Drive	Hos	Houses	Pl	Place	Thea	Theatre
of E	Church of England	Dws	Dwellings	Hosp	Hospital	Pol	Police	Trd	Trading
ath	Cathedral	E	East	Hts	Heights	Prec	Precinct	Twr	Tower
em	Cemetery	Ed	Education	Ind	Industrial	Prim	Primary	Twrs	Towers
en	Central, Centre	Elec	Electricity	Int	International	Prom	Promenade	Uni	University
ft	Croft	Embk	Embankment	Junct	Junction	Pt	Point	Vil	Villa, Villas
fts	Crofts	Est	Estate	La	Lane	Quad	Quadrant	Vw	View
h	Church	Ex	Exchange	Las	Lanes	RC	Roman Catholic	W	West
hyd	Churchyard	Exhib	Exhibition	Lib	Library	Rd	Road	Wd	Wood
in	Cinema	FB	Footbridge	Lo	Lodge	Rds	Roads	Wds	Woods
irc	Circus	FC	Football Club	Lwr	Lower	Rec	Recreation	Wf	Wharf
l/Clo	Close	Fld	Field	Mag	Magistrates	Res	Reservoir	Wk	Walk
o	County	Flds	Fields	Mans	Mansions	Ri	Rise	Wks	Works
oll	College	Fm	Farm	Mem	Memorial	S	South	Yd	Yard
omm	Community	Gall	Gallery	Mkt	Market	Sch	School		
onv	Convent	Gar	Garage	Mkts	Markets	Sec	Secondary		

Post Town Abbreviations

bb.L.	Abbots Langley	Dart.	Dartford	Mord.	Morden	Sutt.	Sutton
dd.	Addlestone	Dor.	Dorking	N.Mal.	New Malden	Swan.	Swanley
mer.	Amersham	E.Mol.	East Molesey	Nthlt.	Northolt	Swans.	Swanscombe
shf.	Ashford	Eden.	Edenbridge	Nthwd.	Northwood	T.Ditt.	Thames Ditton
sh.	Ashtead	Edg.	Edgware	Ong.	Ongar	Tad.	Tadworth
ans.	Banstead	Egh.	Egham	Orp.	Orpington	Tedd.	Teddington
ark.	Barking	Enf.	Enfield	Oxt.	Oxted	Th.Hth.	Thornton Heath
arn.	Barnet	Epp.	Epping	Pnr.	Pinner	Til.	Tilbury
eac.	Beaconsfield	Felt.	Feltham	Pot.B.	Potters Bar	Twick.	Twickenham
eck.	Beckenham	Gdse.	Godstone	Pur.	Purley	Upmin.	Upminster
elv.	Belvedere	Ger.Cr.	Gerrards Cross	Purf.	Purfleet	Uxb.	Uxbridge
et.	Betchworth	Grav.	Gravesend	Rad.	Radlett	Vir.W.	Virginia Water
ex.	Bexley	Green.	Greenhithe	Rain.	Rainham	W.Byf.	West Byfleet
exh.	Bexleyheath	Grnf.	Greenford	Red.	Redhill	W.Mol.	West Molesey
orwd.	Borehamwood	Guil.	Guildford	Reig.	Reigate	W.Wick.	West Wickham
rent.	Brentford	Har.	Harrow	Rich.	Richmond	Wal.Abb.	Waltham Abbey
rom.	Bromley	Hat.	Hatfield	Rick.	Rickmansworth	Wal.Cr.	Waltham Cross
rox.	Broxbourne	Hem.H.	Hemel Hempstead	Rom.	Romford	Wall.	Wallington
rwd.	Brentwood	Hert.	Hertford	Ruis.	Ruislip	Walt.	Walton-on-Thames
uck.H.	Buckhurst Hill	Hmptn.	Hampton	S.Croy.	South Croydon	Warl.	Warlingham
ars.	Carshalton	Horn.	Hornchurch	S.le H.	Stanford-le-Hope	Wat.	Watford
at.	Caterham	Houns.	Hounslow	S.Ock.	South Ockendon	Wdf.Grn.	Woodford Green
h.St.G.	Chalfont St. Giles	Ilf.	Ilford	Sev.	Sevenoaks	Well.	Welling
her.	Chertsey	Islw.	Isleworth	Shep.	Shepperton	Wem.	Wembley
hesh.	Chesham	Ken.	Kenley	Sid.	Sidcup	West Dr.	West Drayton
hess.	Chessington	Kes.	Keston	Slou.	Slough	West.	Westerham
hig.	Chigwell	Kings L.	Kings Langley	St.Alb.	St. Albans	Wey.	Weybridge
his.	Chislehurst	Kings.T.	Kingston upon Thames	Stai.	Staines	Whyt.	Whyteleafe
ob.	Cobham	Long.	Longfield	Stan.	Stanmore	Wind.	Windsor
ouls.	Coulsdon	Loug.	Loughton	Sthl.	Southall	Wok.	Woking
roy.	Croydon	Lthd.	Leatherhead	Sun.	Sunbury-on-Thames	Wor.Pk.	Worcester Park
ag.	Dagenham	Mitch.	Mitcham	Surb.	Surbiton		

Notes

A strict word-by-word alphabetical order is followed in the index whereby generic terms such as Avenue, Close, Gardens etc., although abbreviated, are ordered in their expanded form. So, for example, Abbot St comes before Abbots Av, and Abbots Ri comes before Abbots Rd.

Street names preceded by a definite article (i.e. The) are indexed from their second word onwards with the article being placed at the end of the name,
   e.g. Avenue, The, or Lindens, The

The alphabetical order extends to include postal information so that where two or more streets have exactly the same name, London post town references are given first in alpha-numeric order and are followed by non-London post town references in alphabetical order,
   e.g. Abbey Gdns SE16 is followed by Abbey Gdns W6 and then Abbey Gdns, Chertsey.

In some cases there are two or more streets of the same name in the same postal area. In order to aid correct location, extra information is given in brackets,
   e.g. High St, Epsom and High St (Ewell), Epsom.

The street name and postal district or post town of an entry is followed by the page number and grid reference on which the name will be found, e.g. Abbey Road SW19 will be found on page 120 and in square DC94. Likewise, Norfolk Crescent, Sidcup will be found on page 125 and in square ES87 (within postal district DA15).

All streets within the Central London enlarged-scale section (pages 194-205) are shown in **bold type** when named in the index, e.g. **Abbey St SE1** will be found on page **201** and in square **N6**. Certain streets may also be duplicated on parts of pages 82-84 and 100-104. In these cases the Central London section reference is always given first in bold type, followed by the same name in standard type,

e.g. **Abbey Orchard St SW1**	**199**	**N6**
Abbey Orchard St SW1	101	DK76

The index also contains some roads for which there is insufficient space to name on the map. The adjoining, or nearest named thoroughfare to such roads is shown in *italics*, and the reference indicates where the unnamed road is located off the named thoroughfare.
   e.g. Oyster Catchers Close E16 is off *Freemasons Road* and is located off this road on page 86 in square EH72.

A

A.C. Ct, T.Ditt. 137 CG100
Harvest La
Aaron Hill Rd E6 87 EN71
Abberley Ms SW4 101 DH83
Cedars Rd
Abberton Wk, Rain. 89 FE66
Ongar Way
Abbess Cl E6 86 EL71
Oliver Gdns
Abbess Cl SW2 121 DP88
Abbeville Rd N8 65 DK56
Barrington Rd
Abbeville Rd SW4 121 DJ86
Abbey Av, Wem. 80 CL68
Abbey Cl, Hayes 77 BV74
Abbey Cl, Nthlt. 78 BZ69
Invicta Gro
Abbey Cl, Pnr. 59 BV55
Abbey Cl, Rom. 71 FG58
Abbey Cl, Wok. 167 BE116
Abbey Ct, Wal.Abb. 15 EB34
Abbey Cres, Belv. 106 FA77
Abbey Dr SW17 120 DG92
Church La
Abbey Dr, Abb.L. 7 BU32
Abbey Dr, Stai. 134 BJ98
Abbey Gdns NW8 82 DC68
Abbey Gdns SE16 202 C8
Abbey Gdns W6 99 CY79
Abbey Gdns, Cher. 134 BG100
Abbey Gdns, Wal.Abb. 15 EC33
Abbey Grn, Cher. 134 BG100
Abbey Gro SE2 106 EV77
Abbey Ind Est, Wem. 80 CM67
Abbey La E15 85 EC68
Abbey La, Beck. 123 EA94
Abbey Mead Ind Pk, Wal.Abb. 15 EC34
Abbey Ms E17 67 EA57
Leamington Av
Abbey Orchard St SW1 199 N6
Abbey Orchard St SW1 101 DK76
Abbey Par SW19 120 DC94
Merton High St
Abbey Par W5 80 CM69
Hanger La
Abbey Pk, Beck. 123 EA94
Abbey Pl, Dart. 128 FK85
Priory Rd
Abbey Retail Pk, Bark. 87 EP67
Abbey Rd E15 86 EE68
Abbey Rd NW6 82 DB66
Abbey Rd NW8 82 DC68
Abbey Rd NW10 80 CP68
Abbey Rd SE2 106 EX77
Abbey Rd SW19 120 DC94
Abbey Rd, Bark. 87 EQ67
Abbey Rd, Belv. 106 EX77
Abbey Rd, Bexh. 106 EY84
Abbey Rd, Cher. 134 BH101
Abbey Rd, Croy. 141 DP104
Abbey Rd, Enf. 30 DS43
Abbey Rd, Grav. 131 GL88
Abbey Rd, Green. 129 FW85
Abbey Rd, Ilf. 69 ER57
Abbey Rd, Shep. 134 BN102
Abbey Rd, S.Croy. 161 DX110
Abbey Rd, Vir.W. 132 AX99
Abbey Rd, Wal.Cr. 15 DY34
Abbey Rd, Wok. 166 AW117
Abbey Rd Est NW8 82 DB67
Abbey St E13 86 EG70
Abbey St SE1 201 N6
Abbey St SE1 102 DS76
Abbey Ter SE2 106 EW77
Abbey Vw NW7 43 CT48
Abbey Vw, Wal.Abb. 15 EB33
Abbey Vw, Wat. 24 BX36
Abbey Vw Roundabout, Wal.Abb. 15 EB33
Abbey Wk, W.Mol. 136 CB97
Abbey Way SE2 106 EX76
Abbey Wf Ind Est, Bark. 87 ER68
Abbey Wd La, Rain. 90 FK68
Abbey Wd Rd SE2 106 EV77
Abbeydale Rd, Wem. 80 CN67
Abbeyfield Est SE16 102 DW77
Abbeyfield Rd SE16 202 F8
Abbeyfield Rd SE16 102 DW77
Abbeyfields Cl NW10 80 CN68
Abbeyhill Rd, Sid. 126 EW89
Abbot Cl, Stai. 114 BK94
Abbot Cl, W.Byf. 152 BK110
Abbot St E8 84 DT65
Abbots Av, Epsom 156 CN111
Abbots Cl N1 84 DQ65
Alwyne Rd
Abbots Cl, Brwd. 55 GA46
Abbots Cl, Orp. 145 EQ102
Abbots Cl, Rain. 90 FJ68
Abbots Cl, Ruis. 60 BX62
Abbots Dr, Har. 60 CA61
Abbots Dr, Vir.W. 132 AV99
Abbots Fld, Grav. 131 GJ93
Ruffets Wd
Abbots Gdns N2 64 DD56
Abbots Gdns W8 100 DB76
St. Mary's Pl
Abbots Grn, Croy. 161 DX107
Abbots La SE1 201 N3
Abbots La, Ken. 176 DQ116
Abbots Manor Est SW1 199 H9
Abbots Manor Est SW1 101 DH77
Abbots Pk SW2 121 DN88
Abbot's Pl NW6 82 DB67
Abbots Ri, Kings L. 6 BM26
Abbots Ri, Red. 184 DG132
Abbot's Rd E6 86 EK67
Abbots Rd, Abb.L. 7 BS30
Abbots Rd, Edg. 42 CQ52
Abbots Ter N8 65 DL58
Abbots Vw, Kings L. 6 BM27
Abbots Wk W8 100 DB76
St. Mary's Pl
Abbots Wk, Cat. 176 DU122
Tillingdown Hill
Abbots Way, Beck. 143 DY99
Abbotsbury Cl E15 85 EC68
Abbotsbury Cl W14 99 CZ75
Abbotsbury Rd
Abbotsbury Gdns, Pnr. 60 BW58
Abbotsbury Ms SE15 102 DW83
Abbotsbury Rd W14 99 CY75
Abbotsbury Rd, Brom. 144 EF103
Abbotsbury Rd, Mord. 140 DB99
Abbotsford Av N15 66 DQ56
Abbotsford Cl, Wok. 167 BA117
Onslow Cres
Abbotsford Gdns, Wdf.Grn. 48 EG52
Abbotsford Lo, Nthwd. 39 BS50
Abbotsford Rd, Ilf. 70 EU61
Abbotshade Rd SE16 203 J2
Abbotshade Rd SE16 85 DX74
Abbotshall Av N14 45 DJ48
Abbotshall Rd SE6 123 ED88
Abbotsleigh Cl, Sutt. 158 DB108
Abbotsleigh Rd SW16 121 DJ91
Abbotsmede Cl, Twick. 117 CF89
Abbotstone Rd SW15 99 CW83
Abbotswell Rd SE4 123 DZ85
Abbotswood Cl, Belv. 106 EY76
Coptefield Dr
Abbotswood Dr, Wey. 153 BR110
Abbotswood Gdns, Ilf. 69 EM55
Abbotswood Rd SE22 102 DS84
Abbotswood Rd SW16 121 DK90
Abbotswood Way, Hayes 77 BV74
Abbott Av SW20 139 CX96
Abbott Cl, Hmptn. 116 BY93
Abbott Cl, Nthlt. 78 BZ65
Abbott Rd E14 85 EC71
Abbotts Cl SE28 88 EW73
Abbotts Cl, Rom. 71 FB55
Abbotts Cl, Swan. 147 FG98
Abbotts Cl, Uxb. 76 BK71
Abbotts Cres E4 47 ED49
Abbotts Cres, Enf. 29 DP40
Abbotts Dr, Wal.Abb. 16 EG34
Abbotts Dr, Wem. 61 CH61
Abbotts Pk Rd E10 67 EC59
Abbotts Rd, Barn. 28 DB42
Abbotts Rd, Mitch. 141 DJ98
Abbotts Rd, Sthl. 78 BY74
Abbotts Rd, Sutt. 139 CZ104
Abbott's Tilt, Walt. 136 BY104
Abbotts Wk, Bexh. 106 EX80
Abbs Cross Gdns, Horn. 72 FJ60
Abbs Cross La, Horn. 72 FJ62
Abchurch La EC4 197 L10
Abchurch La EC4 84 DR73
Abchurch Yd EC4 197 K10
Abdale Rd W12 81 CV74
Abenberg Way, Brwd. 55 GB47
Aberavon Rd E3 85 DY69
Abercairn Rd SW16 121 DJ94
Aberconway Rd, Mord. 140 DB97
Abercorn Cl NW7 43 CY52
Abercorn Cl NW8 82 DC69
Abercorn Cl, S.Croy. 161 DX112
Abercorn Cres, Har. 60 CB60
Abercorn Gdns, Har. 61 CK59
Abercorn Gdns, Rom. 70 EV58
Abercorn Gro, Ruis. 59 BR56
Abercorn Pl NW8 82 DC69
Abercorn Rd NW7 43 CY52
Abercorn Rd, Stan. 41 CJ52
Abercorn Way SE1 202 B10
Abercorn Way SE1 102 DU78
Abercorn Way, Wok. 166 AU118
Abercrombie Dr, Enf. 30 DU39
Abercrombie St SW11 100 DE82
Aberdale Ct SE16 103 DX75
Garter Way
Aberdale Gdns, Pot.B. 11 CZ33
Aberdare Cl, W.Wick. 143 EC103
Aberdare Gdns NW6 82 DB66
Aberdare Gdns NW7 43 CX52
Aberdare Rd, Enf. 30 DW42
Aberdeen La N5 65 DP64
Aberdeen Par N18 46 DV50
Angel Rd
Aberdeen Pk N5 66 DQ64
Aberdeen Pk Ms N5 66 DQ63
Aberdeen Pl NW8 82 DD70
Aberdeen Rd N5 66 DQ63
Aberdeen Rd N18 46 DV50
Aberdeen Rd NW10 63 CT64
Aberdeen Rd, Croy. 160 DQ105
Aberdeen Rd, Har. 41 CF54
Aberdeen Sq E14 85 DZ74
Westferry Circ
Aberdeen Ter SE3 103 ED82
Aberdour Rd, Ilf. 70 EV62
Aberdour St SE1 201 M8
Aberdour St SE1 102 DS77
Aberfeldy St E14 85 EC72
Aberford Gdns SE18 104 EL81
Aberford Rd, Borwd. 26 CN40
Aberfoyle Rd SW16 121 DK93
Abergeldie Rd SE12 124 EH86
Aberglen Ind Est, Hayes 95 BR75
Abernethy Rd SE13 104 EE84
Abersham Rd E8 66 DT64
Abery St SE18 105 ES77
Abigail Ms, Rom. 52 FM54
King Alfred Rd
Abingdon Cl NW1 83 DK65
Camden Sq
Abingdon Cl SE1 202 A10
Abingdon Cl SW19 120 DC93
Abingdon Cl, Uxb. 76 BM67
Abingdon Cl, Wok. 166 AV118
Abingdon Pl, Pot.B. 12 DB32
Abingdon Rd N3 44 DC54
Abingdon Rd SW16 141 DL96
Abingdon Rd W8 100 DA76
Abingdon St SW1 199 P6
Abingdon St SW1 101 DL76
Abingdon Vil W8 100 DA76
Abingdon Way, Orp. 164 EV105
Abinger Av, Sutt. 157 CW109
Abinger Cl, Bark. 70 EU63
Abinger Cl, Brom. 144 EL97
Abinger Cl, Wall. 159 DL106
Garden Cl
Abinger Gdns, Islw. 97 CE83
Abinger Gro SE8 103 DZ79
Abinger Ms W9 82 DA70
Warlock Rd
Abinger Rd W4 98 CS76
Ablett St SE16 102 DW78
Abney Gdns N16 66 DT61
Stoke Newington High St
Aboyne Dr SW20 139 CU96
Aboyne Est SW17 120 DD90
Aboyne Rd NW10 62 CS62
Aboyne Rd SW17 120 DD90
Abridge Cl, Wal.Cr. 31 DX35
Abridge Gdns, Rom. 50 FA51
Abridge Pk (Abridge), Rom. 34 EU42
Abridge Rd, Chig. 33 ER44
Abridge Rd, Epp. 33 ES36
Abridge Rd (Abridge), Rom. 34 EU39
Abridge Way, Bark. 88 EV69
Abyssinia Cl SW11 100 DE84
Cairns Rd
Acacia Av N17 46 DR52
Acacia Av, Brent. 97 CH80
Acacia Av, Hayes 77 BT72
Acacia Av, Horn. 71 FF61
Acacia Av, Mitch. 141 DH96
Acacia Rd
Acacia Av, Ruis. 59 BU60
Acacia Av, Shep. 134 BN99
Acacia Av, Stai. 92 AY84
Acacia Av, Wem. 62 CL64
Acacia Av, West Dr. 76 BM73
Acacia Av, Wok. 166 AX120
Acacia Cl SE8 203 K9
Acacia Cl SE8 103 DY77
Acacia Cl SE20 142 DU96
Selby Rd
Acacia Cl, Add. 151 BF110
Acacia Cl, Orp. 145 ER99
Acacia Cl, Stan. 41 CE51
Acacia Cl, Wal.Cr. 14 DS27
Acacia Ct, Wal.Abb. 16 EG34
Lamplighters Cl
Acacia Dr, Add. 151 BF110
Acacia Dr, Bans. 157 CX114
Acacia Dr, Sutt. 139 CZ102
Acacia Dr, Upmin. 72 FN63
Acacia Gdns NW8 82 DD68
Acacia Rd
Acacia Gdns, Upmin. 73 FT59
Acacia Gdns, W.Wick. 143 EC103
Acacia Gro SE21 122 DR89
Acacia Gro, N.Mal. 138 CR97
Acacia Ms, West Dr. 94 BK79
Acacia Pl NW8 82 DD68
Acacia Rd E11 68 EE61
Acacia Rd E17 67 DY58
Acacia Rd N22 45 DN53
Acacia Rd NW8 82 DD68
Acacia Rd SW16 141 DL95
Acacia Rd W3 80 CQ73
Acacia Rd, Beck. 143 DZ97
Acacia Rd, Dart. 128 FK88
Acacia Rd, Enf. 30 DR39
Acacia Rd, Green. 129 FS86
Acacia Rd, Hmptn. 116 CA93
Acacia Rd, Mitch. 141 DH96
Acacia Rd, Stai. 114 BH92
Acacia Wk, Swan. 147 FD96
Walnut Way
Acacia Way, Sid. 125 ET88
Academy Gdns, Croy. 142 DT102
Academy Gdns, Nthlt. 78 BX68
Academy Pl SE18 105 EM81
Academy Rd SE18 105 EM81
Acanthus Dr SE1 202 B10
Acanthus Dr SE1 102 DU78
Acanthus Rd SW11 100 DG83
Accommodation La, West Dr. 94 BJ79
Accommodation Rd NW11 63 CZ59
Accommodation Rd, Cher. 132 AX104
Acer Av, Hayes 78 BY71
Acer Av, Rain. 90 FK69
Acer Rd, West. 178 EK116
Acers, St.Alb. 8 CC28
Acfold Rd SW6 100 DB81
Achilles Cl SE1 202 C10
Achilles Cl SE1 102 DU78
Achilles Pl, Wok. 166 AW117
Achilles Rd NW6 64 DA64
Achilles St SE14 103 DY80
Achilles Way W1 198 G3
Acklam Rd W10 81 CZ71
Acklington Dr NW9 42 CS53
Ackmar Rd SW6 100 DA81
Ackroyd Dr E3 85 DZ71
Ackroyd Rd SE23 123 DX87
Acland Cl SE18 105 ER80
Clothworkers Rd
Acland Cres SE5 102 DR84
Acland Rd NW2 81 CV65
Acme Rd, Wat. 23 BU38
Acock Gro, Nthlt. 60 CB64
Dorchester Rd
Acol Cres, Ruis. 59 BV64
Acol Rd NW6 82 DA66
Aconbury Rd, Dag. 88 EV67
Acorn Cl E4 47 EB50
The Lawns
Acorn Cl, Chis. 125 EQ92
Acorn Cl, Enf. 29 DP39
Acorn Cl, Hmptn. 116 CB93
Acorn Cl, Stan. 41 CH52
Acorn Ct, Ilf. 69 ES58
Acorn Gdns SE19 142 DT95
Acorn Gdns W3 80 CR71
Acorn Gro, Hayes 95 BT80
Acorn Gro, Ruis. 59 BT63
Acorn Gro, Tad. 173 CY124
Warren Lo Dr
Acorn Gro, Wok. 166 AY121
Old Sch Pl
Acorn Ind Pk, Dart. 127 FG85
Acorn La (Cuffley), Pot.B. 13 DL29
Acorn Par SE15 102 DV80
Carlton Gro
Acorn Pl, Wat. 23 BU37
Acorn Rd, Dart. 127 FF85
Acorn Wk SE16 203 L2
Acorn Wk SE16 85 DY74
Acorn Way SE23 123 DX90
Acorn Way, Orp. 163 EP105
Acorns, The, Chig. 49 ES49
Acorns Way, Esher 154 CC106
Acre Dr SE22 102 DU84
Acre La SW2 101 DL84
Acre La, Cars. 158 DG105
Acre La, Wall. 158 DG105
Acre Path, Nthlt. 78 BY65
Arnold Rd
Acre Rd SW19 120 DD93
Acre Rd, Dag. 89 FB66
Acre Rd, Kings.T. 138 CL95
Acre Vw, Horn. 72 FL56
Acre Way, Nthwd. 39 BT53
Acrefield Rd (Chalfont St. Peter), Ger.Cr. 56 AX55
Acres End, Amer. 20 AS39
Acres Gdns, Tad. 173 CX119
Acris St SW18 120 DC85
Acton Cl N9 46 DU47
Acton Cl (Cheshunt), Wal.Cr. 15 DY31
Acton Hill Ms W3 80 CP74
Uxbridge Rd
Acton La NW10 80 CS68
Acton La W3 98 CQ75
Acton La W4 98 CR76
Acton Ms E8 84 DT67
Acton Pk Ind Est W3 98 CR75
Acton St WC1 196 B3
Acton St WC1 83 DM69
Acuba Rd SW18 120 DB89
Acworth Cl N9 46 DW45
Turin Rd
Ada Gdns E14 85 ED72
Ada Gdns E15 86 EF67
Ada Pl E2 84 DU67
Ada Rd SE5 102 DS80
Ada Rd, Wem. 61 CK62
Ada St E8 84 DV67
Adair Cl SE25 142 DV97
Adair Rd W10 81 CY70
Adair Twr W10 81 CY70
Appleford Rd
Adam & Eve Ct W1 195 L8
Adam & Eve Ms W8 100 DA76
Adam Ct SW7 100 DC77
Gloucester Rd
Adam Pl N16 66 DT61
Stoke Newington High St
Adam Rd E4 47 DZ51
Adam St WC2 200 A1
Adam St WC2 83 DL73
Adam Wk SW6 99 CW80
Adams Cl N3 44 DA52
Falkland Av
Adams Cl NW9 62 CP61
Adams Cl, Surb. 138 CM100
Adams Ct EC2 197 L8
Adams Gdns Est SE16 202 F4
Adams Pl E14 204 B2
Adams Pl N7 65 DM64
George's Rd
Adams Rd N17 46 DS54
Adams Rd, Beck. 143 DY99
Adams Row W1 198 G1
Adams Row W1 82 DG73
Adams Sq, Bexh. 106 EY83
Regency Way
Adams Wk, Kings.T. 138 CL96
Adams Way, Croy. 142 DT100
Adamsfield, Wal.Cr. 14 DU27
Adamson Rd E16 86 EG72
Adamson Rd NW3 82 DD66
Adamsrill Cl, Enf. 30 DR44
Adamsrill Rd SE26 123 DY91
Adare Wk SW16 121 DM90
Adastral Est NW9 42 CS53
Adcock Wk, Orp. 163 ET105
Borkwood Pk
Adderley Gdns SE9 125 EN91
Adderley Gro SW11 120 DG85
Culmstock Rd
Adderley Rd, Har. 41 CF53
Adderley St E14 85 EC72
Addington Border, Croy. 161 DY110
Addington Ct SW14 98 CR83
Addington Dr N12 44 DC51
Addington Gro SE26 123 DY91
Addington Rd E3 85 EA69
Addington Rd E16 86 EE70
Addington Rd N4 65 DN58
Addington Rd, Croy. 141 DN102
Addington Rd, S.Croy. 160 DU111
Addington Rd, W.Wick. 144 EE103
Addington Sq SE5 102 DQ79
Addington St SE1 200 C5
Addington Village Rd, Croy. 161 EA106
Addis Cl, Enf. 31 DX39
Addiscombe Av, Croy. 142 DU101
Addiscombe Cl, Har. 61 CJ57
Addiscombe Ct Rd, Croy. 142 DS102
Addiscombe Gro, Croy. 142 DR103
Addiscombe Rd, Croy. 142 DS103
Addiscombe Rd, Wat. 23 BV42
Addison Av N14 29 DH44
Addison Av W11 81 CY74
Addison Av, Houns. 96 CC81
Addison Br Pl W14 99 CZ77
Addison Cl, Cat. 176 DR122
Addison Cl, Nthwd. 39 BU53
Addison Cl, Orp. 145 EQ100
Addison Cres W14 99 CY76
Addison Dr SE12 124 EH85
Eltham Rd
Addison Gdns W14 99 CX76
Addison Gdns, Grays 110 GC77
Palmers Dr
Addison Gdns, Surb. 138 CM98
Addison Gro W4 98 CS76
Addison Pl W11 81 CY74
Addison Pl, Sthl. 78 CA73
Longford Av
Addison Rd E11 68 EG58
Addison Rd E17 67 EB57
Addison Rd SE25 142 DU98
Addison Rd W14 99 CZ76
Addison Rd, Brom. 144 EJ99
Addison Rd, Cat. 176 DR121
Addison Rd, Enf. 30 DW39
Addison Rd, Ilf. 49 EQ53
Addison Rd, Tedd. 117 CH93
Addison Rd, Wok. 167 AZ1
Chertsey Rd
Addison Way NW11 63 CZ
Addison Way, Hayes 77 BU
Addison Way, Nthwd. 39 BT
Addison's Cl, Croy. 143 DZ1
Addle Hill EC4 196 G
Addle St EC2 197
Addlestone Moor, Add. 134 BJ1
Addlestone Pk, Add. 152 BH1
Addlestone Rd, Add. 152 BL1
Adecroft Way, W.Mol. 136 CC
Adela Av, N.Mal. 139 CV
Adela St W10 81 CY
Kensal Rd
Adelaide Av SE4 103 DZ
Adelaide Cl, Enf. 30 DT
Adelaide Cl, Stan. 41 CG
Adelaide Cotts W7 97 CF
Adelaide Gdns, Rom. 70 EY
Adelaide Gro W12 81 CU
Adelaide Pl, Wey. 153 BR1
Adelaide Rd E10 67 EC
Adelaide Rd NW3 82 DD
Adelaide Rd SW18 120 DA
Putney Br Rd
Adelaide Rd W13 79 CG
Adelaide Rd, Ashf. 114 BK
Adelaide Rd, Chis. 125 EP
Adelaide Rd, Houns. 96 BY
Adelaide Rd, Ilf. 69 EP
Adelaide Rd, Rich. 98 CM
Adelaide Rd, Sthl. 96 BY
Adelaide Rd, Surb. 138 CL
Adelaide Rd, Tedd. 117 CF
Adelaide Rd, Til. 111 GF
Adelaide Rd, Walt. 135 BU1
Adelaide St WC2 199
Adelaide Ter, Brent. 97 CK
Adelaide Wk SW9 101 DN
Sussex Wk
Adelina Gro E1 84 DW
Adelina Ms SW12 121 DK
King's Av
Adeline Pl WC1 195 N
Adeline Pl WC1 83 DK
Adeliza Cl, Bark. 87 EP
North St
Adelphi Ct SE16 103 DX
Garter Way
Adelphi Cres, Hayes 77 BT
Adelphi Cres, Horn. 71 FG
Adelphi Gdns, Slou. 92 AS
Adelphi Rd, Epsom 156 CR1
Adelphi Ter WC2 200 A
Adelphi Way, Hayes 77 BT
Aden Gro N16 66 DR
Aden Rd, Enf. 31 DY
Aden Rd, Ilf. 69 EP
Aden Ter N16 66 DR
Adeney Cl W6 99 CX
Adenmore Rd SE6 123 EA
Adie Rd W6 99 CW
Adine Rd E13 86 EH
Adler Ind Est, Hayes 95 BR
Adler St E1 84 DU
Adley St E5 67 DY
Adlington Cl N18 46 DS
Admaston Rd SE18 105 EQ
Admiral Cl, Orp. 146 EX
Admiral Ct NW4 63 CU
Barton Cl
Admiral Pl SE16 203
Admiral Pl SE16 85 DY
Admiral Seymour Rd SE9 105 EM
Admiral Sq SW10 100 DD
Admiral St SE8 103 EA
Admiral Wk W9 82 DA
Admirals Cl E18 68 EH
Admirals Wk NW3 64 DC
Admirals Wk, Couls. 175 DM1
Admirals Wk, Couls. 175 DM1
Goodenough Way
Admirals Wk, Green. 129 FV
Admirals Way E14 204 A
Admirals Way E14 103 EA
Admiralty Cl SE8 103 EA
Reginald Sq
Admiralty Rd, Tedd. 117 CF
Adnams Wk, Rain. 89 FF
Lovell Wk
Adolf St SE6 123 EB
Adolphus Rd N4 65 DP
Adolphus St SE8 103 DZ
Adomar Rd, Dag. 70 EX
Adpar St W2 82 DD
Adrian Av NW2 63 CV
North Circular Rd
Adrian Cl (Harefield), Uxb. 38 BK
Adrian Ms SW10 100 DB
Adrian Rd, Abb.L. 7 BS
Adrienne Av, Sthl. 78 BZ
Adstock Ms (Chalfont St. Peter), Ger.Cr. 36 AX
Church La
Adstock Way, Grays 110 FZ
Advance Rd SE27 122 DQ
Advent Ct, Wdf.Grn. 48 EF
Wood La
Advent Way N18 47 DX
Advice Av, Grays 110 GA
Adys Rd SE15 102 DT
Aerodrome Rd NW4 63 CT
Aerodrome Rd NW9 43 CT
Aerodrome Way, Houns. 96 BW
Aeroville NW9 42 CS
Affleck St N1 196 C
Afghan Rd SW11 100 DE
Afton Dr, S.Ock. 91 FV
Agamemnon Rd NW6 63 CZ
Agar Cl, Surb. 138 CM1
Agar Gro NW1 83 DJ
Agar Gro Est NW1 83 DK
Agar Pl NW1 83 DJ
Agar St WC2 199 P
Agar St WC2 83 DL
Agars Plough, Slou. 92 AU
Agate Cl E16 86 EK
Agate Rd W6 99 CW
Agates La, Ash. 171 CK1

Agatha Cl E1 202 E2
Agaton Rd SE9 125 EQ89
Agave Rd NW2 63 CW63
Agdon St EC1 196 F4
Agdon St EC1 83 DP70
Agincourt Rd NW3 64 DF63
Agister Rd, Chig. 50 EU50
Agnes Av, Ilf. 69 EP63
Agnes Cl E6 87 EN73
Agnes Gdns, Dag. 70 EX63
Agnes Rd W3 81 CT74
Agnes Scott Ct, Wey. 135 BP104
Palace Dr
Agnes St E14 85 DZ72
Agnesfield Cl N12 44 DE51
Agnew Rd SE23 123 DX87
Agricola Ct E3 85 DZ67
Parnell Rd
Agricola Pl, Enf. 30 DT43
Aidan Cl, Dag. 70 EY63
Aileen Wk E15 86 EF66
Ailsa Av, Twick. 117 CG85
Ailsa Rd, Twick. 117 CH85
Ailsa St E14 85 EC71
Ainger Ms NW3 82 DF66
Ainger Rd
Ainger Rd NW3 82 DF66
Ainsdale Cl, Orp. 145 ER102
Ainsdale Cres, Pnr. 60 CA55
Ainsdale Dr SE1 102 DU78
Ainsdale Rd W5 79 CK70
Ainsdale Rd, Wat. 40 BW48
Ainsdale Way, Wok. 166 AU118
Ainsley Av, Rom. 71 FB58
Ainsley Cl N9 46 DS46
Ainsley St E2 84 DV69
Ainslie Wk SW12 121 DH87
Ainslie Wd Cres E4 47 EB50
Ainslie Wd Gdns E4 47 EB49
Ainslie Wd Rd E4 47 EA50
Ainsty Est SE16 103 DX75
Ainsworth Cl NW2 63 CU62
Ainsworth Cl SE15 102 DS82
Lyndhurst Gro
Ainsworth Rd E9 84 DW66
Ainsworth Rd, Croy. 141 DP103
Ainsworth Way NW8 82 DC67
Aintree Av E6 86 EL67
Aintree Cl, Grav. 131 GH90
Aintree Cl, Slou. 93 BE81
Aintree Cl, Uxb. 77 BP72
Craig Dr
Aintree Cres, Ilf. 49 EQ54
Aintree Est SW6 99 CY80
Dawes Rd
Aintree Gro, Upmin. 72 FM62
Aintree Rd, Grnf. 79 CH68
Aintree St SW6 99 CY80
Air Links Ind Est, Houns. 96 BW78
Air St W1 199 L1
Air St W1 83 DJ73
Aird Ct, Hmptn. 136 BZ95
Oldfield Rd
Airdrie Cl N1 83 DM66
Airdrie Cl, Hayes 78 BY71
Glencoe Rd
Aire Dr, S.Ock. 91 FV70
Airedale Av W4 99 CT77
Airedale Av S W4 99 CT78
Netheravon Rd S
Airedale Cl, Dart. 128 FQ88
Airedale Rd SW12 120 DF87
Airedale Rd W5 97 CJ76
Airey Neave Ct, Grays 110 GA75
Airfield Way, Horn. 89 FH65
Airlie Gdns W8 100 DA75
Airlie Gdns, Ilf. 69 EP60
Airport Ind Est, West. 162 EK114
Airport Roundabout E16 86 EK74
Connaught Br
Airport Way, Stai. 93 BF84
Airthrie Rd, Ilf. 70 EV61
Aisgill Av W14 99 CZ78
Aisher Rd SE28 88 EW73
Aisher Way, Sev. 190 FE121
Aislibie Rd SE12 104 EE84
Aitken Cl E8 84 DU67
Pownall Rd
Aitken Cl, Mitch. 140 DF101
Aitken Rd SE6 123 EB89
Aitken Rd, Barn. 27 CW43
Ajax Av NW9 62 CS55
Ajax Rd NW6 64 DA64
Akabusi Cl, Croy. 142 DU100
Akehurst La, Sev. 191 FJ125
Akehurst St SW15 119 CU86
Akenside Rd NW3 64 DD64
Akerman Rd SW9 101 DP82
Akerman Rd, Surb. 137 CJ100
Akers Way, Rick. 21 BD44
Alabama St SE18 105 ER80
Alacross Rd W5 97 CJ75
Alamein Gdns, Dart. 129 FR87
Alamein Rd, Swans. 129 FX86
Alan Cl, Dart. 108 FJ84
Alan Dr, Barn. 27 CY44
Alan Gdns, Rom. 70 FA59
Alan Hocken Way E15 86 EE68
Alan Rd SW19 119 CY92
Alan Way, Slou. 74 AY72
Alanbrooke, Grav. 131 GJ87
Aland Ct SE16 203 L7
Alandale Dr, Pnr. 39 BV54
Alander Ms E17 67 EC56
Alanthus Cl SE12 124 EF86
Alaska St SE1 200 D3
Alba Cl, Hayes 78 BX70
Ramulis Dr
Alba Gdns NW11 63 CY58
Alba Pl W11 81 CZ72
Portobello Rd
Albacore Cres SE13 123 EB86
Albain Cres, Ashf. 114 BL89
Alban Cres, Borwd. 26 CP39
Alban Cres (Farningham), Dart. 148 FN102
Alban Highwalk EC2 84 DQ71
London Wall
Albans Vw, Wat. 7 BV33
Albany W1 199 K1
Albany, The, Wdf.Grn. 48 EF49
Albany Cl N15 65 DP56
Albany Cl SW14 98 CP84
Albany Cl, Bex. 126 EW87
Albany Cl, Bushey 25 CD44
Albany Cl, Esher 154 CA109
Albany Cl, Reig. 184 DA132
Albany Cl, Uxb. 58 BN64
Albany Ct E4 31 EB44
Chelwood Cl
Albany Ct, Epp. 17 ET30
Albany Ctyd W1 199 L1
Albany Cres, Edg. 42 CN52
Albany Cres, Esher 155 CE107
Albany Mans SW11 100 DE80
Albany Ms N1 83 DN66
Barnsbury Pk
Albany Ms SE5 102 DQ79
Albany Rd
Albany Ms, Brom. 124 EG93
Avondale Rd
Albany Ms, Kings.T. 117 CK93
Albany Pk Rd
Albany Ms, St.Alb. 8 CA27
North Orbital Rd
Albany Ms, Sutt. 158 DB106
Camden Rd
Albany Pk, Slou. 93 BD81
Albany Pk Av, Enf. 30 DW39
Albany Pk Rd, Kings.T. 118 CL93
Albany Pk Rd, Lthd. 171 CG119
Albany Pas, Rich. 118 CM85
Albany Pl N7 65 DN63
Benwell Rd
Albany Pl, Brent. 98 CL79
Albany Rd
Albany Pl, Egh. 113 BA91
Albany Rd E10 67 EA59
Albany Rd E12 68 EK63
Albany Rd E17 67 DZ58
Albany Rd N4 65 DM58
Albany Rd N18 46 DV50
Albany Rd SE5 102 DR79
Albany Rd SW19 120 DB92
Albany Rd W13 79 CH73
Albany Rd, Belv. 106 EZ79
Albany Rd, Bex. 126 EW87
Albany Rd, Brent. 97 CK79
Albany Rd, Brwd. 54 FV44
Albany Rd, Chis. 125 EP92
Albany Rd, Enf. 31 DX37
Albany Rd, Horn. 71 FG60
Albany Rd, N.Mal. 138 CR98
Albany Rd, Rich. 118 CM85
Albert Rd
Albany Rd, Rom. 70 EZ58
Albany Rd, Walt. 154 BX105
Albany Rd (Old Windsor), Wind. 112 AU85
Albany St NW1 83 DH68
Albany Ter NW1 83 DH70
Marylebone Rd
Albany Vw, Buck.H. 48 EG46
Albanys, The, Reig. 184 DA131
Albatross Gdns, S.Croy. 161 DX111
Albatross St SE18 105 ES80
Albatross Way SE16 103 DX75
Albemarle SW19 119 CX89
Albemarle App, Ilf. 69 EP58
Albemarle Av, Pot.B. 12 DB33
Albemarle Av, Twick. 116 BZ88
Albemarle Av (Cheshunt), Wal.Cr. 14 DW28
Albemarle Cl, Grays 110 GA75
Albemarle Gdns, Ilf. 69 EP58
Albemarle Gdns, N.Mal. 138 CR98
Albemarle Pk, Stan. 41 CJ50
Marsh La
Albemarle Rd, Barn. 44 DE45
Albemarle Rd, Beck. 143 EB95
Albemarle St W1 199 J1
Albemarle St W1 83 DH73
Albemarle Way EC1 196 F5
Alberon Gdns NW11 63 CZ56
Albert Av E4 47 EA49
Albert Av SW8 101 DM80
Albert Av, Cher. 134 BG97
Albert Br SW3 100 DE79
Albert Br SW11 100 DE79
Albert Br Rd SW11 100 DE80
Albert Carr Gdns SW16 121 DL92
Albert Cl E9 84 DV67
Northiam St
Albert Cl N22 45 DK53
Albert Cl, Grays 110 GC76
Albert Cl, Slou. 92 AT76
Albert St
Albert Ct SW7 100 DD75
Albert Cres E4 47 EA49
Albert Dr SW19 119 CY89
Albert Dr, Wok. 151 BD114
Albert Embk SE1 101 DL78
Albert Gdns E1 85 DX72
Albert Gate SW1 198 E4
Albert Gate SW1 100 DF75
Albert Gro SW20 139 CX95
Albert Hall Mans SW7 100 DD75
Kensington Gore
Albert Mans SW11 100 DF81
Albert Br Rd
Albert Ms E14 85 DY73
Narrow St
Albert Ms W8 100 DC76
Victoria Gro
Albert Murray Cl, Grav. 131 GJ87
Armoury Dr
Albert Pl N3 44 DA53
Albert Pl N17 66 DT55
High Rd
Albert Pl W8 100 DB75
Albert Rd E10 67 EC61
Albert Rd E16 86 EL74
Albert Rd E17 67 EA57
Albert Rd E18 68 EH55
Albert Rd N4 65 DM60
Albert Rd N15 66 DS58
Albert Rd N22 45 DJ53
Albert Rd NW4 63 CX56
Albert Rd NW6 81 CZ68
Albert Rd NW7 43 CT50
Albert Rd SE9 124 EL90
Albert Rd SE20 123 DX94
Albert Rd SE25 142 DU98
Albert Rd W5 79 CH70
Albert Rd, Add. 134 BK104
Albert Rd, Ashf. 114 BM92
Albert Rd, Ash. 172 CM118
Albert Rd, Barn. 28 DC42
Albert Rd, Belv. 106 EZ78
Albert Rd, Bex. 126 FA86
Albert Rd, Brom. 144 EK99
Albert Rd, Buck.H. 48 EK47
Albert Rd, Dag. 70 FA60
Albert Rd, Dart. 128 FJ90
Albert Rd, Egh. 112 AX93
Albert Rd, Epsom 157 CT113
Albert Rd, Hmptn. 116 CC92
Albert Rd, Har. 60 CC55
Albert Rd, Hayes 95 BS76
Albert Rd, Houns. 96 CA84
Albert Rd, Ilf. 69 EP62
Albert Rd, Kings.T. 138 CM96
Albert Rd, Mitch. 140 DF97
Albert Rd, N.Mal. 139 CT98
Albert Rd, Orp. 164 EU106
Albert Rd (St. Mary Cray), Orp. 146 EV100
Albert Rd, Red. 185 DJ129
Albert Rd, Rich. 118 CL85
Albert Rd, Rom. 71 FF57
Albert Rd, Sthl. 96 BX76
Albert Rd, Sutt. 158 DD106
Albert Rd, Swans. 130 FZ86
Albert Rd, Tedd. 117 CF93
Albert Rd, Twick. 117 CF88
Albert Rd, Warl. 177 DZ117
Albert Rd, West Dr. 76 BL74
Albert Rd Est, Belv. 106 EZ78
Albert Rd N, Reig. 183 CZ133
Albert Rd N, Wat. 23 BV41
Albert Rd S, Wat. 23 BV41
Albert Sq E15 68 EE64
Albert Sq SW8 101 DM80
Albert St N12 44 DC50
Albert St NW1 83 DH67
Albert St, Brwd. 54 FW50
Albert St, Slou. 92 AT76
Albert Ter NW1 82 DG67
Albert Ter NW10 80 CR67
Albert Ter, Buck.H. 48 EK47
Albert Ter Ms NW1 82 DG67
Regents Pk Rd
Albert Way SE15 102 DV80
Alberta Av, Sutt. 157 CY105
Alberta Est SE17 200 G10
Alberta Est SE17 101 DP78
Alberta Rd, Enf. 30 DT44
Alberta Rd, Erith 107 FC81
Alberta St SE17 200 F10
Alberta St SE17 101 DP78
Albertine Cl, Epsom 173 CV116
Rose Bushes
Albion Av N10 44 DG53
Albion Av SW8 101 DK82
Albion Bldgs EC1 84 DQ71
Bartholomew Cl
Albion Cl W2 194 C10
Albion Cl, Rom. 71 FD58
Albion Cl, Slou. 74 AU74
Albion Cres, Ch.St.G. 36 AV48
Albion Dr E8 84 DT66
Albion Est SE16 203 H5
Albion Est SE16 103 DX75
Albion Gdns W6 99 CV77
Albion Gro N16 66 DS63
Albion Hill SE13 103 EB82
Albion Hill, Loug. 32 EJ43
Albion Ho, Slou. 93 BB78
Albion Ho, Wok. 167 AZ117
Albion Ms N1 83 DN67
Albion Ms NW6 81 CZ66
Kilburn High Rd
Albion Ms W2 194 C9
Albion Ms W2 82 DE72
Albion Ms W6 99 CV77
Galena Rd
Albion Par N16 66 DR63
Albion Rd
Albion Par, Grav. 131 GK86
Albion Pk, Loug. 32 EK43
Albion Pl EC1 196 F6
Albion Pl EC1 83 DP71
Albion Pl SE25 142 DU97
High St
Albion Pl W6 99 CV77
Albion Rd E17 67 EC55
Albion Rd N16 66 DR63
Albion Rd N17 46 DT54
Albion Rd, Bexh. 106 EZ84
Albion Rd, Ch.St.G. 36 AV47
Albion Rd, Grav. 131 GJ87
Albion Rd, Hayes 77 BS72
Albion Rd, Houns. 96 CA84
Albion Rd, Kings.T. 138 CQ95
Albion Rd, Sutt. 158 DD107
Albion Rd, Twick. 117 CE88
Albion Sq E8 84 DT66
Albion St SE16 202 G5
Albion St SE16 102 DW75
Albion St W2 194 C9
Albion St W2 82 DE72
Albion St, Croy. 141 DP102
Albion Ter E8 84 DT66
Albion Ter, Grav. 131 GJ86
Albion Vil Rd SE26 122 DW90
Albion Way EC1 197 H7
Albion Way SE13 103 EC84
Albion Way, Wem. 62 CP62
North End Rd
Albright Ind Est, Rain. 89 FF71
Albrighton Rd SE22 102 DS83
Albuhera Cl, Enf. 29 DN39
Albury Av, Bexh. 106 EY82
Albury Av, Islw. 97 CF80
Albury Av, Sutt. 157 CW109
Albury Cl, Cher. 132 AU104
Albury Cl, Hmptn. 116 CA93
Albury Dr, Pnr. 40 BX52
Albury Gro Rd (Cheshunt), Wal.Cr. 15 DX30
Albury Ms E12 68 EJ60
Albury Ride (Cheshunt), Wal.Cr. 15 DX31
Albury Rd, Chess. 156 CL106
Albury Rd, Red. 185 DJ129
Albury Rd, Walt. 153 BS107
Albury St SE8 103 EA79
Albury Wk (Cheshunt), Wal.Cr. 15 DX32
Albyfield, Brom. 145 EM97
Albyn Rd SE8 103 EA81
Albyns Cl, Rain. 89 FG66
Albyns La, Rom. 35 FC40
Alcester Cres E5 66 DV61
Alcester Rd, Wall. 159 DH105
Alcock Cl, Wall. 159 DK108
Alcock Rd, Houns. 96 BX80
Alcocks Cl, Tad. 173 CY120
Alcocks La, Tad. 173 CY120
Alconbury Rd E5 66 DU61
Alcorn Cl, Sutt. 140 DA103
Alcott Cl W7 79 CF71
Westcott Cres
Alcuin Ct, Stan. 41 CJ52
Old Ch La
Aldborough Rd, Dag. 89 FC65
Aldborough Rd, Upmin. 72 FM61
Aldborough Rd N, Ilf. 69 ET57
Aldborough Rd S, Ilf. 69 ES60
Aldborough Spur, Slou. 74 AS72
Aldbourne Rd W12 81 CT74
Aldbridge St SE17 201 N10
Aldbridge St SE17 102 DS78
Aldburgh Ms W1 194 G8
Aldbury Av, Wem. 80 CP66
Aldbury Cl, Wat. 24 BX36
Aldbury Ms N9 46 DR45
Aldbury Rd, Rick. 37 BF45
Aldebert Ter SW8 101 DL80
Aldeburgh Cl E5 66 DV61
Southwold Rd
Aldeburgh Pl, Wdf.Grn. 48 EG49
Aldeburgh St SE10 205 M10
Aldeburgh St SE10 104 EG78
Alden Av E15 86 EF69
Aldenham Av, Rad. 25 CG36
Aldenham Dr, Uxb. 77 BP70
Aldenham Gro, Rad. 9 CH34
Aldenham Rd, Borwd. 25 CH42
Aldenham Rd, Bushey 24 BZ41
Aldenham Rd, Rad. 25 CG35
Aldenham Rd, Wat. 24 BX44
Aldenham Rd (Letchmore Heath), Wat. 25 CE39
Aldenham St NW1 195 L1
Aldenham St NW1 83 DK68
Aldenholme, Wey. 153 BS107
Aldensley Rd W6 99 CV76
Alder Av, Upmin. 72 FM63
Alder Cl SE15 102 DT79
Alder Cl, Egh. 112 AY92
Alder Cl, St.Alb. 8 CB28
Alder Dr, S.Ock. 91 FW70
Laburnum Gro
Alder Gro NW2 63 CV61
Alder Ms N19 65 DJ61
Bredgar Rd
Alder Rd SW14 98 CR83
Alder Rd, Iver 75 BC68
Alder Rd, Sid. 125 ET90
Alder Rd (Denham), Uxb. 76 BJ65
Alder Wk, Ilf. 69 EQ64
Alder Wk, Wat. 23 BV35
Aspen Pk Dr
Alder Way, Swan. 147 FD96
Alderbourne La, Iver 57 BA64
Alderbourne La, Slou. 56 AX63
Alderbrook Rd SW12 121 DH86
Alderbury Rd SW13 99 CU79
Alderbury Rd, Slou. 93 AZ75
Alderbury Rd W, Slou. 93 AZ75
Aldercombe La, Cat. 186 DS127
Aldercroft, Couls. 175 DM116
Aldergrove Gdns, Houns. 96 BY82
Bath Rd
Aldergrove Wk, Horn. 90 FJ65
Airfield Way
Alderholt Way SE15 102 DT80
Daniel Gdns
Alderman Av, Bark. 88 EU69
Alderman Judge Mall, Kings.T. 138 CL96
Eden St
Aldermanbury EC2 197 J8
Aldermanbury EC2 84 DQ72
Aldermanbury Sq EC2 197 J7
Aldermans Hill N13 45 DL49
Alderman's Wk EC2 197 M7
Aldermary Rd, Brom. 144 EG95
Aldermoor Rd SE6 123 DZ90
Alderney Av, Houns. 96 CB80
Alderney Gdns, Nthlt. 78 BZ66
Alderney Rd E1 85 DX70
Alderney Rd, Erith 107 FG80
Alderney St SW1 199 J10
Alderney St SW1 101 DH77
Alders, The N21 29 DN44
Alders, The, Felt. 116 BY91
Alders, The, Houns. 96 BZ79
Alders, The, W.Byf. 152 BJ112
Alders, The, W.Wick. 143 EB102
Alders Av, Wdf.Grn. 48 EE51
Alders Cl E11 68 EH61
Aldersbrook Rd
Alders Cl W5 97 CK76
Alders Cl, Edg. 42 CQ50
Alders Gro, E.Mol. 137 CD99
Esher Rd
Alders Rd, Edg. 42 CQ50
Alders Rd, Reig. 184 DB132
Aldersbrook Av, Enf. 30 DS40
Aldersbrook Dr, Kings.T. 118 CM93
Aldersbrook La E12 69 EM62
Aldersbrook Rd E11 68 EH61
Aldersbrook Rd E12 68 EK62
Aldersey Gdns, Bark. 87 ER65
Aldersford Cl SE4 123 DX85
Aldersgate St EC1 197 H8
Aldersgate St EC1 84 DQ71
Aldersgrove, Wal.Abb. 16 EE34
Roundhills
Aldersgrove Av SE9 124 EJ90
Aldershot Rd NW6 81 CZ67
Alderside Wk, Egh. 112 AY92
Aldersmead Av, Croy. 143 DX100
Aldersmead Rd, Beck. 123 DY94
Alderson Pl, Sthl. 78 CC74
Alderson St W10 81 CY70
Kensal Rd
Alderstead Heath, Red. 175 DK124
Alderstead La, Red. 185 DK126
Alderton Cl NW10 62 CR62
Alderton Cl, Brwd. 54 FV43
Alderton Cl, Loug. 33 EN42
Alderton Cres NW4 63 CV57
Alderton Hall La, Loug. 33 EN42
Alderton Hill, Loug. 32 EL43
Alderton Ms, Loug. 33 EN42
Alderton Hall La
Alderton Ri, Loug. 33 EN42
Alderton Rd SE24 102 DQ83
Alderton Rd, Croy. 142 DT101
Alderton Way NW4 63 CV57
Alderton Way, Loug. 33 EM43
Alderville Rd SW6 99 CZ82
Alderwick Dr, Houns. 97 CD83
Alderwood Cl, Cat. 186 DS125
Alderwood Cl, Rom. 34 EV41
Alderwood Dr, Rom. 34 EV41
Alderwood Rd SE9 125 ER86
Aldford St W1 198 F2
Aldford St W1 82 DG74
Aldgate EC3 197 P9
Aldgate EC3 84 DT72
Aldgate Av E1 197 P8
Aldgate High St EC3 197 P9
Aldgate High St EC3 84 DT72
Aldham Dr, S.Ock. 91 FW71
Aldin Av N, Slou. 92 AV75
Aldin Av S, Slou. 92 AU75
Aldine Ct W12 81 CW74
Aldine St
Aldine Pl W12 81 CW74
Uxbridge Rd
Aldine St W12 99 CW75
Aldingham Ct, Horn. 71 FG64
Easedale Dr
Aldingham Gdns, Horn. 71 FG64
Aldington Cl, Dag. 70 EW59
Aldington Rd SE18 104 EK76
Aldis Ms SW17 120 DE92
Aldis St
Aldis St SW17 120 DE92
Aldred Rd NW6 64 DA64
Aldren Rd SW17 120 DC90
Aldrich Cres, Croy. 161 EC109
Aldrich Gdns, Sutt. 139 CZ104
Aldrich Ter SW18 120 DC89
Lidiard Rd
Aldriche Way E4 47 EC51
Aldridge Av, Edg. 42 CP48
Aldridge Av, Enf. 31 EA38
Aldridge Av, Ruis. 60 BX61
Aldridge Av, Stan. 42 CL53
Aldridge Ri, N.Mal. 138 CS101
Aldridge Rd Vil W11 81 CZ71
Aldridge Wk N14 45 DL45
Aldrington Rd SW16 121 DJ92
Aldsworth Cl W9 82 DB70
Aldwick Cl SE9 125 ER90
Aldwick Rd, Croy. 141 DM104
Aldworth Gro SE13 123 EC86
Aldworth Rd E15 86 EE66
Aldwych WC2 196 B10
Aldwych WC2 83 DM73
Aldwych Av, Ilf. 69 EQ56
Aldwych Cl, Horn. 71 FG61
Aldwych Underpass WC2 83 DM72
Kingsway
Alers Rd, Bexh. 126 EX85
Alesia Cl N22 45 DL52
Nightingale Rd
Alestan Beck Rd E16 86 EK72
Fulmer Rd
Alexa Ct W8 100 DA77
Lexham Gdns
Alexander Av NW10 81 CV66
Alexander Cl, Barn. 28 DD42
Alexander Cl, Brom. 144 EG102
Alexander Cl, Sid. 125 ES85
Alexander Cl, Sthl. 78 CC74
Alexander Cl, Twick. 117 CF89
Alexander Ct, Wal.Cr. 15 DX30
Alexander Evans Ms SE23 123 DX88
Sunderland Rd
Alexander Godley Cl, Ash. 172 CM119
Alexander La, Brwd. 55 GB44
Alexander Ms W2 82 DB72
Alexander St
Alexander Pl SW7 198 B8
Alexander Pl SW7 100 DE77
Alexander Rd N19 65 DL62
Alexander Rd, Bexh. 106 EX82
Alexander Rd, Chis. 125 EP92
Alexander Rd, Couls. 175 DH115
Alexander Rd, Egh. 113 BB92
Alexander Rd, Green. 129 FW85
Alexander Rd, St.Alb. 9 CK25
Alexander Sq SW3 198 B8
Alexander Sq SW3 100 DE77
Alexander St W2 82 DA72
Alexanders Wk, Cat. 186 DT126
Alexandra Av N22 45 DK53
Alexandra Av SW11 100 DG81
Alexandra Av W4 98 CR80
Alexandra Av, Har. 60 BZ60
Alexandra Av, Sthl. 78 BZ73
Alexandra Av, Sutt. 140 DA104
Alexandra Av, Warl. 177 DZ117
Alexandra Cl, Ashf. 115 BR94
Alexandra Rd
Alexandra Cl, Grays 111 GH75
Alexandra Cl, Har. 60 CA62
Alexandra Av
Alexandra Cl, Stai. 114 BK93
Alexandra Cl, Swan. 147 FE96
Alexandra Cl, Walt. 135 BU103
Alexandra Cotts SE14 103 DZ81
Alexandra Ct N14 29 DJ43
Alexandra Ct, Ashf. 115 BR93
Alexandra Rd
Alexandra Ct, Wem. 62 CM63
Alexandra Cres, Brom. 124 EF93
Alexandra Dr SE19 122 DS92
Alexandra Dr, Surb. 138 CN101
Alexandra Gdns N10 65 DH56
Alexandra Gdns W4 98 CR80

Alexandra Gdns, Cars. 158 DG109
Alexandra Gdns, Houns. 96 CB82
Alexandra Gro N4 65 DP60
Alexandra Gro N12 44 DB50
Alexandra Ms N2 64 DF55
Fortis Grn
Alexandra Ms SW19 120 DA93
Alexandra Rd
Alexandra Palace N22 45 DK54
Alexandra Palace Way N22 65 DJ55
Alexandra Pk Rd N10 45 DH54
Alexandra Pk Rd N22 45 DK54
Alexandra Pl NW8 82 DC67
Alexandra Pl SE25 142 DR99
Alexandra Pl, Croy. 142 DS102
Alexandra Rd
Alexandra Rd E6 87 EN69
Alexandra Rd E10 67 EC62
Alexandra Rd E17 67 DZ58
Alexandra Rd E18 68 EH55
Alexandra Rd N8 65 DN55
Alexandra Rd N9 46 DV45
Alexandra Rd N10 45 DH52
Alexandra Rd N15 66 DR57
Alexandra Rd NW4 63 CX56
Alexandra Rd NW8 82 DC66
Alexandra Rd SE26 123 DX93
Alexandra Rd SW14 98 CR83
Alexandra Rd SW19 119 CZ93
Alexandra Rd W4 98 CR75
Alexandra Rd, Add. 152 BK105
Alexandra Rd, Ashf. 115 BR94
Alexandra Rd, Borwd. 26 CR38
Alexandra Rd, Brent. 97 CK79
Alexandra Rd, Brwd. 54 FW48
Alexandra Rd, Croy. 142 DS102
Alexandra Rd, Egh. 112 AW93
Alexandra Rd, Enf. 31 DX42
Alexandra Rd, Epsom 157 CT113
Alexandra Rd, Erith 107 FF79
Alexandra Rd, Grav. 131 GL87
Alexandra Rd, Houns. 96 CB82
Alexandra Rd, Kings L. 6 BN29
Alexandra Rd (Chipperfield), Kings L. 6 BG30
Alexandra Rd, Kings.T. 118 CN94
Alexandra Rd, Mitch. 120 DE94
Alexandra Rd, Rain. 89 FF67
Alexandra Rd, Rich. 98 CM82
Alexandra Rd, Rick. 22 BG36
Alexandra Rd, Rom. 71 FF58
Alexandra Rd (Chadwell Heath), Rom. 70 EX58
Alexandra Rd, T.Ditt. 137 CF99
Alexandra Rd, Til. 111 GF82
Alexandra Rd, Twick. 117 CJ86
Alexandra Rd, Uxb. 76 BK68
Alexandra Rd, Warl. 177 DY117
Alexandra Rd, Wat. 23 BU40
Alexandra Rd, West. 178 EH119
Alexandra Sq, Mord. 140 DA99
Alexandra St E16 86 EG71
Alexandra St SE14 103 DY80
Alexandra Wk SE19 122 DS92
Alexandra Way, Epsom 156 CN111
Alexandra Way, Wal.Cr. 15 DZ34
Alexandria Rd W13 79 CG73
Alexis St SE16 202 B8
Alexis St SE16 102 DU77
Alfan La, Dart. 127 FD92
Alfearn Rd E5 66 DW63
Alford Grn, Croy. 161 ED107
Alford Pl N1 197 J1
Alford Rd SW8 101 DK81
Alford Rd, Erith 107 FD78
Alfoxton Av N15 65 DP56
Alfred Cl W4 98 CR77
Belmont Rd
Alfred Gdns, Sthl. 78 BY73
Alfred Ms W1 195 M6
Alfred Ms W1 83 DK71
Alfred Pl WC1 195 M6
Alfred Pl WC1 83 DK71
Alfred Pl, Grav. 131 GF88
Alfred Prior Ho E12 69 EN63
Alfred Rd E15 68 EF64
Alfred Rd SE25 142 DU99
Alfred Rd W2 82 DA71
Alfred Rd W3 80 CQ74
Alfred Rd, Belv. 106 EZ78
Alfred Rd, Brwd. 54 FX47
Alfred Rd, Buck.H. 48 EK47
Alfred Rd, Dart. 128 FL91
Alfred Rd, Felt. 116 BW89
Alfred Rd, Grav. 131 GH89
Alfred Rd, Kings.T. 138 CL97
Alfred Rd, S.Ock. 90 FQ74
Alfred Rd, Sutt. 158 DC106
Alfred St E3 85 DZ69
Alfred St, Grays 110 GC79
Alfreda St SW11 101 DH81
Alfred's Gdns, Bark. 87 ES68
Alfreds Way, Bark. 87 EQ69
Alfreds Way Ind Est, Bark. 88 EU67
Alfreton Cl SW19 119 CX90
Alfriston Av, Croy. 141 DL101
Alfriston Av, Har. 60 CA58
Alfriston Cl, Surb. 138 CM99
Alfriston Rd SW11 120 DF85
Algar Cl, Islw. 97 CG83
Algar Rd
Algar Cl, Stan. 41 CF50
Algar Rd, Islw. 97 CG83
Algarve Rd SW18 120 DB88
Algernon Rd NW4 63 CU58
Algernon Rd NW6 82 DA67
Algernon Rd SE13 103 EB84
Algers Cl, Loug. 32 EK43
Algers Mead, Loug. 32 EK43
Algers Rd, Loug. 32 EK43
Algiers Rd SE13 103 EA84
Alibon Gdns, Dag. 70 FA64
Alibon Rd, Dag. 70 FA64
Alice Cl, Barn. 28 DC42
Station App
Alice Ct SW15 99 CZ84
Deodar Rd
Alice Gilliatt Ct W14 99 CZ79
Alice La E3 85 DZ67
Alice Ms, Tedd. 117 CF92
Luther Rd
Alice Ruston Pl, Wok. 166 AW119
Alice St SE1 201 M7
Alice St SE1 102 DS76
Alice Thompson Cl SE12 124 EJ89
Alice Walker Cl SE24 101 DP84
Shakespeare Rd
Alice Way, Houns. 96 CB84
Alicia Av, Har. 61 CH56
Alicia Cl, Har. 61 CJ56
Alicia Gdns, Har. 61 CJ56
Alie St E1 84 DT72
Alington Cres NW9 62 CQ60
Alington Gro, Wall. 159 DJ109
Alison Cl E6 87 EN72
Alison Cl, Croy. 143 DX102
Shirley Oaks Rd
Alison Cl, Wok. 166 AY115
Aliwal Rd SW11 100 DE84
Alkerden La, Green. 129 FW86
Alkerden La, Swans. 129 FW86
Alkerden Rd W4 98 CS78
Alkham Rd N16 66 DT61
All Hallows Rd N17 46 DS53
All Saints Cl N9 46 DT47
All Saints Cl, Chig. 50 EU48
All Saints Cl, Swans. 130 FZ85
High St
All Saints Cres, Wat. 8 BX33
All Saints Dr SE3 104 EE82
All Saints Dr, S.Croy. 160 DT112
All Saints La, Rick. 22 BN44
All Saints Ms, Har. 41 CE51
All Saints Pas SW18 120 DB85
Wandsworth High St
All Saints Rd SW19 120 DC94
All Saints Rd W3 98 CQ76
All Saints Rd W11 81 CZ71
All Saints Rd, Grav. 131 GF88
All Saints Rd, Sutt. 140 DB104
All Saints St N1 83 DM68
All Saints Twr E10 67 EB59
All Souls Av NW10 81 CV68
All Souls Pl W1 195 J7
Allan Barclay Cl N15 66 DT58
High Rd
Allan Cl, N.Mal. 138 CR99
Allan Way W3 80 CQ71
Allandale Av N3 63 CY55
Allandale Cres, Pot.B. 11 CY32
Allandale Pl, Orp. 146 EX104
Allandale Rd, Enf. 31 DX36
Allandale Rd, Horn. 71 FF59
Allard Cl, Orp. 146 EW101
Allard Cl (Cheshunt), Wal.Cr. 14 DT27
Allard Cres, Bushey 40 CC46
Allard Gdns SW4 121 DK85
Allardyce St SW4 101 DM84
Allbrook Cl, Tedd. 117 CE92
Allcot Cl, Felt. 115 BT88
Allcroft Rd NW5 64 DG64
Allen Cl, Mitch. 141 DH95
Allen Cl, Rad. 10 CL32
Russet Dr
Allen Cl, Sun. 135 BV95
Allen Ct, Grnf. 61 CF64
Allen Edwards Dr SW8 101 DL81
Allen Ho Pk, Wok. 166 AW120
Allen Pl, Twick. 117 CG88
Church St
Allen Rd E3 85 DZ68
Allen Rd N16 66 DS63
Allen Rd, Beck. 143 DX96
Allen Rd, Croy. 141 DM101
Allen Rd, Rain. 90 FJ68
Allen Rd, Sun. 135 BV95
Allen St W8 100 DA76
Allenby Av, S.Croy. 160 DQ109
Allenby Cl, Grnf. 78 CA69
Allenby Cres, Grays 110 GB78
Allenby Dr, Horn. 72 FL60
Allenby Rd SE23 123 DY90
Allenby Rd, Sthl. 78 CA72
Allenby Rd, West. 178 EL117
Allendale Av, Sthl. 78 CA72
Allendale Cl SE5 102 DR81
Daneville Rd
Allendale Cl SE26 123 DX92
Allendale Cl, Dart. 129 FR88
Princes Rd
Allendale Rd, Grnf. 79 CH65
Allens Rd, Enf. 30 DW43
Allensbury Pl NW1 83 DK66
Allenswood Rd SE9 104 EL83
Allerford Ct, Har. 60 CB57
Allerford Rd SE6 123 EB91
Allerton Cl, Borwd. 26 CM38
Allerton Ct NW4 43 CX54
Holders Hill Rd
Allerton Rd N16 66 DQ61
Allerton Rd, Borwd. 26 CL38
Allerton Wk N7 65 DM61
Durham Rd
Allestree Rd SW6 99 CY80
Alleyn Cres SE21 122 DR89
Alleyn Pk SE21 122 DR89
Alleyn Pk, Sthl. 96 BZ77
Alleyn Rd SE21 122 DR90
Alleyndale Rd, Dag. 70 EW61
Allfarthing La SW18 120 DB86
Allgood Cl, Mord. 139 CX100
Allgood St E2 84 DT68
Hackney Rd
Allhallows La EC4 201 K1
Allhallows Rd E6 86 EL71
Allhusen Gdns, Slou. 56 AY63
Alderbourne La
Alliance Cl, Wem. 61 CK63
Alliance Rd E13 86 EJ70
Alliance Rd SE18 106 EU79
Alliance Rd W3 80 CP70
Allied Way W3 98 CS75
Larden Rd
Allingham Cl W7 79 CF73
Allingham Ms N1 84 DQ68
Allingham St
Allingham St N1 84 DQ68
Allington Av N17 46 DS51
Allington Cl SW19 119 CX92
High St Wimbledon
Allington Cl, Grav. 131 GM88
Farley Rd
Allington Cl, Grnf. 78 CC66
Allington Ct, Enf. 31 DX43
Allington Ct, Slou. 74 AT73
Myrtle Cres
Allington Rd NW4 63 CV57
Allington Rd W10 81 CY68
Allington Rd, Har. 60 CC57
Allington Rd, Orp. 145 ER103
Allington St SW1 199 K7
Allington St SW1 101 DH76
Allison Cl SE10 103 EC81
Dartmouth Hill
Allison Cl, Wal.Abb. 16 EG32
Allison Gro SE21 122 DS88
Allison Rd N8 65 DN57
Allison Rd W3 80 CQ72
Allitsen Rd NW8 194 B1
Allitsen Rd NW8 82 DE68
Allmains Cl, Wal.Abb. 16 EH25
Allnutt Way SW4 121 DK85
Allnutts Rd, Epp. 18 EU33
Alloa Rd SE8 203 J10
Alloa Rd SE8 103 DX78
Alloa Rd, Ilf. 70 EU61
Allonby Dr, Ruis. 59 BP59
Allonby Gdns, Wem. 61 CJ60
Allotment La, Sev. 191 FJ122
Alloway Cl, Wok. 166 AV118
Inglewood
Alloway Rd E3 85 DY69
Allsop Pl NW1 194 E5
Allsop Pl NW1 82 DF70
Allum Cl, Borwd. 26 CL42
Allum Gro, Tad. 173 CV121
Preston La
Allum La, Borwd. 26 CM42
Allum Way N20 44 DC46
Allwood Cl SE26 123 DX91
Allwood Rd, Wal.Cr. 14 DT27
Allyn Cl, Stai. 113 BF93
Penton Rd
Alma Av E4 47 EC52
Alma Av, Horn. 72 FL63
Alma Cl, Wok. 166 AS118
Alma Cres, Sutt. 157 CY106
Alma Gro SE1 202 A9
Alma Gro SE1 102 DT77
Alma Pl NW10 81 CV69
Harrow Rd
Alma Pl SE19 122 DT94
Alma Pl, Th.Hth. 141 DN99
Alma Rd N10 44 DG52
Alma Rd SW18 120 DC85
Alma Rd, Cars. 158 DE106
Alma Rd, Enf. 31 DY43
Alma Rd, Esher 137 CE102
Alma Rd, Orp. 146 EX103
Alma Rd, Reig. 184 DB133
Alma Rd, Sid. 126 EU90
Alma Rd, Sthl. 78 BY73
Alma Rd, Swans. 130 FZ85
Alma Row, Har. 41 CD53
Alma Sq NW8 82 DC69
Alma St E15 85 ED65
Alma St NW5 83 DH65
Alma Ter SW18 120 DD87
Alma Ter W8 100 DA76
Allen St
Almack Rd E5 66 DW63
Almeida St N1 83 DP66
Almer Rd SW20 119 CU94
Almeric Rd SW11 100 DF84
Almington St N4 65 DM60
Almners Rd, Cher. 133 BC100
Almond Av W5 98 CL76
Almond Av, Cars. 140 DF103
Almond Av, Uxb. 59 BP62
Almond Av, West Dr. 94 BN76
Almond Av, Wok. 166 AX121
Almond Cl SE15 102 DU82
Almond Cl, Brom. 145 EN101
Almond Cl, Egh. 112 AV93
Almond Cl, Felt. 115 BU88
Highfield Rd
Almond Cl, Grays 111 GG76
Almond Cl, Hayes 77 BS73
Almond Cl, Ruis. 59 BT62
Roundways
Almond Cl, Shep. 135 BQ96
Almond Dr, Swan. 147 FD96
Almond Gro, Brent. 97 CH80
Almond Rd N17 46 DU52
Almond Rd SE16 202 E8
Almond Rd SE16 102 DV77
Almond Rd, Dart. 128 FQ87
Almond Rd, Epsom 156 CR111
Almond Way, Borwd. 26 CP42
Almond Way, Brom. 145 EN101
Almond Way, Har. 40 CB54
Almond Way, Mitch. 141 DK99
Almonds Av, Buck.H. 48 EG47
Almons Way, Slou. 74 AV71
Almorah Rd N1 84 DR66
Almorah Rd, Houns. 96 BX81
Alms Heath, Wok. 169 BP121
Almshouse La, Chess. 155 CJ109
Almshouse La, Enf. 30 DV37
Alnwick Gro, Mord. 140 DB98
Bordesley Rd
Alnwick Rd E16 86 EJ72
Alnwick Rd SE12 124 EH87
Alperton La, Grnf. 79 CK69
Alperton La, Wem. 79 CK69
Alperton St W10 81 CY70
Alpha Cl NW1 194 C3
Alpha Ct, Whyt. 176 DU118
Alpha Gro E14 204 A5
Alpha Gro E14 103 EA75
Alpha Pl NW6 82 DA68
Alpha Pl SW3 100 DE79
Alpha Rd E4 47 EB48
Alpha Rd N18 46 DU51
Alpha Rd SE14 103 DZ81
Alpha Rd, Brwd. 55 GD44
Alpha Rd, Croy. 142 DS102
Alpha Rd, Enf. 31 DY42
Alpha Rd, Surb. 138 CM100
Alpha Rd, Tedd. 117 CD92
Alpha Rd, Uxb. 77 BP70
Alpha Rd, Wok. 167 BB116
Alpha Rd (Chobham), Wok. 150 AT110
Alpha St SE15 102 DU82
Alpha St N, Slou. 92 AU75
Alpha St S, Slou. 92 AT76
Alpha Way, Egh. 133 BC95
Alphabet Gdns, Cars. 140 DD100
Alphabet Sq E3 85 EA71
Hawgood St
Alphea Cl SW19 120 DE94
Courtney Rd
Alpine Av, Surb. 138 CQ103
Alpine Cl, Croy. 142 DS104
Alpine Copse, Brom. 145 EN96
Alpine Gro E9 84 DW66
Alpine Rd SE16 203 H10
Alpine Rd SE16 102 DW77
Alpine Rd, Red. 184 DG131
Alpine Rd, Walt. 135 BU101
Alpine Vw, Cars. 158 DE106
Alpine Wk, Stan. 41 CE47
Alpine Way E6 87 EN71
Alric Av NW10 80 CR66
Alric Av, N.Mal. 138 CS97
Alroy Rd N4 65 DN59
Alsace Rd SE17 201 M10
Alsace Rd SE17 102 DS78
Alscot Rd SE1 202 A8
Alscot Rd SE1 102 DT77
Alscot Way SE1 201 P8
Alscot Way SE1 102 DT77
Alsike Rd SE2 106 EX76
Alsike Rd, Erith 106 EY76
Alsom Av, Wor.Pk. 157 CU105
Alsop Cl, St.Alb. 10 CM27
Halsey Pk
Alston Cl, Surb. 137 CH101
Alston Rd N18 46 DV50
Alston Rd SW17 120 DD91
Alston Rd, Barn. 27 CY41
Alt Gro SW19 119 CZ94
St. George's Rd
Altair Cl N17 46 DT51
Altair Way, Nthwd. 39 BT49
Altash Way SE9 125 EM89
Altenburg Av W13 97 CH76
Altenburg Gdns SW11 100 DF84
Alterton Cl, Wok. 166 AU117
Altham Rd, Pnr. 40 BY52
Althea St SW6 100 DB83
Althorne Gdns E18 68 EF56
Althorne Way, Dag. 70 FA61
Althorp Cl, Barn. 43 CU45
Althorp Rd SW17 120 DF88
Althorpe Gro SW11 100 DD81
Westbridge Rd
Althorpe Ms SW11 100 DD81
Westbridge Rd
Althorpe Rd, Har. 60 CC57
Altmore Av E6 87 EM66
Alton Av, Stan. 41 CF52
Alton Cl, Bex. 126 EY88
Alton Cl, Islw. 97 CF82
Alton Ct, Stai. 133 BE95
Alton Gdns, Beck. 123 EA94
Alton Gdns, Twick. 117 CD87
Alton Rd N17 66 DR55
Alton Rd SW15 119 CU88
Alton Rd, Croy. 141 DN104
Alton Rd, Rich. 98 CL84
Alton St E14 85 EB71
Altyre Cl, Beck. 143 DZ99
Altyre Rd, Croy. 142 DR103
Altyre Way, Beck. 143 DZ99
Aluric Cl, Grays 111 GH77
Alva Way, Wat. 40 BX47
Alvanley Gdns NW6 64 DB64
Alverstoke Rd, Rom. 52 FL52
Alverston Gdns SE25 142 DS99
Alverstone Av SW19 120 DA89
Alverstone Av, Barn. 44 DE45
Alverstone Gdns SE9 125 EQ88
Alverstone Rd E12 69 EN63
Alverstone Rd NW2 81 CW66
Alverstone Rd, N.Mal. 139 CT98
Alverstone Rd, Wem. 62 CM60
Alverton St SE8 103 DZ78
Alveston Av, Har. 61 CH55
Alvey Est SE17 201 M9
Alvey Est SE17 102 DS77
Alvey St SE17 201 M10
Alvey St SE17 102 DS78
Alvia Gdns, Sutt. 158 DC105
Alvington Cres E8 66 DT64
Alway Av, Epsom 156 CQ106
Alwen Gro, S.Ock. 91 FV71
Alwold Cres SE12 124 EH86
Alwyn Av W4 98 CR78
Alwyn Cl, Borwd. 26 CM44
Alwyn Cl, Croy. 161 EB108
Alwyn Gdns NW4 63 CU56
Alwyn Gdns W3 80 CP72
Alwyne Av, Brwd. 55 GA44
Alwyne Ct, Wok. 166 AY116
Alwyne La N1 83 DP66
Alwyne Vil
Alwyne Pl N1 84 DQ65
Alwyne Rd N1 84 DQ66
Alwyne Rd SW19 119 CZ93
Alwyne Rd W7 79 CE73
Alwyne Sq N1 84 DQ65
Alwyne Vil N1 83 DP66
Alwyns Cl, Cher. 134 BG100
Alwyns La
Alwyns La, Cher. 133 BF100
Alyth Gdns NW11 64 DA58
Alzette Ho E2 85 DX69
Amalgamated Dr, Brent. 97 CG79
Amanda Cl, Chig. 49 ER51
Amanda Ct, Slou. 92 AX76
Amanda Ms, Rom. 71 FC57
Amazon St E1 84 DV72
Hessel St
Ambassador Cl, Houns. 96 BY82
Ambassador Gdns E6 87 EM71
Ambassador Sq E14 204 B9
Ambassador Sq E14 103 EB77
Ambassador's Ct SW1 199 L3
Amber Av E17 47 DY53
Amber Ct SW17 120 DG91
Brudenell Rd
Amber Ct, Stai. 113 BF92
Laleham Rd
Amber Gro NW2 63 CX60
Prayle Gro
Amber St E15 85 ED65
Salway Rd
Ambercroft Way, Couls. 175 DP119
Amberden Av N3 64 DA55
Ambergate St SE17 200 G10
Ambergate St SE17 101 DP78
Amberley Cl, Orp. 163 ET106
Warnford Rd
Amberley Cl, Pnr. 60 BZ55
Amberley Ct, Sid. 126 EW92
Amberley Dr, Add. 151 BF110
Amberley Gdns, Enf. 46 DS45
Amberley Gdns, Epsom 157 CT105
Amberley Gro SE26 122 DV91
Amberley Gro, Croy. 142 DT101
Amberley Rd E10 67 EB59
Amberley Rd N13 45 DM47
Amberley Rd SE2 106 EX79
Amberley Rd W9 82 DA71
Amberley Rd, Buck.H. 48 EJ46
Amberley Rd, Enf. 46 DT45
Amberley Way, Houns. 116 BW85
Amberley Way, Mord. 139 CZ101
Amberley Way, Rom. 71 FB56
Amberley Way, Uxb. 76 BL69
Amberside Cl, Islw. 117 CD86
Amberwood Ri, N.Mal. 138 CS100
Amblecote, Cob. 154 BY111
Amblecote Cl SE12 124 EH90
Amblecote Meadows SE12 124 EH90
Amblecote Rd SE12 124 EH90
Ambler Rd N4 65 DP62
Ambleside, Brom. 123 ED93
Ambleside, Epp. 18 EU31
Ambleside Av SW16 121 DK91
Ambleside Av, Beck. 143 DY99
Ambleside Av, Horn. 71 FH64
Ambleside Av, Walt. 136 BW102
Ambleside Cl E9 66 DW64
Churchill Wk
Ambleside Cl E10 67 EB59
Ambleside Cres, Enf. 31 DX41
Ambleside Dr, Felt. 115 BT88
Ambleside Gdns SW16 121 DK92
Ambleside Gdns, Ilf. 68 EL56
Ambleside Gdns, S.Croy. 161 DX109
Ambleside Gdns, Sutt. 158 DC107
Ambleside Gdns, Wem. 61 CK60
Ambleside Rd NW10 81 CT66
Ambleside Rd, Bexh. 106 FA82
Ambleside Wk, Uxb. 76 BK67
High St
Ambleside Way, Egh. 113 BB94
Ambrey Way, Wall. 159 DK109
Ambrooke Rd, Belv. 106 FA76
Ambrosden Av SW1 199 L7
Ambrosden Av SW1 101 DJ76
Ambrose Av NW11 63 CY59
Ambrose Cl E6 86 EL71
Lovage App
Ambrose Cl, Dart. 107 FF84
Ambrose Cl, Orp. 145 ET104
Stapleton Rd
Ambrose Ms SW11 100 DE82
Ambrose St SE16 202 D8
Ambrose St SE16 102 DV77
Ambrose Wk E3 85 EA68
Malmesbury Rd
Amelia St SE17 200 G10
Amelia St SE17 101 DP78
Amen Cor EC4 196 G9
Amen Cor SW17 120 DF93
Amen Ct EC4 196 G8
Amenity Way, Mord. 139 CW101
America Sq EC3 197 P10
America St SE1 201 H3
Amerland Rd SW18 119 CZ86
Amersham Av N18 46 DR51
Amersham Cl, Rom. 52 FM51
Amersham Dr, Rom. 52 FL51
Amersham Gro SE14 103 DZ80
Amersham Pl, Amer. 20 AW39
Amersham Rd SE14 103 DZ81
Amersham Rd (Little Chalfont), Amer. 20 AX39
Amersham Rd, Ch.St.G. 20 AU43
Amersham Rd, Croy. 142 DQ100
Amersham Rd, Ger.Cr. 57 BB59
Amersham Rd (Chalfont St. Peter), Ger.Cr. 56 AY55
Amersham Rd, Rick. 21 BB39
Amersham Rd, Rom. 52 FM51
Amersham Vale SE14 103 DZ80
Amersham Wk, Rom. 52 FM51
Amersham Rd
Amersham Way, Amer. 20 AX39
Amery Gdns NW10 81 CV67
Amery Gdns, Rom. 72 FK55
Amery Rd, Har. 61 CG61
Ames Rd, Swans. 130 FY86
Amesbury, Wal.Abb. 16 EG32
Amesbury Av SW2 121 DL89
Amesbury Cl, Epp. 17 ET31
Amesbury Rd
Amesbury Cl, Wor.Pk. 139 CW102
Amesbury Dr E4 31 EB44
Amesbury Rd, Brom. 144 EK97
Amesbury Rd, Dag. 88 EX66
Amesbury Rd, Epp. 17 ET31
Amesbury Rd, Felt. 116 BX89
Amethyst Rd E15 67 ED63
Amey Dr, Lthd. 170 CC124
Amherst Av W13 79 CJ72
Amherst Cl, Orp. 146 EU98
Amherst Dr, Orp. 145 ET98
Amherst Hill, Sev. 190 FE122
Amherst Rd W13 79 CJ72
Amherst Rd, Sev. 191 FH122
Amhurst Gdns, Islw. 97 CF81
Amhurst Par N16 66 DT59
Amhurst Pk
Amhurst Pk N16 66 DR59
Amhurst Pas E8 66 DU64
Amhurst Rd E8 66 DV64
Amhurst Rd N16 66 DT63
Amhurst Ter E8 66 DU63
Amhurst Wk SE28 88 EU74
Pitfield Cres
Amidas Gdns, Dag. 70 EV63
Amiel St E1 84 DW70
Amies St SW11 100 DF83

ina Way SE16 202 B7
is Av, Add. 152 BG111
is Av, Epsom 156 CP107
is Rd, Wok. 166 AS119
ity Gro SW20 139 CW95
ity Rd E15 86 EF67
manford Gdn NW9 62 CS58
Ruthin Cl
ner Rd SW11 120 DG86
or Rd W6 99 CW76
ott Rd SE15 102 DU83
oy Pl E14 85 EA72
pere Way, Croy. 141 DL101
pleforth Rd SE2 106 EV75
pthill Sq Est NW1 195 L1
pton Pl WC1 196 B3
pton St WC1 196 B3
pton St WC1 83 DM69
roth Cl SE23 122 DV88
stel Way, Wok. 166 AT118
sterdam Rd E14 204 E7
sterdam Rd E14 103 EC76
undsen Ct E14 103 EA78
Napier Av
well Cl, Enf. 30 DR43
well Cl, Wat. 24 BY35
Phillipers
well Ct, Wal.Abb. 16 EF33
well Ct Est N4 66 DQ60
well St EC1 196 D2
well St EC1 83 DN69
y Cl, Wall. 159 DL108
Mollison Dr
y Rd, Oxt. 188 EE129
y Warne Cl E6 86 EL70
Evelyn Denington Rd
yand Cotts, Twick. 117 CH86
Amyand Pk Rd
yand La, Twick. 117 CH87
Marble Hill Gdns
yand Pk Gdns, Twick. 117 CH87
Amyand Pk Rd
yand Pk Rd, Twick. 117 CG87
yruth Rd SE4 123 EA85
atola Rd N19 65 DH61
Dartmouth Pk Hill
caster Cres, N.Mal. 139 CU100
caster Ms, Beck. 143 DX97
caster Rd, Beck. 143 DX97
caster St SE18 105 ES80
chor & Hope La SE7 104 EH76
chor Bay Ind Est, Erith 107 FG79
chor Boul, Dart. 108 FQ84
chor Cl, Bark. 87 ES69
Thames Rd
chor Cl (Cheshunt), Wal.Cr. 15 DX28
chor Dr, Rain. 89 FH69
chor Ms SW12 121 DH86
Hazelbourne Rd
chor St SE16 202 D8
chor St SE16 102 DV77
chor Ter E1 84 DW70
Cephas Av
chor Wf E3 85 EB71
Watts Gro
chor Yd EC1 197 J4
chorage Cl SW19 120 DA92
chorage Pt Ind Est SE7 104 EJ76
cill Cl W6 99 CY79
cona Rd NW10 81 CU68
cona Rd SE18 105 ER78
dace Pk Gdns, Brom. 144 EJ95
dalus Rd SW9 101 DL83
der Cl, Wem. 61 CK63
derson Cl N21 29 DM43
derson Cl W3 80 CR72
derson Cl, Epsom 156 CP112
derson Cl, Sutt. 140 DA102
derson Cl (Harefield), Uxb. 38 BG53
derson Dr, Ashf. 115 BQ91
derson Ho, Bark. 87 ER68
The Coverdales
derson Pl, Houns. 96 CB84
derson Rd E9 85 DX65
derson Rd, Rad. 10 CN33
derson Rd, Wey. 135 BR104
derson Rd, Wdf.Grn. 68 EK55
derson St SW3 198 D10
derson St SW3 100 DF78
derson Way, Belv. 107 FB75
derton Cl SE5 102 DR83
dmark Ct, Sthl. 78 BZ74
Herbert Rd
dover Av E16 86 EK72
King George Av
dover Cl, Epsom 156 CR111
dover Cl, Felt. 115 BT88
dover Cl, Grnf. 78 CB70
Ruislip Rd
dover Cl, Uxb. 76 BH68
dover Pl NW6 82 DB68
dover Rd N7 65 DM61
dover Rd, Orp. 145 ER102
dover Rd, Twick. 117 CD88
dre St E8 66 DU64
drea Av, Grays 110 GA75
drew Borde St WC2 195 N8
drew Cl, Dart. 127 FD85
drew Cl, Ilf. 49 ER51
drew Cl (Shenley), Rad. 10 CM33
drew Pl SW8 101 DK81
Cowthorpe Rd
drew St E14 85 EC72
drewes Gdns E6 86 EL72
drewes Ho EC2 197 J7
drews Cl E6 86 EL72
Linton Gdns
drews Cl, Buck.H. 48 EJ47
drews Cl, Epsom 157 CT114
drews Cl, Har. 61 CD59
Bessborough Rd
drews Cl, Orp. 146 EX96
drews Cl, Wor.Pk. 139 CX103
drews Crosse WC2 196 D9
drews La (Cheshunt), Wal.Cr. 14 DU28
drews Pl SE9 125 EP86

Andrew's Rd E8 84 DV67
Andrews Wk SE17 101 DP79
Dale Rd
Andwell Cl SE2 106 EV75
Anerley Gro SE19 122 DT94
Anerley Hill SE19 122 DT93
Anerley Pk SE20 122 DU94
Anerley Pk Rd SE20 122 DV94
Anerley Rd SE19 122 DU94
Anerley Rd SE20 122 DU94
Anerley Sta Rd SE20 142 DV95
Anerley St SW11 100 DF82
Anerley Vale SE19 122 DT94
Anfield Cl SW12 121 DJ87
Belthorn Cres
Angas Ct, Wey. 153 BQ106
Angel All E1 84 DU72
Whitechapel Rd
Angel Cl N18 46 DT49
Angel Cor Par N18 46 DU50
Fore St
Angel Ct EC2 197 L8
Angel Ct EC2 84 DR72
Angel Ct SW1 199 L3
Angel Ct SW17 120 DF91
Angel Gate EC1 196 G2
Angel Hill, Sutt. 140 DB104
Sutton Common Rd
Angel Hill Dr, Sutt. 140 DB104
Angel La E15 85 ED65
Angel La, Hayes 77 BR71
Angel Ms E1 84 DU73
Cable St
Angel Ms N1 196 E1
Angel Ms N1 83 DN68
Angel Ms SW15 119 CU87
Roehampton High St
Angel Pas EC4 201 K1
Angel Pl N18 46 DU50
Angel Pl SE1 201 K4
Angel Rd N18 46 DV50
Angel Rd, Har. 61 CE58
Angel Rd, T.Ditt. 137 CG101
Angel Rd Wks N18 46 DW50
Angel Sq EC1 196 E1
Angel St EC1 197 H8
Angel St EC1 84 DQ72
Angel Wk W6 99 CW77
Angel Way, Rom. 71 FE57
Angelfield, Houns. 96 CB84
Angelica Cl, West Dr. 76 BL72
Lovibonds Av
Angelica Dr E6 87 EN71
Angelica Gdns, Croy. 143 DX102
Angell Pk Gdns SW9 101 DN83
Angell Rd SW9 101 DN83
Angerstein La SE3 104 EF80
Angle Cl, Uxb. 76 BN67
Angle Grn, Dag. 70 EW60
Angle Rd, Grays 109 FX79
Anglers Cl, Rich. 117 CJ91
Locksmeade Rd
Angler's La NW5 83 DH65
Anglers Reach, Surb. 137 CK99
Angles Rd SW16 121 DL91
Anglesea Av SE18 105 EP77
Anglesea Cen, Grav. 131 GH86
New Rd
Anglesea Pl, Grav. 131 GH86
Clive Rd
Anglesea Rd SE18 105 EP77
Anglesea Rd, Kings.T. 137 CK98
Anglesea Rd, Orp. 146 EW100
Anglesea Ter W6 99 CV76
Wellesley Av
Anglesey Cl, Ashf. 114 BN90
Anglesey Ct Rd, Cars. 158 DG107
Anglesey Dr, Rain. 89 FG71
Anglesey Gdns, Cars. 158 DG107
Anglesey Rd, Enf. 30 DV42
Anglesey Rd, Wat. 40 BW50
Anglesmede Cres, Pnr. 60 CA55
Anglesmede Way, Pnr. 60 BZ55
Anglia Cl N17 46 DV52
Park La
Anglia Ct, Dag. 70 EX60
Spring Cl
Anglia Ho E14 85 DY72
Anglia Wk E6 87 EM67
Anglian Cl, Wat. 24 BW40
Anglian Rd E11 67 ED62
Anglo Rd E3 85 DZ68
Anglo Way, Red. 184 DG132
Angrave Ct E8 84 DT67
Angrave Pas E8 84 DT67
Haggerston Rd
Angus Cl, Chess. 156 CN106
Angus Dr, Ruis. 60 BW63
Angus Gdns NW9 42 CR53
Angus Rd E13 86 EJ69
Angus St SE14 103 DY80
Anhalt Rd SW11 100 DE80
Ankerdine Cres SE18 105 EN80
Ankerwycke Priory, Stai. 113 AZ89
Anlaby Rd, Tedd. 117 CE92
Anley Rd W14 99 CX75
Anmersh Gro, Stan. 41 CK53
Ann La SW10 100 DD80
Ann Moss Way SE16 202 F6
Ann Moss Way SE16 102 DW76
Ann St SE18 105 ER77
Anna Cl E8 84 DT67
Anna Neagle Cl E7 68 EG63
Dames Rd
Annabel Cl E14 85 EB72
Annalee Gdns, S.Ock. 91 FV71
Annalee Rd, S.Ock. 91 FV71
Annan Way, Rom. 51 FD53
Annandale Gro, Uxb. 59 BQ62
Thorpland Av
Annandale Rd SE10 104 EF79
Annandale Rd W4 98 CS77
Annandale Rd, Croy. 142 DU103
Annandale Rd, Sid. 125 ES87
Anne Boleyn's Wk, Kings.T. 118 CL92
Anne Boleyn's Wk, Sutt. 157 CX108
Anne Case Ms, N.Mal. 138 CR97
Sycamore Gro
Anne of Cleves Rd, Dart. 128 FK85
Anne St E13 86 EG70
Anne Way, Ilf. 49 EQ51

Anne Way, W.Mol. 136 CB98
Anners Cl, Egh. 133 BC97
Anne's Wk, Cat. 176 DS120
Annesley Av NW9 62 CR55
Annesley Cl NW10 62 CS62
Annesley Dr, Croy. 143 DZ104
Annesley Rd SE3 104 EH81
Annesley Wk N19 65 DJ61
Annett Cl, Shep. 135 BS98
Annett Rd, Walt. 135 BU101
Annette Cl, Har. 41 CE54
Spencer Rd
Annette Cres N1 84 DQ66
Essex Rd
Annette Rd N7 65 DM63
Annie Besant Cl E3 85 DZ67
Annie Brookes Cl, Stai. 113 BD90
Annifer Way, S.Ock. 91 FV71
Anning St EC2 197 N4
Annington Rd N2 64 DF55
Annis Rd E9 85 DY65
Ann's Cl SW1 198 E5
Ann's Pl E1 197 P7
Annsworthy Av, Th.Hth. 142 DR97
Grange Pk Rd
Annsworthy Cres SE25 142 DR96
Grange Rd
Ansdell Rd SE15 102 DW82
Ansdell St W8 100 DB76
Ansdell Ter W8 100 DB76
Ansdell St
Ansell Gro, Cars. 140 DG102
Ansell Rd SW17 120 DE90
Anselm Cl, Croy. 142 DT104
Park Hill Ri
Anselm Rd SW6 100 DA79
Anselm Rd, Pnr. 40 BZ52
Ansford Rd, Brom. 123 EC92
Ansleigh Pl W11 81 CX73
Ansley Cl, S.Croy. 160 DV114
Anslow Gdns, Iver 75 BD68
Anson Cl, Hem.H. 5 AZ27
Anson Cl, Ken. 176 DR120
Anson Cl, Rom. 51 FB54
Anson Rd N7 65 DK63
Anson Rd NW2 63 CX64
Anson Ter, Nthlt. 78 CB65
Anson Wk, Nthwd. 39 BQ49
Anstead Dr, Rain. 89 FG68
Anstey Rd SE15 102 DU83
Anstey Wk N15 65 DP56
Anstice Cl W4 98 CS80
Anstridge Path SE9 125 ER86
Anstridge Rd SE9 125 ER86
Antelope Av, Grays 110 GA76
Hogg La
Antelope Rd SE18 105 EM76
Anthony Cl NW7 42 CS49
Anthony Cl, Sev. 181 FE120
Anthony Cl, Wat. 40 BW46
Anthony La, Swan. 147 FG95
Anthony Rd SE25 142 DU100
Anthony Rd, Borwd. 26 CM40
Anthony Rd, Grnf. 79 CE68
Anthony Rd, Well. 106 EU81
Anthony St E1 84 DV72
Commercial Rd
Anthonys, Wok. 151 BB112
Anthorne Cl, Pot.B. 12 DB31
Anthus Ms, Nthwd. 39 BS52
Antigua Cl SE19 122 DR92
Salters Hill
Antigua Wk SE19 122 DR92
Antill Rd E3 85 DY69
Antill Rd N15 66 DT56
Antill Ter E1 85 DX72
Antlers Hill E4 31 EB43
Antoinette Ct, Abb.L. 7 BT29
Anton Cres, Sutt. 140 DA104
Anton Rd, S.Ock. 91 FV70
Anton St E8 66 DU64
Antoneys Cl, Pnr. 40 BX54
Antrim Gro NW3 82 DF65
Antrim Mans NW3 82 DE65
Antrim Rd NW3 82 DF65
Antrobus Cl, Sutt. 157 CZ106
Antrobus Rd W4 98 CQ77
Anugraha Conference Cen, Egh. 112 AU91
Anvil Cl SW16 121 DJ94
Anvil Cl (Bovingdon), Hem.H. 5 BB28
Yew Tree Dr
Anvil Ct, Slou. 93 BA77
Blacksmith Row
Anvil La, Cob. 153 BU114
Anvil Pl, St.Alb. 8 CA26
Anvil Rd, Sun. 135 BU97
Anworth Cl, Wdf.Grn. 48 EH51
Anyards Rd, Cob. 153 BV113
Apeldoorn Dr, Wall. 159 DL109
Aperdele Rd, Lthd. 171 CG118
Aperfield Rd, Erith 107 FF79
Aperfield Rd, West. 178 EL117
Apers Av, Wok. 167 AZ121
Apex Cl, Beck. 143 EB95
Apex Cl, Wey. 135 BR104
Apex Cor NW7 42 CR49
Apex Retail Pk, Felt. 116 BZ90
Apex Twr, N.Mal. 138 CS97
Aplin Way, Islw. 97 CE81
Apollo Av, Brom. 144 EH95
Rodway Rd
Apollo Av, Nthwd. 39 BU50
Apollo Cl, Horn. 71 FH61
Apollo Pl E11 68 EE62
Apollo Pl SW10 100 DD80
Apollo Pl, Wok. 166 AU119
Church Rd
Apollo Way SE28 105 ER76
Broadwater Rd
Apostle Way, Th.Hth. 141 DP96
Apothecary St EC4 196 F9
Appach Rd SW2 121 DN86
Apple Cotts, Hem.H. 5 BA27
Apple Garth, Brent. 97 CK77
Apple Gro, Chess. 156 CL105
Apple Gro, Enf. 30 DS41
Apple Mkt, Kings.T. 137 CK96
Eden St
Apple Orchard, Swan. 147 FD98
Apple Rd E11 68 EE62
Apple Tree Av, Uxb. 76 BM71

Apple Tree Av, West Dr. 76 BM71
Apple Tree Roundabout, West Dr. 76 BM73
Apple Tree Yd SW1 199 L2
Appleby Cl E4 47 EC51
Appleby Cl N15 66 DR57
Appleby Cl, Twick. 117 CD89
Appleby Dr, Rom. 52 FJ50
Appleby Gdns, Felt. 115 BT88
Appleby Grn, Rom. 52 FJ50
Appleby Dr
Appleby Rd E8 84 DU66
Appleby Rd E16 86 EF72
Appleby St E2 84 DT68
Appleby St (Cheshunt), Wal.Cr. 14 DT26
Applecroft, St.Alb. 8 CB28
Appledore Av, Bexh. 107 FC81
Appledore Av, Ruis. 59 BV62
Appledore Cl SW17 120 DF89
Appledore Cl, Brom. 144 EF99
Appledore Cl, Edg. 42 CN53
Appledore Cl, Rom. 52 FJ53
Appledore Cres, Sid. 125 ES90
Appledown Ri, Couls. 175 DJ115
Applefield, Amer. 20 AW39
Appleford Rd W10 81 CY70
Applegarth, Croy. 161 EB108
Applegarth, Esher 155 CF106
Applegarth Dr, Dart. 128 FL89
Applegarth Dr, Ilf. 69 ET56
Applegarth Rd SE28 88 EV74
Applegarth Rd W14 99 CX76
Applegate, Brwd. 54 FT43
Appleshaw Cl, Grav. 131 GG92
Appleton Cl, Amer. 20 AV40
Appleton Dr, Dart. 127 FH90
Appleton Gdns, N.Mal. 139 CU100
Appleton Rd SE9 104 EL83
Appleton Rd, Loug. 33 EP41
Appleton Sq, Mitch. 140 DE95
Appleton Way, Horn. 72 FK60
Appletree Cl SE20 142 DV95
Jasmine Gro
Appletree Cl, Lthd. 170 CC124
Appletree Gdns, Barn. 28 DE42
Appletree La, Slou. 92 AW76
Appletree Wk, Wat. 7 BV34
Applewood Cl N20 44 DE46
Applewood Cl NW2 63 CV62
Appold St EC2 197 M6
Appold St EC2 84 DS71
Appold St, Erith 107 FF79
Apprentice Way E5 66 DV63
Clarence Rd
Approach, The NW4 63 CX57
Approach, The W3 80 CR72
Approach, The, Enf. 30 DV40
Approach, The, Lthd. 170 BY123
Maddox La
Approach, The, Orp. 145 ET103
Approach, The, Pot.B. 11 CZ32
Approach, The, Upmin. 72 FP62
Approach Cl N16 66 DS64
Cowper Rd
Approach Rd E2 84 DW68
Approach Rd SW20 139 CW96
Approach Rd, Ashf. 115 BQ93
Approach Rd, Barn. 28 DD42
Approach Rd, Pur. 159 DP112
Approach Rd, W.Mol. 136 CA99
Aprey Gdns NW4 63 CW56
April Cl W7 79 CE73
April Cl, Ash. 172 CM117
April Cl, Felt. 115 BU90
April Cl, Orp. 163 ET106
Briarswood Way
April Glen SE23 123 DX90
April St E8 66 DT63
Aprilwood Cl, Add. 151 BF111
Apsledene, Grav. 131 GK93
Miskin Way
Apsley Cl, Har. 60 CC57
Apsley Rd SE25 142 DV98
Apsley Rd, N.Mal. 138 CQ97
Apsley Way NW2 63 CU61
Apsley Way W1 198 G4
Aquarius Business Pk NW2 63 CU60
Aquarius Way, Nthwd. 39 BU50
Aquila Cl, Lthd. 172 CL121
Aquila St NW8 82 DD68
Aquinas St SE1 200 E3
Arabella Dr SW15 98 CS84
Arabia Cl E4 47 ED45
Arabin Rd SE4 103 DY84
Araglen Av, S.Ock. 91 FV71
Aragon Av, Epsom 157 CV109
Aragon Av, T.Ditt. 137 CF99
Aragon Cl, Brom. 145 EM102
Aragon Cl, Croy. 162 EE110
Aragon Cl, Enf. 29 DM38
Aragon Cl, Loug. 32 EL44
Aragon Cl, Rom. 51 FB51
Aragon Cl, Sun. 115 BT94
Aragon Dr, Ilf. 49 EQ52
Aragon Dr, Ruis. 60 BX60
Aragon Ms E1 202 B2
Aragon Rd, Kings.T. 118 CL92
Aragon Rd, Mord. 139 CX100
Aragon Wk, W.Byf. 152 BM113
Aran Ct, Wey. 135 BR103
Mallards Reach
Aran Dr, Stan. 41 CJ49
Aran Hts, Ch.St.G. 36 AV49
Arandora Cres, Rom. 70 EV59
Arbery Rd E3 85 DY69
Arbor Cl, Beck. 143 EB96
Arbor Ct N16 66 DR61
Lordship Rd
Arbor Rd E4 47 ED48
Arborfield Cl SW2 121 DM88
Arborfield Cl, Slou. 92 AS76
Arbour Cl, Brwd. 54 FW50
Arbour Cl, Lthd. 171 CF123
Arbour Rd, Enf. 31 DX42
Arbour Sq E1 85 DX72
Arbour Vw, Amer. 20 AV39
Arbour Way, Horn. 71 FH64
Arbroath Grn, Wat. 39 BU48
Arbroath Rd SE9 104 EL83
Arbrook Chase, Esher 154 CC107
Arbrook Cl, Orp. 146 EU97

Arbrook La, Esher 154 CC107
Arbury Ter SE26 122 DV90
Oaksford Av
Arbuthnot La, Bex. 126 EY86
Arbuthnot Rd SE14 103 DX82
Arbutus St E8 84 DS67
Arcade, The EC2 197 M7
Arcade, The, Croy. 142 DQ104
High St
Arcade Pl, Rom. 71 FE57
Arcadia Av N3 44 DA53
Arcadia Caravans, Stai. 134 BH95
Arcadia Cl, Cars. 158 DG105
Arcadia St E14 85 EA72
Arcadian Av, Bex. 126 EY86
Arcadian Cl, Bex. 126 EY86
Arcadian Gdns N22 45 DM52
Arcadian Rd, Bex. 126 EY86
Arcany Rd, S.Ock. 91 FV70
Arch Rd, Walt. 136 BX104
Arch St SE1 201 H7
Arch St SE1 102 DQ76
Archangel St SE16 203 J5
Archangel St SE16 103 DX75
Archates Av, Grays 110 GA76
Archbishops Pl SW2 121 DM86
Archdale Pl, N.Mal. 138 CP97
Archdale Rd SE22 122 DT85
Archel Rd W14 99 CZ79
Archer Cl, Kings L. 6 BM29
Archer Cl, Kings.T. 118 CL94
Archer Ho SW11 100 DD81
Vicarage Cres
Archer Ms, Hmptn. 116 CC93
Windmill Rd
Archer Rd SE25 142 DV98
Archer Rd, Orp. 146 EU99
Archer St W1 195 M10
Archer Ter, West Dr. 76 BL73
Yew Av
Archer Way, Swan. 147 FF96
Archers Ct, S.Ock. 91 FV71
Archers Dr, Enf. 30 DW40
Archers Wk SE15 102 DT81
Wodehouse Av
Archery Cl W2 194 C9
Archery Cl W2 82 DE72
Archery Cl, Har. 61 CF55
Archery Rd SE9 125 EM85
Arches, The SW6 99 CZ82
Munster Rd
Arches, The WC2 200 A2
Arches, The, Har. 60 CB61
Archibald Ms W1 198 G2
Archibald Ms W1 82 DG74
Archibald Rd N7 65 DK63
Archibald Rd, Rom. 52 FN53
Archibald St E3 85 EA69
Archie Cl, West Dr. 94 BN75
Archway, Rom. 51 FH51
Archway Cl N19 65 DJ61
St. Johns Way
Archway Cl SW19 120 DB91
Archway Cl W10 81 CX71
Archway Cl, Wall. 141 DK104
Archway Mall N19 65 DJ61
Magdala Av
Archway Rd N6 64 DG58
Archway Rd N19 65 DJ60
Archway St SW13 98 CS83
Arcola St E8 66 DT64
Arctic St NW5 64 DG64
Gillies St
Arcus Rd, Brom. 124 EE93
Ardbeg Rd SE24 122 DR86
Arden Cl, Bushey 41 CF45
Arden Cl, Har. 61 CD62
Arden Cl, Hem.H. 5 BA28
Arden Ct Gdns N2 64 DD58
Arden Cres E14 204 A8
Arden Cres E14 103 EA77
Arden Cres, Dag. 88 EW66
Arden Est N1 197 M1
Arden Est N1 84 DS68
Arden Gro, Orp. 163 EP105
Arden Ms E17 67 EB57
Arden Mhor, Pnr. 59 BV56
Arden Rd N3 63 CY55
Arden Rd W13 79 CJ73
Ardent Cl SE25 142 DS97
Ardent Way (Cheshunt), Wal.Cr. 14 DR26
Hammondstreet Rd
Ardesley Wd, Wey. 153 BS105
Ardfern Av SW16 141 DN97
Ardfillan Rd SE6 123 ED88
Ardgowan Rd SE6 124 EE87
Ardilaun Rd N5 66 DQ63
Ardingly Cl, Croy. 143 DX104
Ardleigh Cl, Horn. 72 FK55
Ardleigh Ct, Brwd. 55 FZ45
Ardleigh Gdns, Brwd. 55 GE44
Fairview Av
Ardleigh Gdns, Sutt. 140 DA101
Ardleigh Grn Rd, Horn. 72 FK57
Ardleigh Ho, Bark. 87 EQ67
St. Ann's
Ardleigh Ms, Ilf. 69 EP62
Bengal Rd
Ardleigh Rd E17 47 DZ53
Ardleigh Rd N1 84 DR65
Ardleigh Ter E17 47 DZ53
Ardley Cl NW10 62 CS62
Ardley Cl SE6 123 DY90
Ardley Cl, Ruis. 59 BQ59
Ardlui Rd SE27 122 DQ89
Ardmay Gdns, Surb. 138 CL99
Ardmere Rd SE13 123 ED86
Ardmore La, Buck.H. 48 EH45
Ardmore Pl, Buck.H. 48 EH45
Ardmore Rd, S.Ock. 91 FV70
Ardoch Rd SE6 123 ED89
Ardra Rd N9 47 DX48
Ardross Av, Nthwd. 39 BS50
Ardrossan Gdns, Wor.Pk. 139 CU104
Ardshiel Cl SW15 99 CX83
Bemish Rd
Ardwell Av, Ilf. 69 EQ57
Ardwell Rd SW2 121 DL89
Ardwick Rd NW2 64 DA63
Arena, The, Enf. 31 DZ38
Arewater Grn, Loug. 33 EM39

Argali Ho, Erith 106 EY76
Kale Rd
Argall Av E10 67 DX59
Argall Way E10 67 DX60
Argent Cl, Egh. 113 BC93
Holbrook Meadow
Argent St SE1 200 G4
Argent St, Grays 110 FY79
Argenta Way NW10 80 CP66
Argles Cl, Green. 129 FU85
Cowley Av
Argon Ms SW6 100 DA80
Argon Rd N18 46 DW50
Argosy Gdns, Stai. 113 BF93
Argosy La, Stai. 114 BK87
Argus Cl, Rom. 51 FB53
Argus Way W3 98 CP76
Argus Way, Nthlt. 78 BY69
Argyle Av, Houns. 116 CA86
Argyle Cl W13 79 CG70
Argyle Gdns, Upmin. 73 FR61
Argyle Pas N17 46 DT53
Argyle Pl W6 99 CV77
Argyle Rd E1 85 DX70
Argyle Rd E15 68 EE63
Argyle Rd E16 86 EJ72
Argyle Rd N12 44 DA50
Argyle Rd N17 46 DU53
Argyle Rd N18 46 DU49
Argyle Rd W13 79 CG71
Argyle Rd, Barn. 27 CW42
Argyle Rd, Grnf. 79 CF69
Argyle Rd, Har. 60 CB57
Argyle Rd, Houns. 116 CB85
Argyle Rd, Ilf. 69 EN61
Argyle Rd, Sev. 191 FH125
Argyle Rd, Tedd. 117 CE92
Argyle Sq WC1 196 A2
Argyle Sq WC1 83 DL69
Argyle St WC1 195 P2
Argyle St WC1 83 DL69
Argyle Wk WC1 196 A3
Argyle Way SE16 102 DU78
Argyll Av, Sthl. 78 CB74
Argyll Cl SW9 101 DM83
Dalyell Rd
Argyll Gdns, Edg. 42 CP54
Argyll Rd W8 100 DA75
Argyll Rd, Grays 110 GA78
Argyll St W1 195 K9
Argyll St W1 83 DJ72
Arica Rd SE4 103 DY84
Ariel Cl, Grav. 131 GM91
Ariel Rd NW6 82 DA65
Ariel Way W12 81 CW74
Ariel Way, Houns. 95 BV83
Arisdale Av, S.Ock. 91 FV71
Aristotle Rd SW4 101 DK83
Ark Av, Grays 110 GA76
Arkell Gro SE19 121 DP94
Arkindale Rd SE6 123 EC90
Arkley Cres E17 67 DZ57
Arkley Dr, Barn. 27 CU42
Arkley La, Barn. 27 CU41
Arkley Pk, Barn. 26 CR44
Arkley Rd E17 67 DZ57
Arkley Vw, Barn. 27 CV42
Arklow Ct, Rick. 21 BC42
Station App
Arklow Ms, Surb. 138 CL103
Vale Rd S
Arklow Rd SE14 103 DZ79
Arkwright Rd NW3 64 DC64
Arkwright Rd, Slou. 93 BE82
Arkwright Rd, S.Croy. 160 DT110
Arkwright Rd, Til. 111 GG82
Arlesey Cl SW15 119 CY86
Lytton Gro
Arlesford Rd SW9 101 DL83
Arlingford Rd SW2 121 DN85
Arlingham Ms, Wal.Abb. 15 EC33
Sun St
Arlington N12 44 DA48
Arlington Av N1 84 DQ68
Arlington Cl, Sid. 125 ES87
Arlington Cl, Sutt. 140 DA103
Arlington Cl, Twick. 117 CJ86
Arlington Ct, Hayes 95 BR78
Shepiston La
Arlington Ct, Reig. 184 DB132
Oakfield Dr
Arlington Cres, Wal.Cr. 15 DY34
Arlington Dr, Cars. 140 DF103
Arlington Dr, Ruis. 59 BR58
Arlington Gdns W4 98 CQ78
Arlington Gdns, Ilf. 69 EN60
Arlington Gdns, Rom. 52 FL53
Arlington Lo SW2 101 DM84
Arlington Lo, Wey. 153 BP105
Arlington Ms, Twick. 117 CH86
Arlington Rd
Arlington Pl SE10 103 EC80
Greenwich S St
Arlington Rd N14 45 DH47
Arlington Rd NW1 83 DH67
Arlington Rd W13 79 CH72
Arlington Rd, Ashf. 114 BM92
Arlington Rd, Rich. 117 CK89
Arlington Rd, Surb. 137 CK100
Arlington Rd, Tedd. 117 CF91
Arlington Rd, Twick. 117 CJ86
Arlington Rd, Wdf.Grn. 48 EG53
Arlington Sq N1 84 DQ67
Arlington St SW1 199 K2
Arlington St SW1 83 DJ74
Arlington Way EC1 196 E2
Arlington Way EC1 83 DN69
Arliss Way, Nthlt. 78 BW67
Arlow Rd N21 45 DN46
Armada Ct SE8 103 EA79
Watergate St
Armada Ct, Grays 110 GA76
Hogg La
Armada St SE8 103 EA79
Armada Way E6 87 EQ73
Armadale Cl N17 66 DV56
Armadale Rd SW6 100 DA80
Armadale Rd, Felt. 115 BU85
Armadale Rd, Wok. 166 AU117
Armagh Rd E3 85 DZ67
Armand Cl, Wat. 23 BT38
Armfield Cl, W.Mol. 136 BZ99
Armfield Cres, Mitch. 140 DF96
Armfield Rd, Enf. 30 DR39
Arminger Rd W12 81 CV74
Armistice Gdns SE25 142 DU97
Penge Rd
Armitage Cl, Rick. 22 BK42
Armitage Rd NW11 63 CZ60
Armitage Rd SE10 205 K10
Armitage Rd SE10 104 EF78
Armor Rd, Purf. 109 FR77
Armour Cl N7 83 DM65
Roman Way
Armoury Dr, Grav. 131 GJ87
Armoury Rd SE8 103 EB82
Armoury Way SW18 120 DA85
Armstead Wk, Dag. 88 FA66
Armstrong Av, Wdf.Grn. 48 EE51
Armstrong Cl E6 87 EM72
Porter Rd
Armstrong Cl, Dag. 70 EX60
Palmer Rd
Armstrong Cl, Pnr. 59 BU58
Armstrong Cl, Sev. 181 FB115
Armstrong Cl, Walt. 135 BU100
Sunbury La
Armstrong Cres, Barn. 28 DD41
Armstrong Gdns, Rad. 10 CL32
Armstrong Rd SW7 100 DD76
Armstrong Rd W3 81 CT74
Armstrong Rd, Egh. 112 AW93
Armstrong Rd, Felt. 116 BY92
Armstrong Way, Sthl. 96 CB75
Armytage Rd, Houns. 96 BX80
Arnal Cres SW18 119 CY87
Arncliffe Cl N11 44 DG51
Kettlewell Cl
Arncroft Ct, Bark. 88 EV69
Renwick Rd
Arndale Cen SW18 120 DB86
Arndale Wk SW18 120 DB85
Garratt La
Arndale Way, Egh. 113 BA92
Church Rd
Arne Gro, Orp. 145 ET104
Arne St WC2 196 A9
Arne St WC2 83 DL72
Arne Wk SE3 104 EF84
Arnett Cl, Rick. 22 BG44
Arnett Sq E4 47 DZ51
Silver Birch Av
Arnett Way, Rick. 22 BG44
Arneway St SW1 199 N7
Arneways Av, Rom. 70 EX55
Arnewood Cl SW15 119 CU88
Arnewood Cl, Lthd. 154 CB113
Arney's La, Mitch. 140 DG100
Arngask Rd SE6 123 ED87
Arnhem Av, S.Ock. 90 FQ74
Arnhem Dr, Croy. 161 ED111
Arnhem Pl E14 203 P7
Arnhem Pl E14 103 EA76
Arnhem Way SE22 122 DS85
East Dulwich Gro
Arnhem Wf E14 103 EA76
Arnhem Pl
Arnison Rd, E.Mol. 137 CD98
Arnold Av E, Enf. 31 EA38
Arnold Av W, Enf. 31 DZ38
Arnold Circ E2 197 P3
Arnold Circ E2 84 DT69
Arnold Cl, Har. 62 CM59
Arnold Cres, Islw. 117 CD85
Arnold Dr, Chess. 155 CK107
Arnold Est SE1 202 A5
Arnold Est SE1 102 DT75
Arnold Gdns N13 45 DP50
Arnold Pl, Til. 111 GJ81
Kipling Av
Arnold Rd E3 85 EA69
Arnold Rd N15 66 DT55
Arnold Rd SW17 120 DF94
Arnold Rd, Dag. 88 EZ66
Arnold Rd, Grav. 131 GJ89
Arnold Rd, Nthlt. 78 BX65
Arnold Rd, Stai. 114 BJ94
Arnold Rd, Wal.Abb. 31 EC40
Sewardstone Rd
Arnold Rd, Wok. 167 BB116
Arnolds Av, Brwd. 55 GC43
Arnolds Cl, Brwd. 55 GC43
Arnolds Fm La, Brwd. 55 GE41
Arnolds La (Sutton at Hone), Dart. 128 FN93
Arnos Gro N14 45 DK49
Arnos Rd N11 45 DJ50
Arnott Cl SE28 88 EW73
Applegarth Rd
Arnott Cl W4 98 CR77
Fishers La
Arnould Av SE5 102 DR84
Arnsberg Way, Bexh. 106 FA84
Arnside Gdns, Wem. 61 CK60
Arnside Rd, Bexh. 106 FA81
Arnside St SE17 102 DQ79
Arnulf St SE6 123 EB91
Arnulls Rd SW16 121 DN93
Arodene Rd SW2 121 DM86
Arosa Rd, Twick. 117 CK86
Arragon Gdns SW16 121 DL94
Arragon Gdns, W.Wick. 143 EB104
Arragon Rd E6 86 EK67
Arragon Rd SW18 120 DB88
Arragon Rd, Twick. 117 CG87
Arran Cl, Erith 107 FD79
Arran Cl, Wall. 159 DH105
Arran Dr E12 68 EK60
Arran Grn, Wat. 40 BW46
Prestwick Rd
Arran Ms W5 80 CM74
Arran Rd SE6 123 EB89
Arran Wk N1 84 DQ66
Arran Way, Esher 136 CB103
Arranmore Ct, Bushey 24 BY42
Bushey Hall Rd
Arras Av, Mord. 140 DC99
Arreton Mead, Wok. 150 AY114
Arrol Rd, Beck. 142 DW97
Arrow Rd E3 85 EB69
Arrowscout Wk, Nthlt. 78 BY69
Argus Way
Arrowsmith Cl, Chig. 49 ET50
Arrowsmith Path, Chig. 49 ET50
Arrowsmith Rd, Chig. 49 ES50
Arrowsmith Rd, Loug. 32 EL41
Arsenal Rd SE9 105 EM82
Artemis Cl, Grav. 131 GL87
Arterberry Rd SW20 119 CW94
Arterial Av, Rain. 89 FH70
Arterial Rd N Stifford, Grays 110 FY75
Arterial Rd Purfleet, Purf. 108 FN76
Arterial Rd W Thurrock, Grays 109 FU76
Artesian Cl NW10 80 CR66
Artesian Cl, Horn. 71 FF58
Artesian Gro, Barn. 28 DC42
Artesian Rd W2 82 DA72
Artesian Wk E11 68 EE62
Arthingworth St E15 86 EE67
Arthur Ct W2 82 DB72
Queensway
Arthur Gro SE18 105 EQ77
Arthur Henderson Ho SW6 99 CZ82
Arthur Horsley Wk E7 68 EF64
Magpie Cl
Arthur Rd E6 87 EM68
Arthur Rd N7 65 DM63
Arthur Rd N9 46 DT47
Arthur Rd SW19 120 DA90
Arthur Rd, Kings.T. 118 CN94
Arthur Rd, N.Mal. 139 CV99
Arthur Rd, Rom. 70 EW59
Arthur Rd, West. 178 EJ115
Arthur St EC4 201 L1
Arthur St, Bushey 24 BX42
Arthur St, Erith 107 FF80
Arthur St, Grav. 131 GG87
Arthur St, Grays 110 GC79
Arthur St W, Grav. 131 GG87
Arthur Toft Ho, Grays 110 GB79
New Rd
Arthurdon Rd SE4 123 EA85
Arthur's Br Rd, Wok. 166 AW117
Artichoke Dell, Rick. 21 BE43
Artichoke Hill E1 202 D1
Artichoke Pl SE5 102 DR81
Camberwell Ch St
Artillery Cl, Ilf. 69 EQ58
Horns Rd
Artillery La E1 197 N7
Artillery La E1 84 DS71
Artillery La W12 81 CU72
Artillery Pas E1 197 N7
Artillery Pl SE18 105 EM77
Artillery Pl SW1 199 M7
Artillery Pl, Har. 40 CC52
Chicheley Rd
Artillery Row SW1 199 M7
Artillery Row SW1 101 DK76
Artillery Row, Grav. 131 GJ87
Artington Cl, Orp. 163 EQ105
Artisan Cl E6 87 EP72
Ferndale St
Artizan St E1 197 N8
Arundel Av, Epsom 157 CV110
Arundel Av, Mord. 139 CZ98
Arundel Av, S.Croy. 160 DU110
Arundel Cl E15 68 EE63
Arundel Cl SW11 120 DE85
Chivalry Rd
Arundel Cl, Bex. 126 EZ86
Arundel Cl, Croy. 141 DP104
Arundel Cl, Hmptn. 116 CB92
Arundel Cl (Cheshunt), Wal.Cr. 14 DW29
Arundel Ct N12 44 DE51
Arundel Ct, Har. 60 CA63
Arundel Ct, Slou. 92 AX77
Arundel Dr, Borwd. 26 CQ43
Arundel Dr, Har. 60 BZ63
Arundel Dr, Orp. 164 EV106
Arundel Dr, Wdf.Grn. 48 EG52
Arundel Gdns N21 45 DN46
Arundel Gdns W11 81 CZ73
Arundel Gdns, Edg. 42 CR52
Arundel Gdns, Ilf. 70 EU61
Arundel Gt Ct WC2 196 C10
Arundel Gro N16 66 DS64
Arundel Pl N1 83 DN65
Arundel Rd, Abb.L. 7 BU32
Arundel Rd, Barn. 28 DE41
Arundel Rd, Croy. 142 DR100
Arundel Rd, Dart. 108 FJ84
Arundel Rd, Houns. 96 BW83
Arundel Rd, Kings.T. 138 CP96
Arundel Rd, Rom. 52 FM53
Arundel Rd, Sutt. 157 CZ108
Arundel Rd, Uxb. 76 BH68
Arundel Sq N7 83 DN65
Arundel St WC2 196 C10
Arundel St WC2 83 DM73
Arundel Ter SW13 99 CV79
Arvon Rd N5 65 DN64
Asbaston Ter, Ilf. 69 EQ64
Buttsbury Rd
Ascalon St SW8 101 DJ80
Ascension Rd, Rom. 51 FC51
Ascham Dr E4 47 EB52
Rushcroft Rd
Ascham End E17 47 DY53
Ascham St NW5 65 DJ64
Aschurch Rd, Croy. 142 DT101
Ascot Cl, Borwd. 26 CN43
Ascot Cl, Ilf. 49 ES51
Ascot Cl, Nthlt. 60 CA64
Ascot Gdns, Enf. 30 DW37
Ascot Gdns, Horn. 72 FL63
Ascot Gdns, Sthl. 78 BZ71
Ascot Ms, Wall. 159 DJ109
Ascot Rd E6 87 EM69
Ascot Rd N15 66 DR57
Ascot Rd N18 46 DU49
Ascot Rd SW17 120 DG93
Ascot Rd, Felt. 114 BN88
Ascot Rd, Grav. 131 GH90
Ascot Rd, Orp. 145 ET98
Ascot Rd, Wat. 23 BS43
Ascott Av W5 98 CL75
Ash Cl SE20 142 DW96
Ash Cl, Abb.L. 7 BR32
Ash Cl, Brwd. 54 FT43
Ash Cl, Cars. 140 DF103
Ash Cl, Edg. 42 CQ49
Ash Cl, Hat. 12 DA25
Ash Cl, N.Mal. 138 CR96
Ash Cl, Orp. 145 ER99
Ash Cl, Red. 185 DJ130
Ash Cl, Rom. 51 FB52
Ash Cl, Sid. 126 EV90
Ash Cl, Slou. 93 BB76
Ash Cl, Stan. 41 CG51
Ash Cl, Swan. 147 FC96
Ash Cl (Harefield), Uxb. 38 BK53
Ash Cl, Wat. 23 BV35
Ash Cl, Wok. 166 AY120
Ash Cl (Pyrford), Wok. 168 BG115
Ash Copse, St.Alb. 8 BZ31
Ash Ct, Epsom 156 CQ105
Ash Grn (Denham), Uxb. 76 BH65
Ash Gro E8 84 DV67
Ash Gro N13 46 DQ48
Ash Gro NW2 63 CX63
Ash Gro SE20 142 DW96
Ash Gro W5 98 CL75
Ash Gro, Enf. 46 DS45
Ash Gro, Felt. 115 BS88
Ash Gro, Hayes 77 BR73
Ash Gro, Houns. 96 BX81
Ash Gro, Slou. 74 AT66
Ash Gro, Sthl. 78 CA71
Ash Gro, Stai. 114 BJ93
Ash Gro (Harefield), Uxb. 38 BK53
Ash Gro, Wem. 61 CG63
Ash Gro, West Dr. 76 BM73
Ash Gro, W.Wick. 143 EC103
Ash Hill Cl, Bushey 40 CB46
Ash Hill Dr, Pnr. 60 BW55
Ash Island, E.Mol. 137 CD97
Ash La, Horn. 72 FN56
Southend Arterial Rd
Ash La, Rom. 51 FG51
Ash Ms, Epsom 156 CS113
Ash Platt, The, Sev. 191 FL121
Ash Platt Rd, Sev. 191 FL121
Ash Ride, Enf. 29 DN35
Ash Rd E15 68 EE64
Ash Rd, Croy. 143 EA103
Ash Rd, Dart. 128 FK88
Ash Rd (Hawley), Dart. 128 FM91
Ash Rd, Grav. 131 GJ91
Ash Rd, Orp. 163 ET108
Ash Rd, Shep. 134 BN98
Ash Rd, Sutt. 139 CY101
Ash Rd, West. 189 ER125
Ash Rd, Wok. 166 AX120
Ash Row, Brom. 145 EN101
Ash Tree Cl, Croy. 143 DY100
Ash Tree Cl, Surb. 138 CL102
Ash Tree Dell NW9 62 CQ57
Ash Tree Rd, Wat. 23 BV36
Ash Tree Way, Croy. 143 DY99
Ash Vale, Rick. 37 BD50
Ash Wk SW2 121 DM88
Ash Wk, S.Ock. 91 FX69
Ash Wk, Wem. 61 CJ63
Ashbeam Cl, Brwd. 53 FW51
Canterbury Way
Ashbourne Av E18 68 EH56
Ashbourne Av N20 44 DF47
Ashbourne Av NW11 63 CZ57
Ashbourne Av, Bexh. 106 EY80
Ashbourne Av, Har. 61 CD61
Ashbourne Cl N12 44 DB49
Ashbourne Cl W5 80 CN71
Ashbourne Cl, Couls. 175 DJ118
Ashbourne Ct E5 67 DY63
Daubeney Rd
Ashbourne Gro NW7 42 CR50
Ashbourne Gro SE22 122 DT85
Ashbourne Gro W4 98 CS78
Ashbourne Par W5 80 CM70
Ashbourne Rd
Ashbourne Ri, Orp. 163 ER105
Ashbourne Rd W5 80 CM71
Ashbourne Rd, Mitch. 120 DG93
Ashbourne Rd, Rom. 52 FJ49
Ashbourne Sq, Nthwd. 39 BS51
Ashbourne Ter SW19 120 DA94
Ashbourne Way NW11 63 CZ57
Ashbourne Av
Ashbridge Rd E11 68 EF59
Ashbridge St NW8 194 B5
Ashbridge St NW8 82 DE70
Ashbrook Rd N19 65 DK60
Ashbrook Rd, Dag. 71 FB62
Ashbrook Rd, Wind. 112 AV87
Ashburn Gdns SW7 100 DC77
Ashburn Pl SW7 100 DC77
Ashburnham Av, Har. 61 CF58
Ashburnham Cl N2 64 DD55
Ashburnham Cl, Sev. 191 FJ127
Fiennes Way
Ashburnham Cl, Wat. 39 BU48
Ashburnham Dr
Ashburnham Dr, Wat. 39 BU48
Ashburnham Gdns, Har. 61 CF58
Ashburnham Gdns, Upmin. 72 FP60
Ashburnham Gro SE10 103 EB80
Ashburnham Pk, Esher 154 CC105
Ashburnham Pl SE10 103 EB80
Ashburnham Retreat SE10 103 EB80
Ashburnham Rd NW10 81 CW69
Ashburnham Rd SW10 100 DC80
Ashburnham Rd, Belv. 107 FC77
Ashburnham Rd, Rich. 117 CH90
Ashburton Av, Croy. 142 DV102
Ashburton Av, Ilf. 69 ES63
Ashburton Cl, Croy. 142 DU102
Ashburton Ct, Pnr. 60 BX55
Ashburton Gdns, Croy. 142 DU103
Ashburton Gro N7 65 DN63
Ashburton Rd E16 86 EG72
Ashburton Rd, Croy. 142 DU102
Ashburton Rd, Ruis. 59 BU61
Ashburton Ter E13 86 EG68
Grasmere Rd
Ashbury Dr, Uxb. 59 BP61
Ashbury Gdns, Rom. 70 EX57
Ashbury Pl SW19 120 DC93
Ashbury Rd SW11 100 DF83
Ashby Av, Chess. 156 CN107
Ashby Cl, Horn. 72 FN
Holme Rd
Ashby Gro N1 84 DQ
Ashby Ms SE4 103 DZ
Ashby Rd N15 66 DU
Ashby Rd SE4 103 DZ
Ashby Rd, Wat. 23 BU
Ashby St EC1 196
Ashby Wk, Croy. 142 DQ1
Ashby Way, West Dr. 94 BN
Ashchurch Gro W12 99 CU
Ashchurch Pk Vil W12 99 CU
Ashchurch Ter W12 99 CU
Ashcombe Av, Surb. 137 CK1
Ashcombe Gdns, Edg. 42 CN
Ashcombe Pk NW2 62 CS
Ashcombe Rd SW19 120 DA
Ashcombe Rd, Cars. 158 DG1
Ashcombe Rd, Red. 185 DJ1
Ashcombe Sq, N.Mal. 138 CQ
Ashcombe St SW6 100 DB
Ashcombe Ter, Tad. 173 CV1
Ashcroft, Pnr. 40 CA
Ashcroft Av, Sid. 126 EU
Ashcroft Cres, Sid. 126 EU
Ashcroft Dr (Denham), Uxb. 57 BF
Ashcroft Pk, Cob. 154 BY1
Ashcroft Ri, Couls. 175 DL1
Ashcroft Rd E3 85 DY
Ashcroft Rd, Chess. 138 CM1
Ashcroft Sq W6 99 CW
King St
Ashdale Cl, Stai. 114 BL
Ashdale Cl, Twick. 116 CC
Ashdale Gro, Stan. 41 CF
Ashdale Rd SE12 124 EH
Ashdale Way, Twick. 116 CC
Ashdale Cl
Ashdene SE15 102 DV
Ashdene, Pnr. 60 BW
Ashdene Cl, Ashf. 115 BQ
Ashdon Cl, Brwd. 55 GC
Poplar Dr
Ashdon Cl, S.Ock. 91 FV
Afton Dr
Ashdon Cl, Wdf.Grn. 48 EH
Ashdon Rd NW10 80 CS
Ashdon Rd, Bushey 24 BX
Ashdown Cl, Beck. 143 EB
Ashdown Cl, Bex. 127 FC
Ashdown Cres NW5 64 DG
Queens Cres
Ashdown Cres (Cheshunt), Wal.Cr. 15 DY
Ashdown Dr, Borwd. 26 CL
Ashdown Est E11 68 EE
High Rd Leytonstone
Ashdown Gdns, S.Croy. 176 DV1
Ashdown Rd, Enf. 30 DW
Ashdown Rd, Epsom 157 CT1
Ashdown Rd, Kings.T. 138 CL
Ashdown Rd, Uxb. 76 BN
Ashdown Wk E14 204
Ashdown Wk E14 103 EA
Ashdown Wk, Rom. 51 FB
Ashdown Way SW17 120 DG
Ashen E6 87 EN
Downings
Ashen Dr, Dart. 127 FG
Ashen Gro SW19 120 DA
Ashen Vale, S.Croy. 161 DX1
Ashenden Rd E5 67 DX
Ashentree Ct EC4 196
Asher Loftus Way N11 44 DF
Asher Way E1 202
Asher Way E1 84 DU
Ashfield Av, Bushey 24 CB
Ashfield Av, Felt. 115 BV
Ashfield Cl, Beck. 123 EA
Ashfield Cl, Rich. 118 CL
Ashfield La, Chis. 125 EQ
Ashfield Par N14 45 DK
Ashfield Rd N4 66 DQ
Ashfield Rd N14 45 DJ
Ashfield Rd W3 81 CT
Ashfield St E1 84 DV
Ashfield Yd E1 84 DV
Ashfield St
Ashfields, Loug. 33 EM
Ashfields, Reig. 184 DB1
Ashfields, Wat. 23 BT
Ashford Av N8 65 DL
Ashford Av, Ashf. 115 BP
Ashford Av, Brwd. 54 FV
Ashford Av, Hayes 78 BX
Ashford Cl E17 67 DZ
Ashford Cl, Ashf. 114 BL
Ashford Cres, Ashf. 114 BL
Ashford Cres, Enf. 30 DW
Ashford Gdns, Cob. 170 BX1
Ashford Grn, Wat. 40 BX
Ashford Ind Est, Ashf. 115 BQ
Ashford Rd E6 87 EN
Ashford Rd E18 48 EH
Ashford Rd NW2 63 CX
Ashford Rd, Ashf. 115 BQ
Ashford Rd, Felt. 115 BT
Ashford Rd, Iver 75 BC
Ashford Rd, Stai. 134 BK
Ashford St N1 197 M
Ashgrove Rd, Ashf. 115 BQ
Ashgrove Rd, Brom. 123 ED
Ashgrove Rd, Ilf. 69 ET
Ashgrove Rd, Sev. 190 FG1
Ashingdon Cl E4 47 EC
Ashington Rd SW6 99 CZ
Ashlake Rd SW16 121 DL
Ashland Pl W1 194 F
Ashland Pl W1 82 DG
Ashlar Pl SE18 105 EP
Masons Hill
Ashlea Rd (Chalfont St. Peter), Ger.Cr. 36 AX5
Ashleigh Av, Egh. 113 BC9
Ashleigh Cl, Amer. 20 AS3
Ashleigh Ct, Wal.Abb. 16 EG3
Lamplighters Cl
Ashleigh Gdns, Sutt. 140 DB10
Ashleigh Gdns, Upmin. 73 FR6
Ashleigh Rd SE20 142 DV9
Ashleigh Rd SW14 98 CS8
Ashley Av, Epsom 156 CR11

Ashley Av, Ilf. 49 EP54
Ashley Av, Mord. 140 DA99
Chalgrove Av
Ashley Cen, Epsom 156 CR113
Ashley Cl NW4 43 CW54
Ashley Cl, Pnr. 39 BV54
Ashley Cl, Sev. 191 FH124
Ashley Cl, Walt. 135 BT102
Ashley Ct, Epsom 156 CR113
Ashley Ct, Wok. 166 AT118
Ashley Cres N22 45 DN54
Ashley Cres SW11 100 DG83
Ashley Dr, Bans. 158 DA114
Ashley Dr, Borwd. 26 CQ43
Ashley Dr, Islw. 97 CE79
Ashley Dr, Twick. 116 CB87
Ashley Dr, Walt. 135 BU104
Ashley Gdns N13 46 DQ49
Ashley Gdns SW1 199 L7
Ashley Gdns SW1 101 DJ76
Ashley Gdns, Orp. 163 ES106
Ashley Gdns, Rich. 117 CK90
Ashley Gdns, Wem. 62 CL61
Ashley Gro, Loug. 32 EL41
Staples Rd
Ashley La NW4 43 CW54
Ashley La, Croy. 159 DP105
Ashley Pk Av, Walt. 135 BT103
Ashley Pk Cres, Walt. 135 BT102
Ashley Pk Rd, Walt. 135 BU103
Ashley Pl SW1 199 K7
Ashley Pl SW1 101 DJ76
Ashley Ri, Walt. 153 BU105
Ashley Rd E4 47 EA50
Ashley Rd E7 86 EJ66
Ashley Rd N17 66 DU55
Ashley Rd N19 65 DL60
Ashley Rd SW19 120 DB93
Ashley Rd, Enf. 30 DW40
Ashley Rd, Epsom 156 CR114
Ashley Rd, Hmptn. 136 CA95
Ashley Rd, Rich. 98 CL83
Jocelyn Rd
Ashley Rd, Sev. 191 FH123
Ashley Rd, T.Ditt. 137 CF100
Ashley Rd, Th.Hth. 141 DM98
Ashley Rd, Uxb. 76 BH68
Ashley Rd, Walt. 135 BU102
Ashley Rd, Wok. 166 AT118
Ashley Sq, Epsom 156 CR113
Ashley Wk NW7 43 CW52
Ashleys, Rick. 37 BF45
Ashlin Rd E15 67 ED63
Ashling Rd, Croy. 142 DU102
Ashlone Rd SW15 99 CW83
Ashlyn Cl, Bushey 24 BY42
Ashlyn Gro, Horn. 72 FK55
Ashlyns Pk, Cob. 154 BY113
Ashlyns Rd, Epp. 17 ET30
Ashlyns Way, Chess. 155 CK107
Ashmead N14 29 DJ44
Ashmead Dr (Denham), Uxb. 58 BG61
Ashmead Gate, Brom. 144 EJ95
Ashmead La (Denham), Uxb. 58 BG61
Ashmead Rd SE8 103 EA82
Ashmead Rd, Felt. 115 BU88
Ashmeads Ct (Shenley), Rad. 9 CK33
Porters Pk Dr
Ashmere Av, Beck. 143 ED96
Ashmere Cl, Sutt. 157 CW106
Ashmere Gro SW2 101 DL84
Ashmill St NW1 194 B6
Ashmill St NW1 82 DE71
Ashmole Pl SW8 101 DM79
Ashmole St SW8 101 DM79
Ashmore Ct, Houns. 96 CA79
Wheatlands
Ashmore Gdns, Grav. 130 GD91
Ashmore Gro, Well. 105 ER83
Ashmore La, Kes. 162 EH111
Ashmore Rd W9 81 CZ70
Ashmount Est N19 65 DK59
Ashmount Rd
Ashmount Rd N15 66 DT57
Ashmount Rd N19 65 DJ59
Ashmount Ter W5 97 CK77
Murray Rd
Ashmour Gdns, Rom. 51 FD54
Ashneal Gdns, Har. 61 CD62
Ashness Gdns, Grnf. 79 CH65
Ashness Rd SW11 120 DF85
Ashridge Cl, Har. 61 CJ58
Ashridge Cl, Hem.H. 5 BA28
Ashridge Cres SE18 105 EQ80
Ashridge Dr, St.Alb. 8 BY30
Ashridge Dr, Wat. 40 BW50
Ashridge Gdns N13 45 DK50
Ashridge Gdns, Pnr. 60 BY56
Ashridge Rd, Chesh. 4 AW31
Ashridge Way, Mord. 139 CZ97
Ashridge Way, Sun. 115 BU93
Ashtead Gap, Lthd. 171 CH116
Ashtead Gap, Lthd. 171 CG116
Kingston Rd
Ashtead Rd E5 66 DU59
Ashtead Wds Rd, Ash. 171 CJ117
Ashton Cl, Sutt. 158 DA105
Ashton Cl, Walt. 153 BV107
Ashton Gdns, Houns. 96 BZ84
Ashton Gdns, Rom. 70 EY58
Ashton Rd E15 67 ED64
Ashton Rd, Enf. 31 DY36
Ashton Rd, Rom. 52 FK52
Ashton Rd, Wok. 166 AT117
Ashton St E14 85 EC73
Ashtree Av, Mitch. 140 DE96
Ashtree Cl, Orp. 163 EP105
Broadwater Gdns
Ashtree Ct, Wal.Abb. 16 EG34
Horseshoe Cl
Ashurst Cl SE20 142 DV95
Ashurst Cl, Dart. 107 FF83
Ashurst Cl, Ken. 176 DR115
Ashurst Cl, Nthwd. 39 BS52
Ashurst Dr, Ilf. 69 EP58
Ashurst Dr, Shep. 134 BL99
Ashurst Dr, Tad. 182 CP130
Ashurst Rd N12 44 DE50
Ashurst Rd, Barn. 28 DF43
Ashurst Rd, Tad. 173 CV121
Ashurst Wk, Croy. 142 DV103
Ashvale Dr, Upmin. 73 FS61
Ashvale Gdns, Rom. 51 FD50
Ashvale Gdns, Upmin. 73 FS61
Ashvale Rd SW17 120 DF92
Ashview Cl, Ashf. 114 BL93
Ashview Gdns, Ashf. 114 BL92
Ashville Rd E11 67 ED61
Ashwater Rd SE12 124 EG88
Ashwell Cl E6 86 EL72
Northumberland Rd
Ashwells Rd, Brwd. 54 FS41
Ashwells Way, Ch.St.G. 36 AW47
Ashwick Cl, Cat. 186 DU125
Ashwin St E8 84 DT65
Ashwindham Ct, Wok. 166 AS118
Ashwindham Ct, Wok. 166 AT118
Raglan Rd
Ashwood, Warl. 176 DW120
Ashwood Av, Rain. 89 FH70
Ashwood Av, Uxb. 76 BN72
Ashwood Gdns, Croy. 161 EB107
Ashwood Gdns, Hayes 95 BT77
Cranford Dr
Ashwood Pk, Lthd. 170 CC124
Ashwood Pk, Wok. 167 BA118
Ashwood Pl, Dart. 129 FV90
Bean La
Ashwood Rd E4 47 ED48
Ashwood Rd, Egh. 112 AV93
Ashwood Rd, Pot.B. 12 DB33
Ashwood Rd, Wok. 167 AZ118
Ashworth Cl SE5 102 DR82
Hascombe Ter
Ashworth Rd W9 82 DB69
Aske St N1 197 M2
Askern Cl, Bexh. 106 EX84
Askew Cres W12 99 CT75
Askew Fm La, Grays 110 FY78
Askew Rd W12 81 CT74
Askew Rd, Nthwd. 39 BR47
Askham Ct W12 81 CU74
Askham Rd W12 81 CU74
Askill Dr SW15 119 CY85
Keswick Rd
Askwith Rd, Rain. 89 FD69
Asland Rd E15 86 EE67
Aslett St SW18 120 DB87
Asmar Cl, Couls. 175 DL115
Asmara Rd NW2 63 CY64
Asmuns Hill NW11 64 DA57
Asmuns Pl NW11 63 CZ57
Asolando Dr SE17 201 J9
Aspdin Rd, Grav. 130 GD90
Aspen Cl N19 65 DJ61
Hargrave Pk
Aspen Cl W5 98 CM75
Aspen Cl, Cob. 170 BY116
Aspen Cl, Orp. 164 EU106
Aspen Cl, St.Alb. 8 BY30
Aspen Cl, Stai. 113 BF90
Aspen Cl, Swan. 147 FD95
Aspen Cl, West Dr. 76 BM74
Aspen Copse, Brom. 145 EM96
Aspen Ct, Hayes 95 BS77
Aspen Ct, Vir.W. 132 AY98
Aspen Dr, Wem. 61 CG63
Aspen Gdns W6 99 CV78
Aspen Gdns, Mitch. 140 DG99
Aspen Grn, Erith 106 EZ76
Aspen Gro, Upmin. 72 FN63
Aspen La, Nthlt. 78 BY69
Aspen Pk Dr, Wat. 23 BV35
Aspen Sq, Wey. 135 BR104
Oatlands Dr
Aspen Vale, Whyt. 176 DT118
Whyteleafe Hill
Aspen Way E14 204 A1
Aspen Way E14 85 EB73
Aspen Way, Bans. 157 CX114
Aspen Way, Enf. 31 DX35
Aspen Way, Felt. 115 BV90
Aspen Way, S.Ock. 91 FX69
Aspenlea Rd W6 99 CX79
Aspern Gro NW3 64 DE64
Aspinall Rd SE4 103 DX83
Aspinden Rd SE16 202 E8
Aspinden Rd SE16 102 DV77
Aspley Rd SW18 120 DB85
Asplins Rd N17 46 DU53
Asprey Gro, Cat. 176 DU124
Asprey Pl, Brom. 144 EK96
Chislehurst Rd
Asquith Cl, Dag. 70 EW60
Crystal Way
Ass Ho La, Har. 40 CB49
Assam St E1 84 DU72
White Ch La
Assata Ms N1 83 DP65
St. Paul's Rd
Assembly Pas E1 84 DW71
Assembly Wk, Cars. 140 DE101
Assher Rd, Walt. 136 BY104
Assurance Cotts, Belv. 106 EZ78
Heron Hill
Astall Cl, Har. 41 CE53
Astbury Rd SE15 102 DW81
Aste St E14 204 D5
Aste St E14 103 EC75
Astell St SW3 198 C10
Astell St SW3 100 DE78
Asters, The, Wal.Cr. 14 DR28
Asteys Row N1 83 DP66
River Pl
Asthall Gdns, Ilf. 69 EQ56
Astle St SW11 100 DG82
Astleham Rd, Shep. 134 BL97
Astley, Grays 110 FZ79
Astley Av NW2 63 CW64
Aston Av, Har. 61 CJ59
Aston Cl, Ash. 171 CJ118
Aston Cl, Bushey 24 CC44
Aston Cl, Sid. 126 EU90
Aston Cl, Wat. 24 BW40
Aston Grn, Houns. 96 BW82
Aston Ms, Rom. 70 EW59
Reynolds Av
Aston Rd SW20 139 CW96
Aston Rd W5 79 CK72
Aston Rd, Esher 155 CE106
Aston St E14 85 DY72
Aston Ter SW12 121 DH86
Cathles Rd
Aston Way, Epsom 173 CT116
Aston Way, Pot.B. 12 DD32
Astons Rd, Nthwd. 39 BQ48
Astonville St SW18 120 DA88
Astor Av, Rom. 71 FC58
Astor Cl, Add. 152 BK105
Astor Cl, Kings.T. 118 CP93
Astoria Wk SW9 101 DN83
Astra Cl, Horn. 89 FH65
Astra Dr, Grav. 131 GL92
Astrop Ms W6 99 CW76
Astrop Ter W6 99 CW76
Astwood Ms SW7 100 DB77
Asylum Rd SE15 102 DV80
Atalanta Cl, Pur. 159 DN110
Atalanta St SW6 99 CX81
Atbara Ct, Tedd. 117 CH93
Atbara Rd, Tedd. 117 CH93
Atcham Rd, Houns. 96 CC84
Atcost Rd, Bark. 88 EU71
Atheldene Rd SW18 120 DB88
Athelney St SE6 123 EA90
Athelstan Cl, Rom. 52 FM54
Athelstan Rd
Athelstan Rd, Kings.T. 138 CM98
Athelstan Rd, Rom. 52 FM53
Athelstan Way, Orp. 146 EU95
Athelstane Gro E3 85 DZ68
Athelstane Ms N4 65 DN60
Stroud Grn Rd
Athelstone Rd, Har. 41 CD54
Athena Cl, Har. 61 CE61
Byron Hill Rd
Athena Cl, Kings.T. 138 CM97
Athena Pl, Nthwd. 39 BT53
The Dr
Athenaeum Pl N10 65 DH55
Fortis Grn Rd
Athenaeum Rd N20 44 DC46
Athenlay Rd SE15 123 DX85
Athens Gdns W9 82 DA70
Elgin Av
Atherden Rd E5 66 DW63
Atherfold Rd SW9 101 DL83
Atherley Way, Houns. 116 BZ87
Atherstone Ct W2 82 DB71
Delamere Ter
Atherstone Ms SW7 100 DC77
Atherton Cl, Stai. 114 BK86
Atherton Dr SW19 119 CX91
Atherton Gdns, Grays 111 GJ77
Atherton Hts, Wem. 79 CJ65
Atherton Ms E7 86 EF65
Atherton Pl, Har. 61 CD55
Atherton Pl, Sthl. 78 CB73
Longford Av
Atherton Rd E7 68 EF64
Atherton Rd SW13 99 CU80
Atherton Rd, Ilf. 48 EL54
Atherton St SW11 100 DE82
Athlon Rd, Wem. 79 CK68
Athlone, Esher 155 CE107
Athlone Cl E5 66 DV63
Goulton Rd
Athlone Cl, Rad. 25 CH36
Athlone Rd SW2 121 DM87
Athlone St NW5 82 DG65
Athol Cl, Pnr. 39 BV53
Athol Gdns, Pnr. 39 BV53
Athol Rd, Erith 107 FC78
Athol Sq E14 85 EC72
Athol Way, Uxb. 76 BN69
Athole Gdns, Enf. 30 DS43
Atholl Rd, Ilf. 70 EU59
Atkins Cl, Wok. 166 AU118
Greythorne Rd
Atkins Dr, W.Wick. 143 ED103
Atkins Rd E10 67 EB58
Atkins Rd SW12 121 DK87
Atkinson Cl, Orp. 164 EU106
Martindale Av
Atkinson Rd E16 86 EJ71
Atlanta Boul, Rom. 71 FE58
Atlantic Rd SW9 101 DN84
Atlantis Cl, Bark. 87 ES69
Thames Rd
Atlas Gdns SE7 104 EJ77
Atlas Ms E8 84 DT65
Tyssen St
Atlas Ms N7 83 DM65
Atlas Rd E13 86 EG68
Atlas Rd N11 45 DH51
Atlas Rd NW10 80 CS69
Atlas Rd, Dart. 108 FM83
Cornwall Rd
Atlas Rd, Wem. 62 CQ63
Atley Rd E3 85 EA67
Atlip Rd, Wem. 80 CL67
Atney Rd SW15 99 CY84
Atria Rd, Nthwd. 39 BU50
Attenborough Cl, Wat. 40 BY48
Harrow Way
Atterbury Cl, West. 189 ER126
Atterbury Rd N4 65 DN58
Atterbury St SW1 199 N9
Atterbury St SW1 101 DL77
Attewood Av NW10 62 CS62
Attewood Rd, Nthlt. 78 BY65
Attfield Cl N20 44 DD47
Attle Cl, Uxb. 76 BN68
Attlee Cl, Hayes 77 BV69
Attlee Cl, Th.Hth. 142 DQ100
Attlee Cl, Grays 110 GA76
Attlee Dr, Dart. 128 FN85
Attlee Rd SE28 88 EV73
Attlee Rd, Hayes 77 BU69
Attlee Ter E17 67 EB56
Attneave St WC1 196 D3
Attwood Cl, S.Croy. 160 DV114
Atwater Cl SW2 121 DN88
Atwell Cl E10 67 EB58
Belmont Pk Rd
Atwell Pl, T.Ditt. 137 CF102
Atwell Rd SE15 102 DU82
Rye La
Atwood, Lthd. 170 BY124
Atwood Av, Rich. 98 CN82
Atwood Rd W6 99 CV77
Atwoods All, Rich. 98 CN81
Leyborne Pk
Aubert Pk N5 65 DP63
Aubert Rd N5 65 DP63
Aubretia Cl, Rom. 52 FL53
Aubrey Av, St.Alb. 9 CJ26
Aubrey Pl NW8 82 DC68
Violet Hill
Aubrey Rd E17 67 EA55
Aubrey Rd N8 65 DL57
Aubrey Rd W8 81 CZ74
Aubrey Wk W8 81 CZ74
Aubyn Hill SE27 122 DQ91
Aubyn Sq SW15 99 CU84
Auckland Av, Rain. 89 FF69
Auckland Cl SE19 142 DT95
Auckland Cl, Enf. 30 DV37
Auckland Cl, Til. 111 GG82
Auckland Gdns SE19 142 DS95
Auckland Hill SE27 122 DQ91
Auckland Ri SE19 142 DS95
Auckland Rd E10 67 EB62
Auckland Rd SE19 142 DT95
Auckland Rd SW11 100 DE84
Auckland Rd, Cat. 176 DS122
Auckland Rd, Ilf. 69 EP60
Auckland Rd, Kings.T. 138 CM98
Auckland Rd, Pot.B. 11 CY32
Auckland St SE11 101 DM78
Kennington La
Auden Pl NW1 82 DG67
Audleigh Pl, Chig. 49 EN51
Audley Cl N10 45 DH52
Audley Cl SW11 100 DG83
Audley Cl, Add. 152 BH106
Audley Cl, Borwd. 26 CN41
Audley Ct E18 68 EF56
Audley Ct, Pnr. 40 BW54
Rickmansworth Rd
Audley Dr E16 205 P2
Audley Dr, Warl. 176 DW115
Audley Firs, Walt. 154 BW105
Audley Gdns, Ilf. 69 ET61
Audley Gdns, Loug. 33 EQ40
Audley Gdns, Wal.Abb. 15 EC34
Audley Pl, Sutt. 158 DA108
Audley Rd NW4 63 CV58
Audley Rd W5 80 CM71
Audley Rd, Enf. 29 DP40
Audley Rd, Rich. 118 CM85
Audley Sq W1 198 G2
Audley Wk, Orp. 146 EW100
Audrey Cl, Beck. 143 EB100
Audrey Gdns, Wem. 61 CH61
Audrey Rd, Ilf. 69 EP62
Audrey St E2 84 DU68
Audric Cl, Kings.T. 138 CN95
Audwick Cl (Cheshunt), Wal.Cr. 15 DX28
Augur Cl, Stai. 113 BF92
Augurs La E13 86 EH69
August End, Slou. 74 AY72
Augusta Cl, W.Mol. 136 BZ97
Freeman Dr
Augusta Rd, Twick. 116 CC89
Augusta St E14 85 EB72
Augustine Cl, Slou. 93 BE83
Augustine Ct, Wal.Abb. 15 EB33
Beaulieu Dr
Augustine Rd W14 99 CX76
Augustine Rd, Grav. 131 GJ87
Augustine Rd, Har. 40 CB53
Augustine Rd, Orp. 146 EW97
Augustus Cl, Brent. 97 CJ80
Augustus La, Orp. 146 EU103
Augustus Rd SW19 119 CY88
Augustus St NW1 195 J1
Augustus St NW1 83 DH68
Aulton Pl SE11 101 DN78
Aultone Way, Cars. 140 DF104
Aultone Way, Sutt. 140 DB103
Aurelia Gdns, Croy. 141 DM99
Aurelia Rd, Croy. 141 DL100
Auriel Av, Dag. 89 FD65
Auriga Ms N16 66 DR64
Auriol Cl, Wor.Pk. 138 CS104
Auriol Pk Rd
Auriol Dr, Grnf. 79 CD66
Auriol Dr, Uxb. 76 BN65
Auriol Pk Rd, Wor.Pk. 138 CS104
Auriol Rd W14 99 CY77
Austell Gdns NW7 42 CS48
Austen Cl SE28 88 EV74
Austen Cl, Green. 129 FW85
Austen Cl, Loug. 33 ER41
Austen Cl, Til. 111 GJ82
Coleridge Rd
Austen Gdns, Dart. 108 FM84
Austen Ho NW6 82 DA69
Austen Rd, Erith 107 FB80
Austen Rd, Har. 60 CB61
Austenway (Chalfont St. Peter), Ger.Cr. 56 AX55
Austenwood Cl (Chalfont St. Peter), Ger.Cr. 36 AX54
Austenwood La (Chalfont St. Peter), Ger.Cr. 36 AX54
Austin Av, Brom. 144 EL99
Austin Cl SE23 123 DZ87
Austin Cl, Couls. 175 DP118
Austin Cl, Twick. 117 CJ85
Austin Ct E6 86 EJ67
Kings Rd
Austin Friars EC2 197 L8
Austin Friars EC2 84 DR72
Austin Friars Pas EC2 197 L8
Austin Friars Sq EC2 197 L8
Austin Rd SW11 100 DG81
Austin Rd, Grav. 131 GF88
Austin Rd, Hayes 95 BT75
Austin Rd, Orp. 146 EU100
Austin St E2 197 P3
Austin St E2 84 DT69
Austin Waye, Uxb. 76 BJ67
Austin's La, Uxb. 59 BR63
Austins Mead, Hem.H. 5 BB28
Austral Cl, Sid. 125 ET90
Austral Dr, Horn. 72 FK59
Austral St SE11 200 F8
Austral St SE11 101 DP77
Australia Rd W12 81 CV73
Australia Rd, Slou. 92 AV75
Austyn Gdns, Surb. 138 CP102
Autumn Cl SW19 120 DC93
Autumn Cl, Enf. 30 DU39
Autumn Dr, Sutt. 158 DB109
Autumn St E3 85 EA67
Auxiliaries Way, Uxb. 57 BF57
Avalon Cl SW20 139 CY96
Avalon Cl W13 79 CG71
Avalon Cl, Enf. 29 DN40
Avalon Cl, Orp. 146 EX104
Avalon Cl, Wat. 8 BY32
Avalon Rd SW6 100 DB81
Avalon Rd W13 79 CG70
Avalon Rd, Orp. 146 EW103
Avard Gdns, Orp. 163 EQ105
Avarn Rd SW17 120 DF93
Ave Maria La EC4 196 G9
Ave Maria La EC4 83 DP72
Avebury Ct N1 84 DR67
Poole St
Avebury Pk, Surb. 137 CK101
Avebury Rd E11 67 ED60
Southwest Rd
Avebury Rd SW19 139 CZ95
Avebury Rd, Orp. 145 ER104
Avebury St N1 84 DR67
Poole St
Aveley Bypass, S.Ock. 90 FQ73
Aveley Cl, Erith 107 FF79
Aveley Cl, S.Ock. 91 FR74
Aveley Rd, Rom. 71 FD56
Aveley Rd, Upmin. 90 FP65
Aveline St SE11 200 D10
Aveline St SE11 101 DN78
Aveling Cl, Pur. 159 DM113
Aveling Pk Rd E17 47 EA54
Avelon Rd, Rain. 89 FG67
Avelon Rd, Rom. 51 FD51
Avenell Rd N5 65 DP62
Avening Rd SW18 120 DA87
Brathway Rd
Avening Ter SW18 120 DA86
Avenons Rd E13 86 EG70
Avenue, The E4 47 ED51
Avenue, The (Leytonstone) E11 68 EF61
Avenue, The (Wanstead) E11 68 EF61
Avenue, The N3 44 DA54
Avenue, The N8 65 DN55
Avenue, The N10 45 DJ54
Avenue, The N11 45 DH49
Avenue, The N17 46 DS54
Avenue, The NW6 81 CX67
Avenue, The SE7 104 EJ80
Avenue, The SE10 103 ED80
Avenue, The SW4 120 DG85
Avenue, The SW18 120 DE87
Avenue, The W4 98 CS76
Avenue, The W13 79 CH73
Avenue, The, Add. 152 BG110
Avenue, The, Barn. 27 CY41
Avenue, The, Beck. 143 EB95
Avenue, The, Bet. 182 CN134
Avenue, The, Bex. 126 EX87
Avenue, The, Brwd. 53 FX51
Avenue, The, Brom. 144 EK97
Avenue, The, Bushey 24 BZ42
Avenue, The, Cars. 158 DG108
Avenue, The, Couls. 175 DK115
Avenue, The, Croy. 142 DS104
Avenue, The, Egh. 113 BB91
Avenue, The, Epsom 157 CV108
Avenue, The, Esher 155 CE107
Avenue, The, Grav. 131 GG88
Avenue, The, Green. 109 FV84
Avenue, The, Hmptn. 116 BZ93
Avenue, The, Har. 41 CF53
Avenue, The, Horn. 72 FJ61
Avenue, The, Houns. 116 CB85
Avenue, The (Cranford), Houns. 95 BU81
Avenue, The, Islw. 97 CD79
Avenue, The, Kes. 144 EK104
Avenue, The, Lthd. 155 CF112
Avenue, The, Loug. 32 EK44
Avenue, The, Nthwd. 39 BQ51
Avenue, The, Orp. 145 ET103
Avenue, The (St. Paul's Cray), Orp. 126 EV94
Avenue, The, Pnr. 60 BZ58
Avenue, The (Hatch End), Pnr. 40 CA52
Avenue, The, Pot.B. 11 CZ30
Avenue, The, Rad. 9 CG33
Avenue, The, Rich. 98 CM82
Avenue, The, Rom. 71 FD56
Avenue, The (Datchet), Slou. 92 AV81
Avenue, The, Stai. 134 BH95
Avenue, The (Sunnymeads), Stai. 92 AX83
Avenue, The, Sun. 135 BV95
Avenue, The, Surb. 138 CM100
Avenue, The, Sutt. 157 CZ109
Avenue, The (Cheam), Sutt. 157 CW108
Avenue, The, Tad. 173 CV122
Avenue, The, Twick. 117 CJ85
Avenue, The (Cowley), Uxb. 76 BK70
Avenue, The (Ickenham), Uxb. 58 BN63
Avenue, The, Wal.Abb. 16 EJ25
Avenue, The, Wat. 23 BV40
Avenue, The, Wem. 62 CM61
Avenue, The, West Dr. 94 BL76
Avenue, The, W.Wick. 143 ED101
Avenue, The, West. 179 EP123
Avenue, The, Whyt. 176 DU119
Avenue, The, Wind. 112 AV85
Avenue, The, Wok. 150 AT109
Avenue, The, Wor.Pk. 139 CT103
Avenue App, Kings L. 6 BN30
Avenue Cl N14 29 DJ44
Avenue Cl NW8 82 DE67
Avenue Cl, Houns. 95 BU81
The Av
Avenue Cl, Rom. 52 FM52
Avenue Cl, Tad. 173 CV122
Avenue Cl, West Dr. 94 BK76
Avenue Cres W3 98 CP75
Avenue Cres, Houns. 95 BV80
Avenue Dr, Slou. 75 AZ71
Avenue Elmers, Surb. 138 CL99
Avenue Gdns SE25 142 DU97
Avenue Gdns SW14 98 CS83
Avenue Gdns W3 98 CP75

Avenue Gdns, Houns. 95 BU80
The Av
Avenue Gdns, Tedd. 117 CF94
Avenue Gate, Loug. 32 EJ44
Avenue Ind Est E4 47 DZ51
Avenue Ind Est, Rom. 52 FK54
Avenue Ms N10 65 DH55
Avenue Pk Rd SE27 121 DP89
Avenue Ri, Bushey 24 CA43
Avenue Rd E7 68 EH64
Avenue Rd N6 65 DJ59
Avenue Rd N12 44 DC49
Avenue Rd N14 45 DJ45
Avenue Rd N15 66 DR57
Avenue Rd NW3 82 DD66
Avenue Rd NW8 82 DD67
Avenue Rd NW10 81 CT68
Avenue Rd SE20 142 DW95
Avenue Rd SE25 142 DU96
Avenue Rd SW16 141 DK96
Avenue Rd SW20 139 CV96
Avenue Rd W3 98 CP75
Avenue Rd, Bans. 174 DB115
Avenue Rd, Beck. 142 DW95
Avenue Rd, Belv. 107 FC77
Avenue Rd, Bexh. 106 EY83
Avenue Rd, Brent. 97 CJ78
Avenue Rd, Brwd. 54 FW49
Avenue Rd, Cat. 176 DR122
Avenue Rd, Cob. 170 BX116
Avenue Rd, Epp. 33 ER36
Avenue Rd, Epsom 156 CR114
Avenue Rd, Erith 107 FC80
Avenue Rd, Felt. 115 BT90
Avenue Rd, Hmptn. 136 CB95
Avenue Rd, Islw. 97 CF81
Avenue Rd, Kings.T. 138 CL97
Avenue Rd, N.Mal. 138 CS98
Avenue Rd, Pnr. 60 BY55
Avenue Rd (Chadwell Heath), Rom. 70 EV59
Avenue Rd (Harold Wd), Rom. 52 FM52
Avenue Rd, Sev. 191 FJ123
Avenue Rd, Sthl. 96 BZ75
Avenue Rd, Stai. 113 BD92
Avenue Rd, Sutt. 158 DA110
Avenue Rd, Tedd. 117 CG94
Avenue Rd, Wall. 159 DJ108
Avenue Rd, West. 178 EL120
Avenue Rd, Wdf.Grn. 48 EJ51
Avenue S, Surb. 138 CM101
Avenue Ter, N.Mal. 138 CQ97
Kingston Rd
Avenue Ter, Wat. 24 BY44
Averil Gro SW16 121 DP93
Averill St W6 99 CX79
Avern Gdns, W.Mol. 136 CB98
Avern Rd, W.Mol. 136 CB99
Avery Fm Row SW1 198 G9
Avery Gdns, Ilf. 69 EM57
Avery Hill Rd SE9 125 ER86
Avery Row W1 195 H10
Avery Row W1 83 DH73
Avey La, Loug. 32 EH39
Avey La, Wal.Abb. 31 ED36
Aviary Cl E16 86 EF71
Aviary Rd, Wok. 168 BG116
Aviemore Cl, Beck. 143 DZ99
Aviemore Way, Beck. 143 DY99
Avignon Rd SE4 103 DX83
Avington Ct SE1 102 DS77
Old Kent Rd
Avington Gro SE20 122 DW94
Avington Way SE15 102 DT80
Daniel Gdns
Avion Cres NW9 43 CU53
Avior Dr, Nthwd. 39 BT49
Avis Gro, Croy. 161 DY110
Avis Sq E1 85 DX72
Avoca Rd SW17 120 DG91
Avocet Ms SE28 105 ER76
Avon Cl, Add. 152 BG107
Avon Cl, Grav. 131 GK89
Avon Cl, Hayes 78 BW70
Avon Cl, Sutt. 158 DC105
Avon Cl, Wat. 8 BW34
Avon Cl, Wor.Pk. 139 CU103
Avon Ct, Grnf. 78 CB70
Braund Av
Avon Grn, S.Ock. 91 FV72
Avon Ms, Pnr. 40 BZ53
Avon Path, S.Croy. 160 DQ107
Avon Pl SE1 201 J5
Avon Rd E17 67 ED55
Avon Rd SE4 103 EA83
Avon Rd, Grnf. 78 CA70
Avon Rd, Sun. 115 BT94
Avon Rd, Upmin. 73 FR58
Avon Way E18 68 EG55
Avondale Av N12 44 DB50
Avondale Av NW2 62 CS62
Avondale Av, Barn. 44 DF46
Avondale Av, Esher 137 CG104
Avondale Av, Stai. 113 BF94
Avondale Av, Wor.Pk. 139 CT102
Avondale Cl, Loug. 49 EM45
Avondale Cl, Walt. 154 BW106
Pleasant Pl
Avondale Ct E11 68 EE60
Avondale Ct E16 86 EE71
Avondale Rd
Avondale Ct E18 48 EH53
Avondale Cres, Enf. 31 DY41
Avondale Cres, Ilf. 68 EK57
Avondale Dr, Hayes 77 BU74
Avondale Dr, Loug. 49 EM45
Avondale Gdns, Houns. 116 BZ85
Avondale Ms, Brom. 124 EG93
Avondale Rd
Avondale Pk Gdns W11 81 CY73
Avondale Pk Rd W11 81 CY73
Avondale Pavement SE1 102 DU78
Avondale Sq
Avondale Ri SE15 102 DT83
Avondale Rd E16 86 EE71
Avondale Rd E17 67 EA59
Avondale Rd N3 44 DC53
Avondale Rd N13 45 DN47
Avondale Rd N15 65 DP57
Avondale Rd SE9 124 EL89
Avondale Rd SW14 98 CR83
Avondale Rd SW19 120 DB92
Avondale Rd, Ashf. 114 BK90
Avondale Rd, Brom. 124 EE93
Avondale Rd, Har. 61 CF55
Avondale Rd, S.Croy. 160 DQ107
Avondale Rd, Well. 106 EW82
Avondale Sq SE1 102 DU78
Avonley Rd SE14 102 DW80
Avonmead, Wok. 166 AW118
Silversmiths Way
Avonmore Gdns W14 99 CY77
Avonmore Rd
Avonmore Pl W14 99 CY77
Avonmore Rd
Avonmore Rd W14 99 CZ77
Avonmouth Rd, Dart. 128 FK85
Avonmouth St SE1 201 H6
Avonmouth St SE1 102 DQ76
Avontar Rd, S.Ock. 91 FV70
Avonwick Rd, Houns. 96 CB82
Avril Way E4 47 EC50
Avro Way, Wall. 159 DL108
Avro Way, Wey. 152 BL110
Awlfield Av N17 46 DR53
Awliscombe Rd, Well. 105 ET82
Axe St, Bark. 87 EQ67
Axholme Av, Edg. 42 CN53
Axis Pk, Slou. 93 BB78
Axminster Cres, Well. 106 EW81
Axminster Rd N7 65 DL62
Axtaine Rd, Orp. 146 EX101
Axtane, Grav. 130 FZ94
Axtane Cl (Sutton at Hone), Dart. 148 FQ96
Axwood, Epsom 172 CQ115
Aybrook St W1 194 F7
Aybrook St W1 82 DG71
Aycliffe Cl, Brom. 145 EM98
Aycliffe Rd W12 81 CT74
Aycliffe Rd, Borwd. 26 CL39
Ayebridges Av, Egh. 113 BC94
Aylands Cl, Wem. 62 CL61
Preston Rd
Aylands Rd, Enf. 30 DW36
Ayles Rd, Hayes 77 BV69
Aylesbury Cl E7 86 EF65
Atherton Rd
Aylesbury Est SE17 102 DR78
Villa St
Aylesbury Rd SE17 102 DR78
Aylesbury Rd, Brom. 144 EG97
Aylesbury St EC1 196 F5
Aylesbury St EC1 83 DP70
Aylesbury St NW10 62 CR62
Aylesford Av, Beck. 143 DY99
Aylesford St SW1 199 M10
Aylesford St SW1 101 DK78
Aylesham Cl NW7 43 CU52
Aylesham Rd, Orp. 145 ET101
Aylestone Av NW6 81 CX67
Aylesworth Spur, Wind. 112 AV87
Aylett Rd SE25 142 DV98
Aylett Rd, Islw. 97 CE82
Aylett Rd, Upmin. 72 FQ61
Ayley Cft, Enf. 30 DU43
Ayliffe Cl, Kings.T. 138 CN96
Cambridge Gdns
Aylmer Cl, Stan. 41 CG49
Aylmer Dr, Stan. 41 CG49
Aylmer Par N2 64 DF57
Aylmer Rd
Aylmer Rd E11 68 EF60
Aylmer Rd N2 64 DE57
Aylmer Rd W12 99 CT75
Aylmer Rd, Dag. 70 EY62
Ayloffe Rd, Dag. 88 EZ65
Ayloffs Cl, Horn. 72 FL57
Ayloffs Wk, Horn. 72 FK57
Aylsham Dr, Uxb. 59 BR61
Aylsham La, Rom. 52 FJ49
Aylton Est SE16 202 G5
Aylward Rd SE23 123 DX89
Aylward Rd SW20 139 CZ96
Aylward St E1 84 DW72
Aylwards Ri, Stan. 41 CG49
Aylwyn Est SE1 201 P6
Aylwyn Est SE1 102 DS76
Aymer Cl, Stai. 133 BE95
Aymer Dr, Stai. 133 BE95
Aynho St, Wat. 23 BV43
Aynhoe Rd W14 99 CX77
Aynscombe Angle, Orp. 146 EV101
Aynscombe La SW14 98 CQ83
Aynscombe Path SW14 98 CQ82
Thames Bk
Ayot Path, Borwd. 26 CN37
Ayr Ct W3 80 CN71
Monks Dr
Ayr Grn, Rom. 51 FE52
Ayr Way, Rom. 51 FE52
Ayres Cl E13 86 EG69
Ayres Cres NW10 80 CR66
Ayres St SE1 201 J4
Ayres St SE1 102 DQ75
Ayron Rd, S.Ock. 91 FV70
Ayrsome Rd N16 66 DS62
Ayrton Rd SW7 100 DD76
Wells Way
Aysgarth Rd SE21 122 DS86
Aytoun Pl SW9 101 DM82
Aytoun Rd SW9 101 DM82
Azalea Cl W7 79 CF74
Azalea Cl, Ilf. 69 EP64
Azalea Ct, Wok. 166 AX119
Azalea Ct, Wdf.Grn. 48 EE52
The Bridle Path
Azalea Dr, Swan. 147 FD98
Azalea Wk, Pnr. 59 BV57
Azalea Wk, Sthl. 96 CC75
Navigator Dr
Azalea Way, Slou. 74 AY72
Blinco La
Azenby Rd SE15 102 DT82
Azile Everitt Ho SE18 105 EQ78
Vicarage Pk
Azof St SE10 205 J9
Azof St SE10 104 EE77

B

B.A.T. Export Ho, Wok. 166 AY117
Baalbec Rd N5 65 DP64
Babbacombe Cl, Chess. 155 CK106
Babbacombe Gdns, Ilf. 68 EL56
Babbacombe Rd, Brom. 144 EG95
Baber Dr, Felt. 116 BW86
Babington Ri, Wem. 80 CN65
Babington Rd NW4 63 CV56
Babington Rd SW16 121 DK92
Babington Rd, Dag. 70 EW64
Babington Rd, Horn. 71 FH60
Babmaes St SW1 199 L1
Babylon La, Tad. 184 DA127
Bacchus Wk N1 197 M1
Bachelor's La, Wok. 168 BN124
Baches St N1 197 L3
Baches St N1 84 DR69
Back Ch La E1 84 DU73
Back Grn, Walt. 154 BW107
Back Hill EC1 196 D5
Back Hill EC1 83 DN70
Back La N8 65 DL57
Back La NW3 64 DC63
Heath St
Back La, Bex. 126 FA87
Back La, Brent. 97 CK79
Back La, Ch.St.G. 36 AU48
Back La, Edg. 42 CQ53
Back La, Grays 91 FW74
Back La, Purf. 109 FS76
Back La, Rich. 117 CJ90
Back La, Rick. 21 BB38
Back La, Rom. 70 EY59
St. Chad's Rd
Back La (Godden Grn), Sev. 191 FN124
Back La (Ide Hill), Sev. 190 FC126
Back La, Wat. 25 CE39
Back Path, Red. 186 DQ133
Back Rd, Sid. 126 EU91
Backhouse Pl SE17 201 N9
Backley Gdns SE25 142 DU100
Bacon Gro SE1 201 P7
Bacon Gro SE1 102 DT76
Bacon La NW9 62 CP56
Bacon La, Edg. 42 CN53
Bacon Link, Rom. 51 FB51
Bacon St E1 84 DT70
Bacon St E2 84 DT70
Bacon Ter, Dag. 70 EV64
Fitzstephen Rd
Bacons Dr (Cuffley), Pot.B. 13 DL29
Bacons La N6 64 DG60
Bacons Mead (Denham), Uxb. 58 BG61
Bacton NW5 64 DG64
Bacton St E2 84 DW69
Roman Rd
Badburgham Ct, Wal.Abb. 16 EF33
Baddeley Cl, Enf. 31 EA38
Government Row
Baddow Cl, Dag. 88 FA67
Baddow Cl, Wdf.Grn. 48 EK51
Baddow Wk N1 84 DQ67
Baden Cl, Stai. 114 BG94
Baden Pl SE1 201 K4
Baden Powell Cl, Dag. 88 EY67
Baden Powell Cl, Surb. 138 CM103
Baden Powell Rd, Sev. 190 FE121
Baden Rd N8 65 DK56
Baden Rd, Ilf. 69 EP64
Bader Cl, Ken. 176 DR115
Bader Wk, Grav. 130 GE90
Bader Way, Rain. 89 FG65
Badger Cl, Felt. 115 BU90
Sycamore Cl
Badger Cl, Houns. 96 BW83
Badger Cl, Ilf. 69 EQ59
Badgers Cl, Ashf. 114 BM92
Fordbridge Rd
Badgers Cl, Borwd. 26 CM40
Kingsley Av
Badgers Cl, Enf. 29 DP41
Badgers Cl, Har. 61 CD58
Badgers Cl, Hayes 77 BS73
Badgers Cl, Wok. 166 AW118
Badgers Copse, Orp. 145 ET103
Badgers Copse, Wor.Pk. 139 CT103
Badgers Cft N20 43 CY46
Badgers Cft SE9 125 EN90
Badgers Hill, Vir.W. 132 AW99
Badgers Hole, Croy. 161 DX105
Badgers La, Warl. 176 DW120
Badgers Mt, Grays 111 GF75
Badgers Ri, Sev. 164 FA110
Badgers Rd, Sev. 165 FB110
Badgers Wk, N.Mal. 138 CS96
Badgers Wk, Pur. 159 DK111
Badgers Wk, Rick. 21 BF42
Badgers Wk, Whyt. 176 DT119
Badgers Wd, Cat. 186 DQ125
Badingham Dr, Lthd. 171 CE123
Badlis Rd E17 67 EA55
Badlow Cl, Erith 107 FE80
Badminton Cl, Borwd. 26 CN40
Badminton Cl, Har. 61 CE56
Badminton Cl, Nthlt. 78 CA65
Badminton Ms E16 205 N2
Badminton Rd SW12 120 DG86
Badsworth Rd SE5 102 DQ80
Baffin Way E14 85 EC73
Prestons Rd
Bagley Cl, West Dr. 94 BL75
Bagley's La SW6 100 DB81
Bagleys Spring, Rom. 70 EY56
Bagot Cl, Ash. 172 CM116
Bagshot Ct SE18 105 EN81
Prince Imperial Rd
Bagshot Rd, Egh. 112 AW94
Bagshot Rd, Enf. 46 DT45
Bagshot St SE17 102 DS78
Bahram Rd, Epsom 156 CR110
Baildon St SE8 103 EA80
Watson's St
Bailey Cl E4 47 EC49
Bailey Cl, Chess. 155 CK107
Ashlyns Way
Bailey Cl, Purf. 109 FR77
Gabion Av
Bailey Pl SE26 123 DX93
Baillie Cl, Rain. 89 FH70
Baillies Wk W5 97 CK75
Liverpool Rd
Bainbridge Rd, Dag. 70 EZ63
Bainbridge St WC1 195 N8
Bainbridge St WC1 83 DK72
Baines Cl, S.Croy. 160 DQ106
Brighton Rd
Bainton Mead, Wok. 166 AU117
Baird Av, Sthl. 78 CB73
Baird Cl E10 67 EA60
Church Rd
Baird Cl NW9 62 CQ58
Baird Cl, Bushey 24 CB44
Ashfield Av
Baird Gdns SE19 122 DS91
Baird Rd, Enf. 30 DV42
Baird St EC1 197 J4
Bairstow Cl, Borwd. 26 CL39
Baizdon Rd SE3 104 EE82
Bakeham La, Egh. 112 AW94
Baker Boy La, Croy. 161 DZ112
Baker Hill Cl, Grav. 131 GF91
Baker La, Mitch. 140 DG96
Baker Pas NW10 80 CS67
Acton La
Baker Rd NW10 80 CS67
Baker Rd SE18 104 EL80
Baker St NW1 194 E5
Baker St NW1 82 DF70
Baker St W1 194 E6
Baker St W1 82 DF71
Baker St, Enf. 30 DR41
Baker St, Pot.B. 27 CY35
Baker St, Wey. 152 BN105
Bakers Av E17 67 EB58
Bakers Ct SE25 142 DS97
Bakers End SW20 139 CY96
Bakers Fld N7 65 DK63
Crayford Rd
Bakers Gdns, Cars. 140 DE103
Bakers Hill E5 66 DW60
Bakers Hill, Barn. 28 DB40
Bakers La N6 64 DF57
Bakers La, Epp. 17 ET30
Bakers Mead, Gdse. 186 DW130
Baker's Ms W1 194 F8
Bakers Ms, Orp. 163 ET107
Bakers Pas NW3 64 DC63
Heath St
Baker's Rents E2 197 P3
Bakers Rd, Uxb. 76 BK66
Bakers Rd (Cheshunt), Wal.Cr. 14 DV30
Bakers Row E15 86 EE68
Baker's Row EC1 196 D5
Baker's Row EC1 83 DN70
Bakers Wd (Denham), Uxb. 57 BD60
Baker's Yd EC1 83 DN70
Baker's Row
Baker's Yd, Uxb. 76 BK66
Bakers Rd
Bakery Cl SW9 101 DM81
Bakery Path, Edg. 42 CP51
Station Rd
Bakery Pl SW11 100 DF84
Altenburg Gdns
Bakewell Way, N.Mal. 138 CS96
Bala Gdn NW9 62 CS58
Snowdon Dr
Balaam St E13 86 EG69
Balaams La N14 45 DK47
Balaclava Rd SE1 202 A9
Balaclava Rd SE1 102 DT77
Balaclava Rd, Surb. 137 CJ101
Balcaskie Rd SE9 125 EM85
Balchen Rd SE3 104 EK82
Balchier Rd SE22 122 DV86
Balcombe Cl, Bexh. 106 EX84
Balcombe St NW1 194 D5
Balcombe St NW1 82 DF70
Balcon Ct W5 80 CM72
Boileau Rd
Balcon Way, Borwd. 26 CQ39
Balcorne St E9 84 DW66
Balder Ri SE12 124 EH89
Balderton St W1 194 G9
Balderton St W1 82 DG72
Baldock St E3 85 EB68
Baldock Way, Borwd. 26 CM39
Baldocks Rd, Epp. 33 ES35
Baldry Gdns SW16 121 DL93
Baldwin Cres SE5 102 DQ81
Baldwin Gdns, Houns. 96 CC81
Gresham Rd
Baldwin St EC1 197 K3
Baldwin Ter N1 84 DQ68
Baldwin's Gdns EC1 196 D6
Baldwin's Gdns EC1 83 DN71
Baldwins Hill, Loug. 33 EM40
Baldwins La, Rick. 23 BP42
Baldwyn Gdns W3 80 CR73
Baldwyns Pk, Bex. 127 FD89
Baldwyns Rd, Bex. 127 FD89
Balfe St N1 196 A1
Balfe St N1 83 DL68
Balfern Gro W4 98 CS78
Balfern St SW11 100 DE81
Balfont Cl, S.Croy. 160 DU113
Balfour Av W7 79 CF74
Balfour Av, Wok. 166 AY122
Balfour Gro N20 44 DF48
Balfour Ho W10 81 CX71
St. Charles Sq
Balfour Ms N9 46 DU48
The Bdy
Balfour Ms W1 198 G2
Balfour Pl SW15 99 CV84
Balfour Pl W1 198 G1
Balfour Rd N5 66 DQ63
Balfour Rd SE25 142 DU98
Balfour Rd SW19 120 DB94
Balfour Rd W3 80 CQ71
Balfour Rd W13 97 CG75
Balfour Rd, Brom. 144 EK99
Balfour Rd, Cars. 158 DF108
Balfour Rd, Grays 110 GC77
Balfour Rd, Har. 61 CD57
Balfour Rd, Houns. 96 CB83
Balfour Rd, Ilf. 69 EP61
Balfour Rd, Sthl. 96 BX76
Balfour Rd, Wey. 152 BN105
Balfour St SE17 201 K8
Balfour St SE17 102 DR77
Balgonie Rd E4 47 ED46
Balgores Cres, Rom. 71 FH5
Balgores La, Rom. 71 FH5
Balgores Sq, Rom. 71 FH5
Balgowan Cl, N.Mal. 138 CS9
Balgowan Rd, Beck. 143 DY9
Balgowan St SE18 105 ET7
Balham Continental Mkt SW12 121 DH8
Balham Gro SW12 120 DG8
Balham High Rd SW12 120 DG8
Balham High Rd SW17 120 DG8
Balham Hill SW12 121 DH8
Balham New Rd SW12 121 DH8
Balham Pk Rd SW12 120 DF8
Balham Rd N9 46 DU4
Balham Sta Rd SW12 121 DH8
Balkan Wk E1 202 D
Balladier Wk E14 85 EB7
Ballamore Rd, Brom. 124 EG9
Ballance Rd E9 85 DX6
Ballands N, The, Lthd. 171 CE12
Ballands S, The, Lthd. 171 CE12
Ballantine St SW18 100 DC8
Ballantyne Dr, Tad. 173 CZ12
Ballard Cl, Kings.T. 118 CR9
Ballards Cl, Dag. 89 FB6
Ballards Fm Rd, Croy. 160 DU10
Ballards Fm Rd, S.Croy. 160 DU10
Ballards Grn, Tad. 173 CY11
Ballards La N3 44 DA5
Ballards La N12 44 DA5
Ballards La, Oxt. 188 EJ12
Ballards Ms, Edg. 42 CN5
Ballards Ri, S.Croy. 160 DU10
Ballards Rd NW2 63 CU6
Ballards Rd, Dag. 89 FB6
Ballards Way, Croy. 160 DV10
Ballards Way, S.Croy. 160 DU10
Ballast Quay SE10 204 G1
Ballast Quay SE10 103 ED7
Ballater Cl, Wat. 40 BW4
Ballater Rd SW2 101 DL8
Ballater Rd, S.Croy. 160 DT10
Ballenger Ct, Wat. 23 BV4
Ballina St SE23 123 DX8
Ballingdon Rd SW11 120 DG8
Ballinger Pt E3 85 EB6
Bromley High St
Balliol Av E4 47 ED4
Balliol Rd N17 46 DS5
Balliol Rd W10 81 CW7
Balliol Rd, Well. 106 EV8
Balloch Rd SE6 123 ED8
Ballogie Av NW10 62 CS6
Ballow Cl SE5 102 DS8
Harris St
Balls Pond Pl N1 84 DR6
Balls Pond Rd
Balls Pond Rd N1 84 DR6
Balmain Cl W5 79 CK7
Balmer Rd E3 85 DZ6
Balmes Rd N1 84 DR6
Balmoral Av N11 44 DG5
Balmoral Av, Beck. 143 DY9
Balmoral Cl SW15 119 CX8
Westleigh Av
Balmoral Cl, St.Alb. 8 CC2
Balmoral Cres, W.Mol. 136 CA97
Balmoral Dr, Borwd. 26 CR43
Balmoral Dr, Hayes 77 BU71
Balmoral Dr, Sthl. 78 BZ70
Balmoral Dr, Wok. 167 BC116
Balmoral Gdns W13 97 CG76
Balmoral Gdns, Bex. 126 EZ87
Balmoral Gdns, Couls. 160 DR110
Balmoral Gdns, Ilf. 69 ET60
Balmoral Gro N7 83 DM65
Balmoral Ms W12 99 CT75
Balmoral Rd E7 68 EJ63
Balmoral Rd E10 67 EB61
Balmoral Rd NW2 81 CV65
Balmoral Rd, Abb.L. 7 BU32
Balmoral Rd, Brwd. 54 FV44
Balmoral Rd (Sutton at Hone), Dart. 128 FP94
Balmoral Rd, Enf. 31 DX36
Balmoral Rd, Har. 60 CA63
Balmoral Rd, Horn. 72 FK62
Balmoral Rd, Kings.T. 138 CM98
Balmoral Rd, Rom. 71 FH56
Balmoral Rd, Wat. 24 BW38
Balmoral Rd, Wor.Pk. 139 CV104
Balmoral Way, Sutt. 158 DA110
Balmore Cres, Barn. 28 DG43
Balmore St N19 65 DH61
Balmuir Gdns SW15 99 CW84
Balnacraig Av NW10 62 CS63
Balniel Gate SW1 199 N10
Balniel Gate SW1 101 DK78
Balquhain Cl, Ash. 171 CK117
Baltic Cl SW19 120 DD94
Baltic Ct SE16 203 J4
Baltic Pl N1 84 DS67
Kingsland Rd
Baltic St E EC1 197 H5
Baltic St E EC1 84 DQ70
Baltic St W EC1 197 H5
Baltic St W EC1 84 DQ70
Baltimore Pl, Well. 105 ET82
Balvaird Pl SW1 101 DK78
Balvernie Gro SW18 119 CZ87
Bamber Ho, Bark. 87 EQ67
St. Margarets
Bamborough Gdns W12 99 CW75
Bamford Av, Wem. 80 CM67
Bamford Ct E15 67 EB64
Clays La
Bamford Rd, Bark. 87 EQ65
Bamford Rd, Brom. 123 EC92
Bamford Way, Rom. 51 FB50
Bampfylde Cl, Wall. 141 DJ104
Bampton Dr NW7 43 CU52
Bampton Rd SE23 123 DX90
Bampton Rd, Rom. 52 FL53
Bampton Way, Wok. 166 AU118
Banavie Gdns, Beck. 143 EC95
Banbury Cl, Enf. 29 DP39
Holtwhites Hill
Banbury Ct WC2 195 P10
Banbury Ct, Sutt. 158 DA108
Banbury Enterprise Cen, Croy. 141 DP103
Factory La

Banbury Rd E9 85 DX66
Banbury Rd E17 47 DX52
Banbury St SW11 100 DE82
Banbury St, Wat. 23 BV43
Banbury Wk, Nthlt. 78 CA68
Brabazon Rd
Banchory Rd SE3 104 EH80
Bancroft Av N2 64 DE57
Bancroft Av, Buck.H. 48 EG47
Bancroft Cl, Ashf. 114 BN92
Feltham Hill Rd
Bancroft Ct, Nthlt. 78 BW67
Bancroft Ct, Reig. 184 DB134
Bancroft Gdns, Har. 40 CC53
Bancroft Gdns, Orp. 145 ET102
Bancroft Rd E1 84 DW69
Bancroft Rd, Har. 40 CC54
Bancroft Rd, Reig. 184 DA134
Band La, Egh. 113 AZ92
Bandon Cl, Uxb. 76 BM67
Bandon Ri, Wall. 159 DK106
Bangalore St SW15 99 CW83
Bangor Cl, Nthlt. 60 CB64
Bangors Cl, Iver 75 BE72
Bangors Rd N, Iver 75 BD67
Bangors Rd S, Iver 75 BE71
Banim St W6 99 CV76
Banister Rd W10 81 CX69
Bank, The N6 65 DH60
Cholmeley Pk
Bank Av, Mitch. 140 DD96
Bank Ct, Dart. 128 FL86
High St
Bank End SE1 201 J2
Bank End SE1 84 DQ74
Bank La SW15 118 CS85
Bank La, Kings.T. 118 CL94
Bank Ms, Sutt. 158 DA111
Sutton Ct Rd
Bank Pl, Brwd. 54 FW47
High St
Bank St, Grav. 131 GH86
Bank St, Sev. 191 FH125
Bankfoot, Grays 110 FZ77
Bankfoot Rd, Brom. 124 EE91
Bankhurst Rd SE6 123 DZ87
Banks La, Bexh. 106 EZ84
Banks La, Epp. 18 EY32
Bank's La, Lthd. 169 BV122
Banks Rd, Borwd. 26 CQ40
Banks Way E12 69 EN63
Grantham Rd
Banksia Rd N18 46 DW50
Banksian Wk, Islw. 97 CE81
Bankside SE1 201 H1
Bankside SE1 84 DQ73
Bankside, Enf. 29 DP39
Bankside, Grav. 130 GC86
Bankside, Sev. 190 FE121
Bankside, S.Croy. 160 DT107
Bankside, Sthl. 78 BX74
Bankside, Wok. 166 AV118
Wyndham Rd
Bankside Av, Nthlt. 77 BU68
Townson Av
Bankside Cl, Bex. 127 FD91
Bankside Cl, Cars. 158 DE107
Bankside Cl, Islw. 97 CF84
Bankside Cl, West. 178 EJ118
Bankside Dr, T.Ditt. 137 CH102
Bankside Rd, Ilf. 69 EQ64
Bankside Way SE19 122 DS93
Lunham Rd
Bankton Rd SW2 101 DN84
Bankwell Rd SE13 104 EE84
Bann Cl, S.Ock. 91 FV73
Banner Cl, Purf. 109 FR77
Brimfield Rd
Banner St EC1 197 J5
Banner St EC1 84 DQ70
Bannerman Ho SW8 101 DM79
Banning St SE10 104 EE78
Bannister Cl SW2 121 DN88
Ewen Cres
Bannister Cl, Grnf. 61 CD64
Bannister Cl, Slou. 92 AY75
Bannister Dr, Brwd. 55 GC44
Bannister Gdns, Orp. 146 EW97
Main Rd
Bannister Ho E9 67 DX64
Homerton High St
Bannockburn Rd SE18 105 ES77
Banstead Gdns N9 46 DS48
Banstead Rd, Bans. 157 CX112
Banstead Rd, Cars. 158 DE107
Banstead Rd, Cat. 176 DR121
Banstead Rd, Epsom 157 CV111
Banstead Rd, Pur. 159 DN111
Banstead Rd S, Sutt. 158 DD110
Banstead St SE15 102 DW83
Banstead Way, Wall. 159 DL106
Banstock Rd, Edg. 42 CP51
Banting Dr N21 29 DM43
Banton Cl, Enf. 30 DV40
Central Av
Bantry St SE5 102 DR80
Banwell Rd, Bex. 126 EX86
Woodside La
Banyard Rd SE16 202 E7
Banyards, Horn. 72 FL56
Bapchild Pl, Orp. 146 EW98
Baptist Gdns NW5 82 DG65
Queens Cres
Barandon Wk W11 81 CX73
Barb Ms W6 99 CW76
Barbara Brosnan Ct NW8 82 DD68
Grove End Rd
Barbara Cl, Shep. 135 BP99
Barbara Hucklesby Cl N22 45 DP54
The Sandlings
Barbauld Rd N16 66 DS62
Barbel Cl, Wal.Cr. 15 EA34
Barber Cl N21 45 DN45
Barberry Cl, Rom. 52 FJ52
Barber's All E13 86 EH69
Barbers Rd E15 85 EB68
Barbican, The EC2 197 H6
Barbican, The EC2 84 DQ71
Barbican Rd, Grnf. 78 CB72
Barbon Cl WC1 196 B6
Barbot Cl N9 46 DU48
Barchard St SW18 120 DB85
Barchester Cl W7 79 CF74
Barchester Cl, Uxb. 76 BJ70
Barchester Rd, Har. 41 CD54
Barchester Rd, Slou. 93 AZ75
Barchester St E14 85 EB71
Barclay Cl SW6 100 DA80
Barclay Cl, Lthd. 170 CB123
Barclay Cl, Wat. 23 BU44
Barclay Oval, Wdf.Grn. 48 EG49
Barclay Path E17 67 EC57
Barclay Rd E11 68 EE60
Barclay Rd E13 86 EJ70
Barclay Rd E17 67 EC57
Barclay Rd N18 46 DR51
Barclay Rd SW6 100 DA80
Barclay Rd, Croy. 142 DR104
Barclay Way SE22 122 DU87
Lordship La
Barclay Way, Grays 109 FT78
Barcombe Av SW2 121 DL89
Barcombe Cl, Orp. 145 ET97
Bard Rd W10 81 CX73
Barden Cl (Harefield), Uxb. 38 BJ52
Barden St SE18 105 ES80
Bardeswell Cl, Brwd. 54 FW47
Bardfield Av, Rom. 70 EX55
Bardney Rd, Mord. 140 DB98
Bardolph Av, Croy. 161 DZ109
Bardolph Rd N7 65 DL63
Bardolph Rd, Rich. 98 CM83
St. Georges Rd
Bardon Wk, Wok. 166 AV117
Bampton Way
Bardsey Pl E1 84 DW71
Mile End Rd
Bardsey Wk N1 84 DQ65
Clephane Rd
Bardsley Cl, Croy. 142 DT104
Bardsley La SE10 103 EC79
Barfett St W10 81 CZ70
Barfield (Sutton at Hone), Dart. 148 FP95
Barfield Av N20 44 DE47
Barfield Rd E11 68 EF60
Barfield Rd, Brom. 145 EN97
Barfields, Loug. 33 EN42
Barfields, Red. 185 DP133
Barfields Gdns, Loug. 33 EN42
Barfields
Barfields Path, Loug. 33 EN42
Barford Cl NW4 43 CU53
Barford St N1 83 DN67
Barforth Rd SE15 102 DV83
Barfreston Way SE20 142 DV95
Bargate Cl SE18 105 ET78
Bargate Cl, N.Mal. 139 CU100
Barge Ho Rd E16 87 EP74
Barge Ho St SE1 200 E2
Barge Wk, E.Mol. 137 CK96
Barge Wk, Kings.T. 137 CK95
Barge Wk, Walt. 136 CC96
Bargery Rd SE6 123 EB88
Bargrove Cl SE20 122 DU94
Bargrove Cres SE6 123 DZ89
Elm La
Barham Av, Borwd. 26 CM41
Barham Cl, Brom. 144 EL102
Barham Cl, Chis. 125 EP92
Barham Cl, Grav. 131 GM88
Barham Cl, Rom. 51 FB54
Barham Cl, Wem. 79 CH65
Barham Cl, Wey. 153 BQ105
Barham Rd SW20 119 CU94
Barham Rd, Chis. 125 EP92
Barham Rd, Dart. 128 FN87
Barham Rd, S.Croy. 160 DQ106
Baring Cl SE12 124 EG89
Baring Rd SE12 124 EG87
Baring Rd, Barn. 28 DD41
Baring Rd, Croy. 142 DU102
Baring St N1 84 DR67
Bark Burr Rd, Grays 110 FZ75
Bark Hart Rd, Orp. 146 EV102
Bark Pl W2 82 DB73
Barkantine Shop Par, The E14 103 EA75
The Quarterdeck
Barker Cl, N.Mal. 138 CQ97
California Rd
Barker Cl, Nthwd. 39 BT52
Barker Dr NW1 83 DJ66
Barker Ms SW4 101 DH84
Barker Rd, Cher. 133 BE101
Barker St SW10 100 DC79
Barker Wk SW16 121 DK90
Barker Way SE22 122 DU88
Dulwich Common
Barkham Rd N17 46 DR52
Barking Ind Pk, Bark. 87 ET67
Barking Rd E6 86 EK68
Barking Rd E13 86 EH70
Barking Rd E16 86 EF71
Barkston Gdns SW5 100 DB77
Barkston Path, Borwd. 26 CN38
Barkway Ct N4 66 DQ62
Queens Dr
Barkwood Cl, Rom. 71 FC57
Barkworth Rd SE16 102 DV78
Barlborough St SE14 102 DW80
Barlby Gdns W10 81 CX70
Barlby Rd W10 81 CX71
Barle Gdns, S.Ock. 91 FV72
Barlee Cres, Uxb. 76 BJ71
Barley Cl, Bushey 24 CB43
Barley La, Ilf. 70 EU59
Barley La, Rom. 70 EV58
Barley Mow Ct, Bet. 182 CQ134
Barley Mow Pas EC1 196 G7
Barley Mow Pas W4 98 CR78
Barley Mow Rd, Egh. 112 AW92
Barley Mow Way, Shep. 134 BN98
Barley Shotts Business Pk W10 81 CZ71
St. Ervans Rd
Barleycorn Way E14 85 DZ73
Barleycorn Way, Horn. 72 FM58
Barleyfields Cl, Rom. 70 EV59
Barlow Cl, Wall. 159 DL107
Cobham Cl
Barlow Pl W1 199 J1
Barlow Rd NW6 81 CZ65
Barlow Rd W3 80 CP74
Barlow Rd, Hmptn. 116 CA94
Barlow St SE17 201 L9
Barlow Way, Rain. 89 FD71
Barmeston Rd SE6 123 EB89
Barmor Cl, Har. 40 CB54
Barmouth Av, Grnf. 79 CF68
Barmouth Rd SW18 120 DC86
Barmouth Rd, Croy. 143 DX103
Barn Cl, Ashf. 115 BP92
Barn Cl, Bans. 174 DD115
Barn Cl, Epsom 172 CQ115
Barn Cl, Nthlt. 78 BW68
Barn Cl, Rad. 25 CG35
Barn Cres, Pur. 160 DR113
Barn Cres, Stan. 41 CJ51
Barn Elms Pk SW15 99 CW82
Barn End Dr, Dart. 128 FJ90
Barn End La, Dart. 128 FJ92
Barn Hill, Wem. 62 CP61
Barn Lea, Rick. 38 BG46
Barn Mead, Epp. 33 ES36
Barn Mead, Ong. 19 FE29
Barn Meadow, Epp. 17 ET25
Upland Rd
Barn Meadow La, Lthd. 170 BZ124
Barn Ms, Har. 60 CA62
Barn Ri, Wem. 62 CN60
Barn St N16 66 DS62
Stoke Newington Ch St
Barn Way, Wem. 62 CN60
Barnabas Ct N21 29 DN43
Cheyne Wk
Barnabas Rd E9 67 DX64
Barnaby Cl, Har. 60 CC61
Barnaby Pl SW7 100 DD77
Barnaby Way, Chig. 49 EP48
Barnacre Cl, Uxb. 76 BK72
New Peachey La
Barnacres Rd, Hem.H. 6 BM25
Barnard Cl SE18 105 EN77
Barnard Cl, Chis. 145 ER95
Barnard Cl, Sun. 115 BV94
Oak Gro
Barnard Cl, Wall. 159 DK108
Barnard Ct, Wok. 166 AS118
Raglan Rd
Barnard Gdns, Hayes 77 BV70
Barnard Gdns, N.Mal. 139 CU98
Barnard Gro E15 86 EF66
Vicarage La
Barnard Hill N10 44 DG54
Barnard Ms SW11 100 DE84
Barnard Rd SW11 100 DE84
Barnard Rd, Enf. 30 DV40
Barnard Rd, Mitch. 140 DG97
Barnard Rd, Warl. 177 EB119
Barnardo Dr, Ilf. 69 EQ56
Barnardo St E1 85 DX72
Devonport St
Barnardos Village, Ilf. 69 EQ55
Barnard's Inn EC1 196 E8
Barnards Pl, S.Croy. 159 DP109
Barnato Cl, W.Byf. 152 BL112
Viscount Gdns
Barnby Sq E15 86 EE67
Barnby St
Barnby St E15 86 EE67
Barnby St NW1 195 L1
Barnby St NW1 83 DJ68
Barncroft Cl, Loug. 33 EN43
Barncroft Cl, Uxb. 77 BP71
Harlington Rd
Barncroft Grn, Loug. 33 EN43
Barncroft Rd, Loug. 33 EN43
Barnehurst Av, Bexh. 107 FC81
Barnehurst Av, Erith 107 FC81
Barnehurst Cl, Erith 107 FC81
Barnehurst Rd, Bexh. 107 FC82
Barnes All, Hmptn. 136 CC96
Hampton Ct Rd
Barnes Av SW13 99 CU80
Barnes Av, Sthl. 96 BZ77
Barnes Br SW13 98 CS82
Barnes Br W4 98 CS82
Barnes Cl E12 68 EK63
Barnes Ct E16 86 EJ71
Ridgwell Rd
Barnes Ct, Wdf.Grn. 48 EK50
Barnes Cray Cotts, Dart. 127 FG85
Maiden La
Barnes Cray Rd, Dart. 107 FG84
Barnes End, N.Mal. 139 CU99
Barnes High St SW13 99 CT82
Barnes Ho, Bark. 87 ER67
St. Marys
Barnes La, Kings L. 6 BH27
Barnes Pikle W5 79 CJ73
Barnes Ri, Kings L. 6 BM27
Barnes Rd N18 46 DW49
Barnes Rd, Ilf. 69 EQ64
Barnes St E14 85 DY72
Barnes Ter SE8 103 DZ78
Barnes Wallis Dr, Wey. 152 BL111
Barnes Way, Iver 75 BF73
Barnesbury Ho SW4 121 DK85
Barnesdale Cres, Orp. 146 EU100
Barnet Bypass, Barn. 26 CS41
Barnet Dr, Brom. 144 EL103
Barnet Gate La, Barn. 27 CT44
Barnet Gro E2 84 DU69
Barnet Hill, Barn. 28 DA42
Barnet Ho N20 44 DC47
Barnet La N20 43 CZ46
Barnet La, Barn. 27 CZ44
Barnet La, Borwd. 25 CK44
Barnet Rd (Arkley), Barn. 27 CV43
Barnet Rd, Pot.B. 12 DB34
Barnet Rd, St.Alb. 10 CL27
Barnet Trd Est, Barn. 27 CZ41
Barnet Way NW7 42 CR45
Barnet Wd Rd, Brom. 144 EJ103
Barnett Cl, Erith 107 FF82
Barnett Cl, Lthd. 171 CH119
Barnett St E1 84 DV72
Cannon St Rd
Barnett Wd La, Ash. 171 CJ119
Barnett Wd La, Lthd. 171 CH120
Barnetts Shaw, Oxt. 187 ED127
Barney Cl SE7 104 EJ78
Barnfield, Bans. 158 DB114
Barnfield, Epp. 18 EU28
Barnfield, Grav. 131 GG89
Barnfield, Iver 75 BE72
Barnfield, N.Mal. 138 CS100
Barnfield Av, Croy. 142 DW103
Barnfield Av, Kings.T. 118 CL92
Barnfield Av, Mitch. 141 DH98
Barnfield Cl N4 65 DL59
Crouch Hill
Barnfield Cl SW17 120 DC90
Barnfield Cl, Couls. 176 DQ119
Barnfield Cl, Green. 129 FT86
Barnfield Cl, Swan. 147 FC101
Barnfield Gdns SE18 105 EP79
Plumstead Common Rd
Barnfield Gdns, Kings.T. 118 CL91
Barnfield Pl E14 204 A9
Barnfield Pl E14 103 EA77
Barnfield Rd SE18 105 EP79
Barnfield Rd W5 79 CJ70
Barnfield Rd, Belv. 106 EZ79
Barnfield Rd, Edg. 42 CQ53
Barnfield Rd, Orp. 146 EX97
Barnfield Rd, Sev. 190 FD123
Barnfield Rd, S.Croy. 160 DS109
Barnfield Rd, West. 178 EK120
Barnfield Way, Oxt. 188 EG133
Barnfield Wd Cl, Beck. 143 ED100
Barnfield Wd Rd, Beck. 143 ED100
Barnham Rd, Grnf. 78 CC69
Barnham St SE1 201 N4
Barnham St SE1 102 DS75
Barnhill, Pnr. 60 BW57
Barnhill Av, Brom. 144 EF99
Barnhill La, Hayes 77 BV69
Barnhill Rd, Hayes 77 BV69
Barnhill Rd, Wem. 62 CQ62
Barnhurst Path, Wat. 40 BW50
Barningham Way NW9 62 CR58
Barnlea Cl, Felt. 116 BY89
Barnmead, Wok. 150 AT110
Barnmead Gdns, Dag. 70 EZ64
Barnmead Rd, Beck. 143 DY95
Barnmead Rd, Dag. 70 EZ64
Barnsbury Cl, N.Mal. 138 CQ98
Barnsbury Cres, Surb. 138 CQ102
Barnsbury Est N1 83 DN67
Barnsbury Rd
Barnsbury Gro N7 83 DM66
Barnsbury La, Surb. 138 CP103
Barnsbury Pk N1 83 DN66
Barnsbury Rd N1 83 DN68
Barnsbury Sq N1 83 DN66
Barnsbury St N1 83 DN66
Barnsbury Ter N1 83 DM66
Barnscroft SW20 139 CV97
Barnsdale Av E14 204 A8
Barnsdale Av E14 103 EA77
Barnsdale Cl, Borwd. 26 CM39
Barnsdale Rd W9 81 CZ70
Barnsfield Pl, Uxb. 76 BJ66
Barnsley Rd, Rom. 52 FM52
Barnsley St E1 84 DV70
Barnstaple Path, Rom. 52 FJ50
Barnstaple Rd, Rom. 52 FJ50
Barnstaple Rd, Ruis. 60 BW62
Barnston Wk N1 84 DQ67
Popham St
Barnston Way, Brwd. 55 GC43
Barnsway, Kings L. 6 BL28
Barnway, Egh. 112 AW92
Barnwell Rd SW2 121 DN85
Barnwell Rd, Dart. 108 FM83
Barnwood Cl W9 82 DB70
Barnwood Cl, Ruis. 59 BR61
Lysander Rd
Barnyard, The, Tad. 173 CU124
Baron Cl N11 44 DG50
Balmoral Av
Baron Cl, Sutt. 158 DB110
Baron Gdns, Ilf. 69 EQ55
Baron Gro, Mitch. 140 DE98
Baron Rd, Dag. 70 EX60
Baron St N1 83 DN68
Baron Wk E16 86 EF71
Baron Wk, Mitch. 140 DE98
Baroness Rd E2 84 DT69
Diss St
Baronet Gro N17 46 DU53
St. Paul's Rd
Baronet Rd N17 46 DU53
Barons, The, Twick. 117 CH86
Barons Ct, Wall. 141 DK104
Whelan Way
Barons Ct Rd W14 99 CY78
Barons Gate, Barn. 28 DE44
Barons Hurst, Epsom 172 CQ116
Barons Keep W14 99 CY78
Barons Mead, Har. 61 CE56
Barons Pl SE1 200 E5
Barons Pl SE1 101 DN75
Barons Wk, Croy. 143 DY100
Barons Way, Egh. 113 BD93
Baronsfield Rd, Twick. 117 CH86
Baronsmead Rd SW13 99 CU81
Baronsmede W5 98 CM75
Baronsmere Rd N2 64 DE56
Barque Ms SE8 103 EA79
Watergate St
Barr Rd, Grav. 131 GM89
Barr Rd, Pot.B. 12 DC33
Barra Hall Circ, Hayes 77 BS72
Barra Hall Rd, Hayes 77 BS73
Barrack Path, Wok. 166 AT118
Barrack Rd, Houns. 96 BX84
Barrack Row, Grav. 131 GH86
Barracks, The, Add. 134 BH104
Barracks La, Barn. 27 CY41
High St
Barras Cl, Enf. 31 EA38
Government Row
Barratt Av N22 45 DM54
Barratt Ind Pk, Sthl. 96 CA75
Barratt Way, Har. 61 CD55
Tudor Rd
Barrenger Rd N10 44 DF53
Barrens Brae, Wok. 167 BA118
Barrens Cl, Wok. 167 BA118
Barrens Pk, Wok. 167 BA118
Barrett Cl, Rom. 51 FH52
Barrett Rd E17 67 EC56
Barrett Rd, Lthd. 170 CC124
Barrett St W1 194 G9
Barrett St W1 82 DG72
Barretts Grn Rd NW10 80 CQ68
Barretts Gro N16 66 DS64
Barretts Rd, Sev. 181 FD120
Barrhill Rd SW2 121 DL89
Barricane, Wok. 166 AV119
Barrie Cl, Couls. 175 DJ115
Barrie Est W2 82 DD73
Craven Ter
Barrie Ho W3 98 CP75
Barriedale SE14 103 DY82
Barrier App SE7 104 EK76
Barrier Pt Rd E16 86 EG74
Barringer Sq SW17 120 DG91
Barrington Cl NW5 64 DG64
Barrington Cl, Ilf. 49 EM53
Barrington Cl, Loug. 33 EQ42
Barrington Rd
Barrington Ct, Brwd. 55 GC44
Barrington Dr (Harefield), Uxb. 38 BG52
Barrington Grn, Loug. 33 EQ42
Barrington Lo, Wey. 153 BQ106
Barrington Pk Gdns, Ch.St.G. 36 AX46
Barrington Rd E12 87 EN65
Barrington Rd N8 65 DK57
Barrington Rd SW9 101 DP83
Barrington Rd, Bexh. 106 EX82
Barrington Rd, Loug. 33 EQ41
Barrington Rd, Pur. 159 DJ112
Barrington Rd, Sutt. 140 DA102
Barrington Vil SE18 105 EN81
Barrow Av, Cars. 158 DF108
Barrow Cl N21 45 DP48
Barrow Grn Rd, Oxt. 187 EC128
Barrow Hedges Cl, Cars. 158 DE108
Barrow Hedges Way, Cars. 158 DE108
Barrow Hill, Wor.Pk. 138 CS103
Barrow Hill Cl, Wor.Pk. 138 CS103
Barrow Hill
Barrow Hill Est NW8 82 DE68
Barrow Hill Rd
Barrow Hill Rd NW8 194 B1
Barrow Hill Rd NW8 82 DE68
Barrow La (Cheshunt), Wal.Cr. 14 DT30
Barrow Pt Av, Pnr. 40 BY54
Barrow Pt La, Pnr. 40 BY54
Barrow Rd SW16 121 DK93
Barrow Rd, Croy. 159 DN106
Barrow Wk, Brent. 97 CJ78
Glenhurst Rd
Barrowdene Cl, Pnr. 40 BY54
Paines La
Barrowell Grn N21 45 DP47
Barrowfield Cl N9 46 DV48
Barrowgate Rd W4 98 CQ78
Barrowsfield, S.Croy. 160 DT112
Barrs Rd NW10 80 CR66
Barry Av N15 66 DT58
Craven Pk Rd
Barry Av, Bexh. 106 EY80
Barry Cl, Grays 111 GG75
Barry Cl, Orp. 145 ES104
Barry Cl, St.Alb. 8 CB25
Barry Rd E6 86 EL72
Barry Rd NW10 80 CQ66
Barry Rd SE22 122 DU86
Barset Rd SE15 102 DW83
Barson Cl SE20 122 DW94
Barston Rd SE27 122 DQ90
Barstow Cres SW2 121 DM88
Barter St WC1 196 A7
Barter St WC1 83 DL71
Barters Wk, Pnr. 60 BY55
High St
Barth Rd SE18 105 ES77
Bartholomew Cl EC1 197 H7
Bartholomew Cl EC1 84 DQ71
Bartholomew Cl SW18 100 DC84
Bartholomew Dr, Rom. 52 FK54
Bartholomew La EC2 197 L9
Bartholomew Pl EC1 197 H7
Bartholomew Rd NW5 83 DJ65
Bartholomew Sq E1 84 DV70
Coventry Rd
Bartholomew Sq EC1 197 J4
Bartholomew Sq EC1 84 DQ70
Bartholomew St SE1 201 K7
Bartholomew St SE1 102 DR76
Bartholomew Vil NW5 83 DJ65
Bartholomew Way, Swan. 147 FE97
Bartle Av E6 86 EL68
Bartle Rd W11 81 CY72
Bartlett Cl E14 85 EA72
Bartlett Ct EC4 196 E8
Bartlett Rd, Grav. 131 GG88
Bartlett Rd, West. 189 EQ126
Bartlett St, S.Croy. 160 DR106
Bartletts Pas EC4 196 E8
Bartlow Gdns, Rom. 51 FD53
Barton, The, Cob. 154 BX112
Barton Av, Rom. 71 FB60
Barton Cl E6 87 EM72
Barton Cl E9 66 DW64
Churchill Wk
Barton Cl NW4 63 CU56
Barton Cl SE15 102 DV83
Kirkwood Rd
Barton Cl, Add. 152 BG107
Barton Cl, Bexh. 126 EY85
Barton Cl, Chig. 49 EQ47
Barton Cl, Shep. 135 BP100
Barton Grn, N.Mal. 138 CR96
Barton Meadows, Ilf. 69 EQ56
Barton Rd W14 99 CY78
Barton Rd (Sutton at Hone), Dart. 148 FP95
Barton Rd, Horn. 71 FG60
Barton Rd, Sid. 126 EY93
Barton Rd, Slou. 93 AZ75
Barton St SW1 199 P6
Barton Way, Borwd. 26 CN40
Barton Way, Rick. 23 BP43
Bartons, The, Borwd. 25 CK44
Bartonway NW8 82 DD68
Queen's Ter
Bartram Cl, Uxb. 77 BP70
Lees Rd
Bartram Rd SE4 123 DY85
Bartrams La, Barn. 28 DC38

Bartrop Cl, Wal.Cr. 14 DR28
Poppy Wk
Barville Cl SE4 103 DY84
St. Norbert Rd
Barwell Business Pk, Chess. 155 CK109
Barwick Rd E7 68 EH63
Barwood Av, W.Wick. 143 EB102
Basden Gro, Felt. 116 CA89
Basedale Rd, Dag. 88 EV66
Baseing Cl E6 87 EN73
Bashley Rd NW10 80 CR70
Basil Av E6 86 EL68
Basil Gdns SE27 122 DQ92
Basil Gdns, Croy. 143 DX102
Primrose La
Basil St SW3 198 D6
Basil St SW3 100 DF76
Basildene Rd, Houns. 96 BX82
Basildon Av, Ilf. 49 EN53
Basildon Cl, Sutt. 158 DB109
Basildon Cl, Wat. 23 BQ44
Basildon Rd SE2 106 EU78
Basilon Rd, Bexh. 106 EY82
Basin S E16 87 EP74
Basing Cl, T.Ditt. 137 CF101
Basing Ct SE15 102 DT81
Basing Dr, Bex. 126 EZ86
Basing Hill NW11 63 CZ60
Basing Hill, Wem. 62 CM61
Basing Ho, Bark. 87 ER67
St. Margarets
Basing Ho Yd E2 197 N2
Basing Pl E2 197 N2
Basing Rd, Bans. 157 CZ114
Basing Rd, Rick. 37 BF46
Basing St W11 81 CZ72
Basing Way N3 64 DB55
Basing Way, T.Ditt. 137 CF101
Basingdon Way SE5 102 DR84
Basingfield Rd, T.Ditt. 137 CF101
Basinghall Av EC2 197 K7
Basinghall Av EC2 84 DR71
Basinghall Gdns, Sutt. 158 DB109
Basinghall St EC2 197 K8
Basinghall St EC2 84 DQ71
Basire St N1 84 DQ67
Baskerville Rd SW18 120 DE87
Basket Gdns SE9 124 EL85
Baslow Cl, Har. 41 CD53
Baslow Wk E5 67 DX63
Overbury St
Basnett Rd SW11 100 DG83
Basque Ct SE16 203 H5
Bassano St SE22 122 DT85
Bassant Rd SE18 105 ET79
Bassein Pk Rd W12 99 CT75
Basset Cl, Add. 152 BH110
Bassett Cl, Sutt. 158 DB109
Bassett Dr, Reig. 184 DA133
Bassett Gdns, Epp. 19 FB26
Bassett Gdns, Islw. 96 CC80
Bassett Ho, Dag. 88 EV67
Bassett Rd W10 81 CX72
Bassett Rd, Uxb. 76 BJ66
New Windsor St
Bassett Rd, Wok. 167 BC116
Bassett St NW5 82 DG65
Bassett Way, Grnf. 78 CB72
Bassetts Cl, Orp. 163 EP105
Bassetts Way, Orp. 163 EP105
Bassingham Rd SW18 120 DC87
Bassingham Rd, Wem. 79 CK65
Bassishaw Highwalk EC2 84 DQ71
London Wall
Basswood Cl SE15 102 DV83
Linden Gro
Bastable Av, Bark. 87 ES68
Bastion Highwalk EC2 84 DQ71
London Wall
Bastion Ho EC2 84 DQ71
London Wall
Bastion Rd SE2 106 EU78
Baston Manor Rd, Brom. 144 EH104
Baston Rd, Brom. 144 EH102
Bastwick St EC1 197 H4
Bastwick St EC1 84 DQ70
Basuto Rd SW6 100 DA81
Bat & Ball Rd, Sev. 191 FJ121
Batavia Cl, Sun. 136 BW95
Batavia Ms SE14 103 DY80
Goodwood Rd
Batavia Rd SE14 103 DY80
Batavia Rd, Sun. 135 BV95
Batchelor St N1 83 DN68
Batchwood Grn, Orp. 146 EU97
Batchworth Heath Hill, Rick. 38 BN49
Batchworth Hill, Rick. 38 BM48
Batchworth La, Nthwd. 39 BS50
Batchworth Roundabout, Rick. 38 BK46
Bate St E14 85 DZ73
Three Colt St
Bateman Cl, Bark. 87 EQ65
Glenny Rd
Bateman Ho SE17 101 DP79
Otto St
Bateman Rd E4 47 EA51
Bateman Rd, Rick. 22 BN44
Bateman St W1 195 M9
Bateman's Bldgs W1 195 M9
Bateman's Row EC2 197 N4
Bateman's Row EC2 84 DS70
Bates Cl, Slou. 74 AY72
Bates Cres SW16 121 DJ94
Bates Cres, Croy. 159 DN106
Bates Ind Est, Rom. 52 FP52
Bates Rd, Rom. 52 FN52
Bates Wk, Add. 152 BJ108
Bateson St SE18 105 ES77
Bateson Way, Wok. 151 BC114
Bath Cl SE15 102 DV80
Asylum Rd
Bath Ct EC1 196 D5
Bath Ho Rd, Croy. 141 DL102
Bath Pas, Kings.T. 137 CK96
St. James Rd
Bath Pl EC2 197 M3
Bath Pl, Barn. 27 CZ41
Bath Rd E7 86 EK65
Bath Rd N9 46 DV47
Bath Rd W4 98 CS77
Bath Rd, Dart. 127 FH87
Bath Rd, Hayes 95 BQ81
Bath Rd, Houns. 96 BW81
Bath Rd, Mitch. 140 DD97
Bath Rd, Rom. 70 EY58
Bath Rd (Colnbrook), Slou. 93 BB79
Bath Rd, West Dr. 94 BK81
Bath St EC1 197 J3
Bath St EC1 84 DR69
Bath St, Grav. 131 GH86
Bath Ter SE1 201 H7
Bath Ter SE1 102 DQ76
Bathgate Rd SW19 119 CX90
Baths Rd, Brom. 144 EK98
Bathurst Av SW19 140 DB95
Brisbane Av
Bathurst Cl, Iver 93 BF75
Bathurst Gdns NW10 81 CV68
Bathurst Ms W2 82 DD73
Sussex Pl
Bathurst Rd, Ilf. 69 EP60
Bathurst St W2 82 DD73
Bathurst Wk, Iver 93 BE75
Bathway SE18 105 EN77
Batley Cl, Mitch. 140 DF101
Batley Pl N16 66 DT62
Batley Rd N16 66 DT62
Stoke Newington High St
Batley Rd, Enf. 30 DQ39
Batman Cl W12 81 CV74
Baton Cl, Purf. 109 FR77
Brimfield Rd
Batoum Gdns W6 99 CW76
Batson St W12 99 CU75
Batsworth Rd, Mitch. 140 DD97
Batten Av, Wok. 166 AS119
Batten Cl E6 87 EM72
Savage Gdns
Batten St SW11 100 DE83
Battenburg Wk SE19 122 DS92
Brabourne Cl
Battersby Rd SE6 123 ED89
Battersea Br SW3 100 DD80
Battersea Br SW11 100 DD80
Battersea Br Rd SW11 100 DE80
Battersea Ch Rd SW11 100 DD81
Battersea High St SW11 100 DD81
Battersea Pk SW11 100 DF80
Battersea Pk Rd SW8 101 DH81
Battersea Pk Rd SW11 100 DE82
Battersea Ri SW11 120 DE85
Battersea Sq SW11 100 DD81
Battersea High St
Battery Rd SE28 105 ES75
Battis, The, Rom. 71 FE58
Waterloo Rd
Battishill Gdns N1 83 DP66
Waterloo Ter
Battishill St N1 83 DP66
Waterloo Ter
Battle Br La SE1 201 M3
Battle Br La SE1 84 DS74
Battle Br Rd NW1 195 P1
Battle Br Rd NW1 83 DL68
Battle Cl SW19 120 DC93
North Rd
Battle Rd, Belv. 107 FC77
Battle Rd, Erith 107 FC77
Battlebridge La, Red. 185 DH130
Battledean Rd N5 65 DP64
Battlers Grn Dr, Rad. 25 CE37
Batts Hill, Red. 184 DE132
Batts Hill, Reig. 184 DD132
Batty St E1 84 DU72
Baudwin Rd SE6 124 EE89
Baugh Rd, Sid. 126 EW92
Baulk, The SW18 120 DA87
Bavant Rd SW16 141 DL96
Bavaria Rd N19 65 DL61
Bavdene Ms NW4 63 CV56
The Burroughs
Bavent Rd SE5 102 DQ82
Bawdale Rd SE22 122 DT85
Bawdsey Av, Ilf. 69 ET56
Bawtree Cl, Sutt. 158 DC110
Bawtree Rd SE14 103 DY80
Bawtree Rd, Uxb. 76 BK65
Bawtry Rd N20 44 DF48
Baxendale N20 44 DC47
Baxendale St E2 84 DU69
Baxter Av, Red. 184 DE134
Baxter Cl, Sthl. 96 CB75
Baxter Cl, Uxb. 77 BP69
Baxter Gdns, Rom. 52 FJ48
Cummings Hall La
Baxter Rd E16 86 EJ72
Baxter Rd N1 84 DR65
Baxter Rd N18 46 DV49
Baxter Rd NW10 80 CS70
Baxter Rd, Ilf. 69 EP64
Bay Ct W5 98 CL76
Popes La
Bay Manor La, Grays 109 FT79
Bay Tree Av, Lthd. 171 CG120
Bay Tree Cl, Brom. 144 EJ95
Bayards, Warl. 176 DW118
Baycroft Cl, Pnr. 60 BW55
Baydon Ct, Brom. 144 EF97
Bayes Cl SE26 122 DW92
Bayeux, Tad. 173 CX122
Bayfield Rd SE9 104 EK84
Bayford Ms E8 84 DV66
Bayford St
Bayford Rd NW10 81 CX69
Bayford St E8 84 DV66
Bayham Pl NW1 83 DJ67
Bayham Rd W4 98 CR76
Bayham Rd W13 79 CH73
Bayham Rd, Mord. 140 DB98
Bayham Rd, Sev. 191 FJ123
Bayham St NW1 83 DJ67
Bayhurst Dr, Nthwd. 39 BT51
Bayley St WC1 195 M7
Bayley St WC1 83 DK71
Bayley Wk SE2 106 EY78
Woolwich Rd
Bayleys Mead, Brwd. 55 GC47
Baylin Rd SW18 120 DB86
Garratt La
Baylis Rd SE1 200 D5
Baylis Rd SE1 101 DN75
Bayliss Av SE28 88 EX73
Bayliss Cl N21 29 DL43
Macleod Rd
Bayly Rd, Dart. 128 FN86
Baymans Wd, Brwd. 54 FY47
Bayne Cl E6 87 EM72
Savage Gdns
Baynes Cl, Enf. 30 DU40
Baynes Ms NW3 82 DD65
Belsize La
Baynes St NW1 83 DJ66
Baynham Cl, Bex. 126 EZ86
Bayonne Rd W6 99 CY79
Bayshill Ri, Nthlt. 78 CB65
Bayston Rd N16 66 DT62
Bayswater Rd W2 194 A10
Bayswater Rd W2 82 DB73
Baythorne St E3 85 DZ71
Baytree Cl, St.Alb. 8 CB27
Baytree Cl, Sid. 125 ET88
Baytree Cl, Wal.Cr. 14 DT27
Baytree Ho E4 47 EB45
Dells Cl
Baytree Rd SW2 101 DM84
Baytree Wk, Wat. 23 BT38
Baywood Sq, Chig. 50 EV49
Bazalgette Cl, N.Mal. 138 CR99
Bazalgette Gdns, N.Mal. 138 CR99
Bazely St E14 85 EC73
Bazile Rd N21 29 DN44
Beach Gro, Felt. 116 CA89
Beacham Cl SE7 104 EK78
Beachborough Rd, Brom. 123 EC91
Beachcroft Rd E11 68 EE62
Beachcroft Way N19 65 DK60
Beachy Rd E3 85 EA66
Beacon Cl, Bans. 173 CX116
Beacon Cl (Chalfont St. Peter), Ger.Cr. 36 AY52
Beacon Cl, Uxb. 58 BK64
Beacon Dr, Dart. 129 FV90
Beacon Gate SE14 103 DX83
Beacon Gro, Cars. 158 DG105
Beacon Hill N7 65 DL64
Beacon Hill, Purf. 108 FP78
Beacon Hill, Wok. 166 AW118
Beacon Ri, Sev. 190 FG126
Beacon Rd SE13 123 ED86
Beacon Rd, Erith 107 FH80
Beacon Rd, Houns. 114 BN86
Beacon Rd Roundabout, Houns. 115 BP86
Beacon Way, Bans. 173 CX116
Beacon Way, Rick. 38 BG45
Beaconfield Av, Epp. 17 ET29
Beaconfield Rd, Epp. 17 ET29
Beaconfield Way, Epp. 17 ET29
Beaconfields, Sev. 190 FF126
Beacons, The, Loug. 33 EN38
Beacons Cl E6 86 EL71
Oliver Gdns
Beaconsfield Cl N11 44 DG49
Beaconsfield Cl SE3 104 EG79
Beaconsfield Cl W4 98 CQ78
Beaconsfield Par SE9 124 EL91
Beaconsfield Rd
Beaconsfield Pl, Epsom 156 CS112
Beaconsfield Rd E10 67 EC61
Beaconsfield Rd E16 86 EF70
Beaconsfield Rd E17 67 DZ58
Beaconsfield Rd N9 46 DU49
Beaconsfield Rd N11 44 DG48
Beaconsfield Rd N15 66 DS56
Beaconsfield Rd NW10 81 CT65
Beaconsfield Rd SE3 104 EF80
Beaconsfield Rd SE9 124 EL89
Beaconsfield Rd SE17 102 DR78
Beaconsfield Rd W4 98 CR76
Beaconsfield Rd W5 97 CJ75
Beaconsfield Rd, Bex. 127 FE88
Beaconsfield Rd, Brom. 144 EK97
Beaconsfield Rd, Croy. 142 DR100
Beaconsfield Rd, Enf. 31 DX37
Beaconsfield Rd, Epsom 172 CR119
Beaconsfield Rd, Esher 155 CE108
Beaconsfield Rd, Hayes 78 BW74
Beaconsfield Rd, N.Mal. 138 CR96
Beaconsfield Rd, Sthl. 78 BX74
Beaconsfield Rd, Surb. 138 CM101
Beaconsfield Rd, Twick. 117 CH86
Beaconsfield Rd, Wok. 167 AZ120
Beaconsfield Ter, Rom. 70 EX58
Beaconsfield Ter Rd W14 99 CY76
Beaconsfield Wk E6 87 EN72
East Ham Manor Way
Beaconsfield Wk SW6 99 CZ81
Beacontree Av E17 47 ED53
Beacontree Rd E11 68 EF59
Beadles La, Oxt. 187 ED130
Beadlow Cl, Cars. 140 DD100
Olveston Wk
Beadman Pl SE27 121 DP91
Norwood High St
Beadman St SE27 121 DP91
Beadnell Rd SE23 123 DX88
Beadon Rd W6 99 CW77
Beadon Rd, Brom. 144 EG98
Beads Hall La, Brwd. 54 FV42
Beaford Gro SW20 139 CY97
Beagle Cl, Felt. 115 BV91
Beagle Cl, Rad. 25 CF37
Beagles Cl, Orp. 146 EX103
Beak St W1 195 L10
Beak St W1 83 DJ73
Beal Cl, Well. 106 EU81
Beal Rd, Ilf. 69 EN61
Beale Cl N13 45 DP50
Beale Pl E3 85 DZ68
Beale Rd E3 85 DZ67
Beales La, Wey. 134 BN104
Beam Av, Dag. 89 FB67
Beam Way, Dag. 89 FD66
Beaminster Gdns, Ilf. 49 EP54
Beamish Cl, Epp. 19 FC25
Beamish Dr, Bushey 40 CC46
Beamish Rd N9 46 DU46
Beamish Rd, Orp. 146 EW101
Bean La, Dart. 129 FV89
Bean Rd, Bexh. 106 EX84
Bean Rd, Green. 129 FU88
Beanacre Cl E9 85 DZ65
Beanshaw SE9 125 EN91
Beansland Gro, Rom. 50 EY54
Bear All EC4 196 F8
Bear Cl, Rom. 71 FB58
Bear Gdns SE1 201 H2
Bear Gdns SE1 84 DQ74
Bear La SE1 200 G2
Bear La SE1 83 DP74
Bear Rd, Felt. 116 BX92
Bear St WC2 195 N10
Beard Rd, Kings.T. 118 CM92
Beardell St SE19 122 DT93
Beardow Gro N14 29 DJ44
Beard's Hill, Hmptn. 136 CA95
Beard's Hill Cl, Hmptn. 136 CA95
Beard's Hill
Beards Rd, Ashf. 115 BS93
Beardsfield E13 86 EG67
Valetta Gro
Beardsley Ter, Dag. 70 EV64
Fitzstephen Rd
Beardsley Way W3 98 CR75
Bearfield Rd, Kings.T. 118 CL94
Bearing Cl, Chig. 50 EU49
Bearing Way, Chig. 50 EU49
Bears Den, Tad. 173 CZ122
Bears Rails Pk, Wind. 112 AT87
Bearstead Ri SE4 123 DZ85
Bearstead Ter, Beck. 143 EA95
Copers Cope Rd
Bearwood Cl, Add. 152 BG107
Ongar Pl
Bearwood Cl, Pot.B. 12 DD31
Beasley's Ait La, Sun. 135 BT100
Beasleys Yd, Uxb. 76 BJ66
Warwick Pl
Beaton Cl SE15 102 DT80
Kelly Av
Beaton Cl, Green. 109 FV84
Beatrice Av SW16 141 DM97
Beatrice Av, Wem. 62 CL64
Beatrice Cl E13 86 EG70
Chargeable La
Beatrice Cl, Pnr. 59 BU56
Reid Cl
Beatrice Ct, Buck.H. 48 EK47
Beatrice Gdns, Grav. 130 GE89
Beatrice Pl W8 100 DB76
Beatrice Rd E17 67 EA57
Beatrice Rd N4 65 DN59
Beatrice Rd N9 46 DW45
Beatrice Rd SE1 202 C9
Beatrice Rd SE1 102 DU77
Beatrice Rd, Oxt. 188 EE129
Beatrice Rd, Rich. 118 CM85
Albert Rd
Beatrice Rd, Sthl. 78 BZ74
Beatson Wk SE16 203 K2
Beatson Wk SE16 85 DY74
Beattie Cl, Felt. 115 BT88
Beattie Cl, Lthd. 170 BZ124
Beattock Ri N10 65 DH56
Beatty Rd N16 66 DS63
Beatty Rd, Stan. 41 CJ51
Beatty Rd, Wal.Cr. 15 DZ34
Beatty St NW1 83 DJ68
Beattyville Gdns, Ilf. 69 EN55
Beauchamp Cl W4 98 CQ76
Church Path
Beauchamp Ct, Stan. 41 CJ50
Hardwick Cl
Beauchamp Gdns, Rick. 38 BG46
Beauchamp Pl SW3 198 C6
Beauchamp Pl SW3 100 DE76
Beauchamp Rd E7 86 EH66
Beauchamp Rd SE19 142 DR95
Beauchamp Rd SW11 100 DE84
Beauchamp Rd, E.Mol. 136 CB99
Beauchamp Rd, Sutt. 158 DA106
Beauchamp Rd, Twick. 117 CG87
Beauchamp Rd, W.Mol. 136 CB99
Beauchamp St EC1 196 D7
Beauchamp Ter SW15 99 CV83
Dryburgh Rd
Beauclare Cl, Lthd. 171 CK121
Hatherwood
Beauclerc Rd W6 99 CV76
Beauclerk Cl, Felt. 115 BV88
Florence Rd
Beaudesert Ms, West Dr. 94 BL75
Beaufort E6 87 EN71
Newark Knok
Beaufort Av, Har. 61 CG56
Beaufort Cl E4 47 EB51
Higham Sta Av
Beaufort Cl SW15 119 CV87
Beaufort Cl W5 80 CM71
Beaufort Cl, Epp. 18 FA27
Beaufort Cl, Grays 110 FZ76
Clifford Rd
Beaufort Cl, Reig. 183 CZ133
Beaufort Cl, Rom. 71 FC56
Beaufort Cl, Wok. 167 BC116
Beaufort Ct, Rich. 117 CJ91
Beaufort Rd
Beaufort Dr NW11 64 DA56
Beaufort Gdns NW4 63 CW58
Beaufort Gdns SW3 198 C6
Beaufort Gdns SW3 100 DE76
Beaufort Gdns SW16 121 DM94
Beaufort Gdns, Houns. 96 BY81
Beaufort Gdns, Ilf. 69 EN60
Beaufort Ms SW6 99 CZ79
Lillie Rd
Beaufort Pk NW11 64 DA56
Beaufort Rd W5 80 CM71
Beaufort Rd, Kings.T. 138 CL98
Beaufort Rd, Reig. 183 CZ133
Beaufort Rd, Rich. 117 CJ91
Beaufort Rd, Ruis. 59 BR61
Lysander Rd
Beaufort Rd, Twick. 117 CJ87
Beaufort Rd, Wok. 167 BC116
Beaufort St SW3 100 DD79
Beaufort Way, Epsom 157 CU108
Beauforts, Egh. 112 AW92
Beaufoy Rd N17 46 DS52
Beaufoy Wk SE11 200 C9
Beaufoy Wk SE11 101 DM77
Beaulieu Av E16 205 P2
Beaulieu Av E16 86 EH7
Beaulieu Av SE26 122 DV9
Beaulieu Cl NW9 62 CS5
Beaulieu Cl SE5 102 DR8
Beaulieu Cl, Houns. 116 BZ8
Beaulieu Cl, Mitch. 140 DG9
Beaulieu Cl, Slou. 92 AV8
Beaulieu Cl, Twick. 117 CK8
Beaulieu Cl, Wat. 40 BW4
Beaulieu Dr, Pnr. 60 BX5
Beaulieu Dr, Wal.Abb. 15 EB3
Beaulieu Gdns N21 46 DQ4
Beaulieu Pl W4 98 CQ7
Rothschild Rd
Beauly Way, Rom. 51 FE5
Beaumanor Gdns SE9 125 EN9
Beaumaris Dr, Wdf.Grn. 48 EK5
Beaumont Av W14 99 CZ7
Beaumont Av, Har. 60 CB5
Beaumont Av, Rich. 98 CM8
Beaumont Av, Wem. 61 CJ6
Beaumont Cl, Kings.T. 118 CN9
Beaumont Cl, Rom. 52 FJ5
Beaumont Cres W14 99 CZ7
Beaumont Cres, Rain. 89 FG6
Beaumont Dr, Ashf. 115 BR9
Beaumont Dr, Grav. 130 GE8
Beaumont Gdns NW3 64 DA6
Beaumont Gdns, Brwd. 55 GC4
Bannister Dr
Beaumont Gate, Rad. 25 CH3
Shenley Hill
Beaumont Gro E1 85 DX7
Beaumont Ms W1 194 G6
Beaumont Pl W1 195 L4
Beaumont Pl W1 83 DJ7
Beaumont Pl, Barn. 27 CZ3
Beaumont Pl, Islw. 117 CF8
Beaumont Ri N19 65 DK6
Beaumont Rd E10 67 EB5
Beaumont Rd E13 86 EH6
Beaumont Rd SE19 122 DQ93
Beaumont Rd SW19 119 CY87
Beaumont Rd W4 98 CQ76
Beaumont Rd, Orp. 145 ER100
Beaumont Rd, Pur. 159 DN113
Beaumont Sq E1 85 DX70
Beaumont St W1 194 G6
Beaumont St W1 82 DG71
Beaumont Vw (Cheshunt), Wal.Cr. 14 DR26
Beaumont Wk NW3 82 DF66
Beauvais Ter, Nthlt. 78 BX69
Beauval Rd SE22 122 DT86
Beaver Cl SE20 122 DU94
Lullington Rd
Beaver Cl, Hmptn. 136 CB95
Beaver Gro, Nthlt. 78 BY69
Jetstar Way
Beaver Rd, Ilf. 50 EW50
Beaverbank Rd SE9 125 ER88
Beaverbrook Roundabout, Lthd. 172 CL123
Beavers Cres, Houns. 96 BW84
Beavers La, Houns. 96 BW83
Beavers La Camp, Houns. 96 BW83
Beavers La
Beaverwood Rd, Chis. 125 ES93
Beavor Gro W6 99 CU77
Beavor La
Beavor La W6 99 CU77
Bebbington Rd SE18 105 ES77
Bebletts Cl, Orp. 163 ET106
Bec Cl, Ruis. 60 BX62
Beccles Dr, Bark. 87 ES65
Beccles St E14 85 DZ73
Beck Cl SE13 103 EB81
Beck Ct, Beck. 143 DX97
Beck La, Beck. 143 DX97
Beck River Pk, Beck. 143 EA95
Rectory Rd
Beck Rd E8 84 DV67
Beck Way, Beck. 143 DZ97
Beckenham Business Cen, Beck. 123 DY93
Beckenham Gdns N9 46 DS48
Beckenham Gro, Brom. 143 ED96
Beckenham Hill Rd SE6 123 EB92
Beckenham Hill Rd, Beck. 123 EB92
Beckenham La, Brom. 144 EE96
Beckenham Pl Pk, Beck. 123 EB94
Beckenham Rd, Beck. 143 DX95
Beckenham Rd, W.Wick. 143 EB101
Beckenshaw Gdns, Bans. 174 DE115
Beckers, The N16 66 DU62
Rectory Rd
Becket Av E6 87 EN69
Becket Cl SE25 142 DU100
Becket Cl, Brwd. 53 FW51
Becket Fold, Har. 61 CF57
Courtfield Cres
Becket Rd N18 46 DW49
Becket St SE1 201 K6
Beckett Av, Ken. 175 DP115
Beckett Cl NW10 80 CR65
Beckett Cl SW16 121 DK89
Beckett Cl, Belv. 106 EY76
Tunstock Way
Beckett Wk, Beck. 123 DY93
Becketts Cl, Felt. 115 BV86
Becketts Cl, Orp. 145 ET104
Becketts Pl, Kings.T. 137 CK95
Beckford Dr, Orp. 145 ER101
Beckford Pl SE17 102 DQ78
Walworth Rd
Beckford Rd, Croy. 142 DT100
Becklow Gdns W12 99 CU75
Becklow Rd
Becklow Ms W12 99 CT75
Becklow Rd
Becklow Rd W12 99 CU75
Beckman Cl, Sev. 181 FC115
Becks Rd, Sid. 126 EU90
Beckton Pk Roundabout E16 87 EM73
Royal Albert Way
Beckton Rd E16 86 EF71
Beckway Rd SW16 141 DK96
Beckway St SE17 201 L9

Beckway St SE17 102 DR77
Beckwith Rd SE24 122 DR86
Beclands Rd SW17 120 DG93
Becmead Av SW16 121 DK91
Becmead Av, Har. 61 CH57
Becondale Rd SE19 122 DS92
Becontree Av, Dag. 70 EV63
Bective Pl SW15 99 CZ84
Bective Rd
Bective Rd E7 68 EG63
Bective Rd SW15 99 CZ84
Becton Pl, Erith 107 FB80
Bedale Rd, Enf. 30 DQ38
Bedale Rd, Rom. 52 FN50
Bedale St SE1 201 K3
Bedale St SE1 84 DR74
Bedale Wk, Dart. 128 FP88
Beddington Cross, Croy. 141 DL101
Beddington Fm Rd
Beddington Fm Rd, Croy. 141 DL102
Beddington Gdns, Cars. 158 DG107
Beddington Gdns, Wall. 159 DH107
Beddington Grn, Orp. 145 ET95
Beddington Gro, Wall. 159 DK106
Beddington La, Croy. 141 DJ99
Beddington Path, Orp. 145 ET95
Beddington Rd, Ilf. 69 ET59
Beddington Rd, Orp. 145 ES96
Beddington Trd Pk W, Croy. 141 DL102
Beddlestead La, Warl. 178 EF117
Bede Cl, Pnr. 40 BX53
Bede Rd, Rom. 70 EW58
Bedenham Way SE15 102 DT80
Daniel Gdns
Bedens Rd, Sid. 126 EY93
Bedfont Cl, Felt. 115 BQ86
Bedfont Cl, Mitch. 140 DG96
Bedfont Ct, Stai. 94 BH84
Bedfont Ct Est, Stai. 94 BG83
Bedfont Grn Cl, Felt. 115 BQ88
Bedfont La, Felt. 115 BT87
Bedfont Rd, Felt. 115 BS89
Bedfont Rd, Stai. 114 BL86
Bedford Av WC1 195 N7
Bedford Av WC1 83 DK71
Bedford Av, Amer. 20 AW39
Bedford Av, Barn. 27 CZ43
Bedford Av, Hayes 77 BV72
Bedford Cl N10 44 DG52
Bedford Cl W4 98 CS79
Bedford Cl, Rick. 21 BB38
Bedford Cl, Wok. 166 AW115
Bedford Cor W4 98 CS77
The Av
Bedford Ct WC2 199 P1
Bedford Cres, Enf. 31 DY35
Bedford Gdns W8 82 DA74
Bedford Gdns, Horn. 72 FJ61
Bedford Hill SW12 121 DH88
Bedford Hill SW16 121 DH88
Bedford Ho SW4 101 DK84
Bedford Ms N2 64 DE55
Bedford Rd
Bedford Pk, Croy. 142 DQ102
Bedford Pk Cor W4 98 CS77
Bath Rd
Bedford Pas SW6 99 CY80
Dawes Rd
Bedford Pl W1 195 L6
Bedford Pl WC1 195 P6
Bedford Pl WC1 83 DL71
Bedford Pl, Croy. 142 DR102
Bedford Rd E6 87 EN67
Bedford Rd E17 47 EA54
Bedford Rd E18 48 EG54
Bedford Rd N2 64 DE55
Bedford Rd N8 65 DK58
Bedford Rd N9 46 DV45
Bedford Rd N15 66 DS56
Bedford Rd N22 45 DL53
Bedford Rd NW7 42 CS48
Bedford Rd SW4 101 DL83
Bedford Rd W4 98 CR76
Bedford Rd W13 79 CH73
Bedford Rd, Dart. 128 FN87
Bedford Rd, Grav. 131 GF89
Bedford Rd, Grays 110 GB78
Bedford Rd, Har. 60 CC58
Bedford Rd, Ilf. 69 EP62
Bedford Rd, Nthwd. 39 BQ48
Bedford Rd, Orp. 146 EV103
Bedford Rd, Ruis. 59 BT63
Bedford Rd, Sid. 125 ES90
Bedford Rd, Twick. 117 CD90
Bedford Rd, Wor.Pk. 139 CW103
Bedford Row WC1 196 C6
Bedford Row WC1 83 DM71
Bedford Sq WC1 195 N7
Bedford Sq WC1 83 DK71
Bedford St WC2 195 P10
Bedford St WC2 83 DL73
Bedford St, Wat. 23 BV39
Bedford Ter SW2 121 DL85
Lyham Rd
Bedford Way WC1 195 N5
Bedford Way WC1 83 DK70
Bedfordbury WC2 195 P10
Bedgebury Gdns SW19 119 CY89
Bedgebury Rd SE9 104 EK84
Bedivere Rd, Brom. 124 EG90
Bedlow Way, Croy. 159 DM105
Bedmond La, Abb.L. 7 BV25
Bedmond Rd, Abb.L. 7 BT29
Bedonwell Rd SE2 106 EY79
Bedonwell Rd, Belv. 106 FA79
Bedonwell Rd, Bexh. 106 FA79
Bedser Cl SE11 101 DM79
Harleyford Rd
Bedser Cl, Th.Hth. 142 DQ97
Bedser Cl, Wok. 167 BA116
Bedser Dr, Grnf. 61 CD64
Bedster Gdns, W.Mol. 136 CB96
Bedwardine Rd SE19 122 DS94
Bedwell Gdns, Hayes 95 BS78
Bedwell Rd N17 46 DS53
Bedwell Rd, Belv. 106 FA78
Beeby Rd E16 86 EH71
Beech Av N20 44 DE46
Beech Av W3 80 CS74
Beech Av, Brent. 97 CH80
Beech Av, Brwd. 55 FZ48
Beech Av, Buck.H. 48 EH47
Beech Av, Enf. 29 DN35
Beech Av, Rad. 9 CG33
Beech Av, Ruis. 59 BV60
Beech Av, Sid. 126 EU87
Beech Av, S.Croy. 160 DR111
Beech Av, Swan. 147 FF98
Beech Av, Upmin. 72 FP62
Beech Av, West. 178 EK119
Beech Av, West. 178 EK119
Westmore Rd
Beech Cl N9 30 DU44
Beech Cl SE8 103 DZ79
Clyde St
Beech Cl SW15 119 CU87
Beech Cl SW19 119 CW93
Beech Cl, Ashf. 115 BR92
Beech Cl, Cars. 140 DF103
Beech Cl, Cob. 154 CA112
Beech Cl, Horn. 71 FH62
Beech Cl, Loug. 33 EP40
Cedar Dr
Beech Cl, Stai. 114 BK87
St. Mary's Cres
Beech Cl, Sun. 136 BX96
Harfield Rd
Beech Cl, Walt. 154 BW105
Beech Cl, W.Byf. 152 BL112
Beech Cl, West Dr. 94 BN76
Beech Cl Ct, Cob. 154 BZ111
Beech Copse, Brom. 145 EM96
Beech Copse, S.Croy. 160 DS106
Beech Ct E17 67 ED55
Beech Ct SE9 124 EL86
Beech Ct, Ilf. 69 EN62
Riverdene Rd
Beech Ct, Surb. 138 CL101
Beech Cres, Tad. 182 CQ130
Beech Dell, Kes. 163 EM105
Beech Dr N2 64 DF55
Beech Dr, Borwd. 26 CM40
Beech Dr, Reig. 184 DD134
Beech Dr, Tad. 173 CZ122
Beech Dr, Wok. 168 BG124
Beech Fm Rd, Warl. 177 EC120
Beech Gdns EC2 84 DQ71
Aldersgate St
Beech Gdns W5 98 CL75
Beech Gdns, Dag. 89 FB66
Beech Gdns, Wok. 166 AY115
Beech Gro, Add. 152 BH105
Beech Gro, Cat. 186 DS126
Beech Gro, Croy. 161 DY110
Beech Gro, Epsom 173 CV117
Beech Gro, Ilf. 49 ES51
Beech Gro, Mitch. 141 DK98
Beech Gro, N.Mal. 138 CR97
Beech Gro, S.Ock. 90 FQ74
Beech Gro, Wok. 166 AX123
Beech Hall, Cher. 151 BC108
Beech Hall Cres E4 47 ED52
Beech Hall Rd E4 47 EC52
Beech Hill, Barn. 28 DD38
Beech Hill, Wok. 166 AX123
Beech Hill Av, Barn. 28 DC39
Beech Hill Gdns, Wal.Abb. 32 EH37
Beech Holt, Lthd. 171 CJ122
Beech Ho, Croy. 161 EB107
Beech Ho Rd, Croy. 142 DR104
Beech La, Beac. 36 AS52
Beech La, Buck.H. 48 EH47
Beech Lawns N12 44 DD50
Beech Lo, Stai. 113 BE92
Farm Cl
Beech Pk, Amer. 20 AV39
Beech Pl, Epp. 17 ET31
Beech Rd N11 45 DL51
Beech Rd SW16 141 DL96
Beech Rd, Dart. 128 FK88
Beech Rd, Epsom 173 CT115
Beech Rd, Felt. 115 BS87
Beech Rd, Orp. 164 EU108
Beech Rd, Red. 185 DJ126
Beech Rd, Reig. 184 DA131
Beech Rd, Sev. 191 FH125
Victoria Rd
Beech Rd, Slou. 92 AY75
Beech Rd, Wat. 23 BU37
Beech Rd, West. 178 EH118
Beech Rd, Wey. 153 BR105
St. Marys Rd
Beech Row, Rich. 118 CL91
Beech St EC2 197 H6
Beech St EC2 84 DQ71
Beech St, Rom. 71 FC56
Beech Tree Cl, Stan. 41 CJ50
Beech Tree Glade E4 48 EF46
Forest Side
Beech Tree La, Stai. 134 BH96
Staines Rd
Beech Tree Pl, Sutt. 158 DB106
St. Nicholas Way
Beech Vale, Wok. 167 AZ118
Hill Vw Rd
Beech Wk NW7 42 CS51
Beech Wk, Dart. 107 FG84
Beech Wk, Epsom 157 CU111
Beech Way NW10 80 CR66
Beech Way, Epsom 173 CT115
Beech Way, S.Croy. 161 DX113
Beech Way, Twick. 116 CA90
Beech Waye, Ger.Cr. 57 AZ59
Beechcroft, Ash. 172 CM119
Beechcroft, Chis. 125 EN94
Beechcroft Av NW11 63 CZ59
Beechcroft Av, Bexh. 107 FD81
Beechcroft Av, Har. 60 CA59
Beechcroft Av, Ken. 176 DR115
Beechcroft Av, N.Mal. 138 CQ95
Beechcroft Av, Rick. 23 BQ44
Beechcroft Av, Sthl. 78 BZ74
Beechcroft Cl, Houns. 96 BY80
Beechcroft Cl, Orp. 163 ER105
Beechcroft Gdns, Wem. 62 CM62
Beechcroft Manor, Wey. 135 BR104
Beechcroft Rd E18 48 EH54
Beechcroft Rd SW14 98 CQ83
Elm Rd
Beechcroft Rd SW17 120 DE89
Beechcroft Rd, Bushey 24 BY43
Beechcroft Rd, Chess. 138 CM104
Beechcroft Rd, Orp. 163 ER105
Beechdale N21 45 DM47
Beechdale Rd SW2 121 DM86
Beechdene, Tad. 173 CV122
Beechen Cliff Way, Islw. 97 CF81
Henley Cl
Beechen Gro, Pnr. 60 BZ55
Beechen Gro, Wat. 24 BW42
Beechen La, Tad. 183 CZ125
Beechenlea La, Swan. 147 FH97
Beeches, The, Bans. 174 DB116
Beeches, The, Brwd. 54 FV48
Beeches, The, Houns. 96 CB81
Beeches, The, Lthd. 171 CE124
Beeches, The, Rick. 21 BF43
Beeches, The, St.Alb. 9 CE27
Beeches, The, Til. 111 GH82
Beeches Av, Cars. 158 DE108
Beeches Cl SE20 142 DW95
Genoa Rd
Beeches Cl, Tad. 174 DA123
Beeches Ct, Brom. 124 EG93
Avondale Rd
Beeches Rd SW17 120 DE90
Beeches Rd, Sutt. 139 CY102
Beeches Wk, Cars. 158 DD109
Beeches Wd, Tad. 174 DA122
Beechfield, Bans. 158 DB113
Beechfield, Kings L. 6 BM30
Beechfield Cl, Borwd. 26 CM40
Anthony Rd
Beechfield Cotts, Brom. 144 EJ96
Widmore Rd
Beechfield Gdns, Rom. 71 FC59
Beechfield Rd N4 66 DQ58
Beechfield Rd SE6 123 DZ88
Beechfield Rd, Brom. 144 EJ96
Beechfield Rd, Erith 107 FE80
Beechfield Wk, Wal.Abb. 31 ED35
Beechhill Rd SE9 125 EN85
Beechmeads, Cob. 154 BX113
Beechmont Av, Vir.W. 132 AX99
Beechmont Cl, Brom. 124 EE92
Beechmont Rd, Sev. 191 FH129
Beechmore Gdns, Sutt. 139 CX103
Beechmore Rd SW11 100 DF81
Beechmount Av W7 79 CD71
Beecholm Ms, Wal.Cr. 15 DX28
Beecholme, Bans. 157 CY114
Beecholme Av, Mitch. 141 DH95
Beecholme Est E5 66 DV62
Prout Rd
Beechpark Way, Wat. 23 BS37
Beechtree Av, Egh. 112 AV93
Beechvale Cl N12 44 DE50
Beechway, Bex. 126 EX86
Beechwood Av N3 63 CZ55
Beechwood Av, Amer. 20 AW38
Beechwood Av, Couls. 175 DH115
Beechwood Av, Grnf. 78 CB69
Beechwood Av, Har. 60 CB62
Beechwood Av, Hayes 77 BR73
Beechwood Av, Orp. 163 ES106
Beechwood Av, Pot.B. 12 DB33
Beechwood Av, Rich. 98 CN81
Beechwood Av, Rick. 21 BB42
Beechwood Av, Ruis. 59 BT61
Beechwood Av, Stai. 114 BH93
Beechwood Av, Sun. 115 BU93
Beechwood Av, Tad. 174 DA121
Beechwood Av, Th.Hth. 141 DP98
Beechwood Av, Uxb. 76 BN72
Beechwood Av, Wey. 153 BS105
Beechwood Circle, Har. 60 CB62
Beechwood Gdns
Beechwood Cl NW7 42 CR50
Beechwood Cl, Amer. 20 AW39
Beechwood Cl, Surb. 137 CJ101
Beechwood Cl (Cheshunt), Wal.Cr. 14 DS26
Beechwood Cl, Wey. 153 BS105
Beechwood Cl, Wok. 166 AS117
Beechwood Ct, Cars. 158 DF105
Beechwood Ct, Sun. 115 BU93
Beechwood Cres, Bexh. 106 EX83
Beechwood Dr, Cob. 154 CA111
Beechwood Dr, Kes. 162 EK105
Beechwood Dr, Wdf.Grn. 48 EF50
Beechwood Gdns NW10 80 CM69
St. Annes Gdns
Beechwood Gdns, Cat. 176 DU122
Beechwood Gdns, Har. 60 CB62
Beechwood Gdns, Ilf. 69 EM57
Beechwood Gdns, Rain. 89 FH71
Beechwood Gdns, Slou. 92 AS75
Beechwood Gro W3 80 CS73
East Acton La
Beechwood Gro, Surb. 137 CJ101
Beechwood La, Warl. 177 DX119
Beechwood Manor, Wey. 153 BS105
Beechwood Ms N9 46 DU47
Beechwood Pk E18 68 EG55
Beechwood Pk, Lthd. 171 CJ123
Beechwood Ri, Chis. 125 EP91
Beechwood Ri, Wat. 23 BV36
Beechwood Rd E8 84 DT65
Beechwood Rd N8 65 DK56
Beechwood Rd, Cat. 176 DU122
Beechwood Rd, S.Croy. 160 DS109
Beechwood Rd, Vir.W. 132 AU101
Beechwood Rd, Wok. 166 AS117
Beechwoods Ct SE19 122 DT92
Crystal Palace Par
Beechworth Cl NW3 64 DA61
Beecot La, Walt. 136 BW103
Beecroft Rd SE4 123 DY85
Beehive Cl E8 84 DT66
Beehive Cl, Borwd. 25 CK44
Beehive Cl, Uxb. 76 BM66
Honey Hill
Beehive Ct, Rom. 52 FM52
Arundel Rd
Beehive La, Ilf. 69 EM58
Beehive Pas EC3 197 M9
Beehive Pl SW9 101 DN83
Beehive Rd, Stai. 113 BF92
Beehive Rd (Cheshunt), Wal.Cr. 13 DP28
Beeken Dene, Orp. 163 EQ105
Isabella Dr
Beel Cl, Amer. 20 AW39
Beeleigh Rd, Mord. 140 DB98
Beesfield La (Farningham), Dart. 148 FN101
Beeston Cl E8 66 DU64
Ferncliff Rd
Beeston Cl, Wat. 40 BX49
Beeston Dr, Wal.Cr. 15 DX27
Beeston Pl SW1 199 J7
Beeston Pl SW1 101 DH76
Beeston Rd, Barn. 28 DD44
Beeston Way, Felt. 116 BW86
Beethoven Rd, Borwd. 25 CK44
Beethoven St W10 81 CY69
Beeton Cl, Pnr. 40 CA52
Begbie Rd SE3 104 EJ81
Beggars Bush La, Wat. 23 BR43
Beggars Hill, Epsom 157 CT108
Beggars Hollow, Enf. 30 DR37
Beggars La, West. 189 ER125
Beggars Roost La, Sutt. 158 DA107
Begonia Cl E6 86 EL71
Begonia Pl, Hmptn. 116 CA93
Gresham Rd
Begonia Wk W12 81 CT72
Du Cane Rd
Beira St SW12 121 DH87
Beken Ct, Wat. 24 BW35
Bekesbourne St E14 85 DY72
Ratcliffe La
Bekesbourne Twr, Orp. 146 EY102
Belcroft Cl, Brom. 124 EF94
Hope Pk
Beldam Haw, Sev. 164 FA112
Beldham Gdns, W.Mol. 136 CB97
Belfairs Dr, Rom. 70 EW59
Belfairs Grn, Wat. 40 BX50
Heysham Dr
Belfast Rd N16 66 DT61
Belfast Rd SE25 142 DV98
Belfield Rd, Epsom 156 CR109
Belfont Wk N7 65 DL63
Belford Gro SE18 105 EN77
Belford Rd, Borwd. 26 CM38
Belfort Rd SE15 102 DW82
Belfry Av (Harefield), Uxb. 38 BG53
Belfry Cl SE16 202 E10
Belfry La, Rick. 38 BJ46
Belfry Shop Cen, The, Red. 184 DF133
Belgrade Rd N16 66 DS63
Belgrade Rd, Hmptn. 136 CB95
Belgrave Av, Rom. 72 FJ55
Belgrave Av, Wat. 23 BT43
Belgrave Cl N14 29 DJ43
Prince George Av
Belgrave Cl NW7 42 CR50
Belgrave Cl W3 98 CQ75
Avenue Rd
Belgrave Cl, Orp. 146 EW98
Belgrave Cl, Walt. 153 BV105
Belgrave Cres, Sun. 135 BV95
Belgrave Dr, Kings L. 7 BQ28
Belgrave Gdns N14 29 DK43
Belgrave Gdns NW8 82 DB67
Belgrave Gdns, Stan. 41 CJ50
Copley Rd
Belgrave Manor, Wok. 166 AY119
Belgrave Ms, Uxb. 76 BK70
Belgrave Ms N SW1 198 F5
Belgrave Ms N SW1 100 DG76
Belgrave Ms S SW1 198 G6
Belgrave Ms S SW1 100 DG76
Belgrave Ms W SW1 198 F6
Belgrave Ms W SW1 100 DG76
Belgrave Pl SW1 198 G6
Belgrave Pl SW1 100 DG76
Belgrave Pl, Slou. 92 AV75
Clifton Rd
Belgrave Rd E10 67 EC60
Belgrave Rd E11 68 EG61
Belgrave Rd E13 86 EJ70
Belgrave Rd E17 67 EA57
Belgrave Rd SE25 142 DT98
Belgrave Rd SW1 199 K9
Belgrave Rd SW1 101 DH77
Belgrave Rd SW13 99 CT80
Belgrave Rd, Houns. 96 BZ83
Belgrave Rd, Ilf. 69 EM60
Belgrave Rd, Mitch. 140 DD97
Belgrave Rd, Slou. 74 AS73
Belgrave Rd, Sun. 135 BV95
Belgrave Sq SW1 198 F6
Belgrave Sq SW1 100 DG76
Belgrave St E1 85 DX72
Belgrave Ter, Wdf.Grn. 48 EG48
Belgrave Wk, Mitch. 140 DD97
Belgrave Yd SW1 199 H7
Belgravia Cl, Barn. 27 CZ41
Belgravia Gdns, Brom. 124 EE93
Belgravia Ho SW4 121 DL86
Belgravia Ms, Kings.T. 137 CK98
Belgrove St WC1 195 P2
Belgrove St WC1 83 DL69
Belham Rd, Kings L. 6 BM28
Belham Wk SE5 102 DR81
D'Eynsford Rd
Belhaven Ct, Borwd. 26 CM39
Belinda Rd SW9 101 DP83
Belitha Vil N1 83 DM66
Bell Av, Rom. 51 FH53
Bell Av, West Dr. 94 BM77
Bell Br Rd, Cher. 133 BF102
Bell Cl, Abb.L. 7 BT27
Bell Cl, Green. 129 FT85
Bell Cl, Pnr. 60 BW55
Bell Cl, Ruis. 59 BT62
Bell Cl, Slou. 74 AV71
Bell Common, Epp. 17 ES32
Bell Ct, Surb. 138 CP103
Barnsbury La
Bell Cres, Couls. 175 DH121
Maple Way
Bell Dr SW18 119 CY87
Bell Fm Av, Dag. 71 FC62
Bell Gdns E10 67 EA60
Church Rd
Bell Gdns E17 67 DZ57
Markhouse Rd
Bell Gdns, Orp. 146 EW99
Bell Grn SE26 123 DZ90
Bell Grn, Hem.H. 5 BB27
Bell Grn La SE26 123 DY92
Bell Hill, Croy. 142 DQ104
Surrey St
Bell Ho Rd, Rom. 71 FC60
Bell Inn Yd EC3 197 L9
Bell La E1 197 P7
Bell La E1 84 DT71
Bell La E16 205 M2
Bell La E16 86 EG74
Bell La NW4 63 CX56
Bell La, Abb.L. 7 BT27
Bell La, Amer. 20 AV39
Bell La, Enf. 31 DX38
Bell La, Hat. 12 DA25
Bell La, Lthd. 171 CD123
Bell La, St.Alb. 10 CL29
Bell La, Twick. 117 CG88
The Embk
Bell La, Wem. 61 CK61
Magnet Rd
Bell La Cl, Lthd. 171 CD123
Bell Meadow SE19 122 DS91
Dulwich Wd Av
Bell Meadow, Gdse. 186 DV132
Bell Meadow, Gdse. 186 DV132
Hickmans Cl
Bell Rd, E.Mol. 137 CD99
Bell Rd, Enf. 30 DR39
Bell Rd, Houns. 96 CB84
Bell St NW1 194 B6
Bell St NW1 82 DE71
Bell St, Reig. 184 DA134
Bell Water Gate SE18 105 EN76
Bell Weir Cl, Stai. 113 BB89
Bell Wf La EC4 197 J10
Bell Wf La EC4 84 DQ73
Bell Yd WC2 196 D8
Bell Yd WC2 83 DN72
Bellamy Cl E14 203 P4
Bellamy Cl W14 99 CZ78
Aisgill Av
Bellamy Cl, Edg. 42 CQ48
Bellamy Cl, Uxb. 58 BN62
Bellamy Cl, Wat. 23 BU39
Bellamy Dr, Stan. 41 CH53
Bellamy Rd E4 47 EB51
Bellamy Rd, Enf. 30 DR40
Bellamy Rd (Cheshunt), Wal.Cr. 15 DY29
Bellamy St SW12 121 DH87
Bellasis Av SW2 121 DL89
Bellclose Rd, West Dr. 94 BL75
Belle Vue, Grnf. 79 CD67
Belle Vue Cl, Stai. 134 BG95
Belle Vue Est NW4 63 CW56
Bell La
Belle Vue La, Bushey 41 CD46
Belle Vue Pk, Th.Hth. 142 DQ97
Belle Vue Rd E17 47 ED54
Belle Vue Rd NW4 63 CW56
Bell La
Belle Vue Rd, Orp. 163 EN110
Standard Rd
Bellefield Rd, Orp. 146 EV99
Bellefields Rd SW9 101 DM83
Bellegrove Cl, Well. 105 ET82
Bellegrove Par, Well. 105 ET83
Bellegrove Rd
Bellegrove Rd, Well. 105 ER82
Bellenden Rd SE15 102 DT82
Bellestaines Pleasaunce E4 47 EA47
Belleville Rd SW11 120 DF85
Bellevue Ms N11 44 DG50
Bellevue Rd
Bellevue Par SW17 120 DE88
Bellevue Rd
Bellevue Pl E1 84 DW70
Bellevue Pl, Slou. 92 AT76
Albert St
Bellevue Rd N11 44 DG49
Bellevue Rd SW13 99 CU82
Bellevue Rd SW17 120 DE88
Bellevue Rd W13 79 CH70
Bellevue Rd, Bexh. 126 EZ85
Bellevue Rd, Horn. 72 FM60
Bellevue Rd, Kings.T. 138 CL97
Bellevue Rd, Rom. 51 FC51
Bellevue Ter (Harefield), Uxb. 38 BG52
Bellew St SW17 120 DC90
Bellfield, Croy. 161 DY109
Bellfield Av, Har. 41 CD51
Bellflower Cl E6 86 EL71
Sorrel Gdns
Bellflower Path, Rom. 52 FJ52
Bellgate Ms NW5 65 DH62
York Ri
Bellhouse La, Brwd. 54 FS43
Bellingham Ct, Bark. 88 EV69
Renwick Rd
Bellingham Grn SE6 123 EA90
Bellingham Rd SE6 123 EB90
Bellmaker Ct E3 85 DZ71
St. Paul's Way
Bellman Av, Grav. 131 GL88
Bellmarsh Rd, Add. 152 BH105
Bellmount Wd Av, Wat. 23 BS39
Bello Cl SE24 121 DP87
Bellot Gdns SE10 205 J10
Bellot Gdns SE10 104 EE78
Bellot St SE10 205 J10
Bellot St SE10 104 EE78
Bellring Cl, Belv. 106 FA79
Bells All SW6 100 DA82
Bells Gdn Est SE15 102 DU80
Buller Cl
Bells Hill, Barn. 27 CX43
Bell's Hill, Slou. 74 AU67
Bells Hill Grn, Slou. 74 AU66
Bells La, Slou. 93 BB83
Bellswood La, Iver 75 BB71
Belltrees Gro SW16 121 DM92
Bellwood Rd SE15 103 DX84
Belmarsh Rd SE28 105 ES75
Western Way
Belmont Av N9 46 DU46
Belmont Av N13 45 DL50
Belmont Av N17 66 DQ55
Belmont Av, Barn. 28 DF43
Belmont Av, N.Mal. 139 CU99
Belmont Av, Sthl. 96 BY76
Belmont Av, Upmin. 72 FM61
Belmont Av, Well. 105 ES83

Belmont Av, Wem. 80 CM67
Belmont Circle, Har. 41 CH53
Belmont Cl E4 47 ED50
Belmont Cl N20 44 DB46
Belmont Cl SW4 101 DJ83
Belmont Cl, Barn. 28 DF42
Belmont Cl, Uxb. 76 BK65
Belmont Cl, Wdf.Grn. 48 EH49
Belmont Cotts (Colnbrook), Slou. 93 BC80
High St
Belmont Ct NW11 63 CZ57
Belmont Gro SE13 103 ED83
Belmont Gro W4 98 CR77
Belmont Rd
Belmont Hall Ct SE13 103 ED83
Belmont Gro
Belmont Hill SE13 103 ED83
Belmont La, Chis. 125 EQ92
Belmont La, Stan. 41 CJ52
Belmont Ms SW19 119 CX89
Chapman Sq
Belmont Pk SE13 103 ED84
Belmont Pk Cl SE13 103 ED84
Belmont Pk
Belmont Pk Rd E10 67 EB58
Belmont Ri, Sutt. 157 CZ109
Belmont Rd N15 66 DQ56
Belmont Rd N17 66 DQ56
Belmont Rd SE25 142 DV99
Belmont Rd SW4 101 DJ83
Belmont Rd W4 98 CR77
Belmont Rd, Beck. 143 DZ96
Belmont Rd, Bushey 24 BY43
Belmont Rd, Chis. 125 EP92
Belmont Rd, Erith 106 FA80
Belmont Rd, Grays 110 FZ78
Belmont Rd, Har. 61 CF55
Belmont Rd, Horn. 72 FK62
Belmont Rd, Ilf. 69 EQ62
Belmont Rd, Lthd. 171 CG122
Belmont Rd, Sutt. 158 DA110
Belmont Rd, Twick. 117 CD89
Belmont Rd, Uxb. 76 BK66
Belmont Rd, Wall. 159 DH106
Belmont St NW1 82 DG66
Belmont Ter W4 98 CR77
Belmont Rd
Belmor, Borwd. 26 CN43
Belmore Av, Hayes 77 BU72
Belmore Av, Wok. 167 BD116
Belmore La N7 65 DK64
Belmore St SW8 101 DK81
Beloe Cl SW15 99 CU83
Belper Ct E5 67 DX63
Pedro St
Belsham St E9 84 DW65
Belsize Av N13 45 DM51
Belsize Av NW3 82 DE65
Belsize Av W13 97 CH76
Belsize Ct NW3 64 DE64
Belsize La
Belsize Cres NW3 64 DD64
Belsize Gdns, Sutt. 158 DB105
Belsize Gro NW3 82 DE65
Belsize La NW3 82 DD65
Belsize Ms NW3 82 DD65
Belsize La
Belsize Pk NW3 82 DD65
Belsize Pk Gdns NW3 82 DE65
Belsize Pk Ms NW3 82 DD65
Belsize La
Belsize Pl NW3 82 DD65
Belsize La
Belsize Rd NW6 82 DC66
Belsize Rd, Har. 41 CD52
Belsize Sq NW3 82 DD65
Belsize Ter NW3 82 DD65
Belson Rd SE18 105 EM77
Belswains La, Hem.H. 6 BM25
Beltana Dr, Grav. 131 GL91
Beltane Dr SW19 119 CX90
Belthorn Cres SW12 121 DJ87
Beltinge Rd, Rom. 72 FM55
Belton Rd E7 86 EH66
Belton Rd E11 68 EE63
Belton Rd N17 66 DS55
Belton Rd NW2 81 CU65
Belton Rd, Sid. 126 EU91
Belton Way E3 85 EA71
Beltona Gdns (Cheshunt), Wal.Cr. 15 DX27
Beltran Rd SW6 100 DB82
Beltwood Rd, Belv. 107 FC77
Belvedere Av SW19 119 CY92
Belvedere Av, Ilf. 49 EP54
Belvedere Bldgs SE1 200 G5
Belvedere Cl, Esher 154 CB106
Belvedere Cl, Grav. 131 GJ88
Belvedere Cl, Tedd. 117 CE92
Belvedere Cl, Wey. 152 BN106
Belvedere Ct N2 64 DD57
Belvedere Dr SW19 119 CY92
Belvedere Gdns, St.Alb. 8 CA27
Belvedere Gdns, W.Mol. 136 BZ99
Belvedere Gro SW19 119 CY92
Belvedere Ho, Felt. 115 BU88
Belvedere Ind Est, Belv. 107 FC76
Belvedere Ms SE15 102 DV83
Belvedere Pl SE1 200 G5
Belvedere Pl SE1 101 DP75
Belvedere Rd E10 67 DY60
Belvedere Rd SE1 200 C4
Belvedere Rd SE1 83 DM74
Belvedere Rd SE2 88 EX74
Belvedere Rd SE19 122 DT94
Belvedere Rd W7 97 CF76
Belvedere Rd, Bexh. 106 EZ83
Belvedere Rd, Brwd. 54 FT48
Belvedere Rd, West. 179 EM118
Belvedere Sq SW19 119 CY92
Belvedere Strand NW9 43 CT54
Belvedere Twr, The SW10 100 DC81
Harbour Av
Belvedere Way, Har. 62 CL58
Belvoir Cl SE9 124 EL90
Belvoir Rd SE22 122 DU87
Belvue Cl, Nthlt. 78 CA66
Belvue Rd, Nthlt. 78 CA66
Bembridge Cl NW6 81 CY66
Bembridge Ct, Slou. 92 AT76
Park St
Bembridge Gdns, Ruis. 59 BR61
Bemerton Est N1 83 DM66
Bemerton St N1 83 DM67
Bemish Rd SW15 99 CX83
Bempton Dr, Ruis. 59 BV61
Bemsted Rd E17 67 DZ55
Ben Hale Cl, Stan. 41 CH49
Ben Jonson Rd E1 85 DY71
Ben Smith Way SE16 202 C6
Ben Tillet Cl, Bark. 88 EU66
Ben Tillett Cl E16 87 EM74
Newland St
Benares Rd SE18 105 ET77
Benbow Rd W6 99 CV76
Benbow St SE8 103 EA79
Benbow Waye, Uxb. 76 BJ71
Benbury Cl, Brom. 123 EC92
Bence, The, Egh. 133 BB97
Bench Fld, S.Croy. 160 DT107
Bench Manor Cres (Chalfont St. Peter), Ger.Cr. 36 AW54
Bencombe Rd, Pur. 159 DN114
Bencroft (Cheshunt), Wal.Cr. 14 DU26
Bencroft Rd SW16 121 DJ94
Bencurtis Pk, W.Wick. 143 ED104
Bendall Ms NW1 194 C6
Bendemeer Rd SW15 99 CX83
Bendish Rd E6 86 EL66
Bendmore Av SE2 106 EU78
Bendon Valley SW18 120 DB87
Bendysh Rd, Bushey 24 BY41
Benedict Cl, Belv. 106 EY76
Tunstock Way
Benedict Cl, Orp. 145 ES104
Benedict Dr, Felt. 115 BR87
Benedict Rd SW9 101 DM83
Benedict Rd, Mitch. 140 DD97
Benedict Way N2 64 DC55
Benedictine Gate, Wal.Cr. 15 DY27
Benen-Stock Rd, Stai. 113 BF85
Benenden Grn, Brom. 144 EG99
Benets Rd, Horn. 72 FN60
Benett Gdns SW16 141 DL96
Benfleet Cl, Cob. 154 BY112
Benfleet Cl, Sutt. 140 DC104
Bengal Ct EC3 84 DR72
Birchin La
Bengal Rd, Ilf. 69 EP63
Bengarth Dr, Har. 41 CD54
Bengarth Rd, Nthlt. 78 BX67
Bengeworth Rd SE5 102 DQ83
Bengeworth Rd, Har. 61 CG61
Benham Cl SW11 100 DD83
Benham Cl, Chess. 155 CJ107
Merritt Gdns
Benham Cl, Couls. 175 DP118
Benham Gdns, Houns. 96 BZ84
Benham Rd W7 79 CE71
Benhams Pl NW3 64 DC63
Holly Wk
Benhill Av, Sutt. 158 DB105
Benhill Rd SE5 102 DR80
Benhill Rd, Sutt. 140 DC104
Benhill Wd Rd, Sutt. 140 DC104
Benhilton Gdns, Sutt. 140 DB104
Benhurst Av, Horn. 71 FH62
Benhurst Cl, S.Croy. 161 DX110
Benhurst Ct SW16 121 DN92
Benhurst Gdns, S.Croy. 160 DW110
Benhurst La SW16 121 DN92
Benin St SE13 123 ED87
Benison Ct, Slou. 92 AT76
Osborne St
Benjafield Cl N18 46 DV49
Brettenham Rd
Benjamin Cl E8 84 DU67
Benjamin Cl, Horn. 71 FG58
Benjamin St EC1 196 F6
Benjamin St EC1 83 DP71
Benledi St E14 85 ED72
Benn St E9 85 DY65
Bennerley Rd SW11 120 DE85
Bennet's Hill EC4 196 G10
Bennetsfield Rd, Uxb. 77 BP74
Bennett Cl, Cob. 153 BU113
Bennett Cl, Kings.T. 137 CJ95
Bennett Cl, Nthwd. 39 BT52
Bennett Cl, Well. 106 EU82
Bennett Gro SE13 103 EB81
Bennett Pk SE3 104 EF83
Bennett Rd E13 86 EJ70
Bennett Rd N16 66 DS63
Bennett Rd, Rom. 70 EY58
Bennett St SW1 199 K2
Bennett St W4 98 CS79
Bennett Way, Dart. 129 FR91
Bennetts Av, Croy. 143 DY103
Bennetts Av, Grnf. 79 CE67
Bennetts Castle La, Dag. 70 EW63
Bennetts Cl N17 46 DT51
Bennetts Cl, Mitch. 141 DH95
Bennetts Copse, Chis. 124 EL93
Bennetts Way, Croy. 143 DY103
Bennetts Yd SW1 199 N7
Bennetts Yd, Uxb. 76 BJ66
High St
Benningholme Rd, Edg. 42 CS51
Bennington Rd N17 46 DS53
Bennington Rd, Wdf.Grn. 48 EE52
Bennions Cl, Horn. 90 FK65
Franklin Rd
Bennison Dr, Rom. 52 FK54
Benn's Wk, Rich. 98 CL84
Rosedale Rd
Benrek Cl, Ilf. 49 EQ53
Bensbury Cl SW15 119 CV87
Bensham Cl, Th.Hth. 142 DQ98
Bensham Gro, Th.Hth. 142 DQ96
Bensham La, Croy. 141 DP101
Bensham La, Th.Hth. 141 DP98
Bensham Manor Rd, Th.Hth. 142 DQ98
Bensington Ct, Felt. 115 BR86
Benskin Rd, Wat. 23 BU43
Benskins La (Havering-atte-Bower), Rom. 52 FK46
Bensley Cl N11 44 DF50
Benson Av E6 86 EJ68
Benson Cl, Houns. 96 CA84
Benson Cl, Slou. 74 AU74
Benson Cl, Uxb. 76 BL71
Benson Quay E1 202 F1
Benson Rd SE23 122 DW88
Benson Rd, Croy. 141 DN104
Benson Rd, Grays 110 GB79
Bentfield Gdns SE9 124 EJ90
Aldersgrove Av
Benthal Rd N16 66 DU61
Benthall Gdns, Ken. 176 DQ116
Bentham Av, Wok. 167 BC115
Bentham Ct N1 84 DQ66
Rotherfield St
Bentham Rd E9 85 DX65
Bentham Rd SE28 88 EV73
Bentham Wk NW10 62 CQ64
Bentinck Cl, Ger.Cr. 56 AX57
Bentinck Ms W1 194 G8
Bentinck Pl NW8 194 B1
Bentinck Rd, West Dr. 76 BK74
Bentinck St W1 194 G8
Bentinck St W1 82 DG72
Bentley Dr NW2 63 CZ62
Bentley Dr, Ilf. 69 EQ58
Bentley Dr, Wey. 152 BN109
Bentley Heath La, Barn. 11 CY34
Bentley Ms, Enf. 30 DR44
Bentley Rd N1 84 DS65
Tottenham Rd
Bentley St, Grav. 131 GJ86
Bentley Way, Stan. 41 CG50
Bentley Way, Wdf.Grn. 48 EG47
Benton Rd, Ilf. 69 ER60
Benton Rd, Wat. 40 BX50
Bentons La SE27 122 DQ91
Bentons Ri SE27 122 DR92
Bentry Cl, Dag. 70 EY61
Bentry Rd, Dag. 70 EY61
Bentworth Rd W12 81 CV72
Benwell Ct, Sun. 135 BU95
Benwell Rd N7 65 DN63
Benwick Cl SE16 202 E7
Benwick Cl SE16 102 DV76
Benworth St E3 85 DZ69
Benyon Path, S.Ock. 91 FW68
Tyssen Pl
Benyon Rd N1 84 DR67
Southgate Rd
Beomonds Row, Cher. 134 BG101
Heriot Rd
Berber Rd SW11 120 DF85
Berberis Wk, West Dr. 94 BL77
Berberry Cl, Edg. 42 CQ49
Larkspur Gro
Berceau Wk, Wat. 23 BS39
Bercta Rd SE9 125 EQ89
Bere St E1 85 DX73
Cranford St
Beredens La, Brwd. 73 FT55
Berenger Wk SW10 100 DD80
Blantyre St
Berens Rd NW10 81 CX69
Berens Rd, Orp. 146 EX99
Berens Way, Chis. 145 ET98
Beresford Av N20 44 DF47
Beresford Av W7 79 CD71
Beresford Av, Slou. 74 AW74
Beresford Av, Surb. 138 CP102
Beresford Av, Twick. 117 CJ86
Beresford Av, Wem. 80 CM67
Beresford Dr, Brom. 144 EK97
Beresford Dr, Wdf.Grn. 48 EJ49
Beresford Gdns, Enf. 30 DS42
Beresford Gdns, Houns. 116 BZ85
Beresford Gdns, Rom. 70 EY57
Beresford Rd E4 48 EE46
Beresford Rd E17 47 EB53
Beresford Rd N2 64 DE55
Beresford Rd N5 66 DQ64
Beresford Rd N8 65 DN57
Beresford Rd, Grav. 130 GE87
Beresford Rd, Har. 61 CD57
Beresford Rd, Kings.T. 138 CM95
Beresford Rd, N.Mal. 138 CQ98
Beresford Rd, Rick. 37 BF46
Beresford Rd, Sthl. 78 BX74
Beresford Rd, Sutt. 157 CZ108
Beresford Sq SE18 105 EP77
Beresford St SE18 105 EP76
Beresford Ter N5 66 DQ64
Berestede Rd W6 99 CT78
Bergen Sq SE16 203 L6
Berger Cl, Orp. 145 ER100
Berger Rd E9 85 DX65
Berghem Ms W14 99 CX76
Blythe Rd
Bergholt Av, Ilf. 68 EL57
Bergholt Cres N16 66 DS59
Bergholt Ms NW1 83 DJ66
Rossendale Way
Bering Sq E14 103 EA78
Napier Av
Bering Wk E16 86 EK72
Berisford Ms SW18 120 DC86
Berkeley Av, Bexh. 106 EX81
Berkeley Av, Grnf. 79 CE65
Berkeley Av, Houns. 95 BU82
Berkeley Av, Ilf. 49 EN54
Berkeley Av, Rom. 51 FC52
Berkeley Cl, Abb.L. 7 BT32
Berkeley Cl, Borwd. 26 CN43
Berkeley Cl, Horn. 72 FP61
Berkeley Cl, Kings.T. 118 CL94
Berkeley Cl, Orp. 145 ES101
Berkeley Cl, Pot.B. 11 CY32
Berkeley Cl, Ruis. 59 BU62
Berkeley Cl, Stai. 113 BD89
Berkeley Ct N14 29 DJ44
Berkeley Ct, Wall. 141 DJ104
Berkeley Ct, Wey. 135 BR103
Berkeley Cres, Barn. 28 DD43
Berkeley Cres, Dart. 128 FM88
Berkeley Dr, Horn. 72 FN60
Berkeley Dr, W.Mol. 136 BZ97
Berkeley Gdns N21 46 DR45
Berkeley Gdns W8 82 DA74
Brunswick Gdns
Berkeley Gdns, Esher 155 CG107
Berkeley Gdns, Walt. 135 BT101
Berkeley Gdns, W.Byf. 151 BF114
Berkeley Ho E3 85 EA70
Berkeley Ms W1 194 E8
Berkeley Pl SW19 119 CX93
Berkeley Pl, Epsom 172 CR115
Berkeley Rd E12 68 EL64
Berkeley Rd N8 65 DK57
Berkeley Rd N15 66 DR58
Berkeley Rd NW9 62 CN56
Berkeley Rd SW13 99 CU81
Berkeley Rd, Uxb. 77 BQ66
Berkeley Sq W1 199 J1
Berkeley Sq W1 83 DH73
Berkeley St W1 199 J1
Berkeley St W1 83 DH73
Berkeley Wk N7 65 DM61
Durham Rd
Berkeley Waye, Houns. 96 BX80
Berkeleys, The, Lthd. 171 CE124
Berkhampstead Rd, Belv. 106 FA78
Berkhamsted Av, Wem. 80 CM65
Berkley Av, Wal.Cr. 15 DX34
Berkley Ct, Rick. 23 BR43
Mayfare
Berkley Cres, Grav. 131 GJ86
Milton Rd
Berkley Gro NW1 82 DF66
Berkley Rd
Berkley Rd NW1 82 DF66
Berkley Rd, Grav. 131 GH86
Berks Hill, Rick. 21 BC43
Berkshire Cl, Cat. 176 DR122
Berkshire Gdns N13 45 DN51
Berkshire Gdns N18 46 DV50
Berkshire Rd E9 85 DZ65
Berkshire Sq, Mitch. 141 DL98
Berkshire Way
Berkshire Way, Horn. 72 FN57
Berkshire Way, Mitch. 141 DL98
Bermans Cl, Brwd. 55 GB47
Hanging Hill La
Bermans Way NW10 62 CS63
Bermondsey Sq SE1 201 N6
Bermondsey St SE1 201 M3
Bermondsey St SE1 102 DS75
Bermondsey Wall E SE16 202 C5
Bermondsey Wall E SE16 102 DU75
Bermondsey Wall W SE16 202 B4
Bermondsey Wall W SE16 102 DU75
Bermuda Rd, Til. 111 GG82
Bernal Cl SE28 88 EX73
Haldane Rd
Bernard Ashley Dr SE7 104 EH78
Bernard Av W13 97 CH76
Bernard Cassidy St E16 86 EF71
Bernard Gdns SW19 119 CZ92
Bernard Gro, Wal.Abb. 15 EB33
Beaulieu Dr
Bernard Rd N15 66 DT57
Bernard Rd, Rom. 71 FC59
Bernard Rd, Wall. 159 DH105
Bernard St WC1 195 P5
Bernard St WC1 83 DL70
Bernard St, Grav. 131 GH86
Bernards Cl, Ilf. 49 EQ51
Bernato Cl, W.Byf. 152 BL112
Viscount Gdns
Bernays Cl, Stan. 41 CJ51
Bernays Gro SW9 101 DM84
Berne Rd, Th.Hth. 142 DQ99
Bernel Dr, Croy. 143 DZ104
Berners Dr W13 79 CG72
Berners Ms W1 195 L7
Berners Ms W1 83 DJ71
Berners Pl W1 195 L8
Berners Pl W1 83 DJ72
Berners Rd N1 83 DN67
Berners Rd N22 45 DN53
Berners St W1 195 L7
Berners St W1 83 DJ71
Bernersmede SE3 104 EG83
Blackheath Pk
Berney Rd, Croy. 142 DR101
Bernhart Cl, Edg. 42 CQ52
Orange Hill Rd
Bernice Cl, Rain. 90 FJ70
Bernville Way, Har. 62 CM57
Kenton Rd
Bernwell Rd E4 48 EE48
Berridge Grn, Edg. 42 CN52
Berridge Ms NW6 64 DA64
Hillfield Rd
Berridge Rd SE19 122 DR92
Berriman Rd N7 65 DM62
Berrington Dr, Lthd. 169 BT124
Berriton Rd, Har. 60 BZ60
Berry Av, Wat. 23 BV36
Berry Cl N21 45 DP46
Berry Cl NW10 80 CS66
Berry Cl, Horn. 72 FJ64
Airfield Way
Berry Cl, Rick. 38 BH45
Berry Ct, Houns. 116 BZ85
Berry Gro La, Wat. 24 CA39
Berry Hill, Stan. 41 CK49
Berry La SE21 122 DR91
Berry La, Rick. 38 BH46
Berry La, Walt. 154 BX106
Burwood Rd
Berry Meade, Ash. 172 CM117
Berry Pl EC1 196 G3
Berry St EC1 196 G4
Berry St EC1 83 DP70
Berry Wk, Ash. 172 CM119
Berry Way W5 98 CL76
Berry Way, Rick. 38 BH45
Berrybank Cl E4 47 EC47
Greenbank Cl
Berrydale Rd, Hayes 78 BY70
Berryfield, Slou. 74 AW72
Berryfield Cl E17 67 EB56
Berryfield Cl, Brom. 144 EL95
Berryfield Rd SE17 200 G10
Berryfield Rd SE17 101 DP78
Berryhill SE9 105 EP84
Berryhill Gdns SE9 105 EP84
Berrylands SW20 139 CW97
Berrylands, Orp. 146 EW104
Berrylands, Surb. 138 CN99
Berrylands Rd, Surb. 138 CM100
Berryman Cl, Dag. 70 EW62
Bennetts Castle La
Berrymans La SE26 123 DX91
Berrymead Gdns W3 80 CQ74
Berrymede Rd W4 98 CR76
Berry's Grn Rd, West. 179 EP116
Berry's Hill, West. 179 EP115
Berrys La, W.Byf. 152 BK111
Berryscroft Ct, Stai. 114 BJ94
Berryscroft Rd
Berryscroft Rd, Stai. 114 BJ94
Bersham La, Grays 110 FZ77
Bert Rd, Th.Hth. 142 DQ99
Bertal Rd SW17 120 DD91
Berther Rd, Horn. 72 FK59
Berthold Ms, Wal.Abb. 15 EB33
Berthon St SE8 103 EA80
Bertie Rd NW10 81 CU65
Bertie Rd SE26 123 DX93
Bertram Cotts SW19 120 DA94
Hartfield Rd
Bertram Rd NW4 63 CU58
Bertram Rd, Enf. 30 DU42
Bertram Rd, Kings.T. 118 CN94
Bertram St N19 65 DH61
Bertram Way, Enf. 30 DT42
Bertrand St SE13 103 EB83
Bertrand Way SE28 88 EV73
Berwick Av, Hayes 78 BX72
Berwick Cl, Stan. 41 CF52
Gordon Av
Berwick Cl, Wal.Cr. 15 EA34
Berwick Cres, Sid. 125 ES86
Berwick La, Ong. 35 FF36
Berwick Pond Cl, Rain. 90 FK68
Berwick Pond Rd, Rain. 90 FL68
Berwick Pond Rd, Upmin. 90 FM66
Berwick Rd E16 86 EH72
Berwick Rd N22 45 DP53
Berwick Rd, Borwd. 26 CM38
Berwick Rd, Rain. 90 FK68
Berwick Rd, Well. 106 EV81
Berwick St W1 195 M9
Berwick St W1 83 DK72
Berwick Way, Orp. 146 EU102
Berwick Way, Sev. 191 FH121
Berwyn Av, Houns. 96 CB81
Berwyn Rd SE24 121 DP88
Berwyn Rd, Rich. 98 CP84
Beryl Av E6 86 EL71
Beryl Ho SE18 105 ET78
Spinel Cl
Beryl Rd W6 99 CX78
Berystede, Kings.T. 118 CP94
Besant Ct N1 66 DR64
Newington Grn Rd
Besant Rd NW2 63 CY63
Besant Wk N7 65 DM61
Newington Barrow Way
Besant Way NW10 62 CQ64
Besley St SW16 121 DJ93
Bessant Dr, Rich. 98 CP81
Bessborough Gdns SW1 199 N10
Bessborough Gdns SW1 101 DK78
Bessborough Pl SW1 199 N10
Bessborough Pl SW1 101 DK78
Bessborough Rd SW15 119 CU88
Bessborough Rd, Har. 61 CD60
Bessborough St SW1 199 M10
Bessborough St SW1 101 DK78
Bessels Grn Rd, Sev. 190 FD123
Bessels Meadow, Sev. 190 FD124
Bessels Way, Sev. 190 FC124
Bessemer Rd SE5 102 DQ82
Bessie Lansbury Cl E6 87 EN72
Bessingby Rd, Ruis. 59 BU61
Bessingham Wk SE4 103 DX84
Frendsbury Rd
Besson St SE14 102 DW81
Bessy St E2 84 DW69
Roman Rd
Bestwood St SE8 203 J9
Bestwood St SE8 103 DX77
Beswick Ms NW6 82 DB65
Lymington Rd
Beta Rd, Wok. 167 BB116
Beta Rd (Chobham), Wok. 150 AT110
Beta Way, Egh. 133 BC95
Betam Rd, Hayes 95 BR75
Betchworth Cl, Sutt. 158 DD106
Turnpike La
Betchworth Rd, Ilf. 69 ES61
Betchworth Way, Croy. 161 EC109
Betenson Av, Sev. 190 FF122
Betham Rd, Grnf. 79 CD69
Bethany Waye, Felt. 115 BS87
Bethecar Rd, Har. 61 CE57
Bethel Rd, Sev. 191 FJ123
Bethel Rd, Well. 106 EW83
Bethell Av E16 86 EF70
Bethell Av, Ilf. 69 EN59
Bethersden Cl, Beck. 123 DZ94
Bethnal Grn Rd E1 197 P4
Bethnal Grn Rd E1 84 DT70
Bethnal Grn Rd E2 197 P4
Bethnal Grn Rd E2 84 DT70
Bethune Av N11 44 DF49
Bethune Rd N16 66 DR59
Bethune Rd NW10 80 CR70
Bethwin Rd SE5 101 DP80
Betjeman Cl, Couls. 175 DM117
Betjeman Cl, Pnr. 60 CA56
Betjeman Cl, Wal.Cr. 14 DU28
Rosedale Way
Betley Ct, Walt. 135 BV104
Betony Cl, Croy. 143 DX102
Primrose La
Betony Rd, Rom. 52 FK51
Cloudberry Rd
Betoyne Av E4 48 EE49
Betsham Rd, Erith 107 FF80
Betsham Rd, Grav. 129 FX92
Betsham Rd, Swans. 130 FY87
Betstyle Rd N11 45 DH49
Betterton Dr, Sid. 126 EY89
Betterton Rd, Rain. 89 FE69
Betterton St WC2 195 P9
Betterton St WC2 83 DL72
Bettles Cl, Uxb. 76 BJ68
Wescott Way
Bettons Pk E15 86 EE67

ttridge Rd SW6 99 CZ82
tts Cl, Beck. 143 DY96
Kendall Rd
tts Ms E17 67 DZ58
Queen's Rd
tts Rd E16 86 EH73
Victoria Dock Rd
tts St E1 202 D1
tts Way SE20 142 DV95
tts Way, Surb. 137 CH102
tula Cl, Ken. 176 DR115
tula Wk, Rain. 90 FK69
tween Sts, Cob. 153 BU114
ulah Av, Th.Hth. 141 DM98
Beulah Rd
ulah Cl, Edg. 42 CP48
ulah Cres, Th.Hth. 142 DQ96
ulah Gro, Croy. 142 DQ100
ulah Hill SE19 121 DP93
ulah Path E17 67 EB57
Addison Rd
ulah Rd E17 67 EB57
ulah Rd SW19 119 CZ94
ulah Rd, Epp. 18 EU29
ulah Rd, Horn. 72 FJ62
ulah Rd, Sutt. 158 DA105
ulah Rd, Th.Hth. 142 DQ97
ulah Wk, Cat. 177 DY120
ult Rd, Dart. 107 FG83
ev Callender Cl SW8 101 DH83
Daley Thompson Way
evan Av, Bark. 88 EU66
evan Ct, Croy. 159 DN106
evan Ho, Grays 110 GD75
Laird Av
evan Pl, Swan. 147 FF98
evan Rd SE2 106 EV78
evan Rd, Barn. 28 DF42
evan St N1 84 DQ67
evan Way, Horn. 72 FM63
evans Cl, Green. 129 FW86
Johnsons Way
evenden St N1 197 L2
evenden St N1 84 DR69
evercote Wk, Belv. 106 EZ79
Osborne Rd
everidge Rd NW10 80 CS66
Curzon Cres
everley Av SW20 139 CT95
everley Av, Houns. 96 BZ84
everley Av, Sid. 125 ET87
everley Cl N21 46 DQ46
everley Cl SW11 100 DD84
Maysoule Rd
everley Cl SW13 99 CT82
everley Cl, Add. 152 BK106
everley Cl, Chess. 155 CJ105
everley Cl, Enf. 30 DS42
everley Cl, Epsom 157 CW111
everley Cl, Horn. 72 FM59
everley Cl, Wey. 135 BS103
everley Cotts SW15 118 CR91
Kingston Vale
everley Ct N14 45 DJ45
everley Ct SE4 103 DZ83
everley Ct, Slou. 92 AV75
Dolphin Rd
everley Cres, Wdf.Grn. 48 EH53
everley Dr, Edg. 62 CP55
everley Gdns NW11 63 CY59
everley Gdns SW13 99 CT83
everley Gdns, Horn. 72 FM59
everley Gdns, Stan. 41 CG53
everley Gdns (Cheshunt), Wal.Cr. 14 DT30
everley Gdns, Wem. 62 CM60
everley Gdns, Wor.Pk. 139 CU102
Green La
everley Hts, Reig. 184 DB132
everley Ho NW8 194 B3
everley La SW15 119 CT90
everley La, Kings.T. 118 CS94
everley Ms E4 47 ED51
Beverley Rd
Beverley Path SW13 99 CT82
Beverley Rd E4 47 ED51
Beverley Rd E6 86 EK69
Beverley Rd SE20 142 DV96
Wadhurst Cl
Beverley Rd SW13 99 CT83
Beverley Rd W4 99 CT78
Beverley Rd, Bexh. 107 FC82
Beverley Rd, Brom. 144 EL103
Beverley Rd, Dag. 70 EY63
Beverley Rd, Kings.T. 137 CJ95
Beverley Rd, Mitch. 141 DK98
Beverley Rd, N.Mal. 139 CU98
Beverley Rd, Ruis. 59 BU61
Beverley Rd, Sthl. 96 BY76
Beverley Rd, Sun. 135 BT95
Beverley Rd, Whyt. 176 DS116
Beverley Rd, Wor.Pk. 139 CW103
Beverley Way SW20 139 CT95
Beverley Way, N.Mal. 139 CT95
Beversbrook Rd N19 65 DK62
Beverston Ms W1 194 D7
Beverstone Rd SW2 121 DM85
Beverstone Rd, Th.Hth. 141 DN98
Bevill Allen Cl SW17 120 DF92
Bevill Cl SE25 142 DU97
Bevin Cl SE16 203 K2
Bevin Ct WC1 83 DN69
Holford St
Bevin Rd, Hayes 77 BU69
Bevin Sq SW17 120 DF90
Bevin Way WC1 196 D2
Bevington Rd W10 81 CY71
Bevington Rd, Beck. 143 EB96
Bevington St SE16 202 C5
Bevington St SE16 102 DU75
Bevis Cl, Dart. 128 FQ87
Bevis Marks EC3 197 N8
Bevis Marks EC3 84 DS72
Bewcastle Gdns, Enf. 29 DL42
Bewdley St N1 83 DN66
Bewick St SW8 101 DH82
Bewley Cl (Cheshunt), Wal.Cr. 15 DX31
Bewley St E1 84 DV73
Dellow St
Bewlys Rd SE27 121 DP92
Bexhill Cl, Felt. 116 BY89
Bexhill Rd N11 45 DK50
Bexhill Rd SE4 123 DZ86
Bexhill Rd SW14 98 CQ83
Bexhill Wk E15 86 EE68
Mitre Rd
Bexley Cl, Dart. 127 FE85
Bexley Gdns N9 46 DR48
Bexley Gdns, Rom. 70 EV57
Bexley High St, Bex. 126 FA87
Bexley La, Dart. 127 FE85
Bexley La, Sid. 126 EW90
Bexley Rd SE9 125 EP85
Bexley Rd, Erith 107 FC80
Beynon Rd, Cars. 158 DF106
Bianca Ho N1 84 DS68
Crondall St
Bianca Rd SE15 102 DT79
Bibsworth Rd N3 43 CZ54
Bibury Cl SE15 102 DS79
Bicester Rd, Rich. 98 CN83
Bickenhall St W1 194 E6
Bickenhall St W1 82 DF71
Bickersteth Rd SW17 120 DF93
Bickerton Rd N19 65 DJ61
Bickley Cres, Brom. 144 EL98
Bickley Pk Rd, Brom. 144 EL97
Bickley Rd E10 67 EB59
Bickley Rd, Brom. 144 EK96
Bickley St SW17 120 DE92
Bicknell Rd SE5 102 DQ83
Bickney Way, Lthd. 170 CC122
Bicknoller Cl, Sutt. 158 DB110
Bicknoller Rd, Enf. 30 DT39
Bicknor Rd, Orp. 145 ES101
Bidborough Cl, Brom. 144 EF99
Bidborough St WC1 195 P3
Bidborough St WC1 83 DK69
Biddenden Way SE9 125 EN91
Biddenden Way, Grav. 130 GE94
Biddenham Turn, Wat. 24 BW35
Bidder St E16 86 EE71
Biddestone Rd N7 65 DM63
Biddulph Rd W9 82 DB69
Biddulph Rd, S.Croy. 160 DQ109
Bideford Av, Grnf. 79 CH68
Bideford Cl, Edg. 42 CN53
Bideford Cl, Felt. 116 BZ90
Bideford Cl, Rom. 52 FJ53
Bideford Gdns, Enf. 46 DS45
Bideford Rd, Brom. 124 EF90
Bideford Rd, Enf. 31 DZ38
Bideford Rd, Ruis. 59 BV62
Bideford Rd, Well. 106 EV80
Bidhams Cres, Tad. 173 CW121
Bidwell Gdns N11 45 DJ52
Bidwell St SE15 102 DV81
Big Common La, Red. 185 DP133
Big Hill E5 66 DV60
Bigbury Cl N17 46 DR52
Weir Hall Rd
Bigbury Rd N17 46 DS52
Barkham Rd
Biggerstaff Rd E15 85 EC67
Biggerstaff St N4 65 DN61
Biggin Av, Mitch. 140 DF95
Biggin Hill SE19 121 DP94
Biggin Hill Business Pk, West. 178 EK115
Biggin Hill Cl, Kings.T. 117 CJ92
Biggin La, Grays 111 GH79
Biggin Way SE19 121 DP94
Bigginwood Rd SW16 121 DP94
Biggs Gro Rd (Cheshunt), Wal.Cr. 14 DR26
Hammondstreet Rd
Biggs Row SW15 99 CX83
Felsham Rd
Bigland St E1 84 DV72
Bignell Rd SE18 105 EP78
Bignold Rd E7 68 EG63
Bigwood Rd NW11 64 DB57
Biko Cl, Uxb. 76 BJ72
Sefton Way
Bill Hamling Cl SE9 125 EM89
Bill Nicholson Way N17 66 DT55
High Rd
Billet Cl, Rom. 70 EX55
Billet La, Horn. 72 FK60
Billet La, Iver 75 BB69
Billet La, Slou. 75 BB73
Billet Rd E17 47 DX54
Billet Rd, Rom. 70 EV55
Billet Rd, Stai. 114 BG90
Farnell Rd
Billets Hart Cl W7 97 CE75
Billing Pl SW10 100 DB80
Billing Rd SW10 100 DB80
Billing St SW10 100 DB80
Billingford Cl SE4 103 DX84
Billings Cl, Dag. 88 EW66
Ellerton Rd
Billington Rd SE14 103 DX80
Billiter Sq EC3 197 N10
Billiter St EC3 197 N9
Billiter St EC3 84 DS72
Billockby Cl, Chess. 156 CM107
Billson St E14 204 E9
Billson St E14 103 EC77
Billy Lows La, Pot.B. 12 DA31
Bilsby Gro SE9 124 EK91
Bilton Cl, Slou. 93 BE82
Bilton Rd, Erith 107 FG79
Bilton Rd, Grnf. 79 CJ67
Bilton Way, Enf. 31 DY39
Bilton Way, Hayes 95 BV75
Bina Gdns SW5 100 DC77
Bincote Rd, Enf. 29 DM41
Binden Rd W12 99 CT76
Bindon Grn, Mord. 140 DB98
Binfield Rd SW4 101 DL81
Binfield Rd, S.Croy. 160 DT106
Binfield Rd, W.Byf. 152 BL112
Bingfield St N1 83 DL67
Bingham Cl, S.Ock. 91 FV72
Bingham Ct N1 83 DP66
Halton Rd
Bingham Dr, Stai. 114 BK94
Bingham Dr, Wok. 166 AT118
Bingham Pl W1 194 F6
Bingham Rd, Croy. 142 DU102
Bingham St N1 84 DR65
Bingley Rd E16 86 EJ72
Bingley Rd, Grnf. 78 CC71
Bingley Rd, Sun. 115 BU94
Binney St W1 194 G10
Binney St W1 82 DG72
Binns Rd W4 98 CS78
Binns Ter W4 98 CS78
Binns Rd
Binsey Wk SE2 88 EW74
Binyon Cres, Stan. 41 CF50
Birbetts Rd SE9 125 EM89
Birch Av N13 46 DQ48
Birch Av, Cat. 176 DR124
Birch Av, Lthd. 171 CF120
Birch Av, West Dr. 76 BM72
Birch Cl E16 86 EE71
Birch Cl N19 65 DJ61
Hargrave Pk
Birch Cl SE15 102 DU82
Bournemouth Rd
Birch Cl, Add. 152 BK109
Birch Cl, Amer. 20 AS37
Birch Cl, Brent. 97 CH80
Birch Cl, Buck.H. 48 EK48
Birch Cl, Dart. 148 FK104
Birch Cl, Houns. 97 CD83
Birch Cl, Iver 75 BD68
Birch Cl, Rom. 71 FB55
Birch Cl, Sev. 191 FH123
Birch Cl, S.Ock. 91 FX69
Birch Cl, Tedd. 117 CG92
Birch Cl, Wok. 166 AW119
Birch Copse, St.Alb. 8 BY30
Birch Ct, Nthwd. 39 BQ51
Rickmansworth Rd
Birch Cres, Horn. 72 FL56
Birch Cres, S.Ock. 91 FX69
Birch Cres, Uxb. 76 BM67
Birch Dr, Rick. 37 BD50
Birch Gdns, Amer. 20 AS39
Birch Gdns, Dag. 71 FC62
Birch Grn NW9 42 CS52
Clayton Fld
Birch Grn, Stai. 114 BG91
Birch Gro E11 68 EE62
Birch Gro SE12 124 EF87
Birch Gro W3 80 CN74
Birch Gro, Cob. 154 BW114
Birch Gro, Pot.B. 12 DA32
Birch Gro, Shep. 135 BS96
Birch Gro, Tad. 173 CY124
Birch Gro, Well. 106 EU84
Birch Gro, Wok. 167 BD115
Birch Hill, Croy. 161 DX106
Birch La, Hem.H. 5 BB33
Birch La, Pur. 159 DL111
Birch Mead, Orp. 145 EN103
Birch Pk, Har. 40 CC52
Birch Pl, Green. 129 FS86
Birch Rd, Felt. 116 BX92
Birch Rd, Rom. 71 FB55
Birch Row, Brom. 145 EN101
Birch Tree Av, W.Wick. 162 EF106
Birch Tree Gro, Chesh. 4 AV30
Birch Tree Wk, Wat. 23 BT37
Birch Tree Way, Croy. 142 DV103
Birch Vale, Cob. 154 CA112
Birch Vw, Epp. 18 EV29
Birch Wk, Borwd. 26 CN39
Birch Wk, Erith 107 FC79
Birch Wk, Mitch. 141 DH95
Birch Wk, W.Byf. 152 BG112
Birch Way, St.Alb. 9 CK27
Birch Way, Warl. 177 DY118
Birch Wd, Rad. 10 CN34
Bircham Path SE4 103 DX84
St. Norbert Rd
Birchanger Rd SE25 142 DU99
Birchcroft Cl, Cat. 186 DQ125
Birchdale, Ger.Cr. 56 AX60
Birchdale Cl, W.Byf. 152 BJ111
Birchdale Gdns, Rom. 70 EX59
Birchdale Rd E7 68 EJ64
Birchdene Dr SE28 106 EU75
Birchen Cl NW9 62 CR61
Birchen Gro NW9 62 CR61
Birchend Cl, S.Croy. 160 DR107
Birches, The N21 29 DM44
Birches, The SE7 104 EH79
Birches, The, Brwd. 54 FY48
Birches, The, Bushey 24 CC43
Birches, The, Epp. 19 FB26
Birches, The, Orp. 163 EN105
Birches, The, Swan. 147 FE96
Birches, The, Wok. 167 AZ118
Heathside Rd
Birches Cl, Epsom 172 CS115
Birches Cl, Mitch. 140 DF97
Birches Cl, Pnr. 60 BY57
Birchfield Cl, Add. 152 BH105
Birchfield Cl, Couls. 175 DM116
Birchfield Gro, Epsom 157 CW110
Birchfield Rd (Cheshunt), Wal.Cr. 14 DV29
Birchfield St E14 85 EA73
Birchgate Ms, Tad. 173 CW121
Bidhams Cres
Birchin La EC3 197 L9
Birchin La EC3 84 DR72
Birchington Cl, Bexh. 107 FB81
Birchington Cl, Orp. 146 EW102
Hart Dyke Rd
Birchington Rd N8 65 DK58
Birchington Rd NW6 82 DA67
Birchington Rd, Surb. 138 CM101
Birchlands Av SW12 120 DF87
Birchmead, Wat. 23 BT38
Birchmead Av, Pnr. 60 BW56
Birchmere Row SE3 104 EF82
Birchmore Wk N5 66 DQ62
Birchville Ct, Bushey 41 CE46
Heathbourne Rd
Birchway, Hayes 77 BU74
Birchwood, Wal.Abb. 16 EE34
Roundhills
Birchwood Av N10 64 DG55
Birchwood Av, Beck. 143 DZ98
Birchwood Av, Sid. 126 EV89
Birchwood Av, Wall. 140 DG104
Birchwood Cl, Brwd. 53 FW51
Canterbury Way
Birchwood Cl, Mord. 140 DB98
Birchwood Ct N13 45 DP50
Birchwood Ct, Edg. 42 CQ54
Birchwood Dr NW3 64 DB62
Birchwood Dr, Dart. 127 FE91
Birchwood Dr, W.Byf. 152 BG112
Birchwood Gro, Hmptn. 116 CA93
Birchwood La, Cat. 185 DP125
Birchwood La, Esher 155 CD110
Birchwood La, Lthd. 155 CD110
Birchwood La, Sev. 180 EZ115
Birchwood Pk Av, Swan. 147 FE97
Birchwood Rd SW17 121 DH92
Birchwood Rd, Dart. 127 FE92
Birchwood Rd, Orp. 145 ER98
Birchwood Rd, Swan. 147 FC95
Birchwood Rd, W.Byf. 152 BG112
Birchwood Ter, Swan. 147 FC95
Birchwood Rd
Birchwood Way, St.Alb. 8 CB28
Bird in Bush Rd SE15 102 DU80
Bird La, Brwd. 73 FX55
Bird La, Upmin. 73 FR57
Bird La (Harefield), Uxb. 38 BJ54
Bird St W1 194 G9
Bird Wk, Twick. 116 BZ88
Bird-in-Hand La, Brom. 144 EK96
Bird-in-Hand Pas SE23 122 DW89
Dartmouth Rd
Birdbrook Cl, Brwd. 55 GB44
Birdbrook Cl, Dag. 89 FC66
Birdbrook Rd SE3 104 EJ83
Birdcage Wk SW1 199 L5
Birdcage Wk SW1 101 DJ75
Birdham Cl, Brom. 144 EL99
Birdhouse La, Orp. 179 EN115
Birdhurst Av, S.Croy. 160 DR105
Birdhurst Gdns, S.Croy. 160 DR105
Birdhurst Ri, S.Croy. 160 DS106
Birdhurst Rd SW18 100 DC84
Birdhurst Rd SW19 120 DE93
Birdhurst Rd, S.Croy. 160 DS106
Birdlip Cl SE15 102 DS79
Birds Fm Av, Rom. 51 FB53
Birds Hill Dr, Lthd. 155 CD113
Birds Hill Ri, Lthd. 155 CD113
Birds Hill Rd, Lthd. 155 CD112
Birdsfield La E3 85 DZ67
Birdswood Dr, Wok. 166 AS119
Birdwood Cl, S.Croy. 161 DX111
Birdwood Cl, Tedd. 117 CE91
Birkbeck Av W3 80 CQ73
Birkbeck Av, Grnf. 78 CC67
Birkbeck Gdns, Wdf.Grn. 48 EF47
Birkbeck Gro W3 98 CR75
Birkbeck Hill SE21 121 DP89
Birkbeck Ms E8 66 DT64
Sandringham Rd
Birkbeck Pl SE21 122 DQ88
Birkbeck Rd E8 66 DT64
Birkbeck Rd N8 65 DL56
Birkbeck Rd N12 44 DC50
Birkbeck Rd N17 46 DT53
Birkbeck Rd NW7 43 CT50
Birkbeck Rd SW19 120 DB92
Birkbeck Rd W3 80 CR74
Birkbeck Rd W5 97 CJ77
Birkbeck Rd, Beck. 142 DW96
Birkbeck Rd, Brwd. 55 GD44
Birkbeck Rd, Enf. 30 DR39
Birkbeck Rd, Ilf. 69 ER57
Birkbeck Rd, Rom. 71 FD60
Birkbeck Rd, Sid. 126 EU90
Birkbeck St E2 84 DV69
Birkbeck Way, Grnf. 78 CC67
Birkdale Av, Pnr. 60 CA55
Birkdale Av, Rom. 52 FM52
Birkdale Cl SE16 102 DV78
Masters Dr
Birkdale Cl, Orp. 145 ER101
Birkdale Gdns, Croy. 161 DX105
Birkdale Gdns, Wat. 40 BX48
Birkdale Rd SE2 106 EU77
Birkdale Rd W5 80 CL71
Birken Ms, Nthwd. 39 BP50
Birkenhead Av, Kings.T. 138 CM96
Birkenhead St WC1 196 A2
Birkenhead St WC1 83 DL69
Birkett Way, Ch.St.G. 20 AX41
Birkhall Rd SE6 123 ED88
Birkheads Rd, Reig. 184 DA133
Birkwood Cl SW12 121 DK87
Birley Rd N20 44 DC47
Birley St SW11 100 DG82
Birling Rd, Erith 107 FD80
Birnam Rd N4 65 DM61
Birnham Cl, Wok. 168 BG123
Birse Cres NW10 62 CS63
Birstall Grn, Wat. 40 BX49
Birstall Rd N15 66 DS57
Birtley Path, Borwd. 26 CL39
Biscay Rd W6 99 CX78
Biscoe Cl, Houns. 96 CA79
Biscoe Way SE13 103 ED83
Bisenden Rd, Croy. 142 DS103
Bisham Cl, Cars. 140 DF102
Bisham Gdns N6 64 DG60
Bishop Butt Cl, Orp. 145 ET104
Stapleton Rd
Bishop Cl W4 98 CQ78
Bishop Duppa's Pk, Shep. 135 BR101
Bishop Fox Way, W.Mol. 136 BZ98
Bishop Ken Rd, Har. 41 CF54
Bishop Kings Rd W14 99 CY77
Bishop Rd N14 45 DH45
Bishop St N1 84 DQ67
Bishop Wk, Brwd. 55 FZ47
Bishop Way NW10 80 CS66
Bishop Wilfred Wd Cl SE15 102 DU82
Moncrieff St
Bishop's Av E13 86 EH67
Bishop's Av SW6 99 CX82
Bishops Av, Borwd. 26 CM43
Bishops Av, Brom. 144 EJ96
Bishops Av, Nthwd. 39 BS49
Bishops Av, Rom. 70 EW58
Bishops Av, The N2 64 DD59
Bishops Br W2 82 DC71
Bishops Br Rd W2 82 DC72
Bishops Cl E17 67 EB56
Bishops Cl N19 65 DJ62
Wyndham Cres
Bishops Cl SE9 125 EQ89
Bishops Cl, Barn. 27 CX44
Bishop's Cl, Couls. 175 DN118
Bishops Cl, Enf. 30 DV40
Central Av
Bishops Cl, Rich. 117 CK90
Bishop's Cl, Sutt. 140 DA104
Bishops Cl, Uxb. 76 BN68
Bishop's Ct EC4 196 F8
Bishop's Ct WC2 196 D8
Bishops Ct, Green. 129 FS85
Chalice Way
Bishops Ct, Wal.Cr. 14 DV30
Churchgate
Bishops Dr, Felt. 115 BR86
Bishops Dr, Nthlt. 78 BY67
Bishops Gro N2 64 DD58
Bishops Gro, Hmptn. 116 BZ91
Bishop's Hall, Kings.T. 137 CK96
Bishops Hall Rd, Brwd. 54 FV44
Bishops Hill, Walt. 135 BU101
Bishop's Pk SW6 99 CX82
Bishop's Pk Rd SW6 99 CX82
Bishops Pk Rd SW16 141 DL95
Bishops Pl, Sutt. 158 DC106
Lind Rd
Bishops Rd N6 64 DG58
Bishops Rd SW6 99 CZ81
Bishops Rd W7 97 CE75
Bishops Rd, Croy. 141 DP101
Bishops Rd, Hayes 77 BQ71
Bishops Rd, Slou. 92 AU75
Bishops Ter SE11 200 E8
Bishops Ter SE11 101 DN77
Bishops Wk, Chis. 145 EQ95
Bishops Wk, Croy. 161 DX106
Bishop's Wk, Pnr. 60 BY55
High St
Bishops Way E2 84 DV68
Bishops Way, Egh. 113 BD93
Bishops Wd, Wok. 166 AT117
Bishopsford Rd, Mord. 140 DC101
Bishopsgate EC2 197 N7
Bishopsgate EC2 84 DS72
Bishopsgate Arc EC2 197 N7
Bishopsgate Chyd EC2 197 M8
Bishopsgate Rd, Egh. 112 AT90
Bishopsthorpe Rd SE26 123 DX91
Bishopswood Rd N6 64 DF59
Biskra, Wat. 23 BU39
Bisley Cl, Wal.Cr. 15 DX33
Bisley Cl, Wor.Pk. 139 CW102
Bispham Rd NW10 80 CM69
Bisson Rd E15 85 EC68
Bisterne Av E17 67 ED55
Bittacy Cl NW7 43 CX51
Bittacy Hill NW7 43 CX51
Bittacy Pk Av NW7 43 CX51
Bittacy Ri NW7 43 CW51
Bittacy Rd NW7 43 CX51
Bittams La, Cher. 151 BE105
Bittern Cl, Hayes 78 BX71
Bittern Cl (Cheshunt), Wal.Cr. 14 DQ25
Bittern St SE1 201 H5
Bitterne Dr, Wok. 166 AT117
Bittoms, The, Kings.T. 137 CK97
Bixley Cl, Sthl. 96 BZ77
Black Acre Cl, Amer. 20 AS39
Black Boy La N15 66 DQ57
Black Boy Wd, St.Alb. 8 CA30
Black Eagle Cl, West. 189 EQ127
Black Fan Cl, Enf. 30 DQ39
Black Friars Ct EC4 196 F10
Black Friars La EC4 196 F10
Black Friars La EC4 83 DP73
Black Gates, Pnr. 60 BZ55
Church La
Black Horse Ct SE1 201 L6
Black Horse Pl, Uxb. 76 BJ67
Waterloo Rd
Black Lake Cl, Egh. 133 BA95
Black Lion Hill, Rad. 10 CL32
Black Lion La W6 99 CU77
Black Lion Ms W6 99 CU77
Black Lion La
Black Pk Rd, Slou. 75 AZ68
Black Path E10 67 DX59
Black Prince Cl, W.Byf. 152 BM114
Black Prince Rd SE1 200 B9
Black Prince Rd SE1 101 DM77
Black Prince Rd SE11 200 C9
Black Prince Rd SE11 101 DM77
Black Rod Cl, Hayes 95 BT76
Black Swan Yd SE1 201 N4
Blackacre Rd, Epp. 33 ES37
Blackall St EC2 197 M4
Blackberry Cl, Shep. 135 BS98
Cherry Way
Blackberry Fm Cl, Houns. 96 BY80
Blackberry Fld, Orp. 146 EU95
Blackbird Hill NW9 62 CQ61
Blackbird Yd E2 84 DT69
Ravenscroft St
Blackbirds La, Wat. 25 CD35
Blackborne Rd, Dag. 88 FA65
Blackborough Cl, Reig. 184 DC134
Blackbridge Rd, Wok. 166 AX119
Blackbrook La, Brom. 145 EN97
Blackburn, The, Lthd. 170 BZ124
Little Bookham St
Blackburn Rd NW6 82 DB65
Blackburn Trd Est, Stai. 114 BM86
Blackburne's Ms W1 194 F10
Blackburne's Ms W1 82 DG73
Blackbury Cl, Pot.B. 12 DC31
Blackbush Av, Rom. 70 EX57
Blackbush Cl, Sutt. 158 DB108
Blackdale (Cheshunt), Wal.Cr. 14 DU27
Blackdown Av, Wok. 167 BE115
Blackdown Cl N2 44 DC54
Blackdown Cl, Wok. 167 BC116
Blackdown Ter SE18 105 EN80
Prince Imperial Rd
Blackett Cl, Stai. 133 BE96
Blackett St SW15 99 CX83
Blacketts Wd Dr, Rick. 21 BB43
Blackfen Rd, Sid. 125 ES85
Blackford Cl, S.Croy. 159 DP109
Blackford Rd, Wat. 40 BX50
Blackford's Path SW15 119 CU87
Roehampton High St

Blackfriars Br EC4 196 F10
Blackfriars Br EC4 83 DP73
Blackfriars Br SE1 196 F10
Blackfriars Br SE1 83 DP73
Blackfriars Pas EC4 196 F10
Blackfriars Rd SE1 200 F5
Blackfriars Rd SE1 83 DP74
Blackhall La, Sev. 191 FK123
Blackhall Pl, Sev. 191 FL124
Blackhall La
Blackheath Av SE10 103 ED80
Blackheath Gro SE3 104 EF82
Blackheath Hill SE10 103 EC81
Blackheath Pk SE3 104 EF83
Blackheath Ri SE13 103 EC82
Blackheath Rd SE10 103 EB81
Blackheath Vale SE3 104 EE82
Blackheath Village SE3 104 EF82
Blackhills, Esher 154 CA109
Blackhorse Cl, Amer. 20 AS38
Blackhorse Cres, Amer. 20 AS38
Blackhorse La E17 67 DX56
Blackhorse La, Croy. 142 DU101
Blackhorse La, Epp. 19 FD25
Blackhorse La, Pot.B. 10 CS30
Blackhorse La, Reig. 184 DB129
Blackhorse Ms E17 67 DX55
Blackhorse La
Blackhorse Rd E17 67 DX56
Blackhorse Rd SE8 103 DY78
Blackhorse Rd, Sid. 126 EU91
Blacklands Dr, Hayes 77 BQ70
Blacklands Meadow, Red. 185 DL133
Blacklands Rd SE6 123 EC91
Blacklands Ter SW3 198 D9
Blacklands Ter SW3 100 DF77
Blackley Cl, Wat. 23 BT37
Blackmans Cl, Dart. 128 FJ88
Blackmans La, Warl. 162 EE114
Blackmans Yd E2 84 DU70
Cheshire St
Blackmead, Sev. 190 FE121
Blackmoor La, Wat. 23 BR43
Blackmore Av, Sthl. 79 CD74
Blackmore Cl, Grays 110 GC78
Blackmore Ct, Wal.Abb. 16 EG33
Blackmore Cres, Wok. 167 BB115
Blackmore Rd, Buck.H. 48 EL45
Blackmore Way, Uxb. 76 BK65
Blackmores Gro, Tedd. 117 CG93
Blackness La, Kes. 162 EK109
Blackness La, Wok. 166 AY119
Blackpool Gdns, Hayes 77 BS70
Blackpool Rd SE15 102 DV82
Blacks Rd W6 99 CW77
Queen Caroline St
Blackshaw Pl N1 84 DS66
Hertford Rd
Blackshaw Rd SW17 120 DC91
Blacksmith Cl, Ash. 172 CM119
Rectory La
Blacksmith Row, Slou. 93 BA77
Blacksmiths Cl, Rom. 70 EW58
Blacksmiths Hill, S.Croy. 160 DU113
Blacksmiths La, Cher. 134 BG101
Blacksmiths La, Orp. 146 EW99
Blacksmiths La, Rain. 89 FF67
Blacksmiths La, Stai. 134 BH97
Blacksmiths La (Denham), Uxb. 57 BC61
Blackstock Ms N4 65 DP61
Blackstock Rd
Blackstock Rd N4 65 DP61
Blackstock Rd N5 65 DP61
Blackstone Cl, Red. 184 DE134
Blackstone Est E8 84 DV66
Blackstone Rd NW2 63 CW64
Blackthorn Av, West Dr. 94 BN77
Blackthorn Cl, Wat. 7 BV32
Blackthorn Ct, Houns. 96 BY80
Blackthorn Dell, Slou. 92 AW76
Blackthorn Gro, Bexh. 106 EY83
Blackthorn St E3 85 EA70
Blackthorn Way, Brwd. 54 FX50
Blackthorne Av, Croy. 142 DW101
Blackthorne Cres, Slou. 93 BE82
Blackthorne Rd
Blackthorne Dr E4 47 ED49
Blackthorne Rd, Slou. 93 BE83
Blackthorne Rd, West. 178 EK116
Blacktree Ms SW9 101 DN83
Blackwall La SE10 205 J10
Blackwall La SE10 104 EE78
Blackwall Pier E14 205 H1
Blackwall Pier E14 86 EE73
Blackwall Tunnel E14 204 F1
Blackwall Tunnel E14 85 ED74
Blackwall Tunnel App SE10 205 H5
Blackwall Tunnel App SE10 104 EE75
Blackwall Tunnel Northern App E3 85 EA68
Blackwall Tunnel Northern App E14 85 EA68
Blackwall Way E14 204 E1
Blackwall Way E14 85 EC73
Blackwater Cl E7 68 EF63
Blackwater Cl, Rain. 89 FE71
Blackwater Rd, Sutt. 158 DB105
High St
Blackwater St SE22 122 DT85
Blackwell Cl E5 67 DX63
Blackwell Cl, Har. 41 CD52
Blackwell Dr, Wat. 24 BW44
Blackwell Gdns, Edg. 42 CN48
Blackwell Hall La, Chesh. 4 AW33
Blackwell Rd, Kings L. 6 BN29
Blackwood Cl, W.Byf. 152 BJ112
Blackwood Ct, Brox. 15 DZ26
Groom Rd
Blackwood St SE17 201 K10
Blackwood St SE17 102 DR78
Blade Ms SW15 99 CZ84
Deodar Rd
Bladen Cl, Wey. 153 BR107
Blades Cl, Lthd. 171 CK120
Blades Ct SW15 99 CZ84
Deodar Rd
Bladindon Dr, Bex. 126 EW87
Bladon Gdns, Har. 60 CB58
Blagdens Cl N14 45 DJ47
Blagdens La N14 45 DK47
Blagdon Rd SE13 123 EB86
Blagdon Rd, N.Mal. 139 CT98
Blagdon Wk, Tedd. 117 CJ93
Blagrove Rd W10 81 CY71
Blair Av NW9 62 CS59
Blair Av, Esher 136 CC103
Blair Cl N1 84 DQ65
Blair Cl, Hayes 95 BU77
Blair Cl, Sid. 125 ES85
Blair Dr, Sev. 191 FH123
Blair Rd, Slou. 74 AS74
Blair St E14 85 EC72
Blairderry Rd SW2 121 DL89
Blairhead Dr, Wat. 39 BV48
Blake Av, Bark. 87 ES67
Blake Cl W10 81 CW71
Blake Cl, Cars. 140 DE101
Blake Cl, Rain. 89 FF67
Blake Cl, Well. 105 ES81
Blake Gdns SW6 100 DB81
Blake Gdns, Dart. 108 FM84
Blake Hall Cres E11 68 EG60
Blake Hall Rd E11 68 EG59
Blake Hall Rd, Ong. 19 FG25
Blake Ho, Beck. 123 EA93
Blake Rd E16 86 EF70
Blake Rd N11 45 DJ52
Blake Rd, Croy. 142 DS103
Blake Rd, Mitch. 140 DE97
Blake St SE8 103 EA79
Watergate St
Blakeborough Dr, Rom. 52 FL54
Blakeden Dr, Esher 155 CF107
Blakehall Rd, Cars. 158 DF107
Blakeley Cotts SE10 103 ED75
Tunnel Av
Blakemore Rd SW16 121 DL90
Blakemore Rd, Th.Hth. 141 DM99
Blakemore Way, Belv. 106 EY76
Blakeney Av, Beck. 143 DZ95
Blakeney Cl E8 66 DU64
Ferncliff Rd
Blakeney Cl N20 44 DC46
Blakeney Cl NW1 83 DK66
Rossendale Way
Blakeney Cl, Epsom 156 CR111
Blakeney Rd, Beck. 123 DZ94
Blakenham Rd SW17 120 DF91
Blaker Ct SE7 104 EJ80
Fairlawn
Blaker Rd E15 85 EC67
Blakes Av, N.Mal. 139 CT99
Blake's Grn, W.Wick. 143 EC102
Blakes La, N.Mal. 139 CT99
Blakes Rd SE15 102 DS80
Blakes Ter, N.Mal. 139 CU99
Blakes Way, Til. 111 GJ82
Coleridge Rd
Blakesley Av W5 79 CJ72
Blakesley Wk SW20 139 CZ96
Kingston Rd
Blakesware Gdns N9 46 DR45
Blakewood Cl, Felt. 116 BW91
Blanch Cl SE15 102 DW80
Culmore Rd
Blanchard Cl SE9 124 EL90
Blanchard Way E8 84 DU65
Blanche La, Pot.B. 11 CT34
Blanche St E16 86 EF70
Blanchedowne SE5 102 DR84
Blanchland Rd, Mord. 140 DB99
Blanchmans Rd, Warl. 177 DY118
Bland St SE9 104 EK84
Blandfield Rd SW12 120 DG86
Blandford Av, Beck. 143 DY96
Blandford Av, Twick. 116 CB88
Blandford Cl N2 64 DC56
Blandford Cl, Croy. 141 DL104
Blandford Cl, Rom. 71 FB56
Blandford Cl, Slou. 92 AX76
Blandford Cl, Wok. 167 BB117
Blandford Ct, Slou. 92 AX76
Blandford Rd S
Blandford Cres E4 47 EC45
Blandford Rd W4 98 CS76
Blandford Rd W5 97 CK75
Blandford Rd, Beck. 142 DW96
Blandford Rd, Sthl. 96 CA77
Blandford Rd, Tedd. 117 CD92
Blandford Rd N, Slou. 92 AX76
Blandford Rd S, Slou. 92 AX76
Blandford Sq NW1 194 C5
Blandford Sq NW1 82 DE70
Blandford St W1 194 E8
Blandford St W1 82 DG71
Blandford Way, Hayes 78 BW72
Blaney Cres E6 87 EP69
Blanmerle Rd SE9 125 EP88
Blann Cl SE9 124 EK86
Blantyre St SW10 100 DD80
Blantyre Wk SW10 100 DD80
Blantyre St
Blashford NW3 82 DF66
Blashford St SE13 123 ED87
Blasker Wk E14 204 A10
Blasker Wk E14 103 EA78
Blattner Cl, Borwd. 26 CL42
Blawith Rd, Har. 61 CE56
Blaxland Ter (Cheshunt), Wal.Cr. 15 DX28
Davison Dr
Blaydon Cl N17 46 DV52
Blaydon Cl, Ruis. 59 BS59
Blaydon Wk N17 46 DV52
Blays Cl, Egh. 112 AW93
Blays La, Egh. 112 AV94
Bleak Hill La SE18 105 ET79
Blean Gro SE20 122 DW94
Bleasdale Av, Grnf. 79 CG68
Blechynden St W10 81 CX73
Bramley Rd
Bleddyn Cl, Sid. 126 EW86
Bledlow Cl SE28 88 EW73
Bledlow Ri, Grnf. 78 CC68
Bleeding Heart Yd EC1 196 E7
Blegborough Rd SW16 121 DJ93
Blencarn Cl, Wok. 166 AT116
Blendon Dr, Bex. 126 EX86
Blendon Path, Brom. 124 EF94
Blendon Rd, Bex. 126 EX86
Blendon Ter SE18 105 EQ78
Blendworth Way SE15 102 DS80
Daniel Gdns
Blenheim Av, Ilf. 69 EN58
Blenheim Cl N21 46 DQ46
Elm Pk Rd
Blenheim Cl SW20 139 CW97
Blenheim Cl, Dart. 128 FJ86
Blenheim Cl, Grnf. 79 CD68
Leaver Gdns
Blenheim Cl, Rom. 71 FC56
Blenheim Cl, Slou. 75 AZ74
Blenheim Cl, Upmin. 73 FS60
Blenheim Cl, Wall. 159 DJ108
Blenheim Cl, Wat. 40 BX45
Blenheim Cl, W.Byf. 151 BF113
Madeira Rd
Blenheim Ct N19 65 DL61
Marlborough Rd
Blenheim Ct, Sid. 125 ER90
Blenheim Cres W11 81 CY72
Blenheim Cres, Ruis. 59 BR61
Blenheim Cres, S.Croy. 160 DQ108
Blenheim Dr, Well. 105 ET81
Blenheim Gdns NW2 63 CW64
Blenheim Gdns SW2 121 DM86
Blenheim Gdns, Kings.T. 118 CP94
Blenheim Gdns, S.Croy. 160 DU112
Blenheim Gdns, S.Ock. 90 FP74
Blenheim Gdns, Wall. 159 DJ107
Blenheim Gdns, Wem. 62 CL62
Blenheim Gdns, Wok. 166 AV119
Blenheim Gro SE15 102 DU82
Blenheim Pk Rd, S.Croy. 160 DQ109
Blenheim Pas NW8 82 DC68
Blenheim Ter
Blenheim Ri N15 66 DT56
Talbot Rd
Blenheim Rd E6 86 EK69
Blenheim Rd E15 68 EE63
Blenheim Rd E17 67 DX55
Blenheim Rd NW8 82 DC68
Blenheim Rd SE20 122 DW94
Maple Rd
Blenheim Rd SW20 139 CW97
Blenheim Rd W4 98 CS76
Blenheim Rd, Abb.L. 7 BU33
Blenheim Rd, Barn. 27 CX41
Blenheim Rd, Brwd. 54 FU44
Blenheim Rd, Brom. 144 EL98
Blenheim Rd, Dart. 128 FJ86
Blenheim Rd, Epsom 156 CR111
Blenheim Rd, Har. 60 CB58
Blenheim Rd, Nthlt. 78 CB65
Blenheim Rd, Orp. 146 EW103
Blenheim Rd, Sid. 126 EW88
Blenheim Rd, Slou. 92 AX77
Blenheim Rd, Sutt. 140 DA104
Blenheim St W1 195 H9
Blenheim Ter NW8 82 DC68
Blenheim Way, Epp. 18 FA27
Blenheim Way, Islw. 97 CG81
Blenkarne Rd SW11 120 DF86
Bleriot Rd, Houns. 96 BW80
Blessbury Rd, Edg. 42 CQ53
Blessing Way, Bark. 88 EW69
Blessington Cl SE13 103 ED83
Blessington Rd SE13 103 ED83
Bletchingley Cl, Red. 185 DJ129
Bletchingley Cl, Th.Hth. 141 DP98
Bletchingley Rd, Gdse. 186 DU131
Bletchingley Rd (Bletchingley), Red. 185 DN133
Bletchingley Rd (South Merstham), Red. 185 DJ129
Bletchley Ct N1 197 K1
Bletchley Ct N1 84 DR68
Bletchley St N1 197 J1
Bletchley St N1 84 DQ68
Bletchmore Cl, Hayes 95 BR78
Bletsoe Wk N1 84 DQ68
Cropley St
Blewbury Ho SE2 106 EX75
Yarnton Way
Bligh Rd, Grav. 131 GG86
Blighs Rd, Sev. 191 FH125
Blinco La, Slou. 74 AY72
Blincoe Cl SW19 119 CX89
Blind La, Bans. 174 DE115
Blind La, Loug. 32 EE40
Blind La, Wal.Abb. 16 EJ33
Blindman's La (Cheshunt), Wal.Cr. 15 DX30
Bliss Cres SE13 103 EB82
Coldbath St
Blissett St SE10 103 EC81
Blisworth Cl, Hayes 78 BY70
Braunston Dr
Blithbury Rd, Dag. 88 EV65
Blithdale Rd SE2 106 EU77
Blithfield St W8 100 DB76
Blockhouse Rd, Grays 110 GC79
Blockley Rd, Wem. 61 CH61
Bloemfontein Av W12 81 CV74
Bloemfontein Rd W12 81 CV73
Blomfield Rd W9 82 DC71
Blomfield St EC2 197 L7
Blomfield St EC2 84 DR71
Blomfield Vil W2 82 DB71
Blomville Rd, Dag. 70 EY62
Blondel St SW11 100 DG82
Blondell Cl, West Dr. 94 BK79
Blondin Av W5 97 CJ77
Blondin St E3 85 EA68
Bloom Gro SE27 121 DP90
Bloom Pk Rd SW6 99 CZ80
Bloomburg St SW1 199 L9
Bloomfield Cl, Wok. 166 AS118
Bloomfield Cres, Ilf. 69 EP58
Bloomfield Pl W1 195 J10
Bloomfield Pl W1 83 DH73
Bloomfield Rd N6 64 DG58
Bloomfield Rd SE18 105 EP78
Bloomfield Rd, Brom. 144 EK99
Bloomfield Rd, Kings.T. 138 CL98
Bloomfield Rd (Cheshunt), Wal.Cr. 14 DQ25
Bloomfield Ter SW1 198 G10
Bloomfield Ter SW1 100 DG78
Bloomfield Ter, West. 189 ES125
Bloomhall Rd SE19 122 DR92
Bloomsbury Cl W5 80 CM73
Bloomsbury Cl, Epsom 156 CR110
Bloomsbury Ct WC1 196 A7
Bloomsbury Cl, Pnr. 60 BZ55
Bloomsbury Ho SW4 121 DK86
Bloomsbury Pl SW18 120 DC85
Fullerton Rd
Bloomsbury Pl WC1 196 A6
Bloomsbury Pl WC1 83 DL71
Bloomsbury Sq WC1 196 A7
Bloomsbury Sq WC1 83 DL71
Bloomsbury St WC1 195 N7
Bloomsbury St WC1 83 DK71
Bloomsbury Way WC1 195 P8
Bloomsbury Way WC1 83 DL72
Blore Cl SW8 101 DK81
Thessaly Rd
Blore Ct W1 195 M9
Blossom Cl W5 98 CL75
Almond Av
Blossom Cl, Dag. 88 EZ67
Blossom Cl, S.Croy. 160 DT106
Blossom La, Enf. 30 DQ39
Blossom Pl E1 197 N5
Blossom St E1 197 N6
Blossom St E1 84 DS70
Blossom Way, Uxb. 76 BM66
Blossom Way, West Dr. 94 BN77
Blossom Waye, Houns. 96 BY80
Blount St E14 85 DY71
Bloxam Gdns SE9 124 EL85
Bloxhall Rd E10 67 DZ60
Bloxham Cres, Hmptn. 136 BZ95
Bloxworth Cl, Wall. 141 DJ104
Blucher Rd SE5 102 DQ80
Blue Anchor All, Rich. 98 CL84
Kew Rd
Blue Anchor La SE16 202 C8
Blue Anchor La SE16 102 DU77
Blue Anchor La, Til. 111 GL77
Blue Anchor Yd E1 84 DU73
Blue Ball La, Egh. 113 AZ92
Blue Ball Yd SW1 199 K3
Blue Barn La, Wey. 152 BN111
Blue Cedars, Bans. 157 CX114
Blue Cedars Pl, Cob. 154 BX112
Bluebell Av E12 68 EL64
Bluebell Cl E9 84 DW67
Moulins Rd
Bluebell Cl SE26 122 DT91
Bluebell Cl, Orp. 145 EQ103
Bluebell Cl, Rom. 71 FE61
Bluebell Cl, Wall. 141 DH102
Bluebell Ct, Wok. 166 AX119
Bluebell Dr, Abb.L. 7 BT27
Bluebell Dr, Wal.Cr. 14 DR28
Bluebell Way, Ilf. 87 EP65
Blueberry Cl, Wdf.Grn. 48 EG51
Blueberry Gdns, Couls. 175 DM116
Blueberry La, Sev. 180 EW116
Bluebridge Av, Hat. 11 CZ27
Bluebridge Rd, Hat. 11 CY26
Bluefield Cl, Hmptn. 116 CA92
Bluegates, Epsom 157 CU108
Bluehouse La, Oxt. 188 EG127
Bluehouse Rd E4 48 EE48
Bluett Rd, St.Alb. 9 CK27
Bluewater Parkway (Bluewater), Green. 129 FS87
Blundel La, Cob. 154 CB114
Blundell Rd, Edg. 42 CR53
Blundell St N7 83 DL66
Blunden Cl, Dag. 70 EW60
Blunden Dr, Slou. 93 BB77
Blunesfield, Pot.B. 12 DD31
Blunt Rd, S.Croy. 160 DR106
Blunts Av, West Dr. 94 BN80
Blunts La, St.Alb. 8 BW27
Blunts Rd SE9 125 EN85
Blurton Rd E5 66 DW63
Blyth Cl E14 204 F8
Blyth Cl, Borwd. 26 CM39
Blyth Cl, Twick. 117 CF86
Grimwood Rd
Blyth Rd E17 67 DZ59
Blyth Rd SE28 88 EW73
Blyth Rd, Brom. 144 EF95
Blyth Rd, Hayes 95 BS75
Blyth Wk, Upmin. 73 FS58
Blyth Wd Pk, Brom. 144 EF95
Blyth Rd
Blythe Cl SE6 123 DZ87
Blythe Cl, Iver 75 BF72
Blythe Hill SE6 123 DZ87
Blythe Hill, Orp. 145 ET95
Blythe Hill La SE6 123 DZ87
Blythe Rd W14 99 CX76
Blythe St E2 84 DV69
Blythe Vale SE6 123 DZ88
Blyth's Wf E14 85 DY73
Narrow St
Blythswood Rd, Ilf. 70 EU60
Blythwood Rd N4 65 DL59
Blythwood Rd, Pnr. 40 BX53
Boades Ms NW3 64 DD63
New End
Boadicea St N1 83 DM67
Copenhagen St
Boakes Cl NW9 62 CQ56
Boakes Meadow, Sev. 165 FF111
Boar Cl, Chig. 50 EU50
Board Sch Rd, Wok. 167 AZ116
Boardman Av E4 31 EB43
Boardman Cl, Barn. 27 CY43
Boardwalk Pl E14 85 EC74
Boar's Head Yd, Brent. 97 CK80
Brent Way
Boat Lifter Way SE16 203 L8
Boathouse Wk SE15 102 DT80
Boathouse Wk, Rich. 98 CL81
Bob Anker Cl E13 86 EG69
Chesterton Rd
Bob Marley Way SE24 101 DN84
Mayall Rd
Bobbin Cl SW4 101 DJ83
Bobby Moore Way N10 44 DF52
Bobs La, Rom. 51 FG52
Bocketts La, Lthd. 171 CF124
Bockhampton Rd, Kings.T. 118 CM94
Bocking St E8 84 DV67
Boddicott Cl SW19 119 CY89
Bodell Cl, Grays 110 GB76
Bodiam Cl, Enf. 30 DR40
Bodiam Rd SW16 121 DK94
Bodle Av, Swans. 130 FY
Bodley Cl, Epp. 17 ET
Bodley Cl, N.Mal. 138 CS
Bodley Manor Way SW2 121 DN
Papworth Way
Bodley Rd, N.Mal. 138 CR1
Bodmin Cl, Har. 60 BZ
Bodmin Cl, Orp. 146 EW1
Bodmin Gro, Mord. 140 DB
Bodmin St SW18 120 DA
Bodnant Gdns SW20 139 CU
Bodney Rd E8 66 DV
Boeing Way, Sthl. 95 BV
Boevey Path, Belv. 106 EZ
Bogey La, Orp. 163 EN1
Bognor Gdns, Wat. 40 BW
Bowring Grn
Bognor Rd, Well. 106 EX
Bohemia Pl E8 84 DV
Bohun Gro, Barn. 28 DE
Boileau Par W5 80 CM
Boileau Rd
Boileau Rd SW13 99 CU
Boileau Rd W5 80 CM
Bois Hall Rd, Add. 152 BK1
Bois Hill, Chesh. 4 AS
Bolden St SE8 103 EB
Bolderwood Way, W.Wick. 143 EB1
Boldmere Rd, Pnr. 60 BW
Boleyn Av, Enf. 30 DV
Boleyn Av, Epsom 157 CV1
Boleyn Cl E17 67 EA
Boleyn Cl, Grays 110 FZ
Clifford Rd
Boleyn Cl, Loug. 32 EL
Roding Gdns
Boleyn Cl, Stai. 113 BE
Chertsey La
Boleyn Ct, Buck.H. 48 EG
Boleyn Dr, Ruis. 60 BX
Boleyn Dr, W.Mol. 136 BZ
Boleyn Gdns, Brwd. 55 GA
Boleyn Gdns, Dag. 89 FC
Boleyn Gdns, W.Wick. 143 EB1
Boleyn Gro, W.Wick. 143 EC1
Boleyn Rd E6 86 EK
Boleyn Rd E7 86 EG
Boleyn Rd N16 66 DS
Boleyn Wk, Lthd. 171 CF1
Boleyn Way, Barn. 28 DC
Boleyn Way, Ilf. 49 EQ
Boleyn Way, Swans. 130 FY
Bolina Rd SE16 202 G
Bolina Rd SE16 102 DW
Bolingbroke Gro SW11 100 DE
Bolingbroke Rd W14 99 CX
Bolingbroke Wk SW11 100 DD
Bolingbroke Way, Hayes 77 BR
Bolliger Ct NW10 80 CQ
Park Royal Rd
Bollo Br Rd W3 98 CP
Bollo La W3 98 CP
Bollo La W4 98 CQ
Bolney Gate SW7 198 B
Bolney St SW8 101 DM
Bolney Way, Felt. 116 BY
Bolsover Gro, Red. 185 DL12
Bolsover St W1 195 J
Bolsover St W1 83 DH7
Bolstead Rd, Mitch. 141 DH
Bolt Cellar La, Epp. 17 ES2
Bolt Ct EC4 196 E
Bolters La, Bans. 157 CZ1
Boltmore Cl NW4 63 CX5
Bolton Cl SE20 142 DU
Selby Rd
Bolton Cl, Chess. 155 CK10
Bolton Cres SE5 101 DP7
Bolton Gdns NW10 81 CX6
Bolton Gdns SW5 100 DB7
Bolton Gdns, Brom. 124 EF9
Bolton Gdns, Tedd. 117 CG9
Bolton Gdns Ms SW10 100 DB7
Bolton Rd E15 86 EF6
Bolton Rd N18 46 DT5
Bolton Rd NW8 82 DB6
Bolton Rd NW10 80 CS6
Bolton Rd W4 98 CQ8
Bolton Rd, Chess. 155 CK10
Bolton Rd, Har. 60 CC5
Bolton St W1 199 J
Bolton St W1 83 DH7
Bolton Wk N7 65 DM6
Durham Rd
Boltons, The SW10 100 DC7
Boltons, The, Wem. 61 CF6
Boltons, The, Wdf.Grn. 48 EG4
Boltons Cl, Wok. 168 BG11
Boltons La, Hayes 95 BQ8
Boltons La, Wok. 168 BG11
Boltons Pl SW5 100 DC7
Bombay St SE16 202 D
Bombay St SE16 102 DV7
Bombers La, West. 179 ER11
Bombers La, West. 179 ES12
Grays Rd
Bomer Cl, West Dr. 94 BN8
Bomore Rd W11 81 CX7
Bon Marche Ter Ms SE27 122 DS9
Gipsy Rd
Bonar Pl, Chis. 124 EL9
Bonar Rd SE15 102 DU8
Bonaventure Ct, Grav. 131 GM9
Bonchester Cl, Chis. 125 EN9
Bonchurch Cl, Sutt. 158 DB10
Bonchurch Rd W10 81 CY7
Bonchurch Rd W13 79 CH7
Bond Cl, Sev. 180 EX11
Bond Cl, West Dr. 76 BM7
Bond Ct EC4 197 K
Bond Ct EC4 84 DR7
Bond Gdns, Wall. 159 DJ10
Bond Rd, Mitch. 140 DE9
Bond Rd, Surb. 138 CM10
Bond Rd, Warl. 177 DX11
Bond St E15 68 EE6
Bond St W4 98 CS7
Bond St W5 79 CK7
Bond St, Egh. 112 AV92

Bond St, Grays 110 GC79
Bondfield Av, Hayes 77 BU69
Bondfield Rd E6 86 EL71
Lovage App
Bondfield Wk, Dart. 108 FM84
Bonding Yd Wk SE16 203 L5
Bondway SW8 101 DL79
Bone Mill La, Gdse. 187 DY134
Eastbourne Rd
Boneta Rd SE18 105 EM76
Bonfield Rd SE13 103 EC84
Bonham Gdns, Dag. 70 EX61
Bonham Rd SW2 121 DM85
Bonham Rd, Dag. 70 EX61
Bonheur Rd W4 98 CR75
Bonhill St EC2 197 L5
Bonhill St EC2 84 DR70
Boniface Gdns, Har. 40 CB52
Boniface Rd, Uxb. 59 BP62
Boniface Wk, Har. 40 CB52
Bonington Rd, Horn. 72 FK64
Bonner Hill Rd, Kings.T. 138 CM97
Bonner Rd E2 84 DW68
Bonner St E2 84 DW68
Bonner Wk, Grays 110 FZ76
Clifford Rd
Bonners Cl, Wok. 166 AY122
Bonnersfield Cl, Har. 61 CF58
Bonnersfield La, Har. 61 CG58
Bonnett Ms, Horn. 72 FL60
Bonneville Gdns SW4 121 DJ86
Bonney Gro (Cheshunt), Wal.Cr. 14 DU30
Bonney Way, Swan. 147 FE96
Bonnington Sq SW8 101 DM79
Bonnington Twr, Brom. 144 EL100
Bonningtons, Brwd. 55 GB48
Bonny St NW1 83 DJ66
Bonser Rd, Twick. 117 CF89
Bonsey Cl, Wok. 166 AY121
Bonsey La, Wok. 166 AY121
Bonseys La, Wok. 151 AZ110
Bonsor Dr, Tad. 173 CY122
Bonsor St SE5 102 DS80
Bonville Gdns NW4 63 CU56
Handowe Cl
Bonville Rd, Brom. 124 EF92
Book Ms WC2 195 N9
Bookbinders' Cotts N20 44 DF48
Manor Dr
Booker Cl E14 85 DZ71
Wallwood St
Booker Rd N18 46 DU50
Bookham Ct, Lthd. 170 BZ123
Church Rd
Bookham Ind Est, Lthd. 170 BZ123
Bookham Rd, Cob. 170 BW119
Boone Ct N9 46 DW48
Boone St SE13 104 EE84
Boones Rd SE13 104 EE84
Boord St SE10 205 J6
Boord St SE10 104 EE76
Boot St N1 197 M3
Boot St N1 84 DS69
Booth Cl E9 84 DV67
Victoria Pk Rd
Booth Cl SE28 88 EV73
Booth Dr, Stai. 114 BK93
Booth Rd NW9 42 CS54
Booth Rd, Croy. 141 DP103
Waddon New Rd
Boothby Rd N19 65 DK61
Booth's Ct (Hutton), Brwd. 55 GC44
Poplar Dr
Booth's Pl W1 195 L7
Bordars Rd W7 79 CE71
Bordars Wk W7 79 CE71
Borden Av, Enf. 30 DR44
Border Cres SE26 122 DV92
Border Gdns, Croy. 161 EB105
Border Rd SE26 122 DV92
Bordergate, Mitch. 140 DE95
Borders La, Loug. 33 EN42
Borderside, Slou. 74 AU72
Bordesley Rd, Mord. 140 DB98
Bordon Wk SW15 119 CU87
Boreas Wk N1 196 G1
Boreham Av E16 86 EG72
Boreham Cl E11 67 EC60
Hainault Rd
Boreham Holt, Borwd. 26 CM42
Boreham Rd N22 46 DQ54
Borehamwood Ind Pk, Borwd. 26 CR40
Borgard Rd SE18 105 EM77
Borkwood Pk, Orp. 163 ET105
Borkwood Way, Orp. 163 ES105
Borland Cl, Green. 129 FU85
Steele Av
Borland Rd SE15 102 DW84
Borland Rd, Tedd. 117 CH93
Bornedene, Pot.B. 11 CY31
Borneo St SW15 99 CW83
Borough High St SE1 201 H5
Borough High St SE1 102 DQ75
Borough Hill, Croy. 141 DP104
Borough Rd SE1 200 F6
Borough Rd SE1 101 DP76
Borough Rd, Islw. 97 CE81
Borough Rd, Kings.T. 138 CN95
Borough Rd, Mitch. 140 DE96
Borough Rd, West. 178 EK121
Borough Sq SE1 201 H5
Borough Way, Pot.B. 11 CY32
Borrett Cl SE17 102 DQ78
Penrose St
Borrodaile Rd SW18 120 DB86
Borrowdale Av, Har. 41 CG54
Borrowdale Cl, Egh. 113 BB94
Derwent Rd
Borrowdale Cl, Ilf. 68 EL56
Borrowdale Cl, S.Croy. 160 DT113
Borrowdale Ct, Enf. 30 DQ39
Borrowdale Dr, S.Croy. 160 DT112
Borthwick Ms E15 68 EE63
Borthwick Rd
Borthwick Rd E15 68 EE63
Borthwick Rd NW9 63 CT58
West Hendon Bdy
Borthwick St SE8 103 EA78
Borwick Av E17 67 DZ55
Bosanquet Cl, Uxb. 76 BK70
Bosbury Rd SE6 123 EC90
Boscastle Rd NW5 65 DH62
Bosco Cl, Orp. 163 ET105
Strickland Way
Boscobel Pl SW1 198 G8
Boscobel Pl SW1 100 DG77
Boscobel St NW8 194 A5
Boscobel St NW8 82 DD70
Boscombe Av E10 67 ED59
Boscombe Av, Grays 110 GD77
Boscombe Av, Horn. 72 FK60
Boscombe Cl E5 67 DY64
Boscombe Cl, Egh. 133 BC95
Boscombe Gdns SW16 121 DL93
Boscombe Rd SW17 120 DG93
Boscombe Rd SW19 140 DB95
Boscombe Rd W12 81 CU74
Boscombe Rd, Wor.Pk. 139 CW102
Bosgrove E4 47 EC46
Boshers Gdns, Egh. 113 AZ93
Boss St SE1 201 P4
Bostal Row, Bexh. 106 EZ83
Harlington Rd
Bostall Heath SE2 106 EW78
Bostall Hill SE2 106 EU78
Bostall La SE2 106 EV78
Bostall Manorway SE2 106 EV77
Bostall Pk Av, Bexh. 106 EY80
Bostall Rd, Orp. 126 EV94
Boston Gdns W4 98 CS79
Boston Gdns W7 97 CG77
Boston Gdns, Brent. 97 CG77
Boston Gro, Ruis. 59 BQ58
Boston Manor Rd, Brent. 97 CH77
Boston Pk Rd, Brent. 97 CJ78
Boston Pl NW1 194 D5
Boston Pl NW1 82 DF70
Boston Rd E6 86 EL69
Boston Rd E17 67 EA58
Boston Rd W7 79 CE74
Boston Rd, Croy. 141 DM100
Boston Rd, Edg. 42 CQ52
Boston St E2 84 DU68
Audrey St
Boston Vale W7 97 CG77
Bostonthorpe Rd W7 97 CE75
Bosun Cl E14 204 A4
Bosville Av, Sev. 190 FG123
Bosville Dr, Sev. 190 FG123
Bosville Rd, Sev. 190 FG123
Boswell Cl, Orp. 146 EW100
Killewarren Way
Boswell Cl (Shenley), Rad. 10 CL32
Boswell Ct WC1 196 A6
Boswell Path, Hayes 95 BT77
Croyde Av
Boswell Rd, Th.Hth. 142 DQ98
Boswell St WC1 196 A6
Boswell St WC1 83 DL71
Bosworth Cl E17 47 DZ53
Bosworth Cres, Rom. 52 FJ51
Bosworth Rd N11 45 DK51
Bosworth Rd W10 81 CY70
Bosworth Rd, Barn. 28 DA41
Bosworth Rd, Dag. 70 FA63
Botany Bay La, Chis. 145 EQ96
Botany Cl, Barn. 28 DE42
Botany Rd (Northfleet), Grav. 110 GA83
Botany Way, Purf. 108 FP78
Boteley Cl E4 47 ED47
Botery's Cross, Red. 185 DP133
Botha Rd E13 86 EH71
Botham Cl, Edg. 42 CQ52
Pavilion Way
Bothwell Cl E16 86 EF71
Bothwell Rd, Croy. 161 EC110
Bothwell St W6 99 CX79
Delorme St
Botley La, Chesh. 4 AU30
Botley Rd, Chesh. 4 AT30
Botolph All EC3 197 M10
Botolph La EC3 197 M10
Botsford Rd SW20 139 CY96
Bott Rd, Dart. 128 FM91
Bottom Ho Fm La, Ch.St.G. 36 AT45
Bottom La, Chesh. 4 AT34
Bottom La, Kings L. 22 BH35
Bottrells Cl, Ch.St.G. 36 AT47
Bottrells La, Ch.St.G. 36 AT47
Botts Ms W2 82 DA72
Chepstow Rd
Botts Pas W2 82 DA72
Chepstow Rd
Botwell Common Rd, Hayes 77 BR73
Botwell Cres, Hayes 77 BS72
Botwell La, Hayes 77 BS74
Boucher Cl, Tedd. 117 CF92
Boucher Dr, Grav. 131 GF90
Bouchier Wk, Rain. 89 FG65
Deere Av
Boughton Av, Brom. 144 EF101
Boughton Hall Av, Wok. 167 BF124
Boughton Rd SE28 105 ES76
Boughton Way, Amer. 20 AW38
Boulcott St E1 85 DX72
Boulevard, The SW17 120 DG89
Balham High Rd
Boulevard, The, Pnr. 60 CA56
Pinner Rd
Boulevard, The, Wat. 23 BR43
Boulevard 25 Retail Pk, Borwd. 26 CN41
Boulmer Rd, Uxb. 76 BJ69
Boulogne Rd, Croy. 142 DQ100
Boulter Gdns, Rain. 89 FG65
Boulthurst Way, Oxt. 188 EH132
Boulton Ho, Brent. 98 CL78
Green Dragon La
Boulton Rd, Dag. 70 EY62
Boultwood Rd E6 86 EL72
Bounce Hill (Navestock), Rom. 35 FH38
Mill La
Bounces La N9 46 DV47
Bounces Rd N9 46 DV46
Boundaries Rd SW12 120 DF89
Boundaries Rd, Felt. 116 BW88
Boundary Av E17 67 DZ59
Boundary Cl SE20 142 DU96
Haysleigh Gdns
Boundary Cl, Barn. 27 CZ39
Boundary Cl, Ilf. 69 ES63
Loxford La
Boundary Cl, Kings.T. 138 CP97
Boundary Cl, Sthl. 96 CA78
Boundary Dr, Brwd. 55 GE45
Boundary La E13 86 EK69
Boundary La SE17 102 DQ79
Boundary Pas E2 197 P4
Boundary Rd E13 86 EJ69
Boundary Rd E17 67 DZ59
Boundary Rd N9 30 DW44
Boundary Rd N22 65 DP55
Boundary Rd NW8 82 DB67
Boundary Rd SW19 120 DD93
Boundary Rd, Ashf. 114 BJ92
Boundary Rd, Bark. 87 EQ68
Boundary Rd, Cars. 159 DH107
Boundary Rd (Chalfont St. Peter), Ger.Cr. 36 AX52
Boundary Rd, Pnr. 60 BX58
Boundary Rd, Rom. 71 FG58
Boundary Rd, Sid. 125 ES85
Boundary Rd, Upmin. 72 FN62
Boundary Rd, Wall. 159 DH107
Boundary Rd, Wem. 62 CL62
Boundary Rd, Wok. 167 BA116
Boundary Row SE1 200 F4
Boundary St E2 197 P3
Boundary St E2 84 DT70
Boundary St, Erith 107 FF80
Boundary Way, Croy. 161 EA106
Boundary Way, Wat. 7 BV32
Boundary Way, Wok. 167 BA115
Boundary Yd, Wok. 167 BA116
Boundary Rd
Boundfield Rd SE6 124 EE90
Bounds Grn Rd N11 45 DJ51
Bounds Grn Rd N22 45 DJ51
Bourchier Cl, Sev. 191 FH126
Bourchier St W1 195 M10
Bourdon Pl W1 195 J10
Bourdon Rd SE20 142 DW96
Bourdon St W1 199 H1
Bourdon St W1 83 DH73
Bourke Cl NW10 80 CS65
Mayo Rd
Bourke Cl SW4 121 DL86
Bourke Hill, Couls. 174 DF118
Bourlet Cl W1 195 K7
Bourn Av N15 66 DR56
Bourn Av, Barn. 28 DD43
Bourn Av, Uxb. 76 BN70
Bournbrook Rd SE3 104 EK83
Bourne, The N14 45 DK46
Bourne, The, Hem.H. 5 BA27
Bourne Av N14 45 DL47
Bourne Av, Cher. 134 BG97
Bourne Av, Hayes 95 BQ76
Bourne Av, Ruis. 60 BW64
Bourne Cl, W.Byf. 152 BH113
Bourne Ct, Ruis. 59 BV64
Bourne Dr, Mitch. 140 DD96
Bourne End, Horn. 72 FN59
Bourne End Rd, Nthwd. 39 BS49
Bourne Est EC1 196 D6
Bourne Est EC1 83 DN71
Bourne Gdns E4 47 EB49
Bourne Gro, Ash. 171 CK119
Bourne Hill N13 45 DL46
Bourne Ind Pk, Dart. 127 FE85
Bourne Rd
Bourne La, Cat. 176 DR121
Bourne Mead, Bex. 127 FD85
Bourne Meadow, Egh. 133 BB98
Bourne Pk Cl, Ken. 176 DS115
Bourne Pl W4 98 CR78
Dukes Av
Bourne Rd E7 68 EF62
Bourne Rd N8 65 DL58
Bourne Rd, Bex. 127 FB86
Bourne Rd, Brom. 144 EK98
Bourne Rd, Bushey 24 CA43
Bourne Rd, Dart. 127 FC86
Bourne Rd, Grav. 131 GM89
Bourne Rd, Red. 185 DJ130
Bourne Rd, Vir.W. 132 AX99
Bourne St SW1 198 F9
Bourne St SW1 100 DG77
Bourne St, Croy. 141 DP103
Waddon New Rd
Bourne Ter W2 82 DB71
Bourne Vale, Brom. 144 EG101
Bourne Vw, Grnf. 79 CF65
Bourne Vw, Ken. 176 DR115
Bourne Way, Add. 152 BJ106
Bourne Way, Brom. 144 EF103
Bourne Way, Epsom 156 CQ105
Bourne Way, Sutt. 157 CZ106
Bourne Way, Swan. 147 FC97
Bourne Way, Wok. 166 AX122
Bournebridge Cl, Brwd. 55 GE45
Bournebridge La, Rom. 50 EZ45
Bournefield Rd, Whyt. 176 DT118
Godstone Rd
Bournehall Av, Bushey 24 CA43
Bournehall La, Bushey 24 CA44
Bournehall Rd, Bushey 24 CA44
Bournemead Av, Nthlt. 77 BU68
Bournemead Cl, Nthlt. 77 BU68
Bournemead Way, Nthlt. 77 BV68
Bournemouth Cl SE15 102 DU82
Bournemouth Rd SE15 102 DU82
Bournemouth Rd SW19 140 DA95
Bourneside, Vir.W. 132 AU101
Bourneside Cres N14 45 DK46
Bourneside Gdns SE6 123 EC92
Bourneside Rd, Add. 152 BK105
Bournevale Rd SW16 121 DL91
Bournewood Rd SE18 106 EU80
Bournewood Rd, Orp. 146 EV101
Bournville Rd SE6 123 EA87
Bournwell Cl, Barn. 28 DF41
Bourton Cl, Hayes 77 BU74
Avondale Dr
Bousfield Rd SE14 103 DX82
Bousley Ri, Cher. 151 BD108
Boutflower Rd SW11 100 DE84
Bouverie Gdns, Har. 61 CK58
Bouverie Gdns, Pur. 159 DL114
Bouverie Ms N16 66 DS61
Bouverie Rd
Bouverie Pl W2 194 A8
Bouverie Pl W2 82 DD72
Bouverie Rd N16 66 DS61
Bouverie Rd, Couls. 174 DG118
Bouverie Rd, Har. 60 CC58
Bouverie St EC4 196 E9
Bouverie St EC4 83 DN72
Bouverie Way, Slou. 92 AY78
Bouvier Rd, Enf. 30 DW38
Boveney Rd SE23 123 DX87
Bovey Way, S.Ock. 91 FV71
Bovill Rd SE23 123 DX87
Bovingdon Av, Wem. 80 CN65
Bovingdon Cl N19 65 DJ61
Junction Rd
Bovingdon Cres, Wat. 8 BX34
Bovingdon La NW9 42 CS53
Bovingdon Rd SW6 100 DB81
Bovingdon Sq, Mitch. 141 DL98
Leicester Av
Bow Arrow La, Dart. 128 FN86
Bow Br Est E3 85 EB69
Bow Chyd EC4 197 J9
Bow Common La E3 85 DY70
Bow Ind Pk E15 85 EA66
Bow La EC4 197 J9
Bow La EC4 84 DQ72
Bow La N12 44 DC53
Bow La, Mord. 139 CY100
Bow Rd E3 85 DZ69
Bow St E15 68 EE64
Bow St WC2 196 A9
Bow St WC2 83 DL72
Bowater Cl NW9 62 CR57
Bowater Cl SW2 121 DL86
Bowater Pl SE3 104 EH80
Bowater Ridge, Wey. 153 BR110
Bowater Rd SE18 104 EK76
Bowden Cl, Felt. 115 BS88
Bowden Dr, Horn. 72 FL60
Bowden St SE11 101 DN78
Bowditch SE8 203 M10
Bowditch SE8 103 DZ78
Bowdon Rd E17 67 EA59
Bowen Dr SE21 122 DS90
Bowen Rd, Har. 60 CC59
Bowen St E14 85 EB72
Bowens Wd, Croy. 161 DZ109
Bower Av SE10 104 EE81
Bower Cl, Nthlt. 78 BW68
Bower Cl, Rom. 51 FD52
Bower Ct, Epp. 18 EU32
Bower Ct, Wok. 167 BB116
Princess Rd
Bower Fm Rd (Havering-atte-Bower), Rom. 51 FC48
Bower Hill, Epp. 18 EU32
Bower Hill Ind Est, Epp. 18 EU32
Bower La (Eynsford), Dart. 148 FL104
Bower Rd, Swan. 127 FG94
Bower St E1 85 DX72
Bower Ter, Epp. 18 EU32
Bower Hill
Bower Vale, Epp. 18 EU32
Bowerdean St SW6 100 DB81
Bowerman Av SE14 103 DY79
Bowerman Rd, Grays 111 GG77
Bowers Av, Grav. 131 GF91
Bowers Rd, Sev. 165 FF111
Bowers Wk E6 87 EM72
Bowes Cl, Sid. 126 EV86
Bowes Rd N11 45 DH50
Bowes Rd N13 45 DL50
Bowes Rd W3 80 CS73
Bowes Rd, Dag. 70 EW63
Bowes Rd, Stai. 113 BE92
Bowes Rd, Walt. 135 BV103
Bowfell Rd W6 99 CW79
Bowford Av, Bexh. 106 EY81
Bowhay, Brwd. 55 GA47
Bowhill Cl SW9 101 DN80
Bowie Cl SW4 121 DK87
Bowl Ct EC2 197 N5
Bowl Ct EC2 84 DS70
Bowland Rd SW4 101 DK84
Bowland Rd, Wdf.Grn. 48 EJ51
Bowland Yd SW1 198 E5
Bowlers Orchard, Ch.St.G. 36 AU48
Bowles Grn, Enf. 30 DV36
Bowles Rd SE1 102 DU79
Old Kent Rd
Bowley Cl SE19 122 DT93
Bowley La SE19 122 DT92
Bowling Cl, Uxb. 76 BM67
Birch Cres
Bowling Ct, Wat. 23 BU42
Bowling Grn Cl SW15 119 CV87
Bowling Grn La EC1 196 E4
Bowling Grn La EC1 83 DN70
Bowling Grn Pl SE1 201 K4
Bowling Grn Pl SE1 102 DR75
Bowling Grn Rd, Wok. 150 AS109
Bowling Grn Row SE18 105 EM76
Samuel St
Bowling Grn St SE11 101 DN79
Bowling Grn Wk N1 197 M2
Bowls, The, Chig. 49 ES49
Bowls Cl, Stan. 41 CH50
Bowman Av E16 86 EF73
Bowman Ms SW18 119 CZ88
Bowmans Cl W13 79 CH74
Bowmans Cl, Pot.B. 12 DD32
Bowmans Grn, Wat. 24 BX36
Bowmans Lea SE23 122 DW87
Bowmans Meadow, Wall. 141 DH104
Bowmans Ms E1 84 DU72
Hooper St
Bowmans Ms N7 65 DL62
Seven Sisters Rd
Bowmans Pl N7 65 DL62
Holloway Rd
Bowmans Rd, Dart. 127 FF87
Bowman's Trd Est NW9 62 CM55
Westmoreland Rd
Bowmead SE9 125 EM89
Bowmont Cl, Brwd. 55 GB44
Bowmore Wk NW1 83 DK66
St. Paul's Cres
Bown Cl, Til. 111 GH82
Bowness Cl E8 84 DT65
Beechwood Rd
Bowness Cres SW15 118 CS92
Bowness Dr, Houns. 96 BY84
Bowness Rd SE6 123 EB87
Bowness Rd, Bexh. 107 FB82
Bowness Way, Horn. 71 FG64
Bowood Rd SW11 100 DG84
Bowood Rd, Enf. 31 DX40
Bowring Grn, Wat. 40 BW50
Bowrons Av, Wem. 79 CK66
Bowry Dr, Stai. 113 AZ86
Bowsley Ct, Felt. 115 BU88
Highfield Rd
Bowsprit, The, Cob. 170 BW115
Bowstridge La, Ch.St.G. 36 AW51
Bowyer Cl E6 87 EM71
Bowyer Cres (Denham), Uxb. 57 BF58
Bowyer Pl SE5 102 DR80
Bowyer St SE5 102 DQ80
Bowyers Cl, Ash. 172 CM118
Box La, Bark. 88 EV68
Box Ridge Av, Pur. 159 DM112
Boxall Rd SE21 122 DS86
Boxford Cl, S.Croy. 161 DX112
Boxgrove Rd SE2 106 EW76
Boxhill Rd, Dor. 182 CL133
Boxhill Rd, Tad. 182 CP131
Boxley Rd, Mord. 140 DC98
Boxley St E16 205 P3
Boxley St E16 86 EH74
Boxmoor Rd, Har. 61 CH56
Boxmoor Rd, Rom. 51 FC50
Boxoll Rd, Dag. 70 EZ63
Boxted Cl, Buck.H. 48 EL46
Boxtree La, Har. 40 CC53
Boxtree Rd, Har. 41 CD52
Boxtree Wk, Orp. 146 EX102
Boxwood Cl, West Dr. 94 BM75
Hawthorne Cres
Boxwood Way, Warl. 177 DX117
Boxworth Cl N12 44 DD50
Boxworth Gro N1 83 DM67
Richmond Av
Boyard Rd SE18 105 EP78
Boyce Cl, Borwd. 26 CL39
Boyce St SE1 200 C3
Boyce Way E13 86 EG70
Boycroft Av NW9 62 CQ58
Boyd Av, Sthl. 78 BZ74
Boyd Cl, Kings.T. 118 CN94
Crescent Rd
Boyd Rd SW19 120 DD93
Boyd St E1 84 DU72
Boydell Ct NW8 82 DD66
St. John's Wd Pk
Boyfield St SE1 200 G5
Boyfield St SE1 101 DP75
Boyland Rd, Brom. 124 EF92
Boyle Av, Stan. 41 CG51
Boyle Cl, Uxb. 76 BM68
Boyle Fm Island, T.Ditt. 137 CG100
Boyle Fm Rd, T.Ditt. 137 CG100
Boyle St W1 195 K10
Boyne Av NW4 63 CX56
Boyne Rd SE13 103 EC83
Boyne Rd, Dag. 70 FA62
Boyne Ter Ms W11 81 CZ74
Boyseland Ct, Edg. 42 CQ47
Boyson Rd SE17 102 DR79
Boyton Cl E1 85 DX70
Stayner's Rd
Boyton Cl N8 65 DL55
Boyton Rd N8 65 DL55
Brabant Ct EC3 197 M10
Brabant Rd N22 45 DM54
Brabazon Av, Wall. 159 DL108
Brabazon Rd, Houns. 96 BW80
Brabazon Rd, Nthlt. 78 CA68
Brabazon St E14 85 EB72
Brabourn Gro SE15 102 DW82
Brabourne Cl SE19 122 DS92
Brabourne Cres, Bexh. 106 EZ79
Brabourne Hts NW7 42 CS48
Brabourne Ri, Beck. 143 EC99
Brace Cl (Cheshunt), Wal.Cr. 13 DP25
Bracewell Av, Grnf. 61 CF64
Bracewell Rd W10 81 CW71
Bracewood Gdns, Croy. 142 DT104
Bracey Ms N4 65 DL61
Bracey St
Bracey St N4 65 DL61
Bracken, The E4 47 EC47
Hortus Rd
Bracken Av SW12 120 DG86
Bracken Av, Croy. 143 EB104
Bracken Cl E6 87 EM71
Bracken Cl, Borwd. 26 CP39
Bracken Cl, Lthd. 170 BZ124
Bracken Cl, Sun. 115 BT93
Cavendish Rd
Bracken Cl, Twick. 116 CA87
Hedley Rd
Bracken Cl, Wok. 167 AZ118
Bracken Dr, Chig. 49 EP51
Bracken End, Islw. 117 CD85
Bracken Gdns SW13 99 CU82
Bracken Hill Cl, Brom. 144 EF95
Bracken Hill La
Bracken Hill La, Brom. 144 EF95
Bracken Ind Est, Ilf. 49 ET52
Bracken Ms E4 47 EC47
Hortus Rd
Bracken Ms, Rom. 70 FA58
Bracken Path, Epsom 156 CP113
Bracken Way, Wok. 150 AT110
Brackenbridge Dr, Ruis. 60 BX62
Brackenbury Gdns W6 99 CV76
Brackenbury Rd N2 64 DC55
Brackenbury Rd W6 99 CV76
Brackendale N21 45 DM47
Brackendale, Pot.B. 12 DA33
Brackendale Cl, Houns. 96 CB81
Brackendale Gdns, Upmin. 72 FQ63
Brackendene, Dart. 127 FE91
Brackendene, St.Alb. 8 BZ30
Brackendene Cl, Wok. 167 BA115

Brackenfield Cl E5 66 DV63
Tiger Way
Brackenforde, Slou. 92 AW75
Brackenhill, Cob. 154 CA111
Brackens, The, Enf. 46 DS45
Brackens, The, Orp. 164 EU106
Brackens Dr, Brwd. 54 FW50
Brackenwood, Sun. 135 BU95
Brackley, Wey. 153 BR106
Brackley Cl, Wall. 159 DL108
Brackley Rd W4 98 CS78
Brackley Rd, Beck. 123 DZ94
Brackley Sq, Wdf.Grn. 48 EK52
Brackley St EC1 197 H6
Brackley Ter W4 98 CS78
Bracklyn Cl N1 84 DR68
Parr St
Bracklyn Ct N1 84 DR68
Wimbourne St
Bracklyn St N1 84 DR68
Bracknell Cl N22 45 DN53
Bracknell Gdns NW3 64 DB63
Bracknell Gate NW3 64 DB64
Bracknell Way NW3 64 DB63
Bracondale, Esher 154 CC107
Bracondale Rd SE2 106 EU77
Brad St SE1 200 E3
Bradbery, Rick. 37 BD50
Bradbourne Pk Rd, Sev. 190 FG123
Bradbourne Rd, Bex. 126 FA87
Bradbourne Rd, Grays 110 GB79
Bradbourne Rd, Sev. 191 FH122
Bradbourne St SW6 100 DA82
Bradbourne Vale Rd, Sev. 190 FF122
Bradbury Cl, Borwd. 26 CP39
Bradbury Cl, Sthl. 96 BZ77
Bradbury Gdns, Slou. 56 AX63
Bradbury Ms N16 66 DS64
Bradbury St
Bradbury St N16 66 DS64
Braddock Cl, Islw. 97 CF83
Braddon Rd, Rich. 98 CM83
Braddyll St SE10 104 EE78
Braden St W9 82 DB70
Shirland Rd
Bradenham Av, Well. 106 EU84
Bradenham Cl SE17 102 DR79
Bradenham Rd, Har. 61 CH56
Bradenham Rd, Hayes 77 BS69
Bradenhurst Cl, Cat. 186 DT126
Bradfield Cl, Wok. 166 AY118
Bradfield Dr, Bark. 70 EU64
Bradfield Rd E16 205 N4
Bradfield Rd E16 104 EG75
Bradfield Rd, Ruis. 60 BY64
Bradford Cl N17 46 DS51
Commercial Rd
Bradford Cl SE26 122 DV91
Coombe Rd
Bradford Cl, Brom. 145 EM102
Bradford Dr, Epsom 157 CT107
Bradford Rd W3 98 CS75
Warple Way
Bradford Rd, Ilf. 69 ER60
Bradford Rd, Rick. 37 BC45
Bradgate (Cuffley), Pot.B. 13 DK27
Bradgate Cl (Cuffley), Pot.B. 13 DK28
Bradgate Rd SE6 123 EA86
Brading Cres E11 68 EH61
Brading Rd SW2 121 DM87
Brading Rd, Croy. 141 DM100
Bradiston Rd W9 81 CZ69
Bradleigh Av, Grays 110 GC77
Bradley Cl N7 83 DM65
Sutterton St
Bradley Cl, Sutt. 158 DA110
Station Rd
Bradley Gdns W13 79 CH72
Bradley Ms SW17 120 DF88
Bellevue Rd
Bradley Rd N22 45 DM54
Bradley Rd SE19 122 DQ93
Bradley Rd, Enf. 31 DY38
Bradley Rd, Wal.Abb. 31 EC40
Sewardstone Rd
Bradley Stone Rd E6 87 EM71
Bradley's Cl N1 83 DN68
White Lion St
Bradman Row, Edg. 42 CQ52
Pavilion Way
Bradmead SW8 101 DH80
Bradmore Grn, Couls. 175 DM118
Coulsdon Rd
Bradmore Grn, Hat. 11 CY26
Bradmore Ho E1 84 DW71
Bradmore La, Hat. 11 CW26
Bradmore Pk Rd W6 99 CV76
Bradmore Way, Couls. 175 DL117
Bradmore Way, Hat. 11 CY26
Bradshaw Cl SW19 120 DA93
Bradshaw Rd, Wat. 24 BW39
Bradshawe Waye, Uxb. 76 BL71
Bradshaws Cl SE25 142 DU97
Bradstock Rd E9 85 DX65
Bradstock Rd, Epsom 157 CU106
Bradwell Av, Dag. 70 FA61
Bradwell Cl E18 68 EF56
Bradwell Cl, Horn. 89 FH65
Bradwell Grn, Brwd. 55 GC44
Bradwell Ms N18 46 DU49
Lyndhurst Rd
Bradwell Rd, Buck.H. 48 EL46
Bradwell St E1 85 DX69
Brady Av, Loug. 33 EQ40
Brady St E1 84 DV70
Bradymead E6 87 EP72
Warwall
Braemar Av N22 45 DL53
Braemar Av NW10 62 CR62
Braemar Av SW19 120 DA89
Braemar Av, Bexh. 107 FC84
Braemar Av, S.Croy. 160 DQ109
Braemar Av, Th.Hth. 141 DN97
Braemar Av, Wem. 79 CK66
Braemar Gdns NW9 42 CR53
Braemar Gdns, Horn. 72 FN58
Braemar Gdns, Sid. 125 ER90
Braemar Gdns, W.Wick. 143 EC102
Braemar Rd E13 86 EF70
Braemar Rd N15 66 DS57
Braemar Rd, Brent. 98 CL79
Braemar Rd, Wor.Pk. 139 CV104
Braes St N1 83 DP66
Braeside, Add. 152 BH111
Braeside, Beck. 123 EA92
Braeside Av SW19 139 CY95
Braeside Av, Sev. 190 FF124
Braeside Cl, Pnr. 40 CA52
The Av
Braeside Cl, Sev. 190 FF123
Braeside Cres, Bexh. 107 FC84
Braeside Rd SW16 121 DJ94
Braesyde Cl, Belv. 106 EZ77
Brafferton Rd, Croy. 160 DQ105
Braganza St SE17 200 F10
Braganza St SE17 101 DP78
Bragg Cl, Dag. 88 EV65
Porters Av
Bragmans La, Hem.H. 5 BB34
Bragmans La, Rick. 5 BE33
Braham St E1 84 DT72
Braid, The, Chesh. 4 AS30
Braid Av W3 80 CS72
Braid Cl, Felt. 116 BZ89
Braidwood Rd SE6 123 ED88
Braidwood St SE1 201 M3
Brailsford Cl, Mitch. 120 DE94
Brailsford Rd SW2 121 DN85
Brainton Av, Felt. 115 BV87
Braintree Av, Ilf. 68 EL56
Braintree Rd, Dag. 70 FA62
Braintree Rd, Ruis. 59 BV63
Braintree St E2 84 DW69
Braithwaite Av, Rom. 70 FA59
Braithwaite Gdns, Stan. 41 CJ53
Braithwaite Rd, Enf. 31 DZ41
Brakefield Rd, Grav. 130 GB93
Brakey Hill, Red. 186 DS134
Bramah Grn SW9 101 DN81
Bramalea Cl N6 64 DG58
Bramall Cl E15 68 EF64
Idmiston Rd
Bramber Ct, Brent. 98 CL77
Sterling Pl
Bramber Rd N12 44 DE50
Bramber Rd W14 99 CZ79
Bramble Av, Dart. 129 FW90
Bramble Banks, Cars. 158 DG109
Bramble Cl, Croy. 161 EA105
Bramble Cl, Shep. 135 BR98
Halliford Cl
Bramble Cl, Stan. 41 CK52
Bramble Cl, Uxb. 76 BM71
Bramble Cl, Wat. 7 BU34
Bramble Cft, Erith 107 FC77
Bramble Gdns W12 81 CT73
Wallflower St
Bramble La, Amer. 20 AS41
Bramble La, Hmptn. 116 BZ93
Bramble La, Sev. 191 FH128
Bramble La, Upmin. 90 FQ67
Bramble Mead, Ch.St.G. 36 AU48
Bramble Ri, Cob. 170 BW115
Bramble Wk, Epsom 156 CP114
Bramble Way, Wok. 167 BF124
Brambleacres Cl, Sutt. 158 DA108
Bramblebury Rd SE18 105 EQ78
Brambledene Cl, Wok. 166 AW118
Brambledown, Stai. 134 BG95
Brambledown Cl, W.Wick. 144 EE99
Brambledown Rd, Cars. 158 DG108
Brambledown Rd, S.Croy. 160 DS108
Brambledown Rd, Wall. 159 DH108
Bramblefield Cl, Long. 149 FX97
Brambles, The, Chig. 49 EQ50
Clayside
Brambles, The, Wal.Cr. 15 DX31
Brambles, The, West Dr. 94 BL77
Brambles Cl, Cat. 176 DS122
Brambles Cl, Islw. 97 CH80
Brambles Fm Dr, Uxb. 76 BN69
Bramblewood, Red. 185 DH129
Bramblewood Cl, Cars. 140 DE102
Brambling Cl, Bushey 24 BY42
Bramblings, The E4 47 ED49
Bramcote Av, Mitch. 140 DF98
Bramcote Ct, Mitch. 140 DF98
Bramcote Av
Bramcote Gro SE16 202 F10
Bramcote Gro SE16 102 DW78
Bramcote Rd SW15 99 CV84
Bramdean Cres SE12 124 EG88
Bramdean Gdns SE12 124 EG88
Bramerton Rd, Beck. 143 DZ97
Bramerton St SW3 100 DE79
Bramfield, Wat. 8 BY34
Garston La
Bramfield Ct N4 66 DQ61
Queens Dr
Bramfield Rd SW11 120 DE86
Bramford Ct N14 45 DK47
Bramford Rd SW18 100 DC84
Bramham Gdns SW5 100 DB78
Bramham Gdns, Chess. 155 CK105
Bramhope La SE7 104 EH79
Bramlands Cl SW11 100 DE83
Bramleas, Wat. 23 BT42
Bramley Av, Couls. 175 DJ115
Bramley Cl E17 47 DY54
Bramley Cl N14 29 DH43
Bramley Cl, Cher. 134 BH102
Bramley Cl, Grav. 131 GF94
Bramley Cl, Hayes 77 BU73
Orchard Rd
Bramley Cl, Orp. 145 EP102
Bramley Cl, S.Croy. 159 DP106
Bramley Cl, Stai. 114 BJ93
Bramley Cl, Swan. 147 FE98
Bramley Cl, Twick. 116 CC86
Bramley Ct, Wat. 7 BV31
Orchard Av
Bramley Ct, Well. 106 EV81
Bramley Cres SW8 101 DK80
Pascal St
Bramley Cres, Ilf. 69 EN58
Bramley Gdns, Wat. 40 BW50
Bramley Hill, S.Croy. 159 DP106
Bramley Pl, Dart. 107 FG84
Bramley Rd N14 29 DH43
Bramley Rd W5 97 CJ76
Bramley Rd W10 81 CX73
Bramley Rd, Sutt. 158 DD106
Bramley Rd (Cheam), Sutt. 157 CX109
Bramley Shaw, Wal.Abb. 16 EF33
Bramley Way, Ash. 172 CM117
Bramley Way, Houns. 116 BZ85
Bramley Way, W.Wick. 143 EB103
Brampton Cl E5 66 DV61
Brampton Cl (Cheshunt), Wal.Cr. 14 DU28
Brampton Gdns N15 66 DQ57
Brampton Rd
Brampton Gdns, Walt. 154 BW106
Brampton Gro NW4 63 CV56
Brampton Gro, Har. 61 CG56
Brampton Gro, Wem. 62 CN60
Brampton La NW4 63 CW56
Brampton Pk Rd N22 65 DN55
Brampton Rd E6 86 EK69
Brampton Rd N15 66 DQ57
Brampton Rd NW9 62 CN56
Brampton Rd SE2 106 EW79
Brampton Rd, Bexh. 106 EX80
Brampton Rd, Croy. 142 DT101
Brampton Rd, Uxb. 77 BP68
Brampton Rd, Wat. 39 BU48
Brampton Ter, Borwd. 26 CN38
Bramshaw Gdns, Wat. 40 BX50
Bramshaw Ri, N.Mal. 138 CS100
Bramshaw Rd E9 85 DX65
Bramshill Cl, Chig. 49 ES50
Tine Rd
Bramshill Gdns NW5 65 DH62
Bramshill Rd NW10 81 CT68
Bramshot Av SE7 104 EG79
Bramshot Way, Wat. 39 BU47
Bramston Cl, Ilf. 49 ET51
Bramston Rd NW10 81 CU68
Bramston Rd SW17 120 DC90
Bramwell Cl, Sun. 136 BX96
Bramwell Ms N1 83 DM67
Brancaster Dr NW7 43 CT52
Brancaster La, Pur. 160 DQ112
Brancaster Pl, Loug. 33 EM41
Brancaster Rd E12 69 EM63
Brancaster Rd SW16 121 DL90
Brancaster Rd, Ilf. 69 ER58
Brancepeth Gdns, Buck.H. 48 EG47
Branch Hill NW3 64 DC62
Branch Pl N1 84 DR67
Branch Rd E14 85 DY73
Branch Rd, Ilf. 50 EV50
Branch Rd (Park St), St.Alb. 9 CD27
Branch St SE15 102 DS80
Brancker Cl, Wall. 159 DL108
Brown Cl
Brancker Rd, Har. 61 CK55
Brancroft Way, Enf. 31 DY39
Brand St SE10 103 EC80
Brandlehow Rd SW15 99 CZ84
Brandon Cl, Grays 110 FZ75
Brandon Cl (Cheshunt), Wal.Cr. 14 DS26
Brandon Est SE17 101 DP79
Brandon Gros Av, S.Ock. 91 FW69
Brandon Ms EC2 84 DR71
Moor La
Brandon Rd E17 67 EC55
Brandon Rd N7 83 DL66
Brandon Rd, Dart. 128 FN87
Brandon Rd, Sthl. 96 BZ78
Brandon Rd, Sutt. 158 DB105
Brandon St SE17 201 J9
Brandon St SE17 102 DQ77
Brandon St, Grav. 131 GH87
Brandram Rd SE13 104 EE83
Brandreth Rd E6 87 EM72
Brandreth Rd SW17 121 DH89
Brandries, The, Wall. 141 DK104
Brands Rd, Slou. 93 BB79
Brandville Gdns, Ilf. 69 EP56
Brandville Rd, West Dr. 94 BL75
Brandy Way, Sutt. 158 DA108
Branfill Rd, Upmin. 72 FP61
Brangbourne Rd, Brom. 123 EC92
Brangton Rd SE11 101 DM78
Brangwyn Cres SW19 140 DD95
Branksea St SW6 99 CY80
Branksome Av N18 46 DT50
Branksome Cl, Walt. 136 BX103
Branksome Rd SW2 121 DL85
Branksome Rd SW19 140 DA95
Branksome Way, Har. 62 CL58
Branksome Way, N.Mal. 138 CQ95
Bransby Rd, Chess. 156 CL107
Branscombe Gdns N21 45 DN45
Branscombe St SE13 103 EB83
Bransdale Cl NW6 82 DB67
West End La
Bransell Cl, Swan. 147 FC100
Bransgrove Rd, Edg. 42 CM53
Branston Cres, Orp. 145 ER102
Branstone Rd, Rich. 98 CM81
Branton Rd, Green. 129 FT86
Brants Wk W7 79 CE70
Brantwood Av, Erith 107 FC80
Brantwood Av, Islw. 97 CG84
Brantwood Cl E17 67 EB55
Brantwood Cl, W.Byf. 152 BG113
Brantwood Gdns
Brantwood Ct, W.Byf. 151 BF113
Brantwood Dr
Brantwood Dr, W.Byf. 151 BF113
Brantwood Gdns, Enf. 29 DL42
Brantwood Gdns, Ilf. 68 EL56
Brantwood Gdns, W.Byf. 151 BF113
Brantwood Rd N17 46 DU51
Brantwood Rd SE24 122 DQ85
Brantwood Rd, Bexh. 107 FB82
Brantwood Rd, S.Croy. 160 DQ109
Brantwood Way, Orp. 146 EW97
Brasenose Dr SW13 99 CW79
Brasher Cl, Grnf. 61 CD64
Brass Tally All SE16 203 J5
Brassey Cl, Felt. 115 BU88
Brassey Cl, Oxt. 188 EF129
Westerham Rd
Brassey Hill, Oxt. 188 EG130
Brassey Rd NW6 81 CZ65
Brassey Rd, Oxt. 188 EF130
Brassey Sq SW11 100 DG83
Brassie Av W3 80 CS72
Brasted Cl SE26 122 DW91
Brasted Cl, Bexh. 126 EX85
Brasted Cl, Orp. 146 EU103
Brasted Cl, Sutt. 158 DA110
Brasted Hill, Sev. 180 EU120
Brasted Hill Rd, West. 180 EV121
Brasted La, Sev. 180 EU119
Brasted Rd, Erith 107 FE80
Brasted Rd, West. 189 ES126
Brathway Rd SW18 120 DA87
Bratley St E1 84 DU70
Weaver St
Brattle Wd, Sev. 191 FH129
Braund Av, Grnf. 78 CB70
Braundton Av, Sid. 125 ET88
Braunston Dr, Hayes 78 BY70
Bravington Cl, Shep. 134 BM99
Bravington Pl W9 81 CZ70
Bravington Rd
Bravington Rd W9 81 CZ68
Brawlings La (Chalfont St. Peter), Ger.Cr. 37 BA49
Brawne Ho SE17 101 DP79
Hillingdon St
Braxfield Rd SE4 103 DY84
Braxted Pk SW16 121 DM93
Bray NW3 82 DE66
Bray Cl, Borwd. 26 CQ39
Bray Cres SE16 203 H4
Bray Dr E16 86 EF73
Bray Gdns, Wok. 167 BE116
Bray Pas E16 86 EG73
Bray Pl SW3 198 D9
Bray Pl SW3 100 DF77
Bray Rd NW7 43 CX51
Bray Rd, Cob. 170 BY116
Bray Springs, Wal.Abb. 16 EE34
Roundhills
Brayards Rd SE15 102 DV82
Brayards Rd Est SE15 102 DV82
Braybourne Cl, Uxb. 76 BJ65
Braybourne Dr, Islw. 97 CF80
Braybrook St W12 81 CT71
Braybrooke Gdns SE19 122 DT94
Fox Hill
Brayburne Av SW4 101 DJ82
Braycourt Av, Walt. 135 BV101
Braydon Rd N16 66 DU60
Brayfield Ter N1 83 DN66
Lofting Rd
Brayford Sq E1 84 DW72
Summercourt Rd
Brayton Gdns, Enf. 29 DK42
Braywood Av, Egh. 113 AZ93
Braywood Rd SE9 105 ER84
Brazil Cl, Croy. 141 DL101
Breach Barn Mobile Home Pk, Wal.Abb. 16 EH29
Breach Barns La, Wal.Abb. 16 EF30
Galley Hill
Breach La, Dag. 88 FA69
Breach Rd, Grays 109 FT79
Bread & Cheese La (Cheshunt), Wal.Cr. 14 DR25
Bread St EC4 197 J9
Bread St EC4 84 DQ73
Breakfield, Couls. 175 DL116
Breakneck Hill, Green. 129 FV85
Breakspear Ct, Abb.L. 7 BT30
Breakspear Path (Harefield), Uxb. 58 BJ55
Breakspear Rd, Ruis. 59 BP58
Breakspear Rd N (Harefield), Uxb. 58 BN57
Breakspear Rd S (Ickenham), Uxb. 58 BM62
Breakspeare Cl, Wat. 23 BV38
Breakspeare Rd, Abb.L. 7 BS31
Breakspears Dr, Orp. 146 EU95
Breakspears Ms SE4 103 EA82
Breakspears Rd
Breakspears Rd SE4 103 DZ84
Bream Cl N17 66 DV56
Bream Gdns E6 87 EN69
Bream St E3 85 EA66
Breamore Cl SW15 119 CU88
Breamore Rd, Ilf. 69 ET61
Bream's Bldgs EC4 196 D8
Bream's Bldgs EC4 83 DN72
Breamwater Gdns, Rich. 117 CH90
Brearley Cl, Edg. 42 CQ52
Pavilion Way
Brearley Cl, Uxb. 76 BL65
Breasley Cl SW15 99 CV84
Brechin Pl SW7 100 DC77
Rosary Gdns
Brecknock Rd N7 65 DJ63
Brecknock Rd N19 65 DJ63
Brecknock Rd Est N7 65 DJ63
Breckonmead, Brom. 144 EJ96
Wanstead Rd
Brecon Cl, Mitch. 141 DL97
Brecon Cl, Wor.Pk. 139 CW103
Brecon Rd W6 99 CY79
Brecon Rd, Enf. 30 DW42
Brede Cl E6 87 EN69
Bredgar Rd N19 65 DJ61
Bredhurst Cl SE20 122 DW93
Bredon Rd SE5 102 DQ83
Bredon Rd, Croy. 142 DT101
Bredune, Ken. 176 DR115
Church Rd
Breech La, Tad. 173 CU124
Breer St SW6 100 DB83
Breeze Ter (Cheshunt), Wal.Cr. 15 DX28
Collet Cl
Breezers Hill E1 202 C1
Brember Rd, Har. 60 CC61
Bremer Ms E17 67 EB56
Church La
Bremer Rd, Stai. 114 BG90
Bremner Cl, Swan. 147 FG98
Bremner Rd SW7 100 DC75
Brenchley Av, Grav. 131 GH92
Brenchley Cl, Brom. 144 EF100
Brenchley Cl, Chis. 145 EN95
Brenchley Gdns SE23 122 DW86
Brenchley Rd, Orp. 145 ET95
Brenda Rd SW17 120 DF89
Brenda Ter, Swans. 130 FY87
Manor Rd
Brendans Cl, Horn. 72 FL60
Brende Gdns, W.Mol. 136 CB98
Brendon Av NW10 62 CS63
Brendon Cl, Erith 107 FE81
Brendon Cl, Esher 154 CC107
Brendon Cl, Hayes 95 BQ80
Brendon Ct, Rad. 9 CH34
The Av
Brendon Dr, Esher 154 CC107
Brendon Gdns, Har. 60 CB63
Brendon Gdns, Ilf. 69 ES57
Brendon Gro N2 44 DC54
Brendon Rd SE9 125 ER89
Brendon Rd, Dag. 70 EZ60
Brendon St W1 194 C8
Brendon St W1 82 DE72
Brendon Way, Enf. 46 DS45
Brenley Cl, Mitch. 140 DG97
Brenley Gdns SE9 104 EK84
Brennan Rd, Til. 111 GH82
Brent, The, Dart. 128 FN87
Brent Cl, Bex. 126 EY88
Brent Cl, Dart. 128 FP86
Brent Cres NW10 80 CM68
Brent Cross Gdns NW4 63 CX58
Haley Rd
Brent Cross Shop Cen NW4 63 CW59
Brent Grn NW4 63 CW57
Brent Grn Wk, Wem. 62 CQ62
Brent La, Dart. 128 FM87
Brent Lea, Brent. 97 CJ80
Brent Pk NW10 62 CR64
Brent Pk Rd NW4 63 CV59
Brent Pk Rd NW9 63 CU60
Brent Pl, Barn. 28 DA43
Brent Rd E16 86 EG71
Brent Rd SE18 105 EP80
Brent Rd, Brent. 97 CJ79
Brent Rd, S.Croy. 160 DV109
Brent Rd, Sthl. 96 BW76
Brent Side, Brent. 97 CJ79
Brent St NW4 63 CW56
Brent Ter NW2 63 CW61
Brent Vw Rd NW9 63 CU59
Brent Way N3 44 DA51
Brent Way, Brent. 97 CK80
Brent Way, Dart. 128 FP86
Brent Way, Wem. 80 CP65
Brentcot Cl W13 79 CH70
Brentfield NW10 80 CP66
Brentfield Cl NW10 80 CR65
Normans Mead
Brentfield Gdns NW2 63 CX59
Hendon Way
Brentfield Rd NW10 80 CR65
Brentfield Rd, Dart. 128 FN86
Brentford Business Cen, Brent. 97 CJ80
Brentford Cl, Hayes 78 BX70
Brentham Way W5 79 CK70
Brenthouse Rd E9 84 DV66
Brenthurst Rd NW10 81 CT65
Brentlands Dr, Dart. 128 FN88
Brentmead Cl W7 79 CE73
Brentmead Gdns NW10 80 CM68
Brentmead Pl NW11 63 CX58
North Circular Rd
Brenton St E14 85 DY72
Brentside Cl W13 79 CG70
Brentside Executive Cen, Brent. 97 CH79
Brentvale Av, Sthl. 79 CD74
Brentvale Av, Wem. 80 CM67
Brentwick Gdns, Brent. 98 CL77
Brentwood Bypass, Brwd. 53 FR49
Brentwood Cl SE9 125 EQ88
Brentwood Ct, Add. 152 BH105
Brentwood Ho SE18 104 EK80
Shooter's Hill Rd
Brentwood Pl, Brwd. 54 FX46
Brentwood Rd, Brwd. 55 GA49
Brentwood Rd, Grays 111 GH77
Brentwood Rd, Rom. 71 FF58
Brereton Rd N17 46 DT52
Bressenden Pl SW1 199 J6
Bressenden Pl SW1 101 DH76
Bressey Av, Enf. 30 DU39
Bressey Gro E18 48 EF54
Bretlands Rd, Cher. 133 BE103
Brett Cl N16 66 DS61
Yoakley Rd
Brett Cl, Nthlt. 78 BX69
Broomcroft Av
Brett Ct N9 46 DW47
Brett Cres NW10 80 CR66
Brett Gdns, Dag. 88 EY66
Brett Ho Cl SW15 119 CX86
Putney Heath La
Brett Pas E8 66 DV64
Kenmure Rd
Brett Pl, Wat. 23 BU37
The Harebreaks
Brett Rd E8 66 DV64
Brett Rd, Barn. 27 CW43
Brettell St SE17 102 DR78
Merrow St
Brettenham Av E17 47 EA53
Brettenham Rd E17 47 EA54
Brettenham Rd N18 46 DV49
Brettgrave, Epsom 156 CQ110
Brevet Cl, Purf. 109 FR77
Brewer St W1 195 L10
Brewer St W1 83 DJ73
Brewer St, Red. 186 DQ131
Brewer's Fld, Dart. 128 FJ91
Brewer's Grn SW1 199 M6
Brewers Hall Gdns EC2 197 J7
Brewers La, Rich. 117 CK85
Brewery Cl, Wem. 61 CG64
Brewery La, Sev. 191 FJ125
High St
Brewery La, Twick. 117 CF87
Brewery La, W.Byf. 152 BL113
Brewery Rd N7 83 DL66

Brewery Rd SE18 105 ER78
Brewery Rd, Brom. 144 EL102
Brewery Rd, Wok. 166 AX117
Brewery Sq SE1 84 DT74
Horselydown La
Brewhouse La E1 202 E3
Brewhouse La E1 84 DV74
Brewhouse Rd SE18 105 EM77
Brewhouse St SW15 99 CY83
Brewhouse Wk SE16 203 K3
Brewhouse Wk SE16 85 DY74
Brewhouse Yd EC1 196 F4
Brewhouse Yd, Grav. 131 GH86
Queen St
Brewood Rd, Dag. 88 EV65
Brewster Gdns W10 81 CW71
Brewster Ho E14 85 DZ73
Brewster Rd E10 67 EB60
Brian Av, S.Croy. 160 DS112
Brian Cl, Horn. 71 FH63
Brian Rd, Rom. 70 EW57
Briane Rd, Epsom 156 CQ110
Briant St SE14 103 DX81
Briants Cl, Pnr. 40 BZ54
Briar Av SW16 121 DM94
Briar Banks, Cars. 158 DG109
Briar Cl N2 64 DB55
Briar Cl N13 46 DQ48
Briar Cl, Buck.H. 48 EK47
Briar Cl, Hmptn. 116 BZ92
Briar Cl, Islw. 117 CF85
Briar Cl (Cheshunt), Wal.Cr. 14 DW29
Briar Cl, W.Byf. 152 BJ111
Briar Ct, Sutt. 157 CW105
Briar Cres, Nthlt. 78 CB65
Briar Gdns, Brom. 144 EF102
Briar Gro, S.Croy. 160 DU113
Briar Hill, Pur. 159 DL111
Briar La, Cars. 158 DG109
Briar La, Croy. 161 EB105
Briar Pas SW16 141 DL97
Briar Pl SW16 141 DM97
Briar Rd NW2 63 CW63
Briar Rd SW16 141 DL97
Briar Rd, Bex. 127 FD90
Briar Rd, Har. 61 CJ57
Briar Rd, Rom. 52 FJ52
Briar Rd, Shep. 134 BM99
Briar Rd, Twick. 117 CE88
Briar Rd, Wat. 7 BU34
Briar Rd, Wok. 167 BB123
Briar Wk SW15 99 CV84
Briar Wk W10 81 CY70
Droop St
Briar Wk, Edg. 42 CQ52
Briar Wk, W.Byf. 152 BG112
Briar Way, West Dr. 94 BN75
Briarbank Rd W13 79 CG72
Briardale Gdns NW3 64 DA62
Briarfield Av N3 44 DB54
Briaris Cl N17 46 DV52
Briarleas Gdns, Upmin. 73 FS59
Briars, The, Bushey 41 CE45
Briars, The, Rick. 22 BH36
Briars, The, Slou. 93 AZ78
Briars, The (Cheshunt), Wal.Cr. 15 DY31
Briars Ct, Lthd. 155 CD114
Briars Wk, Rom. 52 FL54
Briarswood, Wal.Cr. 14 DR28
Briarswood Way, Orp. 163 ET106
Briarwood, Bans. 174 DA115
High St
Briarwood Cl NW9 62 CQ58
Briarwood Cl, Felt. 115 BS90
Briarwood Dr, Nthwd. 39 BU54
Briarwood Rd SW4 121 DK85
Briarwood Rd, Epsom 157 CU107
Briary Cl NW3 82 DE66
Fellows Rd
Briary Ct, Sid. 126 EV92
Briary Gdns, Brom. 124 EH92
Briary Gro, Edg. 42 CP54
Briary La N9 46 DT48
Brick Ct EC4 196 D9
Brick Fm Cl, Rich. 98 CP81
Brick Kiln Cl, Wat. 24 BY44
Brick Kiln La, Oxt. 188 EJ131
Brick La E1 84 DT71
Brick La E2 84 DT69
Brick La, Enf. 30 DV40
Brick La, Stan. 41 CK52
Honeypot La
Brick St W1 199 H3
Brick St W1 83 DH74
Brickcroft, Brox. 15 DY26
Brickenden Ct, Wal.Abb. 16 EF33
Brickett Cl, Ruis. 59 BQ57
Brickfield Cl, Brent. 97 CJ80
Brickfield Cotts SE18 105 ET79
Brickfield Fm Gdns, Orp. 163 EQ105
Brickfield La, Barn. 27 CT44
Brickfield La, Hayes 95 BR79
Brickfield Rd SW19 120 DB91
Brickfield Rd, Epp. 18 EX29
Brickfield Rd, Th.Hth. 141 DP95
Brickfields, Har. 61 CD61
Brickfields La, Epp. 18 EX29
Brickfield Rd
Brickfields Way, West Dr. 94 BM76
Bricklayer's Arms SE1 201 N8
Bricklayer's Arms SE1 102 DS77
Brickwall La, Ruis. 59 BS60
Brickwood Cl SE26 122 DV90
Brickwood Rd, Croy. 142 DS103
Bride Ct EC4 196 F9
Bride La EC4 196 F9
Bride St N7 83 DM65
Brideale Cl SE15 102 DT80
Colegrove Rd
Bridel Ms N1 83 DP67
Colebrooke Row
Bridewain St SE1 202 A6
Bridewain St SE1 102 DT76
Bridewell Pl E1 202 E3
Bridewell Pl EC4 196 F9
Bridford Ms W1 195 J6
Bridge, The, Har. 61 CE55
Bridge App NW1 82 DG66
Bridge Av W6 99 CW78
Bridge Av W7 79 CD71
Bridge Av, Upmin. 72 FN61
Bridge Barn La, Wok. 166 AW117
Bridge Cl W10 81 CX72
Kingsdown Cl
Bridge Cl, Brwd. 55 FZ49
Bridge Cl, Enf. 30 DV40
Bridge Cl, Rom. 71 FE58
Bridge Cl, Tedd. 117 CF91
Shacklegate La
Bridge Cl, Walt. 135 BT101
Bridge Cl, W.Byf. 152 BM112
Bridge Cl, Wok. 166 AW117
Bridge Cotts, Upmin. 73 FU64
Bridge Ct, Wok. 166 AX117
Bridge Dr N13 45 DM49
Bridge End E17 47 EC53
Bridge Gdns, Ashf. 115 BQ94
Bridge Gdns, E.Mol. 137 CD98
Bridge Gate N21 46 DQ45
Ridge Av
Bridge Hill, Epp. 17 ET33
Bridge Ho Quay E14 204 E3
Bridge La NW11 63 CY57
Bridge La SW11 100 DE81
Bridge La, Vir.W. 132 AY99
Bridge Meadows SE14 103 DX79
Bridge Ms, Wok. 166 AX117
Bridge Barn La
Bridge Pk SW18 120 DA85
Bridge Pl SW1 199 J8
Bridge Pl SW1 101 DH77
Bridge Pl, Amer. 20 AT38
Bridge Pl, Croy. 142 DR101
Bridge Pl, Wat. 24 BX43
Bridge Rd E6 87 EM66
Bridge Rd E15 85 ED66
Bridge Rd E17 67 DZ59
Bridge Rd N9 46 DU48
The Bdy
Bridge Rd N22 45 DL53
Bridge Rd NW10 80 CS65
Bridge Rd, Beck. 123 DZ94
Bridge Rd, Bexh. 106 EY82
Bridge Rd, Cher. 134 BH101
Bridge Rd, Chess. 156 CL106
Bridge Rd, E.Mol. 137 CE98
Bridge Rd, Epsom 157 CT112
Bridge Rd, Erith 107 FF81
Bridge Rd, Grays 110 GB78
Bridge Rd, Houns. 97 CD83
Bridge Rd, Islw. 97 CD83
Bridge Rd, Kings L. 7 BQ33
Bridge Rd, Orp. 146 EV100
Bridge Rd, Rain. 89 FF70
Bridge Rd, Sthl. 96 BZ75
Bridge Rd, Sutt. 158 DB107
Bridge Rd, Twick. 117 CH86
Bridge Rd, Uxb. 76 BJ68
Bridge Rd, Wall. 159 DJ106
Bridge Rd, Wem. 62 CN62
Bridge Rd, Wey. 152 BM105
Bridge Row, Croy. 142 DR102
Cross Rd
Bridge St SW1 199 P5
Bridge St SW1 101 DL75
Bridge St W4 98 CR77
Bridge St, Lthd. 171 CG122
Bridge St, Pnr. 60 BX55
Bridge St, Rich. 117 CK85
Bridge St, Slou. 93 BD80
Bridge St, Stai. 113 BE91
Bridge St, Walt. 135 BT102
Bridge Ter E15 85 ED66
Bridge Vw W6 99 CW78
Bridge Way N11 45 DJ48
Pymmes Grn Rd
Bridge Way NW11 63 CZ57
Bridge Way, Cob. 153 BT113
Bridge Way, Couls. 174 DE119
Bridge Way, Twick. 116 CC87
Bridge Way, Uxb. 59 BP64
Bridge Wf, Cher. 134 BJ102
Bridge Wf Rd, Islw. 97 CH83
Church St
Bridge Wks, Uxb. 76 BJ70
Bridge Yd SE1 201 L2
Bridgefield Cl, Bans. 173 CW115
Bridgefield Rd, Sutt. 158 DA107
Bridgefoot SE1 101 DL78
Bridgefoot La, Pot.B. 11 CX33
Bridgeham Cl, Wey. 152 BN106
Mayfield Rd
Bridgeland Rd E16 86 EG73
Bridgeman Rd N1 83 DM66
Bridgeman Rd, Tedd. 117 CG93
Bridgeman St NW8 194 B1
Bridgeman St NW8 82 DE68
Bridgen Rd, Bex. 126 EY86
Bridgend Rd SW18 100 DC84
Bridgend Rd, Enf. 30 DW35
Bridgenhall Rd, Enf. 30 DT39
Bridgeport Pl E1 202 C2
Bridger Cl, Wat. 8 BX33
Bridges Ct SW11 100 DD83
Bridges Dr, Dart. 128 FP85
Bridges La, Croy. 159 DL105
Bridges Ms SW19 120 DB93
Bridges Rd
Bridges Pl SW6 99 CZ81
Bridges Rd SW19 120 DB93
Bridges Rd, Stan. 41 CF50
Bridges Rd Ms SW19 120 DB93
Bridges Rd
Bridgetown Cl SE19 122 DS92
St. Kitts Ter
Bridgeview Ct, Ilf. 49 ER51
Bridgewater Cl, Chis. 145 ES97
Bridgewater Ct, Slou. 93 BA78
Bridgewater Gdns, Edg. 42 CM54
Bridgewater Rd, Ruis. 59 BU63
Bridgewater Rd, Wem. 79 CJ66
Bridgewater Rd, Wey. 153 BR107
Bridgewater Sq EC2 197 H6
Bridgewater St EC2 197 H6
Bridgewater Way, Bushey 24 CB44
Bridgeway, Bark. 87 ET66
Bridgeway, Wem. 80 CL66
Bridgeway St NW1 195 M1
Bridgeway St NW1 83 DJ68
Bridgewood Cl SE20 122 DV94
Bridgewood Rd SW16 121 DK94
Bridgewood Rd, Wor.Pk. 157 CU105
Bridgford St SW18 120 DC90
Bridgman Rd W4 98 CQ76
Bridgwater Cl, Rom. 52 FK50
Bridgwater Rd E15 85 EC67
Bridgwater Rd, Rom. 52 FJ50
Bridgwater Wk, Rom. 52 FK50
Bridle Cl, Enf. 31 DZ37
Bridle Cl, Epsom 156 CR106
Bridle Cl, Kings.T. 137 CK98
Bridle Cl, Sun. 135 BU97
Forge La
Bridle End, Epsom 157 CT114
Bridle La W1 195 L10
Bridle La, Cob. 170 CB115
Bridle La, Lthd. 170 CB115
Bridle La, Rick. 22 BK41
Bridle La, Twick. 117 CH86
Crown Rd
Bridle Path, Croy. 141 DM104
Bridle Path, Wat. 23 BV40
Bridle Path, The, Epsom 157 CV110
Bridle Path, The, Wdf.Grn. 48 EE52
Bridle Rd, Croy. 143 EA104
Bridle Rd, Epsom 157 CT113
Bridle Rd, Esher 155 CH107
Bridle Rd, Pnr. 60 BW58
Bridle Rd, The, Pur. 159 DL110
Bridle Way, Croy. 161 EA106
Bridle Way, Orp. 163 EQ105
Bridle Way, The, Croy. 161 DY110
Bridlepath Way, Felt. 115 BS88
Bridleway, The, Wall. 159 DJ105
Bridleway Cl, Epsom 157 CW110
Bridlington Cl, West. 178 EH119
Bridlington Rd N9 46 DV45
Bridlington Rd, Wat. 40 BX48
Bridport Av, Rom. 71 FB58
Bridport Pl N1 84 DR68
Bridport Rd N18 46 DS50
Bridport Rd, Grnf. 78 CB67
Bridport Rd, Th.Hth. 141 DN97
Bridport Ter SW8 101 DK81
Wandsworth Rd
Bridstow Pl W2 82 DA72
Talbot Rd
Brief St SE5 101 DP81
Brier Lea, Tad. 183 CZ126
Brier Rd, Tad. 173 CV119
Brierley, Croy. 161 EB107
Brierley Av N9 46 DW46
Brierley Cl SE25 142 DU98
Brierley Cl, Horn. 72 FJ58
Brierley Rd E11 67 ED63
Brierley Rd SW12 121 DJ89
Brierly Gdns E2 84 DW68
Royston St
Briery Ct, Rick. 22 BG42
Briery Fld, Rick. 22 BG42
Briery Way, Amer. 20 AS37
Brig Ms SE8 103 EA79
Watergate St
Brigade Cl, Har. 61 CD61
Brigade St SE3 104 EF82
Royal Par
Brigadier Av, Enf. 30 DQ39
Brigadier Hill, Enf. 30 DQ38
Briggeford Cl E5 66 DU61
Geldeston Rd
Briggs Cl, Mitch. 141 DH95
Bright Cl, Belv. 106 EX77
Bright St E14 85 EB72
Brightfield Rd SE12 124 EF85
Brightlands, Grav. 130 GE91
Brightlands Rd, Reig. 184 DC132
Brightling Rd SE4 123 DZ86
Brightlingsea Pl E14 85 DZ73
Brightman Rd SW18 120 DD88
Brighton Av E17 67 DZ57
Brighton Cl, Add. 152 BJ106
Brighton Cl, Uxb. 77 BP66
Brighton Dr, Nthlt. 78 CA65
Brighton Gro SE14 103 DY81
New Cross Rd
Brighton Rd E6 87 EN69
Brighton Rd N2 44 DC54
Brighton Rd N16 66 DS63
Brighton Rd, Add. 152 BJ105
Brighton Rd, Bans. 157 CZ114
Brighton Rd, Couls. 175 DJ119
Brighton Rd, Pur. 160 DQ110
Brighton Rd, S.Croy. 160 DQ106
Brighton Rd, Surb. 137 CJ100
Brighton Rd, Sutt. 158 DB109
Brighton Rd, Tad. 173 CY119
Brighton Rd, Wat. 23 BU38
Brighton Ter SW9 101 DM84
Brights Av, Rain. 89 FH70
Brightside, The, Enf. 31 DX39
Brightside Av, Stai. 114 BJ94
Brightside Rd SE13 123 ED86
Brightview Cl, St.Alb. 8 BY29
Brightwell Cl, Croy. 141 DN102
Sumner Rd
Brightwell Cres SW17 120 DF92
Brightwell Rd, Wat. 23 BU43
Brigstock Rd, Belv. 107 FB77
Brigstock Rd, Couls. 175 DH115
Brigstock Rd, Th.Hth. 141 DN99
Brill Pl NW1 195 N1
Brill Pl NW1 83 DK68
Brim Hill N2 64 DC56
Brimfield Rd, Purf. 109 FR77
Brimpsfield Cl SE2 106 EV76
Brimsdown Av, Enf. 31 DY40
Brimsdown Ind Est, Enf. 31 DZ40
Brimshot La, Wok. 150 AS109
Brimstone Cl, Orp. 164 EW108
Brindle Gate, Sid. 125 ES88
Brindles, Horn. 72 FL56
Brindles, The, Bans. 173 CZ117
Brindles Cl, Brwd. 55 GC47
Brindley Cl, Bexh. 107 FB83
Brindley Cl, Wem. 79 CK67
Brindley St SE14 103 DZ81
Brindley Way, Brom. 124 EG92
Brindley Way, Sthl. 78 CB73
Brindwood Rd E4 47 DZ48
Brinkburn Cl SE2 106 EU77
Brinkburn Cl, Edg. 42 CP54
Brinkburn Gdns, Edg. 62 CN55
Brinkley Rd, Wor.Pk. 139 CV103
Brinklow Cres SE18 105 EP80
Brinklow Ho W2 82 DB71
Brinkworth Rd, Ilf. 68 EL55
Brinkworth Way E9 85 DZ65
Brinley Cl (Cheshunt), Wal.Cr. 15 DX31
Brinsdale Rd NW4 63 CX56
Brinsley Rd, Har. 41 CD54
Brinsley St E1 84 DV72
Watney St
Brinsmead (Park St), St.Alb. 9 CE27
Brinsmead Rd, Rom. 52 FN54
Brinsworth Cl, Twick. 117 CD89
Brinton Wk SE1 200 F3
Brion Pl E14 85 EC71
Brisbane Av SW19 140 DB95
Brisbane Ct N10 45 DH52
Sydney Rd
Brisbane Ho, Til. 111 GF81
Leicester Rd
Brisbane Rd E10 67 EB61
Brisbane Rd W13 97 CG75
Brisbane Rd, Ilf. 69 EP59
Brisbane St SE5 102 DR80
Briscoe Cl E11 68 EF61
Briscoe Rd SW19 120 DD93
Briscoe Rd, Rain. 90 FJ68
Briset Rd SE9 104 EK83
Briset St EC1 196 F6
Briset Way N7 65 DM61
Brisson Cl, Esher 154 BZ107
Bristol Cl, Stai. 114 BL86
Bristol Gdns SW15 119 CW87
Portsmouth Rd
Bristol Gdns W9 82 DB70
Bristol Ms W9 82 DB70
Bristol Gdns
Bristol Pk Rd E17 67 DY56
Bristol Rd E7 86 EJ65
Bristol Rd, Grav. 131 GK90
Bristol Rd, Grnf. 78 CB67
Bristol Rd, Mord. 140 DC99
Bristol Way, Slou. 74 AT74
Briston Gro N8 65 DL58
Briston Ms NW7 43 CU52
Bristow Rd SE19 122 DS92
Bristow Rd, Bexh. 106 EY81
Bristow Rd, Croy. 159 DL105
Bristow Rd, Houns. 96 CC83
Britannia Cl SW4 101 DK84
Bowland Rd
Britannia Cl, Nthlt. 78 BX69
Britannia Dr, Grav. 131 GM92
Britannia Gate E16 205 N2
Britannia Gate E16 86 EG74
Britannia Ind Est, Slou. 93 BE82
Britannia La, Twick. 116 CC87
Britannia Rd E14 204 A9
Britannia Rd E14 103 EA77
Britannia Rd N12 44 DC48
Britannia Rd SW6 100 DB80
Britannia Rd, Brwd. 54 FW50
Britannia Rd, Ilf. 69 EP62
Britannia Rd, Surb. 138 CM101
Britannia Rd, Wal.Cr. 15 DZ34
Britannia Row N1 83 DP67
Britannia St WC1 196 B2
Britannia St WC1 83 DM69
Britannia Wk N1 197 K2
Britannia Wk N1 84 DR68
Britannia Way NW10 80 CP70
Britannia Way SW6 100 DB81
Britannia Rd
Britannia Way, Stai. 114 BK87
British Gro W4 99 CT78
British Gro Pas W4 99 CT78
British Gro S W4 99 CT78
British Gro Pas
British Legion Rd E4 48 EF47
British St E3 85 DZ69
Briton Cl, S.Croy. 160 DS111
Briton Cres, S.Croy. 160 DS111
Briton Hill Rd, S.Croy. 160 DS110
Brittain Rd, Dag. 70 EY62
Brittain Rd, Walt. 154 BX106
Brittains La, Sev. 190 FF123
Britten Cl NW11 64 DB60
Britten Cl, Borwd. 25 CK44
Rodgers Cl
Britten Dr, Sthl. 78 CA72
Britten St SW3 100 DE78
Brittenden Cl, Orp. 163 ES107
Britten's Ct E1 202 D1
Britten's Ct E1 84 DV73
Britton Cl SE6 123 ED87
Brownhill Rd
Britton St EC1 196 F5
Britton St EC1 83 DP70
Brixham Cres, Ruis. 59 BU60
Brixham Gdns, Ilf. 69 ES64
Brixham Rd, Well. 106 EX81
Brixham St E16 87 EN74
Brixton Est, Edg. 42 CP54
Brixton Hill SW2 121 DL87
Brixton Hill Pl SW2 121 DL87
Brixton Hill
Brixton Oval SW2 101 DN84
Brixton Rd SW9 101 DN82
Brixton Rd, Wat. 23 BV39
Brixton Sta Rd SW9 101 DN84
Brixton Water La SW2 121 DM85
Broad Acre, St.Alb. 8 BY30
Broad Cl, Walt. 136 BX104
Broad Ct WC2 196 A9
Broad Ditch Rd, Grav. 130 GC94
Broad Grn Av, Croy. 141 DP101
Broad Highway, Cob. 154 BX114
Broad La EC2 197 M6
Broad La EC2 84 DS71
Broad La N8 65 DM57
Tottenham La
Broad La N15 66 DT56
Broad La, Dart. 127 FG91
Broad La, Hmptn. 116 CA93
Broad Lawn SE9 125 EN89
Broad Mead, Ash. 172 CM117
Broad Oak, Sun. 115 BT93
Broad Oak, Wdf.Grn. 48 EH50
Broad Oak Cl E4 47 EA50
Royston Av
Broad Oak Cl, Orp. 146 EU96
Broad Platts, Slou. 92 AX76
Broad Ride, Egh. 132 AU96
Broad Ride, Vir.W. 132 AU96
Broad Rd, Swans. 130 FY86
Broad Sanctuary SW1 199 N5
Broad Sanctuary SW1 101 DK75
Broad St, Dag. 88 FA66
Broad St, Tedd. 117 CF93
Broad St Av EC2 197 M7
Broad St Pl EC2 197 L7
Broad Vw NW9 62 CN58
Broad Wk N21 45 DM47
Broad Wk NW1 195 H3
Broad Wk NW1 83 DH69
Broad Wk SE3 104 EJ82
Broad Wk W1 198 F2
Broad Wk W1 82 DG74
Broad Wk, Cat. 176 DT122
Broad Wk, Couls. 174 DG123
Broad Wk, Croy. 161 DY110
Broad Wk, Epsom 172 CS117
Chalk La
Broad Wk (Burgh Heath), Epsom 173 CX119
Broad Wk, Houns. 96 BX81
Broad Wk, Orp. 146 EX104
Broad Wk, Rich. 98 CM80
Broad Wk, Sev. 191 FL128
Broad Wk, The W8 82 DB74
Broad Wk, The, E.Mol. 137 CF97
Broad Wk La NW11 63 CZ59
Broad Wk N, The, Brwd. 55 GA49
Broad Wk S, The, Brwd. 55 GA49
Broad Water Cres, Wey. 135 BQ104
Churchill Dr
Broad Yd EC1 196 F5
Broadacre, Stai. 114 BG92
Broadacre Cl, Uxb. 59 BP62
Broadbent Cl N6 65 DH60
Broadbent St W1 195 H10
Broadberry Ct N18 46 DV50
Broadbridge Cl SE3 104 EG80
Broadcoombe, S.Croy. 160 DW108
Broadcroft Av, Stan. 41 CK54
Broadcroft Rd, Orp. 145 ER101
Broadfield Cl NW2 63 CW62
Broadfield Cl, Croy. 141 DM103
Progress Way
Broadfield Cl, Rom. 71 FF57
Broadfield Cl, Tad. 173 CW120
Broadfield Ct, Bushey 41 CE47
Broadfield La NW1 83 DL66
Broadfield Rd SE6 124 EE87
Broadfield Sq, Enf. 30 DV40
Broadfield Way, Buck.H. 48 EJ48
Broadfields, E.Mol. 137 CD100
Broadfields, Har. 40 CB54
Broadfields (Cheshunt), Wal.Cr. 13 DP29
Broadfields Av N21 45 DN45
Broadfields Av, Edg. 42 CP49
Broadfields Hts, Edg. 42 CP49
Broadfields La, Wat. 39 BV46
Broadfields Way NW10 63 CT64
Broadford La, Wok. 150 AT112
Broadgate E13 86 EJ68
Broadgate EC2 84 DS71
Liverpool St
Broadgate, Wal.Abb. 16 EF33
Broadgate Circle EC2 197 M6
Broadgate Rd E16 86 EK72
Fulmer Rd
Broadgates Av, Barn. 28 DB39
Broadgates Rd SW18 120 DD88
Ellerton Rd
Broadgreen Rd (Cheshunt), Wal.Cr. 14 DR26
Hammondstreet Rd
Broadham Grn Rd, Oxt. 187 ED132
Broadham Pl, Oxt. 187 ED131
Broadhead Strand NW9 43 CT53
Broadheath Dr, Chis. 125 EM92
Broadhinton Rd SW4 101 DH83
Broadhurst, Ash. 172 CL116
Broadhurst Av, Edg. 42 CP49
Broadhurst Av, Ilf. 69 ET63
Broadhurst Cl NW6 82 DC65
Broadhurst Gdns
Broadhurst Cl, Rich. 118 CM85
Lower Gro Rd
Broadhurst Gdns NW6 82 DB65
Broadhurst Gdns, Chig. 49 EQ49
Broadhurst Gdns, Ruis. 60 BW61
Broadhurst Wk, Rain. 89 FG65
Broadlake Cl, St.Alb. 9 CK27
Broadlands, Felt. 116 BZ90
Broadlands, Grays 110 FZ78
Bankfoot
Broadlands Av SW16 121 DL89
Broadlands Av, Enf. 30 DV41
Broadlands Av, Shep. 135 BQ100
Broadlands Cl N6 64 DG59
Broadlands Cl SW16 121 DL89
Broadlands Cl, Enf. 30 DV41
Broadlands Cl, Wal.Cr. 15 DX34
Broadlands Dr, Warl. 176 DW119
Broadlands Rd N6 64 DF59
Broadlands Rd, Brom. 124 EH91
Broadlands Way, N.Mal. 139 CT100
Broadlawns Ct, Har. 41 CF53
Broadley Gdns (Shenley), Rad. 10 CL32
Queens Way
Broadley St NW8 194 A6
Broadley St NW8 82 DE71
Broadley Ter NW1 194 C5
Broadley Ter NW1 82 DE70
Broadmark Rd, Slou. 74 AV73
Broadmayne SE17 201 K10
Broadmead SE6 123 EA90
Broadmead Av, Wor.Pk. 139 CU101
Broadmead Cl, Hmptn. 116 CA93
Broadmead Cl, Pnr. 40 BY52
Broadmead Est, Wdf.Grn. 48 EJ52
Broadmead Rd, Hayes 78 BY70
Broadmead Rd, Nthlt. 78 BY70
Broadmead Rd, Wok. 167 BB122
Broadmead Rd, Wdf.Grn. 48 EG51

Broadmeads, Wok. 167 BB122
Broadmead Rd
Broadoak Av, Enf. 31 DX35
Broadoak Cl, Dart. 128 FN93
Broadoak Rd, Erith 107 FD80
Broadoaks, Epp. 17 ET31
Broadoaks, Surb. 138 CP102
Broadoaks Cres, W.Byf. 152 BH114
Broadoaks Way, Brom. 144 EF99
Broadstone Pl W1 194 F7
Broadstone Rd, Horn. 71 FG61
Broadstrood, Loug. 33 EN38
Broadview Av, Grays 110 GD75
Broadview Rd SW16 121 DK94
Broadwalk E18 68 EF55
Broadwalk, Har. 60 CA57
Broadwalk, The, Nthwd. 39 BQ54
Broadwall SE1 200 E2
Broadwall SE1 83 DN74
Broadwater, Pot.B. 12 DB30
Broadwater Cl, Stai. 113 AZ87
Broadwater Cl, Walt. 153 BU106
Broadwater Cl, Wok. 151 BD112
Broadwater Gdns, Orp. 163 EP105
Broadwater Gdns (Harefield), Uxb. 58 BH56
Broadwater La (Harefield), Uxb. 58 BH56
Broadwater Pk (Denham), Uxb. 58 BG58
Broadwater Pl, Wey. 135 BS103
Oatlands Dr
Broadwater Rd N17 46 DS53
Broadwater Rd SE28 105 ER76
Broadwater Rd SW17 120 DE91
Broadwater Rd N, Walt. 153 BT106
Broadwater Rd S, Walt. 153 BT106
Broadway E15 85 ED66
Broadway SW1 199 M6
Broadway SW1 101 DK76
Broadway W13 79 CG74
Broadway, Bark. 87 EQ66
Broadway, Bexh. 106 EY84
Broadway, Grays 110 GC79
Broadway, Rain. 89 FG70
Broadway, Rom. 71 FG55
Broadway, Stai. 114 BH92
Kingston Rd
Broadway, Surb. 138 CP102
Broadway, Swan. 147 FC100
Broadway, Til. 111 GF82
Broadway, The E4 47 ED51
Broadway, The E13 86 EH68
Broadway, The N8 65 DL58
Broadway, The N9 46 DU48
Broadway, The N14 45 DK46
Winchmore Hill Rd
Broadway, The N22 45 DN54
Broadway, The NW7 42 CS50
Broadway, The SW13 98 CS82
The Ter
Broadway, The SW19 119 CZ93
Broadway, The W5 79 CK73
Broadway, The W7 79 CE74
Broadway, The, Add. 152 BG110
Broadway, The, Croy. 159 DL105
Croydon Rd
Broadway, The, Dag. 70 EZ61
Whalebone La S
Broadway, The, Grnf. 78 CC70
Broadway, The, Har. 41 CE54
Broadway, The, Horn. 71 FH63
Broadway, The, Loug. 33 EQ42
Broadway, The, Pnr. 40 BZ52
Broadway, The, Sthl. 78 BX73
Broadway, The, Stai. 134 BJ97
Broadway, The, Stan. 41 CJ50
Broadway, The, Sutt. 157 CY107
Broadway, The, T.Ditt. 137 CE102
Hampton Ct Way
Broadway, The, Wat. 24 BW41
Broadway, The, Wem. 62 CL62
East La
Broadway, The, Wok. 167 AZ117
Broadway, The, Wdf.Grn. 48 EH51
Broadway Av, Croy. 142 DR99
Broadway Av, Twick. 117 CH86
Broadway Cl, S.Croy. 160 DV114
Broadway Cl, Wdf.Grn. 48 EH51
Broadway Ct SW19 120 DA93
The Bdy
Broadway E (Denham), Uxb. 58 BG58
Broadway Gdns, Mitch. 140 DE98
Broadway Mkt E8 84 DV67
Broadway Mkt Ms E8 84 DU67
Brougham Rd
Broadway Ms E5 66 DT59
Broadway Ms N13 45 DM50
Elmdale Rd
Broadway Ms N21 45 DP46
Compton Rd
Broadway Par N8 65 DL58
Broadway Par, Horn. 71 FH63
The Bdy
Broadway Pl SW19 119 CZ93
Hartfield Rd
Broadwick St W1 195 L10
Broadwick St W1 83 DJ72
Broadwood, Grav. 131 GH92
Broadwood Av, Ruis. 59 BT58
Broadwood Ter W8 99 CZ77
Pembroke Rd
Brocas Cl NW3 82 DE66
Fellows Rd
Brock Grn, S.Ock. 91 FV72
Cam Grn
Brock Pl E3 85 EB70
Brock Rd E13 86 EH71
Brock St SE15 102 DW83
Evelina Rd
Brock Way, Vir.W. 132 AW99
Brockdish Av, Bark. 69 ET64
Brockenhurst, W.Mol. 136 BZ100
Brockenhurst Av, Wor.Pk. 138 CS102
Brockenhurst Cl, Wok. 151 AZ114
Brockenhurst Gdns NW7 42 CS50
Brockenhurst Gdns, Ilf. 69 EQ64
Brockenhurst Ms N18 46 DU49
Lyndhurst Rd
Brockenhurst Rd, Croy. 142 DV101
Brockenhurst Way SW16 141 DK96
Brocket Cl, Chig. 49 ET50
Burrow Rd
Brocket Rd, Grays 111 GG76
Brocket Way, Chig. 49 ES50
Brockham Cl SW19 119 CZ92
Brockham Cres, Croy. 161 ED108
Brockham Dr SW2 121 DM87
Fairview Pl
Brockham Dr, Ilf. 69 EP58
Brockham La, Bet. 182 CN134
Brockham St SE1 201 J6
Brockham St SE1 102 DQ76
Brockhamhill Pk, Tad. 182 CQ131
Brockhurst Cl, Stan. 41 CF51
Brockill Cres SE4 103 DY84
Brocklebank Ct, Whyt. 176 DU118
Brocklebank Rd SE7 205 P9
Brocklebank Rd SE7 104 EH77
Brocklebank Rd SW18 120 DC87
Brocklehurst St SE14 103 DX80
Brocklesbury Cl, Wat. 24 BW41
Brocklesby Rd SE25 142 DV98
Brockley Av, Stan. 42 CL48
Brockley Cl, Stan. 42 CL49
Brockley Combe, Wey. 153 BR105
Brockley Cres, Rom. 51 FC52
Brockley Cross SE4 103 DY83
Endwell Rd
Brockley Footpath SE15 102 DW84
Brockley Gdns SE4 103 DZ82
Brockley Gro SE4 123 DZ85
Brockley Gro, Brwd. 55 GA46
Brockley Hall Rd SE4 123 DY86
Brockley Hill, Stan. 41 CJ46
Brockley Ms SE4 123 DY85
Brockley Pk SE23 123 DY87
Brockley Ri SE23 123 DY86
Brockley Rd SE4 103 DZ83
Brockley Vw SE23 123 DY87
Brockley Way SE4 123 DX85
Brockleyside, Stan. 41 CK49
Brockman Ri, Brom. 123 ED91
Brocks Dr, Sutt. 139 CY104
Brockshot Cl, Brent. 97 CK78
Brocksparkwood, Brwd. 55 GB48
Brockton Cl, Rom. 71 FF56
Brockway Cl E11 68 EE60
Brockway Ho, Slou. 93 BB78
Brockwell Cl, Orp. 145 ET99
Brockwell Pk Gdns SE24 121 DN87
Brodewater Rd, Borwd. 26 CP40
Brodia Rd N16 66 DS62
Brodie Rd E4 47 EC46
Brodie Rd, Enf. 30 DQ38
Brodie St SE1 202 A10
Brodlove La E1 85 DX73
Brodrick Gro SE2 106 EV77
Brodrick Rd SW17 120 DE89
Brograve Gdns, Beck. 143 EB96
Broke Fm Dr, Orp. 164 EW109
Broke Wk E8 84 DU67
Broken Wf EC4 197 H10
Brokengate La (Denham), Uxb. 57 BC60
Brokes Cres, Reig. 184 DA132
Brokes Rd, Reig. 184 DA132
Brokesley St E3 85 DZ70
Bromar Rd SE5 102 DS83
Bromborough Grn, Wat. 40 BW50
Brome Rd SE9 105 EM83
Bromefield, Stan. 41 CJ53
Bromefield Ct, Wal.Abb. 16 EG33
Bromehead Rd E1 84 DW72
Bromell's Rd SW4 101 DJ84
Bromet Cl, Wat. 23 BT38
Hempstead Rd
Bromfelde Rd SW4 101 DK82
Bromfelde Wk SW4 101 DK82
Bromfield St N1 83 DN68
Bromford Cl, Oxt. 188 EG133
Bromhall Rd, Dag. 88 EV65
Bromhedge SE9 125 EM90
Bromholm Rd SE2 106 EV76
Bromleigh Cl (Cheshunt), Wal.Cr. 15 DY28
Martins Dr
Bromleigh Ct SE23 122 DV89
Lapse Wd Wk
Bromley, Grays 110 FZ79
Bromley Av, Brom. 124 EE94
Bromley Common, Brom. 144 EJ98
Bromley Cres, Brom. 144 EF97
Bromley Cres, Ruis. 59 BT63
Bromley Gdns, Brom. 144 EF97
Bromley Gro, Brom. 143 ED96
Bromley Hall Rd E14 85 EC71
Bromley High St E3 85 EB69
Bromley Hill, Brom. 124 EE93
Bromley La, Chis. 125 EQ94
Bromley Pk, Brom. 144 EF95
London Rd
Bromley Pl W1 195 K6
Bromley Rd E10 67 EB58
Bromley Rd E17 67 EA55
Bromley Rd N17 46 DR48
Bromley Rd N18 46 DT53
Bromley Rd SE6 123 EB88
Bromley Rd, Beck. 143 EB95
Bromley Rd, Brom. 143 EC96
Bromley Rd (Downham), Brom. 123 EC91
Bromley Rd, Chis. 145 EP95
Bromley St E1 85 DX71
Brompton Arc SW3 198 D5
Brompton Cl SE20 142 DU96
Selby Rd
Brompton Cl, Houns. 116 BZ85
Brompton Dr, Erith 107 FH80
Brompton Gro N2 64 DE56
Brompton Pk Cres SW6 100 DB79
Brompton Pl SW3 198 C6
Brompton Pl SW3 100 DE76
Brompton Rd SW1 198 C6
Brompton Rd SW1 100 DE76
Brompton Rd SW3 198 C6
Brompton Rd SW3 100 DE76
Brompton Rd SW7 198 C6
Brompton Rd SW7 100 DE76
Brompton Sq SW3 198 B6
Brompton Sq SW3 100 DE76
Brompton Ter SE18 105 EN81
Prince Imperial Rd
Bromwich Av N6 64 DG61
Bromyard Av W3 80 CS74
Bromyard Ho SE15 102 DV80
Brondesbury Ct NW2 81 CW65
Brondesbury Ms NW6 82 DA66
Willesden La
Brondesbury Pk NW2 81 CV65
Brondesbury Pk NW6 81 CX66
Brondesbury Rd NW6 81 CZ68
Brondesbury Vil NW6 81 CZ68
Bronsart Rd SW6 99 CY80
Bronsdon Way (Denham), Uxb. 57 BF61
Bronson Rd SW20 139 CX96
Bronte Cl E7 68 EG63
Bective Rd
Bronte Cl, Erith 107 FB80
Bronte Cl, Ilf. 69 EN57
Bronte Cl, Til. 111 GJ82
Bronte Gro, Dart. 108 FM84
Bronte Ho NW6 82 DA69
Bronte Vw, Grav. 131 GJ88
Bronti Cl SE17 102 DQ78
Bronze Age Way, Belv. 107 FC76
Bronze Age Way, Erith 107 FC76
Bronze St SE8 103 EA80
Brook Av, Dag. 89 FB66
Brook Av, Edg. 42 CP51
Brook Av, Wem. 62 CN62
Brook Cl NW7 43 CY52
Frith Ct
Brook Cl SW17 120 DG89
Balham High Rd
Brook Cl SW20 139 CV97
Brook Cl W3 80 CN74
West Lo Av
Brook Cl, Borwd. 26 CP41
Brook Cl, Epsom 156 CS109
Brook Cl, Rom. 51 FF53
Brook Cl, Ruis. 59 BS59
Brook Cl, Stai. 114 BM87
Brook Cres E4 47 EA49
Brook Cres N9 46 DV49
Brook Dr SE11 200 E7
Brook Dr SE11 101 DN77
Brook Dr, Har. 60 CC56
Brook Dr, Rad. 9 CF33
Brook Dr, Ruis. 59 BS58
Brook Dr, Sun. 115 BS92
Chertsey Rd
Brook Fm Rd, Cob. 170 BX115
Brook Gdns E4 47 EB49
Brook Gdns SW13 99 CT83
Brook Gdns, Kings.T. 138 CQ95
Brook Gate W1 198 E1
Brook Gate W1 82 DF73
Brook Grn W6 99 CX77
Brook Grn (Chobham), Wok. 150 AT110
Brookleys
Brook Hill, Oxt. 187 EC130
Brook Ind Est, Hayes 78 BX74
Brook La SE3 104 EH82
Brook La, Bex. 126 EX86
Brook La, Brom. 124 EG93
Brook La, Wok. 167 BE122
Brook La N, Brent. 97 CK78
Brook Mead, Epsom 156 CS107
Brook Meadow N12 44 DB49
Brook Meadow Cl, Wdf.Grn. 48 EE51
Brook Ms N W2 82 DD73
Craven Ter
Brook Par, Chig. 49 EP48
High Rd
Brook Pk Cl N21 29 DP44
Brook Path, Loug. 32 EL42
Brook Pl, Barn. 28 DA43
Brook Ri, Chig. 49 EN48
Brook Rd N8 65 DL56
Brook Rd N22 65 DM55
Brook Rd NW2 63 CU61
Brook Rd, Borwd. 26 CN40
Brook Rd, Brwd. 54 FT48
Brook Rd, Buck.H. 48 EG47
Brook Rd, Epp. 18 EU33
Brook Rd, Grav. 130 GE88
Brook Rd, Ilf. 69 ES58
Brook Rd, Loug. 32 EL43
Brook Rd (Merstham), Red. 185 DJ129
Brook Rd, Rom. 51 FF53
Brook Rd, Surb. 138 CL103
Brook Rd, Swan. 147 FD97
Brook Rd, Th.Hth. 142 DQ98
Brook Rd, Twick. 117 CG86
Brook Rd, Wal.Cr. 15 DZ34
Brook Rd S, Brent. 97 CK79
Brook St N17 46 DT54
High Rd
Brook St W1 194 G10
Brook St W1 83 DH72
Brook St W2 194 A10
Brook St W2 82 DD73
Brook St, Belv. 107 FB78
Brook St, Brwd. 54 FS50
Brook St, Erith 107 FB79
Brook St, Kings.T. 138 CL96
Brook Vale, Erith 107 FB81
Brook Wk N2 44 DD53
Brook Wk, Edg. 42 CR51
Brook Way, Chig. 49 EN48
Brook Way, Lthd. 171 CG118
Brook Way, Rain. 89 FH71
Brookbank Av W7 79 CD71
Brookbank Rd SE13 103 EA83
Brookdale N11 45 DJ49
Brookdale Av, Upmin. 72 FN62
Brookdale Cl, Upmin. 72 FP62
Brookdale Rd E17 67 EA55
Brookdale Rd SE6 123 EB86
Brookdale Rd, Bex. 126 EY86
Brookdene Av, Wat. 39 BV45
Brookdene Dr, Nthwd. 39 BT52
Brookdene Rd SE18 105 ET77
Brooke Av, Har. 60 CC62
Brooke Cl, Bushey 40 CC45
Brooke Rd E5 66 DU62
Brooke Rd E17 67 EC56
Brooke Rd N16 66 DT62
Brooke Rd, Grays 110 GA78
Brooke St EC1 196 D7
Brooke St EC1 83 DN71
Brooke Way, Bushey 40 CC45
Richfield Rd
Brookehowse Rd SE6 123 EB90
Brookend Rd, Sid. 125 ES88
Brooker Rd, Wal.Abb. 15 EC34
Brookers Cl, Ash. 171 CJ117
Brooke's Ct EC1 196 D6
Brookes Mkt EC1 196 E6
Brookfield N6 64 DG62
Brookfield, Epp. 18 EW25
Brookfield, Wok. 166 AV116
Brookfield Av E17 67 EC56
Brookfield Av NW7 43 CV51
Brookfield Av W5 79 CK70
Brookfield Av, Sutt. 158 DD105
Brookfield Cen (Cheshunt), Wal.Cr. 15 DX27
Brookfield Cl NW7 43 CV51
Brookfield Cl, Brwd. 55 GC44
Brookfield Cl, Cher. 151 BD107
Brookfield Ct, Grnf. 78 CC69
Brookfield Ct, Har. 61 CK57
Brookfield Cres NW7 43 CV51
Brookfield Cres, Har. 62 CL57
Brookfield Gdns, Esher 155 CF107
Brookfield Gdns (Cheshunt), Wal.Cr. 15 DX27
Brookfield La (Cheshunt), Wal.Cr. 15 DX27
Brookfield La W (Cheshunt), Wal.Cr. 14 DV28
Brookfield Pk NW5 65 DH62
Brookfield Path, Wdf.Grn. 48 EE51
Brookfield Retail Pk (Cheshunt), Wal.Cr. 15 DX26
Brookfield Rd E9 85 DY65
Brookfield Rd N9 46 DU48
Brookfield Rd W4 98 CR75
Brookfields, Enf. 31 DX42
Brookfields Av, Mitch. 140 DE99
Brookhill Cl SE18 105 EP78
Brookhill Cl, Barn. 28 DE43
Brookhill Rd SE18 105 EP78
Brookhill Rd, Barn. 28 DE43
Brookhouse Gdns E4 48 EE49
Brookhurst Rd, Add. 152 BH107
Brooking Rd E7 68 EG64
Brookland Cl NW11 64 DA56
Brookland Garth NW11 64 DB56
Brookland Hill NW11 64 DA56
Brookland Ri NW11 64 DA56
Brooklands, Dart. 128 FL88
Brooklands App, Rom. 71 FD56
Brooklands Av SW19 120 DB89
Brooklands Av, Sid. 125 ER89
Brooklands Business Pk, Wey. 152 BN110
Brooklands Cl, Cob. 170 BY115
Brooklands Cl, Rom. 71 FD56
Marshalls Rd
Brooklands Cl, Sun. 135 BS95
Brooklands Ct, Add. 152 BK110
Brooklands Dr, Grnf. 79 CK67
Brooklands Gdns, Horn. 72 FJ57
Brooklands Gdns, Pot.B. 11 CY32
Brooklands Ind Est, Wey. 152 BL110
Brooklands La, Rom. 71 FD56
Brooklands La, Wey. 152 BM107
Brooklands Pk SE3 104 EG83
Brooklands Rd, Rom. 71 FD56
Brooklands Rd, T.Ditt. 137 CF102
Brooklands Rd, Wey. 153 BP107
Brooklands Way, Red. 184 DE132
Brooklea Cl NW9 42 CS53
Brookleys, Wok. 150 AT110
Brooklyn Av SE25 142 DV98
Brooklyn Av, Loug. 32 EL42
Brooklyn Cl, Cars. 140 DE103
Brooklyn Cl, Wok. 166 AY119
Brooklyn Ct, Wok. 166 AY119
Brooklyn Rd
Brooklyn Gro SE25 142 DV98
Brooklyn Rd SE25 142 DV98
Brooklyn Rd, Brom. 144 EK99
Brooklyn Rd, Wok. 166 AY118
Brooklyn Way, West Dr. 94 BK76
Brookmans Av, Hat. 11 CY26
Brookmans Cl, Upmin. 73 FS59
Brookmarsh Trd Est SE10 103 EB80
Norman Rd
Brookmead Av, Brom. 145 EM99
Brookmead Cl, Orp. 146 EV101
Brookmead Rd, Croy. 141 DJ100
Brookmead Way, Orp. 146 EV100
Brookmeads Est, Mitch. 140 DE99
Brookmill Cl, Wat. 39 BV45
Brookside Rd
Brookmill Rd SE8 103 EA81
Brooks Av E6 87 EM70
Brooks Cl SE9 125 EN89
Brooks Cl, Wey. 152 BN110
Brooks Ct E15 67 EB64
Clays La
Brooks La W4 98 CN79
Brook's Ms W1 195 H10
Brook's Ms W1 83 DH73
Brooks Rd E13 86 EG67
Brooks Rd W4 98 CN78
Brooks Way, Orp. 146 EW96
Brooksbank St E9 85 DX65
Brooksby Ms N1 83 DN66
Brooksby St
Brooksby St N1 83 DN66
Brooksby's Wk E9 67 DX64
Brookscroft, Croy. 161 DY110
Brookscroft Rd E17 47 EB53
Brookshill, Har. 41 CD50
Brookshill Av, Har. 41 CD50
Brookshill Dr, Har. 41 CD50
Brookside N21 29 DM44
Brookside, Barn. 28 DE44
Brookside, Cars. 158 DG106
Brookside, Cher. 133 BE101
Brookside, Horn. 72 FL57
Brookside, Ilf. 49 EQ51
Brookside, Orp. 145 ET101
Brookside, Pot.B. 11 CU32
Brookside, Slou. 93 BC80
Brookside, Uxb. 76 BM66
Brookside, Wal.Abb. 16 EE33
Broomstick Hall Rd
Brookside Av, Ashf. 114 BJ92
Brookside Av, Stai. 92 AY83
Brookside Cl, Barn. 27 CY44
Brookside Cl, Felt. 115 BU90
Sycamore Cl
Brookside Cl, Har. 61 CK57
Brookside Cl (Kenton), Har. 60 BY63
Brookside Cres (Cuffley), Pot.B. 13 DL27
Brookside Cres, Wor.Pk. 139 CU102
Green La
Brookside Gdns, Enf. 30 DV37
Brookside Rd N9 46 DV49
Brookside Rd N19 65 DJ61
Junction Rd
Brookside Rd NW11 63 CY58
Brookside Rd, Grav. 131 GF94
Brookside Rd, Hayes 78 BW73
Brookside Rd, Wat. 39 BV45
Brookside S, Barn. 44 DG45
Brookside Wk N3 43 CY54
Brookside Wk N12 44 DA51
Brookside Wk NW4 63 CY56
Brookside Wk NW11 63 CY56
Brookside Way, Croy. 143 DX100
Brooksville Av NW6 81 CY67
Brookview Rd SW16 121 DJ92
Brookville Rd SW6 99 CZ80
Brookway SE3 104 EG83
Brookwood Av SW13 99 CT82
Brookwood Cl, Brom. 144 EF98
Brookwood Rd SW18 119 CZ88
Brookwood Rd, Houns. 96 CB81
Broom Av, Orp. 146 EV96
Broom Cl, Brom. 144 EL100
Broom Cl, Esher 154 CB106
Broom Cl, Tedd. 117 CK94
Broom Cl (Cheshunt), Wal.Cr. 14 DU27
Broom Gdns, Croy. 143 EA104
Broom Gro, Wat. 23 BU38
Broom Hall, Lthd. 155 CD114
Broom Hill, Slou. 74 AU66
Broom La, Wok. 150 AS109
Broom Lock, Tedd. 117 CJ93
Broom Mead, Bexh. 126 FA85
Broom Pk, Tedd. 117 CK94
Broom Rd, Croy. 143 EA104
Broom Rd, Tedd. 117 CJ93
Broom Water, Tedd. 117 CJ93
Broom Water W, Tedd. 117 CJ92
Broom Way, Wey. 153 BS105
Broomcroft Av, Nthlt. 78 BW69
Broomcroft Cl, Wok. 167 BD116
Broomcroft Dr, Wok. 167 BD115
Broome Cl, Epsom 182 CQ126
Broome Pl, S.Ock. 91 FR74
Broome Rd, Hmptn. 116 BZ94
Broome Way SE5 102 DQ80
Broomer Pl, Wal.Cr. 14 DW29
Broomfield E17 67 DZ59
Broomfield, St.Alb. 8 CC27
Broomfield, Stai. 114 BG93
Broomfield, Sun. 135 BU95
Broomfield Av N13 45 DM50
Broomfield Av, Brox. 15 DY26
Broomfield Av, Loug. 33 EM44
Broomfield Cl, Rom. 51 FD52
Broomfield Ct, Wey. 153 BP107
Broomfield La N13 45 DM49
Broomfield Pl W13 79 CH74
Broomfield Rd
Broomfield Ride, Lthd. 155 CD112
Broomfield Ri, Abb.L. 7 BR32
Broomfield Rd N13 45 DL50
Broomfield Rd W13 79 CH74
Broomfield Rd, Add. 152 BH111
Broomfield Rd, Beck. 143 DY97
Broomfield Rd, Bexh. 126 FA85
Broomfield Rd, Rich. 98 CM81
Broomfield Rd, Rom. 70 EX59
Broomfield Rd, Sev. 190 FF122
Broomfield Rd, Surb. 138 CM102
Broomfield Rd, Swans. 130 FY86
Broomfield Rd, Tedd. 117 CJ93
Melbourne Rd
Broomfield St E14 85 EA71
Broomfields, Esher 154 CC106
Broomgrove Gdns, Edg. 42 CN53
Broomgrove Rd SW9 101 DM82
Broomhall End, Wok. 166 AY116
Broomhall La
Broomhall La, Wok. 166 AY116
Broomhall Rd, S.Croy. 160 DR109
Broomhall Rd, Wok. 166 AY116
Broomhill Ct, Wdf.Grn. 48 EG51
Broomhill Rd
Broomhill Ri, Bexh. 126 FA85
Broomhill Rd SW18 120 DA85
Broomhill Rd, Dart. 127 FH86
Broomhill Rd, Ilf. 70 EU61
Broomhill Rd, Orp. 146 EU101
Broomhill Rd, Wdf.Grn. 48 EG51
Broomhill Wk, Wdf.Grn. 48 EF52
Broomhills, Grav. 130 FY91
Betsham Rd
Broomhouse La SW6 100 DA82
Broomhouse Rd SW6 100 DA82
Broomlands La, Oxt. 188 EJ125
Broomloan La, Sutt. 140 DA103
Broomsleigh St NW6 63 CZ64
Broomstick Hall Rd, Wal.Abb. 16 EE33
Broomstick La, Chesh. 4 AU30
Broomwood Cl, Croy. 143 DX99
Broomwood Gdns, Brwd. 54 FU44
Broomwood Rd SW11 120 DF86
Broomwood Rd, Orp. 146 EV96
Broseley Gdns, Rom. 52 FL49
Broseley Gro SE26 123 DY92
Broseley Rd, Rom. 52 FL49
Broster Gdns SE25 142 DT97

Brough Cl SW8 101 DL80
Kenchester Cl
Brough Cl, Kings.T. 117 CK92
Brougham Rd E8 84 DU67
Brougham Rd W3 80 CQ72
Brougham St SW11 100 DF82
Broughinge Rd, Borwd. 26 CP40
Broughton Av N3 63 CY55
Broughton Av, Rich. 117 CH90
Broughton Dr SW9 101 DN84
Broughton Gdns N6 65 DJ58
Broughton Rd SW6 100 DB82
Broughton Rd W13 79 CH73
Broughton Rd, Orp. 145 ER103
Broughton Rd, Sev. 181 FG116
Broughton Rd, Th.Hth. 141 DN100
Broughton Rd App SW6 100 DB82
Wandsworth Br Rd
Broughton St SW8 100 DG82
Broughton Way, Rick. 38 BG45
Brouncker Rd W3 98 CQ75
Brow, The, Ch.St.G. 36 AX48
Brow, The, Wat. 7 BV33
Brow Cl, Orp. 146 EX101
Brow Cres
Brow Cres, Orp. 146 EW102
Browells La, Felt. 115 BV89
Brown Cl, Wall. 159 DL108
Brown Hart Gdns W1 194 G10
Brown Hart Gdns W1 82 DG73
Brown Rd, Grav. 131 GL88
Brown St W1 194 D8
Brown St W1 82 DF72
Brownacres Towpath, Wey. 135 BP102
Browne Cl, Brwd. 54 FV46
Browne Cl, Rom. 51 FB50
Bamford Way
Brownfield St E14 85 EB72
Browngraves Rd, Hayes 95 BQ80
Brownhill Rd SE6 123 EB87
Browning Av W7 79 CF72
Browning Av, Sutt. 158 DE105
Browning Av, Wor.Pk. 139 CV102
Browning Cl E17 67 EC56
Browning Cl W9 82 DC70
Randolph Av
Browning Cl, Hmptn. 116 BZ91
Browning Cl, Rom. 50 EZ52
Browning Cl, Well. 105 ES81
Browning Est SE17 201 J10
Browning Est SE17 102 DQ78
Browning Ho W12 81 CW72
Wood La
Browning Ms W1 195 H7
Browning Rd E11 68 EF59
Browning Rd E12 87 EM65
Browning Rd, Dart. 108 FM84
Browning Rd, Enf. 30 DR38
Browning St SE17 201 J10
Browning St SE17 102 DQ78
Browning Wk, Til. 111 GJ82
Coleridge Rd
Browning Way, Houns. 96 BX81
Brownlea Gdns, Ilf. 70 EU61
Brownlow Ms WC1 196 C5
Brownlow Ms WC1 83 DM70
Brownlow Rd E7 68 EH63
Woodford Rd
Brownlow Rd E8 84 DT67
Brownlow Rd N3 44 DB52
Brownlow Rd N11 45 DL51
Brownlow Rd NW10 80 CS66
Brownlow Rd W13 79 CG74
Brownlow Rd, Borwd. 26 CN42
Brownlow Rd, Croy. 160 DS105
Brownlow Rd, Red. 184 DE134
Brownlow St WC1 196 C7
Brownrigg Rd, Ashf. 114 BN91
Brown's Bldgs EC3 197 N9
Brown's Bldgs EC3 84 DS72
Browns La NW5 65 DH64
Browns Rd E17 67 EA55
Browns Rd, Surb. 138 CM101
Brownspring Dr SE9 125 EP91
Brownswell Rd N2 44 DD54
Brownswood Rd N4 65 DP62
Brox La, Cher. 151 BD109
Brox Rd, Cher. 151 BC107
Broxash Rd SW11 120 DG86
Broxbourne Av E18 68 EH56
Broxbourne Rd E7 68 EG62
Broxbourne Rd, Orp. 145 ET101
Broxburn Dr, S.Ock. 91 FV73
Broxburn Par, S.Ock. 91 FV73
Broxburn Dr
Broxhill Rd (Havering-atte-Bower), Rom. 51 FH48
Broxholm Rd SE27 121 DN90
Broxted Ms, Brwd. 55 GC44
Bannister Dr
Broxted Rd SE6 123 DZ89
Broxwood Way NW8 82 DE67
Bruce Av, Horn. 72 FK61
Bruce Av, Shep. 135 BQ100
Bruce Castle Rd N17 46 DT53
Bruce Cl W10 81 CY71
Ladbroke Gro
Bruce Cl, Well. 106 EV81
Bruce Cl, W.Byf. 152 BK113
Bruce Dr, S.Croy. 161 DX109
Bruce Gdns N20 44 DF48
Balfour Gro
Bruce Gro N17 46 DS53
Bruce Gro, Orp. 146 EU102
Bruce Gro, Wat. 24 BW38
Bruce Hall Ms SW17 120 DG91
Brudenell Rd
Bruce Rd E3 85 EB69
Bruce Rd NW10 80 CR66
Bruce Rd SE25 142 DR98
Bruce Rd, Barn. 27 CY41
St. Albans Rd
Bruce Rd, Har. 41 CE54
Bruce Rd, Mitch. 120 DG94
Bruce Way, Wal.Cr. 15 DX33
Bruces Wf Rd, Grays 110 GA79
Bruckner St W10 81 CZ69
Brudenell Rd SW17 120 DF90
Bruffs Meadow, Nthlt. 78 BY65
Bruges Pl NW1 83 DJ66
Randolph St
Brumana Cl, Wey. 153 BP106
Elgin Rd
Brumfield Rd, Epsom 156 CQ106
Brummel Cl, Bexh. 107 FC83
Brune St E1 197 P7
Brune St E1 84 DT71
Brunel Cl SE19 122 DT93
Brunel Cl, Houns. 95 BV80
Brunel Cl, Nthlt. 78 BZ69
Brunel Cl, Rom. 71 FE56
Brunel Cl, Til. 111 GH83
Brunel Est W2 82 DA71
Brunel Pl, Sthl. 78 CB72
Brunel Rd E17 67 DY58
Brunel Rd SE16 202 F5
Brunel Rd SE16 102 DW75
Brunel Rd W3 80 CS71
Brunel Rd, Wdf.Grn. 49 EM50
Brunel St E16 86 EF72
Victoria Dock Rd
Brunel Wk N15 66 DS56
Brunel Wk, Twick. 116 CA87
Stephenson Rd
Brunel Way, Slou. 74 AT74
Brunner Cl NW11 64 DC57
Brunner Ct, Cher. 151 BC106
Brunner Rd E17 67 DZ57
Brunner Rd W5 79 CK70
Bruno Pl NW9 62 CQ61
Brunswick Av N11 44 DG48
Brunswick Av, Upmin. 73 FS59
Brunswick Cen WC1 195 P4
Brunswick Cl, Bexh. 106 EX84
Brunswick Cl, Pnr. 60 BY58
Brunswick Cl, T.Ditt. 137 CF102
Brunswick Cl, Twick. 117 CD90
Brunswick Cl, Walt. 136 BW103
Brunswick Ct EC1 83 DP69
Northampton Sq
Brunswick Ct SE1 201 N5
Brunswick Ct SE1 102 DS75
Brunswick Ct, Barn. 28 DD43
Brunswick Ct, Upmin. 73 FS59
Waycross Rd
Brunswick Cres N11 44 DG48
Brunswick Gdns W5 80 CL69
Brunswick Gdns W8 82 DA74
Brunswick Gdns, Ilf. 49 EQ52
Brunswick Gro N11 44 DG48
Brunswick Gro, Cob. 154 BW113
Brunswick Ind Pk N11 45 DH49
Brunswick Ms SW16 121 DK93
Potters La
Brunswick Ms W1 194 E8
Brunswick Pk SE5 102 DR81
Brunswick Pk Gdns N11 44 DG47
Brunswick Pk Rd N11 44 DG47
Brunswick Pl N1 197 L3
Brunswick Pl N1 84 DR69
Brunswick Pl SE19 122 DU94
Brunswick Quay SE16 203 J7
Brunswick Quay SE16 103 DX76
Brunswick Rd E10 67 EC60
Brunswick Rd E14 85 EC72
Blackwall Tunnel Northern App
Brunswick Rd N15 66 DS57
Brunswick Rd W5 79 CK70
Brunswick Rd, Bexh. 106 EX84
Brunswick Rd, Enf. 31 EA38
Brunswick Rd, Kings.T. 138 CN95
Brunswick Rd, Sutt. 158 DB105
Brunswick Sq N17 46 DT51
Brunswick Sq WC1 196 A5
Brunswick Sq WC1 83 DL70
Brunswick St E17 67 EC57
Brunswick Vil SE5 102 DS81
Brunswick Wk, Grav. 131 GK87
Brunswick Way N11 45 DH49
Brunton Pl E14 85 DY72
Brushfield St E1 197 N7
Brushfield St E1 84 DS71
Brushrise, Wat. 23 BU36
Brushwood Dr, Rick. 21 BC42
Brussels Rd SW11 100 DD84
Bruton Cl, Chis. 125 EM94
Bruton La W1 199 J1
Bruton La W1 83 DH73
Bruton Pl W1 199 J1
Bruton Pl W1 83 DH73
Bruton Rd, Mord. 140 DC99
Bruton St W1 199 J1
Bruton St W1 83 DH73
Bruton Way W13 79 CG71
Bryan Av NW10 81 CV66
Bryan Cl, Sun. 115 BU94
Bryan Rd SE16 203 M4
Bryan Rd SE16 103 DZ75
Bryan's All SW6 100 DB82
Wandsworth Br Rd
Bryanston Av, Twick. 116 CB88
Bryanston Cl, Sthl. 96 BZ77
Bryanston Ms E W1 194 D7
Bryanston Ms W W1 194 D7
Bryanston Pl W1 194 D7
Bryanston Pl W1 82 DF71
Bryanston Rd, Til. 111 GJ82
Bryanston Sq W1 194 D7
Bryanston Sq W1 82 DF71
Bryanston St W1 194 D9
Bryanston St W1 82 DF72
Bryanstone Rd N8 65 DK57
Bryanstone Rd, Wal.Cr. 15 DZ34
Bryant Av, Rom. 52 FK53
Bryant Av, Slou. 74 AS71
Bryant Cl, Barn. 27 CZ43
Bryant Ct E2 84 DT68
Bryant Rd, Nthlt. 78 BW69
Bryant Row, Rom. 52 FJ48
Cummings Hall La
Bryant St E15 85 ED66
Bryantwood Rd N7 65 DN64
Bryce Rd, Dag. 70 EW63
Brycedale Cres N14 45 DK49
Bryden Cl SE26 123 DY92
Brydges Pl WC2 199 P1
Brydges Rd E15 67 ED64
Brydon Wk N1 83 DL67
Outram Pl
Bryer Ct EC2 84 DQ71
Aldersgate St
Bryett Rd N7 65 DL62
Brymay Cl E3 85 EA68
Bryn-y-Mawr Rd, Enf. 30 DT42
Brynford Cl, Wok. 166 AY115
Brynmaer Rd SW11 100 DF81
Bryony Cl, Loug. 33 EP42
Bryony Cl, Uxb. 76 BM71
Bryony Rd W12 81 CU73
Bryony Way, Sun. 115 BT93
Bubblestone Rd, Sev. 181 FH116
Buccleuch Rd, Slou. 92 AU80
Buchan Cl, Uxb. 76 BJ69
Buchan Rd SE15 102 DW83
Buchanan Cl N21 29 DM43
Buchanan Cl, S.Ock. 90 FQ74
Buchanan Ct, Borwd. 26 CQ40
Buchanan Gdns NW10 81 CV68
Bucharest Rd SW18 120 DC87
Buck Hill Wk W2 198 A1
Buck La NW9 62 CR57
Buck St NW1 83 DH66
Buck Wk E17 67 ED56
Foresters Dr
Buckbean Path, Rom. 52 FJ52
Clematis Cl
Buckden Cl N2 64 DF56
Southern Rd
Buckden Cl SE12 124 EF86
Upwood Rd
Buckettsland La, Borwd. 26 CR38
Buckfast Rd, Mord. 140 DB98
Buckfast St E2 84 DU69
Buckham Thorns Rd, West. 189 EQ126
Buckhold Rd SW18 120 DA86
Buckhurst Av, Cars. 140 DE102
Buckhurst Av, Sev. 191 FJ125
Buckhurst Cl, Red. 184 DE132
Buckhurst La, Sev. 191 FJ125
Buckhurst Rd, West. 179 EN121
Buckhurst St E1 84 DV70
Buckhurst Way, Buck.H. 48 EK49
Buckingham Arc WC2 200 A1
Buckingham Av N20 44 DC45
Buckingham Av, Felt. 115 BV86
Buckingham Av, Grnf. 79 CG67
Buckingham Av, Th.Hth. 141 DN95
Buckingham Av, Well. 105 ES84
Buckingham Av, W.Mol. 136 CB97
Buckingham Cl W5 79 CJ71
Buckingham Cl, Enf. 30 DS40
Buckingham Cl, Hmptn. 116 BZ92
Buckingham Cl, Horn. 72 FK58
Buckingham Cl, Orp. 145 ES101
Buckingham Ct NW4 63 CU55
Buckingham Ct, Loug. 33 EN40
Rectory La
Buckingham Dr, Chis. 125 EP92
Buckingham Gdns, Edg. 42 CM52
Buckingham Gdns, Slou. 92 AT75
Buckingham Gdns, Th.Hth. 141 DN96
Buckingham Gdns, W.Mol. 136 CB96
Buckingham Av
Buckingham Gate SW1 199 K5
Buckingham Gate SW1 101 DJ76
Buckingham Gro, Uxb. 76 BN68
Buckingham La SE23 123 DY87
Buckingham Ms N1 84 DS65
Buckingham Rd
Buckingham Ms NW10 81 CT68
Buckingham Rd
Buckingham Ms SW1 199 K6
Buckingham Palace Rd SW1 199 H9
Buckingham Palace Rd SW1 101 DH77
Buckingham Pl SW1 199 K6
Buckingham Rd E10 67 EB62
Buckingham Rd E11 68 EJ57
Buckingham Rd E15 68 EF64
Buckingham Rd E18 48 EF53
Buckingham Rd N1 84 DS65
Buckingham Rd N22 45 DL53
Buckingham Rd NW10 81 CT68
Buckingham Rd, Borwd. 26 CR42
Buckingham Rd, Edg. 42 CM52
Buckingham Rd, Grav. 130 GD87
Dover Rd
Buckingham Rd, Hmptn. 116 BZ92
Buckingham Rd, Har. 61 CD57
Buckingham Rd, Ilf. 69 ER61
Buckingham Rd, Kings.T. 138 CM98
Buckingham Rd, Mitch. 141 DL99
Buckingham Rd, Rich. 117 CK89
Buckingham Rd, Wat. 24 BW37
Buckingham St WC2 200 A1
Buckingham Way, Wall. 159 DJ109
Buckland Av, Slou. 92 AV77
Buckland Cres NW3 82 DD66
Buckland La, Bet. 183 CT129
Buckland La, Tad. 183 CT129
Buckland Ri, Pnr. 40 BW53
Buckland Rd E10 67 EC61
Buckland Rd, Chess. 156 CM106
Buckland Rd, Orp. 163 ES105
Buckland Rd, Reig. 183 CX133
Buckland Rd, Sutt. 157 CW110
Buckland Rd, Tad. 183 CZ128
Buckland St N1 197 L1
Buckland St N1 84 DR68
Buckland Wk W3 98 CQ75
Church Rd
Buckland Wk, Mord. 140 DC98
Buckland Way, Wor.Pk. 139 CW102
Bucklands, The, Rick. 38 BG45
Bucklands Rd, Tedd. 117 CJ93
Buckle St E1 84 DT72
Leman St
Buckleigh Av SW20 139 CY97
Buckleigh Rd SW16 121 DK93
Buckleigh Way SE19 142 DT95
Buckler Gdns SE9 125 EM90
Southold Ri
Bucklers All SW6 99 CZ79
Bucklers Ct, Brwd. 54 FW50
Bucklers Way, Cars. 140 DF104
Bucklersbury EC4 197 K9
Bucklersbury EC4 84 DR72
Bucklersbury Pas EC4 197 K9
Buckles Ct, Belv. 106 EX76
Fendyke Rd
Buckles La, S.Ock. 91 FW71
Buckles Way, Bans. 173 CY116
Buckley Cl, Dart. 107 FF82
Buckley Rd NW6 81 CZ66
Buckley St SE1 200 D3
Buckmaster Cl SW9 101 DM83
Stockwell Pk Rd
Buckmaster Rd SW11 100 DE84
Bucknall St WC2 195 N8
Bucknall St WC2 83 DK72
Bucknalls Cl, Wat. 8 BY32
Bucknalls Dr, St.Alb. 8 BZ31
Bucknalls La, Wat. 8 BX32
Bucknell Cl SW2 101 DM84
Buckner Rd SW2 101 DM84
Bucknills Cl, Epsom 156 CP114
Buckrell Rd E4 47 ED47
Bucks Av, Wat. 40 BY45
Bucks Cl, W.Byf. 152 BH114
Bucks Cross Rd, Grav. 131 GF90
Bucks Cross Rd, Orp. 164 EY106
Bucks Hill, Kings L. 6 BK34
Buckstone Cl SE23 122 DW86
Buckstone Rd N18 46 DU50
Buckters Rents SE16 203 K3
Buckters Rents SE16 85 DY74
Buckthorne Ho, Chig. 50 EV49
Buckthorne Rd SE4 123 DY86
Buckton Rd, Borwd. 26 CM38
Budd Cl N12 44 DB49
Buddings Circle, Wem. 62 CQ62
Budd's All, Twick. 117 CJ85
Arlington Cl
Budebury Rd, Stai. 114 BG92
Budge La, Mitch. 140 DF101
Budge Row EC4 197 K10
Budgen Dr, Red. 184 DG131
Budge's Wk W2 82 DC73
Budgin's Hill, Orp. 164 EW112
Budleigh Cres, Well. 106 EW81
Budoch Ct, Ilf. 70 EU61
Budoch Dr, Ilf. 70 EU61
Buer Rd SW6 99 CY82
Buff Av, Bans. 158 DB114
Bug Hill, Cat. 177 DX120
Bugsby's Way SE7 104 EH77
Bugsby's Way SE10 205 K8
Bugsby's Way SE10 104 EF77
Bulganak Rd, Th.Hth. 142 DQ98
Bulinga St SW1 199 P9
Bulinga St SW1 101 DK77
Bulkeley Cl, Egh. 112 AW91
Bull All, Well. 106 EV83
Welling High St
Bull Cl, Grays 110 FZ75
Bull Hill, Dart. 148 FQ98
Bull Hill, Lthd. 171 CG121
Bull Inn Ct WC2 200 A1
Bull La N18 46 DS50
Bull La, Chis. 125 ER94
Bull La, Dag. 71 FB62
Bull La (Chalfont St. Peter), Ger.Cr. 56 AX55
Bull Rd E15 86 EF68
Bull Wf La EC4 197 J10
Bull Yd, Grav. 131 GH86
High St
Bullace La, Dart. 128 FL86
High St
Bullace Row SE5 102 DQ81
Camberwell Rd
Bullards Pl E2 85 DX69
Bullbanks Rd, Belv. 107 FC77
Bullbeggars La, Gdse. 186 DW132
Bullbeggars La, Wok. 166 AV116
Bullen St SW11 100 DE82
Buller Cl SE15 102 DU80
Buller Rd N17 46 DU54
Buller Rd N22 45 DN54
Buller Rd NW10 81 CX69
Chamberlayne Rd
Buller Rd, Bark. 87 ES66
Buller Rd, Th.Hth. 142 DR96
Bullers Cl, Sid. 126 EY92
Bullers Wd Dr, Chis. 124 EL94
Bullescroft Rd, Edg. 42 CN48
Bullfinch Cl, Sev. 190 FD122
Bullfinch Dene, Sev. 190 FD122
Bullfinch La, Sev. 190 FD122
Bullfinch Rd, S.Croy. 161 DX110
Bullhead Rd, Borwd. 26 CQ41
Bullied Way SW1 199 J9
Bullivant Cl, Green. 129 FU85
Bullivant St E14 85 EC73
Bullrush Cl, Croy. 142 DS100
Bullrush Gro, Uxb. 76 BJ70
Bull's All SW14 98 CR82
Bulls Br Ind Est, Sthl. 95 BV76
Hayes Rd
Bulls Br Rd, Sthl. 95 BV76
Bulls Cross, Enf. 30 DU37
Bulls Cross Ride, Wal.Cr. 30 DU35
Bulls Gdns SW3 198 C8
Bull's Head Pas EC3 197 M9
Bullsbrook Rd, Hayes 78 BW74
Bullsland Gdns, Rick. 21 BB44
Bullsland La, Ger.Cr. 37 BB45
Bullsland La, Rick. 21 BB44
Bullsmoor Cl, Wal.Cr. 30 DW35
Bullsmoor Gdns, Wal.Cr. 30 DV35
Bullsmoor La, Enf. 30 DW35
Bullsmoor La, Wal.Cr. 30 DU35
Bullsmoor Ride, Wal.Cr. 30 DW35
Bullsmoor Way, Wal.Cr. 30 DV35
Bullwell Cres (Cheshunt), Wal.Cr. 15 DY29
Bulmer Gdns, Har. 61 CK59
Bulmer Ms W11 82 DA73
Ladbroke Rd
Bulmer Pl W11 82 DA74
Bulmer Wk, Rain. 90 FJ68
Bulow Est SW6 100 DB82
Broughton Rd
Bulstrode Av, Houns. 96 BZ82
Bulstrode Ct, Ger.Cr. 56 AX58
Bulstrode Gdns, Houns. 96 BZ83
Bulstrode La, Hem.H. 6 BG27
Bulstrode La, Kings L. 5 BE29
Bulstrode Pl W1 194 G7
Bulstrode Pl, Slou. 92 AT76
Bulstrode Rd, Houns. 96 CA83
Bulstrode St W1 194 G8
Bulstrode St W1 82 DG72
Bulstrode Way, Ger.Cr. 56 AX57
Bulwer Ct Rd E11 67 ED60
Bulwer Gdns, Barn. 28 DC42
Bulwer Rd
Bulwer Rd E11 67 ED59
Bulwer Rd N18 46 DS49
Bulwer Rd, Barn. 28 DB42
Bulwer St W12 81 CW74
Bumbles Grn La, Wal.Abb. 16 EH25
Bunbury Way, Epsom 173 CV116
Bunby Rd, Slou. 74 AT66
Bunce Dr, Cat. 176 DR123
Bunces La, Wdf.Grn. 48 EF52
Bundys Way, Stai. 113 BF93
Bungalow Rd SE25 142 DS98
Bungalow Rd, Wok. 169 BQ124
Bungalows, The SW16 121 DH94
Bungalows, The, Wall. 159 DH106
Bunhill Row EC1 197 K4
Bunhill Row EC1 84 DR70
Bunhouse Pl SW1 198 F10
Bunhouse Pl SW1 100 DG78
Bunkers Hill NW11 64 DC59
Bunkers Hill, Belv. 106 FA77
Bunkers Hill, Sid. 126 EZ90
Bunkers La, Hem.H. 6 BN25
Bunning Way N7 83 DL66
Bunns La NW7 43 CT51
Bunn's La, Chesh. 4 AU34
Bunsen St E3 85 DY68
Kenilworth Rd
Bunting Cl N9 47 DX46
Dunnock Cl
Bunting Cl, Mitch. 140 DF99
Buntingbridge Rd, Ilf. 69 ER57
Bunton St SE18 105 EN76
Bunyan Ct EC2 84 DQ71
Beech St
Bunyan Rd E17 67 DY55
Bunyard Dr, Wok. 151 BC114
Bunyons Cl, Brwd. 53 FW51
Essex Way
Buonaparte Ms SW1 199 M10
Burbage Cl SE1 201 K7
Burbage Cl SE1 102 DR76
Burbage Cl (Cheshunt), Wal.Cr. 15 DZ31
Burbage Rd SE21 122 DR86
Burbage Rd SE24 122 DQ86
Burberry Cl, N.Mal. 138 CS96
Burbidge Rd, Shep. 134 BN98
Burbridge Way N17 46 DT54
Burch Rd, Grav. 131 GF86
Burcham St E14 85 EB72
Burcharbro Rd SE2 106 EX79
Burchell Ct, Bushey 40 CC45
Catsey La
Burchell Rd E10 67 EB60
Burchell Rd SE15 102 DV81
Burchett Way, Rom. 70 EZ58
Burchetts Way, Shep. 135 BP100
Burchwall Cl, Rom. 51 FC52
Burcote, Wey. 153 BR107
Burcote Rd SW18 120 DD88
Burcott Gdns, Add. 152 BJ107
Burcott Rd, Pur. 159 DN114
Burden Cl, Brent. 97 CJ78
Burden Way E11 68 EH61
Brading Cres
Burdenshott Av, Rich. 98 CP84
Burder Cl N1 84 DS65
Burder Rd N1 84 DS65
Balls Pond Rd
Burdett Av SW20 139 CU95
Burdett Cl W7 97 CF75
Cherington Rd
Burdett Cl, Sid. 126 EY92
Burdett Ms NW3 82 DD65
Belsize Cres
Burdett Ms W2 82 DB72
Hatherley Gro
Burdett Rd E3 85 DZ70
Burdett Rd E14 85 DZ70
Burdett Rd, Croy. 142 DR100
Burdett Rd, Rich. 98 CM83
Burdett St SE1 200 D6
Burdetts Rd, Dag. 88 EZ67
Burdock Cl, Croy. 143 DX102
Burdock Rd N17 66 DU55
Burdon La, Sutt. 157 CY108
Burdon Pk, Sutt. 157 CZ109
Burfield Cl SW17 120 DD91
Burfield Dr, Warl. 176 DW119
Burfield Rd, Rick. 21 BB43
Burfield Rd, Wind. 112 AU86
Burford Cl, Dag. 70 EW62
Burford Cl, Ilf. 69 EQ56
Burford Cl, Uxb. 58 BL63
Burford Gdns N13 45 DM48
Burford La, Epsom 157 CW111
Burford Rd E6 86 EL69
Burford Rd E15 85 ED66
Burford Rd SE6 123 DZ89
Burford Rd, Brent. 98 CL78
Burford Rd, Brom. 144 EL98
Burford Rd, Sutt. 140 DA103
Burford Rd, Wor.Pk. 139 CT101
Burford Wk SW6 100 DB80
Cambria St
Burford Way, Croy. 161 EC107
Burgate Cl, Dart. 107 FF83
Burge St SE1 201 L7
Burge St SE1 102 DR76
Burges Cl, Horn. 72 FM58
Burges Ct E6 87 EN66
Burges Gro SW13 99 CV80
Burges Rd E6 86 EL66
Burges Way, Stai. 114 BG92
Burgess Av NW9 62 CR58
Burgess Cl, Felt. 116 BY91
Burgess Cl (Cheshunt), Wal.Cr. 14 DQ25

Byron Rd, Add. 152 BL105
Byron Rd, Brwd. 55 GD45
Byron Rd, Dart. 108 FP84
Byron Rd, Har. 61 CE58
Byron Rd (Wealdstone), Har. 41 CF54
Byron Rd, S.Croy. 160 DV110
Byron Rd, Wem. 61 CJ62
Byron St E14 85 EC72
St. Leonards Rd
Byron Ter N9 46 DW45
Byron Way, Hayes 77 BT70
Byron Way, Nthlt. 78 BY69
Byron Way, Rom. 52 FJ53
Byron Way, West Dr. 94 BM77
Bysouth Cl N15 66 DR56
Bysouth Cl, Ilf. 49 EP53
Bythorn St SW9 101 DM83
Byton Rd SW17 120 DF93
Byward Av, Felt. 116 BW86
Byward St EC3 201 N1
Byward St EC3 84 DS73
Bywater Pl SE16 203 L2
Bywater Pl SE16 85 DY74
Bywater St SW3 198 D10
Bywater St SW3 100 DF78
Byway, The, Epsom 157 CT105
Byway, The, Pot.B. 12 DA33
Byway, The, Sutt. 158 DD109
Bywell Pl W1 195 K7
Bywood Av, Croy. 142 DW100
Bywood Cl, Ken. 175 DP115
Byworth Wk N19 65 DK60
Courtauld Rd

C

C.I. Twr, N.Mal. 138 CS97
Cabbell Pl, Add. 152 BJ105
Cabbell St NW1 194 B7
Cabbell St NW1 82 DE71
Caberfeigh Pl, Red. 184 DE134
Cabinet Way E4 47 DZ51
Cable Pl SE10 103 EC81
Diamond Ter
Cable St E1 84 DU73
Cable Trade Pk SE7 104 EJ77
Cabot Sq E14 204 A2
Cabot Sq E14 85 EA74
Cabot Way E6 86 EK67
Parr Rd
Cabrera Av, Vir.W. 132 AW100
Cabrera Cl, Vir.W. 132 AX100
Cabul Rd SW11 100 DE82
Cacket's Cotts, Sev. 179 ES115
Cackets La
Cackets La, Sev. 179 ER115
Cactus Cl SE15 102 DS82
Lyndhurst Gro
Cactus Wk W12 81 CT72
Du Cane Rd
Cadbury Cl, Islw. 97 CG81
Cadbury Cl, Sun. 115 BS94
Cadbury Rd, Sun. 115 BS94
Cadbury Way SE16 202 A7
Caddington Cl, Barn. 28 DE43
Caddington Rd NW2 63 CY62
Caddis Cl, Stan. 41 CF52
Daventer Dr
Caddy Cl, Egh. 113 BA92
Cade La, Sev. 191 FJ128
Cade Rd SE10 103 ED81
Cadell Cl E2 84 DT69
Shipton St
Cader Rd SW18 120 DC86
Cadet Dr SE1 202 A10
Cadet Dr SE1 102 DT77
Cadet Pl SE10 205 H10
Cadet Pl SE10 104 EE78
Cadiz Ct, Dag. 89 FD66
Rainham Rd S
Cadiz Rd, Dag. 89 FC66
Cadiz St SE17 102 DQ78
Cadley Ter SE23 122 DW89
Cadlocks Hill, Sev. 164 EZ110
Cadman Cl SW9 101 DP80
Langton Rd
Cadmer Cl, N.Mal. 138 CS98
Cadmore La (Cheshunt), Wal.Cr. 15 DX28
Cadmus Cl SW4 101 DK83
Aristotle Rd
Cadogan Av, Dart. 129 FR87
Cadogan Cl, Beck. 143 ED95
Albemarle Rd
Cadogan Cl, Har. 60 CB63
Cadogan Cl, Tedd. 117 CE92
Cadogan Ct, Sutt. 158 DB107
Cadogan Gdns E18 68 EH55
Cadogan Gdns N3 44 DB53
Cadogan Gdns N21 29 DN43
Cadogan Gdns SW3 198 E8
Cadogan Gdns SW3 100 DF77
Cadogan Gate SW1 198 E8
Cadogan Gate SW1 100 DF77
Cadogan La SW1 198 F7
Cadogan La SW1 100 DG76
Cadogan Pl SW1 198 E7
Cadogan Pl SW1 100 DF76
Cadogan Rd, Surb. 137 CK99
Cadogan Sq SW1 198 E7
Cadogan Sq SW1 100 DF76
Cadogan St SW3 198 D9
Cadogan St SW3 100 DF77
Cadogan Ter E9 85 DZ65
Cadoxton Av N15 66 DT58
Cadwallon Rd SE9 125 EP89
Caedmon Rd N7 65 DM63
Caen Wd Rd, Ash. 171 CJ118
Caenshill Rd, Wey. 152 BN108
Caenwood Cl, Wey. 152 BN107
Caerleon Cl, Sid. 126 EW92
Caerleon Ter SE2 106 EV77
Blithdale Rd
Caernarvon Cl, Horn. 72 FN60
Caernarvon Cl, Mitch. 141 DL97
Caernarvon Dr, Ilf. 49 EN53
Caesars Wk, Mitch. 140 DF99
Caesars Way, Shep. 135 BR100
Cage Pond Rd, Rad. 10 CM33
Cage Yd, Reig. 184 DA134
High St
Cahill St EC1 197 J5
Cahir St E14 204 B9
Cahir St E14 103 EB77
Caillard Rd, W.Byf. 152 BL111
Cains La, Felt. 115 BS85
Caird St W10 81 CY69
Cairn Av W5 79 CK74
Cairn Way, Stan. 41 CF51
Cairndale Cl, Brom. 124 EF94
Cairnfield Av NW2 62 CS62
Cairngorm Cl, Tedd. 117 CG92
Vicarage Rd
Cairns Av, Wdf.Grn. 48 EL51
Cairns Cl, Dart. 128 FK85
Cairns Rd SW11 120 DE85
Cairo New Rd, Croy. 141 DP103
Cairo Rd E17 67 EA56
Caishowe Rd, Borwd. 26 CP39
Caistor Ms SW12 121 DH87
Caistor Rd
Caistor Pk Rd E15 86 EF67
Caistor Rd SW12 121 DH87
Caithness Gdns, Sid. 125 ET86
Caithness Rd W14 99 CX77
Caithness Rd, Mitch. 121 DH94
Calabria Rd N5 83 DP65
Calais Cl, Wal.Cr. 13 DP25
Hammondstreet Rd
Calais Gate SE5 101 DP81
Calais St
Calais St SE5 101 DP81
Calbourne Av, Horn. 71 FH64
Calbourne Rd SW12 120 DF87
Calcott Cl, Brwd. 54 FV46
Calcott Wk SE9 124 EK91
Calcutta Rd, Til. 111 GF82
Caldbeck, Wal.Abb. 15 ED34
Caldbeck Av, Wor.Pk. 139 CU103
Caldecot Av, Wal.Cr. 14 DT29
Caldecot Rd SE5 102 DQ82
Caldecote Gdns, Bushey 25 CE44
Caldecote La, Bushey 25 CF44
Caldecott Way E5 67 DX62
Calder Av, Grnf. 79 CF68
Calder Av, Hat. 12 DB26
Calder Cl, Enf. 30 DS41
Calder Ct, Slou. 93 AZ78
Calder Gdns, Edg. 62 CN55
Calder Rd, Mord. 140 DC99
Calder Way, Slou. 93 BF83
Calderon Pl W10 81 CW71
St. Quintin Gdns
Calderon Rd E11 67 EC63
Caldervale Rd SW4 121 DK85
Calderwood, Grav. 131 GL92
Calderwood St SE18 105 EN77
Caldicot Grn NW9 62 CS58
Snowdon Dr
Caldwell Rd, Wat. 40 BX49
Caldwell St SW9 101 DM80
Caldwell Yd EC4 84 DQ73
Upper Thames St
Caldy Rd, Belv. 107 FB76
Caldy Wk N1 84 DQ65
Clephane Rd
Cale St SW3 198 B10
Cale St SW3 100 DE78
Caleb St SE1 201 H4
Caledon Rd E6 87 EM67
Caledon Rd, St.Alb. 9 CK26
Caledon Rd, Wall. 158 DG105
Caledonia Rd, Stai. 114 BL88
Caledonia St N1 196 A1
Caledonia St N1 83 DL68
Caledonian Cl, Ilf. 70 EV60
Caledonian Rd N1 196 A1
Caledonian Rd N1 83 DM68
Caledonian Rd N7 65 DM64
Caledonian Wf E14 204 F9
Caledonian Wf E14 103 ED77
Caletock Way SE10 205 K10
Caletock Way SE10 104 EF78
Calfstock La (South Darenth), Dart. 148 FL98
Calico Row SW11 100 DC83
York Pl
Calidore Cl SW2 121 DM86
Endymion Rd
California La, Bushey 41 CD46
California Rd, N.Mal. 138 CQ98
Caliph Cl, Grav. 131 GM90
Callaby Ter N1 84 DR65
Wakeham St
Callaghan Cl SE13 104 EE84
Glenton Rd
Callan Gro, S.Ock. 91 FV73
Callander Rd SE6 123 EB89
Callard Av N13 45 DP50
Callcott Rd NW6 81 CZ66
Callcott St W8 82 DA74
Hillgate Pl
Callendar Rd SW7 100 DD76
Calley Down Cres, Croy. 161 ED110
Callingham Cl E14 85 DZ71
Wallwood St
Callis Fm Cl, Stai. 114 BL86
Bedfont Rd
Callis Rd E17 67 DZ58
Callow Fld, Pur. 159 DN113
Callow Hill, Vir.W. 132 AW97
Callow St SW3 100 DD79
Callowland Cl, Wat. 23 BV38
Calluna Ct, Wok. 167 AZ118
Heathside Rd
Calmont Rd, Brom. 123 ED93
Calmore Cl, Horn. 72 FJ64
Calne Av, Ilf. 49 EP53
Calonne Rd SW19 119 CX91
Calshot Av, Grays 110 FZ75
Calshot Rd, Houns. 94 BN82
Calshot St N1 83 DM68
Calshot Way, Enf. 29 DP41
Calshot Way, Houns. 95 BP82
Calshot Rd
Calthorpe Gdns, Edg. 42 CL50
Jesmond Way
Calthorpe Gdns, Sutt. 140 DC104
Calthorpe St WC1 196 C4
Calthorpe St WC1 83 DM70
Calton Av SE21 122 DS85
Calton Rd, Barn. 28 DC44
Calverley Cl, Beck. 123 EB93
Calverley Cres, Dag. 70 FA61
Calverley Gdns, Har. 61 CK59
Calverley Gro N19 65 DK60
Calverley Rd, Epsom 157 CU107
Calvert Av E2 197 N3
Calvert Av E2 84 DS69
Calvert Cl, Belv. 106 FA77
Calvert Cl, Sid. 126 EY93
Calvert Rd SE10 104 EF78
Calvert Rd, Barn. 27 CX40
Calvert St NW1 82 DG67
Chalcot Rd
Calverton SE5 102 DS79
Albany Rd
Calverton Rd E6 87 EN67
Calvert's Bldgs SE1 201 K3
Calvin Cl, Orp. 146 EX97
Calvin St E1 197 P5
Calvin St E1 84 DT70
Calydon Rd SE7 104 EH78
Calypso Way SE16 203 M7
Calypso Way SE16 103 DZ76
Cam Grn, S.Ock. 91 FV72
Cam Rd E15 85 ED67
Camac Rd, Twick. 117 CD88
Cambalt Rd SW15 119 CX85
Camberley Av SW20 139 CV96
Camberley Av, Enf. 30 DS42
Camberley Cl, Sutt. 139 CX104
Camberley Rd, Houns. 94 BN83
Cambert Way SE3 104 EH84
Camberwell Ch St SE5 102 DR81
Camberwell Glebe SE5 102 DR81
Camberwell Grn SE5 102 DR81
Camberwell Gro SE5 102 DR81
Camberwell New Rd SE5 101 DN80
Camberwell Pas SE5 102 DQ81
Camberwell Grn
Camberwell Rd SE5 102 DQ79
Camberwell Sta Rd SE5 102 DQ81
Cambeys Rd, Dag. 71 FB64
Camborne Av W13 97 CH75
Camborne Av, Rom. 52 FL52
Camborne Cl, Houns. 94 BN83
Camborne Rd
Camborne Ms W11 81 CY72
St. Marks Rd
Camborne Rd SW18 120 DA87
Camborne Rd, Croy. 142 DU101
Camborne Rd, Houns. 94 BN83
Camborne Rd, Mord. 139 CX99
Camborne Rd, Sid. 126 EW90
Camborne Rd, Sutt. 158 DA108
Camborne Rd, Well. 105 ET82
Camborne Rd N, Houns. 94 BN83
Camborne Rd
Camborne Way, Houns. 96 CA81
Camborne Way, Rom. 52 FL52
Cambourne Av N9 47 DX45
Cambray Rd SW12 121 DJ88
Cambray Rd, Orp. 145 ET101
Cambria Cl, Houns. 96 CA84
Cambria Cl, Sid. 125 ER88
Cambria Ct, Felt. 115 BV87
Hounslow Rd
Cambria Ct, Slou. 92 AW75
Turner Rd
Cambria Cres, Grav. 131 GL91
Cambria Gdns, Stai. 114 BL87
Cambria Rd SE5 102 DQ83
Cambria St SW6 100 DB80
Cambrian Av, Ilf. 69 ES57
Cambrian Cl SE27 121 DP90
Cambrian Gro, Grav. 131 GG87
Cambrian Rd E10 67 EA59
Cambrian Rd, Rich. 118 CM86
Cambridge Av NW6 82 DA68
Cambridge Av, Grnf. 61 CF64
Cambridge Av, N.Mal. 139 CT96
Cambridge Av, Rom. 72 FJ55
Cambridge Av, Well. 105 ET84
Cambridge Barracks Rd SE18 105 EM77
Cambridge Circ WC2 195 N9
Cambridge Circ WC2 83 DK72
Cambridge Cl E17 67 DZ58
Cambridge Cl N22 45 DN53
Pellatt Gro
Cambridge Cl NW10 62 CQ62
Cambridge Cl SW20 139 CV95
Cambridge Cl, Houns. 96 BY84
Cambridge Cl (Cheshunt), Wal.Cr. 14 DW29
Cambridge Cl, West Dr. 94 BK79
Cambridge Cl, Wok. 166 AT118
Bingham Dr
Cambridge Cotts, Rich. 98 CN79
Cambridge Cres E2 84 DV68
Cambridge Cres, Tedd. 117 CG92
Cambridge Dr SE12 124 EG85
Cambridge Dr, Pot.B. 11 CX31
Cambridge Dr, Ruis. 60 BW61
Cambridge Gdns N10 45 DH53
Cambridge Gdns N13 45 DN50
Cambridge Gdns N17 46 DR52
Great Cambridge Rd
Cambridge Gdns N21 46 DR45
Cambridge Gdns NW6 82 DA68
Cambridge Gdns W10 81 CY72
Cambridge Gdns, Enf. 30 DU40
Cambridge Gdns, Grays 111 GG77
Cambridge Gdns, Kings.T. 138 CN96
Cambridge Gate NW1 195 J3
Cambridge Gate Ms NW1 195 J3
Cambridge Grn SE9 125 EP88
Cambridge Gro SE20 122 DV94
Cambridge Gro W6 99 CV77
Cambridge Gro Rd, Kings.T. 138 CN96
Cambridge Heath Rd E1 84 DV68
Cambridge Heath Rd E2 84 DV68
Cambridge Mans SW11 100 DF81
Cambridge Rd
Cambridge Par, Enf. 30 DU39
Great Cambridge Rd
Cambridge Pk E11 68 EG59
Cambridge Pk, Twick. 117 CK87
Cambridge Pk Rd E11 68 EF59
Cambridge Pk
Cambridge Pl W8 100 DB75
Cambridge Rd E4 47 ED46
Cambridge Rd E11 68 EF58
Cambridge Rd NW6 82 DA69
Cambridge Rd SE20 142 DV97
Cambridge Rd SW11 100 DF81
Cambridge Rd SW13 99 CT82
Cambridge Rd SW20 139 CU95
Cambridge Rd W7 97 CF75
Cambridge Rd, Ashf. 115 BQ94
Cambridge Rd, Bark. 87 EQ66
Cambridge Rd, Brom. 124 EG94
Cambridge Rd, Cars. 158 DE107
Cambridge Rd, Hmptn. 116 BZ94
Cambridge Rd, Har. 60 CA57
Cambridge Rd, Houns. 96 BY84
Cambridge Rd, Ilf. 69 ES60
Cambridge Rd, Kings.T. 138 CM96
Cambridge Rd, Mitch. 141 DJ97
Cambridge Rd, N.Mal. 138 CS98
Cambridge Rd, Rich. 98 CN80
Cambridge Rd, Sid. 125 ES91
Cambridge Rd, Sthl. 78 BZ74
Cambridge Rd, Tedd. 117 CF91
Cambridge Rd, Twick. 117 CK86
Cambridge Rd, Uxb. 76 BK65
Cambridge Rd, Walt. 135 BV100
Cambridge Rd, Wat. 24 BW42
Cambridge Rd, W.Mol. 136 BZ98
Cambridge Rd N W4 98 CP78
Cambridge Rd S W4 98 CP78
Oxford Rd S
Cambridge Row SE18 105 EP78
Cambridge Sq W2 194 B8
Cambridge Sq W2 82 DE72
Cambridge St SW1 199 J9
Cambridge St SW1 101 DH78
Cambridge Ter N13 45 DN50
Cambridge Ter NW1 195 J3
Cambridge Ter Ms NW1 195 J3
Cambstone Cl N11 44 DG47
Cambus Cl, Hayes 78 BY71
Cambus Rd E16 86 EG71
Camdale Rd SE18 105 ET80
Camden Av, Felt. 116 BW89
Camden Av, Hayes 78 BW73
Camden Cl, Chis. 125 EQ94
Camden Cl, Grav. 130 GC88
Camden Cl, Grays 111 GH77
Camden Gdns NW1 83 DH66
Kentish Town Rd
Camden Gdns, Sutt. 158 DB106
Camden Gdns, Th.Hth. 141 DP97
Camden Gro, Chis. 125 EP93
Camden High St NW1 83 DH67
Camden Hill Rd SE19 122 DS93
Camden La N7 83 DK65
Rowstock Gdns
Camden Lock Pl NW1 83 DH66
Chalk Fm Rd
Camden Ms NW1 83 DK65
Camden Pk Rd NW1 83 DK65
Camden Pk Rd, Chis. 125 EM94
Camden Pas N1 83 DP67
Camden Rd E11 68 EH58
Camden Rd E17 67 DZ58
Camden Rd N7 65 DK64
Camden Rd NW1 83 DJ66
Camden Rd, Bex. 126 EZ88
Camden Rd, Cars. 158 DF105
Camden Rd, Grays 110 FY76
Camden Rd, Sev. 191 FH122
Camden Rd, Sutt. 158 DA106
Camden Row SE3 104 EE82
Camden Sq NW1 83 DK65
Camden Sq SE15 102 DT81
Watts St
Camden St NW1 83 DJ66
Camden Ter NW1 83 DK65
North Vil
Camden Wk N1 83 DP67
Camden Way, Chis. 125 EM94
Camden Way, Th.Hth. 141 DP97
Camdenhurst St E14 85 DY72
Camel Gro, Kings.T. 117 CK92
Camel Rd E16 86 EK74
Camelford Wk W11 81 CY72
Lancaster Rd
Camellia Cl, Rom. 52 FL53
Columbine Way
Camellia Ct, Wdf.Grn. 48 EE52
The Bridle Path
Camellia Pl, Twick. 116 CB87
Camellia St SW8 101 DL80
Camelot Cl SE28 105 ER75
Camelot Cl SW19 120 DA91
Camelot Cl, West. 178 EJ116
Camelot St SE15 102 DV80
Bird in Bush Rd
Camera Pl SW10 100 DD79
Cameron Cl N18 46 DV49
Cameron Cl N20 44 DE47
Myddelton Pk
Cameron Cl, Bex. 127 FD90
Cameron Cl, Brwd. 54 FW49
Cameron Dr, Wal.Cr. 15 DX34
Cameron Pl E1 84 DV72
Varden St
Cameron Rd SE6 123 DZ89
Cameron Rd, Brom. 144 EG98
Cameron Rd, Croy. 141 DP100
Cameron Rd, Ilf. 69 ES60
Cameron Sq, Mitch. 140 DE95
Camerton Cl E8 84 DT65
Buttermere Wk
Camgate Cen, Stai. 114 BM86
Camilla Cl, Sun. 115 BS93
Camilla Rd SE16 202 D9
Camilla Rd SE16 102 DV77
Camille Cl SE25 142 DU97
Camlan Rd, Brom. 124 EF91
Camlet St E2 197 P4
Camlet St E2 84 DT70
Camlet Way, Barn. 28 DA40
Camley St NW1 83 DK66
Camm Gdns, Kings.T. 138 CM96
Church Rd
Camm Gdns, T.Ditt. 137 CE101
Camms Ter, Dag. 71 FC64
Camomile Av, Mitch. 140 DF95
Camomile Rd, Rom. 71 FD61
Camomile St EC3 197 M8
Camomile St EC3 84 DS72
Camomile Way, West Dr. 76 BL72
Camp End Rd, Wey. 153 BR110
Camp Rd SW19 119 CW92
Camp Rd, Cat. 177 DY120
Camp Rd, Ger.Cr. 56 AX59
Camp Vw SW19 119 CV92
Campana Rd SW6 100 DA81
Campbell Av, Ilf. 69 EQ56
Campbell Av, Wok. 167 AZ121
Campbell Cl SE18 105 EN81
Moordown
Campbell Cl SW16 121 DK91
Campbell Cl (Havering-atte-Bower), Rom. 51 FE51
Campbell Cl, Ruis. 59 BU58
Campbell Cl, Twick. 117 CD89
Campbell Ct N17 46 DT53
Campbell Cft, Edg. 42 CN50
Campbell Gordon Way NW2 63 CV63
Campbell Rd E3 85 EA69
Campbell Rd E6 86 EL67
Campbell Rd E15 68 EF63
Trevelyan Rd
Campbell Rd E17 67 DZ56
Campbell Rd N17 46 DU53
Campbell Rd W7 79 CE73
Campbell Rd, Cat. 176 DR121
Campbell Rd, Croy. 141 DP101
Campbell Rd, E.Mol. 137 CF97
Hampton Ct Rd
Campbell Rd, Grav. 131 GF88
Campbell Rd, Twick. 117 CD89
Campbell Rd, Wey. 152 BN108
Campbell Wk N1 83 DL67
Outram Pl
Campdale Rd N7 65 DK62
Campden Cres, Dag. 70 EV63
Campden Cres, Wem. 61 CH61
Campden Gro W8 100 DA75
Campden Hill Gdns W8 82 DA74
Campden Hill Gate W8 100 DA75
Duchess of Bedford's Wk
Campden Hill Pl W11 81 CZ74
Holland Pk Av
Campden Hill Rd W8 82 DA74
Campden Hill Sq W8 81 CZ74
Campden Ho Cl W8 100 DA75
Hornton St
Campden Rd, S.Croy. 160 DS106
Campden Rd, Uxb. 58 BM62
Campden St W8 82 DA74
Campen Cl SW19 119 CY89
Queensmere Rd
Camperdown St E1 84 DT72
Leman St
Campfield Rd SE9 124 EK87
Camphill Ct, W.Byf. 152 BG112
Camphill Ind Est, W.Byf. 152 BH111
Camphill Rd, W.Byf. 152 BG112
Campine Cl (Cheshunt), Wal.Cr. 15 DX28
Welsummer Way
Campion Cl E6 87 EM73
Campion Cl, Croy. 160 DS105
Campion Cl, Grav. 130 GE91
Campion Cl, Har. 62 CM58
Campion Cl, Rom. 71 FD61
Campion Cl (Denham), Uxb. 58 BG62
Lindsey Rd
Campion Cl (Hillingdon), Uxb. 76 BM71
Campion Cl, Wat. 7 BU33
Campion Ct, Grays 110 GD79
Campion Dr, Tad. 173 CV120
Campion Gdns, Wdf.Grn. 48 EG50
Campion Pl SE28 88 EV74
Campion Rd SW15 99 CW84
Campion Rd, Islw. 97 CF81
Campion Ter NW2 63 CX62
Campion Way, Edg. 42 CQ49
Campions, Epp. 18 EU28
Campions, Loug. 33 EN38
Campions, The, Borwd. 26 CN38
Campions Cl, Borwd. 26 CP37
Cample La, S.Ock. 91 FU73
Camplin Rd, Har. 62 CL57
Camplin St SE14 103 DX80
Campsbourne, The N8 65 DL56
Rectory Gdns
Campsbourne Rd N8 65 DL55
Campsey Gdns, Dag. 88 EV66
Campsey Rd, Dag. 88 EV66
Campsfield Rd N8 65 DL55
Campsbourne Rd
Campshill Pl SE13 123 EC85
Campshill Rd
Campshill Rd SE13 123 EC85
Campus Rd E17 67 DZ58
Campus Way NW4 63 CV55
Greyhound Hill
Camrose Av, Edg. 42 CM53
Camrose Av, Erith 107 FB79
Camrose Av, Felt. 115 BV91
Camrose Cl, Croy. 143 DY101
Camrose Cl, Mord. 140 DA98
Camrose St SE2 106 EU78
Can Hatch, Tad. 173 CY118
Canada Av N18 46 DQ51
Canada Cres W3 80 CQ71
Canada Est SE16 202 G6
Canada Est SE16 102 DW76
Canada Fm Rd (South Darenth), Dart. 149 FU98
Canada Fm Rd, Long. 149 FU99
Canada Gdns SE13 123 EC85
Canada La, Brox. 15 DY25
Canada Rd W3 80 CQ70
Canada Rd, Cob. 154 BW113
Canada Rd, Erith 107 FH80
Canada Rd, Slou. 92 AV75
Canada Rd, W.Byf. 152 BK111
Canada Sq E14 204 B2
Canada Sq E14 85 EB74

Canada St SE16 203 H5
Canada St SE16 103 DX75
Canada Way W12 81 CV73
Canadas, The, Brox. 15 DY25
Canadian Av SE6 123 EB88
Canadian Mem Av, Egh. 132 AT96
Canal App SE8 103 DY78
Canal Basin, Grav. 131 GK86
Canal Cl E1 85 DY70
Canal Cl W10 81 CX70
Canal Est, Slou. 93 BA75
Canal Gro SE15 102 DU79
Canal Head SE15 102 DU81
Peckham High St
Canal Path E2 84 DT67
Canal Rd E3 85 DY70
Canal Rd, Grav. 131 GJ86
Canal Side (Harefield), Uxb. 38 BG51
Summerhouse La
Canal St SE5 102 DR79
Canal Wk N1 84 DR67
Canal Wk SE26 122 DW92
Canal Wk, Croy. 142 DS100
Canal Way N1 84 DQ68
Packington Sq
Canal Way NW1 194 A4
Canal Way NW8 194 A4
Canal Way NW10 81 CT70
Canal Way W10 81 CX70
Canal Way Wk W10 81 CX70
Canal Wf, Slou. 93 BA75
Canberra Cl NW4 63 CU55
Canberra Cl, Dag. 89 FD66
Canberra Cl, Horn. 72 FJ63
Canberra Cres, Dag. 89 FD66
Canberra Dr, Hayes 78 BW69
Canberra Dr, Nthlt. 78 BW69
Canberra Rd E6 87 EM67
Barking Rd
Canberra Rd SE7 104 EJ79
Canberra Rd W13 79 CG74
Canberra Rd, Bexh. 106 EX79
Canberra Rd, Houns. 94 BN83
Canberra Sq, Til. 111 GG82
Canbury Av, Kings.T. 138 CM95
Canbury Ms SE26 122 DU90
Wells Pk Rd
Canbury Pk Rd, Kings.T. 138 CL95
Canbury Pas, Kings.T. 137 CK95
Canbury Path, Orp. 146 EU98
Cancell Rd SW9 101 DN81
Candahar Rd SW11 100 DE82
Cander Way, S.Ock. 91 FV73
Candler St N15 66 DR58
Candlerush Cl, Wok. 167 BB117
Candlestick La, Wal.Cr. 14 DV27
Park La
Candover Cl, West Dr. 94 BK80
Candover Rd, Horn. 71 FH60
Candover St W1 195 K7
Candy St E3 85 DZ67
Cane Cl, Wall. 159 DL108
Cane Hill, Rom. 52 FK54
Bennison Dr
Caneland Ct, Wal.Abb. 16 EF34
Canewdon Cl, Wok. 166 AY119
Guildford Rd
Caney Ms NW2 63 CX61
Claremont Rd
Canfield Dr, Ruis. 59 BV64
Canfield Gdns NW6 82 DC66
Canfield Pl NW6 82 DC65
Canfield Gdns
Canfield Rd, Rain. 89 FF67
Canfield Rd, Wdf.Grn. 48 EL52
Canford Av, Nthlt. 78 BY67
Canford Cl, Enf. 29 DN40
Canford Dr, Add. 134 BH103
Canford Gdns, N.Mal. 138 CR100
Canford Pl, Tedd. 117 CH93
Canford Rd SW11 120 DG85
Canham Rd SE25 142 DS97
Canham Rd W3 98 CS75
Canmore Gdns SW16 121 DJ94
Cann Hall Rd E11 68 EE63
Canning Cres N22 45 DM53
Canning Cross SE5 102 DS82
Canning Pas W8 100 DC76
Canning Pl W8 100 DC76
Canning Pl Ms W8 100 DC76
Canning Pl
Canning Rd E15 86 EE68
Canning Rd E17 67 DY56
Canning Rd N5 65 DP62
Canning Rd, Croy. 142 DT103
Canning Rd, Har. 61 CF55
Cannington Rd, Dag. 88 EW65
Cannizaro Rd SW19 119 CW93
Cannon Cl SW20 139 CW97
Cannon Cl, Hmptn. 116 CB93
Hanworth Rd
Cannon Cres, Wok. 150 AS111
Cannon Dr E14 203 P1
Cannon Dr E14 85 EA73
Cannon Gro, Lthd. 171 CE121
Cannon Hill N14 45 DK48
Cannon Hill NW6 64 DA64
Cannon Hill La SW20 139 CY97
Cannon La NW3 64 DD62
Cannon La, Pnr. 60 BY60
Cannon Ms, Wal.Abb. 15 EB33
Cannon Pl NW3 64 DD62
Cannon Pl SE7 104 EL78
Cannon Rd N14 45 DL48
Cannon Rd, Bexh. 106 EY81
Cannon Rd, Wat. 24 BW43
Cannon St EC4 197 H9
Cannon St EC4 84 DQ72
Cannon St Rd E1 84 DV72
Cannon Trd Est, Wem. 62 CP63
Cannon Way, Lthd. 171 CE121
Cannon Way, W.Mol. 136 CA98
Cannon Wf Business Cen SE8 103 DY77
Cannonbury Av, Pnr. 60 BX58
Cannonside, Lthd. 171 CE122
Canon Av, Rom. 70 EW57
Canon Beck Rd SE16 202 G4
Canon Beck Rd SE16 102 DW75
Canon Mohan Cl N14 29 DH44
Farm La
Canon Rd, Brom. 144 EJ97
Canon Row SW1 199 P5
Canon Row SW1 101 DL75
Canon St N1 84 DQ67
Canonbie Rd SE23 122 DW87
Canonbury Cres N1 84 DQ66
Canonbury Gro N1 84 DQ66
Canonbury La N1 83 DP66
Canonbury Pk N N1 84 DQ65
Canonbury Pk S N1 84 DQ65
Canonbury Pl N1 83 DP65
Canonbury Rd N1 83 DP65
Canonbury Rd, Enf. 30 DS39
Canonbury Sq N1 83 DP66
Canonbury St N1 84 DQ66
Canonbury Vil N1 83 DP66
Canonbury Yd N1 84 DQ67
New N Rd
Canons Cl N2 64 DD59
Canons Cl, Edg. 42 CM51
Canons Cl, Rad. 25 CH35
Canons Cl, Reig. 183 CZ133
Canons Cor, Edg. 42 CL49
Canons Dr, Edg. 42 CL51
Canons Gate (Cheshunt), Wal.Cr. 15 DZ26
Canon's Hill, Couls. 175 DN117
Canons La, Tad. 173 CY118
Canons Pk Cl, Edg. 42 CL52
Donnefield Av
Canons Wk, Croy. 143 DX104
Canonsleigh Rd, Dag. 88 EV66
Canopus Way, Nthwd. 39 BU49
Canopus Way, Stai. 114 BL87
Canrobert St E2 84 DV69
Cantelowes Rd NW1 83 DK65
Canterbury Av, Ilf. 68 EL59
Canterbury Av, Sid. 126 EW89
Canterbury Av, Upmin. 73 FT60
Canterbury Cl E6 87 EM72
Harper Rd
Canterbury Cl, Amer. 20 AS39
Canterbury Cl, Beck. 143 EB95
Canterbury Cl, Chig. 49 ET48
Canterbury Cl, Dart. 128 FN87
Canterbury Cl, Grnf. 78 CB72
Canterbury Cl, Nthwd. 39 BT51
Canterbury Cres SW9 101 DN83
Canterbury Gro SE27 121 DP90
Canterbury Ms (Oxshott), Lthd. 154 CC113
Steels La
Canterbury Par, S.Ock. 91 FW69
Canterbury Pl SE17 200 G9
Canterbury Pl SE17 101 DP77
Canterbury Rd E10 67 EC59
Canterbury Rd NW6 82 DA68
Canterbury Rd, Borwd. 26 CN40
Canterbury Rd, Croy. 141 DM101
Canterbury Rd, Felt. 116 BY89
Canterbury Rd, Grav. 131 GJ89
Canterbury Rd, Har. 60 CB57
Canterbury Rd, Mord. 140 DC99
Canterbury Rd, Wat. 23 BV40
Canterbury Ter NW6 82 DA68
Canterbury Way, Brwd. 53 FW51
Canterbury Way, Grays 109 FS80
Canterbury Way, Rick. 23 BQ41
Cantley Gdns SE19 142 DT95
Cantley Gdns, Ilf. 69 EQ58
Cantley Rd W7 97 CG76
Canton St E14 85 EA72
Cantrell Rd E3 85 DZ70
Cantwell Rd SE18 105 EP80
Canute Gdns SE16 203 H8
Canute Gdns SE16 103 DX77
Canvey St SE1 200 G2
Cape Cl, Bark. 87 EQ65
North St
Cape Rd N17 66 DU55
High Cross Rd
Cape Yd E1 202 C2
Capel Av, Wall. 159 DM106
Capel Cl N20 44 DC48
Capel Cl, Brom. 144 EL102
Capel Ct EC2 197 L9
Capel Ct SE20 142 DW95
Melvin Rd
Capel Gdns, Ilf. 69 ET63
Capel Gdns, Pnr. 60 BZ56
Capel Pl, Dart. 128 FJ91
Capel Pt E7 68 EH63
Capel Rd E7 68 EH63
Capel Rd E12 68 EJ63
Capel Rd, Barn. 28 DE44
Capel Rd, Enf. 30 DV36
Capel Rd, Wat. 24 BY44
Capel Vere Wk, Wat. 23 BS39
Capell Av, Rick. 21 BC43
Capell Rd, Rick. 21 BC43
Capell Way, Rick. 21 BD43
Capella Rd, Nthwd. 39 BT50
Capener's Cl SW1 198 F5
Capern Rd SW18 120 DC88
Cargill Rd
Capital Business Cen, Wem. 79 CK68
Capital Interchange Way, Brent. 98 CN78
Capital Pl, Croy. 159 DM106
Stafford Rd
Capitol Ind Pk NW9 62 CQ55
Capitol Way NW9 62 CQ55
Capland St NW8 194 A4
Capland St NW8 82 DD70
Caple Par NW10 80 CS68
Harley Rd
Caple Rd NW10 81 CT68
Capon Cl, Brwd. 54 FV46
Capper St WC1 195 L5
Capper St WC1 83 DJ70
Caprea Cl, Hayes 78 BX71
Triandra Way
Capri Rd, Croy. 142 DT102
Capstan Cl, Rom. 70 EV58
Capstan Ct, Dart. 108 FQ84
Capstan Ride, Enf. 29 DN40
Capstan Rd SE8 203 M8
Capstan Rd SE8 103 DZ77
Capstan Sq E14 204 E5
Capstan Sq E14 103 EC75
Capstan Way SE16 203 L3
Capstan Way SE16 85 DY74
Capstan's Wf, Wok. 166 AT118
Capstone Rd, Brom. 124 EF91
Captain Cook Cl, Ch.St.G. 36 AU49
Capthorne Av, Har. 60 BY60
Capuchin Cl, Stan. 41 CH51
Capulet Ms E16 205 N2
Capworth St E10 67 EA60
Caractacus Cottage Vw, Wat. 39 BU45
Caractacus Grn, Wat. 23 BT44
Caradoc Cl W2 82 DA72
Caradoc St SE10 205 H10
Caradoc St SE10 104 EE78
Caradon Cl E11 68 EE61
Brockway Cl
Caradon Cl, Wok. 166 AV118
Caradon Way N15 66 DR56
Caravan La, Rick. 38 BL45
Caravel Cl E14 103 EA76
Tiller Rd
Caravel Cl, Grays 110 FZ76
Caravel Ms SE8 103 EA79
Watergate St
Caravelle Gdns, Nthlt. 78 BX69
Javelin Way
Caraway Cl E13 86 EH71
Caraway Pl, Wall. 141 DH104
Carberry Rd SE19 122 DS93
Carbery Av W3 98 CM75
Carbis Cl E4 47 ED46
Carbis Rd E14 85 DZ72
Carbone Hill, Hert. 13 DK26
Carbone Hill (Cuffley), Pot.B. 13 DJ27
Carbuncle Pas Way N17 46 DU54
Carburton St W1 195 J6
Carburton St W1 83 DH71
Carbury Cl, Horn. 90 FJ65
Cardale St E14 204 D6
Carden Rd SE15 102 DV83
Cardiff Rd W7 97 CG76
Cardiff Rd, Enf. 30 DV42
Cardiff Rd, Wat. 23 BV44
Cardiff St SE18 105 ES80
Cardiff Way, Abb.L. 7 BU32
Cardigan Cl, Wok. 166 AS118
Bingham Dr
Cardigan Gdns, Ilf. 70 EU61
Cardigan Rd E3 85 DZ68
Cardigan Rd SW13 99 CU82
Cardigan Rd SW19 120 DC93
Haydons Rd
Cardigan Rd, Rich. 118 CL86
Cardigan St SE11 200 D10
Cardigan St SE11 101 DN78
Cardigan Wk N1 84 DQ66
Ashby Gro
Cardinal Av, Borwd. 26 CP41
Cardinal Av, Kings.T. 118 CL92
Cardinal Av, Mord. 139 CY100
Cardinal Bourne St SE1 201 L7
Cardinal Bourne St SE1 102 DR76
Cardinal Cl, Chis. 145 ER95
Cardinal Cl, Edg. 42 CR52
Abbots Rd
Cardinal Cl, Mord. 139 CY101
Cardinal Cl, S.Croy. 160 DU113
Cardinal Cl (Cheshunt), Wal.Cr. 14 DT26
Adamsfield
Cardinal Cl, Wor.Pk. 157 CU105
Cardinal Ct, Borwd. 26 CP41
Cardinal Av
Cardinal Cres, N.Mal. 138 CQ96
Cardinal Dr, Ilf. 49 EQ51
Cardinal Dr, Walt. 136 BX102
Cardinal Pl SW15 99 CX84
Cardinal Rd, Felt. 115 BV88
Cardinal Rd, Ruis. 60 BX60
Cardinal Way, Har. 61 CE55
Wolseley Rd
Cardinal Way, Rain. 90 FK68
Cardinals Wk, Hmptn. 116 CC94
Cardinals Wk, Sun. 115 BS93
Cardinals Way N19 65 DK60
Cardine Ms SE15 102 DV80
Cardingham, Wok. 166 AU117
Cardington Sq, Houns. 96 BX84
Cardington St NW1 195 K2
Cardington St NW1 83 DJ69
Cardozo Rd N7 65 DL64
Cardrew Av N12 44 DD50
Cardrew Cl N12 44 DE50
Cardross St W6 99 CV76
Cardwell Rd N7 65 DL63
Cardwell Rd SE18 105 EM77
Carew Cl N7 65 DM61
Carew Cl, Couls. 175 DP119
Carew Rd N17 46 DU54
Carew Rd W13 97 CJ75
Carew Rd, Ashf. 115 BQ93
Carew Rd, Mitch. 140 DG96
Carew Rd, Nthwd. 39 BS51
Carew Rd, Th.Hth. 141 DP97
Carew Rd, Wall. 159 DJ107
Carew St SE5 102 DQ82
Carew Way, Wat. 40 BZ48
Carey Ct, Bexh. 127 FB85
Carey Gdns SW8 101 DJ81
Carey La EC2 197 H8
Carey Pl SW1 199 M9
Carey Rd, Dag. 70 EY63
Carey St WC2 196 C9
Carey St WC2 83 DM72
Carey Way, Wem. 62 CQ63
Carfax Pl SW4 101 DK84
Holwood Pl
Carfax Rd, Hayes 95 BT78
Carfax Rd, Horn. 71 FF63
Carfree Cl N1 83 DN66
Bewdley St
Cargill Rd SW18 120 DB88
Cargreen Pl SE25 142 DT98
Cargreen Rd
Cargreen Rd SE25 142 DT98
Carholme Rd SE23 123 DZ88
Carisbrooke Rd, Brwd. 54 FV44
Carisbrooke Av, Bex. 126 EX88
Carisbrooke Av, Wat. 24 BX39
Carisbrooke Cl, Enf. 30 DT39
Carisbrooke Cl, Horn. 72 FN60
Carisbrooke Cl, Stan. 41 CK54
Carisbrooke Ct, Slou. 74 AT73
Carisbrooke Gdns SE15 102 DT80
Commercial Way
Carisbrooke Rd E17 67 DY56
Carisbrooke Rd, Brom. 144 EJ98
Carisbrooke Rd, Mitch. 141 DK98
Carisbrooke Rd, St.Alb. 8 CB26
Carker's La NW5 65 DH64
Carl Ekman Ho, Grav. 130 GD87
Carleton Av, Wall. 159 DK109
Carleton Cl, Esher 137 CD102
Carleton Pl (Horton Kirby), Dart. 148 FQ98
Carleton Rd N7 65 DK64
Carleton Rd, Dart. 128 FN87
Carleton Rd (Cheshunt), Wal.Cr. 15 DX28
Carleton Vil NW5 65 DJ64
Leighton Gro
Carlile Cl E3 85 DZ68
Carlina Gdns, Wdf.Grn. 48 EH50
Carlingford Gdns, Mitch. 120 DF94
Carlingford Rd N15 65 DP55
Carlingford Rd NW3 64 DD63
Carlingford Rd, Mord. 139 CX100
Carlisle Av EC3 197 N9
Carlisle Av W3 80 CS72
Carlisle Cl, Kings.T. 138 CN95
Carlisle Cl, Pnr. 60 BY59
Carlisle Gdns, Har. 61 CK59
Carlisle Gdns, Ilf. 68 EL58
Carlisle La SE1 200 C7
Carlisle La SE1 101 DM76
Carlisle Ms NW8 194 A6
Carlisle Ms NW8 82 DD71
Carlisle Pl N11 45 DH49
Carlisle Pl SW1 199 K7
Carlisle Pl SW1 101 DJ76
Carlisle Rd E10 67 EA60
Carlisle Rd N4 65 DN59
Carlisle Rd NW6 81 CY67
Carlisle Rd NW9 62 CQ55
Carlisle Rd, Dart. 128 FN86
Carlisle Rd, Hmptn. 116 CB94
Carlisle Rd, Rom. 71 FG57
Carlisle Rd, Sutt. 157 CZ106
Carlisle St W1 195 M9
Carlisle Wk E8 84 DT65
Laurel St
Carlisle Way SW17 120 DG92
Carlos Pl W1 198 G1
Carlos Pl W1 82 DG73
Carlow St NW1 83 DJ68
Arlington Rd
Carlton Av N14 29 DK43
Carlton Av, Felt. 116 BW86
Carlton Av, Green. 129 FS86
Carlton Av, Har. 61 CH57
Carlton Av, Hayes 95 BS77
Carlton Av, S.Croy. 160 DS108
Carlton Av E, Wem. 62 CL60
Carlton Av W, Wem. 61 CH61
Carlton Cl NW3 64 DA61
Carlton Cl, Borwd. 26 CR42
Carlton Cl, Chess. 155 CK107
Carlton Cl, Edg. 42 CN50
Carlton Cl, Nthlt. 60 CC64
Whitton Av W
Carlton Cl, Upmin. 72 FP61
Carlton Cl, Wok. 151 AZ114
Carlton Ct SW9 101 DP81
Carlton Ct, Ilf. 69 ER55
Carlton Ct, Uxb. 76 BK71
Carlton Cres, Sutt. 157 CY105
Carlton Dr SW15 119 CY85
Carlton Dr, Ilf. 69 ER55
Carlton Gdns SW1 199 M3
Carlton Gdns SW1 83 DK74
Carlton Gdns W5 79 CJ72
Carlton Grn, Red. 184 DE131
Carlton Gro SE15 102 DV81
Carlton Hill NW8 82 DB68
Carlton Ho, Felt. 115 BT87
Carlton Ho Ter SW1 199 M3
Carlton Ho Ter SW1 83 DK74
Carlton Par, Orp. 146 EV101
Carlton Par, Sev. 191 FJ122
St. John's Hill
Carlton Pk Av SW20 139 CW96
Carlton Pl, Nthwd. 39 BP50
Carlton Pl, Wey. 153 BP105
Castle Vw Rd
Carlton Rd E11 68 EF60
Carlton Rd E12 68 EK63
Carlton Rd E17 47 DY53
Carlton Rd N4 65 DN59
Carlton Rd N11 44 DG50
Carlton Rd SW14 98 CQ83
Carlton Rd W4 98 CR75
Carlton Rd W5 79 CJ73
Carlton Rd, Erith 107 FB79
Carlton Rd, Grays 111 GF75
Carlton Rd, N.Mal. 138 CS96
Carlton Rd, Red. 184 DF131
Carlton Rd, Reig. 184 DD132
Carlton Rd, Rom. 71 FG57
Carlton Rd, Sid. 125 ET92
Carlton Rd, Slou. 74 AV73
Carlton Rd, S.Croy. 160 DR107
Carlton Rd, Sun. 115 BT94
Carlton Rd, Walt. 135 BV101
Carlton Rd, Well. 106 EV83
Carlton Rd, Wok. 151 BA114
Carlton Sq E1 85 DX70
Argyle Rd
Carlton St SW1 199 M1
Carlton Ter E11 68 EH57
Carlton Ter N18 46 DR48
Carlton Ter SE26 122 DW90
Carlton Twr Pl SW1 198 E6
Carlton Twr Pl SW1 100 DF76
Carlton Vale NW6 82 DB68
Carlton Vil SW15 119 CW85
St. John's Av
Carlwell St SW17 120 DE92
Carlyle Av, Brom. 144 EK97
Carlyle Av, Sthl. 78 BZ73
Carlyle Cl N2 64 DC58
Carlyle Cl NW10 80 CR67
Carlyle Cl, W.Mol. 136 CB96
Carlyle Gdns, Sthl. 78 BZ73
Carlyle Lo (New Barnet), Barn. 28 DC43
Richmond Rd
Carlyle Ms E1 85 DX70
Alderney Rd
Carlyle Pl SW15 99 CX84
Carlyle Rd E12 68 EL63
Carlyle Rd SE28 88 EV73
Carlyle Rd W5 97 CJ78
Carlyle Rd, Croy. 142 DU103
Carlyle Rd, Stai. 113 BF94
Carlyle Sq SW3 100 DD78
Carlyon Av, Har. 60 BZ63
Carlyon Cl, Wem. 80 CL67
Carlyon Rd, Hayes 78 BW72
Carlyon Rd, Wem. 80 CL68
Carmalt Gdns SW15 99 CW84
Carmalt Gdns, Walt. 154 BW106
Carmarthen Gdn NW9 62 CS58
Snowdon Dr
Carmarthen Rd, Slou. 74 AS73
Carmel Cl, Wok. 166 AY118
Carmel Ct W8 100 DB75
Holland St
Carmel Ct, Wem. 62 CP61
Carmelite Cl, Har. 40 CC53
Carmelite Rd, Har. 40 CC53
Carmelite St EC4 196 E10
Carmelite St EC4 83 DN73
Carmelite Wk, Har. 40 CC53
Carmelite Way, Har. 40 CC54
Carmen Ct, Borwd. 26 CM38
Belford Rd
Carmen St E14 85 EB72
Carmichael Cl SW11 100 DD83
Darien Rd
Carmichael Cl, Ruis. 59 BU63
Carmichael Ms SW18 120 DD87
Carmichael Rd SE25 142 DU99
Carminia Rd SW17 121 DH89
Carnaby St W1 195 K9
Carnaby St W1 83 DJ72
Carnac St SE27 122 DR91
Carnach Grn, S.Ock. 91 FV73
Carnanton Rd E17 47 ED53
Carnarvon Av, Enf. 30 DT41
Carnarvon Dr, Hayes 95 BQ76
Carnarvon Rd E10 67 EC58
Carnarvon Rd E15 86 EF65
Carnarvon Rd E18 48 EF53
Carnarvon Rd, Barn. 27 CY41
Carnation Cl, Rom. 71 FE61
Carnation St SE2 106 EV78
Carnbrook Rd SE3 104 EK83
Carnecke Gdns SE9 124 EL85
Carnegie Cl, Surb. 138 CM103
Fullers Av
Carnegie Pl SW19 119 CX90
Carnegie St N1 83 DM67
Carnforth Cl, Epsom 156 CP107
Carnforth Gdns, Horn. 71 FG64
Carnforth Rd SW16 121 DK94
Carnie Lo SW17 121 DH90
Manville Rd
Carnoustie Dr N1 83 DM66
Carnwath Rd SW6 100 DA83
Carol St NW1 83 DJ67
Carolina Cl E15 68 EE64
Carolina Rd, Th.Hth. 141 DP96
Caroline Cl N10 45 DH54
Alexandra Pk Rd
Caroline Cl SW16 121 DM91
Caroline Cl W2 82 DB73
Bayswater Rd
Caroline Cl, Croy. 160 DS105
Brownlow Rd
Caroline Cl, Islw. 97 CD80
Caroline Cl, West Dr. 94 BK75
Caroline Ct, Ashf. 115 BP93
Caroline Ct, Stan. 41 CG51
The Chase
Caroline Gdns SE15 102 DV80
Caroline Pl SW11 100 DG82
Caroline Pl W2 82 DB73
Caroline Pl, Hayes 95 BS80
Caroline Pl, Wat. 24 BY44
Caroline Pl Ms W2 82 DB73
Orme La
Caroline Rd SW19 119 CZ94
Caroline St E1 85 DX72
Caroline Ter SW1 198 F9
Caroline Ter SW1 100 DG77
Caroline Wk W6 99 CY79
Carolyn Cl, Wok. 166 AT119
Carolyn Dr, Orp. 146 EU104
Caroon Dr, Rick. 22 BH36
Carpenders Av, Wat. 40 BY48
Carpenders Pk, Wat. 40 BY47
Carpenter Cl, Epsom 157 CT109
West St
Carpenter Gdns N21 45 DP47
Carpenter Path, Brwd. 55 GD43
Carpenter St W1 199 H1
Carpenter Way, Pot.B. 12 DC33
Carpenters Arms La, Epp. 18 EV25
Carpenters Ct, Twick. 117 CE89
Carpenters Pl SW4 101 DK84
Carpenters Rd E15 85 EB65
Carpenters Rd, Enf. 30 DW36
Carpenters Wd Dr, Rick. 21 BB42
Carr Gro SE18 104 EL77
Carr Rd E17 47 DZ54
Carr Rd, Nthlt. 78 CB65
Carr St E14 85 DY71
Carrara Wk SW9 101 DN84
Somerleyton Rd
Carrara Wf SW6 99 CY83
Ranelagh Gdns
Carriage Dr E SW11 100 DG80
Carriage Dr N SW11 100 DG79
Carriage Dr S SW11 100 DF81
Carriage Dr W SW11 100 DF80
Carriage Ms, Ilf. 69 EQ61
Carriage Pl N16 66 DR62
Carriageway, The, West. 180 EX124
Carrick Cl, Islw. 97 CG83
Carrick Dr, Ilf. 49 EQ53
Carrick Dr, Sev. 191 FH123
Carrick Gdns N17 46 DS52
Flexmere Rd
Carrick Gate, Esher 136 CC104

Carrick Ms SE8 103 EA79
Watergate St
Carrill Way, Belv. 106 EX77
Carrington Av, Borwd. 26 CP43
Carrington Av, Houns. 116 CB85
Carrington Cl, Barn. 27 CU43
Carrington Cl, Borwd. 26 CQ43
Carrington Cl, Croy. 143 DY101
Carrington Cl, Kings.T. 118 CQ92
Carrington Cl, Red. 184 DF133
Carrington Gdns E7 68 EH63
Woodford Rd
Carrington Pl, Esher 154 CC105
Carrington Rd, Dart. 128 FM86
Carrington Rd, Rich. 98 CN84
Carrington Rd, Slou. 74 AS73
Carrington Sq, Har. 40 CC52
Carrington St W1 199 H3
Carrol Cl NW5 65 DH63
Carroll Cl E15 68 EF64
Carroll Hill, Loug. 33 EM41
Carron Cl E14 85 EB72
Carronade Pl SE28 105 EQ76
Carroun Rd SW8 101 DM80
Carrow Rd, Dag. 88 EV66
Carrow Rd, Walt. 136 BX104
Kenilworth Dr
Carroway La, Grnf. 79 CD69
Cowgate Rd
Carrs La N21 30 DQ43
Carshalton Gro, Sutt. 158 DD105
Carshalton Pk Rd, Cars. 158 DF106
Carshalton Pl, Cars. 158 DG105
Carshalton Rd, Bans. 158 DF114
Carshalton Rd, Cars. 158 DC106
Carshalton Rd, Mitch. 140 DG98
Carshalton Rd, Sutt. 158 DC106
Carsington Gdns, Dart. 128 FK89
Carslake Rd SW15 119 CW86
Carson Rd E16 86 EG70
Carson Rd SE21 122 DR89
Carson Rd, Barn. 28 DF42
Carstairs Rd SE6 123 EC90
Carston Cl SE12 124 EG85
Carswell Cl, Brwd. 55 GD44
Carswell Cl, Ilf. 68 EK56
Roding La S
Carswell Rd SE6 123 EC87
Cart La E4 47 ED45
Cart Path, Wat. 8 BW33
Cartbridge Cl, Wok. 167 BB123
Send Rd
Cartel Cl, Purf. 109 FR77
Carter Cl, Rom. 51 FB52
Carter Cl, Wall. 159 DK108
Carter Ct EC4 83 DP72
Carter La
Carter Dr, Rom. 51 FB52
Carter La EC4 196 G9
Carter La EC4 83 DP72
Carter Pl SE17 102 DQ78
Carter Rd E13 86 EH67
Carter Rd SW19 120 DD93
Carter St SE17 102 DQ79
Carteret St SW1 199 M5
Carteret St SW1 101 DK75
Carteret Way SE8 203 L9
Carteret Way SE8 103 DY77
Carterhatch La, Enf. 30 DU40
Carterhatch Rd, Enf. 30 DW40
Carters Cl, Wor.Pk. 139 CX103
Carters Hill, Sev. 191 FP127
Carters Hill Cl SE9 124 EJ88
Carters La SE23 123 DY89
Carters La, Wok. 167 BC120
Carters Rd, Epsom 173 CT115
Carters Row, Grav. 131 GF88
Carters Yd SW18 120 DA85
Wandsworth High St
Cartersfield Rd, Wal.Abb. 15 EC34
Carthew Rd W6 99 CV76
Carthew Vil W6 99 CV76
Carthouse La, Wok. 150 AS114
Carthusian St EC1 197 H6
Carthusian St EC1 84 DQ71
Cartier Circle E14 204 C3
Cartier Circle E14 85 EB74
Carting La WC2 200 A1
Carting La WC2 83 DL73
Cartmel Cl N17 46 DV52
Heybourne Rd
Cartmel Cl, Reig. 184 DE133
Cartmel Gdns, Mord. 140 DC99
Cartmel Rd, Bexh. 106 FA81
Carton St W1 194 E8
Cartwright Gdns WC1 195 P3
Cartwright Gdns WC1 83 DL69
Cartwright Rd, Dag. 88 EZ66
Cartwright St E1 84 DT73
Cartwright Way SW13 99 CV80
Carver Cl W4 98 CQ76
Carver Rd SE24 122 DQ86
Carville Cres, Brent. 98 CL78
Cary Rd E11 68 EE63
Cary Wk, Rad. 9 CH34
Carysfort Rd N8 65 DK57
Carysfort Rd N16 66 DR62
Cascade Av N10 65 DJ56
Cascade Cl, Buck.H. 48 EK47
Cascade Rd
Cascade Cl, Orp. 146 EW97
Cascade Rd, Buck.H. 48 EK47
Cascades, Croy. 161 DZ110
Caselden Cl, Add. 152 BJ106
Casella Rd SE14 103 DX80
Casewick Rd SE27 121 DP91
Casimir Rd E5 66 DV62
Casino Av SE24 122 DQ85
Caspian St SE5 102 DR80
Caspian Wk E16 86 EK72
Caspian Wf E3 85 EB71
Violet Rd
Cassandra Cl, Nthlt. 61 CD63
Cassandra Gate, Wal.Cr. 15 DZ27
Casselden Rd NW10 80 CR66
Cassidy Rd SW6 100 DA80
Cassilda Rd SE2 106 EU77
Cassilis Rd, Twick. 117 CH85
Cassio Rd, Wat. 23 BV41
Cassiobridge, Wat. 23 BR42
Cassiobridge Rd, Wat. 23 BS42
Cassiobury Av, Felt. 115 BT86
Cassiobury Ct, Wat. 23 BT40
Cassiobury Dr, Wat. 23 BT40
Cassiobury Pk, Wat. 23 BS41
Cassiobury Pk Av, Wat. 23 BS41
Cassiobury Rd E17 67 DX57
Cassis Ct, Loug. 33 EQ42
Cassland Rd E9 84 DW66
Cassland Rd, Th.Hth. 142 DR98
Casslee Rd SE6 123 DZ87
Cassocks Sq, Shep. 135 BR100
Casson St E1 84 DU71
Casstine Cl, Swan. 127 FF94
Castalia Sq E14 103 EC75
Roserton St
Castalia St E14 103 EC75
Plevna St
Castano Ct, Abb.L. 7 BS31
Castell Rd, Loug. 33 EQ39
Castellain Rd W9 82 DB70
Castellan Av, Rom. 71 FH55
Castellane Cl, Stan. 41 CF52
Daventer Dr
Castello Av SW15 119 CW85
Castelnau SW13 99 CV79
Castelnau Gdns SW13 99 CV79
Arundel Ter
Castelnau Pl SW13 99 CV79
Castelnau
Castelnau Row SW13 99 CV79
Lonsdale Rd
Casterbridge NW6 82 DB67
Casterbridge Rd SE3 104 EG83
Casterton St E8 84 DV65
Wilton Way
Castile Rd SE18 105 EN77
Castillon Rd SE6 124 EE89
Castlands Rd SE6 123 DZ89
Castle Av E4 47 ED50
Castle Av, Epsom 157 CU109
Castle Av, Rain. 89 FE66
Castle Av, Slou. 92 AU79
Castle Av, West Dr. 76 BL73
Castle Baynard St EC4 196 G10
Castle Cl E9 67 DY64
Swinnerton St
Castle Cl SW19 119 CX90
Castle Cl W3 98 CP75
Park Rd E
Castle Cl, Brom. 144 EE97
Castle Cl, Bushey 24 CB44
Castle Cl, Red. 186 DQ133
Castle Cl, Rom. 52 FJ48
Castle Cl, Sun. 115 BS94
Mill Fm Av
Castle Ct EC3 197 L9
Castle Ct SE26 123 DY91
Champion Rd
Castle Dr, Ilf. 68 EL58
Castle Fm Rd, Sev. 165 FF109
Castle Gdns, Dor. 182 CM134
Castle Grn, Wey. 135 BS104
Castle Hill, Long. 149 FX99
Castle Hill Av, Croy. 161 EB109
Castle Hill Rd, Egh. 112 AV91
Castle La SW1 199 L6
Castle La SW1 101 DJ76
Castle Ms N12 44 DC50
Castle Rd
Castle Ms NW1 83 DH65
Castle Rd
Castle Par, Epsom 157 CU108
Ewell Bypass
Castle Pl NW1 83 DH65
Castle Pl W4 98 CS77
Windmill Rd
Castle Pt E13 86 EJ68
Castle Rd N12 44 DC50
Castle Rd NW1 83 DH65
Castle Rd, Couls. 174 DE120
Castle Rd, Dag. 88 EV67
Castle Rd, Dart. 165 FH107
Castle Rd, Enf. 31 DY39
Castle Rd, Epsom 172 CP115
Castle Rd, Grays 110 FZ79
Castle Rd, Islw. 97 CF82
Castle Rd, Nthlt. 78 CB65
Castle Rd, Sev. 165 FG108
Castle Rd, Sthl. 96 BZ76
Castle Rd, Swans. 130 FZ86
Castle Rd, Wey. 135 BS104
Castle Rd, Wok. 151 AZ114
Castle Sq, Red. 186 DQ133
Castle St E6 86 EJ68
Castle St, Green. 129 FU85
Castle St, Kings.T. 138 CL96
Castle St, Red. 185 DP133
Castle St, Slou. 92 AT76
Castle St, Swans. 130 FZ86
Castle Vw, Epsom 156 CP114
Castle Vw Rd, Wey. 153 BP105
Castle Wk, Reig. 184 DA134
High St
Castle Wk, Sun. 136 BW97
Elizabeth Gdns
Castle Way SW19 119 CX90
Castle Way, Epsom 157 CU109
Castle Av
Castle Way, Felt. 116 BW91
Castle Yd N6 64 DG59
North Rd
Castle Yd SE1 200 G2
Castle Yd, Rich. 117 CK85
Hill St
Castlebar Hill W5 79 CH71
Castlebar Ms W5 79 CJ71
Castlebar Pk W5 79 CH71
Castlebar Rd W5 79 CJ71
Castlebrook Cl SE11 200 F8
Castlebrook Cl SE11 101 DP77
Castlecombe Dr SW19 119 CX87
Castlecombe Rd SE9 124 EL91
Castledine Rd SE20 122 DV94
Castlefield Rd, Reig. 184 DA133
Castleford Av SE9 125 EP88
Castleford Cl N17 46 DT51
Castlegate, Rich. 98 CM83
Castlehaven Rd NW1 83 DH66
Castleleigh Ct, Enf. 30 DR43
Castlemaine Av, Epsom 157 CV109
Castlemaine Av, S.Croy. 160 DT106
Castlemaine Twr SW11 100 DF81
Castlereagh St W1 194 D8
Castleton Av, Bexh. 107 FD81
Castleton Av, Wem. 62 CL63
Castleton Cl, Bans. 174 DA115
Castleton Cl, Croy. 143 DY100
Castleton Dr, Bans. 174 DA115
Castleton Gdns, Wem. 62 CL62
Castleton Rd E17 47 ED54
Castleton Rd SE9 124 EK91
Castleton Rd, Ilf. 70 EU60
Castleton Rd, Mitch. 141 DK98
Castleton Rd, Ruis. 60 BX60
Castletown Rd W14 99 CY78
Castleview Cl N4 66 DQ60
Castleview Gdns, Ilf. 68 EL58
Castleview Rd, Slou. 92 AW77
Castlewood Dr SE9 105 EM82
Castlewood Rd N15 66 DU58
Castlewood Rd N16 66 DU59
Castlewood Rd, Barn. 28 DD41
Castor La E14 204 B1
Castor La E14 85 EB73
Cat Hill, Barn. 28 DE44
Catalin Ct, Wal.Abb. 15 ED33
Howard Cl
Catalina Av (Chafford Hundred), Grays 110 FZ75
Caterham Av, Ilf. 49 EM54
Caterham Bypass, Cat. 176 DV120
Caterham Cl, Cat. 176 DS120
Caterham Ct, Wal.Abb. 16 EF34
Shernbroke Rd
Caterham Dr, Couls. 175 DP118
Caterham Rd SE13 103 EC83
Catesby St SE17 201 L9
Catesby St SE17 102 DR77
Catford Bdy SE6 123 EB87
Catford Hill SE6 123 DZ89
Catford Ms SE6 123 EB87
Holbeach Rd
Catford Rd SE6 123 EA87
Cathall Rd E11 67 ED62
Cathay St SE16 202 E5
Cathay St SE16 102 DV75
Cathay Wk, Nthlt. 78 CA68
Brabazon Rd
Cathcart Dr, Orp. 145 ES103
Cathcart Hill N19 65 DJ62
Cathcart Rd SW10 100 DC79
Cathcart St NW5 83 DH65
Cathedral Piazza SW1 199 K7
Cathedral Pl EC4 197 H8
Cathedral St SE1 201 K2
Cathedral St SE1 84 DR74
Catherall Rd N5 66 DQ62
Catherine Cl, Brwd. 54 FU43
Catherine Cl, Grays 110 FZ75
Catherine Cl, Loug. 33 EM44
Roding Gdns
Catherine Cl, W.Byf. 152 BL114
Catherine Ct N14 29 DJ43
Conisbee Ct
Catherine Dr, Rich. 98 CL84
Catherine Dr, Sun. 115 BT93
Catherine Gdns, Houns. 97 CD84
Catherine Griffiths Ct EC1 196 E4
Catherine Gro SE10 103 EB81
Catherine Howard Ct, Wey. 135 BP104
Old Palace Rd
Catherine Pl SW1 199 K6
Catherine Pl SW1 101 DJ76
Catherine Rd, Enf. 31 DY36
Catherine Rd, Rom. 71 FH57
Catherine Rd, Surb. 137 CK99
Catherine St WC2 196 B10
Catherine St WC2 83 DM73
Catherine Wheel All E1 197 N7
Catherine Wheel Rd, Brent. 97 CK80
Catherine Wheel Yd SW1 199 K3
Catherine's Cl, West Dr. 94 BK76
Money La
Cathles Rd SW12 121 DH86
Cathnor Rd W12 99 CV75
Catisfield Rd, Enf. 31 DY37
Catlin Cres, Shep. 135 BR99
Catlin Gdns, Gdse. 186 DV130
Catlin St SE16 202 C10
Catlin St SE16 102 DU78
Catling Cl SE23 122 DW90
Catlins La, Pnr. 59 BV55
Cato Rd SW4 101 DK83
Cato St W1 194 C7
Cato St W1 82 DE71
Cator Cl, Croy. 162 EE111
Cator Cres, Croy. 161 ED111
Cator La, Beck. 143 DZ96
Cator Rd SE26 123 DX93
Cator Rd, Cars. 158 DF106
Cator St SE15 102 DT79
Catsey La, Bushey 40 CC45
Catsey Wds, Bushey 40 CC45
Catterick Cl N11 44 DG51
Catterick Way, Borwd. 26 CM39
Cattistock Rd SE9 124 EL92
Cattlegate Hill, Pot.B. 13 DK31
Cattlegate Rd, Enf. 13 DL34
Cattlegate Rd, Pot.B. 13 DK31
Cattley Cl, Barn. 27 CY42
Wood St
Cattlins Cl, Wal.Cr. 14 DT29
Catton St WC1 196 B7
Catton St WC1 83 DM71
Caulfield Rd E6 87 EM66
Caulfield Rd SE15 102 DV82
Causeway, The N2 64 DE56
Causeway, The SW18 100 DB84
Causeway, The SW19 119 CX92
Causeway, The, Cars. 140 DG104
Causeway, The, Chess. 156 CL105
Causeway, The, Esher 155 CF108
Causeway, The, Felt. 95 BU84
Causeway, The, Pot.B. 12 DC31
Causeway, The, Stai. 113 BC91
Causeway, The, Sutt. 158 DC109
Causeway, The, Tedd. 117 CF93
Broad St
Causeway Cl, Pot.B. 12 DD31
Causeway Ct, Wok. 166 AT118
Bingham Dr
Causeyware Rd N9 46 DV45
Causton Rd N6 65 DH59
Causton St SW1 199 N9
Causton St SW1 101 DK77
Cautley Av SW4 121 DJ85
Cavalier Cl, Rom. 70 EX56
Cavalier Gdns, Hayes 77 BR72
Hanover Circle
Cavalry Barracks, Houns. 96 BX83
Cavalry Cres, Houns. 96 BX84
Cavalry Gdns SW15 119 CZ85
Upper Richmond Rd
Cavaye Pl SW10 100 DC78
Fulham Rd
Cave Rd E13 86 EH68
Cave Rd, Rich. 117 CJ91
Cave St N1 83 DM68
Carnegie St
Cavell Cres, Dart. 108 FN84
Cavell Cres, Rom. 52 FL54
Cavell Dr, Enf. 29 DN40
Cavell Rd N17 46 DR52
Cavell Rd (Cheshunt), Wal.Cr. 14 DT27
Cavell St E1 84 DV71
Cavell Way, Epsom 156 CN111
Cavendish Av N3 44 DA54
Cavendish Av NW8 194 A1
Cavendish Av NW8 82 DD68
Cavendish Av W13 79 CG71
Cavendish Av, Erith 107 FC79
Cavendish Av, Har. 61 CD63
Cavendish Av, Horn. 89 FH65
Cavendish Av, N.Mal. 139 CV99
Cavendish Av, Ruis. 59 BV64
Cavendish Av, Sev. 190 FG122
Cavendish Av, Sid. 126 EU87
Cavendish Av, Well. 105 ET83
Cavendish Av, Wdf.Grn. 48 EH53
Cavendish Cl N18 46 DV50
Cavendish Rd
Cavendish Cl NW6 81 CZ66
Cavendish Rd
Cavendish Cl NW8 194 A2
Cavendish Cl NW8 82 DD69
Cavendish Cl, Amer. 20 AV39
Cavendish Cl, Hayes 77 BS71
Westacott
Cavendish Cl, Sun. 115 BT93
Cavendish Ct EC3 197 N8
Cavendish Ct, Rick. 23 BR43
Mayfare
Cavendish Ct, Sun. 115 BT93
Cavendish Cres, Borwd. 26 CN42
Cavendish Cres, Horn. 89 FH65
Cavendish Dr E11 67 ED60
Cavendish Dr, Edg. 42 CM51
Cavendish Dr, Esher 155 CE106
Cavendish Gdns, Bark. 69 ES64
Cavendish Gdns, Ilf. 69 EN60
Cavendish Gdns, Red. 184 DG133
Cavendish Gdns, Rom. 70 EY57
Cavendish Ms N W1 195 J6
Cavendish Ms S W1 195 J7
Cavendish Par, Houns. 96 BY82
Bath Rd
Cavendish Pl W1 195 J8
Cavendish Pl W1 83 DH72
Cavendish Rd E4 47 EC51
Cavendish Rd N4 65 DN58
Cavendish Rd N18 46 DV50
Cavendish Rd NW6 81 CY66
Cavendish Rd SW12 121 DH86
Cavendish Rd SW19 120 DD94
Cavendish Rd W4 98 CQ81
Cavendish Rd, Barn. 27 CW41
Cavendish Rd, Croy. 141 DP102
Cavendish Rd, N.Mal. 139 CT99
Cavendish Rd, Red. 184 DG134
Cavendish Rd, Sun. 115 BT93
Cavendish Rd, Sutt. 158 DC108
Cavendish Rd, Wey. 153 BQ108
Cavendish Rd, Wok. 166 AX119
Cavendish Sq W1 195 J8
Cavendish Sq W1 83 DH72
Cavendish Sq, Long. 149 FX97
Cavendish St N1 197 K1
Cavendish St N1 84 DR68
Cavendish Ter, Felt. 115 BU89
High St
Cavendish Way, W.Wick. 143 EB102
Cavenham Cl, Wok. 166 AY119
Cavenham Gdns, Horn. 72 FJ57
Cavenham Gdns, Ilf. 69 ER62
Caverleigh Way, Wor.Pk. 139 CU102
Caversham Av N13 45 DN48
Caversham Av, Sutt. 139 CY103
Caversham Flats SW3 100 DF79
Caversham St
Caversham Rd N15 66 DQ56
Caversham Rd NW5 83 DJ65
Caversham Rd, Kings.T. 138 CM96
Caversham St SW3 100 DF79
Caverswall St W12 81 CW72
Caveside Cl, Chis. 145 EN95
Cavill's Wk, Chig. 50 EW47
Cavill's Wk, Rom. 50 EX47
Cawdor Av, S.Ock. 91 FU73
Cawdor Cres W7 97 CG77
Cawnpore St SE19 122 DS92
Cawsey Way, Wok. 166 AY117
Caxton Av, Add. 152 BG107
Caxton Dr, Uxb. 76 BK68
Chiltern Vw Rd
Caxton Gro E3 85 EA69
Caxton La, Oxt. 188 EL131
Caxton Ms, Brent. 97 CK79
The Butts
Caxton Ri, Red. 184 DG133
Caxton Rd N22 45 DM54
Caxton Rd SW19 120 DC92
Caxton Rd W12 99 CX75
Caxton Rd, Sthl. 96 BX76
Caxton St SW1 199 L6
Caxton St SW1 101 DJ76
Caxton St N E16 86 EF73
Victoria Dock Rd
Caxton Way, Rom. 71 FE56
Caxton Way, Wat. 23 BR44
Caygill Cl, Brom. 144 EF98
Cayley Cl, Wall. 159 DL108
Cayley Rd, Sthl. 96 CB76
McNair Rd
Cayton Pl EC1 197 K3
Cayton Rd, Grnf. 79 CE68
Cayton St EC1 197 K3
Cazenove Rd E17 47 EA53
Cazenove Rd N16 66 DT61
Cearn Way, Couls. 175 DM115
Cearns Ho E6 86 EK67
Cecil Av, Bark. 87 ER66
Cecil Av, Enf. 30 DT42
Cecil Av, Grays 110 FZ75
Cecil Av, Horn. 72 FL55
Cecil Av, Wem. 62 CM64
Cecil Cl W5 79 CK71
Helena Rd
Cecil Cl, Ashf. 115 BQ93
Cecil Cl, Chess. 155 CK105
Cecil Ct WC2 199 N1
Cecil Ct, Barn. 27 CX41
Cecil Pk, Pnr. 60 BY56
Cecil Pl, Mitch. 140 DF99
Cecil Rd E11 68 EE62
Cecil Rd E13 86 EG67
Cecil Rd E17 47 EA53
Cecil Rd N10 45 DH54
Cecil Rd N14 45 DJ46
Cecil Rd NW9 62 CS55
Cecil Rd NW10 80 CS67
Cecil Rd SW19 120 DB94
Cecil Rd W3 80 CQ71
Cecil Rd, Ashf. 115 BQ94
Cecil Rd, Croy. 141 DM100
Cecil Rd, Enf. 30 DR42
Cecil Rd, Grav. 131 GF88
Cecil Rd, Har. 61 CE55
Cecil Rd, Houns. 96 CC82
Cecil Rd, Ilf. 69 EP63
Cecil Rd, Iver 75 BE72
Cecil Rd, Pot.B. 11 CU32
Cecil Rd, Rom. 70 EX59
Cecil Rd, Sutt. 157 CZ107
Cecil Rd (Cheshunt), Wal.Cr. 15 DX32
Cecil St, Wat. 23 BV38
Cecil Way, Brom. 144 EG102
Cecile Pk N8 65 DL58
Cecilia Cl N2 64 DC55
Cecilia Rd E8 66 DU64
Cedar Av, Barn. 44 DE45
Cedar Av, Cob. 170 BW115
Cedar Av, Enf. 30 DW40
Cedar Av, Grav. 131 GJ91
Cedar Av, Hayes 77 BU72
Cedar Av, Rom. 70 EY57
Cedar Av, Ruis. 78 BW65
Cedar Av, Sid. 126 EU87
Cedar Av, Twick. 116 CB86
Cedar Av, Upmin. 72 FN63
Cedar Av, Wal.Cr. 15 DX33
Cedar Av, West Dr. 76 BM74
Cedar Cl SE21 122 DQ88
Cedar Cl SW15 118 CR91
Cedar Cl, Borwd. 26 CP42
Cedar Cl, Brwd. 55 GD45
Cedar Cl, Brom. 144 EL104
Cedar Cl, Buck.H. 48 EK47
Cedar Cl, Cars. 158 DF107
Cedar Cl, E.Mol. 137 CE98
Cedar Rd
Cedar Cl, Epsom 157 CT114
Cedar Cl, Esher 154 BZ108
Cedar Cl, Iver 75 BC66
Thornbridge Rd
Cedar Cl, Pot.B. 12 DA30
Cedar Cl, Rom. 71 FC56
Cedar Cl, Stai. 134 BJ97
Cedar Cl, Swan. 147 FC96
Cedar Cl, Warl. 177 DY118
Cedar Copse, Brom. 145 EM96
Cedar Ct E8 84 DT66
Cedar Ct E11 68 EH57
Grosvenor Rd
Cedar Ct N1 84 DQ66
Essex Rd
Cedar Ct SE9 124 EL86
Cedar Ct SW19 119 CX90
Cedar Ct, Egh. 113 BA91
Cedar Ct, Epp. 18 EU31
Cedar Cres, Brom. 144 EL104
Cedar Dr N2 64 DE56
Cedar Dr (Sutton at Hone), Dart. 148 FP96
Cedar Dr, Lthd. 171 CE123
Cedar Dr, Loug. 33 EP40
Cedar Dr, Pnr. 40 CA51
Cedar Gdns, Sutt. 158 DC107
Cedar Gdns, Upmin. 72 FQ62
Cedar Gdns, Wok. 166 AV118
St. John's Rd
Cedar Gro W5 98 CL76
Cedar Gro, Bex. 126 EW86
Cedar Gro, Sthl. 78 CA71
Cedar Gro, Wey. 153 BQ105
Cedar Hts, Rich. 118 CL88
Cedar Hill, Epsom 172 CQ116
Cedar Ho, Croy. 161 EB107
Cedar Ho, Sun. 115 BT94
Cedar Lawn Av, Barn. 27 CY43
Cedar Mt SE9 124 EK88
Cedar Pk, Chig. 49 EP49
High Rd
Cedar Pk Gdns, Rom. 70 EX59
Cedar Pk Rd, Enf. 30 DQ38
Cedar Pl SE7 104 EJ78
Floyd Rd
Cedar Pl, Nthwd. 39 BQ51
Cedar Ri N14 44 DG45
Cedar Ri, S.Ock. 91 FX70
Sycamore Way
Cedar Rd N17 46 DT53
Cedar Rd NW2 63 CW63
Cedar Rd, Brwd. 55 GD44
Cedar Rd, Brom. 144 EJ96
Cedar Rd, Cob. 153 BV114
Cedar Rd, Croy. 142 DS103
Cedar Rd, Dart. 128 FK88
Cedar Rd, E.Mol. 137 CE98
Cedar Rd, Enf. 29 DP38

Cedar Rd, Erith 107 FG81
Cedar Rd, Felt. 115 BR88
Cedar Rd, Grays 111 GG76
Cedar Rd, Horn. 72 FJ62
Cedar Rd, Houns. 96 BW82
Cedar Rd, Rom. 71 FC56
Cedar Rd, Sutt. 158 DC107
Cedar Rd, Tedd. 117 CG92
Cedar Rd, Wat. 24 BW44
Cedar Rd, Wey. 152 BN105
Cedar Rd, Wok. 166 AV120
Cedar Ter, Rich. 98 CM84
Cedar Ter Rd, Sev. 191 FJ123
Cedar Tree Gro SE27 121 DP92
Cedar Vista, Rich. 98 CL81
Kew Rd
Cedar Wk, Esher 155 CF107
Cedar Wk, Ken. 176 DQ116
Cedar Wk, Tad. 173 CY120
Cedar Wk, Wal.Abb. 15 ED34
Cedar Way NW1 83 DK66
Cedar Way, Slou. 92 AY78
Cedar Way, Sun. 115 BS94
Cedar Wd Dr, Wat. 23 BV35
Cedarcroft Rd, Chess. 156 CM105
Cedarhurst, Brom. 124 EE94
Elstree Hill
Cedarhurst Dr SE9 124 EJ85
Cedarne Rd SW6 100 DB80
Cedars, Bans. 158 DF114
Cedars, The E15 86 EF67
Portway
Cedars, The W13 79 CJ72
Heronsforde
Cedars, The, Buck.H. 48 EG46
Cedars, The, Lthd. 172 CL121
Cedars, The, Reig. 184 DD134
Cedars, The, Tedd. 117 CF93
Adelaide Rd
Cedars, The, W.Byf. 152 BM112
Cedars Av E17 67 EA57
Cedars Av, Mitch. 140 DG98
Cedars Av, Rick. 38 BJ46
Cedars Cl NW4 63 CX55
Cedars Cl (Chalfont St. Peter), Ger.Cr. 36 AY50
Cedars Ct N9 46 DS47
Church St
Cedars Dr, Uxb. 76 BM68
Cedars Ms SW4 101 DH84
Cedars Rd
Cedars Rd E15 86 EE65
Cedars Rd N9 46 DU47
Church St
Cedars Rd N21 45 DP47
Cedars Rd SW4 101 DH83
Cedars Rd SW13 99 CT82
Cedars Rd W4 98 CQ78
Cedars Rd, Beck. 143 DY96
Cedars Rd, Croy. 141 DL104
Cedars Rd, Kings.T. 137 CJ95
Cedars Rd, Mord. 140 DA98
Cedars Wk, Rick. 21 BF42
Cedarville Gdns SW16 121 DM93
Cedra Ct N16 66 DU60
Cedric Av, Rom. 71 FE55
Cedric Rd SE9 125 EQ90
Celadon Cl, Enf. 31 DY41
Celandine Cl E14 85 EA71
Celandine Cl, S.Ock. 91 FW70
Celandine Dr E8 84 DT66
Richmond Rd
Celandine Dr SE28 88 EV74
Celandine Rd, Walt. 154 BY105
Celandine Way E15 86 EE69
Celbridge Ms W2 82 DB72
Porchester Rd
Celedon Cl, Grays 110 FY75
Celestial Gdns SE13 103 ED84
Celia Cres, Ashf. 114 BK93
Celia Rd N19 65 DJ63
Cell Fm Av, Wind. 112 AV85
Celtic Av, Brom. 144 EE97
Celtic Rd, W.Byf. 152 BL114
Celtic St E14 85 EB71
Cement Block Cotts, Grays 110 GC79
Cemetery La SE7 104 EL79
Cemetery La, Shep. 135 BP101
Cemetery La, Wal.Abb. 16 EF25
Cemetery Rd E7 68 EF63
Cemetery Rd N17 46 DS52
Cemetery Rd SE2 106 EV80
Cenacle Cl NW3 64 DA62
Centaur St SE1 200 C6
Centaur St SE1 101 DM76
Centaurs Business Cen, Islw. 97 CG79
Centaury Ct, Grays 110 GD79
Centenary Est, Enf. 31 DZ42
Centenary Rd, Enf. 31 DZ42
Centenary Wk, Loug. 32 EH41
Centenary Way, Amer. 20 AT38
Centennial Av, Borwd. 41 CH45
Centennial Pk, Borwd. 41 CJ45
Central Av E11 67 ED61
Central Av N2 44 DD54
Central Av N9 46 DS48
Central Av SW11 100 DF80
Central Av, Enf. 30 DV40
Central Av, Grav. 131 GH89
Central Av, Grays 109 FT77
Central Av, Hayes 77 BU73
Central Av, Houns. 96 CC84
Central Av, Pnr. 60 BZ58
Central Av, S.Ock. 108 FQ75
Central Av, Til. 111 GG81
Central Av, Wall. 159 DL106
Central Av, Wal.Cr. 15 DY33
Central Av, Well. 105 ET82
Central Av, W.Mol. 136 BZ98
Central Circ NW4 63 CV57
Hendon Way
Central Dr, Horn. 72 FL62
Central Gdns, Mord. 140 DB99
Central Rd
Central Hill SE19 122 DR92
Central Mkts EC1 196 G7
Central Mkts EC1 83 DP71
Central Par, Croy. 161 EC110
Central Par, Felt. 116 BW87
Central Par, Grnf. 79 CG69
Central Par, Houns. 96 CA80
Heston Rd
Central Par, Surb. 138 CL100
St. Mark's Hill
Central Pk Av, Dag. 71 FB62
Central Pk Est, Houns. 116 BX85
Central Pk Rd E6 86 EK68
Central Pl SE25 142 DV98
Portland Rd
Central Rd, Dart. 128 FL85
Central Rd, Mord. 140 DA99
Central Rd, Wem. 61 CH64
Central Rd, Wor.Pk. 139 CU103
Central Sch Footpath SW14 98 CQ83
Central Sq NW11 64 DB58
Central Sq, Wem. 62 CL64
Station Gro
Central Sq, W.Mol. 136 BZ98
Central St EC1 197 H3
Central St EC1 84 DQ69
Central Way NW10 80 CQ68
Central Way SE28 88 EU73
Central Way, Cars. 158 DE108
Central Way, Felt. 115 BV85
Central Way, Oxt. 187 ED127
Centre, The, Felt. 115 BU89
Centre, The, Walt. 135 BT102
Centre Av W3 80 CR74
Centre Av W10 81 CW69
Harrow Rd
Centre Av, Epp. 17 ET32
Centre Cl, Epp. 17 ET32
Centre Av
Centre Common Rd, Chis. 125 EQ93
Centre Dr, Epp. 17 ET32
Centre Grn, Epp. 17 ET32
Centre Av
Centre Rd E7 68 EG61
Centre Rd E11 68 EG61
Centre Rd, Dag. 89 FB68
Centre St E2 84 DV68
Centre Way E17 47 EC52
Centre Way N9 46 DW47
Centrepoint WC2 195 N8
Centrepoint WC2 83 DK72
Centreway, Ilf. 69 EQ61
Centric Cl NW1 83 DH67
Oval Rd
Centurion Cl N7 83 DM66
Centurion Ct, Wall. 141 DH103
Wandle Rd
Centurion La E3 85 DZ68
Libra Rd
Centurion Way, Erith 106 FA76
Centurion Way, Purf. 108 FM77
Century Cl NW4 63 CX57
Century Ms E5 66 DW63
Lower Clapton Rd
Century Rd E17 67 DY55
Century Rd, Stai. 113 BC92
Cephas Av E1 84 DW70
Cephas St E1 84 DW70
Ceres Rd SE18 105 ET77
Cerise Rd SE15 102 DU81
Cerne Cl, Hayes 78 BX73
Cerne Rd, Grav. 131 GL91
Cerne Rd, Mord. 140 DC100
Cerney Ms W2 82 DD73
Gloucester Ter
Cerotus Pl, Cher. 133 BF101
Cervantes Ct W2 82 DB72
Inverness Ter
Cervantes Ct, Nthwd. 39 BT52
Green La
Cervia Way, Grav. 131 GM90
Cester St E2 84 DU67
Whiston Rd
Ceylon Rd W14 99 CX76
Chace Av, Pot.B. 12 DD32
Chadacre Av, Ilf. 69 EM55
Chadacre Rd, Epsom 157 CV107
Chadbourn St E14 85 EB71
Chadd Dr, Brom. 144 EL97
Chadd Grn E13 86 EG67
Chadfields, Til. 111 GG80
Chadview Ct, Rom. 70 EX59
Chadville Gdns, Rom. 70 EX57
Chadway, Dag. 70 EW60
Chadwell Av, Rom. 70 EV59
Chadwell Av (Cheshunt), Wal.Cr. 14 DW28
Chadwell Bypass, Grays 111 GF78
Chadwell Heath La, Rom. 70 EV57
Chadwell Hill, Grays 111 GH78
Chadwell Rd, Grays 110 GC77
Chadwell St EC1 196 E2
Chadwell St EC1 83 DN69
Chadwick Av E4 47 ED49
Chadwick Av N21 29 DM43
Chadwick Av SW19 120 DA93
Chadwick Cl SW15 119 CT87
Chadwick Cl W7 79 CF71
Westcott Cres
Chadwick Cl, Grav. 130 GE89
Chadwick Cl, Tedd. 117 CG93
Chadwick Dr, Rom. 52 FK54
Chadwick Pl, Surb. 137 CJ101
Chadwick Rd E11 68 EE59
Chadwick Rd NW10 81 CT67
Chadwick Rd SE15 102 DT82
Chadwick Rd, Ilf. 69 EP62
Chadwick St SW1 199 N7
Chadwick St SW1 101 DK76
Chadwick Way SE28 88 EX73
Chadwin Rd E13 86 EH71
Chadworth Way, Esher 155 CD106
Chaffers Mead, Ash. 172 CM116
Chaffinch Av, Croy. 143 DX100
Chaffinch Cl N9 47 DX46
Chaffinch Cl, Croy. 143 DX100
Chaffinch Cl, Surb. 138 CN104
Chaffinch La, Wat. 39 BT45
Chaffinch Rd, Beck. 143 DY95
Chafford Wk, Rain. 90 FJ68
Chafford Way, Rom. 70 EW56
Chagford St NW1 194 D5
Chagford St NW1 82 DF70
Chailey Av, Enf. 30 DT40
Chailey Cl, Houns. 96 BX81
Springwell Rd
Chailey Pl, Walt. 154 BY105
Chailey St E5 66 DW62
Chairmans Av (Denham), Uxb. 57 BF58
Chalbury Wk N1 83 DM68
Chalcombe Rd SE2 106 EV76
Chalcot Cl, Sutt. 158 DA108
Chalcot Cres NW1 82 DF67
Chalcot Gdns NW3 82 DF65
Chalcot Ms SW16 121 DL90
Chalcot Rd NW1 82 DG66
Chalcot Sq NW1 82 DG66
Chalcott Gdns, Surb. 137 CJ102
Chalcroft Rd SE13 124 EE85
Chaldon Common Rd, Cat. 176 DQ124
Chaldon Path, Th.Hth. 141 DP98
Chaldon Rd SW6 99 CY80
Chaldon Rd, Cat. 176 DR124
Chaldon Way, Couls. 175 DL117
Chale Rd SW2 121 DL86
Chale Wk, Sutt. 158 DB109
Hulverston Cl
Chalet Cl, Bex. 127 FD91
Chalet Est NW7 43 CU49
Chalfont Av, Amer. 20 AX39
Chalfont Av, Wem. 80 CP65
Chalfont Ct NW9 63 CT55
Chalfont Grn N9 46 DS48
Chalfont La, Ger.Cr. 37 BC51
Chalfont La, Rick. 21 BB43
Chalfont La (Maple Cross), Rick. 37 BC51
Chalfont Pk (Chalfont St. Peter), Ger.Cr. 57 AZ55
Chalfont Rd N9 46 DT48
Chalfont Rd SE25 142 DT97
Chalfont Rd, Ger.Cr. 37 BB48
Chalfont Rd, Hayes 95 BU75
Chalfont Rd, Rick. 37 BD49
Chalfont Sta Rd, Amer. 20 AW40
Chalfont Wk, Pnr. 40 BW54
Willows Cl
Chalfont Way W13 97 CH76
Chalford Cl, W.Mol. 136 CA98
Chalford Rd SE21 122 DR91
Chalford Wk, Wdf.Grn. 48 EK53
Chalforde Gdns, Rom. 71 FH56
Chalgrove Av, Mord. 140 DA99
Chalgrove Cres, Ilf. 48 EL54
Chalgrove Gdns N3 63 CY55
Chalgrove Rd N17 46 DV53
Chalgrove Rd, Sutt. 158 DD108
Chalice Cl, Wall. 159 DK107
Lavender Vale
Chalice Way, Green. 129 FS85
Chalk Fm Rd NW1 82 DG66
Chalk Hill, Wat. 24 BX44
Chalk Hill Rd W6 99 CX77
Shortlands
Chalk La, Ash. 172 CM119
Chalk La, Barn. 28 DF42
Chalk La, Epsom 172 CR115
Chalk Paddock, Epsom 172 CR115
Chalk Pit Av, Orp. 146 EW97
Chalk Pit Rd, Bans. 174 DA117
Chalk Pit Rd, Epsom 172 CQ119
Chalk Pit Way, Sutt. 158 DC106
Chalk Rd E13 86 EJ71
Chalk Wk, Sutt. 158 DB109
Hulverston Cl
Chalkenden Cl SE20 122 DV94
Chalkhill Rd, Wem. 62 CP62
Chalklands, Wem. 62 CQ62
Chalkley Cl, Mitch. 140 DF96
Chalkmill Rd, Enf. 30 DV41
Chalkpit La, Bet. 182 CP133
Chalkpit La, Oxt. 187 EC125
Chalkpit Wd, Oxt. 187 ED127
Chalkstone Cl, Well. 106 EU81
Chalkwell Pk Av, Enf. 30 DS42
Chalky Bk, Grav. 131 GG91
Chalky La, Chess. 155 CK109
Challacombe Cl, Brwd. 55 GB46
Challenge Cl, Grav. 131 GM91
Challenge Rd, Ashf. 115 BQ90
Challice Way SW2 121 DM88
Challin St SE20 142 DW95
Challis Rd, Brent. 97 CK78
Challock Cl, West. 178 EJ116
Challoner Cl N2 44 DD54
Challoner Cres W14 99 CZ78
Challoner St
Challoner St W14 99 CZ78
Challoners Cl, E.Mol. 137 CD98
Chalmers Ct, Rick. 22 BM44
Chalmers Rd, Ashf. 115 BP91
Chalmers Rd, Bans. 174 DD115
Chalmers Rd E, Ashf. 115 BP91
Chalmers Wk SE17 101 DP79
Hillingdon St
Chalmers Way, Felt. 115 BU85
Chaloner Ct SE1 201 K4
Chalsey Rd SE4 103 DZ84
Chalton Dr N2 64 DC58
Chalton St NW1 195 N2
Chalton St NW1 83 DK68
Chalvey Gdns, Slou. 92 AS75
Chalvey Pk, Slou. 92 AS75
Chalvey Rd E, Slou. 92 AS75
Chamber St E1 84 DT73
Chamberlain Cl SE28 105 ER76
Broadwater Rd
Chamberlain Cotts SE5 102 DR81
Camberwell Gro
Chamberlain Cres, W.Wick. 143 EB102
Chamberlain Gdns, Houns. 96 CC81
Gresham Rd
Chamberlain La, Pnr. 59 BU56
Chamberlain Pl E17 67 DY55
Chamberlain Rd N2 44 DC54
Chamberlain Rd N9 46 DU48
Chamberlain Rd W13 97 CG75
Midhurst Rd
Chamberlain St NW1 82 DF66
Regents Pk Rd
Chamberlain Wk, Felt. 116 BY91
Burgess Cl
Chamberlain Way, Pnr. 59 BV55
Chamberlain Way, Surb. 138 CL101
Chamberlayne Rd NW10 81 CX69
Chambers Cl, Green. 129 FU85
Chambers Gdns N2 44 DD53
Chambers La NW10 81 CV66
Chambers Pl, S.Croy. 160 DR108
Rolleston Rd
Chambers Rd N7 65 DL63
Chambers St SE16 202 B4
Chambers St SE16 102 DU75
Chambersbury La, Hem.H. 6 BN25
Chambord St E2 84 DT69
Champion Cres SE26 123 DY91
Champion Gro SE5 102 DR83
Champion Hill SE5 102 DR83
Champion Hill Est SE5 102 DS83
Champion Pk SE5 102 DR82
Champion Pk Est SE5 102 DR83
Denmark Hill
Champion Rd SE26 123 DY91
Champion Rd, Upmin. 72 FP61
Champness Cl SE27 122 DR91
Rommany Rd
Champneys Cl, Sutt. 157 CZ108
Chance Cl, Grays 110 FZ76
Chance St E1 197 P4
Chance St E1 84 DT70
Chance St E2 197 P4
Chance St E2 84 DT70
Chancel St SE1 200 F2
Chancel St SE1 83 DP74
Chancellor Gdns, S.Croy. 159 DP109
Chancellor Gro SE21 122 DQ89
Chancellor Pas E14 204 A3
Chancellor Pl NW9 43 CT54
Chancellor Way, Sev. 190 FG122
Chancellors Rd W6 99 CW78
Chancellors St W6 99 CW78
Chancelot Rd SE2 106 EV77
Chancery Ct, Dart. 128 FN87
Downs Av
Chancery La WC2 196 D8
Chancery La WC2 83 DN71
Chancery La, Beck. 143 EB96
Chancery Ms SW17 120 DE89
Beechcroft Rd
Chanctonbury Chase, Red. 185 DH134
Chanctonbury Cl SE9 125 EP90
Chanctonbury Gdns, Sutt. 158 DB108
Chanctonbury Way N12 43 CZ49
Chandler Av E16 86 EG71
Chandler Cl, Hmptn. 136 CA95
Chandler Rd, Loug. 33 EP39
Chandler St E1 202 E2
Chandler Way SE15 102 DT80
Chandlers Cl, Felt. 115 BT87
Chandlers Dr, Erith 107 FD77
Chandler's La, Rick. 22 BL37
Chandlers Ms E14 203 P4
Chandlers Ms E14 103 EA75
Chandlers Way SW2 121 DN87
Chandlers Way, Rom. 71 FE57
Chandos Av E17 47 EA54
Chandos Av N14 45 DJ48
Chandos Av N20 44 DC46
Chandos Av W5 97 CJ77
Chandos Cl, Amer. 20 AW38
Chandos Cl, Buck.H. 48 EH47
Chandos Cres, Edg. 42 CM52
Chandos Mall, Slou. 92 AT75
High St
Chandos Par, Edg. 42 CM52
Chandos Cres
Chandos Pl WC2 199 P1
Chandos Pl WC2 83 DL73
Chandos Rd E15 67 ED64
Chandos Rd N2 44 DD54
Chandos Rd N17 46 DS54
Chandos Rd NW2 63 CW64
Chandos Rd NW10 80 CS70
Chandos Rd, Borwd. 26 CM40
Chandos Rd, Har. 60 CC57
Chandos Rd, Pnr. 60 BW59
Chandos Rd, Stai. 113 BD92
Chandos St W1 195 J7
Chandos St W1 83 DH71
Chandos Way NW11 64 DB60
Change All EC3 197 L9
Chanlock Path, S.Ock. 91 FV73
Carnach Grn
Channel Cl, Houns. 96 CA81
Channel Gate Rd NW10 81 CT69
Old Oak La
Channelsea Rd E15 85 ED67
Channing Cl, Horn. 72 FM59
Channings, Wok. 166 AY115
Chant Sq E15 85 ED66
Chant St E15 85 ED66
Chanton Dr, Epsom 157 CW110
Chanton Dr, Sutt. 157 CW110
Chantress Cl, Dag. 89 FC67
Chantrey Cl, Ash. 171 CJ119
Chantrey Rd SW9 101 DM83
Chantreywood, Brwd. 55 GA48
Chantry, The, Uxb. 76 BM69
Chantry Cl NW7 27 CT44
Hendon Wd La
Chantry Cl, Enf. 30 DQ38
Bedale Rd
Chantry Cl, Har. 62 CM57
Chantry Cl, Kings L. 6 BN29
Chantry Cl, Sid. 126 EY92
Ellenborough Rd
Chantry Cl, West Dr. 76 BK73
Chantry Ct, Cars. 140 DE104
Plumpton Way
Chantry Ho, Rain. 89 FD68
Chantry Way
Chantry Hurst, Epsom 172 CR115
Chantry La, Brom. 144 EK99
Bromley Common
Chantry La, St.Alb. 9 CK26
Chantry Pl, Har. 40 CB53
Chantry Pt W9 81 CZ70
Chantry Rd, Cher. 134 BJ101
Chantry Rd, Chess. 156 CM106
Chantry Rd, Har. 40 CB53
Chantry Sq W8 100 DB76
St. Mary's Pl
Chantry St N1 83 DP67
Chantry Way, Mitch. 140 DD97
Chantry Way, Rain. 89 FD68
Chapel Av, Add. 152 BH105
Chapel Cl, Dart. 127 FE85
Chapel Cl, Grays 109 FV79
Chapel Cl, Hat. 12 DD27
Chapel Cl, Wat. 7 BT34
Chapel Ct N2 64 DE55
Chapel Ct SE1 201 K4
Chapel Cft, Kings L. 6 BG31
Chapel End (Chalfont St. Peter), Ger.Cr. 36 AX54
Austenwood La
Chapel Fm Rd SE9 125 EM90
Chapel Gro, Add. 152 BH105
Chapel Gro, Epsom 173 CW119
Chapel High Shop Prec, Brwd. 54 FW47
Chapel Hill, Dart. 127 FE85
Chapel Ho St E14 204 C10
Chapel Ho St E14 103 EB78
Chapel La, Chig. 49 ET48
Chapel La, Pnr. 60 BX55
Chapel La, Rom. 70 EX59
Chapel La, Slou. 74 AV66
Chapel La, Uxb. 76 BN72
Chapel Mkt N1 83 DN68
Chapel Pk Rd, Add. 152 BH105
Chapel Path E11 68 EG58
Chapel Pl EC2 197 M3
Chapel Pl N1 83 DN68
Chapel Mkt
Chapel Pl N17 46 DT52
White Hart La
Chapel Pl W1 195 H9
Chapel Pl W1 83 DH72
Chapel Rd SE27 121 DP91
Chapel Rd W13 79 CH74
Chapel Rd, Bexh. 106 FA84
Chapel Rd, Epp. 17 ET30
Chapel Rd, Houns. 96 CB83
Chapel Rd, Ilf. 69 EN62
Chapel Rd, Oxt. 188 EJ130
Chapel Rd, Red. 184 DF134
Chapel Rd, Tad. 173 CW123
Chapel Rd, Twick. 117 CH87
Chapel Rd, Warl. 177 DX118
Chapel Row (Harefield), Uxb. 38 BJ53
Chapel Side W2 82 DB73
Chapel Sq, Vir.W. 132 AY98
Chapel Stones N17 46 DT53
Chapel St NW1 194 B7
Chapel St NW1 82 DE71
Chapel St SW1 198 G6
Chapel St SW1 100 DG76
Chapel St, Enf. 30 DQ41
Chapel St, Slou. 92 AT75
Chapel St, Uxb. 76 BJ67
Trumper Way
Chapel St, Wok. 167 AZ117
Chapel Ter, Loug. 32 EL42
Forest Rd
Chapel Vw, S.Croy. 160 DV107
Chapel Wk NW4 63 CV56
Chapel Wk, Croy. 142 DQ103
Wellesley Rd
Chapel Way N7 65 DM62
Sussex Way
Chapel Way, Abb.L. 7 BT27
Chapel Way, Epsom 173 CW119
Chapel Yd SW18 120 DA85
Wandsworth High St
Chapelmount Rd, Wdf.Grn. 49 EM51
Chaplaincy Gdns, Horn. 72 FL60
Chaplin Cl SE1 200 E4
Chaplin Cl SE1 101 DN75
Chaplin Cres, Sun. 115 BS93
Chaplin Rd E15 86 EE68
Chaplin Rd N17 66 DT55
Chaplin Rd NW2 81 CU65
Chaplin Rd, Dag. 88 EY66
Chaplin Rd, Wem. 79 CJ65
Chaplin Sq N12 44 DD52
Chapman Cl, West Dr. 94 BM76
Chapman Cres, Har. 62 CL57
Chapman Pk Ind Est NW10 81 CT65
Chapman Rd E9 85 DZ65
Chapman Rd, Belv. 106 FA78
Chapman Rd, Croy. 141 DN102
Chapman Sq SW19 119 CX89
Chapman St E1 84 DV73
Chapman's La SE2 106 EW77
Chapman's La, Belv. 106 EX77
Chapmans La, Orp. 146 EX96
Chapmans Rd, Sev. 180 EY124
Chapmans Yd, Wat. 24 BW42
New Rd
Chapone Pl W1 195 M9
Chapter Cl W4 98 CQ76
Beaumont Rd
Chapter Cl, Uxb. 76 BM66
Chapter Ho Ct EC4 197 H9
Chapter Rd NW2 63 CU64
Chapter Rd SE17 101 DP78
Chapter St SW1 199 M9
Chapter St SW1 101 DK77
Chapter Way, Hmptn. 116 CA91
Chara Pl W4 98 CR79
Charcroft Gdns, Enf. 31 DX42
Chardin Rd W4 98 CS77
Elliott Rd
Chardmore Rd N16 66 DU60
Chardwell Cl E6 86 EL72
Northumberland Rd
Charecroft Way W12 99 CX75
Charfield Ct W9 82 DB70
Shirland Rd
Charford Rd E16 86 EG71
Chargate Cl, Walt. 153 BT107
Chargeable La E13 86 EF70
Chargeable St E16 86 EF70
Chargrove Cl SE16 203 J4
Charing Cl, Orp. 163 ET105
Charing Cross SW1 199 P2
Charing Cross Rd WC2 195 N8
Charing Cross Rd WC2 83 DK72
Charlbert St NW8 82 DE68

Cherry Orchard Gdns, Croy. 142 DR103
Oval Rd
Cherry Orchard Gdns, W.Mol. 136 BZ97
Cherry Orchard Rd, Brom. 144 EL103
Cherry Orchard Rd, Croy. 142 DR103
Cherry Orchard Rd, W.Mol. 136 CA97
Cherry Ri, Ch.St.G. 36 AX47
Cherry Rd, Enf. 30 DW38
Cherry St, Rom. 71 FD57
Cherry St, Wok. 166 AY118
Cherry Tree Av, St.Alb. 9 CK26
Cherry Tree Av, Stai. 114 BH93
Cherry Tree Av, West Dr. 76 BM72
Cherry Tree Cl E9 84 DW67
Moulins Rd
Cherry Tree Cl, Grays 110 GC79
Cherry Tree Cl, Rain. 89 FG68
Cherry Tree Cl, Wem. 61 CF63
Cherry Tree Ct NW9 62 CQ56
Cherry Tree Ct, Couls. 175 DM117
Cherry Tree Dr SW16 121 DL90
Cherry Tree Dr, S.Ock. 91 FX70
Cherry Tree Grn, S.Croy. 160 DV114
Cherry Tree La, Dart. 127 FF90
Cherry Tree La, Epsom 156 CN112
Christ Ch Rd
Cherry Tree La, Iver 76 BG67
Cherry Tree La, Pot.B. 12 DB34
Cherry Tree La, Rain. 89 FE69
Cherry Tree La, Rick. 37 BC46
Cherry Tree La, Slou. 75 AZ65
Cherry Tree Ri, Buck.H. 48 EJ49
Cherry Tree Rd E15 68 EE63
Wingfield Rd
Cherry Tree Rd N2 64 DF56
Cherry Tree Rd, Wat. 23 BV36
Cherry Tree Wk EC1 197 J5
Cherry Tree Wk, Beck. 143 DZ98
Cherry Tree Wk, W.Wick. 162 EF105
Cherry Tree Way, Stan. 41 CH51
Cherry Wk, Brom. 144 EG102
Cherry Wk, Grays 111 GG76
Cherry Wk, Rain. 89 FF68
Cherry Wk, Rick. 22 BJ40
Cherry Way, Epsom 156 CR107
Cherry Way, Shep. 135 BR98
Cherry Way, Slou. 93 BC83
Cherry Wd Way W5 80 CN71
Hanger Vale La
Cherrycot Hill, Orp. 163 ER105
Cherrycot Ri, Orp. 163 EQ105
Cherrycroft Gdns, Pnr. 40 BZ52
Westfield Pk
Cherrydale, Wat. 23 BT42
Cherrydown Av E4 47 DZ48
Cherrydown Cl E4 47 DZ48
Cherrydown Rd, Sid. 126 EX89
Cherrydown Wk, Rom. 51 FB54
Cherrytree La (Chalfont St. Peter), Ger.Cr. 36 AX54
Cherrywood Av, Egh. 112 AV93
Cherrywood Cl E3 85 DY69
Cherrywood Cl, Kings.T. 118 CN94
Cherrywood Dr SW15 119 CX85
Cherrywood Dr, Grav. 130 GE90
Cherrywood La, Mord. 139 CY98
Cherston Gdns, Loug. 33 EN42
Cherston Rd
Cherston Rd, Loug. 33 EN42
Chertsey Br Rd, Cher. 134 BK101
Chertsey Cl, Ken. 175 DP115
Chertsey Cres, Croy. 161 EC110
Chertsey Dr, Sutt. 139 CY103
Chertsey La, Cher. 133 BE95
Chertsey La, Epsom 156 CN112
Chertsey La, Stai. 113 BE92
Chertsey Rd E11 67 ED61
Chertsey Rd, Add. 134 BH103
Chertsey Rd, Ashf. 115 BR94
Chertsey Rd, Felt. 115 BS92
Chertsey Rd, Ilf. 69 ER63
Chertsey Rd, Shep. 134 BN101
Chertsey Rd, Sun. 115 BR94
Chertsey Rd, Twick. 117 CF86
Chertsey Rd, W.Byf. 152 BK111
Chertsey Rd, Wok. 151 BA113
Chertsey Rd (Chobham), Wok. 150 AY110
Chertsey St SW17 120 DG92
Chervil Cl, Felt. 115 BU90
Chervil Ms SE28 88 EV74
Cherwell Cl, Rick. 22 BN43
Cherwell Cl, Slou. 93 BB79
Tweed Rd
Cherwell Ct, Epsom 156 CQ105
Cherwell Gro, S.Ock. 91 FV73
Cherwell Way, Ruis. 59 BQ58
Cheryls Cl SW6 100 DB81
Cheseman St SE26 122 DV90
Chesfield Rd, Kings.T. 118 CL94
Chesham Av, Orp. 145 EP100
Chesham Cl SW1 198 F7
Chesham Cl, Rom. 71 FD56
Chesham Cl, Sutt. 157 CY110
Chesham Ct, Nthwd. 39 BT51
Frithwood Av
Chesham Cres SE20 142 DW96
Chesham La, Ch.St.G. 36 AY48
Chesham La (Chalfont St. Peter), Ger.Cr. 36 AY49
Chesham Ms SW1 198 F6
Chesham Ms SW1 100 DG76
Chesham Pl SW1 198 F7
Chesham Pl SW1 100 DG76
Chesham Rd SE20 142 DW96
Chesham Rd SW19 120 DD92
Chesham Rd, Hem.H. 4 AY27
Chesham Rd, Kings.T. 138 CN95
Chesham St NW10 62 CR62
Chesham St SW1 198 F7
Chesham St SW1 100 DG76
Chesham Ter W13 97 CH75
Chesham Way, Wat. 23 BS44
Cheshire Cl E17 47 EB53
Cheshire Cl SE4 103 DZ82
Cheshire Cl, Cher. 151 BC107
Cheshire Cl, Horn. 72 FN57
Cheshire Cl, Mitch. 141 DL97
Cheshire Ct EC4 196 E9
Cheshire Ct, Slou. 92 AV75
Clements Cl
Cheshire Gdns, Chess. 155 CK107
Cheshire Rd N22 45 DM52
Cheshire St E2 84 DT70
Chesholm Rd N16 66 DS62
Cheshunt Link Rd (Cheshunt), Wal.Cr. 14 DW33
Cheshunt Pk (Cheshunt), Wal.Cr. 14 DV26
Cheshunt Rd E7 86 EH65
Cheshunt Rd, Belv. 106 FA78
Cheshunt Wash (Cheshunt), Wal.Cr. 15 DY27
Chesil Ct E2 84 DV68
Chesil Way, Hayes 77 BT69
Chesilton Rd SW6 99 CZ81
Chesley Gdns E6 86 EK68
Cheslyn Gdns, Wat. 23 BT37
Chesney Cres, Croy. 161 EC108
Chesney St SW11 100 DG81
Chesnut Est N17 66 DT55
Chesnut Gro N17 66 DT55
Chesnut Rd
Chesnut Rd N17 66 DT55
Chess Cl, Chesh. 20 AX36
Chess Cl, Rick. 22 BK42
Chess Hill, Rick. 22 BK42
Chess La, Rick. 22 BK42
Chess Vale Ri, Rick. 22 BM44
Chess Valley Wk, Chesh. 20 AU35
Chess Valley Wk, Rick. 22 BL44
Chess Way, Rick. 22 BG41
Chessfield Pk, Amer. 20 AY39
Chessholme Ct, Sun. 115 BS94
Scotts Av
Chessholme Rd, Ashf. 115 BQ93
Chessington Av N3 63 CY55
Chessington Av, Bexh. 106 EY80
Chessington Cl, Epsom 156 CQ107
Chessington Ct, Pnr. 60 BZ56
Chessington Hall Gdns, Chess. 155 CK108
Chessington Hill Pk, Chess. 156 CN106
Chessington Lo N3 63 CZ55
Chessington Rd, Epsom 157 CT109
Chessington Way, W.Wick. 143 EB103
Chesson Rd W14 99 CZ79
Chesswood Way, Pnr. 40 BX54
Chester Av, Rich. 118 CM85
Chester Av, Twick. 116 BZ88
Chester Av, Upmin. 73 FS61
Chester Cl SW1 198 G5
Chester Cl SW1 100 DG75
Chester Cl SW13 99 CV83
Chester Cl, Ashf. 115 BR92
Chester Cl, Loug. 33 EQ39
Chester Cl, Pot.B. 12 DB29
Chester Cl, Sutt. 140 DA103
Chester Cl, Uxb. 77 BP72
Dawley Av
Chester Cl N NW1 195 J2
Chester Cl S NW1 195 J3
Chester Cotts SW1 198 F9
Chester Ct NW1 195 J2
Chester Ct SE5 102 DR80
Chester Cres E8 84 DT65
Ridley Rd
Chester Dr, Har. 60 BZ58
Chester Gdns W13 79 CG72
Chester Gdns, Enf. 30 DV44
Chester Gdns, Mord. 140 DC100
Chester Gate NW1 195 H3
Chester Gate NW1 83 DH69
Chester Grn, Loug. 33 EQ39
Chester Ms SW1 199 H6
Chester Ms SW1 101 DH76
Chester Path, Loug. 33 EQ39
Chester Pl NW1 195 J2
Chester Rd E7 86 EK66
Chester Rd E11 68 EH58
Chester Rd E16 86 EE70
Chester Rd E17 67 DX57
Chester Rd N9 46 DV46
Chester Rd N17 66 DR55
Chester Rd N19 65 DH61
Chester Rd NW1 194 G3
Chester Rd NW1 82 DG69
Chester Rd SW19 119 CW93
Chester Rd, Borwd. 26 CQ41
Chester Rd, Chig. 49 EN48
Chester Rd, Houns. 95 BV83
Chester Rd (Heathrow Airport), Houns. 94 BN83
Chester Rd, Ilf. 69 ET60
Chester Rd, Loug. 33 EP40
Chester Rd, Nthwd. 39 BS52
Chester Rd, Sid. 125 ES85
Chester Rd, Wat. 23 BU43
Chester Row SW1 198 F9
Chester Row SW1 100 DG77
Chester Sq SW1 199 H8
Chester Sq SW1 101 DH76
Chester Sq Ms SW1 199 H7
Chester St E2 84 DU70
Chester St SW1 198 G6
Chester St SW1 100 DG76
Chester Ter NW1 195 H2
Chester Way SE11 200 E9
Chester Way SE11 101 DN77
Chesterfield Cl, Orp. 146 EX98
Chesterfield Dr, Dart. 127 FH85
Chesterfield Dr, Esher 137 CG103
Chesterfield Dr, Sev. 190 FD122
Chesterfield Gdns N4 65 DP57
Chesterfield Gdns SE10 103 ED80
Crooms Hill
Chesterfield Gdns W1 199 H2
Chesterfield Gdns W1 83 DH74
Chesterfield Gro SE22 122 DT85
Chesterfield Hill W1 199 H1
Chesterfield Hill W1 83 DH73
Chesterfield Ms N4 65 DP57
Chesterfield Gdns
Chesterfield Ms, Ashf. 114 BL91
Chesterfield Rd
Chesterfield Rd E10 67 EC58
Chesterfield Rd N3 44 DA51
Chesterfield Rd W4 98 CQ79
Chesterfield Rd, Ashf. 114 BL91
Chesterfield Rd, Barn. 27 CX43
Chesterfield Rd, Enf. 31 DY37
Chesterfield Rd, Epsom 156 CR108
Chesterfield St W1 199 H2
Chesterfield St W1 83 DH74
Chesterfield Wk SE10 103 ED81
Chesterfield Way SE15 102 DW80
Chesterfield Way, Hayes 95 BU75
Chesterford Gdns NW3 64 DB63
Chesterford Ho SE18 104 EK80
Shooter's Hill Rd
Chesterford Rd E12 69 EM64
Chesters, The, N.Mal. 138 CS95
Chesterton Cl SW18 120 DA85
Ericcson Cl
Chesterton Cl, Grnf. 78 CB68
Chesterton Dr, Red. 185 DL128
Chesterton Dr, Stai. 114 BM88
Chesterton Rd E13 86 EG69
Chesterton Rd W10 81 CX71
Chesterton Sq W8 99 CZ77
Pembroke Rd
Chesterton Ter E13 86 EG69
Chesterton Ter, Kings.T. 138 CN96
Chesterton Way, Til. 111 GJ82
Chesthunte Rd N17 46 DQ53
Chestnut All SW6 99 CZ79
Lillie Rd
Chestnut Av E7 68 EH63
Chestnut Av N8 65 DL57
Chestnut Av SW14 98 CR83
Thornton Rd
Chestnut Av, Brent. 97 CK77
Chestnut Av, Brwd. 54 FS45
Chestnut Av, Buck.H. 48 EK48
Chestnut Av, E.Mol. 137 CF97
Chestnut Av, Edg. 42 CL51
Chestnut Av, Epsom 156 CS105
Chestnut Av, Esher 137 CD101
Chestnut Av, Grays 110 GB75
Chestnut Av (Bluewater), Green. 129 FT87
Chestnut Av, Hmptn. 116 CA94
Chestnut Av, Horn. 71 FF61
Chestnut Av, Nthwd. 39 BT54
Chestnut Av, Rick. 22 BG43
Chestnut Av, Slou. 92 AX75
Chestnut Av, Tedd. 137 CF96
Chestnut Av, Vir.W. 132 AT98
Chestnut Av, Walt. 153 BS109
Chestnut Av, Wem. 61 CH64
Chestnut Av, West Dr. 76 BM73
Chestnut Av, W.Wick. 162 EE106
Chestnut Av, West. 178 EK122
Chestnut Av, Wey. 153 BQ108
Chestnut Av N E17 67 EC56
Chestnut Av S E17 67 EC56
Chestnut Cl N14 29 DJ43
Chestnut Cl N16 66 DR61
Lordship Gro
Chestnut Cl SE6 123 EC92
Chestnut Cl SE14 103 DZ83
Shardeloes Rd
Chestnut Cl SW16 121 DN91
Chestnut Cl, Add. 152 BK106
Chestnut Cl, Ashf. 115 BP91
Chestnut Cl, Buck.H. 48 EK47
Chestnut Cl, Cars. 140 DF102
Chestnut Cl, Egh. 112 AW93
Chestnut Cl (Chalfont St. Peter), Ger.Cr. 37 AZ52
Chestnut Cl, Grav. 131 GF86
Burch Rd
Chestnut Cl, Hayes 77 BS73
Chestnut Cl, Horn. 72 FJ63
Lancaster Dr
Chestnut Cl, Orp. 164 EU106
Chestnut Cl, Sid. 126 EU88
Chestnut Cl, Sun. 115 BT93
Chestnut Cl, Tad. 174 DA123
Chestnut Cl, West Dr. 95 BP80
Chestnut Cl, Wok. 168 BG124
Chestnut Copse, Oxt. 188 EG132
Chestnut Ct SW6 99 CZ79
North End Rd
Chestnut Ct, Amer. 20 AS36
Chestnut Ct, Surb. 138 CL101
Penners Gdns
Chestnut Cres, Walt. 153 BS109
Chestnut Av
Chestnut Dr E11 68 EG58
Chestnut Dr, Bexh. 106 EX83
Chestnut Dr, Egh. 112 AX93
Chestnut Dr, Har. 41 CF52
Chestnut Dr, Pnr. 60 BX58
Chestnut Glen, Horn. 71 FF61
Chestnut Gro SE20 122 DW94
Chestnut Gro SW12 120 DG87
Chestnut Gro W5 97 CK76
Chestnut Gro, Barn. 28 DF43
Chestnut Gro, Brwd. 54 FW47
Chestnut Gro, Dart. 127 FD91
Chestnut Gro, Ilf. 49 ES51
Chestnut Gro, Islw. 97 CG84
Chestnut Gro, Mitch. 141 DK98
Chestnut Gro, N.Mal. 138 CR97
Chestnut Gro, S.Croy. 160 DV108
Chestnut Gro, Stai. 114 BJ93
Chestnut Gro, Wem. 61 CH64
Chestnut Gro, Wok. 166 AY120
Chestnut La N20 43 CY46
Chestnut La, Sev. 191 FH124
Chestnut La, Wey. 153 BP106
Chestnut Manor Cl, Stai. 114 BH92
Chestnut Mead, Red. 184 DE133
Oxford Rd
Chestnut Pl, Ash. 172 CL119
Chestnut Pl, Epsom 157 CU111
Chestnut Ri SE18 105 ER79
Chestnut Ri, Bushey 40 CB45
Chestnut Rd SE27 121 DP90
Chestnut Rd SW20 139 CX96
Chestnut Rd, Ashf. 115 BP91
Chestnut Rd, Dart. 128 FK88
Chestnut Rd, Enf. 31 DY36
Chestnut Rd, Kings.T. 118 CL94
Chestnut Rd, Twick. 117 CE89
Chestnut Wk (Chalfont St. Peter), Ger.Cr. 36 AY52
Chestnut Wk, Sev. 191 FL129
Chestnut Wk, Shep. 135 BS99
Chestnut Wk, Walt. 153 BS109
Octagon Rd
Chestnut Wk, Wat. 23 BU37
Chestnut Wk, W.Byf. 152 BL112
Royston Rd
Chestnut Wk, Wdf.Grn. 48 EG50
Chestnut Way, Felt. 115 BV90
Chestnuts, Brwd. 55 GB46
Chestnuts, The SE14 103 DZ81
Chestnuts, The, Rom. 34 EV41
Chestnuts, The, Walt. 135 BU102
Cheston Av, Croy. 143 DY103
Chestwood Gro, Uxb. 76 BM66
Cheswick Cl, Dart. 107 FF84
Chesworth Cl, Erith 107 FE81
Chettle Cl SE1 201 K6
Chettle Ct N8 65 DN58
Chetwode Dr, Epsom 173 CX118
Chetwode Rd SW17 120 DF90
Chetwode Rd, Tad. 173 CW119
Chetwood Wk E6 86 EL72
Chetwynd Av, Barn. 44 DF46
Chetwynd Dr, Uxb. 76 BM68
Chetwynd Rd NW5 65 DH63
Cheval Pl SW7 198 C6
Cheval Pl SW7 100 DE76
Cheval St E14 203 P6
Cheval St E14 103 EA76
Chevalier Cl, Stan. 42 CL49
Cheveley Cl, Rom. 52 FM53
Chelsworth Dr
Chevely Cl, Epp. 18 EX29
Cheveney Wk, Brom. 144 EG97
Marina Cl
Chevening La, Sev. 180 EY115
Chevening Rd NW6 81 CX68
Chevening Rd SE10 104 EF78
Chevening Rd SE19 122 DR93
Chevening Rd, Sev. 180 EZ119
Chevening Rd (Sundridge), Sev. 180 EY123
Chevenings, The, Sid. 126 EW90
Cheverton Rd N19 65 DK60
Chevet St E9 67 DY64
Kenworthy Rd
Chevington Way, . Horn 72 FK63
Cheviot Cl, Bans. 174 DB115
Cheviot Cl, Bexh. 107 FE82
Cheviot Cl, Bushey 24 CC44
Cheviot Cl, Enf. 30 DR40
Cheviot Cl, Hayes 95 BR80
Cheviot Cl, Sutt. 158 DD109
Cheviot Gdns NW2 63 CX61
Cheviot Gdns SE27 121 DP91
Cheviot Gate NW2 63 CY61
Cheviot Rd SE27 121 DN92
Cheviot Rd, Horn. 71 FG60
Cheviot Rd, Slou. 93 BA78
Cheviot Way, Ilf. 69 ES56
Chevron Cl E16 86 EG72
Chevy Rd, Sthl. 96 CC75
Chewton Rd E17 67 DY56
Cheyham Gdns, Sutt. 157 CX110
Cheyham Way, Sutt. 157 CY110
Cheyne Av E18 68 EF55
Cheyne Av, Twick. 116 BZ88
Cheyne Cl NW4 63 CW57
Cheyne Cl, Brom. 144 EL104
Cedar Cres
Cheyne Cl, Ger.Cr. 56 AY60
Cheyne Ct SW3 100 DF79
Flood St
Cheyne Ct, Bans. 174 DB115
Park Rd
Cheyne Gdns SW3 100 DE79
Cheyne Hill, Surb. 138 CM98
Cheyne Ms SW3 100 DE79
Cheyne Path W7 79 CF72
Copley Cl
Cheyne Pl SW3 100 DF79
Cheyne Rd, Ashf. 115 BR93
Cheyne Row SW3 100 DE79
Cheyne Wk N21 29 DP43
Cheyne Wk NW4 63 CW58
Cheyne Wk SW3 100 DE79
Cheyne Wk SW10 100 DD80
Cheyne Wk, Croy. 142 DU103
Cheyne Wk, Long. 149 FX97
Cavendish Sq
Cheyneys Av, Edg. 41 CK51
Chichele Gdns, Croy. 160 DT105
Brownlow Rd
Chichele Rd NW2 63 CX64
Chichele Rd, Oxt. 188 EE128
Chicheley Gdns, Har. 40 CC52
Chicheley Rd, Har. 40 CC52
Chicheley St SE1 200 C4
Chicheley St SE1 101 DM75
Chichester Av, Ruis. 59 BR61
Chichester Cl E6 86 EL72
Chichester Cl SE3 104 EJ81
Chichester Cl, Hmptn. 116 BZ93
Maple Cl
Chichester Cl, S.Ock. 90 FQ74
Chichester Ct, Epsom 157 CT109
Chichester Ct, Slou. 92 AU75
Chichester Ct, Stan. 62 CL55
Chichester Dr, Pur. 159 DM112
Chichester Dr, Sev. 190 FF125
Chichester Gdns, Ilf. 68 EL59
Chichester Ms SE27 121 DN91
Chichester Rents WC2 196 D8
Chichester Ri, Grav. 131 GK91
Chichester Rd E11 68 EE62
Chichester Rd N9 46 DU46
Chichester Rd NW6 82 DA68
Chichester Rd W2 82 DB71
Chichester Rd, Croy. 142 DS104
Chichester Rd, Green. 129 FT85
Chichester St SW1 101 DJ78
Chichester Way E14 204 F8
Chichester Way E14 103 ED77
Chichester Way, Felt. 115 BV87
Chichester Way, Wat. 8 BY33
Chicksand St E1 84 DT71
Chiddingfold N12 44 DA48
Chiddingstone Av, Bexh. 106 E
Chiddingstone Cl, Sutt. 158 DA1
Chiddingstone St SW6 100 DA
Chieftan Dr, Purf. 108 FM
Chieveley Rd, Bexh. 107 FE
Chiffinch Gdns, Grav. 130 GE
Chignell Pl W13 79 CG
Broadway
Chigwell Hill E1 202
Chigwell Hurst Ct, Pnr. 60 BX
Chigwell La, Loug. 33 EQ
Chigwell Pk, Chig. 49 EP
Chigwell Pk Dr, Chig. 49 EN
Chigwell Ri, Chig. 49 EN
Chigwell Rd E18 68 EH
Chigwell Rd, Wdf.Grn. 48 EJ
Chigwell Vw, Rom. 50 FA
Lodge La
Chilberton Dr, Red. 185 DJ1
Chilbrook Rd, Cob. 169 BU1
Chilcot Cl E14 85 EB
Grundy St
Chilcote La, Amer. 20 AV
Chilcott Rd, Wat. 23 BS
Childebert Rd SW17 121 DH
Childeric Rd SE14 103 DY
Childerley St SW6 99 CX
Fulham Palace Rd
Childers, The, Wdf.Grn. 49 EM
Childers St SE8 103 DY
Childs Av (Harefield), Uxb. 38 BJ
Childs Cl, Horn. 72 FJ
Childs Cres, Swans. 129 FX
Childs Hill Wk NW2 63 CZ
Childs La SE19 122 DS
Westow St
Child's Pl SW5 100 DA
Child's St SW5 100 DA
Child's Wk SW5 100 DA
Child's Pl
Childs Way NW11 63 CZ
Chilham Cl, Bex. 126 EZ
Chilham Cl, Grnf. 79 CG
Chilham Rd SE9 124 EL
Chilham Way, Brom. 144 EG1
Chillerton Rd SW17 120 DG
Chillingworth Gdns, Twick. 117 CF
Tower Rd
Chillingworth Rd N7 65 DN
Liverpool Rd
Chilmark Gdns, N.Mal. 139 CT1
Chilmark Gdns, Red. 185 DL1
Chilmark Rd SW16 141 DK
Chilmead La, Red. 185 DK1
Chilsey Grn Rd, Cher. 133 BE1
Chiltern Av, Bushey 24 CC
Chiltern Av, Twick. 116 CA
Chiltern Business Village, Uxb. 76 BH
Chiltern Cl, Bexh. 107 FE
Cumbrian Av
Chiltern Cl, Borwd. 26 CM
Chiltern Cl, Bushey 24 CB
Chiltern Cl, Croy. 142 DS1
Chiltern Cl (Ickenham), Uxb. 59 BP
Chiltern Cl (Cheshunt), Wal.Cr. 13 DP
Chiltern Cl, Wok. 166 AW1
Chiltern Cl, Wor.Pk. 139 CW1
Cotswold Way
Chiltern Dene, Enf. 29 DM
Chiltern Dr, Rick. 37 BF
Chiltern Dr, Surb. 138 CP
Chiltern Gdns NW2 63 CX
Chiltern Gdns, Brom. 144 EF
Chiltern Gdns, Horn. 72 FJ
Chiltern Hill (Chalfont St. Peter), Ger.Cr. 36 AY
Chiltern Rd E3 85 EA
Chiltern Rd, Grav. 130 GE
Chiltern Rd, Ilf. 69 ES
Chiltern Rd, Pnr. 60 BW
Chiltern Rd, Sutt. 158 DB1
Chiltern St W1 194 F
Chiltern St W1 82 DG
Chiltern Vw Rd, Uxb. 76 BJ
Chiltern Way, Wdf.Grn. 48 EG
Chilterns, The, Sutt. 158 DB1
Gatton Cl
Chilthorne Cl SE6 123 DZ
Ravensbourne Pk Cres
Chilton Av W5 97 CK
Chilton Ct, Walt. 153 BU1
Chilton Gro SE8 203 J
Chilton Gro SE8 103 DX
Chilton Rd, Edg. 42 CN
Manor Pk Cres
Chilton Rd, Grays 111 GG
Chilton Rd, Rich. 98 CN
Chilton St E2 84 DT
Chiltonian Ind Est SE12 124 EF
Chiltons, The E18 48 EG
Grove Hill
Chiltons Cl, Bans. 174 DB1
High St
Chilver St SE10 205 L
Chilver St SE10 104 EF
Chilwell Gdns, Wat. 40 BW
Chilworth Ct SW19 119 CX
Windlesham Gro
Chilworth Gdns, Sutt. 140 DC1
Chilworth Ms W2 82 DC
Chilworth St W2 82 DC
Chimes Av N13 45 DN
Chinbrook Cres SE12 124 EH
Chinbrook Est SE9 124 EK
Chinbrook Rd SE12 124 EH
Chinchilla Dr, Houns. 96 BW
Chindits La, Brwd. 54 FW
Chine, The N10 65 DJ
Chine, The N21 29 DP
Chine, The, Wem. 61 CH
Ching Ct WC2 195 P
Ching Way E4 47 DZ5
Chingdale Rd E4 48 EE4
Chingford Av E4 47 EB4
Chingford Hall Est E4 47 DZ5
Chingford Ind Cen E4 47 DY5

Church Ter SE13 104 EE83
Church Ter SW8 101 DK82
Church Ter, Rich. 117 CK85
Church Trd Est, The, Erith 107 FG80
Church Vale N2 64 DF55
Church Vale SE23 122 DW89
Church Vw, S.Ock. 108 FQ75
Church Vw, Swan. 147 FD97
Lime Rd
Church Vw, Upmin. 72 FN61
Church Vil, Sev. 190 FE122
Church Fld
Church Wk N6 64 DG62
Swains La
Church Wk N16 66 DR63
Church Wk NW2 63 CZ62
Church Wk NW4 63 CW55
Church Wk NW9 62 CR61
Church Wk SW13 99 CU81
Church Wk SW15 119 CV85
Church Wk SW16 141 DJ96
Church Wk SW20 139 CW97
Church Wk, Brent. 97 CJ79
Church Wk, Cat. 176 DU124
Church Wk, Cher. 134 BG101
Church Wk, Dart. 128 FK90
Church Wk (Eynsford), Dart. 148 FL104
Church Wk, Enf. 30 DR41
Church La
Church Wk, Grav. 131 GK88
Church Wk, Hayes 77 BT72
Church Wk, Lthd. 171 CH122
The Cres
Church Wk, Red. 186 DR133
Church Wk, Reig. 184 DC134
Reigate Rd
Church Wk, Rich. 117 CK85
Red Lion St
Church Wk, T.Ditt. 137 CF100
Church Wk, Walt. 135 BU102
Church Wk, Wey. 135 BP103
Beales La
Church Wk Shop Cen, Cat. 176 DU124
Church Wk
Church Way N20 44 DE48
Church Way, Barn. 28 DF42
Church Way, Edg. 42 CN51
Church Way, Oxt. 188 EF132
Church Way, S.Croy. 160 DT110
Churchbury Cl, Enf. 30 DS40
Churchbury La, Enf. 30 DR41
Churchbury Rd SE9 124 EK87
Churchbury Rd, Enf. 30 DR40
Churchcroft Cl SW12 120 DG87
Endlesham Rd
Churchdown, Brom. 124 EE91
Churchfield Av N12 44 DC51
Churchfield Cl, Har. 60 CC56
Churchfield Cl, Hayes 77 BT73
West Av
Churchfield Ms, Slou. 74 AU72
Churchfield Path (Cheshunt), Wal.Cr. 14 DW29
Churchfield Rd W3 80 CQ74
Churchfield Rd W7 97 CE75
Churchfield Rd W13 79 CH74
Churchfield Rd (Chalfont St. Peter), Ger.Cr. 36 AX53
Churchfield Rd, Reig. 183 CZ133
Churchfield Rd, Walt. 135 BU102
Churchfield Rd, Well. 106 EU83
Churchfield Rd, Wey. 152 BN105
Churchfields E18 48 EG53
Churchfields SE10 103 EC79
Roan St
Churchfields, Loug. 32 EL42
Churchfields, W.Mol. 136 CA97
Churchfields, Wok. 166 AY116
Churchfields Av, Felt. 116 BZ90
Churchfields Av, Wey. 153 BP105
Churchfields Rd, Beck. 143 DX96
Churchfields Rd, Wat. 23 BT36
Churchgate (Cheshunt), Wal.Cr. 14 DV30
Churchgate Rd (Cheshunt), Wal.Cr. 14 DV29
Churchill Av, Har. 61 CH58
Churchill Av, Uxb. 77 BP69
Churchill Cl, Dart. 128 FP88
Churchill Cl, Felt. 115 BT88
Churchill Cl, Lthd. 171 CE123
Churchill Cl, Uxb. 77 BP69
Churchill Cl, Warl. 176 DW117
Churchill Ct W5 80 CM70
Churchill Ct, Nthlt. 60 CA64
Churchill Ct, Stai. 114 BJ93
Chestnut Gro
Churchill Dr, Wey. 135 BQ104
Churchill Gdns SW1 101 DJ78
Churchill Gdns W3 80 CN72
Churchill Gdns Rd SW1 101 DH78
Churchill Ms, Wdf.Grn. 48 EF51
High Rd Woodford Grn
Churchill Pl E14 204 C2
Churchill Pl E14 85 EB74
Churchill Pl, Har. 61 CE56
Sandridge Cl
Churchill Rd E16 86 EJ72
Churchill Rd NW2 81 CV65
Churchill Rd NW5 65 DH63
Churchill Rd (Horton Kirby), Dart. 148 FQ98
Churchill Rd, Edg. 42 CM51
Churchill Rd, Epsom 156 CN111
Churchill Rd, Grav. 131 GF88
Churchill Rd, Grays 110 GD79
Churchill Rd, Slou. 93 AZ77
Churchill Rd, S.Croy. 160 DQ109
Churchill Ter E4 47 EA49
Churchill Wk E9 66 DW64
Churchill Way, Brom. 144 EG97
Ethelbert Rd
Churchill Way, Sun. 115 BU92
Churchill Way, West. 162 EK113
Churchley Rd SE26 122 DV91
Churchmead Cl, Barn. 28 DE44
Churchmead Rd NW10 81 CU65
Churchmore Rd SW16 141 DJ95
Churchside Cl, West. 178 EJ117
Churchview Rd, Twick. 117 CD88
Churchway NW1 195 N2
Churchway NW1 83 DK69
Churchwell Path E9 66 DW64
Churchwood Gdns, Wdf.Grn. 48 EG49
Churchyard Row SE11 200 G8
Churston Av E13 86 EH67
Churston Cl SW2 121 DP88
Tulse Hill
Churston Dr, Mord. 139 CX99
Churston Gdns N11 45 DJ51
Churton Pl SW1 199 L9
Churton Pl SW1 101 DJ77
Churton St SW1 199 L9
Churton St SW1 101 DJ77
Chusan Pl E14 85 DZ72
Commercial Rd
Chuters Cl, W.Byf. 152 BL112
Chuters Gro, Epsom 157 CT112
Chyne, The, Ger.Cr. 57 AZ57
Chyngton Cl, Sid. 125 ET90
Cibber Rd SE23 123 DX89
Cicada Rd SW18 120 DC85
Cicely Rd SE15 102 DU81
Cimba Wd, Grav. 131 GL91
Cinder Path, Wok. 166 AW119
Cinderford Way, Brom. 124 EE91
Cinema Par W5 80 CM70
Ashbourne Rd
Cinnamon Cl, Croy. 141 DL101
Cinnamon Row SW11 100 DC83
Cinnamon St E1 202 E3
Cinnamon St E1 84 DV74
Cintra Pk SE19 122 DT94
Circle, The NW2 62 CS62
Circle, The NW7 42 CR50
Circle, The, Til. 111 GG81
Toronto Rd
Circle Gdns SW19 140 DA96
Circle Gdns, W.Byf. 152 BM112
High Rd
Circle Rd, Walt. 153 BS109
Circuits, The, Pnr. 60 BW56
Circular Rd N17 66 DT55
Circular Way SE18 105 EM79
Circus Ms W1 194 D6
Circus Pl EC2 197 L7
Circus Rd NW8 82 DD69
Circus St SE10 103 EC80
Cirencester St W2 82 DB71
Cirrus Cres, Grav. 131 GL92
Cissbury Ring N N12 43 CZ50
Cissbury Ring S N12 43 CZ50
Cissbury Rd N15 66 DR57
Citadel Pl SE11 200 B10
Citizen Rd N7 65 DN63
Citron Ter SE15 102 DV83
Nunhead La
City Gdn Row N1 196 G1
City Gdn Row N1 83 DP68
City Rd EC1 196 F1
City Rd EC1 83 DP68
Civic Sq, Til. 111 GG82
Civic Way, Ilf. 69 EQ56
Civic Way, Ruis. 60 BX64
Clabon Ms SW1 198 D7
Clabon Ms SW1 100 DF76
Clack La, Ruis. 59 BQ60
Clack St SE16 202 G5
Clack St SE16 102 DW75
Clacket La, West. 178 EL124
Clacton Rd E6 86 EK69
Clacton Rd E17 67 DY58
Clacton Rd N17 46 DT54
Sperling Rd
Claigmar Gdns N3 44 DB53
Claire Ct N12 44 DC48
Claire Ct, Bushey 41 CD46
Claire Ct, Pnr. 40 BZ52
Westfield Pk
Claire Gdns, Stan. 41 CJ50
Claire Pl E14 204 A6
Claire Pl E14 103 EA76
Clairvale, Horn. 72 FL59
Clairvale Rd, Houns. 96 BX81
Clairview Rd SW16 121 DH92
Clairville Ct, Reig. 184 DD134
Clairville Gdns W7 79 CF74
Clairville Pt SE23 123 DX90
Clammas Way, Uxb. 76 BJ71
Clamp Hill, Stan. 41 CD49
Clancarty Rd SW6 100 DA82
Clandon Av, Egh. 113 BC94
Clandon Cl W3 98 CP75
Avenue Rd
Clandon Cl, Epsom 157 CT107
Clandon Gdns N3 64 DA55
Clandon Rd, Ilf. 69 ES61
Clandon St SE8 103 EA82
Clanfield Way SE15 102 DS80
Diamond St
Clanricarde Gdns W2 82 DA73
Clap La, Dag. 71 FB62
Clapgate Rd, Bushey 24 CB44
Clapham Common N Side SW4 101 DH84
Clapham Common S Side SW4 121 DH85
Clapham Common W Side SW4 100 DG84
Clapham Cres SW4 101 DK84
Clapham High St SW4 101 DK84
Clapham Junct Est SW11 100 DE84
Clapham Manor St SW4 101 DJ83
Clapham Pk Est SW4 121 DK86
Clapham Pk Rd SW4 101 DK84
Clapham Rd SW9 101 DL83
Clapham Rd Est SW4 101 DK83
Claps Gate La E6 87 EP70
Clapton Common E5 66 DT59
Clapton Pk Est E5 67 DY63
Blackwell Cl
Clapton Pas E5 66 DW64
Clapton Sq E5 66 DV64
Clapton Ter N16 66 DU60
Oldhill St
Clapton Way E5 66 DU63
Clara Pl SE18 105 EN77
Clare Cl N2 64 DC55
Thomas More Way
Clare Cl, Borwd. 26 CM44
Clare Cl, W.Byf. 152 BG113
Clare Cor SE9 125 EP87
Clare Cotts, Red. 185 DP133
Clare Ct, Cat. 177 EA123
Clare Ct, Nthwd. 39 BS50
Clare Cres, Lthd. 171 CG118
Clare Gdns E7 68 EG63
Clare Gdns W11 81 CY72
Westbourne Pk Rd
Clare Gdns, Bark. 87 ET65
Clare Gdns, Egh. 113 BA92
Mowbray Cres
Clare Hill, Esher 154 CB107
Clare La N1 84 DQ66
Clare Lawn Av SW14 118 CR85
Clare Mkt WC2 196 B9
Clare Ms SW6 100 DB80
Waterford Rd
Clare Pk, Amer. 20 AS40
Clare Pl SW15 119 CT87
Minstead Gdns
Clare Rd E11 67 ED58
Clare Rd NW10 81 CU66
Clare Rd SE14 103 DZ81
Clare Rd, Grnf. 79 CD65
Clare Rd, Houns. 96 BZ83
Clare Rd, Stai. 114 BL87
Clare St E2 84 DV68
Clare Way, Bexh. 106 EY81
Clare Way, Sev. 191 FJ127
Clare Wd, Lthd. 171 CH118
Claredale, Wok. 166 AY119
Claremont Av
Claredale St E2 84 DU68
Claremont, St.Alb. 8 CA31
Claremont (Cheshunt), Wal.Cr. 14 DT29
Claremont Av, Esher 154 BZ107
Claremont Av, Har. 62 CL57
Claremont Av, N.Mal. 139 CU99
Claremont Av, Sun. 135 BV95
Claremont Av, Walt. 154 BX105
Claremont Av, Wok. 166 AY119
Claremont Cl E16 87 EN74
Claremont Cl N1 196 E1
Claremont Cl N1 83 DN68
Claremont Cl SW2 121 DL88
Streatham Hill
Claremont Cl, Grays 110 GC76
Premier Av
Claremont Cl, Orp. 163 EN105
Claremont Cl, S.Croy. 176 DV115
Claremont Cl, Walt. 154 BW106
Claremont Ct, Surb. 137 CK100
St. James Rd
Claremont Cres, Dart. 107 FE84
Claremont Cres, Rick. 23 BQ43
Claremont Dr, Esher 154 CB108
Claremont Dr, Shep. 135 BP100
Claremont Dr, Wok. 166 AY119
Claremont End, Esher 154 CB107
Claremont Gdns, Ilf. 69 ES61
Claremont Gdns, Surb. 138 CL99
Claremont Gdns, Upmin. 73 FR60
Claremont Gro W4 98 CS80
Edensor Gdns
Claremont Gro, Wdf.Grn. 48 EJ51
Claremont La, Esher 154 CB105
Claremont Pk N3 43 CY53
Claremont Pk Rd, Esher 154 CB107
Claremont Pl, Grav. 131 GH87
Cutmore St
Claremont Rd E7 68 EH64
Claremont Rd E17 47 DY54
Claremont Rd N6 65 DJ59
Claremont Rd NW2 63 CX62
Claremont Rd W9 81 CY68
Claremont Rd W13 79 CG71
Claremont Rd, Barn. 28 DD37
Claremont Rd, Brom. 144 EL98
Claremont Rd, Croy. 142 DU102
Claremont Rd, Esher 155 CE108
Claremont Rd, Har. 41 CE54
Claremont Rd, Horn. 71 FG58
Claremont Rd, Red. 184 DG131
Claremont Rd, Stai. 113 BD92
Claremont Rd, Surb. 138 CL100
Claremont Rd, Swan. 127 FE94
Claremont Rd, Tedd. 117 CF92
Claremont Rd, Twick. 117 CJ86
Claremont Rd, W.Byf. 152 BG112
Claremont Sq N1 196 D1
Claremont Sq N1 83 DN68
Claremont St E16 87 EN74
Claremont St N18 46 DU51
Claremont St SE10 103 EB79
Claremont Way NW2 63 CW60
Claremount Cl, Epsom 173 CW117
Claremount Gdns, Epsom 173 CW117
Clarence Av SW4 121 DK86
Clarence Av, Brom. 144 EL98
Clarence Av, Ilf. 69 EN58
Clarence Av, N.Mal. 138 CQ96
Clarence Av, Upmin. 72 FN61
Clarence Cl, Bushey 41 CF45
Clarence Cl, Walt. 154 BW105
Clarence Ct, Egh. 113 AZ93
Clarence St
Clarence Cres SW4 121 DK86
Clarence Cres, Sid. 126 EV90
Clarence Dr, Egh. 112 AW91
Clarence Gdns NW1 195 J3
Clarence Gdns NW1 83 DH69
Clarence Gate Gdns NW1 82 DF70
Glentworth St
Clarence La SW15 118 CS86
Clarence Ms E5 66 DV64
Clarence Ms SE16 203 H3
Clarence Ms SE16 85 DX74
Clarence Ms SW12 121 DH87
Clarence Pas NW1 195 P1
Clarence Pl E5 66 DV64
Clarence Pl, Grav. 131 GH87
Clarence Rd E5 66 DV63
Clarence Rd E12 68 EK64
Clarence Rd E16 86 EE70
Clarence Rd E17 47 DX54
Clarence Rd N15 66 DQ57
Clarence Rd N22 45 DL52
Clarence Rd NW6 81 CZ66
Clarence Rd SE9 124 EL89
Clarence Rd SW19 120 DB93
Clarence Rd W4 98 CN78
Clarence Rd, Bexh. 106 EY84
Clarence Rd, Brwd. 54 FV44
Clarence Rd, Brom. 144 EK97
Clarence Rd, Croy. 142 DR101
Clarence Rd, Enf. 30 DV43
Clarence Rd, Grays 110 GA79
Clarence Rd, Rich. 98 CM81
Clarence Rd, Sid. 126 EV90
Clarence Rd, Sutt. 158 DB105
Clarence Rd, Tedd. 117 CF93
Clarence Rd, Wall. 159 DH106
Clarence Rd, Walt. 153 BV105
Clarence Rd, West. 179 EM118
Clarence Row, Grav. 131 GH87
Clarence St, Egh. 113 AZ93
Clarence St, Kings.T. 138 CL96
Clarence St, Rich. 98 CL84
Clarence St, Sthl. 96 BX76
Clarence St, Stai. 113 BE91
Clarence Ter NW1 194 E4
Clarence Ter, Houns. 96 CB84
Clarence Wk SW4 101 DL82
Clarence Way NW1 83 DH66
Clarence Way Est NW1 83 DH66
Clarenden Pl, Dart. 127 FD92
Clarendon Cl E9 84 DW66
Clarendon Cl W2 194 B10
Clarendon Cl, Orp. 146 EU97
Clarendon Ct, Slou. 74 AV73
Clarendon Cres, Twick. 117 CD90
Clarendon Cross W11 81 CY73
Portland Rd
Clarendon Dr SW15 99 CW84
Clarendon Gdns NW4 63 CV55
Clarendon Gdns W9 82 DC70
Clarendon Gdns, Dart. 129 FR87
Clarendon Gdns, Ilf. 69 EM60
Clarendon Gdns, Wem. 61 CK62
Clarendon Gate, Cher. 151 BD107
Clarendon Grn, Orp. 146 EU98
Clarendon Gro NW1 195 M2
Clarendon Gro, Mitch. 140 DF97
Clarendon Gro, Orp. 146 EU97
Clarendon Ms W2 194 B9
Clarendon Ms, Bex. 127 FB88
Clarendon Ms, Borwd. 26 CN41
Clarendon Rd
Clarendon Path, Orp. 146 EU97
Clarendon Pl W2 194 B10
Clarendon Pl W2 82 DE73
Clarendon Pl, Sev. 190 FG125
Clarendon Rd
Clarendon Ri SE13 103 EC83
Clarendon Rd E11 67 ED60
Clarendon Rd E17 67 EB58
Clarendon Rd E18 68 EG55
Clarendon Rd N8 65 DM55
Clarendon Rd N15 65 DP56
Clarendon Rd N18 46 DU51
Clarendon Rd N22 45 DM54
Clarendon Rd SW19 120 DE94
Clarendon Rd W5 80 CL70
Clarendon Rd W11 81 CY73
Clarendon Rd, Ashf. 114 BM91
Clarendon Rd, Borwd. 26 CN41
Clarendon Rd, Croy. 141 DP103
Clarendon Rd, Grav. 131 GJ86
Clarendon Rd, Har. 61 CE58
Clarendon Rd, Hayes 95 BT75
Clarendon Rd, Red. 184 DF133
Clarendon Rd, Sev. 190 FG124
Clarendon Rd, Wall. 159 DJ107
Clarendon Rd (Cheshunt), Wal.Cr. 15 DX29
Clarendon Rd, Wat. 23 BV40
Clarendon St SW1 101 DH78
Clarendon Ter W9 82 DC70
Lanark Pl
Clarendon Wk W11 81 CY72
Clarendon Way N21 30 DQ44
Clarendon Way, Chis. 145 ET97
Clarendon Way, Orp. 145 ET97
Clarens St SE6 123 DZ89
Claret Gdns SE25 142 DS98
Clareville Gro SW7 100 DC77
Clareville Rd, Cat. 176 DU124
Clareville Rd, Orp. 145 EQ103
Clareville St SW7 100 DC77
Clarewood Wk SW9 101 DN84
Somerleyton Rd
Clarges Ms W1 199 H2
Clarges Ms W1 83 DH74
Clarges St W1 199 J2
Clarges St W1 83 DH74
Claribel Rd SW9 101 DP82
Clarice Way, Wall. 159 DL109
Claridge Rd, Dag. 70 EX60
Clarina Rd SE20 123 DX94
Evelina Rd
Clarissa Rd, Rom. 70 EX59
Clarissa St E8 84 DT67
Clark Cl, Erith 107 FG81
Forest Rd
Clark St E1 84 DV71
Clark Way, Houns. 96 BX80
Clarke Grn, Wat. 23 BU35
Clarke Path N16 66 DU60
Braydon Rd
Clarke Way, Wat. 23 BU35
Clarkebourne Dr, Grays 110 GD79
Clarkes Av, Wor.Pk. 139 CX102
Clarkes Dr, Uxb. 76 BL71
Clarke's Ms W1 194 G6
Clarkfield, Rick. 38 BH46
Clarks La, Epp. 17 ET31
Clarks La, Sev. 164 EZ112
Clarks La, Warl. 178 EF123
Clarks La, West. 178 EK123
Clarks Mead, Bushey 40 CC45
Clarks Pl EC2 197 M8
Clarks Rd, Ilf. 69 ER61
Clarkson Rd E16 86 EF72
Clarkson Row NW1 83 DH68
Clarkson St E2 84 DV69
Clarksons, The, Bark. 87 EQ68
Classon Cl, West Dr. 94 BL75
Claston Cl, Dart. 107 FE84
Iron Mill La
Claude Rd E10 67 EC61
Claude Rd E13 86 EH
Claude Rd SE15 102 DV
Claude St E14 203
Claude St E14 103 EA
Claudia Jones Way SW2 121 DL
Claudia Pl SW19 119 CY
Claudian Way, Grays 111 GH
Claughton Rd E13 86 EJ
Claughton Way, Brwd. 55 GD
Clauson Av, Nthlt. 60 CB
Clave St E1 202
Clavell St SE10 103 EC
Claverdale Rd SW2 121 DM
Claverhambury Rd, Wal.Abb. 16 EF
Clavering Av SW13 99 CV
Clavering Cl, Twick. 117 CG
Clavering Rd E12 68 EK
Clavering Way, Brwd. 55 GC
Poplar Dr
Claverings Ind Est N9 47 DX
Claverley Gro N3 44 DA
Claverley Vil N3 44 DB
Claverley Gro
Claverton Cl, Hem.H. 5 BA2
Claverton St SW1 101 DJ7
Claxton Gro W6 99 CX7
Clay Av, Mitch. 141 DH
Clay Hill, Enf. 30 DR
Clay La, Bushey 41 CE
Clay La, Edg. 42 CN
Clay La, Epsom 172 CP12
Clay La, Stai. 114 BM
Clay Rd, The, Loug. 32 EL
Clay St W1 194
Clay Tye Rd, Upmin. 73 FW6
Claybank Gro SE13 103 EB
Algernon Rd
Claybourne Ms SE19 122 DS
Church Rd
Claybridge Rd SE12 124 EJ9
Claybrook Cl N2 64 DD5
Claybrook Rd W6 99 CX7
Clayburn Gdns, S.Ock. 91 FV7
Claybury, Bushey 40 CB4
Claybury Bdy, Ilf. 68 EL5
Claybury Rd, Wdf.Grn. 48 EL5
Claydon Dr, Croy. 159 DL10
Claydon End (Chalfont St. Peter), Ger.Cr. 56 AY5
Claydon La (Chalfont St. Peter), Ger.Cr. 56 AY5
Claydon Rd, Wok. 166 AU11
Claydown Ms SE18 105 EN7
Woolwich New Rd
Clayfarm Rd SE9 125 EQ8
Claygate Cl, Horn. 71 FG6
Claygate Cres, Croy. 161 EC10
Claygate La, Esher 137 CG10
Claygate La, T.Ditt. 137 CG10
Claygate La, Wal.Abb. 15 ED3
Claygate Lo Cl, Esher 155 CE10
Claygate Rd W13 97 CH7
Clayhall Av, Ilf. 68 EL5
Clayhall La, Wind. 112 AT8
Clayhill, Surb. 138 CN9
Clayhill Cres SE9 124 EK9
Claylands Pl SW8 101 DN8
Claylands Rd SW8 101 DM7
Claymill Ho SE18 105 EQ7
Claymore Cl, Mord. 140 DA10
Claymore Ct E17 47 DX5
Billet Rd
Claypit Hill, Wal.Abb. 32 EJ3
Claypole Dr, Houns. 96 BY8
Claypole Rd E15 85 EC6
Clayponds Av, Brent. 98 CL7
Clayponds Gdns W5 97 CK7
Clayponds La, Brent. 98 CL7
Clays La E15 67 EB6
Clay's La, Loug. 33 EN3
Clays La Cl E15 67 EB6
Clayside, Chig. 49 EQ5
Clayton Av, Upmin. 72 FP6
Clayton Av, Wem. 80 CL6
Clayton Cl E6 87 EM7
Brandreth Rd
Clayton Cres, Brent. 97 CK7
Clayton Cft Rd, Dart. 127 FG8
Clayton Fld NW9 42 CS5
Clayton Mead, Gdse. 186 DV13
Clayton Ms SE10 103 ED8
Clayton Rd SE15 102 DU8
Clayton Rd, Chess. 155 CJ10
Clayton Rd, Epsom 156 CS11
Clayton Rd, Hayes 95 BS7
Clayton Rd, Islw. 97 CE8
Clayton Rd, Rom. 71 FC6
Clayton St SE11 101 DN7
Clayton Ter, Hayes 78 BX7
Jollys La
Clayton Wk, Amer. 20 AW3
Clayton Way, Uxb. 76 BK7
Claywood Cl, Orp. 145 ES10
Claywood La, Dart. 129 FX9
Clayworth Cl, Sid. 126 EV8
Cleall Av, Wal.Abb. 15 EC3
Quaker La
Cleanthus Cl SE18 105 EP8
Cleanthus Rd
Cleanthus Rd SE18 105 EP8
Clearbrook Way E1 85 DX7
West Arbour St
Cleardown, Wok. 167 BB11
Clearmount (Chobham), Wok. 150 AS10
Clears, The, Reig. 183 CY13
Clearwater Ter W11 99 CX7
Lorne Gdns
Clearwell Dr W9 82 DB7
Cleave Av, Hayes 95 BS7
Cleave Av, Orp. 163 ES10
Cleave Prior, Couls. 174 DE11
Cleaveland Rd, Surb. 137 CK9
Cleaver Sq SE11 200 E1
Cleaver Sq SE11 101 DN78
Cleaver St SE11 200 E1
Cleaver St SE11 101 DN78
Cleaverholme Cl SE25 142 DV100
Cleeve Ct, Felt. 115 BS88
Kilross Rd
Cleeve Hill SE23 122 DV88

eve Pk Gdns, Sid. 126 EV89
eve Rd, Lthd. 171 CF120
eve Way SW15 119 CT87
Danebury Av
gg St E1 202 E2
gg St E13 86 EG68
land Path, Loug. 33 EP39
land Rd (Chalfont St. Peter), Ger.Cr. 36 AX54
m Attlee Ct SW6 99 CZ79
m Attlee Est SW6 99 CZ79
Lillie Rd
m Attlee Par SW6 99 CZ79
Clem Attlee Ct
matis Cl, Rom. 52 FJ52
matis Gdns, Wdf.Grn. 48 EG50
matis St W12 81 CT73
mence Rd, Dag. 89 FC67
mence St E14 85 DZ71
ment Av SW4 101 DK84
ment Cl NW6 81 CW66
ment Cl W4 98 CR77
Acton La
ment Cl, Pur. 175 DP116
Croftleigh Av
ment Gdns, Hayes 95 BS77
ment Rd SW19 119 CY92
ment Rd, Beck. 143 DX96
ment Rd (Cheshunt), Wal.Cr. 15 DY27
ment St, Swan. 128 FK93
ment Way, Upmin. 72 FM62
menthorpe Rd, Dag. 88 EW65
mentina Rd E10 67 DZ60
mentine Cl W13 97 CH75
Balfour Rd
ments Av E16 86 EG73
ments Cl, Slou. 92 AV75
ments Ct, Houns. 96 BX84
ments Ct, Ilf. 69 EP62
Clements La
ment's Inn WC2 196 C9
ment's Inn WC2 83 DM72
ment's Inn Pas WC2 196 C9
ments La EC4 197 L10
ments La EC4 84 DR73
ments La, Ilf. 69 EP62
ments Mead, Lthd. 171 CG119
ments Pl, Brent. 97 CK78
ments Rd E6 87 EM66
ments Rd SE16 202 C7
ments Rd SE16 102 DU76
ments Rd, Ilf. 69 EP62
ments Rd, Rick. 21 BD43
ments Rd, Walt. 135 BV103
nches Fm La, Sev. 190 FG126
nches Fm Rd, Sev. 190 FG126
ndon Way SE18 105 ER77
Polthorne Gro
nnam St SE1 201 J4
nsham La, Sutt. 140 DA103
nston Ms W1 194 D8
phane Rd N1 84 DR65
re St EC2 197 L4
erics Wk, Shep. 135 BR100
Gordon Rd
rkenwell Cl EC1 196 E4
rkenwell Cl EC1 83 DN70
rkenwell Grn EC1 196 E5
rkenwell Grn EC1 83 DP70
rkenwell Rd EC1 196 D5
rkenwell Rd EC1 83 DN70
erks Cft, Red. 186 DR133
erks Piece, Loug. 33 EM41
ermont Rd E9 84 DW67
eve Rd NW6 82 DA66
eve Rd, Sid. 126 EX90
evedon, Wey. 153 BQ106
evedon Cl N16 66 DT62
Smalley Cl
evedon Gdns, Hayes 95 BR76
evedon Gdns, Houns. 95 BV81
evedon Rd SE20 143 DX95
evedon Rd, Kings.T. 138 CN96
evedon Rd, Twick. 117 CK86
evehurst Cl, Slou. 74 AT65
eveland Av SW20 139 CZ96
eveland Av W4 99 CT77
eveland Av, Hmptn. 116 BZ94
eveland Cl, Walt. 135 BV104
eveland Cres, Borwd. 26 CQ43
eveland Dr, Stai. 134 BH96
eveland Gdns N4 66 DQ57
eveland Gdns NW2 63 CX61
eveland Gdns SW13 99 CT82
eveland Gdns W2 82 DC72
eveland Gdns, Wor.Pk. 138 CS103
eveland Gro E1 84 DW70
Cleveland Way
eveland Ms W1 195 K6
eveland Pk, Stai. 114 BL86
Northumberland Cl
eveland Pk Av E17 67 EA56
eveland Pk Cres E17 67 EA56
eveland Pl SW1 199 L2
eveland Ri, Mord. 139 CX101
eveland Rd E18 68 EG55
eveland Rd N1 84 DR66
eveland Rd N9 46 DV45
eveland Rd SW13 99 CT82
eveland Rd W4 98 CQ76
Antrobus Rd
eveland Rd W13 79 CH71
eveland Rd, Ilf. 69 EP62
eveland Rd, Islw. 97 CG84
eveland Rd, N.Mal. 138 CS98
eveland Rd, Uxb. 76 BK68
eveland Rd, Well. 105 ET82
eveland Rd, Wor.Pk. 138 CS103
eveland Row SW1 199 K3
eveland Row SW1 83 DJ74
eveland Sq W2 82 DC72
eveland St W1 195 K5
eveland St W1 83 DH70
eveland Ter W2 82 DC72
eveland Way E1 84 DW70
eveley Cl SE7 104 EK77
eveley Cres W5 80 CL68
eveleys Rd E5 66 DV62
everly Est W12 81 CU74
eves Av, Brwd. 54 FV46
eves Av, Epsom 157 CV109
Cleves Cl, Cob. 153 BV114
Cleves Cl, Loug. 32 EL44
Cleves Cres, Croy. 161 EC111
Cleves Rd E6 86 EK67
Cleves Rd, Rich. 117 CJ90
Cleves Wk, Ilf. 49 EQ52
Cleves Way, Hmptn. 116 BZ94
Cleves Way, Ruis. 60 BX60
Cleves Way, Sun. 115 BT93
Cleves Wd, Wey. 153 BS105
Clewer Cres, Har. 41 CD53
Clewer Ho SE2 106 EX75
Wolvercote Rd
Clichy Est E1 84 DW71
Clifden Rd E5 66 DW64
Clifden Rd, Brent. 97 CK79
Clifden Rd, Twick. 117 CF88
Cliff End, Pur. 159 DP112
Cliff Pl, S.Ock. 91 FX69
Cliff Reach (Bluewater), Green. 129 FS87
Cliff Rd NW1 83 DK65
Cliff Ter SE8 103 EA82
Cliff Vil NW1 83 DK65
Cliff Wk E16 86 EF71
Cliffe Rd, S.Croy. 160 DR106
Cliffe Wk, Sutt. 158 DC106
Turnpike La
Clifford Av SW14 98 CP83
Clifford Av, Chis. 125 EM93
Clifford Av, Ilf. 49 EP53
Clifford Av, Wall. 159 DJ105
Clifford Cl, Nthlt. 78 BY67
Clifford Dr SW9 101 DP84
Clifford Gdns NW10 81 CW68
Clifford Gro, Ashf. 114 BN91
Clifford Rd E16 86 EF70
Clifford Rd E17 47 EC54
Clifford Rd N9 30 DW44
Clifford Rd SE25 142 DU98
Clifford Rd, Barn. 28 DB41
Clifford Rd, Grays 110 FZ75
Clifford Rd, Houns. 96 BX83
Clifford Rd, Rich. 117 CK89
Clifford Rd, Wem. 79 CK67
Clifford St W1 199 K1
Clifford St W1 83 DJ73
Clifford Way NW10 63 CT63
Clifford's Inn Pas EC4 196 D9
Cliffview Rd SE13 103 EA83
Clifton Av E17 67 DX55
Clifton Av N3 43 CZ53
Clifton Av W12 81 CT74
Clifton Av, Felt. 116 BW90
Clifton Av, Stan. 41 CH54
Clifton Av, Sutt. 158 DB111
Clifton Av, Wem. 80 CM65
Clifton Cl, Add. 134 BH103
Clifton Cl, Cat. 176 DR123
Clifton Cl, Orp. 163 EQ106
Clifton Cl (Cheshunt), Wal.Cr. 15 DY29
Clifton Ct N4 65 DN61
Playford Rd
Clifton Ct NW8 82 DD70
Edgware Rd
Clifton Cres SE15 102 DV80
Clifton Est SE15 102 DV81
Consort Rd
Clifton Gdns N15 66 DT58
Clifton Gdns NW11 63 CZ58
Clifton Gdns W4 98 CR77
Dolman Rd
Clifton Gdns W9 82 DC70
Clifton Gdns, Enf. 29 DL42
Clifton Gdns, Uxb. 77 BP68
Clifton Gro E8 84 DU65
Clifton Gro, Grav. 131 GH87
Clifton Hill NW8 82 DB68
Clifton Marine Par, Grav. 131 GF86
Clifton Pk Av SW20 139 CW96
Clifton Pl SE16 202 G4
Clifton Pl W2 194 A10
Clifton Pl W2 82 DD73
Clifton Pl, Bans. 174 DA116
Court Rd
Clifton Ri SE14 103 DY80
Clifton Rd E7 86 EK65
Clifton Rd E16 86 EE71
Clifton Rd N3 44 DC53
Clifton Rd N8 65 DK58
Clifton Rd N22 45 DJ53
Clifton Rd NW10 81 CU68
Clifton Rd SE25 142 DS98
Clifton Rd SW19 119 CX93
Clifton Rd W9 82 DC70
Clifton Rd, Couls. 175 DH115
Clifton Rd, Grav. 131 GG86
Clifton Rd, Grnf. 78 CC70
Clifton Rd, Har. 62 CM57
Clifton Rd, Horn. 71 FG58
Clifton Rd, Houns. 95 BP83
Inner Ring E
Clifton Rd, Ilf. 69 ER58
Clifton Rd, Islw. 97 CE82
Clifton Rd, Kings.T. 118 CM94
Clifton Rd, Loug. 32 EL42
Clifton Rd, Sid. 125 ES91
Clifton Rd, Slou. 92 AV75
Clifton Rd, Sthl. 96 BY77
Clifton Rd, Tedd. 117 CE91
Clifton Rd, Wall. 159 DH106
Clifton Rd, Wat. 23 BV43
Clifton Rd, Well. 106 EW83
Clifton St EC2 197 M5
Clifton St EC2 84 DS70
Clifton Ter N4 65 DN61
Clifton Vil W9 82 DB71
Clifton Wk E6 86 EL72
Clifton Wk W6 99 CV77
King St
Clifton Wk, Dart. 128 FP86
Osbourne Rd
Clifton Way SE15 102 DW80
Clifton Way, Borwd. 26 CN39
Clifton Way, Brwd. 55 GD46
Clifton Way, Wem. 80 CL67
Clifton Way, Wok. 166 AT117
Cliftons La, Reig. 183 CX131
Climb, The, Rick. 22 BH44
Clinch Ct E16 86 EG71
Cline Rd N11 45 DJ51
Clinger Ct N1 84 DS67
Pitfield St
Clink St SE1 201 J2
Clink St SE1 84 DR74
Clinton Av, E.Mol. 136 CC98
Clinton Av, Well. 105 ET84
Clinton Cres, Ilf. 49 ES51
Clinton Rd E3 85 DY69
Clinton Rd E7 68 EG63
Clinton Rd N15 66 DR56
Clinton Rd, Lthd. 171 CJ123
Clinton Ter, Sutt. 158 DC105
Manor La
Clipper Boul, Dart. 109 FS83
Clipper Boul W, Dart. 109 FR83
Clipper Cl SE16 203 H4
Clipper Cres, Grav. 131 GM91
Clipper Way SE13 103 EC84
Clippesby Cl, Chess. 156 CM108
Clipstone Ms W1 195 K5
Clipstone Ms W1 83 DJ70
Clipstone Rd, Houns. 96 CA83
Clipstone St W1 195 J6
Clipstone St W1 83 DJ71
Clissold Cl N2 64 DF55
Clissold Ct N4 66 DQ61
Clissold Cres N16 66 DR62
Clissold Rd N16 66 DR62
Clitheroe Av, Har. 60 CA60
Clitheroe Gdns, Wat. 40 BX48
Clitheroe Rd SW9 101 DL82
Clitheroe Rd, Rom. 51 FC50
Clitherow Av W7 97 CG76
Clitherow Pas, Brent. 97 CJ78
Clitherow Rd, Brent. 97 CJ78
Clitterhouse Cres NW2 63 CW60
Clitterhouse Rd NW2 63 CW60
Clive Av N18 46 DU51
Claremont St
Clive Av, Dart. 127 FF86
Clive Cl, Pot.B. 11 CZ31
Clive Ct W9 82 DC70
Maida Vale
Clive Par, Nthwd. 39 BS52
Maxwell Rd
Clive Pas SE21 122 DR90
Clive Rd
Clive Rd SE21 122 DR90
Clive Rd SW19 120 DE93
Clive Rd, Belv. 106 FA77
Clive Rd, Brwd. 53 FW52
Clive Rd, Enf. 30 DU42
Clive Rd, Esher 154 CB105
Clive Rd, Felt. 115 BU86
Clive Rd, Grav. 131 GH86
Clive Rd, Rom. 71 FH57
Clive Rd, Twick. 117 CF91
Clive Way, Enf. 30 DU42
Clive Way, Wat. 24 BW39
Cliveden Cl N12 44 DC49
Woodside Av
Cliveden Cl, Brwd. 55 FZ45
Cliveden Pl SW1 198 F8
Cliveden Pl SW1 100 DG77
Cliveden Pl, Shep. 135 BP100
Cliveden Rd SW19 139 CZ95
Clivedon Ct W13 79 CH71
Clivedon Rd E4 48 EE50
Clivesdale Dr, Hayes 77 BV74
Cloak La EC4 197 J10
Cloak La EC4 84 DQ73
Clock Ho Cl, W.Byf. 152 BM112
Clock Ho La, Sev. 190 FG123
Clock Ho Mead, Lthd. 154 CB114
Clock Ho Rd, Beck. 143 DY97
Clock Twr Ms N1 84 DQ67
Arlington Av
Clock Twr Ms SE28 88 EV73
Clock Twr Pl N7 83 DL65
Clock Twr Rd, Islw. 97 CF83
Clockhouse Av, Bark. 87 EQ67
Clockhouse Cl SW19 119 CW90
Clockhouse La, Ashf. 114 BN91
Clockhouse La, Felt. 115 BP89
Clockhouse La, Grays 91 FX74
Clockhouse La, Rom. 51 FB52
Clockhouse La E, Egh. 113 BB94
Clockhouse La W, Egh. 113 BA94
Clockhouse Ms, Rick. 21 BD41
Chorleywood Ho Dr
Clockhouse Pl SW15 119 CY85
Clockhouse Pl, Felt. 115 BQ88
Clockhouse Roundabout, Felt. 115 BP88
Cloister Cl, Rain. 89 FH70
Cloister Cl, Tedd. 117 CH92
Cloister Gdns SE25 142 DV100
Cloister Gdns, Edg. 42 CQ50
Cloister Rd NW2 63 CZ62
Cloister Rd W3 80 CQ71
Cloisters, The, Bushey 24 CB44
Cloisters, The, Rick. 38 BL45
Cloisters, The, Wok. 167 BB121
Cloisters Av, Brom. 145 EM99
Cloisters Mall, Kings.T. 137 CK96
Union St
Clonard Way, Pnr. 40 CA51
Clonbrock Rd N16 66 DS63
Cloncurry St SW6 99 CX82
Clonmel Cl, Har. 61 CD60
Clonmel Rd SW6 99 CZ80
Clonmel Rd, Tedd. 117 CD91
Clonmell Rd N17 66 DR55
Clonmore St SW18 119 CZ88
Cloonmore Av, Orp. 163 ET105
Clorane Gdns NW3 64 DA62
Close, The E4 47 EC52
Beech Hall Rd
Close, The N14 45 DK47
Close, The N20 43 CZ47
Close, The SE3 103 ED82
Heath La
Close, The, Barn. 28 DF44
Close, The, Beck. 143 DY98
Close, The, Bex. 126 FA86
Close, The, Brwd. 54 FW48
Close, The, Bushey 24 CB43
Close, The, Cars. 158 DE109
Close, The, Dart. 128 FJ90
Close, The, Grays 110 GC75
Close, The, Har. 40 CC54
Close, The, Hat. 11 CY26
Close, The, Islw. 97 CD82
Close, The, Iver 75 BC69
Close, The, Mitch. 140 DF98
Close, The, N.Mal. 138 CQ96
Close, The, Orp. 145 ES100
Close, The (Eastcote), Pnr. 60 BW59
Close, The (Rayners La), Pnr. 60 BZ59
Close, The, Pot.B. 12 DA32
Close, The (Pampisford Rd), Pur. 159 DP110
Close, The (Russell Hill), Pur. 159 DM110
Close, The, Rad. 9 CF33
Close, The, Rich. 98 CP83
Close, The, Rick. 38 BJ46
Close, The, Rom. 70 EY58
Close, The, Sev. 190 FE124
Close, The, Sid. 126 EV92
Close, The, Sutt. 139 CZ101
Close, The, Uxb. 76 BL66
Close, The (Hillingdon), Uxb. 76 BN67
Close, The, Vir.W. 132 AW99
Close, The (Barnhill Rd), Wem. 62 CQ62
Close, The (Lyon Pk Av), Wem. 80 CL65
Close, The, W.Byf. 152 BG113
Closemead Cl, Nthwd. 39 BQ51
Cloth Ct EC1 196 G7
Cloth Fair EC1 196 G7
Cloth Fair EC1 83 DP71
Cloth St EC1 197 H6
Clothier St E1 197 N8
Clothworkers Rd SE18 105 ER80
Cloudberry Rd, Rom. 52 FK51
Cloudesdale Rd SW17 121 DH89
Cloudesley Pl N1 83 DN67
Cloudesley Rd N1 83 DN67
Cloudesley Rd, Bexh. 106 EZ81
Cloudesley Rd, Erith 107 FF81
Cloudesley Sq N1 83 DN67
Cloudesley St N1 83 DN67
Clouston Cl, Wall. 159 DL106
Clova Rd E7 86 EF65
Clove Cres E14 85 ED73
Clove Hitch Quay SW11 100 DC83
Clove St E13 86 EG70
Barking Rd
Clovelly Av NW9 63 CT56
Clovelly Av, Uxb. 59 BQ63
Clovelly Av, Warl. 176 DV118
Clovelly Cl, Pnr. 59 BV55
Clovelly Cl, Uxb. 59 BQ63
Clovelly Ct, Horn. 72 FN61
Clovelly Gdns SE19 142 DT95
Clovelly Gdns, Enf. 46 DS45
Clovelly Gdns, Rom. 51 FB53
Clovelly Rd N8 65 DK56
Clovelly Rd W4 98 CQ75
Clovelly Rd W5 97 CJ75
Clovelly Rd, Bexh. 106 EY79
Clovelly Rd, Houns. 96 CA82
Clovelly Way E1 84 DW72
Jamaica St
Clovelly Way, Har. 60 BZ61
Clovelly Way, Orp. 145 ET100
Clover Cl E11 67 ED61
Norman Rd
Clover Ct, Grays 110 GD79
Churchill Rd
Clover Ct, Wok. 166 AX118
Clover Hill, Couls. 175 DH121
Clover Leas, Epp. 17 ET30
Clover Ms SW3 100 DF79
Dilke St
Clover Way, Wall. 140 DG102
Cloverdale Gdns, Sid. 125 ET86
Cloverleys, Loug. 32 EK43
Clovers, The, Grav. 130 GE91
Clowders Rd SE6 123 DZ90
Clowser Cl, Sutt. 158 DC106
Turnpike La
Cloyster Wd, Edg. 41 CK52
Cloysters Grn E1 202 B2
Cloysters Grn E1 84 DU74
Club Gdns Rd, Brom. 144 EG101
Club Row E1 197 P4
Club Row E1 84 DT70
Club Row E2 197 P4
Club Row E2 84 DT70
Clump, The, Rick. 22 BG43
Clump Av, Tad. 182 CQ131
Clumps, The, Ashf. 115 BR91
Clunas Gdns, Rom. 72 FK55
Clunbury Av, Sthl. 96 BZ78
Clunbury St N1 197 L1
Cluny Est SE1 201 M6
Cluny Ms SW5 100 DA77
Cluny Pl SE1 201 M6
Cluse Ct N1 84 DQ68
Dame St
Clutterbucks, Rick. 22 BG36
Clutton St E14 85 EB71
Clydach Rd, Enf. 30 DT42
Clyde Av, S.Croy. 176 DV115
Clyde Circ N15 66 DS56
Clyde Cl, Red. 184 DG133
Clyde Ct, Red. 184 DG133
Clyde Cl
Clyde Cres, Upmin. 73 FS58
Clyde Pl E10 67 EB59
Clyde Rd N15 66 DS56
Clyde Rd N22 45 DK53
Clyde Rd, Croy. 142 DT102
Clyde Rd, Stai. 114 BK88
Clyde Rd, Sutt. 158 DA106
Clyde Rd, Wall. 159 DJ106
Clyde St SE8 103 DZ79
Clyde Ter SE23 122 DW89
Clyde Vale SE23 122 DW89
Clyde Way, Rom. 51 FE53
Clydesdale, Enf. 31 DX42
Clydesdale Av, Stan. 61 CK55
Clydesdale Cl, Borwd. 26 CR43
Clydesdale Cl, Islw. 97 CF83
Clydesdale Gdns, Rich. 98 CP84
Clydesdale Ho, Erith 106 EY75
Kale Rd
Clydesdale Rd W11 81 CZ72
Clydesdale Rd, Horn. 71 FF59
Clydesdale Wk, Brox. 15 DZ25
Tarpan Way
Clydon Cl, Erith 107 FE79
Clyfford Rd, Ruis. 59 BT63
Clymping Dene, Felt. 115 BV87
Clyston Rd, Wat. 23 BT44
Clyston St SW8 101 DJ82
Clyve Way, Stai. 133 BE95
Coach & Horses Yd W1 195 J10
Coach Ho La N5 65 DP63
Highbury Hill
Coach Ho La SW19 119 CX91
Coach Ho Ms SE23 123 DX86
Coach Ho Yd SW18 100 DB84
Ebner St
Coach Rd, Bet. 182 CL134
Coach Rd, Cher. 151 BC107
Coach Yd Ms N19 65 DL60
Trinder Rd
Coachhouse Ms SE20 122 DV94
Coal Rd, Grays 111 GL77
Coal Wf Rd W12 99 CX75
Shepherds Bush Pl
Coaldale Wk SE21 122 DQ87
Lairdale Cl
Coalecroft Rd SW15 99 CW84
Coate St E2 84 DU68
Coates Av SW18 120 DD86
Coates Dell, Wat. 8 BY33
Coates Hill Rd, Brom. 145 EN96
Coates Rd, Borwd. 41 CK45
Coates Wk, Brent. 98 CL78
Coates Way, Wat. 8 BX33
Cobb Cl, Borwd. 26 CQ43
Cobb Cl, Slou. 92 AX81
Cobb Grn, Wat. 7 BV32
Cobb St E1 197 P7
Cobb St E1 84 DT71
Cobbett Cl, Enf. 30 DW36
Cobbett Rd SE9 104 EL83
Cobbett Rd, Twick. 116 CA88
Cobbett St SW8 101 DM80
Cobbetts Av, Ilf. 68 EK57
Cobbetts Cl, Wok. 166 AV117
Cobbetts Hill, Wey. 153 BP107
Cobbins, The, Wal.Abb. 16 EE33
Cobbinsend Rd, Wal.Abb. 16 EK29
Cobblers Wk, E.Mol. 137 CG95
Cobblers Wk, Hmptn. 116 CC94
Cobblers Wk, Kings.T. 137 CG95
Cobblers Wk, Tedd. 117 CD94
Cobbles, The, Brwd. 54 FY47
Cobbles, The, Upmin. 73 FT59
Cobblestone Pl, Croy. 142 DQ102
Oakfield Rd
Cobbold Est NW10 81 CT65
Cobbold Ms W12 99 CT75
Cobbold Rd
Cobbold Rd E11 68 EF62
Cobbold Rd NW10 81 CT65
Cobbold Rd W12 99 CT75
Cobb's Ct EC4 83 DP72
Carter La
Cobb's Rd, Houns. 96 BZ84
Cobden Cl, Uxb. 76 BJ67
Cobden Hill, Rad. 25 CH36
Cobden Rd E11 68 EE62
Cobden Rd SE25 142 DU99
Cobden Rd, Orp. 163 ER105
Cobden Rd, Sev. 191 FJ123
Cobham, Grays 110 GB75
Cobham Av, N.Mal. 139 CU99
Cobham Cl SW11 120 DE86
Cobham Cl, Brom. 144 EL101
Cobham Cl, Edg. 42 CP54
Cobham Cl, Enf. 30 DS41
Sketty Rd
Cobham Cl, Sid. 126 EV86
Park Mead
Cobham Cl, Wall. 159 DL107
Cobham Gate, Cob. 153 BV114
Cobham Ho, Bark. 87 EQ67
St. Margarets
Cobham Ms NW1 83 DK66
Agar Gro
Cobham Pk Rd, Cob. 169 BV117
Cobham Pl, Bexh. 126 EX85
Cobham Rd E17 47 EC53
Cobham Rd N22 65 DP55
Cobham Rd, Cob. 170 CA118
Cobham Rd, Houns. 96 BW80
Cobham Rd, Ilf. 69 ES61
Cobham Rd, Kings.T. 138 CN95
Cobham Rd, Lthd. 171 CE122
Cobham St, Grav. 131 GG87
Cobill Cl, Horn. 72 FJ56
Cobland Rd SE12 124 EJ91
Coborn Rd E3 85 DZ69
Coborn St E3 85 DZ69
Cobourg Rd SE5 102 DT79
Cobourg St NW1 195 L3
Cobourg St NW1 83 DJ69
Cobs Way, Add. 152 BJ110
Cobsdene, Grav. 131 GK93
Coburg Cl SW1 199 L8
Coburg Cres SW2 121 DM88
Coburg Gdns, Ilf. 48 EK54
Coburg Rd N22 65 DM55
Cochrane Ms NW8 194 A1
Cochrane Rd SW19 119 CZ94
Cochrane St NW8 194 A1
Cochrane St NW8 82 DD68
Cock Hill E1 197 N7
Cock La EC1 196 F7
Cock La EC1 83 DP71
Cock La, Lthd. 170 CC122
Cockayne Way SE8 203 L10
Cockayne Way SE8 103 DY78
Cocker Rd, Enf. 30 DV36
Cockerell Rd E17 67 DY58
Cockerhurst Rd, Sev. 165 FD107
Cockett Rd, Slou. 92 AY76
Cockfosters Rd, Barn. 28 DF40
Cockle Way, Rad. 10 CL33
Cockmannings La, Orp. 146 EX102
Cockmannings Rd, Orp. 146 EX101
Cockpit Steps SW1 199 N5
Cockpit Yd WC1 196 C6
Cocks Cres, N.Mal. 139 CT98
Cock's Yd, Uxb. 76 BJ66
Bakers Rd
Cocksett Av, Orp. 163 ES107

Cockspur Ct SW1 199 N2
Cockspur St SW1 199 N2
Cockspur St SW1 83 DK74
Cocksure La, Sid. 126 FA90
Code St E1 84 DT70
Codham Hall La, Brwd. 73 FV56
Codicote Dr, Wat. 8 BX34
Codicote Ter N4 66 DQ61
Green Las
Codling Cl E1 202 C3
Codling Way, Wem. 61 CK63
Codmore Cres, Chesh. 4 AS30
Codmore Wd Rd, Chesh. 4 AW33
Codrington Ct, Wok. 166 AS118
Raglan Rd
Codrington Cres, Grav. 131 GJ92
Codrington Gdns, Grav. 131 GK92
Codrington Hill SE23 123 DY87
Codrington Ms W11 81 CY72
Blenheim Cres
Cody Cl, Har. 61 CK55
Cody Cl, Wall. 159 DK108
Alcock Cl
Cody Rd E16 85 ED70
Cody Rd Business Cen E16 85 ED70
Coe Av SE25 142 DU100
Coe's All, Barn. 27 CY42
Wood St
Coffers Circle, Wem. 62 CP62
Coftards, Slou. 74 AW72
Cogan Av E17 47 DY53
Cohen Cl, Wal.Cr. 15 DY31
Coin St SE1 200 D2
Coin St SE1 83 DN74
Coity Rd NW5 82 DG65
Coke St E1 84 DU72
Cokers La SE21 122 DR88
Perifield
Coke's Fm La, Ch.St.G. 20 AV41
Coke's La, Amer. 20 AW41
Coke's La, Ch.St.G. 20 AU42
Colas Ms NW6 82 DA67
Birchington Rd
Colbeck Ms SW7 100 DB77
Colbeck Rd, Har. 60 CC59
Colberg Pl N16 66 DS59
Colborne Way, Wor.Pk. 139 CW104
Colbrook Av, Hayes 95 BR76
Colbrook Cl, Hayes 95 BR76
Colburn Av, Cat. 176 DT124
Colburn Av, Pnr. 40 BY51
Colburn Way, Sutt. 140 DD104
Colby Ms SE19 122 DS92
Gipsy Hill
Colby Rd SE19 122 DS92
Colby Rd, Walt. 135 BU102
Winchester Rd
Colchester Av E12 69 EM62
Colchester Dr, Pnr. 60 BX57
Colchester Rd E10 67 EC59
Colchester Rd E17 67 EA58
Colchester Rd, Edg. 42 CQ52
Colchester Rd, Nthwd. 39 BU54
Colchester Rd, Rom. 52 FP51
Colchester St E1 84 DT72
Braham St
Colcokes Rd, Bans. 174 DA116
Cold Arbor Rd, Sev. 190 FD124
Cold Blow Cres, Bex. 127 FD88
Cold Blow La SE14 103 DX80
Cold Blows, Mitch. 140 DG97
Cold Harbour E14 204 E3
Cold Harbour E14 103 EC75
Coldbath Sq EC1 196 D4
Coldbath St SE13 103 EB81
Coldershaw Rd W13 79 CG74
Coldfall Av N10 44 DF54
Coldham Gro, Enf. 31 DY37
Coldharbour Cl, Egh. 133 BC97
Coldharbour La SE5 101 DN84
Coldharbour La SW9 101 DN84
Coldharbour La, Bushey 24 CB44
Coldharbour La, Egh. 133 BC97
Coldharbour La, Hayes 77 BU73
Coldharbour La, Pur. 159 DN110
Coldharbour La, Rain. 89 FE72
Coldharbour La, Red. 186 DT134
Coldharbour La, Wok. 167 BF115
Coldharbour Pl SE5 102 DQ82
Denmark Hill
Coldharbour Rd, Croy. 159 DN106
Coldharbour Rd, Grav. 130 GE89
Coldharbour Rd, W.Byf. 151 BF114
Coldharbour Rd, Wok. 167 BF115
Coldharbour Way, Croy. 159 DN106
Coldshott, Oxt. 188 EG133
Coldstream Gdns SW18 119 CZ86
Cole Av, Grays 111 GJ77
Cole Cl SE28 88 EV74
Cole Gdns, Houns. 95 BU80
Cole Pk Gdns, Twick. 117 CG86
Cole Pk Rd, Twick. 117 CG86
Cole Pk Vw, Twick. 117 CG86
Hill Vw Rd
Cole Rd, Twick. 117 CG86
Cole Rd, Wat. 23 BV39
Stamford Rd
Cole St SE1 201 J5
Cole St SE1 102 DQ75
Colebeck Ms N1 83 DP65
Colebert Av E1 84 DW70
Colebrook, Cher. 151 BD107
Colebrook Cl SW15 119 CX87
West Hill
Colebrook Gdns, Loug. 33 EP40
Colebrook Ho E14 85 EB72
Brabazon St
Colebrook La, Loug. 33 EP40
Colebrook Path, Loug. 33 EP40
Colebrook Pl, Cher. 151 BB108
Colebrook Rd SW16 141 DL95
Colebrook Way N11 45 DH50
Colebrooke Av W13 79 CH72
Colebrooke Dr E11 68 EH59
Colebrooke Pl N1 83 DP67
St. Peters St
Colebrooke Ri, Brom. 144 EE96
Colebrooke Rd, Red. 184 DE132
Colebrooke Row N1 196 F1
Colebrooke Row N1 83 DP68
Coleby Path SE5 102 DR80
Harris St
Colechurch Ho SE1 102 DU78
Coledale Dr, Stan. 41 CJ53
Coleford Rd SW18 120 DC85
Colegrave Rd E15 67 ED64
Colegrove Rd SE15 102 DT80
Coleherne Ct SW5 100 DB78
Coleherne Ms SW10 100 DB78
Coleherne Rd SW10 100 DB78
Colehill Gdns SW6 99 CY82
Fulham Palace Rd
Colehill La SW6 99 CY81
Coleman Cl SE25 142 DU96
Warminster Rd
Coleman Flds N1 84 DQ67
Coleman Rd SE5 102 DS80
Coleman Rd, Belv. 106 FA77
Coleman Rd, Dag. 88 EY65
Coleman St EC2 197 K8
Coleman St EC2 84 DR72
Colemans Heath SE9 125 EP90
Colemans La, Ong. 19 FH30
Coleman's La, Wal.Abb. 15 ED26
Colenso Dr NW7 43 CU52
Bunns La
Colenso Rd E5 66 DW63
Colenso Rd, Ilf. 69 ES60
Colepits Wd Rd SE9 125 EQ85
Coleraine Rd N8 65 DN55
Coleraine Rd SE3 104 EF79
Coleridge Av E12 86 EL65
Coleridge Av, Sutt. 158 DE105
Coleridge Cl SW8 101 DH82
Coleridge Cl (Cheshunt), Wal.Cr. 14 DT27
Peakes La
Coleridge Cres, Slou. 93 BE81
Coleridge Gdns NW6 82 DC66
Fairhazel Gdns
Coleridge La N8 65 DL58
Coleridge Rd
Coleridge Rd E17 67 DZ56
Coleridge Rd N4 65 DN61
Coleridge Rd N8 65 DK58
Coleridge Rd N12 44 DC50
Coleridge Rd, Ashf. 114 BL91
Coleridge Rd, Croy. 142 DW101
Coleridge Rd, Dart. 108 FN84
Coleridge Rd, Rom. 52 FH52
Coleridge Rd, Til. 111 GJ82
Coleridge Sq W13 79 CG72
Berners Dr
Coleridge Wk NW11 64 DA56
Coleridge Wk, Brwd. 55 GC45
Coleridge Way, Hayes 77 BU72
Coleridge Way, Orp. 146 EU100
Coleridge Way, West Dr. 94 BM77
Coles Cres, Har. 60 CB61
Coles Grn, Bushey 40 CC46
Coles Grn, Loug. 33 EN39
Coles Grn Ct NW2 63 CU61
Coles Grn Rd NW2 63 CU60
Coles La, West. 180 EW123
Colesburg Rd, Beck. 143 DZ97
Colescroft Hill, Pur. 175 DN115
Colesdale (Cuffley), Pot.B. 13 DL30
Coleshill Rd, Tedd. 117 CE93
Colesmead Rd, Red. 184 DF131
Colestown St SW11 100 DE82
Colet Cl N13 45 DP51
Colet Gdns W14 99 CX77
Colet Rd, Brwd. 55 GC43
Colets Orchard, Sev. 181 FH116
Coley Av, Wok. 167 BA118
Coley St WC1 196 C5
Coley St WC1 83 DM70
Colfe Rd SE23 123 DY88
Colgate Pl, Enf. 31 EA38
Government Row
Colham Av, West Dr. 76 BL74
Colham Grn Rd, Uxb. 76 BN71
Colham Mill Rd, West Dr. 94 BK75
Colham Rd, Uxb. 76 BM70
Colham Roundabout, Uxb. 76 BN73
Colin Cl NW9 62 CS56
Colin Cl, Croy. 143 DZ104
Colin Cl, Dart. 128 FP86
Colin Cl, W.Wick. 144 EF104
Colin Cres NW9 63 CT56
Colin Dr NW9 63 CT57
Colin Gdns NW9 63 CT57
Colin Par NW9 62 CS56
Edgware Rd
Colin Pk Rd NW9 62 CS56
Colin Rd NW10 81 CU65
Colin Rd, Cat. 176 DU123
Colina Ms N15 65 DP57
Harringay Rd
Colina Rd N15 65 DP57
Colindale Av NW9 62 CR55
Colindale Business Pk NW9 62 CQ55
Colindeep Gdns NW4 63 CU57
Colindeep La NW4 62 CS55
Colindeep La NW9 62 CS55
Colinette Rd SW15 99 CW84
Colinton Rd, Ilf. 70 EV61
Coliston Pas SW18 120 DA87
Coliston Rd
Coliston Rd SW18 120 DA87
Collamore Av SW18 120 DE88
Collapit Cl, Har. 60 CB57
Collard Av, Loug. 33 EQ40
Collard Grn, Loug. 33 EQ40
Collard Av
College App SE10 103 EC79
College Av, Egh. 113 BB93
College Av, Epsom 157 CT114
College Av, Grays 110 GB77
College Av, Har. 41 CE53
College Av, Slou. 92 AS76
College Cl E9 66 DW64
Median Rd
College Cl N18 46 DT50
College Cl, Add. 134 BK104
College Cl, Grays 110 GC77
College Cl, Har. 41 CE52
College Cl, Twick. 117 CD88
Meadway
College Ct (Cheshunt), Wal.Cr. 14 DW30
College Cres NW3 82 DD65
College Cres, Red. 184 DG131
College Cross N1 83 DN66
College Dr, Ruis. 59 BU59
College Gdns E4 47 EB45
College Gdns N18 46 DT50
College Gdns SE21 122 DS88
College Gdns SW17 120 DE89
College Gdns, Enf. 30 DR39
College Gdns, Ilf. 68 EL57
College Gdns, N.Mal. 139 CT99
College Grn SE19 122 DS94
College Gro NW1 83 DK67
St. Pancras Way
College Hill EC4 197 J10
College Hill Rd, Har. 41 CF53
College La NW5 65 DH63
College La, Wok. 166 AW119
College Ms SW1 199 P6
College Ms SW18 120 DB85
St. Ann's Hill
College Pk Cl SE13 103 ED84
College Pk Rd N17 46 DT51
College Rd
College Pl E17 68 EE56
College Pl NW1 83 DJ67
College Pl SW10 100 DC80
Hortensia Rd
College Pt E15 86 EF65
College Rd E17 67 EC57
College Rd N17 46 DT51
College Rd N21 45 DN47
College Rd NW10 81 CW68
College Rd SE19 122 DT92
College Rd SE21 122 DS87
College Rd SW19 120 DD93
College Rd W13 79 CH72
College Rd, Abb.L. 7 BT31
College Rd, Brom. 124 EG94
College Rd, Croy. 142 DR103
College Rd, Enf. 30 DR40
College Rd, Epsom 157 CU114
College Rd, Grav. 130 GB85
College Rd, Grays 110 GC77
College Rd (Harrow on the Hill), Har. 61 CE58
College Rd (Harrow Weald), Har. 41 CE53
College Rd, Islw. 97 CF81
College Rd, Swan. 147 FE95
College Rd (Cheshunt), Wal.Cr. 14 DV30
College Rd, Wem. 61 CK60
College Rd, Wok. 167 BB116
College Row E9 67 DX64
College Slip, Brom. 144 EG95
College St EC4 197 K10
College Ter E3 85 DZ69
College Ter N3 43 CZ54
Hendon La
College Vw SE9 124 EK88
College Wk, Kings.T. 138 CL96
Grange Rd
College Way, Ashf. 114 BM91
College Way, Nthwd. 39 BR51
College Yd NW5 65 DH63
College La
Collent St E9 84 DW65
Coller Cres, Dart. 129 FS91
Colless Rd N15 66 DT57
Collet Cl (Cheshunt), Wal.Cr. 15 DX28
Collet Gdns (Cheshunt), Wal.Cr. 15 DX28
Collet Cl
Collett Rd SE16 202 C7
Collett Rd SE16 102 DU76
Collett Way, Sthl. 78 CB74
Colley Hill La, Slou. 56 AT62
Colley La, Reig. 183 CY132
Colley Manor Dr, Reig. 183 CX133
Colley Way, Reig. 183 CY131
Colleyland, Rick. 21 BD42
Collier Cl E6 87 EP72
Trader Rd
Collier Cl, Epsom 156 CN107
Collier Dr, Edg. 42 CN54
Collier Row La, Rom. 51 FB52
Collier Row Rd, Rom. 50 EZ53
Collier St N1 196 B1
Collier St N1 83 DM68
Colliers, Cat. 186 DU125
Colliers Cl, Wok. 166 AV117
Colliers Shaw, Kes. 162 EK105
Colliers Water La, Th.Hth. 141 DN99
Collindale Av, Erith 107 FB79
Collindale Av, Sid. 126 EU88
Collingbourne Rd W12 81 CV74
Collingham Gdns SW5 100 DB77
Collingham Pl SW5 100 DB77
Collingham Rd SW5 100 DB77
Collings Cl N22 45 DM51
Whittington Rd
Collington Cl, Grav. 130 GE87
Beresford Rd
Collingtree Rd SE26 122 DW91
Collingwood Av N10 64 DG55
Collingwood Av, Surb. 138 CQ102
Collingwood Cl SE20 142 DV95
Collingwood Cl, Twick. 116 CA86
Collingwood Dr, St.Alb. 9 CK25
Collingwood Pl, Walt. 135 BU104
Collingwood Rd E17 67 EA58
Collingwood Rd N15 66 DS56
Collingwood Rd, Mitch. 140 DE96
Collingwood Rd, Sutt. 140 DA104
Collingwood Rd, Uxb. 77 BP70
Collingwood St E1 84 DV70
Collins Av, Stan. 42 CL54
Collins Dr, Ruis. 60 BW61
Collins Rd N5 66 DQ63
Collins Sq SE3 104 EF82
Tranquil Vale
Collins St SE3 104 EE82
Collins Way, Brwd. 55 GE43
Collin's Yd N1 83 DP67
Islington Grn
Collinson St SE1 201 H5
Collinson Wk SE1 201 H5
Collinwood Av, Enf. 30 DW41
Collinwood Gdns, Ilf. 69 EM57
Collis All, Twick. 117 CE88
The Grn
Colls Rd SE15 102 DW81
Collyer Av, Croy. 159 DL105
Collyer Pl SE15 102 DU81
Peckham High St
Collyer Rd, Croy. 159 DL105
Collyer Rd, St.Alb. 9 CJ27
Colman Cl, Epsom 173 CW117
Colman Rd E16 86 EJ71
Colman Way, Red. 184 DE132
Colmar Cl E1 85 DX70
Alderney Rd
Colmer Pl, Har. 41 CD52
Colmer Rd SW16 141 DL95
Colmore Ms SE15 102 DV81
Colmore Rd, Enf. 30 DW42
Colnbridge Cl, Stai. 113 BE91
Clarence St
Colnbrook Bypass, Slou. 93 BF80
Colnbrook Bypass, West Dr. 94 BH80
Colnbrook Cl, St.Alb. 10 CL28
Colnbrook Ct, Slou. 93 BF81
Colnbrook St SE1 200 F7
Colnbrook St SE1 101 DP76
Colndale Rd, Slou. 93 BE82
Colne Av, Rick. 38 BG47
Colne Av, Wat. 23 BV44
Colne Av, West Dr. 94 BJ75
Colne Bk, Slou. 93 BC83
Colne Cl, S.Ock. 91 FW73
Colne Ct, Epsom 156 CQ105
Colne Dr, Rom. 52 FM51
Colne Dr, Walt. 136 BX104
Colne Gdns, St.Alb. 10 CL27
Colne Ho, Bark. 87 EP65
Colne Mead, Rick. 38 BG47
Uxbridge Rd
Colne Orchard, Iver 75 BF72
Colne Pk Caravan Site, West Dr. 94 BJ77
Colne Reach, Stai. 113 BF85
Colne Rd E5 67 DY63
Colne Rd N21 46 DR45
Colne Rd, Twick. 117 CE88
Colne St E13 86 EG69
Grange Rd
Colne Valley, Upmin. 73 FS58
Colne Way, Stai. 113 BB90
Colne Way, Wat. 24 BY37
Colnedale Rd, Uxb. 58 BK64
Colney Hatch La N10 45 DH54
Colney Hatch La N11 44 DF51
Colney Rd, Dart. 128 FM86
Cologne Rd SW11 100 DD84
Colomb St SE10 104 EE78
Colombo Rd, Ilf. 69 EQ60
Colombo St SE1 200 F3
Colombo St SE1 83 DP74
Colonels La, Cher. 134 BG100
Colonels Wk, Enf. 29 DP41
Colonial Av, Twick. 116 CC85
Colonial Rd, Felt. 115 BS87
Colonial Rd, Slou. 92 AU75
Colonial Way, Wat. 24 BX39
Colonnade WC1 195 P5
Colonnade WC1 83 DL70
Colonnade Wk SW1 199 H9
Colonnades, The W2 82 DB72
Colosseum Ter NW1 83 DH70
Albany St
Colson Gdns, Loug. 33 EP42
Colson Rd
Colson Grn, Loug. 33 EP42
Colson Rd
Colson Path, Loug. 33 EN42
Colson Rd, Croy. 142 DS103
Colson Rd, Loug. 33 EP42
Colson Way SW16 121 DJ91
Colsterworth Rd N15 66 DT56
Colston Av, Cars. 158 DE105
Colston Cl, Cars. 158 DF105
West St
Colston Cres (Cheshunt), Wal.Cr. 13 DP27
Colston Rd E7 86 EK65
Colston Rd SW14 98 CQ84
Colthurst Cres N4 66 DQ61
Coltishall Rd, Horn. 90 FJ65
Coltness Cres SE2 106 EV78
Colton Gdns N17 66 DQ55
Colton Rd, Har. 61 CE57
Coltsfoot Ct, Grays 110 GD79
Coltsfoot Dr, West Dr. 76 BL72
Coltsfoot Path, Rom. 52 FJ52
Columbia Av, Edg. 42 CP53
Columbia Av, Ruis. 59 BV60
Columbia Av, Wor.Pk. 139 CT101
Columbia Rd E2 197 P2
Columbia Rd E2 84 DT69
Columbia Rd E13 86 EF70
Columbia Sq SW14 98 CQ84
Upper Richmond Rd W
Columbia Wf Rd, Grays 110 GA79
Columbine Av E6 86 EL71
Columbine Av, S.Croy. 159 DP108
Columbine Way SE13 103 EC82
Columbine Way, Rom. 52 FL53
Columbus Ct SE16 84 DW74
Rotherhithe St
Columbus Ctyd E14 203 P2
Columbus Gdns, Nthwd. 39 BU53
Columbus Sq, Erith 107 FF79
Colva Wk N19 65 DH61
Chester Rd
Colvestone Cres E8 66 DT64
Colview Ct SE9 124 EK88
Mottingham La
Colville Est N1 84 DS67
Colville Gdns W11 81 CZ72
Colville Hos W11 81 CZ72
Colville Ms W11 81 CZ72
Lonsdale Rd
Colville Pl W1 195 L7
Colville Rd E11 67 EC62
Colville Rd E17 47 DY54
Colville Rd N9 46 DV46
Colville Rd W3 98 CP76
Colville Rd W11 81 CZ72
Colville Sq W11 81 CZ72
Colville Sq Ms W11 81 CZ
Portobello Rd
Colville Ter W11 81 CZ
Colvin Cl SE26 122 DW
Colvin Gdns E4 47 EC
Colvin Gdns E11 68 EH
Colvin Gdns, Ilf. 49 EC
Colvin Gdns, Wal.Cr. 31 DX
Colvin Rd E6 86 EL
Colvin Rd, Th.Hth. 141 DN
Colwall Gdns, Wdf.Grn. 48 EG
Colwell Rd SE22 122 DT
Colwick Cl N6 65 DK
Colwith Rd W6 99 CW
Colwood Gdns SW19 120 DD
Colworth Gro SE17 201
Colworth Rd E11 68 EE
Colworth Rd, Croy. 142 DU1
Colwyn Av, Grnf. 79 CF
Colwyn Cl SW16 121 DJ
Colwyn Cres, Houns. 96 CC
Colwyn Grn NW9 62 CS
Snowdon Dr
Colwyn Rd NW2 63 CV
Colyer Cl N1 83 DM
Colyer Cl SE9 125 EF
Colyer Rd, Grav. 130 GC
Colyers Cl, Erith 107 FD
Colyers La, Erith 107 FC
Colyers Wk, Erith 107 FE
Colyers La
Colyton Cl, Well. 106 EX
Colyton Cl, Wem. 79 CJ
Bridgewater Rd
Colyton Cl, Wok. 166 AW
Colyton Rd SE22 122 DV
Colyton Way N18 46 DU
Combe Av SE3 104 EF
Combe Bk Dr, Sev. 180 EY1
Combe La, Walt. 153 BT1
Combe Lo SE7 104 EJ
Elliscombe Rd
Combe Martin, Kings.T. 118 CO
Combe Ms SE3 104 EF
Combe Rd, Wat. 23 BT
Combedale Rd SE10 205 M
Combedale Rd SE10 104 EG
Combemartin Rd SW18 119 CY
Comber Cl NW2 63 CV
Comber Gro SE5 102 DQ
Combermere Rd SW9 101 DM
Combermere Rd, Mord. 140 DB1
Comberton Rd E5 66 DV
Combeside SE18 105 ET
Combwell Cres SE2 106 EU
Comely Bk Rd E17 67 EC
Comer Cres, Sthl. 96 CC
Windmill Av
Comeragh Cl, Wok. 166 AU1
Comeragh Ms W14 99 CY
Comeragh Rd W14 99 CY
Comerford Rd SE4 103 DY
Comet Cl E12 68 EK
Comet Cl, Purf. 108 FN
Comet Cl, Wat. 7 BT
Comet Pl SE8 103 EA
Comet Rd, Stai. 114 BK
Comet St SE8 103 EA
Comfort St SE15 102 DT
St. Georges Way
Comforts Fm Av, Oxt. 188 EF1
Comfrey Ct, Grays 110 GD
Commerce Rd N22 45 DM
Commerce Rd, Brent. 97 CJ
Commerce Way, Croy. 141 DM1
Commercial Pl, Grav. 131 GJ
Commercial Rd E1 84 DU
Commercial Rd E14 84 DW
Commercial Rd N17 46 DS
Commercial Rd N18 46 DS
Commercial Rd, Stai. 114 BG
Commercial St E1 197
Commercial St E1 84 DT
Commercial Way NW10 80 CP
Commercial Way SE15 102 DT
Commercial Way, Wok. 167 AZ1
Commerell St SE10 205 J
Commerell St SE10 104 EE
Commodity Quay E1 202 A
Commodore Sq SW10 100 DD
Commodore St E1 85 DY
Common, The W5 80 CL
Common, The, Kings L. 6 BG
Common, The, Rich. 117 CK
Common, The, Sthl. 96 BW
Common, The, Stan. 41 CE
Common, The, West Dr. 94 BJ
Common Cl, Wok. 150 AX1
Common Gate Rd, Rick. 21 BD
Common La, Add. 152 BJ1
Common La, Dart. 127 FG
Common La, Esher 155 CG1
Common La, Kings L. 6 BM
Common La, Rad. 25 CE
Common La, Wat. 25 CE
Common Rd SW13 99 CU
Common Rd, Brwd. 55 GC
Common Rd, Esher 155 CG1
Common Rd, Lthd. 170 BY12
Common Rd, Rick. 21 BD4
Common Rd (Langley), Slou. 93 BA7
Common Rd, Stan. 41 CD
Commondale SW15 99 CW
Commonfield La SW17 120 DE
Tooting Gro
Commonfield Rd, Bans. 158 DA1
Commonmeadow La, Wat. 8 CB
Commonside, Epsom 172 CN1
Commonside, Kes. 162 EJ1
Commonside, Lthd. 170 CA12
Commonside Cl, Couls. 175 DP12
Coulsdon Rd
Commonside Cl, Sutt. 158 DB1
Downs Rd
Commonside E, Mitch. 140 DF9
Commonside W, Mitch. 140 DF9
Commonwealth Av W12 81 CV7
Commonwealth Av, Hayes 77 BR7

mmonwealth Rd N17 46 DU52
mmonwealth Rd, Cat. 176 DU123
mmonwealth Way SE2 106 EV78
mmonwood La, Kings L. 22 BH35
mmunity Cl, Houns. 95 BV81
mmunity Cl, Uxb. 59 BQ62
mmunity La N7 65 DK64
mmunity Rd E15 67 ED64
mmunity Rd, Grnf. 78 CC67
mmunity Wk, Esher 154 CC105
High St
mmunity Way, Rick. 23 BP43
Barton Way
mo Rd SE23 123 DY89
mo St, Rom. 71 FD57
mpass Hill, Rich. 117 CK86
mpayne Gdns NW6 82 DB66
mport Grn, Croy. 162 EE112
mpton Av E6 86 EK68
mpton Av N1 83 DP65
mpton Av N6 64 DE59
mpton Av, Brwd. 55 GC46
mpton Av, Rom. 71 FH55
mpton Cl E3 85 EA71
ompton Cl NW1 195 J3
ompton Cl NW11 63 CX62
The Vale
ompton Cl W13 79 CG72
ompton Cl, Edg. 42 CQ52
Pavilion Way
ompton Cl, Esher 154 CC106
ompton Ct SE19 122 DS92
Victoria Cres
ompton Cres N17 46 DQ52
ompton Cres W4 98 CQ79
ompton Cres, Chess. 156 CL107
ompton Cres, Nthlt. 78 BX67
ompton Gdns, Add. 152 BH106
Monks Cres
ompton Gdns, St.Alb. 8 CB26
ompton Pas EC1 196 G4
ompton Pl WC1 195 P4
ompton Pl, Erith 107 FF79
ompton Pl, Wat. 40 BY48
ompton Ri, Pnr. 60 BY57
ompton Rd N1 83 DP65
ompton Rd N21 45 DN46
ompton Rd NW10 81 CX69
ompton Rd SW19 119 CZ93
ompton Rd, Croy. 142 DV102
ompton Rd, Hayes 77 BS73
ompton St EC1 196 F4
ompton St EC1 83 DP70
ompton Ter N1 83 DP65
omreddy Cl, Enf. 29 DP39
omus Pl SE17 201 M9
omus Pl SE17 102 DS77
omyn Rd SW11 100 DE84
omyne Rd, Wat. 23 BT36
omyns, The, Bushey 40 CC46
omyns Cl E16 86 EF71
omyns Rd, Dag. 88 FA66
onant Ms E1 84 DU73
Back Ch La
onaways Cl, Epsom 157 CU110
oncanon Rd SW2 101 DM84
oncert Hall App SE1 200 C3
oncert Hall App SE1 83 DM74
oncord Cl, Nthlt. 78 BX69
Britannia Cl
oncord Rd W3 80 CP70
oncord Rd, Enf. 30 DW43
oncorde Cl, Houns. 96 CB82
Lampton Rd
oncorde Cl, Uxb. 76 BL68
oncorde Dr E6 87 EM71
oncourse, The N9 46 DU47
New Rd
oncourse, The NW9 43 CT53
oncrete Cotts, Wok. 168 BL116
Wisley La
ondell Rd SW8 101 DJ81
onder St E14 85 DY72
Salmon La
onderton Rd SE5 102 DQ83
ondor Path, Nthlt. 78 CA68
Brabazon Rd
ondor Rd, Stai. 134 BH97
ondor Wk, Horn. 89 FH66
Heron Flight Av
ondover Cres SE18 105 EP80
ondray Pl SW11 100 DE80
onduit, The, Red. 186 DS129
onduit Av SE10 103 ED81
Crooms Hill
onduit Ct WC2 195 P10
onduit La N18 46 DW50
onduit La, Croy. 160 DU106
onduit La, Enf. 31 DY44
Morson Rd
onduit La, S.Croy. 160 DU106
onduit Ms W2 82 DD72
onduit Pas W2 82 DD72
Conduit Pl
onduit Pl W2 82 DD72
onduit Rd SE18 105 EP78
onduit Rd, Slou. 92 AY78
onduit St W1 195 J10
onduit St W1 83 DH73
onduit Way NW10 80 CQ66
onegar Ct, Slou. 74 AS74
onewood St N5 65 DP62
oney Acre SE21 122 DQ88
oney Burrows E4 48 EE47
Wyemead Cres
oney Gro, Uxb. 76 BN69
oney Hill Rd, W.Wick. 144 EE103
oney Way SW8 101 DM79
oneybury, Red. 186 DS134
oneybury Cl, Warl. 176 DV119
oneygrove Path, Nthlt. 78 BY65
Arnold Rd
onference Cl E4 47 EC47
Greenbank Cl
onference Rd SE2 106 EW77
ongleton Gro SE18 105 EQ78
ongo Rd SE18 105 ER78
ongress Rd SE2 106 EW77
ongreve Rd SE9 105 EM83
ongreve Rd, Wal.Abb. 16 EE33
ongreve St SE17 201 M8
Congreve St SE17 102 DS77
Congreve Wk E16 86 EK71
Conical Cor, Enf. 30 DQ40
Conifer Av, Rom. 51 FB50
Conifer Cl, Orp. 163 ER105
Conifer Cl, Reig. 184 DA132
Conifer Cl, Wal.Cr. 14 DT29
Conifer Dr, Brwd. 54 FX50
Conifer Gdns SW16 121 DL90
Conifer Gdns, Enf. 30 DS44
Conifer Gdns, Sutt. 140 DB103
Conifer La, Egh. 113 BC92
Conifer Way, Hayes 77 BU73
Longmead Rd
Conifer Way, Swan. 147 FC95
Conifer Way, Wem. 61 CJ62
Conifers, Wey. 153 BS105
Conifers, The, Wat. 24 BW35
Conifers Cl, Tedd. 117 CH94
Coniger Rd SW6 100 DA82
Coningesby Dr, Wat. 23 BS39
Coningham Ms W12 81 CU74
Percy Rd
Coningham Rd W12 81 CV74
Coningsby Cotts W5 97 CK75
Coningsby Rd
Coningsby Dr, Pot.B. 12 DD33
Coningsby Gdns E4 47 EB51
Coningsby Rd N4 65 DP59
Coningsby Rd W5 97 CJ75
Coningsby Rd, S.Croy. 160 DQ109
Conington Rd SE13 103 EB82
Conisbee Ct N14 29 DJ43
Conisborough Cres SE6 123 EC90
Coniscliffe Cl, Chis. 145 EN95
Coniscliffe Rd N13 46 DQ48
Conista Ct, Wok. 166 AT116
Roundthorn Way
Coniston Av, Bark. 87 ES66
Coniston Av, Grnf. 79 CH69
Coniston Av, Upmin. 72 FQ63
Coniston Av, Well. 105 ES83
Coniston Cl N20 44 DC48
Coniston Cl SW13 99 CT80
Lonsdale Rd
Coniston Cl SW20 139 CX100
Coniston Cl W4 98 CQ81
Coniston Cl, Bark. 87 ES66
Coniston Av
Coniston Cl, Bexh. 107 FC81
Coniston Cl, Dart. 127 FH88
Coniston Cl, Erith 107 FE80
Coniston Gdns N9 46 DW46
Coniston Gdns NW9 62 CR57
Coniston Gdns, Ilf. 68 EL56
Coniston Gdns, Pnr. 59 BU56
Coniston Gdns, Sutt. 158 DD107
Coniston Gdns, Wem. 61 CJ60
Coniston Ho SE5 102 DQ80
Coniston Rd N10 45 DH54
Coniston Rd N17 46 DU51
Coniston Rd, Bexh. 107 FC81
Coniston Rd, Brom. 124 EE93
Coniston Rd, Couls. 175 DJ116
Coniston Rd, Croy. 142 DU101
Coniston Rd, Kings L. 6 BM28
Coniston Rd, Twick. 116 CB86
Coniston Rd, Wok. 167 BB120
Coniston Wk E9 66 DW64
Clifden Rd
Coniston Way, Chess. 138 CL104
Coniston Way, Egh. 113 BB94
Coniston Way, Horn. 71 FG64
Coniston Way, Reig. 184 DE133
Conistone Way N7 83 DL66
Conlan St W10 81 CY70
Conley Rd NW10 80 CS65
Conley St SE10 205 J10
Connaught Av E4 47 ED45
Connaught Av SW14 98 CQ83
Connaught Av, Ashf. 114 BL91
Connaught Av, Barn. 44 DF46
Connaught Av, Enf. 30 DS40
Connaught Av, Grays 110 GB75
Connaught Av, Houns. 116 BY85
Connaught Av, Loug. 32 EK42
Connaught Br E16 86 EK73
Connaught Cl E10 67 DY61
Connaught Cl W2 194 B9
Connaught Cl, Enf. 30 DS40
Connaught Cl, Sutt. 140 DD103
Connaught Cl, Uxb. 77 BQ70
New Rd
Connaught Dr NW11 64 DA56
Connaught Dr, Wey. 152 BN111
Connaught Gdns N10 65 DH57
Connaught Gdns N13 45 DP49
Connaught Gdns, Mord. 140 DC98
Connaught Hill, Loug. 32 EK42
Connaught La, Ilf. 69 ER61
Connaught Rd
Connaught Ms SE18 105 EN78
Connaught Ms W2 194 D9
Connaught Ms, Ilf. 69 ER61
Connaught Rd
Connaught Pl W2 194 D10
Connaught Pl W2 82 DF73
Connaught Rd E4 48 EE45
Connaught Rd E11 67 ED60
Connaught Rd E16 86 EK74
Connaught Rd E17 67 EA57
Connaught Rd N4 65 DN59
Connaught Rd NW10 80 CS67
Connaught Rd SE18 105 EN78
Connaught Rd W13 79 CH73
Connaught Rd, Barn. 27 CX44
Connaught Rd, Har. 41 CF53
Connaught Rd, Horn. 72 FK62
Connaught Rd, Ilf. 69 ER61
Connaught Rd, N.Mal. 138 CS98
Connaught Rd, Rich. 118 CM85
Albert Rd
Connaught Rd, Slou. 92 AV75
Connaught Rd, Sutt. 140 DD103
Connaught Rd, Tedd. 117 CD92
Connaught Roundabout E16 86 EK73
Connaught Br
Connaught Sq W2 194 D9
Connaught Sq W2 82 DF72
Connaught St W2 194 B9
Connaught St W2 82 DE72
Connaught Way N13 45 DP49
Connell Cres W5 80 CM70
Connemara Cl, Borwd. 26 CR44
Percheron Rd
Connington Cres E4 47 ED48
Connop Rd, Enf. 31 DX38
Connor Cl, Ilf. 49 EM53
Fullwell Av
Connor Rd, Dag. 70 EZ63
Connor St E9 85 DX67
Lauriston Rd
Conolly Rd W7 79 CE74
Conquest Rd, Add. 152 BG106
Conrad Cl, Grays 110 GB75
Conrad Dr, Wor.Pk. 139 CW102
Conrad Gdns, Grays 110 GA75
Conrad Ho N16 66 DS64
Cons St SE1 200 E4
Consfield Av, N.Mal. 139 CU98
Consort Cl, Brwd. 54 FW50
Consort Ms, Islw. 117 CD85
Consort Rd SE15 102 DV81
Consort Way (Denham), Uxb. 57 BF58
Knowland Way
Constable Av E16 205 P2
Constable Cl NW11 64 DB58
Constable Cl, Hayes 77 BQ69
Charville La
Constable Cres N15 66 DU57
Constable Gdns, Edg. 42 CN53
Constable Gdns, Islw. 117 CD85
Constable Ms, Dag. 70 EV63
Stonard Rd
Constable Rd, Grav. 130 GE90
Constable Wk SE21 122 DT90
Constance Cres, Brom. 144 EF101
Constance Rd, Croy. 141 DP101
Constance Rd, Enf. 30 DS44
Constance Rd, Sutt. 158 DC105
Constance Rd, Twick. 116 CB87
Constance St E16 86 EL74
Albert Rd
Constantine Pl, Uxb. 76 BM67
Vine La
Constantine Rd NW3 64 DE63
Constitution Hill SW1 199 H4
Constitution Hill SW1 101 DH75
Constitution Hill, Grav. 131 GJ88
Constitution Hill, Wok. 166 AY119
Constitution Ri SE18 105 EN81
Consul Av, Dag. 89 FC69
Consul Gdns, Swan. 127 FG93
Princes Rd
Content St SE17 201 J9
Content St SE17 102 DR77
Contessa Cl, Orp. 163 ES106
Control Twr Rd, Houns. 94 BN83
Convair Wk, Nthlt. 78 BX69
Kittiwake Rd
Convent Cl, Beck. 123 EC94
Convent Gdns W5 97 CJ77
Convent Gdns W11 81 CZ72
Kensington Pk Rd
Convent Hill SE19 122 DQ93
Convent La, Cob. 153 BS111
Seven Hills Rd
Convent Rd, Ashf. 114 BN92
Convent Way, Sthl. 96 BW77
Conway Cl, Rain. 89 FG66
Conway Cl, Stan. 41 CG51
Conway Cres, Grnf. 79 CE68
Conway Cres, Rom. 70 EW59
Conway Dr, Ashf. 115 BQ93
Conway Dr, Hayes 95 BQ76
Conway Dr, Sutt. 158 DB107
Conway Gdns, Enf. 30 DS38
Conway Gdns, Grays 110 GB80
Conway Gdns, Mitch. 141 DK98
Conway Gdns, Wem. 61 CJ59
Conway Gro W3 80 CR71
Conway Ms W1 195 K5
Conway Rd N14 45 DL48
Conway Rd N15 65 DP57
Conway Rd NW2 63 CW61
Conway Rd SE18 105 ER77
Conway Rd SW20 139 CW95
Conway Rd, Felt. 116 BX92
Conway Rd, Houns. 116 BZ87
Conway Rd (Heathrow Airport), Houns. 95 BP83
Inner Ring E
Conway St E13 86 EG70
Conway St W1 195 K5
Conway St W1 83 DJ71
Conway Wk, Hmptn. 116 BZ93
Fearnley Cres
Conybeare NW3 82 DE66
King Henry's Rd
Conybury Cl, Wal.Abb. 16 EG32
Conyer St E3 85 DY68
Conyers Cl, Walt. 154 BX106
Conyers Cl, Wdf.Grn. 48 EE51
Conyers Rd SW16 121 DK92
Conyers Way, Loug. 33 EP41
Cooden Cl, Brom. 124 EH94
Plaistow La
Cook Ct SE16 84 DW74
Rotherhithe St
Cook Rd, Dag. 88 EY67
Cook Sq, Erith 107 FF80
Cooke Cl E14 85 EA74
Cabot Sq
Cookes Cl E11 68 EF61
Cookes La, Sutt. 157 CY107
Cookham Cl, Sthl. 96 CB75
Cookham Cres SE16 203 J4
Cookham Dene Cl, Chis. 145 ER95
Cookham Hill, Orp. 146 FA104
Cookham Rd, Sid. 126 FA94
Cookham Rd, Swan. 146 FA95
Cookhill Rd SE2 106 EV75
Cooks Cl, Rom. 51 FC53
Cook's Hole Rd, Enf. 29 DP38
Cooks Mead, Bushey 24 CB44
Cook's Rd E15 85 EB68
Cooks Rd SE17 101 DP79
Cookson Gro, Erith 107 FB80
Cool Oak La NW9 62 CS59
Coolfin Rd E16 86 EG72
Coolgardie Av E4 47 EC50
Coolgardie Av, Chig. 49 EN48
Coolgardie Rd, Ashf. 115 BQ92
Coolhurst Rd N8 65 DK58
Coomassie Rd W9 81 CZ70
Bravington Rd
Coombe, The, Bet. 182 CR131
Coombe Av, Croy. 160 DS105
Coombe Av, Sev. 181 FH120
Coombe Bk, Kings.T. 138 CS95
Coombe Cl, Edg. 42 CM54
Coombe Cl, Houns. 96 CA84
Coombe Cor N21 45 DP46
Coombe Cres, Hmptn. 116 BY94
Coombe Dr, Add. 151 BF107
Coombe Dr, Kings.T. 118 CR94
Coombe Dr, Ruis. 59 BV60
Coombe End, Kings.T. 118 CR94
Coombe Gdns SW20 139 CU96
Coombe Gdns, N.Mal. 139 CT98
Coombe Hts, Kings.T. 118 CS94
Coombe Hill Glade, Kings.T. 118 CS94
Coombe Hill Rd, Kings.T. 118 CS94
Coombe Hill Rd, Rick. 38 BG45
Coombe Ho Chase, N.Mal. 138 CR95
Coombe La SW20 139 CV96
Coombe La, Croy. 160 DV106
Coombe La W, Kings.T. 139 CU95
Coombe Lea, Brom. 144 EL97
Coombe Neville, Kings.T. 118 CR94
Coombe Pk, Kings.T. 118 CR92
Coombe Ridings, Kings.T. 118 CQ92
Coombe Ri, Brwd. 55 FZ46
Coombe Ri, Kings.T. 138 CQ95
Coombe Rd N22 45 DN53
Coombe Rd NW10 62 CR62
Coombe Rd SE26 122 DV91
Coombe Rd W4 98 CS78
Coombe Rd W13 97 CH76
Northcroft Rd
Coombe Rd, Bushey 40 CC45
Coombe Rd, Croy. 160 DR105
Coombe Rd, Grav. 131 GJ89
Coombe Rd, Hmptn. 116 BZ93
Coombe Rd, Kings.T. 138 CN95
Coombe Rd, N.Mal. 138 CS96
Coombe Rd, Rom. 72 FM55
Coombe Vale, Ger.Cr. 56 AY60
Coombe Wk, Sutt. 140 DB104
Coombe Way, W.Byf. 152 BM112
Coombe Wd Hill, Pur. 160 DQ112
Coombe Wd Rd, Kings.T. 118 CQ92
Coombefield Cl, N.Mal. 138 CS99
Coombehurst Cl, Barn. 28 DF40
Coombelands La, Add. 152 BG107
Coomber Way, Croy. 141 DK101
Coombes Rd, Dag. 88 EZ67
Coombes Rd, St.Alb. 9 CJ26
Coombewood Dr, Rom. 70 EZ58
Coombfield Dr, Dart. 129 FR91
Coombs St N1 196 G1
Coombs St N1 83 DP68
Coomer Ms SW6 99 CZ79
Coomer Pl
Coomer Pl SW6 99 CZ79
Coomer Rd SW6 99 CZ79
Coomer Pl
Cooms Wk, Edg. 42 CQ53
East Rd
Cooper Av E17 47 DX53
Cooper Cl SE1 200 E5
Cooper Cl, Green. 129 FT85
Cooper Ct E15 67 EB64
Clays La
Cooper Cres, Cars. 140 DF104
Cooper Rd NW4 63 CX58
Cooper Rd NW10 63 CU64
Cooper Rd, Croy. 159 DN105
Cooper St E16 86 EF71
Lawrence St
Cooperage Cl N17 46 DT51
Brantwood Rd
Coopers Cl E1 84 DW70
Coopers Cl, Chig. 50 EV47
Coopers Cl, Dag. 89 FB65
Coopers Cl (South Darenth), Dart. 148 FQ95
Coopers Cl, Stai. 113 BE92
Coopers Cres, Borwd. 26 CQ39
Coopers Hill La, Egh. 112 AY91
Coopers Hill Rd, Red. 185 DM133
Coopers La E10 67 EB60
Coopers La NW1 83 DK68
Cooper's La SE12 124 EH89
Coopers La, Pot.B. 12 DD31
Coopers La Rd, Pot.B. 12 DE31
Coopers Rd SE1 102 DT78
Coopers Rd, Grav. 130 GE88
Coopers Rd, Pot.B. 12 DC30
Cooper's Row EC3 197 P10
Coopers Row, Iver 75 BC70
Coopers Shaw Rd, Til. 111 GK80
Coopers Wk E15 67 ED64
Maryland St
Coopers Wk (Cheshunt), Wal.Cr. 15 DX28
Cooper's Yd SE19 122 DS93
Westow Hill
Coopersale Cl, Wdf.Grn. 48 EJ52
Navestock Cres
Coopersale Common, Epp. 18 EX28
Coopersale La, Epp. 34 EU37
Coopersale Rd E9 67 DX64
Coopersale St, Epp. 18 EW32
Coote Gdns, Dag. 70 EZ62
Coote Rd, Bexh. 106 EZ81
Coote Rd, Dag. 70 EZ62
Cope Pl W8 100 DA76
Cope St SE16 203 H8
Cope St SE16 103 DX77
Copeland Dr E14 204 A8
Copeland Dr E14 103 EA77
Copeland Rd E17 67 EB57
Copeland Rd SE15 102 DU82
Copeman Cl SE26 122 DW92
Copeman Rd, Brwd. 55 GD45
Copenhagen Gdns W4 98 CQ75
Copenhagen Pl E14 85 DZ72
Copenhagen St N1 83 DL67
Copenhagen Way, Walt. 135 BV104
Copers Cope Rd, Beck. 123 DZ93
Copford Cl, Wdf.Grn. 48 EL51
Copford Wk N1 84 DQ67
Popham St
Copgate Path SW16 121 DM93
Copinger Wk, Edg. 42 CP53
North Rd
Copland Av, Wem. 61 CK64
Copland Cl, Wem. 61 CJ64
Copland Ms, Wem. 80 CL65
Copland Rd
Copland Rd, Wem. 80 CL65
Copleigh Dr, Tad. 173 CY120
Copleston Ms SE15 102 DT82
Copleston Rd
Copleston Pas SE15 102 DT83
Copleston Rd SE15 102 DT83
Copley Cl SE17 101 DP79
Hillingdon St
Copley Cl W7 79 CF71
Copley Cl, Red. 184 DE132
Copley Cl, Wok. 166 AS119
Copley Dene, Brom. 144 EK95
Copley Pk SW16 121 DM93
Copley Rd, Stan. 41 CJ50
Copley St E1 85 DX71
Stepney Grn
Copley Way, Tad. 173 CX120
Copmans Wick, Rick. 21 BD43
Copnor Way SE15 102 DS80
Diamond St
Coppard Gdns, Chess. 155 CJ107
Copped Hall SE21 122 DR89
Glazebrook Cl
Coppelia Rd SE3 104 EF84
Coppen Rd, Dag. 70 EZ59
Copper Beech Cl NW3 82 DD65
Daleham Ms
Copper Beech Cl, Grav. 131 GK87
Copper Beech Cl, Ilf. 49 EN53
Copper Beech Cl, Orp. 146 EW99
Rookery Gdns
Copper Beech Cl, Wok. 166 AV121
Copper Beech Ct, Loug. 33 EN39
Copper Beech Rd, S.Ock. 91 FW69
Copper Beeches, Islw. 97 CD81
Eversley Cres
Copper Cl SE19 122 DT94
Auckland Rd
Copper Mead Cl NW2 63 CW62
Copper Mill Dr, Islw. 97 CF82
Copper Mill La SW17 120 DC91
Copper Ridge (Chalfont St. Peter), Ger.Cr. 37 AZ50
Copper Row SE1 201 P3
Copper Row SE1 84 DT74
Copperas St SE8 103 EB79
Copperbeech Cl NW3 64 DD64
Akenside Rd
Copperdale Rd, Hayes 95 BU75
Copperfield, Chig. 49 ER51
Copperfield App, Chig. 49 ER51
Copperfield Av, Uxb. 76 BN71
Copperfield Cl, S.Croy. 160 DQ111
Copperfield Ct, Lthd. 171 CG121
Kingston Rd
Copperfield Ct, Pnr. 60 BZ56
Copperfield Way
Copperfield Dr N15 66 DT56
Copperfield Gdns, Brwd. 54 FV46
Copperfield Ms N18 46 DS50
Copperfield Ri, Add. 151 BF106
Copperfield Rd E3 85 DY70
Copperfield Rd SE28 88 EW72
Copperfield St SE1 200 G4
Copperfield St SE1 101 DP75
Copperfield Ter, Slou. 74 AV73
Mirador Cres
Copperfield Way, Chis. 125 EQ93
Copperfield Way, Pnr. 60 BZ56
Copperfields, Lthd. 170 CC122
Copperfields Way, Rom. 52 FK53
Coppergate Cl, Brom. 144 EH95
Coppergate Ct, Wal.Abb. 16 EG34
Farthingale La
Coppermill La E17 66 DW58
Coppermill La, Rick. 37 BE52
Coppermill La (Harefield), Uxb. 37 BE52
Coppermill Rd, Stai. 113 BA86
Coppetts Cl N12 44 DE52
Coppetts Rd N10 44 DG54
Coppice, The, Ashf. 115 BP93
School Rd
Coppice, The, Enf. 29 DP42
Coppice, The, Wat. 24 BW44
Coppice, The, West Dr. 76 BL72
Coppice Cl SW20 139 CW97
Coppice Cl, Ruis. 59 BR58
Coppice Cl, Stan. 41 CF51
Coppice Dr SW15 119 CV86
Coppice Dr, Stai. 112 AX87
Coppice End, Wok. 167 BE116
Coppice La, Reig. 183 CZ132
Coppice Path, Chig. 50 EV49
Coppice Row, Epp. 33 EM36
Coppice Wk N20 44 DA48
Coppice Way E18 68 EF56
Coppies Gro N11 44 DG49
Copping Cl, Croy. 160 DS105
Tipton Dr
Coppins, The, Croy. 161 EB107
Coppins, The, Har. 41 CE51
Coppins La, Iver 75 BF71
Coppock Cl SW11 100 DE82
Coppsfield, W.Mol. 136 CA97
Hurst Rd
Copse, The E4 48 EF46
Copse, The, Cat. 186 DU126
Tupwood La
Copse, The, Lthd. 170 CB123
Copse Av, W.Wick. 143 EB104
Copse Cl SE7 104 EH79
Copse Cl, Nthwd. 39 BQ54
Copse Cl, West Dr. 94 BK76
Copse Edge Av, Epsom 157 CT113
Copse Glade, Surb. 137 CK102
Copse Hill SW20 119 CV94
Copse Hill, Pur. 159 DL113
Copse Hill, Sutt. 158 DB108

Copse La, Beac. 36 AS52
Copse Rd, Cob. 153 BV113
Copse Rd, Wok. 166 AT118
Copse Vw, S.Croy. 161 DX109
Copse Wd, Iver 75 BD67
Copse Wd Ct, Reig. 184 DE132
Green La
Copse Wd Way, Nthwd. 39 BQ52
Copsem Dr, Esher 154 CB107
Copsem La, Esher 154 CC107
Copsem La, Lthd. 154 CC111
Copsem Way, Esher 154 CC107
Copsen Wd, Lthd. 154 CC111
Copsewood Cl, Sid. 125 ES86
Copsewood Rd, Wat. 23 BV39
Copt Hill La, Tad. 173 CY120
Coptefield Dr, Belv. 106 EX76
Coptfold Rd, Brwd. 54 FW47
Copthall Av EC2 197 L8
Copthall Av EC2 84 DR72
Copthall Bldgs EC2 197 K8
Copthall Cl EC2 197 K8
Copthall Cl (Chalfont St. Peter), Ger.Cr. 37 AZ52
Copthall Cor (Chalfont St. Peter), Ger.Cr. 36 AY52
Copthall Ct EC2 84 DR72
Copthall Dr NW7 43 CU52
Copthall Gdns NW7 43 CU52
Copthall Gdns, Twick. 117 CF88
Copthall La (Chalfont St. Peter), Ger.Cr. 36 AY52
Copthall Rd E, Uxb. 58 BN61
Copthall Rd W, Uxb. 58 BN61
Copthall Way, Add. 151 BF110
Copthorne Av SW12 121 DK87
Copthorne Av, Brom. 145 EM103
Copthorne Av, Ilf. 49 EP51
Copthorne Chase, Ashf. 114 BM91
Ford Rd
Copthorne Cl, Rick. 22 BM43
Copthorne Cl, Shep. 135 BQ100
Copthorne Gdns, Horn. 72 FN57
Copthorne Ms, Hayes 95 BS77
Copthorne Ri, S.Croy. 160 DR113
Copthorne Rd, Lthd. 171 CH120
Copthorne Rd, Rick. 22 BM44
Coptic St WC1 195 P7
Coptic St WC1 83 DL71
Copwood Cl N12 44 DD49
Coral Cl, Rom. 70 EW55
Coral Row SW11 100 DC83
Gartons Way
Coral St SE1 200 E5
Coral St SE1 101 DN75
Coraline Cl, Sthl. 78 BZ69
Coralline Wk SE2 106 EW75
Coram Grn, Brwd. 55 GD44
Coram St WC1 195 P5
Coram St WC1 83 DL70
Coran Cl N9 47 DX45
Corban Rd, Houns. 96 CA83
Corbar Cl, Barn. 28 DD38
Corbden Cl SE15 102 DT81
Lisford St
Corbet Cl, Wall. 140 DG102
Corbet Ct EC3 197 L9
Corbet Pl E1 197 P6
Corbet Rd, Epsom 156 CS110
Corbets Av, Upmin. 72 FP64
Corbets Tey Rd, Upmin. 72 FP63
Corbett Cl, Croy. 161 ED112
Corbett Gro N22 45 DL52
Corbett Ho, Wat. 40 BW48
Corbett Rd E11 68 EJ58
Corbett Rd E17 67 EC55
Corbetts La SE16 202 F9
Corbetts Pas SE16 202 F9
Corbicum E11 68 EE59
Corbiere Ct SW19 119 CX93
Thornton Rd
Corbiere Ho N1 84 DS67
Corbins La, Har. 60 CB62
Corbridge Cres E2 84 DV68
Corby Cl, Egh. 112 AW93
Corby Cl, St.Alb. 8 CA25
Corby Cres, Enf. 29 DL42
Corby Dr, Egh. 112 AV93
Corby Rd NW10 80 CR68
Corby Way E3 85 EA70
Knapp Rd
Corbylands Rd, Sid. 125 ES87
Corbyn St N4 65 DL60
Corcorans, Brwd. 54 FV44
Cord Way E14 204 A6
Cordelia Cl SE24 101 DP84
Cordelia Gdns, Stai. 114 BL87
Cordelia Rd, Stai. 114 BL87
Cordelia St E14 85 EB72
Cordell Cl (Cheshunt), Wal.Cr. 15 DY28
Corderoy Pl, Cher. 133 BE100
Cording St E14 85 EB71
Chrisp St
Cordingley Rd, Ruis. 59 BR61
Cordons Cl (Chalfont St. Peter), Ger.Cr. 36 AX53
Cordova Rd E3 85 DY69
Cordrey Gdns, Couls. 175 DL115
Cordwainers Wk E13 86 EG68
Clegg St
Cordwell Rd SE13 124 EE85
Corelli Rd SE3 104 EL82
Corfe Av, Har. 60 CA63
Corfe Cl, Ash. 171 CJ118
Corfe Cl, Hayes 78 BW72
Corfe Twr W3 98 CP75
Corfield Rd N21 29 DM43
Corfield St E2 84 DV69
Corfton Rd W5 80 CL72
Coriander Av E14 85 ED72
Cories Cl, Dag. 70 EX61
Corinium Cl, Wem. 62 CM63
Corinne Rd N19 65 DJ63
Corinthian Manorway, Erith 107 FD77
Corinthian Rd, Erith 107 FD77
Corinthian Way, Stai. 114 BK87
Clare Rd
Cork Sq E1 202 D2
Cork St W1 199 K1
Cork St W1 83 DJ73
Cork St Ms W1 199 K1
Cork Tree Way E4 47 DY50
Corker Wk N7 65 DM61
Corkran Rd, Surb. 137 CK101
Corkscrew Hill, W.Wick. 143 ED103
Corlett St NW1 194 B6
Corlett St NW1 82 DE71
Cormongers La, Red. 185 DK131
Cormont Rd SE5 101 DP81
Cormorant Cl E17 47 DX53
Banbury Rd
Cormorant Pl, Sutt. 139 CY103
Gander Grn La
Cormorant Rd E7 68 EF64
Cormorant Wk, Horn. 89 FH65
Heron Flight Av
Corn Mill Dr, Orp. 145 ET101
Corn Way E11 67 ED62
Cornbury Rd, Edg. 41 CK52
Cornelia Pl, Erith 107 FE79
Queen St
Cornelia St N7 83 DM65
Cornell Cl, Sid. 126 EY93
Cornell Way, Rom. 50 FA50
Corner, The, W.Byf. 152 BG113
Corner Fm Cl, Tad. 173 CW122
Corner Grn SE3 104 EG82
Corner Ho St WC2 199 P2
Corner Mead NW9 43 CT52
Cornerside, Ashf. 115 BQ94
Corney Reach Way W4 98 CS80
Corney Rd W4 98 CS79
Cornfield Cl, Uxb. 76 BK68
The Greenway
Cornfield Rd, Bushey 24 CB42
Cornflower La, Croy. 143 DX102
Cornflower Ter SE22 122 DV86
Cornflower Way, Rom. 52 FL53
Cornford Cl, Brom. 144 EG99
Cornford Gro SW12 121 DH89
Cornhill EC3 197 L9
Cornhill EC3 84 DR72
Cornhill Cl, Add. 134 BH103
Cornhill Dr, Enf. 31 DY37
Ordnance Rd
Cornish Ct N9 46 DV45
Cornish Gro SE20 122 DV94
Cornish Ho SE17 101 DP79
Otto St
Cornish Ho, Brent. 98 CM78
Green Dragon La
Cornmill, Wal.Abb. 15 EB33
Cornmill La SE13 103 EB83
Cornmill Ms, Wal.Abb. 15 EB33
Highbridge St
Cornmow Dr NW10 63 CT64
Cornshaw Rd, Dag. 70 EX60
Cornsland, Brwd. 54 FX48
Cornsland Ct, Brwd. 54 FW48
Cornthwaite Rd E5 66 DW62
Cornwall Av E2 84 DW69
Cornwall Av N3 44 DA52
Cornwall Av N22 45 DL53
Cornwall Av, Esher 155 CF108
The Causeway
Cornwall Av, Sthl. 78 BZ71
Cornwall Av, Well. 105 ES83
Cornwall Av, W.Byf. 152 BM114
Cornwall Cl, Bark. 87 ET65
Cornwall Cl, Horn. 72 FN56
Cornwall Cl, Wal.Cr. 15 DY33
Cornwall Cres W11 81 CY73
Cornwall Dr, Orp. 126 EW94
Cornwall Gdns NW10 81 CV65
Cornwall Gdns SW7 100 DC76
Cornwall Gdns Wk SW7 100 DB76
Cornwall Gdns
Cornwall Gate, Purf. 108 FN77
Fanns Ri
Cornwall Gro W4 98 CS78
Cornwall Ms S SW7 100 DC76
Cornwall Ms W SW7 100 DB76
Cornwall Gdns
Cornwall Rd N4 65 DN59
Cornwall Rd N15 66 DR57
Cornwall Rd N18 46 DU50
Fairfield Rd
Cornwall Rd SE1 200 D2
Cornwall Rd SE1 83 DN74
Cornwall Rd, Brwd. 54 FV43
Cornwall Rd, Croy. 141 DP103
Cornwall Rd, Dart. 108 FM83
Cornwall Rd, Esher 155 CG108
Cornwall Rd, Har. 60 CC58
Cornwall Rd, Pnr. 40 BZ52
Cornwall Rd, Ruis. 59 BT62
Cornwall Rd, Sutt. 157 CZ108
Cornwall Rd, Twick. 117 CG88
Cornwall Rd, Uxb. 76 BK65
Cornwall Rd, Wind. 112 AU86
Cornwall St E1 84 DV73
Watney St
Cornwall Ter NW1 194 E5
Cornwall Ter Ms NW1 194 E5
Cornwall Way, Stai. 113 BE93
Cornwallis Av N9 46 DV47
Cornwallis Av SE9 125 ER89
Cornwallis Cl, Erith 107 FF79
Cornwallis Gro N9 46 DV47
Cornwallis Rd E17 67 DX56
Cornwallis Rd N9 46 DV47
Cornwallis Rd N19 65 DL61
Cornwallis Rd, Dag. 70 EX63
Cornwallis Sq N19 65 DL61
Cornwallis Wk SE9 105 EM83
Cornwell Av, Grav. 131 GJ90
Cornwood Cl N2 64 DD57
Cornwood Dr E1 84 DW72
Cornworthy Rd, Dag. 70 EW64
Corona Rd SE12 124 EG87
Coronation Av N16 66 DT62
Victorian Rd
Coronation Av, Slou. 74 AY72
Coronation Av, Wind. 92 AT81
Coronation Cl, Bex. 126 EX86
Coronation Cl, Ilf. 69 EQ56
Coronation Dr, Horn. 71 FH63
Coronation Hill, Epp. 17 ET30
Coronation Rd E13 86 EJ69
Coronation Rd NW10 80 CM69
Coronation Rd, Hayes 95 BT77
Coronation Wk, Twick. 116 BZ88
Coronet St N1 197 M3
Coronet St N1 84 DS69
Corporation Av, Houns. 96 BY84
Corporation Row EC1 196 E4
Corporation Row EC1 83 DN70
Corporation St E15 86 EE68
Corporation St N7 65 DL64
Corran Way, S.Ock. 91 FV73
Corrance Rd SW2 101 DL84
Corri Av N14 45 DK49
Corrib Dr, Sutt. 158 DE106
Corrie Gdns, Vir.W. 132 AW101
Corrie Rd, Add. 152 BK105
Corrie Rd, Wok. 167 BC120
Corrigan Av, Couls. 158 DG114
Corringham Ct NW11 64 DB59
Corringham Rd
Corringham Rd NW11 64 DA59
Corringham Rd, Wem. 62 CN61
Corringway NW11 64 DB59
Corringway W5 80 CN70
Corsair Cl, Stai. 114 BK87
Corsair Rd, Stai. 114 BL87
Corscombe Cl, Kings.T. 118 CQ92
Corsehill St SW16 121 DJ93
Corsham St N1 197 L3
Corsham St N1 84 DR69
Corsica St N5 83 DP65
Corsley Way E9 85 DZ65
Osborne Rd
Cortayne Rd SW6 99 CZ82
Cortis Rd SW15 119 CV86
Cortis Ter SW15 119 CV86
Corunna Rd SW8 101 DJ81
Corunna Ter SW8 101 DJ81
Corve La, S.Ock. 91 FV73
Corvette Sq SE10 103 ED79
Feathers Pl
Corwell Gdns, Uxb. 77 BQ72
Corwell La, Uxb. 77 BQ72
Cory Dr, Brwd. 55 GB45
Coryton Path W9 81 CZ70
Ashmore Rd
Cosbycote Av SE24 122 DQ85
Cosdach Av, Wall. 159 DK108
Cosedge Cres, Croy. 159 DN106
Cosgrove Cl N21 46 DQ47
Cosgrove Cl, Hayes 78 BY70
Kingsash Dr
Cosmo Pl WC1 196 A6
Cosmur Cl W12 99 CT76
Cossall Wk SE15 102 DV81
Cosser St SE1 200 D6
Cosser St SE1 101 DN76
Costa St SE15 102 DU82
Costead Manor Rd, Brwd. 54 FV46
Costell's Meadow, West. 189 ER126
Coston Wk SE4 103 DX84
Frendsbury Rd
Costons Av, Grnf. 79 CD69
Costons La, Grnf. 79 CD69
Cosway St NW1 194 C6
Cosway St NW1 82 DE71
Cotall St E14 85 EA72
Coteford Cl, Loug. 33 EP40
Coteford Cl, Pnr. 59 BU57
Coteford St SW17 120 DF91
Cotelands, Croy. 142 DS104
Cotesbach Rd E5 66 DW62
Cotesmore Gdns, Dag. 70 EW63
Cotford Rd, Th.Hth. 142 DQ98
Cotham St SE17 201 J9
Cotherstone, Epsom 156 CR110
Cotherstone Rd SW2 121 DM88
Cotlandswick, St.Alb. 9 CJ26
Cotleigh Av, Bex. 126 EX89
Cotleigh Rd NW6 82 DA66
Cotleigh Rd, Rom. 71 FD58
Cotman Cl NW11 64 DC58
Cotman Cl SW15 119 CX86
Westleigh Av
Cotman Gdns, Edg. 42 CN54
Cotman Ms, Dag. 70 EW64
Highgrove Rd
Cotmandene Cres, Orp. 146 EU96
Cotmans Cl, Hayes 77 BU74
Coton Rd, Well. 106 EU83
Cotsford Av, N.Mal. 138 CQ99
Cotswold Av, Bushey 24 CC44
Cotswold Cl, Bexh. 107 FE82
Cotswold Cl, Esher 137 CF104
Cotswold Cl, Kings.T. 118 CP93
Cotswold Cl, Stai. 114 BG92
Cotswold Cl, Uxb. 76 BJ67
Cotswold Ct N11 44 DG49
Cotswold Gdns E6 86 EK69
Cotswold Gdns NW2 63 CX61
Cotswold Gdns, Brwd. 55 GE45
Cotswold Gdns, Ilf. 69 ER59
Cotswold Gate NW2 63 CY60
Cotswold Gdns
Cotswold Grn, Enf. 29 DM42
Cotswold Way
Cotswold Ms SW11 100 DD81
Battersea High St
Cotswold Ri, Orp. 145 ET100
Cotswold Rd, Grav. 130 GE90
Cotswold Rd, Hmptn. 116 CA93
Cotswold Rd, Rom. 52 FM54
Cotswold Rd, Sutt. 158 DB110
Cotswold St SE27 121 DP91
Norwood High St
Cotswold Way, Enf. 29 DM42
Cotswold Way, Wor.Pk. 139 CW103
Cottage Av, Brom. 144 EL102
Cottage Cl, Cher. 151 BC107
Cottage Cl, Rick. 22 BM44
Scots Hill
Cottage Cl, Ruis. 59 BR60
Cottage Cl, Wat. 23 BT40
Cottage Fm Way, Egh. 133 BC97
Green Rd
Cottage Fld Cl, Sid. 126 EW88
Cottage Gdns, Wal.Cr. 14 DW29
Cottage Grn SE5 102 DR80
Cottage Gro SW9 101 DL83
Cottage Gro, Surb. 137 CK100
Cottage Homes NW7 43 CU49
Cottage Pl SW3 198 B6
Cottage Pl SW3 100 DE76
Cottage Rd, Epsom 156 CR108
Cottage St E14 85 EB73
Cottage Wk N16 66 DT62
Smalley Cl
Cottage Wk SE15 102 DT80
Sumner Est
Cottenham Dr NW9 63 CT55
Cottenham Dr SW20 119 CV94
Cottenham Par SW20 139 CV96
Durham Rd
Cottenham Pk Rd SW20 119 CV94
Cottenham Pl SW20 119 CV94
Cottenham Rd E17 67 DZ56
Cotterill Rd, Surb. 138 CL103
Cottesbrook St SE14 103 DY80
Nynehead St
Cottesbrooke Cl, Slou. 93 BD81
Cottesloe Ms SE1 200 E6
Cottesmore Av, Ilf. 49 EN54
Cottesmore Gdns W8 100 DB76
Cottimore Av, Walt. 135 BV102
Cottimore Cres, Walt. 135 BV101
Cottimore La, Walt. 136 BW102
Cottimore Ter, Walt. 135 BV101
Cottingham Chase, Ruis. 59 BU62
Cottingham Rd SE20 123 DX94
Cottingham Rd SW8 101 DM80
Cottington Rd, Felt. 116 BX91
Cottington St SE11 200 E10
Cottle St SE16 202 F5
Cotton Av W3 80 CR72
Cotton Cl, Dag. 88 EW66
Ellerton Rd
Cotton Hill, Brom. 123 ED91
Cotton La, Dart. 128 FQ86
Cotton La, Green. 128 FQ85
Cotton Rd, Pot.B. 12 DC31
Cotton Row SW11 100 DC83
Cotton St E14 85 EC73
Cottongrass Cl, Croy. 143 DX102
Cornflower La
Cottons App, Rom. 71 FD57
Cottons Ct, Rom. 71 FD57
Cottons Gdns E2 197 N2
Cottons La SE1 201 L2
Cotts Cl W7 79 CF71
Westcott Cres
Couchmore Av, Esher 137 CE103
Couchmore Av, Ilf. 49 EM54
Coulgate St SE4 103 DY83
Coulsdon Common, Cat. 176 DQ121
Coulsdon Ct Rd, Couls. 175 DM116
Coulsdon La, Couls. 174 DF119
Coulsdon Pl, Cat. 176 DR122
Coulsdon Ri, Couls. 175 DL117
Coulsdon Rd, Cat. 176 DQ122
Coulsdon Rd, Couls. 175 DM115
Coulson Cl, Dag. 70 EW59
Coulson St SW3 198 D10
Coulson St SW3 100 DF77
Coulter Cl, Hayes 78 BY70
Coulter Cl (Cuffley), Pot.B. 13 DK27
Coulter Rd W6 99 CV76
Coulton Av, Grav. 130 GE87
Council Av, Grav. 130 GC86
Council Cotts, Wok. 168 BK115
Councillor St SE5 102 DQ80
Counter Ct SE1 84 DR74
Southwark St
Counter St SE1 201 M3
Countess Cl (Harefield), Uxb. 38 BJ54
Countess Rd NW5 65 DJ64
Countisbury Av, Enf. 46 DT45
Countisbury Gdns, Add. 152 BH106
Addlestone Pk
Country Way, Felt. 115 BV93
Country Way, Sun. 115 BV93
County Gdns, Bark. 87 ES68
River Rd
County Gate SE9 125 EQ90
County Gate, Barn. 28 DB44
County Gro SE5 102 DQ81
County Rd E6 87 EP71
County Rd, Th.Hth. 141 DP96
County St SE1 201 J7
County St SE1 102 DR76
Coupland Pl SE18 105 EQ78
Courage Cl, Horn. 72 FJ58
Courage Wk, Brwd. 55 GD44
Courcy Rd N8 65 DN55
Courier Rd, Dag. 89 FC70
Courland Gro SW8 101 DK81
Courland Rd, Add. 134 BH104
Courland St SW8 101 DK81
Course, The SE9 125 EN90
Coursers Rd, St.Alb. 10 CN27
Court, The, Ruis. 60 BY63
Court, The, Warl. 177 DY118
Court Av, Belv. 106 EZ78
Court Av, Couls. 175 DN118
Court Av, Rom. 52 FN52
Court Bushes Rd, Whyt. 176 DU120
Court Cl, Har. 62 CL55
Court Cl, Twick. 116 CB90
Court Cl, Wall. 159 DK108
Court Cl Av, Twick. 116 CB90
Court Cres, Chess. 155 CK106
Court Cres, Swan. 147 FE98
Court Downs Rd, Beck. 143 EB96
Court Dr, Croy. 159 DM105
Court Dr, Stan. 42 CL49
Court Dr, Sutt. 158 DE105
Court Dr, Uxb. 76 BM67
Court Fm Av, Epsom 156 CR106
Court Fm Rd SE9 124 EK89
Court Fm Rd, Nthlt. 78 CA66
Court Fm Rd, Warl. 176 DU118
Court Gdns N7 83 DN65
Court Grn Hts, Wok. 166 AW120
Court Haw, Bans. 174 DE115
Court Hill, Couls. 174 DE118
Court Hill, S.Croy. 160 DS112
Court Ho Gdns N3 44 DA51
Court La SE21 122 DS86
Court La, Epsom 156 CQ113
Court La, Iver 76 BG74
Court La Gdns SE21 122 DS87
Court Mead, Nthlt. 78 BZ69
Court Par, Wem. 61 CH62
Court Rd SE9 124 EL89
Court Rd SE25 142 DT96
Court Rd, Bans. 174 DA116
Court Rd, Cat. 176 DR123
Court Rd, Dart. 129 FS92
Court Rd, Gdse. 186 DW
Court Rd, Orp. 146 EV
Court Rd, Sthl. 96 BZ
Court Rd, Uxb. 59 BF
Court St E1 84 DV
Durward St
Court St, Brom. 144 EG
Court Way NW9 62 CS
Court Way W3 80 CC
Court Way, Ilf. 69 EC
Court Way, Rom. 52 FE
Court Way, Twick. 117 CF
Court Wd Dr, Sev. 190 FG1
Court Wd Gro, Croy. 161 DZ
Court Wd La, Croy. 161 DZ
Court Yd SE9 124 EL
Courtauld Cl SE28 88 EU
Pitfield Cres
Courtauld Rd N19 65 DK
Courtaulds, Kings L. 6 BH
Courtenay Av N6 64 DE
Courtenay Av, Har. 40 CC
Courtenay Av, Sutt. 158 DA
Courtenay Dr, Beck. 143 ED
Courtenay Dr, Grays 110 FZ
Clifford Rd
Courtenay Gdns, Har. 40 CC
Courtenay Gdns, Upmin. 72 FC
Courtenay Ms E17 67 DY
Cranbrook Ms
Courtenay Pl E17 67 DY
Courtenay Rd E11 68 EF
Courtenay Rd E17 67 DX
Courtenay Rd SE20 123 DX
Courtenay Rd, Wem. 61 CK
Courtenay Rd, Wok. 167 BA1
Courtenay Rd, Wor.Pk. 139 CW1
Courtenay Sq SE11 101 DN
Courtenay St
Courtenay St SE11 200 D
Courtenay St SE11 101 DN
Courtens Ms, Stan. 41 CJ
Courtfield W5 79 CJ
Castlebar Hill
Courtfield Av, Har. 61 CF
Courtfield Cres, Har. 61 CF
Courtfield Gdns SW5 100 DB
Courtfield Gdns W13 79 CG
Courtfield Gdns, Ruis. 59 BT
Courtfield Gdns (Denham), Uxb. 58 BG
Courtfield Ms SW5 100 DB
Courtfield Gdns
Courtfield Ri, W.Wick. 143 ED1
Courtfield Rd SW7 100 DB
Courtfield Rd, Ashf. 115 BP
Courthill Rd SE13 103 EC
Courthope Rd NW3 64 DF
Courthope Rd SW19 119 CY
Courthope Rd, Grnf. 79 CD
Courthope Vil SW19 119 CY
Courthouse Rd N12 44 DB
Courtland Av E4 48 EF
Courtland Av NW7 42 CR
Courtland Av SW16 121 DM
Courtland Av, Ilf. 69 EM
Courtland Dr, Chig. 49 EP
Courtland Gro SE28 88 EX
Courtland Rd E6 86 EL
Harrow Rd
Courtlands, Rich. 98 CN
Courtlands Av SE12 124 EH
Courtlands Av, Brom. 144 EF1
Courtlands Av, Esher 154 BZ1
Courtlands Av, Hmptn. 116 BZ
Courtlands Av, Rich. 98 CP
Courtlands Av, Slou. 92 AX
Courtlands Cl, Ruis. 59 BT
Courtlands Cl, S.Croy. 160 DT1
Courtlands Cl, Wat. 23 BS
Courtlands Cres, Bans. 174 DA1
Courtlands Dr, Epsom 156 CS1
Courtlands Dr, Wat. 23 BS
Courtlands Rd, Surb. 138 CN1
Courtleas, Cob. 154 CA1
Courtleet Dr, Erith 107 FB
Courtleigh Av, Barn. 28 DD
Courtleigh Gdns NW11 63 CY
Courtman Rd N17 46 DQ
Courtmead Cl SE24 122 DQ
Courtnell St W2 82 DA
Courtney Cl SE19 122 DS
Courtney Cres, Cars. 158 DF1
Courtney Pl, Cob. 154 BZ1
Courtney Pl, Croy. 141 DN1
Courtney Rd N7 65 DN
Bryantwood Rd
Courtney Rd SW19 120 DE
Courtney Rd, Croy. 141 DN1
Courtney Rd, Grays 111 GJ
Courtney Rd, Houns. 94 BN
Courtney Way, Houns. 94 BN
Courtrai Rd SE23 123 DY
Courtside N8 65 DK
Courtway, Wdf.Grn. 48 EJ
Courtway, The, Wat. 40 BY4
Courtyard, The N1 83 DM
Courtyards, The, Slou. 93 BA
Waterside Dr
Cousin La EC4 201 K
Cousins Cl, West Dr. 76 BL7
Couthurst Rd SE3 104 EH7
Coutts Av, Chess. 156 CL1
Coutts Cres NW5 64 DG
Coval Gdns SW14 98 CP
Coval La SW14 98 CP
Coval Rd SW14 98 CP
Coveham Cres, Cob. 153 BU1
Covelees Wall E6 87 EN7
Covell Ct SE8 103 EA8
Reginald Sq
Covenbrook, Brwd. 55 GB4
Covent Gdn WC2 196 A
Covent Gdn WC2 83 DL7
Coventry Cl E6 87 EM7
Harper Rd
Coventry Cl NW6 82 DA6
Kilburn High Rd
Coventry Cross E3 85 EC7
Gillender St
Coventry Rd E1 84 DV7
Coventry Rd E2 84 DV7

ventry Rd SE25 142 DU98
ventry Rd, Ilf. 69 EP60
ventry St W1 199 M1
ventry St W1 83 DK73
verack Cl N14 29 DJ44
verack Cl, Croy. 143 DY101
verdale Cl, Stan. 41 CH50
verdale Ct, Enf. 31 DY37
Raynton Rd
verdale Gdns, Croy. 142 DT104
Park Hill Ri
verdale Rd N11 44 DG51
verdale Rd NW2 81 CX66
verdale Rd W12 81 CV74
verdales, The, Bark. 87 ER68
verley Cl E1 84 DU71
verley Cl, Brwd. 53 FW51
Wilmot Grn
vert, The, Nthwd. 39 BQ53
vert, The, Orp. 145 ES100
vert Rd, Ilf. 49 ET51
vert Way, Barn. 28 DC40
verton Rd SW17 120 DE92
verts, The, Brwd. 55 GA46
verts Rd, Esher 155 CF109
vet Wd Cl, Orp. 145 ET100
Lockesley Dr
vey Cl SW19 140 DB96
vington Gdns SW16 121 DP94
vington Way SW16 121 DM93
w La, Grnf. 79 CD68
w La, Wat. 24 BW36
w Leaze E6 87 EN72
wan Cl E6 86 EL71
Oliver Gdns
wbridge La, Bark. 87 EP66
wbridge Rd, Har. 62 CM56
wcross St EC1 196 F6
wcross St EC1 83 DP71
wden Rd, Orp. 145 ET101
wden St SE6 123 EA91
wdenbeath Path N1 83 DM67
wdray Rd, Uxb. 77 BQ67
wdray Way, Horn. 71 FF63
wdrey Cl, Enf. 30 DS40
wdrey Ct, Dart. 127 FH87
wdrey Rd SW19 120 DB92
wdry Rd E9 85 DY65
Wick Rd
wen Av, Har. 60 CC61
wgate Rd, Grnf. 79 CD68
wick Rd SW17 120 DF91
wings Mead, Nthlt. 78 BY66
wland Av, Enf. 30 DW42
wleaze Rd, Kings.T. 138 CL95
wles (Cheshunt), Wal.Cr. 14 DT27
owley Av, Cher. 133 BF101
owley Av, Green. 129 FT85
owley Business Pk, Uxb. 76 BJ69
owley Cl, S.Croy. 160 DW109
owley Cres, Uxb. 76 BJ71
owley Cres, Walt. 154 BW105
owley Hill, Borwd. 26 CP37
owley La E11 68 EE62
Cathall Rd
owley La, Cher. 133 BF101
owley Mill Rd, Uxb. 76 BH68
owley Pl NW4 63 CW57
owley Rd E11 68 EH57
owley Rd SW9 101 DN81
owley Rd SW14 98 CS83
owley Rd W3 81 CT74
owley Rd, Ilf. 69 EM59
owley Rd, Rom. 51 FH52
owley Rd, Uxb. 76 BJ68
owley St SW1 199 P6
owling Cl W11 81 CY74
Wilsham St
Cowper Av E6 86 EL66
Cowper Av, Sutt. 158 DD105
Cowper Av, Til. 111 GH81
Cowper Cl, Brom. 144 EK98
Cowper Cl, Cher. 133 BF100
Cowper Cl, Well. 126 EU85
Cowper Ct, Wat. 23 BU37
Cowper Gdns N14 29 DJ44
Cowper Gdns, Wall. 159 DJ107
Cowper Rd N14 45 DH46
Cowper Rd N16 66 DS64
Cowper Rd N18 46 DU50
Cowper Rd SW19 120 DC93
Cowper Rd W3 80 CR74
Cowper Rd W7 79 CF73
Cowper Rd, Belv. 106 FA77
Cowper Rd, Brom. 144 EK98
Cowper Rd, Kings.T. 118 CM92
Cowper Rd, Rain. 89 FG70
Cowper St EC2 197 L4
Cowper St EC2 84 DR70
Cowper Ter W10 81 CX71
St. Marks Rd
Cowslip Cl, Uxb. 76 BL66
Cowslip La, Wok. 166 AV115
Cowslip Rd E18 48 EH54
Cowthorpe Rd SW8 101 DK81
Cox Cl, Rad. 10 CM32
Cox La, Chess. 156 CM105
Cox La, Epsom 156 CP106
Coxdean, Epsom 173 CW119
Coxe Pl, Har. 61 CG56
Coxley Ri, Pur. 160 DQ113
Coxmount Rd SE7 104 EK78
Cox's Wk SE21 122 DU88
Coxson Way SE1 201 P5
Coxwell Rd SE18 105 ER78
Coxwell Rd SE19 122 DS94
Coxwold Path, Chess. 156 CL108
Garrison La
Crab Hill, Beck. 123 ED94
Crab La, Wat. 24 CB35
Crabbs Cft Cl, Orp. 163 EQ106
Ladycroft Way
Crabtree Av, Rom. 70 EX56
Crabtree Av, Wem. 80 CL68
Crabtree Cl E2 197 P1
Crabtree Cl E2 84 DT68
Crabtree Cl, Bushey 24 CB43
Crabtree Ct E15 67 EB64
Clays La
Crabtree Dr, Lthd. 171 CJ124
Crabtree Hill, Rom. 50 EZ45
Crabtree La SW6 99 CX80
Crabtree Manorway N, Belv. 107 FC75
Crabtree Manorway S, Belv. 107 FC76
Crabtree Rd, Egh. 133 BC96
Crabtree Wk SE15 102 DT81
Lisford St
Crace St NW1 195 M2
Craddock Rd, Enf. 30 DT41
Craddock St NW5 82 DG65
Prince of Wales Rd
Craddocks Av, Ash. 172 CL117
Craddocks Par, Ash. 172 CL117
Cradley Rd SE9 125 ER88
Cragg Av, Rad. 25 CF36
Craig Dr, Uxb. 77 BP72
Craig Gdns E18 48 EF54
Craig Mt, Rad. 25 CH35
Craig Pk Rd N18 46 DV50
Craig Rd, Rich. 117 CJ91
Craigdale Rd, Horn. 71 FF58
Craigen Av, Croy. 142 DV102
Craigerne Rd SE3 104 EH80
Craigholm SE18 105 EN82
Craigmore Twr, Wok. 166 AY119
Guildford Rd
Craigmuir Pk, Wem. 80 CM67
Craignair Rd SW2 121 DN87
Craignish Av SW16 141 DM96
Craigs Ct SW1 199 P2
Craigs Wk (Cheshunt), Wal.Cr. 15 DX28
Davison Dr
Craigton Rd SE9 105 EM84
Craigweil Av, Rad. 25 CH35
Craigweil Cl, Stan. 41 CK50
Craigweil Dr, Stan. 41 CK50
Craigwell Av, Felt. 115 BU90
Craigwell Cl, Stai. 133 BE95
Craik Ct NW6 81 CZ68
Carlton Vale
Crail Row SE17 201 L9
Cramer St W1 194 G7
Crammerville Wk, Rain. 89 FH70
Cramond Cl W6 99 CY79
Cramond Ct, Felt. 115 BR88
Kilross Rd
Crampshaw La, Ash. 172 CM119
Crampton Rd SE20 122 DW93
Crampton St SE17 201 H9
Crampton St SE17 102 DQ77
Cramptons Rd, Sev. 181 FH120
Cranberry Cl, Nthlt. 78 BX68
Parkfield Av
Cranberry La E16 86 EE70
Cranborne Av, Sthl. 96 CA77
Cranborne Av, Surb. 138 CN104
Cranborne Cl, Pot.B. 11 CY31
Cranborne Cres, Pot.B. 11 CY31
Cranborne Gdns, Upmin. 72 FP61
Cranborne Ind Est, Pot.B. 11 CY30
Cranborne Rd, Bark. 87 ER67
Cranborne Rd, Pot.B. 11 CY30
Cranborne Rd (Cheshunt), Wal.Cr. 15 DX32
Cranborne Waye, Hayes 78 BW73
Cranbourn All WC2 195 N10
Cranbourn Pas SE16 102 DV75
Marigold St
Cranbourn St WC2 195 N10
Cranbourn St WC2 83 DK73
Cranbourne Av E11 68 EH56
Cranbourne Cl SW16 141 DL97
Cranbourne Dr, Pnr. 60 BX57
Cranbourne Gdns NW11 63 CY57
Cranbourne Gdns, Ilf. 69 EQ55
Cranbourne Rd E12 68 EL64
High St N
Cranbourne Rd E15 67 EC63
Cranbourne Rd N10 45 DH54
Cranbourne Rd, Nthwd. 59 BT55
Cranbrook Cl, Brom. 144 EG100
Cranbrook Dr, Esher 136 CC102
Cranbrook Dr, Rom. 71 FH56
Cranbrook Dr, Twick. 116 CB88
Cranbrook Ms E17 67 DZ57
Cranbrook Pk N22 45 DM53
Cranbrook Ri, Ilf. 69 EM59
Cranbrook Rd SE8 103 EA81
Cranbrook Rd SW19 119 CY94
Cranbrook Rd W4 98 CS78
Cranbrook Rd, Barn. 28 DD44
Cranbrook Rd, Bexh. 106 EZ81
Cranbrook Rd, Houns. 96 BZ84
Cranbrook Rd, Ilf. 69 EN60
Cranbrook Rd, Th.Hth. 142 DQ96
Cranbrook St E2 85 DX68
Mace St
Cranbury Rd SW6 100 DB82
Crane Av W3 80 CQ73
Crane Av, Islw. 117 CG85
Crane Cl, Dag. 88 FA65
Crane Cl, Har. 60 CC62
Crane Ct EC4 196 E9
Crane Ct, Epsom 156 CQ105
Crane Gdns, Hayes 95 BT77
Crane Gro N7 83 DN65
Crane Lo Rd, Houns. 95 BV79
Crane Mead SE16 203 H9
Crane Mead SE16 103 DX77
Crane Pk Rd, Twick. 116 CB89
Crane Rd, Twick. 117 CE88
Crane St SE10 103 ED78
Crane St SE15 102 DT81
Crane Way, Twick. 116 CC87
Cranebrook, Twick. 116 CC89
Manor Rd
Cranefield Dr, Wat. 8 BY32
Craneford Cl, Twick. 117 CF87
Craneford Way, Twick. 117 CE87
Cranell Grn, S.Ock. 91 FV74
Cranes Dr, Surb. 138 CL98
Cranes Pk, Surb. 138 CL98
Cranes Pk Av, Surb. 138 CL98
Cranes Pk Cres, Surb. 138 CM98
Cranes Way, Borwd. 26 CQ43
Cranesbill Cl NW9 62 CR55
Colindale Av
Craneswater, Hayes 95 BT80
Craneswater Pk, Sthl. 96 BZ78
Cranfield Cl SE27 122 DQ90
Dunelm Gro
Cranfield Ct, Wok. 166 AU118
Martindale Rd
Cranfield Cres (Cuffley), Pot.B. 13 DL29
Cranfield Dr NW9 42 CS52
Cranfield Rd SE4 103 DZ83
Cranfield Rd E, Cars. 158 DG109
Cranfield Rd W, Cars. 158 DF109
Cranfield Row SE1 200 E6
Cranford Av N13 45 DL50
Cranford Av, Stai. 114 BL87
Cranford Cl SW20 139 CV95
Cranford Cl, Pur. 160 DQ113
Cranford Cl, Stai. 114 BL87
Canopus Way
Cranford Cotts E1 85 DX73
Cranford St
Cranford Dr, Hayes 95 BT77
Cranford La, Hayes 95 BR79
Cranford La (Cranford), Houns. 95 BT81
Cranford La (Hatton Cross), Houns. 95 BT83
Cranford La (Heston), Houns. 96 BX80
Cranford Pk Rd, Hayes 95 BT77
Cranford Ri, Esher 154 CC106
Cranford Rd, Dart. 128 FL88
Cranford St E1 85 DX73
Cranford Way N8 65 DM57
Cranham Gdns, Upmin. 73 FS60
Cranham Rd, Horn. 71 FH58
Cranhurst Rd NW2 63 CW64
Cranleigh Cl SE20 142 DV96
Cranleigh Cl, Bex. 127 FB86
Cranleigh Cl, Orp. 146 EU104
Cranleigh Cl, S.Croy. 160 DU112
Cranleigh Cl (Cheshunt), Wal.Cr. 14 DU28
Cranleigh Dr, Swan. 147 FE98
Cranleigh Gdns N21 29 DN43
Cranleigh Gdns SE25 142 DS97
Cranleigh Gdns, Bark. 87 ER66
Cranleigh Gdns, Har. 62 CL57
Cranleigh Gdns, Kings.T. 118 CM93
Cranleigh Gdns, Loug. 33 EM44
Cranleigh Gdns, S.Croy. 160 DU112
Cranleigh Gdns, Sthl. 78 BZ72
Cranleigh Gdns, Sutt. 140 DB103
Cranleigh Gdns Ind Est, Sthl. 78 BZ72
Cranleigh Ms SW11 100 DE82
Cranleigh Rd N15 66 DQ57
Cranleigh Rd SW19 140 DA97
Cranleigh Rd, Esher 136 CC102
Cranleigh Rd, Felt. 115 BT91
Cranleigh St NW1 195 L1
Cranleigh St NW1 83 DJ68
Cranley Dene Ct N10 65 DH56
Cranley Dr, Ilf. 69 EQ59
Cranley Dr, Ruis. 59 BT61
Cranley Gdns N10 65 DJ56
Cranley Gdns N13 45 DM48
Cranley Gdns SW7 100 DC78
Cranley Gdns, Wall. 159 DJ108
Cranley Ms SW7 100 DC78
Cranley Par SE9 124 EL91
Beaconsfield Rd
Cranley Pl SW7 100 DD77
Cranley Rd E13 86 EH71
Cranley Rd, Ilf. 69 EQ58
Cranley Rd, Walt. 153 BS106
Cranmer Av W13 97 CH76
Cranmer Cl, Mord. 139 CX100
Cranmer Cl, Pot.B. 12 DB30
Cranmer Cl, Ruis. 60 BX60
Cranmer Cl, Stan. 41 CJ52
Cranmer Cl, Warl. 177 DY117
Cranmer Cl, Wey. 152 BN108
Cranmer Ct SW3 198 C9
Cranmer Ct SW4 101 DK83
Cranmer Ct, Hmptn. 116 CB92
Cranmer Rd
Cranmer Fm Cl, Mitch. 140 DF98
Cranmer Gdns, Dag. 71 FC63
Cranmer Gdns, Warl. 177 DY117
Cranmer Rd E7 68 EH63
Cranmer Rd SW9 101 DN80
Cranmer Rd, Croy. 141 DP104
Cranmer Rd, Edg. 42 CP48
Cranmer Rd, Hmptn. 116 CB92
Cranmer Rd, Hayes 77 BR72
Cranmer Rd, Kings.T. 118 CL92
Cranmer Rd, Mitch. 140 DF98
Cranmer Rd, Sev. 190 FE123
Cranmer Ter SW17 120 DD92
Cranmore Av, Islw. 96 CC80
Cranmore Rd, Brom. 124 EE90
Cranmore Rd, Chis. 125 EM92
Cranmore Way N10 65 DJ56
Cranston Cl, Houns. 96 BY82
Cranston Cl, Uxb. 59 BR61
Cranston Est N1 197 L1
Cranston Est N1 84 DR68
Cranston Gdns E4 47 EB50
Cranston Pk Av, Upmin. 72 FQ63
Cranston Rd SE23 123 DY88
Cranswick Rd SE16 202 E10
Cranswick Rd SE16 102 DV78
Crantock Rd SE6 123 EB89
Cranwell Cl E3 85 EB70
Cranwell Gro, Shep. 134 BM98
Cranwell Rd, Houns. 95 BP82
Cranwich Av N21 46 DR45
Cranwich Rd N16 66 DR59
Cranwood St EC1 197 K3
Cranwood St EC1 84 DR69
Cranworth Cres E4 47 ED46
Cranworth Gdns SW9 101 DN81
Craster Rd SW2 121 DM87
Crathie Rd SE12 124 EH86
Cravan Av, Felt. 115 BU89
Craven Av W5 79 CJ73
Craven Av, Sthl. 78 BZ71
Craven Cl, Hayes 77 BU72
Craven Gdns SW19 120 DA92
Craven Gdns, Bark. 87 ES68
Craven Gdns, Ilf. 49 ER54
Craven Gdns (Collier Row), Rom. 50 FA50
Craven Gdns (Harold Wd), Rom. 52 FQ51
Craven Hill W2 82 DC73
Craven Hill Gdns W2 82 DC73
Craven Hill Ms W2 82 DC73
Craven Ms SW11 100 DG83
Taybridge Rd
Craven Pk NW10 80 CS67
Craven Pk Ms NW10 80 CS67
Craven Pk Rd N15 66 DT58
Craven Pk Rd NW10 80 CS67
Craven Pas WC2 199 P2
Craven Pas WC2 83 DL74
Craven Rd NW10 80 CR67
Craven Rd W2 82 DC73
Craven Rd W5 79 CJ73
Craven Rd, Croy. 142 DV102
Craven Rd, Kings.T. 138 CM95
Craven Rd, Orp. 146 EX104
Craven St WC2 199 P2
Craven St WC2 83 DL74
Craven Ter W2 82 DC73
Craven Wk N16 66 DU59
Crawford Av, Wem. 61 CK64
Crawford Cl, Islw. 97 CE82
Crawford Compton Cl, Horn. 90 FJ65
Crawford Est SE5 102 DQ82
Crawford Gdns N13 45 DP48
Crawford Gdns, Nthlt. 78 BZ69
Crawford Ms W1 194 D7
Crawford Pas EC1 196 D5
Crawford Pl W1 194 C8
Crawford Pl W1 82 DE72
Crawford Rd SE5 102 DQ81
Crawford St W1 194 D7
Crawford St W1 82 DF71
Crawfords, Swan. 127 FE94
Crawley Rd E10 67 EB60
Crawley Rd N22 46 DQ54
Crawley Rd, Enf. 46 DS45
Crawshaw Rd, Cher. 151 BD107
Crawshay Cl, Sev. 190 FG123
Crawshay Ct SW9 101 DN81
Eythorne Rd
Crawthew Gro SE22 102 DT84
Cray Av, Ash. 172 CL116
Cray Av, Orp. 146 EV99
Cray Cl, Dart. 107 FG84
Cray Riverway, Dart. 127 FG85
Cray Rd, Belv. 106 FA79
Cray Rd, Sid. 126 EW94
Cray Rd, Swan. 147 FB100
Cray Valley Rd, Orp. 146 EU99
Craybrooke Rd, Sid. 126 EV91
Crayburne, Grav. 130 FZ92
Craybury End SE9 125 EQ89
Craydene Rd, Erith 107 FF81
Crayfield Ind Pk, Orp. 146 EW96
Crayford Cl E6 86 EL71
Neatscourt Rd
Crayford High St, Dart. 107 FE84
Crayford Rd N7 65 DK63
Crayford Rd, Dart. 127 FF85
Crayford Way, Dart. 127 FF85
Crayke Hill, Chess. 156 CL108
Craylands, Orp. 146 EW97
Craylands La, Swans. 129 FX85
Craylands Sq, Swans. 129 FX85
Craymill Sq, Dart. 107 FF82
Crayonne Cl, Sun. 135 BS95
Crayside Ind Est, Dart. 107 FH84
Thames Rd
Crealock Gro, Wdf.Grn. 48 EF50
Crealock St SW18 120 DB86
Creasey Cl, Horn. 71 FH61
St. Leonards Way
Creasy Cl, Abb.L. 7 BT31
Creasy Est SE1 201 M7
Creasy Est SE1 102 DS76
Crebor St SE22 122 DU86
Credenhall Dr, Brom. 145 EM102
Credenhill St SW16 121 DJ93
Crediton Hill NW6 64 DB64
Crediton Rd E16 86 EG72
Pacific Rd
Crediton Rd NW10 81 CX67
Crediton Way, Esher 155 CG106
Credo Way, Grays 109 FV79
Credon Rd E13 86 EJ68
Credon Rd SE16 202 E10
Credon Rd SE16 102 DV78
Cree Way, Rom. 51 FE52
Creechurch La EC3 197 N9
Creechurch La EC3 84 DS72
Creechurch Pl EC3 197 N9
Creed Ct EC4 83 DP72
Ludgate Hill
Creed La EC4 196 G9
Creek, The, Grav. 130 GB85
Creek, The, Sun. 135 BU99
Creek Rd SE8 103 EA79
Creek Rd SE10 103 EA79
Creek Rd, Bark. 87 ET69
Creek Rd, E.Mol. 137 CE98
Creekside SE8 103 EB80
Creekside, Rain. 89 FE70
Creeland Gro SE6 123 DZ88
Catford Hill
Crefeld Cl W6 99 CX79
Creffield Rd W3 80 CM73
Creffield Rd W5 80 CM73
Creighton Av E6 86 EK68
Creighton Av N2 64 DE55
Creighton Av N10 64 DE55
Creighton Cl W12 81 CV73
Bloemfontein Rd
Creighton Rd N17 46 DS52
Creighton Rd NW6 81 CX68
Creighton Rd W5 97 CK76
Cremer St E2 197 P1
Cremer St E2 84 DT68
Cremorne Est SW10 100 DD79
Milman's St
Cremorne Gdns, Epsom 156 CR109
Cremorne Rd SW10 100 DC80
Cremorne Rd, Grav. 131 GF87
Crescent EC3 197 P10
Crescent, The E17 67 DY57
Crescent, The N11 44 DF49
Crescent, The NW2 63 CV62
Crescent, The SW13 99 CT82
Crescent, The SW19 120 DA90
Crescent, The W3 80 CS72
Crescent, The, Abb.L. 7 BT30
Crescent, The, Ashf. 114 BM92
Crescent, The, Barn. 28 DB41
Crescent, The, Beck. 143 EA95
Crescent, The, Bex. 126 EW87
Crescent, The, Cat. 177 EA123
Crescent, The, Cher. 134 BG97
Western Av
Crescent, The, Croy. 142 DR99
Crescent, The, Egh. 112 AY93
Crescent, The, Epp. 17 ET32
Crescent, The, Epsom 156 CN114
Crescent, The, Grav. 131 GF89
Crescent, The, Green. 129 FW85
Crescent, The, Har. 61 CD60
Crescent, The, Hayes 95 BQ80
Crescent, The, Ilf. 69 EN58
Crescent, The, Lthd. 171 CH122
Crescent, The, Loug. 32 EK43
Crescent, The, N.Mal. 138 CQ96
Crescent, The, Reig. 184 DB134
Chartway
Crescent, The, Rick. 23 BP44
Crescent, The, St.Alb. 8 CA30
Crescent, The, Sev. 191 FK121
Crescent, The, Shep. 135 BT101
Crescent, The, Sid. 125 ET91
Crescent, The, Slou. 92 AS75
Crescent, The, Sthl. 96 BZ75
Crescent, The, Surb. 138 CL99
Crescent, The, Sutt. 158 DD105
Crescent, The (Belmont), Sutt. 158 DA111
Crescent, The, Upmin. 73 FS59
Crescent, The, Wat. 24 BW42
Crescent, The (Aldenham), Wat. 24 CB37
Crescent, The, Wem. 61 CH61
Crescent, The, W.Mol. 136 CA98
Crescent, The, W.Wick. 144 EE100
Crescent, The, Wey. 134 BN104
Crescent Av, Grays 110 GD78
Crescent Av, Horn. 71 FF61
Crescent Cotts, Sev. 181 FE120
Crescent Ct, Surb. 137 CK99
Crescent Dr, Brwd. 54 FY46
Crescent Dr, Orp. 145 EP100
Crescent E, Barn. 28 DC38
Crescent Gdns SW19 120 DA90
Crescent Gdns, Ruis. 59 BV58
Crescent Gdns, Swan. 147 FC96
Crescent Gro SW4 101 DJ84
Crescent Gro, Mitch. 140 DE98
Crescent La SW4 121 DK85
Crescent Ms N22 45 DL53
Palace Gates Rd
Crescent Pl SW3 198 B8
Crescent Pl SW3 100 DE77
Crescent Ri N22 45 DK53
Crescent Ri, Barn. 28 DE43
Crescent Rd E4 48 EE45
Crescent Rd E6 86 EJ67
Crescent Rd E10 67 EB61
Crescent Rd E13 86 EG67
Crescent Rd E18 48 EJ54
Crescent Rd N3 43 CZ53
Crescent Rd N8 65 DK59
Crescent Rd N9 46 DU46
Crescent Rd N11 44 DF49
Crescent Rd N15 65 DP55
Carlingford Rd
Crescent Rd N22 45 DK53
Crescent Rd SE18 105 EP78
Crescent Rd SW20 139 CX95
Crescent Rd, Barn. 28 DE43
Crescent Rd, Beck. 143 EB96
Crescent Rd, Brwd. 54 FV49
Crescent Rd, Brom. 124 EG94
Crescent Rd, Cat. 176 DU124
Crescent Rd, Dag. 71 FB63
Crescent Rd, Enf. 29 DP41
Crescent Rd, Erith 107 FF79
Crescent Rd, Kings.T. 118 CN94
Crescent Rd, Red. 186 DQ133
Crescent Rd, Shep. 135 BQ99
Crescent Rd, Sid. 125 ET90
Crescent Rd, S.Ock. 108 FQ75
Crescent Row EC1 197 H5
Crescent Stables SW15 99 CY84
Upper Richmond Rd
Crescent St N1 83 DM66
Crescent Vw, Loug. 32 EK44
Crescent Wk, S.Ock. 108 FQ75
Crescent Way N12 44 DE51
Crescent Way SE4 103 EA83
Crescent Way SW16 121 DM94
Crescent Way, Orp. 163 ES106
Crescent Way, S.Ock. 91 FR74
Crescent W, Barn. 28 DC38
Crescent Wd Rd SE26 122 DU90
Cresford Rd SW6 100 DB81
Crespigny Rd NW4 63 CV58
Cress End, Rick. 38 BG46
Springwell Av
Cressage Cl, Sthl. 78 CA70
Cressall Cl, Lthd. 171 CH120
Cressall Mead, Lthd. 171 CH120
Cresset Rd E9 84 DW65
Cresset St SW4 101 DK83
Cressfield Cl NW5 64 DG64
Cressida Rd N19 65 DJ60
Cressingham Gro, Sutt. 158 DC105
Cressingham Rd SE13 103 EC83
Cressingham Rd, Edg. 42 CR51
Cressington Cl N16 66 DS64
Wordsworth Rd
Cresswell Gdns SW5 100 DC78
Cresswell Pk SE3 104 EF83
Cresswell Pl SW10 100 DC78
Cresswell Rd SE25 142 DU98
Cresswell Rd, Felt. 116 BY91
Cresswell Rd, Twick. 117 CK86
Cresswell Way N21 45 DN45
Cressy Ct E1 84 DW71
Cressy Pl
Cressy Ct W6 99 CV76
Cressy Pl E1 84 DW71
Cressy Rd NW3 64 DF63
Crest, The N13 45 DN49

Crest, The NW4 63 CW57
Crest, The, Surb. 138 CN99
Crest, The (Cheshunt), Wal.Cr. 13 DP27
Orchard Way
Crest Av, Grays 110 GB80
Crest Cl, Sev. 165 FB111
Crest Dr, Enf. 30 DW38
Crest Gdns, Ruis. 60 BW62
Crest Rd NW2 63 CT62
Crest Rd, Brom. 144 EF101
Crest Rd, S.Croy. 160 DV108
Crest Vw, Green. 109 FU84
Woodland Way
Crest Vw, Pnr. 60 BX56
Crest Vw Dr, Orp. 145 EP99
Cresta Dr, Add. 151 BF110
Crestbrook Av N13 45 DP48
Crestbrook Pl N13 45 DP48
Crestfield St WC1 196 A2
Crestfield St WC1 83 DL69
Cresthill Av, Grays 110 GC77
Creston Av, Wok. 166 AS116
Creston Way, Wor.Pk. 139 CX102
Crestway SW15 119 CV86
Crestwood Way, Houns. 116 BZ85
Creswick Rd W3 80 CP73
Creswick Wk E3 85 EA69
Malmesbury Rd
Creswick Wk NW11 63 CZ56
Crete Hall Rd, Grav. 130 GD86
Creton St SE18 105 EN76
Crewdson Rd SW9 101 DN80
Crewe Pl NW10 81 CT69
Crewe's Av, Warl. 176 DW116
Crewe's Cl, Warl. 176 DW116
Crewe's Fm La, Warl. 177 DX116
Crewe's La, Warl. 177 DX116
Crews St E14 203 P8
Crews St E14 103 EA77
Crewys Rd NW2 63 CZ61
Crewys Rd SE15 102 DV82
Crichton Av, Wall. 159 DK106
Crichton Rd, Cars. 158 DF107
Cricket Fld Rd, Uxb. 76 BK67
Cricket Grn, Mitch. 140 DF97
Cricket Grd Rd, Chis. 145 EP95
Cricket La, Beck. 123 DY93
Cricket Way, Wey. 135 BS103
Cricketers Arms Rd, Enf. 30 DQ40
Cricketers Cl N14 45 DJ45
Cricketers Cl, Chess. 155 CK105
Cricketers Cl, Erith 107 FE78
Cricketers Ct SE11 200 F9
Cricketers Ct SE11 101 DP77
Cricketers Ms SW18 120 DB85
East Hill
Cricketers Ter, Cars. 140 DE104
Wrythe La
Cricketfield Rd E5 66 DV63
Cricketfield Rd, West Dr. 94 BJ77
Cricklade Av SW2 121 DL89
Cricklade Av, Rom. 52 FK51
Cricklewood Bdy NW2 63 CX63
Cricklewood La NW2 63 CX63
Cricklewood Trd Est NW2 63 CY62
Cridland St E15 86 EF67
Church St
Crieff Ct, Tedd. 117 CJ94
Crieff Rd SW18 120 DC86
Criffel Av SW2 121 DK89
Crimp Hill Rd, Egh. 112 AU90
Crimp Hill Rd, Wind. 112 AT87
Crimscott St SE1 201 N7
Crimscott St SE1 102 DS76
Crimsworth Rd SW8 101 DK81
Crinan St N1 83 DL68
Cringle St SW8 101 DJ80
Cripplegate St EC2 197 H6
Cripps Grn, Hayes 77 BV70
Stratford Rd
Crisp Rd W6 99 CW78
Crispe Ho, Bark. 87 ER68
Dovehouse Mead
Crispen Rd, Felt. 116 BY91
Crispian Cl NW10 62 CS63
Crispin Cl, Ash. 172 CM118
Crispin Cl, Croy. 141 DL103
Harrington Cl
Crispin Cres, Croy. 141 DK104
Crispin Rd, Edg. 42 CQ51
Crispin St E1 197 P7
Crispin St E1 84 DT71
Criss Cres, Ger.Cr. 36 AW54
Criss Gro (Chalfont St. Peter), Ger.Cr. 36 AW54
Cristowe Rd SW6 99 CZ82
Criterion Ms N19 65 DK61
Crittall's Cor, Sid. 126 EW94
Sidcup Bypass
Crockenhall Way, Grav. 130 GE94
Crockenhill La, Dart. 148 FJ102
Crockenhill La, Swan. 147 FG101
Crockenhill Rd, Orp. 146 EX99
Crockenhill Rd, Swan. 146 EZ100
Crockerton Rd SW17 120 DF89
Crockford Cl, Add. 152 BJ105
Crockford Pk Rd, Add. 152 BJ106
Crockham Way SE9 125 EN91
Crocus Cl, Croy. 143 DX102
Cornflower La
Crocus Fld, Barn. 27 CZ44
Croffets, Tad. 173 CX121
Croft, The E4 48 EE47
Croft, The NW10 81 CT68
Croft, The W5 80 CL71
Croft, The, Barn. 27 CX42
Croft, The, Houns. 96 BY79
Croft, The, Loug. 33 EN40
Croft, The, Pnr. 60 BZ59
Rayners La
Croft, The, Ruis. 60 BW63
Croft, The, St.Alb. 8 CA25
Croft, The, Swan. 147 FC97
Croft, The, Wem. 61 CJ64
Croft Av, W.Wick. 143 EC102
Croft Cl NW7 42 CS48
Croft Cl, Belv. 106 EZ78
Croft Cl, Chis. 125 EM91
Croft Cl, Hayes 95 BQ80
Croft Cl, Kings L. 6 BG30
Croft Cl, Uxb. 76 BN66
Croft End Cl, Chess. 138 CM104
Ashcroft Rd
Croft End Rd, Kings L. 6 BG30
Croft Fld, Kings L. 6 BG30
Croft Gdns W7 97 CG75
Croft Gdns, Ruis. 59 BT60
Croft La, Kings L. 6 BG30
Croft Lo Cl, Wdf.Grn. 48 EH51
Croft Meadow, Kings L. 6 BG30
Croft Ms N12 44 DC48
Croft Rd SW16 141 DN95
Croft Rd SW19 120 DC94
Croft Rd, Brom. 124 EG93
Croft Rd, Cat. 177 DZ122
Croft Rd, Enf. 31 DY39
Croft Rd (Chalfont St. Peter), Ger.Cr. 36 AY54
Croft Rd, Sutt. 158 DE106
Croft Rd, West. 189 EP126
Croft St SE8 203 K9
Croft St SE8 103 DY77
Croft Way, Sev. 190 FF125
Croft Way, Sid. 125 ES90
Croftdown Rd NW5 64 DG62
Crofters, The, Wind. 112 AU86
Crofters Cl, Islw. 117 CD85
Ploughmans End
Crofters Ct SE8 103 DY77
Croft St
Crofters Mead, Croy. 161 DZ109
Crofters Rd, Nthwd. 39 BS49
Crofters Way NW1 83 DK67
Croftleigh Av, Pur. 175 DN116
Crofton, Ash. 172 CL118
Crofton Av W4 98 CR80
Crofton Av, Bex. 126 EX87
Crofton Av, Orp. 145 EQ103
Crofton Av, Walt. 136 BW104
Crofton Cl, Cher. 151 BC108
Crofton Gro E4 47 ED49
Crofton La, Orp. 145 ES101
Crofton Pk Rd SE4 123 DZ86
Crofton Rd E13 86 EH70
Crofton Rd SE5 102 DS81
Crofton Rd, Grays 110 GE76
Crofton Rd, Orp. 145 EN104
Crofton Ter E5 67 DY64
Studley Cl
Crofton Ter, Rich. 98 CM84
Crofton Way, Barn. 28 DB44
Wycherley Cres
Crofton Way, Enf. 29 DN40
Croftongate Way SE4 123 DY85
Crofts, The, Shep. 135 BS98
Crofts La N22 45 DN52
Glendale Av
Crofts Rd, Har. 61 CG58
Crofts St E1 202 B1
Crofts St E1 84 DU73
Croftside SE25 142 DU97
Sunny Bk
Croftway NW3 64 DA63
Croftway, Rich. 117 CH90
Crogsland Rd NW1 82 DG66
Croham Cl, S.Croy. 160 DS107
Croham Manor Rd, S.Croy. 160 DS108
Croham Mt, S.Croy. 160 DS108
Croham Pk Av, S.Croy. 160 DT106
Croham Rd, S.Croy. 160 DS106
Croham Valley Rd, S.Croy. 160 DT107
Croindene Rd SW16 141 DL95
Cromartie Rd N19 65 DK59
Cromarty Rd, Edg. 42 CP47
Crombie Cl, Ilf. 69 EM57
Crombie Rd, Sid. 125 ER88
Cromer Cl, Uxb. 77 BQ72
Dawley Av
Cromer Pl, Orp. 145 ER102
Andover Rd
Cromer Rd E10 67 ED58
James La
Cromer Rd N17 46 DU54
Cromer Rd SE25 142 DV97
Cromer Rd SW17 120 DG93
Cromer Rd, Barn. 28 DC42
Cromer Rd, Horn. 72 FK59
Cromer Rd, Houns. 94 BN83
Cromer Rd, Rom. 71 FC58
Cromer Rd (Chadwell Heath), Rom. 70 EY58
Cromer Rd, Wat. 24 BW38
Cromer Rd, Wdf.Grn. 48 EG49
Cromer Rd W, Houns. 94 BN83
Cromer St WC1 196 A3
Cromer St WC1 83 DL69
Cromer Ter E8 66 DU64
Ferncliff Rd
Cromer Vil Rd SW18 119 CZ86
Cromford Cl, Orp. 145 ES104
Cromford Path E5 67 DX63
Overbury St
Cromford Rd SW18 120 DA85
Cromford Way, N.Mal. 138 CR95
Cromlix Cl, Chis. 145 EP96
Crompton St W2 82 DD70
Cromwell Av N6 65 DH60
Cromwell Av W6 99 CV78
Cromwell Av, Brom. 144 EH98
Cromwell Av, N.Mal. 139 CT99
Cromwell Av (Cheshunt), Wal.Cr. 14 DU30
Cromwell Cl E1 84 DU74
Vaughan Way
Cromwell Cl N2 64 DD56
Cromwell Cl W3 80 CQ74
High St
Cromwell Cl, Brom. 144 EH98
Cromwell Cl, Ch.St.G. 36 AW48
Cromwell Cl, Walt. 135 BV102
Cromwell Cres SW5 100 DA77
Cromwell Dr, Slou. 74 AS72
Cromwell Gdns SW7 198 A7
Cromwell Gdns SW7 100 DD76
Cromwell Gro W6 99 CW76
Cromwell Gro, Cat. 176 DQ121
Cromwell Ind Est E10 67 DY60
Cromwell Ms SW7 198 A8
Cromwell Ms SW7 100 DD77
Cromwell Pl N6 65 DH60
Cromwell Pl SW7 198 A8
Cromwell Pl SW7 100 DD77
Cromwell Pl SW14 98 CQ83
Cromwell Pl W3 80 CQ74
Grove Pl
Cromwell Rd E7 86 EJ66
Cromwell Rd E17 67 EC57
Cromwell Rd N3 44 DC53
Cromwell Rd N10 44 DG52
Cromwell Rd SW5 100 DB77
Cromwell Rd SW7 100 DB77
Cromwell Rd SW9 101 DP81
Cromwell Rd SW19 120 DA92
Cromwell Rd, Beck. 143 DY96
Cromwell Rd, Borwd. 26 CL39
Cromwell Rd, Brwd. 54 FV49
Cromwell Rd, Cat. 176 DQ121
Cromwell Rd, Croy. 142 DR101
Cromwell Rd, Felt. 115 BV88
Cromwell Rd, Grays 110 GA77
Cromwell Rd, Hayes 77 BR72
Cromwell Rd, Houns. 96 CA84
Cromwell Rd, Kings.T. 138 CL95
Cromwell Rd, Red. 184 DF133
Cromwell Rd, Tedd. 117 CG93
Cromwell Rd (Cheshunt), Wal.Cr. 14 DV28
Cromwell Rd, Walt. 135 BV102
Cromwell Rd, Wem. 80 CL68
Cromwell Rd, Wor.Pk. 138 CR104
Cromwell St, Houns. 96 CA84
Cromwell Twr EC2 197 J6
Cromwell Wk, Red. 184 DF134
Cromwells Mere, Rom. 51 FD51
Havering Rd
Crondace Rd SW6 100 DA81
Crondall St N1 197 L1
Crondall St N1 84 DR68
Cronin St SE15 102 DT80
Crook Log, Bexh. 106 EX83
Crooke Rd SE8 203 K10
Crooke Rd SE8 103 DY78
Crooked Billet SW19 119 CW93
Woodhayes Rd
Crooked Billet Roundabout E17 47 EA52
Crooked Billet Roundabout, Stai. 114 BG91
Crooked Billet Yd E2 84 DS69
Kingsland Rd
Crooked La, Grav. 131 GH86
Crooked Mile, Wal.Abb. 15 EC33
Crooked Mile Roundabout, Wal.Abb. 15 EC33
Crooked Usage N3 63 CY55
Crookham Rd SW6 99 CZ81
Crookston Rd SE9 105 EN83
Croombs Rd E16 86 EJ71
Crooms Hill SE10 103 ED80
Crooms Hill Gro SE10 103 EC80
Cropley Ct N1 84 DR68
Cropley St
Cropley St N1 84 DR68
Croppath Rd, Dag. 70 FA63
Cropthorne Ct W9 82 DC69
Maida Vale
Crosby Cl, Felt. 116 BY91
Crosby Ct SE1 201 K4
Crosby Rd E7 86 EG65
Crosby Rd, Dag. 89 FB68
Crosby Row SE1 201 K5
Crosby Row SE1 102 DR75
Crosby Sq EC3 197 M9
Crosby Wk E8 84 DT65
Laurel St
Crosby Wk SW2 121 DN87
Crosier Rd (Ickenham), Uxb. 59 BQ63
Crosier Way, Ruis. 59 BS62
Crosland Pl SW11 100 DG83
Taybridge Rd
Cross Av SE10 103 ED79
Cross Cl SE15 102 DV81
Gordon Rd
Cross Deep, Twick. 117 CF89
Cross Deep Gdns, Twick. 117 CF89
Cross Keys Cl N9 46 DU47
Balham Rd
Cross Keys Cl W1 194 G7
Cross Keys Cl, Sev. 190 FG127
Cross Keys Cl, Sev. 190 FG127
Brittains La
Cross Keys Sq EC1 197 H7
Cross Lances Rd, Houns. 96 CB84
Cross La EC3 201 M1
Cross La N8 65 DM56
Cross La, Bex. 126 EZ87
Cross La, Cher. 151 BB107
Cross La E, Grav. 131 GH89
Cross La W, Grav. 131 GH89
Cross Las (Chalfont St. Peter), Ger.Cr. 36 AY50
Cross Las Cl (Chalfont St. Peter), Ger.Cr. 37 AZ50
Cross Las
Cross Rd E4 48 EE46
Cross Rd N11 45 DH50
Cross Rd N22 45 DN52
Cross Rd SE5 102 DS82
Cross Rd SW19 120 DA94
Cross Rd, Brom. 144 EL103
Cross Rd, Croy. 142 DR102
Cross Rd, Dart. 128 FJ86
Cross Rd (Hawley), Dart. 128 FM91
Cross Rd, Enf. 30 DS42
Cross Rd, Felt. 116 BY91
Cross Rd, Grav. 131 GF86
Cross Rd, Har. 61 CD56
Cross Rd (South Harrow), Har. 60 CB62
Cross Rd (Wealdstone), Har. 41 CG54
Cross Rd, Kings.T. 118 CM94
Cross Rd, Orp. 146 EV99
Cross Rd, Pur. 159 DP113
Cross Rd, Rom. 70 FA55
Cross Rd (Chadwell Heath), Rom. 70 EW59
Cross Rd, Sid. 126 EV91
Sidcup Hill
Cross Rd, Sutt. 158 DD106
Cross Rd (Belmont), Sutt. 158 DA110
Cross Rd, Tad. 173 CW122
Cross Rd, Uxb. 76 BJ66
New Windsor St
Cross Rd, Wal.Cr. 15 DY33
Cross Rd, Wat. 24 BY44
Cross Rd, Wey. 135 BR104
Cross Rd, Wdf.Grn. 49 EM51
Cross Rds, Loug. 32 EH40
Cross St N1 83 DP67
Cross St SW13 98 CS82
Cross St, Erith 107 FE78
Bexley Rd
Cross St, Hmptn. 116 CC92
Cross St, Uxb. 76 BJ66
Cross St, Wat. 24 BW41
Cross Ter, Wal.Abb. 16 EE34
Stonyshotts
Cross Way, The, Har. 41 CE54
Crossacres, Wok. 167 BE115
Crossbow Rd, Chig. 49 ET50
Crossbrook Rd SE3 104 EL82
Crossbrook St (Cheshunt), Wal.Cr. 15 DX31
Crossfield Pl, Wey. 153 BP108
Crossfield Rd N17 66 DQ55
Crossfield Rd NW3 82 DD66
Crossfield St SE8 103 EA80
Crossfields, Loug. 33 EP43
Crossford St SW9 101 DM82
Crossgate, Edg. 42 CN48
Crossgate, Grnf. 79 CH65
Crossing Rd, Epp. 18 EU32
Crossland Rd, Red. 184 DG134
Crossland Rd, Th.Hth. 141 DP100
Crosslands, Cher. 133 BE104
Crosslands Av W5 80 CM74
Crosslands Av, Sthl. 96 BZ78
Crosslands Rd, Epsom 156 CR107
Crosslet St SE17 201 L8
Crosslet Vale SE10 103 EB81
Blackheath Rd
Crossley Cl, West. 178 EK115
Crossley St N7 83 DN65
Crossleys, Ch.St.G. 36 AW49
Crossmead SE9 125 EM88
Crossmead, Wat. 23 BV44
Crossmead Av, Grnf. 78 CA69
Crossmount Ho SE5 102 DQ80
Crossness La SE28 88 EX73
Crossness Rd, Bark. 87 ET69
Crossoaks La, Borwd. 26 CR35
Crossoaks La (South Mimms), Pot.B. 10 CS34
Crosspath, The, Rad. 25 CG35
Crossthwaite Av SE5 102 DR84
Crosswall EC3 197 P10
Crosswall EC3 84 DT73
Crossway N12 44 DD51
Crossway N16 66 DS64
Crossway NW9 63 CT56
Crossway SE28 88 EW72
Crossway SW20 139 CW98
Crossway W13 79 CG70
Crossway, Chesh. 4 AS30
Crossway, Dag. 70 EW62
Crossway, Enf. 46 DS45
Crossway, Hayes 77 BU74
Crossway, Orp. 145 ER98
Crossway, Pnr. 39 BV54
Crossway, Ruis. 60 BW63
Crossway, Walt. 135 BV103
Crossway, Wdf.Grn. 48 EJ49
Crossway, The N22 45 DP52
Crossway, The SE9 124 EK89
Crossway, The, Uxb. 76 BM68
Crossways N21 30 DQ44
Crossways, Brwd. 55 GA44
Crossways, Egh. 113 BD93
Crossways, Rom. 71 FH55
Crossways, S.Croy. 161 DY108
Crossways, Sun. 115 BT94
Crossways, Sutt. 158 DD109
Crossways, West. 178 EJ120
Crossways, The, Couls. 175 DM119
Crossways, The, Houns. 96 BZ80
Crossways, The, Red. 185 DJ130
Crossways, The, Wem. 62 CN61
Crossways Boul, Dart. 108 FQ84
Crossways Boul, Green. 109 FT84
Crossways Business Pk, Dart. 108 FQ84
Crossways La, Reig. 184 DC128
Crossways Rd, Beck. 143 EA98
Crossways Rd, Mitch. 141 DH97
Crosswell Cl, Shep. 135 BQ96
Croston St E8 84 DU67
Crothall Cl N13 45 DM48
Crouch Av, Bark. 88 EV68
Crouch Cl, Beck. 123 EA93
Abbey La
Crouch Cft SE9 125 EN90
Crouch End Hill N8 65 DK59
Crouch Hall Rd N8 65 DK58
Crouch Hill N4 65 DL58
Crouch Hill N8 65 DL58
Crouch La (Cheshunt), Wal.Cr. 14 DQ28
Crouch Oak La, Add. 152 BJ105
Crouch Rd NW10 80 CR66
Crouch Rd, Grays 111 GG78
Crouch Valley, Upmin. 73 FS59
Crouchman's Cl SE26 122 DT90
Crow Dr, Sev. 181 FC115
Crow Grn La, Brwd. 54 FU43
Crow Grn Rd, Brwd. 54 FT43
Crow La, Rom. 70 EZ59
Crowborough Cl, Warl. 177 DY117
Crowborough Dr, Warl. 177 DY118
Crowborough Path, Wat. 40 BX49
Prestwick Rd
Crowborough Rd SW17 120 DG93
Crowden Way SE28 88 EW73
Crowder St E1 84 DV73
Crowfoot Cl E9 67 DZ64
Lee Conservancy Rd
Crowhurst Cl SW9 101 DN82
Crowhurst Mead, Gdse. 186 DW130
Crowhurst Way, Orp. 146 EW99
Crowland Av, Hayes 95 BS77
Crowland Gdns N14 45 DL45
Crowland Rd N15 66 DT57
Crowland Rd, Th.Hth. 142 DF
Crowland Ter N1 84 DF
Crowland Wk, Mord. 140 DB1
Crowlands Av, Rom. 71 FE
Crowley Cres, Croy. 159 DN
Crowline Wk N1 84 DF
Clephane Rd
Crowmarsh Gdns SE23 122 DW
Tyson Rd
Crown Arc, Kings.T. 137 CK
Union St
Crown Ash Hill, West. 162 EH
Crown Ash La, Warl. 178 EG
Crown Ash La, West. 178 EG
Crown Cl E3 85 EA
Crown Cl NW6 82 DB
Crown Cl NW7 43 CT
Crown Cl, Hayes 95 BT
Station Rd
Crown Cl, Orp. 164 EU1
Crown Cl, Slou. 93 BC
Crown Cl, Walt. 136 BW1
Crown Ct EC2 197
Crown Ct SE12 124 EH
Crown Ct WC2 196
Crown Ct, Brom. 144 EK
Victoria Rd
Crown Dale SE19 121 DP
Crown Hill, Croy. 142 DQ1
Church St
Crown Hill, Epp. 17 EM
Crown Hill, Wal.Abb. 17 EM
Crown La N14 45 DJ
Crown La SW16 121 DN
Crown La, Brom. 144 EK
Crown La, Chis. 145 EQ
Crown La, Mord. 140 DB
Crown La, Vir.W. 132 AX1
Crown La Gdns SW16 121 DN
Crown La
Crown La Spur, Brom. 144 EK1
Crown Meadow, Slou. 93 BB
Crown Ms E13 86 EJ
Waghorn Rd
Crown Ms W6 99 CU
Crown Office Row EC4 196 D
Crown Pas SW1 199
Crown Pas SW1 83 DJ
Crown Pas, Kings.T. 137 CK
Church St
Crown Pas, Wat. 24 BW
The Cres
Crown Pl EC2 197 N
Crown Pl EC2 84 DS
Crown Pl NW5 83 DH
Kentish Town Rd
Crown Pt Par SE19 121 DP
Beulah Hill
Crown Ri, Cher. 133 BF1
Crown Ri, Wat. 8 BW
Crown Rd N10 44 DG
Crown Rd, Borwd. 26 CN
Crown Rd, Enf. 30 DV
Crown Rd, Grays 110 GA
Crown Rd, Ilf. 69 ER
Crown Rd, Mord. 140 DB
Crown Rd, N.Mal. 138 CQ
Crown Rd, Orp. 164 EU1
Crown Rd, Ruis. 60 BX
Crown Rd, Sev. 165 FF1
Crown Rd, Sutt. 158 DB1
Crown Rd, Twick. 117 CH
Crown Rd, Vir.W. 132 AW1
Crown Sq, Wok. 167 AZ1
Commercial Way
Crown St SE5 102 DQ
Crown St W3 80 CP
Crown St, Brwd. 54 FW4
Crown St, Dag. 89 FC6
Crown St, Egh. 113 BA
Crown St, Har. 61 CD6
Crown Ter, Rich. 98 CM
Crown Wk, Uxb. 76 BJ6
Oxford Rd
Crown Wk, Wem. 62 CM6
Crown Way, West Dr. 76 BM7
Crown Wds La SE9 105 EP8
Crown Wds La SE18 105 EP8
Crown Wds Way SE9 125 ER8
Crown Wks E2 84 DV6
Temple St
Crown Yd, Houns. 96 CC8
High St
Crowndale Rd NW1 83 DJ6
Crownfield Av, Ilf. 69 ES5
Crownfield Rd E15 67 ED6
Crownfields, Sev. 191 FH12
Crownhill Rd NW10 81 CT6
Crownhill Rd, Wdf.Grn. 48 EL5
Crownmead Way, Rom. 71 FB5
Crownstone Rd SW2 121 DN8
Crowntree Cl, Islw. 97 CF7
Crows Rd E15 85 ED6
Crows Rd, Epp. 17 ET3
Crowshott Av, Stan. 41 CJ5
Crowstone Rd, Grays 110 GC7
Crowther Av, Brent. 98 CL7
Crowther Rd SE25 142 DU9
Crowthorne Cl SW18 119 CZ8
Crowthorne Rd W10 81 CX7
Croxdale Rd, Borwd. 26 CM4
Croxden Cl, Edg. 62 CM5
Croxden Wk, Mord. 140 DC10
Croxford Gdns N22 45 DP5
Croxford Way, Rom. 71 FD6
Horace Av
Croxley Cl, Orp. 146 EV9
Croxley Grn, Orp. 146 EV9
Croxley Rd W9 81 CZ6
Croxley Vw, Wat. 23 BS4
Croxted Cl SE21 122 DQ8
Croxted Rd SE21 122 DQ8
Croxted Rd SE24 122 DQ8
Croyde Av, Grnf. 78 CC6
Croyde Av, Hayes 95 BS7
Croyde Cl, Sid. 125 ER8
Croydon Flyover, Croy. 159 DP10
Croydon Gro, Croy. 141 DP102
Croydon La, Bans. 158 DB114
Croydon La S, Bans. 158 DB114
Croydon Rd E13 86 EF70
Croydon Rd SE20 142 DV96
Croydon Rd, Beck. 143 DY98

roydon Rd, Brom. 144 EF104
roydon Rd, Cat. 176 DU122
roydon Rd, Croy. 159 DH105
roydon Rd, Houns. 95 BP82
roydon Rd, Kes. 144 EJ104
roydon Rd, Mitch. 140 DG98
roydon Rd, Reig. 184 DB134
roydon Rd, Wall. 159 DH105
roydon Rd, Warl. 177 ED122
roydon Rd, W.Wick. 144 EE104
roydon Rd, West. 179 EM123
royland Rd N9 46 DU46
roylands Dr, Surb. 138 CL101
roysdale Av, Sun. 135 BU97
rozier Dr, S.Croy. 160 DV110
rozier Ter E9 67 DX64
rucible Cl, Rom. 70 EV58
rucifix La SE1 201 M4
rucifix La SE1 102 DS75
ruden Ho SE17 101 DP79
Hillingdon St
ruden Rd, Grav. 131 GM90
ruden St N1 83 DP67
ruick Av, S.Ock. 91 FW73
ruikshank Rd E15 68 EE63
ruikshank St WC1 196 D2
ruikshank St WC1 83 DN69
rummock Gdns NW9 62 CS57
rumpsall St SE2 106 EW77
rundal Twr, Orp. 146 EW102
rundale Av NW9 62 CN57
runden Rd, S.Croy. 160 DR108
rusader Cl, Purf. 108 FN77
Centurion Way
rusader Gdns, Croy. 142 DS104
Cotelands
Crusader Way, Wat. 23 BT44
Crushes Cl, Brwd. 55 GE44
Crusoe Ms N16 66 DR61
Crusoe Rd, Erith 107 FD78
Crusoe Rd, Mitch. 120 DF94
Crutched Friars EC3 197 N10
Crutched Friars EC3 84 DS73
Crutches La, Beac. 36 AS51
Crutchfield La, Walt. 135 BV103
Crutchley Rd SE6 124 EE89
Crystal Av, Horn. 72 FL63
Crystal Ct SE19 122 DT92
College Rd
Crystal Ho SE18 105 ET78
Spinel Cl
Crystal Palace Par SE19 122 DT93
Crystal Palace Pk Rd SE26 122 DU92
Crystal Palace Rd SE22 102 DU84
Crystal Palace Sta Rd SE19 122 DU93
Anerley Hill
Crystal Ter SE19 122 DR93
Crystal Vw Ct, Brom. 123 ED91
Winlaton Rd
Crystal Way, Dag. 70 EW60
Crystal Way, Har. 61 CF57
Cuba Dr, Enf. 30 DW40
Cuba St E14 203 P4
Cuba St E14 103 EA75
Cubitt Sq, Sthl. 78 CC74
Windmill Av
Cubitt Steps E14 204 A2
Cubitt St WC1 196 B3
Cubitt St WC1 83 DM69
Cubitt St, Croy. 159 DM106
Cubitt Ter SW4 101 DJ83
Cubitts Yd WC2 196 A10
Cuckmans Dr, St.Alb. 8 CA25
Cuckoo Av W7 79 CE70
Cuckoo Dene W7 79 CD71
Cuckoo Hall La N9 46 DW45
Cuckoo Hill, Pnr. 60 BW55
Cuckoo Hill Dr, Pnr. 60 BW55
Cuckoo Hill Rd, Pnr. 60 BW56
Cuckoo La W7 79 CE73
Cuckoo Pound, Shep. 135 BS99
Cudas Cl, Epsom 157 CT105
Cuddington Av, Wor.Pk. 139 CT104
Cuddington Cl, Tad. 173 CW120
Cuddington Pk Cl, Bans. 157 CZ113
Cuddington Way, Sutt. 157 CX112
Cudham Cl, Sutt. 158 DA110
Cudham Dr, Croy. 161 EC110
Cudham La N, Orp. 163 ES110
Cudham La N, Sev. 163 ER112
Cudham La S, Sev. 179 EQ115
Cudham Pk Rd, Sev. 163 ES110
Cudham Rd, Orp. 163 EN111
Cudham Rd, West. 178 EL120
Cudham St SE6 123 EC87
Cudworth St E1 84 DV70
Cuff Cres SE9 124 EK86
Cuff Pt E2 197 P2
Cuff Pt E2 84 DT69
Cuffley Av, Wat. 8 BX34
Cuffley Hill (Cheshunt), Wal.Cr. 13 DN29
Cugley Rd, Dart. 128 FQ87
Culford Gdns SW3 198 E9
Culford Gdns SW3 100 DF77
Culford Gro N1 84 DS65
Culford Ms N1 84 DS65
Culford Rd
Culford Rd N1 84 DS66
Culford Rd, Grays 110 GC75
Culgaith Gdns, Enf. 29 DL42
Cullen Sq, S.Ock. 91 FW73
Cullen Way NW10 80 CQ70
Cullera Cl, Nthwd. 39 BT51
Cullerne Cl, Epsom 157 CT110
Cullesden Rd, Ken. 175 DP115
Culling Rd SE16 202 F6
Cullings Ct, Wal.Abb. 16 EF33
Cullington Cl, Har. 61 CG56
Cullingworth Rd NW10 63 CU64
Culloden Cl SE16 102 DU78
Culloden Rd, Enf. 29 DP40
Culloden St E14 85 EC72
Cullum St EC3 197 M10
Culmington Rd W13 97 CJ75
Culmington Rd, S.Croy. 160 DQ109
Culmore Cross SW12 121 DH88
Culmore Rd SE15 102 DV80
Culmstock Rd SW11 120 DG85
Culpeper Cl, Ilf. 49 EP51
Culross Cl N15 66 DQ56
Culross St W1 198 F1
Culross St W1 82 DG73
Culsac Rd, Surb. 138 CL103
Culver Dr, Oxt. 188 EE130
Culver Gro, Stan. 41 CJ54
Culverden Rd SW12 121 DJ89
Culverden Rd, Wat. 39 BV48
Culverhay, Ash. 172 CL116
Culverhouse Gdns SW16 121 DM90
Culverlands Cl, Stan. 41 CH49
Culverley Rd SE6 123 EB88
Culvers Av, Cars. 140 DF103
Culvers Retreat, Cars. 140 DF102
Culvers Way, Cars. 140 DF103
Culverstone Cl, Brom. 144 EF100
Culvert La, Uxb. 76 BH68
Culvert Pl SW11 100 DG82
Culvert Rd N15 66 DS57
Culvert Rd SW11 100 DF82
Culworth St NW8 194 B1
Cumberland Av NW10 80 CP69
Cumberland Av, Grav. 131 GJ87
Cumberland Av, Horn. 72 FL62
Cumberland Av, Well. 105 ES83
Cumberland Cl E8 84 DT65
Cumberland Cl SW20 119 CX94
Lansdowne Rd
Cumberland Cl, Amer. 20 AV39
Cumberland Cl, Epsom 156 CS110
Cumberland Cl, Horn. 72 FL62
Cumberland Cl, Ilf. 49 EQ53
Carrick Dr
Cumberland Cl, Twick. 117 CH86
Westmorland Cl
Cumberland Cres W14 99 CY77
Cumberland Dr, Bexh. 106 EY80
Cumberland Dr, Chess. 138 CM104
Cumberland Dr, Dart. 128 FM87
Cumberland Dr, Esher 137 CG103
Cumberland Gdns NW4 43 CY54
Cumberland Gdns WC1 196 C2
Cumberland Gate W1 194 D10
Cumberland Gate W1 82 DF73
Cumberland Mkt NW1 195 J2
Cumberland Mkt NW1 83 DH69
Cumberland Mkt Est NW1 195 J2
Cumberland Mills Sq E14 204 F10
Cumberland Pk W3 81 CU69
Cumberland Pl NW1 195 H2
Cumberland Pl SE6 124 EF88
Cumberland Pl, Sun. 135 BU98
Cumberland Rd E12 68 EK63
Cumberland Rd E13 86 EH71
Cumberland Rd E17 47 DY54
Cumberland Rd N9 46 DW46
Cumberland Rd N22 45 DM54
Cumberland Rd SE25 142 DV100
Cumberland Rd SW13 99 CT81
Cumberland Rd W3 80 CQ73
Cumberland Rd W7 97 CF75
Cumberland Rd, Ashf. 114 BK90
Cumberland Rd, Brom. 144 EE98
Cumberland Rd, Har. 60 CB57
Cumberland Rd, Rich. 98 CN80
Cumberland Rd, Stan. 62 CM55
Cumberland St SW1 199 J10
Cumberland St SW1 101 DH78
Cumberland St, Stai. 113 BD92
Cumberland Ter NW1 195 H2
Cumberland Ter Ms NW1 195 H1
Cumberland Vil W3 80 CQ73
Cumberland Rd
Cumberlands, Ken. 176 DR115
Cumberlow Av SE25 142 DT97
Cumbernauld Gdns, Sun. 115 BT92
Cumberton Rd N17 46 DR53
Cumbrae Cl, Slou. 74 AU74
St. Pauls Av
Cumbrae Gdns, Surb. 137 CJ102
Cumbrian Av, Bexh. 107 FE81
Cumbrian Gdns NW2 63 CX61
Cumbrian Way, Uxb. 76 BK66
Chippendale Waye
Cumley Rd, Ong. 19 FE30
Cumming St N1 196 B1
Cumming St N1 83 DM68
Cummings Hall La, Rom. 52 FJ48
Cumnor Gdns, Epsom 157 CU107
Cumnor Ri, Ken. 176 DQ117
Cumnor Rd, Sutt. 158 DC107
Cunard Cres N21 30 DR44
Cunard Pl EC3 197 N9
Cunard Rd NW10 80 CR69
Cunard St SE5 102 DS79
Albany Rd
Cunard Wk SE16 203 J8
Cunard Wk SE16 103 DY77
Cundy Rd E16 86 EJ72
Cundy St SW1 198 G9
Cundy St SW1 100 DG77
Cundy St Est SW1 198 G9
Cunliffe Cl, Epsom 172 CP124
Cunliffe Rd, Epsom 157 CT105
Cunliffe St SW16 121 DJ93
Cunningham Av, Enf. 31 DY36
Cunningham Cl, Rom. 70 EW57
Cunningham Cl, W.Wick. 143 EB103
Cunningham Pk, Har. 60 CC57
Cunningham Pl NW8 82 DD70
Cunningham Ri, Epp. 19 FC25
Cunningham Rd N15 66 DU56
Cunningham Rd, Bans. 174 DD115
Cunningham Rd (Cheshunt), Wal.Cr. 15 DY27
Cunnington St W4 98 CQ76
Cupar Rd SW11 100 DG81
Cupola Cl, Brom. 124 EH92
Cureton St SW1 199 N9
Cureton St SW1 101 DK77
Curfew Bell Rd, Cher. 133 BF101
Curfew Ho, Bark. 87 EQ67
St. Ann's
Curlew Cl SE28 88 EX73
Curlew Cl, S.Croy. 161 DX111
Curlew Ct, Surb. 138 CM104
Curlew St SE1 201 P4
Curlew St SE1 102 DT75
Curlew Ter, Ilf. 69 EN55
Tiptree Cres
Curlew Way, Hayes 78 BX71
Curlews, The, Grav. 131 GK89
Curling Cl, Couls. 175 DM120
Curling La, Grays 110 FZ78
Curnick's La SE27 122 DQ91
Chapel Rd
Curnock Est NW1 83 DJ67
Plender St
Curran Av, Sid. 125 ET85
Curran Av, Wall. 140 DG104
Curran Cl, Uxb. 76 BJ70
Currey Rd, Grnf. 79 CD65
Curricle St W3 80 CS74
Currie Hill Cl SW19 119 CZ91
Curry Ri NW7 43 CX51
Cursitor St EC4 196 D8
Cursitor St EC4 83 DN72
Curtain Pl EC2 84 DS69
Curtain Rd
Curtain Rd EC2 197 M5
Curtain Rd EC2 84 DS70
Curthwaite Gdns, Enf. 29 DK42
Curtis Cl, Rick. 38 BG46
Curtis Dr W3 80 CR72
Curtis Fld Rd SW16 121 DM91
Curtis La, Wem. 80 CL65
Montrose Cres
Curtis Mill Grn, Rom. 35 FF42
Curtis Mill La, Rom. 35 FF42
Curtis Rd, Epsom 156 CQ105
Curtis Rd, Horn. 72 FM60
Curtis Rd, Houns. 116 BZ87
Curtis St SE1 201 P8
Curtis St SE1 102 DT77
Curtis Way SE1 201 P8
Curtis Way SE1 102 DT77
Curtis Way SE28 88 EV73
Tawney Rd
Curtismill Cl, Orp. 146 EV97
Curtismill Way, Orp. 146 EV97
Curvan Cl, Epsom 157 CT110
Curve, The W12 81 CU73
Curwen Av E7 68 EH63
Woodford Rd
Curwen Rd W12 99 CU75
Curzon Av, Enf. 31 DX43
Curzon Av, Stan. 41 CG53
Curzon Cl, Orp. 163 ER105
Curzon Cl, Wey. 152 BN105
Curzon Rd
Curzon Cres NW10 81 CT66
Curzon Cres, Bark. 87 ET68
Curzon Dr, Grays 110 GC80
Curzon Gate W1 198 G3
Curzon Gate W1 82 DG74
Curzon Mall, Slou. 92 AT75
High St
Curzon Pl W1 198 G3
Curzon Pl, Pnr. 60 BW57
Curzon Rd N10 45 DH54
Curzon Rd W5 79 CH70
Curzon Rd, Th.Hth. 141 DN100
Curzon Rd, Wey. 152 BN105
Curzon St W1 198 G3
Curzon St W1 82 DG74
Cusack Cl, Twick. 117 CF91
Waldegrave Rd
Cussons Cl (Cheshunt), Wal.Cr. 14 DU29
Custom Ho Quay EC3 84 DS73
Lower Thames St
Custom Ho Reach SE16 203 M5
Custom Ho Reach SE16 103 DZ75
Custom Ho Wk EC3 201 M1
Custom Ho Wk EC3 84 DS73
Cut, The SE1 200 E4
Cut, The SE1 101 DN75
Cut Hills, Egh. 132 AV95
Cut Hills, Vir.W. 132 AV95
Cutcombe Rd SE5 102 DQ82
Cuthberga Cl, Bark. 87 EQ66
George St
Cuthbert Gdns SE25 142 DS97
Cuthbert Rd E17 67 EC55
Cuthbert Rd N18 46 DU50
Fairfield Rd
Cuthbert Rd, Croy. 141 DP103
Cuthbert St W2 82 DD70
Cuthberts Cl, Wal.Cr. 14 DT29
Cuthill Wk SE5 102 DR81
Cutler St E1 197 N8
Cutler St E1 84 DS72
Cutlers Gdns E1 197 N8
Cutlers Gdns Arc EC2 84 DS72
Cutler St
Cutlers Sq E14 204 A9
Cutmore St, Grav. 131 GH87
Cutthroat All, Rich. 117 CJ89
Ham St
Cutty Sark Ct, Green. 129 FU85
Low Cl
Cutty Sark Gdns SE10 103 EC79
King William Wk
Cuxton Cl, Bexh. 126 EY85
Cyclamen Cl, Hmptn. 116 CA93
Gresham Rd
Cyclamen Rd, Swan. 147 FD98
Cyclamen Way, Epsom 156 CP106
Cyclops Ms E14 203 P8
Cyclops Ms E14 103 EA77
Cygnet Av, Felt. 116 BW87
Cygnet Cl NW10 62 CR64
Cygnet Cl, Borwd. 26 CQ39
Cygnet Cl, Nthwd. 39 BQ52
Cygnet Cl, Wok. 166 AV116
Cygnet Gdns, Grav. 131 GF89
Cygnet St E1 84 DT70
Sclater St
Cygnet Vw, Grays 109 FT77
Cygnet Way, Hayes 78 BX71
Cygnets, The, Felt. 116 BY91
Cygnets, The, Stai. 113 BF92
Edgell Rd
Cygnets Cl, Red. 184 DG132
Cygnus Business Cen NW10 81 CT65
Cymbeline Ct, Har. 61 CF58
Cynthia St N1 196 C1
Cynthia St N1 83 DM68
Cyntra Pl E8 84 DV66
Mare St
Cypress Av, Enf. 29 DN35
Cypress Av, Twick. 116 CC87
Cypress Cl, Wal.Abb. 15 ED34
Cypress Ct, Vir.W. 132 AY98
Cypress Gro, Ilf. 49 ES51
Cypress Path, Rom. 52 FK52
Cypress Pl W1 195 L5
Cypress Rd SE25 142 DS96
Cypress Rd, Har. 41 CD54
Cypress Tree Cl, Sid. 125 ET87
White Oak Gdns
Cypress Wk, Egh. 112 AV93
Cypress Wk, Wat. 23 BV35
Cedar Wd Dr
Cypress Way, Bans. 157 CX114
Cyprus Av N3 43 CY54
Cyprus Cl N4 65 DP58
Atterbury Rd
Cyprus Gdns N3 43 CY54
Cyprus Pl E2 84 DW68
Cyprus Pl E6 87 EN73
Cyprus Rd N3 43 CZ54
Cyprus Rd N9 46 DT47
Cyprus Roundabout E16 87 EN73
Royal Albert Way
Cyprus St E2 84 DW68
Cyrena Rd SE22 122 DT86
Cyril Mans SW11 100 DF81
Cyril Rd, Bexh. 106 EY82
Cyril Rd, Orp. 146 EU101
Cyrus St EC1 196 G4
Cyrus St EC1 83 DP70
Czar St SE8 103 EA79

D

Da Gama Pl E14 103 EA78
Napier Av
Dabbling Cl, Erith 107 FH80
Dabbs Hill La, Nthlt. 60 CB64
D'Abernon Cl, Esher 154 CA105
D'Abernon Dr, Cob. 170 BY116
Dabin Cres SE10 103 EC81
Dacca St SE8 103 DZ79
Dace Rd E3 85 EA66
Dacre Av, Ilf. 49 EN54
Dacre Av, S.Ock. 91 FR74
Dacre Cl, Chig. 49 EQ49
Dacre Cl, Grnf. 78 CB68
Dacre Cres, S.Ock. 91 FR74
Dacre Gdns SE13 104 EE84
Dacre Gdns, Borwd. 26 CR43
Dacre Gdns, Chig. 49 EQ49
Dacre Pk SE13 104 EE83
Dacre Pl SE13 104 EE83
Dacre Rd E11 68 EF60
Dacre Rd E13 86 EH67
Dacre Rd, Croy. 141 DL101
Dacre St SW1 199 M6
Dacre St SW1 101 DK76
Dacres Rd SE23 123 DX90
Dade Way, Sthl. 96 BZ78
Daerwood Cl, Brom. 145 EM102
Daffodil Av, Brwd. 54 FV43
Daffodil Cl, Croy. 143 DX102
Primrose La
Daffodil Gdns, Ilf. 69 EP64
Daffodil Pl, Hmptn. 116 CA93
Gresham Rd
Daffodil St W12 81 CT73
Dafforne Rd SW17 120 DG90
Dagenham Av, Dag. 88 EY67
Dagenham Rd E10 67 DZ60
Dagenham Rd, Dag. 71 FC63
Dagenham Rd, Rain. 89 FD66
Dagenham Rd, Rom. 71 FD62
Dagger La, Borwd. 25 CG44
Dagmar Av, Wem. 62 CM63
Dagmar Gdns NW10 81 CX68
Dagmar Ms, Sthl. 96 BY76
Dagmar Rd
Dagmar Pas N1 83 DP67
Cross St
Dagmar Rd N4 65 DN59
Dagmar Rd N15 66 DR56
Cornwall Rd
Dagmar Rd N22 45 DK53
Dagmar Rd SE5 102 DS81
Dagmar Rd SE25 142 DS99
Dagmar Rd, Dag. 89 FC66
Dagmar Rd, Kings.T. 138 CM95
Dagmar Rd, Sthl. 96 BY76
Dagmar Ter N1 83 DP67
Dagnall Cres, Uxb. 76 BJ71
Dagnall Pk SE25 142 DS100
Dagnall Rd SE25 142 DS99
Dagnall St SW11 100 DF82
Dagnam Pk Cl, Rom. 52 FN50
Dagnam Pk Dr, Rom. 52 FL50
Dagnam Pk Gdns, Rom. 52 FN51
Dagnam Pk Sq, Rom. 52 FP51
Dagnan Rd SW12 121 DH87
Dagonet Rd, Brom. 124 EG90
Dahlia Cl (Cheshunt), Wal.Cr. 14 DQ25
Dahlia Dr, Swan. 147 FF96
Dahlia Gdns, Ilf. 87 EP65
Dahlia Gdns, Mitch. 141 DK98
Dahlia Rd SE2 106 EV77
Dahomey Rd SW16 121 DJ93
Daiglen Dr, S.Ock. 91 FU73
Daimler Way, Wall. 159 DL108
Daines Cl E12 69 EM62
Colchester Av
Daines Cl, S.Ock. 91 FU70
Dainford Cl, Brom. 123 ED92
Dainton Cl, Brom. 144 EH95
Daintry Cl, Har. 61 CG56
Daintry Lo, Nthwd. 39 BT52
Daintry Way E9 85 DZ65
Eastway
Dairsie Rd SE9 105 EN83
Dairy Cl NW10 81 CU67
Dairy Cl (Sutton at Hone), Dart. 128 FP94
Dairy Cl, Th.Hth. 142 DQ96
Dairy La SE18 105 EM77
Dairy La, Eden. 189 EN134
Dairy Ms SW9 101 DL83
Dairy Wk SW19 119 CY91
Dairy Way, Abb.L. 7 BT29
Tithe Barn Ct
Dairyglen Av, Wal.Cr. 15 DY31
Dairyman Cl NW2 63 CY62
Claremont Rd
Daisy Cl, Croy. 143 DX102
Primrose La
Daisy Dobbins Wk N19 65 DL59
Hillrise Rd
Daisy La SW6 100 DA83
Daisy Rd E16 86 EE70
Cranberry La
Daisy Rd E18 48 EH54
Dakota Gdns E6 86 EL70
Dakota Gdns, Nthlt. 78 BY69
Argus Way
Dalberg Rd SW2 121 DN85
Dalberg Way SE2 106 EX76
Lanridge Rd
Dalby Rd SW18 100 DC84
Dalby St NW5 83 DH65
Dalcross Rd, Houns. 96 BY82
Dale, The, Kes. 162 EK105
Dale, The, Wal.Abb. 16 EE34
Dale Av, Edg. 42 CM53
Dale Av, Houns. 96 BY83
Dale Cl SE3 104 EG83
Dale Cl, Add. 152 BH106
Dale Cl, Barn. 28 DB44
Dale Cl, Dart. 127 FF86
Dale Cl, Pnr. 39 BV53
Dale Cl, S.Ock. 91 FU72
Dale Dr, Hayes 77 BT70
Dale End, Dart. 127 FF86
Dale Rd
Dale Gdns, Wdf.Grn. 48 EH49
Dale Grn Rd N11 45 DH48
Dale Gro N12 44 DC50
Dale Pk Av, Cars. 140 DF103
Dale Pk Rd SE19 142 DQ95
Dale Rd NW5 64 DG64
Grafton Rd
Dale Rd SE17 101 DP79
Dale Rd, Dart. 127 FF86
Dale Rd, Grav. 130 GA91
Dale Rd, Grnf. 78 CB71
Dale Rd, Pur. 159 DN112
Dale Rd, Sun. 115 BT94
Dale Rd, Sutt. 157 CZ105
Dale Rd, Swan. 147 FC96
Dale Rd, Walt. 135 BT101
Dale Row W11 81 CY72
St. Marks Rd
Dale St W4 98 CS78
Dale Vw, Epsom 172 CP123
Dale Vw, Erith 107 FF82
Dale Vw, Wok. 166 AU118
Dale Vw Av E4 47 EC47
Dale Vw Cres E4 47 EC47
Dale Vw Gdns E4 47 ED48
Dale Wk, Dart. 128 FQ88
Dale Wd Rd, Orp. 145 ES101
Dalebury Rd SW17 120 DE89
Dalegarth Gdns, Pur. 160 DR113
Daleham Av, Egh. 113 BA93
Daleham Dr, Uxb. 77 BP72
Daleham Gdns NW3 64 DD64
Daleham Ms NW3 82 DD65
Dalehead NW1 195 K1
Dalehead NW1 83 DJ68
Dalemain Ms E16 205 N2
Dales Path, Borwd. 26 CR43
Farriers Way
Dales Rd, Borwd. 26 CR43
Daleside, Ger.Cr. 56 AY60
Daleside, Orp. 164 EU106
Daleside Cl, Orp. 164 EU107
Daleside Dr, Pot.B. 11 CZ32
Daleside Gdns, Chig. 49 EQ48
Daleside Rd SW16 121 DH92
Daleside Rd, Epsom 156 CR107
Dalestone Ms, Rom. 51 FH51
Daleview Rd N15 66 DS58
Dalewood Cl, Horn. 72 FM59
Dalewood Gdns, Wor.Pk. 139 CV103
Daley St E9 85 DX65
Daley Thompson Way SW8 101 DH82
Dalgarno Gdns W10 81 CW71
Dalgarno Way W10 81 CW70
Dalgleish St E14 85 DY72
Daling Way E3 85 DY67
Dalkeith Gro, Stan. 41 CK50
Dalkeith Rd SE21 122 DQ88
Dalkeith Rd, Ilf. 69 EQ62
Dallas Rd NW4 63 CU59
Dallas Rd SE26 122 DV91
Dallas Rd W5 80 CM71
Dallas Rd, Sutt. 157 CY107
Dallas Ter, Hayes 95 BT76
Dallega Cl, Hayes 77 BR73
Dawley Rd
Dallin Rd SE18 105 EP80
Dallin Rd, Bexh. 106 EX84
Dalling Rd W6 99 CV76
Dallinger Rd SE12 124 EF86
Dallington Cl, Walt. 154 BW107
Dallington Sq EC1 83 DP70
Dallington St
Dallington St EC1 196 G4
Dallington St EC1 83 DP70
Dalmain Rd SE23 123 DX88
Dalmally Rd, Croy. 142 DT101
Dalmeny Av N7 65 DK63
Dalmeny Av SW16 141 DN96
Dalmeny Cl, Wem. 79 CJ65
Dalmeny Cres, Houns. 97 CD84
Dalmeny Rd N7 65 DK62
Dalmeny Rd, Barn. 28 DC44
Dalmeny Rd, Cars. 158 DG108
Dalmeny Rd, Erith 107 FB81
Dalmeny Rd, Wor.Pk. 139 CV104
Dalmeyer Rd NW10 81 CT65
Dalmore Av, Esher 155 CF107
Dalmore Rd SE21 122 DQ89
Dalroy Cl, S.Ock. 91 FU72
Dalrymple Cl N14 45 DK45
Dalrymple Rd SE4 103 DY84
Dalston Cross Shop Cen E8 84 DT65
Dalston Gdns, Stan. 42 CL53
Dalston La E8 84 DT65

Dalton Av, Mitch. 140 DE96
Dalton Cl, Hayes 77 BR70
Dalton Cl, Orp. 145 ES104
Dalton Cl, Pur. 160 DQ112
Dalton Rd, Har. 41 CD54
Dalton St SE27 121 DP89
Dalton Way, Wat. 24 BX43
Daltons Rd, Orp. 147 FB104
Daltons Rd, Swan. 147 FC102
Dalwood St SE5 102 DS81
Daly Ct E15 67 EC64
Clays La
Dalyell Rd SW9 101 DM83
Damascene Wk SE21 122 DQ88
Lovelace Rd
Damask Cres E16 86 EE70
Cranberry La
Dame St N1 84 DQ68
Damer Ter SW10 100 DC80
Tadema Rd
Dames Rd E7 68 EG62
Dameswick Vw, St.Alb. 8 CA27
Damien St E1 84 DV72
Damigos Rd, Grav. 131 GM88
Damon Cl, Sid. 126 EV90
Damson Ct, Swan. 147 FD98
Damson Way, Cars. 158 DF110
Damsonwood Rd, Sthl. 96 CA76
Dan Leno Wk SW6 100 DB80
Britannia Rd
Danbrook Rd SW16 141 DL95
Danbury Cl, Brwd. 54 FT43
Danbury Cl, Rom. 70 EX55
Danbury Cres, S.Ock. 91 FV72
Danbury Ms, Wall. 159 DH105
Danbury Rd, Loug. 48 EL45
Danbury Rd, Rain. 89 FF67
Danbury St N1 83 DP68
Danbury Way, Wdf.Grn. 48 EJ51
Danby St SE15 102 DT83
Dancer Rd SW6 99 CZ81
Dancer Rd, Rich. 98 CN83
Dancers Hill Rd, Barn. 27 CY36
Dancers La, Barn. 27 CW35
Dandelion Cl, Rom. 71 FE61
Dando Cres SE3 104 EH83
Dandridge Cl SE10 205 L10
Dandridge Cl SE10 104 EF78
Dandridge Cl, Slou. 92 AX76
Dane Cl, Amer. 20 AT41
Dane Cl, Bex. 126 FA87
Dane Cl, Orp. 163 ER106
Dane Ct, Wok. 167 BF115
Dane Pl E3 85 DY68
Roman Rd
Dane Rd N18 46 DW48
Dane Rd SW19 140 DC95
Dane Rd W13 79 CJ74
Dane Rd, Ashf. 115 BQ93
Dane Rd, Ilf. 69 EQ64
Dane Rd, Sev. 181 FE117
Dane Rd, Sthl. 78 BY73
Dane Rd, Warl. 177 DX117
Dane St WC1 196 B7
Danebury, Croy. 161 EB107
Danebury Av SW15 118 CS86
Daneby Rd SE6 123 EB90
Danecourt Gdns, Croy. 142 DT104
Danecroft Rd SE24 122 DQ85
Danehill Wk, Sid. 126 EU90
Hatherley Rd
Danehurst Gdns, Ilf. 68 EL57
Danehurst St SW6 99 CY81
Daneland, Barn. 28 DF44
Danemead Gro, Nthlt. 60 CB64
Danemere St SW15 99 CW83
Danes, The, St.Alb. 8 CC28
Danes Cl, Grav. 130 GC90
Danes Cl, Lthd. 154 CC114
Danes Ct, Wem. 62 CP62
Danes Gate, Har. 61 CE55
Danes Hill, Wok. 167 BA118
Danes Rd, Rom. 71 FC59
Danes Way, Brwd. 54 FU43
Danes Way, Lthd. 155 CD114
Danesbury Rd, Felt. 115 BV88
Danescombe SE12 124 EG88
Winn Rd
Danescourt Cres, Sutt. 140 DC103
Danescroft NW4 63 CX57
Danescroft Av NW4 63 CX57
Danescroft Gdns NW4 63 CX57
Danesdale Rd E9 85 DY65
Danesfield SE5 102 DS79
Albany Rd
Danesfield Cl, Walt. 135 BV104
Daneshill, Red. 184 DE133
Daneshill Cl, Red. 184 DE133
Daneswood Av SE6 123 EC90
Daneswood Cl, Wey. 153 BP106
Danethorpe Rd, Wem. 79 CK65
Danetree Cl, Epsom 156 CQ108
Danetree Rd, Epsom 156 CQ108
Danette Gdns, Dag. 70 EZ61
Daneville Rd SE5 102 DR81
Dangan Rd E11 68 EG58
Daniel Bolt Cl E14 85 EB71
Uamvar St
Daniel Cl N18 46 DW49
Daniel Cl SW17 120 DE93
Daniel Cl, Grays 111 GH76
Daniel Cl (Chafford Hundred), Grays 110 FY75
Daniel Gdns SE15 102 DT80
Daniel Pl NW4 63 CV59
Daniel Rd W5 80 CM73
Daniel Way, Bans. 158 DB114
Daniell Way, Croy. 141 DL102
Daniels La, Warl. 177 DZ116
Daniels Ms SE4 103 DZ84
Daniels Rd SE15 102 DW83
Danley Rd, Grays 110 GB79
Derby Rd
Dansey Pl W1 195 M10
Dansington Rd, Well. 106 EU84
Danson Cres, Well. 106 EV83
Danson La, Well. 106 EV84
Danson Mead, Well. 106 EW83
Danson Pk, Bexh. 106 EW84
Danson Rd, Bex. 126 EX85
Danson Rd, Bexh. 126 EX85
Danson Underpass, Sid. 126 EW86
Danson Rd
Dante Pl SE11 200 G8
Dante Rd SE11 200 F8
Dante Rd SE11 101 DP77
Danube St SW3 198 C10
Danvers Rd N8 65 DK56
Danvers St SW3 100 DD79
Danvers Way, Cat. 176 DQ123
Danyon Cl, Rain. 90 FJ68
Danziger Way, Borwd. 26 CQ39
Daphne Gdns E4 47 EC48
Gunners Gro
Daphne St SW18 120 DC86
Daplyn St E1 84 DU71
Hanbury St
D'Arblay St W1 195 L9
D'Arblay St W1 83 DJ72
Darby Cl, Cat. 176 DQ122
Fairbourne La
Darby Cres, Sun. 136 BW96
Darby Dr, Wal.Abb. 15 EC33
Darby Gdns, Sun. 136 BW96
Darcy Av, Wall. 159 DJ105
Darcy Cl N20 44 DD47
D'Arcy Cl, Brwd. 55 GB45
Darcy Cl, Couls. 175 DP119
Darcy Cl (Cheshunt), Wal.Cr. 15 DY31
D'Arcy Dr, Har. 61 CK56
Darcy Gdns, Dag. 88 EZ67
D'Arcy Gdns, Har. 62 CL56
D'Arcy Pl, Ash. 172 CM117
Darcy Rd SW16 141 DL96
D'Arcy Rd, Ash. 172 CM117
Darcy Rd, Islw. 97 CG81
London Rd
D'Arcy Rd, Sutt. 157 CX105
Dare Gdns, Dag. 70 EY62
Grafton Rd
Darell Rd, Rich. 98 CN83
Darent Ind Pk, Erith 108 FJ79
Darent Mead (Sutton at Hone), Dart. 148 FP95
Darent Valley Path, Dart. 128 FM89
Darent Valley Path, Sev. 181 FG115
Darenth Cl, Sev. 190 FC122
Darenth Gdns, West. 189 ER126
Quebec Av
Darenth Hill, Dart. 128 FQ92
Darenth La, Sev. 190 FE121
Darenth La, S.Ock. 91 FU72
Darenth Pk Av, Dart. 129 FR89
Darenth Rd N16 66 DT59
Darenth Rd, Dart. 128 FM87
Darenth Rd (Darenth), Dart. 128 FP91
Darenth Rd, Well. 106 EU81
Darenth Way, Sev. 165 FG111
Darenth Wd Rd, Dart. 129 FS89
Darfield Rd SE4 123 DZ85
Darfield Way W10 81 CX72
Darfur St SW15 99 CX83
Dargate Cl SE19 122 DT94
Chipstead Cl
Darien Rd SW11 100 DD83
Dark La, Brwd. 53 FU52
Dark La (Cheshunt), Wal.Cr. 14 DU31
Darkes La, Pot.B. 12 DA32
Darlan Rd SW6 99 CZ80
Darlands Dr, Barn. 43 CU45
Mays La
Darlaston Rd SW19 119 CX94
Darley Cl, Add. 152 BJ106
Darley Cl, Croy. 143 DY100
Darley Dr, N.Mal. 138 CR96
Darley Gdns, Mord. 140 DB100
Darley Rd N9 46 DT46
Darley Rd SW11 120 DF86
Darling Rd SE4 103 EA83
Darling Row E1 84 DV70
Darlington Gdns, Rom. 52 FK50
Darlington Path, Rom. 52 FK50
Darlington Gdns
Darlington Rd SE27 121 DP92
Darlton Cl, Dart. 107 FF83
Darmaine Cl, S.Croy. 160 DQ108
Churchill Rd
Darndale Cl E17 47 DZ54
Darnets Fld, Sev. 181 FF117
Darnhills, Rad. 25 CG35
Darnicle Hill (Cheshunt), Wal.Cr. 13 DM25
Darnley Ho E14 85 DY72
Darnley Pk, Wey. 135 BP104
Darnley Rd E9 84 DV65
Darnley Rd, Grav. 131 GG88
Darnley Rd, Grays 110 GB79
Stanley Rd
Darnley Rd, Wdf.Grn. 48 EG53
Darnley St, Grav. 131 GG87
Darnley Ter W11 81 CY74
St. James's Gdns
Darns Hill, Swan. 147 FC101
Darrell Cl, Slou. 93 AZ77
Darrell Rd SE22 122 DU85
Darren Cl N4 65 DM59
Darrick Wd Rd, Orp. 145 ER103
Darrington Rd, Borwd. 26 CL39
Darris Cl, Hayes 78 BY70
Darsley Dr SW8 101 DL81
Dart Cl, Slou. 93 BB78
Dart Cl, Upmin. 73 FR58
Dart Grn, S.Ock. 91 FV71
Dart St W10 81 CY69
Dartfields, Rom. 52 FK51
Dartford Av N9 30 DW44
Dartford Bypass, Dart. 127 FE88
Dartford Gdns, Rom. 70 EV58
Heathfield Pk Dr
Dartford Northern Bypass, Dart. 108 FN83
Dartford Rd, Bex. 127 FC88
Dartford Rd, Dart. 127 FG86
Dartford Rd (Farningham), Dart. 148 FP95
Dartford Rd, Sev. 191 FJ124
Dartford St SE17 102 DQ79
Dartford Trade Pk, Dart. 128 FL89
Dartford Tunnel, Dart. 109 FR83
Dartford Tunnel, Purf. 109 FR83
Dartford Tunnel App Rd, Dart. 128 FN86
Dartmoor Wk E14 204 A8
Dartmouth Av, Wok. 151 BC114
Dartmouth Cl W11 81 CZ72
Dartmouth Grn, Wok. 151 BD114
Dartmouth Grn, Wok. 151 BD114
St. Michael's Rd
Dartmouth Gro SE10 103 EC81
Dartmouth Hill SE10 103 EC81
Dartmouth Pk Av NW5 65 DH62
Dartmouth Pk Hill N19 65 DH60
Dartmouth Pk Hill NW5 65 DH63
Dartmouth Pk Rd NW5 65 DH63
Dartmouth Path, Wok. 151 BD114
Dartmouth Path, Wok. 151 BD114
Dartmouth Av
Dartmouth Pl SE23 122 DW89
Dartmouth Rd
Dartmouth Pl W4 98 CS79
Dartmouth Rd E16 86 EG72
Fords Pk Rd
Dartmouth Rd NW2 81 CX65
Dartmouth Rd NW4 63 CU58
Dartmouth Rd SE23 122 DW90
Dartmouth Rd SE26 122 DW90
Dartmouth Rd, Brom. 144 EG101
Dartmouth Rd, Ruis. 59 BU62
Dartmouth Row SE10 103 EC81
Dartmouth St SW1 199 M5
Dartmouth St SW1 101 DK75
Dartmouth Ter SE10 103 ED81
Dartnell Av, W.Byf. 152 BH112
Dartnell Cl, W.Byf. 152 BH112
Dartnell Ct, W.Byf. 152 BJ112
Dartnell Cres, W.Byf. 152 BH112
Dartnell Pk Rd, W.Byf. 152 BJ111
Dartnell Pl, W.Byf. 152 BH112
Dartnell Rd, Croy. 142 DT101
Dartrey Wk SW10 100 DD80
World's End Est
Dartview Cl, Grays 110 GE77
Darvel Cl, Wok. 166 AU116
Darville Rd N16 66 DT62
Darwell Cl E6 87 EN68
Darwin Cl N11 45 DH48
Darwin Cl, Orp. 163 ER106
Darwin Dr, Sthl. 78 CB72
Darwin Gdns, Wat. 40 BW50
Barnhurst Path
Darwin Rd N22 45 DP53
Darwin Rd W5 97 CJ78
Darwin Rd, Slou. 93 AZ75
Darwin Rd, Til. 111 GF81
Darwin Rd, Well. 105 ET83
Darwin St SE17 201 L8
Darwin St SE17 102 DR77
Darynton Dr, Grnf. 79 CD68
Dashwood Cl, Bexh. 126 FA85
Dashwood Cl, Slou. 92 AW77
Dashwood Cl, W.Byf. 152 BJ112
Dashwood Rd N8 65 DM58
Dashwood Rd, Grav. 131 GG89
Dassett Rd SE27 121 DP92
Datchelor Pl SE5 102 DR81
Datchet Pl, Slou. 92 AV81
Datchet Rd SE6 123 DZ90
Datchet Rd, Slou. 92 AT76
Datchet Rd (Horton), Slou. 93 AZ83
Datchet Rd (Old Windsor), Wind. 92 AU84
Datchworth Ct N4 66 DQ62
Queens Dr
Date St SE17 102 DQ78
Daubeney Gdns N17 46 DQ52
Daubeney Rd E5 67 DY63
Daubeney Rd N17 46 DQ52
Daubeney Twr SE8 203 M9
Daubeney Twr SE8 103 DZ77
Dault Rd SW18 120 DC86
Davall Ho, Grays 110 GA79
Argent St
Davema Cl, Chis. 145 EN95
Brenchley Cl
Davenant Rd N19 65 DK61
Davenant Rd, Croy. 159 DP105
Duppas Hill Rd
Davenant St E1 84 DU71
Davenham Av, Nthwd. 39 BT50
Davenport Cl, Tedd. 117 CG93
Davenport Rd SE6 123 EB86
Davenport Rd, Sid. 126 EX89
Daventer Dr, Stan. 41 CF52
Daventry Av E17 67 EA57
Daventry Cl, Slou. 93 BF81
Daventry Gdns, Rom. 52 FJ50
Daventry Grn, Rom. 52 FJ50
Hailsham Rd
Daventry Rd, Rom. 52 FJ50
Daventry St NW1 194 B6
Daventry St NW1 82 DE71
Davern Cl SE10 205 K9
Davern Cl SE10 104 EF77
Davey Cl N7 83 DM65
Davey Rd E9 85 EA66
Davey St SE15 102 DT79
David Av, Grnf. 79 CE69
David Cl, Hayes 95 BR80
David Dr, Rom. 52 FN51
David Ms W1 194 E6
David Rd, Dag. 70 EY61
David Rd, Slou. 93 BF82
David St E15 85 ED65
Davidge St SE1 200 F5
Davidge St SE1 101 DP75
Davids Rd SE23 122 DW88
David's Way, Ilf. 49 ES52
Davidson Gdns SW8 101 DL80
Davidson La, Har. 61 CF59
Grove Hill
Davidson Rd, Croy. 142 DT100
Davidson Way, Rom. 71 FE58
Davies Cl, Croy. 142 DU100
Davies Cl, Rain. 90 FJ69
Davies La E11 68 EE61
Davies Ms W1 195 H10
Davies St W1 195 H10
Davies St W1 83 DH73
Davington Gdns, Dag. 70 EV64
Davington Rd, Dag. 88 EV65
Davinia Cl, Wdf.Grn. 49 EM51
Deacon Way
Davis Av, Grav. 130 GE88
Davis Cl, Sev. 191 FJ122
Davis Rd W3 81 CT74
Davis Rd, Chess. 156 CN105
Davis Rd, Grays 110 FZ76
Davis Rd, S.Ock. 91 FR74
Davis Rd, Wey. 152 BM110
Davis St E13 86 EH68
Davison Cl, Wal.Cr. 15 DX28
Davison Dr (Cheshunt), Wal.Cr. 15 DX28
Davisville Rd W12 99 CU75
Davos Cl, Wok. 166 AY119
Davys Pl, Grav. 131 GL93
Dawell Dr, West. 178 EJ117
Dawes Av, Horn. 72 FK62
Dawes Av, Islw. 117 CG85
Dawes Cl, Green. 129 FT85
Dawes Ct, Esher 154 CB105
Dawes Ho SE17 201 L9
Dawes La, Rick. 21 BE37
Dawes Moor Cl, Slou. 74 AW72
Dawes Rd SW6 99 CY80
Dawes Rd, Uxb. 76 BL68
Dawes St SE17 201 L10
Dawes St SE17 102 DR78
Dawley Av, Uxb. 77 BQ71
Dawley Grn, S.Ock. 91 FU72
Dawley Par, Hayes 77 BQ73
Dawley Rd
Dawley Ride, Slou. 93 BE81
Dawley Rd, Hayes 95 BS76
Dawlish Av N13 45 DL49
Dawlish Av SW18 120 DB89
Dawlish Av, Grnf. 79 CG68
Dawlish Dr, Ilf. 69 ES63
Dawlish Dr, Pnr. 60 BY57
Dawlish Dr, Ruis. 59 BU61
Dawlish Rd E10 67 EC61
Dawlish Rd N17 66 DU55
Dawlish Rd NW2 81 CX65
Dawlish Wk, Rom. 52 FJ53
Dawn Cl, Houns. 96 BY83
Dawn Cres E15 85 ED67
Bridge Rd
Dawn Redwood Cl, Slou. 93 BA83
Dawnay Gdns SW18 120 DD89
Dawnay Rd SW18 120 DC89
Dawpool Rd NW2 63 CT61
Daws Hill E4 31 EC41
Daws La NW7 43 CT50
Dawson Av, Bark. 87 ET66
Dawson Av, Orp. 146 EV96
Dawson Cl SE18 105 EQ77
Dawson Cl, Hayes 77 BR71
Dawson Dr, Rain. 89 FH66
Dawson Dr, Swan. 127 FE94
Dawson Gdns, Bark. 87 ET66
Dawson Av
Dawson Hts Est SE22 122 DU87
Dawson Pl W2 82 DA73
Dawson Rd NW2 63 CW64
Dawson Rd, Kings.T. 138 CM97
Dawson Rd, W.Byf. 152 BK111
Dawson St E2 84 DT68
Dax Ct, Sun. 136 BW97
Thames St
Daybrook Rd SW19 140 DB96
Daylesford Av SW15 99 CU84
Daylop Dr, Chig. 50 EV48
Daymer Gdns, Pnr. 59 BV56
Daymerslea Ridge, Lthd. 171 CJ121
Days Acre, S.Croy. 160 DT110
Days La, Brwd. 54 FU42
Days La, Sid. 125 ES87
Daysbrook Rd SW2 121 DM88
Dayton Dr, Erith 108 FK78
Dayton Gro SE15 102 DW81
De Barowe Ms N5 65 DP63
Leigh Rd
De Beauvoir Cres N1 84 DS67
De Beauvoir Est N1 84 DR67
De Beauvoir Rd N1 84 DS67
De Beauvoir Sq N1 84 DS66
De Bohun Av N14 29 DH44
De Brome Rd, Felt. 116 BW88
De Burgh Pk, Bans. 174 DB115
De Crespigny Pk SE5 102 DR82
De Frene Rd SE26 123 DX91
De Havilland Ct, Rad. 10 CL32
Armstrong Gdns
De Havilland Dr, Wey. 152 BL111
De Havilland Rd, Edg. 42 CP54
De Havilland Rd, Houns. 96 BW80
De Havilland Rd, Wall. 159 DL108
De Havilland Way, Abb.L. 7 BT32
De Havilland Way, Stai. 114 BK86
De Lapre Cl, Orp. 146 EX101
De Lara Way, Wok. 166 AX118
De Laune St SE17 101 DP78
De Luci Rd, Erith 107 FC78
De Lucy St SE2 106 EV77
De Mandeville Gate, Enf. 30 DU42
Southbury Rd
De Mel Cl, Epsom 156 CN112
Trotter Way
De Montfort Par SW16 121 DL90
Streatham High Rd
De Montfort Rd SW16 121 DL90
De Morgan Rd SW6 100 DB83
De Quincey Ms E16 205 N2
De Quincey Rd N17 46 DR53
De Ros Pl, Egh. 113 BA93
De Salis Rd, Uxb. 77 BQ70
De Vere Cotts W8 100 DC76
Canning Pl
De Vere Gdns W8 100 DC75
De Vere Gdns, Ilf. 69 EM61
De Vere Ms W8 100 DC76
Canning Pl
De Vere Wk, Wat. 23 BS40
De Walden St W1 194 G7
Deacon Cl, Cob. 169 BV119
Deacon Cl, Pur. 159 DL109
Deacon Ms N1 84 DR66
Deacon Pl, Cat. 176 DQ123
Deacon Rd NW2 63 CU64
Deacon Rd, Kings.T. 138 CM95
Deacon Way SE17 201 H8
Deacon Way SE17 102 DQ77
Deacon Way, Wdf.Grn. 49 EM52
Deacons Cl, Borwd. 26 CN4
Deacons Cl, Pnr. 39 BV5
Deacons Hill, Wat. 24 BW4
Deacon's Hill Rd, Borwd. 26 CM4
Deacons Leas, Orp. 163 ER10
Deacons Ri N2 64 DD5
Deacons Wk, Hmptn. 116 BZ9
Bishops Gro
Deadhearn La, Ch.St.G. 36 AY4
Deadman's Ash La, Rick. 22 BH3
Deakin Cl, Wat. 39 BS4
Chenies Way
Deal Ms W5 97 CK7
Darwin Rd
Deal Porters Way SE16 202 G
Deal Porters Way SE16 102 DW7
Deal Rd SW17 120 DG9
Deal St E1 84 DU7
Deal Wk SW9 101 DN8
Mandela St
Deal's Gateway SE10 103 EB8
Blackheath Rd
Dealtry Rd SW15 99 CW8
Dean Bradley St SW1 199 P
Dean Bradley St SW1 101 DL7
Dean Cl E9 66 DW6
Churchill Wk
Dean Cl SE16 203 J
Dean Cl, Uxb. 76 BM6
Dean Cl, Wok. 167 BE11
Dean Ct, Wem. 61 CH6
Dean Dr, Stan. 42 CL5
Dean Farrar St SW1 199 M
Dean Farrar St SW1 101 DK7
Dean Fld, Hem.H. 5 BA2
Dean Gdns E17 67 ED5
Dean Gdns W13 79 CH7
Northfield Av
Dean La, Red. 175 DH12
Dean Rd NW2 81 CW6
Dean Rd SE28 88 EU7
Dean Rd, Croy. 160 DR10
Dean Rd, Hmptn. 116 CA9
Dean Rd, Houns. 116 CB8
Dean Ryle St SW1 199 P
Dean Ryle St SW1 101 DL7
Dean Stanley St SW1 199 P
Dean Stanley St SW1 101 DL7
Dean St E7 68 EG6
Dean St W1 195 M
Dean St W1 83 DK7
Dean Trench St SW1 199 P
Dean Trench St SW1 101 DL7
Dean Wk, Edg. 42 CQ51
Deansbrook Rd
Dean Way, Sthl. 96 CB7
Deanacre Cl (Chalfont St. Peter), Ger.Cr. 36 AY51
Deancroft Rd (Chalfont St. Peter), Ger.Cr. 36 AY51
Deancross St E1 84 DW72
Deane Av, Ruis. 60 BW64
Deane Cft Rd, Pnr. 60 BW58
Deane Way, Ruis. 59 BV58
Deanery Cl N2 64 DE56
Deanery Ms W1 198 G2
Deanery Rd E15 86 EE65
Deanery Rd, Eden. 189 EQ134
Deanery St W1 198 G2
Deanery St W1 82 DG74
Deanhill Rd SW14 98 CP84
Deans Bldgs SE17 201 K9
Deans Bldgs SE17 102 DR77
Deans Cl W4 98 CP79
Deans Cl, Abb.L. 7 BR32
Deans Cl, Amer. 20 AT37
Dean's Cl, Croy. 142 DT104
Deans Cl, Edg. 42 CQ51
Deans Cl, Slou. 74 AV67
Deans Cl, Tad. 173 CV124
Deans La
Deans Ct EC4 196 G9
Deans Dr N13 45 DP51
Deans Dr, Edg. 42 CR50
Dean's Gate Cl SE23 123 DX90
Deans La W4 98 CP79
Deans La, Edg. 42 CQ51
Deans La, Red. 185 DN133
Deans La, Tad. 173 CV124
Deans Ms W1 195 J8
Dean's Pl SW1 199 M10
Dean's Pl SW1 101 DK78
Deans Rd W7 79 CF74
Deans Rd, Brwd. 54 FV49
Deans Rd, Red. 185 DJ130
Deans Rd, Sutt. 140 DB104
Deans Wk, Couls. 175 DN118
Deans Way, Edg. 42 CQ50
Dean's Yd SW1 199 N6
Deansbrook Cl, Edg. 42 CQ52
Deansbrook Rd, Edg. 42 CQ51
Deanscroft Av NW9 62 CQ61
Deansfield, Cat. 186 DT125
Deansway N2 64 DD56
Deansway N9 46 DS48
Deanway, Ch.St.G. 36 AU48
De'Arn Gdns, Mitch. 140 DE97
Dearne Cl, Stan. 41 CG50
Dearsley Ho, Rain. 89 FD68
Dearsley Rd, Enf. 30 DU41
Deason St E15 85 EC67
High St
Debden Cl, Kings.T. 117 CK92
Debden Cl, Wdf.Grn. 48 EJ52
Debden Grn, Loug. 33 EP38
Debden La
Debden La, Loug. 33 EP38
Debden Rd, Loug. 33 EP38
Debden Wk, Horn. 89 FH65
Debenham Rd (Cheshunt), Wal.Cr. 14 DV27
Debnams Rd SE16 202 F9
Deborah Cl, Islw. 97 CE81
Deborah Cres, Ruis. 59 BR59
Debrabant Cl, Erith 107 FD79
Deburgh Rd SW19 120 DC94
Decies Way, Slou. 74 AU67
Decima St SE1 201 M6
Decima St SE1 102 DS76
Deck Cl SE16 203 J4
Decoy Av NW11 63 CY57
Dee Cl, Upmin. 73 FS58
Dee Rd, Rich. 98 CM84

Dee St E14 85 EC72
Dee Way, Epsom 156 CS110
Dee Way, Rom. 51 FE53
Deeley Rd SW8 101 DK81
Deena Cl W3 80 CM72
Deep Fld, Slou. 92 AV80
Deep Pool La, Wok. 150 AV114
Deepdale SW19 119 CX91
Deepdale Av, Brom. 144 EF98
Deepdale Cl N11 44 DG51
Ribblesdale Av
Deepdene W5 80 CM70
Deepdene, Pot.B. 11 CX31
Deepdene Av, Croy. 142 DT104
Deepdene Cl E11 68 EG56
Deepdene Ct N21 29 DP44
Deepdene Gdns SW2 121 DM87
Deepdene Path, Loug. 33 EN42
Deepdene Rd SE5 102 DR84
Deepdene Rd, Loug. 33 EN42
Deepdene Rd, Well. 106 EU83
Deepfield Way, Couls. 175 DL116
Deepwell Cl, Islw. 97 CG81
Deepwood La, Grnf. 79 CD69
Cowgate Rd
Deer Pk Cl, Kings.T. 118 CP94
Deer Pk Gdns, Mitch. 140 DD97
Deer Pk Rd SW19 140 DB96
Deer Pk Wk, Chesh. 4 AS28
Deer Pk Way, Wal.Abb. 31 EC40
Sewardstone Rd
Deer Pk Way, W.Wick. 144 EF103
Deerbrook Rd SE24 121 DP88
Deerdale Rd SE24 102 DQ84
Deere Av, Rain. 89 FG65
Deerhurst Cl, Felt. 115 BU91
Deerhurst Cres, Hmptn. 116 CC92
Deerhurst Rd NW2 81 CX65
Deerhurst Rd SW16 121 DM92
Deerings Dr, Pnr. 59 BU57
Deerings Rd, Reig. 184 DB134
Deerleap Gro E4 31 EB43
Deerleap La, Sev. 164 EX113
Deers Fm Cl, Wok. 168 BL116
Deerswood Cl, Cat. 176 DU124
Deeside Rd SW17 120 DD90
Deeves Hall La, Pot.B. 10 CS33
Defiance Wk SE18 105 EM76
Defiant Way, Wall. 159 DL108
Defoe Av, Rich. 98 CN80
Defoe Cl SE16 203 M5
Defoe Cl SW17 120 DE93
Defoe Cl, Erith 107 FE81
Selkirk Dr
Defoe Ho EC2 197 J6
Defoe Par, Grays 111 GH76
Defoe Rd N16 66 DS61
Defoe Way, Rom. 51 FB51
Degema Rd, Chis. 125 EP92
Dehar Cres NW9 63 CT59
Dehavilland Cl, Nthlt. 78 BX69
Dekker Rd SE21 122 DS86
Delabole Rd, Red. 185 DL129
Delacourt Rd SE3 104 EH80
Old Dover Rd
Delafield Rd SE7 104 EH78
Delafield Rd, Grays 110 GD78
Delaford Cl, Iver 75 BF72
Delaford Rd SE16 202 E10
Delaford Rd SE16 102 DV78
Delaford St SW6 99 CY80
Delagarde Rd, West. 189 EQ126
Delamare Cres, Croy. 142 DW100
Delamare Rd (Cheshunt), Wal.Cr. 15 DZ30
Delamere Gdns NW7 42 CR51
Delamere Rd SW20 139 CX95
Delamere Rd W5 80 CL74
Delamere Rd, Borwd. 26 CP39
Delamere Rd, Hayes 78 BX73
Delamere Ter W2 82 DB71
Delancey Pas NW1 83 DH67
Delancey St
Delancey St NW1 83 DH67
Delaporte Cl, Epsom 156 CS112
Delargy Cl, Grays 111 GH76
Delaware Rd W9 82 DB70
Delawyk Cres SE24 122 DQ86
Delcombe Av, Wor.Pk. 139 CW102
Delderfield, Lthd. 171 CK120
Delft Way SE22 122 DS85
East Dulwich Gro
Delhi Rd, Enf. 46 DT45
Delhi St N1 83 DL67
Delia St SW18 120 DB87
Delisle Rd SE28 105 ES75
Merbury Rd
Delius Cl, Borwd. 25 CJ44
Delius Gro E15 85 ED68
Dell, The SE2 106 EU78
Dell, The SE19 142 DT95
Dell, The, Bex. 127 FE88
Dell, The, Brent. 97 CJ79
Dell, The, Brwd. 53 FV51
Dell, The, Felt. 115 BV87
Harlington Rd W
Dell, The (Chalfont St. Peter), Ger.Cr. 36 AY51
Dell, The, Nthwd. 39 BS47
Dell, The, Pnr. 40 BX54
Dell, The, Rad. 25 CG36
Dell, The, Reig. 184 DA133
Dell, The, Tad. 173 CW121
Dell, The, Wal.Abb. 31 EC40
Sewardstone Rd
Dell, The, Wem. 61 CH64
Dell, The, Wok. 166 AW118
Dell, The, Wdf.Grn. 48 EH48
Dell Cl E15 85 ED67
Dell Cl, Lthd. 171 CE123
Dell Cl, Wall. 159 DK105
Dell Cl, Wdf.Grn. 48 EH48
Dell Fm Rd, Ruis. 59 BR57
Dell La, Epsom 157 CU106
Dell Ri, St.Alb. 8 CB26
Dell Rd, Enf. 30 DW38
Dell Rd, Epsom 157 CU107
Dell Rd, Grays 110 GB77
Dell Rd, Wat. 23 BU37
Dell Rd, West Dr. 94 BM76
Dell Side, Wat. 23 BU37
The Harebreaks
Dell Wk, N.Mal. 138 CS96
Dell Way W13 79 CJ72
Della Path E5 66 DV62
Napoleon Rd
Dellbow Rd, Felt. 115 BV85
Central Way
Dellfield Cl, Beck. 123 EC94
Foxgrove Rd
Dellfield Cl, Rad. 25 CE35
Dellfield Cl, Wat. 23 BU40
Dellfield Cres, Uxb. 76 BJ70
Dellfield Par (Cowley), Uxb. 76 BJ70
High St
Dellmeadow, Abb.L. 7 BS30
Dellors Cl, Barn. 27 CX43
Dellow Cl, Ilf. 69 ER59
Dellow St E1 84 DV73
Dells Cl E4 47 EB45
Dell's Ms SW1 199 L9
Dellside (Harefield), Uxb. 58 BJ57
Dellwood, Rick. 38 BH46
Dellwood Gdns, Ilf. 69 EN55
Delmare Cl SW9 101 DM84
Brighton Ter
Delme Cres SE3 104 EH82
Delmey Cl, Croy. 142 DT104
Radcliffe Rd
Deloraine St SE8 103 EA81
Delorme St W6 99 CX79
Delta Cl, Wok. 150 AT110
Delta Cl, Wor.Pk. 139 CT104
Delta Ct NW2 63 CU61
Delta Gain, Wat. 40 BX47
Delta Gro, Nthlt. 78 BX69
Delta Rd, Brwd. 55 GD44
Delta Rd, Wok. 167 BA116
Delta Rd (Chobham), Wok. 150 AT110
Delta Rd, Wor.Pk. 138 CS104
Delta St E2 84 DU69
Wellington Row
Delta Way, Egh. 133 BC95
Delvan Cl SE18 105 EN80
Ordnance Rd
Delvers Mead, Dag. 71 FC63
Delverton Rd SE17 101 DP78
Delves, Tad. 173 CX121
Heathcote
Delvino Rd SW6 100 DA81
Demesne Rd, Wall. 159 DK106
Demeta Cl, Wem. 62 CQ62
Dempster Cl, Surb. 137 CJ102
Dempster Rd SW18 120 DC85
Den Cl, Beck. 143 ED97
Den Rd, Brom. 143 ED97
Denbar Par, Rom. 71 FC56
Mawney Rd
Denberry Dr, Sid. 126 EV90
Denbigh Cl NW10 80 CS66
Denbigh Cl W11 81 CZ73
Denbigh Cl, Chis. 125 EM93
Denbigh Cl, Horn. 72 FN56
Denbigh Cl, Ruis. 59 BT61
Denbigh Cl, Sthl. 78 BZ72
Denbigh Cl, Sutt. 157 CZ106
Denbigh Dr, Hayes 95 BQ75
Denbigh Gdns, Rich. 118 CM85
Denbigh Ms SW1 199 K9
Denbigh Pl SW1 199 K10
Denbigh Pl SW1 101 DJ78
Denbigh Rd E6 86 EK69
Denbigh Rd W11 81 CZ73
Denbigh Rd W13 79 CH73
Denbigh Rd, Houns. 96 CB82
Denbigh Rd, Sthl. 78 BZ72
Denbigh St SW1 199 K9
Denbigh St SW1 101 DJ77
Denbigh Ter W11 81 CZ73
Denbridge Rd, Brom. 145 EM96
Denby Rd, Cob. 154 BW113
Dendridge Cl, Enf. 30 DV37
Dene, The W13 79 CH71
Dene, The, Croy. 161 DX105
Dene, The, Sev. 191 FH126
Dene, The, Sutt. 157 CZ111
Dene, The, Wem. 62 CL63
Dene, The, W.Mol. 136 BZ99
Dene Av, Houns. 96 BZ83
Dene Av, Sid. 126 EV87
Dene Cl SE4 103 DY83
Dene Cl, Brom. 144 EF102
Dene Cl, Couls. 174 DE119
Dene Cl, Dart. 127 FE91
Dene Cl, Wor.Pk. 139 CT103
Dene Ct, Stan. 41 CJ50
Marsh La
Dene Dr, Orp. 146 EV104
Dene Gdns, Stan. 41 CJ50
Dene Gdns, T.Ditt. 137 CG103
Dene Holm Rd, Grav. 130 GD90
Dene Path, S.Ock. 91 FU72
Dene Pl, Wok. 166 AV118
Dene Rd N11 44 DF46
Dene Rd, Ash. 172 CM119
Dene Rd, Buck.H. 48 EK46
Dene Rd, Dart. 128 FM87
Dene Rd, Nthwd. 39 BS51
Denecroft Cres, Uxb. 77 BP67
Denecroft Gdns, Grays 110 GD76
Denefield Dr, Ken. 176 DR115
Denehurst Gdns NW4 63 CW58
Denehurst Gdns W3 80 CP74
Denehurst Gdns, Rich. 98 CN84
Denehurst Gdns, Twick. 117 CD87
Denehurst Gdns, Wdf.Grn. 48 EH49
Denewood, Barn. 28 DC43
Denewood Cl, Wat. 23 BT37
Denewood Rd N6 64 DF58
Dengie Wk N1 84 DQ67
Basire St
Denham Av (Denham), Uxb. 57 BF61
Denham Cl (Denham), Uxb. 58 BG62
Denham Cl, Well. 106 EW83
Park Vw Rd
Denham Ct Dr (Denham), Uxb. 58 BH63
Denham Cres, Mitch. 140 DF98
Denham Dr, Ilf. 69 EQ58
Denham Gdn Village, Uxb. 57 BF58
Denham Grn La
Denham Grn Cl (Denham), Uxb. 58 BG59
Denham Grn La (Denham), Uxb. 57 BE57
Denham La (Chalfont St. Peter), Ger.Cr. 37 BA53
Denham Rd N20 44 DF48
Denham Rd, Egh. 113 BA91
Denham Rd, Epsom 157 CT112
Denham Rd, Felt. 116 BW86
Denham Rd, Iver 75 BE65
Denham Rd (Denham), Uxb. 75 BE65
Denham St SE10 205 M10
Denham St SE10 104 EG78
Denham Wk (Chalfont St. Peter), Ger.Cr. 37 AZ51
Denham Way, Bark. 87 ES67
Denham Way, Borwd. 26 CR39
Denham Way, Rick. 37 BE52
Denham Way (Denham), Uxb. 58 BG62
Denholme Rd W9 81 CZ69
Denholme Wk, Rain. 89 FF65
Ryder Gdns
Denison Cl N2 64 DC55
Denison Rd SW19 120 DD93
Denison Rd W5 79 CJ70
Denison Rd, Felt. 115 BT91
Deniston Av, Bex. 126 EY88
Denleigh Gdns N21 45 DN46
Denleigh Gdns, T.Ditt. 137 CE100
Denman Dr NW11 64 DA57
Denman Dr, Ashf. 115 BP93
Denman Dr, Esher 155 CG106
Denman Dr N NW11 64 DA57
Denman Dr S NW11 64 DA57
Denman Rd SE15 102 DT81
Denman St W1 199 M1
Denmark Av SW19 119 CY94
Denmark Ct, Mord. 140 DA99
Denmark Gdns, Cars. 140 DG104
Denmark Gro N1 83 DN68
Denmark Hill SE5 102 DR81
Denmark Hill Dr NW9 63 CT56
Denmark Hill Est SE5 102 DR84
Denmark Pl WC2 195 N8
Denmark Rd N8 65 DM56
Denmark Rd NW6 81 CZ68
Denmark Rd SE5 102 DQ81
Denmark Rd SE25 142 DU99
Denmark Rd SW19 119 CX93
Denmark Rd W13 79 CH73
Denmark Rd, Brom. 144 EH95
Denmark Rd, Cars. 140 DF104
Denmark Rd, Kings.T. 138 CL97
Denmark Rd, Twick. 117 CD90
Denmark St E11 68 EE62
High Rd Leytonstone
Denmark St E13 86 EH71
Denmark St N17 46 DV53
Denmark St WC2 195 N9
Denmark St WC2 83 DK72
Denmark St, Wat. 23 BV40
Denmark Wk SE27 122 DQ91
Denmead Cl, Ger.Cr. 56 AY59
Denmead Ho SW15 119 CT86
Highcliffe Dr
Denmead Rd, Croy. 141 DP102
Denmead Way SE15 102 DT80
Pentridge St
Dennan Rd, Surb. 138 CM102
Denne Ter E8 84 DT67
Denner Rd E4 47 EA47
Dennett Rd, Croy. 141 DN101
Dennetts Gro SE14 103 DX82
Dennetts Rd
Dennetts Rd SE14 102 DW81
Dennettsland Rd, Eden. 189 EQ134
Denning Av, Croy. 159 DN105
Denning Cl NW8 82 DC69
Denning Cl, Hmptn. 116 BZ93
Denning Rd NW3 64 DD63
Dennington Cl E5 66 DV61
Detmold Rd
Dennington Pk Rd NW6 82 DA65
Denningtons, The, Wor.Pk. 138 CS103
Dennis Av, Wem. 62 CM64
Dennis Cl, Ashf. 115 BR93
Dennis Cl, Red. 184 DE132
Dennis Gdns, Stan. 41 CJ50
Dennis La, Stan. 41 CH48
Dennis Pk Cres SW20 139 CY95
Dennis Reeve Cl, Mitch. 140 DF95
Dennis Rd, E.Mol. 136 CC98
Dennis Rd, Grav. 131 GG90
Dennis Rd, S.Ock. 91 FU66
Dennis Way SW4 101 DK83
Gauden Rd
Dennises La, Upmin. 91 FS67
Dennison Pt E15 85 EC66
Denny Av, Wal.Abb. 15 ED34
Denny Cl E6 86 EL71
Linton Gdns
Denny Cres SE11 200 E9
Denny Gdns, Dag. 88 EV66
Canonsleigh Rd
Denny Gate, Wal.Cr. 15 DZ27
Denny Rd N9 46 DV46
Denny Rd, Slou. 93 AZ77
Denny St SE11 200 E10
Denny St SE11 101 DN78
Densham Rd E15 86 EE67
Densole Cl, Beck. 143 DY95
Kings Hall Rd
Densworth Gro N9 46 DW47
Dent Cl, S.Ock. 91 FU72
Denton Cl, Barn. 27 CW43
Denton Ct Rd, Grav. 131 GL87
Denton Gro, Walt. 136 BX103
Denton Rd N8 65 DM57
Denton Rd N18 46 DS49
Denton Rd, Bex. 127 FE89
Denton Rd, Dart. 127 FE88
Denton Rd, Twick. 117 CK86
Denton Rd, Well. 106 EW80
Denton St SW18 120 DB86
Denton St, Grav. 131 GL87
Denton Ter, Bex. 127 FE89
Denton Rd
Denton Way E5 67 DX62
Denton Way, Wok. 166 AT118
Dents Gro, Tad. 183 CZ128
Dents Rd SW11 120 DF86
Denvale Wk, Wok. 166 AU118
Denver Cl, Orp. 145 ES100
Denver Ind Est, Rain. 89 FF71
Denver Rd N16 66 DS59
Denver Rd, Dart. 127 FG87
Denyer St SW3 198 C9
Denyer St SW3 100 DE77
Denzil Rd NW10 63 CT64
Denziloe Av, Uxb. 77 BP69
Deodar Rd SW15 99 CY84
Deodara Cl N20 44 DE48
Depot Rd, Epsom 156 CS113
Depot Rd, Houns. 97 CD83
Deptford Br SE8 103 EA81
Deptford Bdy SE8 103 EA81
Deptford Ch St SE8 103 EA79
Deptford Ferry Rd E14 204 A9
Deptford Ferry Rd E14 103 EA77
Deptford Grn SE8 103 EA79
Deptford High St SE8 103 EA79
Deptford Strand SE8 203 N9
Deptford Strand SE8 103 DZ77
Deptford Wf SE8 203 M8
Deptford Wf SE8 103 DZ77
Derby Arms Rd, Epsom 173 CT117
Derby Av N12 44 DC50
Derby Av, Har. 41 CD53
Derby Av, Rom. 71 FC58
Derby Av, Upmin. 72 FM62
Derby Cl, Epsom 173 CV119
Derby Ct E5 67 DX63
Overbury St
Derby Est, Houns. 96 CA84
Derby Gate SW1 199 P4
Derby Hill SE23 122 DW89
Derby Hill Cres SE23 122 DW89
Derby Rd E7 86 EJ66
Derby Rd E9 85 DX67
Derby Rd E18 48 EF53
Derby Rd N18 46 DW50
Derby Rd SW14 98 CP84
Derby Rd SW19 120 DA94
Russell Rd
Derby Rd, Croy. 141 DP103
Derby Rd, Enf. 30 DV43
Derby Rd, Grays 110 GB78
Derby Rd, Grnf. 78 CB67
Derby Rd, Houns. 96 CB84
Derby Rd, Surb. 138 CN102
Derby Rd, Sutt. 157 CZ107
Derby Rd, Uxb. 76 BJ68
Derby Rd, Wat. 24 BW41
Derby Rd Br, Grays 110 GB79
Derby Stables Rd, Epsom 172 CS117
Derby St W1 198 G3
Derbyshire St E2 84 DU69
Dereham Pl EC2 197 N3
Dereham Pl, Rom. 51 FB51
Dereham Rd, Bark. 87 ET65
Derek Av, Epsom 156 CN106
Derek Av, Wall. 159 DH105
Derek Av, Wem. 80 CP66
Derek Cl, Epsom 156 CP106
Derek Walcott Cl SE24 121 DP85
Shakespeare Rd
Derham Gdns, Upmin. 72 FQ62
Deri Av, Rain. 89 FH70
Dericote St E8 84 DU67
Deridene Cl, Stai. 114 BL86
Bedfont Rd
Derifall Cl E6 87 EM71
Dering Pl, Croy. 160 DQ105
Dering Rd, Croy. 160 DQ105
Dering St W1 195 H9
Dering St W1 83 DH72
Dering Way, Grav. 131 GM88
Derinton Rd SW17 120 DF91
Derley Rd, Sthl. 96 BW76
Dermody Gdns SE13 123 ED85
Dermody Rd SE13 123 ED85
Deronda Rd SE24 121 DP88
Deroy Cl, Cars. 158 DF107
Derrick Av, S.Croy. 160 DQ110
Derrick Gdns SE7 104 EJ77
Anchor & Hope La
Derrick Rd, Beck. 143 DZ97
Derry Av, S.Ock. 91 FU72
Derry Downs, Orp. 146 EW100
Derry Rd, Croy. 141 DL104
Derry St W8 100 DB75
Derrydown, Wok. 166 AW121
Dersingham Av E12 69 EN64
Dersingham Rd NW2 63 CY62
Derwent Av N18 46 DR50
Derwent Av NW7 42 CR50
Derwent Av SW15 118 CS91
Derwent Av, Barn. 44 DF46
Derwent Av, Pnr. 40 BY51
Derwent Av, Uxb. 58 BN62
Derwent Cl, Add. 152 BK106
Derwent Cl, Amer. 20 AV39
Derwent Cl, Dart. 127 FH88
Derwent Cl, Esher 155 CE107
Derwent Cl, Felt. 115 BT88
Derwent Cres N20 44 DC48
Derwent Cres, Bexh. 106 FA82
Derwent Cres, Stan. 41 CJ54
Derwent Dr NW9 62 CS57
Derwent Dr, Hayes 77 BS71
Derwent Dr, Orp. 145 ER101
Derwent Dr, Pur. 160 DR113
Derwent Gdns, Ilf. 68 EL56
Derwent Gdns, Wem. 61 CJ59
Derwent Gro SE22 102 DT84
Derwent Par, S.Ock. 91 FV72
Derwent Ri NW9 62 CS58
Derwent Rd N13 45 DM49
Derwent Rd SE20 142 DU96
Derwent Rd SW20 139 CX100
Derwent Rd W5 97 CJ76
Derwent Rd, Egh. 113 BB94
Derwent Rd, Sthl. 78 CA72
Derwent Rd, Twick. 116 CB86
Derwent St SE10 205 H10
Derwent St SE10 104 EE78
Derwent Wk, Wall. 159 DH108
Derwent Way, Horn. 71 FH64
Derwent Yd W5 97 CJ76
Northfield Av
Derwentwater Rd W3 80 CQ74
Desborough Cl W2 82 DB71
Delamere Ter
Desborough Cl, Shep. 134 BN101
Desborough St W2 82 DB71
Cirencester St
Desenfans Rd SE21 122 DS86
Desford Ct, Ashf. 114 BM89
Desford Way
Desford Ms E16 86 EE70
Desford Rd
Desford Rd E16 86 EE70
Desford Way, Ashf. 114 BM89
Desmond Rd, Wat. 23 BT36
Desmond St SE14 103 DY79
Despard Rd N19 65 DJ60
Detillens La, Oxt. 188 EG129
Detling Cl, Horn. 72 FJ64
Detling Rd, Brom. 124 EG92
Detling Rd, Erith 107 FD80
Detling Rd, Grav. 130 GD88
Detmold Rd E5 66 DW61
Devalls Cl E6 87 EN73
Devana End, Cars. 140 DF104
Devas Rd SW20 139 CW95
Devas St E3 85 EB70
Devenay Rd E15 86 EF66
Devenish Rd SE2 106 EU75
Deventer Cres SE22 122 DS85
Deverell St SE1 201 K7
Deverell St SE1 102 DR76
Devereux Ct WC2 196 D9
Devereux Dr, Wat. 23 BS38
Devereux La SW13 99 CV80
Devereux Rd SW11 120 DF86
Devereux Rd, Grays 110 FZ76
Deverill Ct SE20 142 DW95
Deverills Way, Slou. 93 BC77
Deveron Gdns, S.Ock. 91 FU72
Deveron Way, Rom. 51 FE53
Devey Cl, Kings.T. 118 CS94
Devils La, Egh. 113 BD94
Devils La, Stai. 133 BE95
Green La
Devitt Cl, Ash. 172 CN116
Devizes St N1 84 DR67
Poole St
Devoke Way, Walt. 136 BX103
Devon Av, Twick. 116 CC88
Devon Cl N17 66 DT55
Devon Cl, Buck.H. 48 EH47
Devon Cl, Epsom 156 CN112
Devon Cl, Grnf. 79 CJ67
Devon Cl, Ken. 176 DT116
Devon Ct, Dart. 148 FP95
Devon Cres, Red. 184 DD134
Devon Gdns N4 65 DP58
Devon Ri N2 64 DD56
Devon Rd, Bark. 87 ES67
Devon Rd (Sutton at Hone), Dart. 148 FP95
Devon Rd, Red. 185 DJ130
Devon Rd, Sutt. 157 CY109
Devon Rd, Walt. 154 BW105
Devon Rd, Wat. 24 BX39
Devon St SE15 102 DV79
Devon Way, Chess. 155 CJ106
Devon Way, Epsom 156 CP106
Devon Way, Uxb. 76 BM68
Devon Waye, Houns. 96 BZ80
Devoncroft Gdns, Twick. 117 CG87
Devonhurst Pl W4 98 CR78
Heathfield Ter
Devonia Gdns N18 46 DQ51
Devonia Rd N1 83 DP68
Devonport Gdns, Ilf. 69 EM58
Devonport Ms W12 81 CV74
Devonport Rd
Devonport Rd W12 99 CV75
Devonport St E1 84 DW72
Devons Est E3 85 EB69
Devons Rd E3 85 EA71
Devonshire Av, Dart. 127 FH86
Devonshire Av, Sutt. 158 DC108
Devonshire Av, Wok. 151 BC114
Devonshire Cl E15 68 EE63
Devonshire Cl N13 45 DN49
Devonshire Cl W1 195 H6
Devonshire Cl W1 83 DH71
Devonshire Cres NW7 43 CX52
Devonshire Dr SE10 103 EB80
Devonshire Dr, Surb. 137 CK102
Devonshire Gdns N17 46 DQ51
Devonshire Gdns N21 46 DQ45
Devonshire Gdns W4 98 CQ80
Devonshire Gro SE15 102 DV79
Devonshire Hill La N17 46 DQ51
Devonshire Ms W4 98 CS78
Glebe St
Devonshire Ms N W1 195 H6
Devonshire Ms S W1 195 H6
Devonshire Ms S W1 83 DH71
Devonshire Ms W W1 195 H5
Devonshire Ms W W1 83 DH71
Devonshire Pas W4 98 CS78
Devonshire Pl NW2 64 DA62
Devonshire Pl W1 194 G5
Devonshire Pl W1 82 DG70
Devonshire Pl W4 98 CS78
Devonshire Pl W8 100 DB76
St. Mary's Pl
Devonshire Pl Ms W1 194 G5
Devonshire Rd E15 68 EE63
Janson Rd
Devonshire Rd E16 86 EH72
Devonshire Rd E17 67 EA58
Devonshire Rd N9 46 DW46
Devonshire Rd N13 45 DM49
Devonshire Rd N17 46 DQ51
Devonshire Rd NW7 43 CX52
Devonshire Rd SE9 124 EL89
Devonshire Rd SE23 122 DW88
Devonshire Rd SW19 120 DE94
Devonshire Rd W4 98 CS78
Devonshire Rd W5 97 CJ76
Devonshire Rd, Bexh. 106 EY84
Devonshire Rd, Cars. 158 DG105
Devonshire Rd, Croy. 142 DR101
Devonshire Rd, Felt. 116 BY90

Devonshire Rd, Grav. 131 GH88
Devonshire Rd, Grays 110 FY77
Devonshire Rd, Har. 61 CD58
Devonshire Rd, Horn. 72 FJ61
Devonshire Rd, Ilf. 69 ES59
Devonshire Rd, Orp. 146 EU101
Devonshire Rd (Eastcote), Pnr. 60 BW58
Devonshire Rd (Hatch End), Pnr. 40 BZ53
Devonshire Rd, Sthl. 78 CA71
Devonshire Rd, Sutt. 158 DC108
Devonshire Rd, Wey. 152 BN105
Devonshire Row EC2 197 N7
Devonshire Row Ms W1 195 J5
Devonshire Sq EC2 197 N8
Devonshire Sq, Brom. 144 EH98
Devonshire St W1 194 G6
Devonshire St W1 83 DH71
Devonshire St W4 98 CS78
Devonshire Ter W2 82 DC72
Devonshire Way, Croy. 143 DY103
Devonshire Way, Hayes 77 BV72
Dewar St SE15 102 DU83
Dewberry Gdns E6 86 EL71
Dewberry St E14 85 EC71
Dewey Path, Horn. 90 FJ65
Dewey Rd N1 83 DN68
Dewey Rd, Dag. 89 FB65
Dewey St SW17 120 DF92
Dewgrass Gro, Wal.Cr. 31 DX35
Dewhurst Rd W14 99 CX76
Dewhurst Rd (Cheshunt), Wal.Cr. 14 DW29
Dewlands, Gdse. 186 DW131
Dewlands Av, Dart. 128 FP87
Dewlands Ct NW4 43 CX54
Holders Hill Rd
Dewsbury Cl, Pnr. 60 BZ58
Dewsbury Cl, Rom. 52 FL51
Dewsbury Ct W4 98 CQ77
Chiswick Rd
Dewsbury Gdns, Rom. 52 FK51
Dewsbury Gdns, Wor.Pk. 139 CU104
Dewsbury Rd NW10 63 CU64
Dewsbury Rd, Rom. 52 FK51
Dewsbury Ter NW1 83 DH67
Camden High St
Dexter Cl, Grays 110 GA76
Dexter Ho, Erith 106 EY76
Kale Rd
Dexter Rd, Barn. 27 CX44
Dexter Rd (Harefield), Uxb. 38 BJ54
Deyncourt Gdns, Upmin. 72 FQ61
Deyncourt Rd N17 46 DQ53
Deynecourt Gdns E11 68 EJ56
D'Eynsford Rd SE5 102 DR81
Diadem Ct W1 195 M9
Dial Cl, Green. 129 FX85
Knockhall Rd
Dial Wk, The W8 100 DB75
Dialmead, Pot.B. 11 CT34
Crossoaks La
Diamedes Av, Stai. 114 BK87
Diameter Rd, Orp. 145 EP101
Diamond Cl, Dag. 70 EW60
Diamond Cl, Grays 110 FZ76
Diamond Rd, Ruis. 60 BX63
Diamond Rd, Slou. 92 AU75
Diamond Rd, Wat. 23 BU38
Diamond St SE15 102 DS80
Diamond Ter SE10 103 EC81
Diamond Way SE8 103 EA80
Deptford High St
Diana Cl E18 48 EH53
Diana Cl, Grays 110 FZ76
Diana Cl, Slou. 74 AY72
Diana Gdns, Surb. 138 CM103
Diana Ho SW13 99 CT81
Diana Pl NW1 195 J4
Diana Pl NW1 83 DH70
Diana Rd E17 67 DZ55
Dianne Way, Barn. 28 DE43
Dianthus Cl SE2 106 EV78
Carnation St
Dianthus Cl, Cher. 133 BE101
Dianthus Ct, Wok. 166 AX118
Diban Av, Horn. 71 FH63
Dibden Hill, Ch.St.G. 36 AW49
Dibden La, Sev. 190 FE126
Dibden Row SE1 101 DN76
Gerridge St
Dibden St N1 84 DQ67
Dibdin Cl, Sutt. 140 DA104
Dibdin Rd, Sutt. 140 DA104
Diceland Rd, Bans. 173 CZ116
Dicey Av NW2 63 CW64
Dick Turpin Way, Felt. 95 BT84
Dickens Av N3 44 DC53
Dickens Av, Dart. 108 FN84
Dickens Av, Til. 111 GH81
Dickens Av, Uxb. 77 BP72
Dickens Cl, Erith 107 FB80
Dickens Cl, Hayes 95 BS77
Croyde Av
Dickens Cl, Rich. 118 CL89
Dickens Cl, Wal.Cr. 14 DU26
Dickens Dr, Add. 151 BF107
Dickens Dr, Chis. 125 EQ93
Dickens Est SE1 202 B5
Dickens Est SE1 102 DU75
Dickens Est SE16 202 B5
Dickens Est SE16 102 DU75
Dickens La N18 46 DS50
Dickens Ri, Chig. 49 EN48
Dickens Rd E6 86 EK68
Dickens Rd, Grav. 131 GL88
Dickens Sq SE1 201 J6
Dickens Sq SE1 102 DQ76
Dickens St SW8 101 DH82
Dickens Way, Rom. 71 FE56
Dickenson Cl N9 46 DU46
Croyland Rd
Dickenson Rd N8 65 DL59
Dickenson Rd, Felt. 116 BW92
Dickenson St NW5 83 DH65
Dalby St
Dickensons La SE25 142 DU99
Dickensons Pl SE25 142 DU100
Dickenswood Cl SE19 121 DP94
Dickerage La, N.Mal. 138 CQ97
Dickerage Rd, Kings.T. 138 CQ95
Dickerage Rd, N.Mal. 138 CQ95
Dickinson Av, Rick. 22 BN44
Dickinson Sq, Rick. 22 BN44
Dickson (Cheshunt), Wal.Cr. 14 DT27
Dickson Fold, Pnr. 60 BX56
Dickson Rd SE9 104 EL83
Didsbury Cl E6 87 EM67
Barking Rd
Dig Dag Hill (Cheshunt), Wal.Cr. 14 DT27
Digby Cres N4 66 DQ61
Digby Gdns, Dag. 88 FA67
Digby Pl, Croy. 142 DT104
Digby Rd E9 85 DX65
Digby Rd, Bark. 87 ET66
Digby St E2 84 DW69
Digby Wk, Horn. 90 FJ65
Pembrey Way
Digby Way, W.Byf. 152 BM112
High Rd
Digdens Ri, Epsom 172 CQ115
Dighton Ct SE5 102 DQ79
Dighton Rd SW18 120 DC85
Digswell Cl, Borwd. 26 CN38
Digswell St N7 83 DN65
Holloway Rd
Dilhorne Cl SE12 124 EH90
Dilke St SW3 100 DF79
Dillwyn Cl SE26 123 DY91
Dilston Cl, Nthlt. 78 BW69
Yeading La
Dilston Gro SE16 202 F8
Dilston Rd, Lthd. 171 CG119
Dilton Gdns SW15 119 CU88
Dimes Pl W6 99 CV77
King St
Dimmock Dr, Grnf. 61 CD64
Dimmocks La, Rick. 22 BH36
Dimond Cl E7 68 EG63
Dimsdale Dr NW9 62 CQ60
Dimsdale Dr, Enf. 30 DU44
Dimsdale Wk E13 86 EG67
Stratford Rd
Dimson Cres E3 85 EA70
Dingle, The, Uxb. 77 BP68
Dingle Cl, Barn. 27 CT44
Dingle Gdns E14 204 A1
Dingle Gdns E14 85 EA73
Dingle Rd, Ashf. 115 BP92
Dingley La SW16 121 DK89
Dingley Pl EC1 197 J3
Dingley Pl EC1 84 DQ69
Dingley Rd EC1 197 H3
Dingley Rd EC1 84 DQ69
Dingwall Av, Croy. 142 DQ103
Dingwall Gdns NW11 64 DA58
Dingwall Pl, Croy. 142 DR103
Dingwall Rd
Dingwall Rd SW18 120 DC87
Dingwall Rd, Cars. 158 DF109
Dingwall Rd, Croy. 142 DR103
Dinmont St E2 84 DV68
Coate St
Dinmore, Hem.H. 5 AZ28
Dinsdale Cl, Wok. 167 BA118
Dinsdale Gdns SE25 142 DS99
Dinsdale Gdns, Barn. 28 DB43
Dinsdale Rd SE3 104 EF79
Dinsmore Rd SW12 121 DH87
Dinton Rd SW19 120 DD93
Dinton Rd, Kings.T. 118 CM94
Diploma Av N2 64 DE56
Dirdene Cl, Epsom 157 CT112
Dirdene Gdns, Epsom 157 CT112
Dirdene Gro, Epsom 156 CS112
Dirleton Rd E15 86 EF67
Disbrowe Rd W6 99 CY79
Discovery Wk E1 202 D1
Discovery Wk E1 84 DV74
Dishforth La NW9 42 CS53
Disney Ms N4 65 DP57
Chesterfield Gdns
Disney Pl SE1 201 J4
Disney St SE1 201 J4
Dison Cl, Enf. 31 DX39
Disraeli Cl SE28 88 EW74
Disraeli Cl W4 98 CR77
Acton La
Disraeli Ct, Slou. 93 BB79
Sutton Pl
Disraeli Gdns SW15 99 CZ84
Fawe Pk Rd
Disraeli Rd E7 86 EG65
Disraeli Rd NW10 80 CQ68
Disraeli Rd SW15 99 CY84
Disraeli Rd W5 79 CK74
Diss St E2 197 P2
Diss St E2 84 DT69
Distaff La EC4 197 H10
Distaff La EC4 84 DQ73
Distillery La W6 99 CW78
Fulham Palace Rd
Distillery Rd W6 99 CW78
Distillery Wk, Brent. 98 CL79
Pottery Rd
Distin St SE11 200 D9
Distin St SE11 101 DN77
District Rd, Wem. 61 CH64
Ditch All SE10 103 EB81
Ditchburn St E14 204 E1
Ditchburn St E14 85 EC73
Ditches La, Couls. 175 DL120
Ditches Ride, The, Loug. 33 EN37
Ditchfield Rd, Hayes 78 BY70
Dittisham Rd SE9 124 EL91
Ditton Cl, T.Ditt. 137 CG101
Ditton Gra Cl, Surb. 137 CK102
Ditton Gra Dr, Surb. 137 CK102
Ditton Hill, Surb. 137 CJ102
Ditton Hill Rd, Surb. 137 CJ102
Ditton Lawn, T.Ditt. 137 CG102
Ditton Pk, Slou. 92 AX78
Ditton Pk Rd, Slou. 92 AY79
Ditton Pl SE20 142 DV95
Ditton Reach, T.Ditt. 137 CH100
Ditton Rd, Bexh. 126 EX85
Ditton Rd, Slou. 93 AZ79
Ditton Rd (Datchet), Slou. 92 AX81
Ditton Rd, Sthl. 96 BZ77
Ditton Rd, Surb. 138 CL102
Dittoncroft Cl, Croy. 160 DS105
Divis Way SW15 119 CV86
Dixon Clark Ct N1 83 DP65
Canonbury Rd
Dixon Cl E6 87 EM72
Brandreth Rd
Dixon Dr, Wey. 152 BM110
Dixon Pl, W.Wick. 143 EB102
Dixon Rd SE14 103 DY81
Dixon Rd SE25 142 DS97
Dixon's All SE16 202 D5
Dixon's All SE16 102 DV75
Dixons Hill Cl, Hat. 11 CV25
Dixons Hill Rd, Hat. 11 CU25
Dobbin Cl, Har. 41 CG54
Dobell Rd SE9 125 EM85
Dobree Av NW10 81 CV66
Dobson Cl NW6 82 DD66
Dobson Rd, Grav. 131 GL92
Dock Hill Av SE16 203 J4
Dock Hill Av SE16 103 DX75
Dock Rd E16 205 L1
Dock Rd E16 86 EF73
Dock Rd, Brent. 97 CK80
Dock Rd, Grays 110 GD79
Dock Rd, Til. 111 GF82
Dock St E1 84 DU73
Dockers Tanner Rd E14 203 P7
Dockers Tanner Rd E14 103 EA76
Dockett Eddy La, Shep. 134 BM102
Dockhead SE1 202 A5
Dockhead SE1 102 DT75
Dockland St E16 87 EN74
Dockley Rd SE16 202 B7
Dockley Rd SE16 102 DU76
Dockwell Cl, Felt. 95 BU84
Dockyard Ind Est SE18 104 EL76
Woolwich Ch St
Doctor Johnson Av SW17 121 DH90
Doctors Cl SE26 122 DW92
Doctors La, Cat. 175 DN123
Docwra's Bldgs N1 84 DS65
Dod St E14 85 EA72
Dodbrooke Rd SE27 121 DN90
Doddinghurst Rd, Brwd. 54 FW45
Doddington Gro SE17 101 DP79
Doddington Pl SE17 101 DP79
Dodd's Cres, W.Byf. 152 BH114
Dodds La, Ch.St.G. 36 AU47
Dodd's La, Wok. 152 BG114
Dodsley Pl N9 46 DV48
Dodson St SE1 200 E5
Dodson St SE1 101 DN75
Doebury Wk SE18 106 EU79
Prestwood Cl
Doel Cl SW19 120 DC94
Dog Kennel Hill SE22 102 DS83
Dog Kennel Hill Est SE22 102 DS83
Dog Kennel La, Rick. 21 BF42
Dog La NW10 62 CS63
Doggetts Ct, Barn. 28 DE43
Doggett Rd SE6 123 EA87
Doggetts Fm Rd (Denham), Uxb. 57 BC59
Doggetts Wd Cl, Ch.St.G. 20 AV42
Doggetts Wd La, Ch.St.G. 20 AV41
Doghurst Av, Hayes 95 BP80
Doghurst Dr, West Dr. 95 BP80
Doghurst La, Couls. 174 DF120
Dogwood Cl, Grav. 130 GE91
Doherty Rd E13 86 EG70
Dokal Ind Est, Sthl. 96 BY75
Dolben St SE1 200 F3
Dolben St SE1 83 DP74
Dolby Ct EC4 197 J10
Dolby Rd SW6 99 CZ82
Dolland St SE11 101 DM78
Dollis Av N3 43 CZ53
Dollis Brook Wk, Barn. 27 CY44
Dollis Cres, Ruis. 60 BW60
Dollis Hill Av NW2 63 CV62
Dollis Hill Est NW2 63 CU62
Dollis Hill La NW2 63 CV62
Dollis Ms N3 43 CZ53
Dollis Pk
Dollis Pk N3 43 CZ53
Dollis Rd N3 43 CY52
Dollis Rd NW7 43 CY52
Dollis Valley Grn Wk N20 44 DC47
Totteridge La
Dollis Valley Grn Wk, Barn. 27 CY44
Dollis Valley Way, Barn. 27 CZ44
Dolman Cl N3 44 DC54
Avondale Rd
Dolman Rd W4 98 CR77
Dolman St SW4 101 DM84
Dolphin App, Rom. 71 FF56
Dolphin Cl SE16 203 H4
Dolphin Cl SE28 88 EX72
Dolphin Cl, Surb. 137 CK100
Dolphin Ct NW11 63 CY58
Dolphin Ct, Slou. 92 AV75
Dolphin Rd
Dolphin Ct, Stai. 114 BG90
Bremer Rd
Dolphin Ct N, Stai. 114 BG90
Bremer Rd
Dolphin Est, Sun. 135 BS95
Dolphin La E14 204 B1
Dolphin La E14 85 EB73
Dolphin Rd, Nthlt. 78 BZ68
Dolphin Rd, Slou. 92 AV75
Dolphin Rd, Sun. 135 BS95
Dolphin Rd N, Sun. 135 BS95
Dolphin Rd S, Sun. 135 BR95
Dolphin Rd W, Sun. 135 BR95
Dolphin Sq SW1 101 DJ78
Dolphin Sq W4 98 CS80
Dolphin St, Kings.T. 138 CL95
Dolphin Way, Purf. 109 FS78
Dombey St WC1 196 B6
Dombey St WC1 83 DM71
Dome Hill, Cat. 186 DS127
Dome Hill Pk SE26 122 DT91
Dome Hill Peak, Cat. 186 DS126
Dome Way, Red. 184 DF133
Domett Cl SE5 102 DR84
Domfe Pl E5 66 DW63
Rushmore Rd
Domingo St EC1 197 H4
Dominic Ct, Wal.Abb. 15 EB33
Dominica Cl E13 86 EJ68
Dominion Dr, Rom. 51 FB51
Dominion Rd, Croy. 142 DT101
Dominion Rd, Sthl. 96 BY76
Dominion St EC2 197 L6
Dominion Way, Rain. 89 FG69
Domonic Dr SE9 125 EP91
Domville Cl N20 44 DD47
Don Phelan Cl SE5 102 DR81
Don Way, Rom. 51 FE52
Donald Biggs Dr, Grav. 131 GK87
Donald Dr, Rom. 70 EW57
Donald Rd E13 86 EH67
Donald Rd, Croy. 141 DM100
Donald Wds Gdns, Surb. 138 CP103
Donaldson Rd NW6 81 CZ67
Donaldson Rd SE18 105 EN81
Doncaster Dr, Nthlt. 60 BZ64
Doncaster Gdns N4 66 DQ58
Stanhope Gdns
Doncaster Gdns, Nthlt. 60 BZ64
Doncaster Grn, Wat. 40 BW50
Doncaster Rd N9 46 DV45
Doncaster Way, Upmin. 72 FM62
Doncel Ct E4 47 ED45
Donegal St N1 196 C1
Donegal St N1 83 DM68
Doneraile St SW6 99 CX82
Dongola Rd E13 86 EH69
Dongola Rd N17 66 DS55
Dongola Rd W E13 86 EH69
Balaam St
Donington Av, Ilf. 69 EQ57
Donkey All SE22 122 DU87
Donkey La (Farningham), Dart. 148 FP103
Donkey La, Enf. 30 DU40
Donkey La, West Dr. 94 BJ77
Donnay Cl, Ger.Cr. 56 AX58
Donne Ct SE24 122 DQ86
Donne Gdns, Wok. 167 BE115
Donne Pl SW3 198 C8
Donne Pl SW3 100 DE77
Donne Pl, Mitch. 141 DH98
Donne Rd, Dag. 70 EW61
Donnefield Av, Edg. 42 CL52
Donnington Rd NW10 81 CV66
Donnington Rd, Har. 61 CK57
Donnington Rd, Sev. 181 FD120
Donnington Rd, Wor.Pk. 139 CU103
Donnybrook Rd SW16 121 DJ94
Donovan Av N10 45 DH54
Donovan Cl, Epsom 156 CR110
Nimbus Rd
Doods Pk Rd, Reig. 184 DC133
Doods Rd, Reig. 184 DC133
Doods Way, Reig. 184 DD133
Doon St SE1 200 D3
Doone Cl, Tedd. 117 CG93
Dora Rd SW19 120 DA92
Dora St E14 85 DZ72
Dorado Gdns, Orp. 146 EX104
Doral Way, Cars. 158 DF106
Doran Dr, Red. 184 DD134
Doran Gdns, Red. 184 DD134
Doran Gro SE18 105 ES80
Doran Mans N2 64 DF57
Great N Rd
Doran Wk E15 85 EC66
Dorchester Av N13 46 DQ49
Dorchester Av, Bex. 126 EX88
Dorchester Av, Har. 60 CC58
Dorchester Cl, Dart. 128 FM87
Dorchester Cl, Nthlt. 60 CB64
Dorchester Cl, Orp. 126 EU94
Grovelands Rd
Dorchester Ct N14 45 DH45
Dorchester Ct SE24 122 DQ85
Dorchester Ct, Rick. 23 BR43
Mayfare
Dorchester Ct, Wok. 167 BA116
Dorchester Dr SE24 122 DQ85
Dorchester Dr, Felt. 115 BS86
Dorchester Gdns E4 47 EA49
Dorchester Gdns NW11 64 DA56
Dorchester Gro W4 98 CS78
Dorchester Ms, N.Mal. 138 CR98
Elm Rd
Dorchester Ms, Twick. 117 CJ87
Dorchester Rd, Grav. 131 GK90
Dorchester Rd, Mord. 140 DB101
Dorchester Rd, Nthlt. 60 CB64
Dorchester Rd, Wey. 135 BP104
Dorchester Rd, Wor.Pk. 139 CW102
Dorchester Way, Har. 62 CM58
Dorchester Waye, Hayes 78 BW72
Dorcis Av, Bexh. 106 EY82
Dordrecht Rd W3 80 CS74
Dore Av E12 69 EN64
Dore Gdns, Mord. 140 DB101
Doreen Av NW9 62 CR60
Dorell Cl, Sthl. 78 BZ71
Doria Dr, Grav. 131 GL90
Doria Rd SW6 99 CZ82
Dorian Rd, Horn. 71 FG60
Doric Dr, Tad. 173 CZ120
Doric Way NW1 195 M2
Doric Way NW1 83 DK69
Dorien Rd SW20 139 CX96
Dorincourt, Wok. 167 BE115
Doris Av, Erith 107 FC81
Doris Rd E7 86 EG66
Doris Rd, Ashf. 115 BR93
Dorking Cl SE8 103 DZ79
Dorking Cl, Wor.Pk. 139 CX103
Dorking Gdns, Rom. 52 FK50
Dorking Glen, Rom. 52 FK49
Dorking Ri, Rom. 52 FK49
Dorking Rd, Epsom 172 CN116
Dorking Rd, Lthd. 171 CH122
Dorking Rd, Rom. 52 FK49
Dorking Rd, Tad. 173 CX123
Dorking Wk, Rom. 52 FK49
Dorkins Way, Upmin. 73 FS59
Dorlcote Rd SW18 120 DE8
Dorling Dr, Epsom 157 CT11
Dorly Cl, Shep. 135 BS9
Dorma Trd Pk E10 67 DX6
Dorman Pl N9 46 DU4
Balham Rd
Dorman Wk NW10 62 CR6
Garden Way
Dorman Way NW8 82 DD6
Dormans Cl, Nthwd. 39 BR5
Dormay St SW18 120 DB8
Dormer Cl E15 86 EF6
Dormer Cl, Barn. 27 CX4
Dormers Av, Sthl. 78 CA7
Dormers Ri, Sthl. 78 CB7
Dormers Wells La, Sthl. 78 CA7
Dormywood, Ruis. 59 BT5
Dornberg Cl SE3 104 EG8
Dornberg Rd SE3 104 EH8
Banchory Rd
Dorncliffe Rd SW6 99 CY8
Dornels, Slou. 74 AW7
Dorney NW3 82 DE6
Dorney Gro, Wey. 135 BP10
Dorney Ri, Orp. 145 ET9
Dorney Way, Houns. 116 BY8
Dornfell St NW6 63 CZ6
Dornford Gdns, Couls. 176 DQ11
Dornton Rd SW12 121 DH8
Dornton Rd, S.Croy. 160 DR10
Dorothy Av, Wem. 80 CL6
Dorothy Evans Cl, Bexh. 107 FB8
Dorothy Gdns, Dag. 70 EV6
Dorothy Rd SW11 100 DF8
Dorrell Pl SW9 101 DN84
Brixton Rd
Dorrien Wk SW16 121 DK8
Dorrington Ct SE25 142 DS96
Dorrington Gdns, Horn. 72 FK60
Dorrington Pt E3 85 EB69
Bromley High St
Dorrington St EC1 196 D6
Dorrington St EC1 83 DN71
Dorrit Ms N18 46 DS49
Dorrit Way, Chis. 125 EQ93
Dorrofield Cl, Rick. 23 BQ43
Dors Cl NW9 62 CR60
Dorset Av, Hayes 77 BS69
Dorset Av, Rom. 71 FD55
Dorset Av, Sthl. 96 CA77
Dorset Av, Well. 105 ET84
Dorset Bldgs EC4 196 F9
Dorset Cl NW1 194 D6
Dorset Cl, Hayes 77 BS69
Dorset Cres, Grav. 131 GL91
Dorset Dr, Edg. 42 CM51
Dorset Dr, Wok. 167 BB117
Dorset Est E2 84 DT69
Dorset Gdns, Mitch. 141 DM98
Dorset Ms N3 44 DA53
Dorset Ms SW1 199 H6
Dorset Pl E15 85 ED65
Dorset Pl SW1 199 M10
Dorset Ri EC4 196 F9
Dorset Ri EC4 83 DP72
Dorset Rd E7 86 EJ66
Dorset Rd N15 66 DR56
Dorset Rd N22 45 DL53
Dorset Rd SE9 124 EL89
Dorset Rd SW8 101 DM80
Dorset Rd SW19 140 DA95
Dorset Rd W5 97 CJ76
Dorset Rd, Ashf. 114 BK90
Dorset Rd, Beck. 143 DX97
Dorset Rd, Har. 60 CC58
Dorset Rd, Mitch. 140 DE96
Dorset Rd, Sutt. 158 DA110
Dorset Sq NW1 194 D5
Dorset Sq NW1 82 DF70
Dorset Sq, Epsom 156 CR110
Dorset St W1 194 E7
Dorset St W1 82 DG71
Dorset St, Sev. 191 FH125
High St
Dorset Way, Twick. 117 CD88
Dorset Way, Uxb. 76 BM68
Dorset Way, W.Byf. 152 BK110
Dorset Waye, Houns. 96 BZ80
Dorton Cl SE15 102 DT80
Chandler Way
Dorton Dr, Sev. 191 FM122
Dorton Way, Wok. 168 BH121
Dorville Cres W6 99 CV76
Dorville Rd SE12 124 EF85
Dothill Rd SE18 105 ER80
Douai Gro, Hmptn. 136 CC95
Doubleday Rd, Loug. 33 EQ41
Doug Siddons Ct, Grays 110 GC79
Elm Rd
Doughty Ms WC1 196 B5
Doughty Ms WC1 83 DM70
Doughty St WC1 196 B4
Doughty St WC1 83 DM70
Douglas Av E17 47 EA53
Douglas Av, N.Mal. 139 CV98
Douglas Av, Rom. 52 FL54
Douglas Av, Wat. 24 BX37
Douglas Av, Wem. 80 CL66
Douglas Cl, Grays 110 FY76
Douglas Cl, Stan. 41 CG50
Douglas Cl, Wall. 159 DL108
Douglas Ct, Cat. 176 DQ122
Fairbourne La
Douglas Ct, West. 178 EL117
Douglas Cres, Hayes 78 BW70
Douglas Dr, Croy. 143 EA104
Douglas Est N1 84 DQ65
Douglas La, Stai. 113 AZ85
Douglas Ms NW2 63 CY62
Douglas Ms, Bans. 173 CZ116
North Acre
Douglas Rd E4 48 EE45
Douglas Rd E16 86 EG71
Douglas Rd N1 84 DQ66
Douglas Rd N22 45 DN53
Douglas Rd NW6 81 CZ67
Douglas Rd, Add. 134 BH104
Douglas Rd, Esher 136 CB103
Douglas Rd, Horn. 71 FF58
Douglas Rd, Houns. 96 CB83
Douglas Rd, Ilf. 70 EU58
Douglas Rd, Kings.T. 138 CP96

Douglas Rd, Reig. 184 DA133
Douglas Rd, Stai. 114 BK86
Douglas Rd, Surb. 138 CM103
Douglas Rd, Well. 106 EV81
Douglas Sq, Mord. 140 DA100
Douglas St SW1 199 M9
Douglas St SW1 101 DK77
Douglas Ter E17 47 EA53
Douglas Av
Douglas Way SE8 103 DZ80
Doulton Ms NW6 82 DB65
Lymington Rd
Doultons, The, Stai. 114 BG94
Dounesforth Gdns SW18 120 DB88
Dounsell Ct, Brwd. 54 FU44
Ongar Rd
Douro Pl W8 100 DB76
Douro St E3 85 EA68
Douthwaite Sq E1 202 C2
Dove App E6 86 EL71
Dove Cl NW7 43 CT52
Bunns La
Dove Cl, Nthlt. 78 BX70
Wayfarer Rd
Dove Cl, S.Croy. 161 DX111
Dove Ct EC2 197 K9
Dove Ho Gdns E4 47 EA47
Dove La, Pot.B. 12 DB34
Dove Ms SW5 100 DC77
Dove Pk, Pnr. 40 CA52
Dove Pk, Rick. 21 BB44
Dove Rd N1 84 DR65
Dove Row E2 84 DU67
Dove Wk SW1 198 F10
Dove Wk, Horn. 89 FH65
Heron Flight Av
Dovecot Cl, Pnr. 59 BV57
Dovecote Av N22 65 DN55
Dovecote Cl, Wey. 135 BP104
Dovecote Gdns SW14 98 CR83
Avondale Rd
Dovedale Av, Har. 61 CJ58
Dovedale Av, Ilf. 49 EN54
Dovedale Cl (Harefield), Uxb. 38 BJ54
Dovedale Cl, Well. 106 EU82
Dovedale Ri, Mitch. 120 DF94
Dovedale Rd SE22 122 DV85
Dovedale Rd, Dart. 128 FQ88
Dovedon Cl N14 45 DL47
Dovehouse Grn, Wey. 153 BR105
Rosslyn Pk
Dovehouse Mead, Bark. 87 ER68
Dovehouse St SW3 198 B10
Dovehouse St SW3 100 DD78
Doveney Cl, Orp. 146 EW97
Dover Cl NW2 63 CX61
Brent Ter
Dover Cl, Rom. 51 FC54
Dover Flats SE1 102 DS77
Old Kent Rd
Dover Gdns, Cars. 140 DF104
Dover Ho Rd SW15 99 CU84
Dover Pk Dr SW15 119 CV86
Dover Patrol SE3 104 EH82
Kidbrooke Way
Dover Rd E12 68 EJ61
Dover Rd N9 46 DW47
Dover Rd SE19 122 DR93
Dover Rd, Grav. 130 GD87
Dover Rd, Rom. 70 EY58
Dover Rd E, Grav. 130 GE87
Dover St W1 199 J1
Dover St W1 83 DH73
Dover Way, Rick. 23 BQ42
Dover Yd W1 199 K2
Dovercourt Av, Th.Hth. 141 DN98
Dovercourt Est N1 84 DR65
Dovercourt Gdns, Stan. 42 CL50
Dovercourt La, Sutt. 140 DC104
Dovercourt Rd SE22 122 DS86
Doverfield, Wal.Cr. 14 DQ29
Doverfield Rd SW2 121 DL86
Doveridge Gdns N13 45 DP49
Doversmead, Wok. 166 AS116
Doves Cl, Brom. 144 EL103
Dove's Yd N1 83 DN67
Doveton Rd, S.Croy. 160 DR106
Doveton St E1 84 DW70
Malcolm Rd
Dowanhill Rd SE6 123 ED88
Dowdeswell Cl SW15 98 CS84
Dowding Pl, Stan. 41 CG51
Dowding Rd, Uxb. 76 BM66
Dowding Rd, West. 178 EK115
Dowding Wk, Grav. 130 GE90
Dowding Way, Horn. 89 FH66
Dower Av, Wall. 159 DH109
Dowgate Hill EC4 197 K10
Dowgate Hill EC4 84 DR73
Dowland St W10 81 CY68
Dowlas Est SE5 102 DS80
Dowlas St
Dowlas St SE5 102 DS80
Dowlerville Rd, Orp. 163 ET107
Dowman Cl SW19 140 DB95
Nelson Gro Rd
Down Cl, Nthlt. 77 BV68
Down Hall Rd, Kings.T. 137 CK95
Down Pl W6 99 CV77
Down Rd, Tedd. 117 CH93
Down St W1 199 H3
Down St W1 83 DH74
Down St, W.Mol. 136 CA99
Down St Ms W1 199 H3
Down Way, Nthlt. 77 BV69
Downage NW4 63 CW55
Downage, The, Grav. 131 GG89
Downalong, Bushey 41 CD46
Downbank Av, Bexh. 107 FD81
Downbarns Rd, Ruis. 60 BX62
Downbury Ms SW18 120 DA86
Merton Rd
Downderry Rd, Brom. 123 ED90
Downe Av, Sev. 163 EQ112
Downe Cl, Well. 106 EW80
Downe Rd, Kes. 162 EL109
Downe Rd, Mitch. 140 DF96
Downe Rd, Sev. 163 EQ114
Downend SE18 105 EP80
Moordown
Downer Dr, Rick. 22 BG36
Downers Cotts SW4 101 DJ84
The Pavement
Downes Cl, Twick. 117 CH86
St. Margarets Rd
Downes Ct N21 45 DN46
Downfield, Wor.Pk. 139 CT102
Downfield Cl W9 82 DB70
Downfield Rd (Cheshunt), Wal.Cr. 15 DY31
Downham Cl, Rom. 50 FA52
Downham La, Brom. 123 ED92
Downham Way
Downham Rd N1 84 DR66
Downham Way, Brom. 123 ED92
Downhills Av N17 66 DR55
Downhills Pk Rd N17 66 DQ55
Downhills Way N17 66 DQ55
Downhurst Av NW7 42 CR50
Downing Cl, Har. 60 CC55
Downing Dr, Grnf. 79 CD67
Downing Rd, Dag. 88 EZ67
Downing St SW1 199 P4
Downing St SW1 101 DL75
Downings E6 87 EN72
Downings Wd, Rick. 37 BD50
Downland Cl N20 44 DC46
Downland Cl, Couls. 159 DH114
Downland Cl, Epsom 173 CV118
Downland Gdns, Epsom 173 CV118
Downland Way, Epsom 173 CV118
Downlands, Wal.Abb. 16 EE34
Downlands Rd, Pur. 159 DL113
Downleys Cl SE9 124 EL89
Downman Rd SE9 104 EL83
Downs, The SW20 119 CX94
Downs Av, Chis. 125 EM92
Downs Av, Dart. 128 FN87
Downs Av, Epsom 156 CS114
Downs Av, Pnr. 60 BZ58
Downs Br Rd, Beck. 143 ED95
Downs Ct Rd, Pur. 159 DP112
Downs Hill, Beck. 143 ED95
Downs Hill, Grav. 130 GC94
Downs Hill Rd, Epsom 156 CS114
Downs Ho Rd, Epsom 173 CT118
Downs La E5 66 DV63
Downs Rd
Downs La, Lthd. 171 CH123
Downs Pk Rd E5 66 DU64
Downs Pk Rd E8 66 DT64
Downs Rd E5 66 DU63
Downs Rd, Beck. 143 EB96
Downs Rd, Couls. 175 DK118
Downs Rd, Enf. 30 DS42
Downs Rd, Epsom 172 CS115
Downs Rd, Grav. 130 GD91
Downs Rd, Pur. 159 DP111
Downs Rd, Slou. 92 AX75
Downs Rd, Sutt. 158 DB110
Downs Rd, Th.Hth. 142 DQ95
Downs Side, Sutt. 157 CZ111
Downs Vw, Islw. 97 CF80
Downs Vw, Tad. 173 CV121
Downs Way, Epsom 173 CT116
Downs Way, Oxt. 188 EE127
Downs Way, Tad. 173 CV121
Downs Way Cl, Tad. 173 CU121
Downs Wd, Epsom 173 CV117
Downsbury Ms SW18 120 DA85
Merton Rd
Downsell Rd E15 67 EC63
Downsfield Rd E17 67 DY58
Downshall Av, Ilf. 69 ES58
Downshire Hill NW3 64 DD63
Downside, Cher. 133 BF102
Downside, Epsom 156 CS114
Downside, Sun. 135 BU95
Downside, Twick. 117 CF90
Downside Br Rd, Cob. 169 BV115
Downside Cl SW19 120 DC93
Downside Common, Cob. 169 BV118
Downside Common Rd, Cob. 169 BV118
Downside Cres NW3 64 DE64
Downside Cres W13 79 CG70
Downside Orchard, Wok. 167 BA117
Park Rd
Downside Rd, Cob. 169 BV116
Downside Rd, Sutt. 158 DD107
Downside Wk, Nthlt. 78 BZ69
Downsland Dr, Brwd. 54 FW48
Downsview Av, Wok. 167 AZ121
Downsview Cl, Orp. 164 EW110
Downsview Cl, Swan. 147 FF97
Downsview Gdns SE19 121 DP94
Downsview Rd SE19 122 DQ94
Downsview Rd, Sev. 190 FF125
Downsway, Orp. 163 ES106
Downsway, S.Croy. 160 DS111
Downsway, Whyt. 176 DT116
Downsway, The, Sutt. 158 DC109
Downswood, Reig. 184 DE131
Downton Av SW2 121 DL89
Downtown Rd SE16 203 L4
Downtown Rd SE16 103 DY75
Downview Cl, Cob. 169 BV119
Downway N12 44 DE52
Downrey St N1 83 DN67
Richmond Av
Dowry Wk, Wat. 23 BT38
Dowsett Rd N17 46 DT54
Dowson Cl SE5 102 DR84
Doyce St SE1 201 H4
Doyle Cl, Erith 107 FE81
Doyle Gdns NW10 81 CU67
Doyle Rd SE25 142 DU98
Doyle Way, Til. 111 GJ82
Coleridge Rd
D'Oyley St SW1 198 F8
D'Oyley St SW1 100 DG77
D'Oyly Carte Island, Wey. 135 BP102
Doynton St N19 65 DH61
Draco St SE17 102 DQ79
Dragmire La, Mitch. 140 DD98
Dragon La, Wey. 152 BN110
Dragon Rd SE15 102 DS79
Dragonfly Cl E13 86 EH69
Hollybush St
Dragoon Rd SE8 103 DZ78
Dragor Rd NW10 80 CQ70
Drake Av, Cat. 176 DQ122
Drake Av, Slou. 92 AX77
Drake Av, Stai. 113 BF92
Drake Cl SE16 203 J4
Drake Cl, Brwd. 54 FX50
Drake Ct SE19 122 DT92
Drake Ct, Har. 60 BZ60
Drake Cres SE28 88 EW72
Drake Ms, Horn. 89 FG66
Fulmar Rd
Drake Rd SE4 103 EA83
Drake Rd, Chess. 156 CN106
Drake Rd, Croy. 141 DM101
Drake Rd, Grays 110 FY75
Drake Rd, Har. 60 BZ61
Drake Rd, Mitch. 140 DG100
Drake St WC1 196 B7
Drake St, Enf. 30 DR39
Drakefell Rd SE4 103 DX82
Drakefell Rd SE14 103 DX82
Drakefield Rd SW17 120 DG90
Drakeley Ct N5 65 DP63
Highbury Hill
Drakes Cl, Esher 154 CA106
Drakes Cl (Cheshunt), Wal.Cr. 15 DX28
Drakes Ctyd NW6 81 CZ66
Drakes Dr, Nthwd. 39 BP53
Drakes Wk E6 87 EM67
Drakes Way, Wok. 166 AX122
Drakewood Rd SW16 121 DK94
Draper Cl, Belv. 106 EZ77
Draper Cl, Islw. 97 CD80
Thornbury Rd
Draper Pl N1 83 DP67
Essex Rd
Drapers Gdns EC2 84 DR72
Copthall Av
Drapers Rd E15 67 ED63
Drapers Rd N17 66 DT55
Drapers Rd, Enf. 29 DP40
Drappers Way SE16 202 C8
Draven Cl, Brom. 144 EF101
Drawdock Rd SE10 204 G3
Drawdock Rd SE10 85 ED74
Drawell Cl SE18 105 ES78
Drax Av SW20 119 CU94
Draxmont SW19 119 CY93
Dray Gdns SW2 121 DM85
Draycot Rd E11 68 EH58
Draycot Rd, Surb. 138 CN102
Draycott Av SW3 198 C8
Draycott Av SW3 100 DE77
Draycott Av, Har. 61 CH58
Draycott Cl, Har. 61 CH58
Draycott Ms SW6 99 CZ82
New Kings Rd
Draycott Pl SW3 198 D9
Draycott Pl SW3 100 DF77
Draycott Ter SW3 198 E8
Draycott Ter SW3 100 DF77
Drayford Cl W9 81 CZ70
Draymans Way, Islw. 97 CF83
Drayside Ms, Sthl. 96 BZ75
Kingston Rd
Drayson Cl, Wal.Abb. 16 EE32
Drayson Ms W8 100 DA75
Drayton Av W13 79 CG73
Drayton Av, Loug. 33 EM44
Drayton Av, Orp. 145 EP102
Drayton Av, Pot.B. 11 CY32
Drayton Br Rd W7 79 CF73
Drayton Br Rd W13 79 CF73
Drayton Cl, Houns. 116 BZ85
Bramley Way
Drayton Cl, Ilf. 69 ER60
Drayton Cl, Lthd. 171 CE124
Drayton Ford, Rick. 38 BG48
Drayton Gdns N21 45 DP45
Drayton Gdns SW10 100 DC78
Drayton Gdns W13 79 CG73
Drayton Gdns, West Dr. 94 BL75
Drayton Grn W13 79 CG73
Drayton Grn Rd W13 79 CH73
Drayton Gro W13 79 CG73
Drayton Pk N5 65 DN64
Drayton Pk Ms N5 65 DN64
Drayton Pk
Drayton Rd E11 67 ED60
Drayton Rd N17 46 DS54
Drayton Rd NW10 81 CT67
Drayton Rd W13 79 CG73
Drayton Rd, Borwd. 26 CN42
Drayton Rd, Croy. 141 DP103
Drayton Waye, Har. 61 CH58
Drenon Sq, Hayes 77 BT73
Dresden Cl NW6 82 DB65
Dresden Rd N19 65 DK60
Dresden Way, Wey. 153 BQ106
Dressington Av SE4 123 EA86
Drew Av NW7 43 CY51
Drew Gdns, Grnf. 79 CF65
Drew Pl, Cat. 176 DR123
Drew Rd E16 86 EL74
Drewstead Rd SW16 121 DK89
Drey, The (Chalfont St. Peter), Ger.Cr. 36 AY50
Driffield Rd E3 85 DY68
Drift, The, Brom. 144 EK104
Drift La, Cob. 170 BZ117
Drift Rd, Lthd. 169 BT124
Drift Way, Rich. 118 CM88
Drift Way, Slou. 93 BC81
Driftway, The, Bans. 173 CW115
Driftway, The, Lthd. 171 CH123
Downs La
Driftway, The, Mitch. 140 DG95
Driftwood Av, St.Alb. 8 CA26
Driftwood Dr, Ken. 175 DP117
Drill Hall Rd, Cher. 134 BG101
Drinkwater Rd, Har. 60 CB61
Drive, The E4 47 ED45
Drive, The E17 67 EB56
Drive, The E18 68 EG56
Drive, The N3 44 DA52
Drive, The N11 45 DJ51
Drive, The NW10 81 CT67
Longstone Av
Drive, The NW11 63 CY59
Drive, The SW6 99 CY82
Fulham Rd
Drive, The SW16 141 DM97
Drive, The SW20 119 CW94
Drive, The W3 80 CQ72
Drive, The, Ashf. 115 BR94
Drive, The, Bans. 173 CY117
Drive, The, Bark. 87 ET66
Drive, The, Barn. 27 CY41
Drive, The (New Barnet), Barn. 28 DC44
Drive, The, Beck. 143 EA96
Drive, The, Bex. 126 EW86
Drive, The, Brwd. 54 FW50
Drive, The, Buck.H. 48 EJ45
Drive, The, Chis. 145 ET97
Drive, The (Scadbury Pk), Chis. 145 ES95
Drive, The, Cob. 154 BY114
Drive, The, Couls. 159 DL114
Drive, The, Edg. 42 CN50
Drive, The, Enf. 30 DR39
Drive, The, Epsom 157 CT107
Drive, The (Headley), Epsom 172 CN124
Drive, The, Erith 107 FB80
Drive, The, Esher 136 CC102
Drive, The, Felt. 116 BW87
Drive, The (Chalfont St. Peter), Ger.Cr. 36 AY52
Drive, The, Grav. 131 GK91
Drive, The, Har. 60 CA59
Drive, The, Hat. 12 DA25
Drive, The, Houns. 97 CD82
Drive, The, Ilf. 69 EM60
Drive, The, Islw. 97 CD82
Drive, The, Kings.T. 118 CQ94
Drive, The, Lthd. 172 CN124
Drive, The (Fetcham), Lthd. 171 CE122
Drive, The, Loug. 32 EL41
Drive, The, Mord. 140 DD99
Drive, The, Nthwd. 39 BS54
Drive, The, Orp. 145 ET103
Drive, The, Pot.B. 11 CZ33
Drive, The, Rad. 9 CG34
Drive, The, Rick. 22 BJ44
Drive, The, Rom. 51 FC53
Drive, The (Harold Wd), Rom. 52 FL53
Drive, The, St.Alb. 9 CG26
Drive, The, Sev. 191 FH124
Drive, The, Sid. 126 EV90
Drive, The, Slou. 92 AY75
Drive, The (Datchet), Slou. 92 AV81
Drive, The, Stai. 112 AX85
Drive, The, Surb. 138 CL101
Drive, The, Sutt. 157 CZ112
Drive, The, Th.Hth. 142 DR98
Drive, The, Uxb. 58 BL63
Drive, The, Vir.W. 133 AZ99
Drive, The, Wall. 159 DJ110
Drive, The (Cheshunt), Wal.Cr. 13 DP28
Drive, The, Wat. 23 BR37
Drive, The, Wem. 62 CQ61
Drive, The, W.Wick. 143 ED101
Drive, The, Wok. 166 AV120
Drive Mead, Couls. 159 DL114
Drive Rd, Couls. 175 DM119
Drive Spur, Tad. 174 DB121
Driveway, The E17 67 EB58
Hoe St
Driveway, The (Cuffley), Pot.B. 13 DL28
Droitwich Cl SE26 122 DU90
Dromey Gdns, Har. 41 CF52
Dromore Rd SW15 119 CY86
Dronfield Gdns, Dag. 70 EW64
Droop St W10 81 CY70
Drop La, St.Alb. 8 CB30
Drove Way, The, Grav. 130 GE94
Drover La SE15 102 DV80
Drovers Pl SE15 102 DV80
Drovers Rd, S.Croy. 160 DR106
Droveway, Loug. 33 EP40
Druce Rd SE21 122 DS86
Drudgeon Way, Dart. 129 FV90
Druid St SE1 201 N4
Druid St SE1 102 DS75
Druids Cl, Ash. 172 CM120
Druids Way, Brom. 143 ED98
Drum St E1 84 DT72
Whitechapel High St
Drumaline Ridge, Wor.Pk. 138 CS103
Drummond Av, Rom. 71 FD56
Drummond Cl, Erith 107 FE81
Drummond Cres NW1 195 M2
Drummond Cres NW1 83 DK69
Drummond Dr, Stan. 41 CF52
Drummond Gdns, Epsom 156 CP111
Drummond Gate SW1 199 N10
Drummond Gate SW1 101 DK78
Drummond Pl, Rich. 98 CL84
Drummond Pl, Twick. 117 CH86
Drummond Rd E11 68 EJ58
Drummond Rd SE16 202 D6
Drummond Rd SE16 102 DV76
Drummond Rd, Croy. 142 DQ103
Drummond Rd, Rom. 71 FD56
Drummond St NW1 195 K4
Drummond St NW1 83 DJ70
Drummonds, The, Buck.H. 48 EH47
Drummonds, The, Epp. 18 EU30
Drury Cres, Croy. 141 DN103
Drury La WC2 196 A9
Drury La WC2 83 DL72
Drury Rd, Har. 60 CC59
Drury Way NW10 62 CR64
Drury Way Ind Est NW10 62 CQ64
Dryad St SW15 99 CX83
Dryburgh Gdns NW9 62 CN55
Dryburgh Rd SW15 99 CV83
Dryden Av W7 79 CF72
Dryden Cl, Ilf. 49 ET51
Dryden Ct SE11 200 E9
Dryden Ct SE11 101 DN77
Dryden Pl, Til. 111 GH81
Fielding Av
Dryden Rd SW19 120 DC93
Dryden Rd, Enf. 30 DS44
Dryden Rd, Har. 41 CF53
Dryden Rd, Well. 105 ES81
Dryden St WC2 196 A9
Dryden Twrs, Rom. 51 FH52
Dryden Way, Orp. 146 EU102
Dryfield Cl NW10 80 CQ65
Dryfield Rd, Edg. 42 CQ51
Dryfield Wk SE8 103 EA79
New King St
Dryhill La, Sev. 190 FB123
Dryhill Rd, Belv. 106 EZ79
Dryland Av, Orp. 163 ET105
Drylands Rd N8 65 DL58
Drynham Pk, Wey. 135 BS104
Drysdale Av E4 47 EB45
Drysdale Cl, Nthwd. 39 BS52
Northbrook Dr
Drysdale Pl N1 197 N2
Drysdale St N1 197 N2
Drysdale St N1 84 DS69
Du Burstow Ter W7 97 CE75
Du Cane Cl W12 81 CW72
Du Cane Ct SW17 120 DG88
Du Cane Rd W12 81 CT72
Du Cros Dr, Stan. 41 CJ51
Du Cros Rd W3 80 CS74
The Vale
Duarte Pl, Grays 110 FZ76
Dublin Av E8 84 DU67
Ducal St E2 84 DT69
Brick La
Duchess Cl N11 45 DH50
Duchess Cl, Sutt. 158 DC105
Duchess Gro, Buck.H. 48 EH47
Duchess Ms W1 195 J7
Duchess of Bedford's Wk W8 100 DA75
Duchess St W1 195 J7
Duchess St W1 83 DH71
Duchess Wk, Sev. 191 FL125
Duchy Rd, Barn. 28 DD38
Duchy St SE1 200 E2
Duchy St SE1 83 DN74
Ducie St SW4 101 DM84
Duck La W1 195 M9
Duck La, Epp. 18 EW26
Duck Lees La, Enf. 31 DY42
Duckett Ms N4 65 DP58
Duckett Rd
Duckett Rd N4 65 DP58
Duckett St E1 85 DX71
Ducketts Rd, Dart. 127 FF85
Ducking Stool Ct, Rom. 71 FE56
Ducks Hill, Nthwd. 39 BP54
Ducks Hill Rd, Nthwd. 39 BP54
Ducks Hill Rd, Ruis. 39 BP54
Ducks Wk, Twick. 117 CJ85
Dudden Hill La NW10 63 CT63
Duddington Cl SE9 124 EK91
Dudley Av, Har. 61 CJ55
Dudley Av, Wal.Cr. 15 DX32
Dudley Cl, Add. 134 BJ104
Dudley Cl, Grays 110 FY75
Dudley Cl, Hem.H. 5 BA27
Dudley Ct NW11 63 CZ56
Dudley Ct, Slou. 92 AU76
Upton Rd
Dudley Dr, Mord. 139 CY101
Dudley Dr, Ruis. 59 BV64
Dudley Gdns W13 97 CH75
Dudley Gdns, Har. 61 CD60
Dudley Gdns, Rom. 52 FK51
Dudley Rd
Dudley Gro, Epsom 156 CQ114
Dudley Rd E17 47 EA54
Dudley Rd N3 44 DB54
Dudley Rd NW6 81 CY68
Dudley Rd SW19 120 DA93
Dudley Rd, Ashf. 114 BM92
Dudley Rd, Felt. 115 BQ88
Dudley Rd, Grav. 130 GE87
Dudley Rd, Har. 60 CC61
Dudley Rd, Ilf. 69 EP63
Dudley Rd, Kings.T. 138 CM97
Dudley Rd, Rich. 98 CM82
Dudley Rd, Rom. 52 FK51
Dudley Rd, Sthl. 96 BX75
Dudley Rd, Walt. 135 BU100
Dudley St W2 82 DD71
Dudlington Rd E5 66 DW61
Dudmaston Ms SW3 198 A10
Dudsbury Rd, Dart. 127 FG86
Dudsbury Rd, Sid. 126 EV93
Dudset La, Houns. 95 BU81
Duff St E14 85 EB72
Dufferin Av EC1 197 K5
Dufferin St EC1 197 J5
Dufferin St EC1 84 DQ70
Duffield Cl (Daniel Cl), Grays 110 FY75
Duffield Cl (Davis Rd), Grays 110 FZ76
Duffield Cl, Har. 61 CF57
Duffield Dr N15 66 DT56
Copperfield Dr
Duffield La, Slou. 74 AT65
Duffield Pk, Slou. 74 AT69
Duffield Rd, Tad. 173 CV124
Duffins Orchard, Cher. 151 BC108
Dufour's Pl W1 195 L9
Dugard Way SE11 200 F8
Dugard Way SE11 101 DP77
Dugdale Hill La, Pot.B. 11 CY33
Dugdales, Rick. 22 BN42
Duke Gdns, Ilf. 69 ER56
Duke Rd
Duke Humphrey Rd SE3 104 EE81
Duke of Cambridge Cl, Twick. 117 CD86
Duke of Edinburgh Rd, Sutt. 140 DD103
Duke of Wellington Pl SW1 198 G4
Duke of Wellington Pl SW1 100 DG75
Duke of York St SW1 199 L2
Duke of York St SW1 83 DJ74
Duke Rd W4 98 CR78
Duke Rd, Ilf. 69 ER56
Duke Shore Pl E14 203 M1
Duke Shore Wf E14 85 DZ73
Narrow St
Duke St SW1 199 L2
Duke St SW1 83 DJ74

Duke St W1 194 G8
Duke St W1 82 DG72
Duke St, Rich. 97 CK84
Duke St, Sutt. 158 DD105
Duke St, Wat. 24 BW41
Duke St, Wok. 167 AZ117
Duke St Hill SE1 201 L2
Dukes Av N3 44 DB53
Dukes Av N10 65 DJ55
Dukes Av W4 98 CR78
Dukes Av, Edg. 42 CM51
Dukes Av, Epp. 33 ES35
Dukes Av, Grays 110 GA75
Dukes Av, Har. 60 BZ58
Dukes Av (Wealdstone), Har. 61 CE56
Dukes Av, Houns. 96 BY84
Dukes Av, Kings.T. 117 CJ91
Dukes Av, N.Mal. 139 CT97
Dukes Av, Nthlt. 78 BY66
Dukes Av, Rich. 117 CJ91
Dukes Cl, Ashf. 115 BQ91
Dukes Cl, Epp. 19 FB27
Dukes Cl, Ger.Cr. 56 AX60
Dukes Cl, Hmptn. 116 BZ92
Dukes Ct E6 87 EN67
Dukes Ct, Wok. 167 AZ117
Dukes Grn Av, Felt. 115 BU85
Dukes Head Yd N6 65 DH60
Highgate High St
Dukes Hill, Cat. 177 DY120
Dukes Kiln Dr, Ger.Cr. 56 AW60
Dukes La W8 100 DA75
Dukes La, Ger.Cr. 56 AY59
Dukes Lo, Nthwd. 39 BS50
Eastbury Av
Duke's Meadows W4 98 CQ82
Great Chertsey Rd
Dukes Ms N10 65 DH55
Dukes Av
Duke's Ms W1 194 G8
Dukes Orchard, Bex. 127 FC88
Duke's Pas E17 67 EC56
Dukes Pl EC3 197 N9
Dukes Pl EC3 84 DS72
Dukes Ride, Ger.Cr. 56 AY60
Dukes Ride, Uxb. 58 BL63
Dukes Rd E6 87 EN67
Dukes Rd W3 80 CN71
Duke's Rd WC1 195 N3
Duke's Rd WC1 83 DK69
Dukes Rd, Walt. 154 BX106
Dukes Valley, Ger.Cr. 56 AV61
Dukes Way, Uxb. 76 BJ67
Waterloo Rd
Dukes Way, W.Wick. 144 EE104
Dukes Wd Av, Ger.Cr. 56 AY60
Dukes Wd Dr, Ger.Cr. 56 AW60
Duke's Yd W1 194 G10
Dukesthorpe Rd SE26 123 DX91
Dulas St N4 65 DM60
Everleigh St
Dulford St W11 81 CY73
Dulka Rd SW11 120 DF85
Dulverton Rd SE9 125 EQ89
Dulverton Rd, Rom. 52 FK51
Dulverton Rd, Ruis. 59 BU60
Dulverton Rd, S.Croy. 160 DW110
Dulwich Common SE21 122 DS88
Dulwich Common SE22 122 DS88
Dulwich Lawn Cl SE22 122 DT85
Colwell Rd
Dulwich Oaks, The SE21 122 DS90
Dulwich Rd SE24 121 DN85
Dulwich Village SE21 122 DS86
Dulwich Way, Rick. 22 BN43
Dulwich Wd Av SE19 122 DS91
Dulwich Wd Pk SE19 122 DS91
Dumbarton Av, Wal.Cr. 15 DX34
Dumbarton Rd SW2 121 DL86
Dumbleton Cl, Kings.T. 138 CP95
Gloucester Rd
Dumbreck Rd SE9 105 EN84
Dumfries Cl, Wat. 39 BT48
Dumont Rd N16 66 DS62
Dumpton Pl NW1 82 DG66
Gloucester Av
Dumville Dr, Gdse. 186 DV131
Dunally Pk, Shep. 135 BR101
Dunbar Av SW16 141 DN96
Dunbar Av, Beck. 143 DY98
Dunbar Av, Dag. 70 FA62
Dunbar Cl, Hayes 77 BU71
Dunbar Cl, Slou. 74 AU72
Dunbar Ct, Sutt. 158 DD106
Dunbar Ct, Walt. 136 BW103
Dunbar Gdns, Dag. 70 FA64
Dunbar Rd E7 86 EG65
Dunbar Rd N22 45 DN53
Dunbar Rd, N.Mal. 138 CQ98
Dunbar St SE27 122 DQ90
Dunblane Cl, Edg. 42 CP47
Tayside Dr
Dunblane Rd SE9 104 EL83
Dunboe Pl, Shep. 135 BQ101
Dunboyne Rd NW3 64 DF64
Dunbridge St E2 84 DU70
Duncan Cl, Barn. 28 DC42
Duncan Gdns, Stai. 114 BG92
Burges Way
Duncan Gro W3 80 CS72
Duncan Rd E8 84 DV67
Duncan Rd, Rich. 98 CL84
Duncan Rd, Tad. 173 CY119
Duncan St N1 83 DP68
Duncan Ter N1 196 F1
Duncan Ter N1 83 DP68
Duncan Way, Bushey 24 BZ40
Duncannon St WC2 199 P1
Duncannon St WC2 83 DL73
Dunch St E1 84 DV72
Watney St
Duncombe Cl, Amer. 20 AS38
Duncombe Ct, Stai. 113 BF94
Duncombe Hill SE23 123 DY87
Duncombe Rd N19 65 DK60
Duncrievie Rd SE13 123 ED86
Duncroft SE18 105 ES80
Duncroft Cl, Reig. 183 CZ133
Dundalk Rd SE4 103 DY83
Dundas Gdns, W.Mol. 136 CB97
Dundas Rd SE15 102 DW82
Dundee Rd E13 86 EH68
Dundee Rd SE25 142 DV99
Dundee St E1 202 D3
Dundee St E1 84 DV74
Dundee Way, Enf. 31 DY41
Dundela Gdns, Wor.Pk. 157 CV105
Dundonald Cl E6 86 EL72
Northumberland Rd
Dundonald Rd NW10 81 CX67
Dundonald Rd SW19 119 CY94
Dundrey Cres, Red. 185 DL129
Dunedin Dr, Cat. 186 DS125
Dunedin Rd E10 67 EB62
Dunedin Rd, Ilf. 69 EQ60
Dunedin Rd, Rain. 89 FF69
Dunedin Way, Hayes 78 BW70
Dunelm Gro SE27 122 DQ91
Dunelm St E1 85 DX72
Dunfee Way, W.Byf. 152 BL112
Dunfield Gdns SE6 123 EB91
Dunfield Rd SE6 123 EB92
Dunford Rd N7 65 DM63
Dungarvan Av SW15 99 CU84
Dungates La, Bet. 183 CU133
Dunheved Cl, Th.Hth. 141 DN100
Dunheved Rd N, Th.Hth. 141 DN100
Dunheved Rd S, Th.Hth. 141 DN100
Dunheved Rd W, Th.Hth. 141 DN100
Dunholme Grn N9 46 DT48
Dunholme La N9 46 DT48
Dunholme Rd
Dunholme Rd N9 46 DT48
Dunkeld Rd SE25 142 DR98
Dunkeld Rd, Dag. 70 EV61
Dunkellin Gro, S.Ock. 91 FU72
Dunkellin Way
Dunkellin Way, S.Ock. 91 FU72
Dunkery Rd SE9 124 EK91
Dunkin Rd, Dart. 108 FN84
Dunkirk Cl, Grav. 131 GJ92
Dunkirk St SE27 122 DQ91
Waring St
Dunlace Rd E5 66 DW63
Dunleary Cl, Houns. 116 BZ87
Dunley Dr, Croy. 161 EB108
Dunlin Ho W13 79 CF70
Dunloe Av N17 66 DR55
Dunloe St E2 197 P1
Dunloe St E2 84 DT68
Dunlop Pl SE16 202 A7
Dunlop Rd, Til. 111 GF81
Dunmail Dr, Pur. 160 DS114
Dunmore Pt E2 197 P3
Dunmore Rd NW6 81 CY67
Dunmore Rd SW20 139 CW95
Dunmow Cl, Felt. 116 BY91
Dunmow Cl, Loug. 32 EL44
Dunmow Cl, Rom. 70 EW57
Dunmow Dr, Rain. 89 FF67
Dunmow Ho, Dag. 88 EV67
Dunmow Rd E15 67 ED63
Dunmow Wk N1 84 DQ67
Popham St
Dunn Mead NW9 43 CT52
Field Mead
Dunn St E8 66 DT64
Dunnage Cres SE16 203 L8
Dunnets, Wok. 166 AS117
Dunning Cl, S.Ock. 91 FU72
Dent Cl
Dunningford Cl, Horn. 71 FF64
Dunnock Cl N9 47 DX46
Dunnock Cl, Borwd. 26 CN42
Dunnock Rd E6 86 EL72
Dunns Pas WC1 196 A8
Dunny La, Kings L. 5 BE32
Dunnymans Rd, Bans. 173 CZ115
Dunollie Pl NW5 65 DJ64
Dunollie Rd
Dunollie Rd NW5 65 DJ64
Dunoon Rd SE23 122 DW87
Dunraven Dr, Enf. 29 DN40
Dunraven Rd W12 81 CU74
Dunraven St W1 194 E10
Dunraven St W1 82 DF73
Dunsany Rd W14 99 CX76
Dunsborough Pk, Wok. 168 BJ120
Dunsbury Cl, Sutt. 158 DB109
Nettlecombe Cl
Dunsfold Ri, Couls. 159 DK113
Dunsfold Way, Croy. 161 EB108
Dunsford Way SW15 119 CV86
Dover Pk Dr
Dunsmore Cl, Bushey 25 CD44
Dunsmore Cl, Hayes 78 BY70
Kingsash Dr
Dunsmore Rd, Walt. 135 BV100
Dunsmore Way, Bushey 25 CD44
Dunsmure Rd N16 66 DS60
Dunspring La, Ilf. 49 EP54
Dunstable Cl, Rom. 52 FK51
Dunstable Rd
Dunstable Ms W1 194 G6
Dunstable Rd, Rich. 98 CL84
Dunstable Rd, Rom. 52 FK51
Dunstable Rd, W.Mol. 136 BZ98
Dunstall Grn, Wok. 150 AW109
Dunstall Rd SW20 119 CV93
Dunstall Way, W.Mol. 136 CB97
Dunstan Cl N2 64 DC55
Thomas More Way
Dunstan Rd NW11 63 CZ60
Dunstan Rd, Couls. 175 DK117
Dunstans Gro SE22 122 DV86
Dunstans Rd SE22 122 DU87
Dunster Av, Mord. 139 CX102
Dunster Cl, Barn. 27 CX42
Dunster Cl, Rom. 51 FC54
Dunster Cl (Harefield), Uxb. 38 BH53
Dunster Ct EC3 197 N10
Dunster Cres, Horn. 72 FN61
Dunster Dr NW9 62 CQ60
Dunster Gdns NW6 81 CZ66
Dunster Way, Har. 60 BY62
Dunsterville Way SE1 201 L5
Dunston Rd E8 84 DT67
Dunston Rd SW11 100 DG82
Dunston St E8 84 DT67
Dunton Cl, Surb. 138 CL102
Dunton Rd E10 67 EB59
Dunton Rd SE1 201 P10
Dunton Rd SE1 102 DT78
Dunton Rd, Rom. 71 FE56
Duntshill Rd SW18 120 DB88
Dunvegan Cl, W.Mol. 136 CB98
Dunvegan Rd SE9 105 EM84
Dunwich Rd, Bexh. 106 EZ81
Dunworth Ms W11 81 CZ72
Portobello Rd
Duplex Ride SW1 198 E5
Dupont Rd SW20 139 CX96
Dupont St E14 85 DY71
Maroon St
Duppas Av, Croy. 159 DP105
Violet La
Duppas Cl, Shep. 135 BR99
Green La
Duppas Hill La, Croy. 159 DP105
Duppas Hill Rd
Duppas Hill Rd, Croy. 159 DP105
Duppas Hill Ter, Croy. 141 DP104
Duppas Rd, Croy. 141 DN104
Dupre Cl, Grays 110 FY76
Dupree Rd SE7 205 P10
Dupree Rd SE7 104 EH78
Dura Den Cl, Beck. 123 EB94
Durand Cl, Cars. 140 DF102
Durand Gdns SW9 101 DM81
Durand Way NW10 80 CQ66
Durands Wk SE16 203 L4
Durands Wk SE16 103 DZ75
Durant Rd, Swan. 127 FG93
Durant St E2 84 DU69
Durants Pk Av, Enf. 31 DX42
Durants Rd, Enf. 30 DW42
Durban Gdns, Dag. 89 FC66
Durban Rd E15 86 EE69
Durban Rd E17 47 DZ53
Durban Rd N17 46 DS51
Durban Rd SE27 122 DQ91
Durban Rd, Beck. 143 DZ96
Durban Rd, Ilf. 69 ES60
Durban Rd E, Wat. 23 BU42
Durban Rd W, Wat. 23 BU42
Durbin Rd, Chess. 156 CL105
Durdans Rd, Sthl. 78 BZ72
Durell Gdns, Dag. 70 EX64
Durell Rd, Dag. 70 EX64
Durfold Dr, Reig. 184 DC134
Durford Cres SW15 119 CV88
Durham Av, Brom. 144 EF98
Durham Av, Houns. 96 BZ78
Durham Av, Rom. 72 FJ56
Durham Av, Wdf.Grn. 48 EK50
Durham Cl SW20 139 CV96
Durham Rd
Durham Hill, Brom. 124 EF91
Durham Ho St WC2 200 A1
Durham Pl SW3 100 DF78
Smith St
Durham Pl, Ilf. 69 EQ63
Eton Rd
Durham Ri SE18 105 EQ78
Durham Rd E12 68 EK63
Durham Rd E16 86 EE70
Durham Rd N2 64 DE55
Durham Rd N7 65 DM61
Durham Rd N9 46 DU47
Durham Rd SW20 139 CV95
Durham Rd W5 97 CK76
Durham Rd, Borwd. 26 CQ41
Durham Rd, Brom. 144 EF97
Durham Rd, Dag. 71 FC64
Durham Rd, Felt. 116 BW87
Durham Rd, Har. 60 CB57
Durham Rd, Sid. 126 EV92
Durham Row E1 85 DY71
Durham St SE11 101 DM78
Durham Ter W2 82 DB72
Durham Wf, Brent. 97 CJ80
London Rd
Durham Yd E2 84 DV69
Teesdale St
Duriun Way, Erith 107 FH80
Durley Av, Pnr. 60 BY59
Durley Gdns, Orp. 164 EV105
Durley Rd N16 66 DS59
Durlston Rd E5 66 DU61
Durlston Rd, Kings.T. 118 CL93
Durndale La, Grav. 131 GF91
Durnell Way, Loug. 33 EN41
Durnford St N15 66 DS57
Durnford St SE10 103 EC79
Greenwich Ch St
Durning Rd SE19 122 DR92
Durnsford Av SW19 120 DA89
Durnsford Rd N11 45 DK53
Durnsford Rd SW19 120 DA89
Durrant Way, Orp. 163 ER106
Durrant Way, Swans. 130 FY87
Durrants Cl, Rain. 90 FJ68
Durrants Dr, Rick. 23 BQ42
Durrell Rd SW6 99 CZ81
Durrell Way, Shep. 135 BR100
Durrington Av SW20 139 CW95
Durrington Pk Rd SW20 119 CW94
Durrington Rd E5 67 DY63
Dursley Cl SE3 104 EJ82
Dursley Gdns SE3 104 EK81
Dursley Rd SE3 104 EJ82
Durward St E1 84 DV71
Durweston Ms W1 194 E6
Durweston St W1 194 E6
Durweston St W1 82 DF71
Dury Falls Cl, Horn. 72 FM60
Dury Rd, Barn. 27 CZ39
Dutch Barn Cl, Stai. 114 BK86
Dutch Elm Av, Wind. 92 AT80
Dutch Gdns, Kings.T. 118 CP93
Windmill Ri
Dutch Yd SW18 120 DA85
Wandsworth High St
Duthie St E14 204 E1
Dutton St SE10 103 EC81
Dutton Way, Iver 75 BE72
Duxberry Cl, Brom. 144 EL99
Southborough La
Duxford Cl, Horn. 89 FH65
Duxford Ho SE2 106 EX75
Wolvercote Rd
Dwight Ct SW6 99 CY82
Burlington Rd
Dwight Rd, Wat. 39 BR45
Dye Ho La E3 85 EA67
Dyer's Bldgs EC1 196 D7
Dyers Hall Rd E11 68 EE60
Dyers La SW15 99 CV84
Dyers Way, Rom. 51 FH52
Dyke Dr, Orp. 146 EW102
Dykes Path, Wok. 167 BC115
Bentham Av
Dykes Way, Brom. 144 EF97
Dykewood Cl, Bex. 127 FE90
Dylan Cl, Borwd. 41 CK45
Coates Rd
Dylan Rd SE24 101 DP84
Dylan Rd, Belv. 106 FA76
Dylan Thomas Ho N8 65 DM56
Dylways SE5 102 DR84
Dymchurch Cl, Ilf. 49 EN54
Dymchurch Cl, Orp. 163 ES105
Dymes Path SW19 119 CX89
Queensmere Rd
Dymock St SW6 100 DB83
Dymoke Rd, Horn. 71 FF59
Dymond Est SW17 120 DE90
Glenburnie Rd
Dyne Rd NW6 81 CZ66
Dyneley Rd SE12 124 EJ91
Dynevor Rd N16 66 DS62
Dynevor Rd, Rich. 118 CL85
Dynham Rd NW6 82 DA66
Dyott St WC1 195 P8
Dyott St WC1 83 DK72
Dyrham La, Barn. 27 CU36
Dysart Av, Kings.T. 117 CJ92
Dysart St EC2 197 M5
Dyson Rd E11 68 EE58
Dyson Rd E15 86 EF65
Dysons Cl, Wal.Cr. 15 DX33
Dysons Rd N18 46 DV50

E

Eade Rd N4 66 DQ59
Eagans Cl N2 64 DE55
Market Pl
Eagle Av, Rom. 70 EY58
Eagle Cl SE16 102 DW78
Varcoe Rd
Eagle Cl, Amer. 20 AT37
Eagle Cl, Enf. 30 DW42
Eagle Cl, Horn. 89 FH65
Eagle Cl, Wall. 159 DL107
Eagle Cl, Wal.Abb. 16 EG34
Eagle Ct EC1 196 F6
Eagle Ct EC1 83 DP71
Eagle Dr NW9 42 CS54
Eagle Hill SE19 122 DR93
Eagle La E11 68 EG56
Eagle Ms N1 84 DS65
Tottenham Rd
Eagle Pl SW1 199 L1
Eagle Pl SW7 100 DC78
Old Brompton Rd
Eagle Rd, Wem. 79 CK66
Eagle St WC1 196 B7
Eagle St WC1 83 DM71
Eagle Ter, Wdf.Grn. 48 EH52
Eagle Way, Brwd. 53 FV51
Eagle Way, Grav. 130 GA85
Eagle Wf E14 85 EB71
Broomfield St
Eagle Wf Rd N1 84 DQ68
Eagles Dr, West. 178 EK118
Eagles Rd, Green. 109 FV84
Eaglesfield Rd SE18 105 EP80
Ealdham Sq SE9 104 EJ84
Ealing Cl, Borwd. 26 CR39
Ealing Downs Ct, Grnf. 79 CG69
Perivale La
Ealing Grn W5 79 CK74
Ealing Pk Gdns W5 97 CJ77
Ealing Rd, Brent. 97 CK78
Ealing Rd, Nthlt. 78 CA66
Ealing Rd, Wem. 80 CL67
Ealing Village W5 80 CL72
Eamont Cl, Ruis. 59 BP59
Allonby Dr
Eamont St NW8 82 DE68
Eardemont Cl, Dart. 107 FF84
Eardley Cres SW5 100 DA78
Eardley Pt SE18 105 EP77
Wilmount St
Eardley Rd SW16 121 DJ92
Eardley Rd, Belv. 106 FA78
Eardley Rd, Sev. 191 FH124
Earl Cl N11 45 DH50
Earl Ri SE18 105 ER77
Earl Rd SW14 98 CQ84
Elm Rd
Earl Rd, Grav. 130 GE89
Earl St EC2 197 M6
Earl St EC2 84 DR71
Earl St, Wat. 24 BW41
Earldom Rd SW15 99 CW84
Earle Gdns, Kings.T. 118 CL93
Earleswood, Cob. 154 BX112
Earlham Gro E7 68 EF64
Earlham Gro N22 45 DM52
Earlham St WC2 195 N9
Earlham St WC2 83 DK72
Earls Ct Gdns SW5 100 DB77
Earls Ct Rd SW5 100 DA77
Earls Ct Rd W8 100 DA76
Earls Ct Sq SW5 100 DB78
Earls Cres, Har. 61 CE56
Earls La, Pot.B. 10 CS32
Earl's Path, Loug. 32 EJ40
Earls Ter W8 99 CZ76
Earls Wk W8 100 DA76
Earls Wk, Dag. 70 EV63
Earls Way, Orp. 145 ET103
Station Rd
Earlsdown Ho, Bark. 87 ER68
Wheelers Cross
Earlsferry Way N1 83 DM67
Earlsfield Rd SW18 120 DC88
Earlshall Rd SE9 105 EM84
Earlsmead, Har. 60 BZ63
Earlsmead Rd N15 66 DT57
Earlsmead Rd NW10 81 CW68
Earlsthorpe Ms SW12 120 DG86
Earlsthorpe Rd SE26 123 DX91
Earlstoke St EC1 196 F2
Earlston Gro E9 84 DV67
Earlswood Av, Th.Hth. 141 DN99
Earlswood Cl SE10 104 EE78
Earlswood St
Earlswood Gdns, Ilf. 69 EN55
Earlswood St SE10 104 EE78
Early Ms NW1 83 DH67
Arlington Rd
Earnshaw St WC2 195 N8
Earnshaw St WC2 83 DK72
Earsby St W14 99 CY77
Easby Cres, Mord. 140 DB100
Easebourne Rd, Dag. 70 EW64
Easedale Dr, Horn. 71 FG64
Easedale Ho, Islw. 117 CF85
Summerwood Rd
Easington Way, S.Ock. 91 FU71
Easley's Ms W1 194 G8
East Acton La W3 80 CS74
East Arbour St E1 85 DX72
East Av E12 86 EL66
East Av E17 67 EB56
East Av, Hayes 95 BT75
East Av, Sthl. 78 BZ73
East Av, Wall. 159 DM106
East Av, Walt. 153 BT110
Octagon Rd
East Bk N16 66 DS59
East Barnet Rd, Barn. 28 DE44
East Churchfield Rd W3 80 CR74
East Cl W5 80 CN70
East Cl, Barn. 28 DG42
East Cl, Grnf. 78 CC68
East Cl, Rain. 89 FH70
East Cl, St.Alb. 8 CB25
East Common, Ger.Cr. 56 AY59
East Ct, Wem. 61 CJ61
East Cres N11 44 DF49
East Cres, Enf. 30 DT43
East Cres Rd, Grav. 131 GJ86
East Cross Cen E15 85 EA65
Waterden Rd
East Cross Route E3 85 EA67
East Dene Dr, Rom. 52 FK50
East Dr, Cars. 158 DE109
East Dr, Nthwd. 39 BS47
East Dr, Orp. 146 EV100
East Dr, Slou. 74 AS69
East Dr, Vir.W. 132 AU101
East Dr, Wat. 23 BV35
East Duck Lees La, Enf. 31 DY42
East Dulwich Gro SE22 122 DS86
East Dulwich Rd SE15 102 DT84
East Dulwich Rd SE22 102 DT84
East End Rd N2 64 DC55
East End Rd N3 44 DA54
East End Way, Pnr. 60 BY55
East Entrance, Dag. 89 FB68
East Ferry Rd E14 204 C8
East Ferry Rd E14 103 EB76
East Gdns SW17 120 DE93
East Gdns, Wok. 167 BC117
East Gorse, Croy. 161 DY112
East Grn, Hem.H. 6 BM25
East Hall La, Rain. 90 FK72
East Hall Rd, Orp. 146 EY101
East Ham Ind Est E6 86 EL70
East Ham Manor Way E6 87 EN72
East Harding St EC4 196 E8
East Heath Rd NW3 64 DD62
East Hill SW18 120 DB85
East Hill, Dart. 128 FM87
East Hill (South Darenth), Dart. 148 FQ95
East Hill, Oxt. 188 EE129
East Hill, S.Croy. 160 DS110
East Hill, Wem. 62 CN61
East Hill, West. 178 EH118
East Hill, Wok. 167 BC116
East Hill Dr, Dart. 128 FM87
East Hill Rd, Oxt. 188 EE129
East Holme, Erith 107 FD81
East India Dock Rd E14 85 ED72
East Kent Av, Grav. 130 GC86
East La SE16 202 B5
East La SE16 102 DU75
East La, Abb.L. 7 BU29
East La, Dart. 149 FR96
East La, Kings.T. 137 CK97
High St
East La, Wem. 61 CK62
East Lo La, Enf. 29 DK36
East Mascalls SE7 104 EJ79
Mascalls Rd
East Mead, Ruis. 60 BX62
East Mill, Grav. 131 GF86
East Milton Rd, Grav. 131 GK87
East Mt St E1 84 DV71
East Pk Cl, Rom. 70 EX57
East Parkside SE10 205 K5
East Parkside SE10 104 EE75
East Pas EC1 196 G6
East Pier E1 202 D3
East Pl SE27 122 DQ91
Pilgrim Hill
East Poultry Av EC1 196 F7
East Ramp, Houns. 95 BP81
East Ridgeway (Cuffley), Pot.B. 13 DL29
East Rd E15 86 EG67
East Rd N1 197 K3
East Rd N1 84 DR69
East Rd SW19 120 DC93
East Rd, Barn. 44 DG46
East Rd, Edg. 42 CP53
East Rd, Enf. 30 DW38
East Rd, Felt. 115 BR87
East Rd, Kings.T. 138 CL95
East Rd, Reig. 183 CZ133
East Rd (Chadwell Heath), Rom. 70 EY57
East Rd (Rush Grn), Rom. 71 FD59
East Rd, Well. 106 EV82
East Rd, West Dr. 94 BM77
East Rd, Wey. 153 BR108
East Rochester Way SE9 105 ES84
East Rochester Way, Bex. 127 FC87

East Rochester Way, Sid. 105 ES84
East Row E11 68 EG58
East Row W10 81 CY70
East Sheen Av SW14 98 CR84
East Smithfield E1 202 A1
East Smithfield E1 84 DT73
East St SE17 201 J10
East St SE17 102 DQ78
East St, Bark. 87 EQ66
East St, Bexh. 106 FA84
East St, Brent. 97 CJ80
East St, Brom. 144 EG96
East St, Cher. 134 BG101
East St, Epsom 156 CS112
East St, Grays 110 GC79
East St (South Stifford), Grays 110 FY79
East Surrey Gro SE15 102 DT80
East Tenter St E1 84 DT72
East Ter, Grav. 131 GJ86
East Thurrock Rd, Grays 110 GB79
East Twrs, Pnr. 60 BX57
East Vw E4 47 EC50
East Vw, Barn. 27 CZ41
East Wk, Barn. 44 DG45
East Wk, Hayes 77 BU74
East Wk, Reig. 184 DB134
East Way E11 68 EH57
East Way, Brom. 144 EG101
East Way, Croy. 143 DY103
East Way, Hayes 77 BU74
East Way, Ruis. 59 BU60
East Woodside, Bex. 126 EY88
Eastbank Rd, Hmptn. 116 CC92
Eastbourne Av W3 80 CR72
Eastbourne Gdns SW14 98 CQ83
Eastbourne Ms W2 82 DC72
Eastbourne Rd E6 87 EN69
Eastbourne Rd E15 86 EE67
Eastbourne Rd N15 66 DS58
Eastbourne Rd SW17 120 DG93
Eastbourne Rd W4 98 CQ79
Eastbourne Rd, Brent. 97 CJ78
Eastbourne Rd, Felt. 116 BX89
Eastbourne Rd, Gdse. 186 DW132
Eastbourne Ter W2 82 DC72
Eastbournia Av N9 46 DV48
Eastbridge, Slou. 74 AV74
Victoria Rd
Eastbrook Av N9 46 DW45
Eastbrook Av, Dag. 71 FC63
Eastbrook Cl, Wok. 167 BA116
Eastbrook Dr, Rom. 71 FE62
Eastbrook Rd SE3 104 EH80
Eastbrook Rd, Wal.Abb. 16 EE33
Eastbury Av, Bark. 87 ES67
Eastbury Av, Enf. 30 DS39
Eastbury Av, Nthwd. 39 BS50
Eastbury Ct, Bark. 87 ES67
Eastbury Gro W4 98 CS78
Eastbury Ho, Bark. 87 ET67
Eastbury Pl, Nthwd. 39 BT50
Eastbury Av
Eastbury Rd E6 87 EN70
Eastbury Rd, Kings.T. 118 CL94
Eastbury Rd, Nthwd. 39 BS51
Eastbury Rd, Orp. 145 ER100
Eastbury Rd, Rom. 71 FD58
Eastbury Rd, Wat. 39 BV45
Eastbury Sq, Bark. 87 ET67
Eastbury Ter E1 85 DX70
Eastcastle St W1 195 K8
Eastcastle St W1 83 DJ72
Eastcheap EC3 197 L10
Eastcheap EC3 84 DR73
Eastchurch Rd, Houns. 95 BS82
Eastcombe Av SE7 104 EH79
Eastcote, Orp. 145 ET102
Eastcote Av, Grnf. 61 CG64
Eastcote Av, Har. 60 CB61
Eastcote Av, W.Mol. 136 BZ99
Eastcote La, Har. 60 CA62
Eastcote La, Nthlt. 78 CA66
Eastcote La N, Nthlt. 78 BZ65
Eastcote Pl, Pnr. 59 BV58
Eastcote Rd, Har. 60 CC62
Eastcote Rd, Pnr. 60 BX57
Eastcote Rd (Eastcote Village), Pnr. 59 BU58
Eastcote Rd, Ruis. 59 BS59
Eastcote Rd, Well. 105 ER82
Eastcote St SW9 101 DM82
Eastcote Vw, Pnr. 60 BW56
Eastcroft Rd, Epsom 156 CS108
Eastdean Av, Epsom 156 CP113
Eastdown Pk SE13 103 ED84
Eastern Av E11 68 EJ58
Eastern Av, Cher. 134 BG97
Eastern Av, Grays 109 FT78
Eastern Av, Ilf. 68 EL58
Eastern Av, Pnr. 60 BX59
Eastern Av, Rom. 70 EW56
Eastern Av, S.Ock. 90 FQ74
Eastern Av, Wal.Cr. 15 DY33
Eastern Av E, Rom. 71 FD55
Eastern Av W, Rom. 70 EY56
Eastern Ind Est, Erith 106 FA75
Eastern Pathway, Horn. 90 FJ67
Eastern Perimeter Rd, Houns. 95 BT83
Eastern Rd E13 86 EH68
Eastern Rd E17 67 EC57
Eastern Rd N2 64 DF55
Eastern Rd N22 45 DL53
Eastern Rd SE4 103 EA84
Eastern Rd, Grays 110 GD77
Eastern Rd, Rom. 71 FE57
Eastern Vw, West. 178 EJ117
Eastern Way SE2 88 EX74
Eastern Way SE28 106 EU75
Eastern Way, Belv. 107 FB75
Eastern Way, Erith 88 EX74
Eastern Way, Grays 110 GA79
Easternville Gdns, Ilf. 69 EQ58
Eastfield Av, Wat. 24 BX39
Eastfield Cl, Slou. 92 AU76
St. Laurence Way
Eastfield Cotts, Hayes 95 BS78
Eastfield Gdns, Dag. 70 FA63
Eastfield Par, Pot.B. 12 DD32
Eastfield Rd E17 67 EA56
Eastfield Rd N8 65 DL55
Eastfield Rd, Brwd. 54 FX47
Eastfield Rd, Dag. 70 FA63
Eastfield Rd, Enf. 31 DX38
Eastfield Rd, Wal.Cr. 15 DY32
Eastfields, Pnr. 60 BW57
Eastfields Rd W3 80 CQ71
Eastfields Rd, Mitch. 140 DG96
Eastgate, Bans. 157 CY114
Eastgate Cl SE28 88 EX72
Eastglade, Nthwd. 39 BS50
Eastglade, Pnr. 60 BY55
Eastham Cl, Barn. 27 CY43
Eastham Cres, Brwd. 55 GA49
Eastholm NW11 64 DB56
Eastholme, Hayes 77 BU74
Eastlake Rd SE5 101 DP82
Eastlands Cl, Oxt. 187 ED127
Eastlands Way
Eastlands Cres SE21 122 DT86
Eastlands Way, Oxt. 187 ED127
Eastlea Av, Wat. 24 BY37
Eastlea Ms E16 86 EE70
Desford Rd
Eastleigh Av, Har. 60 CB61
Eastleigh Cl NW2 62 CS62
Eastleigh Cl, Sutt. 158 DB108
Eastleigh Rd E17 47 DZ54
Eastleigh Rd, Bexh. 107 FC82
Eastleigh Rd, Houns. 95 BT83
Cranford La
Eastleigh Wk SW15 119 CU87
Eastleigh Way, Felt. 115 BU88
Eastman Rd W3 80 CR74
Eastmead, Wok. 166 AV117
Eastmead Av, Grnf. 78 CB69
Eastmead Cl, Brom. 144 EL96
Eastmearn Rd SE21 122 DQ89
Eastmont Rd, Esher 137 CE103
Eastmoor Pl SE7 104 EK76
Eastmoor St
Eastmoor St SE7 104 EK76
Eastney Rd, Croy. 141 DP102
Eastney St SE10 103 ED78
Eastnor, Hem.H. 5 BA28
Eastnor Rd SE9 125 EQ88
Easton Gdns, Borwd. 26 CR42
Easton St WC1 196 D3
Eastry Av, Brom. 144 EF100
Eastry Rd, Erith 106 FA80
Eastside Rd NW11 63 CZ56
Eastview Av SE18 105 ES80
Eastville Av NW11 63 CZ58
Eastway E9 85 DZ65
Eastway E10 67 EC63
Eastway E15 67 EA64
Eastway, Epsom 156 CQ112
Eastway, Mord. 139 CX99
Eastway, Wall. 159 DJ105
Eastway Commercial Cen E9 67 EA64
Eastwell Cl, Beck. 143 DY95
Eastwick Cres, Rick. 37 BF47
Eastwick Dr, Lthd. 170 CA123
Eastwick Pk Av, Lthd. 170 CB124
Eastwick Rd, Walt. 153 BV106
Eastwood Cl E18 48 EG54
George La
Eastwood Cl N17 46 DV52
Northumberland Gro
Eastwood Dr, Rain. 89 FH72
Eastwood Rd E18 48 EG54
Eastwood Rd N10 44 DG54
Eastwood Rd, Ilf. 70 EU59
Eastwood Rd, West Dr. 94 BN75
Eastwood St SW16 121 DJ93
Eastworth Rd, Cher. 134 BG102
Eatington Rd E10 67 ED57
Eaton Cl SW1 198 F9
Eaton Cl SW1 100 DG77
Eaton Cl, Stan. 41 CH49
Eaton Dr SW9 101 DP84
Eaton Dr, Kings.T. 118 CN94
Eaton Dr, Rom. 51 FB52
Eaton Gdns, Dag. 88 EY66
Eaton Gate SW1 198 F8
Eaton Gate SW1 100 DG77
Eaton Gate, Nthwd. 39 BQ51
Eaton La SW1 199 J7
Eaton La SW1 101 DH76
Eaton Ms N SW1 198 F8
Eaton Ms N SW1 100 DG76
Eaton Ms S SW1 198 G8
Eaton Ms S SW1 101 DH76
Eaton Ms W SW1 198 G8
Eaton Ms W SW1 100 DG77
Eaton Pk, Cob. 154 BY114
Eaton Pk Rd N13 45 DN47
Eaton Pk Rd, Cob. 154 BY114
Eaton Pl SW1 198 F7
Eaton Pl SW1 100 DG76
Eaton Ri E11 68 EJ57
Eaton Ri W5 79 CK72
Eaton Rd NW4 63 CW57
Eaton Rd, Enf. 30 DS41
Eaton Rd, Houns. 97 CD84
Eaton Rd, Sid. 126 EX89
Eaton Rd, Sutt. 158 DD107
Eaton Rd, Upmin. 73 FS61
Eaton Row SW1 199 H7
Eaton Row SW1 101 DH76
Eaton Sq SW1 199 H6
Eaton Sq SW1 100 DG77
Eaton Sq, Long. 149 FX97
Bramblefield Cl
Eaton Ter SW1 198 F8
Eaton Ter SW1 100 DG77
Eaton Ter Ms SW1 198 F8
Eaton Wk SE15 102 DT80
Sumner Est
Eatons Mead E4 47 EA47
Eatonville Rd SW17 120 DF89
Eatonville Vil SW17 120 DF89
Eatonville Rd
Ebbas Way, Epsom 172 CP115
Ebbisham Dr SW8 101 DM79
Ebbisham La, Tad. 173 CT121
Ebbisham Rd, Epsom 156 CP114
Ebbisham Rd, Wor.Pk. 139 CW103
Ebbsfleet Ind Est, Grav. 130 GA85
Ebbsfleet Rd NW2 63 CY63
Ebbsfleet Wk, Grav. 130 GB86
Ebdon Way SE3 104 EH83
Ebenezer St N1 197 K2
Ebenezer St N1 84 DR69
Ebenezer Wk SW16 141 DJ95
Ebley Cl SE15 102 DT79
Ebner St SW18 120 DB85
Ebor St E1 197 P4
Ebor St E1 84 DT70
Ebrington Rd, Har. 61 CK58
Ebsworth St SE23 123 DX87
Eburne Rd N7 65 DL62
Ebury Br SW1 199 H10
Ebury Br SW1 101 DH78
Ebury Br Est SW1 199 H10
Ebury Br Est SW1 101 DH78
Ebury Br Rd SW1 100 DG78
Ebury Cl, Kes. 144 EL104
Ebury Cl, Nthwd. 39 BQ50
Ebury Ms SE27 121 DP90
Ebury Ms SW1 199 H8
Ebury Ms SW1 101 DH77
Ebury Ms E SW1 199 H8
Ebury Rd, Rick. 38 BK46
Ebury Rd, Wat. 24 BW41
Ebury Sq SW1 198 G9
Ebury Sq SW1 100 DG77
Ebury St SW1 199 H8
Ebury St SW1 100 DG77
Ebury Way Cycle Path, The, Rick. 39 BP45
Ebury Way Cycle Path, The, Wat. 39 BP45
Eccles Rd SW11 100 DF84
Ecclesbourne Cl N13 45 DN50
Ecclesbourne Gdns N13 45 DN50
Ecclesbourne Rd N1 84 DQ66
Ecclesbourne Rd, Th.Hth. 142 DQ99
Eccleston Br SW1 199 J8
Eccleston Br SW1 101 DH77
Eccleston Cl, Barn. 28 DF42
Eccleston Cl, Orp. 145 ER102
Eccleston Cres, Rom. 70 EU59
Eccleston Ms SW1 198 G7
Eccleston Ms SW1 100 DG76
Eccleston Pl SW1 199 H8
Eccleston Pl SW1 101 DH77
Eccleston Rd W13 79 CG73
Eccleston Sq SW1 199 J9
Eccleston Sq SW1 101 DH77
Eccleston Sq Ms SW1 199 K9
Eccleston St SW1 199 H7
Eccleston St SW1 100 DG76
Ecclestone Ct, Wem. 62 CL64
St. John's Rd
Ecclestone Pl, Wem. 62 CM64
Echelforde Dr, Ashf. 114 BN91
Echo Hts E4 47 EB46
Mount Echo Dr
Echo Sq, Grav. 131 GJ89
Old Rd E
Eckersley St E1 84 DU70
Buxton St
Eckford St N1 83 DN68
Eckstein Rd SW11 100 DE84
Eclipse Rd E13 86 EH71
Ecton Rd, Add. 152 BH105
Ector Rd SE6 124 EE89
Edbrooke Rd W9 82 DA70
Eddiscombe Rd SW6 99 CZ82
Eddy Cl, Rom. 71 FB58
Eddystone Rd SE4 123 DY85
Eddystone Wk, Stai. 114 BL87
Ede Cl, Houns. 96 BZ83
Eden Cl NW3 64 DA61
Eden Cl W8 100 DA76
Adam & Eve Ms
Eden Cl, Add. 152 BH110
Eden Cl, Bex. 127 FD91
Eden Cl, Slou. 93 BA78
Eden Cl, Wem. 79 CK67
Eden Grn, S.Ock. 91 FV71
Bovey Way
Eden Gro E17 67 EB57
Eden Gro N7 65 DM64
Eden Gro Rd, W.Byf. 152 BL113
Eden Ms SW17 120 DC90
Huntspill St
Eden Pk Av, Beck. 143 DY98
Eden Pl, Grav. 131 GH87
Lord St
Eden Rd E17 67 EB57
Eden Rd SE27 121 DP92
Eden Rd, Beck. 143 DY98
Eden Rd, Bex. 127 FC91
Eden Rd, Croy. 160 DR105
Eden St, Kings.T. 137 CK96
Eden Wk, Kings.T. 138 CL96
Eden St
Eden Way, Beck. 143 DZ99
Eden Way, Warl. 177 DY118
Edenbridge Cl SE16 102 DV78
Masters Dr
Edenbridge Cl, Orp. 146 EX98
Edenbridge Rd E9 85 DX66
Edenbridge Rd, Enf. 30 DS44
Edencourt Rd SW16 121 DH93
Edendale Rd, Bexh. 107 FD81
Edenfield Gdns, Wor.Pk. 139 CT104
Edenhall Cl, Rom. 52 FJ50
Edenhall Glen, Rom. 52 FJ50
Edenhall Rd, Rom. 52 FJ50
Edenham Way W10 81 CZ71
Elkstone Rd
Edenhurst Av SW6 99 CZ83
Edenside Rd, Lthd. 170 BZ124
Edensor Gdns W4 98 CS80
Edensor Rd W4 98 CS80
Edenvale Cl, Mitch. 120 DG94
Edenvale Rd
Edenvale Rd, Mitch. 120 DG94
Edenvale St SW6 100 DB82
Ederline Av SW16 141 DM97
Edgar Cl, Swan. 147 FF97
Edgar Kail Way SE22 102 DS84
Edgar Rd E3 85 EB69
Edgar Rd, Houns. 116 BZ87
Edgar Rd, Rom. 70 EX59
Edgar Rd, S.Croy. 160 DR109
Edgar Rd, West Dr. 76 BL73
Edgar Rd, West. 178 EK121
Edgarley Ter SW6 99 CY81
Edgbaston Dr, Rad. 10 CL32
Edgbaston Rd, Wat. 39 BV48
Edge Cl, Wey. 152 BN108
Edge Hill SE18 105 EP79
Edge Hill SW19 119 CX94
Edge Hill Av N3 64 DA55
Edge Hill Ct SW19 119 CX94
Edge St W8 82 DA74
Kensington Ch St
Edgeborough Way, Brom. 124 EK94
Edgebury, Chis. 125 EP91
Edgebury Wk, Chis. 125 EQ91
Edgecombe Ho SW19 119 CY88
Edgecoombe, S.Croy. 160 DW108
Edgecoombe Cl, Kings.T. 118 CR94
Edgecot Gro N15 66 DR57
Oulton Rd
Edgecote Cl W3 80 CQ74
Cheltenham Pl
Edgefield Av, Bark. 87 ET66
Edgefield Cl, Dart. 128 FP88
Edgehill Ct, Walt. 136 BW102
St. Johns Dr
Edgehill Gdns, Dag. 70 FA63
Edgehill Rd W13 79 CJ71
Edgehill Rd, Chis. 125 EQ90
Edgehill Rd, Mitch. 141 DH95
Edgehill Rd, Pur. 159 DN110
Edgel St SW18 100 DB84
Ferrier St
Edgeley, Lthd. 170 BY124
Edgeley La SW4 101 DK83
Edgeley Rd
Edgeley Rd SW4 101 DK83
Edgell Cl, Vir.W. 133 AZ97
Edgell Rd, Stai. 113 BF92
Edgepoint Cl SE27 121 DP92
Knights Hill
Edgewood Dr, Orp. 163 ET106
Edgewood Grn, Croy. 143 DX102
Edgeworth Av NW4 63 CU57
Edgeworth Cl NW4 63 CU57
Edgeworth Cl, Whyt. 176 DU118
Edgeworth Cres NW4 63 CU57
Edgeworth Rd SE9 104 EJ84
Edgeworth Rd, Barn. 28 DE42
Edgington Rd SW16 121 DK93
Edgington Way, Sid. 126 EW94
Edgware Ct, Edg. 42 CN51
Cavendish Dr
Edgware Rd NW2 63 CV60
Edgware Rd NW9 62 CR55
Edgware Rd W2 194 C8
Edgware Rd W2 82 DE72
Edgware Rd Sub W2 82 DE71
Edgware Rd
Edgware Way, Edg. 42 CM49
Edgwarebury Gdns, Edg. 42 CN50
Edgwarebury La, Borwd. 42 CL45
Edgwarebury La, Edg. 42 CN49
Edinburgh Av, Rick. 22 BG44
Edinburgh Cl E2 84 DW68
Russia La
Edinburgh Cl, Pnr. 60 BX59
Edinburgh Cl, Uxb. 59 BP63
Edinburgh Ct SW20 139 CX99
Edinburgh Cres, Wal.Cr. 15 DY33
Edinburgh Dr, Abb.L. 7 BU32
Edinburgh Dr, Rom. 71 FC56
Eastern Av W
Edinburgh Dr, Stai. 114 BK93
Edinburgh Dr (Denham), Uxb. 57 BF58
Edinburgh Dr (Ickenham), Uxb. 59 BP63
Edinburgh Gate SW1 198 D4
Edinburgh Gate SW1 100 DF75
Edinburgh Ho W9 82 DC69
Edinburgh Ms, Til. 111 GH82
Edinburgh Rd E13 86 EH68
Edinburgh Rd E17 67 EA57
Edinburgh Rd N18 46 DU50
Edinburgh Rd W7 97 CF75
Edinburgh Rd, Sutt. 140 DC103
Edington Rd SE2 106 EV76
Edington Rd, Enf. 30 DW40
Edis St NW1 82 DG67
Edison Av, Horn. 71 FF61
Edison Cl E17 67 EA57
Exeter Rd
Edison Cl, Horn. 71 FF60
Edison Av
Edison Dr, Sthl. 78 CB72
Edison Gro SE18 105 ET80
Edison Rd N8 65 DK58
Edison Rd, Brom. 144 EG96
Edison Rd, Enf. 31 DZ40
Edison Rd, Well. 105 ET81
Edith Cavell Cl N19 65 DK59
Hornsey Ri Gdns
Edith Gdns, Surb. 138 CP101
Edith Gro SW10 100 DC79
Edith Rd E6 86 EK66
Edith Rd E15 67 ED64
Chandos Rd
Edith Rd N11 45 DK52
Edith Rd SE25 142 DR99
Edith Rd SW19 120 DB93
Edith Rd W14 99 CY77
Edith Rd, Orp. 164 EU106
Edith Rd, Rom. 70 EX58
Edith Row SW6 100 DB81
Edith St E2 84 DU68
Edith Ter SW10 100 DC80
Edith Turbeville Ct N19 65 DL59
Hillrise Rd
Edith Vil W14 99 CZ77
Edith Yd SW10 100 DC80
World's End Est
Edithna St SW9 101 DL83
Edmansons Cl N17 46 DS53
Bruce Gro
Edmeston Cl E9 85 DY65
Edmond Halley Way SE10 205 J5
Edmond Halley Way SE10 104 EE75
Edmonds Ct, W.Mol. 136 CB98
Avern Rd
Edmonton Grn N9 46 DV47
Hertford Rd
Edmund Gro, Felt. 116 BZ89
Edmund Hurst Dr E6 87 EN71
Winsor Ter
Edmund Rd (Chafford Hundred), Grays 109 FX75
Edmund Rd, Mitch. 140 DE97
Edmund Rd, Orp. 146 EW100
Edmund Rd, Rain. 89 FE68
Edmund Rd, Well. 106 EU83
Edmund St SE5 102 DR80
Edmunds Av, Orp. 146 EX97
Edmunds Cl, Hayes 78 BW71
Edmunds Wk N2 64 DD56
Edmunds Way, Slou. 74 AV71
Edna Rd SW20 139 CX96
Edna St SW11 100 DE81
Edric Rd SE14 103 DX80
Edrich Ho SW4 101 DL81
Edrick Rd, Edg. 42 CQ51
Edrick Wk, Edg. 42 CQ51
Edridge Cl, Bushey 24 CC43
Edridge Cl, Horn. 72 FK64
Edridge Rd, Croy. 142 DQ104
Edulf Rd, Borwd. 26 CP39
Edward Amey Cl, Wat. 24 BW36
Edward Av E4 47 EB51
Edward Av, Mord. 140 DD99
Edward Cl N9 46 DT45
Edward Cl, Abb.L. 7 BT32
Edward Cl (Chafford Hundred), Grays 109 FX76
Edward Cl, Hmptn. 116 CC92
Edward Rd
Edward Cl, Nthlt. 78 BW68
Edward Cl, Rom. 72 FJ55
Edward Ct E16 86 EG71
Alexandra St
Edward Ct, Stai. 114 BJ93
Elizabeth Av
Edward Ct, Wal.Abb. 16 EF33
Edward Gro, Barn. 28 DD43
Edward Ms NW1 195 J1
Edward Pauling Ho, Felt. 115 BT87
Westmacott Dr
Edward Pl SE8 103 DZ79
Edward Rd E17 67 DX56
Edward Rd SE20 123 DX94
Edward Rd, Barn. 28 DD43
Edward Rd, Brom. 124 EH94
Edward Rd, Chis. 125 EP92
Edward Rd, Couls. 175 DK115
Edward Rd, Croy. 142 DS101
Edward Rd, Felt. 115 BR85
Edward Rd, Hmptn. 116 CC92
Edward Rd, Har. 60 CC55
Edward Rd, Nthlt. 78 BW68
Edward Rd, Rom. 70 EY58
Edward Rd, West. 178 EL118
Edward II Av, W.Byf. 152 BM114
Edward Sq N1 83 DM67
Caledonian Rd
Edward Sq SE16 203 L2
Edward St E16 86 EG70
Edward St SE8 103 DZ79
Edward St SE14 103 DY80
Edward Temme Av E15 86 EF66
Edward Tyler Rd SE12 124 EH89
Edward Way, Ashf. 114 BM89
Edwardes Pl W8 99 CZ76
Edwardes Sq
Edwardes Sq W8 100 DA76
Edward's Av, Ruis. 77 BV65
Edwards Cl, Brwd. 55 GE44
Edwards Cl, Wor.Pk. 139 CX103
Edwards Cotts N1 83 DP65
Compton Av
Edwards Ct, Slou. 92 AS75
Edwards Dr N11 45 DK52
Gordon Rd
Edwards Gdns, Swan. 147 FD98
Ladds Way
Edwards La N16 66 DR61
Edwards Ms N1 83 DN66
Edwards Ms W1 194 F9
Edwards Ms W1 82 DG72
Edwards Rd, Belv. 106 FA77
Edwards Way, Brwd. 55 GE44
Edwards Yd, Wem. 80 CL67
Mount Pleasant
Edwin Av E6 87 EN68
Edwin Cl, Bexh. 106 EZ79
Edwin Cl, Rain. 89 FF69
Edwin Pl, Croy. 142 DR102
Cross Rd
Edwin Rd, Dart. 127 FH90
Edwin Rd, Edg. 42 CR51
Edwin Rd, Twick. 117 CF88
Edwin St E1 84 DW70
Edwin St E16 86 EG71
Edwin St, Grav. 131 GH87
Edwina Gdns, Ilf. 68 EL57
Edwin's Mead E9 67 DY63
Lindisfarne Way
Edwyn Cl, Barn. 27 CW44
Eel Brook Studios SW6 100 DA80
Moore Pk Rd
Eel Pie Island, Twick. 117 CH88
Effie Pl SW6 100 DA80
Effie Rd SW6 100 DA80
Effingham Cl, Sutt. 158 DB108
Effingham Common, Lthd. 169 BU123
Effingham Common Rd, Lthd. 169 BU123
Effingham Ct, Wok. 166 AY118
Constitution Hill
Effingham Rd N8 65 DN57
Effingham Rd SE12 124 EE85
Effingham Rd, Croy. 141 DM101
Effingham Rd, Surb. 137 CH101
Effort St SW17 120 DE92
Effra Par SW2 121 DN85
Effra Rd SW2 101 DN84
Effra Rd SW19 120 DB93
Egan Way, Hayes 77 BS73
Egbert St NW1 82 DG67
Egdean Wk, Sev. 191 FJ123
Egerton Av, Swan. 127 FF94
Egerton Cl, Dart. 127 FH88
Egerton Cl, Pnr. 59 BU56
Egerton Cres SW3 198 C8
Egerton Cres SW3 100 DE77

Egerton Dr SE10 103 EB81
Egerton Gdns NW4 63 CV56
Egerton Gdns NW10 81 CW67
Egerton Gdns SW3 198 B7
Egerton Gdns SW3 100 DE76
Egerton Gdns W13 79 CH72
Egerton Gdns, Ilf. 69 ET62
Egerton Gdns Ms SW3 198 C7
Egerton Gdns Ms SW3 100 DE76
Egerton Pl SW3 198 C7
Egerton Pl SW3 100 DE76
Egerton Pl, Wey. 153 BQ107
Egerton Rd N16 66 DT59
Egerton Rd SE25 142 DS97
Egerton Rd, N.Mal. 139 CT98
Egerton Rd, Twick. 117 CE87
Egerton Rd, Wem. 80 CM66
Egerton Rd, Wey. 153 BQ107
Egerton Ter SW3 198 C7
Egerton Ter SW3 100 DE76
Egerton Way, Hayes 95 BP80
Egg Hall, Epp. 18 EU29
Eggardon Ct, Nthlt. 78 CC65
Lancaster Rd
Egham Bypass, Egh. 113 AZ92
Egham Cl SW19 119 CY89
Winterfold Cl
Egham Cl, Sutt. 139 CY103
Egham Cres, Sutt. 139 CX104
Egham Hill, Egh. 112 AX93
Egham Rd E13 86 EH71
Eglantine La (Horton Kirby), Dart. 148 FN101
Eglantine Rd SW18 120 DC85
Egleston Rd, Mord. 140 DB100
Egley Dr, Wok. 166 AX122
Egley Rd, Wok. 166 AX122
Eglington Ct SE17 102 DQ79
Carter St
Eglington Rd E4 47 ED45
Eglinton Hill SE18 105 EP79
Eglinton Rd SE18 105 EN79
Eglinton Rd, Swans. 130 FZ86
Eglise Rd, Warl. 177 DY117
Egliston Ms SW15 99 CW83
Egliston Rd SW15 99 CW83
Eglon Ms NW1 82 DF66
Berkley Rd
Egmont Av, Surb. 138 CM102
Egmont Pk Rd, Tad. 183 CU125
Egmont Rd, N.Mal. 139 CT98
Egmont Rd, Surb. 138 CM102
Egmont Rd, Sutt. 158 DC108
Egmont Rd, Walt. 135 BV101
Egmont St SE14 103 DX80
Egmont Way, Tad. 173 CY119
Oatlands Rd
Egremont Rd SE27 121 DN90
Egret Way, Hayes 78 BX71
Eider Cl E7 68 EF64
Eider Cl, Hayes 78 BX71
Cygnet Way
Eighteenth Rd, Mitch. 141 DL98
Eighth Av E12 69 EM63
Eighth Av, Hayes 77 BU74
Eileen Rd SE25 142 DR99
Eindhoven Cl, Cars. 140 DG102
Eisenhower Dr E6 86 EL71
Elaine Gro NW5 64 DG64
Elam Cl SE5 101 DP82
Elam St SE5 101 DP82
Elan Rd, S.Ock. 91 FU71
Eland Pl, Croy. 141 DP104
Eland Rd
Eland Rd SW11 100 DF83
Eland Rd, Croy. 141 DP104
Elba Pl SE17 201 J8
Elbe St SW6 100 DC82
Elberon Av, Croy. 141 DJ100
Elborough Rd SE25 142 DU99
Elborough St SW18 120 DA88
Elbow Meadow, Slou. 93 BF81
Elbury Dr E16 86 EG72
Elcho St SW11 100 DE80
Elcot Av SE15 102 DV80
Elder Av N8 65 DL57
Elder Cl, Sid. 125 ET88
Elder Cl, West Dr. 76 BL73
Yew Av
Elder Ct, Bushey 41 CE47
Elder Gdns SE27 122 DQ91
Gladstone Ter
Elder Oak Cl SE20 142 DV95
Elder Rd SE27 122 DQ92
Elder St E1 197 P5
Elder St E1 84 DT71
Elder Wk N1 83 DP67
Essex Rd
Elder Way, Rain. 90 FK69
Elder Way, Slou. 93 AZ75
Elderbek Cl, Wal.Cr. 14 DU28
Elderberry Gro SE27 122 DQ92
Linton Gro
Elderberry Rd W5 98 CL75
Elderberry Way, Wat. 23 BV35
Elderfield Pl SW17 121 DH91
Elderfield Rd E5 66 DW63
Elderfield Rd, Slou. 74 AT65
Elderfield Wk E11 68 EH57
Elderflower Way E15 86 EE66
Eldersley Cl, Red. 184 DF132
Elderslie Cl, Beck. 143 EB99
Elderslie Rd SE9 125 EN85
Elderton Rd SE26 123 DY91
Eldertree Pl, Mitch. 141 DJ95
Eldertree Way
Eldertree Way, Mitch. 141 DH95
Elderwood Pl SE27 122 DQ92
Elder Rd
Eldon Av, Borwd. 26 CN40
Eldon Av, Croy. 142 DW103
Eldon Av, Houns. 96 CA80
Eldon Gro NW3 64 DD64
Eldon Pk SE25 142 DV98
Eldon Rd E17 67 DZ56
Eldon Rd N9 46 DW47
Eldon Rd N22 45 DP53
Eldon Rd W8 100 DB76
Eldon Rd, Cat. 176 DR121
Eldon St EC2 197 L7
Eldon St EC2 84 DR71
Eldon Way NW10 80 CP68
Eldred Dr, Orp. 146 EW103
Eldred Gdns, Upmin. 73 FS59
Eldred Rd, Bark. 87 ES67
Eldrick Ct, Felt. 115 BR88
Kilross Rd
Eldridge Cl, Felt. 115 BU88
Eleanor Av, Epsom 156 CR110
Eleanor Cl N15 66 DT55
Arnold Rd
Eleanor Cl SE16 203 H4
Eleanor Cl SE16 103 DX75
Eleanor Cres NW7 43 CX49
Eleanor Cross Rd, Wal.Cr. 15 DY34
Eleanor Gdns, Barn. 27 CX43
Eleanor Gdns, Dag. 70 EZ62
Eleanor Gro SW13 98 CS83
Eleanor Gro (Ickenham), Uxb. 59 BP62
Eleanor Rd E8 84 DV66
Eleanor Rd E15 86 EF65
Eleanor Rd N11 45 DL51
Eleanor Rd (Chalfont St. Peter), Ger.Cr. 36 AW53
Eleanor Rd, Wal.Cr. 15 DY33
Eleanor St E3 85 EA69
Eleanor Wk SE18 105 EM77
Samuel St
Eleanor Way, Brwd. 54 FX50
Eleanor Way, Wal.Cr. 15 DZ33
Electric Av SW9 101 DN84
Electric Av, Enf. 31 DZ36
Electric La SW9 101 DN84
Electric Par, Surb. 137 CK100
Elephant & Castle SE1 200 G7
Elephant & Castle SE1 101 DP77
Elephant La SE16 202 F4
Elephant La SE16 102 DW75
Elephant Rd SE17 201 H8
Elephant Rd SE17 102 DQ77
Elers Rd W13 97 CJ75
Elers Rd, Hayes 95 BR77
Eleven Acre Ri, Loug. 33 EM41
Eley Est N18 46 DW50
Eley Rd N18 47 DX50
Elf Row E1 84 DW73
Elfin Gro, Tedd. 117 CF92
Broad St
Elfindale Rd SE24 122 DQ85
Elford Cl SE3 104 EH84
Elfort Rd N5 65 DN63
Elfrida Cres SE6 123 EA91
Elfrida Rd, Wat. 24 BW43
Elfwine Rd W7 79 CE71
Elgal Cl, Orp. 163 EP106
Orchard Rd
Elgar Av NW10 80 CR65
Mitchellbrook Way
Elgar Av SW16 141 DL97
Elgar Av W5 98 CL75
Elgar Av, Surb. 138 CP101
Elgar Cl E13 86 EJ68
Bushey Rd
Elgar Cl SE8 103 EA80
Comet St
Elgar Cl, Borwd. 41 CK45
Elgar Cl, Buck.H. 48 EK47
Elgar Cl, Uxb. 58 BN61
Elgar Gdns, Til. 111 GH81
Elgar St SE16 203 L6
Elgar St SE16 103 DY76
Elgin Av W9 82 DB69
Elgin Av, Ashf. 115 BQ93
Elgin Av, Har. 41 CH54
Elgin Av, Rom. 52 FP52
Elgin Cres W11 81 CZ72
Elgin Cres, Cat. 176 DU122
Elgin Cres, Houns. 95 BS82
Eastern Perimeter Rd
Elgin Dr, Nthwd. 39 BS52
Elgin Ms W11 81 CY72
Ladbroke Gro
Elgin Ms N W9 82 DB69
Randolph Av
Elgin Ms S W9 82 DB69
Randolph Av
Elgin Rd N22 45 DJ54
Elgin Rd, Croy. 142 DT102
Elgin Rd, Ilf. 69 ES60
Elgin Rd, Sutt. 140 DC104
Elgin Rd, Wall. 159 DJ107
Elgin Rd (Cheshunt), Wal.Cr. 14 DW30
Elgin Rd, Wey. 152 BN106
Elgood Av, Nthwd. 39 BU51
Elgood Cl W11 81 CY73
Avondale Pk Rd
Elham Cl, Brom. 124 EK94
Elia Ms N1 196 F1
Elia Ms N1 83 DP68
Elia St N1 196 F1
Elia St N1 83 DP68
Elias Pl SW8 101 DN79
Elibank Rd SE9 105 EN84
Elim Est SE1 201 M6
Elim Est SE1 102 DS76
Elim Way E13 86 EF69
Eliot Bk SE23 122 DV89
Eliot Cotts SE3 104 EE82
Eliot Pl
Eliot Ct N15 66 DT56
Tynemouth Rd
Eliot Dr, Har. 60 CB61
Eliot Gdns SW15 99 CU84
Eliot Hill SE13 103 EC82
Eliot Ms NW8 82 DC68
Eliot Pk SE13 103 EC83
Eliot Pl SE3 104 EE82
Eliot Rd, Dag. 70 EX63
Eliot Rd, Dart. 128 FP85
Eliot Vale SE3 103 ED82
Elizabeth Av N1 84 DQ66
Elizabeth Av, Amer. 20 AV39
Elizabeth Av, Enf. 29 DP41
Elizabeth Av, Ilf. 69 ER61
Elizabeth Av, Stai. 114 BJ93
Elizabeth Blackwell Ho N22 45 DN53
Progress Way
Elizabeth Br SW1 199 H9
Elizabeth Br SW1 101 DH77
Elizabeth Cl E14 85 EB72
Grundy St
Elizabeth Cl W9 82 DC70
Randolph Av
Elizabeth Cl, Barn. 27 CX41
Elizabeth Cl, Rom. 51 FB53
Elizabeth Cl, Sutt. 157 CZ105
Elizabeth Cl, Til. 111 GH82
Elizabeth Clyde Cl N15 66 DS56
Elizabeth Cotts, Rich. 98 CM81
Elizabeth Ct SW1 199 N7
Elizabeth Ct, Grav. 131 GG86
St. James's Rd
Elizabeth Ct, Wat. 23 BT38
Elizabeth Dr, Epp. 33 ES36
Elizabeth Est SE17 102 DR79
Elizabeth Fry Rd E8 84 DV66
Lamb La
Elizabeth Gdns W3 81 CT74
Elizabeth Gdns, Stan. 41 CJ51
Elizabeth Gdns, Sun. 136 BW97
Elizabeth Huggins Cotts, Grav. 131 GG89
Elizabeth Ms NW3 82 DE65
Elizabeth Pl N15 66 DR56
Elizabeth Ride N9 46 DV45
Elizabeth Rd E6 86 EK67
Elizabeth Rd N15 66 DS57
Elizabeth Rd, Brwd. 54 FV44
Elizabeth Rd, Grays 110 FZ76
Elizabeth Rd, Rain. 89 FH71
Elizabeth Sq SE16 203 K1
Elizabeth St SW1 198 G8
Elizabeth St SW1 100 DG77
Elizabeth St, Green. 129 FS85
Elizabeth Ter SE9 125 EM86
Elizabeth Way SE19 122 DR94
Elizabeth Way, Felt. 116 BW91
Elizabeth Way, Orp. 146 EW99
Elizabeth Way, Slou. 74 AT67
Elizabethan Cl, Stai. 114 BK87
Elizabethan Way
Elizabethan Way, Stai. 114 BK87
Elkanette Ms N20 44 DC47
Ridgeview Rd
Elkington Rd E13 86 EH70
Elkins, The, Rom. 51 FE54
Elkins Rd, Slou. 56 AS61
Elkstone Rd W10 81 CZ71
Ella Rd N8 65 DL59
Ellaline Rd W6 99 CX79
Ellanby Cres N18 46 DV50
Elland Rd SE15 102 DW84
Elland Rd, Walt. 136 BX103
Ellement Cl, Pnr. 60 BX57
Ellen Cl, Brom. 144 EK97
Ellen Ct N9 46 DW47
Densworth Gro
Ellen St E1 84 DU72
Ellen Webb Dr, Har. 61 CE55
Ellenborough Pl SW15 99 CU84
Ellenborough Rd N22 46 DQ53
Ellenborough Rd, Sid. 126 EX92
Ellenbridge Way, S.Croy. 160 DS109
Ellenbrook Cl, Wat. 23 BV39
Hatfield Rd
Elleray Rd, Tedd. 117 CF93
Ellerby St SW6 99 CX81
Ellerdale Cl NW3 64 DC63
Ellerdale Rd
Ellerdale Rd NW3 64 DC64
Ellerdale St SE13 103 EB84
Ellerdine Rd, Houns. 96 CC84
Ellerker Gdns, Rich. 118 CL86
Ellerman Av, Twick. 116 BZ88
Ellerman Rd, Til. 111 GF82
Ellerslie, Grav. 131 GK87
Ellerslie Gdns NW10 81 CU67
Ellerslie Rd W12 81 CV74
Ellerslie Sq Ind Est SW2 121 DL85
Ellerton Gdns, Dag. 88 EW66
Ellerton Rd SW13 99 CU81
Ellerton Rd SW18 120 DD88
Ellerton Rd SW20 119 CU94
Ellerton Rd, Dag. 88 EW66
Ellerton Rd, Surb. 138 CM103
Ellery Rd SE19 122 DR94
Ellery St SE15 102 DV82
Ellesborough Cl, Wat. 40 BW50
Ellesmere Av NW7 42 CR48
Ellesmere Av, Beck. 143 EB96
Ellesmere Cl E11 68 EF57
Ellesmere Cl, Ruis. 59 BQ59
Ellesmere Dr, S.Croy. 160 DV114
Ellesmere Gdns, Ilf. 68 EL57
Ellesmere Gro, Barn. 27 CZ43
Ellesmere Pl, Walt. 153 BS106
Ellesmere Rd E3 85 DY68
Ellesmere Rd NW10 63 CU64
Ellesmere Rd W4 98 CR79
Ellesmere Rd, Grnf. 78 CC70
Ellesmere Rd, Twick. 117 CJ86
Ellesmere Rd, Wey. 153 BR107
Ellesmere St E14 85 EB72
Ellice Rd, Oxt. 188 EF129
Elliman Av, Slou. 74 AS73
Ellingfort Rd E8 84 DV66
Ellingham Rd E15 67 ED63
Ellingham Rd W12 99 CU75
Ellingham Rd, Chess. 155 CK107
Ellington Rd N10 65 DH56
Ellington Rd, Felt. 115 BT91
Ellington Rd, Houns. 96 CB82
Ellington St N7 83 DN65
Ellington Way, Epsom 173 CV117
Elliot Cl E15 86 EE66
Elliot Rd NW4 63 CV58
Elliot Rd, Stan. 41 CG51
Elliott Av, Ruis. 59 BV61
Elliott Cl, Wem. 62 CM62
Elliott Gdns, Rom. 51 FH53
Elliott Gdns, Shep. 134 BN98
Elliott Rd SW9 101 DP80
Elliott Rd W4 98 CS77
Elliott Rd, Brom. 144 EK98
Elliott Rd, Th.Hth. 141 DP98
Elliott Sq NW3 82 DE66
Elliott St, Grav. 131 GK87
Elliotts Cl (Cowley), Uxb. 76 BJ71
Elliotts La, West. 180 EW124
Elliott's Pl N1 83 DP67
St. Peters St
Elliotts Row SE11 200 F8
Elliotts Row SE11 101 DP77
Ellis Av (Chalfont St. Peter), Ger.Cr. 37 AZ53
Ellis Av, Rain. 89 FG71
Ellis Av, Slou. 92 AS75
Ellis Cl NW10 81 CV65
High Rd
Ellis Cl SE9 125 EQ89
Ellis Cl, Couls. 175 DM120
Ellis Ct W7 79 CF71
Ellis Fm Cl, Wok. 166 AX122
Ellis Ms SE7 104 EJ79
Ellis Rd, Couls. 175 DM120
Ellis Rd, Mitch. 140 DF100
Ellis Rd, Sthl. 78 CC74
Ellis St SW1 198 E8
Ellis St SW1 100 DF77
Ellis Way, Dart. 128 FM89
Elliscombe Rd SE7 104 EJ78
Ellisfield Dr SW15 119 CT87
Ellison Gdns, Sthl. 96 BZ77
Ellison Rd SW13 99 CT82
Ellison Rd SW16 121 DK94
Ellison Rd, Sid. 125 ER88
Elliston Ho SE18 105 EN77
Ellmore Cl, Rom. 51 FH53
Ellora Rd SW16 121 DK92
Ellsworth St E2 84 DV69
Ellwood Ct W9 82 DB70
Clearwell Dr
Ellwood Gdns, Wat. 7 BV34
Ellwood Ri, Ch.St.G. 36 AW47
Elm Av W5 80 CL74
Elm Av, Cars. 158 DF110
Elm Av, Ruis. 59 BU60
Elm Av, Upmin. 72 FP62
Elm Av, Wat. 40 BY45
Elm Bk, Brom. 144 EK96
Elm Bk Gdns SW13 98 CS82
Elm Cl E11 68 EH58
Elm Cl N19 65 DJ61
Hargrave Pk
Elm Cl NW4 63 CX57
Elm Cl SW20 139 CW98
Grand Dr
Elm Cl, Buck.H. 48 EK47
Elm Cl, Cars. 140 DF102
Elm Cl, Dart. 128 FJ88
Elm Cl, Har. 60 CB58
Elm Cl, Hayes 77 BU72
Elm Cl, Lthd. 171 CH122
Elm Cl, Rom. 51 FB54
Elm Cl, S.Croy. 160 DS107
Elm Cl, Stai. 114 BK88
Elm Cl, Surb. 138 CQ101
Elm Cl, Tad. 182 CQ130
Elm Cl, Twick. 116 CB89
Elm Cl, Wal.Abb. 15 ED34
Elm Cl, Warl. 177 DX117
Elm Cl, Wok. 166 AX115
Elm Cl (Send Marsh), Wok. 168 BG124
Elm Ct EC4 196 D10
Elm Ct, Mitch. 140 DF96
Armfield Cres
Elm Ct, Sun. 115 BT94
Elm Cres W5 80 CL74
Elm Cres, Kings.T. 138 CL95
Elm Cft, Slou. 92 AW81
Elm Dr, Har. 60 CB58
Elm Dr, Lthd. 171 CH122
Elm Dr, Sun. 136 BW96
Elm Dr, Swan. 147 FD96
Elm Dr (Cheshunt), Wal.Cr. 15 DY28
Elm Dr, Wok. 150 AT110
Elm Fm Caravan Pk, Cher. 133 BC101
Elm Friars Wk NW1 83 DK66
Elm Gdns N2 64 DC55
Elm Gdns, Enf. 30 DR38
Elm Gdns, Epp. 19 FB26
Elm Gdns, Epsom 173 CW119
Elm Gdns, Esher 155 CF107
Elm Gdns, Mitch. 141 DK98
Elm Grn W3 80 CS72
Elm Gro N8 65 DL58
Elm Gro NW2 63 CX63
Elm Gro SE15 102 DT82
Elm Gro SW19 119 CY94
Elm Gro, Cat. 176 DS122
Elm Gro, Epsom 156 CQ114
Elm Gro, Erith 107 FD80
Elm Gro, Har. 60 CA59
Elm Gro, Horn. 72 FL58
Elm Gro, Kings.T. 138 CL95
Elm Gro, Orp. 145 ET102
Elm Gro, Sutt. 158 DB105
Elm Gro, Wat. 23 BU37
Elm Gro, West Dr. 76 BM73
Willow Av
Elm Gro, Wdf.Grn. 48 EF50
Elm Gro Par, Wall. 140 DG104
Butter Hill
Elm Gro Rd SW13 99 CU82
Elm Gro Rd W5 98 CL75
Elm Gro Rd, Cob. 170 BX116
Elm Hall Gdns E11 68 EH57
Elm La SE6 123 DZ89
Elm La, Wok. 169 BP118
Elm Lawn Cl, Uxb. 76 BL66
Park Rd
Elm Ms, Rich. 118 CM86
Grove Rd
Elm Par, Horn. 71 FH63
St. Nicholas Av
Elm Pk SW2 121 DM86
Elm Pk, Stan. 41 CH50
Elm Pk Av N15 66 DT57
Elm Pk Av, Horn. 71 FG63
Elm Pk Ct, Pnr. 60 BW55
Elm Pk Gdns NW4 63 CX57
Elm Pk Gdns SW10 100 DD78
Elm Pk La SW3 100 DD78
Elm Pk Mans SW10 100 DC79
Park Wk
Elm Pk Rd E10 67 DY60
Elm Pk Rd N3 43 CZ52
Elm Pk Rd N21 46 DQ45
Elm Pk Rd SE25 142 DT97
Elm Pk Rd SW3 100 DD79
Elm Pk Rd, Pnr. 40 BW54
Elm Pl SW7 100 DD7
Elm Quay Ct SW8 101 DK7
Elm Rd E7 86 EF6
Elm Rd E11 67 ED6
Elm Rd E17 67 EC5
Elm Rd N22 45 DP5
Granville Rd
Elm Rd SW14 98 CQ8
Elm Rd, Barn. 27 CZ4
Elm Rd, Beck. 143 DZ9
Elm Rd, Chess. 156 CL10
Elm Rd, Dart. 128 FK8
Elm Rd, Epsom 157 CT10
Elm Rd, Erith 107 FG81
Elm Rd, Esher 155 CF10
Elm Rd, Felt. 115 BR8
Elm Rd, Grav. 131 GJ9
Elm Rd, Grays 110 GC7
Elm Rd, Green. 129 FS8
Elm Rd, Kings.T. 138 CM9
Elm Rd, Lthd. 171 CH12
Elm Rd, N.Mal. 138 CR9
Elm Rd, Orp. 164 EU10
Elm Rd, Pur. 159 DP11
Elm Rd, Red. 184 DE134
Elm Rd, Rom. 51 FB54
Elm Rd, Sid. 126 EU91
Elm Rd, S.Ock. 90 FQ74
Elm Rd, Th.Hth. 142 DR98
Elm Rd, Wall. 140 DG102
Elm Rd, Warl. 177 DX117
Elm Rd, Wem. 62 CL64
Elm Rd, West. 189 ES125
Elm Rd, Wok. 166 AX118
Elm Rd (Horsell), Wok. 167 AZ115
Elm Rd W, Sutt. 139 CZ101
Elm Row NW3 64 DC62
Elm St WC1 196 C5
Elm St WC1 83 DM70
Elm Ter NW2 64 DA62
Elm Ter NW3 64 DE63
Constantine Rd
Elm Ter SE9 125 EN86
Elm Ter, Grays 109 FV79
Elm Ter, Har. 41 CD52
Elm Tree Av, Esher 137 CD101
Elm Tree Cl NW8 82 DD69
Elm Tree Cl, Ashf. 115 BP92
Convent Rd
Elm Tree Cl, Cher. 133 BE103
Elm Tree Cl, Nthlt. 78 BZ68
Elm Tree Rd NW8 82 DD69
Elm Tree Wk, Rick. 21 BF42
Elm Wk NW3 64 DA61
Elm Wk SW20 139 CW98
Elm Wk, Orp. 145 EM104
Elm Wk, Rad. 25 CF36
Elm Wk, Rom. 71 FG55
Elm Way N11 44 DG51
Elm Way NW10 62 CS63
Elm Way, Brwd. 54 FU48
Elm Way, Epsom 156 CR106
Elm Way, Rick. 38 BH46
Elm Way, Wor.Pk. 139 CW104
Elmar Rd N15 66 DR56
Elmbank N14 45 DL45
Elmbank Av, Barn. 27 CW42
Elmbank Av, Egh. 112 AV93
Elmbank Way W7 79 CD71
Elmbourne Dr, Belv. 107 FB77
Elmbourne Rd SW17 120 DG90
Elmbridge Av, Surb. 138 CP99
Elmbridge Cl, Ruis. 59 BU58
Elmbridge Dr, Ruis. 59 BT57
Elmbridge La, Wok. 167 AZ119
Elmbridge Rd, Ilf. 50 EU51
Elmbridge Wk E8 84 DU66
Wilman Gro
Elmbrook Cl, Sun. 135 BV95
Elmbrook Gdns SE9 104 EL84
Elmbrook Rd, Sutt. 157 CZ105
Elmcote Way, Rick. 22 BM44
Elmcourt Rd SE27 121 DP89
Elmcroft N8 65 DM57
Elmcroft, Lthd. 170 CA124
Elmcroft Av E11 68 EH57
Elmcroft Av N9 30 DV44
Elmcroft Av NW11 63 CZ59
Elmcroft Av, Sid. 125 ET86
Elmcroft Cl E11 68 EH56
Elmcroft Cl W5 79 CK72
Elmcroft Cl, Chess. 138 CL104
Elmcroft Cl, Felt. 115 BT86
Elmcroft Cres NW11 63 CY59
Elmcroft Cres, Har. 60 CA55
Elmcroft Dr, Ashf. 114 BN92
Elmcroft Dr, Chess. 138 CL104
Elmcroft Gdns NW9 62 CN57
Elmcroft Rd, Orp. 146 EU101
Elmcroft St E5 66 DW63
Elmdale Rd N13 45 DM50
Elmdene, Surb. 138 CQ102
Elmdene Av, Horn. 72 FM57
Elmdene Cl, Beck. 143 DZ99
Elmdene Ct, Wok. 166 AY118
Constitution Hill
Elmdene Rd SE18 105 EP78
Elmdon Rd, Houns. 96 BX82
Elmdon Rd (Hatton Cross), Houns. 95 BT83
Elmer Av (Havering-atte-Bower), Rom. 51 FE48
Elmer Cl, Enf. 29 DM41
Elmer Cl, Rain. 89 FG66
Elmer Cotts, Lthd. 171 CG123
Elmer Gdns, Edg. 42 CP52
Elmer Gdns, Islw. 97 CD83
Elmer Gdns, Rain. 89 FG66
Elmer Ms, Lthd. 171 CG123
Elmer Rd SE6 123 EC87
Elmers Dr, Tedd. 117 CH93
Kingston Rd
Elmers End Rd SE20 142 DW96
Elmers End Rd, Beck. 142 DW96
Elmers Rd SE25 142 DU101
Elmerside Rd, Beck. 143 DY98
Elmfield, Lthd. 170 CA123
Elmfield Av N8 65 DL57
Elmfield Av, Mitch. 140 DG95
Elmfield Av, Tedd. 117 CF92
Elmfield Cl, Grav. 131 GH88
Elmfield Cl, Har. 61 CE61
Elmfield Cl, Pot.B. 11 CY33

Elmfield Pk, Brom. 144 EG97
Elmfield Rd E4 47 EC47
Elmfield Rd E17 67 DX58
Elmfield Rd N2 64 DD55
Elmfield Rd SW17 120 DG89
Elmfield Rd, Brom. 144 EG97
Elmfield Rd, Pot.B. 11 CY33
Elmfield Rd, Sthl. 96 BY76
Elmfield Way W9 82 DA71
Elmfield Way, S.Croy. 160 DT109
Elmgate Av, Felt. 115 BV90
Elmgate Gdns, Edg. 42 CR50
Elmgreen Cl E15 86 EE67
Church St N
Elmgrove Cres, Har. 61 CF57
Elmgrove Gdns, Har. 61 CG57
Elmgrove Rd, Croy. 142 DV101
Elmgrove Rd, Har. 61 CF57
Elmgrove Rd, Wey. 152 BN105
Elmhurst, Belv. 106 EY79
Elmhurst Av N2 64 DD55
Elmhurst Av, Mitch. 121 DH94
Elmhurst Dr E18 48 EG54
Elmhurst Dr, Horn. 72 FJ60
Elmhurst Gdns E18 48 EH53
Elmhurst Dr
Elmhurst Rd E7 86 EH66
Elmhurst Rd N17 46 DT54
Elmhurst Rd SE9 124 EL89
Elmhurst Rd, Enf. 30 DW37
Elmhurst Rd, Slou. 93 BA76
Elmhurst St SW4 101 DK83
Elmhurst Vil SE15 102 DW84
Cheltenham Rd
Elmhurst Way, Loug. 49 EM45
Elmington Cl, Bex. 127 FB86
Elmington Est SE5 102 DR80
Elmington Rd SE5 102 DR81
Elmira St SE13 103 EB83
Elmlea Dr, Hayes 77 BS71
Grange Rd
Elmlee Cl, Chis. 125 EM93
Elmley Cl E6 86 EL71
Northumberland Rd
Elmley St SE18 105 ER77
Elmore Cl, Wem. 80 CL68
Elmore Rd E11 67 EC62
Elmore Rd, Couls. 174 DF121
Elmore Rd, Enf. 31 DX39
Elmore St N1 84 DQ66
Elmores, Loug. 33 EN41
Elmpark Gdns, S.Croy. 160 DW110
Elmroyd Av, Pot.B. 11 CZ33
Elmroyd Cl, Pot.B. 11 CZ33
Elms, The SW13 99 CT83
Elms Av N10 65 DH55
Elms Av NW4 63 CX57
Elms Ct, Wem. 61 CF63
Elms Cres SW4 121 DJ86
Elms Fm Rd, Horn. 72 FJ64
Elms Gdns, Dag. 70 EZ63
Elms Gdns, Wem. 61 CG63
Elms La, Wem. 61 CG63
Elms Ms W2 82 DD73
Elms Pk Av, Wem. 61 CG63
Elms Rd SW4 121 DJ85
Elms Rd (Chalfont St. Peter), Ger.Cr. 36 AY52
Elms Rd, Har. 41 CE52
Elmscott Gdns N21 30 DQ44
Elmscott Rd, Brom. 124 EF92
Elmscroft Gdns, Pot.B. 11 CY32
Elmsdale Rd E17 67 DZ56
Elmshaw Rd SW15 119 CU85
Elmshorn, Epsom 173 CW116
Elmshurst Cres N2 64 DD56
Elmside, Croy. 161 EB107
Elmside Rd, Wem. 62 CN62
Elmsleigh Av, Har. 61 CH56
Elmsleigh Cen, The, Stai. 113 BF91
Elmsleigh Ct, Sutt. 140 DB104
Elmsleigh Rd, Stai. 113 BF92
Elmsleigh Rd, Twick. 117 CD89
Elmslie Cl, Epsom 156 CQ114
Elmslie Cl, Wdf.Grn. 49 EM51
Elmslie Pt E3 85 DZ71
Elmstead Av, Chis. 125 EM92
Elmstead Av, Wem. 62 CL60
Elmstead Cl N20 44 DA47
Elmstead Cl, Epsom 156 CS106
Elmstead Cl, Sev. 190 FE122
Elmstead Cres, Well. 106 EW79
Elmstead Gdns, Wor.Pk. 139 CU104
Elmstead Glade, Chis. 125 EM93
Elmstead La, Chis. 125 EM92
Elmstead Rd, Erith 107 FE81
Elmstead Rd, Ilf. 69 ES61
Elmstead Rd, W.Byf. 152 BG113
Elmstone Rd SW6 100 DA81
Elmsway, Ashf. 114 BM92
Elmswood, Lthd. 170 BZ124
Elmsworth Av, Houns. 96 CB82
Elmton Way E5 66 DU62
Rendlesham Rd
Elmtree Cl, W.Byf. 152 BL113
Elmtree Rd, Tedd. 117 CE91
Elmwood Av N13 45 DL50
Elmwood Av, Borwd. 26 CP42
Elmwood Av, Felt. 115 BU89
Elmwood Av, Har. 61 CG57
Elmwood Cl, Ash. 171 CK117
Elmwood Cl, Epsom 157 CU108
Elmwood Cl, Wall. 140 DG103
Elmwood Ct, Ash. 171 CK117
Elmwood Cl
Elmwood Ct, Wem. 61 CG62
Elmwood Cres NW9 62 CQ56
Elmwood Dr, Bex. 126 EY87
Elmwood Dr, Epsom 157 CU107
Elmwood Gdns W7 79 CE72
Elmwood Pk, Ger.Cr. 56 AY60
Elmwood Rd SE24 122 DR85
Elmwood Rd W4 98 CQ79
Elmwood Rd, Croy. 141 DP101
Elmwood Rd, Mitch. 140 DF97
Elmwood Rd, Red. 184 DG130
Elmwood Rd, Slou. 74 AV73
Elmworth Gro SE21 122 DR89
Elnathan Ms W9 82 DB70
Shirland Rd
Elphinstone Rd E17 47 DZ54
Elphinstone St N5 65 DP63
Avenell Rd
Elrick Cl, Erith 107 FE79
Queen St
Elrington Rd E8 84 DU65
Elrington Rd, Wdf.Grn. 48 EG50
Elruge Cl, West Dr. 94 BK76
Elsa Rd, Well. 106 EV82
Elsa St E1 85 DY71
Elsdale St E9 84 DW65
Elsden Ms E2 84 DW68
Old Ford Rd
Elsden Rd N17 46 DT53
Elsdon Rd, Wok. 166 AU117
Elsenham Rd E12 69 EN64
Elsenham St SW18 119 CZ88
Elsham Rd E11 68 EE62
Elsham Rd W14 99 CY75
Elsham Ter W14 99 CY75
Elsie Rd SE22 102 DT84
Elsiedene Rd N21 46 DQ45
Elsiemaud Rd SE4 123 DZ85
Elsinge Rd, Enf. 30 DV36
Elsinore Av, Stai. 114 BL87
Elsinore Gdns NW2 63 CY62
Elsinore Rd SE23 123 DY88
Elsinore Way, Rich. 98 CP83
Lower Richmond Rd
Elsley Rd SW11 100 DF83
Elspeth Rd SW11 100 DF84
Elspeth Rd, Wem. 62 CL64
Elsrick Av, Mord. 140 DA99
Chalgrove Av
Elstan Way, Croy. 143 DY101
Elsted St SE17 201 L9
Elsted St SE17 102 DR77
Elstow Cl SE9 125 EN85
Elstow Cl, Ruis. 60 BX59
Elstow Gdns, Dag. 88 EY67
Elstow Rd, Dag. 88 EY66
Elstree Gdns N9 46 DV46
Elstree Gdns, Belv. 106 EY77
Elstree Gdns, Ilf. 69 EQ64
Elstree Hill, Brom. 124 EE94
Elstree Hill N, Borwd. 25 CK44
Elstree Hill S, Borwd. 41 CJ45
Elstree Pk, Borwd. 26 CR44
Elstree Rd, Borwd. 25 CG44
Elstree Rd, Bushey 41 CD45
Elstree Way, Borwd. 26 CP41
Elswick Rd SE13 103 EB82
Elswick St SW6 100 DC82
Elsworth Cl, Felt. 115 BS88
Elsworthy, T.Ditt. 137 CE100
Elsworthy Ri NW3 82 DE66
Elsworthy Rd NW3 82 DE67
Elsworthy Ter NW3 82 DE66
Elsynge Rd SW18 120 DD85
Eltham Grn SE9 124 EJ85
Eltham Grn Rd SE9 104 EJ84
Eltham High St SE9 125 EM86
Eltham Hill SE9 124 EK85
Eltham Palace Rd SE9 124 EJ86
Eltham Pk Gdns SE9 105 EN84
Eltham Rd SE9 124 EJ85
Eltham Rd SE12 124 EF85
Elthiron Rd SW6 100 DA81
Elthorne Av W7 97 CF75
Elthorne Ct, Felt. 116 BW88
Elthorne Pk Rd W7 97 CF75
Elthorne Rd N19 65 DK61
Elthorne Rd NW9 62 CR59
Elthorne Rd, Uxb. 76 BK68
Elthorne Way NW9 62 CR58
Elthruda Rd SE13 123 ED86
Eltisley Rd, Ilf. 69 EP63
Elton Av, Barn. 27 CZ43
Elton Av, Grnf. 79 CF65
Elton Av, Wem. 61 CH64
Elton Cl, Kings.T. 117 CJ94
Elton Ho E3 85 DZ67
Elton Pk, Wat. 23 BV40
Elton Pl N16 66 DS64
Elton Rd, Kings.T. 138 CM95
Elton Rd, Pur. 159 DJ112
Elton Way, Wat. 24 CB40
Eltringham St SW18 100 DC84
Elvaston Ms SW7 100 DC76
Elvaston Pl SW7 100 DC76
Elveden Cl, Wok. 168 BH117
Elveden Pl NW10 80 CN68
Elveden Rd NW10 80 CN68
Elvedon Rd, Cob. 153 BV111
Elvendon Rd N13 45 DL51
Elver Gdns E2 84 DU68
St. Peter's Cl
Elverson Rd SE8 103 EB82
Elverton St SW1 199 M8
Elverton St SW1 101 DK77
Elvet Av, Rom. 72 FJ56
Elvington Grn, Brom. 144 EF99
Elvington La NW9 42 CS53
Elvino Rd SE26 123 DY92
Elvis Rd NW2 81 CW65
Elwell Cl, Egh. 113 BA92
Mowbray Cres
Elwick Rd, S.Ock. 91 FW72
Elwill Way, Beck. 143 EC98
Elwin St E2 84 DU69
Elwood St N5 65 DP62
Elwyn Gdns SE12 124 EG87
Ely Cl, Amer. 20 AS39
Ely Cl, Erith 107 FF82
Ely Cl, N.Mal. 139 CT96
Ely Ct EC1 196 E7
Ely Gdns, Borwd. 26 CR43
Ely Gdns, Dag. 71 FC62
Ely Gdns, Ilf. 68 EL59
Canterbury Av
Ely Pl EC1 196 E7
Ely Pl, Wdf.Grn. 49 EN51
Ely Rd E10 67 EC58
Ely Rd, Croy. 142 DR99
Ely Rd (Heathrow Airport), Houns. 95 BT82
Eastern Perimeter Rd
Ely Rd (Hounslow W), Houns. 96 BW83
Elyne Rd N4 65 DN58
Elysian Av, Orp. 145 ET100
Elysium Pl SW6 99 CZ82
Fulham Pk Gdns
Elysium St SW6 99 CZ82
Fulham Pk Gdns
Elystan Business Cen, Hayes 78 BW73
Elystan Cl, Wall. 159 DH109
Elystan Pl SW3 198 C10
Elystan Pl SW3 100 DE78
Elystan St SW3 198 B9
Elystan St SW3 100 DE77
Elystan Wk N1 83 DN67
Cloudesley Rd
Emanuel Av W3 80 CQ72
Emanuel Dr, Hmptn. 116 BZ92
Emba St SE16 202 C5
Emba St SE16 102 DU75
Embankment SW15 99 CX82
Embankment, The, Stai. 112 AW87
Embankment, The, Twick. 117 CG88
Embankment Gdns SW3 100 DF79
Embankment Pl WC2 200 A2
Embankment Pl WC2 83 DL74
Embassy Ct, Sid. 126 EV90
Embassy Ct, Well. 106 EV83
Welling High St
Embassy Gdns, Beck. 143 DZ95
Blakeney Rd
Ember Cen, Walt. 136 BY103
Ember Cl, Add. 152 BK106
Ember Cl, Orp. 145 EQ101
Ember Fm Av, E.Mol. 137 CD100
Ember Fm Way, E.Mol. 137 CD100
Ember Gdns, T.Ditt. 137 CE101
Ember La, E.Mol. 137 CD102
Ember La, Esher 137 CD101
Ember Rd, Slou. 93 BB76
Embercourt Rd, T.Ditt. 137 CE100
Emberson Way, Epp. 19 FC26
Emberton SE5 102 DS79
Albany Rd
Embleton Rd SE13 103 EB83
Embleton Rd, Wat. 39 BU48
Embleton Wk, Hmptn. 116 BZ93
Fearnley Cres
Embley Pt E5 66 DV63
Tiger Way
Embry Cl, Stan. 41 CG49
Embry Dr, Stan. 41 CG51
Embry Way, Stan. 41 CG50
Emden Cl, West Dr. 94 BN75
Emden St SW6 100 DB81
Emerald Cl E16 86 EL72
Emerald Cl, Slou. 92 AS75
Emerald Gdns, Dag. 70 FA60
Emerald Sq, Sthl. 96 BX76
Emerald St WC1 196 B6
Emerald St WC1 83 DM71
Emerson Dr, Horn. 72 FK59
Emerson Gdns, Har. 62 CM58
Emerson Rd, Ilf. 69 EN59
Emerson St SE1 201 H2
Emerson St SE1 84 DQ74
Emersons Av, Swan. 127 FF94
Emerton Cl, Bexh. 106 EY84
Emerton Rd, Lthd. 170 CC120
Emery Hill St SW1 199 L7
Emery Hill St SW1 101 DJ76
Emery St SE1 200 E6
Emes Rd, Erith 107 FC80
Emilia Cl, Enf. 30 DV43
Emily Davidson Dr, Epsom 173 CV118
Emily Jackson Cl, Sev. 191 FH124
Emily Pl N7 65 DN63
Emley Rd, Add. 134 BG104
Emlyn Gdns W12 98 CS75
Emlyn La, Lthd. 171 CG122
Emlyn Rd W12 98 CS76
Emma Rd E13 86 EF68
Emma St E2 84 DV68
Emmanuel Lo, Wal.Cr. 14 DW30
College Rd
Emmanuel Rd SW12 121 DJ88
Emmanuel Rd, Nthwd. 39 BT52
Emmaus Way, Chig. 49 EN50
Emmett Cl (Shenley), Rad. 10 CL33
Emmetts Cl, Wok. 166 AW117
Emmott Av, Ilf. 69 EQ57
Emmott Cl E1 85 DY70
Emmott Cl NW11 64 DC58
Emms Pas, Kings.T. 137 CK96
High St
Emperor's Gate SW7 100 DB76
Empire Av N18 46 DQ50
Empire Cen, Wat. 24 BW39
Empire Ct, Wem. 62 CP62
Empire Rd, Grnf. 79 CJ67
Empire Sq N7 65 DL62
Holloway Rd
Empire Way, Wem. 62 CM63
Empire Wf Rd E14 204 F9
Empire Wf Rd E14 103 ED77
Empire Yd N7 65 DL62
Holloway Rd
Empress Av E4 47 EA52
Empress Av E12 68 EJ61
Empress Av, Ilf. 69 EM61
Empress Av, Wdf.Grn. 48 EF52
Empress Dr, Chis. 125 EP93
Empress Pl SW6 100 DA78
Empress Rd, Grav. 131 GL87
Empress St SE17 102 DQ79
Empson St E3 85 EB70
Emsworth Cl N9 46 DW46
Emsworth Rd, Ilf. 49 EP54
Emsworth St SW2 121 DM89
Emu Rd SW8 101 DH82
Ena Rd SW16 141 DL97
Enborne Grn, S.Ock. 91 FU71
Elan Rd
Enbrook St W10 81 CY69
Endale Cl, Cars. 140 DF103
Endeavour Rd (Cheshunt), Wal.Cr. 15 DY27
Endeavour Way SW19 120 DB91
Endeavour Way, Bark. 88 EU68
Endeavour Way, Croy. 141 DK101
Endell St WC2 195 P8
Endell St WC2 83 DL72
Enderby St SE10 205 H10
Enderby St SE10 104 EE78
Enderley Cl, Har. 41 CE53
Enderley Rd
Enderley Rd, Har. 41 CE53
Endersby Rd, Barn. 27 CW43
Endersleigh Gdns NW4 63 CU56
Endlebury Rd E4 47 EC47
Endlesham Rd SW12 120 DG87
Endsleigh Cl, S.Croy. 160 DW110
Endsleigh Gdns WC1 195 M4
Endsleigh Gdns WC1 83 DK70
Endsleigh Gdns, Ilf. 69 EM61
Endsleigh Gdns, Surb. 137 CJ100
Endsleigh Gdns, Walt. 154 BW106
Endsleigh Pl WC1 195 N4
Endsleigh Pl WC1 83 DK70
Endsleigh Rd W13 79 CG73
Endsleigh Rd, Red. 185 DJ129
Endsleigh Rd, Sthl. 96 BY77
Endsleigh St WC1 195 M4
Endsleigh St WC1 83 DK70
Endway, Surb. 138 CN101
Endwell Rd SE4 103 DY82
Endymion Rd N4 65 DN59
Endymion Rd SW2 121 DM86
Energen Cl NW10 80 CS65
Enfield Cl, Uxb. 76 BK68
Villier St
Enfield Retail Pk, Enf. 30 DV41
Enfield Rd N1 84 DS66
Enfield Rd W3 98 CP75
Enfield Rd, Brent. 97 CK78
Enfield Rd, Enf. 29 DK42
Enfield Rd, Houns. 95 BS82
Eastern Perimeter Rd
Enfield Wk, Brent. 97 CK78
Enford St W1 194 D6
Enford St W1 82 DF71
Engadine Cl, Croy. 142 DT104
Engadine St SW18 119 CZ88
Engate St SE13 103 EC84
Engayne Gdns, Upmin. 72 FP60
Engel Pk NW7 43 CW51
Engineer Cl SE18 105 EN79
Engineers Way, Wem. 62 CN63
England Way, N.Mal. 138 CQ97
California Rd
Englands La NW3 82 DF65
Englands La, Loug. 33 EN40
Englefield Cl, Croy. 142 DQ100
Queen's Rd
Englefield Cl, Enf. 29 DN40
Englefield Cl, Orp. 145 ET98
Englefield Cres, Orp. 145 ET98
Englefield Grn, Egh. 112 AW91
Englefield Path, Orp. 145 ET98
Englefield Rd N1 84 DR65
Englefield Rd, Orp. 146 EU98
Engleheart Dr, Felt. 115 BT86
Engleheart Rd SE6 123 EB87
Englehurst, Egh. 112 AW93
Englemere Pk (Oxshott), Lthd. 154 CB114
Englewood Rd SW12 121 DH86
Engliff La, Wok. 167 BF116
English Gdns, Stai. 92 AX84
English Grds SE1 201 M3
English St E3 85 DZ70
Enid Cl, St.Alb. 8 BZ31
Enid St SE16 202 A6
Enid St SE16 102 DT76
Enmore Av SE25 142 DU99
Enmore Gdns SW14 118 CR85
Enmore Rd SE25 142 DU99
Enmore Rd SW15 99 CW84
Enmore Rd, Sthl. 78 CA70
Ennerdale Av, Horn. 71 FG64
Ennerdale Av, Stan. 61 CJ55
Ennerdale Cl, Felt. 115 BT88
Ennerdale Cl (Cheam), Sutt. 157 CZ105
Ennerdale Dr NW9 62 CS57
Ennerdale Gdns, Wem. 61 CK60
Ennerdale Ho E3 85 DZ70
Ennerdale Rd, Bexh. 106 FA81
Ennerdale Rd, Rich. 98 CM82
Ennersdale Rd SE13 123 ED85
Ennis Rd N4 65 DN60
Ennis Rd SE18 105 EQ79
Ennismore Av W4 99 CT77
Ennismore Av, Grnf. 79 CE65
Ennismore Gdns SW7 198 B5
Ennismore Gdns SW7 100 DE75
Ennismore Gdns, T.Ditt. 137 CE100
Ennismore Gdns Ms SW7 198 B6
Ennismore Gdns Ms SW7 100 DE76
Ennismore Ms SW7 198 B5
Ennismore Ms SW7 100 DE75
Ennismore St SW7 198 B6
Ennismore St SW7 100 DE76
Ensign Cl, Pur. 159 DN110
Ensign Cl, Stai. 114 BK88
Ensign Dr N13 46 DQ48
Ensign St E1 84 DU73
Ensign Way, Stai. 114 BK88
Enslin Rd SE9 125 EN86
Ensor Ms SW7 100 DD78
Cranley Gdns
Enstone Rd, Enf. 31 DY41
Enstone Rd, Uxb. 58 BM62
Enterdent Rd, Gdse. 186 DW134
Enterprise Cl, Croy. 141 DN102
Enterprise Way NW10 81 CU69
Enterprise Way SW18 100 DA84
Enterprise Way, Tedd. 117 CF92
Enterprize Way SE8 203 M8
Enterprize Way SE8 103 DZ77
Eothen Cl, Cat. 176 DU124
Eothen Hts, Cat. 176 DU124
Epirus Ms SW6 100 DA80
Epirus Rd SW6 99 CZ80
Epping Cl E14 204 A8
Epping Cl E14 103 EA77
Epping Cl, Rom. 71 FB55
Epping Glade E4 31 EC44
Epping La, Rom. 34 EV40
Epping New Rd, Buck.H. 48 EH47
Epping New Rd, Loug. 32 EH43
Epping Pl N1 83 DN65
Liverpool Rd
Epping Rd, Epp. 33 EM35
Epping Rd (Epping Grn), Epp. 17 ER27
Epping Rd (North Weald Bassett), Epp. 18 EW28
Epping Rd (Toot Hill), Ong. 19 FC30
Epping Way E4 31 EB44
Epple Rd SW6 99 CZ81
Epsom Cl, Bexh. 107 FB83
Epsom Cl, Nthlt. 60 BZ64
Epsom Downs, Epsom 173 CU118
Epsom Downs Metro Cen, Tad. 173 CV120
Waterfield
Epsom Gap, Lthd. 171 CH115
Epsom La N, Epsom 173 CV118
Epsom La N, Tad. 173 CV118
Epsom La S, Tad. 173 CW121
Epsom Rd E10 67 EC58
Epsom Rd, Ash. 172 CM118
Epsom Rd, Croy. 159 DN105
Epsom Rd, Epsom 157 CT110
Epsom Rd, Ilf. 69 ET58
Epsom Rd, Lthd. 171 CH121
Epsom Rd, Mord. 139 CZ100
Epsom Rd, Sutt. 139 CZ101
Epsom Sq, Houns. 95 BT82
Eastern Perimeter Rd
Epsom Way, Horn. 72 FM63
Epstein Rd SE28 88 EU74
Epworth Rd, Islw. 97 CH80
Epworth St EC2 197 L5
Epworth St EC2 84 DR70
Equity Sq E2 84 DT69
Shacklewell St
Erasmus St SW1 199 N9
Erasmus St SW1 101 DK77
Erconwald St W12 81 CT72
Eresby Dr, Beck. 143 EA102
Eresby Pl NW6 82 DA66
Eric Clarke La, Bark. 87 EP70
Eric Cl E7 68 EG63
Eric Rd E7 68 EG63
Eric Rd NW10 81 CT65
Church Rd
Eric Rd, Rom. 70 EX59
Eric Steele Ho, St.Alb. 8 CB27
Eric St E3 85 DZ70
Erica Ct, Swan. 147 FE98
Azalea Dr
Erica Ct, Wok. 166 AX118
Erica Gdns, Croy. 161 EB105
Erica St W12 81 CU73
Ericcson Cl SW18 120 DA85
Eridge Grn Cl, Orp. 146 EW102
Petten Gro
Eridge Rd W4 98 CR76
Erin Cl, Brom. 124 EE94
Erin Cl, Ilf. 70 EU58
Erindale SE18 105 ER79
Erindale Ter SE18 105 ER79
Eriswell Cres, Walt. 153 BS107
Eriswell Rd, Walt. 153 BT105
Erith Ct, Purf. 108 FN77
Thamley
Erith Cres, Rom. 51 FC53
Erith High St, Erith 107 FE78
Erith Rd, Belv. 106 FA78
Erith Rd, Bexh. 107 FB84
Erith Rd, Erith 107 FB84
Erkenwald Cl, Cher. 133 BE101
Erlanger Rd SE14 103 DX81
Erlesmere Gdns W13 97 CG76
Ermine Cl, Houns. 96 BW82
Ermine Cl (Cheshunt), Wal.Cr. 14 DV31
Ermine Ho N17 46 DT52
Moselle St
Ermine Rd N15 66 DT58
Ermine Rd SE13 103 EB83
Ermine Side, Enf. 30 DU43
Ermington Rd SE9 125 EQ89
Ermyn Cl, Lthd. 171 CK121
Ermyn Way, Lthd. 171 CK121
Ernald Av E6 86 EL68
Ernan Cl, S.Ock. 91 FU71
Ernan Rd, S.Ock. 91 FU71
Erncroft Way, Twick. 117 CF86
Ernest Av SE27 121 DP91
Ernest Cl, Beck. 143 EA99
Ernest Gdns W4 98 CP79
Ernest Gro, Beck. 143 DZ99
Ernest Rd, Horn. 72 FL58
Ernest Rd, Kings.T. 138 CP96
Ernest Sq, Kings.T. 138 CP96
Ernest St E1 85 DX70
Ernle Rd SW20 119 CV94
Ernshaw Pl SW15 119 CY85
Carlton Dr
Erpingham Rd SW15 99 CW83
Erridge Rd SW19 140 DA96
Erriff Dr, S.Ock. 91 FT71
Errington Cl, Grays 111 GH76
Cedar Rd
Errington Rd W9 81 CZ70
Errol Gdns, Hayes 77 BV70
Errol Gdns, N.Mal. 139 CU98
Errol St EC1 197 J5
Errol St EC1 84 DQ70
Erroll Rd, Rom. 71 FF56
Erskine Cl, Sutt. 140 DE104
Erskine Cres N17 66 DV56
Erskine Hill NW11 64 DA57
Erskine Ms NW3 82 DF66
Erskine Rd
Erskine Rd E17 67 DZ56
Erskine Rd NW3 82 DF66
Erskine Rd, Sutt. 158 DD105
Erskine Rd, Wat. 40 BW48
Erwood Rd SE7 104 EL78
Esam Way SW16 121 DN92
Escot Way, Barn. 27 CW43
Escott Gdns SE9 124 EL91
Escott Pl, Cher. 151 BC107
Escreet Gro SE18 105 EN77
Esdaile Gdns, Upmin. 73 FR59
Esher Av, Rom. 71 FC58
Esher Av, Sutt. 139 CX104
Esher Av, Walt. 135 BU101
Esher Bypass, Chess. 155 CJ105
Esher Bypass, Cob. 155 CH108
Esher Bypass, Esher 154 CA110
Esher Cl, Bex. 126 EY88

Esher Cl, Esher 154 CB106
Esher Cres, Houns. 95 BS82
Eastern Perimeter Rd
Esher Gdns SW19 119 CX89
Esher Grn, Esher 154 CB105
Esher Ms, Mitch. 140 DF97
Esher Pk Av, Esher 154 CC105
Esher Pl Av, Esher 154 CB105
Esher Rd, E.Mol. 137 CD100
Esher Rd, Ilf. 69 ES62
Esher Rd, Walt. 154 BX106
Esk Rd E13 86 EG70
Esk Way, Rom. 51 FD52
Eskdale, St.Alb. 10 CM27
Eskdale Av, Nthlt. 78 BZ67
Eskdale Cl, Dart. 128 FQ89
Eskdale Cl, Wem. 61 CK61
Eskdale Gdns, Pur. 160 DR114
Eskdale Rd, Bexh. 106 FA82
Eskdale Rd, Uxb. 76 BH68
Eskley Gdns, S.Ock. 91 FV70
Eskmont Ridge SE19 122 DS94
Esmar Cres NW9 63 CU59
Esme Ho SW15 99 CT84
Esmeralda Rd SE1 202 C9
Esmeralda Rd SE1 102 DU77
Esmond Cl, Rain. 89 FH66
Dawson Dr
Esmond Rd NW6 81 CZ67
Esmond Rd W4 98 CR77
Esmond St SW15 99 CY84
Esparto St SW18 120 DB87
Essenden Rd, Belv. 106 FA78
Essenden Rd, S.Croy. 160 DS108
Essendene Cl, Cat. 176 DS123
Essendene Rd, Cat. 176 DS123
Essendine Rd W9 82 DA70
Essex Av, Islw. 97 CE83
Essex Cl E17 67 DY56
Essex Cl, Add. 152 BJ105
Essex Cl, Mord. 139 CX101
Essex Cl, Rom. 71 FB56
Essex Cl, Ruis. 60 BX60
Essex Ct EC4 196 D9
Essex Ct SW13 99 CT82
Essex Gdns N4 65 DP58
Essex Gdns, Horn. 72 FN57
Essex Gro SE19 122 DR93
Essex Ho E14 85 EB72
Giraud St
Essex La, Kings L. 7 BS33
Essex Pk N3 44 DB51
Essex Pk Ms W3 80 CS74
Essex Pl W4 98 CQ77
Essex Pl Sq W4 98 CR77
Essex Pl
Essex Rd E4 48 EE46
Essex Rd E10 67 EC58
Essex Rd E12 68 EL64
Essex Rd E17 67 DY58
Essex Rd E18 48 EH54
Essex Rd N1 83 DP67
Essex Rd NW10 80 CS66
Essex Rd W3 80 CQ73
Essex Rd W4 98 CR77
Belmont Rd
Essex Rd, Bark. 87 ER66
Essex Rd, Borwd. 26 CN41
Essex Rd, Dag. 71 FC64
Essex Rd, Dart. 128 FK86
Essex Rd, Enf. 30 DR42
Essex Rd, Grav. 131 GG88
Essex Rd, Grays 109 FU79
Essex Rd, Long. 149 FX96
Essex Rd, Rom. 71 FB56
Essex Rd (Chadwell Heath), Rom. 70 EW59
Essex Rd, Wat. 23 BU40
Essex Rd S E11 67 ED59
Essex St E7 68 EG64
Essex St WC2 196 D10
Essex Twr SE20 142 DV95
Essex Vil W8 100 DA75
Essex Way, Brwd. 53 FW51
Essex Way, Epp. 18 EV32
Essex Way, Ong. 19 FF29
Essex Wf E5 67 DX61
Essian St E1 85 DY71
Essoldo Way, Edg. 62 CM55
Estate Way E10 67 DZ60
Estcourt Rd SE25 142 DV100
Estcourt Rd SW6 99 CZ80
Estcourt Rd, Wat. 24 BW41
Este Rd SW11 100 DE83
Estella Av, N.Mal. 139 CV98
Estelle Rd NW3 64 DF63
Esterbrooke St SW1 199 M9
Esterbrooke St SW1 101 DK77
Esther Cl N21 45 DN45
Esther Rd E11 68 EE59
Estoria Cl SW2 121 DN87
Estreham Rd SW16 121 DK93
Estridge Cl, Houns. 96 CA84
Estuary Cl, Bark. 88 EV69
Eswyn Rd SW17 120 DF91
Etchingham Pk Rd N3 44 DB52
Etchingham Rd E15 67 EC63
Eternit Wk SW6 99 CW81
Etfield Gro, Sid. 126 EV92
Ethel Bailey Cl, Epsom 156 CN112
Christ Ch Rd
Ethel Rd E16 86 EH72
Ethel Rd, Ashf. 114 BL92
Ethel St SE17 201 H9
Ethel Ter, Orp. 164 EW109
Ethelbert Cl, Brom. 144 EG97
Ethelbert Gdns, Ilf. 69 EM57
Ethelbert Rd SW20 139 CX95
Ethelbert Rd, Brom. 144 EG97
Ethelbert Rd, Dart. 128 FL91
Ethelbert Rd, Erith 107 FC80
Ethelbert Rd, Orp. 146 EX97
Ethelbert St SW12 121 DH88
Fernlea Rd
Ethelburga Rd, Rom. 52 FM53
Ethelburga St SW11 100 DE81
Amery Gdns
Ethelden Rd W12 81 CV74
Etheldene Av N10 65 DJ56
Ethelwine Pl, Abb.L. 7 BT30
The Cres
Etheridge Grn, Loug. 33 EQ41
Etheridge Rd
Etheridge Rd NW2 63 CW59
Etheridge Rd, Loug. 33 EP40
Etherley Rd N15 66 DQ57
Etherow St SE22 122 DU86
Etherstone Grn SW16 121 DN91
Etherstone Rd
Etherstone Rd SW16 121 DN91
Ethnard Rd SE15 102 DV79
Ethorpe Cl, Ger.Cr. 56 AY57
Ethorpe Cres, Ger.Cr. 56 AY57
Ethronvi Rd, Bexh. 106 EY83
Etloe Rd E10 67 EA61
Eton Av N12 44 DC52
Eton Av NW3 82 DD66
Eton Av, Barn. 28 DE44
Eton Av, Houns. 96 BZ79
Eton Av, N.Mal. 138 CR99
Eton Av, Wem. 61 CH63
Eton Cl SW18 120 DB87
Eton Cl, Slou. 92 AU79
Eton Coll Rd NW3 82 DF65
Eton Ct NW3 82 DD66
Eton Av
Eton Ct, Stai. 113 BF92
Richmond Rd
Eton Ct, Wem. 61 CJ63
Eton Av
Eton Garages NW3 82 DE65
Lambolle Pl
Eton Gro NW9 62 CN55
Eton Gro SE13 104 EE83
Eton Hall NW3 82 DF65
Eton Coll Rd
Eton Pl NW3 82 DG66
Haverstock Hill
Eton Ri NW3 82 DF65
Eton Coll Rd
Eton Rd NW3 82 DF66
Eton Rd, Hayes 95 BT80
Eton Rd, Ilf. 69 EQ64
Eton Rd, Orp. 164 EV105
Eton Rd, Slou. 92 AT78
Eton St, Rich. 118 CL85
Eton Vil NW3 82 DF65
Eton Way, Dart. 108 FJ84
Etta St SE8 103 DY79
Etton Cl, Horn. 72 FL61
Ettrick St E14 85 EC72
Etwell Pl, Surb. 138 CM100
Euclid Way, Grays 109 FU77
Eugene Cl, Rom. 72 FJ56
Eugenia Rd SE16 202 G9
Eugenia Rd SE16 102 DW77
Eureka Rd, Kings.T. 138 CN96
Washington Rd
Europa Pl EC1 197 H3
Europa Trd Est, Erith 107 FD78
Europe Rd SE18 105 EM76
Eustace Rd E6 86 EL69
Eustace Rd SW6 100 DA80
Eustace Rd, Rom. 70 EX59
Euston Av, Wat. 23 BT43
Euston Cen NW1 83 DJ70
Triton Sq
Euston Gro NW1 195 M3
Euston Gro NW1 83 DK69
Euston Rd N1 195 P2
Euston Rd N1 83 DK70
Euston Rd NW1 195 J5
Euston Rd NW1 83 DH70
Euston Rd, Croy. 141 DN102
Euston Sq NW1 195 M3
Euston Sq NW1 83 DK69
Euston Sta Colonnade NW1 195 M3
Euston St NW1 195 L4
Euston St NW1 83 DJ69
Eva Rd, Rom. 70 EW59
Evandale Rd SW9 101 DN82
Evangelist Rd NW5 65 DH63
Evans Av, Wat. 23 BT35
Evans Cl E8 84 DT65
Buttermere Wk
Evans Cl, Green. 129 FU85
Evans Cl, Rick. 22 BN43
New Rd
Evans Gro, Felt. 116 CA89
Evans Rd SE6 124 EE89
Evansdale, Rain. 89 FF69
New Zealand Way
Evanston Av E4 47 EC52
Evanston Gdns, Ilf. 68 EL58
Eve Rd E11 68 EE63
Eve Rd E15 86 EE68
Eve Rd N17 66 DS55
Eve Rd, Islw. 97 CG84
Eve Rd, Wok. 167 BB115
Evelina Rd SE15 102 DW83
Evelina Rd SE20 123 DX94
Eveline Lowe Est SE16 202 B7
Eveline Lowe Est SE16 102 DU76
Eveline Rd, Mitch. 140 DF95
Evelyn Av NW9 62 CR56
Evelyn Av, Ruis. 59 BT58
Evelyn Cl, Twick. 116 CB87
Evelyn Cl, Wok. 166 AX120
Evelyn Ct N1 197 K1
Evelyn Cres, Sun. 135 BT95
Evelyn Denington Rd E6 86 EL70
Evelyn Dr, Pnr. 40 BX52
Evelyn Fox Ct W10 81 CW71
Evelyn Gdns SW7 100 DD78
Evelyn Gdns, Gdse. 186 DW130
Evelyn Gdns, Rich. 98 CL84
Kew Rd
Evelyn Gro W5 80 CM74
Evelyn Gro, Sthl. 78 BZ72
Evelyn Rd E16 205 P2
Evelyn Rd E16 86 EH74
Evelyn Rd E17 67 EC56
Evelyn Rd SW19 120 DB92
Evelyn Rd W4 98 CR76
Evelyn Rd, Barn. 28 DF42
Evelyn Rd, Rich. 98 CL83
Evelyn Rd (Ham), Rich. 117 CJ90
Evelyn Sharp Cl, Rom. 72 FK55
Amery Gdns
Evelyn St SE8 203 K9
Evelyn St SE8 103 DY78
Evelyn Ter, Rich. 98 CL83
Evelyn Wk N1 197 K1
Evelyn Wk N1 84 DR68
Evelyn Wk, Brwd. 53 FW51
Evelyn Way, Cob. 170 BZ116
Evelyn Way, Epsom 156 CN111
Evelyn Way, Sun. 135 BT95
Evelyn Way, Wall. 159 DK105
Evelyn Yd W1 195 M8
Evelyns Cl, Uxb. 76 BN72
Evening Hill, Beck. 123 EC94
Evensyde, Wat. 23 BR44
Evenwood Cl SW15 119 CY85
Everard Av, Brom. 144 EG102
Everard Av, Slou. 92 AS75
Everard La, Cat. 176 DU122
Tillingdown Hill
Everard Way, Wem. 62 CL62
Everatt Cl SW18 119 CZ86
Amerland Rd
Everdon Rd SW13 99 CU79
Everest Cl, Grav. 130 GE90
Everest Ct, Wok. 166 AS116
Langmans Way
Everest Pl E14 85 EC71
Everest Pl, Swan. 147 FD98
Everest Rd SE9 125 EM85
Everest Rd, Stai. 114 BK87
Everett Cl, Bushey 41 CE46
Everett Cl, Pnr. 59 BT55
Everett Cl (Cheshunt), Wal.Cr. 14 DQ26
Everett Wk, Belv. 106 EZ78
Osborne Rd
Everglade, West. 178 EK118
Everglade Strand NW9 43 CT53
Evergreen Ct, Stai. 114 BK87
Evergreen Way
Evergreen Oak Av, Wind. 92 AU83
Evergreen Way, Hayes 77 BT73
Evergreen Way, Stai. 114 BK87
Everilda St N1 83 DM67
Evering Rd E5 66 DT62
Evering Rd N16 66 DT62
Everington Rd N10 44 DF54
Everington St W6 99 CX79
Everitt Rd NW10 80 CR69
Everlands Cl, Wok. 166 AY118
Everleigh St N4 65 DM60
Eversfield Gdns NW7 42 CS52
Eversfield Rd, Reig. 184 DB134
Eversfield Rd, Rich. 98 CM82
Evershed Wk W4 98 CR77
Eversholt St NW1 83 DJ68
Evershot Rd N4 65 DM60
Eversleigh Gdns, Upmin. 73 FR60
Eversleigh Rd E6 86 EK67
Eversleigh Rd N3 43 CZ52
Eversleigh Rd SW11 100 DG82
Eversleigh Rd, Barn. 28 DC43
Eversley Av, Bexh. 107 FD82
Eversley Av, Wem. 62 CN61
Eversley Cl N21 29 DM44
Eversley Cres N21 29 DM44
Eversley Cres, Islw. 97 CD81
Eversley Cres, Ruis. 59 BS61
Eversley Cross, Bexh. 107 FE82
Eversley Mt N21 29 DM44
Eversley Pk SW19 119 CV92
Eversley Pk Rd N21 29 DM44
Eversley Rd SE7 104 EH79
Eversley Rd SE19 122 DR94
Eversley Rd, Surb. 138 CM98
Eversley Way, Croy. 161 EA105
Eversley Way, Egh. 133 BC96
Everthorpe Rd SE15 102 DT83
Everton Bldgs NW1 195 K3
Everton Dr, Stan. 62 CM55
Everton Rd, Croy. 142 DU102
Evesham Av E17 47 EA54
Evesham Cl, Grnf. 78 CB68
Evesham Cl, Reig. 183 CZ133
Evesham Cl, Sutt. 158 DA108
Evesham Grn, Mord. 140 DB100
Evesham Rd E15 86 EF67
Evesham Rd N11 45 DJ50
Evesham Rd, Felt. 116 BW87
Sparrow Fm Dr
Evesham Rd, Grav. 131 GK89
Evesham Rd, Mord. 140 DB100
Evesham Rd, Reig. 183 CZ134
Evesham Rd N, Reig. 183 CZ133
Evesham St W11 81 CX73
Evesham Wk SE5 102 DR82
Love Wk
Evesham Wk SW9 101 DN82
Evesham Way SW11 100 DG83
Evesham Way, Ilf. 69 EN55
Evreham Rd, Iver 75 BE72
Evry Rd, Sid. 126 EW93
Ewald Rd SW6 99 CZ82
Ewan Rd, Rom. 52 FK54
Ewanrigg Ter, Wdf.Grn. 48 EJ50
Ewart Gro N22 45 DN53
Ewart Pl E3 85 DZ68
Ewart Rd SE23 123 DX87
Ewe Cl N7 83 DL65
Ewell Bypass, Epsom 157 CU108
Ewell Ct Av, Epsom 156 CS106
Ewell Downs Rd, Epsom 157 CU111
Ewell Ho Gro, Epsom 157 CT110
Ewell Pk Gdns, Epsom 157 CU108
Ewell Pk Way, Epsom 157 CU107
Ewell Rd, Surb. 138 CL100
Ewell Rd (Long Ditton), Surb. 137 CH101
Ewell Rd, Sutt. 157 CY107
Ewellhurst Rd, Ilf. 48 EL54
Ewelme Rd SE23 122 DW88
Ewen Cres SW2 121 DN88
Ewer St SE1 201 H3
Ewer St SE1 84 DQ74
Ewhurst Av, S.Croy. 160 DT109
Ewhurst Cl, Sutt. 157 CW109
Ewhurst Ho E1 84 DW71
Ewhurst Rd SE4 123 DZ86
Exbury Rd SE6 123 EA89
Excel Ct WC2 199 N1
Excelsior Cl, Kings.T. 138 CN96
Washington Rd
Excelsior Gdns SE13 103 EC82
Exchange Arc EC2 197 N6
Exchange Bldgs E1 84 DS72
Cutler St
Exchange Ct WC2 200 A1
Exchange Pl EC2 197 M6
Exchange Rd, Wat. 23 BV42
Exchange Sq EC2 197 M6
Exchange Sq EC2 84 DS71
Exchange St, Rom. 71 FE57
Exchequer Ct EC3 84 DS72
St. Mary Axe
Exeforde Av, Ashf. 114 BN91
Exeter Cl E6 87 EM72
Harper Rd
Exeter Cl, Wat. 24 BW40
Exeter Gdns, Ilf. 68 EL60
Exeter Ho SW15 119 CW86
Putney Heath
Exeter Ms NW6 82 DB65
West Hampstead Ms
Exeter Rd E16 86 EG71
Exeter Rd E17 67 EA57
Exeter Rd N9 46 DW47
Exeter Rd N14 45 DH46
Exeter Rd NW2 63 CY64
Exeter Rd, Croy. 142 DS101
Exeter Rd, Dag. 89 FB65
Exeter Rd, Enf. 31 DX41
Exeter Rd, Felt. 116 BZ90
Exeter Rd, Grav. 131 GK90
Exeter Rd, Har. 60 BY61
Exeter Rd, Houns. 95 BS82
Exeter Rd, Well. 105 ET82
Exeter St WC2 196 A10
Exeter St WC2 83 DL73
Exeter Way SE14 103 DZ80
Exeter Way, Houns. 95 BS83
Exford Gdns SE12 124 EH88
Exford Rd SE12 124 EH89
Exhibition Cl W12 81 CW73
Exhibition Rd SW7 198 A5
Exhibition Rd SW7 100 DD75
Exmoor Cl, Ilf. 49 EQ53
Exmoor St W10 81 CX70
Exmouth Mkt EC1 196 D4
Exmouth Mkt EC1 83 DN70
Exmouth Ms NW1 195 L3
Exmouth Pl E8 84 DV66
Exmouth Rd E17 67 DZ57
Exmouth Rd, Brom. 144 EH97
Exmouth Rd, Grays 110 GB79
Exmouth Rd, Hayes 77 BS69
Exmouth Rd, Ruis. 60 BW62
Exmouth Rd, Well. 106 EW81
Exmouth St E1 84 DW72
Commercial Rd
Exning Rd E16 86 EF70
Exon St SE17 201 M10
Exon St SE17 102 DS78
Explorer Av, Stai. 114 BL88
Explorer Dr, Wat. 23 BT44
Express Dr, Ilf. 70 EV60
Exton Cres NW10 80 CQ66
Exton Gdns, Dag. 70 EW64
Exton St SE1 200 D3
Exton St SE1 83 DN74
Eyebright Cl, Croy. 143 DX102
Primrose La
Eyhurst Av, Horn. 71 FG62
Eyhurst Cl NW2 63 CU61
Eyhurst Cl, Tad. 173 CZ123
Eyhurst Pk, Tad. 174 DC123
Eyhurst Spur, Tad. 173 CZ124
Eylewood Rd SE27 122 DQ92
Eynella Rd SE22 122 DT87
Eynham Rd W12 81 CW72
Eynsford Cl, Orp. 145 EQ101
Eynsford Cres, Bex. 126 EW88
Eynsford Rd, Green. 129 FW85
Eynsford Rd, Ilf. 69 ES61
Eynsford Rd, Sev. 165 FH108
Eynsford Rd, Swan. 147 FD100
Eynsham Dr SE2 106 EU77
Eynswood Dr, Sid. 126 EV92
Eyot Gdns W6 99 CT78
Eyot Grn W4 99 CT79
Chiswick Mall
Eyre Cl, Rom. 71 FH56
Eyre Ct NW8 82 DD68
Finchley Rd
Eyre St Hill EC1 196 D5
Eyston Dr, Wey. 152 BN110
Eythorne Rd SW9 101 DN81
Ezra St E2 84 DT69

F

Faber Gdns NW4 63 CU57
Fabian Rd SW6 99 CZ80
Fabian St E6 87 EM70
Fackenden La, Sev. 165 FH113
Factory La N17 46 DT54
Factory La, Croy. 141 DN102
Factory Rd E16 86 EL74
Factory Rd, Grav. 130 GC86
Factory Sq SW16 121 DL93
Factory Yd W7 79 CE74
Uxbridge Rd
Faesten Way, Bex. 127 FE90
Faggotts Cl, Rad. 25 CJ35
Faggs Rd, Felt. 115 BU85
Fagus Av, Rain. 90 FK69
Faints Cl, Wal.Cr. 14 DT29
Fair Acres, Brom. 144 EG99
Fair Cl, Bushey 40 CB45
Claybury
Fair La, Couls. 184 DC125
Fair St SE1 201 N4
Fair St, Houns. 96 CC83
High St
Fairacre, N.Mal. 138 CS97
Fairacres SW15 99 CU84
Fairacres, Cob. 154 BX112
Fairacres, Croy. 161 DZ109
Fairacres, Ruis. 59 BT59
Fairacres, Tad. 173 CW121
Fairacres Cl, Pot.B. 11 CZ33
Fairbairn Cl, Pur. 159 DN113
Fairbairn Grn SW9 101 DN81
Fairbank Av, Orp. 145 EP103
Fairbank Est N1 84 DR68
East Rd
Fairbanks Rd N17 66 DT55
Fairbourne, Cob. 154 BX113
Fairbourne Cl, Wok. 166 AU118
Abercorn Way
Fairbourne La, Cat. 176 DQ122
Fairbourne Rd N17 66 DS55
Fairbridge Rd N19 65 DK61
Fairbrook Cl N13 45 DN50
Fairbrook Rd N13 45 DN51
Fairburn Cl, Borwd. 26 CN39
Fairburn Ct SW15 119 CY85
Mercier Rd
Fairby Rd SE12 124 EH85
Faircharm Trd Est SE8 103 EB80
Fairchild Cl SW11 100 DD82
Wye St
Fairchild Pl EC2 197 N5
Fairchild St EC2 197 N5
Fairchildes Av, Croy. 161 ED112
Fairchildes La, Warl. 161 ED114
Fairclough St E1 84 DU72
Faircross Av, Bark. 87 EQ65
Faircross Av, Rom. 51 FD52
Fairdale Gdns SW15 99 CV84
Fairdale Gdns, Hayes 77 BU74
Fairdene Rd, Couls. 175 DK117
Fairey Av, Hayes 95 BT77
Fairfax Av, Epsom 157 CV109
Fairfax Av, Red. 184 DE133
Fairfax Cl, Walt. 135 BV102
Fairfax Gdns SE3 104 EK81
Fairfax Ms E16 205 P2
Fairfax Ms SW15 99 CW84
Upper Richmond Rd
Fairfax Pl NW6 82 DC66
Fairfax Rd N8 65 DN56
Fairfax Rd NW6 82 DC66
Fairfax Rd W4 98 CS76
Fairfax Rd, Grays 110 GB78
Fairfax Rd, Tedd. 117 CG93
Fairfax Rd, Til. 111 GF81
Fairfax Rd, Wok. 167 BB120
Fairfax Way N10 44 DG52
Cromwell Rd
Fairfield App, Stai. 112 AX86
Fairfield Av NW4 63 CV58
Fairfield Av, Edg. 42 CP51
Fairfield Av, Ruis. 59 BQ59
Fairfield Av, Slou. 92 AW80
Fairfield Av, Stai. 113 BF91
Fairfield Av, Twick. 116 CB88
Fairfield Av, Upmin. 72 FQ62
Fairfield Av, Wat. 40 BW48
Fairfield Cl N12 44 DC49
Fairfield Cl, Enf. 31 DY42
Scotland Grn Rd N
Fairfield Cl, Epsom 156 CS106
Fairfield Cl, Horn. 71 FG60
Fairfield Cl, Mitch. 120 DE94
Fairfield Cl, Nthwd. 39 BP50
Thirlmere Gdns
Fairfield Cl, Rad. 25 CE37
Fairfield Cl, Sid. 125 ET86
Fairfield Cl, Slou. 92 AX80
Fairfield Ct NW10 81 CU67
Fairfield Ct, Nthwd. 39 BU54
Windsor Cl
Fairfield Cres, Edg. 42 CP51
Fairfield Dr SW18 120 DB85
Fairfield Dr, Grnf. 79 CJ67
Fairfield Dr, Har. 60 CC55
Fairfield E, Kings.T. 138 CL96
Fairfield Gdns N8 65 DL57
Elder Av
Fairfield Gro SE7 104 EK78
Fairfield Ind Est, Kings.T. 138 CM97
Fairfield N, Kings.T. 138 CL96
Fairfield Pk, Cob. 154 BX114
Fairfield Path, Croy. 142 DR104
Fairfield Pathway, Horn. 90 FJ66
Fairfield Pl, Kings.T. 138 CL97
Fairfield Rd E3 85 EA68
Fairfield Rd E17 47 DY54
Fairfield Rd N8 65 DL57
Fairfield Rd N18 46 DU49
Fairfield Rd W7 97 CG76
Fairfield Rd, Beck. 143 EA96
Fairfield Rd, Bexh. 106 EZ82
Fairfield Rd, Brwd. 54 FW48
Fairfield Rd, Brom. 124 EG94
Fairfield Rd, Croy. 142 DS104
Fairfield Rd, Epp. 18 EV29
Fairfield Rd, Ilf. 87 EP65
Fairfield Rd, Kings.T. 138 CL96
Fairfield Rd, Lthd. 171 CH121
Fairfield Rd, Orp. 145 ER100
Fairfield Rd, Sthl. 78 BZ72
Fairfield Rd, Stai. 112 AX86
Fairfield Rd, Uxb. 76 BK65
Fairfield Rd, West Dr. 76 BL74
Fairfield Rd, Wdf.Grn. 48 EG51
Fairfield S, Kings.T. 138 CL96
Fairfield St SW18 120 DB85
Fairfield Wk, Lthd. 171 CH121
Fairfield Rd
Fairfield Wk (Cheshunt), Wal.Cr. 15 DY28
Fairfield Way, Barn. 28 DA43
Fairfield Way, Couls. 159 DK114
Fairfield Way, Epsom 156 CS106
Fairfield W, Kings.T. 138 CL96
Fairfields, Cher. 134 BG102
Fairfields, Grav. 131 GL92
Fairfields Cl NW9 62 CQ57
Fairfields Cres NW9 62 CQ56
Fairfields Rd, Houns. 96 CC83
Fairfolds, Wat. 24 BY36
Fairfoot Rd E3 85 EA70
Fairford Av, Bexh. 107 FD81
Fairford Av, Croy. 143 DX99
Fairford Cl, Croy. 143 DY99
Fairford Cl, Reig. 184 DC132
Fairford Cl, Rom. 52 FP51
Fairford Way
Fairford Cl, W.Byf. 151 BF114
Fairford Gdns, Wor.Pk. 139 CT103
Fairford Way, Rom. 52 FP51
Fairgreen, Barn. 28 DF41
Fairgreen E, Barn. 28 DF41
Fairgreen Rd, Th.Hth. 141 DP99
Fairham Av, S.Ock. 91 FU73
Fairhaven, Egh. 113 AZ92
Fairhaven Av, Croy. 143 DX100
Fairhaven Cres, Wat. 39 BU48
Fairhaven Rd, Red. 184 DG130

Fairhazel Gdns NW6 82 DB65
Fairholme, Felt. 115 BR87
Fairholme Av, Rom. 71 FG57
Fairholme Cl N3 63 CY56
Fairholme Cres, Ash. 171 CJ117
Fairholme Cres, Hayes 77 BT70
Fairholme Gdns N3 63 CY55
Fairholme Gdns, Upmin. 73 FT59
Fairholme Rd W14 99 CY78
Fairholme Rd, Ashf. 114 BL92
Fairholme Rd, Croy. 141 DN101
Fairholme Rd, Har. 61 CF57
Fairholme Rd, Ilf. 69 EM59
Fairholme Rd, Sutt. 157 CZ107
Fairholt Cl N16 66 DS60
Fairholt Rd N16 66 DR60
Fairholt St SW7 198 C6
Fairkytes Av, Horn. 72 FK60
Fairland Rd E15 86 EF65
Fairlands Av, Buck.H. 48 EG47
Fairlands Av, Sutt. 140 DA103
Fairlands Av, Th.Hth. 141 DM98
Fairlands Ct SE9 125 EN86
North Pk
Fairlawn SE7 104 EJ79
Fairlawn, Lthd. 170 BZ124
Fairlawn Av N2 64 DE56
Fairlawn Av W4 98 CQ77
Fairlawn Av, Bexh. 106 EX82
Fairlawn Cl N14 29 DJ44
Fairlawn Cl, Esher 155 CF107
Fairlawn Cl, Felt. 116 BZ91
Fairlawn Cl, Kings.T. 118 CQ93
Fairlawn Dr, Wdf.Grn. 48 EG52
Fairlawn Gdns, Sthl. 78 BZ73
Fairlawn Gro W4 98 CQ77
Fairlawn Gro, Bans. 158 DD113
Fairlawn Pk SE26 123 DY92
Fairlawn Pk, Wok. 150 AY114
Fairlawn Rd SW19 119 CZ94
Fairlawn Rd, Bans. 158 DD112
Fairlawn Rd, Cars. 158 DC111
Fairlawns, Add. 151 BF111
Fairlawns, Brwd. 54 FU48
Fairlawns, Pnr. 40 BW54
Fairlawns, Sun. 135 BU97
Fairlawns, Twick. 117 CJ86
Fairlawns, Wat. 23 BT38
Langley Rd
Fairlawns, Wey. 153 BS106
Fairlawns Cl, Horn. 72 FM59
Fairlawns Cl, Stai. 114 BH93
Fairlea Pl W5 79 CK70
Fairley Way (Cheshunt), Wal.Cr. 14 DV28
Fairlie Gdns SE23 122 DW87
Fairlight Av E4 47 ED47
Fairlight Av NW10 80 CS68
Fairlight Av, Wdf.Grn. 48 EG51
Fairlight Cl E4 47 ED47
Fairlight Cl, Wor.Pk. 157 CW105
Fairlight Dr, Uxb. 76 BK65
Fairlight Rd SW17 120 DD91
Fairlop Cl, Horn. 89 FH65
Fairlop Gdns, Ilf. 49 EQ52
Fairlop Rd E11 67 ED59
Fairlop Rd, Ilf. 49 EQ54
Fairmark Dr, Uxb. 76 BN65
Fairmead, Brom. 145 EM98
Fairmead, Surb. 138 CP102
Fairmead, Wok. 166 AW118
Fairmead Cl, Brom. 145 EM98
Fairmead Cl, Houns. 96 BX80
Fairmead Cl, N.Mal. 138 CR97
Fairmead Cres, Edg. 42 CQ48
Fairmead Gdns, Ilf. 68 EL57
Fairmead Rd N19 65 DK62
Fairmead Rd, Croy. 141 DM102
Fairmead Rd, Loug. 32 EH42
Fairmead Side, Loug. 32 EJ43
Fairmeads, Cob. 154 BZ113
Fairmeads, Loug. 33 EP40
Fairmile Av SW16 121 DK92
Fairmile Av, Cob. 154 BY114
Fairmile La, Cob. 154 BX112
Fairmile Pk Copse, Cob. 154 BZ112
Fairmile Pk Rd, Cob. 154 BZ113
Fairmont Cl, Belv. 106 EZ78
Lullingstone Rd
Fairmount Rd SW2 121 DM86
Fairoak Cl, Ken. 175 DP115
Fairoak Cl, Lthd. 155 CD112
Fairoak Cl, Orp. 145 EP101
Fairoak Dr SE9 125 ER85
Fairoak Gdns, Rom. 51 FE54
Fairoak La, Chess. 154 CC112
Fairoak La, Lthd. 155 CF111
Fairs Rd, Lthd. 171 CG119
Fairseat Cl, Bushey 41 CE47
Hive Rd
Fairstead Wk N1 84 DQ67
Popham Rd
Fairthorn Rd SE7 205 N10
Fairthorn Rd SE7 104 EG78
Fairtrough Rd, Orp. 164 EV112
Fairview, Epsom 157 CW111
Fairview, Erith 107 FF80
Guild Rd
Fairview, Pot.B. 12 DB29
Hawkshead Rd
Fairview Av, Brwd. 55 GE45
Fairview Av, Rain. 90 FK68
Fairview Av, Wem. 79 CK65
Fairview Av, Wok. 166 AY118
Fairview Cl E17 47 DY53
Fairview Cl, Chig. 49 ES49
Fairview Cl, Wok. 167 AZ118
Fairview Av
Fairview Ct, Ashf. 114 BN92
Fairview Cres, Har. 60 CA60
Fairview Dr, Chig. 49 ES49
Fairview Dr, Orp. 163 ER105
Fairview Dr, Shep. 134 BM99
Fairview Dr, Wat. 23 BS36
Fairview Gdns, Wdf.Grn. 48 EH53
Fairview Ind Est, Oxt. 188 EG133
Fairview Ind Pk, Rain. 89 FE71
Fairview Pl SW2 121 DM87
Fairview Rd N15 66 DT57
Fairview Rd SW16 141 DM95
Fairview Rd, Chig. 49 ES49
Fairview Rd, Enf. 29 DN39
Fairview Rd, Epsom 157 CT111
Fairview Rd, Grav. 130 GD94
Fairview Rd, Sutt. 158 DD106
Fairview Way, Edg. 42 CN49
Fairwater Av, Well. 106 EU84
Fairwater Dr, Add. 152 BK109
Fairway SW20 139 CW97
Fairway, Bexh. 126 EY85
Fairway, Cars. 158 DC111
Fairway, Cher. 134 BH102
Fairway, Orp. 145 ER99
Fairway, Vir.W. 132 AV100
Fairway, Wdf.Grn. 48 EJ50
Fairway, The N13 46 DQ48
Fairway, The N14 29 DH44
Fairway, The NW7 42 CR48
Fairway, The W3 80 CS72
Fairway, The, Abb.L. 7 BR32
Fairway, The, Barn. 28 DB44
Fairway, The, Brom. 145 EM99
Fairway, The, Grav. 131 GG89
Fairway, The, Lthd. 171 CG118
Fairway, The, N.Mal. 138 CR95
Fairway, The, Nthlt. 78 CC65
Fairway, The, Nthwd. 39 BS49
Fairway, The, Ruis. 60 BX62
Fairway, The, Upmin. 72 FQ59
Fairway, The, Uxb. 76 BM68
Fairway, The, Wem. 61 CH62
Fairway, The, W.Mol. 136 CB97
Fairway, The, Wey. 152 BN111
Fairway Av NW9 62 CP55
Fairway Av, Borwd. 26 CP40
Fairway Av, West Dr. 76 BJ74
Fairway Cl NW11 64 DC59
Fairway Cl, Croy. 143 DY99
Fairway Cl, Epsom 156 CQ105
Fairway Cl, Houns. 116 BW85
Fairway Cl, St.Alb. 8 CC27
Fairway Cl, West Dr. 76 BK74
Fairway Av
Fairway Cl, Wok. 166 AU119
Fairway Ct NW7 42 CR48
The Fairway
Fairway Dr SE28 88 EX72
Fairway Dr, Dart. 128 FP87
Fairway Dr, Grnf. 78 CB66
Fairway Gdns, Beck. 143 ED100
Fairway Gdns, Ilf. 69 EQ64
Fairways, Ashf. 115 BP93
Fairways, Ken. 176 DQ117
Fairways, Stan. 42 CL54
Fairways, Tedd. 117 CK94
Fairways, Wal.Abb. 16 EE34
Fairways, Wal.Cr. 15 DX26
Fairweather Cl N15 66 DS56
Fairweather Rd N16 66 DU58
Fairwyn Rd SE26 123 DY91
Fakenham Cl NW7 43 CU52
Fakenham Cl, Nthlt. 78 CA65
Goodwood Dr
Fakruddin St E1 84 DU70
Falaise, Egh. 112 AY92
Falcon Av, Brom. 144 EL98
Falcon Av, Grays 110 GB79
Falcon Cl SE1 200 G2
Falcon Cl W4 98 CQ79
Sutton La S
Falcon Cl, Dart. 128 FM85
Falcon Cl, Nthwd. 39 BS52
Falcon Cl, Wal.Abb. 16 EG34
Kestrel Rd
Falcon Ct EC4 196 D9
Falcon Ct EC4 83 DN72
Falcon Ct, Wok. 151 BC114
Blackmore Cres
Falcon Cres, Enf. 31 DX43
Falcon Dr, Stai. 114 BK86
Falcon Gro SW11 100 DE83
Falcon Ho W13 79 CF70
Falcon La SW11 100 DE83
Falcon Ms, Grav. 130 GE88
Falcon Pk Ind Est NW10 63 CT64
Falcon Rd SW11 100 DE82
Falcon Rd, Enf. 31 DX43
Falcon Rd, Hmptn. 116 BZ94
Falcon St E13 86 EG70
Falcon Ter SW11 100 DE83
Falcon Way E11 68 EG56
Falcon Way E14 204 C8
Falcon Way E14 103 EB77
Falcon Way NW9 42 CS54
Falcon Way, Felt. 115 BV85
Falcon Way, Har. 62 CL57
Falcon Way, Horn. 89 FG66
Falcon Way, Sun. 135 BS96
Falcon Way, Wat. 8 BY34
Falconberg Ct W1 195 N8
Falconberg Ms W1 195 M8
Falconer Rd, Bushey 24 BZ44
Falconer Rd, Ilf. 50 EV50
Falconer Wk N7 65 DM61
Newington Barrow Way
Falconhurst, Lthd. 171 CD115
Falcons Cl, West. 178 EK117
Falconwood, Egh. 112 AY92
Falconwood, Lthd. 171 CF120
Falconwood Av, Well. 105 ER82
Falconwood Par, Well. 105 ES84
Falconwood Rd, Croy. 161 EA108
Falcourt Cl, Sutt. 158 DB106
Falkirk Cl, Horn. 72 FN60
Falkirk Gdns, Wat. 40 BX50
Blackford Rd
Falkirk Ho W9 82 DB69
Falkirk St N1 197 N1
Falkirk St N1 84 DS68
Falkland Av N3 44 DA52
Falkland Av N11 44 DG49
Falkland Pk Av SE25 142 DS97
Falkland Pl NW5 65 DJ64
Falkland Rd
Falkland Rd N8 65 DN56
Falkland Rd NW5 65 DJ64
Falkland Rd, Barn. 27 CY40
Fallaize Av, Ilf. 69 EP63
Riverdene Rd
Falling La, West Dr. 76 BL73
Falloden Way NW11 64 DA56
Fallow Cl, Chig. 49 ET50
Fallow Ct SE16 102 DU78
Argyle Way
Fallow Ct Av N12 44 DC52
Fallow Flds, Loug. 48 EJ45
Fallowfield, Dart. 129 FV90
Fallowfield, Stan. 41 CG48
Fallowfield Cl (Harefield), Uxb. 38 BJ53
Fallowfield Ct, Stan. 41 CG48
Fallowfields Dr N12 44 DE51
Fallows Cl N2 44 DC54
Fallsbrook Rd SW16 121 DJ94
Falman Cl N9 46 DU46
Croyland Rd
Falmer Rd E17 67 EB55
Falmer Rd N15 66 DQ57
Falmer Rd, Enf. 30 DS42
Falmouth Av E4 47 ED50
Falmouth Cl N22 45 DM52
Truro Rd
Falmouth Cl SE12 124 EF85
Falmouth Gdns, Ilf. 68 EL57
Falmouth Rd SE1 201 J6
Falmouth Rd SE1 102 DQ76
Falmouth Rd, Walt. 154 BW105
Falmouth St E15 67 ED64
Falstaff Ms, Hmptn. 117 CD92
Hampton Rd
Falstone, Wok. 166 AV118
Fambridge Cl SE26 123 DZ91
Fambridge Rd, Dag. 70 FA60
Famet Av, Pur. 160 DQ113
Famet Cl, Pur. 160 DQ113
Famet Wk, Pur. 160 DQ113
Fane St W14 99 CZ79
North End Rd
Fangrove Caravan Pk, Cher. 133 BB102
Fann St EC1 197 H5
Fann St EC1 84 DQ70
Fann St EC2 197 H5
Fann St EC2 84 DQ70
Fanns Ri, Purf. 108 FN77
Fanshaw St N1 197 M2
Fanshaw St N1 84 DS69
Fanshawe Av, Bark. 87 EQ65
Fanshawe Cres, Dag. 70 EY64
Fanshawe Cres, Horn. 72 FK58
Fanshawe Rd, Grays 111 GG76
Fanshawe Rd, Rich. 117 CJ91
Fanthorpe St SW15 99 CW83
Faraday Av, Sid. 126 EU89
Faraday Cl N7 83 DM65
Bride St
Faraday Cl, Wat. 23 BR44
Faraday Rd E15 86 EF65
Faraday Rd SW19 120 DA93
Faraday Rd W3 80 CQ73
Faraday Rd W10 81 CY71
Faraday Rd, Sthl. 78 CB73
Faraday Rd, Well. 106 EU83
Faraday Rd, W.Mol. 136 CA98
Faraday Way SE18 104 EK76
Faraday Way, Croy. 141 DM102
Ampere Way
Faraday Way, Orp. 146 EV98
Fareham Rd, Felt. 116 BW87
Fareham St W1 195 M8
Farewell Pl, Mitch. 140 DE95
Faringdon Av, Brom. 145 EP100
Faringdon Av, Rom. 52 FJ53
Faringford Cl, Pot.B. 12 DD31
Faringford Rd E15 86 EE66
Farington Acres, Wey. 135 BR104
Faris Barn Dr, Add. 151 BF112
Faris La, Add. 151 BF111
Farjeon Rd SE3 104 EK81
Farleigh Av, Brom. 144 EF100
Farleigh Border, Croy. 161 DY112
Farleigh Ct Rd, Warl. 161 DZ114
Farleigh Dean Cres, Croy. 161 EB111
Farleigh Pl N16 66 DT63
Farleigh Rd
Farleigh Rd N16 66 DT63
Farleigh Rd, Add. 152 BG111
Farleigh Rd, Warl. 177 DX118
Farleton Cl, Wey. 153 BR107
Farley Common, West. 189 EP126
Farley Dr, Ilf. 69 ES60
Farley La, West. 189 EP127
Farley Nursery, West. 189 EQ127
Farley Pk, Oxt. 187 ED130
Farley Pl SE25 142 DU98
Farley Rd SE6 123 EB87
Farley Rd, Grav. 131 GM88
Farley Rd, S.Croy. 160 DV108
Farleycroft, West. 189 EQ126
Farlington Pl SW15 119 CV87
Roehampton La
Farlow Cl, Grav. 131 GF90
Farlow Rd SW15 99 CX83
Farlton Rd SW18 120 DB87
Farm Av NW2 63 CY62
Farm Av SW16 121 DL91
Farm Av, Har. 60 BZ59
Farm Av, Swan. 147 FC97
Farm Av, Wem. 79 CJ65
Farm Cl, Amer. 20 AX39
Farm Cl, Barn. 27 CW43
Farm Cl, Borwd. 25 CK38
Farm Cl, Brwd. 55 GC45
Farm Cl, Buck.H. 48 EJ48
Farm Cl, Cher. 133 BA100
Farm Cl, Couls. 174 DF120
Farm Cl, Dag. 89 FC66
Farm Cl (Fetcham), Lthd. 171 CD124
Farm Cl (Cuffley), Pot.B. 13 DK27
Farm Cl, Rad. 10 CL30
Farm Cl, Shep. 134 BN101
Farm Cl, Sthl. 78 CB73
Farm Cl, Stai. 113 BE92
Farm Cl, Sutt. 158 DD108
Farm Cl, Uxb. 59 BP61
Farm Cl, Wall. 159 DJ110
Farm Cl (Cheshunt), Wal.Cr. 14 DW30
Farm Cl, W.Byf. 152 BM112
Farm Cl, W.Wick. 144 EE104
Farm Ct NW4 63 CU55
Farm Cres, Slou. 74 AV71
Farm Dr, Croy. 143 DZ103
Farm Dr, Pur. 159 DK112
Farm End E4 32 EE43
Farm End, Nthwd. 39 BP53
Drakes Dr
Farm Fld, Wat. 23 BS38
Farm Flds, S.Croy. 160 DS111
Farm Hill Rd, Wal.Abb. 15 EC34
Farm Ho Cl, Brox. 15 DZ25
Farm La N14 28 DG44
Farm La SW6 100 DA79
Farm La, Add. 152 BG107
Farm La, Ash. 172 CN116
Farm La, Cars. 158 DF110
Farm La, Croy. 143 DZ103
Farm La, Epsom 172 CP119
Farm La, Pur. 159 DJ110
Farm La, Rick. 22 BH41
Farm La, Wok. 167 BC124
Farm Pl W8 82 DA74
Uxbridge St
Farm Pl, Dart. 107 FG84
Farm Rd N21 46 DQ46
Farm Rd, Edg. 42 CP51
Farm Rd, Esher 136 CB102
Farm Rd, Grays 111 GF75
Farm Rd, Houns. 116 BY88
Farm Rd, Mord. 140 DB99
Farm Rd, Nthwd. 39 BQ50
Farm Rd, Rain. 90 FJ69
Farm Rd, Rick. 21 BA42
Farm Rd, Sev. 191 FJ121
Farm Rd, Stai. 114 BH93
Farm Rd, Sutt. 158 DD108
Farm Rd, Warl. 177 DY119
Farm Rd, Wok. 167 BB120
Farm St W1 199 H1
Farm St W1 83 DH73
Farm Vale, Bex. 127 FB86
Farm Vw, Tad. 183 CZ127
Farm Wk NW11 63 CZ57
Farm Way, Buck.H. 48 EJ49
Farm Way, Bushey 24 CB42
Farm Way, Horn. 71 FH63
Farm Way, Nthwd. 39 BS49
Farm Way, Stai. 113 BF86
Farm Way, Wor.Pk. 139 CW104
Farman Gro, Nthlt. 78 BX69
Wayfarer Rd
Farmborough Cl, Har. 61 CD59
Pool Rd
Farmcote Rd SE12 124 EG88
Farmcroft, Grav. 131 GG89
Farmdale Rd SE10 205 N10
Farmdale Rd SE10 104 EG78
Farmdale Rd, Cars. 158 DE108
Farmer Rd E10 67 EB60
Farmer St W8 82 DA74
Uxbridge St
Farmers Cl, Wat. 7 BV33
Farmers Ct, Wal.Abb. 16 EG33
Winters Way
Farmers Rd SE5 101 DP80
Farmers Rd, Stai. 113 BE92
Farmfield Rd, Brom. 124 EE92
Farmhouse Cl, Wok. 167 BD115
Farmhouse Rd SW16 121 DJ94
Farmilo Rd E17 67 DZ59
Farmington Av, Sutt. 140 DD104
Farmland Wk, Chis. 125 EP92
Farmlands, Enf. 29 DN39
Farmlands, Pnr. 59 BU56
Farmlands, The, Nthlt. 78 BZ65
Farmleigh N14 45 DJ45
Farmleigh Gro, Walt. 153 BT106
Farmstead Rd SE6 123 EB91
Farmstead Rd, Har. 41 CD53
Farmview, Cob. 170 BX116
Farmway, Dag. 70 EW63
Farnaby Dr, Sev. 190 FF126
Farnaby Rd SE9 104 EJ84
Farnaby Rd, Brom. 123 ED94
Farnan Av E17 47 EA54
Farnan Rd SW16 121 DL92
Farnborough Av E17 67 DY55
Farnborough Av, S.Croy. 161 DX108
Farnborough Cl, Wem. 62 CP61
Chalkhill Rd
Farnborough Common, Orp. 145 EM104
Farnborough Cres, Brom. 144 EF102
Saville Row
Farnborough Cres, S.Croy. 161 DY109
Farnborough Hill, Orp. 163 ER106
Farnborough Way SE15 102 DT80
Chandler Way
Farnborough Way, Orp. 163 EQ105
Farncombe St SE16 202 C5
Farncombe St SE16 102 DU75
Farndale Av N13 45 DP48
Farndale Cres, Grnf. 78 CC69
Farnell Ms SW5 100 DB78
Earls Ct Sq
Farnell Rd, Islw. 97 CD83
Farnell Rd, Stai. 114 BG90
Farnes Dr, Rom. 52 FJ54
Farnham Cl N20 44 DC45
Farnham Cl, Hem.H. 5 BA28
Farnham Gdns SW20 139 CV96
Farnham Pl SE1 200 G3
Farnham Rd, Ilf. 69 ET59
Farnham Rd, Rom. 52 FK50
Farnham Rd, Well. 106 EW82
Farnham Royal SE11 101 DM78
Farningham Cres, Cat. 176 DU123
Commonwealth Rd
Farningham Hill Rd (Farningham), Dart. 148 FJ99
Farningham Rd N17 46 DU52
Farningham Rd, Cat. 176 DU123
Farnley, Wok. 166 AT117
Farnley Rd E4 48 EE45
Farnley Rd SE25 142 DR98
Farnol Rd, Dart. 108 FN84
Faro Cl, Brom. 145 EN96
Faroe Rd W14 99 CX76
Farorna Wk, Enf. 29 DN39
Farquhar Rd SE19 122 DT92
Farquhar Rd SW19 120 DA90
Farquharson Rd, Croy. 142 DQ102
Farr Av, Bark. 88 EU68
Farr Rd, Enf. 30 DR39
Farraline Rd, Wat. 23 BV42
Farrance Rd, Rom. 70 EY58
Farrance St E14 85 DZ72
Farrans Ct, Har. 61 CH59
Farrant Av N22 45 DN54
Farrant Cl, Orp. 164 EU108
Farrant Way, Borwd. 26 CL39
Farrell Ho E1 84 DW72
Farren Rd SE23 123 DY89
Farrer Ms N8 65 DJ56
Farrer Rd
Farrer Rd N8 65 DJ56
Farrer Rd, Har. 62 CL57
Farrer's Pl, Croy. 161 DX105
Farrier Cl, Sun. 135 BU98
Farrier Cl, Uxb. 76 BN72
Horseshoe Dr
Farrier Rd, Nthlt. 78 CA68
Farrier St NW1 83 DH66
Farrier Wk SW10 100 DC79
Farriers Cl, Epsom 156 CS112
Portland Pl
Farriers Cl, Grav. 131 GM88
Farriers Cl (Bovingdon), Hem.H. 5 BB28
Chipperfield Rd
Farriers Ct, Sutt. 157 CY108
Forge La
Farriers Ct, Wat. 7 BV32
Farriers End, Brox. 15 DZ26
Farriers Rd, Epsom 156 CS112
Farriers Way, Borwd. 26 CQ44
Farringdon La EC1 196 E5
Farringdon La EC1 83 DN70
Farringdon Rd EC1 196 D4
Farringdon Rd EC1 83 DN70
Farringdon St EC4 196 F8
Farringdon St EC4 83 DP71
Farringford Cl, St.Alb. 8 CA26
Farrington Av, Orp. 146 EV97
Farrington Pl, Chis. 125 ER94
Farrington Pl, Nthwd. 39 BT49
Farrins Rents SE16 203 K3
Farrins Rents SE16 85 DY74
Farrow La SE14 102 DW80
Farrow Pl SE16 203 K6
Farthing All SE1 202 B5
Farthing Cl, Dart. 108 FM84
Farthing Flds E1 202 E2
Farthing Grn La, Slou. 74 AU68
Farthing St, Orp. 163 EM108
Farthingale Ct, Wal.Abb. 16 EG34
Farthingale La, Wal.Abb. 16 EG34
Farthingale Wk E15 85 ED66
Farthings, Wok. 166 AS116
Farthings, The, Kings.T. 138 CN95
Brunswick Rd
Farthings Cl E4 48 EE48
Farthings Cl, Pnr. 59 BV58
Farwell Rd, Sid. 126 EV90
Farwig La, Brom. 144 EF95
Fashion St E1 197 P7
Fashion St E1 84 DT71
Fashoda Rd, Brom. 144 EK98
Fassett Rd E8 84 DU65
Fassett Rd, Kings.T. 138 CL98
Fassett Sq E8 84 DU65
Fassnidge Way, Uxb. 76 BJ66
Oxford Rd
Fauconberg Rd W4 98 CQ79
Faulkner Cl, Dag. 70 EX59
Faulkner St SE14 102 DW81
Faulkner's All EC1 196 F6
Faulkners Rd, Walt. 154 BW106
Fauna Cl, Rom. 70 EW59
Faunce St SE17 101 DP78
Harmsworth St
Favart Rd SW6 100 DA81
Faverolle Grn, Wal.Cr. 15 DX28
Faversham Av E4 48 EE46
Faversham Av, Enf. 30 DR44
Faversham Cl, Chig. 50 EV47
Faversham Rd SE6 123 DZ87
Faversham Rd, Beck. 143 DZ96
Faversham Rd, Mord. 140 DB100
Fawcett Cl SW11 100 DD82
Fawcett Cl SW16 121 DN91
Fawcett Est E5 66 DU60
Fawcett Rd NW10 81 CT67
Fawcett Rd, Croy. 141 DP104
Fawcett St SW10 100 DC79
Fawcus Cl, Esher 155 CF107
Dalmore Av
Fawe Pk Rd SW15 99 CZ84
Fawe St E14 85 EB71
Fawke Common, Sev. 191 FP127
Fawke Common Rd, Sev. 191 FP126
Fawkes Av, Dart. 128 FM89
Fawkham Grn Rd (Fawkham Grn), Long. 149 FV104
Fawkham Rd, Long. 149 FX97
Fawley Rd NW6 64 DB64
Fawn Rd E13 86 EJ68
Fawn Rd, Chig. 49 ET50
Fawnbrake Av SE24 121 DP85
Fawns Manor Cl, Felt. 115 BQ88
Fawns Manor Rd, Felt. 115 BR88
Fawood Av NW10 80 CR66
Fawsley Cl, Slou. 93 BE80
Fawters Cl, Brwd. 55 GD44
Fay Grn, Abb.L. 7 BR33
Fayerfield, Pot.B. 12 DD31
Faygate Cres, Bexh. 126 FA85
Faygate Rd SW2 121 DM89
Fayland Av SW16 121 DJ92
Faymore Gdns, S.Ock. 91 FU72
Fearney Mead, Rick. 38 BG46
Fearnley Cres, Hmptn. 116 BZ92
Fearnley St, Wat. 23 BV42
Fearns Mead, Brwd. 54 FW50
Bucklers Ct
Fearon St SE10 205 M10
Fearon St SE10 104 EG78
Featherbed La, Abb.L. 7 BV26
Sergehill La
Featherbed La, Croy. 161 DZ108
Featherbed La, Rom. 50 EY45
Featherbed La, Warl. 161 ED113

Feathers La, Stai. 113 BA89
Feathers Pl SE10 103 ED79
Featherstone Av SE23 122 DV89
Featherstone Gdns, Borwd. 26 CQ42
Featherstone Ind Est, Sthl. 96 BY75
Featherstone Rd NW7 43 CV51
Featherstone Rd, Sthl. 96 BY76
Featherstone St EC1 197 K4
Featherstone St EC1 84 DR70
Featherstone Ter, Sthl. 96 BY76
Featley Rd SW9 101 DP83
Federal Rd, Grnf. 79 CJ68
Federal Way, Wat. 24 BW38
Federation Rd SE2 106 EV77
Fee Fm Rd, Esher 155 CF108
Feenan Highway, Til. 111 GH80
Felbridge Av, Stan. 41 CG53
Felbridge Cl SW16 121 DN91
Felbridge Cl, Sutt. 158 DC109
Felbrigge Rd, Ilf. 69 ET61
Felcott Cl, Walt. 136 BW104
Felcott Rd, Walt. 136 BW104
Felday Rd SE13 123 EB86
Felden Cl, Pnr. 40 BY52
Felden Cl, Wat. 8 BX34
Felden St SW6 99 CZ81
Feldman Cl N16 66 DU60
Felgate Ms W6 99 CV77
Felhampton Rd SE9 125 EP89
Felhurst Cres, Dag. 71 FB63
Felicia Way, Grays 111 GH77
Felipe Rd, Grays 109 FW76
Felix Av N8 65 DL58
Felix La, Shep. 135 BS100
Felix Rd W13 79 CG73
Felix Rd, Walt. 135 BU100
Felix St E2 84 DV68
Hackney Rd
Felixstowe Ct E16 105 EP75
Barge Ho Rd
Felixstowe Rd N9 46 DU49
Felixstowe Rd N17 66 DT55
Felixstowe Rd NW10 81 CV69
Felixstowe Rd SE2 106 EV76
Fell Rd, Croy. 142 DQ104
Fell Wk, Edg. 42 CP53
East Rd
Fellbrigg Rd SE22 122 DT85
Fellbrigg St E1 84 DV70
Headlam St
Fellbrook, Rich. 117 CH90
Fellmongers Yd, Croy. 142 DQ103
Surrey St
Fellowes Cl, Hayes 78 BX70
Paddington Cl
Fellowes Rd, Cars. 140 DE104
Fellows Ct E2 197 P1
Fellows Ct E2 84 DT68
Fellows Rd NW3 82 DD66
Felltram Way SE7 205 N10
Felmersham Cl SW4 101 DK84
Haselrigge Rd
Felmingham Rd SE20 142 DW96
Felnex Trd Est, Wall. 140 DG103
Fels Cl, Dag. 71 FB62
Fels Fm Av, Dag. 71 FC62
Felsberg Rd SW2 121 DL86
Felsham Rd SW15 99 CX83
Felspar Cl SE18 105 ET78
Felstead Av, Ilf. 49 EN53
Felstead Cl, Brwd. 55 GC44
Felstead Gdns E14 103 EC78
Ferry St
Felstead Rd E11 68 EG59
Felstead Rd, Epsom 156 CR111
Felstead Rd, Loug. 48 EL45
Felstead Rd, Orp. 146 EU103
Felstead Rd, Rom. 51 FC51
Felstead Rd, Wal.Cr. 15 DY32
Felstead St E9 85 DZ65
Felsted Rd E16 86 EK72
Feltham Av, E.Mol. 137 CE98
Feltham Business Complex, Felt. 115 BV89
Feltham Hill Rd, Ashf. 115 BP92
Feltham Hill Rd, Felt. 115 BU91
Feltham Rd, Ashf. 115 BP91
Feltham Rd, Mitch. 140 DF96
Felthambrook Way, Felt. 115 BV90
Felton Cl, Borwd. 26 CL38
Felton Cl, Brox. 15 DZ25
Felton Cl, Orp. 145 EP100
Felton Gdns, Bark. 87 ES67
Sutton Rd
Felton Lea, Sid. 125 ET92
Felton Rd W13 97 CJ75
Camborne Av
Felton Rd, Bark. 87 ES68
Sutton Rd
Felton St N1 84 DR67
Fen Cl, Brwd. 55 GC42
Fen Ct EC3 197 M10
Fen Gro, Sid. 125 ET86
Fen La, Upmin. 73 FW64
Fen St E16 86 EF73
Victoria Dock Rd
Fencepiece Rd, Chig. 49 EQ50
Fencepiece Rd, Ilf. 49 EQ50
Fenchurch Av EC3 197 M9
Fenchurch Av EC3 84 DS72
Fenchurch Bldgs EC3 197 N9
Fenchurch Pl EC3 197 N10
Fenchurch St EC3 197 M10
Fenchurch St EC3 84 DS73
Fendall Rd, Epsom 156 CQ106
Fendall St SE1 201 N7
Fendall St SE1 102 DS76
Fendt Cl E16 86 EF73
Bowman Av
Fendyke Rd, Belv. 106 EX76
Fenelon Pl W14 99 CZ77
Fengates Rd, Red. 184 DE134
Fenham Rd SE15 102 DU80
Fenman Ct N17 46 DV53
Shelbourne Rd
Fenman Gdns, Ilf. 70 EV60
Fenn Cl, Brom. 124 EG93
Fenn St E9 66 DW64
Fennel Cl E16 86 EE70
Cranberry La
Fennel Cl, Croy. 143 DX102
Primrose La
Fennel St SE18 105 EN79
Fennells Mead, Epsom 157 CT109
Fenner Cl SE16 202 E8
Fenner Ho, Walt. 153 BU105
Fenner Rd, Grays 109 FW77
Fenner Sq SW11 100 DD83
Thomas Baines Rd
Fenning St SE1 201 M4
Fenns Way, Wok. 166 AY115
Fens Way, Swan. 127 FG93
Fenstanton Av N12 44 DD50
Fenswood Cl, Bex. 126 FA85
Fentiman Rd SW8 101 DL79
Fentiman Way, Horn. 72 FL60
Fenton Av, Stai. 114 BJ93
Fenton Cl E8 84 DT65
Laurel St
Fenton Cl SW9 101 DM82
Fenton Cl, Chis. 125 EM92
Fenton Cl, Red. 184 DG134
Fenton Rd N17 46 DQ52
Fenton Rd, Red. 184 DG134
Fentons Av E13 86 EH68
Fenwick Cl SE18 105 EN79
Ritter St
Fenwick Cl, Wok. 166 AV118
Fenwick Gro SE15 102 DU83
Fenwick Path, Borwd. 26 CM38
Fenwick Pl SW9 101 DL83
Fenwick Rd SE15 102 DU83
Ferdinand Pl NW1 82 DG66
Ferdinand St
Ferdinand St NW1 82 DG65
Fergus Rd N5 65 DP64
Calabria Rd
Ferguson Av, Grav. 131 GJ91
Ferguson Av, Rom. 52 FJ54
Ferguson Av, Surb. 138 CM99
Ferguson Cl E14 204 A9
Ferguson Cl E14 103 EA77
Ferguson Cl, Brom. 143 EC97
Ferguson Ct, Rom. 52 FK54
Ferguson Dr W3 80 CR72
Ferme Pk Rd N4 65 DL57
Ferme Pk Rd N8 65 DL57
Fermor Rd SE23 123 DY88
Fermoy Rd W9 81 CZ70
Fermoy Rd, Grnf. 78 CB70
Fern Av, Mitch. 141 DK98
Fern Cl, Erith 107 FH81
Hollywood Way
Fern Cl, Warl. 177 DY118
Fern Dene W13 79 CH71
Templewood
Fern Gro, Felt. 115 BV87
Fern La, Houns. 96 BZ78
Fern St E3 85 EA70
Fern Twrs, Cat. 186 DU125
Fern Wk SE16 102 DU78
Argyle Way
Fern Wk, Ashf. 114 BK92
Ferndale Rd
Fern Way, Wat. 23 BU35
Fernbank, Buck.H. 48 EH46
Fernbank Av, Horn. 72 FJ63
Fernbank Av, Walt. 136 BY101
Fernbank Av, Wem. 61 CF63
Fernbank Ms SW12 121 DJ86
Fernbank Rd, Add. 152 BG106
Fernbrook Av, Sid. 125 ES85
Blackfen Rd
Fernbrook Cres SE13 124 EE86
Fernbrook Dr, Har. 60 CB59
Fernbrook Rd SE13 124 EE86
Ferncliff Rd E8 66 DU64
Ferncroft Av N12 44 DE51
Ferncroft Av NW3 64 DA62
Ferncroft Av, Ruis. 60 BW61
Ferndale, Brom. 144 EJ96
Ferndale Av E17 67 ED57
Ferndale Av, Cher. 133 BE104
Ferndale Av, Houns. 96 BY83
Ferndale Cl, Bexh. 106 EY81
Ferndale Ct SE3 104 EF80
Ferndale Cres, Uxb. 76 BJ69
Ferndale Rd E7 86 EH66
Ferndale Rd E11 68 EE61
Ferndale Rd N15 66 DT58
Ferndale Rd SE25 142 DV99
Ferndale Rd SW4 101 DL84
Ferndale Rd SW9 101 DM83
Ferndale Rd, Ashf. 114 BK92
Ferndale Rd, Bans. 173 CZ116
Ferndale Rd, Enf. 31 DY37
Ferndale Rd, Grav. 131 GH89
Ferndale Rd, Rom. 51 FC54
Ferndale Rd, Wok. 167 AZ116
Ferndale St E6 87 EP73
Ferndale Ter, Har. 61 CF56
Ferndale Way, Orp. 163 ER106
Ferndell Av, Bex. 127 FD90
Fernden Way, Rom. 71 FB58
Ferndene, St.Alb. 8 BZ31
Ferndene Rd SE24 102 DQ84
Ferndown, Horn. 72 FM58
Ferndown, Nthwd. 39 BU54
Ferndown Av, Orp. 145 ER102
Ferndown Cl, Pnr. 40 BY52
Ferndown Cl, Sutt. 158 DD107
Ferndown Gdns, Cob. 154 BW113
Ferndown Rd SE9 124 EK87
Ferndown Rd, Wat. 40 BW48
Fernery, The, Stai. 113 BE92
Fernes Cl, Uxb. 76 BJ72
Ferney Ct, W.Byf. 152 BK112
Ferney Rd
Ferney Meade Way, Islw. 97 CG82
Ferney Rd, Barn. 44 DG45
Ferney Rd (Cheshunt), Wal.Cr. 14 DR26
Hammondstreet Rd
Ferney Rd, W.Byf. 152 BK112
Fernhall Dr, Ilf. 68 EK57
Fernhall La, Wal.Abb. 16 EK31
Fernham Rd, Th.Hth. 142 DQ97
Fernhead Rd W9 81 CZ70
Fernheath Way, Dart. 127 FD92
Fernhill, Lthd. 155 CD114
Fernhill Cl, Wok. 166 AW120
Fernhill Ct E17 47 ED54
Fernhill Gdns, Kings.T. 117 CK92
Fernhill La, Wok. 166 AW120
Fernhill Pk, Wok. 166 AW120
Fernhill St E16 87 EM74
Fernhills, Kings L. 7 BR33
Fernholme Rd SE15 123 DX85
Fernhurst Gdns, Edg. 42 CN51
Fernhurst Rd SW6 99 CY81
Fernhurst Rd, Ashf. 115 BQ91
Fernhurst Rd, Croy. 142 DU101
Fernie Cl, Chig. 50 EU50
Fernihough Cl, Wey. 152 BN111
Fernlands Cl, Cher. 133 BE104
Fernlea, Lthd. 170 CB123
Fernlea Rd SW12 121 DH88
Fernlea Rd, Mitch. 140 DG96
Fernleigh Cl, Croy. 159 DN105
Stafford Rd
Fernleigh Cl, Walt. 135 BV104
Fernleigh Ct, Har. 40 CB54
Fernleigh Ct, Wem. 62 CL61
Fernleigh Rd N21 45 DN47
Ferns Cl, Enf. 31 DY36
Ferns Cl, S.Croy. 160 DV110
Ferns Rd E15 86 EF65
Fernsbury St WC1 196 D3
Fernshaw Rd SW10 100 DC79
Fernside NW11 64 DA61
Finchley Rd
Fernside, Buck.H. 48 EH46
Fernside Av NW7 42 CR48
Fernside Av, Felt. 115 BV91
Fernside La, Sev. 191 FJ129
Fernside Rd SW12 120 DF88
Fernsleigh Cl (Chalfont St. Peter), Ger.Cr. 36 AY51
Fernthorpe Rd SW16 121 DJ93
Ferntower Rd N5 66 DR64
Fernways, Ilf. 69 EP63
Cecil Rd
Fernwood Av SW16 121 DK91
Fernwood Av, Wem. 61 CJ64
Bridgewater Rd
Fernwood Cl, Brom. 144 EJ96
Fernwood Cres N20 44 DF48
Ferny Hill, Barn. 28 DF38
Ferranti Cl SE18 104 EK76
Ferraro Cl, Houns. 96 CA79
Ferrers Av, Wall. 159 DK105
Ferrers Av, West Dr. 94 BK75
Ferrers Rd SW16 121 DK92
Ferrestone Rd N8 65 DM56
Ferriby Cl N1 83 DN66
Bewdley St
Ferrier Pt E16 86 EH71
Forty Acre La
Ferrier St SW18 100 DB84
Ferriers Way, Epsom 173 CW119
Ferring Cl, Har. 60 CC60
Ferrings SE21 122 DS89
Ferris Av, Croy. 143 DZ104
Ferris Rd SE22 102 DU84
Ferro Rd, Rain. 89 FG70
Ferron Rd E5 66 DV62
Ferrour Ct N2 64 DD55
Ferry Av, Stai. 113 BE94
Ferry La N17 66 DV56
Ferry La SW13 99 CT79
Ferry La, Brent. 98 CL79
Ferry La, Cher. 134 BH98
Ferry La, Rain. 89 FE72
Ferry La, Rich. 98 CM79
Ferry La, Shep. 134 BN102
Ferry La (Hythe End), Stai. 113 BB89
Ferry La (Laleham), Stai. 134 BJ97
Ferry Pl SE18 105 EN76
Woolwich High St
Ferry Rd SW13 99 CU80
Ferry Rd, Tedd. 117 CH92
Ferry Rd, T.Ditt. 137 CH100
Ferry Rd, Til. 111 GG83
Ferry Rd, Twick. 117 CH88
Ferry Rd, W.Mol. 136 CA97
Ferry Sq, Brent. 97 CK79
Ferry Sq, Shep. 135 BP101
Ferry St E14 204 D10
Ferry St E14 103 EC78
Ferryhills Cl, Wat. 40 BW48
Ferrymead Av, Grnf. 78 CA69
Ferrymead Dr, Grnf. 78 CA68
Ferrymead Gdns, Grnf. 78 CC68
Ferrymoor, Rich. 117 CH90
Feryby Rd, Grays 111 GH76
Festing Rd SW15 99 CX83
Festival Cl, Bex. 126 EX88
Festival Cl, Erith 107 FF80
Betsham Rd
Festival Cl, Uxb. 77 BP67
Festival Path, Wok. 166 AT119
Festival Wk, Cars. 158 DF106
Fetcham Common La, Lthd. 170 CB121
Fetcham Pk Dr, Lthd. 171 CE123
Fetherstone Cl, Pot.B. 12 DD32
Fetter La EC4 196 E9
Fetter La EC4 83 DN72
Ffinch St SE8 103 EA80
Fiddicroft Av, Bans. 158 DB114
Fiddlers Cl, Green. 109 FV84
Fidler Pl, Bushey 24 CB44
Ashfield Av
Field Cl E4 47 EB51
Field Cl, Brom. 144 EJ96
Field Cl, Buck.H. 48 EJ48
Field Cl, Chesh. 4 AS28
Field Cl, Chess. 155 CJ106
Field Cl, Hayes 95 BQ80
Field Cl, Houns. 95 BV81
Field Cl, Rom. 34 EV41
Field Cl, Ruis. 59 BQ60
Field Way
Field Cl, S.Croy. 160 DV114
Field Cl, W.Mol. 136 CB99
Field Ct WC1 196 C7
Field Ct, Oxt. 188 EE127
Silkham Rd
Field End, Barn. 27 CV42
Field End, Couls. 159 DK114
Field End, Nthlt. 78 BX65
Field End, Ruis. 78 BW65
Field End, Twick. 117 CF91
Field End Cl, Wat. 40 BY45
Field End Rd, Pnr. 59 BV58
Field End Rd, Ruis. 60 BY63
Field La, Brent. 97 CJ80
Field La, Tedd. 117 CG92
Field Mead NW7 42 CS52
Field Mead NW9 42 CS52
Field Pl, N.Mal. 139 CT100
Field Rd E7 68 EG63
Field Rd N17 66 DR55
Field Rd W6 99 CY78
Field Rd, Felt. 115 BV86
Field Rd, S.Ock. 90 FQ74
Field Rd (Denham), Uxb. 57 BE63
Field Rd, Wat. 24 BY44
Field St WC1 196 B2
Field St WC1 83 DM69
Field Vw, Egh. 113 BC92
Field Vw, Felt. 115 BR91
Field Vw Ri, St.Alb. 8 BY29
Field Vw Rd, Pot.B. 12 DA33
Field Way NW10 80 CQ66
Twybridge Way
Field Way, Croy. 161 EB107
Field Way (Chalfont St. Peter), Ger.Cr. 36 AX52
Field Way, Grnf. 78 CB67
Field Way, Hem.H. 5 BA27
Field Way, Rick. 38 BH46
Field Way, Ruis. 59 BQ60
Field Way, Uxb. 76 BK70
Fieldcommon La, Walt. 136 BZ101
Fieldend Rd SW16 141 DJ95
Fielders Cl, Enf. 30 DS42
Woodfield Cl
Fielders Cl, Har. 60 CC60
Fielders Way (Shenley), Rad. 10 CL33
Fieldfare Rd SE28 88 EW73
Fieldgate La, Mitch. 140 DE97
Fieldgate St E1 84 DU71
Fieldhouse Cl E18 48 EG53
Fieldhouse Rd SW12 121 DJ88
Fieldhurst, Slou. 93 AZ78
Fieldhurst Cl, Add. 152 BH106
Fielding Av, Til. 111 GH81
Fielding Av, Twick. 116 CC90
Fielding Gdns, Slou. 92 AW75
Fielding Ho NW6 82 DA69
Fielding Ms SW13 99 CV79
Castelnau
Fielding Rd W4 98 CR76
Fielding Rd W14 99 CX76
Fielding St SE17 102 DQ79
Fielding Wk W13 97 CH76
Fielding Way, Brwd. 55 GC44
Fieldings, The SE23 122 DW88
Fieldings, The, Wok. 166 AT116
Fieldings Rd (Cheshunt), Wal.Cr. 15 DZ29
Fields Ct, Pot.B. 12 DD33
Fields Est E8 84 DU66
Fields Pk Cres, Rom. 70 EX57
Fieldsend Rd, Sutt. 157 CY106
Fieldside Cl, Orp. 163 EQ105
State Fm Av
Fieldside Rd, Brom. 123 ED92
Fieldview SW18 120 DD88
Fieldview Ct, Stai. 114 BG93
Burges Way
Fieldway, Dag. 70 EV63
Fieldway, Orp. 145 ER100
Fieldway Cres N5 65 DN64
Fiennes Cl, Dag. 70 EW60
Fiennes Way, Sev. 191 FJ127
Fiesta Dr, Dag. 89 FC70
Fife Rd E16 86 EG71
Fife Rd N22 45 DP52
Fife Rd SW14 118 CQ85
Fife Rd, Kings.T. 138 CL96
Fife Ter N1 83 DM68
Fifehead Cl, Ashf. 114 BL93
Fifield Path SE23 123 DX90
Bampton Rd
Fifth Av E12 69 EM63
Fifth Av W10 81 CY69
Fifth Av, Grays 109 FU79
Fifth Av, Hayes 77 BT74
Fifth Av, Wat. 24 BX35
Fifth Cross Rd, Twick. 117 CD89
Fifth Way, Wem. 62 CP63
Fig St, Sev. 190 FF129
Fig Tree Cl NW10 80 CS67
Craven Pk
Figges Rd, Mitch. 120 DG94
Filby Rd, Chess. 156 CM107
Filey Av N16 66 DU60
Filey Cl, Sutt. 158 DC108
Filey Cl, West. 178 EH119
Filey Waye, Ruis. 59 BU61
Filigree Ct SE16 203 M3
Fillebrook Av, Enf. 30 DS40
Fillebrook Rd E11 67 ED60
Filmer La, Sev. 191 FL121
Filmer Rd SW6 99 CY81
Filston La, Sev. 165 FE113
Filston Rd, Erith 107 FB78
Riverdale Rd
Finborough Rd SW10 100 DB78
Finborough Rd SW17 120 DF93
Finch Av SE27 122 DR91
Finch Cl NW10 62 CR64
Finch Cl, Barn. 28 DA43
Finch Dr, Felt. 116 BX87
Finch Grn, Rick. 21 BF42
Finch La EC3 197 L9
Finch La, Amer. 20 AV40
Finch La, Bushey 24 CA43
Finch Ms SE15 102 DT80
Finchale Rd SE2 106 EU76
Fincham Cl, Uxb. 59 BQ61
Aylsham Dr
Finchdean Way SE15 102 DT80
Daniel Gdns
Finchingfield Av, Wdf.Grn. 48 EJ52
Finchley Cl, Dart. 128 FN86
Finchley Ct N3 44 DB51
Finchley La NW4 63 CW56
Finchley Pk N12 44 DC49
Finchley Pl NW8 82 DD68
Finchley Rd NW2 64 DA62
Finchley Rd NW3 82 DC65
Finchley Rd NW8 82 DD67
Finchley Rd NW11 63 CZ58
Finchley Rd, Grays 110 GB79
Finchley Way N3 44 DA52
Finck St SE1 200 C5
Finden Rd E7 68 EH64
Findhorn Av, Hayes 77 BV71
Findhorn St E14 85 EC72
Findon Cl SW18 120 DA86
Wimbledon Pk Rd
Findon Cl, Har. 60 CB62
Findon Gdns, Rain. 89 FG71
Findon Rd N9 46 DV46
Findon Rd W12 99 CU75
Fine Bush La (Harefield), Uxb. 59 BP58
Fingal St SE10 205 L10
Fingal St SE10 104 EF78
Finglesham Cl, Orp. 146 EX102
Westwell Cl
Finians Cl, Uxb. 76 BM66
Finland Quay SE16 203 L7
Finland Quay SE16 103 DY76
Finland Rd SE4 103 DY83
Finland St SE16 203 L7
Finland St SE16 103 DY76
Finlay Gdns, Add. 152 BJ105
Finlay St SW6 99 CX81
Finlays Cl, Chess. 156 CN106
Finnart Cl, Wey. 153 BQ105
Finnart Ho Dr, Wey. 153 BQ105
Vaillant Rd
Finnis St E2 84 DV69
Finnymore Rd, Dag. 88 EY66
Finsbury Av EC2 197 L7
Finsbury Circ EC2 197 L7
Finsbury Circ EC2 84 DR71
Finsbury Cotts N22 45 DL52
Clarence Rd
Finsbury Ct, Wal.Cr. 15 DY34
Parkside
Finsbury Est EC1 196 F3
Finsbury Est EC1 83 DN69
Finsbury Ho N22 45 DL53
Finsbury Mkt EC2 197 M5
Finsbury Mkt EC2 84 DS70
Finsbury Pk Av N4 66 DQ58
Finsbury Pk Rd N4 65 DP62
Finsbury Pavement EC2 197 L6
Finsbury Pavement EC2 84 DR71
Finsbury Rd N22 45 DM53
Finsbury Sq EC2 197 L6
Finsbury Sq EC2 84 DR71
Finsbury St EC2 197 K6
Finsbury St EC2 84 DR71
Finsbury Way, Bex. 126 EZ86
Finsen Rd SE5 102 DQ83
Finstock Rd W10 81 CX72
Finucane Dr, Orp. 146 EW101
Finucane Gdns, Rain. 89 FG65
Finucane Ri, Bushey 40 CC47
Finway Ct, Wat. 23 BT43
Whippendell Rd
Fiona Cl, Lthd. 170 CA124
Fir Cl, Walt. 135 BU101
Fir Dene, Orp. 145 EM104
Fir Gra Av, Wey. 153 BP106
Fir Gro, N.Mal. 139 CT100
Fir Gro, Wok. 166 AU119
Fir Rd, Felt. 116 BX92
Fir Rd, Sutt. 139 CZ102
Fir Tree Av, Mitch. 140 DG96
Fir Tree Av, Slou. 74 AT70
Fir Tree Av, West Dr. 94 BN76
Fir Tree Cl SW16 121 DJ92
Fir Tree Cl W5 80 CL72
Fir Tree Cl, Epsom 173 CW115
Fir Tree Cl (Ewell), Epsom 157 CT105
Fir Tree Cl, Esher 154 CC106
Fir Tree Cl, Grays 110 GD79
Fir Tree Cl, Lthd. 171 CJ123
Fir Tree Cl, Orp. 163 ET106
Highfield Av
Fir Tree Cl, Rom. 71 FD55
Fir Tree Gdns, Croy. 161 EA105
Fir Tree Gro, Cars. 158 DF108
Fir Tree Hill, Rick. 22 BM38
Fir Tree Pl, Ashf. 114 BN92
Percy Av
Fir Tree Rd, Bans. 157 CW114
Fir Tree Rd, Epsom 173 CV116
Fir Tree Rd, Houns. 96 BY84
Fir Tree Rd, Lthd. 171 CJ123
Fir Tree Wk, Dag. 71 FC62
Wheel Fm Dr
Fir Tree Wk, Enf. 30 DR41
Fir Tree Wk, Reig. 184 DD134
Fir Trees, Rom. 34 EV41
Fir Trees Cl SE16 203 L3
Fir Trees Cl SE16 85 DY74
Firbank Cl E16 86 EK71
Firbank Cl, Enf. 30 DQ42
Gladbeck Way
Firbank Dr, Wat. 40 BY45
Firbank Dr, Wok. 166 AV119
Firbank La, Wok. 166 AV119
Firbank Pl, Egh. 112 AV93
Firbank Rd SE15 102 DV82
Firbank Rd, Rom. 51 FB50
Fircroft Cl, Slou. 74 AU65
Fircroft Cl, Wok. 167 AZ118
Fircroft Cl
Fircroft Gdns, Har. 61 CE62
Fircroft Rd SW17 120 DF89
Fircroft Rd, Chess. 156 CM105
Firdene, Surb. 138 CQ102
Fire Bell All, Surb. 138 CL100
Fire Sta All, Barn. 27 CZ40
Christchurch La
Firecrest Dr NW3 64 DB62
Firefly Cl, Wall. 159 DL108
Firefly Gdns E6 86 EL70
Jack Dash Way
Firethorn Cl, Edg. 42 CQ49
Larkspur Gro
Firfield Rd, Add. 152 BG105
Firfields, Wey. 153 BP107
Firham Pk Av, Rom. 52 FN52
Firhill Rd SE6 123 EA91
Firlands, Wey. 153 BS107

Firmin Rd, Dart. 128 FJ85
Firmingers Rd, Orp. 165 FB106
Firs, The E17 67 DY57
Leucha Rd
Firs, The N20 44 DD46
Firs, The W5 79 CK71
Firs, The, Bex. 127 FD88
Dartford Rd
Firs, The, Brwd. 54 FU44
Firs, The, Cat. 176 DR122
Yorke Gate Rd
Firs, The, Tad. 183 CZ126
Brighton Rd
Firs, The, Wal.Cr. 14 DS27
Firs Av N10 64 DG55
Firs Av N11 44 DG51
Firs Av SW14 98 CQ84
Firs Cl N10 64 DG55
Firs Av
Firs Cl SE23 123 DX87
Firs Cl, Esher 155 CE107
Firs Cl, Iver 75 BC67
Thornbridge Rd
Firs Cl, Mitch. 141 DH96
Firs Dr, Houns. 95 BV80
Firs Dr, Loug. 33 EN39
Firs Dr, Slou. 75 AZ74
Firs End (Chalfont St. Peter), Ger.Cr. 56 AY55
Firs End (Chalfont St. Peter), Ger.Cr. 56 AY55
Southside
Firs La N13 46 DQ48
Firs La N21 46 DQ47
Firs La, Pot.B. 12 DB33
Firs Pk Av N21 46 DR46
Firs Pk Gdns N21 46 DQ46
Firs Rd, Ken. 175 DP115
Firs Wk, Nthwd. 39 BR51
Firs Wk, Wdf.Grn. 48 EG50
Firs Wd Cl, Pot.B. 12 DF32
Firsby Av, Croy. 143 DX102
Firsby Rd N16 66 DT60
Firscroft N13 46 DQ48
Firsdene Cl, Cher. 151 BD107
Slade Rd
Firsgrove Cres, Brwd. 54 FV49
Firsgrove Rd, Brwd. 54 FV49
Firside Gro, Sid. 125 ET88
First Av E12 68 EL63
First Av E13 86 EG69
First Av E17 67 EA57
First Av N18 46 DW49
First Av NW4 63 CW56
First Av SW14 98 CS83
First Av W3 81 CT74
First Av W10 81 CZ70
First Av, Bexh. 106 EW80
First Av, Dag. 89 FB68
First Av, Enf. 30 DT44
First Av, Epsom 156 CS109
First Av, Grav. 130 GE88
First Av, Grays 109 FU79
First Av, Hayes 77 BT74
First Av, Rom. 70 EW57
First Av, Walt. 135 BV100
First Av, Wat. 24 BW35
First Av, Wem. 61 CK61
First Av, W.Mol. 136 BZ98
First Cl, W.Mol. 136 CC97
First Cross Rd, Twick. 117 CE89
First Dr NW10 80 CQ66
First Slip, Lthd. 171 CG118
First St SW3 198 C8
First St SW3 100 DE77
First Way, Wem. 62 CP63
Firstway SW20 139 CW96
Firswood Av, Epsom 157 CT106
Firth Gdns SW6 99 CY81
Firtree Ct, Borwd. 26 CM42
Firwood Cl, Wok. 166 AS119
Firwood Rd, Vir.W. 132 AS100
Fish St Hill EC3 197 L10
Fish St Hill EC3 84 DR73
Fisher Cl, Croy. 142 DT102
Grant Rd
Fisher Cl, Grnf. 78 CA69
Gosling Cl
Fisher Cl, Kings L. 6 BN29
Fisher Cl, Walt. 153 BV105
Fisher Rd, Har. 41 CF54
Fisher St E16 86 EG71
Fisher St WC1 196 B7
Fisher St WC1 83 DM71
Fisherman Cl, Rich. 117 CJ91
Locksmeade Rd
Fishermans Dr SE16 203 J4
Fishermans Dr SE16 103 DX75
Fishermans Hill, Grav. 130 GB85
Fisherman's Wk E14 203 P2
Fisherman's Wk E14 85 EA74
Fishermans Wk SE28 105 ES75
Tugboat St
Fishers Cl, Bushey 24 BY41
Fishers Cl, Wal.Cr. 15 EA34
Fishers Ct SE14 103 DX81
Besson St
Fishers La W4 98 CR77
Fishers La, Epp. 17 ES32
Fishers Way, Belv. 89 FC74
Fishersdene, Esher 155 CG108
Fisherton St NW8 82 DD70
Fishguard Spur, Slou. 92 AV75
Fishguard Way E16 105 EP75
Barge Ho Rd
Fishing Temple, Stai. 133 BF95
Fishponds Rd SW17 120 DE91
Fishponds Rd, Kes. 162 EK106
Fisons Rd E16 205 M3
Fisons Rd E16 86 EG74
Fitzalan Rd N3 63 CY55
Fitzalan Rd, Esher 155 CE108
Fitzalan St SE11 200 C8
Fitzalan St SE11 101 DM77
Fitzgeorge Av W14 99 CY77
Fitzgeorge Av, N.Mal. 138 CR95
Fitzgerald Av SW14 98 CS83
Fitzgerald Cl E11 68 EG57
Fitzgerald Rd
Fitzgerald Ho E14 85 EB72
Fitzgerald Ho, Hayes 77 BV74
Fitzgerald Rd E11 68 EG57
Fitzgerald Rd SW14 98 CR83
Fitzgerald Rd, T.Ditt. 137 CG100
Fitzhardinge St W1 194 F8
Fitzhardinge St W1 82 DG72
Fitzherbert Ho, Rich. 118 CM86
Kingsmead
Fitzhugh Gro SW18 120 DD86
Fitzhugh Gro Est SW18 120 DD86
Fitzilian Av, Rom. 52 FM53
Fitzjames Av W14 99 CY77
Fitzjames Av, Croy. 142 DU103
Fitzjohn Av, Barn. 27 CY43
Fitzjohn's Av NW3 64 DD64
Fitzmaurice Pl W1 199 J2
Fitzmaurice Pl W1 83 DH73
Fitzneal St W12 81 CT72
Fitzrobert Pl, Egh. 113 BA93
Fitzroy Cl N6 64 DF60
Fitzroy Ct W1 195 L5
Fitzroy Cres W4 98 CR80
Fitzroy Gdns SE19 122 DS94
Fitzroy Ms W1 195 K5
Fitzroy Pk N6 64 DF60
Fitzroy Rd NW1 82 DG67
Fitzroy Sq W1 195 K5
Fitzroy Sq W1 83 DJ70
Fitzroy St W1 195 K5
Fitzroy St W1 83 DJ70
Fitzroy Yd NW1 82 DG67
Fitzroy Rd
Fitzstephen Rd, Dag. 70 EV64
Fitzwarren Gdns N19 65 DJ60
Fitzwilliam Av, Rich. 98 CM82
Fitzwilliam Ms E16 205 M2
Fitzwilliam Rd SW4 101 DJ83
Fitzwygram Cl, Hmptn. 116 CC92
Five Acre NW9 43 CT53
Five Acres, Kings L. 6 BM29
Five Acres, St.Alb. 9 CK25
Five Acres Av, St.Alb. 8 BZ29
Five Bell All E14 85 DZ73
Three Colt St
Five Elms Rd, Brom. 144 EH104
Five Elms Rd, Dag. 70 EZ62
Five Flds Cl, Wat. 40 BZ48
Five Oaks, Add. 151 BF107
Five Oaks La, Chig. 50 EY51
Five Points, Iver 75 BC69
Five Wents, Swan. 147 FG96
Fiveacre Cl, Th.Hth. 141 DN100
Fiveash Rd, Grav. 131 GF87
Fives Ct SE11 200 F8
Fiveways Rd SW9 101 DP82
Fladbury Rd N15 66 DR58
Fladgate Rd E11 68 EE58
Flag Cl, Croy. 143 DX102
Flag Wk, Pnr. 59 BU58
Eastcote Rd
Flagstaff Cl, Wal.Abb. 15 EB33
Flagstaff Rd, Wal.Abb. 15 EB33
Flambard Rd, Har. 61 CG58
Flamborough Cl, West. 178 EH119
Flamborough Rd, Ruis. 59 BU62
Flamborough St E14 85 DY72
Flamingo Gdns, Nthlt. 78 BY69
Jetstar Way
Flamingo Wk, Horn. 89 FG65
Flamstead End Rd (Cheshunt), Wal.Cr. 14 DV28
Flamstead Gdns, Dag. 88 EW66
Flamstead Rd
Flamstead Rd, Dag. 88 EW66
Flamsted Av, Wem. 80 CN65
Flamsteed Rd SE7 104 EL78
Flanchford Rd W12 99 CT76
Flanchford Rd, Reig. 183 CX134
Flanders Ct, Egh. 113 BC92
Flanders Cres SW17 120 DF94
Flanders Rd E6 87 EM68
Flanders Rd W4 98 CS77
Flanders Way E9 85 DX65
Flank St E1 84 DU73
Dock St
Flash La, Enf. 29 DP37
Flask Cotts NW3 64 DD63
New End Sq
Flask Wk NW3 64 DD63
Flat Iron Sq SE1 84 DQ74
Union St
Flaunden Bottom, Chesh. 20 AY36
Flaunden Bottom, Hem.H. 20 AY35
Flaunden Hill, Hem.H. 5 AZ33
Flaunden La, Hem.H. 5 BB32
Flaunden La, Rick. 5 BD33
Flaunden Pk, Hem.H. 5 BA32
Flavell Ms SE10 205 J10
Flavell Ms SE10 104 EE78
Flaxen Cl E4 47 EB48
Flaxen Rd
Flaxen Rd E4 47 EB48
Flaxley Rd, Mord. 140 DB100
Flaxman Ct W1 195 M9
Flaxman Rd SE5 101 DP82
Flaxman Ter WC1 195 N3
Flaxman Ter WC1 83 DK69
Flaxton Rd SE18 105 ER81
Flecker Cl, Stan. 41 CF50
Fleece Dr N9 46 DU49
Fleece Rd, Surb. 137 CJ102
Fleece Wk N7 83 DL65
Manger Rd
Fleeming Cl E17 47 DZ54
Pennant Ter
Fleeming Rd E17 47 DZ54
Fleet Av, Dart. 128 FQ88
Fleet Av, Upmin. 73 FR58
Fleet Cl, Ruis. 59 BQ58
Fleet Cl, Upmin. 73 FR58
Fleet Cl, W.Mol. 136 BZ99
Fleet La, W.Mol. 136 BZ100
Fleet Pl EC4 83 DN72
Farringdon St
Fleet Rd NW3 64 DE64
Fleet Rd, Dart. 128 FQ88
Fleet Rd, Grav. 130 GC90
Fleet Sq WC1 196 B3
Fleet St EC4 196 D9
Fleet St EC4 83 DN72
Fleet St Hill E1 84 DU70
Weaver St
Fleetdale Par, Dart. 128 FQ88
Fleet Av
Fleetside, W.Mol. 136 BZ100
Fleetway, Egh. 133 BC97
Fleetway Business Pk, Grnf. 79 CH68
Fleetwood Cl E16 86 EK71
Fleetwood Cl, Ch.St.G. 36 AU49
Fleetwood Cl, Chess. 155 CK108
Fleetwood Cl, Croy. 142 DS104
Chepstow Ri
Fleetwood Cl, Tad. 173 CW120
Fleetwood Ct E6 87 EM71
Evelyn Denington Rd
Fleetwood Ct, W.Byf. 152 BG113
Fleetwood Gro W3 80 CS73
East Acton La
Fleetwood Rd NW10 63 CU64
Fleetwood Rd, Kings.T. 138 CP97
Fleetwood Rd, Slou. 74 AT74
Fleetwood Sq, Kings.T. 138 CP97
Fleetwood St N16 66 DS61
Stoke Newington Ch St
Fleetwood Way, Wat. 40 BW49
Fleming Cl (Cheshunt), Wal.Cr. 14 DU26
Fleming Ct W2 82 DD71
St. Marys Ter
Fleming Ct, Croy. 159 DN106
Fleming Dr N21 29 DM43
Sydenham Av
Fleming Gdns, Rom. 52 FK54
Bartholomew Dr
Fleming Gdns, Til. 111 GJ81
Fielding Av
Fleming Mead, Mitch. 120 DE94
Fleming Rd SE17 101 DP79
Fleming Rd, Grays 109 FW77
Fleming Rd, Sthl. 78 CB72
Fleming Way SE28 88 EX73
Fleming Way, Islw. 97 CF83
Flemings, Brwd. 53 FW51
Flemish Flds, Cher. 134 BG101
Flemming Av, Ruis. 59 BV60
Flempton Rd E10 67 DY60
Fletcher Cl E6 87 EP72
Trader Rd
Fletcher Cl, Cher. 151 BE107
Fletcher La E10 67 EC59
Fletcher Path SE8 103 EA80
New Butt La
Fletcher Rd W4 98 CQ76
Fletcher Rd, Cher. 151 BD107
Fletcher Rd, Chig. 49 ET50
Fletcher St E1 84 DU73
Cable St
Fletchers Cl, Brom. 144 EH98
Fletching Rd E5 66 DW62
Fletching Rd SE7 104 EJ79
Fletton Rd N11 45 DL52
Fleur de Lis St E1 197 N5
Fleur de Lis St E1 84 DS70
Fleur Gates SW19 119 CX87
Princes Way
Flexmere Gdns N17 46 DR53
Flexmere Rd
Flexmere Rd N17 46 DR53
Flight App NW9 43 CT54
Flimwell Cl, Brom. 124 EE92
Flint Cl, Bans. 158 DB114
Flint Cl, Red. 184 DF133
Flint Down Cl, Orp. 146 EU95
Flint St SE17 201 L9
Flint St SE17 102 DR77
Flint St, Grays 109 FV79
Flintlock Cl, Stai. 94 BG84
Flintmill Cres SE3 104 EL82
Flinton St SE17 201 N10
Flinton St SE17 102 DS78
Flitcroft St WC2 195 N8
Floats, The, Sev. 190 FE121
Flock Mill Pl SW18 120 DB88
Flockton St SE16 202 B5
Flodden Rd SE5 102 DQ81
Flood La, Twick. 117 CG88
Church La
Flood Pas SE18 105 EM77
Samuel St
Flood St SW3 100 DE78
Flood Wk SW3 100 DE79
Flora Cl E14 85 EB72
Flora Gdns W6 99 CV77
Ravenscourt Rd
Flora Gdns, Croy. 161 EC111
Flora Gdns, Rom. 70 EW58
Flora St, Belv. 106 EZ78
Victoria St
Floral Ct, Ash. 171 CJ118
Rosedale
Floral Dr, St.Alb. 9 CK26
Floral St WC2 195 P10
Floral St WC2 83 DL73
Florence Av, Add. 152 BG111
Florence Av, Enf. 30 DQ41
Florence Av, Mord. 140 DC99
Florence Cantwell Wk N19 65 DL59
Hillrise Rd
Florence Cl, Grays 110 FY79
Florence Cl, Horn. 72 FL61
Florence Cl, Walt. 135 BV101
Florence Rd
Florence Cl, Wat. 23 BU35
Florence Dr, Enf. 30 DQ41
Florence Elson Cl E12 69 EN63
Grantham Rd
Florence Gdns W4 98 CQ79
Florence Gdns, Rom. 70 EW59
Roxy Av
Florence Gdns, Stai. 114 BH94
Florence Nightingale Ho N1 84 DR65
Clephane Rd
Florence Rd E6 86 EJ67
Florence Rd E13 86 EF68
Florence Rd N4 65 DN60
Florence Rd SE2 106 EW76
Florence Rd SE14 103 DZ81
Florence Rd SW19 120 DB93
Florence Rd W4 98 CR76
Florence Rd W5 80 CL73
Florence Rd, Beck. 143 DX96
Florence Rd, Brom. 144 EG95
Florence Rd, Felt. 115 BV88
Florence Rd, Kings.T. 118 CM94
Florence Rd, S.Croy. 160 DR109
Florence Rd, Sthl. 96 BX77
Florence Rd, Walt. 135 BV101
Florence St E16 86 EF70
Florence St N1 83 DP66
Florence St NW4 63 CW56
Florence Ter SE14 103 DZ81
Florence Way SW12 120 DF88
Florfield Pas E8 84 DV65
Reading La
Florfield Rd E8 84 DV65
Reading La
Florian Av, Sutt. 158 DD105
Florian Rd SW15 99 CY84
Florida Cl, Bushey 41 CD47
Florida Rd, Th.Hth. 141 DP95
Florida St E2 84 DU69
Floriston Av, Uxb. 77 BQ66
Floriston Cl, Stan. 41 CH53
Floriston Gdns, Stan. 41 CH53
Floss St SW15 99 CW82
Flower & Dean Wk E1 84 DT71
Thrawl St
Flower Cres, Cher. 151 BB107
Flower La NW7 43 CT50
Flower La, Gdse. 187 DY128
Flower Pot Cl N15 66 DT58
St. Ann's Rd
Flower Wk, The SW7 100 DC75
Flowerfield, Sev. 181 FF117
Flowerhill Way, Grav. 130 GE94
Flowers Ms N19 65 DJ61
Tollhouse Way
Flowersmead SW17 120 DG89
Floyd Rd SE7 104 EJ78
Floyds La, Wok. 168 BG116
Fludyer St SE13 104 EE84
Flux's La, Epp. 18 EU33
Flyer's Way, The, West. 189 ER126
Foley Ms, Esher 155 CE108
Foley Rd, Esher 155 CE108
Foley Rd, West. 178 EK118
Foley St W1 195 K7
Foley St W1 83 DJ71
Folgate St E1 197 N6
Folgate St E1 84 DS71
Foliot St W12 81 CT72
Folkes La, Upmin. 73 FT57
Folkestone Ct, Slou. 93 BA78
Folkestone Rd E6 87 EN68
Folkestone Rd E17 67 EB56
Folkestone Rd N18 46 DU49
Folkingham La NW9 42 CR53
Folkington Cor N12 43 CZ50
Follet Dr, Abb.L. 7 BT31
Follett Cl, Wind. 112 AV86
Follett St E14 85 EC72
Folly Cl, Rad. 25 CF36
Folly La E4 47 DZ52
Folly La E17 47 DY53
Folly Ms W11 81 CZ72
Portobello Rd
Folly Pathway, Rad. 25 CF35
Folly Wall E14 204 E5
Folly Wall E14 103 EC75
Follyfield Rd, Bans. 158 DA114
Font Hills N2 44 DC54
Fontaine Rd SW16 121 DM94
Fontarabia Rd SW11 100 DG84
Fontayne Av, Chig. 49 EQ49
Fontayne Av, Rain. 89 FE66
Fontayne Av, Rom. 51 FE54
Fontenoy Rd SW12 121 DH89
Fonteyne Gdns, Wdf.Grn. 48 EK54
Lechmere Av
Fonthill Cl SE20 142 DU96
Selby Rd
Fonthill Ms N4 65 DN61
Lennox Rd
Fonthill Rd N4 65 DM60
Fontley Way SW15 119 CU87
Fontmell Cl, Ashf. 114 BN92
Fontmell Pk, Ashf. 114 BM92
Fontwell Cl, Har. 41 CE52
Fontwell Cl, Nthlt. 78 CA65
Fontwell Dr, Brom. 145 EN99
Fontwell Pk Gdns, Horn. 72 FL63
Foord Cl, Dart. 129 FS89
Football La, Har. 61 CE60
Footbury Hill Rd, Orp. 146 EU101
Footpath, The SW15 119 CU85
Foots Cray High St, Sid. 126 EW93
Foots Cray La, Sid. 126 EW88
Footscray Rd SE9 125 EN86
Footway, The SE9 125 EQ87
Forbench Cl, Wok. 168 BH122
Forbes Av, Pot.B. 12 DD33
Forbes Cl NW2 63 CU62
Forbes Cl, Horn. 71 FH60
St. Leonards Way
Forbes Ct SE19 122 DS92
Forbes St E1 84 DU72
Ellen St
Forbes Way, Ruis. 59 BV61
Forburg Rd N16 66 DU60
Force Grn La, West. 179 ER124
Ford Cl E3 85 DY68
Roman Rd
Ford Cl, Ashf. 114 BL93
Ford Cl, Bushey 24 CC42
Ford Cl, Har. 61 CD59
Ford Cl, Rain. 89 FF66
Ford Cl, Shep. 134 BN98
Ford Cl, Th.Hth. 141 DP100
Ford End (Denham), Uxb. 57 BF61
Ford End, Wdf.Grn. 48 EH51
Ford La, Iver 76 BG72
Ford La, Rain. 89 FF66
Ford Rd E3 85 DY67
Ford Rd, Ashf. 114 BM91
Ford Rd, Cher. 134 BH102
Ford Rd, Dag. 88 EZ66
Ford Rd, Grav. 130 GB85
Ford Rd (Old Woking), Wok. 167 BB120
Ford Sq E1 84 DV71
Ford St E3 85 DY67
Ford St E16 86 EF72
Fordbridge Cl, Cher. 134 BH102
Fordbridge Rd, Ashf. 114 BL93
Fordbridge Rd, Shep. 135 BS100
Fordbridge Rd, Sun. 135 BS100
Fordcroft Rd, Orp. 146 EV99
Forde Av, Brom. 144 EJ97
Fordel Rd SE6 123 ED88
Fordham Cl, Barn. 28 DE41
Fordham Cl, Horn. 72 FN59
Fordham Rd, Barn. 28 DD41
Fordham St E1 84 DU72
Fordhook Av W5 80 CM73
Fordingley Rd W9 81 CZ69
Fordington Rd N6 64 DF57
Fordmill Rd SE6 123 EA89
Fords Gro N21 46 DQ46
Fords Pk Rd E16 86 EG72
Fordwater Rd, Cher. 134 BH102
Fordwater Trd Est, Cher. 134 BJ102
Fordwich Cl, Orp. 145 ET101
Fordwych Rd NW2 63 CY64
Fordyce Cl, Horn. 72 FM59
Fordyce Rd SE13 123 EC86
Fordyke Rd, Dag. 70 EZ61
Fore St EC2 197 J7
Fore St EC2 84 DQ71
Fore St N9 46 DU50
Fore St N18 46 DT51
Fore St, Pnr. 59 BU57
Fore St Av EC2 197 K7
Forefield, St.Alb. 8 CA27
Foreland Ct NW4 43 CY53
Foreland St SE18 105 ER77
Plumstead Rd
Foreman Ct W6 99 CW77
Hammersmith Bdy
Foremark Cl, Ilf. 49 ET50
Foreshore SE8 203 N9
Foreshore SE8 103 DZ77
Forest, The E11 68 EE56
Forest App E4 48 EE45
Forest App, Wdf.Grn. 48 EF52
Forest Av E4 48 EE45
Forest Av, Chig. 49 EN50
Forest Business Pk E17 67 DX59
Forest Cl E11 68 EF57
Forest Cl, Chis. 145 EN95
Forest Cl, Wal.Abb. 32 EH37
Forest Cl, Wok. 167 BD115
Forest Cl, Wdf.Grn. 48 EH48
Forest Ct E4 48 EF46
Forest Ct E11 68 EE56
Forest Cres, Ash. 172 CN116
Forest Cft SE23 122 DV89
Forest Dr E12 68 EK62
Forest Dr, Epp. 33 ES36
Forest Dr, Kes. 162 EL105
Forest Dr, Sun. 115 BT94
Forest Dr, Tad. 173 CZ121
Forest Dr, Wdf.Grn. 47 ED52
Forest Dr E E11 67 ED59
Forest Dr W E11 67 EC59
Forest Edge, Buck.H. 48 EJ49
Forest Gdns N17 46 DT54
Forest Gate NW9 62 CS57
Forest Glade E4 48 EE49
Forest Glade E11 68 EE58
Forest Glade, Epp. 18 EY27
Forest Gro E8 84 DT66
Forest Hts, Buck.H. 48 EG47
Forest Hill Business Cen SE23 122 DW89
Forest Hill Ind Est SE23 122 DW89
Perry Vale
Forest Hill Rd SE22 122 DV85
Forest Hill Rd SE23 122 DV85
Forest Ind Pk, Ilf. 49 ES53
Forest La E7 68 EE64
Forest La E15 68 EE64
Forest La, Chig. 49 EN50
Forest La, Lthd. 169 BT124
Forest Mt Rd, Wdf.Grn. 47 ED52
Forest Ridge, Beck. 143 EA97
Forest Ridge, Kes. 162 EL105
Forest Ri E17 67 ED57
Forest Rd E7 68 EG63
Forest Rd E8 84 DT65
Forest Rd E11 67 ED59
Forest Rd E17 66 DW56
Forest Rd N9 46 DV46
Forest Rd N17 66 DW56
Forest Rd, Enf. 31 DY36
Forest Rd, Erith 107 FG81
Forest Rd, Felt. 116 BW89
Forest Rd, Ilf. 49 ES53
Forest Rd, Lthd. 169 BU123
Forest Rd, Loug. 32 EK41
Forest Rd, Rich. 98 CN80
Forest Rd, Rom. 71 FB55
Forest Rd, Sutt. 140 DA102
Forest Rd (Cheshunt), Wal.Cr. 15 DX29
Forest Rd, Wat. 7 BV33
Forest Rd, Wok. 167 BD115
Forest Rd, Wdf.Grn. 67 EB55
Forest Side E4 48 EF45
Forest Side E7 68 EH63
Capel Rd
Forest Side, Buck.H. 48 EJ46
Forest Side, Epp. 17 ER33
Forest Side, Wal.Abb. 32 EJ36
Forest Side, Wor.Pk. 139 CT102
Forest St E7 68 EG64
Forest Vw E4 47 ED45
Forest Vw E11 68 EF59
High Rd Leytonstone
Forest Vw Av E10 67 ED57
Forest Vw Rd E12 68 EL63
Forest Vw Rd E17 47 EC53
Forest Vw Rd, Loug. 32 EK42
Forest Wk, Bushey 24 BZ39
Millbrook Rd
Forest Way N19 65 DJ61
Hargrave Pk
Forest Way, Ash. 172 CM117
Forest Way, Loug. 32 EK35
Forest Way, Orp. 145 ET99
Forest Way, Sid. 125 ER87
Forest Way, Wal.Abb. 32 EK35
Forest Way, Wdf.Grn. 48 EH49
Forestdale N14 45 DK49
Forester Rd SE15 102 DV84
Foresters Cl, Wall. 159 DK108
Foresters Cl, Wal.Cr. 14 DS27

Foresters Cl, Wok. 166 AT118
Foresters Cres, Bexh. 107 FB84
Foresters Dr E17 67 ED56
Foresters Dr, Wall. 159 DK108
Forestholme Cl SE23 122 DW89
Forfar Rd N22 45 DP53
Forfar Rd SW11 100 DG81
Forge Av, Couls. 175 DN120
Forge Br La, Couls. 175 DH121
Forge Cl, Brom. 144 EG102
Forge Cl, Hayes 95 BR79
High St
Forge Cl, Kings L. 6 BG31
Forge Cotts W5 79 CK74
Ealing Grn
Forge Dr, Esher 155 CG108
Forge End, St.Alb. 8 CA26
Forge End, Wok. 166 AY117
Forge End, Wok. 166 AY117
Vale Fm Rd
Forge La (Horton Kirby), Dart. 148 FQ98
Forge La, Felt. 116 BY92
Forge La, Grav. 131 GM89
Forge La, Nthwd. 39 BS52
Forge La, Sun. 135 BU97
Forge La, Sutt. 157 CY108
Forge Ms, Sun. 135 BU97
Forge La
Forge Pl NW1 82 DG65
Malden Cres
Forge Way, Sev. 165 FF111
Forgefield, West. 178 EK116
Main Rd
Forlong Path, Nthlt. 78 BY65
Arnold Rd
Forman Pl N16 66 DT63
Farleigh Rd
Formby Av, Stan. 61 CJ55
Formby Cl, Slou. 93 BC77
Formosa St W9 82 DB70
Formunt Cl E16 86 EF71
Vincent St
Forres Gdns NW11 64 DA58
Forrest Gdns SW16 141 DM97
Forrester Path SE26 123 DX91
Forris Av, Hayes 77 BT74
Forset St W1 194 C8
Forset St W1 82 DE72
Forstal Cl, Brom. 144 EG97
Ridley Rd
Forster Rd E17 67 DY58
Forster Rd N17 66 DT55
Forster Rd SW2 121 DL87
Forster Rd, Beck. 143 DY97
Forster Rd, Croy. 142 DQ101
Windmill Rd
Forsters Cl, Rom. 70 EZ58
Forster's Way SW18 120 DB88
Forsters Way, Hayes 77 BV72
Forston St N1 84 DR68
Cropley St
Forsyte Cres SE19 142 DS95
Forsyth Gdns SE17 101 DP79
Forsyth Path, Wok. 151 BD113
Forsyth Pl, Enf. 30 DS43
Forsyth Rd, Wok. 151 BC114
Forsythia Cl, Ilf. 69 EP64
Forsythia Gdns, Slou. 92 AY76
Fort La, Reig. 184 DB130
Fort Rd SE1 202 A9
Fort Rd SE1 102 DT77
Fort Rd, Nthlt. 78 CA66
Fort Rd, Sev. 181 FC115
Fort Rd, Tad. 182 CP131
Fort Rd, Tad. 182 CP131
Boxhill Rd
Fort Rd, Til. 111 GH84
Fort St E1 197 N7
Fort St E16 86 EH74
Forterie Gdns, Ilf. 70 EU62
Fortescue Av E8 84 DV66
Mentmore Ter
Fortescue Av, Twick. 116 CC90
Fortescue Rd SW19 120 DD94
Fortescue Rd, Edg. 42 CR53
Fortescue Rd, Wey. 152 BM105
Fortess Gro NW5 65 DH64
Fortess Rd
Fortess Rd NW5 65 DH64
Fortess Wk NW5 65 DH64
Fortess Rd
Forth Rd, Upmin. 73 FR58
Forthbridge Rd SW11 100 DG84
Fortin Cl, S.Ock. 91 FU73
Fortin Path, S.Ock. 91 FU73
Fortin Way, S.Ock. 91 FU73
Fortis Cl E16 86 EJ72
Fortis Grn N2 64 DE56
Fortis Grn N10 64 DE56
Fortis Grn Av N2 64 DF55
Fortis Grn Rd N10 64 DG55
Fortismere Av N10 64 DG55
Fortnam Rd N19 65 DK61
Fortnums Acre, Stan. 41 CF51
Fortrose Gdns SW2 121 DK88
New Pk Rd
Fortrye Cl, Grav. 130 GE89
Fortuna Cl N7 83 DM65
Vulcan Way
Fortune Gate Rd NW10 80 CS67
Fortune Grn Rd NW6 64 DA63
Fortune La, Borwd. 25 CK44
Fortune St EC1 197 J5
Fortune St EC1 84 DQ70
Fortune Wk SE28 105 ER76
Broadwater Rd
Fortune Way NW10 81 CU69
Fortunes Mead, Nthlt. 78 BY65
Forty Acre La E16 86 EG71
Forty Av, Wem. 62 CM62
Forty Cl, Wem. 62 CM61
Forty Footpath SW14 98 CQ83
Forty Hill, Enf. 30 DT38
Forty La, Wem. 62 CP61
Fortyfoot Rd, Lthd. 171 CJ121
Forum, The, W.Mol. 136 CB98
Forum Way, Edg. 42 CN51
High St
Forumside, Edg. 42 CN51
High St
Forval Cl, Mitch. 140 DF99
Forward Dr, Har. 61 CF56
Fosbury Ms W2 82 DB73
Inverness Ter
Foscote Ms W9 82 DA71
Amberley Rd
Foscote Rd NW4 63 CV58
Foskett Rd SW6 99 CZ82
Foss Av, Croy. 159 DN106
Foss Rd SW17 120 DD91
Fossdene Rd SE7 104 EH78
Fossdyke Cl, Hayes 78 BY71
Fosse Way W13 79 CG71
Fosse Way, W.Byf. 151 BF113
Brantwood Dr
Fossil Rd SE13 103 EA83
Fossington Rd, Belv. 106 EX77
Fossway, Dag. 70 EW61
Foster Cl (Cheshunt), Wal.Cr. 15 DX30
Foster La EC2 197 H8
Foster La EC2 84 DQ72
Foster Rd E13 86 EG70
Foster Rd W3 80 CS73
Foster Rd W4 98 CR78
Foster St NW4 63 CW56
Foster Wk NW4 63 CW56
New Brent St
Fosterdown, Gdse. 186 DV129
Fosters Cl E18 48 EH53
Fosters Cl, Chis. 125 EM92
Fothergill Cl E13 86 EG68
Fothergill Dr N21 29 DM43
Fotheringham Rd, Enf. 30 DT42
Fotherley Rd, Rick. 37 BF47
Foubert's Pl W1 195 K9
Foubert's Pl W1 83 DJ72
Foulden Rd N16 66 DT63
Foulden Ter N16 66 DT63
Foulden Rd
Foulis Ter SW7 198 A10
Foulis Ter SW7 100 DD78
Foulser Rd SW17 120 DF90
Foulsham Rd, Th.Hth. 142 DQ97
Founder Cl E6 87 EP72
Trader Rd
Founders Ct EC2 197 K8
Founders Dr (Denham), Uxb. 57 BF58
Founders Gdns SE19 122 DQ94
Foundry Cl SE16 203 K2
Foundry Cl SE16 85 DY74
Foundry La, Slou. 93 BB83
Foundry Ms NW1 195 L4
Fount St SW8 101 DK80
Fountain Cl, Uxb. 77 BQ71
New Rd
Fountain Ct EC4 196 D10
Fountain Dr SE19 122 DT91
Fountain Dr, Cars. 158 DF109
Fountain Grn Sq SE16 102 DU75
Bermondsey Wall E
Fountain La, Sev. 191 FP122
Fountain Ms N5 66 DQ63
Kelross Rd
Fountain Pl SW9 101 DN81
Fountain Pl, Wal.Abb. 15 EC34
Fountain Rd SW17 120 DD92
Fountain Rd, Th.Hth. 142 DQ96
Fountain Sq SW1 199 H8
Fountain Sq SW1 101 DH77
Fountain St E2 84 DT69
Columbia Rd
Fountain Wk, Grav. 130 GE86
Fountains, The, Loug. 48 EJ45
Fallow Flds
Fountains Av, Felt. 116 BZ90
Fountains Cl, Felt. 116 BZ89
Fountains Cres N14 45 DL45
Fountayne Rd N15 66 DU56
Fountayne Rd N16 66 DU61
Four Acres, Cob. 154 BY113
Four Seasons Cl E3 85 EA68
Four Seasons Cres, Sutt. 139 CZ103
Kimpton Rd
Four Tubs, The, Bushey 41 CD45
Four Wents, Cob. 153 BV113
Four Wents, The E4 47 ED47
Kings Rd
Fouracres SW12 121 DH89
Little Dimocks
Fouracres, Enf. 31 DY39
Fourland Wk, Edg. 42 CQ51
Fournier St E1 197 P6
Fournier St E1 84 DT71
Fourth Av E12 69 EM63
Fourth Av W10 81 CY70
Fourth Av, Grays 109 FU79
Fourth Av, Hayes 77 BT74
Fourth Av, Rom. 71 FD60
Fourth Av, Wat. 24 BX35
Fourth Cross Rd, Twick. 117 CD89
Fourth Dr, Couls. 175 DK116
Fourth Way, Wem. 62 CQ63
Fowey Av, Ilf. 68 EK57
Fowey Cl E1 202 D2
Fowler Cl SW11 100 DD83
Fowler Rd E7 68 EG63
Fowler Rd N1 83 DP66
Halton Rd
Fowler Rd, Ilf. 50 EV51
Fowler Rd, Mitch. 140 DG96
Fowlers Cl, Sid. 126 EY92
Thursland Rd
Fowlers Mead, Wok. 150 AS109
Windsor Rd
Fowlers Wk W5 79 CK70
Fowley Cl, Wal.Cr. 15 DZ34
Fowley Mead Pk, Wal.Cr. 15 EA34
Fownes St SW11 100 DE83
Fox & Knot St EC1 196 G6
Fox Cl E1 84 DW70
Fox Cl E16 86 EG71
Fox Cl, Borwd. 25 CK44
Rodgers Cl
Fox Cl, Bushey 24 CB42
Fox Cl, Orp. 164 EU106
Fox Cl, Rom. 51 FB50
Fox Cl, Wey. 153 BR106
Fox Cl, Wok. 167 BD115
Fox Covert, Lthd. 171 CD124
Fox Gro, Walt. 135 BV101
Fox Hill SE19 122 DT94
Fox Hill, Kes. 162 EJ106
Fox Hill Gdns SE19 122 DT94
Fox Hollow Cl SE18 105 ES78
Fox Hollow Dr, Bexh. 106 EX83
Fox Ho Rd, Belv. 107 FB77
Fox La N13 45 DM48
Fox La W5 80 CL70
Fox La, Cat. 175 DP121
Fox La, Kes. 162 EH106
Fox La, Lthd. 170 BY124
Fox La, Reig. 184 DB131
Fox La N, Cher. 133 BF102
Fox La S, Cher. 133 BF102
Guildford St
Fox Manor Way, Grays 109 FV79
Fox Rd E16 86 EF71
Fox Rd, Slou. 92 AX77
Foxacre, Cat. 176 DS122
Town End Cl
Foxberry Rd SE4 103 DY83
Foxberry Wk, Grav. 130 GD91
Rowmarsh Cl
Foxborough Cl, Slou. 93 AZ78
Foxborough Gdns SE4 123 EA85
Foxbourne Rd SW17 120 DG89
Foxburrow Rd, Chig. 50 EX50
Foxbury Av, Chis. 125 ER93
Foxbury Cl, Brom. 124 EH93
Foxbury Cl, Orp. 164 EU106
Foxbury Dr
Foxbury Dr, Orp. 164 EU107
Foxbury Rd, Brom. 124 EG93
Foxcombe, Croy. 161 EB107
Foxcombe Cl E6 86 EK68
Boleyn Rd
Foxcombe Rd SW15 119 CU88
Alton Rd
Foxcote SE5 102 DS78
Foxcroft Rd SE18 105 EP81
Foxdell, Nthwd. 39 BR51
Foxdell Way (Chalfont St. Peter), Ger.Cr. 36 AY50
Foxearth Cl, West. 178 EL118
Foxearth Rd, S.Croy. 160 DW110
Foxearth Spur, S.Croy. 160 DW109
Foxes Dale SE3 104 EG83
Foxes Dale, Brom. 143 ED97
Foxes Dr, Wal.Cr. 14 DU29
Foxes Grn, Grays 111 GG75
Foxes La (Cuffley), Pot.B. 13 DL28
Tolmers Rd
Foxfield Cl, Nthwd. 39 BT51
Foxfield Rd, Orp. 145 ER103
Foxglove Cl, Sthl. 78 BY73
Foxglove Cl, Stai. 114 BK88
Foxglove Gdns E11 68 EJ56
Foxglove Gdns, Pur. 159 DL111
Foxglove La, Chess. 156 CN105
Foxglove Rd, Rom. 71 FE61
Foxglove Rd, S.Ock. 91 FW71
Foxglove St W12 81 CT73
Foxglove Way, Wall. 141 DH102
Foxgrove N14 45 DL48
Foxgrove Av, Beck. 123 EB94
Foxgrove Dr, Wok. 167 BA115
Foxgrove Path, Wat. 40 BX50
Foxgrove Rd, Beck. 123 EB94
Foxhall Rd, Upmin. 72 FQ64
Foxham Rd N19 65 DK62
Foxhanger Gdns, Wok. 167 BA116
Oriental Rd
Foxherne, Slou. 92 AW75
Foxhill, Wat. 23 BU36
Foxhills, Wok. 166 AW117
Foxhills Cl, Cher. 151 BB107
Foxhills Rd, Cher. 151 BA105
Foxhole Rd SE9 124 EL85
Foxholes, Wey. 153 BR106
Foxholt Gdns NW10 80 CQ66
Foxhome Cl, Chis. 125 EN93
Foxhounds La, Grav. 130 GA90
Foxlake Rd, W.Byf. 152 BM112
Foxlands Cl, Wat. 7 BU34
Foxlands Cres, Dag. 71 FC64
Foxlands La, Dag. 71 FC64
Foxlands Rd, Dag. 71 FC64
Foxlees, Wem. 61 CG63
Foxley Cl E8 66 DU64
Ferncliff Rd
Foxley Cl, Loug. 33 EP40
Foxley Gdns, Pur. 159 DP113
Foxley Hill Rd, Pur. 159 DN112
Foxley La, Pur. 159 DK111
Foxley Rd SW9 101 DN80
Foxley Rd, Ken. 159 DP114
Foxley Rd, Th.Hth. 141 DP98
Foxley Sq SW9 101 DP80
Cancell Rd
Foxleys, Wat. 40 BY48
Foxmead Cl, Enf. 29 DM41
Foxmoor Ct (Denham), Uxb. 58 BG58
North Orbital Rd
Foxmore St SW11 100 DF81
Foxon Cl, Cat. 176 DS121
Foxon La, Cat. 176 DR121
Foxon La Gdns, Cat. 176 DS121
Fox's Path, Mitch. 140 DE96
Foxton Gro, Mitch. 140 DD96
Foxton Rd, Grays 109 FX79
Foxwarren, Esher 155 CF109
Foxwell Ms SE4 103 DY83
Foxwell St
Foxwell St SE4 103 DY83
Foxwood Chase, Wal.Abb. 31 EC40
Sewardstone Rd
Foxwood Cl NW7 42 CS49
Foxwood Cl, Felt. 115 BV90
Foxwood Grn Cl, Enf. 30 DS44
Foxwood Gro, Grav. 130 GE88
Foxwood Gro, Orp. 164 EW110
Foxwood Rd SE3 104 EF84
Foxwood Rd, Dart. 129 FV90
Foyle Dr, S.Ock. 91 FU71
Foyle Rd N17 46 DU53
Foyle Rd SE3 104 EF79
Frailey Cl, Wok. 167 BB116
Frailey Hill, Wok. 167 BB116
Framewood Rd, Slou. 74 AW66
Framfield Cl N12 44 DA48
Framfield Ct, Enf. 30 DS44
Framfield Rd N5 65 DP64
Framfield Rd W7 79 CE72
Framfield Rd, Mitch. 120 DG94
Framlingham Cl E5 66 DW61
Detmold Rd
Framlingham Cres SE9 124 EL91
Frampton Cl, Sutt. 158 DA108
Frampton Pk Rd E9 84 DW65
Frampton Rd, Epp. 18 EU28
Frampton Rd, Houns. 116 BY85
Frampton Rd, Pot.B. 12 DC30
Frampton St NW8 82 DD70
Francemary Rd SE4 123 EA85
Frances Av (Chafford Hundred), Grays 109 FW77
Frances Gdns, S.Ock. 91 FT72
Frances Rd E4 47 EA51
Frances St SE18 105 EM77
Franche Ct Rd SW17 120 DC90
Francis Av, Bexh. 106 FA82
Francis Av, Felt. 115 BU90
Francis Av, Ilf. 69 ER61
Francis Barber Cl SW16 121 DM91
Well Cl
Francis Chichester Way SW11 100 DG81
Francis Cl E14 204 F8
Francis Cl, Epsom 156 CR105
Francis Cl, Shep. 134 BN98
Francis Gro SW19 119 CZ93
Francis Rd E10 67 EC60
Francis Rd N2 64 DF56
Lynmouth Rd
Francis Rd, Cat. 176 DR122
Francis Rd, Croy. 141 DP101
Francis Rd, Dart. 128 FK85
Francis Rd, Grnf. 79 CJ67
Francis Rd, Har. 61 CG57
Francis Rd, Houns. 96 BX82
Francis Rd, Ilf. 69 ER61
Francis Rd, Orp. 146 EX97
Francis Rd, Pnr. 60 BW57
Francis Rd, Wall. 159 DJ107
Francis Rd, Wat. 23 BV42
Francis St E15 68 EE64
Francis St SW1 199 K8
Francis St SW1 101 DJ77
Francis St, Ilf. 69 ER61
Francis Ter N19 65 DJ62
Junction Rd
Francis Wk N1 83 DM67
Bingfield St
Franciscan Rd SW17 120 DF92
Francisco Cl (Chafford Hundred), Grays 109 FW76
Francklyn Gdns, Edg. 42 CN48
Francombe Gdns, Rom. 71 FG58
Franconia Rd SW4 121 DJ85
Frank Bailey Wk E12 69 EN64
Gainsborough Av
Frank Burton Cl SE7 104 EH78
Victoria Way
Frank Dixon Cl SE21 122 DS88
Frank Dixon Way SE21 122 DS88
Frank Martin Ct, Wal.Cr. 14 DU30
Frank St E13 86 EG70
Frank Towell Ct, Felt. 115 BU88
Frankfurt Rd SE24 122 DQ85
Frankham St SE8 103 EA80
Frankland Cl SE16 202 F8
Frankland Cl SE16 102 DW77
Frankland Cl, Rick. 38 BN45
Frankland Cl, Wdf.Grn. 48 EJ50
Frankland Rd E4 47 EA50
Frankland Rd SW7 100 DD76
Frankland Rd, Rick. 23 BP44
Franklands Dr, Add. 151 BF108
Franklin Av (Cheshunt), Wal.Cr. 14 DV30
Franklin Cl N20 44 DC45
Franklin Cl SE13 103 EB81
Franklin Cl SE27 121 DP90
Franklin Cl, Kings.T. 138 CN97
Franklin Cres, Mitch. 141 DJ98
Franklin Ho NW9 63 CT59
Franklin Pas SE9 104 EL83
Franklin Rd SE20 122 DW94
Franklin Rd, Bexh. 106 EY81
Franklin Rd, Grav. 131 GK92
Franklin Rd, Horn. 90 FJ65
Franklin Rd, Wat. 23 BV40
Franklin Sq W14 99 CZ78
Marchbank Rd
Franklin St E3 85 EB69
St. Leonards St
Franklin St N15 66 DS58
Franklin Way, Croy. 141 DL101
Franklins Ms, Har. 60 CC61
Franklin's Row SW3 198 E10
Franklin's Row SW3 100 DF78
Franklyn Gdns, Ilf. 49 ER51
Franklyn Rd NW10 81 CT66
Franklyn Rd, Walt. 135 BU100
Franks Av, N.Mal. 138 CQ98
Franks La (Horton Kirby), Dart. 148 FN98
Frankswood Av, Orp. 145 EP99
Frankswood Av, West Dr. 76 BM72
Franlaw Cres N13 46 DQ49
Franmil Rd, Horn. 71 FG60
Fransfield Gro SE26 122 DV90
Frant Cl SE20 122 DW94
Frant Rd, Th.Hth. 141 DP99
Franthorne Way SE6 123 EB89
Fraser Cl E6 86 EL72
Linton Gdns
Fraser Cl, Bex. 127 FC88
Dartford Rd
Fraser Ho, Brent. 98 CM78
Green Dragon La
Fraser Rd E17 67 EB57
Fraser Rd N9 46 DV48
Fraser Rd, Erith 107 FC78
Fraser Rd, Grnf. 79 CH67
Fraser Rd (Cheshunt), Wal.Cr. 15 DY28
Fraser St W4 98 CS78
Frating Cres, Wdf.Grn. 48 EG51
Frays Av, West Dr. 94 BK75
Frays Cl, West Dr. 94 BK76
Frays Lea, Uxb. 76 BJ68
Frays Waye, Uxb. 76 BJ67
Frazer Av, Ruis. 60 BW64
Frazer Cl, Rom. 71 FF59
Frazier St SE1 200 D5
Frazier St SE1 101 DN75
Frean St SE16 202 B6
Frean St SE16 102 DU76
Fred Wigg Twr E11 68 EF61
Freda Corbett Cl SE15 102 DU80
Bird in Bush Rd
Frederic Ms SW1 198 E5
Frederic St E17 67 DY57
Frederica Rd E4 47 ED45
Frederica St N7 83 DM66
Caledonian Rd
Frederick Andrews Ct, Grays 110 GD79
Frederick Cl W2 194 D10
Frederick Cl W2 82 DE73
Frederick Cl, Sutt. 157 CZ105
Frederick Ct NW2 63 CY62
Douglas Ms
Frederick Cres SW9 101 DP80
Frederick Cres, Enf. 30 DW40
Frederick Gdns, Sutt. 157 CZ106
Frederick Pl SE18 105 EP78
Frederick Rd SE17 101 DP78
Chapter Rd
Frederick Rd, Rain. 89 FD68
Frederick Rd, Sutt. 157 CZ106
Frederick Sq SE16 203 K1
Frederick St WC1 196 B3
Frederick St WC1 83 DM69
Frederick Ter E8 84 DT67
Haggerston Rd
Frederick Vil W7 79 CE74
Lower Boston Rd
Frederick's Pl EC2 197 K9
Fredericks Pl N12 44 DC49
Frederick's Row EC1 196 F2
Fredora Av, Hayes 77 BT70
Free Prae Rd, Cher. 134 BG102
Free Trade Wf E1 84 DU73
The Highway
Freeborne Gdns, Rain. 89 FG65
Mungo Pk Rd
Freedom Cl E17 67 DY56
Freedom Rd N17 46 DR54
Freedom St SW11 100 DF82
Freedown La, Sutt. 158 DC113
Freegrove Rd N7 65 DL64
Freeland Pk NW4 43 CY54
Freeland Rd W5 80 CM73
Freeland Way, Erith 107 FG81
Slade Grn Rd
Freelands Av, S.Croy. 161 DX109
Freelands Gro, Brom. 144 EH95
Freelands Rd, Brom. 144 EH95
Freelands Rd, Cob. 153 BV114
Freeling St N1 83 DM66
Caledonian Rd
Freeman Cl, Nthlt. 78 BY66
Freeman Cl, Shep. 135 BS98
Freeman Ct N7 65 DL62
Tollington Way
Freeman Dr, W.Mol. 136 BZ97
Freeman Rd, Grav. 131 GL90
Freeman Rd, Mord. 140 DD99
Freeman Way, Horn. 72 FL58
Freemans Cl, Slou. 74 AT65
Freemans La, Hayes 77 BS73
Freemantle Av, Enf. 31 DX43
Freemantle St SE17 201 M10
Freemantle St SE17 102 DS78
Freemasons Rd E16 86 EH71
Freemasons Rd, Croy. 142 DS102
Freesia Cl, Orp. 163 ET106
Briarswood Way
Freethorpe Cl SE19 142 DR95
Freezeland Way, Uxb. 76 BN65
Western Av
Freightmaster Est, Rain. 107 FG76
Freke Rd SW11 100 DG83
Fremantle Ho, Til. 111 GF81
Leicester Rd
Fremantle Rd, Belv. 106 FA77
Fremantle Rd, Ilf. 49 EQ54
Fremont St E9 84 DW67
French Apartments, The, Pur. 159 DN112
Lansdowne Rd
French Gdns, Cob. 154 BW114
French Ordinary Ct EC3 197 N10
French Pl E1 197 N3
French St, Sun. 136 BW96
French St, West. 189 ES128
Frenchaye, Add. 152 BJ106
Frenches, The, Red. 184 DG132
Frenches Ct, Red. 184 DG132
Frenches Rd
Frenches Dr, Red. 184 DG132
The Frenches
Frenches Rd, Red. 184 DG132
French's Wells, Wok. 166 AV117
Frendsbury Rd SE4 103 DY84
Frensham (Cheshunt), Wal.Cr. 14 DT27
Frensham Cl, Sthl. 78 BZ70
Frensham Ct, Mitch. 140 DD97
Phipps Br Rd
Frensham Dr SW15 119 CU89
Frensham Dr, Croy. 161 EC108
Frensham Rd SE9 125 ER89
Frensham Rd, Ken. 159 DP114
Frensham St SE15 102 DU79
Frensham Way, Epsom 173 CW116
Frere St SW11 100 DE82
Fresh Wf Rd, Bark. 87 EP67
Freshfield Av E8 84 DT66
Freshfield Cl SE13 103 ED84
Marischal Rd
Freshfield Dr N14 45 DH45
Freshfields, Croy. 143 DZ101
Freshfields Av, Upmin. 72 FP64
Freshford St SW18 120 DC90
Freshmount Gdns, Epsom 156 CP111
Freshwater Cl SW17 120 DG93
Freshwater Rd SW17 120 DG93
Freshwater Rd, Dag. 70 EX60
Freshwell Av, Rom. 70 EW56
Freshwood Cl, Beck. 143 EB95

Freshwood Way, Wall. 159 DH109
Freston Gdns, Barn. 28 DG43
Freston Pk N3 43 CZ54
Freston Rd W10 81 CX73
Freston Rd W11 81 CX73
Freta Rd, Bexh. 126 EZ85
Frewin Rd SW18 120 DD88
Friar Ms SE27 121 DP90
Prioress Rd
Friar Rd, Hayes 78 BX70
Friar Rd, Orp. 146 EU99
Friar St EC4 196 G9
Friars, The, Chig. 49 ES49
Friars Av N20 44 DE48
Friars Av SW15 119 CT90
Friars Av, Brwd. 55 GA46
Friars Cl E4 47 EC48
Friars Cl N2 64 DD56
Friars Cl, Brwd. 55 FZ45
Friars Cl, Nthlt. 78 BX69
Broomcroft Av
Friars Gdns W3 80 CR72
St. Dunstans Av
Friars Gate Cl, Wdf.Grn. 48 EG49
Friars La, Rich. 117 CK85
Friars Mead E14 204 E7
Friars Mead E14 103 EC76
Friars Ms SE9 125 EN85
Friars Orchard, Lthd. 171 CD121
Friars Pl La W3 80 CR73
Friars Ri, Wok. 167 BA118
Friars Rd E6 86 EK67
Friars Rd, Vir.W. 132 AX98
Friars Stile Pl, Rich. 118 CL86
Friars Stile Rd
Friars Stile Rd, Rich. 118 CL86
Friars Wk N14 45 DH46
Friars Wk SE2 106 EX78
Friars Way W3 80 CR72
Friars Way, Bushey 24 BZ39
Friars Way, Cher. 134 BG100
Friars Way, Kings L. 6 BN30
Friars Wd, Croy. 161 DY109
Friary, The, Wind. 112 AV86
Friary Cl N12 44 DE50
Friary Ct SW1 199 L3
Friary Ct, Wok. 166 AT118
Friary Est SE15 102 DU79
Friary Island, Stai. 112 AW86
Friary La, Wdf.Grn. 48 EG49
Friary Rd N12 44 DD49
Friary Rd SE15 102 DU80
Friary Rd W3 80 CQ72
Friary Rd, Stai. 112 AW86
Friary Way N12 44 DE49
Friday Hill E4 48 EE47
Friday Hill E E4 48 EE48
Friday Hill W E4 48 EE47
Friday Rd, Erith 107 FD78
Friday Rd, Mitch. 120 DF94
Friday St EC4 197 H9
Friday St EC4 84 DQ72
Frideswide Pl NW5 65 DJ64
Islip St
Friend St EC1 196 F2
Friend St EC1 83 DP69
Friendly Pl SE13 103 EB81
Lewisham Rd
Friendly St SE8 103 EA81
Friendly St Ms SE8 103 EA82
Friendly St
Friends Av, Wal.Cr. 15 DX31
Friends Rd, Croy. 142 DR104
Friends Rd, Pur. 159 DP112
Friends Wk, Stai. 113 BF92
Friends Wk, Uxb. 76 BK66
Bakers Rd
Friendship Wk, Nthlt. 78 BX69
Wayfarer Rd
Friern Barnet La N11 44 DE49
Friern Barnet La N20 44 DE49
Friern Barnet Rd N11 44 DF50
Friern Br Retail Pk N11 45 DH51
Friern Ct N20 44 DD48
Friern Mt Dr N20 44 DC45
Friern Pk N12 44 DC50
Friern Rd SE22 122 DU86
Friern Watch Av N12 44 DC49
Frigate Ms SE8 103 EA79
Watergate St
Frimley Av, Horn. 72 FN60
Frimley Av, Wall. 159 DL106
Frimley Cl SW19 119 CY89
Frimley Cl, Croy. 161 EC108
Frimley Ct, Sid. 126 EV92
Frimley Cres, Croy. 161 EC108
Frimley Gdns, Mitch. 140 DE97
Frimley Rd, Chess. 156 CL106
Frimley Rd, Ilf. 69 ES62
Frimley Way E1 85 DX70
Fringewood Cl, Nthwd. 39 BP53
Frinsted Cl, Orp. 146 EX98
Frinsted Rd, Erith 107 FD80
Frinton Cl, Wat. 39 BV47
Frinton Dr, Wdf.Grn. 47 ED52
Frinton Ms, Ilf. 69 EN58
Bramley Cres
Frinton Rd E6 86 EK69
Frinton Rd N15 66 DS58
Frinton Rd SW17 120 DG93
Frinton Rd, Rom. 50 EZ52
Frinton Rd, Sid. 126 EY89
Friston Path, Chig. 49 ES50
Friston St SW6 100 DB82
Friswell Pl, Bexh. 106 FA84
Frith Ct NW7 43 CY52
Frith Knowle, Walt. 153 BV106
Frith La NW7 43 CY52
Frith Rd E11 67 EC63
Frith Rd, Croy. 142 DQ103
Frith St W1 195 M9
Frith St W1 83 DK72
Fritham Cl, N.Mal. 138 CS100
Frithe, The, Slou. 74 AV72
Friths Dr, Reig. 184 DB131
Frithville Gdns W12 81 CW74
Frithwald Rd, Cher. 133 BF101
Frithwood Av, Nthwd. 39 BS51
Frizlands La, Dag. 71 FB63
Frobisher Cl, Ken. 176 DR117
Hayes La
Frobisher Cl, Pnr. 60 BX59
Frobisher Cres, Stai. 114 BL87
Frobisher Gdns, Stai. 114 BL87
Frobisher Pas E14 204 A2
Frobisher Rd E6 87 EM72
Frobisher Rd N8 65 DN56
Frobisher Rd, Erith 107 FF80
Frobisher St SE10 104 EE79
Frobisher Way, Grav. 131 GL92
Frobisher Way, Green. 109 FV84
Frog La, Rain. 89 FD71
Froggy La (Denham), Uxb. 57 BD62
Froghall La, Chig. 49 ER49
Froghole La, Eden. 189 ER132
Frogley Rd SE22 102 DT84
Frogmoor La, Rick. 38 BK47
Frogmore SW18 120 DA85
Frogmore, St.Alb. 9 CD27
Frogmore Av, Hayes 77 BS70
Frogmore Cl, Sutt. 139 CX104
Frogmore Dr, Wind. 92 AS81
Frogmore Est, Ruis. 60 BX64
Frogmore Gdns, Hayes 77 BS70
Frogmore Gdns, Sutt. 157 CY105
Frogmore Home Pk, St.Alb. 9 CD28
Frogmore Ind Est NW10 80 CQ69
Frognal NW3 64 DC64
Frognal Av, Har. 61 CF56
Frognal Av, Sid. 126 EU93
Frognal Cl NW3 64 DC64
Frognal Ct NW3 82 DC65
Frognal Gdns NW3 64 DC63
Frognal La NW3 64 DB64
Frognal Par NW3 82 DC65
Frognal Ct
Frognal Pl, Sid. 126 EU93
Frognal Ri NW3 64 DC63
Frognal Way NW3 64 DC63
Froissart Rd SE9 124 EK85
Frome Rd N22 65 DP55
Westbury Av
Frome St N1 84 DQ68
Fromondes Rd, Sutt. 157 CY106
Front La, Upmin. 73 FS59
Frostic Wk E1 84 DT71
Froude St SW8 101 DH82
Frowyke Cres, Pot.B. 11 CU32
Fruen Rd, Felt. 115 BT87
Fry Cl, Rom. 50 FA50
Fry Rd E6 86 EK66
Fry Rd NW10 81 CT67
Fryatt Rd N17 46 DR52
Fryatt St E14 86 EE72
Orchard Pl
Fryent Cl NW9 62 CN58
Fryent Cres NW9 62 CS58
Fryent Flds NW9 62 CS58
Fryent Gro NW9 62 CS58
Fryent Way NW9 62 CN58
Fryern Wd, Cat. 176 DQ124
Frye's Bldgs N1 83 DN68
Upper St
Frying Pan All E1 197 P7
Fryston Av, Couls. 159 DH114
Fryston Av, Croy. 142 DU103
Fuchsia Cl, Rom. 71 FE61
Fuchsia St SE2 106 EV78
Fulbeck Dr NW9 42 CS53
Fulbeck Wk, Edg. 42 CP47
Bushfield Cres
Fulbeck Way, Har. 40 CC54
Fulbourne Cl, Red. 184 DE132
Dennis Cl
Fulbourne Rd E17 47 EC53
Fulbourne St E1 84 DV71
Durward St
Fulbrook Av, Add. 152 BG111
Fulbrook La, S.Ock. 91 FT73
Fulbrook Ms N19 65 DJ63
Junction Rd
Fulbrook Rd N19 65 DJ63
Junction Rd
Fulford Gro, Wat. 39 BV47
Fulford Rd, Cat. 176 DR121
Fulford Rd, Epsom 156 CR108
Fulford St SE16 202 E5
Fulford St SE16 102 DV75
Fulham Bdy SW6 100 DA80
Fulham Cl, Uxb. 77 BQ70
Uxbridge Rd
Fulham Ct SW6 100 DA80
Fulham Rd
Fulham High St SW6 99 CY82
Fulham Palace Rd SW6 99 CX80
Fulham Palace Rd W6 99 CW78
Fulham Pk Gdns SW6 99 CZ82
Fulham Pk Rd SW6 99 CZ82
Fulham Rd SW3 100 DC79
Fulham Rd SW6 99 CY82
Fulham Rd SW10 100 DB80
Fullarton Cres, S.Ock. 91 FT72
Fullbrooks Av, Wor.Pk. 139 CT102
Fuller Cl E2 84 DU70
St. Matthew's Row
Fuller Cl, Orp. 163 ET106
Fuller Gdns, Wat. 23 BV37
Fuller Rd
Fuller Rd, Dag. 70 EV62
Fuller Rd, Wat. 23 BV37
Fuller St NW4 63 CW56
Fuller Ter, Ilf. 69 EQ64
Oaktree Gro
Fuller Way, Hayes 95 BT78
Fuller Way, Rick. 22 BN43
Fullers Av, Surb. 138 CM103
Fullers Av, Wdf.Grn. 48 EF52
Fullers Cl, Rom. 51 FC52
Fullers Cl, Wal.Abb. 16 EG33
Fullers Hill, West. 189 ER126
High St
Fullers La, Rom. 51 FC52
Fullers Rd E18 48 EF53
Fullers Way N, Surb. 138 CM104
Fullers Way S, Chess. 156 CL105
Fullers Wd, Croy. 161 EA106
Fullers Wd La, Red. 185 DJ134
Fullerton Cl, W.Byf. 152 BM114
Fullerton Dr, W.Byf. 152 BL114
Fullerton Rd SW18 120 DC85
Fullerton Rd, Cars. 158 DE109
Fullerton Rd, Croy. 142 DT101
Fullerton Rd, W.Byf. 152 BM114
Fullerton Way, W.Byf. 152 BL114
Fullmer Way, Add. 151 BF110
Fullwell Av, Ilf. 49 EM53
Fullwell Cross Roundabout, Ilf. 49 ER54
Fencepiece Rd
Fullwoods Ms N1 197 L2
Fulmar Ct, Surb. 138 CM100
Fulmar Rd, Horn. 89 FG66
Fulmead St SW6 100 DB81
Fulmer Cl, Hmptn. 116 BY92
Fulmer Common Rd, Iver 75 AZ65
Fulmer Common Rd, Slou. 75 AZ65
Fulmer Dr, Ger.Cr. 56 AW60
Fulmer La, Ger.Cr. 57 BB60
Fulmer La, Slou. 56 AY62
Fulmer Ri Est, Slou. 75 AZ65
Fulmer Rd E16 86 EK71
Fulmer Rd, Ger.Cr. 56 AY62
Fulmer Rd, Slou. 56 AY63
Fulmer Way W13 97 CH76
Fulmer Way, Ger.Cr. 56 AY58
Fulready Rd E10 67 ED57
Fulstone Cl, Houns. 96 BZ84
Fulthorp Rd SE3 104 EF82
Fulton Ms W2 82 DC73
Porchester Ter
Fulton Rd, Wem. 62 CN62
Fulwell Pk Av, Twick. 116 CB89
Fulwell Rd, Tedd. 117 CD91
Fulwich Rd, Dart. 128 FM86
Fulwood Av, Wem. 80 CM67
Fulwood Cl, Hayes 77 BT72
Fulwood Gdns, Twick. 117 CF86
Fulwood Pl WC1 196 C7
Fulwood Pl WC1 83 DM71
Fulwood Wk SW19 119 CY88
Furber St W6 99 CV76
Furham Feild, Pnr. 40 CA52
Furley Rd SE15 102 DU80
Furlong Cl, Wall. 140 DG102
Furlong Rd N7 83 DN65
Furlough, The, Wok. 167 BA117
Pembroke Rd
Furmage St SW18 120 DB87
Furneaux Av SE27 121 DP92
Furner Cl, Dart. 107 FF83
Furness Cl, Grays 111 GH78
Furness Rd NW10 81 CU68
Furness Rd SW6 100 DB82
Furness Rd, Har. 60 CB59
Furness Rd, Mord. 140 DB101
Furness Way, Horn. 71 FG64
Furnival Cl, Vir.W. 132 AX100
Furnival St EC4 196 D8
Furnival St EC4 83 DN72
Furrow La E9 66 DW64
Furrows, The (Harefield), Uxb. 58 BJ57
Furrows, The, Walt. 136 BW103
Furrows Pl, Cat. 176 DT123
Fursby Av N3 44 DA51
Further Acre NW9 43 CT54
Further Grn Rd SE6 124 EE87
Furtherfield, Abb.L. 7 BS32
Furtherfield Cl, Croy. 141 DN100
Furze Cl, Red. 184 DF133
Furze Cl, Wat. 40 BW50
Furze Fm Cl, Rom. 50 EY54
Furze Fld, Lthd. 155 CD113
Furze Gro, Tad. 173 CZ121
Furze Hill, Pur. 159 DL111
Furze Hill, Red. 184 DE133
Linkfield La
Furze Hill, Tad. 173 CZ120
Furze La, Pur. 159 DL111
Furze Rd, Add. 151 BF107
Furze Rd, Th.Hth. 142 DQ97
Furze St E3 85 EA71
Furze Vw, Rick. 21 BC44
Furzebushes La, St.Alb. 8 BY25
Furzedown Dr SW17 121 DH92
Furzedown Rd SW17 121 DH92
Furzedown Rd, Sutt. 158 DC111
Furzefield (Cheshunt), Wal.Cr. 14 DV28
Furzefield Cl, Chis. 125 EP93
Furzefield Rd SE3 104 EH79
Furzeground Way, Uxb. 77 BQ74
Furzeham Rd, West Dr. 94 BL75
Furzehill Rd, Borwd. 26 CN42
Furzewood, Sun. 135 BU95
Fuschia Ct, Wdf.Grn. 48 EE52
The Bridle Path
Fusedale Way, S.Ock. 91 FT73
Fyfe Way, Brom. 144 EG96
Widmore Rd
Fyfield Cl, Brom. 143 ED98
Fyfield Ct E7 86 EG65
Fyfield Rd E17 67 ED55
Fyfield Rd SW9 101 DN83
Fyfield Rd, Enf. 30 DS41
Fyfield Rd, Rain. 89 FF67
Fyfield Rd, Wdf.Grn. 48 EJ52
Fynes St SW1 199 M8
Fynes St SW1 101 DK77

G

G.E.C. Est, Wem. 61 CK62
Gabion Av, Purf. 109 FR77
Gable Cl, Abb.L. 7 BS32
Gable Cl, Dart. 127 FG85
Gable Cl, Pnr. 40 CA52
Gable Ct SE26 122 DV92
Lawrie Pk Av
Gables, The, Bans. 173 CZ117
Gables, The, Lthd. 154 CC112
Gables, The, Wem. 62 CM63
Gables Av, Ashf. 114 BM92
Gables Av, Borwd. 26 CM41
Gables Cl SE5 102 DS81
Gables Cl SE12 124 EG88
Gables Cl (Chalfont St. Peter), Ger.Cr. 36 AY49
Gables Cl, Slou. 92 AU79
Gables Cl, Wok. 167 AZ120
Kingfield Rd
Gables Ct, Wok. 167 AZ120
Kingfield Rd
Gabriel Cl, Felt. 116 BX91
Gabriel Cl (Chafford Hundred), Grays 109 FW76
Gabriel Cl, Rom. 51 FC52
Gabriel Spring Rd (Fawkham Grn), Long. 149 FR103
Gabriel Spring Rd (East), Long. 149 FS103
Gabriel St SE23 123 DX87
Gabrielle Cl, Wem. 62 CM62
Gabrielle Ct NW3 82 DD65
Gabriels Gdns, Grav. 131 GL92
Gad Cl E13 86 EH69
Gaddesden Av, Wem. 80 CM65
Gaddesden Cres, Wat. 8 BX34
Gade Av, Wat. 23 BS42
Gade Bk, Rick. 23 BR42
Gade Cl, Hayes 77 BV74
Gade Cl, Wat. 23 BS42
Gade Twr, Hem.H. 6 BN25
Gade Valley Cl, Kings L. 6 BN28
Gade Vw Gdns, Kings L. 7 BQ32
Gadesden Rd, Epsom 156 CQ107
Gadsbury Cl NW9 63 CT58
Gadsden Cl, Upmin. 73 FS58
Gadswell Cl, Wat. 24 BX36
Gadwall Cl E16 86 EH72
Freemasons Rd
Gadwall Way SE28 105 ER75
Gage Rd E16 86 EE71
Malmesbury Rd
Gage St WC1 196 A6
Gainford St N1 83 DN67
Richmond Av
Gainsboro Gdns, Grnf. 61 CE64
Gainsborough Av E12 69 EN64
Gainsborough Av, Dart. 128 FJ85
Gainsborough Av, Til. 111 GG81
Gainsborough Cl, Beck. 123 EA94
Gainsborough Cl, Esher 137 CE102
Lime Tree Av
Gainsborough Ct N12 44 DB50
Gainsborough Ct W12 99 CW75
Lime Gro
Gainsborough Ct, Walt. 153 BU105
Gainsborough Dr, Grav. 130 GD90
Gainsborough Dr, S.Croy. 160 DU113
Gainsborough Gdns NW3 64 DD62
Gainsborough Gdns NW11 63 CZ59
Gainsborough Gdns, Edg. 42 CM54
Gainsborough Gdns, Islw. 117 CD85
Gainsborough Ms SE26 122 DV90
Panmure Rd
Gainsborough Pl, Chig. 49 ET48
Gainsborough Rd E11 68 EE59
Gainsborough Rd E15 86 EE69
Gainsborough Rd N12 44 DB50
Gainsborough Rd W4 99 CT77
Gainsborough Rd, Dag. 70 EV63
Gainsborough Rd, Epsom 156 CQ110
Gainsborough Rd, Hayes 77 BQ68
Gainsborough Rd, N.Mal. 138 CR101
Gainsborough Rd, Rain. 89 FG67
Gainsborough Rd, Rich. 98 CM83
Gainsborough Rd, Wdf.Grn. 48 EL51
Gainsborough Sq, Bexh. 106 EX83
Regency Way
Gainsford Rd E17 67 DZ56
Gainsford St SE1 201 P4
Gainsford St SE1 102 DT75
Gairloch Rd SE5 102 DS82
Gaisford St NW5 83 DJ65
Gaist Av, Cat. 176 DU122
Gaitskell Rd SE9 125 EQ88
Galahad Rd, Brom. 124 EG90
Galata Rd SW13 99 CU80
Galatea Sq SE15 102 DV83
Scylla Rd
Galbraith St E14 204 D6
Galbraith St E14 103 EC76
Galdana Av, Barn. 28 DC41
Gale Cl, Hmptn. 116 BY93
Stewart Cl
Gale Cl, Mitch. 140 DD97
Gale Cres, Bans. 174 DA117
Gale St E3 85 EA71
Gale St, Dag. 88 EX67
Galeborough Av, Wdf.Grn. 47 ED52
Galen Cl, Epsom 156 CN111
Williams Evans Rd
Galen Pl WC1 196 A7
Galena Ho SE18 105 ET78
Grosmont Rd
Galena Rd W6 99 CV77
Gales Gdns E2 84 DV69
Gales Way, Wdf.Grn. 48 EL52
Galesbury Rd SW18 120 DC86
Galey Grn, S.Ock. 91 FV71
Bovey Way
Galgate Cl SW19 119 CY88
Gallants Fm Rd, Barn. 44 DE45
Galleon Boul, Dart. 109 FR84
Galleon Cl SE16 202 G4
Galleon Cl, Erith 107 FD77
Galleon Rd, Grays 109 FW77
Galleons Dr, Bark. 87 ES69
Thames Rd
Galleons La, Slou. 74 AX71
Gallery Gdns, Nthlt. 78 BX68
Gallery Rd SE21 122 DR88
Galley Hill, Wal.Abb. 16 EF30
Galley Hill Rd, Grav. 130 FZ85
Galley Hill Rd, Swans. 130 FZ85
Galley La, Barn. 27 CV41
Galleymead Rd, Slou. 93 BF81
Galleywall Rd SE16 202 D9
Galleywall Rd SE16 102 DV77
Galleywood Cres, Rom. 51 FD51
Gallia Rd N5 65 DP64
Galliard Cl N9 30 DW44
Galliard Rd N9 46 DU46
Gallions Cl, Bark. 88 EU69
Gallions Rd E16 87 EP73
Gallions Rd SE7 104 EH77
Gallions Roundabout E16 87 EP73
Gallions Vw Rd SE28 105 ER75
Goldfinch Rd
Gallon Cl SE7 104 EJ77
Gallop, The, S.Croy. 160 DV108
Gallop, The, Sutt. 158 DC108
Gallops, The, Tad. 183 CV126
Gallosson Rd SE18 105 ES77
Galloway Chase, Slou. 74 AU73
Galloway Cl, Brox. 15 DZ26
Galloway Path, Croy. 160 DR105
Galloway Rd W12 81 CU74
Gallows Cor, Rom. 52 FK53
Gallows Hill, Kings L. 7 BQ31
Gallows Hill La, Abb.L. 7 BQ32
Gallus Cl N21 29 DM44
Gallus Sq SE3 104 EH83
Galpins Rd, Th.Hth. 141 DM98
Galsworthy Av, Rom. 70 EV59
Galsworthy Cl SE28 88 EV74
Galsworthy Cres SE3 104 EJ81
Merriman Rd
Galsworthy Rd NW2 63 CY63
Galsworthy Rd, Cher. 134 BG101
Galsworthy Rd, Kings.T. 118 CP94
Galsworthy Rd, Til. 111 GJ81
Galsworthy Ter N16 66 DS62
Hawksley Rd
Galton St W10 81 CY70
Galva Cl, Barn. 28 DG42
Galvani Way, Croy. 141 DM102
Ampere Way
Galveston Rd SW15 119 CZ85
Galway Cl SE16 102 DV78
Masters Dr
Galway St EC1 197 J3
Galway St EC1 84 DQ69
Gambetta St SW8 101 DH82
Gambia St SE1 200 G3
Gambles La, Wok. 168 BJ124
Gambole Rd SW17 120 DE91
Games Rd, Barn. 28 DF41
Gamlen Rd SW15 99 CX84
Gammons Fm Cl, Wat. 23 BT36
Gammons La, Brox. 14 DT25
Gammons La, Wat. 23 BV38
Gamuel Cl E17 67 EA58
Gander Grn Cres, Hmptn. 136 CA95
Gander Grn La, Sutt. 139 CY103
Ganders Ash, Wat. 7 BU33
Gandhi Cl E17 67 EA58
Gandolfi St SE15 102 DS79
St. Georges Way
Gangers Hill, Cat. 187 EA127
Gangers Hill, Gdse. 187 EA127
Gant Ct, Wal.Abb. 16 EF34
Ganton St W1 195 K10
Ganton Wk, Wat. 40 BY49
Woodhall La
Gantshill Cres, Ilf. 69 EN57
Gantshill Cross, Ilf. 69 EN58
Eastern Av
Gap Rd SW19 120 DA92
Garage Rd W3 80 CN72
Garbrand Wk, Epsom 157 CT109
Garbutt Pl W1 194 G6
Garbutt Rd, Upmin. 72 FQ61
Gard St EC1 196 G2
Garden Av, Bexh. 106 FA83
Garden Av, Mitch. 121 DH94
Garden City, Edg. 42 CN51
Garden Cl E4 47 EA50
Garden Cl SE12 124 EH90
Garden Cl SW15 119 CV87
Garden Cl, Add. 152 BK105
Garden Cl, Ashf. 115 BQ93
Garden Cl, Bans. 174 DA115
Garden Cl, Barn. 27 CW42
Garden Cl, Hmptn. 116 BZ92
Garden Cl, Lthd. 171 CJ124
Garden Cl, Nthlt. 78 BY67
Garden Cl, Ruis. 59 BS61
Garden Cl, Wall. 159 DL106
Garden Cl, Wat. 23 BT40
Garden Cotts, Orp. 146 EW96
Main Rd
Garden Ct EC4 196 D10
Garden Ct SE15 102 DT81
Sumner Est
Garden Ct, Rich. 98 CM81
Lichfield Rd
Garden Ct, Stan. 41 CJ50
Marsh La
Garden Ct, W.Mol. 136 CB98
Avern Rd
Garden End, Amer. 20 AS37
Garden La SW2 121 DM88
Christchurch Rd
Garden La, Brom. 124 EH93
Garden Ms W2 82 DA73
Linden Gdns
Garden Ms, Slou. 74 AT74
Littledown Rd
Garden Pl, Dart. 128 FK90
Garden Reach, Ch.St.G. 20 AX41
Garden Rd NW8 82 DC69
Garden Rd SE20 142 DW95
Garden Rd, Abb.L. 7 BS31
Garden Rd, Brom. 124 EH94
Garden Rd, Rich. 98 CN83
Garden Rd, Sev. 191 FK122
Garden Rd, Walt. 135 BV100
Garden Row SE1 200 F7
Garden Row SE1 101 DP76
Garden Row, Grav. 131 GF90
Garden St E1 85 DX71
Garden Ter SW1 199 M10
Garden Wk EC2 197 M3
Garden Wk, Beck. 143 DZ95
Hayne Rd
Garden Wk, Couls. 175 DH123
Garden Way NW10 80 CQ65
Garden Way, Loug. 33 EN38
Gardeners Cl N11 44 DG47
Gardeners Rd, Croy. 141 DP102
Gardenia Rd, Enf. 30 DS44

Gar-Gil This index reads in the sequence: Street Name / Postal District or Post Town / Map Page Reference / Grid Reference

Gardenia Way, Wdf.Grn. 48 EG50
Gardens, The SE22 102 DU84
Gardens, The, Beck. 143 EC96
Gardens, The, Esher 154 CA105
Gardens, The, Felt. 115 BR85
Gardens, The, Har. 60 CC58
Gardens, The, Hat. 11 CY27
Gardens, The, Pnr. 60 BZ58
Gardens, The, Wat. 23 BT40
Gardiner Av NW2 63 CW64
Gardiner Cl, Dag. 70 EX63
Gardiner Cl, Enf. 31 DX44
Gardiner Cl, Orp. 146 EW96
Gardner Cl E11 68 EH58
Gardner Gro, Felt. 116 BZ89
Gardner Rd E13 86 EH70
Gardners La EC4 197 H10
Gardnor Rd NW3 64 DD63
Flask Wk
Garendon Gdns, Mord. 140 DB101
Garendon Rd, Mord. 140 DB101
Gareth Cl, Wor.Pk. 139 CX103
Burnham Dr
Gareth Gro, Brom. 124 EG91
Garfield Ms SW11 100 DG83
Garfield Rd
Garfield Rd E4 47 ED46
Garfield Rd E13 86 EF70
Garfield Rd SW11 100 DG83
Garfield Rd SW19 120 DC92
Garfield Rd, Add. 152 BJ106
Garfield Rd, Enf. 30 DW42
Garfield Rd, Twick. 117 CG88
Garfield St, Wat. 23 BV38
Garford St E14 203 P1
Garford St E14 85 EA73
Garganey Wk SE28 88 EX73
Garibaldi St SE18 105 ES77
Garland Cl, Wal.Cr. 15 DY31
Garland Rd SE18 105 ER80
Garland Rd, Stan. 42 CL53
Garland Way, Cat. 176 DR122
Garland Way, Horn. 72 FL56
Garlands Ct, Croy. 160 DR105
Chatsworth Rd
Garlands Rd, Lthd. 171 CH121
Garlichill Rd, Epsom 173 CV117
Garlick Hill EC4 197 J10
Garlick Hill EC4 84 DQ73
Garlies Rd SE23 123 DY90
Garlinge Rd NW2 81 CZ65
Garman Cl N18 46 DR50
Garman Rd N17 46 DW52
Garnault Ms EC1 196 E3
Garnault Pl EC1 196 E3
Garnault Rd, Enf. 30 DT38
Garner Dr, Brox. 15 DY26
Garner Rd E17 47 EC53
Garner St E2 84 DU68
Coate St
Garners Cl (Chalfont St. Peter), Ger.Cr. 36 AY51
Garners End (Chalfont St. Peter), Ger.Cr. 36 AY51
Garners Rd (Chalfont St. Peter), Ger.Cr. 36 AY51
Garnet Rd NW10 80 CS65
Garnet Rd, Th.Hth. 142 DR98
Garnet St E1 202 F1
Garnet St E1 84 DW73
Garnet Wk E6 86 EL71
Kingfisher St
Garnett Cl SE9 105 EM83
Garnett Cl, Wat. 24 BX37
Garnett Dr, St.Alb. 8 BZ29
Garnett Rd NW3 64 DF64
Garnett Way E17 47 DY53
McEntee Av
Garnham Cl N16 66 DT61
Garnham St
Garnham St N16 66 DT61
Garnies Cl SE15 102 DT80
Garnon Mead, Epp. 18 EX28
Garrad's Rd SW16 121 DK90
Garrard Cl, Bexh. 106 FA83
Garrard Cl, Chis. 125 EP92
Garrard Rd, Bans. 174 DA116
Garrard Wk NW10 80 CS65
Garnet Rd
Garratt Cl, Croy. 159 DL105
Garratt La SW17 120 DD91
Garratt La SW18 120 DB85
Garratt Rd, Edg. 42 CN52
Garratt Ter SW17 120 DE91
Garratts La, Bans. 173 CZ116
Garratts Rd, Bushey 40 CC45
Garrett Cl W3 80 CR71
Jenner Av
Garrett St EC1 197 J4
Garrick Av NW11 63 CY58
Garrick Cl SW18 100 DC84
Garrick Cl W5 80 CL70
Garrick Cl, Rich. 117 CK85
The Grn
Garrick Cl, Stai. 114 BG94
Garrick Cl, Walt. 153 BV105
Garrick Cres, Croy. 142 DS103
Garrick Dr NW4 43 CW54
Garrick Dr SE28 105 ER76
Broadwater Rd
Garrick Gdns, W.Mol. 136 CA97
Garrick Pk NW4 43 CX54
Garrick Rd NW9 63 CT58
Garrick Rd, Grnf. 78 CB70
Garrick Rd, Rich. 98 CN82
Garrick St WC2 195 P10
Garrick St WC2 83 DL73
Garrick St, Grav. 131 GH86
Barrack Row
Garrick Way NW4 63 CX56
Garrison Cl SE18 105 EN80
Red Lion La
Garrison Cl, Houns. 116 BZ85
Garrison La, Chess. 155 CK108
Garrison Par, Purf. 108 FN77
Comet Cl
Garrolds Cl, Swan. 147 FD96
Garron La, S.Ock. 91 FT72
Garry Cl, Rom. 51 FE52
Garry Way, Rom. 51 FE52
Garsdale Cl N11 44 DG51
Garside Cl SE28 105 ER76
Goosander Way
Garside Cl, Hmptn. 116 CB93
Garsington Ms SE4 103 DZ83
Garsmouth Way, Wat. 24 BX36
Garson Cl, Esher 154 BZ107
Garson Rd
Garson La, Stai. 112 AX87
Garson Mead, Esher 154 BZ106
Garson Rd, Esher 154 BZ107
Garston Cres, Wat. 8 BW34
Garston Dr, Wat. 8 BW34
Garston Gdns, Ken. 176 DR115
Godstone Rd
Garston La, Ken. 160 DR114
Garston La, Wat. 8 BX34
Garston Pk Par, Wat. 8 BX34
Garter Way SE16 203 H5
Garth, The, Abb.L. 7 BR33
Garth, The, Cob. 154 BY113
Garth, The, Hmptn. 116 CB93
Uxbridge Rd
Garth, The, Har. 62 CM58
Garth Cl W4 98 CR78
Garth Cl, Kings.T. 118 CM92
Garth Cl, Mord. 139 CX101
Garth Cl, Ruis. 60 BX60
Garth Ct W4 98 CR78
Garth Rd
Garth Ms W5 80 CL70
Greystoke Gdns
Garth Rd NW2 63 CZ61
Garth Rd W4 98 CR79
Garth Rd, Kings.T. 118 CM92
Garth Rd, Mord. 139 CW100
Garth Rd, Sev. 191 FJ128
Garth Rd, S.Ock. 91 FW70
Garth Rd Ind Cen, Mord. 139 CX101
Garthland Dr, Barn. 27 CV43
Garthorne Rd SE23 123 DX87
Garthside, Rich. 118 CL92
Garthway N12 44 DE51
Gartlett Rd, Wat. 24 BW41
Gartmoor Gdns SW19 119 CZ88
Gartmore Rd, Ilf. 69 ET60
Garton Pl SW18 120 DC86
Gartons Cl, Enf. 30 DW43
Gartons Way SW11 100 DC83
Garvary Rd E16 86 EH72
Garvock Dr, Sev. 190 FG126
Garway Rd W2 82 DB72
Gascoigne Gdns, Wdf.Grn. 48 EE52
Gascoigne Pl E2 197 P3
Gascoigne Pl E2 84 DT69
Gascoigne Rd, Bark. 87 EQ67
Gascoigne Rd, Croy. 161 EC110
Gascoigne Rd, Wey. 135 BP104
Gascony Av NW6 82 DA66
Gascoyne Cl, Pot.B. 11 CU32
Gascoyne Cl, Rom. 52 FK52
Gascoyne Dr, Dart. 107 FF82
Gascoyne Rd E9 85 DX66
Gaselee St E14 204 E1
Gaselee St E14 85 EC73
Gasholder Pl SE11 101 DM78
Kennington La
Gaskarth Rd SW12 121 DH86
Gaskarth Rd, Edg. 42 CQ53
Gaskell Rd N6 64 DF58
Gaskell St SW4 101 DL82
Gaskin St N1 83 DP67
Gaspar Cl SW5 100 DB77
Courtfield Gdns
Gaspar Ms SW5 100 DB77
Courtfield Gdns
Gassiot Rd SW17 120 DF91
Gassiot Way, Sutt. 140 DD104
Gasson Rd, Swans. 130 FY86
Gastein Rd W6 99 CX79
Gaston Bell Cl, Rich. 98 CM83
Gaston Br Rd, Shep. 135 BS99
Gaston Rd, Mitch. 140 DG97
Gaston Way, Shep. 135 BR99
Gataker St SE16 202 E6
Gataker St SE16 102 DV76
Gatcombe Rd E16 205 N2
Gatcombe Rd E16 86 EG74
Gatcombe Rd N19 65 DK62
Gatcombe Way, Barn. 28 DF41
Gate Cl, Borwd. 26 CQ39
Gate End, Nthwd. 39 BU52
Gate Ms SW7 198 C5
Gate Ms SW7 100 DE75
Gate St WC2 196 B8
Gateforth St NW8 194 B5
Gateforth St NW8 82 DE70
Gatehill Rd, Nthwd. 39 BT52
Gatehope Dr, S.Ock. 91 FT72
Gatehouse Cl, Kings.T. 118 CQ94
Gatehouse Sq SE1 84 DQ74
Southwark Br Rd
Gateley Rd SW9 101 DM83
Gater Dr, Enf. 30 DR39
Gates Grn Rd, Kes. 162 EG105
Gates Grn Rd, W.Wick. 144 EF104
Gatesborough St EC2 197 M4
Gatesden Cl, Lthd. 170 CC123
Gatesden Rd, Lthd. 170 CC123
Gateshead Rd, Borwd. 26 CM39
Gateside Rd SW17 120 DF90
Gatestone Rd SE19 122 DS93
Gateway SE17 102 DQ79
Gateway, Wey. 135 BP104
Palace Dr
Gateway, The, Wok. 151 BB114
Gateway Arc N1 83 DP68
Islington High St
Gateway Cl, Nthwd. 39 BQ51
Gateway Ind Est NW10 81 CT69
Gateway Ms E8 66 DT64
Shacklewell La
Gateway Rd E10 67 EB62
Gateways, The SW3 198 C9
Gateways, The SW3 100 DF77
Gateways, The, Wal.Cr. 14 DR28
Gatewick Cl, Slou. 74 AS74
Gatfield Gro, Felt. 116 CA89
Gathorne Rd N22 45 DN54
Gathorne St E2 85 DX68
Mace St
Gatley Av, Epsom 156 CP106
Gatliff Rd SW1 101 DH78
Gatling Rd SE2 106 EU78
Gatonby St SE15 102 DT80
Kelly Av
Gatting Cl, Edg. 42 CQ52
Pavilion Way
Gatting Way, Uxb. 76 BL65
Gatton Bottom, Red. 185 DH127
Gatton Bottom, Reig. 184 DE128
Gatton Cl, Reig. 184 DC131
Gatton Cl, Sutt. 158 DB109
Gatton Pk, Reig. 184 DF129
Gatton Pk, Reig. 184 DF128
Rocky La
Gatton Pk Rd, Red. 184 DD132
Gatton Pk Rd, Reig. 184 DD132
Gatton Rd SW17 120 DE91
Gatton Rd, Reig. 184 DC131
Gattons Way, Sid. 126 EZ91
Gatward Cl N21 29 DP44
Gatward Grn N9 46 DS47
Gatwick Rd SW18 119 CZ87
Gatwick Rd, Grav. 131 GH90
Gatwick Way, Horn. 72 FM63
Haydock Cl
Gauden Cl SW4 101 DK83
Gauden Rd SW4 101 DK82
Gaumont App, Wat. 23 BV41
Gaumont Ter W12 99 CW75
Lime Gro
Gaunt St SE1 201 H6
Gauntlet Cl, Nthlt. 78 BY66
Gauntlet Cres, Ken. 176 DR120
Gauntlett Ct, Wem. 61 CH64
Gauntlett Rd, Sutt. 158 DD106
Gautrey Rd SE15 102 DW82
Gautrey Sq E6 87 EM72
Gavel St SE17 201 L8
Gavell Rd, Cob. 153 BU113
Gavenny Path, S.Ock. 91 FT72
Gaveston Cl, W.Byf. 152 BM113
Gaveston Rd, Lthd. 171 CG120
Gavestone Cres SE12 124 EH87
Gavestone Rd SE12 124 EH87
Gaviller Pl E5 66 DV63
Clarence Rd
Gavin St SE18 105 ES77
Gavina Cl, Mord. 140 DE99
Gaviots Cl, Ger.Cr. 57 AZ60
Gaviots Grn, Ger.Cr. 56 AY60
Gaviots Way, Ger.Cr. 56 AY59
Gawber St E2 84 DW69
Gawsworth Cl E15 68 EE64
Ash Rd
Gawthorne Av NW7 43 CY50
Lane App
Gawthorne Ct E3 85 EA68
Mostyn Gro
Gay Cl NW2 63 CV64
Gay Gdns, Dag. 71 FC63
Gay Rd E15 85 ED68
Gay St SW15 99 CX83
Gaydon Ho W2 82 DB71
Gaydon La NW9 42 CS53
Gayfere Rd, Epsom 157 CU106
Gayfere Rd, Ilf. 69 EM55
Gayfere St SW1 199 P7
Gayfere St SW1 101 DL76
Gayford Rd W12 99 CT75
Gayhurst SE17 102 DR79
Hopwood Rd
Gayhurst Rd E8 84 DU66
Gayler Cl, Red. 186 DT133
Gaylor Rd, Nthlt. 60 BZ64
Gaylor Rd, Til. 110 GE81
Gaynes Ct, Upmin. 72 FP63
Gaynes Hill Rd, Wdf.Grn. 48 EL51
Gaynes Pk, Epp. 18 EY31
Gaynes Pk Rd, Upmin. 72 FN63
Gaynes Rd, Upmin. 72 FP61
Gaynesford Rd SE23 123 DX89
Gaynesford Rd, Cars. 158 DF108
Gaysham Av, Ilf. 69 EN57
Gaysham Hall, Ilf. 69 EP55
Gayton Cl, Amer. 20 AS35
Gayton Cl, Ash. 172 CL118
Gayton Ct, Har. 61 CF58
Gayton Cres NW3 64 DD63
Gayton Rd NW3 64 DD63
Gayton Rd SE2 106 EW76
Florence Rd
Gayton Rd, Har. 61 CF58
Gayville Rd SW11 120 DF86
Gaywood Av (Cheshunt), Wal.Cr. 15 DX30
Gaywood Cl SW2 121 DM88
Gaywood Est SE1 200 G7
Gaywood Est SE1 101 DP76
Gaywood Rd E17 67 EA55
Gaywood Rd, Ash. 172 CM118
Gaywood St SE1 200 G7
Gaza St SE17 101 DP78
Braganza St
Gazelda Vil, Wat. 24 BX43
Lower High St
Gazelle Glade, Grav. 131 GM92
Geariesville Gdns, Ilf. 69 EP56
Geary Dr, Brwd. 54 FW46
Geary Rd NW10 63 CU64
Geary St N7 65 DM64
Geddes Pl, Bexh. 106 FA84
Market Pl
Geddes Rd, Bushey 24 CC42
Gedeney Rd N17 46 DQ53
Gedling Pl SE1 202 A6
Gedling Pl SE1 102 DT75
Gee St EC1 197 H4
Gee St EC1 84 DQ70
Geere Rd E15 86 EF67
Gees Ct W1 194 G9
Geffrye Ct N1 197 N1
Geffrye Est N1 84 DS68
Stanway St
Geffrye St E2 84 DT68
Geisthorp Ct, Wal.Abb. 16 EG33
Winters Way
Geldart Rd SE15 102 DV80
Geldeston Rd E5 66 DU61
Gell Cl, Uxb. 58 BM62
Gellatly Rd SE14 102 DW82
Gelsthorpe Rd, Rom. 51 FB52
Gemini Gro, Nthlt. 78 BY69
Javelin Way
General Gordon Pl SE18 105 EP77
General Wolfe Rd SE10 103 ED81
Generals Wk, The, Enf. 31 DY37
Genesis Business Pk, Wok. 167 BC115
Genesis Cl (Stanwell), Stai. 114 BM88
Genesta Rd SE18 105 EP79
Geneva Cl, Shep. 135 BS96
Geneva Dr SW9 101 DN84
Geneva Gdns, Rom. 70 EY57
Geneva Rd, Kings.T. 138 CL98
Geneva Rd, Th.Hth. 142 DQ99
Genever Cl E4 47 EA50
Genista Rd N18 46 DV50
Genoa Av SW15 119 CW85
Genoa Rd SE20 142 DW95
Genotin Rd, Enf. 30 DR41
Genotin Ter, Enf. 30 DR41
Genotin Rd
Gentian Row SE13 103 EC81
Sparta St
Gentlemans Row, Enf. 30 DQ41
Gentry Gdns E13 86 EG70
Whitwell Rd
Geoffrey Av, Rom. 52 FN51
Geoffrey Cl SE5 102 DQ82
Geoffrey Gdns E6 86 EL68
Geoffrey Rd SE4 103 DZ83
George Avey Cft, Epp. 19 FB26
George Beard Rd SE8 203 M9
George Beard Rd SE8 103 DZ77
George Comberton Wk E12 69 EN64
Gainsborough Av
George Ct WC2 200 A1
George Cres N10 44 DG52
George Crook's Ho, Grays 110 GB79
New Rd
George Downing Est N16 66 DT61
Cazenove Rd
George V Av, Pnr. 60 CA55
George V Cl, Pnr. 60 CA55
George V Av
George V Way, Grnf. 79 CH67
George V Way, Rick. 22 BG36
George Gange Way, Har. 61 CE55
George Grn Dr, Slou. 75 AZ71
George Grn Rd, Slou. 74 AX72
George Gro Rd SE20 142 DU95
George Inn Yd SE1 201 K3
George La E18 48 EG54
George La SE13 123 EC86
George La, Brom. 144 EH102
George Lansbury Ho N22 45 DN53
Progress Way
George Loveless Ho E2 84 DT69
Diss St
George Lowe Ct W2 82 DB71
Bourne Ter
George Mathers Rd SE11 200 F8
George Mathers Rd SE11 101 DP77
George Ms NW1 195 K3
George Ms, Enf. 30 DR41
Sydney Rd
George Pl N17 66 DS55
Dongola Rd
George Rd E4 47 EA51
George Rd, Kings.T. 118 CP94
George Rd, N.Mal. 139 CT98
George Row SE16 202 B5
George Row SE16 102 DU75
George Sq SW19 139 CZ97
Mostyn Rd
George St E16 86 EF72
George St W1 194 E8
George St W1 82 DG72
George St W7 79 CE74
The Bdy
George St, Bark. 87 EQ66
George St, Croy. 142 DR103
George St, Grays 110 GA79
George St, Houns. 96 BZ82
George St, Rich. 117 CK85
George St, Rom. 71 FF58
George St, Sthl. 96 BY77
George St, Stai. 113 BF91
George St, Sutt. 158 DB106
George St, Uxb. 76 BK66
George St, Wat. 24 BW42
George Tilbury Ho, Grays 111 GH75
George Wyver Cl SW19 119 CY87
Beaumont Rd
George Yd EC3 197 L9
George Yd W1 194 G10
George Yd W1 82 DG73
Georgelands (Ripley), Wok. 168 BH121
Georges Cl, Orp. 146 EW97
Georges Dr, Brwd. 54 FT43
Georges Mead, Borwd. 25 CK44
George's Rd N7 65 DM64
Georges Rd, West. 178 EK120
Georges Sq SW6 99 CZ79
North End Rd
Georges Ter, Cat. 176 DQ122
Coulsdon Rd
George's Wd Rd, Hat. 12 DA26
Georgetown Cl SE19 122 DR92
St. Kitts Ter
Georgette Pl SE10 103 EC80
King George St
Georgeville Gdns, Ilf. 69 EP56
Georgewood Rd, Hem.H. 6 BM25
Georgia Rd, N.Mal. 138 CQ98
Georgia Rd, Th.Hth. 141 DP95
Georgian Cl, Brom. 144 EH101
Georgian Cl, Stai. 114 BH91
Georgian Cl, Stan. 41 CG52
Georgian Cl, Uxb. 58 BL63
Georgian Ct SW16 121 DL91
Gleneldon Rd
Georgian Ct, Wem. 80 CN65
Georgian Way, Har. 61 CD61
Georgiana St NW1 83 DJ67
Georgina Gdns E2 84 DT69
Columbia Rd
Geraint Rd, Brom. 124 EG91
Gerald Ms SW1 198 G8
Gerald Rd E16 86 EF70
Gerald Rd SW1 198 G8
Gerald Rd SW1 100 DG77
Gerald Rd, Dag. 70 EZ61
Gerald Rd, Grav. 131 GL87
Geraldine Rd SW18 120 DC85
Geraldine Rd W4 98 CN79
Geraldine St SE11 200 F7
Geraldine St SE11 101 DP76
Geralds Gro, Bans. 157 CX114
Gerard Av, Houns. 116 CA87
Redfern Av
Gerard Gdns, Rain. 89 FE68
Gerard Rd SW13 99 CT81
Gerard Rd, Har. 61 CG58
Gerards Cl SE16 102 DW78
Gerda Rd SE9 125 EQ89
Gerdview Dr, Dart. 128 FJ91
Germander Way E15 86 EE69
Gernon Cl, Rain. 90 FK68
Jordans Way
Gernon Rd E3 85 DY68
Geron Way NW2 63 CV60
Gerpins La, Upmin. 90 FM68
Gerrard Cres, Brwd. 54 FV48
Gerrard Gdns, Pnr. 59 BU57
Gerrard Pl W1 195 N10
Gerrard Rd N1 83 DP68
Gerrard St W1 195 M10
Gerrard St W1 83 DK73
Gerrards Cl N14 29 DJ43
Gerrards Cross Rd, Slou. 74 AU66
Gerrards Mead, Bans. 173 CZ117
Garratts La
Gerridge St SE1 200 E5
Gerridge St SE1 101 DN76
Gerry Raffles Sq E15 85 ED65
Salway Rd
Gertrude Rd, Belv. 106 FA77
Gertrude St SW10 100 DC79
Gervase Cl, Wem. 62 CQ62
Gervase Rd, Edg. 42 CQ53
Gervase St SE15 102 DV80
Gews Cor (Cheshunt), Wal.Cr. 15 DX29
Ghent St SE6 123 EA89
Ghent Way E8 84 DT65
Tyssen St
Giant Arches Rd SE24 122 DQ87
Giant Tree Hill, Bushey 41 CD46
Gibbard Ms SW19 119 CX92
Gibbfield Cl, Rom. 70 EY55
Gibbins Rd E15 85 EC66
Gibbon Rd SE15 102 DW82
Gibbon Rd W3 80 CS73
Gibbon Rd, Kings.T. 138 CL95
Gibbon Wk SW15 99 CU84
Swinburne Rd
Gibbons Cl, Borwd. 26 CL39
Gibbons Rd NW10 80 CR65
Gibbs Av SE19 122 DR92
Gibbs Cl SE19 122 DR92
Gibbs Cl (Cheshunt), Wal.Cr. 15 DX29
Gibbs Couch, Wat. 40 BX48
Gibbs Grn W14 99 CZ78
Gibbs Grn, Edg. 42 CQ50
Gibbs Rd N18 46 DW49
Gibbs Sq SE19 122 DR92
Gibraltar Cl, Brwd. 53 FW51
Essex Way
Gibraltar Cres, Epsom 156 CS110
Gibraltar Ho, Brwd. 53 FW51
Gibraltar Wk E2 84 DT69
Gibson Cl E1 84 DW70
Colebert Av
Gibson Cl N21 29 DN44
Gibson Cl, Chess. 155 CJ107
Gibson Cl, Epp. 19 FC25
Beamish Cl
Gibson Cl, Grav. 131 GF90
Gibson Cl, Islw. 97 CD83
Gibson Ct, Slou. 93 AZ78
Gibson Gdns N16 66 DT61
Northwold Rd
Gibson Pl, Stai. 114 BJ86
Gibson Rd SE11 200 C9
Gibson Rd SE11 101 DM77
Gibson Rd, Dag. 70 EW60
Gibson Rd, Sutt. 158 DB106
Gibson Rd, Uxb. 58 BM63
Gibson Sq N1 83 DN67
Gibson St SE10 104 EE78
Gibson's Hill SW16 121 DN93
Gidd Hill, Couls. 174 DG116
Gidea Av, Rom. 71 FG55
Gidea Cl, Rom. 71 FG55
Gidea Cl, S.Ock. 91 FW69
Tyssen Pl
Gideon Cl, Belv. 107 FB77
Gideon Ms W5 97 CK75
Gideon Rd SW11 100 DG83
Gidian Ct, St.Alb. 9 CD27
Giesbach Rd N19 65 DJ61
Giffard Rd N18 46 DS50
Giffin St SE8 103 EA80
Gifford Gdns W7 79 CD71
Gifford Pl, Brwd. 54 FX50
Blackthorn Way
Gifford St N1 83 DL66
Giffordside, Grays 111 GH78
Gift La E15 86 EE67
Giggs Hill, Orp. 146 EU96
Giggs Hill Gdns, T.Ditt. 137 CG102
Giggs Hill Rd, T.Ditt. 137 CG101
Gilbert Cl SE18 105 EM81
Gilbert Cl, Swans. 129 FX86
Gilbert Gro, Edg. 42 CR53
Gilbert Ho EC2 84 DQ71
Fore St
Gilbert Ho SE8 103 EA79
McMillan St
Gilbert Pl WC1 195 P7
Gilbert Rd SE11 200 E9
Gilbert Rd SE11 101 DN77

Gilbert Rd SW19 120 DC94
Gilbert Rd, Belv. 106 FA76
Gilbert Rd, Brom. 124 EG94
Gilbert Rd, Grays 109 FW76
Gilbert Rd, Pnr. 60 BX56
Gilbert Rd, Rom. 71 FF56
Gilbert Rd (Harefield), Uxb. 38 BK54
Gilbert St E15 68 EE63
Gilbert St W1 194 G10
Gilbert St W1 82 DG72
Gilbert St, Enf. 30 DW37
Gilbert St, Houns. 96 CC83
High St
Gilbert Way, Croy. 141 DL102
Beddington Fm Rd
Gilbey Cl, Uxb. 59 BP63
Gilbey Rd SW17 120 DE91
Gilbeys Yd NW1 83 DH67
Oval Rd
Gilbourne Rd SE18 105 ET79
Gilda Av, Enf. 31 DY43
Gilda Cres N16 66 DU60
Gildea Cl, Pnr. 40 CA52
Gildea St W1 195 J7
Gilden Cres NW5 64 DG64
Gildenhill Rd, Swan. 128 FJ94
Gilders Rd, Chess. 156 CM107
Gildersome St SE18 105 EN79
Nightingale Vale
Giles Cl, Rain. 90 FK68
Giles Coppice SE19 122 DT91
Giles Travers Cl, Egh. 133 BC97
Gilfrid Cl, Uxb. 77 BP72
Craig Dr
Gilhams Av, Bans. 157 CY112
Gilkes Cres SE21 122 DS86
Gilkes Pl SE21 122 DS86
Gill Av E16 86 EG72
Gill Cl, Wat. 23 BQ44
Gill Cres, Grav. 131 GF90
Gill St E14 85 DZ72
Gillam Way, Rain. 89 FG65
Gillan Grn, Bushey 40 CC47
Gillards Ms E17 67 EA56
Gillards Way
Gillards Way E17 67 EA56
Gillender St E3 85 EC70
Gillender St E14 85 EC70
Gillespie Rd N5 65 DN62
Gillett Av E6 86 EL68
Gillett Pl N16 66 DS64
Gillett St
Gillett Rd, Th.Hth. 142 DR98
Gillett St N16 66 DS64
Gillette Cor, Islw. 97 CG80
Gillfoot NW1 195 L1
Gillfoot NW1 83 DJ68
Gillham Ter N17 46 DU51
Gilliam Gro, Pur. 159 DN110
Gillian Cres, Rom. 52 FJ54
Gillian Pk Rd, Sutt. 139 CZ102
Gillian St SE13 123 EB85
Gilliat Cl, Iver 75 BE72
Dutton Way
Gilliat Rd, Slou. 74 AS73
Gilliat's Grn, Rick. 21 BD42
Gillies St NW5 64 DG64
Gilling Ct NW3 82 DE65
Gillingham Ms SW1 199 K8
Gillingham Rd NW2 63 CY62
Gillingham Row SW1 199 K8
Gillingham St SW1 199 K8
Gillingham St SW1 101 DH77
Gillison Wk SE16 202 C6
Gillman Dr E15 86 EF67
Gillmans Rd, Orp. 146 EV102
Gills Hill, Rad. 25 CF35
Gills Hill La, Rad. 25 CF36
Gills Hollow, Rad. 25 CF36
Gill's Rd, Dart. 149 FS95
Gillum Cl, Barn. 44 DF46
Gilmore Cl, Slou. 92 AW75
Gilmore Cl, Uxb. 58 BN62
Gilmore Cres, Ashf. 114 BN92
Gilmore Rd SE13 103 ED84
Gilmour Cl, Wal.Cr. 30 DU35
Gilpin Av SW14 98 CR84
Gilpin Cl W2 82 DC71
Porteus Rd
Gilpin Cl, Mitch. 140 DE96
Gilpin Cres N18 46 DT50
Gilpin Cres, Twick. 116 CB87
Gilpin Rd E5 67 DY63
Gilpin Way, Hayes 95 BR80
Gilroy Cl, Rain. 89 FF65
Gilroy Way, Orp. 146 EV101
Gilsland, Wal.Abb. 32 EE35
Gilsland Rd, Th.Hth. 142 DR98
Gilstead Ho, Bark. 88 EV68
Gilstead Rd SW6 100 DB82
Gilston Rd SW10 100 DC78
Gilton Rd SE6 124 EE90
Giltspur St EC1 196 G8
Giltspur St EC1 83 DP72
Gilwell Cl E4 31 EB42
Antlers Hill
Gilwell La E4 31 EC42
Gilwell Pk E4 31 EC41
Gimcrack Hill, Lthd. 171 CH123
Dorking Rd
Gippeswyck Cl, Pnr. 40 BX53
Uxbridge Rd
Gipsy Hill SE19 122 DS92
Gipsy La SW15 99 CU83
Gipsy La, Grays 110 GC79
Gipsy Rd SE27 122 DQ91
Gipsy Rd, Well. 106 EX81
Gipsy Rd Gdns SE27 122 DQ91
Giralda Cl E16 86 EK71
Fulmer Rd
Giraud St E14 85 EB72
Girdlers Rd W14 99 CX77
Girdlestone Wk N19 65 DJ61
Girdwood Rd SW18 119 CY87
Girling Way, Felt. 95 BU83
Girona Cl (Chafford Hundred), Grays 109 FW76
Gironde Rd SW6 99 CZ80
Girtin Rd, Bushey 24 CB43
Girton Av NW9 62 CN55
Girton Cl, Nthlt. 78 CC65
Girton Ct, Wal.Cr. 15 DY30
Girton Gdns, Croy. 143 EA104
Girton Rd SE26 123 DX92
Girton Rd, Nthlt. 78 CC65
Girton Vil W10 81 CX72
Girton Way, Rick. 23 BQ43
Gisborne Gdns, Rain. 89 FF69
Gisbourne Cl, Wall. 141 DK104
Gisburn Rd N8 65 DM56
Gisburne Way, Wat. 23 BU37
Gissing Wk N1 83 DN66
Lofting Rd
Gittens Cl, Brom. 124 EF91
Given Wilson Wk E13 86 EF68
Glacier Way, Wem. 79 CK68
Gladbeck Way, Enf. 29 DP42
Gladding Rd E12 68 EK63
Gladding Rd (Cheshunt), Wal.Cr. 13 DP25
Glade, The N21 29 DM44
Glade, The SE7 104 EJ80
Glade, The, Brwd. 55 GA46
Glade, The, Brom. 144 EK96
Glade, The, Couls. 175 DN119
Glade, The, Croy. 143 DX99
Glade, The, Enf. 29 DN41
Glade, The, Epsom 157 CU106
Glade, The, Ger.Cr. 56 AX60
Glade, The, Ilf. 49 EM53
Glade, The, Lthd. 170 CA122
Glade, The, Sev. 191 FH123
Glade, The, Stai. 114 BH94
Glade, The, Sutt. 157 CY109
Glade, The, Tad. 174 DA121
Glade, The, Upmin. 72 FQ64
Glade, The, W.Byf. 151 BE113
Glade, The, W.Wick. 143 EB104
Glade, The, Wdf.Grn. 48 EH48
Glade Cl, Surb. 137 CK103
Glade Ct, Ilf. 49 EM53
The Glade
Glade Gdns, Croy. 143 DY101
Glade La, Sthl. 96 CB75
Glade Spur, Tad. 174 DB121
Glades, The, Grav. 131 GK93
Glades Pl, Brom. 144 EG96
Widmore Rd
Glades Shop Cen, The, Brom. 144 EG96
Gladeside N21 29 DM44
Gladeside, Croy. 143 DX100
Gladeside Cl, Chess. 155 CK108
Leatherhead Rd
Gladeside Ct, Warl. 176 DV120
Gladesmore Rd N15 66 DT58
Gladeswood Rd, Belv. 107 FB77
Gladeway, The, Wal.Abb. 15 ED33
Gladiator St SE23 123 DY86
Glading Ter N16 66 DT62
Gladioli Cl, Hmptn. 116 CA93
Gresham Rd
Gladsdale Dr, Pnr. 59 BU56
Gladsmuir Cl, Walt. 136 BW103
Gladsmuir Rd N19 65 DJ60
Gladsmuir Rd, Barn. 27 CY40
Gladstone Av E12 86 EL66
Gladstone Av N22 45 DN54
Gladstone Av, Felt. 115 BU86
Gladstone Av, Twick. 117 CD87
Gladstone Gdns, Houns. 96 CC81
Gresham Rd
Gladstone Ms NW6 81 CZ66
Cavendish Rd
Gladstone Ms SE20 122 DW94
Gladstone Par NW2 63 CV60
Edgware Rd
Gladstone Pk Gdns NW2 63 CV62
Gladstone Pl E3 85 DZ68
Roman Rd
Gladstone Pl, Barn. 27 CX42
Gladstone Rd SW19 120 DA94
Gladstone Rd W4 98 CR76
Acton La
Gladstone Rd, Ash. 171 CK118
Gladstone Rd, Buck.H. 48 EH46
Gladstone Rd, Croy. 142 DR101
Gladstone Rd, Dart. 128 FM86
Gladstone Rd, Kings.T. 138 CN97
Gladstone Rd, Orp. 163 EQ106
Gladstone Rd, Sthl. 96 BY76
Gladstone Rd, Surb. 137 CK103
Gladstone Rd, Wat. 24 BW41
Gladstone St SE1 200 F6
Gladstone St SE1 101 DP76
Gladstone Ter SE27 122 DQ91
Gladstone Ter SW8 101 DH81
Gladstone Way, Har. 61 CE55
Gladwell Rd N8 65 DM58
Gladwell Rd, Brom. 124 EG93
Gladwyn Rd SW15 99 CX83
Gladys Rd NW6 82 DA66
Glaisyer Way, Iver 75 BC68
Glamis Cl (Cheshunt), Wal.Cr. 14 DU29
Glamis Cres, Hayes 95 BQ76
Glamis Dr, Horn. 72 FL60
Glamis Pl E1 84 DW73
Glamis Rd E1 84 DW73
Glamis Way, Nthlt. 78 CC65
Glamorgan Cl, Mitch. 141 DL97
Glamorgan Rd, Kings.T. 117 CJ94
Glanfield Rd, Beck. 143 DZ98
Glanleam Rd, Stan. 41 CK49
Glanmead, Brwd. 54 FY46
Glanmor Rd, Slou. 74 AV73
Glanthams Cl, Brwd. 54 FY47
Glanthams Rd, Brwd. 55 FZ47
Glanty, The, Egh. 113 BB91
Glanville Dr, Horn. 72 FM60
Glanville Rd SW2 121 DL85
Glanville Rd, Brom. 144 EH97
Glasbrook Av, Twick. 116 BZ88
Glasbrook Rd SE9 124 EK87
Glaserton Rd N16 66 DS59
Glasford St SW17 120 DF93
Glasgow Ho W9 82 DB68
Glasgow Rd E13 86 EH68
Glasgow Rd N18 46 DV50
Aberdeen Rd
Glasgow Ter SW1 101 DJ78
Glass St E2 84 DV70
Coventry Rd
Glass Yd SE18 105 EN76
Woolwich High St
Glasse Cl W13 79 CG73
Glasshill St SE1 200 G4
Glasshill St SE1 101 DP75
Glasshouse All EC4 196 E9
Glasshouse Flds E1 85 DX73
Glasshouse St W1 199 L1
Glasshouse St W1 83 DJ73
Glasshouse Wk SE11 200 A10
Glasshouse Wk SE11 101 DL78
Glasshouse Yd EC1 197 H6
Glasslyn Rd N8 65 DK57
Glassmill La, Brom. 144 EF96
Glastonbury Av, Wdf.Grn. 48 EK52
Glastonbury Cl, Orp. 146 EW102
Glastonbury Rd N9 46 DT46
Glastonbury Rd, Mord. 140 DA101
Glastonbury St NW6 63 CZ64
Glaucus St E3 85 EB71
Glazbury Rd W14 99 CY77
Glazebrook Cl SE21 122 DR89
Glazebrook Rd, Tedd. 117 CF94
Glebe, The SE3 104 EE83
Glebe, The SW16 121 DK91
Glebe, The, Chis. 145 EQ95
Glebe, The, Kings L. 6 BN29
Glebe, The, Wat. 8 BW33
Glebe, The, West Dr. 94 BM77
Glebe, The, Wor.Pk. 139 CT102
Glebe Av, Enf. 29 DP41
Glebe Av, Har. 62 CL55
Glebe Av, Mitch. 140 DE96
Glebe Av, Ruis. 77 BV65
Glebe Av, Uxb. 59 BQ63
Glebe Av, Wdf.Grn. 48 EG51
Glebe Cl W4 98 CS78
Glebe St
Glebe Cl (Chalfont St. Peter), Ger.Cr. 36 AX52
Glebe Cl, S.Croy. 160 DT111
Glebe Cl, Uxb. 59 BQ63
Glebe Cotts, Sutt. 158 DB105
Vale Rd
Glebe Cotts, West. 180 EV123
Glebe Ct W7 79 CD73
Glebe Ct, Mitch. 140 DF97
Glebe Ct, Sev. 191 FH126
Oak La
Glebe Ct, Stan. 41 CJ50
Glebe Rd
Glebe Cres NW4 63 CW56
Glebe Cres, Har. 62 CL55
Glebe Gdns, N.Mal. 138 CS101
Glebe Gdns, W.Byf. 152 BK114
Glebe Ho Dr, Brom. 144 EH102
Glebe Hyrst SE19 122 DT91
Giles Coppice
Glebe Hyrst, S.Croy. 160 DT112
Glebe La, Barn. 27 CU43
Glebe La, Har. 62 CL56
Glebe La, Sev. 191 FH126
Glebe Path, Mitch. 140 DE97
Glebe Pl SW3 100 DE79
Glebe Pl (Horton Kirby), Dart. 148 FQ98
Glebe Rd E8 84 DT66
Middleton Rd
Glebe Rd N3 44 DC53
Glebe Rd N8 65 DM56
Glebe Rd NW10 81 CT65
Glebe Rd SW13 99 CU82
Glebe Rd, Ash. 171 CK118
Glebe Rd, Brom. 144 EG95
Glebe Rd, Cars. 158 DF107
Glebe Rd, Dag. 89 FB65
Glebe Rd, Egh. 113 BC93
Glebe Rd (Chalfont St. Peter), Ger.Cr. 36 AW53
Glebe Rd, Grav. 131 GF88
Glebe Rd, Hayes 77 BT74
Glebe Rd, Rain. 90 FJ69
Glebe Rd, Red. 175 DH124
Glebe Rd, Stai. 114 BH93
Glebe Rd, Stan. 41 CJ50
Glebe Rd, Sutt. 157 CY109
Glebe Rd, Uxb. 76 BJ68
Glebe Rd, Warl. 177 DX117
Glebe Rd, Wind. 112 AV85
Glebe Side, Twick. 117 CF86
Glebe St W4 98 CS78
Glebe Ter E3 85 EA69
Bow Rd
Glebe Way, Erith 107 FE79
Glebe Way, Felt. 116 CA90
Glebe Way, Horn. 72 FL59
Glebe Way, S.Croy. 160 DT111
Glebe Way, W.Wick. 143 EC103
Glebefield, The, Sev. 190 FF123
Glebeland Gdns, Shep. 135 BQ100
Glebelands, Chig. 50 EV48
Glebelands, Dart. 107 FF84
Glebelands, Esher 155 CF109
Glebelands, W.Mol. 136 CB99
Glebelands Av E18 48 EG54
Glebelands Av, Ilf. 69 ER59
Glebelands Cl SE5 102 DS83
Grove Hill Rd
Glebelands Rd, Felt. 115 BU87
Glebeway, Wdf.Grn. 48 EJ50
Gledhow Gdns SW5 100 DC77
Gledhow Wd, Tad. 174 DB121
Gledstanes Rd W14 99 CY78
Gledwood Av, Hayes 77 BT71
Gledwood Cres, Hayes 77 BT71
Gledwood Dr, Hayes 77 BT71
Gledwood Gdns, Hayes 77 BT71
Gleed Av, Bushey 41 CD47
Gleeson Dr, Orp. 163 ET106
Gleeson Ms, Add. 152 BJ105
Glegg Pl SW15 99 CX84
Glen, The, Add. 151 BF106
Glen, The, Brom. 144 EE96
Glen, The, Croy. 143 DX103
Glen, The, Enf. 29 DP42
Glen, The, Nthwd. 39 BR52
Glen, The, Orp. 145 EM104
Glen, The, Pnr. 60 BY59
Glen, The (Eastcote), Pnr. 59 BV57
Glen, The, Rain. 90 FJ70
Glen, The, Slou. 92 AW77
Glen, The, Sthl. 96 BZ78
Glen, The, Wem. 61 CK63
Glen Albyn Rd SW19 119 CX89
Glen Av, Ashf. 114 BN91
Glen Cl, Shep. 134 BN98
Glen Cl, Tad. 173 CY123
Glen Cres, Wdf.Grn. 48 EH51
Glen Gdns, Croy. 141 DN104
Glen Ri, Wdf.Grn. 48 EH51
Glen Rd E13 86 EJ70
Glen Rd E17 67 DZ57
Glen Rd, Chess. 138 CL104
Glen Rd End, Wall. 159 DH109
Glen Ter E14 204 E4
Glen Vw, Grav. 131 GJ88
Glen Wk, Islw. 117 CD85
Glen Way, Wat. 23 BS38
Glena Mt, Sutt. 158 DC105
Glenaffric Av E14 204 F9
Glenaffric Av E14 103 ED77
Glenalla Rd, Ruis. 59 BT59
Glenalmond Rd, Har. 62 CL56
Glenalvon Way SE18 104 EL77
Glenarm Rd E5 66 DW64
Glenavon Cl, Esher 155 CG108
Glenavon Gdns, Slou. 92 AW77
Glenavon Rd E15 86 EE66
Glenbarr Cl SE9 105 EP83
Dumbreck Rd
Glenbow Rd, Brom. 124 EE93
Glenbrook N, Enf. 29 DM42
Glenbrook Rd NW6 64 DA64
Glenbrook S, Enf. 29 DM42
Glenbuck Ct, Surb. 137 CK100
Glenbuck Rd
Glenbuck Rd, Surb. 137 CK100
Glenburnie Rd SW17 120 DF90
Glencairn Dr W5 79 CJ70
Glencairn Rd SW16 121 DL94
Glencairne Cl E16 86 EK71
Glencoe Av, Ilf. 69 ER59
Glencoe Dr, Dag. 70 FA63
Glencoe Rd, Bushey 24 CA44
Glencoe Rd, Hayes 78 BX71
Glencoe Rd, Wey. 134 BN104
Glencorse Grn, Wat. 40 BX49
Caldwell Rd
Glendale, Swan. 147 FF99
Glendale Av N22 45 DN52
Glendale Av, Edg. 42 CM49
Glendale Av, Rom. 70 EW59
Glendale Cl SE9 105 EN83
Dumbreck Rd
Glendale Cl, Brwd. 54 FY45
Glendale Cl, Wok. 166 AW118
Glendale Dr SW19 119 CZ92
Glendale Gdns, Wem. 61 CK60
Glendale Ms, Beck. 143 EB95
Glendale Ri, Ken. 175 DP115
Glendale Rd, Erith 107 FC77
Glendale Rd, Grav. 130 GE91
Glendale Wk (Cheshunt), Wal.Cr. 15 DY30
Glendale Way SE28 88 EW73
Glendall St SW9 101 DM84
Glendarvon St SW15 99 CX83
Glendevon Cl, Edg. 42 CP48
Tayside Dr
Glendish Rd N17 46 DV53
Glendor Gdns NW7 42 CR49
Glendower Cres, Orp. 146 EU100
Glendower Gdns SW14 98 CR83
Glendower Rd
Glendower Pl SW7 100 DD77
Glendower Rd E4 47 ED46
Glendower Rd SW14 98 CR83
Glendown Rd SE2 106 EU78
Glendun Rd W3 80 CS73
Gleneagle Ms SW16 121 DK92
Ambleside Av
Gleneagle Rd SW16 121 DK92
Gleneagles, Stan. 41 CH51
Gleneagles Cl SE16 102 DV78
Ryder Dr
Gleneagles Cl, Orp. 145 ER102
Gleneagles Cl, Rom. 52 FM52
Gleneagles Cl, Stai. 114 BK86
Gleneagles Cl, Wat. 40 BX49
Gleneagles Grn, Orp. 145 ER102
Tandridge Dr
Gleneagles Twr, Sthl. 78 CC72
Gleneldon Ms SW16 121 DL91
Gleneldon Rd SW16 121 DL91
Glenelg Rd SW2 121 DL85
Glenesk Rd SE9 105 EN83
Glenfarg Rd SE6 123 ED88
Glenfield Cres, Ruis. 59 BR59
Glenfield Rd SW12 121 DJ88
Glenfield Rd W13 97 CH75
Glenfield Rd, Ashf. 115 BP93
Glenfield Rd, Bans. 174 DB115
Glenfield Ter W13 97 CH75
Glenfinlas Way SE5 101 DP80
Glenforth St SE10 205 L10
Glenforth St SE10 104 EF78
Glengall Causeway E14 203 P6
Glengall Causeway E14 103 EA76
Glengall Gro E14 204 D6
Glengall Gro E14 103 EC76
Glengall Rd NW6 81 CZ67
Glengall Rd SE15 102 DT79
Glengall Rd, Bexh. 106 EY83
Glengall Rd, Edg. 42 CP48
Glengall Rd, Wdf.Grn. 48 EG51
Glengall Ter SE15 102 DT79
Glengarnock Av E14 204 E9
Glengarnock Av E14 103 EC77
Glengarry Rd SE22 122 DS85
Glenham Dr, Ilf. 69 EP57
Glenhaven Av, Borwd. 26 CN41
Glenhead Cl SE9 105 EP83
Dumbreck Rd
Glenheadon Cl, Lthd. 171 CK123
Glenheadon Ri
Glenheadon Ri, Lthd. 171 CK123
Glenhill Cl N3 44 DA54
Glenhouse Rd SE9 125 EN85
Glenhurst Av NW5 64 DG63
Glenhurst Av, Bex. 126 EZ88
Glenhurst Av, Ruis. 59 BQ59
Glenhurst Ct SE19 122 DT92
Glenhurst Ri SE19 122 DQ94
Glenhurst Rd N12 44 DD50
Glenhurst Rd, Brent. 97 CJ79
Glenilla Rd NW3 82 DE65
Glenister Ho, Hayes 77 BV74
Glenister Pk Rd SW16 121 DK94
Glenister Rd SE10 205 K10
Glenister Rd SE10 104 EF78
Glenister St E16 87 EN74
Glenlea Rd SE9 125 EM85
Glenlion Ct, Wey. 135 BS104
Glenloch Rd NW3 82 DE65
Glenloch Rd, Enf. 30 DW40
Glenluce Rd SE3 104 EG79
Glenlyon Rd SE9 125 EN85
Glenmere Av NW7 43 CU52
Glenmill, Hmptn. 116 BZ92
Glenmore Cl, Add. 134 BH104
Glenmore Gdns, Abb.L. 7 BU32
Stewart Cl
Glenmore Rd NW3 82 DE65
Glenmore Rd, Well. 105 ET81
Glenmore Way, Bark. 88 EU68
Glenmount Path SE18 105 EQ78
Raglan Rd
Glenn Av, Pur. 159 DP111
Glennie Rd SE27 121 DN90
Glenny Rd, Bark. 87 EQ65
Glenorchy Cl, Hayes 78 BY71
Glenparke Rd E7 86 EH65
Glenrosa Gdns, Grav. 131 GM92
Glenrosa St SW6 100 DC82
Glenrose Ct, Sid. 126 EV92
Glenroy St W12 81 CW72
Glensdale Rd SE4 103 DZ83
Glenshee Cl, Nthwd. 39 BQ51
Rickmansworth Rd
Glenshiel Rd SE9 125 EN85
Glenside, Chig. 49 EP51
Glenside Cotts, Slou. 92 AT76
Glentanner Way SW17 120 DD90
Aboyne Rd
Glentham Gdns SW13 99 CV79
Glentham Rd
Glentham Rd SW13 99 CU79
Glenthorne Av, Croy. 142 DV102
Glenthorne Cl, Sutt. 140 DA102
Glenthorne Cl, Uxb. 76 BN69
Uxbridge Rd
Glenthorne Gdns, Ilf. 69 EN55
Glenthorne Gdns, Sutt. 140 DA102
Glenthorne Ms W6 99 CV77
Glenthorne Rd
Glenthorne Rd E17 67 DY57
Glenthorne Rd N11 44 DF50
Glenthorne Rd W6 99 CW77
Glenthorne Rd, Kings.T. 138 CM98
Glenthorpe Rd, Mord. 139 CX99
Glenton Cl, Rom. 51 FE51
Glenton Rd SE13 104 EE84
Glenton Way, Rom. 51 FE52
Glentrammon Av, Orp. 163 ET107
Glentrammon Cl, Orp. 163 ET107
Glentrammon Gdns, Orp. 163 ET107
Glentrammon Rd, Orp. 163 ET107
Glentworth St NW1 194 E5
Glentworth St NW1 82 DF70
Glenure Rd SE9 125 EN85
Glenview SE2 106 EX79
Glenview Rd, Brom. 144 EK96
Glenville Av, Enf. 30 DQ38
Glenville Gro SE8 103 DZ80
Glenville Ms SW18 120 DB87
Glenville Rd, Kings.T. 138 CN95
Glenwood Av NW9 62 CS60
Glenwood Av, Rain. 89 FH70
Glenwood Cl, Har. 61 CF57
Glenwood Dr, Rom. 71 FG56
Glenwood Gdns, Ilf. 69 EN57
Glenwood Gro NW9 62 CQ60
Glenwood Rd N15 65 DP57
Glenwood Rd NW7 42 CS48
Glenwood Rd SE6 123 DZ88
Glenwood Rd, Epsom 157 CU107
Glenwood Rd, Houns. 97 CD83
Glenwood Way, Croy. 143 DX100
Glenworth Av E14 204 F9
Glenworth Av E14 103 ED77
Gliddon Rd W14 99 CY77
Glimpsing Grn, Erith 106 EY76
Glisson Rd, Uxb. 76 BN68
Gload Cres, Orp. 146 EX103
Global App E3 85 EB68
Hancock Rd
Globe Ind Estates, Grays 110 GC78
Globe Pond Rd SE16 203 K3
Globe Pond Rd SE16 85 DY74
Globe Rd E1 84 DW69
Globe Rd E2 202 E5
Globe Rd E2 84 DW69
Globe Rd E15 68 EF64
Globe Rd, Horn. 71 FG58
Globe Rd, Wdf.Grn. 48 EJ51
Globe Rope Wk E14 204 D9
Globe Rope Wk E14 103 EC77
Globe St SE1 201 J6
Globe St SE1 102 DR76
Globe Ter E2 84 DW69
Globe Rd
Globe Yd W1 195 H9
Glossop Rd, S.Croy. 160 DR109
Gloster Rd, N.Mal. 138 CS98
Gloster Rd, Wok. 167 BA120
Gloucester Arc SW7 100 DC77
Gloucester Rd
Gloucester Av NW1 82 DG66
Gloucester Av, Grays 110 GC75
Gloucester Av, Horn. 72 FN56
Gloucester Av, Sid. 125 ES89
Gloucester Av, Wal.Cr. 15 DY33
Gloucester Av, Well. 105 ET84
Gloucester Circ SE10 103 EC80
Gloucester Cl NW10 80 CR66
Gloucester Cl, S.Ock. 91 FW69
South Rd
Gloucester Ct, T.Ditt. 137 CG102
Gloucester Ct EC3 201 N1
Gloucester Ct, Rich. 98 CN80
Gloucester Ct, Til. 111 GF82
Dock Rd

Gloucester Ct (Denham), Uxb. 58 BG58
Moorfield Rd
Gloucester Cres NW1 83 DH67
Gloucester Cres, Stai. 114 BK93
Gloucester Dr N4 65 DP61
Gloucester Dr NW11 64 DA56
Gloucester Dr, Stai. 113 BC90
Gloucester Gdns NW11 63 CZ59
Gloucester Gdns W2 82 DC72
Bishops Br Rd
Gloucester Gdns, Barn. 28 DG42
Gloucester Gdns, Ilf. 68 EL59
Gloucester Gdns, Sutt. 140 DB103
Gloucester Gate NW1 83 DH68
Gloucester Gate Ms NW1 83 DH68
Gloucester Gate
Gloucester Gro, Edg. 42 CR53
Gloucester Gro Est SE15 102 DS79
Gloucester Ho N7 65 DL62
Gloucester Ho NW6 82 DA68
Gloucester Ms E10 67 EA59
Gloucester Rd
Gloucester Ms W2 82 DC72
Gloucester Ms W W2 82 DC72
Cleveland Ter
Gloucester Par, Sid. 126 EU85
Gloucester Pl NW1 194 D4
Gloucester Pl NW1 82 DF70
Gloucester Pl W1 194 E6
Gloucester Pl W1 82 DF71
Gloucester Pl, Enf. 30 DQ40
Chase Side
Gloucester Pl Ms W1 194 E7
Gloucester Rd E10 67 EA59
Gloucester Rd E11 68 EH57
Gloucester Rd E12 69 EM62
Gloucester Rd E17 47 DX54
Gloucester Rd N17 46 DR54
Gloucester Rd N18 46 DT50
Gloucester Rd SW7 100 DC77
Gloucester Rd W3 98 CQ75
Gloucester Rd W5 97 CJ75
Gloucester Rd, Barn. 28 DC43
Gloucester Rd, Belv. 106 EZ78
Gloucester Rd, Brwd. 54 FV43
Gloucester Rd, Croy. 142 DR100
Gloucester Rd, Dart. 127 FH87
Gloucester Rd, Enf. 30 DQ38
Gloucester Rd, Felt. 116 BW88
Gloucester Rd, Grav. 131 GJ91
Gloucester Rd, Hmptn. 116 CB94
Gloucester Rd, Har. 60 CB57
Gloucester Rd, Houns. 96 BY84
Gloucester Rd, Kings.T. 138 CP96
Gloucester Rd, Red. 184 DF133
Gloucester Rd, Rich. 98 CN80
Gloucester Rd, Rom. 71 FE58
Gloucester Rd, Tedd. 117 CE92
Gloucester Rd, Twick. 116 CC88
Gloucester Sq E2 84 DU67
Whiston Rd
Gloucester Sq W2 194 A9
Gloucester Sq W2 82 DD72
Gloucester Sq, Wok. 166 AY117
Church St E
Gloucester St SW1 101 DJ78
Gloucester Ter W2 82 DD73
Gloucester Wk W8 100 DA75
Gloucester Wk, Wok. 167 AZ117
Gloucester Wk, Wok. 167 AZ117
Church St E
Gloucester Way EC1 196 E3
Gloucester Way EC1 83 DN69
Glover Cl SE2 106 EW77
Glover Cl, Wal.Cr. 14 DT27
Allwood Rd
Glover Dr N18 46 DW51
Glover Rd, Pnr. 60 BX58
Glovers Gro, Ruis. 59 BP59
Gloxinia Rd, Grav. 130 GB93
Gloxinia Wk, Hmptn. 116 CA93
Glycena Rd SW11 100 DF83
Glyn Av, Barn. 28 DD42
Glyn Cl SE25 142 DS96
Glyn Cl, Epsom 157 CU109
Glyn Ct SW16 121 DN90
Glyn Davies Cl, Sev. 181 FE120
Glyn Dr, Sid. 126 EV91
Glyn Rd E5 67 DX63
Glyn Rd, Enf. 30 DW42
Glyn Rd, Wor.Pk. 139 CX103
Glyn St SE11 101 DM78
Kennington La
Glynde Ms SW3 198 C7
Glynde Rd, Bexh. 106 EX83
Glynde St SE4 123 DZ86
Glyndebourne Pk, Orp. 145 EP103
Glyndon Rd SE18 105 EQ77
Glynfield Rd NW10 80 CS66
Glynne Rd N22 45 DN54
Glynswood (Chalfont St. Peter), Ger.Cr. 37 AZ52
Glynwood Ct SE23 122 DW89
Goat La, Enf. 30 DT38
Goat La, Surb. 137 CJ103
Goat Rd, Mitch. 140 DG101
Goat St SE1 201 P4
Goat Wf, Brent. 98 CL79
Goaters All SW6 99 CZ80
Goatsfield Rd, West. 178 EJ120
Goatswood La, Rom. 51 FH45
Gobions Av, Rom. 51 FD52
Gobions Way, Pot.B. 12 DB28
Swanley Bar La
Godalming Av, Wall. 159 DL106
Godalming Rd E14 85 EB71
Godbold Rd E15 86 EE69
Goddard Cl, Shep. 134 BM97
Magdalene Rd
Goddard Rd, Beck. 143 DX98
Goddards Way, Ilf. 69 ER60
Goddington Chase, Orp. 164 EV105
Goddington La, Orp. 146 EU104
Godfrey Av, Nthlt. 78 BY67
Godfrey Av, Twick. 117 CD87
Godfrey Hill SE18 104 EL77
Godfrey Rd SE18 105 EM77
Godfrey St E15 85 EC68
Godfrey St SW3 198 C10
Godfrey St SW3 100 DE78
Godfrey Way, Houns. 116 BZ87
Goding St SE11 101 DL78
Godley Rd SW18 120 DD88
Godley Rd, W.Byf. 152 BM113
Godliman St EC4 197 H9
Godliman St EC4 84 DQ72
Godman Rd SE15 102 DV82
Godman Rd, Grays 111 GG76
Godolphin Cl N13 45 DP51
Godolphin Cl, Sutt. 157 CZ111
Godolphin Pl W3 80 CR73
Vyner Rd
Godolphin Rd W12 99 CV75
Godolphin Rd, Wey. 153 BR107
Godric Cres, Croy. 161 ED110
Godson Rd, Croy. 141 DN104
Godson St N1 83 DN68
Godstone Bypass, Gdse. 186 DW129
Godstone Grn, Gdse. 186 DV131
Godstone Grn Rd, Gdse. 186 DV131
Godstone Hill, Gdse. 186 DV127
Godstone Rd, Cat. 176 DU124
Godstone Rd, Ken. 159 DN112
Godstone Rd, Oxt. 187 EA131
Godstone Rd, Pur. 159 DN112
Godstone Rd, Red. 186 DR133
Godstone Rd, Sutt. 158 DC105
Godstone Rd, Twick. 117 CH86
Godstone Rd, Whyt. 176 DT116
Godstow Rd SE2 106 EW75
Godwin Cl E4 31 EC38
Godwin Cl N1 84 DQ68
Napier Gro
Godwin Cl, Epsom 156 CQ107
Godwin Ct NW1 83 DJ68
Crowndale Rd
Godwin Rd E7 68 EH63
Godwin Rd, Brom. 144 EJ97
Goffers Rd SE3 103 ED81
Goffs Cres (Cheshunt), Wal.Cr. 13 DP29
Goffs La (Cheshunt), Wal.Cr. 14 DR29
Goffs Oak Av (Cheshunt), Wal.Cr. 13 DP28
Goffs Rd, Ashf. 115 BR93
Gogmore Fm Cl, Cher. 133 BF101
Gogmore La, Cher. 134 BG101
Goidel Cl, Wall. 159 DK105
Golborne Gdns W10 81 CZ70
Golborne Rd
Golborne Ms W10 81 CY71
Portobello Rd
Golborne Rd W10 81 CY71
Gold Hill, Edg. 42 CR51
Gold Hill E (Chalfont St. Peter), Ger.Cr. 36 AX54
Gold Hill N (Chalfont St. Peter), Ger.Cr. 36 AW53
Gold Hill W (Chalfont St. Peter), Ger.Cr. 36 AW53
Gold La, Edg. 42 CR51
Golda Cl, Barn. 27 CX44
Goldace, Grays 110 FZ79
Goldbeaters Gro, Edg. 42 CS51
Goldcliff Cl, Mord. 140 DA100
Goldcrest Cl E16 86 EK71
Sheerwater Rd
Goldcrest Cl SE28 88 EW73
Goldcrest Ms W5 79 CK71
Montpelier Av
Goldcrest Way, Bushey 40 CC46
Goldcrest Way, Croy. 161 ED109
Goldcrest Way, Pur. 159 DK110
Golden Ct, Rich. 117 CK85
George St
Golden Cres, Hayes 77 BT74
Golden Cross Ms W11 81 CZ72
Basing St
Golden La EC1 197 H5
Golden La EC1 84 DQ70
Golden La Est EC1 197 H5
Golden Manor W7 79 CE73
Golden Plover Cl E16 86 EH72
Maplin Rd
Golden Sq W1 195 L10
Golden Sq W1 83 DJ73
Golden Yd NW3 64 DC63
Heath St
Golders Cl, Edg. 42 CP50
Golders Gdns NW11 63 CY59
Golders Grn Cres NW11 63 CZ59
Golders Grn Rd NW11 63 CY58
Golders Manor Dr NW11 63 CX58
Golders Pk Cl NW11 64 DB60
Golders Ri NW4 63 CX57
Golders Way NW11 63 CZ59
Goldfinch Cl, Orp. 164 EU106
Goldfinch Rd SE28 105 ER76
Goldfinch Rd, S.Croy. 161 DY110
Goldfinch Way, Borwd. 26 CN42
Goldfort Wk, Wok. 166 AS116
Langmans Way
Goldhawk Ms W12 99 CV75
Devonport Rd
Goldhawk Rd W6 99 CT77
Goldhawk Rd W12 99 CU76
Goldhaze Cl, Wdf.Grn. 48 EK52
Goldhurst Ter NW6 82 DB66
Golding Cl, Chess. 155 CJ107
Coppard Gdns
Golding Rd, Sev. 191 FJ122
Golding St E1 84 DU72
Golding Ter SW11 100 DG82
Longhedge St
Goldingham Av, Loug. 33 EQ40
Goldings, The, Wok. 166 AT116
Goldings Hill, Loug. 33 EN39
Goldings Ri, Loug. 33 EN39
Goldings Rd, Loug. 33 EN39
Goldington Cres NW1 83 DK68
Goldington St NW1 83 DK68
Goldman Cl E2 84 DU70
Goldney Rd W9 82 DA70
Goldrill Dr N11 44 DG47
Goldrings Rd, Lthd. 154 CC113
Goldsboro Rd SW8 101 DK81
Goldsborough Cres E4 47 EB47
Goldsdown Cl, Enf. 31 DY40
Goldsdown Rd, Enf. 31 DX40
Goldsel Rd, Swan. 147 FD99
Goldsmid St SE18 105 ES78
Sladedale Rd
Goldsmith, Grays 110 FZ79
Goldsmith Av E12 86 EL65
Goldsmith Av NW9 63 CT58
Goldsmith Av W3 80 CR73
Goldsmith Av, Rom. 70 FA59
Goldsmith Cl W3 80 CS74
East Acton La
Goldsmith Cl, Har. 60 CB60
Goldsmith La NW9 62 CP56
Goldsmith Rd E10 67 EA60
Goldsmith Rd E17 47 DX54
Goldsmith Rd N11 44 DF50
Goldsmith Rd SE15 102 DU81
Goldsmith Rd W3 80 CR74
Goldsmith St EC2 197 J8
Goldsmiths Bottom, . Sev 190 FE127
Goldsmiths Cl, Wok. 166 AW118
Goldsmith's Row E2 84 DU68
Goldsmith's Sq E2 84 DU68
Goldsworth Orchard, Wok. 166 AU118
St. John's Rd
Goldsworth Pk Trd Est, Wok. 166 AV116
Goldsworth Rd, Wok. 166 AW118
Goldsworthy Gdns SE16 202 G9
Goldsworthy Gdns SE16 102 DW77
Goldwell Rd, Th.Hth. 141 DM98
Goldwin Cl SE14 102 DW81
Goldwing Cl E16 86 EG72
Golf Cl, Bushey 24 BX41
Golf Cl, Stan. 41 CJ52
Golf Cl, Th.Hth. 141 DN95
Kensington Av
Golf Cl, Wok. 151 BE114
Golf Club Dr, Kings.T. 118 CR94
Golf Club Rd, Hat. 12 DA26
Golf Club Rd, Wey. 153 BP109
Golf Club Rd, Wok. 166 AU120
Golf Ho Rd, Oxt. 188 EJ129
Golf Links Av, Grav. 131 GH92
Golf Ride, Enf. 29 DN35
Golf Rd W5 80 CM72
Boileau Rd
Golf Rd, Brom. 145 EN97
Golf Rd, Ken. 176 DR118
Golf Side, Sutt. 157 CY111
Golf Side, Twick. 117 CD90
Golfe Rd, Ilf. 69 ER62
Golfside Cl N20 44 DE48
Golfside Cl, N.Mal. 138 CS96
Goliath Cl, Wall. 159 DL108
Gollogly Ter SE7 104 EJ78
Gomer Gdns, Tedd. 117 CG93
Gomer Pl, Tedd. 117 CG93
Gomm Rd SE16 202 F7
Gomm Rd SE16 102 DW76
Gomshall Av, Wall. 159 DL106
Gomshall Gdns, Ken. 176 DS115
Gomshall Rd, Sutt. 157 CW110
Gondar Gdns NW6 63 CZ64
Gonson Pl SE8 103 EA79
Gonson St SE8 103 EB79
Gonston Cl SW19 119 CY89
Boddicott Cl
Gonville Av, Rick. 23 BP44
Gonville Cres, Nthlt. 78 CB65
Gonville Rd, Th.Hth. 141 DM99
Gonville St SW6 99 CY83
Putney Br App
Goodall Rd E11 67 EC62
Gooden Ct, Har. 61 CE62
Goodenough Cl, Couls. 175 DN120
Goodenough Rd SW19 119 CZ94
Goodenough Way, Couls. 175 DM120
Gooderham Ho, Grays 111 GH75
Goodge Pl W1 195 L7
Goodge St W1 195 L7
Goodge St W1 83 DJ71
Goodhall St NW10 80 CS69
Goodhart Pl E14 85 DY73
Goodhart Way, W.Wick. 144 EE101
Goodhew Rd, Croy. 142 DU100
Gooding Cl, N.Mal. 138 CQ98
Goodinge Cl N7 83 DL65
Goodlake Ct (Denham), Uxb. 57 BF59
Goodley Stock, West. 189 EP129
Goodley Stock Rd, Eden. 189 EP131
Goodley Stock Rd, West. 189 EP128
Goodman Cres SW2 121 DK89
Goodman Pk, Slou. 74 AW74
Goodman Pl, Stai. 113 BF91
Goodman Rd E10 67 EC59
Goodmans Ct, Wem. 61 CK63
Goodman's Stile E1 84 DU72
Goodmans Yd E1 197 P10
Goodmans Yd E1 84 DT73
Goodmayes Av, Ilf. 70 EU60
Goodmayes La, Ilf. 70 EU63
Goodmayes Rd, Ilf. 70 EU60
Goodmead Rd, Orp. 146 EU101
Goodrich Cl, Wat. 23 BU35
Goodrich Rd SE22 122 DT86
Goods Way NW1 83 DL68
Goodson Rd NW10 80 CS66
Goodway Gdns E14 85 ED72
Goodwin Cl SE16 202 A7
Goodwin Cl SE16 102 DU76
Goodwin Cl, Mitch. 140 DD97
Goodwin Ct, Wal.Cr. 15 DY28
Goodwin Dr, Sid. 126 EX90
Goodwin Gdns, Croy. 159 DP107
Goodwin Rd N9 46 DW46
Goodwin Rd W12 99 CU75
Goodwin Rd, Croy. 159 DP106
Goodwin St N4 65 DN61
Fonthill Rd
Goodwins Ct WC2 195 P10
Goodwood Av, Brwd. 55 GE44
Goodwood Av, Enf. 30 DW37
Goodwood Av, Horn. 72 FL63
Goodwood Av, Wat. 23 BS35
Goodwood Cl, Mord. 140 DA98
Goodwood Cl, Stan. 41 CJ50
Goodwood Cres, Grav. 131 GJ93
Goodwood Dr, Nthlt. 78 CA65
Goodwood Path, Borwd. 26 CN41
Stratfield Rd
Goodwood Rd SE14 103 DY80
Goodwood Rd, Red. 184 DF132
Goodwyn Av NW7 42 CS50
Goodwyns Vale N10 44 DG53
Goodyers Av, Rad. 9 CF33
Goodyers Gdns NW4 63 CX57
Goosander Way SE28 105 ER76
Goose Acre, Chesh. 4 AT30
Goose Grn, Cob. 169 BU119
Goose Grn Cl, Orp. 146 EU96
Goose La, Wok. 166 AV122
Goose Sq E6 87 EM72
Harper Rd
Gooseacre La, Har. 61 CK57
Goosefields, Rick. 22 BJ44
Gooseley La E6 87 EN69
Goosens Cl, Sutt. 158 DC106
Turnpike La
Gooshays Dr, Rom. 52 FL50
Gooshays Gdns, Rom. 52 FL51
Gophir La EC4 197 K10
Gopsall St N1 84 DR67
Goral Mead, Rick. 38 BK46
Gordon Av E4 48 EE51
Gordon Av SW14 98 CS84
Gordon Av, Horn. 71 FF61
Gordon Av, S.Croy. 160 DQ110
Gordon Av, Stan. 41 CH51
Gordon Av, Twick. 117 CG85
Gordon Cl E17 67 EA58
Gordon Cl N19 65 DJ60
Highgate Hill
Gordon Cl, Cher. 133 BE104
Gordon Cl, Stai. 114 BH93
Gordon Ct W12 81 CW72
Gordon Cres, Croy. 142 DS102
Gordon Cres, Hayes 95 BU76
Gordon Dr, Cher. 133 BE104
Gordon Dr, Shep. 135 BR100
Gordon Gdns, Edg. 42 CP54
Gordon Gro SE5 101 DP82
Gordon Hill, Enf. 30 DQ39
Gordon Ho Rd NW5 64 DG63
Gordon Pl W8 100 DA75
Gordon Pl, Grav. 131 GJ86
East Ter
Gordon Prom, Grav. 131 GJ86
Gordon Prom E, Grav. 131 GJ86
Gordon Rd E4 48 EE45
Gordon Rd E11 68 EG58
Gordon Rd E15 67 EC63
Gordon Rd E18 48 EH53
Gordon Rd N3 43 CZ52
Gordon Rd N9 46 DV47
Gordon Rd N11 45 DK52
Gordon Rd SE15 102 DV82
Gordon Rd W4 98 CP79
Gordon Rd W5 79 CJ73
Gordon Rd W13 79 CH73
Gordon Rd, Ashf. 114 BL90
Gordon Rd, Bark. 87 ES67
Gordon Rd, Beck. 143 DZ97
Gordon Rd, Belv. 107 FC77
Gordon Rd, Brwd. 55 GA46
Gordon Rd, Cars. 158 DF107
Gordon Rd, Cat. 176 DR121
Gordon Rd, Dart. 128 FK87
Gordon Rd, Enf. 30 DQ39
Gordon Rd, Esher 155 CE107
Gordon Rd, Grav. 130 GE87
Gordon Rd, Grays 111 GF75
Gordon Rd, Har. 61 CE55
Gordon Rd, Houns. 96 CC84
Gordon Rd, Ilf. 69 ER62
Gordon Rd, Kings.T. 138 CM95
Gordon Rd, Red. 184 DG131
Gordon Rd, Rich. 98 CM82
Gordon Rd, Rom. 70 EZ58
Gordon Rd, Sev. 191 FH125
Gordon Rd, Shep. 135 BR100
Gordon Rd, Sid. 125 ES85
Gordon Rd, Sthl. 96 BY77
Gordon Rd, Stai. 113 BC91
Gordon Rd, Surb. 138 CM101
Gordon Rd, Wal.Abb. 15 EA34
Gordon Rd, West Dr. 76 BL73
Gordon Sq WC1 195 N5
Gordon Sq WC1 83 DK70
Gordon St E13 86 EG69
Grange Rd
Gordon St WC1 195 M4
Gordon St WC1 83 DK70
Gordon Way, Barn. 27 CZ42
Gordon Way, Brom. 144 EG95
Gordon Way, Ch.St.G. 36 AV48
Gordonbrock Rd SE4 123 EA85
Gordondale Rd SW19 120 DA89
Gordons Way, Oxt. 187 ED128
Gore Cl (Harefield), Uxb. 58 BH56
Gore Ct NW9 62 CN57
Gore Rd E9 84 DW67
Gore Rd SW20 139 CW96
Gore Rd, Dart. 128 FQ89
Gore St SW7 100 DC76
Gorefield Pl NW6 82 DA68
Gorelands La, Ch.St.G. 37 AZ47
Goresbrook Rd, Dag. 88 EV67
Goresbrook Village, Dag. 88 EV67
Goresbrook Rd
Gorham Pl W11 81 CY73
Mary Pl
Goring Cl, Rom. 51 FC53
Goring Gdns, Dag. 70 EW63
Goring Rd N11 45 DL51
Goring Rd, Dag. 89 FD65
Goring Rd, Stai. 113 BD92
Goring St EC3 197 N8
Goring St EC3 84 DS72
Goring Way, Grnf. 78 CC68
Gorings Sq, Stai. 113 BE91
Gorle Cl, Wat. 7 BU34
Gorleston Rd N15 66 DR57
Gorleston St W14 99 CY77
Gorman Rd SE18 105 EM77
Gorringe Av (South Darenth), Dart. 149 FR96
Gorringe Pk Av, Mitch. 120 DF94
Gorse Cl E16 86 EG72
Gorse Cl, Tad. 173 CV120
Gorse Hill (Farningham), Dart. 148 FL100
Gorse Hill La, Vir.W. 132 AX98
Gorse Hill Rd, Vir.W. 132 AX98
Gorse La, Wok. 150 AS108
Gorse Ri SW17 120 DG92
Gorse Rd, Croy. 161 EA105
Gorse Rd, Orp. 146 FA103
Gorse Wk, West Dr. 76 BL72
Gorselands Cl, W.Byf. 152 BJ111
Gorseway, Rom. 71 FE61
Gorst Rd NW10 80 CQ70
Gorst Rd SW11 120 DF86
Gorsuch Pl E2 197 P2
Gorsuch St E2 197 P2
Gorsuch St E2 84 DT69
Gosberton Rd SW12 120 DG88
Gosbury Hill, Chess. 156 CL105
Gosfield Rd, Dag. 70 FA61
Gosfield Rd, Epsom 156 CR112
Gosfield St W1 195 K6
Gosfield St W1 83 DJ71
Gosford Gdns, Ilf. 69 EM57
Gosforth La, Wat. 40 BW48
Gosforth Path, Wat. 39 BU48
Goshawk Gdns, Hayes 77 BS69
Goslett Yd WC2 195 N9
Gosling Cl, Grnf. 78 CA69
Gosling Grn, Slou. 92 AY76
Gosling Rd, Slou. 92 AY76
Gosling Way SW9 101 DN81
Gospatrick Rd N17 46 DQ53
Gospel Oak Est NW5 64 DF64
Gosport Dr, Horn. 90 FJ65
Gosport Rd E17 67 DZ57
Gosport Wk N17 66 DV57
Yarmouth Cres
Gosport Way SE15 102 DT80
Pentridge St
Goss Hill, Dart. 128 FJ93
Goss Hill, Swan. 128 FJ93
Gossage Rd SE18 105 ER78
Ancona Rd
Gossage Rd, Uxb. 76 BM66
Gossamers, The, Wat. 24 BY36
Gosset St E2 84 DT69
Gosshill Rd, Chis. 145 EN96
Gossington Cl, Chis. 125 EP91
Beechwood Ri
Gosterwood St SE8 103 DY79
Gostling Rd, Twick. 116 CA88
Goston Gdns, Th.Hth. 141 DN97
Goswell Rd EC1 197 H5
Goswell Rd EC1 83 DP69
Gothic Cl, Dart. 128 FK90
Gothic Ct, Hayes 95 BR79
Sipson La
Gothic Rd, Twick. 117 CD89
Gottfried Ms NW5 65 DJ63
Fortess Rd
Goudhurst Rd, Brom. 124 EE92
Gouge Av, Grav. 130 GE88
Gough Rd E15 68 EF63
Gough Rd, Enf. 30 DV40
Gough Sq EC4 196 E8
Gough Sq EC4 83 DN72
Gough St WC1 196 C4
Gough St WC1 83 DM70
Gough Wk E14 85 EA72
Saracen St
Gould Ct SE19 122 DT92
Gould Rd, Felt. 115 BS87
Gould Rd, Twick. 117 CE88
Gould Ter E8 66 DV64
Kenmure Rd
Goulding Gdns, Th.Hth. 141 DP96
Goulds Grn, Uxb. 77 BP72
Goulston St E1 197 P8
Goulston St E1 84 DT72
Goulton Rd E5 66 DV63
Gourley Pl N15 66 DS57
Gourley St
Gourley St N15 66 DS57
Gourock Rd SE9 125 EN85
Govan St E2 84 DU67
Whiston Rd
Government Row, Enf. 31 EA38
Governors Av (Denham), Uxb. 57 BF57
Governors Cl, Amer. 20 AT37
Govett Av, Shep. 135 BQ99
Govier Cl E15 86 EE66
Gowan Av SW6 99 CY81
Gowan Rd NW10 81 CV65
Gowar Fld, Pot.B. 11 CU32
Gower, The, Egh. 133 BB97
Gower Cl SW4 121 DJ86
Gower Ct WC1 195 M4
Gower Ms WC1 195 M7
Gower Ms WC1 83 DK71
Gower Pl WC1 195 L4
Gower Pl WC1 83 DJ70
Gower Rd E7 86 EG65
Gower Rd, Islw. 97 CF79
Gower Rd, Wey. 153 BR107
Gower St WC1 195 M5
Gower St WC1 83 DJ70
Gowers, The, Amer. 20 AS36
Gowers La, Grays 111 GF75
Gower's Wk E1 84 DU72
Gowland Pl, Beck. 143 DZ96
Gowlett Rd SE15 102 DU83
Gowrie Rd SW11 100 DG83
Graburn Way, E.Mol. 137 CD97
Grace Av, Bexh. 106 EZ82
Grace Av (Shenley), Rad. 9 CK33
Grace Cl SE9 124 EK90
Grace Cl, Borwd. 26 CR39
Grace Cl, Edg. 42 CQ52
Pavilion Way
Grace Cl, Ilf. 49 ET51
Grace Jones Cl E8 84 DU65
Parkholme Rd
Grace Path SE26 122 DW91
Silverdale
Grace Pl E3 85 EB69
St. Leonards St
Grace Rd, Croy. 142 DQ100
Grace St E3 85 EB69

Gracechurch St EC3 197 L10
Gracechurch St EC3 84 DR73
Gracedale Rd SW16 121 DH92
Gracefield Gdns SW16 121 DL90
Grace's All E1 84 DU73
Graces Ms SE5 102 DS82
Graces Rd SE5 102 DS82
Gracious La, Sev. 190 FG130
Gracious La End, Sev. 190 FF130
Gracious Pond Rd, Wok. 150 AT108
Gradient, The SE26 122 DU91
Graeme Rd, Enf. 30 DR40
Graemesdyke Av SW14 98 CP84
Grafton Cl W13 79 CG72
Grafton Cl, Houns. 116 BY88
Grafton Cl, Slou. 74 AY72
Grafton Cl, W.Byf. 151 BF113
Madeira Rd
Grafton Cl, Wor.Pk. 138 CS104
Grafton Ct, Felt. 115 BR88
Loxwood Cl
Grafton Cres NW1 83 DH65
Grafton Gdns N4 66 DQ58
Grafton Gdns, Dag. 70 EY61
Grafton Ho E3 85 EA69
Grafton Ms W1 195 K5
Grafton Pk Rd, Wor.Pk. 138 CS103
Grafton Pl NW1 195 M3
Grafton Pl NW1 83 DK69
Grafton Rd NW5 64 DG64
Grafton Rd W3 80 CQ73
Grafton Rd, Croy. 141 DN102
Grafton Rd, Dag. 70 EY61
Grafton Rd, Enf. 29 DM41
Grafton Rd, Har. 60 CC57
Grafton Rd, N.Mal. 138 CS97
Grafton Rd, Wor.Pk. 138 CR104
Grafton Sq SW4 101 DJ83
Grafton St W1 199 J1
Grafton St W1 83 DH73
Grafton Ter NW5 64 DF64
Grafton Way W1 195 K5
Grafton Way W1 83 DJ70
Grafton Way WC1 195 K5
Grafton Way WC1 83 DJ70
Grafton Way, W.Mol. 136 BZ98
Grafton Yd NW5 83 DH65
Prince of Wales Rd
Graftons, The NW2 64 DA62
Hermitage La
Graham Av W13 97 CH75
Graham Av, Mitch. 140 DG95
Graham Cl, Brwd. 55 GC43
Graham Cl, Croy. 143 EA103
Graham Gdns, Surb. 138 CL102
Graham Rd E8 84 DU65
Graham Rd E13 86 EG70
Graham Rd N15 65 DP55
Graham Rd NW4 63 CV58
Graham Rd SW19 119 CZ94
Graham Rd W4 98 CR76
Graham Rd, Bexh. 106 FA84
Graham Rd, Hmptn. 116 CA91
Graham Rd, Har. 61 CE55
Graham Rd, Mitch. 140 DG95
Graham Rd, Pur. 159 DN113
Graham St N1 196 G1
Graham St N1 83 DP68
Graham Ter SW1 198 F9
Graham Ter SW1 100 DG77
Grahame Pk Est NW9 43 CT53
Grahame Pk Way NW7 43 CT52
Grahame Pk Way NW9 43 CT54
Grainger Cl, Nthlt. 60 CC64
Lancaster Rd
Grainger Rd N22 46 DQ53
Grainger Rd, Islw. 97 CF82
Grainge's Yd, Uxb. 76 BJ66
Cross St
Gramer Cl E11 67 ED61
Norman Rd
Grampian Cl, Hayes 95 BR80
Grampian Cl, Orp. 145 ET100
Cotswold Ri
Grampian Gdns NW2 63 CY60
Grampian Way, Slou. 93 BA78
Granard Av SW15 119 CV85
Granard Rd SW12 120 DF87
Granaries, The, Wal.Abb. 16 EE34
Granary Cl N9 46 DW45
Turin Rd
Granary Rd E1 84 DV70
Granary St NW1 83 DK67
Granby Bldgs SE11 200 B9
Granby Pk Rd (Cheshunt), Wal.Cr. 14 DT28
Granby Rd SE9 105 EM82
Granby Rd, Grav. 130 GD86
Granby St E2 84 DT70
Granby Ter NW1 195 K1
Granby Ter NW1 83 DJ68
Grand Arc N12 44 DC50
Ballards La
Grand Av EC1 196 G6
Grand Av N10 64 DG56
Grand Av, Surb. 138 CP99
Grand Av, Wem. 62 CN64
Grand Av E, Wem. 62 CP64
Grand Dep Rd SE18 105 EN78
Grand Dr SW20 139 CW96
Grand Dr, Sthl. 96 CC75
Grand Junct Wf N1 197 H1
Grand Junct Wf N1 84 DQ68
Grand Par Ms SW15 119 CY85
Upper Richmond Rd
Grand Stand Rd, Epsom 173 CT117
Grand Union Canal Wk W7 97 CE76
Grand Union Cl W9 81 CZ71
Woodfield Rd
Grand Union Cres E8 84 DU66
Grand Union Ind Est NW10 80 CP68
Grand Union Wk NW1 83 DH66
Grand Vw Av, West. 178 EJ117
Grand Wk E1 85 DY70
Solebay St
Granden Rd SW16 141 DL96
Grandfield Av, Wat. 23 BT39
Grandis Cotts, Wok. 168 BH122
Grandison Rd SW11 120 DF85
Grandison Rd, Wor.Pk. 139 CW103
Granfield St SW11 100 DD81
Grange, The N2 44 DD54
Central Av
Grange, The N20 44 DC46
Grange, The SE1 201 P6
Grange, The SE1 102 DT76
Grange, The SW19 119 CX93
Grange, The, Croy. 143 DZ103
Grange, The, Dart. 149 FR95
Grange, The, Walt. 135 BV103
Grange, The, Wem. 80 CN66
Grange, The, Wind. 112 AV85
Grange, The, Wok. 150 AS110
Grange, The, Wor.Pk. 138 CR104
Grange Av N12 44 DC50
Grange Av N20 43 CY45
Grange Av SE25 142 DS96
Grange Av, Barn. 44 DE46
Grange Av, Stan. 41 CH54
Grange Av, Twick. 117 CE89
Grange Av, Wdf.Grn. 48 EG51
Grange Cl, Brwd. 55 GC50
Grange Cl, Edg. 42 CQ50
Grange Cl (Chalfont St. Peter), Ger.Cr. 36 AY53
Grange Cl, Hayes 77 BS71
Grange Cl, Houns. 96 BZ79
Grange Cl, Lthd. 171 CK120
Grange Cl (Bletchingley), Red. 186 DR133
Grange Cl (Merstham), Red. 185 DH128
Grange Cl, Sid. 126 EU90
Grange Cl, Stai. 112 AY86
Grange Cl, Wat. 23 BU39
Grange Cl, W.Mol. 136 CB98
Grange Cl, West. 189 EQ126
Grange Cl, Wdf.Grn. 48 EG52
Grange Ct E8 84 DT66
Grange Ct WC2 196 C9
Grange Ct, Chig. 49 EQ47
Grange Ct, Loug. 32 EK43
Grange Ct, Nthlt. 78 BW68
Grange Ct, Stai. 114 BG92
Grange Ct, Wal.Abb. 15 EC34
Grange Ct, Walt. 135 BU103
Grange Cres SE28 88 EW72
Grange Cres, Chig. 49 ER50
Grange Cres, Dart. 128 FP86
Grange Dr, Chis. 124 EL93
Grange Dr, Orp. 164 EW109
Rushmore Hill
Grange Dr, Red. 185 DH128
London Rd S
Grange Dr, Wok. 150 AY114
Grange Fm Cl, Har. 60 CC61
Grange Flds (Chalfont St. Peter), Ger.Cr. 36 AY53
Lower Rd
Grange Gdns N14 45 DK46
Grange Gdns NW3 64 DB62
Grange Gdns SE25 142 DS96
Grange Gdns, Bans. 158 DB113
Grange Gdns, Pnr. 60 BZ56
Grange Gro N1 84 DQ65
Grange Hill SE25 142 DS96
Grange Hill, Edg. 42 CQ50
Grange Ho, Bark. 87 ER67
St. Margarets
Grange La SE21 122 DT89
Grange La, Wat. 25 CD39
Grange Mans, Epsom 157 CT108
Grange Meadow, Bans. 158 DB113
Grange Ms SE10 103 ED80
Crooms Hill
Grange Pk W5 80 CL74
Grange Pk, Wok. 166 AY115
Grange Pk Av N21 29 DP44
Grange Pk Pl SW20 119 CV94
Grange Pk Rd E10 67 EB60
Grange Pk Rd, Th.Hth. 142 DR98
Grange Pl NW6 82 DA66
Grange Pl, Stai. 134 BJ96
Grange Rd E10 67 EA60
Grange Rd E13 86 EF69
Grange Rd E17 67 DY57
Grange Rd N6 64 DG58
Grange Rd N17 46 DU51
Grange Rd N18 46 DU51
Grange Rd NW10 81 CV65
Grange Rd SE1 201 N7
Grange Rd SE1 102 DS76
Grange Rd SE19 142 DR98
Grange Rd SE25 142 DR98
Grange Rd SW13 99 CU81
Grange Rd W4 98 CP78
Grange Rd W5 79 CK74
Grange Rd, Add. 152 BG110
Grange Rd, Borwd. 26 CM43
Grange Rd, Bushey 24 BY43
Grange Rd, Cat. 186 DU125
Grange Rd, Chess. 156 CL105
Grange Rd, Edg. 42 CR51
Grange Rd, Egh. 113 AZ92
Grange Rd (Chalfont St Peter), Ger.Cr. 36 AY53
Grange Rd, Grav. 131 GG87
Grange Rd, Grays 110 GB79
Grange Rd, Har. 61 CG58
Grange Rd (South Harrow), Har. 61 CD61
Grange Rd, Hayes 77 BS72
Grange Rd, Ilf. 69 EP63
Grange Rd, Kings.T. 138 CL97
Grange Rd, Lthd. 171 CK120
Grange Rd, Orp. 145 EQ103
Grange Rd, Rom. 51 FH51
Grange Rd, Sev. 190 FG127
Grange Rd, S.Croy. 160 DQ110
Grange Rd, S.Ock. 90 FQ74
Grange Rd, Sthl. 96 BY75
Grange Rd, Sutt. 158 DA108
Grange Rd, Th.Hth. 142 DR98
Grange Rd, Walt. 154 BY105
Grange Rd, W.Mol. 136 CB98
Grange Rd, Wok. 150 AY114
Grange St N1 84 DR67
Grange Vale, Sutt. 158 DB108
Grange Vw Rd N20 44 DC46
Grange Wk SE1 201 N6
Grange Wk SE1 102 DS76
Grange Way, Erith 107 FH80
Grange Way, Iver 75 BF72
Grange Yd SE1 201 P7
Grange Yd SE1 102 DT76
Grangecliffe Gdns SE25 142 DS96
Grangecourt Rd N16 66 DS60
Grangedale Cl, Nthwd. 39 BS53
Grangehill Pl SE9 105 EM83
Westmount Rd
Grangehill Rd SE9 105 EM83
Grangemill Rd SE6 123 EA90
Grangemill Way SE6 123 EA89
Grangemount, Lthd. 171 CK120
Granger Way, Rom. 71 FG58
Grangeway N12 44 DB49
Grangeway NW6 82 DA66
Messina Av
Grangeway, Wdf.Grn. 48 EJ49
Grangeway, The N21 29 DP44
Grangeway Gdns, Ilf. 68 EL57
Grangeways Cl, Grav. 131 GF91
Grangewood, Bex. 126 EZ88
Hurst Rd
Grangewood, Pot.B. 12 DB30
Grangewood, Slou. 74 AW71
Grangewood Av, Grays 110 GE76
Grangewood Av, Rain. 90 FJ70
Grangewood Cl, Brwd. 55 GA48
Knight's Way
Grangewood Cl, Pnr. 59 BU57
Grangewood Dr, Sun. 115 BT94
Forest Dr
Grangewood La, Beck. 123 DZ93
Grangewood St E6 86 EJ67
Grangewood Ter SE25 142 DR97
Grange Rd
Granham Gdns N9 46 DT47
Granite St SE18 105 ET78
Granleigh Rd E11 68 EE61
Gransden Av E8 84 DV66
Gransden Rd W12 99 CT75
Wendell Rd
Grant Av, Slou. 74 AS72
Grant Cl N14 45 DJ45
Grant Cl, Shep. 135 BP100
Grant Pl, Croy. 142 DT102
Grant Rd SW11 100 DD84
Grant Rd, Croy. 142 DT102
Grant Rd, Har. 61 CF55
Grant St E13 86 EG69
Grant St N1 83 DN68
Chapel Mkt
Grant Way, Islw. 97 CG79
Grantbridge St N1 83 DP68
Grantchester Cl, Har. 61 CF62
Grantham Cl, Edg. 42 CL48
Grantham Gdns, Rom. 70 EZ58
Grantham Grn, Borwd. 26 CQ43
Grantham Pl W1 199 H3
Grantham Rd E12 69 EN63
Grantham Rd SW9 101 DL82
Grantham Rd W4 98 CS80
Grantley Pl, Esher 154 CB106
Grantley Rd, Houns. 96 BW82
Grantley St E1 85 DX69
Grantock Rd E17 47 ED53
Granton Av, Upmin. 72 FM61
Granton Rd SW16 141 DJ95
Granton Rd, Ilf. 70 EU60
Granton Rd, Sid. 126 EW93
Grants Cl NW7 43 CW52
Grants La, Oxt. 188 EJ132
Grantully Rd W9 82 DB69
Granville Av N9 46 DW48
Granville Av, Felt. 115 BU89
Granville Av, Houns. 116 CA85
Granville Cl, Croy. 142 DS103
Granville Cl, W.Byf. 152 BM113
Church Rd
Granville Cl, Wey. 153 BQ107
Granville Ct N1 84 DR67
Granville Dene, Hem.H. 5 BA27
Granville Gdns SW16 141 DM95
Granville Gdns W5 80 CM74
Granville Gro SE13 103 EC83
Granville Ms, Sid. 126 EU91
Granville Pk SE13 103 EC83
Granville Pl (North Finchley) N12 44 DC52
High Rd
Granville Pl W1 194 F9
Granville Pl W1 82 DG72
Granville Pl, Pnr. 40 BX54
Elm Pk Rd
Granville Rd E17 67 EB58
Granville Rd E18 48 EH54
Granville Rd N4 65 DM58
Granville Rd N12 44 DB52
Granville Rd N13 45 DM51
Russell Rd
Granville Rd N22 45 DP53
Granville Rd NW2 63 CZ61
Granville Rd NW6 82 DA68
Granville Rd SW18 120 DA87
Granville Rd SW19 120 DA94
Russell Rd
Granville Rd, Barn. 27 CW42
Granville Rd, Epp. 18 EV29
Granville Rd, Grav. 131 GF87
Granville Rd, Hayes 95 BT77
Granville Rd, Ilf. 69 EP60
Granville Rd, Oxt. 188 EF129
Granville Rd, Sev. 190 FG124
Granville Rd, Sid. 126 EU91
Granville Rd, Uxb. 77 BP65
Granville Rd, Wat. 24 BW42
Granville Rd, Well. 106 EW83
Granville Rd, West. 189 EQ126
Granville Rd, Wey. 153 BQ107
Granville Rd, Wok. 167 AZ120
Granville Sq SE15 102 DS80
Granville Sq WC1 196 C3
Granville Sq WC1 83 DM69
Granville St WC1 196 C3
Grape St WC2 195 P8
Graphite Sq SE11 200 B10
Grapsome Cl, Chess. 155 CK107
Ashlyns Way
Grasdene Rd SE18 106 EU80
Grasholm Way, Slou. 93 BC77
Grasmere Av SW15 118 CR91
Grasmere Av SW19 140 DA97
Grasmere Av W3 80 CQ73
Grasmere Av, Houns. 116 CB86
Grasmere Av, Orp. 145 EP104
Grasmere Av, Ruis. 59 BQ59
Grasmere Av, Slou. 74 AU73
Grasmere Av, Wem. 61 CK59
Grasmere Cl, Egh. 113 BB94
Keswick Rd
Grasmere Cl, Felt. 115 BT88
Grasmere Cl, Loug. 33 EM40
Grasmere Cl, Wat. 7 BV32
Grasmere Ct N22 45 DM51
Palmerston Rd
Grasmere Gdns, Har. 41 CG54
Grasmere Gdns, Ilf. 69 EM57
Grasmere Gdns, Orp. 145 EP104
Grasmere Rd E13 86 EG68
Grasmere Rd N10 45 DH53
Grasmere Rd N17 46 DU51
Grasmere Rd SE25 142 DV100
Grasmere Rd SW16 121 DM92
Grasmere Rd, Bexh. 107 FC81
Grasmere Rd, Brom. 144 EF95
Grasmere Rd, Orp. 145 EP104
Grasmere Rd, Pur. 159 DP111
Grasmere Way, W.Byf. 152 BM112
Grass Pk N3 43 CZ53
Grassfield Cl, Couls. 175 DH119
Grassingham End (Chalfont St. Peter), Ger.Cr. 36 AY52
Grassingham Rd (Chalfont St. Peter), Ger.Cr. 36 AY52
Grassington Cl N11 44 DG51
Ribblesdale Av
Grassington Cl, St.Alb. 8 CA30
Grassington Rd, Sid. 126 EU91
Grassmere Rd, Horn. 72 FM56
Grassmount SE23 122 DV89
Grassmount, Pur. 159 DJ110
Grassway, Wall. 159 DJ105
Grassy La, Sev. 191 FH126
Grasvenor Av, Barn. 28 DA44
Grately Way SE15 102 DT80
Daniel Gdns
Gratton Rd W14 99 CY76
Gratton Ter NW2 63 CX62
Gravel Cl, Chig. 50 EU47
Gravel Hill N3 43 CZ54
Gravel Hill, Bexh. 127 FB85
Gravel Hill, Croy. 161 DX107
Gravel Hill (Chalfont St. Peter), Ger.Cr. 36 AY53
Gravel Hill, Lthd. 171 CH121
North St
Gravel Hill, Loug. 32 EG38
Gravel Hill, Uxb. 58 BK64
Gravel Hill Cl, Bexh. 127 FB85
Gravel La E1 197 P8
Gravel La, Chig. 50 EU46
Gravel Pit La SE9 125 EQ85
Gravel Pit Way, Orp. 146 EU103
Gravel Rd, Brom. 144 EL103
Gravel Rd, Dart. 128 FP94
Gravel Rd, Twick. 117 CE88
Graveley Av, Borwd. 26 CQ42
Gravelly Hill, Cat. 186 DS128
Gravelly Ride SW19 119 CV91
Gravelwood Cl, Chis. 125 EQ90
Graveney Gro SE20 122 DW94
Graveney Rd SW17 120 DE91
Gravesend Rd W12 81 CU73
Gray Av, Dag. 70 EZ60
Gray Gdns, Rain. 89 FG65
Gray Pl, Cher. 151 BC107
Clarendon Gate
Gray St SE1 200 E5
Grayburn Cl, Ch.St.G. 36 AU47
Grayham Cres, N.Mal. 138 CR98
Grayham Rd, N.Mal. 138 CR98
Grayland Cl, Brom. 144 EK95
Graylands, Epp. 33 ER37
Graylands, Wok. 166 AY116
Graylands Cl, Wok. 166 AY116
Grayling Cl E16 86 EE70
Cranberry La
Grayling Rd N16 66 DR61
Grayling Sq E2 84 DU69
Graylings, The, Abb.L. 7 BR33
Grays End Cl, Grays 110 GA76
Grays Fm Rd, Orp. 146 EV95
Gray's Inn WC1 196 C6
Gray's Inn WC1 83 DN71
Gray's Inn Pl WC1 196 C7
Gray's Inn Rd WC1 196 B3
Gray's Inn Rd WC1 83 DM70
Gray's Inn Sq WC1 196 C6
Grays La, Ashf. 115 BP91
Gray's La, Ash. 172 CM119
Gray's La, Epsom 172 CP121
Shepherds' Wk
Grays Pk Rd, Slou. 74 AU68
Grays Pl, Slou. 74 AT74
Grays Rd, Slou. 74 AT74
Grays Rd, Uxb. 76 BL67
Grays Rd, West. 179 EP121
Grays Wk, Brwd. 55 GD45
Gray's Yd W1 194 G9
Grayscroft Rd SW16 121 DK94
Grayshott Rd SW11 100 DG82
Grayswood Gdns SW20 139 CV96
Farnham Gdns
Graywood Ct N12 44 DC52
Grazebrook Rd N16 66 DR61
Grazeley Cl, Bexh. 127 FC85
Grazeley Ct SE19 122 DS91
Gipsy Hill
Great Acre Ct SW4 101 DK84
St. Alphonsus Rd
Great Bell All EC2 197 K8
Great Benty, West Dr. 94 BL77
Great Brownings SE21 122 DT91
Great Bushey Dr N20 44 DB46
Great Cambridge Rd N9 46 DT46
Great Cambridge Rd N17 46 DR50
Great Cambridge Rd N18 46 DR50
Great Cambridge Rd, Brox. 15 DY26
Great Cambridge Rd, Enf. 30 DU42
Great Cambridge Rd (Cheshunt), Wal.Cr. 14 DW34
Great Castle St W1 195 J8
Great Castle St W1 83 DJ72
Great Cen Av, Ruis. 60 BW64
Great Cen St NW1 194 D6
Great Cen St NW1 82 DF71
Great Cen Way NW10 62 CS64
Great Cen Way, Wem. 62 CQ63
Great Chapel St W1 195 M8
Great Chapel St W1 83 DK72
Great Chertsey Rd W4 98 CQ82
Great Chertsey Rd, Felt. 116 CA90
Great Ch La W6 99 CX78
Great Coll St SW1 199 P6
Great Coll St SW1 101 DL76
Great Cross Av SE10 104 EE80
Great Cullings, Rom. 71 FE61
Great Cumberland Ms W1 194 D9
Great Cumberland Pl W1 194 D8
Great Cumberland Pl W1 82 DF72
Great Dover St SE1 201 J5
Great Dover St SE1 102 DR75
Great Eastern Rd E15 85 ED66
Great Eastern Rd, Brwd. 54 FW49
Great Eastern St EC2 197 M3
Great Eastern St EC2 84 DS69
Great Eastern Wk EC2 197 N7
Great Ellshams, Bans. 174 DA116
Great Elms Rd, Brom. 144 EJ98
Great Fld NW9 42 CS53
Great Fleete Way, Bark. 88 EW68
Great Galley Cl, Bark. 88 EV69
Great Gdns Rd, Horn. 71 FH58
Great George St SW1 199 N5
Great George St SW1 101 DK75
Great Gregories La, Epp. 17 ES33
Great Gro, Bushey 24 CB42
Great Gros, Wal.Cr. 14 DS28
Great Guildford St SE1 201 H2
Great Guildford St SE1 84 DQ74
Great Harry Dr SE9 125 EN90
Great James St WC1 196 B5
Great James St WC1 83 DM71
Great Julians, Rick. 22 BN42
Grove Cres
Great Marlborough St W1 195 K9
Great Marlborough St W1 83 DJ72
Great Maze Pond SE1 201 L4
Great Maze Pond SE1 102 DR75
Great Nelmes Chase, Horn. 72 FM57
Great New St EC4 196 E8
Great Newport St WC2 83 DK73
Cranbourn St
Great N Rd N2 64 DE56
Great N Rd N6 64 DE56
Great N Rd, Barn. 27 CZ38
Great N Rd (New Barnet), Barn. 28 DA43
Great N Rd, Hat. 12 DB27
Great N Rd, Pot.B. 12 DB27
Great N Way NW4 43 CW54
Great Oaks, Brwd. 55 GB44
Great Oaks, Chig. 49 EQ49
Great Ormond St WC1 196 A6
Great Ormond St WC1 83 DL71
Great Owl Rd, Chig. 49 EN48
Great Pk, Kings L. 6 BM30
Great Percy St WC1 196 C2
Great Percy St WC1 83 DM69
Great Peter St SW1 199 M7
Great Peter St SW1 101 DK76
Great Pettits Ct, Rom. 51 FE54
Great Portland St W1 195 J6
Great Portland St W1 83 DH71
Great Pulteney St W1 195 L10
Great Pulteney St W1 83 DJ73
Great Queen St WC2 196 A9
Great Queen St WC2 83 DL72
Great Queen St, Dart. 128 FM87
Great Ropers La, Brwd. 53 FU51
Great Russell St WC1 195 N8
Great Russell St WC1 83 DL71
Great St. Helens EC3 197 M8
Great St. Helens EC3 84 DS72
Great St. Thomas Apostle EC4 197 J10
Great Scotland Yd SW1 199 P3
Great Scotland Yd SW1 83 DL74
Great Slades, Pot.B. 11 CZ33
Great Smith St SW1 199 N6
Great Smith St SW1 101 DK76
Great South-West Rd, Felt. 115 BQ87
Great South-West Rd, Houns. 95 BT84
Great Spilmans SE22 122 DS85
Great Stockwood Rd (Cheshunt), Wal.Cr. 14 DR26
Hammondstreet Rd
Great Strand NW9 43 CT53
Great Suffolk St SE1 200 G3
Great Suffolk St SE1 101 DP75
Great Sutton St EC1 196 G5
Great Sutton St EC1 83 DP70
Great Swan All EC2 197 K8
Great Tattenhams, Epsom 173 CV118
Great Thrift, Orp. 145 EQ98
Great Till Cl, Sev. 181 FE116
Great Titchfield St W1 195 K8
Great Titchfield St W1 83 DJ72
Great Twr St EC3 197 M10
Great Twr St EC3 84 DS73
Great Trinity La EC4 197 J10
Great Turnstile WC1 196 C7
Great Warley St, Brwd. 53 FU53
Great W Rd W4 98 CP78
Great W Rd W6 99 CT78
Great W Rd, Brent. 98 CP78
Great W Rd, Houns. 96 BX82
Great W Rd, Islw. 97 CF80
Great Western Rd W2 81 CZ71
Great Western Rd W9 81 CZ71
Great Western Rd W11 81 CZ71
Great Wf Rd E14 85 EB74
Churchill Pl

Great Winchester St EC2 197 L8
Great Winchester St EC2 84 DR72
Great Windmill St W1 195 M10
Great Windmill St W1 83 DK73
Great Woodcote Dr, Pur. 159 DK110
Great Woodcote Pk, Pur. 159 DK110
Great Yd SE1 201 N4
Greatdown Rd W7 79 CF70
Greatfield Av E6 87 EM70
Greatfield Cl N19 65 DJ63
Warrender Rd
Greatfield Cl SE4 103 EA84
Greatfields Dr, Uxb. 76 BN71
Greatfields Rd, Bark. 87 ER67
Greatham Rd, Bushey 24 BX41
Greatham Wk SW15 119 CU88
Greathurst End, Lthd. 170 BZ124
Greatness La, Sev. 191 FJ121
Greatness Rd, Sev. 191 FJ121
Greatorex St E1 84 DU71
Greatwood, Chis. 125 EN94
Greatwood Cl, Cher. 151 BC109
Greaves Cl, Bark. 87 ES66
Norfolk Rd
Greaves Pl SW17 120 DE91
Grebe Av, Hayes 78 BX72
Cygnet Way
Grebe Cl E7 68 EF64
Cormorant Rd
Grebe Cl E17 47 DY52
Grebe Cl, Bark. 87 ES69
Thames Rd
Grebe Ct, Sutt. 139 CY103
Gander Grn La
Grebe Crest, Grays 109 FU77
Grecian Cres SE19 121 DP93
Greding Wk, Brwd. 55 GB47
Gredo Ho, Bark. 88 EV69
Greek Ct W1 195 N9
Greek St W1 195 N9
Greek St W1 83 DK72
Greek Yd WC2 195 P10
Green, The E4 47 EC46
Green, The E11 68 EH58
Green, The E15 86 EE65
Green, The N9 46 DU47
Green, The N14 45 DK48
Green, The N21 45 DN45
Green, The SW14 98 CQ83
Green, The SW19 119 CX92
Green, The W3 80 CS72
Green, The W5 79 CK74
High St
Green, The, Bexh. 106 FA81
Green, The, Brom. 144 EG101
Green, The, Cars. 158 DG105
Green, The, Cat. 177 EA123
Green, The, Ch.St.G. 36 AW47
High St
Green, The, Croy. 161 DZ109
Green, The, Dart. 129 FR89
Green, The, Epp. 33 ES37
Green, The, Epsom 157 CU111
Green, The, Esher 155 CF107
Green, The, Felt. 115 BV89
Green, The, Hayes 77 BS72
Wood End
Green, The, Hem.H. 5 BA29
Green, The, Houns. 96 CA79
Heston Rd
Green, The, Lthd. 171 CD124
Green, The, Mord. 139 CY98
Green, The, N.Mal. 138 CQ97
Green, The (Pratt's Bottom), Orp. 164 EW110
Rushmore Hill
Green, The (St. Paul's Cray), Orp. 126 EV94
The Av
Green, The, Rain. 90 FL73
Green, The, Rich. 117 CK85
Green, The (Croxley Grn), Rick. 22 BN44
Green, The (Sarratt), Rick. 22 BG35
Green, The, Rom. 51 FE48
Green, The, Sev. 191 FK122
Green, The, Shep. 135 BS98
Green, The, Sid. 126 EU91
Green, The (Datchet), Slou. 92 AV80
Green, The, S.Ock. 91 FW69
Green, The, Sthl. 96 BY76
Green, The, Stai. 112 AY86
Green, The, Sutt. 140 DB104
Green, The, Tad. 173 CY119
Green, The, Til. 111 GL79
Green, The, Twick. 117 CE88
Green, The (Harefield), Uxb. 38 BJ53
Green, The (Ickenham), Uxb. 59 BQ61
Green, The, Wal.Abb. 15 EC34
Sewardstone Rd
Green, The (Cheshunt), Wal.Cr. 14 DW28
Green, The, Walt. 153 BS110
Octagon Rd
Green, The, Warl. 177 DX117
Green, The, Wat. 25 CE39
Green, The, Well. 105 ES84
Green, The, Wem. 61 CG61
Green, The, West Dr. 94 BK76
Green, The, West. 189 ER126
Green, The, Wok. 168 BH121
Green, The, Wdf.Grn. 48 EG50
Green Acres, Croy. 142 DT104
Green Arbour Ct EC1 196 F8
Green Av NW7 42 CR49
Green Av W13 97 CH76
Green Bk E1 202 D3
Green Bk E1 84 DV74
Green Bk N12 44 DB49
Green Cl NW9 62 CQ58
Green Cl NW11 64 DC59
Green Cl, Brom. 144 EE97
Green Cl, Cars. 140 DF103
Green Cl, Felt. 116 BY92
Green Cl, Hat. 11 CY26
Station Rd
Green Cl (Cheshunt), Wal.Cr. 15 DY32
Green Ct Rd, Swan. 147 FD99
Green Cft, Edg. 42 CQ50
Deans La
Green Curve, Bans. 157 CZ114
Green Dale SE5 102 DR84
Green Dale SE22 122 DS85
Green Dale Cl SE22 122 DS85
Green Dale
Green Dragon Ct SE1 201 K2
Green Dragon La N21 29 DP44
Green Dragon La, Brent. 98 CL78
Green Dragon Yd E1 84 DU71
Old Montague St
Green Dr, Slou. 92 AY77
Green Dr, Slou. 92 AY77
London Rd
Green Dr, Sthl. 78 CA74
Green Dr, Wok. 167 BF123
Green E Rd, Beac. 36 AS52
Green Edge, Wat. 23 BU35
Clarke Grn
Green End N21 45 DP47
Green End, Chess. 156 CL105
Green Gdns, Orp. 163 EQ106
Green Glade, Epp. 33 ES37
Green Glades, Horn. 72 FM58
Green Hill, Buck.H. 48 EJ46
Green Hill, Orp. 162 EL112
Green Hill La, Warl. 177 DY117
Green Hill La, Warl. 177 DY117
Sunny Bk
Green Hundred Rd SE15 102 DU79
Green La E4 32 EE41
Green La NW4 63 CX57
Green La SE9 125 EN89
Green La SE20 123 DX94
Green La SW16 121 DM94
Green La W7 97 CE75
Green La, Add. 134 BG104
Green La, Amer. 20 AS38
Green La, Ash. 171 CJ117
Green La, Brwd. 54 FU46
Greenshaw
Green La (Pilgrim's Hatch), Brwd. 54 FV43
Green La (Warley), Brwd. 53 FU52
Green La, Cat. 176 DQ122
Green La, Cher. 133 BE103
Green La, Chesh. 4 AV33
Green La, Chess. 156 CL109
Green La, Chig. 49 ER47
Green La, Chis. 125 EP91
Green La, Cob. 154 BY112
Green La, Couls. 184 DA125
Green La, Dag. 70 EX61
Green La, Edg. 42 CN50
Green La, Egh. 113 BB91
Green La (Thorpe), Egh. 133 BD95
Green La, Felt. 116 BY92
Green La, Har. 61 CE62
Green La (Bovingdon), Hem.H. 5 AZ28
Green La, Houns. 95 BV83
Green La, Ilf. 69 EQ61
Green La, Lthd. 171 CK121
Green La, Mord. 140 DB100
Green La, N.Mal. 138 CQ99
Green La, Nthwd. 39 BT52
Green La, Pur. 159 DJ111
Green La, Red. 184 DE132
Green La (Bletchingley), Red. 186 DS131
Green La, Reig. 183 CZ134
Green La, Rick. 22 BM43
Green La, Shep. 135 BQ100
Green La (Datchet), Slou. 92 AV81
Green La, S.Ock. 91 FR69
Green La, Stai. 133 BE95
Green La, Stan. 41 CH49
Green La, Sun. 115 BT94
Green La, Tad. 183 CZ126
Green La, Th.Hth. 141 DN95
Green La, Upmin. 91 FR68
Green La, Uxb. 77 BQ71
Green La, Wal.Abb. 16 EJ34
Green La, Walt. 153 BV107
Green La, Warl. 177 DY116
Green La, Wat. 40 BW46
Green La, W.Byf. 152 BM112
Green La, W.Mol. 136 CB99
Green La (Chobham), Wok. 150 AT110
Green La (Mayford), Wok. 166 AV121
Copper Beech Cl
Green La (Ockham), Wok. 169 BP124
Green La, Wor.Pk. 139 CU102
Green La Av, Walt. 154 BW106
Green La Cl, Cher. 133 BE103
Green La Cl, W.Byf. 152 BM112
Green La Gdns, Th.Hth. 142 DQ96
Green Las N4 66 DQ60
Green Las N8 65 DP55
Green Las N13 45 DM51
Green Las N15 65 DP55
Green Las N16 66 DQ62
Green Las N21 45 DP46
Green Las, Epsom 156 CS109
Green Lawns, Ruis. 60 BW60
Green Leaf Av, Wall. 159 DK105
Green Leas, Sun. 115 BT93
Green Leas, Wal.Abb. 15 ED34
Roundhills
Green Leas Cl, Sun. 115 BT93
Green Leas
Green Man Gdns W13 79 CG73
Green Man La W13 79 CG74
Green Man La, Felt. 95 BU84
Green Man Pas W13 79 CG73
Green Man Roundabout E11 68 EF59
Green Manor Way, Grav. 110 FZ84
Green Mead, Esher 154 BZ107
Winterdown Gdns
Green Meadow, Pot.B. 12 DA30
Green Moor Link N21 45 DP45
Green N Rd, Beac. 36 AS51
Green Pk, Stai. 113 BE90
Green Pk Way, Grnf. 79 CE67
Green Pl, Dart. 127 FE85
Green Pt E15 86 EE65
Green Pond Cl E17 67 DZ55
Green Pond Rd E17 67 DY55
Green Ride, Epp. 33 EP35
Green Ride, Loug. 32 EG43
Green Rd N14 29 DH44
Green Rd N20 44 DC48
Green Rd, Egh. 133 BB98
Green Sand Rd, Red. 184 DG133
Noke Dr
Green Shield Ind Est E16 86 EG74
Bradfield Rd
Green St E7 86 EH65
Green St E13 86 EJ67
Green St W1 194 F10
Green St W1 82 DG73
Green St, Borwd. 26 CN36
Green St, Enf. 30 DW40
Green St, Rad. 26 CN36
Green St, Rick. 21 BC40
Green St, Sun. 135 BU95
Green St Grn Rd, Dart. 128 FP88
Green Tiles La (Denham), Uxb. 57 BF58
Green Vale W5 80 CM72
Green Vale, Bexh. 126 EX85
Green Verges, Stan. 41 CK52
Green Vw, Chess. 156 CM108
Green Vw Cl, Hem.H. 5 BA29
Green Wk NW4 63 CX57
Green Wk SE1 201 M7
Green Wk, Buck.H. 48 EL45
Green Wk, Dart. 107 FF84
Green Wk, Hmptn. 116 BZ93
Orpwood Cl
Green Wk, Ruis. 59 BT60
Green Wk, Sthl. 96 CA78
Green Wk, Wdf.Grn. 48 EL51
Green Wk, The E4 47 EC46
Green Way SE9 124 EK85
Green Way, Brom. 144 EL100
Green Way, Red. 184 DE132
Green Way, Sun. 135 BU98
Green W Rd, Beac. 36 AS52
Green Wrythe Cres, Cars. 140 DE102
Green Wrythe La, Cars. 140 DD100
Greenacre, Dart. 128 FL89
Oakfield La
Greenacre, Wok. 166 AS116
Mead Ct
Greenacre Cl, Barn. 27 CZ38
Greenacre Cl, Nthlt. 60 BZ64
Eastcote La
Greenacre Cl, Swan. 147 FE98
Greenacre Ct, Egh. 112 AW93
Greenacre Gdns E17 67 EC56
Greenacre Pl, Wall. 141 DH103
Park Rd
Greenacre Sq SE16 203 J4
Greenacre Wk N14 45 DL48
Greenacres SE9 125 EN86
Greenacres, Bushey 41 CD47
Greenacres, Epp. 17 ET29
Greenacres, Lthd. 170 CB124
Greenacres, Oxt. 188 EE127
Greenacres Av, Uxb. 58 BM62
Greenacres Cl, Orp. 163 EQ105
Greenacres Cl, Rain. 90 FL69
Greenacres Dr, Stan. 41 CH52
Greenall Cl (Cheshunt), Wal.Cr. 15 DY30
Greenaway Gdns NW3 64 DB63
Greenbank (Cheshunt), Wal.Cr. 14 DV28
Greenbank Av, Wem. 61 CG64
Greenbank Cl E4 47 EC47
Greenbank Cl, Rom. 52 FK48
Greenbank Cres NW4 63 CY56
Greenbank Rd, Wat. 23 BR36
Greenbanks, Dart. 128 FL89
Greenbanks, Upmin. 73 FS60
Greenbay Rd SE7 104 EK80
Greenberry St NW8 194 B1
Greenberry St NW8 82 DE68
Greenbrook Av, Barn. 28 DC39
Greenbury Cl, Rick. 21 BC41
Green St
Greencoat Pl SW1 199 L8
Greencoat Pl SW1 101 DJ77
Greencoat Row SW1 199 L7
Greencourt Av, Croy. 142 DV103
Greencourt Av, Edg. 42 CP53
Greencourt Gdns, Croy. 142 DV102
Greencourt Rd, Orp. 145 ER99
Greencrest Pl NW2 63 CV62
Dollis Hill La
Greencroft Av, Ruis. 60 BW61
Greencroft Cl E6 86 EL71
Neatscourt Rd
Greencroft Gdns NW6 82 DB66
Greencroft Gdns, Enf. 30 DS41
Greencroft Rd, Houns. 96 BZ81
Greendale Ms, Slou. 74 AU73
Greendale Wk, Grav. 130 GE90
Greene Fielde End, Stai. 114 BK94
Greenend Rd W4 98 CS75
Greenfarm Cl, Orp. 163 ET106
Greenfield Av, Surb. 138 CP101
Greenfield Av, Wat. 40 BX47
Greenfield End (Chalfont St. Peter), Ger.Cr. 36 AY51
Greenfield Gdns NW2 63 CY61
Greenfield Gdns, Dag. 88 EX67
Greenfield Gdns, Orp. 145 ER101
Greenfield Link, Couls. 175 DL115
Greenfield Rd E1 84 DU71
Greenfield Rd N15 66 DS57
Greenfield Rd, Dag. 88 EW67
Greenfield Rd, Dart. 127 FD92
Greenfield St, Wal.Abb. 15 EC34
Greenfield Way, Har. 60 CB55
Greenfields, Loug. 33 EN42
Greenfields (Cuffley), Pot.B. 13 DL30
South Dr
Greenfields Cl, Brwd. 53 FW51
Essex Way
Greenfields Cl, Loug. 33 EN42
Greenford Av W7 79 CE70
Greenford Av, Sthl. 78 BZ73
Greenford Gdns, Grnf. 78 CB69
Greenford Rd, Grnf. 78 CC71
Greenford Rd, Har. 79 CD68
Greenford Rd, Sthl. 78 CC74
Greenford Rd, Sutt. 158 DB105
Greengate, Grnf. 79 CH65
Greengate St E13 86 EH68
Greenhalgh Wk N2 64 DC56
Greenham Cl SE1 200 D5
Greenham Cl SE1 101 DN75
Greenham Cres E4 47 DZ51
Greenham Rd N10 44 DG54
Greenham Wk, Wok. 166 AW118
Greenhayes Av, Bans. 158 DA114
Greenhayes Cl, Reig. 184 DC134
Greenhayes Gdns, Bans. 174 DA115
Greenheys Cl, Nthwd. 39 BS53
Greenheys Dr E18 68 EF55
Greenheys Pl, Wok. 167 AZ118
White Rose La
Greenhill NW3 64 DD63
Hampstead High St
Greenhill SE18 105 EM78
Greenhill, Sutt. 140 DC103
Greenhill, Wem. 62 CP61
Greenhill Av, Cat. 176 DV121
Greenhill Cres, Wat. 23 BS44
Greenhill Gdns, Nthlt. 78 BZ68
Greenhill Gro E12 68 EL63
Greenhill Pk NW10 80 CS67
Greenhill Pk, Barn. 28 DB43
Greenhill Rd NW10 80 CS67
Greenhill Rd, Grav. 131 GF89
Greenhill Rd, Har. 61 CE58
Greenhill Ter SE18 105 EM78
Greenhill Ter, Nthlt. 78 BZ68
Greenhill Way, Croy. 161 DX111
Greenhill Way, Har. 61 CE58
Greenhill Way, Wem. 62 CP61
Greenhills Cl, Rick. 22 BH43
Greenhill's Rents EC1 196 G6
Greenhills Ter N1 84 DR65
Baxter Rd
Greenhithe Cl, Sid. 125 ES87
Greenholm Rd SE9 125 EP85
Greenhurst La, Oxt. 188 EG132
Greenhurst Rd SE27 121 DN92
Greening St SE2 106 EW77
Greenland Cres, Sthl. 96 BW76
Greenland Ms SE8 103 DX78
Trundleys Rd
Greenland Pl NW1 83 DH67
Greenland Rd
Greenland Quay SE16 203 J8
Greenland Quay SE16 103 DX77
Greenland Rd NW1 83 DJ67
Greenland Rd, Barn. 27 CW44
Greenland St NW1 83 DH67
Camden High St
Greenlands Rd, Stai. 114 BG91
Greenlands Rd, Wey. 135 BP104
Greenlaw Gdns, N.Mal. 139 CT101
Greenlaw St SE18 105 EN76
Greenlea Pk SW19 140 DD95
Greenleaf Cl SW2 121 DN87
Tulse Hill
Greenleaf Rd E6 86 EJ67
Redclyffe Rd
Greenleaf Rd E17 67 DZ55
Greenleafe Dr, Ilf. 69 EP56
Greenleaves Ct, Ashf. 115 BP93
Redleaves Av
Greenleigh Av, Orp. 146 EV98
Greenman St N1 84 DQ66
Greenmead Cl SE25 142 DU99
Greenmeads, Wok. 166 AY122
Greenmoor Rd, Enf. 30 DW40
Greeno Cres, Shep. 134 BN99
Greenoak Pl, Barn. 28 DF41
Cockfosters Rd
Greenoak Ri, West. 178 EJ118
Greenoak Way SW19 119 CX91
Greenock Rd SW16 141 DK95
Greenock Rd W3 98 CP76
Greenock Way, Rom. 51 FE51
Greenpark Ct, Wem. 79 CJ66
Greens Cl, The, Loug. 33 EN40
Green's Ct W1 195 M10
Green's End SE18 105 EP77
Greensand Cl (South Merstham), Red. 185 DK128
Greensand Rd, Red. 184 DG133
Greenshank Cl E17 47 DY52
Banbury Rd
Greenshaw, Brwd. 54 FV46
Greenside, Bex. 126 EY88
Greenside, Borwd. 26 CN38
Greenside, Dag. 70 EW60
Greenside, Swan. 147 FD96
Greenside Cl N20 44 DD47
Greenside Cl SE6 123 ED89
Greenside Rd W12 99 CU76
Greenside Rd, Croy. 141 DN101
Greenside Rd, Wey. 135 BP104
Greenside Wk, West. 178 EH118
Kings Rd
Greenslade Av, Ash. 172 CP119
Greenslade Rd, Bark. 87 ER66
Greenstead Av, Wdf.Grn. 48 EJ52
Greenstead Cl, Brwd. 55 GE45
Greenstead Cl, Wdf.Grn. 48 EJ51
Greenstead Gdns
Greenstead Gdns SW15 119 CU85
Greenstead Gdns, Wdf.Grn. 48 EJ51
Greensted Rd, Loug. 48 EL45
Greensted Rd, Ong. 19 FG28
Greenstone Ms E11 68 EG58
Greensward, Bushey 24 CB44
Greentrees, Epp. 18 EU31
Greenvale Rd SE9 105 EM84
Greenview Av, Beck. 143 DY100
Greenview Av, Croy. 143 DY10
Greenview Ct, Ashf. 114 BM9
Village Way
Greenway N14 45 DL4
Greenway N20 44 DA4
Greenway SW20 139 CW9
Greenway, Brwd. 55 GA4
Greenway, Chis. 125 EN9
Greenway, Dag. 70 EW6
Greenway, Har. 62 CL5
Greenway, Hayes 77 BV7
Greenway, Lthd. 170 CB12
Greenway, Pnr. 39 BV5
Greenway, Rom. 52 FP5
Greenway, Wall. 159 DJ10
Greenway, West. 178 EJ12
Greenway, Wdf.Grn. 48 EJ5
Greenway, The NW9 42 CR5
Greenway, The, Enf. 31 DX3
Greenway, The, Epsom 172 CN11
Greenway, The (Chalfont St. Peter), Ger.Cr. 56 AX5
Greenway, The, Har. 41 CE5
Greenway, The, Houns. 96 BZ8
Greenway, The, Orp. 146 EV10
Greenway, The, Oxt. 188 EH13
Greenway, The, Pnr. 60 BZ5
Greenway, The, Pot.B. 12 DA3
Greenway, The, Rick. 38 BG4
Greenway, The, Uxb. 76 BJ6
Greenway, The (Ickenham), Uxb. 59 BQ6
Greenway Av E17 67 ED5
Greenway Cl N4 66 DQ6
Greenway Cl N11 44 DG5
Greenway Cl N15 66 DT5
Copperfield Dr
Greenway Cl N20 44 DA4
Greenway Cl NW9 42 CR5
Greenway Cl, W.Byf. 152 BG11
Greenway Dr, Stai. 134 BK9
Greenway Gdns NW9 42 CR5
Greenway Gdns, Croy. 143 DZ10
Greenway Gdns, Grnf. 78 CA6
Greenway Gdns, Har. 41 CE5
Greenways, Abb.L. 7 BS3
Greenways, Beck. 143 EA9
Greenways, Egh. 112 AY9
Greenways, Esher 155 CE10
Greenways, Tad. 183 CV12
Greenways (Cheshunt), Wal.Cr. 13 DP2
Greenways, Wok. 167 BA11
Pembroke Rd
Greenways, The, Twick. 117 CG8
South Western Rd
Greenwell Cl, Gdse. 186 DV13
Greenwell St W1 195 J5
Greenwell St W1 83 DH70
Greenwich Ch St SE10 103 EC79
Greenwich Ct, Wal.Cr. 15 DY34
Parkside
Greenwich Cres E6 86 EL71
Swan App
Greenwich Foot Tunnel E14 103 EC78
Greenwich Foot Tunnel SE10 103 EC78
Greenwich High Rd SE10 103 EB81
Greenwich Ind Est SE7 205 P9
Greenwich Ind Est SE7 104 EH77
Greenwich Mkt SE10 103 EC79
Greenwich Mkt SE10 103 EC79
Greenwich Pk SE10 104 EE80
Greenwich Pk St SE10 103 ED78
Greenwich S St SE10 103 EB81
Greenwich Vw Pl E14 204 B7
Greenwich Vw Pl E14 103 EB76
Greenwich Way, Wal.Abb. 31 EC40
Sewardstone Rd
Greenwood Av, Dag. 71 FB63
Greenwood Av, Enf. 31 DY40
Greenwood Av (Cheshunt), Wal.Cr. 14 DV31
Greenwood Cl, Add. 151 BF111
Greenwood Cl, Amer. 20 AS37
Greenwood Cl, Bushey 41 CE45
Langmead Dr
Greenwood Cl, Mord. 139 CY98
Greenwood Cl, Orp. 145 ES100
Greenwood Cl, Sid. 126 EU89
Hurst Rd
Greenwood Cl, T.Ditt. 137 CG102
Greenwood Cl (Cheshunt), Wal.Cr. 14 DV31
Greenwood Av
Greenwood Ct SW1 199 K10
Greenwood Ct SW1 101 DJ78
Greenwood Dr E4 47 EC50
Avril Way
Greenwood Dr, Wat. 7 BV34
Greenwood Gdns N13 45 DP48
Greenwood Gdns, Cat. 186 DU125
Greenwood Gdns, Ilf. 49 EQ52
Greenwood Gdns (Shenley), Rad. 10 CL33
Greenwood Ho, Grays 110 GA79
Argent St
Greenwood La, Hmptn. 116 CB92
Greenwood Pk, Kings.T. 118 CS94
Greenwood Pl NW5 65 DH64
Highgate Rd
Greenwood Rd E8 84 DU65
Greenwood Rd E13 86 EF68
Maud Rd
Greenwood Rd, Bex. 127 FD91
Greenwood Rd, Chig. 50 EV49
Greenwood Rd, Croy. 141 DP101
Greenwood Rd, Islw. 97 CE83
Greenwood Rd, Mitch. 141 DK97
Greenwood Rd, T.Ditt. 137 CG102
Greenwood Rd, Wok. 166 AS120
Greenwood Ter NW10 80 CR67
Greenwood Way, Sev. 190 FF125
Greenwoods, The, Har. 60 CC61
Sherwood Rd
Greenyard, Wal.Abb. 15 EC33
Greer Rd, Har. 40 CC53
Greet St SE1 200 E3
Greet St SE1 83 DN74
Greg Cl E10 67 EC58

Gregor Ms SE3 104 EG80
Gregory Av, Pot.B. 12 DC33
Gregory Cl, Wok. 166 AW117
Gregory Cres SE9 124 EK87
Gregory Dr, Wind. 112 AV86
Gregory Ms, Wal.Abb. 15 EB33
Beaulieu Dr
Gregory Pl W8 100 DB75
Gregory Rd, Rom. 70 EX56
Gregory Rd, Sthl. 96 CA76
Gregson Cl, Borwd. 26 CQ39
Gregson's Ride, Loug. 33 EN38
Greig Cl N8 65 DL57
Greig Ter SE17 101 DP79
Lorrimore Sq
Grena Gdns, Rich. 98 CM84
Grena Rd, Rich. 98 CM84
Grenaby Av, Croy. 142 DR101
Grenaby Rd, Croy. 142 DR101
Grenada Rd SE7 104 EJ80
Grenade St E14 85 DZ73
Grenadier St E16 87 EN74
Grenadine Cl, Wal.Cr. 14 DT27
Allwood Rd
Grendon Gdns, Wem. 62 CN61
Grendon St NW8 194 B4
Grendon St NW8 82 DE70
Grenfell Av, Horn. 71 FF60
Grenfell Cl, Borwd. 26 CQ39
Grenfell Gdns, Har. 62 CL59
Grenfell Rd W11 81 CX73
Grenfell Rd, Mitch. 120 DF93
Grenfell Twr W11 81 CX73
Grenfell Wk W11 81 CX73
Grennell Cl, Sutt. 140 DD103
Grennell Rd, Sutt. 140 DC103
Grenoble Gdns N13 45 DN51
Grenville Cl N3 43 CZ53
Grenville Cl, Cob. 154 BX113
Grenville Cl, Surb. 138 CQ102
Grenville Cl, Wal.Cr. 15 DX32
Grenville Gdns, Wdf.Grn. 48 EJ53
Grenville Ms SW7 100 DC77
Grenville Ms, Hmptn. 116 CB92
Grenville Pl NW7 42 CR50
Grenville Pl SW7 100 DC76
Grenville Rd N19 65 DL60
Grenville Rd, Croy. 161 EC109
Grenville St WC1 196 A5
Grenville St WC1 83 DL70
Gresham Av N20 44 DF49
Gresham Av, Warl. 177 DY118
Gresham Cl, Bex. 126 EY86
Gresham Cl, Brwd. 54 FW48
Gresham Cl, Enf. 30 DQ41
Gresham Cl, Oxt. 188 EF128
Gresham Dr, Rom. 70 EV57
Gresham Gdns NW11 63 CY60
Gresham Rd E6 87 EM68
Gresham Rd E16 86 EH72
Gresham Rd NW10 62 CR64
Gresham Rd SE25 142 DU98
Gresham Rd SW9 101 DN83
Gresham Rd, Beck. 143 DY96
Gresham Rd, Brwd. 54 FW48
Gresham Rd, Edg. 42 CM51
Gresham Rd, Hmptn. 116 CA93
Gresham Rd, Houns. 96 CC81
Gresham Rd, Oxt. 188 EF128
Gresham Rd, Stai. 113 BF92
Gresham Rd, Uxb. 76 BN68
Gresham St EC2 197 H8
Gresham St EC2 84 DQ72
Gresham Way SW19 120 DA90
Gresley Cl E17 67 DY58
Gresley Cl N15 66 DR56
Clinton Rd
Gresley Ct, Pot.B. 12 DC29
Gresley Rd N19 65 DJ60
Gresse St W1 195 M7
Gresse St W1 83 DK71
Gressenhall Rd SW18 119 CZ86
Gresswell Cl, Sid. 126 EU90
Greswell St SW6 99 CX81
Gretton Rd N17 46 DS52
Greville Av, S.Croy. 161 DX110
Greville Cl, Ash. 172 CL119
Greville Cl, Twick. 117 CH87
Greville Hall NW6 82 DB68
Greville Ms NW6 82 DB68
Greville Rd
Greville Pk Av, Ash. 172 CL118
Greville Pk Rd, Ash. 172 CL118
Greville Pl NW6 82 DB68
Greville Rd E17 67 EC56
Greville Rd NW6 82 DB67
Greville Rd, Rich. 118 CM86
Greville St EC1 196 E7
Greville St EC1 83 DN71
Grey Alders, Bans. 157 CW114
High Beeches
Grey Cl NW11 64 DC58
Grey Eagle St E1 197 P6
Grey Eagle St E1 84 DT71
Grey Twrs Av, Horn. 72 FK60
Grey Twrs Gdns, Horn. 72 FK60
Grey Twrs Av
Greycaine Rd, Wat. 24 BX37
Greycoat Pl SW1 199 M7
Greycoat Pl SW1 101 DK76
Greycoat St SW1 199 M7
Greycoat St SW1 101 DK76
Greycot Rd, Beck. 123 EA92
Greyfell Cl, Stan. 41 CH50
Coverdale Cl
Greyfields Cl, Pur. 159 DP113
Greyfriars, Brwd. 55 GB45
Greyfriars Pas EC1 196 G8
Greyfriars Rd, Wok. 168 BG124
Greyhound Hill NW4 63 CU55
Greyhound La SW16 121 DK93
Greyhound La, Grays 111 GG75
Greyhound La, Pot.B. 11 CU33
Greyhound Rd N17 66 DS55
Greyhound Rd NW10 81 CV69
Greyhound Rd W6 99 CX79
Greyhound Rd W14 99 CX79
Greyhound Rd, Sutt. 158 DC106
Greyhound Ter SW16 141 DJ95
Greyhound Way, Dart. 127 FE86
Greys Pk Cl, Kes. 162 EJ106
Greystead Rd SE23 122 DW87
Greystoke Av, Pnr. 60 CA55
Greystoke Dr, Ruis. 59 BP58
Greystoke Gdns W5 80 CL70
Greystoke Gdns, Enf. 29 DK42
Greystoke Pk Ter W5 79 CK69
Greystoke Pl EC4 196 D8
Greystone Cl, S.Croy. 160 DW111
Greystone Gdns, Har. 61 CJ58
Greystone Gdns, Ilf. 49 EQ54
Greystone Path E11 68 EF59
Grove Rd
Greystones Dr, Reig. 184 DC132
Greyswood St SW16 121 DH93
Greythorne Rd, Wok. 166 AU118
Grice Av, West. 162 EH113
Gridiron Pl, Upmin. 72 FP62
Grierson Rd SE23 123 DX87
Grieves Rd, Grav. 131 GF90
Griffin Av, Upmin. 73 FS58
Griffin Cen, The, Felt. 115 BV85
Griffin Cl NW10 63 CV64
Griffin Manor Way SE28 105 ER76
Griffin Rd N17 46 DS54
Griffin Rd SE18 105 ER78
Griffin Wk, Green. 129 FT85
Church Rd
Griffin Way, Sun. 135 BU96
Griffins, The, Grays 110 GB75
Griffith Cl, Dag. 70 EW60
Gibson Rd
Griffiths Cl, Wor.Pk. 139 CV103
Griffiths Rd SW19 120 DA94
Grifon Rd, Grays 109 FW76
Griggs App, Ilf. 69 EQ61
Griggs Gdns, Horn. 72 FJ64
Tylers Cres
Griggs Pl SE1 201 N7
Griggs Rd E10 67 EC58
Grilse Cl N9 46 DV49
Grimsby Gro E16 105 EP75
Barge Ho Rd
Grimsby St E2 84 DU70
Cheshire St
Grimsdyke Cres, Barn. 27 CW41
Grimsdyke Rd, Pnr. 40 BY52
Grimsel Path SE5 101 DP80
Laxley Cl
Grimshaw Cl N6 64 DG59
Grimshaw Way, Rom. 71 FF57
Grimston Rd SW6 99 CZ82
Grimstone Cl, Rom. 51 FB51
Grimwade Av, Croy. 142 DU104
Grimwade Cl SE15 102 DW83
Grimwade Cres SE15 102 DW83
Evelina Rd
Grimwood Rd, Twick. 117 CF87
Grindal St SE1 200 D5
Grindall Cl, Croy. 159 DP105
Hillside Rd
Grindleford Av N11 44 DG47
Grindley Gdns, Croy. 142 DT100
Grinling Pl SE8 103 EA79
Grinstead Rd SE8 103 DY78
Grisedale Cl, Pur. 160 DS114
Grisedale Gdns, Pur. 160 DS114
Grittleton Av, Wem. 80 CP65
Grittleton Rd W9 82 DA70
Grizedale Ter SE23 122 DV89
Grobars Av, Wok. 166 AW115
Grocer's Hall Ct EC2 197 K9
Grogan Cl, Hmptn. 116 BZ93
Groom Cres SW18 120 DD87
Groom Pl SW1 198 G6
Groom Pl SW1 100 DG76
Groom Rd, Brox. 15 DZ26
Groombridge Cl, Walt. 153 BV106
Groombridge Cl, Well. 126 EU85
Groombridge Rd E9 85 DX66
Groomfield Cl SW17 120 DG91
Grooms Cotts, Chesh. 4 AV30
Grooms Dr, Pnr. 59 BU57
Grosmont Rd SE18 105 ET78
Grosse Way SW15 119 CV86
Grosvenor Av N5 66 DQ64
Grosvenor Av SW14 98 CS83
Grosvenor Av, Cars. 158 DF107
Grosvenor Av, Har. 60 CB58
Grosvenor Av, Hayes 77 BS68
Grosvenor Av, Kings L. 7 BQ28
Grosvenor Av, Rich. 118 CL85
Grosvenor Rd
Grosvenor Cl, Iver 75 BD69
Grosvenor Cl, Loug. 33 EP39
Grosvenor Cotts SW1 198 F8
Grosvenor Ct N14 45 DJ45
Grosvenor Ct, Rick. 23 BR43
Mayfare
Grosvenor Ct, Slou. 74 AS72
Stoke Poges La
Grosvenor Cres NW9 62 CN56
Grosvenor Cres SW1 198 G5
Grosvenor Cres SW1 100 DG75
Grosvenor Cres, Dart. 128 FK85
Grosvenor Cres, Uxb. 77 BP66
Grosvenor Cres Ms SW1 198 F5
Grosvenor Cres Ms SW1 100 DG75
Grosvenor Dr, Horn. 72 FJ60
Grosvenor Dr, Loug. 33 EP39
Grosvenor Est SW1 199 N8
Grosvenor Est SW1 101 DK77
Grosvenor Gdns E6 86 EK69
Grosvenor Gdns N10 65 DJ55
Grosvenor Gdns N14 29 DK43
Grosvenor Gdns NW2 63 CW64
Grosvenor Gdns NW11 63 CZ58
Grosvenor Gdns SW1 199 H6
Grosvenor Gdns SW1 101 DH76
Grosvenor Gdns SW14 98 CS83
Grosvenor Gdns, Kings.T. 117 CK93
Grosvenor Gdns, Upmin. 73 FR60
Grosvenor Gdns, Wall. 159 DJ108
Grosvenor Gdns, Wdf.Grn 48 EG51
Grosvenor Gdns Ms E SW1 199 J6
Grosvenor Gdns Ms N SW1 199 H7
Grosvenor Gdns Ms S SW1 199 J7
Grosvenor Gate W1 198 E1
Grosvenor Gate W1 82 DF73
Grosvenor Hill SW19 119 CY93
Grosvenor Hill W1 195 H10
Grosvenor Hill W1 83 DH73
Grosvenor Pk SE5 102 DQ79
Grosvenor Pk Rd E17 67 EA57
Grosvenor Path, Loug. 33 EP39
Grosvenor Pl SW1 198 G5
Grosvenor Pl SW1 100 DG75
Grosvenor Pl, Wey. 135 BR104
Vale Rd
Grosvenor Ri E E17 67 EB57
Grosvenor Rd E6 86 EK67
Grosvenor Rd E7 86 EH65
Grosvenor Rd E10 67 EC60
Grosvenor Rd E11 68 EG57
Grosvenor Rd N3 43 CZ52
Grosvenor Rd N9 46 DV46
Grosvenor Rd N10 45 DH53
Grosvenor Rd SE25 142 DU98
Grosvenor Rd SW1 101 DH79
Grosvenor Rd W4 98 CP78
Grosvenor Rd W7 79 CG74
Grosvenor Rd, Belv. 106 FA79
Grosvenor Rd, Bexh. 126 EX85
Grosvenor Rd, Borwd. 26 CN41
Grosvenor Rd, Brent. 97 CK79
Grosvenor Rd, Dag. 70 EZ60
Grosvenor Rd, Epsom 172 CR119
Grosvenor Rd, Houns. 96 BZ83
Grosvenor Rd, Ilf. 69 EQ62
Grosvenor Rd, Nthwd. 39 BT50
Grosvenor Rd, Orp. 145 ES100
Grosvenor Rd, Rich. 118 CL85
Grosvenor Rd, Rom. 71 FD59
Grosvenor Rd, Sthl. 96 BZ76
Grosvenor Rd, Stai. 114 BG94
Grosvenor Rd, Twick. 117 CG87
Grosvenor Rd, Wall. 159 DH107
Grosvenor Rd, Wat. 24 BW42
Grosvenor Rd, W.Wick. 143 EB102
Grosvenor Sq W1 194 G10
Grosvenor Sq W1 82 DG73
Grosvenor Sq, Kings L. 7 BQ28
Grosvenor Av
Grosvenor St W1 195 H10
Grosvenor St W1 83 DH73
Grosvenor Ter SE5 101 DP80
Grosvenor Vale, Ruis. 59 BT61
Grosvenor Way E5 66 DW61
Grosvenor Wf Rd E14 204 F9
Grosvenor Wf Rd E14 103 ED77
Grote's Bldgs SE3 104 EE82
Grote's Pl SE3 104 EE82
Groton Rd SW18 120 DB89
Grotto Pas W1 194 G6
Grotto Rd, Twick. 117 CF89
Grotto Rd, Wey. 135 BP104
Grove, The E15 86 EE65
Grove, The N3 44 DA53
Grove, The N4 65 DM59
Grove, The N6 64 DG60
Grove, The N8 65 DK57
Grove, The N13 45 DN49
Grove, The N14 29 DJ43
Grove, The NW9 62 CR57
Grove, The NW11 63 CY59
Grove, The W5 79 CK74
Grove, The, Add. 152 BH106
Grove, The, Bexh. 106 EX84
Grove, The, Brwd. 54 FT49
Grove, The, Cat. 175 DP121
Grove, The, Chesh. 20 AX36
Grove, The, Couls. 175 DK115
Grove, The, Edg. 42 CP49
Grove, The, Egh. 113 BA92
Grove, The, Enf. 29 DN40
Grove, The, Epsom 156 CS113
Grove, The (Ewell), Epsom 157 CT110
Grove, The, Esher 136 CB102
Grove, The, Grav. 131 GH87
Grove, The, Grnf. 78 CC72
Grove, The, Hat. 12 DA27
Grove, The, Islw. 97 CE81
Grove, The, Pot.B. 12 DC32
Grove, The, Rad. 9 CG34
Grove, The, Sid. 126 EY91
Grove, The, Slou. 92 AU75
Grove, The, Stan. 41 CG47
Grove, The, Swan. 147 FF97
Grove, The, Swans. 130 FZ85
Grove, The, Tedd. 117 CG91
Grove, The, Twick. 117 CH86
Bridge Rd
Grove, The, Upmin. 72 FP63
Grove, The, Uxb. 58 BN64
Grove, The, Walt. 135 BV101
Grove, The, Wat. 23 BQ37
Grove, The, W.Wick. 143 EB104
Grove, The, West. 178 EK118
Grove, The, Wok. 167 AZ116
Grove Av N3 44 DA52
Grove Av N10 45 DJ54
Grove Av W7 79 CE72
Grove Av, Epsom 156 CS113
Grove Av, Pnr. 60 BY56
Grove Av, Sutt. 158 DA107
Grove Av, Twick. 117 CF88
Grove Bk, Wat. 40 BX46
Grove Cl N14 45 DH45
Avenue Rd
Grove Cl SE23 123 DX88
Grove Cl, Brom. 144 EG103
Grove Cl, Felt. 116 BY91
Grove Cl (Chalfont St. Peter), Ger.Cr. 36 AW53
Grove La
Grove Cl, Kings.T. 138 CM98
Grove Cl, Slou. 92 AU76
Alpha St S
Grove Cl, Uxb. 58 BN64
Grove Cl, Wind. 112 AV87
Grove Cotts SW3 100 DE79
Grove Ct SE3 104 EG81
Grove Ct, E.Mol. 137 CD99
Walton Rd
Grove Ct, Wal.Abb. 15 EB33
Highbridge St
Grove Cres E18 48 EF54
Grove Cres NW9 62 CQ56
Grove Cres SE5 102 DS82
Grove Cres, Felt. 116 BY91
Grove Cres, Kings.T. 138 CL97
Grove Cres, Rick. 22 BN42
Grove Cres, Walt. 135 BV101
Grove Cres Rd E15 85 ED65
Grove End E18 48 EF54
Grove Hill
Grove End NW5 65 DH63
Chetwynd Rd
Grove End (Chalfont St. Peter), Ger.Cr. 36 AW53
Grove End Gdns NW8 82 DD68
Grove End Rd
Grove End La, Esher 137 CD102
Grove End Rd NW8 82 DD69
Grove Fm Ct, Mitch. 140 DF98
Brookfields Av
Grove Fm Pk, Nthwd. 39 BR50
Grove Footpath, Surb. 138 CL98
Grove Gdns E15 86 EE65
Grove Gdns NW4 63 CU56
Grove Gdns NW8 194 C3
Grove Gdns, Dag. 71 FC62
Grove Gdns, Enf. 31 DX39
Grove Gdns, Tedd. 117 CG91
Grove Grn Rd E11 67 EC62
Grove Hall Ct NW8 82 DC69
Hall Rd
Grove Hall Rd, Bushey 24 BY42
Grove Heath, Wok. 168 BJ124
Grove Heath Ct, Wok. 168 BJ124
Grove Heath N, Wok. 168 BH122
Grove Heath Rd (Ripley), Wok. 168 BJ123
Grove Hill E18 48 EF54
Grove Hill (Chalfont St. Peter), Ger.Cr. 36 AW52
Grove Hill, Har. 61 CE59
Grove Hill Rd SE5 102 DS83
Grove Hill Rd, Har. 61 CE59
Grove Ho Rd N8 65 DL56
Grove La SE5 102 DR81
Grove La, Chesh. 4 AV27
Grove La, Chig. 49 ET48
Grove La, Couls. 158 DG113
Grove La, Epp. 18 EU30
High St
Grove La (Chalfont St. Peter), Ger.Cr. 36 AW53
Grove La, Kings.T. 138 CL98
Grove La, Uxb. 76 BM70
Grove La Ter SE5 102 DS83
Grove La
Grove Mkt Pl SE9 125 EM86
Grove Ms W6 99 CW76
Grove Ms W11 81 CZ72
Portobello Rd
Grove Mill La, Wat. 23 BP37
Grove Mill Pl, Cars. 140 DG104
Grove Pk E11 68 EH58
Grove Pk NW9 62 CQ56
Grove Pk SE5 102 DS82
Grove Pk Av E4 47 EB52
Grove Pk Br W4 98 CQ80
Grove Pk Gdns W4 98 CP79
Grove Pk Ms W4 98 CQ80
Grove Pk Rd N15 66 DS56
Grove Pk Rd SE9 124 EJ90
Grove Pk Rd W4 98 CP80
Grove Pk Rd, Rain. 89 FG67
Grove Pk Ter W4 98 CP79
Grove Pas E2 84 DV68
Grove Pas, Tedd. 117 CG92
Grove Path (Cheshunt), Wal.Cr. 14 DU31
Grove Pl NW3 64 DD63
Christchurch Hill
Grove Pl SW12 121 DH86
Cathles Rd
Grove Pl W3 80 CQ74
Grove Pl W5 79 CK74
The Gro
Grove Pl, Bans. 158 DF112
Grove Pl, Bark. 87 EQ67
Clockhouse Av
Grove Pl, Wat. 24 CB39
Hartspring La
Grove Pl, Wey. 153 BQ106
Princes Rd
Grove Rd E3 85 DX67
Grove Rd E4 47 EB49
Grove Rd E11 68 EF59
Grove Rd E17 67 EB57
Grove Rd E18 48 EF54
Grove Rd N11 45 DH50
Grove Rd N12 44 DD50
Grove Rd N15 66 DS57
Grove Rd NW2 81 CW65
Grove Rd SW13 99 CT82
Grove Rd SW19 120 DC94
Grove Rd W3 80 CQ74
Grove Rd W5 79 CK73
Grove Rd, Amer. 20 AT37
Grove Rd, Ash. 172 CM118
Grove Rd, Barn. 28 DE41
Grove Rd, Belv. 106 EZ79
Grove Rd, Bexh. 107 FC84
Grove Rd, Borwd. 26 CN39
Grove Rd, Brent. 97 CJ78
Grove Rd, Cher. 133 BF100
Grove Rd, E.Mol. 137 CD98
Grove Rd, Edg. 42 CN51
Grove Rd, Epsom 156 CS113
Grove Rd, Grav. 130 GB85
Grove Rd, Grays 110 GC79
Grove Rd, Houns. 96 CA84
Grove Rd, Islw. 97 CE81
Grove Rd, Mitch. 141 DH96
Grove Rd, Nthwd. 39 BR50
Grove Rd, Oxt. 187 EC134
Southlands La
Grove Rd, Pnr. 60 BZ57
Grove Rd, Rich. 118 CM86
Grove Rd, Rick. 38 BG47
Grove Rd, Rom. 70 EV59
Grove Rd, Sev. 191 FJ121
Grove Rd (Seal), Sev. 191 FN122
Grove Rd, Shep. 135 BQ100
Grove Rd, Surb. 137 CK99
Grove Rd, Sutt. 158 DB107
Grove Rd, Th.Hth. 141 DN98
Grove Rd, Twick. 117 CD90
Grove Rd, Uxb. 76 BK66
Grove Rd, West. 178 EJ120
Grove Rd, Wok. 167 AZ116
Grove Rd W, Enf. 30 DW37
Grove Shaw, Tad. 173 CY124
Grove St N18 46 DT51
Grove St SE8 203 M8
Grove St SE8 103 DZ77
Grove Ter NW5 65 DH62
Grove Ter, Tedd. 117 CG91
Grove Ter Ms NW5 65 DH62
Grove Ter
Grove Vale SE22 102 DT84
Grove Vale, Chis. 125 EN93
Grove Vil E14 85 EB73
Grove Way, Esher 136 CC101
Grove Way, Rick. 21 BB42
Grove Way, Uxb. 76 BK66
Grove Way, Wem. 62 CP64
Grove Wd Hill, Couls. 159 DK114
Grovebarns, Stai. 114 BG93
Grovebury Cl, Erith 107 FD79
Grovebury Gdns, St.Alb. 8 CC27
Grovebury Rd SE2 106 EV75
Grovedale Cl (Cheshunt), Wal.Cr. 14 DT30
Grovedale Rd N19 65 DK61
Groveherst Rd, Dart. 108 FM83
Grovehill Rd, Red. 184 DE134
Groveland Av SW16 121 DM94
Groveland Ct EC4 197 J9
Groveland Rd, Beck. 143 DZ97
Groveland Way, N.Mal. 138 CQ99
Grovelands, St.Alb. 8 CB27
Grovelands, W.Mol. 136 CA98
Grovelands Cl SE5 102 DS82
Grovelands Cl, Har. 60 CB62
Grovelands Ct N14 45 DK45
Grovelands Rd N13 45 DM49
Grovelands Rd N15 66 DU58
Grovelands Rd, Orp. 126 EU94
Grovelands Rd, Pur. 159 DL112
Grovelands Way, Grays 110 FZ78
Groveley Rd, Sun. 115 BT92
Grover Rd, Wat. 40 BX45
Groveside Cl W3 80 CN72
Groveside Cl, Cars. 140 DE103
Groveside Rd E4 48 EE47
Grovestile Waye, Felt. 115 BR87
Groveway SW9 101 DM81
Groveway, Dag. 70 EX63
Grovewood, Rich. 98 CN81
Sandycombe Rd
Grovewood Cl, Rick. 21 BB43
Grovewood Pl, Wdf.Grn. 49 EM51
Grubb St, Oxt. 188 EJ128
Grummant Rd SE15 102 DT81
Grundy St E14 85 EB72
Gruneisen Rd N3 44 DB52
Guardian Cl, Horn. 71 FH60
Guardsman Cl, Brwd. 54 FX50
Gubbins La, Rom. 52 FM52
Gubyon Av SE24 121 DP85
Guerin Sq E3 85 DZ69
Malmesbury Rd
Guernsey Cl, Houns. 96 CA81
Guernsey Fm Dr, Wok. 166 AX115
Guernsey Gro SE24 122 DQ87
Guernsey Rd E11 67 ED60
Guibal Rd SE12 124 EH87
Guild Rd SE7 104 EK78
Guild Rd, Erith 107 FF80
Guildersfield Rd SW16 121 DL94
Guildford Av, Felt. 115 BT89
Guildford Gdns, Rom. 52 FL51
Guildford Gro SE10 103 EB81
Guildford La, Wok. 166 AX120
Guildford Rd E6 86 EL72
Guildford Rd E17 47 EC53
Guildford Rd SW8 101 DL81
Guildford Rd, Cher. 133 BE102
Guildford Rd, Croy. 142 DR100
Guildford Rd, Ilf. 69 ES61
Guildford Rd, Lthd. 171 CG122
Guildford Rd, Rom. 52 FL51
Guildford Rd, Wok. 166 AY119
Guildford Rd (Mayford), Wok. 166 AX122
Guildford St, Cher. 134 BG101
Guildford St, Stai. 114 BG93
Guildford Way, Wall. 159 DL106
Guildhall Bldgs EC2 84 DR72
Basinghall St
Guildhall Yd EC2 197 K8
Guildhouse St SW1 199 K8
Guildhouse St SW1 101 DJ77
Guildown Av N12 44 DB49
Guildsway E17 47 DZ53
Guileshill La, Wok. 168 BL123
Guilford Av, Surb. 138 CM99
Guilford Pl WC1 196 B5
Guilford Pl WC1 83 DM70
Guilford St WC1 195 P5
Guilford St WC1 83 DL70
Guilford Vil, Surb. 138 CM100
Alpha Rd
Guilsborough Cl NW10 80 CS66
Guinevere Gdns, Wal.Cr. 15 DY31
Guinness Bldgs SE1 201 M7
Guinness Bldgs SE1 102 DS77
Guinness Cl E9 85 DY66
Guinness Cl, Hayes 95 BR76
Guinness Ct, Wok. 166 AT118
Iveagh Rd
Guinness Sq SE1 201 M8
Guinness Trust Bldgs SE11 200 G10
Guinness Trust Bldgs SE11 101 DP78
Guinness Trust Bldgs SW3 198 D9
Guinness Trust Bldgs SW9 101 DP84
Guinness Trust Est N16 66 DS60
Holmleigh Rd
Guion Rd SW6 99 CZ82
Gull Cl, Wall. 159 DL108

Gul-Ham This index reads in the sequence: Street Name / Postal District or Post Town / Map Page Reference / Grid Reference

Gull Wk, Horn. 89 FH66
Heron Flight Av
Gulland Cl, Bushey 24 CC43
Gulland Wk N1 84 DQ65
Clephane Rd
Gullet Wd Rd, Wat. 23 BU35
Gulliver Cl, Nthlt. 78 BZ67
Gulliver Rd, Sid. 125 ES89
Gulliver St SE16 203 M6
Gulliver St SE16 103 DZ76
Gulston Wk SW3 198 E9
Gulston Wk W11 81 CZ72
Basing St
Gumleigh Rd W5 97 CJ77
Gumley Gdns, Islw. 97 CG83
Gumley Rd, Grays 109 FX79
Gumping Rd, Orp. 145 EQ103
Gun Hill, Til. 111 GK79
Gun St E1 197 P7
Gun St E1 84 DT71
Gundulph Rd, Brom. 144 EJ97
Gunfleet Cl, Grav. 131 GL87
Gunmakers La E3 85 DY67
Gunn Rd, Swans. 130 FY86
Gunnell Cl SE26 122 DU92
Gunnell Cl, Croy. 142 DU100
Gunner Dr, Enf. 31 EA38
Government Row
Gunner La SE18 105 EN78
Gunners Gro E4 47 EC48
Gunners Rd SW18 120 DD89
Gunnersbury Av W3 98 CN76
Gunnersbury Av W4 98 CN76
Gunnersbury Av W5 80 CM74
Gunnersbury Cl W4 98 CP78
Grange Rd
Gunnersbury Ct W3 98 CP75
Bollo La
Gunnersbury Cres W3 98 CN75
Gunnersbury Dr W5 98 CM75
Gunnersbury Gdns W3 98 CN75
Gunnersbury La W3 98 CN76
Gunnersbury Ms W4 98 CP78
Chiswick High Rd
Gunnersbury Pk W3 98 CM77
Gunnersbury Pk W5 98 CM77
Gunning Rd, Grays 110 GD78
Gunning St SE18 105 ES77
Gunpowder Sq EC4 196 E8
Gunstor Rd N16 66 DS63
Gunter Gro SW10 100 DC79
Gunter Gro, Edg. 42 CR53
Gunterstone Rd W14 99 CY77
Gunthorpe St E1 84 DT72
Gunton Rd E5 66 DV62
Gunton Rd SW17 120 DG93
Gunwhale Cl SE16 203 J3
Gunwhale Cl SE16 85 DX74
Gurdon Rd SE7 104 EG78
Gurnard Cl, West Dr. 76 BK73
Trout Rd
Gurnell Gro W13 79 CF70
Gurney Cl E15 68 EE64
Gurney Rd
Gurney Cl E17 47 DX53
Gurney Cl, Bark. 87 EP65
Gurney Cres, Croy. 141 DM102
Gurney Dr N2 64 DC57
Gurney Rd E15 68 EE64
Gurney Rd, Cars. 158 DG105
Gurney Rd, Nthlt. 77 BV69
Guthrie St SW3 198 B10
Gutter La EC2 197 J8
Gutter La EC2 84 DQ72
Gutteridge La, Rom. 35 FC44
Guy Barnett Gro SE3 104 EG83
Casterbridge Rd
Guy Rd, Wall. 141 DK104
Guy St SE1 201 L4
Guy St SE1 102 DR75
Guyatt Gdns, Mitch. 140 DG96
Ormerod Gdns
Guyscliff Rd SE13 123 EC85
Guysfield Cl, Rain. 89 FG67
Guysfield Dr, Rain. 89 FG67
Gwalior Rd SW15 99 CX83
Felsham Rd
Gwendolen Av SW15 119 CX85
Gwendolen Cl SW15 119 CX85
Gwendoline Av E13 86 EH67
Gwendwr Rd W14 99 CY78
Gwent Cl, Wat. 8 BX34
Gwillim Cl, Sid. 126 EU85
Gwydor Rd, Beck. 143 DX98
Gwydyr Rd, Brom. 144 EF97
Gwyn Cl SW6 100 DC80
Gwynn Rd, Grav. 130 GC89
Gwynne Av, Croy. 143 DX101
Gwynne Cl W4 99 CT79
Gwynne Pk Av, Wdf.Grn. 49 EM51
Gwynne Pl WC1 196 C3
Gwynne Rd SW11 100 DD82
Gwynne Rd, Cat. 176 DR123
Gyfford Wk, Wal.Cr. 14 DV31
Gylcote Cl SE5 102 DR84
Gyles Pk, Stan. 41 CJ53
Gyllyngdune Gdns, Ilf. 69 ET61
Gypsy La, Kings L. 23 BR35
Gypsy La, Slou. 56 AS63

H

Ha-Ha Rd SE18 105 EM79
Haarlem Rd W14 99 CX76
Haberdasher Est N1 84 DR69
Haberdasher St
Haberdasher Pl N1 197 L2
Haberdasher St N1 197 L2
Haberdasher St N1 84 DR69
Habgood Rd, Loug. 32 EL41
Haccombe Rd SW19 120 DC93
Haydons Rd
Hackbridge Grn, Wall. 140 DG103
Hackbridge Pk Gdns, Cars. 140 DG103
Hackbridge Rd, Wall. 140 DG103
Hacketts La, Wok. 151 BF114
Hackford Rd SW9 101 DM81
Hackforth Cl, Barn. 27 CV43
Hackington Cres, Beck. 123 EA93
Hackney Cl, Borwd. 26 CR43
Hackney Gro E8 84 DV65
Reading La
Hackney Rd E2 197 P3
Hackney Rd E2 84 DT69
Hacton Dr, Horn. 72 FK63
Hacton La, Horn. 72 FM64
Hacton La, Upmin. 72 FM64
Hadden Rd SE28 105 ES76
Hadden Way, Grnf. 79 CD65
Haddestoke Gate (Cheshunt), Wal.Cr. 15 DZ26
Haddington Rd, Brom. 123 ED90
Haddo St SE10 103 EB79
Haddon Cl, Borwd. 26 CN41
Haddon Cl, Enf. 30 DU44
Haddon Cl, N.Mal. 139 CT99
Haddon Cl, Wey. 135 BR104
Haddon Gro, Sid. 126 EU87
Haddon Rd, Orp. 146 EW99
Haddon Rd, Rick. 21 BC43
Haddon Rd, Sutt. 158 DB105
Haddonfield SE8 203 J9
Haddonfield SE8 103 DX77
Hadfield Cl, Sthl. 78 BZ69
Adrienne Av
Hadfield Rd, Stai. 114 BK86
Hadlands Cl, Hem.H. 5 AZ26
Hadleigh Cl E1 84 DW70
Mantus Rd
Hadleigh Cl SW20 139 CZ96
Hadleigh Dr, Sutt. 158 DA109
Hadleigh Rd N9 46 DV45
Hadleigh St E2 84 DW70
Hadleigh Wk E6 86 EL72
Hadley Cl N21 29 DN44
Hadley Cl, Borwd. 26 CM44
Hadley Common, Barn. 28 DA40
Hadley Gdns W4 98 CR78
Hadley Gdns, Sthl. 96 BZ78
Hadley Grn, Barn. 27 CZ40
Hadley Grn Rd, Barn. 27 CZ40
Hadley Grn W, Barn. 27 CZ40
Hadley Gro, Barn. 27 CY40
Hadley Highstone, Barn. 27 CZ39
Hadley Pl, Wey. 152 BN108
Hadley Ridge, Barn. 27 CZ41
Hadley Rd (Hadley Wd), Barn. 29 DH38
Hadley Rd (New Barnet), Barn. 28 DB42
Hadley Rd, Belv. 106 EZ77
Hadley Rd, Enf. 29 DL38
Hadley Rd, Mitch. 141 DK98
Hadley St NW1 83 DH65
Hadley Way N21 29 DN44
Hadley Wd Ri, Ken. 175 DP115
Hadlow Pl SE19 122 DU94
Hadlow Rd, Sid. 126 EU91
Hadlow Rd, Well. 106 EW80
Hadlow Way, Grav. 130 GE94
Hadrian Cl, Stai. 114 BL88
Hadrian Way
Hadrian Cl, Wall. 159 DL108
Hadrian Est E2 84 DU68
Hadrian St SE10 104 EE78
Hadrian Way, Stai. 114 BL87
Hadrians Ride, Enf. 30 DT43
Hadyn Pk Rd W12 99 CU75
Hafer Rd SW11 100 DF84
Hafton Rd SE6 124 EE88
Hagden La, Wat. 23 BT43
Haggard Rd, Twick. 117 CH87
Haggerston Rd E8 84 DT66
Haggerston Rd, Borwd. 26 CL38
Hague St E2 84 DU69
Derbyshire St
Haig Gdns, Grav. 131 GJ87
Haig Pl, Mord. 140 DA100
Green La
Haig Rd, Grays 111 GG76
Haig Rd, Stan. 41 CJ50
Haig Rd, Uxb. 77 BP71
Haig Rd, West. 178 EL117
Haig Rd E E13 86 EJ69
Haig Rd W E13 86 EJ69
Haigville Gdns, Ilf. 69 EP56
Hailes Cl SW19 120 DC93
North Rd
Hailey Rd, Erith 106 FA75
Haileybury Av, Enf. 30 DT44
Haileybury Rd, Orp. 164 EU105
Hailsham Av SW2 121 DM89
Hailsham Cl, Rom. 52 FJ50
Hailsham Cl, Surb. 137 CK101
Hailsham Dr, Har. 61 CD55
Hailsham Gdns, Rom. 52 FJ50
Hailsham Rd SW17 120 DG93
Hailsham Rd, Rom. 52 FJ50
Hailsham Ter N18 46 DQ50
Haimo Rd SE9 124 EK85
Hainault Ct E17 67 ED56
Hainault Gore, Rom. 70 EY57
Hainault Gro, Chig. 49 EQ49
Hainault Ind Est, Ilf. 50 EW50
Hainault Rd E11 67 EC60
Hainault Rd, Chig. 49 EP48
Hainault Rd, Rom. 51 FC54
Hainault Rd (Chadwell Heath), Rom. 70 EZ58
Hainault Rd (Hainault), Rom. 70 EV55
Hainault St SE9 125 EP88
Hainault St, Ilf. 69 EP61
Haines Ct, Wey. 153 BR106
St. George's Lo
Haines Wk, Mord. 140 DB101
Dorchester Rd
Haines Way, Wat. 7 BU34
Hainford Cl SE4 103 DX84
Haining Cl W4 98 CN78
Wellesley Rd
Hainthorpe Rd SE27 121 DP90
Hainton Cl E1 84 DV72
Halberd Ms E5 66 DV61
Knightland Rd
Halbutt Gdns, Dag. 70 EZ62
Halbutt St, Dag. 70 EZ63
Halcomb St N1 84 DS67
Halcot Av, Bexh. 127 FB85
Halcrow St E1 84 DV71
Newark St
Halcyon Ct, Wem. 62 CP62
Coffers Circle
Halcyon Way, Horn. 72 FM60
Haldan Rd E4 47 EC51
Haldane Cl N10 45 DH52
Haldane Gdns, Grav. 130 GC88
Haldane Pl SW18 120 DB88
Haldane Rd E6 86 EK69
Haldane Rd SE28 88 EX73
Haldane Rd SW6 99 CZ80
Haldane Rd, Sthl. 78 CC72
Haldon Cl, Chig. 49 ES50
Arrowsmith Rd
Haldon Rd SW18 119 CZ85
Hale, The E4 47 ED52
Hale, The N17 66 DU56
Hale Cl E4 47 EC48
Hale Cl, Edg. 42 CQ50
Hale Cl, Orp. 163 EQ105
Hale Dr NW7 42 CQ51
Hale End, Rom. 51 FH51
Hale End, Wok. 166 AV121
Hale End Cl, Ruis. 59 BU58
Hale End Rd E4 47 ED51
Hale End Rd E17 47 ED53
Hale End Rd, Wdf.Grn. 47 ED52
Hale Gdns N17 66 DU55
Hale Gdns W3 80 CN74
Hale Gro Gdns NW7 42 CR50
Hale La NW7 42 CR50
Hale La, Edg. 42 CP50
Hale La, Sev. 181 FE117
Hale Path SE27 121 DP91
Hale Rd E6 86 EL70
Hale Rd N17 66 DU55
Hale St E14 85 EB73
Hale St, Stai. 113 BE91
Hale Wk W7 79 CE71
Halefield Rd N17 46 DU53
Hales St SE8 103 EA80
Deptford High St
Halesowen Rd, Mord. 140 DB101
Haleswood, Cob. 153 BV114
Halesworth Cl E5 66 DW61
Theydon Rd
Halesworth Cl, Rom. 52 FL52
Halesworth Rd SE13 103 EB83
Halesworth Rd, Rom. 52 FL51
Haley Rd NW4 63 CW58
Half Acre, Brent. 97 CK79
Half Acre Rd W7 79 CE74
Half Moon Ct EC1 197 H7
Half Moon Cres N1 83 DM68
Half Moon La SE24 122 DQ86
Half Moon La, Epp. 17 ET31
Half Moon Pas E1 84 DT72
Braham St
Half Moon St W1 199 J2
Half Moon St W1 83 DH74
Halfacre Hill (Chalfont St. Peter), Ger.Cr. 36 AY53
Halfhide La (Cheshunt), Wal.Cr. 15 DX27
Halfhides, Wal.Abb. 15 ED33
Halford Cl, Edg. 42 CP54
Halford Rd E10 67 ED57
Halford Rd SW6 100 DA79
Halford Rd, Rich. 118 CL85
Halford Rd, Uxb. 58 BN64
Halfway Ct, Purf. 108 FN77
Thamley
Halfway Grn, Walt. 135 BV104
Halfway St, Sid. 125 ER87
Haliburton Rd, Twick. 117 CG85
Haliday Wk N1 84 DR65
Balls Pond Rd
Halidon Cl E9 66 DW64
Urswick Rd
Halidon Ri, Rom. 52 FP51
Halifax Rd, Enf. 30 DQ40
Halifax Rd, Grnf. 78 CB67
Halifax Rd, Rick. 37 BC45
Halifax St SE26 122 DV91
Halifield Dr, Belv. 106 EY76
Haling Down Pas, S.Croy. 160 DQ109
Haling Gro, S.Croy. 160 DQ108
Haling Pk, S.Croy. 160 DQ107
Haling Pk Gdns, S.Croy. 159 DP107
Haling Pk Rd, S.Croy. 159 DP106
Haling Rd, S.Croy. 160 DR107
Halings La (Denham), Uxb. 57 BE56
Halkin Arc SW1 198 F6
Halkin Arc SW1 100 DG76
Halkin Ms SW1 198 F6
Halkin Pl SW1 198 F6
Halkin Pl SW1 100 DG76
Halkin St SW1 198 G5
Halkin St SW1 100 DG75
Halkingcroft, Slou. 92 AW75
Hall, The SE3 104 EG83
Hall Av N18 46 DR51
Weir Hall Av
Hall Av, S.Ock. 90 FQ74
Hall Cl W5 80 CL71
Hall Cl, Rick. 38 BG46
Hall Ct, Slou. 92 AV80
Hall Ct, Tedd. 117 CF92
Teddington Pk
Hall Cres, S.Ock. 108 FQ75
Hall Dr SE26 122 DW92
Hall Dr W7 79 CE72
Hall Dr (Harefield), Uxb. 38 BJ53
Hall Fm Cl, Stan. 41 CH49
Hall Fm Dr, Twick. 117 CD87
Hall Gdns E4 47 DZ49
Hall Gate NW8 82 DC69
Hall Rd
Hall Grn La, Brwd. 55 GC45
Hall Hill, Oxt. 187 ED131
Hall Hill, Sev. 191 FP123
Hall La E4 47 DY50
Hall La NW4 43 CU53
Hall La, Brwd. 55 FZ44
Hall La, Hayes 95 BR80
Hall La, S.Ock. 91 FX68
Hall La, Upmin. 72 FQ60
Hall Oak Wk NW6 81 CZ65
Maygrove Rd
Hall Pk Rd, Upmin. 72 FQ64
Hall Pl W2 82 DD70
Hall Pl, Wok. 167 BA116
Hall Pl Cres, Bex. 127 FC85
Hall Pl Dr, Wey. 153 BS106
Hall Rd E6 87 EM67
Hall Rd E15 67 ED63
Hall Rd NW8 82 DC69
Hall Rd, Dart. 108 FM84
Hall Rd, Grav. 130 GC90
Hall Rd, Islw. 117 CD85
Hall Rd, Rom. 70 EW58
Hall Rd (Gidea Pk), Rom. 71 FH55
Hall Rd, S.Ock. 108 FQ75
Hall Rd, Wall. 159 DH109
Hall St EC1 196 G2
Hall St EC1 83 DP69
Hall St N12 44 DC50
Hall Ter, Rom. 52 FN52
Hall Ter, S.Ock. 109 FR75
Hall Vw SE9 124 EK89
Hall Way, Pur. 159 DP113
Hallam Cl, Chis. 125 EM92
Hallam Cl, Wat. 24 BW40
Hallam Gdns, Pnr. 40 BY52
Hallam Ms W1 195 J6
Hallam Rd N15 65 DP56
Hallam Rd SW13 99 CV83
Hallam St W1 195 J5
Hallam St W1 83 DH71
Halland Way, Nthwd. 39 BR51
Halley Gdns SE13 103 ED84
Halley Rd E7 86 EJ65
Halley Rd E12 86 EK65
Halley Rd, Wal.Abb. 31 EC40
Sewardstone Rd
Halley St E14 85 DY71
Halleys App, Wok. 166 AU118
Halleys Ct, Wok. 166 AU118
Halleys App
Halleys Wk, Add. 152 BK108
Hallfield Est W2 82 DC72
Hallford Way, Dart. 128 FJ85
Halliards, The, Walt. 135 BU100
Felix Rd
Halliday Cl (Shenley), Rad. 10 CL32
Halliday Sq, Sthl. 79 CD74
Halliford Cl, Shep. 135 BR98
Halliford Rd, Shep. 135 BS99
Halliford Rd, Sun. 135 BS99
Halliford St N1 84 DQ66
Hallingbury Ct E17 67 EB55
Hallington Cl, Wok. 166 AV117
Halliwell Rd SW2 121 DM86
Halliwick Rd N10 44 DG53
Hallmark Trd Est NW10 62 CQ63
Great Cen Way
Hallmead Rd, Sutt. 140 DB104
Hallowell Av, Croy. 159 DL105
Hallowell Cl, Mitch. 140 DG97
Hallowell Rd, Nthwd. 39 BS52
Hallowes Cres, Wat. 39 BU48
Hayling Rd
Hallowfield Way, Mitch. 140 DE97
Hallside Rd, Enf. 30 DT38
Hallsland Way, Oxt. 188 EF133
Hallsville Rd E16 86 EF72
Hallswelle Rd NW11 63 CZ57
Hallwood Cres, Brwd. 54 FY45
Hallywell Cres E6 87 EM71
Halons Rd SE9 125 EN87
Halpin Pl SE17 201 L9
Halsbrook Rd SE3 104 EK83
Halsbury Cl, Stan. 41 CH49
Halsbury Rd W12 81 CV74
Halsbury Rd E, Nthlt. 60 CC63
Halsbury Rd W, Nthlt. 60 CB64
Halsend, Hayes 77 BV74
Halsey Ms SW3 198 D8
Halsey Pk, St.Alb. 10 CM27
Halsey Pl, Wat. 23 BV38
Halsey Rd, Wat. 23 BV41
Halsey St SW3 198 D8
Halsey St SW3 100 DF77
Halsham Cres, Bark. 87 ET65
Halsmere Rd SE5 101 DP81
Halstead Cl, Croy. 142 DQ104
Charles St
Halstead Ct N1 197 L1
Halstead Gdns N21 46 DR46
Halstead Hill (Cheshunt), Wal.Cr. 14 DS29
Halstead La, Sev. 164 EZ114
Halstead Rd E11 68 EG57
Halstead Rd N21 46 DQ46
Halstead Rd, Enf. 30 DS42
Halstead Rd, Erith 107 FE81
Halstead Way, Brwd. 55 GC44
Halston Cl SW11 120 DF86
Halstow Rd NW10 81 CX69
Halstow Rd SE10 104 EG78
Halsway, Hayes 77 BU74
Halt Robin La, Belv. 107 FB77
Halt Robin Rd
Halt Robin Rd, Belv. 106 FA77
Halter Cl, Borwd. 26 CR43
Clydesdale Cl
Halton Cross St N1 83 DP67
Halton Pl N1 84 DQ67
Dibden St
Halton Rd N1 83 DP66
Halton Rd, Grays 111 GJ76
Ham, The, Brent. 97 CJ80
Ham Cl, Rich. 117 CJ90
Ham Common, Rich. 118 CM91
Ham Fm Rd, Rich. 117 CK91
Ham Gate Av, Rich. 117 CK90
Ham Island, Wind. 92 AX84
Ham La, Egh. 112 AV91
Ham La, Wind. 92 AX84
Ham Pk Rd E7 86 EF66
Ham Pk Rd E15 86 EF66
Ham Ridings, Rich. 118 CM92
Ham St, Rich. 117 CJ89
Ham Vw, Croy. 143 DY100
Ham Yd W1 195 M10
Hambalt Rd SW4 121 DJ85
Hamble Cl, Ruis. 59 BS61
Chichester Av
Hamble Cl, Wok. 166 AU117
Hamble Ct, Kings.T. 117 CK94
Hamble La, S.Ock. 91 FT71
Hamble St SW6 100 DB83
Hamble Wk, Nthlt. 78 CA68
Brabazon Rd
Hamble Wk, Wok. 166 AU118
Hamble Wk, Wok. 166 AU118
Denton Way
Hambledon Cl, Uxb. 77 BP71
Aldenham Dr
Hambledon Gdns SE25 142 DT97
Hambledon Hill, Epsom 172 CQ116
Hambledon Pl SE21 122 DS88
Hambledon Rd SW18 119 CZ87
Hambledon Rd, Cat. 176 DR123
Hambledon Vale, Epsom 172 CQ116
Hambledown Rd, Sid. 125 ER87
Hambleton Cl, Wor.Pk. 139 CW103
Cotswold Way
Hamblings Cl, Rad. 9 CK33
Hambridge Way SW2 121 DN87
Hambro Av, Brom. 144 EG102
Hambro Rd SW16 121 DK93
Hambro Rd, Brwd. 54 FX47
Hambrook Rd SE25 142 DV97
Hamburgh Rd, Sthl. 78 BY74
Hamburgh Ct, Wal.Cr. 15 DX28
Hamden Cres, Dag. 71 FB62
Hamel Cl, Har. 61 CK55
Hamelin St E14 85 EC72
St. Leonards Rd
Hamer Cl, Hem.H. 5 BA28
Hamerton Rd, Grav. 130 GB85
Hameway E6 87 EN70
Hamfield Cl, Oxt. 187 EC127
Hamfrith Rd E15 86 EF65
Hamhaugh Island, Shep. 134 BN103
Hamilton Av N9 46 DU45
Hamilton Av, Cob. 153 BU113
Hamilton Av, Ilf. 69 EP56
Hamilton Av, Rom. 51 FD54
Hamilton Av, Surb. 138 CP102
Hamilton Av, Sutt. 139 CY103
Hamilton Av, Wok. 167 BE115
Hamilton Cl N17 66 DT55
Hamilton Cl NW8 82 DD69
Hamilton Cl SE16 203 L5
Hamilton Cl, Barn. 28 DE42
Hamilton Cl, Cher. 133 BF102
Hamilton Cl, Epsom 156 CQ112
Hamilton Cl, Felt. 115 BT92
Hamilton Cl, Pot.B. 11 CU33
Hamilton Cl, Pur. 159 DP112
Hamilton Cl, St.Alb. 8 CA30
Hamilton Cl, Stan. 41 CF47
Hamilton Ct W5 80 CM73
Hamilton Ct W9 82 DC69
Maida Vale
Hamilton Cres N13 45 DN49
Hamilton Cres, Brwd. 54 FW49
Hamilton Cres, Har. 60 BZ62
Hamilton Cres, Houns. 116 CB85
Hamilton Dr, Rom. 52 FL54
Hamilton Gdns NW8 82 DC69
Hamilton La N5 65 DP63
Hamilton Pk
Hamilton Mead, Hem.H. 5 BA27
Hamilton Ms W1 199 H4
Hamilton Pk N5 65 DP63
Hamilton Pk W N5 65 DP63
Hamilton Pl N19 65 DK62
Wedmore St
Hamilton Pl W1 198 G3
Hamilton Pl W1 82 DG74
Hamilton Pl, Sun. 115 BV94
Hamilton Pl, Tad. 173 CZ122
Hamilton Rd E15 86 EE69
Hamilton Rd E17 47 DY54
Hamilton Rd N2 64 DC55
Hamilton Rd N9 46 DU45
Hamilton Rd NW10 63 CU64
Hamilton Rd NW11 63 CX59
Hamilton Rd SE27 122 DR91
Hamilton Rd SW19 120 DB94
Hamilton Rd W4 98 CS75
Hamilton Rd W5 80 CL73
Hamilton Rd, Barn. 28 DE42
Hamilton Rd, Bexh. 106 EY82
Hamilton Rd, Brent. 97 CK79
Hamilton Rd, Felt. 115 BT91
Hamilton Rd, Grays 109 FW78
Hamilton Rd, Har. 61 CE57
Hamilton Rd, Hayes 77 BV73
Hamilton Rd, Ilf. 69 EP63
Hamilton Rd, Kings L. 7 BQ33
Hamilton Rd, Rom. 71 FH57
Hamilton Rd, Sid. 126 EU91
Hamilton Rd, Sthl. 78 BZ74
Hamilton Rd, Th.Hth. 142 DR97
Hamilton Rd, Twick. 117 CE88
Hamilton Rd, Uxb. 76 BK71
Hamilton Rd, Wat. 39 BV48
Hamilton Sq SE1 201 L4
Hamilton St SE8 103 EA79
Deptford High St
Hamilton St, Wat. 24 BW43
Hamilton Ter NW8 82 DB68
Hamilton Wk, Erith 107 FF80
Hamilton Way N3 44 DA51
Hamilton Way N13 45 DP49
Hamilton Way, Wall. 159 DK109
Hamlea Cl SE12 124 EF85
Hamlet, The SE5 102 DR83
Hamlet Cl SE13 104 EE84
Old Rd
Hamlet Cl, Rom. 50 FA52
Hamlet Gdns W6 99 CU77
Hamlet Rd SE19 122 DT94
Hamlet Rd, Rom. 50 FA52
Hamlet Sq NW2 63 CY62
The Vale
Hamlet Way SE1 201 L4
Hamlets Way E3 85 DZ70
Hamlin Cres, Pnr. 60 BW57
Hamlin Rd, Sev. 190 FE121
Hamlyn Cl, Edg. 42 CL48
Hamlyn Gdns SE19 122 DS94
Hamm Ct, Wey. 134 BL103
Hamm Moor La, Add. 152 BL106
Hammelton Grn SW9 101 DP81
Cromwell Rd
Hammelton Rd, Brom. 144 EF95
Hammer Par, Wat. 7 BU33
Hammers Gate, St.Alb. 8 CA25
Hammers La NW7 43 CU50
Hammersmith Br SW13 99 CV78

Harrier Rd NW9 42 CS54
Harrier Way E6 87 EM71
Harrier Way, Wal.Abb. 16 EG34
Harriers Cl W5 80 CL73
Harries Rd, Hayes 78 BW70
Harriescourt, Wal.Abb. 16 EG32
Harriet Cl E8 84 DU67
Harriet Gdns, Croy. 142 DU103
Harriet St SW1 198 E5
Harriet Tubman Cl SW2 121 DN87
Harriet Wk SW1 198 E5
Harriet Wk SW1 100 DF75
Harriet Way, Bushey 41 CD45
Harringay Gdns N8 65 DP56
Harringay Rd N15 65 DP57
Harrington Cl NW10 62 CR62
Harrington Cl, Croy. 141 DL103
Harrington Ct W10 81 CZ69
Dart St
Harrington Gdns SW7 100 DB77
Harrington Hill E5 66 DV60
Harrington Rd E11 68 EE60
Harrington Rd SE25 142 DV98
Harrington Rd SW7 100 DD77
Harrington Sq NW1 195 K1
Harrington Sq NW1 83 DJ68
Harrington St NW1 195 K2
Harrington St NW1 83 DJ69
Harrington Way SE18 104 EK76
Harriott Cl SE10 104 EF77
Harriotts Cl, Ash. 171 CJ120
Harriotts La
Harriotts La, Ash. 171 CJ119
Harris Cl, Enf. 29 DP39
Harris Cl, Grav. 130 GE90
Harris Cl, Houns. 96 CA81
Harris Cl, Rom. 52 FL52
Alverstoke Rd
Harris La, Rad. 10 CN34
Harris Rd, Bexh. 106 EY81
Harris Rd, Dag. 70 EZ64
Harris Rd, Wat. 23 BU35
Harris St E17 67 DZ59
Harris St SE5 102 DR80
Harris Way, Sun. 135 BS95
Harrison Cl N20 44 DE46
Harrison Cl, Brwd. 55 GD43
Harrison Cl, Nthwd. 39 BQ51
Harrison Ct, Shep. 135 BP99
Greeno Cres
Harrison Dr, Epp. 19 FB26
Harrison Rd, Dag. 89 FB65
Harrison St WC1 196 A3
Harrison St WC1 83 DL69
Harrison Wk (Cheshunt), Wal.Cr. 15 DX30
Harrison Way, Sev. 190 FG122
Harrison Way, Wal.Abb. 31 EC40
Sewardstone Rd
Harrisons Ri, Croy. 141 DP104
Harrisons Wf, Purf. 108 FN78
Harrogate Ct, Slou. 93 BA78
Harrogate Rd, Wat. 40 BW48
Harrold Rd, Dag. 70 EV64
Harrow Av, Enf. 30 DT44
Harrow Bottom Rd, Vir.W. 133 AZ100
Harrow Cl, Add. 134 BH103
Harrow Cl, Chess. 155 CK108
Harrow Cres, Rom. 51 FH52
Harrow Dr N9 46 DT46
Harrow Dr, Horn. 71 FH59
Harrow Flds Gdns, Har. 61 CE62
Harrow Gdns, Orp. 164 EV105
Harrow Gdns, Warl. 177 DZ115
Harrow Grn E11 68 EE62
Harrow Rd
Harrow La E14 204 D1
Harrow La E14 85 EC73
Harrow Manorway SE2 88 EW74
Harrow Mkt, Slou. 93 BA76
Harrow Pk, Har. 61 CE61
Harrow Pas, Kings.T. 137 CK96
Market Pl
Harrow Pl E1 197 N8
Harrow Pl E1 84 DS72
Harrow Rd E6 86 EL67
Harrow Rd E11 68 EE62
Harrow Rd NW10 81 CV69
Harrow Rd W2 81 CZ70
Harrow Rd W9 81 CZ70
Harrow Rd W10 81 CX70
Harrow Rd, Bark. 87 ES67
Harrow Rd, Cars. 158 DE106
Harrow Rd, Felt. 114 BN88
Harrow Rd, Ilf. 69 EQ63
Harrow Rd, Sev. 180 EY115
Harrow Rd, Slou. 93 AZ76
Harrow Rd, Warl. 177 DZ115
Harrow Rd, Wem. 61 CJ64
Harrow Rd (Tokyngton), Wem. 80 CP65
Harrow Vw, Har. 61 CD56
Harrow Vw, Hayes 77 BU72
Harrow Vw, Uxb. 77 BQ69
Harrow Vw Rd W5 79 CH70
Harrow Way, Shep. 135 BQ96
Harrow Way, Wat. 40 BY48
Harrow Weald Pk, Har. 41 CD51
Harroway Rd SW11 100 DD82
Harrowby Gdns, Grav. 130 GE89
Harrowby St W1 194 C8
Harrowby St W1 82 DE72
Harrowdene Cl, Wem. 61 CK63
Harrowdene Gdns, Tedd. 117 CG93
Harrowdene Rd, Wem. 61 CK62
Harrowes Meade, Edg. 42 CN48
Harrowgate Rd E9 85 DY65
Harston Dr, Enf. 31 EA38
Hart Cl, Red. 186 DT134
Hart Cor, Grays 109 FX78
Hart Cres, Chig. 49 ET50
Hart Dyke Cres, Swan. 147 FD97
Hart Dyke Rd
Hart Dyke Rd, Orp. 146 EW102
Hart Dyke Rd, Swan. 147 FD97
Hart Gro W5 80 CN74
Hart Gro, Sthl. 78 CA71
Hart Rd, W.Byf. 152 BL113
Hart St EC3 197 N10
Hart St, Brwd. 54 FW47
Harte Rd, Houns. 96 BZ82
Hartfield Av, Borwd. 26 CN43
Hartfield Av, Nthlt. 77 BV68
Hartfield Cl, Borwd. 26 CN43
Hartfield Cres SW19 119 CZ94
Hartfield Cres, W.Wick. 144 EG104
Hartfield Gro SE20 142 DV95
Hartfield Pl, Grav. 130 GD87
Hartfield Rd SW19 119 CZ94
Hartfield Rd, Chess. 155 CK106
Hartfield Rd, W.Wick. 162 EG105
Hartfield Ter E3 85 EA68
Hartford Av, Har. 61 CG55
Hartford Rd, Bex. 126 FA86
Hartford Rd, Epsom 156 CN107
Hartforde Rd, Borwd. 26 CN40
Harthall La, Hem.H. 7 BS26
Harthall La, Kings L. 7 BP28
Hartham Cl N7 65 DL64
Hartham Cl, Islw. 97 CG81
Hartham Rd N7 65 DL64
Hartham Rd N17 46 DT54
Hartham Rd, Islw. 97 CF81
Harting Rd SE9 124 EL91
Hartington Cl, Har. 61 CE63
Hartington Ct W4 98 CP80
Hartington Pl, Reig. 184 DA132
Hartington Rd E16 86 EH72
Hartington Rd E17 67 DY58
Hartington Rd SW8 101 DL81
Hartington Rd W4 98 CP80
Hartington Rd W13 79 CH73
Hartington Rd, Sthl. 96 BY75
Hartington Rd, Twick. 117 CH87
Hartismere Rd SW6 99 CZ80
Hartlake Rd E9 85 DX65
Hartland Cl N21 30 DQ44
Elmscott Gdns
Hartland Cl, Add. 152 BJ110
Hartland Cl, Edg. 42 CN47
Hartland Dr, Edg. 42 CN47
Hartland Dr, Ruis. 59 BV62
Hartland Rd E15 86 EF66
Hartland Rd N11 44 DF50
Hartland Rd NW1 83 DH66
Hartland Rd NW6 81 CZ68
Hartland Rd, Add. 152 BG108
Hartland Rd, Epp. 18 EU31
Hartland Rd, Hmptn. 116 CB91
Hartland Rd, Horn. 71 FG61
Hartland Rd, Islw. 97 CG83
Hartland Rd, Mord. 140 DA101
Hartland Rd (Cheshunt), Wal.Cr. 15 DX30
Hartland Way, Croy. 143 DY103
Hartland Way, Mord. 139 CZ101
Hartlands Cl, Bex. 126 EZ86
Hartlepool Ct E16 105 EP75
Barge Ho Rd
Hartley Av E6 86 EL67
Hartley Av NW7 43 CT50
Hartley Cl NW7 43 CT50
Hartley Cl, Brom. 145 EM96
Hartley Cl, Slou. 74 AW67
Hartley Copse, Wind. 112 AU86
Hartley Down, Pur. 159 DM113
Hartley Fm Est, Pur. 175 DM115
Hartley Hill, Pur. 175 DM115
Hartley Old Rd, Pur. 159 DM114
Hartley Rd E11 68 EF60
Hartley Rd, Croy. 141 DP101
Hartley Rd, Well. 106 EW80
Hartley Rd, West. 189 ER125
Hartley St E2 84 DW69
Hartley Way, Pur. 175 DM115
Hartmann Rd E16 86 EK74
Hartmoor Ms, Enf. 31 DX37
Hartnoll St N7 65 DM64
Eden Gro
Harton Cl, Brom. 144 EK95
Harton Rd N9 46 DV47
Harton St SE8 103 EA81
Harts Cl, Bushey 24 CA40
Harts Gro, Wdf.Grn. 48 EG50
Harts La SE14 103 DY80
Harts La, Bark. 87 EP65
Hartsbourne Av, Bushey 40 CC47
Hartsbourne Cl, Bushey 41 CD47
Hartsbourne Rd, Bushey 41 CD47
Hartscroft, Croy. 161 DY109
Hartshill Cl, Uxb. 76 BN65
Hartshill Rd, Grav. 131 GF89
Hartshill Wk, Wok. 166 AV116
Hartshill Wk, Wok. 166 AV116
Sythwood
Hartshorn All EC3 197 N9
Hartshorn Gdns E6 87 EN70
Hartslands Rd, Sev. 191 FJ123
Hartslock Dr SE2 106 EX75
Hartsmead Rd SE9 125 EM89
Hartspring La, Bushey 24 CA39
Hartspring La, Wat. 24 CA39
Hartsway, Enf. 30 DW42
Hartswood Cl, Brwd. 54 FY49
Hartswood Gdns W12 99 CT76
Hartswood Grn, Bushey 41 CD47
Hartswood Rd W12 99 CT75
Hartswood Rd, Brwd. 54 FY49
Hartsworth Cl E13 86 EF68
Hartville Rd SE18 105 ES77
Hartwell Dr E4 47 EC51
Hartwell St E8 84 DT65
Dalston La
Harvard Hill W4 98 CP79
Harvard La W4 98 CP78
Harvard Rd SE13 123 EC85
Harvard Rd W4 98 CP78
Harvard Rd, Islw. 97 CE81
Harvard Wk, Horn. 71 FG63
Harvel Cl, Orp. 146 EU97
Harvel Cres SE2 106 EX78
Harvest Bk Rd, W.Wick. 144 EF104
Harvest Ct, Shep. 134 BN98
Harvest End, Wat. 24 BX36
Harvest La, Loug. 48 EJ45
Fallow Flds
Harvest La, T.Ditt. 137 CG100
Harvest Rd, Bushey 24 CB42
Harvest Rd, Egh. 112 AX92
Harvest Rd, Felt. 115 BU91
Harvest Way, Swan. 147 FD101
Harvester Rd, Epsom 156 CR110
Harvesters Cl, Islw. 117 CD85
Harvey, Grays 110 GB75
Harvey Dr, Hmptn. 136 CB95
Harvey Gdns E11 68 EF60
Harvey Rd
Harvey Gdns SE7 104 EK77
Harvey Gdns, Loug. 33 EP41
Harvey Ho, Brent. 98 CL78
Green Dragon La
Harvey Pt E16 86 EH71
Fife Rd
Harvey Rd E11 68 EF60
Harvey Rd N8 65 DM57
Harvey Rd SE5 102 DR81
Harvey Rd, Houns. 116 BZ87
Harvey Rd, Ilf. 69 EP64
Harvey Rd, Nthlt. 78 BW66
Harvey Rd, Rick. 22 BN44
Harvey Rd, St.Alb. 9 CJ26
Harvey Rd, Slou. 93 BB76
Harvey Rd, Uxb. 76 BN68
Harvey Rd, Walt. 135 BU101
Harvey St N1 84 DR67
Harveyfields, Wal.Abb. 15 EC34
Harveys La, Rom. 71 FD61
Harvil Rd (Harefield), Uxb. 58 BK58
Harvil Rd (Ickenham), Uxb. 58 BL60
Harvill Rd, Sid. 126 EX92
Harvington Wk E8 84 DU66
Wilman Gro
Harvist Est N7 65 DN63
Harvist Rd NW6 81 CX68
Harwater Dr, Loug. 33 EM40
Harwell Cl, Ruis. 59 BR60
Harwell Pas N2 64 DF56
Harwich La EC2 197 N6
Harwich La EC2 84 DS71
Harwood Av, Brom. 144 EH96
Harwood Av, Horn. 72 FL55
Harwood Av, Mitch. 140 DE97
Harwood Cl N12 44 DE51
Summerfields Av
Harwood Cl, Wem. 61 CK63
Harrowdene Rd
Harwood Dr, Uxb. 76 BM67
Harwood Gdns, Wind. 112 AV87
Harwood Hall La, Upmin. 90 FP65
Harwood Rd SW6 100 DA80
Harwood Ter SW6 100 DB81
Harwoods Rd, Wat. 23 BU42
Harwoods Yd N21 45 DN45
Wades Hill
Hascombe Ter SE5 102 DR82
Haselbury Rd N9 46 DS49
Haselbury Rd N18 46 DS49
Haseldine Rd, St.Alb. 9 CK26
Haseley End SE23 122 DW87
Tyson Rd
Haselrigge Rd SW4 101 DK84
Haseltine Rd SE26 123 DZ91
Haselwood Dr, Enf. 29 DP42
Haskard Rd, Dag. 70 EX63
Haskell Ho NW10 80 CR67
Hasker St SW3 198 C8
Hasker St SW3 100 DE77
Haslam Av, Sutt. 139 CY102
Haslam Cl N1 83 DN66
Haslam Cl, Uxb. 59 BQ61
Haslam St SE15 102 DT80
Haslemere Av NW4 63 CX58
Haslemere Av SW18 120 DB89
Haslemere Av W7 97 CG76
Haslemere Av W13 97 CG76
Haslemere Av, Barn. 44 DF46
Haslemere Av, Houns. 96 BW82
Haslemere Av, Mitch. 140 DD96
Haslemere Cl, Hmptn. 116 BZ92
Haslemere Cl, Wall. 159 DL106
Stafford Rd
Haslemere Gdns N3 63 CZ55
Haslemere Heathrow Est, Houns. 95 BV82
Haslemere Rd N8 65 DK59
Haslemere Rd N21 45 DP47
Haslemere Rd, Bexh. 106 EZ82
Haslemere Rd, Ilf. 69 ET61
Haslemere Rd, Th.Hth. 141 DP99
Hasler Cl SE28 88 EV73
Haslett Rd, Shep. 135 BS96
Hasluck Gdns, Barn. 28 DC44
Hassard St E2 84 DT68
Hackney Rd
Hassendean Rd SE3 104 EH79
Hassett Rd E9 85 DX65
Hassock Wd, Kes. 162 EK105
Hassocks Cl SE26 122 DV90
Hassocks Rd SW16 141 DK95
Hassop Rd NW2 63 CX63
Hassop Wk SE9 124 EL91
Hasted Cl, Green. 129 FW86
Hasted Rd SE7 104 EK78
Hastings Av, Ilf. 69 EQ56
Hastings Cl SE15 102 DU80
Hastings Cl, Barn. 28 DC42
Leicester Rd
Hastings Cl, Grays 110 FY79
Hastings Dr, Surb. 137 CJ100
Hastings Ho SE18 105 EM77
Hastings Rd N11 45 DJ50
Hastings Rd N17 66 DR55
Hastings Rd W13 79 CH73
Hastings Rd, Brom. 144 EL102
Hastings Rd, Croy. 142 DT102
Hastings Rd, Rom. 71 FH57
Hastings St WC1 195 P3
Hastings St WC1 83 DL69
Hastings Way, Bushey 24 BY42
Hastings Way, Rick. 23 BP42
Hastingwood Trd Est N18 47 DX51
Hastoe Cl, Hayes 78 BY70
Kingsash Dr
Hat and Mitre Ct EC1 196 G5
Hatch, The, Enf. 31 DX39
Hatch Cl, Add. 134 BH104
Hatch Gdns, Tad. 173 CX120
Hatch Gro, Rom. 70 EY56
Hatch La E4 47 ED49
Hatch La, Cob. 169 BP119
Hatch La, Couls. 174 DG115
Hatch La, West Dr. 94 BK80
Hatch La, Wok. 169 BP120
Hatch Pl, Kings.T. 118 CM92
Hatch Rd SW16 141 DL96
Hatch Rd, Brwd. 54 FU43
Hatch Side, Chig. 49 EN50
Hatcham Pk Ms SE14 103 DX81
Hatcham Pk Rd
Hatcham Pk Rd SE14 103 DX81
Hatcham Rd SE15 102 DW79
Hatchard Rd N19 65 DK61
Hatchcroft NW4 63 CV55
Hatchett Rd, Felt. 115 BQ88
Hatchlands Rd, Red. 184 DE134
Hatchwood Cl, Wdf.Grn. 48 EF49
Sunset Av
Hatcliffe Cl SE3 104 EF83
Hatcliffe St SE10 205 K10
Hatfield Cl SE14 103 DX80
Reaston St
Hatfield Cl, Brwd. 55 GD45
Hatfield Cl, Horn. 72 FK64
Hatfield Cl, Ilf. 69 EP55
Hatfield Cl, Mitch. 140 DD98
Hatfield Cl, Sutt. 158 DA109
Hatfield Cl, W.Byf. 152 BH112
Hatfield Mead, Mord. 140 DA99
Central Rd
Hatfield Rd E15 68 EE64
Hatfield Rd W4 98 CR75
Hatfield Rd W13 79 CG74
Hatfield Rd, Ash. 172 CM119
Hatfield Rd, Dag. 88 EY66
Hatfield Rd, Grays 109 FW78
Hatfield Rd, Pot.B. 12 DC30
Hatfield Rd, Slou. 92 AU75
Hatfield Rd, Wat. 23 BV39
Hatfields SE1 200 E2
Hatfields SE1 83 DP74
Hatfields, Loug. 33 EP41
Hathaway Cl, Brom. 145 EM102
Hathaway Cl, Ruis. 59 BT63
Stafford Rd
Hathaway Cl, Stan. 41 CG50
Hathaway Cres E12 87 EM65
Hathaway Gdns W13 79 CF71
Hathaway Gdns, Grays 110 GB76
Hathaway Rd
Hathaway Gdns, Rom. 70 EX57
Hathaway Rd, Croy. 141 DP101
Hathaway Rd, Grays 110 GB77
Hatherleigh Cl, Chess. 155 CK106
Hatherleigh Cl, Mord. 140 DA98
Hatherleigh Gdns, Pot.B. 12 DD32
Hatherleigh Rd, Ruis. 59 BU61
Hatherleigh Way, Rom. 52 FK53
Hatherley Cres, Sid. 126 EU89
Hatherley Gdns E6 86 EK69
Hatherley Gdns N8 65 DL58
Hatherley Gro W2 82 DB72
Hatherley Ms E17 67 EA56
Hatherley Rd E17 67 DZ56
Hatherley Rd, Rich. 98 CM82
Hatherley Rd, Sid. 126 EU91
Hatherley St SW1 199 L8
Hathern Gdns SE9 125 EN91
Hatherop Rd, Hmptn. 116 BZ94
Hatherwood, Lthd. 171 CK121
Hathorne Cl SE15 102 DV82
Hathway St SE15 102 DW82
Gibbon Rd
Hathway Ter SE14 102 DW82
Gibbon Rd
Hatley Av, Ilf. 69 EQ56
Hatley Cl N11 44 DF50
Hatley Rd N4 65 DM61
Hatteraick St SE16 202 G4
Hatters La, Wat. 23 BR44
Hattersfield Cl, Belv. 106 EZ77
Hatton Cl SE18 105 ER80
Hatton Cl, Grav. 130 GE90
Hatton Cl (Chafford Hundred), Grays 109 FX76
Hatton Ct E5 67 DY63
Gilpin Rd
Hatton Gdn EC1 196 E6
Hatton Gdn EC1 83 DN71
Hatton Gdns, Mitch. 140 DF99
Hatton Grn, Felt. 95 BU84
Hatton Gro, West Dr. 94 BK75
Hatton Ho E1 84 DU73
Wellclose Sq
Hatton Pl EC1 196 E5
Hatton Pl EC1 83 DN70
Hatton Rd, Croy. 141 DN102
Hatton Rd, Felt. 115 BS85
Hatton Rd (Cheshunt), Wal.Cr. 15 DX29
Hatton Row NW8 194 A5
Hatton St NW8 194 A5
Hatton Wall EC1 196 D6
Hatton Wall EC1 83 DN71
Haunch of Venison Yd W1 195 H9
Havana Cl, Rom. 71 FE57
Havana Rd SW19 120 DA89
Havannah St E14 204 A5
Havannah St E14 103 EA75
Havant Rd E17 67 EC55
Havant Way SE15 102 DT80
Daniel Gdns
Havelock Pl, Har. 61 CE58
Havelock Rd N17 46 DU54
Havelock Rd SW19 120 DC92
Havelock Rd, Belv. 106 EZ77
Havelock Rd, Brom. 144 EJ98
Havelock Rd, Croy. 142 DT102
Havelock Rd, Dart. 127 FH87
Havelock Rd, Grav. 131 GF88
Havelock Rd, Har. 61 CE55
Havelock Rd, Kings L. 6 BN28
Havelock Rd, Sthl. 96 BZ76
Havelock St N1 83 DL67
Havelock St, Ilf. 69 EP61
Havelock Ter SW8 101 DH80
Havelock Wk SE23 122 DW88
Haven, The SE26 122 DV92
Springfield Rd
Haven, The, Grays 111 GF78
Haven, The, Rich. 98 CN8
Haven Cl SE9 125 EM9
Haven Cl SW19 119 CX9
Haven Cl, Grav. 131 GF9
Haven Cl, Hayes 77 BS7
Haven Cl, Sid. 126 EV9
Haven Cl, Swan. 147 FF9
Haven Grn W5 79 CK7
Haven Grn Ct W5 79 CK7
Haven Grn
Haven La W5 80 CL7
Haven Pl W5 79 CK7
The Bdy
Haven Pl, Grays 110 GC7
Haven Rd, Ashf. 115 BP9
Haven St NW1 83 DH6
Castlehaven Rd
Haven Ter W5 79 CK7
The Bdy
Havengore Av, Grav. 131 GL8
Havenhurst Ri, Enf. 29 DN4
Havensfield, Kings L. 6 BH3
Nunfield
Havenwood, Wem. 62 CP6
Havenwood Cl, Brwd. 53 FW5
Wilmot Grn
Haverfield Gdns, Rich. 98 CN8
Haverfield Rd E3 85 DY6
Haverford Way, Edg. 42 CM5
Haverhill Rd E4 47 EC4
Haverhill Rd SW12 121 DJ8
Havering Dr, Rom. 71 FE5
Havering Gdns, Rom. 70 EW5
Havering Rd, Rom. 71 FD5
Havering St E1 85 DX7
Devonport St
Havering Way, Bark. 88 EV6
Havers Av, Walt. 154 BX10
Haversfield Est, Brent. 98 CL7
Haversham Cl, Twick. 117 CK8
Haversham Pl N6 64 DF6
Haverstock Ct, Orp. 146 EU9
Haverstock Hill NW3 64 DE6
Haverstock Rd NW5 64 DG6
Haverstock St N1 196 G
Haverstock St N1 83 DP6
Haverthwaite Rd, Orp. 145 ER10
Havil St SE5 102 DS8
Havisham Pl SE19 121 DP9
Hawarden Gro SE24 122 DQ8
Hawarden Hill NW2 63 CU6
Hawarden Rd E17 67 DX5
Hawarden Rd, Cat. 176 DQ12
Hawbridge Rd E11 67 ED6
Hawes Cl, Nthwd. 39 BT5
Hawes La E4 31 EC3
Hawes La, W.Wick. 143 ED10
Hawes Rd N18 46 DV5
Hawes Rd, Brom. 144 EH9
Hawes Rd, Tad. 173 CX12
Hatch Gdns
Hawes St N1 83 DP6
Haweswater Dr, Wat. 8 BW3
Haweswater Ho, Islw. 117 CF8
Summerwood Rd
Hawfield Bk, Orp. 146 EX10
Hawfield Gdns, St.Alb. 9 CD2
Hawgood St E3 85 EA7
Hawk Cl, Wal.Abb. 16 EG3
Hawk Ter, Ilf. 69 EN5
Tiptree Cres
Hawkdene E4 31 EB4
Hawke Pk Rd N22 65 DP5
Hawke Pl SE16 203 J
Hawke Rd SE19 122 DS9
Hawker Cl, Wall. 159 DL10
Hawkes Cl, Grays 110 GB7
New Rd
Hawke's Pl, Sev. 190 FG12
Hawkes Rd, Mitch. 140 DE9
Hawkesbury Rd SW15 119 CV8
Hawkesfield Rd SE23 123 DY8
Hawkesley Cl, Twick. 117 CG9
Hawkesworth Cl, Nthwd. 39 BS5
Hawkewood Rd, Sun. 135 BU9
Hawkhirst Rd, Ken. 176 DR11
Hawkhurst, Cob. 154 CA11
Hawkhurst Gdns, Chess. 156 CL10
Hawkhurst Gdns, Rom. 51 FD5
Hawkhurst Rd SW16 141 DK9
Hawkhurst Way, N.Mal. 138 CR9
Hawkhurst Way, W.Wick. 143 EB10
Hawkinge Wk, Orp. 146 EV9
Hawkinge Way, Horn. 90 FJ6
Hawkins Av, Grav. 131 GJ9
Hawkins Cl NW7 42 CR5
Hale La
Hawkins Cl, Borwd. 26 CQ4
Banks Rd
Hawkins Cl, Har. 61 CD5
Hawkins Rd, Tedd. 117 CH9
Hawkins Way SE6 123 EA9
Hawkins Way, Hem.H. 5 BA2
Hawkley Gdns SE27 121 DP8
Hawkridge Cl, Rom. 70 EW5
Hawkridge Dr, Grays 110 GD7
Hawks Hill, Epp. 18 FA2
Hawk's Hill, Lthd. 171 CF12
Hawk's Hill, Lthd. 171 CF12
Guildford Rd
Hawks Hill Cl, Lthd. 171 CF12
Hawks Ms SE10 103 EC8
Luton Pl
Hawks Rd, Kings.T. 138 CM9
Hawksbrook La, Beck. 143 EB10
Hawkshaw Cl SW2 121 DL8
Tierney Rd
Hawkshead Cl, Brom. 124 EE9
Hawkshead La, Hat. 11 CW2
Hawkshead Rd NW10 81 CT6
Hawkshead Rd W4 98 CS7
Hawkshead Rd, Pot.B. 12 DB2
Hawkshill Cl, Esher 154 CA10
Hawkshill Way, Esher 154 BZ10
Hawkslade Rd SE15 123 DX8
Hawksley Rd N16 66 DS6
Hawksmead Cl, Enf. 31 DX3
Hawksmoor, Rad. 10 CN3
Hawksmoor Cl E6 86 EL7
Allhallows Rd

Hawksmoor Cl SE18 105 ES78
Hawksmoor Grn, Brwd. 55 GD43
Hawksmoor Ms E1 84 DV73
Cable St
Hawksmoor St W6 99 CX79
Hawksmouth E4 47 EB45
Hawkstone Rd SE16 202 G8
Hawkstone Rd SE16 102 DW77
Hawksview, Cob. 154 CA113
Hawksway, Stai. 113 BF90
Hawkswell Cl, Wok. 166 AT117
Hawkswell Wk, Wok. 166 AS117
Lockfield Dr
Hawkswood Gro, Slou. 75 AZ65
Hawkswood La, Ger.Cr. 57 AZ64
Hawkwell Ct E4 47 EC48
Colvin Gdns
Hawkwell Ho, Dag. 70 FA60
Hawkwell Wk N1 84 DQ67
Basire St
Hawkwood Cres E4 31 EB44
Hawkwood La, Chis. 145 EQ95
Hawkwood Mt E5 66 DV60
Hawlands Dr, Pnr. 60 BY59
Hawley Cl, Hmptn. 116 BZ93
Hawley Cres NW1 83 DH66
Hawley Ms NW1 83 DH66
Hawley St
Hawley Rd N18 47 DX50
Hawley Rd NW1 83 DH66
Hawley Rd, Dart. 128 FL89
Hawley St NW1 83 DH66
Hawley Way, Ashf. 114 BN92
Haws La, Stai. 114 BG86
Hawstead La, Orp. 164 EZ106
Hawstead Rd SE6 123 EB86
Hawsted, Buck.H. 48 EH45
Hawthorn Av N13 45 DL50
Hawthorn Av, Brwd. 55 FZ48
Hawthorn Av, Cars. 158 DG108
Hawthorn Av, Rain. 89 FH70
Hawthorn Av, Rich. 98 CL82
Kew Rd
Hawthorn Av, Th.Hth. 141 DP95
Hawthorn Cen, Har. 61 CF56
Hawthorn Cl, Abb.L. 7 BU32
Magnolia Av
Hawthorn Cl, Bans. 157 CY114
Hawthorn Cl, Grav. 131 GH91
Hawthorn Cl, Hmptn. 116 CA92
Hawthorn Cl, Houns. 95 BV80
Hawthorn Cl, Iver 75 BD68
Hawthorn Cl, Orp. 145 ER100
Hawthorn Cl, Wat. 23 BT38
Hawthorn Cl, Wok. 166 AY120
Hawthorn Cotts, Well. 106 EU83
Hook La
Hawthorn Ct, Rich. 98 CP81
West Hall Rd
Hawthorn Cres SW17 120 DG92
Hawthorn Cres, S.Croy. 160 DW111
Hawthorn Dr, Har. 60 BZ58
Hawthorn Dr (Denham), Uxb. 76 BJ65
Hawthorn Dr, W.Wick. 162 EE105
Hawthorn Gdns W5 97 CK76
Hawthorn Gro SE20 122 DV94
Hawthorn Gro, Barn. 27 CT44
Hawthorn Gro, Enf. 30 DR38
Hawthorn Hatch, Brent. 97 CH80
Hawthorn La, Sev. 190 FF122
Hawthorn Ms NW7 43 CY53
Holders Hill Rd
Hawthorn Pl, Erith 107 FC78
Hawthorn Rd N8 65 DK55
Hawthorn Rd N18 46 DT50
Hawthorn Rd NW10 81 CU66
Hawthorn Rd, Bexh. 106 EZ84
Hawthorn Rd, Brent. 97 CH80
Hawthorn Rd, Buck.H. 48 EK49
Hawthorn Rd, Dart. 128 FK88
Hawthorn Rd, Sutt. 158 DE107
Hawthorn Rd, Wall. 159 DH108
Hawthorn Rd, Wok. 166 AX120
Hawthorn Rd (Send Marsh), Wok. 168 BG124
Hawthorn Wk W10 81 CY70
Droop St
Hawthorn Way, Add. 152 BJ110
Hawthorn Way, Shep. 135 BR98
Hawthornden Cl N12 44 DE51
Fallowfields Dr
Hawthorndene Cl, Brom. 144 EG103
Hawthorndene Rd, Brom. 144 EF103
Hawthorne Av, Har. 61 CG58
Hawthorne Av, Mitch. 140 DD96
Hawthorne Av, Ruis. 59 BV58
Hawthorne Av (Cheshunt), Wal.Cr. 14 DV31
Hawthorne Av, West. 178 EK115
Hawthorne Cl N1 84 DS65
Hawthorne Cl, Brom. 145 EM97
Hawthorne Cl, Sutt. 140 DB103
Aultone Way
Hawthorne Cl (Cheshunt), Wal.Cr. 14 DV31
Hawthorne Ct, Nthwd. 39 BU54
Ryefield Cres
Hawthorne Ct, Walt. 136 BX103
Ambleside Av
Hawthorne Cres, Slou. 74 AS71
Hawthorne Cres, West Dr. 94 BM75
Hawthorne Fm Av, Nthlt. 78 BY67
Hawthorne Gro NW9 62 CQ59
Hawthorne Ms, Grnf. 78 CC72
Greenford Rd
Hawthorne Pl, Epsom 156 CS112
Hawthorne Pl, Hayes 77 BT73
Hawthorne Rd E17 67 EA55
Hawthorne Rd, Brom. 145 EM97
Hawthorne Rd, Rad. 9 CG34
Hawthorne Rd, Stai. 113 BC92
Hawthorne Way N9 46 DS47
Hawthorne Way, Stai. 114 BK87
Hawthorns, Wdf.Grn. 48 EG48
Hawthorns, The, Ch.St.G. 20 AW40
Hawthorns, The, Epsom 157 CT107
Ewell Bypass
Hawthorns, The, Loug. 33 EN42
Hawthorns, The, Oxt. 188 EG133
Hawthorns, The, Rick. 37 BD50
Hawthorns, The, Slou. 93 BF81
Hawtrees, Rad. 25 CF35
Hawtrey Av, Nthlt. 78 BX68
Hawtrey Cl, Slou. 92 AV75
Hawtrey Dr, Ruis. 59 BU59
Hawtrey Rd NW3 82 DE66
Haxted Rd, Brom. 144 EH95
North Rd
Hay Cl E15 86 EE66
Hay Cl, Borwd. 26 CQ40
Hay Currie St E14 85 EB72
Hay Hill W1 199 J1
Hay Hill W1 83 DH73
Hay La NW9 62 CR56
Hay La, Slou. 56 AX63
Hay St E2 84 DU67
Hayburn Way, Horn. 71 FF60
Haycroft Cl, Couls. 175 DP118
Caterham Dr
Haycroft Gdns NW10 81 CU67
Haycroft Rd SW2 121 DL85
Haycroft Rd, Surb. 138 CL104
Hayday Rd E16 86 EG71
Hayden Ct, Add. 152 BH111
Hayden Rd, Wal.Abb. 31 EC40
Sewardstone Rd
Hayden Way, Rom. 51 FC54
Haydens Cl, Orp. 146 EV100
Haydens Pl W11 81 CZ72
Portobello Rd
Haydn Av, Pur. 159 DN114
Haydns Ms W3 80 CQ72
Emanuel Av
Haydock Av, Nthlt. 78 CA65
Haydock Cl, Horn. 72 FM63
Haydock Grn, Nthlt. 78 CA65
Haydock Av
Haydon Cl NW9 62 CQ56
Haydon Cl, Enf. 30 DS44
Mortimer Dr
Haydon Dr, Pnr. 59 BU56
Haydon Pk Rd SW19 120 DB92
Haydon Rd, Dag. 70 EW61
Haydon Rd, Wat. 24 BY44
Haydon St EC3 197 P10
Haydon Wk E1 84 DT73
Mansell St
Haydon Way SW11 100 DD84
St. John's Hill
Haydons Rd SW19 120 DB92
Hayes, The, Epsom 172 CR119
Hayes Barton, Wok. 167 BD116
Hayes Bypass, Hayes 78 BX70
Hayes Chase, W.Wick. 144 EE99
Hayes Cl, Brom. 144 EG103
Hayes Cl, Grays 109 FW79
Hayes Ct SW2 121 DL88
Hayes Cres NW11 63 CZ57
Hayes Cres, Sutt. 157 CX105
Hayes Dr, Rain. 89 FH66
Hayes End Cl, Hayes 77 BR70
Hayes End Dr, Hayes 77 BR70
Hayes End Rd, Hayes 77 BR70
Hayes Gdn, Brom. 144 EG103
Hayes Hill, Brom. 144 EE102
Hayes Hill Rd, Brom. 144 EF102
Hayes La, Beck. 143 EC97
Hayes La, Brom. 144 EG99
Hayes La, Ken. 160 DQ114
Hayes Mead Rd, Brom. 144 EE102
Hayes Metro Cen, Hayes 78 BW73
Hayes Pk, Hayes 77 BS70
Hayes Pl NW1 194 C5
Hayes Rd, Brom. 144 EG98
Hayes Rd, Green. 129 FS87
Hayes Rd, Sthl. 95 BV77
Hayes St, Brom. 144 EH102
Hayes Wk, Brox. 15 DZ25
Landau Way
Hayes Wk, Pot.B. 12 DB33
Hyde Av
Hayes Way, Beck. 143 EC98
Hayes Wd Av, Brom. 144 EH102
Hayesford Pk Dr, Brom. 144 EF99
Hayfield Cl, Bushey 24 CB42
Hayfield Pas E1 84 DW70
Stepney Grn
Hayfield Rd, Orp. 146 EU99
Hayfield Yd E1 84 DW70
Mile End Rd
Haygarth Pl SW19 119 CX92
Haygreen Cl, Kings.T. 118 CP93
Hayland Cl NW9 62 CR56
Hayles St SE11 200 F8
Hayles St SE11 101 DP77
Haylett Gdns, Kings.T. 137 CK98
Anglesea Rd
Hayling Av, Felt. 115 BU90
Hayling Cl N16 66 DS64
Pellerin Rd
Hayling Rd, Wat. 39 BV47
Haymaker Cl, Uxb. 76 BM66
Honey Hill
Hayman Cres, Hayes 77 BR68
Hayman St N1 83 DP66
Cross St
Haymarket SW1 199 M1
Haymarket SW1 83 DK73
Haymarket Arc SW1 199 M1
Haymeads Dr, Esher 154 CC107
Haymer Gdns, Wor.Pk. 139 CU104
Haymerle Rd SE15 102 DU79
Haymill Cl, Grnf. 79 CF69
Hayne Rd, Beck. 143 DZ96
Hayne St EC1 196 G6
Haynes Cl N11 44 DG48
Haynes Cl N17 46 DV52
Haynes Cl SE3 104 EE83
Haynes Cl, Slou. 93 AZ78
Haynes Cl, Wok. 168 BH122
Haynes La SE19 122 DS93
Haynes Rd, Grav. 131 GF90
Haynes Rd, Horn. 72 FK57
Haynes Rd, Wem. 80 CL66
Haynt Wk SW20 139 CY97
Hay's La SE1 201 M3
Hay's Ms W1 199 H1
Hay's Ms W1 83 DH73
Hays Wk, Sutt. 157 CX110
Haysleigh Gdns SE20 142 DU96
Haysoms Cl, Rom. 71 FE56
Haystall Cl, Hayes 77 BS68
Hayter Rd SW2 121 DL85
Hayton Cl E8 84 DT65
Buttermere Wk
Haywain, Oxt. 187 ED130
Hayward Cl SW19 140 DB95
Hayward Cl, Dart. 127 FD85
Hayward Dr, Dart. 128 FM89
Hayward Gdns SW15 119 CW86
Hayward Rd N20 44 DC47
Hayward Rd, T.Ditt. 137 CG102
Haywards Cl, Brwd. 55 GE44
Haywards Cl, Rom. 70 EV57
Hayward's Pl EC1 196 F4
Haywood Cl, Pnr. 40 BX54
Haywood Ct, Wal.Abb. 16 EF34
Haywood Pk, Rick. 21 BF43
Haywood Ri, Orp. 163 ES105
Haywood Rd, Brom. 144 EK98
Hayworth Cl, Enf. 31 DY40
Green St
Hazel Av, West Dr. 94 BN76
Hazel Cl N13 46 DR48
Hazel Cl N19 65 DJ61
Hargrave Pk
Hazel Cl SE15 102 DU82
Hazel Cl, Brent. 97 CH80
Hazel Cl, Croy. 143 DX101
Hazel Cl, Egh. 112 AV93
Hazel Cl, Horn. 71 FH62
Hazel Cl, Mitch. 141 DK98
Hazel Cl, Twick. 116 CC87
Hazel Cl, Wal.Cr. 14 DS26
The Laurels
Hazel Dr, Erith 107 FH81
Hazel Dr, S.Ock. 91 FX69
Hazel End, Swan. 147 FE99
Hazel Gdns, Edg. 42 CP49
Hazel Gdns, Grays 110 GE76
Hazel Gro SE26 123 DX91
Hazel Gro, Enf. 30 DU44
Dimsdale Dr
Hazel Gro, Orp. 145 EP103
Hazel Gro, Rom. 70 EY55
Hazel Gro, Stai. 114 BH93
Hazel Gro, Wat. 23 BV35
Cedar Wd Dr
Hazel Gro, Wem. 80 CL67
Carlyon Rd
Hazel Gro Est SE26 123 DX91
Hazel La, Rich. 118 CL89
Hazel Mead, Barn. 27 CV43
Hazel Mead, Epsom 157 CU110
Hazel Ri, Horn. 72 FJ58
Hazel Rd E15 68 EE64
Wingfield Rd
Hazel Rd NW10 81 CW69
Hazel Rd, Dart. 128 FK89
Hazel Rd, Erith 107 FG81
Hazel Rd, St.Alb. 8 CB28
Hazel Rd, W.Byf. 152 BG114
Hazel Tree Rd, Wat. 23 BV37
Hazel Wk, Brom. 145 EN100
Hazel Way E4 47 DZ51
Hazel Way SE1 201 P8
Hazel Way, Couls. 174 DF119
Hazel Way, Lthd. 170 CC122
Hazelbank, Surb. 138 CQ102
Hazelbank Ct, Cher. 134 BJ102
Hazelbank Rd SE6 123 ED89
Hazelbank Rd, Cher. 134 BJ102
Hazelbourne Rd SW12 121 DH86
Hazelbrouck Gdns, Ilf. 49 ER52
Hazelbury Av, Abb.L. 7 BQ32
Hazelbury Cl SW19 140 DA96
Hazelbury Grn N9 46 DS48
Hazelbury La N9 46 DS48
Hazelcroft, Pnr. 40 CA51
Hazelcroft Cl, Uxb. 76 BM66
Hazeldean Rd NW10 80 CR66
Hazeldene, Add. 152 BJ106
Hazeldene, Wal.Cr. 15 DY32
Hazeldene Ct, Ken. 176 DR115
Hazeldene Dr, Pnr. 60 BW55
Hazeldene Gdns, Uxb. 77 BQ67
Hazeldene Rd, Ilf. 70 EV61
Hazeldene Rd, Well. 106 EW82
Hazeldon Rd SE4 123 DY85
Hazeleigh, Brwd. 55 GB48
Hazeleigh Gdns, Wdf.Grn. 48 EL50
Hazelgreen Cl N21 45 DP46
Hazelhurst, Beck. 143 ED95
Hazelhurst Rd SW17 120 DC91
Hazell Cres, Rom. 51 FB53
Hazell Way, Slou. 74 AT65
Hazells Rd, Grav. 130 GD92
Hazellville Rd N19 65 DK59
Hazelmere Cl, Felt. 115 BR86
Hazelmere Cl, Lthd. 171 CH119
Hazelmere Cl, Nthlt. 78 BZ68
Hazelmere Dr, Nthlt. 78 BZ68
Hazelmere Gdns, Horn. 71 FH57
Hazelmere Rd NW6 82 DA67
Hazelmere Rd, Nthlt. 78 BZ68
Hazelmere Rd, Orp. 145 EQ98
Hazelmere Wk, Nthlt. 78 BZ68
Hazelmere Way, Brom. 144 EG100
Hazeltree La, Nthlt. 78 BY69
Hazelwood, Loug. 32 EK43
Hazelwood Av, Mord. 140 DB98
Hazelwood Cl W5 98 CL75
Hazelwood Cl, Har. 60 CB56
Hazelwood Ct NW10 62 CS62
Neasden La N
Hazelwood Cres N13 45 DN49
Hazelwood Cft, Surb. 138 CL100
Hazelwood Dr, Pnr. 39 BV54
Hazelwood Gdns, Brwd. 54 FU44
Hazelwood Gro, S.Croy. 160 DV113
Hazelwood Hts, Oxt. 188 EG131
Hazelwood La N13 45 DN49
Hazelwood La, Abb.L. 7 BQ32
Hazelwood La, Couls. 174 DF119
Hazelwood Pk Cl, Chig. 49 ES50
Hazelwood Rd E17 67 DY57
Hazelwood Rd, Enf. 30 DT44
Hazelwood Rd, Oxt. 188 EH132
Hazelwood Rd, Rick. 23 BQ44
Hazelwood Rd, Sev. 163 ER112
Hazelwood Rd, Wok. 166 AS118
Hazlebury Rd SW6 100 DB82
Hazledean Rd, Croy. 142 DR103
Hazledene Rd W4 98 CQ79
Hazlemere Gdns, Wor.Pk. 139 CV102
Hazlemere Rd, Slou. 74 AW74
Hazlewell Rd SW15 119 CW85
Hazlewood Cl E5 67 DY62
Mandeville St
Hazlewood Cres W10 81 CY70
Hazlitt Ms W14 99 CY76
Hazlitt Rd
Hazlitt Rd W14 99 CY76
Hazon Way, Epsom 156 CR112
Heacham Av, Uxb. 59 BQ62
Head St E1 85 DX72
Headcorn Pl, Th.Hth. 141 DM98
Headcorn Rd
Headcorn Rd N17 46 DT52
Headcorn Rd, Brom. 124 EF92
Headcorn Rd, Th.Hth. 141 DM98
Headfort Pl SW1 198 G5
Headfort Pl SW1 100 DG75
Headingley Cl, Ilf. 49 ET51
Headingley Cl, Rad. 10 CL32
Headingley Cl (Cheshunt), Wal.Cr. 14 DT26
Holbeck La
Headington Rd SW18 120 DC89
Headlam Rd SW4 121 DK86
Headlam St E1 84 DV70
Headley App, Ilf. 69 EN57
Headley Av, Wall. 159 DM106
Headley Chase, Brwd. 54 FW49
Headley Cl, Epsom 156 CN107
Headley Common, Brwd. 53 FV52
Warley Gap
Headley Common Rd, Epsom 182 CR127
Headley Common Rd, Tad. 182 CR127
Headley Ct SE26 122 DV92
Headley Dr, Croy. 161 EB108
Headley Dr, Epsom 173 CV119
Headley Dr, Ilf. 69 EP58
Headley Gro, Tad. 173 CV120
Headley Heath App, Dor. 182 CP130
Ashurst Dr
Headley Heath App, Tad. 182 CP130
Headley Rd (Tyrrell's Wd), Epsom 172 CN123
Headley Rd (Woodcote), Epsom 172 CP118
Headley Rd, Lthd. 171 CK123
Head's Ms W11 82 DA72
Artesian Rd
Headstone Dr, Har. 61 CE55
Headstone Gdns, Har. 60 CC56
Headstone La, Har. 60 CB56
Headstone Rd, Har. 61 CE57
Headway, The, Epsom 157 CT109
Headway Cl, Rich. 117 CJ91
Locksmeade Rd
Heald St SE14 103 DZ81
Healey Dr, Orp. 163 ET105
Healey Rd, Wat. 23 BT44
Healey St NW1 83 DH65
Heanor Ct E5 67 DX62
Pedro St
Heards La, Brwd. 55 FZ41
Hearn Ri, Nthlt. 78 BX67
Hearn Rd, Rom. 71 FF58
Hearn St EC2 197 N5
Hearn St EC2 84 DS70
Hearne Ct, Ch.St.G. 36 AV48
Gordon Way
Hearne Rd W4 98 CN79
Hearn's Bldgs SE17 201 L9
Hearn's Rd, Orp. 146 EW98
Hearnville Rd SW12 120 DG88
Heath, The W7 79 CE74
Lower Boston Rd
Heath, The, Cat. 176 DQ124
Heath, The, Rad. 9 CG33
Heath Av, Bexh. 106 EX79
Heath Brow NW3 64 DC62
North End Way
Heath Cl NW11 64 DB59
Heath Cl W5 80 CM70
Heath Cl, Bans. 158 DB114
Heath Cl, Hayes 95 BR80
Heath Cl, Orp. 146 EW100
Sussex Rd
Heath Cl, Pot.B. 12 DB30
Heath Cl, Rom. 71 FG55
Heath Cl, Stai. 114 BJ86
Heath Cl, Vir.W. 132 AX98
Heath Cotts, Pot.B. 12 DB30
Heath Rd
Heath Ct, Houns. 96 BZ84
Heath Ct, Uxb. 76 BL66
Heath Dr NW3 64 DB63
Heath Dr SW20 139 CW98
Heath Dr, Epp. 33 ES35
Heath Dr, Pot.B. 12 DA30
Heath Dr, Rom. 51 FG53
Heath Dr, Sutt. 158 DC109
Heath Dr, Tad. 183 CU125
Heath Dr, Wok. 167 BB122
Heath Fm Ct, Wat. 23 BR37
Grove Mill La
Heath Gdns, Twick. 117 CF88
Heath Gro SE20 122 DW94
Maple Rd
Heath Gro, Sun. 115 BT94
Heath Hurst Rd NW3 64 DE63
Heath La SE3 103 ED82
Heath La (Lower), Dart. 128 FJ88
Heath La (Upper), Dart. 127 FG89
Heath Mead SW19 119 CX90
Heath Pk Ct, Rom. 71 FG57
Heath Pk Rd
Heath Pk Dr, Brom. 144 EL97
Heath Pk Rd, Rom. 71 FG57
Heath Pas NW3 64 DB61
Heath Ridge Grn, Cob. 154 CA113
Heath Ri SW15 119 CX86
Heath Ri, Brom. 144 EF100
Heath Ri, Vir.W. 132 AX98
Heath Ri, Wok. 168 BH123
Heath Rd SW8 101 DH82
Heath Rd, Bex. 127 FC88
Heath Rd, Cat. 176 DR123
Heath Rd, Dart. 127 FF86
Heath Rd, Har. 60 CC59
Heath Rd, Houns. 96 CB84
Heath Rd, Lthd. 154 CC112
Heath Rd, Pot.B. 12 DA30
Heath Rd, Rom. 70 EX59
Heath Rd, Th.Hth. 142 DQ97
Heath Rd, Twick. 117 CF88
Heath Rd, Uxb. 77 BQ70
Heath Rd, Wat. 40 BX45
Heath Rd, Wey. 152 BN106
Heath Rd, Wok. 167 AZ115
Heath Side NW3 64 DD63
Heath Side, Orp. 145 EQ102
Heath St NW3 64 DC63
Heath St, Dart. 128 FK87
Heath Vw N2 64 DC56
Heath Vw Cl N2 64 DC56
Heath Vw Gdns, Grays 110 GC75
Heath Vw Rd, Grays 110 GC75
Heath Vil SE18 105 ET78
Heath Vil SW18 120 DC88
Cargill Rd
Heath Way, Erith 107 FC81
Heathacre, Slou. 93 BE81
Park St
Heatham Pk, Twick. 117 CF87
Heathbourne Rd, Bushey 41 CE47
Heathbourne Rd, Stan. 41 CE47
Heathbridge, Wey. 152 BN108
Heathclose Av, Dart. 127 FH87
Heathclose Rd, Dart. 127 FG88
Heathcock Ct WC2 83 DL73
Strand
Heathcote, Tad. 173 CX121
Heathcote Av, Ilf. 49 EM54
Heathcote Gro E4 47 EC48
Heathcote Rd, Epsom 156 CR114
Heathcote Rd, Twick. 117 CH86
Heathcote St WC1 196 B4
Heathcote St WC1 83 DM70
Heathcote Way, West Dr. 76 BK74
Tavistock Rd
Heathcroft NW11 64 DB60
Heathcroft W5 80 CM70
Heathcroft Av, Sun. 115 BT94
Heathcroft Gdns E17 47 ED53
Hale End Rd
Heathdale Av, Houns. 96 BY83
Heathdene, Tad. 173 CY119
Canons La
Heathdene Dr, Belv. 107 FB77
Heathdene Rd SW16 121 DM94
Heathdene Rd, Wall. 159 DH108
Heathdown Rd, Wok. 167 BD115
Heathedge SE26 122 DV89
Heathend Rd, Bex. 127 FE88
Heather Av, Rom. 51 FD54
Heather Cl E6 87 EP72
Heather Cl SE13 123 ED87
Heather Cl SW8 101 DH83
Heather Cl, Abb.L. 7 BU32
Magnolia Av
Heather Cl, Add. 152 BH110
Heather Cl, Brwd. 54 FV43
Heather Cl, Hmptn. 136 BZ95
Heather Cl, Islw. 117 CD85
Harvesters Cl
Heather Cl, Red. 185 DH130
Heather Cl, Rom. 51 FD53
Heather Cl, Tad. 173 CY122
Heather Cl, Uxb. 76 BM71
Violet Av
Heather Cl, Wok. 166 AW115
Heather Dr, Dart. 127 FG87
Heather Dr, Enf. 29 DP40
Chasewood Av
Heather Dr, Rom. 51 FD54
Heather End, Swan. 147 FD98
Heather Gdns NW11 63 CY58
Heather Gdns, Rom. 51 FD54
Heather Gdns, Sutt. 158 DA107
Heather Glen, Rom. 51 FD54
Heather La, Wat. 23 BT35
Heather La, West Dr. 76 BL72
Heather Pk Dr, Wem. 80 CN66
Heather Pl, Esher 154 CB105
Park Rd
Heather Ri, Bushey 24 BZ40
Heather Rd E4 47 DZ51
Heather Rd NW2 63 CT61
Heather Rd SE12 124 EG89
Heather Wk W10 81 CY70
Droop St
Heather Wk, Edg. 42 CP50
Heather Wk, Twick. 116 CA87
Stephenson Rd
Heather Wk, Walt. 153 BT110
Octagon Rd
Heather Way, Pot.B. 11 CZ32
Heather Way, Rom. 51 FD54
Heather Way, S.Croy. 161 DX109
Heather Way, Stan. 41 CF51
Heather Way, Wok. 150 AS108
Heatherbank SE9 105 EM82
Heatherbank, Chis. 145 EN96
Heatherbank Cl, Dart. 127 FE86
Heatherdale Cl, Kings.T. 118 CN93
Heatherden Grn, Iver 75 BC67
Heatherdene Cl N12 44 DC53
Bow La
Heatherdene Cl, Mitch. 140 DE98
Heatherfields, Add. 152 BH110
Heatherfold Way, Pnr. 59 BT55
Heatherlands, Sun. 115 BU93
Heatherley Dr, Ilf. 68 EL55
Heathers, The, Stai. 114 BM87
Heatherset Cl, Esher 154 CC106
Heatherset Gdns SW16 121 DM94
Heatherside Dr, Vir.W. 132 AU100
Heatherside Rd, Epsom 156 CR108
Heatherside Rd, Sid. 126 EX90
Wren Rd
Heathervale Caravan Pk, Add. 152 BJ110
Heathervale Rd, Add. 152 BH110

Heatherwood Cl E12 68 EJ61
Heatherwood Dr, Hayes 77 BR68
Charville La
Heathfield E4 47 EC48
Heathfield, Chis. 125 EQ93
Heathfield, Cob. 154 CA114
Heathfield Av SW18 120 DD87
Heathfield Rd
Heathfield Av, S.Croy. 161 DY109
Heathfield Cl E16 86 EK71
Heathfield Cl, Kes. 162 EJ106
Heathfield Cl, Pot.B. 12 DB30
Heathfield Cl, Wok. 167 BA118
Heathfield Dr, Mitch. 140 DE95
Heathfield Gdns NW11 63 CX58
Heathfield Gdns SW18 120 DD86
Heathfield Rd
Heathfield Gdns W4 98 CQ78
Heathfield Gdns, Croy. 160 DR105
Coombe Rd
Heathfield La, Chis. 125 EP93
Heathfield N, Twick. 117 CF87
Heathfield Pk NW2 81 CW65
Heathfield Pk Dr, Rom. 70 EV57
Heathfield Ri, Ruis. 59 BQ59
Heathfield Rd SW18 120 DC86
Heathfield Rd W3 98 CP75
Heathfield Rd, Bexh. 106 EZ84
Heathfield Rd, Brom. 124 EF94
Heathfield Rd, Bushey 24 BY42
Heathfield Rd, Croy. 160 DR105
Heathfield Rd, Kes. 162 EJ106
Heathfield Rd, Sev. 190 FF122
Heathfield Rd, Walt. 154 BY105
Heathfield Rd, Wok. 167 BA118
Heathfield S, Twick. 117 CF87
Heathfield Sq SW18 120 DD87
Heathfield St W11 81 CY73
Portland Rd
Heathfield Ter SE18 105 ET79
Heathfield Ter W4 98 CQ78
Heathfield Vale, S.Croy. 161 DX109
Heathfields Ct, Houns. 116 BY85
Frampton Rd
Heathgate NW11 64 DB58
Heathgate Pl NW3 64 DF64
Agincourt Rd
Heathhurst Rd, S.Croy. 160 DS109
Heathland Rd N16 66 DS60
Heathlands, Tad. 173 CX122
Heathlands Cl, Sun. 135 BU96
Heathlands Cl, Twick. 117 CF89
Heathlands Cl, Wok. 150 AY114
Heathlands Ri, Dart. 127 FH86
Heathlands Way, Houns. 116 BY85
Frampton Rd
Heathlee Rd SE3 104 EF84
Heathlee Rd, Dart. 127 FE86
Heathley End, Chis. 125 EQ93
Heathmans Rd SW6 99 CZ81
Heathrow Cl, West Dr. 94 BH81
Heathrow Interchange, Hayes 78 BW74
Heathrow Int Trd Est, Houns. 95 BV83
Heathrow Tunnel App, Houns. 95 BP83
Heathrow Vehicle Tunnel, Houns. 95 BP81
Heaths Cl, Enf. 30 DS40
Heathside, Esher 137 CE104
Heathside, Houns. 116 BZ87
Heathside, Wey. 153 BP106
Heathside Av, Bexh. 106 EY81
Heathside Cl, Esher 137 CE104
Heathside Cl, Nthwd. 39 BR50
Heathside Ct, Tad. 173 CV123
Heathside Cres, Wok. 167 AZ117
Heathside Gdns, Wok. 167 BA117
Heathside Pk Rd, Wok. 167 AZ118
Heathside Pl, Epsom 173 CX118
Heathside Rd, Nthwd. 39 BR49
Heathside Rd, Wok. 167 AZ118
Heathstan Rd W12 81 CU72
Heathview Av, Dart. 127 FE86
Heathview Ct SW19 119 CX89
Heathview Cres, Dart. 127 FG88
Heathview Dr SE2 106 EX79
Heathview Gdns SW15 119 CW87
Heathview Rd, Th.Hth. 141 DN98
Heathville Rd N19 65 DL59
Heathwall St SW11 100 DF83
Heathway SE3 104 EF80
Heathway, Cat. 186 DQ125
Heathway, Croy. 143 DZ104
Heathway, Dag. 88 FA66
Heathway, Iver 75 BD68
Heathway, Lthd. 169 BT124
Heathway, Wdf.Grn. 48 EJ49
Heathway Ind Est, Dag. 71 FB63
Manchester Way
Heathwood Gdns SE7 104 EL77
Heathwood Gdns, Swan. 147 FC96
Heathwood Wk, Bex. 127 FE88
Heaton Av, Rom. 51 FH52
Heaton Cl E4 47 EC48
Friars Cl
Heaton Cl, Rom. 52 FJ52
Heaton Ct, Wal.Cr. 15 DX29
Heaton Gra Rd, Rom. 51 FF54
Heaton Rd SE15 102 DU83
Heaton Rd, Mitch. 120 DG94
Heaton Way, Rom. 52 FJ52
Heaver Rd SW11 100 DD83
Wye St
Heavitree Cl SE18 105 ER78
Heavitree Rd SE18 105 ER78
Hebden Ct E2 84 DT67
Laburnum St
Hebden Ter N17 46 DS51
Commercial Rd
Hebdon Rd SW17 120 DE90
Heber Rd NW2 63 CX64
Heber Rd SE22 122 DT86
Hebron Rd W6 99 CV76
Hecham Cl E17 47 DY54
Heckfield Pl SW6 100 DA80
Fulham Rd
Heckford Cl, Wat. 23 BQ44
Heckford St E1 85 DX73
The Highway
Hector St SE18 105 ES77
Heddington Gro N7 65 DM64
Heddon Cl, Islw. 97 CG84
Heddon Ct Av, Barn. 28 DF43
Heddon Rd, Barn. 28 DF43
Heddon St W1 195 K10
Heddon St W1 83 DJ73
Hedge Hill, Enf. 29 DP39
Hedge La N13 45 DP48
Hedge Pl Rd, Green. 129 FT86
Hedge Wk SE6 123 EB91
Hedgeley, Ilf. 69 EM56
Hedgemans Rd, Dag. 88 EX66
Hedgemans Way, Dag. 88 EY65
Hedger St SE11 200 F8
Hedgerley Ct, Wok. 166 AW117
Hedgerley Gdns, Grnf. 78 CC68
Hedgerley Grn, Slou. 56 AT58
Hedgerley La, Ger.Cr. 56 AV59
Hedgerley La, Slou. 56 AS58
Hedgerow (Chalfont St. Peter), Ger.Cr. 36 AY51
Hedgerow Wk, Wal.Cr. 15 DX30
Hedgerows, The, Grav. 130 GE89
Hedgers Cl, Loug. 33 EN42
Newmans La
Hedgers Gro E9 85 DY65
Hedgeside Rd, Nthwd. 39 BQ50
Hedgewood Gdns, Ilf. 69 EN57
Hedgley St SE12 124 EF85
Hedingham Cl N1 84 DQ66
Popham Rd
Hedingham Rd, Dag. 70 EV64
Hedingham Rd, Grays 109 FW78
Hedingham Rd, Horn. 72 FN60
Hedley Av, Grays 109 FW80
Hedley Cl, Rom. 71 FE57
High St
Hedley Rd, Twick. 116 CA87
Hedley Row N5 66 DR64
Poets Rd
Hedworth Av, Wal.Cr. 15 DX33
Heenan Cl, Bark. 87 EQ65
Glenny Rd
Heene Rd, Enf. 30 DR39
Heideck Gdns, Brwd. 55 GB47
Victors Cres
Heidegger Cres SW13 99 CV79
Trinity Ch Rd
Heigham Rd E6 86 EK66
Heighton Gdns, Croy. 159 DP106
Heights, The SE7 104 EJ78
Heights, The, Beck. 123 EC94
Heights, The, Loug. 33 EM40
Heights, The, Nthlt. 60 BZ64
Heights, The, Wal.Abb. 16 EH25
Heights, The, Wey. 152 BN110
Heights Cl SW20 119 CV94
Heights Cl, Bans. 173 CY116
Heiron St SE17 101 DP79
Helby Rd SW4 121 DK86
Helder Gro SE12 124 EF87
Helder St, S.Croy. 160 DR107
Heldmann Cl, Houns. 97 CD84
Helen Av, Felt. 115 BV87
Helen Cl N2 64 DC55
Thomas More Way
Helen Cl, Dart. 127 FH87
Helen Cl, W.Mol. 136 CB98
Helen Rd, Horn. 72 FK55
Helen St SE18 105 EP77
Wilmount St
Helena Cl, Barn. 28 DD38
Helena Cl, Wall. 159 DL108
Helena Pl E9 84 DW67
Fremont St
Helena Rd E13 86 EF68
Helena Rd E17 67 EA57
Helena Rd NW10 63 CV64
Helena Rd W5 79 CK71
Helena Sq SE16 203 K1
Helens Gate, Wal.Cr. 15 DZ26
Helen's Pl E2 84 DW69
Roman Rd
Helenslea Av NW11 63 CZ60
Helford Cl, Ruis. 59 BS61
Chichester Av
Helford Wk, Wok. 166 AU118
Helford Way, Upmin. 73 FR58
Helgiford Gdns, Sun. 115 BS94
Helix Gdns SW2 121 DM86
Helix Rd
Helix Rd SW2 121 DM86
Helleborine, Grays 110 FZ78
Hellings St E1 202 C3
Helm Cl, Epsom 156 CN112
Helme Cl SW19 119 CZ92
Helmet Row EC1 197 J4
Helmet Row EC1 84 DQ70
Helmsdale, Wok. 166 AV118
Winnington Way
Helmsdale Cl, Hayes 78 BY70
Berrydale Rd
Helmsdale Cl, Rom. 51 FE52
Helmsdale Rd SW16 141 DJ95
Helmsdale Rd, Rom. 51 FE52
Helmsley Pl E8 84 DV66
Helsinki Sq SE16 203 L6
Helston Cl, Pnr. 40 BZ52
Helston Pl, Abb.L. 7 BT32
Shirley Rd
Helvellyn Cl, Egh. 113 BB94
Helvetia St SE6 123 DZ89
Hemans St SW8 101 DK80
Hemberton Rd SW9 101 DL83
Hemery Rd, Grnf. 61 CD64
Heming Rd, Edg. 42 CP52
Hemingford Cl N12 44 DD50
Hemingford Rd N1 83 DM67
Hemingford Rd, Sutt. 157 CW105
Hemingford Rd, Wat. 23 BS36
Hemington Av N11 44 DF50
Hemlock Cl, Tad. 173 CY123
Hemlock Cl, Tad. 173 CY124
Warren Lo Dr
Hemlock Rd W12 81 CT73
Hemmen La, Hayes 77 BT72
Hemming Cl, Hmptn. 136 CA95
Chandler Cl
Hemming St E1 84 DU70
Hemming Way, Wat. 23 BU35
Hemmings Cl, Sid. 126 EV89
Hemnall St, Epp. 17 ET31
Hemp Wk SE17 201 L8
Hemp Wk SE17 102 DR77
Hempshaw Av, Bans. 174 DF116
Hempson Av, Slou. 92 AW76
Hempstead Cl, Buck.H. 48 EG47
Hempstead Rd E17 47 ED54
Hempstead Rd, Hem.H. 5 BA27
Hempstead Rd, Kings L. 6 BM26
Hempstead Rd, Wat. 23 BT39
Hemsby Rd, Chess. 156 CM107
Hemstal Rd NW6 82 DA66
Hemsted Rd, Erith 107 FE80
Hemswell Dr NW9 42 CS53
Hemsworth Ct N1 84 DS68
Hemsworth St
Hemsworth St N1 84 DS68
Hemus Pl SW3 100 DE78
Chelsea Manor St
Hen & Chicken Ct EC4 83 DN72
Fleet St
Henbane Path, Rom. 52 FK52
Clematis Cl
Henbit Cl, Tad. 173 CV119
Henbury Way, Wat. 40 BX48
Henchman St W12 81 CT72
Hencroft St N, Slou. 92 AT75
Hencroft St S, Slou. 92 AT76
Hencroft St S, Slou. 92 AT76
Osborne St
Hendale Av NW4 63 CU55
Henderson Cl NW10 80 CQ65
Henderson Cl, Horn. 71 FH61
St. Leonards Way
Henderson Dr NW8 82 DD70
Cunningham Pl
Henderson Dr, Dart. 108 FM84
Henderson Pl, Abb.L. 7 BT27
Henderson Rd E7 86 EJ65
Henderson Rd N9 46 DV46
Henderson Rd SW18 120 DE87
Henderson Rd, Croy. 142 DR100
Henderson Rd, Hayes 77 BU69
Henderson Rd, West. 162 EJ112
Hendham Rd SW17 120 DE89
Hendon Av N3 43 CY53
Hendon Gdns, Rom. 51 FC51
Hendon Hall Ct NW4 63 CX55
Hendon La N3 63 CY55
Hendon Pk Row NW11 63 CZ58
Hendon Rd N9 46 DU47
Hendon Way NW2 63 CZ62
Hendon Way NW4 63 CV58
Hendon Way, Stai. 114 BK86
Hendon Wd La NW7 27 CT44
Hendre Rd SE1 201 N9
Hendren Cl, Grnf. 61 CD64
Dimmock Dr
Hendrick Av SW12 120 DF87
Heneage Cres, Croy. 161 EC110
Heneage La EC3 197 N9
Heneage St E1 84 DT71
Henfield Cl N19 65 DJ60
Henfield Cl, Bex. 126 FA86
Henfield Rd SW19 139 CZ95
Hengelo Gdns, Mitch. 140 DD98
Hengist Rd SE12 124 EH87
Hengist Rd, Erith 107 FB80
Hengist Way, Brom. 144 EE98
Hengrave Rd SE23 123 DX87
Hengrove Ct, Bex. 126 EY88
Hurst Rd
Hengrove Cres, Ashf. 114 BK90
Henhurst Rd, Grav. 131 GK94
Henley Av, Sutt. 139 CY104
Henley Cl, Grnf. 78 CC68
Henley Cl, Islw. 97 CF81
Henley Ct N14 45 DJ45
Henley Ct, Wok. 167 BB120
Henley Cross SE3 104 EH83
Henley Deane, Grav. 130 GE91
Henley Dr SE1 202 A8
Henley Dr SE1 102 DT77
Henley Dr, Kings.T. 119 CT94
Henley Gdns, Pnr. 59 BV55
Henley Gdns, Rom. 70 EY57
Henley Rd E16 105 EM75
Henley Rd N18 46 DS49
Henley Rd NW10 81 CW67
Henley Rd, Ilf. 69 EQ63
Henley St SW11 100 DG82
Henley Way, Felt. 116 BX92
Henlow Pl, Rich. 117 CK89
Sandpits Rd
Hennel Cl SE23 122 DW90
Hennessy Ct, Wok. 151 BC113
Henniker Gdns E6 86 EK69
Henniker Ms SW3 100 DD79
Callow St
Henniker Pt E15 68 EE64
Henniker Rd E15 67 ED64
Henning St SW11 100 DE81
Henningham Rd N17 46 DR53
Henrietta Cl SE8 103 EA79
Henrietta Ms WC1 196 A4
Henrietta Pl W1 195 H9
Henrietta Pl W1 83 DH72
Henrietta St E15 67 EC64
Henrietta St WC2 196 A10
Henrietta St WC2 83 DL73
Henriques St E1 84 DU72
Henry Addlington Cl E6 87 EN71
Winsor Ter
Henry Cl, Enf. 30 DS38
Henry Cooper Way SE9 124 EK90
Henry Darlot Dr NW7 43 CX50
Henry Dickens Ct W11 81 CX74
Henry Doulton Dr SW17 121 DH91
Henry Jackson Rd SW15 99 CX83
Henry Macaulay Av, Kings.T. 137 CK95
Henry Rd E6 86 EL68
Henry Rd N4 66 DQ60
Henry Rd, Barn. 28 DD43
Henry St, Brom. 144 EH95
Henry St, Grays 110 GC79
East Thurrock Rd
Henry's Av, Wdf.Grn. 48 EF50
Henry's Wk, Ilf. 49 ER52
Henryson Rd SE4 123 EA85
Hensford Gdns SE26 122 DV91
Wells Pk Rd
Henshall St N1 84 DR65
Henshaw St SE17 201 K8
Henshaw St SE17 102 DR77
Henshawe Rd, Dag. 70 EX62
Henshill Pt E3 85 EB69
Bromley High St
Henslow Way, Wok. 151 BD114
Henslowe Rd SE22 122 DU85
Henson Av NW2 63 CW64
Henson Cl, Orp. 145 EP103
Henson Path, Har. 61 CK55
Henson Pl, Nthlt. 78 BW67
Henstridge Pl NW8 82 DE68
Hensworth Rd, Ashf. 114 BK93
Henty Cl SW11 100 DE80
Henty Wk SW15 119 CV85
Henville Rd, Brom. 144 EH95
Henwick Rd SE9 104 EK83
Henwood Side, Wdf.Grn. 49 EM51
Love La
Hepburn Cl (Chafford Hundred), Grays 109 FW77
Hepburn Gdns, Brom. 144 EE102
Hepburn Ms SW11 120 DF85
Webbs Rd
Hepple Cl, Islw. 97 CH82
Hepplestone Cl SW15 119 CV86
Dover Pk Dr
Hepscott Rd E9 85 EA66
Hepworth Ct, Bark. 70 EU64
Hepworth Gdns, Bark. 70 EU64
Hepworth Rd SW16 121 DL94
Hepworth Wk NW3 64 DE64
Haverstock Hill
Hepworth Way, Walt. 135 BT102
Heracles Cl, Wall. 159 DL108
Herald Gdns, Wall. 141 DH104
Herald St E2 84 DV70
Three Colts La
Herald Wk, Dart. 128 FM85
Temple Hill Sq
Herald's Ct SE11 200 F9
Herald's Pl SE11 200 E8
Herbal Hill EC1 196 E5
Herbal Hill EC1 83 DN70
Herbert Cres SW1 198 E6
Herbert Cres, Wok. 166 AS117
Herbert Gdns NW10 81 CV68
Herbert Gdns W4 98 CP79
Magnolia Rd
Herbert Gdns, Rom. 70 EX59
Herbert Pl SE18 105 EP79
Plumstead Common Rd
Herbert Rd E12 68 EL63
Herbert Rd E17 67 DZ59
Herbert Rd N11 45 DL52
Herbert Rd N15 66 DT57
Herbert Rd NW9 63 CU58
Herbert Rd SE18 105 EN80
Herbert Rd SW19 119 CZ94
Herbert Rd, Bexh. 106 EY82
Herbert Rd, Brom. 144 EK99
Herbert Rd, Horn. 72 FL59
Herbert Rd, Ilf. 69 ES61
Herbert Rd, Kings.T. 138 CM97
Herbert Rd, Sthl. 78 BZ74
Herbert Rd, Swan. 127 FH93
Herbert Rd, Swans. 130 FZ86
Herbert St E13 86 EG68
Herbert St NW5 82 DG65
Herbert Ter SE18 105 EP79
Herbert Rd
Herbrand St WC1 195 P4
Herbrand St WC1 83 DL70
Hercies Rd, Uxb. 76 BM66
Hercules Pl N7 65 DL62
Hercules St
Hercules Rd SE1 200 C7
Hercules Rd SE1 101 DM76
Hercules St N7 65 DL62
Hercules Twr SE14 103 DY79
Milton Ct Rd
Hereford Av, Barn. 44 DF46
Hereford Cl, Epsom 156 CR113
Hereford Cl, Stai. 134 BH95
Hereford Copse, Wok. 166 AV119
Hereford Gdns SE13 124 EE85
Longhurst Rd
Hereford Gdns, Ilf. 68 EL59
Hereford Gdns, Pnr. 60 BY57
Hereford Gdns, Twick. 116 CC88
Hereford Ho NW6 82 DA68
Hereford Ms W2 82 DA72
Hereford Rd
Hereford Pl SE14 103 DZ80
Hereford Retreat SE15 102 DU80
Bird in Bush Rd
Hereford Rd E11 68 EH57
Hereford Rd W2 82 DA72
Hereford Rd W3 80 CP73
Hereford Rd W5 97 CJ76
Hereford Rd, Felt. 116 BW88
Hereford Sq SW7 100 DC77
Hereford St E2 84 DU70
Hereford Way, Chess. 155 CJ106
Herent Dr, Ilf. 69 EM55
Hereward Av, Pur. 159 DN111
Hereward Cl, Wal.Abb. 15 ED32
Hereward Gdns N13 45 DN50
Hereward Grn, Loug. 33 EQ39
Hereward Rd SW17 120 DF91
Herga Ct, Har. 61 CE62
Herga Ct, Wat. 23 BU40
Herga Rd, Har. 61 CF56
Herington Gro, Brwd. 55 GA45
Heriot Av E4 47 EA47
Heriot Rd NW4 63 CW57
Heriot Rd, Cher. 134 BG101
Heriots Cl, Stan. 41 CG49
Heritage Cl SW9 101 DP83
Heritage Cl, Uxb. 76 BJ70
Heritage Hill, Kes. 162 EJ106
Heritage Vw, Har. 61 CF62
Heritage Wk, Rick. 21 BE41
Chenies Rd
Herkomer Cl, Bushey 24 CB44
Herkomer Rd, Bushey 24 CA43
Herlwyn Av, Ruis. 59 BS62
Herlwyn Gdns SW17 120 DF91
Hermes Pt W9 82 DA70
Hermes St N1 196 D1
Hermes Wk, Nthlt. 78 CA68
Hotspur Rd
Hermes Way, Wall. 159 DK108
Hermiston Av N8 65 DL57
Hermit Pl NW6 82 DB67
Belsize Rd
Hermit Rd E16 86 EF71
Hermit St EC1 196 F2
Hermit St EC1 83 DP69
Hermitage, The SE23 122 DW88
Hermitage, The SW13 99 CT81
Hermitage, The, Felt. 115 BT90
Hermitage, The, Rich. 117 CK85
Hermitage, The, Uxb. 76 BL65
Hermitage Cl E18 68 EF56
Hermitage Cl, Enf. 29 DP40
Hermitage Cl, Esher 155 CG107
Hermitage Cl, Shep. 134 BN98
Hermitage Cl, Slou. 92 AW76
Hermitage Ct E18 68 EG56
Hermitage Ct NW2 64 DA62
Hermitage La
Hermitage Ct, Pot.B. 12 DC33
Southgate Rd
Hermitage Gdns NW2 64 DA62
Hermitage Gdns SE19 122 DQ93
Hermitage La N18 46 DR50
Hermitage La NW2 64 DA62
Hermitage La SE25 142 DU100
Hermitage La SW16 121 DM94
Hermitage La, Croy. 142 DU100
Hermitage Path SW16 141 DL95
Hermitage Rd N4 65 DP59
Hermitage Rd N15 65 DP59
Hermitage Rd SE19 122 DQ94
Hermitage Rd, Ken. 176 DQ116
Hermitage Rd, Wok. 166 AT119
Hermitage Row E8 66 DU64
Hermitage St W2 82 DD71
Hermitage Wk E18 68 EF56
Hermitage Wall E1 202 C3
Hermitage Wall E1 84 DU74
Hermitage Way, Stan. 41 CG53
Hermitage Wds Cres, Wok. 166 AS119
Hermon Gro, Hayes 77 BU74
Hermon Hill E11 68 EG57
Hermon Hill E18 68 EG57
Herndon Cl, Egh. 113 BA91
Herndon Rd SW18 120 DC85
Herne Cl NW10 62 CR64
North Circular Rd
Herne Hill SE24 122 DQ86
Herne Hill Rd SE24 102 DQ83
Herne Ms N18 46 DU49
Lyndhurst Rd
Herne Pl SE24 121 DP85
Herne Rd, Bushey 24 CB44
Herne Rd, Surb. 137 CK103
Heron Cl E17 47 DZ54
Heron Cl NW10 80 CS65
Heron Cl, Buck.H. 48 EG46
Heron Cl, Rick. 38 BK47
Heron Cl, Sutt. 139 CY103
Gander Grn La
Heron Cl, Uxb. 76 BK65
Heron Ct, Brom. 144 EJ98
Heron Cres, Sid. 125 ES90
Heron Dale, Add. 152 BK106
Heron Dr N4 66 DQ61
Heron Dr, Slou. 93 BB77
Heron Flight Av, Horn. 89 FG66
Heron Hill, Belv. 106 EZ77
Heron Ms, Ilf. 69 EP61
Balfour Rd
Heron Pl SE16 203 L2
Heron Pl SE16 85 DY74
Heron Quay E14 203 P3
Heron Quay E14 85 EA74
Heron Rd SE24 102 DQ84
Heron Rd, Croy. 142 DS103
Tunstall Rd
Heron Rd, Twick. 97 CG84
Heron Sq, Rich. 117 CK85
Bridge St
Heron Wk, Nthwd. 39 BS49
Heron Wk, Wok. 151 BC114
Blackmore Cres
Heron Way, Grays 109 FV78
Heron Way, Upmin. 73 FS60
Herondale, S.Croy. 161 DX109
Herondale Av SW18 120 DD88
Heronfield, Egh. 112 AV93
Heronfield, Pot.B. 12 DC30
Herongate Rd E12 68 EJ61
Herongate Rd, Swan. 127 FE93
Herongate Rd (Cheshunt), Wal.Cr. 15 DY27
Heronry, The, Walt. 153 BU107
Herons, The E11 68 EF58
Herons Cft, Wey. 153 BR107
Heron's Pl, Islw. 97 CH83
Herons Ri, Barn. 28 DE42
Heronsforde W13 79 CJ72
Heronsgate, Edg. 42 CN50
Heronsgate Rd, Rick. 21 BB44
Heronslea, Wat. 24 BW36
Heronslea Dr, Stan. 42 CL50
Heronswood, Wal.Abb. 16 EE34
Roundhills
Heronway, Brwd. 55 GA46
Heronway, Wdf.Grn. 48 EJ49
Herrick Rd N5 66 DQ62
Herrick St SW1 199 N8
Herrick St SW1 101 DK77
Herries St W10 81 CY68
Herringham Rd SE7 104 EJ76
Herrings La, Cher. 134 BG100
Herrongate Cl, Enf. 30 DT40
Hersant Cl NW10 81 CU67
Herschel Pk Dr, Slou. 92 AT75
Herschel St, Slou. 92 AT75
Herschell Rd SE23 123 DY87
Hersham Bypass, Walt. 153 BV106
Hersham Cl SW15 119 CU87
Hersham Gdns, Walt. 154 BW105
Hersham Rd, Walt. 154 BW105
Hertford Av SW14 118 CS85
Hertford Cl, Barn. 28 DD41
Hertford Pl W1 195 K5

Hertford Rd N1 84 DS67
Hertford Rd N2 64 DE55
Hertford Rd N9 46 DV47
Hertford Rd, Bark. 87 EP66
Hertford Rd, Barn. 28 DC41
Hertford Rd, Enf. 30 DW41
Hertford Rd, Ilf. 69 ES58
Hertford Rd, Wal.Cr. 31 DX36
Hertford Sq, Mitch. 141 DL98
Hertford Way
Hertford St W1 199 H2
Hertford St W1 83 DH74
Hertford Wk, Belv. 106 FA78
Hoddesdon Rd
Hertford Way, Mitch. 141 DL98
Hertslet Rd N7 65 DM62
Hertsmere Rd E14 203 P1
Hertsmere Rd E14 85 EA73
Hervey Cl N3 44 DA53
Hervey Pk Rd E17 67 DY56
Hervey Rd SE3 104 EH81
Hesa Rd, Hayes 77 BU72
Hesewall Cl SW4 101 DJ82
Brayburne Av
Hesiers Hill, Warl. 178 EE117
Hesiers Rd, Warl. 178 EE117
Hesketh Av, Dart. 128 FP88
Hesketh Pl W11 81 CY73
Hesketh Rd E7 68 EG62
Heslop Rd SW12 120 DF88
Hesper Ms SW5 100 DB78
Hesperus Cres E14 204 B9
Hesperus Cres E14 103 EB77
Hessel Rd W13 97 CG75
Hessel St E1 84 DV72
Hesselyn Dr, Rain. 89 FH66
Hessle Gro, Epsom 157 CT111
Hester Rd N18 46 DU50
Hester Rd SW11 100 DE80
Hester Ter, Rich. 98 CN83
Chilton Rd
Hestercombe Av SW6 99 CY82
Hesterman Way, Croy. 141 DM102
Heston Av, Houns. 96 BY80
Heston Gra La, Houns. 96 BZ79
Heston Ind Mall, Houns. 96 BZ80
Heston Rd, Houns. 96 CA80
Heston St SE14 103 DZ81
Heswell Grn, Wat. 39 BU48
Fairhaven Cres
Hetherington Rd SW4 101 DL84
Hetherington Rd, Shep. 135 BQ96
Hetherington Way, Uxb. 58 BL63
Hethersett Cl, Reig. 184 DC131
Hetley Gdns SE19 122 DT94
Fox Hill
Hetley Rd W12 81 CV74
Heton Gdns NW4 63 CU56
Heusden Way, Ger.Cr. 57 AZ60
Hevelius Cl SE10 205 K10
Hevelius Cl SE10 104 EF78
Hever Ct Rd, Grav. 131 GK93
Hever Cft SE9 125 EN91
Hever Gdns, Brom. 145 EN97
Heverham Rd SE18 105 ES77
Heversham Rd, Bexh. 106 FA82
Hewens Rd, Hayes 77 BQ70
Hewens Rd, Uxb. 77 BQ70
Hewer St W10 81 CX71
Hewers Way, Tad. 173 CV120
Hewett Cl, Stan. 41 CH49
Hewett Pl, Swan. 147 FD98
Hewett Rd, Dag. 70 EX63
Hewett St EC2 197 N5
Hewins Cl, Wal.Abb. 16 EE33
Broomstick Hall Rd
Hewish Rd N18 46 DS49
Hewison St E3 85 DZ68
Hewitt Av N22 45 DP54
Hewitt Cl, Croy. 143 EA104
Hewitt Rd N8 65 DN57
Hewitts Rd, Orp. 164 EZ108
Hewlett Rd E3 85 DY68
Hexagon, The N6 64 DF60
Hexal Rd SE6 124 EE90
Hexham Gdns, Islw. 97 CG80
Hexham Rd SE27 122 DQ89
Hexham Rd, Barn. 28 DB42
Hexham Rd, Mord. 140 DB102
Hextalls La, Red. 186 DR128
Heybourne Rd N17 46 DV52
Heybridge Av SW16 121 DL94
Heybridge Dr, Ilf. 69 ER55
Heybridge Way E10 67 DY59
Heyford Av SW8 101 DL80
Heyford Av SW20 139 CZ97
Heyford Rd, Mitch. 140 DE96
Heyford Rd, Rad. 25 CF37
Heyford Ter SW8 101 DL80
Heyford Av
Heygate St SE17 201 H9
Heygate St SE17 102 DQ77
Heylyn Sq E3 85 DZ69
Malmesbury Rd
Heymede, Lthd. 171 CJ123
Heynes Rd, Dag. 70 EW63
Heysham Dr, Wat. 40 BW50
Heysham La NW3 64 DB62
Heysham Rd N15 66 DR58
Heythorp Cl, Wok. 166 AT117
Heythorp St SW18 119 CZ88
Heythrop Dr (Ickenham), Uxb. 58 BM63
Heywood Av NW9 42 CS53
Heyworth Rd E5 66 DV63
Heyworth Rd E15 68 EF64
Hibbert Av, Wat. 24 BX38
Hibbert Lo, Ger.Cr. 36 AX54
Gold Hill E
Hibbert Rd E17 67 DZ59
Hibbert Rd, Har. 41 CF54
Hibbert St SW11 100 DD83
Hibberts Way, Ger.Cr. 56 AY56
North Pk
Hibbs Cl, Swan. 147 FD96
Hibernia Dr, Grav. 131 GM90
Hibernia Gdns, Houns. 96 CA84
Hibernia Pt SE2 106 EX75
Wolvercote Rd
Hibernia Rd, Houns. 96 CA84
Hibiscus Cl, Edg. 42 CQ49
Campion Way
Hichisson Rd SE15 122 DW85
Hickin Cl SE7 104 EK77
Hickin St E14 204 D6
Hickling Rd, Ilf. 69 EP64
Hickman Av E4 47 EC51
Hickman Cl E16 86 EK71
Hickman Rd, Rom. 70 EW59
Hickmans Cl, Gdse. 186 DW132
Hickmore Wk SW4 101 DJ83
Hickory Cl N9 46 DU45
Hicks Av, Grnf. 79 CD69
Hicks Cl SW11 100 DE83
Hicks St SE8 203 K10
Hicks St SE8 103 DY78
Hidcote Cl, Wok. 167 BB116
Hidcote Gdns SW20 139 CV97
Hide E6 87 EN72
Downings
Hide Pl SW1 199 M9
Hide Pl SW1 101 DK77
Hide Rd, Har. 61 CD56
Hideaway, The, Abb.L. 7 BU31
Hides St N7 83 DM65
Sheringham Rd
Higgins Rd (Cheshunt), Wal.Cr. 14 DR26
Hammondstreet Rd
Higgins Wk, Hmptn. 116 BY93
Abbott Cl
High Acres, Abb.L. 7 BR32
High Beech, S.Croy. 160 DS108
High Beech Rd, Loug. 32 EK42
High Beeches, Bans. 157 CX114
High Beeches, Ger.Cr. 56 AX60
High Beeches, Orp. 164 EU107
High Beeches, Sid. 126 EY92
High Beeches Cl, Pur. 159 DK110
High Br SE10 103 ED78
High Br Wf SE10 103 ED78
High Broom Cres, W.Wick. 143 EB101
High Canons, Borwd. 26 CQ37
High Cedar Dr SW20 119 CV94
High Cl, Rick. 22 BJ43
High Coombe Pl, Kings.T. 118 CR93
High Cross, Wat. 25 CD37
High Cross Cen N15 66 DU56
High Cross Rd N17 66 DU55
High Dr, Cat. 177 DZ122
High Dr, Lthd. 155 CD114
High Dr, N.Mal. 138 CQ95
High Elms, Chig. 49 ES49
High Elms, Upmin. 73 FS60
High Elms, Wdf.Grn. 48 EG50
High Elms Cl, Nthwd. 39 BR51
High Elms La, Wat. 7 BV31
High Elms Rd, Orp. 163 EP110
High Firs, Rad. 25 CF35
High Firs, Swan. 147 FE98
High Foleys, Esher 155 CH108
High Gables, Loug. 32 EK43
High Garth, Esher 154 CC107
High Gro SE18 105 ER80
High Gro, Brom. 144 EJ95
High Hill Est E5 66 DV60
Mount Pleasant La
High Hill Ferry E5 66 DV60
High Hill Rd, Warl. 177 EC115
High Holborn WC1 196 A8
High Holborn WC1 83 DL72
High Ho La, Til. 111 GJ75
High La W7 79 CD72
High La, Cat. 177 DZ119
High La, Warl. 177 DZ118
High Lawns, Har. 61 CE62
High Level Dr SE26 122 DU91
High Mead, Chig. 49 EQ47
High Mead, Har. 61 CE57
High Mead, W.Wick. 143 ED103
High Meadow Cl, Pnr. 59 BV56
Daymer Gdns
High Meadow Cres NW9 62 CR57
High Meadow Pl, Cher. 133 BF100
High Meadows, Chig. 49 ER50
High Meads Rd E16 86 EK72
Fulmer Rd
High Mt NW4 63 CU58
High Oaks, Enf. 29 DM38
High Pk Av, Rich. 98 CN81
High Pk Rd, Rich. 98 CN81
High Path SW19 140 DB95
High Pine Cl, Wey. 153 BQ106
High Pines, Warl. 176 DW119
High Pt N6 64 DG59
High Pt SE9 125 EP90
High Pt, Wey. 152 BN106
High Ridge (Cuffley), Pot.B. 13 DL27
High Ridge Cl, Hem.H. 6 BK25
High Ridge Rd, Hem.H. 6 BK25
High Rd N2 44 DD54
High Rd N11 45 DH50
High Rd N12 44 DC51
High Rd N15 66 DT58
High Rd N17 46 DT53
High Rd N20 44 DC45
High Rd N22 65 DN55
High Rd (Willesden) NW10 81 CT65
High Rd, Buck.H. 48 EH47
High Rd, Bushey 41 CD46
High Rd, Chig. 49 EM50
High Rd, Couls. 174 DF121
High Rd (Wilmington), Dart. 128 FJ90
High Rd, Epp. 17 ER32
High Rd (North Weald Bassett), Epp. 19 FB27
High Rd (Thornwood), Epp. 18 EV28
High Rd (Harrow Weald), Har. 41 CE52
High Rd, Ilf. 69 EP62
High Rd (Seven Kings), Ilf. 69 ET60
High Rd, Loug. 48 EJ45
High Rd, Pnr. 59 BV56
High Rd, Reig. 184 DD126
High Rd (Chadwell Heath), Rom. 70 EV60
High Rd, Uxb. 76 BJ71
High Rd, Wat. 23 BT35
High Rd, Wem. 61 CK64
High Rd, W.Byf. 152 BM112
High Rd Ickenham, Uxb. 59 BP62
High Rd Leyton E10 67 EB60
High Rd Leyton E15 67 EC62
High Rd Leytonstone E11 68 EE63
High Rd Leytonstone E15 68 EE63
High Rd Turnford, Brox. 15 DY25
High Rd Woodford Grn E18 48 EG54
High Rd Woodford Grn, Wdf.Grn. 48 EF52
High Silver, Loug. 32 EK42
High Standing, Cat. 186 DQ125
High St E11 68 EG57
High St E13 86 EG68
High St E15 85 EC68
High St E17 67 DZ57
High St N8 65 DL56
High St N14 45 DK46
High St NW7 43 CV49
High St (Harlesden) NW10 81 CT68
High St SE20 122 DV93
High St (South Norwood) SE25 142 DT98
High St W3 80 CP74
High St W5 79 CK73
High St, Abb.L. 6 BN29
High St (Bedmond), Abb.L. 7 BS31
High St, Add. 152 BH105
High St, Bans. 174 DA115
High St, Barn. 27 CY41
High St, Beck. 143 EA95
High St (Elstree), Borwd. 25 CK44
High St, Brent. 97 CK79
High St, Brwd. 54 FW47
High St, Brom. 144 EG96
High St, Bushey 24 CA44
High St, Cars. 158 DG105
High St, Cat. 176 DS123
High St, Ch.St.G. 36 AW48
High St, Chis. 125 EP93
High St, Cob. 153 BV114
High St, Croy. 142 DQ103
High St, Dart. 128 FL86
High St (Bean), Dart. 129 FV90
High St (Eynsford), Dart. 148 FL103
High St (Farningham), Dart. 148 FM100
High St, Edg. 42 CN51
High St, Egh. 113 BA92
High St (Ponders End), Enf. 30 DW42
High St, Epp. 17 ET31
High St, Epsom 156 CR113
High St (Ewell), Epsom 157 CT110
High St, Esher 154 CB105
High St (Claygate), Esher 155 CF107
High St, Felt. 115 BU90
High St (Chalfont St. Peter), Ger.Cr. 36 AY53
High St, Gdse. 186 DV131
High St, Grav. 131 GH86
High St (Northfleet), Grav. 130 GB86
High St, Grays 110 GA79
High St, Green. 109 FV84
High St, Hmptn. 116 CC93
High St, Har. 61 CE60
High St (Wealdstone), Har. 61 CE55
High St, Hayes 95 BS78
High St (Bovingdon), Hem.H. 5 BA27
High St, Horn. 72 FK60
High St, Houns. 96 CC83
High St (Cranford), Houns. 95 BU81
High St, Ilf. 49 EQ54
High St, Iver 75 BE72
High St, Kings L. 7 BT27
High St, Kings.T. 137 CK96
High St (Hampton Wick), Kings.T. 137 CJ95
High St, Lthd. 171 CH122
High St (Oxshott), Lthd. 155 CD113
High St, N.Mal. 138 CS97
High St, Nthwd. 39 BT53
High St, Orp. 146 EU102
High St (Downe), Orp. 163 EN111
High St (Farnborough), Orp. 163 EP106
High St (Green St Grn), Orp. 163 ET108
High St (St. Mary Cray), Orp. 146 EW98
High St, Oxt. 187 ED130
High St (Limpsfield), Oxt. 188 EG128
High St, Pnr. 60 BY55
High St, Pot.B. 12 DC33
High St, Purf. 108 FN78
London Rd Purfleet
High St, Pur. 159 DN111
High St, Red. 184 DF134
High St (Bletchingley), Red. 186 DQ133
High St (Merstham), Red. 185 DH128
High St (Nutfield), Red. 185 DM133
High St, Reig. 184 DA134
High St, Rick. 38 BK46
High St, Rom. 71 FE57
High St, Ruis. 59 BS59
High St (London Colney), St.Alb. 9 CJ25
High St, Sev. 191 FJ125
High St (Chipstead), Sev. 190 FC122
High St (Kemsing), Sev. 191 FL121
High St (Otford), Sev. 181 FF116
High St (Shoreham), Sev. 165 FF110
High St, Shep. 135 BP100
High St, Slou. 92 AU75
High St (Colnbrook), Slou. 93 BC80
High St (Datchet), Slou. 92 AV81
High St (Langley), Slou. 93 AZ78
High St, S.Ock. 91 FR74
High St, Sthl. 78 BZ74
High St, Stai. 113 BF91
High St (Stanwell), Stai. 114 BK86
High St (Wraysbury), Stai. 112 AY86
High St, Sutt. 158 DB105
High St (Cheam), Sutt. 157 CY107
High St, Swan. 147 FF98
High St, Swans. 130 FZ85
High St, Tad. 173 CW123
High St, Tedd. 117 CG92
High St, T.Ditt. 137 CG101
High St, Th.Hth. 142 DQ98
High St (Whitton), Twick. 116 CC87
High St, Uxb. 76 BK67
High St (Cowley), Uxb. 76 BJ70
High St (Harefield), Uxb. 38 BJ54
High St, Wal.Cr. 15 DY34
High St (Cheshunt), Wal.Cr. 15 DX29
High St, Walt. 135 BU102
High St, Wat. 23 BV42
High St, Wem. 62 CM63
High St, West Dr. 94 BK79
High St (Yiewsley), West Dr. 76 BK74
High St, W.Mol. 136 CA98
High St, W.Wick. 143 EB102
High St, West. 189 EQ127
High St, Wey. 152 BN105
High St, Wok. 166 AY117
High St (Chobham), Wok. 150 AS111
High St (Horsell), Wok. 166 AV115
High St (Old Woking), Wok. 167 BB121
High St (Ripley), Wok. 168 BJ121
High St Colliers Wd SW19 120 DD94
High St Ms SW19 119 CY92
High St N E6 86 EL67
High St N E12 68 EL64
High St S E6 87 EM68
High St Wimbledon SW19 119 CX92
High Timber St EC4 197 H10
High Timber St EC4 84 DQ73
High Tor Cl, Brom. 124 EH94
Babbacombe Rd
High Tree Cl, Add. 151 BF106
High Tree Ct W7 79 CE73
High Trees SW2 121 DN88
High Trees, Barn. 28 DE43
High Trees, Croy. 143 DY102
High Trees Cl, Cat. 176 DT123
High Trees Ct, Brwd. 54 FW49
Warley Mt
High Vw, Ch.St.G. 36 AX47
High Vw, Pnr. 60 BW56
High Vw, Rick. 22 BG42
High Vw, Sutt. 157 CZ111
High Vw, Wat. 23 BT44
High Vw Av, Grays 110 GC78
High Vw Cl SE19 142 DT96
High Vw Cl, Loug. 32 EJ43
High Vw Rd E18 68 EF55
High Worple, Har. 60 BZ59
Higham Hill Rd E17 47 DY54
Higham Pl E17 67 DY55
Higham Rd N17 66 DR55
Higham Rd, Wdf.Grn. 48 EG51
Higham Sta Av E4 47 EB51
Higham St E17 67 DY55
Higham Vw, Epp. 19 FB26
Highams Ct E4 47 ED48
Friars Cl
Highams Lo Business Cen E17 67 DY55
Highams Pk Ind Est E4 47 EC51
Highbank Way N8 65 DN58
Highbanks Cl, Well. 106 EV80
Highbanks Rd, Pnr. 40 CB50
Highbarns, Hem.H. 6 BN25
Highbarrow Rd, Croy. 142 DU101
Highbridge Ind Est, Uxb. 76 BJ66
Highbridge Rd, Bark. 87 EP67
Highbridge St, Wal.Abb. 15 EA33
Highbrook Rd SE3 104 EK83
Highbury Av, Th.Hth. 141 DN96
Highbury Cl, N.Mal. 138 CQ98
Highbury Cl, W.Wick. 143 EB103
Highbury Cor N5 83 DN65
Highbury Cres N5 65 DN64
Highbury Est N5 66 DQ64
Highbury Gdns, Ilf. 69 ES61
Highbury Gra N5 65 DP63
Highbury Gro N5 83 DP65
Highbury Hill N5 65 DN62
Highbury Ms N7 83 DN65
Holloway Rd
Highbury New Pk N5 66 DQ64
Highbury Pk N5 65 DP62
Highbury Pk Ms N5 66 DQ63
Highbury Gra
Highbury Pl N5 83 DP65
Highbury Quad N5 66 DQ62
Highbury Rd SW19 119 CY92
Highbury Sta Rd N1 83 DN65
Highbury Ter N5 65 DP64
Highbury Ter Ms N5 65 DP64
Highclere Cl, Ken. 176 DQ115
Highclere Rd, N.Mal. 138 CR97
Highclere St SE26 123 DY91
Highcliffe Dr SW15 119 CT86
Highcliffe Gdns, Ilf. 68 EL57
Highcombe SE7 104 EH79
Highcombe Cl SE9 124 EK88
Highcroft NW9 62 CR57
Highcroft Av, Wem. 80 CN67
Highcroft Ct, Lthd. 170 CA123
Highcroft Gdns NW11 63 CZ58
Highcroft Rd N19 65 DL59
Highcroft Rd, Hem.H. 6 BG25
Highcross Rd, Grav. 129 FX92
Highcross Way SW15 119 CU88
Highdaun Dr SW16 141 DM98
Highdown, Wor.Pk. 139 CT103
Highdown La, Sutt. 158 DB111
Highdown Rd SW15 119 CV86
Higher Dr, Bans. 157 CX112
Higher Dr, Pur. 159 DN113
Higher Grn, Epsom 157 CU113
Highfield, Bans. 174 DE117
Highfield, Ch.St.G. 36 AX47
Highfield, Felt. 115 BU88
Highfield, Kings L. 6 BL28
Highfield, Wat. 40 BZ48
Highfield Av NW9 62 CQ57
Highfield Av NW11 63 CX59
Highfield Av, Erith 107 FB79
Highfield Av, Grnf. 61 CE64
Highfield Av, Orp. 163 ET106
Highfield Av, Pnr. 60 BZ57
Highfield Av, Wem. 62 CM62
Highfield Cl N22 45 DN53
Highfield Cl NW9 62 CQ57
Highfield Cl SE13 123 ED87
Highfield Cl, Egh. 112 AW93
Highfield Cl, Lthd. 155 CD111
Highfield Cl, Nthwd. 39 BS53
Highfield Cl, Rom. 51 FC51
Highfield Cl, Surb. 137 CJ102
Highfield Cl, W.Byf. 152 BG113
Highfield Ct N14 29 DJ44
Highfield Cres, Horn. 72 FM61
Highfield Cres, Nthwd. 39 BS53
Highfield Dr, Brom. 144 EE98
Highfield Dr, Cat. 176 DU122
Highfield Dr, Epsom 157 CT108
Highfield Dr (Ickenham), Uxb. 58 BL63
Highfield Dr, W.Wick. 143 EB103
Highfield Gdns NW11 63 CY58
Highfield Gdns, Grays 110 GD75
Highfield Grn, Epp. 17 ES31
Highfield Hill SE19 122 DR94
Highfield Link, Rom. 51 FC51
Highfield Pl, Epp. 17 ES31
Highfield Rd N21 45 DP47
Highfield Rd NW11 63 CY58
Highfield Rd W3 80 CP71
Highfield Rd, Bexh. 126 EZ85
Highfield Rd, Brom. 145 EM98
Highfield Rd, Bushey 24 BY43
Highfield Rd, Cat. 176 DU122
Highfield Rd, Cher. 134 BG102
Highfield Rd, Chis. 145 ET97
Highfield Rd, Dart. 128 FK87
Highfield Rd, Felt. 115 BU89
Highfield Rd, Horn. 72 FM61
Highfield Rd, Islw. 97 CF81
Highfield Rd, Nthwd. 39 BS53
Highfield Rd, Pur. 159 DM110
Highfield Rd, Rom. 51 FC52
Highfield Rd, Sun. 135 BT98
Highfield Rd, Surb. 138 CQ101
Highfield Rd, Sutt. 158 DE106
Highfield Rd (Cheshunt), Wal.Cr. 14 DS26
Highfield Rd, Walt. 135 BU102
Highfield Rd, W.Byf. 152 BG113
Highfield Rd, West. 178 EJ117
Highfield Rd, Wdf.Grn. 48 EL52
Highfield Rd S, Dart. 128 FK87
Highfield Twr, Rom. 51 FD50
Highfield Way, Horn. 72 FM61
Highfield Way, Pot.B. 12 DB32
Highfield Way, Rick. 22 BH44
Highfields, Ash. 171 CK119
Highfields, Lthd. 171 CD124
Highfields (Cuffley), Pot.B. 13 DL28
Highfields, Rad. 25 CF35
Highfields Gro N6 64 DF60
Highgate Av N6 65 DH58
Highgate Cl N6 64 DG59
Highgate High St N6 64 DG60
Highgate Hill N6 65 DH60
Highgate Hill N19 65 DH60
Highgate Rd NW5 65 DH63
Highgate Wk SE23 122 DW89
Highgate W Hill N6 64 DG61
Highgrove, Brwd. 54 FV44
Highgrove Cl N11 44 DG50
Balmoral Av
Highgrove Cl, Chis. 144 EL95
Highgrove Ct, Beck. 123 EA94
Park Rd
Highgrove Ms, Cars. 140 DF104
Highgrove Ms, Grays 110 GC78
Highgrove Rd, Dag. 70 EW64
Highgrove Way, Ruis. 59 BU58
Highland Av W7 79 CE72
Highland Av, Brwd. 54 FW46
Highland Av, Dag. 71 FC62
Highland Av, Loug. 32 EL44
Highland Cotts, Wall. 159 DH105
Highland Ct E18 48 EH53
Highland Cft, Beck. 123 EB92
Highland Dr, Bushey 40 CC45
Highland Pk, Felt. 115 BT91
Highland Rd SE19 122 DS93
Highland Rd, Bexh. 126 FA85
Highland Rd, Brom. 144 EF95
Highland Rd, Nthwd. 39 BT54
Highland Rd, Pur. 159 DN114
Highland Rd, Sev. 165 FB111
Highlands, Ash. 171 CJ119
Highlands, Wat. 40 BW46
Highlands, The, Edg. 42 CP54
Highlands, The, Pot.B. 28 DB43
Highlands, The, Rick. 38 BH45
Highlands Av N21 29 DM43
Highlands Av W3 80 CQ73
Highlands Av, Lthd. 171 CJ122
Highlands Cl N4 65 DL59
Mount Vw Rd
Highlands Cl (Chalfont St. Peter), Ger.Cr. 37 AZ52
Highlands Cl, Houns. 96 CB81
Highlands Cl, Lthd. 171 CH122
Highlands End (Chalfont St. Peter), Ger.Cr. 36 AY52
Highlands Gdns, Ilf. 69 EM60

Highlands Heath SW15 119 CW87
Highlands Hill, Swan. 147 FG96
Highlands La (Chalfont St. Peter), Ger.Cr. 37 AZ51
Highlands La, Wok. 166 AY122
Highlands Pk, Lthd. 171 CK123
Highlands Pk, Sev. 191 FL121
Highlands Rd, Barn. 28 DA43
Highlands Rd, Lthd. 171 CH122
Highlands Rd, Orp. 146 EV101
Highlands Rd, Reig. 184 DD133
Highlea Cl NW9 42 CS53
Highlever Rd W10 81 CW71
Highmead SE18 105 ET80
Highmead Cres, Wem. 80 CM66
Highmore Rd SE3 104 EE79
Highridge Cl, Epsom 172 CS115
Highshore Rd SE15 102 DT82
Highstead Cres, Erith 107 FE81
Highstone Av E11 68 EG58
Highview, Cat. 176 DS124
Highview, Nthlt. 78 BY69
Highview, Wok. 166 AS117
Mulgrave Way
Highview Av, Edg. 42 CQ49
Highview Av, Wall. 159 DM106
Highview Cl, Pot.B. 12 DC33
Highview Cres, Brwd. 55 GC44
Highview Gdns N3 63 CY55
Highview Gdns N11 45 DJ50
Highview Gdns, Edg. 42 CQ49
Highview Gdns, Pot.B. 12 DC33
Highview Gdns, Upmin. 72 FP61
Highview Ho, Rom. 70 EY56
Highview Path, Bans. 174 DA115
Highview Rd SE19 122 DR93
Highview Rd W13 79 CG71
Highview Rd, Sid. 126 EV91
Highway, The E1 202 C1
Highway, The E1 84 DV73
Highway, The E14 202 D1
Highway, The E14 84 DV73
Highway, The, Orp. 164 EW106
Highway, The, Stan. 41 CF53
Highway, The, Sutt. 158 DC109
Highwold, Couls. 174 DG118
Highwood, Brom. 144 EE97
Highwood Av N12 44 DC49
Highwood Av, Bushey 24 BZ39
Highwood Cl, Brwd. 54 FV45
Highwood Cl, Ken. 176 DQ117
Highwood Cl, Orp. 145 EQ103
Highwood Dr, Orp. 145 EQ103
Highwood Gdns, Ilf. 69 EM57
Highwood Gro NW7 42 CR50
Highwood Hall La, Hem.H. 7 BQ25
Highwood Hill NW7 43 CT48
Highwood La, Loug. 33 EN43
Highwood Rd N19 65 DL62
Highwoods, Cat. 186 DS125
Highwoods, Lthd. 171 CJ121
Highworth Rd N11 45 DK51
Hilary Av, Mitch. 140 DG97
Hilary Cl SW6 100 DB80
Hilary Cl, Erith 107 FC81
Hilary Cl, Horn. 72 FK64
Hilary Rd W12 81 CT72
Hilary Rd, Slou. 92 AY76
Hilbert Rd, Sutt. 139 CX104
Hilborough Way, Orp. 163 ER106
Hilda May Av, Swan. 147 FE97
Hilda Rd E6 86 EK66
Hilda Rd E16 86 EE70
Hilda Ter SW9 101 DN82
Hilda Vale Cl, Orp. 163 EP105
Hilda Vale Rd, Orp. 163 EN105
Hilden Dr, Erith 107 FH80
Hildenborough Gdns, Brom. 124 EE93
Hildenlea Pl, Brom. 144 EE96
Hildenley Cl, Red. 185 DK128
Malmstone Av
Hilders, The, Ash. 172 CP117
Hildreth St SW12 121 DH88
Hildyard Rd SW6 100 DA79
Hiley Rd NW10 81 CW69
Hilfield La, Wat. 25 CD41
Hilfield La S, Bushey 25 CF44
Hilgrove Rd NW6 82 DC66
Hiliary Gdns, Stan. 41 CJ54
Hiljon Cres (Chalfont St. Peter), Ger.Cr. 36 AY53
Hill, The, Cat. 176 DT124
Hill, The, Grav. 130 GC86
Hill Barn, S.Croy. 160 DS111
Hill Brow, Brom. 144 EK95
Hill Brow, Dart. 127 FF86
Hill Cl NW2 63 CV62
Hill Cl NW11 64 DA58
Hill Cl, Barn. 27 CW43
Hill Cl, Chis. 125 EP92
Hill Cl, Cob. 154 CA112
Hill Cl, Grav. 130 GE94
Hill Cl, Har. 61 CE62
Hill Cl, Pur. 160 DQ113
Hill Cl, Stan. 41 CH49
Hill Cl, Wok. 166 AX115
Hill Ct, Nthlt. 60 CA64
Hill Cres N20 44 DB47
Hill Cres, Bex. 127 FC88
Hill Cres, Har. 61 CG57
Hill Cres, Horn. 72 FJ58
Hill Cres, Surb. 138 CM99
Hill Cres, Wor.Pk. 139 CW103
Hill Crest, Pot.B. 12 DC34
Hill Crest, Sev. 190 FG122
Hill Crest, Sid. 126 EU87
Hill Dr NW9 62 CQ60
Hill Dr SW16 141 DM97
Hill End, Orp. 145 ET103
The App
Hill End Rd (Harefield), Uxb. 38 BH51
Hill Fm Av, Wat. 7 BU33
Hill Fm Cl, Wat. 7 BU33
Hill Fm Ind Est, Wat. 7 BT33
Hill Fm La, Ch.St.G. 36 AT46
Hill Fm Rd W10 81 CW71
Hill Fm Rd (Chalfont St. Peter), Ger.Cr. 36 AY52
Hill Fm Rd, Uxb. 59 BR63
Austin's La
Hill Gro, Felt. 116 BZ89
Watermill Way
Hill Gro, Rom. 71 FE55
Hill Ho Av, Stan. 41 CF52
Hill Ho Cl N21 45 DN45
Hill Ho Cl (Chalfont St. Peter), Ger.Cr. 36 AY52
Rickmansworth La
Hill Ho Dr, Hmptn. 136 CA95
Hill Ho Dr, Wey. 152 BN111
Hill Ho Rd SW16 121 DM92
Hill La, Ruis. 59 BQ60
Hill La, Tad. 173 CY121
Hill Leys (Cuffley), Pot.B. 13 DL28
Hill Pk Dr, Lthd. 171 CF119
Hill Path SW16 121 DM92
Valley Rd
Hill Ri N9 30 DV44
Hill Ri NW11 64 DB56
Hill Ri SE23 122 DV88
London Rd
Hill Ri, Dart. 129 FR92
Hill Ri, Esher 137 CH103
Hill Ri (Chalfont St. Peter), Ger.Cr. 36 AX54
Hill Ri, Grnf. 78 CC66
Hill Ri, Pot.B. 12 DC34
Hill Ri (Cuffley), Pot.B. 13 DK27
Hill Ri, Rich. 117 CK85
Hill Ri, Rick. 22 BH44
Hill Ri, Ruis. 59 BQ60
Hill Ri, Slou. 93 BA79
Hill Ri, Upmin. 72 FN61
Hill Ri Cres (Chalfont St. Peter), Ger.Cr. 36 AY54
Hill Rd N10 44 DF53
Hill Rd NW8 82 DC68
Hill Rd, Brwd. 54 FU48
Hill Rd, Cars. 158 DE107
Hill Rd, Dart. 128 FL89
Hill Rd, Epp. 33 ES37
Hill Rd, Har. 61 CG57
Hill Rd, Lthd. 170 CB122
Hill Rd, Mitch. 141 DH95
Hill Rd, Nthwd. 39 BR51
Hill Rd, Pnr. 60 BY57
Hill Rd, Pur. 159 DM112
Hill Rd, Sutt. 158 DB106
Hill Rd, Wem. 61 CH62
Hill St W1 198 G2
Hill St W1 83 DH74
Hill St, Rich. 117 CK85
Hill Top NW11 64 DB56
Hill Top, Loug. 33 EN40
Hill Top, Mord. 140 DA100
Hill Top, Sutt. 139 CZ101
Hill Top Cl, Loug. 33 EN41
Hill Top Pl, Loug. 33 EN41
Hill Top Vw, Wdf.Grn. 49 EM51
Hill Vw Cl, Tad. 173 CW121
Shelvers Way
Hill Vw Cres, Orp. 145 ET102
Hill Vw Dr, Well. 105 ES82
Hill Vw Gdns NW9 62 CR57
Hill Vw Rd, Esher 155 CG108
Hill Vw Rd, Orp. 145 ET102
Hill Vw Rd, Stai. 112 AX86
Hill Vw Rd, Twick. 117 CG86
Hill Vw Rd, Wok. 167 AZ118
Hill Waye, Ger.Cr. 57 AZ58
Hillars Heath Rd, Couls. 175 DL115
Hillary Av, Grav. 130 GE90
Hillary Cres, Walt. 136 BW102
Hillary Ri, Barn. 28 DA42
Hillary Rd, Sthl. 96 CA76
Hillbeck Cl SE15 102 DW80
Hillbeck Way, Grnf. 79 CD67
Hillborne Cl, Hayes 95 BU78
Hillborough Av, Sev. 191 FK122
Hillborough Cl SW19 120 DC94
Hillbrook Gdns, Wey. 152 BN108
Hillbrook Rd SW17 120 DF90
Hillbrow, N.Mal. 139 CT97
Hillbrow Cl, Bex. 127 FD91
Hillbrow Cotts, Gdse. 186 DW132
Hillbrow Ct, Gdse. 186 DW132
Hillbrow Rd, Brom. 124 EE94
Hillbrow Rd, Esher 154 CC105
Hillbury Av, Har. 61 CH57
Hillbury Cl, Warl. 176 DV118
Hillbury Gdns, Warl. 176 DW118
Hillbury Rd SW17 121 DH90
Hillbury Rd, Warl. 176 DU117
Hillbury Rd, Whyt. 176 DU117
Hillcote Av SW16 121 DN94
Hillcourt Av N12 44 DB51
Hillcourt Est N16 66 DR60
Hillcourt Rd SE22 122 DV86
Hillcrest N6 64 DG59
Hillcrest N21 45 DP45
Hillcrest, Wey. 153 BP105
Hillcrest Av NW11 63 CY57
Hillcrest Av, Cher. 151 BE105
Hillcrest Av, Edg. 42 CP49
Hillcrest Av, Grays 109 FU79
Hillcrest Av, Pnr. 60 BX56
Hillcrest Cl SE26 122 DU91
Hillcrest Cl, Beck. 143 DZ99
Hillcrest Cl, Epsom 173 CT115
Hillcrest Dr, Green. 129 FV85
Riverview Rd
Hillcrest Gdns N3 63 CY56
Hillcrest Gdns NW2 63 CU62
Hillcrest Gdns, Esher 137 CF104
Hillcrest Par, Couls. 159 DH114
Hillcrest Rd E17 47 ED54
Hillcrest Rd E18 48 EF54
Hillcrest Rd W3 80 CN74
Hillcrest Rd W5 80 CL71
Hillcrest Rd, Brom. 124 EG92
Hillcrest Rd, Dart. 127 FF87
Hillcrest Rd, Horn. 71 FG59
Hillcrest Rd, Loug. 32 EK44
Hillcrest Rd, Ong. 19 FE30
Hillcrest Rd, Orp. 146 EU103
Hillcrest Rd, Pur. 159 DM110
Hillcrest Rd, Rad. 10 CN33
Hillcrest Rd, West. 178 EK116
Hillcrest Rd, Whyt. 176 DT117
Hillcrest Vw, Beck. 143 DZ100
Hillcrest Way, Epp. 18 EU31
Hillcrest Waye, Ger.Cr. 57 AZ59
Hillcroft, Loug. 33 EN40
Hillcroft Av, Pnr. 60 BZ58
Hillcroft Av, Pur. 159 DJ113
Hillcroft Cres W5 80 CL72
Hillcroft Cres, Ruis. 60 BX62
Hillcroft Cres, Wat. 39 BV46
Hillcroft Cres, Wem. 62 CM63
Hillcroft Rd E6 87 EP71
Hillcroome Rd, Sutt. 158 DD107
Hillcross Av, Mord. 139 CZ99
Hilldale Rd, Sutt. 157 CZ105
Hilldeane Rd, Pur. 159 DN109
Hilldene Av, Rom. 52 FJ51
Hilldene Cl, Rom. 52 FK50
Hilldown Rd SW16 121 DL94
Hilldown Rd, Brom. 144 EE102
Hilldrop Cres N7 65 DK64
Hilldrop Est N7 65 DK64
Hilldrop La N7 65 DK64
Hilldrop Rd N7 65 DK64
Hilldrop Rd, Brom. 124 EG93
Hillend SE18 105 EN81
Hillersdon, Slou. 74 AV71
Hillersdon Av SW13 99 CU82
Hillersdon Av, Edg. 42 CM50
Hillery Cl SE17 201 L9
Hilley Fld La, Lthd. 170 CC122
Hillfield Av N8 65 DL57
Hillfield Av NW9 62 CS57
Hillfield Av, Wem. 80 CL66
Hillfield Cl, Har. 60 CC56
Hillfield Cl, Red. 184 DG134
Hillfield Ct NW3 64 DE64
Hillfield Par, Mord. 140 DE100
Hillfield Pk N10 65 DH56
Hillfield Pk N21 45 DN47
Hillfield Pk Ms N10 65 DH56
Hillfield Rd NW6 63 CZ64
Hillfield Rd (Chalfont St. Peter), Ger.Cr. 36 AY52
Hillfield Rd, Hmptn. 116 BZ94
Hillfield Rd, Red. 184 DG134
Hillfield Rd, Sev. 181 FE120
Hillfield Sq (Chalfont St. Peter), Ger.Cr. 36 AY52
Hillfoot Av, Rom. 51 FC53
Hillfoot Rd, Rom. 51 FC53
Hillgate Pl SW12 121 DH87
Hillgate Pl W8 82 DA74
Hillgate St W8 82 DA74
Hillgrove (Chalfont St. Peter), Ger.Cr. 37 AZ53
Hillhouse, Wal.Abb. 16 EF33
Hillhouse Rd, Dart. 128 FQ87
Hillhurst Gdns, Cat. 176 DS120
Hilliard Rd, Nthwd. 39 BT53
Hilliards Ct E1 202 E2
Hilliards Rd, Uxb. 76 BK72
Hillier Cl, Barn. 28 DB44
Hillier Gdns, Croy. 159 DN106
Crowley Cres
Hillier Pl, Chess. 155 CJ107
Hillier Rd SW11 120 DF86
Hilliers Av, Uxb. 76 BN69
Harlington Rd
Hilliers La, Croy. 141 DL104
Hillingdale, West. 178 EH118
Hillingdon Av, Sev. 191 FJ121
Hillingdon Av, Stai. 114 BL88
Hillingdon Hill, Uxb. 76 BL69
Hillingdon Ri, Sev. 191 FK122
Hillingdon Rd, Bexh. 107 FC82
Hillingdon Rd, Grav. 131 GG89
Hillingdon Rd, Uxb. 76 BL67
Hillingdon Rd, Wat. 7 BU34
Hillingdon St SE5 101 DP79
Hillingdon St SE17 101 DP79
Hillington Gdns, Wdf.Grn. 48 EK54
Hillman Cl, Horn. 72 FK55
Hillman Cl, Uxb. 58 BL64
Hillman Dr W10 81 CW70
Hillman St E8 84 DV65
Hillmarton Rd N7 65 DL64
Hillmead Dr SW9 101 DP84
Hillmont Rd, Esher 137 CE104
Hillmore Gro SE26 123 DX92
Hillmount, Wok. 166 AY119
Constitution Hill
Hillreach SE18 105 EM78
Hillrise, Walt. 135 BT101
Hillrise Av, Wat. 24 BX38
Hillrise Rd N19 65 DL59
Hillrise Rd, Rom. 51 FC51
Hills Chace, Brwd. 54 FW49
Hills La, Nthwd. 39 BS53
Hills Ms W5 80 CL73
Hills Pl W1 195 K9
Hills Rd, Buck.H. 48 EH46
Hillsborough Grn, Wat. 39 BU48
Ashburnham Dr
Hillsborough Rd SE22 122 DS85
Hillsgrove, Well. 106 EW80
Hillside NW9 62 CR56
Hillside NW10 80 CQ67
Hillside SW19 119 CX93
Hillside, Bans. 173 CY115
Hillside, Barn. 28 DC43
Hillside, Dart. 129 FS92
Hillside (Farningham), Dart. 148 FM101
Hillside, Erith 107 FD77
Hillside, Grays 110 GD77
Hillside, Slou. 92 AS75
Hillside (Harefield), Uxb. 58 BJ57
Hillside, Vir.W. 132 AW100
Hillside, Wok. 166 AX120
Hillside, The, Orp. 164 EV109
Hillside Av N11 44 DF51
Hillside Av, Borwd. 26 CP42
Hillside Av, Grav. 131 GK89
Hillside Av, Pur. 159 DP113
Hillside Av (Cheshunt), Wal.Cr. 15 DX31
Hillside Av, Wem. 62 CM63
Hillside Av, Wdf.Grn. 48 EJ50
Hillside Cl NW8 82 DB68
Hillside Cl, Abb.L. 7 BS32
Hillside Cl, Bans. 173 CY116
Hillside Cl, Ch.St.G. 36 AV48
Hillside Cl (Chalfont St. Peter), Ger.Cr. 36 AY51
Hillside Cl, Mord. 139 CY98
Hillside Cl, Wdf.Grn. 48 EJ50
Hillside Ct, Swan. 147 FG98
Hillside Cres, Enf. 30 DR38
Hillside Cres, Har. 60 CC60
Hillside Cres, Nthwd. 39 BU53
Hillside Cres (Cheshunt), Wal.Cr. 15 DX31
Hillside Cres, Wat. 24 BY44
Hillside Dr, Edg. 42 CN51
Hillside Dr, Grav. 131 GK89
Hillside Est N15 66 DT58
Hillside Gdns E17 67 ED55
Hillside Gdns N6 64 DG58
Hillside Gdns SW2 121 DN89
Hillside Gdns, Add. 151 BF107
Hillside Gdns, Barn. 27 CY42
Hillside Gdns, Bet. 182 CN134
Hillside Gdns, Edg. 42 CM49
Hillside Gdns, Har. 62 CL59
Hillside Gdns, Nthwd. 39 BU52
Hillside Gdns, Wall. 159 DJ108
Hillside Gro N14 45 DK45
Hillside Gro NW7 43 CU52
Hillside La, Brom. 144 EG103
Hillside Pas SW2 121 DM89
Hillside Ri, Nthwd. 39 BU52
Hillside Rd N15 66 DS59
Hillside Rd SW2 121 DN89
Hillside Rd W5 80 CL71
Hillside Rd, Ash. 172 CM117
Hillside Rd, Brom. 144 EF97
Hillside Rd, Bushey 24 BY43
Hillside Rd, Couls. 175 DM118
Hillside Rd, Croy. 159 DP106
Hillside Rd, Dart. 127 FG86
Hillside Rd, Epsom 157 CW110
Hillside Rd, Nthwd. 39 BU52
Hillside Rd, Pnr. 39 BV52
Hillside Rd, Rad. 25 CH35
Hillside Rd, Rick. 21 BC43
Hillside Rd, Sev. 191 FK123
Hillside Rd, Sthl. 78 CA70
Hillside Rd, Surb. 138 CM99
Hillside Rd, Sutt. 157 CZ108
Hillside Rd, West. 178 EL119
Hillside Rd, Whyt. 176 DU118
Hillside Wk, Brwd. 54 FU48
Hillsleigh Rd W8 81 CZ74
Hillsmead Way, S.Croy. 160 DU113
Hillstowe St E5 66 DW61
Hilltop Cl, Lthd. 171 CJ123
Hilltop Cl (Cheshunt), Wal.Cr. 14 DT26
Hilltop Gdns NW4 43 CV53
Great N Way
Hilltop Gdns, Dart. 128 FM85
Hilltop Gdns, Orp. 145 ES103
Hilltop La, Cat. 185 DN126
Hilltop La, Red. 185 DN126
Hilltop Rd NW6 82 DA66
Hilltop Rd, Grays 109 FV79
Hilltop Rd, Kings L. 7 BR27
Hilltop Rd, Whyt. 176 DS117
Hilltop Wk, Cat. 177 DY120
Hilltop Way, Stan. 41 CG48
Hillview SW20 119 CV94
Hillview, Mitch. 141 DL98
Hillview Av, Har. 62 CL57
Hillview Av, Horn. 72 FJ58
Hillview Cl, Pnr. 40 BZ51
Hillview Cl, Pur. 159 DP111
Hillview Ct, Wok. 167 AZ118
Hillview Cres, Ilf. 69 EM58
Hillview Gdns NW4 63 CX56
Hillview Gdns, Har. 60 CA55
Hillview Gdns (Cheshunt), Wal.Cr. 15 DX27
Hillview Rd NW7 43 CX49
Hillview Rd, Chis. 125 EN92
Hillview Rd, Pnr. 40 BZ52
Hillview Rd, Sutt. 140 DC104
Hillway N6 64 DG61
Hillway NW9 62 CS60
Hillwood Cl, Brwd. 55 GB46
Hillwood Gro, Brwd. 55 GB46
Hillworth Rd SW2 121 DN87
Hilly Flds Cres SE4 103 EA83
Hillyard Rd W7 79 CE71
Hillyard St SW9 101 DN81
Hillyfield E17 67 DY55
Hillyfields, Loug. 33 EN40
Hilperton Rd, Slou. 92 AS75
Hilsea St E5 66 DW63
Hilton Av N12 44 DD50
Hilton Cl, Uxb. 76 BH68
Hilton Way, S.Croy. 176 DV115
Hilversum Cres SE22 122 DS85
East Dulwich Gro
Himalayan Way, Wat. 23 BT44
Himley Rd SW17 120 DE92
Hinchcliffe Cl, Wall. 159 DM108
Hinchley Cl, Esher 137 CF104
Hinchley Dr, Esher 137 CF104
Hinchley Way, Esher 137 CG104
Hinckley Rd SE15 102 DU84
Hind Cl, Chig. 49 ET50
Hind Ct EC4 196 E9
Hind Cres, Erith 107 FD79
Hind Gro E14 85 EA72
Hind Ter, Grays 109 FX78
Mill La
Hinde Ms W1 82 DG72
Marylebone La
Hinde St W1 194 G8
Hinde St W1 82 DG72
Hindes Rd, Har. 61 CD57
Hindhead Cl N16 66 DS60
Hindhead Cl, Uxb. 77 BP71
Aldenham Dr
Hindhead Gdns, Nthlt. 78 BY67
Hindhead Grn, Wat. 40 BW50
Hindhead Way, Wall. 159 DL106
Hindmans Rd SE22 122 DU85
Hindmans Way, Dag. 88 EZ70
Hindmarsh Cl E1 84 DU73
Cable St
Hindrey Rd E5 66 DV64
Hindsley's Pl SE23 122 DW89
Hinkler Cl, Wall. 159 DL108
Hinkler Rd, Har. 61 CK55
Hinkley Cl (Harefield), Uxb. 58 BJ56
Hinksey Cl, Slou. 93 BB76
Hinksey Path SE2 106 EX76
Hinstock Rd SE18 105 EQ79
Hinton Av, Houns. 96 BX84
Hinton Cl SE9 124 EL88
Hinton Rd N18 46 DS49
Hinton Rd SE24 101 DP83
Hinton Rd, Uxb. 76 BJ67
Hinton Rd, Wall. 159 DJ107
Hipley St, Wok. 167 BB121
Hippodrome Ms W11 81 CY73
Portland Rd
Hippodrome Pl W11 81 CY73
Hiscocks Ho NW10 80 CQ66
Hitcham Rd E17 67 DZ59
Hitchcock Cl, Shep. 134 BM97
Hitchen Hatch La, Sev. 190 FG124
Hitchin Cl, Rom. 52 FJ49
Hitchin Sq E3 85 DY68
Hither Fm Rd SE3 104 EJ83
Hither Grn La SE13 123 EC85
Hither Meadow (Chalfont St. Peter), Ger.Cr. 36 AY53
Lower Rd
Hitherbroom Rd, Hayes 77 BU74
Hitherfield Rd SW16 121 DM89
Hitherfield Rd, Dag. 70 EY61
Hitherlands SW12 121 DH89
Hithermoor Rd, Stai. 114 BG85
Hitherwell Dr, Har. 41 CD53
Hitherwood Cl, Horn. 72 FK63
Swanbourne Dr
Hitherwood Cl, Reig. 184 DD132
Hitherwood Dr SE19 122 DT91
Hive, The (Northfleet), Grav. 130 GB85
Fishermans Hill
Hive Cl, Brwd. 54 FU47
Hive Cl, Bushey 41 CD47
Hive La, Grav. 130 GB86
Hive Rd, Bushey 41 CD47
Hoadly Rd SW16 121 DK90
Hobart Cl N20 44 DE47
Oakleigh Rd N
Hobart Cl, Hayes 78 BX70
Hobart Dr, Hayes 78 BX70
Hobart Gdns, Th.Hth. 142 DR97
Hobart La, Hayes 78 BX70
Hobart Pl SW1 199 H6
Hobart Pl SW1 101 DH76
Hobart Pl, Rich. 118 CM86
Chisholm Rd
Hobart Rd, Dag. 70 EX63
Hobart Rd, Hayes 78 BX70
Hobart Rd, Ilf. 49 EQ54
Hobart Rd, Til. 111 GG81
Hobart Rd, Wor.Pk. 139 CV104
Hobarts Dr (Denham), Uxb. 57 BF58
Hobbayne Rd W7 79 CD72
Hobbes Wk SW15 119 CV85
Hobbs Cl (Cheshunt), Wal.Cr. 15 DX29
Hobbs Cl, W.Byf. 152 BH113
Hobbs Cross Rd, Epp. 34 EW35
Hobbs Grn N2 64 DC55
Hobbs Ms, Ilf. 69 ET61
Ripley Rd
Hobbs Pl Est N1 84 DS67
Pitfield St
Hobbs Rd SE27 122 DQ91
Hobby Horse Cl (Cheshunt), Wal.Cr. 14 DR26
Hammondstreet Rd
Hobday St E14 85 EB71
Hobill Wk, Surb. 138 CM100
Hoblands End, Chis. 125 ES93
Hobsons Pl E1 84 DU71
Hanbury St
Hobury St SW10 100 DC79
Hockenden La, Swan. 147 FB96
Hocker St E2 197 P3
Hockering Gdns, Wok. 167 BA117
Hockering Rd, Wok. 167 BA118
Hockett Cl SE8 203 L8
Hockett Cl SE8 103 DY77
Hockley Av E6 86 EL68
Hockley Dr, Rom. 51 FH54
Hockley La, Slou. 74 AV67
Hockley Ms, Bark. 87 ES68
Hocroft Av NW2 63 CZ62
Hocroft Rd NW2 63 CZ63
Hocroft Wk NW2 63 CZ62
Hodder Dr, Grnf. 79 CF68
Hoddesdon Rd, Belv. 106 FA78
Hoddesdon Rd, Brox. 15 DX27
Hodford Rd NW11 63 CZ61
Hodgemoor Vw, Ch.St.G. 36 AT48
Hodges Way, Wat. 23 BU44
Hodgkin Cl SE28 88 EX73
Fleming Way
Hodister Cl SE5 102 DQ80
Badsworth Rd
Hodnet Gro SE16 203 H8
Hodnet Gro SE16 103 DX77
Hodsoll Ct, Orp. 146 EX100
Hodson Cl, Har. 60 BZ62
Hodson Cres, Orp. 146 EX100
Hoe, The, Wat. 40 BX47
Hoe La, Enf. 30 DU38
Hoe La, Rom. 34 EV43
Hoe St E17 67 EA56
Hoebrook Cl, Wok. 166 AX121
Hofland Rd W14 99 CX76
Hog Hill Rd, Rom. 50 EZ52
Hog Pits, Hem.H. 5 BB32
Hogan Ms W2 82 DD71
Porteus Rd
Hogan Way E5 66 DU61
Geldeston Rd
Hogarth Av, Ashf. 115 BQ93
Hogarth Av, Brwd. 54 FY48
Hogarth Cl E16 86 EK71
Hogarth Cl W5 80 CL71
Hogarth Ct EC3 197 N10
Hogarth Ct SE19 122 DT91
Fountain Dr
Hogarth Ct, Bushey 40 CB45
Steeplands
Hogarth Cres SW19 140 DD95

Hogarth Cres, Croy. 142 DQ101
Hogarth Gdns, Houns. 96 CA80
Hogarth Hill NW11 63 CZ56
Hogarth La W4 98 CS79
Hogarth Pl SW5 100 DB77
Hogarth Rd
Hogarth Reach, Loug. 33 EM43
Hogarth Rd SW5 100 DB77
Hogarth Rd, Dag. 70 EV64
Hogarth Rd, Edg. 42 CN54
Hogarth Roundabout 98 CS79
Hogarth Roundabout W4 98 CS79
Flyover W4
Burlington La
Hogarth Way, Hmptn. 136 CC95
Hogg La, Borwd. 25 CG42
Hogg La, Grays 110 GA76
Hogg La Roundabout, Grays 110 FZ75
Hogpits Bottom, Hem.H. 5 BA32
Hogs La, Grav. 130 GD90
Hogs Orchard, Swan. 147 FH95
Hogscross La, Couls. 174 DF123
Hogshead Pas E1 202 E1
Hogshill La, Cob. 154 BX112
Hogsmill Way, Epsom 156 CQ106
Hogtrough Hill, West. 179 ET120
Hogtrough La, Gdse. 187 EA128
Hogtrough La, Oxt. 187 EB128
Holbeach Gdns, Sid. 125 ES86
Holbeach Ms SW12 121 DH88
Harberson Rd
Holbeach Rd SE6 123 EA87
Holbeck La (Cheshunt), Wal.Cr. 14 DT26
Holbeck Row SE15 102 DU80
Holbein Gate, Nthwd. 39 BS50
Holbein Ms SW1 198 F10
Holbein Ms SW1 100 DG78
Holbein Pl SW1 198 F9
Holbein Pl SW1 100 DG77
Holbein Ter, Dag. 70 EV63
Marlborough Rd
Holberton Gdns NW10 81 CV69
Holborn EC1 196 D7
Holborn EC1 83 DN71
Holborn Circ EC1 196 E7
Holborn Pl WC1 196 B7
Holborn Rd E13 86 EH70
Holborn Viaduct EC1 196 E7
Holborn Viaduct EC1 83 DN71
Holborn Way, Mitch. 140 DF96
Holbreck Pl, Wok. 167 AZ118
Heathside Rd
Holbrook Cl N19 65 DH60
Dartmouth Pk Hill
Holbrook Cl, Enf. 30 DT39
Holbrook La, Chis. 125 ER93
Holbrook Meadow, Egh. 113 BC93
Holbrook Rd E15 86 EF68
Holbrook Way, Brom. 145 EM100
Holbrooke Ct N7 65 DL63
Holbrooke Pl, Rich. 117 CK85
Hill Ri
Holburne Cl SE3 104 EJ81
Holburne Gdns SE3 104 EK81
Holburne Rd SE3 104 EJ81
Holcombe Hill NW7 43 CU48
Highwood Hill
Holcombe Rd N17 66 DT55
Holcombe Rd, Ilf. 69 EN59
Holcombe St W6 99 CV77
Holcon Ct, Red. 184 DG131
Holcote Cl, Belv. 106 EY76
Blakemore Way
Holcroft Rd E9 84 DW66
Holdbrook N, Wal.Cr. 15 DZ34
Eleanor Way
Holdbrook S, Wal.Cr. 15 DZ34
Queens Way
Holdbrook Way, Rom. 52 FM54
Holden Av N12 44 DB50
Holden Av NW9 62 CQ60
Holden Cl, Dag. 70 EV62
Holden Gdns, Brwd. 54 FX50
Holden Pl, Cob. 153 BV114
Holden Pt E15 85 ED65
Waddington Rd
Holden Rd N12 44 DB50
Holden St SW11 100 DG82
Holden Way, Upmin. 73 FR59
Holdenby Rd SE4 123 DY85
Holdenhurst Av N12 44 DB52
Holder Cl N3 44 DB52
Holderness Way SE27 121 DP92
Holdernesse Cl, Islw. 97 CG81
Holdernesse Rd SW17 120 DF90
Holders Hill Av NW4 43 CX54
Holders Hill Circ NW7 43 CY52
Dollis Rd
Holders Hill Cres NW4 43 CX54
Holders Hill Dr NW4 63 CX55
Holders Hill Gdns NW4 43 CY54
Holders Hill Rd NW4 43 CX54
Holders Hill Rd NW7 43 CY53
Holdgate St SE7 104 EK76
Westmoor St
Hole Fm La, Brwd. 53 FU54
Holecroft, Wal.Abb. 16 EE34
Holford Pl WC1 196 C2
Holford Rd NW3 64 DC62
Holford Rd, Grays 111 GK76
Holford Rd, S.le H. 111 GL75
Holford St WC1 196 D2
Holford St WC1 83 DN69
Holgate Av SW11 100 DD83
Holgate Gdns, Dag. 70 FA64
Holgate Rd, Dag. 70 FA64
Holland Av SW20 139 CT95
Holland Av, Sutt. 158 DA109
Holland Cl, Barn. 44 DD45
Holland Cl, Brom. 144 EF103
Holland Cl, Red. 184 DF134
Holland Cl, Rom. 71 FC57
Holland Cl, Stan. 41 CH50
Holland Cres, Oxt. 188 EG133
Holland Dr SE23 123 DY90
Holland Gdns W14 99 CY76
Holland Gdns, Egh. 133 BF96
Holland Gdns, Wat. 24 BW35
Holland Gro SW9 101 DN80
Holland La, Oxt. 188 EG133
Holland Pk W8 99 CZ75
Holland Pk W11 99 CZ75
Holland Pk Av W11 99 CY75
Holland Pk Av, Ilf. 69 ES58
Holland Pk Gdns W14 81 CY74
Holland Pk Ms W11 81 CY74
Holland Pk Rd W14 99 CZ76
Holland Pas N1 84 DQ67
Basire St
Holland Pl W8 100 DB75
Kensington Ch St
Holland Rd E6 87 EM67
Holland Rd E15 86 EE69
Holland Rd NW10 81 CU67
Holland Rd SE25 142 DU99
Holland Rd W14 99 CX75
Holland Rd, Oxt. 188 EG133
Holland Rd, Wem. 79 CK65
Holland St SE1 200 G2
Holland St SE1 83 DP74
Holland St W8 100 DA75
Holland Vil Rd W14 99 CY75
Holland Wk N19 65 DK60
Duncombe Rd
Holland Wk W8 99 CZ75
Holland Wk, Stan. 41 CG50
Holland Way, Brom. 144 EF103
Hollands, The, Felt. 116 BX91
Hollands, The, Wok. 166 AY118
Montgomery Rd
Hollands, The, Wor.Pk. 139 CT102
Hollar Rd N16 66 DT62
Stoke Newington High St
Hollen St W1 195 M8
Hollen St W1 83 DJ72
Holles Cl, Hmptn. 116 CA93
Holles St W1 195 J8
Holles St W1 83 DH72
Holley Rd W3 98 CS75
Hollickwood Av N12 44 DF51
Holliday Sq SW11 100 DD83
Fowler Cl
Hollidge Way, Dag. 89 FB65
Hollies, The E11 68 EG57
Hollies, The N20 44 DD46
Oakleigh Pk N
Hollies, The, Grav. 131 GK93
Hollies, The, Har. 61 CG56
Hollies, The, Hem.H. 5 BA29
Hollies Av, Sid. 125 ET89
Hollies Av, W.Byf. 151 BF113
Hollies Cl SW16 121 DN93
Hollies Cl, Twick. 117 CF89
Hollies Ct, Add. 152 BJ106
Hollies End NW7 43 CV50
Hollies Rd W5 97 CJ77
Hollies Way SW12 120 DG87
Bracken Av
Hollies Way, Pot.B. 12 DC31
Holligrave Rd, Brom. 144 EG95
Hollingbourne Av, Bexh. 106 EZ80
Hollingbourne Gdns W13 79 CH71
Hollingbourne Rd SE24 122 DQ85
Hollingbourne Twr, Orp. 146 EX102
Hollingsworth Rd, Croy. 160 DV107
Hollington Cres, N.Mal. 139 CT100
Hollington Rd E6 87 EM69
Hollington Rd N17 46 DU54
Hollingworth Cl, W.Mol. 136 BZ98
Hollingworth Rd, Orp. 145 EP100
Hollingworth Way, West. 189 ER126
Hollis Pl, Grays 110 GA77
Ward Av
Hollman Gdns SW16 121 DP93
Hollow, The, Wdf.Grn. 48 EF49
Hollow Cotts, Purf. 108 FN78
Hollow Hill La, Iver 75 BB73
Hollow La, Vir.W. 132 AY97
Hollow Wk, Rich. 98 CL80
Kew Rd
Hollow Way La, Amer. 20 AS35
Hollow Way La, Chesh. 20 AS35
Holloway Cl, West Dr. 94 BL78
Holloway Dr, Vir.W. 132 AY98
Holloway Hill, Cher. 133 BC104
Holloway La, Rick. 21 BD36
Holloway La, West Dr. 94 BL79
Holloway Rd E6 87 EM69
Holloway Rd E11 68 EE62
Holloway Rd N7 83 DN65
Holloway Rd N19 65 DK61
Holloway St, Houns. 96 CB83
Hollowfield Av, Grays 110 GD77
Hollowfield Wk, Nthlt. 78 BY65
Hollows, The, Brent. 98 CM79
Kew Br Rd
Holly Av, Add. 152 BG110
Holly Av, Stan. 42 CL54
Holly Av, Walt. 136 BX102
Holly Bk Rd, Wok. 166 AV121
Holly Bush Hill NW3 64 DC63
Holly Bush La, Hmptn. 116 BZ94
Holly Bush La, Sev. 191 FJ123
Holly Bush Steps NW3 64 DC63
Heath St
Holly Bush Vale NW3 64 DC63
Heath St
Holly Cl NW10 80 CS66
Holly Cl, Buck.H. 48 EK48
Holly Cl, Cher. 132 AU104
Holly Cl, Egh. 112 AV93
Holly Cl, Felt. 116 BY92
Holly Cl, Wall. 159 DH108
Holly Cl, Wok. 166 AV119
Holly Cottage Ms, Uxb. 76 BN71
Pield Heath Rd
Holly Cres, Beck. 143 DZ99
Holly Cres, Wdf.Grn. 47 ED52
Holly Dr E4 47 EB45
Holly Dr, Brent. 97 CG79
Holly Dr, Pot.B. 12 DB33
Holly Dr, S.Ock. 91 FX70
Holly Dr, Wind. 112 AS85
Holly Fm Rd, Sthl. 96 BY78
Holly Gdns, West Dr. 94 BM75
Holly Grn, Wey. 135 BR104
Holly Gro NW9 62 CQ59
Holly Gro SE15 102 DT82
Holly Gro, Bushey 41 CD45
Holly Gro, Pnr. 40 BY53
Holly Hedge Ter SE13 123 ED85
Holly Hedges La, Hem.H. 5 BC30
Holly Hedges La, Rick. 5 BC30
Holly Hill N21 29 DM44
Holly Hill NW3 64 DC63
Holly Hill Dr, Bans. 174 DA116
Holly Hill Rd, Belv. 107 FB78
Holly Hill Rd, Erith 107 FB78
Holly Ho, Brwd. 54 FX46
Sawyers Hall La
Holly La, Bans. 174 DA116
Holly La E, Bans. 174 DA116
Holly La W, Bans. 174 DA117
Holly Lo, Tad. 183 CY126
Holly Lo Gdns N6 64 DG61
Holly Ms SW10 100 DC78
Drayton Gdns
Holly Mt NW3 64 DC63
Holly Bush Hill
Holly Pk N3 63 CZ55
Holly Pk N4 65 DM59
Holly Pk Est N4 65 DM59
Blythwood Rd
Holly Pk Gdns N3 64 DA55
Holly Pk Rd N11 44 DG50
Holly Pk Rd W7 79 CF74
Holly Pl NW3 64 DC63
Holly Wk
Holly Rd E11 68 EF59
Holly Rd W4 98 CR77
Dolman Rd
Holly Rd, Dart. 128 FK88
Holly Rd, Enf. 31 DX36
Holly Rd, Hmptn. 116 CC93
Holly Rd, Houns. 96 CB84
Holly Rd, Orp. 164 EU108
Holly Rd, Twick. 117 CG88
Holly St E8 84 DT65
Holly St Est E8 84 DT66
Holly Ter N6 64 DG60
Highgate W Hill
Holly Ter N20 44 DC47
Swan La
Holly Tree Av, Swan. 147 FE96
Holly Tree Cl, Chesh. 4 AV31
Holly Tree Rd, Cat. 176 DS122
Elm Gro
Holly Vw Cl NW4 63 CU58
Holly Village N6 65 DH61
Swains La
Holly Wk NW3 64 DC63
Holly Wk, Enf. 30 DR41
Holly Wk, Rich. 98 CL82
Holly Way, Mitch. 141 DK98
Hollybank Cl, Hmptn. 116 CA92
Hollybank Rd, W.Byf. 152 BG114
Hollyberry La NW3 64 DC63
Holly Wk
Hollybrake Cl, Chis. 125 ER94
Hollybush Cl E11 68 EG57
Hollybush Cl, Har. 41 CE53
Hollybush Cl, Sev. 191 FJ124
Hollybush Cl, Wat. 40 BW45
Hollybush Ct, Sev. 191 FJ124
Hollybush Gdns E2 84 DV69
Hollybush Hill E11 68 EF58
Hollybush Hill, Slou. 74 AU66
Hollybush La, Iver 75 BB72
Hollybush La, Orp. 164 FA107
Hollybush La (Denham), Uxb. 57 BE63
Hollybush La, Wok. 168 BK119
Hollybush Pl E2 84 DV69
Bethnal Grn Rd
Hollybush Rd, Grav. 131 GJ89
Hollybush Rd, Kings.T. 118 CL92
Hollybush St E13 86 EH69
Hollybush Wk SW9 101 DP84
Hollybush Way, Wal.Cr. 14 DU28
Hollycombe, Egh. 112 AW91
Hollycroft Av NW3 64 DA62
Hollycroft Av, Wem. 62 CM61
Hollycroft Cl, S.Croy. 160 DS106
Hollycroft Cl, West Dr. 94 BN79
Hollycroft Gdns, West Dr. 94 BN79
Hollydale Cl, Nthlt. 60 CB63
Dorchester Rd
Hollydale Dr, Brom. 145 EM104
Hollydale Rd SE15 102 DW81
Hollydene SE15 102 DV81
Hollydown Way E11 67 ED62
Hollyfield Av N11 44 DF50
Hollyfield Rd, Surb. 138 CM101
Hollyfields, Brox. 15 DY26
Hollyhedge Rd, Cob. 153 BV114
Hollymead, Cars. 140 DF104
Hollymead Rd, Couls. 174 DG118
Hollymeoak Rd, Couls. 175 DH119
Hollymoor La, Epsom 156 CR110
Hollymount Cl SE10 103 EC81
Hollytree Cl SW19 119 CX88
Hollytree Cl (Chalfont St. Peter), Ger.Cr. 36 AY50
Hollywood Ct, Borwd. 26 CM42
Deacon's Hill Rd
Hollywood Gdns, Hayes 77 BV72
Hollywood Ms SW10 100 DC79
Hollywood Rd
Hollywood Rd E4 47 DY50
Hollywood Rd SW10 100 DC79
Hollywood Way, Erith 107 FH81
Hollywood Way, Wdf.Grn. 47 ED52
Hollywoods, Croy. 161 DZ109
Holm Cl, Add. 151 BE112
Holm Gro, Uxb. 76 BN66
Holm Oak Cl SW15 119 CZ86
West Hill
Holm Oak Ms SW4 121 DL85
King's Av
Holm Wk SE3 104 EG82
Blackheath Pk
Holman Rd SW11 100 DD82
Holman Rd, Epsom 156 CQ106
Holmbank Dr, Shep. 135 BS98
Holmbridge Gdns, Enf. 31 DX42
Holmbrook Dr NW4 63 CX57
Holmbury Ct SW17 120 DF90
Holmbury Ct SW19 120 DE94
Cavendish Rd
Holmbury Gdns, Hayes 77 BT74
Church Rd
Holmbury Gro, Croy. 161 DZ108
Holmbury Pk, Brom. 124 EL94
Holmbury Vw E5 66 DV60
Holmbush Rd SW15 119 CY86
Holmcote Gdns N5 66 DQ64
Holmcroft, Tad. 183 CV125
Holmcroft Way, Brom. 145 EM99
Holmdale Cl, Borwd. 26 CM40
Holmdale Gdns NW4 63 CX57
Holmdale Rd NW6 64 DA64
Holmdale Rd, Chis. 125 EQ92
Holmdale Ter N15 66 DS59
Holmdene Av NW7 43 CU51
Holmdene Av SE24 122 DQ85
Holmdene Av, Har. 60 CB55
Holmdene Cl, Beck. 143 EC96
Holme Chase, Wey. 153 BQ107
Holme Cl (Cheshunt), Wal.Cr. 15 DY31
Holme Lacey Rd SE12 124 EF86
Holme Lea, Wat. 8 BW34
Kingsway
Holme Pk, Borwd. 26 CM40
Holme Rd E6 86 EL67
Holme Rd, Horn. 72 FN60
Holme Way, Stan. 41 CF51
Holmead Rd SW6 100 DB80
Holmebury Cl, Bushey 41 CE47
Holmedale, Slou. 74 AW73
Holmefield Ct NW3 82 DE65
Holmes Av E17 67 DZ55
Holmes Av NW7 43 CY50
Holmes Cl, Wok. 167 AZ121
Holmes Pl SW10 100 DC79
Fulham Rd
Holmes Rd NW5 65 DH64
Holmes Rd SW19 120 DC94
Holmes Rd, Twick. 117 CF89
Holmes Ter SE1 200 D4
Holmes Ter SE1 101 DN75
Holmesdale, Wal.Cr. 31 DX35
Holmesdale Av SW14 98 CP83
Holmesdale Cl SE25 142 DT97
Holmesdale Hill (South Darenth), Dart. 148 FQ95
Holmesdale Rd N6 65 DH59
Holmesdale Rd SE25 142 DR99
Holmesdale Rd, Bexh. 106 EX82
Holmesdale Rd, Croy. 142 DR99
Holmesdale Rd (South Darenth), Dart. 148 FQ95
Holmesdale Rd, Reig. 184 DA133
Holmesdale Rd, Rich. 98 CM81
Holmesdale Rd, Sev. 191 FJ123
Holmesdale Rd, Tedd. 117 CJ93
Holmesley Rd SE23 123 DY86
Holmethorpe Av, Red. 185 DH131
Holmethorpe Ind Est, Red. 185 DH131
Holmethorpe Av
Holmewood Gdns SW2 121 DM87
Holmewood Rd SE25 142 DS97
Holmewood Rd SW2 121 DL87
Holmfield Av NW4 63 CX57
Holmhurst Rd, Belv. 107 FB78
Holmlea Rd, Slou. 92 AX81
Holmlea Wk, Slou. 92 AW81
Holmleigh Av, Dart. 108 FJ84
Holmleigh Rd N16 66 DS60
Holmleigh Rd Est N16 66 DT60
Holmleigh Rd
Holms St E2 84 DU68
Holmsdale Cl, Iver 75 BF72
Holmsdale Gro, Bexh. 107 FE82
Holmshaw Cl SE26 123 DY91
Holmshill La, Borwd. 26 CS36
Holmside Ri, Wat. 39 BV48
Holmside Rd SW12 120 DG86
Holmsley Cl, N.Mal. 139 CT100
Holmstall Av, Edg. 62 CQ55
Holmwood Av, Brwd. 55 GA44
Holmwood Av, S.Croy. 160 DT113
Holmwood Cl, Add. 152 BG106
Holmwood Cl, Har. 60 CC55
Holmwood Cl, Nthlt. 78 CB65
Holmwood Cl, Sutt. 157 CX109
Holmwood Gdns N3 44 DA54
Holmwood Gdns, Wall. 159 DH107
Holmwood Gro NW7 42 CR50
Holmwood Rd, Chess. 155 CK106
Holmwood Rd, Enf. 31 DX36
Holmwood Rd, Ilf. 69 ES61
Holmwood Rd, Sutt. 157 CW110
Holmwood Vil SE7 205 N10
Holne Chase N2 64 DC58
Holne Chase, Mord. 139 CZ100
Holness Rd E15 86 EF65
Holroyd Cl, Esher 155 CF109
Holroyd Rd SW15 99 CW84
Holroyd Rd, Esher 155 CF109
Holstein Av, Wey. 152 BN105
Holstein Way, Erith 106 EY76
Holstock Rd, Ilf. 69 EQ62
Holsworth Cl, Har. 60 CC57
Holsworthy Sq WC1 196 C5
Holsworthy Way, Chess. 155 CJ106
Holt, The, Ilf. 49 EQ51
Holt, The, Wall. 159 DJ105
Holt Cl N10 64 DG56
Holt Cl SE28 88 EV73
Holt Cl, Borwd. 26 CM42
Holt Cl, Chig. 49 ET50
Holt Ct E15 67 EC64
Clays La
Holt Rd E16 86 EL74
Holt Rd, Rom. 52 FL52
Alverstoke Rd
Holt Rd, Wem. 61 CH62
Holt Way, Chig. 49 ET50
Holton St E1 85 DX70
Holtsmere Cl, Wat. 24 BW35
Holtwhite Av, Enf. 30 DQ40
Holtwhites Hill, Enf. 29 DP39
Holtwood Rd, Lthd. 154 CC113
Holwell Pl, Pnr. 60 BY56
Holwood Cl, Walt. 136 BW103
Holwood Pk Av, Orp. 163 EM105
Holwood Pl SW4 101 DK84
Holybourne Av SW15 119 CU87
Holyfield Rd, Wal.Abb. 15 EC29
Holyhead Cl E3 85 EA69
Holyhead Cl E6 87 EM71
Valiant Way
Holyoak Rd SE11 200 F8
Holyoake Av, Wok. 166 AW117
Holyoake Ct SE16 203 L4
Holyoake Cres, Wok. 166 AW117
Holyoake Ter, Sev. 190 FG124
Holyoake Wk N2 64 DC55
Holyoake Wk W5 79 CJ70
Holyport Rd SW6 99 CW80
Holyrood Av, Har. 60 BY63
Holyrood Gdns, Edg. 62 CP55
Holyrood Gdns, Grays 111 GJ77
Holyrood Ms E16 205 N2
Holyrood Rd, Barn. 28 DC44
Holyrood St SE1 201 M3
Holywell Cl SE3 104 EG79
Holywell Cl SE16 202 E10
Holywell Cl, Stai. 114 BL88
Holywell Ind Est, Wat. 23 BR44
Holywell La EC2 197 N4
Holywell La EC2 84 DS70
Holywell Rd, Wat. 23 BU43
Holywell Row EC2 197 M5
Holywell Row EC2 84 DS70
Holywell Way, Stai. 114 BL88
Home Cl, Cars. 140 DF103
Home Cl, Lthd. 171 CD121
Home Cl, Nthlt. 78 BZ69
Home Ct, Felt. 115 BU88
Home Fm Cl, Cher. 151 BA108
Home Fm Cl, Esher 154 CB107
Home Fm Cl, Shep. 135 BS98
Home Fm Cl, Tad. 173 CX117
Home Fm Cl, T.Ditt. 137 CF101
Home Fm Gdns, Walt. 136 BW103
Home Fm Rd, Rick. 38 BN49
Home Fm Way, Slou. 74 AW67
Home Gdns, Dag. 71 FC62
Home Gdns, Dart. 128 FL86
Home Hill, Swan. 127 FF94
Home Lea, Orp. 163 ET106
Home Mead, Stan. 41 CJ53
Home Mead Cl, Grav. 131 GH87
Home Meadow, Bans. 174 DA116
Home Orchard, Dart. 128 FL86
Home Pk, Oxt. 188 EG131
Home Pk Mill Link Rd, Kings L. 7 BP31
Home Pk Rd SW19 120 DA90
Home Pk Wk, Kings.T. 137 CK98
Home Rd SW11 100 DE82
Home Way, Rick. 37 BF46
Homecroft Gdns, Loug. 33 EP42
Homecroft Rd N22 46 DQ53
Homecroft Rd SE26 122 DW92
Homedean Rd, Sev. 190 FC122
Homefarm Rd W7 79 CE72
Homefield, Hem.H. 5 BB28
Homefield, Wal.Abb. 16 EG32
Homefield, Walt. 154 BX105
Homefield Av, Ilf. 69 ES57
Homefield Cl NW10 80 CQ65
Homefield Cl, Add. 151 BE112
Homefield Cl, Epp. 18 EU30
Homefield Cl, Hayes 78 BW70
Homefield Cl, Lthd. 171 CJ121
Homefield Cl, Orp. 146 EV98
Homefield Cl, Swan. 147 FF97
Homefield Fm Rd, Dart. 148 FM96
Homefield Gdns N2 64 DD55
Homefield Gdns, Mitch. 140 DC96
Homefield Gdns, Tad. 173 CW120
Homefield Ms, Beck. 143 EA95
Homefield Pk, Sutt. 158 DB107
Homefield Ri, Orp. 146 EU102
Homefield Rd SW19 119 CX93
Homefield Rd W4 99 CT77
Homefield Rd, Brom. 144 EJ95
Homefield Rd, Bushey 24 CA43
Homefield Rd, Couls. 175 DP119
Homefield Rd, Edg. 42 CR51
Homefield Rd, Rad. 25 CF37
Homefield Rd, Rick. 21 BC42
Green St
Homefield Rd, Sev. 190 FE122
Homefield Rd, Walt. 136 BY101
Homefield Rd, Warl. 176 DW119
Homefield Rd, Wem. 61 CG63
Homefield St N1 197 M1
Homefield St N1 84 DS68
Homeland Dr, Sutt. 158 DB109
Homelands, Lthd. 171 CJ121
Homelands Dr SE19 122 DS94
Homeleigh Ct, Wal.Cr. 14 DV29
Homeleigh Rd SE15 123 DX85
Homemead SW12 121 DJ89
Homemead Rd, Brom. 145 EM99
Homemead Rd, Croy. 141 DJ100
Homer Cl, Bexh. 107 FC81
Homer Dr E14 203 P8
Homer Dr E14 103 EA77
Homer Rd E9 85 DY65
Homer Rd, Croy. 143 DX100
Homer Row W1 194 C7
Homer Row W1 82 DE71
Homer St W1 194 C7
Homer St W1 82 DE71
Homersham Rd, Kings.T. 138 CN96
Homerton Gro E9 67 DX64
Homerton High St E9 66 DW64
Homerton Rd E9 67 DY64
Homerton Row E9 66 DW64
Homerton Ter E9 84 DW65
Morning La
Homesdale Cl E11 68 EG57
Homesdale Rd, Brom. 144 EJ98
Homesdale Rd, Cat. 176 DR123
Homesdale Rd, Orp. 145 ES101
Homesfield NW11 64 DA57
Homestall Rd SE22 122 DW85
Homestead, The N11 45 DH49
Homestead, The, Dart. 128 FJ86
Homestead Cl, St.Alb. 8 CC27
Homestead Gdns, Esher 155 CE106
Homestead Paddock N14 29 DH43
Homestead Pk NW2 63 CT62
Homestead Rd SW6 99 CZ80
Homestead Rd, Cat. 176 DR123
Homestead Rd, Dag. 70 EZ61
Homestead Rd, Orp. 164 EV108

Homestead Rd, Rick. 38 BK45
Park Rd
Homestead Rd, Stai. 114 BH93
Homestead Way, Croy. 161 EC111
Homewaters Av, Sun. 135 BT95
Homeway, Rom. 52 FP51
Homewillow Cl N21 29 DP44
Homewood, Slou. 74 AX72
Homewood Av (Cuffley), Pot.B. 13 DL27
Homewood Cl, Hmptn. 116 BZ93
Fearnley Cres
Homewood Cres, Chis. 125 ES93
Homewood La, Pot.B. 13 DJ27
Homewood Pk, Cher. 151 BC105
Honduras St EC1 197 H4
Honey Brook, Wal.Abb. 16 EE33
Honey Cl, Dag. 89 FB65
Honey Hill, Uxb. 76 BM66
Honey La EC2 197 J9
Honey La, Wal.Abb. 32 EG35
Honeybourne Rd NW6 64 DB64
Honeybourne Way, Orp. 145 ER102
Honeybrook Rd SW12 121 DJ87
Honeycroft, Loug. 33 EN42
Honeycroft Hill, Uxb. 76 BL66
Honeyden Rd, Sid. 126 EY93
Honeyman Cl NW6 81 CX66
Honeypot Cl NW9 62 CM56
Honeypot La NW9 62 CM55
Honeypot La, Brwd. 54 FU48
Honeypot La, Stan. 62 CM55
Honeypots Rd, Wok. 166 AX122
Honeysett Rd N17 46 DT54
Reform Row
Honeysuckle Cl, Brwd. 54 FV43
Honeysuckle Cl, Iver 75 BC72
Honeysuckle Cl, Rom. 52 FK51
Cloudberry Rd
Honeysuckle Cl, Sthl. 78 BY73
Honeysuckle Gdns, Croy. 143 DX102
Primrose La
Honeywell Rd SW11 120 DF86
Honeywood Cl, Pot.B. 12 DE33
Honeywood Rd NW10 81 CT68
Honeywood Rd, Islw. 97 CG84
Honeywood Wk, Cars. 158 DF105
Honister Cl, Stan. 41 CH53
Honister Gdns, Stan. 41 CH52
Honister Hts, Pur. 160 DR114
Honister Pl, Stan. 41 CH53
Honiton Rd NW6 81 CZ68
Honiton Rd, Rom. 71 FD58
Honiton Rd, Well. 105 ET82
Honley Rd SE6 123 EB87
Honnor Gdns, Islw. 96 CC83
London Rd
Honnor Rd, Stai. 114 BK94
Honor Oak Pk SE23 122 DW86
Honor Oak Ri SE23 122 DW86
Honor Oak Rd SE23 122 DW88
Hood Av N14 29 DH44
Hood Av SW14 118 CQ85
Hood Av, Orp. 146 EV99
Hood Cl, Croy. 141 DP102
Parson's Mead
Hood Ct EC4 196 E9
Hood Rd SW20 119 CT94
Hood Rd, Rain. 89 FE67
Hood Wk, Rom. 51 FB53
Hoodcote Gdns N21 45 DP45
Hook, The, Barn. 28 DD44
Hook Fm Rd, Brom. 144 EK99
Hook Gate, Enf. 30 DV36
Hook Grn La, Dart. 127 FF90
Hook Grn Rd, Grav. 130 FY94
Hook Heath Av, Wok. 166 AV119
Hook Heath Gdns, Wok. 166 AT121
Hook Heath Rd, Wok. 166 AW121
Hook Hill, S.Croy. 160 DS110
Hook Hill La, Wok. 166 AV121
Hook Hill Pk, Wok. 166 AV121
Hook La, Pot.B. 12 DF32
Hook La, Rom. 34 EZ44
Hook La, Well. 125 ET85
Hook Ri N, Surb. 138 CN104
Hook Ri S, Surb. 138 CN104
Hook Ri S Ind Pk, Surb. 138 CN104
Hook Rd, Chess. 155 CK106
Hook Rd, Epsom 156 CR111
Hook Rd, Surb. 138 CL104
Hook Wk, Edg. 42 CQ51
Hookers Rd E17 67 DX55
Hookfield, Epsom 156 CQ113
Hookfields, Grav. 130 GE90
Hooking Grn, Har. 60 CB57
Hooks Cl SE15 102 DV81
Woods Rd
Hooks Hall Dr, Dag. 71 FC62
Hooks Way SE22 122 DU88
Dulwich Common
Hookstone Way, Wdf.Grn. 48 EK52
Hookwood Cor, Oxt. 188 EH128
Hookwood La
Hookwood La, Oxt. 188 EH128
Hookwood Rd, Orp. 164 EW111
Hoop La NW11 63 CZ59
Hooper Rd E16 86 EG72
Hooper Sq E1 84 DU73
Hooper St
Hooper St E1 84 DU72
Hooper's Ct SW3 198 D5
Hoopers Yd, Sev. 191 FJ126
Hop Gdns WC2 199 P1
Hope Cl N1 84 DQ65
Wallace Rd
Hope Cl SE12 124 EH90
Hope Cl, Sutt. 158 DC106
Hope Cl, Wdf.Grn. 48 EJ51
West Gro
Hope Grn, Wat. 7 BU33
Hope Pk, Brom. 124 EF94
Hope Rd, Swans. 130 FZ86
Hope St SW11 100 DD83
Hope Ter, Grays 109 FX78
Hope Wf SE16 102 DW75
St. Marychurch St
Hopedale Rd SE7 104 EH79
Hopefield Av NW6 81 CY68
Hopes Cl, Houns. 96 CA79
Old Cote Dr
Hopetown St E1 84 DT71
Brick La
Hopewell Dr, Grav. 131 GM92
Hopewell St SE5 102 DR80
Hopewell Yd SE5 102 DR80
Hopewell St
Hopfield, Wok. 166 AY116
Hopfield Av, W.Byf. 152 BL112
Hopgarden La, Sev. 190 FG128
Hopgood St W12 81 CW74
Macfarlane Rd
Hopkins Cl N10 44 DG52
Cromwell Rd
Hopkins Cl, Rom. 72 FJ55
Hopkins Ms E15 86 EF67
West Rd
Hopkins St W1 195 L9
Hopkinsons Pl NW1 82 DG67
Fitzroy Rd
Hoppers Rd N13 45 DN47
Hoppers Rd N21 45 DN47
Hoppett Rd E4 48 EE48
Hoppety, The, Tad. 173 CX122
Hopping La N1 83 DP65
St. Mary's Gro
Hoppingwood Av, N.Mal. 138 CS97
Hoppit Rd, Wal.Abb. 15 EB32
Hoppner Rd, Hayes 77 BQ68
Hopton Gdns SE1 200 G2
Hopton Gdns SE1 83 DP74
Hopton Gdns, N.Mal. 139 CU100
Hopton Rd SW16 121 DL92
Hopton St SE1 200 G2
Hopton St SE1 83 DP74
Hopwood Cl SW17 120 DC90
Hopwood Cl, Wat. 23 BR36
Hopwood Rd SE17 102 DR79
Hopwood Wk E8 84 DU66
Wilman Gro
Horace Av, Rom. 71 FC60
Horace Rd E7 68 EH63
Horace Rd, Ilf. 69 EQ55
Horace Rd, Kings.T. 138 CM97
Horatio Ct SE16 84 DW74
Rotherhithe St
Horatio Pl E14 204 E3
Horatio Pl SW19 120 DA94
Kingston Rd
Horatio St E2 84 DT68
Horatius Way, Croy. 159 DM106
Horbury Cres W11 82 DA73
Horbury Ms W11 81 CZ73
Ladbroke Rd
Horder Rd SW6 99 CY81
Hordle Prom E SE15 102 DT80
Daniel Gdns
Hordle Prom N SE15 102 DT80
Daniel Gdns
Hordle Prom S SE15 102 DT80
Pentridge St
Hordle Prom W SE15 102 DS80
Diamond St
Horizon Way SE7 104 EH77
Horksley Gdns, Brwd. 55 GC44
Bannister Dr
Horle Wk SE5 101 DP82
Lilford Rd
Horley Cl, Bexh. 126 FA85
Horley Rd SE9 124 EL91
Hormead Rd W9 81 CZ70
Horn La SE10 205 M9
Horn La SE10 104 EG77
Horn La W3 80 CQ73
Horn La, Wdf.Grn. 48 EG51
Horn Link Way SE10 205 M8
Horn Link Way SE10 104 EG77
Horn Pk Cl SE12 124 EH85
Horn Pk La SE12 124 EH85
Hornbeam Av, Upmin. 72 FN63
Hornbeam Chase, S.Ock. 91 FX69
Hornbeam Cl NW7 43 CT48
Marsh La
Hornbeam Cl SE11 200 D8
Hornbeam Cl, Borwd. 26 CN39
Hornbeam Cl, Brwd. 55 GB48
Hornbeam Cl, Buck.H. 48 EK48
Hornbeam Rd
Hornbeam Cl, Epp. 33 ES37
Hornbeam Cl, Ilf. 69 ER64
Hornbeam Cl, Nthlt. 60 BZ64
Hornbeam Cres, Brent. 97 CH80
Hornbeam Gdns, Slou. 92 AU76
Upton Rd
Hornbeam Gro E4 48 EE48
Hornbeam La E4 32 EE43
Hornbeam La, Bexh. 107 FC82
Hornbeam Rd, Buck.H. 48 EK48
Hornbeam Rd, Epp. 33 ER37
Hornbeam Rd, Hayes 78 BW71
Hornbeam Ter, Cars. 140 DE102
Hornbeam Twr E11 67 ED62
Hollydown Way
Hornbeam Wk, Rich. 118 CM90
Hornbeam Wk, Walt. 153 BT109
Octagon Rd
Hornbeam Way, Brom. 145 EN100
Hornbeam Way, Wal.Cr. 14 DT29
Hornbeams, St.Alb. 8 BZ30
Hornbeams Av, Enf. 30 DW35
Hornbeams Ri N11 44 DG51
Hornbill Cl, Uxb. 76 BK72
Hornblower Cl SE16 203 K8
Hornbuckle Cl, Har. 61 CD61
Hornby Cl NW3 82 DD66
Horncastle Cl SE12 124 EG87
Horncastle Rd SE12 124 EG87
Hornchurch Cl, Kings.T. 117 CK91
Hornchurch Hill, Whyt. 176 DT117
Hornchurch Rd, Horn. 71 FG60
Horndean Cl SW15 119 CU88
Bessborough Rd
Horndon Cl, Rom. 51 FC53
Horndon Grn, Rom. 51 FC53
Horndon Rd, Rom. 51 FC54
Horne Rd, Shep. 134 BN98
Horne Way SW15 99 CW82
Horner La, Mitch. 140 DD96
Hornets, The, Wat. 23 BV42
Hornfair Rd SE7 104 EJ79
Hornford Way, Rom. 71 FE59
Hornhill Rd, Ger.Cr. 37 BB50
Hornhill Rd, Rick. 37 BD50
Horniman Dr SE23 122 DV88
Horning Cl SE9 124 EL91
Hornminster Glen, Horn. 72 FN61
Horns End Pl, Pnr. 60 BW56
Horns Rd, Ilf. 69 EQ58
Hornsby La, Grays 111 GG75
Hornsey La N6 65 DH60
Hornsey La N19 65 DJ59
Hornsey La Est N19 65 DK59
Hornsey La
Hornsey La Gdns N6 65 DJ59
Hornsey Pk Rd N8 65 DM55
Hornsey Ri N19 65 DK59
Hornsey Ri Gdns N19 65 DK59
Hornsey Rd N7 65 DL61
Hornsey Rd N19 65 DL61
Hornsey St N7 65 DM64
Hornshay St SE15 102 DW79
Hornton Pl W8 100 DA75
Hornton St W8 100 DA75
Horsa Cl, Wall. 159 DL108
Horsa Rd SE12 124 EJ87
Horsa Rd, Erith 107 FC80
Horse & Dolphin Yd W1 195 N10
Horse Fair, Kings.T. 137 CK96
Horse Guards Av SW1 199 P3
Horse Guards Av SW1 83 DL74
Horse Guards Rd SW1 199 N3
Horse Guards Rd SW1 83 DK74
Horse Hill, Chesh. 4 AX32
Horse Leaze E6 87 EN72
Horse Ride SW1 199 M3
Horse Ride SW1 83 DJ74
Horse Ride, Tad. 183 CY125
Horse Rd E7 68 EH62
Centre Rd
Horse Shoe Cres, Nthlt. 78 CA68
Horse Shoe Grn, Sutt. 140 DB103
Aultone Way
Horse Yd N1 83 DP67
Essex Rd
Horsebridge Cl, Dag. 88 EY67
Horsecroft, Bans. 173 CZ117
Lyme Regis Rd
Horsecroft Cl, Orp. 146 EV102
Horsecroft Rd, Edg. 42 CR52
Horseferry Pl SE10 103 EC79
Horseferry Rd E14 85 DY73
Horseferry Rd SW1 199 M7
Horseferry Rd SW1 101 DK77
Horsell Birch, Wok. 166 AV115
Horsell Common, Wok. 150 AX114
Horsell Common Rd, Wok. 150 AW114
Horsell Ct, Cher. 134 BH101
Stepgates
Horsell Moor, Wok. 166 AX117
Horsell Pk, Wok. 166 AX116
Horsell Pk Cl, Wok. 166 AX116
Horsell Ri, Wok. 166 AX115
Horsell Ri Cl, Wok. 166 AX115
Horsell Rd N5 65 DN64
Horsell Rd, Orp. 146 EV95
Horsell Vale, Wok. 166 AY115
Horsell Way, Wok. 166 AW116
Horselydown La SE1 201 P4
Horselydown La SE1 102 DT75
Horseman Side, Brwd. 51 FH45
Horsemans Ride, St.Alb. 8 CA26
Horsemoor Cl, Slou. 93 BA77
Parlaunt Rd
Horsenden Av, Grnf. 61 CE64
Horsenden Cres, Grnf. 61 CF64
Horsenden La N, Grnf. 79 CF65
Horsenden La S, Grnf. 79 CG68
Horseshoe, The, Bans. 173 CZ115
Horseshoe, The, Couls. 159 DK113
Horseshoe Cl E14 204 D10
Horseshoe Cl NW2 63 CV61
Horseshoe Cl, Wal.Abb. 16 EG34
Horseshoe Dr, Uxb. 76 BN72
Horseshoe Hill, Wal.Abb. 16 EJ33
Horseshoe La N20 43 CX46
Horseshoe La, Enf. 30 DQ41
Chase Side
Horseshoe La, Wat. 7 BV32
Horseshoe Ridge, Wey. 153 BQ111
Horsfeld Gdns SE9 124 EL85
Horsfeld Rd SE9 124 EK85
Horsfield Cl, Dart. 128 FQ87
Horsford Rd SW2 121 DM85
Horsham Av N12 44 DE50
Horsham Rd, Bexh. 126 FA85
Horsham Rd, Felt. 115 BQ86
Horsley Cl, Epsom 156 CR113
Horsley Dr, Croy. 161 EC108
Horsley Dr, Kings.T. 117 CK92
Horsley Rd E4 47 EC47
Horsley Rd, Brom. 144 EH95
Palace Rd
Horsley Rd, Cob. 169 BV119
Horsley St SE17 102 DR79
Horsleys, Rick. 37 BD50
Horsmonden Cl, Orp. 145 ES101
Horsmonden Rd SE4 123 DZ85
Hortensia Rd SW10 100 DC80
Horticultural Pl W4 98 CR78
Heathfield Ter
Horton Av NW2 63 CY63
Horton Br Rd, West Dr. 76 BM74
Horton Cl, West Dr. 76 BM74
Horton Footpath, Epsom 156 CQ111
Horton Gdns, Epsom 156 CQ111
Horton Hill
Horton Hill, Epsom 156 CQ111
Horton Ind Pk, West Dr. 76 BM74
Horton La, Epsom 156 CP110
Horton Rd E8 84 DV65
Horton Rd (Horton Kirby), Dart. 148 FQ97
Horton Rd, Slou. 93 BA81
Horton Rd (Datchet), Slou. 92 AW81
Horton Rd (Poyle), Slou. 93 BE83
Horton Rd, Stai. 114 BG85
Horton Rd, West Dr. 76 BN74
Horton St SE13 103 EB83
Horton Way, Croy. 143 DX99
Horton Way (Farningham), Dart. 148 FM101
Hortons Way, West. 189 ER126
Hortus Rd E4 47 EC47
Hortus Rd, Sthl. 96 BZ75
Horvath Cl, Wey. 153 BR105
Horwood Cl, Rick. 38 BG45
Thellusson Way
Horwood Ct, Wat. 24 BX37
Hosack Rd SW17 120 DF89
Hoser Av SE12 124 EG89
Hosey Common La, West. 189 ES130
Hosey Common Rd, Eden. 189 EQ133
Hosey Common Rd, West. 189 ER130
Hosey Hill, West. 189 ER127
Hosier La EC1 196 F7
Hosier La EC1 83 DP71
Hoskins Cl E16 86 EJ72
Hoskins Cl, Hayes 95 BT78
Cranford Dr
Hoskins Rd, Oxt. 188 EE129
Hoskins St SE10 103 ED78
Hoskins Wk, Oxt. 188 EE129
Hospital Br Rd, Twick. 116 CB87
Hospital Rd E9 67 DX64
Homerton Row
Hospital Rd, Houns. 96 CA83
Hospital Rd, Sev. 191 FJ121
Hotham Cl (Sutton at Hone), Dart. 128 FP94
Hotham Cl, Swan. 147 FH95
Hotham Cl, W.Mol. 136 CA97
Garrick Gdns
Hotham Rd SW15 99 CW83
Hotham Rd SW19 120 DC94
Hotham Rd Ms SW19 120 DC94
Haydons Rd
Hotham St E15 86 EE67
Hothfield Pl SE16 202 G7
Hotspur Rd, Nthlt. 78 CA68
Hotspur St SE11 200 D10
Hotspur St SE11 101 DN78
Houblon Rd, Rich. 118 CL85
Houblons Hill, Epp. 18 EW31
Houghton Cl E8 84 DT65
Buttermere Wk
Houghton Cl, Hmptn. 116 BY93
Houghton Rd N15 66 DT57
West Grn Rd
Houghton St WC2 196 C9
Houlder Cres, Croy. 159 DP107
Houndsden Rd N21 29 DM44
Houndsditch EC3 197 N8
Houndsditch EC3 84 DS72
Houndsfield Rd N9 46 DV45
Hounslow Av, Houns. 116 CB85
Hounslow Gdns, Houns. 116 CB85
Hounslow Rd (Feltham), Felt. 115 BV88
Hounslow Rd (Hanworth), Felt. 116 BX91
Hounslow Rd, Twick. 116 CC86
Houseman Way SE5 102 DR80
Hopewell St
Houston Pl, Esher 137 CE102
Lime Tree Av
Houston Rd SE23 123 DY89
Houston Rd, Surb. 137 CH100
Hove Av E17 67 DZ57
Hove Cl, Brwd. 55 GC47
Hove Gdns, Sutt. 140 DB102
Hoveden Rd NW2 63 CY64
Hoveton Rd SE28 88 EW72
How La, Couls. 174 DG117
How Wd, St.Alb. 8 CB28
Howard Agne Cl, Hem.H. 5 BA27
Howard Av, Bex. 126 EW88
Howard Av, Epsom 157 CU110
Howard Business Pk, Wal.Abb. 15 ED33
Howard Cl
Howard Cl N11 44 DG47
Howard Cl NW2 63 CY63
Howard Cl W3 80 CP72
Howard Cl, Ash. 172 CM118
Howard Cl, Bushey 41 CE45
Howard Cl, Hmptn. 116 CC93
Howard Cl, Lthd. 171 CJ123
Windmill Dr
Howard Cl, Loug. 32 EL44
Howard Cl, Sun. 115 BT93
Catherine Dr
Howard Cl, Tad. 183 CT125
Howard Cl, Wal.Abb. 15 ED34
Howard Cl, Wat. 23 BU37
Howard Ct, Reig. 184 DC133
Howard Dr, Borwd. 26 CR42
Howard Ms N5 65 DP63
Hamilton Pk
Howard Pl SW1 199 K7
Howard Pl, Reig. 184 DA132
Howard Rd E6 87 EM68
Howard Rd E11 68 EE62
Howard Rd E17 67 EA55
Howard Rd N15 66 DS58
Howard Rd N16 66 DR63
Howard Rd NW2 63 CX63
Howard Rd SE20 142 DW95
Howard Rd SE25 142 DU99
Howard Rd, Bark. 87 ER67
Howard Rd, Brom. 124 EG94
Howard Rd, Couls. 175 DJ115
Howard Rd, Dart. 128 FN86
Howard Rd, Grays 109 FW76
Howard Rd, Ilf. 69 EP63
Howard Rd, Islw. 97 CF83
Howard Rd, Lthd. 169 BU122
Howard Rd, N.Mal. 138 CS97
Howard Rd, Sthl. 78 CB72
Howard Rd, Surb. 138 CM100
Howard Rd, Upmin. 72 FQ61
Howard St, T.Ditt. 137 CH101
Howard Wk N2 64 DC56
Howard Way, Barn. 27 CX43
Howards Cl, Pnr. 39 BV54
Howards Cl, Wok. 167 BA120
Howards Crest Cl, Beck. 143 EC96
Howards La SW15 99 CV84
Howards La, Add. 151 BE10
Howards Rd E13 86 EG6
Howards Rd, Wok. 167 AZ12
Howards Thicket, Ger.Cr. 56 AW6
Howards Wd Dr, Ger.Cr. 56 AX6
Howarth Ct E15 67 EC6
Clays La
Howarth Rd SE2 106 EU7
Howberry Cl, Edg. 41 CK5
Howberry Rd, Edg. 41 CK5
Howberry Rd, Stan. 41 CK5
Howberry Rd, Th.Hth. 142 DR9
Howbury La, Erith 107 FG8
Howbury Rd SE15 102 DW8
Howcroft Cres N3 44 DA5
Howcroft La, Grnf. 79 CD6
Cowgate Rd
Howden Cl SE28 88 EX7
Howden Rd SE25 142 DT9
Howden St SE15 102 DU8
Howe Cl, Rad. 10 CL3
Howe Cl, Rom. 50 FA5
Howe Dr, Cat. 176 DR12
Yorke Gate Rd
Howell Cl, Rom. 70 EX5
Howell Hill Cl, Epsom 157 CW11
Howell Hill Gro, Epsom 157 CW11
Howell Wk SE1 200 G
Howes Cl N3 64 DA5
Howes Rd, Wal.Abb. 31 EC4
Sewardstone Rd
Howfield Pl N17 66 DT5
Howgate Rd SW14 98 CR8
Howick Pl SW1 199 L7
Howick Pl SW1 101 DJ76
Howie St SW11 100 DE80
Howitt Cl NW3 82 DE65
Howitt Rd
Howitt Rd NW3 82 DE65
Howitts Cl, Esher 154 CA107
Howland Est SE16 202 G6
Howland Est SE16 102 DW76
Howland Ms E W1 195 L6
Howland St W1 195 K6
Howland St W1 83 DJ71
Howland Way SE16 203 L5
Howland Way SE16 103 DY75
Howletts La, Ruis. 59 BQ57
Howletts Rd SE24 122 DQ86
Howley Pl W2 82 DC71
Howley Rd, Croy. 141 DP104
Hows Cl, Uxb. 76 BJ67
Hows Rd
Hows Rd, Uxb. 76 BJ67
Hows St E2 84 DT68
Howsman Rd SW13 99 CU79
Howson Rd SE4 103 DY84
Howson Ter, Rich. 118 CL86
Howton Pl, Bushey 41 CD46
Hoxton Mkt N1 197 M3
Hoxton Sq N1 197 M3
Hoxton Sq N1 84 DS69
Hoxton St N1 197 N3
Hoxton St N1 84 DS67
Hoy St E16 86 EF72
Hoy Ter, Grays 109 FX78
Hoylake Cres (Ickenham), Uxb. 59 BP61
Hoylake Gdns, Mitch. 141 DJ97
Hoylake Gdns, Rom. 52 FN53
Hoylake Gdns, Ruis. 59 BV60
Hoylake Gdns, Wat. 40 BX49
Hoylake Rd W3 80 CS72
Hoyland Cl SE15 102 DV80
Commercial Way
Hoyle Rd SW17 120 DE92
Hubbard Dr, Chess. 155 CJ107
Hubbard Rd SE27 122 DQ91
Hubbard St E15 86 EE67
Hubbards Chase, Horn. 72 FN57
Hubbards Cl, Horn. 72 FN57
Hubbards Cl, Uxb. 76 BM72
West Drayton Rd
Hubbards Rd, Rick. 21 BD43
Hubbinet Ind Est, Rom. 71 FC55
Hubert Gro SW9 101 DL83
Hubert Rd E6 86 EK69
Hubert Rd, Brwd. 54 FV48
Hubert Rd, Rain. 89 FF69
Hubert Rd, Slou. 92 AX76
Hucknall Cl, Rom. 52 FM51
Huddart St E3 85 EA71
Huddleston Cl E2 84 DW68
Huddleston Rd N7 65 DK63
Huddlestone Cres, Red. 185 DK128
Huddlestone Rd E7 68 EF63
Huddlestone Rd NW2 81 CV65
Hudons Cl, Grays 109 FT78
Hudson Av (Denham), Uxb. 57 BF58
Hudson Cl, Wat. 23 BT36
Hudson Ct E14 103 EA78
Napier Av
Hudson Ct SW19 120 DB94
Hudson Gdns, Orp. 163 ET107
Superior Dr
Hudson Pl SE18 105 EQ78
Hudson Rd, Bexh. 106 EZ82
Hudson Rd, Hayes 95 BR79
Hudsons, Tad. 173 CX121
Hudson's Pl SW1 199 J8
Huggin Ct EC4 197 J10
Huggin Hill EC4 197 J10
Huggins Pl SW2 121 DM88
Roupell Rd
Hugh Dalton Av SW6 99 CZ79
Hugh Gaitskell Cl SW6 99 CZ79
Hugh Ms SW1 199 J9
Hugh Pl SW1 199 M8
Hugh St SW1 199 J9
Hugh St SW1 101 DH77
Hughan Rd E15 67 ED64
Hughenden Av, Har. 61 CH57
Hughenden Gdns, Nthlt. 78 BW69
Hughenden Rd, Wor.Pk. 139 CU101
Hughenden Ter E15 67 EC63
Westdown Rd
Hughes Rd, Ashf. 115 BQ94
Hughes Rd, Grays 111 GG76
Hughes Rd, Hayes 77 BV73
Hughes Wk, Croy. 142 DQ101
St. Saviours Rd
Hugo Gdns, Rain. 89 FG65

Hugo Gryn Way, Rad. 10 CL31
Farm Cl
Hugo Rd N19 65 DJ63
Hugon Rd SW6 100 DB83
Huguenot Pl E1 84 DT71
Huguenot Pl SW18 120 DC85
Huguenot Sq SE15 102 DV83
Scylla Rd
Hull Cl SE16 203 J4
Hull Cl SE16 103 DX75
Hull Cl, Sutt. 158 DB110
Yarbridge Cl
Hull Cl (Cheshunt), Wal.Cr. 14 DR26
Hammondstreet Rd
Hull Pl E16 105 EP75
Barge Ho Rd
Hull St EC1 197 H3
Hullbridge Ms N1 84 DR67
Sherborne St
Hulletts La, Brwd. 54 FS41
Hulse Av, Bark. 87 ER65
Hulse Av, Rom. 51 FB53
Hulse Ter, Ilf. 69 EQ64
Buttsbury Rd
Hulsewood Cl, Dart. 127 FH90
Hulton Cl, Lthd. 171 CJ123
Windmill Dr
Hulverston Cl, Sutt. 158 DB110
Humber Av, S.Ock. 91 FT72
Humber Cl, West Dr. 76 BK74
Humber Dr W10 81 CX70
Humber Dr, Upmin. 73 FR58
Humber Rd NW2 63 CV61
Humber Rd SE3 104 EF79
Humber Rd, Dart. 128 FK85
Humber Way, Slou. 93 BA77
Humberstone Rd E13 86 EJ69
Humberton Cl E9 67 DY64
Marsh Hill
Humbolt Rd W6 99 CY79
Hume Av, Til. 111 GG83
Hume Ter E16 86 EJ72
Prince Regent La
Hume Way, Ruis. 59 BU58
Humes Av W7 97 CE76
Hummer Rd, Egh. 113 BA91
Humphrey Cl, Ilf. 49 EM53
Humphrey Cl, Lthd. 170 CC122
Humphrey St SE1 201 P10
Humphrey St SE1 102 DT78
Humphries Cl, Dag. 70 EZ63
Hundred Acre NW9 43 CT54
Hungerdown E4 47 EC46
Hungerford Av, Slou. 74 AS71
Hungerford Br SE1 200 A2
Hungerford Br SE1 83 DL74
Hungerford Br WC2 200 A2
Hungerford Br WC2 83 DL74
Hungerford La WC2 199 P2
Hungerford Rd N7 65 DL64
Hungerford Sq, Wey. 153 BR105
Rosslyn Pk
Hungerford St E1 84 DV72
Commercial Rd
Hungry Hill, Wok. 168 BK124
Hungry Hill La
Hungry Hill La, Wok. 168 BK124
Hunsdon Cl, Dag. 88 EY65
Hunsdon Dr, Sev. 191 FH123
Hunsdon Rd SE14 103 DX79
Hunslett St E2 84 DW68
Royston St
Hunstanton Cl, Slou. 93 BC80
Hunston Rd, Mord. 140 DB102
Hunt Rd, Grav. 130 GE90
Hunt Rd, Sthl. 96 CA76
Hunt St W11 81 CX74
Hunt Way SE22 122 DU88
Dulwich Common
Hunter Av, Brwd. 55 GA44
Hunter Cl SE1 201 L7
Hunter Cl SW12 120 DG88
Balham Pk Rd
Hunter Cl, Borwd. 26 CQ43
Hunter Cl, Pot.B. 12 DB33
Hunter Dr, Horn. 72 FJ63
Hunter Ho, Felt. 115 BU88
Hunter Rd SW20 139 CW95
Hunter Rd, Ilf. 69 EP64
Hunter Rd, Th.Hth. 142 DR97
Hunter St WC1 196 A4
Hunter St WC1 83 DL70
Hunter Wk E13 86 EG68
Hunter Wk, Borwd. 26 CQ43
Ashley Dr
Huntercrombe Gdns, Wat. 40 BW49
Hunters, The, Beck. 143 EC95
Hunters Cl, Bex. 127 FE90
Hunters Cl, Epsom 156 CQ113
Marshalls Cl
Hunters Cl, Hem.H. 5 BA29
Hunters Ct, Rich. 117 CK85
Friars La
Hunters Gro, Har. 61 CJ56
Hunters Gro, Hayes 77 BU74
Hunters Gro, Orp. 163 EP105
Hunters Gro, Rom. 51 FB50
Hunters Hall Rd, Dag. 70 FA63
Hunters Hill, Ruis. 60 BW62
Hunters La, Wat. 7 BT33
Hunters Meadow SE19 122 DS91
Dulwich Wd Av
Hunters Reach, Wal.Cr. 14 DT29
Hunters Ride, St.Alb. 8 CA31
Hunters Rd, Chess. 138 CL104
Hunters Sq, Dag. 70 FA63
Hunters Wk, Sev. 164 EY114
Hunters Way, Croy. 160 DS105
Brownlow Rd
Hunters Way, Enf. 29 DN39
Huntersfield Cl, Reig. 184 DB131
Hunting Cl, Esher 154 CA105
Hunting Gate Cl, Enf. 29 DN41
Hunting Gate Dr, Chess. 156 CL108
Hunting Gate Ms, Sutt. 140 DB104
Hunting Gate Ms, Twick. 117 CE88
Colne Rd
Huntingdon Cl, Mitch. 141 DL97
Huntingdon Gdns W4 98 CQ80
Huntingdon Gdns, Wor.Pk. 139 CW104
Huntingdon Rd N2 64 DE55
Huntingdon Rd N9 46 DW46
Huntingdon Rd, Red. 184 DF134
Huntingdon Rd, Wok. 166 AT117
Huntingdon St E16 86 EF72
Huntingdon St N1 83 DM66
Huntingfield, Croy. 161 DZ108
Huntingfield Rd SW15 119 CU85
Huntingfield Way, Egh. 113 BD94
Huntings Rd, Dag. 88 FA65
Huntland Cl, Rain. 89 FH71
Huntley Av, Grav. 130 GB86
Huntley Dr N3 44 DA51
Huntley St WC1 195 L5
Huntley St WC1 83 DJ70
Huntley Way SW20 139 CU96
Huntly Rd SE25 142 DS98
Hunton Br Hill, Kings L. 7 BQ33
Hunton St E1 84 DU70
Hunt's Cl SE3 104 EG82
Hunt's Ct WC2 199 N1
Hunts La E15 85 EC68
Hunts Mead, Enf. 31 DX41
Hunts Mead Cl, Chis. 125 EM94
Hunts Slip Rd SE21 122 DS90
Huntsman Cl, Warl. 176 DW119
Huntsman Rd, Ilf. 50 EU51
Huntsman St SE17 201 L9
Huntsman St SE17 102 DR77
Huntsmans Cl, Felt. 115 BV91
Huntsmans Cl, Lthd. 171 CD124
The Grn
Huntsmans Dr, Upmin. 72 FQ64
Huntsmoor Rd, Epsom 156 CR106
Huntspill St SW17 120 DC90
Huntsworth Ms NW1 194 D5
Hurdwick Pl NW1 83 DJ68
Harrington Sq
Hurley Cl, Walt. 135 BV103
Hurley Cres SE16 203 J4
Hurley Rd SE11 200 E9
Hurley Rd SE11 101 DN77
Hurley Rd, Grnf. 78 CB72
Hurlfield, Dart. 128 FJ90
Hurlford, Wok. 166 AU117
Hurlingham Ct SW6 99 CZ83
Hurlingham Gdns SW6 99 CZ83
Hurlingham Rd SW6 99 CZ82
Hurlingham Rd, Bexh. 106 EZ80
Hurlingham Sq SW6 100 DB83
Peterborough Rd
Hurlock St N5 65 DP62
Hurlstone Rd SE25 142 DR99
Hurn Ct Rd, Houns. 96 BX82
Renfrew Rd
Hurnford Cl, S.Croy. 160 DS110
Huron Cl, Orp. 163 ET107
Winnipeg Dr
Huron Rd SW17 120 DG89
Hurren Cl SE3 104 EE83
Hurricane Way, Abb.L. 7 BU32
Abbey Dr
Hurricane Way, Epp. 18 EZ27
Hurricane Way, Slou. 93 BB79
Sutton La
Hurry Cl E15 86 EE66
Hursley Rd, Chig. 49 ET50
Tufter Rd
Hurst Av E4 47 EA49
Hurst Av N6 65 DJ58
Hurst Cl E4 47 EA48
Hurst Cl NW11 64 DB58
Hurst Cl, Brom. 144 EF102
Hurst Cl, Chess. 156 CN106
Hurst Cl, Nthlt. 60 BZ64
Hurst Cl, Wok. 166 AW120
Hurst Dr, Tad. 183 CU126
Hurst Dr, Wal.Cr. 15 DX34
Hurst Est SE2 106 EX78
Hurst Grn Cl, Oxt. 188 EG132
Hurst Grn Rd, Oxt. 188 EF132
Hurst Gro, Walt. 135 BT102
Hurst La SE2 106 EX78
Hurst La, E.Mol. 136 CC98
Hurst La, Egh. 133 BA96
Hurst La, Epsom 172 CQ124
Hurst Pk Av, Horn. 72 FL63
Newmarket Way
Hurst Pl, Nthwd. 39 BP53
Hurst Ri, Barn. 28 DA41
Hurst Rd E17 67 EB55
Hurst Rd N21 45 DN46
Hurst Rd, Bex. 126 EX88
Hurst Rd, Buck.H. 48 EK46
Hurst Rd, Croy. 160 DR106
Hurst Rd, E.Mol. 136 CB97
Hurst Rd, Epsom 156 CR111
Hurst Rd (Headley), Epsom 172 CR123
Hurst Rd, Erith 107 FC80
Hurst Rd, Sid. 126 EU89
Hurst Rd, Tad. 172 CR123
Hurst Rd, Walt. 136 BW99
Hurst Rd, W.Mol. 136 BY97
Hurst Springs, Bex. 126 EY88
Hurst St SE24 121 DP86
Hurst Vw Rd, S.Croy. 160 DS108
Hurst Way, Sev. 191 FJ127
Hurst Way, S.Croy. 160 DS107
Hurst Way, Wok. 151 BE114
Hurstbourne, Esher 155 CF107
Hurstbourne Gdns, Bark. 87 ES65
Hurstbourne Rd SE23 123 DY88
Hurstcourt Rd, Sutt. 140 DB103
Hurstdene Av, Brom. 144 EF102
Hurstdene Av, Stai. 114 BH93
Hurstdene Gdns N15 66 DS59
Hurstfield, Brom. 144 EG99
Hurstfield Cres, Hayes 77 BS70
Hurstfield Rd, W.Mol. 136 CA97
Hurstlands, Oxt. 188 EG132
Hurstlands Cl, Horn. 72 FJ59
Hurstleigh Cl, Red. 184 DF132
Hurstleigh Dr, Red. 184 DF132
Hurstleigh Gdns, Ilf. 49 EM53
Hurstmead Ct, Edg. 42 CP49
Hurstway Wk W11 81 CX73
Hurstwood Av E18 68 EH56
Hurstwood Av, Bex. 126 EY88
Hurstwood Av, Bexh. 107 FE81
Hurstwood Av, Brwd. 54 FV45
Ongar Rd
Hurstwood Av, Erith 107 FE81
Hurstwood Ct, Upmin. 72 FQ60
Hurstwood Dr, Brom. 145 EM97
Hurstwood Rd NW11 63 CY56
Hurtwood Rd, Walt. 136 BZ101
Hurworth Rd, Slou. 92 AW76
Huson Cl NW3 82 DE66
Hussars Cl, Houns. 96 BY83
Husseywell Cres, Brom. 144 EG102
Hutchings St E14 203 P5
Hutchings St E14 103 EA75
Hutchings Wk NW11 64 DB56
Hutchingsons Rd, Croy. 161 EC111
Hutchins Cl E15 85 EC66
Gibbins Rd
Hutchins Cl, Horn. 72 FL62
Hutchins Rd SE28 88 EU73
Hutchinson Ter, Wem. 61 CK62
Hutton Cl, Grnf. 61 CD64
Mary Peters Dr
Hutton Cl, Wdf.Grn. 48 EH51
Hutton Dr, Brwd. 55 GD45
Hutton Gdns, Har. 40 CC52
Hutton Gate, Brwd. 55 GB45
Hutton Gro N12 44 DB50
Hutton La, Har. 40 CC52
Hutton Rd, Brwd. 55 FZ45
Hutton Row, Edg. 42 CQ52
Pavilion Way
Hutton St EC4 196 E9
Hutton Village, Brwd. 55 GE45
Hutton Wk, Har. 40 CC52
Huxbear St SE4 123 DZ85
Huxley Cl, Nthlt. 78 BY67
Huxley Cl, Uxb. 76 BK70
Huxley Dr, Rom. 70 EV59
Huxley Gdns NW10 80 CM69
Huxley Par N18 46 DR50
Huxley Pl N13 45 DP49
Huxley Rd E10 67 EC61
Huxley Rd N18 46 DR49
Huxley Rd, Well. 105 ET83
Huxley Sayze N18 46 DR50
Huxley St W10 81 CY69
Hyacinth Cl, Hmptn. 116 CA93
Gresham Rd
Hyacinth Cl, Ilf. 87 EP65
Hyacinth Ct, Pnr. 60 BW55
Tulip Ct
Hyacinth Dr, Uxb. 76 BL66
Hyacinth Rd SW15 119 CU88
Hyburn Cl, St.Alb. 8 BZ30
Hycliffe Gdns, Chig. 49 EQ49
Hyde, The NW9 62 CS57
Hyde Av, Pot.B. 12 DB33
Hyde Cl E13 86 EG68
Hyde Cl, Ashf. 115 BS93
Hyde Ter
Hyde Cl, Barn. 27 CZ41
Hyde Cl (Chafford Hundred), Grays 109 FX76
Hyde Ct N20 44 DD48
Hyde Ct, Wal.Cr. 15 DY34
Parkside
Hyde Cres NW9 62 CS57
Hyde Dr, Orp. 146 EV98
Hyde Est Rd NW9 63 CT57
Hyde Ho NW9 62 CS57
Hyde La SW11 100 DE81
Battersea Br Rd
Hyde La, Hem.H. 7 BR26
Hyde La (Bovingdon), Hem.H. 5 BA27
Hyde La, St.Alb. 9 CE28
Hyde La, Wok. 168 BN120
Hyde Meadows, Hem.H. 5 BA28
Hyde Pk SW7 198 B2
Hyde Pk SW7 82 DF74
Hyde Pk W1 198 B2
Hyde Pk W1 82 DF74
Hyde Pk W2 198 B2
Hyde Pk W2 82 DF74
Hyde Pk Av N21 46 DQ47
Hyde Pk Cor W1 198 G4
Hyde Pk Cor W1 100 DG75
Hyde Pk Cres W2 194 B9
Hyde Pk Cres W2 82 DE72
Hyde Pk Gdns N21 46 DQ46
Hyde Pk Gdns W2 194 A10
Hyde Pk Gdns W2 82 DD73
Hyde Pk Gdns Ms W2 194 A10
Hyde Pk Gate SW7 100 DC75
Hyde Pk Gate Ms SW7 100 DC75
Hyde Pk Gate
Hyde Pk Pl W2 194 C10
Hyde Pk Pl W2 82 DE73
Hyde Pk Sq W2 194 B9
Hyde Pk Sq W2 82 DE72
Hyde Pk Sq Ms W2 194 B9
Hyde Pk St W2 194 B9
Hyde Pk St W2 82 DE72
Hyde Rd N1 84 DR67
Hyde Rd, Bexh. 106 EZ82
Hyde Rd, Rich. 118 CM85
Albert Rd
Hyde Rd, S.Croy. 160 DS113
Hyde Rd, Wat. 23 BU40
Hyde St SE8 103 EA79
Deptford High St
Hyde Ter, Ashf. 115 BS93
Hyde Vale SE10 103 EC80
Hyde Wk, Mord. 140 DA101
Hyde Way N9 46 DT47
Hyde Way, Hayes 95 BT77
Hydefield Cl N21 46 DR46
Hydefield Ct N9 46 DS47
Hyder Rd, Grays 111 GJ76
Hyderabad Way E15 86 EE66
Hydes Pl N1 83 DP66
Compton Av
Hydeside Gdns N9 46 DT47
Hydethorpe Av N9 46 DT47
Hydethorpe Rd SW12 121 DJ88
Hyland Cl, Horn. 71 FH59
Hyland Way, Horn. 71 FH59
Hylands Cl, Epsom 172 CQ115
Hylands Ms, Epsom 172 CQ115
Hylands Rd E17 47 ED54
Hylands Rd, Epsom 172 CQ115
Hylton St SE18 105 ET77
Hyndewood SE23 123 DX90
Hyndman St SE15 102 DV79
Hynton Rd, Dag. 70 EW61
Hyperion Pl, Epsom 156 CR109
Hyrons Cl, Amer. 20 AS38
Hyrstdene, S.Croy. 159 DP105
Hyson Rd SE16 202 E10
Hythe, The, Stai. 113 BE92
Hythe Av, Bexh. 106 EZ80
Hythe Cl N18 46 DU49
Hythe Cl, Orp. 146 EW98
Sandway Rd
Hythe End Rd, Stai. 113 BA89
Hythe Fld Av, Egh. 113 BD93
Hythe Pk Rd, Egh. 113 BC92
Hythe Path, Th.Hth. 142 DR97
Hythe Rd NW10 81 CU70
Hythe Rd, Stai. 113 BD92
Hythe Rd, Th.Hth. 142 DR96
Hythe St, Dart. 128 FL86
Hythe St Lwr, Dart. 128 FL85
Hyver Hill NW7 26 CR44

I

Ian Sq, Enf. 31 DX39
Lansbury Rd
Ibbetson Path, Loug. 33 EP41
Ibbotson Av E16 86 EF72
Ibbott St E1 84 DW70
Mantus Rd
Iberian Av, Wall. 159 DK105
Ibis La W4 98 CQ81
Ibis Way, Hayes 78 BX72
Cygnet Way
Ibscott Cl, Dag. 89 FC65
Ibsley Gdns SW15 119 CU88
Ibsley Way, Barn. 28 DE43
Ice Wf Marina N1 83 DL68
New Wf Rd
Icehouse Wd, Oxt. 188 EE131
Iceland Rd E3 85 EA67
Iceni Ct E3 85 DZ67
Roman Rd
Ickburgh Est E5 66 DV62
Ickburgh Rd
Ickburgh Rd E5 66 DV62
Ickenham Cl, Ruis. 59 BR61
Ickenham Rd, Ruis. 59 BR60
Ickenham Rd (Ickenham), Uxb. 59 BQ61
Ickleton Rd SE9 124 EL91
Icklingham Gate, Cob. 154 BW112
Icklingham Rd, Cob. 154 BW112
Icknield Dr, Ilf. 69 EP57
Ickworth Pk Rd E17 67 DY56
Ida Rd N15 66 DR57
Ida St E14 85 EC72
Iden Cl, Brom. 144 EE97
Idlecombe Rd SW17 120 DG93
Idmiston Rd E15 68 EF64
Idmiston Rd SE27 122 DQ90
Idmiston Rd, Wor.Pk. 139 CT101
Idmiston Sq, Wor.Pk. 139 CT101
Idol La EC3 201 M1
Idonia St SE8 103 DZ80
Iffley Cl, Uxb. 76 BK66
Iffley Rd W6 99 CV76
Ifield Rd SW10 100 DB79
Ifield Way, Grav. 131 GK93
Ifor Evans Pl E1 85 DX70
Mile End Rd
Ightham Rd, Erith 106 FA80
Ikea Twr NW10 62 CR64
Ikona Ct, Wey. 153 BQ106
Ilbert St W10 81 CX69
Ilchester Gdns W2 82 DB73
Ilchester Pl W14 99 CZ76
Ilchester Rd, Dag. 70 EV64
Ildersly Gro SE21 122 DR89
Ilderton Rd SE15 102 DW80
Ilderton Rd SE16 202 F10
Ilderton Rd SE16 102 DV78
Ilex Cl, Egh. 112 AV94
Ilex Cl, Sun. 136 BW96
Oakington Dr
Ilex Ho N4 65 DM59
Ilex Rd NW10 81 CT65
Ilex Way SW16 121 DN92
Ilford Hill, Ilf. 69 EN62
Ilford La, Ilf. 69 EP62
Ilfracombe Cres, Horn. 72 FJ63
Ilfracombe Gdns, Rom. 70 EV59
Ilfracombe Rd, Brom. 124 EF90
Iliffe St SE17 200 G10
Iliffe St SE17 101 DP78
Iliffe Yd SE17 200 G10
Ilkeston Ct E5 67 DX63
Overbury St
Ilkley Cl SE19 122 DR93
Ilkley Rd E16 86 EJ71
Ilkley Rd, Wat. 40 BX50
Illingworth Cl, Mitch. 140 DD97
Illingworth Way, Enf. 30 DS42
Ilmington Rd, Har. 61 CK58
Ilminster Gdns SW11 100 DE84
Imber Cl N14 45 DJ45
Imber Cl, Esher 137 CD102
Ember La
Imber Ct Trd Est, E.Mol. 137 CD100
Imber Gro, Esher 137 CD101
Imber Pk Rd, Esher 137 CD102
Imber St N1 84 DR67
Imer Pl, T.Ditt. 137 CF101
Imperial Av N16 66 DT62
Victorian Rd
Imperial Business Est, Grav. 131 GF86
Imperial Cl, Har. 60 CA58
Imperial Coll Rd SW7 100 DD76
Imperial Cres, Wey. 135 BQ104
Churchill Dr
Imperial Dr, Grav. 131 GM92
Imperial Dr, Har. 60 CA59
Imperial Gdns, Mitch. 141 DH97
Imperial Ms E6 86 EJ68
Central Pk Rd
Imperial Retail Pk, Grav. 131 GG86
Imperial Rd N22 45 DL53
Imperial Rd SW6 100 DC81
Imperial Rd, Felt. 115 BS87
Imperial Sq SW6 100 DB81
Imperial St E3 85 EC69
Imperial Way, Chis. 125 EQ90
Imperial Way, Croy. 159 DM107
Imperial Way, Har. 62 CL58
Imperial Way, Wat. 24 BW39
Imre Cl W12 81 CV74
Ellerslie Rd
Inca Dr SE9 125 EP87
Ince Rd, Walt. 153 BS107
Inchmery Rd SE6 123 EB89
Inchwood, Croy. 161 EB105
Independent Pl E8 66 DT64
Downs Pk Rd
Independents Rd SE3 104 EF83
Blackheath Village
Inderwick Rd N8 65 DM57
Indescon Ct E14 204 A5
Indescon Ct E14 103 EB75
India Pl WC2 196 B10
India Rd, Slou. 92 AV75
India St EC3 197 P9
India Way W12 81 CV73
Indigo Ms E14 85 EC73
Ashton St
Indigo Ms N16 66 DR62
Indus Rd SE7 104 EJ80
Industry Ter SW9 101 DN83
Canterbury Cres
Ingal Rd E13 86 EG70
Ingate Pl SW8 101 DH81
Ingatestone Rd E12 68 EJ60
Ingatestone Rd SE25 142 DV98
Ingatestone Rd, Wdf.Grn. 48 EG52
Ingelow Rd SW8 101 DH82
Ingels Mead, Epp. 17 ET29
Ingersoll Rd W12 81 CV74
Ingersoll Rd, Enf. 30 DW38
Ingestre Pl W1 195 L9
Ingestre Rd E7 68 EG63
Ingestre Rd NW5 65 DH63
Ingham Cl, S.Croy. 161 DX109
Ingham Rd NW6 64 DA63
Ingham Rd, S.Croy. 160 DW109
Ingle Cl, Pnr. 60 BY55
Inglebert St EC1 196 D2
Ingleboro Dr, Pur. 160 DR113
Ingleborough St SW9 101 DN82
Ingleby Dr, Har. 61 CD62
Ingleby Gdns, Chig. 50 EV48
Ingleby Rd, Dag. 89 FB65
Ingleby Rd, Grays 111 GH76
Ingleby Rd, Ilf. 69 EP60
Ingleby Way, Chis. 125 EN92
Ingleby Way, Wall. 159 DK109
Ingledew Rd SE18 105 ER78
Inglefield, Pot.B. 12 DA30
Ingleglen, Horn. 72 FN59
Inglehurst, Add. 152 BH110
Inglehurst Gdns, Ilf. 69 EM57
Inglemere Rd SE23 123 DX90
Inglemere Rd, Mitch. 120 DF94
Inglesham Wk E9 85 DZ65
Ingleside, Slou. 93 BE81
Ingleside Cl, Beck. 123 EA94
Ingleside Gro SE3 104 EF79
Inglethorpe St SW6 99 CX81
Ingleton Av, Well. 126 EU85
Ingleton Rd N18 46 DU51
Ingleton Rd, Cars. 158 DE109
Ingleton St SW9 101 DN82
Ingleway N12 44 DD51
Inglewood, Cher. 133 BF104
Inglewood, Croy. 161 DY109
Inglewood, Wok. 166 AV118
Inglewood Cl E14 204 A8
Inglewood Cl E14 103 EA77
Inglewood Cl, Horn. 72 FK63
Inglewood Cl, Ilf. 49 ET51
Inglewood Copse, Brom. 144 EL96
Inglewood Rd NW6 64 DA64
Inglewood Rd, Bexh. 107 FD84
Inglis Barracks NW7 43 CY51
Inglis Rd W5 80 CM73
Inglis Rd, Croy. 142 DT102
Inglis St SE5 101 DP81
Ingoldsby Rd, Grav. 131 GL88
Ingram Av NW11 64 DC59
Ingram Cl SE11 200 C8
Ingram Cl, Stan. 41 CJ50
Ingram Rd N2 64 DE56
Ingram Rd, Dart. 128 FL88
Ingram Rd, Grays 110 GD77
Ingram Rd, Th.Hth. 142 DQ95
Ingram Way, Grnf. 79 CD67
Ingrams Cl, Walt. 154 BW106
Ingrave Ho, Dag. 88 EV67
Ingrave Rd, Brwd. 54 FX47
Ingrave Rd, Rom. 71 FD56
Ingrave St SW11 100 DD83
Ingrebourne Gdns, Upmin. 72 FQ60
Ingrebourne Rd, Rain. 89 FH70
Ingrebourne Valley Grn Way, Horn. 72 FK64
Ingress Gdns, Green. 129 FX85
Ingress St W4 98 CS78
Devonshire Rd
Ingreway, Rom. 52 FP52
Inigo Jones Rd SE7 104 EL80
Inigo Pl WC2 195 P10
Inkerman Rd NW5 83 DH65
Inkerman Rd, Wok. 166 AS118
Inkerman Ter W8 100 DA76
Allen St
Inkerman Way, Wok. 166 AS118
Inks Grn E4 47 EC50
Inman Rd NW10 80 CS67
Inman Rd SW18 120 DC87
Inmans Row, Wdf.Grn. 48 EG49
Inner Circle NW1 194 F2
Inner Circle NW1 82 DG69
Inner Pk Rd SW19 119 CX88
Inner Ring E, Houns. 95 BP83
Inner Ring W, Houns. 94 BN83
Inner Temple La EC4 196 D9
Innes Cl SW20 139 CY96
Innes Gdns SW15 119 CV86
Innes Yd, Croy. 142 DQ104
Whitgift St
Inniskilling Rd E13 86 EJ68
Innova Business Pk, Enf. 31 DZ36
Innova Way, Enf. 31 DZ36
Innovation Cl, Wem. 80 CL67

Inskip Cl E10 67 EB61
Inskip Dr, Horn. 72 FL60
Inskip Rd, Dag. 70 EX60
Institute Pl E8 66 DV64
Amhurst Rd
Institute Rd, Epp. 18 EX29
Instone Cl, Wall. 159 DL108
Instone Rd, Dart. 128 FK87
Integer Gdns E11 67 ED59
Forest Rd
Interchange E Ind Est E5 66 DW60
Theydon Rd
International Av, Houns. 96 BW78
International Trd Est, Sthl. 95 BV76
Inver Cl E5 66 DW61
Theydon Rd
Inver Ct W2 82 DB72
Inverness Ter
Inveraray Pl SE18 105 ER79
Old Mill Rd
Inverclyde Gdns, Rom. 70 EX56
Inveresk Gdns, Wor.Pk. 139 CT104
Inverforth Cl NW3 64 DC61
North End Way
Inverforth Rd N11 45 DH50
Inverine Rd SE7 104 EH78
Invermore Pl SE18 105 EQ77
Inverness Av, Enf. 30 DS39
Inverness Dr, Ilf. 49 ES51
Inverness Gdns W8 82 DB74
Vicarage Gate
Inverness Ms E16 105 EP75
Barge Ho Rd
Inverness Ms W2 82 DB73
Inverness Ter
Inverness Pl W2 82 DB73
Inverness Rd N18 46 DV50
Aberdeen Rd
Inverness Rd, Houns. 96 BZ84
Inverness Rd, Sthl. 96 BY77
Inverness Rd, Wor.Pk. 139 CX102
Inverness St NW1 83 DH67
Inverness Ter W2 82 DB73
Inverton Rd SE15 103 DX84
Invicta Cl, Chis. 125 EN92
Invicta Cl, Felt. 115 BT88
Westmacott Dr
Invicta Gro, Nthlt. 78 BZ69
Invicta Plaza SE1 200 F2
Invicta Rd SE3 104 EG80
Invicta Rd, Dart. 128 FP86
Inville Rd SE17 102 DR78
Inwen Ct SE8 103 DY78
Inwood Av, Couls. 175 DN120
Inwood Av, Houns. 96 CC83
Inwood Cl, Croy. 143 DY103
Inwood Ct, Walt. 136 BW103
Inwood Rd, Houns. 96 CB84
Inworth St SW11 100 DE82
Inworth Wk N1 84 DQ67
Popham St
Ion Sq E2 84 DU68
Hackney Rd
Iona Cl SE6 123 EA87
Iona Cl, Mord. 140 DB101
Ipswich Rd SW17 120 DG93
Ireland Cl E6 87 EM71
Bradley Stone Rd
Ireland Pl N22 45 DL52
Whittington Rd
Ireland Yd EC4 196 G9
Ireland Yd EC4 83 DP72
Irene Rd SW6 100 DA81
Irene Rd, Cob. 154 CA114
Irene Rd, Orp. 145 ET101
Ireton Av, Walt. 135 BS103
Ireton Cl N10 44 DG52
Cromwell Rd
Ireton Pl, Grays 110 GA77
Russell Rd
Ireton St E3 85 EA70
Tidworth Rd
Iris Av, Bex. 126 EY85
Iris Cl E6 86 EL70
Iris Cl, Brwd. 54 FV43
Iris Cl, Croy. 143 DX102
Iris Cl, Surb. 138 CM101
Iris Ct, Pnr. 60 BW55
Iris Cres, Bexh. 106 EZ79
Iris Path, Rom. 52 FJ52
Clematis Cl
Iris Rd, Epsom 156 CP106
Iris Wk, Edg. 42 CQ49
Ash Cl
Iris Way E4 47 DZ51
Irkdale Av, Enf. 30 DT39
Iron Br Cl NW10 62 CS64
Iron Br Cl, Sthl. 78 CC74
Iron Br Rd, Uxb. 94 BN75
Iron Br Rd, West Dr. 94 BN75
Iron Mill La, Dart. 107 FE84
Iron Mill Pl SW18 120 DB86
Garratt La
Iron Mill Pl, Dart. 107 FF84
Iron Mill Rd SW18 120 DB86
Ironmonger La EC2 197 K9
Ironmonger Pas EC1 197 J4
Ironmonger Row EC1 197 J4
Ironmonger Row EC1 84 DQ69
Ironmongers Pl E14 204 A9
Irons Way, Rom. 51 FC52
Ironside Cl SE16 203 H4
Irvine Av, Har. 61 CG55
Irvine Cl N20 44 DE47
Irvine Gdns, S.Ock. 91 FT72
Irvine Pl, Vir.W. 132 AY99
Irvine Way, Orp. 145 ET101
Irving Av, Nthlt. 78 BX67
Irving Gro SW9 101 DM82
Irving Rd W14 99 CX76
Irving St WC2 195 N10
Irving St WC2 83 DK73
Irving Wk, Swans. 130 FY87
Irving Way NW9 63 CT57
Irving Way, Swan. 147 FD96
Irwin Av SE18 105 ES80
Irwin Cl, Uxb. 58 BN62
Irwin Gdns NW10 81 CV67
Isabel Gate (Cheshunt), Wal.Cr. 15 DZ26
Isabel Hill Cl, Hmptn. 136 CB95
Upper Sunbury Rd
Isabel St SW9 101 DM81
Isabella Cl N14 45 DJ45
Isabella Ct, Rich. 118 CM86
Grove Rd
Isabella Dr, Orp. 163 EQ105
Isabella Rd E9 66 DW64
Isabella St SE1 200 F3
Isabella St SE1 83 DP74
Isabelle Cl, Wal.Cr. 14 DQ29
Isambard Cl, Uxb. 76 BK69
Isambard Ms E14 204 E7
Isambard Ms E14 103 EC76
Isambard Pl SE16 202 G3
Isbell Gdns, Rom. 51 FE52
Isel Way SE22 122 DS85
East Dulwich Gro
Isham Rd SW16 141 DL96
Isis Cl SW15 99 CW84
Isis Cl, Ruis. 59 BQ58
Isis Dr, Upmin. 73 FS58
Isis St SW18 120 DC89
Isla Rd SE18 105 EQ79
Island, The, Stai. 113 BA90
Island, The, West Dr. 94 BH81
Island Cl, Stai. 113 BE91
Island Fm Av, W.Mol. 136 BZ99
Island Fm Rd, W.Mol. 136 BZ99
Island Rd, Mitch. 120 DF94
Island Row E14 85 DZ72
Commercial Rd
Islay Gdns, Houns. 116 BX85
Islay Wk N1 84 DQ66
Douglas Rd
Isledon Rd N7 65 DN62
Islehurst Cl, Chis. 145 EN95
Isleworth Business Complex, Islw. 97 CF82
St. John's Rd
Isleworth Prom, Twick. 97 CH84
Islington Grn N1 83 DP67
Islington High St N1 196 E1
Islington High St N1 83 DP68
Islington Pk Ms N1 83 DN66
Islington Pk St
Islington Pk St N1 83 DN66
Islip Gdns, Edg. 42 CR52
Islip Gdns, Nthlt. 78 BY66
Islip Manor Rd, Nthlt. 78 BY66
Islip St NW5 65 DJ64
Ismailia Rd E7 86 EH66
Ismay Ct, Slou. 74 AS73
Elliman Av
Isom Cl E13 86 EJ70
Belgrave Rd
Istead Ri, Grav. 131 GF94
Itchingwood Common Rd, Oxt. 188 EJ133
Ivanhoe Cl, Uxb. 76 BK71
Ivanhoe Dr, Har. 61 CG55
Ivanhoe Rd SE5 102 DT83
Ivanhoe Rd, Houns. 96 BX83
Ivatt Pl W14 99 CZ78
Ivatt Way N17 65 DP55
Ive Fm Cl E10 67 EA61
Ive Fm La E10 67 EA61
Iveagh Av NW10 80 CN68
Iveagh Cl E9 85 DX67
Iveagh Cl NW10 80 CN68
Iveagh Cl, Nthwd. 39 BP53
Iveagh Rd, Wok. 166 AT118
Iveagh Ter NW10 80 CN68
Iveagh Av
Ivedon Rd, Well. 106 EW82
Iveley Rd SW4 101 DJ82
Iver La, Iver 76 BH71
Iver La, Uxb. 76 BH71
Iver Rd, Brwd. 54 FV44
Iver Rd, Iver 76 BG72
Iverdale Cl, Iver 75 BC73
Ivere Dr, Barn. 28 DB44
Iverhurst Cl, Bexh. 126 EX85
Iverna Ct W8 100 DA76
Iverna Gdns W8 100 DA76
Iverna Gdns, Felt. 115 BR85
Ivers Way, Croy. 161 EB108
Iverson Rd NW6 81 CZ65
Ives Gdns, Rom. 71 FF56
Sims Cl
Ives Rd E16 86 EE71
Ives Rd, Slou. 93 AZ76
Ives St SW3 198 C8
Ives St SW3 100 DE77
Ivestor Ter SE23 122 DW87
Ivimey St E2 84 DU69
Ivinghoe Cl, Enf. 30 DS40
Ivinghoe Cl, Wat. 24 BX35
Ivinghoe Rd, Bushey 41 CD45
Ivinghoe Rd, Dag. 70 EV64
Ivinghoe Rd, Rick. 38 BG45
Ivor Gro SE9 125 EP88
Ivor Pl NW1 194 D5
Ivor Pl NW1 82 DF70
Ivor St NW1 83 DJ66
Ivory Sq SW11 100 DC83
Gartons Way
Ivorydown, Brom. 124 EG91
Ivy Bower Cl, Green. 129 FV85
Riverview Rd
Ivy Chimneys Rd, Epp. 17 ES32
Ivy Cl, Dart. 128 FN87
Ivy Cl, Grav. 131 GJ90
Ivy Cl, Har. 60 BZ63
Ivy Cl, Pnr. 60 BW59
Ivy Cl, Sun. 136 BW96
Ivy Cotts E14 85 EB73
Grove Vil
Ivy Ct SE16 102 DU78
Argyle Way
Ivy Cres W4 98 CQ77
Ivy Gdns N8 65 DL58
Ivy Gdns, Mitch. 141 DK97
Ivy Ho La, Sev. 181 FD118
Ivy Ho Rd, Uxb. 59 BP62
Ivy La, Houns. 96 BZ84
Ivy La, Sev. 180 EY116
Ivy La, Wok. 167 BB118
Ivy Lea, Rick. 38 BG46
Springwell Av
Ivy Lo La, Rom. 52 FP53
Ivy Mill Cl, Gdse. 186 DV132
Ivy Mill La, Gdse. 186 DU132
Ivy Pl, Surb. 138 CM100
Alpha Rd
Ivy Rd E16 86 EG72
Pacific Rd
Ivy Rd E17 67 EA58
Ivy Rd N14 45 DJ45
Ivy Rd NW2 63 CW63
Ivy Rd SE4 103 DZ84
Ivy Rd SW17 120 DE92
Tooting High St
Ivy Rd, Houns. 96 CB84
Ivy Rd, Surb. 138 CN102
Ivy St N1 84 DS68
Ivy Wk, Dag. 88 EY65
Ivybridge Cl, Twick. 117 CG86
Ivybridge Cl, Uxb. 76 BL69
Ivybridge Est, Islw. 117 CF85
Ivybridge La WC2 200 A1
Ivychurch Cl SE20 122 DW94
Ivychurch La SE17 201 P10
Ivydale Rd SE15 103 DX83
Ivydale Rd, Cars. 140 DF103
Ivyday Gro SW16 121 DM90
Ivydene, W.Mol. 136 BZ99
Ivydene Cl, Sutt. 158 DC105
Ivyhouse Rd, Dag. 88 EX65
Ivymount Rd SE27 121 DN90
Ixworth Pl SW3 198 B10
Ixworth Pl SW3 100 DE78
Izane Rd, Bexh. 106 EZ84

J

Jacaranda Cl, N.Mal. 138 CS97
Jacaranda Gro E8 84 DT66
Queensbridge Rd
Jack Barnett Way N22 45 DM54
Jack Clow Rd E15 86 EE68
Jack Cornwell St E12 69 EN63
Jack Dash Way E6 86 EL70
Jack Walker Ct N5 65 DP63
Jackass La, Kes. 162 EH107
Jackass La, Oxt. 187 DZ131
Jackets La, Nthwd. 39 BP53
Jackets La (Harefield), Uxb. 38 BN52
Jacketts Fld, Abb.L. 7 BT31
Jacklin Grn, Wdf.Grn. 48 EG49
Jackman Ms NW10 62 CS62
Jackman St E8 84 DV67
Jackmans La, Wok. 166 AU119
Jacks La (Harefield), Uxb. 38 BG53
Jackson Cl E9 84 DW66
Jackson Cl, Epsom 156 CR114
Jackson Cl, Green. 129 FU85
Cowley Av
Jackson Cl, Horn. 72 FM56
Jackson Cl, Uxb. 76 BL66
Jackson Rd
Jackson Rd N7 65 DM63
Jackson Rd, Bark. 87 ER67
Jackson Rd, Barn. 28 DE44
Jackson Rd, Brom. 144 EL103
Jackson Rd, Uxb. 76 BL66
Jackson St SE18 105 EN79
Jackson Way, Sthl. 96 CB75
Jacksons Dr, Wal.Cr. 14 DU28
Jacksons La N6 64 DG59
Jacksons Pl, Croy. 142 DR102
Cross Rd
Jacksons Way, Croy. 143 EA104
Jacob Ho, Erith 106 EX75
Kale Rd
Jacob St SE1 202 A4
Jacob St SE1 102 DU75
Jacobs Av, Rom. 52 FL54
Jacobs Cl, Dag. 71 FB63
Jacobs Ho E13 86 EJ69
Jacobs La, Dart. 148 FQ97
Jacob's Well Ms W1 194 G8
Jacqueline Cl, Nthlt. 78 BZ67
Canford Av
Jade Cl E16 86 EK72
Jade Cl NW2 63 CX59
Marble Dr
Jade Cl, Dag. 70 EW60
Jaffe Rd, Ilf. 69 EQ60
Jaffray Pl SE27 121 DP91
Chapel Rd
Jaffray Rd, Brom. 144 EK98
Jaggard Way SW12 120 DF87
Jagger Cl, Dart. 128 FQ87
Jago Cl SE18 105 EQ79
Jago Wk SE5 102 DR80
Jail La (Biggin Hill), West. 178 EK116
Jamaica Rd SE1 202 A5
Jamaica Rd SE1 102 DU75
Jamaica Rd SE16 202 D6
Jamaica Rd SE16 102 DV75
Jamaica Rd, Th.Hth. 141 DP100
Jamaica St E1 84 DW72
James Av NW2 63 CW64
James Av, Dag. 70 EZ60
James Bedford Cl, Pnr. 40 BW54
James Boswell Cl SW16 121 DN91
Curtis Fld Rd
James Cl E13 86 EG68
Richmond St
James Cl NW11 63 CY58
Woodlands
James Cl, Bushey 24 BY43
Aldenham Rd
James Cl, Rom. 71 FG57
James Collins Cl W9 81 CZ70
Fermoy Rd
James Ct N1 84 DQ66
Morton Rd
James Dudson Ct NW10 80 CQ66
James Gdns N22 45 DP52
James Hammett Ho E2 84 DT69
Ravenscroft St
James Joyce Wk SE24 101 DP84
Shakespeare Rd
James La E10 67 ED59
James La E11 67 ED58
James Martin Cl (Denham), Uxb. 58 BG58
James Newman Ct SE9 125 EN90
Great Harry Dr
James Pl N17 46 DT53
James Rd, Dart. 127 FG87
James Sinclair Pt E13 86 EJ67
James St W1 194 G8
James St W1 82 DG72
James St WC2 196 A10
James St, Bark. 87 EQ66
James St, Enf. 30 DT43
James St, Epp. 17 ET28
James St, Houns. 97 CD83
James Ter SW14 98 CR83
Addington Ct
James Yd E4 47 ED51
Larkshall Rd
Jameson Cl W3 98 CQ75
Acton La
Jameson Ct E2 84 DW68
Russia La
Jameson St W8 82 DA74
James's Cotts, Rich. 98 CN80
Kew Rd
Jamestown Rd NW1 83 DH67
Jamestown Way E14 204 G1
Jamestown Way E14 85 ED73
Jamieson Ho, Houns. 116 BZ87
Jamnagar Cl, Stai. 113 BF93
Jane St E1 84 DV72
Commercial Rd
Janet St E14 204 A6
Janet St E14 103 EA76
Janeway Pl SE16 202 D5
Janeway St SE16 202 C5
Janeway St SE16 102 DU75
Janice Ms, Ilf. 69 EP62
Oakfield Rd
Janmead, Brwd. 55 GB45
Janoway Hill La, Wok. 166 AW119
Janoway Hill La, Wok. 166 AW119
Firbank La
Jansen Wk SW11 100 DD84
Hope St
Janson Cl E15 68 EE64
Janson Rd
Janson Cl NW10 62 CR62
Janson Rd E15 68 EE64
Jansons Rd N15 66 DS55
Japan Cres N4 65 DM59
Japan Rd, Rom. 70 EX58
Japonica Cl, Wok. 166 AW118
Jardine Rd E1 85 DX73
Jarrah Cotts, Purf. 109 FR79
London Rd Purfleet
Jarrett Cl SW2 121 DP88
Jarrow Cl, Mord. 140 DB99
Jarrow Rd N17 66 DV56
Jarrow Rd SE16 202 F9
Jarrow Rd SE16 102 DW77
Jarrow Rd, Rom. 70 EW58
Jarrow Way E9 67 DY63
Jarvis Cleys (Cheshunt), Wal.Cr. 14 DT26
Jarvis Cl, Bark. 87 ER67
Westbury Rd
Jarvis Cl, Barn. 27 CX43
Jarvis Rd SE22 102 DS84
Melbourne Gro
Jarvis Rd, S.Croy. 160 DR107
Jarvis Way, Rom. 52 FL54
Jasmin Cl, Nthwd. 39 BT53
Jasmin Rd, Epsom 156 CP106
Jasmine Cl, Ilf. 69 EP64
Jasmine Cl, Orp. 145 EP103
Jasmine Cl, Sthl. 78 BY73
Jasmine Cl, Wok. 166 AT116
Jasmine Gdns, Croy. 143 EB104
Jasmine Gdns, Har. 60 CA61
Jasmine Gro SE20 142 DV95
Jasmine Rd, Rom. 71 FE61
Jasmine Ter, West Dr. 94 BN75
Jasmine Way, E.Mol. 137 CE98
Hampton Ct Way
Jason Cl, Brwd. 54 FT49
Jason Cl, Wey. 153 BQ106
Jason Ct W1 82 DG72
Marylebone La
Jason Wk SE9 125 EN91
Jasons Hill, Chesh. 4 AV30
Jasper Cl, Enf. 30 DW38
Jasper Pas SE19 122 DT93
Jasper Rd E16 86 EK72
Jasper Rd SE19 122 DT92
Jasper Wk N1 197 K2
Javelin Way, Nthlt. 78 BX69
Jay Gdns, Chis. 125 EM91
Jay Ms SW7 100 DC75
Jaycroft, Enf. 29 DN39
The Ridgeway
Jays Covert, Couls. 174 DG119
Jebb Av SW2 121 DL86
Jebb St E3 85 EA68
Jedburgh Rd E13 86 EJ69
Jedburgh St SW11 100 DG84
Jeddo Rd W12 99 CT75
Jefferson Cl W13 97 CH76
Jefferson Cl, Ilf. 69 EP57
Jefferson Cl, Slou. 93 BA77
Jefferson Wk SE18 105 EN79
Kempt St
Jeffreys Pl NW1 83 DJ66
Jeffreys St
Jeffreys Rd SW4 101 DL82
Jeffreys Rd, Enf. 31 DZ41
Jeffreys St NW1 83 DH66
Jeffreys Wk SW4 101 DL82
Jeffries Ho NW10 80 CR67
Jeffs Cl, Hmptn. 116 CB93
Uxbridge Rd
Jeffs Rd, Sutt. 157 CZ105
Jeger Av E2 84 DT67
Jeken Rd SE9 104 EJ84
Jelf Rd SW2 121 DN85
Jellicoe Av, Grav. 131 GJ90
Jellicoe Av W, Grav. 131 GJ90
Kitchener Av
Jellicoe Gdns, Stan. 41 CF51
Jellicoe Rd E13 86 EG70
Jutland Rd
Jellicoe Rd N17 46 DR52
Jellicoe Rd, Wat. 23 BU44
Jemmett Cl, Kings.T. 138 CP95
Jengar Cl, Sutt. 158 DB105
Jenkins Av, St.Alb. 8 BY30
Jenkins La E6 87 EN68
Jenkins La, Bark. 87 EP68
Jenkins Rd E13 86 EH70
Jenner Av W3 80 CR71
Jenner Ho SE3 104 EE79
Jenner Pl SW13 99 CV79
Jenner Rd N16 66 DT61
Jennett Rd, Croy. 141 DN104
Jennifer Rd, Brom. 124 EF90
Jennings Cl, Add. 152 BJ109
Woodham La
Jennings Cl, Surb. 137 CJ101
Jennings Rd SE22 122 DT86
Jennings Way, Barn. 27 CW41
Jenningtree Rd, Erith 107 FH80
Jenningtree Way, Belv. 107 FC75
Jenny Hammond Cl E11 68 EF62
Newcomen Rd
Jenny Path, Rom. 52 FK52
Jenson Way SE19 122 DT94
Jenton Av, Bexh. 106 EY81
Jephson Rd E7 86 EJ66
Jephson St SE5 102 DR81
Grove La
Jephtha Rd SW18 120 DA86
Jeppos La, Mitch. 140 DF98
Jepps Cl, Wal.Cr. 13 DP25
Hammondstreet Rd
Jerdan Pl SW6 100 DA80
Jeremiah St E14 85 EB72
Jeremys Grn N18 46 DV49
Jermyn St SW1 199 K2
Jermyn St SW1 83 DK73
Jerningham Av, Ilf. 49 EP54
Jerningham Rd SE14 103 DY82
Jerome Cres NW8 194 B4
Jerome Cres NW8 82 DE70
Jerome St E1 197 P6
Jerrard St N1 197 N1
Jerrard St SE13 103 EB83
Jersey Av, Stan. 41 CH54
Jersey Cl, Cher. 133 BF104
Jersey Dr, Orp. 145 ER100
Jersey Par, Houns. 96 CB81
Jersey Rd E11 67 ED60
Jersey Rd E16 86 EJ72
Prince Regent La
Jersey Rd SW17 121 DH93
Jersey Rd W7 97 CG75
Jersey Rd, Houns. 96 CB81
Jersey Rd, Ilf. 69 EP63
Jersey Rd, Islw. 97 CE79
Jersey Rd, Rain. 89 FG66
Jersey St E2 84 DV69
Bethnal Grn Rd
Jerusalem Pas EC1 196 F5
Jervis Av, Enf. 31 DY35
Jervis Ct W1 195 J9
Jerviston Gdns SW16 121 DN93
Jesmond Av, Wem. 80 CM65
Jesmond Cl, Mitch. 141 DH97
Jesmond Rd, Croy. 142 DT101
Jesmond Way, Stan. 42 CL50
Jessam Av E5 66 DV60
Jessamine Pl, Dart. 128 FQ87
Jessamine Rd W7 79 CE74
Jessamine Ter, Swan. 147 FC95
Birchwood Rd
Jessamy Rd, Wey. 135 BP103
Jesse Rd E10 67 EC60
Jessel Dr, Loug. 33 EQ39
Jessett Cl, Erith 107 FD77
West St
Jessica Rd SW18 120 DC86
Jessie Blythe La N19 65 DL59
Jessiman Ter, Shep. 134 BN99
Jessop Av, Sthl. 96 BZ77
Jessop Rd SE24 101 DP84
Milkwood Rd
Jessop Sq E14 85 EA74
Heron Quay
Jessops Way, Croy. 141 DJ100
Jessup Cl SE18 105 EQ77
Jetstar Way, Nthlt. 78 BY69
Jetty Wk, Grays 110 GA79
Jevington Way SE12 124 EH88
Jewel Rd E17 67 EA55
Jewels Hill, West. 162 EG112
Jewry St EC3 197 P9
Jewry St EC3 84 DT72
Jew's Row SW18 100 DC84
Jews Wk SE26 122 DV91
Jeymer Av NW2 63 CV64
Jeymer Dr, Grnf. 78 CC67
Jeypore Pas SW18 120 DC86
Jeypore Rd
Jeypore Rd SW18 120 DC87
Jillian Cl, Hmptn. 116 CA94
Jim Bradley Cl SE18 105 EN77
John Wilson St
Joan Cres SE9 124 EK87
Joan Gdns, Dag. 70 EY61
Joan Rd, Dag. 70 EY61
Joan St SE1 200 F3
Joan St SE1 83 DP74
Jocelyn Rd, Rich. 98 CL83
Jocelyn St SE15 102 DU81
Jockey's Flds WC1 196 C6
Jockey's Flds WC1 83 DM71
Jodane St SE8 203 M9
Jodane St SE8 103 DZ77
Jodrell Cl, Islw. 97 CG81
Jodrell Rd E3 85 DZ67
Jodrell Way, Grays 109 FT78
Joel St, Nthwd. 59 BU55
Joel St, Pnr. 59 BU55
Johanna St SE1 200 D5
John Adam St WC2 200 A1
John Adam St WC2 83 DL73
John Aird Ct W2 82 DC71
John Archer Way SW18 120 DD86
John Ashby Cl SW2 121 DL86
John Austin Cl, Kings.T. 138 CM95
Queen Elizabeth Rd
John Barnes Wk E15 86 EF65
John Bradshaw Rd N14 45 DK46
High St
John Burns Dr, Bark. 87 ES66
John Campbell Rd N16 66 DS64
John Carpenter St EC4 196 F10
John Carpenter St EC4 83 DP73
John Cobb Rd, Wey. 152 BN108
John Cornwell VC Ho E12 69 EN63
John Felton Rd SE16 202 B5
John Felton Rd SE16 102 DU75

281

Kendrick Rd, Slou. 92 AV76
Kenelm Cl, Har. 61 CG62
Kenerne Dr, Barn. 27 CY43
Kenford Cl, Wat. 7 BV32
Kenia Wk, Grav. 131 GM90
Kenilford Rd SW12 121 DH87
Kenilworth Av E17 47 EA54
Kenilworth Av SW19 120 DA92
Kenilworth Av, Cob. 154 CB114
Kenilworth Av, Har. 60 BZ63
Kenilworth Av, Rom. 52 FP50
Kenilworth Cl, Bans. 174 DB116
Kenilworth Cl, Borwd. 26 CQ41
Kenilworth Cl, Slou. 92 AT76
Kenilworth Ct SW15 99 CX83
Lower Richmond Rd
Kenilworth Ct, Wat. 23 BU39
Hempstead Rd
Kenilworth Cres, Enf. 30 DS39
Kenilworth Dr, Borwd. 26 CQ41
Kenilworth Dr, Rick. 23 BP42
Kenilworth Dr, Walt. 136 BX104
Kenilworth Gdns SE18 105 EP82
Kenilworth Gdns, Hayes 77 BT71
Kenilworth Gdns, Horn. 72 FJ62
Kenilworth Gdns, Ilf. 69 ET61
Kenilworth Gdns, Loug. 33 EM44
Kenilworth Gdns, Sthl. 78 BZ69
Kenilworth Gdns, Stai. 114 BJ92
Kenilworth Gdns, Wat. 40 BW50
Kenilworth Rd E3 85 DY68
Kenilworth Rd NW6 81 CZ67
Kenilworth Rd SE20 143 DX95
Kenilworth Rd W5 80 CL74
Kenilworth Rd, Ashf. 114 BK90
Kenilworth Rd, Edg. 42 CQ48
Kenilworth Rd, Epsom 157 CU107
Kenilworth Rd, Orp. 145 EQ100
Kenley Av NW9 42 CS53
Kenley Cl, Barn. 28 DE42
Kenley Cl, Bex. 126 FA87
Kenley Cl, Cat. 176 DR120
Kenley Cl, Chis. 145 ES97
Kenley Gdns, Horn. 72 FM61
Kenley Gdns, Th.Hth. 141 DP98
Kenley La, Ken. 160 DQ114
Kenley Rd SW19 139 CZ96
Kenley Rd, Kings.T. 138 CP96
Kenley Rd, Twick. 117 CG86
Kenley Wk W11 81 CY73
Kenley Wk, Sutt. 157 CX105
Kenlor Rd SW17 120 DD92
Kenmare Dr, Mitch. 120 DF94
Kenmare Gdns N13 45 DP49
Kenmare Rd, Th.Hth. 141 DN100
Kenmere Gdns, Wem. 80 CN67
Kenmere Rd, Well. 106 EW82
Kenmont Gdns NW10 81 CV69
Kenmore Av, Har. 61 CG56
Kenmore Cl, Rich. 98 CN80
Kent Rd
Kenmore Cres, Hayes 77 BT69
Kenmore Gdns, Edg. 42 CP54
Kenmore Rd, Har. 61 CK55
Kenmore Rd, Ken. 159 DP114
Kenmure Rd E8 66 DV64
Kenmure Yd E8 66 DV64
Kenmure Rd
Kennacraig Cl E16 205 N3
Kennard Rd E15 85 ED66
Kennard Rd N11 44 DF50
Kennard St E16 87 EM74
Kennard St SW11 100 DG82
Kennedy Av, Enf. 30 DW44
Kennedy Cl E13 86 EG68
Kennedy Cl, Mitch. 140 DG96
Kennedy Cl, Orp. 145 ER102
Kennedy Cl, Pnr. 40 BZ51
Kennedy Cl (Cheshunt), Wal.Cr. 15 DX28
Kennedy Gdns, Sev. 191 FJ123
Kennedy Path W7 79 CF70
Harp Rd
Kennedy Rd W7 79 CE71
Kennedy Rd, Bark. 87 ES67
Kennedy Wk SE17 102 DR77
Flint St
Kennel Cl, Lthd. 170 CC124
Kennel La, Lthd. 170 CC122
Kennelwood Cres, Croy. 161 ED111
Kennet Cl SW11 100 DD84
Maysoule Rd
Kennet Cl, Upmin. 73 FS58
Kennet Grn, S.Ock. 91 FV73
Kennet Rd W9 81 CZ70
Kennet Rd, Dart. 107 FG83
Kennet Rd, Islw. 97 CF83
Kennet Sq, Mitch. 140 DE95
Kennet St E1 202 C2
Kennet St E1 84 DU74
Kennet Wf La EC4 197 J10
Kenneth Av, Ilf. 69 EP63
Kenneth Cres NW2 63 CV64
Kenneth Gdns, Stan. 41 CG51
Kenneth More Rd, Ilf. 69 EP62
Oakfield Rd
Kenneth Rd, Bans. 174 DD115
Kenneth Rd, Rom. 70 EX59
Kenneth Robbins Ho N17 46 DV52
Kennett Ct, Swan. 147 FE97
Kennett Dr, Hayes 78 BY71
Kennett Rd, Slou. 93 BB76
Kenning St SE16 202 G4
Kenning Ter N1 84 DS67
Kenninghall Rd E5 66 DU62
Kenninghall Rd N18 46 DW50
Kennings Way SE11 200 F10
Kennings Way SE11 101 DN78
Kennington Grn SE11 101 DN78
Montford Pl
Kennington Gro SE11 101 DM79
Oval Way
Kennington La SE11 200 E10
Kennington La SE11 101 DM78
Kennington Oval SE11 101 DM79
Kennington Pk Est SE11 101 DN79
Harleyford St
Kennington Pk Gdns SE11 101 DP79
Kennington Pk Pl SE11 101 DN79
Kennington Pk Rd SE11 101 DN79
Kennington Rd SE1 200 D6
Kennington Rd SE1 101 DN76
Kennington Rd SE11 200 D7
Kennington Rd SE11 101 DN77
Kenny Dr, Cars. 158 DF108
Fountain Dr
Kenny Rd NW7 43 CY50
Kennylands Rd, Ilf. 50 EU52
Forest Rd
Kenrick Pl W1 194 F6
Kenrick Sq, Red. 186 DS133
Kensal Rd W10 81 CY70
Kensington Av E12 86 EL65
Kensington Av, Th.Hth. 141 DN95
Kensington Av, Wat. 23 BT42
Kensington Ch Ct W8 100 DB75
Kensington Ch St W8 82 DA74
Kensington Ch Wk W8 100 DB75
Kensington Cl N11 44 DG51
Kensington Ct W8 100 DB75
Kensington Ct Gdns W8 100 DB76
Kensington Ct Pl
Kensington Ct Ms W8 100 DB75
Kensington Ct Pl
Kensington Ct Pl W8 100 DB76
Kensington Dr, Wdf.Grn. 48 EK53
Kensington Gdns W2 82 DC74
Kensington Gdns, Ilf. 69 EM60
Kensington Gdns, Kings.T. 137 CK97
Portsmouth Rd
Kensington Gdns Sq W2 82 DB72
Kensington Gate W8 100 DC76
Kensington Gore SW7 100 DD75
Kensington Hall Gdns W14 99 CZ78
Beaumont Av
Kensington High St W8 100 DA76
Kensington High St W14 99 CY77
Kensington Mall W8 82 DA74
Kensington Palace Gdns W8 82 DB74
Kensington Pk Gdns W11 81 CZ73
Kensington Pk Ms W11 81 CZ72
Kensington Pk Rd
Kensington Pk Rd W11 81 CZ73
Kensington Pl W8 82 DA74
Kensington Rd SW7 198 A5
Kensington Rd SW7 100 DD75
Kensington Rd W8 100 DB75
Kensington Rd, Brwd. 54 FU44
Kensington Rd, Nthlt. 78 CA69
Kensington Rd, Rom. 71 FC58
Kensington Sq W8 100 DB75
Kensington Ter, S.Croy. 160 DR108
Sanderstead Rd
Kent Av W13 79 CH71
Kent Av, Dag. 88 FA70
Kent Av, Well. 125 ET85
Kent Cl, Borwd. 26 CR38
Kent Cl, Mitch. 141 DL98
Kent Cl, Orp. 163 ES107
Kent Cl, Stai. 114 BK93
Kent Cl, Uxb. 76 BJ65
Kent Dr, Barn. 28 DG42
Kent Dr, Horn. 72 FK63
Kent Dr, Tedd. 117 CE92
Kent Gdns W13 79 CH71
Kent Gdns, Ruis. 59 BV58
Kent Gate Way, Croy. 161 EA106
Kent Hatch Rd, Eden. 189 EM131
Kent Hatch Rd, Oxt. 188 EJ129
Kent Ho La, Beck. 123 DY92
Kent Ho Rd SE26 143 DX95
Kent Ho Rd, Beck. 123 DY92
Kent Pas NW1 194 D4
Kent Pas NW1 82 DF69
Kent Rd N21 46 DR46
Kent Rd W4 98 CQ76
Kent Rd, Dag. 71 FB64
Kent Rd, Dart. 128 FK86
Kent Rd, E.Mol. 136 CC98
Kent Rd, Grav. 131 GG88
Kent Rd, Grays 110 GC79
Kent Rd, Kings.T. 137 CK97
The Bittoms
Kent Rd, Long. 149 FX96
Kent Rd, Orp. 146 EV100
Kent Rd, Rich. 98 CN80
Kent Rd, W.Wick. 143 EB102
Kent Rd, Wok. 167 BB116
Kent St E2 84 DT68
Kent St E13 86 EJ69
Kent Ter NW1 194 C3
Kent Ter NW1 82 DE69
Kent Twr SE20 122 DV94
Kent Vw, S.Ock. 108 FQ75
Kent Vw Gdns, Ilf. 69 ES61
Kent Wk SW9 101 DP84
Moorland Rd
Kent Way SE15 102 DT81
Sumner Est
Kent Way, Surb. 138 CL104
Kent Yd SW7 198 C5
Kentford Way, Nthlt. 78 BY67
Kentish Bldgs SE1 201 K3
Kentish La, Hat. 12 DC25
Kentish Rd, Belv. 106 FA77
Kentish Town Rd NW1 83 DH66
Kentish Town Rd NW5 83 DH66
Kentish Way, Brom. 144 EG96
Kentmere Rd SE18 105 ES77
Kenton Av, Har. 61 CF59
Kenton Av, Sthl. 78 CA73
Kenton Av, Sun. 136 BY96
Kenton Ct W14 99 CZ76
Kensington High St
Kenton Gdns, Har. 61 CJ57
Kenton La, Har. 61 CJ55
Kenton Pk Av, Har. 61 CK56
Kenton Pk Cl, Har. 61 CJ56
Kenton Pk Cres, Har. 61 CK56
Kenton Pk Rd, Har. 61 CJ56
Kenton Rd E9 85 DX65
Kenton Rd, Har. 61 CK57
Kenton St WC1 195 P4
Kenton St WC1 83 DL70
Kenton Way, Hayes 77 BS69
Exmouth Rd
Kenton Way, Wok. 166 AT117
Kents Pas, Hmptn. 136 BZ95
Kentwode Grn SW13 99 CU80
Kenver Av N12 44 DD51
Kenward Rd SE9 124 EJ85
Kenway, Rain. 90 FJ69
Kenway, Rom. 51 FC54
Kenway Cl, Rain. 90 FJ69
Kenway
Kenway Dr, Amer. 20 AV39
Kenway Rd SW5 100 DB77
Kenway Wk, Rain. 90 FK69
Kenway
Kenwood Av N14 29 DK43
Kenwood Av SE14 103 DX81
Besson St
Kenwood Cl NW3 64 DD60
Kenwood Cl, West Dr. 94 BN79
Kenwood Dr, Beck. 143 EC97
Kenwood Dr, Rick. 37 BF47
Kenwood Dr, Walt. 153 BV107
Kenwood Gdns E18 68 EH55
Kenwood Gdns, Ilf. 69 EN56
Kenwood Pk, Wey. 153 BR107
Kenwood Ridge, Ken. 175 DP117
Kenwood Rd N6 64 DF58
Kenwood Rd N9 46 DU46
Kenworth Cl, Wal.Cr. 15 DX33
Kenworthy Rd E9 67 DY64
Kenwyn Dr NW2 62 CS62
Kenwyn Rd SW4 101 DK84
Kenwyn Rd SW20 139 CW95
Kenwyn Rd, Dart. 128 FK85
Kenya Rd SE7 104 EK80
Kenyngton Dr, Sun. 115 BU92
Kenyngton Pl, Har. 61 CJ57
Kenyon St SW6 99 CX81
Keogh Rd E15 86 EE65
Kepler Rd SW4 101 DL84
Keppel Rd E6 87 EM66
Keppel Rd, Dag. 70 EY63
Keppel Row SE1 201 H3
Keppel Spur, Wind. 112 AV87
Keppel St WC1 195 N6
Keppel St WC1 83 DK71
Kerbela St E2 84 DU70
Cheshire St
Kerbey St E14 85 EB72
Kerdistone Cl, Pot.B. 12 DB30
Kerfield Cres SE5 102 DR81
Kerfield Pl SE5 102 DR81
Kernow Cl, Horn. 72 FL61
Kerri Cl, Barn. 27 CW42
Kerridge Ct N1 84 DS65
Kerrill Av, Couls. 175 DN119
Kerrison Pl W5 79 CK74
Kerrison Rd E15 85 ED67
Kerrison Rd SW11 100 DE83
Kerrison Rd W5 79 CK74
Kerrison Vil W5 79 CK74
Kerrison Pl
Kerry Av, S.Ock. 108 FM75
Kerry Av, Stan. 41 CK49
Kerry Cl E16 86 EH72
Kerry Cl N13 45 DM47
Kerry Cl, Upmin. 73 FT59
Kerry Ct, Stan. 41 CK49
Kerry Dr, Upmin. 73 FT59
Kerry Path SE14 103 DZ79
Kerry Rd
Kerry Rd SE14 103 DZ79
Kerry Ter, Wok. 167 BB116
Kersey Dr, S.Croy. 160 DW112
Kersey Gdns SE9 124 EL91
Kersey Gdns, Rom. 52 FL53
Kersfield Rd SW15 119 CX86
Kershaw Cl SW18 120 DD86
Westover Rd
Kershaw Cl (Chafford Hundred), Grays 109 FW77
Kershaw Cl, Horn. 72 FL59
Kershaw Rd, Dag. 70 FA62
Kersley Ms SW11 100 DF82
Kersley Rd N16 66 DS62
Kersley St SW11 100 DF82
Kerstin Cl, Hayes 77 BT73
St. Mary's Rd
Kerswell Cl N15 66 DS57
Kerwick Cl N7 83 DM66
Sutterton St
Keslake Rd NW6 81 CX68
Kessock Cl N17 66 DV57
Kesteven Cl, Ilf. 49 ET51
Kestlake Rd, Bex. 126 EW86
East Rochester Way
Keston Av, Add. 152 BG111
Keston Av, Couls. 175 DN119
Keston Av, Kes. 162 EJ106
Keston Cl N18 46 DR48
Keston Cl, Well. 106 EW80
Keston Gdns, Kes. 162 EJ105
Keston Ms, Wat. 23 BV40
Nascot Rd
Keston Pk Cl, Kes. 145 EM104
Keston Rd N17 66 DR55
Keston Rd SE15 102 DU83
Keston Rd, Th.Hth. 141 DN100
Kestrel Av E6 86 EL71
Swan App
Kestrel Av SE24 121 DP85
Kestrel Av, Stai. 113 BF90
Kestrel Cl NW9 42 CS54
Kestrel Cl NW10 62 CR64
Kestrel Cl, Epsom 156 CN112
Kestrel Cl, Horn. 89 FH66
Kestrel Cl, Ilf. 50 EW49
Kestrel Cl, Kings.T. 117 CK91
Kestrel Cl, Wat. 8 BY34
Kestrel Ho EC1 197 H2
Kestrel Ho EC1 83 DP69
Kestrel Ho W13 79 CF70
Kestrel Pl SE14 103 DY79
Milton Ct Rd
Kestrel Rd, Wal.Abb. 16 EG34
Kestrel Way, Croy. 161 ED109
Kestrels, The, St.Alb. 8 BZ31
Bucknalls Dr
Keswick Av SW15 118 CS92
Keswick Av SW19 140 DA96
Keswick Av, Horn. 72 FK60
Keswick Bdy SW15 119 CY85
Upper Richmond Rd
Keswick Cl, Sutt. 158 DC105
Keswick Ct, Slou. 74 AT73
Stoke Rd
Keswick Dr, Enf. 30 DW36
Keswick Gdns, Ilf. 68 EL57
Keswick Gdns, Ruis. 59 BR58
Keswick Gdns, Wem. 62 CL63
Keswick Ms W5 80 CL74
Keswick Rd SW15 119 CY85
Keswick Rd, Bexh. 106 FA82
Keswick Rd, Egh. 113 BB94
Keswick Rd, Orp. 145 ET102
Keswick Rd, Twick. 116 CC86
Keswick Rd, W.Wick. 144 EE103
Kett Gdns SW2 121 DM85
Kettering Rd, Enf. 31 DX37
Beaconsfield Rd
Kettering Rd, Rom. 52 FL52
Kettering St SW16 121 DJ93
Kettlebaston Rd E10 67 DZ60
Kettlewell Cl N11 44 DG51
Kettlewell Cl, Wok. 150 AX114
Kettlewell Ct, Swan. 147 FF96
Kettlewell Dr, Wok. 150 AY114
Kettlewell Hill, Wok. 150 AY114
Ketton Grn, Red. 185 DK128
Malmstone Av
Kevan Dr, Wok. 167 BE124
Kevan Ho SE5 102 DQ80
Kevelioc Rd N17 46 DQ53
Kevin Cl, Houns. 96 BX82
Kevington Cl, Orp. 145 ET98
Kevington Dr, Chis. 145 ET98
Kevington Dr, Orp. 145 ET98
Kew Br, Brent. 98 CM79
Kew Br, Rich. 98 CM79
Kew Br Arches, Rich. 98 CM79
Kew Br
Kew Br Ct W4 98 CN78
Kew Br Rd, Brent. 98 CM79
Kew Cres, Sutt. 139 CY104
Kew Foot Rd, Rich. 98 CL84
Kew Gdns Rd, Rich. 98 CM80
Kew Grn, Rich. 98 CN79
Kew Meadow Path, Rich. 98 CN81
Kew Palace, Rich. 98 CL80
Kew Rd, Rich. 98 CL83
Kewferry Dr, Nthwd. 39 BP50
Kewferry Rd, Nthwd. 39 BQ51
Key Cl E1 84 DV70
Keybridge Ho SW8 101 DL79
Keyes Rd NW2 63 CX64
Keyes Rd, Dart. 108 FM84
Keymer Cl, West. 178 EK116
Keymer Rd SW2 121 DM89
Keynes Cl N2 64 DF55
Keynsham Av, Wdf.Grn. 48 EE49
Keynsham Gdns SE9 124 EL85
Keynsham Rd SE9 124 EK85
Keynsham Rd, Mord. 140 DB102
Keynsham Wk, Mord. 140 DB102
Keys, The, Brwd. 53 FW51
Eagle Way
Keyse Rd SE1 201 P7
Keysham Av, Houns. 95 BU81
The Av
Keystone Cres N1 196 A1
Keywood Dr, Sun. 115 BU93
Keyworth Cl E5 67 DY63
Keyworth St SE1 200 G6
Keyworth St SE1 101 DP76
Kezia St SE8 103 DY78
Trundleys Rd
Khalsa Av, Grav. 131 GJ87
Khama Rd SW17 120 DE91
Khartoum Pl, Grav. 131 GJ86
Khartoum Rd E13 86 EH69
Khartoum Rd SW17 120 DD91
Khartoum Rd, Ilf. 69 EP64
Khyber Rd SW11 100 DE82
Kibworth St SW8 101 DM80
Kidbrooke Gdns SE3 104 EG82
Kidbrooke Gro SE3 104 EG81
Kidbrooke La SE9 104 EL84
Kidbrooke Pk Cl SE3 104 EH81
Kidbrooke Pk Rd SE3 104 EH81
Kidbrooke Way SE3 104 EH82
Kidd Pl SE7 104 EL78
Kidderminster Pl, Croy. 141 DP102
Kidderminster Rd
Kidderminster Rd, Croy. 141 DP102
Kidderpore Av NW3 64 DA63
Kidderpore Gdns NW3 64 DA63
Kidlington Way NW9 42 CS54
Kielder Cl, Ilf. 49 ET51
Kiffen St EC2 197 L4
Kilberry Cl, Islw. 97 CD81
Kilburn Br NW6 81 CZ66
Kilburn High Rd
Kilburn Gate NW6 82 DB68
Kilburn Priory
Kilburn High Rd NW6 81 CZ66
Kilburn La W9 81 CX69
Kilburn La W10 81 CX69
Kilburn Pk Rd NW6 82 DA69
Kilburn Pl NW6 82 DA67
Kilburn Priory NW6 82 DB67
Kilburn Sq NW6 82 DA67
Kilburn High Rd
Kilburn Vale NW6 82 DB67
Belsize Rd
Kilby Cl, Wat. 24 BX35
Kilcorral Cl, Epsom 157 CU114
Kildare Cl, Ruis. 60 BW60
Kildare Gdns W2 82 DA72
Kildare Rd E16 86 EG71
Kildare Ter W2 82 DA72
Kildare Wk E14 85 EA72
Farrance St
Kildonan Cl, Wat. 23 BT39
Kildoran Rd SW2 121 DL85
Kildowan Rd, Ilf. 70 EU60
Kilgour Rd SE23 123 DY86
Kilkie St SW6 100 DC82
Killarney Rd SW18 120 DC86
Killasser Ct, Tad. 173 CW123
Killburns Mill Cl, Wall. 159 DH105
London Rd
Killearn Rd SE6 123 ED88
Killester Gdns, Wor.Pk. 157 CV105
Killewarren Way, Orp. 146 EW100
Killick Cl, Sev. 190 FE121
Killick St N1 83 DM68
Killieser Av SW2 121 DL89
Killip Cl E16 86 EF72
Killowen Av, Nthlt. 60 CC64
Killowen Rd E9 85 DX65
Killy Hill, Wok. 150 AS108
Killy Hill, Wok. 150 AS108
Broom La
Killyon Rd SW8 101 DJ82
Killyon Ter SW8 101 DJ82
Kilmaine Rd SW6 99 CY80
Kilmarnock Gdns, Dag. 70 EW62
Lindsey Rd
Kilmarnock Pk, Reig. 184 DB133
Kilmarnock Rd, Wat. 40 BX49
Kilmarsh Rd W6 99 CW77
Kilmartin Av SW16 141 DM97
Kilmartin Rd, Ilf. 70 EU61
Kilmartin Way, Horn. 71 FH64
Kilmeston Way SE15 102 DT80
Daniel Gdns
Kilmington Cl, Brwd. 55 GB47
Kilmington Rd SW13 99 CU79
Kilmiston Av, Shep. 135 BQ100
Kilmorey Gdns, Twick. 117 CH85
Kilmorey Rd, Twick. 97 CH84
Kilmorie Rd SE23 123 DY88
Kiln Av, Amer. 20 AW38
Kiln Cl, Hayes 95 BR79
Brickfield La
Kiln La, Chesh. 4 AV31
Kiln La, Epsom 156 CS111
Kiln La, Wok. 168 BH124
Kiln Ms SW17 120 DD92
Kiln Pl NW5 64 DG64
Kiln Rd, Epp. 18 FA27
Kiln Way, Grays 110 FZ78
Kiln Way, Nthwd. 39 BS51
Kiln Wd La, Rom. 51 FD50
Kilndown, Grav. 131 GK93
Kilner St E14 85 EA71
Kilnside, Esher 155 CG108
Kilnwood, Sev. 164 EZ113
Kilpatrick Way, Hayes 78 BY71
Kilravock St W10 81 CY69
Kilross Rd, Felt. 115 BR88
Kilrue La, Walt. 153 BT105
Kilrush Ter, Wok. 167 BA116
Kilsby Wk, Dag. 88 EV65
Rugby Rd
Kilsha Rd, Walt. 135 BV100
Kilsmore La, Wal.Cr. 15 DX28
Kilvinton Dr, Enf. 30 DR38
Kilworth Av, Brwd. 55 GA44
Kimbell Gdns SW6 99 CY81
Kimbell Pl SE3 104 EJ84
Tudway Rd
Kimber Rd SW18 120 DA87
Kimberley Av E6 86 EL68
Kimberley Av SE15 102 DV82
Kimberley Av, Ilf. 69 ER59
Kimberley Av, Rom. 71 FC58
Kimberley Cl, Slou. 93 AZ77
Kimberley Dr, Sid. 126 EX89
Kimberley Gdns N4 65 DP57
Kimberley Gdns, Enf. 30 DT41
Kimberley Gate, Brom. 124 EF94
Oaklands Rd
Kimberley Pl, Pur. 159 DN111
Brighton Rd
Kimberley Ride, Cob. 154 CB113
Kimberley Rd E4 48 EE46
Kimberley Rd E11 67 ED61
Kimberley Rd E16 86 EF70
Kimberley Rd E17 47 DZ53
Kimberley Rd N17 46 DU54
Kimberley Rd N18 46 DV51
Kimberley Rd NW6 81 CY67
Kimberley Rd SW9 101 DL82
Kimberley Rd, Beck. 143 DX96
Kimberley Rd, Croy. 141 DP100
Kimberley Way E4 48 EE46
Kimble Cl, Wat. 23 BS44
Kimble Cres, Bushey 40 CC45
Kimble Rd SW19 120 DD93
Kimbolton Cl SE12 124 EF86
Kimbolton Grn, Borwd. 26 CQ42
Kimbolton Row SW3 198 B9
Kimmeridge Gdns SE9 124 EL91
Kimmeridge Rd SE9 124 EL91
Kimpton Av, Brwd. 54 FV45
Kimpton Pl, Wat. 8 BX34
Kimpton Rd SE5 102 DR81
Kimpton Rd, Sutt. 139 CZ103
Kimpton Trade Business Cen, Sutt. 139 CZ103
Kimptons Cl, Pot.B. 11 CX33
Kimptons Mead, Pot.B. 11 CX32
Kinburn Dr, Egh. 112 AY92
Kinburn St SE16 203 H4
Kinburn St SE16 103 DX75
Kincaid Rd SE15 102 DV80
Kincardine Gdns W9 81 CZ70
Harrow Rd
Kinch Gro, Wem. 62 CM59
Kincraig Dr, Sev. 190 FG124
Kinder Cl SE28 88 EX73
Kinder St E1 84 DV72
Cannon St Rd
Kindersley Way, Abb.L. 7 BQ31
Kinetic Cres, Enf. 31 DZ36
Kinfauns Av, Horn. 72 FJ58
Kinfauns Rd SW2 121 DN89
Kinfauns Rd, Ilf. 70 EU60
King Acre Ct, Stai. 113 BE90
Victoria Rd
King Alfred Av SE6 123 EA90
King Alfred Rd, Rom. 52 FM54
King & Queen Cl SE9 124 EL91
St. Keverne Rd
King & Queen St SE17 201 J9
King & Queen St SE17 102 DQ78
King Arthur Cl SE15 102 DW80
King Arthur Ct, Wal.Cr. 15 DX31
King Charles Cres, Surb. 138 CM101
King Charles Rd, Rad. 10 CL32
King Charles Rd, Surb. 138 CM99
King Charles St SW1 199 N4
King Charles St SW1 101 DK75
King Charles Ter E1 202 E1
King Charles Wk SW19 119 CY88
Princes Way
King David La E1 84 DW73
King Edward Av, Dart. 128 FK86
King Edward Av, Rain. 90 FK68

King Edward Dr, Chess. 138 CL104
Kelvin Gro
King Edward Dr, Grays 110 GE75
King Edward Ms SW13 99 CU81
King Edward Rd E10 67 EC60
King Edward Rd E17 67 DY55
King Edward Rd, Barn. 28 DA42
King Edward Rd, Brwd. 54 FW48
King Edward Rd, Green. 129 FU85
King Edward Rd, Rad. 10 CM33
King Edward Rd, Rom. 71 FF58
King Edward Rd, Wal.Cr. 15 DY33
King Edward Rd, Wat. 24 BY44
King Edward VII Av, Wind. 92 AS80
King Edward St EC1 197 H8
King Edward St EC1 84 DQ72
King Edward III Ms SE16 202 E5
King Edward Wk SE1 200 E6
King Edward Wk SE1 101 DN76
King Edward's Gdns W3 80 CN74
King Edwards Gro, Tedd. 117 CH93
King Edward's Pl W3 80 CN74
King Edward's Gdns
King Edwards Rd E9 84 DV67
King Edwards Rd N9 46 DV45
King Edwards Rd, Bark. 87 ER67
King Edward's Rd, Enf. 31 DX42
King Edwards Rd, Ruis. 59 BR60
King Frederik IX Twr SE16 203 M6
King Gdns, Croy. 159 DP106
King George Av E16 86 EK72
King George Av, Bushey 24 CB44
King George Av, Ilf. 69 ER57
King George Av, Walt. 136 BX102
King George Cl, Rom. 71 FC55
King George Cl, Sun. 115 BT92
Groveley Rd
King George Rd, Wal.Abb. 15 EC34
King George VI Av, Mitch. 140 DF98
King George VI Av, West. 178 EK116
King George Sq, Rich. 118 CM86
King George St SE10 103 EC80
King Georges Av, Wat. 23 BS43
King Georges Dr, Add. 152 BG110
King Georges Dr, Sthl. 78 BZ71
King Georges Rd, Brwd. 54 FV44
King George's Trd Est, Chess. 156 CN105
King Harolds Way, Bexh. 106 EX80
King Henry Ms, Orp. 163 ET106
Osgood Av
King Henry St N16 66 DS64
King Henry Ter E1 202 E1
King Henry's Ct, Wal.Abb. 31 EC40
Sewardstone Rd
King Henry's Dr, Croy. 161 EC109
King Henry's Ms, Enf. 31 EA37
King Henry's Rd NW3 82 DE66
King Henry's Rd, Kings.T. 138 CP97
King Henry's Wk N1 84 DS65
King James Av (Cuffley), Pot.B. 13 DL29
King James Ct SE1 101 DP75
Borough Rd
King James St SE1 200 G5
King James St SE1 101 DP75
King John Ct EC2 197 N4
King John St E1 85 DX71
King John's Cl, Stai. 112 AW86
King Johns Wk SE9 124 EK88
King Sq EC1 197 H3
King Stairs Cl SE16 202 E4
King St E13 86 EG70
King St EC2 197 J9
King St EC2 84 DQ72
King St N2 64 DD55
King St N17 46 DT53
King St SW1 199 L3
King St SW1 83 DJ74
King St W3 80 CP74
King St W6 99 CU77
King St WC2 195 P10
King St WC2 83 DL73
King St, Cher. 134 BG102
King St, Grav. 131 GH86
King St, Rich. 117 CK85
King St, Sthl. 96 BY76
King St, Twick. 117 CG88
King St, Wat. 24 BW42
King William Ct, Wal.Abb. 31 EC40
Sewardstone Rd
King William IV Gdns SE20 122 DW93
St. John's Rd
King William La SE10 104 EE78
Orlop St
King William St EC4 201 L1
King William St EC4 84 DR73
King William Wk SE10 103 EC79
Kingaby Gdns, Rain. 89 FG66
Kingcup Cl, Croy. 143 DX102
Primrose La
Kingdon Rd NW6 82 DA65
Kingfield Cl, Wok. 167 AZ120
Kingfield Dr, Wok. 167 AZ120
Kingfield Gdns, Wok. 167 AZ120
Kingfield Grn, Wok. 167 AZ120
Kingfield Rd W5 79 CK70
Kingfield Rd, Wok. 166 AY120
Kingfield St E14 204 E9
Kingfield St E14 103 EC77
Kingfisher Av E11 68 EH58
Eastern Av
Kingfisher Cl SE28 88 EW73
Kingfisher Cl, Brwd. 55 GA45
Kingfisher Cl, Har. 41 CF52
Kingfisher Cl, Nthwd. 39 BP53
Kingfisher Cl, Orp. 146 EX98
Kingfisher Cl, Walt. 154 BY106
Old Esher Rd
Kingfisher Ct SW19 119 CY89
Queensmere Rd
Kingfisher Ct, Enf. 29 DM38
Mount Vw
Kingfisher Ct, Surb. 138 CM101
Ewell Rd
Kingfisher Ct, Sutt. 139 CY103
Gander Grn La
Kingfisher Ct, Wok. 151 BC114
Blackmore Cres
Kingfisher Dr, Red. 184 DG131
Kingfisher Dr, Rich. 117 CH91
Kingfisher Dr, Stai. 113 BF91
Kingfisher Gdns, S.Croy. 161 DX111
Kingfisher Lure, Kings L. 7 BP29
Kingfisher Lure, Rick. 22 BH42
Kingfisher Rd, Upmin. 73 FT60
Kingfisher Sq SE8 103 DZ79
Kingfisher St E6 86 EL71
Kingfisher Wk NW9 42 CS54
Eagle Dr
Kingfisher Way NW10 80 CR65
Kingfisher Way, Beck. 143 DX99
Kingham Cl SW18 120 DC87
Kingham Cl W11 99 CY75
Kinghorn St EC1 197 H7
Kinglake Ct, Wok. 166 AS118
Raglan Rd
Kinglake Est SE17 201 N10
Kinglake St SE17 102 DS78
Kingly Ct W1 195 K10
Kingly St W1 195 K9
Kingly St W1 83 DJ72
Kings Arbour, Sthl. 96 BY78
Kings Arms Ct E1 84 DU71
Old Montague St
Kings Arms Yd EC2 197 K8
Kings Av N10 64 DG55
Kings Av N21 45 DP46
King's Av SW4 121 DK87
King's Av SW12 121 DK88
Kings Av W5 79 CK72
Kings Av, Brom. 124 EF93
Kings Av, Buck.H. 48 EK47
Kings Av, Cars. 158 DE108
Kings Av, Grnf. 78 CB72
Kings Av, Houns. 96 CB81
Kings Av, N.Mal. 138 CS98
Kings Av, Rom. 70 EZ58
Kings Av, Sun. 115 BT92
Kings Av, Wat. 23 BT42
Kings Av, W.Byf. 152 BK112
Kings Av, Wdf.Grn. 48 EH50
Kings Bench St SE1 200 G4
Kings Bench Wk EC4 196 E9
Kings Chace Vw, Enf. 29 DN40
Crofton Way
Kings Chase, Brwd. 54 FW48
Kings Chase, E.Mol. 136 CC97
Kings Cl E10 67 EB59
Kings Cl NW4 63 CX56
Kings Cl, Ch.St.G. 36 AX47
Kings Cl, Dart. 107 FE84
Kings Cl, Kings L. 6 BH31
Kings Cl, Nthwd. 39 BT51
Kings Cl, Stai. 114 BK94
Kings Cl, T.Ditt. 137 CG100
Kings Cl, Walt. 135 BV102
King's Cl, Wat. 23 BV42
Lady's Cl
Kings Coll Rd NW3 82 DE66
Kings Coll Rd, Ruis. 59 BT58
Kings Ct E13 86 EH67
Kings Ct W6 99 CU77
King St
Kings Ct, Tad. 173 CW122
Kings Ct, Wem. 62 CP61
Kings Ct S SW3 100 DE78
Chelsea Manor Gdns
Kings Cres N4 66 DQ62
Kings Cres Est N4 66 DQ61
King's Cross Br N1 196 A2
King's Cross Rd WC1 196 C2
King's Cross Rd WC1 83 DM69
Kings Dr, Edg. 42 CM49
Kings Dr, Grav. 131 GH90
Kings Dr, Surb. 138 CN101
Kings Dr, Tedd. 117 CD92
Kings Dr, T.Ditt. 137 CH100
Kings Dr, Wem. 62 CP61
Kings Dr, The, Walt. 153 BT109
Kings Fm Av, Rich. 98 CN84
Kings Fm Rd, Rick. 21 BD44
Kings Gdns NW6 82 DA66
West End La
Kings Gdns, Ilf. 69 ER60
Kings Gdns, Upmin. 73 FS59
King's Garth Ms SE23 122 DW89
London Rd
Kings Grn, Loug. 32 EL41
Kings Gro SE15 102 DV80
Kings Gro, Rom. 71 FG57
Kings Hall Rd, Beck. 123 DY94
Kings Head Hill E4 47 EB45
Kings Head La, W.Byf. 152 BK111
Kings Head Yd SE1 201 K3
Kings Highway SE18 105 ES79
Kings Hill, Loug. 32 EL40
Kings Keep, Kings.T. 138 CL98
Beaufort Rd
Kings La, Egh. 112 AU92
Kings La, Kings L. 6 BG31
Kings La, Sutt. 158 DD107
Kings Langley Bypass, Kings L. 6 BK28
Kings Lynn Cl, Rom. 52 FK51
Kings Lynn Dr
Kings Lynn Dr, Rom. 52 FK51
Kings Lynn Path, Rom. 52 FK51
Kings Lynn Dr
Kings Mead Pk, Esher 155 CE108
Kings Meadow, Kings L. 6 BN28
Kings Ms SW4 121 DL85
King's Av
King's Ms WC1 196 C5
King's Ms WC1 83 DM71
Kings Ms, Chig. 49 EQ47
Kings Oak, Rom. 70 FA55
King's Orchard SE9 124 EL86
King's Paddock, Hmptn. 136 CC95
Kings Par, Cars. 140 DE104
Wrythe La
King's Pas E11 68 EE59
Kings Pas, Kings.T. 137 CK96
Kings Pl SE1 201 H5
Kings Pl W4 98 CQ78
Kings Pl, Buck.H. 48 EJ47
Kings Pl, Loug. 48 EJ45
Fallow Flds
King's Reach Twr SE1 200 E2
King's Reach Twr SE1 83 DN74
Kings Ride Gate, Rich. 98 CN84
Kings Rd E4 47 ED46
Kings Rd E6 86 EJ67
Kings Rd E11 68 EE59
King's Rd N17 46 DT53
Kings Rd N18 46 DU50
Kings Rd N22 45 DM53
Kings Rd NW10 81 CV66
Kings Rd SE25 142 DU97
King's Rd SW1 198 C10
King's Rd SW1 100 DF78
King's Rd SW3 198 C10
King's Rd SW3 100 DF78
King's Rd SW6 100 DB81
King's Rd SW10 100 DB81
Kings Rd SW14 98 CR83
Kings Rd SW19 120 DA93
Kings Rd W5 79 CK71
Kings Rd, Add. 152 BH110
Kings Rd, Bark. 87 EQ66
North St
Kings Rd, Barn. 27 CW41
Kings Rd, Brwd. 54 FW48
Kings Rd, Ch.St.G. 36 AX47
Kings Rd, Egh. 113 BA91
Kings Rd, Felt. 116 BW88
Kings Rd, Har. 60 BZ61
Kings Rd, Kings.T. 118 CL94
Kings Rd, Mitch. 140 DG97
Kings Rd, Orp. 163 ET105
Kings Rd, Rich. 118 CM85
Kings Rd, Rom. 71 FG57
Kings Rd (London Colney), St.Alb. 9 CJ26
Kings Rd, Slou. 92 AS76
Kings Rd, Surb. 137 CJ102
Kings Rd, Sutt. 158 DA110
Kings Rd, Tedd. 117 CD92
Kings Rd, Twick. 117 CH86
King's Rd, Uxb. 76 BK68
Kings Rd, Wal.Cr. 15 DY34
Kings Rd, Walt. 135 BV103
Kings Rd, West Dr. 94 BM75
Kings Rd, West. 178 EJ116
Kings Rd, Wok. 167 BA116
Kings Rd Bungalows, Har. 60 BZ62
Kings Rd
King's Scholars' Pas SW1 199 K8
King's Ter NW1 83 DJ67
Plender St
Kings Ter, Islw. 97 CG83
Worple Rd
Kings Wk, Grays 110 GA79
King's Wk, Kings.T. 137 CK95
Kings Wk, S.Croy. 160 DV114
Kings Warren (Oxshott), Lthd. 154 CC111
Kings Way, Har. 61 CE56
Kingsand Rd SE12 124 EG89
Kingsash Dr, Hayes 78 BY70
Kingsbridge Av W3 98 CM75
Kingsbridge Circ, Rom. 52 FL51
Kingsbridge Cl, Rom. 52 FL51
Kingsbridge Cres, Sthl. 78 BZ71
Kingsbridge Rd W10 81 CW72
Kingsbridge Rd, Bark. 87 ER68
Kingsbridge Rd, Mord. 139 CX101
Kingsbridge Rd, Rom. 52 FL51
Kingsbridge Rd, Sthl. 96 BZ77
Kingsbridge Rd, Walt. 135 BV101
Kingsbridge Way, Hayes 77 BS69
Kingsbrook, Lthd. 171 CG118
Ryebrook Rd
Kingsbury Circle NW9 62 CN57
Kingsbury Cres, Stai. 113 BD91
Kingsbury Dr, Wind. 112 AV86
Kingsbury Rd N1 84 DS65
Kingsbury Rd NW9 62 CP57
Kingsbury Ter N1 84 DS65
Kingsbury Trd Est NW9 62 CR58
Kingsclere Cl SW15 119 CU87
Kingsclere Ct, Barn. 28 DC43
Gloucester Rd
Kingsclere Pl, Enf. 30 DQ40
Chase Side
Kingscliffe Gdns SW19 119 CZ88
Kingscote Rd W4 98 CR76
Kingscote Rd, Croy. 142 DV101
Kingscote Rd, N.Mal. 138 CR97
Kingscote St EC4 196 F10
Kingscourt Rd SW16 121 DK90
Kingscroft Rd NW2 81 CZ65
Kingscroft Rd, Bans. 174 DD115
Kingscroft Rd, Lthd. 171 CH120
Kingsdale Ct, Wal.Abb. 16 EG34
Lamplighters Cl
Kingsdale Gdns W11 81 CX74
Kingsdale Rd SE18 105 ET80
Kingsdale Rd SE20 123 DX94
Kingsdene, Tad. 173 CV121
Kingsdown Av W3 80 CS73
Kingsdown Av W13 97 CH75
Kingsdown Av, S.Croy. 159 DP109
Kingsdown Cl SE16 102 DV78
Masters Dr
Kingsdown Cl W10 81 CX72
Kingsdown Cl, Grav. 131 GM88
Farley Rd
Kingsdown Rd E11 68 EE62
Kingsdown Rd N19 65 DL61
Kingsdown Rd, Epsom 157 CU113
Kingsdown Rd, Sutt. 157 CY106
Kingsdown Way, Brom. 144 EG101
Kingsdowne Rd, Surb. 138 CL101
Kingsend, Ruis. 59 BR60
Kingsfield Av, Har. 60 CB56
Kingsfield Ct, Wat. 40 BX45
Kingsfield Dr, Enf. 31 DX35
Kingsfield Ho SE9 124 EK90
Kingsfield Rd, Har. 61 CD59
Kingsfield Rd, Wat. 40 BX45
Kingsfield Ter, Dart. 128 FK86
Priory Rd
Kingsfield Way, Enf. 31 DX35
Kingsford Av, Wall. 159 DL108
Kingsford St NW5 64 DF64
Kingsford Way E6 87 EM71
Kingsgate, Wem. 62 CQ62
Kingsgate Av N3 64 DA55
Kingsgate Cl, Bexh. 106 EY81
Kingsgate Cl, Orp. 146 EW97
Main Rd
Kingsgate Pl NW6 82 DA66
Kingsgate Rd NW6 82 DA66
Kingsgate Rd, Kings.T. 138 CL95
Kingsground SE9 124 EL87
Kingshall Ms SE13 103 EC83
Lewisham Rd
Kingshill Av, Har. 61 CH56
Kingshill Av, Hayes 77 BS69
Kingshill Av, Nthlt. 77 BU69
Kingshill Av, Rom. 51 FC51
Kingshill Av, Wor.Pk. 139 CU101
Kingshill Dr, Har. 61 CH55
Kingshold Rd E9 84 DW66
Kingsholm Gdns SE9 104 EK84
Kingshurst Rd SE12 124 EG87
Kingsland NW8 82 DE67
Broxwood Way
Kingsland, Pot.B. 11 CZ33
Kingsland Grn E8 84 DS65
Kingsland High St E8 66 DT64
Kingsland Pas E8 84 DS65
Kingsland Grn
Kingsland Rd E2 197 N2
Kingsland Rd E2 84 DS68
Kingsland Rd E8 84 DS68
Kingsland Rd E13 86 EJ69
Kingslawn Cl SW15 119 CV85
Howards La
Kingslea, Lthd. 171 CG120
Kingsleigh Pl, Mitch. 140 DF97
Chatsworth Pl
Kingsleigh Wk, Brom. 144 EF98
Stamford Dr
Kingsley Av W13 79 CG72
Kingsley Av, Bans. 174 DA115
Kingsley Av, Borwd. 26 CM40
Kingsley Av, Dart. 128 FN85
Kingsley Av, Egh. 112 AV93
Kingsley Av, Houns. 96 CC82
Kingsley Av, Sthl. 78 CA73
Kingsley Av, Sutt. 158 DD105
Kingsley Av (Cheshunt), Wal.Cr. 14 DV29
Kingsley Cl N2 64 DC57
Kingsley Cl, Dag. 71 FB63
Kingsley Ct, Edg. 42 CP47
Kingsley Dr, Wor.Pk. 139 CT103
Badgers Copse
Kingsley Flats SE1 102 DS77
Old Kent Rd
Kingsley Gdns E4 47 EA50
Kingsley Gdns, Horn. 72 FK56
Kingsley Ms E1 202 E1
Kingsley Ms W8 100 DB76
Stanford Rd
Kingsley Ms, Chis. 125 EP93
Kingsley Pl N6 64 DG59
Kingsley Rd E7 86 EG66
Kingsley Rd E17 47 EC54
Kingsley Rd N13 45 DN49
Kingsley Rd NW6 81 CZ67
Kingsley Rd SW19 120 DB92
Kingsley Rd, Brwd. 55 GD45
Kingsley Rd, Croy. 141 DN102
Kingsley Rd, Har. 60 CC63
Kingsley Rd, Houns. 96 CC82
Kingsley Rd, Ilf. 49 EQ53
Kingsley Rd, Loug. 33 ER41
Kingsley Rd, Orp. 163 ET108
Kingsley Rd, Pnr. 60 BZ56
Kingsley St SW11 100 DF83
Kingsley Wk, Grays 111 GG77
Kingsley Way N2 64 DC58
Kingsley Wd Dr SE9 125 EM90
Kingslyn Cres SE19 142 DS95
Kingsman Par SE18 105 EM76
Woolwich Ch St
Kingsman St SE18 105 EM76
Kingsmead, Barn. 28 DA42
Kingsmead (Cuffley), Pot.B. 13 DL28
Kingsmead, Rich. 118 CM86
Kingsmead, Wal.Cr. 15 DX28
Kingsmead, West. 178 EK116
Kingsmead Av N9 46 DV46
Kingsmead Av NW9 62 CR59
Kingsmead Av, Mitch. 141 DJ97
Kingsmead Av, Rom. 71 FE58
Kingsmead Av, Sun. 136 BW97
Kingsmead Av, Surb. 138 CN103
Kingsmead Av, Wor.Pk. 139 CV104
Kingsmead Cl, Epsom 156 CR108
Kingsmead Cl, Sid. 126 EU89
Kingsmead Cl, Tedd. 117 CG93
Kingsmead Dr, Nthlt. 78 BZ66
Kingsmead Est E9 67 DY63
Kingsmead Way
Kingsmead Rd SW2 121 DN89
Kingsmead Way E9 67 DY63
Kingsmere Cl SW15 99 CY83
Felsham Rd
Kingsmere Pk NW9 62 CP60
Kingsmere Rd SW19 119 CX89
Kingsmill Gdns, Dag. 70 EZ64
Kingsmill Rd, Dag. 70 EZ64
Kingsmill Ter NW8 82 DD68
Kingsnympton Pk, Kings.T. 118 CP93
Kingspark Ct E18 68 EG55
Kingsridge SW19 119 CY89
Kingsridge Gdns, Dart. 128 FK86
Kingsthorpe Rd SE26 123 DX91
Kingston Av, Felt. 115 BS86
Kingston Av, Lthd. 171 CH121
Kingston Av, Sutt. 139 CY104
Kingston Av, West Dr. 76 BM73
Kingston Br, Kings.T. 137 CK96
Kingston Bypass SW15 118 CS91
Kingston Bypass SW20 118 CS91
Kingston Bypass, Esher 137 CG104
Kingston Bypass, N.Mal. 139 CT95
Kingston Bypass, Surb. 138 CL104
Kingston Cl, Nthlt. 78 BZ67
Kingston Cl, Rom. 70 EY55
Kingston Cl, Tedd. 117 CH93
Kingston Ct N4 66 DQ58
Wiltshire Gdns
Kingston Ct, Grav. 130 GB85
Kingston Cres, Ashf. 114 BJ92
Kingston Cres, Beck. 143 DZ95
Kingston Gdns, Croy. 141 DL104
Wandle Rd
Kingston Hall Rd, Kings.T. 137 CK97
Kingston Hill, Kings.T. 118 CQ93
Kingston Hill Av, Rom. 70 EY55
Kingston Hill Pl, Kings.T. 118 CQ91
Kingston Ho Gdns, Lthd. 171 CG121
Upper Fairfield Rd
Kingston La, Tedd. 117 CG92
Kingston La, Uxb. 76 BL69
Kingston La, West Dr. 94 BM75
Kingston Pk Est, Kings.T. 118 CP93
Kingston Pl, Har. 41 CF52
Richmond Gdns
Kingston Ri, Add. 152 BG110
Kingston Rd N9 46 DU47
Kingston Rd SW15 119 CU88
Kingston Rd SW19 139 CZ95
Kingston Rd SW20 139 CX96
Kingston Rd, Ashf. 114 BM93
Kingston Rd, Barn. 28 DD43
Kingston Rd, Epsom 156 CS106
Kingston Rd, Ilf. 69 EP63
Kingston Rd, Kings.T. 138 CP97
Kingston Rd, Lthd. 171 CG117
Kingston Rd, N.Mal. 138 CR98
Kingston Rd, Rom. 71 FF56
Kingston Rd, Sthl. 96 BZ75
Kingston Rd, Stai. 114 BH93
Kingston Rd, Surb. 138 CP103
Kingston Rd, Tedd. 117 CH92
Kingston Rd, Wor.Pk. 138 CP103
Kingston Sq SE19 122 DR92
Kingston Vale SW15 118 CR91
Kingstown St NW1 82 DG67
Kingswater Pl SW11 100 DE80
Battersea Ch Rd
Kingsway N12 44 DC51
Kingsway SW14 98 CP83
Kingsway WC2 196 B8
Kingsway WC2 83 DM72
Kingsway, Croy. 159 DM106
Kingsway, Enf. 30 DV43
Kingsway (Chalfont St. Peter), Ger.Cr. 56 AY55
Kingsway, Hayes 77 BQ71
Kingsway, Iver 75 BE72
High St
Kingsway, N.Mal. 139 CW98
Kingsway, Orp. 145 ES99
Kingsway (Cuffley), Pot.B. 13 DL30
Kingsway, Stai. 114 BK88
Kingsway, Wat. 8 BW34
Kingsway, Wem. 62 CL63
Kingsway, W.Wick. 144 EE104
Kingsway, Wok. 166 AX118
Kingsway, Wdf.Grn. 48 EJ50
Kingsway, The, Epsom 157 CT111
Kingsway Av, S.Croy. 160 DW109
Kingsway Av, Wok. 166 AX118
Kingsway Business Pk, Hmptn. 136 BZ95
Kingsway Cres, Har. 60 CC56
Kingsway Pl EC1 76 BJ70
Sans Wk
Kingsway Rd, Sutt. 157 CY108
Kingswear Rd NW5 65 DH62
Kingswear Rd, Ruis. 59 BU61
Kingswell Ride (Cuffley), Pot.B. 13 DL30
Kingswood Av NW6 81 CY67
Kingswood Av, Belv. 106 EZ77
Kingswood Av, Brom. 144 EE97
Kingswood Av, Hmptn. 116 CB93
Kingswood Av, Houns. 96 BZ81
Kingswood Av, S.Croy. 176 DV115
Kingswood Av, Swan. 147 FF98
Kingswood Av, Th.Hth. 141 DN99
Kingswood Cl N20 28 DC44
Kingswood Cl SW8 101 DL80
Kingswood Cl, Dart. 128 FJ86
Kingswood Cl, Egh. 112 AX91
Kingswood Cl, Enf. 30 DS43
Kingswood Cl, N.Mal. 139 CT100
Motspur Pk
Kingswood Cl, Orp. 145 ER101
Kingswood Cl, Surb. 138 CL101
Kingswood Cl, Wey. 153 BP108
Kingswood Creek, Stai. 112 AX85
Kingswood Dr SE19 122 DS91
Kingswood Dr, Cars. 140 DF102
Kingswood Dr, Sutt. 158 DB109
Kingswood Est SE21 122 DS91
Bowen Dr
Kingswood La, S.Croy. 160 DW113
Kingswood La, Warl. 176 DW115
Kingswood Pk N3 43 CZ54
Kingswood Pl SE13 104 EE84
Kingswood Ri, Egh. 112 AX92
Kingswood Rd E11 67 ED61
Grove Grn Rd
Kingswood Rd SE20 122 DW93
Kingswood Rd SW2 121 DL86
Kingswood Rd SW19 119 CZ94
Kingswood Rd W4 98 CQ76
Kingswood Rd, Brom. 143 ED98
Kingswood Rd, Ilf. 70 EU60
Kingswood Rd, Sev. 181 FE120
Kingswood Rd, Tad. 173 CV121
Kingswood Rd, Wat. 7 BV34
Kingswood Rd, Wem. 62 CN62
Kingswood Ter W4 98 CQ76
Kingswood Rd
Kingswood Way, S.Croy. 160 DW113
Kingswood Way, Wall. 159 DL106
Kingsworth Cl, Beck. 143 DY99
Kingsworthy Cl, Kings.T. 138 CM97
Kingthorpe Rd NW10 80 CR66

Kingthorpe Ter NW10 80 CR65
Kingwell Rd, Barn. 28 DD38
Kingwood Rd SW6 99 CY81
Kinlet Rd SE18 105 EQ81
Kinloch Dr NW9 62 CS59
Kinloch St N7 65 DM62
Hornsey Rd
Kinloss Ct N3 63 CZ56
Haslemere Gdns
Kinloss Gdns N3 63 CZ56
Kinloss Rd, Cars. 140 DC101
Kinnaird Av W4 98 CQ80
Kinnaird Av, Brom. 124 EF93
Kinnaird Cl, Brom. 124 EF93
Kinnaird Way, Wdf.Grn. 49 EM51
Kinnear Rd W12 99 CT75
Kinnerton Pl N SW1 198 E5
Kinnerton Pl S SW1 198 E5
Kinnerton St SW1 198 F5
Kinnerton St SW1 100 DG75
Kinnerton Yd SW1 198 E5
Kinnoul Rd W6 99 CY79
Kinross Av, Wor.Pk. 139 CU103
Kinross Cl, Edg. 42 CP47
Tayside Dr
Kinross Cl, Har. 62 CM57
Kinross Cl, Sun. 115 BT92
Kinross Dr, Sun. 115 BT92
Kinsale Rd SE15 102 DU83
Kintore Way SE1 201 P8
Kintyre Cl SW16 141 DM97
Kinveachy Gdns SE7 104 EL78
Kinver Rd SE26 122 DW91
Kipings, Tad. 173 CX122
Kipling Av, Til. 111 GH81
Kipling Dr SW19 120 DD93
Kipling Est SE1 201 L5
Kipling Est SE1 102 DR75
Kipling Pl, Stan. 41 CF51
Uxbridge Rd
Kipling Rd, Bexh. 106 EY81
Kipling Rd, Dart. 128 FP85
Kipling St SE1 201 L5
Kipling St SE1 102 DR75
Kipling Ter N9 46 DR48
Kipling Twrs, Rom. 51 FH52
Kippington Cl, Sev. 190 FF124
Kippington Dr SE9 124 EK88
Kippington Ho, Sev. 190 FG126
Kippington Rd
Kippington Rd, Sev. 190 FG124
Kirby Cl, Epsom 157 CT106
Kirby Cl, Ilf. 49 ES51
Kirby Cl, Loug. 48 EL45
Kirby Cl, Nthwd. 39 BT51
Kirby Cl, Rom. 52 FN50
Kirby Est SE16 202 D6
Kirby Est SE16 102 DV76
Kirby Gro SE1 201 M4
Kirby Gro SE1 102 DS75
Kirby Rd, Dart. 128 FQ87
Kirby Rd, Wok. 166 AW117
Kirby St EC1 196 E6
Kirby Way, Walt. 136 BW100
Kirchen Rd W13 79 CH73
Kirk Ct, Sev. 190 FG123
Kirk La SE18 105 EQ79
Kirk Ri, Sutt. 140 DB104
Kirk Rd E17 67 DZ58
Kirkby Cl N11 44 DG51
Coverdale Rd
Kirkcaldy Grn, Wat. 40 BW48
Trevose Way
Kirkdale SE26 122 DV89
Kirkdale Rd E11 68 EE60
Kirkfield Cl W13 79 CH74
Broomfield Rd
Kirkham Rd E6 86 EL72
Kirkham St SE18 105 ES79
Kirkland Av, Ilf. 49 EN54
Kirkland Av, Wok. 166 AS116
Kirkland Cl, Sid. 125 ES86
Kirkland Wk E8 84 DT65
Kirkleas Rd, Surb. 138 CL102
Kirklees Rd, Dag. 70 EW64
Kirklees Rd, Th.Hth. 141 DN99
Kirkley Rd SW19 140 DA95
Kirkly Cl, S.Croy. 160 DS109
Kirkman Pl W1 195 M7
Kirkmichael Rd E14 85 EC72
Dee St
Kirks Pl E14 85 DZ71
Rhodeswell Rd
Kirkside Rd SE3 104 EG79
Kirkstall Av N17 66 DR56
Kirkstall Gdns SW2 121 DL88
Kirkstall Rd SW2 121 DK88
Kirkstead Ct E5 67 DY62
Mandeville St
Kirksted Rd, Mord. 140 DB102
Kirkstone Way, Brom. 124 EE94
Kirkton Rd N15 66 DS56
Kirkwall Pl E2 84 DW69
Kirkwall Spur, Slou. 74 AS71
Kirkwood Rd SE15 102 DV82
Kirn Rd W13 79 CH73
Kirchen Rd
Kirrane Cl, N.Mal. 139 CT99
Kirtley Rd SE26 123 DY91
Kirtling St SW8 101 DJ80
Kirton Cl W4 98 CR77
Dolman Rd
Kirton Cl, Horn. 90 FJ65
Kirton Gdns E2 84 DT69
Chambord St
Kirton Rd E13 86 EJ68
Kirton Wk, Edg. 42 CQ52
Kirwyn Way SE5 101 DP80
Kitcat Ter E3 85 EA69
Kitchener Av, Grav. 131 GJ90
Kitchener Rd E7 86 EH65
Kitchener Rd E17 47 EB53
Kitchener Rd N2 64 DE55
Kitchener Rd N17 66 DR55
Kitchener Rd, Dag. 89 FB65
Kitchener Rd, Th.Hth. 142 DR97
Kite Pl E2 84 DU69
Nelson Gdns
Kite Yd SW11 100 DF81
Cambridge Rd
Kitley Gdns SE19 142 DT95
Kitsmead La, Cher. 132 AX103
Kitson Rd SE5 102 DR80
Kitson Rd SW13 99 CU81
Kitswell Way, Rad. 9 CF33
Kitters Grn, Abb.L. 7 BS31
High St
Kittiwake Cl, S.Croy. 161 DY110
Kittiwake Pl, Sutt. 139 CY103
Gander Grn La
Kittiwake Rd, Nthlt. 78 BX69
Kittiwake Way, Hayes 78 BX71
Kitto Rd SE14 103 DX82
Kitt's End Rd, Barn. 27 CX36
Kiver Rd N19 65 DK61
Kiwi Cl, Twick. 117 CH86
Crown Rd
Klea Av SW4 121 DJ86
Knapdale Cl SE23 122 DV89
Knapmill Rd SE6 123 EA89
Knapmill Way SE6 123 EB89
Knapp Cl NW10 80 CS65
Knapp Rd E3 85 EA70
Knapp Rd, Ashf. 114 BM91
Knapton Ms SW17 120 DG93
Seely Rd
Knaresborough Dr SW18 120 DB88
Knaresborough Pl SW5 100 DB77
Knatchbull Rd NW10 80 CR67
Knatchbull Rd SE5 102 DQ81
Knebworth Av E17 47 EA53
Knebworth Path, Borwd. 26 CR42
Knebworth Rd N16 66 DS63
Nevill Rd
Knee Hill SE2 106 EW77
Knee Hill Cres SE2 106 EW77
Kneller Gdns, Islw. 117 CD85
Kneller Rd SE4 103 DY84
Kneller Rd, N.Mal. 138 CS101
Kneller Rd, Twick. 116 CC86
Knighten St E1 202 C3
Knighten St E1 84 DU74
Knightland Rd E5 66 DV61
Knighton Cl, Rom. 71 FD58
Knighton Cl, S.Croy. 159 DP108
Knighton Cl, Wdf.Grn. 48 EH49
Knighton Dr, Wdf.Grn. 48 EG49
Knighton La, Buck.H. 48 EH47
Knighton Pk Rd SE26 123 DX92
Knighton Rd E7 68 EG62
Knighton Rd, Rom. 71 FC58
Knighton Rd, Sev. 181 FF116
Knighton Way La (Denham), Uxb. 76 BH65
Knightrider Ct EC4 197 H10
Knightrider St EC4 84 DQ73
Godliman St
Knights Arc SW1 198 D5
Knights Av W5 98 CL75
Knights Cl E9 66 DW64
Churchill Wk
Knights Cl, Egh. 113 BD93
Knights Ct, Kings.T. 138 CL97
Knights Ct, Rom. 70 EY58
Knights Hill SE27 121 DP92
Knights Hill Sq SE27 121 DP91
Knights Hill
Knights La N9 46 DU48
Knights Manor Way, Dart. 128 FM86
Knights Pk, Kings.T. 138 CL97
Knights Pl, Red. 184 DG133
Noke Dr
Knights Ridge, Orp. 164 EV106
Stirling Dr
Knights Rd E16 205 N4
Knights Rd E16 104 EG75
Knights Rd, Stan. 41 CJ49
Knights Wk SE11 200 F9
Knights Wk, Rom. 34 EV41
Knight's Way, Brwd. 55 GA48
Knights Way, Ilf. 49 EQ51
Knightsbridge SW1 198 E5
Knightsbridge SW1 100 DF75
Knightsbridge SW7 198 C5
Knightsbridge SW7 100 DE75
Knightsbridge Cres, Stai. 114 BH93
Knightsbridge Gdns, Rom. 71 FD57
Knightsbridge Grn SW1 198 D5
Knightsbridge Grn SW1 100 DF75
Knightswood, Wok. 166 AT118
Knightswood Cl, Edg. 42 CQ47
Knightwood Cres, N.Mal. 138 CS100
Knipp Hill, Cob. 154 BZ113
Knivet Rd SW6 100 DA79
Knobs Hill Rd E15 85 EB67
Knockhall Chase, Green. 129 FV85
Knockhall Rd, Green. 129 FW86
Knockholt Cl, Sutt. 158 DB110
Knockholt Main Rd, Sev. 180 EY115
Knockholt Rd SE9 124 EK85
Knockholt Rd, Sev. 164 EZ113
Knole, The SE9 125 EN91
Knole, The, Grav. 130 GE94
Knole Cl, Croy. 142 DW100
Stockbury Rd
Knole Gate, Sid. 125 ES90
Woodside Cres
Knole La, Sev. 191 FJ126
Knole Rd, Dart. 127 FG87
Knole Rd, Sev. 191 FK123
Knole Way, Sev. 191 FJ125
Knoll, The W13 79 CJ71
Knoll, The, Beck. 143 EB95
Knoll, The, Brom. 144 EG103
Knoll, The, Cher. 133 BF102
Knoll, The, Cob. 154 CA113
Knoll, The, Lthd. 171 CJ120
Knoll Ct SE19 122 DT92
Knoll Cres, Nthwd. 39 BS53
Knoll Dr N14 44 DG45
Knoll Pk Rd, Cher. 133 BF102
Knoll Ri, Orp. 145 ET102
Knoll Rd SW18 120 DC85
Knoll Rd, Bex. 126 FA87
Knoll Rd, Sid. 126 EV92
Knollmead, Surb. 138 CQ102
Knolls, The, Epsom 173 CW116
Knolls Cl, Wor.Pk. 139 CV104
Knollys Cl SW16 121 DN90
Knollys Rd SW16 121 DN90
Knolton Way, Slou. 74 AW72
Knottisford St E2 84 DW69
Knotts Grn Ms E10 67 EB58
Knotts Grn Rd E10 67 EB58
Knotts Pl, Sev. 190 FG124
Knowl Hill, Wok. 167 BB119
Knowl Pk, Borwd. 26 CL43
Knowl Way, Borwd. 26 CM42
Knowland Way (Denham), Uxb. 57 BF58
Knowle, The, Tad. 173 CW121
Knowle Av, Bexh. 106 EY80
Knowle Cl SW9 101 DN83
Knowle Gdns, W.Byf. 151 BF113
Madeira Rd
Knowle Grn, Stai. 114 BG92
Knowle Gro, Vir.W. 132 AW101
Knowle Gro Cl, Vir.W. 132 AW101
Knowle Hill, Vir.W. 132 AV101
Knowle Pk, Cob. 170 BY115
Knowle Pk Av, Stai. 114 BH93
Knowle Rd, Brom. 144 EL103
Knowle Rd, Twick. 117 CE88
Knowles Cl, West Dr. 76 BL74
Knowles Hill Cres SE13 123 ED85
Knowles Wk SW4 101 DJ83
Knowlton Grn, Brom. 144 EF99
Knowsley Av, Sthl. 78 CA74
Knowsley Rd SW11 100 DF82
Knox Rd E7 86 EF65
Knox St W1 194 D6
Knox St W1 82 DF71
Knoxfield Caravan Pk, Dart. 129 FS90
Knoyle St SE14 103 DY79
Chubworthy St
Knutsford Av, Wat. 24 BX38
Koh-i-noor Av, Bushey 24 CA44
Kohat Rd SW19 120 DB92
Koonowla Cl, West. 178 EK115
Kooringa, Warl. 176 DV119
Korda Cl, Shep. 134 BM97
Kossuth St SE10 205 H10
Kossuth St SE10 104 EE78
Kotree Way SE1 202 C9
Kramer Ms SW5 100 DA78
Kempsford Gdns
Kreedman Wk E8 66 DU64
Kreisel Wk, Rich. 98 CM79
Kuala Gdns SW16 141 DM95
Kuhn Way E7 68 EG64
Forest La
Kydbrook Cl, Orp. 145 ER101
Kylemore Cl E6 86 EK68
Parr Rd
Kylemore Rd NW6 82 DA66
Kymberley Rd, Har. 61 CE58
Kyme Rd, Horn. 71 FF58
Kynance Cl, Rom. 52 FJ48
Kynance Gdns, Stan. 41 CJ53
Kynance Ms SW7 100 DB76
Kynance Pl SW7 100 DC76
Kynaston Av N16 66 DT62
Dynevor Rd
Kynaston Av, Th.Hth. 142 DQ99
Kynaston Cl, Har. 41 CD52
Kynaston Cres, Th.Hth. 142 DQ99
Kynaston Rd N16 66 DS62
Kynaston Rd, Brom. 124 EG92
Kynaston Rd, Enf. 30 DR39
Kynaston Rd, Orp. 146 EV101
Kynaston Rd, Th.Hth. 142 DQ99
Kynaston Wd, Har. 41 CD52
Kynersley Cl, Cars. 140 DF104
William St
Kynock Rd N18 46 DW49
Kyrle Rd SW11 120 DG85
Kytes Dr, Wat. 8 BX33
Kytes Est, Wat. 8 BX33
Kyverdale Rd N16 66 DT61

L

La Plata Gro, Brwd. 54 FV48
La Roche Cl, Slou. 92 AW76
La Tourne Gdns, Orp. 145 EQ104
Laburnham Cl, Upmin. 73 FU59
Laburnham Gdns, Upmin. 73 FT59
Laburnum Av N9 46 DS47
Laburnum Av N17 46 DR52
Laburnum Av, Dart. 128 FJ88
Laburnum Av, Horn. 71 FF62
Laburnum Av, Sutt. 140 DE104
Laburnum Av, Swan. 147 FC97
Laburnum Av, West Dr. 76 BM73
Laburnum Cl E4 47 DZ51
Laburnum Cl N11 44 DG51
Laburnum Cl SE15 102 DW80
Clifton Way
Laburnum Cl (Cheshunt), Wal.Cr. 15 DX31
Laburnum Ct E2 84 DT67
Laburnum St
Laburnum Ct, Stan. 41 CJ49
Laburnum Cres, Sun. 135 BV95
Batavia Rd
Laburnum Gdns N21 46 DQ47
Laburnum Gdns, Croy. 143 DX101
Laburnum Gro N21 46 DQ47
Laburnum Gro NW9 62 CQ59
Laburnum Gro, Grav. 130 GD87
Laburnum Gro, Houns. 96 BZ84
Laburnum Gro, N.Mal. 138 CR96
Laburnum Gro, Ruis. 59 BR58
Laburnum Gro, St.Alb. 8 CB25
Laburnum Gro, Slou. 93 BB79
Laburnum Gro, S.Ock. 91 FW69
Laburnum Gro, Sthl. 78 BZ70
Laburnum Ho, Dag. 70 FA61
Bradwell Av
Laburnum Pl, Egh. 112 AV93
Laburnum Rd SW19 120 DC94
Laburnum Rd, Cher. 134 BG102
Laburnum Rd, Epp. 18 EW29
Laburnum Rd, Epsom 156 CS113
Laburnum Rd, Hayes 95 BT77
Laburnum Rd, Mitch. 140 DG96
Laburnum Rd, Wok. 166 AX120
Laburnum St E2 84 DT67
Laburnum Wk, Horn. 72 FJ64
Laburnum Way, Brom. 145 EN101
Laburnum Way, Stai. 114 BM88
Laburnum Way (Cheshunt), Wal.Cr. 13 DP28
Millcrest Rd
Lacebark Cl, Sid. 125 ET87
Lacey Av, Couls. 175 DN120
Lacey Cl N9 46 DU47
Lacey Cl, Egh. 113 BD94
Lacey Dr, Couls. 175 DN120
Lacey Dr, Dag. 70 EV63
Lacey Dr, Edg. 42 CL49
Lacey Dr, Hmptn. 136 BZ95
Lacey Grn, Couls. 175 DN120
Lacey Wk E3 85 EA68
Lackford Rd, Couls. 174 DF118
Lackington St EC2 197 L6
Lackington St EC2 84 DR71
Lackmore Rd, Enf. 30 DW35
Lacock Cl SW19 120 DC93
Lacon Rd SE22 102 DU84
Lacy Rd SW15 99 CX84
Ladas Rd SE27 122 DQ91
Ladbroke Ct, Red. 184 DG132
Ladbroke Rd
Ladbroke Cres W11 81 CY72
Ladbroke Gro
Ladbroke Gdns W11 81 CZ73
Ladbroke Gro W10 81 CX70
Ladbroke Gro W11 81 CY72
Ladbroke Gro, Red. 184 DG133
Ladbroke Ms W11 81 CY74
Ladbroke Rd
Ladbroke Rd W11 81 CZ74
Ladbroke Rd, Enf. 30 DT44
Ladbroke Rd, Epsom 156 CR114
Ladbroke Rd, Red. 184 DG133
Ladbroke Sq W11 81 CZ73
Ladbroke Ter W11 81 CZ73
Ladbroke Wk W11 81 CZ74
Ladbrook Cl, Pnr. 60 BZ57
Ladbrook Rd SE25 142 DR97
Ladbrooke Cl, Pot.B. 12 DA32
Strafford Gate
Ladbrooke Cres, Sid. 126 EX90
Ladbrooke Dr, Pot.B. 12 DA32
Ladderstile Ride, Kings.T. 118 CP92
Ladderswood Way N11 45 DJ50
Ladds Way, Swan. 147 FD98
Lady Booth Rd, Kings.T. 138 CL96
Lady Docker Path SE16 203 K5
Lady Hay, Wor.Pk. 139 CT103
Lady Margaret Rd N19 65 DJ63
Lady Margaret Rd NW5 65 DJ64
Lady Margaret Rd, Sthl. 78 BZ71
Lady Somerset Rd NW5 65 DH63
Ladybower Ct E5 67 DY63
Gilpin Rd
Ladycroft Gdns, Orp. 163 EQ106
Ladycroft Rd SE13 103 EB83
Ladycroft Wk, Stan. 41 CK53
Ladycroft Way, Orp. 163 EQ106
Ladyfield Cl, Loug. 33 EP42
Ladyfields, Grav. 131 GF91
Ladyfields, Loug. 33 EP42
Ladygate La, Ruis. 59 BP58
Ladygrove, Croy. 161 DY109
Ladymeadow, Kings L. 6 BK27
Lady's Cl, Wat. 23 BV42
Ladysmith Av E6 86 EL68
Ladysmith Av, Ilf. 69 ER59
Ladysmith Rd E16 86 EF69
Ladysmith Rd N17 46 DU54
Ladysmith Rd N18 46 DV50
Ladysmith Rd SE9 125 EN86
Ladysmith Rd, Enf. 30 DS41
Ladysmith Rd, Har. 41 CE54
Ladythorpe Cl, Add. 152 BH105
Church Rd
Ladywalk, Rick. 37 BE50
Ladywell Cl SE4 103 DZ84
Adelaide Av
Ladywell Hts SE4 123 DZ86
Ladywell Rd SE13 123 EA85
Ladywell St E15 86 EF67
Plaistow Gro
Ladywood Av, Orp. 145 ES99
Ladywood Cl, Rick. 22 BH41
Ladywood Rd, Dart. 129 FS92
Ladywood Rd, Surb. 138 CN103
Lafone Av, Felt. 116 BW88
Alfred Rd
Lafone St SE1 201 P4
Lafone St SE1 102 DT75
Lagado Ms SE16 203 J3
Lagado Ms SE16 85 DX74
Lagger, The, Ch.St.G. 36 AV48
Lagger Cl, Ch.St.G. 36 AV48
Laglands Cl, Reig. 184 DC132
Lagonda Av, Ilf. 49 ET51
Lagonda Way, Dart. 108 FJ84
Arundel Rd
Lagoon Rd, Orp. 146 EV99
Laidlaw Dr N21 29 DM43
Chadwick Av
Laing Cl, Ilf. 49 ER51
Laing Dean, Nthlt. 78 BW67
Laings Av, Mitch. 140 DF96
Lainlock Pl, Houns. 96 CB81
Spring Gro Rd
Lainson St SW18 120 DA87
Laird Av, Grays 110 GD75
Laird Ho SE5 102 DQ80
Lairdale Cl SE21 122 DQ88
Lairs Cl N7 83 DL65
Manger Rd
Laitwood Rd SW12 121 DH88
Lake, The, Bushey 40 CC46
Lake Av, Brom. 124 EG93
Lake Av, Rain. 90 FK68
Lake Cl SW19 119 CZ92
Lake Rd
Lake Cl, W.Byf. 152 BK112
Lake Dr, Bushey 40 CC47
Lake Gdns, Dag. 70 FA64
Lake Gdns, Rich. 117 CH89
Lake Gdns, Wall. 141 DH104
Lake Ho Rd E11 68 EG62
Lake Ri, Grays 109 FU77
Lake Ri, Rom. 71 FF55
Lake Rd SW19 119 CZ92
Lake Rd, Croy. 143 DZ103
Lake Rd, Rom. 70 EX56
Lake Rd, Vir.W. 132 AV98
Lake Vw, Edg. 42 CM50
Lake Vw, Pot.B. 12 DC33
Lake Vw Rd, Sev. 190 FG122
Lakedale Rd SE18 105 ES79
Lakefield Rd N22 45 DP54
Lakefields Cl, Rain. 90 FK68
Lakehall Gdns, Th.Hth. 141 DP99
Lakehall Rd, Th.Hth. 141 DP99
Lakehurst Rd, Epsom 156 CS106
Lakeland Cl, Chig. 50 EV49
Lakeland Cl, Har. 41 CD51
Lakenheath N14 29 DK44
Laker Pl SW15 119 CZ86
Lakers Ri, Bans. 174 DE116
Lakes Rd, Kes. 162 EJ106
Lakeside N3 44 DB54
Lakeside W13 79 CJ72
Edgehill Rd
Lakeside, Beck. 143 EB97
Lakeside, Enf. 29 DK42
Lakeside, Rain. 90 FL68
Lakeside, Red. 184 DG132
Lakeside, Wall. 141 DH104
Derek Av
Lakeside, Wey. 135 BS103
Lakeside, Wok. 166 AS119
Lakeside Av SE28 88 EU74
Lakeside Av, Ilf. 68 EK56
Lakeside Cl SE25 142 DU96
Lakeside Cl, Chig. 49 ET49
Lakeside Cl, Ruis. 59 BR56
Lakeside Cl, Sid. 126 EW85
Lakeside Cl, Wok. 166 AS119
Lakeside Ct N4 65 DP61
Lakeside Ct, Borwd. 26 CN43
Cavendish Cres
Lakeside Cres, Barn. 28 DF43
Lakeside Cres, Brwd. 54 FX48
Lakeside Cres, Wey. 135 BQ104
Churchill Dr
Lakeside Dr, Brom. 144 EL104
Lakeside Dr, Esher 154 CC107
Lakeside Dr, Slou. 74 AS67
Lakeside Gra, Wey. 135 BQ104
Lakeside Pl, St.Alb. 9 CK27
Lakeside Rd N13 45 DM49
Lakeside Rd W14 99 CX76
Lakeside Rd, Slou. 93 BF80
Lakeside Rd (Cheshunt), Wal.Cr. 14 DW28
Lakeside Way, Wem. 62 CN63
Lakeswood Rd, Orp. 145 EP100
Lakeview Ct SW19 119 CY89
Victoria Dr
Lakeview Rd SE27 121 DN92
Lakeview Rd, Well. 106 EV84
Lakis Cl NW3 64 DC63
Flask Wk
Laleham Av NW7 42 CR48
Laleham Cl, Stai. 134 BH95
Worple Rd
Laleham Ct, Wok. 166 AY116
Laleham Pk, Stai. 134 BJ98
Laleham Reach, Cher. 134 BH96
Laleham Rd SE6 123 EC86
Laleham Rd, Shep. 134 BM98
Laleham Rd, Stai. 113 BF92
Lalor St SW6 99 CY82
Lamb Cl, Til. 111 GJ82
Coleridge Rd
Lamb Cl, Wat. 8 BW34
Lamb La E8 84 DV66
Lamb St E1 197 P6
Lamb St E1 84 DT71
Lamb Wk SE1 201 M5
Lamb Yd, Wat. 24 BX43
Lambarde Av SE9 125 EN91
Lambarde Dr, Sev. 190 FG123
Lambarde Rd, Sev. 190 FG122
Lambardes Cl, Orp. 164 EW110
Lamberhurst Cl, Orp. 146 EX102
Lamberhurst Rd SE27 121 DN91
Lamberhurst Rd, Dag. 70 EZ60
Lambert Av, Rich. 98 CP83
Lambert Av, Slou. 92 AY75
Lambert Cl, West. 178 EK116
Lambert Ct, Bushey 24 BX42
Lambert Jones Ms EC2 84 DQ71
Beech St
Lambert Rd E16 86 EH72
Lambert Rd N12 44 DD50
Lambert Rd SW2 121 DL85
Lambert Rd, Bans. 158 DA114
Lambert St N1 83 DN66
Lambert Wk, Wem. 61 CK62
Lambert Way N12 44 DC50
Woodhouse Rd
Lamberts Pl, Croy. 142 DR102
Lamberts Rd, Surb. 138 CL99
Lambeth Br SE1 200 A8
Lambeth Br SE1 101 DL77
Lambeth Br SW1 200 A8
Lambeth Br SW1 101 DL77
Lambeth High St SE1 200 B9
Lambeth High St SE1 101 DM77
Lambeth Hill EC4 197 H10
Lambeth Hill EC4 84 DQ73
Lambeth Palace Rd SE1 200 B7
Lambeth Palace Rd SE1 101 DM76
Lambeth Rd SE1 200 C7
Lambeth Rd SE1 101 DM77
Lambeth Rd SE11 200 C7
Lambeth Rd SE11 101 DM77
Lambeth Rd, Croy. 141 DN101
Lambeth Wk SE11 200 C8
Lambeth Wk SE11 101 DM77
Lamble St NW5 64 DG64
Lambley Rd, Dag. 88 EV65
Lambly Hill, Vir.W. 132 AY97
Lambolle Pl NW3 82 DE65
Lambolle Rd NW3 82 DE65
Lambourn Chase, Rad. 25 CF36
Lambourn Cl W7 97 CF75
Lambourn Rd SW4 101 DH83
Lambourne Av SW19 119 CZ91
Lambourne Cl, Chig. 50 EV47
Lambourne Rd
Lambourne Cres, Chig. 50 EV47
Lambourne Cres, Wok. 151 BD113
Lambourne Dr, Brwd. 55 GE45
Lambourne Dr, Cob. 170 BX115
Lambourne Gdns E4 47 EA47

Larkin Cl, Brwd. 55 GC45
Larkin Cl, Couls. 175 DM117
Larkings La, Slou. 74 AV67
Larks Gro, Bark. 87 ES66
Larksfield, Egh. 112 AW94
Larksfield Gro, Enf. 30 DV39
Larkshall Ct, Rom. 51 FC54
Larkshall Cres E4 47 EC49
Larkshall Rd E4 47 EC50
Larkspur Cl E6 86 EL71
Larkspur Cl N17 46 DR52
Fryatt Rd
Larkspur Cl NW9 62 CP57
Larkspur Cl, Orp. 146 EW103
Larkspur Cl, Ruis. 59 BQ59
Larkspur Cl, S.Ock. 91 FW69
Larkspur Gro, Edg. 42 CQ49
Larkspur Way, Epsom 156 CQ106
Larkswood Cl, Erith 107 FG81
Larkswood Ct E4 47 ED50
Larkswood Ri, Pnr. 60 BW56
Larkswood Rd E4 47 EA49
Larkway Cl NW9 62 CR56
Larmans Rd, Enf. 30 DW36
Larnach Rd W6 99 CX79
Larne Rd, Ruis. 59 BT59
Larner Rd, Erith 107 FE80
Larpent Av SW15 119 CW85
Larsen Dr, Wal.Abb. 15 ED34
Larwood Cl, Grnf. 61 CD64
Las Palmas Est, Shep. 135 BQ101
Lascelles Av, Har. 61 CD59
Lascelles Cl E11 67 ED61
Lascelles Cl, Brwd. 54 FU43
Lascelles Rd, Slou. 92 AV76
Lascotts Rd N22 45 DM51
Lassa Rd SE9 124 EL85
Lassell St SE10 103 ED78
Lasseter Pl SE3 104 EF79
Vanbrugh Hill
Lasswade Rd, Cher. 133 BF101
Latchett Rd E18 48 EH53
Latchford Pl, Chig. 50 EV49
Manford Way
Latching Cl, Rom. 52 FK49
Troopers Dr
Latchingdon Ct E17 67 DX56
Latchingdon Gdns, Wdf.Grn. 48 EL51
Latchmere Cl, Rich. 118 CL92
Latchmere La, Kings.T. 118 CM93
Latchmere Pas SW11 100 DE82
Cabul Rd
Latchmere Rd SW11 100 DF82
Latchmere Rd, Kings.T. 118 CL94
Latchmere St SW11 100 DF82
Latchmoor Av (Chalfont St. Peter), Ger.Cr. 56 AX56
Latchmoor Gro (Chalfont St. Peter), Ger.Cr. 56 AX56
Latchmoor Way (Chalfont St. Peter), Ger.Cr. 56 AX56
Lateward Rd, Brent. 97 CK79
Latham Cl E6 86 EL72
Oliver Gdns
Latham Cl, Dart. 129 FS89
Latham Cl, Twick. 117 CG87
Latham Cl, West. 178 EJ116
Latham Ho E1 85 DX72
Latham Rd, Bexh. 126 FA85
Latham Rd, Twick. 117 CF87
Lathams Way, Croy. 141 DM102
Lathkill Cl, Enf. 46 DU45
Lathom Rd E6 87 EM66
Latimer SE17 102 DS78
Beaconsfield Rd
Latimer Av E6 87 EM67
Latimer Cl, Amer. 20 AW39
Latimer Cl, Pnr. 40 BW53
Latimer Cl, Wat. 39 BS45
Latimer Cl, Wok. 167 BB116
Latimer Cl, Wor.Pk. 157 CV105
Latimer Dr, Horn. 72 FK62
Latimer Gdns, Pnr. 40 BW53
Latimer Pl W10 81 CW72
Latimer Rd E7 68 EH63
Latimer Rd N15 66 DS58
Latimer Rd SW19 120 DB93
Latimer Rd W10 81 CW72
Latimer Rd, Barn. 28 DB41
Latimer Rd, Chesh. 20 AU36
Latimer Rd, Croy. 141 DP104
Abbey Rd
Latimer Rd, Rick. 21 BB38
Latimer Rd, Tedd. 117 CF92
Latona Dr, Grav. 131 GM92
Latona Rd SE15 102 DU79
Lattimer Pl W4 98 CS79
Latton Cl, Esher 154 CB105
Latton Cl, Walt. 136 BY101
Latymer Cl, Wey. 153 BQ105
Latymer Ct W6 99 CX77
Latymer Rd N9 46 DT46
Latymer Way N9 46 DR47
Laud St SE11 200 B10
Laud St, Croy. 142 DQ104
Lauder Cl, Nthlt. 78 BX68
Lauderdale Dr, Rich. 117 CK90
Lauderdale Pl EC2 84 DQ71
Beech St
Lauderdale Rd W9 82 DB69
Lauderdale Rd, Kings L. 7 BQ33
Lauderdale Twr EC2 197 H6
Laughton Ct, Borwd. 26 CR40
Banks Rd
Laughton Rd, Nthlt. 78 BX67
Launcelot Rd, Brom. 124 EG91
Launcelot St SE1 200 D5
Launceston Cl, Rom. 52 FJ53
Launceston Gdns, Grnf. 79 CJ67
Launceston Pl W8 100 DC76
Launceston Rd, Grnf. 79 CJ67
Launch St E14 204 D6
Launch St E14 103 EC76
Launders La, Rain. 90 FM69
Laundress La N16 66 DU62
Laundry La N1 84 DQ67
Greenman St
Laundry La, Wal.Abb. 16 EE25
Laundry Rd W6 99 CY79
Laura Cl E11 68 EJ57
Laura Cl, Enf. 30 DS43
Laura Dr, Swan. 127 FG94
Laura Pl E5 66 DW63
Lauradale Rd N2 64 DF56
Laurel Av, Egh. 112 AV92
Laurel Av, Grav. 131 GJ89
Laurel Av, Pot.B. 11 CZ32
Laurel Av, Slou. 92 AY75
Laurel Av, Twick. 117 CF88
Laurel Bk Gdns SW6 99 CZ82
New Kings Rd
Laurel Bk Rd, Enf. 30 DQ39
Laurel Bk Vil W7 79 CE74
Lower Boston Rd
Laurel Cl N19 65 DJ61
Hargrave Pk
Laurel Cl SW17 120 DE92
Laurel Cl, Brwd. 55 GB43
Laurel Cl, Dart. 128 FJ88
Willow Rd
Laurel Cl, Ilf. 49 EQ51
Laurel Cl, Sid. 126 EU90
Laurel Cl, Slou. 93 BE80
Laurel Cl, Wok. 151 BD113
Laurel Ct (Cuffley), Pot.B. 13 DM29
Station Rd
Laurel Cres, Croy. 143 EA104
Laurel Cres, Rom. 71 FE60
Laurel Cres, Wok. 151 BC113
Laurel Dr N21 45 DN45
Laurel Dr, Oxt. 188 EF131
Laurel Dr, S.Ock. 91 FX70
Laurel Flds, Pot.B. 11 CZ31
Laurel Gdns E4 47 EB45
Laurel Gdns NW7 42 CR48
Laurel Gdns W7 79 CE74
Laurel Gdns, Houns. 96 BY84
Laurel Gro SE20 122 DV94
Laurel Gro SE26 123 DX91
Laurel La, Horn. 72 FL61
Station La
Laurel La, West Dr. 94 BL77
Laurel Lo La, Barn. 27 CW36
Laurel Pk, Har. 41 CF52
Laurel Rd SW13 99 CU82
Laurel Rd SW20 139 CV95
Laurel Rd (Chalfont St. Peter), Ger.Cr. 36 AX53
Laurel Rd, Hmptn. 117 CD92
Laurel St E8 84 DT65
Laurel Vw N12 44 DB48
Laurel Way E18 68 EF56
Laurel Way N20 44 DA48
Laurels, The, Bans. 173 CZ117
Laurels, The, Cob. 170 BY115
Laurels, The, Dart. 128 FJ90
Laurels, The, Wal.Cr. 14 DS27
Laurels, The, Wey. 135 BR104
Laurels Rd, Iver 75 BD68
Laurence Ms W12 99 CU75
Askew Rd
Laurence Pountney Hill EC4 197 K10
Laurence Pountney La EC4 197 K10
Laurie Gro SE14 103 DY81
Laurie Rd W7 79 CE71
Laurie Wk, Rom. 71 FE57
Laurier Rd NW5 65 DH62
Laurier Rd, Croy. 142 DT101
Laurimel Cl, Stan. 41 CH51
September Way
Laurino Pl, Bushey 40 CC47
Lauriston Rd E9 85 DX67
Lauriston Rd SW19 119 CX93
Lausanne Rd N8 65 DN56
Lausanne Rd SE15 102 DW81
Lauser Rd, Stai. 114 BJ87
Lavell St N16 66 DR63
Lavender Av NW9 62 CQ60
Lavender Av, Brwd. 54 FV43
Lavender Av, Mitch. 140 DE95
Lavender Av, Wor.Pk. 139 CW104
Lavender Cl SW3 100 DD79
Danvers St
Lavender Cl, Brom. 144 EL100
Lavender Cl, Cars. 158 DG105
Lavender Cl, Cat. 186 DQ125
Lavender Cl, Couls. 175 DJ119
Lavender Cl, Rom. 52 FK52
Lavender Cl (Cheshunt), Wal.Cr. 14 DT27
Lavender Ct, W.Mol. 136 CB97
Molesham Way
Lavender Dr, Uxb. 76 BM71
Lavender Gdns SW11 100 DF84
Lavender Gdns, Enf. 29 DP39
Lavender Gdns, Har. 41 CE51
Uxbridge Rd
Lavender Gro E8 84 DT66
Lavender Gro, Mitch. 140 DE95
Lavender Hill SW11 100 DE84
Lavender Hill, Enf. 29 DN39
Lavender Hill, Swan. 147 FD97
Lavender Ms, Wall. 159 DL107
Lavender Pk Rd, W.Byf. 152 BG112
Lavender Pl, Ilf. 69 EP64
Lavender Ri, West Dr. 94 BN75
Lavender Rd SE16 203 K2
Lavender Rd SE16 85 DY74
Lavender Rd SW11 100 DD83
Lavender Rd, Cars. 158 DG105
Lavender Rd, Croy. 141 DM100
Lavender Rd, Enf. 30 DR39
Lavender Rd, Epsom 156 CP106
Lavender Rd, Sutt. 158 DD105
Lavender Rd, Uxb. 76 BM71
Lavender Rd, Wok. 167 BB116
Lavender Sq E11 67 ED62
Anglian Rd
Lavender St E15 86 EE65
Manbey Gro
Lavender Sweep SW11 100 DF84
Lavender Ter SW11 100 DE83
Falcon Rd
Lavender Vale, Wall. 159 DK107
Lavender Wk SW11 100 DF84
Lavender Wk, Mitch. 140 DG97
Lavender Way, Croy. 143 DX100
Lavengro Rd SE27 122 DQ89
Lavenham Rd SW18 119 CZ89
Lavernock Rd, Bexh. 106 FA82
Lavers Rd N16 66 DS62
Laverstoke Gdns SW15 119 CU87
Laverton Ms SW5 100 DB77
Laverton Pl
Laverton Pl SW5 100 DB77
Lavidge Rd SE9 124 EL89
Lavina Gro N1 83 DM68
Wharfdale Rd
Lavington Rd W13 79 CH74
Lavington Rd, Croy. 141 DM104
Lavington St SE1 200 G3
Lavington St SE1 83 DP74
Lavinia Av, Wat. 8 BX34
Lavinia Rd, Dart. 128 FM86
Lavrock La, Rick. 38 BM45
Law Ho, Bark. 88 EU68
Law St SE1 201 L6
Law St SE1 102 DR76
Lawdons Gdns, Croy. 159 DP105
Lawford Av, Rick. 21 BC44
Lawford Cl, Horn. 72 FJ63
Lawford Cl, Rick. 21 BC44
Lawford Cl, Wall. 159 DL109
Lawford Gdns, Dart. 128 FJ85
Lawford Gdns, Ken. 176 DQ116
Lawford Rd N1 84 DS66
Lawford Rd NW5 83 DJ65
Lawford Rd W4 98 CQ80
Lawless St E14 85 EB73
Lawley Rd N14 45 DH45
Lawley St E5 66 DW63
Lawn, The, Sthl. 96 CA78
Lawn Av, West Dr. 94 BJ75
Lawn Cl N9 46 DT45
Lawn Cl, Brom. 124 EH93
Lawn Cl, N.Mal. 138 CS96
Lawn Cl, Ruis. 59 BT62
Lawn Cl, Slou. 92 AW80
Lawn Cl, Swan. 147 FC96
Lawn Cres, Rich. 98 CN82
Lawn Fm Gro, Rom. 70 EY56
Lawn Gdns W7 79 CE74
Lawn Ho Cl E14 204 D4
Lawn Ho Cl E14 103 EC75
Lawn La SW8 101 DL79
Lawn Pk, Sev. 191 FH127
Lawn Pl SE15 102 DT81
Sumner Est
Lawn Rd NW3 64 DF64
Lawn Rd, Beck. 123 DZ94
Lawn Rd, Grav. 130 GC86
Lawn Rd, Uxb. 76 BJ66
New Windsor St
Lawn Ter SE3 104 EE83
Lawn Vale, Pnr. 40 BX54
Lawnfield NW2 81 CX66
Coverdale Rd
Lawns, The E4 47 EA50
Lawns, The SE3 104 EE83
Lee Ter
Lawns, The SE19 142 DR95
Lawns, The, Pnr. 40 CB52
Lawns, The (Shenley), Rad. 10 CL33
Lawns, The, Sid. 126 EV91
Lawns, The, Sutt. 157 CY108
Lawns Ct, Wem. 62 CM61
The Av
Lawns Cres, Grays 110 GD79
Lawns Way, Rom. 51 FC52
Lawnside SE3 104 EF84
Lawrance Gdns (Cheshunt), Wal.Cr. 15 DX28
Lawrence Av E12 69 EN63
Lawrence Av E17 47 DX53
Lawrence Av N13 45 DP49
Lawrence Av NW7 42 CS49
Lawrence Av, N.Mal. 138 CR100
Lawrence Bldgs N16 66 DT62
Lawrence Campe Cl N20 44 DD48
Friern Barnet La
Lawrence Cl E3 85 EA68
Lawrence Cl N15 66 DS55
Lawrence Rd
Lawrence Ct NW7 42 CS50
Lawrence Cres, Dag. 71 FB62
Lawrence Cres, Edg. 42 CN54
Lawrence Dr, Uxb. 59 BQ63
Lawrence Gdns NW7 43 CT48
Lawrence Gdns, Til. 111 GH80
Lawrence Hill E4 47 EA47
Lawrence Hill Gdns, Dart. 128 FJ86
Lawrence Hill Rd, Dart. 128 FJ86
Lawrence La EC2 197 J9
Lawrence La, Bet. 183 CV131
Lawrence Pl N1 83 DL67
Outram Pl
Lawrence Rd E6 86 EK67
Lawrence Rd E13 86 EH67
Lawrence Rd N15 66 DS56
Lawrence Rd N18 46 DV49
Lawrence Rd SE25 142 DT98
Lawrence Rd W5 97 CK77
Lawrence Rd, Erith 107 FB80
Lawrence Rd, Hmptn. 116 BZ94
Lawrence Rd, Hayes 77 BQ68
Lawrence Rd, Houns. 96 BW84
Lawrence Rd, Pnr. 60 BX57
Lawrence Rd, Rich. 117 CJ91
Lawrence Rd, Rom. 71 FH57
Lawrence Rd, W.Wick. 162 EG105
Lawrence Sq, Grav. 131 GF90
Haynes Rd
Lawrence St E16 86 EF71
Lawrence St NW7 43 CT49
Lawrence St SW3 100 DE79
Lawrence Way NW10 62 CQ63
Lawrence Weaver Cl, Mord. 140 DB100
Green La
Lawrie Pk Av SE26 122 DV92
Lawrie Pk Cres SE26 122 DV92
Lawrie Pk Gdns SE26 122 DV91
Lawrie Pk Rd SE26 122 DV93
Lawson Cl E16 86 EJ71
Lawson Cl SW19 119 CX90
Lawson Est SE1 201 K7
Lawson Est SE1 102 DR76
Lawson Gdns, Dart. 128 FK85
Lawson Gdns, Pnr. 59 BV55
Lawson Rd, Dart. 108 FK84
Lawson Rd, Enf. 30 DW39
Lawson Rd, Sthl. 78 BZ70
Lawson Wk, Cars. 158 DF108
Fountain Dr
Lawton Rd E3 85 DY69
Lawton Rd E10 67 EC60
Lawton Rd, Barn. 28 DD41
Lawton Rd, Loug. 33 EP41
Laxcon Cl NW10 62 CQ64
Laxey Rd, Orp. 163 ET107
Laxley Cl SE5 101 DP80
Laxton Gdns (Shenley), Rad. 10 CL32
Porters Pk Dr
Laxton Gdns, Red. 185 DK128
Laxton Pl NW1 195 J4
Layard Rd SE16 202 E8
Layard Rd SE16 102 DV77
Layard Rd, Enf. 30 DT39
Layard Rd, Th.Hth. 142 DR96
Layard Sq SE16 202 D8
Layard Sq SE16 102 DV77
Layborne Av, Rom. 52 FJ48
Cummings Hall La
Layburn Cres, Slou. 93 BB79
Laycock St N1 83 DN65
Layer Gdns W3 80 CN73
Layfield Cl NW4 63 CV59
Layfield Cres NW4 63 CV59
Layfield Rd NW4 63 CV59
Layhams Rd, Kes. 162 EF106
Layhams Rd, W.Wick. 143 ED104
Laymarsh Cl, Belv. 106 EZ76
Laymead Cl, Nthlt. 78 BY65
Laystall St EC1 196 D5
Laystall St EC1 83 DN70
Layters Av (Chalfont St. Peter), Ger.Cr. 36 AW54
Layters Av S (Chalfont St. Peter), Ger.Cr. 36 AW54
Layters Cl (Chalfont St. Peter), Ger.Cr. 36 AW54
Layters End (Chalfont St. Peter), Ger.Cr. 36 AW54
Layters Grn La (Chalfont St. Peter), Ger.Cr. 56 AU55
Layters Way, Ger.Cr. 56 AX56
Layton Ct, Wey. 153 BP105
Castle Vw Rd
Layton Cres, Croy. 159 DN106
Layton Rd N1 83 DN68
Parkfield St
Layton Rd, Brent. 97 CK78
Layton Rd, Houns. 96 CB84
Laytons Bldgs SE1 201 J4
Laytons La, Sun. 135 BT96
Layzell Wk SE9 124 EK88
Mottingham La
Lazar Wk N7 65 DM61
Briset Way
Le Corte Cl, Kings L. 6 BM29
Le May Av SE12 124 EH90
Le Personne Rd, Cat. 176 DR122
Lea, The, Egh. 133 BB95
Lea Br Rd E5 66 DW62
Lea Br Rd E10 67 DY60
Lea Br Rd E17 67 ED56
Lea Bushes, Wat. 24 BY35
Lea Cl, Bushey 24 CB43
Lea Cres, Ruis. 59 BT63
Lea Gdns, Wem. 62 CL63
Lea Hall Rd E10 67 EA60
Lea Mt, Wal.Cr. 14 DS28
Lea Rd, Beck. 143 EA96
Fairfield Rd
Lea Rd, Enf. 30 DR39
Lea Rd, Grays 111 GG78
Lea Rd, Sev. 191 FJ127
Lea Rd, Sthl. 96 BY77
Lea Rd, Wal.Abb. 15 EA34
Lea Vale, Dart. 107 FD84
Lea Valley Rd E4 31 DX43
Lea Valley Rd, Enf. 31 DX43
Lea Valley Trd Est N18 47 DX50
Lea Valley Viaduct E4 47 DX50
Lea Valley Viaduct N18 47 DX50
Lea Valley Wk E3 85 EC70
Lea Valley Wk E9 67 DZ64
Lea Valley Wk E10 67 DY62
Lea Valley Wk E14 85 EC70
Lea Valley Wk E15 85 EC70
Lea Valley Wk E17 46 DW53
Lea Valley Wk N9 46 DW53
Lea Valley Wk N17 46 DW53
Lea Valley Wk N18 46 DW53
Lea Valley Wk, Enf. 31 DZ41
Lea Valley Wk, Wal.Abb. 15 DZ30
Lea Valley Wk, Wal.Cr. 15 DZ30
Lea Vw Hos E5 66 DV60
Springfield
Leabank Cl, Har. 61 CE62
Leabank Sq E9 85 EA65
Leabank Vw N15 66 DU58
Leabourne Rd N16 66 DU58
Leach Gro, Lthd. 171 CJ122
Leachcroft (Chalfont St. Peter), Ger.Cr. 36 AV53
Leacroft, Stai. 114 BH91
Leacroft Av SW12 120 DF87
Leacroft Cl, Ken. 176 DQ116
Leacroft Cl, Stai. 114 BH91
Leacroft Cl, West Dr. 76 BL72
Leacroft Rd, Iver 75 BD72
Leadale Av E4 47 EA47
Leadale Rd N15 66 DU58
Leadale Rd N16 66 DU58
Leadbeaters Cl N11 44 DF50
Goldsmith Rd
Leadenhall Mkt EC3 197 M9
Leadenhall Pl EC3 197 M9
Leadenhall St EC3 197 M9
Leadenhall St EC3 84 DS72
Leader Av E12 69 EN64
Leadings, The, Wem. 62 CQ62
Leaf Cl, Nthwd. 39 BR52
Leaf Cl, T.Ditt. 137 CE99
Leaf Gro SE27 121 DN92
Leafield Cl SW16 121 DP93
Leafield Cl, Wok. 166 AV118
Winnington Way
Leafield La, Sid. 126 EZ91
Leafield Rd SW20 139 CZ97
Leafield Rd, Sutt. 140 DA103
Leaford Cres, Wat. 23 BT37
Leaforis Rd, Wal.Cr. 14 DU28
Leafy Gro, Croy. 161 DY111
Leafy Gro, Kes. 162 EJ106
Leafy Oak Rd SE12 124 EJ90
Leafy Way, Brwd. 55 GD46
Leafy Way, Croy. 142 DT103
Leagrave St E5 66 DW62
Leaholme Way, Ruis. 59 BP58
Leahurst Rd SE13 123 ED85
Leake Ct SE1 200 C5
Leake St SE1 200 C4
Leake St SE1 101 DM75
Lealand Rd N15 66 DT58
Leamington Av E17 67 EA57
Leamington Av, Brom. 124 EJ92
Leamington Av, Mord. 139 CZ98
Leamington Av, Orp. 163 ES105
Leamington Cl E12 68 EL64
Leamington Cl, Brom. 124 EJ92
Leamington Cl, Houns. 116 CC85
Leamington Cl, Rom. 52 FM51
Leamington Cres, Har. 60 BY62
Leamington Gdns, Ilf. 69 ET61
Leamington Pk W3 80 CR71
Leamington Pl, Hayes 77 BT70
Leamington Rd, Rom. 52 FN50
Leamington Rd, Sthl. 96 BX77
Leamington Rd Vil W11 81 CZ71
Leamore St W6 99 CV77
Leamouth Rd E6 86 EL72
Remington Rd
Leamouth Rd E14 85 ED72
Leander Ct SE8 103 EA81
Leander Dr, Grav. 131 GM91
Leander Gdns, Wat. 24 BY37
Leander Rd SW2 121 DM86
Leander Rd, Nthlt. 78 CA68
Leander Rd, Th.Hth. 141 DM98
Learner Dr, Har. 60 CA61
Learoyd Gdns E6 87 EN73
Leas, The, Bushey 24 BZ39
Leas, The, Stai. 114 BG91
Raleigh Ct
Leas, The, Upmin. 73 FR59
Leas Cl, Chess. 156 CM108
Leas Dale SE9 125 EN90
Leas Dr, Iver 75 BE72
Leas Grn, Chis. 125 ET93
Leas La, Warl. 177 DX118
Leas Rd, Warl. 177 DX118
Leaside, Lthd. 170 CA123
Leaside Av N10 64 DG55
Leaside Ct, Uxb. 77 BP69
The Larches
Leaside Rd E5 66 DW60
Leasowes Rd E10 67 EA60
Leasway, Brwd. 54 FX48
Leasway, Upmin. 72 FQ62
Leathart Cl, Horn. 89 FH66
Dowding Way
Leather Bottle La, Belv. 106 EY77
Leather Cl, Mitch. 140 DG96
Leather Gdns E15 86 EE67
Abbey Rd
Leather La EC1 196 E7
Leather La EC1 83 DN71
Leather La, Horn. 72 FK60
North St
Leatherbottle Grn, Erith 106 EZ76
Leatherdale St E1 84 DW70
Portelet Rd
Leatherhead Bypass Rd, Lthd. 171 CH120
Leatherhead Cl N16 66 DT60
Leatherhead Rd, Ash. 171 CK121
Leatherhead Rd, Chess. 155 CJ110
Leatherhead Rd, Lthd. 171 CK121
Leatherhead Rd (Oxshott), Lthd. 155 CD114
Leathermarket Ct SE1 201 M5
Leathermarket Ct SE1 102 DS75
Leathermarket St SE1 201 M5
Leathermarket St SE1 102 DS75
Leathersellers Cl, Barn. 27 CY42
The Av
Leathsail Rd, Har. 60 CB62
Leathwaite Rd SW11 100 DF84
Leathwell Rd SE8 103 EB82
Leaveland Cl, Beck. 143 EA98
Leaver Gdns, Grnf. 79 CD68
Leaves Grn Cres, Kes. 162 EJ111
Leaves Grn Rd, Kes. 162 EK111
Leavesden Rd, Stan. 41 CG51
Leavesden Rd, Wat. 23 BV38
Leavesden Rd, Wey. 153 BP106
Leaview, Wal.Abb. 15 EB33
Leaway E10 67 DX60
Leazes Av, Cat. 175 DN123
Leazes La, Cat. 175 DN123
Lebanon Av, Felt. 116 BX92
Lebanon Cl, Wat. 23 BR36
Lebanon Ct, Twick. 117 CH87
Lebanon Dr, Cob. 154 CA113
Lebanon Gdns SW18 120 DA86
Lebanon Gdns, West. 178 EK117
Lebanon Pk, Twick. 117 CH87
Lebanon Rd SW18 120 DA85
Lebanon Rd, Croy. 142 DS102
Lebrun Sq SE3 104 EH83
Lechmere App, Wdf.Grn. 48 EJ54
Lechmere Av, Chig. 49 EQ49
Lechmere Av, Wdf.Grn. 48 EK54
Lechmere Rd NW2 81 CV65
Leckford Rd SW18 120 DC89
Leckwith Av, Bexh. 106 EY79
Lecky St SW7 100 DD78
Leconfield Av SW13 99 CT83
Leconfield Rd N5 66 DR63
Leconfield Wk, Horn. 90 FJ65
Airfield Way
Leda Av, Enf. 31 DX39
Leda Rd SE18 105 EM76
Ledbury Est SE15 102 DV80
Ledbury Ms N W11 82 DA73
Ledbury Rd
Ledbury Ms W W11 82 DA73
Ledbury Rd
Ledbury Pl, Croy. 160 DQ105
Ledbury Rd
Ledbury Rd W11 81 CZ72
Ledbury Rd, Croy. 160 DQ105
Ledbury Rd, Reig. 183 CZ133
Ledbury St SE15 102 DU80

Ledger Dr, Add. 151 BF106
Ledgers Rd, Warl. 177 EB117
Ledrington Rd SE19 122 DU93
Anerley Hill
Ledway Dr, Wem. 62 CM59
Lee, The, Nthwd. 39 BT50
Lee Av, Rom. 70 EY58
Lee Br SE13 103 EC83
Lee Ch St SE13 104 EE84
Lee Cl E17 47 DX53
Lee Cl, Barn. 28 DC42
Lee Conservancy Rd E9 67 DZ64
Lee Fm Cl, Chesh. 4 AU30
Lee Gdns Av, Horn. 72 FN60
Lee Grn, Orp. 146 EU99
Lee Grn La, Epsom 172 CP124
Lee Gro, Chig. 49 EN47
Lee High Rd SE12 103 ED83
Lee High Rd SE13 103 ED83
Lee Pk SE3 104 EF84
Lee Pk Way N9 47 DX49
Lee Pk Way N18 47 DX49
Lee Rd NW7 43 CX52
Lee Rd SE3 104 EF83
Lee Rd SW19 140 DB95
Lee Rd, Enf. 30 DU44
Lee Rd, Grnf. 79 CJ67
Lee St E8 84 DT67
Lee Ter SE3 104 EE83
Lee Ter SE13 104 EE83
Lee Valley Cycle Route, Wal.Abb. 15 EC26
Lee Valley Technopark N17 66 DU55
Lee Vw, Enf. 29 DP39
Leech La, Epsom 182 CQ126
Leech La, Lthd. 182 CQ126
Leechcroft Av, Sid. 125 ET85
Leechcroft Av, Swan. 147 FF97
Leechcroft Rd, Wall. 140 DG104
Leecroft Rd, Barn. 27 CY43
Leeds Cl, Orp. 146 EX103
Leeds Pl N4 65 DM61
Tollington Pk
Leeds Rd, Ilf. 69 ER60
Leeds Rd, Slou. 74 AS73
Leeds St N18 46 DU50
Leefe Way, Pot.B. 13 DK28
Leefern Rd W12 99 CU75
Leegate SE12 124 EF85
Leegate Cl, Wok. 166 AV116
Sythwood
Leeke St WC1 196 B2
Leeke St WC1 83 DM69
Leeland Rd W13 79 CG74
Leeland Ter W13 79 CG74
Leeland Way NW10 63 CT63
Leeming Rd, Borwd. 26 CM39
Leerdam Dr E14 204 E7
Leerdam Dr E14 103 EC76
Lees, The, Croy. 143 DZ103
Lees Av, Nthwd. 39 BT53
Lees Pl W1 194 F10
Lees Pl W1 82 DG73
Lees Rd, Uxb. 77 BP70
Leeside, Barn. 27 CY43
Leeside, Pot.B. 12 DD31
Wayside
Leeside Cres NW11 63 CZ58
Leeside Rd N17 46 DV51
Leeson Rd SE24 101 DN84
Leesons Hill, Chis. 145 ET97
Leesons Hill, Orp. 146 EU97
Leesons Way, Orp. 145 ET96
Leeward Gdns SW19 119 CZ93
Leeway SE8 203 M10
Leeway SE8 103 DZ78
Leeway Cl, Pnr. 40 BZ52
Leewood Cl SE12 124 EF86
Upwood Rd
Leewood Pl, Swan. 147 FD98
Lefevre Wk E3 85 EA67
Lefroy Rd W12 99 CT75
Legard Rd N5 65 DP62
Legatt Rd SE9 124 EK85
Leggatt Rd E15 85 EC68
Leggatts Cl, Wat. 23 BT36
Leggatts Ri, Wat. 23 BU35
Leggatts Way, Wat. 23 BT36
Leggatts Wd Av, Wat. 23 BV36
Legge St SE13 123 EC85
Leghorn Rd NW10 81 CT68
Leghorn Rd SE18 105 ER78
Legion Cl N1 83 DN65
Legion Ct, Mord. 140 DA100
Legion Rd, Grnf. 78 CC67
Legion Way N12 44 DE52
Legon Av, Rom. 71 FC60
Legrace Av, Houns. 96 BX82
Leicester Av, Mitch. 141 DL98
Leicester Cl, Wor.Pk. 157 CW105
Leicester Ct WC2 195 N10
Leicester Gdns, Ilf. 69 ES59
Leicester Pl WC2 195 N10
Leicester Rd E11 68 EH57
Leicester Rd N2 64 DE55
Leicester Rd NW10 80 CR66
Leicester Rd, Barn. 28 DB43
Leicester Rd, Croy. 142 DS101
Leicester Rd, Til. 111 GF81
Leicester Sq WC2 199 N1
Leicester Sq WC2 83 DK73
Leicester St WC2 195 N10
Leigh Av, Ilf. 68 EK56
Leigh Cl, Add. 151 BF108
Leigh Cl, N.Mal. 138 CR98
Leigh Cor, Cob. 154 BW114
Leigh Hill Rd
Leigh Ct SE4 103 EA82
Lewisham Way
Leigh Ct, Borwd. 26 CR40
Banks Rd
Leigh Ct, Har. 61 CE60
Leigh Ct Cl, Cob. 154 BW114
Leigh Cres, Croy. 161 EB108
Leigh Dr, Rom. 52 FK49
Leigh Gdns NW10 81 CW68
Leigh Hill Rd, Cob. 154 BW114
Leigh Hunt Dr N14 45 DK46
Leigh Hunt St SE1 201 H4
Leigh Orchard Cl SW16 121 DM90
Leigh Pk, Slou. 92 AV80
Leigh Pl EC1 196 D6
Leigh Pl, Cob. 170 BW115
Leigh Pl, Well. 106 EU82
Leigh Pl La, Gdse. 187 DY132
Leigh Rd E6 87 EN65
Leigh Rd E10 67 EC59
Leigh Rd N5 65 DP63
Leigh Rd, Cob. 153 BV113
Leigh Rd, Grav. 131 GH89
Leigh Rd, Houns. 97 CD84
Leigh Rodd, Wat. 40 BZ48
Leigh St WC1 195 P4
Leigh St WC1 83 DL70
Leigh Ter, Orp. 146 EV97
Saxville Rd
Leigham Av SW16 121 DL90
Leigham Ct, Wall. 159 DJ107
Stafford Rd
Leigham Ct Rd SW16 121 DL89
Leigham Dr, Islw. 97 CE80
Leigham Vale SW2 121 DM90
Leigham Vale SW16 121 DM90
Leighton Av E12 69 EN64
Leighton Av, Pnr. 60 BY55
Leighton Cl, Edg. 42 CN54
Leighton Cres NW5 65 DJ64
Leighton Gro
Leighton Gdns NW10 81 CV68
Leighton Gdns, S.Croy. 160 DV113
Leighton Gdns, Til. 111 GG80
Leighton Gro NW5 65 DJ64
Leighton Pl NW5 65 DJ64
Leighton Rd NW5 65 DK64
Leighton Rd W13 97 CG75
Leighton Rd, Enf. 30 DT43
Leighton Rd, Har. 41 CD54
Leighton St, Croy. 141 DP102
Leighton Way, Epsom 156 CR114
Leila Parnell Pl SE7 104 EJ79
Leinster Av SW14 98 CQ83
Leinster Gdns W2 82 DC72
Leinster Ms W2 82 DC73
Leinster Pl W2 82 DC72
Leinster Rd N10 65 DH56
Leinster Rd NW6 82 DA69
Stafford Rd
Leinster Sq W2 82 DA72
Leinster Ter W2 82 DC73
Leiston Spur, Slou. 74 AS72
Leisure La, W.Byf. 152 BH112
Leisure Way N12 44 DD52
Leith Cl NW9 62 CR60
Leith Cl, Slou. 74 AU74
Leith Hill, Orp. 146 EU95
Leith Hill Grn, Orp. 146 EU95
Leith Hill
Leith Pk Rd, Grav. 131 GH88
Leith Rd N22 45 DP53
Leith Rd, Epsom 156 CS112
Leith Yd NW6 82 DA67
Quex Rd
Leithcote Gdns SW16 121 DM91
Leithcote Path SW16 121 DM90
Lela Av, Houns. 96 BW82
Lelitia Cl E8 84 DU67
Pownall Rd
Leman St E1 84 DT72
Lemark Cl, Stan. 41 CJ50
Lemmon Rd SE10 104 EE79
Lemna Rd E11 68 EE59
Lemonfield Dr, Wat. 8 BY32
Lemonwell Ct SE9 125 EQ85
Lemonwell Dr
Lemonwell Dr SE9 125 EQ85
Lemsford Cl N15 66 DU57
Lemsford Ct N4 66 DQ61
Brownswood Rd
Lemsford Ct, Borwd. 26 CQ42
Lemuel St SW18 120 DB86
Len Freeman Pl SW6 99 CZ80
John Smith Av
Lena Gdns W6 99 CW76
Lena Kennedy Cl E4 47 EB51
Lenanton Steps E14 204 A4
Lendal Ter SW4 101 DK83
Lenelby Rd, Surb. 138 CN102
Lenham Rd SE12 104 EF84
Lenham Rd, Bexh. 106 EZ79
Lenham Rd, Sutt. 158 DB105
Lenham Rd, Th.Hth. 142 DR96
Lenmore Av, Grays 110 GC76
Lennard Av, W.Wick. 144 EE103
Lennard Cl, W.Wick. 144 EE103
Lennard Rd SE20 122 DW93
Lennard Rd, Beck. 123 DX93
Lennard Rd, Brom. 145 EM102
Lennard Rd, Croy. 142 DQ102
Lennard Rd, Sev. 181 FE120
Lennard Row, S.Ock. 91 FR74
Lennon Rd NW2 63 CW64
Lennox Av, Grav. 131 GF86
Lennox Cl, Rom. 71 FF58
Lennox Gdns NW10 63 CT63
Lennox Gdns SW1 198 D7
Lennox Gdns SW1 100 DF76
Lennox Gdns, Croy. 159 DP105
Lennox Gdns, Ilf. 69 EM60
Lennox Gdns Ms SW1 198 D7
Lennox Gdns Ms SW1 100 DF76
Lennox Rd E17 67 DZ58
Lennox Rd N4 65 DM61
Lennox Rd, Grav. 131 GF86
Lennox Rd E, Grav. 131 GG87
Lenor Cl, Bexh. 106 EY84
Lens Rd E7 86 EJ66
Lensbury Cl (Cheshunt), Wal.Cr. 15 DY28
Ashdown Cres
Lensbury Way SE2 106 EW76
Lenthall Av, Grays 110 GA75
Lenthall Rd E8 84 DU66
Lenthall Rd, Loug. 33 ER42
Lenthorp Rd SE10 205 K10
Lenthorp Rd SE10 104 EF77
Lentmead Rd, Brom. 124 EF90
Lenton Path SE18 105 ER79
Lenton Ri, Rich. 98 CL83
Evelyn Ter
Lenton St SE18 105 ER77
Leo St SE15 102 DV80
Leo Yd EC1 196 G5
Leof Cres SE6 123 EB92
Leominster Rd, Mord. 140 DC100
Leominster Wk, Mord. 140 DC100
Leonard Av, Mord. 140 DC99
Leonard Av, Rom. 71 FD60
Leonard Av, Sev. 181 FH116
Leonard Av, Swans. 130 FY87
Leonard Rd E4 47 EA51
Leonard Rd E7 68 EG63
Leonard Rd N9 46 DT48
Leonard Rd SW16 141 DJ95
Leonard Rd, Sthl. 96 BX76
Leonard Robbins Path SE28 88 EV73
Tawney Rd
Leonard St E16 86 EL74
Leonard St EC2 197 L4
Leonard St EC2 84 DR70
Leonard Way, Brwd. 54 FS49
Leontine Cl SE15 102 DU80
Leopards Ct EC1 196 D6
Leopold Av SW19 119 CZ92
Leopold Ms E9 84 DW67
Fremont St
Leopold Rd E17 67 EA57
Leopold Rd N2 64 DD55
Leopold Rd N18 46 DV50
Leopold Rd NW10 80 CS66
Leopold Rd SW19 119 CZ91
Leopold Rd W5 80 CM74
Leopold St E3 85 DZ71
Leopold Ter SW19 120 DA92
Dora Rd
Leppoc Rd SW4 121 DK85
Leret Way, Lthd. 171 CH121
Leroy St SE1 201 M8
Leroy St SE1 102 DS77
Lerwick Dr, Slou. 74 AS71
Lescombe Cl SE23 123 DY90
Lescombe Rd SE23 123 DY90
Lesley Cl, Bex. 127 FB87
Lesley Cl, Grav. 131 GF94
Lesley Cl, Swan. 147 FD97
Leslie Gdns, Sutt. 158 DA108
Leslie Gro, Croy. 142 DS102
Leslie Gro Pl, Croy. 142 DR102
Leslie Gro
Leslie Pk Rd, Croy. 142 DS102
Leslie Rd E11 67 EC63
Leslie Rd E16 86 EH72
Leslie Rd N2 64 DD55
Leslie Smith Sq SE18 105 EN79
Nightingale Vale
Lesney Fm Est, Erith 107 FD80
Lesney Pk, Erith 107 FD79
Lesney Pk Rd, Erith 107 FD79
Lessar Av SW4 121 DJ85
Lessing St SE23 123 DY87
Lessingham Av SW17 120 DF91
Lessingham Av, Ilf. 69 EN55
Lessington Av, Rom. 71 FC58
Lessness Av, Bexh. 106 EX80
Lessness Pk, Belv. 106 EZ78
Lessness Rd, Belv. 106 FA78
Stapley Rd
Lessness Rd, Mord. 140 DC100
Lester Av E15 86 EE69
Leston Cl, Rain. 89 FG69
Leswin Pl N16 66 DT62
Leswin Rd
Leswin Rd N16 66 DT62
Letchfield, Chesh. 4 AV31
Letchford Gdns NW10 81 CU69
Letchford Ms NW10 81 CU69
Letchford Gdns
Letchford Ter, Har. 40 CB53
Letchmore Rd, Rad. 25 CG36
Letchworth Av, Felt. 115 BT87
Letchworth Cl, Brom. 144 EG99
Letchworth Cl, Wat. 40 BX50
Letchworth Dr, Brom. 144 EG99
Letchworth St SW17 120 DF91
Lethbridge Cl SE13 103 EC81
Lett Rd E15 85 ED66
Letter Box La, Sev. 191 FJ129
Letterstone Rd SW6 99 CZ80
Varna Rd
Lettice St SW6 99 CZ81
Lettsom St SE5 102 DS82
Lettsom Wk E13 86 EG68
Leucha Rd E17 67 DY57
Levana Cl SW19 119 CY88
Levehurst Way SW4 101 DL82
Leven Cl, Wal.Cr. 15 DX33
Leven Cl, Wat. 40 BX50
Leven Dr, Wal.Cr. 15 DX33
Leven Rd E14 85 EC71
Leven Way, Hayes 77 BS72
Levendale Rd SE23 123 DY89
Lever Sq, Grays 111 GG77
Lever St EC1 196 G3
Lever St EC1 83 DP69
Leveret Cl, Croy. 161 ED111
Leveret Cl, Wat. 7 BU34
Leverett St SW3 198 C8
Leverholme Gdns SE9 125 EN90
Leverson St SW16 121 DJ93
Leverton Pl NW5 65 DJ64
Leverton St
Leverton St NW5 65 DJ64
Leverton Way, Wal.Abb. 15 EC33
Leveson Rd, Grays 111 GH76
Levett Gdns, Ilf. 69 ET63
Levett Rd, Bark. 87 ES65
Levett Rd, Lthd. 171 CH120
Levine Gdns, Bark. 88 EX68
Levison Way N19 65 DK61
Grovedale Rd
Lewes Cl, Nthlt. 78 CA65
Lewes Rd N12 44 DE50
Lewes Rd, Brom. 144 EK96
Lewes Rd, Rom. 52 FJ49
Lewes Way, Rick. 23 BQ42
Lewesdon Cl SW19 119 CX88
Leweston Pl N16 66 DT59
Lewey Ho E3 85 DZ70
Lewgars Av NW9 62 CQ58
Lewin Rd SW14 98 CR83
Lewin Rd SW16 121 DK93
Lewin Rd, Bexh. 106 EY84
Lewins Rd, Epsom 156 CP114
Lewins Rd (Chalfont St. Peter), Ger.Cr. 56 AX55
Lewis Av E17 47 EA53
Lewis Cl N14 45 DJ45
Orchid Rd
Lewis Cl, Add. 152 BJ105
Lewis Cl, Brwd. 55 FZ45
Lewis Cl (Harefield), Uxb. 38 BJ54
Lewis Cres NW10 62 CQ64
Lewis Gdns N2 44 DD54
Lewis Gro SE13 103 EC83
Lewis La (Chalfont St. Peter), Ger.Cr. 36 AY53
Lewis Rd, Horn. 72 FJ58
Lewis Rd, Mitch. 140 DD96
Lewis Rd, Rich. 117 CK85
Red Lion St
Lewis Rd, Sid. 126 EW90
Lewis Rd, Sthl. 96 BY75
Lewis Rd, Sutt. 158 DB105
Lewis Rd, Swans. 130 FY86
Lewis Rd, Well. 106 EW83
Lewis St NW1 83 DH66
Lewis Way, Dag. 89 FB65
Lewisham High St SE13 103 EC83
Lewisham Hill SE13 103 EC82
Lewisham Pk SE13 123 EB86
Lewisham Rd SE13 103 EB81
Lewisham St SW1 199 N5
Lewisham Way SE4 103 DZ81
Lewisham Way SE14 103 DZ81
Lexden Dr, Rom. 70 EV58
Lexden Rd W3 80 CP73
Lexden Rd, Mitch. 141 DK98
Lexham Ct, Grnf. 79 CD67
Lexham Gdns W8 100 DB76
Lexham Gdns Ms W8 100 DB76
Lexham Ho, Bark. 87 ER67
St. Margarets
Lexham Ms W8 100 DA77
Lexham Wk W8 100 DB76
Lexham Gdns
Lexington Cl, Borwd. 26 CM41
Lexington Ct, Pur. 160 DQ110
Lexington St W1 195 L9
Lexington St W1 83 DJ72
Lexington Way, Barn. 27 CX42
Lexington Way, Upmin. 73 FT58
Lexton Gdns SW12 121 DK88
Ley Hill Rd, Hem.H. 4 AX30
Ley St, Ilf. 69 EP61
Leyborne Av W13 97 CH75
Leyborne Pk, Rich. 98 CN81
Leybourne Av, W.Byf. 152 BM113
Leybourne Cl, Brom. 144 EG100
Leybourne Cl, W.Byf. 152 BM113
Leybourne Av
Leybourne Rd E11 68 EF60
Leybourne Rd NW1 83 DH66
Leybourne Rd NW9 62 CN57
Leybourne Rd, Uxb. 77 BQ67
Leybourne St NW1 83 DH66
Hawley St
Leybridge Ct SE12 124 EG85
Leyburn Cl E17 67 EB56
Church La
Leyburn Cres, Rom. 52 FL52
Leyburn Gdns, Croy. 142 DS103
Leyburn Gro N18 46 DU51
Leyburn Rd N18 46 DU51
Leyburn Rd, Rom. 52 FL52
Leycroft Cl, Loug. 33 EN43
Leycroft Gdns, Erith 107 FH81
Leyden St E1 197 P7
Leydenhatch La, Swan. 147 FC95
Leydon Cl SE16 203 J3
Leyfield, Wor.Pk. 138 CS102
Leyhill Cl, Swan. 147 FE99
Leyland Av, Enf. 31 DY40
Leyland Cl (Cheshunt), Wal.Cr. 14 DW28
Leyland Gdns, Wdf.Grn. 48 EJ50
Leyland Rd SE12 124 EG85
Leylands La, Stai. 113 BF85
Leylang Rd SE14 103 DX80
Leys, The N2 64 DC56
Leys, The, Har. 62 CM58
Leys Av, Dag. 89 FC66
Leys Cl, Dag. 89 FC66
Leys Cl, Har. 61 CD57
Leys Cl (Harefield), Uxb. 38 BK53
Leys Gdns, Barn. 28 DG43
Leys Rd, Lthd. 155 CD112
Leys Rd E, Enf. 31 DY39
Leys Rd W, Enf. 31 DY39
Leysdown Av, Bexh. 107 FC84
Leysdown Rd SE9 124 EL89
Leysfield Rd W12 99 CU75
Leyspring Rd E11 68 EF60
Leyswood Dr, Ilf. 69 ES57
Leythe Rd W3 98 CQ75
Leyton Business Cen E10 67 EA61
Leyton Cross Rd, Dart. 127 FF90
Leyton Gra E10 67 EB60
Goldsmith Rd
Leyton Gra Est E10 67 EB60
Leyton Grn Rd E10 67 EC58
Leyton Ind Village E10 67 DX59
Leyton Pk Rd E10 67 EC62
Leyton Rd E15 67 ED64
Leyton Rd SW19 120 DC94
Leyton Way E11 68 EE59
Leytonstone Rd E15 68 EE64
Leywick St E15 86 EE68
Leywood Cl, Amer. 20 AS40
Lezayre Rd, Orp. 163 ET107
Liardet St SE14 103 DY79
Liberia Rd N5 83 DP65
Liberty, The, Rom. 71 FE57
Liberty Av SW19 140 DD95
Liberty Hall Rd, Add. 152 BG106
Liberty La, Add. 152 BG106
Liberty Ms SW12 121 DH86
Liberty Ri, Add. 152 BG107
Liberty St SW9 101 DM81
Libra Rd E3 85 DZ67
Libra Rd E13 86 EG68
Library Hill, Brwd. 54 FX47
Coptfold Rd
Library Pl E1 84 DV73
Cable St
Library St SE1 200 F5
Library St SE1 101 DP75
Library Way, Twick. 116 CC87
Nelson Rd
Licenced Victuallers Nat Homes, Uxb. 57 BF58
Denham Grn La
Lichfield Cl, Barn. 28 DF41
Lichfield Gdns, Rich. 98 CL84
Lichfield Gro N3 44 DB54
Lichfield Rd E3 85 DY69
Lichfield Rd E6 86 EK69
Lichfield Rd N9 46 DU47
Winchester Rd
Lichfield Rd NW2 63 CY63
Lichfield Rd, Dag. 70 EV63
Lichfield Rd, Houns. 96 BW83
Lichfield Rd, Nthwd. 59 BU55
Lichfield Rd, Rich. 98 CM81
Lichfield Rd, Wdf.Grn. 48 EE49
Lichfield Sq, Rich. 98 CL84
Lichfield Gdns
Lichfield Ter, Upmin. 73 FS61
Lichfield Way, S.Croy. 161 DX110
Lichlade Cl, Orp. 163 ET105
Lidbury Rd NW7 43 CY51
Lidcote Gdns SW9 101 DN82
Liddall Way, West Dr. 76 BM74
Liddell Cl, Har. 61 CK55
Liddell Gdns NW10 81 CW68
Liddell Rd NW6 82 DA65
Lidding Rd, Har. 61 CK57
Liddington Rd E15 86 EF67
Liddon Rd E13 86 EH69
Liddon Rd, Brom. 144 EJ97
Liden Cl E17 67 DZ60
Hitcham Rd
Lidfield Rd N16 66 DR63
Lidgate Rd SE15 102 DT80
Chandler Way
Lidiard Rd SW18 120 DC89
Lidlington Pl NW1 195 L1
Lidlington Pl NW1 83 DJ68
Lido Sq N17 46 DR54
Lidstone Cl, Wok. 166 AV117
Lidyard Rd N19 65 DJ60
Lieutenant Ellis Way, Wal.Cr. 14 DT31
Liffler Rd SE18 105 ES78
Lifford St SW15 99 CX84
Liffords Pl SW13 99 CT82
Lightcliffe Rd N13 45 DN49
Lighter Cl SE16 203 L8
Lighter Cl SE16 103 DY77
Lighterman Ms E1 85 DX72
Lightermans Rd E14 204 A5
Lightermans Rd E14 103 EA75
Lightermans Wk SW18 100 DA84
Lightfoot Rd N8 65 DL57
Lightley Cl, Wem. 80 CM66
Stanley Av
Lightswood Cl (Cheshunt), Wal.Cr. 14 DR26
Hammondstreet Rd
Ligonier St E2 197 P4
Lila Pl, Swan. 147 FE98
Lilac Av, Enf. 30 DW36
Lilac Av, Wok. 166 AX120
Lilac Cl E4 47 DZ51
Lilac Cl, Brwd. 54 FV43
Magnolia Way
Lilac Cl (Cheshunt), Wal.Cr. 14 DV31
Greenwood Av
Lilac Gdns W5 97 CK76
Lilac Gdns, Croy. 143 EA104
Lilac Gdns, Hayes 77 BS72
Lilac Gdns, Rom. 71 FE60
Lilac Gdns, Swan. 147 FD97
Lilac Pl SE11 200 B9
Lilac Pl SE11 101 DM77
Lilac Pl, West Dr. 76 BM73
Cedar Av
Lilac St W12 81 CU73
Lilburne Gdns SE9 124 EL85
Lilburne Rd SE9 124 EL85
Lilburne Wk NW10 80 CQ65
Lile Cres W7 79 CE71
Lilestone Est NW8 82 DD70
Fisherton St
Lilestone St NW8 194 B4
Lilestone St NW8 82 DE70
Lilford Rd SE5 101 DP82
Lilian Barker Cl SE12 124 EG85
Lilian Board Way, Grnf. 61 CD64
Lilian Cl N16 66 DS62
Barbauld Rd
Lilian Cres, Brwd. 55 GC47
Lilian Gdns, Wdf.Grn. 48 EH53
Lilian Rd SW16 141 DJ95
Lillechurch Rd, Dag. 88 EV65
Lilleshall Rd, Mord. 140 DD100
Lilley Cl E1 202 C3
Lilley Cl, Brwd. 54 FT49
Lilley Dr, Tad. 174 DB122
Lilley La NW7 42 CR50
Lillian Av W3 98 CN75
Lillian Rd SW13 99 CU79
Lillie Rd SW6 99 CY80
Lillie Rd, West. 178 EK118
Lillie Yd SW6 100 DA79
Lillieshall Rd SW4 101 DH83
Lillington Gdns Est SW1 199 L9
Lilliots La, Lthd. 171 CG119
Kingston Rd
Lilliput Av, Nthlt. 78 BZ67
Lilliput Rd, Rom. 71 FD59
Lily Cl W14 99 CY77
Lily Dr, West Dr. 94 BK76
Wise La
Lily Gdns, Wem. 79 CJ68
Lily Pl EC1 196 E6
Lily Pl EC1 83 DN71
Lily Rd E17 67 EA58
Lilyville Rd SW6 99 CZ81
Limbourne Av, Dag. 70 EZ59
Limburg Rd SW11 100 DF84
Lime Av, Brwd. 55 FZ48
Lime Av, Grav. 130 GD87
Lime Av, Upmin. 72 FN63
Lime Av, West Dr. 76 BM73
Lime Av, Wind. 92 AT80
Lime Cl E1 202 C2
Lime Cl E1 84 DU74

Lime Cl, Brom. 144 EL98
Lime Cl, Buck.H. 48 EK48
Lime Cl, Cars. 140 DF103
Lime Cl, Har. 41 CG54
Lime Cl, Pnr. 59 BT55
Lime Cl, Rom. 71 FC56
Lime Cl, S.Ock. 91 FW69
Lime Cl, Wat. 40 BX45
Lime Ct, Mitch. 140 DD96
Lewis Rd
Lime Cres, Sun. 136 BW96
Lime Gro E4 47 DZ51
Burnside Av
Lime Gro N20 43 CZ46
Lime Gro W12 99 CW75
Lime Gro, Add. 152 BG105
Lime Gro, Hayes 77 BR73
Lime Gro, Ilf. 49 ET51
Lime Gro, N.Mal. 138 CR97
Lime Gro, Orp. 145 EP103
Lime Gro, Ruis. 59 BV59
Lime Gro, Sid. 125 ET86
Lime Gro, Twick. 117 CF86
Lime Gro, Warl. 177 DY118
Lime Gro, Wok. 166 AY121
Lime Meadow Av, S.Croy. 160 DU113
Lime Pit La, Sev. 181 FC117
Lime Rd, Epp. 17 ET31
Lime Rd, Rich. 98 CM84
St. Mary's Gro
Lime Rd, Swan. 147 FD97
Lime Row, Erith 106 EZ76
Northwood Pl
Lime St E17 67 DY56
Lime St EC3 197 M10
Lime St EC3 84 DS73
Lime St Pas EC3 197 M9
Lime Ter W7 79 CE73
Manor Ct Rd
Lime Tree Av, Esher 137 CD102
Lime Tree Av (Bluewater), Green. 129 FU88
Lime Tree Av, T.Ditt. 137 CD102
Lime Tree Cl, Lthd. 170 CA124
Lime Tree Gro, Croy. 143 DZ104
Lime Tree Pl, Mitch. 141 DH95
Lime Tree Rd, Houns. 96 CB81
Lime Tree Ter SE6 123 DZ88
Winterstoke Rd
Lime Tree Wk, Amer. 20 AT39
Lime Tree Wk, Bushey 41 CE46
Lime Tree Wk, Enf. 30 DQ38
Lime Tree Wk, Rick. 22 BH43
Lime Tree Wk, Sev. 191 FH125
Lime Tree Wk, Vir.W. 132 AY98
Lime Tree Wk, W.Wick. 162 EF105
Lime Wk E15 86 EE67
Church St N
Lime Wk (Denham), Uxb. 58 BJ64
Lime Wks Rd, Red. 185 DJ126
Limeburner La EC4 196 F9
Limeburner La EC4 83 DP72
Limebush Cl, Add. 152 BJ109
Limecroft Cl, Epsom 156 CR108
Limedene Cl, Pnr. 40 BX53
Limeharbour E14 204 C5
Limeharbour E14 103 EB76
Limehouse Causeway E14 85 DZ73
Limehouse Flds Est E14 85 DY71
Limehouse Link E14 85 DY73
Limekiln Dr SE7 104 EH79
Limekiln Pl SE19 122 DT94
Limerick Cl SW12 121 DJ87
Limerick Gdns, Upmin. 73 FT59
Limerston St SW10 100 DC79
Limes, The W2 82 DA73
Linden Gdns
Limes, The, Brwd. 55 FZ48
Limes, The, Brom. 144 EL103
Limes, The, Har. 41 CF54
Limes, The, Purf. 108 FN78
Tank Hill Rd
Limes, The, Wok. 166 AX115
Limes Av E11 68 EH56
Limes Av N12 44 DC49
Limes Av NW7 42 CS51
Limes Av NW11 63 CY59
Limes Av SE20 122 DV94
Limes Av SW13 99 CT82
Limes Av, Cars. 140 DF102
Limes Av, Chig. 49 ER51
Limes Av, Croy. 141 DN104
Limes Av, The N11 45 DH50
Limes Cl, Ashf. 114 BN92
Limes Ct, Brwd. 54 FX46
Sawyers Hall La
Limes Fld Rd SW14 98 CS83
White Hart La
Limes Gdns SW18 120 DA86
Limes Gro SE13 103 EC84
Limes Pl, Croy. 142 DR101
Limes Rd, Beck. 143 EB96
Limes Rd, Croy. 142 DR100
Limes Rd, Egh. 113 AZ92
Limes Rd (Cheshunt), Wal.Cr. 15 DX32
Limes Rd, Wey. 152 BN105
Limes Row, Orp. 163 EP106
Orchard Rd
Limes Wk SE15 102 DV84
Limes Wk W5 97 CK75
Chestnut Gro
Limesdale Gdns, Edg. 42 CQ54
Limesford Rd SE15 103 DX84
Limestone Wk, Erith 106 EX76
Limetree Cl SW2 121 DM88
Limetree Ter, Well. 106 EU83
Hook La
Limetree Wk SW17 120 DG92
Church La
Limewood Cl E17 67 DZ56
Limewood Cl W13 79 CH72
St. Stephens Rd
Limewood Ct, Ilf. 69 EM57
Limewood Rd, Erith 107 FC80
Limpsfield Av SW19 119 CX89
Limpsfield Av, Th.Hth. 141 DM99
Limpsfield Rd, S.Croy. 160 DU112
Limpsfield Rd, Warl. 176 DW116
Linacre Ct W6 99 CX78
Linacre Rd NW2 81 CV65
Linberry Wk SE8 203 M9
Linberry Wk SE8 103 DZ77
Linchfield Rd, Slou. 92 AW81
Linchmere Rd SE12 124 EF87
Lincoln Av N14 45 DJ48
Lincoln Av SW19 119 CX90
Lincoln Av, Rom. 71 FD60
Lincoln Av, Twick. 116 CC89
Lincoln Cl SE25 142 DU100
Woodside Grn
Lincoln Cl, Erith 107 FF82
Lincoln Cl, Grnf. 78 CC67
Lincoln Cl, Har. 60 BZ57
Lincoln Cl, Horn. 72 FN57
Lincoln Ct N16 66 DR59
Lincoln Ct, Borwd. 26 CR43
Lincoln Cres, Enf. 30 DS43
Lincoln Dr, Rick. 23 BP42
Lincoln Dr, Wat. 40 BW48
Lincoln Dr, Wok. 167 BE115
Lincoln Gdns, Ilf. 68 EL59
Lincoln Grn Rd, Orp. 145 ET99
Lincoln Ms NW6 81 CZ67
Willesden La
Lincoln Ms SE21 122 DR88
Lincoln Pk, Amer. 20 AS39
Lincoln Rd E7 86 EK65
Lincoln Rd E13 86 EH70
Lincoln Rd E18 48 EG53
Grove Rd
Lincoln Rd N2 64 DE55
Lincoln Rd SE25 142 DV97
Lincoln Rd, Enf. 30 DU43
Lincoln Rd, Erith 107 FF82
Lincoln Rd, Felt. 116 BZ90
Lincoln Rd (Chalfont St. Peter), Ger.Cr. 36 AY53
Lincoln Rd, Har. 60 BZ57
Lincoln Rd, Mitch. 141 DL99
Lincoln Rd, N.Mal. 138 CQ97
Lincoln Rd, Nthwd. 59 BT55
Lincoln Rd, Sid. 126 EV92
Lincoln Rd, Wem. 79 CK65
Lincoln Rd, Wor.Pk. 139 CV102
Lincoln St E11 68 EE61
Lincoln St SW3 198 D9
Lincoln St SW3 100 DF77
Lincoln Wk, Epsom 156 CR110
Hollymoor La
Lincoln Way, Enf. 30 DV43
Lincoln Way, Rick. 23 BP42
Lincoln Way, Sun. 135 BS95
Lincolns, The NW7 43 CT48
Lincolns Flds, Epp. 17 ET29
Lincoln's Inn WC2 196 C8
Lincoln's Inn WC2 83 DN72
Lincoln's Inn Flds WC2 196 B8
Lincoln's Inn Flds WC2 83 DM72
Lincolnshott, Grav. 130 GB92
Lincombe Rd, Brom. 124 EF90
Lind Rd, Sutt. 158 DC106
Lind St SE8 103 EB82
Lindal Cres, Enf. 29 DL42
Lindal Rd SE4 123 DZ85
Lindale Cl, Vir.W. 132 AT98
Lindales, The N17 46 DT51
Brantwood Rd
Lindbergh Rd, Wall. 159 DL109
Linden Av NW10 81 CX68
Linden Av, Couls. 175 DH116
Linden Av, Dart. 128 FJ88
Linden Av, Enf. 30 DU39
Linden Av, Houns. 116 CB85
Linden Av, Ruis. 59 BU60
Linden Av, Th.Hth. 141 DP98
Linden Av, Wem. 62 CM64
Linden Chase Rd, Sev. 191 FH122
Linden Cl N14 29 DJ44
Linden Cl, Add. 152 BG111
Linden Cl, Orp. 164 EU106
Linden Cl, Purf. 108 FQ79
Linden Cl, Ruis. 59 BU60
Linden Cl, Stan. 41 CH50
Linden Cl, Tad. 173 CX120
Linden Cl, T.Ditt. 137 CF101
Linden Cl, Wal.Cr. 14 DV30
Linden Ct W12 81 CW74
Linden Ct, Egh. 112 AV93
Linden Ct, Lthd. 171 CH121
Linden Cres, Grnf. 79 CF65
Linden Cres, Kings.T. 138 CM96
Linden Cres, Wdf.Grn. 48 EH51
Linden Dr, Cat. 176 DQ124
Linden Dr (Chalfont St. Peter), Ger.Cr. 36 AY54
Woodside Hill
Linden Gdns W2 82 DA73
Linden Gdns W4 98 CR78
Linden Gdns, Enf. 30 DU39
Linden Gdns, Lthd. 171 CJ121
Linden Gro SE15 102 DW83
Linden Gro SE26 122 DW93
Linden Gro, N.Mal. 138 CS97
Linden Gro, Tedd. 117 CF92
Waldegrave Rd
Linden Gro, Walt. 135 BT103
Linden Gro, Warl. 177 DY118
Linden Ho, Slou. 93 BB78
Linden Lawns, Wem. 62 CM63
Linden Lea N2 64 DC57
Linden Lea, Wat. 7 BU33
Linden Leas, W.Wick. 143 ED103
Linden Ms N1 66 DR64
Mildmay Gro N
Linden Ms W2 82 DA73
Linden Gdns
Linden Pas W4 98 CR78
Linden Gdns
Linden Pit Path, Lthd. 171 CH121
Linden Pl, Epsom 156 CS112
East St
Linden Pl, Mitch. 140 DE98
Linden Ri, Brwd. 54 FX50
Linden Rd E17 67 DZ57
High St
Linden Rd N10 65 DH56
Linden Rd N11 44 DF47
Linden Rd N15 66 DQ56
Linden Rd, Hmptn. 116 CA94
Linden Rd, Lthd. 171 CH121
Linden Rd, Wey. 153 BQ109
Linden Sq, Sev. 190 FE122
London Rd
Linden St, Rom. 71 FD56
Linden Wk N19 65 DJ61
Hargrave Pk
Linden Way N14 29 DJ44
Linden Way, Pur. 159 DJ110
Linden Way, Shep. 135 BQ99
Linden Way, Wok. 167 AZ121
Linden Way, Wok. 167 AZ121
St. Martha's Av
Linden Way (Send Marsh), Wok. 167 BF124
Lindenfield, Chis. 145 EP96
Lindens, The N12 44 DD50
Lindens, The W4 98 CQ81
Hartington Rd
Lindens, The, Croy. 161 EC107
Lindens, The, Loug. 33 EM43
Lindeth Cl, Stan. 41 CJ51
Old Ch La
Lindfield Gdns NW3 64 DB64
Lindfield Rd W5 79 CJ70
Lindfield Rd, Croy. 142 DT100
Lindfield Rd, Rom. 52 FL50
Lindfield St E14 85 EA72
Lindhill Cl, Enf. 31 DX39
Lindisfarne Cl, Grav. 131 GL89
St. Benedict's Av
Lindisfarne Rd SW20 119 CU94
Lindisfarne Rd, Dag. 70 EW62
Lindisfarne Way E9 67 DY63
Lindley Est SE15 102 DU80
Bird in Bush Rd
Lindley Rd E10 67 EB61
Lindley Rd, Gdse. 186 DW130
Lindley Rd, Walt. 136 BX104
Lindley St E1 84 DW71
Lindo St SE15 102 DW82
Selden Rd
Lindore Rd SW11 100 DF84
Lindores Rd, Cars. 140 DC101
Lindrop St SW6 100 DC82
Lindsay Cl, Chess. 156 CL108
Lindsay Cl, Epsom 156 CQ113
Lindsay Cl, Stai. 114 BK85
Lindsay Dr, Har. 62 CL58
Lindsay Dr, Shep. 135 BR100
Lindsay Pl, Wal.Cr. 14 DV30
Lindsay Rd, Add. 152 BG110
Lindsay Rd, Hmptn. 116 CB91
Lindsay Rd, Wor.Pk. 139 CV103
Lindsay Sq SW1 199 N10
Lindsay Sq SW1 101 DK78
Lindsell St SE10 103 EC81
Lindsey Cl, Brwd. 54 FU49
Lindsey Cl, Brom. 144 EK97
Lindsey Cl, Mitch. 141 DL98
Lindsey Gdns, Felt. 115 BR87
Lindsey Ms N1 84 DQ66
Lindsey Rd, Dag. 70 EW63
Lindsey Rd (Denham), Uxb. 58 BG62
Lindsey St EC1 196 G6
Lindsey St EC1 83 DP71
Lindsey St, Epp. 17 ER28
Lindsey Way, Horn. 72 FJ57
Lindum Rd, Tedd. 117 CJ94
Lindvale, Wok. 166 AY115
Lindway SE27 121 DP92
Lindwood Cl E6 86 EL71
Northumberland Rd
Linfield Cl NW4 63 CW55
Linfield Cl, Walt. 153 BV106
Linfields, Amer. 20 AW40
Linford Rd E17 67 EC55
Linford Rd, Grays 111 GH78
Linford St SW8 101 DJ81
Ling Rd E16 86 EG71
Ling Rd, Erith 107 FC79
Lingards Rd SE13 103 EC84
Lingey Cl, Sid. 125 ET89
Lingfield Av, Dart. 128 FP87
Lingfield Av, Kings.T. 138 CL98
Lingfield Av, Upmin. 72 FM62
Lingfield Cl, Enf. 30 DS44
Lingfield Cl, Nthwd. 39 BS52
Lingfield Cres SE9 105 ER84
Lingfield Gdns N9 46 DV45
Lingfield Gdns, Couls. 175 DP119
Lingfield Rd SW19 119 CX92
Lingfield Rd, Grav. 131 GH89
Lingfield Rd, Wor.Pk. 139 CW104
Lingfield Way, Wat. 23 BT38
Lingham St SW9 101 DL82
Lingholm Way, Barn. 27 CX43
Lingmere Cl, Chig. 49 EQ47
Lingmoor Dr, Wat. 8 BW33
Lingrove Gdns, Buck.H. 48 EH47
Beech La
Lings Coppice SE21 122 DR89
Lingwell Rd SW17 120 DE90
Lingwood Gdns, Islw. 97 CE80
Lingwood Rd E5 66 DU59
Linhope St NW1 194 D4
Linhope St NW1 82 DF70
Linington Av, Chesh. 4 AU30
Link, The SE9 125 EN90
Link, The W3 80 CP72
Link, The, Enf. 31 DY39
Link, The, Nthlt. 60 BZ64
Eastcote La
Link, The, Pnr. 60 BW59
Link, The, Slou. 74 AV72
Link, The, Wem. 61 CJ60
Nathans Rd
Link Av, Wok. 167 BD115
Link La, Wall. 159 DK107
Link Rd N11 44 DG49
Link Rd, Add. 152 BL105
Weybridge Rd
Link Rd, Dag. 89 FB68
Link Rd, Felt. 115 BT87
Link Rd, Slou. 92 AW80
Link Rd, Wall. 140 DG102
Link Rd, Wat. 24 BX40
Link St E9 84 DW65
Link Way, Brom. 144 EL101
Link Way, Horn. 72 FL60
Link Way, Pnr. 40 BX53
Link Way, Stai. 114 BH93
Link Way (Denham), Uxb. 58 BG58
Link Way Rd, Brwd. 54 FT48
Linkfield, Brom. 144 EG100
Linkfield, W.Mol. 136 CA97
Linkfield Cor, Red. 184 DE133
Hatchlands Rd
Linkfield Gdns, Red. 184 DE134
Hatchlands Rd
Linkfield La, Red. 184 DE133
Linkfield Rd, Islw. 97 CF82
Linkfield St, Red. 184 DE134
Linklea Cl NW9 42 CS52
Links, The E17 67 DY56
Links, The (Cheshunt), Wal.Cr. 15 DX26
Links, The, Walt. 135 BU103
Links Av, Mord. 140 DA98
Links Av, Rom. 51 FH54
Links Brow, Lthd. 171 CE124
Links Cl, Ash. 171 CJ117
Links Dr N20 44 DA46
Links Dr, Borwd. 26 CM41
Links Dr, Rad. 9 CF33
Links Gdns SW16 121 DN94
Links Grn Way, Cob. 154 CA114
Links Pl, Ash. 171 CK117
Links Rd NW2 63 CT61
Links Rd SW17 120 DG93
Links Rd W3 80 CN72
Links Rd, Ashf. 114 BL92
Links Rd, Ash. 171 CJ118
Links Rd, Epsom 157 CU113
Links Rd, W.Wick. 143 EC102
Links Rd, Wdf.Grn. 48 EG50
Links Side, Enf. 29 DN41
Links Vw N3 43 CZ52
Links Vw, Dart. 128 FJ88
Links Vw Av, Bet. 182 CN134
Links Vw Cl, Stan. 41 CG51
Links Vw Rd, Croy. 143 EA104
Links Vw Rd, Hmptn. 116 CC92
Links Way, Beck. 143 EA100
Links Way, Rick. 23 BQ41
Links Yd E1 84 DU71
Spelman St
Linkscroft Av, Ashf. 115 BP93
Linkside N12 43 CZ51
Linkside, Chig. 49 EQ50
Linkside, N.Mal. 138 CS96
Linkside Cl, Enf. 29 DM41
Linkside Gdns, Enf. 29 DM41
Linksway NW4 43 CX54
Linksway, Nthwd. 39 BQ53
Linkway N4 66 DQ59
Linkway SW20 139 CV97
Linkway, Dag. 70 EW63
Linkway, Rich. 117 CH89
Linkway, Wok. 167 BC117
Linkway, The, Barn. 28 DB44
Linkway, The, Sutt. 158 DD109
Linkwood Wk NW1 83 DK66
Maiden La
Linley Cres, Rom. 71 FB55
Linley Rd N17 46 DS54
Linnell Cl NW11 64 DB58
Linnell Dr NW11 64 DB58
Linnell Rd N18 46 DU50
Fairfield Rd
Linnell Rd SE5 102 DS82
Linnet Cl N9 47 DX46
Linnet Cl SE28 88 EW73
Linnet Cl, Bushey 40 CC45
Linnet Cl, S.Croy. 161 DX110
Linnet Ms SW12 120 DG87
Linnet Rd, Abb.L. 7 BU31
Linnet Ter, Ilf. 69 EN55
Tiptree Cres
Linnet Way, Purf. 108 FP78
Linnett Cl E4 47 EC49
Linom Rd SW4 101 DL84
Linscott Rd E5 66 DW63
Linsdell Rd, Bark. 87 EQ67
Linsey St SE16 202 B8
Linsey St SE16 102 DU77
Linslade Cl, Houns. 116 BY85
Frampton Rd
Linslade Cl, Pnr. 59 BV55
Linslade Rd, Orp. 164 EU107
Linstead Ct SE9 125 ES86
Linstead St NW6 82 DA66
Linstead Way SW18 119 CY87
Linster Gro, Borwd. 26 CQ43
Lintaine Cl W6 99 CY79
Moylan Rd
Linthorpe Av, Wem. 79 CJ65
Linthorpe Rd N16 66 DS59
Linthorpe Rd, Barn. 28 DE41
Linton Av, Borwd. 26 CM39
Linton Cl, Mitch. 140 DF101
Linton Cl, Well. 106 EV81
Anthony Rd
Linton Gdns E6 86 EL72
Linton Glade, Croy. 161 DY109
Linton Gro SE27 121 DP92
Linton Rd, Bark. 87 EQ66
Linton St N1 84 DQ67
Lintons, The, Bark. 87 EQ66
Lintons La, Epsom 156 CS112
Lintott Ct, Stai. 114 BK86
Linver Rd SW6 100 DA82
Linwood Cl SE5 102 DT82
Linwood Cres, Enf. 30 DU39
Linwood Way SE15 102 DT80
Daniel Gdns
Linzee Rd N8 65 DL56
Lion Av, Twick. 117 CF88
Lion Rd
Lion Cl SE4 123 EA86
Lion Cl, Shep. 134 BL97
Lion Ct, Borwd. 26 CQ39
Lion Gate Gdns, Rich. 98 CM83
Lion Grn Rd, Couls. 175 DK115
Lion La, Red. 184 DF133
Lion Pk Av, Chess. 156 CN105
Lion Plaza EC2 84 DR72
Threadneedle St
Lion Rd E6 87 EM71
Lion Rd N9 46 DU47
Lion Rd, Bexh. 106 EZ84
Lion Rd, Croy. 142 DQ99
Lion Rd, Twick. 117 CF88
Lion Way, Brent. 97 CK80
Lion Wf Rd, Islw. 97 CH83
Lion Yd SW4 101 DK84
Tremadoc Rd
Lionel Gdns SE9 124 EK85
Lionel Ms W10 81 CY71
Telford Rd
Lionel Oxley Ho, Grays 110 GB79
New Rd
Lionel Rd SE9 124 EK85
Lionel Rd, Brent. 98 CM78
Lions Cl SE9 124 EJ90
Liphook Cl, Horn. 71 FF63
Petworth Way
Liphook Cres SE23 122 DW87
Liphook Rd, Wat. 40 BX49
Lippitts Hill, Loug. 32 EE39
Lipsham Cl, Bans. 158 DD113
Lipton Cl SE28 88 EW73
Aisher Rd
Lipton Rd E1 85 DX72
Bower St
Lisbon Av, Twick. 116 CC89
Lisburne Rd NW3 64 DF63
Lisford St SE15 102 DT81
Lisgar Ter W14 99 CZ77
Liskeard Cl, Chis. 125 EQ93
Liskeard Gdns SE3 104 EG81
Liskeard Lo, Cat. 186 DU126
Lisle Cl SW17 121 DH91
Lisle Pl, Grays 110 GA76
Lisle St WC2 195 N10
Lisle St WC2 83 DK73
Lismore Circ NW5 64 DG64
Lismore Cl, Islw. 97 CG82
Lismore Pk, Slou. 74 AT72
Lismore Rd N17 66 DR55
Lismore Rd, S.Croy. 160 DS107
Lismore Wk N1 84 DQ65
Clephane Rd
Liss Way SE15 102 DT80
Pentridge St
Lissenden Gdns NW5 64 DG63
Lissoms Rd, Couls. 174 DG118
Lisson Grn Est NW8 194 B3
Lisson Grn Est NW8 82 DE69
Lisson Gro NW1 194 B5
Lisson Gro NW1 82 DE70
Lisson Gro NW8 194 A3
Lisson Gro NW8 82 DD69
Lisson St NW1 194 B6
Lisson St NW1 82 DE71
Lister Av, Rom. 52 FK54
Lister Cl W3 80 CR71
Lister Cl, Mitch. 140 DE95
Lister Gdns N18 46 DQ50
Lister Ho SE3 104 EE79
Lister Rd E11 68 EE60
Lister Rd, Til. 111 GG82
Lister St E13 86 EG69
Sewell St
Lister Wk SE28 88 EX73
Haldane Rd
Liston Rd N17 46 DU53
Liston Rd SW4 101 DJ83
Liston Way, Wdf.Grn. 48 EJ52
Listowel Cl SW9 101 DN80
Mandela St
Listowel Rd, Dag. 70 FA62
Listria Pk N16 66 DS61
Litchfield Av E15 86 EE65
Litchfield Av, Mord. 139 CZ101
Litchfield Gdns NW10 81 CU65
Litchfield Rd, Sutt. 158 DC105
Litchfield St WC2 195 N10
Litchfield St WC2 83 DK73
Litchfield Way NW11 64 DB57
Lithos Rd NW3 82 DB65
Little Acre, Beck. 143 EA97
Little Albany St NW1 195 J4
Little Argyll St W1 195 K9
Little Aston Rd, Rom. 52 FM52
Little Belhus Cl, S.Ock. 91 FU70
Little Benty, West Dr. 94 BK78
Little Birch Cl, Add. 152 BK109
Little Birches, Sid. 125 ES89
Little Boltons, The SW5 100 DB78
Little Boltons, The SW10 100 DB78
Little Bookham Common, Lthd. 170 BY122
Little Bookham St, Lthd. 170 BZ124
Little Bornes SE21 122 DS91
Little Britain EC1 196 G7
Little Britain EC1 83 DP71
Little Brownings SE23 122 DV89
Little Bury St N9 46 DR46
Little Bushey La, Bushey 25 CD44
Little Bushey La Footpath, Bushey 41 CD45
Little Bushey La
Little Cedars N12 44 DC49
Woodside Av
Little Chester St SW1 198 G6
Little Chester St SW1 101 DH76
Little Cloisters SW1 101 DK76
Tufton St
Little Coll La EC4 84 DR73
Garlick Hill
Little Coll St SW1 199 P6
Little Common, Stan. 41 CG48
Little Common La, Red. 185 DP132
Little Ct, W.Wick. 144 EE103
Little Dean's Yd SW1 199 P6
Little Dimocks SW12 121 DH89
Little Dormers, Ger.Cr. 57 AZ56
Little Dorrit Ct SE1 201 J4
Little Dorrit Ct SE1 102 DQ75
Little Dragons, Loug. 32 EK42
Little Ealing La W5 97 CJ77
Little Edward St NW1 195 J2
Little Elms, Hayes 95 BR80
Little Essex St WC2 196 D10
Little Ferry Rd, Twick. 117 CH88
Ferry Rd
Little Friday Rd E4 48 EE47
Little Gaynes Gdns, Upmin. 72 FP63
Little Gaynes La, Upmin. 72 FM63
Little Gearies, Ilf. 69 EP56
Little George St SW1 199 P5
Little Gerpins La, Upmin. 90 FM67
Little Gra, Grnf. 79 CG69
Perivale La
Little Graylings, Abb.L. 7 BS33

Little Grn, Rich. 97 CK84
Little Grn La, Cher. 133 BE104
Little Grn La, Rick. 23 BP41
Little Grn St NW5 65 DH63
College La
Little Gregories La, Epp. 33 ER35
Little Gro, Bushey 24 CB42
Little Gro Av, Wal.Cr. 13 DP25
Hammondstreet Rd
Little Halliards, Walt. 135 BU100
Felix Rd
Little Hayes, Kings L. 6 BN29
Little Heath SE7 104 EL79
Little Heath, Rom. 70 EV56
Little Heath La, Wok. 150 AS109
Little Heath Rd, Bexh. 106 EZ81
Little Heath Rd, Wok. 150 AS109
Little Hill, Rick. 21 BC44
Little How Cft, Abb.L. 7 BQ31
Little Ilford La E12 69 EM63
Little Julians Hill, Sev. 190 FG128
Little Marlborough St W1 195 K9
Little Martins, Bushey 24 CB43
Little Mead, Wok. 166 AT116
Little Moreton Cl, W.Byf. 152 BH112
Little Moss La, Pnr. 40 BY54
Little New St EC4 196 E8
Little Newport St WC2 195 N10
Little Newport St WC2 83 DK73
Little Orchard, Add. 151 BF111
Little Orchard, Wok. 151 BA114
Little Orchard Cl, Abb.L. 7 BR32
Little Orchard Cl, Pnr. 40 BY54
Barrow Pt La
Little Oxhey La, Wat. 40 BX50
Little Pk, Hem.H. 5 BA28
Little Pk Dr, Felt. 116 BX89
Little Pk Gdns, Enf. 30 DQ41
Little Pastures, Brwd. 54 FT49
Tern Way
Little Pipers Cl (Cheshunt), Wal.Cr. 13 DP29
Little Plucketts Way, Buck.H. 48 EJ46
Little Portland St W1 195 K8
Little Portland St W1 83 DH72
Little Potters, Bushey 41 CD45
Little Queen St, Dart. 128 FM87
Little Queens Rd, Tedd. 117 CF93
Little Redlands, Brom. 144 EL96
Little Reeves Av, Amer. 20 AT39
Little Riding, Wok. 167 BB116
Little Rd, Croy. 142 DS102
Lower Addiscombe Rd
Little Rd, Hayes 95 BT75
Little Roke Av, Ken. 159 DP114
Little Roke Rd, Ken. 160 DQ114
Little Russell St WC1 195 P7
Little Russell St WC1 83 DL71
Little Russets, Brwd. 55 GE45
Hutton Village
Little St. James's St SW1 199 K3
Little St. James's St SW1 83 DJ74
Little St. Leonards SW14 98 CQ83
Little Sanctuary SW1 199 N5
Little Smith St SW1 199 N6
Little Somerset St E1 197 P9
Little Strand NW9 43 CT54
Little Stream Cl, Nthwd. 39 BS50
Little St, Wal.Abb. 31 EC40
Sewardstone Rd
Little Sutton La, Slou. 93 BC78
Little Thrift, Orp. 145 EQ98
Little Titchfield St W1 195 K7
Little Trinity La EC4 197 J10
Little Turnstile WC1 196 B7
Little Windmill Hill, Kings L. 5 BE32
Little Wd Cl, Orp. 146 EU95
Little Woodcote Est, Cars. 158 DG111
Woodmansterne La
Little Woodcote Est, . Wall 158 DG111
Woodmansterne La
Little Woodcote La, Cars. 159 DH112
Little Woodcote La, Pur. 159 DH112
Little Woodcote La, Wall. 159 DH112
Littlebrook Cl, Croy. 143 DX100
Littlebrook Gdns (Cheshunt), Wal.Cr. 14 DW30
Littlebrook Manor Way, Dart. 128 FN85
Littlebury Rd SW4 101 DK83
Littlecombe SE7 104 EH79
Littlecombe Cl SW15 119 CX86
Littlecote Cl SW19 119 CX87
Littlecote Pl, Pnr. 40 BY53
Littlecourt Rd, Sev. 190 FG124
Littlecroft SE9 105 EN83
Littlecroft, Grav. 130 GE94
Littlecroft Rd, Egh. 113 AZ92
Littledale SE2 106 EU79
Littledale, Dart. 128 FQ90
Littledown Rd, Slou. 74 AT74
Littlefield Cl N19 65 DJ63
Tufnell Pk Rd
Littlefield Cl, Kings.T. 138 CL96
Fairfield W
Littlefield Rd, Edg. 42 CQ52
Littlegrove, Barn. 28 DE44
Littleheath La, Cob. 154 CA114
Littleheath Rd, S.Croy. 160 DV108
Littlejohn Rd W7 79 CF72
Littlejohn Rd, Orp. 146 EU100
Littlemead, Esher 155 CD105
Littlemede SE9 125 EM90
Littlemoor Rd, Ilf. 69 ER62
Littlemore Rd SE2 106 EU75
Littleport Spur, Slou. 74 AS72
Littlers Cl SW19 140 DD95
Runnymede
Littlestock Rd (Cheshunt), Wal.Cr. 14 DR26
Hammondstreet Rd
Littlestone Cl, Beck. 123 EA93
Abbey La
Littleton Av E4 48 EF46
Littleton Cres, Har. 61 CF61
Littleton La, Shep. 134 BK101
Littleton Rd, Ashf. 115 BQ94
Littleton Rd, Har. 61 CF61
Littleton St SW18 120 DC89
Littlewick Rd, Wok. 150 AW114
Littlewood SE13 123 EC85
Littlewood, Sev. 191 FJ122
Littlewood Cl W13 97 CH76
Littleworth Av, Esher 155 CD106
Littleworth Common Rd, Esher 137 CD104
Littleworth La, Esher 155 CD105
Littleworth Pl, Esher 155 CD105
Littleworth Rd, Esher 155 CE105
Livermere Rd E8 84 DT67
Liverpool Gro SE17 102 DR78
Liverpool Rd E10 67 EC58
Liverpool Rd E16 86 EE71
Liverpool Rd N1 83 DN68
Liverpool Rd N7 65 DN64
Liverpool Rd W5 97 CK75
Liverpool Rd, Kings.T. 118 CN94
Liverpool Rd, Th.Hth. 142 DQ97
Liverpool Rd, Wat. 23 BV43
Liverpool St EC2 197 M7
Liverpool St EC2 84 DS71
Livesey Cl, Kings.T. 138 CM97
Livesey Pl SE15 102 DU79
Peckham Pk Rd
Livingston Coll Twrs E10 67 EC58
Essex Rd
Livingstone Ct, Barn. 27 CY40
Christchurch La
Livingstone Gdns, Grav. 131 GK92
Livingstone Pl E14 103 EC78
Ferry St
Livingstone Rd E15 85 EC67
Livingstone Rd E17 67 EB58
Livingstone Rd N13 45 DL51
Livingstone Rd SW11 100 DD83
Winstanley Rd
Livingstone Rd, Cat. 176 DR122
Livingstone Rd, Grav. 131 GK92
Livingstone Rd, Houns. 96 CC84
Livingstone Rd, Sthl. 78 BX73
Livingstone Rd, Th.Hth. 142 DQ96
Livingstone Ter, Rain. 89 FE67
Livingstone Wk SW11 100 DD83
Livonia St W1 195 L9
Lizard St EC1 197 J3
Lizard St EC1 84 DQ69
Lizban St SE3 104 EH80
Llanbury Cl (Chalfont St. Peter), Ger.Cr. 36 AY52
Llanelly Rd NW2 63 CZ61
Llanover Rd SE18 105 EN79
Llanover Rd, Wem. 61 CK62
Llanthony Rd, Mord. 140 DD100
Llanvanor Rd NW2 63 CZ61
Llewellyn St SE16 202 C5
Lloyd Av SW16 141 DL95
Lloyd Av, Couls. 158 DG114
Lloyd Baker St WC1 196 C3
Lloyd Baker St WC1 83 DM69
Lloyd Ct, Pnr. 60 BX57
Lloyd Pk Av, Croy. 160 DT105
Lloyd Rd E6 87 EM67
Lloyd Rd E17 67 DX56
Lloyd Rd, Dag. 88 EZ65
Lloyd Rd, Wor.Pk. 139 CW104
Lloyd Sq WC1 196 D2
Lloyd Sq WC1 83 DN69
Lloyd St WC1 196 D2
Lloyd St WC1 83 DN69
Lloyd's Av EC3 197 N9
Lloyd's Av EC3 84 DS72
Lloyds Pl SE3 104 EE82
Lloyd's Row EC1 196 E3
Lloyds Way, Beck. 143 DY99
Loampit Hill SE13 103 EA82
Loampit Vale SE13 103 EB83
Loanda Cl E8 84 DT67
Clarissa St
Loates La, Wat. 24 BW41
Loats Rd SW2 121 DL86
Lobelia Cl E6 86 EL71
Sorrel Gdns
Local Board Rd, Wat. 24 BW43
Locarno Rd W3 80 CQ74
High St
Locarno Rd, Grnf. 78 CC70
Lochaber Rd SE13 104 EE84
Lochaline St W6 99 CW79
Lochan Cl, Hayes 78 BY70
Lochinvar St SW12 121 DH87
Lochmere Cl, Erith 107 FB79
Lochnagar St E14 85 EC71
Lock Chase SE3 104 EF83
Lock Cl, Add. 151 BE113
Lock Cl, Sthl. 96 CC75
Navigator Dr
Lock Island, Shep. 134 BN103
Lock La, Wok. 168 BH116
Lock Rd, Rich. 117 CJ91
Locke Cl, Rain. 89 FF65
Locke Gdns, Slou. 92 AW75
Locke King Cl, Wey. 152 BN108
Locke King Rd, Wey. 152 BN108
Locke Way, Wok. 167 AZ117
The Bdy
Lockesfield Pl E14 204 C10
Lockesfield Pl E14 103 EB78
Lockesley Dr, Orp. 145 ET100
Lockesley Sq, Surb. 137 CK100
Locket Rd, Har. 61 CE55
Lockfield Av, Enf. 31 DY40
Lockfield Dr, Wok. 166 AT118
Lockgate Cl E9 67 DZ64
Lee Conservancy Rd
Lockhart Cl N7 83 DM65
Lockhart Cl, Enf. 30 DV43
Derby Rd
Lockhart Rd, Cob. 154 BW113
Lockhart St E3 85 DZ70
Lockhurst St E5 67 DX63
Lockie Pl SE25 142 DU97
Lockier Wk, Wem. 61 CK62
Lockington Rd SW8 101 DH81
Lockmead Rd N15 66 DU58
Lockmead Rd SE13 103 EC83
Locks La, Mitch. 140 DF95
Locksley Dr, Wok. 166 AT118
Robin Hood Rd
Locksley Est E14 85 DZ72
Locksley St E14 85 DZ71
Locksmeade Rd, Rich. 117 CJ91
Lockswood Cl, Barn. 28 DF42
Lockwood Cl SE26 123 DX91
Lockwood Ind Pk N17 66 DV55
Lockwood Path, Wok. 151 BD113
Lockwood Sq SE16 202 D6
Lockwood Sq SE16 102 DV76
Lockwood Wk, Rom. 71 FE57
Lockwood Way E17 47 DX54
Lockwood Way, Chess. 156 CN106
Lockyer Est SE1 201 L4
Lockyer Rd, Purf. 108 FQ79
Lockyer St SE1 201 L5
Loddiges Rd E9 84 DW66
Loddon Spur, Slou. 74 AS73
Loder Cl, Wok. 151 BD113
Loder St SE15 102 DW81
Lodge Av SW14 98 CS83
Lodge Av, Borwd. 26 CM43
Lodge Av, Croy. 141 DN104
Lodge Av, Dag. 88 EU67
Lodge Av, Dart. 128 FJ86
Lodge Av, Har. 62 CL56
Lodge Av, Rom. 71 FG56
Lodge Cl N18 46 DQ50
Lodge Cl, Brwd. 55 GE45
Lodge Cl, Chig. 50 EU48
Lodge Cl, Cob. 170 BZ115
Lodge Cl, Edg. 42 CM51
Lodge Cl, Egh. 112 AX92
Lodge Cl, Epsom 157 CW110
Howell Hill Gro
Lodge Cl, Islw. 97 CH81
Lodge Cl, Lthd. 171 CD122
Lodge Cl, Orp. 146 EV102
Lodge Cl, Uxb. 76 BJ70
Lodge Cl, Wall. 140 DG102
Lodge Ct, Horn. 72 FL61
Lodge Ct, Wem. 62 CL64
Lodge Cres, Orp. 146 EV102
Lodge Cres, Wal.Cr. 15 DX34
Lodge Dr N13 45 DN49
Lodge Dr, Rick. 22 BJ42
Lodge End, Rad. 9 CH34
Lodge End, Rick. 23 BR42
Lodge Gdns, Beck. 143 DZ99
Lodge Hill SE2 106 EV80
Lodge Hill, Ilf. 68 EL56
Lodge Hill, Pur. 175 DN115
Lodge Hill, Well. 106 EV80
Lodge La N12 44 DC50
Lodge La, Bex. 126 EX86
Lodge La, Ch.St.G. 21 AZ41
Lodge La, Croy. 161 EA107
Lodge La, Grays 110 GA75
Lodge La, Rom. 50 FA52
Lodge La, Wal.Abb. 31 ED35
Lodge La, West. 189 EQ127
Lodge Pl, Sutt. 158 DB106
Lodge Rd NW4 63 CW56
Lodge Rd NW8 194 A3
Lodge Rd NW8 82 DD69
Lodge Rd, Brom. 124 EH94
Lodge Rd, Croy. 141 DP100
Lodge Rd, Lthd. 170 CC122
Lodge Rd, Sutt. 158 DB106
Throwley Way
Lodge Rd, Wall. 159 DH106
Lodge Vil, Wdf.Grn. 48 EF52
Lodge Way, Ashf. 114 BL89
Lodge Way, Shep. 135 BQ96
Lodgebottom Rd, Lthd. 182 CM127
Lodgehill Pk Cl, Har. 60 CB61
Lodore Gdns NW9 62 CS57
Lodore Grn, Uxb. 58 BL62
Lodore St E14 85 EC72
Loewen Rd, Grays 111 GG76
Lofthouse Pl, Chess. 155 CJ107
Loftie St SE16 202 C5
Loftie St SE16 102 DU75
Lofting Rd N1 83 DM66
Loftus Rd W12 81 CV74
Logan Cl, Enf. 31 DX39
Logan Cl, Houns. 96 BZ83
Logan Ms W8 100 DA77
Logan Pl W8 100 DA77
Logan Rd N9 46 DV47
Logan Rd, Wem. 62 CL61
Loggetts, The SE21 122 DS89
Logs Hill, Brom. 124 EL94
Logs Hill, Chis. 124 EL94
Logs Hill Cl, Chis. 144 EL95
Lois Dr, Shep. 135 BP99
Lolesworth Cl E1 84 DT71
Commercial St
Lollard St SE11 200 C8
Lollard St SE11 101 DM77
Loman Path, S.Ock. 91 FT72
Loman St SE1 200 G4
Loman St SE1 101 DP75
Lomas Cl, Croy. 161 EC108
Lomas Ct E8 84 DT66
Lomas St E1 84 DU71
Lombard Av, Enf. 30 DW39
Lombard Av, Ilf. 69 ES60
Lombard Business Pk SW19 140 DC96
Lombard Ct EC3 197 L10
Lombard Ct W3 80 CP74
Crown St
Lombard La EC4 196 E9
Lombard Rd N11 45 DH50
Lombard Rd SW11 100 DD82
Lombard Rd SW19 140 DB96
Lombard St EC3 197 L9
Lombard St EC3 84 DR72
Lombard St, Dart. 148 FQ99
Lombard Wall SE7 205 P7
Lombard Wall SE7 104 EH76
Lombards, The, Horn. 72 FM59
Lombardy Cl, Wok. 166 AT117
Nethercote Av
Lombardy Pl W2 82 DB73
Bark Pl
Lombardy Way, Borwd. 26 CL39
Lomond Cl N15 66 DS56
Lomond Cl, Wem. 80 CM66
Lomond Gdns, S.Croy. 161 DY108
Lomond Gro SE5 102 DR80
Loncin Mead Av, Add. 152 BJ109
Loncroft Rd SE5 102 DS79
Londesborough Rd N16 66 DS63
London Br EC4 201 L2
London Br EC4 84 DR74
London Br SE1 201 L2
London Br SE1 84 DR74
London Br St SE1 201 K3
London Br St SE1 84 DR74
London Br Wk SE1 201 L2
London Br Wk SE1 84 DS74
London City Airport E16 87 EM74
London Colney Bypass, St.Alb. 9 CK25
London Flds E8 84 DV66
London Flds E Side E8 84 DV66
London Flds W Side E8 84 DU66
London La E8 84 DV66
London La, Brom. 124 EF94
London Ms W2 194 A9
London Rd E13 86 EG68
London Rd SE1 200 F6
London Rd SE1 101 DP76
London Rd SE23 122 DU88
London Rd SW16 141 DM95
London Rd SW17 140 DF96
London Rd, Ashf. 114 BH90
London Rd, Bark. 87 EP66
London Rd, Borwd. 10 CN34
London Rd, Brent. 97 CJ80
London Rd, Brwd. 54 FT49
London Rd, Brom. 124 EF94
London Rd, Bushey 24 BY44
London Rd, Cat. 176 DR123
London Rd, Ch.St.G. 36 AW47
London Rd, Croy. 141 DP101
London Rd, Dart. 128 FP87
London Rd (Crayford), Dart. 127 FD85
London Rd (Farningham), Dart. 148 FL100
London Rd, Egh. 132 AV95
London Rd, Enf. 30 DR41
London Rd, Epsom 157 CT109
London Rd, Felt. 114 BH90
London Rd, Grav. 130 GD86
London Rd, Grays 109 FW79
London Rd, Green. 129 FS86
London Rd, Har. 61 CE61
London Rd, Houns. 97 CD83
London Rd, Islw. 97 CF82
London Rd, Kings.T. 138 CM96
London Rd, Mitch. 140 DF96
London Rd (Beddington Cor), Mitch. 140 DG101
London Rd, Mord. 140 DA99
London Rd, Ong. 35 FH36
London Rd, Rad. 10 CM33
London Rd, Red. 184 DG132
London Rd, Reig. 184 DA134
London Rd, Rick. 38 BM47
London Rd, Rom. 70 FA58
London Rd (Abridge), Rom. 33 ET42
London Rd (Stapleford Tawney), Rom. 35 FC40
London Rd, Sev. 190 FF123
London Rd (Halstead), Sev. 165 FB112
London Rd (Longford), Sev. 181 FD117
London Rd, Slou. 93 AZ78
London Rd (Datchet), Slou. 92 AX80
London Rd, S.Ock. 90 FM74
London Rd, Stai. 113 BF91
London Rd, Stan. 41 CJ50
London Rd, Sutt. 139 CX104
London Rd, Swan. 147 FC96
London Rd, Swans. 129 FV85
London Rd, Th.Hth. 141 DN99
London Rd, Til. 111 GH82
London Rd, Twick. 117 CG85
London Rd, Vir.W. 132 AV95
London Rd, Wall. 159 DH105
London Rd, Wem. 80 CL65
London Rd, West. 189 ER125
London Rd E, Amer. 20 AT42
London Rd N, Red. 185 DH125
London Rd Purfleet, Purf. 108 FN78
London Rd S, Red. 184 DG130
London Rd W Thurrock, Grays 109 FS79
London Stile W4 98 CN78
Wellesley Rd
London St EC3 197 N10
London St W2 194 A9
London St W2 82 DD72
London St, Cher. 134 BG101
London Wall EC2 197 J7
London Wall EC2 84 DQ71
London Wall Bldgs EC2 197 L7
Londons Cl, Upmin. 72 FQ64
Lonesome Way SW16 141 DH95
Long Acre WC2 195 P10
Long Acre WC2 83 DL73
Long Acre, Orp. 146 EX103
Long Barn Cl, Wat. 7 BV32
Long Copse Cl, Lthd. 170 CB123
Long Ct, Purf. 108 FN77
Thamley
Long Deacon Rd E4 48 EE46
Long Dr W3 80 CS72
Long Dr, Grnf. 78 CB67
Long Dr, Ruis. 60 BX63
Long Elmes, Har. 40 CB53
Long Elms, Abb.L. 7 BR33
Long Elms Cl, Abb.L. 7 BR33
Long Elms
Long Fallow, St.Alb. 8 CA27
Long Fld NW9 42 CS52
Long Grn, Chig. 49 ES49
Long Gro, Rom. 52 FL54
Long Gro Rd, Epsom 156 CP110
Long Hedges, Houns. 96 CA81
Long Hill, Cat. 177 DX121
Long La EC1 196 G6
Long La EC1 83 DP71
Long La N2 44 DC54
Long La N3 44 DC54
Long La SE1 201 K5
Long La SE1 102 DR75
Long La, Bexh. 106 EX80
Long La, Croy. 142 DW99
Long La, Grays 110 GA75
Long La, Hem.H. 5 AZ31
Long La, Rick. 37 BF47
Long La (Heronsgate), Rick. 21 BC44
Long La, Stai. 114 BM89
Long La, Uxb. 76 BN69
Long Leys E4 47 EB51
Long Lo Dr, Walt. 136 BW104
Long Mark Rd E16 86 EK71
Fulmer Rd
Long Mead NW9 43 CT53
Long Meadow NW5 65 DK64
Torriano Av
Long Meadow, Brwd. 55 GC47
Long Meadow, Rom. 52 FJ48
Long Meadow, Sev. 190 FD121
Long Meadow Cl, W.Wick. 143 EC101
Long Pond Rd SE3 104 EE81
Long Reach, Wok. 168 BN123
Long Reach Ct, Bark. 87 ER68
Long Ridings Av, Brwd. 55 GB43
Long Rd SW4 101 DJ84
Long Shaw, Lthd. 171 CG119
Long St E2 197 P2
Long St E2 84 DT69
Long St, Wal.Abb. 16 EL32
Long Wk SE1 201 N6
Long Wk SE18 105 EP79
Long Wk SW13 98 CS82
Long Wk, Ch.St.G. 20 AX41
Long Wk, Epsom 173 CX119
Long Wk, N.Mal. 138 CQ97
Long Wk, Wal.Abb. 15 EA30
Long Wk, W.Byf. 152 BJ114
Long Wd Dr, Beac. 36 AT51
Long Yd WC1 196 B5
Long Yd WC1 83 DM70
Longacre Pl, Cars. 158 DG107
Beddington Gdns
Longacre Rd E17 47 ED53
Longaford Way, Brwd. 55 GB46
Longbeach Rd SW11 100 DF83
Longberrys NW2 63 CZ62
Longboat Row, Sthl. 78 BZ72
Longbourne Way, Cher. 133 BF100
Longboyds, Cob. 153 BV114
Longbridge Rd, Bark. 87 EQ66
Longbridge Rd, Dag. 70 EU63
Longbridge Way SE13 123 EC85
Longbridge Way, Uxb. 76 BH68
Longbury Cl, Orp. 146 EV97
Longbury Dr, Orp. 146 EV97
Longcliffe Path, Wat. 39 BU48
Gosforth La
Longcroft SE9 125 EM90
Longcroft, Wat. 39 BV45
Longcroft Av, Bans. 158 DC114
Longcroft Dr, Wal.Cr. 15 DZ34
Longcroft La, Hem.H. 5 BC28
Longcroft Ri, Loug. 33 EN43
Longcroft Rd, Rick. 37 BD50
Longcrofte Rd, Edg. 41 CK52
Longcrofts, Wal.Abb. 16 EE34
Roundhills
Longcross Rd, Cher. 132 AY104
Longdon Wd, Kes. 162 EL105
Longdown La N, Epsom 157 CU114
Longdown La S, Epsom 157 CU114
Longdown Rd SE6 123 EA91
Longdown Rd, Epsom 157 CU114
Longfellow Dr, Brwd. 55 GC45
Longfellow Rd E17 67 DZ58
Longfellow Rd, Wor.Pk. 139 CU103
Longfellow Way SE1 202 A9
Longfield, Brom. 144 EF95
Longfield, Loug. 32 EJ43
Longfield Av E17 67 DY56
Longfield Av NW7 43 CU52
Longfield Av W5 79 CJ73
Longfield Av, Enf. 30 DW37
Longfield Av, Horn. 71 FF59
Longfield Av, Wall. 140 DG102
Longfield Av, Wem. 62 CL60
Longfield Cres SE26 122 DW90
Longfield Cres, Tad. 173 CW120
Longfield Dr SW14 118 CP85
Longfield Dr, Mitch. 120 DE94
Longfield Est SE1 202 A9
Longfield Est SE1 102 DT77
Longfield La (Cheshunt), Wal.Cr. 14 DU27
Longfield Rd W5 79 CJ73
Longfield St SW18 120 DA87
Longfield Wk W5 79 CJ72
Longford Av, Felt. 115 BS86
Longford Av, Sthl. 78 CA73
Longford Av, Stai. 114 BL88
Longford Cl, Hmptn. 116 CA91
Longford Cl, Hayes 78 BX73
Longford Gdns
Longford Ct E5 67 DX63
Pedro St
Longford Ct NW4 63 CX56
Longford Ct, Epsom 156 CQ105
Longford Gdns, Hayes 78 BX73
Longford Gdns, Sutt. 140 DC104
Longford Rd, Twick. 116 CA88
Longford Roundabout, West Dr. 94 BH81
Longford St NW1 195 J4
Longford St NW1 83 DH70
Longford Wk SW2 121 DN87
Longford Way, Stai. 114 BL88
Longhayes Av, Rom. 70 EX56
Longhayes Ct, Rom. 70 EX56
Longhayes Av
Longheath Gdns, Croy. 142 DW99
Longhedge Ho SE26 122 DT91
Longhedge St SW11 100 DG82
Longhill Rd SE6 123 ED89
Longhook Gdns, Nthlt. 77 BU68
Longhope Cl SE15 102 DS79
Longhouse Rd, Grays 111 GH76
Longhurst Rd SE13 123 ED85

udlow Rd, Felt. 115 BU91
udlow St EC1 197 H4
udlow Way N2 64 DC56
udlow Way, Rick. 23 BQ42
udovick Wk SW15 98 CS84
udwick Ms SE14 103 DY80
uffield Rd SE2 106 EV76
uffman Rd SE12 124 EH90
ugard Rd SE15 102 DV82
ugg App E12 69 EN62
uke Ho E1 84 DV72
uke St EC2 197 M4
uke St EC2 84 DS70
ukin Cres E4 47 ED48
ukin St E1 84 DW72
ukintone Cl, Loug. 32 EL44
ullarook Cl, West. 178 EJ116
ullingstone Av, Swan. 147 FF97
ullingstone Cl, Orp. 126 EV94
Lullingstone Cres
ullingstone Cres, Orp. 126 EU94
ullingstone La SE13 123 ED87
ullingstone La (Eynsford), Dart. 148 FJ104
ullingstone Rd, Belv. 106 EZ79
ullington Garth N12 43 CZ50
ullington Garth, Borwd. 26 CP43
ullington Garth, Brom. 124 EE94
ullington Rd SE20 122 DU94
ullington Rd, Dag. 88 EY66
ulot Gdns N19 65 DH61
ulworth SE17 201 K10
ulworth Av, Houns. 96 CB80
ulworth Av (Cheshunt), Wal.Cr. 13 DP29
ulworth Av, Wem. 61 CJ59
ulworth Cl, Har. 60 BZ62
ulworth Cres, Mitch. 140 DE96
ulworth Dr, Pnr. 60 BX58
ulworth Dr, Rom. 51 FB50
ulworth Gdns, Har. 60 BY61
ulworth Rd SE9 124 EL89
ulworth Rd SE15 102 DV82
ulworth Rd, Well. 105 ET82
ulworth Waye, Hayes 78 BW72
umen Rd, Wem. 61 CK61
umley Cl, Belv. 106 FA79
umley Ct WC2 200 A1
umley Gdns, Sutt. 157 CY106
umley Rd, Sutt. 157 CY107
umley St W1 194 G9
una Rd, Th.Hth. 142 DQ97
unar Cl, West. 178 EK116
unar Ho, Croy. 142 DQ102
undin Wk, Wat. 40 BX49
Woodhall La
undy Dr, Hayes 95 BS77
undy Wk N1 84 DQ65
Clephane Rd
unedale Rd, Dart. 128 FQ88
unedale Wk, Dart. 128 FP88
Lunedale Rd
Lunghurst Rd, Cat. 177 DZ120
Lunham Rd SE19 122 DS93
Lupin Cl SW2 121 DP89
Palace Rd
Lupin Cl, Croy. 143 DX102
Primrose La
Lupin Cl, Rom. 71 FD61
Lupin Cl, West Dr. 94 BK78
Magnolia St
Lupin Cres, Ilf. 69 EP64
Bluebell Way
Luppit Cl, Brwd. 55 GA46
Lupton Cl SE12 124 EH90
Lupton St NW5 65 DJ63
Lupus St SW1 199 L10
Lupus St SW1 101 DH79
Luralda Gdns E14 204 E10
Lurgan Av W6 99 CX79
Lurline Gdns SW11 100 DG81
Luscombe Ct, Brom. 144 EE96
Luscombe Way SW8 101 DL80
Lushes Ct, Loug. 33 EP43
Lushes Rd
Lushes Rd, Loug. 33 EP43
Lushington Dr, Cob. 153 BV114
Lushington Rd NW10 81 CV68
Lushington Rd SE6 123 EB92
Lushington Ter E8 66 DU64
Wayland Av
Lusted Hall La, West. 178 EJ120
Lusted Rd, Sev. 181 FE120
Luther Cl, Edg. 42 CQ47
Luther King Cl E17 67 DY58
Luther Rd, Tedd. 117 CF92
Luton Pl SE10 103 EC80
Luton Rd E17 67 DZ55
Luton Rd, Sid. 126 EW90
Luton St NW8 194 A5
Luton St NW8 82 DD70
Lutton Ter NW3 64 DD63
Flask Wk
Luttrell Av SW15 119 CV85
Lutwyche Rd SE6 123 DZ89
Luxborough La, Chig. 48 EL48
Luxborough St W1 194 F6
Luxborough St W1 82 DG70
Luxemburg Gdns W6 99 CX77
Luxfield Rd SE9 124 EL88
Luxford St SE16 203 H9
Luxford St SE16 103 DX77
Luxmore St SE4 103 DZ81
Luxor St SE5 102 DQ83
Luxted Rd, Orp. 163 EN112
Lyal Rd E3 85 DY68
Lyall Av SE21 122 DS90
Lyall Ms SW1 198 F7
Lyall Ms SW1 100 DG76
Lyall Ms W SW1 198 F7
Lyall St SW1 198 F7
Lyall St SW1 100 DG76
Lycett Pl W12 99 CU75
Becklow Rd
Lych Gate, Wat. 8 BX33
Lych Gate Rd, Orp. 146 EU102
Lych Gate Wk, Hayes 77 BT73
Lych Way, Wok. 166 AX116
Lyconby Gdns, Croy. 143 DY101
Lydd Cl, Sid. 125 ES90
Lydd Rd, Bexh. 106 EZ80
Lydden Ct SE9 125 ES86
Lydden Gro SW18 120 DB87
Lydden Rd SW18 120 DB87
Lydeard Rd E6 87 EM66
Lydele Cl, Wok. 167 AZ115
Lydford Cl N16 66 DS64
Pellerin Rd
Lydford Rd N15 66 DR57
Lydford Rd NW2 81 CX65
Lydford Rd W9 81 CZ70
Lydhurst Av SW2 121 DM89
Lydia Rd, Erith 107 FF79
Lydney Cl SE15 102 DS80
Lydney Cl SW19 119 CY89
Princes Way
Lydon Rd SW4 101 DJ83
Lydstep Rd, Chis. 125 EN91
Lye, The, Tad. 173 CW122
Lye La, St.Alb. 8 CA30
Lyfield, Lthd. 154 CB114
Lyford Rd SW18 120 DD87
Lygon Pl SW1 199 H7
Lyham Cl SW2 121 DL86
Lyham Rd SW2 121 DL85
Lyle Cl, Mitch. 140 DG101
Lyle Pk, Sev. 191 FH123
Lymbourne Cl, Sutt. 158 DA110
Lyme Fm Rd SE12 104 EG84
Lyme Gro E9 84 DW66
St. Thomas's Sq
Lyme Regis Rd, Bans. 173 CZ117
Lyme Rd, Well. 106 EV81
Lyme St NW1 83 DJ66
Lyme Ter NW1 83 DJ66
Royal Coll St
Lymer Av SE19 122 DT92
Lymescote Gdns, Sutt. 140 DA103
Lyminge Cl, Sid. 125 ET91
Lyminge Gdns SW18 120 DE88
Lymington Av N22 45 DN54
Lymington Cl E6 87 EM71
Valiant Way
Lymington Cl SW16 141 DK96
Lymington Dr, Ruis. 59 BR61
Lymington Gdns, Epsom 157 CT106
Lymington Rd NW6 82 DB65
Lymington Rd, Dag. 70 EX60
Lympstone Gdns SE15 102 DU80
Lyn Ms E3 85 DZ69
Tredegar Sq
Lynbridge Gdns N13 45 DP49
Lynbrook Cl SE15 102 DS80
Blakes Rd
Lynbrook Cl, Rain. 89 FD68
Lynceley Gra, Epp. 18 EU29
Lynch, The, Uxb. 76 BJ67
New Windsor St
Lynch Cl, Uxb. 76 BJ66
New Windsor St
Lynch Wk SE8 103 DZ79
Prince St
Lynchen Cl, Houns. 95 BU81
The Av
Lyncott Cres SW4 101 DH84
Lyncroft Av, Pnr. 60 BY57
Lyncroft Gdns NW6 64 DA64
Lyncroft Gdns W13 97 CJ75
Lyncroft Gdns, Epsom 157 CT109
Lyncroft Gdns, Houns. 96 CC84
Lyndale NW2 63 CZ63
Lyndale Av NW2 63 CZ62
Lyndale Cl SE3 104 EF79
Lyndale Ct, W.Byf. 152 BG113
Parvis Rd
Lyndale Est, Grays 109 FV79
Lyndale Rd, Red. 184 DF131
Lynden Way, Swan. 147 FC97
Lyndhurst Av N12 44 DF51
Lyndhurst Av NW7 42 CS51
Lyndhurst Av SW16 141 DK96
Lyndhurst Av, Pnr. 39 BV53
Lyndhurst Av, Sthl. 78 CB74
Lyndhurst Av, Sun. 135 BU97
Lyndhurst Av, Surb. 138 CP102
Lyndhurst Av, Twick. 116 BZ88
Lyndhurst Cl NW10 62 CR62
Lyndhurst Cl, Bexh. 107 FB83
Lyndhurst Cl, Croy. 142 DT104
Lyndhurst Cl, Orp. 163 EP105
Lyndhurst Cl, Wok. 166 AX115
Lyndhurst Ct, Sutt. 158 DA108
Overton Rd
Lyndhurst Dr E10 67 EC59
Lyndhurst Dr, Horn. 72 FJ60
Lyndhurst Dr, N.Mal. 138 CS100
Lyndhurst Dr, Sev. 190 FE124
Lyndhurst Gdns N3 43 CY53
Lyndhurst Gdns NW3 64 DD64
Lyndhurst Gdns, Bark. 87 ES65
Lyndhurst Gdns, Enf. 30 DS42
Lyndhurst Gdns, Ilf. 69 ER58
Lyndhurst Gdns, Pnr. 39 BV53
Lyndhurst Gro SE15 102 DS82
Lyndhurst Ri, Chig. 49 EN49
Lyndhurst Rd E4 47 EC52
Lyndhurst Rd N18 46 DU49
Lyndhurst Rd N22 45 DM51
Lyndhurst Rd NW3 64 DD64
Lyndhurst Rd, Bexh. 107 FB83
Lyndhurst Rd, Couls. 174 DG116
Lyndhurst Rd, Grnf. 78 CB70
Lyndhurst Rd, Th.Hth. 141 DN98
Lyndhurst Sq SE15 102 DT81
Lyndhurst Ter NW3 64 DD64
Lyndhurst Way SE15 102 DT81
Lyndhurst Way, Brwd. 55 GC45
Lyndhurst Way, Cher. 133 BE104
Lyndhurst Way, Sutt. 158 DA108
Lyndon Av, Pnr. 40 BY51
Lyndon Av, Sid. 125 ET85
Lyndon Av, Wall. 140 DG104
Lyndon Rd, Belv. 106 FA77
Lyndwood Dr, Wind. 112 AU86
Lyne Cl, Vir.W. 133 AZ100
Lyne Cres E17 47 DZ53
Lyne Crossing Rd, Cher. 133 BA100
Lyne La, Cher. 133 BA100
Lyne La, Egh. 133 BA99
Lyne La, Vir.W. 133 BA100
Lyne Rd, Vir.W. 132 AX100
Lynegrove Av, Ashf. 115 BQ92
Lyneham Wk E5 67 DY64
Lyneham Wk, Pnr. 59 BT55
Lynett Rd, Dag. 70 EX61
Lynette Av SW4 121 DH86
Lynford Cl, Barn. 27 CT43
Rowley La
Lynford Cl, Edg. 42 CQ52
Lynford Gdns, Edg. 42 CP48
Lynford Gdns, Ilf. 69 ET61
Lynhurst Cres, Uxb. 77 BQ66
Lynhurst Rd, Uxb. 77 BQ66
Lynmere Rd, Well. 106 EV82
Lynmouth Av, Enf. 30 DT44
Lynmouth Av, Mord. 139 CX101
Lynmouth Dr, Ruis. 59 BV61
Lynmouth Gdns, Grnf. 79 CH67
Lynmouth Gdns, Houns. 96 BX81
Lynmouth Ri, Orp. 146 EV98
Lynmouth Rd E17 67 DY58
Lynmouth Rd N2 64 DF55
Lynmouth Rd N16 66 DT60
Lynmouth Rd, Grnf. 79 CH67
Lynn Cl, Ashf. 115 BR92
Goffs Rd
Lynn Cl, Har. 41 CD54
Lynn Ms E11 68 EE61
Lynn Rd
Lynn Rd E11 68 EE61
Lynn Rd SW12 121 DH87
Lynn Rd, Ilf. 69 ER59
Lynn St, Enf. 30 DR39
Lynne Cl, Orp. 163 ET107
Lynne Cl, S.Croy. 160 DW111
Lynne Wk, Esher 154 CC106
Lynne Way NW10 80 CS65
Lynne Way, Nthlt. 78 BX68
Lynross Cl, Rom. 52 FM54
Lynscott Way, S.Croy. 159 DP109
Lynsted Cl, Bexh. 127 FB85
Lynsted Cl, Brom. 144 EJ96
Lynsted Ct, Beck. 143 DY96
Churchfields Rd
Lynsted Gdns SE9 104 EK83
Lynton Av N12 44 DD49
Lynton Av NW9 63 CT56
Lynton Av W13 79 CG72
Lynton Av, Orp. 146 EV98
Lynton Av, Rom. 50 FA53
Lynton Cl NW10 62 CS64
Lynton Cl, Chess. 156 CL105
Lynton Cl, Islw. 97 CF84
Lynton Cres, Ilf. 69 EP58
Lynton Crest, Pot.B. 12 DA32
Strafford Gate
Lynton Est SE1 202 B9
Lynton Gdns N11 45 DK51
Lynton Gdns, Enf. 46 DS45
Lynton Mead N20 44 DA48
Lynton Par, Wal.Cr. 15 DX30
Turners Hill
Lynton Rd E4 47 EB50
Lynton Rd N8 65 DK57
Lynton Rd NW6 81 CZ67
Lynton Rd SE1 202 A9
Lynton Rd SE1 102 DT77
Lynton Rd W3 80 CN73
Lynton Rd, Croy. 141 DN100
Lynton Rd, Grav. 131 GG88
Lynton Rd, Har. 60 BY61
Lynton Rd, N.Mal. 138 CR99
Lynton Rd S, Grav. 131 GG88
Lynton Ter W3 80 CQ72
Lynton Rd
Lynton Wk, Hayes 77 BS69
Lynwood Av, Couls. 175 DH115
Lynwood Av, Egh. 112 AY93
Lynwood Av, Epsom 157 CT114
Lynwood Av, Slou. 92 AX76
Lynwood Cl E18 48 EJ53
Lynwood Cl, Har. 60 BY62
Lynwood Cl, Rom. 51 FB51
Lynwood Cl, Wok. 151 BD113
Lynwood Dr, Nthwd. 39 BT53
Lynwood Dr, Rom. 51 FB51
Lynwood Dr, Wor.Pk. 139 CU103
Lynwood Gdns, Croy. 159 DM105
Lynwood Gdns, Sthl. 78 BZ72
Lynwood Gro N21 45 DN46
Lynwood Gro, Orp. 145 ES101
Lynwood Hts, Rick. 22 BH43
Lynwood Rd SW17 120 DF90
Lynwood Rd W5 80 CL70
Lynwood Rd, Epsom 157 CT114
Lynwood Rd, Red. 184 DG132
Lynwood Rd, T.Ditt. 137 CF103
Lyon Business Pk, Bark. 87 ES68
Lyon Meade, Stan. 41 CJ53
Lyon Pk Av, Wem. 80 CL65
Lyon Rd SW19 140 DC95
Lyon Rd, Har. 61 CF58
Lyon Rd, Rom. 71 FF59
Lyon Rd, Walt. 136 BY103
Lyon St N1 83 DM66
Caledonian Rd
Lyon Way, Grnf. 79 CE67
Lyons Pl NW8 82 DD70
Lyons Wk W14 99 CY77
Lyonsdene, Tad. 183 CZ127
Lyonsdene, Tad. 183 CZ127
Smithy La
Lyonsdown Av, Barn. 28 DC44
Lyonsdown Rd, Barn. 28 DC44
Lyoth Rd, Orp. 145 EQ103
Lyric Dr, Grnf. 78 CB70
Lyric Rd SW13 99 CT81
Lysander Cl, Hem.H. 5 AZ27
Lysander Gdns, Surb. 138 CM100
Ewell Rd
Lysander Gro N19 65 DK60
Lysander Rd, Croy. 159 DM107
Lysander Rd, Ruis. 59 BR61
Lysander Way, Abb.L. 7 BU32
Lysander Way, Orp. 145 EQ104
Lysia St SW6 99 CX80
Lysias Rd SW12 120 DG86
Lysley Pl, Hat. 12 DC27
Lysons Wk SW15 119 CU85
Swinburne Rd
Lyster Ms, Cob. 153 BV113
Lytchet Rd, Brom. 124 EH94
Lytchet Way, Enf. 30 DW39
Lytchgate Cl, S.Croy. 160 DS108
Lytcott Dr, W.Mol. 136 BZ97
Freeman Dr
Lytcott Gro SE22 122 DT85
Lyte St E2 84 DW68
Bishops Way
Lytham Av, Wat. 40 BX50
Lytham Gro W5 80 CL69
Lytham St SE17 102 DR78
Lyttelton Cl NW3 82 DE66
Lyttelton Rd E10 67 EB62
Lyttelton Rd N2 64 DC57
Lyttleton Rd N8 65 DN55
Lytton Av N13 45 DN47
Lytton Av, Enf. 31 DY38
Lytton Cl N2 64 DD57
Lytton Cl, Loug. 33 ER41
Lytton Cl, Nthlt. 78 BZ66
Lytton Gdns, Wall. 159 DK105
Lytton Gro SW15 119 CX85
Lytton Pk, Cob. 154 BZ112
Lytton Rd E11 68 EE59
Lytton Rd, Barn. 28 DC42
Lytton Rd, Grays 111 GG77
Lytton Rd, Pnr. 40 BY52
Lytton Rd, Rom. 71 FH57
Lytton Rd, Wok. 167 BB116
Lytton Strachey Path SE28 88 EV73
Titmuss Av
Lyveden Rd SE3 104 EH80
Lyveden Rd SW17 120 DE93
Lywood Cl, Tad. 173 CW122

M

Mabbotts, Tad. 173 CX121
Mabbutt Cl, St.Alb. 8 BY30
Mabel Rd, Swan. 127 FG93
Mabel St, Wok. 166 AX117
Maberley Cres SE19 122 DU94
Maberley Rd SE19 142 DT95
Maberley Rd, Beck. 143 DX97
Mabledon Pl WC1 195 N3
Mabledon Pl WC1 83 DK69
Mablethorpe Rd SW6 99 CY80
Mabley St E9 85 DY65
Macaret Cl N20 44 DB45
MacArthur Cl E7 86 EG65
MacArthur Ter SE7 104 EL79
Macaulay Av, Esher 137 CF103
Macaulay Ct SW4 101 DH83
Macaulay Rd E6 86 EK68
Macaulay Rd SW4 101 DH83
Macaulay Rd, Cat. 176 DS122
Macaulay Sq SW4 101 DH84
Macaulay Way SE28 88 EV73
Booth Cl
Macauley Ms SE13 103 EC82
Macbean St SE18 105 EN76
Macbeth St W6 99 CV78
Macclesfield Br NW1 82 DE68
Macclesfield Rd EC1 197 H2
Macclesfield Rd EC1 84 DQ69
Macclesfield Rd SE25 142 DV99
Macclesfield St W1 195 N10
Macclesfield St W1 83 DK73
Macdonald Av, Dag. 71 FB62
Macdonald Av, Horn. 72 FL56
Macdonald Rd E7 68 EG63
Macdonald Rd E17 47 EC54
Macdonald Rd N11 44 DF50
Macdonald Rd N19 65 DJ61
Macdonald Way, Horn. 72 FL56
Macdonnell Gdns, Wat. 23 BT35
High Rd
Macduff Rd SW11 100 DG81
Mace Cl E1 202 D2
Mace Ct, Grays 110 GE79
Mace La, Sev. 163 ER113
Mace St E2 85 DX68
MacFarlane La, Islw. 97 CF79
Macfarlane Rd W12 81 CW74
Macfarren Pl NW1 194 G5
Macgregor Rd E16 86 EJ71
Machell Rd SE15 102 DW83
Macintosh Cl, Wal.Cr. 14 DR26
Mackay Rd SW4 101 DH83
Mackennal St NW8 194 C1
Mackennal St NW8 82 DE68
Mackenzie Mall, Slou. 92 AT75
High St
Mackenzie Rd N7 83 DM65
Mackenzie Rd, Beck. 142 DW96
Mackenzie St, Slou. 74 AT74
Mackenzie Wk E14 204 A3
Mackenzie Wk E14 85 EA74
Mackenzie Way, Grav. 131 GK93
Mackeson Rd NW3 64 DF63
Mackie Rd SW2 121 DN87
Mackintosh La E9 67 DX64
Homerton High St
Macklin St WC2 196 A8
Macklin St WC2 83 DL72
Mackrow Wk E14 85 EC73
Robin Hood La
Macks Rd SE16 202 C8
Macks Rd SE16 102 DU77
Mackworth St NW1 195 K2
Mackworth St NW1 83 DJ69
Maclaren Ms SW15 99 CW84
Clarendon Dr
Maclean Rd SE23 123 DY86
Maclennan Av, Rain. 90 FK69
Macleod Cl, Grays 110 GD77
Macleod Rd N21 29 DL43
Macleod St SE17 102 DQ78
Maclise Rd W14 99 CY76
Macmillan Gdns, Dart. 108 FN84
Macoma Rd SE18 105 ER79
Macoma Ter SE18 105 ER79
Macon Way, Upmin. 73 FT59
Maconochies Rd E14 204 B10
Maconochies Rd E14 103 EB78
Macquarie Way E14 204 C9
Macquarie Way E14 103 EB77
Macready Pl N7 65 DL63
Warlters Rd
Macroom Rd W9 81 CZ69
Mada Rd, Orp. 145 EP104
Madan Rd, West. 189 ER125
Madans Wk, Epsom 156 CR114
Maddams St E3 85 EB70
Madden Cl, Swans. 129 FX86
Maddison Cl, Tedd. 117 CF93
Maddock Way SE17 101 DP79
Maddocks Cl, Sid. 126 EY92
Maddox La, Lthd. 170 BY123
Maddox Pk, Lthd. 170 BY123
Maddox St W1 195 J10
Maddox St W1 83 DH73
Madeira Av, Brom. 124 EE94
Madeira Cl, W.Byf. 152 BG113
Brantwood Gdns
Madeira Cres, W.Byf. 152 BG113
Brantwood Gdns
Madeira Gro, Wdf.Grn. 48 EJ51
Madeira Rd E11 67 ED60
Madeira Rd N13 45 DP49
Madeira Rd SW16 121 DL92
Madeira Rd, Mitch. 140 DF98
Madeira Rd, W.Byf. 151 BF113
Madeira Wk, Brwd. 54 FY48
Madeira Wk, Reig. 184 DD133
Madeley Rd W5 80 CL72
Madeline Gro, Ilf. 69 ER64
Madeline Rd SE20 142 DU95
Madells, Epp. 17 ET31
Madge Gill Way E6 86 EL67
Ron Leighton Way
Madinah Rd E8 84 DU65
Madison Cres, Bexh. 106 EW80
Madison Gdns, Bexh. 106 EW80
Madison Gdns, Brom. 144 EF97
Madison Way, Sev. 190 FF123
Madras Pl N7 83 DN65
Madras Rd, Ilf. 69 EP63
Madresfield Ct, Rad. 10 CL32
Russet Dr
Madrid Rd SW13 99 CU81
Madrigal La SE5 101 DP80
Madron St SE17 201 N10
Madron St SE17 102 DS78
Maesmaur Rd, West. 178 EK121
Mafeking Av E6 86 EK68
Mafeking Av, Brent. 98 CL79
Mafeking Av, Ilf. 69 ER59
Mafeking Rd E16 86 EF70
Mafeking Rd N17 46 DU54
Mafeking Rd, Enf. 30 DT41
Mafeking Rd, Stai. 113 BB89
Magazine Pl, Lthd. 171 CH122
Magazine Rd, Cat. 175 DP122
Magdala Av N19 65 DH61
Magdala Rd, Islw. 97 CG83
Magdala Rd, S.Croy. 160 DR108
Napier Rd
Magdalen Cl, W.Byf. 152 BL114
Magdalen Cres, W.Byf. 152 BL114
Magdalen Gdns, Brwd. 55 GE44
Magdalen Gro, Orp. 164 EV105
Magdalen Pas E1 84 DT73
Prescot St
Magdalen Rd SW18 120 DC88
Magdalen St SE1 201 M3
Magdalen St SE1 84 DS74
Magdalene Cl SE15 102 DV82
Heaton Rd
Magdalene Gdns E6 87 EN70
Magdalene Rd, Shep. 134 BM98
Magee St SE11 101 DN79
Magellan Pl E14 103 EA78
Napier Av
Maggie Blake's Cause SE1 201 P3
Magna Carta La, Stai. 112 AX88
Magna Rd, Egh. 112 AV93
Magnaville Rd, Bushey 41 CE45
Magnet Est, Grays 109 FW78
Magnet Rd, Grays 109 FW79
Magnet Rd, Wem. 61 CK61
Magnin Cl E8 84 DU67
Wilde Cl
Magnolia Av, Abb.L. 7 BU32
Magnolia Cl E10 67 EA61
Magnolia Cl, Kings.T. 118 CQ93
Magnolia Cl, St.Alb. 9 CD27
Magnolia Ct, Har. 62 CM59
Magnolia Ct, Rich. 98 CP81
West Hall Rd
Magnolia Dr, West. 178 EK116
Magnolia Gdns, Edg. 42 CQ49
Ash Cl
Magnolia Gdns, Slou. 92 AW76
Magnolia Pl SW4 121 DL85
Magnolia Pl W5 80 CL71
Montpelier Rd
Magnolia Rd W4 98 CP79
Magnolia St, West Dr. 94 BK77
Magnolia Way, Brwd. 54 FV43
Magnolia Way, Epsom 156 CQ106
Magnum Cl, Rain. 90 FJ70
Magpie All EC4 196 E9
Magpie Cl E7 68 EF64
Magpie Cl NW9 42 CS54
Eagle Dr
Magpie Cl, Couls. 175 DJ118
Ashbourne Cl
Magpie Cl, Enf. 30 DU39
Magpie Hall Cl, Brom. 144 EL100
Magpie Hall La, Brom. 145 EM99
Magpie Hall Rd, Bushey 41 CE47
Magpie La, Brwd. 53 FW54
Magpie Pl SE14 103 DY79
Milton Ct Rd
Magri Wk E1 84 DW71
Ashfield St
Maguire Dr, Rich. 117 CJ91
Maguire St SE1 202 A4
Maguire St SE1 102 DT75
Mahatma Gandhi Ho, Wem. 62 CN64
Mahlon Av, Ruis. 59 BV64
Mahogany Cl SE16 203 L3
Mahogany Cl SE16 85 DY74
Mahon Cl, Enf. 30 DT39
Maida Av E4 47 EB45
Maida Av W2 82 DC71
Maida Rd, Belv. 106 FA76
Maida Vale W9 82 DB68
Maida Vale Rd, Dart. 127 FG85
Maida Way E4 47 EB45
Maiden Erlegh Av, Bex. 126 EY88
Maiden La NW1 83 DK66
Maiden La SE1 201 J2
Maiden La WC2 200 A1
Maiden La WC2 83 DL73
Maiden La, Dart. 107 FG83

Maiden Rd E15 86 EE66
Maidenshaw Rd, Epsom 156 CR112
Maidenstone Hill SE10 103 EC81
Maids of Honour Row, Rich. 117 CK85
The Grn
Maidstone Av, Rom. 51 FC54
Maidstone Bldgs SE1 201 J3
Maidstone Ho E14 85 EB72
Carmen St
Maidstone Rd N11 45 DK51
Maidstone Rd, Grays 110 GA79
Maidstone Rd, Sev. 190 FE122
Maidstone Rd (Seal), Sev. 191 FN121
Maidstone Rd, Sid. 126 EX93
Maidstone Rd, Swan. 147 FB95
Maidstone St E2 84 DU68
Audrey St
Main Av, Enf. 30 DT43
Main Av, Nthwd. 39 BQ48
Main Dr, Ger.Cr. 56 AW57
Main Dr, Iver 93 BE77
Main Dr, Wem. 61 CK62
Main Par, Rick. 21 BC42
Whitelands Av
Main Par Flats, Rick. 21 BC42
Whitelands Av
Main Ride, Egh. 112 AS93
Main Rd (Farningham), Dart. 148 FL100
Main Rd (Sutton at Hone), Dart. 128 FP93
Main Rd, Eden. 189 EQ134
Main Rd, Long. 149 FX96
Main Rd, Orp. 146 EW95
Main Rd, Rom. 71 FF56
Main Rd (Sundridge), Sev. 180 EX124
Main Rd, Sid. 125 ES90
Main Rd, Swan. 127 FF94
Main Rd (Crockenhill), Swan. 147 FD100
Main Rd, West. 162 EJ113
Main St, Felt. 116 BX92
Mainridge Rd, Chis. 125 EN91
Maisemore St SE15 102 DU80
Peckham Pk Rd
Maisie Webster Cl, Stai. 114 BK87
Lauser Rd
Maitland Cl SE10 103 EB80
Maitland Cl, Houns. 96 BZ83
Maitland Cl, Walt. 136 BY103
Maitland Cl, W.Byf. 152 BG113
Maitland Pk Est NW3 82 DF65
Maitland Pk Rd NW3 82 DF65
Maitland Pk Vil NW3 82 DF65
Maitland Pl E5 66 DV63
Clarence Rd
Maitland Rd E15 86 EF65
Maitland Rd SE26 123 DX93
Maize Row E14 85 DZ73
Commercial Rd
Maizey Ct, Brwd. 54 FU43
Danes Way
Majendie Rd SE18 105 ER78
Majestic Way, Mitch. 140 DF96
Major Rd E15 67 ED64
Major Rd SE16 202 C6
Majors Fm Rd, Slou. 92 AX80
Makepeace Av N6 64 DG61
Makepeace Rd E11 68 EG56
Makepeace Rd, Nthlt. 78 BY68
Makins St SW3 198 C9
Makins St SW3 100 DE77
Malabar St E14 203 P5
Malabar St E14 103 EA75
Malam Gdns E14 85 EB73
Wades Pl
Malan Cl, West. 178 EL117
Malan Sq, Rain. 89 FH65
Malbrook Rd SW15 99 CV84
Malcolm Ct, Stan. 41 CJ50
Malcolm Cres NW4 63 CU58
Malcolm Dr, Surb. 138 CL102
Malcolm Pl E2 84 DW70
Malcolm Rd E1 84 DW70
Malcolm Rd SE20 122 DW94
Malcolm Rd SE25 142 DU100
Malcolm Rd SW19 119 CY93
Malcolm Rd, Couls. 175 DK115
Malcolm Rd, Uxb. 58 BM63
Malcolm Way E11 68 EG57
Malcolms Way N14 29 DJ43
Malden Av SE25 142 DV98
Malden Av, Grnf. 61 CE64
Malden Cl, Amer. 20 AT38
Malden Cres NW1 82 DG65
Malden Grn Av, Wor.Pk. 139 CT102
Malden Hill, N.Mal. 139 CT97
Malden Hill Gdns, N.Mal. 139 CT97
Malden Pk, N.Mal. 139 CT100
Malden Pl NW5 64 DG64
Grafton Ter
Malden Rd NW5 64 DG64
Malden Rd, Borwd. 26 CN41
Malden Rd, N.Mal. 138 CS99
Malden Rd, Sutt. 157 CX105
Malden Rd, Wat. 23 BV40
Malden Rd, Wor.Pk. 139 CT101
Malden Way, N.Mal. 139 CT99
Maldon Cl E15 67 ED64
David St
Maldon Cl N1 84 DQ67
Maldon Cl SE5 102 DS83
Maldon Ct, Wall. 159 DJ106
Maldon Rd
Maldon Rd N9 46 DT48
Maldon Rd W3 80 CQ73
Maldon Rd, Rom. 71 FC59
Maldon Rd, Wall. 159 DH106
Maldon Wk, Wdf.Grn. 48 EJ51
Malet Cl, Egh. 113 BD93
Malet Pl WC1 195 M5
Malet Pl WC1 83 DK70
Malet St WC1 195 M5
Malet St WC1 83 DK70
Maley Av SE27 121 DP89
Malford Ct E18 48 EG54
Malford Gro E18 68 EF56
Malfort Rd SE5 102 DS83
Malham Cl N11 44 DG51
Catterick Cl
Malham Rd SE23 123 DX88
Malins Cl, Barn. 27 CV43
Mall, The E15 85 ED66
Mall, The N14 45 DL48
Mall, The SW1 199 L4
Mall, The SW1 101 DJ75
Mall, The SW14 118 CQ85
Mall, The W5 80 CL73
Mall, The, Brom. 144 EG97
High St
Mall, The, Croy. 142 DQ103
Mall, The, Har. 62 CM58
Mall, The, Horn. 71 FH60
Mall, The, St.Alb. 8 CC27
Mall, The, Surb. 137 CK99
Mall Rd W6 99 CV78
Mallams Ms SW9 101 DP83
St. James's Cres
Mallard Cl E9 85 DZ65
Mallard Cl NW6 82 DA68
Mallard Cl W7 97 CE75
Mallard Cl, Barn. 28 DD44
The Hook
Mallard Cl, Dart. 128 FM85
Mallard Cl, Red. 184 DG131
Mallard Cl, Twick. 116 CA87
Stephenson Rd
Mallard Cl, Upmin. 73 FT59
Mallard Path SE28 105 ER76
Mallard Pl, Twick. 117 CG90
Mallard Rd, Abb.L. 7 BU31
Mallard Rd, S.Croy. 161 DX110
Mallard Wk, Beck. 143 DX99
Mallard Wk, Sid. 126 EW92
Mallard Way NW9 62 CQ59
Mallard Way, Brwd. 55 GB45
Mallard Way, Nthwd. 39 BQ52
Mallard Way, Wall. 159 DJ109
Mallard Way, Wat. 24 BY37
Mallards, The, Stai. 134 BH96
Thames Side
Mallards Reach, Wey. 135 BR103
Mallards Rd, Bark. 87 ES69
Thames Rd
Mallards Rd, Wdf.Grn. 48 EH52
Mallet Dr, Nthlt. 60 BZ64
Mallet Rd SE13 123 ED86
Malling Cl, Croy. 142 DW100
Malling Gdns, Mord. 140 DC100
Malling Way, Brom. 144 EF101
Mallinson Cl, Horn. 72 FJ64
Mallinson Rd SW11 120 DE85
Mallinson Rd, Croy. 141 DK104
Mallion Ct, Wal.Abb. 16 EF33
Mallord St SW3 100 DD79
Mallory Cl SE4 103 DY84
Mallory Gdns, Barn. 44 DG45
Mallory St NW8 194 C4
Mallory St NW8 82 DE70
Mallow Cl, Croy. 143 DX102
Marigold Way
Mallow Cl, Grav. 130 GE91
Mallow Cl, Tad. 173 CV119
Mallow Ct, Grays 110 GD79
Mallow Mead NW7 43 CY52
Mallow St EC1 197 K4
Mallow Wk, Wal.Cr. 14 DR28
Mallows, The, Uxb. 59 BP62
Mallys Pl, Dart. 148 FQ95
Malm Cl, Rick. 38 BK47
Malmains Cl, Beck. 143 ED99
Malmains Way, Beck. 143 EC98
Malmesbury Cl, Pnr. 59 BT56
Malmesbury Rd E3 85 DZ69
Malmesbury Rd E16 86 EE71
Malmesbury Rd E18 48 EF53
Malmesbury Rd, Mord. 140 DC101
Malmesbury Ter E16 86 EF71
Malmstone Av, Red. 185 DJ128
Malpas Dr, Pnr. 60 BX57
Malpas Rd E8 84 DV65
Malpas Rd SE4 103 DZ82
Malpas Rd, Dag. 88 EX65
Malpas Rd, Grays 111 GJ76
Malpas Rd, Slou. 74 AV73
Malt Hill, Egh. 112 AY92
Malt Ho Cl, Wind. 112 AV87
Malt La, Rad. 25 CG35
Malt St SE1 102 DU79
Malta Rd E10 67 EA60
Malta Rd, Til. 111 GF82
Malta St EC1 196 G4
Maltby Cl, Orp. 146 EU102
Vinson Cl
Maltby Dr, Enf. 30 DV38
Maltby Rd, Chess. 156 CN107
Maltby St SE1 201 P5
Maltby St SE1 102 DT75
Malthouse Dr W4 98 CS79
Malthouse Dr, Felt. 116 BX92
Malthouse Pas SW13 98 CS82
The Ter
Malthouse Pl, Rad. 9 CG34
Malthus Path SE28 88 EW74
Owen Cl
Malting Ho E14 85 DZ73
Malting Way, Islw. 97 CF83
Maltings, The, Kings L. 7 BQ33
Maltings, The, Orp. 145 ET102
Maltings, The, Oxt. 188 EF131
Maltings, The, Rom. 71 FF59
Maltings, The, Stai. 113 BE91
Church St
Maltings, The, W.Byf. 152 BM113
Maltings Cl SW13 98 CS82
Cleveland Gdns
Maltings Dr, Epp. 18 EU29
Palmers Hill
Maltings La, Epp. 18 EU29
Maltings Ms, Sid. 126 EU90
Station Rd
Maltings Pl SW6 100 DC81
Maltmans La (Chalfont St. Peter), Ger.Cr. 56 AW55
Malton Ms SE18 105 ES79
Malton St
Malton Ms W10 81 CY72
Cambridge Gdns
Malton Rd W10 81 CY72
St. Marks Rd
Malton St SE18 105 ES79
Maltravers St WC2 196 C10
Malus Cl, Add. 151 BF108
Malus Dr, Add. 151 BF108
Malva Cl SW18 120 DB85
St. Ann's Hill
Malvern Av E4 47 ED52
Malvern Av, Bexh. 106 EY80
Malvern Av, Har. 60 BY62
Malvern Cl SE20 142 DU96
Derwent Rd
Malvern Cl W10 81 CZ71
Malvern Cl, Cher. 151 BC107
Malvern Cl, Mitch. 141 DJ97
Malvern Cl, Surb. 138 CL102
Malvern Cl, Uxb. 59 BP61
Malvern Ct SE14 102 DW80
Avonley Rd
Malvern Ct SW7 198 A9
Malvern Ct SW7 100 DD77
Malvern Ct, Slou. 93 BA79
Hill Ri
Malvern Dr, Felt. 116 BX92
Malvern Dr, Ilf. 69 ET63
Malvern Dr, Wdf.Grn. 48 EJ50
Malvern Gdns NW2 63 CY61
Malvern Gdns NW6 81 CZ68
Carlton Vale
Malvern Gdns, Har. 62 CL55
Malvern Gdns, Loug. 33 EM44
Malvern Ms NW6 82 DA69
Malvern Rd
Malvern Pl NW6 81 CZ69
Malvern Rd E6 86 EL67
Malvern Rd E8 84 DU66
Malvern Rd E11 68 EE61
Malvern Rd N8 65 DM55
Malvern Rd N17 66 DU55
Malvern Rd NW6 82 DA69
Malvern Rd, Enf. 31 DY37
Malvern Rd, Grays 110 GD77
Malvern Rd, Hmptn. 116 CA94
Malvern Rd, Hayes 95 BS80
Malvern Rd, Horn. 71 FG58
Malvern Rd, Orp. 164 EV105
Malvern Rd, Surb. 138 CL103
Malvern Rd, Th.Hth. 141 DN98
Malvern Ter N1 83 DN67
Malvern Ter N9 46 DT46
Latymer Rd
Malvern Way W13 79 CH71
Templewood
Malvern Way, Rick. 23 BP43
Malvina Av, Grav. 131 GH89
Malwood Rd SW12 121 DH86
Malyons, The, Shep. 135 BR100
Gordon Rd
Malyons Rd SE13 123 EB85
Malyons Rd, Swan. 127 FF94
Malyons Ter SE13 123 EB85
Managers St E14 204 E3
Manatee Pl, Wall. 141 DK104
Croydon Rd
Manaton Cl SE15 102 DV83
Manaton Cres, Sthl. 78 CA72
Manbey Gro E15 86 EE65
Manbey Pk Rd E15 86 EE65
Manbey Rd E15 86 EE65
Manbey St E15 86 EE65
Manbre Rd W6 99 CW79
Manbrough Av E6 87 EM69
Manchester Dr W10 81 CY70
Manchester Gro E14 204 D10
Manchester Gro E14 103 EC78
Manchester Ms W1 194 F7
Manchester Rd E14 204 D10
Manchester Rd E14 103 EC78
Manchester Rd N15 66 DR58
Manchester Rd, Th.Hth. 142 DQ97
Manchester Sq W1 194 F8
Manchester Sq W1 82 DG72
Manchester St W1 194 F7
Manchester St W1 82 DG71
Manchester Way, Dag. 71 FB63
Manchuria Rd SW11 120 DG86
Manciple St SE1 201 K5
Manciple St SE1 102 DR76
Mandalay Rd SW4 121 DJ85
Mandarin St E14 85 EA73
Salter St
Mandarin Way, Hayes 78 BX71
Mandela Cl NW10 80 CQ66
Mandela Rd E16 86 EG72
Mandela St NW1 83 DJ67
Mandela St SW9 101 DN80
Mandela Way SE1 201 P9
Mandela Way SE1 102 DS77
Mandeville Cl SE3 104 EF80
Vanbrugh Pk
Mandeville Cl SW20 139 CY95
Mandeville Cl, Wat. 23 BT38
Mandeville Ct E4 47 DY49
Mandeville Ct, Egh. 113 BA91
Mandeville Dr, Surb. 137 CK102
Mandeville Pl W1 194 G8
Mandeville Pl W1 82 DG72
Mandeville Rd N14 45 DH47
Mandeville Rd, Enf. 31 DX36
Mandeville Rd, Islw. 97 CG82
Mandeville Rd, Nthlt. 78 CA66
Mandeville Rd, Pot.B. 12 DC32
Mandeville Rd, Shep. 134 BN99
Mandeville St E5 67 DY62
Mandeville Wk, Brwd. 55 GE44
Mandrake Rd SW17 120 DF90
Mandrake Way E15 86 EE66
Mandrell Rd SW2 121 DL85
Manette St W1 195 N9
Manette St W1 83 DK72
Manford Cl, Chig. 50 EU49
Manford Cross, Chig. 50 EU50
Manford Ind Est, Erith 107 FG79
Manford Way, Chig. 49 ES50
Manfred Rd SW15 119 CZ85
Manger Rd N7 83 DL65
Mangold Way, Erith 106 EY76
Manhattan Wf E16 205 M4
Manhattan Wf E16 104 EG75
Manilla St E14 203 P4
Manilla St E14 103 EA75
Manister Rd SE2 106 EU76
Manitoba Ct SE16 102 DW75
Renforth St
Manitoba Gdns, Orp. 163 ET107
Superior Dr
Manley Ct N16 66 DT62
Stoke Newington High St
Manley St NW1 82 DG67
Manly Dixon Dr, Enf. 31 DY37
Mann Cl, Croy. 142 DQ104
Salem Pl
Mannamead, Epsom 172 CS119
Mannamead Cl, Epsom 172 CS119
Mannamead
Mannin Rd, Rom. 70 EV59
Manning Gdns, Har. 61 CK59
Manning Pl, Rich. 118 CM86
Grove Rd
Manning Rd E17 67 DY57
Southcote Rd
Manning Rd, Dag. 88 FA65
Manning Rd, Orp. 146 EX99
Manning St, S.Ock. 90 FQ74
Manningford Cl EC1 196 F2
Manningtree Cl SW19 119 CY88
Manningtree Rd, Ruis. 59 BV63
Manningtree St E1 84 DU72
White Ch La
Mannock Dr, Loug. 33 EQ40
Mannock Rd N22 65 DP55
Mannock Rd, Dart. 108 FM83
Barnwell Rd
Manns Cl, Islw. 117 CF85
Manns Rd, Edg. 42 CN51
Manoel Rd, Twick. 116 CC89
Manor Av SE4 103 DZ82
Manor Av, Cat. 176 DS124
Manor Av, Horn. 72 FJ57
Manor Av, Houns. 96 BX83
Manor Av, Nthlt. 78 BZ66
Manor Chase, Wey. 153 BP106
Manor Cl E17 47 DY54
Manor Rd
Manor Cl NW7 42 CR50
Manor Dr
Manor Cl NW9 62 CP57
Manor Cl SE28 88 EW73
Manor Cl, Barn. 27 CY42
Manor Cl, Dag. 89 FD65
Manor Cl (Crayford), Dart. 107 FD84
Manor Cl (Wilmington), Dart. 127 FG90
Manor Cl, Rom. 71 FG57
Manor Rd
Manor Cl, Ruis. 59 BT60
Manor Cl, S.Ock. 90 FQ74
Manor Cl, Warl. 177 DY117
Manor Cl, Wok. 167 BF116
Manor Cl, Wor.Pk. 138 CS102
Manor Cl S, S.Ock. 90 FQ74
Manor Cl
Manor Cotts, Nthwd. 39 BT53
Manor Cotts App N2 44 DC54
Manor Ct E10 67 EB60
Grange Pk Rd
Manor Ct N2 64 DF57
Manor Ct SW6 100 DB81
Bagley's La
Manor Ct, Enf. 30 DV36
Manor Ct, Rad. 25 CF38
Manor Ct, Twick. 116 CC89
Manor Ct, Wem. 62 CL64
Manor Ct, Wey. 153 BP105
Manor Ct Rd W7 79 CE73
Manor Cres, Epsom 156 CN112
Manor Cres, Horn. 72 FJ57
Manor Cres, Surb. 138 CN100
Manor Cres, W.Byf. 152 BM113
Manor Dr N14 45 DH45
Manor Dr N20 44 DE48
Manor Dr NW7 42 CR50
Manor Dr, Add. 152 BG110
Manor Dr, Epsom 156 CS107
Manor Dr, Esher 137 CF103
Manor Dr, Felt. 116 BX92
Lebanon Av
Manor Dr, St.Alb. 8 CA27
Manor Dr, Sun. 135 BU96
Manor Dr, Surb. 138 CM100
Manor Dr, Wem. 62 CM63
Manor Dr, The, Wor.Pk. 138 CS102
Manor Dr N, N.Mal. 138 CR101
Manor Dr N, Wor.Pk. 138 CS102
Manor Est SE16 202 D9
Manor Est SE16 102 DV77
Manor Fm (Farningham), Dart. 148 FM101
Manor Fm Av, Shep. 135 BP100
Manor Fm Cl, Wor.Pk. 138 CS102
Manor Fm Dr E4 48 EE48
Manor Fm Est, Stai. 112 AX86
Manor Fm La, Egh. 113 BA92
Manor Fm Rd, Enf. 30 DV35
Manor Fm Rd, Th.Hth. 141 DN96
Manor Fm Rd, Wem. 79 CK68
Manor Flds SW15 119 CX86
Manor Gdns N7 65 DL62
Manor Gdns SW20 139 CZ96
Manor Gdns W3 98 CN77
Manor Gdns W4 98 CS78
Devonshire Rd
Manor Gdns, Hmptn. 116 CB94
Manor Gdns, Rich. 98 CM84
Manor Gdns, Ruis. 60 BW64
Manor Gdns, S.Croy. 160 DT107
Manor Gdns, Sun. 135 BU96
Manor Gate, Nthlt. 78 BY66
Manor Grn Rd, Epsom 156 CP113
Manor Gro SE15 102 DW79
Manor Gro, Beck. 143 EB96
Manor Gro, Rich. 98 CN84
Manor Hall Av NW4 43 CW54
Manor Hall Dr NW4 43 CX54
Manor Ho Ct, Epsom 156 CQ113
Manor Ho Ct, Shep. 135 BP101
Manor Ho Dr NW6 81 CX66
Manor Ho Dr, Nthwd. 39 BP52
Manor Ho Dr, Walt. 153 BT105
Eriswell Rd
Manor Ho Est, Stan. 41 CH51
Old Ch La
Manor Ho Gdns, Abb.L. 7 BR31
Manor Ho La, Slou. 92 AV80
Horton Rd
Manor Ho Way, Islw. 97 CH83
Manor La SE12 124 EE8
Manor La SE13 104 EE8
Manor La, Felt. 115 BU8
Manor La, Ger.Cr. 56 AX5
Manor La, Hayes 95 BR7
Manor La (Fawkham Grn), Long. 149 FW10
Manor La, Sev. 149 FW10
Manor La, Sun. 135 BU9
Manor La, Sutt. 158 DC10
Manor La, Tad. 184 DA12
Manor La Ter SE13 104 EE8
Manor Leaze, Egh. 113 BB9
Manor Ms NW6 82 DA6
Cambridge Av
Manor Ms SE4 103 EA8
Manor Mt SE23 122 DW8
Manor Par NW10 81 CT6
Station Rd
Manor Pk SE13 103 ED8
Manor Pk, Chis. 145 ER9
Manor Pk, Rich. 98 CM8
Manor Pk, Stai. 113 BD9
Manor Pk Cl, W.Wick. 143 EB10
Manor Pk Cres, Edg. 42 CN5
Manor Pk Dr, Har. 60 CB5
Manor Pk Gdns, Edg. 42 CN5
Manor Pk Par SE13 103 ED8
Lee High Rd
Manor Pk Rd E12 68 EK6
Manor Pk Rd N2 64 DD5
Manor Pk Rd NW10 81 CT6
Manor Pk Rd, Chis. 145 EQ9
Manor Pk Rd, Sutt. 158 DC10
Manor Pk Rd, W.Wick. 143 EB10
Manor Pl SE17 101 DP7
Manor Pl, Chis. 145 ER9
Manor Pl, Dart. 128 FL8
Highfield Rd S
Manor Pl, Felt. 115 BU8
Manor Pl, Mitch. 141 DJ9
Manor Pl, Stai. 114 BH9
Manor Pl, Sutt. 158 DB10
Manor Pl, Walt. 135 BT10
Manor Rd
Manor Rd E10 67 EA5
Manor Rd E15 86 EE6
Manor Rd E16 86 EE6
Manor Rd E17 47 DY5
Manor Rd N16 66 DR6
Manor Rd N17 46 DU5
Manor Rd N22 45 DL51
Manor Rd SE25 142 DU9
Manor Rd SW20 139 CZ9
Manor Rd W13 79 CG7
Manor Rd, Ashf. 114 BM9
Manor Rd, Bark. 87 ET6
Manor Rd, Barn. 27 CY4
Manor Rd, Beck. 143 EB9
Manor Rd, Bex. 127 FB8
Manor Rd, Chig. 49 EP5
Manor Rd, Dag. 89 FC6
Manor Rd, Dart. 107 FE8
Manor Rd, E.Mol. 137 CD9
Manor Rd, Enf. 30 DR40
Manor Rd, Erith 107 FF79
Manor Rd, Grav. 131 GH86
Manor Rd, Grays 110 GC79
Manor Rd (West Thurrock), Grays 109 FW79
Manor Rd, Har. 61 CG58
Manor Rd, Hayes 77 BU72
Manor Rd, Loug. 32 EH44
Manor Rd (High Beach), Loug. 32 EH38
Manor Rd, Mitch. 141 DJ98
Manor Rd, Pot.B. 11 CZ31
Manor Rd, Red. 185 DJ129
Manor Rd, Reig. 183 CZ132
Manor Rd, Rich. 98 CM83
Manor Rd, Rom. 71 FG57
Manor Rd (Chadwell Heath), Rom. 70 EX58
Manor Rd (Lambourne End), Rom. 50 EW47
Manor Rd, Ruis. 59 BR60
Manor Rd (London Colney), St.Alb. 9 CJ26
Manor Rd, Sev. 180 EX124
Manor Rd, Sid. 125 ET90
Manor Rd, Sutt. 157 CZ108
Manor Rd, Swans. 129 FX86
Manor Rd, Tedd. 117 CH92
Manor Rd, Til. 111 GG82
Manor Rd, Twick. 116 CC89
Manor Rd, Wall. 159 DH105
Manor Rd, Wal.Abb. 15 ED33
Manor Rd, Walt. 135 BT101
Manor Rd, Wat. 23 BV39
Manor Rd, W.Wick. 143 EB103
Manor Rd, West. 178 EL120
Manor Rd, Wok. 166 AW116
Manor Rd (Send Marsh), Wok. 167 BF123
Manor Rd, Wdf.Grn. 49 EM51
Manor Rd N, Esher 137 CF104
Manor Rd N, T.Ditt. 137 CG103
Manor Rd N, Wall. 159 DH105
Manor Rd S, Esher 155 CE105
Manor Sq, Dag. 70 EX61
Manor Vale, Brent. 97 CJ78
Manor Vw N3 44 DB54
Manor Wk, Wey. 153 BP106
Manor Way E4 47 ED49
Manor Way NW9 62 CS55
Manor Way SE3 104 EF84
Manor Way SE28 88 EW74
Manor Way, Bans. 174 DF116
Manor Way, Beck. 143 EA96
Manor Way, Bex. 126 FA88
Manor Way, Bexh. 107 FD83
Manor Way, Borwd. 26 CQ42
Manor Way, Brwd. 54 FU48
Manor Way, Brom. 144 EL100
Manor Way, Egh. 113 AZ93
Manor Way, Grays 110 GB80
Manor Way, Har. 60 CB56
Manor Way, Lthd. 170 CC116
Manor Way, Mitch. 141 DJ97
Manor Way, Orp. 145 EQ98
Manor Way, Pot.B. 12 DA30
Manor Way, Pur. 159 DL112
Manor Way, Rain. 89 FE71

Manor Way, Rick. 22 BN42
Manor Way, Ruis. 59 BS59
Manor Way, S.Croy. 160 DS107
Manor Way, Sthl. 96 BX77
Manor Way, Swans. 109 FX84
Manor Way (Cheshunt), Wal.Cr. 15 DY31
Russells Ride
Manor Way, Wok. 167 BB121
Manor Way, Wor.Pk. 138 CS102
Manor Way, The, Wall. 159 DH105
Manor Way Ind Est, Grays 110 GC80
Manor Waye, Uxb. 76 BK67
Manor Wd Rd, Pur. 159 DL113
Manorbrook SE3 104 EG84
Manorcrofts Rd, Egh. 113 BA93
Manordene Cl, T.Ditt. 137 CG102
Manordene Rd SE28 88 EW72
Manorfield Cl N19 65 DJ63
Tufnell Pk Rd
Manorfields Cl, Chis. 145 ET97
Manorgate Rd, Kings.T. 138 CN95
Manorhall Gdns E10 67 EA60
Manorside, Barn. 27 CY42
Manorside Cl SE2 106 EW77
Manorway, Enf. 46 DS45
Manorway, Wdf.Grn. 48 EJ50
Manpreet Ct E12 69 EM64
Morris Av
Manresa Rd SW3 100 DE78
Mansard Beeches SW17 120 DG92
Mansard Cl, Horn. 71 FG61
Mansard Cl, Pnr. 60 BX55
Manse Cl, Hayes 95 BR79
Manse Rd N16 66 DT62
Manse Way, Swan. 147 FG98
Mansel Cl, Slou. 74 AV71
Mansel Gro E17 47 EA53
Mansel Rd SW19 119 CY93
Mansell Rd W3 98 CR75
Mansell Rd, Grnf. 78 CB71
Mansell St E1 202 A1
Mansell St E1 84 DT72
Mansell Way, Cat. 176 DR122
Manser Rd, Rain. 89 FE69
Mansergh Cl SE18 104 EL80
Mansfield Av N15 66 DR56
Mansfield Av, Barn. 28 DF44
Mansfield Av, Ruis. 59 BV60
Mansfield Cl N9 30 DU44
Mansfield Cl, Orp. 146 EX101
Mansfield Cl, Wey. 153 BP106
Mansfield Dr, Hayes 77 BS70
Mansfield Dr, Red. 185 DK128
Mansfield Gdns, Horn. 72 FK61
Mansfield Hill E4 47 EB46
Mansfield Ms W1 195 H7
Mansfield Pl NW3 64 DC63
New End
Mansfield Rd E11 68 EH58
Mansfield Rd E17 67 DZ56
Mansfield Rd NW3 64 DF64
Mansfield Rd W3 80 CP70
Mansfield Rd, Chess. 155 CJ106
Mansfield Rd, Ilf. 69 EN61
Mansfield Rd, S.Croy. 160 DR107
Mansfield Rd, Swan. 127 FE93
Mansfield St W1 195 H7
Mansfield St W1 83 DH71
Mansford St E2 84 DU68
Manship Rd, Mitch. 120 DG94
Mansion Cl SW9 101 DN81
Cowley Rd
Mansion Gdns NW3 64 DB62
Mansion Ho EC4 197 K9
Mansion Ho EC4 84 DR72
Mansion Ho Pl EC4 197 K9
Mansion Ho St EC4 197 K9
Mansion La, Iver 75 BC74
Manson Ms SW7 100 DC77
Manson Pl SW7 100 DD77
Manstead Gdns, Rain. 89 FH72
Mansted Gdns, Rom. 70 EW59
Manston Av, Sthl. 96 CA77
Manston Cl SE20 142 DW95
Garden Rd
Manston Cl (Cheshunt), Wal.Cr. 14 DW30
Manston Gro, Kings.T. 117 CK92
Manston Way, Horn. 89 FH65
Manstone Rd NW2 63 CY64
Manthorp Rd SE18 105 EQ78
Mantilla Rd SW17 120 DG91
Mantle Rd SE4 103 DY83
Mantle Way E15 86 EE66
Romford Rd
Mantlet Cl SW16 121 DJ94
Manton Av W7 97 CF75
Manton Cl, Hayes 77 BS73
Manton Rd SE2 106 EU77
Mantua St SW11 100 DD83
Mantus Cl E1 84 DW70
Mantus Rd
Mantus Rd E1 84 DW70
Manus Way N20 44 DC47
Blakeney Cl
Manville Gdns SW17 121 DH89
Manville Rd SW17 120 DG89
Manwood Rd SE4 123 DZ85
Manwood St E16 87 EM74
Manygate La, Shep. 135 BQ101
Manygates SW12 121 DH89
Mape St E2 84 DV70
Mapesbury Rd NW2 81 CY65
Mapeshill Pl NW2 81 CW65
Maple Av E4 47 DZ50
Maple Av W3 80 CS74
Maple Av, Har. 60 CB61
Maple Av, Upmin. 72 FP62
Maple Av, West Dr. 76 BL73
Maple Cl N3 44 DA51
Maple Cl N16 66 DU58
Maple Cl SW4 121 DK86
Maple Cl, Brwd. 55 FZ48
Cherry Av
Maple Cl, Buck.H. 48 EK48
Maple Cl, Bushey 24 BY40
Maple Cl, Epp. 33 ER37
Loughton La
Maple Cl, Hmptn. 116 BZ93
Maple Cl, Hayes 78 BX69
Maple Cl, Horn. 71 FH62
Maple Cl, Ilf. 49 ES50
Maple Cl, Mitch. 141 DH95
Maple Cl, Orp. 145 ER99
Maple Cl, Ruis. 59 BV58
Maple Cl, Swan. 147 FE96
Maple Cl, Whyt. 176 DT117
Maple Ct, Egh. 112 AV93
Ashwood Rd
Maple Ct, N.Mal. 138 CS97
Maple Cres, Sid. 126 EU86
Maple Cres, Slou. 74 AV73
Maple Cross Ind Est, Rick. 37 BF49
Maple Dr, S.Ock. 91 FX70
Maple Gdns, Edg. 42 CS52
Maple Gdns, Stai. 114 BL89
Maple Gate, Loug. 33 EN40
Maple Gro NW9 62 CQ59
Maple Gro W5 97 CK76
Maple Gro, Brent. 97 CH80
Maple Gro, Sthl. 78 BZ71
Maple Gro, Wat. 23 BU39
Maple Gro, Wok. 166 AY121
Maple Hill, Hem.H. 4 AX30
Ley Hill Rd
Maple Ind Est, Felt. 115 BU90
Maple Way
Maple Leaf Cl, Abb.L. 7 BU32
Magnolia Av
Maple Leaf Cl, West. 178 EK116
Main Rd
Maple Leaf Dr, Sid. 125 ET88
Maple Leaf Sq SE16 203 J4
Maple Lo Cl, Rick. 37 BE49
Maple Ms NW6 82 DB68
Kilburn Pk Rd
Maple Ms SW16 121 DM92
Maple Pl W1 195 L5
Maple Pl, Bans. 157 CX114
Maple Pl, West Dr. 76 BM73
Maple Av
Maple Rd E11 68 EE58
Maple Rd SE20 142 DV95
Maple Rd, Ash. 171 CK119
Maple Rd, Dart. 128 FJ88
Maple Rd, Grav. 131 GJ91
Maple Rd, Grays 110 GC79
Maple Rd, Hayes 78 BW69
Maple Rd, Surb. 138 CL99
Maple Rd, Whyt. 176 DT117
Maple Rd, Wok. 168 BG124
Maple Springs, Wal.Abb. 16 EG33
Maple St W1 195 K6
Maple St W1 83 DJ71
Maple St, Rom. 71 FC56
Maple Wk W10 81 CX70
Droop St
Maple Wk, Sutt. 158 DB110
Maple Way, Couls. 175 DH121
Maple Way, Felt. 115 BV90
Maplecroft Cl E6 86 EL72
Allhallows Rd
Mapledale Av, Croy. 142 DU103
Mapledene, Chis. 125 EQ92
Kemnal Rd
Mapledene Rd E8 84 DT66
Maplefield, St.Alb. 8 CB29
Maplefield La, Ch.St.G. 20 AV41
Maplehurst, Lthd. 171 CD123
Maplehurst Cl, Kings.T. 138 CL98
Mapleleaf Cl, S.Croy. 161 DX111
Mapleleafe Gdns, Ilf. 69 EP55
Maples, The, Bans. 158 DB114
Maples, The, Cher. 151 BB107
Maples, The (Claygate), Esher 155 CG108
Stevens La
Maples, The, Wal.Cr. 14 DS28
Maples Pl E1 84 DV71
Raven Row
Maplescombe La (Farningham), Dart. 148 FN104
Maplestead Rd SW2 121 DM87
Maplestead Rd, Dag. 88 EV67
Maplethorpe Rd, Th.Hth. 141 DP98
Mapleton Cl, Brom. 144 EG100
Mapleton Cres SW18 120 DB86
Mapleton Cres, Enf. 30 DW38
Mapleton Rd E4 47 EC48
Mapleton Rd SW18 120 DB86
Mapleton Rd, Eden. 189 ET133
Mapleton Rd, Enf. 30 DV40
Mapleton Rd, West. 189 ES130
Maplin Cl N21 29 DM44
Maplin Ho SE2 106 EX75
Wolvercote Rd
Maplin Pk, Slou. 93 BC75
Maplin Rd E16 86 EG72
Maplin St E3 85 DZ69
Mapperley Dr, Wdf.Grn. 48 EE52
Forest Dr
Mar Rd, S.Ock. 91 FW70
Maran Way, Erith 106 EX75
Marban Rd W9 81 CZ69
Marble Arch W1 194 E10
Marble Arch W1 82 DF73
Marble Cl W3 80 CP74
Marble Dr NW2 63 CX59
Marble Hill Cl, Twick. 117 CH87
Marble Hill Gdns, Twick. 117 CH87
Marble Ho SE18 105 ET78
Felspar Cl
Marble Quay E1 202 B2
Marble Quay E1 84 DU74
Marbles Way, Tad. 173 CX119
Marbrook Ct SE12 124 EJ90
Marcellina Way, Orp. 145 ES104
Marcet Rd, Dart. 128 FJ85
March Rd, Twick. 117 CG87
March Rd, Wey. 152 BN106
Marchant Rd E11 67 ED61
Marchant St SE14 103 DY79
Sanford St
Marchbank Rd W14 99 CZ79
Marchmant Cl, Horn. 72 FJ62
Marchmont Gdns, Rich. 118 CM85
Marchmont Rd
Marchmont Rd, Rich. 118 CM85
Marchmont Rd, Wall. 159 DJ108
Marchmont St WC1 195 P4
Marchmont St WC1 83 DL70
Marchside Cl, Houns. 96 BX81
Springwell Rd
Marchwood Cl SE5 102 DS80
Marchwood Cres W5 79 CJ72
Marcia Rd SE1 201 N9
Marcia Rd SE1 102 DS77
Marcilly Rd SW18 120 DD85
Marco Rd W6 99 CW76
Marcon Pl E8 84 DV65
Marconi Rd E10 67 EA60
Marconi Rd, Grav. 130 GD90
Marconi Way, Sthl. 78 CB72
Marcourt Lawns W5 80 CL70
Marcus Ct E15 86 EE67
Marcus Garvey Ms SE22 122 DV85
St. Aidan's Rd
Marcus Garvey Way SE24 101 DN84
Marcus Rd, Dart. 127 FG87
Marcus St E15 86 EF67
Marcus St SW18 120 DB86
Marcus Ter SW18 120 DB86
Marcuse Rd, Cat. 176 DR123
Mardale Dr NW9 62 CR57
Mardell Rd, Croy. 143 DX99
Marden Av, Brom. 144 EG100
Marden Cl, Chig. 50 EV47
Marden Cres, Bex. 127 FC85
Marden Cres, Croy. 141 DM100
Marden Pk, Cat. 187 DZ125
Marden Rd N17 66 DS55
Marden Rd, Croy. 141 DM100
Marden Rd, Rom. 71 FE58
Kingsmead Av
Marden Sq SE16 202 D7
Marden Sq SE16 102 DV76
Marder Rd W13 97 CG75
Mardyke Ho, Rain. 89 FD68
Lower Mardyke Av
Mare St E8 84 DV67
Marechal Niel Av, Sid. 125 ER90
Maresfield, Croy. 142 DS104
Maresfield Gdns NW3 64 DC64
Marfleet Cl, Cars. 140 DE103
Margaret Av E4 31 EB44
Margaret Av, Brwd. 55 FZ45
Margaret Bondfield Av, Bark. 88 EU66
Margaret Bldgs N16 66 DT60
Margaret Rd
Margaret Cl, Abb.L. 7 BT32
Margaret Cl, Epp. 18 EU29
Margaret Rd
Margaret Cl, Pot.B. 12 DC33
Margaret Cl, Rom. 71 FH57
Margaret Rd
Margaret Cl, Stai. 114 BK93
Charles Rd
Margaret Cl, Wal.Abb. 15 ED33
Margaret Ct W1 195 K8
Margaret Dr, Horn. 72 FM60
Margaret Gardner Dr SE9 125 EM89
Margaret Ingram Cl SW6 99 CZ79
John Smith Av
Margaret Lockwood Cl, Kings.T. 138 CM98
Margaret Rd N16 66 DT60
Margaret Rd, Barn. 28 DD42
Margaret Rd, Bex. 126 EX86
Margaret Rd, Epp. 18 EU29
Margaret Rd, Rom. 71 FH57
Margaret Sq, Uxb. 76 BJ67
Margaret St W1 195 J8
Margaret St W1 83 DH72
Margaret Way, Couls. 175 DP118
Margaret Way, Ilf. 68 EL58
Margaretta Ter SW3 100 DE79
Margaretting Rd E12 68 EJ60
Margate Rd SW2 121 DL85
Margeholes, Wat. 40 BY47
Margery Gro, Tad. 183 CY129
Margery La, Tad. 183 CZ129
Margery Pk Rd E7 86 EG65
Margery Rd, Dag. 70 EX62
Margery St WC1 196 D3
Margery St WC1 83 DN69
Margherita Pl, Wal.Abb. 16 EF34
Margherita Rd, Wal.Abb. 16 EG34
Margin Dr SW19 119 CX92
Margravine Gdns W6 99 CX78
Margravine Rd W6 99 CX79
Marham Gdns SW18 120 DE88
Marham Gdns, Mord. 140 DC100
Maria Cl SE1 202 D8
Maria Ter E1 85 DX70
Maria Theresa Cl, N.Mal. 138 CR99
Mariam Gdns, Horn. 72 FM61
Marian Cl, Hayes 78 BX70
Marian Ct, Sutt. 158 DB106
Marian Pl E2 84 DV68
Marian Rd SW16 141 DJ95
Marian Sq E2 84 DU68
Pritchard's Rd
Marian St E2 84 DV68
Hackney Rd
Marian Way NW10 81 CT66
Maricas Av, Har. 41 CD53
Marie Lloyd Gdns N19 65 DL59
Hornsey Ri Gdns
Marie Lloyd Wk E8 84 DU65
Forest Rd
Mariette Way, Wall. 159 DL109
Marigold All SE1 200 F1
Marigold Cl, Sthl. 78 BY73
Lancaster Rd
Marigold Rd N17 46 DW52
Marigold St SE16 202 D5
Marigold St SE16 102 DV75
Marigold Way E4 47 DZ51
Silver Birch Av
Marigold Way, Croy. 143 DX102
Marina App, Hayes 78 BY71
Marina Av, N.Mal. 139 CV99
Marina Cl, Brom. 144 EG97
Marina Cl, Cher. 134 BH102
Marina Dr, Dart. 128 FN88
Marina Dr, Grav. 131 GF87
Marina Dr, Well. 105 ES82
Marina Gdns, Rom. 71 FC58
Marina Gdns (Cheshunt), Wal.Cr. 14 DW30
Marina Way, Iver 75 BF73
Marina Way, Tedd. 117 CK94
Fairways
Marine Dr SE18 105 EM77
Marine Dr, Bark. 87 ES69
Thames Rd
Marine St SE16 202 B6
Marine St SE16 102 DU76
Marinefield Rd SW6 100 DB82
Mariner Gdns, Rich. 117 CJ90
Mariner Rd E12 69 EM63
Dersingham Av
Mariners Ct, Green. 109 FV84
High St
Mariners Ms E14 204 F8
Mariners Ms E14 103 ED77
Mariners Wk, Erith 107 FF79
Frobisher Rd
Marion Av, Shep. 135 BP99
Marion Cl, Bushey 24 BZ39
Marion Cl, Ilf. 49 ER52
Marion Cres, Orp. 146 EU99
Marion Gro, Wdf.Grn. 48 EE50
Marion Rd NW7 43 CU50
Marion Rd, Th.Hth. 142 DQ99
Marischal Rd SE13 103 ED83
Marisco Cl, Grays 111 GH77
Marish La (Denham), Uxb. 57 BC56
Marish Wf, Slou. 92 AY75
Maritime Cl, Green. 129 FV85
Maritime Quay E14 204 A10
Maritime Quay E14 103 EA78
Maritime St E3 85 DZ70
Marius Pas SW17 120 DG89
Marius Rd
Marius Rd SW17 120 DG89
Marjorams Av, Loug. 33 EM40
Marjorie Gro SW11 100 DF84
Marjorie Ms E1 85 DX72
Arbour Sq
Mark Av E4 31 EB44
Mark Cl, Bexh. 106 EY81
Mark Cl, Sthl. 78 CB74
Longford Av
Mark Dr (Chalfont St. Peter), Ger.Cr. 36 AX49
Mark La EC3 197 N10
Mark La EC3 84 DS73
Mark La, Grav. 131 GL86
Mark Oak La, Lthd. 170 CA122
Mark Rd N22 45 DP54
Mark Sq EC2 197 M4
Mark St E15 86 EE66
Mark St EC2 197 M4
Mark St, Reig. 184 DB133
Mark Way, Swan. 147 FG99
Markab Rd, Nthwd. 39 BT50
Marke Cl, Kes. 162 EL105
Markedge La, Couls. 174 DE124
Markedge La, Red. 184 DF126
Markeston Grn, Wat. 40 BX49
Market Ct W1 195 K8
Market Est N7 83 DL65
Market Hill SE18 105 EN76
Market La, Edg. 42 CQ53
Market La, Iver 93 BC75
Market La, Slou. 93 BC75
Market Link, Rom. 71 FE56
Market Meadow, Orp. 146 EW98
Market Ms W1 199 H3
Market Ms W1 83 DH74
Market Pl N2 64 DE55
Market Pl NW11 64 DC56
Market Pl SE16 202 C8
Market Pl W1 195 K8
Market Pl W1 83 DJ72
Market Pl W3 80 CQ74
Market Pl, Bexh. 106 FA84
Market Pl, Brent. 97 CJ80
Market Pl, Dart. 128 FL87
Market St
Market Pl, Enf. 30 DR41
The Town
Market Pl (Chalfont St. Peter), Ger.Cr. 36 AX53
Market Pl, Kings.T. 137 CK96
Market Pl, Rom. 71 FE57
Market Pl (Abridge), Rom. 34 EV41
Market Pl, Til. 111 GF82
Market Rd N7 83 DL65
Market Rd, Rich. 98 CN83
Market Row SW9 101 DN84
Atlantic Rd
Market Sq E2 197 P2
Market Sq E14 85 EB72
Chrisp St
Market Sq N9 46 DU47
New Rd
Market Sq, Brom. 144 EG96
Market Sq, Stai. 113 BE91
Clarence St
Market Sq, Uxb. 76 BJ66
High St
Market Sq, Wal.Abb. 15 EC33
Leverton Way
Market Sq, West. 189 EQ127
Market Sq, Wok. 166 AY117
Cawsey Way
Market St E6 87 EM68
Market St SE18 105 EN77
Market St, Dart. 128 FL87
Market St, Wat. 23 BV42
Market Way E14 85 EB72
Kerbey St
Market Way, Wem. 62 CL64
Turton Rd
Market Way, West. 189 ER126
Costell's Meadow
Marketfield Rd, Red. 184 DF134
Marketfield Way, Red. 184 DF134
Markfield, Croy. 161 DZ110
Markfield Gdns E4 47 EB45
Markfield Rd N15 66 DU56
Markfield Rd, Cat. 186 DV126
Markham Pl SW3 198 D10
Markham Rd (Cheshunt), Wal.Cr. 14 DQ26
Markham Sq SW3 198 D10
Markham Sq SW3 100 DF78
Markham St SW3 198 C10
Markham St SW3 100 DE78
Markhole Cl, Hmptn. 116 BZ94
Priory Rd
Markhouse Av E17 67 DY58
Markhouse Rd E17 67 DZ57
Markmanor Av E17 67 DY59
Marks Rd, Rom. 71 FC57
Marks Rd, Warl. 177 DY118
Marks Sq, Grav. 131 GF91
Marksbury Av, Rich. 98 CN83
Markville Gdns, Cat. 186 DU125
Markway, Sun. 136 BW96
Markwell Cl SE26 122 DV91
Longton Gro
Markyate Rd, Dag. 70 EV64
Marl Rd SW18 100 DB84
Marl St SW18 100 DC84
Marl Rd
Marlands Rd, Ilf. 68 EL55
Marlborough Av E8 84 DU67
Marlborough Av N14 45 DJ48
Marlborough Av, Edg. 42 CP48
Marlborough Av, Ruis. 59 BQ58
Marlborough Bldgs SW3 198 C8
Marlborough Bldgs SW3 100 DE77
Marlborough Cl N20 44 DF48
Marlborough Gdns
Marlborough Cl SE17 200 G9
Marlborough Cl SW19 120 DE93
Marlborough Cl, Grays 110 GC75
Marlborough Cl, Orp. 145 ET101
Aylesham Rd
Marlborough Cl, Upmin. 73 FS60
Marlborough Cl, Walt. 136 BX104
Arch Rd
Marlborough Ct W1 195 K9
Marlborough Ct W8 100 DA77
Marlborough Ct, Wall. 159 DJ108
Cranley Gdns
Marlborough Cres W4 98 CR76
Marlborough Cres, Sev. 190 FE124
Marlborough Dr, Ilf. 68 EL55
Marlborough Dr, Wey. 135 BQ104
Marlborough Gdns N20 44 DF48
Marlborough Gdns, Upmin. 73 FR60
Marlborough Gate Ho W2 82 DD73
Elms Ms
Marlborough Gro SE1 102 DU78
Marlborough Hill NW8 82 DC67
Marlborough Hill, Har. 61 CF56
Marlborough La SE7 104 EJ79
Marlborough Pk Av, Sid. 126 EU87
Marlborough Pl NW8 82 DC68
Marlborough Rd E4 47 EA51
Marlborough Rd E7 86 EJ66
Marlborough Rd E15 68 EE63
Borthwick Rd
Marlborough Rd E18 68 EG55
Marlborough Rd N9 46 DT46
Marlborough Rd N19 65 DK61
Marlborough Rd N22 45 DL52
Marlborough Rd SW1 199 L3
Marlborough Rd SW1 83 DJ74
Marlborough Rd SW19 120 DD93
Marlborough Rd W4 98 CQ78
Marlborough Rd W5 97 CK75
Marlborough Rd, Ashf. 114 BK92
Marlborough Rd, Bexh. 106 EX83
Marlborough Rd, Brwd. 54 FU44
Marlborough Rd, Brom. 144 EJ98
Marlborough Rd, Dag. 70 EV63
Marlborough Rd, Dart. 128 FJ86
Marlborough Rd, Felt. 116 BX89
Marlborough Rd, Hmptn. 116 CA93
Marlborough Rd, Islw. 97 CH81
Marlborough Rd, Rich. 118 CL86
Marlborough Rd, Rom. 70 FA56
Marlborough Rd, Slou. 92 AX77
Marlborough Rd, S.Croy. 160 DQ108
Marlborough Rd, Sthl. 96 BW76
Marlborough Rd, Sutt. 140 DA104
Marlborough Rd, Uxb. 77 BP70
Marlborough Rd, Wat. 23 BV42
Marlborough Rd, Wok. 167 BA116
Marlborough St SW3 198 B9
Marlborough St SW3 100 DE77
Marlborough Yd N19 65 DK61
Marlborough Rd
Marld, The, Ash. 172 CM118
Marle Gdns, Wal.Abb. 15 EC32
Marler Rd SE23 123 DY88
Marlescroft Way, Loug. 33 EP43
Marley Av, Bexh. 106 EX79
Marley Cl N15 65 DP56
Stanmore Rd
Marley Cl, Add. 151 BF107
Marley Cl, Grnf. 78 CA69
Marley Wk NW2 63 CW64
Lennon Rd
Marlin Cl, Sun. 115 BT93
Marlin Sq, Abb.L. 7 BT31
Marling Way, Grav. 131 GL92
Marlingdene Cl, Hmptn. 116 CA93
Marlings Cl, Chis. 145 ES98
Marlings Cl, Whyt. 176 DS117
Marlings Pk Av, Chis. 145 ES98
Marlins, The, Nthwd. 39 BT51
Marlins Cl, Rick. 21 BE40
Marlins Cl, Sutt. 158 DC106
Turnpike La
Marlins Meadow, Wat. 23 BR44
Marloes Cl, Wem. 61 CK63
Marloes Rd W8 100 DB76
Marlow Av, Purf. 108 FN77
Marlow Cl SE20 142 DV97
Marlow Ct NW6 81 CX66
Marlow Ct NW9 63 CT55
Marlow Cres, Twick. 117 CF86
Marlow Dr, Sutt. 139 CX103
Marlow Gdns, Hayes 95 BR76
Marlow Rd E6 87 EM69
Marlow Rd SE20 142 DV97
Marlow Rd, Sthl. 96 BZ76

Marlow Way SE16 203 H4
Marlow Way SE16 103 DX75
Marlowe Cl, Chis. 125 ER93
Marlowe Cl, Ilf. 49 EQ53
Marlowe Gdns SE9 125 EN86
Marlowe Gdns, Rom. 52 FJ53
Shenstone Gdns
Marlowe Rd E17 67 EC56
Marlowe Sq, Mitch. 141 DJ98
Marlowe Way, Croy. 141 DL103
Marlowes, The NW8 82 DD67
Marlowes, The, Dart. 107 FD84
Marlpit Av, Couls. 175 DL117
Marlpit La, Couls. 175 DK116
Marlton St SE10 205 L10
Marlwood Cl, Sid. 125 ES89
Marlyon Rd, Ilf. 50 EV50
Marmadon Rd SE18 105 ET77
Marmion App E4 47 EA49
Marmion Av E4 47 DZ49
Marmion Cl E4 47 DZ49
Marmion Ms SW11 100 DG83
Taybridge Rd
Marmion Rd SW11 100 DG84
Marmont Rd SE15 102 DU81
Marmora Rd SE22 122 DW86
Marmot Rd, Houns. 96 BX83
Marne Av N11 45 DH49
Marne Av, Well. 106 EU83
Marne St W10 81 CY69
Marnell Way, Houns. 96 BX83
Marney Rd SW11 100 DG84
Marneys Cl, Epsom 172 CN115
Marnfield Cres SW2 121 DM87
Marnham Av NW2 63 CY63
Marnham Cres, Grnf. 78 CB69
Marnock Rd SE4 123 DY85
Maroon St E14 85 DY71
Maroons Way SE6 123 EA92
Marquess Rd N1 84 DR65
Marquis Cl, Wem. 80 CM66
Marquis Rd N4 65 DM60
Marquis Rd N22 45 DM51
Marquis Rd NW1 83 DK65
Marrabon Cl, Sid. 126 EU88
Marram Ct, Grays 110 GE79
Medlar Rd
Marrick Cl SW15 99 CU84
Marrilyne Av, Enf. 31 DZ38
Marriot Ter, Rick. 21 BF42
Marriots Cl NW9 63 CT58
Marriott Cl, Felt. 115 BR86
Marriott Lo Cl, Add. 152 BJ105
Marriott Rd E15 86 EE67
Marriott Rd N4 65 DM60
Marriott Rd N10 44 DF53
Marriott Rd, Barn. 27 CX41
Marriott Rd, Dart. 128 FN87
Marrowells, Wey. 135 BT104
Marryat Pl SW19 119 CY91
Marryat Rd SW19 119 CX92
Marryat Rd, Enf. 30 DV35
Marryat Sq SW6 99 CY81
Marsala Rd SE13 103 EB84
Marsden Rd N9 46 DV47
Marsden Rd SE15 102 DT83
Marsden St NW5 82 DG65
Marsden Way, Orp. 163 ET105
Marsh Av, Epsom 156 CS110
Marsh Av, Mitch. 140 DG96
Marsh Cl NW7 43 CT48
Marsh Cl, Wal.Cr. 15 DZ33
Marsh Ct SW19 140 DC95
Marsh Dr NW9 63 CT58
Marsh Fm Rd, Twick. 117 CF88
Marsh Grn Rd, Dag. 88 FA67
Marsh Hill E9 67 DY64
Marsh La E10 67 EA61
Marsh La N17 46 DV52
Marsh La NW7 42 CS49
Marsh La, Add. 152 BH105
Marsh La, Stan. 41 CJ50
Marsh Rd, Pnr. 60 BY56
Marsh Rd, Wem. 79 CK68
Marsh St E14 204 B9
Marsh St, Dart. 108 FN82
Marsh Ter, Orp. 146 EX98
Buttermere Rd
Marsh Wall E14 203 P3
Marsh Wall E14 85 EA74
Marsh Way, Rain. 89 FD72
Marshall Cl SW18 120 DC86
Allfarthing La
Marshall Cl, Har. 61 CD59
Bowen Rd
Marshall Cl, Houns. 116 BZ85
Marshall Cl, S.Croy. 160 DU113
Marshall Dr, Hayes 77 BT71
Marshall Path SE28 88 EV73
Attlee Rd
Marshall Pl, Add. 152 BJ109
Marshall Rd E10 67 EB62
Marshall Rd N17 46 DR53
Marshall St W1 195 L9
Marshall St W1 83 DJ72
Marshalls Cl N11 45 DH49
Marshalls Cl, Epsom 156 CQ113
Marshalls Dr, Rom. 71 FE55
Marshall's Gro SE18 104 EL77
Marshalls Pl SE16 202 A7
Marshalls Rd, Rom. 71 FD56
Marshall's Rd, Sutt. 158 DB105
Marshalsea Rd SE1 201 J4
Marshalsea Rd SE1 102 DQ75
Marsham Cl, Chis. 125 EP92
Marsham La, Ger.Cr. 56 AY58
Marsham Lo, Ger.Cr. 56 AY58
Marsham St SW1 199 N7
Marsham St SW1 101 DK76
Marsham Way, Ger.Cr. 56 AY57
Marshbrook Cl SE3 104 EK83
Marshcroft Dr (Cheshunt), Wal.Cr. 15 DY30
Marshe Cl, Pot.B. 12 DD32
Marshfield, Slou. 92 AW81
Marshfield St E14 204 D6
Marshfield St E14 103 EC76
Marshfoot Rd, Grays 110 GE78
Marshgate La E15 85 EB67
Marshgate Path SE28 105 EQ77
Tom Cribb Rd
Marshgate Sidings E15 85 EB66
Marshgate La
Marshside Cl N9 46 DW46
Marsland Cl SE17 101 DP78
Marston, Epsom 156 CQ111
Marston Av, Chess. 156 CL107
Marston Av, Dag. 70 FA61
Marston Cl NW6 82 DC66
Fairfax Rd
Marston Cl, Dag. 70 FA62
Marston Ct, Walt. 136 BW102
St. Johns Dr
Marston Dr, Warl. 177 DY118
Marston Ho, Grays 110 GA79
Marston Rd, Ilf. 48 EL53
Marston Rd, Tedd. 117 CH92
Marston Rd, Wok. 166 AV117
Marston Way SE19 121 DP94
Marsworth Av, Pnr. 40 BX53
Marsworth Cl, Hayes 78 BY71
Marsworth Cl, Wat. 23 BS44
Mart St WC2 196 A9
Martaban Rd N16 66 DS61
Martel Pl E8 84 DT65
Dalston La
Martell Rd SE21 122 DR90
Martello St E8 84 DV66
Martello Ter E8 84 DV66
Marten Rd E17 47 EA54
Martens Av, Bexh. 107 FC84
Martens Cl, Bexh. 107 FC84
Martha Ct E2 84 DV68
Cambridge Heath Rd
Martha Rd E4 47 DZ51
Martha Rd E15 86 EE65
Martha St E1 84 DV72
Martham Cl SE28 88 EX73
Marthorne Cres, Har. 41 CD54
Martin Bowes Rd SE9 105 EM83
Martin Cl N9 47 DX46
Martin Cl, S.Croy. 161 DX111
Martin Cl, Uxb. 76 BL68
Valley Rd
Martin Cl, Warl. 176 DV116
Martin Cres, Croy. 141 DN102
Martin Dene, Bexh. 126 EZ85
Martin Dr, Dart. 128 FQ86
Martin Dr, Nthlt. 60 BZ64
Martin Dr, Rain. 89 FH70
Martin Gdns, Dag. 70 EW63
Martin Gro, Mord. 140 DA97
Martin La EC4 197 L10
Martin Ri, Bexh. 126 EZ85
Martin Rd, Dag. 70 EW63
Martin Rd, Dart. 128 FJ90
Martin Rd, Slou. 92 AS76
Martin Rd, S.Ock. 91 FR73
Martin St SE28 105 ES75
Merbury Rd
Martin Way SW20 139 CY97
Martin Way, Mord. 139 CY97
Martin Way, Wok. 166 AU118
Martinbridge Ind Est, Enf. 30 DU43
Martindale SW14 118 CQ85
Martindale, Iver 75 BD70
Martindale Av E16 86 EG73
Martindale Av, Orp. 164 EU106
Martindale Rd SW12 121 DH87
Martindale Rd, Houns. 96 BY83
Martindale Rd, Wok. 166 AT118
Martineau Cl, Esher 155 CD105
Martineau Ms N5 65 DP63
Martineau Rd
Martineau Rd N5 65 DP63
Martineau St E1 84 DW73
Martingale Cl, Sun. 135 BU98
Martingales Cl, Rich. 117 CK90
Martins Cl, Orp. 146 EX97
Martins Cl, Rad. 25 CE36
Martins Cl, W.Wick. 143 ED102
Martins Dr (Cheshunt), Wal.Cr. 15 DY28
Martins Mt, Barn. 28 DA42
Martin's Plain, Slou. 74 AS69
Martins Rd, Brom. 144 EE96
Martins Shaw, Sev. 190 FC122
Martins Wk N10 44 DG53
Martins Wk, Borwd. 26 CN42
Siskin Cl
Martinsfield Cl, Chig. 49 ES49
Martinstown Cl, Horn. 72 FN58
Martinsyde, Wok. 167 BC117
Martlesham Cl, Horn. 72 FJ64
Martlet Gro, Nthlt. 78 BX69
Javelin Way
Martlett Ct WC2 196 A9
Martley Dr, Ilf. 69 EP57
Martock Cl, Har. 61 CG56
Marton Cl SE6 123 EA90
Marton Rd N16 66 DS61
Martyrs La, Wok. 151 BB112
Martys Yd NW3 64 DD63
Hampstead High St
Marvell Av, Hayes 77 BU71
Marvels Cl SE12 124 EH89
Marvels La SE12 124 EH89
Marville Rd SW6 99 CZ80
Marvin St E8 84 DV65
Sylvester Rd
Marwell, West. 189 EP126
Marwell Cl, Rom. 71 FG57
Marwell Cl, W.Wick. 144 EF103
Deer Pk Way
Marwood Cl, Kings L. 6 BN29
Marwood Cl, Well. 106 EV83
Mary Adelaide Cl SW15 118 CS91
Mary Ann Gdns SE8 103 EA79
Mary Cl, Stan. 62 CM56
Mary Datchelor Cl SE5 102 DR81
Mary Grn NW8 82 DB67
Mary Kingsley Ct N19 65 DL59
Hillrise Rd
Mary Lawrenson Pl SE3 104 EF80
Mary Macarthur Ho W6 99 CY79
Field Rd
Mary Peters Dr, Grnf. 61 CD64
Mary Pl W11 81 CY73
Mary Rose Cl, Hmptn. 136 CA95
Ashley Rd
Mary Rose Mall E6 87 EN71
Frobisher Rd
Mary Seacole Cl E8 84 DT67
Clarissa St
Mary St E16 86 EF71
Barking Rd
Mary St N1 84 DQ67
Mary Ter NW1 83 DH67
Maryatt Av, Har. 60 CB61
Marybank SE18 105 EM77
Maryfield Cl, Bex. 127 FE90
Marygold Wk, Amer. 20 AV39
Maryhill Cl, Ken. 176 DQ117
Maryland Ind Est E15 67 ED64
Maryland Rd
Maryland Pk E15 68 EE64
Maryland Pt E15 86 EE65
Leytonstone Rd
Maryland Rd E15 67 ED64
Maryland Rd N22 45 DM51
Maryland Rd, Th.Hth. 141 DP95
Maryland Sq E15 68 EE64
Maryland St E15 67 ED64
Maryland Wk N1 84 DQ67
Popham St
Maryland Way, Sun. 135 BU96
Marylands Rd W9 82 DA70
Marylebone Flyover NW1 194 A7
Marylebone Flyover W2 194 A7
Marylebone High St W1 194 G6
Marylebone High St W1 82 DG71
Marylebone La W1 195 H9
Marylebone La W1 82 DG72
Marylebone Ms W1 195 H7
Marylebone Ms W1 83 DH71
Marylebone Pas W1 195 L8
Marylebone Rd NW1 194 C6
Marylebone Rd NW1 82 DE71
Marylebone St W1 194 G7
Marylebone St W1 82 DG71
Marylee Way SE11 200 C10
Marylee Way SE11 101 DM77
Maryon Gro SE7 104 EL77
Maryon Ms NW3 64 DE63
South End Rd
Maryon Rd SE7 104 EL77
Maryon Rd SE18 104 EL77
Maryrose Way N20 44 DD46
Mary's Ter, Twick. 117 CG87
Maryside, Slou. 92 AY75
Masbro Rd W14 99 CX76
Mascalls Ct SE7 104 EJ79
Victoria Way
Mascalls Gdns, Brwd. 54 FT49
Mascalls La, Brwd. 54 FT49
Mascalls Rd SE7 104 EJ79
Mascotte Rd SW15 99 CX84
Mascotts Cl NW2 63 CV62
Masefield Av, Borwd. 26 CP43
Masefield Av, Sthl. 78 CA73
Masefield Av, Stan. 41 CF50
Masefield Cl, Erith 107 FF81
Masefield Cl, Rom. 52 FJ53
Masefield Ct, Brwd. 54 FW49
Masefield Cres N14 29 DJ44
Masefield Cres, Rom. 52 FJ53
Masefield Dr, Upmin. 72 FQ59
Masefield Gdns E6 87 EN70
Masefield La, Hayes 77 BV70
Masefield Rd, Dart. 128 FP85
Masefield Rd, Grav. 130 GD90
Masefield Rd, Grays 110 GE75
Masefield Rd, Hmptn. 116 BZ91
Wordsworth Rd
Masefield Vw, Orp. 145 EQ104
Masefield Way, Stai. 114 BM88
Masham Ho, Erith 106 EX75
Kale Rd
Mashie Rd W3 80 CS72
Mashiters Hill, Rom. 51 FD53
Mashiters Wk, Rom. 71 FE55
Maskall Cl SW2 121 DN88
Maskani Wk SW16 121 DJ94
Bates Cres
Maskell Rd SW17 120 DC90
Maskelyne Cl SW11 100 DE81
Mason Bradbear Ct N1 84 DR65
St. Paul's Rd
Mason Cl E16 86 EG73
Mason Cl SE16 202 C10
Mason Cl SW20 139 CX95
Mason Cl, Bexh. 107 FB83
Mason Cl, Borwd. 26 CQ40
Mason Cl, Hmptn. 136 BZ95
Mason Dr, Rom. 52 FL54
Whitmore Av
Mason Rd, Sutt. 158 DB106
Manor Pl
Mason Rd, Wdf.Grn. 48 EE49
Mason St SE17 201 L8
Mason St SE17 102 DR77
Mason Way, Wal.Abb. 16 EF34
Masonic Hall Rd, Cher. 133 BF100
Masons Arms Ms W1 195 J9
Masons Av EC2 197 K8
Masons Av, Croy. 142 DQ104
Masons Av, Har. 61 CF56
Masons Ct, Wem. 62 CN61
Mayfields
Masons Grn La W3 80 CN71
Masons Hill SE18 105 EP77
Masons Hill, Brom. 144 EG97
Mason's Pl EC1 196 G2
Mason's Pl EC1 83 DP69
Masons Pl, Mitch. 140 DF95
Masons Rd, Enf. 30 DW36
Mason's Yd SW1 199 L2
Mason's Yd SW19 119 CX92
High St Wimbledon
Massey Cl N11 45 DH50
Grove Rd
Massie Rd E8 84 DU65
Graham Rd
Massingberd Way SW17 121 DH91
Massinger St SE17 201 M9
Massingham St E1 85 DX70
Masson Av, Ruis. 78 BW65
Mast Ho Ter E14 204 A9
Mast Ho Ter E14 103 EA77
Mast Leisure Pk SE16 203 J7
Mast Leisure Pk SE16 103 DX76
Master Cl, Oxt. 188 EE129
Church La
Master Gunner Pl SE18 104 EL80
Masterman Ho SE5 102 DR80
Masterman Rd E6 86 EL69
Masters Dr SE16 102 DV78
Masters St E1 85 DX71
Masthead Cl, Dart. 108 FQ84
Mastmaker Rd E14 204 A5
Mastmaker Rd E14 103 EA75
Maswell Pk Cres, Houns. 116 CC85
Maswell Pk Rd, Houns. 116 CB85
Matcham Rd E11 68 EE62
Matchless Dr SE18 105 EN80
Matfield Cl, Brom. 144 EG99
Matfield Rd, Belv. 106 FA79
Matham Gro SE22 102 DT84
Matham Rd, E.Mol. 137 CD99
Matheson Rd W14 99 CZ77
Mathews Av E6 87 EN68
Mathews Pk Av E15 86 EF65
Mathias Cl, Epsom 156 CQ113
Mathisen Way, Slou. 93 BE81
Matilda Cl SE19 122 DR94
Elizabeth Way
Matilda St N1 83 DM67
Matlock Cl SE24 102 DQ84
Matlock Cl, Barn. 27 CX44
Matlock Ct SE5 102 DR84
Denmark Hill Est
Matlock Cres, Sutt. 157 CY105
Matlock Cres, Wat. 40 BW48
Matlock Gdns, Horn. 72 FL62
Matlock Gdns, Sutt. 157 CY105
Matlock Pl, Sutt. 157 CY105
Matlock Rd E10 67 EC58
Matlock Rd, Cat. 176 DS121
Matlock St E14 85 DY72
Matlock Way, N.Mal. 138 CR95
Matrimony Pl SW8 101 DJ82
Matson Ct, Wdf.Grn. 48 EE52
The Bridle Path
Matthew Arnold Cl, Cob. 153 BU114
Matthew Arnold Cl, Stai. 114 BJ93
Elizabeth Av
Matthew Cl W10 81 CX70
Matthew Ct, Mitch. 141 DK99
Matthew Parker St SW1 199 N5
Matthew Parker St SW1 101 DK75
Matthews Cl (Havering-atte-Bower), Rom. 52 FM53
Oak Rd
Matthews Gdns, Croy. 161 ED111
Matthews Rd, Grnf. 61 CD64
Matthews St SW11 100 DF82
Matthews Yd WC2 195 P9
Matthias Rd N16 66 DR64
Mattingley Way SE15 102 DT80
Daniel Gdns
Mattison Rd N4 65 DN58
Mattock La W5 79 CH74
Mattock La W13 79 CH74
Maud Cashmore Way SE18 105 EM76
Maud Gdns E13 86 EF67
Maud Gdns, Bark. 87 ET68
Maud Rd E10 67 EC62
Maud Rd E13 86 EF68
Maud St E16 86 EF71
Maude Cres, Wat. 23 BV37
Maude Rd E17 67 DY57
Maude Rd SE5 102 DS81
Maude Rd, Swan. 127 FG93
Maude Ter E17 67 DY56
Maudesville Cotts W7 79 CE74
The Bdy
Maudlin's Grn E1 202 B2
Maudslay Rd SE9 105 EM83
Maudsley Ho, Brent. 98 CL78
Green Dragon La
Mauleverer Rd SW2 121 DL85
Maundeby Wk NW10 80 CS65
Neasden La
Maunder Rd W7 79 CF74
Maunsel St SW1 199 M8
Maunsel St SW1 101 DK77
Maurice Av N22 45 DP54
Maurice Av, Cat. 176 DR122
Maurice Brown Cl NW7 43 CX50
Maurice St W12 81 CV72
Maurice Wk NW11 64 DC56
Maurier Cl, Nthlt. 78 BW67
Mauritius Rd SE10 205 J9
Mauritius Rd SE10 104 EE77
Maury Rd N16 66 DU61
Mavelstone Cl, Brom. 144 EL95
Mavelstone Rd, Brom. 144 EL95
Maverton Rd E3 85 EA67
Mavis Av, Epsom 156 CS106
Mavis Cl, Epsom 156 CS106
Mavis Gro, Horn. 72 FL61
Mavis Wk E6 86 EL71
Mawbey Est SE1 102 DU78
Mawbey Pl SE1 102 DT78
Mawbey Rd SE1 102 DT78
Old Kent Rd
Mawbey Rd, Cher. 151 BD107
Mawbey St SW8 101 DL80
Mawney Cl, Rom. 51 FB54
Mawney Rd, Rom. 71 FC56
Mawson Cl SW20 139 CY96
Mawson La W4 99 CT79
Great W Rd
Maxey Gdns, Dag. 70 EY63
Maxey Rd SE18 105 EQ77
Maxey Rd, Dag. 70 EY63
Maxfield Cl N20 44 DC45
Maxilla Gdns W10 81 CX72
Cambridge Gdns
Maxilla Wk W10 81 CX72
Kingsdown Cl
Maxim Rd N21 29 DN44
Maxim Rd, Dart. 127 FE85
Maxim Rd, Erith 107 FE77
Maximfeldt Rd, Erith 107 FE78
Maxted Pk, Har. 61 CE59
Maxted Rd SE15 102 DT83
Maxwell Cl, Croy. 141 DL102
Maxwell Cl, Rick. 38 BG47
Maxwell Dr, W.Byf. 152 BJ111
Maxwell Gdns, Orp. 145 ET104
Maxwell Ri, Wat. 40 BY45
Maxwell Rd SW6 100 DB80
Maxwell Rd, Ashf. 115 BQ93
Maxwell Rd, Borwd. 26 CP41
Maxwell Rd, Nthwd. 39 BR52
Maxwell Rd, Well. 106 EU83
Maxwell Rd, West Dr. 94 BM77
Maxwelton Av NW7 42 CR50
Maxwelton Cl NW7 42 CR50
May Av, Grav. 131 GF88
Dover Rd E
May Av, Orp. 146 EV99
May Bate Av, Kings.T. 137 CK95
May Cl, Chess. 156 CM107
May Cotts, Wat. 24 BW43
May Ct SW19 140 DC95
May Ct, Grays 110 GE79
Medlar Rd
May Gdns, Wem. 79 CJ68
May Rd E4 47 EA51
May Rd E13 86 EG68
May Rd, Dart. 128 FM91
May Rd, Twick. 117 CE88
May St W14 99 CZ78
North End Rd
May Tree La, Stan. 41 CF52
May Wk E13 86 EH68
Maya Angelou Ct E4 47 EC49
Bailey Cl
Maya Rd N2 64 DC56
Mayall Rd SE24 121 DP85
Maybank Av E18 48 EH54
Maybank Av, Horn. 72 FJ64
Maybank Av, Wem. 61 CF64
Maybank Gdns, Pnr. 59 BU57
Maybank Lo, Horn. 72 FJ64
Maybank Rd E18 48 EH53
Maybells Commercial Est, Bark. 88 EX68
Mayberry Pl, Surb. 138 CM101
Maybourne Cl SE26 122 DV92
Maybourne Ri, Wok. 166 AX124
Maybrick Rd, Horn. 72 FJ58
Maybrook Meadow Est, Bark. 88 EU66
Maybury Av, Dart. 128 FQ88
Maybury Av (Cheshunt), Wal.Cr. 14 DV28
Maybury Cl, Enf. 30 DV38
Maybury Cl, Loug. 33 EP42
Maybury Cl, Orp. 145 EP99
Maybury Cl, Tad. 173 CY119
Ballards Grn
Maybury Gdns NW10 81 CV65
Maybury Hill, Wok. 167 BB116
Maybury Ms N6 65 DJ59
Maybury Rd E13 86 EJ70
Maybury Rd, Bark. 87 ET68
Maybury Rd, Wok. 167 AZ117
Maybury St SW17 120 DE92
Maybush Rd, Horn. 72 FL59
Maychurch Cl, Stan. 41 CK52
Maycock Gro, Nthwd. 39 BT51
Maycroft, Pnr. 39 BV54
Maycroft Av, Grays 110 GD78
Maycroft Gdns, Grays 110 GD78
Maycroft Rd (Cheshunt), Wal.Cr. 14 DS26
Maycross Av, Mord. 139 CZ97
Mayday Gdns SE3 104 EL82
Mayday Rd, Th.Hth. 141 DP100
Maydwell Lo, Borwd. 26 CM40
Mayell Cl, Lthd. 171 CJ123
Mayer Rd, Wal.Abb. 31 EC40
Sewardstone Rd
Mayerne Rd SE9 124 EK85
Mayes Cl, Swan. 147 FG98
Mayes Cl, Warl. 177 DX118
Mayes Rd N22 45 DN54
Mayesbrook Rd, Bark. 87 ET67
Mayesbrook Rd, Dag. 70 EU62
Mayesbrook Rd, Ilf. 70 EU62
Mayesford Rd, Rom. 70 EW59
Mayeswood Rd SE12 124 EJ90
Mayfair Av, Bexh. 106 EX81
Mayfair Av, Ilf. 69 EM61
Mayfair Av, Rom. 70 EX58
Mayfair Av, Twick. 116 CC87
Mayfair Av, Wor.Pk. 139 CU102
Mayfair Cl, Beck. 143 EB95
Mayfair Cl, Surb. 138 CL102
Mayfair Gdns N17 46 DR51
Mayfair Gdns, Wdf.Grn. 48 EG52
Mayfair Ms NW1 82 DF66
Regents Pk Rd
Mayfair Pl W1 199 J2
Mayfair Pl W1 83 DH74
Mayfair Rd, Dart. 128 FK85
Mayfair Ter N14 45 DK45
Mayfare, Rick. 23 BR43
Mayfield, Bexh. 106 EZ83
Mayfield, Wal.Abb. 15 ED34
Mayfield Av N12 44 DC49
Mayfield Av N14 45 DK47
Mayfield Av W4 98 CS77
Mayfield Av W13 97 CH76
Mayfield Av, Add. 152 BH110
Mayfield Av, Ger.Cr. 56 AX56
Mayfield Av, Har. 61 CH57
Mayfield Av, Orp. 145 ET102
Mayfield Av, Wdf.Grn. 48 EG52
Mayfield Cl E8 84 DT65
Forest Rd
Mayfield Cl SW4 121 DK85
Mayfield Cl, Add. 152 BJ110
Mayfield Cl, Ashf. 115 BP93
Mayfield Cl, T.Ditt. 137 CH102
Mayfield Cl, Uxb. 77 BP69
Mayfield Cl, Walt. 153 BU105
Mayfield Cres N9 30 DV44
Mayfield Cres, Th.Hth. 141 DM98
Mayfield Dr, Pnr. 60 BZ56
Mayfield Gdns NW4 63 CX58
Mayfield Gdns W7 79 CD72
Mayfield Gdns, Brwd. 54 FV46
Mayfield Gdns, Stai. 113 BF93
Mayfield Gdns, Walt. 153 BU105
Mayfield Mans SW18 119 CX87
West Hill
Mayfield Pk, West Dr. 94 BJ76
Mayfield Rd E4 47 EC47

Mayfield Rd E8 84 DT66
Mayfield Rd E13 86 EF70
Mayfield Rd E17 47 DY54
Mayfield Rd N8 65 DM58
Mayfield Rd SW19 139 CZ95
Mayfield Rd W3 80 CP73
Mayfield Rd W12 98 CS75
Mayfield Rd, Belv. 107 FC77
Mayfield Rd, Brom. 144 EL99
Mayfield Rd, Dag. 70 EW60
Mayfield Rd, Enf. 31 DX40
Mayfield Rd, Grav. 131 GF87
Mayfield Rd, S.Croy. 160 DR109
Mayfield Rd, Sutt. 158 DD107
Mayfield Rd, Th.Hth. 141 DM98
Mayfield Rd, Walt. 153 BU105
Mayfield Rd, Wey. 152 BM106
Mayfields, Grays 110 GC75
Mayfields, Swans. 130 FY86
Madden Cl
Mayfields, Wem. 62 CN61
Mayfields Cl, Wem. 62 CN61
Mayflower Cl SE16 203 J8
Mayflower Cl, Ruis. 59 BQ58
Leaholme Way
Mayflower Cl, S.Ock. 91 FW70
Mayflower Ct SE16 102 DW75
St. Marychurch St
Mayflower Path, Brwd. 53 FW51
Eagle Way
Mayflower Rd SW9 101 DL83
Mayflower Rd, Grays 109 FW78
Mayflower Rd, St.Alb. 8 CB27
Mayflower St SE16 202 F5
Mayflower St SE16 102 DW75
Mayfly Cl, Orp. 146 EX98
Mayfly Cl, Pnr. 60 BW59
Mayfly Gdns, Nthlt. 78 BX69
Ruislip Rd
Mayford Cl SW12 120 DF87
Mayford Cl, Beck. 143 DX97
Mayford Cl, Wok. 166 AX122
Mayford Grn, Wok. 166 AW122
Smarts Heath Rd
Mayford Rd SW12 120 DF87
Maygood St N1 83 DM68
Maygoods Cl, Uxb. 76 BK71
Maygoods Grn, Uxb. 76 BK71
Worcester Rd
Maygoods La, Uxb. 76 BK71
Maygoods Vw, Uxb. 76 BJ71
Benbow Waye
Maygreen Cres, Horn. 71 FG59
Maygrove Rd NW6 81 CZ65
Mayhew Cl E4 47 EA48
Mayhill Rd SE7 104 EH79
Mayhill Rd, Barn. 27 CY44
Mayhurst Av, Wok. 167 BC116
Mayhurst Cl, Wok. 167 BC116
Mayhurst Cres, Wok. 167 BC116
Maylands Av, Horn. 71 FH63
Maylands Dr, Sid. 126 EX90
Maylands Dr, Uxb. 76 BK65
Maylands Rd, Wat. 40 BW49
Maylands Way, Rom. 52 FQ51
Maynard Cl N15 66 DS56
Brunswick Rd
Maynard Cl SW6 100 DB80
Cambria St
Maynard Cl, Erith 107 FF80
Maynard Cl, Wal.Abb. 16 EF34
Maynard Path E17 67 EC57
Maynard Rd
Maynard Pl, Pot.B. 13 DL29
Maynard Rd E17 67 EC57
Maynards, Horn. 72 FL59
Maynards Quay E1 202 F1
Maynooth Gdns, Cars. 140 DF101
Middleton Rd
Mayo Cl (Cheshunt), Wal.Cr. 14 DW28
Mayo Rd NW10 80 CS65
Mayo Rd, Croy. 142 DR99
Mayo Rd, Walt. 135 BT101
Mayola Rd E5 66 DW63
Mayor's La, Dart. 128 FJ92
Mayow Rd SE23 123 DX90
Mayow Rd SE26 123 DX91
Mayplace Av, Dart. 107 FG84
Mayplace Cl, Bexh. 107 FB83
Mayplace La SE18 105 EP80
Mayplace Rd E, Bexh. 107 FB83
Mayplace Rd E, Dart. 107 FC83
Mayplace Rd W, Bexh. 106 FA84
Maypole Cres, Erith 108 FK79
Maypole Cres, Ilf. 49 ER52
Maypole Dr, Chig. 50 EU48
Maypole Rd, Grav. 131 GM88
Maypole Rd, Orp. 164 EZ106
Mayroyd Av, Surb. 138 CN103
Mays Cl, Wey. 152 BM110
Mays Ct WC2 199 P1
Mays Gro, Wok. 167 BD123
Mays Hill Rd, Brom. 144 EE96
Mays La E4 47 ED47
Mays La, Barn. 43 CV45
Mays Rd, Tedd. 117 CD92
Maysfield Rd, Wok. 167 BD123
Maysoule Rd SW11 100 DD84
Mayston Ms SE10 104 EG78
Westcombe Hill
Mayswood Gdns, Dag. 89 FC65
Maythorne Cl, Wat. 23 BS42
Mayton St N7 65 DM62
Maytree Cl, Edg. 42 CQ48
Maytree Cl, Rain. 89 FE68
Maytree Cres, Wat. 23 BT35
Maytree Gdns W5 97 CK75
South Ealing Rd
Maytree Wk SW2 121 DN89
Maytrees, Rad. 25 CG37
Mayville Est N16 66 DS64
King Henry St
Mayville Rd E11 68 EE62
Mayville Rd, Ilf. 69 EP64
Maywater Cl, S.Croy. 160 DR111
Maywin Dr, Horn. 72 FM60
Maywood Cl, Beck. 123 EB94
Maze Hill SE3 104 EE79
Maze Hill SE10 104 EE79
Maze Rd, Rich. 98 CN80
Mazenod Av NW6 82 DA66
McAdam Dr, Enf. 29 DP40
Rowantree Rd
McAuley Cl SE1 200 D6
McAuley Cl SE1 101 DN76
McAuley Cl SE9 125 EP85
McCall Cl SW4 101 DL82
Jeffreys Rd
McCall Cres SE7 104 EL78
McCarthy Rd, Felt. 116 BX92
McCoid Way SE1 201 H5
McCrone Ms NW3 82 DD65
Belsize La
McCudden Rd, Dart. 108 FM83
Cornwall Rd
McCullum Rd E3 85 DZ67
McDermott Cl SW11 100 DE83
McDermott Rd SE15 102 DU83
McDonough Cl, Chess. 156 CL105
McDowall Cl E16 86 EF71
McDowall Rd SE5 102 DQ81
McEntee Av E17 47 DY53
McEwen Way E15 85 ED67
McGrath Rd E15 86 EF65
McGredy (Cheshunt), Wal.Cr. 14 DV29
McGregor Rd W11 81 CZ72
McIntosh Cl, Rom. 71 FE55
McIntosh Cl, Wall. 159 DL108
McIntosh Rd, Rom. 71 FE55
McKay Rd SW20 119 CV94
McKay Trd Est, Slou. 93 BE82
McKellar Cl, Bushey 40 CC47
McKerrell Rd SE15 102 DU81
McLeod Rd SE2 106 EV77
McLeod's Ms SW7 100 DB77
McMillan Cl, Grav. 131 GJ91
McMillan St SE8 103 EA79
McNair Rd, Sthl. 96 CB75
McNeil Rd SE5 102 DS82
McNicol Dr NW10 80 CQ68
McRae La, Mitch. 140 DF101
Mead, The N2 44 DC54
Mead, The W13 79 CH71
Mead, The, Ash. 172 CL119
Mead, The, Beck. 143 EC95
Mead, The, Uxb. 58 BN61
Mead, The, Wall. 159 DK107
Mead, The (Cheshunt), Wal.Cr. 14 DW29
Mead, The, Wat. 40 BY48
Mead, The, W.Wick. 143 ED102
Mead Av, Slou. 93 BB75
Mead Cl, Egh. 113 BB93
Mead Cl, Grays 110 GB75
Mead Cl, Har. 41 CD53
Mead Cl, Loug. 33 EP40
Mead Cl, Red. 184 DG131
Mead Cl, Rom. 51 FG54
Mead Cl, Slou. 93 BB75
Mead Cl, Swan. 147 FG99
Mead Cl (Denham), Uxb. 58 BG61
Mead Ct NW9 62 CQ57
Mead Ct, Egh. 113 BC93
Holbrook Meadow
Mead Ct, Wal.Abb. 15 EB34
Mead Ct, Wok. 166 AS116
Mead Cres E4 47 EC49
Mead Cres, Dart. 128 FK88
Beech Rd
Mead Cres, Sutt. 158 DE105
Mead End, Ash. 172 CM116
Mead Fld, Har. 60 BZ62
Kings Rd
Mead Gro, Rom. 70 EY55
Mead Ho La, Hayes 77 BR70
Mead La, Cher. 134 BH102
Mead La Caravan Pk, Cher. 134 BJ102
Mead Path SW17 120 DC92
Mead Pl E9 84 DW65
Mead Pl, Croy. 141 DP102
Mead Pl, Rick. 38 BH46
Mead Plat NW10 80 CQ65
Mead Rd, Cat. 176 DT123
Mead Rd, Chis. 125 EQ93
Mead Rd, Dart. 128 FK88
Mead Rd, Edg. 42 CN51
Mead Rd, Grav. 131 GH89
Mead Rd, Rad. 10 CM33
Mead Rd, Rich. 117 CJ90
Mead Rd, Uxb. 76 BK66
Mead Rd, Walt. 154 BY105
Mead Row SE1 200 D6
Mead Ter, Wem. 61 CK63
Meadow Way
Mead Wk, Slou. 93 BB75
Mead Way, Brom. 144 EF100
Mead Way, Bushey 24 BY40
Mead Way, Couls. 175 DL118
Mead Way, Croy. 143 DY103
Meadcroft Rd SE11 101 DP79
Meade Cl W4 98 CN79
Meade Ct, Tad. 173 CU124
Meades, The, Wey. 153 BQ107
Meadfield, Edg. 42 CP47
Meadfield Av, Slou. 93 BA76
Meadfield Grn, Edg. 42 CP47
Meadfield Rd, Slou. 93 BA76
Meadfoot Rd SW16 121 DJ94
Meadgate Av, Wdf.Grn. 48 EL50
Meadhurst Rd, Cher. 134 BH102
Meadlands Dr, Rich. 117 CK89
Meadow, The, Chis. 125 EQ93
Meadow Av, Croy. 143 DX100
Meadow Bk N21 29 DM44
Meadow Cl E4 47 EB46
Mount Echo Av
Meadow Cl E9 67 DZ64
Meadow Cl SE6 123 EA92
Meadow Cl SW20 139 CW98
Meadow Cl, Barn. 27 CZ44
Meadow Cl, Bexh. 126 EZ85
Meadow Cl, Chis. 125 EP92
Meadow Cl, Enf. 31 DY38
Meadow Cl, Esher 137 CF104
Meadow Cl, Houns. 116 CA86
Meadow Cl, Nthlt. 78 CA68
Meadow Cl, Pur. 159 DK113
Meadow Cl, Rich. 118 CL88
Meadow Cl, Ruis. 59 BT58
Meadow Cl (Bricket Wd), St.Alb. 8 CA29
Meadow Cl (London Colney), St.Alb. 9 CK27
Meadow Cl, Sev. 190 FG123
Meadow Cl, Sutt. 140 DB103
Aultone Way
Meadow Cl, Walt. 154 BZ105
Meadow Cl, Wind. 112 AV86
Meadow Ct, Epsom 156 CQ113
Meadow Ct, Stai. 113 BE90
Moor La
Meadow Dr N10 65 DH55
Meadow Dr NW4 43 CW54
Meadow Dr, Amer. 20 AS37
Meadow Dr, Wok. 167 BF123
Meadow Gdns, Edg. 42 CP51
Meadow Gdns, Stai. 113 BD92
Meadow Garth NW10 80 CQ65
Meadow Hill, Couls. 159 DJ113
Meadow Hill, N.Mal. 138 CS100
Meadow Hill, Pur. 159 DJ113
Meadow La, Lthd. 170 CC121
Meadow Ms SW8 101 DM79
Meadow Pl SW8 101 DL80
Meadow Pl W4 98 CS80
Edensor Rd
Meadow Ri, Couls. 159 DK113
Meadow Rd SW8 101 DM79
Meadow Rd SW19 120 DC94
Meadow Rd, Ashf. 115 BR92
Meadow Rd, Ash. 172 CL117
Meadow Rd, Bark. 87 ET66
Meadow Rd, Borwd. 26 CP40
Meadow Rd, Brom. 144 EE95
Meadow Rd, Bushey 24 CB43
Meadow Rd, Dag. 88 EZ65
Meadow Rd, Epp. 18 EU29
Meadow Rd, Esher 155 CE107
Meadow Rd, Felt. 116 BY89
Meadow Rd, Grav. 131 GG89
Meadow Rd, Loug. 32 EL43
Meadow Rd, Pnr. 60 BX56
Meadow Rd, Rom. 71 FC60
Meadow Rd, Slou. 92 AY77
Meadow Rd, Sthl. 78 BZ73
Meadow Rd, Sutt. 158 DE106
Meadow Rd, Vir.W. 132 AS99
Meadow Rd, Wat. 7 BU34
Meadow Row SE1 201 H7
Meadow Row SE1 102 DQ76
Meadow Stile, Croy. 142 DQ104
High St
Meadow Vw, Ch.St.G. 36 AU48
Meadow Vw, Har. 61 CE60
Meadow Vw, Sid. 126 EV87
Meadow Vw, Stai. 113 BF85
Meadow Vw Rd, Hayes 77 BQ70
Meadow Vw Rd, Th.Hth. 141 DP99
Meadow Wk E18 68 EG56
Meadow Wk, Dag. 88 EZ65
Meadow Wk, Dart. 128 FJ91
Meadow Wk, Epsom 156 CS107
Meadow Wk, Tad. 173 CV124
Meadow Wk, Wall. 141 DH104
Meadow Way NW9 62 CR57
Meadow Way, Abb.L. 7 BT27
Meadow Way, Add. 152 BH105
Meadow Way, Chess. 156 CL106
Meadow Way, Chig. 49 EQ48
Meadow Way, Dart. 128 FQ87
Meadow Way, Kings L. 6 BN30
Meadow Way (Great Bookham), Lthd. 170 CB123
Meadow Way, Orp. 145 EN104
Meadow Way, Pot.B. 12 DA34
Meadow Way, Rick. 38 BJ45
Meadow Way, Ruis. 59 BV58
Meadow Way, Tad. 173 CY118
Meadow Way, Upmin. 72 FQ62
Meadow Way, Wem. 61 CK63
Meadow Way, Wind. 112 AV86
Meadow Way, The, Har. 41 CE53
Meadow Waye, Houns. 96 BY79
Meadowbank NW3 82 DF66
Meadowbank SE3 104 EF83
Meadowbank, Kings L. 6 BN30
Meadowbank, Surb. 138 CM100
Meadowbank, Wat. 40 BW45
Meadowbank Cl SW6 99 CW80
Meadowbank Cl, Barn. 27 CT43
Meadowbank Gdns, Houns. 95 BU82
Meadowbank Rd NW9 62 CR59
Meadowbanks, Barn. 27 CU43
Barnet Rd
Meadowbrook, Oxt. 187 EC130
Meadowbrook Cl, Slou. 93 BF82
Meadowcourt Rd SE3 104 EF84
Meadowcroft, Brom. 145 EM97
Meadowcroft, Bushey 24 CB44
Meadowcroft (Chalfont St. Peter), Ger.Cr. 36 AX54
Meadowcroft Rd N13 45 DN47
Meadowcross, Wal.Abb. 16 EE34
Meadowlands, Cob. 153 BU113
Meadowlands, Horn. 72 FL59
Meadowlands, Oxt. 188 EG134
Meadowlands Pk, Add. 134 BL104
Meadowlea Cl, West Dr. 94 BK79
Meadows, The, Amer. 20 AS39
Meadows, The, Orp. 164 EW107
Meadows, The, Sev. 164 EZ113
Meadows, The, Warl. 177 DX117
Meadows Cl E10 67 EA61
Meadows End, Sun. 135 BU95
Meadows Leigh Cl, Wey. 135 BQ104
Meadowside SE9 104 EJ84
Meadowside, Beac. 36 AT52
Meadowside, Dart. 128 FK88
Meadowside, Lthd. 170 CA123
Meadowside, Walt. 136 BW103
Meadowside Rd, Sutt. 157 CY109
Meadowside Rd, Upmin. 72 FQ64
Meadowsweet Cl E16 86 EK71
Monarch Dr
Meadowview, Orp. 146 EW97
Meadowview Rd SE6 123 DZ92
Meadowview Rd, Bex. 126 EY86
Meadowview Rd, Epsom 156 CS109
Meads, The, Edg. 42 CR51
Meads, The, St.Alb. 8 BZ29
Meads, The, Sutt. 139 CY104
Meads, The, Upmin. 73 FS61
Meads, The, Uxb. 76 BL70
Meads La, Ilf. 69 ES59
Meads Rd N22 45 DP54
Meads Rd, Enf. 31 DY39
Meadsway, Brwd. 53 FV51
Meadvale Rd W5 79 CH70
Meadvale Rd, Croy. 142 DT101
Meadway N14 45 DK47
Meadway NW11 64 DB58
Meadway SW20 139 CW98
Meadway, Ashf. 114 BN91
Meadway, Barn. 28 DA42
Meadway, Beck. 143 EC95
Meadway, Enf. 30 DW36
Meadway, Epsom 156 CQ112
Meadway, Esher 154 CB109
Meadway, Grays 110 GD77
Meadway, Ilf. 69 ES63
Meadway (Oxshott), Lthd. 155 CD114
Meadway, Rom. 51 FG54
Meadway, Ruis. 59 BR58
Meadway, Sev. 164 EZ113
Meadway, Stai. 114 BG94
Meadway, Surb. 138 CQ102
Meadway, Twick. 117 CD88
Meadway, Warl. 176 DW115
Meadway, Wdf.Grn. 48 EJ50
Meadway, The SE3 103 ED82
Heath La
Meadway, The, Buck.H. 48 EK46
Meadway, The, Loug. 33 EM44
Meadway, The, Orp. 164 EV106
Meadway, The (Cuffley), Pot.B. 13 DM28
Meadway, The, Sev. 190 FF122
Meadway Cl NW11 64 DB58
Meadway Cl, Barn. 28 DA42
Meadway Cl, Pnr. 40 CB51
Highbanks Rd
Meadway Cl, Stai. 113 BF94
Meadway Ct NW11 64 DB58
Meadway Dr, Add. 152 BJ108
Meadway Dr, Wok. 166 AW116
Meadway Gdns, Ruis. 59 BR58
Meadway Gate NW11 64 DA58
Meadway Pk, Ger.Cr. 56 AX60
Meaford Way SE20 122 DV94
Meakin Est SE1 201 M6
Meakin Est SE1 102 DS76
Meanley Rd E12 68 EL63
Meard St W1 195 M9
Meard St W1 83 DK72
Meare Cl, Tad. 173 CW123
Meath Cl, Orp. 146 EV99
Meath Rd E15 86 EF68
Meath Rd, Ilf. 69 EQ62
Meath St SW11 101 DH81
Mechanics Path SE8 103 EA80
Deptford High St
Mecklenburgh Pl WC1 196 B4
Mecklenburgh Pl WC1 83 DM70
Mecklenburgh Sq WC1 196 B4
Mecklenburgh Sq WC1 83 DM70
Mecklenburgh St WC1 196 B4
Medburn St NW1 83 DK68
Medbury Rd, Grav. 131 GM88
Medcalf Rd, Enf. 31 DZ37
Medcroft Gdns SW14 98 CQ84
Mede Cl, Stai. 112 AX88
Mede Fld, Lthd. 171 CD124
Medebourne Cl SE3 104 EG83
Medesenge Way N13 45 DP51
Medfield St SW15 119 CV87
Medhurst Cl E3 85 DY68
Arbery Rd
Medhurst Cl, Wok. 150 AT109
Medhurst Cres, Grav. 131 GM89
Medhurst Gdns, Grav. 131 GM90
Medhurst Rd E3 85 DY68
Arbery Rd
Median Rd E5 66 DW64
Medick Ct, Grays 110 GE79
Medina Av, Esher 137 CE104
Medina Gro N7 65 DN62
Medina Rd
Medina Rd N7 65 DN62
Medina Rd, Grays 110 GD77
Medlake Rd, Egh. 113 BC93
Medland Cl, Wall. 140 DG102
Medlar Cl, Nthlt. 78 BY68
Parkfield Av
Medlar Ct, Slou. 74 AW74
Medlar Rd, Grays 110 GD79
Medlar St SE5 102 DQ81
Medley Rd NW6 82 DA65
Medman Cl, Uxb. 76 BJ68
Chiltern Vw Rd
Medora Rd SW2 121 DM87
Medora Rd, Rom. 71 FD56
Medow Mead, Rad. 9 CF33
Medusa Rd SE6 123 EB86
Medway Bldgs E3 85 DY68
Medway Rd
Medway Cl, Croy. 142 DW100
Medway Cl, Ilf. 69 EQ64
Medway Cl, Wat. 8 BW34
Medway Dr, Grnf. 79 CF68
Medway Gdns, Wem. 61 CG63
Medway Ms E3 85 DY68
Medway Rd
Medway Par, Grnf. 79 CF68
Medway Rd E3 85 DY68
Medway Rd, Dart. 107 FG83
Medway St SW1 199 N7
Medway St SW1 101 DK76
Medwin St SW4 101 DM84
Meerbrook Rd SE3 104 EJ83
Meeson Rd E15 86 EF67
Meeson St E5 67 DY63
Meesons La, Grays 110 FZ77
Meeting Flds Path E9 84 DW65
Morning La
Meeting Ho La SE15 102 DV81
Meetinghouse All E1 202 E2
Megg La, Kings L. 6 BH29
Mehetabel Rd E9 84 DW65
Meister Cl, Ilf. 69 ER60
Melancholy Wk, Rich. 117 CJ89
Melanda Cl, Chis. 125 EM92
Melanie Cl, Bexh. 106 EY81
Melba Gdns, Til. 111 GG80
Melba Way SE13 103 EB81
Melbourne Av N13 45 DM51
Melbourne Av W13 79 CG74
Melbourne Av, Pnr. 60 CB55
Melbourne Cl, Orp. 145 ES101
Melbourne Cl, Uxb. 58 BN63
Melbourne Cl, Wall. 159 DJ106
Melbourne Rd
Melbourne Ct E5 67 DY63
Daubeney Rd
Melbourne Ct N10 45 DH52
Sydney Rd
Melbourne Ct SE20 122 DU94
Melbourne Gdns, Rom. 70 EY57
Melbourne Gro SE22 102 DS84
Melbourne Ho, Hayes 78 BW70
Melbourne Ms SE6 123 EC87
Melbourne Ms SW9 101 DN81
Melbourne Pl WC2 196 C10
Melbourne Pl WC2 83 DM72
Melbourne Rd E6 87 EM67
Melbourne Rd E10 67 EB59
Melbourne Rd E17 67 DY56
Melbourne Rd SW19 140 DA95
Melbourne Rd, Bushey 24 CB44
Melbourne Rd, Ilf. 69 EP60
Melbourne Rd, Tedd. 117 CJ93
Melbourne Rd, Til. 110 GE81
Melbourne Rd, Wall. 159 DH106
Melbourne Sq SW9 101 DN81
Melbourne Ms
Melbourne Ter SW6 100 DB80
Waterford Rd
Melbourne Way, Enf. 30 DT44
Melbury Av, Sthl. 96 CB76
Melbury Cl, Cher. 134 BG101
Melbury Cl, Chis. 125 EM93
Melbury Cl, Esher 155 CH107
Melbury Cl, W.Byf. 152 BG114
Melbury Ct W8 99 CZ76
Melbury Dr SE5 102 DS80
Sedgmoor Pl
Melbury Gdns SW20 139 CV95
Melbury Rd W14 99 CZ76
Melbury Rd, Har. 62 CM57
Melbury Ter NW1 194 C5
Melbury Ter NW1 82 DE70
Melcombe Gdns, Har. 62 CM58
Melcombe Pl NW1 194 D6
Melcombe Pl NW1 82 DF71
Melcombe St NW1 194 E5
Melcombe St NW1 82 DF70
Meldex Cl NW7 43 CW51
Meldon Cl SW6 100 DB81
Bagley's La
Meldone Cl, Surb. 138 CP100
Meldrum Cl, Orp. 146 EW100
Killewarren Way
Meldrum Cl, Oxt. 188 EF132
Meldrum Rd, Ilf. 70 EU61
Melfield Gdns SE6 123 EB91
Melford Av, Bark. 87 ES65
Melford Cl, Chess. 156 CM106
Melford Rd E6 87 EM70
Melford Rd E11 68 EE61
Melford Rd E17 67 DY56
Melford Rd SE22 122 DU87
Melford Rd, Ilf. 69 ER61
Melfort Av, Th.Hth. 141 DP97
Melfort Rd, Th.Hth. 141 DP97
Melgund Rd N5 65 DN64
Melina Cl, Hayes 77 BR71
Middleton Rd
Melina Pl NW8 82 DD69
Melina Rd W12 99 CV75
Melior Pl SE1 201 M4
Melior St SE1 201 L4
Melior St SE1 102 DR75
Meliot Rd SE6 123 ED89
Melksham Cl, Rom. 52 FM52
Melksham Dr, Rom. 52 FM52
Melksham Gdns
Melksham Gdns, Rom. 52 FL52
Melksham Grn, Rom. 52 FM52
Melksham Gdns
Mell St SE10 104 EE78
Trafalgar Rd
Meller Cl, Croy. 141 DL104
Melling Dr, Enf. 30 DU39
Melling St SE18 105 ES79
Mellish Cl, Bark. 87 ET67
Mellish Gdns, Wdf.Grn. 48 EG50
Mellish Ind Est SE18 104 EL76
Harrington Way
Mellish St E14 203 P6
Mellish St E14 103 EA76
Mellison Rd SW17 120 DE92
Mellitus St W12 81 CT72
Mellor Cl, Walt. 136 BZ101
Mellow Cl, Bans. 158 DB114
Mellow La E, Hayes 77 BQ69
Mellow La W, Uxb. 77 BQ69
Mellows Rd, Ilf. 69 EM55
Mellows Rd, Wall. 159 DK106
Mells Cres SE9 125 EM91
Melody La N5 65 DP64
Melody Rd SW18 120 DC85
Melody Rd, West. 178 EJ118
Melon Pl W8 100 DA75
Kensington Ch St
Melon Rd E11 68 EE62
Melon Rd SE15 102 DU81
Melrose Av N22 45 DP53
Melrose Av NW2 63 CW64
Melrose Av SW16 141 DM97
Melrose Av SW19 120 DA89
Melrose Av, Borwd. 26 CP43
Melrose Av, Grnf. 78 CB68
Melrose Av, Mitch. 121 DH94
Melrose Av, Pot.B. 12 DB32
Melrose Av, Twick. 116 CB87
Melrose Cl SE12 124 EG88
Melrose Cl, Grnf. 78 CB68
Melrose Cl, Hayes 77 BU71
Melrose Cres, Orp. 163 ER105
Melrose Dr, Sthl. 78 CA74
Melrose Gdns W6 99 CW76

ill La, Ch.St.G. 36 AU47
ill La, Croy. 141 DM104
ill La (Eynsford), Dart. 148 FL102
ill La, Egh. 133 BC98
ill La, Epsom 157 CT109
ill La, Ger.Cr. 57 AZ58
ill La, Grays 109 FX78
ill La, Kings L. 6 BN29
ill La, Lthd. 171 CG122
ill La (Toot Hill), Ong. 19 FE29
ill La (Downe), Orp. 163 EN110
ill La, Oxt. 188 EF132
ill La (Limpsfield Chart), Oxt. 189 EM131
ill La, Red. 185 DJ131
ill La, Rick. 23 BQ44
Watford Rd
ill La (Chadwell Heath), Rom. 70 EY58
ill La (Navestock), Rom. 35 FH40
ill La, Sev. 191 FJ121
ill La (Shoreham), Sev. 165 FF110
Mill La, Slou. 93 BB83
Mill La, Wal.Cr. 15 DY28
Mill La, W.Byf. 152 BM113
Mill La, West. 189 EQ127
Mill La, Wok. 168 BK119
Mill La, Wdf.Grn. 48 EF50
Mill La Trd Est, Croy. 141 DM104
Mill Mead, Stai. 113 BF91
Mill Mead Rd N17 66 DV55
Mill Pk Av, Horn. 72 FL61
Mill Pl E14 85 DZ72
East India Dock Rd
Mill Pl, Chis. 145 EP95
Mill Pl, Dart. 107 FG84
Mill Pl, Kings.T. 138 CM97
Mill Pl, Slou. 92 AX82
Mill Pl Caravan Pk, Slou. 92 AW82
Mill Plat, Islw. 97 CG82
Mill Plat Av, Islw. 97 CG82
Mill Pond Cl, Sev. 191 FK121
Mill Pond Rd, Dart. 128 FL86
Mill Ridge, Edg. 42 CM50
Mill Rd E16 86 EH74
Mill Rd SE13 103 EC83
Loampit Vale
Mill Rd SW19 120 DC94
Mill Rd, Cob. 170 BW115
Mill Rd, Dart. 128 FM91
Mill Rd, Epsom 157 CT112
Mill Rd, Erith 107 FC80
Mill Rd, Esher 136 CA103
Mill Rd, Grav. 130 GE87
Mill Rd, Ilf. 69 EN62
Mill Rd, Purf. 108 FP79
Mill Rd, Sev. 190 FE121
Mill Rd, S.Ock. 90 FQ73
Mill Rd, Tad. 173 CX123
Mill Rd, Twick. 116 CC89
Mill Rd, West Dr. 94 BJ76
Mill Row N1 84 DS67
Mill Shaw, Oxt. 188 EF132
Mill Shot Cl SW6 99 CW80
Mill St SE1 202 A5
Mill St SE1 102 DT75
Mill St W1 195 K10
Mill St W1 83 DJ73
Mill St, Kings.T. 138 CL97
Mill St, Slou. 74 AT74
Mill St (Colnbrook), Slou. 93 BD80
Mill St, West. 189 ER127
Mill Vale, Brom. 144 EF96
Mill Vw, St.Alb. 9 CD27
Park St
Mill Vw Cl, Epsom 157 CT108
Mill Vw Gdns, Croy. 143 DX104
Mill Way, Bushey 24 BY40
Mill Way, Felt. 115 BV85
Mill Way, Lthd. 172 CM124
Mill Way, Rick. 37 BF46
Mill Yd E1 84 DU73
Cable St
Millais Av E12 69 EN64
Millais Gdns, Edg. 42 CN54
Millais Pl, Til. 111 GG80
Millais Rd E11 67 EC63
Millais Rd, Enf. 30 DT43
Millais Rd, N.Mal. 138 CS100
Millais Way, Epsom 156 CQ105
Millan Cl, Add. 152 BH110
Milland Ct, Borwd. 26 CR39
Millard Cl N16 66 DS64
Boleyn Rd
Millard Ter, Dag. 88 FA65
Church Elm La
Millbank SW1 199 P7
Millbank SW1 101 DL76
Millbank, Stai. 114 BH92
Millbank Twr SW1 199 P9
Millbank Twr SW1 101 DL77
Millbank Way SE12 124 EG85
Millbourne Rd, Felt. 116 BY91
Millbro, Swan. 127 FG94
Millbrook, Wey. 153 BS105
Millbrook Av, Well. 105 ER84
Millbrook Gdns, Rom. 51 FE54
Millbrook Gdns (Chadwell Heath), Rom. 70 EZ58
Millbrook Pl NW1 83 DJ68
Hampstead Rd
Millbrook Rd N9 46 DV46
Millbrook Rd SW9 101 DP83
Millbrook Rd, Bushey 24 BZ39
Millbrook Way, Slou. 93 BE82
Millcrest Rd (Cheshunt), Wal.Cr. 13 DP28
Millender Wk SE16 202 G9
Millender Wk SE16 102 DW77
Millennium Cl E16 86 EG72
Russell Rd
Millennium Cl, Uxb. 76 BJ67
Waterloo Rd
Millennium Dr E14 204 F8
Millennium Dr E14 103 ED77
Millennium Mile SE1 200 B3
Millennium Mile SE1 83 DP73
Millennium Pl E2 84 DV68
Millennium Pt E14 103 EA75
Millennium Sq SE1 202 A4
Millennium Way SE10 205 H4
Millennium Way SE10 104 EE75
Miller Cl, Mitch. 140 DF101
Miller Cl, Pnr. 40 BW54
Miller Pl, Ger.Cr. 56 AX57
Miller Rd SW19 120 DD93
Miller Rd, Croy. 141 DM102
Miller St NW1 83 DJ68
Miller Wk SE1 200 E3
Miller Wk SE1 83 DN74
Miller's Av E8 66 DT64
Millers Cl NW7 43 CU49
Millers Cl, Chig. 50 EV47
Millers Cl, Rick. 21 BE41
Millers Cl, Stai. 114 BH92
Millers Copse, Epsom 172 CR119
Millers Ct W4 99 CT78
Chiswick Mall
Millers Grn Cl, Enf. 29 DP41
Miller's La, Chig. 50 EV46
Millers La, Wind. 112 AT86
Millers Meadow Cl SE3 124 EF85
Meadowcourt Rd
Miller's Ter E8 66 DT64
Millers Way W6 99 CW75
Millet Rd, Grnf. 78 CB69
Millfield, Sun. 135 BR95
Millfield Av E17 47 DY53
Millfield Dr, Grav. 130 GE89
Millfield La N6 64 DF61
Millfield La, Tad. 183 CZ125
Millfield Pl N6 64 DG61
Millfield Rd, Edg. 42 CQ54
Millfield Rd, Houns. 116 BY88
Millfields Cl, Orp. 146 EV97
Millfields Cotts, Orp. 146 EV98
Millfields Cl
Millfields Est E5 67 DX62
Denton Way
Millfields Rd E5 66 DW63
Millford, Wok. 166 AV117
Millgrove St SW11 100 DG82
Millharbour E14 204 B5
Millharbour E14 103 EB76
Millhaven Cl, Rom. 70 EV58
Millhedge Cl, Cob. 170 BY116
Millhoo Ct, Wal.Abb. 16 EF34
Millhouse La, Abb.L. 7 BT27
Millhouse Pl SE27 121 DP91
Millicent Rd E10 67 DZ60
Milligan St E14 203 N1
Milligan St E14 85 DZ73
Milliners Ct, Loug. 33 EN40
The Cft
Milling Rd, Edg. 42 CR52
Millington Rd, Hayes 95 BS76
Millman Ms WC1 196 B5
Millman Ms WC1 83 DM70
Millman Pl WC1 83 DM70
Millman St
Millman St WC1 196 B5
Millman St WC1 83 DM70
Millmark Gro SE14 103 DY82
Millmarsh La, Enf. 31 DZ40
Millmead, W.Byf. 152 BM112
Millpond Ct, Add. 152 BL106
Millpond Est SE16 202 D5
Mills Cl, Uxb. 76 BN68
Mills Ct EC2 197 N3
Mills Gro E14 85 EC71
Dewberry St
Mills Gro NW4 63 CX55
Mills Rd, Walt. 154 BW106
Mills Row W4 98 CR77
Mills Spur, Wind. 112 AV87
Mills Way, Brwd. 55 GC46
Millside, Cars. 140 DF103
Millside Ct, Iver 94 BH75
Millside Ind Est, Dart. 108 FK84
Millside Pl, Islw. 97 CH82
Millsmead Way, Loug. 33 EM40
Millson Cl N20 44 DD47
Millstead Cl, Tad. 173 CV122
Millstone Cl (South Darenth), Dart. 148 FQ96
Millstone Ms, Dart. 148 FQ95
Millstream Cl N13 45 DN50
Millstream Rd SE1 201 P5
Millstream Rd SE1 102 DT75
Millthorne Cl, Rick. 22 BM43
Millview Cl, Reig. 184 DD132
Millwall Dock Rd E14 203 P6
Millwall Dock Rd E14 103 EA76
Millway NW7 42 CS50
Millway, Reig. 184 DD134
Millway Gdns, Nthlt. 78 BZ65
Millwell Cres, Chig. 49 ER50
Millwood Rd, Houns. 116 CC85
Millwood Rd, Orp. 146 EW97
Millwood St W10 81 CY71
St. Charles Sq
Milman Cl, Pnr. 60 BX55
Milman Rd NW6 81 CY68
Milman's St SW10 100 DD79
Milmead Ind Cen N17 46 DV54
Milne Feild, Pnr. 40 CA52
Milne Gdns SE9 124 EL85
Milne Pk E, Croy. 161 ED111
Milne Pk W, Croy. 161 ED111
Milne Way (Harefield), Uxb. 38 BH53
Milner App, Cat. 176 DU121
Milner Cl, Cat. 176 DT121
Milner Cl, Wat. 7 BV34
Milner Ct, Bushey 24 CB44
Milner Dr, Cob. 154 BZ112
Milner Dr, Twick. 117 CD87
Milner Pl N1 83 DN67
Milner Pl, Cars. 158 DG105
High St
Milner Rd E15 86 EE69
Milner Rd SW19 140 DB95
Milner Rd, Cat. 176 DU122
Milner Rd, Dag. 70 EW61
Milner Rd, Kings.T. 137 CK97
Milner Rd, Mord. 140 DD99
Milner Rd, Th.Hth. 142 DR97
Milner Sq N1 83 DP66
Milner St SW3 198 D8
Milner St SW3 100 DF77
Milner Wk SE9 125 ER88
Milnthorpe Rd W4 98 CR79
Milo Rd SE22 122 DT86
Milroy Av, Grav. 130 GE89
Milroy Wk SE1 200 F2
Milson Rd W14 99 CY76
Milton Av E6 86 EK66
Milton Av N6 65 DJ59
Milton Av NW9 62 CQ55
Milton Av NW10 80 CQ67
Milton Av, Barn. 27 CZ43
Milton Av, Croy. 142 DR101
Milton Av (Chalfont St. Peter), Ger.Cr. 56 AX56
Milton Av, Grav. 131 GJ88
Milton Av, Horn. 71 FF61
Milton Av, Sev. 165 FB110
Milton Av, Sutt. 140 DD104
Milton Cl N2 64 DC57
Milton Cl SE1 201 P9
Milton Cl SE1 102 DT77
Milton Cl, Hayes 77 BU72
Milton Cl, Slou. 93 BA83
Milton Cl, Sutt. 140 DD104
Milton Ct EC2 197 K6
Milton Ct, Uxb. 59 BP62
Milton Ct, Wal.Abb. 15 EC34
Milton Ct Rd SE14 103 DY79
Milton Cres, Ilf. 69 EQ59
Milton Dr, Borwd. 26 CP43
Milton Dr, Shep. 134 BL98
Milton Flds, Ch.St.G. 36 AV48
Milton Gdn Est N16 66 DS63
Milton Gro
Milton Gdns, Epsom 156 CS114
Milton Gdns, Stai. 114 BM88
Chesterton Dr
Milton Gdns, Til. 111 GH81
Milton Gro N11 45 DJ50
Milton Gro N16 66 DR63
Milton Hall Rd, Grav. 131 GK88
Milton Hill, Ch.St.G. 36 AV48
Milton Pk N6 65 DJ59
Milton Pl N7 65 DN64
George's Rd
Milton Pl, Grav. 131 GJ86
Milton Rd E17 67 EA56
Milton Rd N6 65 DJ59
Milton Rd N15 65 DP56
Milton Rd NW7 43 CU50
Milton Rd NW9 63 CU59
West Hendon Bdy
Milton Rd SE24 121 DP86
Milton Rd SW14 98 CR83
Milton Rd SW19 120 DC93
Milton Rd W3 80 CR74
Milton Rd W7 79 CF73
Milton Rd, Add. 152 BG107
Milton Rd, Belv. 106 FA77
Milton Rd, Brwd. 54 FV49
Milton Rd, Cat. 176 DR121
Milton Rd, Croy. 142 DR102
Milton Rd, Egh. 113 AZ92
Milton Rd, Grav. 131 GJ86
Milton Rd, Grays 110 GB78
Milton Rd, Hmptn. 116 CA94
Milton Rd, Har. 61 CE56
Milton Rd, Mitch. 120 DG94
Milton Rd, Rom. 71 FG58
Milton Rd, Sev. 190 FE121
Milton Rd, Sutt. 140 DA104
Milton Rd, Swans. 130 FY86
Milton Rd, Uxb. 59 BP63
Milton Rd, Wall. 159 DJ107
Milton Rd, Walt. 136 BX104
Milton Rd, Well. 105 ET81
Milton St EC2 197 K6
Milton St EC2 84 DR71
Milton St, Swans. 129 FX86
Milton St, Wal.Abb. 15 EC34
Milton St, Wat. 23 BV38
Milton Way, West Dr. 94 BM77
Milverton Dr, Uxb. 59 BQ63
Milverton Gdns, Ilf. 69 ET61
Milverton Rd NW6 81 CW66
Milverton St SE11 101 DN78
Milverton Way SE9 125 EN91
Milward St E1 84 DV71
Stepney Way
Milward Wk SE18 105 EN79
Spearman St
Mimms Hall Rd, Pot.B. 11 CX31
Mimms La, Pot.B. 10 CQ33
Mimms La, Rad. 10 CN33
Mimosa Cl, Brwd. 54 FV43
Mimosa Cl, Orp. 146 EW104
Berrylands
Mimosa Cl, Rom. 52 FJ52
Mimosa Rd, Hayes 78 BW71
Mimosa St SW6 99 CZ81
Mina Av, Slou. 92 AX75
Mina Rd SE17 102 DS78
Mina Rd SW19 140 DA95
Minard Rd SE6 124 EE87
Minchenden Cres N14 45 DJ48
Minchin Cl, Lthd. 171 CG122
Mincing La EC3 197 M10
Mincing La EC3 84 DS73
Mincing La, Wok. 150 AT108
Minden Rd SE20 142 DV95
Minden Rd, Sutt. 139 CZ103
Minehead Rd SW16 121 DM92
Minehead Rd, Har. 60 CA62
Minera Ms SW1 198 G8
Minera Ms SW1 100 DG77
Mineral St SE18 105 ES77
Minerva Cl SW9 101 DN80
Minerva Cl, Sid. 125 ES90
Minerva Dr, Wat. 23 BS36
Minerva Rd E4 47 EB52
Minerva Rd NW10 80 CQ69
Minerva Rd, Kings.T. 138 CM96
Minerva St E2 84 DV68
Minet Av NW10 80 CS68
Minet Dr, Hayes 77 BU74
Minet Gdns NW10 80 CS68
Minet Gdns, Hayes 77 BU74
Minet Rd SW9 101 DP82
Minford Gdns W14 99 CX75
Ming St E14 85 EA73
Mingard Wk N7 65 DM61
Hornsey Rd
Ministry Way SE9 125 EM89
Miniver Pl EC4 84 DQ73
Garlick Hill
Mink Ct, Houns. 96 BW83
Minniedale, Surb. 138 CM99
Minnow St SE17 102 DS77
East St
Minnow Wk SE17 201 N9
Minorca Rd, Wey. 152 BN105
Minories EC3 197 P10
Minories EC3 84 DT72
Minshull Pl, Beck. 123 EA94
Minshull St SW8 101 DK81
Wandsworth Rd
Minson Rd E9 85 DX67
Minstead Gdns SW15 119 CT87
Minstead Way, N.Mal. 138 CS100
Minster Av, Sutt. 140 DA103
Leafield Rd
Minster Ct EC3 84 DR73
Mincing La
Minster Ct, Horn. 72 FN61
Minster Ct, St.Alb. 9 CE28
Minster Dr, Croy. 160 DS105
Minster Gdns, W.Mol. 136 BZ99
Molesey Av
Minster Pavement EC3 84 DR73
Mincing La
Minster Rd NW2 63 CY64
Minster Rd, Brom. 124 EH94
Minster Wk N8 65 DL56
Lightfoot Rd
Minster Way, Horn. 72 FM60
Minster Way, Slou. 93 AZ75
Minsterley Av, Shep. 135 BS98
Minstrel Gdns, Surb. 138 CM98
Mint Business Pk E16 86 EG71
Butchers Rd
Mint Cl, Uxb. 77 BP69
Mint La, Tad. 184 DA129
Mint Rd, Bans. 174 DC116
Mint Rd, Wall. 159 DH105
Mint St SE1 201 H4
Mint Wk, Croy. 142 DQ104
High St
Mint Wk, Warl. 177 DX118
Mint Wk, Wok. 166 AS117
Mintern Cl N13 45 DP48
Mintern St N1 84 DR68
Minterne Av, Sthl. 96 CA77
Minterne Rd, Har. 62 CM57
Minterne Waye, Hayes 78 BW72
Minton Ms NW6 82 DB65
Lymington Rd
Mirabel Rd SW6 99 CZ80
Mirador Cres, Slou. 74 AV73
Miramar Way, Horn. 72 FK64
Miranda Cl E1 84 DW71
Sidney St
Miranda Ct W3 80 CM72
Queens Dr
Miranda Rd N19 65 DJ60
Mirfield St SE7 104 EK77
Miriam Rd SE18 105 ES78
Mirravale Trd Est, Dag. 70 EZ59
Mirren Cl, Har. 60 BZ63
Mirrie La (Denham), Uxb. 57 BC57
Mirror Path SE9 124 EJ90
Lambscroft Av
Misbourne Av (Chalfont St. Peter), Ger.Cr. 36 AY50
Misbourne Cl (Chalfont St. Peter), Ger.Cr. 36 AY50
Misbourne Ct, Slou. 93 BA77
High St
Misbourne Meadows, Uxb. 57 BC60
Misbourne Rd, Uxb. 76 BN67
Misbourne Vale (Chalfont St. Peter), Ger.Cr. 36 AX50
Miskin Rd, Dart. 128 FJ87
Miskin Way, Grav. 131 GK93
Missenden Cl, Felt. 115 BT88
Missenden Gdns, Mord. 140 DC100
Mission Gro E17 67 DY57
Mission Pl SE15 102 DU81
Mission Sq, Brent. 98 CL79
Mistletoe Cl, Croy. 143 DX102
Marigold Way
Misty's Fld, Walt. 136 BW102
Mitali Pas E1 84 DU72
Back Ch La
Mitcham Gdn Village, Mitch. 140 DG99
Mitcham Ind Est, Mitch. 140 DG95
Mitcham La SW16 121 DJ93
Mitcham Pk, Mitch. 140 DF98
Mitcham Rd E6 86 EL69
Mitcham Rd SW17 120 DF92
Mitcham Rd, Croy. 141 DL100
Mitcham Rd, Ilf. 69 ET59
Mitchell Av, Grav. 130 GD89
Mitchell Cl SE2 106 EW77
Mitchell Cl, Abb.L. 7 BU32
Mitchell Cl, Belv. 107 FC76
Mitchell Cl, Dart. 128 FL89
Mitchell Cl, Hem.H. 5 AZ27
Mitchell Cl, Rain. 90 FJ68
Mitchell Rd N13 45 DP50
Mitchell Rd, Orp. 163 ET105
Mitchell St EC1 197 H4
Mitchell St EC1 84 DQ70
Mitchell Wk E6 86 EL71
Mitchell Wk, Amer. 20 AS38
Mitchell Wk, Swans. 130 FY87
Mitchell Way NW10 80 CQ65
Mitchell Way, Brom. 144 EG95
Mitchellbrook Way NW10 80 CR65
Mitchell's Pl SE21 122 DS87
Dulwich Village
Mitchison Rd N1 84 DR65
Mitchley Av, Pur. 160 DQ113
Mitchley Av, S.Croy. 160 DQ113
Mitchley Gro, S.Croy. 160 DU113
Mitchley Hill, S.Croy. 160 DT113
Mitchley Rd N17 66 DU55
Mitchley Vw, S.Croy. 160 DU113
Mitford Cl, Chess. 155 CJ107
Merritt Gdns
Mitford Rd N19 65 DL61
Mitre, The E14 85 DZ73
Three Colt St
Mitre Av E17 67 DZ55
Greenleaf Rd
Mitre Cl, Brom. 144 EF96
Beckenham La
Mitre Cl, Shep. 135 BR100
Gordon Dr
Mitre Cl, Sutt. 158 DC108
Mitre Ct EC2 197 J8
Mitre Ct EC4 196 E9
Mitre Rd E15 86 EE68
Mitre Rd SE1 200 E4
Mitre Rd SE1 101 DN75
Mitre Sq EC3 197 N9
Mitre St EC3 197 N9
Mitre St EC3 84 DS72
Mitre Way W10 81 CV70
Mixbury Gro, Wey. 153 BR107
Mixnams La, Cher. 134 BG97
Mizen Cl, Cob. 154 BX114
Mizen Way, Cob. 170 BW115
Moat, The, N.Mal. 138 CS95
Moat, The, Ong. 19 FF29
Moat Cl, Bushey 24 CB43
Moat Cl, Orp. 163 ET107
Moat Cl, Sev. 190 FB123
Moat Ct, Ash. 172 CL117
Moat Cres N3 64 DB55
Moat Cft, Well. 106 EW83
Moat Dr E13 86 EJ68
Boundary Rd
Moat Dr, Har. 60 CC56
Moat Dr, Ruis. 59 BS59
Moat Dr, Slou. 74 AW71
Moat Fm Rd, Nthlt. 78 BZ65
Moat La, Erith 107 FG81
Moat Pl SW9 101 DM83
Moat Pl W3 80 CP72
Moat Pl (Denham), Uxb. 58 BH63
Moated Fm Dr, Add. 152 BJ108
Moatfield Rd, Bushey 24 CB43
Moatside, Enf. 31 DX42
Moatside, Felt. 116 BW91
Moatview Ct, Bushey 24 CB43
Moberley Rd SW4 121 DK87
Modbury Gdns NW5 82 DG65
Queens Cres
Modder Pl SW15 99 CX84
Model Cotts SW14 98 CQ84
Upper Richmond Rd W
Model Fm Cl SE9 124 EL90
Modling Ho E2 85 DX68
Moelwyn Hughes Ct N7 65 DK64
Hilldrop Cres
Moelyn Ms, Har. 61 CG57
Moffat Rd N13 45 DL51
Moffat Rd SW17 120 DE91
Moffat Rd, Th.Hth. 142 DQ96
Moffats Cl, Hat. 12 DA26
Moffats La, Hat. 11 CZ26
Mogador Cotts, Tad. 183 CX128
Mogador Rd
Mogador Rd, Tad. 183 CX128
Mogden La, Islw. 117 CE85
Mohmmad Khan Rd E11 68 EF60
Harvey Rd
Moir Cl, S.Croy. 160 DU109
Moira Cl N17 46 DS54
Moira Rd SE9 105 EM84
Moland Mead SE16 203 H10
Molash Rd, Orp. 146 EX98
Molasses Row SW11 100 DC83
Cinnamon Row
Mole Abbey Gdns, W.Mol. 136 CA97
New Rd
Mole Business Pk, Lthd. 171 CG121
Mole Ct, Epsom 156 CQ105
Mole Rd, Lthd. 171 CD121
Mole Rd, Walt. 154 BX106
Mole Valley Pl, Ash. 171 CK119
Molember Ct, E.Mol. 137 CE99
Molember Rd, E.Mol. 137 CE99
Moles Hill, Lthd. 155 CD111
Molescroft SE9 125 EQ90
Molesey Av, W.Mol. 136 BZ98
Molesey Cl, Walt. 154 BY105
Molesey Dr, Sutt. 139 CY103
Molesey Pk Av, W.Mol. 136 CB99
Molesey Pk Cl, E.Mol. 136 CC99
Molesey Pk Rd, E.Mol. 137 CD99
Molesey Pk Rd, W.Mol. 136 CB99
Molesey Rd, Walt. 154 BX106
Molesey Rd, W.Mol. 136 BY99
Molesford Rd SW6 100 DA81
Molesham Cl, W.Mol. 136 CB97
Molesham Way, W.Mol. 136 CB97
Molesworth Rd, Cob. 153 BU113
Molesworth St SE13 103 EC83
Molineaux Pl, Tedd. 117 CG92
Mollands La, S.Ock. 91 FW70
Mollison Av, Enf. 31 DY40
Mollison Dr, Wall. 159 DL107
Mollison Ri, Grav. 131 GL92
Mollison Way, Edg. 42 CN54
Molloy Ct, Wok. 167 BA116
Courtenay Rd
Molly Huggins Cl SW12 121 DJ87
Molteno Rd, Wat. 23 BU39
Molyneaux Av, Hem.H. 5 AZ27
Molyneux Dr SW17 121 DH91
Molyneux Rd, Wey. 152 BN106
Molyneux St W1 194 C7
Molyneux St W1 82 DE71
Mona Rd SE15 102 DW82
Mona St E16 86 EF71
Monahan Av, Pur. 159 DM112
Monarch Cl, Felt. 115 BS87
Monarch Cl, Til. 111 GH82
Monarch Cl, W.Wick. 162 EF105
Monarch Dr E16 86 EK71
Monarch Ms E17 67 EB57
Monarch Ms SW16 121 DN92
Monarch Pl, Buck.H. 48 EJ47
Monarch Rd, Belv. 106 FA76
Monarchs Way, Ruis. 59 BR60
Monarchs Way, Wal.Cr. 15 DY34
Monastery Gdns, Enf. 30 DR40
Monaveen Gdns, W.Mol. 136 CA97
Monck St SW1 199 N7
Monck St SW1 101 DK76
Monclar Rd SE5 102 DR84

Moncorvo Cl SW7 198 B5
Moncrieff Cl E6 86 EL72
Linton Gdns
Moncrieff Pl SE15 102 DU82
Rye La
Moncrieff St SE15 102 DU82
Mondial Way, Hayes 95 BQ80
Monega Rd E7 86 EJ65
Monega Rd E12 86 EK65
Money Av, Cat. 176 DR122
Money Hill Rd, Rick. 38 BJ46
Money La, West Dr. 94 BK76
Money Rd, Cat. 176 DR122
Moneyhill Par, Rick. 38 BH46
Uxbridge Rd
Mongers La, Epsom 157 CT110
Monica Cl, Wat. 24 BW40
Monier Rd E3 85 EA66
Monivea Rd, Beck. 123 DZ94
Monk Dr E16 86 EG72
Monk Pas E16 86 EG73
Monk Dr
Monk St SE18 105 EN77
Monkchester Cl, Loug. 33 EN39
Monkfrith Av N14 29 DH44
Monkfrith Cl N14 45 DH45
Monkfrith Way N14 44 DG45
Monkhams Av, Wdf.Grn. 48 EG50
Monkhams Dr, Wdf.Grn. 48 EH49
Monkhams La, Buck.H. 48 EH48
Monkhams La, Wdf.Grn. 48 EG50
Monkleigh Rd, Mord. 139 CY97
Monks Av, Barn. 28 DC44
Monks Av, W.Mol. 136 BZ99
Monks Chase, Brwd. 55 GC50
Monks Cl SE2 106 EX77
Monks Cl, Enf. 30 DQ40
Monks Cl, Har. 60 CB61
Monks Cl, Ruis. 60 BX63
Monks Cres, Add. 152 BH106
Monks Cres, Walt. 135 BV102
Monks Dr W3 80 CN71
Monks Grn, Lthd. 170 CC121
Monks Orchard, Dart. 128 FJ89
Monks Orchard Rd, Beck. 143 EA102
Monks Pk, Wem. 80 CQ65
Monks Pk Gdns, Wem. 80 CP65
Monks Pl, Cat. 176 DU122
Tillingdown Hill
Monks Rd, Bans. 174 DA116
Monks Rd, Enf. 30 DQ40
Monks Rd, Vir.W. 132 AX98
Monks Wk, Cher. 133 BE98
Monks Wk, Grav. 130 GA93
Monk's Wk, Reig. 184 DB134
Monks Way NW11 63 CZ56
Hurstwood Rd
Monks Way, Beck. 143 EA99
Monks Way, Orp. 145 EQ102
Monks Way, Stai. 114 BK94
Monks Way, West Dr. 94 BL79
Harmondsworth La
Monksdene Gdns, Sutt. 140 DB104
Monksgrove, Loug. 33 EN43
Monksmead, Borwd. 26 CQ42
Monkswell Ct N10 44 DG53
Pembroke Rd
Monkswell La, Couls. 174 DB124
Monkswood Av, Wal.Abb. 15 ED33
Monkswood Gdns, Borwd. 26 CR42
Monkswood Gdns, Ilf. 69 EN55
Monkton Rd, Well. 105 ET82
Monkton St SE11 200 E8
Monkton St SE11 101 DN77
Monkville Av NW11 63 CZ56
Monkwell Sq EC2 197 J7
Monkwood Cl, Rom. 71 FG57
Monmouth Av E18 68 EH55
Monmouth Av, Kings.T. 117 CJ94
Monmouth Cl W4 98 CR76
Beaumont Rd
Monmouth Cl, Mitch. 141 DL98
Recreation Way
Monmouth Cl, Well. 106 EU84
Monmouth Gro, Brent. 98 CL77
Sterling Pl
Monmouth Pl W2 82 DA72
Monmouth Rd
Monmouth Rd E6 87 EM69
Monmouth Rd N9 46 DV47
Monmouth Rd W2 82 DB72
Monmouth Rd, Dag. 70 EZ64
Monmouth Rd, Hayes 95 BS77
Monmouth Rd, Wat. 23 BV41
Monmouth St WC2 195 P9
Monmouth St WC2 83 DL73
Monnery Rd N19 65 DJ62
Monnow Grn, S.Ock. 90 FQ73
Monnow Rd
Monnow Rd SE1 202 B9
Monnow Rd SE1 102 DU77
Monnow Rd, S.Ock. 90 FQ73
Mono La, Felt. 115 BV89
Monoux Gro E17 47 EA53
Monro Gdns, Har. 41 CE52
Monroe Cres, Enf. 30 DV39
Monroe Dr SW14 118 CP85
Mons Wk, Egh. 113 BC92
Mons Way, Brom. 144 EL100
Monsal Ct E5 67 DX63
Redwald Rd
Monsell Gdns, Stai. 113 BE92
Monsell Rd N4 65 DP62
Monson Rd NW10 81 CU68
Monson Rd SE14 103 DX80
Monson Rd, Red. 184 DF130
Montacute Rd SE6 123 DZ87
Montacute Rd, Bushey 41 CE45
Montacute Rd, Croy. 161 EC109
Montacute Rd, Mord. 140 DD100
Montagu Cres N18 46 DV49
Montagu Gdns N18 46 DV49
Montagu Gdns, Wall. 159 DJ105
Montagu Mans W1 194 E6
Montagu Ms N W1 194 E7
Montagu Ms N W1 82 DF71
Montagu Ms S W1 194 E8
Montagu Ms W W1 194 E8
Montagu Pl W1 194 D7
Montagu Pl W1 82 DF71
Montagu Rd N9 46 DW48
Montagu Rd N18 46 DV50
Montagu Rd NW4 63 CU58
Montagu Rd Ind Est N18 46 DW49
Montagu Row W1 194 E7
Montagu Sq W1 194 E7
Montagu Sq W1 82 DF71
Montagu St W1 194 E8
Montagu St W1 82 DF72
Montague Av SE4 103 DZ84
Montague Av W7 79 CF74
Montague Av, S.Croy. 160 DS112
Montague Cl SE1 201 K2
Montague Cl SE1 84 DR74
Montague Cl, Walt. 135 BU101
Montague Dr, Cat. 176 DQ122
Drake Av
Montague Gdns W3 80 CN73
Montague Hall Pl, Bushey 24 CA44
Montague Pl WC1 195 N6
Montague Pl WC1 83 DK71
Montague Rd E8 66 DU64
Montague Rd E11 68 EF61
Montague Rd N8 65 DM57
Montague Rd N15 66 DU56
Montague Rd SW19 120 DB94
Montague Rd W7 79 CF74
Montague Rd W13 79 CH72
Montague Rd, Croy. 141 DP102
Montague Rd, Houns. 96 CB83
Montague Rd, Rich. 118 CL86
Montague Rd, Slou. 74 AT73
Montague Rd (Datchet), Slou. 92 AV81
Montague Rd, Sthl. 96 BY77
Montague Rd, Uxb. 76 BK66
Montague Sq SE15 102 DW80
Clifton Way
Montague St EC1 197 H7
Montague St EC1 84 DQ71
Montague St WC1 195 P6
Montague St WC1 83 DL71
Montague Waye, Sthl. 96 BY76
Montalt Rd, Wdf.Grn. 48 EF50
Montana Cl, S.Croy. 160 DR110
Montana Gdns SE26 123 DZ91
Worsley Br Rd
Montana Gdns, Sutt. 158 DC106
Lind Rd
Montana Rd SW17 120 DG91
Montana Rd SW20 139 CW95
Montayne Rd (Cheshunt), Wal.Cr. 15 DX32
Montbelle Rd SE9 125 EP90
Montbretia Cl, Orp. 146 EW98
Montcalm Cl, Brom. 144 EG100
Montcalm Cl, Hayes 77 BV69
Ayles Rd
Montcalm Rd SE7 104 EK80
Montclare St E2 197 P3
Monteagle Av, Bark. 87 EQ65
Monteagle Way E5 66 DU62
Rendlesham Rd
Monteagle Way SE15 102 DV83
Montefiore St SW8 101 DH82
Montego Cl SE24 101 DN84
Railton Rd
Monteith Rd E3 85 DZ67
Montem Rd SE23 123 DZ87
Montem Rd, N.Mal. 138 CS98
Montem St N4 65 DM60
Thorpedale Rd
Montenotte Rd N8 65 DJ57
Monterey Cl, Bex. 127 FC89
Montesole Ct, Pnr. 40 BW54
Montevetro SW11 100 DD81
Battersea Ch Rd
Montford Pl SE11 101 DN78
Montford Rd, Sun. 135 BU98
Montfort Gdns, Ilf. 49 EQ51
Montfort Pl SW19 119 CX88
Montgolfier Wk, Nthlt. 78 BY69
Jetstar Way
Montgomery Av, Esher 137 CE104
Montgomery Cl, Grays 110 GC75
Montgomery Cl, Mitch. 141 DL98
Montgomery Cl, Sid. 125 ET86
Montgomery Cres, Rom. 52 FJ50
Montgomery Dr (Cheshunt), Wal.Cr. 15 DY28
Montgomery Rd W4 98 CQ77
Montgomery Rd (South Darenth), Dart. 149 FR95
Montgomery Rd, Edg. 42 CM51
Montgomery Rd, Wok. 166 AY118
Montholme Rd SW11 120 DF86
Monthope Rd E1 84 DU71
Casson St
Montolieu Gdns SW15 119 CV85
Montpelier Av W5 79 CJ71
Montpelier Av, Bex. 126 EX87
Montpelier Cl, Uxb. 76 BN67
Montpelier Gdns E6 86 EK69
Montpelier Gdns, Rom. 70 EW59
Montpelier Gro NW5 65 DJ64
Montpelier Ms SW7 198 C6
Montpelier Pl E1 84 DW72
Montpelier Pl SW7 198 C6
Montpelier Pl SW7 100 DE76
Montpelier Ri NW11 63 CY59
Montpelier Ri, Wem. 61 CK60
Montpelier Rd N3 44 DC53
Montpelier Rd SE15 102 DV81
Montpelier Rd W5 79 CK71
Montpelier Rd, Pur. 159 DP110
Montpelier Rd, Sutt. 158 DC105
Montpelier Row SE3 104 EF82
Montpelier Row, Twick. 117 CJ87
Montpelier Sq SW7 198 C5
Montpelier Sq SW7 100 DE75
Montpelier St SW7 198 C5
Montpelier St SW7 100 DE75
Montpelier Ter SW7 198 C5
Montpelier Vale SE3 104 EF82
Montpelier Wk SW7 198 C6
Montpelier Wk SW7 100 DE76
Montpelier Way NW11 63 CY59
Montrave Rd SE20 122 DW93
Montreal Pl WC2 196 B10
Montreal Rd, Ilf. 69 EQ59
Montreal Rd, Sev. 190 FE123
Montreal Rd, Til. 111 GG82
Montrell Rd SW2 121 DL88
Montrose Av NW6 81 CY68
Montrose Av, Edg. 42 CQ54
Montrose Av, Rom. 52 FJ54
Montrose Av, Sid. 126 EU87
Montrose Av (Datchet), Slou. 92 AW80
Montrose Av, Twick. 116 CB87
Montrose Av, Well. 105 ES83
Montrose Cl, Ashf. 115 BQ93
Montrose Cl, Well. 105 ET83
Montrose Cl, Wdf.Grn. 48 EG49
Montrose Ct SW7 198 A5
Montrose Ct SW7 100 DD75
Montrose Cres N12 44 DC51
Montrose Cres, Wem. 80 CL65
Montrose Gdns, Lthd. 155 CD112
Montrose Gdns, Mitch. 140 DF97
Montrose Gdns, Sutt. 140 DB103
Montrose Pl SW1 198 G5
Montrose Pl SW1 100 DG75
Montrose Rd, Felt. 115 BR86
Montrose Rd, Har. 41 CE54
Montrose Wk, Wey. 135 BP104
Montrose Way SE23 123 DX88
Montrose Way, Slou. 92 AX81
Montrouge Cres, Epsom 173 CW116
Montserrat Av, Wdf.Grn. 47 ED52
Montserrat Cl SE19 122 DR92
Montserrat Rd SW15 99 CY84
Monument Gdns SE13 123 EC85
Monument Grn, Wey. 135 BP104
Monument Hill, Wey. 153 BP105
Monument La (Chalfont St. Peter), Ger.Cr. 36 AY51
Monument Rd, Wey. 153 BP105
Monument Rd, Wok. 151 BA114
Monument St EC3 197 L10
Monument St EC3 84 DR73
Monument Way N17 66 DT55
Monument Way E, Wok. 167 BB115
Monument Way W, Wok. 167 BA115
Monza St E1 202 F1
Monza St E1 84 DW73
Moodkee St SE16 202 G6
Moodkee St SE16 102 DW76
Moody Rd SE15 102 DT81
Moody St E1 85 DX69
Moon La, Barn. 27 CZ41
Moon St N1 83 DP67
Moor La EC2 197 K7
Moor La EC2 84 DR71
Moor La, Chess. 156 CL105
Moor La, Rick. 38 BM47
Moor La (Sarratt), Rick. 21 BE36
Moor La, Stai. 113 BE90
Moor La, Upmin. 73 FS60
Moor La, West Dr. 94 BJ79
Moor La, Wok. 166 AY122
Moor La Crossing, Wat. 39 BQ46
Moor Mead Rd, Twick. 117 CG86
Moor Mill La, St.Alb. 9 CE29
Moor Pk Est, Nthwd. 39 BQ49
Moor Pk Gdns, Kings.T. 118 CS94
Moor Pk Ind Est, Wat. 39 BQ45
Moor Pk Mansion, Rick. 38 BN48
Moor Pk Rd, Nthwd. 39 BR50
Moor Pl EC2 197 K7
Moor Rd, The, Sev. 181 FH120
Moor St W1 195 N9
Moor Vw, Wat. 39 BU45
Moorcroft Gdns, Brom. 144 EL99
Southborough Rd
Moorcroft La, Uxb. 76 BN71
Moorcroft Rd SW16 121 DL90
Moorcroft Way, Pnr. 60 BY57
Moordown SE18 105 EN81
Moore Av, Grays 110 FY78
Moore Av, Til. 111 GH82
Moore Cl SW14 98 CQ83
Little St. Leonards
Moore Cl, Add. 152 BH106
Moore Cl, Dart. 129 FR89
Moore Cl, Mitch. 141 DH96
Moore Cl, Wall. 159 DL109
Brabazon Av
Moore Cres, Dag. 88 EV67
Moore Gro Cres, Egh. 112 AY94
Moore Pk Rd SW6 100 DB80
Moore Rd SE19 122 DQ93
Moore Rd, Swans. 130 FY86
Moore St SW3 198 D8
Moore St SW3 100 DF77
Moore Wk E7 68 EG63
Stracey Rd
Moore Way SE22 122 DU88
Lordship La
Moore Way, Sutt. 158 DA109
Moorefield Rd N17 46 DT54
Moorehead Way SE3 104 EH83
Mooreland Rd, Brom. 124 EF94
Moores Pl, Brwd. 54 FX47
Moorey Cl E15 86 EF67
Stephen's Rd
Moorfield Av W5 79 CK70
Moorfield Rd, Chess. 156 CL106
Moorfield Rd, Enf. 30 DW39
Moorfield Rd, Orp. 146 EU101
Moorfield Rd, Uxb. 76 BK72
Moorfield Rd (Harefield), Uxb. 58 BG59
Moorfields EC2 197 K7
Moorfields EC2 84 DR71
Moorfields Cl, Stai. 133 BE95
Moorfields Highwalk EC2 84 DR71
Fore St
Moorgate EC2 197 K8
Moorgate EC2 84 DR72
Moorgate Pl EC2 197 K8
Moorhall Rd (Harefield), Uxb. 58 BH58
Moorhayes Dr, Stai. 134 BJ97
Moorhen Cl, Erith 107 FH80
Moorholme, Wok. 166 AY119
Oakbank
Moorhouse Rd W2 82 DA72
Moorhouse Rd, Har. 61 CK55
Moorhouse Rd, Oxt. 189 EM131
Moorhouse Rd, West. 189 EM128
Moorhurst Av (Cheshunt), Wal.Cr. 13 DN29
Moorings SE28 88 EV73
Moorings, The, Wind. 112 AW87
Straight Rd
Moorland Cl, Rom. 51 FB52
Moorland Cl, Twick. 116 CA87
Telford Rd
Moorland Rd SW9 101 DP84
Moorland Rd, West Dr. 94 BJ79
Moorlands, St.Alb. 9 CE28
Frogmore
Moorlands, The, Wok. 167 AZ121
Moorlands Av NW7 43 CV51
Moorlands Est SW9 101 DN84
Moormead Dr, Epsom 156 CS106
Moormede Cres, Stai. 113 BF91
Moorside Rd, Brom. 124 EE90
Moorsom Way, Couls. 175 DK117
Moorstown Ct, Slou. 92 AS75
Moortown Rd, Wat. 40 BW49
Moot Ct NW9 62 CN57
Mora Rd NW2 63 CW63
Mora St EC1 197 J3
Mora St EC1 84 DQ69
Moran Cl, St.Alb. 8 BZ31
Morant Gdns, Rom. 51 FB50
Morant Pl N22 45 DM53
Commerce Rd
Morant Rd, Grays 111 GH76
Morant St E14 85 EA73
Morants Ct Rd, Sev. 181 FC118
Morat St SW9 101 DM81
Moravian Pl SW10 100 DD79
Milman's St
Moravian St E2 84 DW69
Moray Av, Hayes 77 BT74
Moray Cl, Edg. 42 CP47
Pentland Av
Moray Cl, Rom. 51 FE52
Moray Dr, Slou. 74 AU72
Moray Ms N7 65 DM61
Durham Rd
Moray Rd N4 65 DM61
Moray Way, Rom. 51 FD52
Mordaunt Gdns, Dag. 88 EY66
Mordaunt Ho NW10 80 CR67
Mordaunt Rd NW10 80 CR67
Mordaunt St SW9 101 DM83
Morden Cl SE13 103 EC82
Morden Cl, Tad. 173 CX120
Marbles Way
Morden Ct, Mord. 140 DB98
Morden Gdns, Grnf. 61 CF64
Morden Gdns, Mitch. 140 DD98
Morden Hall Rd, Mord. 140 DB97
Morden Hill SE13 103 EC82
Morden La SE13 103 EC81
Morden Rd SE3 104 EG82
Morden Rd SW19 140 DB95
Morden Rd, Mitch. 140 DC98
Morden Rd, Rom. 70 EY59
Morden Rd Ms SE3 104 EG82
Morden St SE13 103 EB81
Morden Way, Sutt. 140 DA101
Morden Wf Rd SE10 205 H7
Morden Wf Rd SE10 104 EE76
Mordon Rd, Ilf. 69 ET59
Mordred Rd SE6 124 EE89
More Cl E16 86 EF72
More Cl W14 99 CY77
More Cl, Pur. 159 DN111
More La, Esher 136 CB103
Moreau Wk, Slou. 74 AY72
Alan Way
Morecambe Cl E1 85 DX71
Morecambe Cl, Horn. 71 FH64
Morecambe Gdns, Stan. 41 CK49
Morecambe St SE17 201 J9
Morecambe St SE17 102 DQ77
Morecambe Ter N18 46 DR49
Morecoombe Cl, Kings.T. 118 CP94
Moree Way N18 46 DU49
Morel Ct, Sev. 191 FH122
Moreland Av, Grays 110 GC75
Moreland Av, Slou. 93 BC80
Moreland Cl, Slou. 93 BC80
Moreland Av
Moreland Dr, Ger.Cr. 57 AZ59
Moreland St EC1 196 G2
Moreland St EC1 83 DP69
Moreland Way E4 47 EB48
Morell Cl, Barn. 28 DC41
Galdana Av
Morella Cl, Vir.W. 132 AW98
Morella Rd SW12 120 DF87
Morello Av, Uxb. 77 BP71
Morello Cl, Swan. 147 FD98
Morello Dr, Slou. 75 AZ74
Moremead, Wal.Abb. 15 ED33
Moremead Rd SE6 123 DZ91
Morena St SE6 123 EB87
Moresby Av, Surb. 138 CP101
Moresby Rd E5 66 DV60
Moresby Wk SW8 101 DJ82
Moretaine Rd, Ashf. 114 BK90
Hengrove Cres
Moreton Av, Islw. 97 CE81
Moreton Cl E5 66 DW61
Moreton Cl N15 66 DR58
Moreton Cl NW7 43 CW51
Moreton Cl SW1 101 DJ78
Moreton Ter
Moreton Cl, Swan. 147 FE96
Bonney Way
Moreton Cl (Cheshunt), Wal.Cr. 14 DV27
Moreton Gdns, Wdf.Grn. 48 EL50
Moreton Ind Est, Swan. 147 FH98
Moreton Pl SW1 199 L10
Moreton Pl SW1 101 DJ78
Moreton Rd N15 66 DR58
Moreton Rd, S.Croy. 160 DR106
Moreton Rd, Wor.Pk. 139 CU103
Moreton St SW1 199 L10
Moreton St SW1 101 DK78
Moreton Ter SW1 199 L10
Moreton Ter SW1 101 DJ7
Moreton Ter Ms N SW1 199 L1
Moreton Ter Ms S SW1 199 L1
Moreton Twr W3 80 CP7
Morewood Cl, Sev. 190 FF12
Morewood Cl Ind Pk, Sev. 190 FF12
Morewood Cl
Morford Cl, Ruis. 59 BV5
Morford Way, Ruis. 59 BV5
Morgan Av E17 67 ED5
Morgan Cl, Dag. 88 FA6
Morgan Cl, Nthwd. 39 BT5
Morgan Cres, Epp. 33 ER3
Morgan Dr, Green. 129 FS8
Morgan Gdns, Wat. 24 CB3
Morgan Rd N7 65 DN6
Morgan Rd W10 81 CZ7
Morgan Rd, Brom. 124 EG9
Morgan St E3 85 DY6
Morgan St E16 86 EF7
Morgan Way, Rain. 90 FJ6
Morgan Way, Wdf.Grn. 48 EL5
Morgans La SE1 201 M
Morgans La SE1 84 DS7
Morgans La, Hayes 77 BR7
Moriatry Cl N7 65 DL6
Morie St SW18 120 DB8
Morieux Rd E10 67 DZ6
Moring Rd SW17 120 DG9
Morkyns Wk SE21 122 DS9
Morland Av, Croy. 142 DS10
Morland Av, Dart. 127 FH8
Morland Cl NW11 64 DB6
Morland Cl, Hmptn. 116 BZ9
Morland Cl, Mitch. 140 DE9
Morland Gdns NW10 80 CR6
Morland Gdns, Sthl. 78 CB7
Morland Ms N1 83 DN6
Lofting Rd
Morland Rd E17 67 DX5
Morland Rd SE20 123 DX9
Morland Rd, Croy. 142 DS10
Morland Rd, Dag. 88 FA6
Morland Rd, Har. 62 CL5
Morland Rd, Ilf. 69 EP6
Morland Rd, Sutt. 158 DC10
Morland Way (Cheshunt), Wal.Cr. 15 DY28
Morley Av E4 47 ED52
Morley Av N18 46 DU4
Morley Av N22 45 DN54
Morley Cl, Orp. 145 EP103
Morley Cl, Slou. 93 AZ75
Morley Cres, Edg. 42 CQ47
Morley Cres, Ruis. 60 BW61
Morley Cres E, Stan. 41 CJ54
Morley Cres W, Stan. 41 CJ54
Morley Hill, Enf. 30 DR38
Morley Rd E10 67 EC60
Morley Rd E15 86 EF68
Morley Rd SE13 103 EC84
Morley Rd, Bark. 87 ER67
Morley Rd, Chis. 145 EQ95
Morley Rd, Rom. 70 EY57
Morley Rd, S.Croy. 160 DT110
Morley Rd, Sutt. 139 CZ102
Morley Rd, Twick. 117 CK86
Morley Sq, Grays 111 GG77
Morley St SE1 200 E6
Morley St SE1 101 DN75
Morna Rd SE5 102 DQ82
Morning La E9 84 DW65
Morning Ri, Rick. 22 BK41
Morningside Rd, Wor.Pk. 139 CV103
Mornington Av W14 99 CZ77
Mornington Av, Brom. 144 EJ97
Mornington Av, Ilf. 69 EN59
Mornington Cl, West. 178 EK117
Mornington Cl, Wdf.Grn. 48 EG49
Mornington Ct, Bex. 127 FC88
Mornington Cres NW1 83 DJ68
Mornington Cres, Houns. 95 BV81
Mornington Gro E3 85 EA69
Mornington Ms SE5 102 DQ81
Mornington Pl NW1 83 DH68
Mornington Ter
Mornington Rd E4 47 ED45
Mornington Rd E11 68 EF60
Mornington Rd SE8 103 DZ80
Mornington Rd, Ashf. 115 BQ92
Mornington Rd, Grnf. 78 CB71
Mornington Rd, Loug. 33 EQ41
Mornington Rd, Rad. 9 CG34
Mornington Rd, Wdf.Grn. 48 EF49
Mornington St NW1 83 DH68
Mornington Ter NW1 83 DH67
Mornington Wk, Rich. 117 CK91
Morocco St SE1 201 M5
Morocco St SE1 102 DS75
Morpeth Av, Borwd. 26 CM38
Morpeth Gro E9 85 DX67
Morpeth Rd E9 84 DW67
Morpeth St E2 85 DX69
Morpeth Ter SW1 199 K7
Morpeth Ter SW1 101 DJ76
Morpeth Wk N17 46 DV52
West Rd
Morrab Gdns, Ilf. 69 ET62
Morrice Cl, Slou. 93 AZ77
Morris Av E12 69 EM64
Morris Cl, Croy. 143 DY100
Morris Cl (Chalfont St. Peter), Ger.Cr. 37 AZ53
Morris Cl, Orp. 145 ES104
Morris Ct E4 47 EB48
Flaxen Rd
Morris Ct, Wal.Abb. 16 EF34
Morris Gdns SW18 120 DA87
Morris Gdns, Dart. 128 FN85
Morris Pl N4 65 DN61
Morris Rd E14 85 EB71
Morris Rd E15 68 EE63
Morris Rd, Dag. 70 EZ61
Morris Rd, Islw. 97 CF83
Morris Rd, Rom. 51 FH52
Morris St E1 84 DV72
Morris Way, St.Alb. 10 CL26
Morrish Rd SW2 121 DL87

Morrison Av N17 66 DS55
Morrison Rd, Bark. 88 EY68
Morrison Rd, Hayes 77 BV69
Morrison St SW11 100 DG83
Morriston Cl, Wat. 40 BW50
Morse Cl E13 86 EG69
Morse Cl (Harefield), Uxb. 38 BJ54
Morshead Rd W9 82 DA69
Morson Rd, Enf. 31 DY44
Morston Cl, Tad. 173 CV120
Waterfield
Morston Gdns SE9 125 EM91
Morten Cl SW4 121 DK86
Morten Gdns (Denham), Uxb. 58 BG59
Morteyne Rd N17 46 DR53
Mortgramit Sq SE18 105 EN76
Powis St
Mortham St E15 86 EE67
Mortimer Cl NW2 63 CZ62
Mortimer Cl SW16 121 DK89
Mortimer Cl, Bushey 24 CB44
Mortimer Cres NW6 82 DB67
Mortimer Cres, Wor.Pk. 138 CR104
Mortimer Dr, Enf. 30 DS43
Mortimer Est NW6 82 DB67
Mortimer Gate, Wal.Cr. 15 DZ27
Mortimer Mkt WC1 195 L5
Mortimer Pl NW6 82 DB67
Mortimer Rd E6 87 EM69
Mortimer Rd N1 84 DS66
Mortimer Rd NW10 81 CW69
Mortimer Rd W13 79 CJ72
Mortimer Rd, Erith 107 FD79
Mortimer Rd, Mitch. 140 DF95
Mortimer Rd, Orp. 146 EU103
Mortimer Rd, Slou. 92 AX76
Mortimer Rd, West. 162 EJ112
Mortimer Sq W11 81 CX73
St. Anns Rd
Mortimer St W1 195 K7
Mortimer St W1 83 DJ72
Mortimer Ter NW5 65 DH63
Gordon Ho Rd
Mortlake Cl, Croy. 141 DL104
Richmond Rd
Mortlake Dr, Mitch. 140 DE95
Mortlake High St SW14 98 CR83
Mortlake Rd E16 86 EH72
Mortlake Rd, Ilf. 69 EQ63
Mortlake Rd, Rich. 98 CN80
Mortlake Ter, Rich. 98 CN80
Kew Rd
Mortlock Cl SE15 102 DV81
Cossall Wk
Morton, Tad. 173 CX121
Hudsons
Morton Cl, Wok. 166 AW115
Morton Cres N14 45 DK49
Morton Gdns, Wall. 159 DJ106
Morton Ms SW5 100 DB77
Earls Ct Gdns
Morton Pl SE1 200 D7
Morton Rd E15 86 EF66
Morton Rd N1 84 DQ66
Morton Rd, Mord. 140 DD99
Morton Rd, Wok. 166 AW115
Morton Way N14 45 DJ48
Morval Rd SW2 121 DN85
Morvale Cl, Belv. 106 EZ77
Morven Cl, Pot.B. 12 DC31
Morven Rd SW17 120 DF90
Morville St E3 85 EA68
Morwell St WC1 195 N7
Mosbach Gdns, Brwd. 55 GB47
Moscow Pl W2 82 DB73
Moscow Rd
Moscow Rd W2 82 DA73
Moselle Av N22 45 DN54
Moselle Cl N8 65 DM55
Miles Rd
Moselle Ho N17 46 DT52
William St
Moselle Pl N17 46 DT52
High Rd
Moselle Rd, West. 178 EL118
Moselle St N17 46 DT52
Mospey Cres, Epsom 173 CT115
Moss Bk, Grays 110 FZ78
Moss Cl E1 84 DU71
Old Montague St
Moss Cl, Pnr. 40 BZ54
Moss Cl, Rick. 38 BK47
Moss Gdns, Felt. 115 BU89
Moss Gdns, S.Croy. 161 DX108
Warren Av
Moss Hall Cres N12 44 DB51
Moss Hall Gro N12 44 DB51
Moss La, Pnr. 60 BZ55
Moss La, Rom. 71 FF58
Wheatsheaf Rd
Moss Rd, Dag. 88 FA66
Moss Rd, S.Ock. 91 FW71
Moss Rd, Wat. 7 BV34
Moss Side, St.Alb. 8 BZ30
Moss Way, Dart. 129 FR91
Mossborough Cl N12 44 DB51
Mossbury Rd SW11 100 DE83
Mossdown Cl, Belv. 106 FA77
Mossendew Cl (Harefield), Uxb. 38 BK53
Mossfield, Cob. 153 BU113
Mossford Ct, Ilf. 69 EP55
Mossford Grn, Ilf. 69 EP55
Mossford La, Ilf. 49 EP54
Mossford St E3 85 DZ70
Mossington Gdns SE16 202 F9
Mosslea Rd SE20 122 DW93
Mosslea Rd, Brom. 144 EK99
Mosslea Rd, Orp. 145 EQ104
Mosslea Rd, Whyt. 176 DT116
Mossop St SW3 198 C8
Mossop St SW3 100 DE77
Mossville Gdns, Mord. 139 CZ97
Moston Cl, Hayes 95 BT78
Fuller Way
Mostyn Av, Wem. 62 CM64
Mostyn Gdns NW10 81 CX68
Mostyn Gro E3 85 DZ68
Mostyn Rd SW9 101 DN81
Mostyn Rd SW19 139 CZ95
Mostyn Rd, Bushey 24 CC43
Mostyn Rd, Edg. 42 CR52
Mosul Way, Brom. 144 EL100
Mosyer Dr, Orp. 146 EX103
Motcomb St SW1 198 E6
Motcomb St SW1 100 DG76
Mothers' Sq E5 66 DV63
Motherwell Way, Grays 109 FU78
Motley Av EC2 84 DS70
Scrutton St
Motley St SW8 101 DJ82
St. Rule St
Motspur Pk, N.Mal. 139 CT100
Mott St E4 31 ED38
Mott St, Loug. 32 EF39
Mottingham Gdns SE9 124 EK88
Mottingham La SE9 124 EJ88
Mottingham La SE12 124 EJ88
Mottingham Rd N9 31 DX44
Mottingham Rd SE9 124 EL89
Mottisfont Rd SE2 106 EU76
Motts Hill La, Tad. 173 CU123
Mouchotte Cl, West. 162 EH112
Moulins Rd E9 84 DW67
Moultain Hill, Swan. 147 FG98
Moulton Av, Houns. 96 BY82
Moultrie Way, Upmin. 73 FS59
Mound, The SE9 125 EN90
Moundfield Rd N16 66 DU58
Mount, The N20 44 DC47
Mount, The NW3 64 DC63
Heath St
Mount, The W3 80 CQ74
High St
Mount, The, Brwd. 54 FW48
Mount, The, Couls. 174 DG115
Mount, The (Ewell), Epsom 157 CT110
Mount, The, Esher 154 CA107
Mount, The, Lthd. 171 CE123
Mount, The, N.Mal. 139 CT97
Mount, The, Pot.B. 12 DB30
Mount, The, Rick. 22 BJ44
Mount, The, Rom. 52 FJ48
Mount, The, Tad. 183 CZ126
Mount, The, Vir.W. 132 AX100
Mount, The (Cheshunt), Wal.Cr. 14 DR26
Mount, The, Warl. 176 DU119
Mount, The, Wem. 62 CP61
Mount, The, Wey. 135 BS103
Mount, The, Wok. 166 AX118
Mount, The (St. John's), Wok. 166 AU119
Mount, The, Wor.Pk. 157 CV105
Mount Adon Pk SE22 122 DU87
Mount Angelus Rd SW15 119 CT87
Mount Ararat Rd, Rich. 118 CL85
Mount Ash Rd SE26 122 DV90
Mount Av E4 47 EA48
Mount Av W5 79 CK71
Mount Av, Brwd. 55 GB45
Mount Av, Cat. 176 DQ124
Mount Av, Rom. 52 FQ51
Mount Av, Sthl. 78 CA72
Mount Cl W5 79 CJ71
Mount Cl, Barn. 28 DG42
Mount Cl, Brom. 144 EL95
Mount Cl, Cars. 158 DG109
Mount Cl, Ken. 176 DQ116
Mount Cl, Lthd. 171 CE123
Mount Cl, Sev. 190 FF123
Mount Cl, Wok. 166 AV121
Mount Cl, The, Vir.W. 132 AX100
Mount Cor, Felt. 116 BX89
Mount Ct SW15 99 CY83
Weimar St
Mount Ct, W.Wick. 144 EE103
Mount Cres, Brwd. 54 FX49
Mount Culver Av, Sid. 126 EX93
Mount Dr, Bexh. 126 EY85
Mount Dr, Har. 60 BZ57
Mount Dr, St.Alb. 9 CD25
Mount Dr, Wem. 62 CQ61
Mount Dr, The, Reig. 184 DC132
Mount Echo Av E4 47 EB47
Mount Echo Dr E4 47 EB46
Mount Ephraim La SW16 121 DK90
Mount Ephraim Rd SW16 121 DK90
Mount Est, The E5 66 DV61
Mount Pleasant La
Mount Felix, Walt. 135 BT102
Mount Gdns SE26 122 DV90
Mount Grace Rd, Pot.B. 12 DA31
Mount Gro, Edg. 42 CQ48
Mount Harry Rd, Sev. 190 FG123
Mount Hermon Cl, Wok. 166 AX118
Mount Hermon Rd, Wok. 166 AX119
Mount Hill La, Ger.Cr. 56 AV60
Mount La (Denham), Uxb. 57 BD61
Mount Lee, Egh. 112 AY92
Mount Ms, Hmptn. 136 CB95
Mount Mills EC1 196 G3
Mount Nod Rd SW16 121 DM90
Mount Pk, Cars. 158 DG109
Mount Pk Av, Har. 61 CD61
Mount Pk Av, S.Croy. 159 DP109
Mount Pk Cres W5 79 CK72
Mount Pk Rd W5 79 CK71
Mount Pk Rd, Har. 61 CD62
Mount Pk Rd, Pnr. 59 BU57
Mount Pl W3 80 CP74
High St
Mount Pleasant SE27 122 DQ91
Mount Pleasant WC1 196 C5
Mount Pleasant WC1 83 DN70
Mount Pleasant, Barn. 28 DE42
Mount Pleasant, Epsom 157 CT110
Mount Pleasant, Ruis. 60 BW61
Mount Pleasant (Harefield), Uxb. 38 BG53
Mount Pleasant, Wem. 80 CL67
Mount Pleasant, West. 178 EK117
Mount Pleasant, Wey. 134 BN104
Mount Pleasant Av, Brwd. 55 GE44
Mount Pleasant Cres N4 65 DM59
Mount Pleasant Hill E5 66 DW61
Mount Pleasant La E5 66 DV61
Mount Pleasant La, St.Alb. 8 BY30
Mount Pleasant Pl SE18 105 ER77
Orchard Rd
Mount Pleasant Rd E17 47 DY54
Mount Pleasant Rd N17 46 DS54
Mount Pleasant Rd NW10 81 CW66
Mount Pleasant Rd SE13 123 EB86
Mount Pleasant Rd W5 79 CJ70
Mount Pleasant Rd, Cat. 176 DU123
Mount Pleasant Rd, Chig. 49 ER49
Mount Pleasant Rd, Dart. 128 FM86
Mount Pleasant Rd, N.Mal. 138 CQ97
Mount Pleasant Rd, Rom. 51 FD51
Mount Pleasant Vil N4 65 DM59
Mount Pleasant Wk, Bex. 127 FC85
Mount Rd NW2 63 CV62
Mount Rd NW4 63 CU58
Mount Rd SE19 122 DR93
Mount Rd SW19 120 DA89
Mount Rd, Barn. 28 DE43
Mount Rd, Bexh. 126 EX85
Mount Rd, Chess. 156 CM106
Mount Rd, Dag. 70 EZ60
Mount Rd, Dart. 127 FF86
Mount Rd, Epp. 18 EW32
Mount Rd, Felt. 116 BY90
Mount Rd, Hayes 95 BU75
Mount Rd, Ilf. 69 EP64
Mount Rd, Mitch. 140 DE96
Mount Rd, N.Mal. 138 CR97
Mount Rd, Wok. 166 AV121
Mount Rd (Chobham), Wok. 150 AV112
Mount Row W1 199 H1
Mount Row W1 83 DH73
Mount Sq, The NW3 64 DC62
Heath St
Mount Stewart Av, Har. 61 CK58
Mount St W1 198 G1
Mount St W1 82 DG73
Mount Ter E1 84 DV71
New Rd
Mount Vernon NW3 64 DC63
Mount Vw NW7 42 CR48
Mount Vw W5 79 CK70
Mount Vw, Enf. 29 DM38
Mount Vw, Rick. 38 BH46
Mount Vw, St.Alb. 10 CL27
Mount Vw Rd E4 47 EC45
Mount Vw Rd N4 65 DL59
Mount Vw Rd NW9 62 CR56
Mount Vil SE27 121 DP90
Mount Way, Cars. 158 DG109
Mountacre Cl SE26 122 DT91
Mountague Pl E14 85 EC73
Mountain Ct (Eynsford), Dart. 148 FL103
Pollyhaugh
Mountbatten Cl SE18 105 ES79
Mountbatten Cl SE19 122 DS92
Mountbatten Cl, Slou. 92 AU76
Mountbatten Ct SE16 84 DW74
Rotherhithe St
Mountbatten Ct, Buck.H. 48 EK47
Mountbatten Gdns, Beck. 143 DY98
Balmoral Av
Mountbatten Ms SW18 120 DC88
Inman Rd
Mountbel Rd, Stan. 41 CG53
Mountcombe Cl, Surb. 138 CL101
Mountearl Gdns SW16 121 DM90
Mountfield Cl SE6 123 ED87
Mountfield Rd E6 87 EN68
Mountfield Rd N3 64 DA55
Mountfield Rd W5 79 CK72
Mountfield Way, Orp. 146 EW98
Mountford St E1 84 DU72
Adler St
Mountfort Cres N1 83 DN66
Barnsbury Sq
Mountfort Ter N1 83 DN66
Barnsbury Sq
Mountgrove Rd N5 65 DP62
Mounthurst Rd, Brom. 144 EF101
Mountington Pk Cl, Har. 61 CK58
Mountjoy Cl SE2 106 EV75
Mountjoy Ho EC2 84 DQ71
The Barbican
Mountnessing Bypass, Brwd. 55 GD41
Mounts Pond Rd SE3 103 ED82
Mounts Rd, Green. 129 FV85
Mountsfield Cl, Stai. 114 BG86
Mountsfield Ct SE13 123 ED86
Mountside, Felt. 116 BY90
Hampton Rd W
Mountside, Stan. 41 CF53
Mountview, Nthwd. 39 BT51
Mountview Ct N8 65 DP56
Green Las
Mountview Rd, Esher 155 CH108
Mountview Rd, Orp. 146 EU101
Mountview Rd (Cheshunt), Wal.Cr. 14 DS26
Mountway, Pot.B. 12 DA30
Mountwood, W.Mol. 136 CA97
Mountwood Cl, S.Croy. 160 DV110
Movers La, Bark. 87 ES68
Mowat Ind Est, Wat. 24 BW38
Mowatt Cl N19 65 DK60
Mowbray Av, W.Byf. 152 BL113
Mowbray Cres, Egh. 113 BA92
Mowbray Rd NW6 81 CY66
Mowbray Rd SE19 142 DT95
Mowbray Rd, Barn. 28 DC42
Mowbray Rd, Edg. 42 CN49
Mowbray Rd, Rich. 117 CJ90
Mowbrays Cl, Rom. 51 FC53
Mowbrays Rd, Rom. 51 FC54
Mowbrey Gdns, Loug. 33 EQ40
Mowlem St E2 84 DV68
Mowlem Trd Est N17 46 DW52
Mowll St SW9 101 DN80
Moxom Av (Cheshunt), Wal.Cr. 15 DY30
Moxon Cl E13 86 EF68
Whitelegg Rd
Moxon St W1 194 F7
Moxon St W1 82 DG71
Moxon St, Barn. 27 CZ41
Moye Cl E2 84 DU67
Dove Row
Moyers Rd E10 67 EC59
Moylan Rd W6 99 CY79
Moyne Ct, Wok. 166 AT118
Iveagh Rd
Moyne Pl NW10 80 CN68
Moynihan Dr N21 29 DL43
Moys Cl, Croy. 141 DL100
Moyser Rd SW16 121 DH92
Mozart St W10 81 CZ69
Mozart Ter SW1 198 G9
Mozart Ter SW1 100 DG77
Muchelney Rd, Mord. 140 DC100
Muckhatch La, Egh. 133 BB97
Muckingford Rd, S.le H. 111 GM77
Muckingford Rd, Til. 111 GL77
Mud La W5 79 CK71
Muddy La, Slou. 74 AS71
Muggeridge Cl, S.Croy. 160 DR106
Muggeridge Rd, Dag. 71 FB63
Muir Dr SW18 120 DD86
Muir Rd E5 66 DU63
Muir St E16 87 EM74
Newland St
Muirdown Av SW14 98 CR84
Muirfield W3 80 CS72
Muirfield Cl SE16 102 DV78
Ryder Dr
Muirfield Cl, Wat. 40 BW49
Muirfield Cres E14 204 B6
Muirfield Grn, Wat. 40 BW49
Muirfield Rd, Wat. 40 BX49
Muirfield Rd, Wok. 166 AU118
Muirkirk Rd SE6 123 EC88
Mulberry Av, Stai. 114 BL88
Mulberry Av, Wind. 92 AT83
Mulberry Cl E4 47 EA47
Mulberry Cl N8 65 DL57
Mulberry Cl NW3 64 DD63
Hampstead High St
Mulberry Cl NW4 63 CW55
Mulberry Cl SE7 104 EK79
Mulberry Cl SE22 122 DU85
Mulberry Cl SW3 100 DD79
Beaufort St
Mulberry Cl SW16 121 DJ91
Mulberry Cl, Amer. 20 AT39
Mulberry Cl, Barn. 28 DD42
Mulberry Cl, Nthlt. 78 BY68
Parkfield Av
Mulberry Cl, Rom. 71 FH56
Mulberry Cl, St.Alb. 8 CB28
Mulberry Cl, Wey. 135 BP104
Mulberry Cl, Wok. 150 AY114
Mulberry Ct, Bark. 87 ET66
Westrow Dr
Mulberry Cres, Brent. 97 CH80
Mulberry Cres, West Dr. 94 BN75
Mulberry Dr, Purf. 108 FM77
Mulberry Dr, Slou. 92 AY78
Mulberry Gdns (Shenley), Rad. 10 CL33
Mulberry Hill, Brwd. 55 FZ45
Mulberry La, Croy. 142 DT102
Mulberry Ms, Wall. 159 DJ107
Ross Rd
Mulberry Par, West Dr. 94 BN76
Mulberry Pl W6 99 CU78
Chiswick Mall
Mulberry Rd E8 84 DT66
Mulberry Rd, Grav. 130 GE90
Mulberry St E1 84 DU72
Adler St
Mulberry Trees, Shep. 135 BQ101
Mulberry Wk SW3 100 DD79
Mulberry Way E18 48 EH54
Mulberry Way, Belv. 107 FC75
Mulberry Way, Ilf. 69 EQ56
Mulgrave Rd NW10 63 CT63
Mulgrave Rd SW6 99 CZ79
Mulgrave Rd W5 79 CK69
Mulgrave Rd, Croy. 142 DR104
Mulgrave Rd, Har. 61 CG61
Mulgrave Rd, Sutt. 158 DA107
Mulgrave Way, Wok. 166 AS118
Mulholland Cl, Mitch. 141 DH96
Mulkern Rd N19 65 DK60
Mull Wk N1 84 DQ65
Clephane Rd
Mullards Cl, Mitch. 140 DF102
Mullein Ct, Grays 110 GD79
Mullens Rd, Egh. 113 BB92
Muller Rd SW4 121 DK86
Mullet Gdns E2 84 DU68
St. Peter's Cl
Mullins Path SW14 98 CR83
Mullion Cl, Har. 40 CB53
Mullion Wk, Wat. 40 BX49
Ormskirk Rd
Mulready St NW8 194 B5
Multi Way W3 98 CS75
Valetta Rd
Multon Rd SW18 120 DD87
Mulvaney Way SE1 201 L5
Mulvaney Way SE1 102 DR75
Mumford Ct EC2 197 J8
Mumford Rd SE24 121 DP85
Railton Rd
Mumfords La (Chalfont St. Peter), Ger.Cr. 56 AU55
Muncaster Cl, Ashf. 114 BN91
Muncaster Rd SW11 120 DF85
Muncaster Rd, Ashf. 115 BP92
Muncies Ms SE6 123 EC89
Mund St W14 99 CZ78
Mundania Rd SE22 122 DV86
Munday Rd E16 86 EG72
Mundells, Wal.Cr. 14 DU27
Munden Dr, Wat. 24 BY37
Munden Gro, Wat. 24 BW38
Munden St W14 99 CY77
Munden Vw, Wat. 24 BX36
Mundesley Cl, Wat. 40 BW49
Mundesley Spur, Slou. 74 AS72
Mundford Rd E5 66 DW61
Mundon Gdns, Ilf. 69 ER60
Mundy St N1 197 M2
Mundy St N1 84 DS69
Munford Dr, Swans. 130 FY87
Mungo Pk Cl, Bushey 40 CC47
Mungo Pk Rd, Grav. 131 GK92
Mungo Pk Rd, Rain. 89 FG65
Mungo Pk Way, Orp. 146 EW101
Munnery Way, Orp. 145 EN104
Munnings Gdns, Islw. 117 CD85
Munro Dr N11 45 DJ51
Munro Ms W10 81 CY71
Munro Rd, Bushey 24 CB43
Munro Ter SW10 100 DD80
Munslow Gdns, Sutt. 158 DD105
Munster Av, Houns. 96 BZ84
Munster Ct, Tedd. 117 CJ93
Munster Gdns N13 45 DP49
Munster Ms SW6 99 CY80
Munster Rd
Munster Rd SW6 99 CZ81
Munster Rd, Tedd. 117 CJ93
Munster Sq NW1 195 J4
Munster Sq NW1 83 DH69
Munton Rd SE17 201 J8
Munton Rd SE17 102 DQ77
Murchison Av, Bex. 126 EX88
Murchison Rd E10 67 EC61
Murdoch Cl, Stai. 114 BG92
Murdock Cl E16 86 EF72
Rogers Rd
Murdock St SE15 102 DV79
Murfett Cl SW19 119 CY89
Murfitt Way, Upmin. 72 FN63
Muriel Av, Wat. 24 BW43
Muriel St N1 83 DM68
Murillo Rd SE13 103 ED84
Murphy St SE1 200 D5
Murphy St SE1 101 DN75
Murray Av, Brom. 144 EH96
Murray Av, Houns. 116 CB85
Murray Business Cen, Orp. 146 EV97
Murray Cres, Pnr. 40 BX53
Murray Grn, Wok. 151 BC114
Bunyard Dr
Murray Gro N1 197 K1
Murray Gro N1 84 DQ68
Murray Ms NW1 83 DK66
Murray Rd SW19 119 CX93
Murray Rd W5 97 CJ77
Murray Rd, Cher. 151 BC107
Murray Rd, Nthwd. 39 BS53
Murray Rd, Orp. 146 EV97
Murray Rd, Rich. 117 CH89
Murray Sq E16 86 EG72
Murray St NW1 83 DK66
Murray Ter NW3 64 DD63
Flask Wk
Murray Ter W5 97 CK77
Murray Rd
Murrays La, W.Byf. 152 BK114
Murrells Wk, Lthd. 170 CA123
Murreys, The, Ash. 171 CK118
Mursell Est SW8 101 DM81
Murthering La, Rom. 35 FG43
Murtwell Dr, Chig. 49 EQ51
Musard Rd W6 99 CY79
Musard Rd W14 99 CY79
Musbury St E1 84 DW72
Muscal W6 99 CY79
Muscatel Pl SE5 102 DS81
Dalwood St
Muschamp Rd SE15 102 DT83
Muschamp Rd, Cars. 140 DE103
Muscovy Ho, Erith 106 EY75
Kale Rd
Muscovy St EC3 201 N1
Museum La SW7 100 DD76
Exhibition Rd
Museum Pas E2 84 DV69
Victoria Pk Sq
Museum St WC1 195 P7
Museum St WC1 83 DL72
Musgrave Cl, Barn. 28 DC39
Musgrave Cl, Wal.Cr. 14 DT27
Allwood Rd
Musgrave Cres SW6 100 DA81
Musgrave Rd, Islw. 97 CF81
Musgrove Rd SE14 103 DX81
Musjid Rd SW11 100 DD82
Kambala Rd
Muskalls Cl (Cheshunt), Wal.Cr. 14 DU27
Musket Cl, Barn. 28 DD43
East Barnet Rd
Musquash Way, Houns. 96 BW82
Mussenden La (Horton Kirby), Dart. 148 FQ99
Mussenden La (Fawkham Grn), Long. 149 FS101
Muston Rd E5 66 DV61
Mustow Pl SW6 99 CZ82
Munster Rd
Muswell Av N10 45 DH54
Muswell Hill N10 65 DH55
Muswell Hill Bdy N10 65 DH55
Muswell Hill Pl N10 65 DH56
Muswell Hill Rd N6 64 DG58
Muswell Hill Rd N10 64 DG56
Muswell Ms N10 65 DH55
Muswell Rd
Muswell Rd N10 65 DH55
Mutchetts Cl, Wat. 8 BY33
Mutrix Rd NW6 82 DA67
Mutton La, Pot.B. 11 CY31
Mutton Pl NW1 83 DH65
Harmood St
Muybridge Rd, N.Mal. 138 CQ96
Myatt Rd SW9 101 DP81
Myatt's Flds N SW9 101 DN81
Eythorne Rd
Myatt's Flds S SW9 101 DN82
Mycenae Rd SE3 104 EG80
Myddelton Av, Enf. 30 DS38
Myddelton Cl, Enf. 30 DT39
Myddelton Gdns N21 45 DP45
Myddelton Pk N20 44 DD48
Myddelton Pas EC1 196 E2
Myddelton Rd N8 65 DL56
Myddelton Sq EC1 196 E2
Myddelton Sq EC1 83 DN69

Myddelton St EC1 196 E3
Myddelton St EC1 83 DN69
Myddleton Av N4 66 DQ61
Myddleton Ms N22 45 DL52
Myddleton Path (Cheshunt), Wal.Cr. 14 DV31
Myddleton Rd N22 45 DL52
Myddleton Rd, Uxb. 76 BJ67
Myers La SE14 103 DX79
Mygrove Cl, Rain. 90 FK68
Mygrove Gdns, Rain. 90 FK68
Mygrove Rd, Rain. 90 FK68
Myles Ct, Wal.Cr. 14 DQ29
Mylis Cl SE26 122 DV91
Mylius Cl SE14 102 DW81
Kender St
Mylne Cl, Wal.Cr. 14 DW27
Mylne St EC1 196 D1
Mylne St EC1 83 DN69
Mylor Cl, Wok. 150 AY114
Mymms Dr, Hat. 12 DA26
Mynns Cl, Epsom 156 CP114
Myra St SE2 106 EU77
Myrdle St E1 84 DU71
Myrke, The, Slou. 92 AT77
Myrna Cl SW19 120 DE94
Myron Pl SE13 103 EC83
Myrtle Av, Felt. 95 BS84
Myrtle Av, Ruis. 59 BU59
Myrtle Cl, Barn. 44 DF46
Myrtle Cl, Erith 107 FE80
Myrtle Cl, Slou. 93 BE81
Myrtle Cl, Uxb. 76 BM71
Violet Av
Myrtle Cl, West Dr. 94 BM76
Myrtle Cres, Slou. 74 AT73
Myrtle Gdns W7 79 CE74
Myrtle Gro, Enf. 30 DR38
Myrtle Gro, N.Mal. 138 CQ96
Myrtle Gro, S.Ock. 108 FQ75
Myrtle Pl, Dart. 129 FR87
Myrtle Rd E6 86 EL67
Myrtle Rd E17 67 DY58
Myrtle Rd N13 46 DQ48
Myrtle Rd W3 80 CQ74
Myrtle Rd, Brwd. 54 FW48
Myrtle Rd, Croy. 143 EA104
Myrtle Rd, Dart. 128 FK88
Myrtle Rd, Hmptn. 116 CC93
Myrtle Rd, Houns. 96 CC82
Myrtle Rd, Ilf. 69 EP61
Myrtle Rd, Rom. 52 FJ51
Myrtle Rd, Sutt. 158 DC106
Myrtle Wk N1 197 M1
Myrtle Wk N1 84 DS68
Myrtleberry Cl E8 84 DT65
Beechwood Rd
Myrtledene Rd SE2 106 EU78
Myrtleside Cl, Nthwd. 39 BR52
Mysore Rd SW11 100 DF83
Myton Rd SE21 122 DR90

N

Nadine St SE7 104 EJ78
Nafferton Ri, Loug. 32 EK43
Nagle Cl E17 47 ED54
Nag's Head Ct EC1 197 H5
Nags Head La, Brwd. 53 FR51
Nags Head La, Upmin. 52 FQ53
Nags Head La, Well. 106 EV83
Nags Head Rd, Enf. 30 DW42
Nailsworth Cres, Red. 185 DK129
Nailzee Cl, Ger.Cr. 56 AY59
Nairn Ct, Til. 111 GF82
Dock Rd
Nairn Grn, Wat. 39 BU48
Nairn Rd, Ruis. 78 BW65
Nairn St E14 85 EC71
Nairne Gro SE24 122 DR85
Naish Ct N1 83 DL67
Nallhead Rd, Felt. 116 BW92
Namba Roy Cl SW16 121 DM91
Valley Rd
Namton Dr, Th.Hth. 141 DM98
Nan Clark's La NW7 43 CT47
Nancy Downs, Wat. 40 BW45
Nankin St E14 85 EA72
Nansen Rd SW11 100 DG84
Nansen Rd, Grav. 131 GK91
Nant Rd NW2 63 CZ61
Nant St E2 84 DV69
Cambridge Heath Rd
Nantes Cl SW18 100 DC84
Nantes Pas E1 197 P6
Naoroji St WC1 196 D3
Nap, The, Kings L. 6 BN29
Napier Av E14 204 A10
Napier Av E14 103 EA78
Napier Av SW6 99 CZ83
Napier Cl SE8 103 DZ80
Amersham Vale
Napier Cl W14 99 CZ76
Napier Rd
Napier Cl, Horn. 71 FH60
St. Leonards Way
Napier Cl, St.Alb. 9 CK25
Napier Cl, West Dr. 94 BM76
Napier Ct SW6 99 CZ83
Ranelagh Gdns
Napier Ct (Cheshunt), Wal.Cr. 14 DV28
Flamstead End Rd
Napier Dr, Bushey 24 BY42
Napier Gro N1 197 J1
Napier Gro N1 84 DQ68
Napier Ho, Rain. 89 FF69
Napier Pl W14 99 CZ76
Napier Rd E6 87 EN67
Napier Rd E11 68 EE63
Napier Rd E15 86 EE68
Napier Rd N17 66 DS55
Napier Rd NW10 81 CV69
Napier Rd SE25 142 DV98
Napier Rd W14 99 CZ76
Napier Rd, Ashf. 115 BR94
Napier Rd, Belv. 106 EZ77
Napier Rd, Brom. 144 EH98
Napier Rd, Enf. 31 DX43
Napier Rd, Grav. 131 GF88
Napier Rd, Houns. 94 BK81
Napier Rd, Islw. 97 CG84
Napier Rd, S.Croy. 160 DR108
Napier Rd, Wem. 61 CK64
Napier Ter N1 83 DP66
Napoleon Rd E5 66 DV62
Napoleon Rd, Twick. 117 CH87
Napsbury Av, St.Alb. 9 CJ26
Napton Cl, Hayes 78 BY70
Kingsash Dr
Narbonne Av SW4 121 DJ85
Narboro Ct, Rom. 71 FG57
Manor Rd
Narborough Cl, Uxb. 59 BQ61
Aylsham Dr
Narborough St SW6 100 DB82
Narcissus Rd NW6 64 DA64
Narcot La, Ch.St.G. 36 AU48
Narcot La (Chalfont St. Peter), Ger.Cr. 36 AV52
Narcot Rd, Ch.St.G. 36 AU48
Narcot Way, Ch.St.G. 36 AU49
Nare Rd, S.Ock. 90 FQ73
Naresby Fold, Stan. 41 CJ51
Bernays Cl
Narford Rd E5 66 DU62
Narrow La, Warl. 176 DV119
Narrow St E14 203 M1
Narrow St E14 85 DY73
Narrow Way, Brom. 144 EL100
Nascot Pl, Wat. 23 BV39
Nascot Rd, Wat. 23 BV40
Nascot St W12 81 CW72
Nascot St, Wat. 23 BV40
Nascot Wd Rd, Wat. 23 BT37
Naseby Cl NW6 82 DC66
Fairfax Rd
Naseby Cl, Islw. 97 CE81
Naseby Ct, Walt. 136 BW103
Clements Rd
Naseby Rd SE19 122 DR93
Naseby Rd, Dag. 70 FA62
Naseby Rd, Ilf. 49 EM53
Nash Cl, Borwd. 26 CM42
Nash Cl, Sutt. 140 DD104
Nash Ct E14 204 B3
Nash Cft, Grav. 130 GE91
Nash Dr, Red. 184 DF132
Nash Gdns, Red. 184 DF132
Nash Grn, Brom. 124 EG93
Nash Grn, Hem.H. 6 BM25
Nash La, Kes. 162 EG106
Nash Mills La, Hem.H. 6 BM26
Nash Rd N9 46 DW47
Nash Rd SE4 103 DY84
Nash Rd, Rom. 70 EX56
Nash Rd, Slou. 93 AZ77
Nash St NW1 195 J3
Nash Way, Har. 61 CH58
Nash's Yd, Uxb. 76 BK66
Bakers Rd
Nasmyth St W6 99 CV76
Nassau Path SE28 88 EW74
Disraeli Cl
Nassau Rd SW13 99 CT81
Nassau St W1 195 K7
Nassau St W1 83 DJ71
Nassington Rd NW3 64 DE63
Natal Rd N11 45 DL51
Natal Rd SW16 121 DK93
Natal Rd, Ilf. 69 EP63
Natal Rd, Th.Hth. 142 DR97
Natalie Cl, Felt. 115 BR87
Natalie Ms, Twick. 117 CD90
Sixth Cross Rd
Nathan Cl, Upmin. 73 FS60
Nathan Way SE28 105 ES77
Nathaniel Cl E1 84 DT71
Thrawl St
Nathans Rd, Wem. 61 CJ60
Nation Way E4 47 EC46
Naunton Way, Horn. 72 FK62
Naval Row E14 85 EC73
Naval Wk, Brom. 144 EG97
High St
Navarino Gro E8 84 DU65
Navarino Rd E8 84 DU65
Navarre Gdns, Rom. 51 FB51
Navarre Rd E6 86 EL68
Navarre St E2 197 P4
Navarre St E2 84 DT70
Navenby Wk E3 85 EA70
Rounton Rd
Navestock Cl E4 47 EC48
Mapleton Rd
Navestock Cres, Wdf.Grn. 48 EJ53
Navestock Ho, Bark. 88 EV68
Navigator Dr, Sthl. 96 CC75
Navy St SW4 101 DK83
Naylor Gro, Enf. 31 DX43
South St
Naylor Rd N20 44 DC47
Naylor Rd SE15 102 DV80
Naylor Ter (Colnbrook), Slou. 93 BC80
Vicarage Way
Nazareth Gdns SE15 102 DV82
Nazeing Wk, Rain. 89 FE67
Ongar Way
Nazrul St E2 197 P2
Nazrul St E2 84 DT69
Neagle Cl, Borwd. 26 CQ39
Balcon Way
Neal Av, Sthl. 78 BZ70
Neal Cl, Ger.Cr. 57 BB60
Neal Cl, Nthwd. 39 BU53
Neal Ct, Wal.Abb. 16 EF33
Neal St WC2 195 P9
Neal St WC2 83 DL72
Neal St, Wat. 24 BW43
Nealden St SW9 101 DM83
Neale Cl N2 64 DC55
Neal's Yd WC2 195 P9
Near Acre NW9 43 CT53
Neasden Cl NW10 62 CS64
Neasden La NW10 62 CS63
Neasden La N NW10 62 CR62
Neasham Rd, Dag. 70 EV64
Neate St SE5 102 DT79
Neath Gdns, Mord. 140 DC100
Neathouse Pl SW1 199 K8
Neats Acre, Ruis. 59 BR59
Neatscourt Rd E6 86 EK71
Neave Cres, Rom. 52 FJ53
Neb Cor Rd, Oxt. 187 EC131
Nebraska St SE1 201 K5
Nebraska St SE1 102 DR75
Neckinger SE16 202 A6
Neckinger SE16 102 DT76
Neckinger Est SE16 202 A6
Neckinger Est SE16 102 DT76
Neckinger St SE1 202 A5
Neckinger St SE1 102 DT75
Nectarine Way SE13 103 EB82
Needham Rd W11 82 DA72
Westbourne Gro
Needham Ter NW2 63 CX62
Needleman St SE16 203 H5
Needleman St SE16 103 DX75
Needles Bk, Gdse. 186 DV131
Neela Cl, Uxb. 59 BP63
Neeld Cres NW4 63 CV57
Neeld Cres, Wem. 62 CN64
Neeld Par, Wem. 62 CN64
Harrow Rd
Neil Cl, Ashf. 115 BQ92
Neil Wates Cres SW2 121 DN88
Nelgarde Rd SE6 123 EA87
Nell Gwynn Cl, Rad. 10 CL32
Nell Gwynne Av, Shep. 135 BR100
Nell Gwynne Cl, Epsom 156 CN111
Ripley Way
Nella Rd W6 99 CX79
Nelldale Rd SE16 202 F8
Nelldale Rd SE16 102 DW77
Nellgrove Rd, Uxb. 77 BP70
Nello James Gdns SE27 122 DR91
Nelmes Cl, Horn. 72 FM57
Nelmes Cres, Horn. 72 FL57
Nelmes Rd, Horn. 72 FL59
Nelmes Way, Horn. 72 FL56
Nelson Cl, Brwd. 54 FX50
Nelson Cl, Croy. 141 DP102
Nelson Cl, Felt. 115 BT88
Nelson Cl, Rom. 51 FB53
Nelson Cl, Slou. 92 AX77
Nelson Cl, Uxb. 77 BP69
Nelson Cl, Walt. 135 BV102
Nelson Cl, West. 178 EL117
Nelson Ct SE16 84 DW74
Brunel Rd
Nelson Gdns E2 84 DU69
Nelson Gdns, Houns. 116 CA86
Nelson Gro Rd SW19 140 DB95
Nelson La, Uxb. 77 BP69
Nelson Rd
Nelson Mandela Cl N10 44 DG54
Nelson Mandela Rd SE3 104 EJ83
Nelson Pas EC1 197 J3
Nelson Pl N1 196 G1
Nelson Pl N1 83 DP68
Nelson Pl, Sid. 126 EU91
Nelson Rd E4 47 EB51
Nelson Rd E11 68 EG56
Nelson Rd N8 65 DM57
Nelson Rd N9 46 DV47
Nelson Rd N15 66 DS56
Nelson Rd SE10 103 EC79
Nelson Rd SW19 120 DB94
Nelson Rd, Ashf. 114 BL92
Nelson Rd, Belv. 106 EZ78
Nelson Rd, Brom. 144 EJ98
Nelson Rd, Cat. 176 DR123
Nelson Rd, Dart. 128 FJ86
Nelson Rd, Enf. 31 DX44
Nelson Rd, Grav. 131 GF89
Nelson Rd, Har. 61 CD60
Nelson Rd, Houns. 116 CC87
Nelson Rd (Heathrow Airport), Houns. 94 BM81
Nelson Rd, N.Mal. 138 CR99
Nelson Rd, Rain. 89 FF68
Nelson Rd, Sid. 126 EU91
Nelson Rd, S.Ock. 91 FW68
Nelson Rd, Stan. 41 CJ51
Nelson Rd, Twick. 116 CC86
Nelson Rd, Uxb. 77 BP69
Nelson Sq SE1 200 F4
Nelson Sq SE1 101 DP75
Nelson St E1 84 DV72
Nelson St E6 87 EM68
Nelson St E16 86 EF73
Huntingdon St
Nelson Ter N1 196 G1
Nelson Ter N1 83 DP68
Nelson Trd Est SW19 140 DB95
Nelson Wk SE16 203 L3
Nelson's Row SW4 101 DK84
Nelsons Yd NW1 83 DJ68
Mornington Cres
Nelwyn Av, Horn. 72 FM57
Nemoure Rd W3 80 CQ73
Nene Gdns, Felt. 116 BZ89
Nene Rd, Houns. 95 BP81
Nepaul Rd SW11 100 DE82
Nepean St SW15 119 CU86
Neptune Rd, Har. 61 CD58
Neptune Rd (Heathrow Airport), Houns. 95 BR81
Neptune St SE16 202 F6
Neptune St SE16 102 DW76
Neptune Wk, Erith 107 FD77
Nesbit Rd SE9 104 EK84
Nesbitt Cl SE3 104 EE83
Hurren Cl
Nesbitt Sq SE19 122 DS94
Coxwell Rd
Nesbitts All, Barn. 27 CZ41
Bath Pl
Nesham St E1 202 B2
Nesham St E1 84 DU74
Ness Rd, Erith 108 FK79
Ness St SE16 202 B6
Nesta Rd, Wdf.Grn. 48 EE51
Nestles Av, Hayes 95 BT76
Neston Rd, Wat. 24 BW37
Nestor Av N21 29 DP44
Nethan Dr, S.Ock. 90 FQ73
Nether Cl N3 44 DA52
Nether St N3 44 DA53
Nether St N12 44 DA52
Netheravon Rd W4 99 CT77
Netheravon Rd W7 79 CF74
Netheravon Rd S W4 99 CT78
Netherbury Rd W5 97 CK76
Netherby Gdns, Enf. 29 DL42
Netherby Pk, Wey. 153 BS106
Netherby Rd SE23 122 DW87
Nethercote Av, Wok. 166 AT117
Nethercourt Av N3 44 DA51
Netherfield Gdns, Bark. 87 ER65
Netherfield Rd N12 44 DB50
Netherfield Rd SW17 120 DG90
Netherford Rd SW4 101 DJ82
Netherhall Gdns NW3 82 DC65
Netherhall Way NW3 64 DC64
Netherhall Gdns
Netherlands, The, Couls. 175 DJ119
Netherlands Rd, Barn. 28 DD44
Netherleigh Cl N6 65 DH60
Nethern Ct Rd, Cat. 177 EA123
Netherne La, Couls. 175 DK121
Netherne La, Red. 175 DJ123
Netherpark Dr, Rom. 51 FF54
Netherton Gro SW10 100 DC79
Netherton Rd N15 66 DR58
Netherton Rd, Twick. 117 CH85
Netherwood N2 44 DD54
Netherwood Pl W14 99 CX76
Netherwood Rd
Netherwood Rd W14 99 CX76
Netherwood St NW6 81 CZ66
Netley Cl, Croy. 161 EC108
Netley Cl, Sutt. 157 CX106
Netley Dr, Walt. 136 BZ101
Netley Gdns, Mord. 140 DC101
Netley Rd E17 67 DZ57
Netley Rd, Brent. 98 CL79
Netley Rd (Heathrow Airport), Houns. 95 BR81
Netley Rd, Ilf. 69 ER57
Netley Rd, Mord. 140 DC101
Netley St NW1 195 K3
Nettlecombe Cl, Sutt. 158 DB109
Nettleden Av, Wem. 80 CN65
Nettlefold Pl SE27 121 DP90
Nettlestead Cl, Beck. 123 DZ94
Copers Cope Rd
Nettleton Rd SE14 103 DX81
Nettleton Rd, Houns. 95 BP81
Nettleton Rd, Uxb. 58 BM63
Nettlewood Rd SW16 121 DK94
Neuchatel Rd SE6 123 DZ89
Nevada Cl, N.Mal. 138 CQ98
Georgia Rd
Nevada St SE10 103 EC79
Nevell Rd, Grays 111 GH76
Nevern Pl SW5 100 DA77
Nevern Rd SW5 100 DA77
Nevern Sq SW5 100 DA78
Nevil Cl, Nthwd. 39 BQ50
Nevill Gro, Wat. 23 BV39
Nevill Rd N16 66 DS63
Nevill Way, Loug. 48 EL45
Valley Hill
Neville Av, N.Mal. 138 CR95
Neville Cl E11 68 EF62
Neville Cl NW1 195 N1
Neville Cl NW6 81 CZ68
Neville Cl SE15 102 DU80
Neville Cl W3 98 CQ75
Acton La
Neville Cl, Bans. 158 DB114
Neville Cl, Esher 154 BZ107
Neville Cl, Houns. 96 CB82
Neville Cl, Pot.B. 11 CZ31
Neville Cl, Sid. 125 ET91
Neville Cl, Slou. 74 AT65
Neville Dr N2 64 DC58
Neville Gdns, Dag. 70 EX62
Neville Gill Cl SW18 120 DA86
Neville Pl N22 45 DM53
Neville Rd E7 86 EG66
Neville Rd NW6 81 CZ68
Neville Rd W5 79 CK70
Neville Rd, Croy. 142 DR101
Neville Rd, Dag. 70 EX61
Neville Rd, Ilf. 49 EQ53
Neville Rd, Kings.T. 138 CN96
Neville Rd, Rich. 117 CJ90
Neville St SW7 100 DD78
Neville Ter SW7 100 DD78
Neville Wk, Cars. 140 DE101
Green Wrythe La
Nevilles Ct NW2 63 CU62
Nevin Dr E4 47 EB46
Nevinson Cl SW18 120 DD86
Nevis Cl, Rom. 51 FE51
Nevis Rd SW17 120 DG89
New Arc, Uxb. 76 BK67
High St
New Ash Cl N2 64 DD55
Oakridge Dr
New Atlas Wf E14 203 N7
New Barn La, Beac. 36 AS49
New Barn La, Sev. 179 EQ116
New Barn La, West. 179 EQ118
New Barn La, Whyt. 176 DS117
New Barn Rd, Swan. 147 FE95
New Barn St E13 86 EG70
New Barns Av, Mitch. 141 DK98
New Barns Way, Chig. 49 EP48
New Battlebridge La, Red. 185 DH130
New Berry La, Walt. 154 BX106
New Bond St W1 195 J10
New Bond St W1 83 DH73
New Brent St NW4 63 CW57
New Br St EC4 196 F9
New Br St EC4 83 DP72
New Broad St EC2 197 M7
New Broad St EC2 84 DS71
New Bdy W5 79 CK73
New Bdy, Hmptn. 117 CD92
Hampton Rd
New Burlington Ms W1 195 K10
New Burlington Pl W1 195 K10
New Burlington St W1 195 K10
New Burlington St W1 83 DJ73
New Butt La SE8 103 EA80
New Butt La N SE8 103 EA80
Reginald Rd
New Cavendish St W1 195 J6
New Cavendish St W1 82 DG71
New Change EC4 197 H9
New Change EC4 84 DQ72
New Chapel Sq, Felt. 115 BV88
New Charles St EC1 196 G2
New Ch Ct SE19 122 DU9
Waldegrave Rd
New Ch Rd SE5 102 DQ8
New City Rd E13 86 EJ6
New Cl SW19 140 DC9
New Cl, Felt. 116 BY9
New Coll Ct NW3 82 DC6
College Cres
New Coll Ms N1 83 DN6
Islington Pk St
New Coll Par NW3 82 DD6
College Cres
New Compton St WC2 195 N
New Compton St WC2 83 DK7
New Coppice, Wok. 166 AS11
New Cotts, Rain. 90 FJ7
New Ct EC4 196 D1
New Ct, Add. 134 BJ10
New Covent Gdn Mkt SW8 101 DK8
New Coventry St W1 199 N
New Crane Pl E1 202 F
New Cross Rd SE14 102 DW8
New End NW3 64 DC6
New End Sq NW3 64 DD6
New Era Est N1 84 DS6
Phillipp St
New Fm Av, Brom. 144 EG9
New Fm Dr, Rom. 34 EV4
New Fm La, Nthwd. 39 BS5
New Ferry App SE18 105 EN7
New Fetter La EC4 196 E
New Fetter La EC4 83 DN7
New Ford Rd, Wal.Cr. 15 DZ3
New Forest La, Chig. 49 EN5
New Gdn Dr, West Dr. 94 BL7
Drayton Gdns
New Globe Wk SE1 201 H
New Globe Wk SE1 84 DQ7
New Goulston St E1 197 P
New Grn Pl SE19 122 DS9
Hawke Rd
New Hall Cl, Hem.H. 5 BA2
New Hall Dr, Rom. 52 FL5
New Haw Rd, Add. 152 BJ10
New Heston Rd, Houns. 96 BZ8
New Horizons Ct, Brent. 97 CG7
Shield Dr
New Ho La, Grav. 131 GF9
New Inn Bdy EC2 197 N
New Inn Pas WC2 196 C
New Inn St EC2 197 N
New Inn Yd EC2 197 N
New Inn Yd EC2 84 DS7
New James Ct SE15 102 DV8
Nunhead La
New Jersey Ct SE15 102 DV8
New Jubilee Ct, Wdf.Grn. 48 EG5
Grange Av
New Kent Rd SE1 201 H7
New Kent Rd SE1 102 DQ76
New King St SE8 103 EA79
New Kings Rd SW6 99 CZ82
New La, Guil. 166 AY122
New Lo Dr, Oxt. 188 EF128
New London St EC3 197 N10
New Lydenburg St SE7 104 EJ76
New Mill Rd, Orp. 146 EW95
New Mt St E15 85 ED66
Bridge Rd
New N Pl EC2 197 M5
New N Rd N1 197 L1
New N Rd N1 84 DR68
New N Rd, Ilf. 49 ER52
New N St WC1 196 B6
New N St WC1 83 DM71
New Oak Rd N2 44 DC54
New Orleans Wk N19 65 DK59
New Oxford St WC1 195 N8
New Oxford St WC1 83 DK72
New Par, Ashf. 114 BM91
Church Rd
New Par, Rick. 21 BC42
Whitelands Av
New Par Flats, Rick. 21 BC42
Whitelands Av
New Pk Av N13 46 DQ48
New Pk Cl, Nthlt. 78 BY65
New Pk Ct SW2 121 DL87
New Pk Par SW2 121 DL86
Doverfield Rd
New Pk Rd SW2 121 DK88
New Pk Rd, Ashf. 115 BQ92
New Pk Rd (Harefield), Uxb. 38 BJ53
New Peachey La, Uxb. 76 BK72
New Pl Gdns, Upmin. 73 FR61
New Pl Sq SE16 202 D6
New Pl Sq SE16 102 DV76
New Plaistow Rd E15 86 EE67
New Printing Ho Sq WC1 83 DM70
Gray's Inn Rd
New Priory Ct NW6 82 DA66
Mazenod Av
New Quebec St W1 194 E9
New Quebec St W1 82 DF72
New Ride SW7 198 D4
New Ride SW7 100 DE75
New River Ct (Cheshunt), Wal.Cr. 14 DV30
Pengelly Cl
New River Cres N13 45 DP49
New River Trd Est (Cheshunt), Wal.Cr. 15 DX26
New River Wk N1 84 DQ65
New River Way N4 66 DR59
New Rd E1 84 DV71
New Rd E4 47 EB49
New Rd N8 65 DL57
New Rd N9 46 DU48
New Rd N17 46 DT53
New Rd N22 46 DQ53
New Rd NW7 43 CY52
New Rd (Barnet Gate) NW7 43 CT45
New Rd SE2 106 EX77
New Rd, Amer. 20 AS37
New Rd, Borwd. 25 CK44
New Rd, Brent. 97 CK79
New Rd, Brwd. 54 FX47
New Rd, Ch.St.G. 20 AY41

Norfolk Rd, Har. 60 CB57
Norfolk Rd, Ilf. 69 ES60
Norfolk Rd, Rick. 38 BL46
Norfolk Rd, Rom. 71 FC58
Norfolk Rd, Th.Hth. 142 DQ97
Norfolk Rd, Upmin. 72 FN62
Norfolk Rd, Uxb. 76 BK65
Norfolk Row SE1 200 B8
Norfolk Sq W2 194 A9
Norfolk Sq W2 82 DD72
Norfolk Sq Ms W2 194 A9
Norfolk St E7 68 EG63
Norfolk Ter W6 99 CY78
Field Rd
Norgrove Pk, Ger.Cr. 56 AY56
Norgrove St SW12 120 DG87
Norheads La, Warl. 178 EG119
Norheads La, West. 178 EJ116
Norhyrst Av SE25 142 DT97
Nork Gdns, Bans. 157 CY114
Nork Ri, Bans. 173 CX116
Nork Way, Bans. 173 CY115
Norland Pl W11 81 CY74
Norland Rd W11 81 CX74
Norland Sq W11 81 CY74
Norlands Cres, Chis. 145 EP95
Norlands Gate, Chis. 145 EP95
Norlands La, Egh. 133 BE97
Norley Vale SW15 119 CU88
Norlington Rd E10 67 EC60
Norlington Rd E11 67 EC60
Norman Av N22 45 DP53
Norman Av, Epsom 157 CT112
Norman Av, Felt. 116 BY89
Norman Av, S.Croy. 160 DQ110
Norman Av, Sthl. 78 BY73
Norman Av, Twick. 117 CH87
Norman Cl, Epsom 173 CW119
Merland Ri
Norman Cl, Orp. 145 EQ104
Norman Cl, Rom. 51 FB54
Norman Cl, Wal.Abb. 15 ED33
Norman Ct, Ilf. 69 ER59
Norman Ct, Pot.B. 12 DC30
Norman Cres, Brwd. 55 GA48
Norman Cres, Houns. 96 BX81
Norman Cres, Pnr. 40 BW53
Norman Gro E3 85 DY68
Norman Rd E6 87 EM70
Norman Rd E11 67 ED61
Norman Rd N15 66 DT57
Norman Rd SE10 103 EB80
Norman Rd SW19 120 DC94
Norman Rd, Ashf. 115 BR93
Norman Rd, Belv. 107 FB76
Norman Rd, Dart. 128 FL88
Norman Rd, Horn. 71 FG59
Norman Rd, Ilf. 69 EP64
Norman Rd, Sutt. 158 DA106
Norman Rd, Th.Hth. 141 DP99
Norman St EC1 197 H3
Norman Way N14 45 DL47
Norman Way W3 80 CP71
Normanby Cl SW15 119 CZ85
Manfred Rd
Normanby Rd NW10 63 CT63
Normand Gdns W14 99 CY79
Greyhound Rd
Normand Ms W14 99 CY79
Normand Rd
Normand Rd W14 99 CZ79
Normandy Av, Barn. 27 CZ43
Normandy Dr, Hayes 77 BQ72
Normandy Rd SW9 101 DN81
Normandy Ter E16 86 EH72
Normandy Wk, Egh. 113 BC92
Mullens Rd
Normandy Way, Erith 107 FE81
Normanhurst, Ashf. 114 BN92
Normanhurst, Brwd. 55 GC44
Normanhurst Av, Bexh. 106 EX81
Normanhurst Dr, Twick. 117 CH85
St. Margarets Rd
Normanhurst Rd SW2 121 DM89
Normanhurst Rd, Orp. 146 EV96
Normanhurst Rd, Walt. 136 BX103
Normans, The, Slou. 74 AV72
Norman's Bldgs EC1 84 DQ69
Ironmonger Row
Normans Cl NW10 80 CR65
Normans Cl, Grav. 131 GG87
Normans Cl, Uxb. 76 BL71
Normans Mead NW10 80 CR65
Normansfield Av, Tedd. 117 CJ94
Normansfield Cl, Bushey 40 CB45
Normanshire Av E4 47 EC49
Normanshire Dr E4 47 EA49
Normanton Av SW19 120 DA89
Normanton Pk E4 48 EE48
Normanton Rd, S.Croy. 160 DS107
Normanton St SE23 123 DX89
Normington Cl SW16 121 DN92
Norrice Lea N2 64 DD57
Norris Rd, Stai. 113 BF91
Norris St SW1 199 M1
Norris Way, Dart. 107 FF83
Norroy Rd SW15 99 CX84
Norrys Cl, Barn. 28 DF43
Norrys Rd, Barn. 28 DF42
Norseman Cl, Ilf. 70 EV60
Norseman Way, Grnf. 78 CB67
Olympic Way
Norstead Pl SW15 119 CU89
Norsted La, Orp. 164 EU110
North Access Rd E17 67 DX58
North Acre NW9 42 CS53
North Acre, Bans. 173 CZ116
North Acton Rd NW10 80 CR68
North App, Nthwd. 39 BQ47
North App, Wat. 23 BU35
North Audley St W1 194 F9
North Audley St W1 82 DG72
North Av N18 46 DU49
North Av W13 79 CH72
North Av, Brwd. 53 FR45
North Av, Cars. 158 DF108
North Av, Har. 60 CB58
North Av, Hayes 77 BU73
North Av, Rad. 10 CL32
North Av, Rich. 98 CN81
Sandycombe Rd
North Av, Sthl. 78 BZ73
North Av, Walt. 153 BS109
North Bk NW8 194 B3
North Bk NW8 82 DE69
North Birkbeck Rd E11 67 ED62
North Branch Av W10 81 CW69
Harrow Rd
North Carriage Dr W2 194 B10
North Carriage Dr W2 82 DD73
North Circular Rd E4 47 DZ52
North Circular Rd E18 48 EJ54
North Circular Rd N3 64 DB55
North Circular Rd N12 44 DD53
North Circular Rd N13 45 DN50
North Circular Rd NW2 62 CS62
North Circular Rd NW10 80 CQ66
North Circular Rd NW11 63 CY56
North Cl, Barn. 27 CW43
North Cl, Bexh. 106 EX84
North Cl, Chig. 50 EU50
North Cl, Dag. 88 FA67
North Cl, Felt. 115 BR86
North Rd
North Cl, Mord. 139 CY98
North Cl, St.Alb. 8 CB25
North Colonnade E14 204 A2
North Colonnade E14 85 EA74
North Common, Wey. 153 BP105
North Common Rd W5 80 CL73
North Common Rd, Uxb. 58 BK64
North Cotts, St.Alb. 9 CG25
North Countess Rd E17 47 DZ53
North Ct W1 195 L6
North Ct, Rick. 38 BG46
Hall Cl
North Cray Rd, Bex. 126 EZ90
North Cray Rd, Sid. 126 EY93
North Cres E16 85 ED70
North Cres N3 43 CZ54
North Cres WC1 195 M6
North Cres WC1 83 DK71
North Cross Rd SE22 122 DT85
North Cross Rd, Ilf. 69 EQ56
North Dene NW7 42 CR48
North Dene, Houns. 96 CB81
North Down, S.Croy. 160 DS111
North Downs Cres, Croy. 161 EB110
North Downs Rd, Croy. 161 EB110
North Downs Way, Bet. 183 CU130
North Downs Way, Cat. 185 DN126
North Downs Way, Gdse. 187 DY128
North Downs Way, Oxt. 188 EE126
North Downs Way, Red. 184 DG128
North Downs Way, Reig. 184 DD130
North Downs Way, Sev. 181 FD118
North Downs Way, Tad. 183 CX130
North Downs Way, West. 179 ER121
North Dr SW16 121 DJ91
North Dr, Houns. 96 CC82
North Dr, Orp. 163 ES105
North Dr, Rom. 72 FJ55
North Dr, Ruis. 59 BS59
North Dr, Slou. 74 AS69
North Dr, Vir.W. 132 AS100
North End NW3 64 DC61
North End, Buck.H. 48 EJ45
North End, Croy. 142 DQ103
North End, Rom. 52 FJ47
North End Av NW3 64 DC61
North End Cres W14 99 CZ77
North End Ho W14 99 CY77
North End La, Orp. 163 EN110
North End Par W14 99 CY77
North End Rd
North End Rd NW11 64 DA60
North End Rd SW6 99 CZ79
North End Rd W14 99 CY77
North End Rd, Wem. 62 CN62
North End Way NW3 64 DC61
North Eyot Gdns W6 99 CT78
St. Peter's Sq
North Flockton St SE16 202 B4
North Gdn E14 85 DZ74
Westferry Circ
North Gdns SW19 120 DD94
North Glade, The, Bex. 126 EZ87
North Gower St NW1 195 L3
North Gower St NW1 83 DJ69
North Grn NW9 42 CS52
Clayton Fld
North Grn, Slou. 74 AS73
North Gro N6 64 DG59
North Gro N15 66 DR57
North Gro, Cher. 133 BF100
North Hatton Rd (Heathrow Airport), Houns. 95 BR81
North Hill N6 64 DF58
North Hill, Rick. 21 BE40
North Hill Av N6 64 DG58
North Hill Dr, Rom. 52 FK48
North Hill Grn, Rom. 52 FK49
North Hyde Gdns, Hayes 95 BU77
North Hyde La, Houns. 96 BY78
North Hyde La, Sthl. 96 BY78
North Hyde Rd, Hayes 95 BT76
North Kent Av, Grav. 130 GC86
North La, Tedd. 117 CF93
North Lo Cl SW15 119 CX85
Westleigh Av
North Mall N9 46 DV47
St. Martins Rd
North Mead, Red. 184 DF131
North Ms WC1 196 C5
North Ms WC1 83 DM70
North Mymms Pk, Hat. 11 CT25
North Orbital Rd, Rick. 37 BE50
North Orbital Rd, St.Alb. 10 CL25
North Orbital Rd (Denham), Uxb. 57 BF55
North Orbital Rd, Wat. 7 BU34
North Par, Chess. 156 CL106
North Pk SE9 125 EM86
North Pk, Ger.Cr. 56 AY56
North Pk, Iver 93 BC76
North Pk La, Gdse. 186 DU129
North Pas SW18 100 DA84
North Peckham Est SE15 102 DT80
North Perimeter Rd, Uxb. 76 BL69
Kingston La
North Pl, Mitch. 120 DF94
North Pl, Tedd. 117 CF93
North Pl, Wal.Abb. 15 EB33
Highbridge St
North Pole La, Kes. 162 EF107
North Pole Rd W10 81 CW71
North Ride W2 198 B1
North Ride W2 82 DE73
North Riding, St.Alb. 8 CA30
North Rd N6 64 DG59
North Rd N7 83 DL65
North Rd N9 46 DV46
North Rd SE18 105 ES77
North Rd SW19 120 DC93
North Rd W5 97 CK76
North Rd, Belv. 107 FB76
North Rd, Brent. 98 CL79
North Rd, Brwd. 54 FW46
North Rd, Brom. 144 EH95
North Rd, Dart. 127 FF86
North Rd, Edg. 42 CP53
North Rd, Felt. 115 BR86
North Rd, Hayes 77 BR71
North Rd, Ilf. 69 ES61
North Rd, Purf. 109 FR77
North Rd, Rich. 98 CN83
North Rd, Rick. 21 BD43
North Rd, Rom. 70 EY57
North Rd (Havering-atte-Bower), Rom. 51 FE48
North Rd, S.Ock. 91 FW68
North Rd, Sthl. 78 CA73
North Rd, Surb. 137 CK100
North Rd, Wal.Cr. 15 DY33
North Rd, Walt. 154 BW106
North Rd, West Dr. 94 BM76
North Rd, W.Wick. 143 EB102
North Rd, Wok. 167 BA116
North Rd Av, Brwd. 54 FW46
North Row W1 194 E10
North Row W1 82 DF73
North Service Rd, Brwd. 54 FW47
North Several SE3 103 ED82
Orchard Dr
North Side Wandsworth Common SW18 120 DD85
North Sq N9 46 DV47
St. Martins Rd
North Sq NW11 64 DA57
North St E13 86 EH68
North St NW4 63 CW57
North St SW4 101 DJ83
North St, Bark. 87 EP65
North St, Bexh. 106 FA84
North St, Brom. 144 EG95
North St, Cars. 140 DF104
North St, Dart. 128 FK87
North St, Egh. 113 AZ92
North St, Grav. 131 GH87
South St
North St, Horn. 72 FK59
North St, Islw. 97 CG83
North St, Lthd. 171 CG121
North St, Red. 184 DF133
North St, Rom. 71 FD55
North St Pas E13 86 EH68
North Tenter St E1 84 DT72
North Ter SW3 198 B7
North Ter SW3 100 DE76
North Verbena Gdns W6 99 CU78
St. Peter's Sq
North Vw SW19 119 CV92
North Vw W5 79 CJ70
North Vw, Ilf. 50 EU52
North Vw, Pnr. 60 BW59
North Vw Av, Til. 111 GG81
North Vw Cres, Epsom 173 CV117
North Vw Dr, Wdf.Grn. 48 EK54
North Vw Rd N8 65 DK55
North Vw Rd, Sev. 191 FJ121
Seal Rd
North Vil NW1 83 DK65
North Wk W2 82 DC73
Bayswater Rd
North Wk, Croy. 161 EB106
North Way N9 46 DW47
North Way N11 45 DJ51
North Way NW9 62 CP55
North Way, Pnr. 60 BW55
North Way, Uxb. 76 BL66
North Weald Airfield, Epp. 18 EZ26
North Western Av, Wat. 24 BW36
North Wf Rd W2 82 DD71
North Wd Ct SE25 142 DU97
Regina Rd
North Woolwich Rd E16 205 L2
North Woolwich Rd E16 86 EG74
North Woolwich Roundabout E16 86 EK74
North Woolwich Rd
North Worple Way SW14 98 CR83
Northall Rd, Bexh. 107 FC82
Northallerton Way, Rom. 52 FK50
Northampton Gro N1 66 DR64
Northampton Pk N1 84 DQ65
Northampton Rd EC1 196 E4
Northampton Rd EC1 83 DN70
Northampton Rd, Croy. 142 DU103
Northampton Rd, Enf. 31 DY42
Northampton Sq EC1 196 F3
Northampton Sq EC1 83 DP69
Northampton St N1 84 DQ66
Northanger Rd SW16 121 DL93
Northaw Pl, Pot.B. 12 DD30
Northaw Rd E (Cuffley), Pot.B. 13 DK31
Northaw Rd W, Pot.B. 12 DG30
Northbank Rd E17 47 EC54
Northborough Rd SW16 141 DK97
Northbourne, Brom. 144 EG101
Northbourne Rd SW4 101 DK84
Northbrook Dr, Nthwd. 39 BS53
Northbrook Rd N22 45 DL52
Northbrook Rd SE13 123 ED85
Northbrook Rd, Barn. 27 CY44
Northbrook Rd, Croy. 142 DR99
Northbrook Rd, Ilf. 69 EN61
Northburgh St EC1 196 G4
Northburgh St EC1 83 DP70
Northchurch SE17 201 L10
Northchurch Rd N1 84 DR66
Northchurch Rd, Wem. 80 CM65
Northchurch Ter N1 84 DS66
Northcliffe Cl, Wor.Pk. 138 CS104
Northcliffe Dr N20 43 CZ46
Northcote, Add. 152 BK105
Northcote, Lthd. 154 CC114
Northcote, Pnr. 40 BW54
Northcote Av W5 80 CL73
Northcote Av, Islw. 117 CG85
Northcote Av, Sthl. 78 BY73
Northcote Av, Surb. 138 CN101
Northcote Rd E17 67 DY56
Northcote Rd NW10 80 CS66
Northcote Rd SW11 100 DE84
Northcote Rd, Croy. 142 DR100
Northcote Rd, Grav. 131 GF88
Northcote Rd, N.Mal. 138 CQ97
Northcote Rd, Sid. 125 ES91
Northcote Rd, Twick. 117 CG85
Northcott Av N22 45 DL53
Northcotts, Abb.L. 7 BR33
Long Elms
Northcroft Cl, Egh. 112 AV92
Northcroft Gdns, Egh. 112 AV92
Northcroft Rd W13 97 CH75
Northcroft Rd, Egh. 112 AV92
Northcroft Rd, Epsom 156 CR108
Northcroft Ter W13 97 CH75
Northcroft Rd
Northcroft Vil, Egh. 112 AV92
Northdene, Chig. 49 ER50
Northdene Gdns N15 66 DT58
Northdown Cl, Ruis. 59 BT62
Northdown Gdns, Ilf. 69 ES57
Northdown Rd, Cat. 177 EA123
Northdown Rd (Chalfont St. Peter), Ger.Cr. 36 AY51
Northdown Rd, Horn. 71 FH59
Northdown Rd, Long. 149 FX96
Northdown Rd, Sutt. 158 DA110
Northdown Rd, Well. 106 EV82
Northdown St N1 83 DM68
Northend, Brwd. 54 FW50
Northend Rd, Dart. 107 FF81
Northend Rd, Erith 107 FF80
Northend Trd Est, Erith 107 FE81
Northern Av N9 46 DT47
Northern Perimeter Rd, Houns. 95 BQ81
Northern Perimeter Rd W, Houns. 94 BK81
Northern Relief Rd, Bark. 87 EP66
Northern Rd E13 86 EH67
Northern Service Rd, Barn. 27 CY41
Northernhay Wk, Mord. 139 CY98
Northey Av, Sutt. 157 CZ110
Northey St E14 85 DY73
Northfield, Loug. 32 EK42
Northfield Av W5 97 CH75
Northfield Av W13 97 CH75
Northfield Av, Orp. 146 EW100
Northfield Av, Pnr. 60 BX56
Northfield Cl, Brom. 144 EL95
Northfield Cl, Hayes 95 BT76
Northfield Ct, Stai. 134 BH95
Northfield Cres, Sutt. 157 CY105
Northfield Gdns, Dag. 70 EZ63
Northfield Rd
Northfield Gdns, Wat. 24 BW37
Northfield Pk, Hayes 95 BT76
Northfield Path, Dag. 70 EZ62
Northfield Pl, Wey. 153 BP108
Northfield Rd E6 87 EM66
Northfield Rd N16 66 DS59
Northfield Rd W13 97 CH75
Northfield Rd, Barn. 28 DE41
Northfield Rd, Borwd. 26 CP39
Northfield Rd, Cob. 153 BU113
Northfield Rd, Dag. 70 EZ63
Northfield Rd, Enf. 30 DV43
Northfield Rd, Houns. 96 BX79
Northfield Rd, Stai. 134 BH95
Northfield Rd, Wal.Cr. 15 DY32
Northfields SW18 100 DA84
Northfields, Ash. 172 CL119
Northfields, Grays 110 GC77
Northfields Ind Est, Wem. 80 CN67
Northfields Rd W3 80 CP71
Northfleet Grn Rd, Grav. 130 GC93
Northfleet Ind Est, Grav. 110 FZ84
Northgate, Nthwd. 39 BQ52
Northgate Dr NW9 62 CS58
Northgate Path, Borwd. 26 CM39
Northiam N12 44 DA48
Northiam St E9 84 DV67
Northington St WC1 196 C5
Northington St WC1 83 DM70
Northlands, Pot.B. 12 DD31
Northlands Av, Orp. 163 ES105
Northlands St SE5 102 DQ82
Northolm, Edg. 42 CR49
Northolme Cl, Grays 110 GC76
Premier Av
Northolme Gdns, Edg. 42 CN53
Northolme Ri, Orp. 145 ES103
Northolme Rd N5 66 DQ63
Northolt Av, Ruis. 59 BV64
Northolt Gdns, Grnf. 61 CF64
Northolt Rd, Har. 60 CB63
Northolt Rd, Houns. 94 BK81
Northolt Way, Horn. 90 FJ65
Northover, Brom. 124 EF90
Northport St N1 84 DR67
Northridge Rd, Grav. 131 GJ90
Northrop Rd, Houns. 95 BS81
Northside Rd, Brom. 144 EG95
Mitchell Way
Northspur Rd, Sutt. 140 DA104
Northstead Rd SW2 121 DN89
Northumberland All EC3 197 N
Northumberland All EC3 84 DS72
Northumberland Av E12 68 EJ6
Northumberland Av WC2 199 P2
Northumberland Av WC2 83 DL74
Northumberland Av, Enf. 30 DV39
Northumberland Av, Horn. 72 FJ57
Northumberland Av, Islw. 97 CF81
Northumberland Av, Well. 105 ES84
Northumberland Cl, Erith 107 FC80
Northumberland Cl, Stai. 114 BL86
Northumberland Cres, Felt. 115 BS86
Northumberland Gdns N9 46 DT48
Northumberland Gdns, Brom. 145 EN98
Northumberland Gdns, Islw. 97 CG80
Northumberland Gdns, Mitch. 141 DK99
Northumberland Gro N17 46 DV52
Northumberland Pk N17 46 DT52
Northumberland Pk, Erith 107 FC80
Northumberland Pl W2 82 DA72
Northumberland Pl, Rich. 117 CK85
Northumberland Rd E6 86 EL72
Northumberland Rd E17 67 EA59
Northumberland Rd, Barn. 28 DC44
Northumberland Rd, Grav. 131 GF94
Northumberland Rd, Har. 60 BZ57
Northumberland Row, Twick. 117 CE88
Colne Rd
Northumberland St WC2 199 P2
Northumberland St WC2 83 DL74
Northumberland Way, Erith 107 FC81
Northumbria St E14 85 EA72
Northview, Swan. 147 FE96
Northview Cres NW10 63 CT63
Northway NW11 64 DB57
Northway, Mord. 139 CY97
Northway, Rick. 38 BK45
Northway, Wall. 159 DJ105
Northway Circ NW7 42 CR49
Northway Cres NW7 42 CR49
Northway Rd SE5 102 DQ83
Northway Rd, Croy. 142 DT100
Northways Par NW3 82 DD66
College Cres
Northweald La, Kings.T. 117 CK92
Northwest Pl N1 83 DN68
Chapel Mkt
Northwick Av, Har. 61 CG58
Northwick Circle, Har. 61 CJ58
Northwick Cl NW8 82 DD70
Northwick Ter
Northwick Pk Rd, Har. 61 CF58
Northwick Rd, Wat. 40 BW49
Northwick Rd, Wem. 79 CK67
Northwick Ter NW8 82 DD70
Northwick Wk, Har. 61 CF59
Northwold Dr, Pnr. 60 BW55
Cuckoo Hill
Northwold Est E5 66 DU61
Northwold Rd E5 66 DT61
Northwold Rd N16 66 DT61
Northwood, Grays 111 GH75
Northwood Av, Horn. 71 FG63
Northwood Av, Pur. 159 DN113
Northwood Cl, Wal.Cr. 14 DT27
Northwood Gdns N12 44 DD50
Northwood Gdns, Grnf. 61 CF64
Northwood Gdns, Ilf. 69 EN56
Northwood Hall N6 65 DJ59
Northwood Ho SE27 122 DR91
Northwood Pl, Erith 106 EZ76
Northwood Rd N6 65 DH59
Northwood Rd SE23 123 DZ88
Northwood Rd, Cars. 158 DG107
Northwood Rd, Houns. 94 BK81
Northwood Rd, Th.Hth. 141 DP96
Northwood Rd (Harefield), Uxb. 38 BJ53
Northwood Way SE19 122 DR93
Roman Ri
Northwood Way, Nthwd. 39 BU52
Northwood Way (Harefield), Uxb. 38 BK53
Nortoft Rd (Chalfont St. Peter), Ger.Cr. 37 AZ51
Norton Av, Surb. 138 CP101
Norton Cl E4 47 EA50
Norton Cl, Borwd. 26 CN39
Norton Cl, Enf. 30 DV40
Brick La
Norton Folgate E1 197 N6
Norton Folgate E1 84 DS71
Norton Gdns SW16 141 DL96
Norton La, Cob. 169 BT119
Norton Rd E10 67 DZ60
Norton Rd, Dag. 89 FD65
Norton Rd, Uxb. 76 BK69
Norton Rd, Wem. 79 CK65
Norval Rd, Wem. 61 CH61
Norway Dr, Slou. 74 AV71
Norway Gate SE16 203 L6
Norway Gate SE16 103 DY76
Norway Pl E14 85 DZ72
East India Dock Rd
Norway St SE10 103 EB79

Norway Wk, Rain. 90 FJ70
The Glen
Norwich Ho E14 85 EB72
Cordelia St
Norwich Ms, Ilf. 70 EU60
Ashgrove Rd
Norwich Pl, Bexh. 106 FA84
Norwich Rd E7 68 EG64
Norwich Rd, Dag. 88 FA68
Norwich Rd, Grnf. 78 CB67
Norwich Rd, Nthwd. 59 BT55
Norwich Rd, Th.Hth. 142 DQ97
Norwich St EC4 196 D8
Norwich St EC4 83 DN72
Norwich Wk, Edg. 42 CQ52
Norwich Way, Rick. 23 BP41
Norwood Av, Rom. 71 FE59
Norwood Av, Wem. 80 CM67
Norwood Cl, Sthl. 96 CA77
Norwood Cl, Twick. 117 CD89
Fourth Cross Rd
Norwood Cres, Houns. 95 BQ81
Norwood Dr, Har. 60 BZ58
Norwood Fm La, Cob. 153 BU111
Norwood Gdns, Hayes 78 BW70
Norwood Gdns, Sthl. 96 BZ77
Norwood Grn Rd, Sthl. 96 CA77
Norwood High St SE27 121 DP90
Norwood La, Iver 75 BD70
Norwood Pk Rd SE27 122 DQ92
Norwood Rd SE24 121 DP88
Norwood Rd SE27 121 DP89
Norwood Rd, Sthl. 96 BZ77
Norwood Rd (Cheshunt), Wal.Cr. 15 DY30
Norwood Ter, Sthl. 96 CB77
Tentelow La
Nota Ms N3 44 DA53
Station Rd
Notley End, Egh. 112 AW93
Notley St SE5 102 DR80
Notre Dame Est SW4 101 DJ84
Notson Rd SE25 142 DV98
Notting Barn Rd W10 81 CX70
Notting Hill Gate W11 82 DA74
Nottingdale Sq W11 81 CY74
Wilsham St
Nottingham Av E16 86 EJ71
Nottingham Cl, Wat. 7 BU33
Nottingham Cl, Wok. 166 AT118
Nottingham Ct WC2 195 P9
Nottingham Ct, Wok. 166 AT118
Nottingham Cl
Nottingham Pl W1 194 F5
Nottingham Pl W1 82 DG70
Nottingham Rd E10 67 EC58
Nottingham Rd SW17 120 DF88
Nottingham Rd, Islw. 97 CF82
Nottingham Rd, Rick. 37 BC45
Nottingham Rd, S.Croy. 160 DQ105
Nottingham St W1 194 F6
Nottingham St W1 82 DG71
Nottingham Ter NW1 194 F5
Nova Ms, Sutt. 139 CY102
Nova Rd, Croy. 141 DP101
Novar Cl, Orp. 145 ET101
Novar Rd SE9 125 EQ88
Novello St SW6 100 DA81
Novello Way, Borwd. 26 CR39
Nowell Rd SW13 99 CU79
Nower, The, Sev. 179 ET119
Nower Hill, Pnr. 60 BZ56
Noyna Rd SW17 120 DF90
Nuding Cl SE13 103 EA83
Nuffield Rd, Swan. 127 FG93
Nugent Ind Pk, Orp. 146 EW99
Nugent Rd N19 65 DL60
Nugent Rd SE25 142 DT97
Nugent Ter NW8 82 DC68
Nugents Ct, Pnr. 40 BY53
St. Thomas' Dr
Nugents Pk, Pnr. 40 BY53
Nun Ct EC2 197 K8
Nunappleton Way, Oxt. 188 EG132
Nuneaton Rd, Dag. 88 EX66
Nunfield, Kings L. 6 BH31
Nunhead Cres SE15 102 DV83
Nunhead Est SE15 102 DV83
Nunhead Grn SE15 102 DV83
Nunhead Grn (Denham), Uxb. 57 BF58
Nunhead Gro SE15 102 DV83
Nunhead La SE15 102 DV83
Nunhead Pas SE15 102 DU83
Peckham Rye
Nunnington Cl SE9 124 EL90
Nunns Rd, Enf. 30 DQ40
Nunns Way, Grays 110 GD77
Nuns Wk, Vir.W. 132 AX99
Nunsbury Dr, Brox. 15 DY25
Nupton Dr, Barn. 27 CW44
Nursery, The, Erith 107 FF80
Nursery Av N3 44 DC54
Nursery Av, Bexh. 106 EZ83
Nursery Av, Croy. 143 DX103
Nursery Cl SE4 103 DZ82
Nursery Cl SW15 99 CX84
Nursery Cl, Add. 151 BF110
Nursery Cl, Amer. 20 AS39
Nursery Cl, Croy. 143 DX103
Nursery Cl, Dart. 128 FQ87
Nursery Cl, Enf. 31 DX39
Nursery Cl, Epsom 156 CS110
Nursery Cl, Felt. 115 BV87
Nursery Cl, Orp. 146 EU101
Nursery Cl, Rom. 70 EX58
Nursery Cl, Sev. 191 FJ122
Nursery Cl, S.Ock. 91 FW70
Nursery Cl, Swan. 147 FC96
Nursery Cl, Tad. 183 CU125
Nursery Cl, Wok. 166 AW116
Nursery Cl, Wdf.Grn. 48 EH50
Nursery Ct N17 46 DT52
Nursery St
Nursery Gdns, Chis. 125 EP93
Nursery Gdns, Enf. 31 DX39
Nursery Gdns, Houns. 116 BZ85
Nursery Gdns, Stai. 114 BH94
Nursery Gdns, Sun. 135 BT96
Nursery Gdns, Wal.Cr. 14 DR28
Nursery La E2 84 DT67
Nursery La E7 86 EG65
Nursery La W10 81 CW71
Nursery La, Slou. 74 AW74
Nursery La, Uxb. 76 BK70
Nursery Pl, Sev. 190 FD122
Nursery Rd E9 84 DW65
Morning La
Nursery Rd N2 44 DD53
Nursery Rd N14 45 DJ45
Nursery Rd SW9 101 DM84
Nursery Rd, Brox. 15 DY25
Nursery Rd, Loug. 32 EJ43
Nursery Rd (High Beach), Loug. 32 EH39
Nursery Rd, Pnr. 60 BW55
Nursery Rd, Sun. 135 BS96
Nursery Rd, Sutt. 158 DC105
Nursery Rd, Tad. 183 CU125
Nursery Rd, Th.Hth. 142 DR98
Nursery Rd Merton SW19 140 DB96
Nursery Rd Mitcham, Mitch. 140 DE97
Nursery Rd Wimbledon SW19 119 CY94
Worple Rd
Nursery Row SE17 201 K9
Nursery Row SE17 102 DR77
Nursery Row, Barn. 27 CY41
St. Albans Rd
Nursery St N17 46 DT52
Nursery Wk NW4 63 CV55
Nursery Wk, Rom. 71 FD59
Nursery Way, Stai. 112 AX86
Nursery Waye, Uxb. 76 BK67
Nurserymans Rd N11 44 DG47
Nurstead Rd, Erith 106 FA80
Nut Tree Cl, Orp. 146 EX104
Nutberry Av, Grays 110 GA75
Nutberry Cl, Grays 110 GA75
Long La
Nutbourne St W10 81 CY69
Nutbrook St SE15 102 DU83
Nutbrowne Rd, Dag. 88 EZ67
Nutcroft Gro, Lthd. 171 CE121
Nutcroft Rd SE15 102 DV80
Nutfield Cl N18 46 DU51
Nutfield Cl, Cars. 140 DE104
Nutfield Gdns, Ilf. 69 ET61
Nutfield Gdns, Nthlt. 78 BW68
Nutfield Marsh Rd, Red. 185 DJ130
Nutfield Rd E15 67 EC63
Nutfield Rd NW2 63 CU61
Nutfield Rd SE22 122 DT85
Nutfield Rd, Couls. 174 DG116
Nutfield Rd, Red. 184 DG134
Nutfield Rd (South Merstham), Red. 185 DJ129
Nutfield Rd, Th.Hth. 141 DP98
Nutfield Way, Orp. 145 EN103
Nutford Pl W1 194 C8
Nutford Pl W1 82 DF72
Nuthatch Cl, Stai. 114 BM88
Nuthatch Gdns SE28 105 ER75
Nuthurst Av SW2 121 DM89
Nutkin Wk, Uxb. 76 BL66
Park Rd
Nutley Cl, Swan. 147 FF95
Nutley Ct, Reig. 183 CZ134
Nutley La
Nutley La, Reig. 183 CZ133
Nutley Ter NW3 82 DC65
Nutmead Cl, Bex. 127 FC88
Nutmeg Cl E16 86 EE70
Cranberry La
Nutmeg La E14 85 ED72
Nutt Gro, Edg. 41 CK47
Nutt St SE15 102 DT80
Nuttall St N1 84 DS68
Nutter La E11 68 EJ58
Nuttfield Cl, Rick. 23 BP44
Nutty La, Shep. 135 BQ98
Nutwell St SW17 120 DE92
Nutwood Gdns (Cheshunt), Wal.Cr. 14 DR26
Hammondstreet Rd
Nuxley Rd, Belv. 106 EZ79
Nyanza St SE18 105 ER79
Nye Bevan Est E5 67 DX62
Nye Way, Hem.H. 5 BA28
Nyefield Pk, Tad. 183 CU126
Nylands Av, Rich. 98 CN81
Nymans Gdns SW20 139 CV97
Hidcote Gdns
Nynehead St SE14 103 DY80
Nyon Gro SE6 123 DZ89
Nyssa Cl, Wdf.Grn. 49 EM51
Gwynne Pk Av
Nyth Cl, Upmin. 73 FR58
Nyton Cl N19 65 DL60
Courtauld Rd

O

Oak Apple Ct SE12 124 EG89
Oak Av N8 65 DL56
Oak Av N10 45 DH52
Oak Av N17 46 DR52
Oak Av, Croy. 143 EA103
Oak Av, Egh. 113 BC94
Oak Av, Enf. 29 DM38
Oak Av, Hmptn. 116 BY92
Oak Av, Houns. 96 BX80
Oak Av, St.Alb. 8 CA30
Oak Av, Sev. 191 FH128
Oak Av, Upmin. 72 FP62
Oak Av, Uxb. 59 BP61
Oak Av, West Dr. 94 BN76
Oak Bk, Croy. 161 EC107
Oak Cl N14 45 DH45
Oak Cl, Dart. 107 FE84
Oak Cl, Sutt. 140 DC103
Oak Cl, Tad. 182 CP130
Oak Cl, Wal.Abb. 15 ED34
Oak Cottage Cl SE6 124 EF88
Oak Cres E16 86 EE71
Oak Dene W13 79 CH71
The Dene
Oak Dr, Tad. 182 CP130
Oak End Dr, Iver 75 BC68
Oak End Way, Add. 151 BE112
Oak End Way, Ger.Cr. 56 AY57
Oak Fm, Borwd. 26 CQ43
Oak Gdns, Croy. 143 EA103
Oak Gdns, Edg. 42 CQ54
Oak Glade, Epp. 18 EX29
Coopersale Common
Oak Glade, Epsom 156 CN112
Christ Ch Rd
Oak Glade, Nthwd. 39 BP53
Oak Glen, Horn. 72 FL55
Oak Grn, Abb.L. 7 BS32
Oak Grn Way, Abb.L. 7 BS32
Oak Gro NW2 63 CY63
Oak Gro, Ruis. 59 BV60
Oak Gro, Sun. 115 BV94
Oak Gro, W.Wick. 143 EC103
Oak Gro Rd SE20 142 DW95
Oak Hall Rd E11 68 EH58
Oak Hill, Epsom 172 CR116
Oak Hill, Surb. 138 CL101
Oak Hill, Wdf.Grn. 47 ED52
Oak Hill Cl, Wdf.Grn. 47 ED52
Oak Hill Cres, Surb. 138 CL101
Oak Hill Cres, Wdf.Grn. 47 ED52
Oak Hill Gdns, Wdf.Grn. 48 EE53
Oak Hill Gro, Surb. 138 CL100
Oak Hill Pk NW3 64 DB63
Oak Hill Pk Ms NW3 64 DC63
Oak Hill Rd, Rom. 51 FD45
Oak Hill Rd, Sev. 190 FG124
Oak Hill Rd, Surb. 138 CL100
Oak Hill Way NW3 64 DC63
Oak La E14 85 DZ73
Oak La N2 44 DD54
Oak La N11 45 DK51
Oak La, Egh. 112 AW90
Oak La, Islw. 97 CE84
Oak La (Cuffley), Pot.B. 13 DM28
Oak La, Sev. 190 FG127
Oak La, Twick. 117 CG87
Oak La, Wok. 167 BC116
Beaufort Rd
Oak La, Wdf.Grn. 48 EF49
Oak Leaf Cl, Epsom 156 CQ112
Oak Lo Av, Chig. 49 ER50
Oak Lo Cl, Stan. 41 CJ50
Dennis La
Oak Lo Cl, Walt. 154 BW106
Oak Lo Dr, W.Wick. 143 EB101
Oak Lo La, West. 189 ER125
Oak Manor Dr, Wem. 62 CM64
Oakington Manor Dr
Oak Pk, W.Byf. 151 BE113
Oak Pk Gdns SW19 119 CX87
Oak Path, Bushey 24 CB44
Ashfield Av
Oak Piece, Epp. 19 FC25
Oak Pl SW18 120 DB85
East Hill
Oak Ri, Buck.H. 48 EK48
Oak Rd W5 79 CK73
The Bdy
Oak Rd, Cat. 176 DS122
Oak Rd, Cob. 170 BX115
Oak Rd, Epp. 17 ET30
Oak Rd (Northumberland Heath), Erith 107 FC80
Oak Rd (Slade Grn), Erith 107 FG81
Oak Rd, Grav. 131 GJ90
Oak Rd, Grays 110 GC79
Oak Rd, Green. 129 FS86
Oak Rd, Lthd. 171 CG118
Oak Rd, N.Mal. 138 CR96
Oak Rd, Orp. 164 EU108
Oak Rd, Reig. 184 DB133
Oak Rd, Rom. 52 FM53
Oak Rd, West. 189 ER125
Oak Row SW16 141 DJ96
Oak Sq, Sev. 191 FJ126
High St
Oak St, Rom. 71 FC57
Oak Tree Av (Bluewater), Green. 129 FT87
Oak Tree Cl W5 79 CJ72
Pinewood Gro
Oak Tree Cl, Abb.L. 7 BR32
Oak Tree Cl, Loug. 33 EQ39
Oak Tree Cl, Stan. 41 CJ52
Oak Tree Cl, Vir.W. 132 AX101
Oak Tree Ct, Borwd. 25 CK44
Barnet La
Oak Tree Dell NW9 62 CQ57
Oak Tree Dr N20 44 DB46
Oak Tree Dr, Egh. 112 AW92
Oak Tree Gdns, Brom. 124 EH92
Oak Tree Rd NW8 194 A3
Oak Tree Rd NW8 82 DE69
Oak Village NW5 64 DG63
Oak Way N14 45 DH45
Oak Way W3 80 CS74
Oak Way, Ash. 172 CN116
Oak Way, Croy. 143 DX100
Oak Way, Felt. 115 BS88
Oakapple Cl, S.Croy. 160 DV114
Oakbank, Brwd. 55 GE43
Oakbank, Lthd. 170 CC123
Oakbank, Wok. 166 AY119
Oakbank Av, Walt. 136 BZ101
Oakbank Gro SE24 102 DQ84
Oakbrook Cl, Brom. 124 EH91
Oakbury Rd SW6 100 DB82
Oakcombe Cl, N.Mal. 138 CS95
Traps La
Oakcroft Cl, Pnr. 39 BV54
Oakcroft Cl, W.Byf. 151 BF114
Oakcroft Rd SE13 103 ED82
Oakcroft Rd, Chess. 156 CM105
Oakcroft Rd, W.Byf. 151 BF114
Oakcroft Vil, Chess. 156 CM105
Oakdale N14 45 DH46
Oakdale Av, Har. 62 CL57
Oakdale Av, Nthwd. 39 BU54
Oakdale Cl, Wat. 40 BW49
Oakdale Gdns E4 47 EC50
Oakdale La, Eden. 189 EP133
Oakdale Rd E7 86 EH66
Oakdale Rd E11 67 ED61
Oakdale Rd E18 48 EH54
Oakdale Rd N4 66 DQ58
Oakdale Rd SE15 102 DW83
Oakdale Rd SW16 121 DL92
Oakdale Rd, Epsom 156 CR109
Oakdale Rd, Wat. 40 BW48
Oakdale Rd, Wey. 134 BN104
Oakdale Way, Mitch. 140 DG101
Wolseley Rd
Oakden St SE11 200 E8
Oakden St SE11 101 DN77
Oakdene SE15 102 DV81
Carlton Gro
Oakdene, Rom. 52 FM54
Oakdene, Tad. 173 CY120
Oakdene (Cheshunt), Wal.Cr. 15 DY30
Oakdene, Wok. 150 AT110
Oakdene Av, Chis. 125 EN92
Oakdene Av, Erith 107 FC79
Oakdene Av, T.Ditt. 137 CG102
Oakdene Cl, Horn. 71 FH58
Oakdene Cl, Pnr. 40 BZ52
Oakdene Dr, Surb. 138 CQ101
Oakdene Ms, Sutt. 139 CZ102
Oakdene Par, Cob. 153 BV114
Anyards Rd
Oakdene Pk N3 43 CZ52
Oakdene Rd, Cob. 153 BV114
Oakdene Rd, Lthd. 170 BZ124
Oakdene Rd, Orp. 145 ET99
Oakdene Rd, Red. 184 DE134
Oakdene Rd, Sev. 190 FG122
Oakdene Rd, Uxb. 77 BP68
Oakdene Rd, Wat. 23 BV36
Oake Ct SW15 119 CY85
Oaken Coppice, Ash. 172 CN119
Oaken Dr, Esher 155 CF107
Oaken La, Esher 155 CE106
Oakenholt Ho SE2 106 EX75
Hartslock Dr
Oakenshaw Cl, Surb. 138 CL101
Oakes Cl E6 87 EM72
Savage Gdns
Oakeshott Av N6 64 DG61
Oakey La SE1 200 D6
Oakey La SE1 101 DN76
Oakfield E4 47 EB50
Oakfield, Rick. 37 BF45
Oakfield, Wok. 166 AS116
Oakfield Av, Har. 61 CH55
Oakfield Cl, N.Mal. 139 CT99
Blakes La
Oakfield Cl, Pot.B. 11 CZ31
Oakfield Cl, Ruis. 59 BT58
Oakfield Cl, Wey. 153 BQ105
Oakfield Ct N8 65 DL59
Oakfield Ct NW2 63 CX59
Hendon Way
Oakfield Ct, Borwd. 26 CP41
Oakfield Dr, Reig. 184 DA132
Oakfield Gdns N18 46 DS49
Oakfield Gdns SE19 122 DS92
Oakfield Gdns, Beck. 143 EA99
Oakfield Gdns, Cars. 140 DE102
Oakfield Gdns, Grnf. 79 CD70
Oakfield Glade, Wey. 153 BQ105
Oakfield La, Bex. 127 FE89
Oakfield La, Dart. 127 FG89
Oakfield La, Kes. 162 EJ105
Oakfield Pk Rd, Dart. 128 FK89
Oakfield Pl, Dart. 128 FK89
Oakfield Rd E6 86 EL67
Oakfield Rd E17 47 DY54
Oakfield Rd N3 44 DB53
Oakfield Rd N4 65 DN58
Oakfield Rd N14 45 DL48
Oakfield Rd SE20 122 DV94
Oakfield Rd SW19 119 CX90
Oakfield Rd, Ashf. 115 BP92
Oakfield Rd, Ash. 171 CK117
Oakfield Rd, Cob. 153 BV113
Oakfield Rd, Croy. 142 DQ102
Oakfield Rd, Ilf. 69 EP61
Oakfield Rd, Orp. 146 EU101
Goodmead Rd
Oakfield St SW10 100 DC79
Oakfields, Sev. 191 FH126
Oakfields, Walt. 135 BU102
Oakfields, W.Byf. 152 BH114
Oakfields Rd NW11 63 CY58
Oakford Rd NW5 65 DJ63
Oakhall Ct E11 68 EH58
Oakhall Dr, Sun. 115 BT92
Oakham Cl SE6 123 DZ89
Rutland Wk
Oakham Cl, Barn. 28 DF41
Oakham Dr, Brom. 144 EF98
Oakhampton Rd NW7 43 CX52
Oakhill, Esher 155 CG107
Oakhill Av NW3 64 DB63
Oakhill Av, Pnr. 40 BY54
Oakhill Cl, Ash. 171 CJ118
Oakhill Cl, Rick. 37 BE49
Oakhill Ct SW19 119 CX94
Oakhill Dr, Surb. 138 CL101
Oakhill Gdns, Wey. 135 BS103
Oakhill Path, Surb. 138 CL100
Oakhill Pl SW15 120 DA85
Oakhill Rd
Oakhill Rd SW15 119 CZ85
Oakhill Rd SW16 141 DL95
Oakhill Rd, Add. 151 BF107
Oakhill Rd, Ash. 171 CJ118
Oakhill Rd, Beck. 143 EC96
Oakhill Rd, Orp. 145 ET102
Oakhill Rd, Purf. 108 FP78
Oakhill Rd, Rick. 37 BD49
Oakhill Rd, Sutt. 140 DB104
Oakhouse Rd, Bexh. 126 FA85
Oakhurst, Wok. 150 AS109
Oakhurst Av, Barn. 44 DE45
Oakhurst Av, Bexh. 106 EY80
Oakhurst Cl E17 68 EE56
Oakhurst Cl, Ilf. 49 EQ53
Oakhurst Cl, Tedd. 117 CE92
Oakhurst Gdns E4 48 EF46
Oakhurst Gdns E17 68 EE56
Oakhurst Gdns, Bexh. 106 EY80
Oakhurst Gro SE22 102 DU84
Oakhurst Pl, Wat. 23 BT42
Cherrydale
Oakhurst Ri, Cars. 158 DE110
Oakhurst Rd, Enf. 31 DX36
Oakhurst Rd, Epsom 156 CQ107
Oakington Av, Amer. 20 AY39
Oakington Av, Har. 60 CA59
Oakington Av, Hayes 95 BR77
Oakington Av, Wem. 62 CM62
Oakington Dr, Sun. 136 BW96
Oakington Manor Dr, Wem. 62 CN64
Oakington Rd W9 82 DA70
Oakington Way N8 65 DL58
Oakland Gdns, Brwd. 55 GC43
Oakland Pl, Buck.H. 48 EG47
Oakland Rd E15 67 ED63
Oakland Way, Epsom 156 CR107
Oaklands N21 45 DM47
Oaklands, Ken. 160 DQ114
Oaklands, Lthd. 171 CD124
Oaklands, Twick. 116 CC87
Oaklands Av N9 30 DV44
Oaklands Av, Esher 137 CD102
Oaklands Av, Hat. 11 CY27
Oaklands Av, Islw. 97 CF79
Oaklands Av, Rom. 71 FE55
Oaklands Av, Sid. 125 ET87
Oaklands Av, Th.Hth. 141 DN98
Oaklands Av, Wat. 39 BV46
Oaklands Av, W.Wick. 143 EB104
Oaklands Cl, Bexh. 126 EZ85
Oaklands Cl, Chess. 155 CJ105
Oaklands Cl, Orp. 145 ES100
Oaklands Ct, Add. 134 BH104
Oaklands Ct, Wat. 23 BU39
Oaklands Ct, Wem. 61 CK64
Oaklands Dr, S.Ock. 91 FW71
Oaklands Est SW4 121 DJ86
Oaklands Gdns, Ken. 160 DQ114
Oaklands Gate, Nthwd. 39 BS51
Green La
Oaklands Gro W12 81 CU74
Oaklands La, Barn. 27 CV42
Oaklands La, West. 162 EH113
Oaklands Pk Av, Ilf. 69 ER61
High Rd
Oaklands Pl SW4 101 DJ84
St. Alphonsus Rd
Oaklands Rd N20 43 CZ45
Oaklands Rd NW2 63 CX63
Oaklands Rd SW14 98 CR83
Oaklands Rd W7 97 CF75
Oaklands Rd, Bexh. 106 EZ84
Oaklands Rd, Brom. 124 EE94
Oaklands Rd, Dart. 128 FP88
Oaklands Rd, Grav. 131 GF91
Oaklands Rd (Cheshunt), Wal.Cr. 14 DS26
Oaklands Way, Tad. 173 CW122
Oaklands Way, Wall. 159 DK108
Oaklawn Rd, Lthd. 171 CE118
Oaklea Pas, Kings.T. 137 CK97
Oakleafe Gdns, Ilf. 69 EP55
Oakleigh Av N20 44 DD47
Oakleigh Av, Edg. 42 CP54
Oakleigh Av, Surb. 138 CN102
Oakleigh Cl N20 44 DF48
Oakleigh Cl, Swan. 147 FE97
Oakleigh Ct, Barn. 28 DE44
Church Hill Rd
Oakleigh Ct, Edg. 42 CQ54
Oakleigh Cres N20 44 DE48
Oakleigh Dr, Rick. 23 BQ44
Oakleigh Gdns N20 44 DC46
Oakleigh Gdns, Edg. 42 CM50
Oakleigh Gdns, Orp. 163 ES105
Oakleigh Ms N20 44 DC47
Oakleigh Rd N
Oakleigh Pk Av, Chis. 145 EN95
Oakleigh Pk N N20 44 DD46
Oakleigh Pk S N20 44 DE47
Oakleigh Ri, Epp. 18 EU32
Bower Hill
Oakleigh Rd, Pnr. 40 BZ51
Oakleigh Rd, Uxb. 77 BQ66
Oakleigh Rd N N20 44 DD47
Oakleigh Rd S N11 44 DG48
Oakleigh Way, Mitch. 141 DH95
Oakleigh Way, Surb. 138 CN102
Oakley Av W5 80 CN73
Oakley Av, Bark. 87 ET66
Oakley Av, Croy. 159 DL105
Oakley Cl E4 47 EC48
Mapleton Rd
Oakley Cl E6 86 EL72
Northumberland Rd
Oakley Cl W7 79 CE73
Oakley Cl, Add. 152 BK105
Oakley Cl, Grays 109 FW79
Oakley Cl, Islw. 97 CD81
Oakley Ct, Loug. 33 EN40
Hillyfields
Oakley Ct, Mitch. 140 DG102
London Rd
Oakley Cres EC1 196 G1
Oakley Cres, Slou. 74 AS73
Oakley Dr SE9 125 ER88
Oakley Dr SE13 123 EC85
Hither Grn La
Oakley Dr, Brom. 144 EL104
Oakley Dr, Rom. 52 FN50
Oakley Gdns N8 65 DM57
Oakley Gdns SW3 100 DE79
Oakley Gdns, Bans. 174 DB115
Oakley Pk, Bex. 126 EW87
Oakley Pl SE1 102 DT78
Oakley Rd N1 84 DR66
Oakley Rd SE25 142 DV99
Oakley Rd, Brom. 144 EL104
Oakley Rd, Har. 61 CE58
Oakley Rd, Warl. 176 DU118
Oakley Sq NW1 83 DJ68
Oakley St SW3 100 DE79
Oakley Wk W6 99 CX79
Oakley Yd E2 84 DT70
Bacon St
Oaklodge Way NW7 43 CT51
Oakmead Av, Brom. 144 EG100
Oakmead Gdns, Edg. 42 CR49
Oakmead Grn, Epsom 172 CP115
Oakmead Pl, Mitch. 140 DE95
Oakmead Rd SW12 120 DG88
Oakmead Rd, Croy. 141 DK100
Oakmeade, Pnr. 40 CA51
Oakmere Av, Pot.B. 12 DC33
Oakmere Cl, Pot.B. 12 DD31
Oakmere La, Pot.B. 12 DC32
Oakmere Rd SE2 106 EU79
Oakmoor Way, Chig. 49 ES50
Oakmount Pl, Orp. 145 ER102
Oakridge, St.Alb. 8 BZ29
Oakridge Av, Rad. 9 CF34

Oakridge Dr N2 64 DD55
Oakridge La, Brom. 123 ED92
Downham Way
Oakridge La, Rad. 9 CF33
Oakridge La, Wat. 25 CD35
Oakridge Rd, Brom. 123 ED91
Oakroyd Av, Pot.B. 11 CZ33
Oakroyd Cl, Pot.B. 11 CZ34
Oaks, The N12 44 DB49
Oaks, The SE18 105 EQ78
Oaks, The, Epsom 157 CT114
Oaks, The, Hayes 77 BQ68
Charville La
Oaks, The, Ruis. 59 BS59
Oaks, The, Stai. 113 BF91
Moormede Cres
Oaks, The, Swan. 147 FE96
Oaks, The, Tad. 173 CW123
Oaks, The, Wat. 40 BW46
Oaks, The, W.Byf. 152 BG113
Oaks, The, Wdf.Grn. 48 EE51
Oaks Av SE19 122 DS92
Oaks Av, Felt. 116 BY89
Oaks Av, Rom. 51 FC54
Oaks Av, Wor.Pk. 139 CV104
Oaks Cl, Lthd. 171 CG121
Oaks Cl, Rad. 25 CF35
Oaks Gro E4 48 EE47
Oaks La, Croy. 142 DW104
Oaks La, Ilf. 69 ES57
Oaks Rd, Croy. 160 DV106
Oaks Rd, Ken. 159 DP114
Oaks Rd, Reig. 184 DC133
Oaks Rd, Stai. 114 BK86
Oaks Rd, Wok. 166 AY117
Oaks Track, Cars. 158 DF111
Oaks Track, Wall. 159 DH110
Oaks Way, Cars. 158 DF108
Oaks Way, Epsom 173 CV119
Epsom La N
Oaks Way, Ken. 160 DQ114
Oaks Way, Surb. 137 CK103
Oaksford Av SE26 122 DV90
Oakshade Rd, Brom. 123 ED91
Oakshade Rd, Lthd. 154 CC114
Oakshaw, Oxt. 187 ED127
Oakshaw Rd SW18 120 DB87
Oakside (Denham), Uxb. 76 BH65
Oakthorpe Rd N13 45 DN50
Oaktree Av N13 45 DP48
Oaktree Cl, Brwd. 55 FZ49
Hawthorn Av
Oaktree Cl, Wal.Cr. 13 DP28
Oaktree Gro, Ilf. 69 ER64
Oakview Cl, Wal.Cr. 14 DV28
Oakview Gdns N2 64 DD56
Oakview Gro, Croy. 143 DY102
Oakview Rd SE6 123 EB92
Oakway SW20 139 CW98
Oakway, Brom. 143 ED96
Oakway, Wok. 166 AS119
Oakway Cl, Bex. 126 EY86
Oakway Pl, Rad. 9 CG34
Watling St
Oakways SE9 125 EP86
Oakwell Dr, Pot.B. 13 DH32
Oakwood, Wall. 159 DH109
Oakwood, Wal.Abb. 31 ED35
Roundhills
Oakwood Av N14 45 DK45
Oakwood Av, Beck. 143 EC96
Oakwood Av, Borwd. 26 CP42
Oakwood Av, Brwd. 55 GE44
Oakwood Av, Brom. 144 EH97
Oakwood Av, Mitch. 140 DD96
Oakwood Av, Pur. 159 DP112
Oakwood Av, Sthl. 78 CA73
Oakwood Chase, Horn. 72 FM58
Oakwood Cl N14 29 DJ44
Oakwood Cl, Chis. 125 EM93
Oakwood Cl, Dart. 128 FP88
Oakwood Cl, Red. 184 DG134
Oakwood Cl, Wdf.Grn. 48 EL51
Green Wk
Oakwood Ct W14 99 CZ76
Oakwood Cres N21 29 DL44
Oakwood Cres, Grnf. 79 CG65
Oakwood Dr SE19 122 DR93
Oakwood Dr, Bexh. 107 FD84
Oakwood Dr, Edg. 42 CQ51
Oakwood Dr, Sev. 191 FH123
Oakwood Gdns, Ilf. 69 ET61
Oakwood Gdns, Orp. 145 EQ103
Oakwood Gdns, Sutt. 140 DA103
Oakwood Hill, Loug. 33 EM44
Oakwood Hill Ind Est, Loug. 33 EQ43
Oakwood La W14 99 CZ76
Oakwood Pk Rd N14 45 DK45
Oakwood Pl, Croy. 141 DN100
Oakwood Ri, Cat. 186 DS125
Oakwood Rd NW11 64 DB57
Oakwood Rd SW20 139 CU95
Oakwood Rd, Croy. 141 DN100
Oakwood Rd, Orp. 145 EQ103
Oakwood Rd, Pnr. 39 BV54
Oakwood Rd, Red. 185 DN129
Oakwood Rd, St.Alb. 8 BZ29
Oakwood Rd, Vir.W. 132 AW99
Oakwood Rd, Wok. 166 AS119
Oakwood Vw N14 29 DK44
Oakworth Rd W10 81 CW71
Oarsman Pl, E.Mol. 137 CE98
Oast Ho Cl, Stai. 112 AY87
Oast Rd, Oxt. 188 EF131
Oasthouse Way, Orp. 146 EV98
Oat La EC2 197 H8
Oat La EC2 84 DQ72
Oates Cl, Brom. 143 ED97
Oates Rd, Rom. 51 FB50
Oatfield Rd, Orp. 145 ET102
Oatfield Rd, Tad. 173 CV120
Oatland Ri E17 47 DY54
Oatlands Av, Wey. 153 BR106
Oatlands Chase, Wey. 135 BS104
Oatlands Cl, Wey. 153 BQ105
Oatlands Dr, Wey. 135 BR104
Oatlands Grn, Wey. 135 BR104
Oatlands Dr
Oatlands Mere, Wey. 135 BR104
Oatlands Rd, Enf. 30 DW39
Oatlands Rd, Tad. 173 CY119

Oban Cl E13 86 EJ70
Oban Ho, Bark. 87 ER68
Wheelers Cross
Oban Rd E13 86 EJ69
Oban Rd SE25 142 DR98
Oban St E14 85 ED72
Obelisk Ride, Egh. 112 AS93
Oberon Cl, Borwd. 26 CQ39
Oberon Way, Shep. 134 BL97
Oberstein Rd SW11 100 DD84
Oborne Cl SE24 121 DP85
Observatory Gdns W8 100 DA75
Observatory Ms E14 204 F8
Observatory Rd SW14 98 CQ84
Observatory Wk, Red. 184 DF134
Lower Br Rd
Occupation La SE18 105 EP81
Occupation La W5 97 CK77
Occupation Rd SE17 201 H10
Occupation Rd SE17 102 DQ78
Occupation Rd W13 97 CH75
Occupation Rd, Wat. 23 BV43
Ocean Est E1 85 DX70
Ocean St E1 85 DX71
Ocean Wf E14 203 P5
Ocean Wf E14 103 EA75
Ockenden Cl, Wok. 167 AZ118
Ockenden Rd
Ockenden Gdns, Wok. 167 AZ118
Ockenden Rd
Ockenden Rd, Wok. 167 AZ118
Ockendon Rd N1 84 DR65
Ockendon Rd, Upmin. 72 FQ64
Ockham Dr, Lthd. 169 BR124
Ockham Dr, Orp. 126 EU94
Ockham La, Cob. 169 BT118
Ockham La, Wok. 169 BP120
Ockham Rd N, Lthd. 169 BQ124
Ockham Rd N, Wok. 168 BN121
Ockley Rd SW16 121 DL90
Ockley Rd, Croy. 141 DM101
Ockleys Mead, Gdse. 186 DW129
Octagon Arc EC2 197 M7
Octagon Rd, Walt. 153 BS109
Octavia Cl, Mitch. 140 DE99
Octavia Rd, Islw. 97 CF82
Octavia St SW11 100 DE81
Octavia Way SE28 88 EV73
Booth Cl
Octavia Way, Stai. 114 BG93
Octavius St SE8 103 EA80
Odard Rd, W.Mol. 136 CA98
Down St
Oddesey Rd, Borwd. 26 CP39
Odessa Rd E7 68 EF63
Odessa Rd NW10 81 CU68
Odessa St SE16 203 M5
Odessa St SE16 103 DZ75
Odger St SW11 100 DF82
Odhams Wk WC2 195 P9
Odyssey Business Pk, Ruis. 59 BV64
Offa's Mead E9 67 DY63
Lindisfarne Way
Offenbach Ho E2 85 DX68
Offenham Rd SE9 125 EM91
Offerton Rd SW4 101 DJ83
Offham Slope N12 43 CZ50
Offley Pl, Islw. 97 CD80
Thornbury Rd
Offley Rd SW9 101 DN80
Offord Cl N17 46 DU52
Offord Rd N1 83 DM66
Offord St N1 83 DM66
Ogilby St SE18 105 EM77
Oglander Rd SE15 102 DT84
Ogle St W1 195 K6
Ogle St W1 83 DJ71
Oglethorpe Rd, Dag. 70 EZ62
Ohio Rd E13 86 EF70
Oil Mill La W6 99 CU78
Okeburn Rd SW17 120 DG92
Okehampton Cl N12 44 DD50
Okehampton Cres, Well. 106 EV81
Okehampton Rd NW10 81 CW67
Okehampton Rd, Rom. 52 FJ51
Okehampton Sq, Rom. 52 FJ51
Okemore Gdns, Orp. 146 EW98
Olaf St W11 81 CX73
Old Acre, Wok. 152 BG114
Old Amersham Rd, Ger.Cr. 57 BB60
Old Av, W.Byf. 151 BE113
Old Av, Wey. 153 BR107
Old Av Cl, W.Byf. 151 BE113
Old Bailey EC4 196 G9
Old Bailey EC4 83 DP72
Old Barge Ho All SE1 200 D2
Old Barn Cl, Sutt. 157 CY108
Old Barn La, Ken. 176 DT116
Old Barn La, Rick. 22 BM43
Old Barn Rd, Epsom 172 CQ117
Old Barn Way, Bexh. 107 FD83
Old Barrack Yd SW1 198 F5
Old Barrowfield E15 86 EE67
New Plaistow Rd
Old Bath Rd, Slou. 93 BE81
Old Bellgate Wf E14 203 P7
Old Bellgate Wf E14 103 EA76
Old Bethnal Grn Rd E2 84 DU69
Old Bexley La, Bex. 127 FD89
Old Bexley La, Dart. 127 FF88
Old Bond St W1 199 K1
Old Bond St W1 83 DJ73
Old Brewers Yd WC2 195 P9
Old Brewery Ms NW3 64 DD63
Hampstead High St
Old Br Cl, Nthlt. 78 CA68
Old Br St, Kings.T. 137 CK96
Old Broad St EC2 197 L9
Old Broad St EC2 84 DR72
Old Bromley Rd, Brom. 123 ED92
Old Brompton Rd SW5 100 DA78
Old Brompton Rd SW7 100 DA78
Old Bldgs WC2 196 D8
Old Burlington St W1 195 K10
Old Burlington St W1 83 DJ73
Old Carriageway, The, Sev. 190 FC123
Old Castle St E1 197 P8
Old Castle St E1 84 DT72
Old Cavendish St W1 195 H8

Old Cavendish St W1 83 DH72
Old Change Ct EC4 84 DQ72
Carter La
Old Chapel Rd, Swan. 147 FC101
Old Charlton Rd, Shep. 135 BQ99
Old Chelsea Ms SW3 100 DD79
Danvers St
Old Chertsey Rd, Wok. 150 AV110
Old Chestnut Av, Esher 154 CA107
Old Ch La NW9 62 CQ61
Old Ch La, Brwd. 55 GE42
Old Ch La, Grnf. 79 CG69
Perivale La
Old Ch La, Stan. 41 CJ52
Old Ch Path, Esher 154 CB105
High St
Old Ch Rd E1 85 DX72
Old Ch Rd E4 47 EA49
Old Ch St SW3 100 DD78
Old Claygate La, Esher 155 CG107
Old Clem Sq SE18 105 EN79
Kempt St
Old Coach Rd, Cher. 133 BD99
Old Common Rd, Cob. 153 BU112
Old Compton St W1 195 M10
Old Compton St W1 83 DK73
Old Cote Dr, Houns. 96 CA79
Old Ct, Ash. 172 CL119
Old Ct Pl W8 100 DB75
Old Dartford Rd (Farningham), Dart. 148 FM100
Old Dean, Hem.H. 5 BA27
Old Deer Pk Gdns, Rich. 98 CL83
Old Devonshire Rd SW12 121 DH87
Old Dock App Rd, Grays 110 GE77
Old Dock Cl, Rich. 98 CN79
Watcombe Cotts
Old Dover Rd SE3 104 EH80
Old Esher Cl, Walt. 154 BX106
Old Esher Rd
Old Esher Rd, Walt. 154 BX106
Old Farleigh Rd, S.Croy. 160 DW110
Old Farleigh Rd, Warl. 161 DY113
Old Fm Av N14 45 DJ45
Old Fm Av, Sid. 125 ER88
Old Fm Cl, Houns. 96 BZ84
Old Fm Gdns, Swan. 147 FF97
Old Fm Pas, Hmptn. 136 CC95
Old Fm Rd N2 44 DD53
Old Fm Rd, Hmptn. 116 BZ93
Old Fm Rd, West Dr. 94 BK75
Old Fm Rd E, Sid. 126 EU89
Old Fm Rd W, Sid. 125 ET89
Old Farmhouse Dr, Lthd. 171 CD115
Old Ferry Dr, Stai. 112 AW86
Old Fld Cl, Amer. 20 AY39
Old Fish St Hill EC4 197 H10
Old Fleet La EC4 196 F8
Old Fold Cl, Barn. 27 CZ39
Old Fold La
Old Fold La, Barn. 27 CZ39
Old Fold Vw, Barn. 27 CW41
Old Ford Rd E2 84 DW68
Old Ford Rd E3 85 DY68
Old Forge Cl, Stan. 41 CG49
Old Forge Cl, Wat. 7 BU33
Old Forge Cres, Shep. 135 BP100
Old Forge Ms W12 99 CV75
Goodwin Rd
Old Forge Rd, Enf. 30 DT38
Old Forge Way, Sid. 126 EV91
Old Fox Cl, Cat. 175 DP121
Old Fox Footpath, S.Croy. 160 DS108
Essenden Rd
Old Gannon Cl, Nthwd. 39 BQ50
Old Gdn, The, Sev. 190 FD123
Old Gloucester St WC1 196 A6
Old Gloucester St WC1 83 DL71
Old Gro Cl (Cheshunt), Wal.Cr. 14 DR26
Hammondstreet Rd
Old Hall Cl, Pnr. 40 BY53
Old Hall Dr, Pnr. 40 BY53
Old Harrow La, West. 179 EQ119
Old Hatch Manor, Ruis. 59 BT59
Old Hill, Chis. 145 EN95
Old Hill, Orp. 163 ER107
Old Hill, Wok. 166 AX120
Old Homesdale Rd, Brom. 144 EJ98
Old Hosp Cl SW12 120 DF88
Old Ho Cl SW19 119 CY92
Old Ho Cl, Epsom 157 CT110
Old Ho Gdns, Twick. 117 CJ85
Old Ho La, Kings L. 22 BL35
Old Howlett's La, Ruis. 59 BQ58
Old Jamaica Rd SE16 202 B6
Old Jamaica Rd SE16 102 DU76
Old James St SE15 102 DV83
Old Jewry EC2 197 K9
Old Jewry EC2 84 DR72
Old Kent Rd SE1 201 M8
Old Kent Rd SE1 102 DS77
Old Kent Rd SE15 102 DS77
Old Kenton La NW9 62 CP57
Old Kingston Rd, Wor.Pk. 138 CQ104
Old La, Cob. 169 BP117
Old La, West. 178 EK121
Old La Gdns, Cob. 169 BT122
Old Lo La, Ken. 175 DN115
Old Lo La, Pur. 159 DM114
Old Lo Pl, Twick. 117 CH86
St. Margarets Rd
Old Lo Way, Stan. 41 CG50
Old London Rd, Epsom 173 CU118
Old London Rd, Sev. 164 FA110
Old London Rd (Knockholt Pound), Sev. 180 EY115
Old Maidstone Rd, Sid. 126 EZ94
Old Malden La, Wor.Pk. 138 CR103
Old Malt Way, Wok. 166 AX117
Old Manor Dr, Grav. 131 GJ88
Old Manor Dr, Islw. 116 CC86
Old Manor Ho Ms, Shep. 134 BN97
Squires Br Rd
Old Manor Rd, Sthl. 96 BW77
Western Rd
Old Manor Way, Bexh. 107 FD82
Old Manor Way, Chis. 125 EM92

Old Manor Yd SW5 100 DB77
Earls Ct Rd
Old Mkt Sq E2 84 DT69
Diss St
Old Marylebone Rd NW1 194 C7
Old Marylebone Rd NW1 82 DE71
Old Mead (Chalfont St. Peter), Ger.Cr. 36 AY51
Old Ms, Har. 61 CE57
Hindes Rd
Old Mill Cl (Eynsford), Dart. 148 FL102
Old Mill Ct E18 68 EJ55
Old Mill La, Red. 185 DH128
Old Mill La, Uxb. 76 BH72
Old Mill Pl, Rom. 71 FD58
Old Mill Rd SE18 105 ER79
Old Mill Rd, Kings L. 7 BQ33
Old Mill Rd (Denham), Uxb. 58 BG62
Old Mitre Ct EC4 83 DN72
Fleet St
Old Montague St E1 84 DU71
Old Nichol St E2 197 P4
Old Nichol St E2 84 DT70
Old N St WC1 196 B6
Old Oak Av, Couls. 174 DE119
Old Oak Cl, Chess. 156 CM105
Old Oak Common La NW10 80 CS70
Old Oak Common La W3 80 CS71
Old Oak La NW10 80 CS69
Old Oak Rd W3 81 CT73
Old Oaks, Wal.Abb. 16 EE32
Old Orchard, St.Alb. 8 CC26
Old Orchard, Sun. 136 BW96
Old Orchard, W.Byf. 152 BM112
Old Orchard, The NW3 64 DF63
Nassington Rd
Old Orchard Cl, Barn. 28 DD38
Old Orchard Cl, Uxb. 76 BN72
Old Otford Rd, Sev. 181 FH117
Old Palace La, Rich. 117 CJ85
Old Palace Rd, Croy. 141 DP104
Old Palace Rd, Wey. 135 BP104
Old Palace Ter, Rich. 117 CK85
King St
Old Palace Yd SW1 199 P6
Old Palace Yd SW1 101 DL76
Old Palace Yd, Rich. 117 CJ85
Old Paradise St SE11 200 B8
Old Paradise St SE11 101 DM77
Old Pk Av SW12 120 DG86
Old Pk Av, Enf. 30 DQ42
Old Pk Gro, Enf. 30 DQ42
Old Pk La W1 198 G3
Old Pk La W1 82 DG74
Old Pk Ms, Houns. 96 BZ80
Old Pk Ride, Wal.Cr. 14 DT33
Old Pk Ridings N21 29 DP44
Old Pk Rd N13 45 DM49
Old Pk Rd SE2 106 EU78
Old Pk Rd, Enf. 29 DP41
Old Pk Rd S, Enf. 29 DP42
Old Pk Vw, Enf. 29 DN41
Old Parkbury La, St.Alb. 9 CF30
Old Parvis Rd, W.Byf. 152 BK112
Old Perry St, Chis. 125 ES94
Old Perry St, Grav. 130 GE89
Old Polhill, Sev. 181 FD115
Old Pound Cl, Islw. 97 CG81
Old Priory (Harefield), Uxb. 59 BP59
Old Pye St SW1 199 M6
Old Pye St SW1 101 DK76
Old Quebec St W1 194 E9
Old Quebec St W1 82 DF72
Old Queen St SW1 199 N5
Old Queen St SW1 101 DK75
Old Rectory Cl, Tad. 173 CU124
Old Rectory Gdns, Edg. 42 CN51
Old Rectory La (Denham), Uxb. 57 BE59
Old Redding, Har. 40 CC49
Old Reigate Rd, Bet. 182 CP134
Old Reigate Rd, Dor. 182 CL134
Old Rd SE13 104 EE84
Old Rd, Add. 151 BF108
Old Rd, Bet. 182 CR134
Old Rd, Dart. 107 FD84
Old Rd, Enf. 30 DW39
Old Rd E, Grav. 131 GH88
Old Rd W, Grav. 131 GF88
Old Rope Wk, Sun. 135 BV97
The Av
Old Royal Free Pl N1 83 DN67
Liverpool Rd
Old Royal Free Sq N1 83 DN67
Old Ruislip Rd, Nthlt. 78 BX68
Old Savill's Cotts, Chig. 49 EQ49
The Chase
Old Sch Cl SW19 140 DA96
Old Sch Cl, Beck. 143 DX96
Old Sch Ct, Stai. 112 AY87
Old Sch Cres E7 86 EF65
Old Sch Ms, Wey. 153 BR105
Old Sch Pl, Wok. 166 AY121
Old Sch Rd, Uxb. 76 BM71
Royal La
Old Sch Sq, T.Ditt. 137 CF100
Old Schools La, Epsom 157 CT109
Old Seacoal La EC4 196 F8
Old Shire La, Ger.Cr. 37 BA46
Old Shire La, Rick. 21 BB44
Old Shire La, Wal.Abb. 32 EG35
Old Slade La, Iver 93 BE76
Old Solesbridge La, Rick. 22 BG41
Old S Cl, Pnr. 40 BX53
Old S Lambeth Rd SW8 101 DL80
Old Spitalfields Mkt E1 197 P6
Old Spitalfields Mkt E1 84 DT71
Old Sq WC2 196 C8
Old Sq WC2 83 DM72
Old Sta App, Lthd. 171 CG121
Old Sta Rd, Hayes 95 BT76
Old Sta Rd, Loug. 32 EL43
Old Stockley Rd, West Dr. 95 BP75
Old St E13 86 EH68

Old St EC1 197 H
Old St EC1 84 DQ7
Old Swan Yd, Cars. 158 DF10
Old Tilburstow Rd, Gdse. 186 DW13
Old Town SW4 101 DJ8
Old Town, Croy. 141 DP10
Old Tram Yd SE18 105 ES7
Lakedale Rd
Old Tye Av, West. 178 EL11
Old Uxbridge Rd, Rick. 37 BE5
Old Wk, The, Sev. 181 FH11
Old Watford Rd, St.Alb. 8 BY3
Old Watling St, Grav. 131 GG9
Old Westhall Cl, Warl. 176 DW11
Old Windsor Lock, Wind. 112 AW8
Old Woking Rd, W.Byf. 151 BF11
Old Woking Rd, Wok. 167 BE11
Old Woolwich Rd SE10 103 ED7
Old York Rd SW18 120 DB8
Oldacre Ms SW12 121 DH8
Balham Gro
Oldberry Rd, Edg. 42 CR5
Oldborough Rd, Wem. 61 CJ6
Oldbury Cl, Cher. 133 BE10
Oldbury Rd
Oldbury Cl, Orp. 146 EX9
Oldbury Pl W1 194 G
Oldbury Pl W1 82 DG7
Oldbury Rd, Cher. 133 BE10
Oldbury Rd, Enf. 30 DU4
Oldchurch Gdns, Rom. 71 FD5
Oldchurch Ri, Rom. 71 FD5
Oldchurch Rd, Rom. 71 FD5
Olden La, Pur. 159 DN11
Oldfield Cl, Brom. 145 EM9
Oldfield Cl, Grnf. 61 CE6
Oldfield Cl, Stan. 41 CG5
Oldfield Cl (Cheshunt), Wal.Cr. 15 DY2
Oldfield Dr (Cheshunt), Wal.Cr. 15 DY2
Oldfield Fm Gdns, Grnf. 79 CD6
Oldfield Gdns, Ash. 171 CK11
Oldfield Gro SE16 203 H
Oldfield Gro SE16 103 DX7
Oldfield La N, Grnf. 79 CE6
Oldfield La S, Grnf. 78 CC7
Oldfield Ms N6 65 DJ5
Oldfield Rd N16 66 DS6
Oldfield Rd NW10 81 CT6
Oldfield Rd SW19 119 CY9
Oldfield Rd W3 99 CT7
Valetta Rd
Oldfield Rd, Bexh. 106 EY8
Oldfield Rd, Brom. 145 EM9
Oldfield Rd, Hmptn. 136 BZ9
Oldfield Rd, St.Alb. 9 CK2
Oldfield Wd, Wok. 167 BB11
Maybury Hill
Oldfields Circ, Nthlt. 78 CC6
Oldfields Rd, Sutt. 139 CZ10
Oldfields Trd Est, Sutt. 140 DA10
Oldfields Rd
Oldham Ter W3 80 CQ7
Oldhill St N16 66 DU6
Oldridge Rd SW12 120 DG8
Olds App, Wat. 39 BP4
Olds Cl, Wat. 39 BP4
Oldstead Rd, Brom. 123 ED9
Oleander Cl, Orp. 163 ER10
O'Leary Sq E1 84 DW7
Olinda Rd N16 66 DT5
Oliphant St W10 81 CX6
Olive Rd E13 86 EJ6
Olive Rd NW2 63 CW6
Olive Rd SW19 120 DC9
Norman Rd
Olive Rd W5 97 CK7
Olive Rd, Dart. 128 FK8
Olive St, Rom. 71 FD5
Oliver Av SE25 142 DT9
Oliver Cl E10 67 EB6
Oliver Rd
Oliver Cl W4 98 CP7
Oliver Cl, Add. 152 BG10
Oliver Cl, Grays 109 FT8
Oliver Cl, St.Alb. 9 CD2
Oliver Cres (Farningham), Dart. 148 FM10
Oliver Gdns E6 86 EL7
Oliver Gro SE25 142 DT9
Oliver Rd E10 67 EB6
Oliver Rd E17 67 EC5
Oliver Rd, Brwd. 55 GA4
Oliver Rd, Grays 109 FT8
Oliver Rd, N.Mal. 138 CQ9
Oliver Rd, Rain. 89 FF6
Oliver Rd, Sutt. 158 DD10
Oliver Rd, Swan. 147 FD9
Oliver-Goldsmith Est SE15 102 DU8
Olivers Yd EC1 197
Olivette St SW15 99 CX8
Olivia Gdns (Harefield), Uxb. 38 BJ5
Ollards Gro, Loug. 32 EK4
Olleberrie La, Rick. 5 BD3
Ollerton Grn E3 85 DZ6
Ollerton Rd N11 45 DK5
Olley Cl, Wall. 159 DL10
Ollgar Cl W12 81 CT7
Olliffe St E14 204 E
Olliffe St E14 103 EC7
Olmar St SE1 102 DU7
Olney Rd SE17 101 DP7
Olron Cres, Bexh. 126 EX8
Olven Rd SE18 105 EQ8
Olveston Wk, Cars. 140 DD10
Olwen Ms, Pnr. 40 BX5
Olyffe Av, Well. 106 EU8
Olyffe Dr, Beck. 143 EC9
Olympia Ms W2 82 DB7
Queensway
Olympia Way W14 99 CY7
Olympic Retail Pk, Wem. 62 CP6
Olympic Way, Grnf. 78 CB6
Olympic Way, Wem. 62 CN6
Olympus Sq E5 66 DU6
Nolan Way
Oman Av NW2 63 CW6
O'Meara St SE1 201

O'Meara St SE1 84 DQ74
Omega Cl E14 204 B6
Omega Pl N1 196 A1
Omega Rd, Wok. 167 BA115
Omega St SE14 103 EA81
Omega Way, Egh. 133 BC95
Ommaney Rd SE14 103 DX81
Omnibus Way E17 47 EA54
On The Hill, Wat. 40 BY47
Ondine Rd SE15 102 DT84
One Tree Cl SE23 122 DW86
Onega Gate SE16 203 K6
Onega Gate SE16 103 DY76
O'Neill Path SE18 105 EN79
Kempt St
Ongar Cl, Add. 151 BF107
Ongar Cl, Rom. 70 EW57
Ongar Hill, Add. 152 BG107
Ongar Pl, Add. 152 BG107
Ongar Rd SW6 100 DA79
Ongar Rd, Add. 152 BG106
Ongar Rd, Brwd. 54 FV45
Ongar Rd (Pilgrim's Hatch), Brwd. 54 FS42
Ongar Rd, Rom. 34 EW40
Ongar Way, Rain. 89 FE67
Onra Rd E17 67 EA59
Onslow Av, Rich. 118 CL85
Onslow Av, Sutt. 157 CZ110
Onslow Cl E4 47 EC47
Onslow Cl, T.Ditt. 137 CE102
Onslow Cl, Wok. 167 BA117
Onslow Cres, Chis. 145 EP95
Onslow Cres, Wok. 167 BA117
Onslow Dr, Sid. 126 EX89
Onslow Gdns E18 68 EH55
Onslow Gdns N10 65 DH57
Onslow Gdns N21 29 DN43
Onslow Gdns SW7 100 DD78
Onslow Gdns, S.Croy. 160 DU112
Onslow Gdns, T.Ditt. 137 CE102
Onslow Gdns, Wall. 159 DJ107
Onslow Ms, Cher. 134 BG100
Onslow Ms E SW7 100 DD77
Cranley Pl
Onslow Ms W SW7 100 DD77
Cranley Pl
Onslow Rd, Croy. 141 DM101
Onslow Rd, N.Mal. 139 CU98
Onslow Rd, Rich. 118 CL85
Onslow Rd, Walt. 153 BT105
Onslow Sq SW7 198 A8
Onslow Sq SW7 100 DD77
Onslow St EC1 196 E5
Onslow Way, T.Ditt. 137 CE102
Onslow Way, Wok. 167 BF115
Ontario St SE1 200 G7
Ontario St SE1 101 DP76
Ontario Way E14 203 P1
Ontario Way E14 85 EA73
Opal Cl E16 86 EK72
Opal Ct, Slou. 74 AV70
Wexham St
Opal Ms NW6 81 CZ67
Priory Pk Rd
Opal Ms, Ilf. 69 EP61
Ley St
Opal St SE11 200 F9
Opal St SE11 101 DP77
Openshaw Rd SE2 106 EV77
Openview SW18 120 DC88
Ophelia Gdns NW2 63 CY62
The Vale
Ophir Ter SE15 102 DU81
Opossum Way, Houns. 96 BW82
Oppenheim Rd SE13 103 EC82
Oppidans Ms NW3 82 DF66
Meadowbank
Oppidans Rd NW3 82 DF66
Orange Ct E1 202 C3
Orange Ct La, Orp. 163 EN109
Orange Gro E11 68 EE62
Orange Gro, Chig. 49 EQ51
Orange Hill Rd, Edg. 42 CQ52
Orange Pl SE16 202 G7
Orange St WC2 199 M1
Orange St WC2 83 DK73
Orange Tree Hill (Havering-atte-Bower), Rom. 51 FD50
Orange Yd W1 195 N9
Orangery, The, Rich. 117 CJ89
Orangery La SE9 125 EM85
Oratory La SW3 198 A10
Orb St SE17 201 K9
Orb St SE17 102 DR77
Orbain Rd SW6 99 CY80
Orbel St SW11 100 DE81
Orbital Cres, Wat. 23 BT35
Orbital One, Dart. 128 FP89
Orchard, The N14 29 DH43
Orchard, The N21 30 DR44
Orchard, The NW11 64 DA57
Orchard, The SE3 103 ED82
Orchard, The W4 98 CR77
Orchard, The W5 79 CK71
Orchard, The, Bans. 174 DA116
Orchard, The, Epsom 157 CT108
Orchard, The (Ewell), Epsom 157 CT110
Tayles Hill Dr
Orchard, The, Houns. 96 CC82
Orchard, The, Kings L. 6 BN29
Orchard, The, Rick. 22 BM43
Green La
Orchard, The, Sev. 181 FE120
Orchard, The, Swan. 147 FD96
Orchard, The, Vir.W. 132 AY99
Orchard, The, Wey. 153 BP105
Orchard, The, Wok. 166 AY122
Orchard Av N3 64 DA55
Orchard Av N14 29 DJ44
Orchard Av N20 44 DD47
Orchard Av, Add. 151 BF111
Orchard Av, Ashf. 115 BQ93
Orchard Av, Belv. 106 EY79
Orchard Av, Brwd. 55 FZ48
Orchard Av, Croy. 143 DY101
Orchard Av, Dart. 127 FH87
Orchard Av, Felt. 115 BR85
Orchard Av, Grav. 131 GH92
Orchard Av, Houns. 96 BY80
Orchard Av, Mitch. 140 DG102
Orchard Av, N.Mal. 138 CS96
Orchard Av, Rain. 90 FJ70
Orchard Av, Sthl. 78 BY74
Orchard Av, T.Ditt. 137 CG102
Orchard Av, Wat. 7 BV32
Orchard Cl E4 47 EA49
Chingford Mt Rd
Orchard Cl E11 68 EH56
Orchard Cl N1 84 DQ66
Morton Rd
Orchard Cl NW2 63 CU62
Orchard Cl SE23 122 DW86
Brenchley Gdns
Orchard Cl SW20 139 CW98
Grand Dr
Orchard Cl W10 81 CY71
Orchard Cl, Ashf. 115 BQ93
Orchard Cl, Bans. 158 DB114
Orchard Cl, Bexh. 106 EY81
Orchard Cl, Borwd. 26 CM42
Orchard Cl, Bushey 41 CD46
Orchard Cl, Edg. 42 CL51
Orchard Cl, Egh. 113 BB92
Orchard Cl, Epsom 156 CP107
Orchard Cl, Lthd. 171 CF119
Orchard Cl (Effingham), Lthd. 169 BT124
Orchard Cl (Fetcham), Lthd. 171 CD122
Orchard Cl, Nthlt. 60 CC64
Orchard Cl (Cuffley), Pot.B. 13 DL28
Orchard Cl, Rad. 25 CE37
Orchard Cl, Rick. 21 BD42
Orchard Cl, Ruis. 59 BQ59
Orchard Cl, S.Ock. 91 FW70
Orchard Cl, Surb. 137 CH101
Orchard Cl (Denham), Uxb. 76 BH65
Orchard Cl, Walt. 135 BV101
Garden Rd
Orchard Cl, Wat. 23 BT40
Orchard Cl, Wem. 80 CL67
Orchard Cl, Wok. 167 BB116
Orchard Ct, Hem.H. 5 BA27
Orchard Ct, Islw. 97 CD81
Thornbury Av
Orchard Ct, Twick. 117 CD89
Orchard Ct, Wor.Pk. 139 CU102
The Av
Orchard Cres, Edg. 42 CQ50
Orchard Cres, Enf. 30 DT39
Orchard Dr SE3 104 EE82
Orchard Dr, Ash. 171 CK120
Orchard Dr, Edg. 42 CM50
Orchard Dr, Epp. 33 ES36
Orchard Dr, Grays 110 GA75
Orchard Dr, Rick. 21 BC41
Orchard Dr, St.Alb. 8 CB27
Orchard Dr, Uxb. 76 BK70
Orchard Dr, Wat. 23 BT39
Orchard Dr, Wok. 167 AZ115
Orchard End, Cat. 176 DS122
Orchard End, Lthd. 170 CC124
Orchard End, Wey. 135 BS103
Orchard End Av, Amer. 20 AT39
Orchard Gdns, Chess. 156 CL105
Orchard Gdns, Epsom 156 CQ114
Orchard Gdns, Sutt. 158 DA106
Orchard Gdns, Wal.Abb. 15 EC34
Orchard Gate NW9 62 CS56
Orchard Gate, Esher 137 CD102
Orchard Gate, Grnf. 79 CH65
Orchard Grn, Orp. 145 ES103
Orchard Gro SE20 122 DU94
Orchard Gro, Croy. 143 DY101
Orchard Gro, Edg. 42 CN53
Orchard Gro (Chalfont St. Peter), Ger.Cr. 36 AW53
Orchard Gro, Har. 62 CM57
Orchard Gro, Orp. 145 ET103
Orchard Hill SE13 103 EB82
Coldbath St
Orchard Hill, Cars. 158 DF106
Orchard Hill, Dart. 127 FE85
Orchard La SW20 139 CV95
Orchard La, Brwd. 54 FT43
Orchard La, E.Mol. 137 CD100
Orchard La, Wdf.Grn. 48 EJ49
Orchard Lea Cl, Wok. 167 BE115
Orchard Leigh, Chesh. 4 AU28
Orchard Mains, Wok. 166 AW119
Orchard Ms N1 84 DR66
Southgate Gro
Orchard Path, Slou. 75 BA72
Orchard Pl E14 86 EE73
Orchard Pl N17 46 DT52
Orchard Pl, Sev. 180 EY124
Orchard Pl, Wal.Cr. 15 DX30
Turners Hill
Orchard Ri, Croy. 143 DY102
Orchard Ri, Kings.T. 138 CQ95
Orchard Ri, Pnr. 59 BT55
Orchard Ri, Rich. 98 CP84
Orchard Ri E, Sid. 125 ET85
Orchard Ri W, Sid. 125 ES85
Orchard Rd N6 65 DH59
Orchard Rd SE3 104 EE82
Eliot Pl
Orchard Rd SE18 105 ER77
Orchard Rd, Barn. 27 CZ42
Orchard Rd, Belv. 106 FA77
Orchard Rd, Brent. 97 CJ79
Orchard Rd, Brom. 144 EJ95
Orchard Rd, Ch.St.G. 36 AW47
Orchard Rd, Chess. 156 CL105
Orchard Rd, Dag. 88 FA67
Orchard Rd, Enf. 30 DW43
Orchard Rd, Grav. 130 GC89
Orchard Rd, Hmptn. 116 BZ94
Orchard Rd, Hayes 77 BT73
Orchard Rd, Houns. 116 BZ85
Orchard Rd, Kings.T. 138 CL96
Orchard Rd, Mitch. 140 DG102
Orchard Rd (Farnborough), Orp. 163 EP106
Orchard Rd (Pratt's Bottom), Orp. 164 EW110
Orchard Rd, Reig. 184 DB134
Orchard Rd, Rich. 98 CN83
Orchard Rd, Rom. 51 FB53
Orchard Rd (Otford), Sev. 181 FF116
Orchard Rd (Riverhead), Sev. 190 FE122
Orchard Rd, Sid. 125 ES91
Orchard Rd, S.Croy. 160 DV114
Orchard Rd, S.Ock. 91 FW70
Orchard Rd, Sun. 115 BV94
Hanworth Rd
Orchard Rd, Sutt. 158 DA106
Orchard Rd, Swans. 130 FY85
Orchard Rd, Twick. 117 CG85
Orchard Rd, Well. 106 EV83
Orchard Rd, Wind. 112 AV86
Orchard Sq W14 99 CZ78
Sun Rd
Orchard St E17 67 DY56
Orchard St W1 194 F9
Orchard St W1 82 DG72
Orchard St, Dart. 128 FL86
Orchard Ter, Enf. 30 DU44
Great Cambridge Rd
Orchard Vw, Uxb. 76 BK70
Orchard Vil, Sid. 126 EW93
Cray Rd
Orchard Way, Add. 152 BH106
Orchard Way, Ashf. 114 BM89
Orchard Way, Beck. 143 DY99
Orchard Way, Chig. 50 EU48
Orchard Way, Croy. 143 DY101
Orchard Way, Dart. 128 FK90
Orchard Way, Enf. 30 DS41
Orchard Way, Esher 154 CC107
Orchard Way, Hem.H. 5 BA28
Orchard Way, Oxt. 188 EG133
Orchard Way, Pot.B. 12 DB28
Orchard Way, Rick. 38 BG45
Orchard Way, Slou. 74 AY74
Orchard Way, Sutt. 158 DD105
Orchard Way, Tad. 183 CZ126
Orchard Way (Cheshunt), Wal.Cr. 13 DP27
Orchard Waye, Uxb. 76 BK68
Orchardleigh, Lthd. 171 CH122
Orchardleigh Av, Enf. 30 DW40
Orchardmede N21 30 DR44
Orchards, The, Epp. 18 EU32
Orchards Cl, W.Byf. 152 BG114
Orchards Residential Pk, The, Slou. 75 AZ74
Orchards Shop Cen, Dart. 128 FL86
Orchardson St NW8 82 DD70
Orchehill Av, Ger.Cr. 56 AX56
Orchehill Ct, Ger.Cr. 56 AY57
Orchehill Ri, Ger.Cr. 56 AY57
Orchid Cl E6 86 EL71
Orchid Cl, Rom. 34 EV41
Orchid Cl, Sthl. 78 BY72
Orchid Ct, Egh. 113 BB91
Orchid Ct, Rom. 71 FE61
Orchid Rd N14 45 DJ45
Orchid St W12 81 CU73
Orchis Gro, Grays 110 FZ78
Orchis Way, Rom. 52 FM51
Orde Hall St WC1 196 B5
Orde Hall St WC1 83 DM70
Ordell Rd E3 85 DZ68
Ordnance Cl, Felt. 115 BU90
Ordnance Cres SE10 204 G4
Ordnance Cres SE10 103 ED75
Ordnance Hill NW8 82 DD67
Ordnance Ms NW8 82 DD68
St. Ann's Ter
Ordnance Rd E16 86 EF71
Ordnance Rd SE18 105 EN79
Ordnance Rd, Enf. 31 DX37
Ordnance Rd, Grav. 131 GJ86
Oregano Cl, West Dr. 76 BM72
Camomile Way
Oregano Dr E14 85 ED72
Oregon Av E12 69 EM63
Oregon Cl, N.Mal. 138 CQ98
Georgia Rd
Oregon Sq, Orp. 145 ER102
Orestes Ms NW6 64 DA64
Aldred Rd
Oreston Rd, Rain. 90 FK69
Orford Ct SE27 121 DP89
Orford Gdns, Twick. 117 CF89
Orford Rd E17 67 EA57
Orford Rd E18 68 EH55
Orford Rd SE6 123 EB90
Organ Hall Rd, Borwd. 26 CL39
Organ La E4 47 EC47
Oriel Cl, Mitch. 141 DK98
Oriel Ct NW3 64 DC63
Heath St
Oriel Dr SW13 99 CV79
Oriel Gdns, Ilf. 69 EM55
Oriel Pl NW3 64 DC63
Heath St
Oriel Rd E9 85 DX65
Oriel Way, Nthlt. 78 CB66
Orient Ind Pk E10 67 EA61
Orient St SE11 200 F8
Orient Way E5 67 DX62
Orient Way E10 67 DY61
Oriental Cl, Wok. 167 BA117
Oriental Rd
Oriental Rd E16 86 EK74
Oriental Rd, Wok. 167 BA117
Oriole Cl, Abb.L. 7 BU31
Oriole Way SE28 88 EV73
Orion Rd N11 45 DH51
Orion Way, Nthwd. 39 BT49
Orissa Rd SE18 105 ES78
Orkney St SW11 100 DG82
Orlando Gdns, Epsom 156 CR110
Orlando Rd SW4 101 DJ83
Orleans Cl, Esher 137 CD103
Orleans Rd SE19 122 DR93
Orleans Rd, Twick. 117 CH87
Orleston Ms N7 83 DN65
Orleston Rd N7 83 DN65
Orlestone Gdns, Orp. 164 EY106
Orley Fm Rd, Har. 61 CE62
Orlop St SE10 104 EE78
Ormanton Rd SE26 122 DU91
Orme Ct W2 82 DB73
Orme Ct Ms W2 82 DB73
Orme La
Orme La W2 82 DB73
Orme Rd, Kings.T. 138 CP96
Orme Sq W2 82 DB73
Bayswater Rd
Ormeley Rd SW12 121 DH88
Ormerod Gdns, Mitch. 140 DG96
Ormesby Cl SE28 88 EX73
Wroxham Rd
Ormesby Dr, Pot.B. 11 CX32
Ormesby Way, Har. 62 CM58
Ormiston Gro W12 81 CV74
Ormiston Rd SE10 104 EG78
Ormond Av, Hmptn. 136 CB95
Ormond Av, Rich. 117 CK85
Ormond Rd
Ormond Cl WC1 196 A6
Ormond Cl, Rom. 52 FK54
Chadwick Dr
Ormond Cres, Hmptn. 136 CB95
Ormond Dr, Hmptn. 116 CB94
Ormond Ms WC1 196 A5
Ormond Rd N19 65 DL60
Ormond Rd, Rich. 117 CK85
Ormond Yd SW1 199 L2
Ormonde Av, Epsom 156 CR109
Ormonde Av, Orp. 145 EQ103
Ormonde Gate SW3 100 DF78
Ormonde Pl SW1 198 F9
Ormonde Ri, Buck.H. 48 EJ46
Ormonde Rd SW14 98 CP83
Ormonde Rd, Nthwd. 39 BR49
Ormonde Rd, Wok. 166 AW116
Ormonde Ter NW8 82 DF67
Ormsby Gdns, Grnf. 78 CC68
Ormsby Pl N16 66 DT62
Victorian Gro
Ormsby Pt SE18 105 EP77
Troy Ct
Ormsby St E2 84 DT68
Ormside St SE15 102 DW79
Ormside Way, Red. 185 DH130
Ormskirk Rd, Wat. 40 BX49
Ornan Rd NW3 64 DE64
Oronsay Wk N1 84 DQ65
Clephane Rd
Orpen Wk N16 66 DS62
Orphanage Rd, Wat. 24 BW40
Orpheus St SE5 102 DR81
Orpin Rd, Red. 185 DH130
Orpington Bypass, Orp. 146 EV103
Orpington Bypass, Sev. 164 FA109
Orpington Gdns N18 46 DS48
Orpington Rd N21 45 DP46
Orpington Rd, Chis. 145 ES97
Orpwood Cl, Hmptn. 116 BZ92
Orsett Heath Cres, Grays 111 GG76
Orsett Rd, Grays 110 GA78
Orsett St SE11 200 C10
Orsett St SE11 101 DM78
Orsett Ter W2 82 DC72
Orsett Ter, Wdf.Grn. 48 EJ53
Orsman Rd N1 84 DS67
Orton St E1 202 B3
Orville Rd SW11 100 DD82
Orwell Cl, Hayes 77 BS73
Orwell Cl, Rain. 89 FD71
Orwell Ct N5 66 DQ63
Orwell Rd E13 86 EJ68
Osbaldeston Rd N16 66 DU61
Osbert St SW1 199 M9
Osberton Rd SE12 124 EG85
Osborn Cl E8 84 DU67
Osborn Gdns NW7 43 CX52
Osborn La SE23 123 DY87
Osborn St E1 84 DT71
Osborn Ter SE3 104 EF84
Lee Rd
Osborne Av, Stai. 114 BL88
Osborne Cl, Barn. 28 DF41
Osborne Cl, Beck. 143 DY98
Osborne Cl, Felt. 116 BX92
Osborne Cl, Horn. 71 FH58
Osborne Ct, Pot.B. 12 DB29
Osborne Gdns, Pot.B. 12 DB30
Osborne Gdns, Th.Hth. 142 DQ96
Osborne Gro E17 67 DZ56
Osborne Gro N4 65 DN60
Osborne Ms E17 67 DZ56
Osborne Gro
Osborne Pl, Sutt. 158 DD106
Osborne Rd E7 68 EH64
Osborne Rd E9 85 DZ65
Osborne Rd E10 67 EB62
Osborne Rd N4 65 DN60
Osborne Rd N13 45 DN48
Osborne Rd NW2 81 CV65
Osborne Rd W3 98 CP76
Osborne Rd, Belv. 106 EZ78
Osborne Rd, Brwd. 54 FU44
Osborne Rd, Buck.H. 48 EH46
Osborne Rd, Dag. 70 EZ64
Osborne Rd, Egh. 113 AZ93
Osborne Rd, Enf. 31 DY40
Osborne Rd, Horn. 71 FH58
Osborne Rd, Houns. 96 BZ83
Osborne Rd, Kings.T. 118 CL94
Osborne Rd, Pot.B. 12 DB30
Osborne Rd, Red. 184 DG131
Osborne Rd, Sthl. 78 CC72
Osborne Rd, Th.Hth. 142 DQ96
Osborne Rd, Uxb. 76 BJ66
Oxford Rd
Osborne Rd, Wal.Cr. 15 DY27
Osborne Rd, Walt. 135 BU102
Osborne Rd, Wat. 24 BW38
Osborne Sq, Dag. 70 EZ63
Osborne St, Slou. 92 AT75
Osborne Ter SW17 120 DG92
Church La
Osbourne Av, Kings L. 6 BM28
Osbourne Rd, Dart. 128 FP86
Oscar St SE8 103 EA81
Oseney Cres NW5 83 DJ65
Osgood Av, Orp. 163 ET106
Osgood Gdns, Orp. 163 ET106
O'Shea Gro E3 85 DZ67
Osidge La N14 44 DG46
Osier Ms W4 99 CT79
Osier Pl, Egh. 113 BC93
Osier St E1 84 DW70
Osier Way E10 67 EB62
Osier Way, Bans. 157 CY114
Osier Way, Mitch. 140 DE99
Osiers Rd SW18 100 DA84
Oslac Rd SE6 123 EB92
Oslo Ct NW8 194 B1
Oslo Sq SE16 203 L6
Osman Cl N15 66 DR58
Tewkesbury Rd
Osman Rd N9 46 DU48
Osman Rd W6 99 CW76
Batoum Gdns
Osmond Cl, Har. 60 CC61
Osmond Gdns, Wall. 159 DJ106
Osmund St W12 81 CT72
Braybrook St
Osnaburgh St NW1 195 J5
Osnaburgh St NW1 83 DH70
Osnaburgh Ter NW1 195 J4
Osney Ho SE2 106 EX75
Hartslock Dr
Osney Wk, Cars. 140 DD100
Osney Way, Grav. 131 GM89
Osprey Cl E6 86 EL71
Dove App
Osprey Cl E11 68 EG56
Osprey Cl E17 47 DY52
Osprey Cl, Sutt. 139 CY103
Gander Grn La
Osprey Cl, Wat. 8 BY34
Falcon Way
Osprey Cl, West Dr. 94 BL75
Osprey Ct, Wal.Abb. 16 EG34
Osprey Gdns, S.Croy. 161 DX110
Osprey Ms, Enf. 30 DV43
Osprey Rd, Wal.Abb. 16 EG34
Ospringe Cl SE20 122 DW94
Ospringe Ct SE9 125 ER86
Alderwood Rd
Ospringe Rd NW5 65 DJ63
Osram Rd, Wem. 61 CK62
Osric Path N1 197 M1
Osric Path N1 84 DS68
Ossian Ms N4 65 DM59
Ossian Rd N4 65 DM59
Ossington Bldgs W1 194 F6
Ossington Cl W2 82 DB73
Ossington St
Ossington St W2 82 DB73
Ossory Rd SE1 102 DU78
Ossulston St NW1 195 M1
Ossulston St NW1 83 DK69
Ossulton Pl N2 64 DC55
East End Rd
Ossulton Way N2 64 DC56
Ostade Rd SW2 121 DM87
Osten Ms SW7 100 DB76
McLeod's Ms
Oster Ter E17 67 DX57
Southcote Rd
Osterberg Rd, Dart. 108 FM84
Osterley Av, Islw. 97 CD80
Osterley Cl, Orp. 146 EU95
Leith Hill
Osterley Ct, Islw. 97 CD81
Osterley Cres, Islw. 97 CE81
Osterley Gdns, Th.Hth. 142 DQ96
Osterley Ho E14 85 EB72
Giraud St
Osterley La, Islw. 97 CE78
Osterley La, Sthl. 96 CA78
Osterley Pk, Islw. 97 CD78
Osterley Pk Rd, Sthl. 96 BZ76
Osterley Pk Vw Rd W7 97 CE75
Osterley Rd N16 66 DS63
Osterley Rd, Islw. 97 CE80
Osterley Views, Sthl. 78 CC74
West Pk Rd
Ostliffe Rd N13 45 DP50
Oswald Cl, Lthd. 170 CC122
Oswald Rd, Lthd. 170 CC122
Oswald Rd, Sthl. 78 BY74
Oswald St E5 67 DX62
Oswald Ter NW2 63 CW62
Temple Rd
Oswald's Mead E9 67 DY63
Lindisfarne Way
Osward, Croy. 161 DZ109
Osward Pl N9 46 DV47
Osward Rd SW17 120 DF89
Oswell Ho E1 202 E2
Oswell Ho E1 84 DV74
Oswin St SE11 200 G8
Oswin St SE11 101 DP77
Oswyth Rd SE5 102 DS82
Otford Cl SE20 142 DW95
Otford Cl, Bex. 127 FB86
Southwold Rd
Otford Cl, Brom. 145 EN97
Otford Cres SE4 123 DZ86
Otford La, Sev. 164 EZ112
Otford Rd, Sev. 181 FH118
Othello Cl SE11 200 F10
Otis St E3 85 EC69
Otley App, Ilf. 69 EP58
Otley Dr, Ilf. 69 EP57
Otley Rd E16 86 EJ72
Otley Ter E5 67 DX61
Otley Way, Wat. 40 BW48
Otlinge Cl, Orp. 146 EX98
Ottawa Gdns, Dag. 89 FD66
Ottawa Rd, Til. 111 GG82
Ottaway St E5 66 DU62
Stellman Cl
Ottenden Cl, Orp. 163 ES105
Southfleet Rd
Otter Cl, Cher. 151 BB107
Otter Meadow, Lthd. 171 CF119
Otter Rd, Grnf. 78 CC70
Otterbourne Rd E4 47 ED48
Otterbourne Rd, Croy. 142 DQ103
Otterburn Gdns, Islw. 97 CG80
Otterburn Ho SE5 102 DQ80
Otterburn St SW17 120 DF93
Otterden St SE6 123 EA91
Otterfield Rd, West Dr. 76 BL73
Ottermead La, Cher. 151 BC107
Otters Cl, Orp. 146 EX98
Otterspool La, Wat. 24 BY38
Otterspool Service Rd, Wat. 24 BZ39
Otterspool Way, Wat. 24 BY37
Otto Cl SE26 122 DV90
Otto St SE17 101 DP79
Ottoman Ter, Wat. 24 BW41
Ebury Rd
Ottways Av, Ash. 171 CK119

Ottways La, Ash. 171 CK120
Otway Gdns, Bushey 41 CE45
Otways Cl, Pot.B. 12 DB32
Oulton Cl E5 66 DW61
Mundford Rd
Oulton Cl SE28 88 EW72
Rollesby Way
Oulton Cres, Bark. 87 ET65
Oulton Cres, Pot.B. 11 CX32
Oulton Rd N15 66 DR57
Oulton Way, Wat. 40 BY49
Oundle Av, Bushey 24 CC44
Ousden Cl (Cheshunt), Wal.Cr. 15 DY30
Ousden Dr (Cheshunt), Wal.Cr. 15 DY30
Ouseley Rd SW12 120 DF88
Ouseley Rd, Stai. 112 AW87
Ouseley Rd, Wind. 112 AW87
Outer Circle NW1 194 F5
Outer Circle NW1 83 DH68
Outfield Rd (Chalfont St. Peter), Ger.Cr. 36 AX52
Outgate Rd NW10 81 CT66
Outlook Dr, Ch.St.G. 36 AX48
Outram Pl N1 83 DL67
Outram Pl, Wey. 153 BQ106
Outram Rd E6 86 EL67
Outram Rd N22 45 DK53
Outram Rd, Croy. 142 DT102
Outwich St EC3 197 N8
Outwood La, Couls. 174 DF118
Outwood La, Tad. 174 DB122
Oval, The E2 84 DV68
Oval, The, Bans. 158 DA114
Oval, The, Brox. 15 DY25
Oval, The, Sid. 126 EU87
Oval Gdns, Grays 110 GC76
Oval Pl SW8 101 DM80
Oval Rd NW1 83 DH67
Oval Rd, Croy. 142 DS102
Oval Rd N, Dag. 89 FB67
Oval Rd S, Dag. 89 FB68
Oval Way SE11 101 DM78
Oval Way, Ger.Cr. 56 AY56
Ovenden Rd, Sev. 180 EX120
Over The Misbourne, Ger.Cr. 57 BA58
Over The Misbourne (Denham), Uxb. 57 BC58
Overbrae, Beck. 123 EA93
Overbrook Wk, Edg. 42 CN52
Overbury Av, Beck. 143 EB97
Overbury Cres, Croy. 161 EC110
Overbury Rd N15 66 DR58
Overbury St E5 67 DX63
Overcliff Rd SE13 103 EA83
Overcliff Rd, Grays 110 GD78
Overcliffe, Grav. 131 GG86
Overcourt Cl, Sid. 126 EV86
Overdale, Ash. 172 CL115
Overdale, Red. 186 DQ133
Overdale Av, N.Mal. 138 CQ96
Overdale Rd W5 97 CJ76
Overdown Rd SE6 123 EA91
Overhill, Warl. 176 DW119
Overhill Rd SE22 122 DU87
Overhill Rd, Pur. 159 DN109
Overhill Way, Beck. 143 ED99
Overlea Rd E5 66 DU59
Overmead, Sid. 125 ER87
Overmead, Swan. 147 FE99
Oversley Ho W2 82 DA71
Overstand Cl, Beck. 143 EA99
Overstone Gdns, Croy. 143 DZ101
Overstone Rd W6 99 CW76
Overstream, Rick. 22 BH42
Overthorpe Cl, Wok. 166 AS117
Overton Cl NW10 80 CQ65
Overton Cl, Islw. 97 CF81
Avenue Rd
Overton Ct E11 68 EG59
Overton Dr E11 68 EH59
Overton Dr, Rom. 70 EW59
Overton Rd E10 67 DY60
Overton Rd N14 29 DL43
Overton Rd SE2 106 EW76
Overton Rd SW9 101 DN82
Overton Rd, Sutt. 158 DA107
Overton Rd E SE2 106 EX76
Overtons Yd, Croy. 142 DQ104
Overy St, Dart. 128 FL86
Ovesdon Av, Har. 60 BZ60
Ovett Cl SE19 122 DS93
Ovex Cl E14 204 E5
Ovex Cl E14 103 EC75
Ovington Ct, Wok. 166 AT116
Roundthorn Way
Ovington Gdns SW3 198 C7
Ovington Gdns SW3 100 DE76
Ovington Ms SW3 198 C7
Ovington Ms SW3 100 DE76
Ovington Sq SW3 198 C7
Ovington Sq SW3 100 DE76
Ovington St SW3 198 C7
Ovington St SW3 100 DE76
Owen Cl SE28 88 EW74
Owen Cl, Croy. 142 DR100
Owen Cl, Hayes 77 BV69
Owen Cl, Rom. 51 FB51
Owen Gdns, Wdf.Grn. 48 EL51
Owen Pl, Lthd. 171 CH122
Church Rd
Owen Rd N13 46 DQ50
Owen Rd, Hayes 77 BV69
Owen St EC1 196 F1
Owen Wk SE20 122 DU94
Sycamore Gro
Owen Waters Ho, Ilf. 49 EM53
Owen Way NW10 80 CQ65
Owenite St SE2 106 EV77
Owen's Ct EC1 196 F2
Owen's Row EC1 196 F2
Owens Way SE23 123 DY87
Owens Way, Rick. 22 BN43
Owgan Cl SE5 102 DR80
Benhill Rd
Owl Cl, S.Croy. 161 DX110
Owl Pk, Loug. 32 EF40
Owlets Hall Cl, Horn. 72 FM55
Prospect Rd
Ownstead Gdns, S.Croy. 160 DT111
Ownsted Hill, Croy. 161 EC110
Ox La, Epsom 157 CU109
Church St
Oxberry Av SW6 99 CY82
Oxdowne Cl, Cob. 154 CB114
Oxenden Wd Rd, Orp. 164 EV107
Oxendon St SW1 199 M1
Oxendon St SW1 83 DK73
Oxenford St SE15 102 DT83
Oxenholme NW1 195 L1
Oxenholme NW1 83 DJ68
Oxenpark Av, Wem. 62 CL59
Oxestalls Rd SE8 203 L10
Oxestalls Rd SE8 103 DY78
Oxford Av SW20 139 CY96
Oxford Av, Grays 111 GG77
Oxford Av, Hayes 95 BT80
Oxford Av, Horn. 72 FN56
Oxford Av, Houns. 96 CA78
Oxford Circ Av W1 195 K9
Oxford Cl N9 46 DV47
Oxford Cl, Ashf. 115 BQ94
Oxford Cl, Grav. 131 GM89
Oxford Cl, Mitch. 141 DJ97
Oxford Cl, Nthwd. 39 BQ49
Oxford Cl (Cheshunt), Wal.Cr. 15 DX29
Oxford Ct EC4 197 K10
Oxford Ct W3 80 CN72
Oxford Ct, Brwd. 54 FX49
Oxford Ct, Felt. 116 BX91
Oxford Way
Oxford Cres, N.Mal. 138 CR100
Oxford Dr, Ruis. 60 BW61
Oxford Gdns N20 44 DD46
Oxford Gdns N21 46 DQ45
Oxford Gdns W4 98 CN78
Oxford Gdns W10 81 CY72
Oxford Gdns (Denham), Uxb. 57 BF62
Oxford Gate W6 99 CX77
Oxford Ms, Bex. 126 FA87
Bexley High St
Oxford Pl NW10 62 CR62
Neasden La N
Oxford Rd E15 85 ED65
Oxford Rd N4 65 DN60
Oxford Rd N9 46 DV47
Oxford Rd NW6 82 DA68
Oxford Rd SE19 122 DR93
Oxford Rd SW15 99 CY84
Oxford Rd W5 79 CK73
Oxford Rd, Cars. 158 DE107
Oxford Rd, Enf. 30 DV43
Oxford Rd, Ger.Cr. 57 BA60
Oxford Rd, Har. 60 CC58
Oxford Rd (Wealdstone), Har. 61 CF55
Oxford Rd, Ilf. 69 EQ63
Oxford Rd, Red. 184 DE133
Oxford Rd, Rom. 52 FM51
Oxford Rd, Sid. 126 EV92
Oxford Rd, Tedd. 117 CD92
Oxford Rd, Uxb. 76 BJ66
Oxford Rd, Wall. 159 DJ106
Oxford Rd, Wdf.Grn. 48 EJ50
Oxford Rd N W4 98 CP78
Oxford Rd S W4 98 CN78
Oxford Sq W2 194 C9
Oxford Sq W2 82 DE72
Oxford St W1 194 F9
Oxford St W1 83 DH72
Oxford St, Wat. 23 BV43
Oxford Wk, Sthl. 78 BZ74
Oxford Way, Felt. 116 BX91
Oxgate Gdns NW2 63 CV62
Oxgate La NW2 63 CV61
Oxhawth Cres, Brom. 145 EN99
Oxhey Av, Wat. 40 BX45
Oxhey Dr, Nthwd. 39 BV50
Oxhey Dr, Wat. 40 BW48
Oxhey La, Har. 40 CB50
Oxhey La, Pnr. 40 CB50
Oxhey La, Wat. 40 BZ48
Oxhey Ridge Cl, Nthwd. 39 BU50
Oxhey Rd, Wat. 40 BW45
Oxleas E6 87 EP72
Oxleas Cl, Well. 105 ER82
Oxleay Ct, Har. 60 CA60
Oxleay Rd, Har. 60 CA60
Oxleigh Cl, N.Mal. 138 CS99
Oxley Cl SE1 202 A10
Oxley Cl SE1 102 DT78
Oxley Cl, Rom. 52 FJ54
Oxleys Rd NW2 63 CV62
Oxleys Rd, Wal.Abb. 16 EG32
Oxlip Cl, Croy. 143 DX102
Marigold Way
Oxlow La, Dag. 70 FA63
Oxonian St SE22 102 DT84
Oxshott Ri, Cob. 154 BX113
Oxshott Rd, Lthd. 171 CE115
Oxshott Way, Cob. 170 BY115
Oxted Cl, Mitch. 140 DD97
Oxted Rd, Gdse. 186 DW130
Oxtoby Way SW16 141 DK96
Oyster Catcher Ter, Ilf. 69 EN55
Tiptree Cres
Oyster Catchers Cl E16 86 EH72
Freemasons Rd
Oyster La, W.Byf. 152 BK110
Oyster Row E1 84 DW72
Lukin St
Ozolins Way E16 86 EG72

P

Pablo Neruda Cl SE24 101 DP84
Shakespeare Rd
Pace Pl E1 84 DV72
Bigland St
Paceheath Cl, Rom. 51 FD51
Pachesham Dr, Lthd. 171 CF116
Oxshott Rd
Pachesham Pk, Lthd. 171 CG117
Pacific Cl, Felt. 115 BT88
Pacific Rd E16 86 EG72
Packet Boat La, Uxb. 76 BH72
Packham Cl, Orp. 146 EW104
Berrylands
Packham Rd, Grav. 131 GF90
Packhorse La, Borwd. 26 CS37
Packhorse La, Pot.B. 10 CR31
Packhorse Rd (Chalfont St. Peter), Ger.Cr. 56 AY58
Packhorse Rd, Sev. 190 FC123
Packington Rd W3 98 CQ76
Packington Sq N1 84 DQ67
Packington St N1 83 DP67
Packmores Rd SE9 125 ER85
Padbrook, Oxt. 188 EG129
Padbrook Cl, Oxt. 188 EH128
Padbury SE17 102 DS78
Padbury Cl, Felt. 115 BR88
Padbury Ct E2 84 DT69
Padcroft Rd, West Dr. 76 BK74
Paddenswick Rd W6 99 CU76
Paddington Cl, Hayes 78 BX70
Paddington Grn W2 194 A6
Paddington Grn W2 82 DD71
Paddington St W1 194 F6
Paddington St W1 82 DG71
Paddock, The (Chalfont St. Peter), Ger.Cr. 36 AY50
Paddock, The, Slou. 92 AV81
Paddock, The (Ickenham), Uxb. 59 BP63
Paddock, The, West. 189 EQ126
Paddock Cl SE3 104 EG82
Paddock Cl SE26 123 DX91
Paddock Cl (South Darenth), Dart. 148 FQ95
Paddock Cl, Nthlt. 78 CA68
Paddock Cl, Orp. 163 EP105
State Fm Av
Paddock Cl, Oxt. 188 EF131
Paddock Cl, Wat. 24 BY44
Paddock Cl, Wor.Pk. 138 CS102
Paddock Gdns SE19 122 DS93
Westow St
Paddock Rd NW2 63 CU62
Paddock Rd, Bexh. 106 EY84
Paddock Rd, Ruis. 60 BX62
Paddock Wk, Warl. 176 DV119
Paddock Way, Chis. 125 ER94
Paddock Way, Oxt. 188 EF131
Paddock Way, Wok. 151 BB114
Paddocks, The, Add. 152 BH110
Paddocks, The, Barn. 28 DF41
Paddocks, The, Rick. 21 BF42
Paddocks, The, Rom. 35 FF44
Paddocks, The, Sev. 191 FK124
Paddocks, The, Vir.W. 132 AY100
Paddocks, The, Wem. 62 CP61
Paddocks, The, Wey. 135 BS104
Paddocks Cl, Ash. 172 CL118
Paddocks Cl, Cob. 154 BW114
Paddocks Cl, Har. 60 CB63
Paddocks Cl, Orp. 146 EX103
Paddocks Mead, Wok. 166 AS116
Paddocks Way, Ash. 172 CL118
Paddocks Way, Cher. 134 BH102
Padfield Rd SE5 102 DQ83
Padgets, The, Wal.Abb. 16 EE34
Rochford Av
Padnall Ct, Rom. 70 EX55
Padnall Rd
Padnall Rd, Rom. 70 EX56
Padstow Cl, Orp. 163 ET105
Padstow Cl, Slou. 92 AY76
Padstow Rd, Enf. 29 DP40
Padstow Wk, Felt. 115 BT88
Padua Rd SE20 142 DW95
Pagden St SW8 101 DH81
Page Cl, Dag. 70 EY64
Page Cl, Dart. 129 FW90
Page Cl, Hmptn. 116 BY93
Page Cl, Har. 62 CM58
Page Cres, Croy. 159 DN106
Page Cres, Erith 107 FF80
Page Grn Rd N15 66 DU57
Page Grn Ter N15 66 DT57
Page Heath La, Brom. 144 EK97
Page Heath Vil, Brom. 144 EK97
Page Meadow NW7 43 CU52
Page Rd, Felt. 115 BR86
Page St NW7 43 CU53
Page St SW1 199 N8
Page St SW1 101 DL77
Pageant Av NW9 42 CR53
Pageant Cl, Til. 111 GJ81
Pageant Cres SE16 203 L2
Pageant Wk, Croy. 142 DS104
Pageantmaster Ct EC4 196 F9
Pagehurst Rd, Croy. 142 DV101
Pages Hill N10 44 DG54
Pages La N10 44 DG54
Pages La, Rom. 52 FP54
Pages La, Uxb. 76 BJ65
Pages Wk SE1 201 M8
Pages Wk SE1 102 DS77
Pages Yd W4 98 CS79
Church St
Paget Av, Sutt. 140 DD104
Paget Cl, Hmptn. 117 CD91
Paget Gdns, Chis. 145 EP95
Paget La, Islw. 97 CD83
Paget Pl, Kings.T. 118 CQ93
Paget Pl, T.Ditt. 137 CG102
Brooklands Rd
Paget Ri SE18 105 EN80
Paget Rd N16 66 DR60
Paget Rd, Ilf. 69 EP63
Paget Rd, Slou. 93 AZ77
Paget Rd, Uxb. 77 BQ70
Paget St EC1 196 F2
Paget Ter SE18 105 EN79
Pagette Way, Grays 110 GA77
Pagitts Gro, Barn. 28 DB39
Paglesfield, Brwd. 55 GC44
Pagnell St SE14 103 DZ80
Pagoda Av, Rich. 98 CM83
Pagoda Gdns SE3 103 ED82
Pagoda Vista, Rich. 98 CM82
Paignton Rd N15 66 DS58
Paignton Rd, Ruis. 59 BU62
Paines Brook Rd, Rom. 52 FM51
Paines Brook Way
Paines Brook Way, . Rom 52 FM51
Paines Cl, Pnr. 60 BY55
Paines La, Pnr. 40 BY53
Pains Cl, Mitch. 141 DH96
Pains Hill, Oxt. 188 EJ132
Painsthorpe Rd N16 66 DS62
Oldfield Rd
Painters Ash La, Grav. 130 GD90
Painters La, Enf. 31 DY35
Painters Rd, Ilf. 69 ET55
Paisley Rd N22 45 DP53
Paisley Rd, Cars. 140 DD102
Pakeman St N7 65 DM62
Pakenham Cl SW12 120 DG88
Balham Pk Rd
Pakenham St WC1 196 C4
Pakenham St WC1 83 DM69
Pakes Way, Epp. 33 ES37
Palace Av W8 82 DB74
Palace Cl, Kings L. 6 BM30
Palace Ct NW3 64 DB64
Palace Ct W2 82 DB73
Palace Ct, Brom. 144 EH95
Palace Gro
Palace Ct, Har. 62 CL58
Palace Ct Gdns N10 65 DJ55
Palace Dr, Wey. 135 BP104
Palace Gdns, Buck.H. 48 EK46
Palace Gdns, Enf. 30 DR41
Palace Gdns Ms W8 82 DA74
Palace Gdns Ter W8 82 DA74
Palace Gate W8 100 DC75
Palace Gates Rd N22 45 DK53
Palace Grn W8 100 DB75
Palace Grn, Croy. 161 DZ108
Palace Gro SE19 122 DT94
Palace Gro, Brom. 144 EH95
Palace Ms E17 67 DZ56
Palace Ms SW1 198 G9
Palace Ms SW6 99 CZ80
Hartismere Rd
Palace of Industry, Wem. 62 CN63
Palace Par E17 67 EA56
High St
Palace Pl SW1 199 K6
Palace Rd N8 65 DK57
Palace Rd N11 45 DL52
Palace Rd SE19 122 DT94
Palace Rd SW2 121 DM88
Palace Rd, Brom. 144 EH95
Palace Rd, E.Mol. 137 CD97
Palace Rd, Kings.T. 137 CK98
Palace Rd, Ruis. 60 BY63
Palace Rd, West. 179 EN121
Chestnut Av
Palace Rd Est SW2 121 DM88
Palace Sq SE19 122 DT94
Palace St SW1 199 K6
Palace St SW1 101 DJ76
Palace Vw SE12 124 EG89
Palace Vw, Brom. 144 EG97
Palace Vw, Croy. 161 DZ105
Palace Vw Rd E4 47 EB50
Palace Way, Wey. 135 BP104
Palace Dr
Palamos Rd E10 67 EA60
Palatine Av N16 66 DT63
Stoke Newington Rd
Palatine Rd N16 66 DS63
Palermo Rd NW10 81 CU68
Palestine Gro SW19 140 DD95
Palewell Cl, Orp. 146 EV96
Palewell Common Dr SW14 118 CR85
Palewell Pk SW14 118 CR85
Paley Gdns, Loug. 33 EQ41
Palfrey Pl SW8 101 DM80
Palgrave Av, Sthl. 78 CA73
Palgrave Rd W12 99 CT76
Palissy St E2 197 P3
Pall Mall SW1 199 L3
Pall Mall SW1 83 DJ74
Pall Mall E SW1 199 N2
Pall Mall E SW1 83 DK74
Pall Mall Pl SW1 199 L3
Pall Mall Pl SW1 83 DJ74
Palladino Ho SW17 120 DE92
Laurel Cl
Pallant Way, Orp. 145 EN104
Pallet Way SE18 104 EL81
Palliser Dr, Rain. 89 FG71
Palliser Rd W14 99 CY78
Palliser Rd, Ch.St.G. 36 AU48
Palm Av, Sid. 126 EX93
Palm Cl E10 67 EB62
Palm Gro W5 98 CL76
Palm Rd, Rom. 71 FC57
Palmar Cres, Bexh. 106 FA83
Palmar Rd, Bexh. 106 FA82
Palmarsh Cl, Orp. 146 EX98
Wotton Grn
Palmeira Rd, Bexh. 106 EX83
Palmer Av, Bushey 24 CB43
Palmer Av, Grav. 131 GK91
Palmer Av, Sutt. 157 CW105
Palmer Cl, Houns. 96 CA81
Palmer Cl, W.Wick. 143 ED104
Palmer Cres, Cher. 151 BD107
Palmer Cres, Kings.T. 138 CL97
Palmer Gdns, Barn. 27 CX43
Palmer Pl N7 65 DN64
Palmer Rd E13 86 EH70
Palmer Rd, Dag. 70 EX60
Palmer St SW1 199 M5
Palmer St SW1 101 DK76
Palmers Av, Grays 110 GC78
Palmers Dr, Grays 110 GC77
Palmers Gro, W.Mol. 136 CA98
Palmers Hill, Epp. 18 EU29
Palmers La, Enf. 30 DV39
Palmers Moor La, Iver 76 BG70
Palmers Orchard, Sev. 165 FF111
Palmers Pas SW14 98 CQ83
Palmers Rd
Palmers Rd E2 85 DX68
Palmers Rd N11 45 DJ50
Palmers Rd SW14 98 CQ83
Palmers Rd SW16 141 DM96
Palmers Rd, Borwd. 26 CP39
Palmers Way (Cheshunt), Wal.Cr. 15 DY29
Palmersfield Rd, Bans. 158 DA114
Palmerston Av, Slou. 92 AV76
Palmerston Cl, Wok. 151 AZ114
Palmerston Cres N13 45 DM50
Palmerston Cres SE18 105 EQ79
Palmerston Gdns, Grays 109 FX78
Palmerston Gro SW19 120 DA94
Palmerston Rd E7 68 EH64
Palmerston Rd E17 67 DZ5
Palmerston Rd N22 45 DM5
Palmerston Rd NW6 82 DA6
Palmerston Rd SW14 98 CQ8
Palmerston Rd SW19 120 DA9
Palmerston Rd W3 98 CQ7
Palmerston Rd, Buck.H. 48 EH4
Palmerston Rd, Cars. 158 DF10
Palmerston Rd, Croy. 142 DR9
Palmerston Rd, Grays 109 FX7
Palmerston Rd, Har. 61 CF5
Palmerston Rd, Houns. 96 CC8
Gresham Rd
Palmerston Rd, Orp. 163 EQ10
Palmerston Rd, Rain. 90 FJ6
Palmerston Rd, Sutt. 158 DC10
Vernon Rd
Palmerston Rd, Twick. 117 CF8
Palmerston Way SW8 101 DH8
Bradmead
Palmerstone Ct, Vir.W. 132 AY9
Sandhills La
Pamela Gdns, Pnr. 59 BV5
Pamela Wk E8 84 DU6
Marlborough Av
Pampisford Rd, Pur. 159 DN11
Pampisford Rd, S.Croy. 159 DP10
Pams Way, Epsom 156 CR10
Pancras La EC4 197 J
Pancras Rd NW1 83 DK6
Pancroft, Rom. 34 EV4
Pandora Rd NW6 82 DA6
Panfield Ms, Ilf. 69 EN5
Cranbrook Rd
Panfield Rd SE2 106 EU7
Pangbourne Av W10 81 CW7
Pangbourne Dr, Stan. 41 CK5
Panhard Pl, Sthl. 78 CB7
Pank Av, Barn. 28 DC4
Pankhurst Cl SE14 103 DX8
Briant St
Pankhurst Cl, Islw. 97 CF8
Pankhurst Rd, Walt. 136 BW10
Panmuir Rd SW20 139 CV9
Panmure Cl N5 65 DP6
Panmure Rd SE26 122 DV9
Pannells Cl, Cher. 133 BF10
Pansy Gdns W12 81 CU7
Panters, Swan. 127 FF9
Panther Dr NW10 62 CR6
Pantile Rd, Wey. 153 BR10
Pantile Row, Slou. 93 BA7
Pantile Wk, Uxb. 76 BJ6
High St
Pantiles, The NW11 63 CZ5
Willifield Way
Pantiles, The, Bexh. 106 EZ8
Pantiles, The, Brom. 144 EL9
Pantiles, The, Bushey 41 CD4
Pantiles Cl N13 45 DP5
Pantiles Cl, Wok. 166 AV11
Panton St SW1 199 M
Panyer All EC4 197 H
Papercourt La, Wok. 167 BF12
Papermill Cl, Cars. 158 DG10
Papillons Wk SE3 104 EG8
Papworth Gdns N7 65 DM6
Liverpool Rd
Papworth Way SW2 121 DN8
Parade, The SW11 100 DF8
Parade, The, Brwd. 54 FW4
Kings Rd
Parade, The, Dart. 127 FF8
Crayford Way
Parade, The, Epsom 156 CR11
Parade, The, Esher 155 CE10
Parade, The, Hmptn. 117 CD9
Hampton Rd
Parade, The, Rom. 52 FP5
Parade, The, S.Ock. 108 FQ7
Parade, The, Sun. 115 BT9
Parade, The, Vir.W. 132 AX10
Parade, The, Wat. 23 BV4
Parade, The (Carpenders Pk), Wat. 40 BY4
Parade Ms SE27 121 DP8
Norwood Rd
Paradise Cl (Cheshunt), Wal.Cr. 14 DV2
Paradise Pas N7 65 DN6
Paradise Pl SE18 104 EL7
Woodhill
Paradise Rd SW4 101 DL8
Paradise Rd, Rich. 117 CK8
Paradise Rd, Wal.Abb. 15 EC3
Paradise Row E2 84 DV6
Bethnal Grn Rd
Paradise St SE16 202 D
Paradise St SE16 102 DV7
Paradise Wk SW3 100 DF7
Paragon, The SE3 104 EF8
Paragon Cl E16 86 EG7
Paragon Gro, Surb. 138 CM10
Paragon Ms SE1 201 L
Paragon Pl SE3 104 EF8
Paragon Pl, Surb. 138 CM10
Berrylands Rd
Paragon Rd E9 84 DV6
Parbury Ri, Chess. 156 CL10
Parbury Rd SE23 123 DY8
Parchment Cl, Amer. 20 AS3
Parchmore Rd, Th.Hth. 141 DP9
Parchmore Way, Th.Hth. 141 DP9
Pardon St EC1 196 G
Pardoner St SE1 201 L
Pardoner St SE1 102 DR7
Pares Cl, Wok. 166 AX11
Parfett St E1 84 DU7
Parfitt Cl NW3 64 DC6
North End
Parfour Dr, Ken. 176 DQ11
Parfrey St W6 99 CW7
Parham Dr, Ilf. 69 EP5
Parham Way N10 45 DJ5
Paris Gdn SE1 200 F
Paris Gdn SE1 83 DP7
Parish Cl, Horn. 71 FH6
St. Leonards Way
Parish Gate Dr, Sid. 125 ES8
Parish La SE20 123 DX9
Parish Ms SE20 123 DX9
Parish Wf Pl SE18 104 EL7
Woodhill

Park, The N6 64 DG58
Park, The NW11 64 DB60
Park, The SE19 122 DS94
Park, The SE23 122 DV88
Park Hill
Park, The W5 79 CK74
Park, The, Cars. 158 DF106
Park, The, Lthd. 170 CA123
Park, The, Sid. 125 ET92
Park App, Well. 106 EV84
Park Av E6 87 EN67
Park Av E15 86 EE65
Park Av N3 44 DB53
Park Av N13 45 DN48
Park Av N18 46 DU49
Park Av N22 45 DL54
Park Av NW2 81 CV65
Park Av NW10 80 CM69
Park Av NW11 64 DB60
Park Av SW14 98 CR84
Park Av, Bark. 87 EQ65
Park Av, Brwd. 55 GC46
Park Av, Brom. 124 EF93
Park Av, Bushey 24 BZ40
Park Av, Cars. 158 DG107
Park Av, Cat. 176 DS124
Park Av, Egh. 113 BC93
Park Av, Enf. 30 DS44
Park Av, Grav. 131 GJ88
Park Av (Perry St), Grav. 130 GE88
Park Av, Grays 109 FU79
Park Av, Houns. 116 CB86
Park Av, Ilf. 69 EN60
Park Av, Mitch. 121 DH94
Park Av, Orp. 146 EU103
Park Av (Farnborough), Orp. 145 EM104
Park Av, Pot.B. 12 DC34
Park Av, Rad. 9 CH33
Park Av, Rick. 22 BG43
Park Av, Ruis. 59 BR58
Park Av, Sthl. 78 CA74
Park Av, Stai. 113 BF93
Park Av (Sunnymeads), Stai. 112 AX85
Park Av, Upmin. 73 FS59
Park Av, Wat. 23 BU42
Park Av, W.Wick. 143 EC103
Park Av, Wdf.Grn. 48 EH50
Park Av E, Epsom 157 CU107
Park Av Ms, Mitch. 121 DH94
Park Av
Park Av N N8 65 DK55
Park Av N NW10 63 CV64
Park Av Rd N17 46 DV52
Park Av S N8 65 DK56
Park Av W, Epsom 157 CU107
Park Boul, Rom. 51 FF53
Park Chase, Wem. 62 CM63
Park Cl E9 84 DW67
Park Cl NW2 63 CV62
Park Cl NW10 80 CM69
Park Cl SW1 198 D5
Park Cl SW1 100 DF75
Park Cl W4 98 CR78
Park Cl W14 99 CZ76
Park Cl, Add. 152 BH110
Park Cl, Bushey 24 BX41
Park Cl, Cars. 158 DF107
Park Cl, Epp. 18 FA27
Park Cl, Esher 154 CA107
Park Cl, Hmptn. 136 CC95
Park Cl, Har. 41 CE53
Park Cl (Brookmans Pk), Hat. 11 CZ26
Park Cl, Houns. 116 CC85
Park Cl, Kings.T. 138 CN95
Park Cl, Lthd. 171 CD124
Park Cl, Rick. 39 BP49
Park Cl, Walt. 135 BT103
Park Cor Rd, Grav. 130 FZ91
Park Ct SE26 122 DV93
Park Ct, Kings.T. 137 CJ95
Park Ct, N.Mal. 138 CR98
Park Ct, Wem. 62 CL64
Park Ct, W.Byf. 152 BG113
Park Ct, Wok. 167 AZ118
Park Dr
Park Cres N3 44 DB52
Park Cres W1 195 H5
Park Cres W1 83 DH70
Park Cres, Borwd. 26 CM41
Park Cres, Enf. 30 DR42
Park Cres, Erith 107 FD79
Park Cres, Har. 41 CE53
Park Cres, Horn. 71 FG59
Park Cres, Twick. 117 CD88
Park Cres Ms E W1 195 J5
Park Cres Ms W W1 195 H6
Park Cres Rd, Erith 107 FD79
Park Cft, Edg. 42 CQ53
Park Dale N11 45 DK51
Park Dr N21 30 DQ44
Park Dr NW11 64 DB60
Park Dr SE7 104 EL79
Park Dr SW14 98 CR84
Park Dr W3 98 CN76
Park Dr, Ash. 172 CN118
Park Dr, Dag. 71 FC62
Park Dr, Har. 60 CA59
Park Dr (Harrow Weald), Har. 41 CE51
Park Dr, Pot.B. 12 DA31
Park Dr, Rom. 71 FD56
Park Dr, Upmin. 72 FQ63
Park Dr, Wey. 153 BP106
Park Dr, Wok. 167 AZ118
Park Dr Cl SE7 104 EL78
Park End NW3 64 DE63
South Hill Pk
Park End, Brom. 144 EF95
Park End Rd, Rom. 71 FE56
Park Fm Cl N2 64 DC55
Park Fm Cl, Pnr. 59 BV57
Field End Rd
Park Fm Rd, Brom. 144 EK95
Park Fm Rd, Kings.T. 118 CL94
Park Fm Rd, Upmin. 72 FM64
Park Gdns NW9 62 CP55
Park Gdns, Erith 107 FD77
Valley Rd
Park Gdns, Kings.T. 118 CN92
Park Gate N2 64 DD55
Park Gate N21 45 DM45
Park Gate W5 79 CK71
Mount Av
Park Gates, Har. 60 CA63
Park Gra Gdns, Sev. 191 FJ127
Solefields Rd
Park Grn, Lthd. 170 CA124
Park Gro E15 86 EG67
Park Gro N11 45 DK52
Park Gro, Bexh. 107 FC84
Park Gro, Brom. 144 EH95
Park Gro, Ch.St.G. 20 AX41
Park Gro, Edg. 42 CM50
Park Gro Rd E11 68 EE61
Park Hall Rd N2 64 DE56
Park Hall Rd SE21 122 DQ90
Park Hall Rd, Reig. 184 DA132
Park Hill SE23 122 DV89
Park Hill SW4 121 DK85
Park Hill W5 79 CK71
Park Hill, Brom. 144 EL98
Park Hill, Cars. 158 DE107
Park Hill, Loug. 32 EK43
Park Hill, Rich. 118 CM86
Park Hill Cl, Cars. 158 DE106
Park Hill Ct SW17 120 DF90
Beeches Rd
Park Hill Ri, Croy. 142 DS103
Park Hill Rd, Brom. 144 EE96
Park Hill Rd, Croy. 160 DS105
Park Hill Rd, Epsom 157 CT111
Park Hill Rd, Wall. 159 DH108
Park Ho N21 45 DM45
Park Ho Gdns, Twick. 117 CJ86
Park Ind Est, St.Alb. 9 CE27
Park La E15 85 ED67
High St
Park La N9 46 DT48
Park La N17 46 DU52
Park La W1 198 G3
Park La W1 82 DG73
Park La, Ash. 172 CM118
Park La, Bans. 174 DD118
Park La, Cars. 158 DG105
Park La, Couls. 175 DK121
Park La, Croy. 142 DR104
Park La, Har. 60 CB62
Park La, Hayes 77 BS71
Park La, Horn. 71 FG58
Park La (Elm Pk), Horn. 89 FH65
Park La, Houns. 95 BU80
Park La, Rich. 97 CK84
Park La (Chadwell Heath), Rom. 70 EX58
Park La, Sev. 191 FJ124
Park La (Seal), Sev. 191 FN121
Park La, Slou. 92 AV76
Park La (Horton), Slou. 93 BA83
Park La, S.Ock. 91 FR74
Park La, Stan. 41 CG48
Park La, Sutt. 157 CY107
Park La, Swan. 148 FJ96
Park La, Tedd. 117 CF93
Park La (Harefield), Uxb. 38 BG53
Park La, Wall. 158 DG105
Park La, Wal.Cr. 14 DW33
Park La (Cheshunt), Wal.Cr. 14 DU26
Park La, Wem. 62 CL64
Park La Cl N17 46 DU52
Park Lawn Rd, Wey. 153 BQ105
Park Lawns, Wem. 62 CM63
Park Ley Rd, Cat. 177 DX120
Park Mead, Har. 60 CB62
Park Mead, Sid. 126 EV85
Park Ms SE24 122 DQ86
Croxted Rd
Park Ms, Chis. 125 EP93
Park Ms, E.Mol. 136 CC98
Park Ms, Hmptn. 116 CC92
Park Rd
Park Ms, Rain. 89 FG65
Sowrey Av
Park Nook Gdns, Enf. 30 DR37
Park Par NW10 81 CT68
Park Pl E14 203 P2
Park Pl E14 85 EA74
Park Pl SW1 199 K3
Park Pl SW1 83 DJ74
Park Pl W3 98 CN77
Park Pl W5 79 CK74
Park Pl, Amer. 20 AT38
Park Pl, Grav. 131 GJ86
Park Pl, Hmptn. 116 CC93
Park Pl, St.Alb. 9 CD27
Park Pl, Sev. 190 FD123
Park Pl, Wem. 62 CM63
Park Pl, Wok. 167 AZ118
Park Dr
Park Pl Vil W2 82 DC71
Park Ridings N8 65 DN55
Park Ri SE23 123 DY88
Park Ri, Har. 41 CE53
Park Ri, Lthd. 171 CH121
Park Ri Cl, Lthd. 171 CH121
Park Ri Rd SE23 123 DY88
Park Rd E6 86 EJ67
Park Rd E10 67 EA60
Park Rd E12 68 EH60
Park Rd E15 86 EG67
Park Rd E17 67 DZ57
Park Rd N2 64 DD55
Park Rd N8 65 DJ56
Park Rd N11 45 DK52
Park Rd N14 45 DK45
Park Rd N15 65 DP56
Park Rd N18 46 DT49
Park Rd NW1 194 B2
Park Rd NW1 82 DE69
Park Rd NW4 63 CU59
Park Rd NW8 194 B2
Park Rd NW8 82 DE69
Park Rd NW9 62 CR59
Park Rd NW10 80 CS67
Park Rd SE25 142 DS98
Park Rd SW19 120 DD93
Park Rd W4 98 CQ80
Park Rd W7 79 CF73
Park Rd, Amer. 20 AT37
Park Rd, Ashf. 115 BP92
Park Rd, Ash. 172 CL118
Park Rd, Bans. 174 DB115
Park Rd, Barn. 27 CZ42
Park Rd (New Barnet), Barn. 28 DE42
Park Rd, Beck. 123 DZ94
Park Rd, Brwd. 54 FV46
Park Rd, Brom. 144 EH95
Park Rd, Bushey 24 CA44
Park Rd, Cat. 176 DS123
Park Rd, Chis. 125 EP93
Park Rd, Dart. 128 FN87
Park Rd, E.Mol. 136 CC98
Park Rd, Egh. 113 BA91
Park Rd, Enf. 31 DY36
Park Rd, Esher 154 CB105
Park Rd, Felt. 116 BX91
Park Rd, Grav. 131 GH88
Park Rd, Grays 110 GB78
Park Rd, Hmptn. 116 CB91
Park Rd, Hayes 77 BS71
Park Rd, Houns. 96 CC84
Park Rd, Ilf. 69 ER62
Park Rd, Islw. 97 CH81
Park Rd, Ken. 175 DP115
Park Rd, Kings.T. 118 CM92
Park Rd (Hampton Wick), Kings.T. 117 CF93
Park Rd, N.Mal. 138 CR98
Park Rd, Orp. 146 EW99
Park Rd, Oxt. 188 EF128
Park Rd, Pot.B. 12 DG30
Park Rd, Rad. 25 CG35
Park Rd, Red. 184 DF132
Park Rd, Rich. 118 CM86
Park Rd, Rick. 38 BK45
Park Rd, Shep. 134 BN102
Park Rd, Stai. 114 BH86
Park Rd, Sun. 115 BV94
Park Rd, Surb. 138 CM99
Park Rd, Sutt. 157 CY107
Park Rd, Swan. 147 FF97
Park Rd, Swans. 130 FY86
Park Rd, Tedd. 137 CJ95
Park Rd, Twick. 117 CJ86
Park Rd, Uxb. 76 BL66
Park Rd, Wall. 159 DH106
Park Rd (Hackbridge), Wall. 141 DH103
Park Rd, Wal.Cr. 15 DX33
Park Rd, Warl. 162 EE114
Park Rd, Wat. 23 BU39
Park Rd, Wem. 80 CL65
Park Rd, Wok. 167 BA117
Park Rd E W3 98 CP75
Park Rd E, Uxb. 76 BK68
Hillingdon Rd
Park Rd N W3 98 CP75
Park Rd N W4 98 CR78
Park Row SE10 103 ED79
Park Royal Rd NW10 80 CQ69
Park Royal Rd W3 80 CQ69
Park Sq, Esher 154 CB105
Park Rd
Park Sq E NW1 195 H4
Park Sq E NW1 83 DH70
Park Sq Ms NW1 195 H4
Park Sq Ms NW1 83 DH70
Park Sq W NW1 195 H4
Park Sq W NW1 83 DH70
Park St SE1 201 H2
Park St SE1 84 DQ74
Park St W1 194 F10
Park St W1 82 DG73
Park St, Croy. 142 DQ103
Park St, St.Alb. 9 CD26
Park St, Slou. 92 AT76
Park St (Colnbrook), Slou. 93 BD80
Park St, Tedd. 117 CE93
Park St La, St.Alb. 8 CB30
Park Ter, Green. 129 FV85
Park Ter (Sundridge), Sev. 180 EX124
Main Rd
Park Ter, Wor.Pk. 139 CU102
Park Vw N21 45 DM45
Park Vw W3 80 CQ71
Park Vw, N.Mal. 139 CT97
Park Vw, Pnr. 40 BZ53
Park Vw, Pot.B. 12 DC33
Park Vw, S.Ock. 91 FR74
Park Vw, Wem. 62 CP64
Park Vw Ct, Ilf. 69 ES58
Brancaster Rd
Park Vw Ct, Wok. 166 AY119
Park Vw Cres N11 45 DH49
Park Vw Est E2 85 DX68
Park Vw Gdns NW4 63 CW57
Park Vw Gdns, Bark. 87 ES68
River Rd
Park Vw Gdns, Grays 110 GB78
Park Vw Gdns, Ilf. 69 EM56
Park Vw Rd N3 44 DB53
Park Vw Rd N17 66 DU55
Park Vw Rd NW10 63 CT63
Park Vw Rd W5 80 CL71
Park Vw Rd, Cat. 177 DY122
Park Vw Rd, Pnr. 39 BV52
Park Vw Rd, Sthl. 78 CA74
Park Vw Rd, Uxb. 76 BN72
Park Vw Rd, Well. 106 EW83
Park Village E NW1 83 DH68
Park Village W NW1 83 DH68
Park Vil, Rom. 70 EX58
Park Vista SE10 103 ED79
Park Wk N6 64 DG59
North Rd
Park Wk SE10 103 ED80
Crooms Hill
Park Wk SW10 100 DC79
Park Wk, Ash. 172 CM119
Rectory La
Park Way N20 44 DF49
Park Way NW11 63 CY57
Park Way, Bex. 127 FE90
Park Way, Brwd. 55 FZ46
Park Way, Edg. 42 CP53
Park Way, Enf. 29 DN40
Park Way, Felt. 115 BV87
Park Way, Lthd. 170 CA123
Park Way, Rick. 38 BJ46
Park Way, Ruis. 59 BU60
Park Way, W.Mol. 136 CB97
Park W W2 194 C9
Park W Pl W2 194 C8
Park Wks Rd, Red. 185 DM133
Parkcroft Rd SE12 124 EF87
Parkdale Cres, Wor.Pk. 138 CR104
Parkdale Rd SE18 105 ES78
Parke Rd SW13 99 CU81
Parke Rd, Sun. 135 BU98
Parker Av, Til. 111 GJ81
Parker Cl E16 86 EL74
Parker Ms WC2 196 A8
Parker Rd, Croy. 160 DQ105
Parker Rd, Grays 110 FZ78
Parker St E16 86 EL74
Parker St WC2 196 A8
Parker St WC2 83 DL72
Parker St, Wat. 23 BV39
Parkers Cl, Ash. 172 CL119
Parkers Hill, Ash. 172 CL119
Parkers La, Ash. 172 CL119
Parkers Row SE1 202 A5
Parkes Rd, Chig. 49 ES50
Parkfield, Rick. 21 BF42
Parkfield, Sev. 191 FM123
Parkfield Av SW14 98 CS84
Parkfield Av, Felt. 115 BU90
Parkfield Av, Har. 40 CC54
Parkfield Av, Nthlt. 78 BX68
Parkfield Av, Uxb. 77 BP69
Parkfield Cl, Edg. 42 CP51
Parkfield Cl, Nthlt. 78 BY68
Parkfield Cres, Felt. 115 BU90
Parkfield Cres, Har. 40 CC54
Parkfield Cres, Ruis. 60 BY62
Parkfield Dr, Nthlt. 78 BX68
Parkfield Gdns, Har. 60 CB55
Parkfield Rd NW10 81 CU66
Parkfield Rd SE14 103 DZ81
Parkfield Rd, Felt. 115 BU90
Parkfield Rd, Har. 60 CC62
Parkfield Rd, Nthlt. 78 BY68
Parkfield Rd (Ickenham), Uxb. 59 BP61
Parkfield St N1 83 DN68
Parkfield Way, Brom. 145 EM100
Parkfields SW15 99 CW84
Parkfields, Croy. 143 DZ102
Parkfields, Lthd. 155 CD111
Parkfields Av NW9 62 CR60
Parkfields Av SW20 139 CV95
Parkfields Cl, Cars. 158 DG105
Devonshire Rd
Parkfields Rd, Kings.T. 118 CM92
Parkgate SE3 104 EF83
Parkgate Av, Barn. 28 DC39
Parkgate Cl, Kings.T. 118 CP93
Warboys App
Parkgate Cres, Barn. 28 DC40
Parkgate Gdns SW14 118 CR85
Parkgate Ms N6 65 DJ59
Stanhope Rd
Parkgate Rd SW11 100 DE80
Parkgate Rd, Orp. 165 FB105
Parkgate Rd, Wall. 158 DG106
Parkgate Rd, Wat. 24 BW37
Parkham Ct, Brom. 144 EE96
Parkham St SW11 100 DE81
Parkhill Cl, Horn. 72 FJ62
Parkhill Rd E4 47 EC46
Parkhill Rd NW3 64 DF64
Parkhill Rd, Bex. 126 EZ87
Parkhill Rd, Sid. 125 ER90
Parkhill Wk NW3 64 DF64
Parkholme Rd E8 84 DT65
Parkhouse St SE5 102 DR80
Parkhurst, Epsom 156 CQ110
Parkhurst Av E16 86 EH74
Wesley Av
Parkhurst Gdns, Bex. 126 FA87
Parkhurst Rd E12 69 EN63
Parkhurst Rd E17 67 DY56
Parkhurst Rd N7 65 DL63
Parkhurst Rd N11 44 DG49
Parkhurst Rd N17 46 DU54
Parkhurst Rd N22 45 DM52
Parkhurst Rd, Bex. 126 FA87
Parkhurst Rd, Sutt. 158 DD105
Parkland Av, Rom. 71 FE55
Parkland Av, Slou. 92 AX77
Parkland Av, Upmin. 72 FP64
Parkland Cl, Chig. 49 EQ48
Parkland Cl, Sev. 191 FJ129
Parkland Gdns SW19 119 CX88
Parkland Gro, Ashf. 114 BN91
Parkland Rd N22 45 DM54
Parkland Rd, Ashf. 114 BN91
Parkland Rd, Wdf.Grn. 48 EG52
Parkland Wk N4 65 DM59
Parkland Wk N6 65 DK59
Parkland Wk N10 65 DH56
Parklands N6 65 DH59
Parklands, Add. 152 BJ106
Parklands, Chig. 49 EQ48
Parklands, Epp. 18 EX29
Parklands, Lthd. 170 CA123
Parklands, Oxt. 188 EE131
Parklands, Surb. 138 CM99
Parklands, Wal.Abb. 15 ED32
Parklands Cl SW14 118 CQ85
Parklands Cl, Barn. 28 DD38
Parklands Ct, Houns. 96 BX82
Parklands Dr N3 63 CY55
Parklands Rd SW16 121 DH92
Parklands Way, Wor.Pk. 138 CS104
Parklawn Av, Epsom 156 CP113
Parklea Cl NW9 42 CS53
Parkleigh Rd SW19 140 DB96
Parkleys, Rich. 117 CK91
Parkmead SW15 119 CV86
Parkmead, Loug. 33 EN43
Parkmead Gdns NW7 43 CT51
Parkmore Cl, Wdf.Grn. 48 EG49
Parkshot, Rich. 98 CL84
Parkside N3 44 DB53
Parkside NW2 63 CV62
Parkside NW7 43 CU51
Parkside SE3 104 EF80
Parkside SW19 119 CX91
Parkside, Add. 152 BH110
Parkside, Buck.H. 48 EH47
Parkside (Chalfont St. Peter), Ger.Cr. 57 AZ56
Lower Rd
Parkside, Grays 110 GE76
Parkside, Hmptn. 117 CD92
Parkside, Pot.B. 12 DC32
High St
Parkside, Sev. 164 EZ113
Parkside, Sid. 126 EV89
Parkside, Sutt. 157 CY107
Parkside, Wal.Cr. 15 DY34
Parkside, Wat. 24 BW44
Parkside Av SW19 119 CX92
Parkside Av, Bexh. 107 FD82
Parkside Av, Brom. 144 EL98
Parkside Av, Rom. 71 FD55
Parkside Av, Til. 111 GH82
Parkside Cl SE20 122 DW94
Parkside Ct, Wey. 152 BN105
Parkside Cres N7 65 DN62
Parkside Cres, Surb. 138 CQ100
Parkside Cross, Bexh. 107 FE82
Parkside Dr, Edg. 42 CN48
Parkside Dr, Wat. 23 BS40
Parkside Est E9 84 DW67
Rutland Rd
Parkside Gdns SW19 119 CX91
Parkside Gdns, Barn. 44 DF46
Parkside Gdns, Couls. 175 DH117
Parkside Ho, Dag. 71 FC62
Parkside Rd SW11 100 DG81
Parkside Rd, Belv. 107 FC77
Parkside Rd, Houns. 116 CB85
Parkside Rd, Nthwd. 39 BT50
Parkside Ter N18 46 DR49
Great Cambridge Rd
Parkside Wk SE10 205 H7
Parkside Wk SE10 104 EE78
Parkside Wk, Slou. 92 AU76
Parkside Way, Har. 60 CB56
Parkstead Rd SW15 119 CU85
Parkstone Av N18 46 DT50
Parkstone Av, Horn. 72 FL58
Parkstone Rd E17 67 EC55
Parkstone Rd SE15 102 DU82
Rye La
Parkthorne Cl, Har. 60 CB58
Parkthorne Dr, Har. 60 CA58
Parkthorne Rd SW12 121 DK87
Parkview Ct SW18 120 DA86
Broomhill Rd
Parkview Dr, Mitch. 140 DD96
Parkview Rd SE9 125 EP89
Parkview Rd, Croy. 142 DU102
Parkville Rd SW6 99 CZ80
Parkway N14 45 DL47
Parkway NW1 83 DH67
Parkway SW20 139 CX98
Parkway, Croy. 161 EC109
Parkway, Erith 106 EY76
Parkway, Ilf. 69 ET62
Parkway, Rain. 89 FG70
Upminster Rd S
Parkway, Rom. 71 FF55
Parkway, Uxb. 76 BN66
Parkway, Wey. 153 BR105
Parkway, Wdf.Grn. 48 EJ50
Parkway, The, Hayes 78 BW72
Parkway, The (Cranford), Houns. 95 BV82
Parkway, The, Iver 75 BC68
Parkway, The, Nthlt. 78 BX69
Parkway, The, Sthl. 95 BU78
Parkway Trd Est, Houns. 96 BW79
Parkwood N20 44 DF48
Parkwood, Beck. 143 EA95
Parkwood Av, Esher 136 CC102
Parkwood Cl, Bans. 173 CX115
Parkwood Gro, Sun. 135 BU97
Parkwood Ms N6 65 DH58
Parkwood Rd SW19 119 CZ92
Parkwood Rd, Bans. 173 CX115
Parkwood Rd, Bex. 126 EZ87
Parkwood Rd, Islw. 97 CF81
Parkwood Rd, Red. 185 DL133
Parkwood Rd, West. 178 EL121
Parkwood Vw, Bans. 173 CW116
Parlaunt Rd, Slou. 93 BA77
Parley Dr, Wok. 166 AW117
Parliament Ct E1 84 DS71
Sandy's Row
Parliament Hill NW3 64 DE63
Parliament Ms SW14 98 CQ82
Thames Bk
Parliament Sq SW1 199 P5
Parliament Sq SW1 101 DL75
Parliament St SW1 199 P5
Parliament St SW1 101 DL75
Parma Cres SW11 100 DF84
Parmiter St E2 84 DV68
Parnell Cl, Abb.L. 7 BT30
Parnell Cl, Edg. 42 CP49
Parnell Gdns, Wey. 152 BN111
Parnell Rd E3 85 DZ67
Parnham St E14 85 DY72
Blount St
Parolles Rd N19 65 DJ60
Paroma Rd, Belv. 106 FA76
Parr Av, Epsom 157 CV109
Parr Cl N9 46 DV49
Parr Cl N18 46 DV49
Parr Cl, Lthd. 171 CF120
Parr Ct, Felt. 116 BW91
Parr Rd E6 86 EK67
Parr Rd, Stan. 41 CK53
Parr St N1 84 DR68
Parrock, The, Grav. 131 GJ88
Parrock Av, Grav. 131 GJ88
Parrock Rd, Grav. 131 GJ88
Parrock St, Grav. 131 GH87
Parrotts Cl, Rick. 22 BN42
Parrs Cl, S.Croy. 160 DR109
Florence Rd
Parrs Pl, Hmptn. 116 CA94
Parry Av E6 87 EM72
Parry Cl, Epsom 157 CU108
Parry Dr, Wey. 152 BN110
Parry Grn N, Slou. 93 AZ77
Parry Grn S, Slou. 93 BA77
Parry Pl SE18 105 EP77
Parry Rd SE25 142 DS97
Parry Rd W10 81 CY69
Parry St SW8 101 DL79
Parsifal Rd NW6 64 DA64
Parsley Gdns, Croy. 143 DX102
Primrose La

Parsloes Av, Dag. 70 EX63
Parson St NW4 63 CW56
Parsonage Cl, Abb.L. 7 BS30
Parsonage Cl, Hayes 77 BT72
Parsonage Cl, Warl. 177 DY116
Parsonage Gdns, Enf. 30 DQ40
Parsonage La (South Darenth), Dart. 128 FP93
Parsonage La, Enf. 30 DR40
Parsonage La, Sid. 126 EZ91
Parsonage Manorway, Belv. 106 FA79
Parsonage Rd, Ch.St.G. 36 AV48
Parsonage Rd, Egh. 112 AX92
Parsonage Rd, Grays 109 FW79
Parsonage Rd, Rain. 90 FJ68
Parsonage Rd, Rick. 38 BK45
Parsonage St E14 204 E9
Parsonage St E14 103 EC77
Parsons Cres, Edg. 42 CN48
Parsons Grn SW6 100 DA81
Parsons Grn La SW6 100 DA81
Parsons Gro, Edg. 42 CN48
Parsons Hill SE18 105 EN76
Powis St
Parson's Ho W2 82 DD70
Parsons La, Dart. 127 FH90
Parson's Mead, Croy. 141 DP102
Parsons Mead, E.Mol. 136 CC97
Parsons Pightle, Couls. 175 DN120
Coulsdon Rd
Parsons Rd E13 86 EJ68
Old St
Parsonsfield Cl, Bans. 173 CX115
Parsonsfield Rd, Bans. 173 CX116
Parthenia Rd SW6 100 DA81
Parthia Cl, Tad. 173 CV119
Partingdale La NW7 43 CX50
Partington Cl N19 65 DK60
Partridge Cl E16 86 EK71
Fulmer Rd
Partridge Cl, Barn. 27 CW44
Partridge Cl, Bushey 40 CB46
Partridge Cl, Chesh. 4 AS28
Partridge Cl, Stan. 42 CL49
Partridge Ct EC1 83 DP70
Percival St
Partridge Dr, Orp. 145 EQ104
Partridge Grn SE9 125 EN90
Partridge Knoll, Pur. 159 DP112
Partridge Mead, Bans. 173 CW116
Partridge Rd, Hmptn. 116 BZ93
Partridge Rd, Sid. 125 ES90
Partridge Sq E6 86 EL71
Nightingale Way
Partridge Way N22 45 DL53
Parvills, Wal.Abb. 15 ED32
Parvin St SW8 101 DK81
Parvis Rd, W.Byf. 152 BH113
Pasadena Cl, Hayes 95 BV75
Pasadena Cl Trd Est, Hayes 95 BV75
Pasadena Cl
Pascal St SW8 101 DK80
Pascoe Rd SE13 123 ED85
Pasfield, Wal.Abb. 15 ED33
Pasley Cl SE17 102 DQ78
Penrose St
Pasquier Rd E17 67 DY55
Passey Pl SE9 125 EM86
Passfield Dr E14 85 EB71
Uamvar St
Passfield Path SE28 88 EV73
Booth Cl
Passing All EC1 196 G5
Passmore Gdns N11 45 DK51
Passmore St SW1 198 F9
Passmore St SW1 100 DG77
Pastens Rd, Oxt. 188 EJ131
Pasteur Cl NW9 42 CS54
Pasteur Dr, Rom. 52 FK54
Pasteur Gdns N18 45 DP50
Paston Cl E5 67 DX62
Caldecott Way
Paston Cl, Wall. 141 DJ104
Paston Cres SE12 124 EH87
Pastor St SE11 200 G8
Pastor St SE11 101 DP77
Pasture Cl, Bushey 40 CC45
Pasture Cl, Wem. 61 CH62
Pasture Rd SE6 124 EF88
Pasture Rd, Dag. 70 EZ63
Pasture Rd, Wem. 61 CH61
Pastures, The N20 43 CZ46
Pastures, The, Wat. 40 BW45
Pastures Mead, Uxb. 76 BN65
Patch, The, Sev. 190 FE122
Patch Cl, Uxb. 76 BM67
Patcham Ct, Sutt. 158 DC109
Patcham Ter SW8 101 DH81
Pater St W8 100 DA76
Paternoster Cl, Wal.Abb. 16 EF33
Paternoster Hill, Wal.Abb. 16 EF32
Paternoster Row EC4 197 H9
Paternoster Row (Havering-atte-Bower), Rom. 52 FJ47
Paternoster Sq EC4 196 G8
Paterson Rd, Ashf. 114 BK92
Pates Manor Dr, Felt. 115 BR87
Path, The SW19 140 DB95
Pathfield Rd SW16 121 DK93
Pathway, The, Rad. 25 CF36
Pathway, The, Wat. 40 BX46
Anthony Cl
Patience Rd SW11 100 DE82
Patio Cl SW4 121 DK86
Patmore Est SW8 101 DJ81
Patmore La, Walt. 153 BT107
Patmore Rd, Wal.Abb. 16 EE34
Patmore St SW8 101 DJ81
Patmore Way, Rom. 51 FB50
Patmos Rd SW9 101 DP80
Paton Cl E3 85 EA69
Paton St EC1 197 H3
Patricia Ct, Chis. 145 ER95
Manor Pk Rd
Patricia Ct, Well. 106 EV80
Patricia Dr, Horn. 72 FL60
Patricia Gdns, Sutt. 158 DA111
The Cres
Patrick Connolly Gdns E3 85 EB69
Talwin St
Patrick Gro, Wal.Abb. 15 EB33
Beaulieu Dr
Patrick Pas SW11 100 DE82
Patrick Rd E13 86 EJ69
Patrington Cl, Uxb. 76 BJ69
Boulmer Rd
Patriot Sq E2 84 DV68
Patrol Pl SE6 123 EB86
Patrons Dr (Denham), Uxb. 57 BF58
Patshull Pl NW5 83 DJ65
Patshull Rd
Patshull Rd NW5 83 DJ65
Patten All, Rich. 117 CK85
The Hermitage
Patten Rd SW18 120 DE87
Pattenden Rd SE6 123 DZ88
Patterdale Cl, Brom. 124 EF93
Patterdale Rd SE15 102 DW80
Patterdale Rd, Dart. 129 FR88
Patterson Ct SE19 122 DT94
Patterson Rd SE19 122 DT93
Pattina Wk SE16 85 DZ74
Pattison Pt E16 86 EG71
Fife Rd
Pattison Rd NW2 64 DA62
Pattison Wk SE18 105 EQ78
Paul Cl E15 86 EE66
Paul St
Paul Gdns, Croy. 142 DT103
Paul Julius Cl E14 204 F1
Paul Julius Cl E14 85 ED73
Paul Robeson Cl E6 87 EN69
Eastbourne Rd
Paul St E15 85 ED67
Paul St EC2 197 L5
Paul St EC2 84 DR70
Paulet Rd SE5 101 DP82
Paulhan Rd, Har. 61 CK56
Paulin Dr N21 45 DN45
Pauline Cres, Twick. 116 CC88
Paulinus Cl, Orp. 146 EW96
Pauls Grn, Wal.Cr. 15 DY33
Eleanor Rd
Paul's Pl, Ash. 172 CP119
Paul's Wk EC4 196 G10
Paul's Wk EC4 84 DQ73
Paultons Sq SW3 100 DD79
Paultons St SW3 100 DD79
Pauntley St N19 65 DJ60
Paved Ct, Rich. 117 CK85
Paveley Dr SW11 100 DE80
Paveley St NW8 194 C4
Paveley St NW8 82 DE70
Pavement, The SW4 101 DJ84
Pavement, The W5 98 CL76
Popes La
Pavement Ms, Rom. 70 EX59
Clarissa Rd
Pavement Sq, Croy. 142 DU102
Pavet Cl, Dag. 89 FB65
Pavilion Gdns, Stai. 114 BH94
Pavilion Ms N3 44 DA54
Windermere Av
Pavilion Rd SW1 198 E7
Pavilion Rd SW1 100 DF75
Pavilion Rd, Ilf. 69 EM59
Pavilion St SW1 198 E7
Pavilion Ter, E.Mol. 137 CF98
Pavilion Ter, Ilf. 69 ES57
Southdown Cres
Pavilion Way, Amer. 20 AW39
Pavilion Way, Edg. 42 CP52
Pavilion Way, Ruis. 60 BW61
Pavilions, The, Epp. 19 FC25
Pawleyne Cl SE20 122 DW94
Pawsey Cl E13 86 EG67
Plashet Rd
Pawson's Rd, Croy. 142 DQ100
Paxford Rd, Wem. 61 CH61
Paxton Cl, Rich. 98 CM82
Paxton Cl, Walt. 136 BW101
Shaw Dr
Paxton Gdns, Wok. 151 BE112
Paxton Pl SE27 122 DS91
Paxton Rd N17 46 DT52
Paxton Rd SE23 123 DY90
Paxton Rd W4 98 CS79
Paxton Rd, Brom. 124 EG94
Paxton Ter SW1 101 DH79
Payne Rd E3 85 EB68
Payne St SE8 103 DZ79
Paynell Ct SE3 104 EE83
Lawn Ter
Paynes Wk W6 99 CY79
Paynesfield Av SW14 98 CR83
Paynesfield Rd, Bushey 41 CF45
Paynesfield Rd, West. 178 EJ121
Pea La, Upmin. 91 FU66
Peabody Av SW1 199 H10
Peabody Cl SE10 103 EB81
Devonshire Dr
Peabody Cl SW1 101 DH79
Lupus St
Peabody Cl, Croy. 142 DW102
Shirley Rd
Peabody Dws WC1 195 P4
Peabody Est EC1 197 J5
Peabody Est N17 46 DS53
Peabody Est SE1 200 E3
Peabody Est SE24 122 DQ87
Peabody Est SW3 100 DE79
Margaretta Ter
Peabody Est W6 99 CW78
The Sq
Peabody Est W10 81 CW71
Peabody Hill SE21 121 DP88
Peabody Hill Est SE21 121 DP87
Peabody Sq N1 83 DP67
Essex Rd
Peabody Sq SE1 200 F5
Peabody Sq SE1 101 DP75
Peabody Trust SE1 201 H3
Peabody Trust SE1 84 DQ74
Peabody Yd N1 84 DQ67
Greenman St
Peace Cl N14 29 DH43
Peace Cl SE25 142 DS98
Peace Cl, Wal.Cr. 14 DU29
Goffs La
Peace Gro, Wem. 62 CP62
Peace Prospect, Wat. 23 BU41
Peace Rd, Iver 75 BA68
Peace Rd, Slou. 75 BA68
Peace St SE18 105 EP79
Nightingale Vale
Peach Cft, Grav. 130 GE90
Peach Rd W10 81 CX69
Peach Tree Av, West Dr. 76 BM72
Pear Tree Av
Peaches Cl, Sutt. 157 CY108
Peachey Cl, Uxb. 76 BK72
Peachey La, Uxb. 76 BK71
Peachum Rd SE3 104 EF79
Peacock Av, Felt. 115 BR88
Peacock Cl, Horn. 72 FL56
Peacock Gdns, S.Croy. 161 DY110
Peacock St SE17 200 G9
Peacock St, Grav. 131 GJ87
Peacock Wk E16 86 EH72
Peacock Wk, Abb.L. 7 BU31
Peacock Yd SE17 200 G9
Peacocks Cen, The, Wok. 166 AY117
Peak, The SE26 122 DW90
Peak Hill SE26 122 DW91
Peak Hill Av SE26 122 DW91
Peak Hill Gdns SE26 122 DW91
Peakes La (Cheshunt), Wal.Cr. 14 DT27
Peakes Way (Cheshunt), Wal.Cr. 14 DT27
Peaketon Av, Ilf. 68 EK56
Peaks Hill, Pur. 159 DK110
Peaks Hill Ri, Pur. 159 DL110
Peal Gdns W13 79 CG70
Ruislip Rd E
Peall Rd, Croy. 141 DM100
Pear Cl NW9 62 CR56
Pear Cl SE14 103 DY80
Southerngate Way
Pear Pl SE1 200 D4
Pear Rd E11 67 ED62
Pear Tree Av, West Dr. 76 BM72
Pear Tree Cl E2 84 DT67
Pear Tree Cl, Add. 152 BG106
Pear Tree Rd
Pear Tree Cl, Amer. 20 AT39
Orchard End Av
Pear Tree Cl, Chess. 156 CN106
Pear Tree Cl, Mitch. 140 DE96
Pear Tree Cl, Swan. 147 FD96
Pear Tree Ct EC1 196 E4
Pear Tree Ct EC1 83 DN70
Pear Tree Rd, Add. 152 BG106
Pear Tree Rd, Ashf. 115 BQ92
Pear Tree St EC1 196 G4
Pear Tree St EC1 83 DP70
Pear Tree Wk (Cheshunt), Wal.Cr. 14 DR26
Pearce Cl, Mitch. 140 DG96
Pearce Rd, W.Mol. 136 CB97
Pearcefield Av SE23 122 DW88
Pearcroft Rd E11 67 ED61
Pearcy Cl, Rom. 52 FL52
Alverstoke Rd
Peardon St SW8 101 DH82
Peareswood Gdns, Stan. 41 CK53
Peareswood Rd, Erith 107 FF81
Pearfield Rd SE23 123 DY90
Pearl Cl E6 87 EN72
Pearl Cl NW2 63 CX59
Marble Dr
Pearl Ct, Wok. 166 AS116
Langmans Way
Pearl Rd E17 67 EA55
Pearl St E1 202 E2
Pearmain Cl, Shep. 135 BP99
Pearman St SE1 200 E6
Pearman St SE1 101 DN75
Pears Rd, Houns. 96 CC83
Pearscroft Ct SW6 100 DB81
Pearscroft Rd SW6 100 DB81
Pearse St SE15 102 DS79
Dragon Rd
Pearson Ms SW4 101 DK83
Edgeley Rd
Pearson St E2 84 DT68
Pearson Way, Dart. 128 FM89
Pearsons Av SE14 103 EA81
Tanners Hill
Peartree Av SW17 120 DC90
Peartree Cl, Erith 107 FD81
Peartree Cl, S.Croy. 160 DV114
Peartree Cl, S.Ock. 91 FW68
Peartree Gdns, Dag. 70 EV63
Peartree Gdns, Rom. 51 FB54
Peartree La E1 202 G1
Peartree Rd, Enf. 30 DS41
Peartree Way SE10 205 M8
Peartree Way SE10 104 EG77
Peary Pl E2 84 DW69
Kirkwall Pl
Pease Cl, Horn. 89 FH66
Dowding Way
Peatfield Cl, Sid. 125 ES90
Woodside Rd
Peatmore Av, Wok. 168 BG116
Peatmore Cl, Wok. 168 BG116
Pebble Cl, Tad. 182 CS128
Pebble Hill Rd, Bet. 182 CS131
Pebble Hill Rd, Tad. 182 CS131
Pebble La, Epsom 172 CN121
Pebble La, Lthd. 182 CL125
Pebble Way W3 80 CP74
Pebworth Rd, Har. 61 CG61
Peckarmans Wd SE26 122 DU90
Peckett Sq N5 66 DQ63
Highbury Gra
Peckford Pl SW9 101 DN82
Peckham Gro SE15 102 DS80
Peckham High St SE15 102 DU81
Peckham Hill St SE15 102 DU80
Peckham Pk Rd SE15 102 DU80
Peckham Rd SE5 102 DS81
Peckham Rd SE15 102 DS81
Peckham Rye SE15 102 DU83
Peckham Rye SE22 102 DU84
Pecks Yd E1 197 P6
Peckwater St NW5 65 DJ64
Pedham Pl Ind Est, Swan. 147 FG99
Pedlars Wk N7 83 DL65
Pedley Rd, Dag. 70 EW60
Pedley St E1 84 DT70
Pedro St E5 67 DX62
Pedworth Gdns SE16 202 F9
Peek Cres SW19 119 CX92
Peel Cl E4 47 EB47
Peel Cl N9 46 DU48
Plevna Rd
Peel Dr NW9 63 CT55
Peel Dr, Ilf. 68 EL55
Peel Gro E2 84 DW68
Peel Pas W8 82 DA74
Peel St
Peel Pl, Ilf. 48 EL54
Peel Prec NW6 82 DA68
Peel Rd E18 48 EF53
Peel Rd NW6 81 CZ69
Peel Rd, Har. 61 CF55
Peel Rd, Orp. 163 EQ106
Peel Rd, Wem. 61 CK62
Peel St W8 82 DA74
Peel Way, Rom. 52 FM54
Peel Way, Uxb. 76 BL71
Peerage Way, Horn. 72 FL59
Peerless Dr (Harefield), Uxb. 58 BJ57
Peerless St EC1 197 K3
Peerless St EC1 84 DR69
Pegamoid Rd N18 46 DW48
Pegasus Cl N16 66 DR63
Green Las
Pegasus Ct, Abb.L. 7 BT32
Furtherfield
Pegasus Ct, Grav. 131 GJ90
Pegasus Pl SE11 101 DN79
Clayton St
Pegasus Way N11 45 DH51
Pegelm Gdns, Horn. 72 FM59
Pegg Rd, Houns. 96 BX80
Peggotty Way, Uxb. 77 BP72
Dickens Av
Pegley Gdns SE12 124 EG89
Pegmire La, Wat. 24 CC39
Pegwell St SE18 105 ES80
Peket Cl, Stai. 133 BE95
Pekin Cl E14 85 EA72
Pekin St
Pekin St E14 85 EA72
Peldon Ct, Rich. 98 CM84
Peldon Pas, Rich. 98 CM84
Worple Way
Peldon Wk N1 83 DP67
Britannia Row
Pelham Av, Bark. 87 ET67
Pelham Cl SE5 102 DS82
Pelham Cres SW7 198 B9
Pelham Cres SW7 100 DE77
Pelham Pl SW7 198 B9
Pelham Pl SW7 100 DE77
Pelham Rd E18 68 EH55
Pelham Rd N15 66 DT56
Pelham Rd N22 45 DN54
Pelham Rd SW19 120 DA94
Pelham Rd, Beck. 142 DW96
Pelham Rd, Bexh. 106 FA83
Pelham Rd, Grav. 131 GF87
Pelham Rd, Ilf. 69 ER61
Pelham Rd S, Grav. 131 GF88
Pelham St SW7 198 A8
Pelham St SW7 100 DE77
Pelham Ter, Grav. 131 GF87
Campbell Rd
Pelhams, The, Wat. 24 BX35
Pelhams Cl, Esher 154 CA105
Pelhams Wk, Esher 136 CA104
Pelican Est SE15 102 DT81
Pelican Pas E1 84 DW70
Cambridge Heath Rd
Pelican Wk SW9 101 DP84
Loughborough Pk
Pelier St SE17 102 DQ79
Langdale Cl
Pelinore Rd SE6 124 EE89
Pellant Rd SW6 99 CY80
Pellatt Gro N22 45 DN53
Pellatt Rd SE22 122 DT85
Pellatt Rd, Wem. 61 CK61
Pellerin Rd N16 66 DS64
Pelling Hill, Wind. 112 AV87
Pelling St E14 85 EA72
Pellipar Cl N13 45 DN48
Pellipar Gdns SE18 105 EM78
Pelly Ct, Epp. 17 ET31
Pelly Rd E13 86 EG68
Pelter St E2 197 P2
Pelter St E2 84 DT69
Pelton Av, Sutt. 158 DB110
Pelton Rd SE10 205 H10
Pelton Rd SE10 104 EE78
Pembar Av E17 67 DY55
Pember Rd NW10 81 CX69
Pemberley Chase (West Ewell), Epsom 156 CP106
Pemberley Cl (West Ewell), Epsom 156 CP106
Ruxley Cl
Pemberton Av, Rom. 71 FH55
Pemberton Gdns N19 65 DJ62
Pemberton Gdns, Rom. 70 EY57
Pemberton Gdns, Swan. 147 FE97
Pemberton Ho SE26 122 DU91
High Level Dr
Pemberton Pl E8 84 DV66
Mare St
Pemberton Pl, Esher 136 CC104
Carrick Gate
Pemberton Rd N4 65 DN57
Pemberton Rd, E.Mol. 136 CC98
Pemberton Row EC4 196 E8
Pemberton Ter N19 65 DJ62
Pembrey Way, Horn. 90 FJ65
Pembridge Av, Twick. 116 BZ88
Pembridge Chase, Hem.H. 5 BA28
Pembridge Cl
Pembridge Cl, Hem.H. 5 AZ28
Pembridge Cres W11 82 DA73
Pembridge Gdns W2 82 DA73
Pembridge Ms W11 82 DA73
Pembridge Pl SW15 120 DA85
Oakhill Rd
Pembridge Pl W2 82 DA73
Pembridge Rd W11 82 DA73
Pembridge Rd, Hem.H. 5 BA28
Pembridge Sq W2 82 DA73
Pembridge Vil W2 82 DA73
Pembridge Vil W11 82 DA73
Pembroke Av, Enf. 30 DV38
Pembroke Av, Har. 61 CG55
Pembroke Av, Pnr. 60 BX60
Pembroke Av, Surb. 138 CP99
Pembroke Av, Walt. 154 BX105
Pembroke Cl SW1 198 G5
Pembroke Cl SW1 100 DG75
Pembroke Cl, Bans. 174 DB117
Pembroke Cl, Erith 107 FD77
Pembroke Rd
Pembroke Cl, Horn. 72 FM56
Pembroke Cotts W8 100 DA76
Pembroke Sq
Pembroke Dr (Cheshunt), Wal.Cr. 13 DP29
Pembroke Gdns W8 99 CZ77
Pembroke Gdns, Dag. 71 FB62
Pembroke Gdns, Wok. 167 BA118
Pembroke Gdns Cl W8 100 DA76
Pembroke Ms E3 85 DY69
Morgan St
Pembroke Ms N10 44 DG53
Pembroke Rd
Pembroke Ms W8 100 DA76
Earls Wk
Pembroke Ms, Sev. 191 FH125
Pembroke Rd
Pembroke Pl W8 100 DA76
Pembroke Pl (Sutton at Hone), Dart. 148 FP95
Pembroke Pl, Edg. 42 CN52
Pembroke Pl, Islw. 97 CE82
Thornbury Rd
Pembroke Rd E6 87 EM71
Pembroke Rd E17 67 EB57
Pembroke Rd N8 65 DL56
Pembroke Rd N10 44 DG53
Pembroke Rd N13 46 DQ48
Pembroke Rd N15 66 DT57
Pembroke Rd SE25 142 DS98
Pembroke Rd W8 100 DA77
Pembroke Rd, Brom. 144 EJ96
Pembroke Rd, Erith 107 FC78
Pembroke Rd, Grnf. 78 CB70
Pembroke Rd, Ilf. 69 ET60
Pembroke Rd, Mitch. 140 DG96
Pembroke Rd, Nthwd. 39 BQ48
Pembroke Rd, Ruis. 59 BT60
Pembroke Rd, Sev. 191 FH125
Pembroke Rd, Wem. 61 CK62
Pembroke Rd, Wok. 167 BA118
Pembroke Sq W8 100 DA76
Pembroke St N1 83 DL66
Pembroke Studios W8 99 CZ76
Pembroke Vil W8 100 DA77
Pembroke Vil, Rich. 97 CK84
Pembroke Wk W8 100 DA77
Pembroke Way, Hayes 95 BQ76
Pembury Av, Wor.Pk. 139 CU101
Pembury Cl, Brom. 144 EF101
Pembury Cl, Couls. 158 DG114
Pembury Ct, Hayes 95 BR79
Pembury Cres, Sid. 126 EY89
Pembury Pl E5 66 DV64
Pembury Rd E5 66 DV64
Pembury Rd N17 46 DT54
Pembury Rd SE25 142 DU98
Pembury Rd, Bexh. 106 EY80
Pemdevon Rd, Croy. 141 DN101
Pemell Cl E1 84 DW70
Colebert Av
Pemerich Cl, Hayes 95 BT78
Pempath Pl, Wem. 61 CK61
Penally Pl N1 84 DR67
Shepperton Rd
Penang St E1 202 E2
Penang St E1 84 DV74
Penard Rd, Sthl. 96 CA76
Penarth St SE15 102 DW79
Penates, Esher 155 CD105
Penberth Rd SE6 123 EC88
Penbury Rd, Sthl. 96 BZ77
Pencombe Ms W11 81 CZ73
Denbigh Rd
Pencraig Way SE15 102 DV79
Pencroft Dr, Dart. 128 FJ87
Shepherds La
Penda Rd, Erith 107 FB80
Pendall Cl, Barn. 28 DE42
Pendarves Rd SW20 139 CW95
Penda's Mead E9 67 DY63
Lindisfarne Way
Pendell Av, Hayes 95 BT8
Pendell Rd, Red. 185 DP13
Pendennis Cl, W.Byf. 152 BG114
Pendennis Rd N17 66 DR55
Pendennis Rd SW16 121 DL9
Pendennis Rd, Orp. 146 EW10
Pendennis Rd, Sev. 191 FH12
Penderel Rd, Houns. 116 CA85
Penderry Ri SE6 123 ED8
Penderyn Way N7 65 DK6
Pendle Rd SW16 121 DH9
Pendlestone Rd E17 67 EB5
Pendragon Rd, Brom. 124 EF9
Pendragon Wk NW9 62 CS58
Pendrell Rd SE4 103 DY82
Pendrell St SE18 105 ER80
Pendula Dr, Hayes 78 BX70
Pendulum Ms E8 66 DT64
Birkbeck Rd
Penerley Rd SE6 123 EB88
Penerley Rd, Rain. 89 FH7
Penfold Cl, Croy. 141 DN10
Epsom Rd
Penfold La, Bex. 126 EX8
Penfold Pl NW1 194 B
Penfold Pl NW1 82 DE7
Penfold Rd N9 47 DX4
Penfold St NW1 194 A
Penfold St NW1 82 DD7
Penfold St NW8 194 A
Penfold St NW8 82 DD7
Penford Gdns SE9 104 EK8
Penford St SE5 101 DP8

Street	Page	Grid
Pengarth Rd, Bex.	126	EX85
Penge Ho SW11 *Wye St*	100	DD83
Penge La SE20	122	DW94
Penge Rd E13	86	EJ66
Penge Rd SE20	142	DU97
Penge Rd SE25	142	DU97
Pengelly Cl (Cheshunt), Wal.Cr.	14	DV30
Penhall Rd SE7	104	EK77
Penhill Rd, Bex.	126	EW87
Penhurst, Wok.	151	AZ114
Penhurst Rd, Ilf.	49	EP52
Penifather La, Grnf.	79	CD69
Peninsular Cl, Felt.	115	BR86
Peninsular Pk Rd SE7	**205**	**N9**
Peninsular Pk Rd SE7	104	EG77
Penistone Rd SW16	121	DL94
Penistone Wk, Rom. *Okehampton Rd*	52	FJ51
Penketh Dr, Har.	61	CD62
Penman Cl, St.Alb.	8	CA27
Penman's Grn, Kings L.	6	BG32
Penmon Rd SE2	106	EU76
Penn Cl, Grnf.	78	CB68
Penn Cl, Har.	61	CJ56
Penn Cl, Rick.	21	BD44
Penn Cl, Uxb.	76	BK70
Penn Dr (Denham), Uxb.	57	BF58
Penn Gdns, Chis.	145	EP96
Penn Gdns, Rom.	50	FA52
Penn Gaskell La (Chalfont St. Peter), Ger.Cr.	37	AZ50
Penn La, Bex.	126	EX85
Penn Meadow, Slou.	74	AT67
Penn Pl, Rick. *Northway*	38	BK45
Penn Rd N7	65	DL64
Penn Rd (Chalfont St. Peter), Ger.Cr.	36	AX53
Penn Rd, Rick.	37	BF46
Penn Rd, St.Alb.	8	CC27
Penn Rd (Datchet), Slou.	92	AX81
Penn Rd, Wat.	23	BV39
Penn St N1	84	DR67
Penn Way, Rick.	21	BD44
Pennack Rd SE15	102	DT79
Pennant Ms W8	100	DB77
Pennant Ter E17	47	DZ54
Pennard Rd W12	99	CW75
Pennards, The, Sun.	136	BW96
Penne Cl, Rad.	9	CF34
Penner Cl SW19 *Victoria Dr*	119	CY89
Penners Gdns, Surb.	138	CL101
Pennethorne Cl E9 *Victoria Pk Rd*	84	DW67
Pennethorne Rd SE15	102	DV80
Penney Cl, Dart.	128	FK87
Pennine Dr NW2	63	CY61
Pennine La NW2 *Pennine Dr*	63	CY61
Pennine Way, Bexh.	107	FE81
Pennine Way, Grav.	130	GE90
Pennine Way, Hayes	95	BR80
Pennington Cl SE27 *Hamilton Rd*	122	DR91
Pennington Cl, Rom.	50	FA50
Pennington Dr N21	29	DL43
Pennington Dr, Wey.	135	BS104
Pennington Rd (Chalfont St. Peter), Ger.Cr.	36	AX52
Pennington St E1	**202**	**C1**
Pennington St E1	84	DU73
Pennington Way SE12	124	EH89
Penningtons, The, Amer.	20	AS37
Pennis La (Fawkham Grn), Long.	149	FX100
Penniston Cl N17	46	DQ54
Penny Cl, Rain.	89	FH69
Penny La, Shep.	135	BS101
Penny Ms SW12 *Caistor Rd*	121	DH87
Penny Rd NW10	80	CP69
Pennycroft, Croy.	161	DY109
Pennyfather La, Enf.	30	DQ41
Pennyfield, Cob.	153	BU113
Pennyfields E14	85	EA73
Pennyfields, Brwd.	54	FW49
Pennylets Grn, Slou.	74	AT66
Pennymoor Wk W9 *Ashmore Rd*	81	CZ69
Pennyroyal Av E6	87	EN72
Penpoll Rd E8	84	DV65
Penpool La, Well.	106	EV83
Penrhyn Av E17	47	DZ53
Penrhyn Cres E17	47	EA53
Penrhyn Cres SW14	98	CQ84
Penrhyn Gro E17	47	EA53
Penrhyn Rd, Kings.T.	138	CL97
Penrith Cl SW15	119	CY85
Penrith Cl, Beck. *Albemarle Rd*	143	EB95
Penrith Cl, Reig.	184	DE133
Penrith Cl, Uxb. *Chippendale Waye*	76	BK66
Penrith Cres, Rain.	71	FG64
Penrith Pl SE27 *Harpenden Rd*	121	DP89
Penrith Rd N15	66	DR57
Penrith Rd, Ilf.	49	ET51
Penrith Rd, N.Mal.	138	CR98
Penrith Rd, Rom.	52	FN51
Penrith Rd, Th.Hth.	142	DQ96
Penrith St SW16	121	DJ93
Penrose Av, Wat.	40	BX47
Penrose Dr, Epsom	156	CN111
Penrose Gro SE17	102	DQ78
Penrose Ho SE17	102	DQ78
Penrose Rd, Lthd.	170	CC122
Penrose St SE17	102	DQ78
Penry St SE1	**201**	**N9**
Penryn St NW1	83	DK68
Pensbury Pl SW8	101	DJ82
Pensbury St SW8	101	DJ82
Penscroft Gdns, Borwd.	26	CR42
Pensford Av, Rich.	98	CN82
Penshurst Av, Sid.	126	EU86
Penshurst Cl (Chalfont St. Peter), Ger.Cr.	36	AX54
Penshurst Gdns, Edg.	42	CP50
Penshurst Grn, Brom.	144	EF99
Penshurst Rd E9	85	DX66
Penshurst Rd N17	46	DT52
Penshurst Rd, Bexh.	106	EZ81
Penshurst Rd, Pot.B.	12	DD31
Penshurst Rd, Th.Hth.	141	DP99
Penshurst Wk, Brom. *Hayesford Pk Dr*	144	EF99
Penshurst Way, Orp. *Star La*	146	EW98
Penshurst Way, Sutt.	158	DA108
Pensilver Cl, Barn.	28	DE42
Pensons La, Ong.	19	FG28
Penstemon Cl N3	44	DA52
Penstock Footpath N22	65	DL55
Pentavia Retail Pk NW7 *Bunns La*	43	CT52
Pentelow Gdns, Felt.	115	BU86
Pentire Cl, Upmin.	73	FS58
Pentire Rd E17	47	ED53
Pentland Av, Edg.	42	CP47
Pentland Av, Shep.	134	BN99
Pentland Cl NW11	63	CY61
Pentland Gdns SW18 *St. Ann's Hill*	120	DC86
Pentland Pl, Nthlt.	78	BY67
Pentland Rd, Bushey	24	CC44
Pentland St SW18	120	DC86
Pentland Way, Uxb.	59	BQ62
Pentlands Cl, Mitch.	141	DH97
Pentlow St SW15	99	CW83
Pentlow Way, Buck.H.	48	EL45
Pentney Rd E4	47	ED46
Pentney Rd SW12	121	DJ88
Pentney Rd SW19 *Midmoor Rd*	139	CY95
Penton Av, Stai.	113	BF94
Penton Dr (Cheshunt), Wal.Cr.	15	DX29
Penton Gro N1	**196**	**D1**
Penton Hall Dr, Stai.	134	BG95
Penton Hook Rd, Stai.	114	BG94
Penton Ho SE2 *Hartslock Dr*	106	EX75
Penton Pk, Cher.	134	BG97
Penton Pl SE17	**200**	**G10**
Penton Pl SE17	101	DP78
Penton Ri WC1	**196**	**C2**
Penton Ri WC1	83	DM69
Penton Rd, Stai.	113	BF94
Penton St N1	83	DN68
Pentonville Rd N1	**196**	**B1**
Pentonville Rd N1	83	DM68
Pentrich Av, Enf.	30	DU38
Pentridge St SE15	102	DT80
Pentyre Av N18	46	DR50
Penwerris Av, Islw.	96	CC80
Penwith Rd SW18	120	DB89
Penwith Wk, Wok. *Wych Hill Pk*	166	AX119
Penwood End, Wok.	166	AV121
Penwortham Rd SW16	121	DH93
Penwortham Rd, S.Croy.	160	DQ110
Penylan Pl, Edg.	42	CN52
Penywern Rd SW5	100	DA78
Penzance Cl (Harefield), Uxb.	38	BK53
Penzance Gdns, Rom.	52	FN51
Penzance Pl W11	81	CY74
Penzance Rd, Rom.	52	FN51
Penzance St W11	81	CY74
Peony Cl, Brwd.	54	FV44
Peony Ct, Wdf.Grn. *The Bridle Path*	48	EE52
Peony Gdns W12	81	CU73
Peplins Cl, Hat.	11	CY26
Peplins Way, Hat.	11	CY25
Peploe Rd NW6	81	CX68
Peplow Cl, West Dr. *Tavistock Rd*	76	BK74
Pepper All, Loug.	32	EG39
Pepper Cl E6	87	EM71
Pepper Cl, Cat.	186	DS125
Pepper Hill, Grav.	130	GC90
Pepper St E14	**204**	**B6**
Pepper St E14	103	EB76
Pepper St SE1	**201**	**H4**
Pepperhill La, Grav.	130	GC90
Peppermead Sq SE13	123	EA85
Peppermint Cl, Croy.	141	DL101
Peppermint Pl E11 *Birch Gro*	68	EE62
Peppie Cl N16 *Bouverie Rd*	66	DS61
Pepys Cl, Ash.	172	CN117
Pepys Cl, Dart.	108	FN84
Pepys Cl, Grav.	130	GD90
Pepys Cl, Slou.	93	BB79
Pepys Cl, Til.	111	GJ81
Pepys Cl, Uxb.	59	BP63
Pepys Cres E16	**205**	**N2**
Pepys Cres, Barn.	27	CW43
Pepys Ri, Orp.	145	ET102
Pepys Rd SE14	103	DX81
Pepys Rd SW20	139	CW95
Pepys St EC3	**197**	**N10**
Pepys St EC3	84	DS73
Perceval Av NW3	64	DE64
Perch St E8	66	DT63
Percheron Cl, Islw.	97	CG83
Percheron Rd, Borwd.	26	CR44
Percival Cl, Lthd.	154	CB107
Percival Ct N17 *High Rd*	46	DT52
Percival Ct, Nthlt.	60	CA64
Percival Gdns, Rom.	70	EW58
Percival Rd SW14	98	CQ84
Percival Rd, Enf.	30	DT42
Percival Rd, Felt.	115	BT89
Percival Rd, Horn.	72	FJ58
Percival Rd, Orp.	145	EP103
Percival St EC1	**196**	**F4**
Percival St EC1	83	DP70
Percival Way, Epsom	156	CQ105
Percy Av, Ashf.	114	BN92
Percy Bryant Rd, Sun.	115	BS94
Percy Bush Rd, West Dr.	94	BM76
Percy Circ WC1	**196**	**C2**
Percy Circ WC1	83	DM69
Percy Gdns, Enf.	31	DX43
Percy Gdns, Hayes	77	BS69
Percy Gdns, Islw.	97	CG82
Percy Gdns, Wor.Pk.	138	CS102
Percy Ms W1	**195**	**M7**
Percy Pas W1	**195**	**L7**
Percy Pl, Slou.	92	AV81
Percy Rd E11	68	EE59
Percy Rd E16	86	EE71
Percy Rd N12	44	DC50
Percy Rd N21	46	DQ45
Percy Rd NW6 *Stafford Rd*	82	DA69
Percy Rd SE20	143	DX95
Percy Rd SE25	142	DU99
Percy Rd W12	99	CU75
Percy Rd, Bexh.	106	EY82
Percy Rd, Hmptn.	116	CA94
Percy Rd, Ilf.	70	EU59
Percy Rd, Islw.	97	CG84
Percy Rd, Mitch.	140	DG101
Percy Rd, Rom.	71	FB55
Percy Rd, Twick.	116	CB88
Percy Rd, Wat.	23	BV42
Percy St W1	**195**	**M7**
Percy St W1	83	DK71
Percy St, Grays	110	GC79
Percy Ter, Ch.St.G. *Sycamore Rd*	36	AU48
Percy Way, Twick.	116	CC88
Percy Yd WC1	**196**	**C2**
Peregrine Cl NW10	62	CR64
Peregrine Cl, Wat.	8	BY34
Peregrine Ct SW16 *Leithcote Gdns*	121	DM91
Peregrine Ct, Well.	105	ET81
Peregrine Gdns, Croy.	143	DY103
Peregrine Ho EC1	**196**	**G2**
Peregrine Ho EC1	83	DP69
Peregrine Rd, Ilf.	50	EV50
Peregrine Rd, Sun.	135	BT96
Peregrine Rd, Wal.Abb.	16	EG34
Peregrine Wk, Horn. *Heron Flight Av*	89	FH65
Peregrine Way SW19	119	CW94
Perham Rd W14	99	CY78
Perham Way, St.Alb.	9	CK26
Peridot St E6	86	EL71
Perifield SE21	122	DQ88
Perimeade Rd, Grnf.	79	CJ68
Periton Rd SE9	104	EK84
Perivale Gdns W13 *Bellevue Rd*	79	CH70
Perivale Gdns, Wat.	7	BV34
Perivale Gra, Grnf.	79	CG69
Perivale Ind Pk, Grnf.	79	CH68
Perivale La, Grnf.	79	CG69
Perivale New Business Cen, Grnf.	79	CH68
Perkin Cl, Wem.	61	CH64
Perkins Cl, Green.	129	FT85
Perkins Ct, Ashf.	114	BM92
Perkin's Rents SW1	**199**	**M6**
Perkin's Rents SW1	101	DK76
Perkins Rd, Ilf.	69	ER57
Perkins Sq SE1	**201**	**J2**
Perks Cl SE3 *Hurren Cl*	104	EE83
Perleybrooke La, Wok. *Bampton Way*	166	AU117
Permain Cl (Shenley), Rad.	9	CK33
Perpins Rd SE9	125	ES86
Perram Cl, Brox.	15	DY26
Perran Rd SW2 *Christchurch Rd*	121	DP89
Perran Wk, Brent.	98	CL78
Perren St NW5 *Ryland Rd*	83	DH65
Perrers Rd W6	99	CV77
Perrin Cl, Ashf. *Fordbridge Rd*	114	BM92
Perrin Ct, Wok. *Blackmore Cres*	167	BB115
Perrin Rd, Wem.	61	CG63
Perrins Ct NW3 *Hampstead High St*	64	DC63
Perrins La NW3	64	DC63
Perrin's Wk NW3	64	DC63
Perriors Cl (Cheshunt), Wal.Cr.	14	DU27
Perrott St SE18	105	EQ77
Perry Av W3	80	CR72
Perry Cl, Rain. *Lowen Rd*	89	FD68
Perry Cl, Uxb. *Harlington Rd*	77	BQ72
Perry Ct E14 *Napier Av*	103	EA78
Perry Ct N15 *Albert Rd*	66	DS58
Perry Gdns N9 *Deansway*	46	DS48
Perry Garth, Nthlt.	78	BW67
Perry Gro, Dart.	108	FN84
Perry Hall Cl, Orp.	146	EU101
Perry Hall Rd, Orp.	145	ET100
Perry Hill SE6	123	DZ90
Perry Ho, Rain. *Lowen Rd*	89	FD68
Perry How, Wor.Pk.	139	CT102
Perry Mead, Bushey	40	CB45
Perry Mead, Enf.	29	DP40
Perry Oaks Dr (Heathrow Airport), Houns.	94	BH82
Perry Oaks Dr, West Dr.	94	BH82
Perry Ri SE23	123	DY90
Perry Rd, Dag.	88	EZ70
Perry St, Chis.	125	ER93
Perry St, Dart.	107	FE84
Perry St, Grav.	130	GE88
Perry St Gdns, Chis. *Old Perry St*	125	ES93
Perry Vale SE23	122	DW89
Perry Way, S.Ock.	90	FQ73
Perryfield Way NW9	63	CT58
Perryfield Way, Rich.	117	CH89
Perryman Ho, Bark. *The Shaftesburys*	87	EQ67
Perrymans Fm Rd, Ilf.	69	ER58
Perrymead St SW6	100	DA81
Perryn Rd SE16	**202**	**D6**
Perryn Rd W3	80	CR73
Perrys La, Sev.	164	EV113
Perrys Pl W1	**195**	**M8**
Perrysfield Rd (Cheshunt), Wal.Cr.	15	DY27
Persant Rd SE6	124	EE89
Perseverance Cotts (Ripley), Wok.	168	BJ121
Perseverance Cotts (Ripley), Wok. *High St*	168	BJ121
Perseverance Pl SW9	101	DN80
Perseverance Pl, Rich. *Shaftesbury Rd*	98	CL83
Persfield Cl, Epsom	157	CU110
Pershore Cl, Ilf.	69	EP57
Pershore Gro, Cars.	140	DD100
Pert Cl N10	45	DH52
Perth Av NW9	62	CR59
Perth Av, Hayes	78	BW70
Perth Cl SW20 *Huntley Way*	139	CU96
Perth Rd E10	67	DY60
Perth Rd E13	86	EH68
Perth Rd N4	65	DN60
Perth Rd N22	45	DP53
Perth Rd, Bark.	87	ER68
Perth Rd, Beck.	143	EC96
Perth Rd, Ilf.	69	EN58
Perth Ter, Ilf.	69	EQ59
Perwell Av, Har.	60	BZ60
Perwell Ct, Har.	60	BZ60
Peter Av NW10	81	CV66
Peter Av, Oxt.	187	ED129
Peter James Business Cen, Hayes	95	BU75
Peter St W1	**195**	**L10**
Peter St W1	83	DK73
Peter St, Grav.	131	GH87
Peterboat Cl SE10	**205**	**J8**
Peterborough Av, Upmin.	73	FS60
Peterborough Gdns, Ilf.	68	EL59
Peterborough Ms SW6	100	DA82
Peterborough Rd E10	67	EC57
Peterborough Rd SW6	100	DA82
Peterborough Rd, Cars.	140	DE100
Peterborough Rd, Har.	61	CE60
Peterborough Vil SW6	100	DB81
Peterchurch Ho SE15 *Commercial Way*	102	DV79
Petergate SW11	100	DC84
Peterhead Ms, Slou. *Grampian Way*	93	BA78
Peterhill Cl (Chalfont St. Peter), Ger.Cr.	36	AY50
Peters Av, St.Alb.	9	CJ26
Peters Cl, Dag.	70	EX60
Peters Cl, Stan.	41	CK51
Peters Cl, Well.	105	ES82
Peters Hill EC4	**197**	**H10**
Peter's La EC1	**196**	**G6**
Peters Path SE26	122	DV91
Petersfield Av, Rom.	52	FL51
Petersfield Av, Slou.	74	AU74
Petersfield Av, Stai.	114	BJ92
Petersfield Cl N18	46	DQ50
Petersfield Cl, Rom.	52	FN51
Petersfield Cres, Couls.	175	DL115
Petersfield Ri SW15	119	CV88
Petersfield Rd W3	98	CQ75
Petersfield Rd, Stai.	114	BJ92
Petersham Av, W.Byf.	152	BL112
Petersham Cl, Rich.	117	CK89
Petersham Cl, Sutt.	158	DA106
Petersham Cl, W.Byf.	152	BL112
Petersham Dr, Orp.	145	ET96
Petersham Gdns, Orp.	145	ET96
Petersham La SW7	100	DC76
Petersham Ms SW7	100	DC76
Petersham Pl SW7	100	DC76
Petersham Rd, Rich.	118	CL86
Petersham Ter, Croy. *Richmond Grn*	141	DL104
Peterslea, Kings L.	7	BP29
Petersmead Cl, Tad. *The Av*	173	CW123
Peterstone Rd SE2	106	EV76
Peterstow Cl SW19	119	CY89
Peterwood Way, Croy.	141	DM103
Petherton Rd N5	66	DQ64
Petley Rd W6	99	CW79
Peto Pl NW1	**195**	**J4**
Peto Pl NW1	83	DH70
Peto St N E16 *Victoria Dock Rd*	86	EF73
Petrie Cl NW2	81	CY65
Pett Cl, Horn. *St. Leonards Way*	71	FH61
Pett St SE18	104	EL77
Petten Cl, Orp.	146	EX102
Petten Gro, Orp.	146	EW102
Petters Rd, Ash.	172	CM116
Petticoat La E1	**197**	**N7**
Petticoat La E1	84	DS71
Petticoat Sq E1	**197**	**P8**
Petticoat Sq E1	84	DT72
Pettits Boul, Rom.	51	FE53
Pettits Cl, Rom.	51	FE54
Pettits La, Rom.	51	FE54
Pettits La N, Rom.	51	FD53
Pettits Pl, Dag.	70	FA64
Pettits Rd, Dag.	70	FA64
Pettiward Cl SW15	99	CW84
Pettley Gdns, Rom.	71	FD57
Pettman Cres SE28	105	ER76
Petts Hill, Nthlt.	60	CB64
Petts La, Shep.	134	BN98
Petts Wd Rd, Orp.	145	EQ99
Pettsgrove Av, Wem.	61	CJ64
Petty France SW1	**199**	**L6**
Petty France SW1	101	DJ76
Pettys Cl (Cheshunt), Wal.Cr.	15	DX28
Petworth Cl, Couls.	175	DJ119
Petworth Cl, Nthlt.	78	BZ66
Petworth Gdns SW20 *Hidcote Gdns*	139	CV97
Petworth Gdns, Uxb.	77	BQ67
Petworth Rd N12	44	DE50
Petworth Rd, Bexh.	126	FA85
Petworth St SW11	100	DE81
Petworth Way, Horn.	71	FF63
Petyt Pl SW3 *Old Ch St*	100	DE79
Petyward SW3	**198**	**C9**
Petyward SW3	100	DE77
Pevel Ho, Dag.	70	FA61
Pevensey Av N11	45	DK50
Pevensey Av, Enf.	30	DR40
Pevensey Cl, Islw.	96	CC80
Pevensey Rd E7	68	EF63
Pevensey Rd SW17	120	DD91
Pevensey Rd, Felt.	116	BY88
Peverel E6 *Downings*	87	EN72
Peveret Cl N11 *Woodland Rd*	45	DH50
Peveril Dr, Tedd.	117	CD92
Pewsey Cl E4	47	EA50
Peyton Pl SE10	103	EC80
Peyton's Cotts, Red.	185	DM132
Peyton's Cotts, Red. *Nutfield Marsh Rd*	185	DM132
Pharaoh Cl, Mitch.	140	DF101
Pharaoh's Island, Shep.	134	BM103
Pheasant Cl E16 *Maplin Rd*	86	EG72
Pheasant Cl, Pur. *Partridge Knoll*	159	DP113
Pheasant Hill, Ch.St.G.	36	AW47
Pheasant Wk (Chalfont St. Peter), Ger.Cr.	36	AX49
Pheasants Way, Rick.	38	BH45
Phelp St SE17	102	DR79
Phelps Way, Hayes	95	BT77
Phene St SW3	100	DE79
Phil Brown Pl SW8 *Heath Rd*	101	DH82
Philan Way, Rom.	51	FD51
Philbeach Gdns SW5	100	DA78
Philchurch Pl E1 *Ellen St*	84	DU72
Philimore Cl SE18	105	ES78
Philip Av, Rom.	71	FD60
Philip Av, Swan.	147	FD98
Philip Cl, Brwd.	54	FV44
Philip Cl, Rom. *Philip Av*	71	FD60
Philip Gdns, Croy.	143	DZ103
Philip La N15	66	DR56
Philip Rd SE15 *Peckham Rye*	102	DU83
Philip Rd, Rain.	89	FE69
Philip Rd, Stai.	114	BK93
Philip St E13	86	EG70
Philip Wk SE15	102	DU83
Philipot Path SE9	125	EM86
Philippa Gdns SE9	124	EK85
Philippa Way, Grays	111	GH77
Philips Cl, Cars.	140	DG102
Phillida Rd, Rom.	52	FN54
Phillimore Gdns NW10	81	CW67
Phillimore Gdns W8	100	DA75
Phillimore Gdns Cl W8 *Phillimore Gdns*	100	DA76
Phillimore Pl W8	100	DA75
Phillimore Pl, Rad.	25	CE36
Phillimore Wk W8	100	DA76
Phillipers, Wat.	24	BY35
Phillipp St N1	84	DS67
Phillips Cl, Dart.	127	FH86
Philpot La EC3	**197**	**M10**
Philpot La, Wok.	150	AV113
Philpot Path, Ilf. *Sunnyside Rd*	69	EQ62
Philpot Sq SW6 *Peterborough Rd*	100	DB83
Philpot St E1	84	DV72
Philpots Cl, West Dr.	76	BK73
Phineas Pett Rd SE9	104	EL83
Phipp St EC2	**197**	**M4**
Phipp St EC2	84	DS70
Phipps Br Rd SW19	140	DC96
Phipps Br Rd, Mitch.	140	DC96
Phipps Hatch La, Enf.	30	DQ38
Phipp's Ms SW1	**199**	**H7**
Phoebeth Rd SE4	123	EA85
Phoenix Cl E8 *Stean St*	84	DT67
Phoenix Cl, Epsom *Queen Alexandra's Way*	156	CN112
Phoenix Cl, Nthwd.	39	BT49
Phoenix Cl, W.Wick.	144	EE103
Phoenix Dr, Kes.	144	EK104
Phoenix Pk, Brent.	97	CK78
Phoenix Pl WC1	**196**	**C4**
Phoenix Pl WC1	83	DM70
Phoenix Pl, Dart.	128	FK87
Phoenix Rd NW1	**195**	**M2**
Phoenix Rd NW1	83	DK69
Phoenix Rd SE20	122	DW93
Phoenix St WC2	**195**	**N9**
Phoenix Way, Houns.	96	BW79
Phoenix Wf SE10	**205**	**K4**
Phoenix Wf SE10	104	EF75
Phoenix Wf Rd SE1	**202**	**A5**
Phygtle, The (Chalfont St. Peter), Ger.Cr.	36	AY51
Phyllis Av, N.Mal.	139	CV99
Physic Pl SW3 *Royal Hosp Rd*	100	DF79
Piazza, The WC2 *Covent Gdn*	83	DL73
Picardy Manorway, Belv.	107	FB76
Picardy Rd, Belv.	106	FA77
Picardy St, Belv.	106	FA76
Piccadilly W1	**199**	**J3**
Piccadilly W1	83	DH74
Piccadilly Arc SW1	**199**	**K2**
Piccadilly Circ W1	**199**	**M1**
Piccadilly Circ W1	83	DK73
Piccadilly Pl W1	**199**	**L1**
Pick Hill, Wal.Abb.	16	EF32
Pickard St EC1	**196**	**G2**
Pickering Av E6	87	EN68
Pickering Cl E9 *Cassland Rd*	85	DX66
Pickering Gdns, Croy.	142	DT100
Pickering Ms W2 *Bishops Br Rd*	82	DB72
Pickering Pl SW1	**199**	**L3**
Pickering St N1 *Essex Rd*	83	DP67
Pickets Cl, Bushey	41	CD46
Pickets St SW12	121	DH87
Pickett Cft, Stan.	41	CK53

Picketts Lock La N9 46 DW47
Pickford Cl, Bexh. 106 EY82
Pickford Dr, Slou. 75 AZ74
Pickford La, Bexh. 106 EY82
Pickford Rd, Bexh. 106 EY83
Pickfords Wf N1 197 H1
Pickfords Wf N1 84 DQ68
Pickhurst Grn, Brom. 144 EF101
Pickhurst La, Brom. 144 EF102
Pickhurst La, W.Wick. 144 EE100
Pickhurst Mead, Brom. 144 EF101
Pickhurst Pk, Brom. 144 EE99
Pickhurst Ri, W.Wick. 143 EC101
Pickins Piece, Slou. 93 BA82
Pickle Herring St SE1 84 DS74
Tooley St
Pickmoss La, Sev. 181 FH116
Pickwick Cl, Houns. 116 BY85
Dorney Way
Pickwick Ct SE9 124 EL88
West Pk
Pickwick Gdns, Grav. 130 GD90
Pickwick Ms N18 46 DS50
Pickwick Pl, Har. 61 CE59
Pickwick Rd SE21 122 DR87
Pickwick St SE1 201 H5
Pickwick Ter, Slou. 74 AV73
Maple Cres
Pickwick Way, Chis. 125 EQ93
Pickworth Cl SW8 101 DL80
Kenchester Cl
Picquets Way, Bans. 173 CY116
Picton Pl W1 194 G9
Picton Pl, Surb. 138 CN102
Picton St SE5 102 DR80
Piedmont Rd SE18 105 ER78
Pield Heath Av, Uxb. 76 BN70
Pield Heath Rd, Uxb. 76 BM71
Pier Head E1 202 D3
Pier Par E16 105 EN75
Pier Rd
Pier Rd E16 105 EM75
Pier Rd, Erith 107 FE79
Pier Rd, Felt. 115 BV85
Pier Rd, Grav. 131 GF86
Pier Rd, Green. 109 FV84
Pier St E14 204 E8
Pier St E14 103 EC77
Pier Ter SW18 100 DC84
Jew's Row
Pier Wk, Grays 110 GA80
Pier Way SE28 105 ER76
Piercing Hill, Epp. 33 ER35
Piermont Grn SE22 122 DV85
Piermont Pl, Brom. 144 EL96
Piermont Rd SE22 122 DV85
Pierrepoint Arc N1 83 DP68
Islington High St
Pierrepoint Rd W3 80 CP73
Pierrepoint Row N1 83 DP68
Islington High St
Pigeon La, Hmptn. 116 CA91
Pigeonhouse La, Couls. 184 DC125
Piggs Cor, Grays 110 GC76
Piggy La, Rick. 21 BB44
Pigott St E14 85 EA72
Pike Cl, Brom. 124 EH92
Pike Cl, Uxb. 76 BM67
Pike La, Upmin. 73 FT64
Pike Rd NW7 42 CR49
Ellesmere Av
Pike Way, Epp. 18 FA27
Pikes End, Pnr. 59 BV56
Pikes Hill, Epsom 156 CS113
Pikestone Cl, Hayes 78 BY70
Berrydale Rd
Pilgrim Cl, Mord. 140 DB101
Pilgrim Cl, St.Alb. 8 CC27
Pilgrim Hill SE27 122 DQ91
Pilgrim Hill, Orp. 146 EY96
Pilgrim St EC4 196 F9
Pilgrimage St SE1 201 K5
Pilgrimage St SE1 102 DR75
Pilgrims Cl N13 45 DM49
Pilgrims Cl, Brwd. 54 FT43
Pilgrims Cl, Nthlt. 60 CC64
Pilgrims Cl, Wat. 8 BX33
Kytes Dr
Pilgrims Ct SE3 104 EG81
Pilgrim's La NW3 64 DD63
Pilgrims La, Cat. 185 DM125
Pilgrims La, Grays 91 FW74
Pilgrims La, Oxt. 188 EH125
Pilgrims La, West. 178 EL123
Pilgrims Ms E14 85 EC73
Blackwall Way
Pilgrims Pl NW3 64 DD63
Hampstead High St
Pilgrims Pl, Reig. 184 DA132
Pilgrims Ri, Barn. 28 DE43
Pilgrims Rd, Swans. 110 FY84
Pilgrims Vw, Green. 129 FW86
Pilgrims Way E6 86 EL67
High St N
Pilgrims Way N19 65 DK60
Pilgrims' Way, Bet. 182 CQ133
Chalkpit La
Pilgrims' Way, Bet. 183 CY131
Pilgrims' Way, Cat. 185 DN126
Pilgrims Way, Dart. 128 FN88
Pilgrims' Way, Red. 185 DJ127
Pilgrims Way, Reig. 184 DA131
Pilgrims Way (Chevening), Sev. 180 EV121
Pilgrims Way, S.Croy. 160 DT106
Pilgrim's Way, Wem. 62 CP60
Pilgrims Way, West. 179 EM123
Pilgrims Way W, Sev. 181 FD116
Pilkington Rd SE15 102 DV82
Pilkington Rd, Orp. 145 EQ103
Pillions La, Hayes 77 BR70
Pilots Pl, Grav. 131 GJ86
Pilsdon Cl SW19 119 CX88
Inner Pk Rd
Piltdown Rd, Wat. 40 BX49
Pilton Est, The, Croy. 141 DP103
Pitlake
Pilton Pl SE17 201 J10
Pilton Pl SE17 102 DQ78
Pimento Ct W5 97 CK76
Olive Rd
Pimlico Rd SW1 198 F10
Pimlico Rd SW1 100 DG78
Pimlico Wk N1 197 M2
Pimpernel Way, Rom. 52 FK51
Pinchbeck Rd, Orp. 163 ET107
Pinchfield, Rick. 37 BE50
Pinchin St E1 84 DU73
Pincott Pl SE4 103 DX83
Billingford Cl
Pincott Rd SW19 140 DC95
Pincott Rd, Bexh. 126 FA85
Pindar St EC2 197 M6
Pindar St EC2 84 DS71
Pindock Ms W9 82 DB70
Warwick Av
Pine Av E15 67 ED64
Pine Av, Grav. 131 GK88
Pine Av, W.Wick. 143 EB102
Pine Cl E10 67 EB61
Walnut Rd
Pine Cl N14 45 DJ45
Pine Cl N19 65 DJ61
Hargrave Pk
Pine Cl SE20 142 DW95
Pine Cl, Add. 152 BH111
Pine Cl, Ken. 176 DR117
Pine Cl, Stan. 41 CH49
Pine Cl, Swan. 147 FF98
Pine Cl (Cheshunt), Wal.Cr. 15 DX28
Pine Cl, Wok. 166 AW117
Pine Coombe, Croy. 161 DX105
Pine Ct, Upmin. 72 FN63
Pine Cres, Brwd. 55 GD43
Pine Cres, Cars. 158 DD111
Pine Gdns, Ruis. 59 BV60
Pine Gdns, Surb. 138 CN100
Pine Glade, Orp. 163 EM105
Pine Gro N4 65 DL61
Pine Gro N20 43 CZ46
Pine Gro SW19 119 CZ92
Pine Gro, Bushey 24 BZ40
Pine Gro, Hat. 12 DB25
Pine Gro, St.Alb. 8 BZ30
Pine Gro, Wey. 153 BP106
Pine Gro Ms, Wey. 153 BQ106
Pine Hill, Epsom 172 CR115
Pine Ms NW10 81 CX68
Clifford Gdns
Pine Pl, Bans. 157 CX114
Pine Pl, Hayes 77 BT70
Pine Ridge, Cars. 158 DG109
Pine Rd N11 44 DG47
Pine Rd NW2 63 CW63
Pine Rd, Wok. 166 AW120
Pine St EC1 196 D4
Pine St EC1 83 DN70
Pine Tree Cl, Houns. 95 BV81
Pine Tree Hill, Wok. 167 BD116
Pine Trees Dr, Uxb. 58 BL63
Pine Vw Manor, Epp. 18 EU30
Pine Wk, Bans. 174 DF117
Pine Wk, Brom. 144 EJ95
Pine Wk, Cars. 158 DD110
Pine Wk, Cat. 176 DT122
Pine Wk, Cob. 154 BX114
Pine Wk, Surb. 138 CN100
Pine Way, Egh. 112 AV93
Ashwood Rd
Pine Wd, Sun. 135 BU95
Pineapple Ct SW1 199 K6
Pineapple Rd, Amer. 20 AT39
Pinecrest Gdns, Orp. 163 EP105
Pinecroft, Brwd. 55 GB45
Pinecroft, Rom. 72 FJ56
Pinecroft Cres, Barn. 27 CY42
Hillside Gdns
Pinedene SE15 102 DV81
Meeting Ho La
Pinefield Cl E14 85 EA73
Pinehurst, Sev. 191 FL121
Pinehurst Cl, Abb.L. 7 BS32
Pinehurst Cl, Tad. 174 DA122
Pinehurst Wk, Orp. 145 ES102
Pinel Cl, Vir.W. 132 AY98
Pinelands Cl SE3 104 EF80
St. John's Pk
Pinemartin Cl NW2 63 CW62
Pineneedle La, Sev. 191 FH123
Pines, The N14 29 DJ43
Pines, The, Borwd. 26 CM40
Anthony Rd
Pines, The, Couls. 175 DH118
Pines, The, Pur. 159 DP113
Pines, The, Sun. 135 BU97
Pines, The, Wok. 151 AZ114
Pines, The, Wdf.Grn. 48 EG48
Pines Av, Enf. 30 DV36
Pines Cl, Nthwd. 39 BS51
Pines Rd, Brom. 144 EL96
Pinetree Cl (Chalfont St. Peter), Ger.Cr. 36 AW52
Pinewood Av, Add. 152 BJ109
Pinewood Av, Pnr. 40 CB51
Pinewood Av, Rain. 89 FH70
Pinewood Av, Sev. 191 FK121
Pinewood Av, Sid. 125 ES88
Pinewood Av, Uxb. 76 BM72
Pinewood Cl, Borwd. 26 CR39
Pinewood Cl, Croy. 143 DY104
Pinewood Cl, Ger.Cr. 56 AY59
Dukes Wd Av
Pinewood Cl, Iver 75 BC66
Pinewood Cl, Nthwd. 39 BV50
Pinewood Cl, Orp. 145 ER102
Pinewood Cl, Pnr. 40 CB51
Pinewood Cl, Wat. 23 BU39
Pinewood Cl, Wok. 151 BA114
Pinewood Dr, Orp. 163 ES106
Pinewood Dr, Pot.B. 11 CZ31
Pinewood Dr, Stai. 114 BG92
Cotswold Cl
Pinewood Grn, Iver 75 BC66
Pinewood Gro W5 79 CJ72
Pinewood Gro, Add. 152 BH110
Pinewood Pk, Add. 152 BH111
Pinewood Ride, Iver 75 BA68
Pinewood Ride, Slou. 75 BA65
Fulmer Common Rd
Pinewood Rd SE2 106 EX79
Pinewood Rd, Brom. 144 EG98
Pinewood Rd, Felt. 115 BV90
Pinewood Rd, Iver 75 BB65
Pinewood Rd (Havering-atte-Bower), Rom. 51 FC49
Pinewood Rd, Vir.W. 132 AU98
Pinewood Way, Brwd. 55 GD43
Pinfold Rd SW16 121 DL91
Pinfold Rd, Bushey 24 BZ40
Pinglestone Cl, West Dr. 94 BL80
Pinkcoat Cl, Felt. 115 BV90
Tanglewood Way
Pinkerton Pl SW16 121 DK91
Riggindale Rd
Pinkham Way N11 44 DG52
Pinks Hill, Swan. 147 FE99
Pinkwell Av, Hayes 95 BR77
Pinkwell La, Hayes 95 BQ77
Pinley Gdns, Dag. 88 EV67
Stamford Rd
Pinn Cl, Uxb. 76 BK72
High Rd
Pinn Way, Ruis. 59 BS59
Pinnacle Hill, Bexh. 107 FB84
Pinnacle Hill N, Bexh. 107 FB83
Pinnacles, Wal.Abb. 16 EE34
Pinnell Pl SE9 104 EK84
Pinnell Rd SE9 104 EK84
Pinner Ct, Pnr. 60 CA56
Pinner Grn, Pnr. 40 BW54
Pinner Gro, Pnr. 60 BY56
Pinner Hill, Pnr. 40 BW53
Pinner Hill Rd, Pnr. 40 BW54
Pinner Pk, Pnr. 40 CA53
Pinner Pk Av, Har. 60 CB55
Pinner Pk Gdns, Har. 40 CC54
Pinner Rd, Har. 60 CB57
Pinner Rd, Nthwd. 39 BT53
Pinner Rd, Pnr. 60 BZ56
Pinner Rd, Wat. 24 BX44
Pinner Vw, Har. 60 CC58
Pinnocks Av, Grav. 131 GH88
Pinstone Way, Ger.Cr. 57 BB61
Pintail Cl E6 86 EL71
Swan App
Pintail Rd, Wdf.Grn. 48 EH52
Pintail Way, Hayes 78 BX71
Pinto Cl, Borwd. 26 CR44
Percheron Rd
Pinto Way SE3 104 EH84
Pioneer Pl, Croy. 161 EA109
Featherbed La
Pioneer St SE15 102 DU81
Pioneer Way W12 81 CV72
Du Cane Rd
Pioneer Way, Swan. 147 FE97
Pioneer Way, Wat. 23 BT44
Pioneers Ind Pk, Croy. 141 DL102
Piper Cl N7 65 DM64
Piper Rd, Kings.T. 138 CN97
Pipers Cl, Cob. 170 BX115
Pipers End, Vir.W. 132 AX97
Piper's Gdns, Croy. 143 DY101
Pipers Grn NW9 62 CQ57
Pipers Grn La, Edg. 42 CL48
Pipewell Rd, Cars. 140 DE100
Pippin Cl NW2 63 CV62
Pippin Cl, Croy. 143 DZ102
Pippin Cl (Shenley), Rad. 9 CK33
Pippins, The, Slou. 75 AZ74
Pickford Dr
Pippins Cl, West Dr. 94 BK76
Pippins Ct, Ashf. 115 BP93
Piquet Rd SE20 142 DW96
Pirbright Cres, Croy. 161 EC107
Pirbright Rd SW18 119 CZ88
Pirie Cl SE5 102 DR83
Denmark Hill
Pirie St E16 86 EH74
Pirrip Cl, Grav. 131 GM89
Pitcairn Cl, Rom. 70 FA56
Pitcairn Rd, Mitch. 120 DF94
Pitcairn's Path, Har. 60 CC62
Eastcote Rd
Pitchfont La, Oxt. 178 EF124
Pitchford St E15 85 ED66
Pitfield Cres SE28 88 EU74
Pitfield Est N1 197 L2
Pitfield Est N1 84 DR69
Pitfield St N1 197 M2
Pitfield St N1 84 DS69
Pitfield Way NW10 80 CQ65
Pitfield Way, Enf. 30 DW39
Pitfold Cl SE12 124 EG86
Pitfold Rd SE12 124 EG86
Pitlake, Croy. 141 DP103
Pitman St SE5 102 DQ80
Pitsea Pl E1 85 DX72
Pitsea St
Pitsea St E1 85 DX72
Pitshanger La W5 79 CH70
Pitshanger Pk W13 79 CJ69
Pitson Cl, Add. 152 BK105
Pitt Cres SW19 120 DB91
Pitt Pl, Epsom 156 CS114
Pitt Rd, Croy. 142 DQ99
Pitt Rd, Epsom 156 CS114
Pitt Rd, Orp. 163 EQ105
Pitt Rd, Th.Hth. 142 DQ99
Pitt St W8 100 DA75
Pittman Cl, Brwd. 55 GC50
Pittman Gdns, Ilf. 69 EQ64
Pitt's Head Ms W1 198 G3
Pitt's Head Ms W1 82 DG74
Pittsmead Av, Brom. 144 EG101
Pittville Gdns SE25 142 DU97
Pittwood, Brwd. 55 GA46
Pitwood Grn, Tad. 173 CW120
Pitwood Pk Ind Est, Tad. 173 CV120
Waterfield
Pixfield Ct, Brom. 144 EF96
Beckenham La
Pixley St E14 85 DZ72
Pixton Way, Croy. 161 DY109
Place Fm Av, Orp. 145 ER102
Place Fm Rd, Red. 186 DR130
Placehouse La, Couls. 175 DM119
Plain, The, Epp. 18 EV29
Plaistow Gro E15 86 EF67
Plaistow Gro, Brom. 124 EH94
Plaistow La, Brom. 124 EH94
Plaistow Pk Rd E13 86 EH68
Plaistow Rd E13 86 EF67
Plaistow Rd E15 86 EF67
Plaitford Cl, Rick. 38 BL47
Plane Av, Grav. 130 GD87
Plane St SE26 122 DV90
Plane Tree Cres, Felt. 115 BV90
Plane Tree Wk SE19 122 DS93
Central Hill
Planes, The, Cher. 134 BJ101
Plantaganet Pl, Wal.Abb. 15 EB33
Plantagenet Cl, Wor.Pk. 156 CR105
Plantagenet Gdns, Rom. 70 EX59
Broomfield Rd
Plantagenet Pl, Rom. 70 EX59
Broomfield Rd
Plantagenet Rd, Barn. 28 DC42
Plantain Gdns E11 67 ED62
Hollydown Way
Plantain Pl SE1 201 K4
Plantation, The SE3 104 EG82
Plantation Cl, Green. 129 FT86
Plantation Dr, Orp. 146 EX102
Plantation La, Warl. 177 DY119
Plantation Rd, Amer. 20 AS37
Plantation Rd, Erith 107 FG81
Plantation Rd, Swan. 127 FG94
Plantation Way, Amer. 20 AS37
Plantation Wf SW11 100 DC83
Plasel Ct E13 86 EG67
Plashet Rd
Plashet Gdns, Brwd. 55 GA49
Plashet Gro E6 86 EJ67
Plashet Rd E13 86 EG67
Plassy Rd SE6 123 EB87
Platford Grn, Horn. 72 FL56
Platina St EC2 197 L4
Plato Rd SW2 101 DL84
Platt, The SW15 99 CX83
Platt St NW1 83 DK68
Platts Av, Wat. 23 BV41
Platt's Eyot, Hmptn. 136 CA96
Platt's La NW3 64 DA63
Platts Rd, Enf. 30 DW39
Plawsfield Rd, Beck. 143 DX95
Plaxtol Cl, Brom. 144 EJ95
Plaxtol Rd, Erith 106 FA80
Plaxton Ct E11 68 EF62
Woodhouse Rd
Playfair St W6 99 CW78
Winslow Rd
Playfield Av, Rom. 51 FC53
Playfield Cres SE22 122 DT85
Playfield Rd, Edg. 42 CQ54
Playford Rd N4 65 DM61
Playgreen Way SE6 123 EA91
Playground Cl, Beck. 143 DX96
Churchfields Rd
Playhouse Yd EC4 196 F9
Plaza Par NW6 82 DB68
Kilburn High Rd
Plaza W, Houns. 96 CB81
Pleasance, The SW15 99 CV84
Pleasance Rd SW15 119 CV85
Pleasance Rd, Orp. 146 EV96
Pleasant Gro, Croy. 143 DZ104
Pleasant Pl N1 83 DP66
Pleasant Pl, Rick. 37 BE52
Pleasant Pl, Walt. 154 BW107
Pleasant Row NW1 83 DH67
Pleasant Vw, Erith 107 FE78
Pleasant Vw Pl, Orp. 163 EP106
High St
Pleasant Way, Wem. 79 CJ68
Pleasure Pit Rd, Ash. 172 CP118
Plender St NW1 83 DJ67
Plender St Est NW1 83 DJ67
Plender St
Pleshey Rd N7 65 DK63
Plesman Way, Wall. 159 DL109
Plevna Cres N15 66 DS58
Plevna Rd N9 46 DU48
Plevna Rd, Hmptn. 136 CB95
Plevna St E14 204 D6
Plevna St E14 103 EC76
Pleydell Av SE19 122 DT94
Pleydell Av W6 99 CT77
Pleydell Ct EC4 196 E9
Pleydell Est EC1 84 DQ69
Radnor St
Pleydell St EC4 196 E9
Plimsoll Cl E14 85 EB72
Grundy St
Plimsoll Rd N4 65 DN62
Plough Ct EC3 197 L10
Plough Fm Cl, Ruis. 59 BR58
Plough Hill (Cuffley), Pot.B. 13 DL28
Plough Ind Est, Lthd. 171 CH119
Plough Ind Est, Lthd. 171 CG120
Kingston Rd
Plough La SE22 122 DT86
Plough La SW17 120 DB92
Plough La SW19 120 DB92
Plough La, Cob. 169 BU116
Plough La, Pur. 159 DL109
Plough La, Rick. 5 BF33
Plough La, Slou. 74 AV67
Plough La, Tedd. 117 CG92
Plough La (Harefield), Uxb. 38 BJ51
Plough La, Wall. 159 DL105
Plough La Cl, Wall. 159 DL106
Plough Ms SW11 100 DD84
Plough Ter
Plough Pl EC4 196 E8
Plough Ri, Upmin. 73 FS59
Plough Rd SW11 100 DD83
Plough Rd, Epsom 156 CR109
Plough St E1 84 DT72
Leman St
Plough Ter SW11 100 DD84
Plough Way SE16 203 J8
Plough Way SE16 103 DX77
Plough Yd EC2 197 N5
Plough Yd EC2 84 DS70
Ploughlees La, Slou. 74 AS73
Ploughmans Cl NW1 83 DK67
Crofters Way
Ploughmans End, Islw. 117 CD85
Plover Cl, Stai. 113 BF90
Waters Dr
Plover Gdns, Upmin. 73 FT60
Plover Way SE16 203 L6
Plover Way SE16 103 DY76
Plover Way, Hayes 78 BX72
Plowden Bldgs EC4 83 DN7
Middle Temple La
Plowman Cl N18 46 DR5
Plowman Way, Dag. 70 EW6
Plum Cl, Felt. 115 BU8
Highfield Rd
Plum Garth, Brent. 97 CK7
Plum La SE18 105 EP8
Plumbers Row E1 84 DU7
Plumbridge St SE10 103 EC8
Blackheath Hill
Plummer La, Mitch. 140 DF9
Plummer Rd SW4 121 DK8
Plummers Cft, Sev. 190 FE12
Plumpton Av, Horn. 72 FL6
Plumpton Cl, Nthlt. 78 CA6
Plumpton Way, Cars. 140 DE10
Plumstead Common Rd SE18 105 EP7
Plumstead High St SE18 105 ES7
Plumstead Rd SE18 105 EP7
Plumtree Cl, Dag. 89 FB6
Plumtree Cl, Wall. 159 DK10
Plumtree Ct EC4 196 E
Plumtree Mead, Loug. 33 EN4
Plymouth Dr, Sev. 191 FJ12
Plymouth Ho, Rain. 89 FF6
Plymouth Pk, Sev. 191 FJ12
Plymouth Rd E16 86 EG7
Plymouth Rd, Brom. 144 EH9
Plymouth Wf E14 204 F
Plymouth Wf E14 103 ED7
Plympton Av NW6 81 CZ6
Plympton Cl, Belv. 106 EY7
Halifield Dr
Plympton Pl NW8 194 B
Plympton Rd NW6 81 CZ6
Plympton St NW8 194 B
Plympton St NW8 82 DE7
Plymstock Rd, Well. 106 EW8
Pocketsdell La, Hem.H. 4 AX2
Pocklington Cl NW9 42 CS5
Pocock Av, West Dr. 94 BM7
Pocock St SE1 200 F
Pocock St SE1 101 DP7
Pococks La (Eton), Wind. 92 AS7
Podmore Rd SW18 100 DC8
Poets Gate, Wal.Cr. 14 DS2
Poets Rd N5 66 DR6
Poets Way, Har. 61 CE5
Blawith Rd
Point, The, Ruis. 59 BU6
Bedford Rd
Point Cl SE10 103 EC8
Point Hill
Point Hill SE10 103 EC8
Point of Thomas Path E1 202 G
Point Pl, Wem. 80 CP6
Point Pleasant SW18 100 DA8
Pointalls Cl N3 44 DC5
Pointer Cl SE28 88 EX7
Pointers, The, Ash. 172 CL12
Pointers Cl E14 204 B1
Pointers Cl E14 103 EB7
Pointers Rd, Cob. 169 BQ11
Poland St W1 195 L
Poland St W1 83 DJ7
Pole Cat All, Brom. 144 EF10
Pole Hill Rd E4 47 EC4
Pole Hill Rd, Hayes 77 BQ6
Pole Hill Rd, Uxb. 77 BQ6
Polebrook Rd SE3 104 EJ8
Polecroft La SE6 123 DZ8
Polehamptons, The, Hmptn. 116 CC9
High St
Poles Hill, Rick. 5 BE3
Polesden Gdns SW20 139 CV9
Polesden La, Wok. 167 BF12
Polesteeple Hill, West. 178 EK11
Polesworth Ho W2 82 DA7
Polesworth Rd, Dag. 88 EX6
Polhill, Sev. 181 FC11
Police Sta La, Bushey 40 CB4
Sparrows Herne
Police Sta Rd, Walt. 154 BW10
Pollard Av (Denham), Uxb. 57 BF5
Pollard Cl E16 86 EG7
Pollard Cl N7 65 DM6
Pollard Cl, Chig. 50 EU5
Pollard Cl, Wind. 112 AV8
Pollard Rd N20 44 DE4
Pollard Rd, Mord. 140 DD9
Pollard Rd, Wok. 167 BB11
Pollard Row E2 84 DU6
Pollard St E2 84 DU6
Pollard Wk, Sid. 126 EW9
Pollards, Rick. 37 BD5
Pollards Cl, Loug. 32 EJ4
Pollards Cl (Cheshunt), Wal.Cr. 14 DQ2
Pollards Cres SW16 141 DL9
Pollards Hill E SW16 141 DM9
Pollards Hill N SW16 141 DL9
Pollards Hill S SW16 141 DL9
Pollards Hill W SW16 141 DL9
Pollards Oak Cres, Oxt. 188 EG13
Pollards Oak Rd, Oxt. 188 EG13
Pollards Wd Hill, Oxt. 188 EH13
Pollards Wd Rd SW16 141 DL9
Pollards Wd Rd, Oxt. 188 EH13
Pollen St W1 195 J
Pollitt Dr NW8 82 DD7
Cunningham Pl
Pollyhaugh (Eynsford), Dart. 148 FL10
Polperro Cl, Orp. 145 ET10
Cotswold Ri
Polsted Rd SE6 123 DZ8
Polthorne Est SE18 105 ER7
Polthorne Gro SE18 105 EQ7
Polworth Rd SW16 121 DL9
Polygon, The SW4 101 DJ8
Old Town
Polygon Rd NW1 195 M
Polygon Rd NW1 83 DK6
Polytechnic St SE18 105 EN7
Pomell Way E1 84 DT7
Commercial St
Pomeroy Cres, Wat. 23 BV3

Priest Ct EC2 197 H8
Priest Hill, Egh. 112 AW90
Priest Hill, Wind. 112 AW90
Priest Pk Av, Har. 60 CA61
Priestfield Rd SE23 123 DY90
Priestlands Pk Rd, Sid. 125 ET90
Priestley Cl N16 66 DT59
Ravensdale Rd
Priestley Gdns, Rom. 70 EV58
Priestley Rd, Mitch. 140 DG96
Priestley Way E17 67 DX55
Priestley Way NW2 63 CU60
Priestly Gdns, Wok. 167 BA120
Priests Av, Rom. 51 FD54
Priests Br SW14 98 CS83
Priests Br SW15 98 CS83
Priests Fld, Brwd. 55 GC50
Priests La, Brwd. 54 FY47
Prima Rd SW9 101 DN80
Primrose Av, Enf. 30 DR39
Primrose Av, Rom. 70 EV59
Primrose Cl SE6 123 EC92
Primrose Cl, Har. 60 BZ63
Primrose Cl, Wall. 141 DH102
Primrose Dr, West Dr. 94 BK76
Wise La
Primrose Gdns NW3 82 DE65
Primrose Gdns, Bushey 40 CB45
Primrose Gdns, Ruis. 60 BW64
Primrose Glen, Horn. 72 FL56
Primrose Hill EC4 196 E9
Primrose Hill, Brwd. 54 FW48
Primrose Hill, Kings L. 7 BP28
Primrose Hill Ct NW3 82 DF66
Primrose Hill Rd NW3 82 DE66
Primrose Hill Studios NW1 82 DG67
Fitzroy Rd
Primrose La, Croy. 143 DX102
Primrose Ms NW1 82 DF66
Sharpleshall St
Primrose Ms SE3 104 EH80
Primrose Ms W5 97 CK75
St. Mary's Rd
Primrose Path (Cheshunt), Wal.Cr. 14 DU31
Primrose Rd E10 67 EB60
Primrose Rd E18 48 EH54
Primrose Rd, Walt. 154 BW106
Primrose Sq E9 84 DW66
Primrose St EC2 197 M6
Primrose St EC2 84 DS71
Primrose Wk, Epsom 157 CT108
Primrose Way, Wem. 79 CK68
Primula St W12 81 CU72
Prince Albert Rd NW1 194 C1
Prince Albert Rd NW1 82 DE68
Prince Albert Rd NW8 194 C1
Prince Albert Rd NW8 82 DE68
Prince Alberts Wk, Wind. 92 AU81
Prince Arthur Ms NW3 64 DC63
Perrins La
Prince Arthur Rd NW3 64 DC64
Prince Charles Av (South Darenth), Dart. 149 FR96
Prince Charles Dr NW4 63 CW59
Prince Charles Rd SE3 104 EF81
Prince Charles Way, Wall. 141 DH104
Prince Consort Dr, Chis. 145 ER95
Prince Consort Rd SW7 100 DC76
Prince Edward Rd E9 85 DZ65
Prince George Av N14 29 DJ43
Prince George Duke of Kent Ct, Chis. 125 ER94
Holbrook La
Prince George Rd N16 66 DS63
Prince George's Av SW20 139 CW96
Prince George's Rd SW19 140 DD95
Prince Henry Rd SE7 104 EK80
Prince Imperial Rd SE18 105 EM81
Prince Imperial Rd, Chis. 125 EP94
Prince John Rd SE9 124 EL85
Prince of Orange La SE10 103 EC80
Greenwich High Rd
Prince of Wales Cl NW4 63 CV56
Church Ter
Prince of Wales Dr SW8 101 DH80
Prince of Wales Dr SW11 100 DF81
Prince of Wales Footpath, Enf. 31 DY38
Prince of Wales Gate SW7 198 B4
Prince of Wales Gate SW7 100 DE75
Prince of Wales Pas NW1 195 K3
Prince of Wales Rd NW5 82 DG65
Prince of Wales Rd SE3 104 EF81
Prince of Wales Rd, Sutt. 140 DD103
Prince of Wales Ter W4 98 CS78
Prince of Wales Ter W8 100 DB75
Kensington Rd
Prince Regent Ct SE16 85 DY74
Rotherhithe St
Prince Regent La E13 86 EH69
Prince Regent La E16 86 EJ71
Prince Regent Ms NW1 83 DJ69
Hampstead Rd
Prince Regent Rd, Houns. 96 CC83
Prince Rd SE25 142 DS99
Prince Rupert Rd SE9 105 EM84
Prince St SE8 103 DZ79
Prince St, Wat. 24 BW41
Princedale Rd W11 81 CY74
Princelet St E1 84 DT71
Prince's Arc SW1 199 L2
Princes Av N3 44 DA53
Princes Av N10 64 DG55
Princes Av N13 45 DN50
Princes Av N22 45 DK53
Princes Av NW9 62 CP56
Princes Av W3 98 CN76
Princes Av, Cars. 158 DF108
Princes Av, Dart. 128 FP88
Princes Av, Enf. 31 DY36
Princes Av, Grnf. 78 CB72
Princes Av, Orp. 145 ES99
Princes Av, S.Croy. 176 DV115
Princes Av, Surb. 138 CN102
Princes Av, Wat. 23 BT43
Princes Av, Wdf.Grn. 48 EH49
Princes Cl N4 65 DP60
Princes Cl NW9 62 CN56
Princes Cl SW4 101 DJ83
Old Town
Princes Cl, Edg. 42 CN50
Princes Cl, Epp. 19 FC25
Princes Cl, Sid. 126 EX90
Princes Cl, S.Croy. 176 DV115
Princes Cl, Tedd. 117 CD91
Princes Ct E1 202 E1
Princes Ct E1 84 DV73
Princes Ct SE16 203 M7
Princes Ct SE16 103 DZ76
Princes Ct, Wem. 62 CL64
Princes Dr, Har. 61 CE55
Prince's Dr, Lthd. 155 CE112
Princes Gdns SW7 198 A6
Princes Gdns SW7 100 DD76
Princes Gdns W3 80 CN71
Princes Gdns W5 79 CJ70
Princes Gate NW1 82 DE69
Park Rd
Princes Gate SW7 198 B5
Princes Gate SW7 100 DE75
Princes Gate Ct SW7 198 A5
Princes Gate Ms SW7 198 A6
Princes Gate Ms SW7 100 DD76
Princes La N10 65 DH55
Princes Ms W2 82 DA73
Hereford Rd
Princes Par, Pot.B. 12 DC32
High St
Princes Pk, Rain. 89 FG66
Princes Pk Av NW11 63 CY58
Princes Pk Av, Hayes 77 BR73
Princes Pk Circle, Hayes 77 BR73
Princes Pk Cl, Hayes 77 BR73
Princes Pk La, Hayes 77 BR73
Princes Pk Par, Hayes 77 BR73
Princes Pl SW1 199 L2
Princes Pl W11 81 CY74
Princes Plain, Brom. 144 EL101
Princes Ri SE13 103 EC82
Princes Riverside Rd SE16 203 H2
Princes Riverside Rd SE16 85 DX74
Princes Rd N18 46 DW49
Princes Rd SE20 123 DX93
Princes Rd SW14 98 CR83
Princes Rd SW19 120 DA93
Princes Rd W13 79 CH74
Broomfield Rd
Princes Rd, Ashf. 114 BM92
Princes Rd, Buck.H. 48 EJ47
Princes Rd, Dart. 127 FG86
Princes Rd, Egh. 113 AZ93
Princes Rd, Felt. 115 BT89
Princes Rd, Grav. 131 GJ90
Princes Rd, Ilf. 69 ER56
Princes Rd, Kings.T. 118 CN94
Princes Rd, Rich. 118 CM85
Princes Rd (Kew), Rich. 98 CM80
Princes Rd, Rom. 71 FG57
Princes Rd, Swan. 127 FG93
Princes Rd, Tedd. 117 CD91
Princes Rd, Wey. 153 BP106
Princes Sq W2 82 DB73
Princes St EC2 197 K9
Princes St EC2 84 DR72
Princes St N17 46 DS51
Queen St
Princes St W1 195 J9
Princes St W1 83 DH72
Princes St, Bexh. 106 EZ84
Princes St, Grav. 131 GH86
Princes St, Rich. 118 CL85
Sheen Rd
Princes St, Slou. 92 AV75
Princes St, Sutt. 158 DD105
Princes Ter E13 86 EH67
Princes Vw, Dart. 128 FN88
Princes Way SW19 119 CX87
Princes Way, Brwd. 55 GA46
Princes Way, Buck.H. 48 EJ47
Princes Way, Croy. 159 DM106
Princes Way, Ruis. 60 BY63
Princes Way, W.Wick. 162 EF105
Princes Yd W11 81 CY74
Princedale Rd
Princesfield Rd, Wal.Abb. 16 EH33
Princess Alice Way SE28 105 ER75
Princess Av, Wem. 62 CL61
Princess Cres N4 65 DP61
Princess Gdns, Wok. 167 BB116
Princess La, Ruis. 59 BS60
Princess Louise Cl W2 82 DD71
Church St
Princess Mary's Rd, Add. 152 BJ105
Princess May Rd N16 66 DS63
Princess Ms NW3 82 DD65
Belsize Cres
Princess Par, Orp. 145 EN104
Crofton Rd
Princess Pk Manor N11 44 DG50
Princess Rd NW1 82 DG67
Princess Rd NW6 82 DA68
Princess Rd, Croy. 142 DQ100
Princess Rd, Wok. 167 BB116
Princess St SE1 200 G7
Princess St SE1 101 DP76
Princess Way, Red. 184 DG133
Princesses Wk, Rich. 98 CL80
Kew Rd
Princethorpe Ho W2 82 DB71
Princethorpe Rd SE26 123 DX91
Princeton Ct SW15 99 CX83
Felsham Rd
Princeton St WC1 196 B6
Princeton St WC1 83 DM71
Pringle Gdns SW16 121 DJ91
Pringle Gdns, Pur. 159 DM110
Print Village SE15 102 DT82
Chadwick Rd
Printer St EC4 196 E8
Printers Inn Ct EC4 196 D8
Printing Ho La, Hayes 95 BS75
Printing Ho Yd E2 197 N2
Priolo Rd SE7 104 EJ78
Prior Av, Sutt. 158 DE108
Prior Bolton St N1 83 DP65
Prior Chase, Grays 110 FZ77
Prior Rd, Ilf. 69 EN62
Prior St SE10 103 EC80
Prioress Rd SE27 121 DP90
Prioress St SE1 201 L7
Prioress St SE1 102 DR76
Priors, The, Ash. 171 CK119
Priors Cl, Slou. 92 AU76
Priors Ct, Wok. 166 AU118
Priors Cft E17 47 DY54
Priors Cft, Wok. 167 BA120
Priors Fld, Nthlt. 78 BY65
Arnold Rd
Priors Gdns, Ruis. 60 BW64
Priors Mead, Enf. 30 DS39
Priors Pk, Horn. 72 FJ62
Priorsford Av, Orp. 146 EU98
Priory, The SE3 104 EF84
Priory, The, Gdse. 186 DV131
Priory Av E4 47 DZ48
Priory Av E17 67 EA57
Priory Av N8 65 DK56
Priory Av W4 98 CS77
Priory Av, Orp. 145 ER100
Priory Av, Sutt. 157 CX105
Priory Av (Harefield), Uxb. 58 BJ56
Priory Av, Wem. 61 CF63
Priory Cl E4 47 DZ48
Priory Cl E18 48 EG53
Priory Cl N3 43 CZ53
Church Cres
Priory Cl N14 29 DH43
Priory Cl N20 43 CZ45
Priory Cl SW19 140 DB95
High Path
Priory Cl, Beck. 143 DY97
Priory Cl, Brwd. 54 FU43
Priory Cl, Chis. 145 EM95
Priory Cl, Dart. 128 FJ85
Priory Cl, Hmptn. 136 BZ95
Priory Gdns
Priory Cl, Hayes 77 BV73
Priory Cl, Ruis. 59 BT60
Priory Cl, Stan. 41 CF48
Priory Cl, Sun. 115 BU94
Staines Rd E
Priory Cl (Denham), Uxb. 58 BG62
Priory Cl (Harefield), Uxb. 58 BH56
Priory Cl, Walt. 135 BU104
Priory Cl (Sudbury), Wem. 61 CF63
Priory Cl, Wok. 151 BD113
Priory Ct E17 67 DZ55
Priory Ct EC4 83 DP72
Ludgate Hill
Priory Ct SW8 101 DK81
Priory Ct, Bushey 40 CC46
Sparrows Herne
Priory Ct Est E17 47 DZ54
Priory Cres SE19 122 DQ94
Priory Cres, Sutt. 157 CX105
Priory Cres, Wem. 61 CG62
Priory Dr SE2 106 EX78
Priory Dr, Stan. 41 CF48
Priory Fld Dr, Edg. 42 CP49
Priory Flds (Farningham), Dart. 148 FM103
Priory Gdns N6 65 DH58
Priory Gdns SE25 142 DT98
Priory Gdns SW13 99 CT83
Priory Gdns W4 98 CS77
Priory Gdns W5 80 CL69
Hanger La
Priory Gdns, Ashf. 115 BR92
Priory Gdns, Dart. 128 FK85
Priory Gdns, Hmptn. 116 BZ94
Priory Gdns (Harefield), Uxb. 58 BJ56
Priory Gdns, Wem. 61 CG63
Priory Gate, Wal.Cr. 15 DZ27
Priory Grn, Stai. 114 BH92
Priory Grn Est N1 83 DM68
Priory Gro SW8 101 DL81
Priory Gro, Rom. 52 FL48
Priory Hill, Dart. 128 FK85
Priory Hill, Wem. 61 CG63
Priory La SW15 118 CS86
Priory La (Farningham), Dart. 148 FM102
Priory La, Rich. 98 CN80
Forest Rd
Priory La, W.Mol. 136 CB98
Priory Ms SW8 101 DK81
Priory Ms, Horn. 71 FH60
Priory Ms, Stai. 114 BH92
Chestnut Manor Cl
Priory Pk SE3 104 EF83
Priory Pk Rd NW6 81 CZ67
Priory Pk Rd, Wem. 61 CG63
Priory Path, Rom. 52 FL48
Priory Pl, Dart. 128 FK86
Priory Pl, Walt. 135 BU104
Priory Rd E6 86 EK67
Priory Rd N8 65 DK56
Priory Rd NW6 82 DB67
Priory Rd SW19 120 DD94
Priory Rd W4 98 CR76
Priory Rd, Bark. 87 ER66
Priory Rd, Chess. 138 CL104
Priory Rd, Croy. 141 DN101
Priory Rd, Dart. 108 FK84
Priory Rd (Chalfont St. Peter), Ger.Cr. 56 AW55
Priory Rd, Hmptn. 116 BZ94
Priory Rd, Houns. 116 CC85
Priory Rd, Loug. 32 EL42
Priory Rd, Rich. 98 CN79
Priory Rd, Rom. 52 FL48
Priory Rd, Sutt. 157 CX105
Priory Shop Cen, Dart. 128 FL86
Priory St E3 85 EB69
St. Leonards St
Priory Ter NW6 82 DB67
Priory Ter, Sun. 115 BU94
Staines Rd E
Priory Vw, Bushey 41 CE45
Priory Wk SW10 100 DC78
Priory Way (Chalfont St. Peter), Ger.Cr. 56 AX55
Priory Way, Har. 60 CB56
Priory Way, Slou. 92 AV80
Priory Way, Sthl. 96 BX76
Priory Way, West Dr. 94 BL79
Pritchard's Rd E2 84 DU67
Priter Rd SE16 202 C7
Priter Rd SE16 102 DU76
Priter Way SE16 102 DU76
Dockley Rd
Private Rd, Enf. 30 DS43
Probert Rd SW2 121 DN85
Probyn Rd SW2 121 DP89
Procter St WC1 196 B7
Procter St WC1 83 DM71
Proctor Cl, Mitch. 140 DG95
Proctors Cl, Felt. 115 BU88
Profumo Rd, Walt. 154 BX106
Progress Business Pk, Croy. 141 DM103
Progress Way N22 45 DN53
Progress Way, Croy. 141 DM103
Progress Way, Enf. 30 DU43
Promenade, The W4 98 CS81
Promenade App Rd W4 98 CS80
Promenade de Verdun, Pur. 159 DK111
Promenade Mans, Edg. 42 CP50
Hale La
Prospect Business Pk, Loug. 33 EQ42
Prospect Cl SE26 122 DV91
Prospect Cl, Belv. 106 FA77
Prospect Cl, Houns. 96 BZ81
Prospect Cl, Ruis. 60 BX59
Prospect Cotts SW18 100 DA84
Point Pleasant
Prospect Cres, Twick. 116 CC86
Prospect Gro, Grav. 131 GK87
Prospect Hill E17 67 EB56
Prospect La, Egh. 112 AT92
Prospect Pl E1 202 F2
Prospect Pl E1 84 DW74
Prospect Pl N2 64 DD56
Prospect Pl N17 46 DS53
Prospect Pl NW2 63 CZ62
Ridge Rd
Prospect Pl NW3 64 DC63
Holly Wk
Prospect Pl, Brom. 144 EH97
Prospect Pl, Dart. 128 FL86
Prospect Pl, Epsom 156 CS113
Clayton Rd
Prospect Pl, Grav. 131 GK87
Prospect Pl, Grays 110 GB79
Prospect Pl, Rom. 51 FC54
Prospect Pl, Stai. 113 BF92
Prospect Quay SW18 100 DA84
Point Pleasant
Prospect Ring N2 64 DD55
Prospect Rd NW2 63 CZ62
Prospect Rd, Barn. 28 DA43
Prospect Rd, Horn. 72 FM55
Prospect Rd, Sev. 191 FJ123
Prospect Rd, Surb. 137 CJ100
Prospect Rd (Cheshunt), Wal.Cr. 14 DW29
Prospect Rd, Wdf.Grn. 48 EJ50
Prospect St SE16 202 E6
Prospect Vale SE18 104 EL77
Prospect Way, Brwd. 55 GE42
Prospero Rd N19 65 DJ60
Prossers, Tad. 173 CX121
Croffets
Protea Cl E16 86 EF70
Hermit Rd
Prothero Gdns NW4 63 CV57
Prothero Ho NW10 80 CR66
Prothero Rd SW6 99 CY80
Prout Gro NW10 62 CS63
Prout Rd E5 66 DV62
Provence St N1 84 DQ68
St. Peters St
Providence Ct W1 194 G10
Providence Ct W1 82 DG73
Providence La, Hayes 95 BR80
Providence Pl N1 83 DP67
Upper St
Providence Pl, Epsom 156 CS112
Providence Pl, Rom. 50 EZ54
Providence Pl, Wok. 152 BG114
Providence Rd, West Dr. 76 BL74
Providence Row N1 196 B1
Providence Row Cl E2 84 DV69
Ainsley St
Providence Sq SE1 102 DT75
Mill St
Providence St N1 84 DQ68
St. Peters St
Providence St, Green. 129 FU85
Providence Yd E2 84 DU69
Ezra St
Provident Ind Est, Hayes 95 BU75
Provost Est N1 197 K2
Provost Est N1 84 DR68
Provost Rd NW3 82 DF66
Provost St N1 197 K3
Provost St N1 84 DR69
Prowse Av, Bushey 40 CC47
Prowse Pl NW1 83 DH66
Bonny St
Pruden Cl N14 45 DJ47
Prudent Pas EC2 197 J8
Prune Hill, Egh. 112 AX94
Prusom St E1 202 E3
Prusom St E1 84 DV74
Pryor Cl, Abb.L. 7 BT32
Pryors, The NW3 64 DD62
Puck La, Wal.Abb. 15 ED29
Puddenhole Cotts, Bet. 182 CN133
Pudding La EC3 201 L1
Pudding La EC3 84 DR73
Pudding La, Chig. 49 ET46
Pudding La, Sev. 191 FN121
Church St
Pudding Mill La E15 85 EB67
Puddle Dock EC4 196 G10
Puddledock La, Dart. 127 FE9
Puddledock La, West. 189 ET13
Puers La, Beac. 36 AS5
Puffin Cl, Bark. 87 ES6
Thames Rd
Puffin Cl, Beck. 143 DX9
Puffin Ter, Ilf. 69 EN5
Tiptree Cres
Pulborough Rd SW18 119 CZ8
Pulborough Way, Houns. 96 BW8
Pulford Rd N15 66 DR5
Pulham Av N2 64 DC5
Puller Rd, Barn. 27 CY4
Pulleyns Av E6 86 EL6
Pullman Ct SW2 121 DL8
Pullman Gdns SW15 119 CW8
Pullman Pl SE9 124 EL8
Pullmans Pl, Stai. 114 BG9
Pulross Rd SW9 101 DM8
Pulteney Cl E3 85 DZ6
Pulteney Gdns E18 68 EH5
Pulteney Rd
Pulteney Rd E18 68 EH5
Pulteney Ter N1 83 DM6
Pulton Pl SW6 100 DA8
Puma Ct E1 197 F
Pump All, Brent. 97 CK8
Pump Cl, Nthlt. 78 CA6
Union Rd
Pump Ct EC4 196 D
Pump Hill, Loug. 33 EM4
Pump Ho Cl, Brom. 144 EF9
Pump La SE14 102 DW8
Farrow La
Pump La, Chesh. 4 AS3
Pump La, Hayes 95 BU7
Pump La, Orp. 165 FB10
Pump Pail N, Croy. 142 DQ10
Old Town
Pump Pail S, Croy. 142 DQ10
Southbridge Rd
Pumping Sta Rd W4 98 CS8
Pundersons Gdns E2 84 DV
Punjab La, Sthl. 78 BZ
Herbert Rd
Purbeck Av, N.Mal. 139 CT10
Purbeck Cl, Red. 185 DK12
Purbeck Dr NW2 63 CY6
Purbeck Dr, Wok. 151 AZ1
Purbeck Rd, Horn. 71 FG6
Purberry Gro, Epsom 157 CT1
Purbrock Av, Wat. 24 BW3
Purbrook Est SE1 201 N
Purbrook St SE1 201 N
Purbrook St SE1 102 DS7
Purcell Cl, Borwd. 25 CK3
Purcell Cl, Ken. 160 DR1
Purcell Cres SW6 99 CY8
Purcell Ms NW10 80 CS
Suffolk Rd
Purcell Rd, Grnf. 78 CB7
Purcell St N1 84 DS
Purcells Av, Edg. 42 CN
Purcells Cl, Ash. 172 CM1
Albert Rd
Purchese St NW1 83 DK
Purdy St E3 85 EB7
Purelake Ms SE13 103 ED
Purfleet Bypass, Purf. 108 FP7
Purfleet Deep Wf, Purf. 108 FQ
Purfleet Ind Pk, S.Ock. 108 FM7
Purfleet Rd, S.Ock. 108 FN
Purland Cl, Dag. 70 EZ
Purland Rd SE28 105 ET
Purleigh Av, Wdf.Grn. 48 EL
Purley Av NW2 63 CY
Purley Bury Av, Pur. 160 DQ1
Purley Bury Cl, Pur. 160 DQ1
Purley Cl, Ilf. 49 EN
Purley Downs Rd, Pur. 160 DQ1
Purley Downs Rd, S.Croy. 160 DR1
Purley Hill, Pur. 159 DP1
Purley Knoll, Pur. 159 DM1
Purley Oaks Rd, S.Croy. 160 DR1
Purley Par, Pur. 159 DN1
High St
Purley Pk Rd, Pur. 159 DP1
Purley Pl N1 83 DP
Islington Pk St
Purley Ri, Pur. 159 DM1
Purley Rd N9 46 DR
Purley Rd, Pur. 159 DN1
Purley Rd, S.Croy. 160 DR1
Purley Vale, Pur. 159 DP1
Purley Way, Croy. 141 DM1
Purley Way, Pur. 159 DN1
Purley Way Cres, Croy. 141 DM1
Purley Way
Purlieu Way, Epp. 33 ES
Purlings Rd, Bushey 24 CB
Purneys Rd SE9 104 EK
Purrett Rd SE18 105 ET
Purser's Cross Rd SW6 99 CZ
Pursewardens Cl W13 79 CJ
Pursley Gdns, Borwd. 26 CN
Pursley Rd NW7 43 CV
Purves Rd NW10 81 CW
Puteaux Ho E2 85 DX
Putney Br SW6 99 CY
Putney Br SW15 99 CY
Putney Br App SW6 99 CY
Putney Br Rd SW15 99 CY
Putney Br Rd SW18 120 DA
Putney Common SW15 99 CW
Putney Gdns, Rom. 70 EV
Heathfield Pk Dr
Putney Heath SW15 119 CW
Putney Heath La SW15 119 CX
Putney High St SW15 99 CX
Putney Hill SW15 119 CX
Putney Pk Av SW15 99 CU
Putney Pk La SW15 99 CV
Putney Rd, Enf. 31 DX
Puttenham Cl, Wat. 40 BW
Pycroft Way N9 46 DT
Pye Cl, Cat. 176 DR1
St. Lawrence Way
Pyecombe Cor N12 43 CZ
Pyghtle, The (Denham), Uxb. 58 BG
Pylbrook Rd, Sutt. 140 DA1

Pyle Hill, Wok. 166 AX124
Pylon Way, Croy. 141 DL102
Pym Cl, Barn. 28 DD43
Pym Orchard, West. 180 EW124
Pym Pl, Grays 110 GA77
Pymers Mead SE21 122 DQ88
Pymmes Cl N13 45 DM50
Pymmes Cl N17 46 DV53
Pymmes Gdns N N9 46 DT48
Pymmes Gdns S N9 46 DT48
Pymmes Grn Rd N11 45 DH49
Pymmes Rd N13 45 DL51
Pymms Brook Dr, Barn. 28 DE42
Pynchester Cl, Uxb. 58 BN61
Pyne Rd, Surb. 138 CN102
Pyne Ter SW19 119 CX88
Windlesham Gro
Pynest Grn La, Wal.Abb. 32 EG38
Pynfolds SE16 202 E5
Pynham Cl SE2 106 EU76
Pynnacles Cl, Stan. 41 CH50
Pyrcroft La, Wey. 153 BP106
Pyrcroft Rd, Cher. 133 BF101
Pyrford Common Rd, Wok. 167 BD116
Pyrford Ct, Wok. 167 BE117
Pyrford Heath, Wok. 167 BF116
Pyrford Lock, Wok. 168 BJ116
Pyrford Rd, W.Byf. 152 BG113
Pyrford Rd, Wok. 152 BG114
Pyrford Wds Cl, Wok. 167 BF115
Pyrford Wds Rd, Wok. 167 BE115
Pyrland Rd N5 66 DR64
Pyrland Rd, Rich. 118 CM86
Pyrles Grn, Loug. 33 EP39
Pyrles La, Loug. 33 EP40
Pyrmont Gro SE27 121 DP90
Pyrmont Rd W4 98 CN79
Pyrmont Rd, Ilf. 69 EQ61
High Rd
Pytchley Cres SE19 122 DQ93
Pytchley Rd SE22 102 DS83

Q

Quad Rd, Wem. 61 CK62
Courtenay Rd
Quadrangle, The W2 194 B8
Quadrangle Ms, Stan. 41 CJ52
Quadrant, The SE24 122 DQ85
Herne Hill
Quadrant, The SW20 139 CY95
Quadrant, The, Bexh. 106 EX80
Quadrant, The, Epsom 156 CS113
Quadrant, The, Purf. 108 FQ77
Quadrant, The, Rich. 98 CL84
Quadrant, The, Sutt. 158 DC107
Quadrant Arc W1 199 L1
Quadrant Arc, Rom. 71 FE57
Quadrant Gro NW5 64 DF64
Quadrant Rd, Rich. 97 CK84
Quadrant Rd, Th.Hth. 141 DP98
Quadrant Way, Wey. 152 BM105
Portmore Pk Rd
Quaggy Wk SE3 104 EG84
Quail Gdns, S.Croy. 161 DY110
Quainton St NW10 62 CR62
Quaker Cl, Sev. 191 FK123
Quaker Ct E1 197 P5
Quaker La, Sthl. 96 CA76
Quaker La, Wal.Abb. 15 EC34
Quaker St E1 197 P5
Quaker St E1 84 DT70
Quakers Course NW9 43 CT53
Quakers Hall La, Sev. 191 FJ122
Quakers La, Islw. 97 CG81
Quakers La, Pot.B. 12 DB30
Quaker's Pl E7 68 EK64
Quakers Wk N21 30 DR44
Quality Ct WC2 196 D8
Quality Ct WC2 83 DN72
Quality St, Red. 185 DH128
Quantock Cl, Hayes 95 BR80
Quantock Cl, Slou. 93 BA78
Quantock Dr, Wor.Pk. 139 CW103
Quantock Gdns NW2 63 CX61
Quantock Rd, Bexh. 107 FE82
Cumbrian Av
Quarles Cl, Rom. 50 FA52
Quarley Way SE15 102 DT80
Daniel Gdns
Quarr Rd, Cars. 140 DD100
Quarrendon St SW6 100 DA82
Quarry, The, Bet. 182 CS132
Station Rd
Quarry Cl, Lthd. 171 CK121
Quarry Cl, Oxt. 188 EE130
Quarry Cotts, Sev. 190 FG123
Quarry Gdns, Lthd. 171 CK121
Quarry Hill, Grays 110 GA78
Quarry Hill, Sev. 191 FK123
Quarry Hill Pk, Reig. 184 DC131
Quarry Ms, Purf. 108 FN77
Fanns Ri
Quarry Pk Rd, Sutt. 157 CZ107
Quarry Ri, Sutt. 157 CZ107
Quarry Rd SW18 120 DC86
Quarry Rd, Gdse. 186 DW128
Quarry Rd, Oxt. 188 EE130
Quarryside Business Pk, Red. 185 DH130
Quarter Mile La E10 67 EB63
Quarterdeck, The E14 203 P5
Quarterdeck, The E14 103 EA75
Quartermaine Av, Wok. 167 AZ122
Quaves Rd, Slou. 92 AV76
Quay La, Green. 109 FV84
Quay W, Tedd. 117 CH92
Quebec Av, West. 189 ER126
Quebec Ms W1 194 E9
Quebec Rd, Hayes 78 BW73
Quebec Rd, Ilf. 69 EP59
Quebec Rd, Til. 111 GG82
Quebec Sq, West. 189 ER126
Quebec Way SE16 203 J5
Quebec Way SE16 103 DX75
Queen Adelaide Rd SE20 122 DW93
Queen Alexandra's Ct SW19 119 CZ92
Queen Alexandra's Way, Epsom 156 CN112
Queen Anne Av N15 66 DT57
Suffield Rd
Queen Anne Av, Brom. 144 EF97
Queen Anne Dr, Esher 155 CE108
Queen Anne Ms W1 195 J7
Queen Anne Rd E9 85 DX65
Queen Anne St W1 195 H8
Queen Anne St W1 83 DH72
Queen Anne Ter E1 202 E1
Queen Anne's Cl, Twick. 117 CD90
Queen Anne's Gdns W4 98 CS76
Queen Annes Gdns W5 98 CL75
Queen Annes Gdns, Enf. 30 DS44
Queen Annes Gdns, Lthd. 171 CH121
Upper Fairfield Rd
Queen Anne's Gdns, Mitch. 140 DF97
Queen Anne's Gate SW1 199 M5
Queen Anne's Gate SW1 101 DK75
Queen Anne's Gate, Bexh. 106 EX83
Queen Anne's Gro W4 98 CS76
Queen Annes Gro W5 98 CL75
Queen Annes Gro, Enf. 46 DR45
Queen Anne's Ms, Lthd. 171 CH121
Fairfield Rd
Queen Annes Pl, Enf. 30 DS44
Queen Annes Ter, Lthd. 171 CH121
Upper Fairfield Rd
Queen Anne's Wk WC1 83 DL70
Guilford St
Queen Caroline Est W6 99 CW78
Queen Caroline St W6 99 CW77
Queen Elizabeth Ct, Brox. 15 DZ26
Groom Rd
Queen Elizabeth Ct, Wal.Abb. 31 EC40
Sewardstone Rd
Queen Elizabeth Gdns, Mord. 140 DA98
Queen Elizabeth Pl, Til. 111 GG84
Queen Elizabeth Rd E17 67 DY55
Queen Elizabeth Rd, Kings.T. 138 CM95
Queen Elizabeth II Br, Dart. 109 FR82
Queen Elizabeth II Br, Grays 109 FR82
Queen Elizabeth St SE1 201 N4
Queen Elizabeth St SE1 102 DT75
Queen Elizabeth Wk SW13 99 CV81
Queen Elizabeth Wk, Wind. 92 AS82
Queen Elizabeth Way, Wok. 167 AZ119
Queen Elizabeths Cl N16 66 DR61
Queen Elizabeths Dr N14 45 DL46
Queen Elizabeth's Dr, Croy. 161 ED110
Queen Elizabeth's Gdns, Croy. 161 ED110
Queen Elizabeth's Dr
Queen Elizabeths Wk N16 66 DR61
Queen Elizabeth's Wk, Wall. 159 DK105
Queen Margaret's Gro N1 66 DS64
Queen Mary Av, Mord. 139 CX99
Queen Mary Cl, Rom. 71 FF58
Queen Mary Cl, Surb. 138 CN104
Queen Mary Cl, Wok. 167 BC116
Queen Mary Rd SE19 121 DP93
Queen Mary Rd, Shep. 135 BQ96
Queen Mary's Av, Cars. 158 DF108
Queen Marys Av, Wat. 23 BS42
Queen Marys Ct, Wal.Abb. 31 EC40
Sewardstone Rd
Queen Marys Dr, Add. 151 BF110
Queen Mother's Dr (Denham), Uxb. 57 BF58
Queen of Denmark Ct SE16 203 M6
Queen of Denmark Ct SE16 103 DZ76
Queen Sq WC1 196 A5
Queen Sq WC1 83 DL70
Queen Sq Pl WC1 196 A5
Queen St EC4 197 J10
Queen St EC4 84 DQ73
Queen St N17 46 DS51
Queen St W1 199 H2
Queen St W1 83 DH74
Queen St, Bexh. 106 EZ83
Queen St, Brwd. 54 FW50
Queen St, Cher. 134 BG102
Queen St, Croy. 142 DQ104
Church Rd
Queen St, Erith 107 FE79
Queen St, Grav. 131 GH86
Queen St, Kings L. 6 BG32
Queen St, Rom. 71 FD58
Queen St Pl EC4 201 J1
Queen Victoria Av, Wem. 79 CK66
Queen Victoria St EC4 196 G10
Queen Victoria St EC4 83 DP73
Queen Victoria Ter E1 202 E1
Queen Victoria's Wk, Wind. 92 AS81
Queenborough Gdns, Chis. 125 ER93
Queenborough Gdns, Ilf. 69 EN56
Queendale Ct, Wok. 166 AT116
Roundthorn Way
Queenhill Rd, S.Croy. 160 DV110
Queenhithe EC4 197 J10
Queenhithe EC4 84 DQ73
Queens Acre, Sutt. 157 CX108
Queens All, Epp. 17 ET31
Queens Av N3 44 DC52
Queens Av N10 64 DG55
Queens Av N20 44 DD47
Queen's Av N21 45 DP46
Queens Av, Felt. 116 BW91
Queens Av, Grnf. 78 CB72
Queens Av, Stan. 61 CJ55
Queens Av, Wat. 23 BT42
Queens Av, W.Byf. 152 BK112
Queens Av, Wdf.Grn. 48 EH50
Queen's Circ SW8 101 DH80
Queenstown Rd
Queen's Circ SW11 101 DH80
Queenstown Rd
Queens Cl, Edg. 42 CN50
Queens Cl, Tad. 173 CU124
Queens Cl, Wall. 159 DH106
Queens Rd
Queens Cl, Wind. 112 AU85
Queens Club Gdns W14 99 CY79
Queens Ct SE23 122 DW88
Queens Ct, Rich. 118 CM86
Queens Ct, Slou. 74 AT73
Queens Ct, Wey. 153 BR106
Queens Ct, Wok. 167 AZ118
Hill Vw Rd
Queens Ct Ride, Cob. 153 BU113
Queens Cres NW5 82 DG65
Queens Cres, Rich. 118 CM85
Queens Dr E10 67 EA59
Queens Dr N4 65 DP61
Queens Dr W3 80 CM72
Queens Dr W5 80 CM72
Queens Dr, Abb.L. 7 BT32
Queens Dr, Lthd. 154 CC111
Queen's Dr, Slou. 75 AZ66
Queens Dr, Surb. 138 CN101
Queens Dr, T.Ditt. 137 CG101
Queens Dr, Wal.Cr. 15 EA34
Queens Dr, The, Rick. 37 BF45
Queens Elm Par SW3 100 DD78
Old Ch St
Queen's Elm Sq SW3 100 DD78
Old Ch St
Queens Gdns NW4 63 CW57
Queens Gdns W2 82 DC73
Queens Gdns W5 79 CJ70
Queens Gdns, Dart. 128 FP88
Queen's Gdns, Houns. 96 BY81
Queens Gdns, Rain. 89 FD68
Queens Gdns, Upmin. 73 FT58
Queen's Gate SW7 100 DC76
Queen's Gate Gdns SW7 100 DC76
Queens Gate Gdns SW15 99 CV84
Upper Richmond Rd
Queen's Gate Ms SW7 100 DC75
Queen's Gate Pl SW7 100 DC76
Queen's Gate Pl Ms SW7 100 DC76
Queen's Gate Ter SW7 100 DC76
Queen's Gro NW8 82 DD67
Queen's Gro Ms NW8 82 DD67
Queens Gro Rd E4 47 ED46
Queen's Head St N1 83 DP67
Queens Head Yd SE1 201 K3
Queens Ho, Tedd. 117 CF93
Queens La N10 65 DH55
Queens La, Ashf. 114 BM91
Clarendon Rd
Queens Mkt E13 86 EJ67
Green St
Queens Ms W2 82 DB73
Queens Par N11 44 DF50
Colney Hatch La
Queens Par W5 80 CM72
Queens Par Cl N11 44 DF50
Colney Hatch La
Queens Pk Ct W10 81 CX69
Queens Pk Gdns, Felt. 115 BU90
Vernon Rd
Queens Pk Rd, Cat. 176 DS123
Queens Pk Rd, Rom. 52 FM53
Queens Pas, Chis. 125 EP93
High St
Queens Pl, Mord. 140 DA98
Queens Pl, Wat. 24 BW41
Queen's Prom, Kings.T. 137 CK97
Portsmouth Rd
Queens Reach, E.Mol. 137 CE98
Queens Ride SW13 99 CU83
Queens Ride SW15 99 CU83
Queen's Ride, Rich. 118 CP88
Queens Ri, Rich. 118 CM86
Queens Rd E11 67 ED59
Queens Rd E13 86 EH67
Queen's Rd E17 67 DZ58
Queens Rd N3 44 DC53
Queens Rd N9 46 DV48
Queen's Rd N11 45 DL52
Queens Rd NW4 63 CW57
Queens Rd SE14 102 DV81
Queens Rd SE15 102 DV81
Queens Rd SW14 98 CR83
Queens Rd SW19 119 CZ93
Queens Rd W5 80 CL72
Queens Rd, Bark. 87 EQ65
Queens Rd, Barn. 27 CX41
Queens Rd, Beck. 143 DY96
Queens Rd, Brwd. 54 FW48
Queens Rd, Brom. 144 EG96
Queens Rd, Buck.H. 48 EH47
Queens Rd, Chis. 125 EP93
Queen's Rd, Croy. 141 DP100
Queens Rd, Egh. 113 AZ93
Queens Rd, Enf. 30 DS42
Queens Rd, Epp. 19 FB26
Queen's Rd, Erith 107 FE79
Queens Rd, Felt. 115 BV88
Queens Rd, Grav. 131 GJ90
Queens Rd, Hmptn. 116 CB91
Queens Rd, Hayes 77 BS72
Queen's Rd, Houns. 96 CB83
Queens Rd, Kings.T. 118 CN94
Queens Rd, Loug. 32 EL41
Queens Rd, Mitch. 140 DD97
Queens Rd, Mord. 140 DA98
Queens Rd, N.Mal. 139 CT98
Queens Rd, Rich. 118 CL87
Queen's Rd, Slou. 74 AT73
Queens Rd (Datchet), Slou. 92 AU81
Queens Rd, Sthl. 96 BX75
Queens Rd, Sutt. 158 DA110
Queen's Rd, Tedd. 117 CF93
Queen's Rd, T.Ditt. 137 CF99
Queens Rd, Twick. 117 CF88
Queen's Rd, Uxb. 76 BJ69
Queens Rd, Wall. 159 DH106
Queens Rd, Wal.Cr. 15 DY34
Queens Rd, Walt. 153 BV106
Queens Rd, Wat. 24 BW42
Queen's Rd, Well. 106 EV82
Queens Rd, West Dr. 94 BM75
Queens Rd, Wey. 153 BQ105
Queens Rd W E13 86 EG68
Queen's Row SE17 102 DR79
Queens Ter E13 86 EH67
Queen's Ter NW8 82 DD68
Queens Ter, Islw. 97 CG84
Queens Ter Cotts W7 97 CE75
Boston Rd
Queens Wk E4 47 ED46
The Grn Wk
Queens Wk NW9 62 CQ61
Queen's Wk SW1 199 K3
Queen's Wk SW1 83 DJ74
Queens Wk W5 79 CJ70
Queens Wk, Ashf. 114 BK91
Queen's Wk, Har. 61 CE56
Queens Wk, Ruis. 60 BX62
Queen's Wk, The SE1 201 N2
Queen's Wk, The SE1 84 DS74
Queens Way NW4 63 CW57
Queens Way, Croy. 159 DM107
Queens Way, Felt. 116 BW91
Queens Way, Rad. 10 CL32
Queens Way, Wal.Cr. 15 DZ34
Queens Well Av N20 44 DE48
Queen's Wd Rd N10 65 DH58
Queens Yd WC1 195 L5
Queensberry Ms W SW7 100 DD77
Queen's Gate
Queensberry Pl SW7 100 DD77
Queensberry Way SW7 100 DD77
Harrington Rd
Queensborough Ms W2 82 DC73
Porchester Ter
Queensborough Pas W2 82 DC73
Porchester Ter
Queensborough S Bldgs W2 82 DC73
Porchester Ter
Queensborough Studios W2 82 DC73
Porchester Ter
Queensborough Ter W2 82 DB73
Queensbridge Pk, Islw. 117 CE85
Queensbridge Rd E2 84 DT67
Queensbridge Rd E8 84 DT66
Queensbury Circle Par, Har. 62 CL55
Streatfield Rd
Queensbury Circle Par, Stan. 62 CL55
Streatfield Rd
Queensbury Pl, Rich. 117 CK85
Friars La
Queensbury Rd NW9 62 CR59
Queensbury Rd, Wem. 80 CM68
Queensbury Sta Par, Edg. 62 CM55
Queensbury St N1 84 DQ66
Queenscourt, Wem. 62 CL63
Queenscroft Rd SE9 124 EK85
Queensdale Cres W11 81 CX74
Queensdale Pl W11 81 CY74
Queensdale Rd W11 81 CX74
Queensdale Wk W11 81 CY74
Queensdown Rd E5 66 DV63
Queensferry Wk N17 66 DV56
Jarrow Rd
Queensgate, Cob. 154 BX112
Queensgate, Wal.Cr. 15 DZ34
Queensgate Gdns, Chis. 145 ER95
Queensgate Pl NW6 82 DA66
Queensland Av N18 46 DQ51
Queensland Av SW19 140 DB95
Queensland Pl N7 65 DN63
Queensland Rd
Queensland Rd N7 65 DN63
Queensmead NW8 82 DD67
Queensmead, Lthd. 154 CC111
Queensmead, Slou. 92 AV81
Queensmead Av, Epsom 157 CV110
Queensmead Rd, Brom. 144 EF96
Queensmere Cl SW19 119 CX89
Queensmere Rd SW19 119 CX89
Queensmere Rd, Slou. 92 AU75
Wellington St
Queensmere Shop Cen, Slou. 92 AT75
Queensmere Shop Cen, Slou. 92 AT75
High St
Queensmill Rd SW6 99 CX80
Queensthorpe Rd SE26 123 DX91
Queenstown Gdns, Rain. 89 FF69
Queenstown Ms SW8 101 DH82
Queenstown Rd
Queenstown Rd SW8 101 DH79
Queensville Rd SW12 121 DK87
Queensway W2 82 DB72
Queensway, Enf. 30 DV42
Queensway, Orp. 145 EQ99
Queensway, Red. 184 DF133
Queensway, Sun. 135 BV96
Queensway, W.Wick. 144 EE104
Queensway, The (Chalfont St. Peter), Ger.Cr. 56 AX55
Queensway N, Walt. 154 BW105
Robinsway
Queensway S, Walt. 154 BW106
Trenchard Cl
Queenswood Av E17 47 EC53
Queenswood Av, Brwd. 55 GD43
Queenswood Av, Hmptn. 116 CB93
Queenswood Av, Houns. 96 BZ82
Queenswood Av, Th.Hth. 141 DN99
Queenswood Av, Wall. 159 DK105
Queenswood Cres, Wat. 7 BU33
Queenswood Gdns E11 68 EH60
Queenswood Pk N3 43 CY54
Queenswood Rd SE23 123 DX90
Queenswood Rd, Sid. 125 ET85
Quemerford Rd N7 65 DM64
Quendon Dr, Wal.Abb. 15 ED33
Quennel Way, Brwd. 55 GC45
Quennell Cl, Ash. 172 CL119
Parkers La
Quentin Pl SE13 104 EE83
Quentin Rd SE13 104 EE83
Quentin Way, Vir.W. 132 AV98
Quernmore Cl, Brom. 124 EG93
Quernmore Rd N4 65 DN58
Quernmore Rd, Brom. 124 EG93
Querrin St SW6 100 DC82
Quex Ms NW6 82 DA67
Quex Rd
Quex Rd NW6 82 DA67
Quick Pl N1 83 DP67
Quick Rd W4 98 CS78
Quick St N1 196 G1
Quick St N1 83 DP68
Quick St Ms N1 196 F1
Quickley La, Rick. 21 BB44
Quickley Ri, Rick. 21 BC44
Quickmoor La, Kings L. 6 BH33
Quicks Rd SW19 120 DB94
Quickswood NW3 82 DE66
King Henry's Rd
Quickwood Cl, Rick. 22 BG44
Quiet Cl, Add. 152 BG105
Quiet Nook, Brom. 144 EK104
Croydon Rd
Quill Hall La, Amer. 20 AT37
Quill La SW15 99 CX84
Quill St N4 65 DN62
Quill St W5 80 CL69
Quillot, The, Walt. 153 BT106
Quilp St SE1 201 H4
Quilter Gdns, Orp. 146 EW102
Quilter Rd, Orp. 146 EW102
Quilter St E2 84 DU69
Quilter St SE18 105 ET78
Quilting Ct SE16 103 DX75
Garter Way
Quinbrookes, Slou. 74 AW72
Quince Tree Cl, S.Ock. 91 FW70
Quincy Rd, Egh. 113 BA92
Quinta Dr, Barn. 27 CV43
Quintin Av SW20 139 CZ95
Quintin Cl, Pnr. 59 BV57
High Rd
Quinton Cl, Beck. 143 EC97
Quinton Cl, Houns. 95 BV80
Quinton Cl, Wall. 159 DH105
Quinton Rd, T.Ditt. 137 CG102
Quinton St SW18 120 DC89
Quintrell Cl, Wok. 166 AV117
Quixley St E14 85 ED73
Quorn Rd SE22 102 DS84

R

Raans Rd, Amer. 20 AT38
Rabbit La, Walt. 153 BU108
Rabbit Row W8 82 DA74
Kensington Mall
Rabbits Rd E12 68 EL63
Rabbits Rd (South Darenth), Dart. 149 FR96
Rabies Heath Rd, Gdse. 186 DU134
Rabies Heath Rd, Red. 186 DS133
Rabournmead Dr, Nthlt. 60 BY64
Raby Rd, N.Mal. 138 CR98
Raby St E14 85 DY72
Salmon La
Raccoon Way, Houns. 96 BW82
Rachel Cl, Ilf. 69 ER55
Rachel Pt E5 66 DU63
Muir Rd
Rackham Cl, Well. 106 EV82
Rackham Ms SW16 121 DJ93
Westcote Rd
Racton Rd SW6 100 DA79
Radbourne Av W5 97 CJ77
Radbourne Cl E5 67 DX63
Overbury St
Radbourne Cres E17 47 ED54
Radbourne Rd SW12 121 DJ87
Radcliffe Av NW10 81 CU68
Radcliffe Av, Enf. 30 DQ39
Radcliffe Gdns, Cars. 158 DE108
Radcliffe Ms, Hmptn. 116 CC92
Taylor Cl
Radcliffe Path SW8 101 DJ82
St. Rule St
Radcliffe Rd N21 45 DP46
Radcliffe Rd SE1 201 N6
Radcliffe Rd, Croy. 142 DT103
Radcliffe Rd, Har. 41 CG54
Radcliffe Sq SW15 119 CX86
Radcliffe Way, Nthlt. 78 BX69
Radcot Av, Slou. 93 BB76
Radcot Pt SE23 123 DX90
Radcot St SE11 101 DN78
Raddington Rd W10 81 CY71
Radfield Way, Sid. 125 ER87
Radford Rd SE13 123 EC86
Radford Way, Bark. 87 ET69
Radipole Rd SW6 99 CZ81
Radius Pk, Felt. 95 BT84
Radland Rd E16 86 EF72
Radlet Av SE26 122 DV90
Radlett Cl E7 86 EF65
Radlett La, Rad. 25 CK35
Radlett Pk Rd, Rad. 9 CG34
Radlett Pl NW8 82 DE67
Radlett Rd, St.Alb. 9 CE28
Radlett Rd, Wat. 24 BW41
Radlett Rd (Aldenham), Wat. 25 CD36
Radley Av, Ilf. 69 ET63
Radley Cl, Felt. 115 BT88
Radley Ct SE16 203 J4
Radley Gdns, Har. 62 CL56
Radley Ho SE2 106 EX75
Wolvercote Rd
Radley Ms W8 100 DA76
Radley Rd N17 46 DS54

Radley's La E18 48 EG54
Radleys Mead, Dag. 89 FB65
Radlix Rd E10 67 EA60
Radnor Av, Har. 61 CE57
Radnor Av, Well. 126 EV85
Radnor Cl, Chis. 125 ES93
Homewood Cres
Radnor Cl, Mitch. 141 DL98
Radnor Cres SE18 106 EU80
Radnor Cres, Ilf. 69 EM57
Radnor Gdns, Enf. 30 DS39
Radnor Gdns, Twick. 117 CF89
Radnor Gro, Uxb. 76 BN68
Charnwood Rd
Radnor Ms W2 194 A9
Radnor Pl W2 194 B9
Radnor Pl W2 82 DE72
Radnor Rd NW6 81 CY67
Radnor Rd SE15 102 DU80
Radnor Rd, Har. 61 CD57
Radnor Rd, Twick. 117 CF89
Radnor Rd, Wey. 134 BN104
Radnor St EC1 197 J3
Radnor St EC1 84 DQ69
Radnor Ter W14 99 CZ77
Radnor Wk E14 204 A8
Radnor Wk SW3 100 DE78
Radnor Wk, Croy. 143 DZ100
Radnor Way NW10 80 CP70
Radnor Way, Slou. 92 AY77
Radolphs, Tad. 173 CX122
Heathcote
Radstock Av, Har. 61 CG55
Radstock St SW11 100 DE80
Radstock Way, Red. 185 DK128
Radstone Ct, Wok. 167 AZ118
Radwell Path, Borwd. 26 CL39
Cromwell Rd
Raebarn Gdns, Barn. 27 CV43
Raeburn Av, Dart. 127 FH85
Raeburn Av, Surb. 138 CP100
Raeburn Cl NW11 64 DC58
Raeburn Cl, Kings.T. 117 CK94
Raeburn Ct, Wok. 166 AU118
Martin Way
Raeburn Rd, Edg. 42 CN53
Raeburn Rd, Hayes 77 BR68
Raeburn Rd, Sid. 125 ES86
Raeburn St SW2 101 DL84
Rafford Way, Brom. 144 EH96
Raft Rd SW18 100 DA84
North Pas
Rag Hill Cl, West. 178 EL121
Rag Hill Rd, West. 178 EK121
Raggleswood, Chis. 145 EN95
Raglan Av, Wal.Cr. 15 DX34
Raglan Cl, Houns. 116 BY85
Vickers Way
Raglan Cl, Reig. 184 DC132
Raglan Ct SE12 124 EG85
Raglan Ct, S.Croy. 159 DP106
Raglan Ct, Wem. 62 CM63
Raglan Gdns, Wat. 39 BV46
Raglan Prec, Cat. 176 DS122
Raglan Rd E17 67 EC57
Raglan Rd SE18 105 EQ78
Raglan Rd, Belv. 106 EZ77
Raglan Rd, Brom. 144 EJ98
Raglan Rd, Enf. 46 DS45
Raglan Rd, Reig. 184 DB131
Raglan Rd, Wok. 166 AS118
Raglan St NW5 83 DH65
Raglan Ter, Har. 60 CB63
Raglan Way, Nthlt. 78 CC65
Ragley Cl W3 98 CQ75
Church Rd
Rags La (Cheshunt), Wal.Cr. 14 DS27
Rahn Rd, Epp. 18 EU31
Raider Cl, Rom. 50 FA53
Railey Ms NW5 65 DJ64
Railpit La, Warl. 178 EE115
Railshead Rd, Islw. 97 CH84
Railton Rd SE24 121 DN85
Railway App N4 65 DN58
Wightman Rd
Railway App SE1 201 L2
Railway App SE1 84 DR74
Railway App, Har. 61 CF56
Railway App, Twick. 117 CG87
Railway App, Wall. 159 DH107
Railway Av SE16 202 G4
Railway Av SE16 102 DW75
Railway Cotts, Wat. 23 BV39
Railway Ms E3 85 EA69
Wellington Way
Railway Ms W10 81 CY72
Ladbroke Gro
Railway Pas, Tedd. 117 CG93
Victoria Rd
Railway Pl SW19 119 CZ93
Hartfield Rd
Railway Pl, Belv. 106 FA76
Railway Pl, Grav. 131 GH87
Windmill St
Railway Ri SE22 102 DS84
Grove Vale
Railway Rd, Tedd. 117 CF91
Railway Rd, Wal.Cr. 15 DY33
Railway Side SW13 98 CS83
Railway Sq, Brwd. 54 FW48
Fairfield Rd
Railway St N1 196 A1
Railway St N1 83 DL68
Railway St, Grav. 130 GA85
Railway St, Rom. 70 EW60
Railway Ter SE13 123 EB85
Ladywell Rd
Railway Ter, Felt. 115 BU88
Railway Ter, Kings L. 6 BN27
Railway Ter, Slou. 74 AT74
Railway Ter, Stai. 113 BD92
Railway Ter, West. 189 ER125
Rainborough Cl NW10 80 CQ65
Rainbow Av E14 204 B10
Rainbow Av E14 103 EB78
Rainbow Ct, Wat. 24 BW44
Oxhey Rd
Rainbow Ct, Wok. 166 AS116
Langmans Way
Rainbow Ind Est, West Dr. 76 BK73
Rainbow Quay SE16 203 L7
Rainbow Quay SE16 103 DY76
Rainbow Rd, Grays 109 FW77
Rainbow St SE5 102 DS80
Raine St E1 202 E2
Raine St E1 84 DV74
Rainer Cl (Cheshunt), Wal.Cr. 15 DX29
Rainham Cl SE9 125 ER86
Rainham Cl SW11 120 DE86
Rainham Rd NW10 81 CW69
Rainham Rd, Rain. 89 FF66
Rainham Rd N, Dag. 71 FB61
Rainham Rd S, Dag. 71 FB63
Rainhill Way E3 85 EA69
Rainsborough Av SE8 203 K9
Rainsborough Av SE8 103 DY77
Rainsford Cl, Stan. 41 CJ50
Coverdale Cl
Rainsford Rd NW10 80 CP69
Rainsford St W2 194 B8
Rainsford Way, Horn. 71 FG60
Rainton Rd SE7 205 N10
Rainton Rd SE7 104 EG78
Rainville Rd W6 99 CW79
Raisins Hill, Pnr. 60 BW55
Raith Av N14 45 DK48
Raleana Rd E14 204 E2
Raleana Rd E14 85 EC74
Raleigh Av, Hayes 77 BV71
Raleigh Av, Wall. 159 DK105
Raleigh Cl NW4 63 CW57
Raleigh Cl, Erith 107 FF79
Raleigh Cl, Pnr. 60 BX59
Raleigh Cl, Ruis. 59 BT61
Raleigh Ct SE16 85 DX74
Rotherhithe St
Raleigh Ct, Stai. 114 BG91
Raleigh Ct, Wall. 159 DH107
Raleigh Dr N20 44 DE48
Raleigh Dr, Esher 155 CD106
Raleigh Dr, Surb. 138 CQ102
Raleigh Gdns SW2 121 DM86
Brixton Hill
Raleigh Gdns, Mitch. 140 DF96
Raleigh Ms N1 83 DP67
Queen's Head St
Raleigh Ms, Orp. 163 ET106
Osgood Av
Raleigh Rd N8 65 DN56
Raleigh Rd SE20 123 DX94
Raleigh Rd, Enf. 30 DR42
Raleigh Rd, Felt. 115 BT89
Raleigh Rd, Rich. 98 CM83
Raleigh Rd, Sthl. 96 BY78
Raleigh St N1 83 DP67
Raleigh Way N14 45 DK46
Raleigh Way, Felt. 116 BW92
Ralliwood Rd, Ash. 172 CN119
Ralph Ct W2 82 DB72
Queensway
Ralph Perring Ct, Beck. 143 EA98
Ralston St SW3 100 DF78
Tedworth Sq
Ralston Way, Wat. 40 BX47
Ram Pas, Kings.T. 137 CK96
High St
Ram Pl E9 84 DW65
Chatham Pl
Ram St SW18 120 DB85
Rama Cl SW16 121 DK94
Rama Ct, Har. 61 CE61
Ramac Way SE7 205 P9
Ramac Way SE7 104 EH77
Rambler Cl SW16 121 DJ91
Rambler La, Slou. 92 AW76
Rame Cl SW17 120 DG92
Ramilles Cl SW2 121 DL86
Ramillies Pl W1 195 K9
Ramillies Pl W1 83 DJ72
Ramillies Rd NW7 42 CS47
Ramillies Rd W4 98 CR77
Ramillies Rd, Sid. 126 EV86
Ramillies St W1 195 K9
Ramney Dr, Enf. 31 DY37
Ramornie Cl, Walt. 154 BZ106
Rampart St E1 84 DV72
Commercial Rd
Rampayne St SW1 199 M10
Rampayne St SW1 101 DK78
Rampton Cl E4 47 EA48
Rams Gro, Rom. 70 EY56
Ramsay Gdns, Rom. 52 FJ53
Ramsay Ms SW3 100 DE79
King's Rd
Ramsay Pl, Har. 61 CE60
Ramsay Rd E7 68 EE63
Ramsay Rd W3 98 CQ76
Ramscroft Cl N9 46 DS45
Ramsdale Rd SW17 120 DG92
Ramsden Cl, Orp. 146 EW102
Ramsden Dr, Rom. 50 FA52
Ramsden Rd N11 44 DF50
Ramsden Rd SW12 120 DG86
Ramsden Rd, Erith 107 FD80
Ramsden Rd, Orp. 146 EV101
Ramsey Cl NW9 63 CT58
West Hendon Bdy
Ramsey Cl, Grnf. 60 CC64
Ramsey Cl, Hat. 12 DD27
Ramsey Ho, Wem. 80 CL65
Ramsey Ms N4 65 DP62
Monsell Rd
Ramsey Rd, Th.Hth. 141 DM100
Ramsey St E2 84 DU70
Ramsey Wk N1 84 DR65
Clephane Rd
Ramsey Way N14 45 DJ45
Ramsgate Cl E16 205 P3
Ramsgate St E8 84 DT65
Dalston La
Ramsgill App, Ilf. 69 ET56
Ramsgill Dr, Ilf. 69 ET57
Ramulis Dr, Hayes 78 BX70
Ramus Wd Av, Orp. 163 ES106
Rancliffe Gdns SE9 104 EL84
Rancliffe Rd E6 86 EL68
Randall Av NW2 63 CT62
Randall Cl SW11 100 DE81
Randall Cl, Erith 107 FC79
Randall Cl, Slou. 93 AZ78
Randall Dr, Horn. 72 FJ63
Randall Pl SE10 103 EC80
Randall Rd SE11 200 B10
Randall Rd SE11 101 DM77
Randall Row SE11 200 B9
Randalls Cres, Lthd. 171 CG120
Randalls Dr, Brwd. 55 GE44
Randalls Pk Av, Lthd. 171 CG120
Randalls Pk Dr, Lthd. 171 CG121
Randalls Rd
Randalls Rd, Lthd. 171 CE119
Randalls Way, Lthd. 171 CG121
Randell's Rd N1 83 DL67
Randle Rd, Rich. 117 CJ91
Randles La, Sev. 180 EX115
Randlesdown Rd SE6 123 EA91
Randolph App E16 86 EK72
Randolph Av W9 82 DC70
Randolph Cl, Bexh. 107 FC83
Randolph Cl, Cob. 170 CA115
Randolph Cl, Kings.T. 118 CQ92
Randolph Cl, Wok. 166 AS117
Creston Av
Randolph Cres W9 82 DC70
Randolph Gdns NW6 82 DB68
Randolph Gro, Rom. 70 EW57
Donald Dr
Randolph Ho, Croy. 142 DQ102
Randolph Ms W9 82 DC70
Randolph Rd E17 67 EB57
Randolph Rd W9 82 DC70
Randolph Rd, Epsom 157 CT114
Randolph Rd, Slou. 92 AY76
Randolph Rd, Sthl. 96 BZ75
Randolph St NW1 83 DJ66
Randolph's La, West. 189 EP126
Randon Cl, Har. 40 CB54
Ranelagh Av SW6 99 CZ83
Ranelagh Av SW13 99 CU82
Ranelagh Br W2 82 DB71
Gloucester Ter
Ranelagh Cl, Edg. 42 CN49
Ranelagh Dr, Edg. 42 CN49
Ranelagh Dr, Twick. 117 CH85
Ranelagh Gdns E11 68 EJ57
Ranelagh Gdns SW6 99 CZ83
Ranelagh Gdns W4 98 CQ80
Grove Pk Gdns
Ranelagh Gdns W6 99 CT76
Ranelagh Gdns, Grav. 131 GF87
Ranelagh Gdns, Ilf. 69 EN60
Ranelagh Gro SW1 198 G10
Ranelagh Gro SW1 100 DG78
Ranelagh Ms W5 97 CK75
Ranelagh Rd
Ranelagh Pl, N.Mal. 138 CS99
Rodney Rd
Ranelagh Rd E6 87 EN67
Ranelagh Rd E11 68 EE63
Ranelagh Rd E15 86 EE67
Ranelagh Rd N17 66 DS55
Ranelagh Rd N22 45 DM53
Ranelagh Rd NW10 81 CT68
Ranelagh Rd SW1 101 DJ78
Lupus St
Ranelagh Rd W5 97 CK75
Ranelagh Rd, Red. 184 DE134
Ranelagh Rd, Sthl. 78 BX74
Ranelagh Rd, Wem. 61 CK64
Ranfurly Rd, Sutt. 140 DA103
Range Rd, Grav. 131 GL87
Range Way, Shep. 134 BN101
Rangefield Rd, Brom. 124 EE92
Rangemoor Rd N15 66 DT57
Ranger Wk, Add. 152 BH106
Monks Cres
Rangers Rd E4 48 EE45
Rangers Rd, Loug. 48 EE45
Rangers Sq SE10 103 ED81
Rangeworth Pl, Sid. 125 ET90
Priestlands Pk Rd
Rangoon St EC3 84 DT72
Northumberland All
Rankin Cl NW9 62 CS55
Ranleigh Gdns, Bexh. 106 EZ80
Ranmere St SW12 121 DH88
Ormeley Rd
Ranmoor Cl, Har. 61 CD56
Ranmoor Gdns, Har. 61 CD56
Ranmore Av, Croy. 142 DT104
Ranmore Cl, Red. 184 DG131
Ranmore Path, Orp. 146 EU98
Ranmore Rd, Sutt. 157 CX109
Rannoch Cl, Edg. 42 CP47
Rannoch Rd W6 99 CW79
Rannock Av NW9 62 CS59
Ranskill Rd, Borwd. 26 CN39
Ransom Cl, Wat. 40 BW45
Ransom Rd SE7 104 EJ78
Harvey Gdns
Ransom Wk SE7 104 EJ78
Woolwich Rd
Ranston Cl (Denham), Uxb. 57 BF58
Nightingale Way
Ranston St NW1 194 B6
Ranulf Rd NW2 63 CZ63
Ranwell Cl E3 85 DZ67
Beale Rd
Ranwell St E3 85 DZ67
Ranworth Cl, Erith 107 FE82
Ranworth Rd N9 46 DW47
Ranyard Cl, Chess. 138 CM104
Raphael Av, Rom. 71 FF55
Raphael Av, Til. 111 GG80
Raphael Cl, Rad. 10 CL32
Raphael Dr, T.Ditt. 137 CF101
Raphael Dr, Wat. 24 BX40
Raphael Rd, Grav. 131 GK87
Raphael St SW7 198 D5
Raphael St SW7 100 DF75
Rapier Cl, Purf. 108 FN77
Rasehill Cl, Rick. 22 BJ43
Rashleigh St SW8 101 DH82
Peardon St
Rashleigh Way (Horton Kirby), Dart. 148 FQ98
Rasper Rd N20 44 DC47
Rastell Av SW2 121 DK89
Ratcliff Rd E7 68 EJ64
Ratcliffe Cl SE12 124 EG87
Ratcliffe Cl, Uxb. 76 BK69
Ratcliffe Cross St E1 85 DX72
Ratcliffe La E14 85 DY72
Ratcliffe Orchard E1 85 DX73
Rathbone Mkt E16 86 EF71
Barking Rd
Rathbone Pl W1 195 M8
Rathbone Pl W1 83 DK72
Rathbone Pt E5 66 DU63
Nolan Way
Rathbone St E16 86 EF71
Rathbone St W1 195 L7
Rathbone St W1 83 DJ71
Rathcoole Av N8 65 DM56
Rathcoole Gdns N8 65 DM57
Rathfern Rd SE6 123 DZ88
Rathgar Av W13 79 CH74
Rathgar Cl N3 43 CZ54
Rathgar Rd SW9 101 DP83
Coldharbour La
Rathlin Wk N1 84 DQ65
Clephane Rd
Rathmell Dr SW4 121 DK86
Rathmore Rd SE7 104 EH78
Rathmore Rd, Grav. 131 GH87
Rathwell Path, Borwd. 26 CL39
Rats La, Loug. 32 EH38
Rattray Rd SW2 101 DN84
Raul Rd SE15 102 DU81
Ravel Gdns, S.Ock. 90 FQ72
Ravel Rd, S.Ock. 90 FQ72
Raveley St NW5 65 DJ63
Raven Cl NW9 42 CS54
Eagle Dr
Raven Cl, Rick. 38 BJ45
Raven Ct E5 66 DU62
Stellman Cl
Raven Rd E18 48 EJ54
Raven Row E1 84 DV71
Ravencroft, Grays 111 GH75
Alexandra Cl
Ravendale Rd, Sun. 135 BT96
Ravenet St SW11 101 DH81
Strasburg Rd
Ravenfield, Egh. 112 AW93
Ravenfield Rd SW17 120 DF90
Ravenhill Rd E13 86 EJ68
Ravenna Rd SW15 119 CX85
Ravenoak Way, Chig. 49 ES50
Ravenor Pk Rd, Grnf. 78 CB69
Ravens Cl, Brom. 144 EF96
Ravens Cl, Enf. 30 DS40
Ravens Cl, Red. 184 DF132
Ravens Ms SE12 124 EG85
Ravens Way
Ravens Way SE12 124 EG85
Ravensbourne Av, Beck. 123 ED94
Ravensbourne Av, Brom. 123 ED94
Ravensbourne Av, Stai. 114 BL88
Ravensbourne Cres, Rom. 72 FM55
Ravensbourne Gdns W13 79 CH71
Ravensbourne Gdns, Ilf. 49 EN53
Ravensbourne Pk SE6 123 EA87
Ravensbourne Pk Cres SE6 123 DZ87
Ravensbourne Pl SE13 103 EB82
Ravensbourne Rd SE6 123 DZ87
Ravensbourne Rd, Brom. 144 EG97
Ravensbourne Rd, Dart. 107 FG83
Ravensbourne Rd, Twick. 117 CJ86
Ravensbury Av, Mord. 140 DC99
Ravensbury Ct, Mitch. 140 DD98
Ravensbury Gro
Ravensbury Gro, Mitch. 140 DD98
Ravensbury La, Mitch. 140 DD98
Ravensbury Path, Mitch. 140 DD98
Ravensbury Rd SW18 120 DA89
Ravensbury Rd, Orp. 145 ET98
Ravensbury Ter SW18 120 DB88
Ravenscar Rd, Brom. 124 EE91
Ravenscar Rd, Surb. 138 CM103
Ravenscourt, Sun. 135 BT95
Ravenscourt Av W6 99 CU77
Ravenscourt Cl, Horn. 72 FL62
Ravenscourt Dr
Ravenscourt Cl, Ruis. 59 BQ59
Ravenscourt Dr, Horn. 72 FL62
Ravenscourt Gdns W6 99 CU77
Ravenscourt Gro, Horn. 72 FL61
Ravenscourt Pk W6 99 CU76
Ravenscourt Pl W6 99 CV77
Ravenscourt Rd W6 99 CV77
Ravenscourt Rd, Orp. 146 EU97
Ravenscourt Sq W6 99 CU76
Ravenscraig Rd N11 45 DH49
Ravenscroft, Wat. 8 BY34
Ravenscroft Av NW11 63 CZ59
Ravenscroft Av, Wem. 62 CM60
Ravenscroft Cl E16 86 EG71
Ravenscroft Cres SE9 125 EM90
Ravenscroft Pk, Barn. 27 CX42
Ravenscroft Rd E16 86 EG71
Ravenscroft Rd W4 98 CQ77
Ravenscroft Rd, Beck. 142 DW96
Ravenscroft Rd, Wey. 153 BQ111
Ravenscroft St E2 84 DT68
Ravensdale Av N12 44 DC49
Ravensdale Gdns SE19 122 DR94
Ravensdale Gdns, Houns. 96 BY83
Ravensdale Ms, Stai. 114 BH93
Worple Rd
Ravensdale Rd N16 66 DT59
Ravensdale Rd, Houns. 96 BY83
Ravensdon St SE11 101 DN78
Ravensfield, Slou. 92 AX75
Ravensfield Cl, Dag. 70 EX63
Ravensfield Gdns, Epsom 156 CS106
Ravenshaw St NW6 63 CZ64
Ravenshead Cl, S.Croy. 160 DW111
Ravenshill, Chis. 145 EP95
Ravenshurst Av NW4 63 CW56
Ravenside Cl N18 47 DX51
Ravenside Retail Pk N18 47 DX50
Ravenslea Rd SW12 120 DF87
Ravensmead (Chalfont St. Peter), Ger.Cr. 37 AZ50
Ravensmead Rd, Brom. 123 ED94
Ravensmede Way W4 99 CT77
Ravensmere, Epp. 18 EU31
Ravenstone SE17 102 DS78
Ravenstone Rd N8 65 DN55
Ravenstone Rd NW9 63 CT58
West Hendon Bdy
Ravenstone St SW12 120 DG88
Ravenswold, Ken. 176 DQ115
Ravenswood, Bex. 126 EY88
Ravenswood Av, Surb. 138 CM103
Ravenswood Av, W.Wick. 143 EC102
Ravenswood Cl, Cob. 170 BX115
Ravenswood Cl, Rom. 51 FB50
Ravenswood Ct, Kings.T. 118 CP93
Ravenswood Ct, Wok. 167 AZ118
Ravenswood Cres, Har. 60 BZ61
Ravenswood Cres, W.Wick. 143 EC102
Ravenswood Gdns, Islw. 97 CE81
Ravenswood Pk, Nthwd. 39 BU51
Ravenswood Rd E17 67 EB56
Ravenswood Rd SW12 121 DH87
Ravenswood Rd, Croy. 141 DP104
Ravensworth Rd NW10 81 CV69
Ravensworth Rd SE9 125 EM91
Ravent Rd SE11 200 C9
Ravent Rd SE11 101 DM77
Ravey St EC2 197 M4
Ravine Gro SE18 105 ES79
Rawlings Cl, Orp. 164 EU106
Rawlings St SW3 198 D8
Rawlings St SW3 100 DF77
Rawlins Cl N3 63 CY55
Rawlins Cl, S.Croy. 161 DY108
Rawnsley Av, Mitch. 140 DD99
Rawreth Wk N1 84 DQ67
Basire St
Rawson St SW11 100 DG81
Strasburg Rd
Rawsthorne Cl E16 87 EM74
Kennard St
Rawstone Wk E13 86 EG68
Rawstorne Pl EC1 196 F2
Rawstorne St EC1 196 F2
Rawstorne St EC1 83 DP69
Ray Cl, Chess. 155 CJ107
Merritt Gdns
Ray Gdns, Bark. 88 EU68
Ray Gdns, Stan. 41 CH50
Ray Lamb Way, Erith 107 FH79
Ray Lo Rd, Wdf.Grn. 48 EJ51
Ray Massey Way E6 86 EL67
Ron Leighton Way
Ray Rd, Rom. 51 FB50
Ray Rd, W.Mol. 136 CB99
Ray St EC1 196 E5
Ray St EC1 83 DN70
Ray St Br EC1 196 E5
Ray Wk N7 65 DM61
Andover Rd
Rayburn Rd, Horn. 72 FN59
Raydean Rd, Barn. 28 DB43
Raydon Rd (Cheshunt), Wal.Cr. 15 DX32
Raydon St N19 65 DH61
Raydons Gdns, Dag. 70 EY64
Raydons Rd, Dag. 70 EY64
Rayfield, Epp. 18 EU30
Rayfield Cl, Brom. 144 EL100
Rayford Av SE12 124 EF87
Rayford Cl, Dart. 128 FJ85
Raylands Mead, Ger.Cr. 56 AW57
Bull La
Rayleas Cl SE18 105 EP81
Rayleigh Av, Tedd. 117 CE93
Rayleigh Cl N13 46 DR48
Rayleigh Rd
Rayleigh Cl, Brwd. 55 GC44
Rayleigh Ct, Kings.T. 138 CM96
Rayleigh Ri, S.Croy. 160 DS107
Rayleigh Rd E16 86 EH74
Wesley Av
Rayleigh Rd N13 46 DQ48
Rayleigh Rd SW19 139 CZ95
Rayleigh Rd, Brwd. 55 GC44
Rayleigh Rd, Wdf.Grn. 48 EJ51
Raymead NW4 63 CW56
Tenterden Gro
Raymead Av, Th.Hth. 141 DN99
Raymead Cl, Lthd. 171 CE122
Raymead Way, Lthd. 171 CE122
Raymere Gdns SE18 105 ER80
Raymond Av E18 68 EF55
Raymond Av W13 97 CG76
Raymond Bldgs WC1 196 C6
Raymond Cl SE26 122 DW92
Raymond Cl, Abb.L. 7 BR32
Raymond Cl, Slou. 93 BE81
Raymond Ct N10 44 DG52
Pembroke Rd
Raymond Ct, Pot.B. 12 DC34
St. Francis Cl
Raymond Gdns, Chig. 50 EV48
Raymond Rd E13 86 EJ66
Raymond Rd SW19 119 CY93
Raymond Rd, Beck. 143 DY98
Raymond Rd, Ilf. 69 ER59
Raymond Rd, Slou. 93 BA76
Raymond Way, Esher 155 CG107
Raymouth Rd SE16 202 E8
Raymouth Rd SE16 102 DV77
Rayne Ct E18 68 EF56
Rayner Twr E10 67 EA59
Rayners Cl, Slou. 93 BC80
Rayners Cl, Wem. 61 CK64
Rayners Ct, Grav. 130 GB86
Rayners Ct, Har. 60 CA60
Rayners Cres, Nthlt. 77 BV69
Rayners Gdns, Nthlt. 77 BV68
Rayners La, Har. 60 CB61
Rayners La, Pnr. 60 BZ58
Rayners Rd SW15 119 CY85
Raynes Av E11 68 EJ59
Raynham Av N18 46 DU51
Raynham Rd N18 46 DU50
Raynham Rd W6 99 CV77
Raynham Ter N18 46 DU50
Raynor Cl, Sthl. 78 BZ74
Raynor Pl N1 84 DQ67
Elizabeth Av
Raynton Cl, Har. 60 BY60

Raynton Cl, Hayes 77 BT70
Raynton Dr, Hayes 77 BT70
Raynton Rd, Enf. 31 DX37
Rays Av N18 46 DW49
Rays Hill, Dart. 148 FQ98
Rays Rd N18 46 DW49
Rays Rd, W.Wick. 143 EC101
Raywood Cl, Hayes 95 BQ80
Reachview Cl NW1 83 DJ66
Baynes St
Read Cl, T.Ditt. 137 CG101
Read Ct, Wal.Abb. 16 EG33
Read Rd, Ash. 171 CK117
Read Way, Grav. 131 GK92
Reade Ct, Slou. 74 AV72
Victoria Rd
Reade Wk NW10 80 CS66
Denbigh Cl
Readens, The, Bans. 174 DF116
Reading Arch Rd, Red. 184 DF134
Reading La E8 84 DV65
Reading Rd, Nthlt. 60 CB64
Reading Rd, Sutt. 158 DC106
Reading Way NW7 43 CX50
Readings, The, Rick. 21 BF41
Reads Cl, Ilf. 69 EP62
Chapel Rd
Reads Rest La, Tad. 173 CZ119
Reapers Cl NW1 83 DK67
Crofters Way
Reapers Way, Islw. 117 CD85
Hall Rd
Reardon Ct N21 46 DQ47
Cosgrove Cl
Reardon Path E1 202 E3
Reardon Path E1 84 DV74
Reardon St E1 202 D2
Reardon St E1 84 DV74
Reaston St SE14 103 DX80
Reckitt Rd W4 98 CS78
Record St SE15 102 DW79
Recovery St SW17 120 DE92
Recreation Av, Rom. 71 FC57
Recreation Av (Harold Wd), Rom. 52 FM54
Recreation Rd SE26 123 DX91
Recreation Rd, Brom. 144 EF96
Recreation Rd, Sid. 125 ES90
Woodside Rd
Recreation Rd, Sthl. 96 BY77
Recreation Way, Mitch. 141 DK97
Rector St N1 84 DQ67
Rectory Chase, Brwd. 73 FX56
Rectory Cl E4 47 EA48
Rectory Cl N3 43 CZ53
Rectory Cl SW20 139 CW97
Rectory Cl, Ash. 172 CM119
Rectory Cl, Dart. 107 FE84
Rectory Cl, Shep. 134 BN97
Rectory Cl, Sid. 126 EV91
Rectory Cl, Stan. 41 CH51
Rectory Cl, Surb. 137 CJ102
Rectory Cl, W.Byf. 152 BL113
Rectory Cres E11 68 EJ58
Rectory Fm Rd, Enf. 29 DM38
Rectory Fld Cres SE7 104 EJ80
Rectory Gdns N8 65 DL56
Rectory Gdns SW4 101 DJ83
Rectory Gdns, Ch.St.G. 36 AV48
Rectory Gdns, Nthlt. 78 BZ67
Rectory Gdns, Upmin. 73 FR61
Rectory Grn, Beck. 143 DZ95
Rectory Gro SW4 101 DJ83
Rectory Gro, Croy. 141 DP103
Rectory Gro, Hmptn. 116 BZ91
Rectory La SW17 120 DG93
Rectory La, Ash. 172 CM118
Rectory La, Bans. 158 DF114
Rectory La, Bet. 183 CT131
Rectory La, Edg. 42 CN51
Rectory La, Kings L. 6 BN28
Rectory La, Loug. 33 EN40
Rectory La, Rad. 10 CN33
Rectory La, Rick. 38 BK46
Rectory La, Sev. 191 FJ126
Rectory La, Sid. 126 EV91
Rectory La, Stan. 41 CH50
Rectory La, Surb. 137 CJ102
Rectory La, Wall. 159 DJ105
Rectory La, W.Byf. 152 BL113
Rectory La, West. 178 EL123
Rectory La (Brasted), West. 180 EW123
Rectory Meadow, Grav. 130 GA93
Rectory Orchard SW19 119 CY91
Rectory Pk, S.Croy. 160 DS113
Rectory Pk Av, Nthlt. 78 BZ69
Rectory Pl SE18 105 EN77
Rectory Rd E12 69 EM64
Rectory Rd E17 67 EB55
Rectory Rd N16 66 DT62
Rectory Rd SW13 99 CU82
Rectory Rd W3 80 CP74
Rectory Rd, Beck. 143 EA95
Rectory Rd, Couls. 184 DD125
Rectory Rd, Dag. 88 FA66
Rectory Rd, Grays 110 GD76
Rectory Rd, Hayes 77 BU72
Rectory Rd, Houns. 95 BV81
Rectory Rd, Kes. 162 EK108
Rectory Rd, Rick. 38 BK46
Rectory Rd, Sthl. 96 BZ76
Rectory Rd, Sutt. 140 DA104
Rectory Rd, Swans. 130 FY87
Rectory Rd, Til. 111 GK79
Rectory Sq E1 85 DX71
Rectory Way, Uxb. 59 BP62
Reculver Ms N18 46 DU49
Lyndhurst Rd
Reculver Rd SE16 203 H10
Reculver Rd SE16 103 DX78
Red Anchor Cl SW3 100 DE79
Old Ch St
Red Barracks Rd SE18 105 EM77
Red Cedars Rd, Orp. 145 ES101
Red Cottage Ms, Slou. 92 AW76
Red Ct, Slou. 74 AS74
Red Hill, Chis. 125 EN92
Red Hill (Denham), Uxb. 57 BD61
Red Ho La, Bexh. 106 EX84
Red Ho La, Walt. 135 BU103
Red Ho Sq N1 84 DQ65
Clephane Rd
Red La, Esher 155 CG107
Red La, Oxt. 188 EH133
Red Leaf Cl, Slou. 75 AZ74
Pickford Dr
Red Lion Cl SE17 102 DQ79
Red Lion Row
Red Lion Cl, Orp. 146 EW100
Red Lion Ct EC4 196 E8
Red Lion Hill N2 44 DD54
Red Lion La SE18 105 EN80
Red Lion La, Hem.H. 6 BM26
Red Lion La, Rick. 22 BG35
Red Lion La, Wok. 150 AS109
Red Lion La, Wok. 150 AS109
Red Lion Rd
Red Lion Pl SE18 105 EN81
Shooter's Hill Rd
Red Lion Rd, Surb. 138 CM103
Red Lion Rd, Wok. 150 AS109
Red Lion Row SE17 102 DQ79
Red Lion Sq SW18 120 DA85
Wandsworth High St
Red Lion Sq WC1 196 B7
Red Lion Sq WC1 83 DM71
Red Lion St WC1 196 B6
Red Lion St WC1 83 DM71
Red Lion St, Rich. 117 CK85
Red Lion Yd W1 198 G2
Red Lion Yd, Wat. 24 BW42
High St
Red Lo Cres, Bex. 127 FD90
Red Lo Rd, Bex. 127 FD90
Red Lo Rd, W.Wick. 143 ED100
Red Oak Cl, Orp. 145 EP104
Red Oaks Mead, Epp. 33 ER37
Red Path E9 85 DZ65
Red Pl W1 194 F10
Red Post Hill SE21 122 DR85
Red Post Hill SE24 102 DR84
Red Rd, Borwd. 26 CM41
Red Rd, Brwd. 54 FV49
Red St, Grav. 130 GA93
Redan Pl W2 82 DB72
Redan St W14 99 CX76
Redan Ter SE5 102 DQ82
Flaxman Rd
Redbarn Cl, Pur. 159 DP111
Whytecliffe Rd S
Redberry Gro SE26 122 DW90
Redbourne Av N3 44 DA53
Redbridge Enterprise Cen, Ilf. 69 EQ61
Redbridge Gdns SE5 102 DS80
Redbridge La E, Ilf. 68 EK58
Redbridge La W E11 68 EH58
Redburn St SW3 100 DF79
Redbury Cl, Rain. 89 FH70
Deri Av
Redcar Cl, Nthlt. 60 CB64
Redcar Rd, Rom. 52 FM50
Redcar St SE5 102 DQ80
Redcastle Cl E1 84 DW73
Redchurch St E2 197 P4
Redchurch St E2 84 DT70
Redcliffe Cl SW5 100 DB78
Warwick Rd
Redcliffe Gdns SW5 100 DB78
Redcliffe Gdns SW10 100 DB78
Redcliffe Gdns, Ilf. 69 EN60
Redcliffe Ms SW10 100 DB78
Redcliffe Pl SW10 100 DC79
Redcliffe Rd SW10 100 DC78
Redcliffe Sq SW10 100 DB78
Redcliffe St SW10 100 DB79
Redclose Av, Mord. 140 DA99
Chalgrove Av
Redclyffe Rd E6 86 EJ67
Redcourt, Wok. 167 BD115
Redcroft Rd, Sthl. 78 CC73
Redcross Way SE1 201 J4
Redcross Way SE1 102 DQ75
Redden Ct Rd, Rom. 72 FL55
Redding Cl, Dart. 129 FS89
Reddings, The NW7 43 CT48
Reddings, The, Borwd. 26 CM41
Reddings Av, Bushey 24 CB43
Reddings Cl NW7 43 CT49
Reddington Cl, S.Croy. 160 DR109
Reddington Dr, Slou. 92 AY76
Reddins Rd SE15 102 DU79
Reddons Rd, Beck. 123 DY94
Reddown Rd, Couls. 175 DK118
Reddy Rd, Erith 107 FF79
Rede Ct, Wey. 135 BP104
Old Palace Rd
Rede Pl W2 82 DA72
Chepstow Pl
Redesdale Gdns, Islw. 97 CG80
Redesdale St SW3 100 DF79
Redfern Av, Houns. 116 CA87
Redfern Cl, Uxb. 76 BJ67
Redfern Gdns, Rom. 52 FK54
Redfern Rd NW10 80 CS66
Redfern Rd SE6 123 EC87
Redfield La SW5 100 DA77
Redfield Ms SW5 100 DA77
Redfield La
Redford Av, Couls. 159 DH114
Redford Av, Th.Hth. 141 DM98
Redford Av, Wall. 159 DL107
Redford Cl, Felt. 115 BT89
Redford Wk N1 83 DP67
Britannia Row
Redford Way, Uxb. 76 BJ66
Redgate Dr, Brom. 144 EH103
Redgate Ter SW15 119 CX86
Lytton Gro
Redgrave Cl, Croy. 142 DT100
Redgrave Rd SW15 99 CX83
Redhall Ct, Cat. 176 DR123
Redhall La, Rick. 22 BL39
Redheath Cl, Wat. 23 BT35
Redhill Dr, Edg. 42 CQ54
Redhill Rd, Cob. 153 BP113
Redhill St NW1 195 J2
Redhill St NW1 83 DH68
Redhouse Rd, Croy. 141 DK100
Redhouse Rd, West. 178 EJ120
Redington Gdns NW3 64 DB63
Redington Rd NW3 64 DB63
Redland Gdns, W.Mol. 136 BZ98
Dunstable Rd
Redlands, Couls. 175 DL116
Redlands Ct, Brom. 124 EF94
Redlands Rd, Enf. 31 DY39
Redlands Rd, Sev. 190 FF124
Redlands Way SW2 121 DM87
Redleaf Cl, Belv. 106 FA79
Redleaves Av, Ashf. 115 BP93
Redlees Cl, Islw. 97 CG84
Redman Cl, Nthlt. 78 BW68
Redmans La, Sev. 165 FE107
Redman's Rd E1 84 DW71
Redmead La E1 202 B3
Redmead Rd, Hayes 95 BS77
Redmore Rd W6 99 CV77
Redpoll Way, Erith 106 EX76
Redriff Est SE16 203 M6
Redriff Est SE16 103 DZ76
Redriff Rd SE16 203 J7
Redriff Rd SE16 103 DX77
Redriff Rd, Rom. 51 FB54
Redriffe Rd E13 86 EF67
Redroofs Cl, Beck. 143 EB95
Redruth Cl N22 45 DM52
Palmerston Rd
Redruth Gdns, Rom. 52 FM50
Redruth Rd E9 85 DX67
Redruth Rd, Rom. 52 FM50
Redruth Wk, Rom. 52 FN50
Redstart Cl E6 86 EL71
Columbine Av
Redstart Cl SE14 103 DY80
Southerngate Way
Redstart Cl, Croy. 161 ED110
Redston Rd N8 65 DK56
Redstone Hill, Red. 184 DG134
Redstone Manor, Red. 184 DG134
Redstone Pk, Red. 184 DG134
Redvers Rd N22 45 DN54
Redvers Rd, Warl. 176 DW118
Redvers St N1 197 N1
Redwald Rd E5 67 DX63
Redway Dr, Twick. 116 CC87
Redwing Cl, S.Croy. 161 DX111
Redwing Gdns, W.Byf. 152 BH112
Redwing Gro, Abb.L. 7 BU31
Redwing Path SE28 105 ER75
Redwood, Egh. 133 BE96
Redwood Chase, S.Ock. 91 FW70
Redwood Cl N14 45 DK45
The Vale
Redwood Cl SE16 203 L3
Redwood Cl SE16 85 DY74
Redwood Cl, Ken. 160 DQ114
Redwood Cl, Sid. 126 EU87
Redwood Cl, Uxb. 77 BP68
The Larches
Redwood Cl, Wat. 40 BW49
Redwood Ct NW6 81 CY66
The Av
Redwood Est, Houns. 95 BV79
Redwood Gdns E4 31 EB44
Redwood Gdns, Chig. 50 EU50
Redwood Ms SW4 101 DH83
Hannington Rd
Redwood Mt, Reig. 184 DA131
Redwood Ri, Borwd. 26 CN37
Redwood Twr E11 67 ED62
Hollydown Way
Redwood Wk, Surb. 137 CK102
Redwood Way, Barn. 27 CX43
Redwoods SW15 119 CU88
Redwoods Cl, Buck.H. 48 EH47
Beech La
Ree La Cotts, Loug. 33 EN40
Englands La
Reece Ms SW7 100 DD77
Reed Av, Orp. 145 ES104
Reed Cl E16 86 EG71
Reed Cl SE12 124 EG85
Reed Cl, Iver 75 BE72
Reed Cl, St.Alb. 10 CL27
Reed Pl, Shep. 134 BM102
Reed Pl, W.Byf. 151 BE113
Reed Pond Wk, Rom. 51 FF54
Reed Rd N17 46 DT54
Reede Gdns, Dag. 71 FB64
Reede Rd, Dag. 88 FA65
Reede Way, Dag. 89 FB65
Reedham Cl N17 66 DV56
Reedham Cl, St.Alb. 8 CA29
Reedham Dr, Pur. 159 DN113
Reedham Pk Av, Pur. 175 DN116
Reedham St SE15 102 DU82
Reedholm Vil N16 66 DR63
Winston Rd
Reeds Cres, Wat. 24 BW40
Reeds Pl NW1 83 DJ66
Royal Coll St
Reeds Wk, Wat. 24 BW40
Reedsfield Cl, Ashf. 115 BP91
The Yews
Reedsfield Rd, Ashf. 115 BP91
Reedworth St SE11 200 E9
Reedworth St SE11 101 DN77
Reenglass Rd, Stan. 41 CK49
Rees Dr, Stan. 42 CL49
Rees Gdns, Croy. 142 DT100
Rees St N1 84 DQ67
Reesland Cl E12 69 EN64
Reets Fm Cl NW9 62 CS58
Reeves Av NW9 62 CR59
Reeves Cor, Croy. 141 DP103
Roman Way
Reeves Cres, Swan. 147 FD97
Reeves Ms W1 198 F1
Reeves Ms W1 82 DG73
Reeves Rd E3 85 EB70
Reeves Rd SE18 105 EP79
Reform Row N17 46 DT54
Reform St SW11 100 DF82
Regal Cl E1 84 DU71
Old Montague St
Regal Cl W5 79 CK71
Regal Ct N18 46 DT50
College Cl
Regal Cres, Wall. 141 DH104
Regal Dr N11 45 DH50
Regal La NW1 82 DG67
Regents Pk Rd
Regal Pl E3 85 DZ69
Coborn St
Regal Pl SW6 100 DB80
Maxwell Rd
Regal Row SE15 102 DW81
Queens Rd
Regal Way, Har. 62 CL58
Regal Way, Wat. 24 BW38
Regan Way N1 197 M1
Regan Way N1 84 DS68
Regarder Rd, Chig. 50 EU50
Regarth Av, Rom. 71 FE58
Regency Cl W5 80 CL72
Regency Cl, Chig. 49 EQ50
Regency Cl, Hmptn. 116 BZ92
Regency Ct, Brwd. 54 FW47
Regency Cres NW4 43 CX54
Regency Dr, Ruis. 59 BS60
Regency Dr, W.Byf. 151 BF113
Regency Gdns, Horn. 72 FJ59
Regency Gdns, Walt. 136 BW102
Regency Lo, Buck.H. 48 EK47
Regency Ms NW10 81 CU65
High Rd
Regency Ms, Beck. 143 EC95
Regency Ms, Islw. 117 CE85
Queensbridge Pk
Regency Pl SW1 199 N8
Regency St SW1 199 N8
Regency St SW1 101 DK77
Regency Ter SW7 100 DD78
Fulham Rd
Regency Wk, Croy. 143 DY100
Regency Wk, Rich. 118 CL86
Friars Stile Rd
Regency Way, Bexh. 106 EX83
Regency Way, Wok. 167 BD115
Regent Av, Uxb. 77 BP66
Regent Cl N12 44 DC50
Nether St
Regent Cl, Add. 152 BK109
Regent Cl, Grays 110 GC75
Regent Cl, Har. 62 CL58
Regent Cl, Houns. 95 BV81
Regent Ct, Red. 185 DJ129
Regent Ct, Slou. 74 AS72
Stoke Poges La
Regent Cres, Red. 184 DF132
Regent Gdns, Ilf. 70 EU58
Regent Gate, Wal.Cr. 15 DY34
Regent Pk, Lthd. 171 CG118
Regent Pl SW19 120 DB92
Haydons Rd
Regent Pl W1 195 L10
Regent Pl, Croy. 142 DT102
Grant Rd
Regent Rd SE24 121 DP86
Regent Rd, Epp. 17 ET30
Regent Rd, Surb. 138 CM99
Regent Sq E3 85 EB69
Regent Sq WC1 196 A3
Regent Sq WC1 83 DL69
Regent Sq, Belv. 107 FB77
Regent St NW10 81 CX69
Wellington Rd
Regent St SW1 199 M1
Regent St SW1 83 DK73
Regent St W1 195 J8
Regent St W1 83 DH72
Regent St W4 98 CN78
Regent St, Wat. 23 BV38
Regents Av N13 45 DM50
Regents Br Gdns SW8 101 DL80
Regents Cl, Hayes 77 BS71
Park Rd
Regents Cl, Rad. 9 CG34
Regents Cl, S.Croy. 160 DS107
Regents Cl, Whyt. 176 DS118
Regents Dr, Kes. 162 EK106
Regents Ms NW8 82 DC68
Langford Pl
Regent's Pk NW1 194 E1
Regent's Pk NW1 82 DG68
Regent's Pk Est NW1 195 K3
Regents Pk Rd N3 63 CZ55
Regents Pk Rd NW1 82 DF67
Regents Pk Ter NW1 83 DH67
Oval Rd
Regent's Pl NW1 195 K4
Regent's Pl NW1 83 DJ70
Regent's Pl SE3 104 EG82
Regents Pl, Loug. 48 EJ45
Fallow Flds
Regents Row E8 84 DU67
Regina Cl, Barn. 27 CX41
Regina Rd N4 65 DM60
Regina Rd SE25 142 DU97
Regina Rd W13 79 CG74
Regina Rd, Sthl. 96 BY77
Regina Ter W13 79 CH74
Reginald Rd E7 86 EG66
Reginald Rd SE8 103 EA80
Reginald Rd, Nthwd. 39 BT53
Reginald Rd, Rom. 52 FN53
Reginald Sq SE8 103 EA80
Regis Pl SW2 101 DM84
Regis Rd NW5 65 DH64
Regnart Bldgs NW1 195 L4
Reid Av, Cat. 176 DR121
Reid Cl, Couls. 175 DH116
Reid Cl, Pnr. 59 BU56
Reidhaven Rd SE18 105 ES77
Reigate Av, Sutt. 140 DA102
Reigate Business Ms, Reig. 183 CZ133
Albert Rd N
Reigate Hill, Reig. 184 DB130
Reigate Hill Cl, Reig. 184 DA131
Reigate Rd, Bet. 182 CS132
Reigate Rd, Brom. 124 EF90
Reigate Rd, Epsom 157 CT110
Reigate Rd, Ilf. 69 ET61
Reigate Rd, Lthd. 171 CJ122
Reigate Rd, Red. 184 DB134
Reigate Rd, Reig. 184 DB134
Reigate Rd, Tad. 173 CX117
Reigate Way, Wall. 159 DL106
Reighton Rd E5 66 DU62
Relay Rd W12 81 CW73
Relf Rd SE15 102 DU83
Relko Ct, Epsom 156 CR110
Relko Gdns, Sutt. 158 DD106
Relton Ms SW7 198 C6
Rembrandt Cl E14 204 F7
Rembrandt Cl E14 103 ED76
Rembrandt Cl SW1 198 F9
Rembrandt Ct, Epsom 157 CT107
Rembrandt Dr, Grav. 130 GD90
Rembrandt Rd SE13 104 EE84
Rembrandt Rd, Edg. 42 CN54
Rembrandt Way, Walt. 135 BV104
Remington Rd E6 86 EL72
Remington Rd N15 66 DR58
Remington St N1 196 G1
Remington St N1 83 DP68
Remnant St WC2 196 B8
Rempstone Ms N1 84 DR68
Mintern St
Remus Rd E3 85 EA66
Monier Rd
Rendle Cl, Croy. 142 DT99
Rendlesham Av, Rad. 25 CF37
Rendlesham Rd E5 66 DU63
Rendlesham Rd, Enf. 29 DP39
Rendlesham Way, Rick. 21 BC44
Renforth St SE16 202 G5
Renforth St SE16 102 DW75
Renfree Way, Shep. 134 BM101
Renfrew Cl E6 87 EN73
Renfrew Rd SE11 200 F8
Renfrew Rd SE11 101 DP77
Renfrew Rd, Houns. 96 BX82
Renfrew Rd, Kings.T. 118 CP94
Renmans, The, Ash. 172 CM116
Renmuir St SW17 120 DF93
Rennell St SE13 103 EC83
Rennels Way, Islw. 97 CE82
St. John's Rd
Renness Rd E17 67 DY55
Rennets Cl SE9 125 ES85
Rennets Wd Rd SE9 125 ER85
Rennie Cl, Ashf. 114 BK90
Rennie Est SE16 202 E9
Rennie Est SE16 102 DV77
Rennie St SE1 200 F2
Rennie St SE1 83 DP74
Rennison Cl, Wal.Cr. 14 DT27
Allwood Rd
Renown Cl, Croy. 141 DP102
Renown Cl, Rom. 50 FA53
Rensburg Rd E17 67 DX57
Renshaw Cl, Belv. 106 EZ79
Grove Rd
Renters Av NW4 63 CW58
Renton Dr, Orp. 146 EX101
Renwick Ind Est, Bark. 88 EV67
Renwick Rd, Bark. 88 EV70
Repens Way, Hayes 78 BX70
Stipularis Dr
Rephidim St SE1 201 M7
Replingham Rd SW18 119 CZ88
Reporton Rd SW6 99 CY81
Repository Rd SE18 105 EM79
Repton Av, Hayes 95 BR77
Repton Av, Rom. 71 FG55
Repton Av, Wem. 61 CJ63
Repton Cl, Cars. 158 DE106
Repton Ct, Beck. 143 EB95
Repton Dr, Rom. 71 FG56
Repton Gdns, Rom. 71 FG55
Repton Gro, Ilf. 49 EM53
Repton Pl, Amer. 20 AU39
Repton Rd, Har. 62 CM56
Repton Rd, Orp. 146 EU104
Repton St E14 85 DY72
Repton Way, Rick. 22 BN43
Repulse Cl, Rom. 51 FB53
Reservoir Cl, Th.Hth. 142 DR98
Reservoir Rd N14 29 DJ43
Reservoir Rd SE4 103 DY82
Reservoir Rd, Ruis. 59 BQ56
Resolution Wk SE18 105 EM76
Restavon Pk, West. 179 EP116
Restell Cl SE3 104 EE79
Restmor Way, Wall. 140 DG103
Reston Cl, Borwd. 26 CN38
Reston Path, Borwd. 26 CN38
Reston Pl SW7 100 DC75
Hyde Pk Gate
Restons Cres SE9 125 ER86
Restormel Cl, Houns. 116 CA85
Retcar Cl N19 65 DH61
Dartmouth Pk Hill
Retcar Pl N19 65 DH61
Retford Cl, Borwd. 26 CN38
The Campions
Retford Cl, Rom. 52 FN51
Retford Path, Rom. 52 FN51
Retford Rd, Rom. 52 FN51
Retford St N1 197 N1
Retingham Way E4 47 EB47
Retreat, The NW9 62 CR57
Retreat, The SW14 98 CS83
South Worple Way
Retreat, The, Abb.L. 7 BQ31
Abbots Rd
Retreat, The, Add. 152 BK106
Retreat, The, Amer. 20 AY39
Retreat, The, Brwd. 54 FV46
Costead Manor Rd
Retreat, The (Hutton), Brwd. 55 GB44
Retreat, The, Egh. 112 AX92
Retreat, The, Grays 110 GB79
Retreat, The, Har. 60 CA59
Retreat, The, Kings L. 7 BQ31
Retreat, The, Orp. 164 EV107
Retreat, The, Surb. 138 CM100
Retreat, The, Th.Hth. 142 DR98
Retreat, The, Wor.Pk. 139 CV103
Retreat Cl, Har. 61 CJ57
Retreat Pl E9 84 DW65
Retreat Rd, Rich. 117 CK85
Retreat Way, Chig. 50 EV48
Reubens Rd, Brwd. 55 GB44
Reunion Row E1 202 E1
Reveley Sq SE16 203 L5
Revell Cl, Lthd. 170 CB122
Revell Dr, Lthd. 170 CB122
Revell Ri SE18 105 ET79
Revell Rd, Kings.T. 138 CP95
Revell Rd, Sutt. 157 CZ107
Revelon Rd SE4 103 DY84
Revelstoke Rd SW18 119 CZ89
Reventlow Rd SE9 125 EQ88
Reverdy Rd SE1 202 B9
Reverdy Rd SE1 102 DU77
Reverend Cl, Har. 60 CB62

Revesby Rd, Cars. 140 DD100
Review Rd NW2 63 CT61
Review Rd, Dag. 89 FB67
Rewell St SW6 100 DC80
Rewley Rd, Cars. 140 DD100
Rex Av, Ashf. 114 BN92
Rex Cl, Rom. 51 FB52
Rex Pl W1 198 G1
Reydon Av E11 68 EJ58
Reynard Cl SE4 103 DY83
Foxwell St
Reynard Cl, Brom. 145 EM97
Reynard Dr SE19 122 DT94
Reynard Pl SE14 103 DY79
Milton Ct Rd
Reynards Way, St.Alb. 8 BZ29
Reynardson Rd N17 46 DQ52
Reynolds Av E12 69 EN64
Reynolds Av, Chess. 156 CL108
Reynolds Av, Rom. 70 EW59
Reynolds Cl NW11 64 DB59
Reynolds Cl SW19 140 DD95
Reynolds Cl, Cars. 140 DF102
Reynolds Ct E11 68 EF62
Cobbold Rd
Reynolds Ct, Rom. 70 EX55
Reynolds Dr, Edg. 62 CM55
Reynolds Pl SE3 104 EH80
Reynolds Pl, Rich. 118 CM86
Cambrian Rd
Reynolds Rd SE15 122 DW85
Reynolds Rd W4 98 CQ76
Reynolds Rd, Hayes 78 BW70
Reynolds Rd, N.Mal. 138 CR101
Reynolds Way, Croy. 160 DS105
Rheidol Ms N1 84 DQ68
Rheidol Ter
Rheidol Ter N1 83 DP68
Rheingold Way, Wall. 159 DL109
Rheola Cl N17 46 DT53
Rhoda St E2 84 DT70
Brick La
Rhodes Av N22 45 DJ53
Rhodes Cl, Egh. 113 BC92
Mullens Rd
Rhodes Moorhouse Ct, Mord. 140 DA100
Rhodes St N7 65 DM64
Mackenzie Rd
Rhodes Way, Wat. 24 BX40
Rhodesia Rd E11 67 ED61
Rhodesia Rd SW9 101 DL82
Rhodeswell Rd E14 85 DZ72
Rhododendron Ride, Egh. 112 AT94
Rhododendron Ride, Slou. 75 AZ69
Rhodrons Av, Chess. 156 CL106
Rhondda Gro E3 85 DY69
Rhyl Rd, Grnf. 79 CF68
Rhyl St NW5 82 DG65
Rhys Av N11 45 DK52
Rialto Rd, Mitch. 140 DG96
Ribble Cl, Wdf.Grn. 48 EJ51
Prospect Rd
Ribbledale, St.Alb. 10 CM27
Ribblesdale Av N11 44 DG51
Ribblesdale Av, Nthlt. 78 CB65
Ribblesdale Rd N8 65 DM56
Ribblesdale Rd SW16 121 DH93
Ribblesdale Rd, Dart. 128 FQ88
Ribbon Dance Ms SE5 102 DR81
Camberwell Gro
Ribchester Av, Grnf. 79 CF69
Ribston Cl, Brom. 145 EM102
Ribston Cl, Rad. 9 CK33
Wayside
Ricardo Path SE28 88 EW74
Byron Cl
Ricardo Rd, Wind. 112 AV86
Meadow Way
Ricardo St E14 85 EB72
Ricards Rd SW19 119 CZ92
Rich La SW5 100 DB78
Warwick Rd
Rich St E14 85 DZ73
Richard Cl SE18 104 EL77
Richard Foster Cl E17 67 DZ59
Richard Ho Dr E16 86 EK72
Richard St E1 84 DV72
Commercial Rd
Richards Av, Rom. 71 FC57
Richards Cl, Bushey 41 CD45
Richards Cl, Har. 61 CG57
Richards Cl, Hayes 95 BR79
Richards Cl, Uxb. 76 BN67
Richards Fld, Epsom 156 CR109
Richards Pl E17 67 EA55
Richards Pl SW3 198 C8
Richards Rd, Cob. 154 CB114
Richardson Cl E8 84 DT67
Clarissa St
Richardson Cl, Green. 129 FU85
Steele Av
Richardson Cl, St.Alb. 10 CL27
Richardson Cres (Cheshunt), Wal.Cr. 13 DP26
Richardson Rd E15 86 EE68
Richardson's Ms W1 195 K5
Richbell Cl, Ash. 171 CK118
Richbell Pl WC1 196 B6
Richborne Ter SW8 101 DM80
Richborough Cl, Orp. 146 EX98
Richborough Rd NW2 63 CX63
Richens Cl, Houns. 97 CD82
Riches Rd, Ilf. 69 EQ61
Richfield Rd, Bushey 40 CC45
Richford Rd E15 86 EF67
Richford St W6 99 CW75
Richings Way, Iver 93 BF76
Richland Av, Couls. 158 DG114
Richlands Av, Epsom 157 CU105
Richmer Rd, Erith 107 FG80
Richmond Av E4 47 ED50
Richmond Av N1 83 DM67
Richmond Av NW10 81 CW65
Richmond Av SW20 139 CY95
Richmond Av, Felt. 115 BS86
Richmond Av, Uxb. 77 BP65
Richmond Br, Rich. 117 CK86
Richmond Br, Twick. 117 CK86
Richmond Bldgs W1 195 M9
Richmond Cl E17 67 DZ58
Richmond Cl, Amer. 20 AT38
Richmond Cl, Borwd. 26 CR43
Richmond Cl, Epsom 156 CS114
Richmond Cl, Lthd. 170 CC124
Richmond Cl (Cheshunt), Wal.Cr. 14 DW29
Richmond Cl, West. 178 EH119
Richmond Ct, Pot.B. 12 DC31
Richmond Cres E4 47 ED50
Richmond Cres N1 83 DM67
Richmond Cres N9 46 DU46
Richmond Cres, Slou. 74 AU74
Richmond Cres, Stai. 113 BF92
Richmond Dr, Grav. 131 GL89
Richmond Dr, Shep. 135 BQ100
Richmond Dr, Wat. 23 BS39
Richmond Gdns NW4 63 CU57
Richmond Gdns, Har. 41 CF51
Richmond Grn, Croy. 141 DL104
Richmond Gro N1 83 DP66
Richmond Gro, Surb. 138 CM100
Richmond Hill, Rich. 118 CL86
Richmond Hill Ct, Rich. 118 CL86
Richmond Ms W1 195 M9
Richmond Ms, Tedd. 117 CF93
Broad St
Richmond Pk, Kings.T. 118 CQ87
Richmond Pk, Loug. 48 EJ45
Fallow Flds
Richmond Pk, Rich. 118 CQ87
Richmond Pk Rd SW14 118 CQ85
Richmond Pk Rd, Kings.T. 118 CL94
Richmond Pl SE18 105 EQ77
Richmond Rd E4 47 ED46
Richmond Rd E7 68 EH64
Richmond Rd E8 84 DT66
Richmond Rd E11 67 ED61
Richmond Rd N2 44 DC54
Richmond Rd N11 45 DL51
Richmond Rd N15 66 DS58
Richmond Rd SW20 139 CV95
Richmond Rd W5 98 CL75
Richmond Rd, Barn. 28 DB43
Richmond Rd, Couls. 175 DH115
Richmond Rd, Croy. 141 DL104
Richmond Rd, Grays 110 GC79
Richmond Rd, Ilf. 69 EQ62
Richmond Rd, Islw. 97 CG83
Richmond Rd, Kings.T. 117 CK92
Richmond Rd, Pot.B. 12 DC31
Richmond Rd, Rom. 71 FF58
Richmond Rd, Stai. 113 BF92
Richmond Rd, Th.Hth. 141 DP97
Richmond Rd, Twick. 117 CJ86
Richmond St E13 86 EG68
Richmond Ter SW1 199 P4
Richmond Ter SW1 101 DL75
Richmond Ter Ms SW1 101 DL75
Parliament St
Richmond Way E11 68 EG61
Richmond Way W12 99 CX75
Richmond Way W14 99 CX76
Richmond Way, Lthd. 170 CB123
Richmond Way, Rick. 23 BQ42
Richmount Gdns SE3 104 EG83
Rick Roberts Way E15 85 EC67
Rickard Cl NW4 63 CV56
Rickard Cl SW2 121 DM88
Rickard Cl, West Dr. 94 BK76
Rickards Cl, Surb. 138 CL102
Rickett St SW6 100 DA79
Ricketts Hill Rd, West. 178 EK118
Rickman Cres, Add. 134 BH104
Rickman Hill, Couls. 175 DH118
Rickman Hill Rd, Couls. 175 DH118
Rickman St E1 84 DW69
Mantus Rd
Rickmans La, Slou. 56 AS64
Rickmansworth La (Chalfont St. Peter), Ger.Cr. 37 AZ50
Rickmansworth Pk, Rick. 38 BK45
Rickmansworth Rd, Nthwd. 39 BR52
Rickmansworth Rd, Pnr. 39 BV54
Rickmansworth Rd, Rick. 21 BE41
Rickmansworth Rd (Harefield), Uxb. 38 BJ53
Rickmansworth Rd, Wat. 23 BS42
Rickthorne Rd N19 65 DL61
Landseer Rd
Rickyard Path SE9 104 EL84
Ridding La, Grnf. 61 CF64
Riddings, The, Cat. 186 DT125
Riddlesdown Av, Pur. 160 DQ112
Riddlesdown Rd, Pur. 160 DQ111
Riddons Rd SE12 124 EJ90
Ride, The, Brent. 97 CH78
Ride, The, Enf. 30 DW41
Rideout St SE18 105 EM77
Rider Cl, Sid. 125 ES86
Riders Way, Gdse. 186 DW131
Ridgdale St E3 85 EB68
Ridge, The, Bex. 126 EZ87
Ridge, The, Cat. 187 EB126
Ridge, The, Couls. 159 DL114
Ridge, The, Epsom 172 CP117
Ridge, The, Lthd. 171 CD124
Ridge, The, Orp. 145 ER103
Ridge, The, Pur. 159 DJ110
Ridge, The, Surb. 138 CN99
Ridge, The, Twick. 117 CD87
Ridge, The, Wok. 167 BB117
Ridge Av N21 46 DQ45
Ridge Av, Dart. 127 FF86
Ridge Cl NW4 43 CX54
Ridge Cl NW9 62 CR56
Ridge Cl SE28 105 ER75
Ridge Cl, Wok. 166 AV121
Ridge Crest, Enf. 29 DM39
Ridge Hill NW11 63 CY60
Ridge La, Wat. 23 BS36
Ridge Langley, S.Croy. 160 DU110
Ridge Pk, Pur. 159 DK110
Ridge Rd N8 65 DM58
Ridge Rd N21 46 DQ46
Ridge Rd NW2 63 CZ62
Ridge Rd, Mitch. 121 DH94
Ridge Rd, Sutt. 139 CY102
Ridge St, Wat. 23 BV38
Ridge Way SE19 122 DS93
Central Hill
Ridge Way, Dart. 127 FF86
Ridge Way, Felt. 116 BY90
Ridge Way, Iver 75 BE74
Ridgebrook Rd SE3 104 EJ83
Ridgecroft Cl, Bex. 127 FC88
Ridgefield, Wat. 23 BS37
Ridgegate Cl, Reig. 184 DD132
Ridgehurst Av, Wat. 7 BT34
Ridgelands, Lthd. 171 CD124
Ridgemead Rd, Egh. 112 AU90
Ridgemont Gdns, Edg. 42 CQ49
Ridgemount, Wey. 135 BS103
Oatlands Dr
Ridgemount Av, Couls. 175 DH117
Ridgemount Av, Croy. 143 DX102
Ridgemount Cl SE20 122 DV94
Anerley Pk
Ridgemount End (Chalfont St. Peter), Ger.Cr. 36 AY50
Ridgemount Gdns, Enf. 29 DP40
Ridgeview Cl, Barn. 27 CX44
Ridgeview Lo, St.Alb. 10 CM28
Ridgeview Rd N20 44 DB48
Ridgeway SE28 105 ER77
Pettman Cres
Ridgeway, Brwd. 55 GB46
Ridgeway, Brom. 144 EG103
Ridgeway, Dart. 129 FS92
Ridgeway, Epsom 156 CQ112
Ridgeway, Grays 110 GE77
Ridgeway, Rick. 38 BH45
Ridgeway, Vir.W. 132 AY99
Ridgeway, Wok. 166 AX115
Ridgeway, Wdf.Grn. 48 EJ49
Ridgeway, The E4 47 EB47
Ridgeway, The N3 44 DB52
Ridgeway, The N11 44 DF49
Ridgeway, The N14 45 DL47
Ridgeway, The NW7 43 CV49
Ridgeway, The NW9 62 CS56
Ridgeway, The NW11 63 CZ60
Ridgeway, The W3 98 CN76
Ridgeway, The, Croy. 141 DM104
Ridgeway, The, Enf. 29 DN39
Ridgeway, The (Chalfont St. Peter), Ger.Cr. 56 AX55
Ridgeway, The, Har. 60 BZ57
Ridgeway, The (Kenton), Har. 61 CJ58
Ridgeway, The, Lthd. 154 CC114
Ridgeway, The (Oxshott), Lthd. 171 CD123
Ridgeway, The, Pot.B. 12 DD34
Ridgeway, The (Cuffley), Pot.B. 12 DE28
Ridgeway, The, Rad. 25 CF37
Ridgeway, The (Gidea Pk), Rom. 71 FG56
Ridgeway, The (Harold Wd), Rom. 52 FL53
Ridgeway, The, Ruis. 60 CA58
Ridgeway, The, S.Croy. 160 DS110
Ridgeway, The, Stan. 41 CJ51
Ridgeway, The, Walt. 135 BT102
Ridgeway, The, Wat. 23 BS37
Ridgeway Av, Barn. 28 DF44
Ridgeway Av, Grav. 131 GH90
Ridgeway Cl, Lthd. 154 CC114
Ridgeway Cl, Wok. 166 AX116
Ridgeway Ct, Red. 184 DF134
Ridgeway Rd
Ridgeway Cres, Orp. 145 ES104
Ridgeway Cres Gdns, Orp. 145 ES103
Ridgeway Dr, Brom. 124 EH91
Ridgeway E, Sid. 125 ET85
Ridgeway Est, The, Iver 75 BF74
Ridgeway Gdns N6 65 DJ59
Ridgeway Gdns, Ilf. 68 EL57
Ridgeway Gdns, Wok. 166 AX115
Ridgeway Rd SW9 101 DP83
Ridgeway Rd, Islw. 97 CE80
Ridgeway Rd, Red. 184 DE134
Ridgeway Rd N, Islw. 97 CE79
Ridgeway Wk, Nthlt. 78 BY65
Fortunes Mead
Ridgeway W, Sid. 125 ES85
Ridgewell Cl N1 84 DQ67
Basire St
Ridgewell Cl SE26 123 DZ91
Ridgewell Cl, Dag. 89 FB67
Ridgmount Gdns WC1 195 M5
Ridgmount Pl WC1 195 M6
Ridgmount Rd SW18 120 DB85
Ridgmount St WC1 195 M6
Ridgway SW19 119 CX93
Ridgway, Wok. 168 BG115
Ridgway, The, Sutt. 158 DD108
Ridgway Gdns SW19 119 CX94
Ridgway Pl SW19 119 CY93
Ridgway Rd, Wok. 167 BF115
Ridgwell Rd E16 86 EJ71
Riding, The NW11 63 CZ59
Golders Grn Rd
Riding, The, Wok. 151 BB114
Riding Ct Rd, Slou. 92 AW80
Riding Hill, S.Croy. 160 DU113
Riding Ho St W1 195 K7
Riding Ho St W1 83 DH71
Ridings, The W5 80 CM70
Ridings, The, Add. 151 BF107
Ridings, The, Ash. 171 CK117
Ridings, The, Chesh. 20 AX36
Ridings, The, Chig. 50 EV49
Manford Way
Ridings, The, Cob. 154 CA112
Ridings, The, Epsom 172 CS115
Ridings, The (Ewell), Epsom 157 CT109
Ridings, The, Iver 93 BF77
Ridings, The, Reig. 184 DD131
Ridings, The, Sun. 135 BU95
Ridings, The, Surb. 138 CN99
Ridings, The, Tad. 173 CZ120
Ridings, The, West. 178 EL117
Ridings, The, Wok. 168 BG123
Ridings Av N21 29 DP42
Ridings Cl N6 65 DJ59
Hornsey La Gdns
Ridings La, Wok. 168 BN123
Ridlands Gro, Oxt. 188 EL130
Ridlands La, Oxt. 188 EK130
Ridlands Ri, Oxt. 188 EL130
Ridler Rd, Enf. 30 DS38
Ridley Av W13 97 CH76
Ridley Cl, Rom. 51 FH53
Ridley Rd E7 68 EJ63
Ridley Rd E8 66 DT64
Ridley Rd NW10 81 CU68
Ridley Rd SW19 120 DB94
Ridley Rd, Brom. 144 EF97
Ridley Rd, Warl. 176 DW118
Ridley Rd, Well. 106 EV81
Ridley Several SE3 104 EH82
Blackheath Pk
Ridsdale Rd SE20 142 DV95
Ridsdale Rd, Wok. 166 AV117
Riefield Rd SE9 105 EQ84
Riesco Dr, Croy. 160 DW107
Riffel Rd NW2 63 CW64
Riffhams, Brwd. 55 GB48
Rifle Butts All, Epsom 173 CT115
Rifle Pl SE11 101 DN79
Rifle Pl W11 81 CX74
Rifle St E14 85 EB71
Rigault Rd SW6 99 CY82
Rigby Cl, Croy. 141 DN104
Rigby Gdns, Grays 111 GH77
Rigby La, Hayes 95 BR75
Rigby Ms, Ilf. 69 EP61
Cranbrook Rd
Rigby Pl, Enf. 31 EA38
Government Row
Rigden St E14 85 EB72
Rigeley Rd NW10 81 CU69
Rigg App E10 67 DX60
Rigge Pl SW4 101 DK84
Riggindale Rd SW16 121 DK92
Riley Rd SE1 201 N6
Riley Rd SE1 102 DT76
Riley Rd, Enf. 30 DW38
Riley St SW10 100 DD79
Rinaldo Rd SW12 121 DH87
Ring, The W2 194 B10
Ring, The W2 82 DD73
Ring Cl, Brom. 124 EH94
Garden Rd
Ring Rd W12 81 CW73
Ringcroft St N7 65 DN64
Ringers Rd, Brom. 144 EG97
Ringford Rd SW18 119 CZ85
Ringlet Cl E16 86 EH72
Ringlewell Cl, Enf. 30 DV40
Central Av
Ringley Pk Rd, Reig. 184 DC134
Ringmer Av SW6 99 CY81
Ringmer Gdns N19 65 DL61
Sussex Way
Ringmer Pl N21 30 DR43
Ringmer Way, Brom. 145 EM99
Ringmore Ri SE23 122 DV87
Ringmore Rd, Walt. 136 BW104
Ringshall Rd, Orp. 146 EU97
Ringslade Rd N22 45 DM54
Ringstead Rd SE6 123 EB87
Ringstead Rd, Sutt. 158 DD105
Ringway N11 45 DJ51
Ringway, Sthl. 96 BY78
Ringway Rd, St.Alb. 8 CB27
Ringwold Cl, Beck. 123 DY94
Ringwood Av N2 44 DF54
Ringwood Av, Croy. 141 DL101
Ringwood Av, Horn. 72 FK61
Ringwood Av, Orp. 164 EW110
Ringwood Av, Red. 184 DF131
Ringwood Cl, Pnr. 60 BW55
Ringwood Gdns E14 204 A8
Ringwood Gdns SW15 119 CU89
Ringwood Rd E17 67 DZ58
Ringwood Way N21 45 DP46
Ringwood Way, Hmptn. 116 CA91
Ripley Av, Egh. 112 AY93
Ripley Bypass, Wok. 168 BK122
Ripley Cl, Brom. 145 EM99
Ringmer Way
Ripley Cl, Croy. 161 EC107
Ripley Cl, Slou. 92 AY77
Ripley Gdns SW14 98 CR83
Ripley Gdns, Sutt. 158 DC105
Ripley La, Wok. 168 BL123
Ripley Ms E11 68 EE59
Wadley Rd
Ripley Rd E16 86 EJ72
Ripley Rd, Belv. 106 FA77
Ripley Rd, Enf. 30 DQ39
Ripley Rd, Hmptn. 116 CA94
Ripley Rd, Ilf. 69 ET61
Ripley Vw, Loug. 33 EP38
Ripley Vil W5 79 CJ72
Castlebar Rd
Ripley Way, Epsom 156 CN111
Ripley Way (Cheshunt), Wal.Cr. 14 DV30
Riplington Ct SW15 119 CU87
Longwood Dr
Ripon Cl, Nthlt. 60 CA64
Ripon Gdns, Chess. 155 CJ106
Ripon Gdns, Ilf. 68 EL58
Ripon Rd N9 46 DV45
Ripon Rd N17 66 DR55
Ripon Rd SE18 105 EP79
Ripon Way, Borwd. 26 CQ43
Rippersley Rd, Well. 106 EU81
Ripple Rd, Bark. 87 EQ66
Ripple Rd, Dag. 88 EV67
Rippleside Commercial Est, Bark. 88 EW68
Ripplevale Gro N1 83 DM66
Rippolson Rd SE18 105 ET78
Ripston Rd, Ashf. 115 BR92
Risborough Dr, Wor.Pk. 139 CU101
Risborough St SE1 200 G4
Risdon St SE16 202 G5
Rise, The E11 68 EG57
Rise, The N13 45 DN49
Rise, The NW7 43 CT51
Rise, The NW10 62 CR63
Rise, The, Bex. 126 EW87
Rise, The, Borwd. 26 CM43
Rise, The, Buck.H. 48 EK45
Rise, The, Dart. 107 FF84
Rise, The, Edg. 42 CP50
Rise, The, Epsom 157 CT110
Rise, The, Grav. 131 GL9
Rise, The, Grnf. 61 CG6
Rise, The, St.Alb. 9 CD2
Rise, The, Sev. 191 FJ12
Rise, The, S.Croy. 160 DW10
Rise, The, Tad. 173 CW12
Rise, The, Uxb. 76 BM6
Rise Pk Boul, Rom. 51 FF5
Rise Pk Par, Rom. 51 FE5
Pettits La N
Risebridge Chase, Rom. 51 FF5
Risebridge Rd, Rom. 51 FF5
Risedale Rd, Bexh. 107 FB8
Riseldine Rd SE23 123 DY8
Riseway, Brwd. 54 FY4
Rising Hill Cl, Nthwd. 39 BQ5
Ducks Hill Rd
Rising Sun Ct EC1 196 G
Risinghill St N1 83 DM6
Risingholme Cl, Bushey 40 CB4
Risingholme Cl, Har. 41 CE5
Risingholme Rd, Har. 41 CE5
Risings, The E17 67 ED5
Risley Av N17 46 DQ5
Rita Rd SW8 101 DL8
Ritches Rd N15 66 DQ5
Ritchie Rd, Croy. 142 DV10
Ritchie St N1 83 DN6
Ritchings Av E17 67 DY5
Ritherdon Rd SW17 120 DG8
Ritson Rd E8 84 DU6
Ritter St SE18 105 EN7
Ritz Ct, Pot.B. 12 DA3
Ritz Par W5 80 CM7
Connell Cres
Rivaz Pl E9 84 DW6
Rivenhall Gdns E18 68 EF5
River Ash Est, Shep. 135 BT10
River Av N13 45 DP4
River Av, T.Ditt. 137 CG10
River Bk N21 46 DQ4
River Bk, E.Mol. 137 CD9
River Bk, T.Ditt. 137 CF9
River Bk, W.Mol. 136 BZ9
River Barge Cl E14 204 E
River Brent Business Pk W7 97 CE7
River Cl E11 68 EJ5
River Cl, Rain. 89 FH7
River Cl, Ruis. 59 BT5
River Cl, Sthl. 96 CC7
River Cl, Surb. 137 CK9
Catherine Rd
River Cl, Wal.Cr. 15 EA3
River Crane Wk, Felt. 116 BX8
River Crane Wk, Houns. 116 BX8
River Crane Way, Felt. 116 BZ8
Watermill Way
River Dr, Upmin. 72 FQ5
River Front, Enf. 30 DR4
River Gdns, Cars. 140 DG10
River Gdns, Felt. 95 BV8
River Gro Pk, Beck. 143 DZ9
River Hill, Cob. 169 BV11
River Island Cl, Lthd. 171 CD12
River La, Lthd. 171 CD12
River La, Rich. 117 CK8
River Pk Av, Stai. 113 BD9
River Pk Gdns, Brom. 123 ED9
River Pk Rd N22 45 DM5
River Pl N1 84 DQ6
River Reach, Tedd. 117 CJ9
River Rd, Bark. 87 ES6
River Rd, Brwd. 54 FS4
River Rd, Buck.H. 48 EL4
River Rd, Stai. 133 BF9
River Rd Business Pk, Bark. 87 ET6
River St EC1 196 D
River St EC1 83 DN6
River Ter W6 99 CW7
Crisp Rd
River Vw, Enf. 30 DQ41
Chase Side
River Vw, Grays 111 GG77
River Wk (Denham), Uxb. 58 BJ64
River Wk, Walt. 135 BU100
River Way, Epsom 156 CR106
River Way, Loug. 33 EN44
River Way, Twick. 116 CB89
River Wey Navigation, Wok. 167 BB122
Riverbank, Stai. 113 BF93
Riverbank Way, Brent. 97 CJ79
Rivercourt Rd W6 99 CV77
Riverdale SE13 103 EC83
Lewisham High St
Riverdale Cl, Bark. 87 ES69
Thames Rd
Riverdale Dr SW18 120 DB88
Strathville Rd
Riverdale Dr, Wok. 167 AZ121
Riverdale Gdns, Twick. 117 CJ86
Riverdale Rd SE18 105 ET78
Riverdale Rd, Bex. 126 EZ87
Riverdale Rd, Erith 107 FB78
Riverdale Rd, Felt. 116 BY91
Riverdale Rd, Twick. 117 CJ86
Riverdene, Edg. 42 CQ48
Riverdene Rd, Ilf. 69 EN62
Riverfield Rd, Stai. 113 BF93
Riverhead Cl E17 47 DX54
Riverhead Dr, Sutt. 158 DA110
Riverhill, Sev. 191 FL130
Riverholme Dr, Epsom 156 CR109
Rivermead, E.Mol. 136 CC97
Rivermead, W.Byf. 152 BM113
Rivermead Cl, Add. 152 BJ108
Rivermead Cl, Tedd. 117 CH92
Rivermead Ct SW6 99 CZ83
Rivermeads Av, Twick. 116 CA90
Rivermount, Walt. 135 BT101
Rivernook Cl, Walt. 136 BW99
Riversdale, Grav. 130 GE89
Riversdale Rd N5 65 DP62
Riversdale Rd, Rom. 51 FB52
Riversdale Rd, T.Ditt. 137 CG99
Riversdell Cl, Cher. 133 BF101
Riversfield Rd, Enf. 30 DS41
Riverside NW4 63 CV59
Riverside SE7 104 EH76

Riverside, Cher. 134 BG97
Riverside (Eynsford), Dart. 148 FK103
Riverside (Runnymede), Egh. 113 BA90
Windsor Rd
Riverside (London Colney), St.Alb. 10 CL27
Riverside, Shep. 135 BS101
Riverside, Stai. 133 BF95
Riverside (Wraysbury), Stai. 112 AW87
Riverside, Twick. 117 CH88
Riverside, The, E.Mol. 137 CD97
Riverside Av, E.Mol. 137 CD99
Riverside Business Cen SW18 120 DB88
Riverside Cl E5 66 DW60
Riverside Cl W7 79 CE70
Riverside Cl, Kings L. 7 BP29
Riverside Cl, Kings.T. 137 CK98
Riverside Cl, Orp. 146 EW96
Riverside Cl, Stai. 133 BF95
Riverside Cl, Wall. 141 DH104
Riverside Ct E4 31 EB44
Chelwood Cl
Riverside Ct SW8 101 DK79
Riverside Dr NW11 63 CY58
Riverside Dr W4 98 CR80
Riverside Dr, Esher 154 CA105
Riverside Dr, Mitch. 140 DE99
Riverside Dr, Rich. 117 CH89
Riverside Dr, Rick. 38 BK46
Riverside Dr, Stai. 133 BF95
Riverside Dr (Egham Hythe), Stai. 113 BE92
Riverside Gdns N3 63 CY55
Riverside Gdns W6 99 CV78
Riverside Gdns, Enf. 30 DQ40
Riverside Gdns, Wem. 80 CL68
Riverside Gdns, Wok. 167 BB121
Riverside Ind Est, Bark. 88 EU69
Riverside Ind Est, Enf. 31 DY44
Riverside Mans E1 202 F2
Riverside Ms, Croy. 141 DL104
Wandle Rd
Riverside Path (Cheshunt), Wal.Cr. 15 DY29
Church La
Riverside Pl, Stai. 114 BK86
Riverside Rd E15 85 EC68
Riverside Rd N15 66 DU58
Riverside Rd SW17 120 DB91
Riverside Rd, Sid. 126 EY90
Riverside Rd, Stai. 113 BF94
Riverside Rd (Stanwell), Stai. 114 BK85
Riverside Rd, Walt. 154 BX105
Riverside Rd, Wat. 23 BV44
Riverside Wk SE1 200 B3
Riverside Wk SE1 83 DM74
Riverside Wk, Bex. 126 EW87
Riverside Wk, Islw. 97 CE83
Riverside Wk, Kings.T. 137 CK96
High St
Riverside Wk, Loug. 33 EP44
Riverside Way, Dart. 128 FL85
Riverside Way, St.Alb. 9 CD32
Riverside Way, Uxb. 76 BH67
Riverside W SW18 100 DB84
Smugglers Way
Riverton Cl W9 81 CZ69
Riverview Gdns SW13 99 CV79
Riverview Gdns, Cob. 153 BU113
Riverview Gdns, Twick. 117 CF89
Riverview Gro W4 98 CP79
Riverview Pk SE6 123 EA89
Riverview Rd W4 98 CP79
Riverview Rd, Epsom 156 CQ105
Riverview Rd, Green. 129 FU85
Riverway N13 45 DN50
Riverway, Stai. 134 BH95
Riverwood La, Chis. 145 ER95
Rivey Cl, W.Byf. 151 BF114
Rivington Av, Wdf.Grn. 48 EK54
Rivington Ct NW10 81 CU67
Rivington Cres NW7 43 CT52
Rivington Pl EC2 197 N3
Rivington St EC2 197 M3
Rivington St EC2 84 DS69
Rivington Wk E8 84 DU67
Wilde Cl
Rivulet Rd N17 46 DQ52
Rixon Cl, Slou. 74 AY72
Rixon Ho SE18 105 EP79
Barnfield Rd
Rixon St N7 65 DN62
Rixsen Rd E12 68 EL64
Roach Rd E3 85 EA66
Roads Pl N19 65 DL61
Hornsey Rd
Roakes Av, Add. 134 BH103
Roan St SE10 103 EC79
Robarts Cl, Pnr. 59 BV57
Field End Rd
Robb Rd, Stan. 41 CG51
Robert Adam St W1 194 F8
Robert Adam St W1 82 DG72
Robert Cl W9 82 DC70
Randolph Av
Robert Cl, Chig. 49 ET50
Robert Cl, Pot.B. 11 CY33
Robert Cl, Walt. 153 BV106
Robert Dashwood Way SE17 201 H9
Robert Dashwood Way SE17 102 DQ77
Robert Gentry Ho W14 99 CY78
Comeragh Rd
Robert Keen Cl SE15 102 DU81
Cicely Rd
Robert Lowe Cl SE14 103 DX80
Robert Owen Ho SW6 99 CX81
Robert St E16 87 EP74
Robert St NW1 195 J3
Robert St NW1 83 DH69
Robert St SE18 105 ER77
Robert St WC2 200 A1
Robert St, Croy. 142 DQ104
High St
Roberta St E2 84 DU69
Roberton Dr, Brom. 144 EJ95
Roberts Cl SE9 125 ER88
Roberts Cl, Orp. 146 EW99
Roberts Cl, Rom. 51 FH53
Roberts Cl, Stai. 114 BJ86
Roberts Cl, Sutt. 157 CX108
Roberts Cl (Cheshunt), Wal.Cr. 15 DY30
Norwood Rd
Roberts Cl, West Dr. 76 BL74
Roberts La (Chalfont St. Peter), Ger.Cr. 37 BA50
Roberts Ms SW1 198 F7
Roberts Ms, Orp. 146 EU102
Robert's Pl EC1 196 E4
Roberts Rd E17 47 EB53
Roberts Rd NW7 43 CY51
Roberts Rd, Belv. 106 FA78
Roberts Rd, Wat. 24 BW43
Tucker St
Roberts Way, Egh. 112 AW94
Roberts Wd Dr (Chalfont St. Peter), Ger.Cr. 37 AZ50
Robertsbridge Rd, Cars. 140 DC102
Robertson Cl, Brox. 15 DY26
Robertson Ct, Wok. 166 AS118
Raglan Rd
Robertson Rd E15 85 EC67
Robertson St SW8 101 DH82
Robeson St E3 85 DZ71
Ackroyd Dr
Robeson Way, Borwd. 26 CQ39
Robin Cl NW7 42 CS48
Robin Cl, Add. 152 BK106
Robin Cl, Hmptn. 116 BY92
Robin Cl, Rom. 51 FD52
Robin Ct SE16 202 B8
Robin Ct SE16 102 DU77
Robin Cres E6 86 EK71
Robin Gdns, Red. 184 DG131
Robin Gro N6 64 DG61
Robin Gro, Brent. 97 CJ79
Robin Gro, Har. 62 CM58
Robin Hill Dr, Chis. 124 EL93
Robin Hood Cl, Wok. 166 AT118
Robin Hood Cres, Wok. 166 AS117
Robin Hood Dr, Bushey 24 BZ39
Robin Hood Dr, Har. 41 CF52
Robin Hood Grn, Orp. 146 EU99
Robin Hood La E14 85 EC73
Robin Hood La SW15 118 CS91
Robin Hood La, Bexh. 126 EY85
Robin Hood La, Guil. 167 AZ124
Robin Hood La, Sutt. 158 DA106
Robin Hood Rd SW19 119 CV92
Robin Hood Rd, Brwd. 54 FV45
Robin Hood Rd, Wok. 166 AT118
Robin Hood Way SW15 118 CS91
Robin Hood Way SW20 118 CS91
Robin Hood Way, Grnf. 79 CF65
Robin Way, Orp. 146 EV97
Robin Way (Cuffley), Pot.B. 13 DL28
Robin Way, Stai. 113 BF90
Robin Willis Way, Wind. 112 AU86
Robina Cl, Bexh. 106 EX84
Robina Cl, Nthwd. 39 BT53
Robinhood Cl, Mitch. 141 DJ97
Robinhood La, Mitch. 141 DJ97
Robinia Av, Grav. 130 GD87
Robinia Cl, Ilf. 49 ES51
Robinia Cres E10 67 EB61
Robins Cl, St.Alb. 10 CL27
High St
Robins Cl, Uxb. 76 BJ71
Newcourt
Robins Ct SE12 124 EJ90
Robins Gro, W.Wick. 144 EG104
Robins La, Epp. 33 EQ36
Robins Orchard (Chalfont St. Peter), Ger.Cr. 36 AY51
Robinscroft Ms SE10 103 EB81
Sparta St
Robinson Av (Cheshunt), Wal.Cr. 13 DP28
Robinson Cl, Horn. 89 FH66
Robinson Cres, Bushey 40 CC46
Robinson Rd E2 84 DW68
Robinson Rd SW17 120 DE93
Robinson Rd, Dag. 70 FA63
Robinson St SW3 100 DF79
Christchurch St
Robinsons Cl W13 79 CG71
Robinsway, Wal.Abb. 16 EE34
Roundhills
Robinsway, Walt. 154 BW105
Robinwood Gro, Uxb. 76 BM70
Robinwood Pl SW15 118 CR91
Roborough Wk, Horn. 90 FJ65
Robsart St SW9 101 DM82
Robson Av NW10 81 CU67
Robson Cl E6 86 EL72
Linton Gdns
Robson Cl, Enf. 29 DP40
Robson Cl (Chalfont St. Peter), Ger.Cr. 36 AY50
Robson Rd SE27 121 DP90
Robsons Cl, Wal.Cr. 14 DW29
Robyns Cft, Grav. 130 GE90
Robyns Way, Sev. 190 FF122
Roch Av, Edg. 42 CM54
Rochdale Rd E17 67 EA59
Rochdale Rd SE2 106 EV78
Rochdale Way SE8 103 EA80
Octavius St
Roche Rd SW16 141 DM95
Roche Wk, Cars. 140 DD100
Rochelle Cl SW11 100 DD84
Rochelle St E2 197 P3
Rochemont Wk E8 84 DT67
Pownall Rd
Rochester Av E13 86 EJ67
Rochester Av, Brom. 144 EH96
Rochester Av, Felt. 115 BT89
Rochester Cl SW16 121 DL94
Rochester Cl, Enf. 30 DS39
Rochester Cl, Sid. 126 EV86
Rochester Dr, Bex. 126 EZ86
Rochester Dr, Pnr. 60 BX57
Rochester Dr, Wat. 8 BW34
Rochester Gdns, Cat. 176 DS122
Rochester Gdns, Croy. 142 DS104
Rochester Gdns, Ilf. 69 EM59
Rochester Ms NW1 83 DJ66
Rochester Pl NW1 83 DJ65
Rochester Rd NW1 83 DJ65
Rochester Rd, Cars. 158 DF105
Rochester Rd, Dart. 128 FN87
Rochester Rd, Grav. 131 GL87
Rochester Rd, Nthwd. 59 BT55
Rochester Rd, Stai. 113 BD92
Rochester Row SW1 199 L8
Rochester Row SW1 101 DJ77
Rochester Sq NW1 83 DJ66
Rochester St SW1 199 M7
Rochester St SW1 101 DK76
Rochester Ter NW1 83 DJ65
Rochester Wk SE1 201 K2
Rochester Way SE3 104 EH81
Rochester Way SE9 105 EM83
Rochester Way, Dart. 127 FD87
Rochester Way, Rick. 23 BP42
Rochester Way Relief Rd SE3 104 EH81
Rochester Way Relief Rd SE9 104 EL84
Rochford Av, Brwd. 55 GA43
Rochford Av, Loug. 33 EQ41
Rochford Av, Rom. 70 EW57
Rochford Av, Wal.Abb. 15 ED33
Rochford Cl E6 86 EK68
Boleyn Rd
Rochford Cl, Brox. 15 DY26
Rochford Cl, Horn. 89 FH65
Rochford Grn, Loug. 33 EQ41
Rochford St NW5 64 DF64
Rochford Wk E8 84 DU66
Wilman Gro
Rochford Way, Croy. 141 DL100
Rochfords Gdns, Slou. 74 AW74
Rock Av SW14 98 CR83
South Worple Way
Rock Gdns, Dag. 71 FB64
Rock Gro Way SE16 202 C8
Rock Hill SE26 122 DT91
Rock Hill, Orp. 164 FA107
Rock St N4 65 DN61
Rockall Ct, Slou. 93 BB76
Rockbourne Rd SE23 123 DX88
Rockchase Gdns, Horn. 72 FL58
Rockdale Rd, Sev. 191 FH125
Rockells Pl SE22 122 DV86
Rockfield Cl, Oxt. 188 EF131
Rockfield Rd, Oxt. 188 EF129
Rockford Av, Grnf. 79 CG68
Rockhall Rd NW2 63 CX63
Rockhampton Cl SE27 121 DN91
Rockhampton Rd
Rockhampton Rd SE27 121 DN91
Rockhampton Rd, S.Croy. 160 DS107
Rockingham Av, Horn. 71 FH58
Rockingham Cl SW15 99 CT84
Rockingham Cl, Uxb. 76 BJ67
Rockingham Est SE1 201 H7
Rockingham Est SE1 102 DQ76
Rockingham Par, Uxb. 76 BJ66
Rockingham Rd, Uxb. 76 BH67
Rockingham St SE1 201 H7
Rockingham St SE1 102 DQ76
Rockland Rd SW15 99 CY84
Rocklands Dr, Stan. 41 CH54
Rockleigh Ct, Brwd. 55 GA45
Hutton Rd
Rockley Rd W14 99 CX75
Rockliffe Av, Kings L. 6 BN30
Rockmount Rd SE18 105 ET78
Rockmount Rd SE19 122 DR93
Rocks La SW13 99 CU81
Rockshaw Rd, Red. 185 DM127
Rockware Av, Grnf. 79 CD67
Rockways, Barn. 27 CT44
Rockwell Gdns SE19 122 DS92
Rockwell Rd, Dag. 71 FB64
Rockwood Pl W12 99 CW75
Rocky La, Reig. 184 DF128
Rocliffe St N1 196 G1
Rocombe Cres SE23 122 DW87
Rocque La SE3 104 EF83
Rodborough Rd NW11 64 DA60
Roden Ct N6 65 DK59
Hornsey La
Roden Gdns, Croy. 142 DS100
Roden St N7 65 DM62
Roden St, Ilf. 69 EN62
Rodenhurst Rd SW4 121 DJ86
Rodeo Cl, Erith 107 FH81
Roderick Rd NW3 64 DF63
Rodgers Cl, Borwd. 25 CK44
Roding Av, Wdf.Grn. 48 EL51
Roding Gdns, Loug. 32 EL44
Roding La, Buck.H. 48 EL46
Roding La, Chig. 49 EN46
Roding La N, Wdf.Grn. 48 EK54
Roding La S, Ilf. 68 EK56
Roding La S, Wdf.Grn. 68 EK56
Roding Ms E1 202 C2
Roding Rd E5 67 DX63
Roding Rd E6 87 EP71
Roding Rd, Loug. 32 EL43
Roding Trd Est, Bark. 87 EP66
Roding Vw, Buck.H. 48 EK46
Roding Way, Rain. 90 FK68
Rodings, The, Upmin. 73 FR58
Rodings, The, Wdf.Grn. 48 EJ51
Rodings Row, Barn. 27 CY43
Leecroft Rd
Rodmarton St W1 194 E7
Rodmarton St W1 82 DF71
Rodmell Cl, Hayes 78 BY70
Rodmell Slope N12 43 CZ50
Rodmere St SE10 104 EE78
Trafalgar Rd
Rodmill La SW2 121 DL87
Rodney Cl, Croy. 141 DP102
Rodney Cl, N.Mal. 138 CS99
Rodney Cl, Pnr. 60 BY59
Rodney Cl, Walt. 136 BW102
Rodney Rd
Rodney Ct W9 82 DC70
Maida Vale
Rodney Gdns, Pnr. 59 BV57
Rodney Gdns, W.Wick. 162 EG105
Rodney Grn, Walt. 136 BW103
Rodney Pl E17 47 DY54
Rodney Pl SE17 201 J8
Rodney Pl SE17 102 DQ77
Rodney Pl SW19 140 DC95
Rodney Rd E11 68 EH56
Rodney Rd SE17 201 J8
Rodney Rd SE17 102 DR77
Rodney Rd, Mitch. 140 DE96
Rodney Rd, N.Mal. 138 CS99
Rodney Rd, Twick. 116 CA86
Rodney Rd, Walt. 136 BW103
Rodney St N1 83 DM68
Rodney Way, Rom. 50 FA53
Rodney Way, Slou. 93 BE81
Rodona Rd, Wey. 153 BR111
Rodway Rd SW15 119 CU87
Rodway Rd, Brom. 144 EH95
Rodwell Cl, Ruis. 60 BW59
Rodwell Ct, Add. 152 BJ105
Garfield Rd
Rodwell Pl, Edg. 42 CN51
Whitchurch La
Rodwell Rd SE22 122 DT86
Roe End NW9 62 CQ56
Roe Grn NW9 62 CQ57
Roe La NW9 62 CP56
Roe Way, Wall. 159 DL108
Roebourne Way E16 105 EN75
Roebuck Cl, Ash. 172 CL120
Roebuck Cl, Felt. 115 BV91
Roebuck Cl, Reig. 184 DB134
Roebuck La N17 46 DT51
High Rd
Roebuck La, Buck.H. 48 EJ45
Roebuck Rd, Chess. 156 CN106
Roebuck Rd, Ilf. 50 EV50
Roedean Av, Enf. 30 DW39
Roedean Cl, Enf. 30 DW39
Roedean Cl, Orp. 164 EV105
Roedean Cres SW15 118 CS86
Roedean Dr, Rom. 71 FE56
Roehampton Cl SW15 99 CU84
Roehampton Cl, Grav. 131 GL87
Roehampton Dr, Chis. 125 EQ93
Roehampton Gate SW15 118 CS86
Roehampton High St SW15 119 CV87
Roehampton La SW15 99 CU84
Roehampton Vale SW15 118 CS90
Rofant Rd, Nthwd. 39 BS51
Roffes La, Cat. 176 DR124
Roffey Cl, Pur. 175 DP116
Roffey St E14 204 D5
Roffey St E14 103 EC75
Roffords, Wok. 166 AV117
Rogate Ho E5 66 DU62
Muir Rd
Roger Dowley Ct E2 84 DW68
Russia La
Roger St WC1 196 C5
Roger St WC1 83 DM70
Rogers Cl, Cat. 176 DV122
Tillingdown Hill
Rogers Cl, Couls. 175 DP118
Rogers Cl (Cheshunt), Wal.Cr. 14 DR26
Hammondstreet Rd
Rogers Ct, Swan. 147 FG98
Rogers Gdns, Dag. 70 FA64
Rogers La, Slou. 74 AT67
Rogers La, Warl. 177 DZ118
Rogers Mead, Gdse. 186 DV132
Ivy Mill La
Rogers Rd E16 86 EF72
Rogers Rd SW17 120 DD91
Rogers Rd, Dag. 70 FA64
Rogers Rd, Grays 110 GC77
Rogers Ruff, Nthwd. 39 BQ53
Rogers Wk N12 44 DB48
Brook Meadow
Rojack Rd SE23 123 DX88
Roke Cl, Ken. 160 DQ114
Roke Lo Rd, Ken. 159 DP113
Roke Rd, Ken. 176 DQ115
Rokeby Ct, Wok. 166 AT117
Rokeby Gdns, Wdf.Grn. 48 EG53
Rokeby Pl SW20 119 CV94
Rokeby Rd SE4 103 DZ82
Rokeby St E15 86 EE67
Roker Pk Av, Uxb. 58 BL63
Rokesby Cl, Well. 105 ER82
Rokesby Pl, Wem. 61 CK64
Rokesly Av N8 65 DL57
Roland Gdns SW7 100 DC78
Roland Gdns, Felt. 116 BZ90
Hampton Rd W
Roland Ms E1 85 DX71
Stepney Grn
Roland Rd E17 67 ED56
Roland Way SE17 102 DR78
Roland Way SW7 100 DC78
Roland Gdns
Roland Way, Wor.Pk. 139 CT103
Roles Gro, Rom. 70 EX56
Rolfe Cl, Barn. 28 DE42
Rolinsden Way, Kes. 162 EK105
Roll Gdns, Ilf. 69 EN57
Rollesby Rd, Chess. 156 CN107
Rollesby Way SE28 88 EW73
Rolleston Av, Orp. 145 EP100
Rolleston Cl, Orp. 145 EP101
Rolleston Rd, S.Croy. 160 DR108
Rollins St SE15 102 DW79
Rollit Cres, Houns. 116 CA85
Rollit St N7 65 DM64
Hornsey Rd
Rollo Rd, Swan. 127 FF94
Rolls Bldgs EC4 196 D8
Rolls Pk Av E4 47 EA51
Rolls Pk Rd E4 47 EB50
Rolls Pas EC4 196 D8
Rolls Rd SE1 202 A10
Rolls Rd SE1 102 DT78
Rollscourt Av SE24 122 DQ85
Rolt St SE8 103 DY79
Rolvenden Gdns, Brom. 124 EK94
Rolvenden Pl N17 46 DU53
Manor Rd
Rom Cres, Rom. 71 FF59
Rom Valley Way, Rom. 71 FE59
Roma Read Cl SW15 119 CV87
Bessborough Rd
Roma Rd E17 67 DY55
Roman Cl W3 98 CP75
Avenue Gdns
Roman Cl, Felt. 116 BW85
Roman Cl, Rain. 89 FD68
Roman Cl (Harefield), Uxb. 38 BH53
Roman Gdns, Kings L. 7 BP30
Roman Ho, Rain. 89 FD68
Roman Cl
Roman Ind Est, Croy. 142 DS101
Roman Ri SE19 122 DR93
Roman Rd E2 84 DW69
Roman Rd E3 85 DY68
Roman Rd E6 86 EL70
Roman Rd N10 45 DH52
Roman Rd NW2 63 CW62
Roman Rd W4 99 CT77
Roman Rd, Grav. 130 GC90
Roman Rd, Ilf. 87 EP65
Roman Sq SE28 88 EU74
Roman Vil Rd (South Darenth), Dart. 128 FQ92
Roman Way N7 83 DM65
Roman Way SE15 102 DW80
Clifton Way
Roman Way, Cars. 158 DF108
Fountain Dr
Roman Way, Croy. 141 DP103
Roman Way, Dart. 127 FE85
Roman Way, Enf. 30 DT43
Roman Way, Wal.Abb. 31 EC40
Sewardstone Rd
Roman Way Ind Est N1 83 DM66
Offord St
Romanfield Rd SW2 121 DM87
Romanhurst Av, Brom. 144 EE98
Romanhurst Gdns, Brom. 144 EE98
Romans Way, Wok. 168 BG115
Romany Gdns E17 47 DY53
McEntee Av
Romany Gdns, Sutt. 140 DA101
Romany Ri, Orp. 145 EQ102
Romberg Rd SW17 120 DG90
Romborough Gdns SE13 123 EC85
Romborough Way SE13 123 EC85
Romeland, Borwd. 25 CK44
Romeland, Wal.Abb. 15 EC33
Romero Cl SW9 101 DM83
Stockwell Rd
Romero Sq SE3 104 EJ84
Romeyn Rd SW16 121 DM90
Romford Rd E7 68 EH64
Romford Rd E12 68 EL63
Romford Rd E15 86 EE66
Romford Rd, Chig. 50 EU48
Romford Rd, Rom. 50 EY52
Romford Rd, S.Ock. 90 FQ73
Romford St E1 84 DU71
Romilly Dr, Wat. 40 BY48
Romilly Rd N4 65 DP61
Romilly St W1 195 M10
Romilly St W1 83 DK73
Rommany Rd SE27 122 DR91
Romney Chase, Horn. 72 FM58
Romney Cl N17 46 DV53
Romney Cl NW11 64 DC60
Romney Cl SE14 102 DW80
Kender St
Romney Cl, Ashf. 115 BQ92
Romney Cl, Chess. 156 CL105
Romney Cl, Har. 60 CA59
Romney Dr, Brom. 124 EK94
Romney Dr, Har. 60 CA59
Romney Gdns, Bexh. 106 EZ81
Romney Lock, Wind. 92 AS79
Romney Ms W1 194 F6
Romney Par, Hayes 77 BR68
Romney Rd
Romney Rd SE10 103 EC79
Romney Rd, Grav. 130 GE90
Romney Rd, Hayes 77 BR68
Romney Rd, N.Mal. 138 CR100
Romney Row NW2 63 CX61
Brent Ter
Romney St SW1 199 N7
Romney St SW1 101 DL76
Romola Rd SE24 121 DP88
Romsey Cl, Orp. 163 EP105
Romsey Cl, Slou. 93 AZ76
Romsey Gdns, Dag. 88 EX67
Romsey Rd W13 79 CG73
Romsey Rd, Dag. 88 EX67
Ron Leighton Way E6 86 EL67
Rona Rd NW3 64 DG63
Rona Wk N1 84 DR65
Clephane Rd
Ronald Av E15 86 EE69
Ronald Cl, Beck. 143 DZ98
Ronald Rd, Rom. 52 FN53
Ronald St E1 84 DW72
Devonport St
Ronalds Rd N5 65 DN64
Ronalds Rd, Brom. 144 EG95
Ronaldsay Spur, Slou. 74 AS71
Ronaldstone Rd, Sid. 125 ES86
Ronart St, Har. 61 CF55
Stuart Rd
Rondu Rd NW2 63 CY64
Ronelean Rd, Surb. 138 CM104
Roneo Cor, Horn. 71 FF60
Roneo Link, Horn. 71 FF60
Ronfearn Av, Orp. 146 EX99
Ronneby Cl, Wey. 135 BS104
Ronson Way, Lthd. 171 CG121
Randalls Rd
Ronver Rd SE12 124 EF87
Rood La EC3 197 M10
Rood La EC3 84 DS73
Rook Cl, Horn. 89 FG66
Rook La, Cat. 175 DM124
Rook Wk E6 86 EL72
Allhallows Rd
Rookby Ct N21 45 DP47
Carpenter Gdns
Rookdean, Sev. 190 FC122
Rooke Way SE10 205 K10
Rooke Way SE10 104 EF78
Rookeries Cl, Felt. 115 BV90
Rookery, The, Grays 109 FU79
Rookery Cl NW9 63 CT57
Rookery Cl, Lthd. 171 CE124
Rookery Ct, Grays 109 FU79
Rookery Cres, Dag. 89 FB66

Rowland Gro SE26 122 DV90
Dallas Rd
Rowland Hill Av N17 46 DQ52
Rowland Hill St NW3 64 DE64
Rowland Wk (Havering-atte-Bower), Rom. 51 FE48
Rowland Way SW19 140 DB95
Hayward Cl
Rowland Way, Ashf. 115 BQ94
Littleton Rd
Rowlands Av, Pnr. 40 CA51
Rowlands Cl N6 64 DG58
North Hill
Rowlands Cl NW7 43 CU52
Rowlands Cl (Cheshunt), Wal.Cr. 15 DX30
Rowlands Flds (Cheshunt), Wal.Cr. 15 DX29
Rowlands Rd, Dag. 70 EZ61
Rowlatt Cl, Dart. 128 FJ91
Rowlett Rd, Dart. 128 FJ91
Whitehead Cl
Rowley Av, Sid. 126 EV87
Rowley Cl, Wat. 24 BY44
Lower Paddock Rd
Rowley Cl, Wem. 80 CM66
Rowley Cl, Wok. 168 BG116
Rowley Ct, Cat. 176 DR122
Fairbourne La
Rowley Gdns N4 66 DQ59
Rowley Gdns (Cheshunt), Wal.Cr. 15 DX28
Warwick Dr
Rowley Grn Rd, Barn. 27 CT43
Rowley Ind Pk W3 98 CP76
Rowley La, Barn. 27 CT43
Rowley La, Borwd. 26 CR39
Rowley La, Slou. 74 AW67
Rowley Mead, Epp. 18 EW25
Rowley Rd N15 66 DQ57
Rowley Way NW8 82 DB67
Rowlheys Pl, West Dr. 94 BL76
Rowlls Rd, Kings.T. 138 CM97
Rowmarsh Cl, Grav. 130 GD91
Rowney Gdns, Dag. 88 EW65
Rowney Rd, Dag. 88 EV65
Rowntree Clifford Cl E13 86 EH69
Liddon Rd
Rowntree Path SE28 88 EV73
Booth Cl
Rowntree Rd, Twick. 117 CE88
Rowse Cl E15 85 EC66
Rowsley Av NW4 63 CW55
Rowstock Gdns N7 65 DK64
Rowton Rd SE18 105 EQ80
Rowtown, Add. 151 BF108
Rowzill Rd, Swan. 127 FF93
Roxborough Av, Har. 61 CD59
Roxborough Av, Islw. 97 CF80
Roxborough Pk, Har. 61 CE59
Roxborough Rd, Har. 61 CD57
Roxbourne Cl, Nthlt. 78 BX65
Roxburgh Av, Upmin. 72 FQ62
Roxburgh Rd SE27 121 DP92
Roxburn Way, Ruis. 59 BT62
Roxby Pl SW6 100 DA79
Roxeth Ct, Ashf. 114 BN92
Roxeth Grn Av, Har. 60 CB62
Roxeth Gro, Har. 60 CB63
Roxeth Hill, Har. 61 CD61
Roxford Cl, Shep. 135 BS99
Roxley Rd SE13 123 EB86
Roxton Gdns, Croy. 161 EA106
Roxwell Gdns, Brwd. 55 GC43
Roxwell Rd W12 99 CU75
Roxwell Rd, Bark. 88 EU68
Roxwell Trd Pk E10 67 DY59
Roxwell Way, Wdf.Grn. 48 EJ52
Roxy Av, Rom. 70 EW59
Roy Gdns, Ilf. 69 ES56
Roy Gro, Hmptn. 116 CB93
Roy Rd, Nthwd. 39 BT52
Roy Sq E14 85 DY73
Narrow St
Royal Albert Dock E16 87 EM73
Royal Albert Roundabout E16 86 EL73
Royal Albert Way
Royal Albert Way E16 86 EK73
Royal Arc W1 199 K1
Royal Artillery Barracks SE18 105 EN78
Repository Rd
Royal Av SW3 198 D10
Royal Av SW3 100 DF78
Royal Av, Wal.Cr. 15 DY33
Royal Av, Wor.Pk. 138 CS103
Royal Circ SE27 121 DN90
Royal Cl N16 66 DS60
Manor Rd
Royal Cl, Ilf. 70 EU59
Royal Cl, Uxb. 76 BM72
Royal Cl, Wor.Pk. 138 CS103
Royal Coll St NW1 83 DJ66
Royal Ct EC3 84 DR72
Cornhill
Royal Ct SE16 203 M6
Royal Ct SE16 103 DZ76
Royal Cres W11 81 CX74
Royal Cres, Ruis. 60 BY63
Royal Cres Ms W11 81 CX74
Queensdale Rd
Royal Docks Rd E6 87 EP72
Royal Dr N11 44 DG50
Royal Dr, Epsom 173 CV118
Royal Ex EC3 197 L9
Royal Ex EC3 84 DR72
Royal Ex Av EC3 197 L9
Royal Ex Bldgs EC3 197 L9
Royal Ex Steps EC3 84 DR72
Cornhill
Royal Gdns W7 97 CG76
Royal Herbert Pavilions SE18 105 EM81
Gilbert Cl
Royal Hill SE10 103 EC80
Royal Horticultural Society Cotts, Wok. 168 BL116
Wisley La
Royal Hosp Rd SW3 100 DF79
Royal La, Uxb. 76 BM69
Royal La, West Dr. 76 BM72
Royal London Est, The N17 46 DV51
Royal Ms, The SW1 199 J6
Royal Ms, The SW1 101 DH76
Royal Mint Ct EC3 202 A1
Royal Mint Ct EC3 84 DT73
Royal Mint Pl E1 84 DT73
Blue Anchor Yd
Royal Mint St E1 84 DT73
Royal Mt Ct, Twick. 117 CE90
Royal Naval Pl SE14 103 DZ80
Royal Oak Ct N1 84 DS69
Pitfield St
Royal Oak Pl SE22 122 DV86
Royal Oak Rd E8 84 DV65
Royal Oak Rd, Bexh. 126 EZ85
Royal Oak Rd, Wok. 166 AW118
Royal Opera Arc SW1 199 M2
Royal Opera Arc SW1 83 DK74
Royal Orchard Cl SW18 119 CY87
Royal Par SE3 104 EE82
Royal Par SW6 99 CY80
Dawes Rd
Royal Par W5 80 CL69
Western Av
Royal Par, Chis. 125 EQ94
Royal Par, Rich. 98 CN81
Station App
Royal Par Ms SE3 104 EF82
Royal Par
Royal Par Ms, Chis. 125 EQ94
Royal Pier Ms, Grav. 131 GH86
Royal Pier Rd
Royal Pier Rd, Grav. 131 GH86
Royal Pl SE10 103 EC80
Royal Rd E16 86 EK72
Royal Rd SE17 101 DP79
Royal Rd, Dart. 128 FN92
Royal Rd, Sid. 126 EX90
Royal Rd, Tedd. 117 CD92
Royal Route, Wem. 62 CM63
Royal St SE1 200 C6
Royal St SE1 101 DM76
Royal Victor Pl E3 85 DX68
Royal Victoria Dock E16 86 EH73
Royal Victoria Patriotic Building SW18 120 DD86
Fitzhugh Gro
Royal Victoria Pl E16 86 EH74
Wesley Av
Royal Wk, Wall. 141 DH104
Prince Charles Way
Royal Windsor Ct, Surb. 138 CN102
Royalty Ms W1 195 M9
Roycraft Av, Bark. 87 ET68
Roycraft Cl, Bark. 87 ET68
Roycroft Cl E18 48 EH53
Roycroft Cl SW2 121 DN88
Roydene Rd SE18 105 ES79
Roydon Cl SW11 101 DH81
Reform St
Roydon Cl, Loug. 48 EL45
Roydon Ct, Walt. 153 BU105
Roydon St SW11 101 DH81
Southolm St
Royle Cl (Chalfont St. Peter), Ger.Cr. 37 AZ52
Royle Cl, Rom. 71 FH57
Royle Cres W13 79 CG70
Royston Av E4 47 EA50
Royston Av, Sutt. 140 DD104
Royston Av, Wall. 159 DK105
Royston Av, W.Byf. 152 BL112
Royston Cl, Houns. 95 BV81
Royston Cl, Walt. 135 BU102
Royston Ct SE24 122 DQ86
Burbage Rd
Royston Ct, Rich. 98 CM81
Lichfield Rd
Royston Ct, Surb. 138 CN104
Hook Ri N
Royston Gdns, Ilf. 68 EK58
Royston Gro, Pnr. 40 BZ51
Royston Par, Ilf. 68 EK58
Royston Pk Rd, Pnr. 40 BZ51
Royston Rd SE20 143 DX95
Royston Rd, Dart. 127 FF86
Royston Rd, Rich. 118 CL85
Royston Rd, Rom. 52 FN52
Royston Rd, W.Byf. 152 BL112
Royston St E2 84 DW68
Roystons, The, Surb. 138 CP99
Rozel Ct N1 84 DS67
Rozel Rd SW4 101 DJ82
Rubastic Rd, Sthl. 95 BV76
Rubens Rd, Nthlt. 78 BW68
Rubens St SE6 123 DZ89
Ruberoid Rd, Enf. 31 DZ41
Ruby Ms E17 67 EA55
Ruby Rd
Ruby Rd E17 67 EA55
Ruby St SE15 102 DV79
Ruby Triangle SE15 102 DV79
Sandgate St
Ruckholt Cl E10 67 EB62
Ruckholt Rd E10 67 EA63
Rucklers La, Kings L. 6 BK27
Rucklidge Av NW10 81 CT68
Rudall Cres NW3 64 DD63
Willoughby Rd
Ruddington Cl E5 67 DY63
Ruddock Cl, Edg. 42 CQ52
Orange Hill Rd
Ruddstreet Cl SE18 105 EP77
Ruddy Way NW7 43 CU51
Flower La
Ruden Way, Epsom 173 CV116
Rudge Ri, Add. 151 BF106
Rudland Rd, Bexh. 107 FB83
Rudloe Rd SW12 121 DJ87
Rudolf Pl SW8 101 DL79
Miles St
Rudolph Ct SE22 122 DU87
Rudolph Rd E13 86 EF68
Rudolph Rd NW6 82 DA68
Rudolph Rd, Bushey 24 CA44
Rudsworth Cl, Slou. 93 BD80
Rudyard Gro NW7 42 CQ51
Rue de St. Lawrence, Wal.Abb. 15 EC34
Quaker La
Ruffets Wd, Grav. 131 GJ93
Ruffetts, The, S.Croy. 160 DV108
Ruffetts Cl, S.Croy. 160 DV108
Ruffetts Way, Tad. 173 CY118
Ruffle Cl, West Dr. 76 BL69
Kingston La
Rufford Cl, Har. 61 CG58
Rufford Cl, Wat. 23 BT37
Rufford St N1 83 DL67
Rufford Twr W3 80 CP74
Rufus Cl, Ruis. 60 BY62
Rufus St N1 197 M3
Rugby Av N9 46 DT46
Rugby Av, Grnf. 79 CD65
Rugby Av, Wem. 61 CH64
Rugby Cl, Har. 61 CE57
Rugby Gdns, Dag. 88 EW65
Rugby La, Sutt. 157 CX109
Nonsuch Wk
Rugby Rd NW9 62 CP56
Rugby Rd W4 98 CS75
Rugby Rd, Dag. 88 EV66
Rugby Rd, Twick. 117 CE86
Rugby St WC1 196 B5
Rugby St WC1 83 DM70
Rugby Way, Rick. 23 BP43
Rugg St E14 85 EA73
Rugged La, Wal.Abb. 16 EK33
Ruggles-Brise Rd, Ashf. 114 BK92
Ruislip Cl, Grnf. 78 CB70
Ruislip Ct, Ruis. 59 BT61
Courtfield Gdns
Ruislip Rd, Grnf. 78 CA69
Ruislip Rd, Nthlt. 78 BX69
Ruislip Rd, Sthl. 78 CA69
Ruislip Rd E W7 79 CE70
Ruislip Rd E W13 79 CD70
Ruislip Rd E, Grnf. 78 CA69
Ruislip St SW17 120 DF91
Rum Cl E1 202 F1
Rum Cl E1 84 DW73
Rumania Wk, Grav. 131 GM90
Rumbold Rd SW6 100 DB80
Rumsey Cl, Hmptn. 116 BZ93
Rumsey Ms N4 65 DP62
Monsell Rd
Rumsey Rd SW9 101 DM83
Rumsley, Wal.Cr. 14 DU27
Runbury Circle NW9 62 CR61
Runciman Cl, Orp. 164 EW110
Runcorn Cl N17 66 DV56
Runcorn Pl W11 81 CY73
Rundell Cres NW4 63 CV57
Runes Cl, Mitch. 140 DD98
Runnel Fld, Har. 61 CE62
Runnemede Rd, Egh. 113 BA91
Running Horse Yd, Brent. 98 CL79
Pottery Rd
Running Waters, Brwd. 55 GA49
Runnymede SW19 140 DD95
Runnymede Cl, Twick. 116 CB86
Runnymede Ct, Croy. 142 DT103
Runnymede Ct, Egh. 113 BA91
Runnymede Cres SW16 141 DK95
Runnymede Gdns, Grnf. 79 CD68
Runnymede Gdns, Twick. 116 CB86
Runnymede Rd, Twick. 116 CB86
Runrig Hill, Amer. 20 AS35
Runway, The, Ruis. 59 BV64
Rupack St SE16 202 F5
Rupert Av, Wem. 62 CL64
Rupert Ct W1 195 M10
Rupert Ct, W.Mol. 136 CA98
St. Peter's Rd
Rupert Gdns SW9 101 DP82
Rupert Rd N19 65 DK62
Holloway Rd
Rupert Rd NW6 81 CZ68
Rupert Rd W4 98 CS76
Rupert St W1 195 M10
Rupert St W1 83 DK73
Rural Cl, Horn. 71 FH60
Rural Vale, Grav. 130 GE87
Rural Way SW16 121 DH94
Rural Way, Red. 184 DG134
Ruscoe Dr, Wok. 167 BA117
Pembroke Rd
Ruscoe Rd E16 86 EF72
Ruscombe Dr, St.Alb. 8 CB26
Ruscombe Gdns, Slou. 92 AU80
Ruscombe Way, Felt. 115 BT87
Rush, The SW19 139 CZ95
Kingston Rd
Rush Dr, Wal.Abb. 31 EC40
Sewardstone Rd
Rush Grn Gdns, Rom. 71 FC60
Rush Grn Rd, Rom. 71 FC60
Rush Gro St SE18 105 EM77
Rush Hill Ms SW11 100 DG83
Rush Hill Rd
Rush Hill Rd SW11 100 DG83
Rusham Pk Av, Egh. 113 AZ93
Rusham Rd SW12 120 DF86
Rusham Rd, Egh. 113 AZ93
Rushbrook Cres E17 47 DZ53
Rushbrook Rd SE9 125 EQ89
Rushcroft Rd E4 47 EA52
Rushcroft Rd SW2 101 DN84
Rushden Cl SE19 122 DR94
Rushden Gdns NW7 43 CW51
Rushden Gdns, Ilf. 69 EN55
Rushdene SE2 106 EX76
Rushdene Av, Barn. 44 DE45
Rushdene Cl, Nthlt. 78 BW69
Rushdene Cres, Nthlt. 78 BW68
Rushdene Rd, Brwd. 54 FW45
Rushdene Rd, Pnr. 60 BX58
Rushdene Wk, West. 178 EK117
Rushdon Cl, Grays 110 GA76
Rushdon Cl, Rom. 71 FG57
Rushen Wk, Cars. 140 DD102
Paisley Rd
Rushes Mead, Uxb. 76 BJ67
Frays Waye
Rushet Rd, Orp. 146 EU96
Rushett Cl, T.Ditt. 137 CH102
Rushett La, Chess. 155 CJ111
Rushett La, Epsom 155 CJ111
Rushett Rd, T.Ditt. 137 CH101
Rushey Cl, N.Mal. 138 CR98
Rushey Grn SE6 123 EB87
Rushey Hill, Enf. 29 DM42
Rushey Mead SE4 123 EA85
Rushfield, Pot.B. 11 CX33
Rushford Rd SE4 123 DZ86
Rushgrove Av NW9 63 CT57
Rushleigh Av (Cheshunt), Wal.Cr. 15 DX31
Rushley Cl, Kes. 162 EK105
Rushmead E2 84 DV69
Florida St
Rushmead, Rich. 117 CH90
Rushmead Cl, Croy. 160 DT105
Rushmere Av, Upmin. 72 FQ62
Rushmere Ct, Wor.Pk. 139 CU103
The Av
Rushmere La, Chesh. 4 AU28
Rushmere La, Hem.H. 4 AU28
Rushmere Pl SW19 119 CX92
Rushmoor Cl, Pnr. 59 BV56
Rushmoor Cl, Rick. 38 BK47
Rushmore Cl, Brom. 144 EL97
Rushmore Cres E5 67 DX63
Rushmore Rd
Rushmore Hill, Orp. 164 EW110
Rushmore Hill, Sev. 164 EX112
Rushmore Rd E5 66 DW63
Rusholme Av, Dag. 70 FA62
Rusholme Gro SE19 122 DS92
Rusholme Rd SW15 119 CY86
Rushout Av, Har. 61 CH58
Rushton Av, Wat. 23 BU35
Rushton St N1 84 DR68
Rushworth Av NW4 63 CU55
Rushworth Gdns
Rushworth Gdns NW4 63 CU56
Rushworth Rd, Reig. 184 DA133
Rushworth St SE1 200 G4
Rushworth St SE1 101 DP75
Rushy Meadow La, Cars. 140 DE103
Ruskin Av E12 86 EL65
Ruskin Av, Felt. 115 BT86
Ruskin Av, Rich. 98 CN80
Ruskin Av, Upmin. 72 FQ59
Ruskin Av, Wal.Abb. 16 EE34
Ruskin Av, Well. 106 EU82
Ruskin Cl NW11 64 DB58
Ruskin Cl (Cheshunt), Wal.Cr. 14 DS26
Ruskin Dr, Orp. 145 ES104
Ruskin Dr, Well. 106 EU83
Ruskin Dr, Wor.Pk. 139 CV103
Ruskin Gdns W5 79 CK70
Ruskin Gdns, Har. 62 CM56
Ruskin Gdns, Rom. 51 FH52
Ruskin Gro, Dart. 128 FN85
Ruskin Gro, Well. 106 EU82
Ruskin Pk Ho SE5 102 DR83
Ruskin Rd N17 46 DT53
Ruskin Rd, Belv. 106 FA77
Ruskin Rd, Cars. 158 DF106
Ruskin Rd, Croy. 141 DP103
Ruskin Rd, Grays 111 GG77
Ruskin Rd, Islw. 97 CF83
Ruskin Rd, Sthl. 78 BY73
Ruskin Rd, Stai. 113 BF94
Ruskin Wk N9 46 DU47
Durham Rd
Ruskin Wk SE24 122 DQ85
Ruskin Wk, Brom. 145 EM100
Ruskin Way SW19 140 DD95
Rusland Av, Orp. 145 ER104
Rusland Hts, Har. 61 CE56
Rusland Pk Rd
Rusland Pk Rd, Har. 61 CE56
Rusper Cl NW2 63 CW62
Rusper Cl, Stan. 41 CJ49
Rusper Rd N22 46 DQ54
Rusper Rd, Dag. 88 EW65
Russell Av N22 45 DP54
Russell Cl NW10 80 CQ66
Russell Cl SE7 104 EJ80
Russell Cl W4 99 CT79
Russell Cl, Amer. 20 AX39
Russell Cl, Beck. 143 EB97
Russell Cl, Bexh. 106 FA84
Russell Cl, Brwd. 54 FV45
Russell Cl, Dart. 107 FG83
Russell Cl, Nthwd. 39 BQ50
Russell Cl, Ruis. 60 BW61
Russell Cl, Tad. 183 CU125
Russell Cl, Wok. 166 AW115
Russell Ct SW1 199 L3
Russell Ct, Lthd. 171 CH122
Russell Ct, St.Alb. 8 CA30
Russell Cres, Wat. 23 BT35
High Rd
Russell Dr, Stai. 114 BK86
Russell Gdns N20 44 DE47
Russell Gdns NW11 63 CY58
Russell Gdns W14 99 CY76
Russell Gdns, Rich. 117 CJ89
Russell Gdns, West Dr. 94 BN78
Russell Gdns Ms W14 99 CY75
Russell Grn Cl, Pur. 159 DN110
Russell Gro NW7 42 CS50
Russell Gro SW9 101 DN80
Russell Hill, Pur. 159 DM110
Russell Hill Pl, Pur. 159 DN111
Purley Way
Russell Hill Rd, Pur. 159 DN110
Russell Kerr Cl W4 98 CQ80
Burlington La
Russell La N20 44 DE47
Russell La, Wat. 23 BR36
Russell Mead, Har. 41 CF53
Russell Pl NW3 64 DE64
Aspern Gro
Russell Pl SE16 203 K7
Russell Pl (Sutton at Hone), Dart. 148 FN95
Russell Rd E4 47 DZ49
Russell Rd E10 67 EB58
Russell Rd E16 86 EG72
Russell Rd E17 67 DZ55
Russell Rd N8 65 DK58
Russell Rd N13 45 DM51
Russell Rd N15 66 DS57
Russell Rd N20 44 DE47
Russell Rd NW9 63 CT58
Russell Rd SW19 120 DA94
Russell Rd W14 99 CY76
Russell Rd, Buck.H. 48 EH46
Russell Rd, Enf. 30 DT38
Russell Rd, Grav. 131 GK86
Russell Rd, Grays 110 GA77
Russell Rd, Mitch. 140 DE97
Russell Rd, Nthlt. 60 CC64
Russell Rd, Nthwd. 39 BQ49
Russell Rd, Shep. 135 BQ101
Russell Rd, Til. 110 GE81
Russell Rd, Twick. 117 CF86
Russell Rd, Walt. 135 BU100
Russell Rd, Wok. 166 AW115
Russell Sq WC1 195 P5
Russell Sq WC1 83 DK71
Russell Sq, Long. 149 FX97
Cavendish Sq
Russell St WC2 196 A10
Russell St WC2 83 DM72
Russell Wk, Rich. 118 CM86
Park Hill
Russell Way, Sutt. 158 DA106
Russell Way, Wat. 39 BV45
Russells, Tad. 173 CX122
Russell's Footpath SW16 121 DL92
Russells Ride (Cheshunt), Wal.Cr. 15 DY31
Russet Cl, Stai. 113 BF86
Russet Cl, Uxb. 77 BQ70
Uxbridge Rd
Russet Cl, Walt. 136 BX104
Russet Cres N7 65 DM64
Stock Orchard Cres
Russet Dr, Croy. 143 DY102
Russet Dr, Rad. 10 CL32
Russets, The (Chalfont St. Peter), Ger.Cr. 36 AX54
Austenwood Cl
Russets Cl E4 47 ED49
Larkshall Rd
Russett Cl, Orp. 164 EV106
Russett Cl, Wal.Cr. 14 DS26
Russett Ct, Cat. 186 DU125
Russett Hill (Chalfont St. Peter), Ger.Cr. 56 AY55
Russett Way SE13 103 EB82
Conington Rd
Russett Way, Swan. 147 FD96
Russetts, Horn. 72 FL56
Russetts Cl, Wok. 167 AZ115
Russetts Cl, Wok. 167 AZ115
Orchard Dr
Russia Ct EC2 197 J8
Russia Dock Rd SE16 203 L3
Russia Dock Rd SE16 85 DY74
Russia La E2 84 DW68
Russia Row EC2 197 J9
Russia Wk SE16 203 K5
Russia Wk SE16 103 DY75
Russington Rd, Shep. 135 BR100
Rust Sq SE5 102 DR80
Rusthall Av W4 98 CR77
Rusthall Cl, Croy. 142 DW100
Rustic Av SW16 121 DH94
Rustic Cl, Upmin. 73 FS60
Rustic Pl, Wem. 61 CK63
Rustic Wk E16 86 EH72
Lambert Rd
Rustington Wk, Mord. 139 CZ101
Ruston Av, Surb. 138 CP101
Ruston Gdns N14 28 DG44
Farm La
Ruston Ms W11 81 CY72
St. Marks Rd
Ruston Rd SE18 104 EL76
Ruston St E3 85 DZ67
Rutford Rd SW16 121 DL92
Ruth Cl, Stan. 62 CM56
Ruthen Cl, Epsom 156 CP114
Rutherford Cl, Borwd. 26 CQ40
Rutherford Cl, Sutt. 158 DD107
Rutherford Cl, Uxb. 76 BM71
Royal La
Rutherford St SW1 199 M8
Rutherford St SW1 101 DK77
Rutherford Twr, Sthl. 78 CB72
Rutherford Way, Bushey 41 CD46
Rutherford Way, Wem. 62 CN63
Rutherglen Rd SE2 106 EU79
Rutherwick Ri, Couls. 175 DL117
Rutherwyk Rd, Cher. 133 BE101
Rutherwyke Cl, Epsom 157 CU107
Ruthin Cl NW9 62 CS58
Ruthin Rd SE3 104 EG79
Ruthven Av, Wal.Cr. 15 DX33
Ruthven St E9 85 DX67
Lauriston Rd
Rutland App, Horn. 72 FN57
Rutland Av, Sid. 126 EU87
Rutland Cl SW14 98 CQ83
Rutland Cl SW19 120 DE94
Rutland Rd
Rutland Cl, Ash. 172 CL117
Rutland Cl, Bex. 126 EX88
Rutland Cl, Chess. 156 CM107
Rutland Cl, Dart. 128 FK87
Rutland Cl, Epsom 156 CR110
Rutland Cl, Red. 184 DF133
Rutland Ct, Enf. 30 DW43
Rutland Dr, Horn. 72 FN57
Rutland Dr, Mord. 139 CZ100
Rutland Dr, Rich. 117 CK88
Rutland Gdns N4 65 DP58
Rutland Gdns SW7 198 C5
Rutland Gdns SW7 100 DE75
Rutland Gdns W13 79 CG71
Rutland Gdns, Croy. 160 DS105
Rutland Gdns, Dag. 70 EW64
Rutland Gdns Ms SW7 198 C5
Rutland Gate SW7 198 C5
Rutland Gate SW7 100 DE75
Rutland Gate, Belv. 107 FB78
Rutland Gate, Brom. 144 EF98
Rutland Gate Ms SW7 198 B5
Rutland Gro W6 99 CV78
Rutland Ms NW8 82 DB67
Boundary Rd
Rutland Ms E SW7 198 B6
Rutland Ms S SW7 198 B6
Rutland Ms W SW7 100 DE76
Ennismore St
Rutland Pk NW2 81 CW65
Rutland Pk SE6 123 DZ89
Rutland Pk Gdns NW2 81 CW65
Rutland Pk

This index reads in the sequence: Street Name / Postal District or Post Town / Map Page Reference / Grid Reference **St.F-St.M**

St. Francis Rd (Denham), Uxb. 57 BF58
St. Francis Twr E4 47 DZ51
Iris Way
St. Francis Way, Grays 111 GJ77
St. Francis Way, Ilf. 69 ES63
St. Frideswides Ms E14 85 EC72
Lodore St
St. Gabriel's Cl E11 68 EH60
St. Gabriels Rd NW2 63 CX64
St. George St W1 195 J9
St. George St W1 83 DH72
St. Georges Av E7 86 EH66
St. Georges Av N7 65 DK63
St. Georges Av NW9 62 CQ56
St. George's Av W5 97 CK75
St. Georges Av, Grays 110 GC77
St. Georges Av, Horn. 72 FM59
St. Georges Av, Sthl. 78 BZ73
St. George's Av, Wey. 153 BP107
St. Georges Circ SE1 200 F6
St. Georges Circ SE1 101 DP76
St. Georges Cl NW11 63 CZ58
St. George's Cl SW8 101 DJ81
Patmore Est
St. Georges Cl, Wem. 61 CG62
St. George's Cl, Wey. 153 BQ106
St. Georges Ct E6 87 EM70
St. Georges Ct EC4 196 F8
St. Georges Ct SW7 100 DC76
Gloucester Rd
St. Georges Cres, Grav. 131 GK91
St. George's Dr SW1 199 K10
St. George's Dr SW1 101 DH77
St. Georges Dr, Uxb. 58 BM62
St. Georges Dr, Wat. 40 BY48
St. George's Est, Amer. 20 AU39
St. Georges Flds W2 194 C9
St. Georges Flds W2 82 DE72
St. Georges Gdns, Epsom 157 CT114
Lynwood Rd
St. George's Gdns, Surb. 138 CP103
Hamilton Av
St. Georges Gro SW17 120 DD90
St. Georges Gro Est SW17 120 DD90
St. Georges Ind Est, Kings.T. 117 CK92
St. Georges La EC3 197 M10
St. George's Lo, Wey. 153 BR106
St. Georges Ms NW1 82 DF66
Regents Pk Rd
St. Georges Pl, Twick. 117 CG88
Church St
St. Georges Rd E7 86 EH65
St. Georges Rd E10 67 EC62
St. Georges Rd N9 46 DU48
St. Georges Rd N13 45 DM48
St. Georges Rd NW11 63 CZ58
St. Georges Rd SE1 200 E6
St. Georges Rd SE1 101 DN76
St. George's Rd SW19 119 CZ93
St. Georges Rd W4 98 CS75
St. Georges Rd W7 79 CF74
St. Georges Rd, Add. 152 BJ105
St. George's Rd, Beck. 143 EB95
St. Georges Rd, Brom. 145 EM96
St. Georges Rd, Dag. 70 EY64
St. Georges Rd, Enf. 30 DT38
St. George's Rd, Felt. 116 BX91
St. Georges Rd, Ilf. 69 EM59
St. George's Rd, Kings.T. 118 CN94
St. George's Rd, Mitch. 141 DH97
St. George's Rd, Orp. 145 ER100
St. Georges Rd, Rich. 98 CM83
St. Georges Rd, Sev. 191 FH122
St. George's Rd, Sid. 126 EX93
St. Georges Rd, Swan. 147 FF98
St. Georges Rd, Twick. 117 CH85
St. Georges Rd, Wall. 159 DH106
St. Georges Rd, Wat. 23 BV38
St. George's Rd, Wey. 153 BR107
St. Georges Rd W, Brom. 144 EL95
St. Georges Shop Cen, Grav. 131 GH86
St. Georges Sq E7 86 EH66
St. Georges Sq E14 85 DY73
Narrow St
St. Georges Sq SE8 203 M8
St. Georges Sq SE8 103 DZ77
St. George's Sq SW1 199 M10
St. Georges Sq SW1 101 DK78
St. George's Sq, N.Mal. 138 CS97
High St
St. George's Sq Ms SW1 101 DK78
St. Georges Ter NW1 82 DF66
Regents Pk Rd
St. Georges Wk, Croy. 142 DQ104
St. Georges Way SE15 102 DS79
St. Gerards Cl SW4 121 DJ85
St. German's Pl SE3 104 EG81
St. Germans Rd SE23 123 DY88
St. Giles Av, Dag. 89 FB66
St. Giles Av, Pot.B. 11 CV33
St. Giles Av, Uxb. 59 BQ63
St. Giles Cl, Dag. 89 FB66
St. Giles Av
St. Giles Cl, Orp. 163 ER106
St. Giles Ct WC2 83 DL72
St. Giles High St
St. Giles High St WC2 195 N8
St. Giles High St WC2 83 DK72
St. Giles Pas WC2 195 N9
St. Giles Rd SE5 102 DS80
St. Gilles Ho E2 85 DX68
St. Gothard Rd SE27 122 DR91
St. Gregory Cl, Ruis. 60 BW63
St. Gregorys Cres, Grav. 131 GL89
St. Helena Rd SE16 203 H9
St. Helena Rd SE16 103 DX77
St. Helena St WC1 196 D3
St. Helens Cl, Uxb. 76 BK72
St. Helens Ct, Epp. 18 EU30
Hemnall St
St. Helens Ct, Rain. 89 FG70
St. Helens Cres SW16 141 DM95
St. Helens Rd
St. Helens Gdns W10 81 CX72
St. Helens Pl EC3 197 M8
St. Helens Rd SW16 141 DM95
St. Helen's Rd W13 79 CH74
Dane Rd
St. Helens Rd, Erith 106 EX75
St. Helens Rd, Ilf. 69 EM58
St. Helier Av, Mord. 140 DC101
St. Heliers Av, Houns. 116 CA85
St. Heliers Rd E10 67 EC58
St. Hildas Av, Ashf. 114 BL92
St. Hildas Cl NW6 81 CX66
St. Hildas Cl SW17 120 DE89
St. Hilda's Rd SW13 99 CV79
St. Hilda's Way, Grav. 131 GK91
St. Huberts Cl, Ger.Cr. 56 AY60
St. Huberts La, Ger.Cr. 57 AZ61
St. Hughe's Cl SW17 120 DE89
College Gdns
St. Hughs Rd SE20 142 DV95
Ridsdale Rd
St. Ives Cl, Rom. 52 FM52
St. Ivians Dr, Rom. 71 FG55
St. James Av N20 44 DE48
St. James Av W13 79 CG74
St. James Av, Epsom 157 CT111
St. James Av, Sutt. 158 DA106
St. James Cl N20 44 DE48
St. James Cl SE18 105 EQ78
Congleton Gro
St. James Cl, Barn. 28 DD42
St. James Cl, Epsom 156 CS114
St. James Cl, N.Mal. 139 CT99
St. James Cl, Ruis. 60 BW61
St. James Cl, Wok. 166 AU118
St. James Ct, Green. 129 FT86
St. James Gdns, Wem. 79 CK66
St. James Gate NW1 83 DK66
St. Paul's Cres
St. James Gro SW11 100 DF82
Reform St
St. James La, Green. 129 FS88
St. James Ms E14 204 E7
St. James Ms E14 103 EC76
St. James Ms E17 67 DY57
St. James's St
St. James Ms, Wey. 153 BP105
St. James Pl, Dart. 128 FK86
Spital St
St. James Rd E15 68 EF64
St. James Rd N9 46 DV47
Queens Rd
St. James Rd, Brwd. 54 FW48
St. James Rd, Cars. 140 DE104
St. James Rd, Kings.T. 138 CL96
St. James Rd, Mitch. 120 DG94
St. James Rd, Pur. 159 DP113
St. James Rd, Sev. 191 FH122
St. James Rd, Surb. 137 CK100
St. James Rd, Sutt. 158 DA106
St. James Rd (Cheshunt), Wal.Cr. 14 DQ28
St. James Rd, Wat. 23 BV43
St. James St W6 99 CW78
St. James Wk SE15 102 DT80
Commercial Way
St. James Wk, Iver 93 BE75
St. James Way, Sid. 126 EY92
St. James's SE14 103 DY81
St. James's Av E2 84 DW68
St. James's Av, Beck. 143 DY97
St. James's Av, Grav. 131 GG87
St. James's Av, Hmptn. 116 CC92
St. James's Cl SW17 120 DF89
St. James's Dr
St. James's Cotts, Rich. 117 CK85
Paradise Rd
St. James's Ct SW1 199 L6
St. James's Ct SW1 101 DJ76
St. James's Cres SW9 101 DN83
St. James's Dr SW12 120 DF88
St. James's Dr SW17 120 DF88
St. James's Gdns W11 81 CY74
St. James's La N10 65 DH56
St. James's Mkt SW1 199 M1
St. James's Palace SW1 199 L4
St. James's Palace SW1 83 DJ74
St. James's Pk SW1 199 M4
St. James's Pk SW1 101 DK75
St. James's Pk, Croy. 142 DQ101
St. James's Pas EC3 197 N9
St. James's Pl SW1 199 K3
St. James's Pl SW1 83 DJ74
St. James's Rd SE1 202 C10
St. James's Rd SE1 102 DU78
St. James's Rd SE16 202 C6
St. James's Rd SE16 102 DU76
St. James's Rd, Croy. 141 DP101
St. James's Rd, Grav. 131 GG86
St. James's Rd, Hmptn. 116 CB92
St. James's Row EC1 196 E4
St. James's Sq SW1 199 L2
St. James's Sq SW1 83 DJ74
St. James's St E17 67 DY57
St. James's St SW1 199 K2
St. James's St SW1 83 DJ74
St. James's St, Grav. 131 GG86
St. James's Ter NW8 82 DF68
Prince Albert Rd
St. James's Ter Ms NW8 82 DF67
St. James's Wk EC1 196 F4
St. James's Wk EC1 83 DP70
St. Jeromes Gro, Hayes 77 BQ72
St. Joans Rd N9 46 DT46
St. John Fisher Rd, Erith 106 EX76
St. John St EC1 196 G5
St. John St EC1 83 DP70
St. Johns Av N11 44 DF50
St. John's Av NW10 81 CT67
St. John's Av SW15 119 CX85
St. Johns Av, Brwd. 54 FX49
St. John's Av, Epsom 157 CT112
St. Johns Av, Lthd. 171 CH121
St. John's Ch Rd E9 66 DW64
St. Johns Cl N14 29 DJ44
Chase Rd
St. John's Cl SW6 100 DA80
Dawes Rd
St. Johns Cl, Lthd. 171 CJ120
St. John's Cl, Pot.B. 12 DC33
St. John's Cl, Rain. 89 FG66
St. John's Cl, Uxb. 76 BH67
St. John's Cl, Wem. 62 CL64
St. John's Cotts SE20 122 DW94
Maple Rd
St. Johns Cotts, Rich. 98 CL84
Kew Foot Rd
St. Johns Ct, Buck.H. 48 EH46
St. John's Ct, Egh. 113 BA92
St. John's Ct, Islw. 97 CF82
St. Johns Ct, Nthwd. 39 BS53
Murray Rd
St. Johns Ct, Wok. 166 AU119
St. Johns Hill Rd
St. John's Cres SW9 101 DN83
St. Johns Dr SW18 120 DB88
St. Johns Dr, Walt. 136 BW102
St. John's Est N1 197 L1
St. John's Est N1 84 DR68
St. John's Est SE1 201 P4
St. John's Gdns W11 81 CZ73
St. Johns Gro N19 65 DJ61
St. Johns Gro SW13 99 CT82
Terrace Gdns
St. Johns Gro, Rich. 98 CL84
Kew Foot Rd
St. John's Hill SW11 100 DD84
St. John's Hill, Couls. 175 DN117
St. John's Hill, Pur. 175 DN116
St. John's Hill, Sev. 191 FJ123
St. John's Hill Gro SW11 100 DD84
St. Johns Hill Rd, Wok. 166 AU119
St. John's La EC1 196 F5
St. John's La EC1 83 DP70
St. John's Lye, Wok. 166 AT119
St. John's Ms W11 82 DA72
Ledbury Rd
St. Johns Ms, Wok. 166 AU119
St. Johns Par, Sid. 126 EU91
Church Rd
St. John's Pk SE3 104 EF80
St. John's Pas SW19 119 CY93
Ridgway Pl
St. John's Path EC1 196 F5
St. Johns Pathway SE23 122 DW88
Devonshire Rd
St. John's Pl EC1 196 F5
St. Johns Ri, Wok. 166 AV119
St. John's Rd E4 47 EB48
St. John's Rd E6 86 EL67
Ron Leighton Way
St. Johns Rd E16 86 EG72
St. John's Rd E17 47 EB54
St. John's Rd N15 66 DS58
St. Johns Rd NW11 63 CZ58
St. John's Rd SE20 122 DW94
St. John's Rd SW11 100 DE84
St. John's Rd SW19 119 CY94
St. John's Rd, Bark. 87 ES67
St. John's Rd, Cars. 140 DE104
St. Johns Rd, Croy. 141 DP104
Sylverdale Rd
St. John's Rd, Dart. 128 FQ87
St. John's Rd, E.Mol. 137 CD98
St. John's Rd, Epp. 17 ET30
St. John's Rd, Erith 107 FD78
St. John's Rd, Felt. 116 BY91
St. Johns Rd, Grav. 131 GK87
St. John's Rd, Grays 111 GH78
St. John's Rd, Har. 61 CF58
St. Johns Rd, Ilf. 69 ER59
St. John's Rd, Islw. 97 CF82
St. John's Rd, Kings.T. 137 CJ96
St. Johns Rd, Lthd. 171 CJ121
St. Johns Rd, Loug. 33 EM40
St. Johns Rd, N.Mal. 138 CQ97
St. John's Rd, Orp. 145 ER100
St. John's Rd, Rich. 98 CL84
St. Johns Rd, Rom. 51 FC50
St. John's Rd, Sev. 191 FH121
St. John's Rd, Sid. 126 EV91
St. Johns Rd, Slou. 74 AU74
St. Johns Rd, Sthl. 96 BY76
St. Johns Rd, Sutt. 140 DA103
St. Johns Rd, Uxb. 76 BH67
St. Johns Rd, Wat. 23 BV40
St. John's Rd, Well. 106 EV83
St. John's Rd, Wem. 61 CK63
St. John's Rd, Wok. 166 AV118
St. John's Sq EC1 196 F5
St. Johns Ter E7 86 EH65
St. Johns Ter SE18 105 EQ79
St. Johns Ter SW15 118 CR91
Kingston Vale
St. Johns Ter W10 81 CX70
Harrow Rd
St. Johns Ter, Enf. 30 DR37
St. Johns Vale SE8 103 EA82
St. Johns Vil N19 65 DK61
St. John's Vil W8 100 DB76
St. Mary's Pl
St. Johns Way N19 65 DK60
St. John's Wd Ct NW8 194 A3
St. John's Wd High St NW8 194 A1
St. John's Wd High St NW8 82 DD68
St. John's Wd Pk NW8 82 DD67
St. John's Wd Rd NW8 82 DD70
St. John's Wd Ter NW8 82 DD68
St. Josephs Cl W10 81 CY71
Bevington Rd
St. Joseph's Cl, Orp. 163 ET105
St. Joseph's Ct SE7 104 EH79
St. Josephs Dr, Sthl. 78 BY74
St. Joseph's Gro NW4 63 CV56
St. Josephs Rd N9 46 DV45
St. Joseph's Rd, Wal.Cr. 15 DY33
St. Joseph's Vale SE3 103 ED82
St. Jude St N16 66 DS64
St. Judes Cl, Egh. 112 AW92
St. Jude's Rd E2 84 DV68
St. Jude's Rd, Egh. 112 AW90
St. Julians, Sev. 191 FN128
St. Julian's Cl SW16 121 DN91
St. Julian's Fm Rd SE27 121 DN91
St. Julian's Rd NW6 81 CZ66
St. Justin Cl, Orp. 146 EX97
St. Katharines Prec NW1 83 DH68
Outer Circle
St. Katharine's Way E1 202 A2
St. Katharine's Way E1 84 DT74
St. Katherines Rd, Cat. 186 DU125
St. Katherines Rd, Erith 106 EX75
St. Katherine's Row EC3 197 N9
St. Katherine's Wk W11 81 CX73
Hunt St
St. Keverne Rd SE9 124 EL91
St. Kilda Rd W13 79 CG74
St. Kilda Rd, Orp. 145 ET102
St. Kilda's Rd N16 66 DR60
St. Kilda's Rd, Brwd. 54 FV45
St. Kilda's Rd, Har. 61 CE58
St. Kitts Ter SE19 122 DS92
St. Laurence Cl NW6 81 CX67
St. Laurence Cl, Orp. 146 EX97
St. Laurence Cl, Uxb. 76 BJ71
St. Laurence Way, Slou. 92 AU76
St. Lawrence Cl, Abb.L. 7 BS30
St. Lawrence Cl, Edg. 42 CM52
St. Lawrence Cl, Hem.H. 5 BA27
St. Lawrence Dr, Pnr. 59 BV58
St. Lawrence Rd, Upmin. 72 FQ61
St. Lawrence St E14 204 E2
St. Lawrence St E14 85 EC74
St. Lawrence Ter W10 81 CY71
St. Lawrence Way SW9 101 DN82
St. Lawrence Way, Cat. 176 DQ123
St. Lawrence Way, St.Alb. 8 BZ30
St. Lawrence's Way, Reig. 184 DA134
Church St
St. Leonards Av E4 48 EE51
St. Leonards Av, Har. 61 CJ56
St. Leonards Cl, Bushey 24 BY42
St. Leonard's Cl, Well. 106 EU83
Hook La
St. Leonards Ct N1 197 J2
St. Leonards Ct N1 84 DR69
St. Leonard's Gdns, Houns. 96 BY80
St. Leonards Gdns, Ilf. 69 EQ64
St. Leonards Ri, Orp. 163 ES105
St. Leonards Rd E14 85 EB71
St. Leonards Rd NW10 80 CR70
St. Leonard's Rd SW14 98 CP83
St. Leonards Rd W13 79 CJ73
St. Leonards Rd, Amer. 20 AS35
St. Leonards Rd, Croy. 141 DP104
St. Leonards Rd, Epsom 173 CW119
St. Leonards Rd, Esher 155 CF107
St. Leonard's Rd, Surb. 137 CK99
St. Leonards Rd, T.Ditt. 137 CG100
St. Leonards Rd, Wal.Abb. 16 EE25
St. Leonards Sq NW5 82 DG65
St. Leonard's Sq, Surb. 137 CK99
St. Leonard's Rd
St. Leonards St E3 85 EB69
St. Leonard's Ter SW3 100 DF78
St. Leonards Wk SW16 121 DM94
St. Leonards Wk, Iver 93 BF76
St. Leonards Way, Horn. 71 FH61
St. Loo Av SW3 100 DE79
St. Louis Rd SE27 122 DQ91
St. Loy's Rd N17 46 DS54
St. Lucia Dr E15 86 EF67
St. Luke Cl, Uxb. 76 BK72
St. Luke's Av SW4 101 DK84
St. Lukes Av, Enf. 30 DR38
St. Luke's Av, Ilf. 69 EP64
St. Lukes Cl EC1 84 DQ70
Old St
St. Luke's Cl SE25 142 DV100
St. Lukes Cl, Dart. 129 FS92
St. Lukes Cl, Swan. 147 FD96
St. Luke's Est EC1 197 K3
St. Luke's Est EC1 84 DR69
St. Lukes Ms W11 81 CZ72
Basing St
St. Lukes Pas, Kings.T. 138 CM95
St. Lukes Rd W11 81 CZ71
St. Lukes Rd, Uxb. 76 BL66
St. Lukes Rd, Whyt. 176 DT118
Whyteleafe Hill
St. Lukes Rd, Wind. 112 AU86
St. Lukes Sq E16 86 EF72
St. Luke's St SW3 198 B10
St. Luke's St SW3 100 DE78
St. Luke's Yd W9 81 CZ68
St. Malo Av N9 46 DW48
St. Margaret Dr, Epsom 156 CR114
St. Margarets, Bark. 87 ER67
St. Margarets Av N15 65 DP56
St. Margarets Av N20 44 DC47
St. Margarets Av, Ashf. 115 BP91
St. Margarets Av, Har. 60 CC62
St. Margarets Av, Sid. 125 ER90
St. Margaret's Av, Sutt. 139 CY104
St. Margarets Av, Uxb. 76 BN70
St. Margarets Cl, Dart. 129 FR89
St. Margarets Cl, Iver 75 BD68
St. Margarets Gate
St. Margarets Cl, Orp. 164 EV105
St. Margaret's Ct SE1 201 J3
St. Margarets Cres SW15 119 CV85
St. Margaret's Cres, Grav. 131 GL90
St. Margaret's Dr, Twick. 117 CH85
St. Margarets Gate, Iver 75 BD68
St. Margaret's Gro E11 68 EF62
St. Margaret's Gro SE18 105 EQ79
St. Margarets Gro, Twick. 117 CG86
St. Margarets La W8 100 DB76
St. Margarets Pas SE13 104 EE83
Church Ter
St. Margarets Rd E12 68 EJ61
St. Margaret's Rd N17 66 DS55
St. Margaret's Rd NW10 81 CW69
St. Margarets Rd SE4 103 DZ84
St. Margarets Rd W7 97 CE75
St. Margarets Rd, Couls. 175 DH121
St. Margarets Rd (South Darenth), Dart. 129 FS93
St. Margarets Rd, Edg. 42 CP50
St. Margaret's Rd, Grav. 130 GE89
St. Margarets Rd, Islw. 97 CH84
St. Margaret's Rd, Ruis. 59 BR58
St. Margarets Rd, Twick. 97 CH84
St. Margarets Sq SE4 103 DZ84
Adelaide Av
St. Margaret's St SW1 199 P5
St. Margaret's St SW1 101 DK77
St. Margaret's Ter SE18 105 EQ78
St. Mark St E1 84 DT72
St. Marks Av, Grav. 131 GF87
St. Marks Cl SE10 103 EC80
Ashburnham Gro
St. Marks Cl W11 81 CY72
Lancaster Rd
St. Mark's Cl, Barn. 28 DB41
St. Marks Cres NW1 82 DG67
St. Marks Gate E9 85 DZ66
Cadogan Ter
St. Mark's Gro SW10 100 DB79
St. Mark's Hill, Surb. 138 CL100
St. Mark's Pl SW19 119 CZ93
Wimbledon Hill Rd
St. Marks Pl W11 81 CY72
St. Marks Ri E8 66 DT64
St. Marks Rd SE25 142 DU98
Coventry Rd
St. Mark's Rd W5 80 CL74
The Common
St. Marks Rd W7 97 CE75
St. Marks Rd W10 81 CX72
St. Marks Rd W11 81 CY72
St. Marks Rd, Brom. 144 EH97
St. Marks Rd, Enf. 30 DT44
St. Mark's Rd, Epsom 173 CW118
St. Marks Rd, Mitch. 140 DF96
St. Mark's Rd, Tedd. 117 CH94
St. Marks Sq NW1 82 DG67
St. Martha's Av, Wok. 167 AZ121
St. Martin Cl, Uxb. 76 BK72
St. Martins App, Ruis. 59 BS59
St. Martins Av E6 86 EK68
St. Martins Av, Epsom 156 CS114
St. Martins Cl NW1 83 DJ67
St. Martins Cl, Enf. 30 DV39
St. Martins Cl, Epsom 156 CS113
Church Rd
St. Martins Cl, Erith 106 EX75
St. Helens Rd
St. Martin's Cl, Wat. 40 BW49
Muirfield Rd
St. Martin's Cl, West Dr. 94 BK76
St. Martin's Rd
St. Martin's Ct WC2 83 DK73
St. Martin's La
St. Martin's Ct, Ashf. 114 BJ92
St. Martins Dr, Walt. 136 BW104
St. Martins Est SW2 121 DN88
St. Martin's La WC2 195 P10
St. Martin's La WC2 83 DL73
St. Martins Meadow, West. 180 EW123
St. Martin's Ms WC2 199 P1
St. Martins Ms, Wok. 168 BG116
St. Martin's Pl WC2 199 P1
St. Martin's Pl WC2 83 DL73
St. Martins Rd N9 46 DV47
St. Martin's Rd SW9 101 DM82
St. Martins Rd, Dart. 128 FM86
St. Martin's Rd, West Dr. 94 BJ76
St. Martin's St WC2 199 N1
St. Martins Way SW17 120 DC90
St. Martin's-le-Grand EC1 197 H8
St. Martin's-le-Grand EC1 84 DQ72
St. Mary Abbots Pl W8 99 CZ76
St. Mary Abbots Ter W14 99 CZ76
St. Mary at Hill EC3 201 M1
St. Mary at Hill EC3 84 DS73
St. Mary Av, Wall. 140 DG104
St. Mary Axe EC3 197 M9
St. Mary Axe EC3 84 DS72
St. Mary Rd E17 67 EA56
St. Mary St SE18 105 EM77
St. Marychurch St SE16 202 F5
St. Marychurch St SE16 102 DW75
St. Marys, Bark. 87 ER67
St. Marys App E12 69 EM64
St. Marys Av E11 68 EH58
St. Mary's Av N3 43 CY54
St. Marys Av, Brwd. 55 GA43
St. Mary's Av, Brom. 144 EE97
St. Mary's Av, Nthwd. 39 BS50
St. Mary's Av, Stai. 114 BK87
St. Mary's Av, Tedd. 117 CF93
St. Mary's Av Cen, Sthl. 96 CB77
St. Mary's Av N, Sthl. 96 CB77
St. Mary's Av S, Sthl. 96 CB77
St. Mary's Cl N17 46 DT53
Kemble Rd
St. Marys Cl, Chess. 156 CM108
St. Marys Cl, Epsom 157 CU108
St. Mary's Cl, Grav. 131 GJ89
St. Mary's Cl, Grays 110 GD79
Dock Rd
St. Mary's Cl, Lthd. 171 CD123
St. Marys Cl, Orp. 146 EV96
St. Mary's Cl, Oxt. 188 EE129
St. Mary's Cl, Stai. 114 BK87
St. Mary's Cl, Sun. 135 BU98
Green Way
St. Mary's Cl (Harefield), Uxb. 58 BH55
St. Marys Cl, Wat. 23 BV42
George St
St. Marys Ct E6 87 EM70
St. Mary's Ct SE7 104 EK80
St. Mary's Ct W5 97 CK75
St. Mary's Rd
St. Mary's Cres NW4 63 CV55
St. Mary's Cres, Hayes 77 BT73
St. Marys Cres, Islw. 97 CD80
St. Mary's Cres, Stai. 114 BK87
St. Marys Dr, Felt. 115 BQ87
St. Mary's Dr, Sev. 190 FE123
St. Mary's Gdns SE11 200 E8
St. Mary's Gdns SE11 101 DN77
St. Mary's Gate W8 100 DB76
St. Marys Grn N2 64 DC55
Thomas More Way
St. Marys Grn, West. 178 EJ118
St. Mary's Gro N1 83 DP65
St. Mary's Gro SW13 99 CV83

St. Mary's Gro W4 98 CP79
St. Mary's Gro, Rich. 98 CM84
St. Marys Gro, West. 178 EJ118
St. Mary's La, Upmin. 72 FN61
St. Marys Mans W2 82 DC71
St. Mary's Ms NW6 82 DB66
Priory Rd
St. Mary's Ms, Rich. 117 CJ90
Back La
St. Mary's Mt, Cat. 176 DT124
St. Marys Path N1 83 DP67
St. Mary's Pl SE9 125 EN86
Eltham High St
St. Mary's Pl W5 97 CK75
St. Mary's Rd
St. Mary's Pl W8 100 DB76
St. Marys Rd E10 67 EC62
St. Marys Rd E13 86 EH68
St. Marys Rd N8 65 DL56
High St
St. Marys Rd N9 46 DW46
St. Mary's Rd NW10 80 CS67
St. Marys Rd NW11 63 CY59
St. Mary's Rd SE15 102 DW81
St. Mary's Rd SE25 142 DS97
St. Mary's Rd (Wimbledon) SW19 119 CY92
St. Mary's Rd W5 97 CK75
St. Mary's Rd, Barn. 44 DF45
St. Mary's Rd, Bex. 127 FC88
St. Marys Rd, E.Mol. 137 CD99
St. Mary's Rd, Grays 111 GH77
St. Mary's Rd, Green. 129 FS85
St. Mary's Rd, Hayes 77 BT73
St. Marys Rd, Ilf. 69 EQ61
St. Marys Rd, Lthd. 171 CH122
St. Mary's Rd, Slou. 74 AY74
St. Mary's Rd, S.Croy. 160 DR110
St. Marys Rd, Surb. 137 CK100
St. Marys Rd (Long Ditton), Surb. 137 CJ101
St. Marys Rd, Swan. 147 FD98
St. Mary's Rd (Denham), Uxb. 57 BF58
St. Mary's Rd (Harefield), Uxb. 58 BH56
St. Mary's Rd (Cheshunt), Wal.Cr. 14 DW29
St. Mary's Rd, Wat. 23 BV42
St. Marys Rd, Wey. 153 BR105
St. Mary's Rd, Wok. 166 AW117
St. Mary's Rd, Wor.Pk. 138 CS103
St. Marys Sq W2 82 DD71
St. Mary's Sq W5 97 CK75
St. Mary's Rd
St. Marys Ter W2 82 DD71
St. Marys Vw, Har. 61 CJ57
St. Mary's Wk SE11 200 E8
St. Mary's Wk SE11 101 DN77
St. Mary's Wk, Hayes 77 BT73
St. Mary's Rd
St. Mary's Wk, Red. 186 DR133
St. Mary's Way, Chig. 49 EN50
St. Mary's Way (Chalfont St. Peter), Ger.Cr. 36 AX54
St. Matthew Cl, Uxb. 76 BK72
St. Matthew St SW1 199 M7
St. Matthew's Av, Surb. 138 CL102
St. Matthews Cl, Rain. 89 FG66
St. Matthews Cl, Wat. 24 BX44
St. Matthew's Dr, Brom. 145 EM97
St. Matthew's Rd SW2 101 DM84
St. Matthews Rd W5 80 CL74
The Common
St. Matthew's Rd, Red. 184 DF133
St. Matthew's Row E2 84 DU69
St. Matthias Cl NW9 63 CT57
St. Maur Rd SW6 99 CZ81
St. Merryn Cl SE18 105 ER80
St. Michael's All EC3 197 L9
St. Michaels Av N9 46 DW45
St. Michael's Av, Wem. 80 CN65
St. Michaels Cl E16 86 EK71
Fulmer Rd
St. Michael's Cl N3 43 CZ54
St. Michaels Cl N12 44 DE50
St. Michaels Cl, Brom. 144 EL97
St. Michaels Cl, Erith 106 EX75
St. Helens Rd
St. Michaels Cl, S.Ock. 90 FQ73
St. Michaels Cl, Walt. 136 BW103
St. Michaels Cl, Wor.Pk. 139 CT103
St. Michaels Cres, Pnr. 60 BY58
St. Michaels Dr, Wat. 7 BV33
St. Michaels Gdns W10 81 CY71
St. Lawrence Ter
St. Michaels Rd NW2 63 CW63
St. Michael's Rd SW9 101 DM82
St. Michael's Rd, Ashf. 114 BN92
St. Michaels Rd, Cat. 176 DR122
St. Michaels Rd, Croy. 142 DQ102
St. Michaels Rd, Grays 111 GH78
St. Michaels Rd, Wall. 159 DJ107
St. Michaels Rd, Well. 106 EV83
St. Michael's Rd, Wok. 151 BD114
St. Michaels St W2 194 A8
St. Michaels St W2 82 DE71
St. Michaels Ter N22 45 DL54
St. Michaels Way, Pot.B. 12 DB30
St. Mildred's Ct EC2 84 DR72
Poultry
St. Mildreds Rd SE12 124 EE87
St. Monica's Rd, Tad. 173 CZ121
St. Nazaire Cl, Egh. 113 BC92
Mullens Rd
St. Neots Cl, Borwd. 26 CN38
St. Neots Rd, Rom. 52 FM52
St. Nicholas Av, Horn. 71 FG62
St. Nicholas Cl, Amer. 20 AV39
St. Nicholas Cl, Borwd. 25 CK44
St. Nicholas Cl, Uxb. 76 BK72
St. Nicholas Cres, Wok. 168 BG116
St. Nicholas Dr, Sev. 191 FH126
St. Nicholas Dr, Shep. 134 BN101
St. Nicholas Glebe SW17 120 DG93
St. Nicholas Gro, Brwd. 55 GC50
St. Nicholas Hill, Lthd. 171 CH122
St. Nicholas Rd SE18 105 ET78
St. Nicholas Rd, Sutt. 158 DB106
St. Nicholas Rd, T.Ditt. 137 CF100
St. Nicholas St SE8 103 EA81
Lucas St
St. Nicholas Way, Sutt. 158 DB105
St. Nicolas La, Chis. 144 EL95
St. Ninian's Ct N20 44 DF48
St. Norbert Grn SE4 103 DY84
St. Norbert Rd SE4 103 DY84
St. Normans Way, Epsom 157 CU110
St. Olaf's Rd SW6 99 CY80
St. Olaves Cl, Stai. 113 BF94
St. Olaves Ct EC2 197 K9
St. Olave's Est SE1 201 N4
St. Olaves Gdns SE11 200 D8
St. Olaves Rd E6 87 EN67
St. Olave's Wk SW16 141 DJ96
St. Olav's Sq SE16 202 F6
St. Olav's Sq SE16 102 DW76
St. Oswald's Pl SE11 101 DM78
St. Oswald's Rd SW16 141 DP95
St. Oswulf St SW1 199 N9
St. Pancras Way NW1 83 DJ66
St. Patrick's Ct, Wdf.Grn. 48 EE52
St. Patrick's Gdns, Grav. 131 GK90
St. Patricks Pl, Grays 111 GJ77
St. Paul Cl, Uxb. 76 BK71
St. Paul St N1 84 DQ67
St. Paul's All EC4 83 DP72
St. Paul's Chyd
St. Paul's Av NW2 81 CV65
St. Paul's Av SE16 203 J2
St. Paul's Av SE16 85 DX74
St. Pauls Av, Har. 62 CM57
St. Pauls Av, Slou. 74 AT73
St. Paul's Chyd EC4 196 G9
St. Paul's Chyd EC4 83 DP72
St. Paul's Cl SE7 104 EK78
St. Paul's Cl W5 80 CM74
St. Pauls Cl, Add. 152 BG106
St. Paul's Cl, Ashf. 115 BQ92
St. Paul's Cl, Cars. 140 DE102
St. Pauls Cl, Chess. 155 CK105
St. Pauls Cl, Hayes 95 BR78
St. Paul's Cl, Houns. 96 BY82
St. Pauls Cl, S.Ock. 90 FQ73
St. Pauls Cl, Swans. 130 FY87
Swanscombe St
St. Paul's Ct W14 99 CX77
Colet Gdns
St. Pauls Ctyd SE8 103 EA80
Deptford High St
St. Pauls Cray Rd, Chis. 145 ER95
St. Paul's Cres NW1 83 DK66
St. Pauls Dr E15 67 ED64
St. Paul's Ms NW1 83 DK66
St. Paul's Cres
St. Paul's Pl N1 84 DR65
St. Pauls Pl, S.Ock. 90 FQ73
St. Pauls Ri N13 45 DP51
St. Paul's Rd N1 83 DP65
St. Paul's Rd N17 46 DU52
St. Paul's Rd, Bark. 87 EQ67
St. Paul's Rd, Brent. 97 CK79
St. Paul's Rd, Erith 107 FC80
St. Paul's Rd, Rich. 98 CM83
St. Paul's Rd, Stai. 113 BD92
St. Paul's Rd, Th.Hth. 142 DQ97
St. Pauls Rd, Wok. 167 BA117
St. Paul's Shrubbery N1 84 DR65
St. Pauls Sq, Brom. 144 EG96
St. Paul's Ter SE17 101 DP79
Westcott Rd
St. Pauls Twr E10 67 EB59
St. Pauls Wk, Kings.T. 118 CN94
Alexandra Rd
St. Paul's Way E3 85 DZ71
St. Paul's Way E14 85 DZ71
St. Paul's Way N3 44 DB52
St. Pauls Way, Wal.Abb. 15 ED33
Rochford Av
St. Pauls Way, Wat. 24 BW40
St. Pauls Wd Hill, Orp. 145 ES96
St. Peter's All EC3 197 L9
St. Peter's Av E2 84 DU68
St. Peter's Cl
St. Peter's Av E17 68 EE56
St. Peters Av N18 46 DU49
St. Peter's Cl E2 84 DU68
St. Peters Cl SW17 120 DE89
College Gdns
St. Peter's Cl, Barn. 27 CV43
St. Peters Cl, Bushey 41 CD46
St. Peters Cl, Chis. 125 ER94
St. Peters Cl (Chalfont St. Peter), Ger.Cr. 36 AY53
Lewis La
St. Peters Cl, Ilf. 69 ES56
St. Peters Cl, Rick. 38 BH46
St. Peter's Cl, Ruis. 60 BX61
St. Peters Cl, Stai. 113 BF93
St. Peters Cl, Swans. 130 FZ87
Keary Rd
St. Peters Cl, Wind. 112 AU85
Church Rd
St. Peters Cl, Wok. 167 BC120
St. Peter's Ct NW4 63 CW57
St. Peters Ct SE3 104 EF84
Eltham Rd
St. Peters Ct SE4 103 DZ82
Wickham Rd
St. Peters Ct (Chalfont St. Peter), Ger.Cr. 36 AY53
High St
St. Peters Ct, W.Mol. 136 CA98
St. Peter's Gdns SE27 121 DN90
St. Peter's Gro W6 99 CU77
St. Peters La, Orp. 146 EU96
St. Peter's Pl W9 82 DB70
Shirland Rd
St. Peters Rd N9 46 DW46
St. Peter's Rd W6 99 CU78
St. Peters Rd, Brwd. 54 FV49
Crescent Rd
St. Peter's Rd, Croy. 160 DR105
St. Peter's Rd, Grays 111 GH77
St. Peters Rd, Kings.T. 138 CN96
St. Peters Rd, Sthl. 78 CA71
St. Peters Rd, Twick. 117 CH85
St. Peters Rd, Uxb. 76 BK71
St. Peter's Rd, W.Mol. 136 CA98
St. Peters Rd, Wok. 167 BB121
St. Peter's Sq E2 84 DU68
St. Peter's Cl
St. Peter's Sq W6 99 CU78
St. Peters St N1 83 DP67
St. Peter's St, S.Croy. 160 DR106
St. Peters Ter SW6 99 CY80
St. Peter's Vil W6 99 CU77
St. Peter's Way N1 84 DS66
St. Peters Way W5 79 CK71
St. Peter's Way, Add. 134 BG104
St. Peter's Way, Cher. 151 BD105
St. Peters Way, Hayes 95 BR78
St. Peters Way, Rick. 21 BB43
St. Petersburgh Ms W2 82 DB73
St. Petersburgh Pl W2 82 DB73
St. Philip Sq SW8 101 DH82
St. Philip St SW8 101 DH82
St. Philip's Av, Wor.Pk. 139 CV103
St. Philip's Rd E8 84 DU65
St. Philips Rd, Surb. 137 CK100
St. Philip's Way N1 84 DQ67
Linton St
St. Pinnock Av, Stai. 134 BG95
St. Quentin Rd, Well. 105 ET83
St. Quintin Av W10 81 CW71
St. Quintin Gdns W10 81 CW71
St. Quintin Rd E13 86 EH68
St. Raphael's Way NW10 62 CQ64
St. Regis Cl N10 45 DH54
St. Ronan's Cl, Barn. 28 DD38
St. Ronans Cres, Wdf.Grn. 48 EG52
St. Rule St SW8 101 DJ82
St. Saviour's Est SE1 201 P6
St. Saviour's Est SE1 102 DT76
St. Saviour's Rd SW2 121 DM85
St. Saviours Rd, Croy. 142 DQ100
St. Silas Pl NW5 82 DG65
St. Silas St Est NW5 82 DG65
St. Simon's Av SW15 119 CW85
St. Stephens Av E17 67 EC57
St. Stephens Av W12 99 CV75
St. Stephens Av W13 79 CH72
St. Stephen's Av, Ash. 172 CL116
St. Stephens Cl E17 67 EB57
St. Stephens Cl NW8 82 DE67
St. Stephens Cl, Sthl. 78 CA71
St. Stephens Cres W2 82 DA72
St. Stephens Cres, Brwd. 55 GA49
St. Stephens Cres, Th.Hth. 141 DN97
St. Stephens Gdn Est W2 82 DA72
Shrewsbury Rd
St. Stephens Gdns SW15 119 CZ85
Manfred Rd
St. Stephens Gdns W2 82 DA72
St. Stephens Gdns, Twick. 117 CJ86
St. Stephens Gro SE13 103 EC83
St. Stephens Ms W2 82 DA71
Chepstow Rd
St. Stephen's Par E7 86 EJ66
Green St
St. Stephen's Pas, Twick. 117 CJ86
Richmond Rd
St. Stephen's Rd E3 85 DZ68
St. Stephens Rd E6 86 EJ66
St. Stephen's Rd E17 67 EB57
Grove Rd
St. Stephens Rd W13 79 CH72
St. Stephen's Rd, Barn. 27 CX43
St. Stephens Rd, Enf. 31 DX37
St. Stephens Rd, Houns. 116 CA86
St. Stephen's Rd, West Dr. 76 BK74
St. Stephens Row EC4 197 K9
St. Stephens Ter SW8 101 DM80
St. Stephen's Wk SW7 100 DC77
St. Swithin's La EC4 197 K10
St. Swithin's La EC4 84 DR73
St. Swithun's Rd SE13 123 ED85
St. Teresa Wk, Grays 111 GH76
St. Theresa Cl, Epsom 156 CQ114
St. Theresa's Rd, Felt. 95 BT84
St. Thomas' Cl, Surb. 138 CM102
St. Thomas Cl, Wok. 166 AW117
St. Mary's Rd
St. Thomas Ct, Bex. 126 FA87
St. Thomas Dr, Orp. 145 EQ102
St. Thomas' Dr, Pnr. 40 BY53
St. Thomas Gdns, Ilf. 87 EQ65
St. Thomas Pl NW1 83 DK66
St. Thomas Rd E16 86 EG72
St. Thomas Rd N14 45 DK45
St. Thomas' Rd W4 98 CQ79
St. Thomas Rd, Belv. 107 FC75
St. Thomas Rd, Brwd. 54 FX47
St. Thomas Rd, Grav. 131 GF89
Beatrice Gdns
St. Thomas St SE1 201 K3
St. Thomas St SE1 84 DR74
St. Thomas Wk, Slou. 93 BD80
St. Thomas's Av, Grav. 131 GH88
St. Thomas's Cl, Wal.Abb. 16 EH33
St. Thomas's Gdns NW5 82 DG65
Queens Cres
St. Thomas's Pl E9 84 DW66
St. Thomas's Rd N4 65 DN61
St. Thomas's Rd NW10 80 CS67
St. Thomas's Sq E9 84 DV66
St. Thomas's Way SW6 99 CZ80
St. Timothy's Ms, Brom. 144 EH95
Wharton Rd
St. Ursula Gro, Pnr. 60 BX57
St. Ursula Rd, Sthl. 78 CA72
St. Vincent Cl SE27 121 DP92
St. Vincent Rd, Twick. 116 CC86
St. Vincent Rd, Walt. 135 BV104
St. Vincent St W1 194 G7
St. Vincents Av, Dart. 128 FN85
St. Vincents Rd, Dart. 128 FN86
St. Vincents Way, Pot.B. 12 DC33
St. Wilfrids Cl, Barn. 28 DE43
St. Wilfrids Rd, Barn. 28 DD43
St. Winefride's Av E12 69 EM64
St. Winifreds, Ken. 176 DQ115
St. Winifreds Cl, Chig. 49 EQ50
St. Winifred's Rd, Tedd. 117 CH93
St. Winifred's Rd, West. 179 EM118
Saints Cl SE27 121 DP91
Wolfington Rd
Saints Dr E7 68 EK64
Saints Wk, Grays 111 GJ77
Saladin Dr, Purf. 108 FN77
Salamanca Pl SE1 200 B9
Salamanca St SE1 200 A9
Salamanca St SE1 101 DM77
Salamander Cl, Kings.T. 117 CJ92
Salamander Quay (Harefield), Uxb. 38 BG52
Coppermill La
Salamons Way, Rain. 89 FE72
Salcombe Dr, Mord. 139 CX102
Salcombe Dr, Rom. 70 EZ58
Salcombe Gdns NW7 43 CW51
Salcombe Pk, Loug. 32 EK43
High Rd
Salcombe Rd E17 67 DZ59
Salcombe Rd N16 66 DS64
Salcombe Rd, Ashf. 114 BL91
Salcombe Way, Hayes 77 BS69
Portland Rd
Salcombe Way, Ruis. 59 BU61
Salcot Cres, Croy. 161 EC110
Salcote Rd, Grav. 131 GL92
Salcott Rd SW11 120 DE85
Salcott Rd, Croy. 141 DL104
Sale Pl W2 194 B7
Sale Pl W2 82 DE71
Sale St E2 84 DU70
Hereford St
Salehurst Cl, Har. 62 CL57
Salehurst Rd SE4 123 DZ86
Salem Pl, Croy. 142 DQ104
Salem Pl, Grav. 130 GD87
Salem Rd W2 82 DB73
Salford Rd SW2 121 DK88
Salhouse Cl SE28 88 EW72
Rollesby Way
Salisbury Av N3 63 CZ55
Salisbury Av, Bark. 87 ES66
Salisbury Av, Sutt. 157 CZ107
Salisbury Av, Swan. 147 FG98
Salisbury Cl SE17 201 K8
Salisbury Cl, Amer. 20 AS39
Salisbury Cl, Pot.B. 12 DC32
Salisbury Cl, Upmin. 73 FT61
Canterbury Av
Salisbury Cl, Wor.Pk. 139 CT104
Salisbury Ct EC4 196 F9
Salisbury Ct EC4 83 DP72
Salisbury Cres (Cheshunt), Wal.Cr. 15 DX32
Salisbury Gdns SW19 119 CY94
Salisbury Gdns, Buck.H. 48 EK47
Salisbury Hall Gdns E4 47 EA51
Salisbury Ho E14 85 EB72
Hobday St
Salisbury Ms SW6 99 CZ80
Dawes Rd
Salisbury Ms, Brom. 144 EL99
Salisbury Rd
Salisbury Pl SW9 101 DP80
Salisbury Pl W1 194 D6
Salisbury Pl W1 82 DF71
Salisbury Pl, W.Byf. 152 BJ111
Salisbury Rd E4 47 EA48
Salisbury Rd E7 86 EG65
Salisbury Rd E10 67 EC61
Salisbury Rd E12 68 EK64
Salisbury Rd E17 67 EC57
Salisbury Rd N4 65 DP57
Salisbury Rd N9 46 DU48
Salisbury Rd N22 45 DP53
Salisbury Rd SE25 142 DU100
Salisbury Rd SW19 119 CY94
Salisbury Rd W13 97 CG75
Salisbury Rd, Bans. 158 DB114
Salisbury Rd, Barn. 27 CY41
Salisbury Rd, Bex. 126 FA88
Salisbury Rd, Brom. 144 EL99
Salisbury Rd, Cars. 158 DF107
Salisbury Rd, Dag. 89 FB65
Salisbury Rd, Dart. 128 FQ88
Salisbury Rd, Enf. 31 DZ37
Salisbury Rd, Felt. 116 BW88
Salisbury Rd, Gdse. 186 DW131
Salisbury Rd, Grav. 131 GF88
Salisbury Rd, Grays 110 GC79
Salisbury Rd, Har. 61 CD57
Salisbury Rd, Houns. 96 BW83
Salisbury Rd (Heathrow Airport), Houns. 115 BQ85
Salisbury Rd, Ilf. 69 ES61
Salisbury Rd, N.Mal. 138 CR97
Salisbury Rd, Pnr. 59 BU56
Salisbury Rd, Rich. 98 CL84
Salisbury Rd, Rom. 71 FH57
Salisbury Rd, Sthl. 96 BY77
Salisbury Rd, Uxb. 76 BH68
Salisbury Rd, Wat. 23 BV38
Salisbury Rd, Wok. 166 AY119
Salisbury Rd, Wor.Pk. 139 CT104
Salisbury Sq EC4 196 E9
Salisbury St NW8 194 B5
Salisbury St NW8 82 DE70
Salisbury St W3 98 CQ75
Salisbury Ter SE15 102 DW83
Salisbury Wk N19 65 DJ61
Salix Cl, Sun. 115 BV94
Oak Gro
Salix Rd, Grays 110 GD79
Salliesfield, Twick. 117 CD86
Sally Murray Cl E12 69 EN63
Grantham Rd
Salmen Rd E13 86 EF68
Salmon La E14 85 DY72
Salmon Rd, Belv. 106 FA78
Salmon Rd, Dart. 108 FM83
Salmon St E14 85 DZ72
Salmon La
Salmon St NW9 62 CP60
Salmond Cl, Stan. 41 CG51
Robb Rd
Salmonds Gro, Brwd. 55 GC50
Salmons La, Whyt. 176 DU119
Salmons La W, Cat. 176 DS120
Salmons Rd N9 46 DU46
Salmons Rd, Chess. 155 CK107
Salomons Rd E13 86 EJ71
Chalk Rd
Salop Rd E17 67 DX58
Salt Box Hill, West. 162 EH113
Saltash Cl, Sutt. 157 CZ105
Saltash Rd, Ilf. 49 ER52
Saltash Rd, Well. 106 EW81
Saltcoats Rd W4 98 CS75
Saltcroft Cl, Wem. 62 CP60
Salter Cl, Har. 60 BZ62
Salter Rd SE16 203 H3
Salter Rd SE16 85 DX74
Salter St E14 85 EA73
Salter St NW10 81 CU69
Salterford Rd SW17 120 DG93
Salters Cl, Rick. 38 BL46
Salters Gdns, Wat. 23 BU39
Salters Hall Ct EC4 197 K10
Salters Hill SE19 122 DR92
Salters Rd E17 67 ED56
Salters Rd W10 81 CX70
Salterton Rd N7 65 DL62
Saltford Cl, Erith 107 FE78
Salthill Cl, Uxb. 58 BL64
Saltley Cl E6 86 EL72
Dunnock Rd
Saltoun Rd SW2 101 DN84
Saltram Cl N15 66 DT56
Saltram Cres W9 81 CZ69
Saltwell St E14 85 EA73
Saltwood Cl, Orp. 164 EW105
Saltwood Gro SE17 102 DR78
Merrow St
Salusbury Rd NW6 81 CY67
Salutation Rd SE10 205 J8
Salutation Rd SE10 104 EE77
Salvia Gdns, Grnf. 79 CG68
Selborne Gdns
Salvin Rd SW15 99 CX83
Salway Cl, Wdf.Grn. 48 EF52
Salway Pl E15 86 EE65
Broadway
Salway Rd E15 85 ED65
Sam Bartram Cl SE7 104 EJ78
Samantha Cl E17 67 DZ59
Samantha Ms (Havering-atte-Bower), Rom. 51 FE48
Sambruck Ms SE6 123 EB88
Samels Ct W6 99 CU78
South Black Lion La
Samford St NW8 194 A5
Samford St NW8 82 DD70
Samos Rd SE20 142 DV96
Samphire Ct, Grays 110 GE80
Salix Rd
Sampson Av, Barn. 27 CX43
Sampson Cl, Belv. 106 EX76
Carrill Way
Sampson St E1 202 C3
Sampson St E1 84 DU74
Sampsons Ct, Shep. 135 BQ99
Linden Way
Samson St E13 86 EJ68
Samuel Cl E8 84 DT67
Pownall Rd
Samuel Cl SE14 103 DX79
Samuel Cl SE18 104 EL77
Samuel Gray Gdns, Kings.T. 137 CK95
Samuel Johnson Cl SW16 121 DN91
Curtis Fld Rd
Samuel Lewis Trust Dws E8 66 DU63
Amhurst Rd
Samuel Lewis Trust Dws N1 83 DN66
Liverpool Rd
Samuel Lewis Trust Dws SW3 198 B9
Samuel Lewis Trust Dws SW6 100 DA80
Samuel St SE15 102 DT80
Samuel St SE18 105 EM77
Samuels Cl W6 99 CU78
South Black Lion La
Sancroft Cl NW2 63 CV62
Sancroft Rd, Har. 41 CF54
Sancroft St SE11 200 C10
Sancroft St SE11 101 DM78
Sanctuary, The SW1 199 N5
Sanctuary, The, Bex. 126 EX86
Sanctuary, The, Mord. 140 DA100
Sanctuary Cl, Dart. 128 FJ86
Sanctuary Cl (Harefield), Uxb. 38 BJ52
Sanctuary Rd, Houns. 114 BN86
Sanctuary St SE1 201 J5
Sandal Rd N18 46 DU50
Sandal Rd, N.Mal. 138 CR99
Sandal St E15 86 EE67
Sandale Cl N16 66 DR62
Stoke Newington Ch St
Sandall Cl W5 80 CL70
Sandall Rd NW5 83 DJ65
Sandall Rd W5 80 CL70
Sandalwood Av, Cher. 133 BD104
Sandalwood Cl E1 85 DY70
Solebay St
Sandalwood Dr, Ruis. 59 BQ59
Sandalwood Rd, Felt. 115 BV90
Sandbach Pl SE18 105 EQ77
Sandbanks, Felt. 115 BT88
Sandbanks Hill, Dart. 129 FV93
Sandbourne Av SW19 140 DB97
Sandbourne Rd SE4 103 DY82
Sandbrook Cl NW7 42 CR51
Sandbrook Rd N16 66 DS62
Sandby Grn SE9 104 EL83
Sandcliff Rd, Erith 107 FD77
Sandcroft Cl N13 45 DP51
Sandell St SE1 200 D4
Sandells Av, Ashf. 115 BQ91
Sanders Cl, Hmptn. 116 CC92
Sanders Cl, St.Alb. 9 CK27
Sanders La NW7 43 CX52
Sanders Way N19 65 DK60
Sussex Way
Sandersfield Gdns, Bans. 174 DA115
Sandersfield Rd, Bans. 174 DB115
Sanderson Av, Sev. 164 FA110
Sanderson Cl NW5 65 DH63
Sanderson Rd, Uxb. 76 BJ65
Sanderstead Av NW2 63 CY61
Sanderstead Cl SW12 121 DJ87
Atkins Rd
Sanderstead Ct Av, S.Croy. 160 DU113

Sanderstead Hill, S.Croy. 160 DS111
Sanderstead Rd E10 67 DY60
Sanderstead Rd, Orp. 146 EV100
Sanderstead Rd, S.Croy. 160 DR108
Sandes Pl, Lthd. 171 CG118
Sandfield Gdns, Th.Hth. 141 DP97
Sandfield Pas, Th.Hth. 142 DQ97
Sandfield Rd, Th.Hth. 141 DP97
Sandfields, Wok. 167 BD124
Sandford Av N22 46 DQ52
Sandford Av, Loug. 33 EQ41
Sandford Cl E6 87 EM70
Sandford Ct N16 66 DS60
Sandford Rd E6 86 EL70
Sandford Rd, Bexh. 106 EY84
Sandford Rd, Brom. 144 EG98
Sandford St SW6 100 DB80
King's Rd
Sandgate Cl, Rom. 71 FD59
Sandgate La SW18 120 DE88
Sandgate Rd, Well. 106 EW80
Sandgate St SE15 102 DV79
Sandham Pt SE18 105 EP77
Troy Ct
Sandhills, Wall. 159 DK105
Sandhills La, Vir.W. 132 AY99
Sandhills Meadow, Shep. 135 BQ101
Sandhurst Av, Har. 60 CB58
Sandhurst Av, Surb. 138 CP101
Sandhurst Cl NW9 62 CN55
Sandhurst Cl, S.Croy. 160 DS109
Sandhurst Dr, Ilf. 69 ET63
Sandhurst Rd N9 30 DW44
Sandhurst Rd NW9 62 CN55
Sandhurst Rd SE6 123 ED88
Sandhurst Rd, Bex. 126 EX85
Sandhurst Rd, Orp. 146 EU104
Sandhurst Rd, Sid. 125 ET90
Sandhurst Rd, Til. 111 GJ82
Sandhurst Way, S.Croy. 160 DS108
Sandiford Rd, Sutt. 139 CZ103
Sandiland Cres, Brom. 144 EF103
Sandilands, Croy. 142 DU103
Sandilands, Sev. 190 FD122
Sandilands Rd SW6 100 DB81
Sandison St SE15 102 DT83
Sandland St WC1 196 C7
Sandland St WC1 83 DM71
Sandlands Gro, Tad. 173 CU123
Sandlands Rd, Tad. 173 CU123
Sandling Ri SE9 125 EN90
Sandlings, The N22 45 DN54
Sandlings Cl SE15 102 DV82
Pilkington Rd
Sandmere Rd SW4 101 DL84
Sandon Cl, Esher 137 CD101
Sandon Rd (Cheshunt), Wal.Cr. 14 DW30
Sandow Cres, Hayes 95 BT76
Sandown Av, Dag. 89 FC65
Sandown Av, Esher 154 CC106
Sandown Av, Horn. 72 FK61
Sandown Cl, Houns. 95 BU81
Sandown Dr, Cars. 158 DG109
Sandown Gate, Esher 136 CC104
Sandown Ind Pk, Esher 136 CA103
Sandown Rd SE25 142 DV99
Sandown Rd, Couls. 174 DG116
Sandown Rd, Esher 154 CC105
Sandown Rd, Grav. 131 GJ93
Sandown Rd, Wat. 24 BW38
Sandown Way, Nthlt. 78 BY65
Sandpiper Cl E17 47 DX53
Sandpiper Cl SE16 203 M4
Sandpiper Cl SE16 103 DZ75
Sandpiper Dr, Erith 107 FH80
Sandpiper Rd, S.Croy. 161 DX111
Sandpiper Rd, Sutt. 139 CY103
Gander Grn La
Sandpiper Way, Orp. 146 EX98
Sandpipers, The, Grav. 131 GK89
Sandpit Hall Rd, Wok. 150 AU112
Sandpit La, Brwd. 54 FT46
Sandpit Pl SE7 104 EL78
Sandpit Rd, Brom. 124 EE92
Sandpit Rd, Dart. 108 FJ84
Sandpits Rd, Croy. 161 DX105
Sandpits Rd, Rich. 117 CK89
Sandra Cl N22 46 DQ53
New Rd
Sandra Cl, Houns. 116 CB85
Sandridge Cl, Har. 61 CE56
Sandridge Ct N4 66 DQ62
Queens Dr
Sandridge St N19 65 DJ61
Sandringham Av SW20 139 CY96
Sandringham Cl SW19 119 CX88
Sandringham Cl, Enf. 30 DS40
Sandringham Cl, Ilf. 69 EQ55
Sandringham Cl, Wok. 168 BG116
Sandringham Ct W9 82 DC69
Maida Vale
Sandringham Cres, Har. 60 CA61
Sandringham Dr, Ashf. 114 BK91
Sandringham Dr, Well. 105 ES82
Sandringham Gdns N8 65 DL58
Sandringham Gdns N12 44 DD51
Sandringham Gdns, Houns. 95 BU81
Sandringham Gdns, Ilf. 69 EQ55
Sandringham Ms W5 79 CK73
High St
Sandringham Pk, Cob. 154 BZ112
Sandringham Rd E7 68 EJ64
Sandringham Rd E8 66 DT64
Sandringham Rd E10 67 ED58
Sandringham Rd N22 66 DQ55
Sandringham Rd NW2 81 CV65
Sandringham Rd NW11 63 CY59
Sandringham Rd, Bark. 87 ET65
Sandringham Rd, Brwd. 54 FV43
Sandringham Rd, Brom. 124 EG92
Sandringham Rd, Houns. 114 BL85
Sandringham Rd, Nthlt. 78 CA66
Sandringham Rd, Pot.B. 12 DB30
Sandringham Rd, Th.Hth. 142 DQ99
Sandringham Rd, Wat. 24 BW37
Sandringham Rd, Wor.Pk. 139 CU104
Sandringham Way, Wal.Cr. 15 DX34
Sandrock Pl, Croy. 161 DX105
Sandrock Rd SE13 103 EA83
Sandroyd Way, Cob. 154 CA113
Sand's End La SW6 100 DB81
Sands Way, Wdf.Grn. 48 EL51
Sandstone Pl N19 65 DH61
Sandstone Rd SE12 124 EH89
Sandtoft Rd SE7 104 EH79
Sandway Path, Orp. 146 EW98
Okemore Gdns
Sandway Rd, Orp. 146 EW98
Sandwell Cres NW6 82 DA65
Sandwich St WC1 195 P3
Sandwich St WC1 83 DL69
Sandwick Cl NW7 43 CU52
Sebergham Gro
Sandy Bk Rd, Grav. 131 GH88
Sandy Bury, Orp. 145 ER104
Sandy Cl, Wok. 167 BB117
Sandy La
Sandy Dr, Cob. 154 CA111
Sandy Dr, Felt. 115 BS88
Sandy Hill Av SE18 105 EP78
Sandy Hill Rd SE18 105 EP78
Sandy Hill Rd, Wall. 159 DJ109
Sandy La, Bushey 24 CC41
Sandy La, Cob. 154 BZ112
Sandy La, Dart. 129 FW89
Sandy La (Chadwell St. Mary), Grays 111 GH79
Sandy La (West Thurrock), Grays 109 FV79
London Rd
Sandy La, Har. 62 CM58
Sandy La, Kings.T. 117 CG94
Sandy La, Lthd. 154 CA112
Sandy La, Mitch. 140 DG95
Sandy La, Nthwd. 39 BU50
Sandy La, Orp. 146 EU101
Sandy La (St. Paul's Cray), Orp. 146 EX95
Sandy La, Oxt. 187 EC129
Sandy La (Limpsfield), Oxt. 188 EH127
Sandy La (Bletchingley), Red. 185 DP132
Sandy La, Rich. 117 CJ89
Sandy La, Sev. 191 FJ123
Sandy La, Sid. 126 EX94
Sandy La, S.Ock. 90 FM73
Sandy La, Sutt. 157 CY108
Sandy La, Tad. 173 CZ124
Sandy La, Tedd. 117 CG94
Sandy La, Vir.W. 132 AY98
Sandy La, Walt. 135 BV100
Sandy La, Wat. 24 CC41
Sandy La, West. 189 ER125
Sandy La, Wok. 167 BC116
Sandy La (Chobham), Wok. 150 AS109
Sandy La (Pyrford), Wok. 167 BF117
Sandy La (Send), Wok. 167 BC123
Sandy La Est, Rich. 117 CK89
Sandy La N, Wall. 159 DK106
Sandy La S, Wall. 159 DK107
Sandy Lo La, Nthwd. 39 BR47
Sandy Lo Rd, Rick. 39 BP47
Sandy Lo Way, Nthwd. 39 BS50
Sandy Ridge, Chis. 125 EN93
Sandy Ri (Chalfont St. Peter), Ger.Cr. 36 AY53
Sandy Rd NW3 64 DB62
Sandy Rd, Add. 152 BG107
Sandy Way, Cob. 154 CA112
Sandy Way, Croy. 143 DZ104
Sandy Way, Walt. 135 BT102
Sandy Way, Wok. 167 BC117
Sandycombe Rd, Felt. 115 BU88
Sandycombe Rd, Rich. 98 CN83
Sandycoombe Rd, Twick. 117 CJ86
Sandycroft SE2 106 EU79
Sandycroft, Epsom 157 CW110
Sandycroft Rd, Amer. 20 AV39
Sandyhill Rd, Ilf. 69 EP63
Sandymount Av, Stan. 41 CJ50
Sandy's Row E1 197 N7
Sandy's Row E1 84 DS71
Sanford La N16 66 DT61
Lawrence Bldgs
Sanford St SE14 103 DY79
Sanford Ter N16 66 DT62
Sanford Wk N16 66 DT61
Sanford Ter
Sanford Wk SE14 103 DY79
Cold Blow La
Sanger Av, Chess. 156 CL106
Sanger Dr, Wok. 167 BC123
Sangley Rd SE6 123 EB87
Sangley Rd SE25 142 DS98
Sangora Rd SW11 100 DD84
Sans Wk EC1 196 E4
Sans Wk EC1 83 DN70
Sansom Rd E11 68 EE61
Sansom St SE5 102 DR80
Santers La, Pot.B. 11 CY33
Santley St SW4 101 DM84
Santos Rd SW18 120 DA85
Santway, The, Stan. 41 CE50
Sanway Cl, W.Byf. 152 BL114
Sanway Rd, W.Byf. 152 BL114
Sapcote Trd Cen NW10 63 CT64
Saperton Wk SE11 200 C8
Saperton Wk SE11 101 DM77
Sapho Pk, Grav. 131 GM91
Saphora Cl, Orp. 163 ER106
Oleander Cl
Sapphire Cl E6 87 EN72
Sapphire Cl, Dag. 70 EW60
Sapphire Rd SE8 203 L9
Sapphire Rd SE8 103 DY77
Sappho Ct, Wok. 166 AS116
Langmans Way
Sara Ct, Beck. 143 EB95
Albemarle Rd
Sara Cres, Green. 109 FU84
Sara Pk, Grav. 131 GL91
Saracen Cl, Croy. 142 DR100
Saracen St E14 85 EA72
Saracen's Head Yd EC3 197 P9
Sarah Ho SW15 99 CT84
Sarah St N1 197 N2
Saratoga Rd E5 66 DW63
Sardinia St WC2 196 B9
Sargeant Cl, Uxb. 76 BK69
Ratcliffe Cl
Sarita Cl, Har. 41 CD54
Sarjant Path SW19 119 CX89
Queensmere Rd
Sark Cl, Houns. 96 CA80
Sark Wk E16 86 EH72
Sarnesfield Ho SE15 102 DV79
Pencraig Way
Sarnesfield Rd, Enf. 30 DR41
Church St
Sarratt Bottom, Rick. 21 BE36
Sarratt La, Rick. 22 BH40
Sarratt Rd, Rick. 22 BM41
Sarre Av, Horn. 90 FJ65
Sarre Rd NW2 63 CZ64
Sarre Rd, Orp. 146 EW99
Sarsby Dr, Stai. 113 BA89
Feathers La
Sarsen Av, Houns. 96 BZ82
Sarsfeld Rd SW12 120 DF88
Sarsfield Rd, Grnf. 79 CH68
Sartor Rd SE15 103 DX84
Sarum Complex, Uxb. 76 BH68
Sarum Grn, Wey. 135 BS104
Sarum Ter E3 85 DZ70
Satanita Cl E16 86 EK72
Fulmer Rd
Satchell Mead NW9 43 CT53
Satchwell Rd E2 84 DU69
Satis Ct, Epsom 157 CT111
Windmill Av
Sauls Grn E11 68 EE62
Napier Rd
Saunder Cl, Wal.Cr. 15 DX27
Welsummer Way
Saunders Cl E14 203 N1
Saunders Cl, Grav. 130 GE89
Saunders Copse, Wok. 166 AV122
Saunders La, Wok. 166 AS122
Saunders Ness Rd E14 204 E10
Saunders Ness Rd E14 103 EC78
Saunders Rd SE18 105 ET78
Saunders Rd, Uxb. 76 BM66
Saunders St SE11 200 D8
Saunders St SE11 101 DN77
Saunders Way SE28 88 EV73
Oriole Way
Saunders Way, Dart. 128 FM89
Saunderton Rd, Wem. 61 CH64
Saunton Av, Hayes 95 BT80
Saunton Rd, Horn. 71 FG61
Savage Gdns E6 87 EM72
Savage Gdns EC3 197 N10
Savay Cl (Denham), Uxb. 58 BG59
Savay La (Denham), Uxb. 58 BG58
Savernake Rd N9 30 DU44
Savernake Rd NW3 64 DF63
Savery Dr, Surb. 137 CJ101
Savile Cl, N.Mal. 138 CS99
Savile Cl, T.Ditt. 137 CF102
Savile Gdns, Croy. 142 DT103
Savile Row W1 195 K10
Savile Row W1 83 DJ73
Savill Cl (Cheshunt), Wal.Cr. 14 DQ25
Markham Rd
Savill Gdns SW20 139 CU97
Bodnant Gdns
Savill Row, Wdf.Grn. 48 EF51
Saville Cres, Ashf. 115 BR93
Saville Rd E16 86 EL74
Saville Rd W4 98 CR76
Saville Rd, Rom. 70 EZ58
Saville Rd, Twick. 117 CF88
Saville Row, Brom. 144 EF102
Saville Row, Enf. 31 DX40
Savona Cl SW19 119 CY94
Savona Est SW8 101 DJ80
Savona St SW8 101 DJ80
Savoy Av, Hayes 95 BS78
Savoy Bldgs WC2 200 B1
Savoy Cl E15 86 EE67
Arthingworth St
Savoy Cl, Edg. 42 CN50
Savoy Cl (Harefield), Uxb. 38 BK54
Savoy Ct WC2 200 A1
Savoy Hill WC2 200 B1
Savoy Pl WC2 200 A1
Savoy Pl WC2 83 DL73
Savoy Rd, Dart. 128 FK85
Savoy Row WC2 196 B10
Savoy Steps WC2 83 DM73
Savoy St
Savoy St WC2 196 B10
Savoy St WC2 83 DM73
Savoy Way WC2 200 B1
Sawbill Cl, Hayes 78 BX71
Sawkins Cl SW19 119 CY89
Sawley Rd W12 81 CU74
Sawtry Cl, Cars. 140 DE101
Sawtry Way, Borwd. 26 CN38
Sawyer Cl N9 46 DU47
Lion Rd
Sawyer St SE1 201 H4
Sawyer St SE1 102 DQ75
Sawyers Chase, Rom. 34 EV41
Sawyers Cl, Dag. 89 FC65
Sawyers Hall La, Brwd. 54 FW45
Sawyer's Hill, Rich. 118 CP87
Sawyers La, Borwd. 25 CH40
Sawyers La, Pot.B. 11 CX34
Sawyers Lawn W13 79 CF72
Saxby Rd SW2 121 DL87
Saxham Rd, Bark. 87 ET67
Saxlingham Rd E4 47 ED48
Saxon Av, Felt. 116 BZ89
Saxon Cl E17 67 EA59
Saxon Cl, Brwd. 55 GA48
Saxon Cl, Grav. 130 GC90
Saxon Cl, Rom. 52 FM54
Saxon Cl, Sev. 181 FF117
Saxon Cl, Slou. 93 AZ75
Saxon Cl, Surb. 137 CK100
Saxon Cl, Uxb. 76 BM71
Saxon Ct, Borwd. 26 CL40
Saxon Dr W3 80 CP72
Saxon Gdns, Sthl. 78 BY73
Saxon Rd
Saxon Pl (Horton Kirby), Dart. 148 FQ99
Saxon Rd E3 85 DZ68
Saxon Rd E6 87 EM70
Saxon Rd N22 45 DP53
Saxon Rd SE25 142 DR99
Saxon Rd, Ashf. 115 BR93
Saxon Rd, Brom. 124 EF94
Saxon Rd, Dart. 128 FL91
Saxon Rd, Ilf. 87 EP65
Saxon Rd, Sthl. 78 BY74
Saxon Rd, Walt. 136 BX104
Saxon Rd, Wem. 62 CQ62
Saxon Shore Way, Grav. 131 GM86
Saxon Wk, Sid. 126 EW93
Saxon Way N14 29 DK44
Saxon Way, Reig. 183 CZ133
Saxon Way, Wal.Abb. 15 EC33
Saxon Way, West Dr. 94 BJ79
Saxon Way, Wind. 112 AV86
Saxonbury Av, Sun. 135 BV97
Saxonbury Cl, Mitch. 140 DD97
Saxonbury Gdns, Surb. 137 CJ102
Saxonfield Cl SW2 121 DM87
Saxons, Tad. 173 CX121
Saxony Par, Hayes 77 BQ71
Saxton Cl SE13 103 ED83
Saxville Rd, Orp. 146 EV97
Sayer Cl, Green. 129 FU85
Sayers Cl, Lthd. 170 CC124
Sayers Wk, Rich. 118 CM87
Stafford Pl
Sayes Ct SE8 103 DZ78
Sayes Ct St
Sayes Ct, Add. 152 BJ106
Sayes Ct Fm Dr, Add. 152 BH106
Sayes Ct Rd, Orp. 146 EU98
Sayes Ct St SE8 103 DZ79
Sayesbury La N18 46 DU50
Scadbury Pk, Chis. 125 ET93
Scads Hill Cl, Orp. 145 ET100
Scala St W1 195 L6
Scala St W1 83 DJ71
Scales Rd N17 66 DT55
Scammel Way, Wat. 23 BT44
Scampston Ms W10 81 CX72
Scampton Rd, Houns. 114 BM86
Southampton Rd
Scandrett St E1 202 D3
Scandrett St E1 84 DV74
Scarba Wk N1 84 DR65
Marquess Rd
Scarborough Cl, Sutt. 157 CZ111
Scarborough Cl, West. 178 EJ118
Scarborough Rd E11 67 ED60
Scarborough Rd N4 65 DN59
Scarborough Rd N9 46 DW45
Scarborough Rd, Houns. 115 BQ86
Southern Perimeter Rd
Scarborough St E1 84 DT72
West Tenter St
Scarbrook Rd, Croy. 142 DQ104
Scarle Rd, Wem. 79 CK65
Scarlet Cl, Orp. 146 EV98
Scarlet Rd SE6 124 EE90
Scarlett Cl, Wok. 166 AT118
Bingham Dr
Scarlette Manor Way SW2 121 DN87
Papworth Way
Scarsbrook Rd SE3 104 EK83
Scarsdale Pl W8 100 DB76
Wrights La
Scarsdale Rd, Har. 60 CC62
Scarsdale Vil W8 100 DA76
Scarth Rd SW13 99 CT83
Scatterdells La, Kings L. 5 BF30
Scawen Cl, Cars. 158 DG105
Scawen Rd SE8 103 DY78
Scawfell St E2 84 DT68
Scaynes Link N12 44 DA50
Sceaux Est SE5 102 DS81
Sceaux Gdns SE5 102 DT81
Sceptre Rd E2 84 DW69
Schofield Wk SE3 104 EH80
Dornberg Cl
Scholars Rd E4 47 EC46
Scholars Rd SW12 121 DJ88
Scholars Wk (Chalfont St. Peter), Ger.Cr. 36 AY51
Scholars Way, Amer. 20 AT38
Scholefield Rd N19 65 DK60
Schonfeld Sq N16 66 DR61
School Cres, Dart. 107 FF84
School Grn La, Epp. 19 FC25
School Hill, Red. 185 DJ128
School Ho La, Tedd. 117 CH94
School La SE23 122 DV89
School La, Add. 152 BG105
School La, Bushey 40 CB45
School La, Cat. 186 DT126
School La, Ch.St.G. 36 AV47
School La, Dart. 129 FW90
School La (Horton Kirby), Dart. 148 FQ98
School La, Egh. 113 BA92
School La (Chalfont St. Peter), Ger.Cr. 36 AX54
School La, Kings.T. 137 CJ95
School Rd
School La, Lthd. 171 CD122
School La, Long. 149 FT100
School La, Pnr. 60 BY56
School La, St.Alb. 8 CA31
School La (Seal), Sev. 191 FM121
School La, Shep. 135 BP100
School La, Slou. 74 AV67
School La, Surb. 138 CN102
School La, Swan. 147 FH95
School La, Tad. 183 CU125
Chequers La
School La, Well. 106 EV83
School La, Wok. 169 BP122
School Mead, Abb.L. 7 BS32
School Pas, Kings.T. 138 CM96
School Pas, Sthl. 78 BZ74
School Rd E12 69 EM63
School Rd NW10 80 CR70
School Rd, Ashf. 115 BP93
School Rd, Chis. 145 EQ95
School Rd, Dag. 88 FA67
School Rd, E.Mol. 137 CD98
School Rd, Hmptn. 116 CC93
School Rd, Houns. 96 CC83
School Rd, Kings.T. 137 CJ95
School Rd, Ong. 19 FG32
School Rd, Pot.B. 12 DC30
School Rd, West Dr. 94 BK79
School Rd Av, Hmptn. 116 CC93
School Wk, Slou. 74 AV73
Grasmere Av
School Wk, Sun. 135 BT98
School Way N12 44 DC49
High Rd
School Way, Dag. 70 EW62
Schoolbell Ms E3 85 DY68
Arbery Rd
Schoolfield Rd, Grays 109 FU79
Schoolhouse Gdns, Loug. 33 EP42
Schoolhouse La E1 85 DX73
Schoolway N12 44 DD51
Schooner Cl E14 204 F7
Schooner Cl E14 103 ED76
Schooner Cl SE16 203 H4
Schooner Cl, Bark. 87 ES69
Thames Rd
Schooner Ct, Dart. 108 FQ84
Schroder Ct, Egh. 112 AV92
Schubert Rd SW15 119 CZ85
Schubert Rd, Borwd. 25 CK44
Scilla Ct, Grays 110 GD79
Sclater St E1 197 P4
Sclater St E1 84 DT70
Scoble Pl N16 66 DT63
Amhurst Rd
Scoles Cres SW2 121 DN88
Scoresby St SE1 200 F3
Scoresby St SE1 83 DP74
Scorton Av, Grnf. 79 CG68
Scot Gro, Pnr. 40 BX52
Scotch Common W13 79 CG71
Scoter Cl, Wdf.Grn. 48 EH52
Mallards Rd
Scotia Rd SW2 121 DN87
Scotland Br Rd, Add. 152 BG111
Scotland Grn N17 46 DU54
Scotland Grn Rd, Enf. 31 DX43
Scotland Grn Rd N, Enf. 31 DX42
Scotland Pl SW1 199 P2
Scotland Rd, Buck.H. 48 EJ46
Scotney Wk, Horn. 72 FK64
Bonington Rd
Scots Hill, Rick. 22 BM44
Scots Hill Cl, Rick. 22 BM44
Scots Hill
Scotscraig, Rad. 25 CF35
Scotsdale Cl, Orp. 145 ES98
Scotsdale Cl, Sutt. 157 CY108
Scotsdale Rd SE12 124 EH85
Scotshall La, Warl. 161 EC114
Scotsmill La, Rick. 22 BM44
Scotswood St EC1 196 E4
Scotswood Wk N17 46 DU52
Scott Cl SW16 141 DM95
Scott Cl, Epsom 156 CQ106
Scott Cl, West Dr. 94 BM77
Scott Ct W3 98 CQ75
Petersfield Rd
Scott Cres, Erith 107 FF81
Cloudesley Rd
Scott Cres, Har. 60 CB60
Scott Ellis Gdns NW8 82 DD69
Scott Fm Cl, T.Ditt. 137 CH102
Scott Gdns, Houns. 96 BX80
Scott Ho N18 46 DU50
Scott Lidgett Cres SE16 202 B5
Scott Lidgett Cres SE16 102 DU75
Scott Rd, Grav. 131 GK92
Scott Rd, Grays 111 GG77
Scott Russell Pl E14 204 B10
Scott St E1 84 DV70
Scott Trimmer Way, Houns. 96 BY82
Scottes La, Dag. 70 EX60
Valence Av
Scotts Av, Brom. 143 ED96
Scotts Av, Sun. 115 BS94
Scotts Cl, Horn. 72 FJ64
Rye Cl
Scotts Cl, Stai. 114 BK88
Scotts Dr, Hmptn. 116 CB94
Scotts Fm Rd, Epsom 156 CQ107
Scotts La, Brom. 143 ED97
Scotts La, Walt. 154 BX105
Scotts Rd E10 67 EC60
Scotts Rd W12 99 CV75
Scotts Rd, Brom. 124 EG94
Scotts Rd, Sthl. 96 BW76
Scotts Way, Sev. 190 FE122
Scotts Way, Sun. 115 BS93
Scott's Yd EC4 197 K10
Scottswood Cl, Bushey 24 BY40
Scottswood Rd
Scottswood Rd, Bushey 24 BY40
Scottwell Dr NW9 63 CT57
Crossway
Scoulding Rd E16 86 EF72
Scouler St E14 204 F1
Scout App NW10 62 CS63
Scout La SW4 101 DJ83
Old Town
Scout Way NW7 42 CR49
Scovell Cres SE1 201 H5
Scovell Rd SE1 201 H5
Scratchers La (Fawkham Grn), Long. 149 FR103
Scrattons Ter, Bark. 88 EX68
Scriven St E8 84 DT67
Scrooby St SE6 123 EB86
Scrubbitts Pk Rd, Rad. 25 CG35
Scrubbitts Sq, Rad. 25 CG36
The Dell
Scrubs La NW10 81 CU69
Scrubs La W10 81 CU69
Scrutton Cl SW12 121 DK87
Scrutton St EC2 197 M5
Scrutton St EC2 84 DS70
Scudamore La NW9 62 CQ55

Scudders Hill (Fawkham Gr), Long. 149 FV100
Scutari Rd SE22 122 DW85
Scylla Cres, Houns. 115 BP87
Scylla Pl, Wok. 166 AU119
Church Rd
Scylla Rd SE15 102 DV83
Scylla Rd, Houns. 115 BP86
Seaborough Rd, Grays 111 GJ76
Seabright St E2 84 DV69
Bethnal Grn Rd
Seabrook Dr, W.Wick. 144 EE103
Seabrook Gdns, Rom. 70 FA59
Seabrook Rd, Dag. 70 EX62
Seabrook Rd, Kings L. 7 BR27
Seabrooke Ri, Grays 110 GB79
Seaburn Cl, Rain. 89 FE68
Seacole Cl W3 80 CR71
Seacourt Rd SE2 106 EX75
Seacourt Rd, Slou. 93 BB77
Seacroft Gdns, Wat. 40 BX48
Seafield Rd N11 45 DK49
Seaford Cl, Ruis. 59 BR61
Seaford Rd E17 67 EB55
Seaford Rd N15 66 DR57
Seaford Rd W13 79 CH74
Seaford Rd, Enf. 30 DS42
Seaford Rd, Houns. 114 BK85
Seaford St WC1 196 A3
Seaford St WC1 83 DL69
Seaforth Av, N.Mal. 139 CV99
Seaforth Cl, Rom. 51 FE52
Seaforth Cres N5 66 DQ64
Seaforth Dr, Wal.Cr. 15 DX34
Seaforth Gdns N21 45 DM45
Seaforth Gdns, Epsom 157 CT105
Seaforth Gdns, Wdf.Grn. 48 EJ50
Seaforth Pl SW1 101 DJ76
Buckingham Gate
Seagrave Rd SW6 100 DA79
Seagry Rd E11 68 EG58
Seagull Cl, Bark. 87 ES69
Thames Rd
Seal Dr, Sev. 191 FM121
Seal Hollow Rd, Sev. 191 FJ124
Seal Rd, Sev. 191 FJ121
Seal St E8 66 DT63
Sealand Rd, Houns. 114 BN86
Sealand Wk, Nthlt. 78 BY69
Wayfarer Rd
Seaman Cl, St.Alb. 9 CD25
Searches La, Abb.L. 7 BV28
Searchwood Rd, Warl. 176 DV118
Searle Pl N4 65 DM60
Evershot Rd
Searles Cl SW11 100 DE80
Searles Dr E6 87 EN71
Winsor Ter
Searles Rd SE1 201 L8
Searles Rd SE1 102 DR77
Sears St SE5 102 DR80
Seasprite Cl, Nthlt. 78 BX69
Seaton Av, Ilf. 69 ES64
Seaton Cl E13 86 EH70
New Barn St
Seaton Cl SE11 200 E10
Seaton Cl SE11 101 DN78
Seaton Cl SW15 119 CV88
Seaton Cl, Twick. 117 CD86
Seaton Dr, Ashf. 114 BL89
Seaton Gdns, Ruis. 59 BU62
Seaton Pl NW1 83 DJ70
Triton Sq
Seaton Pt E5 66 DU63
Nolan Way
Seaton Rd, Dart. 127 FG87
Seaton Rd, Hayes 95 BR77
Seaton Rd, Mitch. 140 DE96
Seaton Rd, St.Alb. 9 CK26
Seaton Rd, Twick. 116 CC86
Seaton Rd, Well. 106 EW80
Seaton Rd, Wem. 80 CL68
Seaton St N18 46 DU50
Sebastian Av, Brwd. 55 GA44
Sebastian St EC1 196 G3
Sebastian St EC1 83 DP69
Sebastopol Rd N9 46 DU49
Sebbon St N1 83 DP66
Sebergham Gro NW7 43 CU52
Sebert Rd E7 68 EH64
Sebright Pas E2 84 DU68
Hackney Rd
Sebright Rd, Barn. 27 CX40
Secker Cres, Har. 40 CC53
Secker St SE1 200 D3
Second Av E12 68 EL63
Second Av E13 86 EG69
Second Av E17 67 EA57
Second Av N18 46 DW49
Second Av NW4 63 CX56
Second Av SW14 98 CS83
Second Av W3 81 CT74
Second Av W10 81 CY70
Second Av, Dag. 89 FB67
Second Av, Enf. 30 DT43
Second Av, Grays 109 FU79
Second Av, Hayes 77 BT74
Second Av, Rom. 70 EW57
Second Av, Walt. 135 BV100
Second Av, Wat. 24 BX35
Second Av, Wem. 61 CK61
Second Cl, W.Mol. 136 CC98
Second Cross Rd, Twick. 117 CE89
Second Way, Wem. 62 CP63
Sedan Way SE17 201 M10
Sedcombe Cl, Sid. 126 EV91
Knoll Rd
Sedcote Rd, Enf. 30 DW43
Sedding St SW1 198 F8
Sedding St SW1 100 DG77
Seddon Ho EC2 84 DQ71
The Barbican
Seddon Rd, Mord. 140 DD99
Seddon St WC1 196 C3
Sedge Ct, Grays 110 GE80
Sedge Rd N17 46 DW52
Sedgebrook Rd SE3 104 EK82
Sedgecombe Av, Har. 61 CJ57
Sedgefield Cl, Rom. 52 FM49
Sedgefield Cres, Rom. 52 FM49
Sedgeford Rd W12 81 CT74
Sedgehill Rd SE6 123 EA91
Sedgemere Av N2 64 DC55
Sedgemere Rd SE2 106 EW76
Sedgemoor Dr, Dag. 70 FA63
Sedgeway SE6 124 EF88
Sedgewick Av, Uxb. 77 BP66
Sedgewood Cl, Brom. 144 EF101
Sedgmoor Pl SE5 102 DS80
Sedgwick Rd E10 67 EC61
Sedgwick St E9 67 DX64
Sedleigh Rd SW18 119 CZ86
Sedlescombe Rd SW6 99 CZ79
Sedley, Grav. 130 GA93
Sedley Cl, Enf. 30 DV38
Sedley Gro (Harefield), Uxb. 58 BJ56
Sedley Pl W1 195 H9
Sedley Ri, Loug. 33 EM40
Sedum Cl NW9 62 CP57
Seeley Dr SE21 122 DS91
Seelig Av NW9 63 CU59
Seely Rd SW17 120 DG93
Seer Grn La, Beac. 36 AS52
Seething La EC3 201 N1
Seething La EC3 84 DS73
Seething Wells La, Surb. 137 CJ100
Sefton Av NW7 42 CR50
Sefton Av, Har. 41 CD53
Sefton Cl, Orp. 145 ET98
Sefton Cl, Slou. 74 AT66
Sefton Paddock, Slou. 74 AU66
Sefton Pk, Slou. 74 AU66
Sefton Rd, Croy. 142 DU102
Sefton Rd, Epsom 156 CR110
Sefton Rd, Orp. 145 ET98
Sefton St SW15 99 CW82
Sefton Way, Uxb. 76 BJ72
Segal Cl SE23 123 DY87
Segrave Cl, Wey. 152 BN108
Sekforde St EC1 196 F5
Sekforde St EC1 83 DP70
Sekhon Ter, Felt. 116 CA90
Selah Dr, Swan. 147 FC95
Selan Gdns, Hayes 77 BV71
Selbie Av NW10 63 CT64
Selborne Av E12 69 EN63
Walton Rd
Selborne Av, Bex. 126 EY88
Selborne Gdns NW4 63 CU56
Selborne Gdns, Grnf. 79 CG67
Selborne Rd E17 67 DZ57
Selborne Rd N14 45 DL48
Selborne Rd N22 45 DM53
Selborne Rd SE5 102 DR82
Denmark Hill
Selborne Rd, Croy. 142 DS104
Selborne Rd, Ilf. 69 EN61
Selborne Rd, N.Mal. 138 CS96
Selborne Rd, Sid. 126 EV91
Selborne Wk E17 67 DZ56
Selbourne Av, Add. 152 BH110
Selbourne Av, Surb. 138 CM103
Selbourne Cl, Add. 152 BH109
Selbourne Sq, Gdse. 186 DW130
Selby Chase, Ruis. 59 BV61
Selby Cl E6 86 EL71
Linton Gdns
Selby Cl, Chess. 156 CL108
Selby Cl, Chis. 125 EN93
Selby Gdns, Sthl. 78 CA70
Selby Grn, Cars. 140 DE101
Selby Rd E11 68 EE62
Selby Rd E13 86 EH71
Selby Rd N17 46 DS51
Selby Rd SE20 142 DU96
Selby Rd W5 79 CH70
Selby Rd, Ashf. 115 BQ93
Selby Rd, Cars. 140 DE101
Selby St E1 84 DU70
Selby Wk, Wok. 166 AV118
Wyndham Rd
Selcroft Rd, Pur. 159 DP112
Selden Rd SE15 102 DW82
Selden Wk N7 65 DM61
Durham Rd
Selhurst Cl SW19 119 CX88
Selhurst Cl, Wok. 167 AZ115
Selhurst New Rd SE25 142 DS100
Selhurst Pl SE25 142 DS100
Selhurst Rd N9 46 DR48
Selhurst Rd SE25 142 DS99
Selinas La, Dag. 70 EY59
Selkirk Dr, Erith 107 FE81
Selkirk Rd SW17 120 DE91
Selkirk Rd, Twick. 116 CC89
Sell Cl (Cheshunt), Wal.Cr. 13 DP26
Gladding Rd
Sellers Cl, Borwd. 26 CQ39
Sellers Hall Cl N3 44 DA52
Sellincourt Rd SW17 120 DE92
Sellindge Cl, Beck. 123 DZ94
Sellon Ms SE11 200 C9
Sellons Av NW10 81 CT67
Sellwood Dr, Barn. 27 CX43
Selsdon Av, S.Croy. 160 DR107
Selsdon Rd
Selsdon Cl, Rom. 51 FC53
Selsdon Cl, Surb. 138 CL99
Selsdon Cres, S.Croy. 160 DW109
Selsdon Pk Rd, S.Croy. 161 DX109
Selsdon Rd E11 68 EG59
Selsdon Rd E13 86 EJ67
Selsdon Rd NW2 63 CT61
Selsdon Rd SE27 121 DP90
Selsdon Rd, Add. 152 BG111
Selsdon Rd, S.Croy. 160 DR106
Selsdon Rd Ind Est, S.Croy. 160 DR107
Selsdon Rd
Selsdon Way E14 204 C7
Selsdon Way E14 103 EB76
Selsea Pl N16 66 DS64
Crossway
Selsey Cres, Well. 106 EX81
Selsey St E14 85 EA71
Selvage La NW7 42 CR50
Selway Cl, Pnr. 59 BV56
Selwood Cl, Stai. 114 BJ86
Selwood Gdns, Stai. 114 BJ86
Selwood Pl SW7 100 DD78
Selwood Rd, Brwd. 54 FT48
Selwood Rd, Chess. 155 CK105
Selwood Rd, Croy. 142 DV103
Selwood Rd, Sutt. 139 CZ102
Selwood Rd, Wok. 167 BB120
Selwood Ter SW7 100 DD78
Neville Ter
Selworthy Cl E11 68 EG57
Selworthy Rd SE6 123 DZ90
Selwyn Av E4 47 EC51
Selwyn Av, Ilf. 69 ES58
Selwyn Av, Rich. 98 CL83
Selwyn Cl, Houns. 96 BY84
Selwyn Ct SE3 104 EE83
Selwyn Ct, Edg. 42 CP52
Camrose Av
Selwyn Cres, Well. 106 EV84
Selwyn Pl, Orp. 146 EV97
Selwyn Rd E3 85 DZ68
Selwyn Rd E13 86 EH67
Selwyn Rd NW10 80 CR66
Selwyn Rd, N.Mal. 138 CR99
Selwyn Rd, Til. 111 GF82
Dock Rd
Semley Gate E9 85 DZ65
Eastway
Semley Pl SW1 198 G9
Semley Pl SW1 100 DG77
Semley Rd SW16 141 DL96
Semper Cl, Wok. 166 AS117
Semper Rd, Grays 111 GJ75
Senate St SE15 102 DW82
Senator Wk SE28 105 ER76
Broadwater Rd
Send Barns La, Wok. 167 BD124
Send Cl, Wok. 167 BC123
Send Marsh Rd, Wok. 167 BF123
Send Par Cl, Wok. 167 BC123
Send Rd
Send Rd, Wok. 167 BB122
Seneca Rd, Th.Hth. 142 DQ98
Senga Rd, Wall. 140 DG102
Senhouse Rd, Sutt. 139 CX104
Senior St W2 82 DB71
Senlac Rd SE12 124 EH88
Sennen Rd, Enf. 46 DT45
Sennen Wk SE9 124 EL90
Senrab St E1 85 DX72
Sentinel Cl, Nthlt. 78 BY70
Sentinel Sq NW4 63 CW56
Sentis Ct, Nthwd. 39 BS51
Carew Rd
September Way, Stan. 41 CH51
Sequoia Cl, Bushey 41 CD46
Giant Tree Hill
Sequoia Gdns, Orp. 145 ET101
Sequoia Pk, Pnr. 40 CB51
Serbin Cl E10 67 EC59
Sergeants Grn La, Wal.Abb. 16 EJ33
Sergehill La, Abb.L. 7 BT27
Serjeants Inn EC4 196 E9
Serle St WC2 196 C8
Serle St WC2 83 DM72
Sermed Ct, Slou. 74 AW74
Sermon Dr, Swan. 147 FC97
Sermon La EC4 197 H9
Serpentine Ct, Sev. 191 FK122
Serpentine Grn, Red. 185 DK129
Malmstone Av
Serpentine Rd W2 198 D3
Serpentine Rd W2 82 DF74
Serpentine Rd, Sev. 191 FJ123
Service Rd, The, Pot.B. 12 DA32
Serviden Dr, Brom. 144 EK95
Setchell Rd SE1 201 P8
Setchell Way SE1 201 P8
Seth St SE16 202 G5
Seton Gdns, Dag. 88 EW66
Settle Pt E13 86 EG68
London Rd
Settle Rd E13 86 EG68
London Rd
Settle Rd, Rom. 52 FN49
Settles St E1 84 DU71
Settrington Rd SW6 100 DB82
Seven Acres, Cars. 140 DE103
Seven Acres, Nthwd. 39 BU51
Seven Acres, Swan. 147 FD100
Seven Arches App, Wey. 152 BM108
Seven Arches Rd, Brwd. 54 FX48
Seven Hills Cl, Walt. 153 BS109
Seven Hills Rd, Cob. 153 BS111
Seven Hills Rd, Iver 75 BC65
Seven Hills Rd, Walt. 153 BS109
Seven Hills Rd S, Cob. 153 BS113
Seven Kings Rd, Ilf. 69 ET61
Seven Sisters Rd N4 65 DM62
Seven Sisters Rd N7 65 DM62
Seven Sisters Rd N15 66 DR58
Seven Stars Cor W12 99 CU76
Goldhawk Rd
Sevenoaks Business Cen, Sev. 191 FJ121
Sevenoaks Bypass, Sev. 190 FC123
Sevenoaks Cl, Bexh. 107 FC84
Sevenoaks Cl, Rom. 52 FJ49
Sevenoaks Cl, Sutt. 158 DA110
Sevenoaks Ct, Nthwd. 39 BQ52
Sevenoaks Ho SE25 142 DU97
Sevenoaks Rd SE4 123 DY86
Sevenoaks Rd, Orp. 163 ET105
Sevenoaks Rd (Green St Grn), Orp. 163 ET108
Sevenoaks Rd (Otford), Sev. 181 FH116
Sevenoaks Way, Orp. 126 EW94
Sevenoaks Way, Sid. 126 EW94
Seventh Av E12 69 EM63
Seventh Av, Hayes 77 BU74
Severn Av, Rom. 71 FH55
Severn Cres, Slou. 93 BB78
Severn Dr, Enf. 30 DU38
Severn Dr, Esher 137 CG103
Severn Dr, Upmin. 73 FR58
Severn Dr, Walt. 136 BX103
Severn Rd, S.Ock. 90 FQ72
Severn Way NW10 63 CT64
Severn Way, Wat. 8 BW34
Severnake Cl E14 204 A8
Severnake Cl E14 103 EA77
Severns Fld, Epp. 18 EU29
Severnvale, St.Alb. 10 CM27
Thamesdale
Severus Rd SW11 100 DE84
Seville Ms N1 84 DS66
Seville St SW1 198 E5
Seville St SW1 100 DF75
Sevington Rd NW4 63 CV58
Sevington St W9 82 DB70
Seward Rd W7 97 CG75
Seward Rd, Beck. 143 DX96
Seward St EC1 196 G4
Seward St EC1 84 DQ69
Sewardstone Gdns E4 31 EB43
Sewardstone Rd E2 84 DW68
Sewardstone Rd E4 47 EB45
Sewardstone Rd, Wal.Abb. 31 EC38
Sewardstone Roundabout, Wal.Abb. 31 EC35
Sewardstone St, Wal.Abb. 15 EC34
Sewdley St E5 67 DX62
Sewell Rd SE2 106 EU76
Sewell St E13 86 EG69
Sextant Av E14 204 F8
Sextant Av E14 103 ED77
Sexton Cl, Rain. 89 FF67
Blake Cl
Sexton Cl (Cheshunt), Wal.Cr. 14 DQ25
Shambrook Rd
Sexton Rd, Til. 111 GF81
Seymer Rd, Rom. 71 FD55
Seymour Av N17 46 DU54
Seymour Av, Cat. 176 DQ122
Fairbourne La
Seymour Av, Epsom 157 CV109
Seymour Av, Mord. 139 CX101
Seymour Cl, E.Mol. 136 CC99
Seymour Cl, Loug. 32 EL44
Seymour Cl, Pnr. 40 BZ53
Seymour Ct E4 48 EF47
Seymour Dr, Brom. 145 EM102
Seymour Gdns SE4 103 DY83
Seymour Gdns, Felt. 116 BW91
Seymour Gdns, Ilf. 69 EM60
Seymour Gdns, Ruis. 60 BX60
Seymour Gdns, Surb. 138 CM99
Seymour Gdns, Twick. 117 CH87
Seymour Ms W1 194 F8
Seymour Ms W1 82 DG72
Seymour Pl SE25 142 DV98
Seymour Pl W1 194 D7
Seymour Pl W1 82 DE71
Seymour Rd E4 47 EB46
Seymour Rd E6 86 EK68
Seymour Rd E10 67 DZ60
Seymour Rd N3 44 DB52
Seymour Rd N8 65 DN57
Seymour Rd N9 46 DV47
Seymour Rd SW18 119 CZ87
Seymour Rd SW19 119 CX89
Seymour Rd W4 98 CQ77
Seymour Rd, Cars. 158 DG106
Seymour Rd, Ch.St.G. 36 AW49
Seymour Rd, E.Mol. 136 CC99
Seymour Rd, Grav. 131 GF88
Seymour Rd, Hmptn. 116 CC92
Seymour Rd, Kings.T. 137 CK95
Seymour Rd, Mitch. 140 DG101
Seymour Rd, Til. 111 GF81
Seymour St W1 194 D9
Seymour St W1 82 DF72
Seymour St W2 194 D9
Seymour St W2 82 DF72
Seymour Ter SE20 142 DV95
Seymour Vil SE20 142 DV95
Seymour Wk SW10 100 DC79
Seymour Wk, Swans. 130 FY87
Seymour Way, Sun. 115 BS93
Seymours, The, Loug. 33 EN39
Seyssel St E14 103 EC77
Shaa Rd W3 80 CR73
Shacklands Rd, Sev. 165 FB111
Shackleford Rd, Wok. 167 BA121
Shacklegate La, Tedd. 117 CE91
Shackleton Cl SE23 122 DV89
Featherstone Av
Shackleton Ct E14 103 EA78
Napier Av
Shackleton Rd, Slou. 74 AT73
Shackleton Rd, Sthl. 78 BZ73
Shackleton Way, Abb.L. 7 BU32
Lysander Way
Shacklewell Grn E8 66 DT63
Shacklewell La E8 66 DT64
Shacklewell Rd N16 66 DT63
Shacklewell Row E8 66 DT63
Shacklewell St E2 84 DT70
Shad Thames SE1 201 P3
Shad Thames SE1 84 DT74
Shadbolt Av E4 47 DY50
Shadbolt Cl, Wor.Pk. 139 CT103
Shadwell Ct, Nthlt. 78 BZ68
Shadwell Dr
Shadwell Dr, Nthlt. 78 BZ69
Shadwell Gdns E1 84 DW72
Martha St
Shadwell Pierhead E1 202 G1
Shadwell Pl E1 84 DW73
Sutton St
Shady Bush Cl, Bushey 40 CC45
Richfield Rd
Shady La, Wat. 23 BV40
Shaef Way, Tedd. 117 CG94
Shafter Rd, Dag. 89 FC65
Shaftesbury, Loug. 32 EK41
Shaftesbury Av W1 195 M10
Shaftesbury Av W1 83 DK73
Shaftesbury Av WC2 195 M10
Shaftesbury Av WC2 83 DK73
Shaftesbury Av, Barn. 28 DC42
Shaftesbury Av, Enf. 31 DX40
Shaftesbury Av, Felt. 115 BU86
Shaftesbury Av, Har. 60 CB60
Shaftesbury Av (Kenton), Har. 61 CK58
Shaftesbury Av, Sthl. 96 CA77
Shaftesbury Circle, Har. 60 CC60
Shaftesbury Av
Shaftesbury Ct N1 84 DR68
Shaftesbury St
Shaftesbury Cres, Stai. 114 BK94
Shaftesbury Gdns NW10 80 CS70
Shaftesbury La, Dart. 108 FP84
Shaftesbury Ms SW4 121 DJ85
Clapham Common S Side
Shaftesbury Ms W8 100 DA76
Stratford Rd
Shaftesbury Pl W14 99 CZ77
Warwick Rd
Shaftesbury Pt E13 86 EH68
High St
Shaftesbury Rd E4 47 ED46
Shaftesbury Rd E7 86 EJ66
Shaftesbury Rd E10 67 EA60
Shaftesbury Rd E17 67 EB58
Shaftesbury Rd N18 46 DS51
Shaftesbury Rd N19 65 DL60
Shaftesbury Rd, Beck. 143 DZ96
Shaftesbury Rd, Cars. 140 DD101
Shaftesbury Rd, Epp. 17 ET29
Shaftesbury Rd, Rich. 98 CL83
Shaftesbury Rd, Rom. 71 FF58
Shaftesbury Rd, Wat. 24 BW41
Shaftesbury Rd, Wok. 167 BA117
Shaftesbury St N1 197 J1
Shaftesbury St N1 84 DQ68
Shaftesbury Way, Kings L. 7 BQ28
Shaftesbury Way, Twick. 117 CD90
Shaftesbury Waye, Hayes 77 BV71
Shaftesburys, The, Bark. 87 EN66
Shafto Ms SW1 198 D7
Shafton Rd E9 85 DX67
Shaggy Calf La, Slou. 74 AU73
Shakespeare Av N11 45 DJ50
Shakespeare Av NW10 80 CR67
Shakespeare Av, Felt. 115 BU86
Shakespeare Av, Hayes 77 BV70
Shakespeare Av, Til. 111 GH82
Shakespeare Cres E12 87 EM65
Shakespeare Cres NW10 80 CR67
Shakespeare Dr, Har. 62 CN58
Shakespeare Gdns N2 64 DF56
Shakespeare Ho N14 45 DK47
High St
Shakespeare Rd E17 47 DX54
Shakespeare Rd N3 44 DA53
Popes Dr
Shakespeare Rd NW7 43 CT49
Shakespeare Rd SE24 121 DP85
Shakespeare Rd W3 80 CQ74
Shakespeare Rd W7 79 CF73
Shakespeare Rd, Add. 152 BK105
Shakespeare Rd, Bexh. 106 EY81
Shakespeare Rd, Dart. 108 FN84
Shakespeare Rd, Rom. 71 FF58
Shakespeare Sq, Ilf. 49 EQ51
Shakespeare St, Wat. 23 BV38
Shakespeare Twr EC2 84 DQ71
Beech St
Shakespeare Way, Felt. 116 BW91
Shakspeare Ms N16 66 DS63
Shakspeare Wk
Shakspeare Wk N16 66 DS63
Shalcomb St SW10 100 DC79
Shalcross Dr (Cheshunt), Wal.Cr. 15 DZ30
Shaldon Dr, Mord. 139 CY99
Shaldon Dr, Ruis. 60 BW62
Shaldon Rd, Edg. 42 CM53
Shaldon Way, Walt. 136 BW104
Shale Grn, Red. 185 DK129
Bletchingley Rd
Shalfleet Dr W10 81 CX73
Shalford Cl, Orp. 163 EQ105
Shalimar Gdns W3 80 CQ73
Shalimar Rd W3 80 CQ73
Hereford Rd
Shallons Rd SE9 125 EP91
Shalston Vil, Surb. 138 CM100
Shalstone Rd SW14 98 CP83
Shambrook Rd (Cheshunt), Wal.Cr. 13 DP25
Shamrock Cl, Lthd. 171 CD121
Shamrock Rd, Croy. 141 DM100
Shamrock Rd, Grav. 131 GL87
Shamrock St SW4 101 DK83
Shamrock Way N14 45 DH46
Shand St SE1 201 N4
Shand St SE1 102 DS75
Shandon Rd SW4 121 DJ86
Shandy St E1 85 DX71
Shanklin Cl, Wal.Cr. 14 DT29
Hornbeam Way
Shanklin Gdns, Wat. 40 BW49
Shanklin Rd N8 65 DK57
Shanklin Rd N15 66 DU56
Shanklin Way SE15 102 DT80
Pentridge St
Shannon Cl NW2 63 CX62
Shannon Cl, Sthl. 96 BX78
Shannon Gro SW9 101 DM84
Shannon Pl NW8 82 DE68
Allitsen Rd
Shannon Way, Beck. 123 EB93
Shannon Way, S.Ock. 90 FQ73
Shantock Hall La, Hem.H. 4 AY29
Shantock La, Hem.H. 4 AX30
Shap Cres, Cars. 140 DF102
Shapland Way N13 45 DM50
Shardcroft Av SE24 121 DP85
Shardeloes Rd SE14 103 DZ82
Sharland Cl, Th.Hth. 141 DN100
Dunheved Rd N
Sharland Rd, Grav. 131 GJ89
Sharman Ct, Sid. 126 EU91
Sharnbrooke Cl, Well. 106 EW83
Sharney Av, Slou. 93 BB76
Sharon Cl, Epsom 156 CQ113
Sharon Cl, Lthd. 170 CA124
Sharon Cl, Surb. 137 CK102
Sharon Gdns E9 84 DW67
Sharon Rd W4 98 CR78
Sharon Rd, Enf. 31 DY40
Sharp Way, Dart. 108 FM83
Sharpe Cl W7 79 CF71
Templeman Rd
Sharpleshall St NW1 82 DF66

Sharpness Cl, Hayes 78 BY71
Sharps La, Ruis. 59 BR59
Sharratt St SE15 102 DW79
Sharsted St SE17 101 DP78
Sharvel La, Nthlt. 77 BU67
Shavers Pl SW1 199 M1
Shaw Av, Bark. 88 EY68
Shaw Cl SE28 88 EV74
Shaw Cl, Bushey 41 CE47
Shaw Cl, Cher. 151 BC107
Shaw Cl, Epsom 157 CT111
Shaw Cl, Horn. 71 FH60
Shaw Cl, S.Croy. 160 DT112
Shaw Cl (Cheshunt), Wal.Cr. 14 DW28
Shaw Ct, Wind. 112 AU85
Shaw Cres, Brwd. 55 GD43
Shaw Cres, S.Croy. 160 DT112
Shaw Cres, Til. 111 GH81
Shaw Dr, Walt. 136 BW101
Shaw Gdns, Bark. 88 EY68
Shaw Rd SE22 102 DS84
Shaw Rd, Brom. 124 EF90
Shaw Rd, Enf. 31 DX39
Shaw Rd, West. 178 EJ120
Shaw Sq E17 47 DY53
Shaw Way, Wall. 159 DL108
Shawbrooke Rd SE9 124 EJ85
Shawbury Rd SE22 122 DT85
Shawfield Ct, West Dr. 94 BL76
Shawfield Pk, Brom. 144 EK96
Shawfield St SW3 100 DE78
Shawford Ct SW15 119 CU87
Shawford Rd, Epsom 156 CR107
Shawley Cres, Epsom 173 CW118
Shawley Way, Epsom 173 CV118
Shaws Cotts SE23 123 DY90
Shaxton Cres, Croy. 161 EC109
Shearing Dr, Cars. 140 DC101
Stavordale Rd
Shearling Way N7 83 DL65
Shearman Rd SE3 104 EF84
Shears Ct, Sun. 115 BS94
Staines Rd W
Shearsmith Ho E1 84 DU73
Cable St
Shearwater Cl, Bark. 87 ES69
Thames Rd
Shearwater Rd, Sutt. 139 CY103
Gander Grn La
Shearwater Way, Hayes 78 BX72
Shearwood Cres, Dart. 107 FF83
Sheath's La, Lthd. 154 CB113
Sheaveshill Av NW9 62 CS56
Sheehy Way, Slou. 74 AV73
Sheen Common Dr, Rich. 98 CN84
Sheen Ct, Rich. 98 CN84
Sheen Ct Rd, Rich. 98 CN84
Sheen Gate Gdns SW14 98 CQ84
Sheen Gro N1 83 DN67
Richmond Av
Sheen La SW14 98 CQ83
Sheen Pk, Rich. 98 CM84
Sheen Rd, Orp. 145 ET98
Sheen Rd, Rich. 118 CL85
Sheen Way, Wall. 159 DM106
Sheen Wd SW14 118 CQ85
Sheendale Rd, Rich. 98 CM84
Sheenewood SE26 122 DV92
Sheep La E8 84 DV67
Sheep Wk, Epsom 172 CR122
Sheep Wk, Reig. 183 CY131
Sheep Wk, Shep. 134 BM101
Sheep Wk, The, Wok. 167 BE118
Sheep Wk Ms SW19 119 CX93
Sheepbarn La, Warl. 162 EF112
Sheepcot Dr, Wat. 8 BW34
Sheepcot La, Wat. 7 BV34
Sheepcote Cl, Houns. 95 BU80
Sheepcote Gdns (Denham), Uxb. 58 BG58
Sheepcote La SW11 100 DF82
Sheepcote La, Orp. 146 EZ99
Sheepcote La, Swan. 146 EZ98
Sheepcote Rd, Har. 61 CF58
Sheepcotes Rd, Rom. 70 EX56
Sheephouse Way, N.Mal. 138 CS101
Sheerness Ms E16 105 EP75
Barge Ho Rd
Sheerwater Av, Add. 151 BE112
Sheerwater Business Cen, Wok. 151 BC114
Sheerwater Rd E16 86 EK71
Sheerwater Rd, Add. 151 BE112
Sheerwater Rd, W.Byf. 151 BE112
Sheffield Dr, Rom. 52 FN50
Sheffield Gdns, Rom. 52 FN50
Sheffield Rd, Houns. 115 BR85
Southern Perimeter Rd
Sheffield Sq E3 85 DZ69
Malmesbury Rd
Sheffield St WC2 196 B9
Sheffield Ter W8 82 DA74
Shefton Ri, Nthwd. 39 BU52
Sheila Cl, Rom. 51 FB52
Sheila Rd, Rom. 51 FB52
Sheilings, The, Horn. 72 FM57
Shelbourne Cl, Pnr. 60 BZ55
Shelbourne Pl, Beck. 123 EA94
Park Rd
Shelbourne Rd N17 46 DV54
Shelburne Rd N7 65 DM63
Shelbury Cl, Sid. 126 EU90
Shelbury Rd SE22 122 DV85
Sheldon Av N6 64 DE59
Sheldon Av, Ilf. 49 EP54
Sheldon Cl SE12 124 EH85
Sheldon Cl SE20 142 DV95
Sheldon Cl (Cheshunt), Wal.Cr. 14 DS26
Sheldon Rd N18 46 DS49
Sheldon Rd NW2 63 CX63
Sheldon Rd, Bexh. 106 EZ81
Sheldon Rd, Dag. 88 EY66
Sheldon St, Croy. 142 DQ104
Wandle Rd
Sheldrake Cl E16 87 EM74
Newland St
Sheldrake Pl W8 99 CZ75
Sheldrick Cl SW19 140 DD96
Shelduck Cl E15 68 EF64
Sheldwich Ter, Brom. 144 EL100
Shelford Pl N16 66 DR62
Stoke Newington Ch St
Shelford Ri SE19 122 DT94
Shelford Rd, Barn. 27 CW44
Shelgate Rd SW11 120 DF85
Shell Cl, Brom. 145 EM100
Shell Rd SE13 103 EB83
Shellbank La, Dart. 129 FU93
Shellduck Cl NW9 42 CS54
Swan Dr
Shelley Av E12 86 EL65
Shelley Av, Grnf. 79 CD69
Shelley Av, Horn. 71 FF61
Shelley Cl SE15 102 DV82
Shelley Cl, Bans. 173 CX115
Shelley Cl, Couls. 175 DM117
Shelley Cl, Edg. 42 CN49
Shelley Cl, Grnf. 79 CD69
Shelley Cl, Hayes 77 BU71
Shelley Cl, Nthwd. 39 BT50
Shelley Cl, Orp. 145 ES104
Shelley Cl, Slou. 93 AZ78
Shelley Cres, Houns. 96 BX82
Shelley Cres, Sthl. 78 BZ72
Shelley Dr, Well. 105 ES81
Shelley Gdns, Wem. 61 CJ61
Shelley Gro, Loug. 33 EM42
Shelley La (Harefield), Uxb. 38 BG53
Shelley Pl, Til. 111 GH81
Kipling Av
Shelley Rd, Brwd. 55 GD45
Shelley Way SW19 120 DD93
Shelleys La, Sev. 179 ET116
Shellfield Cl, Stai. 114 BG85
Shellness Rd E5 66 DV64
Shellwood Rd SW11 100 DF82
Shelmerdine Cl E3 85 EA71
Shelson Av, Felt. 115 BT90
Shelton Av, Warl. 176 DW117
Shelton Cl, Warl. 176 DW117
Shelton Ct, Slou. 92 AW76
London Rd
Shelton Rd SW19 140 DA95
Shelton St WC2 195 P9
Shelton St WC2 83 DL72
Shelvers Grn, Tad. 173 CW121
Shelvers Hill, Tad. 173 CW121
Ashurst Rd
Shelvers Spur, Tad. 173 CW121
Shelvers Way, Tad. 173 CW121
Shenden Cl, Sev. 191 FJ128
Shenden Way, Sev. 191 FJ128
Shenfield Cl, Couls. 175 DJ119
Woodfield Cl
Shenfield Common, Brwd. 54 FY48
Shenfield Cres, Brwd. 54 FY47
Shenfield Gdns, Brwd. 55 GB44
Shenfield Grn, Brwd. 55 GA45
Hutton Rd
Shenfield Ho SE18 104 EK80
Shooter's Hill Rd
Shenfield Pl, Brwd. 54 FY45
Shenfield Rd, Brwd. 54 FX46
Shenfield Rd, Wdf.Grn. 48 EH52
Shenfield St N1 197 N1
Shenfield St N1 84 DS68
Shenley Av, Ruis. 59 BT61
Shenley Hill, Rad. 25 CG35
Shenley La, St.Alb. 9 CJ27
Shenley Manor (Shenley), Rad. 9 CK33
Shenley Rd SE5 102 DS81
Shenley Rd, Borwd. 26 CN42
Shenley Rd, Dart. 128 FN86
Shenley Rd, Houns. 96 BY81
Shenley Rd, Rad. 9 CH34
Shenleybury, Rad. 10 CL30
Shenleybury Cotts, Rad. 10 CL31
Shenstone Cl, Dart. 107 FD84
Shenstone Gdns, Rom. 52 FJ53
Shepcot Ho N14 29 DJ44
Shepherd Cl W1 82 DG73
Lees Pl
Shepherd Cl, Abb.L. 7 BT30
Shepherd Mkt W1 199 H2
Shepherd St W1 199 H3
Shepherd St, Grav. 130 GD87
Shepherdess Pl N1 197 J2
Shepherdess Wk N1 84 DQ68
Shepherds Bush Grn W12 99 CW75
Shepherds Bush Mkt W12 99 CW75
Shepherds Bush Pl W12 99 CX75
Shepherds Bush Rd W6 99 CW77
Shepherds Cl N6 65 DH58
Shepherds Cl, Lthd. 172 CL124
Shepherds Cl, Orp. 145 ET104
Stapleton Rd
Shepherds Cl, Rom. 70 EX57
Shepherds Cl, Shep. 135 BP100
Shepherds Cl (Cowley), Uxb. 76 BJ70
High St
Shepherds Ct W12 99 CX75
Shepherds Grn, Chis. 125 ER94
Shepherds Hill N6 65 DH58
Shepherds Hill, Red. 185 DJ126
Shepherds Hill, Rom. 52 FN54
Shepherds La E9 67 DX64
Shepherd's La, Brwd. 54 FS45
Shepherds La, Dart. 127 FG88
Shepherds La, Rick. 37 BF45
Shepherds Path, Nthlt. 78 BY65
Fortunes Mead
Shepherds Pl W1 194 F10
Shepherds Pl W1 82 DG73
Shepherds Rd, Wat. 23 BT41
Shepherds Wk NW2 63 CU61
Shepherds Wk NW3 64 DD64
Shepherds Wk, Bushey 41 CD47
Shepherds' Wk, Epsom 172 CP121
Shepherds Way, Hat. 12 DC27
Shepherds Way, Rick. 38 BH45
Shepherds Way, S.Croy. 161 DX108
Shepiston La, Hayes 95 BR77
Shepiston La, West Dr. 95 BQ77
Shepley Cl, Cars. 140 DG104
Shepley Cl, Horn. 72 FK64
Chevington Way
Shepley Ms, Enf. 31 EA37
Sheppard Cl, Enf. 30 DV39
Sheppard Cl, Kings.T. 138 CL98
Beaufort Rd
Sheppard Dr SE16 202 D10
Sheppard Dr SE16 102 DV78
Sheppard St E16 86 EF70
Shepperton Business Pk, Shep. 135 BQ99
Shepperton Cl, Borwd. 26 CR39
Shepperton Ct, Shep. 135 BP100
Shepperton Ct Dr, Shep. 135 BP99
Shepperton Rd N1 84 DQ67
Shepperton Rd, Orp. 145 EQ100
Shepperton Rd, Stai. 134 BJ97
Sheppey Cl, Erith 107 FH80
Sheppey Gdns, Dag. 88 EW66
Sheppey Rd
Sheppey Rd, Dag. 88 EV66
Sheppey Wk N1 84 DQ66
Clephane Rd
Shepppeys La, Abb.L. 7 BS28
Sheppy Pl, Grav. 131 GH87
Sherard Ct N7 65 DL62
Manor Gdns
Sherard Rd SE9 124 EL85
Sheraton Business Cen, Grnf. 79 CH68
Sheraton Cl, Borwd. 26 CM43
Sheraton Dr, Epsom 156 CQ113
Sheraton Ms, Wat. 23 BS42
Sheraton St W1 195 M9
Sherborne Av, Enf. 30 DW40
Sherborne Av, Sthl. 96 CA77
Sherborne Cl, Epsom 173 CW117
Sherborne Cl, Hayes 78 BW72
Sherborne Cl, Slou. 93 BE81
Sherborne Cres, Cars. 140 DE101
Sherborne Gdns NW9 62 CN55
Sherborne Gdns W13 79 CH72
Sherborne Gdns, Rom. 50 FA50
Sherborne La EC4 197 K10
Sherborne Pl, Nthwd. 39 BR51
Sherborne Rd, Chess. 156 CL106
Sherborne Rd, Felt. 115 BR87
Sherborne Rd, Orp. 145 ET98
Sherborne Rd, Sutt. 140 DA103
Sherborne St N1 84 DR67
Sherborne Wk, Lthd. 171 CJ121
Windfield
Sherborne Way, Rick. 23 BP42
Sherboro Rd N15 66 DT58
Ermine Rd
Sherbourne Cotts, Wat. 24 BW43
Watford Fld Rd
Sherbourne Gdns, Shep. 135 BS101
Sherbourne Pl, Stan. 41 CG51
The Chase
Sherbrook Gdns N21 45 DP45
Sherbrooke Cl, Bexh. 106 FA84
Sherbrooke Rd SW6 99 CZ80
Shere Av, Sutt. 157 CW110
Shere Cl, Chess. 155 CK106
Shere Rd, Ilf. 69 EN57
Sheredan Rd E4 47 ED50
Sherfield Av, Rick. 38 BK47
Sherfield Cl, N.Mal. 138 CQ97
California Rd
Sherfield Gdns SW15 119 CT86
Sherfield Rd, Grays 110 GB79
Sheridan Cl, Rom. 51 FH52
Sheridan Cl, Swan. 147 FF97
Willow Av
Sheridan Cl, Uxb. 77 BQ70
Alpha Rd
Sheridan Ct, Houns. 116 BZ85
Vickers Way
Sheridan Cres, Chis. 145 EP96
Sheridan Dr, Reig. 184 DB132
Sheridan Gdns, Har. 61 CK58
Sheridan Ms E11 68 EG58
Woodbine Pl
Sheridan Pl SW13 99 CT82
Brookwood Av
Sheridan Pl, Hmptn. 136 CB95
Sheridan Rd E7 68 EF62
Sheridan Rd E12 68 EL64
Sheridan Rd SW19 139 CZ95
Sheridan Rd, Belv. 106 FA77
Sheridan Rd, Bexh. 106 EY83
Sheridan Rd, Rich. 117 CJ90
Sheridan Rd, Wat. 40 BX45
Sheridan St E1 84 DV72
Watney St
Sheridan Ter, Nthlt. 60 CB64
Whitton Av W
Sheridan Wk NW11 64 DA58
Sheridan Wk, Cars. 158 DF106
Carshalton Pk Rd
Sheridan Way, Beck. 143 DZ95
Turners Meadow Way
Sheriff Way, Wat. 7 BU33
Sheringham Av E12 69 EM63
Sheringham Av N14 29 DK43
Sheringham Av, Felt. 115 BU90
Sheringham Av, Rom. 71 FC58
Sheringham Av, Twick. 116 BZ88
Sheringham Dr, Bark. 69 ET64
Sheringham Rd N7 83 DM65
Sheringham Rd SE20 142 DV97
Sheringham Twr, Sthl. 78 CB73
Sherington Av, Pnr. 40 CA52
Sherington Rd SE7 104 EH79
Sherland Rd, Twick. 117 CF88
Sherlies Av, Orp. 145 ES103
Sherlock Ms W1 194 F6
Sherman Rd, Brom. 144 EG95
Sherman Rd, Slou. 74 AS71
Shermanbury Pl, Erith 107 FF80
Betsham Rd
Shernbroke Rd, Wal.Abb. 16 EF34
Shernhall St E17 67 EC57
Sherrard Rd E7 86 EJ65
Sherrard Rd E12 68 EK64
Sherrards Way, Barn. 28 DA43
Sherrick Grn Rd NW10 63 CV64
Sherriff Rd NW6 82 DA65
Sherrin Rd E10 67 EA63
Sherringham Av N17 46 DU54
Sherrock Gdns NW4 63 CU56
Sherry Ms, Bark. 87 ER66
Cecil Av
Sherwin Rd SE14 103 DX81
Sherwood Av E18 68 EH55
Sherwood Av SW16 121 DK94
Sherwood Av, Grnf. 79 CE65
Sherwood Av, Hayes 77 BV70
Sherwood Av, Pot.B. 11 CY32
Sherwood Av, Ruis. 59 BS58
Sherwood Cl SW13 99 CV83
Lower Common S
Sherwood Cl W13 79 CH74
Sherwood Cl, Bex. 126 EW86
Sherwood Cl, Lthd. 170 CC122
Sherwood Cl, Slou. 92 AY76
Sherwood Gdns E14 204 A8
Sherwood Gdns E14 103 EA77
Sherwood Gdns SE16 102 DU78
Sherwood Gdns, Bark. 87 ER66
Sherwood Pk Av, Sid. 126 EU87
Sherwood Pk Rd, Mitch. 141 DJ98
Sherwood Pk Rd, Sutt. 158 DA106
Sherwood Rd NW4 63 CW55
Sherwood Rd SW19 119 CZ94
Sherwood Rd, Couls. 175 DJ116
Sherwood Rd, Croy. 142 DV101
Sherwood Rd, Hmptn. 116 CC92
Sherwood Rd, Har. 60 CC61
Sherwood Rd, Ilf. 69 ER56
Sherwood Rd, Well. 105 ES82
Sherwood Rd, Wok. 166 AS117
Sherwood St N20 44 DD48
Sherwood St W1 195 L10
Sherwood Ter N20 44 DD48
Green Rd
Sherwood Way, W.Wick. 143 EB103
Sherwoods Rd, Wat. 40 BY45
Shetland Cl, Borwd. 26 CR44
Percheron Rd
Shetland Rd E3 85 DZ68
Shevon Way, Brwd. 54 FT49
Shewens Rd, Wey. 153 BR105
Shey Copse, Wok. 167 BC117
Shield Dr, Brent. 97 CG79
Shield Rd, Ashf. 115 BQ91
Shieldhall St SE2 106 EW77
Shifford Path SE23 123 DX90
Shilburn Way, Wok. 166 AU118
Shillibeer Pl W1 194 C6
Shillibeer Wk, Chig. 49 ET48
Shillingford St N1 83 DP66
Cross St
Shillitoe Av, Pot.B. 11 CX32
Shinfield St W12 81 CW72
Shingle Ct, Wal.Abb. 16 EG33
Shinglewell Rd, Erith 106 FA80
Shinners Cl SE25 142 DU99
Ship All W4 98 CN79
Thames Rd
Ship & Mermaid Row SE1 201 L4
Ship Hill, West. 178 EJ121
Ship La SW14 98 CQ82
Ship La, Brwd. 55 GE42
Ship La (Sutton at Hone), Dart. 148 FK95
Ship La, Purf. 109 FS76
Ship La, S.Ock. 109 FR75
Ship La, Swan. 148 FK95
Ship La Caravan Site, S.Ock. 109 FR76
Ship St SE8 103 EA81
Ship Tavern Pas EC3 197 M10
Ship Yd E14 204 B10
Ship Yd, Wey. 153 BP105
High St
Shipfield Cl, West. 178 EJ121
Shipka Rd SW12 121 DH88
Shipman Rd E16 86 EH72
Shipman Rd SE23 123 DX89
Shipton Cl, Dag. 70 EX62
Shipton St E2 84 DT69
Shipwright Rd SE16 203 K5
Shipwright Rd SE16 103 DY75
Shirburn Cl SE23 122 DW87
Tyson Rd
Shirbutt St E14 85 EB73
Shire Cl, Brox. 15 DZ26
Groom Rd
Shire Ct, Epsom 157 CT108
Shire Ct, Erith 106 EX76
St. John Fisher Rd
Shire Horse Way, Islw. 97 CF83
Shire La (Chalfont St. Peter), Ger.Cr. 37 BD54
Shire La, Kes. 163 EM108
Shire La, Orp. 163 EM108
Shire La, Rick. 21 BB43
Shire La (Denham), Uxb. 57 BE55
Shire Pl SW18 120 DC87
Whitehead Cl
Shirebrook Rd SE3 104 EK83
Shirehall Cl NW4 63 CX58
Shirehall Gdns NW4 63 CX58
Shirehall La NW4 63 CX58
Shirehall Pk NW4 63 CX58
Shirehall Rd, Dart. 128 FK92
Shiremeade, Borwd. 26 CM43
Shires, The, Rich. 118 CL91
Shires Cl, Ash. 171 CK118
Shires Ho, W.Byf. 152 BL113
Eden Gro Rd
Shirland Ms W9 81 CZ69
Shirland Rd W9 82 DA70
Shirley Av, Bex. 126 EX87
Shirley Av, Couls. 175 DP119
Shirley Av, Croy. 142 DW102
Shirley Av, Sutt. 158 DE105
Shirley Av (Cheam), Sutt. 157 CZ109
Shirley Ch Rd, Croy. 143 DX104
Shirley Cl E17 67 EB57
Addison Rd
Shirley Cl, Dart. 108 FJ84
Shirley Cl, Houns. 116 CC85
Shirley Cl (Cheshunt), Wal.Cr. 14 DW29
Shirley Ct, Croy. 143 DX104
Shirley Cres, Beck. 143 DY98
Shirley Dr, Houns. 116 CC85
Shirley Gdns W7 79 CG74
Shirley Gdns, Bark. 87 ES65
Shirley Gdns, Horn. 72 FJ61
Shirley Gro N9 46 DW45
Shirley Gro SW11 100 DG83
Shirley Hts, Wall. 159 DJ109
Shirley Hills Rd, Croy. 161 DX106
Shirley Ho Dr SE7 104 EJ80
Shirley Oaks Rd, Croy. 143 DX102
Shirley Pk Rd, Croy. 142 DV102
Shirley Rd E15 86 EE66
Shirley Rd W4 98 CR75
Shirley Rd, Abb.L. 7 BT32
Shirley Rd, Croy. 142 DV101
Shirley Rd, Enf. 30 DQ41
Shirley Rd, Sid. 125 ES90
Shirley Rd, Wall. 159 DJ109
Shirley St E16 86 EF72
Shirley Way, Croy. 143 DY104
Shirlock Rd NW3 64 DF63
Shobden Rd N17 46 DR53
Shobroke Cl NW2 63 CW62
Shoe La EC4 196 E8
Shoe La EC4 83 DN72
Shoebury Rd E6 87 EM66
Sholden Gdns, Orp. 146 EW99
Sholto Rd, Houns. 114 BM85
Shonks Mill Rd, Rom. 35 FG37
Shoot Up Hill NW2 63 CY64
Shooters Av, Har. 61 CJ56
Shooter's Hill SE18 105 EN81
Shooter's Hill, Well. 105 EN81
Shooter's Hill Rd SE3 104 EH80
Shooter's Hill Rd SE10 103 ED81
Shooter's Hill Rd SE18 104 EH80
Shooters Rd, Enf. 29 DP39
Shord Hill, Ken. 176 DR116
Shore, The (Northfleet), Grav. 130 GC85
Shore, The (Rosherville), Grav. 131 GF86
Shore Cl, Felt. 115 BU87
Shore Cl, Hmptn. 116 BY92
Stewart Cl
Shore Gro, Felt. 116 CA89
Shore Pl E9 84 DW66
Shore Rd E9 84 DW66
Shorediche Cl, Uxb. 58 BM62
Shoreditch High St E1 197 N3
Shoreditch High St E1 84 DS70
Shoreham Cl SW18 120 DB85
Ram St
Shoreham Cl, Bex. 126 EX88
Stansted Cres
Shoreham Cl, Croy. 142 DW100
Shoreham La, Orp. 164 FA107
Shoreham La, Sev. 190 FF122
Shoreham La (Halstead), Sev. 164 EZ112
Shoreham Pl, Sev. 165 FG112
Shoreham Rd, Orp. 146 EV95
Shoreham Rd, Sev. 165 FH111
Shoreham Rd E, Houns. 114 BL85
Shoreham Rd W, Houns. 114 BL85
Shoreham Way, Brom. 144 EG100
Shores Rd, Wok. 150 AY114
Shorncliffe Rd SE1 201 P10
Shorncliffe Rd SE1 102 DT78
Shorndean St SE6 123 EC88
Shorne Cl, Orp. 146 EX98
Shorne Cl, Sid. 126 EV86
Shornefield Cl, Brom. 145 EN97
Shornells Way SE2 106 EW78
Willrose Cres
Shorrolds Rd SW6 99 CZ80
Short Hedges, Houns. 96 CB81
Short Hill, Har. 61 CE60
High St
Short La, Oxt. 188 EH132
Short La, St.Alb. 8 BZ30
Short La, Stai. 114 BM88
Short Path SE18 105 EP79
Westdale Rd
Short Rd E11 68 EE61
Short Rd E15 85 ED67
Short Rd W4 98 CS79
Short Rd, Houns. 114 BL86
Short St NW4 63 CW56
New Brent St
Short St SE1 200 E4
Short Wall E15 85 EC69
Short Way SE9 104 EL83
Short Way, Twick. 116 CC87
Shortacres, Red. 185 DM133
Shortcroft Rd, Epsom 157 CT108
Shortcrofts Rd, Dag. 88 EZ65
Shorter Av, Brwd. 55 FZ44
Shorter St E1 197 P10
Shorter St E1 84 DT73
Shortfern, Slou. 74 AW72
Shortgate N12 43 CZ49
Shortlands W6 99 CX77
Shortlands, Hayes 95 BR79
Shortlands Cl N18 46 DR48
Shortlands Cl, Belv. 106 EZ76
Shortlands Gdns, Brom. 144 EE96
Shortlands Gro, Brom. 143 ED97
Shortlands Rd E10 67 EB59
Shortlands Rd, Brom. 143 ED97
Shortlands Rd, Kings.T. 118 CM94
Shortmead Dr (Cheshunt), Wal.Cr. 15 DY31
Shorts Cft NW9 62 CP56
Shorts Gdns WC2 195 P9
Shorts Gdns WC2 83 DL72
Shorts Rd, Cars. 158 DE105
Shortway N12 44 DE51
Shortwood Av, Stai. 114 BH90
Shortwood Common, Stai. 114 BH91
Shotfield, Wall. 159 DH107
Shothanger Way, Hem.H. 5 BC26
Shott Cl, Sutt. 158 DC106
Turnpike La
Shottendane Rd SW6 100 DA81
Shottery Cl SE9 124 EL90
Shottfield Av SW14 98 CS84
Shoulder of Mutton All E14 85 DY73
Narrow St
Shouldham St W1 194 C7
Shouldham St W1 82 DE71
Showers Way, Hayes 77 BU74

326

Solna Av SW15 119 CW85
Solna Rd N21 46 DR46
Solomon Av N9 46 DU49
Solomons Hill, Rick. 38 BK45
Northway
Solomon's Pas SE15 102 DV84
Solom's Ct Rd, Bans. 174 DE117
Solon New Rd SW4 101 DL84
Solon New Rd Est SW4 101 DL84
Solon New Rd
Solon Rd SW2 101 DL84
Solway Cl E8 84 DT65
Buttermere Wk
Solway Cl, Houns. 96 BY83
Solway Rd N22 45 DP53
Solway Rd SE22 102 DU84
Somaford Gro, Barn. 28 DD44
Somali Rd NW2 63 CZ63
Somerby Rd, Bark. 87 ER66
Somercoates Cl, Barn. 28 DE41
Somerden Rd, Orp. 146 EX101
Somerfield Cl, Tad. 173 CY119
Somerfield Rd N4 65 DP61
Somerford Cl, Pnr. 59 BU56
Somerford Gro N16 66 DT63
Somerford Gro N17 46 DU52
Somerford Gro Est N16 66 DT63
Somerford Gro
Somerford St E1 84 DV70
Somerford Way SE16 203 K5
Somerford Way SE16 103 DY75
Somerhill Av, Sid. 126 EV87
Somerhill Rd, Well. 106 EV82
Somerleyton Pas SW9 101 DP84
Somerleyton Rd SW9 101 DN84
Somers Cl NW1 83 DK68
Platt St
Somers Cl, Reig. 184 DA133
Somers Cres W2 194 B9
Somers Cres W2 82 DE72
Somers Ms W2 194 B9
Somers Pl SW2 121 DM87
Somers Pl, Reig. 184 DA133
Somers Rd E17 67 DZ56
Somers Rd SW2 121 DM86
Somers Rd, Reig. 183 CZ133
Somers Way, Bushey 40 CC45
Somersby Gdns, Ilf. 69 EM57
Somerset Av SW20 139 CV96
Somerset Av, Chess. 155 CK105
Somerset Av, Well. 125 ET85
Somerset Cl N17 46 DR54
Somerset Cl, Epsom 156 CS109
Somerset Cl, N.Mal. 138 CS100
Somerset Cl, Walt. 153 BV106
Queens Rd
Somerset Cl, Wdf.Grn. 48 EG53
Somerset Est SW11 100 DD81
Somerset Gdns N6 64 DG59
Somerset Gdns N17 46 DS52
Somerset Gdns SE13 103 EB82
Somerset Gdns SW16 141 DM97
Somerset Gdns, Horn. 72 FN60
Somerset Gdns, Tedd. 117 CE92
Somerset Rd E17 67 EA57
Somerset Rd N17 66 DT55
Somerset Rd N18 46 DT50
Somerset Rd NW4 63 CW56
Somerset Rd SW19 119 CY91
Somerset Rd W4 98 CR76
Somerset Rd W13 79 CH74
Somerset Rd, Barn. 28 DB43
Somerset Rd, Brent. 97 CJ79
Somerset Rd, Dart. 127 FH86
Somerset Rd, Enf. 31 EA38
Somerset Rd, Har. 60 CC57
Somerset Rd, Kings.T. 138 CM96
Somerset Rd, Orp. 146 EU101
Somerset Rd, Sthl. 78 BZ71
Somerset Rd, Tedd. 117 CE92
Somerset Sq W14 99 CY75
Somerset Way, Iver 93 BF75
Somerset Waye, Houns. 96 BY79
Somersham Rd, Bexh. 106 EY82
Somerton Av, Rich. 98 CP83
Somerton Cl, Pur. 175 DN115
Somerton Rd NW2 63 CY62
Somerton Rd SE15 102 DV84
Somertrees Av SE12 124 EH89
Somervell Rd, Har. 60 BZ64
Somerville Av SW13 99 CV79
Somerville Rd SE20 123 DX94
Somerville Rd, Cob. 154 CA114
Somerville Rd, Dart. 128 FM86
Somerville Rd, Rom. 70 EW58
Sonderburg Rd N7 65 DM61
Sondes St SE17 102 DR79
Sonia Cl, Wat. 40 BW45
Sonia Ct, Har. 61 CF58
Sonia Gdns N12 44 DC49
Woodside Av
Sonia Gdns NW10 63 CT63
Sonia Gdns, Houns. 96 CA80
Sonnet Wk, West. 178 EH118
Kings Rd
Sonning Gdns, Hmptn. 116 BY93
Sonning Rd SE25 142 DU100
Soper Cl E4 47 DZ50
Soper Dr, Cat. 176 DR123
Hambledon Rd
Soper Ms, Enf. 31 EA38
Harston Dr
Sopers Rd (Cuffley), Pot.B. 13 DM29
Sophia Cl N7 83 DM65
Mackenzie Rd
Sophia Rd E10 67 EB60
Sophia Rd E16 86 EH72
Sophia Sq SE16 203 K1
Sopwith Av, Chess. 156 CL106
Sopwith Cl, Kings.T. 118 CM92
Sopwith Cl, West. 178 EK116
Sopwith Dr, W.Byf. 152 BL111
Sopwith Dr, Wey. 152 BL111
Sopwith Rd, Houns. 96 BW80
Sopwith Way SW8 101 DH80
Sopwith Way, Kings.T. 138 CL95
Sorbie Cl, Wey. 153 BQ107
Sorrel Bk, Croy. 161 DY110
Sorrel Cl SE28 88 EU74
Sorrel Cl, Grays 110 GD79
Salix Rd
Sorrel Gdns E6 86 EL71
Sorrel La E14 85 ED72
Sorrel Wk, Rom. 71 FF55
Sorrel Way, Grav. 130 GE91
Sorrell Cl SE14 103 DY80
Southerngate Way
Sorrento Rd, Sutt. 140 DB104
Sotheby Rd N5 65 DP62
Sotheran Cl E8 84 DU67
Sotheron Rd SW6 100 DB80
Sotheron Rd, Wat. 24 BW40
Soudan Rd SW11 100 DF81
Souldern Rd W14 99 CX76
Souldern St, Wat. 23 BU43
Sounds Lo, Swan. 147 FC100
South Access Rd E17 67 DY59
South Acre NW9 42 CS54
South Africa Rd W12 81 CV74
South Albert Rd, Reig. 183 CZ133
South App, Nthwd. 39 BR49
South Audley St W1 198 G1
South Audley St W1 82 DG73
South Av E4 47 EB45
South Av, Cars. 158 DF108
South Av, Egh. 113 BC93
South Av, Rich. 98 CN82
Sandycombe Rd
South Av, Sthl. 78 BZ73
South Av, Walt. 153 BS110
South Av Gdns, Sthl. 78 BZ73
South Bk, Chis. 125 EQ91
South Bk, Surb. 138 CL100
South Bk, West. 189 ER126
South Bk Ter, Surb. 138 CL100
South Birkbeck Rd E11 67 ED62
South Black Lion La W6 99 CU78
South Bolton Gdns SW5 100 DB78
South Border, The, Pur. 159 DK111
South Carriage Dr SW1 198 D4
South Carriage Dr SW1 100 DE75
South Carriage Dr SW7 198 A5
South Carriage Dr SW7 100 DE75
South Cl N6 65 DH58
South Cl, Barn. 27 CZ41
South Cl, Bexh. 106 EX84
South Cl, Dag. 88 FA67
South Cl, Mord. 140 DB100
Green La
South Cl, Pnr. 60 BZ59
South Cl, St.Alb. 8 CB25
South Cl, Twick. 116 CA90
South Cl, West Dr. 94 BM76
South Cl, Wok. 166 AW116
South Cl Grn, Red. 185 DH129
South Colonnade E14 204 A2
South Colonnade E14 85 EA74
South Common Rd, Uxb. 76 BL65
South Cottage Dr, Rick. 21 BF43
South Cottage Gdns, Rick. 21 BF43
South Countess Rd E17 67 DZ55
South Cres E16 85 ED70
South Cres WC1 195 M7
South Cres WC1 83 DK71
South Cft, Egh. 112 AV92
South Cross Rd, Ilf. 69 EQ57
South Croxted Rd SE21 122 DR90
South Dene NW7 42 CR48
South Dr, Bans. 158 DE113
South Dr, Brwd. 54 FX49
South Dr, Couls. 175 DK115
South Dr, Orp. 163 ES106
South Dr (Cuffley), Pot.B. 13 DL30
South Dr, Rom. 72 FJ55
South Dr, Ruis. 59 BS60
South Dr, Sutt. 157 CY110
South Dr, Vir.W. 132 AU102
South Ealing Rd W5 97 CK75
South Eastern Av N9 46 DT48
South Eaton Pl SW1 198 G8
South Eaton Pl SW1 100 DG77
South Eden Pk Rd, Beck. 143 EB100
South Edwardes Sq W8 99 CZ76
South End W8 100 DB76
St. Albans Gro
South End, Croy. 160 DQ105
South End Cl NW3 64 DE63
South End Grn NW3 64 DE63
South End Rd
South End Rd NW3 64 DE63
South End Rd, Horn. 89 FH65
South End Rd, Rain. 89 FG67
South End Row W8 100 DB76
South Esk Rd E7 86 EJ65
South Gdns SW19 120 DD94
South Gipsy Rd, Well. 106 EX83
South Glade, The, Bex. 126 EZ88
South Grn NW9 42 CS53
Clayton Fld
South Grn, Slou. 74 AS73
South Gro E17 67 DZ57
South Gro N6 64 DG60
South Gro N15 66 DR57
South Gro, Cher. 133 BF100
South Gro Ho N6 64 DG60
Highgate W Hill
South Hall Cl, Dart. 148 FM101
South Hall Dr, Rain. 89 FH71
South Hill, Chis. 125 EM93
South Hill Av, Har. 60 CC62
South Hill Gro, Har. 61 CE63
South Hill Pk NW3 64 DE63
South Hill Pk Gdns NW3 64 DE63
South Hill Rd, Brom. 144 EE97
South Hill Rd, Grav. 131 GH88
South Huxley N18 46 DR50
South Island Pl SW9 101 DM80
South Kensington Sta Arc SW7 100 DD77
Pelham St
South Kent Av, Grav. 130 GC86
South Lambeth Pl SW8 101 DL79
South Lambeth Rd SW8 101 DL80
South La, Kings.T. 137 CK97
South La, N.Mal. 138 CR98
South La W, N.Mal. 138 CR98
South Lo Av, Mitch. 141 DL98
South Lo Cres, Enf. 29 DK42
South Lo Dr N14 29 DL43
South Lo Rd, Walt. 153 BU109
South Mall N9 46 DU48
Plevna Rd
South Mead NW9 43 CT53
South Mead, Epsom 156 CS108
South Mead, Red. 184 DF131
South Meadows, Wem. 62 CM64
South Molton La W1 195 H9
South Molton La W1 83 DH72
South Molton Rd E16 86 EG72
South Molton St W1 195 H9
South Molton St W1 83 DH72
South Norwood Hill SE25 142 DS96
South Oak Rd SW16 121 DM91
South Ordnance Rd, Enf. 31 EA37
South Par SW3 198 A10
South Par SW3 100 DD78
South Par W4 98 CR77
South Par, Wal.Abb. 15 EC33
Sun St
South Pk SW6 100 DA82
South Pk, Ger.Cr. 57 AZ57
South Pk, Sev. 191 FH125
South Pk Av, Rick. 21 BF43
South Pk Cres SE6 124 EF88
South Pk Cres, Ger.Cr. 56 AY56
South Pk Cres, Ilf. 69 ER62
South Pk Dr, Bark. 69 ES63
South Pk Dr, Ger.Cr. 56 AY56
South Pk Dr, Ilf. 69 ES63
South Pk Gro, N.Mal. 138 CQ98
South Pk Hill Rd, S.Croy. 160 DR106
South Pk Ms SW6 100 DB83
South Pk Rd SW19 120 DA93
South Pk Rd, Ilf. 69 ER62
South Pk Ter, Ilf. 69 ES62
South Pk Vw, Ger.Cr. 57 AZ56
South Pk Way, Ruis. 78 BW65
South Penge Pk Est SE20 142 DV96
South Perimeter Rd, Uxb. 76 BL69
Kingston La
South Pl EC2 197 L6
South Pl EC2 84 DR71
South Pl, Enf. 30 DW43
South Pl, Surb. 138 CM101
South Pl Ms EC2 197 L7
South Ridge, Wey. 153 BP110
South Riding, St.Alb. 8 CA30
South Ri, Cars. 158 DE109
South Ri Way SE18 105 ER78
South Rd N9 46 DU46
South Rd SE23 123 DX89
South Rd SW19 120 DC93
South Rd W5 97 CK77
South Rd, Edg. 42 CP53
South Rd, Egh. 112 AW93
South Rd, Erith 107 FF79
South Rd, Felt. 116 BX92
South Rd, Hmptn. 116 BY93
South Rd, Rick. 21 BC43
South Rd (Chadwell Heath), Rom. 70 EW57
South Rd (Little Heath), Rom. 70 EY58
South Rd, S.Ock. 91 FW72
South Rd, Sthl. 96 BZ75
South Rd, Twick. 117 CD90
South Rd, West Dr. 94 BN76
South Rd, Wey. 153 BQ106
South Rd (St. George's Hill), Wey. 153 BP109
South Rd, Wok. 150 AX114
South Row SE3 104 EF82
South Sea St SE16 203 M6
South Sea St SE16 103 DZ76
South Side W6 99 CT76
South Sq NW11 64 DB58
South Sq WC1 196 D7
South St W1 198 G2
South St W1 82 DG74
South St, Brwd. 54 FW47
South St, Brom. 144 EG96
South St, Enf. 31 DX43
South St, Epsom 156 CR113
South St, Grav. 131 GH87
South St, Islw. 97 CG83
South St, Rain. 89 FC68
South St, Rom. 71 FE57
South St, Stai. 113 BF92
South Tenter St E1 84 DT73
South Ter SW7 198 B8
South Ter SW7 100 DE77
South Ter, Surb. 138 CL100
South Vale SE19 122 DS93
South Vale, Har. 61 CE63
South Vw, Brom. 144 EH96
South Vw Av, Til. 111 GG81
South Vw Ct, Wok. 166 AY118
Constitution Hill
South Vw Dr E18 68 EH55
South Vw Dr, Upmin. 72 FN62
South Vw Rd N8 65 DK55
South Vw Rd, Ash. 171 CK119
South Vw Rd, Dart. 128 FK90
South Vw Rd, Ger.Cr. 56 AX56
South Vw Rd, Grays 109 FW79
South Vw Rd, Loug. 33 EM44
South Vw Rd, Pnr. 39 BV51
South Vil NW1 83 DK65
South Wk, Hayes 77 BR71
Middleton Rd
South Wk, Reig. 184 DB134
Church St
South Wk, W.Wick. 144 EE104
South Way N9 46 DW47
South Way N11 45 DJ51
Ringway
South Way, Abb.L. 7 BT33
South Way, Brom. 144 EG101
South Way, Croy. 143 DY104
South Way, Har. 60 CA56
South Way, Purf. 109 FS76
South Way, Wem. 62 CN64
South Weald Dr, Wal.Abb. 15 ED33
South Weald Rd, Brwd. 54 FU48
South W India Dock Entrance E14 103 EC75
Prestons Rd
South Western Rd, Twick. 117 CG86
South Wf Rd W2 82 DD72
South Woodford to Barking Relief Rd E11 68 EJ56
South Woodford to Barking Relief Rd E12 69 EN62
South Woodford to Barking Relief Rd E18 68 EJ56
South Woodford to Barking Relief Rd, Bark. 69 EN62
South Woodford to Barking Relief Rd, Ilf. 69 EN62
South Worple Av SW14 98 CS83
South Worple Way SW14 98 CR83
Southacre Way, Pnr. 40 BW53
Southall La, Houns. 95 BV79
Southall La, Sthl. 96 BW77
Southall Pl SE1 201 K5
Southall Pl SE1 102 DR75
Southall Way, Brwd. 54 FT49
Southam St W10 81 CY70
Southampton Bldgs WC2 196 D8
Southampton Gdns, Mitch. 141 DL99
Southampton Ms E16 205 P2
Southampton Pl WC1 196 A7
Southampton Pl WC1 83 DL71
Southampton Rd NW5 64 DF64
Southampton Rd, Houns. 114 BN86
Southampton Row WC1 196 A6
Southampton Row WC1 83 DL71
Southampton St WC2 196 A10
Southampton St WC2 83 DL73
Southampton Way SE5 102 DR80
Southbank, T.Ditt. 137 CH101
Southborough Cl, Surb. 137 CK102
Southborough La, Brom. 144 EL99
Southborough Rd E9 84 DW67
Southborough Rd, Brom. 144 EL97
Southborough Rd, Surb. 138 CL102
Southbourne, Brom. 144 EG101
Southbourne Av NW9 42 CQ54
Southbourne Cl, Pnr. 60 BY59
Southbourne Cres NW4 63 CY56
Southbourne Gdns SE12 124 EH85
Southbourne Gdns, Ilf. 69 EQ64
Southbourne Gdns, Ruis. 59 BV60
Southbridge Pl, Croy. 160 DQ105
Southbridge Rd, Croy. 160 DQ105
Southbridge Way, Sthl. 96 BY75
Southbrook Dr (Cheshunt), Wal.Cr. 15 DX28
Southbrook Ms SE12 124 EF86
Southbrook Rd SE12 124 EF86
Southbrook Rd SW16 141 DL95
Southbury Av, Enf. 30 DU43
Southbury Cl, Horn. 72 FK64
Southbury Rd, Enf. 30 DR41
Southchurch Rd E6 87 EM68
Southcliffe Dr (Chalfont St. Peter), Ger.Cr. 36 AY50
Southcombe St W14 99 CY77
Southcote, Wok. 166 AX115
Southcote Av, Felt. 115 BT89
Southcote Av, Surb. 138 CP101
Southcote Ri, Ruis. 59 BR59
Southcote Rd E17 67 DX57
Southcote Rd N19 65 DJ63
Southcote Rd SE25 142 DV100
Southcote Rd, Red. 185 DJ129
Southcote Rd, S.Croy. 160 DS110
Southcroft Av, Well. 105 ES83
Southcroft Av, W.Wick. 143 EC103
Southcroft Rd SW16 120 DG93
Southcroft Rd SW17 120 DG93
Southcroft Rd, Orp. 145 ES104
Southdale, Chig. 49 ER51
Southdean Gdns SW19 119 CZ89
Southdene, Sev. 164 EY113
Southdown Av W7 97 CG76
Southdown Cres, Har. 60 CB60
Southdown Cres, Ilf. 69 ES57
Southdown Dr SW20 119 CX94
Crescent Rd
Southdown Rd SW20 139 CX95
Southdown Rd, Cars. 158 DG109
Southdown Rd, Cat. 177 DZ122
Southdown Rd, Horn. 71 FH59
Southdown Rd, Walt. 154 BY105
Southdowns (South Darenth), Dart. 149 FR96
Southend Arterial Rd, Brwd. 73 FV57
Southend Arterial Rd, Horn. 52 FK54
Southend Arterial Rd, Rom. 52 FK54
Southend Arterial Rd, Upmin. 73 FR57
Southend Cl SE9 125 EP86
Southend Cres SE9 125 EN86
Southend La SE6 123 DZ91
Southend La SE26 123 DZ91
Southend La, Wal.Abb. 16 EH34
Southend Rd E4 47 DY50
Southend Rd E6 87 EM66
Southend Rd E17 47 EB53
Southend Rd E18 48 EG53
Southend Rd, Beck. 123 EA94
Southend Rd, Grays 110 GC77
Southend Rd, Wdf.Grn. 48 EJ54
Southerland Cl, Wey. 153 BQ105
Southern Av SE25 142 DT97
Southern Av, Felt. 115 BU88
Southern Dr, Loug. 33 EM44
Southern Gro E3 85 DZ69
Southern Perimeter Rd, Houns. 115 BR85
Southern Pl, Swan. 147 FD98
Southern Rd E13 86 EH68
Southern Rd N2 64 DF56
Southern Row W10 81 CY70
Southern St N1 83 DM68
Southern Way, Rom. 70 FA58
Southerngate Way SE14 103 DY80
Southernhay, Loug. 32 EK43
Southerns La, Couls. 184 DC125
Southerton Rd W6 99 CW76
Southerton Way (Shenley), Rad. 10 CL33
Southey Ms E16 205 N2
Southey Rd N15 66 DS57
Southey Rd SW9 101 DN81
Southey Rd SW19 120 DA94
Southey St SE20 123 DX94
Southey Wk, Til. 111 GH81
Southfield, Barn. 27 CX44
Southfield Av, Wat. 24 BW38
Southfield Cl, Uxb. 76 BN69
Southfield Cotts W7 97 CF75
Oaklands Rd
Southfield Gdns, Twick. 117 CF91
Southfield Pk, Har. 60 CB56
Southfield Pl, Wey. 153 BP108
Southfield Rd N17 46 DS54
The Av
Southfield Rd W4 98 CS76
Southfield Rd, Chis. 145 ET97
Southfield Rd, Enf. 30 DV44
Southfield Rd, Wal.Cr. 15 DY32
Southfields NW4 43 CU54
Southfields, E.Mol. 137 CE100
Southfields, Swan. 127 FE94
Southfields Av, Ashf. 115 BP93
Southfields Ct SW19 119 CY88
Southfields Pas SW18 120 DA86
Southfields Rd SW18 120 DA86
Southfields Rd, Cat. 177 EB123
Southfleet Rd, Dart. 129 FW91
Southfleet Rd, Grav. 131 GF89
Southfleet Rd, Orp. 145 ES104
Southfleet Rd, Swans. 130 FZ87
Southgate, Purf. 108 FQ77
Southgate Av, Felt. 115 BR91
Southgate Circ N14 45 DK46
The Bourne
Southgate Gro N1 84 DR66
Southgate Rd N1 84 DR66
Southgate Rd, Pot.B. 12 DC33
Southholme Cl SE19 142 DS95
Southill La, Pnr. 59 BU56
Southill Rd, Chis. 124 EL94
Southill St E14 85 EB72
Chrisp St
Southland Rd SE18 105 ET80
Southland Way, Houns. 117 CD85
Southlands Av, Orp. 163 ER105
Southlands Cl, Couls. 175 DM117
Southlands Dr SW19 119 CX89
Southlands Gro, Brom. 144 EL97
Southlands La, Oxt. 187 EB134
Southlands Rd, Brom. 144 EJ98
Southlands Rd, Iver 57 BF64
Southlands Rd (Denham), Uxb. 57 BF63
Southlea Rd, Slou. 92 AV81
Southlea Rd, Wind. 92 AU84
Southly Cl, Sutt. 140 DA104
Southmead Cres (Cheshunt), Wal.Cr. 15 DY30
Southmead Rd SW19 119 CY88
Southmont Rd, Esher 137 CE103
Southmoor Way E9 85 DZ65
Southold Ri SE9 125 EM90
Southolm St SW11 101 DH81
Southover N12 44 DA49
Southover, Brom. 124 EG92
Southport Rd SE18 105 ER77
Southridge Pl SW20 119 CX94
Southsea Av, Wat. 23 BU42
Southsea Rd, Kings.T. 138 CL98
Southside (Chalfont St. Peter), Ger.Cr. 56 AX55
Southside Common SW19 119 CW93
Southspring, Sid. 125 ER87
Southvale Rd SE3 104 EE82
Southview Av NW10 63 CT64
Southview Cl SW17 120 DG92
Southview Cl, Bex. 126 EZ86
Southview Cl, Swan. 147 FF98
Southview Cl (Cheshunt), Wal.Cr. 14 DS26
Southview Cres, Ilf. 69 EP58
Southview Gdns, Wall. 159 DJ108
Southview Rd, Brom. 123 ED91
Southview Rd, Cat. 177 EB124
Southview Rd, Warl. 176 DU119
Southviews, S.Croy. 161 DX109
Southville SW8 101 DK81
Southville Cl, Epsom 156 CR109
Southville Cl, Felt. 115 BS88
Southville Cres, Felt. 115 BS88
Southville Rd, Felt. 115 BS88
Southville Rd, T.Ditt. 137 CH101
Southwark Br EC4 201 J2
Southwark Br EC4 84 DQ74
Southwark Br SE1 201 J2
Southwark Br SE1 84 DQ74
Southwark Br Rd SE1 200 G6
Southwark Br Rd SE1 101 DP76
Southwark Gro SE1 201 H3
Southwark Pk Est SE16 202 D8
Southwark Pk Est SE16 102 DV77
Southwark Pk Rd SE16 202 A8
Southwark Pk Rd SE16 102 DT77
Southwark Pl, Brom. 145 EM97
St. Georges Rd
Southwark St SE1 200 G2
Southwark St SE1 83 DP74
Southwater Cl E14 85 DZ72
Southwater Cl, Beck. 123 EB94
Southway N20 44 DA47
Southway NW11 64 DB58
Southway SW20 139 CW98
Southway, Cars. 158 DD110
Southway, Wall. 159 DJ105
Southwell Av, Nthlt. 78 CA65
Southwell Gdns SW7 100 DC77
Southwell Gro Rd E11 68 EE61
Southwell Rd SE5 102 DQ83
Southwell Rd, Croy. 141 DN100
Southwell Rd, Har. 61 CK58
Southwest Rd E11 67 ED60
Southwick Ms W2 194 A8
Southwick Pl W2 194 B9
Southwick Pl W2 82 DE72

Southwick St W2 194 B8
Southwick St W2 82 DE72
Southwold Dr, Bark. 70 EU64
Southwold Rd E5 66 DV61
Southwold Rd, Bex. 127 FB86
Southwold Rd, Wat. 24 BW38
Southwold Spur, Slou. 93 BC75
Southwood Av, Cher. 151 BC108
Southwood Av N6 65 DH59
Southwood Av, Couls. 175 DJ115
Southwood Av, Kings.T. 138 CQ95
Southwood Cl, Brom. 145 EM98
Southwood Cl, Wor.Pk. 139 CX102
Southwood Dr, Surb. 138 CQ101
Southwood Gdns, 137 CG104
Esher
Southwood Gdns, Ilf. 69 EP56
Southwood La N6 64 DG59
Southwood Lawn Rd 64 DG59
N6
Southwood Rd SE9 125 EP89
Southwood Rd SE28 88 EV74
Southwood Smith St N1 83 DN67
Barford St
Soval Ct, Nthwd. 39 BR52
Maxwell Rd
Sovereign Cl E1 202 E1
Sovereign Cl E1 84 DV73
Sovereign Cl W5 79 CJ71
Sovereign Cl, Pur. 159 DM110
Sovereign Cl, Ruis. 59 BS60
Sovereign Ct, Brom. 145 EM99
Sovereign Ct, W.Mol. 136 BZ98
Sovereign Cres SE16 85 DY74
Rotherhithe St
Sovereign Gro, Wem. 61 CK62
Sovereign Ms E2 84 DT68
Pearson St
Sovereign Pk NW10 80 CP70
Sovereign Pl, Kings L. 6 BN29
Sovereign Rd, Bark. 88 EW69
Sowerby Cl SE9 124 EL85
Sowrey Av, Rain. 89 FF65
Soyer Ct, Wok. 166 AS118
Raglan Rd
Spa Cl SE25 142 DS95
Spa Dr, Epsom 156 CN114
Spa Grn Est EC1 196 E2
Spa Grn Est EC1 83 DN69
Spa Hill SE19 142 DR95
Spa Rd SE16 201 P7
Spa Rd SE16 102 DT76
Space Waye, Felt. 115 BU85
Spafield St EC1 196 D4
Spalding Cl, Edg. 42 CS52
Blundell Rd
Spalding Cl NW4 63 CW58
Spalding Rd SW17 121 DH92
Spalt Cl, Brwd. 55 GB47
Spanby Rd E3 85 EA70
Spaniards Cl NW11 64 DD60
Spaniards End NW3 64 DC60
Spaniards Rd NW3 64 DC61
Spanish Pl W1 194 G7
Spanish Pl W1 82 DG72
Spanish Rd SW18 120 DC85
Spareleaze Hill, Loug. 33 EM43
Sparepenny La 148 FL102
(Eynsford), Dart.
Sparkbridge Rd, Har. 61 CE56
Sparks Cl W3 80 CR72
Joseph Av
Sparks Cl, Dag. 70 EX61
Sparks Cl, Hmptn. 116 BY93
Victors Dr
Sparrow Cl, Hmptn. 116 BY93
Sparrow Dr, Orp. 145 EQ102
Sparrow Fm Dr, Felt. 116 BX87
Sparrow Fm Rd, Epsom 157 CU105
Sparrow Grn, Dag. 71 FB62
Sparrows Herne, 40 CB45
Bushey
Sparrows La SE9 125 EQ87
Sparrows Mead, Red. 184 DG131
Sparrows Way, Bushey 40 CC46
Sparrows Herne
Sparsholt Rd N19 65 DM60
Sparsholt Rd, Bark. 87 ES67
Sparta St SE10 103 EB81
Spear Ms SW5 100 DA77
Spearman St SE18 105 EN79
Spearpoint Gdns, Ilf. 69 ET56
Spears Rd N19 65 DL60
Speart La, Houns. 96 BY80
Spedan Cl NW3 64 DB62
Speed Ho EC2 197 K6
Speedbird Way, 94 BH80
West Dr.
Speedgate Hill 149 FU103
(Fawkham Grn), Long.
Speedwell Ct, Grays 110 GE80
Speedwell St SE8 103 EA80
Comet St
Speedy Pl WC1 195 P3
Speer Rd, T.Ditt. 137 CF99
Speirs Cl, N.Mal. 139 CT100
Speke Ho SE5 102 DQ80
Speke Rd, Th.Hth. 142 DR96
Spekehill SE9 125 EM90
Speldhurst Cl, Brom. 144 EF99
Speldhurst Rd E9 85 DX66
Speldhurst Rd W4 98 CR76
Spellbrook Wk N1 84 DQ67
Basire St
Spelman St E1 84 DU71
Spelthorne Gro, Sun. 115 BT94
Spelthorne La, Ashf. 135 BQ95
Spence Av, W.Byf. 152 BL114
Spence Cl SE16 203 M5
Spencer Av N13 45 DM51
Spencer Av, Hayes 77 BU71
Spencer Av (Cheshunt), 14 DS26
Wal.Cr.
Spencer Cl N3 44 DA54
Spencer Cl NW10 80 CM69
Spencer Cl, Epsom 172 CS119
Spencer Cl, Orp. 145 ES103
Spencer Cl, Uxb. 76 BJ69
Spencer Cl, Wok. 151 BC113
Spencer Cl, Wdf.Grn. 48 EJ50
Spencer Ct NW8 82 DC68
Marlborough Pl
Spencer Dr N2 64 DC58

Spencer Gdns SE9 125 EM85
Spencer Gdns SW14 118 CQ85
Spencer Gdns, Egh. 112 AX92
Spencer Hill SW19 119 CY93
Spencer Hill Rd SW19 119 CY94
Spencer Ms SW8 101 DM81
Lansdowne Way
Spencer Ms W6 99 CY79
Greyhound Rd
Spencer Pk SW18 120 DD85
Spencer Pas E2 84 DV68
Pritchard's Rd
Spencer Pl N1 83 DP66
Canonbury La
Spencer Pl, Croy. 142 DR101
Gloucester Rd
Spencer Ri NW5 65 DH63
Spencer Rd E6 86 EK67
Spencer Rd E17 47 EC53
Spencer Rd N8 65 DM57
Spencer Rd N11 45 DH49
Spencer Rd N17 46 DU53
Spencer Rd SW18 100 DD84
Spencer Rd SW20 139 CV95
Spencer Rd W3 80 CQ74
Spencer Rd W4 98 CQ80
Spencer Rd, Brom. 124 EE94
Spencer Rd, Cat. 176 DR121
Spencer Rd, Cob. 169 BV115
Spencer Rd, E.Mol. 136 CC99
Spencer Rd, Har. 41 CE54
Spencer Rd, Ilf. 69 ET60
Spencer Rd, Islw. 97 CD81
Spencer Rd, Mitch. 140 DG97
Spencer Rd 140 DG101
(Beddington Cor), Mitch.
Spencer Rd, Rain. 89 FD69
Spencer Rd, Slou. 93 AZ76
Spencer Rd, S.Croy. 160 DS106
Spencer Rd, Twick. 117 CE90
Spencer Rd, Wem. 61 CJ61
Spencer St EC1 196 F3
Spencer St EC1 83 DP69
Spencer St, Grav. 131 GG87
Spencer St, Sthl. 96 BX75
Spencer Wk NW3 64 DC63
Hampstead High St
Spencer Wk SW15 99 CX84
Spencer Wk, Rick. 22 BJ43
Spencer Wk, Til. 111 GG82
Spenser Av, Wey. 152 BN108
Spenser Cres, Upmin. 72 FQ59
Spenser Gro N16 66 DS63
Spenser Ms SE21 122 DR88
Croxted Rd
Spenser Rd SE24 121 DN85
Spenser St SW1 199 L6
Spenser St SW1 101 DJ76
Spensley Wk N16 66 DR62
Clissold Rd
Speranza St SE18 105 ET78
Sperling Rd N17 46 DS54
Spert St E14 85 DY73
Spey St E14 85 EC71
Spey Way, Rom. 51 FE52
Speyhawk Pl, Pot.B. 11 CZ28
Hawkshead Rd
Speyside N14 29 DJ44
Spezia Rd NW10 81 CU68
Spicer Cl SW9 101 DP82
Spicer Cl, Walt. 136 BW100
Spicers Fld, Lthd. 155 CD113
Spicersfield (Cheshunt), 14 DU27
Wal.Cr.
Spice's Yd, Croy. 160 DQ105
Spielman Rd, Dart. 108 FM84
Spigurnell Rd N17 46 DR53
Spikes Br Rd, Sthl. 78 BY72
Spilsby Cl NW9 42 CS54
Kenley Av
Spilsby Rd, Rom. 52 FK52
Spindle Cl SE18 104 EL76
Spindles, Til. 111 GG80
Spindlewood Gdns, 160 DS105
Croy.
Spindlewoods, Tad. 173 CV122
Spindrift Av E14 204 B8
Spindrift Av E14 103 EB77
Spinel Cl SE18 105 ET78
Spingate Cl, Horn. 72 FK64
Spinnaker Cl, Bark. 87 ES69
Thames Rd
Spinnells Rd, Har. 60 BZ60
Spinney, The N21 45 DN45
Spinney, The SW16 121 DK90
Spinney, The, Barn. 28 DB40
Spinney, The, Brwd. 55 GC44
Spinney, The, Epsom 173 CV119
Spinney, The, Lthd. 154 CC112
Spinney, The (Great 170 CB124
Bookham), Lthd.
Spinney, The, Pot.B. 12 DD31
Spinney, The, Pur. 159 DP111
Spinney, The, Sid. 126 EY92
Spinney, The, Stan. 42 CL49
Spinney, The, Sun. 135 BU95
Spinney, The, Sutt. 157 CW105
Spinney, The, Swan. 147 FE96
Spinney, The, Wat. 23 BU39
Spinney, The, Wem. 61 CG62
Spinney Cl, Cob. 154 CA111
Spinney Cl, N.Mal. 138 CS99
Spinney Cl, Rain. 89 FE68
Spinney Cl, West Dr. 76 BL73
Yew Av
Spinney Cl, Wor.Pk. 139 CT103
Spinney Dr, Felt. 115 BQ87
Spinney Gdns SE19 122 DT92
Spinney Gdns, Dag. 70 EY64
Spinney Hill, Add. 151 BE106
Spinney Oak, Brom. 144 EL96
Spinney Oak, Cher. 151 BD107
Spinney Way, Sev. 163 ER111
Spinneycroft, Lthd. 171 CD115
Spinneys, The, Brom. 145 EM96
Spire Cl, Grav. 131 GH88
Spires, The, Dart. 128 FK89
Spirit Quay E1 202 C2
Spital La, Brwd. 54 FT48
Spital Sq E1 197 N6
Spital Sq E1 84 DS71
Spital St E1 84 DU70
Spital St, Dart. 128 FK86

Spital Yd E1 197 N6
Spitfire Est, Houns. 96 BW78
Spitfire Way, Houns. 96 BW78
Splendour Wk SE16 102 DW78
Verney Rd
Spode Wk NW6 82 DB65
Lymington Rd
Spondon Rd N15 66 DU56
Spoonbill Way, Hayes 78 BX71
Spooner Wk, Wall. 159 DK106
Spooners Dr, St.Alb. 8 CC27
Spooners Ms W3 80 CR74
Churchfield Rd
Sportsbank St SE6 123 EC87
Spottons Gro N17 46 DQ53
Gospatrick Rd
Spout Hill, Croy. 161 EA106
Spout La, Eden. 189 EQ134
Spout La, Stai. 114 BG85
Spout La N, Stai. 94 BH84
Spratt Hall Rd E11 68 EG58
Spratts All, Cher. 151 BE107
Spratts La, Cher. 151 BE107
Spray La, Twick. 117 CE86
Spray St SE18 105 EP77
Spreighton Rd, W.Mol. 136 CB98
Spriggs Oak, Epp. 18 EU29
Palmers Hill
Sprimont Pl SW3 198 D10
Sprimont Pl SW3 100 DF78
Spring Av, Egh. 112 AY93
Spring Bottom La, Red. 185 DN127
Spring Br Ms W5 79 CK73
Spring Br Rd
Spring Br Rd W5 79 CK73
Spring Cl, Barn. 27 CX43
Spring Cl, Borwd. 26 CN39
Spring Cl, Chesh. 20 AX36
Spring Cl, Dag. 70 EX60
Spring Cl (Harefield), 38 BK53
Uxb.
Spring Cl La, Sutt. 157 CY107
Spring Cotts, Surb. 137 CK99
St. Leonard's Rd
Spring Ct, Sid. 126 EU90
Station Rd
Spring Ct Rd, Enf. 29 DN38
Spring Cfts, Bushey 24 CA43
Spring Dr, Pnr. 59 BU58
Eastcote Rd
Spring Fm Cl, Rain. 90 FK69
Spring Gdns N5 66 DQ64
Grosvenor Av
Spring Gdns SW1 199 N2
Spring Gdns, Horn. 71 FH63
Spring Gdns, Orp. 164 EV107
Spring Gdns, Rom. 71 FC57
Spring Gdns, Wall. 159 DJ106
Spring Gdns, W.Mol. 136 CC99
Spring Gdns, West. 178 EJ118
Spring Gdns, Wdf.Grn. 48 EJ52
Spring Gdns Ind Est, 71 FC57
Rom.
Spring Gro SE19 122 DT94
Alma Pl
Spring Gro W4 98 CN78
Spring Gro, Grav. 131 GH88
Spring Gro, Hmptn. 136 BC95
Plevna Rd
Spring Gro, Lthd. 170 CB123
Spring Gro, Loug. 32 EK44
Spring Gro, Mitch. 140 DG95
Spring Gro Cres, 96 CC81
Houns.
Spring Gro Rd, Houns. 96 CC81
Spring Gro Rd, Islw. 96 CC81
Spring Gro Rd, Rich. 118 CM85
Spring Hill E5 66 DU59
Spring Hill SE26 122 DW91
Spring Lake, Stan. 41 CH49
Spring La E5 66 DV60
Spring La N10 64 DG55
Spring La SE25 142 DV100
Spring La, Oxt. 187 ED131
Spring Ms W1 194 E6
Spring Ms, Epsom 157 CT109
Old Schools La
Spring Pk Av, Croy. 143 DX103
Spring Pk Dr N4 66 DQ60
Spring Pk Rd, Croy. 143 DX103
Spring Pas SW15 99 CX83
Embankment
Spring Path NW3 64 DD64
Spring Pl NW5 65 DH64
Spring Ri, Egh. 112 AY93
Spring Rd, Felt. 115 BT90
Spring Shaw Rd, Orp. 146 EU95
Spring St W2 82 DD72
Spring St, Epsom 157 CT109
Spring Ter, Rich. 118 CL85
Spring Vale, Bexh. 107 FB84
Spring Vale, Green. 129 FW86
Spring Vale Cl, Swan. 147 FF95
Spring Vale N, Dart. 128 FK87
Spring Vale S, Dart. 128 FK87
Spring Vil Rd, Edg. 42 CN52
Spring Wk E1 84 DU71
Old Montague St
Spring Wds, Vir.W. 132 AV98
Springall St SE15 102 DV80
Springate Fld, Slou. 92 AY75
Springbank N21 29 DM44
Springbank Av, Horn. 72 FJ64
Springbank Rd SE13 123 ED86
Springbank Wk NW1 83 DK66
St. Paul's Cres
Springbourne Ct, Beck. 143 EC95
Springcroft Av N2 64 DF56
Springdale Ms N16 66 DR63
Springdale Rd
Springdale Rd N16 66 DR63
Springfield E5 66 DV60
Springfield, Bushey 41 CD46
Springfield, Epp. 17 ET32
Springfield, Oxt. 187 ED130
Springfield Av N10 65 DJ55
Springfield Av SW20 139 CZ97
Springfield Av, Brwd. 55 GE45
Springfield Av, Hmptn. 116 CB93
Springfield Av, Swan. 147 FF98
Springfield Cl N12 44 DB50
Springfield Cl, Pot.B. 12 DD31

Springfield Cl, Rick. 23 BP43
Springfield Cl, Stan. 41 CG48
Springfield Cl, Wok. 166 AS118
Springfield Dr, Ilf. 69 EQ58
Springfield Dr, Lthd. 171 CE119
Springfield Gdns E5 66 DV60
Springfield Gdns NW9 62 CR57
Springfield Gdns, Brom. 145 EM98
Springfield Gdns, Ruis. 59 BV60
Springfield Gdns, 72 FQ62
Upmin.
Springfield Gdns, 143 EB103
W.Wick.
Springfield Gdns, 48 EJ52
Wdf.Grn.
Springfield Gro SE7 104 EJ79
Springfield Gro, Sun. 135 BT95
Springfield La NW6 82 DB67
Springfield La, Wey. 153 BP105
Springfield Meadows, 153 BP105
Wey.
Springfield Mt NW9 62 CS57
Springfield Pl, N.Mal. 138 CQ98
Springfield Ri SE26 122 DV90
Springfield Rd E4 48 EE46
Springfield Rd E6 87 EM66
Springfield Rd E15 86 EE69
Springfield Rd E17 67 DZ58
Springfield Rd N11 45 DH50
Springfield Rd N15 66 DU56
Springfield Rd NW8 82 DC67
Springfield Rd SE26 122 DV92
Springfield Rd SW19 119 CZ92
Springfield Rd W7 79 CE74
Springfield Rd, Ashf. 114 BM92
Springfield Rd, Bexh. 107 FB83
Springfield Rd, Brom. 145 EM98
Springfield Rd, Epsom 157 CW110
Springfield Rd, Grays 110 GD75
Springfield Rd, Har. 61 CE58
Springfield Rd, Hayes 78 BW74
Springfield Rd, Kings.T. 138 CL97
Springfield Rd, Slou. 93 BB80
Springfield Rd, Tedd. 117 CG92
Springfield Rd, Th.Hth. 142 DQ95
Springfield Rd, Twick. 116 CA88
Springfield Rd, Wall. 159 DH106
Springfield Rd 15 DY32
(Cheshunt), Wal.Cr.
Springfield Rd, Wat. 7 BV33
Haines Way
Springfield Rd, Well. 106 EV83
Springfield Wk NW6 82 DB67
Springfield Wk, Orp. 145 ER102
Place Fm Av
Springfields, Wal.Abb. 16 EE34
Springfields Cl, Cher. 134 BH102
Springhead Enterprise 130 GC88
Pk, Grav.
Springhead Rd, Erith 107 FF79
Springhead Rd, Grav. 130 GC87
Springhill Cl SE5 102 DR83
Springholm Cl, West. 178 EJ118
Springhurst Cl, Croy. 161 DZ105
Springpark Dr, Beck. 143 EC97
Springpond Rd, Dag. 70 EY64
Springrice Rd SE13 123 ED86
Springs, The, Brox. 15 DY25
Springshaw Cl, Sev. 190 FD123
Springvale Av, Brent. 97 CK78
Springvale Est W14 99 CY76
Blythe Rd
Springvale Retail Pk, 146 EW97
Orp.
Springvale Ter W14 99 CX76
Springvale Way, Orp. 146 EW97
Springwater Cl SE18 105 EN81
Springway, Har. 61 CD59
Springwell Av NW10 81 CT67
Springwell Av, Rick. 38 BG47
Springwell Cl SW16 121 DN91
Etherstone Rd
Springwell Ct, Houns. 96 BX82
Springwell Hill 38 BH51
(Harefield), Uxb.
Springwell La, Rick. 38 BG49
Springwell La 38 BG49
(Harefield), Uxb.
Springwell Rd SW16 121 DN91
Springwell Rd, Houns. 96 BX81
Springwood (Cheshunt), 14 DU26
Wal.Cr.
Springwood Cl 38 BK53
(Harefield), Uxb.
Springwood Cres, Edg. 42 CP47
Springwood Way, Rom. 71 FG57
Sprowston Ms E7 86 EG65
Sprowston Rd E7 68 EG64
Spruce Cl, Red. 184 DF133
Spruce Ct W5 98 CL76
Elderberry Rd
Spruce Hills Rd E17 47 EC54
Spruce Pk, Brom. 144 EF98
Cumberland Rd
Spruce Rd, West. 178 EK116
Spruce Way, St.Alb. 8 CB27
Sprucedale Cl, Swan. 147 FE96
Sprucedale Gdns, Croy. 161 DX105
Sprucedale Gdns, Wall. 159 DK109
Sprules Rd SE4 103 DY82
Spur, The (Cheshunt), 15 DX28
Wal.Cr.
Welsummer Way
Spur Cl, Abb.L. 7 BR33
Spur Cl, Rom. 34 EV41
Spur Rd N15 66 DR56
Philip La
Spur Rd SE1 200 D4
Spur Rd SW1 199 K5
Spur Rd SW1 101 DJ75
Spur Rd, Bark. 87 EQ69
Spur Rd, Edg. 42 CL49
Spur Rd, Felt. 115 BV85
Spur Rd, Islw. 97 CH80
Spur Rd, Orp. 146 EU103
Spur Rd Est, Edg. 42 CM49
Spurfield, W.Mol. 136 CB97
Spurgate, Brwd. 55 GA47
Spurgeon Av SE19 142 DR95
Spurgeon Rd SE19 142 DR95
Spurgeon St SE1 201 K7
Spurgeon St SE1 102 DR76

Spurling Rd SE22 102 DT84
Spurling Rd, Dag. 88 EZ65
Spurrell Av, Bex. 127 FD91
Spurstowe Rd E8 84 DV65
Marcon Pl
Spurstowe Ter E8 66 DV64
Squadrons App, Horn. 90 FJ65
Square, The W6 99 CW78
Square, The, Cars. 158 DG106
Square, The, Hayes 77 BR74
Square, The, Ilf. 69 EN59
Square, The, Rich. 117 CK85
Square, The, Sev. 190 FE122
Amherst Hill
Square, The, Swan. 147 FD97
Square, The, Wat. 23 BV37
The Harebreaks
Square, The, West Dr. 94 BH81
Square, The, West. 178 EJ120
Square, The, Wey. 153 BQ105
Square, The, Wok. 168 BL110
Square Rigger Row 100 DC83
SW11
York Pl
Squarey St SW17 120 DC90
Squerryes Mede, West. 189 EQ127
Squire Gdns NW8 82 DD69
St. John's Wd Rd
Squires Br Rd, Shep. 134 BM98
Squires Ct SW19 120 DA91
Springfields Cl
Squires Fld, Swan. 147 FF95
Squires La N3 44 DB54
Squires Mt NW3 64 DD62
East Heath Rd
Squires Rd, Shep. 134 BM98
Squires Wk, Ashf. 115 BR94
Napier Rd
Squires Way, Dart. 127 FD91
Squires Wd Dr, Chis. 124 EL94
Squirrel Cl, Houns. 96 BW82
Squirrel Keep, W.Byf. 152 BH112
Squirrel Ms W13 79 CG73
Squirrel Wd, W.Byf. 152 BH112
Squirrels, The SE13 103 ED83
Belmont Hill
Squirrels, The, Bushey 25 CD44
Squirrels, The, Pnr. 60 BZ55
Squirrels Chase, Grays 111 GG75
Hornsby La
Squirrels Cl N12 44 DC49
Woodside Av
Squirrels Cl, Uxb. 76 BN66
Squirrels Grn, Lthd. 170 CA123
Squirrels Grn, Wor.Pk. 139 CT102
Squirrels Heath Av, 71 FH55
Rom.
Squirrels Heath La, 72 FJ56
Horn.
Squirrels Heath La, 72 FJ56
Rom.
Squirrels Heath Rd, 72 FL55
Rom.
Squirrels La, Buck.H. 48 EK48
Squirrels Trd Est, The, 95 BU76
Hayes
Squirrels Way, Epsom 172 CR115
Squirries St E2 84 DU69
Stable Cl, Nthlt. 78 CA68
Stable Wk N2 44 DD53
Old Fm Rd
Stable Way W10 81 CW72
Latimer Rd
Stable Yd SW1 199 K4
Stable Yd SW1 101 DM82
Broomgrove Rd
Stable Yd SW15 99 CW83
Danemere St
Stable Yd Rd SW1 199 K3
Stable Yd Rd SW1 83 DJ74
Stables, The, Buck.H. 48 EJ45
Stables, The, Cob. 154 BZ114
Stables, The, Swan. 147 FH95
Stables End, Orp. 145 EQ104
Stables Ms SE27 122 DQ92
Stables Way SE11 200 D10
Stables Way SE11 101 DN78
Stacey Av N18 46 DW49
Stacey Cl E10 67 ED57
Halford Rd
Stacey Cl, Grav. 131 GL92
Stacey St N7 65 DN62
Stacey St WC2 195 N9
Stacey St WC2 83 DK72
Stack Rd, Dart. 149 FR97
Stackhouse St SW3 198 D6
Stacy Path SE5 102 DS80
Harris St
Stadium Rd NW2 63 CW59
Stadium Rd SE18 105 EM80
Stadium St SW10 100 DC80
Stadium Way, Dart. 127 FE85
Stadium Way, Wem. 62 CM63
Staff St EC1 197 L3
Staffa Rd E10 67 DY60
Stafford Av, Horn. 72 FK55
Stafford Cl E17 67 DZ58
Stafford Cl N14 29 DJ43
Stafford Cl NW6 82 DA69
Stafford Cl, Cat. 176 DT123
Stafford Cl (Chafford 109 FW77
Hundred), Grays
Stafford Cl, Green. 129 FT85
Stafford Cl, Sutt. 157 CY107
Stafford Cl (Cheshunt), 14 DV29
Wal.Cr.
Stafford Ct W8 100 DA76
Stafford Cross, Croy. 159 DM106
Stafford Gdns, Croy. 159 DM106
Stafford Pl SW1 199 K6
Stafford Pl SW1 101 DJ76
Stafford Pl, Rich. 118 CM87
Stafford Rd E3 85 DZ68
Stafford Rd E7 86 EJ66
Stafford Rd NW6 82 DA69
Stafford Rd, Cat. 176 DT122
Stafford Rd, Croy. 159 DN105
Stafford Rd, Har. 40 CC52
Stafford Rd, N.Mal. 138 CQ97
Stafford Rd, Ruis. 59 BT63
Stafford Rd, Sid. 125 ES91

Stafford Rd, Wall. 159 DJ107
Stafford Sq, Wey. 153 BR105
Rosslyn Pk
Stafford St W1 199 K2
Stafford St W1 83 DJ74
Stafford Ter W8 100 DA76
Stafford Way, Sev. 191 FJ127
Staffordshire St SE15 102 DU81
Stag Cl, Edg. 42 CQ54
Stag La NW9 42 CP54
Stag La SW15 119 CT89
Stag La, Buck.H. 48 EH47
Stag La, Edg. 42 CP54
Stag La, Rick. 21 BC44
Stag Leys, Ash. 172 CL120
Stag Leys Cl, Bans. 174 DD115
Stag Pl SW1 199 K6
Stag Pl SW1 101 DJ76
Stag Ride SW19 119 CT90
Stagbury Av, Couls. 174 DE118
Stagbury Cl, Couls. 174 DE119
Stagg Hill, Barn. 28 DD35
Stagg Hill, Pot.B. 28 DD35
Staggart Grn, Chig. 49 ET51
Stags Way, Islw. 97 CF79
Stainash Cres, Stai. 114 BH92
Stainash Par, Stai. 114 BH92
Kingston Rd
Stainbank Rd, Mitch. 141 DH97
Stainby Cl, West Dr. 94 BL76
Stainby Rd N15 66 DT56
Stainer Rd, Borwd. 25 CK39
Stainer St SE1 201 L3
Stainer St SE1 84 DR74
Staines Av, Sutt. 139 CX103
Staines Br, Stai. 113 BE92
Staines Bypass, Ashf. 114 BK92
Staines Bypass, Stai. 114 BH91
Staines La, Cher. 133 BF99
Staines La Cl, Cher. 133 BF100
Staines Rd, Cher. 133 BF97
Staines Rd, Felt. 115 BR87
Staines Rd, Houns. 96 CB83
Staines Rd, Ilf. 69 ER63
Staines Rd, Stai. 134 BH95
Staines Rd (Wraysbury), Stai. 112 AY87
Staines Rd, Twick. 116 CA90
Staines Rd E, Sun. 115 BU94
Staines Rd W, Ashf. 115 BP93
Staines Rd W, Sun. 115 BP93
Staines Wk, Sid. 126 EW93
Evry Rd
Stainford Cl, Ashf. 115 BR92
Stainforth Rd E17 67 EA56
Stainforth Rd, Ilf. 69 ER59
Staining La EC2 197 J8
Staining La EC2 84 DQ72
Stainmore Cl, Chis. 145 ER95
Stains Cl (Cheshunt), Wal.Cr. 15 DY28
Stainsbury St E2 84 DW68
Royston St
Stainsby Pl E14 85 EA72
Stainsby Rd
Stainsby Rd E14 85 EA72
Stainton Rd SE6 123 ED86
Stainton Rd, Enf. 30 DW39
Stainton Wk, Wok. 166 AW118
Inglewood
Stairfoot La, Sev. 190 FC122
Staithes Way, Tad. 173 CV120
Stalbridge St NW1 194 C6
Stalham St SE16 202 E7
Stalham St SE16 102 DV76
Stalisfield Pl, Orp. 163 EN110
Mill La
Stambourne Way SE19 122 DS94
Stambourne Way, W.Wick. 143 EC104
Stamford Brook Av W6 99 CT76
Stamford Brook Rd W6 99 CT76
Stamford Cl N15 66 DU56
Stamford Cl NW3 64 DC63
Heath St
Stamford Cl, Har. 41 CE52
Stamford Cl, Pot.B. 12 DD32
Stamford Cl, Sthl. 78 CA73
Stamford Cotts SW10 100 DB80
Billing St
Stamford Ct W6 99 CT77
Goldhawk Rd
Stamford Dr, Brom. 144 EF98
Stamford Gdns, Dag. 88 EW66
Stamford Grn Rd, Epsom 156 CP113
Stamford Gro E N16 66 DU60
Oldhill St
Stamford Gro W N16 66 DU60
Oldhill St
Stamford Hill N16 66 DT61
Stamford Hill Est N16 66 DT60
Stamford Rd E6 86 EL67
Stamford Rd N1 84 DS66
Stamford Rd N15 66 DU57
Stamford Rd, Dag. 88 EV67
Stamford Rd, Walt. 136 BX104
Kenilworth Dr
Stamford Rd, Wat. 23 BV40
Stamford St SE1 200 D3
Stamford St SE1 83 DN74
Stamp Pl E2 197 P2
Stamp Pl E2 84 DT69
Stanard Cl N16 66 DS59
Stanborough Av, Borwd. 26 CN37
Stanborough Cl, Borwd. 26 CN38
Stanborough Cl, Hmptn. 116 BZ93
Stanborough Pk, Wat. 23 BV35
Stanborough Pas E8 84 DT65
Abbot St
Stanborough Rd, Houns. 97 CD83
Stanbridge Pl N21 45 DP47
Stanbridge Rd SW15 99 CW83
Stanbrook Rd SE2 106 EV75
Stanbrook Rd, Grav. 131 GF88
Stanbury Av, Wat. 23 BS37
Stanbury Rd SE15 102 DV81
Stancroft NW9 62 CS56
Standale Gro, Ruis. 59 BQ57
Standard Ind Est E16 105 EM75
Standard Pl EC2 197 N3
Standard Rd NW10 80 CQ70
Standard Rd, Belv. 106 FA78
Standard Rd, Bexh. 106 EY84
Standard Rd, Enf. 31 DY38
Standard Rd, Houns. 96 BY83
Standard Rd, Orp. 163 EN110
Standen Av, Horn. 72 FK62
Standen Rd SW18 119 CZ87
Standfield, Abb.L. 7 BS31
Standfield Gdns, Dag. 88 FA65
Standfield Rd
Standfield Rd, Dag. 70 FA64
Standish Rd W6 99 CU77
Standlake Pt SE23 123 DX90
Stane Cl SW19 140 DB95
Hayward Cl
Stane St, Lthd. 172 CM124
Reigate Rd
Stane St, Lthd. 182 CL126
Stane Way SE18 104 EK80
Stane Way, Epsom 157 CU110
Stanfield Rd E3 85 DY68
Stanford Cl, Hmptn. 116 BZ93
Stanford Cl, Rom. 71 FB58
Stanford Cl, Ruis. 59 BQ58
Stanford Cl, Wdf.Grn. 48 EL50
Stanford Ct, Wal.Abb. 16 EG33
Stanford Gdns, S.Ock. 91 FR74
Stanford Ho, Bark. 88 EV68
Stanford Pl SE17 201 M9
Stanford Rd N11 44 DF50
Stanford Rd SW16 141 DK96
Stanford Rd W8 100 DB76
Stanford Rd, Grays 110 GD76
Stanford St SW1 199 M9
Stanford Way SW16 141 DK96
Stangate Cres, Borwd. 26 CS43
Stangate Gdns, Stan. 41 CH49
Stanger Rd SE25 142 DU98
Stanham Pl, Dart. 107 FG84
Crayford Way
Stanham Rd, Dart. 128 FJ85
Stanhope Av N3 63 CZ55
Stanhope Av, Brom. 144 EF102
Stanhope Av, Har. 41 CD53
Stanhope Cl SE16 203 J4
Stanhope Gdns N4 65 DP58
Stanhope Gdns N6 65 DH58
Stanhope Gdns NW7 43 CT50
Stanhope Gdns SW7 100 DC77
Stanhope Gdns, Dag. 70 EZ62
Stanhope Gdns, Ilf. 69 EM60
Stanhope Gate W1 198 G2
Stanhope Gate W1 82 DG74
Stanhope Gro, Beck. 143 DZ99
Stanhope Heath, Stai. 114 BJ86
Stanhope Ms E SW7 100 DC77
Stanhope Ms S SW7 100 DC77
Gloucester Rd
Stanhope Ms W SW7 100 DC77
Stanhope Par NW1 195 K2
Stanhope Pk Rd, Grnf. 78 CC70
Stanhope Pl W2 194 D9
Stanhope Pl W2 82 DF72
Stanhope Rd E17 67 EB57
Stanhope Rd N6 65 DJ58
Stanhope Rd N12 44 DC50
Stanhope Rd, Barn. 27 CW44
Stanhope Rd, Bexh. 106 EY82
Stanhope Rd, Cars. 158 DG108
Stanhope Rd, Croy. 142 DS104
Stanhope Rd, Dag. 70 EZ61
Stanhope Rd, Grnf. 78 CC71
Stanhope Rd, Rain. 89 FG68
Stanhope Rd, Sid. 126 EU91
Stanhope Rd, Swans. 130 FZ85
Stanhope Rd, Wal.Cr. 15 DY33
Stanhope Row W1 199 H3
Stanhope St NW1 195 K3
Stanhope St NW1 83 DJ69
Stanhope Ter W2 194 A10
Stanhope Ter W2 82 DD73
Stanhope Way, Sev. 190 FD122
Stanhope Way, Stai. 114 BJ86
Stanhopes, Oxt. 188 EH128
Stanier Cl W14 99 CZ78
Aisgill Av
Staniland Dr, Wey. 152 BM110
Stanlake Ms W12 81 CW74
Stanlake Rd W12 81 CV74
Stanlake Vil W12 81 CV74
Stanley Av, Bark. 87 ET68
Stanley Av, Beck. 143 EC96
Stanley Av, Dag. 70 EZ60
Stanley Av, Grnf. 78 CC67
Stanley Av, N.Mal. 139 CU99
Stanley Av, Rom. 71 FG56
Stanley Av, St.Alb. 8 CA25
Stanley Av, Wem. 80 CL66
Stanley Cl SW8 101 DM79
Stanley Cl, Couls. 175 DM117
Stanley Cl, Green. 129 FS85
Stanley Cl, Horn. 72 FJ61
Stanley Rd
Stanley Cl, Rom. 71 FG56
Stanley Cl, Uxb. 76 BK67
Stanley Cl, Wem. 80 CL66
Stanley Cotts, Slou. 74 AT74
Stanley Cres W11 81 CZ73
Stanley Cres, Grav. 131 GK92
Stanley Gdns NW2 63 CW64
Stanley Gdns W3 80 CS74
Stanley Gdns W11 81 CZ73
Stanley Gdns, Borwd. 26 CL39
Stanley Gdns, Mitch. 120 DG93
Ashbourne Rd
Stanley Gdns, S.Croy. 160 DU112
Stanley Gdns, Wall. 159 DJ107
Stanley Gdns, Walt. 154 BW107
Stanley Gdns Ms W11 81 CZ73
Stanley Cres
Stanley Gdns Rd, Tedd. 117 CE92
Stanley Grn E, Slou. 93 AZ77
Stanley Grn W, Slou. 93 AZ77
Stanley Gro SW8 100 DG82
Stanley Gro, Croy. 141 DN100
Stanley Pk Dr, Wem. 80 CM66
Stanley Pk Rd, Cars. 158 DF108
Stanley Pk Rd, Wall. 159 DH107
Stanley Pas NW1 195 P1
Stanley Rd E4 47 ED46
Stanley Rd E10 67 EB58
Stanley Rd E12 68 EL64
Stanley Rd E15 85 ED67
Stanley Rd E18 48 EF53
Stanley Rd N2 64 DD55
Stanley Rd N9 46 DT46
Stanley Rd N10 45 DH52
Stanley Rd N11 45 DK51
Stanley Rd N15 65 DP56
Stanley Rd NW9 63 CU59
West Hendon Bdy
Stanley Rd SW14 98 CP84
Stanley Rd SW19 120 DA94
Stanley Rd W3 98 CQ76
Stanley Rd, Ashf. 114 BL92
Stanley Rd, Brom. 144 EH98
Stanley Rd, Cars. 158 DG108
Stanley Rd, Croy. 141 DN101
Stanley Rd, Enf. 30 DS41
Stanley Rd, Grav. 130 GE88
Stanley Rd, Grays 110 GB78
Stanley Rd, Har. 60 CC61
Stanley Rd, Horn. 72 FJ61
Stanley Rd, Houns. 96 CC84
Stanley Rd, Ilf. 69 ER61
Stanley Rd, Mitch. 120 DG94
Stanley Rd, Mord. 140 DA98
Stanley Rd, Nthwd. 39 BU53
Stanley Rd, Orp. 146 EU102
Stanley Rd, Sid. 126 EU90
Stanley Rd, Sthl. 78 BY73
Stanley Rd, Sutt. 158 DB107
Stanley Rd, Swans. 130 FZ86
Stanley Rd, Tedd. 117 CE91
Stanley Rd, Twick. 117 CD90
Stanley Rd, Wat. 24 BW41
Stanley Rd, Wem. 80 CM65
Stanley Rd, Wok. 167 AZ116
Stanley Rd N, Rain. 89 FE67
Stanley Rd S, Rain. 89 FF68
Stanley Sq, Cars. 158 DF109
Stanley St SE8 103 DZ80
Stanley St, Cat. 176 DQ122
Coulsdon Rd
Stanley Ter N19 65 DL61
Stanley Way, Orp. 146 EV99
Stanleycroft Cl, Islw. 97 CE81
Stanmer St SW11 100 DE81
Stanmore Gdns, Rich. 98 CM83
Stanmore Gdns, Sutt. 140 DC104
Stanmore Hall, Stan. 41 CH48
Stanmore Hill, Stan. 41 CG48
Stanmore Pk, Stan. 41 CH50
Stanmore Pl NW1 83 DH67
Arlington Rd
Stanmore Rd E11 68 EF60
Stanmore Rd N15 65 DP56
Stanmore Rd, Belv. 107 FC77
Stanmore Rd, Rich. 98 CM83
Stanmore Rd, Wat. 23 BV39
Stanmore St N1 83 DM67
Caledonian Rd
Stanmore Ter, Beck. 143 EA96
Stanmore Way, Loug. 33 EN39
Stanmount Rd, St.Alb. 8 CA25
Stannard Ms E8 84 DU65
Stannard Rd E8 84 DU65
Stannary Pl SE11 101 DN78
Stannary St SE11 101 DN79
Stannet Way, Wall. 159 DJ105
Stannington Path, Borwd. 26 CN39
Stansfeld Rd E6 86 EK71
Stansfield Rd SW9 101 DM83
Stansfield Rd, Houns. 95 BV82
Stansgate Rd, Dag. 70 FA61
Stanstead Cl, Brom. 144 EF99
Stanstead Gro SE6 123 DZ88
Catford Hill
Stanstead Manor, Sutt. 158 DA107
Stanstead Rd E11 68 EH57
Stanstead Rd SE6 123 DX88
Stanstead Rd SE23 123 DX88
Stanstead Rd, Cat. 186 DR125
Stanstead Rd, Houns. 114 BM86
Stansted Cl, Horn. 89 FH65
Stansted Cres, Bex. 126 EX88
Stanswood Gdns SE5 102 DS80
Sedgmoor Pl
Stanthorpe Cl SW16 121 DL92
Stanthorpe Rd
Stanthorpe Rd SW16 121 DL92
Stanton Av, Tedd. 117 CE92
Stanton Cl, Epsom 156 CP106
Stanton Cl, Orp. 146 EW101
Stanton Cl, Wor.Pk. 139 CX102
Stanton Rd SE26 123 DZ91
Stanton Way
Stanton Rd SW13 99 CT82
Stanton Rd SW20 139 CX96
Stanton Rd, Croy. 142 DQ101
Stanton Sq SE26 123 DZ91
Stanton Way
Stanton Way SE26 123 DZ91
Stanton Way, Slou. 92 AY77
Stanway Cl, Chig. 49 ES50
Stanway Ct N1 84 DS68
Hoxton St
Stanway Gdns W3 80 CN74
Stanway Gdns, Edg. 42 CQ50
Stanway Rd, Wal.Abb. 16 EG33
Stanway St N1 84 DS68
Stanwell Cl, Stai. 114 BK86
Stanwell Gdns, Stai. 114 BK86
Stanwell Moor Rd, Stai. 114 BH85
Stanwell Moor Rd, West Dr. 94 BH81
Stanwell New Rd, Stai. 114 BH90
Stanwell Rd, Ashf. 114 BL91
Stanwell Rd, Felt. 115 BQ87
Stanwell Rd, Slou. 93 BA83
Stanwick Rd W14 99 CZ77
Stanworth St SE1 201 P5
Stanworth St SE1 102 DT75
Stanwyck Dr, Chig. 49 EQ50
Stanwyck Gdns, Rom. 51 FH50
Stapenhill Rd, Wem. 61 CH62
Staple Cl, Bex. 127 FD90
Staple Hill Rd, Wok. 150 AS105
Staple Inn WC1 196 D7
Staple Inn Bldgs WC1 196 D7
Staple Inn Bldgs WC1 83 DN71
Staple St SE1 201 L5
Staple St SE1 102 DR75
Staplefield Cl SW2 121 DL88
Staplefield Cl, Pnr. 40 BY52
Stapleford Av, Ilf. 69 ES57
Stapleford Cl E4 47 EC48
Stapleford Cl SW19 119 CY87
Stapleford Cl, Kings.T. 138 CN97
Stapleford Ct, Sev. 190 FF123
Stapleford Gdns, Rom. 50 FA51
Stapleford Rd, Rom. 35 FB42
Stapleford Rd, Wem. 79 CK66
Stapleford Tawney, Ong. 19 FC32
Stapleford Tawney, Rom. 35 FD35
Stapleford Way, Bark. 88 EV69
Staplehurst Rd SE13 124 EE85
Staplehurst Rd, Cars. 158 DE108
Staples Cl SE16 203 K2
Staples Cl SE16 85 DY74
Staples Cor NW2 63 CV60
Staples Cor Business Pk NW2 63 CV60
Staples Rd, Loug. 32 EL41
Stapleton Cl, Pot.B. 12 DD31
Stapleton Cres, Rain. 89 FG65
Stapleton Gdns, Croy. 159 DN106
Stapleton Hall Rd N4 65 DM59
Stapleton Rd SW17 120 DG90
Stapleton Rd, Bexh. 106 EZ80
Stapleton Rd, Borwd. 26 CN38
Stapleton Rd, Orp. 145 ET104
Stapley Rd, Belv. 106 FA78
Stapylton Rd, Barn. 27 CY41
Star & Garter Hill, Rich. 118 CL88
Star Hill, Dart. 127 FE85
Star Hill, Wok. 166 AW119
Star Hill Rd, Sev. 180 EZ116
Star La E16 86 EE70
Star La, Couls. 174 DG122
Star La, Epp. 18 EU30
Star La, Orp. 146 EY98
Star Path, Nthlt. 78 CA68
Brabazon Rd
Star Pl E1 202 A1
Star Rd W14 99 CZ79
Star Rd, Islw. 97 CD82
Star Rd, Uxb. 77 BQ70
Star St E16 86 EF71
Star St W2 194 A8
Star St W2 82 DE71
Star Yd WC2 196 D8
Starboard Av, Green. 129 FV86
Starboard Way E14 204 B6
Starboard Way E14 103 EA76
Starch Ho La, Ilf. 49 ER54
Starcross St NW1 195 L3
Starcross St NW1 83 DJ69
Starfield Rd W12 99 CU75
Starkey Cl (Cheshunt), Wal.Cr. 14 DQ25
Shambrook Rd
Starling Cl, Buck.H. 48 EG46
Starling Cl, Pnr. 60 BW55
Starling La (Cuffley), Pot.B. 13 DM28
Starling Ms SE28 105 ER75
Whinchat Rd
Starling Wk, Hmptn. 116 BY93
Oak Av
Starlings, The, Lthd. 154 CC113
Starmans Cl, Dag. 88 EY67
Starrock La, Couls. 174 DF120
Starrock Rd, Couls. 175 DH119
Starts Cl, Orp. 145 EN104
Starts Hill Av, Orp. 163 EP105
Starts Hill Rd, Orp. 145 EN104
Starveall Cl, West Dr. 94 BM76
Starwood Cl, W.Byf. 152 BJ111
Starwood Ct, Slou. 92 AW76
London Rd
State Fm Av, Orp. 163 EP105
Staten Gdns, Twick. 117 CF88
Lion Rd
Statham Gro N16 66 DQ63
Green Las
Statham Gro N18 46 DS50
Station App (Highams Pk) E4 47 ED51
The Av
Station App E7 68 EH63
Woodford Rd
Station App (Snaresbrook) E11 68 EG57
High St
Station App N11 45 DH50
Friern Barnet Rd
Station App N12 44 DB50
Holden Rd
Station App (Woodside Pk) N12 44 DB49
Station App (Stoke Newington) N16 66 DT61
Stamford Hill
Station App NW10 81 CT69
Station Rd
Station App SE1 200 C5
Station App SE1 101 DN75
Station App SE3 104 EH83
Kidbrooke Pk Rd
Station App (Mottingham) SE9 125 EM88
Station App (Lower Sydenham) SE26 123 DZ92
Worsley Br Rd
Station App (Sydenham) SE26 122 DW91
Sydenham Rd
Station App SW6 99 CY83
Station App SW16 121 DK92
Station App W7 79 CE74
Station App (Little Chalfont), Amer. 20 AX39
Chalfont Sta Rd
Station App, Ashf. 114 BL91
Station App, Barn. 28 DC42
Station App, Bex. 126 FA87
Bexley High St
Station App, Bexh. 106 EY82
Avenue Rd
Station App (Barnehurst), Bexh. 107 FC82
Station App, Brom. 144 EG102
Station App, Buck.H. 48 EK49
Cherry Tree Ri
Station App, Chis. 145 EN95
Station App (Elmstead Wds), Chis. 124 EL93
Station App, Couls. 175 DK116
Station App (Chipstead), Couls. 174 DF118
Station App, Dart. 128 FL86
Station App (Crayford), Dart. 127 FF86
Station App (Theydon Bois), Epp. 33 ES36
Coppice Row
Station App, Epsom 156 CR113
Station App (Ewell E), Epsom 157 CV110
Station App (Ewell W), Epsom 157 CT109
Chessington Rd
Station App (Stoneleigh), Epsom 157 CU106
Station App (Hinchley Wd), Esher 137 CF104
Station App, Ger.Cr. 56 AY57
Station App, Grays 110 GA79
Station App, Grnf. 79 CD66
Station App, Hmptn. 136 CA95
Milton Rd
Station App, Har. 61 CE59
Station App, Hayes 95 BT75
Station App, Ken. 160 DQ114
Hayes La
Station App, Kings.T. 138 CN95
Station App, Lthd. 171 CG121
Station App (Oxshott), Lthd. 154 CC113
Station App, Loug. 32 EL43
Station App (Debden), Loug. 33 EQ42
Station App, Nthwd. 39 BS52
Station App, Orp. 145 ET103
Station App (Chelsfield), Orp. 164 EV106
Station App (St. Mary Cray), Orp. 146 EV98
Station App, Oxt. 188 EE128
Station App, Pnr. 60 BY55
Station App (Hatch End), Pnr. 40 CA52
Uxbridge Rd
Station App, Pot.B. 11 CZ32
Wyllyotts Pl
Station App, Pur. 159 DN111
Whytecliffe Rd S
Station App, Rad. 25 CG35
Shenley Hill
Station App, Rich. 98 CN81
Station App, Rick. 21 BC42
Station App, Ruis. 59 BV64
Station App, Shep. 135 BQ100
Station App, S.Croy. 160 DR109
Sanderstead Rd
Station App, Stai. 114 BG92
Station App, Sun. 135 BU95
Station App (Belmont), Sutt. 158 DB110
Brighton Rd
Station App (Cheam), Sutt. 157 CY108
Station App, Swan. 147 FE98
Station App, Upmin. 72 FQ61
Station App (Denham), Uxb. 57 BD59
Middle Rd
Station App, Vir.W. 132 AX98
Station App, Wal.Cr. 15 DY34
Station App (Cheshunt), Wal.Cr. 15 DZ30
Station App, Wat. 23 BT41
Cassiobury Pk Av
Station App (Carpenders Pk), Wat. 40 BX48
Prestwick Rd
Station App, Well. 105 ET82
Station App, Wem. 79 CH65
Station App, W.Byf. 152 BG112
Station App, West Dr. 76 BL74
Station App, Wey. 152 BN107
Station App, Whyt. 176 DU117
Station App, Wok. 167 AZ117
Station App N, Sid. 126 EU89
Station App Rd W4 98 CQ80
Station App Rd, Couls. 175 DK115
Station App Rd, Tad. 173 CW122
Station App Rd, Til. 111 GG84
Station Av SW9 101 DP83
Coldharbour La
Station Av, Cat. 176 DU124
Station Av, Epsom 156 CS109
Station Av, N.Mal. 138 CS97
Station Av, Rich. 98 CN81
Station Par
Station Av, Walt. 153 BU105
Station Cl N3 44 DA53
Station Cl (Woodside Pk) N12 44 DB49
Station Cl, Hmptn. 136 CB95
Station Cl, Hat. 11 CY26
Station Rd
Station Cl, Pot.B. 11 CZ31
Station Cres N15 66 DR56
Station Cres SE3 104 EG78
Station Cres, Ashf. 114 BK90
Station Cres, Wem. 79 CH65
Station Est, Beck. 143 DX98
Elmers End Rd
Station Est Rd, Felt. 115 BV88
Station Footpath, Kings L. 7 BP31
Station Gar Ms SW16 121 DK93
Estreham Rd
Station Gdns W4 98 CQ80
Station Gro, Wem. 80 CL65
Station Hill, Brom. 144 EG103
Station Ho Ms N9 46 DU49
Fore St
Station La, Horn. 72 FK62
Station Par E11 68 EG57
Station Par N14 45 DK46
High St
Station Par NW2 81 CW65

Station Par SW12 120 DG88
Balham High Rd
Station Par W3 80 CN72
Station Par, Ashf. 114 BM91
Woodthorpe Rd
Station Par, Bark. 87 EQ66
Station Par, Felt. 115 BV87
Station Par, Horn. 71 FH63
Rosewood Av
Station Par, Rich. 98 CN81
Station Par, Sev. 190 FG124
London Rd
Station Par (Denham), Uxb. 58 BG59
Station Par, Vir.W. 132 AX98
Station Pas E18 48 EH54
Maybank Rd
Station Pas SE15 102 DV81
Asylum Rd
Station Path E8 84 DV65
Amhurst Rd
Station Path, Stai. 113 BF91
Station Pl N4 65 DN61
Seven Sisters Rd
Station Ri SE27 121 DP89
Norwood Rd
Station Rd (Chingford) E4 47 ED46
Station Rd E7 68 EG63
Station Rd E12 68 EK63
Station Rd E17 67 DY58
Station Rd N3 44 DA53
Station Rd N11 45 DH50
Station Rd N17 66 DU55
Hale Rd
Station Rd N19 65 DJ62
Station Rd N21 45 DP46
Station Rd N22 45 DM54
Station Rd NW4 63 CU58
Station Rd NW7 42 CS50
Station Rd NW10 81 CT68
Station Rd SE13 103 EC83
Station Rd SE20 122 DW93
Station Rd (Norwood Junct) SE25 142 DT98
Station Rd SW13 99 CU83
Station Rd SW19 140 DC95
Station Rd W5 80 CM72
Station Rd (Hanwell) W7 79 CE74
Station Rd, Add. 152 BJ105
Station Rd, Ashf. 114 BM91
Station Rd, Barn. 28 DB43
Station Rd, Belv. 106 FA76
Station Rd, Bet. 182 CS131
Station Rd, Bexh. 106 EY83
Station Rd, Borwd. 26 CN42
Station Rd, Brent. 97 CJ79
Station Rd, Brom. 144 EG95
Station Rd (Shortlands), Brom. 144 EE96
Station Rd, Cars. 158 DF105
Station Rd, Cat. 177 DZ123
Station Rd, Cher. 133 BF102
Station Rd, Chess. 156 CL106
Station Rd, Chig. 49 EP48
Station Rd, Cob. 170 BY117
Station Rd (East Croydon), Croy. 142 DR103
Station Rd (West Croydon), Croy. 142 DQ102
Station Rd (Crayford), Dart. 127 FF86
Station Rd (Eynsford), Dart. 148 FK104
Station Rd (South Darenth), Dart. 148 FP96
Station Rd, Edg. 42 CN51
Station Rd, Egh. 113 BA92
Station Rd, Epp. 18 EU31
Station Rd (North Weald Bassett), Epp. 19 FB27
Station Rd, Esher 137 CD103
Station Rd (Claygate), Esher 155 CD106
Station Rd, Ger.Cr. 56 AY57
Station Rd (Betsham), Grav. 130 GA91
Station Rd (Northfleet), Grav. 130 GB86
Station Rd, Green. 129 FU85
Station Rd, Hmptn. 136 CA95
Station Rd, Har. 61 CF59
Station Rd (North Harrow), Har. 60 CB57
Station Rd, Hat. 11 CX25
Station Rd, Hayes 95 BT76
Station Rd, Houns. 96 CB84
Station Rd, Ilf. 69 EP62
Station Rd (Barkingside), Ilf. 69 ER55
Station Rd, Ken. 160 DQ114
Station Rd, Kings L. 7 BP29
Station Rd, Kings.T. 138 CN95
Station Rd (Hampton Wick), Kings.T. 137 CJ95
Station Rd, Lthd. 171 CG121
Station Rd, Loug. 32 EL42
Station Rd (Motspur Pk), N.Mal. 139 CV99
Station Rd, Orp. 145 ET103
Station Rd (St. Mary Cray), Orp. 146 EW98
Station Rd (Cuffley), Pot.B. 13 DM29
Station Rd, Rad. 25 CG35
Station Rd, Red. 184 DG133
Station Rd (Merstham), Red. 185 DJ128
Station Rd, Rick. 38 BK45
Station Rd (Chadwell Heath), Rom. 70 EX59
Station Rd (Gidea Pk), Rom. 71 FH56
Station Rd (Harold Wd), Rom. 52 FM53
Station Rd (Bricket Wd), St.Alb. 8 CA31
Station Rd (Dunton Grn), Sev. 181 FE120
Station Rd (Halstead), Sev. 164 EZ111
Station Rd (Otford), Sev. 181 FH116
Station Rd (Shoreham), Sev. 165 FG111
Station Rd, Shep. 135 BQ99
Station Rd, Sid. 126 EU91
Station Rd (Langley), Slou. 93 BA76
Station Rd (Wraysbury), Stai. 113 AZ86
Station Rd, Sun. 115 BU94
Station Rd (Belmont), Sutt. 158 DA110
Station Rd, Swan. 147 FE98
Station Rd, Tedd. 117 CF92
Station Rd, T.Ditt. 137 CF101
Station Rd, Twick. 117 CF88
Station Rd, Upmin. 72 FQ61
Station Rd, Uxb. 76 BJ70
Station Rd, Wal.Cr. 15 EA34
Station Rd, Wat. 23 BV40
Station Rd, W.Byf. 152 BG112
Station Rd, West Dr. 76 BL74
Station Rd, W.Wick. 143 EC102
Station Rd, West. 180 EV123
Station Rd, Whyt. 176 DT118
Station Rd, Wok. 150 AT111
Station Rd E, Oxt. 188 EE128
Station Rd N, Belv. 107 FB76
Station Rd N, Egh. 113 BA92
Station Rd N, Red. 185 DJ128
Station Rd S, Red. 185 DJ128
Station Rd W, Oxt. 188 EE129
Station Sq (Petts Wd), Orp. 145 EQ99
Station Sq (St. Mary Cray), Orp. 146 EV98
Station Sq, Rom. 71 FH56
Station St E15 85 ED66
Station St E16 87 EP74
Station Ter NW10 81 CX68
Station Ter SE5 102 DQ81
Station Ter, St.Alb. 9 CD26
Park St
Station Vw, Grnf. 79 CD67
Station Way SE15 102 DU82
Rye La
Station Way (Roding Valley), Buck.H. 48 EJ49
Station Way (Epsom), Epsom 156 CR113
Station Way (Claygate), Esher 155 CE107
Station Way (Cheam), Sutt. 157 CY107
Station Yd, Twick. 117 CG87
Stationers Hall Ct EC4 83 DP72
Ludgate Hill
Staunton Rd, Kings.T. 118 CL93
Staunton St SE8 103 DZ79
Stave Yd Rd SE16 203 K3
Stave Yd Rd SE16 85 DY74
Staveley Cl E9 66 DW64
Churchill Wk
Staveley Cl N7 65 DL63
Penn Rd
Staveley Cl SE15 102 DV81
Asylum Rd
Staveley Gdns W4 98 CR81
Staveley Rd W4 98 CR80
Staveley Rd, Ashf. 115 BR93
Staveley Way, Wok. 166 AS117
Staverton Rd NW2 81 CW66
Staverton Rd, Horn. 72 FK58
Stavordale Rd N5 65 DP63
Stavordale Rd, Cars. 140 DC101
Stayne End, Vir.W. 132 AU98
Stayner's Rd E1 85 DX70
Stayton Rd, Sutt. 140 DA104
Stead St SE17 201 K9
Stead St SE17 102 DR77
Steadfast Rd, Kings.T. 137 CK95
Steam Fm La, Felt. 95 BT84
Stean St E8 84 DT67
Stebbing Way, Bark. 88 EU68
Stebondale St E14 204 E9
Stebondale St E14 103 EC78
Stedham Pl WC1 195 P8
Stedman Cl, Bex. 127 FE90
Stedman Cl, Uxb. 58 BN62
Steed Cl, Horn. 71 FH61
St. Leonards Way
Steedman St SE17 201 H9
Steeds Rd N10 44 DF53
Steeds Way, Loug. 32 EL41
Steele Av, Green. 129 FT85
Steele Rd E11 68 EE63
Steele Rd N17 66 DS55
Steele Rd NW10 80 CQ68
Steele Rd W4 98 CQ76
Steele Rd, Islw. 97 CG84
Steele Wk, Erith 107 FB79
Steeles Ms N NW3 82 DF65
Steeles Rd
Steeles Ms S NW3 82 DF65
Steeles Rd
Steeles Rd NW3 82 DF65
Steel's La E1 84 DW72
Devonport St
Steels La, Lthd. 154 CB114
Steelyard Pas EC4 84 DR73
Upper Thames St
Steen Way SE22 122 DS85
East Dulwich Gro
Steep Cl, Orp. 163 ET107
Steep Hill SW16 121 DK90
Steep Hill, Croy. 160 DS105
Steeplands, Bushey 40 CB45
Steeple Cl SW6 99 CY82
Steeple Cl SW19 119 CY92
Steeple Ct E1 84 DV70
Coventry Rd
Steeple Gdns, Add. 152 BH106
Weatherall Cl
Steeple Hts Dr, West. 178 EK117
Steeple Wk N1 84 DQ67
Basire St
Steeplestone Cl N18 46 DQ50
Steerforth St SW18 120 DB89
Steers Mead, Mitch. 140 DF95
Steers Way SE16 203 L5
Steers Way SE16 103 DY75
Stella Rd SW17 120 DF93
Stellar Ho N17 46 DT51
Stelling Rd, Erith 107 FD80
Stellman Cl E5 66 DU62
Stembridge Rd SE20 142 DV96
Sten Cl, Enf. 31 EA38
Government Row
Stents La, Cob. 170 BZ120
Stepbridge Path, Wok. 166 AX117
Goldsworth Rd
Stepgates, Cher. 134 BH101
Stepgates Cl, Cher. 134 BH101
Stephan Cl E8 84 DU67
Stephen Av, Rain. 89 FG65
Stephen Cl, Egh. 113 BC93
Stephen Cl, Orp. 145 ET104
Stephen Ms W1 195 M7
Stephen Rd, Bexh. 107 FC83
Stephen St W1 195 M7
Stephen St W1 83 DK71
Stephendale Rd SW6 100 DB82
Stephens Cl, Rom. 52 FJ50
Stephen's Rd E15 86 EE67
Stephenson Av, Til. 111 GG81
Stephenson Rd E17 67 DY57
Stephenson Rd W7 79 CF72
Stephenson Rd, Twick. 116 CA87
Stephenson St E16 86 EE70
Stephenson St NW10 80 CS69
Stephenson Way NW1 195 L4
Stephenson Way NW1 83 DJ70
Stephenson Way, Wat. 24 BX41
Stepney Causeway E1 85 DX72
Stepney Grn E1 84 DW71
Stepney High St E1 85 DX71
Stepney Way E1 84 DV71
Sterling Av, Edg. 42 CM49
Sterling Av, Pnr. 60 BY59
Sterling Av, Wal.Cr. 15 DX34
Sterling Cl, Pnr. 60 BX60
Sterling Gdns SE14 103 DY79
Sterling Ind Est, Dag. 71 FB63
Sterling Pl W5 98 CL77
Sterling Rd, Enf. 30 DR38
Sterling St SW7 198 C6
Sterling Way N18 46 DR50
Stern Cl, Bark. 88 EY69
Choats Rd
Sterndale Rd W14 99 CX76
Sterndale Rd, Dart. 128 FM87
Sterne St W12 99 CX75
Sternhall La SE15 102 DU83
Sternhold Av SW2 121 DK89
Sterry Cres, Dag. 70 FA64
Alibon Rd
Sterry Dr, Epsom 156 CS105
Sterry Dr, T.Ditt. 137 CE100
Sterry Gdns, Dag. 88 FA65
Sterry Rd, Bark. 87 ET67
Sterry Rd, Dag. 70 FA63
Sterry St SE1 201 K5
Sterry St SE1 102 DR75
Steucers La SE23 123 DY87
Steve Biko La SE6 123 EA91
Steve Biko Rd N7 65 DN62
Steve Biko Way, Houns. 96 CA83
Stevedale Rd, Well. 106 EW82
Stevedore St E1 202 D2
Stevenage Cres, Borwd. 26 CL39
Stevenage Rd E6 87 EN65
Stevenage Rd SW6 99 CX80
Stevens Av E9 84 DW65
Stevens Cl, Beck. 123 EA93
Stevens Cl, Bex. 127 FD91
Steven's Cl, Dart. 129 FS92
Stevens Cl, Epsom 156 CS113
Upper High St
Stevens Cl, Hmptn. 116 BZ93
Stevens Cl, Pnr. 60 BW57
Bridle Rd
Stevens Grn, Bushey 40 CC46
Stevens La, Esher 155 CG108
Stevens Pl, Pur. 159 DP113
Stevens Rd, Dag. 70 EV62
Stevens St SE1 201 N6
Steven's Wk, Croy. 161 DY111
Stevens Way, Chig. 49 ES49
Stevenson Cl, Barn. 28 DD44
Stevenson Cl, Erith 107 FH80
Stevenson Cres SE16 202 C10
Stevenson Cres SE16 102 DV78
Steventon Rd W12 81 CT73
Stew La EC4 197 H10
Steward Cl (Cheshunt), Wal.Cr. 15 DY30
Steward St E1 197 N7
Steward St E1 84 DS71
Stewards Cl, Epp. 18 EU33
Stewards Grn La, Epp. 18 EV32
Stewards Grn Rd, Epp. 18 EU33
Stewards Holte Wk N11 45 DH49
Coppies Gro
Stewards Wk, Rom. 71 FE57
Stewart, Tad. 173 CX121
Stewart Av, Shep. 134 BN98
Stewart Av, Slou. 74 AT71
Stewart Av, Upmin. 72 FP62
Stewart Cl NW9 62 CQ58
Stewart Cl, Abb.L. 7 BT32
Stewart Cl, Chis. 125 EP92
Stewart Cl, Hmptn. 116 BY92
Stewart Cl, Wok. 166 AT117
Nethercote Av
Stewart Rainbird Ho E12 69 EN64
Stewart Rd E15 67 ED63
Stewart St E14 204 E5
Stewart St E14 103 EC75
Stewart's Gro SW3 198 A10
Stewart's Gro SW3 100 DD77
Stewart's Rd SW8 101 DJ80
Stewartsby Cl N18 46 DQ50
Steyne Rd W3 80 CQ74
Steyning Cl, Ken. 175 DP116
Steyning Gro SE9 125 EM91
Steyning Way, Houns. 96 BW84
Steynings Way N12 44 DA50
Steynton Av, Bex. 126 EX89
Stickland Rd, Belv. 106 FA77
Picardy Rd
Stickleton Cl, Grnf. 78 CB69
Stifford Hill (North Stifford), Grays 91 FX74
Stifford Hill, S.Ock. 91 FW73
Stifford Rd, S.Ock. 91 FR74
Stile Hall Gdns W4 98 CN78
Stile Hall Par W4 98 CN78
Chiswick High Rd
Stile Path, Sun. 135 BU97
Stile Rd, Slou. 92 AX76
Stilecroft Gdns, Wem. 61 CH62
Stiles Cl, Brom. 145 EM100
Stiles Cl, Erith 107 FB78
Riverdale Rd
Stillingfleet Rd SW13 99 CU79
Stillington St SW1 199 L8
Stillington St SW1 101 DJ77
Stillness Rd SE23 123 DY86
Stilton Cres NW10 80 CQ66
Stilton Path, Borwd. 26 CN38
Stilwell Dr, Uxb. 76 BM71
Royal La
Stilwell Roundabout, Uxb. 76 BN73
Stipularis Dr, Hayes 78 BX70
Stirling Cl SW16 141 DJ95
Stirling Cl, Bans. 173 CZ117
Stirling Cl, Rain. 89 FH69
Stirling Cl, Uxb. 76 BJ69
Ferndale Cres
Stirling Cor, Barn. 26 CR44
Stirling Cor, Borwd. 26 CR44
Stirling Dr, Orp. 164 EV106
Stirling Gro, Houns. 96 CC82
Stirling Rd E13 86 EH68
Stirling Rd E17 67 DY55
Stirling Rd N17 46 DU53
Stirling Rd N22 45 DP53
Stirling Rd SW9 101 DL82
Stirling Rd W3 98 CP76
Stirling Rd, Har. 61 CF55
Stirling Rd, Hayes 77 BV73
Stirling Rd, Houns. 114 BM86
Stirling Rd, Twick. 116 CA87
Stirling Rd Path E17 67 DY55
Stirling Wk, N.Mal. 138 CQ99
Stirling Wk, Surb. 138 CP100
Stirling Way, Abb.L. 7 BU32
Stirling Way, Borwd. 26 CR44
Stirling Way, Croy. 141 DL101
Stites Hill Rd, Couls. 175 DP120
Stiven Cres, Har. 60 BZ62
Stoats Nest Rd, Couls. 159 DL114
Stoats Nest Village, Couls. 175 DL115
Stock Hill, West. 178 EK116
Stock La, Dart. 128 FJ91
Stock Orchard Cres N7 65 DM64
Stock Orchard St N7 65 DM64
Stock St E13 86 EG68
Stockbury Rd, Croy. 142 DW100
Stockdale Rd, Dag. 70 EZ61
Stockdove Way, Grnf. 79 CF69
Stocker Gdns, Dag. 88 EW66
Ellerton Rd
Stockers Fm Rd, Rick. 38 BK48
Stockers La, Wok. 167 AZ120
Stockfield Rd SW16 121 DM90
Stockfield Rd, Esher 155 CE106
Stockham's Cl, S.Croy. 160 DR111
Stockholm Rd SE16 102 DW78
Stockholm Way E1 202 B2
Stockholm Way E1 84 DU74
Stockhurst Cl SW15 99 CW82
Stockingswater La, Enf. 31 DY41
Stockland Rd, Rom. 71 FD58
Stockley Cl, West Dr. 95 BP75
Stockley Fm Rd, West Dr. 95 BP76
Stockley Rd
Stockley Pk, Uxb. 77 BP74
Stockley Pk Roundabout, Uxb. 77 BP74
Stockley Rd, Uxb. 77 BP73
Stockley Rd, West Dr. 95 BP77
Stockport Rd SW16 141 DK95
Stockport Rd, Rick. 37 BC45
Stocks Pl E14 85 DZ73
Grenade St
Stocksfield Rd E17 67 EC55
Stockton Gdns N17 46 DQ52
Stockton Rd
Stockton Gdns NW7 42 CS48
Stockton Rd N17 46 DQ52
Stockton Rd N18 46 DU51
Stockwell Av SW9 101 DM83
Stockwell Cl, Brom. 144 EH96
Stockwell Cl (Cheshunt), Wal.Cr. 14 DU28
Stockwell Gdns SW9 101 DM82
Stockwell Gdns Est SW9 101 DL82
Stockwell Grn SW9 101 DM82
Stockwell La SW9 101 DM82
Stockwell La (Cheshunt), Wal.Cr. 14 DU28
Stockwell Ms SW9 101 DM82
Stockwell Rd
Stockwell Pk Cres SW9 101 DM82
Stockwell Pk Est SW9 101 DN82
Stockwell Pk Rd SW9 101 DM81
Stockwell Pk Wk SW9 101 DM83
Stockwell Rd SW9 101 DM82
Stockwell St SE10 103 EC79
Stockwell Ter SW9 101 DM81
Stodart Rd SE20 142 DW95
Stofield Gdns SE9 124 EK90
Aldersgrove Av
Stoford Cl SW19 119 CY87
Stoke Av, Ilf. 50 EU51
Stoke Cl, Cob. 170 BZ116
Stoke Common Rd, Slou. 56 AU63
Stoke Ct Dr, Slou. 74 AS67
Stoke Gdns, Slou. 74 AS74
Stoke Grn, Slou. 74 AU70
Stoke Newington Ch St N16 66 DR62
Stoke Newington Common N16 66 DT62
Stoke Newington High St N16 66 DT62
Stoke Newington Rd N16 66 DT64
Stoke Pl NW10 81 CT69
Stoke Poges La, Slou. 74 AS72
Stoke Rd, Cob. 170 BW115
Stoke Rd, Kings.T. 118 CQ94
Stoke Rd, Rain. 90 FK68
Stoke Rd, Slou. 74 AT71
Stoke Rd, Walt. 136 BW104
Stoke Wd, Slou. 56 AT63
Stokenchurch St SW6 100 DB81
Stokes Ridings, Tad. 173 CX123
Stokes Rd E6 86 EL70
Stokes Rd, Croy. 143 DX100
Stokesay, Slou. 74 AT73
Stokesby Rd, Chess. 156 CM107
Stokesheath Rd, Lthd. 155 CD111
Stokesley St W12 81 CT72
Stoll Cl NW2 63 CW62
Stompond La, Walt. 135 BU103
Stoms Path SE6 123 EA92
Stonard Rd N13 45 DN48
Stonard Rd, Dag. 70 EV64
Stonards Hill, Epp. 18 EW31
Stonards Hill, Loug. 33 EM44
Stondon Pk SE23 123 DY87
Stondon Wk E6 86 EK68
Stone Bldgs WC2 196 C7
Stone Bldgs WC2 83 DM71
Stone Cl SW4 101 DJ82
Larkhall Ri
Stone Cl, Dag. 70 EZ61
Stone Cl, West Dr. 76 BM74
Stone Cres, Felt. 115 BT87
Stone Hall Gdns W8 100 DB76
St. Mary's Gate
Stone Hall Pl W8 100 DB76
St. Mary's Gate
Stone Hall Rd N21 45 DM45
Stone Ho Ct EC3 197 M8
Stone Ness Rd, Grays 109 FV79
Stone Pk Av, Beck. 143 EA98
Stone Pl, Wor.Pk. 139 CU103
Stone Pl Rd, Green. 129 FS85
Stone Rd, Brom. 144 EF99
Stone St, Croy. 159 DN106
Stone St, Grav. 131 GH86
Stonebanks, Walt. 135 BU101
Stonebridge Common E8 84 DT66
Mayfield Rd
Stonebridge Pk NW10 80 CR66
Stonebridge Rd N15 66 DS57
Stonebridge Rd, Grav. 130 GA85
Stonebridge Way, Wem. 80 CP65
Stonechat Sq E6 86 EL71
Peridot St
Stonecot Cl, Sutt. 139 CY102
Stonecot Hill, Sutt. 139 CY102
Stonecroft Av, Iver 75 BE72
Stonecroft Cl, Barn. 27 CV42
Stonecroft Rd, Erith 107 FC80
Stonecroft Way, Croy. 141 DL101
Stonecrop Cl NW9 62 CR55
Colindale Av
Stonecutter Ct EC4 83 DP72
Stonecutter St
Stonecutter St EC4 196 F8
Stonecutter St EC4 83 DP72
Stonefield Cl, Bexh. 106 FA83
Stonefield Cl, Ruis. 60 BY64
Stonefield St N1 83 DN67
Stonefield Way SE7 104 EK80
Greenbay Rd
Stonefield Way, Ruis. 60 BY63
Stonegate Cl, Orp. 146 EW97
Main Rd
Stonegrove, Edg. 42 CL49
Stonegrove Est, Edg. 42 CM49
Stonegrove Gdns, Edg. 42 CM50
Stonehall Av, Ilf. 68 EL58
Stoneham Rd N11 45 DJ51
Stonehill Cl SW14 118 CR85
Stonehill Cres, Cher. 150 AY107
Stonehill Grn, Dart. 127 FC94
Stonehill Rd SW14 118 CQ85
Stonehill Rd W4 98 CN78
Wellesley Rd
Stonehill Rd, Cher. 151 BA105
Stonehill Rd, Wok. 150 AW108
Stonehill Wds Caravan Pk, Sid. 127 FB93
Stonehills Ct SE21 122 DS90
Stonehorse Rd, Enf. 30 DW43
Stonehouse Gdns, Cat. 186 DS125
Stonehouse La, Purf. 109 FS79
Stonehouse La, Sev. 164 EX109
Stonehouse Rd, Sev. 164 EW110
Stoneings La, Sev. 179 ET118
Stoneleigh Av, Enf. 30 DV39
Stoneleigh Av, Wor.Pk. 157 CU105
Stoneleigh Bdy, Epsom 157 CU106
Stoneleigh Cl, Wal.Cr. 15 DX33
Stoneleigh Cres, Epsom 157 CT106
Stoneleigh Pk, Wey. 153 BQ106
Stoneleigh Pk Av, Croy. 143 DX100
Stoneleigh Pk Rd, Epsom 157 CT107
Stoneleigh Pl W11 81 CX73
Stoneleigh Rd N17 66 DT55
Stoneleigh Rd, Cars. 140 DE101
Stoneleigh Rd, Ilf. 68 EL55
Stoneleigh Rd, Oxt. 188 EL130
Stoneleigh St W11 81 CX73
Stoneleigh Ter N19 65 DH61
Stonells Rd SW11 120 DF85
Chatham Rd
Stonemasons Cl N15 66 DR56
Stonenest St N4 65 DM60
Stones All, Wat. 23 BV42
Stones Cross Rd, Swan. 147 FC99
Stones End St SE1 201 H5
Stones End St SE1 102 DQ75
Stones Rd, Epsom 156 CS112
Stoneswood Rd, Oxt. 188 EH130
Stonewall E6 87 EN71
Stonewood, Dart. 129 FW90
Stonewood Rd, Erith 107 FE78
Stoney All SE18 105 EN82
Stoney La E1 197 N8
Stoney La SE19 122 DT93
Church Rd
Stoney La, Hem.H. 5 BB27
Stoney La, Kings L. 5 BE30
Stoney St SE1 201 K2
Stoney St SE1 84 DR74
Stoneyard La E14 204 B1
Stoneycroft Cl SE12 124 EF87
Stoneycroft Rd, Wdf.Grn. 48 EL51

Stoneydeep, Tedd. 117 CG91
Twickenham Rd
Stoneydown E17 67 DY56
Stoneydown Av E17 67 DY56
Stoneyfield Rd, Couls. 175 DM117
Stoneyfields Gdns, Edg. 42 CQ49
Stoneyfields La, Edg. 42 CQ50
Stoneylands Ct, Egh. 113 AZ92
Stoneylands Rd, Egh. 113 AZ92
Stonhouse St SW4 101 DK83
Stonny Cft, Ash. 172 CM117
Stonor Rd W14 99 CZ77
Stony La, Amer. 20 AY38
Stony Path, Loug. 33 EM40
Stonycroft Cl, Enf. 31 DY40
Brimsdown Av
Stonyshotts, Wal.Abb. 16 EE34
Stoop Ct, W.Byf. 152 BH112
Stopes St SE15 102 DT80
Stopford Rd E13 86 EG67
Stopford Rd SE17 101 DP78
Store Rd E16 105 EN75
Store St E15 67 ED64
Store St WC1 195 M7
Store St WC1 83 DK71
Storers Quay E14 204 F9
Storers Quay E14 103 ED77
Storey Rd E17 67 DZ56
Storey Rd N6 64 DF58
Storey St E16 87 EN74
Storey's Gate SW1 199 N5
Storey's Gate SW1 101 DK75
Stories Ms SE5 102 DS82
Stories Rd SE5 102 DS83
Stork Rd E7 86 EF65
Storks Rd SE16 202 C7
Storks Rd SE16 102 DU76
Storksmead Rd, Edg. 42 CS52
Stormont Rd N6 64 DF59
Stormont Rd SW11 100 DG83
Stormont Way, Chess. 155 CJ106
Stormount Dr, Hayes 95 BQ75
Stornaway Rd, Slou. 93 BC77
Stornaway Strand, Grav. 131 GM91
Storr Gdns, Brwd. 55 GD43
Storrington Rd, Croy. 142 DT102
Story St N1 83 DM66
Carnoustie Dr
Stothard Pl EC2 84 DS71
Bishopsgate
Stothard St E1 84 DW70
Colebert Av
Stott Cl SW18 120 DD86
Stoughton Av, Sutt. 157 CX106
Stoughton Cl SE11 200 C9
Stoughton Cl SW15 119 CU88
Bessborough Rd
Stour Av, Sthl. 96 CA76
Stour Cl, Kes. 162 EJ105
Stour Rd E3 85 EA66
Stour Rd, Dag. 70 FA61
Stour Rd, Dart. 107 FG83
Stour Rd, Grays 111 GG78
Stour Way, Upmin. 73 FS58
Stourcliffe St W1 194 D9
Stourcliffe St W1 82 DF72
Stourhead Cl SW19 119 CX87
Castlecombe Dr
Stourhead Gdns SW20 139 CU97
Stourton Av, Felt. 116 BZ91
Stow Cres E17 47 DY52
Stowage SE8 103 EA79
Stowe Ct, Dart. 128 FQ87
Stowe Cres, Ruis. 59 BP58
Stowe Gdns N9 46 DT46
Latymer Rd
Stowe Pl N15 66 DS55
Stowe Rd W12 99 CV75
Stowe Rd, Orp. 164 EV105
Stowell Av, Croy. 161 ED110
Stowting Rd, Orp. 163 ES105
Stox Mead, Har. 41 CD53
Stracey Rd E7 68 EG63
Stracey Rd NW10 80 CR67
Strachan Pl SW19 119 CW93
Woodhayes Rd
Stradbroke Dr, Chig. 49 EN51
Stradbroke Gro, Buck.H. 48 EK46
Stradbroke Gro, Ilf. 68 EL55
Stradbroke Pk, Chig. 49 EP51
Stradbroke Rd N5 66 DQ63
Stradbrook Cl, Har. 60 BZ62
Stiven Cres
Stradella Rd SE24 122 DQ86
Strafford Av, Ilf. 49 EN54
Strafford Cl, Pot.B. 12 DA32
Strafford Gate
Strafford Gate, Pot.B. 12 DA32
Strafford Rd W3 98 CQ75
Strafford Rd, Barn. 27 CY41
Strafford Rd, Houns. 96 BZ83
Strafford Rd, Twick. 117 CG87
Strafford St E14 203 P4
Strafford St E14 103 EA75
Strahan Rd E3 85 DY69
Straight, The, Sthl. 96 BX75
Straight Rd, Rom. 52 FJ52
Straight Rd, Wind. 112 AU85
Straightsmouth SE10 103 EC80
Strait Rd E6 86 EL73
Straker's Rd SE15 102 DV84
Strand WC2 199 P1
Strand WC2 83 DL73
Strand Cl, Epsom 172 CR119
Strand La WC2 196 C10
Strand on the Grn W4 98 CN79
Strand Pl N18 46 DR49
Strand Sch App W4 98 CN79
Thames Rd
Strandfield Cl SE18 105 ES78
Strangeways, Wat. 23 BS36
Strangways Ter W14 99 CZ76
Melbury Rd
Stranraer Gdns, Slou. 74 AS74
Stranraer Rd, Houns. 114 BL86
Stranraer Way N1 83 DL66
Strasburg Rd SW11 101 DH81
Stratfield Pk Cl N21 45 DP45
Stratfield Rd, Borwd. 26 CN41
Stratfield Rd, Slou. 92 AU75
Stratford Av W8 100 DA76
Stratford Rd
Stratford Av, Uxb. 76 BM68
Stratford Cen, The E15 85 ED66
Stratford Cl, Bark. 88 EU66
Stratford Cl, Dag. 89 FC66
Stratford Ct, N.Mal. 138 CR98
Kingston Rd
Stratford Gro SW15 99 CX84
Stratford Ho Av, Brom. 144 EL97
Stratford Pl W1 195 H9
Stratford Pl W1 83 DH72
Stratford Rd E13 86 EF67
Stratford Rd NW4 63 CX56
Stratford Rd W8 100 DA76
Stratford Rd, Hayes 77 BV70
Stratford Rd, Houns. 115 BP86
Stratford Rd, Sthl. 96 BY77
Stratford Rd, Th.Hth. 141 DN98
Stratford Rd, Wat. 23 BU40
Stratford Vil NW1 83 DJ66
Stratford Way, St.Alb. 8 BZ29
Stratford Way, Wat. 23 BT40
Strath Ter SW11 100 DE84
Strathan Cl SW18 119 CY86
Strathaven Rd SE12 124 EH86
Strathblaine Rd SW11 100 DD84
Strathbrook Rd SW16 121 DM94
Strathcona Rd, Wem. 61 CK61
Strathdale SW16 121 DM92
Strathdon Dr SW17 120 DD90
Strathearn Av, Hayes 95 BT80
Strathearn Av, Twick. 116 CB88
Strathearn Pl W2 194 A10
Strathearn Pl W2 82 DE73
Strathearn Rd SW19 120 DA92
Strathearn Rd, Sutt. 158 DA106
Stratheden Par SE3 104 EG80
Stratheden Rd
Stratheden Rd SE3 104 EG81
Strathfield Gdns, Bark. 87 ER65
Strathleven Rd SW2 121 DL85
Strathmore Cl, Cat. 176 DS121
Strathmore Gdns N3 44 DB53
Strathmore Gdns W8 82 DA74
Palace Gdns Ter
Strathmore Gdns, Edg. 42 CP54
Strathmore Gdns, Horn. 71 FF60
Strathmore Rd SW19 120 DA90
Strathmore Rd, Croy. 142 DQ101
Strathmore Rd, Tedd. 117 CE91
Strathnairn St SE1 202 C9
Strathnairn St SE1 102 DU77
Strathray Gdns NW3 82 DE65
Strathville Rd SW18 120 DB89
Strathyre Av SW16 141 DN97
Stratton Av, Enf. 30 DR37
Stratton Av, Wall. 159 DK109
Stratton Chase Dr, Ch.St.G. 36 AU47
Stratton Cl SW19 140 DA96
Stratton Cl, Bexh. 106 EY83
Stratton Cl, Edg. 42 CM51
Stratton Cl, Houns. 96 BZ81
Stratton Cl, Walt. 136 BW102
St. Johns Dr
Stratton Dr, Bark. 69 ET64
Stratton Gdns, Sthl. 78 BZ72
Stratton Rd SW19 140 DA96
Stratton Rd, Bexh. 106 EY83
Stratton Rd, Rom. 52 FN50
Stratton Rd, Sun. 135 BT96
Stratton St W1 199 J2
Stratton St W1 83 DH74
Stratton Ter, West. 189 EQ127
High St
Stratton Wk, Rom. 52 FN50
Strattondale St E14 204 D6
Strattondale St E14 103 EC76
Strauss Rd W4 98 CR75
Straw Cl, Cat. 176 DQ123
Strawberry Flds, Swan. 147 FE95
Strawberry Hill, Twick. 117 CF90
Strawberry Hill Cl, Twick. 117 CF90
Strawberry Hill Rd, Twick. 117 CF90
Strawberry La, Cars. 140 DF104
Strawberry Vale N2 44 DD53
Strawberry Vale, Twick. 117 CG90
Strayfield Rd, Enf. 29 DP37
Streakes Fld Rd NW2 63 CU61
Stream Cl, W.Byf. 152 BK112
Stream La, Edg. 42 CP50
Streamdale SE2 106 EU79
Streamside Cl N9 46 DT46
Streamside Cl, Brom. 144 EG98
Streamway, Belv. 106 FA79
Streatfield Av E6 87 EM67
Streatfield Rd, Har. 61 CK55
Streatham Cl SW16 121 DL89
Streatham Common N SW16 121 DL92
Streatham Common S SW16 121 DL93
Streatham Ct SW16 121 DL90
Streatham High Rd SW16 121 DL92
Streatham Hill SW2 121 DL89
Streatham Pl SW2 121 DL87
Streatham Rd SW16 140 DG95
Streatham Rd, Mitch. 140 DG95
Streatham St WC1 195 N8
Streatham St WC1 83 DK72
Streatham Vale SW16 121 DJ94
Streathbourne Rd SW17 120 DG89
Streatley Pl NW3 64 DC63
New End Sq
Streatley Rd NW6 81 CZ66
Street, The, Ash. 172 CL119
Street, The, Dart. 148 FP98
Street, The, Kings L. 6 BG31
Street, The, Lthd. 171 CD122
Streeters La, Wall. 141 DK104
Streetfield Ms SE3 104 EG83
Streimer Rd E15 85 EC68
Strelley Way W3 80 CS73
Stretton Pl, Amer. 20 AT38
Stretton Rd, Croy. 142 DS101
Stretton Rd, Rich. 117 CJ89
Stretton Way, Borwd. 26 CL38
Strickland Av, Dart. 108 FL83
Strickland Row SW18 120 DD87
Strickland St SE8 103 EA82
Strickland Way, Orp. 163 ET105
Stride Rd E13 86 EF68
Stringhams Copse, Wok. 167 BF124
Stripling Way, Wat. 23 BU44
Strode Cl N10 44 DG52
Pembroke Rd
Strode Rd E7 68 EG63
Strode Rd N17 46 DS54
Strode Rd NW10 81 CU65
Strode Rd SW6 99 CX80
Strode St, Egh. 113 BA91
Strodes Coll La, Egh. 113 AZ92
Strodes Cres, Stai. 114 BJ92
Strone Rd E7 86 EJ65
Strone Rd E12 86 EK65
Strone Way, Hayes 78 BY70
Strongbow Cres SE9 125 EM85
Strongbow Rd SE9 125 EM85
Strongbridge Cl, Har. 60 CA60
Stronsa Rd W12 99 CT75
Strood Av, Rom. 71 FD60
Stroud Cres SW15 119 CU90
Stroud Fld, Nthlt. 78 BY65
Stroud Gate, Har. 60 CB63
Stroud Grn Gdns, Croy. 142 DW101
Stroud Grn Rd N4 65 DM60
Stroud Grn Way, Croy. 142 DV101
Stroud Rd SE25 142 DU100
Stroud Rd SW19 120 DA90
Stroud Way, Ashf. 115 BP93
Courtfield Rd
Stroude Rd, Egh. 113 BA93
Stroude Rd, Vir.W. 132 AY98
Stroudes Cl, Wor.Pk. 138 CS101
Stroudley Wk E3 85 EB69
Strouds Cl (Chadwell Heath), Rom. 70 EV57
Stroudwater Pk, Wey. 153 BP107
Strouts Pl E2 197 P2
Struan Gdns, Wok. 166 AY115
Strutton Grd SW1 199 M6
Strutton Grd SW1 101 DK76
Struttons Av, Grav. 131 GF89
Strype St E1 197 P7
Stuart Av NW9 63 CU59
Stuart Av W5 80 CM74
Stuart Av, Brom. 144 EG102
Stuart Av, Har. 60 BZ62
Stuart Av, Walt. 135 BV102
Stuart Cl, Brwd. 54 FV43
Stuart Cl, Swan. 127 FF94
Stuart Cl, Uxb. 76 BN65
Stuart Ct (Elstree), Borwd. 25 CK44
High St
Stuart Cres N22 45 DM53
Stuart Cres, Croy. 143 DZ104
Stuart Cres, Hayes 77 BQ72
Stuart Evans Cl, Well. 106 EW83
Stuart Gro, Tedd. 117 CE92
Stuart Mantle Way, Erith 107 FD80
Stuart Pl, Mitch. 140 DF95
Stuart Rd NW6 82 DA69
Stuart Rd SE15 102 DW84
Stuart Rd SW19 120 DA90
Stuart Rd W3 80 CQ74
Stuart Rd, Bark. 87 ET66
Stuart Rd, Barn. 44 DE45
Stuart Rd, Grav. 131 GG86
Stuart Rd, Grays 110 GB78
Stuart Rd, Har. 41 CF54
Stuart Rd, Rich. 117 CH89
Stuart Rd, Th.Hth. 142 DQ98
Stuart Rd, Warl. 176 DV120
Stuart Rd, Well. 106 EV81
Stuart Twr W9 82 DC69
Stuart Way, Stai. 114 BH93
Stuart Way, Vir.W. 132 AU97
Stuart Way (Cheshunt), Wal.Cr. 14 DV31
Stubbers La, Upmin. 91 FR65
Stubbings Hall La, Wal.Abb. 15 EB28
Stubbs Dr SE16 202 D10
Stubbs Dr SE16 102 DV78
Stubbs End Cl, Amer. 20 AS37
Stubbs Hill, Sev. 164 EW113
Stubbs La, Tad. 183 CZ128
Stubbs Ms, Dag. 70 EV63
Marlborough Rd
Stubbs Pt E13 86 EH70
Stubbs Way SW19 140 DD95
Brangwyn Cres
Stubbs Wd, Amer. 20 AS36
Stucley Pl NW1 83 DH66
Hawley Cres
Stucley Rd, Houns. 96 CC80
Stud Grn, Wat. 7 BV32
Studd St N1 83 DP67
Studdridge St SW6 100 DA82
Studholme Ct NW3 64 DA63
Studholme St SE15 102 DV80
Studio Ct, Borwd. 26 CQ40
Studio Pl SW1 198 E5
Studio Way, Borwd. 26 CQ40
Studios, The, Bushey 24 CA44
Studios Rd, Shep. 134 BM97
Studland SE17 201 K10
Studland Cl, Sid. 125 ET90
Studland Rd SE26 123 DX92
Studland Rd W7 79 CD72
Studland Rd, Kings.T. 118 CL93
Studland Rd, W.Byf. 152 BM113
Studland St W6 99 CV77
Studley Av E4 47 ED52
Studley Cl E5 67 DY64
Studley Ct, Sid. 126 EV92
Studley Dr, Ilf. 68 EK58
Studley Est SW4 101 DL81
Studley Gra Rd W7 97 CE75
Studley Rd E7 86 EH65
Studley Rd SW4 101 DL81
Studley Rd, Dag. 88 EX66
Stukeley Rd E7 86 EH66
Stukeley St WC2 196 A8
Stukeley St WC2 83 DL72
Stump Rd, Epp. 18 EW27
Stumps Hill La, Beck. 123 EA93
Stumps La, Whyt. 176 DS117
Sturdy Rd SE15 102 DV82
Sturge Av E17 47 EB54
Sturge St SE1 201 H4
Sturgeon Rd SE17 102 DQ78
Sturges Fld, Chis. 125 ER93
Sturgess Av NW4 63 CV59
Sturlas Way, Wal.Cr. 15 DX33
Sturmer Way N7 65 DM64
Stock Orchard Cres
Sturminster Cl, Hayes 78 BW72
Sturrock Cl N15 66 DR56
Sturry St E14 85 EB72
Sturt St N1 197 J1
Sturt St N1 84 DQ68
Sturts La, Tad. 183 CT127
Stutfield St E1 84 DU72
Stychens Cl, Red. 186 DQ133
Stychens La, Red. 186 DQ132
Stylecroft Rd, Ch.St.G. 36 AX47
Styles Gdns SW9 101 DP83
Styles Way, Beck. 143 EC98
Styventon Pl, Cher. 133 BF101
Subrosa Dr, Red. 185 DH130
Succombs Hill, Warl. 176 DV120
Succombs Hill, Whyt. 176 DV120
Succombs Pl, Warl. 176 DV120
Sudbourne Rd SW2 121 DL85
Sudbrook Gdns, Rich. 117 CK90
Sudbrook La, Rich. 118 CL88
Sudbrooke Rd SW12 120 DF86
Sudbury E6 87 EN72
Newark Knok
Sudbury Av, Wem. 61 CK62
Sudbury Ct E5 67 DY63
Sudbury Ct Dr, Har. 61 CF62
Sudbury Ct Rd, Har. 61 CF62
Sudbury Cres, Brom. 124 EG93
Sudbury Cres, Wem. 61 CH64
Sudbury Cft, Wem. 61 CF63
Sudbury Gdns, Croy. 160 DS105
Langton Way
Sudbury Hts Av, Grnf. 61 CF64
Sudbury Hill, Har. 61 CE61
Sudbury Hill Cl, Wem. 61 CE63
Sudbury Rd, Bark. 69 ET64
Sudeley St N1 196 G1
Sudeley St N1 83 DP68
Sudicamps Ct, Wal.Abb. 16 EG33
Sudlow Rd SW18 100 DA84
Sudrey St SE1 201 H5
Suez Av, Grnf. 79 CF68
Suez Rd, Enf. 31 DY42
Suffield Cl, S.Croy. 161 DX112
Suffield Rd E4 47 EB48
Suffield Rd N15 66 DT57
Suffield Rd SE20 142 DW96
Suffolk Cl, Borwd. 26 CR43
Clydesdale Cl
Suffolk Cl, St.Alb. 9 CJ25
Suffolk Ct E10 67 EA59
Suffolk Ct, Ilf. 69 ES58
Suffolk Ct, Surb. 137 CK100
St. James Rd
Suffolk La EC4 197 K10
Suffolk Pk Rd E17 67 DY56
Suffolk Pl SW1 199 N2
Suffolk Rd E13 86 EF69
Suffolk Rd N15 66 DR58
Suffolk Rd NW10 80 CS66
Suffolk Rd SE25 142 DT98
Suffolk Rd SW13 99 CT80
Suffolk Rd, Bark. 87 ER66
Suffolk Rd, Dag. 71 FC64
Suffolk Rd, Dart. 128 FL86
Suffolk Rd, Enf. 30 DV43
Suffolk Rd, Grav. 131 GK86
Suffolk Rd, Har. 60 BZ58
Suffolk Rd, Ilf. 69 ES58
Suffolk Rd, Pot.B. 11 CY32
Suffolk Rd, Sid. 126 EW93
Suffolk Rd, Wor.Pk. 139 CT103
Suffolk St E7 68 EG64
Suffolk St SW1 199 N2
Suffolk Way, Horn. 72 FN56
Suffolk Way, Sev. 191 FJ125
Sugar Bakers Ct EC3 84 DS72
Creechurch La
Sugar Ho La E15 85 EC68
Sugar Loaf Wk E2 84 DW69
Victoria Pk Sq
Sugar Quay Wk EC3 201 N1
Sugar Quay Wk EC3 84 DS73
Sugden Rd SW11 100 DG83
Sugden Rd, T.Ditt. 137 CH102
Sugden Way, Bark. 87 ET68
Sulgrave Gdns W6 99 CW75
Sulgrave Rd
Sulgrave Rd W6 99 CW75
Sulina Rd SW2 121 DL87
Sulivan Ct SW6 100 DA83
Sulivan Rd SW6 100 DA83
Sullivan Av E16 86 EK71
Sullivan Cl SW11 100 DE83
Sullivan Cl, Dart. 127 FH86
Sullivan Cl, W.Mol. 136 CA97
Victoria Av
Sullivan Cres (Harefield), Uxb. 38 BK54
Sullivan Rd SE11 200 E8
Sullivan Rd SE11 101 DP77
Sullivan Rd, Til. 111 GG81
Sullivan Way, Borwd. 25 CJ44
Sullivans Reach, Walt. 135 BT101
Sultan Rd E11 68 EH56
Sultan St SE5 102 DQ80
Sultan St, Beck. 143 DX96
Sumatra Rd NW6 64 DA64
Sumburgh Rd SW12 120 DG86
Sumburgh Way, Slou. 74 AS71
Summer Av, E.Mol. 137 CE99
Summer Gdns, E.Mol. 137 CE99
Summer Gro, Borwd. 25 CK44
Summer Hill, Borwd. 26 CN43
Summer Hill, Chis. 145 EN96
Summer Hill Vil, Chis. 145 EN95
Summer Rd, E.Mol. 137 CE99
Summer Rd, T.Ditt. 137 CF99
Summer St EC1 196 D5
Summer Trees, Sun. 135 BV95
The Av
Summercourt Rd E1 84 DW72
Summerene Cl SW16 121 DJ94
Bates Cres
Summerfield, Ash. 171 CK119
Summerfield Av NW6 81 CY68
Summerfield Cl, Add. 151 BF106
Spinney Hill
Summerfield Cl, St.Alb. 9 CJ26
Summerfield La, Surb. 137 CK103
Summerfield Pl, Cher. 151 BD107
Crawshaw Rd
Summerfield Rd W5 79 CH70
Summerfield Rd, Loug. 32 EK44
Summerfield Rd, Wat. 23 BU35
Summerfield St SE12 124 EF87
Summerfields Av N12 44 DE51
Summerhayes Cl, Wok. 150 AY114
Summerhays, Cob. 154 BX113
Summerhill Cl, Orp. 145 ES104
Summerhill Gro, Enf. 30 DS44
Summerhill Rd N15 66 DR56
Summerhill Rd, Dart. 128 FK87
Summerhill Way, Mitch. 140 DG95
Summerhouse Av, Houns. 96 BY81
Summerhouse Dr, Bex. 127 FD91
Summerhouse Dr, Dart. 127 FD91
Summerhouse La (Harefield), Uxb. 38 BG52
Summerhouse La, Wat. 24 CC40
Summerhouse La, West Dr. 94 BK79
Summerhouse Rd N16 66 DS61
Summerhouse Way, Abb.L. 7 BT30
Summerland Gdns N10 65 DH55
Summerlands Av W3 80 CQ73
Summerlay Cl, Tad. 173 CY120
Summerlee Av N2 64 DF56
Summerlee Gdns N2 64 DF56
Summerley St SW18 120 DB89
Summerly Av, Reig. 184 DA133
Burnham Dr
Summers Cl, Sutt. 158 DA108
Overton Rd
Summers Cl, Wem. 62 CP60
Summers Cl, Wey. 152 BN111
Summers La N12 44 DD52
Summers Row N12 44 DE51
Summersby Rd N6 65 DH58
Summerstown SW17 120 DC90
Summerswood Cl, Ken. 176 DR116
Longwood Rd
Summerswood La, Borwd. 10 CS34
Summerton Way SE28 88 EX72
Summerville Gdns, Sutt. 157 CZ107
Summerwood Rd, Islw. 117 CF85
Summit, The, Loug. 33 EM39
Summit Av NW9 62 CR57
Summit Cl N14 45 DJ47
Summit Cl NW9 62 CR56
Summit Cl, Edg. 42 CN52
Summit Ct NW2 63 CY64
Summit Dr, Wdf.Grn. 48 EK54
Summit Est N16 66 DU59
Summit Pl, Wey. 152 BN108
Caenshill Rd
Summit Rd E17 67 EB56
Summit Rd, Nthlt. 78 CA66
Summit Rd, Pot.B. 11 CY30
Summit Way N14 45 DH47
Summit Way SE19 122 DS94
Sumner Av SE15 102 DT81
Sumner Rd
Sumner Cl, Lthd. 171 CD124
Sumner Cl, Orp. 163 EQ105
Sumner Est SE15 102 DT80
Sumner Gdns, Croy. 141 DN102
Sumner Pl SW7 198 A9
Sumner Pl SW7 100 DD77
Sumner Pl, Add. 152 BG106
Sumner Pl Ms SW7 198 A9
Sumner Rd SE15 102 DT80
Sumner Rd, Croy. 141 DN102
Sumner Rd, Har. 60 CC59
Sumner Rd S, Croy. 141 DN102
Sumner St SE1 200 G2
Sumner St SE1 84 DQ74
Sumpter Cl NW3 82 DC65
Sun All, Rich. 98 CL84
Kew Rd
Sun Ct EC3 197 L9
Sun Ct, Erith 107 FF82
Sun Hill (Fawkham Grn), Long. 149 FU104
Sun Hill, Wok. 166 AU121
Sun La SE3 104 EH80
Sun La, Grav. 131 GJ89
Sun Pas SE16 202 B6
Sun Rd W14 99 CZ78
Sun Rd, Swans. 130 FZ86
Sun St EC2 197 M7
Sun St EC2 84 DR71
Sun St, Wal.Abb. 15 EC33
Sun St Pas EC2 197 M7
Sun Wk E1 202 B1
Sunbeam Cres W10 81 CW70
Sunbeam Rd NW10 80 CQ70
Sunbury Av NW7 42 CR50
Sunbury Av SW14 98 CR84
Sunbury Ct, Sun. 136 BX96
Sunbury Ct Island, Sun. 136 BX97
Sunbury Ct Ms, Sun. 136 BX96
Lower Hampton Rd
Sunbury Ct Rd, Sun. 136 BW96
Sunbury Cres, Felt. 115 BT91
Ryland Cl
Sunbury Gdns NW7 42 CR50
Sunbury La SW11 100 DD81
Sunbury La, Walt. 135 BU100
Sunbury Lock Ait, Walt. 135 BV98
Sunbury Rd, Felt. 115 BT90
Sunbury Rd, Sutt. 139 CX104
Sunbury St SE18 105 EM76
Sunbury Way, Felt. 116 BW92
Suncroft Pl SE26 122 DW90
Sundale Av, S.Croy. 160 DW110
Sunderland Ct SE22 122 DU87
Sunderland Mt SE23 123 DX89
Sunderland Rd
Sunderland Rd SE23 123 DX88
Sunderland Rd W5 97 CK76
Sunderland Ter W2 82 DB72
Sunderland Way E12 68 EK61

Sundew Av W12 81 CU73
Sundew Ct, Grays 110 GD79
Salix Rd
Sundial Av SE25 142 DT97
Sundon Cres, Vir.W. 132 AV99
Sundorne Rd SE7 104 EJ78
Sundown Av, S.Croy. 160 DT111
Sundown Rd, Ashf. 115 BQ92
Sundra Wk E1 85 DX70
Beaumont Gro
Sundridge Av, Brom. 124 EK94
Sundridge Av, Chis. 124 EK94
Sundridge Av, Well. 105 ER82
Sundridge Cl, Dart. 128 FN86
Sundridge Ho, Brom. 124 EH92
Burnt Ash La
Sundridge La, Sev. 180 EV117
Sundridge Pl, Croy. 142 DU102
Inglis Rd
Sundridge Rd, Croy. 142 DT101
Sundridge Rd, Sev. 180 FA120
Sundridge Rd, Wok. 167 BA119
Sunfields Pl SE3 104 EH80
Sunflower Way, Rom. 52 FK53
Sunkist Way, Wall. 159 DL109
Sunland Av, Bexh. 106 EY84
Sunleigh Rd, Wem. 80 CL67
Sunley Gdns, Grnf. 79 CG67
Sunlight Cl SW19 120 DC93
Sunlight Sq E2 84 DV69
Sunmead Cl, Lthd. 171 CF122
Sunmead Rd, Sun. 135 BU97
Sunna Gdns, Sun. 135 BV96
Sunning Hill, Grav. 130 GE89
Sunningdale N14 45 DK50
Wilmer Way
Sunningdale Av W3 80 CS73
Sunningdale Av, Bark. 87 ER67
Sunningdale Av, Felt. 116 BY89
Sunningdale Av, Rain. 89 FH70
Sunningdale Av, Ruis. 60 BW60
Sunningdale Cl E6 87 EM69
Ascot Rd
Sunningdale Cl SE16 102 DV78
Ryder Dr
Sunningdale Cl SE28 88 EY72
Sunningdale Cl, Stan. 41 CG52
Sunningdale Cl, Surb. 138 CL103
Culsac Rd
Sunningdale Gdns NW9 62 CQ57
Sunningdale Gdns W8 100 DA76
Lexham Ms
Sunningdale Rd, Brom. 144 EL98
Sunningdale Rd, Rain. 89 FG66
Sunningdale Rd, Sutt. 157 CZ105
Sunningfields Cres NW4 43 CV54
Sunningfields Rd NW4 43 CV54
Sunninghill Rd SE13 103 EB82
Sunnings La, Upmin. 90 FQ65
Sunningvale Av, West. 178 EJ115
Sunningvale Cl, West. 178 EK116
Sunny Bk SE25 142 DU97
Sunny Bk, Warl. 177 DY117
Sunny Cres NW10 80 CQ66
Sunny Gdns Par NW4 43 CW54
Great N Way
Sunny Gdns Rd NW4 43 CV54
Sunny Hill NW4 63 CV55
Sunny Nook Gdns, S.Croy. 160 DR107
Selsdon Rd
Sunny Ri, Cat. 176 DR124
Sunny Rd, The, Enf. 31 DX39
Sunny Vw NW9 62 CR57
Sunny Way N12 44 DE52
Sunnybank, Epsom 172 CQ116
Sunnybank Rd, Pot.B. 12 DA33
Sunnybank Vil, Red. 186 DT132
Sunnycroft Gdns, Upmin. 73 FT59
Sunnycroft Rd SE25 142 DU97
Sunnycroft Rd, Houns. 96 CB82
Sunnycroft Rd, Sthl. 78 CA71
Sunnydale, Orp. 145 EN103
Sunnydale Gdns NW7 42 CR51
Sunnydale Rd SE12 124 EH85
Sunnydell, St.Alb. 8 CB26
Sunnydene Av E4 47 ED50
Sunnydene Av, Ruis. 59 BU61
Sunnydene Cl, Rom. 52 FM52
Sunnydene Gdns, Wem. 79 CJ65
Sunnydene Rd, Pur. 159 DP113
Sunnydene St SE26 123 DY91
Sunnyfield NW7 43 CT49
Sunnyfield Rd, Chis. 146 EU97
Sunnyhill Cl E5 67 DY63
Sunnyhill Rd SW16 121 DL91
Sunnyhill Rd, Rick. 37 BD51
Sunnyhurst Cl, Sutt. 140 DA104
Sunnymead Av, Mitch. 141 DJ97
Sunnymead Rd NW9 62 CR59
Sunnymead Rd SW15 119 CV85
Sunnymede, Chig. 50 EV48
Sunnymede Av, Cars. 158 DD111
Sunnymede Av, Chesh. 4 AS28
Sunnymede Av, Epsom 156 CS109
Sunnymede Dr, Ilf. 69 EP56
Sunnyside NW2 63 CZ62
Sunnyside SW19 119 CY93
Sunnyside, Walt. 136 BW99
Sunnyside Cotts, Chesh. 4 AU26
Sunnyside Dr E4 47 EC45
Sunnyside Gdns, Upmin. 72 FQ61
Sunnyside Pas SW19 119 CY93
Sunnyside Pl SW19 119 CY93
Sunnyside
Sunnyside Rd E10 67 EA60
Sunnyside Rd N19 65 DK59
Sunnyside Rd W5 79 CK74
Sunnyside Rd, Epp. 17 ET32
Sunnyside Rd, Ilf. 69 EQ62
Sunnyside Rd, Tedd. 117 CD91
Sunnyside Rd E N9 46 DU48
Sunnyside Rd N N9 46 DT48
Sunnyside Rd S N9 46 DT48
Sunnyside Ter NW9 62 CR55
Edgware Rd
Sunray Av SE24 102 DR84
Sunray Av, Brwd. 55 GE44
Sunray Av, Brom. 144 EL100
Sunray Av, Surb. 138 CP103
Sunray Av, West Dr. 94 BK75
Sunrise Av, Horn. 72 FJ62
Sunrise Cl, Felt. 116 BZ90
Exeter Rd
Sunset Av E4 47 EB46
Sunset Av, Wdf.Grn. 48 EF49
Sunset Cl, Erith 107 FH81
Sunset Dr (Havering-atte-Bower), Rom. 51 FH50
Sunset Gdns SE25 142 DT96
Sunset Rd SE5 102 DQ84
Sunset Rd SE28 106 EU75
Sunset Vw, Barn. 27 CY40
Sunshine Way, Mitch. 140 DF96
Sunstone Gro, Red. 185 DL129
Sunwell Cl SE15 102 DV81
Cossall Wk
Superior Dr, Orp. 163 ET107
Surbiton Ct, Surb. 137 CJ100
Surbiton Cres, Kings.T. 138 CL98
Surbiton Hall Cl, Kings.T. 138 CL98
Surbiton Hill Pk, Surb. 138 CN99
Surbiton Hill Rd, Surb. 138 CL98
Surbiton Par, Surb. 138 CL100
St. Mark's Hill
Surbiton Rd, Kings.T. 138 CL98
Surlingham Cl SE28 88 EX73
Surma Cl E1 84 DV70
Surman Cres, Brwd. 55 GC45
Surmans Cl, Dag. 88 EV67
Goresbrook Rd
Surr St N7 65 DL64
Surrendale Pl W9 82 DA70
Surrey Canal Rd SE14 102 DW79
Surrey Canal Rd SE15 102 DW79
Surrey Cres W4 98 CN78
Surrey Dr, Horn. 72 FN56
Surrey Gdns N4 66 DQ58
Finsbury Pk Av
Surrey Gdns, Lthd. 169 BT123
Surrey Gro SE17 102 DS78
Surrey Sq
Surrey Gro, Sutt. 140 DD104
Surrey Hills, Tad. 182 CP130
Surrey Hills Av, Tad. 182 CQ130
Surrey La SW11 100 DE81
Surrey La Est SW11 100 DE81
Surrey Lo SE1 200 D7
Surrey Ms SE27 122 DS91
Hamilton Rd
Surrey Mt SE23 122 DV88
Surrey Quays Rd SE16 203 H5
Surrey Quays Rd SE16 103 DX75
Surrey Rd SE15 123 DX85
Surrey Rd, Bark. 87 ES67
Surrey Rd, Dag. 71 FB64
Surrey Rd, Har. 60 CC57
Surrey Rd, W.Wick. 143 EB102
Surrey Row SE1 200 F4
Surrey Row SE1 101 DP75
Surrey Sq SE17 201 M10
Surrey Sq SE17 102 DS78
Surrey St E13 86 EH69
Surrey St WC2 196 C10
Surrey St WC2 83 DM73
Surrey St, Croy. 142 DQ104
Surrey Ter SE17 201 N10
Surrey Ter SE17 102 DS78
Surrey Twr SE20 122 DW94
Surrey Twrs, Add. 152 BJ106
Garfield Rd
Surrey Water Rd SE16 203 J3
Surrey Water Rd SE16 85 DX74
Surridge Cl, Rain. 90 FJ69
Surridge Gdns SE19 122 DR93
Hancock Rd
Susan Cl, Rom. 71 FC55
Susan Rd SE3 104 EH82
Susan Wd, Chis. 145 EN95
Susannah St E14 85 EB72
Sussex Av, Islw. 97 CE83
Sussex Av, Rom. 52 FM52
Sussex Cl N19 65 DL61
Cornwallis Rd
Sussex Cl, Ch.St.G. 36 AV47
Sussex Cl, Ilf. 69 EM57
Sussex Cl, N.Mal. 138 CS98
Sussex Cl, Slou. 92 AV75
Sussex Cl, Twick. 117 CH86
Westmorland Cl
Sussex Cres, Nthlt. 78 CA65
Sussex Gdns N4 66 DQ57
Sussex Gdns N6 64 DF57
Great N Rd
Sussex Gdns W2 82 DD72
Sussex Gdns, Chess. 155 CK107
Sussex Keep, Slou. 92 AV75
Sussex Cl
Sussex Ms E W2 194 A9
Sussex Ms W W2 194 A10
Sussex Pl NW1 194 D4
Sussex Pl NW1 82 DF70
Sussex Pl W2 194 A9
Sussex Pl W2 82 DD72
Sussex Pl W6 99 CW78
Sussex Pl, Erith 107 FB80
Sussex Pl, N.Mal. 138 CS98
Sussex Pl, Slou. 92 AV75
Sussex Ring N12 44 DA50
Sussex Rd E6 87 EN67
Sussex Rd, Brwd. 54 FV49
Sussex Rd, Cars. 158 DF107
Sussex Rd, Dart. 128 FN87
Sussex Rd, Erith 107 FB80
Sussex Rd, Har. 60 CC57
Sussex Rd, Mitch. 141 DL99
Lincoln Rd
Sussex Rd, N.Mal. 138 CS98
Sussex Rd, Orp. 146 EW100
Sussex Rd, Sid. 126 EV92
Sussex Rd, S.Croy. 160 DR107
Sussex Rd, Sthl. 96 BX76
Sussex Rd, Uxb. 59 BQ63
Sussex Rd, Wat. 23 BU38
Sussex Rd, W.Wick. 143 EB102
Sussex Sq W2 194 A10
Sussex Sq W2 82 DD73
Sussex St E13 86 EH69
Sussex St SW1 101 DH78
Sussex Wk SW9 101 DP84
Sussex Way N7 65 DL61
Sussex Way N19 65 DL60
Sussex Way, Barn. 28 DG43
Sussex Way (Denham), Uxb. 57 BF57
Sutcliffe Cl NW11 64 DB57
Sutcliffe Cl, Bushey 24 CC42
Sutcliffe Ho, Hayes 77 BU72
Sutcliffe Rd SE18 105 ES79
Sutcliffe Rd, Well. 106 EW82
Sutherland Av W9 82 DC69
Sutherland Av W13 79 CH72
Sutherland Av, Hayes 95 BU77
Sutherland Av, Orp. 145 ET100
Sutherland Av (Cuffley), Pot.B. 13 DK28
Sutherland Av, Sun. 135 BT96
Sutherland Av, Well. 105 ES84
Sutherland Av, West. 178 EK117
Sutherland Cl, Barn. 27 CY42
Sutherland Cl, Green. 129 FT85
Sutherland Ct NW9 62 CP57
Sutherland Dr SW19 140 DD95
Willow Vw
Sutherland Gdns SW14 98 CS83
Sutherland Gdns, Sun. 135 BT96
Sutherland Av
Sutherland Gdns, Wor.Pk. 139 CV102
Sutherland Gro SW18 119 CY86
Sutherland Gro, Tedd. 117 CE92
Sutherland Pl W2 82 DA72
Sutherland Pt E5 66 DV63
Tiger Way
Sutherland Rd E17 47 DX54
Sutherland Rd N9 46 DU46
Sutherland Rd N17 46 DU52
Sutherland Rd W4 98 CS79
Sutherland Rd W13 79 CG72
Sutherland Rd, Belv. 106 FA76
Sutherland Rd, Croy. 141 DN101
Sutherland Rd, Enf. 31 DX43
Sutherland Rd, Sthl. 78 BZ72
Sutherland Rd Path E17 67 DX55
Sutherland Row SW1 199 J10
Sutherland Row SW1 101 DH78
Sutherland Sq SE17 102 DQ78
Sutherland St SW1 199 H10
Sutherland St SW1 101 DH78
Sutherland Wk SE17 102 DQ78
Sutherland Way (Cuffley), Pot.B. 13 DK28
Sutlej Rd SE7 104 EJ80
Sutterton St N7 83 DM65
Sutton Av, Slou. 92 AW75
Sutton Av, Wok. 166 AS119
Sutton Cl, Beck. 143 EB95
Albemarle Rd
Sutton Cl, Loug. 48 EL45
Sutton Cl, Pnr. 59 BU57
Sutton Common Rd, Sutt 139 CZ101
Sutton Ct W4 98 CQ79
Sutton Ct Rd E13 86 EJ69
Sutton Ct Rd W4 98 CQ80
Sutton Ct Rd, Sutt. 158 DC107
Sutton Ct Rd, Uxb. 77 BP67
Sutton Cres, Barn. 27 CX43
Sutton Dene, Houns. 96 CB81
Sutton Est SW3 198 C10
Sutton Est SW3 100 DE78
Sutton Est W10 81 CW71
Sutton Est, The N1 83 DP66
Sutton Gdns, Bark. 87 ES67
Sutton Rd
Sutton Gdns, Croy. 142 DT99
Sutton Gdns, Red. 185 DK129
Sutton Grn, Bark. 87 ES67
Sutton Rd
Sutton Gro, Sutt. 158 DD105
Sutton Hall Rd, Houns. 96 CA80
Sutton La, Bans. 174 DB115
Sutton La, Houns. 96 BZ83
Sutton La, Slou. 93 BC78
Sutton La, Sutt. 158 DB111
Sutton La N W4 98 CQ78
Sutton La S W4 98 CQ79
Sutton Par NW4 63 CW56
Church Rd
Sutton Pk Rd, Sutt. 158 DB107
Sutton Path, Borwd. 26 CN40
Stratfield Rd
Sutton Pl E9 66 DW64
Sutton Pl, Slou. 93 BB79
Sutton Rd E13 86 EF70
Sutton Rd E17 47 DX53
Sutton Rd N10 44 DG54
Sutton Rd, Bark. 87 ES68
Sutton Rd, Houns. 96 CA81
Sutton Rd, Wat. 24 BW41
Sutton Row W1 195 N8
Sutton Row W1 83 DK72
Sutton Sq E9 66 DW64
Urswick Rd
Sutton Sq, Houns. 96 BZ81
Sutton St E1 84 DW72
Sutton Way W10 81 CW71
Sutton Way, Houns. 96 BZ81
Suttons Av, Horn. 72 FJ62
Suttons Gdns, Horn. 72 FK62
Suttons La, Horn. 72 FK64
Sutton's Way EC1 197 J5
Swabey Rd, Slou. 93 BA77
Swaby Rd SW18 120 DC88
Swaffham Way N22 45 DP52
White Hart La
Swaffield Rd SW18 120 DB87
Swaffield Rd, Sev. 191 FJ122
Swain Cl SW16 121 DH93
Swain Rd, Th.Hth. 142 DQ99
Swains Cl, West Dr. 94 BL75
Swains La N6 64 DG62
Swains Rd SW17 120 DF94
Swainson Rd W3 99 CT75
Swaisland Dr, Dart. 127 FF85
Swaisland Rd, Dart. 127 FH85
Swakeleys Dr, Uxb. 58 BN63
Swakeleys Rd (Ickenham), Uxb. 58 BM62
Swale Cl, S.Ock. 90 FQ72
Swale Rd, Dart. 107 FG83
Swaledale Cl N11 44 DG51
Ribblesdale Av
Swaledale Rd, Dart. 128 FQ88
Swallands Rd SE6 123 EA90
Swallow Cl SE14 102 DW81
Swallow Cl, Bushey 40 CC46
Swallow Cl, Erith 107 FE81
Swallow Cl (Chafford Hundred), Grays 109 FW77
Swallow Cl, Green. 129 FT85
Swallow Cl, Rick. 38 BJ45
Swallow Cl, Stai. 113 BF91
Swallow Dr NW10 80 CR65
Kingfisher Way
Swallow Dr, Nthlt. 78 CA68
Swallow Gdns SW16 121 DK92
Swallow Pas W1 195 J9
Swallow Pl W1 195 J9
Swallow St E6 86 EL71
Swallow St W1 199 L1
Swallow St, Iver 75 BD69
Swallow Wk, Horn. 89 FH65
Heron Flight Av
Swallowdale, Iver 75 BD69
Swallowdale, S.Croy. 161 DX109
Swallowfield, Egh. 112 AV93
Heronfield
Swallowfield Rd SE7 104 EH78
Swallowfield Way, Hayes 95 BR75
Swallowfields, Grav. 130 GE90
Hillary Av
Swallows Oak, Abb.L. 7 BT31
Swallowtail Cl, Orp. 146 EX98
Swan & Pike Rd, Enf. 31 EA38
Swan App E6 86 EL71
Swan Av, Upmin. 73 FT60
Swan Cl E17 47 DY53
Swan Cl, Croy. 142 DS101
Swan Cl, Felt. 116 BY91
Swan Cl, Orp. 146 EU97
Swan Cl, Rick. 38 BK45
Parsonage Rd
Swan Ct SW3 100 DE78
Flood St
Swan Dr NW9 42 CS54
Swan La EC4 201 K1
Swan La N20 44 DC48
Swan La, Dart. 127 FF87
Swan La, Loug. 48 EJ45
Swan Mead SE1 201 M7
Swan Mead SE1 102 DS76
Swan Pas E1 84 DT73
Cartwright St
Swan Path E10 67 EC60
Jesse Rd
Swan Pl SW13 99 CT82
Swan Rd SE16 202 G4
Swan Rd SE16 102 DW75
Swan Rd SE18 104 EK76
Swan Rd, Felt. 116 BY92
Swan Rd, Iver 75 BF72
Swan Rd, Sthl. 78 CB72
Swan Rd, West Dr. 94 BK75
Swan St SE1 201 J6
Swan St SE1 102 DQ76
Swan St, Islw. 97 CH83
Swan Wk SW3 100 DF79
Swan Wk, Rom. 71 FE57
Swan Wk, Shep. 135 BS101
Swan Way, Enf. 31 DX40
Swan Yd N1 83 DP65
Highbury Sta Rd
Swanage Rd E4 47 EC52
Swanage Rd SW18 120 DC86
Swanage Waye, Hayes 78 BW72
Swanbourne Dr, Horn. 72 FJ64
Swanbridge Rd, Bexh. 106 FA81
Swandon Way SW18 100 DB84
Swanfield Rd, Wal.Cr. 15 DY33
Swanfield St E2 197 P3
Swanfield St E2 84 DT69
Swanland Rd, Hat. 11 CV31
Swanland Rd, Pot.B. 11 CV33
Swanley Bar La, Pot.B. 12 DB28
Swanley Bypass, Sid. 147 FC97
Swanley Bypass, Swan. 147 FC97
Swanley Cen, Swan. 147 FE97
Swanley Cres, Pot.B. 12 DB29
Swanley La, Swan. 147 FF97
Swanley Rd, Well. 106 EW81
Swanley Village Rd, Swan. 147 FH95
Swanscombe Rd W4 98 CS78
Swanscombe Rd W11 81 CX74
Swanscombe St, Swans. 130 FY87
Swansea Ct E16 105 EP75
Barge Ho Rd
Swansea Rd, Enf. 30 DW42
Swansea Rd, Houns. 115 BQ86
Southern Perimeter Rd
Swanshope, Loug. 33 EP40
Swansland Gdns E17 47 DY53
McEntee Av
Swanston Path, Wat. 40 BW48
Swanton Gdns SW19 119 CX88
Swanton Rd, Erith 107 FB80
Swanwick Cl SW15 119 CT87
Sward Rd, Orp. 146 EU100
Swaton Rd E3 85 EA70
Swaylands Rd, Belv. 106 FA79
Swaynesland Rd, Eden. 189 EM134
Swaythling Cl N18 46 DV49
Sweden Gate SE16 203 L8
Sweden Gate SE16 103 DY76
Swedenborg Gdns E1 84 DU73
Sweeney Cres SE1 202 A5
Sweeney Cres SE1 102 DT75
Sweeps Ditch Cl, Stai. 134 BG95
Sweeps La, Egh. 113 AZ92
Sweeps La, Orp. 146 EX99
Sweet Briar Grn N9 46 DT48
Sweet Briar Gro N9 46 DT48
Sweet Briar La, Epsom 156 CR114
Sweet Briar Wk N18 46 DT49
Sweetcroft La, Uxb. 76 BN66
Sweetmans Av, Pnr. 60 BX55
Sweets Way N20 44 DD47
Swete St E13 86 EG68
Swetenham Wk SE18 105 EQ78
Sandbach Pl
Sweyn Pl SE3 104 EG82
Sweyne Rd, Swans. 130 FY86
Swievelands Rd, West. 178 EH119
Swift Cl E17 47 DY52
Swift Cl, Har. 60 CB61
Swift Cl, Hayes 77 BT72
Church Rd
Swift Cl, Upmin. 73 FS60
Swift Rd, Felt. 116 BY90
Swift Rd, Sthl. 96 BZ76
Swift St SW6 99 CZ81
Swiftsden Way, Brom. 124 EE93
Swiftsure Rd (Chafford Hundred), Grays 109 FW77
Swinbrook Rd W10 81 CY71
Swinburne Ct SE5 102 DR84
Basingdon Way
Swinburne Cres, Croy. 142 DW100
Swinburne Gdns, Til. 111 GH82
Swinburne Rd SW15 99 CU84
Swinderby Rd, Wem. 80 CL65
Swindon Cl, Ilf. 69 ES61
Salisbury Rd
Swindon Cl, Rom. 52 FM50
Swindon Gdns, Rom. 52 FM50
Swindon La, Rom. 52 FM50
Swindon Rd, Houns. 115 BQ85
Swindon St W12 81 CV74
Swinfield Cl, Felt. 116 BY91
Swinford Gdns SW9 101 DP83
Swingate La SE18 105 ES79
Swinnerton St E9 67 DY64
Swinton Cl, Wem. 62 CP60
Swinton Pl WC1 196 B2
Swinton Pl WC1 83 DM69
Swinton St WC1 196 B2
Swinton St WC1 83 DM69
Swires Shaw, Kes. 162 EK105
Swiss Av, Wat. 23 BS42
Swiss Cl, Wat. 23 BS41
Swiss Ter NW6 82 DD66
Swithland Gdns SE9 125 EN91
Swyncombe Av W5 97 CH77
Swynford Gdns NW4 63 CU56
Handowe Cl
Sybil Ms N4 65 DP58
Lothair Rd N
Sybil Phoenix Cl SE8 203 J10
Sybil Phoenix Cl SE8 103 DX78
Sybil Thorndike Ho N1 84 DQ65
Clephane Rd
Sybourn St E17 67 DZ59
Sycamore App, Rick. 23 BQ43
Sycamore Av W5 97 CK76
Sycamore Av, Hayes 77 BS73
Sycamore Av, Sid. 125 ET86
Sycamore Av, Upmin. 72 FN62
Sycamore Cl E16 86 EE70
Clarence Rd
Sycamore Cl N9 46 DU49
Pycroft Way
Sycamore Cl SE9 124 EL89
Sycamore Cl W3 80 CS74
Bromyard Av
Sycamore Cl, Barn. 28 DD44
Sycamore Cl, Bushey 24 BY40
Sycamore Cl, Cars. 158 DF105
Sycamore Cl, Ch.St.G. 36 AU48
Sycamore Cl, Edg. 42 CQ49
Ash Cl
Sycamore Cl, Felt. 115 BU90
Sycamore Cl, Grav. 131 GK87
Sycamore Cl, Lthd. 171 CE123
Sycamore Cl, Loug. 33 EP40
Cedar Dr
Sycamore Cl, Nthlt. 78 BY67
Sycamore Cl, Wal.Cr. 14 DT27
Sycamore Cl, Wat. 23 BV35
Sycamore Cl, West Dr. 76 BM73
Whitethorn Av
Sycamore Ct, Surb. 138 CL101
Penners Gdns
Sycamore Dr, Brwd. 54 FW46
Copperfield Gdns
Sycamore Dr, St.Alb. 9 CD27
Sycamore Dr, Swan. 147 FE97
Sycamore Gdns W6 99 CV75
Sycamore Gdns, Mitch. 140 DD96
Sycamore Gro NW9 62 CQ59
Sycamore Gro SE6 123 EC86
Sycamore Gro SE20 122 DU94
Sycamore Gro, N.Mal. 138 CR97
Sycamore Hill N11 44 DG51
Sycamore Ms SW4 101 DJ83
Sycamore Ri, Bans. 157 CX114
Sycamore Ri, Ch.St.G. 36 AU48
Sycamore Rd SW19 119 CW93
Sycamore Rd, Ch.St.G. 36 AU48
Sycamore Rd, Dart. 128 FK88
Sycamore Rd, Rick. 23 BQ43
Sycamore St EC1 197 H5
Sycamore Wk W10 81 CY70
Fifth Av
Sycamore Wk, Egh. 112 AV93
Sycamore Wk, Ilf. 69 EQ56
Civic Way
Sycamore Wk, Slou. 74 AY72
Sycamore Way, S.Ock. 91 FX70
Sycamore Way, Tedd. 117 CJ93
Sycamore Way, Th.Hth. 141 DN99
Sycamores, The, Rad. 9 CH34
The Av
Sycamores, The, S.Ock. 91 FR74
Dacre Av
Sydenham Av N21 29 DM43
Sydenham Av SE26 122 DV92
Sydenham Cl, Rom. 71 FF56
Sydenham Cotts SE12 124 EJ89
Sydenham Hill SE23 122 DV88
Sydenham Hill SE26 122 DU90
Sydenham Hill Est SE26 122 DU90
Sydenham Pk SE26 122 DW90
Sydenham Pk Rd SE26 122 DW90
Sydenham Ri SE23 122 DV89
Sydenham Rd SE26 122 DW92
Sydenham Rd, Croy. 142 DR101
Sydmons Ct SE23 122 DW87
Sydner Ms N16 66 DT63
Sydner Rd
Sydner Rd N16 66 DT63
Sydney Av, Pur. 159 DM112
Sydney Cl SW3 198 A9
Sydney Cl SW3 100 DD77
Sydney Cres, Ashf. 115 BP93
Sydney Gro NW4 63 CW57
Sydney Ms SW3 198 A9
Sydney Ms SW3 100 DD77
Sydney Pl SW7 198 A9

Sydney Pl SW7 100 DD77
Sydney Rd E11 68 EH58
Mansfield Rd
Sydney Rd N8 65 DN56
Sydney Rd N10 44 DG53
Sydney Rd SE2 106 EW76
Sydney Rd SW20 139 CX96
Sydney Rd W13 79 CG74
Sydney Rd, Bexh. 106 EX84
Sydney Rd, Enf. 30 DR42
Sydney Rd, Felt. 115 BU88
Sydney Rd, Ilf. 49 EQ54
Sydney Rd, Rich. 98 CL84
Sydney Rd, Sid. 125 ES91
Sydney Rd, Sutt. 158 DA105
Sydney Rd, Tedd. 117 CF92
Sydney Rd, Til. 111 GG82
Sydney Rd, Wat. 23 BS43
Sydney Rd, Wdf.Grn. 48 EG49
Sydney St SW3 198 B10
Sydney St SW3 100 DE77
Syke Cluan, Iver 93 BE75
Syke Ings, Iver 93 BE76
Sykes Dr, Stai. 114 BH92
Sylvan Av N3 44 DA54
Sylvan Av N22 45 DM52
Sylvan Av NW7 43 CT51
Sylvan Av, Horn. 72 FL58
Sylvan Av, Rom. 70 EZ58
Sylvan Cl, Grays 110 FY77
Warren La
Sylvan Cl, Oxt. 188 EH129
Sylvan Cl, S.Croy. 160 DV110
Sylvan Cl, Wok. 167 BB117
Sylvan Est SE19 142 DT95
Sylvan Gdns, Surb. 137 CK101
Sylvan Gro NW2 63 CX63
Sylvan Gro SE15 102 DV79
Sylvan Hill SE19 142 DS95
Sylvan Rd E7 86 EG65
Sylvan Rd E11 68 EG57
Sylvan Rd E17 67 EA57
Sylvan Rd SE19 142 DT95
Sylvan Rd, Ilf. 69 EQ61
Hainault St
Sylvan Wk, Brom. 145 EM97
Sylvan Way, Chig. 50 EV48
Sylvan Way, Dag. 70 EV62
Sylvan Way, W.Wick. 162 EE105
Sylvana Cl, Uxb. 76 BM67
Sylverdale Rd, Croy. 141 DP104
Sylverdale Rd, Pur. 159 DP113
Sylvester Av, Chis. 125 EM93
Sylvester Gdns, Ilf. 50 EV50
Sylvester Path E8 84 DV65
Sylvester Rd
Sylvester Rd E8 84 DV65
Sylvester Rd E17 67 DZ59
Sylvester Rd N2 44 DC54
Sylvester Rd, Wem. 61 CJ64
Sylvestres, Sev. 190 FD121
Sylvestrus Cl, Kings.T. 138 CN95
Sylvia Av, Brwd. 55 GC47
Sylvia Av, Pnr. 40 BZ51
Sylvia Ct, Wem. 80 CP66
Harrow Rd
Sylvia Gdns, Wem. 80 CP66
Symes Ms NW1 83 DJ68
Camden High St
Symonds Ct (Cheshunt), Wal.Cr. 15 DX28
High St
Symons St SW3 198 E9
Symons St SW3 100 DF77
Syon Gate Way, Brent. 97 CG80
Syon La, Islw. 97 CH80
Syon Pk Gdns, Islw. 97 CF80
Syon Vista, Rich. 97 CK81
Syracuse Av, Rain. 90 FL69
Syringa Ct, Grays 110 GD80
Sythwood, Wok. 166 AV117

T

Tabard Cen SE1 102 DR76
Prioress St
Tabard Gdn Est SE1 201 L5
Tabard Gdn Est SE1 102 DR75
Tabard St SE1 201 K5
Tabard St SE1 102 DR75
Tabarin Way, Epsom 173 CW116
Tabernacle Av E13 86 EG70
Barking Rd
Tabernacle St EC2 197 L5
Tabernacle St EC2 84 DR70
Tableer Av SW4 121 DK85
Tabley Rd N7 65 DL63
Tabor Gdns, Sutt. 157 CZ107
Tabor Gro SW19 119 CY94
Tabor Rd W6 99 CV76
Tabors Ct, Brwd. 55 FZ45
Shenfield Rd
Tabrums Way, Upmin. 73 FS59
Tachbrook Est SW1 101 DK78
Tachbrook Ms SW1 199 K8
Tachbrook Rd, Felt. 115 BT87
Tachbrook Rd, Sthl. 96 BX77
Tachbrook Rd, Uxb. 76 BJ68
Tachbrook St SW1 199 L9
Tachbrook St SW1 101 DJ77
Tack Ms SE4 103 EA83
Tadema Rd SW10 100 DC80
Tadlows Cl, Upmin. 72 FP64
Tadmor Cl, Sun. 135 BT98
Tadmor St W12 81 CX74
Tadorne Rd, Tad. 173 CW121
Tadworth Av, N.Mal. 139 CT99
Tadworth Cl, Tad. 173 CX122
Tadworth Par, Horn. 71 FH63
Maylands Av
Tadworth Rd NW2 63 CU61
Tadworth St, Tad. 173 CW123
Taeping St E14 204 B8
Taeping St E14 103 EB77
Taffy's How, Mitch. 140 DE97
Taft Way E3 85 EB69
St. Leonards St
Tagalie Pl (Shenley), Rad. 10 CL32
Porters Pk Dr
Tagg's Island, Hmptn. 137 CD96
Tailworth St E1 84 DU71
Chicksand St
Tait Rd, Croy. 142 DS101
Takeley Cl, Rom. 51 FD54
Takeley Cl, Wal.Abb. 15 ED33
Takhar Ms SW11 100 DE82
Cabul Rd
Talacre Rd NW5 82 DG65
Talbot Av N2 64 DD55
Talbot Av, Slou. 93 AZ76
Talbot Av, Wat. 40 BY45
Talbot Cl N15 66 DT56
Talbot Ct EC3 197 L10
Talbot Cres NW4 63 CU57
Talbot Gdns, Ilf. 70 EU61
Talbot Ho E14 85 EB72
Giraud St
Talbot Pl SE3 104 EE82
Talbot Pl, Slou. 92 AW81
Talbot Rd E6 87 EN68
Talbot Rd E7 68 EG63
Talbot Rd N6 64 DG58
Talbot Rd N15 66 DT56
Talbot Rd N22 45 DJ54
Talbot Rd SE22 102 DS84
Talbot Rd W2 81 CZ72
Talbot Rd W11 81 CZ72
Talbot Rd W13 79 CG73
Talbot Rd, Ashf. 114 BK92
Talbot Rd, Brom. 144 EH98
Masons Hill
Talbot Rd, Cars. 158 DG106
Talbot Rd, Dag. 88 EZ65
Talbot Rd, Har. 41 CF54
Talbot Rd, Islw. 97 CG84
Talbot Rd, Rick. 38 BL46
Talbot Rd, Sthl. 96 BY77
Talbot Rd, Th.Hth. 142 DR98
Talbot Rd, Twick. 117 CE88
Talbot Rd, Wem. 61 CK64
Talbot Sq W2 194 A9
Talbot Sq W2 82 DD72
Talbot Wk NW10 80 CS65
Garnet Rd
Talbot Wk W11 81 CY72
Talbot Yd SE1 201 K3
Talbrook, Brwd. 54 FT48
Taleworth Cl, Ash. 171 CK120
Taleworth Pk, Ash. 171 CK120
Taleworth Rd, Ash. 171 CK119
Talfourd Pl SE15 102 DT81
Talfourd Rd SE15 102 DT81
Talgarth Rd W6 99 CY78
Talgarth Rd W14 99 CY78
Talgarth Wk NW9 62 CS57
Talisman Cl, Ilf. 70 EV60
Talisman Sq SE26 122 DU91
Talisman Way, Epsom 173 CW116
Talisman Way, Wem. 62 CM62
Tall Elms Cl, Brom. 144 EF99
Tall Trees SW16 141 DM97
Tall Trees, Slou. 93 BE81
Tall Trees Cl, Horn. 72 FK58
Tallack Cl, Har. 41 CE52
College Hill Rd
Tallack Rd E10 67 DZ60
Tallents Cl (Sutton at Hone), Dart. 128 FP94
Tallis Cl E16 86 EH72
Tallis Gro SE7 104 EH79
Tallis St EC4 196 E10
Tallis St EC4 83 DN73
Tallis Vw NW10 80 CR65
Tallis Way, Borwd. 25 CK39
Tallon Rd, Brwd. 55 GE43
Tally Ho Cor N12 44 DC50
Tally Rd, Oxt. 188 EL131
Talma Gdns, Twick. 117 CE86
Talma Rd SW2 101 DN84
Talmage Cl SE23 122 DW87
Tyson Rd
Talman Gro, Stan. 41 CK51
Talus Cl, Purf. 109 FR77
Brimfield Rd
Talwin St E3 85 EB69
Tamar Cl E3 85 DZ67
Lefevre Wk
Tamar Cl, Upmin. 73 FS58
Tamar Dr, S.Ock. 90 FQ72
Tamar Sq, Wdf.Grn. 48 EH51
Tamar St SE7 104 EL76
Woolwich Rd
Tamar Way N17 66 DU55
Tamar Way, Slou. 93 BB78
Tamarind Yd E1 202 C2
Tamarisk Cl, S.Ock. 91 FW70
Tamarisk Rd, S.Ock. 91 FW69
Tamarisk Sq W12 81 CT73
Tamerton Sq, Wok. 166 AY119
Tamesis Gdns, Wor.Pk. 138 CS102
Tamesis Strand, Grav. 131 GL92
Tamian Way, Houns. 96 BW84
Tamworth Av, Wdf.Grn. 48 EE51
Tamworth La, Mitch. 141 DH96
Tamworth Pk, Mitch. 141 DH98
Tamworth Pl, Croy. 142 DQ103
Tamworth Rd, Croy. 141 DP103
Tamworth St SW6 100 DA79
Tancred Rd N4 65 DP58
Tandridge Ct, Cat. 176 DU122
Tandridge Dr, Orp. 145 ER102
Tandridge Gdns, S.Croy. 160 DT113
Tandridge Hill La, Gdse. 187 DZ128
Tandridge La, Oxt. 187 EA131
Tandridge Pl, Orp. 145 ER101
Tandridge Dr
Tandridge Rd, Warl. 177 DX119
Tanfield Av NW2 63 CT63
Tanfield Cl, Wal.Cr. 14 DU27
Tanfield Rd, Croy. 160 DQ105
Tangent Link, Rom. 52 FK53
Tangent Rd, Rom. 52 FK53
Ashton Rd
Tangier Rd, Rich. 98 CP83
Tangier Way, Tad. 173 CY117
Tangier Wd, Tad. 173 CY118
Tangle Tree Cl N3 44 DB54
Tanglebury Cl, Brom. 145 EM98
Tanglewood Cl, Cher. 132 AV104
Tanglewood Cl, Croy. 142 DW104
Tanglewood Cl, Stan. 41 CE47
Tanglewood Cl, Uxb. 76 BN69
Tanglewood Cl, Wok. 167 BD116
Tanglewood Way, Felt. 115 BV90
Tangley Gro SW15 119 CT86
Tangley Pk Rd, Hmptn. 116 BZ93
Tanglyn Av, Shep. 135 BP99
Tangmere Cres, Horn. 89 FH65
Tangmere Gdns, Nthlt. 78 BW68
Tangmere Gro, Kings.T. 117 CK92
Tangmere Way NW9 42 CS54
Tanhouse Rd, Oxt. 187 ED132
Tanhurst Wk SE2 106 EX76
Alsike Rd
Tank Hill Rd, Purf. 108 FN78
Tank La, Purf. 108 FN77
Tankerton Rd, Surb. 138 CM103
Tankerton St WC1 196 A3
Tankerville Rd SW16 121 DK93
Tankridge Rd NW2 63 CV61
Tanner St SE1 201 N5
Tanner St SE1 102 DS75
Tanner St, Bark. 87 EQ65
Tanners Cl, Walt. 135 BV100
Tanners Dean, Lthd. 171 CJ122
Tanners End La N18 46 DS49
Tanners Hill SE8 103 DZ81
Tanners Hill, Abb.L. 7 BT31
Tanners La, Ilf. 69 EQ55
Tanners Wd Cl, Abb.L. 7 BS32
Tanners Wd La
Tanners Wd La, Abb.L. 7 BS32
Tannery, The, Red. 184 DE134
Oakdene Rd
Tannery Cl, Beck. 143 DX99
Tannery Cl, Dag. 71 FB62
Tannery La, Wok. 167 BF122
Tannington Ter N5 65 DN62
Tannsfeld Rd SE26 123 DX92
Tansley Cl N7 65 DK64
Hilldrop Rd
Tanswell Est SE1 200 E5
Tanswell St SE1 200 D5
Tansy Cl E6 87 EN72
Tansy Cl, Rom. 52 FL51
Tant Av E16 86 EF72
Tantallon Rd SW12 120 DG88
Tantony Gro, Rom. 70 EX55
Tanworth Cl, Nthwd. 39 BQ51
Tanworth Gdns, Pnr. 39 BV54
Tanyard La, Bex. 126 FA87
Bexley High St
Tanza Rd NW3 64 DF63
Tapestry Cl, Sutt. 158 DB108
Taplow NW3 82 DD66
Taplow SE17 102 DS78
Thurlow St
Taplow Rd N13 46 DQ49
Taplow St N1 197 J1
Taplow St N1 84 DQ68
Tapp St E1 84 DV70
Tappesfield Rd SE15 102 DW83
Tapster St, Barn. 27 CZ42
Taransay Wk N1 84 DR65
Marquess Rd
Tarbert Rd SE22 122 DS85
Tarbert Wk E1 84 DW73
Juniper St
Target Cl, Felt. 115 BS86
Tariff Cres SE8 203 M8
Tariff Cres SE8 103 DZ77
Tariff Rd N17 46 DU51
Tarleton Gdns SE23 122 DV88
Tarling Cl, Sid. 126 EV90
Tarling Rd E16 86 EF72
Tarling Rd N2 44 DC54
Tarling St E1 84 DV72
Tarling St Est E1 84 DW72
Tarmac Way, West Dr. 94 BH80
Tarn St SE1 201 H7
Tarnbank, Enf. 29 DL43
Tarnwood Pk SE9 125 EM88
Tarnworth Rd, Rom. 52 FN50
Tarpan Way, Brox. 15 DZ26
Tarquin Ho SE26 122 DU91
Tarragon Cl SE14 103 DY80
Tarragon Gro SE26 123 DX93
Tarrant Pl W1 194 D7
Tarrington Cl SW16 121 DK90
Tarry La SE8 203 K8
Tarry La SE8 103 DY77
Tartar Rd, Cob. 154 BW113
Tarver Rd SE17 101 DP78
Tarves Way SE10 103 EB80
Tash Pl N11 45 DH50
Woodland Rd
Tasker Cl, Hayes 95 BQ80
Tasker Ho, Bark. 87 ER68
Dovehouse Mead
Tasker Rd NW3 64 DF64
Tasker Rd, Grays 111 GH76
Tasman Ct, Sun. 115 BS94
Tasman Rd SW9 101 DL83
Tasman Wk E16 86 EK72
Royal Rd
Tasmania Ho, Til. 111 GG81
Hobart Rd
Tasmania Ter N18 46 DQ51
Tasso Rd W6 99 CY79
Tatam Rd NW10 80 CQ66
Tate & Lyle Jetty E16 104 EL75
Tate Cl, Lthd. 171 CJ123
Windmill Dr
Tate Rd E16 87 EM74
Newland St
Tate Rd (Chalfont St. Peter), Ger.Cr. 37 AZ50
Tate Rd, Sutt. 158 DA106
Tatnell Rd SE23 123 DY86
Tatsfield App Rd, West. 178 EH123
Tatsfield La, West. 179 EM121
Tattenham Cor Rd, Epsom 173 CT117
Tattenham Cres, Epsom 173 CU118
Tattenham Gro, Epsom 173 CV118
Tattenham Way, Tad. 173 CX118
Tattersall Cl SE9 124 EL85
Tatton Cres N16 66 DT59
Clapton Common
Tatum St SE17 201 L9
Tatum St SE17 102 DR77
Tauber Cl, Borwd. 26 CM42
Tauheed Cl N4 66 DQ61
Taunton Av SW20 139 CV96
Taunton Av, Cat. 176 DT123
Taunton Av, Houns. 96 CC82
Taunton Cl, Bexh. 107 FD82
Taunton Cl, Ilf. 49 ET51
Taunton Cl, Sutt. 140 DA102
Taunton Dr N2 44 DC54
Taunton Dr, Enf. 29 DN41
Taunton La, Couls. 175 DN119
Taunton Ms NW1 194 D5
Taunton Pl NW1 194 D4
Taunton Pl NW1 82 DF70
Taunton Rd SE12 124 EE85
West End Rd
Taunton Rd, Grav. 130 GA85
Taunton Rd, Grnf. 78 CB67
Taunton Rd, Rom. 52 FJ49
Taunton Vale, Grav. 131 GK90
Taunton Way, Stan. 62 CL55
Tavern Cl, Cars. 140 DE101
Tavern La SW9 101 DN82
Taverner Sq N5 66 DQ63
Highbury Gra
Taverners Cl W11 81 CY74
Addison Av
Taverners Way E4 48 EE46
Douglas Rd
Tavistock Av E17 67 DY55
Tavistock Av, Grnf. 79 CG68
Tavistock Cl N16 66 DS64
Crossway
Tavistock Cl, Pot.B. 12 DD31
Tavistock Cl, Rom. 52 FK53
Tavistock Cl, Stai. 114 BK94
Tavistock Cres W11 81 CZ71
Tavistock Cres, Mitch. 141 DL98
Tavistock Gdns, Ilf. 69 ES63
Tavistock Gate, Croy. 142 DR102
Tavistock Gro, Croy. 142 DR101
Tavistock Ms E18 68 EG56
Avon Way
Tavistock Ms W11 81 CZ72
Lancaster Rd
Tavistock Pl E18 68 EG55
Avon Way
Tavistock Pl N14 45 DH45
Chase Side
Tavistock Pl WC1 195 N4
Tavistock Pl WC1 83 DL70
Tavistock Rd E7 68 EF63
Tavistock Rd E15 86 EF65
Tavistock Rd E18 68 EG55
Tavistock Rd N4 66 DR58
Tavistock Rd NW10 81 CT68
Tavistock Rd W11 81 CZ71
Tavistock Rd, Brom. 144 EF98
Tavistock Rd, Cars. 140 DD102
Tavistock Rd, Croy. 142 DR102
Tavistock Rd, Edg. 42 CN53
Tavistock Rd, Uxb. 59 BQ64
Tavistock Rd, Wat. 24 BX39
Tavistock Rd, Well. 106 EW81
Tavistock Rd, West Dr. 76 BK74
Tavistock Sq WC1 195 N4
Tavistock Sq WC1 83 DK70
Tavistock St WC2 196 A10
Tavistock St WC2 83 DL73
Tavistock Ter N19 65 DK62
Tavistock Twr SE16 203 K7
Tavistock Wk, Cars. 140 DD102
Tavistock Rd
Taviton St WC1 195 M4
Taviton St WC1 83 DK70
Tavy Cl SE11 200 E10
Tavy Cl SE11 101 DN78
Tawney Common, Epp. 18 FA32
Tawney Rd SE28 88 EV73
Tawny Av, Upmin. 72 FP64
Tawny Cl W13 79 CH74
Tawny Cl, Felt. 115 BU90
Chervil Cl
Tawny Way SE16 203 J8
Tawny Way SE16 103 DX77
Tay Way, Rom. 51 FF53
Tayben Av, Twick. 117 CE86
Taybridge Rd SW11 100 DG83
Tayburn Cl E14 85 EC72
Tayfield Cl, Uxb. 59 BQ62
Tayler Cotts, Pot.B. 11 CT34
Crossoaks La
Tayles Hill, Epsom 157 CT110
Tayles Hill Dr
Tayles Hill Dr, Epsom 157 CT110
Taylor Av, Rich. 98 CP82
Taylor Cl N17 46 DU52
Taylor Cl, Epsom 156 CN111
Williams Evans Rd
Taylor Cl, Hmptn. 116 CC92
Taylor Cl, Houns. 96 CC81
Taylor Cl, Orp. 163 ET105
Taylor Cl, Rom. 50 FA52
Taylor Cl, Uxb. 38 BJ53
High St
Taylor Ct E15 67 EC64
Clays La
Taylor Rd, Ash. 171 CK117
Taylor Rd, Mitch. 120 DE94
Taylor Rd, Wall. 159 DH106
Taylor Row, Dart. 128 FJ90
Taylor Row, Rom. 52 FJ48
Cummings Hall La
Taylors Bldgs SE18 105 EP77
Spray St
Taylors Cl, Sid. 125 ET91
Taylors Grn W3 80 CS72
Long Dr
Taylors La NW10 80 CS66
Taylors La SE26 122 DV91
Taylors La, Barn. 27 CZ39
Taymount Ri SE23 122 DW89
Taynton Dr, Red. 185 DK129
Tayport Cl N1 83 DL66
Tayside Dr, Edg. 42 CP48
Taywood Rd, Nthlt. 78 BZ69
Teak Cl SE16 203 L3
Teak Cl SE16 85 DY74
Teal Av, Orp. 146 EX98
Teal Cl E16 86 EK71
Fulmer Rd
Teal Cl, S.Croy. 161 DX111
Teal Dr, Nthwd. 39 BQ52
Teal Pl, Sutt. 139 CY103
Gander Grn La
Teale St E2 84 DU68
Tealing Dr, Epsom 156 CR105
Teardrop Ind Est, Swan. 147 FH99
Teasel Cl, Croy. 143 DX102
Teasel Way E15 86 EE69
Teazle Wd Hill, Lthd. 171 CE117
Teazle Wd Hill, Lthd. 171 CE117
Oaklawn Rd
Teazlewood Pk, Lthd. 171 CG117
Tebworth Rd N17 46 DT52
Teck Cl, Islw. 97 CG82
Tedder Cl, Chess. 155 CJ106
Tedder Cl, Ruis. 59 BV64
West End Rd
Tedder Cl, Uxb. 76 BM66
Tedder Rd, S.Croy. 160 DW108
Teddington Cl, Epsom 156 CR110
Teddington Lock, Tedd. 117 CH91
Teddington Pk, Tedd. 117 CF92
Teddington Pk Rd, Tedd. 117 CF91
Tedworth Gdns SW3 100 DF78
Tedworth Sq
Tedworth Sq SW3 100 DF78
Tee, The W3 80 CS72
Tees Av, Grnf. 79 CE68
Tees Cl, Upmin. 73 FR59
Tees Dr, Rom. 52 FK48
Teesdale Av, Islw. 97 CG81
Teesdale Cl E2 84 DV68
Teesdale Gdns SE25 142 DS96
Teesdale Gdns, Islw. 97 CG81
Teesdale Rd E11 68 EF58
Teesdale Rd, Dart. 128 FQ88
Teesdale St E2 84 DV68
Teesdale Yd E2 84 DV68
Teesdale St
Teeswater Ct, Erith 106 EX76
Middle Way
Teevan Cl, Croy. 142 DU101
Teevan Rd, Croy. 142 DU101
Teggs La, Wok. 167 BF116
Teignmouth Cl SW4 101 DK84
Teignmouth Cl, Edg. 42 CM54
Teignmouth Gdns, Grnf. 79 CG68
Teignmouth Rd NW2 63 CX64
Teignmouth Rd, Well. 106 EW82
Telcote Way, Ruis. 60 BW59
Woodlands Av
Telegraph Hill NW3 64 DB62
Telegraph La, Esher 155 CF107
Telegraph Ms, Ilf. 70 EU60
Telegraph Pl E14 204 B8
Telegraph Pl E14 103 EB77
Telegraph Rd SW15 119 CV87
Telegraph St EC2 197 K8
Telegraph Track, Cars. 158 DG110
Telemann Sq SE3 104 EH83
Telephone Pl SW6 99 CZ79
Lillie Rd
Telfer Cl W3 98 CQ75
Church Rd
Telferscot Rd SW12 121 DK88
Telford Av SW2 121 DL88
Telford Cl E17 67 DY59
Telford Cl SE19 122 DT93
St. Aubyn's Rd
Telford Cl, Wat. 24 BX35
Telford Dr, Walt. 136 BW101
Telford Rd N11 45 DJ51
Telford Rd NW9 63 CU58
West Hendon Bdy
Telford Rd SE9 125 ER89
Telford Rd W10 81 CY71
Telford Rd, St.Alb. 9 CJ27
Telford Rd, Sthl. 78 CB73
Telford Rd, Twick. 116 CA87
Telford Ter SW1 101 DJ79
Telford Way W3 80 CS71
Telford Way, Hayes 78 BY71
Telfords Yd E1 202 C1
Telham Rd E6 87 EN68
Tell Gro SE22 102 DT84
Tellisford, Esher 154 CB105
Tellson Av SE18 104 EK81
Telscombe Cl, Orp. 145 ES103
Telston La, Sev. 181 FF117
Temeraire St SE16 202 G5
Temperley Rd SW12 120 DG87
Tempest Av, Pot.B. 12 DC32
Tempest Mead, Epp. 17 ET30
Station Rd
Tempest Rd, Egh. 113 BC93
Tempest Way, Rain. 89 FG65
Templar Dr SE28 88 EX72
Templar Dr, Grav. 131 GG92
Templar Ho NW2 81 CZ65
Shoot Up Hill
Templar Ho, Rain. 89 FD68
Chantry Way
Templar Pl, Hmptn. 116 CA94
Templar St SE5 101 DP82
Templars Av NW11 63 CZ58
Templars Cres N3 44 DA54
Templars Dr, Har. 41 CD51
Temple EC4 83 DN73
Temple Av EC4 196 E10
Temple Av EC4 83 DN73
Temple Av N20 44 DD45
Temple Av, Croy. 143 DZ103
Temple Av, Dag. 70 FA60
Temple Bar Rd, Wok. 166 AT119
Temple Cl E11 68 EE59
Wadley Rd
Temple Cl N3 43 CZ54
Cyprus Rd
Temple Cl SE28 105 EQ76
Temple Cl, Epsom 156 CR112
Temple Cl (Cheshunt), Wal.Cr. 14 DU31
Temple Cl, Wat. 23 BT40
Temple Ct E1 85 DX71
Rectory Sq
Temple Ct, Pot.B. 11 CY31
Temple Fortune Hill NW11 64 DA57
Temple Fortune La NW11 64 DA58
Temple Fortune Par NW11 63 CZ57
Finchley Rd
Temple Gdns N21 45 DP47
Barrowell Grn
Temple Gdns NW11 63 CZ58
Temple Gdns, Dag. 70 EX62
Temple Gdns, Rick. 39 BP49
Temple Gdns, Stai. 133 BF95

Thornton Rd, Croy. 141 DM101
Thornton Rd, Ilf. 69 EP63
Thornton Rd, Pot.B. 12 DC30
Thornton Rd, Th.Hth. 141 DM101
Thornton Rd E SW19 119 CX93
Thornton Rd
Thornton Rd Retail Pk, Croy. 141 DM100
Thornton Row, Th.Hth. 141 DN99
London Rd
Thornton St SW9 101 DN82
Thornton Way NW11 64 DB57
Thorntons Fm Av, Rom. 71 FD60
Thorntree Rd SE7 104 EK78
Thornville Gro, Mitch. 140 DC96
Thornville St SE8 103 EA81
Thornwood Cl E18 48 EH54
Thornwood Rd SE13 124 EE85
Thornwood Rd, Epp. 18 EV29
Thorogood Gdns E15 68 EE64
Thorogood Way, Rain. 89 FE67
Thorold Cl, S.Croy. 161 DX110
Thorold Rd N22 45 DL52
Thorold Rd, Ilf. 69 EP61
Thoroughfare, The, Tad. 183 CU125
Thoroughfare, The, Tad. 183 CU125
Chequers La
Thorparch Rd SW8 101 DK81
Thorpe Bypass, Egh. 133 BB96
Thorpe Cl W10 81 CY72
Cambridge Gdns
Thorpe Cl, Croy. 161 EC111
Thorpe Cl, Orp. 145 ES103
Thorpe Cres E17 47 DZ54
Thorpe Cres, Wat. 40 BW45
Thorpe Hall Rd E17 47 EC53
Thorpe Ind Est, Egh. 133 BC96
Thorpe Lea Rd, Egh. 113 BB93
Thorpe Lo, Horn. 72 FL59
Thorpe Rd E6 87 EM67
Thorpe Rd E7 68 EF63
Thorpe Rd E17 47 EC54
Thorpe Rd N15 66 DS58
Thorpe Rd, Bark. 87 ER66
Thorpe Rd, Cher. 133 BD99
Thorpe Rd, Kings.T. 118 CL94
Thorpe Rd, Stai. 113 BD93
Thorpebank Rd W12 81 CU74
Thorpedale Gdns, Ilf. 69 EN56
Thorpedale Rd N4 65 DL60
Thorpeside Cl, Stai. 133 BE96
Thorpewood Av SE26 122 DV89
Thorpland Av, Uxb. 59 BQ62
Thorsden Cl, Wok. 166 AY118
Thorsden Ct, Wok. 166 AY118
Guildford Rd
Thorsden Way SE19 122 DS91
Oaks Av
Thorverton Rd NW2 63 CY62
Thoydon Rd E3 85 DY68
Thrale Rd SW16 121 DJ92
Thrale St SE1 201 J3
Thrale St SE1 84 DQ74
Thrasher Cl E8 84 DT67
Stean St
Thrawl St E1 84 DT71
Threadneedle St EC2 197 L9
Threadneedle St EC2 84 DR72
Three Barrels Wk EC4 197 J10
Three Colt St E14 85 DZ73
Three Colts Cor E2 84 DU70
Weaver St
Three Colts La E2 84 DV70
Three Cors, Bexh. 107 FB82
Three Cups Yd WC1 196 C7
Three Forests Way, Chig. 50 EW48
Three Forests Way, Loug. 32 EK38
The Clay Rd
Three Forests Way, Rom. 50 EW48
Three Forests Way, Wal.Abb. 32 EK36
Three Gates Rd (Fawkham Grn), Long. 149 FU102
Three Households, Ch.St.G. 36 AT49
Three Kings Rd, Mitch. 140 DG97
Three Kings Yd W1 195 H10
Three Kings Yd W1 83 DH73
Three Mill La E3 85 EC69
Three Oak La SE1 201 P4
Three Oaks Cl, Uxb. 58 BM62
Threshers Pl W11 81 CY73
Thriffwood SE26 122 DW90
Thrift, The, Dart. 129 FW90
Thrift Fm La, Borwd. 26 CP40
Thrift Grn, Brwd. 55 GA48
Knight's Way
Thrift La, Sev. 179 ER117
Thrifts Mead, Epp. 33 ES37
Thrigby Rd, Chess. 156 CM107
Throckmorten Rd E16 86 EH72
Throgmorton Av EC2 197 L8
Throgmorton Av EC2 84 DR72
Throgmorton St EC2 197 L8
Throgmorton St EC2 84 DR72
Throwley Cl SE2 106 EW76
Throwley Rd, Sutt. 158 DB106
Throwley Way, Sutt. 158 DB105
Thrums, The, Wat. 23 BV37
Thrupp Cl, Mitch. 141 DH96
Thrupps Av, Walt. 154 BX106
Thrupps La, Walt. 154 BX106
Thrush Grn, Har. 60 CA56
Thrush Grn, Rick. 38 BJ45
Thrush La (Cuffley), Pot.B. 13 DL28
Thrush St SE17 201 H10
Thruxton Way SE15 102 DT80
Daniel Gdns
Thunderer Rd, Dag. 88 EY70
Thurbarn Rd SE6 123 EB92
Thurland Rd SE16 202 B6
Thurland Rd SE16 102 DU76
Thurlby Cl, Har. 61 CG58
Gayton Rd
Thurlby Cl, Wdf.Grn. 49 EM50
Thurlby Rd SE27 121 DN91
Thurlby Rd, Wem. 79 CK65
Thurleigh Av SW12 120 DG86
Thurleigh Rd SW12 120 DG86
Thurleston Av, Mord. 139 CY99
Thurlestone Av N12 44 DF51
Thurlestone Av, Ilf. 69 ET63
Thurlestone Cl, Shep. 135 BQ100
Thurlestone Rd SE27 121 DN90
Thurloe Cl SW7 198 B8
Thurloe Cl SW7 100 DE76
Thurloe Gdns, Rom. 71 FF58
Thurloe Pl SW7 198 A8
Thurloe Pl SW7 100 DD77
Thurloe Pl Ms SW7 198 A8
Thurloe Sq SW7 198 B8
Thurloe Sq SW7 100 DE77
Thurloe St SW7 198 A8
Thurloe St SW7 100 DD77
Thurloe Wk, Grays 110 GA76
Thurlow Cl E4 47 EB51
Higham Sta Av
Thurlow Gdns, Ilf. 49 ER51
Thurlow Gdns, Wem. 61 CK64
Thurlow Hill SE21 122 DQ88
Thurlow Pk Rd SE21 121 DP88
Thurlow Rd NW3 64 DD64
Thurlow Rd W7 97 CG75
Thurlow St SE17 201 L10
Thurlow St SE17 102 DR78
Thurlow Ter NW5 64 DG64
Thurlstone Rd, Ruis. 59 BU62
Thurlton Ct, Wok. 166 AY116
Chobham Rd
Thurnby Ct, Twick. 117 CE90
Thurnham Way, Tad. 173 CW120
Thurrock Lakeside, Grays 109 FV77
Thurrock Pk Ind Est, Til. 110 GD80
Thurrock Pk Way, Til. 110 GD80
Thursby Rd, Wok. 166 AU118
Thursland Rd, Sid. 126 EY92
Thursley Cres, Croy. 161 ED108
Thursley Gdns SW19 119 CX89
Thursley Rd SE9 125 EM90
Thurso Cl, Rom. 52 FP51
Thurso St SW17 120 DD91
Thurstan Rd SW20 119 CV94
Thurston Rd SE13 103 EB82
Thurston Rd, Sthl. 78 BZ72
Thurtle Rd E2 84 DT67
Thwaite Cl, Erith 107 FC79
Thyer Cl, Orp. 163 EQ105
Isabella Dr
Thyra Gro N12 44 DB51
Tibbatts Rd E3 85 EB70
Tibbenham Wk E13 86 EF68
Tibberton Sq N1 84 DQ66
Popham Rd
Tibbets Cl SW19 119 CX88
Tibbet's Cor SW15 119 CX87
Tibbet's Cor Underpass SW15 119 CX87
West Hill
Tibbet's Ride SW15 119 CX87
Tibbles Cl, Wat. 24 BY35
Tibbs Hill Rd, Abb.L. 7 BT30
Tiber Gdns N1 83 DM67
Treaty St
Ticehurst Cl, Orp. 126 EU94
Grovelands Rd
Ticehurst Rd SE23 123 DY89
Tichborne, Rick. 37 BD50
Tichmarsh, Epsom 156 CQ110
Tickford Cl SE2 106 EW75
Ampleforth Rd
Tidal Basin Rd E16 205 L1
Tidal Basin Rd E16 86 EF73
Tidenham Gdns, Croy. 142 DS104
Tideswell Rd SW15 119 CW85
Tideswell Rd, Croy. 143 EA104
Tideway Cl, Rich. 117 CH91
Locksmeade Rd
Tidey St E3 85 EA71
Tidford Rd, Well. 105 ET82
Tidworth Rd E3 85 EA70
Tidy's La, Epp. 18 EV29
Tiepigs La, Brom. 144 EE103
Tiepigs La, W.Wick. 144 EE103
Tierney Rd SW2 121 DL88
Tiger La, Brom. 144 EH98
Tiger Way E5 66 DV63
Tilbrook Rd SE3 104 EJ83
Tilburstow Hill Rd, Gdse. 186 DW132
Tilbury Cl SE15 102 DT80
Willowbrook Rd
Tilbury Cl, Orp. 146 EV96
Tilbury Docks, Til. 110 GE84
Tilbury Gdns, Til. 111 GG84
Tilbury Hotel Rd, Til. 111 GG84
Tilbury Rd E6 87 EM68
Tilbury Rd E10 67 EC59
Tildesley Rd SW15 119 CW86
Tile Fm Rd, Orp. 145 ER104
Tile Kiln La N6 65 DH60
Winchester Rd
Tile Kiln La N13 46 DQ50
Tile Kiln La, Bex. 127 FC89
Tile Kiln La (Harefield), Uxb. 59 BP59
Tile Yd E14 85 DZ72
Commercial Rd
Tilehouse Cl, Borwd. 26 CM41
Tilehouse La, Ger.Cr. 37 BE53
Tilehouse La, Rick. 37 BE53
Tilehouse La (Denham), Uxb. 57 BE58
Tilehouse Way (Denham), Uxb. 57 BF59
Tilehurst Pt SE2 106 EW75
Yarnton Way
Tilehurst Rd SW18 120 DD88
Tilehurst Rd, Sutt. 157 CY106
Tilekiln Cl, Wal.Cr. 14 DT29
Tileyard Rd N7 83 DL66
Tilford Av, Croy. 161 EC109
Tilford Gdns SW19 119 CX89
Tilia Cl, Sutt. 157 CZ106
Tilia Rd E5 66 DV63
Clarence Rd
Tilia Wk SW9 101 DP84
Moorland Rd
Till Av (Farningham), Dart. 148 FM102
Tiller Rd E14 203 P6
Tiller Rd E14 103 EA76
Tillett Cl NW10 80 CQ65
Tillett Sq SE16 203 L5
Tillett Way E2 84 DU69
Gosset St
Tilley La, Epsom 172 CQ123
Tillgate Common, Red. 186 DQ133
Tilling Rd NW2 63 CW60
Tilling Way, Wem. 61 CK61
Tillingbourne Gdns N3 63 CZ55
Tillingbourne Grn, Orp. 146 EU98
Tillingbourne Way N3 63 CZ55
Tillingbourne Gdns
Tillingdown Hill, Cat. 176 DU122
Tillingdown La, Cat. 176 DV124
Tillingham Ct, Wal.Abb. 16 EG33
Tillingham Way N12 44 DA49
Tillman St E1 84 DV72
Bigland St
Tilloch St N1 83 DM66
Carnoustie Dr
Tillotson Rd N9 46 DT47
Tillotson Rd, Har. 40 CB52
Tillotson Rd, Ilf. 69 EN59
Tilly's La, Stai. 113 BF91
Tilmans Mead (Farningham), Dart. 148 FM101
Tilney Ct EC1 197 J4
Tilney Dr, Buck.H. 48 EG47
Tilney Gdns N1 84 DR65
Tilney Rd, Dag. 88 EZ65
Tilney Rd, Sthl. 96 BW77
Tilney St W1 198 G2
Tilney St W1 82 DG74
Tilson Gdns SW2 121 DL87
Tilson Ho SW2 121 DL87
Tilson Gdns
Tilson Rd N17 46 DU53
Tilt Cl, Cob. 170 BY116
Tilt Meadow, Cob. 170 BY116
Tilt Rd, Cob. 170 BW115
Tilt Yd App SE9 125 EM86
Tilton St SW6 99 CY79
Tiltwood, The W3 80 CQ73
Acacia Rd
Timber Cl, Chis. 145 EN96
Timber Cl, Wok. 151 BF114
Hacketts La
Timber Hill Rd, Cat. 176 DU124
Timber La, Cat. 176 DU124
Timber Hill Rd
Timber Mill Way SW4 101 DK83
Timber Pond Rd SE16 203 J3
Timber Pond Rd SE16 103 DX75
Timber Ridge, Rick. 22 BK42
Timber St EC1 197 H4
Timbercroft, Epsom 156 CS105
Timbercroft La SE18 105 ES79
Timberdene NW4 43 CX54
Timberdene Av, Ilf. 49 EP53
Timberhill, Ash. 172 CL119
Ottways La
Timberland Rd E1 84 DV72
Timberling Gdns, S.Croy. 160 DR109
Sanderstead Rd
Timberslip Dr, Wall. 159 DK109
Timbertop Rd, West. 178 EJ118
Timberwharf Rd N16 66 DU58
Timbrell Pl SE16 203 M3
Time Sq E8 66 DT64
Times Sq, Sutt. 158 DB106
Timothy Cl SW4 121 DJ85
Elms Rd
Timothy Cl, Bexh. 126 EY85
Timothy Ho, Erith 106 EY75
Kale Rd
Timothy Rd E3 85 DZ71
Timperley Gdns, Red. 184 DE132
Timsbury Wk SW15 119 CU88
Timsway, Stai. 113 BF92
Tindal St SW9 101 DP81
Tindale Cl, S.Croy. 160 DR111
Tindall Cl, Rom. 52 FM54
Tinderbox All SW14 98 CR83
Tine Rd, Chig. 49 ES50
Tingeys Top La, Enf. 29 DN36
Tinniswood Cl N5 65 DN64
Drayton Pk
Tinsey Cl, Egh. 113 BB92
Tinsley Rd E1 84 DW71
Tintagel Cl, Epsom 157 CT114
Tintagel Cres SE22 102 DT84
Tintagel Dr, Stan. 41 CK49
Tintagel Gdns SE22 102 DT84
Oxonian St
Tintagel Rd, Orp. 146 EW103
Tintagel Way, Wok. 167 BA116
Tintern Av NW9 62 CP55
Tintern Cl SW15 119 CY85
Tintern Cl SW19 120 DC94
Tintern Gdns N14 45 DL45
Tintern Path NW9 62 CS58
Ruthin Cl
Tintern Rd N22 46 DQ53
Tintern Rd, Cars. 140 DD102
Tintern St SW4 101 DL84
Tintern Way, Har. 60 CB60
Tinto Rd E16 86 EG70
Tinwell Ms, Borwd. 26 CQ43
Cranes Way
Tinworth St SE11 200 A10
Tinworth St SE11 101 DM78
Tippendell La, St.Alb. 8 CB26
Tippetts Cl, Enf. 30 DQ39
Tipthorpe Rd SW11 100 DG83
Tipton Cotts, Add. 152 BG105
Oliver Cl
Tipton Dr, Croy. 160 DS105
Tiptree Cl E4 47 EC48
Mapleton Rd
Tiptree Cl, Horn. 72 FN60
Tiptree Cres, Ilf. 69 EN55
Tiptree Dr, Enf. 30 DR42
Tiptree Est, Ilf. 69 EN55
Tiptree Rd, Ruis. 59 BV63
Tirlemont Rd, S.Croy. 160 DQ108
Tirrell Rd, Croy. 142 DQ100
Tisbury Ct W1 83 DK73
Rupert St
Tisbury Rd SW16 141 DL96
Tisdall Pl SE17 201 L9
Tisdall Pl SE17 102 DR77
Titan Rd, Grays 110 GA78
Titchborne Row W2 194 C9
Titchfield Rd NW8 82 DF67
Titchfield Rd, Cars. 140 DD102
Titchfield Rd, Enf. 31 DY37
Titchfield Wk, Cars. 140 DD101
Titchfield Rd
Titchwell Rd SW18 120 DD87
Tite Hill, Egh. 112 AX92
Tite St SW3 100 DF78
Tithe Barn Cl, Kings.T. 138 CM95
Tithe Barn Ct, Abb.L. 7 BT29
Tithe Barn Way, Nthlt. 77 BV69
Tithe Cl NW7 43 CU53
Tithe Cl, Hayes 77 BT71
Gledwood Dr
Tithe Cl, Walt. 135 BV100
Tithe Ct, Slou. 93 BA77
Tithe Fm Av, Har. 60 CA62
Tithe Fm Cl, Har. 60 CA62
Tithe La, Stai. 113 BA86
Tithe Meadow, Wat. 23 BR44
Tithe Meadows, Vir.W. 132 AX100
Tithe Wk NW7 43 CU53
Tithepit Shaw La, Warl. 176 DV115
Titian Av, Bushey 41 CE45
Titley Cl E4 47 EA50
Titmus Cl, Uxb. 77 BQ72
Titmuss Av SE28 88 EV73
Titmuss St W12 99 CV75
Titsey Hill, Oxt. 178 EF123
Titsey Rd, Oxt. 188 EH125
Tiverton Av, Ilf. 69 EN55
Tiverton Dr SE9 125 EQ88
Tiverton Gro, Rom. 52 FN50
Tiverton Rd N15 66 DR58
Tiverton Rd N18 46 DS50
Tiverton Rd NW10 81 CX67
Tiverton Rd, Edg. 42 CM54
Tiverton Rd, Houns. 96 CC82
Tiverton Rd, Pot.B. 12 DD31
Tiverton Rd, Ruis. 59 BU62
Tiverton Rd, Th.Hth. 141 DN99
Willett Rd
Tiverton Rd, Wem. 80 CL68
Tiverton St SE1 201 H7
Tiverton St SE1 102 DQ76
Tiverton Way, Chess. 155 CJ106
Tivoli Ct SE16 203 M4
Tivoli Ct SE16 103 DZ75
Tivoli Gdns SE18 104 EL77
Tivoli Rd N8 65 DK57
Tivoli Rd SE27 122 DQ92
Tivoli Rd, Houns. 96 BY84
Toad La, Houns. 96 BZ84
Tobacco Quay E1 202 D1
Tobago St E14 203 P4
Tobin Cl NW3 82 DE66
Toby La E1 85 DY70
Toby Way, Surb. 138 CP103
Todd Cl, Rain. 90 FK70
Todds Wk N7 65 DM61
Andover Rd
Toft Av, Grays 110 GD77
Token Yd SW15 99 CY84
Montserrat Rd
Tokenhouse Yd EC2 197 K8
Tokyngton Av, Wem. 80 CN65
Toland Sq SW15 119 CU85
Tolcarne Dr, Pnr. 59 BV55
Toldene Ct, Couls. 175 DM120
Toley Av, Wem. 62 CL59
Tollbridge Cl W10 81 CY70
Kensal Rd
Tolldene Cl, Wok. 166 AS117
Robin Hood Rd
Tollers La, Couls. 175 DM119
Tollesbury Gdns, Ilf. 69 ER55
Tollet St E1 85 DX70
Tollgate Cl, Rick. 21 BF41
Tollgate Dr SE21 122 DS89
Tollgate Dr, Hayes 78 BX73
Delamere Rd
Tollgate Gdns NW6 82 DB68
Tollgate Rd E6 86 EK71
Tollgate Rd E16 86 EJ71
Tollgate Rd, Dart. 129 FR87
Tollgate Rd, Wal.Cr. 31 DX35
Tollhouse La, Wall. 159 DJ109
Tollhouse Way N19 65 DJ61
Tollington Pk N4 65 DM61
Tollington Pl N4 65 DM61
Tollington Rd N7 65 DM63
Tollington Way N7 65 DL62
Tolmers Av (Cuffley), Pot.B. 13 DL28
Tolmers Gdns (Cuffley), Pot.B. 13 DL29
Tolmers Ms, Hert. 13 DL25
Tolmers Pk, Hert. 13 DL25
Tolmers Rd (Cuffley), Pot.B. 13 DL27
Tolmers Sq NW1 195 L4
Tolpits Cl, Wat. 23 BT43
Tolpits La, Wat. 23 BT44
Tolpuddle Av E13 86 EJ67
Rochester Av
Tolpuddle St N1 83 DN68
Tolsford Rd E5 66 DV64
Tolson Rd, Islw. 97 CG83
Tolvaddon, Wok. 166 AU117
Cardingham
Tolverne Rd SW20 139 CW95
Tolworth Cl, Surb. 138 CP102
Tolworth Gdns, Rom. 70 EX57
Tolworth Pk Rd, Surb. 138 CM103
Tolworth Ri N, Surb. 138 CQ101
Elmbridge Av
Tolworth Ri S, Surb. 138 CQ102
Warren Dr S
Tolworth Rd, Surb. 138 CL103
Tolworth Twr, Surb. 138 CP103
Tom Coombs Cl SE9 104 EL84
Well Hall Rd
Tom Cribb Rd SE28 105 EQ76
Tom Gros Cl E15 67 ED64
Maryland St
Tom Hood Cl E15 67 ED64
Maryland St
Tom Jenkinson Rd E16 205 N2
Tom Jenkinson Rd E16 86 EG74
Tom Mann Cl, Bark. 87 ES67
Tom Nolan Cl E15 86 EE68
Tom Smith Cl SE10 104 EE79
Maze Hill
Tom Thumbs Arch E3 85 EA68
Malmesbury Rd
Tomahawk Gdns, Nthlt. 78 BX69
Javelin Way
Tomkins Cl, Borwd. 26 CL39
Tallis Way
Tomkyns La, Upmin. 73 FR56
Tomlin Cl, Epsom 156 CR111
Tomlins Gro E3 85 EA69
Tomlins Orchard, Bark. 87 EQ67
Tomlins Ter E14 85 DZ71
Rhodeswell Rd
Tomlins Wk N7 65 DM61
Briset Way
Tomlinson Cl E2 84 DT69
Tomlinson Cl W4 98 CP78
Oxford Rd N
Tomlyns Cl, Brwd. 55 GE44
Tomo Ind Est, Uxb. 76 BJ72
Tompion St EC1 196 F3
Toms Hill, Kings L. 6 BJ33
Bucks Hill
Toms Hill, Rick. 22 BL36
Toms La, Abb.L. 7 BR28
Toms La, Kings L. 7 BP29
Tomswood Ct, Ilf. 49 EQ53
Tomswood Hill, Ilf. 49 EP52
Tomswood Rd, Chig. 49 EN51
Tonbridge Cl, Bans. 158 DF114
Tonbridge Cres, Har. 62 CL56
Tonbridge Ho SE25 142 DU97
Tonbridge Rd, Rom. 52 FK52
Tonbridge Rd, Sev. 191 FJ127
Tonbridge Rd, W.Mol. 136 BY98
Tonbridge St WC1 195 P2
Tonbridge St WC1 83 DL69
Tonbridge Wk WC1 83 DL69
Tonbridge St
Tonfield Rd, Sutt. 139 CZ102
Tonge Cl, Beck. 143 EA99
Tonsley Hill SW18 120 DB85
Tonsley Pl SW18 120 DB85
Tonsley Rd SW18 120 DB85
Tonsley St SW18 120 DB85
Tonstall Rd, Epsom 156 CR110
Tonstall Rd, Mitch. 140 DG96
Tony Cannell Ms E3 85 DZ69
Maplin St
Tooke Cl, Pnr. 40 BY53
Tookey Cl, Har. 62 CM59
Arnold Cl
Took's Ct EC4 196 D8
Tooley St SE1 201 L2
Tooley St SE1 84 DR74
Tooley St, Grav. 130 GD87
Toorack Rd, Har. 41 CD54
Toot Hill Rd, Ong. 19 FF29
Tooting Bec Gdns SW16 121 DK91
Tooting Bec Rd SW16 120 DG90
Tooting Bec Rd SW17 120 DG90
Tooting Gro SW17 120 DE92
Tooting High St SW17 120 DE93
Tootswood Rd, Brom. 144 EE99
Tooveys Mill Cl, Kings L 6 BN28
Top Dartford Rd, Dart. 127 FF94
Top Dartford Rd, Swan. 127 FF94
Top Ho Ri E4 47 EC45
Parkhill Rd
Top Pk, Beck. 144 EE99
Top Pk, Ger.Cr. 56 AW58
Topaz Wk NW2 63 CX59
Marble Dr
Topcliffe Dr, Orp. 163 ER105
Topham Sq N17 46 DQ53
Topham St EC1 196 D4
Topiary, The, Ash. 172 CL120
Topiary Sq, Rich. 98 CM83
Topland Rd (Chalfont St. Peter), Ger.Cr. 36 AX52
Toplands Av, S.Ock. 90 FP74
Topley St SE9 104 EK84
Topmast Pt E14 203 P5
Topmast Pt E14 103 EA75
Topp Wk NW2 63 CW61
Topping La, Uxb. 76 BK69
Topsfield Cl N8 65 DK57
Wolseley Rd
Topsfield Par N8 65 DL57
Tottenham La
Topsfield Rd N8 65 DL57
Topsham Rd SW17 120 DF90
Tor Gdns W8 100 DA75
Tor La, Wey. 153 BQ111
Tor Rd, Well. 106 EW81
Torbay Rd NW6 81 CZ66
Torbay Rd, Har. 60 BY61
Torbay St NW1 83 DH66
Hawley Rd
Torbitt Way, Ilf. 69 ET57
Torbridge Cl, Edg. 42 CL52
Torbrook Cl, Bex. 126 EY86
Torcross Dr SE23 122 DW89
Torcross Rd, Ruis. 59 BV62
Torin Ct, Egh. 112 AW92
Torland Dr, Lthd. 155 CD114
Tormead Cl, Sutt. 158 DA107
Tormount Rd SE18 105 ES79
Toronto Av E12 69 EM63
Toronto Rd E11 67 ED63
Toronto Rd, Ilf. 69 EP60
Toronto Rd, Til. 111 GG82
Torquay Gdns, Ilf. 68 EK56
Torquay St W2 82 DB71
Harrow Rd
Torr Rd SE20 123 DX94
Torrance Cl, Horn. 71 FH60
Torre Wk, Cars. 140 DE102
Torrens Rd E15 86 EF65
Torrens Rd SW2 121 DM85
Torrens Sq E15 86 EE65
Torrens St EC1 196 E1
Torrens St EC1 83 DN68
Torrens Wk, Grav. 131 GL92
Torres Sq E14 103 EA78
Napier Av
Torriano Av NW5 65 DK64
Torriano Cotts NW5 65 DJ64
Torriano Av
Torriano Ms NW5 65 DK64
Torriano Av
Torridge Gdns SE15 102 DW84

Torridge Rd, Slou. 93 BB79
Torridge Rd, Th.Hth. 141 DP99
Torridon Cl, Wok. 166 AV117
Torridon Rd SE6 123 ED88
Torridon Rd SE13 123 ED87
Torrington Av N12 44 DD50
Torrington Cl N12 44 DD49
Torrington Cl, Esher 155 CE107
Torrington Dr, Har. 60 CB63
Torrington Dr, Loug. 33 EQ42
Torrington Dr, Pot.B. 12 DD32
Torrington Gdns N11 45 DJ51
Torrington Gdns, Grnf. 79 CJ66
Torrington Gdns, Loug. 33 EQ42
Torrington Gro N12 44 DE50
Torrington Pk N12 44 DD50
Torrington Pl E1 202 C3
Torrington Pl E1 84 DU74
Torrington Pl WC1 195 M6
Torrington Pl WC1 83 DK71
Torrington Rd E18 68 EG55
Torrington Rd, Dag. 70 EZ60
Torrington Rd, Esher 155 CE107
Torrington Rd, Grnf. 79 CJ67
Torrington Rd, Ruis. 59 BT62
Torrington Sq WC1 195 N5
Torrington Sq WC1 83 DK70
Torrington Sq, Croy. 142 DR101
Tavistock Gro
Torrington Way, Mord. 140 DA100
Torver Rd, Har. 61 CE56
Torver Way, Orp. 145 ER104
Torwood La, Whyt. 176 DT120
Torwood Rd SW15 119 CU85
Torworth Rd, Borwd. 26 CM39
Tothill St SW1 199 M5
Tothill St SW1 101 DK75
Totnes Rd, Well. 106 EV80
Totnes Wk N2 64 DD56
Tottan Ter E1 85 DX72
Tottenhall Rd N13 45 DN51
Tottenham Ct Rd W1 195 L5
Tottenham Ct Rd W1 83 DJ70
Tottenham Grn E N15 66 DT56
Tottenham La N8 65 DL57
Tottenham Ms W1 195 L6
Tottenham Rd N1 84 DS65
Tottenham St W1 195 L7
Tottenham St W1 83 DJ71
Totterdown St SW17 120 DF91
Totteridge Common N20 43 CU47
Totteridge Grn N20 44 DA47
Totteridge Ho SW11 100 DD82
Yelverton Rd
Totteridge La N20 44 DA47
Totteridge Rd, Enf. 31 DX37
Totteridge Village N20 43 CY46
Totternhoe Cl, Har. 61 CJ57
Totton Rd, Th.Hth. 141 DN97
Toulmin St SE1 201 H5
Toulmin St SE1 102 DQ75
Toulon St SE5 102 DQ80
Tournay Rd SW6 99 CZ80
Toussaint Wk SE16 202 C6
Tovey Cl, St.Alb. 9 CK26
Tovil Cl SE20 142 DU96
Towcester Rd E3 85 EB70
Tower Br E1 201 P3
Tower Br E1 84 DT74
Tower Br SE1 201 P3
Tower Br SE1 84 DT74
Tower Br App E1 201 P2
Tower Br App E1 84 DT74
Tower Br Piazza SE1 84 DT74
Horselydown La
Tower Br Rd SE1 201 M7
Tower Br Rd SE1 102 DS76
Tower Cl NW3 64 DD64
Lyndhurst Rd
Tower Cl SE20 122 DV94
Tower Cl, Grav. 131 GL92
Tower Cl, Ilf. 49 EP51
Tower Cl, Orp. 145 ET103
Tower Cl, Wok. 166 AX117
Tower Ct WC2 195 P9
Tower Ct, Brwd. 54 FV47
Tower Cft (Eynsford), Dart. 148 FL103
High St
Tower Gdns, Esher 155 CG108
Tower Gdns Rd N17 46 DQ53
Tower Gro, Wey. 135 BS103
Tower Hamlets Rd E7 68 EF63
Tower Hamlets Rd E17 67 EA55
Tower Hill EC3 201 N1
Tower Hill EC3 84 DS73
Tower Hill, Brwd. 54 FW47
Tower Hill, Kings L. 5 BE29
Tower Hill Ter EC3 84 DS73
Byward St
Tower La, Wem. 61 CK62
Main Dr
Tower Ms E17 67 EA56
Tower Mill Rd SE15 102 DS79
Wells Way
Tower Pk Rd, Dart. 127 FE85
Crayford Rd
Tower Pier EC3 201 N2
Tower Pier EC3 84 DT74
Tower Pl EC3 201 N1
Tower Pt, Enf. 30 DR42
Tower Retail Pk, Dart. 127 FE85
Crayford Rd
Tower Ri, Rich. 98 CL83
Jocelyn Rd
Tower Rd NW10 81 CU66
Tower Rd, Belv. 107 FC77
Tower Rd, Bexh. 107 FB84
Tower Rd, Dart. 128 FJ86
Tower Rd, Epp. 17 ES30
Tower Rd, Orp. 145 ET103
Tower Rd, Tad. 173 CW123
Tower Rd, Twick. 117 CF90
Tower Royal EC4 197 J10
Tower St WC2 195 N9
Tower St WC2 83 DK72
Tower Ter N22 45 DM54
Mayes Rd
Tower Vw, Croy. 143 DX101
Towers, The, Ken. 176 DQ115
Towers Av, Uxb. 77 BQ69
Towers Pl, Rich. 118 CL85
Eton St
Towers Rd, Grays 110 GC78
Towers Rd, Pnr. 40 BY53
Towers Rd, Sthl. 78 CA70
Towers Wk, Wey. 153 BP107
Towers Wd, Dart. 149 FR95
Towfield Rd, Felt. 116 BZ89
Towing Path Wk N1 83 DK67
York Way
Town, The, Enf. 30 DR41
Town Ct Path N4 66 DQ60
Town End, Cat. 176 DS122
Town End Cl, Cat. 176 DS122
Town Fm Way, Stai. 114 BK87
Town La
Town Fld La, Ch.St.G. 36 AW48
Town Fld Way, Islw. 97 CG82
Town Hall App N16 66 DS63
Milton Gro
Town Hall App Rd N15 66 DT56
Town Hall Av W4 98 CR78
Town Hall Rd SW11 100 DF83
Town La, Stai. 114 BK86
Town Meadow, Brent. 97 CK80
Town Path, Egh. 113 BA92
Town Pier, Grav. 131 GH86
West St
Town Quay, Bark. 87 EP67
Town Rd N9 46 DV47
Town Sq, Erith 107 FE79
Pier Rd
Town Sq, Wok. 167 AZ117
Church St E
Town Sq Cres (Bluewater), Green. 129 FT87
Town Tree Rd, Ashf. 114 BN92
Towncourt Cres, Orp. 145 EQ99
Towncourt La, Orp. 145 ER100
Towney Mead, Nthlt. 78 BZ68
Towney Mead Ct, Nthlt. 78 BZ68
Towney Mead
Townfield, Rick. 38 BJ45
Townfield Cor, Grav. 131 GJ88
Townfield Rd, Hayes 77 BT74
Townfield Sq, Hayes 77 BT73
Towngate, Cob. 170 BY115
Townholm Cres W7 97 CF76
Townley Ct E15 86 EF65
Townley Rd SE22 122 DS85
Townley Rd, Bexh. 126 EZ85
Townley St SE17 201 K10
Townmead, Red. 186 DR133
Townmead Rd SW6 100 DC82
Townmead Rd, Rich. 98 CP82
Townmead Rd, Wal.Abb. 15 EC34
Townsend Av N14 45 DK49
Townsend Ind Est NW10 80 CR68
Townsend La NW9 62 CR59
Townsend La, Wok. 167 BB121
St. Peters Rd
Townsend Rd N15 66 DT57
Townsend Rd, Ashf. 114 BL92
Townsend Rd, Sthl. 78 BY74
Townsend St SE17 201 L9
Townsend St SE17 102 DR77
Townsend Way, Nthwd. 39 BT52
Townsend Yd N6 65 DH60
Townshend Cl, Sid. 126 EV93
Townshend Est NW8 82 DE68
Townshend Rd NW8 82 DE67
Townshend Rd, Chis. 125 EP92
Townshend Rd, Rich. 98 CM84
Townshend Ter, Rich. 98 CM84
Townslow La, Wok. 168 BJ116
Townson Av, Nthlt. 77 BU69
Townson Way, Nthlt. 77 BU68
Townson Av
Towpath, Shep. 134 BM103
Towpath Wk E9 67 DZ64
Towpath Way, Croy. 142 DT100
Towton Rd SE27 122 DQ89
Toynbec Cl, Chis. 125 EP91
Beechwood Ri
Toynbee Rd SW20 139 CY95
Toynbee St E1 197 P7
Toynbee St E1 84 DT71
Toyne Way N6 64 DF58
Gaskell Rd
Tracery, The, Bans. 174 DB115
Tracey Av NW2 63 CW64
Tracious Cl, Wok. 166 AV116
Sythwood
Tracious La, Wok. 166 AV116
Tracy Ct, Stan. 41 CJ52
Trade Cl N13 45 DN49
Trader Rd E6 87 EP72
Tradescant Rd SW8 101 DL80
Trading Est Rd NW10 80 CQ70
Trafalgar Av N17 46 DS51
Trafalgar Av SE15 102 DT78
Trafalgar Av, Wor.Pk. 139 CX102
Trafalgar Business Cen, Bark. 87 ET70
Trafalgar Cl SE16 203 K8
Trafalgar Ct, Cob. 153 BU113
Trafalgar Dr, Walt. 135 BV104
Trafalgar Gdns E1 85 DX71
Trafalgar Gdns W8 100 DB76
South End Row
Trafalgar Gro SE10 103 ED79
Trafalgar Pl E11 68 EG56
Trafalgar Pl N18 46 DU50
Trafalgar Rd SE10 103 ED79
Trafalgar Rd SW19 120 DB94
Trafalgar Rd, Dart. 128 FL89
Trafalgar Rd, Grav. 131 GG87
Trafalgar Rd, Rain. 89 FF68
Trafalgar Rd, Twick. 117 CD89
Trafalgar Sq SW1 199 N2
Trafalgar Sq SW1 83 DK74
Trafalgar Sq WC2 199 N2
Trafalgar Sq WC2 83 DK74
Trafalgar St SE17 201 K10
Trafalgar St SE17 102 DR78
Trafalgar Ter, Har. 61 CE60
Nelson Rd
Trafalgar Way E14 204 D2
Trafalgar Way E14 85 EC74
Trafalgar Way, Croy. 141 DM103
Trafford Cl E15 67 EB64
Trafford Cl, Ilf. 49 ET51
Trafford Cl, Rad. 10 CL32
Trafford Rd, Th.Hth. 141 DM99
Tralee Ct SE16 202 E10
Tramway Av E15 86 EE66
Tramway Av N9 46 DV45
Tramway Path, Mitch. 140 DF99
Tranby Pl E9 67 DX64
Homerton High St
Tranley Ms NW3 64 DE63
Fleet Rd
Tranmere Rd N9 46 DT45
Tranmere Rd SW18 120 DC89
Tranmere Rd, Twick. 116 CB87
Tranquil Dale, Bet. 183 CT132
Tranquil Pas SE3 104 EF82
Tranquil Vale
Tranquil Ri, Erith 107 FE78
West St
Tranquil Vale SE3 104 EE82
Transay Wk N1 84 DR65
Marquess Rd
Transept St NW1 194 B7
Transept St NW1 82 DE71
Transmere Cl, Orp. 145 EQ100
Transmere Rd, Orp. 145 EQ100
Transom Cl SE16 203 L8
Transom Sq E14 204 B10
Transom Sq E14 103 EB77
Transport Av, Brent. 97 CH78
Tranton Rd SE16 202 C6
Tranton Rd SE16 102 DU76
Traps Hill, Loug. 33 EM41
Traps La, N.Mal. 138 CS95
Travellers Way, Houns. 96 BW82
Travers Cl E17 47 DX53
Travers Rd N7 65 DN62
Treacy Cl, Bushey 40 CC47
Treadgold St W11 81 CX73
Treadway St E2 84 DV68
Treadwell Rd, Epsom 172 CS115
Treaty Rd, Houns. 96 CB83
Hanworth Rd
Treaty St N1 83 DM67
Trebble Rd, Swans. 130 FY86
Trebeck St W1 199 H2
Trebovir Rd SW5 100 DA78
Treby St E3 85 DZ70
Trecastle Way N7 65 DK63
Carleton Rd
Tredegar Ms E3 85 DZ69
Tredegar Ter
Tredegar Rd E3 85 DZ68
Tredegar Rd N11 45 DK52
Tredegar Rd, Dart. 127 FG89
Tredegar Sq E3 85 DZ69
Tredegar Ter E3 85 DZ69
Trederwen Rd E8 84 DU67
Tredown Rd SE26 122 DW92
Tredwell Cl SW2 121 DM89
Hillside Rd
Tredwell Cl, Brom. 144 EL98
Tredwell Rd SE27 121 DP91
Tree Cl, Rich. 117 CK88
Tree Rd E16 86 EJ72
Tree Tops, Brwd. 54 FW46
Tree Way, Reig. 184 DB131
Treebourne Rd, West. 178 EJ117
Treen Av SW13 99 CT83
Treeside Cl, West Dr. 94 BK77
Treetops, Grav. 131 GH92
Treetops, Whyt. 176 DU118
Treetops Cl SE2 106 EY78
Treetops Cl, Nthwd. 39 BR50
Treetops Vw, Loug. 32 EJ44
High Rd
Treeview Cl SE19 142 DS95
Treewall Gdns, Brom. 124 EH91
Trefgarne Rd, Dag. 70 FA61
Trefil Wk N7 65 DL63
Trefoil Ho, Erith 106 EY75
Kale Rd
Trefoil Rd SW18 120 DC85
Trefusis Wk, Wat. 23 BS39
Tregaron Av N8 65 DL58
Tregaron Gdns, N.Mal. 138 CS98
Avenue Rd
Tregarth Pl, Wok. 166 AT117
Tregarthen Pl, Lthd. 171 CJ121
Tregarvon Rd SW11 100 DG84
Tregenna Av, Har. 60 BZ63
Tregenna Cl N14 29 DJ43
Tregenna Ct, Har. 60 CA63
Trego Rd E9 85 EA66
Tregothnan Rd SW9 101 DL83
Tregunter Rd SW10 100 DC79
Trehearn Rd, Ilf. 49 ER52
Trehern Rd SW14 98 CR83
Treherne Ct SW9 101 DN81
Eythorne Rd
Treherne Ct SW17 120 DG91
Trehurst St E5 67 DY64
Trelawn Cl, Cher. 151 BC108
Trelawn Rd E10 67 EC62
Trelawn Rd SW2 121 DN85
Trelawney Av, Slou. 92 AX76
Trelawney Cl E17 67 EB56
Orford Rd
Trelawney Est E9 84 DW65
Trelawney Gro, Wey. 152 BN107
Trelawney Rd, Ilf. 49 ER52
Trellick Twr W10 81 CZ70
Trellis Sq E3 85 DZ69
Malmesbury Rd
Treloar Gdns SE19 122 DR93
Hancock Rd
Tremadoc Rd SW4 101 DK84
Tremaine Cl SE4 103 EA82
Tremaine Rd SE20 142 DV96
Trematon Pl, Tedd. 117 CJ94
Tremlett Gro N19 65 DJ62
Tremlett Ms N19 65 DJ62
Trenance, Wok. 166 AU117
Cardingham
Trenance Gdns, Ilf. 70 EU62
Trench Yd Ct, Mord. 140 DB100
Green La
Trenchard Av, Ruis. 59 BV63
Trenchard Cl NW9 42 CS53
Fulbeck Dr
Trenchard Cl, Stan. 41 CG51
Trenchard Cl, Walt. 154 BW106
Trenchard Ct, Mord. 140 DB100
Green La
Trenchard St SE10 103 ED78
Trenches La, Slou. 75 BA73
Trenchold St SW8 101 DL79
Trenham Dr, Warl. 176 DW116
Trenholme Cl SE20 122 DV94
Trenholme Ct, Cat. 176 DU122
Trenholme Rd SE20 122 DV94
Trenholme Ter SE20 122 DV94
Trenmar Gdns NW10 81 CV69
Trent Av W5 97 CJ76
Trent Av, Upmin. 73 FR58
Trent Cl, Rad. 10 CL32
Edgbaston Dr
Trent Gdns N14 29 DH44
Trent Rd SW2 121 DM85
Trent Rd, Buck.H. 48 EH46
Trent Rd, Slou. 93 BB79
Trent Way, Hayes 77 BS68
Trent Way, Wor.Pk. 139 CW104
Trentbridge Cl, Ilf. 49 ET51
Trentham Cres, Wok. 167 BA121
Trentham Dr, Orp. 146 EU98
Trentham St SW18 120 DA88
Trentwood Side, Enf. 29 DM41
Treport St SW18 120 DB87
Tresco Cl, Brom. 124 EE93
Tresco Gdns, Ilf. 70 EU61
Tresco Rd SE15 102 DV84
Trescoe Gdns, Har. 60 BY59
Trescoe Gdns, Rom. 51 FC50
Tresham Cres NW8 194 B4
Tresham Cres NW8 82 DE70
Tresham Rd, Bark. 87 ET66
Tresham Wk E9 66 DW64
Churchill Wk
Tresilian Av N21 29 DM43
Tresillian Way, Wok. 166 AU116
Tressell Cl N1 83 DP66
Sebbon St
Tressillian Cres SE4 103 EA83
Tressillian Rd SE4 103 DZ84
Tresta Wk, Wok. 166 AU115
Trestis Cl, Hayes 78 BY71
Jollys La
Treston Ct, Stai. 113 BF92
Treswell Rd, Dag. 88 EY67
Tretawn Gdns NW7 42 CS49
Tretawn Pk NW7 42 CS49
Trevanion Rd W14 99 CY78
Treve Av, Har. 60 CC59
Trevellance Way, Wat. 8 BW33
Trevelyan Av E12 69 EM63
Trevelyan Cl, Dart. 108 FM84
Trevelyan Cres, Har. 61 CK59
Trevelyan Gdns NW10 81 CW67
Trevelyan Rd E15 68 EF63
Trevelyan Rd SW17 120 DE92
Trevereux Hill, Oxt. 189 EM131
Treveris St SE1 200 F3
Treverton St W10 81 CX70
Treves Cl N21 29 DM43
Treville St SW15 119 CV87
Treviso Rd SE23 123 DX89
Farren Rd
Trevithick Cl, Felt. 115 BT88
Trevithick Dr, Dart. 108 FM84
Trevithick St SE8 103 EA78
Trevone Gdns, Pnr. 60 BY58
Trevor Cl, Barn. 28 DD43
Trevor Cl, Brom. 144 EF101
Trevor Cl, Har. 41 CF52
Kenton La
Trevor Cl, Islw. 117 CF85
Trevor Cl, Nthlt. 78 BW68
Trevor Cres, Ruis. 59 BT63
Trevor Gdns, Edg. 42 CR53
Trevor Gdns, Nthlt. 78 BW68
Trevor Gdns, Ruis. 59 BU63
Clyfford Rd
Trevor Pl SW7 198 C5
Trevor Pl SW7 100 DE75
Trevor Rd SW19 119 CY94
Trevor Rd, Edg. 42 CR53
Trevor Rd, Hayes 95 BS75
Trevor Rd, Wdf.Grn. 48 EG52
Trevor Sq SW7 198 D5
Trevor Sq SW7 100 DF75
Trevor St SW7 198 C5
Trevor St SW7 100 DE75
Trevor Wk SW7 100 DF75
Trevor Sq
Trevose Av, W.Byf. 151 BF114
Trevose Rd E17 47 ED53
Trevose Way, Wat. 40 BW48
Trewarden Av, Iver 75 BD68
Trewenna Dr, Chess. 155 CK106
Trewenna Dr, Pot.B. 12 DD32
Trewince Rd SW20 139 CW95
Trewint St SW18 120 DC89
Trewsbury Ho SE2 106 EX75
Hartslock Dr
Trewsbury Rd SE26 123 DX92
Triandra Way, Hayes 78 BX71
Triangle, The EC1 83 DP70
Goswell Rd
Triangle, The N13 45 DN49
Lodge Dr
Triangle, The, Bark. 87 EQ65
Tanner St
Triangle, The, Hmptn. 136 CC95
High St
Triangle, The, Kings.T. 138 CQ96
Kenley Rd
Triangle, The, Wok. 166 AW118
Triangle, The, Wok. 166 AW118
St. John's Rd
Triangle Ct E16 86 EK71
Tollgate Rd
Triangle Pas, Barn. 28 DC42
Triangle Pl SW4 101 DK84
Triangle Rd E8 84 DV67
Trident Gdns, Nthlt. 78 BX69
Jetstar Way
Trident Ind Est, Slou. 93 BE83
Trident Rd, Wat. 7 BT34
Trident St SE16 203 J8
Trident St SE16 103 DX77
Trident Way, Sthl. 95 BV76
Trig La EC4 197 H10
Trigg's Cl, Wok. 166 AX119
Trigg's La, Wok. 166 AW118
Trigo Ct, Epsom 156 CR11
Blakeney Cl
Trigon Rd SW8 101 DM8
Trilby Rd SE23 123 DX8
Trim St SE14 103 DZ7
Trimmer Wk, Brent. 98 CL7
Trinder Gdns N19 65 DL6
Trinder Rd
Trinder Rd N19 65 DL6
Trinder Rd, Barn. 27 CW4
Tring Av W5 80 CM7
Tring Av, Sthl. 78 BZ7
Tring Av, Wem. 80 CN6
Tring Cl, Ilf. 69 EQ5
Tring Cl, Rom. 52 FM4
Tring Gdns, Rom. 52 FL4
Tring Grn, Rom. 52 FM4
Tring Wk, Rom. 52 FL4
Tring Gdns
Tringham Cl, Cher. 151 BC10
Trinidad Gdns, Dag. 89 FD6
Trinidad St E14 85 DZ7
Trinity Av N2 64 DD5
Trinity Av, Enf. 30 DT4
Trinity Buoy Wf E14 205 K1
Trinity Buoy Wf E14 86 EF7
Trinity Ch Pas SW13 99 CV7
Trinity Ch Rd SW13 99 CV7
Trinity Ch Sq SE1 201 J
Trinity Ch Sq SE1 102 DQ7
Trinity Cl E8 84 DT6
Trinity Cl E11 68 EE6
Trinity Cl NW3 64 DD6
Hampstead High St
Trinity Cl SE13 103 ED84
Wisteria Rd
Trinity Cl, Brom. 144 EL102
Trinity Cl, Houns. 96 BY84
Trinity Cl, Nthwd. 39 BS51
Trinity Cl, S.Croy. 160 DS109
Trinity Cl, Stai. 114 BJ86
Trinity Cotts, Rich. 98 CM83
Trinity Rd
Trinity Ct N1 84 DS66
Downham Rd
Trinity Ct SE7 104 EK77
Charlton La
Trinity Cres SW17 120 DF89
Trinity Gdns E16 86 EF70
Cliff Wk
Trinity Gdns SW9 101 DM84
Trinity Gdns, Dart. 128 FK86
Summerhill Rd
Trinity Gro SE10 103 EC81
Trinity Hall Cl, Wat. 24 BW41
Trinity La, Wal.Cr. 15 DY32
Trinity Ms SE20 142 DV95
Trinity Ms W10 81 CX72
Cambridge Gdns
Trinity Path SE26 122 DW90
Trinity Pl, Bexh. 106 EZ84
Trinity Ri SW2 121 DN88
Trinity Rd N2 64 DD55
Trinity Rd N22 45 DL53
Trinity Rd SW17 120 DF89
Trinity Rd SW18 120 DD85
Trinity Rd SW19 120 DA93
Trinity Rd, Grav. 131 GJ87
Trinity Rd, Ilf. 69 EQ55
Trinity Rd, Rich. 98 CM83
Trinity Rd, Sthl. 78 BY74
Trinity Sq EC3 201 N1
Trinity Sq EC3 84 DS73
Trinity St E16 86 EG71
Vincent St
Trinity St SE1 201 J5
Trinity St SE1 102 DQ75
Trinity St, Enf. 30 DQ40
Trinity Wk NW3 82 DC65
Trinity Way E4 47 DZ51
Trinity Way W3 80 CS73
Trio Pl SE1 201 J5
Tripps Hill, Ch.St.G. 36 AU48
Tripps Hill Cl, Ch.St.G. 36 AU48
Tristan Sq SE3 104 EE83
Tristram Cl E17 67 ED55
Tristram Rd, Brom. 124 EF91
Triton Sq NW1 195 K4
Triton Sq NW1 83 DJ70
Tritton Av, Croy. 159 DL105
Tritton Rd SE21 122 DR90
Trittons, Tad. 173 CW121
Triumph Cl (Chafford Hundred), Grays 109 FW77
Triumph Cl, Hayes 95 BQ80
Triumph Ho, Bark. 88 EV69
Triumph Rd E6 87 EM72
Trivett Cl, Green. 129 FU85
Trojan Ct NW6 81 CY66
Willesden La
Trojan Way, Croy. 141 DM104
Trolling Down Hill, Dart. 128 FP89
Troon Cl SE16 202 E10
Troon St E1 85 DY72
Troopers Dr, Rom. 52 FK49
Trosley Av, Grav. 131 GH89
Trosley Rd, Belv. 106 FA79
Trossachs Rd SE22 122 DS85
Trothy Rd SE1 202 C8
Trotsworth Av, Vir.W. 132 AX98
Trotsworth Ct, Vir.W. 132 AY98
Trott Rd N10 44 DF52
Trott St SW11 100 DE81
Trotter Way, Epsom 156 CN112
Trotters Bottom, Barn. 27 CU37
Trotters La, Wok. 150 AV112
Trotts La, West. 189 EQ127
Trotwood, Chig. 49 ER51
Trotwood Cl, Brwd. 54 FY46
Middleton Rd
Troughton Rd SE7 205 P10
Troughton Rd SE7 104 EH78
Trout La, West Dr. 76 BJ73
Trout Ri, Rick. 22 BH41
Trout Rd, West Dr. 76 BK74
Troutbeck Cl, Slou. 74 AU73
Troutbeck Rd SE14 103 DY81
Troutstream Way, Rick. 22 BH42
Trouville Rd SW4 121 DJ86
Trowbridge Est E9 85 DZ65
Osborne Rd
Trowbridge Rd E9 85 DZ65
Trowbridge Rd, Rom. 52 FK51

Trowers Way, Red. 185 DH131
Trowley Ri, Abb.L. 7 BS31
Trowlock Av, Tedd. 117 CJ93
Trowlock Island, Tedd. 117 CK92
Trowlock Way, Tedd. 117 CK93
Troy Cl, Tad. 173 CV120
Troy Ct SE18 105 EP77
Troy Rd SE19 122 DR93
Troy Town SE15 102 DU83
Trubshaw Rd, Sthl. 96 CB76
Havelock Rd
Truesdale Dr (Harefield), Uxb. 58 BJ57
Truesdale Rd E6 87 EM72
Trulock Ct N17 46 DU52
Trulock Rd N17 46 DU52
Truman Cl, Edg. 42 CP52
Pavilion Way
Truman's Rd N16 66 DS64
Trump St EC2 197 J9
Trumper Way, Uxb. 76 BJ67
Trumpers Way W7 97 CE76
Trumpington Rd E7 68 EF63
Trumps Grn Av, Vir.W. 132 AX100
Trumps Grn Cl, Vir.W. 132 AY99
Trumps Grn Rd
Trumps Grn Rd, Vir.W. 132 AX100
Trumps Mill La, Vir.W. 133 AZ100
Trundle St SE1 201 H4
Trundlers Way, Bushey 41 CE46
Trundleys Rd SE8 203 J10
Trundleys Rd SE8 103 DX78
Trundleys Ter SE8 203 J9
Trundleys Ter SE8 103 DX77
Trunks All, Swan. 147 FB96
Truro Gdns, Ilf. 68 EL59
Truro Rd E17 67 DZ56
Truro Rd N22 45 DL52
Truro Rd, Grav. 131 GK90
Truro St NW5 82 DG65
Truro Wk, Rom. 52 FJ51
Saddleworth Rd
Truro Way, Hayes 77 BS69
Portland Rd
Truslove Rd SE27 121 DN92
Trussley Rd W6 99 CW76
Trust Rd, Wal.Cr. 15 DY34
Trust Wk SE21 121 DP88
Peabody Hill
Trustees Way (Denham), Uxb. 57 BF57
Trustons Gdns, Horn. 71 FG59
Tryfan Cl, Ilf. 68 EK57
Tryon St SW3 198 D10
Tryon St SW3 100 DF78
Trys Hill, Cher. 133 AZ103
Trystings Cl, Esher 155 CG107
Tuam Rd SE18 105 ER79
Tubbenden Cl, Orp. 145 ES103
Tubbenden Dr, Orp. 163 ER105
Tubbenden La, Orp. 145 ES104
Tubbenden La S, Orp. 163 ER106
Tubbs Rd NW10 81 CT68
Tubs Hill Par, Sev. 190 FG124
Tubwell Rd, Slou. 74 AV67
Tuck Rd, Rain. 89 FG65
Tucker Rd, Cher. 151 BD107
Tucker St, Wat. 24 BW43
Tuckey Gro, Wok. 167 BF124
Tudor Av, Hmptn. 116 CA93
Tudor Av, Rom. 71 FG55
Tudor Av (Cheshunt), Wal.Cr. 14 DU31
Tudor Av, Wat. 24 BX37
Tudor Av, Wor.Pk. 139 CV104
Tudor Cl N6 65 DJ59
Tudor Cl NW3 64 DE64
Tudor Cl NW7 43 CU51
Tudor Cl NW9 62 CQ61
Tudor Cl SW2 121 DM86
Elm Pk
Tudor Cl, Ashf. 114 BL91
Tudor Cl, Bans. 173 CY115
Tudor Cl, Brwd. 55 FZ44
Tudor Cl, Chess. 156 CL106
Tudor Cl, Chig. 49 EN49
Tudor Cl, Chis. 145 EM95
Tudor Cl, Cob. 154 BZ113
Tudor Cl, Couls. 175 DN118
Tudor Cl, Dart. 127 FH86
Tudor Cl, Epsom 157 CT110
Tudor Cl, Grav. 130 GE88
Tudor Cl, Lthd. 170 CA124
Tudor Cl, Pnr. 59 BU57
Tudor Cl, S.Croy. 176 DV115
Tudor Cl, Sutt. 157 CX106
Tudor Cl, Wall. 159 DJ108
Tudor Cl (Cheshunt), Wal.Cr. 14 DV31
Tudor Cl, Wok. 167 BA117
Tudor Cl, Wdf.Grn. 48 EH50
Tudor Ct E17 67 DY59
Tudor Ct, Borwd. 26 CL40
Tudor Ct, Felt. 116 BW91
Tudor Ct, Swan. 147 FC101
Tudor Ct N, Wem. 62 CN64
Tudor Ct S, Wem. 62 CN64
Tudor Cres, Enf. 29 DP39
Tudor Cres, Ilf. 49 EP51
Tudor Dr, Kings.T. 118 CL92
Tudor Dr, Mord. 139 CX100
Tudor Dr, Rom. 71 FG56
Tudor Dr, Walt. 136 BX102
Tudor Dr, Wat. 24 BX38
Tudor Est NW10 80 CP68
Tudor Gdns NW9 62 CQ61
Tudor Gdns SW13 98 CS83
Treen Av
Tudor Gdns W3 80 CN72
Tudor Gdns, Har. 41 CD54
Tudor Rd
Tudor Gdns, Rom. 71 FG56
Tudor Gdns, Twick. 117 CF88
Tudor Gdns, Upmin. 72 FQ61
Tudor Gdns, W.Wick. 143 EC104
Tudor Gro E9 84 DW66
Tudor Gro N20 44 DE48
Church Cres
Tudor La, Wind. 112 AW87
Tudor Manor Gdns, Wat. 8 BX32
Tudor Ms, Rom. 71 FF57
Eastern Rd
Tudor Par, Rick. 38 BG45
Berry La
Tudor Pl W1 195 M8
Tudor Pl, Mitch. 120 DE94
Tudor Rd E4 47 EB51
Tudor Rd E6 86 EJ67
Tudor Rd E9 84 DV67
Tudor Rd N9 46 DV45
Tudor Rd SE19 122 DT94
Tudor Rd SE25 142 DV99
Tudor Rd, Ashf. 115 BR93
Tudor Rd, Bark. 87 ET67
Tudor Rd, Barn. 28 DA41
Tudor Rd, Beck. 143 EB97
Tudor Rd, Hmptn. 116 CA94
Tudor Rd, Har. 41 CD54
Tudor Rd, Hayes 77 BR72
Tudor Rd, Houns. 97 CD84
Tudor Rd, Kings.T. 118 CN94
Tudor Rd, Pnr. 40 BW54
Tudor Rd, Sthl. 78 BY73
Tudor Sq, Hayes 77 BR71
Tudor St EC4 196 E10
Tudor St EC4 83 DN73
Tudor Wk, Bex. 126 EY86
Tudor Wk, Lthd. 171 CF120
Tudor Wk, Wat. 24 BX37
Tudor Wk, Wey. 135 BP104
West Palace Gdns
Tudor Way N14 45 DK46
Tudor Way W3 98 CN75
Tudor Way, Orp. 145 ER100
Tudor Way, Rick. 38 BG46
Tudor Way, Uxb. 76 BN65
Tudor Way, Wal.Abb. 15 ED33
Tudor Well Cl, Stan. 41 CH50
Tudors, The, Reig. 184 DC131
Tudorwalk, Grays 110 GA76
Thurloe Wk
Tudway Rd SE3 104 EH83
Tufnail Rd, Dart. 128 FM86
Tufnell Pk Rd N7 65 DJ63
Tufnell Pk Rd N19 65 DJ63
Tufter Rd, Chig. 49 ET50
Tufton Gdns, W.Mol. 136 CB96
Tufton Rd E4 47 EA49
Tufton St SW1 199 N6
Tufton St SW1 101 DK76
Tugboat St SE28 105 ES75
Tugela Rd, Croy. 142 DR100
Tugela St SE6 123 DZ89
Tugmutton Cl, Orp. 163 EP105
Acorn Way
Tuilerie St E2 84 DU68
Tulip Cl E6 87 EM71
Bradley Stone Rd
Tulip Cl, Brwd. 54 FV43
Poppy Cl
Tulip Cl, Croy. 143 DX102
Tulip Cl, Hmptn. 116 BZ93
Partridge Rd
Tulip Cl, Rom. 52 FK51
Cloudberry Rd
Tulip Cl, Sthl. 96 CC75
Chevy Rd
Tulip Ct, Pnr. 60 BW55
Tulip Gdns, Ilf. 87 EP65
Tulip Way, West Dr. 94 BK76
Wise La
Tull St, Mitch. 140 DF101
Tulse Cl, Beck. 143 EC97
Tulse Hill SW2 121 DN86
Tulse Hill Est SW2 121 DN86
Tulsemere Rd SE27 122 DQ89
Tulyar Cl, Tad. 173 CV120
Tumber St, Epsom 182 CQ125
Tumblewood Rd, Bans. 173 CY116
Tumbling Bay, Walt. 135 BU100
Tummons Gdns SE25 142 DS96
Tun Yd SW8 101 DH82
Peardon St
Tuncombe Rd N18 46 DS49
Tunis Rd W12 81 CV74
Tunley Grn E14 85 DZ71
Burdett Rd
Tunley Rd NW10 80 CS67
Tunley Rd SW17 120 DG88
Tunmarsh La E13 86 EJ69
Tunmers End (Chalfont St. Peter), Ger.Cr. 36 AW53
Tunnan Leys E6 87 EN72
Tunnel Av SE10 204 G4
Tunnel Av SE10 103 ED75
Tunnel Gdns N11 45 DJ52
Tunnel Rd SE16 202 F4
Tunnel Rd, Reig. 184 DA133
Church St
Tunnel Wd Cl, Wat. 23 BT37
Tunnel Wd Rd, Wat. 23 BT37
Tunstall Av, Ilf. 50 EU51
Tunstall Cl, Orp. 163 ES105
Tunstall Rd SW9 101 DM84
Tunstall Rd, Croy. 142 DS102
Tunstall Wk, Brent. 98 CL79
Tunstock Way, Belv. 106 EY76
Tunworth Cl NW9 62 CQ58
Tunworth Cres SW15 119 CT86
Tupelo Rd E10 67 EB61
Tupwood Ct, Cat. 186 DU125
Tupwood La, Cat. 186 DU125
Tupwood Scrubbs Rd, Cat. 186 DU128
Turenne Cl SW18 100 DC84
Turfhouse La, Wok. 150 AS109
Turin Rd N9 46 DW45
Turin St E2 84 DU69
Turkey Oak Cl SE19 142 DS95
Turkey St, Enf. 30 DV37
Turks Cl, Uxb. 76 BN69
Harlington Rd
Turk's Head Yd EC1 196 F6
Turks Row SW3 198 E10
Turks Row SW3 100 DF78
Turle Rd N4 65 DM60
Turle Rd SW16 141 DL96
Turlewray Cl N4 65 DM60
Turley Cl E15 86 EE67
Turnagain La EC4 196 F8
Turnagain La, Dart. 127 FG90
Turnage Rd, Dag. 70 EY60
Turnberry Cl NW4 43 CX54
Turnberry Cl SE16 102 DV78
Ryder Dr
Turnberry Ct, Wat. 40 BW48
Turnberry Dr, St.Alb. 8 BY30
Turnberry Quay E14 204 C6
Turnberry Way, Orp. 145 ER102
Turnbull Cl, Green. 129 FS87
Turnbury Cl SE28 88 EX72
Turnchapel Ms SW4 101 DH83
Cedars Rd
Turner Av N15 66 DS56
Turner Av, Mitch. 140 DF95
Turner Av, Twick. 116 CC90
Turner Cl NW11 64 DB58
Turner Cl SW9 101 DP81
Langton Rd
Turner Cl, Hayes 77 BQ68
Charville La
Turner Cl, Wem. 61 CK64
Turner Ct, Dart. 128 FJ85
Wilmot Rd
Turner Dr NW11 64 DB58
Turner Rd E17 67 EC55
Turner Rd, Bushey 24 CC42
Turner Rd, Dart. 129 FV90
Turner Rd, Edg. 62 CM55
Turner Rd, N.Mal. 138 CR101
Turner Rd, Slou. 92 AW75
Turner Rd, West. 162 EJ112
Turner St E1 84 DV71
Turner St E16 86 EF72
Turners Cl, Stai. 114 BH92
Turners Gdns, Sev. 191 FJ128
Turners Hill (Cheshunt), Wal.Cr. 15 DX30
Turners La, Walt. 153 BV107
Turners Meadow Way, Beck. 143 DZ95
Turners Rd E3 85 DZ71
Turners Way, Croy. 141 DN103
Turners Wd NW11 64 DC59
Turners Wd Dr, Ch.St.G. 36 AX48
Turneville Rd W14 99 CZ79
Turney Rd SE21 122 DR87
Turneys Orchard, Rick. 21 BD43
Turnham Grn Ter W4 98 CS77
Turnham Grn Ter Ms W4 98 CS77
Turnham Grn Ter
Turnham Rd SE4 123 DY85
Turnmill St EC1 196 E5
Turnmill St EC1 83 DN70
Turnoak Av, Wok. 166 AY120
Turnoak La, Wok. 166 AY119
Wych Hill La
Turnpike Cl SE8 103 DZ80
Amersham Vale
Turnpike Dr, Orp. 164 EW109
Turnpike Ho EC1 196 G3
Turnpike Ho EC1 83 DP69
Turnpike La N8 65 DM56
Turnpike La, Sutt. 158 DC106
Turnpike La, Til. 111 GK78
Turnpike La, Uxb. 76 BL69
Turnpike Link, Croy. 142 DS103
Turnpike Way, Islw. 97 CG81
Turnpin La SE10 103 EC79
Turnstone Cl E13 86 EG69
Turnstone Cl NW9 42 CS54
Kestrel Cl
Turnstone Cl, S.Croy. 161 DY110
Turnstone Cl (Ickenham), Uxb. 59 BP64
Turnstones, The, Grav. 131 GK89
Turnstones, The, Wat. 24 BY36
Turp Av, Grays 110 GC75
Turpentine La SW1 199 J10
Turpin Av, Rom. 50 FA52
Turpin Cl, Enf. 31 EA38
Government Row
Turpin La, Erith 107 FG80
Turpin Rd, Felt. 115 BT86
Staines Rd
Turpin Way N19 65 DK61
Elthorne Rd
Turpin Way, Wall. 159 DH108
Turpington Cl, Brom. 144 EL100
Turpington La, Brom. 144 EL101
Turpins La, Wdf.Grn. 49 EM50
Turquand St SE17 201 J9
Turret Gro SW4 101 DJ83
Turton Rd, Wem. 62 CL64
Turville St E2 197 P4
Tuscan Rd SE18 105 ER78
Tuskar St SE10 104 EE78
Tustin Est SE15 102 DW79
Tuttlebee La, Buck.H. 48 EG47
Tuxford Cl, Borwd. 26 CL38
Twankhams All, Epp. 18 EU30
Hemnall St
Tweed Glen, Rom. 51 FD52
Tweed Grn, Rom. 51 FE52
Tweed Rd, Slou. 93 BA79
Tweed Way, Rom. 51 FD52
Tweedale Ct E15 67 EC64
Tweeddale Gro, Uxb. 59 BQ62
Tweeddale Rd, Cars. 140 DD102
Tweedmouth Rd E13 86 EH68
Tweedy Cl, Enf. 30 DT43
Tweedy Rd, Brom. 144 EG95
Tweezer's All WC2 196 D10
Twelve Acre Cl, Lthd. 170 BZ124
Twelvetrees Cres E3 85 EC70
Twentyman Cl, Wdf.Grn. 48 EG50
Twickenham Br, Rich. 117 CJ85
Twickenham Br, Twick. 117 CJ85
Twickenham Cl, Croy. 141 DM104
Twickenham Gdns, Grnf. 61 CG64
Twickenham Gdns, Har. 41 CE52
Twickenham Rd E11 67 ED61
Twickenham Rd, Felt. 116 BZ90
Twickenham Rd, Islw. 97 CG83
Twickenham Rd, Rich. 97 CJ84
Twickenham Rd, Tedd. 117 CG92
Twickenham Trd Est, Twick. 117 CF86
Twig Folly Cl E2 85 DX68
Roman Rd
Twigg Cl, Erith 107 FE80
Twilley St SW18 120 DB87
Twin Tumps Way SE28 88 EU73
Twine Cl, Bark. 88 EV69
Thames Rd
Twine Ct E1 84 DW73
Twine Ter E3 85 DZ70
Ropery St
Twineham Grn N12 44 DA49
Tillingham Way
Twining Av, Twick. 116 CC90
Twinn Rd NW7 43 CY51
Twinoaks, Cob. 154 CA113
Twisden Rd NW5 65 DH63
Twisleton Ct, Dart. 128 FK86
Priory Hill
Twitchells La, Beac. 36 AT51
Twitton La, Sev. 181 FD115
Twitton Meadows, Sev. 181 FE116
Two Rivers Retail Pk, Stai. 113 BE91
Twybridge Way NW10 80 CQ66
Twycross Ms SE10 205 J9
Twyford Abbey Rd NW10 80 CM69
Twyford Av N2 64 DF55
Twyford Av W3 80 CN73
Twyford Cres W3 80 CN74
Twyford Pl WC2 196 B8
Twyford Rd, Cars. 140 DD102
Twyford Rd, Har. 60 CB60
Twyford Rd, Ilf. 69 EQ64
Twyford St N1 83 DM67
Tyas Rd E16 86 EF70
Tybenham Rd SW19 140 DA97
Tyberry Rd, Enf. 30 DV41
Tyburn La, Har. 61 CE59
Tyburn Way W1 194 E10
Tyburn Way W1 82 DF73
Tyburns, The, Brwd. 55 GC47
Tycehurst Hill, Loug. 33 EM42
Tydcombe Rd, Warl. 176 DW119
Tye La, Epsom 182 CR127
Tye La, Epsom 182 CR126
Headley Common Rd
Tye La, Orp. 163 EQ106
Tye La, Tad. 183 CT128
Dorking Rd
Tyers Est SE1 201 M4
Tyers Est SE1 102 DS75
Tyers Gate SE1 201 M4
Tyers St SE11 200 B10
Tyers St SE11 101 DM78
Tyers Ter SE11 101 DM78
Tyeshurst Cl SE2 106 EY78
Tyfield Cl (Cheshunt), Wal.Cr. 14 DW30
Tykeswater La, Borwd. 25 CJ39
Tyle Grn, Horn. 72 FL56
Tyle Pl, Wind. 112 AU85
Tylecroft Rd SW16 141 DL96
Tylehurst Gdns, Ilf. 69 EQ64
Tyler Cl E2 84 DT68
Tyler Gdns, Add. 152 BJ105
Tyler Gro, Dart. 108 FM84
Spielman Rd
Tyler St SE10 104 EE78
Tyler Way, Brwd. 54 FV46
Tylers Cl, Gdse. 186 DV130
Tylers Cl, Kings L. 6 BL28
Tylers Cl, Loug. 48 EL45
Tyler's Ct W1 195 M9
Tylers Cres, Horn. 72 FJ64
Tylers Gate, Har. 62 CL58
Tylers Grn Rd, Swan. 147 FC100
Tylers Hill Rd, Chesh. 4 AT30
Tylers Path, Cars. 158 DF105
Rochester Rd
Tylers Way, Wat. 25 CD42
Tylersfield, Abb.L. 7 BT31
Tylney Av SE19 122 DT92
Tylney Rd E7 68 EJ63
Tylney Rd, Brom. 144 EK96
Tynan Cl, Felt. 115 BU88
Sandycombe Rd
Tyndale Ct E14 204 B10
Tyndale Ct E14 103 EB78
Tyndale La N1 83 DP66
Upper St
Tyndale Ter N1 83 DP66
Canonbury La
Tyndall Rd E10 67 EC61
Tyndall Rd, Well. 105 ET83
Tyne Cl, Upmin. 73 FR58
Tyne Gdns, S.Ock. 90 FQ73
Tyne St E1 84 DT72
Old Castle St
Tynedale, St.Alb. 10 CM27
Thamesdale
Tynedale Cl, Dart. 129 FR88
Tyneham Rd SW11 100 DG82
Tynemouth Cl E6 87 EP72
Covelees Wall
Tynemouth Dr, Enf. 30 DU38
Tynemouth Rd N15 66 DT56
Tynemouth Rd SE18 105 ET78
Tynemouth Rd, Mitch. 120 DG94
Tynemouth St SW6 100 DC82
Type St E2 85 DX68
Tyrawley Rd SW6 100 DB81
Tyrell Cl, Har. 61 CE63
Tyrell Ct, Cars. 158 DF105
Tyrell Ri, Brwd. 54 FW50
Tyrells Cl, Upmin. 72 FN61
Tyrols Rd SE23 123 DX88
Wastdale Rd
Tyron Way, Sid. 125 ES91
Tyrone Rd E6 87 EM68
Tyrrel Way NW9 63 CT59
Tyrrell Av, Well. 126 EU85
Tyrrell Rd SE22 102 DU84
Tyrrell Sq, Mitch. 140 DE95
Tyrrells Hall Cl, Grays 110 GD79
Tyrwhitt Rd SE4 103 EA83
Tysea Hill, Rom. 51 FF45
Tysoe Av, Enf. 31 DZ36
Tysoe St EC1 196 D3
Tyson Rd SE23 122 DW87
Tyssen Pas E8 84 DT65
Tyssen Pl, S.Ock. 91 FW69
Tyssen Rd N16 66 DT62
Tyssen St E8 84 DT65
Tyssen St N1 197 N1
Tytherton Rd N19 65 DK62

U

Uamvar St E14 85 EB71
Uckfield Gro, Mitch. 140 DG95
Uckfield Rd, Enf. 31 DX37
Udall Gdns, Rom. 50 FA51
Udall St SW1 199 L9
Udney Pk Rd, Tedd. 117 CG92
Uffington Rd NW10 81 CU67
Uffington Rd SE27 121 DN91
Ufford Cl, Har. 40 CB52
Ufford Rd
Ufford Rd, Har. 40 CB52
Ufford St SE1 200 E4
Ufford St SE1 101 DN75
Ufton Gro N1 84 DR66
Ufton Rd N1 84 DS66
Uhura Sq N16 66 DS62
Ujima Ct SW16 121 DL91
Sunnyhill Rd
Ullathorne Rd SW16 121 DJ91
Ulleswater Rd N14 45 DL49
Ullin St E14 85 EC71
St. Leonards Rd
Ullswater Business Pk, Couls. 175 DL116
Ullswater Cl SW15 118 CR91
Ullswater Cl, Brom. 124 EE93
Ullswater Cl, Hayes 77 BS68
Ullswater Ct, Har. 60 CA59
Oakington Av
Ullswater Cres SW15 118 CR91
Ullswater Cres, Couls. 175 DL116
Ullswater Rd SE27 121 DP89
Ullswater Rd SW13 99 CU80
Ullswater Way, Horn. 71 FG64
Ulstan Cl, Cat. 177 EA123
Ulster Gdns N13 46 DQ49
Ulster Pl NW1 195 H5
Ulster Ter NW1 195 H4
Ulundi Rd SE3 104 EE79
Ulva Rd SW15 119 CX85
Ravenna Rd
Ulverscroft Rd SE22 122 DT85
Ulverston Rd E17 47 ED54
Ulverstone Rd SE27 121 DP89
Ulwin Av, W.Byf. 152 BL113
Ulysses Rd NW6 63 CZ64
Umberston St E1 84 DV72
Hessel St
Umbria St SW15 119 CU86
Umfreville Rd N4 65 DP58
Undercliff Rd SE13 103 EA83
Underhill, Barn. 28 DA43
Underhill Pk Rd, Reig. 184 DA131
Underhill Pas NW1 83 DH67
Camden High St
Underhill Rd SE22 122 DV86
Underhill St NW1 83 DH67
Camden High St
Underne Av N14 45 DH47
Underriver Ho Rd, Sev. 191 FP130
Undershaft EC3 197 M9
Undershaft EC3 84 DS72
Undershaw Rd, Brom. 124 EE90
Underwood, Croy. 161 EC106
Underwood, The SE9 125 EM89
Underwood Rd E1 84 DU70
Underwood Rd E4 47 EB50
Underwood Rd, Cat. 186 DS126
Underwood Rd, Wdf.Grn. 48 EK52
Underwood Row N1 197 J2
Underwood Row N1 84 DQ69
Underwood St N1 197 J2
Underwood St N1 84 DQ69
Undine Rd E14 204 C8
Undine Rd E14 103 EB77
Undine St SW17 120 DF92
Uneeda Dr, Grnf. 79 CD67
Unicorn Wk, Green. 129 FT85
Union Cl E11 67 ED63
Union Cotts E15 86 EE66
Welfare Rd
Union Ct EC2 197 M8
Union Ct, Rich. 118 CL85
Eton St
Union Dr E1 85 DY70
Canal Cl
Union Gro SW8 101 DK82
Union Pk NW10 80 CQ69
Acton La
Union Rd N11 45 DK51
Union Rd SW4 101 DK82
Union Rd SW8 101 DK82
Union Rd, Brom. 144 EK99
Union Rd, Croy. 142 DQ101
Union Rd, Nthlt. 78 CA68
Union Rd, Wem. 80 CL65
Union Sq N1 84 DQ67
Union St E15 85 EC67
Union St SE1 200 G3
Union St SE1 83 DP74
Union St, Barn. 27 CY42
Union St, Kings.T. 137 CK96
Union Wk E2 197 N2
Unity Cl NW10 81 CU65
Unity Cl SE19 122 DQ92
Crown Dale
Unity Cl, Croy. 161 EB109
Castle Hill Av
Unity Rd, Enf. 30 DW37
Unity Way SE18 104 EK76
Unity Wf SE1 202 A4
University Cl NW7 43 CT52
University Cl, Bushey 24 CA42
University Gdns, Bex. 126 EZ87
University Pl, Erith 107 FB80
Belmont Rd
University Rd SW19 120 DD93
University St WC1 195 L5
University St WC1 83 DJ70
University Way E16 87 EN73
University Way, Dart. 108 FJ84
Unwin Av, Felt. 115 BS85
Unwin Cl SE15 102 DU79
Unwin Rd SW7 198 A6
Unwin Rd, Islw. 97 CE83
Up Cor, Ch.St.G. 36 AW47

Up Cor Cl, Ch.St.G. 36 AV47
Upbrook Ms W2 82 DC72
Chilworth St
Upcerne Rd SW10 100 DC80
Upchurch Cl SE20 122 DV94
Upcroft Av, Edg. 42 CQ50
Updale Cl, Pot.B. 11 CY33
Updale Rd, Sid. 125 ET91
Upfield, Croy. 142 DV103
Upfield Rd W7 79 CF70
Upgrove Manor Way SW2 121 DN87
Trinity Ri
Uphall Rd, Ilf. 69 EP64
Upham Pk Rd W4 98 CS77
Uphill Dr NW7 42 CS50
Uphill Dr NW9 62 CQ57
Uphill Gro NW7 42 CS49
Uphill Rd NW7 42 CS49
Upland Ct Rd, Rom. 52 FM54
Upland Dr, Hat. 12 DB25
Upland Ms SE22 122 DU85
Upland Rd
Upland Rd E13 86 EF70
Sutton Rd
Upland Rd SE22 122 DU85
Upland Rd, Bexh. 106 EZ83
Upland Rd, Cat. 177 EB120
Upland Rd, Epp. 17 ET25
Upland Rd, S.Croy. 160 DR106
Upland Rd, Sutt. 158 DD108
Upland Way, Epsom 173 CW118
Uplands, Ash. 171 CK120
Uplands, Beck. 143 EA96
Uplands, Rick. 22 BM44
Uplands, The, Ger.Cr. 56 AY60
Uplands, The, Loug. 33 EM41
Uplands, The, Ruis. 59 BU60
Uplands, The, St.Alb. 8 BY30
Uplands Av E17 47 DX54
Blackhorse La
Uplands Business Pk E17 47 DX54
Uplands Cl SW14 118 CP85
Monroe Dr
Uplands Cl, Ger.Cr. 56 AY60
Uplands Cl, Sev. 190 FF123
Uplands Dr, Lthd. 155 CD113
Uplands End, Wdf.Grn. 48 EL52
Uplands Pk Rd, Enf. 29 DN41
Uplands Rd N8 65 DM57
Uplands Rd, Barn. 44 DG46
Uplands Rd, Brwd. 54 FY50
Uplands Rd, Ken. 176 DQ116
Uplands Rd, Orp. 146 EV102
Uplands Rd, Rom. 70 EX55
Uplands Rd, Wdf.Grn. 48 EL52
Uplands Way N21 29 DN43
Uplands Way, Sev. 190 FF123
Upminster Rd, Horn. 72 FM61
Upminster Rd, Upmin. 72 FM61
Upminster Rd N, Rain. 90 FJ69
Upminster Rd S, Rain. 89 FG70
Upminster Trd Pk, Upmin. 73 FX59
Upney Cl, Horn. 72 FJ64
Tylers Cres
Upney La, Bark. 87 ES65
Upnor Way SE17 201 N10
Uppark Dr, Ilf. 69 EQ58
Upper Abbey Rd, Belv. 106 EZ77
Upper Addison Gdns W14 99 CY75
Upper Bardsey Wk N1 84 DQ65
Clephane Rd
Upper Belgrave St SW1 198 G6
Upper Belgrave St SW1 100 DG76
Upper Berkeley St W1 194 D9
Upper Berkeley St W1 82 DF72
Upper Beulah Hill SE19 142 DS95
Upper Brentwood Rd, Rom. 72 FJ56
Upper Br Rd, Red. 184 DE134
Upper Brighton Rd, Surb. 137 CK100
Upper Brockley Rd SE4 103 DZ82
Upper Brook St W1 198 F1
Upper Brook St W1 82 DG73
Upper Butts, Brent. 97 CJ79
Upper Caldy Wk N1 84 DQ65
Clephane Rd
Upper Camelford Wk W11 81 CY72
Lancaster Rd
Upper Cavendish Av N3 64 DA55
Upper Cheyne Row SW3 100 DE79
Upper Ch Hill, Green. 129 FS85
Upper Clapton Rd E5 66 DV60
Upper Clarendon Wk W11 81 CY72
Lancaster Rd
Upper Cornsland, Brwd. 54 FX48
Upper Ct Rd, Cat. 177 EA123
Upper Ct Rd, Epsom 156 CQ111
Upper Dengie Wk N1 84 DQ67
Popham Rd
Upper Dr, West. 178 EJ118
Upper Dunnymans, Bans. 157 CZ114
Basing Rd
Upper Elmers End Rd, Beck. 143 DY98
Upper Fairfield Rd, Lthd. 171 CH121
Upper Fm Rd, W.Mol. 136 BZ98
Upper Fosters NW4 63 CW57
New Brent St
Upper Grn E, Mitch. 140 DF97
Upper Grn W, Mitch. 140 DF97
London Rd
Upper Grenfell Wk W11 81 CX73
Whitchurch Rd
Upper Grosvenor St W1 198 F1
Upper Grosvenor St W1 82 DG73
Upper Grotto Rd, Twick. 117 CF89
Upper Grd SE1 200 D2
Upper Grd SE1 83 DP74
Upper Gro SE25 142 DS98
Upper Gro Rd, Belv. 106 EZ79
Upper Guild Hall (Bluewater), Green. 129 FU88
Bluewater Parkway
Upper Gulland Wk N1 84 DQ65
Clephane Rd
Upper Halliford Bypass, Shep. 135 BS99
Upper Halliford Grn, Shep. 135 BS98
Holmbank Dr
Upper Halliford Rd, Shep. 135 BS96
Upper Ham Rd, Kings.T. 117 CK91
Upper Ham Rd, Rich. 117 CK91
Upper Handa Wk N1 84 DR65
Clephane Rd
Upper Harley St NW1 194 G4
Upper Harley St NW1 82 DG70
Upper Hawkwell Wk N1 84 DQ67
Popham Rd
Upper High St, Epsom 156 CS113
Upper Highway, Abb.L. 7 BR33
Upper Highway, Kings L. 7 BQ32
Upper Hill Ri, Rick. 22 BH44
Upper Hitch, Wat. 40 BY46
Upper Holly Hill Rd, Belv. 107 FB78
Upper James St W1 195 L10
Upper John St W1 195 L10
Upper Lismore Wk N1 84 DQ65
Clephane Rd
Upper Mall W6 99 CU78
Upper Marsh SE1 200 C6
Upper Marsh SE1 101 DM76
Upper Montagu St W1 194 D6
Upper Montagu St W1 82 DF71
Upper Mulgrave Rd, Sutt. 157 CZ108
Upper N St E14 85 EA71
Upper Paddock Rd, Wat. 24 BY44
Upper Palace Rd, E.Mol. 137 CD97
Upper Pk, Loug. 32 EK42
Upper Pk Rd N11 45 DH50
Upper Pk Rd NW3 64 DF64
Upper Pk Rd, Belv. 107 FB77
Upper Pk Rd, Brom. 144 EH95
Upper Pk Rd, Kings.T. 118 CN93
Upper Phillimore Gdns W8 100 DA75
Upper Pillory Down, Cars. 158 DG113
Upper Pines, Bans. 174 DF117
Upper Rainham Rd, Horn. 71 FF63
Upper Ramsey Wk N1 84 DR65
Clephane Rd
Upper Rawreth Wk N1 84 DQ67
Popham Rd
Upper Richmond Rd SW15 99 CY84
Upper Richmond Rd W SW14 98 CP84
Upper Richmond Rd W, Rich. 98 CN84
Upper Rd E13 86 EG69
Upper Rd (Denham), Uxb. 57 BD59
Upper Rd, Wall. 159 DK106
Upper Rose Gall (Bluewater), Green. 129 FU88
Bluewater Parkway
Upper Ryle, Brwd. 54 FV45
Upper St. Martin's La WC2 195 P10
Upper Sawley Wd, Bans. 157 CZ114
Upper Selsdon Rd, S.Croy. 160 DT108
Upper Sheppey Wk N1 84 DQ66
Clephane Rd
Upper Sheridan Rd, Belv. 106 FA77
Coleman Rd
Upper Shirley Rd, Croy. 142 DW103
Upper Shott (Cheshunt), Wal.Cr. 14 DT26
Upper Sq, Islw. 97 CG83
North St
Upper Sta Rd, Rad. 25 CG35
Upper St N1 83 DN68
Upper Sunbury Rd, Hmptn. 136 BY95
Upper Sutton La, Houns. 96 CA80
Upper Swaines, Epp. 17 ET30
Upper Tachbrook St SW1 199 K8
Upper Tachbrook St SW1 101 DJ77
Upper Tail, Wat. 40 BY48
Upper Talbot Wk W11 81 CY72
Lancaster Rd
Upper Teddington Rd, Kings.T. 137 CJ95
Upper Ter NW3 64 DC62
Upper Thames St EC4 196 G10
Upper Thames St EC4 84 DQ73
Upper Thames Wk (Bluewater), Green. 129 FU88
Bluewater Parkway
Upper Tollington Pk N4 65 DN60
Upper Tooting Pk SW17 120 DF89
Upper Tooting Rd SW17 120 DF91
Upper Town Rd, Grnf. 78 CB70
Upper Tulse Hill SW2 121 DM87
Upper Vernon Rd, Sutt. 158 DD106
Upper Wk, Vir.W. 132 AY98
Upper Walthamstow Rd E17 67 ED56
Upper W St, Reig. 183 CZ134
Upper Wickham La, Well. 106 EV80
Upper Wimpole St W1 195 H6
Upper Wimpole St W1 82 DG71
Upper Woburn Pl WC1 195 N3
Upper Woburn Pl WC1 83 DK69
Upper Woodcote Village, Pur. 159 DK112
Upperton Rd, Sid. 125 ET92
Upperton Rd E E13 86 EJ69
Inniskilling Rd
Upperton Rd W E13 86 EJ69
Uppingham Av, Stan. 41 CH53
Upsdell Av N13 45 DN51
Upshire Rd, Wal.Abb. 16 EF32
Upshirebury Grn, Wal.Abb. 16 EK33
Horseshoe Hill
Upshott La, Wok. 167 BF117
Upstall St SE5 101 DP81
Upton, Wok. 166 AV117
Upton Av E7 86 EG66
Upton Cl, Bex. 126 EZ86
Upton Cl, St.Alb. 9 CD25
Upton Cl, Slou. 92 AT76
Upton Ct SE20 122 DW94
Blean Gro
Upton Ct Rd, Slou. 92 AU76
Upton Dene, Sutt. 158 DB108
Upton Gdns, Har. 61 CH57
Upton La E7 86 EG66
Upton Lo Cl, Bushey 40 CC45
Upton Pk, Slou. 92 AT76
Upton Pk Rd E7 86 EH66
Upton Rd N18 46 DU50
Upton Rd SE18 105 EQ79
Upton Rd, Bex. 126 EZ86
Upton Rd, Bexh. 106 EY84
Upton Rd, Houns. 96 CA83
Upton Rd, Slou. 92 AU76
Upton Rd, Th.Hth. 142 DR96
Upton Rd, Wat. 23 BV42
Upton Rd S, Bex. 126 EZ86
Upway N12 44 DE52
Upway (Chalfont St. Peter), Ger.Cr. 37 AZ53
Upwood Rd SE12 124 EG86
Upwood Rd SW16 141 DL95
Urban Av, Horn. 72 FJ62
Urlwin St SE5 102 DQ79
Urlwin Wk SW9 101 DN82
Urmston Dr SW19 119 CY88
Ursula Ms N4 66 DQ60
Portland Ri
Ursula St SW11 100 DE81
Urswick Gdns, Dag. 88 EY66
Urswick Rd
Urswick Rd E9 66 DW64
Urswick Rd, Dag. 88 EX66
Usborne Ms SW8 101 DM80
Usher Rd E3 85 DZ68
Usherwood Cl, Tad. 182 CP131
Usk Rd SW11 100 DC84
Usk Rd, S.Ock. 90 FQ72
Usk St E2 85 DX69
Utopia Village NW1 82 DG67
Chalcot Rd
Uvedale Cl, Croy. 161 ED111
Uvedale Cres
Uvedale Cres, Croy. 161 ED111
Uvedale Rd, Dag. 70 FA62
Uvedale Rd, Enf. 30 DR43
Uvedale Rd, Oxt. 188 EF129
Uverdale Rd SW10 100 DC80
Uxbridge Gdns, Felt. 116 BX89
Marlborough Rd
Uxbridge Rd W3 80 CL73
Uxbridge Rd W5 80 CL73
Uxbridge Rd W7 79 CF74
Uxbridge Rd W12 81 CU74
Uxbridge Rd W13 79 CF74
Uxbridge Rd, Felt. 116 BW89
Uxbridge Rd, Hmptn. 116 CA91
Uxbridge Rd, Har. 40 CC52
Uxbridge Rd, Hayes 78 BW73
Uxbridge Rd, Iver 74 AY71
Uxbridge Rd, Kings.T. 137 CK98
Uxbridge Rd, Pnr. 40 CB52
Uxbridge Rd, Rick. 37 BF47
Uxbridge Rd, Slou. 92 AU75
Uxbridge Rd, Sthl. 78 CA74
Uxbridge Rd, Stan. 41 CF51
Uxbridge Rd, Uxb. 77 BV72
Uxbridge St W8 82 DA74
Uxendon Cres, Wem. 62 CL60
Uxendon Hill, Wem. 62 CM60

V

Vache La, Ch.St.G. 36 AW47
Vache Ms, Ch.St.G. 36 AX46
Vaillant Rd, Wey. 153 BQ105
Valan Leas, Brom. 144 EE97
Valance Av E4 48 EF46
Vale, The N10 44 DG53
Vale, The N14 45 DK45
Vale, The NW11 63 CX62
Vale, The SW3 100 DD79
Vale, The W3 80 CR74
Vale, The, Brwd. 54 FW46
Vale, The, Couls. 159 DK114
Vale, The, Croy. 143 DX103
Vale, The, Felt. 115 BV86
Vale, The (Chalfont St. Peter), Ger.Cr. 36 AX53
Vale, The, Houns. 96 BY79
Vale, The, Ruis. 60 BW63
Vale, The, Sun. 115 BU93
Ashridge Way
Vale, The, Wdf.Grn. 48 EG52
Vale Av, Borwd. 26 CP43
Vale Border, Croy. 161 DX111
Vale Cl N2 64 DF55
Church Vale
Vale Cl W9 82 DC69
Maida Vale
Vale Cl, Brwd. 54 FT43
Vale Cl (Chalfont St. Peter), Ger.Cr. 36 AX53
Vale Cl, Orp. 163 EN105
Vale Cl, Wey. 135 BR104
Vale Cl, Wok. 166 AY116
The Larches
Vale Cotts SW15 118 CR91
Kingston Vale
Vale Ct W9 82 DC69
Maida Vale
Vale Ct, Wey. 135 BR104
Vale Cres SW15 118 CS90
Vale Cft, Esher 155 CE108
Vale Cft, Pnr. 60 BY57
Vale Dr, Barn. 27 CZ42
Vale End SE22 102 DS84
Grove Vale
Vale Fm Rd, Wok. 166 AX117
Vale Gro N4 66 DQ59
Vale Gro W3 80 CR74
The Vale
Vale Gro, Slou. 92 AS76
Vale Ind Est, Wat. 39 BQ46
Vale La W3 80 CN71
Vale of Health NW3 64 DD62
East Heath Rd
Vale Par SW15 118 CR91
Kingston Vale
Vale Ri NW11 63 CZ60
Vale Rd E7 86 EH65
Vale Rd N4 66 DQ59
Vale Rd, Brom. 145 EN96
Vale Rd, Bushey 24 BY43
Vale Rd, Dart. 127 FH88
Vale Rd, Epsom 157 CT105
Vale Rd, Esher 155 CE109
Vale Rd, Grav. 130 GD87
Vale Rd, Mitch. 141 DK97
Vale Rd, Sutt. 158 DB105
Vale Rd, Wey. 135 BR104
Vale Rd, Wor.Pk. 157 CT105
Vale Rd N, Surb. 138 CL103
Vale Rd S, Surb. 138 CL103
Vale Row N5 65 DP62
Gillespie Rd
Vale Royal N7 83 DL66
Vale St SE27 122 DR90
Vale Ter N4 66 DQ58
Valence Av, Dag. 70 EX62
Valence Circ, Dag. 70 EX62
Valence Dr (Cheshunt), Wal.Cr. 14 DU28
Valence Rd, Erith 107 FD80
Valence Wd Rd, Dag. 70 EX62
Valencia Rd, Stan. 41 CJ49
Valency Cl, Nthwd. 39 BT49
Valentia Pl SW9 101 DN84
Brixton Sta Rd
Valentine Av, Bex. 126 EY89
Valentine Ct SE23 123 DX89
Valentine Pl SE1 200 F4
Valentine Pl SE1 101 DP75
Valentine Rd E9 85 DX65
Valentine Rd, Har. 60 CC62
Valentine Row SE1 200 F5
Valentine Row SE1 101 DP75
Valentine Way, Ch.St.G. 36 AX48
Valentines Rd, Ilf. 69 EP60
Valentines Way, Rom. 71 FE61
Valentyne Cl, Croy. 162 EE111
Warbank Cres
Valerian Way E15 86 EE69
Valerie Ct, Bushey 40 CC45
Valeswood Rd, Brom. 124 EF92
Valetta Gro E13 86 EG68
Valetta Rd W3 98 CS75
Valette St E9 84 DV65
Valiant Cl, Nthlt. 78 BX69
Ruislip Rd
Valiant Cl, Rom. 50 FA54
Valiant Ho SE7 104 EJ78
Valiant Path NW9 42 CS52
Blundell Rd
Valiant Way E6 87 EM71
Vallance Rd E1 84 DU70
Vallance Rd E2 84 DU69
Vallance Rd N22 45 DJ54
Vallentin Rd E17 67 EC56
Valley Av N12 44 DD49
Valley Cl, Dart. 127 FF86
Valley Cl, Loug. 33 EM44
Valley Cl, Pnr. 39 BV54
Alandale Dr
Valley Cl, Wal.Abb. 15 EC32
Valley Ct, Cat. 176 DU122
Beechwood Gdns
Valley Ct, Ken. 160 DQ114
Hayes La
Valley Dr NW9 62 CN58
Valley Dr, Grav. 131 GK89
Valley Dr, Sev. 191 FH125
Valley Flds Cres, Enf. 29 DN40
Valley Gdns SW19 120 DD94
Valley Gdns, Wem. 80 CM66
Valley Gro SE7 104 EJ78
Valley Hill, Loug. 48 EL45
Valley Link Ind Est, Enf. 31 DY44
Valley Ms, Twick. 117 CG89
Cross Deep
Valley Ri, Wat. 7 BV33
Valley Rd SW16 121 DM91
Valley Rd, Belv. 107 FB77
Valley Rd, Brom. 144 EE96
Valley Rd, Dart. 127 FF86
Valley Rd, Erith 107 FD77
Valley Rd, Ken. 176 DR115
Valley Rd (Fawkham Grn), Long. 149 FV102
Valley Rd, Orp. 146 EV95
Valley Rd, Rick. 22 BG43
Valley Rd, Uxb. 76 BL68
Valley Side E4 47 EA47
Valley Side Par E4 47 EA47
Valley Side
Valley Vw, Barn. 27 CY44
Valley Vw, Green. 129 FV86
Valley Vw (Cheshunt), Wal.Cr. 14 DQ28
Valley Vw, West. 178 EJ118
Valley Vw Gdns, Ken. 176 DS115
Godstone Rd
Valley Wk, Croy. 142 DW103
Valley Wk, Rick. 23 BQ43
Valley Way, Ger.Cr. 56 AW58
Valleyfield Rd SW16 121 DM92
Valliere Rd NW10 81 CV69
Valliers Wd Rd, Sid. 125 ER88
Vallis Way W13 79 CG71
Vallis Way, Chess. 155 CK105
Valmar Rd SE5 102 DQ81
Valnay St SW17 120 DF92
Valognes Av E17 47 DY53
Valonia Gdns SW18 119 CZ86
Vambery Rd SE18 105 EQ79
Van Dyck Av, N.Mal. 138 CR101
Vanbrough Cres, Nthlt. 78 BW67
Vanbrugh Cl E16 86 EK71
Fulmer Rd
Vanbrugh Dr, Walt. 136 BW101
Vanbrugh Flds SE3 104 EF80
Vanbrugh Hill SE3 104 EF78
Vanbrugh Hill SE10 104 EF78
Vanbrugh Pk SE3 104 EF80
Vanbrugh Pk Rd SE3 104 EF80
Vanbrugh Pk Rd W SE3 104 EF80
Vanbrugh Rd W4 98 CR76
Vanbrugh Ter SE3 104 EF81
Vanburgh Cl, Orp. 145 ES102
Vancouver Cl, Epsom 156 CQ111
Vancouver Rd SE23 123 DY89
Vancouver Rd, Edg. 42 CP53
Vancouver Rd, Hayes 77 BV70
Vancouver Rd, Rich. 117 CJ91
Vanderbilt Rd SW18 120 DC88
Vanderville Gdns N2 44 DC54
Tarling Rd
Vandome Cl E16 86 EH72
Vandon Pas SW1 199 L6
Vandon St SW1 199 L6
Vandon St SW1 101 DJ76
Vandy St EC2 197 M5
Vandyke Cl SW15 119 CX87
Vandyke Cl, Red. 184 DF131
Vandyke Cross SE9 124 EL85
Vane Cl NW3 64 DD63
Vane Cl, Har. 62 CM58
Vane St SW1 199 L8
Vanessa Cl, Belv. 106 FA78
Vanessa Wk, Grav. 131 GM92
Vanessa Way, Bex. 127 FD90
Vanguard Cl E16 86 EG71
Vanguard Cl, Croy. 141 DP102
Vanguard Cl, Rom. 51 FB54
Vanguard St SE8 103 EA81
Vanguard Way, Cat. 177 EB121
Slines Oak Rd
Vanguard Way, Wall. 159 DL108
Vanguard Way, Warl. 177 EB121
Vanguard Way, Warl. 177 EC120
Croydon Rd
Vanneck Sq SW15 119 CU85
Vanners Par, W.Byf. 152 BL113
Brewery La
Vanoc Gdns, Brom. 124 EG90
Vanquisher Wk, Grav. 131 GM90
Vansittart Rd E7 68 EF63
Vansittart St SE14 103 DY80
Vanston Pl SW6 100 DA80
Vant Rd SW17 120 DF92
Vantage Ms E14 204 E3
Varcoe Rd SE16 102 DV78
Varden St E1 84 DV72
Vardens Rd SW11 100 DD84
Vardon Cl N3 43 CY53
Claremont Pk
Vardon Cl W3 80 CR72
Varley Par NW9 62 CS56
Varley Rd E16 86 EH72
Varley Way, Mitch. 140 DD96
Varna Rd SW6 99 CY80
Varna Rd, Hmptn. 136 CB95
Varndell St NW1 195 K2
Varndell St NW1 83 DJ69
Varney Cl (Cheshunt), Wal.Cr. 14 DU27
Varsity Dr, Twick. 117 CE85
Varsity Row SW14 98 CQ82
William's La
Vartry Rd N15 66 DR58
Vassall Rd SW9 101 DN80
Vauban Est SE16 202 A7
Vauban Est SE16 102 DU76
Vauban St SE16 202 A7
Vauban St SE16 102 DT76
Vaughan Av NW4 63 CU57
Vaughan Av W6 99 CT77
Vaughan Av, Horn. 72 FK63
Vaughan Cl, Hmptn. 116 BY93
Oak Av
Vaughan Gdns, Ilf. 69 EM59
Vaughan Rd E15 86 EF65
Vaughan Rd SE5 102 DQ83
Vaughan Rd, Har. 60 CC59
Vaughan Rd, T.Ditt. 137 CH101
Vaughan Rd, Well. 105 ET82
Vaughan St SE16 203 M5
Vaughan St SE16 103 DZ75
Vaughan Way E1 202 B1
Vaughan Way E1 84 DU73
Vaughan Williams Cl SE8 103 EA80
Watson's St
Vaux Cres, Walt. 153 BV107
Vauxhall Br SE1 101 DL78
Vauxhall Br SW1 101 DL78
Vauxhall Br Rd SW1 199 L8
Vauxhall Br Rd SW1 101 DJ77
Vauxhall Cl, Grav. 131 GF87
Vauxhall Gdns, S.Croy. 160 DQ107
Vauxhall Gro SW8 101 DM79
Vauxhall Pl, Dart. 128 FL87
Vauxhall St SE11 101 DM78
Vauxhall Wk SE11 200 B10
Vauxhall Wk SE11 101 DM78
Vawdrey Cl E1 84 DW70
Veals Mead, Mitch. 140 DE95
Vectis Gdns SW17 121 DH93
Vectis Rd
Vectis Rd SW17 121 DH93
Veda Rd SE13 103 EA84
Vega Cres, Nthwd. 39 BT50
Vega Rd, Bushey 40 CC45
Vegal Cres, Egh. 112 AW92
Velde Way SE22 122 DS85
East Dulwich Gro
Veldene Way, Har. 60 BZ62
Velletri Ho E2 85 DX68
Vellum Dr, Cars. 140 DG104
Venables Cl, Dag. 71 FB63
Venables St NW8 194 A6
Venables St NW8 82 DD70
Vencourt Pl W6 99 CU78
Venetia Rd N4 65 DP58
Venetia Rd W5 97 CK75
Venetian Rd SE5 102 DQ82
Venette Cl, Rain. 89 FH71
Venn St SW4 101 DJ84
Venner Rd SE26 122 DW93
Venners Cl, Bexh. 107 FE82
Ventnor Av, Stan. 41 CH53
Ventnor Dr N20 44 DB48
Ventnor Gdns, Bark. 87 ES65
Ventnor Rd SE14 103 DX80

Ventnor Rd, Sutt. 158 DB108
Venton Cl, Wok. 166 AV117
Ventura Pk, St.Alb. 9 CF29
Venture Cl, Bex. 126 EY87
Venue St E14 85 EC71
Venus Hill, Hem.H. 5 BA31
Venus Rd SE18 105 EM76
Veny Cres, Horn. 72 FK64
Vera Av N21 29 DN43
Vera Ct, Wat. 40 BX45
Vera Lynn Cl E7 68 EG63
Dames Rd
Vera Rd SW6 99 CY81
Verbena Cl E16 86 EF70
Cranberry La
Verbena Cl, S.Ock. 91 FW72
Verbena Cl, West Dr. 94 BK78
Magnolia St
Verbena Gdns W6 99 CU78
Verdant La SE6 124 EE88
Verdayne Av, Croy. 143 DX102
Verdayne Gdns, Warl. 176 DW116
Vereders Rd, Chig. 50 EU50
Verdun Rd SE18 106 EU79
Verdun Rd SW13 99 CU79
Verdure Cl, Wat. 8 BY32
Vere Rd, Loug. 33 EQ42
Vere St W1 195 H9
Vere St W1 83 DH72
Vereker Dr, Sun. 135 BU97
Vereker Rd W14 99 CY78
Verity Cl W11 81 CY72
Vermeer Gdns SE15 102 DW84
Elland Rd
Vermont Cl, Enf. 29 DP42
Vermont Rd SE19 122 DR93
Vermont Rd SW18 120 DB86
Vermont Rd, Sutt. 140 DB104
Verney Gdns, Dag. 70 EY63
Verney Rd SE16 102 DU79
Verney Rd, Dag. 70 EY64
Verney Rd, Slou. 93 BA77
Verney St NW10 62 CR62
Verney Way SE16 102 DV78
Vernham Rd SE18 105 EQ79
Vernon Av E12 69 EM63
Vernon Av SW20 139 CX96
Vernon Av, Enf. 31 DY36
Vernon Av, Wdf.Grn. 48 EH52
Vernon Cl, Cher. 151 BD107
Vernon Cl, Epsom 156 CQ107
Vernon Cl, Orp. 146 EV97
Vernon Ct, Stan. 41 CH53
Vernon Dr
Vernon Cres, Barn. 28 DG44
Vernon Cres, Brwd. 55 GA48
Vernon Dr, Stan. 41 CG53
Vernon Dr (Harefield), Uxb. 38 BJ53
Vernon Ms E17 67 DZ56
Vernon Rd
Vernon Ms W14 99 CY77
Vernon St
Vernon Pl WC1 196 A7
Vernon Pl WC1 83 DL71
Vernon Ri WC1 196 C2
Vernon Ri WC1 83 DM69
Vernon Ri, Grnf. 61 CD64
Vernon Rd E3 85 DZ68
Vernon Rd E11 68 EE60
Vernon Rd E15 86 EE66
Vernon Rd E17 67 DZ57
Vernon Rd N8 65 DN55
Vernon Rd SW14 98 CR83
Vernon Rd, Bushey 24 BY43
Vernon Rd, Felt. 115 BT89
Vernon Rd, Ilf. 69 ET60
Vernon Rd, Rom. 51 FC50
Vernon Rd, Sutt. 158 DC106
Vernon Rd, Swans. 130 FZ86
Vernon Sq WC1 196 C2
Vernon St W14 99 CY77
Vernon Wk, Tad. 173 CX120
Vernon Way, Cat. 176 DQ122
Wellington Rd
Vernon Yd W11 81 CZ73
Portobello Rd
Veroan Rd, Bexh. 106 EY82
Verona Cl, Uxb. 76 BJ71
Verona Dr, Surb. 138 CL103
Verona Gdns, Grav. 131 GL91
Verona Rd E7 86 EG66
Upton La
Veronica Cl, Rom. 52 FJ52
Veronica Gdns SW16 141 DJ95
Veronica Rd SW17 121 DH90
Veronique Gdns, Ilf. 69 EP57
Verralls, Wok. 167 BB117
Verran Rd SW12 121 DH87
Balham Gro
Versailles Rd SE20 122 DU94
Verulam Av E17 67 DZ58
Verulam Av, Pur. 159 DJ112
Verulam Bldgs WC1 196 C6
Verulam Pas, Wat. 23 BV40
Verulam Rd, Grnf. 78 CA70
Verulam St WC1 196 D6
Verwood Dr, Barn. 28 DF41
Verwood Rd, Har. 40 CC54
Veryan, Wok. 166 AU117
Veryan Cl, Orp. 146 EW98
Vesey Path E14 85 EB72
East India Dock Rd
Vespan Rd W12 99 CU75
Vesta Rd SE4 103 DY82
Vestris Rd SE23 123 DX89
Vestry Ms SE5 102 DS81
Vestry Rd E17 67 EB56
Vestry Rd SE5 102 DS81
Vestry St N1 197 K2
Vestry St N1 84 DR69
Vevey St SE6 123 DZ89
Vexil Cl, Purf. 109 FR77
Veysey Gdns, Dag. 70 FA62
Viaduct Pl E2 84 DV69
Viaduct St
Viaduct St E2 84 DV69
Vian Av, Enf. 31 DY35
Vian St SE13 103 EB83
Vibart Gdns SW2 121 DM87
Vibart Wk N1 83 DL67
Outram Pl
Vicarage Av SE3 104 EG81
Vicarage Av, Egh. 113 BB93
Vicarage Cl, Brwd. 54 FS49
Vicarage Cl, Erith 107 FC79
Vicarage Cl, Nthlt. 78 BZ66
Vicarage Cl, Pot.B. 12 DF30
Vicarage Cl, Ruis. 59 BR59
Vicarage Cl, Tad. 173 CY124
Vicarage Cl, Wor.Pk. 138 CS102
Vicarage Ct W8 100 DB75
Vicarage Gate
Vicarage Ct, Egh. 113 BB93
Vicarage Ct, Felt. 115 BQ87
Vicarage Cres SW11 100 DD81
Vicarage Cres, Egh. 113 BB92
Vicarage Dr SW14 118 CR85
Vicarage Dr, Bark. 87 EQ66
Vicarage Dr, Beck. 143 EA95
Vicarage Dr, Grav. 130 GC86
Vicarage Fm Rd, Houns. 96 BY82
Vicarage Flds, Walt. 136 BW100
Vicarage Gdns SW14 118 CQ85
Vicarage Rd
Vicarage Gdns W8 82 DA74
Vicarage Gdns, Mitch. 140 DE97
Vicarage Gate W8 100 DB75
Vicarage Gate Ms, Tad. 173 CY124
Vicarage Gate Ms, Tad. 173 CY124
Warren Lo Dr
Vicarage Gro SE5 102 DR81
Vicarage Hill, West. 189 ER126
Vicarage La E6 87 EM69
Vicarage La E15 86 EE66
Vicarage La, Chig. 49 EQ47
Vicarage La, Epsom 157 CU109
Vicarage La, Hem.H. 5 BB26
Vicarage La, Ilf. 69 ER60
Vicarage La, Kings L. 6 BM29
Vicarage La, Lthd. 171 CH122
Vicarage La, Sev. 181 FD119
London Rd
Vicarage La (Laleham), Stai. 134 BH97
Vicarage La (Wraysbury), Stai. 112 AY88
Vicarage Pk SE18 105 EQ78
Vicarage Path N8 65 DL59
Vicarage Pl, Slou. 92 AU76
Vicarage Rd E10 67 EB60
Vicarage Rd E15 86 EF66
Vicarage Rd N17 46 DU52
Vicarage Rd NW4 63 CU58
Vicarage Rd SE18 105 EQ78
Vicarage Rd SW14 118 CQ85
Vicarage Rd, Bex. 127 FB88
Vicarage Rd, Croy. 141 DN104
Vicarage Rd, Dag. 89 FB65
Vicarage Rd, Egh. 113 BB93
Vicarage Rd, Epp. 18 EW29
Vicarage Rd, Horn. 71 FG60
Vicarage Rd, Kings.T. 137 CK96
Vicarage Rd (Hampton Wick), Kings.T. 137 CJ95
Vicarage Rd, Stai. 113 BE91
Vicarage Rd, Sun. 115 BT92
Vicarage Rd, Sutt. 158 DB105
Vicarage Rd, Tedd. 117 CG92
Vicarage Rd, Twick. 117 CE89
Vicarage Rd (Whitton), Twick. 116 CC86
Vicarage Rd, Wat. 23 BU44
Vicarage Rd, Wok. 167 AZ121
Vicarage Rd, Wdf.Grn. 48 EL52
Vicarage Sq, Grays 110 GA79
Vicarage Wk, Reig. 184 DB134
Chartway
Vicarage Way NW10 62 CR62
Vicarage Way, Ger.Cr. 57 AZ58
Vicarage Way, Har. 60 CA59
Vicarage Way, Slou. 93 BC80
Vicars Br Cl, Wem. 80 CL68
Vicars Cl E9 84 DW67
Northiam St
Vicars Cl E15 86 EG67
Vicars Cl, Enf. 30 DS40
Vicars Hill SE13 103 EB84
Vicars Moor La N21 45 DN45
Vicars Oak Rd SE19 122 DS93
Vicars Rd NW5 64 DG64
Vicars Wk, Dag. 70 EV62
Viceroy Cl N2 64 DE56
Market Pl
Viceroy Ct NW8 82 DE68
Prince Albert Rd
Viceroy Par N2 64 DE55
High Rd
Viceroy Rd SW8 101 DL81
Vickers Dr N, Wey. 152 BL110
Vickers Dr S, Wey. 152 BL111
Vickers Rd, Erith 107 FD78
Vickers Way, Houns. 116 BY85
Victor App, Horn. 72 FK60
Abbs Cross Gdns
Victor Cl, Horn. 72 FK60
Victor Ct, Horn. 72 FK60
Victor Ct, Rain. 89 FD68
Askwith Rd
Victor Gdns, Horn. 72 FK60
Victor Gro, Wem. 80 CL66
Victor Rd NW10 81 CV69
Victor Rd SE20 123 DX94
Victor Rd, Har. 60 CC55
Victor Rd, Tedd. 117 CE91
Victor Smith Ct, St.Alb. 8 CA31
Victor Vil N9 46 DR48
Victor Wk NW9 42 CS54
Booth Rd
Victor Wk, Horn. 72 FK60
Abbs Cross Gdns
Victoria Arc SW1 101 DH76
Terminus Pl
Victoria Av E6 86 EK67
Victoria Av EC2 197 N7
Victoria Av N3 43 CZ53
Victoria Av, Barn. 28 DD42
Victoria Av, Grav. 131 GH87
Sheppy Pl
Victoria Av, Grays 110 GC75
Victoria Av, Houns. 116 BZ85
Victoria Av, Rom. 51 FB51
Victoria Av, S.Croy. 160 DQ110
Victoria Av, Surb. 137 CK101
Victoria Av, Uxb. 77 BP66
Victoria Av, Wall. 140 DG104
Victoria Av, Wem. 80 CP65
Victoria Av, W.Mol. 136 CA97
Victoria Cl, Barn. 28 DD42
Victoria Cl, Grays 110 GC75
Victoria Cl, Hayes 77 BR72
Commonwealth Av
Victoria Cl, Rick. 38 BK45
Nightingale Rd
Victoria Cl, Wal.Cr. 15 DX30
Victoria Cl, W.Mol. 136 CA97
Victoria Av
Victoria Cl, Wey. 135 BR104
Victoria Cotts, Rich. 98 CM81
Victoria Ct, Wem. 80 CN65
Victoria Cres N15 66 DS57
Victoria Cres SE19 122 DS93
Victoria Cres SW19 119 CZ94
Victoria Cres, Iver 76 BG73
Victoria Dock Rd E16 86 EG73
Victoria Dr SW19 119 CX87
Victoria Dr (South Darenth), Dart. 149 FR96
Victoria Embk EC4 200 B1
Victoria Embk EC4 83 DM73
Victoria Embk SW1 200 A4
Victoria Embk SW1 101 DL75
Victoria Embk WC2 200 B1
Victoria Embk WC2 101 DL75
Victoria Gdns W11 82 DA74
Victoria Gdns, Houns. 96 BY81
Victoria Gdns, West. 178 EJ115
Victoria Gro N12 44 DC50
Victoria Gro W8 100 DC76
Victoria Gro Ms W2 82 DB73
Ossington St
Victoria Hill Rd, Swan. 147 FF95
Victoria Ind Est NW10 80 CS69
Victoria Ind Pk, Dart. 128 FL85
Victoria La, Barn. 27 CZ42
Victoria La, Hayes 95 BQ78
Victoria Ms NW6 82 DA67
Victoria Ms SW4 101 DH84
Victoria Ri
Victoria Ms SW18 120 DC88
Victoria Pk E9 85 DY66
Victoria Pk Rd E9 84 DW67
Victoria Pk Sq E2 84 DW69
Victoria Pas NW8 82 DD70
Cunningham Pl
Victoria Pas, Wat. 23 BV42
Victoria Pl, Epsom 156 CS112
Victoria Pl, Rich. 117 CK85
Victoria Pt E13 86 EG68
Victoria Rd
Victoria Retail Pk, Ruis. 60 BY64
Victoria Ri SW4 101 DH83
Victoria Rd E4 48 EE46
Victoria Rd E11 68 EE63
Victoria Rd E13 86 EG68
Victoria Rd E17 47 EC54
Victoria Rd E18 48 EH54
Victoria Rd N4 65 DM59
Victoria Rd N9 46 DT49
Victoria Rd N15 66 DU56
Victoria Rd N18 46 DT49
Victoria Rd N22 45 DJ53
Victoria Rd NW4 63 CW56
Victoria Rd NW6 81 CZ67
Victoria Rd NW7 43 CT50
Victoria Rd NW10 80 CR71
Victoria Rd SW14 98 CR83
Victoria Rd W3 80 CR71
Victoria Rd W5 79 CH71
Victoria Rd W8 100 DC76
Victoria Rd, Add. 152 BK105
Victoria Rd, Bark. 87 EP65
Victoria Rd, Barn. 28 DD42
Victoria Rd, Bexh. 106 FA84
Victoria Rd, Brwd. 54 FW49
Victoria Rd, Brom. 144 EK99
Victoria Rd, Buck.H. 48 EK47
Victoria Rd, Bushey 40 CB46
Victoria Rd, Chis. 125 EN92
Victoria Rd, Couls. 175 DK115
Victoria Rd, Dag. 71 FB64
Victoria Rd, Dart. 128 FK85
Victoria Rd, Erith 107 FE79
Victoria Rd, Felt. 115 BV88
Victoria Rd, Grav. 131 GF88
Victoria Rd, Kings.T. 138 CM96
Victoria Rd, Mitch. 120 DE94
Victoria Rd, Rom. 71 FE58
Victoria Rd, Ruis. 60 BW64
Victoria Rd, Sev. 191 FH125
Victoria Rd, Sid. 125 ET90
Victoria Rd, Slou. 74 AV74
Victoria Rd, Sthl. 96 BZ76
Victoria Rd, Stai. 113 BE90
Victoria Rd, Surb. 137 CK100
Victoria Rd, Sutt. 158 DD106
Victoria Rd, Tedd. 117 CG93
Victoria Rd, Twick. 117 CG87
Victoria Rd, Uxb. 76 BJ66
New Windsor St
Victoria Rd, Wal.Abb. 15 EC34
Victoria Rd, Wat. 23 BV38
Victoria Rd, Wey. 135 BR104
Victoria Rd, Wok. 166 AY117
Victoria Sq SW1 199 J6
Victoria Sta SW1 199 J8
Victoria Sta SW1 101 DH77
Victoria Steps, Brent. 98 CM79
Kew Br Rd
Victoria St E15 86 EE66
Victoria St SW1 199 K7
Victoria St SW1 101 DJ76
Victoria St, Belv. 106 EZ78
Victoria St, Egh. 112 AW93
Victoria St, Slou. 92 AT75
Victoria Ter N4 65 DN60
Victoria Ter NW10 80 CS69
Old Oak La
Victoria Ter, Har. 61 CE60
Victoria Vil, Rich. 98 CM83
Victoria Way SE7 205 P10
Victoria Way SE7 104 EH78
Victoria Way, Wey. 135 BR104
Victoria Way, Wok. 166 AY117
Victoria Wf E14 203 L1
Victoria Wf E14 85 DY73
Victoria Yd E1 84 DU72
Fairclough St
Victorian Gro N16 66 DS62
Victorian Rd N16 66 DS62
Victors Cres, Brwd. 55 GB47
Victors Dr, Hmptn. 116 BY93
Victors Way, Barn. 27 CZ41
Victory Av, Mord. 140 DC99
Victory Business Cen, Islw. 97 CF83
Victory Pk Rd, Add. 152 BJ105
Victory Pl E14 85 DY73
Northey St
Victory Pl SE17 201 J8
Victory Pl SE17 102 DQ77
Victory Pl SE19 122 DS93
Westow St
Victory Rd E11 68 EH56
Victory Rd SW19 120 DC94
Victory Rd, Cher. 134 BG102
Victory Rd, Grays 109 FW78
Victory Rd, Rain. 89 FG68
Victory Rd Ms SW19 120 DC94
Victory Rd
Victory Wk SE8 103 EA81
Ship St
Victory Way SE16 203 L5
Victory Way SE16 103 DY75
Victory Way, Houns. 96 BW78
Victory Way, Rom. 51 FB54
Vidler Cl, Chess. 155 CJ107
Merritt Gdns
Vienna Cl, Ilf. 48 EL54
Coburg Gdns
View, The SE2 106 EY78
View Cl N6 64 DF59
View Cl, Chig. 49 ER50
View Cl, Har. 61 CD56
View Cl, West. 178 EJ116
View Rd N6 64 DF59
View Rd, Pot.B. 12 DC32
Viewfield Cl, Har. 62 CL59
Viewfield Rd SW18 119 CZ86
Viewfield Rd, Bex. 126 EW88
Viewland Rd SE18 105 ET78
Viewlands Av, West. 179 ES120
Viga Rd N21 29 DN44
Vigerons Way, Grays 111 GH77
Viggory La, Wok. 166 AW115
Vigilant Cl SE26 122 DU91
Vigilant Way, Grav. 131 GL92
Vignoles Rd, Rom. 70 FA59
Vigo St W1 199 K1
Vigo St W1 83 DJ73
Viking Cl E3 85 DY68
Selwyn Rd
Viking Ct SW6 100 DA79
Viking Gdns E6 86 EL70
Jack Dash Way
Viking Pl E10 67 DZ60
Viking Rd, Grav. 130 GC90
Viking Rd, Sthl. 78 BY73
Viking Way, Brwd. 54 FV45
Viking Way, Erith 107 FC76
Viking Way, Rain. 89 FG70
Villa Ct, Dart. 128 FL89
Greenbanks
Villa Rd SW9 101 DN83
Villa St SE17 102 DR78
Villacourt Rd SE18 106 EU80
Village, The SE7 104 EJ79
Village, The (Bluewater), Green. 129 FT87
Village Arc E4 47 ED46
Station Rd
Village Cl E4 47 EC50
Village Cl NW3 64 DE64
Ornan Rd
Village Cl, Wey. 135 BR104
Oatlands Dr
Village Gdns, Epsom 157 CT110
Village Grn Av, West. 178 EL117
Village Grn Rd, Dart. 107 FG84
Village Grn Way, West. 178 EL117
Main Rd
Village Hts, Wdf.Grn. 48 EF50
Village Ms NW9 62 CR61
Village Pk Cl, Enf. 30 DS44
Village Rd N3 43 CY53
Village Rd, Egh. 133 BC97
Village Rd, Enf. 30 DS44
Village Rd (Denham), Uxb. 57 BF61
Village Row, Sutt. 158 DA108
Village Way NW10 62 CR63
Village Way SE21 122 DR86
Village Way, Amer. 20 AX40
Village Way, Ashf. 114 BM91
Village Way, Beck. 143 EA96
Village Way, Pnr. 60 BY59
Village Way, S.Croy. 160 DU113
Village Way E, Har. 60 BZ59
Villas Rd SE18 105 EQ77
Villier Ct, Uxb. 76 BK68
Villier St
Villier St, Uxb. 76 BK68
Villiers, The, Wey. 153 BR107
Villiers Av, Surb. 138 CM99
Villiers Av, Twick. 116 BZ88
Villiers Cl E10 67 EA61
Villiers Cl, Surb. 138 CM98
Villiers Ct N20 44 DC45
Buckingham Av
Villiers Gro, Sutt. 157 CX109
Villiers Path, Surb. 138 CL99
Villiers Rd NW2 81 CU65
Villiers Rd, Beck. 143 DX96
Villiers Rd, Islw. 97 CE82
Villiers Rd, Kings.T. 138 CM97
Villiers Rd, Sthl. 78 BZ74
Villiers Rd, Wat. 24 BY44
Villiers St WC2 199 P1
Villiers St WC2 83 DL73
Vincam Cl, Twick. 116 CA87
Vince St EC1 197 L3
Vince St EC1 84 DR69
Vincent Av, Cars. 158 DD111
Vincent Av, Croy. 161 DY111
Vincent Av, Surb. 138 CP102
Vincent Cl SE16 203 K5
Vincent Cl SE16 103 DY75
Vincent Cl, Barn. 28 DA41
Vincent Cl, Brom. 144 EH98
Vincent Cl, Cher. 133 BE101
Vincent Cl, Couls. 174 DF120
Vincent Cl, Esher 136 CB104
Vincent Cl, Ilf. 49 EQ51
Vincent Cl, Lthd. 170 CB123
Vincent Cl, Sid. 125 ES88
Vincent Cl (Cheshunt), Wal.Cr. 15 DY28
Vincent Cl, West Dr. 94 BN79
Vincent Dr, Shep. 135 BS97
Vincent Dr, Uxb. 76 BM67
Birch Cres
Vincent Gdns NW2 63 CT62
Vincent Grn, Couls. 174 DF120
High Rd
Vincent Ms E3 85 EA68
Vincent Rd E4 47 ED51
Vincent Rd N15 66 DQ56
Vincent Rd N22 45 DN54
Vincent Rd SE18 105 EP77
Vincent Rd W3 98 CQ76
Vincent Rd, Cher. 133 BE101
Vincent Rd, Cob. 170 BY116
Vincent Rd, Couls. 175 DJ116
Vincent Rd, Croy. 142 DS101
Vincent Rd, Dag. 88 EY66
Vincent Rd, Houns. 96 BX82
Vincent Rd, Islw. 97 CD81
Vincent Rd, Kings.T. 138 CN97
Vincent Rd, Rain. 90 FJ70
Vincent Rd, Wem. 80 CM66
Vincent Row, Hmptn. 116 CC93
Vincent Sq SW1 199 L8
Vincent Sq SW1 101 DJ77
Vincent Sq, West. 162 EJ113
Vincent St E16 86 EF71
Vincent St SW1 199 M8
Vincent St SW1 101 DK77
Vincent Ter N1 83 DP68
Vincents Path, Nthlt. 78 BY65
Arnold Rd
Vine, The, Sev. 191 FH124
Vine Av, Sev. 191 FH124
Vine Cl, Stai. 114 BG85
Vine Cl, Surb. 138 CM100
Vine Cl, Sutt. 140 DC104
Vine Cl, West Dr. 94 BN77
Vine Ct E1 84 DU71
Whitechapel Rd
Vine Ct, Har. 62 CL58
Vine Ct Rd, Sev. 191 FJ124
Vine Gdns, Ilf. 69 EQ64
Vine Gro, Uxb. 76 BN66
Vine Hill EC1 196 D5
Vine La SE1 201 N3
Vine La, Uxb. 76 BM67
Vine Pl W5 80 CL74
The Common
Vine Pl, Houns. 96 CB84
Vine Rd E15 86 EF66
Vine Rd SW13 99 CT83
Vine Rd, E.Mol. 136 CC98
Vine Rd, Orp. 163 ET107
Vine Rd, Slou. 74 AT65
Vine Sq W14 99 CZ78
Vine St EC3 197 P10
Vine St W1 199 L1
Vine St, Rom. 71 FC57
Vine St, Uxb. 76 BK67
Vine St Br EC1 196 E5
Vine St Br EC1 83 DN70
Vine Way, Brwd. 54 FW46
Vine Yd SE1 201 J4
Vinegar All E17 67 EB56
Vinegar St E1 202 D2
Vinegar Yd SE1 201 M4
Viner Cl, Walt. 136 BW100
Vineries, The N14 29 DJ44
Vineries, The, Enf. 30 DS41
Vineries Bk NW7 43 CV50
Vineries Cl, Dag. 88 FA65
Heathway
Vineries Cl, West Dr. 94 BN79
Vines Av N3 44 DB53
Viney Bk, Croy. 161 DZ109
Viney Rd SE13 103 EB83
Vineyard, The, Rich. 118 CL85
Vineyard Av NW7 43 CY52
Vineyard Cl SE6 123 EA88
Vineyard Cl, Kings.T. 138 CM97
Vineyard Gro N3 44 DB53
Vineyard Hill, Pot.B. 12 DG29
Vineyard Hill Rd SW19 120 DA91
Vineyard Pas, Rich. 118 CL85
Paradise Rd
Vineyard Path SW14 98 CR83
Vineyard Rd, Felt. 115 BU90
Vineyard Row, Kings.T. 137 CJ95
Vineyard Wk EC1 196 D4
Vineyard Wk EC1 83 DN70
Vineyards Rd, Pot.B. 12 DG30
Vining St SW9 101 DN84
Vinlake Av, Uxb. 58 BM62
Vinson Cl, Orp. 146 EU102
Vintners Pl EC4 84 DQ73
Upper Thames St
Vintry Ms E17 67 EA56
Cleveland Pk Cres
Viola Av SE2 106 EV77
Viola Av, Felt. 116 BW86
Viola Av, Stai. 114 BK88
Viola Cl, S.Ock. 91 FW69
Viola Sq W12 81 CT73
Violet Av, Enf. 30 DR38
Violet Av, Uxb. 76 BM71
Violet Cl E16 86 EE70
Violet Cl, Wall. 141 DH102
Violet Gdns, Croy. 159 DP106
Violet Hill NW8 82 DC68
Violet La, Croy. 159 DP106
Violet Rd E3 85 EB70
Violet Rd E17 67 EA58
Violet Rd E18 48 EH54
Violet St E2 84 DV70
Three Colts La
Violet Way, Rick. 22 BJ42
Virgil Pl W1 194 D7
Virgil St SE1 200 C6
Virgil St SE1 101 DM76
Virginia Av, Vir.W. 132 AW99
Virginia Beeches, Vir.W. 132 AW97
Virginia Cl, Ash. 171 CK118
Skinners La
Virginia Cl, N.Mal. 138 CQ98
Willow Rd

Warberry Rd N22 45 DM54
Warblers Grn, Cob. 154 BZ114
Warboys App, Kings.T. 118 CP93
Warboys Cres E4 47 EC50
Warboys Rd, Kings.T. 118 CP93
Warburton Cl N1 84 DS65
Culford Rd
Warburton Cl, Har. 41 CD51
Warburton Rd E8 84 DV66
Warburton Rd, Twick. 116 CB88
Warburton St E8 84 DV67
Warburton Rd
Warburton Ter E17 47 EB54
Ward Av, Grays 110 GA77
Ward Cl, Erith 107 FD79
Ward Cl, Iver 75 BF72
Ward Cl, S.Croy. 160 DS106
Ward Cl (Cheshunt), Wal.Cr. 14 DU27
Spicersfield
Ward Gdns, Rom. 52 FK54
Whitmore Av
Ward La, Warl. 176 DW116
Ward Rd E15 85 ED67
Ward Rd N19 65 DJ62
Wardalls Gro SE14 102 DW80
Wardell Cl NW7 42 CS52
Wardell Fld NW9 42 CS53
Warden Av, Har. 60 BZ60
Warden Av, Rom. 51 FC50
Warden Rd NW5 82 DG65
Wardens Fld Cl, Orp. 163 ES107
Wardens Gro SE1 201 H3
Wardle St E9 67 DX64
Wardley St SW18 120 DB87
Garratt La
Wardo Av SW6 99 CY81
Wardour Ms W1 195 L9
Wardour St W1 195 M10
Wardour St W1 83 DK73
Wardrobe Pl EC4 196 G10
Wardrobe Ter EC4 196 G10
Wards La, Borwd. 25 CG40
Ward's Pl, Egh. 113 BC93
Wards Rd, Ilf. 69 ER59
Ware Pt Dr SE28 105 ER75
Wareham Cl, Houns. 96 CB84
Waremead Rd, Ilf. 69 EP57
Warenford Way, Borwd. 26 CN39
Warenne Rd, Lthd. 170 CC122
Warescot Cl, Brwd. 54 FV45
Warescot Rd, Brwd. 54 FV45
Warfield Rd NW10 81 CX69
Warfield Rd, Felt. 115 BS87
Warfield Rd, Hmptn. 136 CB95
Warfield Yd NW10 81 CX69
Warfield Rd
Wargrave Av N15 66 DT58
Wargrave Rd, Har. 60 CC62
Warham Rd N4 65 DN57
Warham Rd, Har. 41 CF54
Warham Rd, Sev. 181 FH116
Warham Rd, S.Croy. 160 DQ106
Warham St SE5 101 DP80
Waring Cl, Orp. 163 ET107
Waring Dr, Orp. 163 ET107
Waring Rd, Sid. 126 EW93
Waring St SE27 122 DQ91
Warkworth Gdns, Islw. 97 CG80
Warkworth Rd N17 46 DR52
Warland Rd SE18 105 ER80
Warley Av, Dag. 70 EZ59
Warley Av, Hayes 77 BU71
Warley Cl E10 67 DZ60
Millicent Rd
Warley Gap, Brwd. 53 FV52
Warley Hill, Brwd. 53 FV51
Warley Mt, Brwd. 54 FW49
Warley Rd N9 46 DW47
Warley Rd, Brwd. 53 FT54
Warley Rd, Hayes 77 BU72
Warley Rd, Ilf. 49 EN53
Warley Rd, Upmin. 52 FQ54
Warley Rd, Wdf.Grn. 48 EH52
Warley St E2 85 DX69
Warley St, Brwd. 73 FW58
Warley St, Upmin. 73 FW58
Warley Wds Cres, Brwd. 54 FV49
Warlingham Rd, Th.Hth. 141 DP98
Warlock Rd W9 82 DA70
Warlters Cl N7 65 DL63
Warlters Rd
Warlters Rd N7 65 DL63
Warltersville Rd N19 65 DL59
Warmington Cl E5 67 DX62
Orient Way
Warmington Rd SE24 122 DQ86
Warmington St E13 86 EG70
Barking Rd
Warminster Gdns SE25 142 DU96
Warminster Rd SE25 142 DT96
Warminster Sq SE25 142 DU96
Warminster Rd
Warminster Way, Mitch. 141 DH95
Warndon St SE16 202 G9
Warndon St SE16 103 DX77
Warne Pl, Sid. 126 EV86
Westerham Dr
Warneford Pl, Wat. 24 BY44
Warneford Rd, Har. 61 CK55
Warneford St E9 84 DV67
Warner Av, Sutt. 139 CY103
Warner Cl E15 68 EE64
Warner Cl NW9 63 CT59
Warner Cl, Hmptn. 116 BZ92
Tangley Pk Rd
Warner Cl, Hayes 95 BR80
Warner Par, Hayes 95 BR80
Warner Pl E2 84 DU68
Warner Rd E17 67 DY56
Warner Rd N8 65 DK56
Warner Rd SE5 102 DQ81
Warner Rd, Brom. 124 EF94
Warner St EC1 196 D5
Warner St EC1 83 DN70
Warner Ter E14 85 EA71
Broomfield St
Warner Yd EC1 196 D5
Warners Cl, Wdf.Grn. 48 EG50
Warners La, Kings.T. 117 CK91
Warners Path, Wdf.Grn. 48 EG50
Warnford Ind Est, Hayes 95 BS75
Warnford Rd, Orp. 163 ET106
Warnham Ct Rd, Cars. 158 DF108
Warnham Rd N12 44 DE50
Warple Ms W3 98 CS75
Warple Way
Warple Way W3 98 CS75
Warren, The E12 68 EL63
Warren, The, Ash. 172 CL119
Warren, The, Cars. 158 DD109
Warren, The (Chalfont St. Peter), Ger.Cr. 37 AZ52
Warren, The, Grav. 131 GK91
Warren, The, Hayes 77 BU72
Warren, The, Houns. 96 BZ80
Warren, The, Lthd. 154 CC112
Warren, The, Rad. 9 CG33
Warren, The, Tad. 173 CY123
Warren, The, Wor.Pk. 156 CR105
Warren Av E10 67 EC62
Warren Av, Brom. 124 EE94
Warren Av, Orp. 163 ET106
Warren Av, Rich. 98 CP84
Warren Av, S.Croy. 161 DX108
Warren Av, Sutt. 157 CZ110
Warren Cl N9 47 DX45
Warren Cl SE21 122 DQ87
Lairdale Cl
Warren Cl, Bexh. 126 FA85
Warren Cl, Esher 154 CB105
Warren Cl, Hayes 78 BW71
Warren Cl, Slou. 92 AY76
Warren Cl, Wem. 61 CK61
Warren Ct, Chig. 49 ER49
Warren Ct, Sev. 191 FJ125
Warren Ct, Wey. 152 BN106
Warren Cres N9 46 DT45
Warren Cutting, Kings.T. 118 CR94
Warren Dr, Grnf. 78 CB70
Warren Dr, Horn. 71 FG62
Warren Dr, Orp. 164 EV106
Warren Dr, Ruis. 60 BX59
Warren Dr, Tad. 173 CZ122
Warren Dr, The E11 68 EJ59
Warren Dr N, Surb. 138 CP102
Warren Dr S, Surb. 138 CQ102
Warren Fld, Epp. 18 EU32
Warren Fld, Iver 75 BC68
Warren Flds, Stan. 41 CJ49
Valencia Rd
Warren Footpath, Twick. 117 CK86
Warren Gdns E15 67 ED64
Ashton Rd
Warren Gdns, Orp. 164 EU106
Warren Gro, Borwd. 26 CR42
Warren Hastings Ct, Grav. 131 GF86
Pier Rd
Warren Hts, Grays 110 FY77
Warren Hill, Epsom 172 CR116
Warren Hill, Loug. 32 EJ44
Warren Ho E3 85 EB69
Bromley High St
Warren La SE18 105 EP76
Warren La, Grays 109 FW77
Warren La, Lthd. 154 CC111
Warren La, Oxt. 188 EF134
Warren La, Stan. 41 CG47
Warren La, Wok. 168 BH118
Warren Lo Dr, Tad. 173 CY124
Warren Mead, Bans. 173 CW115
Warren Ms W1 195 K5
Warren Pk, Kings.T. 118 CQ93
Warren Pk, Warl. 177 DX118
Warren Pk Rd, Sutt. 158 DD107
Warren Pl E1 85 DX72
Pitsea St
Warren Pond Rd E4 48 EF46
Warren Ri, N.Mal. 138 CR95
Warren Rd E4 47 EC47
Warren Rd E10 67 EC62
Warren Rd E11 68 EJ60
Warren Rd NW2 63 CT61
Warren Rd SW19 120 DE93
Warren Rd, Add. 152 BG110
Warren Rd, Ashf. 115 BS94
Warren Rd, Bans. 157 CW114
Warren Rd, Bexh. 126 FA85
Warren Rd, Brom. 144 EG103
Warren Rd, Bushey 40 CC46
Warren Rd, Croy. 142 DS102
Warren Rd, Dart. 128 FK90
Warren Rd, Grav. 130 GB92
Warren Rd, Ilf. 69 ER57
Warren Rd, Kings.T. 118 CQ93
Warren Rd, Orp. 163 ET106
Warren Rd, Pur. 159 DP112
Warren Rd, Reig. 184 DB133
Warren Rd, Sid. 126 EW90
Warren Rd, Twick. 116 CC86
Warren Rd, Uxb. 58 BL63
Warren St W1 195 K5
Warren St W1 83 DJ70
Warren Ter, Grays 109 FX75
Arterial Rd W Thurrock
Warren Ter, Rom. 70 EX56
Warren Wk SE7 104 EJ79
Warren Way NW7 43 CY51
Warren Way, Wey. 153 BQ106
Warren Wd Cl, Brom. 144 EF103
Warrender Rd N19 65 DJ62
Warrender Rd, Chesh. 4 AS29
Warrender Way, Ruis. 59 BU59
Warreners La, Wey. 153 BR109
Warrenfield Cl (Cheshunt), Wal.Cr. 14 DU31
Portland Dr
Warrengate La, Pot.B. 11 CW31
Warrengate Rd, Hat. 11 CW28
Warrenne Way, Reig. 184 DA134
Warrens Shawe La, Edg. 42 CP46
Warriner Av, Horn. 72 FK61
Warriner Dr N9 46 DU48
Warriner Gdns SW11 100 DF81
Warrington Cres W9 82 DC70
Warrington Gdns W9 82 DC70
Warwick Av
Warrington Gdns, Horn. 72 FJ58
Warrington Pl E14 204 E2
Warrington Rd, Croy. 141 DP104
Warrington Rd, Dag. 70 EX61
Warrington Rd, Har. 61 CE57
Warrington Rd, Rich. 117 CK85
Warrington Spur, Wind. 112 AV87
Warrington Sq, Dag. 70 EX61
Warrior Av, Grav. 131 GJ91
Warrior Sq E12 69 EN63
Warsaw Cl, Ruis. 77 BV65
Glebe Av
Warsdale Dr NW9 62 CR57
Mardale Dr
Warspite Rd SE18 104 EL76
Warton Rd E15 85 EC66
Warwall E6 87 EP72
Warwick Av W2 82 DC70
Warwick Av W9 82 DB70
Warwick Av, Edg. 42 CP48
Warwick Av, Egh. 133 BC95
Warwick Av, Har. 60 BZ63
Warwick Av (Cuffley), Pot.B. 13 DK27
Warwick Av, Stai. 114 BJ93
Warwick Cl, Barn. 28 DD43
Warwick Cl, Bex. 126 EZ87
Warwick Cl, Bushey 41 CE45
Magnaville Rd
Warwick Cl, Hmptn. 116 CC94
Warwick Cl, Orp. 146 EU104
Warwick Cl (Cuffley), Pot.B. 13 DK27
Warwick Ct SE15 102 DU82
Warwick Ct WC1 196 C7
Warwick Ct, Rick. 21 BF41
Warwick Ct, Surb. 138 CL103
Hook Rd
Warwick Cres W2 82 DC71
Warwick Cres, Hayes 77 BT70
Warwick Deeping, Cher. 151 BC106
Warwick Dene W5 80 CL74
Warwick Dr SW15 99 CV83
Warwick Dr (Cheshunt), Wal.Cr. 15 DX28
Warwick Est W2 82 DB71
Warwick Gdns N4 66 DQ57
Warwick Gdns W14 99 CZ76
Warwick Gdns, Ash. 171 CJ117
Warwick Gdns, Barn. 27 CZ38
Great N Rd
Warwick Gdns, Ilf. 69 EP60
Warwick Gdns, Rom. 72 FJ55
Warwick Gdns, T.Ditt. 137 CF99
Warwick Gro E5 66 DV60
Warwick Gro, Surb. 138 CM101
Warwick Ho St SW1 199 N2
Warwick Ho St SW1 83 DK74
Warwick La EC4 196 G9
Warwick La EC4 83 DP72
Warwick La, Rain. 90 FM68
Warwick La, Upmin. 90 FP68
Warwick La, Wok. 166 AU119
Warwick Pas EC4 196 G8
Warwick Pl W5 97 CK75
Warwick Rd
Warwick Pl W9 82 DC71
Warwick Pl, Grav. 130 GB85
Warwick Pl, Uxb. 76 BJ66
Warwick Pl N SW1 199 K9
Warwick Pl N SW1 101 DJ77
Warwick Quad Shop Mall, Red. 184 DG133
London Rd
Warwick Rd E4 47 EA50
Warwick Rd E11 68 EH57
Warwick Rd E12 68 EL64
Warwick Rd E15 86 EF65
Warwick Rd E17 47 DZ53
Warwick Rd N11 45 DK51
Warwick Rd N18 46 DS49
Warwick Rd SE20 142 DV97
Warwick Rd SW5 99 CZ77
Warwick Rd W5 97 CK75
Warwick Rd W14 99 CZ77
Warwick Rd, Ashf. 114 BL92
Warwick Rd, Barn. 28 DB42
Warwick Rd, Borwd. 26 CR41
Warwick Rd, Couls. 159 DJ114
Warwick Rd, Enf. 31 DZ37
Warwick Rd, Houns. 95 BV83
Warwick Rd, Kings.T. 137 CJ95
Warwick Rd, N.Mal. 138 CQ97
Warwick Rd, Rain. 90 FJ70
Warwick Rd, Red. 184 DF133
Warwick Rd, Sid. 126 EV92
Warwick Rd, Sthl. 96 BZ76
Warwick Rd, Sutt. 158 DC105
Warwick Rd, T.Ditt. 137 CF99
Warwick Rd, Th.Hth. 141 DN97
Warwick Rd, Twick. 117 CE88
Warwick Rd, Well. 106 EW83
Warwick Rd, West Dr. 76 BL74
Warwick Row SW1 199 J6
Warwick Row SW1 101 DH76
Warwick Sq EC4 196 G8
Warwick Sq SW1 199 K10
Warwick Sq SW1 101 DJ78
Warwick Sq Ms SW1 199 K9
Warwick Sq Ms SW1 101 DJ77
Warwick St W1 195 L10
Warwick St W1 83 DJ73
Warwick Ter SE18 105 ER79
Warwick Way SW1 199 K9
Warwick Way SW1 101 DJ77
Warwick Way, Rick. 23 BQ42
Warwick Wold Rd, Red. 185 DN128
Warwick Yd EC1 197 J5
Warwickshire Path SE8 103 DZ80
Wash La, Pot.B. 11 CV33
Wash Rd, Brwd. 55 GE44
Washington Av E12 68 EL63
Washington Cl E3 85 EC72
Washington Cl, Reig. 184 DA131
Washington Rd E6 86 EJ66
St. Stephens Rd
Washington Rd E18 48 EF54
Washington Rd SW13 99 CU80
Washington Rd, Kings.T. 138 CN96
Washington Rd, Wor.Pk. 139 CV103
Washneys Rd, Orp. 164 EV113
Washpond La, Warl. 177 EC118
Wastdale Rd SE23 123 DX88
Wat Tyler Rd SE3 103 EC82
Wat Tyler Rd SE10 103 EC82
Watchfield Ct W4 98 CQ78
Watchgate, Dart. 129 FR91
Watcombe Cotts, Rich. 98 CN79
Watcombe Pl SE25 142 DV99
Albert Rd
Watcombe Rd SE25 142 DV99
Water Circ (Bluewater), Green. 129 FT88
Water Gdns, Stan. 41 CH51
Water Gdns, The W2 82 DE72
Burwood Pl
Water La E15 86 EE65
Water La EC3 84 DS73
Lower Thames St
Water La N9 46 DV46
Water La NW1 83 DH66
Kentish Town Rd
Water La SE14 102 DW80
Water La, Cob. 170 BY115
Water La, Hem.H. 5 BA29
Water La, Ilf. 69 ES62
Water La, Kings L. 7 BP29
Water La, Kings.T. 137 CK95
Water La, Oxt. 188 EG126
Water La, Purf. 108 FN77
Water La, Red. 185 DP130
Water La, Rich. 117 CK85
Water La, Sev. 165 FF112
Water La, Sid. 126 EZ89
Water La, Twick. 117 CG88
The Embk
Water La, Wat. 24 BW42
Water La, West. 189 ER127
Water Lily Cl, Sthl. 96 CC75
Navigator Dr
Water Ms SE15 102 DW84
Water Mill Way (South Darenth), Dart. 148 FP96
Water Rd, Wem. 80 CM67
Water Side, Kings L. 6 BN29
Water St WC2 196 C10
Water Twr Cl, Uxb. 58 BL64
Water Twr Hill, Croy. 160 DR105
Water Twr Pl N1 83 DN67
Liverpool Rd
Waterbank Rd SE6 123 EB90
Waterbeach Rd, Dag. 88 EW65
Waterbrook La NW4 63 CW57
Watercress Pl N1 84 DS66
Hertford Rd
Watercress Rd (Cheshunt), Wal.Cr. 14 DR26
Hammondstreet Rd
Watercress Way, Wok. 166 AV117
Watercroft Rd, Sev. 164 EZ110
Waterdale Rd SE2 106 EU79
Waterdales, Grav. 130 GD88
Waterdell Pl, Rick. 38 BG47
Uxbridge Rd
Waterden Rd E15 67 EA64
Waterer Gdns, Tad. 173 CX118
Waterer Ri, Wall. 159 DK107
Waterfall Cl N14 45 DJ48
Waterfall Cl, Vir.W. 132 AU97
Waterfall Cotts SW19 120 DD93
Waterfall Rd N11 45 DH49
Waterfall Rd N14 45 DJ48
Waterfall Rd SW19 120 DD93
Waterfall Ter SW17 120 DE93
Waterfield, Rick. 37 BC45
Waterfield, Tad. 173 CV119
Waterfield Cl SE28 88 EV74
Waterfield Cl, Belv. 106 FA76
Waterfield Dr, Warl. 176 DW119
Waterfield Gdns SE25 142 DS99
Waterfield Grn, Tad. 173 CW120
Waterfields, Lthd. 171 CH119
Waterfields Way, Wat. 24 BX42
Waterford Cl, Cob. 154 BY111
Waterford Rd SW6 100 DB81
Watergardens, The, Kings.T. 118 CQ93
Watergate EC4 196 F10
Watergate, The, Wat. 40 BX47
Watergate St SE8 103 EA79
Watergate Wk WC2 200 A2
Waterglade Ind Pk, Grays 109 FT78
Waterhall Av E4 48 EE49
Waterhall Cl E17 47 DX53
Waterhead Cl, Erith 107 FE80
Waterhouse Cl E16 86 EK71
Waterhouse Cl NW3 64 DD64
Lyndhurst Rd
Waterhouse Cl W6 99 CX77
Great Ch La
Waterhouse La, Ken. 176 DQ119
Waterhouse La, Ken. 176 DQ119
Hayes La
Waterhouse La, Red. 186 DT132
Waterhouse La, Tad. 173 CY121
Waterhouse Sq EC1 196 D7
Waterhouse Sq EC1 83 DN71
Wateridge Cl E14 103 EA76
Westferry Rd
Wateringbury Cl, Orp. 146 EV97
Waterloo Br SE1 200 B1
Waterloo Br SE1 83 DM73
Waterloo Br WC2 200 B1
Waterloo Br WC2 83 DM73
Waterloo Cl E9 66 DW64
Churchill Wk
Waterloo Cl, Felt. 115 BT88
Waterloo Est E2 84 DW68
Waterloo Gdns E2 84 DW68
Waterloo Gdns N1 83 DP66
Barnsbury St
Waterloo Gdns, Rom. 71 FD58
Waterloo Pas NW6 82 DA66
Waterloo Pl SW1 199 M2
Waterloo Pl SW1 83 DK74
Waterloo Pl, Rich. 118 CL85
Sheen Rd
Waterloo Pl (Kew), Rich. 98 CN79
Waterloo Rd E6 86 EJ66
Waterloo Rd E7 68 EF64
Wellington Rd
Waterloo Rd E10 67 EA59
Waterloo Rd NW2 63 CU60
Waterloo Rd SE1 200 D4
Waterloo Rd SE1 101 DN75
Waterloo Rd, Brwd. 54 FW46
Waterloo Rd, Epsom 156 CR112
Waterloo Rd, Ilf. 49 EQ54
Waterloo Rd, Rom. 71 FE57
Waterloo Rd, Sutt. 158 DD106
Waterloo Rd, Uxb. 76 BJ67
Waterloo St, Grav. 131 GJ87
Waterloo Ter N1 83 DP66
Waterlow Ct NW11 64 DB59
Heath Cl
Waterlow Rd N19 65 DJ60
Waterman Cl, Wat. 23 BV44
Waterman St SW15 99 CX83
Waterman Way E1 202 D2
Waterman Way E1 84 DV74
Waterman's Cl, Kings.T. 118 CL94
Woodside Rd
Watermans Wk SE16 203 K6
Watermans Wk SE16 103 DY76
Watermans Way, Epp. 18 FA27
Watermead, Felt. 115 BS88
Watermead, Tad. 173 CV120
Watermead, Wok. 166 AT116
Watermead La, Cars. 140 DF101
Watermead Rd SE6 123 EC91
Watermead Way N17 66 DV55
Watermeadow Cl, Erith 107 FH81
Watermeadow La SW6 100 DC82
Watermen's Sq SE20 122 DW94
Watermill Cl, Rich. 117 CJ90
Watermill La N18 46 DS50
Watermill Way SW19 140 DC95
Watermill Way, Felt. 116 BZ89
Watermint Cl, Orp. 146 EX98
Wagtail Way
Watermint Quay N16 66 DU59
Waterperry La, Wok. 150 AT110
Waters Dr, Rick. 38 BL46
Waters Dr, Stai. 113 BF90
Waters Gdns, Dag. 70 FA64
Waters Pl SW15 99 CW82
Danemere St
Waters Rd SE6 124 EE90
Waters Rd, Kings.T. 138 CP96
Waters Sq, Kings.T. 138 CP97
Watersedge, Epsom 156 CQ105
Watersfield Way, Edg. 41 CK52
Waterside, Beck. 143 EA95
Rectory Rd
Waterside, Dart. 127 FE85
Waterside, Rad. 9 CH34
Waterside, St.Alb. 10 CL27
Waterside, Uxb. 76 BJ71
Waterside Cl E3 85 DZ67
Waterside Cl SE16 202 C5
Waterside Cl, Bark. 70 EU63
Waterside Cl, Nthlt. 78 BZ69
Waterside Cl, Rom. 52 FN52
Waterside Cl, Surb. 138 CL103
Culsac Rd
Waterside Ct, Kings L. 7 BP29
Water Side
Waterside Dr, Slou. 93 AZ75
Waterside Dr, Walt. 135 BU99
Waterside Pl NW1 82 DG67
Princess Rd
Waterside Pt SW11 100 DE80
Waterside Rd, Sthl. 96 CA76
Waterside Trd Cen W7 97 CE76
Waterside Way SW17 120 DC91
Waterside Way, Wok. 166 AV118
Winnington Way
Watersmeet Way SE28 88 EW72
Waterson Rd, Grays 111 GH77
Waterson St E2 197 N2
Waterson St E2 84 DS69
Watersplash Cl, Kings.T. 138 CL97
Watersplash La, Hayes 95 BU77
Watersplash La, Houns. 95 BV78
Watersplash Rd, Shep. 134 BN98
Waterton Av, Grav. 131 GL87
Waterview Ho E14 85 DY71
Waterway Rd, Lthd. 171 CG122
Waterworks La E5 67 DX61
Waterworks Rd SW2 121 DM86
Waterworks Yd, Croy. 142 DQ104
Surrey St
Watery La SW20 139 CZ96
Watery La, Cher. 133 BD102
Watery La, Nthlt. 78 BW68
Watery La, St.Alb. 9 CK28
Watery La, Sid. 126 EV93
Wates Way, Brwd. 54 FX46
Wates Way, Mitch. 140 DF100
Wateville Rd N17 46 DQ53
Watford Bypass, Borwd. 41 CG45
Watford Cl SW11 100 DE81
Petworth St
Watford Fld Rd, Wat. 24 BW43
Watford Heath, Wat. 40 BX45
Watford Rd E16 86 EG71
Watford Rd, Borwd. 25 CJ44
Watford Rd, Har. 61 CG61
Watford Rd, Kings L. 7 BP32
Watford Rd, Nthwd. 39 BT51
Watford Rd, Rad. 25 CE36
Watford Rd, Rick. 23 BQ43
Watford Rd, St.Alb. 8 CA27
Watford Rd, Wem. 61 CG61
Watford Way NW4 63 CU56
Watford Way NW7 63 CU56
Watkin Rd, Wem. 62 CP62
Watkinson Rd N7 83 DM65
Watling Av, Edg. 42 CR52
Watling Ct EC4 197 J9
Watling Ct, Borwd. 25 CK44
Watling Fm Cl, Stan. 41 CJ46
Watling Gdns NW2 81 CY65
Watling Knoll, Rad. 9 CF33
Watling St EC4 197 H9
Watling St EC4 84 DQ72
Watling St SE15 102 DS79
Dragon Rd
Watling St, Bexh. 107 FB84
Watling St, Borwd. 25 CJ40
Watling St, Dart. 128 FP87
Watling St, Grav. 130 GC90
Watling St, Rad. 9 CF32
Watling St, St.Alb. 9 CD25
Watling St Caravan Site (Travellers), St.Alb. 8 CC25

Wentland Cl SE6 123 ED89
Wentland Rd SE6 123 ED89
Wentworth Av N3 44 DA52
Wentworth Av, Borwd. 26 CM43
Wentworth Cl N3 44 DB52
Wentworth Cl SE28 88 EX72
Wentworth Cl, Ashf. 115 BP91
Reedsfield Rd
Wentworth Cl, Brom. 144 EG103
Hillside La
Wentworth Cl, Grav. 131 GG92
Wentworth Cl, Mord. 140 DA101
Wentworth Cl, Orp. 163 ES106
Wentworth Cl, Pot.B. 12 DA31
Strafford Gate
Wentworth Cl, Surb. 137 CK103
Wentworth Cl, Wat. 23 BT38
Wentworth Cl, Wok. 168 BH121
Wentworth Ct, Surb. 138 CL103
Culsac Rd
Wentworth Cres SE15 102 DU80
Wentworth Cres, Hayes 95 BR76
Wentworth Dr, Dart. 127 FG86
Wentworth Dr, Pnr. 59 BU57
Wentworth Dr, Vir.W. 132 AT98
Wentworth Gdns N13 45 DP49
Wentworth Hill, Wem. 62 CM60
Wentworth Ms E3 85 DZ70
Eric St
Wentworth Pk N3 44 DA52
Wentworth Pl, Grays 110 GD76
Wentworth Pl, Stan. 41 CH51
Greenacres Dr
Wentworth Rd E12 68 EK63
Wentworth Rd NW11 63 CZ58
Wentworth Rd, Barn. 27 CX41
Wentworth Rd, Croy. 141 DN101
Wentworth Rd, Sthl. 96 BW77
Wentworth St E1 197 P8
Wentworth St E1 84 DT72
Wentworth Way, Pnr. 60 BY56
Wentworth Way, Rain. 89 FH69
Wentworth Way, S.Croy. 160 DU114
Wenvoe Av, Bexh. 107 FB82
Wernbrook St SE18 105 EQ79
Werndee Rd SE25 142 DU98
Werneth Hall Rd, Ilf. 69 EM55
Werrington St NW1 195 L1
Werrington St NW1 83 DJ68
Werter Rd SW15 99 CY84
Wescott Way, Uxb. 76 BJ68
Wesley Av E16 205 P2
Wesley Av E16 86 EG74
Wesley Av NW10 80 CR69
Wesley Av, Houns. 96 BY82
Wesley Cl N7 65 DM61
Wesley Cl SE17 200 G9
Wesley Cl SE17 101 DP77
Wesley Cl, Har. 60 CC61
Wesley Cl, Orp. 146 EW97
Wesley Cl (Cheshunt), Wal.Cr. 14 DQ28
Wesley Dr, Egh. 113 BA93
Wesley Rd E10 67 EC59
Wesley Rd NW10 80 CQ67
Wesley Rd, Hayes 77 BU73
Wesley Sq W11 81 CY72
Bartle Rd
Wesley St W1 194 G7
Wesleyan Pl NW5 65 DH63
Gordon Ho Rd
Wessels, Tad. 173 CX121
Wessex Av SW19 140 DA96
Wessex Cl, Ilf. 69 ES58
Wessex Cl, Kings.T. 138 CP95
Gloucester Rd
Wessex Dr, Erith 107 FE81
Wessex Dr, Pnr. 40 BY52
Wessex Gdns NW11 63 CY60
Wessex La, Grnf. 79 CD68
Wessex Rd, Houns. 94 BK82
Wessex St E2 84 DW69
Wessex Way NW11 63 CY60
West App, Orp. 145 EQ99
West Arbour St E1 85 DX72
West Av E17 67 EB56
West Av N3 44 DA51
West Av NW4 63 CX57
West Av, Hayes 77 BT73
West Av, Pnr. 60 BZ58
West Av, St.Alb. 8 CB25
West Av, Sthl. 78 BZ73
West Av, Wall. 159 DL106
West Av, Walt. 153 BS109
West Av Rd E17 67 EA56
West Bk N16 66 DS59
West Bk, Bark. 87 EP67
Highbridge Rd
West Bk, Enf. 30 DQ40
West Barnes La SW20 139 CV96
West Barnes La, N.Mal. 139 CV97
West Carriage Dr W2 198 A3
West Carriage Dr W2 82 DD73
West Cen St WC1 195 P8
West Cen Av W10 81 CV69
Harrow Rd
West Chantry, Har. 40 CB53
Chantry Rd
West Cl N9 46 DT48
West Cl, Ashf. 114 BL91
West Cl, Barn. 27 CV43
West Cl (Cockfosters), Barn. 28 DG42
West Cl, Grnf. 78 CC68
West Cl, Hmptn. 116 BY93
Oak Av
West Cl, Rain. 89 FH70
West Cl, Wem. 62 CM60
West Common, Ger.Cr. 56 AX57
West Common Cl, Ger.Cr. 56 AY57
West Common Rd, Brom. 144 EG103
West Common Rd, Kes. 162 EH105
West Common Rd, Uxb. 58 BK64
West Cotts NW6 64 DA64
West Ct SE18 105 EM81
Prince Imperial Rd
West Ct, Wem. 61 CJ61
West Cres Rd, Grav. 131 GH86
West Cromwell Rd SW5 99 CZ77
West Cromwell Rd W14 99 CZ77
West Cross Cen, Brent. 97 CG79
West Cross Route W10 81 CX73
West Cross Route W11 81 CX73
West Cross Way, Brent. 97 CH79
West Dene, Sutt. 157 CY107
Park La
West Dene Dr, Rom. 52 FK50
West Drayton Pk Av, West Dr. 94 BL76
West Drayton Rd, Uxb. 77 BQ71
West Dr SW16 121 DJ91
West Dr, Cars. 158 DD110
West Dr, Har. 41 CD51
West Dr (Cheam), Sutt. 157 CX109
West Dr, Tad. 173 CX118
West Dr, Vir.W. 132 AT101
West Dr, Wat. 23 BV36
West Dr Gdns, Har. 41 CD51
West Eaton Pl SW1 198 F8
West Eaton Pl SW1 100 DG77
West Eaton Pl Ms SW1 198 F8
West Ella Rd NW10 80 CS66
West End Av E10 67 EC57
West End Av, Pnr. 60 BX56
West End Ct, Pnr. 60 BX56
West End Ct, Slou. 74 AT67
West End Gdns, Esher 154 BZ106
West End Gdns, Nthlt. 78 BW68
Edward Cl
West End La NW6 82 DA67
West End La, Barn. 27 CX42
West End La, Esher 154 BZ107
West End La, Hayes 95 BQ80
West End La, Pnr. 60 BX55
West End La, Slou. 74 AS67
West End Rd, Nthlt. 78 BW66
West End Rd, Ruis. 59 BV64
West End Rd, Sthl. 78 BY74
West Fm Av, Ash. 171 CJ118
West Fm Cl, Ash. 171 CJ119
West Fm Dr, Ash. 171 CK119
West Gdn Pl W2 194 C9
West Gdns E1 202 E1
West Gdns E1 84 DV73
West Gdns SW17 120 DE93
West Gdns, Epsom 156 CS110
West Gate W5 80 CL69
West Gorse, Croy. 161 DY112
West Grn Pl, Grnf. 79 CD67
Uneeda Dr
West Grn Rd N15 66 DR56
West Gro SE10 103 EC81
West Gro, Walt. 153 BV105
West Gro, Wdf.Grn. 48 EJ51
West Halkin St SW1 198 F6
West Halkin St SW1 100 DG76
West Hall Rd, Rich. 98 CP81
West Hallowes SE9 124 EK88
West Ham La E15 86 EE66
West Ham Pk E7 86 EG66
West Hampstead Ms NW6 82 DB65
West Harding St EC4 196 E8
West Harold, Swan. 147 FD97
West Hatch Manor, Ruis. 59 BT60
West Heath, Oxt. 188 EG130
West Heath Av NW11 64 DA60
West Heath Cl NW3 64 DA62
West Heath Cl, Dart. 127 FF86
West Heath Rd
West Heath Dr NW11 64 DA60
West Heath Gdns NW3 64 DA62
West Heath La, Sev. 191 FH128
West Heath Rd NW3 64 DA61
West Heath Rd SE2 106 EX79
West Heath Rd, Dart. 127 FF86
West Hendon Bdy NW9 63 CT58
West Hill SW15 119 CX87
West Hill SW18 120 DA85
West Hill, Dart. 128 FK86
West Hill, Epsom 156 CQ113
West Hill, Har. 61 CE61
West Hill, Orp. 163 EM112
West Hill, Oxt. 187 ED130
West Hill, S.Croy. 160 DS110
West Hill, Wem. 62 CM60
West Hill Av, Epsom 156 CQ112
West Hill Bk, Oxt. 187 ED130
West Hill Ct N6 64 DG62
West Hill Dr, Dart. 128 FJ86
West Hill Pk N6 64 DF61
Merton La
West Hill Ri, Dart. 128 FK86
West Hill Rd SW18 120 DA86
West Hill Rd, Wok. 166 AX119
West Hill Way N20 44 DB46
West Holme, Erith 107 FC81
West Ho Cl SW19 119 CY88
West Hyde La (Chalfont St. Peter), Ger.Cr. 37 AZ52
West India Av E14 203 P2
West India Av E14 85 EA74
West India Dock Rd E14 85 DZ72
West Kent Av, Grav. 130 GC86
West Kentish Town Est NW5 64 DG64
West La SE16 202 D5
West La SE16 102 DV75
West Lo Av W3 80 CN74
West Mall W8 82 DA74
Palace Gdns Ter
West Malling Way, Horn. 72 FJ64
West Mead, Epsom 156 CS107
West Mead, Ruis. 60 BW63
West Mersea Cl E16 205 P3
West Ms N17 46 DV51
West Ms SW1 199 K9
West Mill, Grav. 131 GF86
West Oak, Beck. 143 ED95
West Palace Gdns, Wey. 135 BP104
West Pk SE9 124 EL89
West Pk Av, Rich. 98 CN81
West Pk Cl, Houns. 96 BZ79
Heston Gra La
West Pk Cl, Rom. 70 EX57
West Pk Hill, Brwd. 54 FU48
West Pk Rd, Epsom 156 CM112
West Pk Rd, Rich. 98 CN81
West Pk Rd, Sthl. 78 CC74
West Parkside SE10 205 L7
West Parkside SE10 104 EE75
West Pier E1 202 D3
West Pl SW19 119 CW92
West Poultry Av EC1 196 F7
West Quarters W12 81 CU72
West Quay Dr, Hayes 78 BY71
West Ramp, Houns. 94 BN81
West Ridge Gdns, Grnf. 78 CC68
West Riding, St.Alb. 8 BZ30
West Rd E15 86 EF67
West Rd N17 46 DV51
West Rd SW3 100 DF79
West Rd SW4 121 DK85
West Rd W5 80 CL71
West Rd, Barn. 44 DG46
West Rd, Chess. 155 CJ112
West Rd, Felt. 115 BR86
West Rd, Kings.T. 138 CQ95
West Rd (Chadwell Heath), Rom. 70 EX58
West Rd (Rush Grn), Rom. 71 FD59
West Rd, S.Ock. 91 FV69
West Rd, West Dr. 94 BM76
West Rd, Wey. 153 BQ108
West Row W10 81 CY70
West Shaw, Long. 149 FX96
West Sheen Vale, Rich. 98 CM84
West Side, Brox. 15 DY25
High Rd Turnford
West Side Common SW19 119 CW92
West Smithfield EC1 196 F7
West Smithfield EC1 83 DP71
West Spur Rd, Uxb. 76 BK69
West Sq SE11 200 F7
West Sq SE11 101 DP76
West Sq, Iver 75 BF72
High St
West St E2 84 DV68
West St E11 68 EE62
West St E17 67 EB57
Grove Rd
West St WC2 195 N9
West St, Bexh. 106 EZ84
West St, Brent. 97 CJ79
West St, Brom. 144 EG95
West St, Cars. 140 DF104
West St, Croy. 160 DQ105
West St, Epsom 156 CR113
West St (Ewell), Epsom 156 CS110
West St, Erith 107 FD77
West St, Grav. 131 GG86
West St, Grays 110 GA79
West St, Har. 61 CD60
West St, Reig. 183 CY133
West St, Sutt. 158 DB106
West St, Wat. 23 BV40
West St, Wok. 167 AZ117
Church St E
West St La, Cars. 158 DF105
West Temple Sheen SW14 98 CP84
West Tenter St E1 84 DT72
West Thamesmead Business Pk SE28 105 ET76
Nathan Way
West Thurrock Way, Grays 109 FT77
West Twrs, Pnr. 60 BX58
West Valley Rd, Hem.H. 6 BJ25
West Vw NW4 63 CW56
West Vw, Felt. 115 BQ87
West Vw, Loug. 33 EM41
West Vw Av, Whyt. 176 DU118
Station Rd
West Vw Ct, Borwd. 25 CK44
High St
West Vw Gdns, Borwd. 25 CK44
High St
West Vw Rd, Dart. 128 FM86
West Vw Rd, Swan. 147 FG98
West Vw Rd (Crockenhill), Swan. 147 FD100
West Wk W5 80 CL71
West Wk, Barn. 44 DG45
West Wk, Hayes 77 BU74
West Walkway, The, Sutt. 158 DB111
Cheam Rd
West Warwick Pl SW1 199 J9
West Warwick Pl SW1 101 DH77
West Way N18 46 DR49
West Way NW10 62 CR62
West Way, Brwd. 54 FU48
West Way, Cars. 158 DD110
West Way, Croy. 143 DY103
West Way, Edg. 42 CP51
West Way, Houns. 96 BZ81
West Way, Pnr. 60 BX56
West Way, Rick. 38 BH46
West Way, Ruis. 59 BT60
West Way, Shep. 135 BR100
West Way, W.Wick. 143 ED100
West Way Gdns, Croy. 143 DX103
West Woodside, Bex. 126 EY87
West World W5 80 CL69
West Yoke, Sev. 149 FX103
Westacott, Hayes 77 BS71
Westacott Cl N19 65 DK60
Westacres, Esher 154 BZ108
Westall Rd, Loug. 33 EP41
Westbank Rd, Hmptn. 116 CC93
Westbeech Rd N22 65 DN55
Westbere Dr, Stan. 41 CK49
Westbere Rd NW2 63 CY64
Westbourne Av W3 80 CR72
Westbourne Av, Sutt. 139 CY103
Westbourne Br W2 82 DC71
Westbourne Cl, Hayes 77 BV70
Westbourne Cres W2 82 DD73
Westbourne Cres Ms W2 82 DD73
Westbourne Cres
Westbourne Dr SE23 123 DX89
Westbourne Dr, Brwd. 54 FT49
Westbourne Gdns W2 82 DB72
Westbourne Gro W2 82 DA72
Westbourne Gro W11 81 CZ73
Westbourne Gro Ms W11 82 DA72
Westbourne Gro
Westbourne Gro Ter W2 82 DB72
Westbourne Pk Ms W2 82 DB72
Westbourne Gdns
Westbourne Pk Pas W2 82 DA71
Westbourne Pk Vil
Westbourne Pk Rd W2 82 DA71
Westbourne Pk Rd W11 81 CY72
Westbourne Pk Vil W2 82 DA71
Westbourne Pl N9 46 DV48
Eastbournia Av
Westbourne Rd N7 83 DN65
Westbourne Rd SE26 123 DX93
Westbourne Rd, Bexh. 106 EY80
Westbourne Rd, Croy. 142 DT100
Westbourne Rd, Felt. 115 BT90
Westbourne Rd, Stai. 114 BH94
Westbourne Rd, Uxb. 77 BP70
Westbourne St W2 82 DD73
Westbourne Ter SE23 123 DX89
Westbourne Dr
Westbourne Ter W2 82 DD72
Westbourne Ter Ms W2 82 DC72
Westbourne Ter Rd W2 82 DC71
Westbridge Rd SW11 100 DD81
Westbrook Av, Hmptn. 116 BZ94
Westbrook Cl, Barn. 28 DD41
Westbrook Cres, Barn. 28 DD41
Westbrook Dr, Orp. 146 EW102
Westbrook Rd SE3 104 EH81
Westbrook Rd, Houns. 96 BZ80
Westbrook Rd, Stai. 113 BF92
South St
Westbrook Rd, Th.Hth. 142 DR95
Westbrook Sq, Barn. 28 DD41
Westbrook Cres
Westbrooke Cres, Well. 106 EW83
Westbrooke Rd, Sid. 125 ER89
Westbrooke Rd, Well. 106 EV83
Westbury Av N22 65 DP55
Westbury Av, Esher 155 CF107
Westbury Av, Sthl. 78 CA70
Westbury Av, Wem. 80 CL66
Westbury Cl, Ruis. 59 BU59
Westbury Cl, Shep. 135 BP100
Burchetts Way
Westbury Cl, Whyt. 176 DS116
Beverley Rd
Westbury Dr, Brwd. 54 FV47
Westbury Gro N12 44 DA51
Westbury La, Buck.H. 48 EJ47
Westbury Lo Cl, Pnr. 60 BX55
Westbury Par SW12 121 DH86
Balham Hill
Westbury Pl, Brent. 97 CK79
Westbury Rd E7 68 EH64
Westbury Rd E17 67 EA56
Westbury Rd N11 45 DL51
Westbury Rd N12 44 DA51
Westbury Rd SE20 143 DX95
Westbury Rd W5 80 CL72
Westbury Rd, Bark. 87 ER67
Westbury Rd, Beck. 143 DY97
Westbury Rd, Brwd. 54 FW47
Westbury Rd, Brom. 144 EK95
Westbury Rd, Buck.H. 48 EJ47
Westbury Rd, Croy. 142 DR100
Westbury Rd, Felt. 116 BX88
Westbury Rd, Ilf. 69 EN61
Westbury Rd, N.Mal. 138 CR98
Westbury Rd, Nthwd. 39 BS49
Westbury Rd (Cheshunt), Wal.Cr. 15 DX30
Turners Hill
Westbury Rd, Wat. 23 BV43
Westbury Rd, Wem. 80 CL66
Westbury St SW8 101 DJ82
Westbury Ter E7 86 EH65
Westbury Ter, Upmin. 73 FS61
Westbury Ter, West. 189 EQ127
Westcar La, Walt. 153 BV107
Westchester Dr NW4 63 CX55
Westcombe Av, Croy. 141 DL100
Westcombe Ct SE3 104 EF80
Westcombe Pk Rd
Westcombe Dr, Barn. 28 DA43
Westcombe Hill SE3 104 EG79
Westcombe Hill SE10 205 M10
Westcombe Hill SE10 104 EG78
Westcombe Lo Dr, Hayes 77 BR71
Westcombe Pk Rd SE3 104 EE79
Westcoombe Av SW20 139 CT95
Westcote Ri, Ruis. 59 BQ59
Westcote Rd SW16 121 DJ92
Westcott Av, Grav. 131 GG90
Westcott Cl N15 66 DT58
Ermine Rd
Westcott Cl, Brom. 144 EL99
Ringmer Way
Westcott Cl, Croy. 161 EB109
Castle Hill Av
Westcott Cres W7 79 CE72
Westcott Rd SE17 101 DP79
Westcott Way, Sutt. 157 CW110
Westcourt, Sun. 135 BV96
Westcroft Cl NW2 63 CY63
Westcroft Cl, Enf. 30 DW38
Westcroft Gdns, Mord. 139 CZ97
Westcroft Rd, Cars. 158 DG105
Westcroft Rd, Wall. 158 DG105
Westcroft Sq W6 99 CU77
Westcroft Way NW2 63 CY63
Westdale Pas SE18 105 EP79
Westdale Rd SE18 105 EP79
Westdean Av SE12 124 EH88
Westdean Cl SW18 120 DB86
Westdene Way, Wey. 135 BS104
Westdown Rd E15 67 EC63
Westdown Rd SE6 123 EA87
Wested La, Swan. 147 FG101
Westerdale Rd SE10 104 EG78
Westerfield Rd N15 66 DT57
Westerfolds Cl, Wok. 167 BC116
Westergate Rd SE2 106 EY78
Westerham Av N9 46 DR48
Westerham Cl, Add. 152 BJ107
Westerham Cl, Sutt. 158 DA110
Westerham Dr, Sid. 126 EV86
Westerham Hill, West. 179 EN121
Westerham Rd E10 67 EB59
Westerham Rd, Kes. 162 EK107
Westerham Rd, Oxt. 188 EF129
Westerham Rd, Sev. 190 FC123
Westerham Rd, West. 189 EM128
Westerley Cres SE26 123 DZ92
Westerley Ware, Rich. 98 CN79
Kew Grn
Western Av NW11 63 CX58
Western Av W3 80 CR71
Western Av W5 80 CM70
Western Av, Brwd. 54 FW46
Western Av, Cher. 134 BG97
Western Av, Dag. 89 FC65
Western Av, Egh. 133 BB97
Western Av, Epp. 17 ET32
Western Av, Grays 109 FT78
Western Av, Grnf. 79 CK69
Western Av, Nthlt. 78 BZ67
Western Av, Rom. 52 FJ54
Western Av, Ruis. 77 BP65
Western Av (Denham), Uxb. 58 BJ63
Western Av (Ickenham), Uxb. 77 BP65
Western Av Underpass W5 80 CM69
Western Av
Western Cl, Cher. 134 BG97
Western Av
Western Ct N3 44 DA51
Huntley Dr
Western Cross Cl, Green. 129 FW86
Johnsons Way
Western Dr, Shep. 135 BR100
Western Gdns W5 80 CN73
Western Gdns, Brwd. 54 FW47
Western Gateway E16 205 N1
Western Gateway E16 86 EG73
Western La SW12 120 DG87
Western Ms W9 81 CZ70
Great Western Rd
Western Pathway, Horn. 90 FJ65
Western Perimeter Rd, Houns. 94 BH83
Western Perimeter Rd, West Dr. 94 BH82
Western Pl SE16 202 G4
Western Rd E13 86 EJ67
Western Rd E17 67 EC57
Western Rd N2 64 DF56
Western Rd N22 45 DM54
Western Rd NW10 80 CQ70
Western Rd SW9 101 DN83
Western Rd SW19 140 DD95
Western Rd W5 79 CK73
Western Rd, Brwd. 54 FW47
Western Rd, Epp. 17 ET32
Western Rd, Mitch. 140 DD95
Western Rd, Rom. 71 FE57
Western Rd, Sthl. 96 BX76
Western Rd, Sutt. 158 DA106
Western Ter W6 99 CU78
Chiswick Mall
Western Trd Est NW10 80 CQ70
Western Vw, Hayes 95 BT75
Station Rd
Western Way SE28 105 ER76
Western Way, Barn. 28 DA44
Westernville Gdns, Ilf. 69 EQ59
Westferry Circ E14 203 P2
Westferry Circ E14 85 DZ74
Westferry Rd E14 203 P1
Westferry Rd E14 85 EA74
Westfield, Ash. 172 CM118
Westfield, Loug. 32 EJ43
Westfield, Reig. 184 DB131
Westfield, Sev. 191 FJ122
Westfield Av, S.Croy. 160 DR113
Westfield Av, Wat. 24 BX37
Westfield Av, Wok. 166 AY121
Westfield Cl NW9 62 CQ55
Westfield Cl SW10 100 DC80
Westfield Cl, Enf. 31 DY41
Westfield Cl, Grav. 131 GJ93
Westfield Cl, Sutt. 157 CZ105
Westfield Cl, Wal.Cr. 15 DZ31
Westfield Common, Wok. 166 AY122
Westfield Dr, Har. 61 CK56
Westfield Dr, Lthd. 170 CA122
Westfield Gdns, Har. 61 CK56
Westfield Gro, Wok. 167 AZ120
Westfield La, Har. 61 CK56
Westfield La, Slou. 74 AX73
Westfield Par, Add. 152 BK110
Westfield Pk, Pnr. 40 BZ52
Westfield Pk Dr, Wdf.Grn. 48 EL51
Westfield Rd NW7 42 CR48
Westfield Rd W13 79 CG74
Westfield Rd, Beck. 143 DZ96
Westfield Rd, Bexh. 107 FC82
Westfield Rd, Croy. 141 DP103
Westfield Rd, Dag. 70 EY63
Westfield Rd, Mitch. 140 DF96
Westfield Rd, Surb. 137 CK99
Westfield Rd, Sutt. 157 CZ105
Westfield Rd, Walt. 136 BY101
Westfield Rd, Wok. 166 AX122
Westfield St SE18 104 EK76
Westfield Wk, Wal.Cr. 15 DZ31
Westfield Cl
Westfield Way E1 85 DY69
Westfield Way, Ruis. 59 BS62
Westfield Way, Wok. 166 AY122
Westfields SW13 99 CT83
Westfields Av SW13 98 CS83
Westfields Rd W3 80 CP71
Westgate Cl, Epsom 172 CR115
Chalk La
Westgate Ct, Wal.Cr. 31 DX35
Holmesdale
Westgate Rd SE25 142 DV98
Westgate Rd, Beck. 143 EB95
Westgate Rd, Dart. 128 FK86
Westgate St E8 84 DV67
Westgate Ter SW10 100 DB78
Westglade Ct, Har. 61 CK57
Westgrove La SE10 103 EC81
Westhall Pk, Warl. 176 DW119
Westhall Rd, Warl. 176 DV119
Westhay Gdns SW14 118 CP85
Westhill Cl, Grav. 131 GH88
Leith Pk Rd
Westholm NW11 64 DB56
Westholme, Orp. 145 ES101

Whitehorse Rd, Croy. 142 DQ101
Whitehorse Rd, Th.Hth. 142 DR100
Whitehouse Av, Borwd. 26 CP41
Whitehouse La, Abb.L. 7 BV26
Whitehouse La, Enf. 30 DQ39
Brigadier Hill
Whitehouse Way N14 45 DH47
Whitehouse Way, Iver 75 BD69
Whitehouse Way, Slou. 92 AW76
Whitelands Av, Rick. 21 BC42
Whitelands Way, Rom. 52 FK54
Whiteledges W13 79 CJ72
Whitelegg Rd E13 86 EF68
Whiteley Rd SE19 122 DR92
Whiteleys Cotts W14 99 CZ77
Whiteleys Way, Felt. 116 CA90
Whiteoaks, Bans. 158 DB113
Whiteoaks La, Grnf. 79 CD68
Whitepost Hill, Red. 184 DE134
Whites Av, Ilf. 69 ES58
Whites Cl, Green. 129 FW86
Whites Grds SE1 201 N5
Whites Grds SE1 102 DS75
Whites Grds Est SE1 201 N4
Whites La, Slou. 92 AV79
White's Row E1 197 P7
White's Row E1 84 DT71
White's Sq SW4 101 DK84
Nelson's Row
Whitestile Rd, Brent. 97 CJ78
Whitestone La NW3 64 DC62
Heath St
Whitestone Wk NW3 64 DC62
North End Way
Whitethorn Av, Couls. 174 DG115
Whitethorn Av, West Dr. 76 BL73
Whitethorn Gdns, Croy. 142 DV103
Whitethorn Gdns, Enf. 30 DR43
Whitethorn Gdns, Horn. 72 FJ58
Whitethorn Pl, West Dr. 76 BM74
Whitethorn Av
Whitethorn St E3 85 EA70
Whiteways Ct, Stai. 114 BH94
Pavilion Gdns
Whitewebbs La, Enf. 30 DS35
Whitewebbs Pk, Enf. 30 DQ35
Whitewebbs Rd, Enf. 29 DP35
Whitewebbs Way, Orp. 145 ET95
Whitewood Cotts, West. 178 EJ120
Whitfield Pl W1 195 K5
Whitfield Rd E6 86 EJ66
Whitfield Rd SE3 103 ED81
Whitfield Rd, Bexh. 106 EZ80
Whitfield St W1 195 M7
Whitfield St W1 83 DK71
Whitfield Way, Rick. 37 BF46
Whitford Gdns, Mitch. 140 DF97
Whitgift Av, S.Croy. 160 DQ106
Whitgift Cen, Croy. 142 DQ103
Whitgift St SE11 200 B8
Whitgift St SE11 101 DM77
Whitgift St, Croy. 142 DQ104
Whiting Av, Bark. 87 EP66
Whitings, Ilf. 69 ER57
Whitings Rd, Barn. 27 CW43
Whitings Way E6 87 EN71
Whitland Rd, Cars. 140 DD102
Whitlars Dr, Kings L. 6 BM28
Whitley Cl, Abb.L. 7 BU32
Whitley Cl, Stai. 114 BL86
Whitley Rd N17 46 DS54
Whitlock Dr SW19 119 CY87
Whitman Rd E3 85 DY70
Whitmead Cl, S.Croy. 160 DS107
Whitmore Av, Rom. 52 FL54
Whitmore Cl N11 45 DH50
Whitmore Est N1 84 DS67
Whitmore Gdns NW10 81 CW68
Whitmore Rd N1 84 DS67
Whitmore Rd, Beck. 143 DZ97
Whitmore Rd, Har. 60 CC59
Whitmores Cl, Epsom 172 CQ115
Whitnell Way SW15 119 CX85
Whitney Av, Ilf. 68 EK56
Whitney Rd E10 67 EB59
Whitney Wk, Sid. 126 EY93
Whitstable Cl, Beck. 143 DZ95
Whitstable Cl, Ruis. 59 BS61
Chichester Av
Whitstable Ho W10 81 CX72
Whitstable Pl, Croy. 160 DQ105
Whitta Rd E12 68 EK63
Whittaker Av, Rich. 117 CK85
Hill St
Whittaker Rd E6 86 EJ66
Whittaker Rd, Sutt. 139 CZ104
Whittaker St SW1 198 F9
Whittaker St SW1 100 DG77
Whittaker Way SE1 202 C9
Whittell Gdns SE26 122 DW90
Whittenham Cl, Slou. 74 AU74
Whittingstall Rd SW6 99 CZ81
Whittington Av EC3 197 M9
Whittington Av, Hayes 77 BT71
Whittington Ct N2 64 DF57
Whittington Ms N12 44 DC49
Fredericks Pl
Whittington Rd N22 45 DL52
Whittington Rd, Brwd. 55 GC44
Whittington Way, Pnr. 60 BY57
Whittle Cl E17 67 DY58
Whittle Cl, Sthl. 78 CB72
Whittle Rd, Houns. 96 BW80
Whittle Rd, Sthl. 96 CB75
Post Rd
Whittlebury Cl, Cars. 158 DF108
Whittlesea Cl, Har. 40 CC52
Whittlesea Path, Har. 40 CC53
Whittlesea Rd, Har. 40 CC53
Whittlesey St SE1 200 D3
Whitton Av E, Grnf. 61 CE64
Whitton Av W, Grnf. 60 CC64
Whitton Av W, Nthlt. 60 CC64
Whitton Cl, Grnf. 79 CH65
Whitton Dene, Houns. 116 CC85
Whitton Dene, Islw. 117 CD85
Whitton Dr, Grnf. 79 CG65
Whitton Manor Rd, Islw. 116 CC85
Whitton Rd, Houns. 96 CB84
Whitton Rd, Twick. 117 CF86
Whitton Wk E3 85 EA68
Whitton Waye, Houns. 116 CA86
Whitwell Rd E13 86 EG69
Whitwell Rd, Wat. 24 BX35
Whitworth Pl SE18 105 EP77
Whitworth Rd SE18 105 EN80
Whitworth Rd SE25 142 DS97
Whitworth St SE10 205 J10
Whitworth St SE10 104 EE78
Whopshott Av, Wok. 166 AW116
Whopshott Cl, Wok. 166 AW116
Whopshott Dr, Wok. 166 AW116
Whorlton Rd SE15 102 DV83
Whybridge Cl, Rain. 89 FE67
Whymark Av N22 65 DN55
Whytebeam Vw, Whyt. 176 DT118
Whytecliffe Rd N, Pur. 159 DP111
Whytecliffe Rd S, Pur. 159 DN111
Whytecroft, Houns. 96 BX80
Whyteleafe Hill, Whyt. 176 DT118
Whyteleafe Rd, Cat. 176 DS120
Whyteville Rd E7 86 EH65
Wichling Cl, Orp. 146 EX102
Wick La E3 85 EA68
Wick La, Egh. 112 AT92
Wick Rd E9 85 DX65
Wick Rd, Egh. 112 AV94
Wick Rd, Tedd. 117 CH94
Wick Sq E9 85 DZ65
Eastway
Wickenden Rd, Sev. 191 FJ122
Wicker St E1 84 DV72
Burslem St
Wickers Oake SE19 122 DT91
Wickersley Rd SW11 100 DG82
Wicket, The, Croy. 161 EA106
Wicket Rd, Grnf. 79 CG69
Wickets, The, Ashf. 114 BL91
Wickets End (Shenley), Rad. 10 CL33
Wickets Way, Ilf. 49 ET51
Wickford Cl, Rom. 52 FM50
Wickford Dr
Wickford Dr, Rom. 52 FM50
Wickford St E1 84 DW70
Wickford Way E17 67 DX56
Wickham Av, Croy. 143 DY103
Wickham Av, Sutt. 157 CW106
Wickham Chase, W.Wick. 143 ED101
Wickham Cl, Enf. 30 DV41
Wickham Cl, N.Mal. 139 CT99
Wickham Cl (Harefield), Uxb. 38 BK53
Wickham Ct Rd, W.Wick. 143 EC103
Wickham Cres, W.Wick. 143 EC103
Wickham Fld, Sev. 181 FF116
Wickham Gdns SE4 103 DZ83
Wickham Ho E1 85 DX71
Wickham La SE2 106 EU78
Wickham La, Egh. 113 BA94
Wickham La, Well. 106 EU78
Wickham Ms SE4 103 DZ82
Wickham Rd E4 47 EC52
Wickham Rd SE4 103 DZ83
Wickham Rd, Beck. 143 EB96
Wickham Rd, Croy. 143 DX103
Wickham Rd, Grays 111 GJ75
Wickham Rd, Har. 41 CD54
Wickham St SE11 200 B10
Wickham St SE11 101 DM78
Wickham St, Well. 105 ES82
Wickham Way, Beck. 143 EC98
Wickliffe Av N3 43 CY54
Wickliffe Gdns, Wem. 62 CP61
Wicklow St WC1 196 B2
Wicklow St WC1 83 DM69
Wicks Cl SE9 124 EK91
Wicksteed Cl, Bex. 127 FD90
Wicksteed Ho, Brent. 98 CM78
Green Dragon La
Wickwood St SE5 101 DP82
Wid Cl, Brwd. 55 GD43
Widdecombe Av, Har. 60 BY61
Widdenham Rd N7 65 DM63
Widdin St E15 85 ED66
Wide Way, Mitch. 141 DK97
Widecombe Cl, Rom. 52 FK53
Widecombe Gdns, Ilf. 68 EL56
Widecombe Rd SE9 124 EL90
Widecombe Way N2 64 DD57
Widecroft Rd, Iver 75 BE72
Widegate St E1 197 N7
Widenham Cl, Pnr. 60 BW57
Bridle Rd
Widgeon Cl E16 86 EH72
Maplin Rd
Widgeon Rd, Erith 107 FH80
Widgeon Way, Wat. 24 BY36
Widley Rd W9 82 DA69
Widmore Lo Rd, Brom. 144 EK96
Widmore Rd, Brom. 144 EG96
Widmore Rd, Uxb. 77 BP70
Widworthy Hayes, Brwd. 55 GB46
Wieland Rd, Nthwd. 39 BU52
Wigan Ho E5 66 DV60
Warwick Gro
Wigeon Path SE28 105 ER76
Wigeon Way, Hayes 78 BX72
Wiggenhall Rd, Wat. 23 BV43
Wiggie La, Red. 184 DG132
Wiggins Mead NW9 43 CT52
Wigginton Av, Wem. 80 CP65
Wigham Ho, Bark. 87 EQ66
Wightman Rd N4 65 DN57
Wightman Rd N8 65 DN56
Wigley Bush La, Brwd. 54 FS47
Wigley Rd, Felt. 116 BX89
Wigmore Pl W1 195 H8
Wigmore Pl W1 83 DH72
Wigmore Rd, Cars. 140 DD103
Wigmore St W1 194 F9
Wigmore St W1 82 DG72
Wigmore Wk, Cars. 140 DD103
Wigram Rd E11 68 EJ58
Wigram Sq E17 67 EC55
Wigston Cl N18 46 DS50
Wigston Rd E13 86 EH70
Wigton Gdns, Stan. 42 CL53
Wigton Pl SE11 101 DN78
Milverton St
Wigton Rd E17 47 DZ53
Wigton Rd, Rom. 52 FL49
Wigton Way, Rom. 52 FL49
Wilberforce Rd N4 65 DP62
Wilberforce Rd NW9 63 CU58
Wilberforce Way SW19 119 CX93
Wilberforce Way, Grav. 131 GK92
Wilbraham Pl SW1 198 E8
Wilbraham Pl SW1 100 DF77
Wilbury Av, Sutt. 157 CZ110
Wilbury Rd, Wok. 166 AX117
Wilbury Way N18 46 DR50
Wilby Ms W11 81 CZ74
Wilcot Av, Wat. 40 BY45
Wilcot Cl, Wat. 40 BY45
Wilcot Av
Wilcox Cl SW8 101 DL80
Wilcox Cl, Borwd. 26 CQ39
Wilcox Gdns, Shep. 134 BM97
Wilcox Pl SW1 199 L7
Wilcox Rd SW8 101 DL80
Wilcox Rd, Sutt. 158 DB105
Wilcox Rd, Tedd. 117 CD91
Wild Ct WC2 196 B8
Wild Ct WC2 83 DM72
Wild Goose Dr SE14 102 DW81
Wild Grn N, Slou. 93 BA77
Verney Rd
Wild Grn S, Slou. 93 BA77
Swabey Rd
Wild Hatch NW11 64 DA58
Wild Oaks Cl, Nthwd. 39 BT51
Wild St WC2 196 A9
Wild St WC2 83 DL72
Wildacres, W.Byf. 152 BJ111
Wildbank Ct, Wok. 167 AZ118
White Rose La
Wildcroft Gdns, Edg. 41 CK51
Wildcroft Rd SW15 119 CW87
Wilde Cl E8 84 DU67
Wilde Cl, Til. 111 GJ82
Coleridge Rd
Wilde Pl N13 45 DP51
Medesenge Way
Wilde Pl SW18 120 DD87
Heathfield Rd
Wilde Rd, Erith 107 FB80
Wilder Cl, Ruis. 59 BV60
Wilderness, The, E.Mol. 136 CC99
Wilderness, The, Hmptn. 116 CB91
Park Rd
Wilderness Rd, Chis. 125 EP94
Wilderness Rd, Oxt. 188 EE130
Wildernesse Av, Sev. 191 FL122
Wildernesse Mt, Sev. 191 FK122
Wilders Cl, Wok. 166 AW118
Wilderton Rd N16 66 DS59
Wildfell Rd SE6 123 EB87
Wild's Rents SE1 201 M6
Wild's Rents SE1 102 DS76
Wildwood, Nthwd. 39 BR51
Wildwood Av, St.Alb. 8 BZ30
Wildwood Cl SE12 124 EF87
Wildwood Cl, Wok. 167 BF115
Wildwood Ct, Ken. 176 DR115
Wildwood Gro NW3 64 DC60
North End Way
Wildwood Ri NW11 64 DC60
Wildwood Rd NW11 64 DC59
Wildwood Ter NW3 64 DC60
Wilford Cl, Enf. 30 DR41
Wilford Cl, Nthwd. 39 BR52
Wilford Rd, Slou. 93 AZ77
Wilfred Av, Rain. 89 FG71
Wilfred Owen Cl SW19 120 DC93
Tennyson Rd
Wilfred St SW1 199 K6
Wilfred St SW1 101 DJ76
Wilfred St, Grav. 131 GH86
Wilfred St, Wok. 166 AX118
Wilfrid Gdns W3 80 CQ71
Wilhelmina Av, Couls. 175 DJ119
Wilkes Rd, Brent. 98 CL79
Wilkes Rd, Brwd. 55 GD43
Wilkes St E1 84 DT71
Wilkie Way SE22 122 DU88
Lordship La
Wilkin St NW5 83 DH65
Wilkin St Ms NW5 83 DH65
Wilkin St
Wilkins Cl, Hayes 95 BT78
Wilkins Cl, Mitch. 140 DE95
Wilkins Way, West. 180 EV124
Wilkinson Cl, Dart. 108 FM84
Wilkinson Cl, Uxb. 77 BP67
Wilkinson Cl (Cheshunt), Wal.Cr. 14 DQ26
Wilkinson Rd E16 86 EJ72
Wilkinson St SW8 101 DM80
Wilkinson Way W4 98 CR75
Wilks Av, Dart. 128 FM89
Wilks Gdns, Croy. 143 DY102
Wilks Pl N1 197 N1
Will Crooks Gdns SE9 104 EJ84
Willan Rd N17 46 DR54
Willan Wall E16 86 EF73
Victoria Dock Rd
Willard St SW8 101 DH83
Willcocks Cl, Chess. 138 CL104
Willcott Rd W3 80 CP74
Willen Fld Rd NW10 80 CQ68
Willenhall Av, Barn. 28 DC44
Willenhall Dr, Hayes 77 BS73
Willenhall Rd SE18 105 EP78
Willersley Av, Orp. 145 ER104
Willersley Av, Sid. 125 ET88
Willersley Cl, Sid. 125 ET88
Willes Rd NW5 83 DH65
Willesden La NW2 81 CX65
Willesden La NW6 81 CX65
Willett Cl, Nthlt. 78 BW69
Broomcroft Av
Willett Cl, Orp. 145 ES100
Willett Pl, Th.Hth. 141 DN99
Willett Rd
Willett Rd, Th.Hth. 141 DN99
Willett Way, Orp. 145 ER99
Willetts La (Denham), Uxb. 57 BF63
Willey Broom La, Cat. 185 DN125
Willey Fm La, Cat. 186 DQ126
Willey La, Cat. 186 DR125
William Barefoot Dr SE9 125 EN91
William Bonney Est SW4 101 DK84
William Booth Rd SE20 142 DU95
William Carey Way, Har. 61 CE59
William Cl N2 64 DD55
King St
William Cl, Rom. 51 FC53
William Cl, Sthl. 96 CC75
Windmill Av
William Cory Prom, Erith 107 FE78
William Covell Cl, Enf. 29 DM38
William Dunbar Ho NW6 81 CZ68
William Dyce Ms SW16 121 DK91
Babington Rd
William Ellis Cl, Wind. 112 AU85
William Ellis Way SE16 202 C7
William IV St WC2 199 P1
William IV St WC2 83 DL73
William Gdns SW15 119 CV85
William Guy Gdns E3 85 EB69
Talwin St
William Margrie Cl SE15 102 DU82
Moncrieff St
William Ms SW1 198 E5
William Morley Cl E6 86 EK67
William Morris Cl E17 67 DZ55
William Morris Way SW6 100 DC83
William Nash Ct, Orp. 146 EW97
Brantwood Way
William Pl E3 85 DZ68
Roman Rd
William Rd NW1 195 J3
William Rd NW1 83 DH69
William Rd SW19 119 CY94
William Rd, Cat. 176 DR122
William Rd, Sutt. 158 DC106
William Russell Ct, Wok. 166 AS118
Raglan Rd
William Saville Ho NW6 81 CZ68
William Sq SE16 203 L1
William St E10 67 EB58
William St N17 46 DT52
William St SW1 198 E5
William St SW1 100 DF75
William St, Bark. 87 EQ66
William St, Bushey 24 BX41
William St, Cars. 140 DE104
William St, Grav. 131 GH87
William St, Grays 110 GB79
William St, Slou. 74 AT74
Williams Av E17 47 DZ53
Williams Bldgs E2 84 DW70
Williams Cl N8 65 DK58
Coolhurst Rd
Williams Cl, Add. 152 BH106
Monks Cres
Williams Evans Rd, Epsom 156 CN111
Williams Gro N22 45 DN53
Williams Gro, Surb. 137 CJ100
William's La SW14 98 CQ82
Williams La, Mord. 140 DC99
Williams Rd W13 79 CG73
Williams Rd, Sthl. 96 BY77
Williams Ter, Croy. 159 DN107
Williams Way, Rad. 25 CJ35
Williamson Cl SE10 205 K10
Williamson Rd N4 65 DP58
Williamson St N7 65 DL63
Williamson Way NW7 43 CY51
Williamson Way, Rick. 38 BG46
Willifield Way NW11 63 CZ57
Willingale Cl, Brwd. 55 GE44
Fairview Av
Willingale Cl, Loug. 33 EQ40
Willingale Rd
Willingale Cl, Wdf.Grn. 48 EK51
Willingale Rd, Loug. 33 EQ41
Willingdon Rd N22 45 DP54
Willinghall Cl, Wal.Abb. 15 ED32
Willingham Cl NW5 65 DJ64
Leighton Rd
Willingham Ter NW5 65 DJ64
Leighton Rd
Willingham Way, Kings.T. 138 CN97
Willington Ct E5 67 DY62
Mandeville St
Willington Rd SW9 101 DL83
Willis Av, Sutt. 158 DE107
Willis Cl, Epsom 156 CP113
Willis Rd E15 86 EF67
Willis Rd, Croy. 142 DQ101
Willis Rd, Erith 107 FC77
Willis St E14 85 EB72
Willmore End SW19 140 DB95
Willoughby Av, Croy. 159 DM105
Willoughby Ct, St.Alb. 9 CK26
Willoughby Dr, Rain. 89 FE66
Willoughby Gro N17 46 DV52
Willoughby Ho EC2 84 DR71
Moor La
Willoughby La N17 46 DV52
Willoughby Ms SW4 101 DH84
Wixs La
Willoughby Pk Rd N17 46 DV52
Willoughby Pas E14 203 P2
Willoughby Pas E14 85 EA74
Willoughby Rd N8 65 DN55
Willoughby Rd NW3 64 DD63
Willoughby Rd, Kings.T. 138 CM95
Willoughby Rd, Slou. 93 BA76
Willoughby Rd, Twick. 117 CK86
Willoughby St WC1 195 P7
Willoughby Way SE7 205 P8
Willoughby Way SE7 104 EH77
Willoughbys, The SW14 98 CS84
Upper Richmond Rd W
Willow Av SW13 99 CT82
Willow Av, Sid. 126 EU86
Willow Av, Swan. 147 FF97
Willow Av (Denham), Uxb. 58 BJ64
Willow Av, West Dr. 76 BM73
Willow Bk SW6 99 CY83
Willow Bk, Rich. 117 CH90
Willow Bk, Wok. 166 AY122
Willow Br Rd N1 84 DQ65
Willow Business Cen, Mitch. 140 DF99
Willow Cl, Add. 151 BF111
Willow Cl, Bex. 126 EZ86
Willow Cl, Brent. 97 CJ79
Willow Cl, Brwd. 55 GB44
Willow Cl, Brom. 145 EM99
Willow Cl, Buck.H. 48 EK48
Willow Cl, Erith 107 FG81
Willow Rd
Willow Cl, Horn. 71 FH62
Willow Cl, Orp. 146 EV101
Willow Cl, Slou. 93 BC80
Willow Cl, Th.Hth. 141 DP100
Willow Cl (Cheshunt), Wal.Cr. 14 DS26
Willow Cotts, Mitch. 141 DJ97
Willow Cotts, Rich. 98 CN79
Kew Grn
Willow Ct EC2 197 M4
Willow Ct, Edg. 42 CL49
Willow Cres E (Denham), Uxb. 58 BJ64
Willow Cres W (Denham), Uxb. 58 BJ64
Willow Dene, Bushey 41 CE45
Willow Dene, Pnr. 40 BX54
Willow Dr, Barn. 27 CY42
Willow Dr, Wok. 168 BG124
Willow Edge, Kings L. 6 BN29
Willow End N20 44 DA47
Willow End, Nthwd. 39 BU51
Willow End, Surb. 138 CL102
Willow Fm La SW15 99 CV83
Queens Ride
Willow Gdns, Houns. 96 CA81
Willow Gdns, Ruis. 59 BT61
Willow Grn NW9 42 CS53
Clayton Fld
Willow Grn, Borwd. 26 CR43
Willow Gro E13 86 EG68
Libra Rd
Willow Gro, Chis. 125 EN93
Willow Gro, Ruis. 59 BT61
Willow La, Amer. 20 AT41
Willow La, Mitch. 140 DF99
Willow La, Wat. 23 BU43
Willow Mead, Chig. 50 EU48
Willow Mt, Croy. 142 DS104
Langton Way
Willow Pk, Sev. 181 FF117
Willow Pk, Slou. 74 AU66
Willow Path, Wal.Abb. 16 EE34
Willow Pl SW1 199 L8
Willow Pl SW1 101 DJ77
Willow Rd NW3 64 DD63
Willow Rd W5 98 CL75
Willow Rd, Dart. 128 FJ88
Willow Rd, Enf. 30 DS41
Willow Rd, Erith 107 FG81
Willow Rd, N.Mal. 138 CQ98
Willow Rd, Rom. 70 EY58
Willow Rd, Slou. 93 BE82
Willow Rd, Wall. 159 DH108
Willow St E4 47 ED45
Willow St EC2 197 M4
Willow St EC2 84 DS70
Willow St, Rom. 71 FC56
Willow Tree Cl E3 85 DZ67
Birdsfield La
Willow Tree Cl SW18 120 DB88
Cargill Rd
Willow Tree Cl, Hayes 78 BW70
Willow Tree Cl, Rom. 34 EV41
Market Pl
Willow Tree Cl, Uxb. 59 BQ62
Willow Tree La, Hayes 78 BW70
Willow Tree Wk, Brom. 144 EH95
Willow Vale W12 81 CU74
Willow Vale, Chis. 125 EP93
Willow Vale, Lthd. 170 CB123
Willow Vw SW19 140 DD95
Willow Wk E17 67 DZ57
Willow Wk N2 44 DD54
Willow Wk N15 65 DP56
Willow Wk N21 29 DM44
Willow Wk SE1 201 N8
Willow Wk SE1 102 DS77
Willow Wk, Cher. 134 BG101
Willow Wk, Dart. 128 FJ85
Willow Wk, Egh. 112 AW92
Willow Wk, Orp. 145 EP104
Willow Wk, Sutt. 139 CZ104
Willow Wk, Tad. 182 CQ130
Oak Dr
Willow Wk, Upmin. 73 FS60
Willow Way N3 44 DB52
Willow Way SE26 122 DV90
Willow Way W11 81 CX74
Freston Rd
Willow Way, Epsom 156 CR107
Willow Way, Gdse. 186 DV132
Willow Way, Pot.B. 12 DB33
Willow Way, Rad. 25 CE36
Willow Way, Rom. 52 FP51
Willow Way, St.Alb. 8 CA27
Willow Way, Sun. 135 BU98
Willow Way, Tad. 182 CP130
Oak Dr
Willow Way, Twick. 116 CB89
Willow Way, Wem. 61 CG62
Willow Way, W.Byf. 152 BJ111
Willow Way, Wok. 166 AX121
Willow Wd Cres SE25 142 DS100
Willowbank Gdns, Tad. 173 CV122
Willowbrook Est SE15 102 DT80
Sumner Rd
Willowbrook Rd SE15 102 DT79
Willowbrook Rd, Sthl. 96 CA76
Willowbrook Rd, Stai. 114 BL89
Willowcourt Av, Har. 61 CH57
Willowdene N6 64 DF59
Denewood Rd
Willowdene, Brwd. 54 FT43
Willowdene, Wal.Cr. 15 DY27
Willowdene Cl, Twick. 116 CC87
Willowdene Ct, Brwd. 54 FW49
Willowfield Cl SE18 45 DL48
Conway Rd
Willowhayne Dr, Walt. 135 BV101
Willowhayne Gdns, Wor.Pk. 139 CW104
Willowherb Wk, Rom. 52 FJ52
Clematis Cl
Willowmead, Stai. 134 BH95
Northfield Rd
Willowmead Cl W5 79 CK71

347

Wych Elm Dr, Brom. 124 EF94
London La
Wych Elm Pas, Kings.T. 118 CM94
Wych Elm Rd, Horn. 72 FN58
Wych Elms, St.Alb. 8 CB28
Wych Hill, Wok. 166 AW119
Wych Hill La, Wok. 166 AY119
Wych Hill Pk, Wok. 166 AX119
Wych Hill Ri, Wok. 166 AW119
Wych Hill Way, Wok. 166 AX120
Wyche Gro, S.Croy. 160 DQ108
Wycherley Cl SE3 104 EF80
Wycherley Cres, Barn. 28 DB44
Wychwood Av, Edg. 41 CK51
Wychwood Av, Th.Hth. 142 DQ97
Wychwood Cl, Edg. 41 CK51
Wychwood Cl, Sun. 115 BU93
Wychwood End N6 65 DJ59
Wychwood Gdns, Ilf. 69 EM56
Wychwood Way SE19 122 DR93
Roman Ri
Wychwood Way, Nthwd. 39 BT52
Wyclif St EC1 196 F3
Wycliffe Cl, Well. 105 ET81
Wycliffe Ct, Abb.L. 7 BS32
Wycliffe Gdns, Red. 185 DJ130
Wycliffe Rd SW11 100 DG82
Wycliffe Rd SW19 120 DB93
Wycliffe Row, Grav. 131 GF88
Wycombe Gdns NW11 64 DA61
Wycombe Pl SW18 120 DC86
Wycombe Rd N17 46 DU53
Wycombe Rd, Ilf. 69 EM57
Wycombe Rd, Wem. 80 CN67
Wydehurst Rd, Croy. 142 DU101
Wydell Cl, Mord. 139 CW100
Wydeville Manor Rd SE12 124 EH91
Wye Cl, Ashf. 115 BP91
Wye Cl, Orp. 145 ET101
Wye Cl, Ruis. 59 BQ58
Wye Rd, Grav. 131 GK89
Wye St SW11 100 DD82
Wyedale, St.Alb. 10 CM27
Wyemead Cres E4 48 EE47
Wyeth's Ms, Epsom 157 CT113
Wyeths Rd, Epsom 157 CT113
Wyevale Cl, Pnr. 59 BU55
Wyfields, Ilf. 49 EP53
Ravensbourne Gdns
Wyfold Ho SE2 106 EX75
Wolvercote Rd
Wyfold Rd SW6 99 CY80
Wyhill Wk, Dag. 89 FC65
Wyke Cl, Islw. 97 CF79
Wyke Gdns W7 97 CG76
Wyke Rd E3 85 EA66
Wyke Rd SW20 139 CW96
Wykeham Av, Dag. 88 EW65
Wykeham Av, Horn. 72 FK58
Wykeham Cl, Grav. 131 GL93
Wykeham Cl, West Dr. 94 BN78
Wykeham Grn, Dag. 88 EW65
Wykeham Hill, Wem. 62 CM60
Wykeham Ri N20 43 CY46
Wykeham Rd NW4 63 CW57
Wykeham Rd, Har. 61 CH56
Wylands Rd, Slou. 93 BA77
Wylchin Cl, Pnr. 59 BT56
Wyld Way, Wem. 80 CP65
Wyldes Cl NW11 64 DC60
Wildwood Rd
Wyldfield Gdns N9 46 DT47
Wyleu St SE23 123 DY87
Wylie Rd, Sthl. 96 CA76
Wyllen Cl E1 84 DW70
Wyllyotts Cl, Pot.B. 11 CZ32
Wyllyotts La, Pot.B. 11 CZ32
Wyllyotts Pl, Pot.B. 11 CZ32
Wylo Dr, Barn. 27 CU44
Wymering Rd W9 82 DA69
Wymond St SW15 99 CW83
Wynan Rd E14 204 B10
Wynan Rd E14 103 EB78
Wynash Gdns, Cars. 158 DE106
Wynaud Ct N22 45 DM51
Palmerston Rd
Wyncham Av, Sid. 125 ES88
Wynchgate N14 45 DK46
Wynchgate N21 45 DL46
Wynchgate, Har. 41 CE52
Wyncote Way, S.Croy. 161 DX109
Wyncroft Cl, Brom. 145 EM97
Wyndale Av NW9 62 CN58
Wyndcliff Rd SE7 104 EH79
Wyndcroft Cl, Enf. 29 DP41
Wyndham Av, Cob. 153 BU113
Wyndham Cl, Orp. 145 EQ102
Wyndham Cl, Sutt. 158 DA108
Wyndham Cres N19 65 DJ62
Wyndham Cres, Houns. 116 CA86
Wyndham Est SE5 102 DQ80
Wyndham Ms W1 194 D7
Wyndham Pl W1 194 D7
Wyndham Pl W1 82 DF71
Wyndham Rd E6 86 EK66
Wyndham Rd SE5 101 DP80
Wyndham Rd W13 97 CH76
Wyndham Rd, Barn. 44 DF46
Wyndham Rd, Kings.T. 118 CM94
Wyndham Rd, Wok. 166 AV118
Wyndham St W1 194 D6
Wyndham St W1 82 DF71
Wyndham Yd W1 194 D7
Wyneham Rd SE24 122 DR85
Wynell Rd SE23 123 DX90
Wynford Gro, Orp. 146 EV97
Wynford Pl, Belv. 106 FA79
Wynford Rd N1 83 DM68
Wynford Way SE9 125 EM90
Wynlie Gdns, Pnr. 39 BV54
Wynn Br Cl, Wdf.Grn. 48 EJ53
Chigwell Rd
Wynndale Rd E18 48 EH53
Wynne Rd SW9 101 DN82
Wynns Av, Sid. 126 EU85
Wynnstay Gdns W8 100 DA76
Wynnstow Pk, Oxt. 188 EF131
Wynter St SW11 100 DC84
Wynton Gdns SE25 142 DT99
Wynton Gro, Walt. 135 BU104
Wynton Pl W3 80 CP72
Wynyard Cl, Rick. 22 BG36
Wynyard Ter SE11 200 C10
Wynyard Ter SE11 101 DM78
Wynyatt St EC1 196 F3
Wyre Gro, Edg. 42 CP48
Wyre Gro, Hayes 95 BU77
Wyresdale Cres, Grnf. 79 CF69
Wyteleaf Cl, Ruis. 59 BQ58
Wythburn Pl W1 194 D9
Wythens Wk SE9 125 EP86
Wythenshawe Rd, Dag. 70 FA62
Wythes Cl, Brom. 145 EM96
Wythes Rd E16 86 EL74
Wythfield Rd SE9 125 EM86
Wyvenhoe Rd, Har. 60 CC62
Wyvern Cl, Dart. 128 FJ87
Wyvern Cl, Orp. 146 EV104
Wyvern Est, N.Mal. 139 CU98
Beverley Way
Wyvern Gro, Hayes 95 BP80
Wyvern Rd, Pur. 159 DP110
Wyvern Way, Uxb. 76 BH66
Wyvil Est SW8 101 DL80
Luscombe Way
Wyvil Rd SW8 101 DL79
Wyvis St E14 85 EB71

Y

Yabsley St E14 204 E2
Yabsley St E14 85 EC74
Yaffle Rd, Wey. 153 BQ110
Yalding Cl, Orp. 146 EX98
Yalding Rd SE16 202 B7
Yalding Rd SE16 102 DU76
Yale Cl, Houns. 116 BZ85
Bramley Way
Yale Way, Horn. 71 FG63
Yarborough Rd SW19 140 DD95
Runnymede
Yarbridge Cl, Sutt. 158 DB110
Yard Mead, Egh. 113 BA90
Yardley Cl E4 31 EB43
Yardley Cl, Reig. 184 DB132
Yardley La E4 31 EB43
Yardley St WC1 196 D3
Yardley St WC1 83 DN69
Yarm Cl, Lthd. 171 CJ123
Yarm Ct Rd, Lthd. 171 CJ123
Yarm Way, Lthd. 171 CJ123
Yarmouth Cres N17 66 DV57
Yarmouth Pl W1 199 H3
Yarmouth Rd, Wat. 24 BW38
Yarnfield Sq SE15 102 DU81
Clayton Rd
Yarnton Way SE2 106 EX75
Yarnton Way, Erith 106 EZ76
Yarrow Cres E6 86 EL71
Yarrowfield, Wok. 166 AX123
Yarrowside, Amer. 20 AV41
Yateley St SE18 104 EK76
Yates Ct NW2 81 CX65
Ye Cor, Wat. 24 BY44
Yeading Av, Har. 60 BY61
Yeading Fork, Hayes 78 BW71
Yeading Gdns, Hayes 77 BV71
Yeading La, Hayes 77 BV72
Yeading La, Nthlt. 78 BW69
Yeames Cl W13 79 CG72
Yeate St N1 84 DR66
Yeatman Rd N6 64 DF58
Yeats Cl NW10 80 CS65
Yeats Cl SE13 103 ED82
Eliot Pk
Yeats Ct N15 66 DT56
Tynemouth Rd
Yeend Cl, W.Mol. 136 CA98
Yeldham Rd W6 99 CX78
Yellow Hammer Ct NW9 42 CS54
Eagle Dr
Yellowpine Way, Chig. 50 EV49
Yelverton Cl, Rom. 52 FK53
Yelverton Rd SW11 100 DD82
Yenston Cl, Mord. 140 DA100
Yeo St E3 85 EB71
Yeoman Cl E6 87 EP73
Ferndale St
Yeoman Cl SE27 121 DP90
Yeoman Rd, Nthlt. 78 BY66
Yeoman St SE8 203 K8
Yeoman St SE8 103 DY77
Yeomanry Cl, Epsom 157 CT112
Dirdene Gdns
Yeomans Acre, Ruis. 59 BU58
Yeomans Keep, Rick. 21 BF41
Rickmansworth Rd
Yeomans Meadow, Sev. 190 FG126
Yeoman's Ms, Islw. 117 CE85
Queensbridge Pk
Yeoman's Row SW3 198 C7
Yeoman's Row SW3 100 DE76
Yeomans Way, Enf. 30 DW40
Yeomans Yd E1 84 DT73
Chamber St
Yeomen Way, Ilf. 49 EQ51
Yeoveney Cl, Stai. 113 BD89
Yeovil Cl, Orp. 145 ES103
Yeovilton Pl, Kings.T. 117 CK92
Yerbury Rd N19 65 DK62
Yester Dr, Chis. 124 EL94
Yester Pk, Chis. 125 EM94
Yester Rd, Chis. 125 EM94
Yevele Way, Horn. 72 FL59
Yew Av, West Dr. 76 BL73
Yew Cl, Buck.H. 48 EK47
Yew Cl, Wal.Cr. 14 DS27
Yew Gro NW2 63 CX63
Yew Pl, Wey. 135 BT104
Yew Tree Bottom Rd, Epsom 173 CV116
Yew Tree Cl N21 45 DN45
Yew Tree Cl, Brwd. 55 GB44
Yew Tree Cl, Chesh. 4 AU30
Botley Rd
Yew Tree Cl, Couls. 174 DF119
Yew Tree Cl, Sev. 190 FD123
Yew Tree Cl, Well. 106 EU81
Yew Tree Cl, Wor.Pk. 138 CS102
Yew Tree Ct, Borwd. 25 CK44
Barnet La
Yew Tree Dr, Cat. 186 DT125
Yew Tree Dr, Hem.H. 5 BB28
Yew Tree Gdns, Epsom 172 CP115
Yew Tree Gdns, Rom. 71 FD57
Yew Tree Gdns (Chadwell Heath), Rom. 70 EY57
Yew Tree La, Reig. 184 DB131
Yew Tree Rd W12 81 CT73
Yew Tree Rd, Slou. 92 AU76
Yew Tree Rd, Uxb. 76 BM67
Yew Tree Wk, Houns. 116 BZ85
Yew Tree Wk, Pur. 160 DQ110
Yew Tree Way, Croy. 161 DY110
Yew Trees, Egh. 133 BC97
Yew Trees, Shep. 134 BM98
Laleham Rd
Yew Wk, Har. 61 CE60
Yewbank Cl, Ken. 176 DR115
Yewdale Cl, Brom. 124 EE93
Yewdells Cl, Bet. 183 CU133
Yewfield Rd NW10 81 CT66
Yewlands Cl, Bans. 174 DC115
Yews, The, Ashf. 115 BP91
Yews, The, Grav. 131 GK88
Yews Av, Enf. 30 DV36
Yewtree Cl N22 45 DJ53
Yewtree Cl, Har. 60 CB56
Yewtree End, St.Alb. 8 CB27
Yewtree Rd, Beck. 143 DZ96
Yoakley Rd N16 66 DS61
Yoke Cl N7 83 DL65
Ewe Cl
Yolande Gdns SE9 124 EL85
Yonge Pk N4 65 DN62
York Av SW14 118 CQ85
York Av W7 79 CE74
York Av, Hayes 77 BQ71
York Av, Sid. 125 ES89
York Av, Stan. 41 CH53
York Br NW1 194 F4
York Br NW1 82 DG70
York Bldgs WC2 200 A1
York Cl E6 87 EM72
Boultwood Rd
York Cl W7 79 CE74
York Av
York Cl, Amer. 20 AT39
York Cl, Brwd. 55 FZ45
York Cl, Kings L. 6 BN29
York Cl, Mord. 140 DB98
York Cl, W.Byf. 152 BL112
York Cres, Borwd. 26 CR40
York Cres, Loug. 32 EL41
York Gdns, Walt. 136 BX103
York Gate N14 45 DL45
York Gate NW1 194 F5
York Gate NW1 82 DG70
York Gro SE15 102 DW81
York Hill SE27 121 DP90
York Hill, Loug. 32 EL41
York Hill Est SE27 121 DP90
York Ho, Wem. 62 CM63
York Ho Pl W8 100 DB75
York Ms NW5 65 DH64
Kentish Town Rd
York Ms, Ilf. 69 EN62
York Rd
York Par, Brent. 97 CK78
York Pl SW11 100 DD83
York Pl WC2 200 A1
York Pl, Dag. 89 FC65
York Pl, Grays 110 GA79
York Pl, Ilf. 69 EN61
York Rd
York Ri NW5 65 DH62
York Ri, Orp. 145 ES102
York Rd E4 47 EA50
York Rd E7 86 EG65
York Rd E10 67 EC62
York Rd E17 67 DX57
York Rd N11 45 DK51
York Rd N18 46 DV51
York Rd N21 46 DR45
York Rd SE1 200 C5
York Rd SE1 101 DM75
York Rd SW11 100 DC83
York Rd SW18 100 DC83
York Rd SW19 120 DC93
York Rd W3 80 CQ72
York Rd W5 97 CJ76
York Rd, Barn. 28 DC43
York Rd, Brent. 97 CK78
York Rd, Brwd. 55 FZ45
York Rd, Croy. 141 DN101
York Rd, Dart. 128 FM87
York Rd, Epp. 18 FA27
York Rd, Grav. 131 GJ90
York Rd (Northfleet), Grav. 130 GD87
York Rd, Houns. 96 CB83
York Rd, Ilf. 69 EN62
York Rd, Kings.T. 118 CM94
York Rd, Nthwd. 39 BU54
York Rd, Rain. 89 FD66
York Rd, Rich. 118 CM85
Albert Rd
York Rd, S.Croy. 161 DX110
York Rd, Sutt. 158 DA107
York Rd, Tedd. 117 CE91
York Rd, Uxb. 76 BK66
York Rd, Wal.Cr. 15 DY34
York Rd, Wat. 24 BW43
York Rd, W.Byf. 152 BK112
York Rd, West. 178 EH119
York Rd, Wey. 153 BQ105
York Rd, Wok. 166 AY118
York Sq E14 85 DY72
York St W1 194 E6
York St W1 82 DF71
York St, Bark. 87 EQ67
Abbey Rd
York St, Mitch. 140 DG101
York St, Twick. 117 CG88
York Ter, Enf. 30 DQ38
York Ter, Erith 107 FC81
York Ter E NW1 194 G5
York Ter E NW1 82 DG70
York Ter W NW1 194 F5
York Ter W NW1 82 DG70
York Way N1 83 DL67
York Way N7 83 DK65
York Way N20 44 DF48
York Way, Borwd. 26 CR40
York Way, Chess. 156 CL108
York Way, Felt. 116 BZ90
York Way, Wat. 24 BY36
York Way Ct N1 83 DL67
York Way Est N7 83 DL65
York Way
Yorke Gdns, Reig. 184 DA133
Yorke Gate Rd, Cat. 176 DR122
Yorke Rd, Reig. 183 CZ133
Yorke Rd, Rick. 22 BN44
Yorkland Av, Well. 105 ET83
Yorkshire Cl N16 66 DS62
Yorkshire Gdns N18 46 DV50
Yorkshire Grey Pl NW3 64 DC63
Heath St
Yorkshire Grey Yd WC1 196 B7
Yorkshire Rd E14 85 DY72
Yorkshire Rd, Mitch. 141 DL99
Yorkton St E2 84 DU68
Young Rd E16 86 EJ72
Young St W8 100 DB75
Youngmans Cl, Enf. 30 DQ39
Young's Bldgs EC1 197 J4
Youngs Rd, Ilf. 69 ER57
Youngstroat La, Wok. 150 AY110
Yoxley App, Ilf. 69 EQ58
Yoxley Dr, Ilf. 69 EQ58
Yukon Rd SW12 121 DH87
Yule Cl, St.Alb. 8 BZ30
Yuletide Cl NW10 80 CS66
Yunus Khan Cl E17 67 EA57

Z

Zampa Rd SE16 102 DW78
Zander Ct E2 84 DU68
St. Peter's Cl
Zangwill Rd SE3 104 EK81
Zealand Av, West Dr. 94 BK80
Zealand Rd E3 85 DY68
Zelah Rd, Orp. 146 EV101
Zennor Rd SW12 121 DJ88
Zenoria St SE22 102 DT84
Zermatt Rd, Th.Hth. 142 DQ98
Zetland St E14 85 EB71
Zig Zag Rd, Ken. 176 DQ116
Zion Pl, Grav. 131 GH87
Zion Pl, Th.Hth. 142 DR98
Zion Rd, Th.Hth. 142 DR98
Zion St, Sev. 191 FM121
Church Rd
Zoar St SE1 201 H2
Zoffany St N19 65 DK61

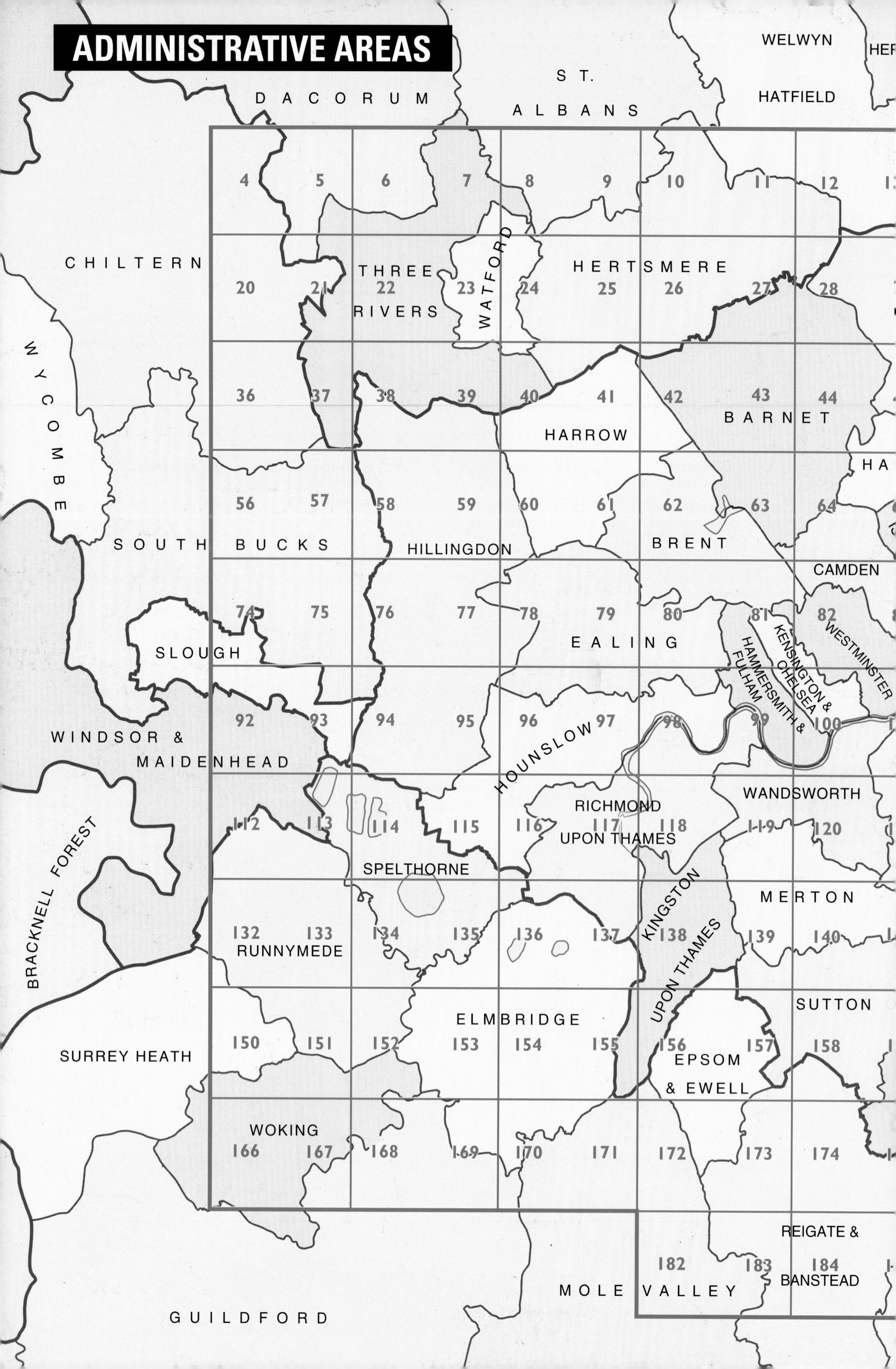

ADMINISTRATIVE AREAS

WELWYN
HER

ST.
ALBANS

HATFIELD

DACORUM

| 4 | 5 | 6 | 7 | 8 | 9 | 10 | 11 | 12 | 13 |

CHILTERN

THREE
RIVERS

WATFORD

HERTSMERE

| 20 | 21 | 22 | 23 | 24 | 25 | 26 | 27 | 28 |

WYCOMBE

| 36 | 37 | 38 | 39 | 40 | 41 | 42 | 43 | 44 |

HARROW

BARNET

HA

SOUTH   BUCKS

| 56 | 57 | 58 | 59 | 60 | 61 | 62 | 63 | 64 |

HILLINGDON

BRENT

CAMDEN

| 74 | 75 | 76 | 77 | 78 | 79 | 80 | 81 | 82 |

SLOUGH

EALING

KENSINGTON &
CHELSEA

HAMMERSMITH &
FULHAM

WESTMINSTER

| 92 | 93 | 94 | 95 | 96 | 97 | 98 | 99 | 100 |

WINDSOR &
MAIDENHEAD

HOUNSLOW

WANDSWORTH

BRACKNELL FOREST

| 112 | 113 | 114 | 115 | 116 | 117 | 118 | 119 | 120 |

RICHMOND
UPON THAMES

SPELTHORNE

MERTON

| 132 | 133 | 134 | 135 | 136 | 137 | 138 | 139 | 140 |

RUNNYMEDE

KINGSTON
UPON THAMES

SUTTON

ELMBRIDGE

EPSOM
& EWELL

SURREY HEATH

| 150 | 151 | 152 | 153 | 154 | 155 | 156 | 157 | 158 |

WOKING

| 166 | 167 | 168 | 169 | 170 | 171 | 172 | 173 | 174 |

REIGATE &

| 182 | 183 | 184 |

MOLE   VALLEY

BANSTEAD

GUILDFORD

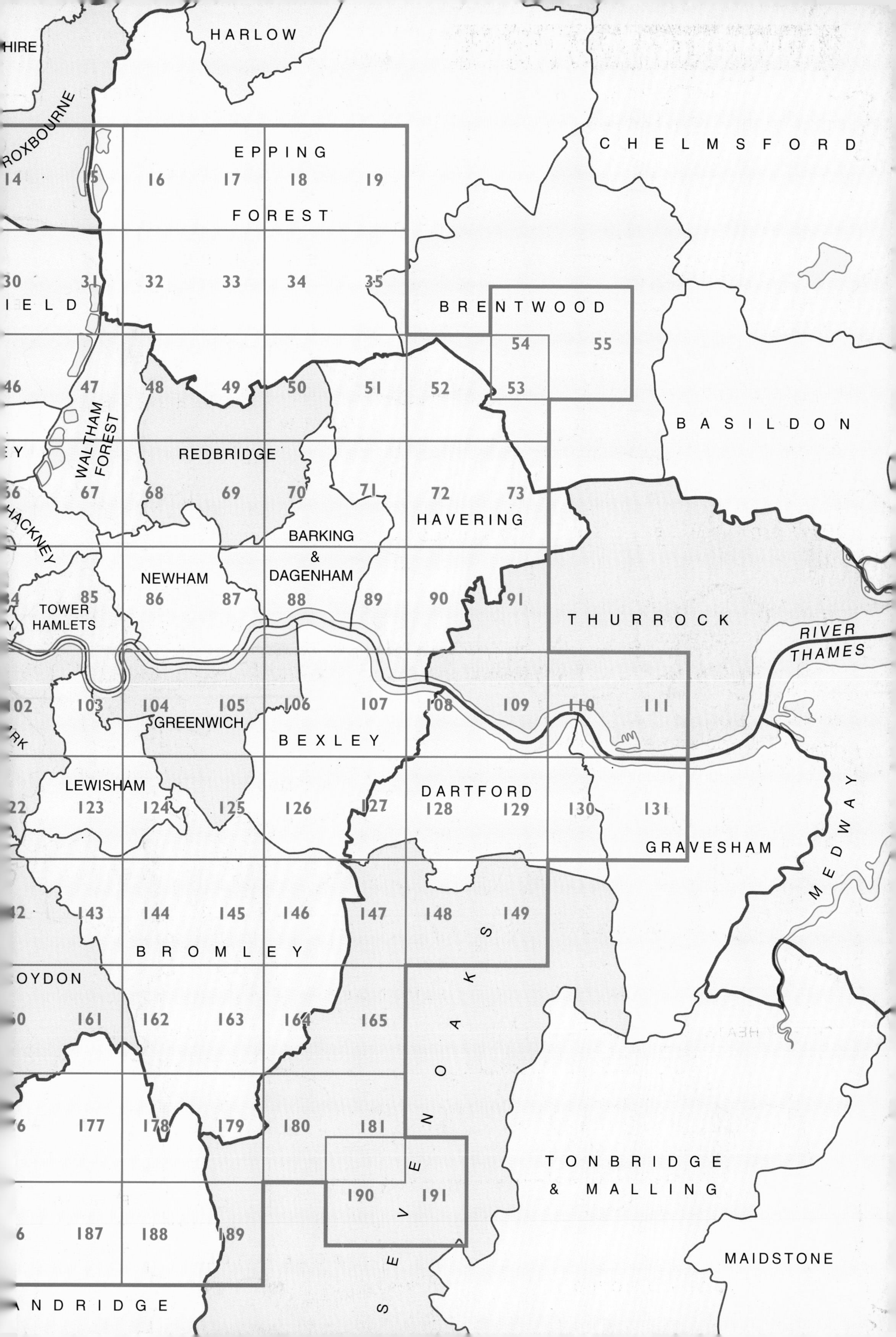

HIRE

HARLOW

CHELMSFORD

ROXBOURNE

EPPING

14 | 15 | 16 | 17 | 18 | 19

FOREST

30 | 31 | 32 | 33 | 34 | 35

BRENTWOOD

IELD

54 | 55

46 | 47 | 48 | 49 | 50 | 51 | 52 | 53

BASILDON

WALTHAM FOREST

REDBRIDGE

Y

66 | 67 | 68 | 69 | 70 | 71 | 72 | 73

HACKNEY

HAVERING

BARKING & DAGENHAM

NEWHAM

84 | 85 | 86 | 87 | 88 | 89 | 90 | 91

Y TOWER HAMLETS

THURROCK

RIVER THAMES

102 | 103 | 104 | 105 | 106 | 107 | 108 | 109 | 110 | 111

RK GREENWICH

BEXLEY

LEWISHAM

DARTFORD

122 | 123 | 124 | 125 | 126 | 127 | 128 | 129 | 130 | 131

GRAVESHAM

M E D W A Y

142 | 143 | 144 | 145 | 146 | 147 | 148 | 149

BROMLEY

S E V E N O A K S

OYDON

160 | 161 | 162 | 163 | 164 | 165

176 | 177 | 178 | 179 | 180 | 181

TONBRIDGE

190 | 191

& MALLING

186 | 187 | 188 | 189

MAIDSTONE

ANDRIDGE